ISBN 978-0-260-16270-0
PIBN 10931814

GRIZZLY GROWLS

(CLARENCE M. HUNT.)

PROPOSING A PLAN, WHICH HAS BEEN approved by financiers of the nation, to ease the credit situation, President Herbert Hoover issued a statement October 7 in which he said: "The prolongation of the depression . . . has produced in some localities in the United States an apprehension wholly unjustified in view of the thousand-fold resources we have for meeting any demand. . . .

"The times call for unity of action on the part of our people. We have met with great difficulties not of our own making. It requires determination to overcome these difficulties and above all to restore and maintain confidence. Our people owe it not only to themselves and in their own interest, but they can, by such an example of stability and purpose, give hope and confidence in our own country and to the rest of the world."

Condemning the "sentimentalism in some people which makes popular heroes out of criminals," the President, in a radio address October 12, said:

"If the police had the vigilant, universal backing of public opinion in their communities, if they had the implacable support of the prosecuting authorities and the courts, if our criminal laws in their endeavor to protect the innocent did not furnish loopholes through which irresponsible, yet clever, criminal lawyers daily find devices of escape for the guilty, I am convinced that our police would stamp out the excessive crime and remove the worldwide disrepute which has disgraced some of our great cities."

Without any doubt, the Federal Congress which convenes in December will be requested to grant immigration quotas to Japan, China and other Oriental nations. And the powerful influences of the United States Chamber of Commerce, the World Peace Foundation, the Federation of Churches of Christ in America and other pro-Jap agencies will be exercised, to the end that the request will be heeded. These agencies are being aided by a nation-wide chain of newspapers, which give their propaganda much prominence.

The scheme has faithful backers, also, in California, among them the Los Angeles Chamber of Commerce and the Southern California Methodist Ministers Association. During the past month, too, the Pacific-Oriental Trades Association was organized to labor and lobby for nullifying the Exclusion Law by granting the quota. Prominent in this latter outfit are William May Garland, William Lacy, Arthur Bent and Orra Monnette of Los Angeles, and William Woods of San Francisco.

The claim being advanced that "sentiment in California now favors a quota for Japan" is a deliberate falsehood! The quota is favored by but a few residents of this state who are apparently more interested in yellow-dollars than the welfare of the White race. The people of California are almost unanimously against the proposed quota, and with all their power the pro-Japists could not muster sufficient encouragement to warrant introduction of a resolution favoring it in the 1931 State Legislature.

On the other hand, the State Legislature of 1923 passed, unanimously, a resolution demanding exclusion of ineligible-to-citizenship aliens. And in 1929 it passed, also unanimously, another resolution opposing the quota. What better evidence that the sentiment in California has not changed?

The Congress, if it considers carefully the welfare of the nation, and particularly the Western states, will not only refuse to grant the quota to Japs and other ineligible-to-citizenship aliens, but it will close the present loopholes through which far too many of them are gaining entrance into this country.

The world suffered a distinct loss when Thomas Elva Edison, the great inventor, died at his West Orange, New Jersey, home October 18. This tribute came from Lee De Forest, inventor:

"In the passing of Thomas Edison humanity has lost its greatest single benefactor since the dawn of history. No individual has ever given himself so continuously, so prodigiously, so beneficially as did Edison. The giver of light and power, he has added infinitely to the light of our intellect and soul and to mankind's power to swiftly progress toward its loftier goals. Were all the world's light and power supply cut off tonight for a single hour in reverent commemoration of its debt to Edison we might perhaps glimpse some faint appreciation of the immeasurable debt we owe to that glorious immortal."

The United States had a Jap population at the time of taking the 1930 census of 138,834; in 1920 they numbered 111,010, a percentage increase of 25.1. Most of them are planted in the Pacific states, where their numbers increased from 93,490 in 1920 to 120,251 in 1930. Their California increase was from 71,952 in 1920 to 97,456 in 1930. The Jap-population figures for this state's cities of 100,000 or more population are quite interesting: Long Beach, 375 (1920), 596 (1930); Los Angeles, 11,618 (1920), 21,081 (1930); Oakland, 2,709 (1920), 2,137 (1930); San Diego, 772 (1920), 911 (1930); San Francisco, 5,358 (1920), 6,250 (1930).

Los Angeles City, incidentally, is pictured in the 1930 census returns as the chief California nesting-place for undesirable ineligible-to-citizenship aliens: 97,116 Mexis and 21,081 Japs. In Sacramento County, the number of Japs jumped from 5,800 in 1920 to 8,114 in 1930.

Do not, for one moment, think that the Japs have congregated at strategic points by accident. They have been put there by Japan for a purpose, which will be impressively evident in the not-far-distant future. It will not be long now until Japs, from certain districts, are members of the State Legislature and representatives in Congress from California.

An effort is being made to stimulate home owning, as it is conceded that the most substantial citizen of any community is the home owner. Not much progress will be made, however, at least in California, until such time as the confiscatory tax burden is very materially lightened.

The tax burden is made up not only of the cost of government, but of special assessments, designed to aid the paving and other trusts. Hundreds of people have lost their homes because of these unjust, if legally lawful, special assessments.

We hear repeatedly that "prosperity is just around the corner." Governor James Rolph could hasten California's negotiation of that corner by calling a special session of the State Legislature to abolish the special assessment evil. When that is done, and not before, there will be a "boom" in home owning.

"The Mexican element in the population has increased very rapidly in certain parts of the United States during the past ten years," says a recent report of the Federal Census Bureau. "By reason of its growing importance it was given a separate classification in the census returns for 1930, having been included for the most part with the White population at prior censuses. The instructions given the enumerators for making this classification were to the effect that all persons born in Mexico or having parents born in Mexico, who are not definitely White, Negro, Indian, Chinese, or Japanese, should be returned as Mexican. Under these instructions, 65,965 persons of Mexican birth or parentage were returned as White and 1,422,533 as Mexicans."

So, a vast majority of the Mexis are considered NOT of the White race. Their numbers in this country increased from an estimated 700,541 in 1920 to 1,422,533 in 1930, a percentage increase of 103.1. The percentage increase in the White population for the same period was but 14.8.

The Mexis who come to this country, being not of the White race, are ineligible for American citizenship. They are not wanted here, except by the interests who employ them at starvation wages, and are not needed. They constitute a decided, and ever-increasing, menace. They have colonized mostly in Texas, California and New Mexico which, at the time of taking the 1930 census, had Mexi populations of 683,681, 368,013 and 114,173, respectively.

The Grizzly Bear Magazine
The ALL California Monthly
OWNED, CONTROLLED, PUBLISHED BY GRIZZLY BEAR PUBLISHING CO.,
(Incorporated)
COMPOSED OF NATIVE SONS.
HERMAN C. LICHTENBERGER, Pres.
JOHN T. NEWELL RAY HOWARD
WM. I. TRAEGER LORENZO F. SOTO
CHAS. R. THOMAS HARRY J. LELANDE
ARTHUR A. SCHMIDT, Vice-Pres.
BOARD OF DIRECTORS

CLARENCE M. HUNT
General Manager and Editor

OFFICIAL ORGAN AND THE ONLY OFFICIAL PUBLICATION OF THE NATIVE SONS AND THE NATIVE DAUGHTERS GOLDEN WEST.

ISSUED FIRST EACH MONTH.
FORMS CLOSE 20th MONTH.
ADVERTISING RATES ON APPLICATION.

SAN FRANCISCO OFFICE:
N.S.G.W. BLDG., 414 MASON ST., RM. 302
(Office Grand Secretary N.S.G.W.)
Telephone: Kearney 1223
SAN FRANCISCO, CALIFORNIA

PUBLICATION OFFICE:
309-15 WILCOX BLDG., 2nd AND SPRING,
Telephone: VAndike 6234
LOS ANGELES, CALIFORNIA

(Entered as second-class matter May 29, 1918, at the Postoffice at Los Angeles, California, under the act of August 24, 1912.)
PUBLISHED REGULARLY SINCE MAY 1907
VOL. L WHOLE NO. 295

In view of the facts revealed by the census, and in order that another color-tragedy may be prevented in this country, the Federal Congress should adopt legislation definitely applying the provisions of the Exclusion Law to Mexico.

United States Senator Hiram W. Johnson, a most valued member of the national lawmaking body, is, like most real Americans, opposed to the slashing of the navy and the reduction of the armaments of the country. In the course of a forceful Navy Day address at San Francisco, he said:

"The cheapest politics today is the politics which raves of peace and yet would take this great nation into any organization abroad from which might spring wars of no concern to us; which bellows of a naval holiday, knowing our absolute inferiority in naval equipment, and would leave us at the mercy of any other first-class power were trouble to arise; which shouts disarmament and means disarmament for us alone, while others continue to arm."

Thursday, November 26, will be Thanksgiving Day. While the people of these United States are having their troubles, they also have much for which to be thankful. Thanks for the numerous blessings should be given the Master Ruler.

The American Legion of Martinez, Contra Costa County, is demanding the immediate dismissal from public service of all married women. Hurrah for the Legion! In this demand, it should have wholehearted support.

The policy of giving employment to married women with able-bodied husbands is all wrong, and is in no small measure responsible for the economic ills so much complained about.

Now is the most opportune time to put a stop, once and for all, to the practice. The American Legion, the Native Sons and other organizations should unite forces and wage a campaign to that end in every county of the state. Such a campaign will be successful, and California and its citizenry will be benefited immeasurably.

In an address at Sacramento October 15, Professor Paul Tanner of the University of Hawaii, Honolulu, declared 72 percent of the Island of Hawaii's population is Japanese, and their number is growing steadily. The public schools are attended only by Orientals; White children are sent to private schools.

(Continued on Page 25)

THE BRODERICK-TERRY DUEL

Peter T. Conmy, M.A.

(Historian Golden Gate Parlor N.S.G.W.)

There has been considerable recent discussion in the daily press regarding the site of the Broderick-Terry duel, famous in California history, the question at issue being whether the site is in San Francisco or San Mateo County. The accompanying article, prepared by Peter T. Conmy, M.A., historian of Golden Gate Parlor No. 29, N.S.G.W., San Francisco, is interesting and enlightening.—Editor.

IN THE HISTORY OF THE UNITED STATES the decade from 1850 to 1860 was characterized by repeated attempts of the South to secure the extension of slavery into the Middle West and Far West. In 1850 when the Northern and the Southern forces were deadlocked in Congress over this matter, the intensity of the situation was broken by a compromise by Henry Clay that admitted California as a free state. In 1853 the Southern element succeeded in breaking down the old Mason-Dixon Line that had for so long separated the slave and the free soil by the Kansas-Nebraska Act, which permitted the territories of Kansas and Nebraska to determine for themselves whether or not they should have slavery. This matter was called to the attention of the nation in a very striking manner in 1858, when it was debated by Lincoln and Douglas in Illinois. This issue, namely, the question of extending slavery into Northern territory, manifested itself in California politics as it had in those of every other state. At that time the Democratic Party was, for all practical purposes, the only party in American politics. The Whig Party was fading out of existence after 1852, and the new Republican Party was not yet of much importance.

In California, as in all other free states, the Democratic Party was divided into two opposing factions—the slave faction and the free-soil faction. Those in favor of extending slavery were known as Lecompton Democrats, and those opposed were called anti-Lecompton Democrats. The leader of the anti-Lecompton group in California was David C. Broderick, a sturdy, self-made young man, born in Washington, the son of an Irish laborer who had worked on the capital building. Broderick had lived in New York City, whence he migrated to California in 1850. The leader of the slave faction was William M. Gwinn, incumbent United States Senator, who had come to California from his home state, Tennessee.

In 1857 Broderick was elected United States Senator from California for a full term. Gwin was re-elected with Broderick's support, but for an unexpired term. In 1858 an attempt was made to carry the state for the Lecompton standard. Broderick toured the state, making speeches everywhere in opposition to the extension of slavery. As the campaign became more intense and more and more bitter, Broderick thought it necessary to unmask the true character of Senator Gwin. To do this, he made public the "scarlet letter," a communication which Gwin had written to Broderick, implying that if Broderick would support his re-election he would not exercise his right to dictate patronage appointments to the president. Broderick supported Gwin's re-election, but Gwin immediately broke his promise. In Washington, Gwin turned the favor of President Buchanan away from Broderick, and as a result Broderick became a strong opponent of the presidential administration. So strong was his opposition in the Senate to the extension of slavery that Southern leaders became most hostile to him.

As a result of this violent opposition to the powers that were, the leaders of the Lecompton group in California marked Broderick as a man to be gotten rid of. Senator Gwin and his friends, who were both ashamed and indignant over the expose of the "scarlet letter," also acquiesced in this. To the honor of these old Californians, it must be said that no attempt was made to murder Broderick. They at least gave him an open chance to defend his life. David C. Terry, a justice of the Supreme Court, challenged Broderick to a duel. After months of letter writing the date was set for September 12, 1859. Terry predicated his challenge upon grounds of certain derogatory remarks about him made by Broderick, but it was an open secret that Terry was really the avenger of his friend, Senator Gwin, and of the Lecompton party.

The duel was to have taken place on Davis Ranch, in San Mateo County. Friends of both men who wished to prevent bloodshed procured warrants from a San Mateo magistrate for the duelists' arrest. The peace officers, in serving the warrants just as the duel was about to start, prevented the shooting. The next morning there was no legal process to interrupt the combatants and they fought it out on the shores of Lake Merced, then in San Francisco but now in San Mateo County. Broderick was mortally wounded and expired three days later. In the passing of David C. Broderick, California lost one of its most able men. His death in the thirty-ninth year of a very promising career was indeed a catastrophe, and public sentiment was so aroused against the Lecompton Party, after the death of Broderick, that the movement for the extension of slavery was lost from then on, in California. During the Civil War this state was one of the most loyal to the Union. Broderick was the first great martyr for the abolition of slavery; Lincoln was the second.

It has long been thought that the Terry-Broderick duel took place on the shores of Lake Merced. In 1917 the N.S.G.W. Historic Landmarks Committee erected a tablet at the site where the duel is believed to have taken place. The spot marked by the committee is in San Mateo County, a few hundred feet over the boundary line between San Francisco and San Mateo Counties. At the time that the duel was fought this spot was in San Francisco County. The San Francisco-San Mateo boundary was fixed in 1856 and amended in 1857. At that time the end of Lake Merced abutted the boundary line. In 1899, by mutual consent of the two counties and with the approval of the State Legislature, the San Mateo area was extended north six or seven hundred feet, so that the location of the duel was put in San Mateo County at that time. Notwithstanding the fact that the place marked by the committee was originally in San Francisco, there is strong evidence to indicate that the duel took place further down in San Mateo County. I have investigated this, in the archives of the Bancroft Library at Berkeley, and find that the newspapers, "Daily Alta' and "'Bulletin," in accounts of the duel state that it took place on a ravine in Davis Ranch in San Mateo County about a mile and a half or two miles south of Lake Merced. This would unquestionably indicate a location different from the one marked by the committee. This evidence is not accepted as conclusive, however. In law, a written document is stronger evidence that human testimony, but writers on historical method are unanimous in urging that written records are to be given precedence over tradition. In spite of this, however, this would seem to be a case where the oral account should be accepted as preponderating the written. The committee employed Herman Schulesler of the Spring Valley Water Company, to whom the land belonged, and he made an exhaustive study of all the records of the company. After he had selected the present place, which is also the traditional spot, he consulted Geo. Green, whose father was keeper of the old Lake Merced boathouse, an eyewitness to the duel. He led Schulesler to this location, saying that his father had years before pointed it out to him as the place where the duel was fought. My personal theory is, that the newspaper reporters confused the duel which was stopped by the peace officers with the one actually fought. Gertrude Atherton says the duel was fought on the shores of the lake, and was witnessed by some seventy-five persons who had journeyed there in wagons, left parked on the shores of the lake. I have visited the monument and studied the contour and vicinity. My inspection convinces me that the water of the lake extended almost to where the monument has been placed, because the soil is marshy nearby and must have been the bed of the lake seventy-two years ago. Unless stronger evidence is found, it is my opinion that the findings of the committee, made in 1917, should stand. The evidence shows that it was intended to fight the duel further down in San Mateo County, September 12, 1859, but the peace officers stopped them; and so the next morning they fought it on the shores of Lake Merced, then in San Francisco County but, since 1899, in San Mateo County.

Farm Bureau Meet—The thirteenth annual convention of the California Farm Bureau Federation will be held at Merced City November 16-18.

Rabbit Show—The Pacific Rabbit Breeders Association will have its fifth annual show at Hayward, Alameda County, November 12-15.

School Bonds—Sacramento City voters have authorized a $1,146,000 bond issue for three new junior high school buildings.

LIFE IN OLD PUEBLO DAYS

DAYS OF UNTROUBLED HAPPINESS and ease, riding over boundless domains or lounging lazily by the adobe walls of the patios; nights of unrestrained but simple gaiety, singing and dancing under the stars—such was the life in early California. This Utopian land has been much eulogized in song and story, for as one writer has commented, "it would be difficult to find in any age or place a community that got more out of life, and with less trouble, with less wear and wickedness than the people of pastoral California."

Regarding amusements among the utilities of life, the early Spaniards devoted a great deal of their time to pleasure-seeking, dancing, horse riding and racing, cockfighting, bull and bear fights, and hunting. For any excuse whatever a fiesta was celebrated with all its various diversions. "Absolutely unconfined, socially and politically, masters of all their eyes surveyed, the beautiful earth and its fruits as free as the sweet air and sunshine, lands unlimited, cattle on a thousand hills, with ready-made servants to tend them, basking here with none to molest or make afraid . . . how should they be else than happy, than lovers of home and country?"

Life was centered on the ranchos, where in the rambling comfortable haciendas hospitality was unlimited. There the caballeros with their families lived a happy life, spending fully half of their time on horseback. Pastoral California was the day of the horseman, for then it was that the Spaniard and his horse were inseparable companions. The cattle industry greatly encouraged this practice; even the women became adept in riding, throwing the lasso and shooting. Training in horsemanship began at an extremely tender age, children of four and five years often being placed on horse and taught to ride at breakneck speed. "Unhorsed, a Californian considered himself but half a man, and he who was not a skilled rider was looked upon with contempt."

Naturally, the Californians developed forms of amusements that could be enjoyed on horseback. One of these was known as "carrera del gallo," or race for the cock, and was one of the most exciting and lively of the games. "A live cock was buried with the head above ground. At a signal a horseman would start at full speed from a distance of about sixty yards, and if by dexterous swoop he could take the bird by the head he was loudly applauded. Should he fail, he was greeted with derisive laughter, and was sometimes unhorsed with violence, or dragged in the dust at the risk of breaking his limbs or neck. Another amusement was to place on the ground a rawhide, and riding at full speed suddenly rein in the horse the moment his forefeet struck the hide."

One of the most popular sports of the day was horse racing, not only for the participants, but for the onlookers as well, who won and lost many a fortune in the betting. There were likewise bull fights and bull and bear fights, but neither of these were as dangerous sports as those enjoyed in Spain or Mexico. In the bull fights no horses were used and the bull was very seldom killed. In the bull and bear fights both animals were fighting animals.

Strength, dexterity and bravery were required and naturally developed in the early colonists, even in their amusements. One game especially requiring these was the "Juego de vara," or the game of rods. "The players formed in a ring, the horses facing inwards. One of the number then rode around the circle, having in his hand a stout rod of quince or other similar wood, which he gave from behind to one of the players. He who received the rod pursued the giver, directing blows at his shoulders which the latter by the exertion of skilful horsemanship endeavored to elude, until by gaining a vacant place in the circle he was exempt from further persecution. This sport was continued for hours, and he who was not a skilled horseman received a good drubbing."

A vital factor in all forms of the Spaniards' amusement was music. "There were songs of the soil, and songs of poets and of troubadours, in this far, lone, beautiful, happy land; and songs that came over from Mother Spain and up from Stepmother Mexico. But everybody sang; and a great many made their own songs, or verses to other songs. 'Not being musical critics, they felt music, and arrived at it; and the folksong of Spanish America is a treasure of inexhaustible beauty and extent. . . . Song then was born of emotion, and never of the commercial itch. It

(Continued on Page 25)

CALIFORNIA HAPPENINGS OF FIFTY YEARS AGO

Thomas R. Jones

(COMPILED EXPRESSLY FOR THE GRIZZLY BEAR.)

THANKSGIVING DAY, NOVEMBER 24, 1881, was observed in California, alike by the godly and the ungodly, with church services, turkey shoots, sporting events and grand balls in many cities and towns. All the saloons did a rushing business; they dispensed "tom and jerry" for coin of the realm, and served free to all imbibers a roast turkey lunch.

Prices of eatables were reasonable: turkeys, 20 cents pound; chickens, 50 cents each; mallard ducks, 50 cents brace; quail, 75 cents dozen; vegetables, 1 cent to 1½ cents pound; apples, 75 cents box; butter, 35 cents pound; eggs, 35 cents dozen; artichokes, 25 cents dozen. Wheat was selling for $1.67 and barley $1.50 a cental, while hay was $12 a ton.

Eighteen eighty-one was a prosperous year for the state. There was no unsalable surplus of products, and no dearth of employment. Everybody was apparently happy. But there was a foreboding of trouble, as the year drew near its close, for those in certain lines of endeavor.

The California Supreme Court decided the state's Sunday closing law was constitutional, and a new movement, backed by the Good Templars and the churches, was organized to see that it was strictly enforced. But one saloon in Sacramento City closed, however, and in Los Angeles, Stockton and San Francisco the booze emporiums defied the law by keeping open on the Sabbath. In the latter city the wholesale liquor dealers organized a "League of Freedom" to fight for "the liberty of the individual."

In some places those seeking to enforce the law went to extremes; for example: At Watsonville, Santa Cruz County, Edward Martin was arrested and found guilty of selling a San Francisco newspaper on Sunday, and Miss James, a telegraph operator, was arrested for keeping the office open two hours on Sunday.

Then, to add to the Sunday closing turmoil, the lowlands met the highlands in court, in injunction array. Farmers on the east side of the Sacramento Valley proceeded to shut down all the hydraulic mines on the tributaries of the American, Yuba, Bear and Feather Rivers. Suit had been brought in Sacramento County against them, and the famous trial of The People versus the Gold Run Hydraulic Mining Company got under way.

Thousands of men in Placer, Nevada, Sierra, Butte and other counties were thrown out of employment, and business became badly depressed. Many families were reported to be emigrating from the hydraulic mining counties. And so began contests between neighboring communities and citizens of the state that became financially hurtful, and trouble loomed large on the horizon.

CHICAGO IMMIGRANTS BRING SMALLPOX.

Burdette Chandler, boring for oil on the Puente rancho in Los Angeles County, struck a gusher at a depth of 165 feet that was yielding a barrel of "black gold" a minute.

A new town, to be named Crockett, was this month laid out in Contra Costa County on the south shore of Carquinez Straits. It is quite a town now.

R. Nadeau of Los Angeles was preparing an acreage for the planting of 1,000,000 grapevines next season.

Pinkeye broke out among the horses of San Francisco, and 200 of the animals were killed in one day.

A band of gray wolves appeared near Sherlock, Mariposa County, and began subsisting on the goats in that vicinity.

The State Health Board decided smallpox was being brought into California by immigrants coming from Chicago via the Central Pacific. Eleven cases, coming from that city during October, were discovered in California North. The board ordered that all cars be inspected in Placer County in future.

Twelve fire companies from adjacent communities participated in a tournament at Hollister, San Benito County. The Pioneer company of the host-town won the first prize.

The Los Angeles District Fair opened November 1 at Los Angeles City. Although the last of the state's numerous district expositions for the year, it was not the least in exhibits, horseracing or attendance.

A Red Bluff, Tehama County, newspaper reporter, writing an account of a fashionable church wedding there, said: "The bride's dainty feet were encased in fairy-sized white slippers." As published the reference read: "The bride's dirty feet," etc. The reporter, of course, had to leave town.

A cloud of cobwebs, about thirty feet above the ground and extending upward about five hundred feet, passed over Nevada City, Nevada County, November 1 and filled the air with gossamerlike threads. Whence it came and whither bound were unknown.

The Marysville, Yuba County, Savings Bank, to the consternation of the citizens, failed November 8. Its liabilities were $446,000 and its paper assets about the same.

G. Barth of Napa City departed for parts unknown November 16, and with him went some $30,000 left with him for safekeeping by confiding friends.

Because he could not read it, the Timbuctoo, Yuba County, postmaster refused to forward a postcard mailed at his office. It was written in Gaelic.

A transit of Mercury, beginning at 2:07 p.m. of November 7, required five hours and twenty minutes for the planet to cross the sun's face. To the skygazers, it looked like a black walnut moving slowly. As far as California was concerned, the show was a success.

UPPER-LIP ADORNMENT CULTIVATED.

The stage from Sonora, Tuolumne County, to Milton was stopped near the former place November 7 by four masked men. They got $3,200 from the express box and robbed the passengers, getting from one $500.

The stage stables at Susanville, Lassen County, burned November 6 and sixty horses were cremated. A loss of $25,000 was sustained.

An Oakland, Alameda County, fire November 8 caused a $50,000 loss, and one at Modesto, Stanislaus County, November 10, in which one man was cremated, caused a $10,000 loss. Several buildings were destroyed by fire at Anaheim, Orange County, November 15. The Wagner House at Coulterville, Mariposa County, burned November 29; loss $10,000.

During the month fires in San Francisco destroyed eighty-two buildings. The losses, totaling $1[illegible],000, were fully covered by insurance.

Captain Edward A. Poole, who came from New Jersey in 1849, died at San Francisco November 8. He established a steamboat line from San Francisco to Sacramento and for many years captained the well-known "Chrysopolis."

An Oroville, Butte County, maiden, being called on at a social function to recite a proverb, gave this: "A kiss untickled by a moustache is like an egg without a yolk." The town's young blades immediately began cultivating an upper-lip adornment.

William H. Patterson, who came in 1857, died at San Francisco November 14. He was a leading attorney.

Dan A. Rice, one of the first locators on Rattlesnake Bar in the '50s, died at Newcastle, Placer County, November 26.

Frank Hudson, a 14-year-old Grass Valley, Nevada County, lad, was killed by the accidental discharge of his shotgun while hunting quail.

Engineer James McGregor was killed at Plymouth, Amador County, November 5, when the boiler at the Empire mine exploded.

(Continued on Page 15)

Passing of the California Pioneer

(Confined to Brief Notices of the Demise of Those Men and Women Who Came to California Prior to 1860.)

JAMES P. TAYLOR, NATIVE OF AUSTRALIA, 85; arrived in California April 1, 1849, and most of the time since resided in San Francisco and Oakland; died at the latter city. He was the oldest surviving member of the Society of California Pioneers, San Francisco, and was the author of "Pioneer Life in California and British Columbia."

Mrs. Claudia Estrada-[illegible]entis, native of Mexico, 91; came in [illegible] and settled in San Benito County; died at San Juan Bautista, survived by eight children. She claimed to have witnessed the raising of the Flag of the United States of America by Captain John C. Fremont atop Fremont Peak, March 4, 1847.

Mrs. Mary McKay-Crocker, native of Wisconsin, 84; came across the plains in 1850 and settled in El Dorado County; died at Sacramento City.

William Pickett, native of Missouri, 83; came in 1852; died at San Francisco. He was a brother of Ina Donna Coolbrith, deceased poet laureate of California.

Mrs. Lurinda Stice-Harris, native of Missouri, 87; came across the plains in 1852 and resided in Solano and Napa Counties; died at Napa City, survived by a daughter.

Mrs. Lydia Mackey-Dunphy, native of England, 82; came in 1853 and long resided in Siskiyou County, the old mining town of Sawyers Bar being her home for many years; died at Yreka, survived by nine children.

Mrs. Mary Elizabeth Foye-Murphy, native of Massachusetts, 85; came in 1853; died at Columbia, Tuolumne County.

Mrs. Olive Ann Wilson, native of New York, 92; came in 1854 and resided in San Francisco and Los Angeles; died at the latter city, survived by a son.

Mrs. Mary Griggs, native of Tennessee, 91; came across the plains in 1855 and settled in Tehama County; died at Red Bluff, survived by a son.

Mrs. Ida F. Livingston, native of New York, 77; came in 1855 and long resided in Stanislaus County; died at San Pablo, Contra Costa County, survived by two children.

Mrs. Mary Ann Ward, native of England, 86; came across the plains in 1855 and resided in El Dorado and Sacramento Counties; died at Sacramento City, survived by seven children.

Benjamin Brooks, native of Connecticut, 89; came in 1856 and resided in San Francisco and San Luis Obispo; died at the latter city. He was a well-known newspaper publisher and editor; his father, the late Benjamin S. Brooks, was a California Pioneer of 1849.

Mrs. Jennie Willey-Strong, 90; came in 1856; died at Los Angeles City.

Alfred C. Howard, native of Missouri, 87; came in 1856; died at Fort Bragg, Mendocino County, survived by a wife and three children.

Mrs. Emelia Ainsworth-Ferguson, native of Missouri, 93; came across the plains in 1857 and settled in Sonoma County; died at Geyserville, survived by four children. She was the widow of Thomas J. Ferguson, California Pioneer of 1849.

Mrs. Mary Ann Bidwell, native of Iowa, 81; came across the plains in 1857 and settled in Shasta County; died at McCloud, Siskiyou County, survived by seven children.

Mrs. Rose Fulda-Hauser, 81; came in 1858 and resided in Los Angeles and San Francisco; died at the former city, survived by two sons, Martin S. Hauser (Ramona Parlor No. 109 N.S.G.W.) of Los Angeles and Herbert Hauser (Fruitvale Parlor No. 252 N.S.G.W.) of Oakland, and a brother, Edward Fulda (California Parlor No. 1 N.S.G.W.) of New York City.

Mrs. Ellen Baley-McCardle, native of Missouri, 84; came via the Santa Fe Trail in 1858 and settled in Fresno County; died at Fresno City, survived by seven children. She was the widow of James McCardle, California Pioneer of 1848 who was well known in Tuolumne, Mariposa and Fresno Counties.

Francis Marion Mecum, native of Michigan, 74; came via the Isthmus of Panama in 1859; died at Chico, Butte County, survived by two children.

Mrs. Caroline Bohna-Dooley, native of Arkansas, 84; came in 1859 and settled in Kern County; died at Bakersfield, survived by seven children.

Mrs. Minneta Everson, native of Illinois, 74; since 1859 a resident of Sacramento County; died at Sacramento City, survived by a husband and two sons.

George D. Webb, born in 1855 while his parents were enroute from Tennessee across the plains; resided in Stanislaus, Calaveras and San Joaquin Counties; died at Stockton.

OLD TIMERS PASS

Colonel James Boon Lankershim, native of Missouri, 81; came in 1860 and resided in San Francisco and Los Angeles; died at Brooklyn, New York, survived by two children.

Milo Miletus Church, native of Vermont, 93; came in 1860; died at Stockton, San Joaquin County, survived by two daughters.

James Clare Pattison, native of Australia, 72; came in 1861; died near Gilroy, Santa Clara County, survived by a wife and three daughters.

Mrs. Amanda Melvina Short-Ward, native of Michigan, 93; since 1862 Sonoma County resident; died at Santa Rosa.

Mrs. Sarah LaVerne Zollars, native of Iowa, 77; came in 1863; died at Diamond Springs, El Dorado County.

Mrs. Mary Buerhle-Davis, native of Ohio, 93; since 1864 Siskiyou County resident; died at Yreka, survived by two daughters.

Edward Weil, 83; came in 1865; died at San Francisco.

John T. Nunes, native of Azores Islands, 84; since 1865 Contra Costa County resident; died at Port Chicago, survived by four daughters.

Mrs. Mary Daly-McKinley, native of Ireland, 88; since 1865 resident San Francisco, where she died; two children survive.

Mrs. Margaret Nance; came in 1866; died near Santa Maria, Santa Barbara County, survived by four children.

Mrs. Agnes Arkley, native of Canada, 86; came in 1866; died at Lompoc, Santa Barbara County, survived by five children.

Mrs. Lydia Harker, 83; came in 1867; died at Santa Rosa, Sonoma County.

William Hamblin Oakes, native of Maine, 75; came in 1869; died at Esparto, Yolo County, survived by seven children.

Charles C. Goodwin, native of New Hampshire, 67; came in 1869 and long resided in Humboldt County; died at Yountville, Napa County.

Henry Hortop, native of Canada, 83; came in 1869 and long resided in Napa County; died at San Francisco, survived by two daughters.

PIONEER NATIVES DEAD

Healdsburg (Sonoma County)—Mrs. Olive Davis-Heitz, born in Napa County in 1858, passed away September 18 survived by a husband and four children.

Bridge House (Sacramento County)—Joseph E. Pratte, born in California in 1853, died September 19.

Eureka (Humboldt County)—Thomas Amen, born in California in 1856, died September 22.

Sacramento City—Frank Farley, born in California in 1859, died September 21.

Oakland (Alameda County)—Mrs. Ellie Hensley-Thornton, born at Sacramento City in 1856, passed away September 22. She was a daughter of Major Samuel J. Hensley, California Pioneer of 1843.

Crescent City (Del Norte County)—Augustus Smith, born in Placer County in 1852, died September 24 survived by two sons.

Irvington (Alameda County)—Miss Mariana Horner, born in California in 1854, passed away September 24.

San Francisco—Mrs. Christian Murray Condon, born in Yuba County in 1856, passed away September 25 survived by four children.

Peralta (Orange County)—Miss Bemigna Peralta, born in this county in 1851, passed away September 26.

San Francisco—Miss Ida M. Kervan, born here in 1854, passed away October 1. She was affiliated with Alta Parlor No. 3 N.D.G.W. and for many years taught in the public schools.

Sacramento City—George H. Fuqua, born in Butte County in 1856, died October 2 survived by a wife and two daughters.

Newcastle (Placer County)—Adolph H. Schnabel, born in this county in 1855, died October 3 survived by a wife and two daughters. He was one of Placer County's best-known fruitgrowers.

Gerber (Tehama County)—Albert E. Brown, born in El Dorado County in 1859, died October 4 survived by a wife and a daughter.

Portland (Oregon State)—Isador Lang, born in Trinity County in 1859, died October 6 survived by a wife and two daughters.

Menlo Park (San Mateo County)—Mrs. Margaret Manuela Buelna, born at San Francisco in 1840, passed away October 7 survived by three children.

Oakland (Alameda County)—Mrs. Julia Hargrave, born in this county in 1848, passed away October 7 survived by two children. She was a

(Continued on Page 26)

VETERAN OF MEXICAN AND CIVIL WARS DIES IN SAN JOAQUIN COUNTY.

Manteca (San Joaquin County)—William Harry Ranes, veteran of the Mexican and the Civil Wars, died at the age of 101, September 29, survived by two daughters. He was born near Lima, Ohio, March 6, 1830.

When the Mexican War broke out he enlisted in Company F, First Ohio Infantry, and was one of the first soldiers to land at Vera Cruz. Then he marched with General Scott's victorious forces into Mexico City. In 1861 he enlisted in Company F, Thirty-eighth Ohio Infantry, and served throughout the Civil War. In 1908 he came to California to reside.

CALIFORNIA'S TAXABLE WEALTH

(CLARENCE M. HUNT.)

THE GRAND TOTAL 1931 ASSESSED value of all taxable property in the State of California is, according to a statement of State Controller Ray L. Riley, $9,402,188,441, a decrease, compared with the 1930 value, $10,203,866,630, of $801,678,189. The total indebtedness of the fifty-eight counties of the state went up from $188,866,324 last year to $201,724,158 this year, an increase of $12,857,834. Here are other comparative figures:

Value of real estate: $3,867,173,026 (1930), $3,786,492,171 (1931); a 1931 decrease of $80,680,855. Value of improvements on real estate: $2,143,372,981 (1930), $2,191,885,304 (1931); a 1931 increase of $48,512,323. Value of personal property: $962,028,425 (1930), $764,220,678 (1931); a 1931 decrease of $197,807,747. Money: $2,591,679 (1930), $2,762,926 (1931); a 1931 increase of $171,247. Solvent credits: $499,841,574 (1930), $358,227,892 (1931); a 1931 decrease of $141,613,682. Stocks, bonds, notes, etc.: $1,334,481,852 (1930), $874,496,022 (1931); a 1931 decrease of $486,985,830.

It will be noted from the figures above that, while the 1931 real estate assessment is decreased $80,680,855, the improvements assessment is increased $48,512,323, so the net decrease on real estate and improvements is but a paltry $32,168,532. On the other hand, the personal property assessment is decreased $197,807,747, the solvent credits assessment $141,613,682, the stocks, bonds and notes assessment $486,985,830, a grand total for these three sources of tax revenue of $826,407,259. From these facts, it is plainly evident that realty is unjustly discriminated against—shamefully and ruinfully tax burdened!

Value of non-operative property: $8,809,489,537 (1930), $7,951,084,993 (1931); a 1931 decrease of $858,404,544. Value of property assessed on operative roll: $1,059,392,248 (1930), $1,134,632,514 (1931); a 1931 increase of $75,240,266. Value of railroads, as assessed by State Board Equalization: $334,984,845 (1930), $316,470,934 (1931); a 1931 decrease of $18,513,911.

Los Angeles continues as the richest county, according to assessment figures, in the state. Its 1931 grand total of all property is $3,943,778,468; the 1930 total was $4,514,261,968; a 1931 decrease of $570,483,500. The peak-year in this county was 1929, when the assessment totaled $4,522,926,824; in two years, therefore, the assessment-figures show a decrease of $579,148,356. The county's indebtedness has increased from $9,952,188 in 1930 to $10,324,601 in 1931. The county's tax rate has been lowered from $1.369 (inside) $1.619 (outside) in 1930 to $1.334 (inside) $1.484 (outside) in 1931. This tax rate, it should be borne in mind, is for Los Angeles County; the total Los Angeles City tax rate for 1931-32 is $4.27 per $100 valuation; for 1930-31 it totaled $4.28. The county has 1,278,434 acres of assessed land. More than 41 percent of the whole state's taxable property is in this one county.

San Francisco, the only combined city-and-county subdivision of California, is the next richest. Its 1931 grand total assessment, $1,640,760,958, is a decrease of $101,698,785, compared with the 1930 total of $1,742,459,743. Last year was San Francisco's peak-assessment year. Its indebtedness has increased from $137,729,400 in 1930 to $152,599,300 in 1931. This year's tax rate, $4.04, is the same as that for last year. San Francisco has but 29,888 acres of assessed land.

These two are the only California counties in the billion-dollar, ten-figure, assessment class. In the nine-figure class are the following counties, with their grand total assessments for 1931 and 1930:

County	1931	1930
Alameda	$587,867,173	$602,733,625
San Diego	253,647,549	278,043,620
Kern	216,814,425	221,391,937
Fresno	204,589,219	211,437,014
Orange	187,226,048	206,832,045
Sacramento	176,771,004	178,394,240
Santa Barbara	156,940,051	160,908,377
Santa Clara	145,812,454	146,760,202
San Bernardino	136,033,314	140,025,917
San Joaquin	134,198,792	149,870,943
Ventura	119,181,867	124,720,684
Contra Costa	112,641,523	116,053,724

All these counties show a decrease for 1931, compared with 1930: Alameda, $14,866,452; San Diego, $24,396,071; Kern, $4,577,512; Fresno, $6,847,795; Orange, $19,605,997; Sac-

(Continued on Page 15)

Native Daughters of the Golden West

HOLLISTER—THE TENTH ANNUAL district meeting of the Parlors of Santa Cruz, Monterey and San Benito Counties at Happy Valley, near Santa Cruz, September 19 and 20, was an outstanding event in the circles of the Order. All the Parlors were well represented. The gathering opened with a Saturday evening dinner at which Supervising Deputy Rose Rhyner was toastmistress. The tables were charmingly decorated in Hallowe'en colors by Santa Cruz No. 26. Each Parlor had been asked to prepare an original "booster" song setting forth the Order's achievements and purposes. These showed great ability on the part of the composers, that submitted by San Juan Bautista No. 179 being particularly well received. An informal meeting followed, and among the speakers were Grand President Evelyn I. Carlson, Grand Secretary Sallie R. Thaler, Past Grand President Bertha A. Briggs, District Deputies Blanche Taix, Pearl Reid and Alta Macaulay.

Adjournment was then taken to the dance hall, where the principles and projects of the Order were presented in pageant form. Copa de Oro No. 105 exemplified the principles upon which the Order is founded—"Love of Home, Veneration of the Pioneers, Devotion to the Flag, and an Abiding Faith in the Existence of God." San Juan Bautista No. 179 exemplified the work the Order is doing in the way of preserving and restoring historic landmarks, directing particular attention to the landmarks of San Benito County. Aleli No. 102 presented Mary E. Brusie, engaged in the splendid work of caring for homeless children; members of the Parlor represented adopted children who have been carefully reared in the homes of foster parents; a wonderful box of dainty garments, made by Aleli girls, manifested keen interest in doing their bit to provide for helpless little tots. Santa Cruz No. 26 exemplified the great work it is doing to assist in caring for veterans of the World War. Games, dancing, a "midnite feed" and the usual serenade during early morning hours closed a happy evening. Sunday opened with a pajama breakfast, after which sports were enjoyed until noontime. During luncheon Grand President Carlson gave a brief talk and commended the Parlors of the district for their activities. Story telling and community singing by the eighty-two in attendance added to the happiness of the occasion.

Past President GENEVIEVE HISKEY (center) of Santa Ana No. 235 presenting flags to Santa Ana American Legion, as recounted in October Grizzly Bear. LEO FROSTIFER (left) and EDDIE CORAN (right), who accepted the flags.

Assists at Neighbor's Reorganization.

Sierraville—Imogen No. 134 had its annual reunion recently for the Pioneers, whose ranks are fast thinning. The guest of honor was "Grandma" Emma Perry, 90 years of age. The festal board was beautifully decorated in a rose-colored scheme. Among the speakers were Past Grand President Emma Lou Humphrey and two of Sierra Valley's Pioneers. Many of the members appeared in old-fashioned garments, ransacked from local storerooms, thus giving an early-day atmosphere to the occasion.

Sixteen members of the Parlor motored to Downieville October 2 to assist in the reorganization of Naomi No. 36. Fifteen candidates were initiated, the officers of Imogen exemplifying the ritual. Officers of Naomi were installed by District Deputy Neva McMahon, Irene Carter becoming president. A chicken supper was served. A color scheme of green was carried out, with a corsage of rosebuds and maidenhair fern at each place. The decorations and corsages were the gift of Past Grand President Humphrey. Thus came to a perfect end a beautiful Indian summer day.

New Parlors in Prospect.

San Bernardino—Lugonia No. 241 had a large attendance at its pot-luck supper October 14. Among the visitors were District Deputy Hazel Hansen and a delegation from Verdugo No. 240 (Glendale). Entertainment followed the dinner, and at the Parlor meeting Mrs. Hansen, who is also vice-chairman of the Grand Parlor Extension of the Order Committee, announced that plans are under way for the formation of parlors in Ontario, Chino, Redlands and Riverside.

October 24 Lugonia had a bridge tea and fashion show for the benefit of its Loyalty Pledge fund; Gladys Baker was in charge. October 28 several candidates were initiated, committees were named for the annual Christmas children's party, and plans for 1932 activities were formulated. The parlor was represented in the October 30 mardigras by a float of humorous nature; a committee headed by Rhoda Smith had charge.

State Flag Given School.

Oakland—The monthly whist of Aloha No. 106 October 13 was largely attended and greatly enjoyed; refreshments were served; Irma S. Murray was chairman of the committee. A tea was sponsored October 24 at the home of Jennie Peterson for the benefit of the Luther Burbank foundation fund. The Parlor joined with Athens No. 195 N.S.G.W. October 27 for a Hallowe'en party; entertainment and refreshments were in keeping with the occasion.

October 16 Aloha presented a California State (Bear) Flag to the Jefferson school in East Oakland. Gladys I. Farley was chairman of the day, and Grand Secretary Sallie R. Thaler made the presentation address. The Parlor has under way plans for an Armistice Day dance November 10, and a dinner at the home of Mary Dowd Reardon November 16.

The Perfect Meeting.

San Jose—Grand President Evelyn I. Carlson was royally received by Vendome No. 100 October 7, the occasion of her official visit. Members of the past presidents club and officers of the Parlor acted as a reception committee. The latter wore white evening gowns and carried arm boquets of long-stemmed yellow chrysanthemums. The Grand President's party included Grand Secretary Sallie Thaler, Grand Trustee Ethel Begley, Grand Outside Sentinel Orinda Giannini, Grand Organist Lola Horgan, Past Grand President Emma G. Foley, Supervising Deputy Clara Gairaud, District Deputies Ida Sweeney, Catherine Derry, Geraldine Brown, Marie Buck, Catherine Keating, Emma O'Meara, Pauline Cleu, Ada May Silva, Augusta Huxol. It was one of the most brilliant affairs in the history of the Parlor, with a record attendance of visitors. Delegations from fifteen Parlors were present, among them being the surprise delegation from the Grand President's Parlor, Dolores No. 169 (San Francisco). Mrs. Carlson was the recipient of gifts and flowers. A dinner preceded the official visit, and refreshments were served at the close of "the perfect meeting," the verdict of those present. Vendome expects to receive a large class of candidates before the close of this term.

The Santa Clara County Pioneer Association was entertained by the Parlor September 30. Luncheon at noon was followed by a program presented by Clara Gairaud and Tillie Brohaska. Dorothy Lorentz, Hazel Haub and Gertrude Mathers were the soloists, while Congressman Arthur Free (Observatory No. 177 N.S.G.W.) and Judge Urban Sontheimer (San Jose No. 22 N.S.G.W.) were the principal speakers. A round table of reminiscences, during which the Pioneers took part, proved extremely interesting. Mrs. Julia Waddington was in charge of the luncheon. A card party was held October 14, with Gertrude Musser as chairman. Hazel Haub was chairman of the annual Hallowe'en party. The one hundred dollar Christmas gift party will be held early in December; Clara Gairaud is the general chairman, and a large crowd is expected.

Contest Losers To Serve Dinner.

Santa Ana—The first of a series of winter Santa Ana No. 235 card parties was given September 22 at the home of Mrs. Wm. West, who was assisted by her daughter, Mrs. Wm. Mize. A silver offering social, the proceeds to go to the fund for the preservation of the Luther Burbank home, was held September 29 at the home of Mrs. Walter Hiskey; bridge and five hundred were played. The Parlor presented a silver cake dish to its recent bride, formerly Marjory Reed, now Mrs. Marjory Hall.

District Deputy Hazel Hansen was a visitor at the September 28 meeting, when announcement was made that the losers in a membership contest would give a dinner for the winners November 1; Mrs. Gertrude Carter is chairman of arrangements. Mrs. Genevieve Hiskey was appointed chairman of the thimble club.

Service One of Life's Highest Goals.

Willows—Youth and age alike enjoyed themselves at Berryessa No. 192's annual entertainment for the oldtimers September 28. The guests were given a warm welcome and were seated at tables attractively decorated with flowers. President Aileen Murphy presided, and Mrs. Edna Knight was the speaker of the evening. "Service for one's fellowman is one of the highest goals one may have in life," said Mrs. Knight, who compared the life led by Father Junipero Serra to the lives of the later Pioneers of California.

After the dinner a puppet show, "Red Riding Hood," was presented under the supervision of Mrs. Marvin Deter, who was assisted by Frances and Vivian Turman, Maxine Jansen, Betty Sanderson and Irene Boyd. Other entertainment features, all of which were greatly enjoyed, were presented by "Chiquita," Edith Smith, Mrs. Frank Turman, "The Victorians," Mrs. Norma Snowden and Mrs. Laura Cummins.

Golden Anniversary Surprise.

San Juan Bautista—San Juan Bautista No.

179 sponsored a delightful surprise party October 7 in honor of Past President Catherine Breen-Nyland's golden wedding anniversary. The color scheme of gold was carried out in every detail. Following delicious refreshments, toasts, presentations of gifts and the singing of songs popular fifty years ago rounded out a happy occasion. Mrs. Nyland, a member of the Parlor, is a daughter of John Breen, who came to California with the Reed-Donner Party.

Mrs. Charlotte Breen-Obenchain, sister of Past President Nyland and Recording Secretary Gertrude Breen of the Parlor, passed away October 15 at Medford, Oregon.

Past Presidents and Grand Officers Guests.

Sacramento—Sutter No. 111 entertained October 6 its past presidents and some of the grand officers. Each past president received a token, and the following grand officers received gifts and flowers: Grand Trustee Edna Briggs, Supervising Deputies Bessie Leitch and Ethel Ludwig, District Deputies Mayme McCormick, Nellie Nordstrom, Doris Fisher and Sadie Brainard. President Lorene Patterson presented to the Parlor a California State (Bear) Flag and fittingly commented on the flag's history. A program was presented by Velverine and Viola Steen, Emilie Lachmann, Ida Merwin, Margaret Nix and the Sutter Parlor glee club.

Lorraine Williams was chairman of the banquet which concluded the occasion. She was assisted by the following hostesses, each of whom presided at a table on which a different color scheme was used in the decorations: Ida Merwin, Lily Tilden, Audrey Brown, Dora Hubert, Hazel Wygant, Emilie Lachmann, Lorene Patterson and Lavinia Bennetts.

New Entertainment Feature.

Oroville—Short talks on the history of California's pioneer families by Mms. Maggie D. Bowers and Sonora Steadman were given at the October 7 meeting of Gold of Ophir No. 190, thus inaugurating a new departure in entertainment features planned by President Jessie Hoover. One candidate was initiated and refreshments were served.

Butte County Past Presidents Association was entertained at the home of Misses Mattie and Irene Lund October 2. In recognition of her fifty-third wedding anniversary Mrs. Mattie Kesseiring was presented with a gift, Mrs. Margaret Hudspeth making the presentation on behalf of the association. The annual banquet of the association will be held at Richardson Springs November 4.

Grand President's Official Itinerary.

San Francisco—During the month of November, Grand President Evelyn I. Carlson will officially visit the following Subordinate Parlors on the dates noted:

2nd—Oakdale No. 125, Oakdale.
3rd—Veritas No. 75, Merced.
4th—Eldora No. 248, Turlock.
9th—Eschol No. 16, Napa.
11th—Placer No. 138, Lincoln.
12th—Eltapome No. 55, Weaverville.
14th—Lassen View No. 98, Shasta; Camellia No. 41, Anderson; Hiawatha No. 140, Redding; Berendos No. 23, Red Bluff; jointly at Redding.
16th—Palo Alto No. 229, Palo Alto.
17th—Richmond No. 147, Richmond.
18th—Minerva No. 2, San Francisco.
19th—Santa Rosa No. 217, Santa Rosa.
24th—Bret Harte No. 232, San Francisco.
30th—San Francisco district meeting.

"How a Woman Keeps a Secret."

Oakland—Piedmont No. 87 September 24 had what it terms "oldtimers night," an evening annually set aside by the Parlor to entertain, in particular, the older members. At the close of the meeting the committee presented a one-act play, "How a Woman Keeps a Secret;" from its title, one may easily judge it was a comedy. After this a mystery bag was set up, and from it a lot of fun was derived. Rose Martinelli and her committee then invited all to the banquet-room, to feast on spaghetti, french bread and home-made cakes.

Interest in Membership Drive.

Fullerton—Grace No. 242 is having a drive for new members. The entire membership is divided under two captains, and much interest is manifest. The losing side will entertain with a dinner at the close of the contest. The Parlor had a public card party October 1, sponsored by the ways and means committee. It was a success, both socially and financially. District Deputy Ora Evans and party from Californiana No. 247 (Los Angeles) were present.

(Continued on Page 17)

Feminine World's Fads and Fancies

PREPARED ESPECIALLY FOR THE GRIZZLY BEAR BY ANNA STOERMER

FASHIONABLE GIRLS LIKE THE SIMple coats. First of all, comfortable and warm coats that they may thoroughly enjoy. For girls from six to fourteen coats are made of tweeds, chinchillas, camel hair, fleeces and some suede-finished fabrics. But in girls' coats, as well as those for adults, the rougher surfaced fabrics are the most fashionable. Sometimes they are fur-trimmed, and sometimes they are not so adorned. Usually durable furs like racoon, opossum, nutria and beaver are used, but occasionally squirrel trims a dressier coat or a tiny touch of leopard is used on the sporty model.

The older girl wears much the same style coat as that of her mother—a monotone tweed with a shawl collar of racoon. The dark tones of the fur blend nicely with brown and biege diagonal tweed. Sometimes the coats are cut with the new deep, roomy armholes. They are dress length, and belted snugly. Some have raglan sleeves, some set-in, and a few, mostly for the bigger girls, have the new dolman sleeve. Some of the sleeves have fullness at the elbow or below, just as do grown-ups' coat sleeves. There are lots of buttons on girls' coats—another good adult fashion for girls, as is the belt. If you want your young daughter to look like the Empress Eugenie, as do many mothers, there are dressy coats with little capelets that look like the tiny capes and yokes that were worn in those days for school wear.

The brown jersey frock for utility is worn beneath the tweed coat and has a pleated skirt and a blouse with detachable collar and cuffs. A bolero frock of crepe-de-chine is equally smart, with its velveteen bolero or without it. Fagoting is used to trim this dainty dress.

Taffeta has an important air, and little girls love to wear it. A dress of this material has a circular skirt with a long-waisted bodice. The joining has a diagonal line finished with two circular tiers at the hip-line. The sash and shoulder bow match the rosebud printed silk. Of course, the little party dresses are adorable with the new puffed sleeves now being worn. Many clever ideas are worked out for the little ones. There is the seamless bolero, which is cut like a bed coat. It adds charm to the youngster's dainty frock. Taffeta not only rustles by itself in frocks for the small child, but is also used under lace for the debutante.

When the new hats first appeared everyone agreed that they would call for special clothes. Period styles have appeared, mostly for evening dresses. Something else happened, also, to make the new clothes look right with the new hats, so wide sleeves came in—the big surprise of the season.

Sleeves are very elaborate, with cuffs applied at any hight. While elbow puffs are on many models, some have detachable sleeves, the removal of which entirely alters the frock. The coat dress is with us again, and may be created of canton crepe or silk-and-wool combination, a splendid style for the stout figure.

It is just a matter of selecting, from all the fashionable things, those that do not emphasize oversize. There is no need for any woman to look as though she had suddenly gained flesh when she puts on this fall's clothes. Some of the styles play into the hands of the large woman. The silhouette is not necessarily very slim. As a matter of fact, it has more curves than it has had for a long time, and wider shoulders.

The smart, large woman, like the women of every size, this year starts selecting her dresses by buying, first, a new corset—one that makes her figure. Then she can wear the new coat dress, the convenient one that goes on and fastens like a coat. It is adjustable and may be wrapped as tight or as loose as is becoming. The smartest coat dress is the one that fastens over in the diagonal closing, and it happens to be the best type for the large woman. The one-sided rever is another smart idea for the coat dress, as it breaks the line at the bust.

The wide crushed belt may be worn when it is the same color and material as the dress. Don't wear contrasting colors in your belts. They emphasize the waist-line and the difference in size. Narrow banding of flat fur is a good trim, because of the soft line it gives around the neck. Avoid wide fur banding or furs that add bulk, as they make one seem heavier. And there are many kinds of new sleeves that help to equalize or balance large parts of the figure, making less marked the difference in sizes between waist, hips and bust.

Smartest new woolens are sheer and fine. Smartest silks are dull finished. Thus they are both helpful to the large figure. Skirts long enough to cover the most of the leg are what every woman wears, whether she be large or small. Satin is a fabric that plays an important role in groups, and while the shiny surface is frequently chosen for the entire frock, there are many examples of the use of crepe satin with both dull and lustrous surfaces. This combination of the two is offered in interesting fashion with alternate bands and curved panels. Often the dull surface is introduced in a yoke that forms the hip-line and waist-line section of the frock, thus giving a slender appearance at that portion of the figure.

Colors are richer. Fewer pastel shades are being worn, the general taste running to wines and carmines, a new bright blue and browns of every hue. Brown combined with fall oak-leaf tones is the principal shade this season for women's suits, dresses and coats. Next in preference is black, green or dark blue.

Coats are plain, and adaptable in soft tweeds with fur trimmings. The line is very neat and the material often contrasts with the material of the dress or hat with which it is worn.

Hats are small but usually have a tiny brim, either turned up cuff-like against the crown or slightly drooping or sloping over one eye. Several models suggest Tyrolean inspiration. Because of this feature, we see the brush and small quill ornament poised high at the side back crown. All felts used are thin, supple and usually plain. Crowns are still shallow and close to the head, and are often fitted with darts or raised tucks.

All trimming motifs are small and perky, ranging from crisp, pointed quills to odd-shaped motifs in flat fur. Broadtail or galyok and ostrich feathers are not only coming into their own again on hats, but are used for fans.

If your new fall dresses don't look good on you, look to your lingerie. It is almost as disastrous to wear last fall's lingerie as last year's dresses. The new lingerie is cut to fit like the new dresses—smooth and sleek. Hips are smoother and narrower, with the fullness taken out. New chemises, slips and panties are cut on the bias and seamed diagonally. They hug the outlines of the figure almost as close as your own skin, and without the use of elastic.

Some of the new panties, in fact, have no fullness, but fit the thighs and are made with flat yoke all around or flat waistband. Chemises and slips are designed much the same through the waist section, with V-shaped cutting and seaming.

Armistice Day—Armistice Day, November 11, a national holiday, will be celebrated in several California towns and cities.

BOOK REVIEWS

(CLARENCE M. HUNT.)

"SWINGING THE CENSER."

By Katherine M. Bell; Finlay Press, Hartford, Connecticut, Publisher; Price $2.75.

"Swinging the Censer" is a collection of selected reminiscences of Old Santa Barbara related by Mrs. Katherine M. Bell, who was born there July 22, 1844, and passed away June 9, 1926. All her life having been spent in that city, she had first-hand knowledge of the events and the personages referred to. Mrs. Bell was the daughter of Dr. Nicholas A. Den, a native of Ireland who reached Santa Barbara July 8, 1836, and Rosa A. Hill, daughter of Daniel Hill, a native of Massachusetts who came to California in 1822 as first officer of the sailing vessel "Rover," and Rafael Luisa Ortega, direct descendant of Jose Maria Ortega who, as commander of Spanish soldiers, came to San Diego in 1799. "Never was Irish, Spanish and Puritan blood better blended than in Katherine M. Bell," writes C. A. Storke.

The volume deals in a most pleasing way with history and romance of early California, particularly that associated with Santa Barbara. Homage is paid to Concepcion Arguello ("La Beata")—San Francisco heroine of a romance of 1806 immortalized by Bret Harte in his poem, "Concepcion de Arguello,"—for some time a resident of Santa Barbara and who the author, "as a child, knew and loved." "Dark Transition Days, Black Pages in the History of Santa Barbara," tells of the career of the notorious Jack Powers and his lawless band. "Santa Barbara's Royal Sunday, October 12, 1919," appeared originally in The Grizzly Bear. Among the many other reminiscences are: "Santa Barbara's First Circus," "A Midnight Reverie," "Memories of Far-off Days" and "The Story of Manuelita, a True Romance of Old California."

Mrs. Bell dedicated these reminiscences to her grandchildren, and her children—Katherine Bell-Cheney, Caroline Bell-Luton, Mary Bell-Cheney and Charles Den Bell—in turn dedicated "Swinging the Censer" to her memory. The memorial volume is embellished with drawings by Margaret Webb and portraits of the author in costumes of various periods.

WINTER VINEYARD

(TED ROBINS.)

As to cold sky the impotent mother lifts
Imploring arms in confident despair,
So the gray earth breaks somnolence with prayer,
Raising her dark dry vines. The pale sand sifts
Through the gnarled fingers and in sullen drifts
Covers the iron-strong wrists, the rusty hair
Of summer grasses. The resentful air
Mourns drowsily late autumn's vanished gifts.

Where is the fire of the grape, the gleam
Presaging passion, the virility
To still the whimpers of the winds that grieve?
Waked from the twilight of a somber dream,
Forced by the sun to new fertility,
The earth, like some lean Sarah, must conceive.

—University California Chronicle.

FEDERAL GOVERNMENT DEVELOPS NEW FROZEN FRUIT PRODUCT.

A new and delicious type of frozen fruit product has been developed by experiments in the United States Department of Agriculture and offers new possibilities for the utilization of various fruits, according to Dr. F. C. Blanck, in charge of the food research division of the bureau of chemistry and soils. Experiments at the bureau's laboratory of fruit and vegetable chemistry in Los Angeles, have included peaches, apricots, plums, cherries, pears, raspberries and strawberries.

"By pulping the pitted fruit, adding a sugar syrup of proper concentration, mixing it thoroughly, and then freezing it at very low temperatures, department chemists have developed a frozen fruit product with a remarkably smooth texture and with the full retention of the original flavor which makes it suitable, and acceptable for direct consumption," says Dr. Blanck.

"If the results measure up to their present promise, this new type of frozen product will offer a new outlet for the fruit grower and packer, besides furnishing the ice-cream manufacturer and soda-fountain operator with a new and highly desirable fruit base, as well as a new frozen fruit product for direct consumption in the frozen state."

Native Sons of the Golden West

AUBURN—THE OLD EMIGRANT TRAIL from Auburn to Lake Tahoe—a line of march vividly reminiscent of the early California rush period, when wagons of emigrant trains crossed the summit of the Sierra at an elevation of more than 8,000 feet to seek the fertile valleys of the interior or to search for gold in the rugged mountains,—has been marked by an expedition sent out on horseback by Auburn No. 59, consisting of Wendell T. Robie, who was in charge, Earl Lukens, Dr. Conrad Briner, Lavelle Shields, William Patrick and Supervisor M. C. Langstaff. Four days were required for the jaunt.

At the summit the party placed a Flag of the United States of America on the monument erected by Robert "Bob" Watson, 80-year-old Tahoe City constable, who made the last two days of the trip, from Robertson's Flat to Tahoe City, with the party. The trail is now marked so clearly that parties desiring to retrace the steps of the hardy Pioneers would have no difficulty in following it from Auburn to the lake. It is a beautiful trip, too, and presents some of the most naturally wonderful views in California.

A committee from the Parlor—Alvin Waddle, Arnold Dorer, Matt Langstaff and Wendell Robie—went to the Placer County Big Tree Grove October 4 and planted several sequoia gigantaea. These California big trees are found only in a few isolated groves. The Placer County grove, the most northern, contains eight mature standing trees, but they are not reproducing themselves.

Admission Day Parade Awards.

Los Angeles—Winners of awards in the Admission Day parade were announced October 13 by Past Grand President Herman C. Lichtenberger as follows:

Most authentic and beautiful float with best presented marching unit—San Francisco Parlors N.S.G.W. and N.D.G.W., and Santa Barbara County Parlors N.S.G.W. and N.D.G.W., grand sweepstakes.

N.S.G.W. marching unit—Guadalupe Parlor No. 231 (San Francisco), first; Marin County Parlors, second; Alameda County Parlors, third.

N.D.G.W. marching unit—Guadalupe Parlor No. 153 (San Francisco), first; Marin County Parlors, second; Alameda County Parlors, third.

N.S.G.W. band—Piedmont Parlor No. 120 (Oakland).

N.S.G.W. drum corps—Napa Parlor No. 62, first; Mount Tamalpais Parlor No. 64 (San Rafael), second.

N.S.G.W. drill team—Castro Parlor No. 232 (San Francisco).

N.D.G.W. drum corps—Tamelpa Parlor No. 231 (Mill Valley), first; Mission Parlor No. 227 (San Francisco), second.

N.D.G.W. drill team—El Carmelo No. 181 (Daly City), first; Twin Peaks Parlor No. 185 (San Francisco), second.

WE REALLY OUGHT TO GO.

There is a brother, O, my brother,
Whose pulse is sinking low;
It is now we ought to see him,
And we really ought to go.

We might be down with sorrow
'Till our backs begin to bow,
But let us see our brother,
For we really ought to go.

For if there comes the reaper
And his life would choose to mow,
We would be very sorry,
So we really ought to go.

And a very little visit
Might cheer a heart that's low
And perhaps would cast some sunshine;
O, we really ought to go.

Let's not sing in sorrow
In the yard where poppies grow,
But at once to see our brother
O, God, do let us go!

And when I get to Heaven
I really want to know
That I've often seen my brother,
For I really ought to go.

There is a place in Heaven
Where the good are known to go
And I am sure it there is written,
You really ought to go.

(The above is published at the request of Los Angeles Parlor No. 45 N.S.G.W. It was written by Owen S. Adams, second vice-president, and by him read before the Parlor at a recent meeting.—Editor.)

Public School Dedicated.

Antioch—Under the auspices of General Winn No. 32 the grand officers dedicated October 11 Antioch's new $145,000 high school in the presence of 500 people. A program was presented, including vocal and instrumental selections, and addresses by Dr. Frank I. Gonzalez, Grand President; William H. Hanlon, superintendent Contra Costa County schools; Mrs. R. L. Knight, president Antioch-Live Oak P.T.A.; Lester J. Bower, commander Harding Post American Legion; Judge Fletcher A. Cutler, Past Grand President.

Commander Bower, on behalf of the American Legion, and Judge Cutler, on behalf of General Winn Parlor, presented, respectively, to the school United States of America and California State (Bear) Flags. They were accepted by Miss Verna Marchetti and Miss Emma Dragon of the student body.

The dedicatory ceremonies were conducted by Grand President Dr. Frank I. Gonzalez, Past Grand President Charles L. Dodge, Grand First Vice-president Seth Millington, Grand Third Vice-president Chas. A. Koenig and Grand Secretary John T. Regan. Grand Trustee Samuel M. Shortridge Jr. was also in attendance.

Humboldt Past Presidents Organize.

Ferndale—Humboldt Past Presidents Assembly No. 13 was instituted at Eureka by officers of the General Assembly. A banquet attended by past presidents of the Humboldt County Parlors—Humboldt No. 14 (Eureka), Arcata No. 20 and Ferndale No. 93—preceded the ceremonies. R. H. Flowers of Ferndale became the first governor. The Assembly meets monthly, alternating between the three Parlors. The next meeting will be at Eureka, with Humboldt No. 14.

A whist tournament between Ferndale and Humboldt has been arranged for the winter. A series of basketball games will be played by Arcata and Ferndale; these contests promise to be big drawing cards.

Membership Standing Largest Parlors.

San Francisco—Grand Secretary John T. Regan reports the standing of the Subordinate Parlors having a membership of over 400 January 1, 1931, as follows, together with their membership figures October 20, 1931:

Parlor	Jan. 1	Oct. 20	Gain	Loss
Ramona No. 109	1163	1168	5	..
South San Francisco No. 157	828	826	..	2
Castro No. 232	690	702	12	..
Stanford No. 76	644	640	..	4
Twin Peaks No. 214	723	634	..	89
Arrowhead No. 110	608	632	24	..
Stockton No. 7	562	560	..	2
Piedmont No. 120	510	521	11	..
Rincon No. 72	463	456	..	7

Initiation at Historic Shrine.

Sacramento—Sacramento No. 3, Sunset No. 26 and La Bandera No. 110 N.D.G.W. had a Hallowe'en party October 16 in honor of La Bandera's drill team, which made its first public appearance. Hallowe'en motifs were used in the decorations. Cards and dancing were in order, and refreshments were served.

Under the auspices of General John A. Sutter Assembly of Past Presidents, the Sacramento County Parlors of Native Sons will conduct a joint class initiation at Sutter Fort, Tuesday night, November 10.

November 14 the Sacramento City Parlors of Native Sons and Native Daughters will have their annual charity ball, for the benefit of the homeless children, at Memorial Auditorium. A. W. Katzenstein heads the general committee of arrangements.

"Days of '49" Celebration.

Sonoma—Sonoma No. 111 will stage its annual "Days of '49" celebration November 13 and 14. Friday night will be given over to a banquet for men only. Saturday night a dance will be featured. Other events, to round out a most complete program, are being arranged, and the carnival spirit will reign throughout the celebration.

The committee in charge is composed of C. E. Bacigalupi (chairman), Emil Andrieux, David J. Eraldi, Joe Andrieux, A. Barrachi, Fred Batto Jr. and Joe Keiser.

CLASSIFIED DIRECTORY
LOS ANGELES NATIVE SONS

ATTORNEYS-AT-LAW.

J. A. ADAIR. J. A. ADAIR JR.
516-18 Fay Bldg., Third and Hill.
Office: MAdison 1141 —Phones— Res.: GLadstone 8042.

HENRY G. BODKIN. V. P. LUCAS.
Chester Williams Bldg., 215 W. 5th St.
Phone: MUtual 5151.

WM. J. HUNSAKER.
458 So. Spring St., Room 1130.
Phone: TRinity 6656.

EDWIN A. MESERVE. SHIRLEY E. MESERVE.
555 So. Flower St.
Phone: TRinity 6161.

THOS. B. REED.
548 So. Spring Street.
Phone: VAndike 0687.

THOMAS P. WHITE.
924 California Bldg., 205 So. Broadway.
Phone: TRinity 6011.

DETECTIVE SERVICE.

LOUIS A. DUNI.
1121 Washington Bldg., 311½ So. Spring.
Phone: TUcker 3013.

PHYSICIAN AND SURGEON.

WILBUR B. PARKER, M.D.
11th Floor Brack Shops, 527 W. 7th St.
Phone: TRinity 5789.
Practice Limited to Urology.

Library Gets Valued Gift.

Livermore—Las Positas No. 96 has presented to the California history section of the local public library an illustrated bound volume of fifty-three typewritten pages dealing with the history of the Livermore Valley. It is a compilation of the essays written by the history students of the Livermore high school in competition in the annual contest sponsored by the Parlor.

The volume is dedicated to Robert Livermore, after whom the valley was named: "In reverent memory of him who had courage to brave the unknown, perseverance to hold his own, willingness to do the right, friendliness for all in plight—Robert Livermore."

Ritual Contest Beneficial.

San Rafael—Marin County Past Presidents Assembly was reorganized through the untiring efforts of James F. Stanley October 5. Ten candidates were initiated by San Francisco Assembly No. 1, Jos. S. Rosa becoming governor. The reorganized Assembly meets alternately, beginning October, the first Monday at the hall of Mount Tamalpais No. 64 in San Rafael, and the first Wednesday at the hall of Sea Point No. 158 in Sausalito. Mount Tamalpais' drum and bugle corps won first prize at the San Francisco Columbus Day celebration October 11.

Much interest is manifest in the ritual contest between Mount Tamalpais and Sea Point, to be held November 17. The trophy, a gavel block surmounted by a bronze bear, is now in possession of the former Parlor. To hold the trophy either Parlor must win two out of three contests. Much interest has been stimulated by these contests, which have been held annually the past four years, and through them an unusually high standard of ritual efficiency is maintained.

Thanksgiving Eve Ball.

Colusa—Colusa No. 69 entertained a large number of guests September 28, including Native Sons and Daughters of Sutter City and members of Colusa No. 194 N.D.G.W. The hall was attractively decorated with the Order's colors. The evening was spent at cards and dancing, after which refreshments were served.

Thanksgiving Eve, November 25, the Parlor will sponsor a dance, proceeds from which will go to the fund being raised to erect a memorial in Will S. Green Park, Colusa's largest public square. The arrangements committee includes Phil Humburg Jr. (chairman), Percy Cooke, Will L. Ash, S. A. Ottenwalter and Erwin Burtis.

Charter Member Dead.

Napa City—Robert Parker Lamdin, a charter member and for forty-six years the treasurer of Napa No. 62, died September 25 survived by a wife. He was born here September 19, 1860, and was one of the best-known and most-respected citizens of Napa County.

Opinions Which Should be Heeded.

Madera—Madera No. 130 entertained San Joaquin Past Presidents Assembly No. 7, September 24, and members of the Order from Fresno, Merced and Madera were present in goodly numbers. A roast pig banquet was served. Great satisfaction was expressed for the wholesome reception given the visitors.

W. J. Mitchell (Fresno No. 25) was the toastmaster. The various speakers expressed the opinion that Native Sons should be foremost in endeavoring to impress on eligibles their duty to California through affiliation with the Order; also, that efforts should be consolidated to impress on members the importance of attending their Parlor meetings and taking an active interest in the Order. At the conclusion of the feast the Assembly had a business session.

Good Cause.

Menlo Park—Menlo No. 185 and Menlo No. 211 N.D.G.W. sponsored a garden party October 18 at the home of Mrs. Peter E. Bush for the benefit of the unemployment fund of Menlo Park. The sale of candy, ice cream, cakes, etc., helped to swell the fund. Prominent among those working for the good cause were Harry Weeden, C. T. Maloney, Phil Blanchard, Eugene Crane, E. J. Derry, Frances Maloney and Catherine Derry.

PINK LEMONS GROW IN CALIFORNIA.

Pink lemons have been found growing on a tree at Burbank, Los Angeles County, according to an announcement of the Federal Agricultural Department. "However, the tree is a rare specimen, and there is little chance of the pink lemonade industry switching to the new lemons for raw material. The tree is a bud sport (or freak) of the variegated Eureka lemon, which was developed from a limb variation of the Eureka lemon, discovered in 1911."

SAN FRANCISCO

THE BIG CITY THAT KNOWS HOW

NAPA CITY—THE ELEVENTH ANNUAL session of the General Assembly of the N.S.G.W. Past Presidents Association was held here October 11, under the auspices of Napa-Solano Counties Assembly No. 11, with fifty officers and delegates in attendance. The reports of the officers showed that during the year Humboldt County Assembly No. 13 had been instituted and Marin County Assembly No. 5 reorganized. Total membership of the General Assembly, as of June 30, 1931, was 829, a gain of twenty-six for the fiscal year.

Resolutions pertaining to immigration were adopted, among them one opposing application of the quota to Asiatics. Sacramento City was named as the meeting place of the 1932 session of the General Assembly, the date being October 15. The following officers were elected:

Louis J. Erb (San Francisco Assembly No. 1), governor general; Arthur J. Cleu (East Bay Assembly No. 3), junior past governor general; J. J. Longshore (General John A. Sutter Assembly No. 10), lieutenant-governor general; James F. Stanley (San Francisco Assembly No. 1), director general; John T. Regan (San Francisco Assembly No. 1), secretary-treasurer general; Frank Roemer (East Bay Assembly No. 3), marshal general; Frank Harrison (Napa-Solano Assembly No. 11), guard general; Frank Wilhelm (San Francisco Assembly No. 1), sentinel general; R. L. P. Bigelow (Fred H. Greely Assembly No. 6), W. A. Strong (San Joaquin Assembly No. 7), A. Gudehus (San Francisco Assembly No. 1), trustees general.

At the conclusion of the business session a banquet was served, with George Wineger as the toastmaster. Speakers included Louis F. Erb; Grand President Dr. Frank I. Gonzalez, Grand Third Vice-president Chas. A. Koenig and Grand Trustee Samuel M. Shortridge Jr., representing the Order of Native Sons; Arthur J. Cleu, J. J. Longshore, James F. Stanley, John T. Regan, Ed. L. Webber and Lowell Palmer. Splendid entertainment features were introduced.

The Past Presidents Association started in San Francisco about thirty years ago, and in time similar organizations came into being in various counties of the state. In 1921, at the suggestion of the parent body, the General Assembly was organized and it now has thirteen subordinate assemblies, all doing effective work for the advancement of the Order of Native Sons of the Golden West.

SALUTES TO ARGONAUTS.

To perpetuate in public interest the achievements of those Argonauts who originated the Society of California Pioneers in San Francisco, the society has arranged a series of salutes. Membership in the society was limited to those Pioneers who arrived in California prior to January 1, 1850. Of the founders, but five are alive—Jules Aroudou and J. H. P. Gedge of San Francisco, Frances Doud of Monterey City, and Sam Brannan Jr. of San Diego City.

The first salute, October 15, honored Louis Sloss. A native of Germany, he arrived at Sacramento in August 1849 and conducted a wholesale grocery there until 1862, when he took up his residence in San Francisco, where he died in 1902. Thirty-six of his descendants attended the function. Among the speakers were Judge M. C. Sloss, C. C. Moore, James N. Gillett, Mayor Angelo J. Rossi, Leland W. Cutler and Dr. Frank I. Gonzalez, Grand President N.S.G.W.

HOMELESS CHILDREN BENEFIT.

The San Francisco N.S.G.W. and N.D.G.W. Homeless Children Committee will hold its annual benefit ball at the Civic Auditorium Thanksgiving Eve, November 25. Officers of the committee have been elected, as follows:

James L. Foley, chairman; Cora Stobing, vice-chairman; Edna A. Urmy, recording secretary; Bertha Mauser, financial secretary; Chas. A. Koenig, treasurer.

HISTORIC SITE MARKED.

Tamalpais Chapter, Daughters of the American Revolution, October 3 unveiled at Clay street and Grant avenue a marker designating the site of San Francisco's first residence. Among the speakers were Mayor Angelo J. Rossi, Police Chief John R. Quinn and Past Grand President Lewis F. Byington of the Native Sons, and Mrs. Frank Phelps Toms, state regent of the D.A.R.

According to the organization's records, this residence was erected in 1836 by Jacob Primer Leese, a native of Ohio who came to California in 1833. The Flag of the United States of America was hoisted over the place—the first time this country's flag was raised in San Francisco. In this residence, too, San Francisco's first White child, Rosalia Vallejo Leese, was born, April 15, 1838.

PERPLEXING QUESTION SOLVED.

Alta Parlor No. 3 N.D.G.W. happily solved the perplexing question of delinquent members by establishing October 12 a relief fund, the nucleus of which is the $35 refunded by the fiesta committee. Under the efficient guidance of District Deputy Annie Franzen the Parlor is preparing for initiation.

Alta has just made a substantial payment on its Loyalty Pledge and plans to complete it before the 1932 Grand Parlor. The Home is a hobby with Grand Trustee Annie C. Thuesen and Elizabeth F. Douglass. Another ardent worker for it is Second Vice-president May L. MacDonald, whose latest donation is a beautiful throw to adorn the baby grand in the lounge of the imposing edifice.

GLEE CLUB ENTERTAINS.

Fremont Parlor No. 59 N.D.G.W. entertained October 6 Grand President Evelyn I. Carlson, who spoke on the homeless children and the Loyalty Pledge. She was handed a check for $100 for the Parlor's pledge. Supervising Deputy May C. Boldeman also spoke, and Grand Organist Lola Horgan and her glee club furnished entertainment. Supper was served to 200 members and guests, the banquetroom being beautifully decorated in red, white and blue.

The arrangements committee included Ella Tait, Katherine McGrath, Julia McDermott, May Grantley, Margaret Carter, Ella Herd, Anita Johnson, Louise Adami, Ella Becker, Hannah Collins and Abby Groom.

SURPRISE FOR ENCOURAGEMENT.

The newly-installed officers of Gabrielle Parlor No. 139 N.D.G.W. were so well pleased with the large number of members that attended the first meeting at which they presided decided to encourage them to come often and gave a surprise party. Mrs. Ruth Koler was chairman. Chicken patties, coffee and delicious homemade cake were served.

Gabrielle, together with Rincon Parlor No. 72 N.S.G.W., had a Hallowe'en party October 28. A Christmas whist party will be held December 7; proceeds are to go to the Loyalty Pledge fund of the Parlor.

UNUSUAL OCCASION.

September 24, El Dorado Parlor No. 52 N.S.G.W. held a ceremony unique in the annals of the Order. It was "Jack Thomas night," in honor of Jack Thomas, a past president and member of Quartz Parlor No. 58 (Grass Valley) for some thirty-three years, but who, during the twenty years he has lived in San Francisco, has faithfully and regularly attended the meetings of El Dorado. Thomas has served on No. 52's committees and has visited its sick time and time again.

In honor of the occasion, National No. 118 and Olympus No. 189 Parlors came in a body. Frank I. Butler extended greetings on behalf of Olympus and President William Brennan expressed the sentiments of National. Past President Robert Donohue made the principal address and presented Jack Thomas with a pen and pencil on behalf of El Dorado. Following this, Secretary Frank A. Bonivert read a communication from Quartz Parlor extending congratulations. Accompanying the letter was a nugget ring of Nevada County gold, a gift to Thomas from his home-Parlor in appreciation of his loyalty to it. Addresses were also made by Past Presidents John Hauer and A. B. Chaquette of El Dorado and Historian Peter Conmy of Golden Gate Parlor No. 29. Following the meeting a midnight supper was enjoyed.

13TH LUCKY DAY.

Presidio Parlor No. 148 N.D.G.W. was honored October 13 by having Grand President Evelyn I. Carlson pay her official visit. So hereafter the members will consider the 13th a lucky day. The Parlor's drill team most colorfully added to the entrance march, and later escorted the Grand

President to a seat of honor. Large palms at various points in the room added both color and beauty when intermingled with the flags.

Among the other grand officers in attendance were Grand Trustees Ethel Begley and Anna Thuesen, Grand Inside Sentinel Orinda G. Giannini, Past Grand Presidents May Boldeman and Margaret Grote-Hill. Grand Organist Lola Horgan, accompanied by the Native Daughter choral, contributed their talents, much to the success of the evening. Visitors from many Parlors were present. Grand President Carlson especially complimented Presidio for its wonderful war veteran welfare work; she also praised the officers on the initiatory and floor work.

SECRETS OF FUTURE REVEALED.

Golden Gate Parlor No. 158 N.D.G.W. had a Hallowe'en party October 26 and great interest was taken in the various styles of costumes worn. Many secrets of the future were revealed by a crystal-gazer. Members are busy working on a layette for the homeless children committee.

A few months ago the Parlor paid $200 toward its Loyalty Pledge. Since then good progress has been made in accumulating the balance, which will soon be paid.

HALLOWE'EN PAJAMA PARTY.

The Native Daughter Home was the setting of a delightful luncheon and bridge October 1, given in honor of Grand President Evelyn I. Carlson by Mrs. Hazel Nelson of Dolores Parlor No. 169 N.D.G.W. Those present were Irene Stelling, Clara Casella, Amelia Silva, Millie Ghirardelli, Erna Lazarus, Emma O'Meara, Mary Krause and Edna Gunther. Two candidates were initiated October 14; dainty refreshments were served.

A picnic was held at New Portola Park October 18 by the Parlor and Dolores Parlor No. 208 N.S.G.W.; games and races were enjoyed. October 20, the Dolores girls were guests of the Dolores boys at a Hallowe'en pajama party. No. 169's sewing club is planning to give a luncheon at the Native Daughter Home Wednesday, November 18.

PLEASING MEMORY.

The official visit of Grand President Evelyn I. Carlson to James Lick Parlor No. 220 N.D.G.W. September 30 is a pleasing memory. Preceding the meeting Mrs. Carlson, Supervising Deputy Mae Boldemann, District Deputy Loretta Cameron, her mother and five candidates were honored guests at a delightful dinner. Elizabeth Richards was chairman of the evening. The meeting was very impressive, with decorations of gold stars on larger pastel stars amongst the foliage. Each officer carried an old-fashioned boquet in blue and gold. Many grand officers, deputies and members visited.

Vocal selections were rendered by Adeline Dryer, and President Lyda Woods presented Grand President Carlson with a boquet of roses. The ritual being exemplified, the Grand President rejoiced over the Parlor's giving $50 toward its Loyalty Pledge and its co-operation in the membership drive. Other grand officers added much to the evening with pleasing remarks. Refreshments were enjoyed after the meeting. The Parlor has in preparation a baby shower for the benefit of the homeless children. An enthusiastic Hallowe'en party was enjoyed under the supervision of Irma Collins.

BRIDE-TO-BE SHOWERED.

Honoring Miss Hilder Nelson of Bret Harte Parlor No. 232 N.D.G.W., fiancee of Christian Eggers, a surprise miscellaneous shower was given October 7 at the home of Mrs. Pearl Wedde. The bride-to-be was the recipient of many lovely gifts.

OLD-LINE PRINTER DEAD.

Thomas C. Russell, one of the last of the old-line printers who used nothing but hand-set type, died at his San Francisco home September 25. At infrequent intervals he issued limited editions of California history works which are gems of the printer's art and have a considerable value.

STATES EXPEND VAST SUM FOR HIGHWAYS; SURFACED MILEAGE INCREASED.

The mileage of State highways in the United States surfaced during 1930 was 27,464, an increase over the preceding year, and state highway departments expended $980,000,000 on roads in the year, an increase of 22 percent over 1929, according to the Federal Agricultural Department's public roads bureau.

Total state income for highway purposes during the year was $1,136,673,437, and only nine states showed a decline in that income. The figures do not include work by counties, townships or other jurisdictions.

Approximately $37,200,000 will be spent on state highways in California during the year 1931, according to data compiled by the State Division of Highways. During the first seven months of this year, contracts were awarded for road construction amounting to $14,400,000. The corresponding figure for 1930 was $11,000,000.

CALIFORNIA'S TAXABLE WEALTH

(Continued from Page 7)

ramento, $1,623,236; Santa Barbara, $3,968,326; Santa Clara, $947,748; San Bernardino, $3,992,603; San Joaquin, $15,672,151; Ventura, $5,538,817; Contra Costa, $3,412,201.

But ten of California's fifty-eight counties show an increased grand total assessment for 1931, compared with 1930: Amador, $8,750,292 (1931), $8,575,305 (1930); $174,987 increase. Calaveras, $9,569,959 (1931), $9,557,105 (1930); $12,854 increase. Imperial, $56,029,605 (1931), $55,893,588 (1930); $136,017 increase. Inyo, $19,988,564 (1931), $19,694,765 (1930); $293,799 increase. Kings, $46,172,072 (1931), $44,248,847 (1930); $1,923,225 increase. Lassen, $26,416,117 (1931), $23,918,890 (1930); $2,497,227 increase. Mono, $6,823,360 (1931), $6,624,202 (1930); $199,158 increase. Placer, $29,766,132 (1931), $29,721,674 (1930); $44,458 increase. Riverside, $94,936,951 (1931), $84,675,560 (1930); $10,261,391 increase. Tuolumne, $12,543,652 (1931), $12,396,544 (1930); $147,108 increase.

Alpine County, with 50,827 acres of assessed land, stands alone in the six-figure grand-total class. Its 1931 assessment, $887,332, is $13,727 less than that of 1930, $901,059. Its indebtedness of $16,000 last year has been reduced to $14,000 this year. It has a tax rate of $2.

Kern County has the largest number of acres of assessed land, 3,847,296. San Bernardino County comes next, with 2,742,828, and then comes Fresno County, with 2,178,000.

The following counties are free of debt: Amador, Calaveras, Humboldt, Inyo, Madera, Mariposa, Mono, Nevada, Placer, Shasta, Sierra, Siskiyou, Tuolumne and Yuba.

FIFTY YEARS AGO

(Continued from Page 5)

Henry T. Showier of Sacramento was accidentally killed while duck hunting November 27.

A cave-in November 29 at the Wakeshaw mine at Ruby Hill, Nevada County, carried William Roberts into a flume, where he drowned.

John M. Boyles and Hugh Galway, old residents of Gridley, Butte County, had an altercation November 5, and Boyles stabbed Galway to death with a pocketknife.

Herbert Osborne, ranch employe of Mrs. Prince, a divorcee, at Marshall Landing, Sonoma County, November 12 beat her to death with a flatiron and then killed himself.

Lawrence Melchor and R. Smith, playing cards in a San Francisco saloon November 24, got into a quarrel, and Melchor shot Smith dead.

RUST ON SNAPDRAGONS.

Snapdragon rust is caused by a fungus that is hard to combat; it is far easier to prevent the rust than to cure it, although not always is either possible. Plants where this rust is liable to occur, such as damp localities along the coast, should be given fertilizer and care to make them as thrifty as possible to resist the disease. Whenever damp weather seems imminent, dust with finely ground sulphur, once every two weeks, or spray with Bordeaux. Snapdragons should be planted where they will get plenty of sun and where there is good air drainage.

"Content is the philosopher's stone that turns all it touches into gold."

Official Directory of Parlors of the N. D. G. W.

ALAMEDA COUNTY.

Angelita No. 32, Livermore—Meets 2nd and 4th Fridays, Foresters Hall; Mrs. Orlena Beck, Rec. Sec., 1109 First St.

Piedmont No. 87, Oakland—Meets Thursdays, Corinthian Hall, Pacific Bldg.; Mrs. Alice E. Miner, Rec. Sec., 421 36th St.

Aloha No. 106, Oakland—Meets Tuesdays, Wigwam Hall, Pacific Bldg.; Gladys I. Farley, Rec. Sec., 4623 Benevides Ave.

Hayward No. 122, Hayward—Meets 1st and 3rd Tuesdays, Bank Hayward Hall, "B" St.; Miss Ruth Gansberger, Rec. Sec., P. O. Box 44, Mount Eden.

Berkeley No. 150, Berkeley—Meets 1st Friday, Masonic Hall; Mrs. Lelia B. Baker, Rec. Sec., 915 Contra Costa Ave.

Bear Flag No. 151, Berkeley—Meets 2nd and 4th Wednesdays, Veterans Memorial Bldg., 1931 Center St.; Mrs. Maud Wagner, Rec. Sec., 317 Alcatraz Ave., Oakland.

Encinal No. 156, Alameda—Meets 2nd and 4th Thursdays, N.S.G.W. Hall; Mrs. Laura E. Fisher, Rec. Sec., 1413 Caroline St.

Brooklyn No. 157, East Oakland—Meets Wednesdays, Masonic Temple, 8th Ave. and E. 14th St.; Mrs. Ruth Cooney, Rec. Sec., 3907 14th Ave.

Argonaut No. 166, Oakland—Meets Tuesdays, Klinkner Hall, 59th and San Pablo; Mrs. Ada Spilman, Rec. Sec., 2905 Ellis St., Berkeley.

Bahia Vista No. 167, Oakland—Meets Thursdays, Wigwam Hall, Pacific Bldg.; Mrs. Minnie E. Raper, Rec. Sec., 3449 Helen St.

Fruitvale No. 177, Oakland—Meets Fridays, W.O.W. Hall; Mrs. Agnes M. Grant, Rec. Sec., 1224 30th Ave.

Laura Loma No. 182, Niles—Meets 1st and 3rd Tuesdays, I.O.O.F. Hall; Mrs. Ethel Fournier, Rec. Sec., P. O. Box 515.

El Cereso No. 207, San Leandro—Meets 2nd and 4th Tuesdays, Masonic Hall; Mrs. Mary Tuttle, Rec. Sec., P. O. Box 56.

Pleasanton No. 237, Pleasanton—Meets 1st and 3rd Tuesdays, I.O.O.F. Hall; Mrs. Myrtle Lanini, Rec. Sec.

Betsy Ross No. 238, Centerville—Meets 1st and 3rd Fridays, Anderson Hall; Miss Constance Lucio, Rec. Sec., P. O. Box 187.

AMADOR COUNTY.

Ursula No. 1, Jackson—Meets 2nd and 4th Tuesdays, N.S.G.W. Hall; Mrs. Emma Boarman-Wright, Rec. Sec., 114 Court St.

Chispa No. 40, Ione—Meets 2nd and 4th Fridays, N.S.G.W. Hall; Mrs. Isabel Ashton, Rec. Sec.

Amapola No. 80, Sutter Creek—Meets 2nd and 4th Thursdays, N.S.G.W. Bldg.; Mrs. Hazel M. Marre, Rec. Sec.

Forrest No. 86, Plymouth—Meets 2nd and 4th Tuesdays, I.O.O.F. Hall; Mrs. Marguerite Davis, Rec. Sec.

BUTTE COUNTY.

Annie K. Bidwell No. 168, Chico—Meets 2nd and 4th Thursdays, I.O.O.F. Hall; Mrs. Irene Henry, Rec. Sec., 3015 Woodland Ave.

Gold of Ophir No. 190, Oroville—Meets 1st and 3rd Wednesdays, Memorial Hall; Mrs. Ruth Brown, Rec. Sec., 1265 Leah Court.

CALAVERAS COUNTY.

Ruby No. 46, Murphys—Meets Fridays, N.S.G.W. Hall; Belle Segale, Rec. Sec.

Princess No. 84, Angels Camp—Meets 2nd Wednesday, I.O.O.F. Hall; Emma May, Rec. Sec.

San Andreas No. 113, San Andreas—Meets 1st Friday, Fraternal Hall; Miss Doris Treat, Rec. Sec.

COLUSA COUNTY.

Colus No. 194, Colusa—Meets 1st and 3rd Mondays, N.S.G.W. Hall; Mrs. Ruby Humburg, 223 Park Hill St.

CONTRA COSTA COUNTY.

Stirling No. 146, Pittsburg—Meets 1st and 3rd Wednesdays, Veteran Memorial Hall; Mrs. Minnie Marcelli, Rec. Sec., 771 E. 12th St.

Richmond No. 147, Richmond—Meets 1st and 3rd Tuesdays, I.O.O.F. Hall, 10th St.; Mrs. Tillie Summers, Rec. Sec., 640 So. 31st St.

Donner No. 193, Byron—Meets 1st and 3rd Wednesdays, I.O.O.F. Hall; Mrs. Anna Pendry, Rec. Sec., P. O. Box 112.

Las Juntas No. 221, Martinez—Meets 1st and 3rd Mondays, Pythias Castle; Mrs. Lola Viera, Rec. Sec., P. O. box 128.

Antioch No. 223, Antioch—Meets 2nd and 4th Tuesdays, I.O.O.F. Hall; Mrs. Estelle Evans, Rec. Sec., 202 E. 5th St., Pittsburg.

Carquinez No. 234, Crockett—Meets 2nd and 4th Wednesdays, I.O.O.F. Hall; Mrs. Cecile Petee, Rec. Sec., 165 Edwards St.

GRAND OFFICERS.

Mrs. Estelle M. Evans........Past Grand President
202 E. Fifth St., Pittsburg

Mrs. Evelyn I. Carlson............Grand President
1965 San Jose Ave., San Francisco

Mrs. Anna M. Armstrong.....Grand Vice-president
Woodland

Mrs. Sallie R. Thaler..............Grand Secretary
555 Baker St., San Francisco

Mrs. Susie K. Christ..............Grand Treasurer
555 Baker St., San Francisco

Mrs. Irma Laird.....................Grand Marshal
Alturas

Mrs. Minna K. Horn.........Grand Inside Sentinel
Etna

Mrs. Orinda G. Giannini.....Grand Outside Sentinel
2142 Filbert St., San Francisco

Mrs. Lola Horgan...................Grand Organist
789 Morse St., San Francisco

GRAND TRUSTEES.

Mrs. Edna Briggs, 1045 Santa Ynez Way, Sacramento
Mrs. Ethel Begley.....1206 Valencia, San Francisco
Mrs. Anna Thuesen....615 38th Ave., San Francisco
Mrs. Gladys Noce.........................Sutter Creek
Mrs. Florence Boyle..............................Oroville
Mrs. Florence Schoneman, 1521 5th Ave., Los Angeles
Mrs. Willow Borba.........................Sebastopol

EL DORADO COUNTY.

Marguerite No. 12, Placerville—Meets 1st and 3rd Wednesdays, Masonic Hall; Mrs. Nettie Leonardi, Rec. Sec., 25 Coloma St.

El Dorado No. 186, Georgetown—Meets 2nd and 4th Saturday afternoons, I.O.O.F. Hall; Mrs. Alta L. Douglas, Rec. Sec.

FRESNO COUNTY.

Fresno No. 187, Fresno—Meets Fridays, Pythian Castle, Cor. "R" and Merced Sts.; Mrs. Lillian Beguhl, Rec. Sec., 749 Echo Ave.

GLENN COUNTY.

Berryessa No. 192, Willows—Meets 1st and 3rd Mondays, I.O.O.F. Hall; Mrs. Leonora Neate, Rec. Sec., 338 No. Lassen St.

HUMBOLDT COUNTY.

Occident No. 28, Eureka—Meets 1st and 3rd Wed-
Rec. Sec., 2309 "B" St.
nesdays, N.S.G.W. Hall; Mrs. Eva L. MacDonald,

Oneonta No. 71, Ferndale—Meets 2nd and 4th Fridays, I.O.O.F. Hall; Mrs. Myra Rumrill, Rec. Sec.

Reichling No. 97, Fortuna—Meets 2nd and 4th Tuesdays, Friendship Hall; Mrs. Grace Swett, Rec. Sec., P. O. Box 328.

KERN COUNTY.

Miocene No. 228, Taft—Meets 1st and 3rd Wednesday afternoons, I.O.O.F. Hall; Mrs. Evalyne Towne, Rec. Sec., P. O. Box 1011.

El Tejon No. 239, Bakersfield—Meets 1st and 3rd Fridays, Castle Hall; Mrs. Grace Dorris, Rec. Sec., 127 Morgan Bldg.

Desert Gold No. 250, Mojave—Meets 2nd and 4th Fridays, I.O.O.F. Hall; Mrs. Mae Coffill, Rec. Sec.

LAKE COUNTY.

Clear Lake No. 135, Middletown—Meets 2nd and 4th Tuesdays, Herrick Hall; Mrs. Retta Reynolds, Rec. Sec., P. O. Box 180.

LASSEN COUNTY.

Nataqua No. 152, Standish—Meets 1st and 3rd Wednesdays, Foresters Hall; Mrs. Olive Bouchard, Rec. Sec.

Mount Lassen No. 215, Bieber—Meets 2nd and 4th Thursdays, I.O.O.F. Hall; Mrs. Angie C. Kenyon, Rec. Sec.

Susanville No. 243, Susanville—Meets 3rd Thursday, I.O.O.F. Hall; Mrs. Georgia Jensen, Rec. Sec., 700 Roop St.

LOS ANGELES COUNTY.

Los Angeles No. 124, Los Angeles—Meets 1st and 3rd Wednesdays, I.O.O.F. Hall, Washington and Oak Sts.; Mrs. Mary K. Corcoran, Rec. Sec., 222 No. Van Ness Ave.

Long Beach No. 154, Long Beach—Meets 1st and 3rd Thursdays, K.P. Hall, 341 Pacific Ave.; Mrs. Alice Waldow, Rec. Sec., 2175 Cedar Ave.

Rudecinda No. 230, San Pedro—Meets 1st and 3rd Fridays, Unity Hall, I.O.O.F. Temple, 10th and Gaffey; Mrs. Carrie E. Lenhouse, Rec. Sec., 1520 So. Pacific.

Verdugo No. 240, Glendale—Meets 2nd and 4th Tuesdays, Masonic Temple, 234 So. Brand Blvd.; Miss Etta Fulkerth, Rec. Sec., 526-A No. Orange St.

Santa Monica Bay No. 245, Ocean Park—Meets 1st and 3rd Mondays, New Eagles Hall, 2823½ Main St.; Mrs. Rosalie Hyde, Rec. Sec., 738 Flower St., Venice.

Californiana No. 247, Los Angeles—Meets 2nd and 4th Tuesday afternoons, Hollywood Studio Club, 1215 Lodi Place; Mrs. Inez Sitton, Rec. Sec., 4223 Berenice St.

MADERA COUNTY.

Madera No 244 Madera—Meets 2nd and 4th Thursdays Masonic Annex; Mrs. Margaret Boyle, Rec. Sec., 225 So. "C" St.

MARIN COUNTY.

Sea Point No. 196, Sausalito—Meets 2nd and 4th Mondays, Perry Hall, 50 Caledonia St.; Mrs. Mary B. Smith, Rec. Sec., 559 Woodward Ave.

Marinita No. 198, San Rafael—Meets 2nd and 4th Mondays, 318 "B" St.; Miss Mollye Y. Spaelti, Rec. Sec., 639 4th St.

Fairfax No. 225, Fairfax—Meets 2nd and 4th Tuesdays, Community Hall; Mrs. Olive A. Greene, Rec. Sec., P. O. Box 277.

Tamelpa No. 231, Mill Valley—Meets 1st and 3rd Tuesdays, I.O.O.F. Hall; Mrs. Delphine M. Todt, Rec. Sec., 400 Grand Ave., San Rafael.

MARIPOSA COUNTY.

Mariposa No. 63, Mariposa—Meets 1st and 3rd Fridays, I.O.O.F. Hall; Mrs. Mamie E. Weston, Rec. Sec.

ATTENTION, SECRETARIES!

THIS DIRECTORY IS PUBLISHED BY AUTHORITY OF THE GRAND PARLOR N.D.G.W., AND ALL NOTICES OF CHANGES MUST BE RECEIVED BY THE GRAND SECRETARY (NOT THE MAGAZINE) ON OR BEFORE THE 20TH OF EACH MONTH TO INSURE CORRECTION IN NEXT PUBLICATION OF DIRECTORY.

MENDOCINO COUNTY.

Fort Bragg No. 210, Fort Bragg—Meets 1st and 3rd Thursdays, I.O.O.F. Hall; Mrs. Ruth W. Fuller, Rec. Sec.

MERCED COUNTY.

Veritas No. 75, Merced—Meets 1st and 3rd Tuesdays, I.O.O.F. Hall; Miss Margaret Thornton, Rec. Sec., 317 18th St.

MODOC COUNTY.

Alturas No. 159, Alturas—Meets 1st Thursday, Alturas Civic Club; Mrs. Irma W. Laird, Rec. Sec.

MONTEREY COUNTY.

Aleli No. 102, Salinas—Meets 2nd and 4th Thursdays, I.O.O.F. Hall; Mrs. Rose Evelyn Rhyner, Rec. Sec., P. O. Box 1274.

Junipero No. 141, Monterey—Meets 1st and 3rd Thursdays, Custom House; Miss Matilda M. Bergschicker, Rec. Sec., 498 Van Buren St.

NAPA COUNTY.

Eschol No. 16, Napa—Meets 2nd and 4th Mondays, N.S.G.W. Hall; Mrs. Ella Ingram, Rec. Sec., 2140 Seminary St.

Calistoga No. 145, Calistoga—Meets 2nd and 4th Mondays, I.O.O.F. Hall; Sadie P. Brooks, Rec. Sec.

La Junta No. 203, Saint Helena—Meets 1st and 3rd Tuesdays, N.S.G.W. Hall; Mrs. Marie Signorelli, Rec. Sec., 1341 Madrona Ave.

NEVADA COUNTY.

Laurel No. 6, Nevada City—Meets 1st and 3rd Wednesdays, I.O.O.F. Hall; Mrs. Nellie E. Clark, Rec. Sec., P. O. Box 212.

Manzanita No. 29, Grass Valley—Meets 1st and 3rd Tuesdays, Auditorium; Mrs. Loraine Keast, Rec. Sec., 123 Race St.

Columbia No. 70, French Corral—Meets Fridays, Farrelley Hall; Mrs. Kate Farrelley-Sullivan, Rec. Sec.

Snow Peak No. 176, Truckee—Meets 2nd and 4th Fridays, I.O.O.F. Hall; Mrs. Henrietta M. Eaton, Rec. Sec., P. O. Box 116.

ORANGE COUNTY.

Santa Ana No. 235, Santa Ana—Meets 2nd and 4th Mondays, K.C. Hall, 4th and French Sts.; Mrs. Matilda S. Lemon, Rec. Sec., 1038 W. Bishop St.

Grace No. 242, Fullerton—Meets 1st and 3rd Thursdays, I.O.O.F. Hall, 116¼ E. Commonwealth; Mrs. Mary Rothaermel, Rec. Sec., 628 Fern Dr.

PLACER COUNTY.

Placer No. 138, Lincoln—Meets 2nd Wednesday, I.O.O.F. Hall; Miss Carrie Parlin, Rec. Sec.

La Rosa No. 191, Roseville—Meets 1st and 3rd Fridays, Eagles Hall; Mrs. Alice Lee West, Rec. Sec., Rocklin.

Auburn No. 233, Auburn—Meets 2nd and 4th Fridays, Foresters Hall; Mrs. Dorothy Reinecke, Rec. Sec., Penryn.

PLUMAS COUNTY.

Plumas Pioneer No. 219, Quincy—Meets 1st and 3rd Mondays, I.O.O.F. Hall; Minnie E. Johnson, Rec. Sec., P. O. Box 243.

SACRAMENTO COUNTY.

Califia No. 22, Sacramento—Meets 2nd and 4th Tuesdays, N.S.G.W. Hall; Miss Lulu Gillis, Rec Sec., 921 8th St.

La Bandera No. 110, Sacramento—Meets 1st and 3rd Fridays, N.S.G.W. Hall; Mrs. Clara Weldon, Rec. Sec., 1310 "O" St.

Sutter No. 111, Sacramento—Meets 1st and 3rd Tuesdays, N.S.G.W. Hall; Mrs. Adele Nix, Rec. Sec., 1238 "S" St.

Fern No. 123, Folsom—Meets 1st and 3rd Tuesdays, K.P. Hall; Mrs. Viola Shumway, Rec. Sec., P. O. Box 48.

Chabolla No. 171, Galt—Meets 2nd and 4th Tuesdays, I.O.O.F. Hall; Mrs. Mary Pritchard, Rec. Sec.

Coloma No. 212, Sacramento—Meets 1st and 3rd Tuesdays, I.O.O.F. Hall, Oak Park; Mrs. Nettie Harry, Rec. Sec., 1217 35th St.

Liberty No. 213, Elk Grove—Meets 2nd and 4th Fridays, I.O.O.F. Hall; Mrs. Frances Wackman, Rec. Sec., P. O. Box 192.

Victory No. 216, Courtland—Meets 1st Saturday and 3rd Monday, N.S.G.W. Hall; Mrs. Agneda Lample, Rec. Sec.

SAN BENITO COUNTY.

Copa de Oro No. 105, Hollister—Meets 2nd and 4th Thursdays, Grangers Union Hall; Mrs. Mollie Daveggio, Rec. Sec., 110 San Benito St.

San Juan Bautista No. 179, San Juan Bautista—Meets 1st Wednesday, Mission Corridor Rooms; Miss Gertrude Breen, Rec. Sec.

SAN BERNARDINO COUNTY.

Lugonia No. 241, San Bernardino—Meets 2nd and 4th Wednesdays, Eagles Hall; Evelyn T. Shaddox, Rec. Sec., 205 Temple St.

SAN DIEGO COUNTY.

San Diego No. 208, San Diego—Meets 2nd and 4th Tuesdays, K.C. Hall, 410 Elm St.; Mrs. Elsie Case, Rec. Sec., 3051 Broadway.

SAN FRANCISCO CITY AND COUNTY.

Minerva No. 2, San Francisco—Meets 1st and 3rd Wednesdays, N.S.G.W. Bldg.; Miss Dorothy Finn, Rec. Sec., 90 Princess St., Sausalito.

Alta No. 3, San Francisco—Meets 2nd and 4th Tuesdays, N.S.G.W. Bldg.; Mrs. Agnese L. Hughes, Rec. Sec., 3980 Sacramento St.

Oro Fino No. 9, San Francisco—Meets 1st and 3rd Thursdays, N.S.G.W. Bldg.; Mrs. Josephine B. Morrisey, Rec. Sec., 4441 20th St.

Golden State No. 50, San Francisco—Meets 1st and 3rd Wednesdays, N.D.G.W. Home; Miss Millie Tietjen, Rec. Sec., 328 Lexington Ave.

Orinda No. 56, San Francisco—Meets 2nd and 4th Fridays, N.D.G.W. Home; Mrs. Anna A. Gruber-Loser, Rec. Sec., 72 Grove Lane, San Anselmo.

Fremont No. 59, San Francisco—Meets 1st and 3rd Tuesdays, N.S.G.W. Bldg.; Miss Hannah Collins, Rec. Sec., 563 Fillmore St.

Buena Vista No. 68, San Francisco—Meets 1st, 3rd and 5th Thursdays, N.D.G.W. Home; Miss Margaret Barrett, Rec. Sec., 3774 20th St.

Las Lomas No. 72, San Francisco—Meets 1st and 3rd Tuesdays, N.D.G.W. Home; Mrs. Marion S. Day, Rec. Sec., 471 Alvarado St.

Yosemite No. 83, San Francisco—Meets 1st and 3rd Tuesdays, American Hall, 20th and Capp Sts.; Miss Mary Bazley, Rec. Sec., 3353 22nd St.

La Estrella No. 89, San Francisco—Meets 2nd and 4th Mondays, N.S.G.W. Bldg.; Miss Birdie Hartman Rec. Sec., 1018 Jackson St.

Sans Souci No. 96, San Francisco—Meets 2nd and 4th Mondays, N.D.G.W. Home; Mrs. Minnie F. Dobbin, Rec. Sec., 1483 43rd Ave.

Calaveras No. 103, San Francisco—Meets 2nd and 4th Tuesdays, Swedish American Hall, 2174 Market St.; Mrs. Lena Lorsheter, Rec. Sec., 492-C 41st St., Oakland.

Darina No. 114, San Francisco—Meets 1st and 3rd Mondays, N.S.G.W. Bldg.; Miss Adele Walsh, Rec. Sec., 479 Page St.

El Vespero No. 118, San Francisco—Meets 2nd and 4th Tuesdays, Masonic Hall, 4705 3rd St.; Mrs. Nell R. Boege, Rec. Sec., 1526 Kirkwood Ave.

Genevieve No. 132, San Francisco—Meets 1st and 3rd Thursdays, N.S.G.W. Bldg.; Miss Branice Peguillan, Rec. Sec., 2434 16th Ave.

Keith No. 137, San Francisco—Meets 2nd and 4th Thursdays, N.S.G.W. Bldg.; Mrs. Helen T. Mann, Rec. Sec., 2265 Sacramento St.

Gabrielle No. 139, San Francisco—Meets 2nd and 4th Wednesdays, N.S.G.W. Bldg.; Mrs. Dorothy Wuesterfeld, Rec. Sec., 1020 Munich St.

Presidio No. 148, San Francisco—Meets 2nd and 4th Tuesdays, N.S.G.W. Bldg.; Mrs. Hattie Gaughran, Rec. Sec., 713 Capp St.

Guadalupe No. 153, San Francisco—Meets 2nd and 4th Mondays, Forester Hall, 170 Valencia St.; Miss May A. McCarthy, Rec. Sec., 336 Elsie St.

Golden Gate No. 158, San Francisco—Meets 2nd and 4th Mondays, N.S.G.W. Bldg.; Mrs. Margaret Ramm, Rec. Sec., 435-A Frederick St.

Dolores No. 169, San Francisco—Meets 2nd and 4th Wednesdays, N.S.G.W. Bldg.; Mrs. Ada Saunders, Rec. Sec., 284 Allison St.

Linda Rosa No. 170, San Francisco—Meets 2nd and 4th Wednesdays, Swedish American Hall, 2174 Market St.; Mrs. Eva P. Tyrrel, Rec. Sec., 2629 Mission St.

Portola No. 172, San Francisco—Meets 1st and 3rd Tuesdays, N.S.G.W. Bldg.; Catherine H. Dolly, Rec. Sec., 4125 23rd St.

Castro No. 178, San Francisco—Meets 1st and 3rd Wednesdays, K.C. Bldg., 150 Golden Gate Ave.; Miss Adeline Sandersfeld, Rec. Sec., 50 Baker St.

Twin Peaks No. 185, San Francisco—Meets 2nd and 4th Fridays, Druids Temple, 44 Page St.; Mrs. Loretta Cameron, Rec. Sec., 3969 Army St.

James Lick No. 220, San Francisco—Meets 1st and 3rd Wednesdays, N.S.G.W. Bldg.; Mrs. Edna Bishop, Rec. Sec., 3841 24th St.

Mission No. 227, San Francisco—Meets 2nd and 4th Fridays, N.S.G.W. Bldg.; Mrs. Ann Dippel, Rec. Sec., 448 Dewey Blvd.

Bret Harte No. 232 San Francisco—Meets 2nd and 4th Tuesdays, Schuberts Hall, 3009 16th St.; Muriele N. Pabst, Rec. Sec., 696 Guerrero St.

La Dorada No. 236, San Francisco—Meets 2nd and 4th Thursdays, N.S.G.W. Hall; Mrs. Theresa R. O'Brien, Rec. Sec., 567 Liberty St.

Balboa No. 249, San Francisco—Meets 1st and 3rd Thursdays, Maccabee Hall, 5th Ave. and Clement St., Jean Moffet, Rec. Sec., 422 Third Ave.

SAN JOAQUIN COUNTY.

Joaquin No. 5, Stockton—Meets 2nd and 4th Tuesdays, N.S.G.W. Hall, 314 E. Main St.; Mrs. Della Garvin, Rec. Sec., 1122 E. Market St.

El Pescadero No. 82, Tracy—Meets 1st and 3rd Fridays, I.O.O.F. Hall; Mrs. Mary A. Hewitson, Rec. Sec., 215 W. 9th St.

Ivy No. 88, Lodi—Meets 1st and 3rd Wednesdays, Eagles Hall; Mrs. Mae Corson, Rec. Sec., 109 So. School St.

Caliz de Oro No. 206, Stockton—Meets 1st and 3rd Tuesdays, N.S.G.W. Hall, 314 E. Main St.; Mrs. Frances Germain, Rec. Sec., 450 No. Regent.

Phoebe A. Hearst No. 214, Manteca—Meets 2nd and 4th Wednesdays, I.O.O.F. Hall; Mrs. Josie M. Frederick, Rec. Sec., Route A, Box 364, Ripon.

SAN LUIS OBISPO COUNTY.

San Miguel No. 94, San Miguel—Meets 2nd and 4th Wednesday afternoons, Clemon Hall; Mrs. Nellie Wickstrom, Rec. Sec.

San Luisita No. 108, San Luis Obispo—Meets 2nd and 4th Thursdays, W.O.W. Hall; Miss Agnes M. Lee, Rec. Sec., P. O. Box 534.

El Pinal No. 163, Cambria—Meets 2nd, 4th and 5th Tuesdays, N.S.G.W. Hall; Kathryn Luchessa, Rec. Sec.

SAN MATEO COUNTY.

Bonita No. 10, Redwood City—Meets 2nd and 4th Thursdays, I.O.O.F. Hall; Mrs. Dora Wilson, Rec. Sec., 518 Middlefield Rd.

Vista del Mar No. 155, Halfmoon Bay—Meets 2nd and 4th Thursdays, I.O.O.F. Hall; Mrs. Grace Griffith, Rec. Sec.

Ano Nuevo No. 180, Pescadero—Meets 1st and 3rd Wednesdays, I.O.O.F. Hall; Mrs. Alice Mattei, Rec. Sec.

El Carmelo No. 181, Daly City—Meets 1st and 3rd Wednesdays, Masonic Hall; Mrs. Hattie Kelly, Rec. Sec., 1179 Brunswick St.

Menlo No. 211, Menlo Park—Meets 2nd and 4th Mondays, Masonic Hall; Mrs. Frances E. Maloney, Rec. Sec., P. O. Box 626.

San Bruno No. 246, San Bruno—Meets 2nd and 4th Fridays, N.D. Hall; Mrs. Evelyn Kelly, Rec. Sec., 353 Hazel Ave.

SANTA BARBARA COUNTY.

Reina del Mar No. 126, Santa Barbara—Meets 1st and 3rd Tuesdays, Pythian Castle, 223 W. Carillo St.; Miss Christina Moller, Rec. Sec., 836 Bath St.

SANTA CLARA COUNTY.

San Jose No. 81, San Jose—Meets Thursdays, Catholic Women Center, 5th and San Fernando Sts.; Mrs. Nellie Fleming, Rec. Sec., Catholic Women's Center.

Vendome No. 100, San Jose—Meets Wednesdays, Scottish Rite Hall; Miss Marie Buck, Rec. Sec., 1114 Ellen St.

El Monte No. 205, Mountain View—Meets 2nd and 4th Fridays, Mockbee Hall; Miss Dolores Collett, Rec. Sec., Route 1, Box 677-A, Los Altos.

Palo Alto No. 229, Palo Alto—Meets 1st and 3rd Mondays, N.S.G.W. Hall; Miss Helena G. Hansen, Rec. Sec., 531 Lytton Ave.

SANTA CRUZ COUNTY.

Santa Cruz No. 26, Santa Cruz—Meets Mondays, N.S.G.W. Hall; Mrs. May L. Williamson, Rec. Sec., 170 Walnut Ave.

El Pajaro No. 35, Watsonville—Meets 1st and 3rd Tuesdays, I.O.O.F. Hall; Miss Ruth E. Wilson, Rec. Sec., 16 Laurel St.

SHASTA COUNTY.

Camellia No. 41, Anderson—Meets 1st and 3rd Tuesdays, Masonic Hall; Mrs. Olga E. Welbourn, Rec. Sec.

Lassen View No. 98, Shasta—Meets 2nd Friday, Masonic Hall; Miss Louise Litsch, Rec. Sec.

Hiawatha No. 140, Redding—Meets 2nd and 4th Wednesdays, Moose Hall; Ruth Presleigh, Rec. Sec., Office County Clerk.

N.D.G.W. OFFICIAL DEATH LIST.

Giving the name, the date of death, and the Subordinate Parlor affiliation of all deceased members as reported to Grand Secretary Sallie R. Thaler from September 18 to October 15:

Wheeler, Emma; September 16; Castro No. 178.
Rupert, Mary K.; September 2; Piedmont No. 87.
Hill, Mary A.; September 15; Darina No. 114.
Fogalsang, Louise; September 11; Colus No. 194.
Dooling, Alida Bastian; September 10; Alta No. 3.
Fricke, Louella B.; August 28; Marguerite No. 12.
Carmichael, Eva Larrison; September 18; Forrest No. 86.
Bidwell, May H.; September 26; Joaquin No. 5.
Mock, Louise; August 31; Santa Ana No. 235.

SIERRA COUNTY.

Naomi No. 36, Downieville—Meets 2nd and 4th Wednesdays, I.O.O.F. Hall; Mrs. Mary Cook, Rec. Sec.

Imogen No. 134, Sierraville—Meets 2nd and 4th Saturday afternoons, Copren Hall; Mrs. Jennie Copren, Rec. Sec.

SISKIYOU COUNTY.

Eschscholtzia No. 112, Etna—Meets 1st and 3rd Wednesdays, Masonic Hall; Mrs. Bernice E. Smith, Rec. Sec.

Mountain Dawn No. 120, Sawyers Bar—Meets 2nd and last Wednesdays, I.O.O.F. Hall; Miss Edith Dunphy, Rec. Sec.

SOLANO COUNTY.

Vallejo No. 195, Vallejo—Meets 1st and 3rd Wednesdays, K.C. Hall, 820 Marin St.; Mrs. Mary Combs, Rec. Sec., 511 York St.

Mary E. Bell No. 224, Dixon—Meets 2nd and 4th Thursdays, I.O.O.F. Hall; Grace McFadyen, Rec. Sec.

SONOMA COUNTY.

Sonoma No 209, Sonoma—Meets 2nd and 4th Mondays, I.O.O.F. Hall; Mrs. Mae Norrbom, Rec. Sec., R.F.D., Box 171.

Santa Rosa No. 217, Santa Rosa—Meets 1st and 3rd Thursdays, N.S.G.W. Hall; Mrs. Clytie Lewis, Rec. Sec., Route 4, Box 345-A.

Petaluma No. 222, Petaluma—Meets 1st and 3rd Tuesdays, Dania Hall; Mrs. Margaret M. Oeltjen, Rec. Sec., 503 Prospect St.

STANISLAUS COUNTY.

Oakdale No. 125, Oakdale—Meets 1st Monday, I.O.O.F. Hall; Mrs. Lou Reeder, Rec. Sec.

Morada No. 199, Modesto—Meets 2nd and 4th Wednesdays, I.O.O.F. Hall; Mrs. Susan Sullivan, Rec. Sec., 517 Semple St.

Eldora No. 248, Turlock—Meets 1st and 3rd Wednesdays, Fraternal Hall; Mrs. Melva Gardner, Rec. Sec., 817 W. Main St.

SUTTER COUNTY.

South Butte No. 226, Sutter—Meets 1st and 3rd Mondays, N.D.G.W. Hall; Mrs. Abbie N. Vagedes, Rec. Sec.

TEHAMA COUNTY.

Berendos No. 23, Red Bluff—Meets 1st and 3rd Tuesdays, W.O.W. Hall, 200 Pine St.; Mrs. Lillie Hammer, Rec. Sec., 636 Jackson St.

TRINITY COUNTY.

Eltapome No. 55, Weaverville—Meets 2nd and 4th Thursdays, N.S.G.W. Hall; Mrs. Lou N. Fetzer, Rec. Sec.

TUOLUMNE COUNTY.

Dardanelle No. 66, Sonora—Meets Fridays, I.O.O.F. Hall; Mrs. Nettie Whitto, Rec. Sec.

Golden Era No. 99, Columbia—Meets 1st and 3rd Thursdays, N.S.G.W. Hall; Miss Irene Ponce, Rec. Sec.

Anona No. 164, Jamestown—Meets 2nd and 4th Tuesdays, I.O.O.F. Hall; Mrs. Rosa A. Beckwith, Rec. Sec., P. O. Box 87.

YOLO COUNTY.

Woodland No. 90, Woodland—Meets 2nd and 4th Tuesdays, N.S.G.W. Hall; Mrs. Maude Heaton, Rec. Sec., 153 College St.

YUBA COUNTY.

Marysville No. 162, Marysville—Meets 2nd and 4th Wednesdays, Liberty Hall; Miss Cecelia C. Gomes, Rec. Sec., 701 6th St.

Camp Far West No. 218, Wheatland—Meets 4th Thursday, I.O.O.F. Hall; Mrs. Ethel C. Brock, Rec. Sec., P. O. Box 285.

AFFILIATED ORGANIZATIONS.

General Assembly Past Presidents—Meetings held annually in April at the home-town of Chief President; Miss Josephine Clark, 824 11th St., Oakland, Chief President; Mrs. Anna G. Loser, 72 Grove Lane, San Anselmo, Chief Secretary.

Past Presidents Association No. 1—Meets 1st and 3rd Mondays, N.S.G.W. Bldg., 414 Mason St., San Francisco; Mrs. Margaret Grote-Hill, Pres.; Mrs. May R. Barry, Rec. Sec., 2319 19th Ave., San Francisco.

Past Presidents Association No. 2—Meets 2nd and 4th Mondays, "Wigwam," Pacific Bldg., 16th and Jefferson, Oakland; Ethel Scheuer, Pres.; Mrs. Elizabeth B. Goodman, Rec. Sec., 134 Juana St., San Leandro.

Past Presidents Association No. 3 (Santa Clara County)—Meets 2nd Tuesday, homes of members; Mrs. Ida Sweeney, Pres.; Amelia S. Hartman, Rec. Sec., 157 Auzerais Ave., San Jose.

Past Presidents Association No. 4 (Sacramento County)—Meets 2nd Monday, Unitarian Hall, 1413 27th St., Sacramento City; Francis Kimball, Pres.; Lily May Tilden, Rec. Sec., 3225 "T" St., Sacramento.

Past Presidents Association No. 5 (Butte County)—Meets 1st Friday, homes of members, Chico and Oroville; Sonora Steadman, Pres.; Ruth Brown, Rec. Sec., 1265 Leah Court, Oroville.

Past Presidents Association No. 6 (Nevada County)—Meets 4th Friday, alternately between Nevada City, Odd Fellows Hall, and Grass Valley, Womens Improvement Clubhouse; Anne Conlin, Pres.; Louise Wales, Rec. Sec., 369 Mill St., Grass Valley.

Past Presidents Association No. 7 (Sonoma County)—Meets 1st Thursday, N.S.G.W. Hall, Santa Rosa; Willow Borba, Pres.; Clytie Lewis, Rec. Sec., R.F.D. No. 4, Box 345-A, Santa Rosa.

Past Presidents Association No. 8 (San Joaquin and Stanislaus Counties)—Meets 1st Thursday, N.S.G.W. Hall, Stockton; Mrs. Mattie M. Stein, Pres.; Mrs. Harriet F. Corr, Rec. Sec., 729 E. Sonora St., Stockton.

Native Sons and Native Daughters Central Committee on Homeless Children—Main Office, 955 Phelan Bldg., San Francisco; Miss Mary E. Brusie, Sec.

(ADVERTISEMENT.)

NATIVE DAUGHTER NEWS

(Continued from Page 9)

The homeless childrens sewing circle of No. 242 is now meeting twice a month. Mamie Hirigoyen and Christine McFarland were October hostesses. The latter was an all-day meeting, with pot-luck luncheon at noon. The Parlor is planning a bazar and a rummage sale in the near future.

Anniversary Celebrated.

Woodland—Woodland No. 90 celebrated its thirty-fifth institution anniversary October 13 with a "kid" party. A covered-dish dinner was served, and games were the principal entertainment feature. Hallowe'en decorations prevailed. Mrs. May Worley, the first president, presided at the meeting, and other charter members in attendance included Mms. May Hutchings, Sadie Clements and Mattie Zimmerman, and Miss Harriett S. Lee. Grand officers present were Grand Vice-president Anna Mixon-Armstrong, Grand Trustee Edna Briggs, Past Grand Presidents Dr. Eva Rasmussen and Louise C. Heilbron, Supervising Deputy Edna G. Richter, District Deputies Emma Bloom, Doris Fisher and Wanda Abele. The charter and veteran members of the Parlor were presented with gifts.

Close to five hundred people had a gay time dancing and playing cards October 3 at the Yolo County Fliers Club, at an affair sponsored by Woodland for the benefit of the Native Daughter Home. Refreshments were served, and a substantial sum was realized.

Anniversary Meeting.

Stockton—The seventeenth anniversary meeting of Caliz de Oro No. 206 was held October 6. An italian dinner was in charge of Henrietta Quevillon. President Ada Javete presided at the business session, at which the high jinks of October 20 was announced. Three candidates were initiated.

Eda Cunningham was in charge of the program, which presented a clever mock stunt. Among those who took part were Buelah Grattan, Clarice Cook, Kathryne Wilde, Roberta Foley, Christene Neeley, Emily Champreux, Maybell McDonald, Florence Carlson, Francis Germain and Ida Stuart. A beautiful basket of chrysanthemums was received from Joaquin No. 5.

Donation for Good Cause.

Hollister—District Deputy Blanche Taix installed the officers of Copa de Oro No. 105 September 24, Elma Chandler becoming president. Community singing was enjoyed and refreshments were served at prettily decorated tables. Ten dollars was donated to the fund being gathered by the local American Legion for the purchase of an inhalator and resusciator for use of the residents of San Benito County. During the evening gifts and flowers were presented District Deputy Taix, President Chandler, Junior Past President Mayme Moran, Josephine Winn and Past Grand President Bertha A. Briggs.

Bride Honor Guest.

Colusa—Mrs. Wm. C. Stokes Jr., a recent bride, was honor guest of Colus No. 194 October 5. A banquet was served, the table being decorated in pink and white; place cards were little brides adorned in most attractive raiment. On an adjoining table was a cottage love nest, built for two, with curtained windows and landscaped yard; a little bride and groom stood guard at the portals. Inside was the Parlor's gift to Mrs. Stokes. There was a wonderful wedding cake, also, from which Freda Yopp drew the hidden wedding ring. Mrs. Warren G. Davison, county chairman California history, reported on the history of Colusa County. The committee in charge for the evening included Ruby Humburg, Vera Jobe and Lillian Clement.

Colus entertained members of Colusa No. 69 N.S.G.W. and their wives at a dance and card party October 12. Stella Bond, Martha Humburg and Christine Humburg had charge.

Three Initiated.

Monterey—Grand President Evelyn I. Carlson was an honored guest of Junipero No. 141 October 9. The ritual was exemplified in a very creditable manner and three candidates were initiated, which makes eight new members this term. Visitors were Mms. Marguerite Sullivan and Marguerite Brown of Alta No. 3 (San Francisco), and Mms. Louise Hattan and Rose Rhyner of Aleli No. 102 (Salinas). A banquet was enjoyed at the close of the meeting.

Homage to Oldtimers.

Middletown—Clear Lake No. 135 paid homage to the oldtimers of this section at a very enjoyable affair October 10. The hall was beautifully

(Concluded on Page 21)

In Memoriam

CLARA MITCHLER.

We, your committee appointed to draft resolutions of respect to the memory of our late beloved sister, Clara Mitchler, respectfully submit the following:

Whereas, The Angel of Death has again entered our Parlor and taken from our midst our beloved sister, Clara Mitchler, we deeply feel the loss of her whose kind and genial manner won the love and esteem of all who knew her, and we realize the still greater loss of those who were nearest and dearest to her. Therefore, be it

Resolved, That we, the members of Murphys Parlor No. 46 N.D.G.W., extend our deepest sympathy to her bereaved family; and be it further resolved, that these resolutions be spread upon the minutes of this Parlor, that a copy be sent to the family of our deceased sister, and that a copy be sent to The Grizzly Bear for publication.

EVALYN M. STEPHENS,
LAURA O. MANUEL,
BELLE SEGALE,
Committee.

Murphys, September 25, 1931.

EVA C. CARMICHAEL.

To the Officers and Members of Forrest Parlor No. 86 N.D.G.W.—We, your committee appointed to draft resolutions of respect to the memory of Eva C. Carmichael, submit the following:

Whereas, In view of the loss we have sustained by the decease of our friend and sister, and of the still greater loss sustained by those who were nearest and dearest to her, therefore be it

Resolved, That it is but a just tribute to the memory of the departed to say, that in regretting her removal from our midst we mourn for one who was in every way worthy of our respect and regard; resolved, that we sincerely condole with the family of the deceased on the dispensation with which it has pleased Divine Providence to afflict them, and commend them for consolation to Him who orders all things for the best and whose chastisements are meant in mercy; be it further resolved, that the charter of our Parlor be draped in mourning for a period of thirty days, that these resolutions be spread upon the minutes, that a copy be sent to the bereaved family, and one to The Grizzly Bear Magazine for publication.

MARGUERITE DAVIS,
SUSIE NOE,
LAURA G. WESTON,
Committee.

Plymouth, September 28, 1931.

LOTTIE GARNSEY GROUARD.

To the Officers and Members of Santa Ana Parlor No. 235 Native Daughters of the Golden West—We, your committee, appointed to draft resolutions of love and respect in memory of our departed sister and charter member, do submit the following:

Once again we bow to the will of Almighty God, who has seen fit to claim His own from amongst our membership and taken to His heavenly home our esteemed sister, pioneer and highly respected citizen of Santa Ana, Lottie Garnsey Grouard; therefore, be it

Resolved, That the sympathy of the Parlor be extended to the bereaved family, and our charter draped in mourning for a period of thirty days; that a copy of these resolutions be sent to the family of the deceased, a copy to The Grizzly Bear for publication, and that a copy be spread upon the minutes of this Parlor.

MATILDA LEMON,
MARGUERITE DICKINSON,
GENEVIEVE HISKEY,
FLORENCE WATSON,
Committee.

Santa Ana, September 28, 1931.

MARY RUPERT.

We, your committee appointed to draft resolutions of respect to the memory of our late beloved sister, Mary Rupert, respectfully submit the following:

Whereas, The Angel of Death has again entered our Parlor and taken from our midst our beloved sister, Mary Rupert, we deeply feel the loss of her whose kind and genial manner won the love and esteem of all who knew her, and we realize the still greater loss of those who were nearest and dearest to her. She has been called from our midst, her body has been returned to the soil of California, and her spirit has been called into the presence of Him, but with us remains the memory of her devotion to our Order. Therefore, be it

Resolved, That we, the members of Piedmont Parlor No. 87 N.D.G.W., extend our deepest sympathy to her bereaved family in the loss of a loving wife and mother; and be it further resolved, that these resolutions be spread upon the minutes of the Parlor, that a copy be sent to the bereaved family of our deceased sister, and that a copy be sent to The Grizzly Bear for publication.

Respectfully submitted,
JOSEPHINE COLLINS,
NELL REALY MOORE,
WINNIE BUCKINGHAM,
Committee.

Oakland, September 30, 1931.

ROBERT P. LAMDIN.

Napa Parlor No. 62 Native Sons of the Golden West deeply regrets the death of Brother Robert P. Lamdin, a charter member of the Parlor, and one of the outstanding Native Sons of Napa County. His many good qualities of mind and heart and his kindly spirit will long be remembered by the members of this Parlor. His attention to his brothers in time of sickness was always keenly manifested by many acts that exhibited his wonderful sympathetic and fraternal spirit. He was always among the first to offer consolation and advice and to extend the hand of brotherly love in time of trouble. In and out of the lodgeroom, his genial spirit was one to cheer the brothers in their fraternal and civic duties, and ever made them appreciate the true spirit and force of brotherly love.

Brother Lamdin had been the treasurer of Napa Parlor for forty-four consecutive years, and during all that time was regarded as one of the staunchest and most painstaking officers which the Parlor had ever honored with official station. It was rarely that he was absent from his post of duty during all of these years, and not until illness overtook him was he compelled to forego the performance of his duties.

Naturally of a most kindly disposition and lovable nature, Brother Lamdin builded among his brethren and in the community a character which distinguished him as a man of the broadest humanitarian ideals, objects and purposes. His noble qualities will always be remembered and cherished by all whose distinction it was to know him; and this community, in which he was born and in which he grew to manhood, will miss him as the years go by.

In all of the affection and kindness which he bestowed upon his friends and brothers, there was always most noticeable that deep devotion which he bore toward his loving wife, for whom he was always solicitous and to whom he gave his undying love and affection unto the day of his death. And it is in this hour of her deep affliction that we extend to her our sympathy and condolence. To her, as well as to his sister and brothers and other relatives, we desire to express our deepest sorrow and extend to each and all of them our sincerest sympathy. Therefore, be it

Resolved, That in the death of Brother Robert P. Lamdin the members of Napa Parlor No. 62 have sustained an irreparable loss of a dear friend and associate, and a place has been made vacant in the community by his passing that will be hard to fill, and he will ever be lovingly remembered by all who knew him.

HENRY C. GESFORD, P.G.P.,
H. J. HOERNLE,
FRANK L. COOMBS, P.G.P.,
Committee.

Napa City, October 6, 1931.

KATHERINE DOLORES HEALY.

To the Officers and Members of Piedmont Parlor No. 87 N.D.G.W.—We, your committee appointed to draft resolutions of respect to the memory of our dearly beloved sister, Katherine Healy, do respectfully submit the following:

Whereas, It has pleased Almighty God, in His infinite wisdom, to release from suffering and remove from our midst our beloved sister, Katherine Healy, whose cheerful smile, loving ways and happy disposition we hold in fond memory; therefore, be it

Resolved, That we, the members of Piedmont Parlor No. 87 N.D.G.W., extend our sincere sympathy to the faithful husband and family; be it further resolved, that a copy of these resolutions be spread upon the minutes of the Parlor, that a copy be forwarded to the family of our deceased sister, and that a copy be sent to The Grizzly Bear Magazine for publication.

Respectfully submitted,
ADDIE L. MOSHER, P.G.P.,
GRETTA MURDEN,
RAMONA HUNTER,
Committee.

Oakland, October 9, 1931.

SARAH KENNEDY.

To the Officers and Members of San Andreas Parlor No. 113 N.D.G.W.—Your committee appointed to prepare resolutions, expressing the sentiments and a deep-felt sympathy of the members of this Parlor on the death of our sister, Sarah Kennedy, respectfully submit the following:

Whereas, By the dispensation of a Divine Providence the angel of death has taken our beloved and esteemed sister, Sarah Kennedy, and summoned her to realms of higher activities; and whereas, our sister has answered the final roll call, leaving her sister members to mourn the loss of one of our devoted and faithful members;

Resolved, That San Andreas Parlor No. 113 N.D.G.W. in the death of our sister has lost one of its honored and respected members, and the community has lost an honest and esteemed neighbor; resolved, that we tender to her family and relatives our heartfelt sympathy in this, their sad hour of affliction; and it is further resolved, that a copy of these resolutions be spread upon the minutes and a copy be sent to the family.

Respectfully submitted,
TILLIE GETCHELL,
GRACE TISCORNIA,
KATE LOEFFLER,
Chairman.

San Andreas, October 3, 1931.

FRANK A. BONIVERT.

Whereas, Our Almighty Father has seen fit to call to the Heavenly Parlor on High our beloved brother, Frank A. Bonivert; and whereas, Brother Bonivert has been an active worker for our Order and our Parlor and has ably filled the office of recording secretary of our Parlor for the past twenty-one years; and whereas, we feel and know that not only El Dorado Parlor, but the entire Order of Native Sons of the Golden West, has by his death lost a loyal and earnest member; now, therefore, be it

Resolved, That El Dorado Parlor No. 52 N.S.G.W. feels most deeply the loss of our brother and extends to his family our heartfelt sympathy; be it further resolved, that a copy of this resolution be sent to the family of our departed brother, that a copy be spread upon the minutes of our Parlor, and that a copy be sent to The Grizzly Bear for publication.

EUGENE HERZOG, President,
ALFRED VLAUTIN, Acting Secretary,
WILLIAM THOMAS, Treasurer.

San Francisco, October 15, 1931.

JASON D. WHITE.

Whereas, It has pleased the Divine Providence to call to his eternal home our beloved brother, Jason D. White; and whereas, this Parlor has sustained the loss of a faithful member, his country a patriotic citizen, and his family a kind and loving father; therefore, be it

Resolved, That this Parlor do extend to his family our most sincere sympathy in their bereavement, and that we most earnestly pray that the Merciful Father may help them bear their loss with Christian fortitude; be it further resolved that, in respect to the memory of our late brother, the charter of this Parlor be draped for a period of thirty days, that a copy of these resolutions be spread upon the minutes, a copy be forwarded to the family of the deceased, and also a copy to The Grizzly Bear Magazine for publication.

C. F. REINDOLLAR,
MONROE LABEL,
LOUIS J. PETER,
Committee on Resolutions.

Adopted by this Parlor Monday evening, October 19, 1931. M. A. ANDRADE, Recording Secretary.

FRANK A. BONIVERT.

To the Officers and Members of Golden Gate Parlor No. 29 N.S.G.W.—The undersigned respectfully submit the following resolution and move its adoption:

Whereas, It has pleased Almighty God to call from our midst on Monday, October 12, 1931, Frank A. Bonivert, a member of El Dorado Parlor No. 52 N.S.G.W., its recording secretary and a past president thereof; and whereas, during the past twenty-one years that Brother Bonivert was a member of El Dorado Parlor he has been one of the stauchest supporters of all the activities of this Order in San Francisco—as an officer of his own Parlor, as an inter-Parlor committeeman, as a delegate to the Grand Parlor, and as a district deputy grand president—to the extent that he was regarded as an outstanding Native Son; therefore, be it

Resolved, That Golden Gate Parlor express and hereby does express sympathy to El Dorado Parlor No. 52 in the terrible loss they are sustaining, and also to the sorrowing family; and be it resolved further, that the regular meeting of Golden Gate Parlor, held this 12th day of October, 1931, be declared closed in respect to the memory of the late Brother Frank A. Bonivert of El Dorado Parlor No. 52.

Respectfully submitted,
THOS. C. CONMY, Past President,
CHAS. A. KOENIG, Grand Third Vice-pres.
PETER T. CONMY, Historian.

The above resolution was unanimously adopted at regular meeting held October 12, 1931, and ordered published in The Grizzly Bear.—ADOLPH EBERHART, Recording Secretary.

ANNA BELLE D. CHAPMAN.

Los Angeles Parlor No. 124 N.D.G.W., in the passing of Anna Belle D. Chapman, has lost a very loyal Native Daughter and a true Californian. Her demise has left a void in the hearts of those nearest and dearest to her. Therefore, be it

Resolved, That Los Angeles Parlor extends sincere sympathy to her husband and bereaved relatives; and further be it resolved, that these resolutions be spread upon the minutes of the Parlor, that a copy be sent to the family of our dear sister, and that a copy be sent to The Grizzly Bear for publication.

ANNIE L. ADAIR,
MARY K. CORCORAN,
EDITH B. SCHALLMO,
Committee.

Los Angeles, October 17, 1931.

THOMAS H. McCOY.

General Winn Parlor No. 32 N.S.G.W.—Brothers: Your committee, appointed to draft resolutions of respect and condolence in the passing of our brother, Thomas H. McCoy, beg leave to submit the following:

Whereas, It has pleased the Almighty Father, to whom the ranks of life report, to remove from our midst our dearly beloved brother, Thomas H. McCoy, to the realm above where beauty, valor and goodness dwell forever with the unnumbered brethren. Mindful of service nobly done, He has called him to everlasting rest. With the faded blossoms of springtime and the withered leaves of autumn He has called him to eternal peace to dwell with the loved ones who have gone before. Therefore, be it

Resolved, That the loss has been great to us, and yet, greater to those of his family. At this time let us pause and bow to our Maker with reverent hearts and in sublime faith, praying that He now hear the sorrow of those who mourn and touch their tired hearts with healing, protecting them with His holy care and keeping clear and bright in memory the splendid flame that now has flickered out. Resolved, that we feel this Parlor of the Native Sons of the Golden West has suffered an irreparable loss; and therefore, be it further resolved, that we extend to the relatives of Brother McCoy our heartfelt sympathy in their bereavement; that a copy of this resolution be spread upon the minutes of General Winn Parlor No. 32 N.S.G.W.; that a copy be sent to the relatives of the deceased, and that a copy be forwarded to The Grizzly Bear Magazine for publication; and be it further resolved, that the Parlor charter be draped in mourning for thirty days.

W. WESLEY FIELD,
F. JUDSON BIGLOW,
JOEL H. FORD,
Committee.

Antioch, October 21, 1931.

REDWOOD, CENTURIES OLD, UNEARTHED.

Watsonville (Santa Cruz County)—A redwood, seven feet in diameter and in a perfect state of preservation, was recently unearthed here by a well driller at a depth of two hundred feet. The forest giant was encrusted in clay.

It is recalled that the California redwoods first were seen in the Pajaro Valley, and it is believed this particular tree fell untold centuries ago. The ocean, which at one time covered this section, is believed to have left deposits over the giant and the shifting top soil did the rest.

School Bonds—Voters of Vallejo, Solano County, have approved a $230,000 bond issue for a new junior high school.

Publishers To Confer—The annual convention of the American Newspaper Publishers Association will be held at Los Angeles City, November 10-13.

GEOLOGIC HISTORY YOSEMITE VALLEY

FEW VALLEYS OR CANYONS ELSEwhere on the earth have aroused more widespread curiosity or have given rise to more speculation and dispute as to the secret of their origin than California's Yosemite Valley. So extraordinary is the valley's appearance, with sheer monumental walls and massive rounded domes, lofty swaying waterfalls and level parklike floor, that it seems in a class by itself, created in some unusual way.

The layman's inclination, not unnaturally, is to appeal to a dramatic, violent cause. Some of the earlier scientists also supposed the strange chasm to have been formed by nothing less than a cataclysm, such as the caving in or rending apart of the earth's crust. Others, however, recognizing on its walls the marks of glacial action, conceived the valley to have been excavated and scoured out by a powerful glacier of the ice age. John Muir, the famous west coast naturalist, was the foremost of these. Still others, denying that glaciers have any notable excavating power, have contended that the Yosemite is primarily a stream-worn canyon, but slightly modified by glacial action. How much of the excavating was done by the Merced River, which flows through the valley, and how much by the ancient glaciers is, indeed, the crux of the Yosemite problem.

This much mooted question is the subject of a publication of the Federal Interior Department entitled "Geologic History of the Yosemite Valley." It is illustrated by numerous photographs showing the striking features of the Yosemite Valley and by several maps, including one on which the ancient glaciers are shown restored. A series of four perspective views helps the reader to visualize the form and character of the valley at each stage of its development. The publication embodies results of investigations begun some years ago, primarily in response to popular demand for information concerning the way in which the beautiful valley was formed. It is from the pen of Francois E. Matthes, also the author of the detailed topographic map of the valley that accompanies the volume. A special chapter on the granitic rocks of the Yosemite region is contributed by Frank C. Calkins.

The new investigations have, in the first place, removed the uncertainty that has always existed as regards the extent and magnitude of the ancient Yosemite Glacier. They have shed new light on the glacial history of the Yosemite region, showing that that region and a large part of the Sierra Nevada were glaciated at least three times, at long intervals, during the ice age. Three important chapters of the preglacial history of the Yosemite Valley, which heretofore has been a sealed book, also stand revealed.

The valley was cut to successively greater depths by the Merced River in consequence of succesive uptilting, amounting to thousands of feet, of the vast earth block that constitutes the Sierra Nevada. The depth of the valley at each of these earlier stages has been determined within narrow limits. The chasm, it is now clear, already had a depth of 3,000 feet when the first glacier invaded it, and so there is fairly definite basis for estimates of the amount of excavation accomplished by the Merced River and the Yosemite Glacier, respectively. The remarkable configuration of the valley, finally, is explained by the fact that the excavating action of the glacier was controlled by the jointed structure of the granite, which is extremely varied.

These general facts and explanations, and many of a more detailed nature relating to individual features of the Yosemite Valley, such as the famous Half Dome, the cliff of El Capitan and the Yosemite Falls, are set forth in language simple enough to be understood by one having no geologic training, yet in sufficient fullness to leave no doubt in the critical reader's mind as to the foundation of observed facts or as to the processes of reasoning whereby the conclusions are reached. Of the nearly half a million people who visit Yosemite annually probably few have failed to ask such questions as are answered in this volume.

Dairy Show—The eleventh annual Pacific Slope Dairy Show is to be held at Oakland, Alameda County, November 9-13.

STATEMENT OF THE OWNERSHIP, MANAGEMENT, CIRCULATION, ETC.,

Required by Act of Congress of August 24, 1912.

of The Grizzly Bear published Monthly
(Insert title of publication.) (State frequency of issue.)

at Los Angeles, California, for October 1, 1931.
(Name of post office and State where publication is entered.) (State whether for April 1 or October 1.)

State of California }
County of Los Angeles } ss.

Before me, a Notary Public in and for the State and County aforesaid, personally appeared Clarence M. Hunt who, having been duly sworn according to law, deposes and says that he is the Managing Editor of the Grizzly Bear Magazine and that the following is, to the best of his
(State whether editor, publisher, business manager or owner.) (Insert title of publication.)
knowledge and belief, a true statement of the ownership, management (and if a daily paper, the circulation), etc., of the aforesaid publication for the date shown in the above caption, required by the Act of August 24, 1912, embodied in section 411, Postal Laws and Regulations, printed on the reverse side of this form, to-wit:

1. That the names and addresses of the publisher, editor, managing editor, and business managers are:

NAME OF—		POST-OFFICE ADDRESS
Publisher,	Grizzly Bear Publishing Co. (Inc.)	Los Angeles, Calif.
Managing Editor,	Clarence M. Hunt	Los Angeles, Calif.

2. That the owner is: (If owned by a corporation, its name and address must be stated and also immediately thereunder the names and addresses of stockholders owning or holding one per cent or more of total amount of stock. If not owned by a corporation, the names and addresses of the individual owners must be given. If owned by a firm, company, or other unincorporated concern, its name and address, as well as those of each individual member, must be given.)
The Grizzly Bear Publishing Co., a Corporation, is the owner. 1261 shares of the 7500 authorized shares of stock have been sold. Names all stockholders, and amount stock held by each, attached hereto.

3. That the known bondholders, mortgagees, and other security holders owning or holding 1 per cent or more of total amount of bonds, mortgages, or other securities are: (If there are none, so state.)
None

4. That the two paragraphs next above, giving the names of the owners, stockholders, and security holders, if any, contain not only the list of stockholders and security holders as they appear upon the books of the company, but also, in cases where the stockholder or security holder appears upon the books of the company as trustee or in any other fiduciary relation, the name of the person or corporation for whom such trustee is acting, is given; also that the said two paragraphs contain statements embracing affiant's full knowledge and belief as to the circumstances and conditions under which stockholders and security holders who do not appear upon the books of the company as trustees, hold stock and securities in a capacity other than that of a bonafide owner; and this affiant has no reason to believe that any other person, association, or corporation has any interest direct or indirect in the said stocks, bonds, or other securities than as so stated by him.

5. That the average number of copies of each issue of this publication sold or distributed, through the mails or otherwise, to paid subscribers during the six months preceding the date shown above is——(This information is required from daily publications only.)

CLARENCE M. HUNT,
Managing Editor.

Sworn to and subscribed before me this 29th day of September, 1931.

HARRY J. LELANDE,
[Seal] Notary Public in and for the County of Los Angeles, State of California.
(My commission expires January, 1932)

STOCKHOLDERS OF THE GRIZZLY BEAR PUBLISHING COMPANY (Inc.)

Following is the list of ALL of the stockholders of the Grizzly Bear Publishing Company, Incorporated, as shown by the Stock Ledger, September 29, 1931:

W. Joseph Ford. 257
Harry J. Lelande, Los Angeles, 24
Warren R. Porter, Watsonville, 10
W. H. Maris, Santa Barbara, 10
C. J. Brown, Los Angeles, 10
C. M. Belshaw, San Francisco, 20
George L. Chanler, Los Angeles, 10
J. N. O. Rech, Los Angeles, 10
J. R. Knowland, Oakland, 15
I. B. Dockweiler, Los Angeles, 15
E. A. Meserve, Los Angeles, 25
W. T. Craig, Los Angeles, 10
Ramona Parlor, N.S.G.W., Los Angeles, 122
M. T. Dooling, Hollister, 5
Corona Parlor, N.S.G.W., Los Angeles, 10
Thomas Monahan, San Jose, 10
Andrew Mocker, San Francisco, 5
Daniel A. Ryan, San Francisco, 10
James D. Phelan, San Francisco, 20
Los Angeles Parlor, N.S.G.W., Los Angeles, 10
Frank H. Dunne, San Francisco, 5
J. Emmett Hayden, San Francisco, 10
W. S. Kingsbury, Sacramento, 10
W. W. Shannon, San Francisco, 5
E. A. Forbes, Marysville, 5
H. C. Lichtenberger, Los Angeles, 12
Frank Hauser, Los Angeles, 10
F. W. Young, Los Angeles, 5
Calvert Wilson, Los Angeles, 3
J. M. Hanley, San Francisco, 1
D. J. Wren, San Francisco, 5
Oakland Parlor, N.S.G.W., Oakland, 25
J. C. Griffin, Merced, 1
E. H. Kraus, Sacramento, 2
Sacramento Parlor, N.S.G.W., Sacramento, 15
Pacific Parlor, N.S.G.W., San Francisco, 10
Napa Parlor, N.S.G.W., Napa, 10
Mt. Tamalpais Parlor, N.S.G.W., San Rafael, 5
Athens Parlor, N.S.G.W., Oakland, 15
Raymond H. Kilborn, San Francisco, 2
Leland E. Kilborn, San Francisco, 3
Benjamin L. McKinley, San Francisco, 1
Sunset Parlor, N.S.G.W., Sacramento, 10
Chico Parlor, N.S.G.W., Chico, 5
Placerville Parlor, N.S.G.W., Placerville, 10
J. B. Amestoy, Los Angeles, 35
F. J. Talamantes, Los Angeles, 5
W. J. Variel, Los Angeles, 2
W. B. Metcalf, Santa Barbara, 2
A. Goux, Santa Barbara, 2
E. M. Bucklue, Los Angeles, 10
P. A. Blair, Los Angeles, 1
W. D. Wagner, San Bernardino, 15
A. A. Schmidt, Los Angeles, 10
P. F. Johnson, Los Angeles, 1
J. D. Smith, Los Angeles, 3
J. B. Masselin, Los Angeles, 1
Wm. Rudolph, Los Angeles, 1
M. G. Jones, Los Angeles, 5
E. M. Lazard, Los Angeles, 2
E. J. Dillon, Los Angeles, 1
Hugh Glassell, Los Angeles, 10
C. Heinzman, Los Angeles, 2
Florence C. Sharp, 11
J. M. Carson, Los Angeles, 5
J. M. Allen, Los Angeles, 5
M. J. Aquirre, Los Angeles, 5
R. C. Monte, Los Angeles, 1
E. H. Hall, Holtville, 1
H. H. Hall, Holtville, 1
E. Zobelein, Los Angeles, 1
Aubry Austin, Los Angeles, 5
Hydraulic Parlor, N.S.G.W., Nevada City, 10
G. A. Burns, Sacramento, 5
Yosemite Parlor, N.S.G.W., Merced, 3
Excelsior Parlor, N.S.G.W., Jackson, 5
F. A. Stephenson, Los Angeles, 10
E. B. Lovie, Los Angeles, 1
San Francisco Parlor, N.S.G.W., San Francisco, 5
W. F. Bryant, Los Angeles, 25
J. M. Hickey, San Francisco, 1
J. E. O'Connell, San Francisco, 8
J. E. Rigney, San Francisco, 1
Golden Gate Parlor, N.S.G.W., San Francisco, 8
Sequoia Parlor, N.S.G.W., San Francisco, 1
Les Henry, Los Angeles, 2
E. O. Edgerton, Los Angeles, 30
Alcalde Parlor, N.S.G.W., San Francisco, 5
George Beebe, Los Angeles, 3
Fletcher Ford, Los Angeles, 15
Ray Howard, Los Angeles, 5
Santa Barbara Parlor, N.S.G.W., Santa Barbara, 10
Fred Eaton, Los Angeles, 2
John T. Newell, Los Angeles, 8
Clarence Jarvis, Sutter Creek, 5
W. A. Hobson, Ventura, 3
Amador Parlor, N.S.G.W., Sutter Creek, 10
John F. Davis, San Francisco, 5
Clarence M. Hunt, Los Angeles, 20
Grant Jackson, Los Angeles, 20
L. H. Valentine, Los Angeles, 8
J. P. Kiefer, Los Angeles, 10
John Castera, Los Angeles, 5
F. J. Palomares, Los Angeles, 1
W. J. McCaffery, Santa Barbara, 2
A. F. Jones, Oroville, 2
San Jose Parlor, N.S.G.W., San Jose, 5
Byron Parlor, N.S.G.W., Byron, 2
Gen. Winn Parlor, N.S.G.W., Antioch, 2
Alameda Parlor, N.S.G.W., Alameda, 1
Georgetown Parlor, N.S.G.W., Georgetown, 5
Precita Parlor, N.S.G.W., San Francisco, 5
Alder Glen Parlor, N.S.G.W., Fort Bragg, 1
Fruitvale Parlor, N.S.G.W., Fruitvale, 1
Quartz Parlor, N.S.G.W., Grass Valley, 5
Selma Parlor, N.S.G.W., Selma, 1
Carquinez Parlor, N.S.G.W., Crockett, 1
H. G. W. Dinkelspiel, San Francisco, 1
Homeless Children's Agency, San Francisco, 1
Bay City Parlor, N.S.G.W., San Francisco, 2
Chas. R. Thomas, Los Angeles, 2
J. D. Hunter, Los Angeles, 3
Daisy E. L. Eckstrom, 10
Irving Baxter, Los Angeles, 5
Harry G. Folsom, Los Angeles, 1
Mrs. Maria Gibson, San Francisco, 10
Stanford Parlor, N.S.G.W., San Francisco, 5
L. F. Soto, Los Angeles, 5
Chas. Stansbury, Los Angeles, 10
Jo V. Snyder, Nevada City, 2
Lon S. McCoy, Los Angeles, 1
William I. Traeger, Los Angeles, 1

Official Directory of Parlors of the N. S. G. W.

ALAMEDA COUNTY.

Alameda No. 47, Alameda City—Guy C. Whitmore, Pres.; Robt. H. Cavanaugh, Sec., 1806 Pacific Ave.; Wednesdays, Native Sons Hall, 1406 Park St.

Oakland No. 50, Oakland—E. A. Rehorst, Pres.; F. M. Norris, Sec., 4280 Terrace St.; Fridays, Native Sons Hall, 11th and Clay Sts.

Las Positas No. 96, Livermore—Delbert L. Johnson, Pres.; John J. Kelly, Sec., P. O. box 341; Thursdays, Foresters Hall.

Eden No. 113, Hayward—William J. Burgess, Pres.; Henry Powell, Sec., 944 Castro St.; 1st and 3rd Wednesdays, Bank, Hayward Hall.

Piedmont No. 120, Oakland—Andrew Costelli, Pres.; Charles Morando, Sec., 906 Vermont St.; Thursdays, Native Sons Hall, 11th and Clay Sts.

Wisteria No. 127, Alvarado—Henry May, Pres.; J. M. Scribner, Sec., Livermore; 1st Thursday, I.O.O.F. Hall.

Halcyon No. 146, Alameda City—T. W. Soule, Pres.; J. C. Bates, Sec., 2139 Buena Vista Ave; 1st and 3rd Tuesdays, I.O.O.F. Hall, 2329 Santa Clara Ave.

Brooklyn No. 151, Oakland—Frank B. Perry, Pres.; E. W. Cooney, Sec., 3907 14th Ave.; Wednesdays, Masonic Temple, 8th Ave. and E. 14th St.

Washington No. 169, Centerville—F. T. Dusterberry, Pres.; Allen G. Norris, Sec., P. O. box 31; 2nd and 4th Tuesdays, Hansen Hall.

Athens No. 195, Oakland—Allan W. Sunkler, Pres.; Harold B. Farley, Sec., 4623 Benevides Ave.; Tuesdays, Native Sons Hall, 11th and Clay Sts.

Berkeley No. 210, Berkeley—Maurice Casey, Pres.; R. J. Garrett, Sec., 1708 Virginia St.; Tuesdays, Native Sons Hall, 2108 Shattuck Ave.

Estudillo No. 223, San Leandro—William G. Lewis, Pres.; Albert G. Pacheco, Sec., 1736 E. 14th St.; 1st and 3rd Tuesdays, Masonic Temple.

Claremont No. 240, Oakland—George F. Davis, Pres.; E. N. Thienger, Sec., 839 Hearst Ave., Berkeley; Tuesdays, Veterans Memorial Bldg., 43rd & Salem Sts., Emeryville.

Pleasanton No. 244, Pleasanton—Peter C. Madsen, Pres.; Ernest W. Schween, Sec.; 2nd and 4th Thursdays, I.O.O.F. Hall.

Niles No. 250, Niles—M. L. Fournier, Pres.; C. E. Martenstein, Sec.; 2nd Thursday, I.O.O.F. Hall.

Fruitvale, No. 252, Oakland—Anthony J. King, Pres.; Ray B. Felton, Sec., 1575 Alice St.; Fridays, W.O.W. Hall, 3256 E. 14th St.

AMADOR COUNTY.

Amador No. 17, Sutter Creek—H. T. Richards, Pres.; F. J. Payne, Sec.; 1st and 3rd Fridays, Native Sons Hall.

Excelsior No. 31, Jackson—Wm. Daugherty, Pres.; William Going, Sec.; 1st and 3rd Wednesdays, Native Sons Hall, 22 Court St.

Ione No. 33, Ione—A. C. Miner, Pres.; Josiah H. Saunders, Sec.; 1st and 3rd Wednesdays, Native Sons Hall.

Plymouth No. 48, Plymouth—B. L. Crain, Pres.; Thos. D. Davis, Sec.; 1st and 3rd Saturdays, I.O.O.F. Hall.

BUTTE COUNTY.

Argonaut No. 8, Oroville—Fred E. Tegrunde, Pres.; Cyril R. Macdonald, Sec., P. O. box 502; 1st and 3rd Wednesdays, Veterans Memorial Hall.

Chico No. 21, Chico—Marcus Choisser, Pres.; Sam Lindsay Adams, Sec., Sacramento Blvd.; 2nd and 4th Thursdays, Elks Hall.

CALAVERAS COUNTY.

Chispa No. 139, Murphys—John Voitich, Pres.; Antone Malaspina, Sec.; Wednesdays, Native Sons Hall.

COLUSA COUNTY.

Colusa No. 69 Colusa City—S. A. Ottenwalter, Pres.; Phil J. Humburg, Sec., 223 Parkhill St.; Tuesdays, First National Bank Bldg.

CONTRA COSTA COUNTY.

General Winn No. 32, Antioch—Edmont T. Uren, Pres.; Joel H. Ford, Sec., P. O. box 311; 2nd and 4th Wednesdays, Union Hall.

Mount Diablo No. 101, Martinez—Melvin Wells, Pres.; G. T. Barkley, Sec.; 1st and 3rd Mondays, I.O.O.F. Hall.

Byron No. 170, Byron—R. R. Houston, Pres.; H. G. Krumland, Sec.; 1st and 3rd Tuesdays, I.O.O.F. Hall.

Carquinez No. 205, Crockett—Thos. Cox, Pres.; Thomas I. Cahalan, Sec.; 1st and 3rd Wednesdays, I.O.O.F. Hall.

Richmond No. 217, Richmond—M. W. Amaral, Pres.; H. D. Mason, Sec.; 11 6th St.; Wednesdays, Redmen Hall, 11th and Neven Ave.

Concord No. 245, Concord—P. M. Soto, Pres.; D. E. Pramberg, Sec., P. O. box 235; 1st Tuesday, I.O.O.F. Hall.

Diamond No. 246, Pittsburg—Horace L. Lucide, Pres.; Francis A. Irving, Sec., 248 E. 5th St.; 1st and 3rd Wednesdays, Veterans Memorial Bldg.

GRAND OFFICERS.

John T. Newell........Junior Past Grand President
4611 Brynhurst, Los Angeles

Dr. Frank I. Gonzalez..............Grand President
Flood Bldg., San Francisco

Seth Millington..............Grand First Vice-pres.
Gridley

Justice Emmet Seawell....Grand Second Vice-pres.
State Bldg., San Francisco

Chas. A. Koenig............Grand Third Vice-pres.
531 35th Ave, San Francisco

John T. Regan.......................Grand Secretary
N.S.G.W. Bldg., 414 Mason St. San Francisco

John A. Corotto......................Grand Treasurer
560 No. 6th St., San Jose

Horace J. Leavitt.......................Grand Marshal
Weaverville

W. B. O'Brien..................Grand Inside Sentinel
2324 Santa Clara St., Alameda

Gam Hurst ....Grand Outside Sentinel
1400 Financial Center Bldg., Oakland

Leslie Maloche........................Grand Organist
467½ 3rd St., San Bernardino

George H. Barron...................Historiographer
241 Frederick St., San Francisco

GRAND TRUSTEES.

George F. McNoble.......California Bldg., Stockton
Samuel M. Shortridge Jr..................Menlo Park
Jesse H. Miller..712 DeYoung Bldg., San Francisco
Joseph J. McShane..419 Flood Bldg., San Francisco
Frank M. Lane.............333 Blackstone, Fresno
John M. Burnett.................................San Jose

EL DORADO COUNTY.

Placerville No. 9, Placerville—Jos. Scherrer, Pres.; Duncan Bathurst, Sec., 12 Gilmore St.; 2nd and 4th Tuesdays, Masonic Hall.

Georgetown No. 91, Georgetown—J. H. Stanton, Pres.; C. F. Irish, Sec.; 2nd and 4th Wednesdays, I.O.O.F. Hall.

FRESNO COUNTY.

Fresno No. 25, Fresno City—E. F. Fitzgerald, Pres.; John W. Cappleman, Sec., 1389 Wilson; Fridays, W.O.W. Hall, 1354 Van Ness Ave.

Selma No. 107, Selma—Chester E. Shepard, Pres.; E. C. Laughlin, Sec.; 1st Wednesday, American Legion Hall.

HUMBOLDT COUNTY.

Humboldt No. 14, Eureka—Percy R. Henry, Pres.; Loren M. Nelson, Sec., P. O. Box 195; 2nd and 4th Mondays, Native Sons Hall.

Arcata No. 20, Arcata—E. L. Henry, Pres.; William Peters, Sec., P. O. box 1117; Thursdays, Native Sons Hall.

Ferndale No. 93, Ferndale—Geo. E. Becker, Pres.; C. H. Rasmussen, Sec., R.F.D. 47-A; 1st and 3rd Mondays, K.P. Hall.

KERN COUNTY

Bakersfield No. 42, Bakersfield—G. E. Taylor, Pres.; Leroy Vandervoort, Sec., P. O. box 1015; Wednesdays, Justice Court, City Hall.

LAKE COUNTY.

Lower Lake No. 159, Lower Lake—Harold S. Anderson, Pres.; Albert Kugelman, Sec.; Thursdays, I.O.O.F. Hall.

LASSEN COUNTY.

Honey Lake No. 198, Standish—N. B. Elledge, Pres.; W. B. Dewitt, Sec., 842 Roop St., Susanville; 1st and 3rd Wednesdays, Wrede Hall.

Big Valley No. 211, Bieber—George Bunselmeier, Pres.; A. W. McKenzie, Sec.; 1st and 3rd Wednesdays, I.O.O.F. Hall.

LOS ANGELES COUNTY.

Los Angeles No. 45, Los Angeles City—Victor D. Kremer, Pres.; Richard W. Fryer, Sec., 1629 Champlain Ter.; Thursdays, Merchant Plumbers Hall, 1832 So. Hope.

Ramona No. 109, Los Angeles City—Charles G. Young, Pres.; John V. Scott, Sec., Patriotic Hall, 1816 So. Figueroa; Fridays, Patriotic Hall, 1816 So. Figueroa.

Hollywood No. 196, Los Angeles City—Fred Gamble Jr., Pres.; E. J. Reilly, Sec., 210 S. Fremont St.; Mondays, Hollywood Conservatory Music, 5402 Hollywood Blvd.

Long Beach No. 239, Long Beach—Francis H. Gentry, Pres.; W. W. Brady, Sec., 801 Jergins Trust Bldg.; 2nd and 4th Thursdays, Moose Hall, Elm and Anaheim.

Sepulveda No. 263, San Pedro—Lawrence Powers, Pres.; Frank I. Markey, Sec., 101 W. 7th St.; 2nd and 4th Fridays, Odd Fellows Temple, 10th and Gaffey Sts.

Glendale No. 264, Glendale—Gustave W. Jorres, Pres.; A. B. Molen, Sec., 508 So. Belmont St.; 1st and 3rd Tuesdays, Masonic Temple, 234 So. Brand Blvd.

Santa Monica Bay No. 267, Ocean Park—Frederick E. Barnes, Pres.; John J. Smith, Sec., 830 Rialto Ave., Venice; 2nd and 4th Mondays, New Eagle Hall, 2823½ Main St.

Cahuenga No. 268, Reseda—Harold C. Trexler, Pres.; Walter A. Knapp, Sec., 7711 Owensmouth Ave., Canoga Park; first Friday, Alton Hall.

MADERA COUNTY.

Madera No. 130, Madera City—Cornelius Noble, Pres.; T. P. Cosgrave, Sec.; 1st and 3rd Thursdays, First National Bank Bldg.

MARIN COUNTY.

Mount Tamalpais No. 64, San Rafael—Walter Mazza, Pres.; Manuel A. Andrade, Sec., 532 Mission Ave.; 1st and 3rd Mondays, Portuguese American Hall.

Sea Point No. 158, Sausalito—Willis B. Garcia, Pres.; Manuel Santos, Sec., 6 Glen Drive; 1st and 3rd Wednesdays, Perry Bldg.

Nicasio No. 183, Nicasio—M. T. Farley, Pres.; R. J. Rogers, Sec.; 2nd and 4th Wednesdays, U.A.O.D. Hall.

MENDOCINO COUNTY.

Ukiah No. 71, Ukiah—Albert T. Bechtol, Pres.; Ben Hofman, Sec., P. O. box 473; 1st and 3rd Mondays, I.O.O.F. Hall.

ATTENTION, SECRETARIES!

THIS DIRECTORY IS PUBLISHED BY AUTHORITY OF THE GRAND PARLOR N.S.G.W., AND ALL NOTICES OF CHANGES MUST BE RECEIVED BY THE GRAND SECRETARY (NOT THE MAGAZINE) ON OR BEFORE THE 20TH OF EACH MONTH TO INSURE CORRECTION IN NEXT ISSUE OF DIRECTORY.

Broderick No. 117, Point Arena—Abel Olsen, Pres.; H. C. Hunter, Sec.; 1st and 3rd Thursdays, Forester Hall.

Alder Glen No. 200, Fort Bragg—T. J. Simpson, Pres.; C. R. Weller, Sec.; 2nd and 4th Fridays, I.O.O.F. Hall.

MERCED COUNTY.

Yosemite No. 24, Merced City—Anthony A. Rodrigues, Pres.; True W. Fowler, Sec., P. O. box 781; 2nd and 4th Mondays, I.O.O.F. Hall.

MONTEREY COUNTY.

Monterey No. 75, Monterey City—John Thomsen, Pres.; W. W. Rodehaver, Sec., 321 Alvarado St.; 1st and 3rd Fridays, Knights Pythias Hall, Main St.

Santa Lucia No. 97, Salinas—E. L. Adcock, Pres.; R. W. Adcock, Sec., Route 2, box 141; Mondays, Native Sons Hall, 32 W. Alisal St.

Gabilan No. 132, Castroville—George Rodrigues, Pres.; R. H. Martin, Sec., P. O. box 81; 1st and 3rd Thursdays, Native Sons Hall.

NAPA COUNTY.

Saint Helena No. 53, Saint Helena—Edward L. Paulson, Pres.; Edw. L. Bonhote, Sec., P. O. box 267; Mondays, Native Sons Hall.

Napa No. 62, Napa City—H. N. Bunce, Pres.; H. J. Hoernle, Sec., 1226 Oak St.; Mondays, Native Sons Hall.

Calistoga No. 86, Calistoga—Rev. T. J. McKeon, Pres.; R. J. Williams, Sec.; 1st and 3rd Mondays, I.O.O.F. Hall.

NEVADA COUNTY.

Hydraulic No. 56, Nevada City—Spencer G. White, Pres.; Dr. C. W. Chapman, Sec.; Tuesdays, Pythian Castle.

Quartz No. 58, Grass Valley—Richard Hoskins, Pres.; H. Ray George, Sec., 151 Conaway Ave.; Mondays, Auditorium Hall.

Donner No. 162, Truckee—J. F. Lichtenberger, Pres.; H. C. Lichtenberger, Sec.; 2nd and 4th Tuesdays, Native Sons Hall.

ORANGE COUNTY.

Santa Ana No. 265, Santa Ana—R. L. Marsile, Pres.; E. F. Marks, Sec., 1124 No. Bristol St.; 1st and 3rd Mondays, K.C. Hall, 4th and French Sts.

PLACER COUNTY.

Auburn No. 59, Auburn—Cosme Vicencio, Pres.; J. G. Walsh, Sec.; 1st and 3rd Fridays, Foresters Hall.

Silver Star No. 63, Lincoln—Frank Meyers, Pres.; Barney G. Barry, Sec., P. O. box 72; 3rd Wednesday, I.O.O.F. Hall.

Rocklin No. 233, Roseville—Thomas Elliott, Pres.; M. E. Reed, Sec., 253 W. Duranta; 2nd and 4th Wednesdays, Eagles Hall.

PLUMAS COUNTY.

Quincy No. 131, Quincy—J. O. Moncur, Pres.; E. C Kelsey, Sec.; 2nd Thursday, I.O.O.F. Hall.

Golden Anchor No. 182, La Porte—R. J. McGrath, Pres.; LeRoy J. Post, Sec.; 2nd and 4th Sunday mornings, Native Sons Hall.

Plumas No. 228, Taylorsville—E. E. Sikes, Pres.; George E. Boyden, Sec.; 1st and 3rd Mondays, Native Sons Hall.

SACRAMENTO COUNTY.

Sacramento No. 3, Sacramento City—John Major, Pres.; J. F. Didion, Sec., 1131 "O" St.; Thursdays, Native Sons Bldg., 11th and "J" Sts.

Sunset No. 26, Sacramento City—Theodore Jacks, Pres.; Edward E. Reese, Sec., County Treasurer Office; Mondays, Native Sons Bldg., 11th and "J" Sts.

Elk Grove No. 41, Elk Grove—Fred Sehlmeyer, Pres.; Walter Martin, Sec.; 2nd and 4th Fridays, Masonic Hall.

Granite No. 83, Folsom—Joe Relvas, Pres.; Frank Showers, Sec.; 2nd and 4th Tuesdays, K.P. Hall.

Courtland No. 106, Courtland—Albert Pyhnan, Pres.; Jos. Green, Sec.; 1st Saturday and 3rd Monday, Native Sons Hall.

Sutter Fort No. 241, Sacramento City—August Lehman, Pres.; C. L. Katzenstein, Sec., P. O. box 914; 2nd and 4th Wednesdays, Native Sons Bldg., 11th and "J" Sts.

Galt No. 243, Galt—Geo. H. May, Pres.; F. W. Harms, Sec.; 1st and 3rd Mondays, I.O.O.F. Hall.

SAN BENITO COUNTY.

Fremont No. 44, Hollister—Chas. B. Arbeleche, Pres.; J. E. Prendergast Jr., Sec., 1064 Monterey St.; 1st and 3rd Thursdays, Grangers Union Hall.

SAN BERNARDINO COUNTY.

Arrowhead No. 110, San Bernardino City—Leslie Maloche, Pres.; R. W. Brazelton, Sec., 462 6th St.; Wednesdays, Eagles Hall, 469 4th St.

SAN DIEGO COUNTY.

San Diego No. 108, San Diego City—Gregory A. McHorney, Pres.; A. V. Mayrhofer, Sec., 1572 2nd St.; Wednesdays, K.C. Hall, 4th and Elm Sts.

SAN FRANCISCO CITY AND COUNTY.

California No. 1, San Francisco—Elmer W. Bruce, Pres.; Ellis A. Blackman, Sec., 126 Front St.; Thursdays, Native Sons Bldg., 414 Mason St.

Pacific No. 10, San Francisco—Charles R. Boden, Pres.; J. Henry Bastein, Sec., 1880 Howard St.; Tuesdays, Native Sons Bldg., 414 Mason St.

Golden Gate No. 29, San Francisco—Clyde D. Bruhn, Pres.; Adolph Eberhart, Sec., 183 Carl St.; Mondays, Native Sons Bldg., 414 Mason St.

Mission No. 38, San Francisco—Leslie Greine Jr., Pres.; Thos. J. Stewart, Sec., 1919 Howard St.; Wednesdays, Redmen Hall, 3053 16th St.

San Francisco No. 49, San Francisco—George Batchelor, Pres.; David Capurro, Sec., 976 Union St.; Thursdays, Native Sons Bldg., 414 Mason St.

El Dorado No. 52, San Francisco—Eugene Herzog, Pres.; Frank A. Bonivert, Sec., 2164 Larkin St.; Thursdays, Native Sons Bldg., 414 Mason St.

Rincon No. 72, San Francisco—Joseph E. Tinney, Pres.; John A. Gilmour, Sec., 2069 Golden Gate Ave.; Wednesdays, Native Sons Bldg., 414 Mason St.

Stanford No. 76, San Francisco—Hubert Caveney, Pres.; Charles T. O'Kane, Sec., 1111 Pine St.; Tuesdays, Native Sons Bldg., 414 Mason St.

Bay City No. 104, San Francisco—Julius J. Glaser, Pres.; Max E. Licht, Sec., 1831 Fulton St.; 2nd and 4th Wednesdays, Native Sons Bldg., 414 Mason St.

Niantic No. 105, San Francisco—A. Furner, Pres.; J. M. Darcy, Sec., 10 Hoffman Ave.; Wednesdays, Native Sons Bldg., 414 Mason St.

National No. 118, San Francisco—William A. Brennan, Pres.; Frank L. Hatfield, Sec., 3990 20th St.; Thursdays, 1160 Eddy St.

Hesperian No. 137, San Francisco—Walter A. Bermingham, Pres.; Albert Carlson, Sec., 379 Justin Dr.; Thursdays, Native Sons Bldg., 414 Mason St.
Alcalde No. 154, San Francisco—John S. La Barbern, Pres.; Harry S. Burke, Sec., 25 Ord St.; 2nd and 4th Wednesdays, Native Sons Bldg., 414 Mason St.
South San Francisco No. 157, San Francisco—James Brady, Pres.; John T. Regan, Sec., 1489 Newcomb Ave.; Wednesdays, Masonic Bldg., 4705 3rd St.
Sequoia No. 160, San Francisco—James L. Vizzard, Pres.; Walter W. Garrett, Sec., 2500 Van Ness Ave.; Mondays, Swedish-American Bldg., 2174 Market St.
Precita No. 187, San Francisco—Geo. T. Butler, Pres.; Edward Tietjen, Sec., 1367 15th Ave.; Thursdays, Mission Masonic Hall, 2668 Mission St.
Olympus No. 189, San Francisco—Louis Helbing, Pres.; Harvey J. Carty, Sec., 1651 Market St., Apt. 505; 2nd and 4th Tuesdays, Independent Redmen Hall, 3053 16th St.
Presidio No. 194, San Francisco—Paul Pasquet, Pres.; George A. Ducker, Sec., 442 21st Ave.; Mondays, Native Sons Bldg., 414 Mason St.
Marshall No. 202, San Francisco—Robert J. Everson, Pres.; Frank Bacigalupi, Sec., 725 Douglas St.; Wednesdays, Native Sons Bldg., 414 Mason St.
Dolores No. 208, San Francisco—George Stelling, Pres.; Eugene O'Donnell, Sec., Mills Bldg.; Tuesdays, Mission Masonic Bldg., 2668 Mission St.
Twin Peaks No. 214, San Francisco—Jos. J. McShane, Pres.; Thos. Pendergast, Sec., 278 Douglas St.; Wednesdays, Willopi Hall, 4061 24th St.
El Capitan No. 222, San Francisco—Frank Rizzo, Pres.; James Hanna, Sec., 2450 27th Ave.; 1st and 3rd Thursdays, King Soloman Hall, 1739 Fillmore St.
Guadalupe No. 231, San Francisco—George Miles, Pres.; Alvin A. Johnson, Sec., 142 Rousseau St.; Tuesdays, Guadalupe Hall, 4551 Mission St.
Castro No. 232, San Francisco—Joseph P. Toboni Jr., Pres.; James H. Hayes, Sec., 4014 18th St.; Tuesdays, Native Sons Bldg., 414 Mason St.
Balboa No. 234, San Francisco—R. W. Fowler, Pres.; E. W. Boyd, Sec., 45 Carl St.; Thursdays, Maccabee Hall, 5th Ave. and Clement St.
James Lick No. 242, San Francisco—J. P. Madden, Pres.; Wm. Band, Sec., 2587 22nd Ave.; 1st and 3rd Tuesdays, Redmen Hall, 3053 16th St.
Bret Harte No. 260, San Francisco—Dr. H. Wider, Pres.; Ivan Ingram, Sec., 926 Oak St.; Tuesdays, West of Twin Peaks Hall, 233 Legion Court.
Utopia No. 270, San Francisco—Daniel Henry, Pres.; Herbert H. Schneider, Sec., 2455 16th Ave.; Tuesdays, American Hall, 20th and Capp Sts.

SAN JOAQUIN COUNTY.

Stockton No. 7, Stockton—Eugene Allison, Pres.; R. D. Dorcey, Sec., P. O. box 388; Mondays, Native Sons Hall.
Lodi No. 18, Lodi—Ray Rodocker, Pres.; Dr. Clyde Bresnan, Sec.; 2nd and 4th Wednesdays, Eagles Hall.
Tracy No. 186, Tracy—Edward J. Shields, Pres.; R. J. Marraccini, Sec., R.F.D. No. 1, box 217; Thursdays, I.O.O.F. Hall.
Manteca No. 271, Manteca—S. A. Whiting, Pres.; Leonard Faria, Sec., R.F.D. No. 1, Lathrop; 1st and 3rd Wednesdays, I.O.O.F. Hall.

SAN LUIS OBISPO COUNTY.

San Miguel No. 150, San Miguel—H. Twisselman, Pres.; George Sonnenberg Jr., Sec.; 1st and 3rd Wednesdays, Fraternal Hall.
Cambria No. 152, Cambria—L. Bernardisca, Pres.; A. S. Gay, Sec.; Wednesdays, Rigdon Hall.

SAN MATEO COUNTY.

Redwood No. 66, Redwood City—Oscar O. Gustafson, Pres.; A. S. Liguori, Sec., P. O. box 212; Thursdays, American Foresters Hall.
Seaside No. 95, Halfmoon Bay—Edward Deeney, Pres.; John G. Gilcrest, Sec.; 2nd and 4th Tuesdays, I.O.O.F. Hall.
Menlo No. 185, Menlo Park—John Bracisco, Pres.; F. W. Johnson, Sec., P. O. box 601; Thursdays, Duff & Doyle Hall.
Pebble Beach No. 230, Pescadero—Bernard Cabral, Pres.; E. A. Shaw, Sec.; 2nd and 4th Wednesdays, I.O.O.F. Hall.
El Carmelo No. 256, Daly City—Leonard J. Mohr, Pres.; Andrew P. Murphy, Sec., 931 Hanover St.; 2nd and 4th Wednesdays, Eagles Hall.
Industrial City No. 269, South San Francisco—John C. Hamilton, Pres.; Geo. A. Roll, Sec., P. O. box 237; 2nd and 4th Mondays, Metropolitan Hall.

SANTA BARBARA COUNTY.

Santa Barbara No. 116, Santa Barbara City—John L. Stewart, Pres.; H. C. Sweetser, Sec., Court House; 1st and 3rd Wednesdays, I.O.O.F. Hall.

SANTA CLARA COUNTY.

San Jose No. 22, San Jose—William Lordge, Pres.; H. W. McComas, Sec., Suite 7, Porter Bldg.; Mondays, I.O.O.F. Hall.
Santa Clara No. 100, Santa Clara City—John J. Trinajstich, Pres.; Clarence Clevenger, Sec., P. O. box 297; 1st and 3rd Wednesdays, Redmen Hall.
Observatory No. 177, San Jose—Norton J. Mahon, Pres.; A. B. Langford, Sec., Hall Records; Tuesdays, Knights Columbus Hall, 40 No. First St.
Mountain View No. 215, Mountain View—Harold M. Chandler, Pres.; C. A. Antonioli, Sec., 948 California St.; 2nd and 4th Fridays, Mockbee Hall.
Palo Alto No. 216, Palo Alto—Marion R. Smith, Pres.; Albert A. Quinn, Sec., 643 High St.; Mondays, Native Sons Bldg., Hamilton Ave. and Emerson St.

SANTA CRUZ COUNTY.

Watsonville No. 65, Watsonville—Cecil McGowan, Pres.; E. R. Tindall, Sec., 408 East Lake Ave.; 2nd and 4th Tuesdays, I.O.O.F. Hall.
Santa Cruz No. 90, Santa Cruz City—Elmer R. Dakan, Pres.; T. V. Mathews, Sec., 105 Pacheco Ave.; Tuesdays, Native Sons Hall, 117 Pacific Ave.

SHASTA COUNTY.

McCloud No. 149, Redding—Albert F. Ross, Pres.; Hugh A. Shuffleton, Sec.; 1st and 3rd Thursdays, Moose Hall.

SIERRA COUNTY.

Downieville No. 92, Downieville—J. M. McMahon, Pres.; H. S. Tibbey, Sec.; 2nd and 4th Mondays, I.O.O.F. Hall.
Golden Nugget No. 94, Sierra City—Leonard Thompson Jr., Pres; Arthur R. Pride, Sec.; last Saturday, Masonic Hall.

SISKIYOU COUNTY.

Etna No. 192, Etna—George Marx, Pres.; Harvey A. Green, Sec.; 1st and 3rd Wednesdays, I.O.O.F. Hall.
Liberty No. 193, Sawyers Bar—Orrin R. Bigelow, Pres.; John M. Barry, Sec.; 1st and 3rd Saturdays, I.O.O.F. Hall.

N.S.G.W. OFFICIAL DEATH LIST.

Containing the name, the date and the place of birth, the date of death, and the Subordinate Parlor affiliation of deceased members reported to Grand Secretary John T. Regan from September 19, 1931, to October 20, 1931:

Haw, Timothy Edward: Sutter Creek, November 15, 1868; September 13, 1931; Placerville No. 9.

Whiteman, George H.: Poverty Bar, January 24, 1862; October 3, 1931; Amador No. 17.

Simon, Charles: San Francisco, July 30, 1865; September 28, 1931; Yosemite No. 24.

McCoy, Thomas H.: Stockton, June 18, 1900; September 30, 1931, General Winn No. 32.

Winterberg, Adolph: San Francisco, September 1, 1863; August 3, 1931; Mission No. 38.

Amillo, Alfred: Los Angeles, December 19, 1875; September 29, 1931; Los Angeles No. 45.

Flynn, John James: Watsonville, February 10, 1865; September 17, 1931; Alameda No. 47.

Bolte, Herman Fred William: San Francisco, July 20, 1877; September 26, 1931; Alameda No. 47.

Morgan, Edward C.: Murphy's Camp, December 6, 1858; September 8, 1931; Quartz No. 58.

SOLANO COUNTY.

Solano No. 39, Suisun—Ralph E. Gilbert, Pres.; J. W. Kinloch, Sec.; 1st and 3rd Tuesdays, I.O.O.F. Hall.
Vallejo No. 77, Vallejo—John J. Combs, Pres.; Werner B. Hallin, Sec., 912 Carolina; 2nd and 4th Tuesdays, San Pablo Hall.

SONOMA COUNTY.

Petaluma No. 27, Petaluma—Wm. Bojorques, Pres.; C. F. Fobes, Sec., 114 Prospect St.; 2nd and 4th Mondays, Druid Hall, Gross Bldg., 41 Main St.
Santa Rosa No. 28, Santa Rosa—Henry T. Stone, Pres.; Leland S. Lewis, Sec., Court House; Thursdays, Native Sons Hall.
Glen Ellen No. 102, Glen Ellen—C. C. Weise, Pres.; Frank Kirch, Sec., Route 3, Santa Rosa; 2nd Monday, N.S.G.W. Hall.
Sonoma No. 111, Sonoma City—Henry Baliros, Pres.; L. H. Green, Sec.; 1st and 3rd Mondays, I.O.O.F. Hall.
Sebastopol No. 143, Sebastopol—W. H. Murray, Pres.; F. G. McFarlane, Sec.; 1st and 3rd Fridays, I.O.O.F. Hall.

STANISLAUS COUNTY.

Modesto No. 11, Modesto—W. B. Mahoney, Pres.; C. C. Eastin Jr., Sec., P. O. box 898; 1st and 3rd Wednesdays, I.O.O.F. Hall.
Oakdale No. 142, Oakdale—D W. Tulloch, Pres.; E. T. Gobin, Sec.; 2nd Monday, Legion Hall.
Orestimba No. 247, Crows Landing—Lloyd W. Fink, Pres.; G. W. Fink, Sec.; 1st and 3rd Wednesdays, Community Club Home.

SUTTER COUNTY.

Sutter No. 261, Sutter City—Stanley R. McLean, Pres.; Glen R. Haynes, Sec., Yuba City; 1st and 3rd Mondays, Brittan Grammar School.

TRINITY COUNTY.

Mount Bally No. 87, Weaverville—M. F. Kay, Pres.; E. V. Ryan, Sec.; 1st and 3rd Mondays, Native Sons Hall.

TUOLUMNE COUNTY.

Tuolumne No. 144, Sonora—Mathew J. Marshall, Pres.; William M. Harrington, Sec., P. O. box 715; 2nd and 4th Fridays, Knights Columbus Hall.
Columbia No. 258, Columbia—Jos. Cadematori, Pres.; Charles E. Grant, Sec.; 2nd and 4th Thursdays, Native Sons Hall.

VENTURA COUNTY.

Cabrillo No. 114, Ventura City—David Bennett, Pres., 1380 Church St.

YOLO COUNTY.

Woodland No. 30, Woodland—J. L. Aronson, Pres.; E. B. Hayward, Sec.; 1st Thursday, Native Sons Hall.

YUBA COUNTY.

Marysville No. 6, Marysville—John McQuaid, Pres.; Verne Fogarty, Sec., 719 6th St.; 2nd and 4th Wednesdays, Foresters Hall.
Rainbow No. 40, Wheatland—W. E. Jones, Pres.; W. A. Bowser, Sec., P. O. box 313; 2nd Thursday, I.O.O.F. Hall.

AFFILIATED ORGANIZATIONS.

Alameda County Extension of the Order Committee, N.S.G.W.—Dr. William C. Freitas, Chmn.; Edgar G. Hansen, Sec., 1260 Russell St., Berkeley; meets 1st and 3rd Mondays, N.S.G.W. Hall, 11th and Clay Sts., Oakland.
Interparlor Committee (Southern District), N.S.G.W. and N.D.G.W.—Burrel D. Neighbours, Chmn.; F. J. Burmester, Sec., 2434 Micheltorena St., Los Angeles; meets 2nd and 4th Fridays, Patriotic Hall, 1816 So. Figueroa St., Los Angeles.
San Francisco Extension of the Order Committee, N.S.G.W.—Harmon D. Skillin, Chmn.; Harold J. Regan, Sec., 414 Mason St., San Francisco; meets 2nd and 4th Fridays, Grizzly Bear Club, 414 Mason St., San Francisco.
San Francisco Assembly No. 1 Past Presidents Association N.S.G.W.—Meets 1st and 3rd Fridays, Native Sons Bldg., 414 Mason St., San Francisco; H. F. Rickleffs, Gov., J. F. Stanley, Sec., 1175 O'Farrell St., San Francisco.
East Bay Counties Assembly No. 3 Past Presidents Association N.S.G.W.—Meets 4th Monday, Native Sons Hall, 11th and Clay Sts., Oakland; Lester O. Bruck, Gov.; Edgar G. Hanson, Sec., 1260 Russell St., Berkeley.
Fred H. Greely Assembly No. 6 Past Presidents Association N.S.G.W.—Meets monthly with different Parlors comprising district; R. L. P. Bigelow, Gov.; Barney Barry, Sec., P. O. box 72, Lincoln.
San Joaquin Assembly No. 7 Past Presidents Association N.S.G.W.—Meets 1st Friday, Native Sons Hall, Stockton; Clyde H. Gregg, Gov.; R. D. Dorcey, Sec., Native Sons Club, Stockton.
Sonoma County Assembly No. 9 Past Presidents Association N.S.G.W.—Meets monthly at different Parlor headquarters in county; Louis Bosch, Gov.; L. S. Lewis, Sec., Court House, Santa Rosa.
General John A. Sutter Assembly No. 10 Past Presidents Association—L. P. Ferron, Gov.; Jas. J. Longshore, Sec., 514 "J" St., Sacramento.
Grizzly Bear Club—Members all Parlors outside San Francisco at all times welcome. Clubrooms top floor Native Sons Bldg., 414 Mason St., San Francisco.
Native Sons and Native Daughters Central Committee on Homeless Children—Main office, 955 Phelan Bldg., San Francisco; Mary E. Brusie, Sec.

(ADVERTISEMENT.)

Rule, Sharon George: Dutch Flat, August 14, 1888; August 4, 1931; Auburn No. 59.

Lamdin, Robert P.: Napa, September 19, 1860; September 25, 1931; Napa No. 62.

Williams, Donald Ward: Gilda Ranch, October 29, 1880; September 25, 1931; Redwood No. 66.

Hall, Norman F.: San Francisco, November 16, 1872; September 2, 1931; Stanford No. 76.

Lawson, Albert W.: San Francisco, May 22, 1885; September 9, 1931; Stanford No. 76.

Cohen, Isaac Lazarus: Oakland, September 4, 1871; October 11, 1931; Brooklyn No. 151.

O'Brien, Matthew Sylvester: San Francisco, January 31, 1876; September 24, 1931; Sequoia No. 160.

Green, Maxwell Talbot: Traver, August 19, 1888; October 14, 1931. Observatory No. 177.

Atkinson, Frank: Redding, April 23, 1877; September 23, 1931; Dolores No. 208.

Unda, Mose M.: Berkeley, February 11, 1858; October 14, 1931; Berkeley No. 210.

Hartwick, Frank: San Francisco, November 12, 1887; October 7, 1931; Twin Peaks No. 214.

O'Shea, Vincent: San Francisco, June 18, 1890; September 25, 1931; Guadalupe No. 231.

Senegar, Edward O.: San Francisco, November 2, 1909; September 14, 1931; Industrial City No. 269.

NATIVE DAUGHTER NEWS

(Continued from Page 17)

decorated with ferns, autumn leaves and flowers, and delicious refreshments were served. Among the guests were the following, with the year of their arrival in California: Mrs. Maggie Mann (1852), Mrs. Martha Copsey (1856), Mrs. Thomas Parker (1864), Mrs. A. S. Armstrong (1863), Mrs. E. Nay (1862), and Thomas Parker (1863). Mrs. C. M. Young (1851) was unable to be present, but was remembered by the Parlor. Charter members in attendance were Ella Parker, the first president, Cora Herrick, Addie Penny, Bertha Brookins and Angie Nelson.

President Florence Elliott extended a welcome to the oldtimers and presented to them tokens of remembrance, twenty-four members of the Parlor appeared in a drill, and a program of songs and readings was presented by Clara Hunt, Merle Bohn, Florence Elliott, Mrs. Jas. Kesey and Belle Farmer.

Pajama Party.

Petaluma—Petaluma No. 222 had a pajama party October 6 and all joined in the fun. Cards were played and refreshments were served. Vacations being over, more activity is apparent and some very interesting meetings are being held. Captain Annie Dickson is busy with the Parlor's drill team, which will take part in the Armistice Day celebration at Santa Rosa.

Officers Praised.

Menlo Park—Menlo No. 211 had the pleasure October 12 of entertaining Grand President Evelyn I. Carlson, who was loud in her praise for the perfect manner in which the Parlor officers presented their charges. The halls were prettily decorated with red and yellow berries, and the officers made a pleasing picture in pastel shaded evening gowns. Among the many visitors was Past Grand President Margaret Grote-Hill.

Grand President Carlson was the recipient of a gift of china, and remembrances were presented Supervising Deputy Rena Mathias, District Deputy Margaret Malone, Emeline McDonald and Past President Laura Bartels.

Promoting State Park.

Alturas—October 1 heralded the opening of Alturas No. 159's social season, and a large group of guests enjoyed the hospitality of the Parlor at bridge. Some time ago the Parlor proposed to the State Park Commission that Blue Lake, situated in the Warner Range between Lassen and Modoc Counties, be made a state park. The commission recently notified Grand Marshal Irma Laird the project had been given favorable consideration and that the state would contribute one-half the $12,000 which the owners of the property are asking for such of their holdings as would be included in the proposed park if Lassen and Modoc Counties would contribute the balance.

The Lassen County supervisors are favorably disposed toward the project, and the Parlor, through a committee headed by Grand Marshal Laird, is urging the Modoc County supervisors to make the necessary contribution. Civic and fraternal organizations are endorsing the project, as is also the U. S. Forest Service. On the occasion of the visit of Governor James Rolph and party to Alturas, October 14, members of Alturas were present to welcome them.

California Has a Chicago—The Federal Postoffice Department has issued an order changing the name of Bay Point, Contra Costa County, to Port Chicago.

LOS ANGELES
CALIFORNIA'S WONDERLAND
CITY AND COUNTY

COSMOPOLITAN LOS ANGELES HAS OFfered a fruitful field for the nutrition worker of the American Red Cross. The city presents more vivid problems to the nutritionist than other large centers of population. Like New York, Chicago, Philadelphia and other metropolitan cities, it has the ever-present poor, and the ever-present rich who, although it is almost unbelievable, are often as untutored in food knowledge as the poorer classes. In addition to metropolitan social and health problems, Los Angeles, because of its geographic proximity, is invaded by Mexicans and Orientals who contribute their problems to the nutritionist to solve. The nutritionist must spend much energy in an educational program and top her obstacles only through the most clever psychology in overcoming emotional and traditional reactions to the new country's new foods.

But the pioneering nutritionist is a courageous soldier. She finds the lair of those who need her most and invades it despite the terrific task it promises. In the Soto-street district of Los Angeles are many Mexicans. The Red Cross nutritionist of the Los Angeles Chapter organized a nutrition class for Mexican mothers in the school of the district as a part of the regular home and americanization program. The Red Cross has conducted three nutrition classes in this school. Two members of the 1930 class attended all the courses. One woman, a Mexican who understood but little English, was given a statement saying that she had attended all the sessions. She was as proud of this statement as any college graduate with her first diploma. The nutritionist in charge had an extra handicap because so few of the Mexican women had a knowledge of English. However, one of the students was a high-school graduate and acted as interpreter for the entire course of eighteen lessons. A volunteer chapter worker also helped by translating the examination questions into Spanish, with which the Mexican women were conversant. A nutrition class was also established at the Frances DePauw school, a school for Mexican girls under the direction of the Methodist Home Mission Board.

Nutrition service in many localities may well be said to meet an emergency situation, for malnutrition in a community is a distinct emergency. The scope of nutrition service in all communities covers prenatal and preschool instruction to mothers and expectant mothers as well as older girls, school nutrition instruction, and teaching adults and teachers. The demands upon the Los Angeles nutrition service caused it to expand rapidly to include all the ramifications sponsored by the national headquarters.

The nutrition service of the American Red Cross is traceable as far back as 1908, when instruction for women and girls in "dietetics and household economy" was authorized. The work was organized and handled through the bureau of dietitian service, then a part of the Red Cross nursing service. The World War gave the work impetus and additional importance in 1917 for, in the words of Miss Clara D. Noyes, national director of Red Cross nursing service, "nutrition workers were a part of Red Cross equipment overseas."

Nutrition left its mother cradle in nursing service and assumed its own separate identity in July 1921. Eleven years after the founding of the Los Angeles Chapter of the American Red Cross in 1916, the chapter established its nutrition department. Like the mother service at national headquarters in Washington, D. C., the Los Angeles nutrition department has been an eager pioneer in a field rich in possibilities—one might say, almost crying out its need for beneficial instruction in foods.

Nutrition is only one of the many services which the American Red Cross extends to the public. It conducts public health service, nursing service, first-aid and life-saving, home hygiene and care of the sick, volunteer service, disaster service and service to war veterans.

The Red Cross got its first impulse nearly three-quarters of a century ago when Henri Dunant, a young Swiss idealist, viewed the battle of Solferino in Lombardy and was moved to compassion by the agony of the wounded and dying. Before the smoke had cleared away the young Swiss determined to administer aid to the dying soldiers, regardless of their nationalities. Hurrying to a nearby town, Dunant summoned all available men and women and appealed to them to join him in his humanitarian mission to the battlefield. Under his leadership the small group labored over the fallen warriors for many hours after hostilities had ceased.

In the years that followed, Dunant devoted his life to the work of awakening Europe to the need of humanitarian service in time of distress. The movement crystalized in 1864 and the Red Cross was founded at Geneva. Finally, May 21, 1881, the Red Cross came into being in this country. Miss Clara Barton, widely known for her unselfish service to soldiers during the Civil War, founded the society at a meeting in her Washington, D. C., home. Fifty well-known men and women attended the organization meeting and elected Miss Barton as the first president of the Red Cross in America. The Federal Government gave its full support to the movement and, in 1905, Congress granted the charter under which the Red Cross operates today.

This year, the fiftieth anniversary of the American Red Cross, marks the twenty-sixth year that Miss Mabel T. Boardman, the director of its volunteer services, has served the organization, and for twenty years she has been national secretary. Judge John Barton Payne, the eminent jurist, has served as national chairman for more than a decade without remuneration. Herbert Hoover, President of the United States, is the society's president.

Want to reach the California buying public? Then consider the advertising columns of The Grizzly Bear, which is the only publication in the state with a California-wide circulation!

Know your home-state, California! Learn of its past history and of its present-day development by reading regularly The Grizzly Bear. $1.50 for one year (12 issues) Subscribe now.

Want to reach the California buying public? Then consider the advertising columns of The Grizzly Bear, which is the only publication in the state with a California-wide circulation!

Since Dunant's service to the wounded in the battle of Solferino, throughout the administration of Clara Barton, down to the present time, the Red Cross has been carried forward by volunteers. All the society's activities have been made possible by individual memberships. There are now more than 4,000,000 members enrolled.

Due to increased demands in the last fiscal year, ended June 30, the Red Cross needs membership more than ever before. That thought will be in the minds of a quarter-million volunteer workers when the annual roll call opens Armistice Day, November 11. The campaign will end Thanksgiving Day, November 26. Between those dates every citizen in the nation will be invited to become a part of the society.

INTERPARLOR DANCE.

The Interparlor N.S.G.W. and N.D.G.W. Committee is sponsoring a series of dances at the Goldberg-Bosley Ballroom, Venice boulevard and Flower street, the proceeds of which will be used toward defraying expenses of Admission Day celebrations and other joint activities of the Native Sons and Native Daughters. The admission fee has been fixed at one dollar per couple.

The first dance will be held Friday, November 6. The presidents of all the Parlors affiliated with the Interparlor Committee will be guests of honor, and special entertainment features will be introduced.

The sub-committee in charge of these dances—Mary Noerenberg (chairman), Grace Norton, Beulah VanLuven, Andrew Vaughn and Eldred Meyer—urges the membership of both Orders to give these dances their wholehearted support.

TO CELEBRATE ANNIVERSARY.

Los Angeles Parlor No. 45 N.S.G.W. will celebrate the forty-seventh anniversary of its institution with a dance November 12. All Natives and their friends are invited. Refreshments will be served. November 19th has been set aside for initiation. At the conclusion of the ceremonies a musical program will be presented under the supervision of Organist Roger Johnson and Anthony Pierce. No meeting November 26th, Thanksgiving Day.

"WORKING TOGETHER IS SUCCESS."

The pot-luck dinner of Los Angeles Parlor No. 124 N.D.G.W. October 7 was thoroughly enjoyed. The second party of the bridge tournament October 14 was largely attended: Grace DuCasse was in charge. The officers of the Parlor went to Ocean Park October 19 and initiated a class of candidates for Santa Monica Bay Parlor No. 245.

The rummage sale conducted jointly with Verdugo Parlor No. 240 October 15, 16 and 17 was well attended: Ruth Ruiz, the chairman, was assisted by Gertrude Allen, Ann Schibusch, Flora Holy, Adeline Waite and Mrs. R. F. Bird. At the invitation of Mrs. Mattie Gara, Mrs. Fuller gave a most interesting talk October 21 on "Desert Wild Flowers." The Hallowe'en dance October 28 was a delightful affair. Good music was supplied and beautiful prizes were awarded. Many of the dancers were in costume. The hall was attractively decorated in conformity with the occasion, and jollity reigned supreme. Leone Clos was chairman of the committee in charge.

"Coming together is a beginning, keeping together is progress, working together is success," says Gertrude Allen, president No. 124. The Parlor's November calendar includes: 4th, initiation large class of candidates. 11th, card party, third in bridge tournament; Mrs. Adeline Waite, chairman. The 25th being Thanksgiving Eve, the hall will be dark.

SEW FOR NOVEMBER BAZAR

Long Beach—Long Beach Parlor No. 154 N.D.G.W. entertained October 1 the grandmothers, each of whom was asked to tell one cute saying of her grandchild; much merriment ensued. Delicious refreshments were served. Mrs. Genevieve Dalton was chairman of the occasion. The sewing club of the Parlor met October 8 at the home of Mrs. Gussie Taber. A covered-dish luncheon was served, and the members sewed on articles for the November bazar.

October 15 a Hallowe'en party was held. The families and friends of the members were invited, and many came in costume. A surprise program was presented, each officer of the Parlor being responsible for one number. The hall was gaily decorated with ghosts, black cats, etc. Following refreshments a general social evening was held. Genevieve Dalton was in charge of the party.

PENCIL SALE FOR HOMELESS CHILDREN.

Ocean Park—Santa Monica Bay Parlor No. 245 N.D.G.W. had as guests October 19 District

RIGHT NOW IS A GOOD TIME TO BECOME A SUBSCRIBER TO THE GRIZZLY BEAR
The ALL California Monthly

LOS ANGELES--CITY and COUNTY

Deputy Flora Holy and a large delegation from Los Angeles Parlor No. 124. At the invitation of President Mary Meyer, President Gertrude Allen of Los Angeles and her corps of officers exemplified the ritual, three candidates being initiated. For being the first to bring in a new member in the campaign now under way, Edna Romero was presented with an emblematic pin. Cordelia Laventhal rendered vocal selections, and the mystery-box went to Matilda Sepulveda. A lot of fun was had pinning the tail on a donkey. Refreshments were served in the banquetroom, decorated in true Hallowe'en fashion. Amada Machado (chairman), Lottie O'Connor and Rea Jones made up the committee of arrangements for the evening.

For the benefit of the homeless children, the El Camino Real Club of the Parlor, Marie Barnes chairman, conducted a successful pencil sale October 24. A shower for the veteran adopted by No. 245 will be held November 2.

OPPOSES IMMIGRATION MODIFICATION.

Hollywood Parlor No. 196 N.S.G.W. adopted the following resolution October 19: "Whereas, Any modification of the present Federal Immigration Act would be detrimental to the best interests of the United States, therefore, be it

"Resolved. That Hollywood Parlor No. 196 N.S.G.W. is unalterably opposed to any modification of the Federal Immigration Act and appeals to the Senate and the House of Representatives of the United States Congress to do everything in their power to prevent any change in said act."

The Parlor is making a drive for new members, and President Fred Gamble Jr. appointed October 5 the following committee to conduct it to a successful conclusion: Lucien Griffin, Edgar Black, Kenneth Case, Harold Thomas and William Hortenstine. A class of candidates will be initiated November 16.

SURROUNDINGS PLEASE.

The season has begun auspiciously for Californiana Parlor No. 247 N.D.G.W., and under the guidance of President Gertrude Tuttle fine meetings, with excellent attendance, are being held at the new headquarters, 1215 Lodi place, Hollywood. The members are greatly pleased with the beautiful surroundings. A private diningroom has been assigned, and here the members enjoy dainty pre-meeting lunches, the program following in the meetingroom.

Charles Horrworth was a recent speaker, giving a very sensible formula for the growth of the state. Miss Marion Graaf sang a group of songs, including some in Spanish. At another meeting Assemblyman Adam gave a description of the State Legislature and its workings. He was followed by Miss Marion Parks, a member of the Parlor who gave insight, most interesting and amusing, to "Early California Law," which she has studied through delving into old official documents in the city and county archives. A large number of applications for membership have been received, and initiation will be held November 10.

The statue of Felipe de Neve, which is to be presented by Californiana to Los Angeles City, which he founded, is now in the hands of a bronzing company, Sculptor Henry Lion having completed his handiwork. Mrs. Ora Evans, chairman of the committee, is planning an interesting program for the presentation. It was intended to have the presentation during La Fiesta, but it was impossible owing to the fact that the statue was not completed, and also because arrangements could not at that time be made for proper recognition of the event.

ANNUAL LOBSTER FEAST.

Ocean Park—"A Night in Old California," sponsored by Santa Monica Bay Parlor No. 267 N.S.G.W., filled the Sea Breeze Beach Club, Santa Monica, October 17. The affair was a roundup of all the old and new timers of the Order, to help celebrate the fifth institution anniversary of the Parlor. Junior Past Grand President John T. Newell was the honor-guest and delivered a brief address. A splendid program was arranged by Norman Manning, and Jimmy Smith, with his specially arranged Native Son song, stole the show. Two orchestras furnished dance music, and a replica of an old-time San Francisco cafe added interest. An elaborate buffet supper was partaken of by 883. The committee in charge of the successful affair included Eldred L. Meyer (chairman), Harry T. Honn, Phil Romero, Elmer Barnes, Arthur Leonard, Douglas McCreery, J. Howard Blanchard, J. Edward McCurdy, Hector Badia, John J. Smith, Dr. A. B. Mayhew, Arthur Giroux, Claud Wiseman, Stanley Tracey, Jack Dailey, Geo. Green and Beldin Sabine.

Monday, November 9, is the correct date for the Parlor's famous annual lobster feast. Chairman Phil Romero says arrangements have been made to take care of a crowd larger than ever. Jack Dailey and Howard Earl are the chefs in charge. Officers of Sepulveda Parlor No. 263 have been invited to exemplify the ritual November 23, when Santa Monica Bay will have a very large class of candidates. Plans are under way for the organization of a Parlor drum corps.

CO-OPERATION APPRECIATED.

Glendale—Following the October 12 meeting of Verdugo No. 240 N.D.G.W., a program presented by Edith Dobson was participated in by Jane Shally, Zessie Tilbury, Alice Rinaldo, Dora Blenkiron, Betty Sanders, Ada Steele and Margaret Hess. A spoon was presented Genevieve Hess, infant daughter of Mrs. Gertrude Hess.

The Parlor's Hallowe'en costume dance October 27 drew a large crowd and everybody had a good time. All neighboring Parlors of both Native Daughters and Native Sons were well represented, an expression of appreciation for Verdugo's hearty co-operation always in all Los Angeles County activities.

INITIATES CLASS.

San Pedro—Sepulveda Parlor No. 263 N.S.G.W. initiated a class of candidates October 23, the ceremonies being followed by a lobster feast. David Main and Francis Fetzer had charge of the entertainment.

Jointly with Rudecinda Parlor No. 230 N.D.G.W., the Parlor had a Hallowe'en dance October 30. Refreshments were served.

"KANGAROO COURT."

Ramona Parlor No. 109 N.S.G.W. is planning a grand Christmas party for the children of its members December 23, and arrangements are being perfected by a committee headed by Walter Slosson. To raise money for the fund, several events are scheduled; in fact, there will be something special in the way of entertainment every Friday night to and including December 18, the last meeting of 1931 for the Parlor. Joseph P. Coyle and Walter Satterwhite are captains of opposing teams in a membership contest. James P. Sex is organizing a drum and bugle corps.

Ramona's calendar for November includes: 6th, "kangaroo court;" loads of fun to swell the Christmas fund. 13th, initiation and first presentation 1932 "Bear Club" pins; buffet lunch. 20th, awards of turkeys, ducks and other fixings for the Thanksgiving dinner. 27th, nomination officers January-July term; more fun for the Christmas party fund.

THE DEATH RECORD.

James H. Steele, father of Clarence C. Steele (Ramona N.S.), died September 24 at Rosemead.

Mrs. Fanny Wilcox-Drake, sister of Alfred H. Wilcox (Ramona N.S.), passed away September 27.

Alfred Amillo, affiliated with Los Angeles Parlor No. 45 N.S.G.W., died September 28, survived by a wife and two sons. He was born at Los Angeles City, December 19, 1875.

Herbert S. Laughlin, father of H. Sidney Laughlin (Ramona N.S.), died September 29.

Mrs. Anna Bell Dedman-Chapman, affiliated

with Los Angeles Parlor No. 124 N.D.G.W., passed away September 30, survived by a husband and two children.

Mrs. Emily D. Fillmore, mother of Hugh H. Fillmore (Ramona N.S.), passed away October 22.

Robert Parker Sheldon, affiliated with Ramona Parlor No. 109 N.S.G.W., died October 23, survived by a wife and a son. He was born at San Francisco, October 29, 1874.

PERSONAL PARAGRAPHS.

Walter Cripe (Sepulveda N.S.) of San Pedro was a recent visitor to Arizona.

Harry W. Frost (Ramona N.S.), has returned from a trip to Seattle, Washington.

A native daughter arrived at the home of Victor D. Kremer (Los Angeles N.S.) October 10.

J. P. Furlong (Sepulveda N.S.) and family of San Pedro recently returned from a trip to Montana.

Native sons recently arrived at the homes of David Main and Frank Ardaiz (both Sepulveda N.S.) of San Pedro.

Mrs. Nellie McNeil and Harry Ganaway (Sepulveda N.S.) were wedded October 10. They are residing in Wilmington.

Ed Schallmo (Ramona N.S.) and wife (Los Angeles N.D.) vacationed last month in San Francisco and Amador County.

Miss Lillian Estes (Los Angeles N.D.) became the bride of Sheldon LeRoy Schultz at Riverside September 4. They are residing in Los Angeles.

Miss Grace S. Stoermer (Past Grand President N.D.) attended last month the annual convention of the Association of Bank Women at Atlantic City.

Herman C. Lichtenberger (Past Grand President N.S.), as a result of too much Admission Day overwork, collapsed following the fiesta, but is on the road to recovery.

The homes of William DeGoede and David Lee (both Ramona N.S.) were recently gladdened by arivals of native sons, and that of Albert Gerwig (Ramona N.S.) by the coming of a native daughter.

GRIZZLY GROWLS

(Continued from Page 3)

Professor Tanner pointed out that the Jap offspring automatically become citizens, but although outside pressure may be applied to change them, they remain Japanese at heart.

He could truthfully have stated, also, that the Jap, wherever born, is loyal, first, last and only, to his worshiped mikado, regardless of protestations otherwise. The impossible is not possible, therefore the serious defect in the law of this nation which bestows citizenship on children born in this country to aliens ineligible to citizenship should be rectified. The correction of this law-defect should not be delayed!

For the period January-October 1931, 1,532 banks of the country, national and state, closed their doors. Their deposits totaled $1,200,784,000. A very large percentage of them, however, 1,202, were not identified with the Federal Reserve.

In the San Francisco Federal Reserve district, which includes all of California as well as other Western states, the closed banks totaled 51, with deposits of $31,554,000. Thirty-one of these institutions were nonmembers of the Reserve.

The State Health Board reports 40,255 live births in California for the first six months of 1931. The Mexis accounted for 6,676, 16.5 percent of the total.

A syndicated story sent out recently from Sacramento City by the United Press said: "San Francisco has the distinction of having the highest tax rate for any incorporated city in the state, $4.04 per $100 on assessed value."

That is not a fact! The San Francisco rate is for the city and the county combined. The combined city-and-county rate for Los Angeles is $4.27 per $100 of assessed value. So, the highest-tax distinction (?) does not belong to the Bay City.

The Los Angeles Chamber of Commerce has been rejoicing because the Metropolitan Water District, which includes Los Angeles City, authorized a $220,000,000 water-bond issue. It failed, however, to mention the fact that while the district had 714,475 registered voters, but 270,763 of them went to the polls. And it is safe to say that a large percentage of those who did vote are not property owners.

Except the dollar-worshipers, no one will find much to crow about in that record! The result indicates a woeful lack of interest on the part of the majority, and that is anything but a good omen.

In a recent letter to the "Sacramento Bee" anent the reapportionment law passed by the State Legislature, E. A. Parsons of that city says: "Thus do we see another foundation-stone laid for state division as the breach widens between the two sections—north against south—and we have but to analyze the various rivalries, contentions and real grievances to reach the logical conclusion that state division is not only inevitable but desirable. This writer is conversant with conditions in both sections and has for years advocated separation, mainly on the ground that we of the north should rely upon our own splendid natural resources."

Parsons' statement that "state division is not only inevitable but desirable," disproves his contention that he "is conversant with conditions in both sections." State division is not desired, except by a few politicians who hope to personally benefit thereby, and there are no real grievances. The north and the south both have splendid natural sources, that is why California, undivided, is such a wonderful state.

O, CALIFORNIA

(ROSALIE F. HYDE.)

California, O California!
Thy children love thee more and more.
Thy lofty mountains,
Their flowery sides,
The waves that break on thy placid shore.

Thy fields aquiver with nodding grain,
Thy golden orchards, thy gentle rain,
Thy hills and valleys, thy desert plain,
Thy snow-tipped Baldy,
Thy poppy's stain.

Thy Tamalpais, thy Shasta's crown,
Thy virgin forests of wide renown,
Thy Emerald Bay at Tahoe's call,
Yosemite and Bridal Fall,
Thy rivers wide and purling streams,
Lead on to grandeur, lead on to dreams.

Thy roadways where the padres trod,
To teach to all the word of God,
Thy missions gleaming in the sun,
Thy cooling winds when day is done,
Thy islands and thy Golden Gate—
Thou all in all, most glorious state!

(Editor's Note—The above came to The Grizzly Bear from Santa Monica Bay Parlor No. 245 N.D.G.W. (Ocean Park), with which Mrs. Rosalie F. Hyde, the author, is affiliated.)

OLD PUEBLO DAYS

(Continued from Page 4)

came from the heart—and it reached the heart." The Spaniard was instilled with the love of music. "If a man who could not ride well was considered only half a man, so he who could not play upon some instrument or sing agreeably was thought to be hardly human."

A natural accompaniment of the love of music was that of dancing, an art in which the Spanish Californians in Pueblo de Los Angeles were especially talented. In fact, dancing was a passion with the Californians. "It affected all," according to Bancroft, "from infancy to old age; grandmothers and grandchildren were seen dancing together; their houses were constructed with reference to this amusement, and most of the interior space was appropriated to the sala, a large, barn-like room. A few chairs and a wooden settee were all its furniture. If a few people got together at any hour of the day, the first thought was to send for a violin and a guitar, and should the violin and guitar be found together, in appropriate hands, that of itself was sufficient reason to send for the dancers." Antonio Coronel has left an excellent description of a ball sponsored by inhabitants of Los Angeles in 1834.

The balls in 1817 normally concluded about ten or eleven o'clock, but the time was gradually extended by the pleasure-loving people until, in 1840, they frequently lasted all night. At many of the nuptial balls dancing and feasting continued for three days and nights. At these lengthy affairs people ate, drank and danced day and night; while some rested or slept, others carried on the festivities. At these balls many a graceful and intricate dance was displayed by the nimble señoritas and agile señores. Among the favorites of the dances was "la jota."

Another popular dance was the fandango, which was danced by a man and a woman. The "bamba" was an intricate dance performed only by the women who were most familiar with it, for the numerous intricate steps changed frequently. The most accomplished señoritas balanced a glass of water on their heads while dancing the "bamba." Handkerchiefs were placed on the floor, with the corners tied together; these the dancer was to take up with her feet and conceal about her person during the dance. This was done without spilling a single drop of water, and when the feat was concluded the dancer took her seat amid frantic applause. Other dances frequently enjoyed by the early inhabitants of Pueblo de Los Angeles were "la zorrita," "los camotes," "el borrego," el burro," "el jarabe," "el caballo" and "la contradanza."

A pleasant and enjoyable feature of some of the balls was the "cascarones," a custom interestingly described in "Spanish Arcadia": "Carnival week preceding Lent was marked by the 'cascarone' balls, a feature of social life as characteristic of California of that day as the mardi gras was of Europe. For weeks previous to the season the housewives would begin to save their eggshells. A hole was carefully broken in one end of the egg, the contents removed, and the dried shell afterwards filled with 'oropel' (gold leaf finely cut), colored paper, cologne water or, as a special extravagance, gold-dust. The hole in the egg was then sealed with wax or paper pasted on. The compliment was to break the eggs lightly over the heads of favored ones, and as the ladies generally wore their hair floating unconfined, the spangles glittering among their raven tresses as they swept through the dance had a very pretty effect. The 'cascarone' season was observed with particular brilliance at Monterey and Los Angeles, the former being the capital and the latter the largest town in the department."

Thus a backward glance at the happy times of the early Californians presents a picturesque and colorful view, as both young and old played and danced their care-free lives away. The entering Americans could only admire such a happy life, and some have left comments upon it. William Heath Davis says, in relating his experiences in Spanish California: "I have often been a guest at such gatherings, which were the sweetest part of my life, and I thought these native Californians of Spanish extraction were, as a rule, as sincere people as ever lived under the canopy of Heaven. I look back almost two generations ago to those merry days with pride and joy, at the kindness which I received and the manliness and simplicity of the welcome of the fathers of families and the womanly deportment of their wives and daughters and their innocent amusements. The native Californians were about the most contented people that I ever saw, as also were the early foreigners who settled among and intermarried with them, adopted their habits and customs, and became, as it were, a part of themselves."

PIONEER NATIVES DEAD

(Continued from Page 6)

daughter of the late Henry C. and Mary Howland Smith, California Pioneers, respectively, of 1845 and 1846, and is claimed to have been the first White child born in Alameda County.

San Quentin (Marin County)—Jason D. White, born in Sacramento County in 1856, died October 8 survived by a wife and a son. He was affiliated with Mount Tamalpais Parlor No. 64 N.S.G.W. (San Rafael), and was the oldest guard at the state prison.

San Francisco—John C. Moore Sr., born in California in 1852, died October 10 survived by a wife and four children.

Roseville (Placer County)—Henry Jones, born in El Dorado County in 1853, died October 11 survived by a wife and two sons.

Redding (Shasta County)—Irving Short, born in California in 1855, died October 12 survived by a wife.

Sonora (Tuolumne County)—Jeremiah Moore, born in this county in 1859, died October 13.

Stent (Tuolumne County)—Mrs. Clara F. Boyle, born at San Francisco in 1850, passed away October 15 survived by a daughter.

Oakland (Alameda County)—Mrs. Mollie Smith, born at San Francisco in 1859, passed away October 16.

McCloud (Siskiyou County)—Mrs. Isabelle Burgess-DeBell, born in this county in 1859, passed away October 19 survived by seven children.

Occidental (Sonoma County)—John W. Blaney, born in Marin County in 1859, died October 20 survived by a wife and three children.

Berkeley (Alameda County)—Mrs. Margaret Sutton-Ainsworth, born at San Francisco in 1853, passed away October 20 survived by a daughter.

Monterey City—Mrs. Ellen Doud-Pardee, born here in 1851, passed away October 21 survived by a daughter. She was a daughter of the late Francis Doud, veteran of the Mexican War.

San Francisco—Mrs. Kate Watson Kirk, born here in 1859, passed away October 21 survived by a husband and two children. She is said to have been a daughter of the late Colonel Jonathan D. Stevenson, California Pioneer of 1847 who brought the first United States troops into this state during the Mexican War.

San Francisco—Clarence D. Steevens, born at Sacramento City in 1857, died October 22 survived by a wife.

Richfield (Tehama County)—Willard Melton Speegle, born in Butte County in 1856, died October 23 survived by two daughters.

NATIVE SON GRAND OFFICERS DEDICATE JUNIOR HIGH SCHOOL.

San Jose (Santa Clara County)—The N.S.G.W. grand officers dedicated October 25 this city's new Peter H. Burnett junior high school. David M. Burnett of the education board presided, and Grand President Dr. Frank I. Gonzalez delivered an address. On behalf of San Jose Parlor No. 22, Past Grand President Judge Fletcher A. Cutler presented the school with United States of America and California State (Bear) Flags, which were accepted by Eldon Fancher. Grand Trustee John M. Burnett presented a picture of Peter H. Burnett, California's first governor, which was accepted by Principal W. P. Cramsie. A splendid musical program was rendered by the student body.

The dedicatory ceremonies were conducted by Grand President Dr. Frank I. Gonzalez, Past Grand President Charles L. Dodge, Grand First Vice-president Seth Millington, Grand Second Vice-president Justice Emmet Seawell, Grand Third Vice-president Chas. A. Koenig and Grand Secretary John T. Regan. Other grand officers in attendance were Grand Treasurer John A. Corotto, Grand Trustee Samuel M. Shortridge Jr. and Past Grand President Thomas Monahan.

N.S. STATE AUTO OFFICIAL DEAD.

Santa Rosa (Sonoma County)—Daniel H. Lafferty, affiliated with Santa Rosa Parlor No. 28 N.S.G.W. and the president of the California State Automobile Association, died October 20 survived by a wife and two sons. He was born at San Francisco, April 19, 1872.

N.S. GRAND OFFICERS TO MEET.

San Francisco—The Board of Grand Officers N.S.G.W. will meet November 7 to select a successor to Grand Trustee A. W. Garcelon, recently resigned.

A BIT O' FARMING

PREPARED EXPRESSLY FOR THE GRIZZLY BEAR BY M. H. ELLIS

WITH THE RAINFALL IN CALIFORNIA below normal for the last few years and the water situation throughout the state really acute this year, much interest attaches to the predictions made at the Scripps Institution of Oceanography, at La Jolla, as to the coming season. Studying the past years, it has been found the rainfall has run in cycles, and that the present cycle of subnormal precipitation is about at the climax. It is believed, from a review of rainfall in past years, that the approaching winter will be a rather dry one, but that those immediately succeeding will have increasing precipitation. Whether this will be borne out by the facts as they are developed, remains to be seen.

But one thing is certain: there are few new sources this year from which to draw water for irrigation, hence there must be care in conservation. Whatever water is available now for irrigation should be used, if the condition of the soil warrants it. Cover crops in the spring should be turned under rather earlier than usual, even though they may not reach the state of maturity desired: water is taken from the soil mainly by transpiration, and cover crops are heavy users. Weeds, of course, must be kept at a minimum. Water should be carefully and sparingly used, and if it becomes apparent to the farmer that there is to be a real shortage next season, the permanent crops, such as trees, should be given the preference.

So, whatever the merit of the prognostication, care in the use of water and the frequent utilization of the soil tube or auger in determining the need, will be well repaid. Some day, it is to be hoped, California will solve its water problem by the conservation of the wasted flood waters: until that time, individual efforts must be looked to for making the present supply go as far as possible.

SOW SWEET CLOVER NOW.

Fall is the best time to grow sweet clover. The seed will germinate well now, and the stand will have a good chance to get rooted before the next dry season. There is no danger of winter killing in any of the farming districts of California, and clover must have moisture if it is to do well. In most districts of the state, irrigation will be necessary: it is imperative in the valleys. In root formation, sweet clover is much the same as alfalfa, and the two require much the same care.

SPANISH MEASLES IN VINES.

If Spanish measles have appeared in the vineyard this year, plan to give the vines treatment during the dormant season. Just after pruning is perhaps the best time. Sodium arsenate, three pounds to fifty gallons of water, makes a spray that should go far toward correcting the trouble. In pruning, give the sick vines special care; forget the crop for next year and prune not for production but for building up of the vines. Cutting hard will give the vines a chance to rest and to revive themselves.

GREENS FOR LAYING FLOCK.

The fall season, when green feed is the hardest to get, is here. Poultrymen will do well to remember that hens must have green feed if they are to produce and keep in condition so that production will be good. Kale is the most popular green feed, and it does well in most districts all winter. However, barley is a good substitute, or any other green feed the hens will eat. Carrots are a good feed for this purpose. If no fresh green feed is available, mix alfalfa meal with the mash, adding two or three pounds to the hundred of mash; or keep dry alfalfa leaves in the hoppers.

GIRDLED CHERRY TREES.

Last winter in California an eight-year-old cherry orchard suddenly showed signs of being in difficulty, and on investigation it was found many of the trees had been girdled. The first thought was that gophers had done the work; closer investigation showed that field mice were far more responsible. In cultivation weeds and trash had been thrown against the tree trunks, making a fine harbor for the nesting rodents. Before winter sets in see that there are no such refuges for mice; clear the field of gophers if possible. When injury appears, open up the trees, paint with asphaltum, and then pile soil, not trash, over the injury. In extreme cases bridge grafting or inarching may be resorted to.

SOME EARLY BERRIES.

Among the earliest of bushes to come into leaf in the spring are currants and gooseberries. For this year, plantings should be made as early in the winter season as possible, and the bushes should be set where they are to bear without danger of further transplantation. Of course, even if they are in full leaf when set out, they will go ahead and make a crop, but the results will not be as good as if they had been transplanted when dormant and given a chance to get their roots into the soil before the growing season.

BLACK END OF PEARS.

. There is no doubt that black end, hard end and some other pear troubles are more likely to be found on trees on Japanese roots than on French roots. Inarching French seedlings into the tree will alleviate the injury, but there will be no entire cure until the trunk is cut from the old roots. But what is to become of the old roots, and what about the wound caused by the cut? That remains to be seen. The economics of the situation, however, point to interplanting with new trees on French roots as the best solution of the problem. As the new trees develop, the old ones can be pulled out. This entails the loss, perhaps, of some pears at harvest, but right now that seems hardly as important as getting an orchard ready for the return of good prices and profits.

CORN SMUT AND EAR WORMS.

This is the time of year to fight the corn ear worm that is so disagreeable in roasting ear time. Clear the field of all rubbish, and burn it. Plow the ground and work it so as to expose and kill the greatest possible number of hibernating pupae. This method will get most of them. Also it is the best method of fighting corn smut, which is caused by a spore. The spore may carry over in the soil, however, and if the crop was badly smutted, use a new piece of ground if available.

VACCINATION AND TUBERCULOSIS.

Despite warnings concerning the futility of vaccination of cattle as a cure for bovine tuberculosis, there still are those who believe, or hope, they may get results. So far, there has been no test made that bears out such belief. The only safe practice at present is to have the cows tested, and isolate the reactors. Better yet, kill or sell them and replace them with healthy cows. Tuberculosis takes a heavy toll in dairy herds; if it is at all possible, the herd should be cleaned up at once, and kept clean. Calves do not inherit the disease from their dams, and if they are taken at once from the cow and fed clean milk, and kept away from tuberculous cattle, they will not contract the disease.

CITRUS ORCHARD HEATING.

Get the orchard heaters ready as soon as possible after November 1, to protect the citrus fruits against possible cold weather damage during the winter. See that they are filled and ready for action, and see, too, that there is at least a four-day supply of fuel readily available. Test the thermometers, and listen for weather forecasts. The best orchard heater gives no protection if it is stored in a shed. The most important part of fighting frost damage is to be ready when the cold nights come.

CONTROL OF OYSTER SHELL SCALE.

Oyster shell scale apparently is on the increase in the orchards of the state, and the best time for control is in the fall or early winter. Spray with oil, the miscible or paste emulsions, before the rains have come in quantity. The scale reaches the egg-laying stage in February, and the control becomes then more difficult. Willows, as well as some domestic fruits and ornamentals, are host to this pest, and their planting in proximity to the orchard is to be avoided.

CITRUS BROWN ROT.

In November, or in the early weeks of December at the latest, the lemon grower should be on the alert to control brown rot. This disease also affects navel oranges. The best preventive is to spray with Bordeaux, covering the tree trunk to a hight of three and a half to four feet, and the ground around the trees. Use pressure enough to give good coverage. The organism causing this disease is present in the soil all the time, but it is active only in cool, moist weather.

SHOT-HOLE FUNGUS.

Nearly every grower of apricots knows shot-hole fungus, recognizable by the small red spots on the fruit, and the holes in the leaves about the size of shot. The control is a three-fold treatment, the first part of which is a spray with Bordeaux, 5-5-50, before or soon after the first rains. This same spray should be used again in the spring, just as the buds are swelling; and Bordeaux 2-3-50 should be administered just as the husks have been shed from the young fruits.

MY MESSAGE

To All Native Born Californians

I, DR. FRANK I. GONZALEZ, GRAND PRESIDENT OF THE ORDER OF NATIVE SONS OF THE GOLDEN WEST, DO HEREBY APPEAL TO ALL NATIVE BORN CALIFORNIANS OF THE WHITE MALE RACE BORN WITHIN THE STATE OF CALIFORNIA, OF THE AGE OF EIGHTEEN YEARS AND UPWARD, OF GOOD HEALTH AND CHARACTER, AND WHO BELIEVE IN THE EXISTENCE OF A SUPREME BEING, TO JOIN OUR FRATERNITY AND THEREBY ASSIST IN THE AIMS AND PURPOSES OF THE ORGANIZATION:

To arouse Loyalty and Patriotism for State and for Nation.

To elevate and improve the Manhood upon which the destiny of our country depends.

To encourage interest in all matters and measures relating to the material upbuilding of the State of California.

To assist in the development of the wonderful natural resources of California.

To protect the forests, conserve the waters, improve the rivers and the harbors, and beautify the towns and the cities.

To collect, make known and preserve the romantic history of California.

To restore and preserve all the historic landmarks of the State.

To provide homes for California's homeless children, regardless of race, creed or color.

To keep this State a paradise for the American Citizen by thwarting the organized efforts of all undesirable peoples to control its destiny.

THE ORDER OF NATIVE SONS OF THE GOLDEN WEST IS THE ONLY FRATERNITY IN EXISTENCE WHOSE MEMBERSHIP IS MADE UP EXCLUSIVELY OF WHITE NATIVE BORN AMERICANS.

. . . Builded upon the Foundation Stones of **Friendship Loyalty Charity**

IT PRESENTS TO THE NATIVE BORN CALIFORNIAN THE MOST PRODUCTIVE FIELD IN WHICH TO SOW HIS ENERGIES, AND IF HE BE A FAITHFUL CULTIVATOR AND DESIRES TO TAKE ADVANTAGE OF THE OPPORTUNITY AFFORDED HIM, HE WILL REAP A RICH HARVEST IN THE KNOWLEDGE THAT HE HAS BEEN FAITHFUL TO CALIFORNIA AND DILIGENT IN PROTECTING ITS WELFARE.

DR. FRANK I. GONZALEZ,
GRAND PRESIDENT N.S.G.W.

The undersigned, having formed a favorable opinion of the Order of Native Sons of the Golden West, desires additional information.

Name ....

Address ....

City or Town..............................

For further information sign the accompanying blank and mail to

GRAND SECRETARY N.S.G.W.,
302 Native Sons Bldg.,
414 Mason St.,
SAN FRANCISCO, California

Grizzly Bear

DECEMBER THE ONLY OFFICIAL PUBLICATION OF THE NATIVE SONS AND DAUGHTERS OF THE GOLDEN WEST 1931

Merry Christmas

Featuring

GENERAL NEWS OF INTEREST CONCERNING ALL CALIFORNIA, and ORDERS NATIVE SONS and NATIVE DAUGHTERS

Price: 15 Cents

—another Native Son!

Every Westerner has a right to be proud of this *California* gasoline—its wonderful records! Made by *special* process by a *California* company from *California* crudes—owned and directed by *California* men—it is *proving* its wonderful mileage and power superiority by an unbroken string of speedway victories and by its steadily increasing sales of thousands of gallons every month! Try *Richfield* in your *own car today—note the difference!*

PARTNERS IN POWER

Gifts . . .

Gifts are sent as tokens of friendship and affection. . .

They may be both appropriate and practical . . .

Street car tokens are always acceptable. They carry a message of safety and freedom from traffic worries.

Los Angeles Railway

Just One Way to KNOW California Intimately
Read REGULARLY The Grizzly Bear
Subscription by the Year, $1.50

Catalina Island!

Where Every Minute Has Pleasure In It

SEE the gorgeous new Casino with its theatre and ballroom . . . free dancing nightly the year 'round; visit the Bird Park and see hundreds of rare birds . . . admission free. Play golf or tennis at the charming Catalina Country Club . . . green fee only $1 for all day play. View the Submarine Gardens through Glass Bottom Boats. Bathe in the crystal waters of Avalon Bay.

Two sailings daily to and from Catalina. $2.25 round trip from Wilmington; $3.00 from Los Angeles. Wide variety of accommodations—Hotel St. Catherine (American Plan), Hotel Atwater (European Plan), Island Villa bungalettes, afford highest type of service.

Fly to Catalina by Amphibion—you're there in 25 minutes. $5.00 each way. Taking off from Catalina Terminal, Wilmington.

SANTA CATALINA ISLAND COMPANY
6th and Main Streets, Los Angeles, Calif.
Phone MAdison 1151
Also Leading Hotels and Travel Bureaus

W

In All the World No Trip Like This

THE GRIZZLY BEAR

AFFORDS AN OPPORTUNITY

TO CONTACT

THROUGH ADVERTISING

MANY THOUSANDS OF

PERMANENT RESIDENTS

OF CALIFORNIA

IN ALL WALKS OF LIFE

STATE-WIDE CIRCULATION

Let The Grizzly Bear Serve You as a Contact Medium

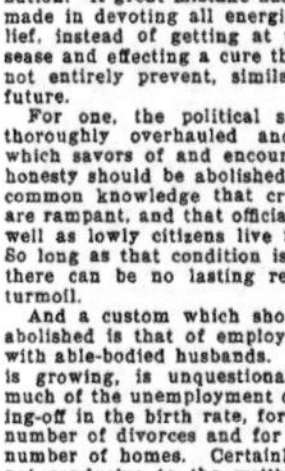

GRIZZLY GROWLS

(CLARENCE M. HUNT.)

DEPRESSION CONTINUES TO OVERshadow the land, and that much-talked-about corner around which, we are daily told, prosperity is patiently waiting to be discovered, has not yet come into view. There is no doubt, however, that the corner is somewhere, and eventually it will be reached. In the meantime we must push forward, otherwise the desired goal cannot be reached.

Good comes from most conditions, not excepting depressions, if we so will. The present depression has afforded an opportunity to abolish customs and cure governmental ills which are, in no small degree, directly responsible for the unhealthy economic condition that afflicts the nation. A great mistake has been, and is being, made in devoting all energies to temporary relief, instead of getting at the root of the disease and effecting a cure that will minimize, if not entirely prevent, similar afflictions in the future.

For one, the political structure should be thoroughly overhauled and every procedure which savors of and encourages graft and dishonesty should be abolished for all time. It is common knowledge that crime and dishonesty are rampant, and that officials and prominent as well as lowly citizens live not within the law. So long as that condition is permitted to exist, there can be no lasting relief from economic turmoil.

And a custom which should be permanently abolished is that of employing married women with able-bodied husbands. This custom, which is growing, is unquestionably responsible for much of the unemployment distress, for the falling-off in the birth rate, for the increase in the number of divorces and for the decrease in the number of homes. Certainly such a custom is not conducive to the wellbeing of the nation, and therefore should not be tolerated.

Just recently the Federal Census Bureau issued an unemployment bulletin. California is listed as having 1,942,155 male gainful workers, 136,252 of whom are able to work but out of a job. There are 558,814 female gainful workers, of whom but 25,435 are out of a job. A conservative estimate of the number of married women with gainfully-employed husbands among the 533,379 females employed in this state is 133,347. If they were compelled to relinquish their positions and males employed in their stead, the number of unemployed males would be inconsequential, and the state would, from every viewpoint, be immeasurably benefited.

Coming from a source always opposed to legislation against the Japs, the "San Francisco Chronicle," the following, which appeared editorially in that paper November 7 under the caption "Japan Caught in the Act," is of decided interest. It substantiates The Grizzly Bear's contention for years that the Japs are not to be trusted, and that in due time this country will pay the full price for the folly of placing any confidence in them:

"Chester Rowell's experience with the Japanese censor at Mukden . . . sheds a flood of light on what the Japanese are doing in Manchuria. They tell us they are merely defending their people and property in Manchuria. Mr. Rowell, a trustworthy person who saw with his own eyes, shows the Japanese attacking the Chinese civil government offices—not military forces—in a strictly Chinese railway zone and deliberately falsifying it to the world.

"The Japanese censor revised Mr. Rowell's account, which told the truth, and put into his mouth a precisely opposite statement, a flat untruth, plainly for the purpose of concealing the facts from the world and to support a false declaration made to the League. The Chinchow incident may not be vastly important in the whole Manchurian situation, but it is important because of the light in which it puts the Japanese claim of honest purpose in that country. It is a very bad light. Honest purpose does not have to falsify its acts to the world . . . .

"Japanese officialdom has no out except of course to disclaim the censor's act and say he 'exceeded his authority.' But this excuse has already been applied to the entire movement in Manchuria. The original attacker at Mukden 'exceeded his authority.' Apparently the Japanese military officials in Manchuria go on 'exceeding their authority.' Is this a handy way to extend the occupation? Japanese must not blame outsiders for concluding that the evident intention of the islanders is to make the most of the results of these 'excesses of authority'."

And here is another very interesting bit of news, sent from Moscow by the Associated Press November 5,—and there is suspicion that it was not published in the pro-Jap American press using that service: "The newspaper 'Pravda,' resuming its attack on the Japanese policies in Manchuria, today published what is described as a secret declaration by Baron Tanaka when he was premier of Japan in 1927, asserting that Japan must crush the United States to capture China. This document, said 'Pravda,' bears out its charge that Japan's present action in Manchuria is a long-planned part of its effort to extend the Japanese hegemony in the Pacific.

"'Japan's aggressive tendencies will not end with China,' said the newspaper. 'It has designs on the Philippines, the Malayan Archipelago, Guam, Tahiti, Samoa and Australia.' Then the editorial quoted the alleged Tanaka statement, which it said had recently been published in China. 'For its own protection,' this document said, 'Japan must remove its difficulties in eastern Asia by establishing a policy of blood and iron. If we intend to win control over China we must first crush the United States. To capture China we must also capture Manchuria and Mongolia'."

The Japs are long on promises and profuse in their protestations of friendship. When they "are caught in the act," they have excuses aplenty; what they cannot invent for themselves, their supporters in this country concoct in their behalf.

And think of it! The United States Chamber of Commerce, the Federation of Churches of Christ in America, the Los Angeles Chamber of Commerce and many similar organizations, as well as several newspapers and numerous individuals, are advocating granting the quota to Japan—aiding that country in its "peaceful invasion" conquest of the Pacific states of these United States.

In fact, these powerful influences will use every means at their command to force the Federal Congress to grant Japan the quota—"to foster the goodwill of those sensitive people," and similar buncombe. The real appeal, of course, is the yellow-dollar! For paltry Jap gold in exchange for American-made goods, the quota advocates would barter the welfare of this nation. Pray God, that there be a sufficient number of White-blooded American citizens in the national law-making body to withstand the onslaughts of the quotaists!

With big headlines, the reactionary daily press last month publicized "The California Plan," promulgated by the State Chamber of Commerce as a so-called "state-wide program to help California build prosperity on a sound, permanent basis." We have little faith in that outfit, for its record suspicions of service first to the "interests," and it has always opposed needed legislation to stop the inflow of Mexis and Japs, and the land-grabbing schemes of the latter.

Any organization which favors allowing ineligible-to-citizenship aliens unhampered access to this nation and this state is not deserving of the moral or the financial support of the masses. The State Chamber of Commerce is not, as the name might imply, a department of the State Government. It was created by various individuals and its main financial support comes from the taxpayers, via the county boards of supervisors. That is one expense which the taxpayers of every county in the state should demand be eliminated, right now!

According to the "Livingston Chronicle," Merced County had, to November 12, shipped back to Mexico at a cost to the taxpayers of $4,200, 265 Mexis. "Almost without exception," said the paper, "every one of the 265 had been, was at the time of shipping, or was likely to become a public charge on the county. One family has been costing the county $180 per month. In another were juvenile court charges who bade fair to cost the county $20 per month each at a state institution until they reached maturity. Nearly all the adults were in a state of health that made it certain they would be 'on the county' for life."

This same condition exists in every county of the state where the Mexis colonize. In the past few months more than 100,000 Mexis have been returned to their homeland from California, some 30,000 from Los Angeles County alone. The expense in all cases is, of course, borne by the taxpayers. These Mexis were brought here by the "big interests" to slave for them, but when they had no more work for them they graciously turned them over to the "deer peeple" to care for. And their care has been, and is, costing the taxpayers millions of dollars annually!

There are additional thousands of these undesirable ineligible-to-citizenship aliens who should be sent back whence they came. The cost to the taxpayers of Los Angeles for the operation of the school department and the general hospital would be materially lessened if every dependent Mexi and his breed were deported, as they should be. And the same is true of all the southern counties.

As frequently remarked in these columns, the great majority of the Mexis who come to this country are not of the White race and are ineligible for American citizenship. The Federal Congress, therefore, should adopt legislation definitely applying the provisions of the National Exclusion Law to Mexico. Unless the Congress does legislate to prevent it, just as soon as the business-sky clears the Mexis will flock back here in greater numbers than ever before. And they will be encouraged to come by the "big interests" and the so-called promotion organizations which are anxious to build up in California a population of quantity without regard to quality.

A survey of California election statistics shows that only one out of every three persons of voting age in this state casts a vote. That is true also as regards most of the states of the nation. And therein is to be found the reason for the many governmental ills so much complained about.

We are minority governed! The minority go to the polls on all election days, and put over their pet bond and other hobbies and favored candidates. The majority stay at home, and then howl continuously and vociferously at the re-

The Grizzly Bear Magazine

The ALL California Monthly

OWNED, CONTROLLED, PUBLISHED BY GRIZZLY BEAR PUBLISHING CO., (Incorporated)

COMPOSED OF NATIVE SONS.

HERMAN C. LICHTENBERGER, Pres.
JOHN T. NEWELL RAY HOWARD
WM. I. TRAEGER LORENZO F. SOTO
CHAS. R. THOMAS HARRY J. LELANDE
ARTHUR A. SCHMIDT, Vice-Pres.
BOARD OF DIRECTORS

CLARENCE M. HUNT
General Manager and Editor

OFFICIAL ORGAN AND THE ONLY OFFICIAL PUBLICATION OF THE NATIVE SONS AND THE NATIVE DAUGHTERS GOLDEN WEST.

ISSUED FIRST EACH MONTH.
FORMS CLOSE 20th MONTH.
ADVERTISING RATES ON APPLICATION.

SAN FRANCISCO OFFICE:
N.S.G.W. BLDG., 414 MASON ST., RM. 302
(Office Grand Secretary N.S.G.W.)
Telephone: Kearney 1223
SAN FRANCISCO, CALIFORNIA

PUBLICATION OFFICE:
309-15 WILCOX BLDG., 2nd AND SPRING,
Telephone: VAndike 6234
LOS ANGELES, CALIFORNIA

(Entered as second-class matter May 29, 1918, at the Postoffice at Los Angeles, California, under the act of August 24, 1912.)

PUBLISHED REGULARLY SINCE MAY 1907

VOL. L WHOLE NO. 296

sults. There can be no hope for a change for the better in government—lessening of the cost, weeding out of incompetents, elimination of grafters and other sorely-needed reforms—until the majority realize their duty as citizens and vote.

"Within the last six months," said the "Sacramento Bee" of November 17, "between twenty and twenty-five Japanese children of the Vacaville, Solano County, vicinity, ranging in age from one to twelve years, have been sent to Japan by their parents. All have secured the necessary papers which will permit their return to this country. Education for a year or two in the Japanese language while they are young is believed to be the objective of the trips."

The surmised objective is another bit of Jap deceit, for there are in California plenty of Jap schools teaching the language of that country, and all Jap children are compelled to attend those schools. All Jap parents in this country, when financially able to do so, send their offspring to Japan. The real objective, however, is to have instilled in their hearts and minds, amid the proper surroundings, loyalty to and reverence for their worshiped mikado.

This situation instances another terrible mistake this country is making—recognizing as a citizen of the United States every child born here, irrespective of the race or citizenship of the parents. Thousands of Japs, born within the United States to parents ineligible to citizenship, are citizens of this nation, although their allegiance is, first, last and always, to Japan.

Will those who have in their keeping the destiny of this country continue to dream, or will they, before it is too late, legislate to extend United States citizenship only to children born here to citizen or eligible-to-citizenship parents? The longer they delay, the sooner will come the day of reckoning!

A humorous, but serious, situation! During recent years hundreds of thousands of the taxpayers' funds have been turned over to promotion bodies by the governing authorities of the cities and the counties of San Francisco and Los Angeles, to be used to induce people to come to California. The paid-for propaganda has even been continued during the depression years, at enormous expense to the taxpayers.

As a result, California, and particularly San Francisco and Los Angeles, have been flooded with a horde seeking employment, and there is no work for them. So, the taxpayers must dig down deeper into their pockets and produce the wherewith to support these people. Now, the governing authorities and the population-promoting bodies want all publicity agencies to urge the previously-advertised-for contingent to stay away.

The Los Angeles Chamber of Commerce is so concerned that it refers to the influx as "floating undesirables," "unwelcome visitors" and "a serious menace." In the "flush" years, however, when increased population was the main concern, the Chamber looked on these comers as desirable, they were heartily welcomed and considered a blessing. Quite a decided change in viewpoint! The harvest, evidently, has fallen short of expectations, at least in quality if not in quantity. The taxpayers should look into this and similar loopholes through which millions of their money are invested in enterprises that produce liabilities requiring the expenditure of additional millions.

"The burden of taxation upon industry has much to do with the present widespread lack of employment and the suffering which follows in its wake," says the California Taxpayers Association. "The era of riotous spending and expansion, which preceded this period of reaction and depression, swelled government to its present inflated condition. The reluctance of the people to allow government to return to its normal position in our economic structure has been and is a serious obstacle to business recovery.

"Further governmental expansion or undertakings, in a country already topheavy with governmental costs, is foolhardy. We must not trust to public works as a means of relieving unemployment. We must stimulate industry—the only agent which can furnish employment for all the people. The most pressing problem before us today is that of controlling and reducing the expenditures of government, for such expenditures take in taxes from industry and business the capital that is their life blood."

Claiming that the California Alien Land Law is being violated by the leasing of land to ineligible-to-citizenship aliens, the Glenn County district attorney has started an investigation. He further declares Americans are aiding the East Indians to lease rice fields. It is to be hoped he will not stop with investigating, as is generally the procedure, but will forcefully prosecute the law's violators, both citizens and aliens.

There are very few counties of the state in which this law is not being openly violated, and there is not a single district attorney who is doing his duty and prosecuting the law's violators. The law does not exist, so far as the enforcement officials are concerned, and the Hindus, the Japs and other ineligible-to-citizenship aliens, aided by dollar-worshiping citizens, continue to entrench themselves through occupancy of the land as owners or lessors.

Here is a field of endeavor in which some organization professing loyalty to the State of California should immediately get to work. Any organization which does, will have the support of a vast majority of the citizenry and will ascend to a "place in the sun" that will never be obscured. There are thousands of the richest acres in this state illegally in the possession of Japs, Hindus, etc. The state law provides a way to dispossess these aliens and have the land escheated to the state. The authorities of the several counties could, but for reasons best known to themselves will not, make any effort to enforce the law and recover the land.

Some organization, therefore, should employ competent help to search the records of each county for every parcel of land, acreage or town lot, illegally possessed by an ineligible-to-citizenship alien, together with the name of the conveyor of title to the property. If, with this necessary information, the authorities still neglect to do their duty, then the best of legal talent should be engaged to enforce the law. The land recovered, and escheated to the state, could, by the state, be turned over to war veterans, citizens of the state.

The Order of Native Sons of the Golden West could, and should, do this work, and take exceptional delight in the doing. All its funds, now diverted to several channels, could be used to finance the battle. Undoubtedly the American Legion would support the movement, and so would numerous individuals who desire that California remain the White man's paradise.

It is a gigantic undertaking, to be sure, but it can, and it is necessary that it should, be done. The greater the undertaking, the greater the reward in its accomplishment. Rout the Japs and the other ineligible-to-citizenship aliens from the lands they illegally possess, and California will be saved. Leave them in possession of their holdings—and the additional holdings they will acquire unless the law be enforced—and California will be lost to the White man, just as certain as day follows night, for the possessors of the soil hold the destiny-key to any country!

THE STAR

(MINNA McGARVEY.)

When Christmas-time is nearing, when cool the air and still,
With piney-laden breezes blowing crisply from the hill,
When long the nights and mystic, and dark the traveled way,
Look up toward the Heavens, and see a star's bright ray.

A star that, gleaming, deepens, as in the long ago
When over distant Bethlehem it shed its steadfast glow;
From plain to highest mountain, from home to foreign shore,
O'er city wide and hamlet, it beacons as of yore.

A blessed star, the symbol and herald of The Light
That to a darkened world was come that calm and holy night;
Eternal in the Heavens, it flashes near and far,
To guide the questing always, our lovely Christmas Star!

PLAN TO CELEBRATE NEXT YEAR WASHINGTON BICENTENNIAL BIRTHDAY

These facts should be emphasized with respect to the celebration of the two hundredth anniversary of the birth of George Washington, first President of the United States, next year:

It is sponsored by the United States Government, Congress creating the United States George Washington Bicentennial Commission, and the President of the United States is its chairman.

It will not be a world's fair or exposition, and it will not be held in any one place. It will be a nation-wide, even a world-wide, series of celebrations in which every state, city and town in this country, together with Americans and others in many foreign countries, will participate. Every community is expected to plan and carry out its own program, in co-operation with the United States commission and the state commissions.

It will last from Washington's Birthday, February 22, 1932, to Thanksgiving Day, November 24, 1932, with special celebrations everywhere on all holidays, anniversaries or other days which can be connected with the life of George Washington.

The United States Bicentennial Commission, Washington building, Washington, D. C., will send literature and suggestions for local programs to any committee, organization or group that will write for them.

COMPLETION RAILWAY HOOKUP MARKS BEGINNING NEW TRANSPORTATION ERA.

Bieber (Lassen County)—The driving of a gold spike here November 10, marking the last work in the uniting of the Great Northern and the Western Pacific Railroads, ushered in a new era in Western transportation of vital importance to California. The event was fittingly celebrated.

Approximately $14,500,000 was spent by the two railroads in the enterprise, 223 miles of trackage being laid over rugged California North mountain country. The Western Pacific built an extension from Keddie, Plumas County, to Bieber, and the Great Northern extended its line from Klamath Falls, Oregon State, to Bieber.

"Those who bring sunshine to the lives of others cannot keep it from themselves."

MONUMENT PERPETUATES MEMORY TUOLUMNE COUNTY PIONEER.

Sonora (Tuolumne County)—A monument in memory of "Dick" Stoker was unveiled November 8 in the Masonic cemetery. The ceremonies were under the auspices of the Sonora Welfare Club, which headed the movement to suitably mark the last resting place of this California Pioneer. The monument's inscription reads:

"Jacob Richard Stoker, 1820-1898. 'His heart was finer metal than any gold his shovel ever brought to light.' Gallant Mexican War veteran. Fought in principal battles. Came to California '49. Jackass Hill '50. Built famous cabin. Intimately associated there with Mark Twain and Gillis Bros. Member Tuolumne Lodge No. 8 F. & A. M. Just and fair. Settled miners' disputes. Helped his fellowmen and community. Famed as 'Dick Baker' in Twain's 'Roughing It.' Hero in 'Jaybird and the Acorn,' 'Burning Shame,' etc."

CALIFORNIA DISTRICT SPARSELY SETTLED.

According to the Federal Census Bureau, Sacramento, California, has the sparest population—274 per square mile—of the nation's metropolitan districts, and New York City has the densest—4,000. Metropolitan districts, for the 1930 census, were established wherever the population of the central city or cities plus that of the adjacent urban territory amounted to 100,000 or more.

Other California districts listed, and their per-square-mile population, are: Los Angeles, 1,572; San Diego, 544; San Francisco-Oakland, 1,562; San Jose, 491.

"Life's highest joy belongs to him who stands, after a struggle, on some spiritual summit and looks first down upon the valley whence he has ascended, and then up to some higher peak which shall become tomorrow's goal."—H. B. Oborn.

Forest Receipts—California benefited to the extent of $280,824 in Federal Government receipts from national forests within the state for the fiscal year ended June 30.

Grape Crop Off—California's 1931 grape harvest is estimated by the State-Federal Crop Reporting Service to be 1,296,000 tons; the 1930 crop totaled 2,182,000 tons.

LOS ANGELES
CALIFORNIA'S WONDERLAND
CITY AND COUNTY

THE CALIFORNIA SOUTH DIVISION OF the President Herbert Hoover's Organization for Unemployment Relief is soliciting, through its industrial committee, co-operation of employers in the consideration of certain of the priorities of employment which are recommended by the national organization. These suggested priorities are:

First, preference to be given to married men with dependents, resident of California for six months or more. Second, preference to single men or women with dependents, similarly resident. Third, preference to single men or women above school age without dependents, but with no other means of support, similarly resident.

In this connection, the committee also invites consideration by employers of the situation presented by married couples, both of whom are working, where no real necessity exists therefore.

The committee asks that a survey be made by each employer and in each industry to determine what may be done towards giving employment to an additional number of workers, either through the shortening of the working week, the working day, by staggering employment or through such other means as may seem appropriate in the various establishments—factory, plant, store or office—under consideration.

The committee suggests that special consideration should be given to the provision of part-time employment at least, for the white-collar class which heretofore has received less than reasonable attention, and which, a survey shows, represents a need and a distress often as acute as that of the industrial worker. The committee also recommends that, in the spread of employment, consideration should be given by each employer to the capacity of each individual employee for self-help.

The above recommendations in regard to priorities as to employment follow closely the issuance of recommended priorities which the public have been asked to observe in the matter of purchases. These are:

First, the people of California South should give initial preference to local products. Second, preference to California products. Third, preference to products of the United States. Fourth, only when American goods are unavailable should foreign products be purchased.

CONTRIBUTE LIBERALLY.

The Los Angeles and Orange Counties N.S.G.W. and N.D.G.W. Joint Homeless Children Committee is sending out the annual Christmas letter asking contributions "to save a child." Irving Baxter is the chairman and Annie L. Adair the secretary of the committee.

"Let's ring the merry Christmas bells and continue the humanitarian work of placing homeless children in childless homes," says the letter. "There'll be an answering ring of gladness in your heart that will match the radiance in the eyes of the child your contribution will help to place in a real home. The need is greater this year than ever! Give whatever you can afford, you know best."

Because of the Native Sons and the Native Daughters, the homeless child is no longer a waif. Four thousand homeless children have been placed in childless homes by the Natives. No Community Chest contributes a nickel to this work. It is deserving of the support of everyone, so contribute liberally. Be a Santa Claus to the homeless children.—C.M.H.

DELIGHTFUL AFFAIR.

The informal dance held by Los Angeles Parlor No. 45 N.S.G.W. in celebration of its forty-seventh institution anniversary November 12 was a delightful affair. There was a good attendance, and excellent music was provided. November 19, Roger Johnson and Anthony Pierce provided a most enjoyable musical entertainment. "Tony" surprised by demonstrating that he is a vocalist of ability.

December 3, Los Angeles will nominate officers and hold initiation. December 10, election of officers. December 24, Christmas Eve, no meeting. December 31, the Parlor plans a dance and watch party. This will be for the womenfolks, as well as the menfolks. Refreshments will be served.

CHRISTMAS PARTY, DECEMBER 16.

Los Angeles Parlor No. 124 N.D.G.W. initiated a class of thirteen candidates November 4. The November 11 card party, in charge of Adeline Waite, was a social and financial success. November 18 officers for the January-July term were nominated; it was decided to retain the present corps, with Gertrude Allen as president. The Spanish lessons are being resumed, the first and third Wednesdays, with Dolores Malin as instructor.

Harriet Martin is chairman of the committee which will convey Christmas cheer from Los Angeles to the veterans at the Sawtelle Soldiers' Home. Flora Holy and Ruth Ruiz are members of the committee preparing baskets for the deserving poor. President Allen, Edith Schallmo and Adeline Waite compose a committee for welfare work among the Parlor's members. A contribution to the restoration fund of San Gabriel Mission has been made.

December 2, Los Angeles will elect officers and will have showers for its latest brides, Matilda Rambean-Besson and Anita Simon-Santos. Edna Trombatore and Dolores Malin will be in charge

When you purchase goods advertised in The Grizzly Bear, or answer an advertisement in this magazine, please be sure to mention The Grizzly Bear. That's co-operation mutually beneficial.

Know your home-state, California! Learn of its past history and of its present-day development by reading regularly The Grizzly Bear. $1.50 for one year (12 issues) Subscribe now.

of the program. December 9, the monthly card party, fourth in the tournament. Vivian Wickser is the chairman. December 16, initiation and Christmas party. The schoolteacher members of the Parlor are arranging the program. All those initiated since July are especially urged to be present.

CHRISTMAS FUND ENRICHED.

Ramona Parlor No. 109 N.S.G.W. initiated a class of candidates November 13, among them being Dr. Rockwell D. Hunt, dean of the graduate students of the University of Southern California and an authority on California history. The first presentation of "1932 Bear Club" pins was made by Walter Slosson. Marshal Charles Straube wants to provide the shut-in members with magazines and books, and any contributions will be thankfully received.

The Christmas fund was considerably enriched last month, and a lot of fun accompanied the "raising of the dough." Judge Louis Valentine conducted a "kangaroo court" November 6, and everyone, including the jury, was found guilty. November 20 a quantity of poultry, contributed by the Drouet boys—three of 'em—and John M. Stahl, was disposed of. Past Grand President Herman C. Lichtenberger showed up after a considerable absence and was given a big "hand," as well as a goose.

December 4, Ramona will elect officers. December 11, Grand Second Vice-president Justice Emmet Seawell will pay an official visit. A class of candidates will be initiated, and refreshments will be served. December 18, a turkey dinner will be served at 6:30 p.m. in the diningroom of Patriotic Hall, where No. 109 holds forth. This will be the Parlor's last meeting of 1931.

Wednesday, December 23, Ramona and Navy Post No. 278 American Legion will have a joint Christmas tree on the second floor of Patriotic Hall. This affair is especially for the children of the members of the Parlor and the Post.

CHRISTMAS WORK PLANNED.

A delightful Thanksgiving program and luncheon were enjoyed by a large number of members and guests of Californiana Parlor No. 247 N.D.G.W. November 24. Decorations appropriate to the festival day were provided by Chairman Edith Adams and the hospitality committee. Mrs. W. K. Chambers, who has not appeared before the Parlor with her inimitable and charming readings for some time, was given an ovation as she rendered a program suitable to the happy occasion. Following the program the regular meeting of the Parlor was held, with President Gertrude Tuttle presiding, and officers were nominated for the coming term.

At the November 10 meeting a shower was held, "a pantry shelf donation," an interesting piece of welfare work for the families of disabled veterans. The goods were delivered Armistice Day. Mrs. Edward Tabor, chairman of the homeless children committee, announced a Christmas party for December 8. A bazar and food sale will be features, and members will donote garments for the babies and also for children of school age. The members always look forward to this party as one of the most delightful of the year. An interesting class of eight, members of prominent and pioneer families, were initiated. The meeting was very largely attended, with delegations from Grace and Santa Ana Parlors, including District Deputy Marguerite Dickinson.

Reports from the very successful bridge breakfast given by the Parlor October 28 showed a profit of $175 which, added to the balance in the fund from last year, will give the committee an opportunity to do some good work during Christmas time. Mrs. Charles Jacobson has been appointed chairman of the philanthropy committee.

OFFICIAL TO VISIT.

Hollywood Parlor No. 196 N.S.G.W. will receive an official visit December 7 from Grand Second vice-president Justice Emmet Seawell. A class of candidates will be initiated, and officers will be elected.

NOTABLE GATHERING.

Long Beach—Long Beach Parlor No. 154 N.D.G.W. had a plunkett dinner November 5, with Mrs. Zella Hodgdon acting as chairman. Bridge and five hundred were played after the dinner, which was a complete social and financial success. A beautiful quilt, made by the thimble club, was awarded President Daisy T. Hansen. November 12 the thimble club met at the home of Mrs. Fannie McPherson. A delicious covered dish luncheon was served. Articles for the bazar held November 21 were completed.

The November 19 meeting of the Parlor was

(Continued on Page 25)

A BIT O' FARMING

PREPARED EXPRESSLY FOR THE GRIZZLY BEAR BY M. H. ELLIS

THERE MAY BE ONE GOOD EFFECT of the economic distress upon the farmers of California,—it has driven them more closely into co-operative organizations to work for their own good, and having tried the co-operation they may like it and stick. It is only through co-operation of the closest kind that permanent prosperity will be brought to agriculture. Co-operation in production and co-operation in marketing must be thorough if it is to be effective.

The farmer, of course, operates in comparatively small units; he is difficult to get into an organization and difficult to hold. Not until he is convinced by actual experience that he is to gain through working with his fellows can he be expected to do so. In the past many farmers have had sad experiences with co-operative organizations of various kinds, but it would be interesting to know what the condition now would be had co-operative organizations never come into being. That is one of the things that cannot be proved; it is one of the things that would be most productive of results if it could.

Co-operation must begin, in truth, before production, in the planning for planting. Production must be co-operative, that surpluses are not piled up with ruinous results. Co-operation must last through the year, with marketing as its climax. If the depression accomplishes this one result, of bringing home to the farmer the necessity of co-operation, it will have been an asset rather than a liability.

GOPHERS AT WORK AGAIN.

With the generous rains of last month, gophers have started their work again. Hard to control in dry weather, they may be exterminated in the fall and winter without much difficulty, in most cases. Cut sweet potatoes, carrots or parsnips, or even apples or prunes, into pieces an inch and a half long and a half-inch square, and dust with powdered strychnine alkaloid to which a small amount of saccharin has been added. An eighth of an ounce of this is enough for four quarts of bait. Put the bait in the main runways. It is necessary to make the baits large enough that the gopher cannot carry them, else he will take them to his storehouse and perhaps escape death. If he has to cut them down in size, he will get the poison.

ALFALFA FOR HOGS.

During the fall and winter, it is a mighty good plan to feed alfalfa to hogs. They will get protein, minerals and vitamins from alfalfa, whether fed as hay or mixed in the ration as meal. In feeding hay, a good plan is to make it available in a rack where the hogs can get what they want, but without waste. Meal should be fed about 10 pounds to 90 of other feeds in a self-feeder. Skim milk, alfalfa and grains are almost perfect insurance against nutritional difficulties with pigs and pregnant sows. Of course, if alfalfa pasture is available, hay need not be used.

SEEDING BURNED OVER PASTURE.

Seeding range that has been burned over has not yet been successfully accomplished. There are some grasses, such as rye, which will grow, but which will die during the dry season. If filaree and bur clover can be started, they will spread naturally, and are the best forage plants for range use. If these can be started, and the seed allowed to mature, it will be spread by the animals that graze the land. A good plan is to try sowing the seed in manure from the corrals; this can be done by mixing it sparsely with the manure when loading. Re-establishment of a bare range is a difficult matter and one that will take years for successful accomplishment.

FERTILIZATION FOR BULB PRODUCTION.

Bulb production requires soil that is fertile, with abundant humus and plenty of nitrogen. Manure turned under in the fall, then a cover crop and a dressing of quickly available nitrogenous commercial fertilizer at planting time, will bring the soil quickly to a degree of fertility that should insure good bulbs. It might be well for the flower grower to remember this, as well: in the home garden cover cropping hardly is feasible, but fertilization is, and good manure will add humus to the soil as well as plant food.

CUTTING TREES BACK.

Whatever may be the reason for the cutting back of trees, whether the annual pruning, for top working on new wood, or the production of new shoots from the old roots, the work should be done in the dormant season. During the summer and fall the tops are busy gathering plant food for storage. If the roots are to be preserved, they must have this food, hence the dormant season is chosen for cutting trees. Pinching back of excessive growth or the training of young trees is an exception. But generally speaking, if the saw or shears is to be used on a tree, it should be done after the leaves have fallen.

HENS IN THE WINTER.

During the winter the hens must be kept warm and dry, but with plenty of fresh air and as much sunshine as possible. If they get wet, the eggs will be soiled from mud on their feet, and the egg check will be smaller. Production will drop, too. The open-front house, facing the south, is probably the best answer to the problem. Keep up the weight of the hens, and if they show a loss in flesh increase the grain and cut down on the mash. Supply plenty of green feed. If sunshine is not available use fish, sardine or cod-liver oil in the mash. None of these, however, is a complete substitute for sunshine.

STORING DAHLIA BULBS.

While dahlia bulbs may be left in the ground all winter, provided the soil is light and well drained, it is a better practice to dig and store them. Dahlias, unlike potatoes, have no eyes on the bulbs and if the crown rots the bulb is destroyed. The bulbs should be carefully dug and packed in moist sand. Then store them in a cool, dark, dry place where the sand will dry gradually, curing the bulbs without injury. If the bulbs are left uncovered, they will dry out and lose much of their vigor before planting time.

THE STRAWBERRY BARREL.

The strawberry barrel is an extremely practical as well as ornamental adjunct to the garden. Quite a crop of berries may be obtained from plants in a barrel. First bore holes, about an inch in diameter, not larger, in the barrel, spacing them irregularly about nine inches to a foot apart. Fill the barrel to the first hole and stick the roots of the plants into the barrel. Pack them snugly about the hole with wet florist moss so that the soil will not wash out. Then add more soil and more plants as the holes are reached. Be sure to spread the roots as much as possible. Be sure, too, that the soil is rich and friable; a core of well-rotted manure may be put in the barrel as the earth is filled in.

SAN JOSE SCALE.

San Jose scale is not a major pest in California. It does not attack citrus fruits at all, and so far has not proved serious on any deciduous fruits save apples and pears. Yet if it is not controlled as it appears, it is entirely conceivable that in time it will become a really serious problem. San Jose scale is easy of control. Lime sulphur, full dormant strength, or good miscible oil applied before growth begins in the spring should bring about satisfactory control.

OIL SPRAY FOR CLEANUP.

Scale, spider eggs, eggs of leaf rollers and those of the various kinds of caterpillars should be killed with a dormant oil spray. Moss and lichen also are controlled by such a spray. The material may be put on at any time during the winter. Now is the proper time, if the ground is dry enough so that the work can be done. Putting off the spraying will not make it more effective, and there is the possibility that this winter may be one of those much-desired seasons where there is an abundance of rainfall which will make orchard work difficult later on.

SUNBURN PROTECTION.

Again the warning against winter sunburn damage. It is more serious than is that caused by the hot sun of the summer, for there are no leaves to shade the trunk and the range of temperature is far greater. On a bright, warm day in winter the bark of a tree will absorb heat that brings it above 90 degrees; yet that night the temperature may be freezing. The result is real injury. This may be prevented by a good coat of whitewash, which will reflect the rays of the sun instead of absorbing them. Whitewashed trees look nice in the summer, but the whitewash will give better returns on the money it cost if it is applied right now.

Growers To Confer—Growers of the state will have a conference with the State Agricultural Department at Sacramento City, December 2 and 3.

"That is not riches, which may be lost; virtue is our true good and the true reward of its possessor."—Da Vinci.

When you purchase goods advertised in The Grizzly Bear, or answer an advertisement in this magazine, please be sure to mention The Grizzly Bear. That's co-operation mutually beneficial.

Native Sons of the Golden West

"TO ALL PARLORS NATIVE SONS OF the Golden West—Dear Sirs and Brothers: The business and financial conditions in this country have not improved any during the year 1931, and in fact, were a little worse than in the previous year. However, we must have faith in the future of our country and those in charge of its affairs, and by exemplifying a spirit of co-operation we will soon be on the road to prosperity, which means better conditions to our fellow Americans.

"President Hoover has caused to be organized throughout the country committees to find ways and means to lead us to better things, and to temporarily offer assistance to those in immediate need. We should lend all the assistance possible to help carry out these plans.

"In our organization we no doubt have members who are suffering through lack of employment and who are unable to keep their dues paid. If you have in your Parlor some members who had been good members but who, through conditions over which they had no control, became delinquent and are liable to suspension, may I ask that you lend a helping hand to these brothers and thereby save them from the stain of being suspended for non-payment of dues, particularly at a time when they are unable to pay. Let us endeavor to hold our membership intact.

"They tell us 'the present depression is near the end and prosperity is around the corner.' I have faith in that statement and believe the year 1932 will find us on the way to prosperity and better conditions. Sincerely and fraternally yours,

"DR. FRANK I. GONZALEZ,
"Grand President N.S.G.W.
"San Francisco, November 23, 1931."

Federal Congress Appealed To.

Many Parlors have passed, and sent to California's representatives in the Federal Congress, resolutions in substance as follows:

Protesting against the proposal to amend the National Exclusion Law, which excludes all ineligible-to-citizenship aliens, so as to apply the quota to the nationals of Japan.

Requesting that the Federal Labor Department be required either to reverse its ruling recognizing Mexican Indians—who make up the great bulk of immigrants to this country from Mexico—as eligible to American citizenship, or to assist in securing a decision from the United States Supreme Court as to their eligibility.

Protesting against further admission into this country for permanent settlement of Filipinos, because of economic, social and political problems thereby created, and recommending independence for the Philippines.

Christmas Greetings

"To the Officers and Members of the Subordinate Parlors Native Sons of the Golden West—My dear Brothers: At this time of the year it is the oldest custom to extend greetings to friends for a Merry Yuletide and a Happy New Year.

"I wish each and every member of our beloved Order Health, Happiness and Prosperity, and an abundance of earthly joys and goodcheer. I hope the little hardships and cares you encountered during this year will disappear in the merry and joyous festivities of your hometide gatherings.

"Health, Benediction and a Merry Christmas!
"DR. FRANK I. GONZALEZ,
"Grand President N.S.G.W.
"San Francisco, November 18, 1931."

Come Out, Oldtimers and Youngsters.

Courtland—Courtland No. 106 will have its annual homeless children benefit dance Saturday night, December 5. Everything is in readiness to make this one of the season's most enjoyable events. This will be a hardtimes dance, featuring both the oldtime and the modern dances. Prizes for the best costumes will be awarded.

"You oldtimers who haven't had the pleasure of hopping to the music of a waltz, quadrille, etc., for many a day, come to Courtland and help make December 5 a big night," urges Third vice-president R. J. Heringer. "And you young people, remember gaiety will reign throughout the evening. Let us all contribute generously to the homeless children!"

County Eligibles Guests.

Santa Ana—As the inauguration of a campaign to increase the membership of the Parlor, Santa Ana No. 265 held an open meeting November 16, to which all eligible natives in Orange County were invited. An interesting program, consisting of spanish and mexican music, was enjoyed, followed by refreshments. During the course of the evening, a past president ring was presented Ed Mueller. The presentation address was made by Mel Head.

The float—entered by this Parlor in conjunction with Santa Ana No. 235 and Grace No. 242 (Fullerton) N.D.G.W.—which, in line with the theme of the parade, represented polo, received honorable mention by the judges of the Armistice Day parade in Santa Ana.

Good Work, Well Done.

Livermore—November 12 Las Positas No. 96 celebrated its forty-fifth institution anniversary with a banquet, the attendance being approximately 100. An affair of this kind has long been conducted annually by the Parlor with the idea of bringing all its members together at least once a year, and it has been most successful in that respect, as well as in providing a splendid social event for the members and invited guests. After the banquet the regular meeting of the Parlor was conducted. Addresses were made by Grand President Dr. Frank I. Gonzalez, Grand Secretary John T. Regan and District Deputy Elwood Fitzgerald.

At this meeting preparations were made for the Parlor's annual Christmas tree party for children of the Livermore valley who might otherwise be overlooked. This affair is one of the big events of the holiday season in Livermore, and at that time some 500 children, regardless of creed, color or nativity, are made happy by Las Positas. The committee handling the affair ascertains, with the aid of the social workers in the community, the names of needy children and extends to them an invitation to be present at the party. Each is given a gift, as well as good things to eat. This is a good work, well done by No. 96!

President Delbert Johnson has named a large committee to handle the Christmas tree details, among them being Carl Clarke, R. J. Ruetz, John Rose, H. W. Hupers, H. L. Wente, J. M. Beazell, Fred Young, E. A. Wente, L. A. Mcvicar, Wm. Medau, Lloyd Gunderson and J. M. Baughman.

Oldtimers Guests.

Placerville—Placerville No. 9 and Marguerite No. 12 N.D.G.W. entertained oldtimers who came to El Dorado County prior to 1870. A delicious chicken dinner was prepared and served by Marguerite, and Placerville had charge of the program, which opened with a welcome address by Louis Mocettini, and continued as follows: Remarks, Mrs. Lloyd Hancock, president Marguerite; accordion selection, Arthur Masten; recitation, Jane McCusker; selection, J. E. Merryman orchestra; vocal solo, Miss Francis Spencer, with piano accompaniment by Mrs. Wright; remarks, District Attorney Henry S. Lyon; vocal solo, Oliver Mann; duet, Mrs. J. Leonardi and Miss Monica McCusker; vocal solos, Mrs. Lena Rantz, George McKee and Mrs. Ovida Forni LeBourveau; duet, Mrs. LeBourveau and George McKee; community singing, oldtime songs.

The oldtimers who answered the rollcall included Henry Veerkamp, Charles Varozza, Mrs. Gilmore, Mrs. and Mr. A. B. Kyburz, Will Clifton, Mrs. Elizabeth Went, Mrs. Carl Herman, Thomas Swansborough, Miss Mary O'Donnell, Mary J. Secombe, Mary Duffy Bathurst, Sara Sexton, Josephine Norris, Mrs. Sara Waddell, Mrs. Masten, Mrs. Elizabeth Killough, Miss M. Reynolds, Mrs. Mary Kent, Henry K. Marks, Miss Etta Bunker, Thomas E. Stacey, Mrs. Fred Engesser, C. E. Holliday, Florence Welch, Mrs. J. N. Rhodes, Frank Wentz, John M. Sellick,

George Swansborough, John B. Sellick, A. E. Chapman, W. H. Carpenter, Marcus Starbuck, W. H. Brewer, A. B. Kyburz, Mrs. Julia Johnson, Sara McCumsey, J. Evans, T. B. Ryan, W. B. McKenzie, Mrs. Ida Sweeney, John J. Duffy, Olivene Stone, Mrs. Kate McNeil, Mrs. Nevada Childs and A. D. Skinner.

Membership Standing Largest Parlors.

San Francisco—Grand Secretary John T. Regan reports the standing of the Subordinate Parlors having a membership of over 400 January 1, 1931, as follows, together with their membership figures November 20, 1931:

Parlor	Jan. 1	Nov. 20	Gain	Loss
Ramona No. 109	1163	1138	..	25
South San Francisco No. 157	828	824	..	4
Castro No. 232	690	702	12	..
Stanford No. 76	644	640	..	4
Twin Peaks No. 214	723	631	..	92
Arrowhead No. 110	608	619	11	..
Stockton No. 7	562	560	..	2
Piedmont No. 120	510	518	8	..
Rincon No. 72	463	456	..	7

Fiftieth Anniversary Celebrated.

Modesto—November 4 Modesto No. 11 celebrated its fiftieth institution anniversary, with approximately 150 members present, representing that Parlor and other Parlors of the San Joaquin Valley. A class of eight candidates were initiated, the ceremony being conducted by a picked team from the Parlor under the supervision of District Deputy Charles W. Gill.

After the meeting a splendid banquet was served, and a very fine entertainment program was presented. Addresses were made by Grand President Dr. Frank I. Gonzalez, Grand Secretary John T. Regan and Grand Trustee George F. McNoble. The general committee of arrangements included Charles D. Blaine, Robert G. Benson, Robert B. Hansen, B. C. Hawkins and C. E. Tucker.

Special Courtesy to Daughters.

Santa Barbara—Santa Barbara No. 116 celebrated Armistice Day with a barbecue and dance at Tucker Grove. More than 300 enjoyed the affair, which was arranged under the general supervision of President John L. Stewart as a special courtesy to Reina del Mar No. 126 N.D.G.W. William McCaffrey prepared the barbecue, and A. C. Dinsmore had charge of the seating arrangements.

San Rafael Natives Capture Trophy.

San Rafael—The annual ritual contest between Mount Tamalpais No. 64 and Sea Point No. 158 (Sausalito) resulted in the trophy, a walnut gavel block surmounted by a bronze bear, being won by the former Parlor with a score of 963 to 823. This trophy was to be awarded permanently to the Parlor whose team scored highest in two out of three contests. Jas. Stanley, J. G. Schroder, Jas. Hayes and D. F. Rickleff judged the contest.

At the banquet following the meeting District Deputy B. J. Brusatori presided, and County Treasurer Charles Redding, in his most elegant manner, presented the trophy to President Walter Mazza, who accepted it for Mount Tamalpais. Grand Trustee Samuel M. Shortridge Jr. said he could not compliment the officers of both teams too highly on the splendid manner in which they acquitted themselves. He stated he was deeply impressed with the great advantages derived by both Parlors from these contests. They are the largest contributing factor in making for the success of these very-much-alive institutions and he will strongly urge all Parlors in his visiting district to have such contests, as he believes those Parlors which take a pride in the ritualistic work are the successful ones, while those which neglect this most important feature are, as a rule, in a moribund condition. Among other speakers were J. Hartley Russell, County Assessor A. F. Pacheco, Sheriff Walter Silmer, Harold J. Haley, Jas. Stanley, J. G. Schroder and Willis B. Garcia. Stanford No. 76's "german" quartet—no, they are not singers,—Messrs. Caveny, Barry, Sullivan and Neely, also spoke briefly, congratulating the officers for their splendid rendition of the work. A committee will get together shortly to arrange for the next series of contests, since this policy has been found to have a most stimulating effect on Nativesonism in Marin County.

Junior High School Dedicated.

San Jose—The grand officers dedicated the Herbert Hoover junior high school November 15. George B. Campbell of the board of education presided, and the speakers included President Bob Wittenberg, who extended greetings on behalf of the student body, Grand President

(Continued on Page 17)

When you purchase goods advertised in The Grizzly Bear, or answer an advertisement in this magazine, please be sure to mention The Grizzly Bear. That's co-operation mutually beneficial.

CALIFORNIA HAPPENINGS OF FIFTY YEARS AGO

Thomas R. Jones

(COMPILED EXPRESSLY FOR THE GRIZZLY BEAR.)

CHRISTMAS DAY 1881 CAME ON A Sunday, so while the Yuletide trees had their inning Saturday, Christmas Eve, the holiday was observed Monday, December 26. This was one of the most prosperous holiday seasons California had ever enjoyed. Money was plentiful, and everybody was happy.

Rain fell heavily Christmas Eve, but Monday was clear and cold. Four storms during December brought a rainfall of 1.88 inches, making the seasonal total 4.71 inches.

Youths of San Francisco became so imbued with the horn-blowing fad during Christmas week nervous citizens complained to the police. All day and all night horns blew incessantly in all parts of the city, and the police chief ordered his men to confiscate all horns found in the possession of blowing lads. Many wagonloads of the noise-instruments were, accordingly, unloaded at the City Hall.

Fresno City was enjoying a real estate "boom." Over 1,000 transactions, at rising prices, were made during the month, the total amount involved approximating $754,000. During the year 1881, 210 houses were constructed.

An oil gusher was struck in Pico Canyon near San Fernando, Los Angeles County.

H. J. Glenn, Colusa County's wheat baron, sowed 30,000 acres to wheat in November and December, and his 1,000 mules were plowing 25,000 additional acres.

San Francisco's Board of Trade started raising a large fund to be used in encouraging immigration from the East to California.

Arrests for violation of the state's Sunday-closing law were being made in many cities and towns. Juries composed of "prominent citizens" were, however, returning not-guilty verdicts, even when saloonkeepers acknowledged their guilt. Accordingly, what was generally regarded as a good law was made ridiculous.

Another temperance organization was born this month, at Oakland, Alameda County. It was named the Order of Good Samaritans, and the initial branch was termed Golden Link Lodge No. 1.

The first through train over the Southern Pacific via Arizona, New Mexico and Texas to New Orleans, Louisiana, left San Francisco December 30.

O. L. Palmer, San Diego City hotel proprietor, was robbed of $1,700 in gold coin which he had concealed under a mattress.

MILLIONS IN COINS FROM COAST MINES.

The treasury of Napa County was found to be $4,600 short. Barth, levanting capitalist of Napa City, had borrowed the amount and left in lieu his promissory note.

Hamilton Hall, the only theater in Grass Valley, Nevada County, burned along with several other buildings December 2, causing a $10,000 loss.

A portion of the Placerville, El Dorado County, Chinatown burned December 20. The same day a Banta, San Joaquin County, hotel was consumed by fire and the Chinese cook was cremated.

The stage from San Luis Obispo City was stopped December 14 near Soledad, Monterey County, by a highwayman who took the express box.

The Downieville, Sierra County, stage was held up near Camptonville, Yuba County, December 16 by a masked road agent. Finding nothing of value in the express box, his blaspheming could be heard for a mile.

The stage from Milton, Calaveras County, to Sonora, Tuolumne County, was stopped near Copperopolis December 29. The robber, hacking open the express box and finding it empty, made off with the mail sack.

Coinage of the United States Mint at San Francisco during 1881 included: 727,000 twenty-dollar gold pieces, valued at $14,540,000; 970,000 ten-dollar gold pieces, valued at $9,700,000; 969,000 five-dollar gold pieces, valued at $4,845,000; 12,700,000 one-dollar silver pieces, valued at $12,700,000. All of the gold and silver in these coins, totaling $41,785,000 in value, came from Pacific Coast mines.

A vein of bituminous coal was found three miles from Ventura City.

In the Boulder mine near Kelsey, El Dorado County, a gold vein eight feet wide was found December 3.

The Bald Mountain Extension Mining Company of Forest City, Sierra County, cleaned up December 9 for the week 170 ounces of gold worth $3,200.

A Fort Jones, Siskiyou County, butcher slaughtered a cow and in its stomach found chispas valued at $14.75.

In the Bald Mountain, Sierra County, claim an eight-ounce nugget was found December 20 shaped like a human being. The legs and feet were in proper position, while the left hand, with but four fingers, was held against the chest.

NOTED HORSETHIEVES ROUNDED UP.

The San Jose, Santa Clara County, electric tower, having six lights of 24,000 candlepower, was put in use December 13. Crowds gathered along the streets to view the then-wonderful illumination.

Mrs. Almina Henley, who came to California from Virginia in 1850, died at Ione, Amador County, December 16.

James C. Symen who, in 1843, settled in Napa valley, died at Napa City, December 28, at the age of 88.

Dr. Joseph Kuhrts, called to accoucheur a Mexican woman named Cruz in Los Angeles City, December 28 delivered her of six female infants.

A. B. Dickhut went for a deer hunt with a party of friends in the mountains west of Orland, Glenn County, December 5. He became lost, and died from exposure in Grindstone Canyon, where his body was found the 18th.

David Evans and Peter Barrow were duck hunting December 8 on San Rafael Creek, Marin County. The boat upset, and Barrow was drowned.

Rev. Charles Wesley Hewes, San Francisco Baptist minister, went suddenly insane December 28 and committed suicide.

Jim Crum, Billy Miner and Billy Miller, noted horsethieves and ex-convicts who operated in the Sacramento and San Joaquin Valleys several years, were arrested after a hard struggle in Yolo County, December 7. November 7 they had robbed a Tuolumne County stage, so they were taken to Sonora for trial for that offense.

(Continued on Page 19)

BOOK REVIEWS

(CLARENCE M. HUNT.)

"THE GREAT TREK."

By Owen Cochran Coy; Powell Publishing Company, Los Angeles, Publisher; Price, $5.00.

The author of this volume, one of the Powell Company's "California" series, is professor of history at the University of Southern California and director of the California Historical Survey Commission. He is also the author of several other California history books, and has contributed numerous articles to The Grizzly Bear.

"There is no more interesting phenomenon in the history of this continent than the westward movement of the American people," says Dr. Coy. "The purpose of this volume is to give the story of that great migration"—following news of the discovery of gold at Coloma, El Dorado County, in 1848,—"which was destined to revolutionize the history of California . . . Our libraries are not supplied with works which treat as a whole the overland emigration at this most important epoch.

"The plan of the author has been to give an account of this movement as nearly as possible in the words of contemporaneous writers. Where a single narrative would not suffice to indicate the variety of hardships encountered or the diversity of routes followed, the diaries of several travelers have been pieced together in a sort of literary mosaic, preserving for the reader as much of the original narrative as possible." So that the reader may follow the various trails, Dr. Coy presents three maps, prepared by himself, showing all the important places mentioned in the text.

"The Great Trek" is illustrated with several drawings specially prepared by Franz Geritz. It has, also, facsimile autographs of the officers of the Covered Wagon Babies Club, and a valuable bibliography. Dr. Coy dedicated the volume "To the memory of my father, Charles Fremont Coy, a lover of history."

"THE PIONEER MINER AND THE PACK MULE EXPRESS."

By Ernest A. Wiltsee; California Historical Society, Publisher, San Francisco; Price, $4.00.

In this work, the fifth of the special publications of the California Historical Society, the author discusses the peculiarities of the situation in which the gold-rush California Pioneers found themselves, with particular reference to the difficulties encountered in obtaining news from home. He describes the forces leading to the development of numerous expresses, at first by individuals and later by organized companies, and relates in detail their methods and development.

The book is profusely illustrated with reproductions of early prints, and of envelopes disclosing the more important types of express franks. Appendices give a list of the California postal stations in 1851, and the names, the locations and the dates of operation of four hundred and forty-six of the early-day expressmen and express companies.

An interesting insert is the "Topographical Map of the Mineral Districts of California, being the first map ever published from actual survey." This map, prepared by John B. Trask in 1853, shows the locations of a large number of the earliest gold camps of California.

"FORTY-NINERS: THE CHRONICLE OF THE CALIFORNIA TRAIL."

By Archer Butler Hulbert; Little, Brown & Co., Boston, Mass., Publisher; Price $3.50.

This volume, an "Atlantic Monthly Press Book," in competition with over five hundred manuscripts won the prize of $5,000 offered by the Atlantic Monthly Press and Little, Brown & Company for the most interesting unpublished work, not fiction, dealing with the American scene. The author has been professor of history and director of the Stewart Commission on Western history at Colorado College since 1925, and since 1927 adjunct professor of American history at Pomona College. Professor Hulbert is also the author of "Historic Highways of America" and several other volumes.

"Forty-Niners" is a chronicle of what happened to the thousands of men and women who came to California via the Overland Trail in the gold-rush days. The record, much of it in the very words of the Argonauts themselves, is alive with humorous and tragic incidents. "To prepare this chronicle of the California gold rush,"

(Continued on Page 15)

Native Daughters of the Golden West

GEORGETOWN—AT ITS ANNUAL DINner, El Dorado No. 186 was hostess to oldtimers of California who came to El Dorado County prior to 1870, members of Georgetown No. 91 N.S.G.W. and other invited guests. Oldtimers answering rollcall were Mrs. Georgia Knox 1852, Mrs. Elizabeth Farnsworth 1853, Peter Morgan 1861, Edward Stanton 1863, Ira Cushman 1865 and Mrs. Florenda Francis 1868. Three generations of Native Daughters, all members of the Parlor, were also present—Mrs. Margaret Roberts; her daughter, Mrs. Ethel Francis, and her granddaughter, Miss Edith Francis. President Hattie Presby welcomed the guests, and the members of El Dorado, attired in quaint pioneer costumes, served a turkey banquet.

At the conclusion of the feast a pageant of California's colorful history, written and directed by Past President Ella Stanton, was presented by the members in costume, Past President Annie Heindel announcing each event. Two oldtime fiddlers, Peter Morgan and Clarence Hotchkiss, accompanied on the piano by Mrs. J. J. Wiley, rendered popular tunes of the early days, and during the spanish period of the pageant Mrs. Budd Polley favored with appropriate guitar selections. Several songs of the mining days were sung by Miss Margaret Kelley, accompanied by Mrs. Wiley.

The affair was Georgetown's fiesta day, and will long be remembered by those so fortunate as to have been guests of the occasion.

Christmas Greetings

"To the Officers and Members of the Subordinate Parlors Native Daughters of the Golden West—Dear Sisters: It gives me great pleasure to call to your attention that the greatest festival of all times will soon be celebrated—the Birthday of the World—CHRISTMAS.

"After nineteen hundred years, the charm of Christmas is just as great and welcome to us of the twentieth century as it was to those who heard the Angelic Choir sing 'Peace on Earth, Good Will Toward Men.'

"How beautiful that night in Bethlehem, when the Shepherds and the Wise Kings traveled from afar to gaze upon the Babe in a lowly manger; a Babe, born to save the world; an answer to all problems and the solution to all difficulties. What a delightful fascination the festival of Christmas has for mankind!

"In a spirit of faith, dear sisters, let us ask HIM to bring peace to the world and ask, especially, that the Temple of Mars be closed forever. Let us forget the bitterness of fears and the anxious thoughts that crowd our lives, and pray to that Babe for the gift of understanding and to make all our moments calm and bright and full of the strength of faith, hope and love. Let us apply the Golden Rule to our everyday life—'Do unto others as we would have them do unto us,'—for such is the spirit of Christmas.

"With just such a spirit, I wish all the blessings, that Heaven alone can give, to each and every member of our Order and their dear ones, and may the new year bring joy and prosperity to every household within our land.

"For I couldn't have a Christmas
That's happy through and through,
Unless I started wishing
A happy one for you.
I couldn't have a minute
That's sunny all the year,
Unless I wished all sunshine
For the members I hold dear.

"Sincerely and fraternally yours, in P.D.F.A.,
"EVELYN I. CARLSON,
"Grand President
"Native Daughters Golden West.
"San Francisco, December 1, 1931."

Grand Parlor Plans Discussed.

Merced—veritas No. 75 received an official visit November 3 from Grand President Evelyn I. Carlson. A large number of members of the Parlor and numerous visitors were in attendance. The evening's extensive program opened with a supper at which President Marie Sorenson presided. In the lodgeroom, decorated in the colors of veritas, gold, white and crimson, the ritual was exemplified, and plans for the Grand Parlor, which meets at Merced in June, were discussed. Following the singing of "I Love You, California," by Marion Pulcifer a gift was presented Grand President Carlson, and corsages were presented Pauline Zirker, charter member, and Supervising Deputies Emma O'Meara, Mae Givens, Eugenia Kahl, Alberta Guard, Margaret Boyle and Katherine Kopf.

veritas had a float, in charge of Hazel Laverty, in the Armistice Day parade, and a committee composed of Zelphia Thomas, Mildred Heinzen, Harriet Hooten and Rhoda Guest has been appointed to take care of a grocery box for welfare work.

"Cast Thy Bread Upon the Waters."

San Jose—vendome No. 100 had an Armistice Day program November 11 with Mrs. Anne Farnsworth in charge. Mrs. Julia Waddington, sewing club chairman, entertained at her home November 13. The Parlor's institution anniversary party November 18 featured a depression dinner. Members came attired in the oldest and worst clothes obtainable. Past presidents, with Mrs. Lotta Koppel as general chairman, had charge of the festivities.

The annual dance sponsored by the San Jose Parlors—San Jose No. 81 and vendome No. 100 N.D.G.W., San Jose No. 22 and Observatory No. 177 N.S.G.W.—for the benefit of the homeless children will be held Saturday evening, December 5.

Vendome's $100 Christmas gift card party, to be held December 9, is in charge of a general committee composed of Mms. Clara Gairaud (chairman), Lotta Koppel and Hazel Haub. Holders of green books are asked to communicate with Mrs. Gairaud before that date. The Parlor recently received a S.O.S. call from a poor family. Without any redtape relief was extended and shoes were provided for five boys and a girl. "Cast thy bread upon the waters and it will come back to thee a hundredfold," is Vendome's motto. Another reason why the green books should be successful.

Memorial Service for Past Grand.

Sacramento—November 10 Califia No. 22 had a memorial service and dedicated a California State (Bear) Flag to the memory of the late Past Grand President Ema Gett. The occasion was also in recognition of the Parlor's institution anniversary and charter members night. Mrs. Gett was a highly esteemed member of Califia and was much loved by all who knew her.

While the members sang "I Love You, California," accompanied at the piano by Miss Oneida Wilhelm, Marshal Maud Cook entered with the flag. "Absent" was sung by a quartet from Sutter No. 111 directed by Miss Ida Thomas. Mrs. Sadie Brainard spoke of Mrs. Gett's life, and Past President Katherine Jones delivered the dedicatory address. First vice-president Sulene Cowan read the following original poem, "In Memory of Mrs. Gett":

"On the highway of life's sweetest memories
We pause from the cares of the day,
To hold in our thoughts, and in spirit,
A loved one we treasure alway.
Time, the great healer of sorrow,
Gives courage and bids 'Carry on.'
The test of the soldier in battle
Is proven when victory is won.
A leader may fall in the conflict,
The colors must still be held high,
To us has this banner fallen,—
Our heritage; dare let it lie?
As the shadows at sunset turn golden,
Weaving tapestries, priceless and rare,
So memory weaves and is holding
A pattern of love we may share.
Enshrined in the folds of this emblem
Are graces and beauties unseen,
But speaking a tender message
From the soul of the giver, serene.
Years cannot dim our devotion,
Service our watchword must be,
This is our test of promotion
If we would share honor with thee.
To one of our state's fairest daughters,
May we honor her memory sublime,
For her loyalty, service, devotion,
To California, your loved state and mine."

Entertains Menfolks.

San Bernardino—November 4, Lugonia No. 241 entertained the husbands of its members and the members of Arrowhead No. 110 N.S.G.W. and their wives at an italian dinner. Gladys Baker was in charge. A short entertainment program followed the dinner. November 25 officers for the January-July term were nominated and a social hour at cards was followed by light refreshments.

Costume Party.

Oakland—Members of Piedmont No. 120 N.S.G.W. were guests of Piedmont No. 87 at a Hallowe'en costume party October 29. A very enjoyable evening was had, there being entertainment, dancing and a banquet. The entertainment consisted of a miniature minstrel show by blackface comedians, and a dancing act. The balance of the evening was spent in dancing. Prizes for the best costumes were awarded Ellen Mullins, Alice Weber, Mae Mead and Merle Wilson. At the close of the evening all repaired to the banquet hall to enjoy pumpkin pie and coffee. Pauline Griswold was chairman of the evening. November 19 No. 87 sponsored a public turkey whist.

Need Homeless Children Funds Stressed.

Halfmoon Bay—Grand President Evelyn I. Carlson paid an official visit to Vista del Mar No. 155 October 22, and was accompanied by Grand Outside Sentinel Orinda Giannini and Supervising Deputy Rena Mathias. Other visitors were District Deputy Dias and delegations from several Parlors.

The address of Mrs. Carlson, a woman of charming personality, was greatly enjoyed. She particularly stressed the necessity of securing funds for continuing the homeless children work, and expressed the hope Vista del Mar and Seaside No. 95 N.S.G.W. would respond this year in the same generous way they have in the past. She also highly commended the officers for the efficient manner in which the Parlor is conducted. A number of other visitors gave short addresses which were much appreciated. At the conclusion of the meeting delicious refreshments were served in the banquetroom, tastefully decorated for the occasion.

Fun for All.

Oroville—Gold of Ophir No. 190 had a Hallowe'en party November 4 at which members of Argonaut No. 8 N.S.G.W. were guests. Entertainment, a laugh-provoking game that brought fun for all, was in charge of Mae Bell Bills, who was assisted by Emma Danforth, Mattie Lund and Irene Lund. Alice Frazier was hostess at a surprise turkey supper. An interesting hour at the festive board was hightened by assembly singing led by Romilda Ralph, with Alta Baldwin at the piano.

State Flags for County Schoolrooms.

Woodland—The official visit of Grand President Evelyn I. Carlson to Woodland No. 90 was the occasion for a largely attended and most interesting session. The evening's first feature was a dinner, which was followed by addresses and the initiation of four candidates. The banquet and meeting rooms had the appearance of an autumn setting, with decorations in the fall motif. Other grand officers in attendance included Grand Vice-president Anna Mixon-Armstrong, Grand Secretary Sallie R. Thaler, Grand Trustee Florence Boyle, Past Grand Presidents Addie Mosher, Mary E. Bell and Dr. Louise C. Heilbron, Supervising Deputies Edna Richter and Ethel Ludwig, District Deputies Inna Bloom, Sadie Brainard, Mamie Davis, Mamie McCormick, Laura Nordstrom, Edna Healey, Bessie Leach and Doris Fisher.

Through the efforts of the Parlor, and with the consent of Mrs. Rowena Norton, county school superintendent, a California State (Bear) Flag will be placed in every Yolo County schoolroom. The first flags were placed October 29 in the West Sacramento school. The program was in charge of Mrs. Edna Richter, chairman of No. 90's history and landmarks committee.

Grand President's Official Itinerary.

San Francisco—During the month of December, Grand President Evelyn I. Carlson will officially visit the following Subordinate Parlors on the dates noted:

1st—La Junta No. 203, Saint Helena.
2nd—Castro No. 178, San Francisco.
3rd—San Jose No. 81, San Jose.
4th—Fruitvale No. 177, Oakland.
5th—Sacramento and Placer Counties district meeting.
7th—Darina No. 114, San Francisco.
8th—Alta No. 3, San Francisco.
10th—Plumas, Glenn and Butte Counties district meeting.
11th—Mission No. 227, San Francisco.
14th—Sonoma No. 209, Sonoma.
15th—Petaluma No. 222, Petaluma.
16th—Golden State No. 50, San Francisco.
18th—El Tejon No. 239, Bakersfield.

Drill Team Gets Trophy.

Petaluma—With President Julia Peroline presiding, Petaluma No. 222 initiated two candidates November 3. With Elizabeth Dillon in charge, refreshments were served at flower bedecked tables following the ceremonies. Large delegations from the Parlor attended the meetings of Eschol No. 16 and Santa Rosa No. 217 when Grand President Evelyn I. Carlson visited those Parlors.

A public card party November 17 was largely attended, and many went home with Thanksgiving turkeys. A twenty-dollar gold piece was also disposed of at a goodly profit. The Parlor's drill team appeared in the Santa Rosa Armistice Day parade and was awarded a trophy. Preparations are being made for the official visit of Grand President Carlson December 15.

"On Armistice Day."

Santa Ana—The benefit card party of Santa Ana No. 235 was well attended and a social success. In charge was a committee composed of Mms. Marguerite Dickinson (chairman), Genevieve Hiskey, Olive Seba, Florence Watson and Muriel Bray. Preceding the November 9 meeting a dinner was served by the losers in a membership drive. Honor guests were District Deputy Hazel Hansen and a delegation from Verdugo No. 240

(Continued on Page 21)

Feminine World's Fads and Fancies

PREPARED ESPECIALLY FOR THE GRIZZLY BEAR BY ANNA STOERMER

SOMEONE HAS HINTED THAT THERE IS not a Santa Claus. If not, who brings the presents to little children—those who still believe with all their wide-eyed wonder in Christmas and know some things so much better than we do? Santy is their hero and, like other heroes of childhood days, he has to suffer many attacks. So does old Father Christmas take many a buffeting in this modern age of skepticism, and over the roof of many a home the tinkle of his reindeers' bells has grown fainter each year.

Streets and stores are gay with excited preparations which prove that Santa Claus does exist, and that there is a Santa Claus will be forcibly impressed on one after a busy day of prowling about and making selections for the youngsters and friends—and always remembering charities. The Christmas spirit cannot be torn apart. "Peace on earth, good will to men," is an ideal that has stayed with us through the centuries.

It is interesting to note that, in common with so many other lines, toys and games are considerably less in price than last year. This means, of course, more Christmas happiness for a larger number of children. The curtain rises on the thrilling drama of dolls and toys, and old Santa himself is smilingly waiting to greet his little friends, in person. He may be found in most of the shops and on the streets from now until Christmas.

This year we see genuine reproductions of furniture for children's playrooms, including four-poster beds, chiffoniers, vanity dressers with benches, drop-leaf and gate-leg tables, windsor chairs, and even an individual toy bathroom, completely equipped with every bathroom accessory. Life-like baby dolls, with composition head, arms and creeping legs, sleeping eyes with long eyelashes and crying voice, are beautifully dressed. The modern couch-hammock, in miniature, is designed for the leisure-loving dolls. It is strongly constructed with steel standard, and is complete with canopy top and awning stripe canvas upholstery.

For the boys, there are the 31-model automobile, all steel body and adjustable pedals, headlights, horn, adjustable windshield, front bumper, toolbox and the new-type ten-inch wheel; a three-car electric train consisting of electric-type locomotive, baggage car and passenger coach, narrow-gauge sectional track with danger signal and semaphore; also a new-type tubular velocipede with chromium-plated handlebars, rubber grip, bell, double coil spring saddle and even the toolbag.

A toy that will be hailed with delight by all "Mickey Mouse" fans is a mechanical orchestra, all metal, key wind, start-and-stop lever; a director, a dancer, a pianist and a drummer all take part.

Toys, the like of which you have never seen before, will greet you on every hand. Amazing mechanical toys that hold small boys, and sometimes the larger ones, spellbound, stand side by side with the most alluring dolls any small girl ever wanted. So it goes. Your progress through the land of make-believe will be a series of surprises.

The Christmas gift of something handmade may be a pajama ensemble, a slumber ensemble, Christmas aprons for tea service or kitchen use, a new wardrobe for dolly, embroidered linens or guest towels. A cloth of which one could be justly proud is embroidered in cutwork with a design of leaves and fruit and has napkins to match. A quilt in an interesting shell design could be made of satin or taffeta, interlined with cozy layers of wool. A small alarm clock for the bedside may be selected in your favored color.

This Christmas will find umbrellas converted into a beautiful costume accessory. There are tailored models as jaunty as a walking stick, and dress types pleasingly keyed to the afternoon mode.

A whole wardrobe of styles are eager for a place among the gifts to one's self and one's friends. Handkerchiefs are always most acceptable, as are hosiery, lovely bags for daytime and evening use, lingerie, handmade slips, panties and chemise, bias-cut nightgowns, low-back slips and one-piece pajamas with lace trimmed coat.

We also find the useful makeup box, with spacious divisions for separate toilet necessities. Boudoir novelties are so attractive—chinese dolls holding powderpuffs; rose pajama cases that look just like a delicate rose in one's bedroom; boudoir pillows; shoe-trees in all the dainty pastel colorings; chiffon sets of handkerchief and garters to match.

We know that more than the gift itself is its association, and a very small gift may be very precious, apart from its intrinsic value. There is a glamour about the holiday sets of perfume, powder and soap. It is not difficult to choose gifts. Maybe something small or something quite impressive—perfume in an elaborate cut-glass bottle, or a makeup box for the woman who travels. There are gifts for every occasion, for young and old.

Accessories to the fact of being well dressed are with us this season in abundant variety. Those little touches—a necklace, a bracelet, a clever clip—all can accentuate and complete the costume, but they must be harmonious and appropriate, otherwise their purpose is defeated. Do not, however, buy tempting trifles unless you have a definite place and use for them. There are pieces and sets of costume jewelry to suit all types, both of beauty and clothes. See that you choose things that set off your outfit.

The most original of all the new designs we have seen is a slip-on glove, with a bracelet

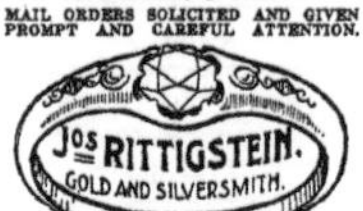

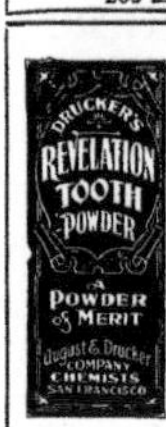

quite rigid at the top of the glove held in place by gold or silver threads. On white and black the thread is silver, and on beige it is gold. You will be glad to know this stunning little bracelet glove comes in daytime shades as well as those for evening wear.

There are many attractive styles in short evening gloves. Some of the newest have little bows on the back of the wrists, some have a tiny gore with stitching and some have turnback all-around cuffs of self-material in the new length. The very latest are the short ones in a variety of styles. However, many women prefer the regulation long gloves for evening wear. If so, you must wear them as if they were shirred, crushed down to the forearm.

Sequin berets to wear with your evening gown are exactly the shape of the every-day model, but the glittering spangles set them worlds apart and make them applicable to the evening formal wear.

Rhinestone buttons and a bow at the waistline are all the trimming required for one of the smartest frocks of the season. The color is a golden beige, and the bodice is draped with a slantwise movement that is clinched with the rhinestone buttons, one near each shoulder and the third one farther down on the right side of the draped neckline. The small bow at the waistline is a continuation of the narrow belt, and looks as though it was also a continuation of the narrow binding around the one-sided peplum. There are tiny little shoulder-cap sleeves over the long ones, and the latter bulge slightly at the wrist.

Fussy clothes are of short duration. The woman who knows her needs, will reserve them for afternoon hours.

BOOK REVIEWS

(Continued from Page 11)

says Professor Hulbert, "the California trail was divided into eight sections. Then every available diary or journal was read for the light it might shed on pioneer experience in the region covered. . . . In addition to consulting this source material the writer has traveled most of the trail himself, mile by mile, several times. Thus a diary of a party of Forty-Niners came into existence. Every material fact in it is from some record left by an Argonaut of the gold-rush days, 1848-1853. . . . Nothing, therefore, is modern in this book except the arrangement."

The work is illustrated with numerous cartoons of the Forty-Niners, and many original drawings of sights and scenes of the time. It also has eight maps of the Overland Trail, and presents the songs sung along the way; these latter, it is stated, are here collected for the first time. A bibliography, always valuable in a California history book, lists the writings of California Argonauts from which the facts in the volume were derived.

SEA GULLS

(MISS ESTHER CRONE.)

Brave rovers of the sea, of billow and lea,
So endowed with grace and motion,
We covet your skill to circle at will
The breakers of God's great ocean.

White heavenly things, with angel-like wings
That can fold or conquer the deep;
And no limit to hights in your tireless flights,
Scaling crag or mountainous steep.

Is the secret you bear, that a Father's care
Makes your life so happy and free?
Do the same hands feed, like the Word we read?
Our brave rovers out on the sea.

LIVING CHRISTMAS TREES SUGGESTED AS CONFIDENCE RESTORER.

"Light an outdoor Christmas tree this year and help to drive away fear and depression," is the message being broadcast by the Outdoor Christmas Tree Association of California.

"It seems that at this particular time, when the world is so full of fear and thoughts of limitation, we should make an extra effort to restore confidence and drive away fear. There is no better way to accomplish this than to decorate outdoor living Christmas trees in front of homes. Living Christmas trees along the highways will also act as beacons to prosperity, and spread a cheerful message of confidence to the visitors from other states as well as to our own citizens."

Depression Discussion—The Institute of Occupational Relations will discuss theories as to the cause of the depression and proposed remedial measures at Los Angeles City, December 14-18.

Official Directory of Parlors of the N. S. G. W.

ALAMEDA COUNTY.

Alameda No. 47, Alameda City—Guy C. Whitmore, Pres.; Robt. H. Cavanaugh, Sec., 1806 Pacific Ave.; Wednesdays, Native Sons Hall, 1406 Park St.

Oakland No. 50, Oakland—E. A. Rehorst, Pres.; F. M. Norris, Sec., 4280 Terrace St.; Fridays, Native Sons Hall, 11th and Clay Sts.

Las Positas No. 96, Livermore—Delbert L. Johnson, Pres.; John J. Kelly, Sec., P. O. box 341; Thursdays, Foresters Hall.

Eden No. 113, Hayward—William J. Burgess, Pres.; Henry Powell, Sec., 944 Castro St.; 1st and 3rd Wednesdays, Bank Hayward Hall.

Piedmont No. 120, Oakland—Andrew Costelli, Pres.; Charles Morando, Sec., 906 Vermont St.; Thursdays, Native Sons Hall, 11th and Clay Sts.

Wisteria No. 127, Alvarado—Henry May, Pres.; J. M. Scribner, Sec., Livermore; 1st Thursday, I.O.O.F. Hall.

Halcyon No. 146, Alameda City—T. W. Soule, Pres.; J. C. Bates, Sec., 2129 Buena Vista Ave; 1st and 3rd Tuesdays, I.O.O.F. Hall, 2329 Santa Clara Ave.

Brooklyn No. 151, Oakland—Frank B. Perry, Pres.; E. W. Cooney, Sec., 3907 14th Ave.; Wednesdays, Masonic Temple, 8th Ave. and E. 14th St.

Washington No. 169, Centerville—F. T. Dusterberry, Pres.; Allen G. Norris, Sec., P. O. box 31; 2nd and 4th Tuesdays, Hansen Hall.

Athens No. 195, Oakland—Allan W. Sunkler, Pres.; Harold B. Farley, Sec., 4623 Benevides Ave.; Tuesdays, Native Sons Hall, 11th and Clay Sts.

Berkeley No. 210, Berkeley—Maurice Casey, Pres.; R. J. Garrett, Sec., 1708 Virginia St.; Tuesdays, Native Sons Hall, 2108 Shattuck Ave.

Estudillo No. 223, San Leandro—William G. Lewis, Pres.; Albert G. Pacheco, Sec., 1735 E. 14th St.; 1st and 3rd Tuesdays, Masonic Temple.

Claremont No. 240, Oakland—George F. Davis, Pres.; E. N. Thienger, Sec., 839 Hearst Ave., Berkeley; Tuesdays, Veterans Memorial Bldg., 43rd & Salem Sts., Emeryville.

Pleasanton No. 244, Pleasanton—Peter C. Madsen, Pres.; Ernest W. Schween, Sec.; 2nd and 4th Thursdays, I.O.O.F. Hall.

Niles No. 250, Niles—M. L. Fournier, Pres.; C. E. Martenstein, Sec.; 2nd Thursday, I.O.O.F. Hall.

Fruitvale, No. 252, Oakland—Anthony J. King, Pres.; Ray B. Felton, Sec., 1575 Alice St.; Fridays, W.O.W. Hall, 3256 E. 14th St.

AMADOR COUNTY.

Amador No. 17, Sutter Creek—H. T. Richards, Pres.; F. J. Payne, Sec.; 1st and 3rd Fridays, Native Sons Hall.

Excelsior No. 31, Jackson—Wm. Daugherty, Pres.; William Going, Sec.; 1st and 3rd Wednesdays, Native Sons Hall, 22 Court St.

Ione No. 33, Ione—A. C. Miner, Pres.; Josiah H. Saunders, Sec.; 1st and 3rd Wednesdays, Native Sons Hall.

Plymouth No. 48, Plymouth—B. L. Crain, Pres.; Thos. D. Davis, Sec.; 1st and 3rd Saturdays, I.O.O.F. Hall.

BUTTE COUNTY.

Argonaut No. 8, Oroville—Fred E. Tegrunde, Pres.; Cyril R. Macdonald, Sec., P. O. box 502; 1st and 3rd Wednesdays, Veterans Memorial Hall.

Chico No. 21, Chico—Marcus Choisser, Pres.; Sam Lindsay Adams, Sec., Sacramento Blvd.; 2nd and 4th Thursdays, Elks Hall.

CALAVERAS COUNTY.

Chispa No. 139, Murphys—John Voitich, Pres.; Antone Malaspina, Sec.; Wednesdays, Native Sons Hall.

COLUSA COUNTY.

Colusa No. 69 Colusa City—S. A. Ottenwalter, Pres.; Phil J. Humburg, Sec. 223 Parkhill St.; Tuesdays, First National Bank Bldg.

CONTRA COSTA COUNTY.

General Winn No. 32, Antioch—Edmont T. Uren, Pres.; Joel H. Ford, Sec, P. O. box 311; 2nd and 4th Wednesdays, Union Hall.

Mount Diablo No. 101, Martinez—Melvin Wells, Pres.; G. T. Barkley, Sec.; 1st and 3rd Mondays, I.O.O.F. Hall.

Byron No. 170, Byron—R. R. Houston, Pres.; H. G. Krumland, Sec.; 1st and 3rd Tuesdays, I.O.O.F. Hall.

Carquinez No. 205, Crockett—Thos. Cox, Pres.; Thomas I. Cahalan, Sec.; 1st and 3rd Wednesdays, I.O.O.F. Hall.

Richmond No. 217, Richmond—M. W. Amaral, Pres.; H. D. Mason, Sec.; 11 6th St.; Wednesdays, Redmen Hall, 11th and Neven Ave.

Concord No. 245, Concord—P. M. Soto, Pres.; D. E. Pramberg, Sec., P. O. box 235; 1st Tuesday, I.O.O.F. Hall.

Diamond No. 246, Pittsburg—Horace L. Lucide, Pres.; Francis A. Irving, Sec., 248 E. 5th St.; 1st and 3rd Wednesdays, Veterans Memorial Bldg.

GRAND OFFICERS.

John T. Newell........Junior Past Grand President
4611 Brynhurst, Los Angeles

Dr. Frank I. Gonzalez.............Grand President
Flood Bldg., San Francisco

Seth Millington.............Grand First Vice-pres.
Gridley

Justice Emmet Seawell....Grand Second Vice-pres.
State Bldg., San Francisco

Chas. A. Koenig...........Grand Third Vice-pres.
531 35th Ave., San Francisco

John T. Regan......................Grand Secretary
N.S.G.W. Bldg., 414 Mason St., San Francisco

John A. Corotto...................Grand Treasurer
560 No. 5th St., San Jose

Horace J. Leavitt..................Grand Marshal
Weaverville

W. B. O'Brien................Grand Inside Sentinel
2324 Santa Clara St., Alameda

Gam Hurst ....Grand Outside Sentinel
1400 Financial Center Bldg., Oakland

Leslie Maloche......................Grand Organist
467½ 3rd St., San Bernardino

George H. Barron.................Historiographer
333 12th Ave., San Francisco

GRAND TRUSTEES.

George F. McNoble......California Bldg., Stockton
Samuel M. Shortridge Jr...............Menlo Park
Jesse H. Miller..712 DeYoung Bldg., San Francisco
Joseph J. McShane..419 Flood Bldg., San Francisco
Frank M. Lane............333 Blackstone, Fresno
John M. Burnett..........................San Jose

EL DORADO COUNTY.

Placerville No. 9, Placerville—Jos. Scherrer, Pres.; Duncan Bathurst, Sec., 12 Gilmore St.; 2nd and 4th Tuesdays, Masonic Hall.

Georgetown No. 91, Georgetown—J. H. Stanton, Pres.; C. F. Irish, Sec.; 2nd and 4th Wednesdays, I.O.O.F. Hall.

FRESNO COUNTY.

Fresno No. 25, Fresno City—E. F. Fitzgerald, Pres.; John W. Cappleman, Sec., 1389 Wilson; Fridays, W.O.W. Hall, 1354 Van Ness Ave.

Selma No. 107, Selma—Chester E. Shepard, Pres.; E. C. Laughlin, Sec.; 1st Wednesday, American Legion Hall.

HUMBOLDT COUNTY.

Humboldt No. 14, Eureka—Percy R. Henry, Pres.; Loren M. Nelson, Sec., P. O. Box 195; 2nd and 4th Mondays, Native Sons Hall.

Arcata No. 20, Arcata—E. L. Henry, Pres.; William Peters, Sec., P. O. box 1117; Thursdays, Native Sons Hall.

Ferndale No. 93, Ferndale—Geo. E. Becker, Pres.; C. H. Rasmussen, Sec., R.F.D. 47-A; 1st and 3rd Mondays, K.P. Hall.

KERN COUNTY

Bakersfield No. 42, Bakersfield—G. E. Taylor, Pres.; Leroy Vandervoort, Sec., 1927 20th St.; Wednesdays, Justice Court, City Hall.

LAKE COUNTY.

Lower Lake No. 159, Lower Lake—Harold S. Anderson, Pres.; Albert Kugelman, Sec.; Thursdays, I.O.O.F. Hall.

LASSEN COUNTY.

Honey Lake No. 198, Standish—N. B. Elledge, Pres.; W. B. Dewitt, Sec., 842 Roop St., Susanville; 1st and 3rd Wednesdays, Wrede Hall.

Big Valley No. 211, Bieber—George Bunselmeier, Pres.; A. W. McKenzie, Sec.; 1st and 3rd Wednesdays, I.O.O.F. Hall.

LOS ANGELES COUNTY.

Los Angeles No. 45, Los Angeles City—Victor D. Kremer, Pres.; Richard W. Fryer, Sec., 1629 Champlain Ter.; Thursdays, Merchant Plumbers Hall, 1832 So. Hone.

Ramona No. 109, Los Angeles City—Charles G. Young, Pres.; John V. Scott, Sec., Patriotic Hall, 1816 So. Figueroa; Fridays, Patriotic Hall, 1816 So. Figueroa.

Hollywood No. 196, Los Angeles City—Fred Gamble Jr., Pres.; E. J. Reilly, Sec., 210 S. Fremont St.; Mondays, Hollywood Conservatory Music, 5402 Hollywood Blvd.

Long Beach No. 239, Long Beach—Francis H. Gentry, Pres.; W. W. Brady, Sec., 801 Jergins Trust Bldg.; 2nd and 4th Thursdays, Moose Hall, Elm and Anaheim.

Sepulveda No. 263, San Pedro—Lawrence Powers, Pres.; Frank I. Markey, Sec., 101 W. 7th St.; 2nd and 4th Fridays, Odd Fellows Temple, 10th and Gaffey Sts.

Glendale No. 264, Glendale—Philip D. Molen, Pres.; Abel B. Molen, Sec., 508 So. Belmont St.; 1st and 3rd Tuesdays, Masonic Temple, 234 So. Brand Blvd.

Santa Monica Bay No. 267, Ocean Park—Frederick E. Barnes, Pres.; John J. Smith, Sec., 830 Rialto Ave., Venice; 2nd and 4th Mondays, New Eagle Hall, 2823¼ Main St.

Cahuenga No. 268, Reseda—Harold C. Trexler, Pres.; Walter A. Knapp, Sec., 7711 Owensmouth Ave., Canoga Park; first Friday, Alton Hall.

MADERA COUNTY.

Madera No. 130, Madera City—Cornelius Noble, Pres.; T. P. Cosgrave, Sec.; 1st and 3rd Thursdays, First National Bank Bldg.

MARIN COUNTY.

Mount Tamalpais No. 64, San Rafael—Walter Mazza, Pres.; Manuel A. Andrade, Sec., 532 Mission Ave.; 1st and 3rd Mondays, Portuguese American Hall.

Sea Point No. 158, Sausalito—Willis B. Garcia, Pres.; Manuel Santos, Sec., 6 Glen Drive; 1st and 3rd Wednesdays, Perry Bldg.

Nicasio No. 183, Nicasio—M. T. Farley, Pres.; R. J. Rogers, Sec.; 2nd and 4th Wednesdays, U.A.O.D. Hall.

MENDOCINO COUNTY.

Ukiah No. 71, Ukiah—Albert T. Bechtol, Pres.; Ben Hofman, Sec., P. O. box 473; 1st and 3rd Mondays, I.O.O.F. Hall.

Broderick No. 117, Point Arena—Abel Olsen, Pres.; H. C. Hunter, Sec.; 1st and 3rd Thursdays, Forester Hall.

Alder Glen No. 200, Fort Bragg—T. J. Simpson, Pres.; C. R. Weller, Sec.; 2nd and 4th Fridays, I.O.O.F. Hall.

MERCED COUNTY.

Yosemite No. 24, Merced City—Anthony A. Rodrigues, Pres.; True W. Fowler, Sec., P. O. box 781; 2nd and 4th Mondays, I.O.O.F. Hall.

MONTEREY COUNTY.

Monterey No. 75, Monterey City—John Thomsen, Pres.; W. W. Rodehaver, Sec., 321 Alvarado St.; 1st and 3rd Fridays, Knights Pythias Hall, Main St.

Santa Lucia No. 97, Salinas—E. L. Adcock, Pres.; R. W. Adcock, Sec., Route 2, box 141; Mondays, Native Sons Hall, 32 W. Alisal St.

Gabilan No. 132, Castroville—George Rodriguez, Pres.; R. H. Martin, Sec., P. O. box 81; 1st and 3rd Thursdays, Native Sons Hall.

NAPA COUNTY.

Saint Helena No. 53, Saint Helena—Edward L. Paulson, Pres.; Edw. L. Bonhote, Sec., P. O. box 267; Mondays, Native Sons Hall.

Napa No. 62, Napa City—H. N. Bunce, Pres.; H. J. Hoernle, Sec., 1226 Oak St.; Mondays, Native Sons Hall.

Calistoga No. 86, Calistoga—Rev. T. J. McKeon, Pres.; Louis Carlenzoli, Sec.; 1st and 3rd Mondays, I.O.O.F. Hall.

NEVADA COUNTY.

Hydraulic No. 56, Nevada City—Spencer G. White, Pres.; Dr. C. W. Chapman, Sec.; Tuesdays, Pythian Castle.

Quartz No. 58, Grass Valley—Richard Hoskins, Pres.; H. Ray George, Sec., 151 Conaway Ave.; Mondays, Auditorium Hall.

Donner No. 162, Truckee—J. F. Lichtenberger, Pres.; H. C. Lichtenberger, Sec.; 2nd and 4th Tuesdays, Native Sons Hall.

ORANGE COUNTY.

Santa Ana No. 265, Santa Ana—R. L. Marsile, Pres.; E. F. Marks, Sec., 1124 No. Bristol St.; 1st and 3rd Mondays, K.C. Hall, 4th and French Sts.

PLACER COUNTY.

Auburn No. 59, Auburn—Cosme Vicencio, Pres.; J. G. Walsh, Sec.; 1st and 3rd Fridays, Foresters Hall.

Silver Star No. 63, Lincoln—Frank Meyers, Pres.; Barney G. Barry, Sec., P. O. box 72; 3rd Wednesday, I.O.O.F. Hall.

Rocklin No. 233, Roseville—Thomas Elliott, Pres.; M. E. Reed, Sec., 253 W. Duranta; 2nd and 4th Wednesdays, Eagles Hall.

PLUMAS COUNTY.

Quincy No. 131, Quincy—J. O. Moncur, Pres.; E. C Kelsey, Sec.; 2nd Thursday, I.O.O.F. Hall.

Golden Anchor No. 182, La Porte—R. J. McGrath, Pres.; LeRoy J. Post, Sec.; 2nd and 4th Sunday mornings, Native Sons Hall.

Plumas No. 228, Taylorsville—E. E. Sikes, Pres.; George E. Boyden, Sec.; 1st and 3rd Mondays, Native Sons Hall.

SACRAMENTO COUNTY.

Sacramento No. 3, Sacramento City—John Major, Pres.; J. F. Didion, Sec., 1131 "O" St.; Thursdays, Native Sons Bldg., 11th and "J" Sts.

Sunset No. 26, Sacramento City—Theodore Jacka, Pres.; Edward E. Reese, Sec., County Treasurer Office; Mondays, Native Sons Bldg., 11th and "J" Sts.

Elk Grove No. 41, Elk Grove—Fred Sehlmeyer, Pres.; Walter Martin, Sec.; 2nd and 4th Fridays, Masonic Hall.

Granite No. 83, Folsom—Joe Relvas, Pres.; Frank Showers, Sec.; 2nd and 4th Tuesdays, K.P. Hall.

Courtland No. 106, Courtland—Albert Pyhnan, Pres.; Jos. Green, Sec.; 1st Saturday and 3rd Monday, Native Sons Hall.

Sutter Fort No. 241, Sacramento City—August Lehman, Pres.; C. L. Katzenstein, Sec., P. O. box 914; 2nd and 4th Wednesdays, Native Sons Bldg., 11th and "J" Sts.

Galt No. 243, Galt—Geo. H. May, Pres.; F. W. Harms, Sec.; 1st and 3rd Mondays, I.O.O.F. Hall.

SAN BENITO COUNTY.

Fremont No. 44, Hollister—Chas. B. Arbeleche, Pres.; J. E. Prendergast Jr., Sec., 1064 Monterey St.; 1st and 3rd Thursdays, Grangers Union Hall.

SAN BERNARDINO COUNTY.

Arrowhead No. 110, San Bernardino City—Leslie Maloche, Pres.; R. W. Brazelton, Sec., 462 6th St.; Wednesdays, Eagles Hall, 469 4th St.

SAN DIEGO COUNTY.

San Diego No. 108, San Diego City—Gregory A. McHorney, Pres.; A. V. Mayrhofer, Sec., 1572 2nd St.; Wednesdays, K.C. Hall, 4th and Elm Sts.

SAN FRANCISCO CITY AND COUNTY.

California No. 1, San Francisco—Elmer W. Bruce, Pres.; Ellis A. Blackman, Sec., 126 Front St.; Thursdays, Native Sons Bldg., 414 Mason St.

Pacific No. 10, San Francisco—Charles R. Boden, Pres.; J. Henry Bastein, Sec., 1880 Howard St.; Tuesdays, Native Sons Bldg., 414 Mason St.

Golden Gate No. 29, San Francisco—Clyde D. Bruhn, Pres.; Adolph Eberhart, Sec., 183 Carl St.; Mondays, Native Sons Bldg., 414 Mason St.

Mission No. 38, San Francisco—Leslie Greine Jr., Pres.; Thos. J. Stewart, Sec., 1919 Howard St.; Wednesdays, Redmen Hall, 3053 16th St.

San Francisco No. 49, San Francisco—George Batchelor, Pres.; David Capurro, Sec., 976 Union St.; Thursdays, Native Sons Bldg., 414 Mason St.

El Dorado No. 52, San Francisco—Eugene Herzog, Pres.; Alfred Vlautin, Sec., 1537 Franklin St.; Thursdays, Native Sons Bldg., 414 Mason St.

Rincon No. 72, San Francisco—Joseph E. Tinney, Pres.; John A. Gilmour, Sec., 2069 Golden Gate Ave.; Wednesdays, Native Sons Bldg., 414 Mason St.

Stanford No. 76, San Francisco—Hubert Caveney, Pres.; Charles T. O'Kane, Sec., 1111 Pine St.; Tuesdays, Native Sons Bldg., 414 Mason St.

Bay City No. 104, San Francisco—Julius J. Glaser, Pres.; Max E. Licht, Sec., 1831 Fulton St.; 2nd and 4th Wednesdays, Native Sons Bldg., 414 Mason St.

Niantic No. 105, San Francisco—A. Furner, Pres.; J. M. Darcy, Sec., 10 Hoffman Ave.; Wednesdays, Native Sons Bldg., 414 Mason St.

National No. 118, San Francisco—William A. Brennan, Pres.; Frank L. Hatfield, Sec., 3990 20th St.; Thursdays, 1160 Eddy St.

ATTENTION, SECRETARIES!

THIS DIRECTORY IS PUBLISHED BY AUTHORITY OF THE GRAND PARLOR N.S.G.W., AND ALL NOTICES OF CHANGES MUST BE RECEIVED BY THE GRAND SECRETARY (NOT THE MAGAZINE) ON OR BEFORE THE 20TH OF EACH MONTH TO INSURE CORRECTION IN NEXT ISSUE OF DIRECTORY.

N.S.G.W. OFFICIAL DEATH LIST.

Containing the name, the date and the place of birth, the date of death, and the Subordinate Parlor affiliation of deceased members reported to Grand Secretary John T. Regan from October 20, 1931, to November 20, 1931:

Loewenthal, Mertyle: Eureka, September 6, 1890; October 19, 1931; Humboldt No. 14.
Sands, John A.: Marysville, October 25, 1859; October 20, 1931; Humboldt No. 14.
Donahue, Felix J.: San Jose, July 11, 1867; October 5, 1931; San Jose No. 22.
Young, Walter Dixon: Sacramento, November 26, 1878; October 1, 1931; Sunset No. 26.
Lafferty, Daniel Henry: San Francisco, April 19, 1872; October 20, 1931; Santa Rosa No. 28.
Swift, Charles Stedman: Dry Creek, September 15, 1861; October 1, 1931; Ione No. 33.
Salomon, Ray John: Los Angeles, March 15, 1908; October 1931; Los Angeles No. 45.
Graham, James: Nevada City, February 22, 1897; October 15, 1931; Hydraulic No. 56.
White, Jason D.: Sacramento, February 15, 1856; October 8, 1931; Mount Tamalpais No. 64.
Albery, Harmon M.: Colusa, May 30, 1884; October 26, 1931; Colusa No. 69.
Sheldon, Robert Parker: San Francisco, October 29, 1874; October 23, 1931; Ramona No. 109.
Holton, Charles H.: San Francisco, September 7, 1870; October 12, 1931; Piedmont No. 120.
White, William Bernard: Oakland, April 13, 1898; October 16, 1931; Piedmont No. 120.
Gallagher, Edward B.: San Francisco, December 9, 1874; October 29; 1931; Precita No. 187.
Boschke, Albert C.: Sacramento, March 15, 1888; October 16, 1931; Hollywood No. 196.
Derby, Harry Cooper: Oakland, August 11, 1871; August 22, 1931; Fruitvale No. 252.
Hamilton, Dr. Jo: Wheatland, December 6, 1874; September 17, 1931; Fruitvale No. 252.

NATIVE SON NEWS

(Continued from Page 9)

Dr. Frank I. Gonzales and Principal R. B. Thompson.

On behalf of Observatory No. 177, Past Grand President Charles A. Thompson presented a California State (Bear) Flag, which was accepted by Jane Gray; Mrs. George F. Smith presented a memorial flag, which was accepted by Billy Gary, and Virginia Tompkins presented a picture of President Herbert Hoover. A splendid program of musical numbers was presented by the student body.

The dedicatory ceremonies were conducted by Grand President Gonzales, Past Grand President Thompson, Grand Third Vice-president Chas. A. Koenig, Grand Secretary John T. Regan and Grand Trustee Jesse H. Miller. Other grand officers in attendance were Grand Trustees John M. Burnett and Samuel M. Shortridge Jr., and Past Grand President Thomas Monahan.

Initiation in Official's Honor.

Santa Rosa—In the Armistice Day parade here the turnout of the Native Sons and the Native Daughters resembled an Admission Day outpouring. The division was led by the drum corps of Mount Tamalpais No. 64 (San Rafael) and then came the drill team of Petaluma No. 222 N.D.G.W., the Sonoma County Past Presidents Associations N.S.G.W. and N.D.G.W., and goodly delegations of members from all the Parlors in Sonoma County. The shetland ponies of Santa Rosa No. 28 were the hit of the parade. Following the march the Parlor had open house and refreshments were served to all the Natives.

November 17, No. 28 initiated a class of candidates in honor of Grand Second Vice-president Justice Emmet Seawell, affiliated with Santa Rosa. A Thanksgiving supper, with turkey and all the trimmings, preceded the meeting. Among the visitors were Grand President Dr. Frank I. Gonzales and Grand Trustee Joseph McShane. The Parlor's good of the order committee has great plans for the annual '49 celebration, to be held New Year Eve, December 31.

Wants Mortgage Moratorium.

San Diego—San Diego No. 108 had a well attended '49 party November 4 which was greatly enjoyed. Among the visitors and speakers were Tallant Tubbs (Presidio No. 194) and Ed. L. Head (Stanford No. 76) of San Francisco.

The Parlor has passed a resolution petitioning Governor James Rolph Jr. (Hesperian No. 137) to declare a year's moratorium on mortgages, and has directed a resolution to the San Diego City Council regarding the wage scale.

Neophytes Trod Rough Trails.

Sonoma—November 16 a class of candidates were initiated for Sonoma No. 111 by the past presidents team of Golden Gate No. 29 (San Francisco). Although it was a very stormy evening and raining hard, twenty-eight members of Golden Gate braved the elements to be in attendance at this affair. The work of this team was conducted in a splendid manner, each officer being almost perfect in the rendition of the ritual. The following conducted the ceremony: Past Presidents Alfred Moore, L. Alvin Werner, Meldron Loudon, John Gibson, Chas. Craig, George Strohmeier, Ralph Young and Arthur Seyden.

After the initiation the neophytes were required to walk over the pioneer trails, including the hot sands of the desert, as did the forefathers when coming into California. The trails were mighty rough and the sands were very hot, which caused a lot of enjoyment for the candidates as well as for the other members assembled. After the meeting a turkey banquet was served. Chas. Craig who, the members of Golden Gate say, is an authority on good food, stated this was one of

(Continued on Page 22)

SAN FRANCISCO
THE BIG CITY THAT KNOWS HOW

WHEN SICKNESS MEANS OPPORTUNITY

(BEULAH WELDON BURHOE.)

ALBERTO HAS BEEN TOLD THAT HE would have to spend one year and possibly two in the tuberculosis sanatorium. He had been told, too, that he could never return to his old job of sheet metal working. He was worried. He knew that the mother's pension allowance would take care of his wife and his three children during the time that he would have to stay in the sanatorium, but he did not know how to face a future in which he could not work at his old trade. During the ten years that Alberto had lived in this country he had worked very hard and he had had little time to spend in study. Little progress had been made in English, beyond an ability to make himself understood.

After he had been in the sanatorium a short time the doctor told him that he was getting along so well he could have the privilege of attending a class in English. He was delighted. He beamed. In broken English he explained that in his trade there were two kinds of jobs: putting up the metal, and "making the pictures on the blue paper." He said he knew how to make the pictures but that the boss would not let him draw because he "could no spick."

For six months now Alberto has been a faithful pupil and has made such progress that he speaks quite good English. He will probably be able to leave the hospital in about three months.

The local tuberculosis association is making arrangements to provide a short course in blueprint drawing. Alberto will then be equipped to take a job in which he can use all thè knowledge gained in his trade and which will be suited to his physical disability. He is no longer worried. His physician believes that improvement has been hastened because of his confidence in the future.

All over the country there is a steadily increasing interest in providing instruction to those who are spending long months in tuberculosis sanatoria. As the toll of tuberculosis is heaviest during the wage-earning period of life—the disease still heads the list of deaths between 18 and 45—it is essential for patients to obtain jobs that are safe for them after leaving sanatoria for their homes. At the present time there are over fifty sanatoria where classes are held for adults. The courses range all the way from instruction to mothers in the conduct of their households and the training of their children, to courses in high school and college subjects. Typing and shorthand are very popular studies.

The local tuberculosis associations, supported entirely through the sale of Christmas seals, are promoting this educational movement so that the months of illness can be changed from a time of boredom to a period of opportunity. The patient discharged from the tuberculosis sanatorium will not only be improved in health, but improved in ability. The Christmas seal is helping to make up the handicap of sickness by providing a chance to acquire greater skill. Aid this worthy cause by purchasing Christmas seals!

N. D. HOME RECEIVES PAINTING.

The annual highjinks of Alta Parlor No. 3 N.D.G.W., to be held December 22, promises to surpass all previous entertainments of that nature. Mrs. Pomeroy is chairman of the committee in charge. Mrs. Lillian Eisien, a member of Alta, has shown a keen interest in the Native Daughter Home. Her gift, a handsome painting in water colors, has been hung in the upper hall between the lounge and the dining-room, where the lighting effect is perfect. The painting is admired by all who enter the beautiful building.

SENTIMENTS EXPRESSED IN SONG.

Orinda Parlor No. 56 N.D.G.W. was hostess to Grand President Evelyn I. Carlson on the occasion of her official visit October 23. The Native Daughter Home, where the meeting was held, received its full measure of praise for being able to accommodate a gathering of over 250 who honored the Grand President and the Parlor. Miss Mildred Gibson sang a song of welcome, the words of which expressed Orinda's sentiments. It was illustrated by the unveiling of a decorated ladder with a doll dressed in white named Evelyn and one costumed in blue named Orinda. Orinda, at the bottom, was extending a hand to Evelyn, at the top. The Native Daughter glee club entertained with several numbers.

Representatives of most of the local and several of the nearby Parlors were in attendance, as were also Grand Secretary Sallie R. Thaler, Grand Trustees Ethel Begley, Anna Thuesen and Willow Barba, Grand Organist Lola Horgan, Grand Outside Sentinel Orinda Giannini, Past Grand Presidents Dr. Mariana Bertola, Genevieve W. Baker, Emma G. Foley, Margaret G. Hill, Addie L. Mosher, Mary E. Bell and Dr. Louise C. Heilbron, District Deputy Helen T. Mann and twenty-six additional deputies. The Parlor presented fifteen of its past presidents, each of whom announced the year of her presidency, commencing with 1894.

Grand President Carlson spoke of the projects of the Order in which she is specially interested, congratulated the Parlor on the acquisition of three new members, expressed pleasure at the welcome extended her, and praised the officers for perfect work and the arrangements committee of the evening for success in creating an at-home atmosphere. Chairman Bertola of the Grand Parlor Home Committee referred to the opportunity the Native Daughters have in being privileged to meet in the Home building and, in doing so, being at home in their own home. She remarked that the Grand President's words about the closeness of one Native Daughter to another was worthy of the head of the Order.

GOLDEN ANNIVERSARY OBSERVED.

Pacific Parlor No. 10 N.S.G.W. had a golden jubilee November 10 in celebration of its fiftieth institution anniversary. Honor guests were James F. Swift, R. D. McElroy, George D. McPherson, S. H. McPherson, C. J. Williams, William Metzner and M. G. Searing, charter members.

Past Grand President Daniel A. Ryan was chairman of the evening, and among the speakers were Dr. Frank I. Gonzalez, Grand President, Charles R. Boden, president of the Parlor, and Bert D. Paolinelli, chairman golden jubilee committee. Several entertainment numbers were presented.

HAPPY EVENING.

Two hundred members of the Order gathered with Buena Vista Parlor No. 68 N.D.G.W. to welcome Grand President Evelyn I. Carlson officially October 29. Prior to the meeting a delectable dinner was prepared and served by Matron L. Hawkins of the Native Daughter Home. The reception and banquet halls were decorated in festoons of black and orange crepe paper, and beautiful boquets of golden flowers carried out the spirit of Hallowe'en. The officers, in pastel shaded gowns, made a pretty picture as they stood in the dimmed lights and perfectly exemplified the ritual.

Officials of the Order present as visitors were Grand Trustees Ethel Begley and Ann Theusen, Grand Organist Lola Horgan, Grand Outside Sentinel Orinda Giannini, Past Grand Presidents Margaret Hill, May C. Boldeman and Dr. Louise C. Heilbron, and District Deputy Lillian O'Claire. Distinguished members of Buena Vista in attendance were Past Grand Presidents Mary E. Bell, Genevieve W. Baker and Dr. Marianna Bertola, and Mrs. Angelo Rossi, wife of San Francisco's mayor. Vocal selections rendered by the Native Daughter glee club were very much appreciated by all assembled. The Parlor added to its roll three new members on this occasion. Much praise was given President L. Mitchell and her able corps of officers for making this a very happy evening for all.

NATIONAL EDUCATION WEEK RECOGNIZED.

For some eleven years the National Education Association has called on civic and fraternal societies to observe the second week of November as national education week. For the first time, a Parlor of Native Sons did so, when Golden Gate No. 29 featured an appropriate program November 9. There was a record attendance, and much enthusiasm was manifest over the interest taken in educational matters.

The program was introduced by Historian Peter T. Conmy, who was the chairman of arrangements. Superior Judge Isadore Harris, a member of the Parlor, spoke on "Education as a Remedy for Crime," which dealt with his experiences on the criminal bench. Deputy School Superintendent Walter C. Nolan made an address on the "Functions of the Public Schools." Vocal selections were rendered by an adult chorus from the Commerce evening high school under the direction of Roy McCarthy. Many members of Golden Gate Parlor No. 158 N.D.G.W. were present, and there were delegations from Presidio, Marshall, El Dorado, Olympus and Quartz Parlors. Grand President Dr. Frank I. Gonzales voiced his approval under good of the order, and Past Grand President Judge Frank H. Dunne, Grand Secretary John T. Regan, Grand Third Vice-president Chas. A. Koenig, Joseph Rose, Harry Gaetjen and Alfred Vlautin also made brief addresses.

OLD COSTUMES AFFORD AMUSEMENT.

November 2 each member of Darina Parlor No. 114 N.D.G.W. appeared at the regular meeting in an old-fashioned costume. These costumes represented the various styles of dress during the past century and were the source of much amusement to those present. District Deputy Dorothy Finn was the guest of honor, and prizes were awarded Misses Esther Stephens and Armida Donati. A most enjoyable evening was brought to a close by the serving of delicious refreshments at daintily decorated tables.

MUSIC KEEPS PARTY AT HIGH PITCH.

With over one hundred members of Gabrielle Parlor No. 139 N.D.G.W. and Rincon Parlor No. 72 N.S.G.W. in attendance, a gay Hallowe'en party was staged. Many bright costumes fitted amongst the strange decorations. A real Hallowe'en supper was served, after which dancing and games of all kinds were indulged in. Pinning the tail on a donkey, which some of the members had never played before, left many helpless.

The officers of Gabrielle were the hostesses, and President Annie Campbell, First Vice-president Ruth Koehler and Past President Lillian McCloskey were given a special vote of thanks for the wonderful decorations, and the classy music which kept the party at a high pitch until the early morning of the next day.

ARMISTICE DAY REMEMBERED.

November 11 Grand First Vice-president Seth Millington made his official visit to South San Francisco Parlor No. 157 N.S.G.W. About two hundred members were present to extend greetings and to provide a pleasant evening for the visitor. One candidate was initiated, and the officers of the Parlor were highly complimented for the efficient manner in which they conducted the initiatory ceremonies. Grand Vice-president Millington also complimented the officers for the manner in which the business was conducted and on the condition of the Parlor in the face of present financial conditions. South San Francisco has a membership of 825 and assets totaling approximately $50,000.

After the meeting a banquet was served in honor of the visiting grand officer and, as well, in commemoration of the thirteenth anniversary of Armistice Day. The Parlor annually holds a banquet on the meeting night nearest November 11, and has been doing so since 1919. All ex-service members of No. 157 are special guests of the evening and wartime songs and stories are sung and related for the entertainment of those assembled. The good of the order committee, headed by Thos. J. O'Rourke, provided a wonderful repast, as well as a splendid entertainment, and few, if any, of the two hundred members present left the banquet hall until the hour of 12:30, at which time the affair came to an end. Addresses were made by Grand President Dr. Frank I. Gonzalez, Grand First Vice-president Seth Millington, Past Grand President William P. Caubu, District Deputy Gustave E. Ritter, Harmon D. Skillin, Judge George Schonfeld and Vincent Lovett, the latter representing all of the ex-service men. Grand Secretary John T. Regan, a member of South Parlor, was the toastmaster.

GRAND PRESIDENT LUNCHEON GUEST.

A Hallowe'en costume party was given by Dolores Parlor No. 169 N.D.G.W. October 28. Refreshments were served at beautifully decorated tables. Pumpkins, witches, owls and cats carried out the spirit of the holiday, and over forty members shared the pleasures of the evening. Prizes were awarded the winners of games and the wearers of the most original and unique costumes. Mrs. Ida Corrigan was chairman of the evening, and District Deputy Agnes McVerry was the honored guest.

The patients in the tubercular ward of Letterman Hospital were guests November 1 of Dolores. The spirit of Hallowe'en was carried out by serving home-made cakes, ice cream, candies, smokes and jellies. Magazines were also passed around. Mrs. Betty Both was hostess, assisted by Miss Juanita Blanchfield and Mrs. Emma O'Meara. A large package of dainty garments, made by the sewing club, was sent to Miss Mary E. Brusie of the Homeless Children Central Committee.

The sewing club gave a most delightful luncheon November 18 at the Native Daughter Home. Grand President Evelyn I. Carlson, who organized the club several years ago, was the honored guest. Mrs. Emma O'Meara acted as hostess, and thirty members sat at tables decorated with Thanksgiving favors.

BUSY WITH HOLIDAY PREPARATIONS.

Castro Parlor No. 178 N.D.G.W. is very busy making preparations for the official visit of Grand President Evelyn I. Carlson, getting ready for the children's Christmas party, the Christmas party for the veterans and the various other activities of the holiday season.

Time was taken, however, to enjoy a little relaxation in the always amusing pranks of Hallowe'en. Mrs. Georgia Nelson presided over the entertainment, and all "sure did have fun." District Deputy Myrtle Ross joined heartily in the festivities and carried away the first prize of the evening. Hallowe'en decorations prevailed, and refreshments were served at prettily decorated tables.

FLAGS PRESENTED SCHOOL.

Bret Harte Parlor No. 260 N.S.G.W. presented United States of America and California State (Bear) Flags to the Farragut school the afternoon of November 10. In the evening the Parlor had its annual Christmas fund indoor circus and dance.

OLD GUARD RETURNS TO LABOR.

Calistoga—At a largely attended meeting of Calistoga Parlor No. 86 N.S.G.W., November 16, four candidates were initiated, a team of veterans exemplifying the ritual. The proceedings of the evening indicated the "old guard" has returned to labor.

The committee arranging the Christmas party, to be held December 7, reported splendid progress. There will be a turkey supper, then the Parlor meeting, and after that a unique entertainment, the nature of which is being kept secret.

FIFTY YEARS AGO

(Continued from Page 10)

They pleaded guilty and were sent to San Quentin for twenty-five years.

Professor George Akern, principal of the Colusa City school, was accidentally killed by the discharge of a pistol December 26. His sad ending was deplored by the entire community.

John Elliott and his wife, residing near Millville, Shasta County, while returning home from that town December 10 attempted to ford Cow Creek in a wagon. A cloudburst caused the water to rise suddenly, the wagon was upset, and both were drowned.

Paul Feberer, San Francisco drug store clerk, was aroused by a burglar, December 5, whom he shot to death. The dead man proved to be Pat McNamar, an ex-convict.

Citrus Millions—During the 1930-31 season more than 83,000 carloads of oranges, lemons and grapefruit were shipped from California. The delivered value of this crop was $145,261,-059, of which amount the growers received $99,520,773.

Official Directory of Parlors of the N. D. G. W.

ALAMEDA COUNTY.

Angelita No. 32, Livermore—Meets 2nd and 4th Fridays, Foresters Hall; Mrs. Orlena Beck, Rec. Sec., 1109 First St.

Piedmont No. 87, Oakland—Meets Thursdays, Corinthian Hall, Pacific Bldg.; Mrs. Alice E. Miner, Rec. Sec., 421 36th St.

Aloha No. 106, Oakland—Meets Tuesdays, Wigwam Hall, Pacific Bldg.; Gladys I. Farley, Rec. Sec., 4623 Benevides Ave.

Hayward No. 122, Hayward—Meets 1st and 3rd Tuesdays, Bank Hayward Hall, "B" St.; Miss Ruth Gansberger, Rec. Sec., P. O. Box 44, Mount Eden.

Berkeley No. 150, Berkeley—Meets 1st Friday, Masonic Hall; Mrs. Lelia B. Baker, Rec. Sec., 915 Contra Costa Ave.

Bear Flag No. 151, Berkeley—Meets 2nd and 4th Wednesdays, Veterans Memorial Bldg., 1931 Center St.; Mrs. Maud Wagner, Rec. Sec., 317 Alcatraz Ave., Oakland.

Encinal No. 156, Alameda—Meets 2nd and 4th Thursdays, N.S.G.W. Hall; Mrs. Laura E. Fisher, Rec. Sec., 1413 Caroline St.

Brooklyn No. 157, East Oakland—Meets Wednesdays, Masonic Temple, 8th Ave. and E. 14th St.; Mrs. Ruth Cooney, Rec. Sec., 3907 14th Ave.

Argonaut No. 166, Oakland—Meets Tuesdays, Klinkner Hall, 59th and San Pablo; Mrs. Ada Spilman, Rec. Sec., 2905 Ellis St., Berkeley.

Bahia Vista No. 167, Oakland—Meets Thursdays, Wigwam Hall, Pacific Bldg.; Mrs. Minnie E. Raper, Rec. Sec., 3449 Helen St.

Fruitvale No. 177, Oakland—Meets Fridays, W.O.W. Hall; Mrs. Agnes M. Grant, Rec. Sec., 1224 30th Ave.

Laura Loma No. 182, Niles—Meets 1st and 3rd Tuesdays, I.O.O.F. Hall; Mrs. Ethel Fournier, Rec. Sec., P. O. Box 515.

El Cereso No. 207, San Leandro—Meets 2nd and 4th Tuesdays, Masonic Hall; Mrs. Mary Tuttle, Rec. Sec., P. O. Box 56.

Pleasanton No. 237, Pleasanton—Meets 1st and 3rd Tuesdays, I.O.O.F. Hall; Mrs. Myrtle Lanini, Rec. Sec.

Betsy Ross No. 238, Centerville—Meets 1st and 3rd Fridays, Anderson Hall; Miss Constance Lucio, Rec. Sec., P. O. Box 187.

AMADOR COUNTY.

Ursula No. 1, Jackson—Meets 2nd and 4th Tuesdays, N.S.G.W. Hall; Mrs. Emma Boarman-Wright, Rec. Sec., 114 Court St.

Chispa No. 40, Ione—Meets 2nd and 4th Fridays, N.S.G.W. Hall; Mrs. Isabel Ashton, Rec. Sec.

Amapola No. 80, Sutter Creek—Meets 2nd and 4th Thursdays, N.S.G.W. Bldg.; Mrs. Hazel M. Marre, Rec. Sec.

Forrest No. 86, Plymouth—Meets 2nd and 4th Tuesdays, I.O.O.F. Hall; Mrs. Marguerite Davis, Rec. Sec.

BUTTE COUNTY.

Annie K. Bidwell No. 168, Chico—Meets 2nd and 4th Thursdays, I.O.O.F. Hall; Mrs. Irene Henry, Rec. Sec., 3015 Woodland Ave.

Gold of Ophir No. 190, Oroville—Meets 1st and 3rd Wednesdays, Memorial Hall; Mrs. Ruth Brown, Rec. Sec., 1265 Leah Court.

CALAVERAS COUNTY.

Ruby No. 46, Murphys—Meets Fridays, N.S.G.W. Hall; Belle Segale, Rec. Sec.

Princess No. 84, Angels Camp—Meets 2nd Wednesday, I.O.O.F. Hall; Emma May, Rec. Sec.

San Andreas No. 113, San Andreas—Meets 1st Friday, Fraternal Hall; Miss Doris Treat, Rec. Sec.

COLUSA COUNTY.

Colus No. 194, Colusa—Meets 1st and 3rd Mondays, N.S.G.W. Hall; Mrs. Ruby Humburg, 223 Park Hill St.

CONTRA COSTA COUNTY.

Stirling No. 146, Pittsburg—Meets 1st and 3rd Wednesdays, Veteran Memorial Hall; Mrs. Minnie Marcelli, Rec. Sec., 771 E. 12th St.

Richmond No. 147, Richmond—Meets 1st and 3rd Tuesdays, I.O.O.F. Hall, 10th St.; Mrs. Tillie Summers, Rec. Sec., 640 So. 31st St.

Donner No. 193, Byron—Meets 1st and 3rd Wednesdays, I.O.O.F. Hall; Mrs. Anna Pendry, Rec. Sec., P. O. Box 112.

Las Juntas No. 221, Martinez—Meets 1st and 3rd Mondays, Pythias Castle; Mrs. Lola Viera, Rec. Sec., P. O. box 128.

Antioch No. 223, Antioch—Meets 2nd and 4th Tuesdays, I.O.O.F. Hall; Mrs. Estelle Evans, Rec. Sec., 202 E. 5th St., Pittsburg.

Carquinez No. 234, Crockett—Meets 2nd and 4th Wednesdays, I.O.O.F. Hall; Mrs. Cecile Petee, Rec. Sec., 465 Edwards St.

GRAND OFFICERS.

Mrs. Estelle M. Evans........Past Grand President
202 E. Fifth St., Pittsburg

Mrs. Evelyn I. Carlson............Grand President
1965 San Jose Ave., San Francisco

Mrs. Anna M. Armstrong.....Grand Vice-president
Woodland

Mrs. Sallie R. Thaler...............Grand Secretary
555 Baker St., San Francisco

Mrs. Susie K. Christ...............Grand Treasurer
555 Baker St., San Francisco

Mrs. Irma Laird.....................Grand Marshal
Alturas

Mrs. Minna K. Horn..........Grand Inside Sentinel
Etna

Mrs. Orinda G. Giannini.....Grand Outside Sentinel
2142 Filbert St., San Francisco

Mrs. Lola Horgan...................Grand Organist
789 Morse St., San Francisco

GRAND TRUSTEES.

Mrs. Edna Briggs, 1045 Santa Ynez Way, Sacramento
Mrs. Ethel Begley......1206 Valencia, San Francisco
Mrs. Anna Thuesen....615 38th Ave., San Francisco
Mrs. Gladys Noce ....Sutter Creek
Mrs. Florence Boyle..............................Oroville
Mrs. Florence Schoneman, 1521 5th Ave., Los Angeles
Mrs. Willow Borba.........................Sebastopol

EL DORADO COUNTY.

Marguerite No. 12, Placerville—Meets 1st and 3rd Wednesdays, Masonic Hall; Mrs. Nettie Leonardi, Rec. Sec., 25 Coloma St.

El Dorado No. 186, Georgetown—Meets 2nd and 4th Saturday afternoons, I.O.O.F. Hall; Mrs. Alta L. Douglas, Rec. Sec.

FRESNO COUNTY.

Fresno No. 187, Fresno—Meets Fridays, Pythian Castle, Cor. "R" and Merced Sts.; Mary Aubery, Rec. Sec., 1040 Delphia Ave.

GLENN COUNTY.

Berryessa No. 192, Willows—Meets 1st and 3rd Mondays, I.O.O.F. Hall; Mrs. Leonora Neate, Rec. Sec., 338 No. Lassen St.

HUMBOLDT COUNTY.

Occident No. 28, Eureka—Meets 1st and 3rd Wed- Rec. Sec., 2309 "B" St. nesdays, N.S.G.W. Hall; Mrs. Eva L. MacDonald,

Oneonta No. 71, Ferndale—Meets 2nd and 4th Fridays, I.O.O.F. Hall; Mrs. Myra Rumrill, Rec. Sec.

Reichling No. 97, Fortuna—Meets 2nd and 4th Tuesdays, Friendship Hall; Mrs. Grace Swett, Rec. Sec., P. O. Box 328.

KERN COUNTY.

Miocene No. 228, Taft—Meets 1st and 3rd Wednesday afternoons, I.O.O.F. Hall; Mrs. Evalyne Towne, Rec. Sec., P. O. Box 1011.

El Tejon No. 239, Bakersfield—Meets 1st and 3rd Fridays, Castle Hall; Mrs. Grace Dorris, Rec. Sec., 127 Morgan Bldg.

Desert Gold No. 250, Mojave—Meets 2nd and 4th Fridays, I.O.O.F. Hall; Mrs. Mae Coffill, Rec. Sec.

LAKE COUNTY.

Clear Lake No. 135, Middletown—Meets 2nd and 4th Tuesdays, Herrick Hall; Mrs. Retta Reynolds, Rec. Sec., P. O. Box 130.

LASSEN COUNTY.

Nataqua No. 152, Standish—Meets 1st and 3rd Wednesdays, Foresters Hall; Mrs. Olive Bouchard, Rec. Sec.

Mount Lassen No. 215, Bieber—Meets 2nd and 4th Thursdays, I.O.O.F. Hall; Mrs. Angie C. Kenyon, Rec. Sec.

Susanville No. 243, Susanville—Meets 3rd Thursday, I.O.O.F. Hall; Mrs. Georgia Jensen, Rec. Sec., 700 Roop St.

LOS ANGELES COUNTY.

Los Angeles No. 124, Los Angeles—Meets 1st and 3rd Wednesdays, I.O.O.F. Hall, Washington and Oak Sts.; Mrs. Mary K. Corcoran, Rec. Sec., 322 No. Van Ness Ave.

Long Beach No. 154, Long Beach—Meets 1st and 3rd Thursdays, K.P. Hall, 341 Pacific Ave.; Mrs. Alice Waldow, Rec. Sec., 2175 Cedar Ave.

Rudecinda No. 230, San Pedro—Meets 1st and 3rd Fridays, Unity Hall, I.O.O.F. Temple, 10th and Gaffey; Mrs. Carrie E. Northway, Rec. Sec., 561 W. 14th St.

Verdugo No. 240, Glendale—Meets 2nd and 4th Tuesdays, Masonic Temple, 234 So. Brand Blvd.; Miss Etta Fulkerth, Rec. Sec., 526-A No. Orange St.

Santa Monica Bay No. 245, Ocean Park—Meets 1st and 3rd Mondays, New Eagles Hall, 2823½ Main St.; Mrs. Rosalie Hyde, Rec. Sec., 738 Flower St., Venice.

Californiana No. 247, Los Angeles—Meets 2nd and 4th Tuesday afternoons, Hollywood Studio Club, 1215 Lodi Place; Mrs. Ines Sitton, Rec. Sec., 4223 Berenice St.

MADERA COUNTY.

Madera No. 244, Madera—Meets 2nd and 4th Thursdays, Masonic Annex; Mrs. Margaret Boyle, Rec. Sec., 225 So. "C" St.

MARIN COUNTY.

Sea Point No. 196, Sausalito—Meets 2nd and 4th Mondays, Perry Hall, 50 Caledonia St.; Mrs. Mary B. Smith, Rec. Sec., 559 Woodward Ave.

Marinita No. 198, San Rafael—Meets 2nd and 4th Mondays, 316 "B" St.; Miss Mollye Y. Spaelti, Rec. Sec., 539 4th St.

Fairfax No. 225, Fairfax—Meets 2nd and 4th Tuesdays, Community Hall; Mrs. Olive A. Greene, Rec. Sec., P. O. Box 277.

Tamelpa No. 231, Mill Valley—Meets 1st and 3rd Tuesdays, I.O.O.F. Hall; Mrs. Delphine M. Todt, Rec. Sec., 400 Grand Ave., San Rafael.

MARIPOSA COUNTY.

Mariposa No. 63, Mariposa—Meets 1st and 3rd Fridays, I.O.O.F. Hall; Mrs. Mamie E. Weston, Rec. Sec.

ATTENTION, SECRETARIES!

THIS DIRECTORY IS PUBLISHED BY AUTHORITY OF THE GRAND PARLOR N.D.G.W., AND ALL NOTICES OF CHANGES MUST BE RECEIVED BY THE GRAND SECRETARY (NOT THE MAGAZINE) ON OR BEFORE THE 20TH OF EACH MONTH TO INSURE CORRECTION IN NEXT PUBLICATION OF DIRECTORY.

MENDOCINO COUNTY.

Fort Bragg No. 210, Fort Bragg—Meets 1st and 3rd Thursdays, I.O.O.F. Hall; Mrs. Ruth W. Fuller, Rec. Sec.

MERCED COUNTY.

Veritas No. 75, Merced—Meets 1st and 3rd Tuesdays, I.O.O.F. Hall; Miss Margaret Thornton, Rec. Sec., 317 18th St.

MODOC COUNTY.

Alturas No. 159, Alturas—Meets 1st Thursday, Alturas Civic Club; Mrs. Irma W. Laird, Rec. Sec.

MONTEREY COUNTY.

Aleli No. 102, Salinas—Meets 2nd and 4th Thursdays, I.O.O.F. Hall; Mrs. Rose Evelyn Rhyner, Rec. Sec., P. O. Box 1274.

Junipero No. 141, Monterey—Meets 1st and 3rd Thursdays, Custom House; Miss Matilda M. Bergschicker, Rec. Sec., 498 Van Buren St.

NAPA COUNTY.

Eschol No. 16, Napa—Meets 2nd and 4th Mondays, N.S.G.W. Hall; Mrs. Ella Ingram, Rec. Sec., 2140 Seminary St.

Calistoga No. 145, Calistoga—Meets 2nd and 4th Mondays, I.O.O.F. Hall; Sadie P. Brooks, Rec. Sec.

La Junta No. 203, Saint Helena—Meets 1st and 3rd Tuesdays, N.S.G.W. Hall; Mrs. Marie Signorelli, Rec. Sec., 1341 Madrona Ave.

NEVADA COUNTY.

Laurel No. 6, Nevada City—Meets 1st and 3rd Wednesdays, I.O.O.F. Hall; Mrs. Nellie E. Clark, Rec. Sec., P. O. Box 212.

Manzanita No. 29, Grass Valley—Meets 1st and 3rd Tuesdays, Auditorium; Mrs. Loraine Keast, Rec. Sec., 123 Race St.

Columbia No. 70, French Corral—Meets Fridays, Farrelley Hall; Mrs. Kate Farrelley-Sullivan, Rec. Sec.

Snow Peak No. 176, Truckee—Meets 2nd and 4th Fridays, I.O.O.F. Hall; Mrs. Henrietta M. Eaton, Rec. Sec., P. O. Box 116.

ORANGE COUNTY.

Santa Ana No. 235, Santa Ana—Meets 2nd and 4th Mondays, K.C. Hall, 4th and French Sts.; Mrs. Matilda S. Lemon, Rec. Sec., 1038 W. Bishop St.

Grace No. 242, Fullerton—Meets 1st and 3rd Thursdays, I.O.O.F. Hall, 116½ E. Commonwealth; Mrs. Mary Rothaermel, Rec. Sec., 628 Fern Dr.

PLACER COUNTY.

Placer No. 138, Lincoln—Meets 2nd Wednesday, I.O.O.F. Hall; Miss Carrie Parlin, Rec. Sec.

La Rosa No. 191, Roseville—Meets 1st and 3rd Fridays, Eagles Hall; Mrs. Alice Lee West, Rec. Sec., Rocklin.

Auburn No. 233, Auburn—Meets 2nd and 4th Fridays, Foresters Hall; Mrs. Dorothy Reinecke, Rec. Sec., Penryn.

PLUMAS COUNTY.

Plumas Pioneer No. 219, Quincy—Meets 1st and 3rd Mondays, I.O.O.F. Hall; Minnie E. Johnson, Rec. Sec., P. O. Box 243.

SACRAMENTO COUNTY.

Califia No. 22, Sacramento—Meets 2nd and 4th Tuesdays, N.S.G.W. Hall; Miss Lulu Gillis, Rec Sec., 921 8th St.

La Bandera No. 110, Sacramento—Meets 1st and 3rd Fridays, N.S.G.W. Hall; Mrs. Clara Weldon, Rec. Sec., 1310 "O" St.

Sutter No. 111, Sacramento—Meets 1st and 3rd Tuesdays, N.S.G.W. Hall; Mrs. Adele Nix, Rec. Sec., 1238 "S" St.

Fern No. 123, Folsom—Meets 1st and 3rd Tuesdays, K.P. Hall; Mrs. Viola Shumway, Rec. Sec., P. O. Box 48.

Chabolla No. 171, Galt—Meets 2nd and 4th Tuesdays, I.O.O.F. Hall; Mrs. Mary Pritchard, Rec. Sec.

Coloma No. 212, Sacramento—Meets 1st and 3rd Tuesdays, I.O.O.F. Hall, Oak Park; Mrs. Nettie Harry, Rec. Sec., 1217 35th St.

Liberty No. 213, Elk Grove—Meets 2nd and 4th Fridays, I.O.O.F. Hall; Mrs. Frances Wackman, Rec. Sec., P. O. Box 192.

Victory No. 216, Courtland—Meets 1st Saturday and 3rd Monday, N.S.G.W. Hall; Mrs. Agneda Lample, Rec. Sec.

SAN BENITO COUNTY.

Copa de Oro No. 105, Hollister—Meets 2nd and 4th Thursdays, Grangers Union Hall; Mrs. Mollie Daveggio, Rec. Sec., 110 San Benito St.

San Juan Bautista No. 179, San Juan Bautista—Meets 1st Wednesday, Mission Corridor Rooms; Miss Gertrude Breen, Rec. Sec.

SAN BERNARDINO COUNTY.

Lugonia No. 241, San Bernardino—Meets 2nd and 4th Wednesdays, Eagles Hall; Evelyn T. Shaddox, Rec. Sec., 205 Temple St.

SAN DIEGO COUNTY.

San Diego No. 208, San Diego—Meets 2nd and 4th Tuesdays, K.C. Hall, 410 Elm St.; Mrs. Elsie Case, Rec. Sec., 3051 Broadway.

SAN FRANCISCO CITY AND COUNTY.

Minerva No. 2, San Francisco—Meets 1st and 3rd Wednesdays, N.S.G.W. Bldg.; Miss Dorothy Finn, Rec. Sec., 90 Princess St., Sausalito.

Alta No. 3, San Francisco—Meets 2nd and 4th Tuesdays, N.S.G.W. Bldg.; Mrs. Agnese L. Hughes, Rec. Sec., 3980 Sacramento St.

Oro Fino No. 9, San Francisco—Meets 1st and 3rd Thursdays, N.S.G.W. Bldg.; Mrs. Josephine B. Morrisey, Rec. Sec., 4441 20th St.

Golden State No. 50, San Francisco—Meets 1st and 3rd Wednesdays, N.D.G.W. Home; Miss Millie Tietjen, Rec. Sec., 328 Lexington Ave.

Orinda No. 56, San Francisco—Meets 2nd and 4th Fridays, N.D.G.W. Home; Mrs. Anna A. Gruber-Loser, Rec. Sec., 72 Grove Lane, San Anselmo.

Fremont No. 59, San Francisco—Meets 1st and 3rd Tuesdays, N.S.G.W. Bldg.; Miss Hannah Collins, Rec. Sec., 563 Fillmore St.

Buena Vista No. 68, San Francisco—Meets 1st, 3rd and 5th Thursdays, N.D.G.W. Home; Miss Margaret Barrett, Rec. Sec., 3774 20th St.

Las Lomas No. 72, San Francisco—Meets 1st and 3rd Tuesdays, N.D.G.W. Home; Mrs. Marion S. Day, Rec. Sec., 471 Alvarado St.

Yosemite No. 83, San Francisco—Meets 1st and 3rd Tuesdays, American Hall, 20th and Capp Sts.; Miss Mary Bazley, Rec. Sec., 3353 22nd St.

La Estrella No. 89, San Francisco—Meets 2nd and 4th Mondays, N.S.G.W. Bldg.; Miss Birdie Hartman, Rec. Sec., 1018 Jackson St.

Sans Souci No. 96, San Francisco—Meets 2nd and 4th Mondays, N.D.G.W. Home; Mrs. Minnie F. Dobbin, Rec. Sec., 1483 43rd Ave.

Calaveras No. 103, San Francisco—Meets 2nd and 4th Tuesdays, Swedish American Hall, 2174 Market St.; Mrs. Lena Lorsheter, Rec. Sec., 492-C 41st St., Oakland.
Darina No. 114, San Francisco—Meets 1st and 3rd Mondays, N.S.G.W. Bldg.; Miss Adele Walsh, Rec. Sec., 479 Page St.
El Vespero No. 118, San Francisco—Meets 2nd and 4th Tuesdays, Masonic Hall, 4705 3rd St.; Mrs. Nell R. Boege, Rec. Sec., 1526 Kirkwood Ave.
Genevieve No. 132, San Francisco—Meets 1st and 3rd Thursdays, N.S.G.W. Bldg.; Miss Branice Peguillan, Rec. Sec., 2434 16th Ave.
Keith No. 137, San Francisco—Meets 2nd and 4th Thursdays, N.S.G.W. Bldg.; Mrs. Helen T. Mann, Rec. Sec., 3265 Sacramento St.
Gabrielle No. 139, San Francisco—Meets 2nd and 4th Wednesdays, N.S.G.W. Bldg.; Mrs. Dorothy Wuesterfeld, Rec. Sec., 1020 Munich St.
Presidio No. 148, San Francisco—Meets 2nd and 4th Tuesdays, N.S.G.W. Bldg.; Mrs. Hattie Gaughran, Rec. Sec., 713 Capp St.
Guadalupe No. 153, San Francisco—Meets 2nd and 4th Mondays, Forester Hall, 170 Valencia St.; Miss May A. McCarthy, Rec. Sec., 336 Elsie St.
Golden Gate No. 158, San Francisco—Meets 2nd and 4th Mondays, N.S.G.W. Bldg.; Mrs. Margaret Ramm, Rec. Sec., 435-A Frederick St.
Dolores No. 169, San Francisco—Meets 2nd and 4th Wednesdays, N.S.G.W. Bldg.; Mrs. Ada Saunders, Rec. Sec., 284 Allison St.
Linda Rosa No. 170, San Francisco—Meets 2nd and 4th Wednesdays, Swedish American Hall, 2174 Market St.; Mrs. Eva P. Tyrrel, Rec. Sec., 2629 Mission St.
Portola No. 172, San Francisco—Meets 1st and 3rd Tuesdays, N.S.G.W. Bldg.; Catherine H. Dolly, Rec. Sec., 4125 23rd St.
Castro No. 178, San Francisco—Meets 1st and 3rd Wednesdays, K.C. Bldg., 150 Golden Gate Ave.; Miss Adeline Sandersfeld, Rec. Sec., 50 Baker St.
Twin Peaks No. 185, San Francisco—Meets 2nd and 4th Fridays, Druids Temple, 44 Page St.; Mrs. Loretta Cameron, Rec. Sec., 3969 Army St.
James Lick No. 220, San Francisco—Meets 1st and 3rd Wednesdays, N.S.G.W. Bldg.; Mrs. Edna Bishop, Rec. Sec., 3841 24th St.
Mission No. 227, San Francisco—Meets 2nd and 4th Fridays, N.S.G.W. Bldg.; Mrs. Ann Dippel, Rec. Sec., 448 Dewey Blvd.
Bret Harte No. 232 San Francisco—Meets 2nd and 4th Tuesdays, Schuberts Hall, 3009 16th St.; Muriele N. Pabst, Rec. Sec., 696 Guerrero St.
La Dorada No. 236, San Francisco—Meets 2nd and 4th Thursdays, N.S.G.W. Hall; Mrs. Theresa R. O'Brien, Rec. Sec., 567 Liberty St.
Balboa No. 249, San Francisco—Meets 1st and 3rd Thursdays, Maccabee Hall, 5th Ave. and Clement St., Jean Moffet, Rec. Sec., 422 Third Ave.

SAN JOAQUIN COUNTY.

Joaquin No. 5, Stockton—Meets 2nd and 4th Tuesdays, N.S.G.W. Hall, 314 E. Main St.; Mrs. Delia Garvin, Rec. Sec., 1122 E. Market St.
El Pescadero No. 82, Tracy—Meets 1st and 3rd Fridays, I.O.O.F. Hall; Mrs. Mary A. Hewitson, Rec. Sec., 215 W. 9th St.
Ivy No. 88, Lodi—Meets 1st and 3rd Wednesdays, Eagles Hall; Mrs. Mae Corson, Rec. Sec., 109 So. School St.
Calis de Oro No. 206, Stockton—Meets 1st and 3rd Tuesdays, N.S.G.W. Hall, 314 E. Main St.; Mrs. Frances Germain, Rec. Sec., 450 No. Regent.
Phoebe A. Hearst No. 214, Manteca—Meets 2nd and 4th Wednesdays, I.O.O.F. Hall; Mrs. Josie M. Frederick, Rec. Sec., Route A, Box 364, Ripon.

SAN LUIS OBISPO COUNTY.

San Miguel No. 94, San Miguel—Meets 2nd and 4th Wednesday afternoons, Clemon Hall; Mrs. Nellie Wickstrom, Rec. Sec.
San Luisita No. 108, San Luis Obispo—Meets 2nd and 4th Thursdays, W.O.W. Hall; Miss Agnes M. Lee, Rec. Sec., P. O. Box 584.
El Pinal No. 163, Cambria—Meets 2nd, 4th and 5th Tuesdays, N.S.G.W. Hall; Kathryn Luchessa, Rec. Sec.

SAN MATEO COUNTY.

Bonita No. 10, Redwood City—Meets 2nd and 4th Thursdays, I.O.O.F. Hall; Mrs. Dora Wilson, Rec. Sec., 518 Middlefield Rd.
Vista del Mar No. 155, Halfmoon Bay—Meets 2nd and 4th Thursdays, I.O.O.F. Hall; Mrs. Grace Griffith, Rec. Sec.
Ano Nuevo No. 180, Pescadero—Meets 1st and 3rd Wednesdays, I.O.O.F. Hall; Mrs. Alice Mattei, Rec. Sec.
El Carmelo No. 181, Daly City—Meets 1st and 3rd Wednesdays, Masonic Hall; Mrs. Hattie Kelly, Rec. Sec., 1179 Brunswick St.
Menlo No. 211, Menlo Park—Meets 2nd and 4th Mondays, Masonic Hall; Mrs. Frances E. Maloney, Rec. Sec., P. O. Box 626.
San Bruno No. 246, San Bruno—Meets 2nd and 4th Fridays, N.D. Hall; Mrs. Evelyn Kelly, Rec. Sec., 353 Hazel Ave.

SANTA BARBARA COUNTY.

Reina del Mar No. 126, Santa Barbara—Meets 1st and 3rd Tuesdays, Pythian Castle, 222 W. Carillo St.; Miss Christina Moller, Rec. Sec., 836 Bath St.

SANTA CLARA COUNTY.

San Jose No. 81, San Jose—Meets Thursdays, Catholic Women Center, 5th and San Fernando Sts.; Mrs. Nellie Fleming, Rec. Sec., Catholic Women's Center.
Vendome No. 100, San Jose—Meets Wednesdays, Scottish Rite Hall; Miss Marie Buck, Rec. Sec., 1414 Ellen St.
El Monte No. 205, Mountain View—Meets 2nd and 4th Fridays, Mockbee Hall; Miss Dolores Collett, Rec. Sec., Route 1, Box 677-A, Los Altos.
Palo Alto No. 229, Palo Alto—Meets 1st and 3rd Mondays, N.S.G.W. Hall; Miss Helena G. Hansen, Rec. Sec., 531 Lytton Ave.

SANTA CRUZ COUNTY.

Santa Cruz No. 26, Santa Cruz—Meets Mondays, N.S.G.W. Hall; Mrs. May L. Williamson, Rec. Sec., 170 Walnut Ave.
El Pajaro No. 35, Watsonville—Meets 1st and 3rd Tuesdays, I.O.O.F. Hall; Miss Ruth E. Wilson, Rec. Sec., 18 Laurel St.

SHASTA COUNTY.

Camellia No. 41, Anderson—Meets 1st and 3rd Tuesdays, Masonic Hall; Mrs. Olga E. Welbourn, Rec. Sec.
Lassen View No. 98, Shasta—Meets 2nd Friday, Masonic Hall; Miss Louise Litsch, Rec. Sec.
Hiawatha No. 140, Redding—Meets 2nd and 4th Wednesdays, Moose Hall; Ruth Presleigh, Rec. Sec., Office County Clerk.

N.D.G.W. OFFICIAL DEATH LIST.

Giving the name, the date of death, and the Subordinate Parlor affiliation of all deceased members as reported to Grand Secretary Sallie R. Thaler from October 15 to November 19:

Longley, Matilda A.; July 7; Santa Cruz No. 26.
Stanton, Elizabeth; October 15; Castro No. 178.
Chapman, Anna Bell A.; September 30; Los Angeles No. 124.
Kervan, Ida Marion; October 1; Alta No. 3.
Dardi, Lina; August 27; Reina del Mar No. 126.
Williams, Carrie R.; June 4; Califia No. 22.
Fournier, Frances C.; October 1; Fruitvale No. 177.

SIERRA COUNTY.

Naomi No. 36, Downieville—Meets 2nd and 4th Wednesdays, I.O.O.F. Hall; Mrs. Mary Cook, Rec. Sec.
Imogen No. 134, Sierraville—Meets 2nd and 4th Saturday afternoons, Copren Hall; Mrs. Jennie Copren, Rec. Sec.

SISKIYOU COUNTY.

Eschscholtzia No. 112, Etna—Meets 1st and 3rd Wednesdays, Masonic Hall; Mrs. Bernice E. Smith, Rec. Sec.
Mountain Dawn No. 120, Sawyers Bar—Meets 2nd and last Wednesdays, I.O.O.F. Hall; Miss Edith Dunphy, Rec. Sec.

SOLANO COUNTY.

Vallejo No. 195, Vallejo—Meets 1st and 3rd Wednesdays, K.C. Hall, 820 Marin St.; Mrs. Mary Combs, Rec. Sec., 511 York St.
Mary E. Bell No. 224, Dixon—Meets 2nd and 4th Thursdays, I.O.O.F. Hall; Grace McFadyen, Rec. Sec.

SONOMA COUNTY.

Sonoma No. 209, Sonoma—Meets 2nd and 4th Mondays, I.O.O.F. Hall; Mrs. Mae Norrbom, Rec. Sec., R.F.D., Box 171.
Santa Rosa No. 217, Santa Rosa—Meets 1st and 3rd Thursdays, N.S.G.W. Hall; Mrs. Clytie Lewis, Rec. Sec., Route 4, Box 345-A.
Petaluma No. 222, Petaluma—Meets 1st and 3rd Tuesdays, Dania Hall; Mrs. Margaret M. Oeltjen, Rec. Sec., 503 Prospect St.

STANISLAUS COUNTY.

Oakdale No. 125, Oakdale—Meets 1st Monday, I.O.O.F. Hall; Mrs. Lou Reeder, Rec. Sec.
Morada No. 199, Modesto—Meets 2nd and 4th Wednesdays, I.O.O.F. Hall; Mrs. Susan Sullivan, Rec. Sec., 517 Semple St.
Eldora No. 248, Turlock—Meets 1st and 3rd Wednesdays, Fraternal Hall; Mrs. Melva Gardner, Rec. Sec., 817 W. Main St.

SUTTER COUNTY.

South Butte No. 226, Sutter—Meets 1st and 3rd Mondays, N.D.G.W. Hall; Mrs. Abbie N. Vagedes, Rec. Sec.

TEHAMA COUNTY.

Berendos No. 23, Red Bluff—Meets 1st and 3rd Tuesdays, W.O.W. Hall, 200 Pine St.; Mrs. Lillie Hammer, Rec. Sec., 636 Jackson St.

TRINITY COUNTY.

Eltapome No. 55, Weaverville—Meets 2nd and 4th Thursdays, N.S.G.W. Hall; Mrs. Lou N. Fetzer, Rec. Sec.

TUOLUMNE COUNTY.

Dardanelle No. 66, Sonora—Meets Fridays, I.O.O.F. Hall; Mrs. Nettie Whitto, Rec. Sec.
Golden Era No. 99, Columbia—Meets 1st and 3rd Thursdays, N.S.G.W. Hall; Miss Irene Ponce, Rec. Sec.
Anona No. 164, Jamestown—Meets 2nd and 4th Tuesdays, I.O.O.F. Hall; Mrs. Rosa A. Beckwith, Rec. Sec., P. O. Box 87.

YOLO COUNTY.

Woodland No. 90, Woodland—Meets 2nd and 4th Tuesdays, N.S.G.W. Hall; Mrs. Maude Heaton, Rec. Sec., 153 College St.

YUBA COUNTY.

Marysville No. 162, Marysville—Meets 2nd and 4th Wednesdays, Liberty Hall; Miss Cecelia C. Gomes, Rec. Sec., 701 6th St.
Camp Far West No. 218, Wheatland—Meets 4th Thursday, I.O.O.F. Hall; Mrs. Ethel C. Brock, Rec. Sec., P. O. Box 285.

AFFILIATED ORGANIZATIONS.

General Assembly Past Presidents—Meetings held annually in April at the home-town of Chief President; Miss Josephine Clark, 824 11th St., Oakland, Chief President; Mrs. Anna G. Loser, 72 Grove Lane, San Anselmo, Chief Secretary.
Past Presidents Association No. 1—Meets 1st and 3rd Mondays, N.S.G.W. Bldg., 414 Mason St., San Francisco; Mrs. Margaret Grote-Hill, Pres.; Mrs. May R. Barry, Rec. Sec., 2319 19th Ave., San Francisco.
Past Presidents Association No. 2—Meets 2nd and 4th Mondays, "Wigwam," Pacific Bldg., 16th and Jefferson, Oakland; Francis McGovern, Pres.; Mrs. Elizabeth B. Goodman, Rec. Sec., 134 Juana St., San Leandro.
Past Presidents Association No. 3 (Santa Clara County)—Meets 2nd Tuesday, homes of members; Mrs. Ida Sweeney, Pres.; Amelia S. Hartman, Rec. Sec., 157 Auzerais Ave., San Jose.
Past Presidents Association No. 4 (Sacramento County)—Meets 2nd Monday, Unitarian Hall, 1413 27th St., Sacramento City; Francis Kimball, Pres.; Lily May Tilden, Rec. Sec., 3225 "T" St., Sacramento.
Past Presidents Association No. 5 (Butte County)—Meets 1st Friday, homes of members, Chico and Oroville; Sonora Steadman, Pres; Ruth Brown, Rec. Sec., 1265 Leah Court, Oroville.
Past Presidents Association No. 6 (Nevada County)—Meets 4th Friday, alternately between Nevada City, Odd Fellows Hall, and Grass Valley, Womens Improvement Clubhouse; Anne Conlin, Pres.; Louise Wales, Rec. Sec., 369 Mill St., Grass Valley.
Past Presidents Association No. 7 (Sonoma County)—Meets 1st Thursday, N.S.G.W. Hall, Santa Rosa; Willow Borba, Pres.; Clytie Lewis, Rec. Sec., R.F.D. No. 4, Box 345-A, Santa Rosa.
Past Presidents Association No. 8 (San Joaquin and Stanislaus Counties)—Meets 2nd Thursday, Red Men Hall, Stockton; Mrs. Mattie M. Stein, Pres.; Mrs. Harriet F. Corr, Rec. Sec., 729 E. Sonora St., Stockton.
Native Sons and Native Daughters Central Committee on Homeless Children—Main Office, 955 Phelan Bldg., San Francisco; Mrs. John W. Stirling, Chmn.; Miss Mary E. Brusie, Sec. Los Angeles branch office, 3924 Sunset Blvd.; Dorothy Schlingman, Sec.

(ADVERTISEMENT.)

Schmidt, Marie; October 24; Gabrielle No. 139.
Mitchler, Clara E.; September 18; Ruby No. 46.
Schmidt, Katherine F.; November 2; Darina No. 114.
Ferm, Mary E.; November 3; Piedmont No. 87.
McDonnell, Dora Blair; August 7; Fresno No. 187.
Kroetz, Mary M.; October 28; Alta No. 3.
Green, Jane L.; November 1; Alta No. 3.

NATIVE DAUGHTER NEWS

(Continued from Page 13)

(Glendale), Grand Trustee Florence Schoneman, and District Deputy Nellie Cline and delegation from Grace No. 242 (Fullerton). Mrs. Hansen announced that a parlor is in process of organization at Riverside.

The thimble club met at the home of Mrs. Walter Moore November 7, and will hold its December 3 meeting at the Greenville home of Mrs. Myrtle Ellis. No. 235 and Santa Ana No. 265 N.S.G.W. had a float depicting a polo field in the Armistice Day parade.

The Parlor has perfected plans for a spanish dinner December 14, when a handsome cedar chest, filled with lovely articles, will be disposed of. December 19 the annual dinner will be held in observance of Santa Ana's institution anniversary. The following lines "On Armistice Day," composed by Recording Secretary Matilda S. Lemon, appear on request of the Parlor:

"Looking back in silent retrospection
Along the thirteen intervening years,
The saddened face of the good old world
Gazed on the Unknown Soldiers' tombs in recollection.
And lo! the rain came down in benediction
As if to wet those mounds with tears.
Tears of love and tenderness to sanctify the grounds
Wherein its sacrifice to War lay, 'neath those mounds.
Out here and yonder, in that land so far away—
Yet, in our hearts and minds are always here to stay;
Tears of thanksgiving that untold human carnage had ended
And what remained of our courageous boys were homeward wended.
Then came the sunshine, glorious with its promise
Of a brighter, better, more Christian view of life,
When all misunderstandings and dissensions
May be settled in more human ways than strife."

Pioneer Mothers Guests.

Colusa — Colus No. 194 feasted and entertained the Pioneer Mothers of Colusa County November 10. Each was presented with a corsage and a dainty handkerchief. Mrs. Warren G. Davison gave the history of Colusa County from the time it was settled by the Colus tribe of Indians, from which the city and the county derived their names.

November 16 the Parlor made plans for the annual Christmas tree and for baskets for the needy. District Deputy Hastings was a visitor. A cake walk was featured in which all the members participated; the cake went to Christine Humberg. Delicious refreshments were served.

Five Initiated.

Modesto—Grand President Evelyn I. Carlson paid her official visit to Morada No. 199 October 28. Among the many in attendance were Past Grand President Dr. Louise C. Heilbron, Supervising Deputy Katherine Kopf, District Deputies Mae F. Givens, Sadie Brainard, Effie Prothero and Tough. The meeting hall was arranged to represent an outdoor rock garden, with flowers and leaves of fall colors adorning the walls. Mrs. Mary Blaine and a committee had charge of the decorations. Five candidates were initiated.

Members of the Parlor gave a handkerchief shower for Mrs. Lottie Islip, who left for Arizona to reside. November 6 the sewing club met at the Ceres home of Mrs. Service. November 18 Morada and Modesto No. 11 N.S.G.W. sponsored a public whist, the proceeds to be used for relief work.

Charming Talk.

Santa Cruz—Grand President Evelyn I. Carlson honored Santa Cruz No. 26 with her presence October 19. The occasion drew a large attendance, including delegations from Watsonville, Salinas, Hollister, Pescadero and Sacramento. The ritualistic work was beautifully done, three new members being received. The Grand President's talk on the projects of the Order was charmingly given and listened to with interest by everyone.

Grand President Carlson, Past Grand Presidents Stella Finkeldey and Bertha Briggs, Supervising Deputy Rose Rhyner and District Deputies Pearl Reid and Alta Maculay received gifts from the Parlor. A sumptuous potluck supper preceded the meeting and during the supper Past President Leona Geyer, accompanied by District Deputy Reid, offered two very lovely vocal numbers. The members who celebrated birthdays in October were honored guests, and a cake with lighted candles was presented them. Chrysanthemums, marigolds and ferns were the effective

(Continued on Page 22)

NATIVE DAUGHTER NEWS

(Continued from Page 21)

decorations in the banquet and meeting rooms. The committee in charge of the supper was Leona Geyer (chairman), Arlette Harris, Mamie Cavanaugh and Mary Gregory.

Anniversary Dinner.

Pittsburg — Stirling No. 146 had its annual birthday dinner in recognition of its twenty-sixth institution anniversary. The table, decorated in Hallowe'en colors, had as a centerpiece a pot of gold. All the decorations were made by Vera Leaderich, chairman of the committee. In attendance were two charter members—Past Grand President Amy V. McAvoy, who is again the president of the Parlor, and Hanna McVay, who has held an office ever since No. 146 was instituted, in 1905, by Ariana Stirling, then Grand President. At the conclusion of the Parlor meeting, which followed the dinner, cards were played and a large birthday cake was served with coffee.

Seven Initiated.

Napa—Grand President Evelyn I. Carlson paid an official visit to Eschol No. 16 November 9. Others in attendance were Grand Trustee Willow Borba, Grand Outside Sentinel Orinda Giannini, Past Grand President Dr. Louise C. Heilbron and visitors from Vallejo, Saint Helena, Petaluma, Santa Rosa, Sacramento and San Rafael. Seven candidates were initiated. A dinner was served prior to the meeting.

Grand President Carlson gave a most interesting talk on the Order's projects. The day being her wedding anniversary, the Parlor presented her with a specially decorated cake and a gift. Flowers were presented the other grand officers. The meeting and banquet rooms were beautifully decorated under the supervision of Ruby Brien and Jane Ezetti.

Pleasing Sum for Worthy Cause.

Hollister—The annual card party of Copa de Oro No. 105 and Fremont No. 44 N.S.G.W. October 22 for the benefit of the homeless kiddies was a brilliant success socially and netted a pleasing sum for this very worthy cause. Thirty-five tables were filled with players of bridge, five hundred and pedro. Attractive prizes were awarded and a neat sum was realized from sales of a small basket of groceries and an exquisite spray of chrysanthemums. The hall was prettily decorated with baskets of autumn blossoms and foliage. Appetizing refreshments were served at the close of the card playing. The net proceeds, amounting to $150, have been forwarded to assist in caring for homeless little ones.

Armistice Day Party.

Santa Barbara—Reina del Mar No. 126 sponsored an Armistice Day party at La Hacienda November 10. Each of the many members and guests deposited, as they entered, a package of cigarets and articles used by the veterans in handicraft work. These will be sent to the San Fernando Hospital. Many attractive features were introduced in the way of entertainment. Miss Marjory Stone and Mrs. Alice Castagna were the general chairmen of arrangements.

Hallowe'en Party.

Chico—Annie K. Bidwell No. 168 had a Hallowe'en party at which a program was presented by Evelyn Boyd, Lila Roohr, Frances Snider, Catherine McEnespy, Margaret Hudspeth and Minnie Westbrook. At supper time the members were seated at a long table, centering which was a pumpkin basket filled with flowers. Placecards and napkins carried out the Hallowe'en motif. Guessing games were introduced, Annie Stoskstill winning the prize. Mrs. Westbrook headed the social committee for the evening.

The Parlor was represented in the Armistice Day, November 11, parade by a float, and has voted to make the usual donation to the Chico Health Center.

Players Complimented.

Sausalito—Sea Point No. 196 entertained the members of Sea Point No. 158 N.S.G.W. and their families at a delightful Hallowe'en party October 26. A one-act comedy, "Crossed Wires," was presented, and the players were highly complimented by the many guests, from San Rafael, Fairfax, Mill Valley and Sausalito. Miss Helen Sullivan was the director. Later in the evening refreshments were served at tables decorated in Hallowe'en favors.

Many congratulations were extended the committee in charge: Mms. Lillian Fancourt, Lillian Azavedo and Alice McGowan; Misses Miriam Bradley, Agnes Brown, Hilda Brown and Alma Burkell.

Responds to Every Appeal.

Palo Alto—Grand President Evelyn I. Carlson officially visited Palo Alto No. 229 November 16. She was accompanied by Supervising Deputy Clara Gairaud, and District Deputies Geraldine Brown, Marie Buck, Catherine Derry and Margaret Malone. Delegations from Orinda, Dolores, Vendome, Ano Nuevo, Bonita and Menlo were also present.

The Grand President commended the Parlor for having responded to every appeal. Following a delightful resume of her aims and ambitions for the Order she was presented with gifts and flowers. The hall was decorated in autumnal flowers in the shades of yellow and russet brown. Refreshments closed a delightful evening.

District Deputies Meet.

Sutter—District Deputies of Yuba, Colusa and Sutter Counties met with South Butte No. 226 October 19, among them being Supervising Deputy Mary Meade, Mrs. Vivian Hastain of Berryessa No. 192, Mrs. Pearl Bowden of Colus No. 194 and Mrs. Josephine Norris of South Butte. Five candidates were initiated into the Parlor. Following the meeting refreshments were served in the prettily decorated banquetroom.

Brides Honored.

Oakland—Aloha No. 106 initiated three candidates November 3, and at the same time honored three new brides—Past Presidents Margaret Bazely and Grace DuPont, and Inside Sentinel Margaret Walker. On behalf of the Parlor, Social Chairman Eda Steuer presented them with gifts. Second Vice-president Thelma Rogers sang "I Love You, California," and a piano duet, "Love Tales of Hoffman," was rendered by Third Vice-president Evelyn Almasy and Outside Sentinel Edith Hoover. Grand Secretary Sallie R. Thaler, District Deputy Mildred Brant and visitors from Bahia Vista No. 167 Encinal No. 156 and Berkeley No. 150 were among those present. Refreshments were served.

November 17 a turkey whist, largely attended, was held jointly with Athens No. 195 N.S.G.W. The proceeds will be used to purchase toys for about eighty poor kiddies who will be guests of the Parlors at the annual Christmas tree December 22. There will be a real Santa Claus, and Ivy Ford's Kiddies will provide entertainment. Irma Murray, whist chairman, announces another turkey whist, for the benefit of the same worthy cause, December 15. With Grace DuPont in charge, a theater party in Berkeley is billed for December 8.

Greatly Enjoyed Party.

Etna—Eschscholtzia No. 112 entertained at a delightful whist party October 23. The following program added pleasure to the evening: piano solo, "Tam O'Shanter," and vocal solo, "Waiting at the Church," Mrs. Minna K. Horn; vocal solos, "Lassie O' Mine" and "Pretty Quadroon," Frank B. Smith; memorized readings, "Accountability" and "A Fish Story," Mrs. Lettie Lewis.

The decorations, the refreshments and the informal fun throughout the evening were in keeping with the spirit of Hallowe'en, and the party was greatly enjoyed by the many members and guests present.

Sew for December Bazar.

Fullerton—Grace No. 242 held a successful rummage sale last month. Preceding the November 17 meeting a pot-luck supper was enjoyed. District Deputy Ora Evans was present, and there were visitors from Santa Ana No. 235.

The homeless children sewing circle spent all day November 16 with Mrs. J. C. Sheppard. The members are busily engaged in sewing for the December bazar. The Parlor is planning to present a California State (Bear) Flag to the Placentia public library.

Death, for the first time, entered the ranks of Grace October 22 and removed Mildred R. Johnson, wife of Edgar Johnson, founder of "The Daily News Tribune." She was born near San Bernardino, January 3, 1869, her parents being Mr. and Mrs. John Ward, covered wagon California Pioneers.

Doings of Past Presidents.

Sacramento—Association No. 4 will entertain twenty-five children of the Sacramento Orphanage with a turkey dinner and Christmas tree December 14. Mrs. Mamie Davis, chairman for the occasion, will be assisted by past presidents of Coloma No. 212.

Chico—Association No. 5 had its fourth annual banquet November 5. Miss Lily Tilden was the principal speaker. Bridge followed the feast.

Stockton—Association No. 8 met at the home of Henrietta Quevillen November 5. Dutch whist was played and refreshments were served. The December 12 meeting will be a costume party.

Poppy Maids Make Favors.

San Jose—San Jose No. 81 will receive Grand President Evelyn I. Carlson December 3. Elaborate plans for a brilliant reception are being made by a committee under the chairmanship of Mrs. Mary C. Newton. A 6:30 dinner will precede the meeting. A very successful card party was held November 19, with Mrs. Kathyrn Nelson as chairman of arrangements.

The Past Presidents of the Parlor entertained November 12. This was a very happy event and brought out a good number of members. A program was given and refreshments were served. Mrs. Matilda Moak, the only charter member present, was presented with a boquet of lovely red rosebuds. Mrs. Myrtle Berins was chairman of the evening. The Poppy Maids sewing club, an auxiliary of the Parlor, has fortnightly meetings which are very enjoyable. Through its efforts the Parlor always has on hand lovely favors for the semi-monthly card parties. Mrs. Elva Dee, the next president of No. 81, is a recent bride, her marriage having occurred in September.

NATIVE SON NEWS

(Continued from Page 17)

the best banquets he ever attended. Addresses were made by Grand Third Vice-president Chas. A. Koenig, Grand Secretary John T. Regan, Al Moore and Harry W. Gaetjen.

Past Presidents Exemplify Ritual.

Fresno—Fresno No. 25 initiated a class of candidates November 27, the ritual being exemplified by a picked team from San Joaquin Past Presidents Assembly headed by Grand Trustee Frank M. Lane. In conjunction with Fresno No. 187 N.D.G.W. a social dance was held November 21.

Grand Trustee Visits.

Alameda—Grand Trustee George F. McNoble paid an official visit November 18 to Alameda No. 47. Grand Inside Sentinel W. B. O'Brien extended greetings on behalf of the Parlor, and a program of entertainment was presented under the supervision of President Guy C. Whitmore.

Past Presidents Enthusiastic.

Sausalito—Marin Past Presidents Assembly No. 5 held the second meeting since its reorganization November 3. A large class of candidates were initiated. Governor-General Louis Erb was in attendance and congratulated the assembly on its rejuvenation, and complimented the members on their enthusiastic spirit. This branch, he says, has a very promising future, and he said several additional assemblies will be instituted soon. He spoke of the great enthusiasm prevailing in the northern district, where he had seen members who came over one hundred miles to attend the meetings. Past Governor-General Victor L. Orengo, Senator Joe Tracy, A. Gudehus, Jas. Stanley, Grand Director-General Chas. Soldavini Jr. and Monroe W. Label were among others who spoke at the banquet following the regular meeting of the Assembly.

Fruit Conference—A conference of deciduous fruit growers is to be held at Hollister, San Benito County, December 10 and 11.

Passing of the California Pioneer

(Confined to Brief Notices of the Demise of Those Men and Women Who Came to California Prior to 1860.)

STEPHEN T. WINCHESTER, NATIVE OF New York, 97; came across the plains to California in 1848 and settled in Nevada County; died at Grass Valley. He was a veteran of the Modoc Indians wars.

Mrs. Ellen E. Ellery, native of Pennsylvania, 84; came across the plains in 1849; died at Eureka, Humboldt County, survived by six children.

Mrs. Elizabeth Larkin, native of Illinois, 85; crossed the plains in 1850; died at Redding, Shasta County, survived by four children.

Jesse Burris, native of Missouri, 81; as a three-months-old infant crossed the plains in 1851 and long resided in Sonoma County; died at San Jose, Santa Clara County.

Mrs. Mary L. Larrabee, native of Rhode Island, 89; came via the Isthmus of Panama in 1850 and settled in San Francisco, where she died; three children survive.

Mrs. Mary Elizabeth Stemmerman-Furlong, native of Louisiana, 92; came across the plains in 1851 and resided in San Mateo, Santa Clara and Monterey Counties; died at Pacific Grove, survived by two sons.

Mrs. Mary Curtis-Richardson, native of New York, 83; came via the Isthmus of Panama in 1852; died at San Francisco. She was a noted artist, two of her best-known paintings being "The Sleeping Child" and "The Young Mother."

Henry McDuffee, native of Vermont, 96; came across the plains in 1852; died at Gilroy, Santa Clara County, survived by a son.

Mrs. Cecelia Mel DeFontenay-Pocock, native of New York, 91; came via the Isthmus of Panama in 1852 and settled in San Francisco, where she died; four children survive.

Mrs. Mary Lowe-McBride, native of Louisiana, 83; came via the Isthmus of Panama in 1852 and three years later settled in Siskiyou County; died near Etna, survived by four children.

Mrs. Susan Edelen Shannon-Verdenal, native of Missouri, 89; came across the plains in 1852 and long resided in San Francisco; died near Fresno City, survived by two daughters.

James William Seawell, native of Missouri, 81; came across the plains in 1853 and resided in Napa, Lake and Sonoma Counties; died at Healdsburg, survived by a wife and a son. He was a brother of Justice Emmet Seawell, Grand Second Vice-president N.S.G.W.

Mrs. Ada Matteson, native of Maine, 88; came across the plains in 1853 and long resided in Tuolumne, Calaveras and San Joaquin Counties; died at Eagle Rock, Los Angeles County, survived by two children.

Henry Petersen, born in 1853 while his parents were enroute to California across the plains; died at San Luis Obispo City, survived by a wife and ten children.

Mrs. Sarah Taylor, native of Wisconsin, 86; came across the plains in 1853 and settled in Shasta County; died at Millville, survived by five children.

William Pallett, 80; came across the plains in 1853 and resided in Los Angeles and Orange Counties; died at Santa Ana, survived by a son.

Mrs. Constance Otto, 90; since 1854 a resident of San Francisco, where she died; five children survive.

Robert Gibbins, native of Arkansas, 90; came in 1854; died at Cloverdale, Sonoma County.

Mrs. Eliza Spray-Moore, native of Iowa, 96; came across the plains in 1854 and for forty years resided in Santa Barbara County; died at Los Angeles City, survived by seven children.

Oliver Morgan, native of Indiana, 83; came across the plains in 1855; died at San Leandro, Alameda County, survived by a wife and two sons.

Mrs. Louisa Kunz, native of Germany, 91; came via Cape Horn in 1856; died at Sacramento City, survived by four children.

Alfred H. Rogers, native of New York, 94; came via the Isthmus of Panama in 1856 and settled in El Dorado County; died at Gold Hill, survived by eight children.

Mrs. Mary A. Fogarty, native of New Hampshire, 92; since 1856 a resident of Oakland, Alameda County, where she died; two children survive.

John McIntire, native of New Hampshire, 88; came in 1856 and after eight years' residence in Amador County settled in Sacramento City, where he died; three children survive. His father, a California Pioneer of 1849, was Amador County's first school superintendent.

Mrs. Margaret Hearn-Brown, native of Missouri, 77; came in 1856 and resided in Sonoma and Colusa Counties; died at Colusa City.

John Hoerl, native of New York, 78; since 1856 San Joaquin County resident; died near Lodi, survived by a wife and a son.

Charles Stevens Murch, native of Michigan, 83; came across the plains in 1857 and resided in Colusa and Placer Counties; died at Hammonton, Yuba County, survived by eleven children.

Mrs. Lena Sander-Haehnlen, native of Louisiana, 84; since 1859 a resident of San Francisco, where she died; three daughters survive.

Bernard Mayer, native of New York, 74; came via the Isthmus of Panama in 1859; died at Mayfield, Santa Clara County, survived by a wife and two children.

Mrs. Helen Walters, native of New York, 81; came via Cape Horn in 1859 and settled in Calaveras County; died at Altaville, survived by a son.

OLD TIMERS PASS

Mrs. Clara Noe, native of Wisconsin, 82; came in 1862; died near Bridge House, Sacramento County. She had resided many years in El Dorado and Amador Counties.

Mack Powers, native of Illinois, 79; came in 1862; died at Susanville, Lassen County, survived by six children. For many years he resided in Plumas County.

Mrs. Sarah Smith-Fearey, native of Scotland, 79; came in 1863; died at Oakland, Alameda County; five children survive.

Mrs. Mary West, native of New Brunswick, 85; came in 1864 and six years later settled in Humboldt County; died at Fortuna, survived by four children.

J. G. Elmore, native of Missouri, 88; since 1865 Stanislaus County resident; died at Salida, survived by a wife and three children.

Mrs. Letitia Kesner-Judy, native of Pennsylvania, 82; came in 1865; died at Roseville, Placer County, survived by two children. She long resided in Yuba County.

Mrs. Mary Bneck-Petersen, native of Germany, 87; came in 1865; died at Dixon, Solano County, survived by four children.

Mrs. Flora E. Leonard, native of Michigan, 73; since 1866 resident Sacramento City, where she died; a husband survives.

Christian A. Beier, native of Denmark, 89; came in 1867; died near Alvarado, Alameda County, survived by a wife and a daughter.

Mrs. Elizabeth Corbally-Dowdell, native of Ireland, 85; since 1868 resident Saint Helena, Napa County, where she died; three children survive.

Mrs. Sarah Pennebaker-Peck, native of Indiana, 94; came in 1868 and long resided in Tulare County; died at Los Angeles City, survived by three sons. She was the grandmother of Judge J. Walter, John W. and Waldo Hanby (all Ramona No. 109 N.S.G.W.).

Antone Piminiel Sr., native of Azores Islands, 84; came in 1868; died at Mendocino City, survived by a wife and seven children.

Mrs. Harriet Newell-Lowrie, native of New Hampshire; since 1868 resident Irvington, Alameda County, where she died; four children survive.

Fredrick Dieckhoff, native of Germany, 86; since 1868 Alameda County resident; died at Livermore, survived by four children.

Mrs. Julia Mahar, native of New York, 87; came in 1869; died at San Francisco, survived by two daughters. For many years she resided in Marin County.

Ferdinand A. Wenzel, native of Germany, 89; since 1869 Tuolumne County resident; died at Sonora, survived by a son.

Warren Ellenwood, native of New York, 89; came in 1869; died at San Jose, Santa Clara County, survived by four children. He long resided in San Joaquin County.

William Thomas Durnford, 72; came in 1869 and long resided in Humboldt County; died at Los Angeles City, survived by three children.

Mrs. Charlotta Bracesco, native of Italy, 82; since 1866 a resident of Menlo Park, San Mateo County, where she died; a husband and five children survive.

PIONEER NATIVES DEAD

Elk River (Humboldt County)—John A. Sands, born in Yuba County in 1859, died October 20 survived by a wife. He was affiliated with Humboldt Parlor No. 14 N.S.G.W. (Eureka).

Colusa City—Benjamin F. Simpson, born in Sutter County in 1857, died October 24 survived by three children.

Hollister (San Benito County)—Mrs. Francisco Ramoni, born in California in 1847, passed away October 25 survived by seven children.

Rocklin (Placer County)—Mrs. Tinnie Glindkamp, born in Sacramento County in 1852, passed away October 26.

Merced City—Mrs. Ellen B. Bobzzen, born in California in 1857, passed away October 26 survived by two children.

Hemet (Riverside County)—Charles E. McGary, born at Sacramento City in 1852, died October 27.

Jamestown (Tuolumne County)—John O'Neill, born here in 1858, died October 28.

Sacramento City—John P. Giamelli, born in Placer County in 1858, died October 28 survived by a wife and a daughter. He was affiliated with Sacramento Parlor No. 3 N.S.G.W.

San Francisco—Dr. Mary M. Kroetz, born here in 1857, passed away October 28 survived by two children. She was affiliated with Alta Parlor No. 3 N.D.G.W.

Sacramento City— Miss Caroline H. Schnabel, born in Placer County in 1858, passed away October 28.

When you purchase goods advertised in The Grizzly Bear, or answer an advertisement in this magazine, please be sure to mention The Grizzly Bear. That's co-operation mutually beneficial.

San Ramon (Contra Costa County)—Miss Loretta Glass, born in this county in 1858, passed away October 29.

Hammonton (Yuba County)—Mrs. America Adkins-Horner, born in California in 1853, passed away October 29 survived by a husband and three children.

Berkeley (Alameda County)—William B. Bayley, born in Solano County in 1859, died October 29 survived by three children.

Santa Rosa (Sonoma County)—Mrs. Mary J. Miller, born in Yolo County in 1855, passed away October 30 survived by three children.

Nipomo (San Luis Obispo County)—David Dana, born here in 1851, died November 1 survived by a wife and six children. He was a son of Captain William G. Dana, early-day California shipmaster, who was a cousin of Richard Henry Dana of "Two Years Before the Mast" fame.

Placerville (El Dorado County)—Charles Edward Fisk, born in California in 1856, died November 1.

Berkeley (Alameda County)—John Holland Mallett, born at San Francisco in 1856, died November 2 survived by a wife and three children.

San Francisco—George Karcher, born at Sacramento City in 1857, died November 3.

Yuba City (Sutter County)—Frank J. Miller, born in California in 1856, died November 7.

Oakland (Alameda County)—Miss Janet Cameron Haight, born at San Francisco in 1858, passed away November 8. She was the daughter of the late Henry H. Haight, California Pioneer of 1849 and tenth governor of California.

San Francisco—August E. Drucker, born here in 1857, died November 8 survived by a wife and two children. He was the head of the August E. Drucker Company, manufacturers of "Revelation" toothpowder.

Hayfork (Trinity County)—Mrs. Jane Adams-Bush, born in Sonoma County in 1856, passed away November 10 survived by four children.

Sacramento City—Frank R. Merrill, born in Nevada County in 1857, died November 10 survived by a wife and five children.

Lower Lake (Lake County)—Eugene Willington Rose, born in Napa County in 1853, died November 18 survived by a wife and a daughter. He was an active member of Lower Lake Parlor No. 159 N.S.G.W. and a delegate to several Grand Parlors.

In Memoriam

MARY E. FERM.

"To the Officers and Members of Piedmont Parlor No. 87 N.D.G.W.: Whereas, It has pleased our Heavenly Father, in His divine wisdom, to remove from our midst and associations our beloved and esteemed sister, Mary E. Ferm; and whereas, in the sudden passing of Sister Ferm Piedmont Parlor No. 87 N.D.G.W. mourns the loss of one of its most loyal and faithful members; therefore, be it

Resolved, That while we will miss our departed sister, the memory of her lovable character and sincere friendship will ever remain fresh in our memory, and we extend the hand of sympathy to the bereaved husband and family in this, their hour of sorrow; and be it further resolved, that these resolutions be spread in full upon the minutes of this Parlor meeting, that a copy be sent to the husband and family of our departed sister, and that a copy be sent to The Grizzly Bear Magazine for publication.

Respectfully submitted,
GRETTA MURDEN, Chairman,
ADDIE L. MOSHER, P.G.P.,
JOSEPHINE COLLINS.
Committee

Oakland, November 12, 1931

MILDRED R. JOHNSON.

To the Officers and Members of Grace Parlor No. 242 N.D.G.W.—Your committee appointed to draft resolutions expressing the sentiments and deep-felt sympathy of the members of this Parlor on the death of our sister, Mildred R. Johnson, respectfully submit the following:

Whereas, It has pleased the Almighty Father to remove from our midst our sister, Mildred R. Johnson, and to summon her to realms of higher activities; and whereas, in her death our Parlor has lost a highly esteemed sister and our community a respected Pioneer citizen; therefore, be it

Resolved, That Grace Parlor extends sincere sympathy to her husband and bereaved relatives; and further be it resolved, that a copy of these resolutions be sent to the family of our sister, that another copy be sent to The Grizzly Bear Magazine for publication, and that a copy be spread upon the minutes of the Parlor.

CARRIE SHEPPARD,
KATE HILL,
MARY ROTHAERMEL,
Committee

Fullerton, November 20, 1931

EUGENE W. ROSE.

"No one hears the door that opens,
When they pass beyond our call;
Soft as loosened leaves of roses
One by one our loved ones fall."

By the death of Eugene W. Rose, our state has lost an honored Pioneer, Lower Lake Parlor No. 159 N.S.G.W. a beloved member, and his family a kind and loving husband and father. The charm of his upright character and kindly disposition won for him the respect and love of our membership, who

Resolved, That this tribute of affection be sent to the bereaved family, that a copy be spread upon our records, and that a copy be sent to The Grizzly Bear for publication.

JOHN H. PEARCE,
ALBERT KUGELMAN,
Committee.

Lower Lake, November 20, 1931.

LOS ANGELES--CITY and COUNTY

LOS ANGELES

(Continued from Page 6)

one of the most brilliant and successful of the entire year. Two candidates were initiated. A beautiful silver gift was presented Mrs. Gertrude Riddle, a recent bride. There was a notable assemblage, representatives of six Parlors, twenty-seven past presidents, five district deputies and Grand Trustee Florence Dodson-Schoneman. The honor guest for the evening was District Deputy Eva Mae Bemis. The tables for the supper were beautifully decorated in autumn leaves and flowers; Mrs. Gertrude Riddle was chairman of the entertainment and supper. Plans are under way for a birthday party in honor of all members having birthdays from July 1 to December 1.

HOMELESS CHILDREN FUND ENRICHED.

Ocean Park—Santa Monica Bay Parlor No. 267 N.S.G.W. entertained some 200 members of the southland Parlors at its annual lobster feast November 9. Phil Romero was chairman of the committee in charge of the "feed," and was assisted by Jack Dailey, Howard Earl and Jack Nelson.

At the Parlor meeting President Barnes invited Past Presidents Eugene W. Biscailuz, J. Howard Blanchard, Dike Freeman, Harold Barden, Phil Romero and Eldred L. Meyer to fill the several stations. Past Grand President John T. Newell was the senior past president of the evening. As first vice-president, in charge of the good of the order, Blanchard extracted a considerable number of shekels from the gang, to the enrichment of the homeless children fund. There were numerous speakers and a lot of good-natured bantering.

At the conclusion of one of the very best of the many successful affairs staged by Santa Monica Bay, an excellent program was presented by Ed. Burke's quartet, the Westerners. November 23 the officers of Sepulveda Parlor No. 263 (San Pedro) were guests of No. 267 and exemplified the ritual for a large class of candidates.

ROUSING MEETING.

Glendale—Glendale No. 264 N.S.G.W. had a rousing good meeting November 2, when three candidates were initiated. Among the large crowd were representatives of seven Parlors. Speakers included Junior Past Grand President John T. Newell, District Deputy Harry Honn, Victor D. Kremer, Charles G. Young, Fred Gamble Jr., Philip Molen, Dr. Joseph A. Kleiser and District Deputy Al Cron. Refreshments were served.

NEIGHBOR VISITED.

San Pedro—A delegation of twenty-two Sepulveda Parlor No. 263 N.S.G.W. members, headed by District Deputy Edward Baldwin, paid a visit to Long Beach Parlor No. 239 October 29, and the officers of No. 263 exemplified the ritual.

The purpose of the visit, suggested by Deputy Baldwin, was to revive the interest of the Long Beach members. President Francis Gentry and Secretary Brady of No. 239 gave assurance that every effort would be made to have that Parlor on the active list at an early date.

INTERPARLOR DANCE.

The first of a series of monthly dances being featured by the Interparlor N.S.G.W. and N.D.G.W. Committee at the Goldberg-Bosley Ballroom, Venice boulevard and Flower street, was held November 6 and was a pleasing success.

The December dance will be held Friday, the 11th. Special features of entertainment will be introduced, including Margaret Nye in a hawaiian dance in costume. Unusually good music is provided by a ten-piece orchestra.

If you want to spend a pleasant evening among congenial friends, give these dances your support. The sub-committee in charge includes Mary Noerenberg (chairman), Grace Norton, Beaulah VanLeuven, Andrew Vaughn and Eldred Meyer.

VETERANS SHOWERED.

Ocean Park—Santa Monica Bay Parlor No. 245 N.D.G.W. had a jam and jelly shower, in charge of President Mary Meyer, for the veterans at Wildwood Sanatorium October 19. Rosalie Hyde gave a report of her visit with Edward Edmiston, adopted by the Parlor. He has been an inmate of the National Soldiers' Home at Sawtelle eleven months.

He was given a shower November 2 and received many lovely gifts. He will be a guest at the Parlor's Christmas tree, which is being arranged for by a committee headed by Mrs. Hyde. A greeting was sent Mrs. D. G. Stephens, "the grand old lady of Santa Monica," who celebrated her ninety-third birthday November 24.

Marie Barnes, chairman of No. 245's homeless children committee, reported the Christmas box ready for delivery, and that the pencil sale was a success. A card party November 30 was in charge of Lottie O'Connor. Refreshments were served by Betty Valencia, Myrtle Barden and Amada Machado. Past President Anna D. Pierce composed the following, entitled "Homeless Children":

Dainty hemstitching, narrow and fine,
Stitches like feathers from white dove's wings,
Tiny french knots like soldiers in line,—
For somebody else's baby things.

A wide, straight hem where the stitches don't show,
A wee, round neck where the fine lace clings,
Small pearl buttons all in a row,—
For somebody else's baby things.

Draw out a thread for each little tuck,
Make a design of three fairy rings,
Keep the seams smooth, don't let them ruck,—
On somebody else's baby things.

Work with your fingers, don't let them stop,
Though your heart's aching, somebody sings;
Keep back the tears, don't let them drop,—
On somebody else's baby things.

THE DEATH RECORD.

Ray John Solomon, affiliated with Los Angeles Parlor No. 45 N.S.G.W., was recently killed in an aeroplane accident in Mexico. He was born at Los Angeles, March 15, 1908, and is survived by a father, Bennie Solomon, also a member of Los Angeles.

Captain David Weldt, brother of Joseph Weldt (Sepulveda N.S.), died recently at Oakland. He was a native of California, aged 78.

Harold Stanley Nichols, brother of Roland Nichols (Los Angeles N.S.), died recently at Calexico, Imperial County.

Mrs. Grace Lopez-Wilson, mother of John J. Wilson (Ramona N.S.), passed away October 25 at San Fernando. She was a native of Los Angeles County, aged 65.

Mrs. Mary E. Coyle, mother of John P. Coyle (Ramona N.S.), passed away October 25 at the age of 75.

John F. Luden, brother of Robert J. Luden (Ramona N.S.), died November 15.

Hilliard W. Lewis, father of Hick Lewis (Los Angeles N.S.), died November 17.

Albert J. Howland, brother of Robert S. Howland (Los Angeles N.S.), died November 18.

PERSONAL PARAGRAPHS.

John V. Scott (Ramona N.S.) was a visitor last month to Imperial Valley.

Emil Plath (Ramona N.S.), who resides in Taft, was a visitor last month.

Miss Matilda Rambeau (Los Angeles N.D.), was wedded November 1 to Marius Besson.

Mrs. Anna E. Van de Sandt (Los Angeles N.D.) and her family are now residing at Roscoe.

Municipal Judge George J. Steiger (Stanford N.S.) of San Francisco was a visitor last month.

Mrs. Julia Waddington (Vendome N.D.) of San Jose is visiting relatives and friends in Los Angeles.

Miss Kathryn Ronan (Los Angeles N.D.) has returned to Death Valley for the winter and the spring.

Granville Pitzer (Sepulveda N.S.) was recently married and is now making his home in Los Angeles.

Vivian Wickser and Erlinda Sepulveda (both Los Angeles N.D.) went to Berkeley to see the football game.

John M. Larronde (Ramona N.S.) has been appointed by Mayor John C. Porter a member of the Los Angeles Fire Commission.

ASSISTING UNEMPLOYED.

Glendale—Verdugo Parlor No. 240 N.D.G.W. had a card party November 19, with Clytelle Hewitt as chairman. President Rose Bartel has appointed Myrteze Tregea head of a special committee to assist in Christmas work at Sawtelle. Nan Hutchinson represents the Parlor in the work being sponsored by the Glendale Chamber of Commerce for the unemployed.

SEASON LIGHT OPERA PROMISED.

The Municipalities Light Opera Association of Southern California, now in process of organization for a season of sixteen weeks of light opera, is developing upon a broader scope than even anticipated, and is now in the process of incorporation upon a national basis, with districts to be allocated throughout the entire United States. California South will always be District No. 1, and general headquarters always will be the parent organization in Los Angeles.

Season books for the eight operas will soon go on sale and the opening performance is hoped to be set for Christmas night. The Municipalities Light Opera Association is a non-profit, nonpartisan and non-sectarian organization, and aside from supplying an outlet for the talents of singers, musicians and composers of California South, will give direct employment to 125 people and indirectly to about 400 more. Officers of the organization are Mrs. Grace Widney Mabee, president; Rex B. Goodcell, treasurer; Frank M. Rainger, director general; W. T. Wyatt, business manager.

DESERVED TESTIMONIAL.

Trustees, alumni, faculty and friends of the University of Southern California, as well as representatives of national and local educational institutions and civic organizations, are joining in a testimonial of respect, gratitude and affection at an anniversary banquet, December 12, honoring President Rufus B. von KleinSmid on the completion of the first ten years of his administration at the Trojan institution. Delegations of students representing the twenty schools and colleges of S.C. also are to pay homage to the educator at the honor function.

Dr. von KleinSmid became president at Southern California in 1921, and 1931 marks the culmination of a decade of service and achievement as educator, organizer and internationalist. Since 1921 the University of Southern California has almost tripled in student enrollment, the faculty has about doubled, seven schools and colleges have been added, and seven new buildings have been erected.

DAD'S NEW FACTORY.

Dad's Cookie Company, makers of the famous "Dad's Original Scotch Oatmeal Cookies," is now located in new quarters at 9309 South Vermont avenue. There was a grand opening November 12, when many people inspected the plant and saw how the cookies are made.

LICENSE RENEWAL TIME APPROACHES; PLATES HAVE CALIFORNIA IN FULL.

Within less than a month renewal of automobile license plates will begin for more than two million California car owners. The renewal period will open December 15 and continue for thirty days. The procedure for renewing registration and obtaining 1932 license plates remains practically unchanged from the method in effect last year.

The white slip certificate of registration is presented with the amount of the fee, which is $3 for all pleasure motor cars. Commercial cars pay a graduated scale of weight fees in addition to the $3. Where the white slip has been lost or mutilated the pink slip is presented and an additional charge of 50 cents is made for issuance of a new white certificate.

In accordance with a new provision enacted by the last Legislature, motorists should give the number of cylinders and serial number of their cars.

After close of the legal registration period, January 15, state officers will investigate cars operated without the new plates and issue citations unless the motorist can show a receipt or other evidence of having applied. In order to allow for transit of new plates in the mails, motorists will have until January 31 to attach them. The plates will have black lettering on an orange background, reversing the 1931 color scheme, and will have the name "California" spelled out instead of abbreviated.

SACRAMENTO NATIVE SONS INITIATE LARGE CLASS; PROMISE BIG THINGS.

(Special to The Grizzly Bear.)

Sacramento City—A class of forty-three candidates were initiated for the following N.S.G.W. Parlors of Sacramento County November 23: Sacramento No. 3, Sunset No. 26, Elk Grove No. 41, Courtland No. 106 and Sutter Fort No. 241. The initiatory ceremony was conducted by a picked team from General John A. Sutter Past Presidents Assembly. Among the initiates was Myril Hoag, Sacramento baseball star who was recently sold to one of the big league clubs for $75,000. There were many visitors from surrounding Parlors.

At the ceremonies' conclusion a banquet was served, with Irving D. Gibson as the toastmaster. Addresses were delivered by Grand President Dr. Frank I. Gonzalez, Grand Secretary John T. Regan, Superior Judge Malcolm C. Glenn and Deputy State Attorney-General Jesse Hession. J. J. Longshore, chairman of the membership campaign committee, stated this class initiation was but the beginning of big things to be accomplished by the Capital City Native Sons.

WASHINGTON BICENTENNIAL STAMPS.

To commemorate the bicentennial anniversary of George Washington, first President of the United States, the Federal Postoffice Department is preparing a series of special postage stamps in twelve denominations from one-half cent to ten cents, both inclusive.

The stamps will be placed on general sale January 2, 1932, and will be kept on sale throughout that year. Each stamp will have as the central design a separate likeness of George Washington.

WHAT IS A CLOUDBURST?

Rain falls during rainfall, but clouds do not burst when there is a "cloudburst." United States Weather Bureau experts say that sometimes strong upward currents of air hold raindrops up from underneath and prevent them from promptly reaching the ground. Then the drops gather in much larger quantities than they usually do. When the upward air currents lessen, or so much water accumulates that the air cannot support it, there occurs the deluge of rain that we call a cloudburst.

"Boosters" Organize—The Shasta-Cascade Wonderland Association has been organized to "boost" the scenic beauties of the Mount Shasta and the Cascade Mountain district.

International Institute—The eighth annual session of the Institute of International Relations will be held December 13-18 at Riverside City.

"Mule in a barnyard, lazy and sick; boy with a pin on end of a stick; boy jabbed the mule, mule gave a lurch; services Monday at the community church."—Exchange.

MY MESSAGE

To All Native Born Californians

I, DR. FRANK I. GONZALEZ, GRAND PRESIDENT OF THE ORDER OF NATIVE SONS OF THE GOLDEN WEST, DO HEREBY APPEAL TO ALL NATIVE BORN CALIFORNIANS OF THE WHITE MALE RACE BORN WITHIN THE STATE OF CALIFORNIA, OF THE AGE OF EIGHTEEN YEARS AND UPWARD, OF GOOD HEALTH AND CHARACTER, AND WHO BELIEVE IN THE EXISTENCE OF A SUPREME BEING, TO JOIN OUR FRATERNITY AND THEREBY ASSIST IN THE AIMS AND PURPOSES OF THE ORGANIZATION:

To arouse Loyalty and Patriotism for State and for Nation.

To elevate and improve the Manhood upon which the destiny of our country depends.

To encourage interest in all matters and measures relating to the material upbuilding of the State of California.

To assist in the development of the wonderful natural resources of California.

To protect the forests, conserve the waters, improve the rivers and the harbors, and beautify the towns and the cities.

To collect, make known and preserve the romantic history of California.

To restore and preserve all the historic landmarks of the State.

To provide homes for California's homeless children, regardless of race, creed or color.

To keep this State a paradise for the American Citizen by thwarting the organized efforts of all undesirable peoples to control its destiny.

THE ORDER OF NATIVE SONS OF THE GOLDEN WEST IS THE ONLY FRATERNITY IN EXISTENCE WHOSE MEMBERSHIP IS MADE UP EXCLUSIVELY OF WHITE NATIVE BORN AMERICANS.

. . . Builded upon the Foundation Stones of — **Friendship, Loyalty, Charity**

IT PRESENTS TO THE NATIVE BORN CALIFORNIAN THE MOST PRODUCTIVE FIELD IN WHICH TO SOW HIS ENERGIES, AND IF HE BE A FAITHFUL CULTIVATOR AND DESIRES TO TAKE ADVANTAGE OF THE OPPORTUNITY AFFORDED HIM, HE WILL REAP A RICH HARVEST IN THE KNOWLEDGE THAT HE HAS BEEN FAITHFUL TO CALIFORNIA AND DILIGENT IN PROTECTING ITS WELFARE.

DR. FRANK I. GONZALEZ,

GRAND PRESIDENT N.S.G.W.

The undersigned, having formed a favorable opinion of the Order of Native Sons of the Golden West, desires additional information.

Name ....

Address ....

City or Town..............................

For further information sign the accompanying blank and mail to

GRAND SECRETARY N.S.G.W.,
302 Native Sons Bldg.,
414 Mason St.,
SAN FRANCISCO, California

nians

OF THE GOLDEN WEST,
LE RACE BORN WITHIN
OF GOOD HEALTH AND
JOIN OUR FRATERNITY

hip

IVE FIELD IN WHICH TO
O TAKE ADVANTAGE OF
E KNOWLEDGE THAT HE
LFARE

LEZ,
PRESIDENT N.S.G.W.

RETARY N.S.G.W.,
CISCO, California

Grizzly Bear

JANUARY — THE ONLY OFFICIAL PUBLICATION OF THE NATIVE SONS AND DAUGHTERS OF THE GOLDEN WEST — 1932

Featuring

GENERAL NEWS OF INTEREST CONCERNING ALL CALIFORNIA, and ORDERS NATIVE SONS and NATIVE DAUGHTERS

Price: 15 Cents

UNCLE JIM'S FARM

William A. Evans

The accompanying story came to The Grizzly Bear from William A. Evans of San Diego City, affiliated with San Diego Parlor No. 108 N.S.G.W., with this notation: "In an unguarded moment I became a native son of this state, therefore it gives me great pleasure to do anything within my power to cheer up those who have found themselves in the same predicament. Hence, this sketch is tendered The Grizzly Bear."—Editor.

WE WERE SEATED AT A TABLE IN the Blue Fox, one of those picturesque little spots that Tiajuana, Mexico, is so full of. My friend, Al, sitting across from me, had been silent for some time. His beer glass was now empty. He was gazing absently at the foamy sediment in the bottom. "And what," I asked, "causes the wrinkles of deep thought on your otherwise noble brow?"

Al was just out from the East, and I had taken it upon myself to show him the sights. Tiajuana had been as good a place as any to start on, so we had flivvered down from San Diego, resolving to commence at the bottom and work upwards, as it were. It was the first day of January, and we were reviewing the remains of an hilarious New Year's Eve. The "remains" being what was disturbing Al, as I am soon to learn.

"It all reminds me of my uncle's farm," he said at last. "My Uncle Jim, in Iowa."

"Come, come," I said. "Are you trying to make fun of my efforts as a rubberneck-wagon spieler?"

"Oh, no," he said hastily. "You're coming along fine. You might tell that bandit to trot out some more beer, however."

"Hey, Pancho Villa," I called to a white-aproned lad who was dashing by. "Another pitcher of beer. A big one this time." The Mexican boy gave me a wan, tired smile, then hurried off. Soon he returned, and we were again looking into the foam that leaves a mustache.

From where we were sitting, you could see the street and all the passersby. All along the outer edge of the sidewalk sat large tubs of garbage, each filling the air with its own individual aroma. Orange rinds, half-eaten sandwiches and all the other forms of remains that follow all successful happenings made up the garbage. It was interesting to watch the people outside fall over these tubs. They always laughed, and some of them even went back to give it another try.

It was now well into the middle of the morning, yet many of the men and women about were attired in evening dress, thinking, no doubt, it was still night. These people must have been from Los Angeles, as the only people in San Diego that wear tuxedos are waiters or fraternity boys. The rest of the population go about in blue serge suits when dressed up. They do this, I have been told, because Will Rogers has a habit of dropping down here from Beverly Hills, unexpectedly, and they always wish to make him feel right at home. It seems that Will is very ticklish about the ribs, and starts to giggle whenever a tailor tries to measure him for a tuxedo. Hence the measurements are always off, so Will just goes without.

Both Al and I felt a little out of it, as we had not yet had time to become as drunk as the rest. However, all comes to he who waits. That is, of course, if he has the price, and a rubber-lined stomach.

Two girls, not more than eighteen years old, if that, came in. They were followed by a pair of elderly looking men. The four had on evening clothes and looked very grand indeed, except for the fact that the girls had a great many liquors stains on the fronts of their otherwise lovely gowns. One of the men must have been the father to the taller of the girls, as we heard her call him "daddy." The other called her escort just plain "honey," and let it go at that.

Al seemed interested in the girl who had "daddy" along, so I said, "Go over and ask her for a dance. She looks like a nice girl. Even your Uncle Jim would approve."

Al looked at me for a moment without answering. Then he said, "It all reminds me of Uncle Jim's farm." "Forget it," I said.

When Al starts in about his uncle, it is time to change the subject. Al is such a devoted nephew, he might rave on forever. Then I would never have a chance to tell him of these sights I am showing off.

Our table was right near the entrance, close by a nice little potted palm that tickled the back of Al's neck whenever he teetered in his chair. Nearly everyone that entered the Blu Fox found it necessary to lurch over in our di rection, then right themselves with the back o my chair, or the table. From us, they always made a beeline for the bar. Here they got on foot (always the left one) hooked over the foot-rail, then commenced to shout loudly for serv ice.

Whenever a group came in together, ther was always one fellow who appeared to be th biggest-hearted man in all the world.

"'son me," he would cry. "What'll it be?' "Atta boy," the rest always cried. "Good ol Smith."

Our pitcher of beer was again empty. Al stil lacked the sparkling eyes that a tourist mus have to enjoy the sights, so I decided to tak more drastic steps.

"How about a shot of old Judge?" I urged "Or maybe you would prefer Three Star Hen esy?"

Al shook his head. "Let's go outside an walk around," he said.

We pushed back our chairs and, after side stepping a party of newcomers who looked a bi sleepy, found ourselves outside close up to th tubs of "remains."

"Let's cross the street," I said. "I want t show you the longest bar in the world, so it' said." This was a sight that, I felt sure, woul make his eyes pop open.

We entered at one end, so as to gaze the ful length of the bar. I had saved this sight unti last, it being my big climax. As far down th line as you could see, ran the mahogany bar. I was at least three city blocks long. The mirror in back of the bartenders reflected the swarm o customers, lined up flank to flank. Some wer tossing off whisky with a flourish. Others wer gulping down foam-topped beer. Still others not drinking at all, were draped over the edg of the bar, their heads resting on any shoulde excepting their own.

Half-way down the bar, a fat woman in a low backed evening gown suddenly sat down on the floor with a bang. This called for a great deal of laughter, and more drinks. The woman was helped to her feet by a nearby man, but sh promptly sat down again.

I stood there in wonder. This is the bar tha all true San Diegans point to with pride. A last, my admiration appeased, I turned to Al

(Continued on Page 5)

GRIZZLY GROWLS

(CLARENCE M. HUNT.)

NOTHING IS BASICALLY WRONG WITH this nation! That may, at first glance, appear as a queer statement,—especially in view of the "magnificent depression" afflicting the country,—but it is, nevertheless, an incontrovertible fact. The ation today has the wealth of limitless reources and of splendid attributes with which t was blessed in the heyday of its "most stounding prosperity." What, then, can the rouble be?

The political system in vogue is all wrong, imply that and nothing more! This governnent, originally of The People, for The People nd by The People, is rapidly degenerating into ne of the politicians, for the classes and by the nterests. The masses have been supplanted by avored classes, and the masses are paying learly for their folly in relinquishing the reins f government. Public officials, generally speakng,—national, state, county, city and township —formerly considered servants of The People, ıave become the slaves of the interests, and ;ive first, last and all consideration to the deigns and wishes of their new masters. Graft, etty and otherwise, law disrespect and incometency are rampant throughout the political ystem.

The People, themselves, are responsible for his damnable system, through the operation of which democracy is proceeding hastily to eventıal doom. They have been cleverly propaganlied into believing that black is white; that the lasses' slaves will, if entrusted with public ofice, be the masses' faithful servants; that, in brief, the impossible is possible. The People have been completely and woefully deceived, and no healthy recovery from existant conditions is possible until they rise in their might and, through the ballot-box, reassume control of government throughout the nation.

The crying need today of these United States is a Moses—not of the political horde, however, —to lead the masses out of the wilderness of depression—the slough of nation-wide putrid political conditions! The selection of a leader must not be entrusted to the major political parties, for they are controlled and operated by one and the same aggregation of higherups whose scheme has always been to, at the opportune times, let loose a smokescreen of supposed party antagonisms and divergence of views, to deceive the masses. And their plans have worked out, to their entire satisfaction; irrespective of how the ballot has gone, they have won, and the masses have lost. Will The People continue to be misled, through cunning and deceit? Surely, this nation must have the needed leader, now and always beyond the reach of the classes, who could and will serve the masses faithfully and well.

"God give us men. The time demands
Strong minds, great hearts, true faith, and ruling hands:
Men whom the lust of office does not kill;
Men whom the spoils of office can not buy;
Men who possess opinions and a will;
Men who have honor; men who will not lie;
Men who can stand before a demagogue
And damn his treacherous flatteries without winking;
Tall men, sun crowned, who live above the fog,
In public duty and in private thinking!
Wrong rules the land, and waiting justice sleeps!"

State Controller Ray Riley reports the cost of the California State Government for the fiscal year ended June 30, 1931, as $124,153,-145, an increase over the preceding year of $5,312,185. Annually since 1924 the cost of state government in California has steadily mounted, increasing $12,846,947 in 1925, $6,-203,953 in 1926, $4,762,504 in 1927, $3,016,-438 in 1928, $20,037,155 in 1929, $8,189,609 in 1930, and $5,312,185 in 1931.

The unwarranted spending orgy of The People's money must cease, for the taxpayers are becoming bankrupt, industry is being crippled and the development of the state is being retarded. Captioned "Political Spending Boosts Taxes," the "San Francisco Chronicle" of December 11 had a commonsense editorial on the tax subject:

"Nation, states, counties, cities—congress, legislatures, boards of supervisors, city councils—have all acquired the easy spending habit. So taxes go up. Industry and business are burdened. So is every individual. . . . The only way to keep taxes down is to spend less. The first place to cut is in the political spending indulged in by congress, legislatures, boards of supervisors and city councils. This kind of spending is the principal tax booster in this and many other countries. Many of the biggest appropriations by legislative bodies of all sorts are chiefly for the purpose of catching votes for the members. . . . Legislators bank on the belief that the voter does not realize that he is also the taxpayer. When the people generally understand that they—all of them —foot the politicians' bills for vote collecting, legislators will have to go slow on this sort of spending. That will cut down taxes. To tax less, spend less!"

Funds are required for the operation of the Federal Government, and taxation provides the sole method for securing needed revenue. Every loyal citizen of these United States should contribute, willingly and promptly, his fair share of the necessary funds. In a recent message to the Congress, President Herbert Hoover suggested various procedures for raising additional tax-funds. One very important source of revenue, however, appears to have been overlooked:

The income-tax exemption, now enjoyed, at the expense of others, by public officeholders and all others in the service of The People, should be eliminated from the provisions of the national income-tax law. No group of citizens are better able than they to contribute to the cost of government. They receive good salaries, promptly, and vast numbers of them are not propertyowners, and pay no direct national or state taxes. Neither are they burdened with the worry of providing the wherewith to meet the cost of their services; that worry is, along with the tax-burden, saddled onto the businessman, the propertyowner, and the other over-burdened direct-taxpayers.

No public servant—national, state, county, city or township—should be exempted from the provisions of the national income-tax law. As a matter of fact, there are today far too many tax-exempt classes of citizens in this country. None should be exempted, excepting those in active service in the Army and the Navy. Now is the opportune time to correct this inequality in taxation, which is unsound in principle. Through its correction, the Federal Government's income-tax revenue would be materially increased, and every citizen with a taxable income would contribute his full share toward the upkeep of the National Government.

Representation without taxation is equally as unjust, burdensome and dangerous as taxation without representation!

"Mexicans are putting the Chinese out of Mexico to make jobs for her own workers," says a communicant to the "Sacramento Bee," and he then inquires: "Why can't California put enough Mexicans out of this state to make jobs for Californians?" Suggest the query be direcfed to the State Chamber of Commerce and its affiliates. They know!

Direct-mail advertising enthusiasts should be interested in this: The Federal Postoffice Department announces that during the 1931 fiscal year they wasted nearly $325,000 in postage, because of obsolete mailing lists; and that 6,-450,164 circulars directed to prospective buyers were disposed of as waste in the dead-letter section. These figures, too, apply only to circulars sent under first-class postage. A much larger amount was lost by those using third-class postage.

A movement for an extra session of the State Legislature, "to deal with the unemployment situation," is gaining momentum, but should be permanently sidetracked. Lawmakers and attaches, not the unemployed, would be the chief beneficiaries therefrom. Use the cost of an extra session for a worthy cause—the relief of distress. If less be expended for commissions and other "overheads" incidental to the investigating of unemployment, more will be available for the unemployed.

The Modesto, Stanislaus County, City Council has issued this edict to municipal employes: "Pay your bills or be fired!" That should be the strictly-enforced policy in every branch of government.

A recent flareup anent the use of California's gasoline-tax monies brought this statement from State Finance Director Roland Vandegrift: "Camouflaged and misleading statements that all state highways are being built and maintained from gasoline taxes and motor-vehicle license fees should be corrected and the facts made known. The facts are, that the interest and redemption of bonds are paid out of general funds."

This referred-to camouflage is just an example of the deceit generally prevalent in governmental circles. Vandegrift's contention, that the principal and interest of highway bonds is an expenditure for highway purposes and therefore should be paid from gas-tax funds, is sound reasoning and should prevail.

Representative French of Idaho has introduced in the Federal Congress a bill to prohibit the advertising of lotteries and gift enterprises by radio. The proposed legislation is, as he contends, "in line with the best thought and practice of the United States." It should be approved by the Congress.

Effort is being put forth to promote home buying by those of moderate means for, as President Herbert Hoover remarked at a recent conference, "Such people are a good risk. They are the very basis of stability to the nation."

(Continued on Page 9)

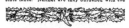

May the Ship that enters Your Harbor during 1932 be filled with a Cargo of Health, Happiness and Success

The Grizzly Bear Magazine
The ALL California Monthly
OWNED, CONTROLLED, PUBLISHED BY GRIZZLY BEAR PUBLISHING CO., (Incorporated)
COMPOSED OF NATIVE SONS.
HERMAN C. LICHTENBERGER, Pres.
JOHN T. NEWELL RAY HOWARD
WM. I. TRAEGER LORENZO F. SOTO
CHAS. R. THOMAS HARRY J. LELANDE
ARTHUR A. SCHMIDT, Vice-Pres.
BOARD OF DIRECTORS
CLARENCE M. HUNT
General Manager and Editor
OFFICIAL ORGAN AND THE ONLY OFFICIAL PUBLICATION OF THE NATIVE SONS AND THE NATIVE DAUGHTERS GOLDEN WEST.
ISSUED FIRST EACH MONTH.
FORMS CLOSE 20th MONTH.
ADVERTISING RATES ON APPLICATION.
SAN FRANCISCO OFFICE:
N.S.G.W. BLDG., 414 MASON ST., RM. 302
(Office Grand Secretary N.S.G.W.)
Telephone: Kearney 1223
SAN FRANCISCO, CALIFORNIA
PUBLICATION OFFICE:
309-15 WILCOX BLDG., 2nd AND SPRING,
Telephone: VAndike 6234
LOS ANGELES, CALIFORNIA
(Entered as second-class matter May 29, 1918, at the Postoffice at Los Angeles, California, under the act of August 24, 1912.)
PUBLISHED REGULARLY SINCE MAY 1907
VOL. L WHOLE NO. 297

THE ROMANCE OF SAN BERNARDINO

Clara M. Barton

This story, which came to The Grizzly Bear from Miss Clara M. Barton of San Bernardino, a member of Lugonia Parlor No. 241 N.D.G.W. of that city, will appear serially. It deals interestingly with the history of the San Bernardino Valley, and is copyrighted by the author. —Editor.

MARCH 14, 1774, JUAN BAUTISTA Anza, the first White man to enter the San Bernardino Valley, led his small train of weary disciples down through the San Gorgonia Pass. They were tired and a little discouraged, and the hardships they faced, as they treked across the Colorado Desert, were vividly marked upon their faces. Some of the children of the caravan were crying, some were laughing, and the smallest of them were finding solace in their mothers' arms. Many of the wagons were scarred with the experiences encountered, and the horses and oxen were exhausted from their long, hard pull. Even the dogs, which had been so faithful, showed signs of the laborious journey.

Anza turned to his little, courageous band, raised his hand in a command to halt and said, "God has been good to us all, dear ones, for He has led us to the end of the rainbow." Little did he know that before him lay one more obstacle which he would have to conquer before he had finally found his resting-place.

One of the riders of a very tired horse cupped his hand over his eyes, looked down into a peaceful valley and turned to Anza and said, "Look, friend, to the serene and welcoming land before us! Yes, it is indeed the end of the rainbow, and a realization of our dreams. Captain Anza, we are all very tired. After we enter this new country, we do not want to go any farther. Why cannot we linger down there for a long rest? Why cannot we build a colony there in which future generations may live?"

Anza looked at the rider, gazed into the distance, nodded his head and said solemnly, "Yes, this looks as if it is a land in which we can establish ourselves. It is a pleasant sight to the eyes, isn't it, to see such a valley that is protected by those majestically built mountains. But come, let us journey on before the dusk sets in." And so Captain Anza continued to lead his train of covered wagons down the steep slopes and trackless ravines.

Several hours later he found himself pushing, pulling, straining every muscle and giving curt orders, as he and the tired but hardy members of his band succeeded in forging the rapid and sandy river of the Santa Ana. The wagons were full of mud and water, and their contents were watersoaked, broken and in a shapeless mass. The horses were dripping with sweat, and the men were breathing hard, when they finally succeeded in landing safely upon the side of the river that was to become their home.

Night had come. Bonfires were built, and in the stillness Anza called his group to gather around the blazing timbers. He offered a prayer of thanksgiving to God, and to the saints who had guided them so kindly and safely to this haven. He thanked his courageous men and women for facing the hardships and disasters, and told them of his faith in and of his deep love for them. Then wishing them a good night's rest, he said, in parting, "God bless you all." Then he left them to receive their much-needed and well-earned rest.

Bright and early the next morning Anza was up and upon his horse. He was riding away from his circle of covered wagons, to explore the country around him. His first thought was to find a spring or flow of water which he could develop for domestic use. He had not gone far, however, when he accosted two fine-looking Indian braves. What took place between them and the lone White man has never been recorded, but Anza brought the Indians into his camp and a friendship was formed, but not of long standing. However, discovering that Anza was becoming their friend, the Indians decided to help him in some way. Since Anza did not understand the sign language nor the Indians the English language, it required grunts and motions of the arms and head, to make him understand that they wished to help him with some valuable information. So he followed them toward a towering mountain, which bore a scar in the shape of a perfect arrowhead.

"What is this?" exclaimed Anza, as he gazed with rapture at the mountain. The Indians answered with more undistinguishable signs, but continuing to point to the ground they were successful in attracting their friend's attention to a flowing stream of warm water.

Anza gazed at it in astonishment. "What a wonderful thing this is!" he exclaimed, as he stooped to let his fingers play in the rippling stream. He found the water warm, and the spring was full. He wended his way back to the camp with the Indians, and knew that this was the beginning of the building of a new empire!

A few days later the majority of the caravan made a final decision to go no further—that this valley, surrounded by majestic mountains and carpeted by fertile soil, should become a settlement.

During the construction of a few crude living quarters, Anza began to wonder. Here were his good people becoming contented in their new achievement and environment. The men working with the timber were singing; the women were happily unpacking their possessions; the children were laughing as they ran after one another in and out of the wagons; the dogs were stretched out full length in the shade of the trees, and the horses and oxen were peacefully grazing on some of the wild grasses near by. Anza did not wonder why his people were trying to forget their hardships, nor why they felt that this was to be their home. He felt that he was at peace with his God, and that all would be well. But here he was with his small band of Pioneers in a most delightful country which bore no name! "This can never do," he thought. But no name came to his mind that would be suitable for such a country as this! In time, however, his thoughts turned to the names of the saints, and the first to enter his mind was that of Saint Joseph. With this thought in mind, and knowing that his settlers would agree with his suggestion, he had them cease their labors and come to him. Mounting the nearby stump of a fallen oak, he told them briefly of his plans and wanted suggestions as to a rightful name.

"We cannot live in a valley of contentment such as this, without giving it a name, can we? No more than your child should go nameless after its birth. So we should not let our colony go unnamed." He looked at each one of his listeners, searching their faces for some sort of an expression. "I have tried," he continued, "to come to some final action as to the best name suitable, and have at last decided there is only one, and that is El Valle de San Jose. It was the good Saint Joseph who guided us out of difficult places, and we can honor him in no better way than this. Are there any other better suggestions? Let no one be silent."

There were slight murmurs from some of the people, and then followed an enthusiastic applause. Anza smiled, descended from the stump, stooped and picked up a handful of soil, again ascended the stump and faced his faithful little group. Turning his face eastward, he raised his hand over his head and, as he let the gravel drop from his fingers, he said reverently, "In the name of the Father, the Son and the Holy Ghost, I name this valley of peace and contentment which lies protected between these mountains and hills, El Valle de San Jose, or the Valley of Saint Joseph." A short prayer followed, and for several years the settlement retained the name of El Valle de San Jose.

Anza found himself not alone in the founding of the valley, as two priests, Fathers Garces and Diaz, led an expedition to the valley in 1775. They and their followers had suffered many hardships. Realizing this, and how much in need of a rest they were, Captain Anza bade the two heroic men and their band a welcome to the camp. Everything was done for them in the way of comfort.

"What a happy surprise this is, Captain Anza," Father Garces remarked after introductions were made and every one had rested. "I never dreamed that we would enter into such a valley as this and find friends like you awaiting us! We came through two beautiful valleys, in one of which we encountered several bears." Little did he know that these two valleys were later to be named Big Bear and Holcomb!

"It was a surprise to us, also, padre," remarked Anza, "because we never expected to see such a land as this! But it is a wonderful surprise to all of us. By the way, did you have any hardships coming?" "Not as many as I expected. The monotony of this trip was somewhat relieved by a few storms, two marriages, one birth and three deaths."

Anza chuckled. "Well, that wasn't so bad. We only had rain, mud, sand and water to go through, two deaths and two births. But since we have arrived and gotten partly settled, it now looks as if there is to be a wedding soon."

Father Garces looked at Anza and smiled. "Shall I remain here for a few days, in case that I am needed?" Anza smiled back at the padre, slowly winked and nodded his head. "It would save a lot of time in trying to find a marrying parson, padre."

Padre Garces nodded to Anza and then proceeded to look at the various shacks being erected. "Do your people plan to remain here long? I see that they are beginning to erect some buildings." Anza also looked in the direction of the construction work. "Yes, father, my people have decided that this country is to be their home."

Looking earnestly at Anza, the padre continued: "I have been establishing missions along the route, and I have been almost convinced that this is one of the best sites in which to build and establish one. I saw several Indians as I entered the valley, and I am sure that this tribe can be taught not only to be friendly with the White man but to learn about God. I want to help you build up a colony that will live!"

Anza reached for the padre's hand. "Father, I am glad that you came, and I shall do all I can to help you." And with this, the foundation of a thriving city was laid.

EPISODE 2.

POLITANA

May 20, 1810, became more than a feast day to the good Father Dumetz. It was a day of victory over impassable róads, through severe storms and deep, shifting sands. He had seen many of his fellowmen die by the wayside, and food and clothing disappear, but he did not become discouraged. He trudged on.

"On this day, we shall be at the Valle de San Jose. There we will find peace and contentment. Do not become discouraged, friends, as I am sure that rest, food and shelter are awaiting us," consoled the padre to his struggling band of fifty men and women.

Father Dumetz left San Gabriel Mission at daybreak two days before, with orders from the good Father Junipero Serra to establish a supply station or mission near or at El Valle de San Jose settlement. This was his goal, and he was nearing it with a strong and brave heart.

It had been twenty-four years since anyone, except Anza and his band, had entered and made his home in this valley. A new generation had taken command of the colony and, like the past generation, was making all newcomers more than welcome. But the dispositions of the Indians had not changed in all these years. The padre found they were preparing for war with the White man!

"We must avert this trouble, if we can," he told his men. "The Indian must be tamed, for he is like a wild colt. My faithful followers, this day is the feast day for the great Saint Bernard, and we must honor his name." With this, the loyal band of Padre Dumetz entered into the Valle de San Jose.

"Father!" exclaimed one of the priests, "this is a wonderful place in which to establish a branch of the San Gabriel. We cannot go much farther. Why can't we settle here for a while? There is no supply station or mission here, and there is need of one." "You are right, padre, and we shall stop here," replied Dumetz.

The few settlers who were toiling the soil saw the train coming and went to meet it. They gave the padres and their band of fifty a warm welcome and the priests then felt that their hard journey had not been in vain.

"You have come to the Valle de San Jose, father, and we bid you welcome! We give you rest and shelter," said one of the settlers. Thus the tired members of the caravan were escorted into the settlement.

Early in the afternoon, Padre Dumetz held an informal conference with the members of his band. "The name of Valle de San Jose should be changed," he told them. "It does not suit this valley. There is a San Jose in the northern part of the state already, and we must avoid conflicting names of our stations. We must have names that can never be erased or discarded. Here it is the feast day of Saint Bernard of Sienna, and to celebrate this day and to honor this splendid saint of ours, I believe that it would be more than appropriate that we change the name of this Valley of San Jose to that of the saint." His listeners made no reply, but all were pondering. They finally agreed that in no more fitting way could they commemorate the name of the saint who had guided them to this prospering territory.

(Continued on Page 23)

A TRAGEDY OF THE PAST

THEY SAY TRUTH IS STRANGER THAN fiction, and after reading the following California news item of seventy-seven years ago, one may well so believe. It was resurrected by James E. Stewart of Auburn, Placer County, who has one of the best collections of original historical material to be found in that vicinity: "THE AUBURN WHIG, M. E. Mills, Editor, Saturday Morning, December 30, 1854. BY TELEGRAPH! Expressly for the Auburn Whig.

"DESPERATE FIGHT! THREE MINERS ATTACKED BY 11 ROBBERS! CONFESSION OF THE ROBBERS! FOUR AMERICANS AND SIX CHINESE ROBBED AND MURDERED. HEROIC CONDUCT OF CAPT. DAVIS. DESTRUCTION OF THE GANG.

"We received the following startling intelligence last night from the office of the MOUNTAIN DEMOCRAT, after our paper had been worked off: Placerville, Dec. 23. Rocky Canon, the place of the tragedy, is a deep and almost inaccessible canon, about forty miles north of this place, near Todd's Valley, and uninhabited.

"Rocky Canon, Dec. 20, 1854. ED. MOUNTAIN DEMOCRAT: No officer having been within a convenient distance to attend to a case of emergency that has just happened near our isolated camp in the mountains here, the undersigned constituted themselves a coroner's jury and held an inquest over the deceased bodies of twelve men that were killed within a mile of our camp on the 19th inst., a full account of which we deemed it our duty to publish. Three of the undersigned were eye witnesses to the whole scene, though too far off to give aid in any way, and the rest of us can readily vouch for their veracity.

"On yesterday, the 19th inst., three men, who afterwards proved to be a Mr. James C. McDonald of Ala., now deceased; a Dr. Boliver A. Sparks of Miss., and a Capt. Jonathan R. Davis of South Carolina, were traveling on foot on a trail within a mile of our camp, to prospect a vein of gold bearing quartz some twenty or thirty miles north of this. As they were passing at the base of a mountain, three of the undersigned, being out on a hunting excursion on its side, saw a party of eleven men, who were concealed in the bushes near the trail, spring up and commence shooting at them. Mr. McDonald had fallen dead ere he fired a pistol, or was even aware of his danger. He and his party had nothing but their revolvers. Dr. Sparks shot twice at the banditti, and then fell severely wounded. In the meantime, Capt. Davis, who was the first to commence shooting, in defense of himself and party, in an instant after the first volley from the robbers, being still unhurt, kept up an incessant firing upon them with his revolver—every ball forcing its victim to bite the dust, until all the loads of both parties seemed to have been discharged.

"The only four surviving robbers made a charge upon Capt. Davis, three with bowie-knives and one with a short sword, or sabre. Capt. D. stood firmly on his ground, until they rushed up abreast within about four steps of him, when he made a spring upon them with a large bowie-knife, warded off their blows as fast as they were aimed at him, gave three of them wounds that soon proved fatal, and having wounded the other one very slightly, and disarmed him by throwing his knife in the air in warding off a blow—as this last man expressed in a tone of gratitude before his death. Capt. D. went to work at once, tearing up his own shirt and binding up all the wounds of the living, both of his friends and his enemies.

"In our examination of the persons of the deceased of those that commenced the attack on Capt. D. and party, we discovered papers, care-

The accompanying came to The Grizzly Bear from Wendell T. Robie of Auburn Parlor No. 59 N.S.G.W., who says the quoted "article is of unquestioned authenticity. Only in a few exceptional cases can the prowess shown by this Captain Davis be matched on the pages of history. Had such a fight been put up for the service of his country, rather than the defense of his life, Captain Davis would have been rewarded with an emblem of valor. It is a decidedly interesting example of the valor of our Pioneers." Permission for the use of the article in The Grizzly Bear was given Robie by Stewart.—Editor.

fully concealed in their pockets, purporting to be a copy of laws by which they were governed. The last of this band thought his wound but slight, and seemed in a fair way to recover until within the last hour, and corroborated all the evidence proven by the papers in their pockets. If Dr. Sparks is well enough to travel, Capt. Davis speaks of moving him down to his friends tomorrow.

"In conclusion, we deem it due to say that shall the evidence be true, Capt. D. and his party acted in self defense. We send this communication to your paper because the bearer, having a very sick family below, will travel post haste all night to Placerville. (Signed) W. C. Thompson, Joseph Hampton, P. L. Robertson, D. W. Hendricks, J. E. Morris Isam, Isaac A. Hart, T. I. Galligus, N. B. Porter, O. B. Wingate, W. L. Newman, J. C. Lewis, L. C. Marshall, T. C. Wallace, A. Hughes, J. Webster, O. C. Clark, and J. K. Tritt.

"Rocky Canon, Dec. 20. TO WM. HENDERSON, PLACERVILLE: Yesterday we had quite an exciting scene to happen within a mile of our camp. Whilst two of my partners and myself were taking a hunt over the hills we heard the reports of guns below us and saw two small parties shooting at each other. Convinced that they were all strangers, we hesitated for a moment before we ventured down to them. A feeling of duty, however, soon prompted us to hasten down. On approaching, we saw two of a little party of three whom we had noticed following the trail unmolested, some half an hour previous, fall in the fight, and the surviving one, a man somewhat above the medium size whom we could readily distinguish from all the rest by his white hat, fighting bravely for his life. Approaching still nearer, we were surprised at the sight of eleven men lying on the ground, seven of them dead, belonging, as they afterwards proved, to a party of robbers; and one dead, and one only wounded of the party of three so recently fired upon from the bushes by the robbers.

"Three of the wounded robbers having died last night, we had ten of them to bury this morning. One survives, who will probably recover. He is marked, however, for life, having lost his nose in toto, and the forefinger of his right hand. Seven of them were shot through the heart. The surviving one, who seems but little hurt, says that their band was composed of two Americans, one Frenchman, five Sydneymen and twelve Mexicans; and that they had commenced operations, having killed six Chinamen three days ago, and four Americans day before yesterday.

"Though we counted twenty-eight bullet holes through Capt. Davis' hat and clothes—seventeen through his hat and eleven through his coat and shirt—he received but two very slight flesh wounds. Yours truly, JOHN WEBSTER."

UNCLE JIM'S FARM

(Continued from Page 2)

He was standing there, his hands in his pockets, a contented grin on his face.

"Say," I said, "this is no time for simpering. You should be filled with awe. Don't you know that this is the longest bar in the—"

"Gosh," broke in Al. "It all reminds me of my Uncle Jim's farm."

"Can't you think of something else besides Uncle Jim's farm?" I exclaimed, exasperated. "It's probably some little truck farm, anyway. What does he raise besides dirty-faced kids?"

"Prize-winning hogs," said Al, still grinning. "And what a wonderful sight it is when they line up at their troughs."

"Enough," I said, "enough! We're going back to San Diego to see Ramona's marriage place."

THE DESERT SUNSET

(E. E. KNAPP.)

On the desert when the sun drops down and brings to close the day,
I love to watch the sunsets and to let my fancies play;
The clouds that low are hanging, tinted by the dying sun,
Form scenes of sublime grandeur where the vivid colors run.

I see forms like galleons with their sails of yellow gold,
Where the buccaneers trod decks of oak and swaggered brave and bold;
I see thin veils of tracery like the spider's silken snare,
And the gem encrusted cloudlets wafted gently here and there.

I see cloud masses piled up high, their tops as white as snow,
Where castles, crags and battlements are formed to quickly go;
The pictures that entrance the eye no artist e'er could paint,
When the bright and golden beams are dimmed to colors rare and faint.

It seems like I am gazing on a sea of azure blue,
Where the clouds form isles of beauty, softly fading from the view;
And when at last the shadows fall and the sun has gone to rest,
The Master Painter draws the veil o'er his canvas in the West.

WESTERNER SIGNALLY HONORED BY IMPORTANT HISTORY SOCIETY.

At the forty-sixth annual meeting of the American Historical Association at Minneapolis, Minnesota, December 28-30, Professor Herbert E. Bolton, head of the history department of the University of California, Berkeley, became the president.

Dr. Bolton has the honor of being the only Westerner, with one exception,—the late Professor Henry Morse Stephens,—to be selected as president of this most important society of historians.

The Pacific Coast branch of the association was in session at Berkeley, December 29 and 30. On the program was Dr. William H. Ellison of the Santa Barbara State Teachers College, who read a paper entitled "From Pierre's Hole to Monterey: A Chapter in the Adventures of George Nidever, Pioneer of the Rocky Mountains and of California."

THE DOG TAKES PRECEDENCE IN CALIFORNIA OWNERSHIP.

If prior residence means anything legally, man's best friend, the dog, takes precedence over either the White man or the Indian in ownership of California. Evidence has just been gathered by the University of California departments of paleontology and geology to show that a primitive form of dog was living in this state about the time that the primitive man-ape ancestor of humans was first learning to walk erect, almost ten million years ago. The evidence is based on a skull found at Crocker Springs, in western Kern County, in February of this year.

V. L. Vanderhoof, field and research assistant in the museum of paleontology, reports that this skull not only represents the earliest fossil of a dog found in California, but is also a new species not yet reported elsewhere. He gives to the new dog the prepossessing name "Borophagus Littoralis." The skull is about eight inches in length.

TREE MOODS

(RUDOLPH ALTROCCHI.)

I hate the weeping-willow, with its strands
Forever drooping and its mawkish tastes,
Slim-leafed newcomer from oriental wastes,
Pale immigrant of melancholy lands.

Our redwood tree I love, primeval tree,
Millennial pioneer upon our shore,
Whose solid limbs still rustle with the lore
On Indian tribesmen in their coned tepee.

With giant arms, deep green and skyward leaping,
It challenges the accident of soil,
Symbol of valiance and of western toil,
Scorning the scion of cemeterial weeping.

—University California Chronicle.

Duck Preserve—The Federal Government has purchased Joyce Island of 1,750 acres, near Suisun, Solano County, for a wild-duck preserve.

Millions Well Invested—California has invested $48,384,200 in homes and farms for veterans, and the amount is being repaid by them.

CALIFORNIA HAPPENINGS OF FIFTY YEARS AGO

Thomas R. Jones

(COMPILED EXPRESSLY FOR THE GRIZZLY BEAR.)

NEW YEAR DAY OF 1882 CAME ON A Sunday, so January 2 was the legal holiday. Beginning New Year Eve, citizens had a three-day celebration. Owing to the optimistic feeling prevailing throughout California, 1881 having been a most prosperous year, paying New Year calls to extend felicitations was at its apex.

A social sensation followed announcement, at Nevada City, Nevada County, that at the New Year ball the hours between 9 and 11 p.m. would be reserved for the bald-headed men, who would have the first choice of dance partners. It was claimed they had not been getting a fair chance in the past.

The weather in January was freakish. A rainstorm the 3rd was followed the 6th by a three-day north wind and freezing temperature. Thermometers in the Sacramento Valley went down to 22 degrees. Rain fell on eight days of the month, and the total fall for the season to date measured 8.89 inches.

California South had a terrific "Santa Ana" January 11. It did great damage, and was followed by a snowstorm. For the first time on record, snow fell at Ventura City, and all the southland hilltops were capped with "the beautiful."

Auburn, Placer County, experienced an earthquake shock at 7 a.m. of January 4, and Alameda County received a shaking at 5:20 p.m. of the 26th. No damage resulted in either instance.

The famous Gold of Ophir rose vine, growing on the Morton farm in Sonoma County, was destroyed by a January 26 gale. The rose encircled and grew over a fifty-foot-high oak tree; the wind blew down the tree and uprooted the vine.

The executive committee of the Veterans Home Association announced January 1 that $30,000 had been subscribed toward building a soldiers' home.

Governor George C. Perkins was delivering in various cities and towns of the state a lecture entitled "The Farmer and His Home."

Twenty cases of smallpox were found aboard an immigrant train at Truckee, Nevada County, January 11. Those afflicted and forty other passengers were put in quarantine, on a sidetrack.

Livermore Valley, Alameda County, was reported as being devastated by immense numbers of wild geese and ducks flocking there to feed on the fields of growing grain.

The California and Nevada Narrow Gauge Railway commenced a survey of a line proposed to run from Modesto, Stanislaus County, to Bodie, Mono County, via Sonora, Tuolumne County, and on eastward.

During the month, 4,289 immigrants arrived in the state by rail and 2,879 by sea; of the latter, 700 were Chinamen. Departures by rail were 2,002 and by sea 2,940.

California's Sunday-closing law continued to agitate the people. The Wholesale Liquor Dealers Association, organized to oppose its enforcement, sent out lecturers to influence public opinion.

FORTY-NINERS HAVE INNING.

At Willow, Glenn County, four saloonkeepers were acquitted of the law's violation January 15. Following the verdict the judge, the jury, the counsel for both sides and several citizens went on an extended spree.

Published statistics showed that California breweries paid the Federal Government a tax on the manufacture of 19,037,387 gallons of lager beer in 1881.

January 10 fire broke out on Main street, opposite the court house, in Los Angeles and destroyed a block of buildings. The loss was $100,000.

The California Flour Mill of San Francisco burned January 26 with a $50,000 loss.

Fire at Truckee, Nevada County, burned January 20 the box factory and lumber yard of Richardson Bros., causing a $20,000 loss.

Several buildings at Colton, San Bernardino County, burned January 30 with a $10,000 loss.

A portion of the Red Bluff, Tehama County, Chinatown was destroyed by fire January 9.

The Hercules Powder Works at Pinole, Contra Costa County, blew up January 11. Two men were killed and seven buildings were wrecked.

The great trial of The People versus the Gold Run Hydraulic Mine and others, being heard at Sacramento City, ended its forty-ninth day January 23, and then was adjourned until February 28 to be resumed for an indefinite time. It was a great inning for '49ers, over a hundred of whom had been called as witnesses. They were first asked how they found the state looking north of Sutter Fort on their arrival and how it now looked; then they were allowed to relate in their own way their early-day experiences. Some had fought Indians; some had come by covered wagon, and others by sea; some had killed grizzly bears; some joined vigilantes to rid communities of desperados; some had paid $1 for an onion; some had mined placers that contained more gold than dirt; all had met with ups and downs, but all were agreed that hydraulic mining was burying the Sacramento Valley with slickens.

One Pioneer related how the word slickens came into use. It was a corruption of a German word, "slaicken-sides," meaning the hanging wall or foot wall of an ore vein. There was no English word for the California miners to apply to this material, so they shortened the German one to "slickens." In time, it was applied to all debris washed from a mine and was in popular usage.

It was estimated that the gold produced in California since the metal's discovery in 1848 to the end of 1881 totaled $2,516,205,000 in value.

A cleanup at the New York Flat hydraulic mine in Yuba County, December 31, 1881, netted 2,000 ounces of gold dust worth $35,000.

The Gold Flat Eureka mine in Nevada County struck a vein of gold quartz that assayed $600 a ton.

Bodie, Mono County, continued to pour its treasure into the world's lap. The gold and silver shipped from there during 1881 amounted to $3,173,000.

SHERIFFS HAVE ROUNDUP.

Mining stocks began the year 1882 with a slump in prices on the San Francisco stock board, and mining company dividends continued to decline.

The stage from Santa Barbara City was stopped January 3 near Los Alamos by three highwaymen, who took the express box.

The stage from Ukiah, Mendocino County, was stopped January 26 by two men, who secured $1,000 from the express box.

Jose J. Vallejo, who had lived at Mission San Jose, Alameda County, since 1838, died at San Jose, Santa Clara County, January 6 at the age of 84. He was a brother of General M. G. Vallejo, Sonoma County Pioneer.

Rev. R. Townsend Huddart, who arrived in San Francisco in 1850 and established the Union College, died there January 13 at the age of 79.

Sheriffs of Merced, Fresno, San Joaquin and other counties had a roundup at Modesto, Stanislaus County, January 20. They had in custody several of the notorious Crum gang of horse thieves and twenty-five stolen horses.

Dr. J. A. Carothers, Hanford, Kings County physician, took an opiate January 27 and to arouse himself stuck his head into a pail of cold water. Unable to withdraw it, he drowned.

Rev. James Cameron, Oakland, Alameda County, Presbyterian minister, was accidentally given a dose of carbolic acid January 5 and died.

Robert Anderson, Auburn, Placer County sportingman, was playing poker January 7 with a stranger. As he was raking in a pot he had won the stranger arose, drew a gun, shot him dead and escaped.

A gang of toughs invaded a January 1 wedding celebration at the home of Charles Rossi, near Watsonville, Santa Cruz County. In the melee that followed, three men were killed and Rossi was dangerously stabbed.

S. Crabtree and Nicholas Couch got into a property dispute at El Monte, Los Angeles County. The mother of the latter entered the controversy. In anger, Crabtree knocked her down, whereupon Couch shot him dead.

W. B. Simmons, 70 years of age, January 17 killed his son-in-law, Albert Bronson, and himself near Hornitos, Mariposa County. They were partners in a farming enterprise.

Flata Gillespie, a 17-year-old lass, was January 20 shot and killed near Lodi, San Joaquin County, by a rejected suitor named Lynde, who committed suicide.

William Sailor, an oldtimer of Camptonville, Yuba County, was killed by a cavein at his mine January 3.

John P. Cassidy, Castroville, Monterey County, constable, arrested G. Tomassini, a saloonkeeper, for violating the Sunday-closing law, and he was convicted. Meeting on the street January 7 both drew guns, and Tomassini was killed.

Mrs. Nannie Ninnes of Grass Valley, Nevada County, went to a dentist January 13 to have several teeth extracted. She was given chloroform, and died in the chair.

Citrus Fair—Cloverdale, Sonoma County, will hold its annual Citrus Fair, February 19 to 22.

Auto Show—San Francisco will hold its annual Pacific Auto Show, January 9 to 16.

A BIT O' FARMING

PREPARED EXPRESSLY FOR THE GRIZZLY BEAR BY M. H. ELLIS

POULTRYMEN LONG HAVE REALIZED they could increase profits if, when buying baby chicks for replacement of hens in laying flocks, they could secure only females. As it is, about half the chicks, of course, turn out to be males, and these must be disposed of at the best price obtainable, which usually shows a loss on the transaction. Even if they had to pay a much higher price for chicks, all of which would prove to be females, the saving in feed, care and trouble would more than offset the additional cost.

Recognizing this trouble, colleges of agriculture in various states have sought to find some means of distinguishing young males from females. In the University of California college an experiment has been under way in an endeavor to breed a new variety of Leghorn chicken, the males of which would be black and the females barred. The new-born chicks then, could be told at once; the black ones would be all black, while those that later would be barred would have an indication of this by the bar on their heads. Unfortunately, the experiment has not worked out well, so far. Colors come true, but production in the strains has not been up to standard. It will be continued, though.

Also, it has been found that male can be told from female baby chicks by close examination of the vent. Whether this can be made practical in commercial hatcheries, where thousands of chicks are handled daily, remains to be seen. But judging from the progress that has been made, as reported to a state-wide conference of poultrymen at Berkeley last month, it is safe to predict that a means of sex determination in baby chicks will be worked out.

POLLINATION OF CHERRIES.

If cherries are to be planted this winter, it will be well to include a few of Black Tartarian among the large sweet varieties, such as Royal Ann, Lambert and 'Bing. Not only are these last named varieties self-sterile and will not pollinate themselves, but they are inter-sterile and will not pollinate each other. Hence, to get good yields some good pollenizer must be included. Pollination of cherries must be provided, and in providing pollenizers be sure the strains used are correct, for even in the Tartarian variety some strains are much better for this work than others.

PROTECT CITRUS BUD UNIONS.

The bud union of a citrus tree is its most vulnerable point. If it is at all prominent, it is quite likely to be injured by implements used in cultivation. If it is below the surface of the ground, much difficulty may result from fungus diseases, such as shell bark of lemons and, to some extent, gummosis in both lemons and oranges. In this event, expose the bud union by digging away the soil and use some means of keeping the soil away. A box built about the trunk will do the work, but a cheaper method is to use a strip of galvanized iron a foot wide. The protector should extend from well above the ground to below the bud union.

RICE HULLS IN THE SOIL.

The use of rice hulls for bedding for animals in the barn has led to an inquiry as to whether they will damage the soil if hauled on and plowed in. While the rice hulls themselves have little value as fertilizer, they certainly can do no damage; they will open up the soil, make it lighter and more pervious to air and water.. After being used as bedding, the hulls will contain more or less manure and this, of course, adds to the value as fertilizer.

CONTROL OF OLIVE KNOT.

Olive knot has been a troublesome problem in nearly every part of the state. However, in the light of recent research, there has appeared a remedy which appears quite sure to control. A solution made of seven parts of light lubricating oil and one part of cresylic acid applied to the knots on trunk and large branches will kill the knots without injuring the bark. On smaller branches, the knots must be cut out with pruning shears; care must be taken to disinfect the shears at every cut. The solution described above will serve well as the disinfectant. Knots may be removed during pruning, but where this method is used, disinfection must be careful if the disease is not spread.

WATCH TREES WHILE PRUNING.

While pruning trees and vines during the winter, the pruners should be instructed to keep an alert watch for any troubles that may be developing in the orchard. Every tree is observed while the pruning is being done, and if those who do it are capable, pests and disease that may not have been suspected may be brought to light. Pruning time offers a splendid chance for careful observation, for with the leaves off the trees, the bark can be more easily inspected.

SPRAY FOR LEAF ROLLER.

Eggs of the leaf roller on the limbs and twigs of fruit trees can be killed, and the insect controlled, by spraying now with miscible oil or a good crude oil spray. If this insect is not now controlled it will be pretty sure to make reappearance next summer, and at that time there is nothing that can be applied to control it, as the caterpillers are rolled in the leaves and well protected.

CONTROL OF NEMATODES.

The nematode problem is one of the most difficult agriculture of this state has to face. Theoretically, the only cure is to put affected soil under clean cultivation for three years, and starve them out. Practically, this does not work out well. In the first place, the use of the land is lost for a term of years and, in the second place, there usually are enough left to start breeding again. Planting of resistant crops is about the only real solution that can be offered. Grains, grasses and corn will thrive despite the nematode. Carbon bisulphide or carbon cyanide may be used by putting it in holes over the area affected, but the cost is almost prohibitive and the cure is not certain.

PREPARE FOR SPRING LAWN.

If a lawn is to be planted next spring, prepare for it now. Either plow or spade, according to the size of the lawn, turning under manure to a good depth. Do not work the soil down too much, but leave it rough, unless there is grading to be done. By spring the manure will have decomposed and plant food will be available for the young grass. Most of the weeds will have sprouted by that time, too, and can be killed before the seed for the lawn is planted, saving much trouble in the young grass. There is no need for further plowing or spading in the spring; level off the surface and work the seed bed down well. Plant the seed when the soil becomes warm enough that it will sprout quickly, so that a good stand may be secured.

STARTING HEATHER PLANTS.

The various kinds of heather have become popular in the state as a means of adding to landscape design. An inquiry as to the propagation of this shrub is answered. Sometime between now and the middle of March cuttings should be made, taking tender young shoots an inch or an inch and a half long. Plant them firmly in sand in a pan or shallow box, covered with a glass frame so they will be warmed by the sun. Bottom heat is not necessary.

When rooted, they should be placed in small pots and given plenty of air and warmth. A glass enclosed porch or greenhouse is best, although they will keep growing in the open if protected from cold and given sunlight. There is much variation in the hardiness of varieties, and the propagator should take the kinds that grow well in his locality, rather than to try those from some other section where there are soil and climatic differences.

PLANTING YOUNG TREES.

Most commercial orchardists have learned, to their sorrow, that in planting young fruit trees it does not do to put them deeper in the soil than they were in the nursery row. Both deciduous and citrus trees are liable to many troubles if the bud union is below the surface of the ground. Time and money must be expended in many instances to remedy the difficulty later. So in planting the tree, see that the bud union is just about where it was in the nursery, no closer to the soil. Any misgivings as to a straight trunk, because of the shape of the union at planting time, are misplaced.

SPRAY FOR SCALE.

Now is the time to get after the scale in the orchards. A good cleanup spray will do away with a lot of troubles later in the year. If possible, choose a date for the spraying after the rainstorms apparently have settled down. Use an oil spray, and cover the wood thoroughly, especially the twigs and smaller limbs. This spraying program is applicable both to citrus and deciduous trees, although in the case of citrus, of course, it is not a guarantee of complete control. On deciduous scale pests, however, a good, thorough spray applied now will be pretty sure to reduce the scale population below the danger point.

TIME TO GRAFT.

Grafting time soon will be here, and any work that is to be done in the changing of the tops of trees by this method should be under consideration now, and scions for use should be secured and laid away. Place the wood to be used in moist, not wet, sand, and store in a cool place for use in top working in the spring.

Passing of the California Pioneer

(Confined to Brief Notices of the Demise of Those Men and Women Who Came to California Prior to 1860.)

SAMUEL BRANNAN JR., NATIVE OF New York, 86; landed in San Francisco July 31, 1846, and was one of the very few surviving senior members of the Society of California Pioneers; died at San Diego City. He came to California aboard the ship "Brooklyn" with his father, Samuel Brannan Sr., one of the state's most noted Pioneers. The elder Brannan preached the first Protestant sermon in San Francisco, August 16, 1846, and in 1847 established a store at New Helvetia, now Sacramento City. At one time he was the richest man in California. There was scarcely an enterprise of moment in which he did not figure, and he was as famous for his charity and open-handed liberality as for his enterprise; unlucky speculations, however, made inroads upon his fortune and his vast wealth melted away.

Peter Nelson, native of Sweden, 94; came via Cape Horn in 1841 and resided since in the San Francisco Bay district; died at Oakland, Alameda County.

William A. Haun, native of Missouri, 83; crossed the plains in 1850 and resided for many years in the Santa Clara Valley and San Luis Obispo County; died at Taft, Kern County, survived by two children.

Mrs. Mary A. Frazier, native of England, 84; came across the plains in 1851 and resided since in the San Francisco Bay region; died at Oakland, Alameda County, survived by four children.

Dan Morris, native of Ireland, 90; came across the plains in 1852 and for many years mined in the northern part of the state; died at Los Angeles City, survived by a wife and four children.

Mrs. Millie Ann Bradford-Geddes, native of Missouri, 82; came across the plains in 1852 and resided in Mariposa and Fresno Counties; died at Arbuckle, Colusa County, survived by seven children.

Andrew Soule Williams, native of Missouri, 83; came across the plains in 1852 and settled in San Jose, Santa Clara County, where he died; four daughters survive.

Mrs. Mary Ellen Barnett-Harvey, native of Ohio, 80; came across the plains in 1854 and settled in Pope Valley, Napa County, where she died; four children survive.

Mrs. Elizabeth Loofbourrow, native of Illinois, 84; came across the plains in 1854 and resided in El Dorado and Alameda Counties; died at Sacramento City, survived by seven children.

Mrs. Anna Tourtelliotte-Bowerman, native of Connecticut, 83; came in 1854 and settled in Trinity County; died at Saratoga, Santa Clara County, survived by a son.

Mrs. Elizabeth Biggs-Roy, native of England, 83; came via Cape Horn in 1854 and resided in San Francisco a half-century; died at Sausalito, Marin County, survived by a son.

Mrs. Annie Brown-Lovett, native of Ohio, 81; came via the Isthmus of Panama in 1855 and resided in Trinity and Tehama Counties; died at Red Bluff, survived by three children. She was a daughter of G. W. Brown, California Pioneer of 1849 who sought his fortune in the Trinity County goldfields.

George W. Hack, native of New York, 85; came via the Isthmus of Panama in 1855 and settled in Sacramento County; died near Sacramento City, survived by a wife.

Mrs. Mary Tate-Hosselkus, native of Ireland, 95; came via the Isthmus of Panama in 1856 and settled in Plumas County; died at Genesee, her home since 1865, survived by four children.

James William Smith, native of Missouri, 79; came across the plains in 1856 and settled in Sutter County; died at Meridian, survived by a wife and eight children.

Charles Clark Haswell, native of Ohio, 78; came in 1857 and resided in San Francisco and Los Angeles; died at the latter city, survived by a wife and three children, among them William Clark Haswell (Ramona Parlor No. 109 N.S.G.W.).

Mrs. Martha Nichols-Langford, native of Georgia, 84; came in 1857 and settled in Amador County; died near Ione, survived by a daughter.

Mrs. Kate Lynch, native of Ireland, 84; came via the Isthmus of Panama in 1858 and settled in San Francisco, where she died; a daughter survives.

William J. Hamm, native of Massachusetts, 75; since 1858 a resident of Sacramento City, where he died; a daughter survives.

John Skedge Borrette, native of Maryland, 79; since 1859 a resident of Lassen County; died at Susanville, survived by a wife and two daughters.

Mrs. Rena Barton-Hilliard, native of Iowa, 77; crossed the plains in 1859; died at Sacramento City.

Mrs. Margaret Clement, native of Germany, 86; came in 1859; died near Brentwood, Contra Costa County.

Mrs. Lucinda Shuey-Blaisdell, native of Illinois, 76; crossed the plains in 1859 and settled in Oakland, Alameda County, where she died; four children survive.

William M. Sparks, native of Missouri, 73; came across the plains in 1859 and settled in Placer County; died at Lincoln, survived by a wife and four children.

Mrs. Angelina Rebecca Bulkley, native of Virginia, 93; came in 1854; died at Palo Alto, Santa Clara County.

William Henry Curnow, native of England, 82; since 1855 Calaveras County resident; died at Mokelumne Hill, survived by a wife.

Mrs. Deborah Bacon-Melendy, native of Oregon, 80; since 1856 San Benito County resident; died in Bear Valley, survived by seven children.

OLD TIMERS PASS

Nathan Henry Dakin, native of Michigan, 91; came in 1861; died at Riverside City, survived by a wife and a son.

Mrs. Josephine VanWalbeck, native of New York, 77; came in 1861; died at Sacramento City, survived by two daughters.

Mrs. S. H. Henry, native of France, 89; since 1861 resident of San Francisco, where she died; four children survive.

John B. McLane, native of Illinois, 74; came in 1861; died at Corning, Tehama County, survived by a wife.

Mrs. Mattie B. Osborn, native of Ohio, 83; came in 1861; died at Atwater, Merced County, survived by two sons.

Henry Thomas Specks, native of Illinois, 77; came in 1861; died at Ferndale, Humboldt County. For many years he resided in Tehama County.

John S. Collins, 85; since 1861 Contra Costa County resident; died at Martinez.

Mrs. Lydia Ann Herrington, native of Illinois, 75; came in 1863; died at Chico, Butte County, survived by two sons.

Albert E. McCombs, native of Kentucky, 94; came in 1863; died at Ukiah, Mendocino County, survived by two children. He was the last Ukiah Valley member of the G.A.R.

Mrs. Soladad Meaghen, native of Mexico, 87; came in 1865; died at Merced Falls, Merced County, survived by a daughter.

Mrs. Annie E. Rhodes, native of Connecticut, 92; since 1865 resident Santa Cruz City, where she died; four children survive.

Edwards Wellen Collins, 84; since 1866 resident Vallejo, Solano County, where he died.

H. W. M. Ogg, native of Canada, 71; since 1866 resident Sacramento City, where he died; two children survive.

Adam Baird, native of Scotland, 85; came in 1867; died at Oakland, Alameda County, survived by five children.

Mrs. Hattie Keagle, native of Iowa, 68; came in 1868; died at Sacramento City, survived by two children. For many years she resided in Amador and San Joaquin Counties.

Frank B. Norton, native of Massachusetts, 84; came in 1869; died at Oakland, Alameda County, survived by a wife and six children.

Z. G. Jameson, native of Missouri, 96; came in 1869; died at San Jose, Santa Clara County, survived by a wife and a son. For many years he resided in Merced County.

Mrs. Alice Lawrence, native of New Hampshire, 72; since 1867 resident Eureka, Humboldt County, where she died.

John Edward Hayman, native of Indiana, 85; came in 1869; died at Napa City. For twenty years he was superintendent of Colusa County schools.

Carlton S. Blodgett, native of Ohio, 74; since 1864 Yolo County resident; died at Zamora, survived by a wife and four children.

Mrs. Selena Richards-Eustice, native of Wisconsin, 80; came in 1862; died at Gilroy, Santa Clara County, survived by a son.

Mrs. Elizabeth Maholm, native of Missouri, 88; since 1861 Sacramento County resident; died at Sheldon, survived by four children.

PIONEER NATIVES DEAD

San Francisco—Joe Marks, born here in 1854, died recently survived by a wife. He resided many years in Tuolumne County.

Fresno City—Mrs. Dora Braverman-Gundelfinger, born at San Francisco in 1856, passed away recently survived by a husband and two children.

San Francisco—Mrs. Ida Thurston Dougherty, born here in 1855, passed away recently survived by a husband and two children. For many years her home was in Alameda County.

Los Angeles City—Mrs. Nellie Clark-Redewill, born at Vallejo, Solano County, in 1857, passed away November 21.

Oroville (Butte County)—Frank Faul, born in Yuba County in 1859, died November 22 survived by a wife and three children.

Monterey City—Edward Allen, born here in 1849, died November 22 survived by a wife and three children.

Chico (Butte County)—Mrs. Florence N. True, born in Yuba County in 1856, passed away November 23. She was affiliated with Annie K. Bidwell Parlor No. 168 N.D.G.W.

La Honda (San Mateo County)—Mrs. Maria Rosalia Evans, born at Pescadero, this county, in 1844, passed away November 24 survived by seven children.

Long Beach (Los Angeles County)—John S. Baker, born in Riverside County in 1855, died

November 25 survived by a wife and four children.

Portland (Oregon State)—Mrs. Ella Hanson-Stout, born in Sutter County in 1857, passed away November 25 survived by two children. She was a daughter of William P. Hanson, California Pioneer of 1849.

Cloverdale (Sonoma County) — Mrs. Susie West-Adams-Zittleman, born in Lake County in 1853, passed away November 26 survived by two children.

Pasadena (Los Angeles County)—Miss Annie Wilson, born in this county in 1858, passed away November 27. She was a daughter of Benjamin D. Wilson, for whom Mount Wilson was named.

Antler (Shasta County)—Jacob Cornish, born in California in 1851, died November 27 survived by a son.

San Francisco—Mrs. Elizabeth Frank-Roseashine, born here in 1858, passed away November 28 survived by four children.

Marysville (Yuba County)—Charles R. Brown, born in Butte County in 1859, died November 29 survived by a wife and five children.

Sacramento City—Charles F. Schwilke, born in El Dorado County in 1858, died December 2 survived by a wife and two daughters. He was affiliated with Sunset Parlor No. 26 N.S.G.W.

Napa City—Gustave Stark, born in Placer County in 1851, died December 5.

San Francisco—George Bailey Davidson, born in Santa Clara County in 1858, died December 5 survived by a wife and two children.

Sacramento City—John Barney Blankenship, born in California in 1854, died December 5 survived by a wife and four children.

San Francisco—Dr. Margaret Mahoney, born here in 1858, passed away December 7. She was affiliated with Oro Fino Parlor No. 9 N.D.G.W., and was a daughter of Denis and Margaret Mahoney, California Pioneers of 1849.

San Luis Obispo City—Willard Jesse, born in California in 1857, died December 10 survived by a wife and three children.

Oakland (Alameda County)—Gabriel Etzel, born in El Dorado County in 1857, died December 12 survived by a wife and a son.

San Francisco—George R. Saddlemire, born in San Joaquin County in 1858, died December 12 survived by a wife.

Sacramento City—Mrs. Emma Wieger, born in California in 1859, passed away December 13 survived by five children.

San Jose (Santa Clara County)—Mrs. Sophia Albee-Baker, born in Humboldt County in 1854, passed away December 13 survived by three daughters.

Sacramento City—Mrs. Lillian Rhiel-Hite, born in Amador County in 1859, passed away December 15 survived by a husband and two daughters.

Yreka (Siskiyou County—William David Doggett, born in this county in 1857, died December 16 survived by a wife and a son.

Placerville (El Dorado County)—Fred Irwin, born at Diamond Springs, this county, in 1859, died December 16 survived by a wife and a daughter. He was affiliated with Placerville Parlor No. 9 N.S.G.W.

Chico (Butte County)—Miss Mary E. Stokes, born in this county in 1859, passed away December 18.

Salinas (Monterey County)—August Henry Lauenstein, born at San Francisco in 1857, died December 19.

Los Angeles City—Mrs. Clara Louise Bacon, born here in 1858, passed away December 19 survived by four children.

GRIZZLY GROWLS

(Continued from Page 3)

The idea is certainly commendable, for the most substantial citizens of any community are the small-home owners. In California, however, any person of moderate means would be foolish, indeed, to attempt to acquire a home until such time as the special assessment evil is completely abolished. Otherwise, the chances are excellent that the investment will be lost to the contracting trust.

"Golden years are fleeting oy;
Youth is passing, too.
Learn to make the most of life,
Lose no happy day.
Time will never bring thee back
Chances swept away."

A copyrighted Associated Press dispatch from Tokio, December 14, quotes Tsuyoshi Inukai, Japan's new premier, as saying: "America is the most powerful nation on the face of the earth. No country would be so foolish as to think even for a moment of attempting war against America in her isolated position. . . . Why, we wouldn't take Manchuria as a gift."

The opposite of the Japs' public declarations is generally their real intention. So, suspicion increases that Japan intends to take, and keep, Manchuria, and that it plans, and is preparing for, war against the United States.

Reports from the National Capital are to the effect that the Congress will apply the immigration quota to Mexico. For the good of this country, the nationals of that country, a great majority of whom are not of the White race and therefore ineligible for American citizenship, should be excluded, just as are the Japs, the Chinks, etc. But, partial protection via the quota from an inundation of undesirable Mexis is preferable to no protection.

The United States Supreme Court held, December 14, that an alien who enters this country without an immigration visa—in violation of the 1924 Immigration Act—may be deported at any time thereafter, the five-year limitation prescribed by section nineteen of the 1917 Immigration Act not being applicable.

This decision should encourage the authorities to round up and deport the thousands of Japs, Mexis and other aliens now illegally here. The country would be greatly benefited by their forced departure.

Married women are barred from teaching in the public schools of more than fifty percent of representative American cities, according to an announcement of the Federal Office of Education. They should be barred from every public school, and also, no married woman with an able-bodied husband should be employed in any capacity.

WELL-KNOWN CONTRA COSTAN DEAD.

Knightsen (Contra Costa County) — George W. Knight, after whom this place was named, died November 30 survived by three daughters. He was a native of Maine, aged 88, and came to California in 1874.

National Orange Show—San Bernardino City is arranging for the Twenty-second National Orange Show, February 18 to 28.

Unemployment Bonds—San Diego City has voted $300,000 bonds to provide work for its unemployed.

Native Sons of the Golden West

SAN FRANCISCO—THE BOARD OF Grand Officers were in session November 28, those in attendance being: Grand President Dr. Frank I. Gonzalez, who presided, Junior Past Grand President John T. Newell, Grand First Vice-president Seth Millington, Grand Second Vice-president Justice Emmet Seawell, Grand Third Vice-president Chas. A. Koenig, Grand Secretary John T. Regan, Grand Trustees George F. McNoble, Samuel M. Shortridge Jr., Jesse H. Miller, Joseph J. McShane, Frank M. Lane and John M. Burnett.

The most important business was the selection of a successor to A. W. Garcelon of Arcata No. 20, recently resigned as Grand Trustee. Candidates for the post were Charles H. Spengemann of Hesperian No. 137 (San Francisco), Edward T. Schnarr of Fruitvale No. 252 (Oakland) and Eldred L. Meyer of Santa Monica Bay No. 267 (Ocean Park). After due consideration Meyer was elected to the vacancy.

Considerable business of a routine nature was disposed of, following which the Board adjourned to the call of the Grand President.

Past Grand Extends Greetings.

Past Grand President Herman C. Lichtenberger, who has been closely pursued by hard luck lately, is again in the hospital, this time with a crushed arm, the result of a fall December 13. So, Herman has not been able to prepare for mailing the season's greetings annually sent to his numerous friends, and has asked The Grizzly Bear to extend his best wishes to all the brethren.—C.M.H.

Annual Rollcall.

Santa Cruz—At the annual rollcall of Santa Cruz No. 90, organized in 1886, three charter members—Reuben Pringle, Ralph Miller and Frank K. Roberts—were honor-guests. President Cliff Kilfoyl introduced Thomas Alzina as toastmaster at the turkey supper, prepared by Enoch Alzina, Hi Faneuf, Ben Crews, Harry Buckhart, Charles Pinkham and Robert Devitt, and served by Joseph Nittler, Ed Blaisdell, Elmer Dakan Jr. and Frank Burns. In addition to the charter members, talks were made by Frank Helms, George S. Tait Jr., W. S. Rodgers, James Bartlett, John C. Geyer, C. E. Canfield, Joseph Aram and others.

History Contest Has Many Entrants.

Sacramento—The annual California history oratorical contest, sponsored by Sacramento No. 3 for the students at the Sacramento high school, was held December 10. Henry Wittpen headed the committee which arranged the details. The judges were Herbert E. White, Superior Judge Malcolm C. Glenn and Thomas Chambers. Milton Rosendahl presided. The school orchestra, Lorraine Hansen student director, rendered selections; Mildred Allen, accompanied by Betty Gaylord, gave a vocal solo, and Margaret Briggs, accompanied by Elva DeMar, a violin solo.

GRAND TRUSTEE ELDRED L. MEYER.

First prize, a silver cup donated by Irving D. Gibson, went to Phoebe Grosch, whose subject was "General Vallejo." Second prize was taken by Betty Gaylord, "Mark Twain, California Author," and third by George Hornstein, "Thomas Starr King." Other contestants, and their subjects, were: Thomas MacBride, "Early History of Sacramento;" Dennis Hession, "Inyo County;" Virginia Simmons, "The Glamorous Decade;" Jack Downey, "The Romance of California Water;" Margaret Lazzarone, "The Manly Party of Death Valley."

Sacramento added many new names to its roster at the initiation conducted by John A. Sutter Past Presidents Assembly recently, and another large class is to be initiated immediately after the holidays. District Deputies Clyde Corcoran and Joseph Lannon will participate in a joint installation of all the Sacramento Parlors in January; dancing will conclude the ceremonies. No. 3 contemplates putting a team in the Municipal Indoor Baseball League, and there is considerable rivalry between the younger members for the eighteen places on the team, of which Frank R. Didion is captain.

Delightful Occasion.

Santa Barbara—Grand Second Vice-president Justice Emmet Seawell officially visited Santa Barbara No. 116 December 15 and the evening was most delightfully spent at a dinner and smoker. Special guests were members of the Santa Barbara Bar Association, Superior Judges S. E. Crow and A. B. Bigler, Mayor Harvey T. Nielson, Supervisor Sam Stanwood and other city and county officials. Vocal selections were rendered by Peace Justice Charles L. Poulsen.

President John L. Stewart of No. 116 was the toastmaster, and President W. P. Butcher and Past President Paul Sweetser extended greetings, respectively, on behalf of the bar association and the Parlor. Justice Seawell's address, in the course of which he appealed for recognition of the important contributions made by California Pioneers towards the development of a great Western empire, was listened to with great interest by the 200 in attendance. "A state should not forget those who, in the past, made the present possible," he concluded. Other speakers were Junior Past Grand President John T. Newell and Grand Trustee Eldred L. Meyer. C. W. McCormick, as president, heads Santa Barbara's newly-elected corps of officers.

Broadcast Sponsored.

Oakland—The Extension of the Order Committee, representing the Alameda County Parlors, assisted by representatives of the Native Daughter Parlors, sponsored December 6 a radio program. Historiographer George H. Barron spoke on the "California Missions," the band of Piedmont No. 120 N.S.G.W. rendered selections, and Mrs. Estelle M. Evans, Past Grand President N.D.G.W., was heard in a group of vocal numbers. The committee which arranged the broadcast included Grand Outside Sentinel Gam Hurst (chairman), Mrs. Sallie R. Thaler, Grand Secretary N.D.G.W., Marion E. White, Lester Steele and Anthony King.

"Kids" Entertained by Oldtimers.

Calistoga—Oldtimers of Calistoga No. 86 sponsored a "kid" party December 7, and it was a huge success. The festivities started with a turkey supper, George Nance being the chef. At the meeting which followed officers were elected, Frank Mariani being selected for president, to succeed Rev. T. J. McKeon, and $20 was contributed to the Calistoga Fire Department for a resuscitator.

Jerome C. Siemsen, chairman of the arrangements committee, took charge under good of the order, and then the fun began. Santa Claus Ed. Light arrived with a large pack of presents for the "kids," and such remembrances! A delightful feature was the presentation of a billfold to R. J. Williams, retiring recording secretary, who has completed a quarter-century of faithful service to the Parlor. Cards and games rounded out one of the most memorable and largest attended occasions in No. 86's history.

Real Assistance Promised.

Ferndale—Ferndale No. 93 elected officers, with O. R. Frame as president, December 7. Following the meeting Humboldt Past Presidents Assembly, which meets alternately in Ferndale, Arcata and Eureka, convened and selected its officers, A. W. McDonald of Humboldt No. 14 being chosen governor. They will be installed at the January 7 meeting in Arcata. The gathering concluded with a clam chowder feast prepared by "Chef" Chas. Kistner.

The Assembly will, during 1932, take over the work of the Humboldt County Central Committee, representing Humboldt No. 14 (Eurkea), Arcata No. 20 and Ferndale No. 93, and hopes to be of real assistance to the Parlors of the county.

Membership Standing Largest Parlors.

San Francisco—Grand Secretary John T. Regan reports the standing of the Subordinate Parlors having a membership of over 400 January 1, 1931, as follows, together with their membership figures December 19, 1931:

Parlor	Jan. 1	Dec. 19	Gain	Loss
Ramona No. 109	1163	1116	..	47
South San Francisco No. 157	828	823	..	5
Castro No. 232	690	702	12	..
Stanford No. 76	644	640	..	4
Twin Peaks No. 214	723	630	..	93
Arrowhead No. 110	608	618	19	..
Stockton No. 7	562	560	..	2
Piedmont No. 120	510	523	12	..
Rincon No. 72	463	449	..	14

Grand President Honor Guest.

Stockton—Grand President Dr. Frank I. Gonzalez and Grand Secretary John T. Regan were

THE GRIZZLY BEAR
IS REGULARLY ON SALE:
SAN FRANCISCO:
Foster & Orear, Ferry News Stand.
N.S.G.W. Bldg., 414 Mason St., Room 302.
OAKLAND:
Fred M. DeWitt, 620 14th St.
LOS ANGELES:
315 Wilcox Bldg., Second and Spring.

Subscription Order Blank
For Your Convenience

Grizzly Bear Magazine,
309-15 Wilcox Bldg.,
206 South Spring St.,
Los Angeles, California.

For the enclosed remittance of $1.50 enter my subscription to The Grizzly Bear Magazine for one year.

Name.................................

Street Address.................................

City or Town.................................

guests at a supper and entertainment staged by Stockton No. 7 December 14 in honor of the Grand President. Included among the many visitors in attendance were representatives of Modesto No. 11, Lodi No. 18, Ione No. 33 and Tuolumne No. 144. Addresses were made by Grand President Gonzalez, Past Grand President Hubert R. McNoble, Grand Secretary Regan and Grand Trustee George F. McNoble.

Shortly after the coming of the new year Stockton will begin preparations for the Grand Parlor, which meets in May in the San Joaquin County government-seat. Plans outlined indicate this will be one of the best Grand Parlors ever held.

Oldtimers Night.

Saint Helena—Saint Helena No. 53 elected officers December 7, Edgar W. Johnson being chosen president. Refreshments were served by a committee composed of Edgar Johnson, Lucas Haus and Gilman Clark. A social dance was sponsored December 12.

January 11 the Parlor will have an oldtimers night, featuring a banquet and numerous surprises. The annual benefit for the homeless children will be held in February. Raymond Palmer, Martin Anderson, Louis D. Vasconi, Gilman Clark and Charles Wagner compose the arrangements committee.

Official Visits.

San Diego—San Diego No. 108 received an official visit December 9 from Grand Second Vice-president Justice Emmet Seawell. There was a good attendance, two candidates were initiated and refreshments were served. Among the speakers of the evening were Justice Seawell, Junior Past Grand President John T. Newell and District Deputy Albert V. Mayrhofer.

Ritual Contest Sponsored.

Napa—At a meeting December 1 of Napa-Solano Past Presidents Assembly No. 11, George Flanagan of Napa No. 62 was elected governor. Officers will be installed January 7. It was decided to sponsor a ritual contest between the Parlors of Napa and Solano Counties and to award a trophy to the best team.

Benefit Nets Neat Sum.

Martinez—Mount Diablo No. 101 and Las Juntas No. 221 N.D.G.W. sponsored a whist party for the benefit of the homeless children. Sixty-seven tables were in operation, and $115 was realized. An added feature was a russian costume dance by Miss Natalie Carr.

The committee conducting the successful affair was: Las Juntas—Mms. Leone Henrichsen (chairman), Nina Keefe, Rose Palmer, Milford Viera, R. Anderson and Frances Upton, and Miss Adele Jones. Mount Diablo—A. E. Goyette, Al Wright, Melvin Wells, R. Anderson and Milford Viera.

Past Presidents to Initiate Large Class.

San Rafael—Officers of Mount Tamalpais No. 64 and Marinita No. 198 N.D.G.W. will be jointly installed January 9, Arthur W. Todt and Miss Gussie Bannister becoming the respective presidents. District deputy B. J. Brusatori will officiate for No. 64.

Marin County Past Presidents Assembly met in San Rafael December 7, Director General James F. Stanley, V. L. Orengo, Henry Rickleffs and other prominent members of San Francisco Assembly No. 1 being in attendance. The next meeting will be at Sausalito, January 6, when a large class of candidates will be initiated and plans will be presented for promoting activities of the Order.

Sheriff Prizewinner.

Antioch—The annual masquerade of General Winn No. 32 for the benefit of the homeless children drew a large crowd. Prizes for the best costumed couple went to Sheriff and Mrs. R. R. Veale, the latter being attired in a costume of colonial design and the former impersonated a spanish don. A chicken supper was served by Antioch No. 223 N.D.G.W.

The committee in charge of the masquerade included Wesley Field, Charles Hornback, F. J. Biglow, Jake Frederickson, Richard J. Trembath, Robert Douglas and Richard Uren.

Generous Donation.

Oroville—Argonaut No. 8 officers, with Thomas R. Cole as president, were elected December 16. They will be installed, jointly with those of Gold of Ophir No. 190 N.D.G.W., January 6. District Deputies Cyril Macdonald and Alice Bass will officiate.

Argonaut has, by resolution approved by the

(Continued on Page 17)

LOS ANGELES
CITY AND COUNTY

"RESIDENTS WHO STRUGGLE ALONG for years, making payments on a small piece of property, supporting local, state and federal governments, giving freely to charity, paying large taxes and assessments, now find out when they are without work, food, and in danger of losing their equities because of no money to make payments, that they cannot get aid from the county welfare department unless they deed their property over to the county," said the Wilmar, Los Angeles County, "Chronicle" of December 10, editorially.

"On the other hand, the county can, and is spending hundreds of thousands of dollars through different organizations in luring more people to this section of the county, a majority of whom either are broke when they get here or go broke soon after arriving. Plenty of funds seem to be available for the care of these people. They soon get on the preferred list and receive county aid. But the good taxpayers, who pay their taxes and support these incompetents in office, continue to pay taxes, go hungry and lose their all.

"It is about time that our lawmaking bodies, and this includes them all from the president down to the supervisors, were doing something for the backbone of the government—the small-home owner—besides talk of moratoriums for Europe and help for the incompetent banker who gambled in stocks and bonds to the loss of the people's money.

"Just so long as the small taxpayer—the one who is being appealed to to loosen up and spend—sees these conditions prevalent everywhere in the country, he would be a bigger sap than he is already to spend one penny for anything except the bare necessities of life. For tomorrow he might be the one trying to get aid from the government which he has faithfully supported with his taxes and moral and physical support."

When you purchase goods advertised in The Grizzly Bear, or answer an advertisement in this magazine, please be sure to mention The Grizzly Bear. That's co-operation mutually beneficial.

1932'S COMING WATCHED.

Los Angeles Parlor No. 45 N.S.G.W. had several visitors December 17, including a large delegation from Sepulveda Parlor No. 263 (San Pedro), Grand Organist Leslie Maloche and C. Y. Stanley of Stanford Parlor No. 76 (San Francisco). Two new members were received. The date was Albert Metz's seventy-fourth birthday anniversary, so in honor of the event he prepared and served refreshments.

The Parlor celebrated the advent of 1932 with a dance and watch party New Year Eve. Good music was provided, and the large crowd had an enjoyable time. Officers of No. 45, with Lee Irwin as president, will be installed January 8 at joint ceremonies at San Pedro.

TO ENTERTAIN NEIGHBORS.

Los Angeles Parlor No. 124 N.D.G.W. initiated a class of twelve candidates December 16, making a total of fifty-one new members received during the July-December term. The annual Christmas party followed the ceremonies and was a wonderful success. It was sponsored by the teacher members. with Ruth Traeger as the chairman, Ramona Thoroughgood the pianist and Jennie Raymond the announcer. A splendid program was presented, including a playlet enacted by the members in costume, and refreshments were served. The electrically-lighted Christmas tree and the fireplace with burning logs formed a pretty scene.

A large delegation of No. 124 members attended the institution of Ontario Parlor No. 251. The Parlor presented the "baby" with a beautiful flag for the president's station. January 4 the Parlor will assist District Deputy Flora Holy in installing the officers of Santa Monica Bay Parlor No. 245.

January 13, Los Angeles will conclude its bridge tournament, which is proving a great success. January 27 these Parlors will be entertained: Rudecinda, Grace, Santa Ana, Californiana, Lugonia, Desert Gold and Ontario. President Gertrude R. Allen who, along with the other officers, has been retained for another term, issued the following Christmas message:

"As we live through the happy holiday season, let us ponder the deeper significance of these two phrases, 'Peace on earth, good will toward men,' and strive to make our lives exemplify them, too. Peace in our own hearts, peace in our Order, our communities, our state and our nation, so that through this sequence we may use the force of our organization to bring about that toward which we are all working—world peace."

THREE INITIATED.

Grand Second Vice-president Justice Emmet Seawell December 7 officially visited Hollywood Parlor No. 196 N.S.G.W. There was a large attendance, including many visitors from all local Parlors. Three candidates were initiated.

Justice Seawell delivered a forceful address, and among the many other speakers were Superior Judge Joseph P. Sproul, Municipal Judge Leo I. Aggeler, District Deputies Albert Cron and Harry Honn, Grand Trustee Eldred L. Meyer and Henry G. Bodkin.

BOYS' CHOIR CHARMS.

The Christmas party of Californiana Parlor No. 247 N.D.G.W., held prior to the December 8 meeting, was a marked success. Mrs. Edward Tabor was in charge and among those who ably assisted were Mms. William Behm, E. B. Loos and Edward H. Anthony. The ball was beautified by the use of gayly-colored flowers. The proceeds were used for Christmas philanthropy.

Officers were elected at the meeting, Mrs. Gertrude Tuttle being retained as president. A delightful program followed the meeting, two talented children, David Leo Tillotson and Adrian Tabor, giving a number of dances in costume. The feature numbers were charmingly presented by the boys' choir—sixteen singers directed by Orel Gardner—of Saint Mary of the Angels Episcopal Church. Tea was served by

the hospitality committee, Mrs. Edith Adams chairman.

CITY GOVERNMENT OVERSTAFFED

The Los Angeles City Unit of the California Taxpayers Association December 14 adopted the following resolution:

"Whereas, The Board of Directors of the Los Angeles City Unit of California Taxpayers Association believes that the departments of the Los Angeles City Government are at this time overstaffed, rather than in need of additional personnel; and

"Whereas, Any additional personnel would incur a tax burden which the people would not be able to stand; now, therefore, be it

"Resolved, That Los Angeles City Unit of California Taxpayers Association go on record as opposed to any increase in the personnel of any department of the city government at this time."

GENUINE CO-OPERATION.

Ocean Park—Santa Monica Bay Parlor No. 245 N.D.G.W. had a royal Christmas party December 21 for the children and other guests. On the extensive program were a charming playlet and a battle of the cascarones. Gifts were distributed by jolly Kris Kringle from a Christmas tree, and ice cream and cake—from Santa's snow mountain and the fairy ovens in the dell—were served. Rosalie Hyde, the general chairman, was assisted by Mary Meyer, Willette Biscailuz, Anna Pierce, Lottie O'Connor, Theresa Henanty, Hazel McCreary, Ethel Mickelson, Marie Barnes, Edith Coe, Hazel Swanson, Rhea Jones, Edna Romero, Grace Abila, Catherine Conterno and Katharine Worsham.

Mrs. Hyde, who is chairman of Santa Monica Bay's veteran welfare committee, attended December 17 a big wrapping event at the National Soldiers Home, Sawtelle. Twenty-eight organizations were represented, and 4,500 packages were prepared for distribution Christmas Eve. Such a sight it was, and such a demonstration of genuine co-operation!

JOINT NATIVE SONS INSTALLATION.

San Pedro — Sepulveda Parlor No. 263 N.S.G.W. is making plans for the joint installation here, January 8, of the officers of all Native Son Parlors in Los Angeles County and vicinity. District Deputy Burrell D. Neighbors will officiate, and an attractive entertainment program will be presented.

Sepulveda is to sponsor a troop of Boy Scouts of America composed of native Californians. Laurence D. Powers will serve as the scoutmaster, and Edwin E. Baldwin and Stanley A. Wheeler will serve with him on the Parlor's scout committee. Francis Fetzer is the newly-elected president of Sepulveda.

PERSONAL PARAGRAPHS.

Miss Eva Williams and Benjamin H. Montey (Ramona N.S.) were recently wedded.

Mrs. Hazel Hansen (Verdugo N.D.) of Glendale was a visitor last month to San Francisco.

C. Y. Stanley (Stanford N.S.) of San Francisco is a visitor and may remain for some time.

Marshal Charles R. Thomas (Ramona N.S.) won the Potrero Country Club golf championship.

Edmund Drouet (Ramona N.S.) of the U. S. Navy sails January 2 for one of the Asiatic stations.

Mrs. Marie McFadyen-Monroe (Long Beach N.D.) of Pendleton, Oregon, spent the holidays with her mother, Mrs. Kate McFadyen (Long Beach N.D.) in Long Beach.

Mrs. Olive Lopez (Californiana N.D.) entertained at her home December 1 in honor of Mr. and Mrs. Refugio Belderrain, who celebrated their fifty-second wedding anniversary.

Ed Schalimo (Ramona N.S.) and wife (Los Angeles N.D.) motored to San Francisco to spend the Christmas holidays with their daughter, Mrs. Adelaide Hickman (Los Angeles N.D.).

THE DEATH RECORD.

Albert William Lyter, affiliated with Ramona Parlor No. 109 N.S.G.W., died recently at Pomona. He was born at San Jose, Santa Clara County, April 21, 1880.

Harrie Lloyd Walker, affiliated with Santa Monica Bay Parlor No. 267 N.S.G.W., died at Beverly Hills November 19. He was born at Oakland, Alameda County, January 18, 1896.

Mrs. Martha K. Boquist, mother of Charles V. Boquist (Ramona N.S.), passed away December 17.

Gottfried Alexander, father of Walter G. Alexander (Ramona N.S.), died December 18.

Mrs. Mary P. Rommel, mother of J. C. Rom-

(Continued on Page 22)

Native Daughters of the Golden West

ONTARIO (SAN BERNARDINO COUNTY)—Ontario No. 251, organized by District Deputy Hazel B. Hansen of Verdugo No. 240 (Glendale), vice-chairman Grand Parlor Extension of the Order Committee, was instituted by Grand President Evelyn I. Carlson December 19 with forty-one charter members. A dinner preceded the ceremonies, the tables being beautifully decorated and brown bears serving as favors. The institution was witnessed by an immense crowd, all surrounding Parlors being well represented. In conducting the ceremonies, the Grand President was assisted by Grand Trustee Florence D. Schoneman, Grand Secretary Sallie R. Thaler, Past Grand Presidents Grace S. Stoermer, Estelle M. Evans, Dr. Louise C. Heilbron and Sue J. Irwin, the district deputies and Marvel Thomas.

The ritual was exemplified by the following: Hazel B. Hansen, president; Marguerite Dickinson, past president; Ruth Ruiz, first vice-president; Helen Anderson, second vice-president; Ora Evans, third vice-president; Marvel Thomas and Flora Holy, marshals; Sallie R. Thaler, recording secretary; Gertrude Allen, financial secretary; Rose Bartel, treasurer; Juanita Lopez, organist; Florence D. Schoneman, Eva Bemis, Daisy Hansen, trustees; Katie Ross, inside sentinel; Clara Fay, outside sentinel; Nellie Cline, junior past president.

Speakers of the evening included Grand President Carlson, Past Grand Presidents Evans, Heilbron and Stoermer, Grand Secretary Thaler, Grand Trustee Schoneman, District Deputy Hansen and Miss Mollie Spaelti of Marinita No. 198 (San Rafael). Nellie Cline, on behalf of the district deputies, presented the new Parlor with the charter fee; Grand President Carlson, a gavel; District Deputy Hazel Hansen, a beautiful hamper—filled with lovely linen from members of the southland Parlors—to be disposed of by the "baby" to secure funds for supplies and paraphernalia. Choice flowers were presented the present and past grand officers.

Officers of Ontario include: Adele Frankish, president; Ethel Baxter, first vice-president; Betty Christian, second vice-president; Maude VanFleet, third vice-president; Esther Kremer, marshal; Helen Hickman, recording secretary; Miss MacDonald, financial secretary; Elizabeth Wanamaker, treasurer; Wilma Poole, outside sentinel; Ruth Cassell, inside sentinel; Jessie Merry, past president; Edith Osgood, Etta Wright, Sidney Herzberg, trustees. On arrival in Ontario, the out-of-town visitors were entertained at tea by Grand Trustee Florence Schoneman, and the following morning District Deputy Hazel Hansen was hostess at breakfast.

Fine Response in Vets' Behalf.

Santa Cruz—As chairman of the Grand Parlor Veterans Welfare Committee for 1931-32, Past Grand President Stella Finkeldey desires to express sincere appreciation for the very fine response from Parlors, grand and past grand officers, past president associations, members and clubs. 132 Parlors have responded to date, making it possible to carry out a program very much along the lines of last year. The hospital at Whipple again requested candy for the holidays and the hospital at Tucson expressed a wish for assistance in recreational work. Miss Finkeldey received the following letter of acknowledgment from the U. S. Veterans Hospital at Whipple, Arizona:

"This will acknowledge receipt, several days ago, of the box of small, hard candies for use Thanksgiving Day. Your assistance in helping us make our tables and trays attractive for Thanksgiving Day is greatly appreciated. Please accept for yourself, and extend to the members of your organization, our thanks for your assistance. With all best wishes to you and your organization. MISS FRANCES MAYNARD, recreational aide. Approved: G. D. Allen, medical officer in charge."

Surprise Shower of Baby Garments.

Fort Bragg—Knowing in advance that a delightful evening was in store, there was a large attendance at the December 2 meeting of Fort Bragg No. 210. Community relief work was discussed, and a committee was appointed to collect food and clothing from the members for the needy. At the conclusion of the meeting all were invited to a delightful supper, prepared by Mms. Lucy Carlson, Clara Mehtian and Burnie.

The tables, arranged around a Christmas tree, were decorated with greens and poinsettias, reminding of the approach of the holiday season. An emblematic pin and a small Christmas tree decorated with handkerchiefs were presented as parting gifts to President Elna Mathews, who is leaving soon for El Centro. The many presents under the tree proved to be a surprise shower of baby garments for Mrs. Lilly Tuomala. Words of thanks from the recipients brought the delightful evening to a close.

Christmas Spirit Prevailed.

Petaluma—The official visit of Grand President Evelyn I. Carlson to Petaluma No. 222 December 15 was the occasion of a largely attended and most interesting meeting. A dinner was held before the meeting, followed by addresses and the initiation of one candidate. The meetinghall was beautifully decorated with a Christmas tree, toyon berries and greens. Other visitors were Grand Trustees Willow Borba and Ethel Begley, Grand Organist Lola Horgan, Grand Outside Sentinel Orinda Giannini, Past Grand President Emma Foley, District Deputy Mae Rose Barry, and delegations from Santa Rosa, Marinita, Fairfax, Portola, Orinda and Mission Parlors. Julia Perolini presided in a very charming manner. Election of officers was held and Elizabeth Dillon was chosen president. A box of clothes on display was sent to the homeless children committee for Christmas, together with a check.

Following the meeting all retired to the banquetroom, where a social time was held. The Christmas spirit prevailed there, also, and refreshments were served by a very active committee headed by Mary Garzoli. Mystery packages were disposed of and were awarded Margaret Colgan, Julia Perolini and Elsie Ricoli. A beautiful gift was presented to Grand President Carlson, and a remembrance to District Deputy Barry for her loyal support to Petaluma.

Birthday Celebrated.

Martinez—A most enjoyable birthday party was given December 7 in honor of the tenth anniversary of Las Juntas No. 221. Mount Diablo No. 101 N.S.G.W. members were the invited guests. Dutch whist was the diversion, awards being given to J. A. Schweinitzer, Mrs. Ethel Keefe and Mrs. Lottie Schaffer.

A sumptuous banquet wound up the evening's entertainment. A huge birthday cake, graced with ten candles, given by Mrs. John Griffin, gave the necessary touch to the festivities. Christmas decorations added color to the affair. Mrs. Ethel Keefe, as chairman and sponsor of the celebration, proved a delightful and able hostess.

Bear Flags Presented Schools.

San Diego—San Diego No. 208 is keeping up its usual pace in activities along the lines of the interests of the Order. Two California State (Bear) Flags recently were presented county schools, San Diego No. 108 N.S.G.W. co-operating. One was given the Emery school at Palm City. Miss Marion S. Stough, introduced by Mrs. Mabel H. Burgert, presented the flag, which was accepted with enthusiastic applause. The other was given the Lakeside school, Edward H. Dowell of No. 108 making the presentation speech. Mrs. Sarah R. Miller appeared on behalf of No. 208. A recent card party netted more than $80, which was turned over to the San Diego Mission restoration fund.

Members of the Past Presidents Association were guests of President Irma A. Heilbron at a dinner party at the home of her sister, Mrs. Alice Damarus, December 11. The January meeting will be held at the home of Mrs. Jane Florentin.

Highly Complimented.

Santa Rosa—The official visit of Grand President Evelyn I. Carlson to Santa Rosa No. 217 was the occasion for a most enjoyable evening. A turkey supper preceded the meeting. The Parlor was highly complimented for the splendid way in which the ritual was exemplified. Mrs. Carlson was presented with a piece of china, and the following grand officers were each presented with a linen handkerchief: Grand Secretary Sallie Thaler, Supervising Deputy Emma Foley, District Deputy Anna Loser, Past Grand President Margaret Grote-Hill, Grand Organist Lola Horgan, Grand Outside Sentinel Orinda Giannini, Grand Trustees Ethel Begley, Willow Borba and Anna Thuesen.

The Grand President, in her usual sweet way, outlined the various projects of the Order, and particularly expressed her "one fond hope, to liquidate the mortgage on the Native Daughter Home." Santa Rosa is 100 percent for that project, and is compiling a cook book, the entire proceeds from which will be turned over to the Home. Delegations from Sonoma, San Rafael, Napa, Vallejo, Calistoga, Mill Valley, Petaluma, Fort Bragg and San Francisco were in attendance. Mrs. Loser, district deputy of Santa Rosa, was highly complimented by the Grand President.

The annual Christmas festivities of No. 217 were held December 17. Baskets were delivered to needy families at Christmas time. January 21 the district meeting of Sonoma and Marin Counties Parlors will be held at Santa Rosa.

Preservation Fund.

San Andreas—San Andreas No. 113 initiated three candidates, and during the social hour following the ceremonies games were played, and Oleta Meyer, Amelia Joy and Kate Loeffler, hostesses for the month, served supper. Doris Treat, Melvina Dalton and Amelia Joy, the committee in charge, report $15.75 has been accumulated for the Luther Burbank home preservation fund of the Parlor.

Charter Members Entertained.

Placerville—Marguerite No. 12 initiated six candidates and entertained the charter members, three of whom were present. The Parlor was instituted June 9, 1887. Eleven of the forty-two original members have retained their membership and reside in various parts of the state. The occasion was greatly enjoyed.

Carol Singers Serenade.

San Jose—The $100 Christmas gift and card

party sponsored by Vendome No. 100 December 9 was a wonderful success. President Adeline Taxiera of Orinda, San Francisco, was called for the trophy. Mrs. Clara Gairaud was the general chairman.

Vendome and Observatory No. 100 N.S.G.W. dispensed cheer and presents to a large number of patients at the U. S. Veteran Hospital at Palo Alto during Christmas week. Mms. Elwin H. Baker, Charles O. Dean and Fred Withycombe from Vendome, and Karl Marten, Chas. Dietz and Lloyd Pinard of Observatory comprised this faithful committee.

December 23 a Christmas tree festival was held by Vendome, with Mrs. William C. Kady as general chairman. A merry time was had killing the word "depression." Santa Claus was there in all his glory, in the person of Miss Tillie Brohaska. Carols were sung under the direction of Mrs. Clara Gairaud, and a Christmas playlet and stories were also enjoyed. The carol singers at the close of the evening drove to the homes of sick members and serenaded them. Many outside of the Order also petitioned for their sweet voices. Four new members were received during December, and a class will be received early in January.

Grand President's Official Itinerary.

San Francisco—During the month of January, Grand President Evelyn I. Carlson will officially visit the following Subordinate Parlors on the dates noted:

5th—Laura Loma No. 182, Niles.
6th—Copa de Oro No. 105, Hollister, and San Juan Bautista No. 179, San Juan, jointly at San Juan.
13th—La Rosa No. 191, Roseville.
14th—Bonita No. 10, Redwood City.
15th—Betsy Ross No. 238, Centerville.
19th—Yosemite No. 83, San Francisco.
20th—Vallejo No. 195, Vallejo.
21st—Sonoma and Marin Counties meeting.
22nd—Twin Peaks No. 185, San Francisco.
25th—Calistoga No. 145, Calistoga.
26th—Argonaut No. 166, Oakland.
27th—Linda Rosa No. 170, San Francisco.
30th—San Mateo District Meeting.

Hundred Children Guests.

Modesto—Morada No. 199 and Modesto No. 11 N.S.G.W. held their eleventh annual Christmas party for the small children December 18. Each member was requested to bring a child. Presents, and stockings filled with candy and nuts were presented the hundred children present. A lovely program of music was also provided. Mrs. Susan Sullivan and Mrs. Emma Smith, assisted by a committee, provided for several needy families at Christmas time. Morada held its annual Christmas party December 21 at the home of Mrs. Ella Turner.

December 11 the sewing club met at the home of Mrs. Emma Smith. Christmas stockings were made and presents were wrapped for the children's party. No. 199 and No. 11 held a public whist party December 9, with 250 present. Proceeds will go to the homeless children and the needy.

Delightful Talk on Co-operation.

San Bernardino—Members of Lugonia No. 241 and their friends were guests December 9 of Arrowhead No. 110 N.S.G.W. Supervisor John Andreson Jr. had charge of the dinner, and short addresses were made by the presidents of both Parlors. The guests voted the affair a complete success. Following the feast No. 241 had its regular meeting, initiated a candidate and elected officers. Installation will be held January 27. President Wixom gave a delightful talk on co-operation.

December 23 Lugonia entertained twenty-five underprivileged children at the annual Christmas party. There was a huge tree, loaded with decorations, gifts and candies, and Santa Claus was present. Later on in the evening the members exchanged inexpensive and humorous gifts. December 31 Lugonia assisted Arrowhead at its annual New Year Eve ball for the benefit of the homeless children.

Butte-Glenn District Meet.

Chico—Native Daughters of Butte and Glenn Counties gathered here December 10 for a district meeting arranged by District Deputy Cora Hintz. Three candidates were initiated, officers of the Parlors represented, with District Deputy Ruth Brown as president, exemplifying the ritual. Grand officers in attendance included Grand President Evelyn I. Carlson, Past Grand President Esther Sullivan and Grand Trustee Gladys Noce. The lodgeroom of Annie K. Bidwell No. 168, where the gathering was held, was beauti-

(Continued on Page 19)

Official Directory of Parlors of the N. S. G. W.

ALAMEDA COUNTY.

Alameda No. 47, Alameda City—Gus Nelson, Pres.; Robt. H. Cavanaugh, Sec., 1806 Pacific Ave.; Wednesdays, Native Sons Hall, 1406 Park St.

Oakland No. 50, Oakland—A. W. Ainger, Pres.; F. M. Norris, Sec., 4280 Terrace St.; Fridays, Native Sons Hall, 11th and Clay Sts.

Las Positas No. 96, Livermore—R. J. Ruetz, Pres.; John J. Kelly, Sec., P. O. box 341; Thursdays, Foresters Hall.

Eden No. 113, Hayward—William J. Burgess, Pres.; Henry Powell, Sec., 944 Castro St.; 1st and 3rd Wednesdays, Bank Hayward Hall.

Piedmont No. 120, Oakland—Walter M. Davis, Pres.; Charles Morando, Sec., 906 Vermont St.; Thursdays, Native Sons Hall, 11th and Clay Sts.

Wisteria No. 127, Alvarado—Henry May, Pres.; J. M. Scribner, Sec., Livermore; 1st Thursday, I.O.O.F. Hall.

Halcyon No. 146, Alameda City—Charles J. Von-Tagen, Pres.; J. C. Bates, Sec., 2139 Buena Vista Ave.; 1st and 3rd Tuesdays, I.O.O.F. Hall, 2329 Santa Clara Ave.

Brooklyn No. 151, Oakland—Frank B. Perry, Pres.; E. W. Cooney, Sec., 3907 14th Ave.; Wednesdays, Masonic Temple, 8th Ave. and E. 14th St.

Washington No. 169, Centerville—F. T. Dusterberry, Pres.; Allen G. Norris, Sec., P. O. box 31; 2nd and 4th Tuesdays, Hansen Hall.

Athens No. 195, Oakland—Henry G. Kroeckel, Pres.; Harold B. Farley, Sec., 4623 Benevides Ave.; Tuesdays, Native Sons Hall, 11th and Clay Sts.

Berkeley No. 210, Berkeley—S. Levy, Pres.; R. J. Garrett, Sec., 1708 Virginia St.; Tuesdays, Native Sons Hall, 2108 Shattuck Ave.

Estudillo No. 223, San Leandro—Frank V. Pacheco, Pres.; Albert G. Pacheco, Sec., 1736 E. 14th St.; 1st and 3rd Tuesdays, Masonic Temple.

Claremont No. 240, Oakland—Fred Bueina, Pres.; E. N. Thienger, Sec., 839 Hearst Ave., Berkeley; Tuesdays, Veterans Memorial Bldg., 43rd & Salem Sts., Emeryville.

Pleasanton No. 244, Pleasanton—Peter C. Madsen, Pres.; Ernest W. Schween, Sec.; 2nd and 4th Thursdays, I.O.O.F. Hall.

Niles No. 250, Niles—M. L. Fournier, Pres.; C. E. Martenstein, Sec.; 2nd Thursday, I.O.O.F. Hall.

Fruitvale No. 252, Oakland—Chester B. Abernethy, Pres.; Ray B. Felton, Sec., 1575 Alice St.; Fridays, W.O.W. Hall, 3256 E. 14th St.

AMADOR COUNTY.

Amador No. 17, Sutter Creek—H. T. Richards, Pres.; F. J. Payne, Sec.; 1st and 3rd Fridays, Native Sons Hall.

Excelsior No. 31, Jackson—Wm. Daugherty, Pres.; William Going, Sec.; 1st and 3rd Wednesdays, Native Sons Hall, 22 Court St.

Ione No. 33, Ione—Marvin Kidd, Pres.; Josiah H. Saunders, Sec.; 1st and 3rd Wednedays, Native Sons Hall.

Plymouth No. 48, Plymouth—L. E. Houston, Pres.; Thos. D. Davis, Sec.; 1st and 3rd Saturdays, I.O.O.F. Hall.

BUTTE COUNTY.

Argonaut No. 8, Oroville—Fred E. Tegrunde, Pres.; Cyril R. Macdonald, Sec., P. O. box 502; 1st and 3rd Wednesdays, Veterans Memorial Hall.

Chico No. 21, Chico—Marcus Cholsser, Pres.; Sam Lindsay Adams, Sec., Sacramento Blvd.; 2nd and 4th Thursdays, Elks Hall.

CALAVERAS COUNTY.

Chispa No. 139, Murphys—John Voitich, Pres.; Antone Malaspina, Sec.; Wednesdays, Native Sons Hall.

COLUSA COUNTY.

Colusa No. 69 Colusa City—S. A. Ottenwalter, Pres.; Phil J. Humburg, Sec., 223 Parkhill St.; Tuesdays, First National Bank Bldg.

CONTRA COSTA COUNTY.

General Winn No. 32, Antioch—Edmont T. Uren, Pres.; Joel H. Ford, Sec., P. O. box 311; 2nd and 4th Wednesdays, Union Hall.

Mount Diablo No. 101, Martinez—R. P. Anderson, Pres.; G. T. Barkley, Sec.; 1st and 3rd Mondays, I.O.O.F. Hall.

Byron No. 170, Byron—R. R. Houston, Pres.; H. G. Krumland, Sec.; 1st and 3rd Tuesdays, I.O.O.F. Hall.

Carquinez No. 205, Crockett—Thos. Cox, Pres.; Thomas I. Cahalan, Sec.; 1st and 3rd Wednesdays, I.O.O.F. Hall.

Richmond No. 217, Richmond—M. W. Amaral, Pres.; H. D. Mason, Sec.; 11 6th St.; Wednesdays, Redmen Hall, 11th and Neven Ave.

Concord No. 245, Concord—P. M. Soto, Pres.; D. E. Pramberg, Sec., P. O. box 235; 1st Tuesday, I.O.O.F. Hall.

Diamond No. 246, Pittsburg—Horace L. Lucide, Pres.; Francis A. Irving, Sec., 248 E. 5th St.; 1st and 3rd Wednesdays, Veterans Memorial Bldg.

GRAND OFFICERS.

John T. Newell........Junior Past Grand President
4611 Brynhurst, Los Angeles

Dr. Frank I. Gonzalez.............Grand President
Flood Bldg., San Francisco

Seth Millington.............Grand First Vice-pres.
Gridley

Justice Emmet Seawell....Grand Second Vice-pres.
State Bldg., San Francisco

Chas. A. Koenig..........Grand Third Vice-pres.
531 35th Ave., San Francisco

John T. Regan....................Grand Secretary
N.S.G.W. Bldg., 414 Mason St., San Francisco

John A. Corotto..................Grand Treasurer
560 No. 5th St., San Jose

Horace J. Leavitt..................Grand Marshal
Weaverville

W. B. O'Brien................Grand Inside Sentinel
2324 Santa Clara St., Alameda

Gam Hurst ....Grand Outside Sentinel
1400 Financial Center Bldg., Oakland

Leslie Maloche.....................Grand Organist
467½ 3rd St., San Bernardino

George H. Barron.................Historiographer
333 12th Ave., San Francisco

GRAND TRUSTEES.

George F. McNoble......California Bldg., Stockton
Samuel M. Shortridge Jr.................Menlo Park
Jesse H. Miller..712 DeYoung Bldg., San Francisco
Joseph J. McShane..419 Flood Bldg., San Francisco
Frank M. Lane............333 Blackstone, Fresno
John M. Burnett............................San Jose
Eldred L. Meyer....922 San Vincente, Santa Monica

EL DORADO COUNTY.

Placerville No. 9, Placerville—Jos. Scherrer, Pres.; Duncan Bathurst, Sec., 12 Gilmore St.; 2nd and 4th Tuesdays, Masonic Hall.

Georgetown No. 91, Georgetown—J. H. Stanton, Pres.; C. F. Irish, Sec.; 2nd and 4th Wednesdays, I.O.O.F. Hall.

FRESNO COUNTY.

Fresno No. 25, Fresno City—E. F. Fitzgerald, Pres.; John W. Cappleman, Sec., 1389 Wilson; Fridays, W.O.W. Hall, 1354 Van Ness Ave.

Selma No. 107, Selma—Chester E. Shepard, Pres.; E. C. Laughlin, Sec.; 1st Wednesday, American Legion Hall.

HUMBOLDT COUNTY.

Humboldt No. 14, Eureka—Edward J. Quinn, Pres.; Loren M. Nelson, Sec., P. O. Box 195; 2nd and 4th Mondays, Native Sons Hall.

Arcata No. 20, Arcata—George Hale, Pres.; William Peters, Sec., P. O. box 1117; Thursdays, Native Sons Hall.

Ferndale No. 93, Ferndale—O. R. Frame, Pres; C. H. Rasmussen, Sec., R.F.D. 47-A; 1st and 3rd Mondays, K.P. Hall.

KERN COUNTY.

Bakersfield No. 42, Bakersfield—G. E. Taylor, Pres.; Leroy Vandervoort, Sec., P. O. Box 1013; Wednesdays, Justice Court, City Hall.

LAKE COUNTY.

Lower Lake No. 159, Lower Lake—Harold S. Anderson, Pres.; Albert Kugelman, Sec.; Thursdays, I.O.O.F. Hall.

LASSEN COUNTY.

Honey Lake No. 198, Standish—N. B. Elledge, Pres.; W. B. Dewitt, Sec., 842 Roop St., Susanville; 1st and 3rd Wednesdays, Wrede Hall.

Big Valley No. 211, Bieber—George Bunselmeier, Pres.; A. W. McKenzie, Sec.; 1st and 3rd Wednesdays, I.O.O.F. Hall.

LOS ANGELES COUNTY.

Los Angeles No. 45, Los Angeles City—Lee E. Erwin, Pres.; Richard W. Fryer, Sec., 1629 Champlain Ter.; Thursdays, Merchant Plumbers Hall, 1332 So. Hope.

Ramona No. 109, Los Angeles City—Chandos E. Bush, Pres.; John V. Scott, Sec., Patriotic Hall, 1816 So. Figueroa; Fridays, Patriotic Hall, 1816 So. Figueroa.

Hollywood No. 196, Los Angeles City—Fred Gamble Jr., Pres.; E. J. Reilly, Sec., 210 S. Fremont St.; Mondays, Hollywood Conservatory Music, 5402 Hollywood Blvd.

Long Beach No. 239, Long Beach—Francis H. Gentry, Pres.; W. W. Brady, Sec., 801 Jergins Trust Bldg.; 2nd and 4th Thursdays, Moose Hall, Elm and Anaheim.

Sepulveda No. 263, San Pedro—Lawrence Powers, Pres.; Frank I. Markey, Sec., 101 W. 7th St.; 2nd and 4th Fridays, Odd Fellows Temple, 10th and Gaffey Sts.

Glendale No. 264, Glendale—Philip D. Molen, Pres.; Abel B. Molen, Sec., 508 So. Belmont St.; 1st and 3rd Tuesdays, Masonic Temple, 234 So. Brand Blvd.

Santa Monica Bay No. 267, Ocean Park—Frederick E. Barnes, Pres.; John J. Smith, Sec., 830 Rialto Ave., Venice; 2nd and 4th Mondays, New Eagle Hall, 2823½ Main St.

Cahuenga No. 268, Reseda—Harold C. Trexler, Pres.; Walter A. Knapp, Sec., 7711 Owensmouth Ave., Canoga Park; first Friday, Alton Hall.

MADERA COUNTY.

Madera No. 130, Madera City—Cornelius Noble, Pres.; T. P. Cosgrave, Sec.; 1st and 3rd Thursdays, First National Bank Bldg.

MARIN COUNTY.

Mount Tamalpais No. 64, San Rafael—Walter Mazza, Pres.; Manuel A. Andrade, Sec., 532 Mission Ave.; 1st and 3rd Mondays, Portuguese American Hall.

Sea Point No. 158, Sausalito—Allyn T. Young, Pres.; Manuel Santos, Sec., 6 Glen Drive; 1st and 3rd Wednesdays, Perry Bldg.

Nicasio No. 183, Nicasio—M. T. Farley, Pres.; R. J. Rogers, Sec.; 2nd and 4th Wednesdays, U.A.O.D. Hall.

MENDOCINO COUNTY.

Ukiah No. 71, Ukiah—Albert T. Bechtol, Pres.; Ben Hofman, Sec., P. O. box 473; 1st and 3rd Mondays, I.O.O.F. Hall.

Broderick No. 117, Point Arena—Sam Reinking, Pres.; H. C. Hunter, Sec.; 1st and 3rd Thursdays, Forester Hall.

Alder Glen No. 200, Fort Bragg—T. J. Simpson, Pres.; C. R. Weller, Sec.; 2nd and 4th Fridays, I.O.O.F. Hall.

ATTENTION, SECRETARIES!

THIS DIRECTORY IS PUBLISHED BY AUTHORITY OF THE GRAND PARLOR N.S.G.W., AND ALL NOTICES OF CHANGES MUST BE RECEIVED BY THE GRAND SECRETARY (NOT THE MAGAZINE) ON OR BEFORE THE 20TH OF EACH MONTH TO INSURE CORRECTION IN NEXT ISSUE OF DIRECTORY.

MERCED COUNTY.

Yosemite No. 24, Merced City—Anthony A. Rodrigues, Pres.; True W. Fowler, Sec., P. O. box 781; 2nd and 4th Mondays, I.O.O.F. Hall.

MONTEREY COUNTY.

Monterey No. 75, Monterey City—John Thomsen, Pres.; T. W. Krieger, Sec., 999 Franklin St.; 1st and 3rd Fridays, Knights Pythias Hall, Main St.

Santa Lucia No. 97, Salinas—E. L. Adcock, Pres.; R. W. Adcock, Sec., Route 2, box 141; Mondays, Native Sons Hall, 32 W. Alisal St.

Gabilan No. 132, Castroville—George Rodriguez, Pres.; R. H. Martin, Sec., P. O. box 81; 1st and 3rd Thursdays, Native Sons Hall.

NAPA COUNTY.

Saint Helena No. 53, Saint Helena—E. W. Johnson, Pres.; Edw. L. Bonhote, Sec., P. O. box 267; Mondays, Native Sons Hall.

Napa No. 62, Napa City—A. G. Boggs, Pres.; H. J. Hoernle, Sec., 1226 Oak St.; Mondays, Native Sons Hall.

Calistoga No. 86, Calistoga—Frank Mariani, Pres.; Louis Carlenzoli, Sec.; 1st and 3rd Mondays, I.O.O.F. Hall.

NEVADA COUNTY.

Hydraulic No. 56, Nevada City—Spencer G. White, Pres.; Dr. C. W. Chapman, Sec.; Tuesdays, Pythian Castle.

Quartz No. 58, Grass Valley—Richard Hoskins, Pres.; H. Ray George, Sec., 151 Conaway Ave.; Mondays, Auditorium Hall.

Donner No. 162, Truckee—J. F. Lichtenberger, Pres.; H. C. Lichtenberger, Sec.; 2nd and 4th Tuesdays, Native Sons Hall.

ORANGE COUNTY.

Santa Ana No. 265, Santa Ana—R. L. Marsile, Pres.; E. F. Marks, Sec., 1124 No. Bristol St.; 1st and 3rd Mondays, K.C. Hall, 4th and French Sts.

PLACER COUNTY.

Auburn No. 59, Auburn—Cosme Vicencio, Pres.; J. G. Walsh, Sec.; 1st and 3rd Fridays, Foresters Hall.

Silver Star No. 63, Lincoln—Frank Meyers, Pres.; Barney G. Barry, Sec., P. O. box 72; 3rd Wednesday, I.O.O.F. Hall.

Rocklin No. 233, Roseville—Thomas Elliott, Pres.; M. E. Reed, Sec., 253 W. Duranta; 2nd and 4th Wednesdays, Eagles Hall.

PLUMAS COUNTY.

Quincy No. 131, Quincy—J. O. Moncur, Pres.; E. C. Kelsey, Sec.; 2nd Thursday, I.O.O.F. Hall.

Golden Anchor No. 182, La Porte—R. J. McGrath, Pres.; LeRoy J. Post, Sec.; 2nd and 4th Sunday mornings, Native Sons Hall.

Plumas No. 228, Taylorsville—E. E. Sikes, Pres.; George E. Boyden, Sec.; 1st and 3rd Mondays, Native Sons Hall.

SACRAMENTO COUNTY.

Sacramento No. 3, Sacramento City—Joseph Hellinge Jr., Pres.; J. F. Didion, Sec., 1131 "O" St.; Thursdays, Native Sons Bldg., 11th and "J" Sts.

Sunset No. 26, Sacramento City—George W. Lial, Pres.; Edward E. Reese, Sec., County Treasurer Office; Mondays, Native Sons Bldg., 11th and "J" Sts.

Elk Grove No. 41, Elk Grove—Fred Sehlmeyer, Pres.; Walter Martin, Sec.; 2nd and 4th Fridays, Masonic Hall.

Granite No. 83, Folsom—Joe Relvas, Pres.; Frank Showers, Sec.; 2nd and 4th Tuesdays, K.P. Hall.

Courtland No. 106, Courtland—Albert Pyhnan, Pres.; Jos. Green, Sec.; 1st Saturday and 3rd Monday, Native Sons Hall.

Sutter Fort No. 241, Sacramento City—August Lehman, Pres.; C. L. Katzenstein, Sec., P. O. box 914; 2nd and 4th Wednesdays, Native Sons Bldg., 11th and "J" Sts.

Galt No. 243, Galt—John Granadas, Pres.; F. W. Harms, Sec.; 1st and 3rd Mondays, I.O.O.F. Hall.

SAN BENITO COUNTY.

Fremont No. 44, Hollister—Chas. B. Arbeleche, Pres.; J. E. Prendergast Jr., Sec., 1064 Monterey St.; 1st and 3rd Thursdays, Grangers Union Hall.

SAN BERNARDINO COUNTY.

Arrowhead No. 110, San Bernardino City—Lynn A. Reed, Pres.; R. W. Brazelton, Sec., 462 6th St.; Wednesdays, Eagles Hall, 469 4th St.

SAN DIEGO COUNTY.

San Diego No. 108, San Diego City—Gregory A. McHorney, Pres.; A. V. Mayrhofer, Sec., 1572 2nd St.; Wednesdays, K.C. Hall, 4th and Elm Sts.

SAN FRANCISCO CITY AND COUNTY.

California No. 1, San Francisco—Sal Juliano, Pres.; Ellis A. Blackman, Sec., 126 Front St.; Thursdays, Native Sons Bldg., 414 Mason St.

Pacific No. 10, San Francisco—John C. Daly, Pres.; J. Henry Bastein, Sec., 1880 Howard St.; Tuesdays, Native Sons Bldg., 414 Mason St.

Golden Gate No. 29, San Francisco—Thomas I. Schlink, Pres.; Adolph Eberhart, Sec., 183 Carl St.; Mondays, Native Sons Bldg., 414 Mason St.

Mission No. 38, San Francisco—Leslie Greine Jr., Pres.; Thos. J. Stewart, Sec., 1919 Howard St.; Wednesdays, Redmen Hall, 3053 16th St.

San Francisco No. 49, San Francisco—Louis L. Ghiotti, Pres.; David Capurro, Sec., 976 Union St.; Thursdays, Native Sons Bldg., 414 Mason St.

El Dorado No. 52, San Francisco—Eugene Herzog, Pres.; Alfred Vlautin, Sec., 1537 Franklin St.; Thursdays, Native Sons Bldg., 414 Mason St.

Rincon No. 72, San Francisco—Michael J. Joyce, Pres.; John A. Gilmour, Sec., 2069 Golden Gate Ave.; Wednesdays, Native Sons Bldg., 414 Mason St.

Stanford No. 76, San Francisco—Albert W. Groskopf, Pres.; Charles T. O'Kane, Sec., 1111 Pine St.; Tuesdays, Native Sons Bldg., 414 Mason St.

Bay City No. 104, San Francisco—Morris Garren, Pres.; Max E. Licht, Sec., 1831 Fulton St.; 2nd and 4th Wednesdays, Native Sons Bldg., 414 Mason St.

Niantic No. 105, San Francisco—A. Furner, Pres.; J. M. Darcy, Sec., 10 Hoffman Ave.; Wednesdays, Native Sons Bldg., 414 Mason St.

National No. 118, San Francisco—Wayne Burke, Pres.; Martin M. Ratigan, Sec., 1325 Page St., Apt. 6.; Thursdays, 1160 Eddy St.

Hesperian No. 137, San Francisco—Walter A. Bermingham, Pres.; Albert Carlson, Sec., 379 Justin Dr.; Thursdays, Native Sons Bldg., 414 Mason St.
Alcalde No. 154, San Francisco—John S. La Barbera, Pres.; Harry S. Burke, Sec., 25 Ord St.; 2nd and 4th Wednesdays, Native Sons Bldg., 414 Mason St.
South San Francisco No. 157, San Francisco—Raymond Conroy, Pres.; John T. Regan, Sec., 1489 Newcomb Ave.; Wednesdays, Masonic Bldg., 4705 3rd St.
Sequoia No. 160, San Francisco—Chester Moreno, Pres.; Walter W. Garrett, Sec., 2500 Van Ness Ave.; Mondays, Swedish-American Bldg., 2174 Market St.
Precita No. 187, San Francisco—Geo. T. Butler, Pres.; Edward Tietjen, Sec., 1367 15th Ave.; Thursdays, Mission Masonic Hall, 2668 Mission St.
Olympus No. 189, San Francisco—Louis Helbing, Pres.; Harvey J. Carty, Sec., 1651 Market St., Apt. 505; 2nd and 4th Tuesdays, Independent Redmen Hall, 3053 16th St.
Presidio No. 194, San Francisco—Paul Pasquet, Pres.; George A. Ducker, Sec., 442 21st Ave.; Mondays, Native Sons Bldg., 414 Mason St.
Marshall No. 202, San Francisco—Arthur Belli, Pres.; Frank Baciglalupi, Sec., 725 Douglas St.; 1st and 3rd Wednesdays, Native Sons Bldg., 414 Mason St.
Dolores No. 208, San Francisco—Daniel Corrigan, Pres.; Eugene O'Donnell, Sec., Mills Bldg.; Tuesdays, Mission Masonic Bldg., 2668 Mission St.
Twin Peaks No. 214, San Francisco—Fred Seeman, Pres.; Thos. Pendergast, Sec., 278 Douglas St.; Wednesdays, Willopi Hall, 4061 24th St.
El Capitan No. 222, San Francisco—Frank Rizzo, Pres.; James Hanna, Sec., 2450 27th Ave.; 1st and 3rd Thursdays, King Soloman Hall, 1739 Fillmore St.
Guadalupe No. 231, San Francisco—George Miles, Pres.; Alvin A. Johnson, Sec., 142 Rousseau St.; Tuesdays, Guadalupe Hall, 4551 Mission St.
Castro No. 232, San Francisco—David A. Simon, Pres.; James H. Hayes, Sec., 4014 18th St.; Tuesdays, Native Sons Bldg., 414 Mason St.
Balboa No. 234, San Francisco—J. LeMer, Pres.; E. W. Boyd, Sec., 45 Carl St.; Thursdays, Maccabee Hall, 6th Ave. and Clement St.
James Lick No. 242, San Francisco—M. G. Mullen, Pres.; Wm. Band, Sec., 2587 22nd Ave.; 1st and 3rd Tuesdays, Redmen Hall, 3053 16th St.
Bret Harte No. 260, San Francisco—J. F. Craig, Pres.; C. J. Eggers, Sec., 194 Prague St.; Tuesdays, West of Twin Peaks Hall, 233 Legion Court.
Utopia No. 270, San Francisco—Joseph Riordan, Pres.; Herbert H. Schneider, Sec., 2455 16th Ave.; Tuesdays, American Hall, 20th and Capp Sts.

SAN JOAQUIN COUNTY.

Stockton No. 7, Stockton—Eugene Allison, Pres.; R. D. Dorcey, Sec., P. O. box 388; Mondays, Native Sons Hall.
Lodi No. 18, Lodi—Ray Rodocker, Pres.; Dr. Clyde Bresnan, Sec.; 2nd and 4th Wednesdays, Eagles Hall.
Tracy No. 186, Tracy—R. J. Marraccini, Pres.; R. J. Marraccini, Sec., R.F.D. No. 1, box 217; Thursdays, I.O.O.F. Hall.
Manteca No. 271, Manteca—S. A. Whiting, Pres.; Leonard Faria, Sec., R.F.D. No. 1, Lathrop; 1st and 3rd Wednesdays, I.O.O.F. Hall.

SAN LUIS OBISPO COUNTY.

San Miguel No. 150, San Miguel—H. Twisselman, Pres.; George Sonnenberg Jr., Sec.; 1st and 3rd Wednesdays, Fraternal Hall.
Cambria No. 152, Cambria—L. Bernardisca, Pres.; A. S. Gay, Sec.; Wednesdays, Rigdon Hall.

SAN MATEO COUNTY.

Redwood No. 66, Redwood City—Oscar O. Gustafson, Pres.; A. S. Liguori, Sec., P. O. box 212; Thursdays, American Foresters Hall.
Seaside No. 95, Halfmoon Bay—Edward Deeney, Pres.; John G. Gilcrest, Sec.; 2nd and 4th Tuesdays, I.O.O.F. Hall.
Menlo No. 185, Menlo Park—John Bracisco, Pres.; F. W. Johnson, Sec., P. O. box 601; Thursdays, Duff & Doyle Hall.
Pebble Beach No. 230, Pescadero—Bernard Cabral, Pres.; E. A. Shaw, Sec.; 2nd and 4th Wednesdays, I.O.O.F. Hall.
El Carmelo No. 256, Daly City—Leonard J. Mohr, Pres.; Andrew P. Murphy, Sec., 931 Hanover St.; 2nd and 4th Wednesdays, Eagles Hall.
Industrial City No. 269, South San Francisco—John C. Hamilton, Pres.; Geo. A. Roll, Sec., P. O. box 237; 2nd and 4th Mondays, Metropolitan Hall.

SANTA BARBARA COUNTY.

Santa Barbara No. 116, Santa Barbara City—John L. Stewart, Pres.; H. C. Sweetser, Sec., Court House; 1st and 3rd Wednesdays, I.O.O.F. Hall.

SANTA CLARA COUNTY.

San Jose No. 22, San Jose—William Lordge, Pres.; H. W. McComas, Sec., Suite 7, Porter Bldg.; Mondays, I.O.O.F. Hall.
Santa Clara No. 100, Santa Clara City—John J. Trinajstich, Pres.; Clarence Clevenger, Sec., P. O. box 297; 1st and 3rd Wednesdays, Redmen Hall.
Observatory No. 177, San Jose—Norton J. Mahon, Pres.; A. B. Langford, Sec., Hall Records; Tuesdays, Knights Columbus Hall, 40 No. First St.
Mountain View No. 215, Mountain View—Gilbert F. McCorkle, Pres.; C. A. Antonioli, Sec., 948 California St.; 2nd and 4th Fridays, Mockbee Hall.
Palo Alto No. 216, Palo Alto—Marion R. Smith, Pres.; Albert A. Quinn, Sec., 643 High St.; Mondays, Native Sons Bldg., Hamilton Ave. and Emerson St.

SANTA CRUZ COUNTY.

Watsonville No. 65, Watsonville—Cecil McGowan, Pres.; E. R. Tindall, Sec., 408 East Lake Ave.; 2nd and 4th Tuesdays, I.O.O.F. Hall.
Santa Cruz No. 90, Santa Cruz City—Elmer R. Dakan, Pres.; T. V. Mathews, Sec., 105 Pacheco Ave.; Tuesdays, Native Sons Hall, 117 Pacific Ave.

SHASTA COUNTY.

McCloud No. 149, Redding—Errol Yank, Pres.; Hugh A. Shuffleton, Sec.; 1st and 3rd Thursdays, Moose Hall.

SIERRA COUNTY.

Downieville No. 92, Downieville—J. M. McMahon, Pres.; H. S. Tibbey, Sec.; 2nd and 4th Mondays, I.O.O.F. Hall.
Golden Nugget No. 94, Sierra City—Leonard Thompson Jr., Pres; Arthur R. Pride, Sec.; last Saturday, Masonic Hall.

SISKIYOU COUNTY.

Etna No. 192, Etna—George Marx, Pres.; Harvey A. Green, Sec.; 1st and 3rd Wednesdays, I.O.O.F. Hall.
Liberty No. 193, Sawyers Bar—Orrin R. Bigelow, Pres.; John M. Barry, Sec.; 1st and 3rd Saturdays, I.O.O.F. Hall.

NATIVE SON NEWS

(Continued from Page 11)

Grand Parlor Board of Control, donated $1,500 toward the Pioneer Memorial building.

Large Class Initiated.

San Leandro—Estudillo No. 223 received an official visit December 15 from Grand Third Vice-president Chas. A. Koenig. There was a very large attendance of members and visitors, and an elaborate program was presented. A large class of candidates were initiated.

SOLANO COUNTY.

Solano No. 39, Suisun—Ralph E. Gilbert, Pres.; J. W. Kinloch, Sec.; 1st and 3rd Tuesdays, I.O.O.F. Hall.
Vallejo No. 77, Vallejo—John J. Combs, Pres.; Werner B. Hallin, Sec., 912 Carolina; 2nd and 4th Tuesdays, San Pablo Hall.

SONOMA COUNTY.

Petaluma No. 27, Petaluma—Wm. Bojorques, Pres.; C. F. Fobes, Sec., 114 Prospect St.; 2nd and 4th Mondays, Druid Hall, Gross Bldg., 41 Main St.
Santa Rosa No. 28, Santa Rosa—Henry T. Stone, Pres.; Leland S. Lewis, Sec., Court House; Tuesdays, Native Sons Hall.
Glen Ellen No. 102, Glen Ellen—C. C. Weise, Pres.; Frank Kirch, Sec., Route 3, Santa Rosa; 2nd Monday, N.S.G.W. Hall.
Sonoma No. 111, Sonoma City—Frederick Bulotti, Pres.; L. H. Green, Sec.; 1st and 3rd Mondays, I.O.O.F. Hall.
Sebastopol No. 143, Sebastopol—W. H. Murray, Pres.; F. G. McFarlane, Sec.; 1st and 3rd Fridays, I.O.O.F. Hall.

STANISLAUS COUNTY.

Modesto No. 11, Modesto—W. B. Mahoney, Pres.; C. C. Eastin Jr., Sec., P. O. box 898; 1st and 3rd Wednesdays, I.O.O.F. Hall.
Oakdale No. 142, Oakdale—D W. Tulloch, Pres.; E. T. Gobin, Sec.; 2nd Monday, Legion Hall.
Orestimba No. 247, Crows Landing—Lloyd W. Fink, Pres.; G. W. Fink, Sec.; 1st and 3rd Wednesdays, Community Club Home.

SUTTER COUNTY.

Sutter No. 261, Sutter City—Stanley R. McLean, Pres.; Glen R. Haynes, Sec., Yuba City; 2nd and 4th Mondays, N.D.G.W. Hall.

TRINITY COUNTY.

Mount Bally No. 87, Weaverville—M. F. Kay, Pres.; E. V. Ryan, Sec.; 1st and 3rd Mondays, Native Sons Hall.

TUOLUMNE COUNTY.

Tuolumne No. 144, Sonora—Mathew J. Marshall, Pres.; William M. Harrington, Sec., P. O. box 715; 2nd and 4th Fridays, Knights Columbus Hall.
Columbia No. 258, Columbia—Jos. Cadematori, Pres.; Charles E. Grant, Sec.; 2nd and 4th Thursdays, Native Sons Hall.

VENTURA COUNTY.

Cabrillo No. 114, Ventura City—David Bennett, Pres., 1380 Church St.

YOLO COUNTY.

Woodland No. 30, Woodland—J. L. Aronson, Pres.; E. B. Hayward, Sec.; 1st Thursday, Native Sons Hall.

YUBA COUNTY.

Marysville No. 6, Marysville—John McQuaid, Pres.; Verne Fogarty, Sec., 719 6th St.; 2nd Friday, Foresters Hall.
Rainbow No. 40, Wheatland—W. E. Jones, Pres.; W. A. Bowser, Sec., P. O. box 313; 2nd Thursday, I.O.O.F. Hall.

AFFILIATED ORGANIZATIONS.

Alameda County Extension of the Order Committee, N.S.G.W.—Dr. William C. Freitas, Chmn.; Edgar G. Hansen, Sec., 1260 Russell St., Berkeley; meets 1st and 3rd Mondays, N.S.G.W. Hall, 11th and Clay Sts., Oakland.
Interparlor Committee (Southern District), N.S.G.W. and N.D.G.W.—Burrel D. Neighbours, Chmn.; F. J. Burmester, Sec., 2434 Micheltorena St., Los Angeles; meets 2nd and 4th Fridays, Patriotic Hall, 1816 So. Figueroa St., Los Angeles.
San Francisco Extension of the Order Committee, N.S.G.W.—Harmon D. Skillin, Chmn.; Harold J. Regan, Sec., 414 Mason St., San Francisco; meets 2nd and 4th Fridays, Grizzly Bear Club, 414 Mason St., San Francisco.
San Francisco Assembly No. 1 Past Presidents Association N.S.G.W.—Meets 1st and 3rd Fridays, Native Sons Bldg., 414 Mason St., San Francisco; H. F. Ricklefts, Gov., J. F. Stanley, Sec., 1175 O'Farrell St., San Francisco.
East Bay Counties Assembly No. 3 Past Presidents Association N.S.G.W.—Meets 4th Monday, Native Sons Hall, 11th and Clay Sts., Oakland; Lester O. Bruck, Gov.; Edgar G. Hanson, Sec., 1260 Russell St., Berkeley.
Marin County Assembly No. 5 Past Presidents Association N.S.G.W.—J. S. Rose Jr., Gov.; L. J. Peter, Sec., Peter Bldg., 4th and "C" Sts., San Rafael.
Fred H. Greely Assembly No. 6 Past Presidents Association N.S.G.W.—Meets monthly with different Parlors comprising district; R. L. P. Bigelow, Gov.; Barney Barry, Sec., P. O. box 72, Lincoln.
San Joaquin Assembly No. 7 Past Presidents Association N.S.G.W.—Meets 1st Friday, Native Sons Hall, Stockton; Clyde H. Gregg, Gov.; R. D. Dorcey, Sec., Native Sons Club, Stockton.
Sonoma County Assembly No. 9 Past Presidents Association N.S.G.W.—Meets monthly at different Parlor headquarters in county; Louis Bosch, Gov.; L. S. Lewis, Sec., Court House, Santa Rosa.
General John A. Sutter Assembly No. 10 Past Presidents Association—L. P. Ferron, Gov.; Jas. J. Longshore, Sec., 514 "J" St., Sacramento.
Grizzly Bear Club—Members all Parlors outside San Francisco at all times welcome. Clubrooms top floor Native Sons Bldg., 414 Mason St., San Francisco.
Native Sons and Native Daughters Central Committee on Homeless Children—Main office, 955 Phelan Bldg., San Francisco; Mrs. John W. Stirling, Chmn.; Miss Mary E. Brusie, Sec. Los Angeles branch office, 3924 Sunset Blvd.; Dorothy Schlingman, Sec.

(ADVERTISEMENT.)

N.S.G.W. OFFICIAL DEATH LIST.

Containing the name, the date and the place of birth, the date of death, and the Subordinate Parlor affiliation of deceased members reported to Grand Secretary John T. Regan from November 20, 1931, to December 19, 1931:

Heilbron, Henry A.; Sacramento, May 19, 1861; September 26, 1931; Sacramento No. 3.
Giannelli, John P.; Sacramento, September 10, 1864; October 29, 1931; Sacramento No. 3.
Miller, John Henry; Sacramento, June 10, 1880; November 25, 1931; Sacramento No. 3.
McLean, Wallace; Freshwater, April 9, 1886; December 1, 1931; Humboldt No. 14.
Schwilke, Charles Frederick; Shaws Flat, November 22, 1858; December 2, 1931; Sunset No. 26.
Brunotte, Paul; San Francisco, October 20, 1864; July 15, 1931; Golden Gate No. 29.
Snyder, William Henry; Sacramento, August 15, 1879; August 15, 1931; Golden Gate No. 29.
Watkins, Harry Newton Hoag; Washington, July 22, 1878; November 9, 1931; Oakland No. 50.
Bonivert, Frank A.; Grass Valley, August 6, 1879; November 9, 1931; El Dorado No. 52.
Zanzi, Paul; San Francisco, June 20, 1870; October 11, 1931; Rincon No. 72.
Clark, Alfred John; San Francisco, June 20, 1869; October 31, 1931; Rincon No. 72.
Houseman, Frank S.; San Francisco, September 21, 1858; December 5, 1931; Vallejo No. 77.
Lyter, Albert William; San Jose, April 21, 1880; July 3, 1931; Ramona No. 109.
Pimentel, William E.; Hayward, June 23, 1867; November 30, 1931; Eden No. 113.
Fitzgerald, John Patrick; Stanislaus, October 12, 1875; November 20, 1931; Oakdale No. 142.
Stumpf, Peter B.; Downieville, March 14, 1868; November 14, 1931; South San Francisco No. 157.
McDonald, John; San Francisco, June 10, 1885; December 11, 1931; Presidio No. 194.
Hartman, Fred William; Oakland, August 14, 1879; November 14, 1931; Athens No. 195.
Hodnett, William James; San Francisco, November 14, 1870; September 9, 1931; Carquinez No. 205.
Kernan, Arthur Thomas; San Francisco, June 7, 1884; November 27, 1931; El Capitan No. 222.
Dawson, Dr. W. C.; St. Helena; February 20, 1884; November 13, 1931; Balboa No. 234.
Smithwick, Sid; Glenville, February 28, 1875; November 23, 1931; Santa Ana No. 265.
Walker, Harrie Lloyd; Oakland, January 18, 1896; November 19, 1931; Santa Monica Bay No. 267.

FLORENCE N. TRUE.

To the Officers and Members of Annie K. Bidwell Parlor No. 168 N.D.G.W.—We, your committee appointed to draft resolutions of respect to the memory of our late sister, Florence N. True, respectfully submit the following:

Whereas, Once again we bow to the will of Almighty God, who has seen fit to claim His own from amongst our membership and taken to His heavenly home our esteemed sister, Florence N. True, organizer and past president of this Parlor. Sister True, as a member of Califia Parlor No. 22 of Sacramento, organized Annie K. Bidwell Parlor on December 17, 1908, and later, on March 25, 1909, transferred her membership to this Parlor.

Resolved, That our charter be draped in mourning; that a copy of these resolutions be spread upon the minutes of our Parlor, and that a copy be sent to The Grizzly Bear for publication.

NORA ARNOLD, Chairman.
MYRTLE BERNARDO,
ETHEL M. ESTES,
Committee.

Chico, December 7, 1931.

Official Directory of Parlors of the N. D. G. W.

ALAMEDA COUNTY.

Angelita No. 32, Livermore—Meets 2nd and 4th Fridays, Foresters Hall; Mrs. Orlena Beck, Rec. Sec., 1109 First St.

Piedmont No. 87, Oakland—Meets Thursdays, Corinthian Hall, Pacific Bldg.; Mrs. Alice E. Miner, Rec. Sec., 421 36th St.

Aloha No. 106, Oakland—Meets Tuesdays, Wigwam Hall, Pacific Bldg.; Gladys L. Farley, Rec. Sec., 4623 Benevides Ave.

Hayward No. 122, Hayward—Meets 1st and 3rd Tuesdays, Bank Hayward Hall, "B" St.; Miss Ruth Gansberger, Rec. Sec., P. O. Box 44, Mount Eden.

Berkeley No. 150, Berkeley—Meets 1st Friday, Masonic Hall; Mrs. Lelia B. Baker, Rec. Sec., 915 Contra Costa Ave.

Bear Flag No. 151, Berkeley—Meets 2nd and 4th Wednesdays, Veterans Memorial Bldg., 1931 Center St.; Mrs. Maud Wagner, Rec. Sec., 317 Alcatraz Ave., Oakland.

Encinal No. 156, Alameda—Meets 2nd and 4th Thursdays, N.S.G.W. Hall; Mrs. Laura E. Fisher, Rec. Sec., 1413 Caroline St.

Brooklyn No. 157, East Oakland—Meets Wednesdays, Masonic Temple, 8th Ave. and E. 14th St.; Mrs. Ruth Cooney, Rec. Sec., 3907 14th Ave.

Argonaut No. 166, Oakland—Meets Tuesdays, Klinkner Hall, 59th and San Pablo; Mrs. Ada Spilman, Rec. Sec., 2905 Ellis St., Berkeley.

Bahia Vista No. 167, Oakland—Meets Thursdays, Wigwam Hall, Pacific Bldg.; Mrs. Minnie E. Raper, Rec. Sec., 3449 Helen St.

Fruitvale No. 177, Oakland—Meets Fridays, W.O.W. Hall; Mrs. Agnes M. Grant, Rec. Sec., 1224 30th Ave.

Laura Loma No. 182, Niles—Meets 1st and 3rd Tuesdays, I.O.O.F. Hall; Mrs. Ethel Fournier, Rec. Sec., P. O. Box 515.

El Cereso No. 207, San Leandro—Meets 2nd and 4th Tuesdays, Masonic Hall; Mrs. Mary Tuttle, Rec. Sec., P. O. Box 56.

Pleasanton No. 237, Pleasanton—Meets 1st and 3rd Tuesdays, I.O.O.F. Hall; Mrs. Myrtle Lanini, Rec. Sec.

Betsy Ross No. 238, Centerville—Meets 1st and 3rd Fridays, Anderson Hall; Miss Constance Lucio, Rec. Sec., P. O. Box 187.

AMADOR COUNTY.

Ursula No. 1, Jackson—Meets 2nd and 4th Tuesdays, N.S.G.W. Hall; Mrs. Emma Boarman-Wright, Rec. Sec., 114 Court St.

Chispa No. 40, Ione—Meets 2nd and 4th Fridays, N.S.G.W. Hall; Mrs. Isabel Ashton, Rec. Sec.

Amapola No. 80, Sutter Creek—Meets 2nd and 4th Thursdays, N.S.G.W. Bldg.; Mrs. Hazel M. Marre, Rec. Sec.

Forrest No. 86, Plymouth—Meets 2nd and 4th Tuesdays, I.O.O.F. Hall; Mrs. Marguerite Davis, Rec. Sec.

BUTTE COUNTY.

Annie K. Bidwell No. 168, Chico—Meets 2nd and 4th Thursdays, I.O.O.F. Hall; Mrs. Irene Henry, Rec. Sec., 3016 Woodland Ave.

Gold of Ophir No. 190, Oroville—Meets 1st and 3rd Wednesdays, Memorial Hall; Mrs. Ruth Brown, Rec. Sec., 1265 Leah Court.

CALAVERAS COUNTY.

Auby No. 46, Murphys—Meets Fridays, N.S.G.W. Hall; Belle Segale, Rec. Sec.

Princess No. 84, Angels Camp—Meets 2nd Wednesday, I.O.O.F. Hall; Emma May, Rec. Sec.

San Andreas No. 113, San Andreas—Meets 1st Friday, Fraternal Hall; Miss Doris Treat, Rec. Sec.

COLUSA COUNTY.

Colus No. 194, Colusa—Meets 1st and 3rd Mondays, N.S.G.W. Hall; Mrs. Ruby Humburg, 223 Park Hill St.

CONTRA COSTA COUNTY.

Stirling No. 146, Pittsburg—Meets 1st and 3rd Wednesdays, Veteran Memorial Hall; Mrs. Minnie Marcelli, Rec. Sec., 771 E. 12th St.

Richmond No. 147, Richmond—Meets 1st and 3rd Tuesdays, I.O.O.F. Hall, 10th St.; Mrs. Tillie Summers, Rec. Sec., 640 So. 31st St.

Donner No. 193, Byron—Meets 1st and 3rd Wednesdays, I.O.O.F. Hall; Mrs. Anna Pendry, Rec. Sec., P. O. Box 112.

Las Juntas No. 221, Martinez—Meets 1st and 3rd Mondays, Pythias Castle; Mrs. Lola Viera, Rec. Sec., P. O. box 128.

Antioch No. 223, Antioch—Meets 2nd and 4th Tuesdays, I.O.O.F. Hall; Mrs. Estelle Evans, Rec. Sec., 202 E. 5th St., Pittsburg.

Carquinez No. 234, Crockett—Meets 2nd and 4th Wednesdays, I.O.O.F. Hall; Mrs. Cecile Petee, Rec. Sec., 465 Edwards St.

GRAND OFFICERS.

Mrs. Estelle M. Evans........Past Grand President
202 E. Fifth St., Pittsburg

Mrs. Evelyn I. Carlson............Grand President
1965 San Jose Ave., San Francisco

Mrs. Anna M. Armstrong.....Grand Vice-president
Woodland

Mrs. Sallie R. Thaler...............Grand Secretary
555 Baker St., San Francisco

Mrs. Susie K. Christ..............Grand Treasurer
555 Baker St., San Francisco

Mrs. Irma Laird.......................Grand Marshal
Alturas

Mrs. Minna K. Horn.........Grand Inside Sentinel
Etna

Mrs. Orinda G. Giannini.....Grand Outside Sentinel
2142 Filbert St., San Francisco

Mrs. Lola Horgan....................Grand Organist
789 Morse St., San Francisco

GRAND TRUSTEES.

Mrs. Edna Briggs, 1045 Santa Ynez Way, Sacramento
Mrs. Ethel Begley.....1206 Valencia, San Francisco
Mrs. Anna Thuesen....615 38th Ave., San Francisco
Mrs. Gladys Noce ....Sutter Creek
Mrs. Florence Boyle............................Oroville
Mrs. Florence Schoneman, 1521 5th Ave., Los Angeles
Mrs. Willow Borba..........................Sebastopol

EL DORADO COUNTY.

Marguerite No. 12, Placerville—Meets 1st and 3rd Wednesdays, Masonic Hall; Mrs. Nettie Leonardi, Rec. Sec., 25 Coloma St.

El Dorado No. 186, Georgetown—Meets 2nd and 4th Saturday afternoons, I.O.O.F. Hall; Mrs. Alta L. Douglas, Rec. Sec.

FRESNO COUNTY.

Fresno No. 187, Fresno—Meets Fridays, Pythian Castle, Cor. "R" and Merced Sts.; Mary Aubery, Rec. Sec., 1040 Delphia Ave.

GLENN COUNTY.

Berryessa No. 192, Willows—Meets 1st and 3rd Mondays, I.O.O.F. Hall; Mrs. Leonora Neate, Rec. Sec., 338 No. Lassen St.

HUMBOLDT COUNTY.

Occident No. 28, Eureka—Meets 1st and 3rd Wed-
Rec. Sec., 2309 "B" St.
nesdays, N.S.G.W. Hall; Mrs. Eva L. MacDonald.

Oneonta No. 71, Ferndale—Meets 2nd and 4th Fridays, I.O.O.F. Hall; Mrs. Myra Rumrill, Rec. Sec.

Reichling No. 97, Fortuna—Meets 2nd and 4th Tuesdays, Friendship Hall; Mrs. Grace Swett, Rec. Sec., P. O. Box 328.

KERN COUNTY.

Miocene No. 228, Taft—Meets 1st and 3rd Wednesday afternoons, I.O.O.F. Hall; Mrs. Evalyne Towne, Rec. Sec., P. O. Box 1011.

El Tejon No. 239, Bakersfield—Meets 1st and 3rd Fridays, Castle Hall; Mrs. Grace Dorris, Rec. Sec., 127 Morgan Bldg.

Desert Gold No. 250, Mojave—Meets 2nd and 4th Fridays, I.O.O.F. Hall; Mrs. Mae Coffill, Rec. Sec.

LAKE COUNTY.

Clear Lake No. 135, Middletown—Meets 2nd and 4th Tuesdays, Herrick Hall; Mrs. Retta Reynolds, Rec. Sec., P. O. Box 180.

LASSEN COUNTY.

Nataqua No. 152, Standish—Meets 1st and 3rd Wednesdays, Foresters Hall; Mrs. Olive Bouchard, Rec. Sec.

Mount Lassen No. 215, Bieber—Meets 2nd and 4th Thursdays, I.O.O.F. Hall; Mrs. Angie C. Kenyon, Rec. Sec.

Susanville No. 243, Susanville—Meets 3rd Thursday, I.O.O.F. Hall; Mrs. Georgia Jensen, Rec. Sec., 706 Roop St.

LOS ANGELES COUNTY.

Los Angeles No. 124, Los Angeles—Meets 1st and 3rd Wednesdays, I.O.O.F. Hall, Washington and Oak Sts.; Mrs. Mary K. Corcoran, Rec. Sec., 322 No. Van Ness Ave.

Long Beach No. 154, Long Beach—Meets 1st and 3rd Thursdays, K.P. Hall, 341 Pacific Ave.; Mrs. Alice Waldow, Rec. Sec., 2175 Cedar Ave.

Rudecinda No. 230, San Pedro—Meets 1st and 3rd Fridays, Unity Hall, I.O.O.F. Temple, 10th and Gaffey; Mrs. Carrie E. Northway, Rec. Sec., 561 W. 14th St.

Verdugo No. 240, Glendale—Meets 2nd and 4th Tuesdays, Masonic Temple, 234 So. Brand Blvd.; Miss Etta Fulkerth, Rec. Sec., 526-A No. Orange St.

Santa Monica Bay No. 245, Ocean Park—Meets 1st and 3rd Mondays, New Eagles Hall, 2823½ Main St.; Mrs. Rosalie Hyde, Rec. Sec., 738 Flower St., Venice.

Californiana No. 247, Los Angeles—Meets 2nd and 4th Tuesday afternoons, Hollywood Studio Club, 1215 Lodi Place; Mrs. Inez Sitton, Rec. Sec., 4223 Berenice St.

MADERA COUNTY.

Madera No 244, Madera—Meets 2nd and 4th Thursdays Masonic Annex; Mrs. Margaret Boyle, Rec. Sec., 225 So. "C" St.

MARIN COUNTY.

Sea Point No. 196, Sausalito—Meets 2nd and 4th Mondays, Perry Hall, 50 Caledonia St.; Mrs. Mary B. Smith, Rec. Sec., 559 Woodward Ave.

Marinita No. 198, San Rafael—Meets 2nd and 4th Mondays, 316 "B" St.; Miss Mollye Y. Spaelti, Rec. Sec., 539 4th St.

Fairfax No. 225, Fairfax—Meets 2nd and 4th Tuesdays, Community Hall; Mrs. Olive A. Greene, Rec. Sec., P. O. Box 277.

Tamelpa No. 231, Mill Valley—Meets 1st and 3rd Tuesdays, I.O.O.F. Hall; Mrs. Delphine M. Todt, Rec. Sec., 400 Grand Ave., San Rafael.

MARIPOSA COUNTY.

Mariposa No. 63, Mariposa—Meets 1st and 3rd Fridays, I.O.O.F. Hall; Mrs. Mamie E. Weston, Rec. Sec.

ATTENTION, SECRETARIES!

THIS DIRECTORY IS PUBLISHED BY AUTHORITY OF THE GRAND PARLOR N.D.G.W., AND ALL NOTICES OF CHANGES MUST BE RECEIVED BY THE GRAND SECRETARY (NOT THE MAGAZINE) ON OR BEFORE THE 20TH OF EACH MONTH TO INSURE CORRECTION IN NEXT PUBLICATION OF DIRECTORY.

MENDOCINO COUNTY.

Fort Bragg No. 210, Fort Bragg—Meets 1st and 3rd Thursdays, I.O.O.F. Hall; Mrs. Ruth W. Fuller, Rec. Sec.

MERCED COUNTY.

Veritas No. 75, Merced—Meets 1st and 3rd Tuesdays, I.O.O.F. Hall; Miss Margaret Thornton, Rec. Sec., 317 18th St.

MODOC COUNTY.

Alturas No. 159, Alturas—Meets 1st Thursday, Alturas Civic Club; Mrs. Irma W. Laird, Rec. Sec.

MONTEREY COUNTY.

Aleli No. 102, Salinas—Meets 2nd and 4th Thursdays, I.O.O.F. Hall; Mrs. Rose Evelyn Rhyner, Rec. Sec., P. O. Box 1274.

Junipero No. 141, Monterey—Meets 1st and 3rd Thursdays, Custom House; Miss Matilda M. Bergschicker, Rec. Sec., 498 Van Buren St.

NAPA COUNTY.

Eschol No. 16, Napa—Meets 2nd and 4th Mondays, N.S.G.W. Hall; Mrs. Ella Ingram, Rec. Sec., 2140 Seminary St.

Calistoga No. 145, Calistoga—Meets 2nd and 4th Mondays, I.O.O.F. Hall; Sadie P. Brooks, Rec. Sec.

La Junta No. 203, Saint Helena—Meets 1st and 3rd Tuesdays, N.S.G.W. Hall; Mrs. Marie Signorelli, Rec. Sec., 1341 Madrona Ave.

NEVADA COUNTY.

Laurel No. 6, Nevada City—Meets 1st and 3rd Wednesdays, I.O.O.F. Hall; Mrs. Nellie E. Clark, Rec. Sec., P. O. Box 212.

Manzanita No. 29, Grass Valley—Meets 1st and 3rd Tuesdays, Auditorium; Mrs. Loraine Keast, Rec. Sec., 123 Race St.

Columbia No. 70, French Corral—Meets Fridays, Farrelley Hall; Mrs. Kate Farrelley-Sullivan, Rec. Sec.

Snow Peak No. 176, Truckee—Meets 2nd and 4th Fridays, I.O.O.F. Hall; Mrs. Henrietta M. Eaton, Rec. Sec., P. O. Box 116.

ORANGE COUNTY.

Santa Ana No. 235, Santa Ana—Meets 2nd and 4th Mondays, K.C. Hall, 4th and French Sts.; Mrs. Matilda S. Lemon, Rec. Sec., 1038 W. Bishop St.

Grace No. 242, Fullerton—Meets 1st and 3rd Thursdays, I.O.O.F. Hall, 116½ E. Commonwealth; Mrs. Mary Rothaermel, Rec. Sec., P. O. Box 235.

PLACER COUNTY.

Placer No. 138, Lincoln—Meets 2nd Wednesday, I.O.O.F. Hall; Miss Carrie Parlin, Rec. Sec.

La Rosa No. 191, Roseville—Meets 1st and 3rd Tuesdays, Eagles Hall; Mrs. Alice Lee West, Rec. Sec., Rocklin.

Auburn No. 233, Auburn—Meets 2nd and 4th Fridays, Foresters Hall; Mrs. Dorothy Reinecke, Rec. Sec., Penryn.

PLUMAS COUNTY.

Plumas Pioneer No. 219, Quincy—Meets 1st and 3rd Mondays, I.O.O.F. Hall; Minnie E. Johnson, Rec. Sec., P. O. Box 243.

SACRAMENTO COUNTY.

Califia No. 22, Sacramento—Meets 2nd and 4th Tuesdays, N.S.G.W. Hall; Miss Lulu Gillis, Rec Sec., 921 8th St.

La Bandera No. 110, Sacramento—Meets 1st and 3rd Fridays, N.S.G.W. Hall; Mrs. Clara Weldon, Rec. Sec., 1310 "O" St.

Sutter No. 111, Sacramento—Meets 1st and 3rd Tuesdays, N.S.G.W. Hall; Mrs. Adele Nix, Rec. Sec., 1238 "S" St.

Fern No. 123, Folsom—Meets 1st and 3rd Tuesdays, K.P. Hall; Mrs. Viola Shumway, Rec. Sec., P. O. Box 48.

Chabolla No. 171, Galt—Meets 2nd and 4th Tuesdays, I.O.O.F. Hall; Mrs. Mary Pritchard, Rec. Sec.

Coloma No. 212, Sacramento—Meets 1st and 3rd Tuesdays, I.O.O.F. Hall, Oak Park; Mrs. Nettie Harry, Rec. Sec., 1217 35th St.

Liberty No. 213, Elk Grove—Meets 2nd and 4th Fridays, I.O.O.F. Hall; Mrs. Frances Wackman, Rec. Sec., P. O. Box 192.

Victory No. 216, Courtland—Meets 1st Saturday and 3rd Monday, N.S.G.W. Hall; Mrs. Agneda Lample, Rec. Sec.

SAN BENITO COUNTY.

Copa de Oro No. 105, Hollister—Meets 2nd and 4th Thursdays, Grangers Union Hall; Mrs. Mollie Daveggio, Rec. Sec., 110 San Benito St.

San Juan Bautista No. 179, San Juan Bautista—Meets 1st Wednesday, Mission Corridor Rooms; Miss Gertrude Breen, Rec. Sec.

SAN BERNARDINO COUNTY.

Lugonia No. 241, San Bernardino—Meets 2nd and 4th Wednesdays, Eagles Hall; Evelyn T. Shaddox, Rec. Sec., 205 Temple St.

Ontario No. 251, Ontario—Meets 1st and 3rd Thursdays, Ontario Hall; Miss Helen Hickman, Rec. Sec.

SAN DIEGO COUNTY.

San Diego No. 208, San Diego—Meets 2nd and 4th Tuesdays, K.C. Hall, 410 Elm St.; Mrs. Elsie Case, Rec. Sec., 3051 Broadway.

SAN FRANCISCO CITY AND COUNTY.

Minerva No. 2, San Francisco—Meets 1st and 3rd Wednesdays, N.S.G.W. Bldg.; Miss Dorothy Finn, Rec. Sec., 90 Princess St., Sausalito.

Alta No. 3, San Francisco—Meets 2nd and 4th Tuesdays, N.S.G.W. Bldg.; Mrs. Agnese L. Hughes, Rec. Sec., 3980 Sacramento St.

Oro Fino No. 9, San Francisco—Meets 1st and 3rd Thursdays, N.S.G.W. Bldg.; Mrs. Josephine B. Morrisey, Rec. Sec., 4441 20th St.

Golden State No. 50, San Francisco—Meets 1st and 3rd Wednesdays, N.D.G.W. Home; Miss Millie Tietjen, Rec. Sec., 328 Lexington Ave.

Orinda No. 56, San Francisco—Meets 2nd and 4th Fridays, N.D.G.W. Home; Mrs. Anna A. Gruber-Loser, Rec. Sec., 72 Grove Lane, San Anselmo.

Fremont No. 59, San Francisco—Meets 1st and 3rd Tuesdays, N.S.G.W. Bldg.; Miss Hannah Collins, Rec. Sec., 563 Fillmore St.

Buena Vista No. 68, San Francisco—Meets 1st, 3rd and 5th Thursdays, N.D.G.W. Home; Miss Margaret Barrett, Rec. Sec., 2774 20th St.

Las Lomas No. 72, San Francisco—Meets 1st and 3rd Tuesdays, N.D.G.W. Home; Mrs. Marion S. Day, Rec. Sec., 471 Alvarado St.

Yosemite No. 83, San Francisco—Meets 1st and 3rd Tuesdays, American Hall, 20th and Capp Sts.; Miss Mary Bazley, Rec. Sec., 3353 22nd St.

La Estrella No. 89, San Francisco—Meets 2nd and 4th Mondays, N.S.G.W. Bldg.; Miss Birdie Hartman, Rec. Sec., 1018 Jackson St.

Sans Souci No. 96, San Francisco—Meets 2nd and 4th Mondays, N.D.G.W. Home; Mrs. Minnie F. Dobbin, Rec. Sec., 1483 43rd Ave.
Calaveras No. 103, San Francisco—Meets 2nd and 4th Tuesdays, Swedish American Hall, 2174 Market St.; Mrs. Lena Lorsheter, Rec. Sec., 492-C 41st St., Oakland.
Darina No. 114, San Francisco—Meets 1st and 3rd Mondays, N.S.G.W. Bldg.; Miss Adele Walsh, Rec. Sec., 479 Page St.
El Vespero No. 118, San Francisco—Meets 2nd and 4th Tuesdays, Masonic Hall, 4705 3rd St.; Mrs. Nell R. Buege, Rec. Sec., 1526 Kirkwood Ave.
Genevieve No. 132, San Francisco—Meets 1st and 3rd Thursdays, N.S.G.W. Bldg.; Miss Branice Peguillan, Rec. Sec., 2434 16th Ave.
Keith No. 137, San Francisco—Meets 2nd and 4th Thursdays, N.S.G.W. Bldg.; Mrs. Helen T. Mann, Rec. Sec., 575 Pierce St., Apt. 206.
Gabrielle No. 139, San Francisco—Meets 2nd and 4th Wednesdays, N.S.G.W. Bldg.; Mrs. Dorothy Wuesterfeld, Rec. Sec., 1020 Munich St.
Presidio No. 148, San Francisco—Meets 2nd and 4th Tuesdays, N.S.G.W. Bldg.; Mrs. Hattie Gaughran, Rec. Sec., 713 Capp St.
Guadalupe No. 153, San Francisco—Meets 2nd and 4th Mondays, Forester Hall, 170 Valencia St.; Miss May A. McCarthy, Rec. Sec., 336 Elsie St.
Golden Gate No. 158, San Francisco—Meets 2nd and 4th Mondays, N.S.G.W. Bldg.; Mrs. Margaret Ramm, Rec. Sec., 435-A Frederick St.
Dolores No. 169, San Francisco—Meets 2nd and 4th Wednesdays, N.S.G.W. Bldg.; Mrs. Ada Saunders, Rec. Sec., 284 Allison St.
Linda Rosa No. 170, San Francisco—Meets 2nd and 4th Wednesdays, Swedish American Hall, 2174 Market St.; Mrs. Eva P. Tyrrel, Rec. Sec., 2629 Mission St.
Portola No. 172, San Francisco—Meets 1st and 3rd Tuesdays, N.S.G.W. Bldg.; Catherine H. Dolly, Rec. Sec., 4125 23rd St.
Castro No. 178, San Francisco—Meets 1st and 3rd Wednesdays, K.C. Bldg., 150 Golden Gate Ave.; Miss Adeline Sandersfeld, Rec. Sec., 50 Baker St.
Twin Peaks No. 185, San Francisco—Meets 2nd and 4th Fridays, Druids Temple, 44 Page St.; Mrs. Loretta Cameron, Rec. Sec., 3969 Army St.
James Lick No. 220, San Francisco—Meets 1st and 3rd Wednesdays, N.S.G.W. Bldg.; Mrs. Edna Bishop, Rec. Sec., 3841 24th St.
Mission No. 227, San Francisco—Meets 2nd and 4th Fridays, N.S.G.W. Bldg.; Mrs. Ann Dippel, Rec. Sec., 448 Dewey Blvd.
Bret Harte No. 232 San Francisco—Meets 2nd and 4th Tuesdays, Schuberts Hall, 3009 16th St.; Muriele N. Pabst, Rec. Sec., 696 Guerrero St.
La Dorada No. 236, San Francisco—Meets 2nd and 4th Thursdays, N.S.G.W. Hall; Mrs. Theresa R. O'Brien, Rec. Sec., 567 Liberty St.
Balboa No. 249, San Francisco—Meets 1st and 3rd Thursdays, Maccabee Hall, 5th Ave. and Clement St., Jean Moffet, Rec. Sec., 422 Third Ave.

SAN JOAQUIN COUNTY.

Joaquin No. 5, Stockton—Meets 2nd and 4th Tuesdays, N.S.G.W. Hall, 314 E. Main St.; Mrs. Delia Garvin, Rec. Sec., 1122 E. Market St.
El Pescadero No. 82, Tracy—Meets 1st and 3rd Fridays, I.O.O.F. Hall; Mrs. Mary A. Hewitson, Rec. Sec., 215 W. 9th St.
Ivy No. 88, Lodi—Meets 1st and 3rd Wednesdays, Eagles Hall; Mrs. Mae Corson, Rec. Sec., 109 So. School St.
Caliz de Oro No. 206, Stockton—Meets 1st and 3rd Tuesdays, N.S.G.W. Hall, 314 E. Main St.; Mrs. Frances Germain, Rec. Sec., 450 No. Regent.
Phoebe A. Hearst No. 214, Manteca—Meets 2nd and 4th Wednesdays, I.O.O.F. Hall; Mrs. Josie M. Frederick, Rec. Sec., Route A, Box 364, Ripon.

SAN LUIS OBISPO COUNTY.

San Miguel No. 94, San Miguel—Meets 2nd and 4th Wednesday afternoons, Clemon Hall; Mrs. Nellie Wickstrom, Rec. Sec.
San Luisita No. 108, San Luis Obispo—Meets 2nd and 4th Thursdays, W.O.W. Hall; Miss Agnes M. Lee, Rec. Sec., P. O. Box 584.
El Pinal No. 163, Cambria—Meets 2nd, 4th and 5th Tuesdays, N.S.G.W. Hall; Kathryn Luchessa, Rec. Sec.

SAN MATEO COUNTY.

Bonita No. 10, Redwood City—Meets 2nd and 4th Thursdays, I.O.O.F. Hall; Mrs. Dora Wilson, Rec. Sec., 518 Middlefield Rd.
Vista del Mar No. 155, Halfmoon Bay—Meets 2nd and 4th Thursdays, I.O.O.F. Hall; Mrs. Grace Griffith, Rec. Sec.
Ano Nuevo No. 180, Pescadero—Meets 1st and 3rd Wednesdays, I.O.O.F. Hall; Mrs. Alice Mattei, Rec. Sec.
El Carmelo No. 181, Daly City—Meets 1st and 3rd Wednesdays, Masonic Hall; Mrs. Hattie Kelly, Rec. Sec., 1179 Brunswick St.
Menlo No. 211, Menlo Park—Meets 2nd and 4th Mondays, Masonic Hall; Mrs. Frances E. Maloney, Rec. Sec., P. O. Box 626.
San Bruno No. 246, San Bruno—Meets 2nd and 4th Fridays, N.D. Hall; Mrs. Evelyn Kelly, Rec. Sec., 353 Hazel Ave.

SANTA BARBARA COUNTY.

Reina del Mar No. 126, Santa Barbara—Meets 1st and 3rd Tuesdays, Pythian Castle, 222 W. Carillo St.; Miss Christina Moller, Rec. Sec., 836 Bath St.

SANTA CLARA COUNTY.

San Jose No. 81, San Jose—Meets Thursdays, Catholic Women Center, 5th and San Fernando Sts.; Mrs. Nellie Fleming, Rec. Sec., Catholic Women's Center.
Vendome No. 100, San Jose—Meets Wednesdays, Scottish Rite Hall; Miss Marie Buck, Rec. Sec., 1114 Ellen St.
El Monte No. 205, Mountain View—Meets 2nd and 4th Fridays, Mockbee Hall; Miss Dolores Collett, Rec. Sec., Route 1, Box 677-A, Los Altos.
Palo Alto No. 229, Palo Alto—Meets 1st and 3rd Mondays, N.S.G.W. Hall; Miss Helena G. Hansen, Rec. Sec., 531 Lytton Ave.

SANTA CRUZ COUNTY.

Santa Cruz No. 26, Santa Cruz—Meets Mondays, N.S.G.W. Hall; Mrs. May L. Williamson, Rec. Sec., 170 Walnut Ave.
El Pajaro No. 35, Watsonville—Meets 1st and 3rd Tuesdays I.O.O.F. Hall; Miss Ruth E. Wilson, Rec. Sec. 16 Laurel St.

SHASTA COUNTY.

Camellia No. 41, Anderson—Meets 1st and 3rd Tuesdays, Masonic Hall; Mrs. Olga E. Welbourn, Rec. Sec.
Lassen View No. 98, Shasta—Meets 2nd Friday, Masonic Hall; Miss Louise Litsch, Rec. Sec.

NATIVE DAUGHTER NEWS

(Continued from Page 15)

fied by Christmas decorations. A hot turkey supper was served, and a minstrel show was staged by Gold of Ophir No. 190. Among others active in arranging details of the affair were Lois Coleman, Ida Weber, Edna Boyd, Margaret Hudspeth and Alta Hengy.

Hiawatha No. 140, Redding—Meets 2nd and 4th Wednesdays, Moose Hall; Ruth Presleigh, Rec. Sec., Office County Clerk.

SIERRA COUNTY.

Naomi No. 36, Downieville—Meets 2nd and 4th Wednesdays, I.O.O.F. Hall; Mrs. Mary Cook, Rec. Sec.
Imogen No. 134, Sierraville—Meets 2nd and 4th Saturday afternoons, Copren Hall; Mrs. Jennie Copren, Rec. Sec.

SISKIYOU COUNTY.

Eschscholtzia No. 112, Etna—Meets 1st and 3rd Wednesdays, Masonic Hall; Mrs. Bernice E. Smith, Rec. Sec.
Mountain Dawn No. 120, Sawyers Bar—Meets 2nd and last Wednesdays, I.O.O.F. Hall; Miss Edith Dunphy, Rec. Sec.

SOLANO COUNTY.

Vallejo No. 195, Vallejo—Meets 1st and 3rd Wednesdays, K.C. Hall, 820 Marin St.; Mrs. Mary Combs, Rec. Sec., 511 York St.
Mary E. Bell No. 224, Dixon—Meets 2nd and 4th Thursdays, I.O.O.F. Hall; Grace McFadyen, Rec. Sec.

SONOMA COUNTY.

Sonoma No. 209, Sonoma—Meets 2nd and 4th Mondays, I.O.O.F. Hall; Mrs. Mae Norrbom, Rec. Sec., R.F.D., Box 171.
Santa Rosa No. 217, Santa Rosa—Meets 1st and 3rd Thursdays, N.S.G.W. Hall; Mrs. Clytie Lewis, Rec. Sec., Route 4, Box 345-A.
Petaluma No. 222, Petaluma—Meets 1st and 3rd Tuesdays, Dania Hall; Mrs. Margaret M. Oeltjen, Rec. Sec., 503 Prospect St.

STANISLAUS COUNTY.

Oakdale No. 125, Oakdale—Meets 1st Monday, I.O.O.F. Hall; Mrs. Lou Reeder, Rec. Sec.
Morada No. 199, Modesto—Meets 2nd and 4th Wednesdays, I.O.O.F. Hall; Mrs. Susan Sullivan, Rec. Sec., 823 10th St.
Eldora No. 248, Turlock—Meets 1st and 3rd Wednesdays, Fraternal Hall; Mrs. Melva Gardner, Rec. Sec., 817 W. Main St.

SUTTER COUNTY.

South Butte No. 226, Sutter—Meets 1st and 3rd Mondays, N.D.G.W. Hall; Mrs. Abbie N. Vagedes, Rec. Sec.

TEHAMA COUNTY.

Berendos No. 23, Red Bluff—Meets 1st and 3rd Tuesdays, W.O.W. Hall, 200 Pine St.; Mrs. Lillie Hammer, Rec. Sec., 636 Jackson St.

TRINITY COUNTY.

Eltapome No. 55, Weaverville—Meets 2nd and 4th Thursdays, N.S.G.W. Hall; Mrs. Lou N. Fetzer, Rec. Sec.

TUOLUMNE COUNTY.

Dardanelle No. 66, Sonora—Meets Fridays, I.O.O.F. Hall; Mrs. Nettie Whitto, Rec. Sec.
Golden Era No. 99, Columbia—Meets 1st and 3rd Thursdays, N.S.G.W. Hall; Miss Irene Ponce, Rec. Sec.
Anona No. 164, Jamestown—Meets 2nd and 4th Tuesdays, I.O.O.F. Hall; Mrs. Rosa A. Beckwith, Rec. Sec., P. O. Box 87.

YOLO COUNTY.

Woodland No. 90, Woodland—Meets 2nd and 4th Tuesdays, N.S.G.W. Hall; Mrs. Maude Heaton, Rec. Sec., 153 College St.

YUBA COUNTY.

Marysville No. 162, Marysville—Meets 2nd and 4th Wednesdays, Liberty Hall; Miss Cecelia C. Gomes, Rec. Sec., 701 6th St.
Camp Far West No. 218, Wheatland—Meets 4th Thursday, I.O.O.F. Hall; Mrs. Ethel C. Brock, Rec. Sec., P. O. Box 285.

AFFILIATED ORGANIZATIONS.

General Assembly Past Presidents—Meetings held annually in April at the home-town of Chief President; Miss Josephine Clark, 824 11th St., Oakland, Chief President; Mrs. Anna G. Loser, 72 Grove Lane, San Anselmo, Chief Secretary.
Past Presidents Association No. 1—Meets 1st and 3rd Mondays, N.S.G.W. Bldg., 414 Mason St., San Francisco; Mrs. Margaret Grote-Hill, Pres.; Mrs. May R. Barry, Rec. Sec., 2319 19th Ave., San Francisco.
Past Presidents Association No. 2—Meets 2nd and 4th Mondays, "Wigwam," Pacific Bldg., 16th and Jefferson, Oakland; Francis McGovern, Pres.; Mrs. Elizabeth B. Goodman, Rec. Sec., 134 Juana St., San Leandro.
Past Presidents Association No. 3 (Santa Clara County)—Meets 2nd Tuesday, homes of members; Mrs. Ida Sweeney, Pres.; Amelia S. Hartman, Rec. Sec., 157 Auzerais Ave., San Jose.
Past Presidents Association No. 4 (Sacramento County)—Meets 2nd Monday, Unitarian Hall, 1413 27th St., Sacramento City; Francis Kimball, Pres.; Lily May Tilden, Rec. Sec., 3225 "T" St., Sacramento.
Past Presidents Association No. 5 (Butte County)—Meets 1st Friday, homes of members, Chico and Oroville; Sonora Steadman, Pres; Ruth Brown, Rec. Sec., 1265 Leah Court, Oroville.
Past Presidents Association No. 6 (Nevada County)—Meets 4th Friday, alternately between Nevada City, Odd Fellows Hall, and Grass Valley, Womens Improvement Clubhouse; Anne Conlin, Pres.; Louise Wales, Rec. Sec., 369 Mill St., Grass Valley.
Past Presidents Association No. 7 (Sonoma County)—Meets 1st Thursday, N.S.G.W. Hall, Santa Rosa; Willow Borba, Pres.; Clytie Lewis, Rec. Sec., R.F.D. No. 4, Box 345-A, Santa Rosa.
Past Presidents Association No. 8 (San Joaquin and Stanislaus Counties)—Meets 2nd Thursday, Red Men Hall, Stockton; Mrs. Mattie M. Stein, Pres.; Mrs. Harriet F. Corr, Rec. Sec., 729 E. Sonora St., Stockton.
Native Sons and Native Daughters Central Committee on Homeless Children—Main Office, 955 Phelan Bldg., San Francisco; Mrs. John W. Stirling, Chmn.; Miss Mary E. Brusie, Sec. Los Angeles branch office, 3924 Sunset Blvd.; Dorothy Schlingman, Sec.

(ADVERTISEMENT.)

Santa Was There.

Susanville—Susanville No. 243 had its annual Christmas party December 15. Members and their families attended. There was a beautiful Christmas tree, and old Santa was there with presents for both young and old. Cards and dancing were enjoyed until midnight, when delicious refreshments were served.

Cascarones for Ball.

Monterey—Junipero No. 141 gave a card party, which was a social and financial success, and is now busy making cascarones for a ball in the near-future. The proceeds will be used for the many worthy projects of the Order. A Christmas box was made up for the homeless children, and the annual donation was also made.

Interesting Departure.

Oroville—At the December 2 meeting of Gold of Ophir No. 190 Mrs. Alice Cundy was elected president. Members of Argonaut No. 8 N.S.G.W. were guests at the refreshment hour following the meeting. Recently Wanda Wilson gave a talk on the early history of the Cherokees, the Indians of this district. This was one in a series of talks being given by daughters and granddaughters of the Pioneers, a departure which is most interesting and informative.

Arizona Veterans Remembered.

San Leandro—Fifteen Christmas boxes were sent by El Cereso No. 207 to veterans at the Whipple Barracks, Arizona. They were prepared by a committee which included Mms. Addie May Silva (chairman), Rose Sanders, Beatrice Passmore, Oliva Kardoza and Julia Freitas. The boxes were sent to Arizona because, it is said, veterans in California hospitals are generally well provided for.

Mrs. Santa There.

Lincoln—Placer No. 138 elected officers December 9, Etta Leavall being chosen president. Among the guests were Past Grand President Dr. Louise C. Heilbron and Supervising Deputy Ethel Ludwig. The annual Christmas party followed the meeting, and Mrs. Santa Claus distributed presents from a beautifully decorated tree. The arrangements committee for the party included Florence Berry (chairman), Carrie Parlin and Phyllis Ramsey.

Past Presidents Doings.

Oakland—Association No. 2 entertained December 15 in honor of Ethel Scheuer, who was presented with a beautiful purse and other gifts. Chairman Winifred Halter and a committee served a turkey supper. December 1 a very successful whist was held at the home of Josephine Clark. December 14 an apron sale was supervised by Helen Cleu. Officers were elected, Freda Reichhold being chosen president. Installation will be held January 11 jointly with East Bay Assembly No. 3 N.S.G.W. Past Presidents.

Oroville—Mms. Cornelia Sank, Florence Boyle and Anna Bernhard were hostesses December 4 to Association No. 5 at the home of the former. Officers were elected, Irene Henry being selected president. A Christmas party followed the meeting and bridge was played.

N.D.G.W. OFFICIAL DEATH LIST.

Giving the name, the date of death, and the Subordinate Parlor affiliation of all deceased members as reported to Grand Secretary Sallie R. Thaler from November 19 to December 18:

Sinnott, Ida J.; November 19; Naomi No. 36.
Calden, Lizzie C.; November 11; Guadalupe No. 153.
Allen, Vera Cecelia; November 17; Twin Peaks No. 185.
Kennedy, Sarah E.; August 30; San Andreas No. 113.
Benson, Lavina C.; October 27; Oneonta No. 71.
Saunders, Nellie G.; November 14; Ursula No. 1.
Mean, Emma; March 25; Buena Vista No. 68.
Christen, Margaret O'Malley; November 4; El Carmelo No. 181.
Watson, Mary E.; November 19; Ivy No. 88.
Davidson, Matilda Blair; November 18; Laurel No. 6.
Adams, Anna C.; November 8; Eltapome No. 55.
True, Florence N.; November 23; Annie K. Bidwell No. 168.
Reynolds, Mary T.; November 19; Plumas Pioneer No. 219.

N. S. CITY OFFICIAL DEAD.

Sacramento City—City Councilman John Henry Miller, affiliated with Sacramento Parlor No. 3 N.S.G.W., died November 25, survived by a wife and two daughters. He was born here June 10, 1880.

"If a man is right, all the bombardment of the world for five, ten, twenty, forty years will only strengthen him in his position. So that all you have to do is to keep yourself right. Never mind the world."—Talmage.

Feminine World's Fads and Fancies

PREPARED ESPECIALLY FOR THE GRIZZLY BEAR BY ANNA STOERMER

INDIVIDUALITY IN SWEATERS IS stressed, with everybody wearing them. One is inclined to wonder if there are enough different styles to go around. There is no excuse, this season, for anybody having one just like her neighbor's; that's a blessing, too.

A slipover sweater has a little turned-down collar, with a loop tie in front that is stitched down, ribbed cuffs and collar, and a waistline. Three contrasting colors are shown, all on brown, green, tile, blue or red. The effect is quite sporty, yet the sweater is nice for general wear and is a style that is practical. Of course, you will have to really see the sweater to appreciate its distinctive air.

There is everything unusual about the sweater ensemble set, with beret and scarf to match the loose, lacy knit. It is made to look hand-done. Four harmonious tones of colors are woven into all three pieces. The sweater itself is an overblouse, with a collarless yoke neckline of a monotone pebble knit. Short sleeves seem to grow right out of it, and it has a metal buckle, matching the metal-button finish at the neck. The scarf is nice and wide, and has fringed ends. A perfect ensemble set for outdoor winter wear anywhere.

Wool suits and frocks are worn by the smartest women for sports wear. Nothing seems to be smarter than the suit of hand-knit wool, a costly fashion, yet essentially a simple one. The most expert workmanship is necessary to give the right "hang" and appearance to the knitted suit, otherwise the result is a sorry-looking affair. It is ideal for walking and sports wear.

The light-weight wool frock, for afternoon wear, is still seen in intriguing versions.

Women are getting more excited than ever about winter sports costumes, and you don't have to go far to enjoy these sports. Having the right costume makes snow sports more enjoyable. Choose dark colors, such as black, navy, dark red or green, because dark colors look smarter against the white backgrounds.

Smart jackets or double-breasted sailor coats look like those of lumberjacks. Trousers and jacket should be of water-proofed gabardine or corduroy. Close-fitting berets or knit caps should be bright or white. Gloves and socks should match.

The winter resort fan will like the gloves of heavy wool. Many prefer the pigskins for sports. Brown ones are always popular. At this time of the year, most everyone is well supplied with gloves, hosiery and scarfs.

Motor toggery is always a lure. In all the shops there are such scores of coats, ensembles and suits, sweaters, jackets, hats and caps that one can scarcely make a choice.

Do not be misled when you hear "Under the coat." It does not mean that one must keep her new togs out of sight. On the contrary, you will be anxious to remove your coat and show the lovely colorings, light or bright, in all the newest shades—bright red, green, blue, and also some new hues of gold, mellon and fuschia.

There is the complete wardrobe for the leisure hours of the modern hostess, whose hobby is home entertainment. Gowns and hostess pajamas both play important roles. The more formal garments are at their loveliest in black or jewel-toned transparent velvet with rayon pile. Glittering lame and satin are individualized in models where exquisite laces are the dominant theme.

A lace and chiffon garment in black has a body of lace with a deep yoke and effective godets set in the skirt of chiffon. The sleeves, of chiffon and lace, are caught in at the wrists by narrow bands of lace. For the tall, slender wearer, long sleeves should be worn with ribbon loops of the material at the wrist and a subtle fullness at the elbow. A cowl neck, form-fitting waist and hips, with the usual graceful flare a little below the knees—this should constitute a gown of elegance and one which should fill the demands of the formal afternoon function.

There are lots of exciting dances, informal supper parties and the like going on, and something more formal than an afternoon frock and less formal than a real dinner or evening gown is needed.

Young girls are starting to busy themselves finding out what is new and smart. First of all, lots of dresses are made in styles and colors that can still be worn over the Easter holidays. They are made with long, sweeping lines, rather full in the skirts, though they hang quite straight and reach all the way down to the ankles. There are sleeves, of course, in all of them, varying from wrist length to the brief little cape, or perhaps a cape collar instead of any sleeves. The very newest type is the three-quarter sleeve. Lovely new colors are the flaming orange, the brilliant green, the new persian shade, the rich sapphire blue and the luscious apricot, as well as a number of others. Flat crepe is the material, though we have seen some garments in sheer crepe, but these do not seem so popular as those of the heavier silks, like canton crepe.

Since we have to supply much of our own brightness these days, it is not surprising that we are ready for red frocks and wraps. Red is a carry-over from last season to the winter, and that seems to be an ample indication that red, in such soft shades as coral and dark, will bloom in the spring.

Accessories for evening still sparkle brightly. Bags and belts are bright and colorful. Gold, silver, kid, metallic and brocaded bags can be carried with many dresses of different colors. Many smart women wear belts and carry bags in ensemble exactly matching, or so nearly alike that they look well together.

Silver and gold bags, slippers and rope belts are new. The belt is made of two ropes of silver or gold metallic cord and fastens with a sparkle buckle.

Peach Conference—A peach products conference is to be held January 8 at the University of California, Berkeley.

SAN FRANCISCO

FOUNDER RELATES HISTORY.

President Gertrude McDonough welcomed Grand President Evelyn I. Carlson on her official visit to Minerva Parlor No. 2 N.D.G.W. There were other guests, among them Mrs. Lillian R. Dyer, Founder of the Order, Grand Trustees Ethel Begley and Willow Borba, Grand Outside Sentinel Orinda G. Giannini, Grand Organist Lola Horgan, Past Grand Presidents Eliza Keith and Margaret Hill, District Deputy Sadie Romick.

Grand President Carlson gave a very interesting talk on all the projects of the Order. Mrs. Dyer related the early history of the Parlor, which was the first to be instituted in San Francisco. She also presented Minerva a badge worn at the celebration of September 9, 1887. Following remarks by the grand officers, all adjourned to the banquethall, where refreshments were served by a committee directed by Lena M. Wall.

MESSAGE AN INSPIRATION.

Honoring Grand President Evelyn I. Carlson, on the occasion of her official visit, Alta Parlor No. 3 N.D.G.W. staged a real Christmas party December 8. Credit for the artistic arrangement of the meetingroom is due Mrs. May L. MacDonald. Among the interesting events was rendition of the "Song of Greeting" by the N.D.G.W. glee club, accompanied by Grand Organist Lola Horgan. This song, composed by Mrs. Claire Bolman of Alta, was dedicated to the Grand President. The initiatory ceremonies were conducted by an efficient corps of officers, "California" being sung by Mrs. Eva Jones.

The message of Grand President Carlson was an inspiration. Beautiful gifts were presented to her. District Deputy Annie Franzen and President Lena Brandt. Grand Trustee Annie C. Thuesen, a special honor-guest, was presented with a handsome electric clock as a mark of appreciation for her ever-faithful service. Entering the banquethall, the guests paused in admiration of the beautiful yuletide scene before them. Miniature Christmas trees, prettily decorated and illuminated, spread cheer while all enjoyed the midnight supper. Mrs. Angeline Vest was chairman of the official visit committee. In addition to visitors from all parts of the state, there were also present: Grand Trustee Willow Borba, Grand Outside Sentinel Orinda Giannini, Past Grand Presidents Dr. Mariana Bertola, May Boldeman, Mary Bell, Margaret G. Hill and Eliza D. Keith.

COURTESIES EXCHANGED.

Members of El Vespero Parlor No. 118 N.D.G.W. were guests of Knights Pythias Lodge No. 45 at an evening of entertainment and dancing which was well attended by both fraternities. A cafeteria-style banquet was greatly enjoyed. These pleasant affairs have become exchanges of courtesies between these two lodges, which meet the same nights in the same hall.

El Vespero's officers-elect, with Miss Anne Godfrey as president, will be installed January 12 by Mrs. Percy Marchant, district deputy. December 22 the Parlor had its annual Christmas tree party, with the customary exchange of presents. Games and dancing were provided and refreshments were served.

MOTHER OF OFFICERS AFFILIATES.

A most interesting meeting was held by Guadalupe Parlor No. 153 N.D.G.W. December 14. Seventy-five members enjoyed a delicious home-cooked turkey dinner prepared by a committee headed by Mrs. Lulu Porter. District Deputy Kathryn Keating, and twenty-one candidates who were later initiated, were guests of honor. One of the initiates, Mrs. Margaret Pyne, is the mother of Miss Margaret Pyne, president, and Miss Florence Pyne, first vice-president of the Parlor.

Guadalupe, as usual, had its Christmas party at Letterman Hospital. Boxes were prepared for all the men in Ward D-1, which the Parlor has adopted and which is visited monthly by a committee headed by Mrs. Carmel Parenti. In order to complete the Loyalty Pledge a card party is to be held in the near-future. Another project dear to the hearts of the Guadalupe girls is the homeless children, and to show their interest in this cause a layette has been started. A committee is making arrangements for the twenty-fifth anniversary banquet, to be held in January.

FAITHFUL SECRETARY ADVANCED.

Golden Gate Parlor No. 158 N.D.G.W. has elected, among other officers for the ensuing term, its beloved recording secretary, Margaret Ramm, to the highest office in the Parlor—that of president. She has served faithfully in the office of secretary for twenty-four years.

December 18 the Parlor held its Christmas tree party for the children of the members. The committee worked hard to give all a good time. December 28 the members had an after-Christmas party for themselves, at which time gifts were exchanged. A committee is working on plans for a celebration of the anniversary of the Parlor, to be held as near January 20 as possible.

CHRISTMAS SEASON THE MOTIF.

The official visit of Grand President Evelyn I. Carlson December 2 will long be remembered by members and guests of Castro Parlor No. 178 N.D.G.W. Previous to the meeting a delightful banquet was enjoyed. The initiatory ceremonies were impressively rendered, four young girls being added to the roll. Grand Organist Lola Horgan and her glee club rendered beautiful selections, thus adding greatly to the pleasure of the evening. Among other grand officers in attendance were Grand Secretary Sallie Thaler, Grand Outside Sentinel Orinda G. Giannini, Grand Trustees Ethel Begley, Anna Thuesen and Willow Borba, Past Grand Presidents Margaret Grote-Hill, Emma G. Foley and Eliza D. Keith. Grand President Carlson gave a most interesting address on the work of the Order. Hand-embroidered pillowcases were disposed of for the benefit of the Loyalty Pledge, which the Parlor will endeavor to complete before the 1932 Grand Parlor.

President Mae Waring, in her gracious manner, invited all present to the banquetroom, where an elaborate repast was served. The room was beautifully decorated, the merry Christmas season being the motif. A large, decorated tree graced the center table and small trees were placed on the other tables. Long streamers of red crepe paper and poinsettias were arranged down the center of the three long tables, giving a festal air to the occasion. Small paper trees were given each guest as a souvenir of the happy night.

"MEE-MO" MYSTIFIES.

Fun ran riot at a novel entertainment staged by La Dorada Parlor No. 236 N.D.G.W. December 10. At the game of "pep" prizes went to Mms. Scherff, Murray, Sanders and Peralta. Dot Ficken appeared in the role of a radio cook. Bernice Braud gave a monologue, "A Lady Buys a Pair of Shoes," and Mildred Beard entertained with clog dances. "Mee-Mo," the mind reader—none other than Outside Sentinel Doris Surbeck—was the evening's sensation, mystifying the audience with feats of telepathy. Following the distribution of gifts by Santa Claus refreshments, prepared by Aileen Buckley and Alice O'Donnell, were served.

HUNDRED CHILDREN REMEMBERED.

Balboa Parlor No. 249 N.D.G.W. is progressing rapidly. Dances, whists and parties have done much for its social and financial success. Although the Parlor is less than a year old the members are very active. A drill team of sixteen has been organized.

At a Christmas tree party given jointly with Balboa No. 234 N.S.G.W. over 100 children were presented with toys and candy. A beautifully decorated tree and the appearance of Santa Claus added to the attractiveness of the evening. Officers will be installed January 21 at a public installation and dance, Marcella Bray becoming president.

Continues as Fair Manager—Charles W. Paine of Sacramento, affiliated with Sacramento Parlor No. 3 N.S.G.W., for the nineteenth consecutive year has been made secretary of the State Agricultural Society, and as such will manage the 1932 California State Fair, to be held September 3 to 10 in the Capital City.

Big Contributor—For the fiscal year ended June 30, 1931, California contributed to the Federal Government in internal revenue taxes $113,066,013; this was 4.65 percent of the total for the nation. The California income tax netted $93,581,718.

When you purchase goods advertised in The Grizzly Bear, or answer an advertisement in this magazine, please be sure to mention The Grizzly Bear. That's co-operation mutually beneficial.

LOS ANGELES--CITY and COUNTY

LOS ANGELES

(Continued from Page 13)

mel (Ramona N.S.), passed away December 20. She was a native of Kentucky, aged 79.

Mrs. Warren Wilson, mother of Douglas Wilson (Ramona N.S.), passed away December 20 at the age of 75.

Robert M. White, father of William W. White (Ramona N.S.), died December 23 at West Hollywood at the age of 74.

CHRISTMAS TREE PARTY.

Long Beach—Long Beach Parlor No. 154 N.D.G.W. initiated two candidates December 3. Officers were elected, Mrs. Violet Tompkins-Henshilwood being chosen president to succeed her sister, Mrs. Daisy Tompkins-Hansen; they are daughters of California Pioneers of 1846. The committee reported the November bazar a success. A check-gift, presented by President Hansen, was voted for Ontario Parlor, instituted December 19. Members whose birthdays come between July 1 and January 1 were honored after the meeting. A tasty lunch was served at beautifully decorated tables and a program was presented. Mrs. Velma Paulstein was in charge.

December 17 the Parlor initiated two additional candidates. A Christmas tree party followed the ceremonies, the members exchanging inexpensive gifts. A turkey, a quilt and a chicken were awarded, respectively, to Mms. Julia Arborn, Mary Stultz and Gussie Taber. The Parlor presented Mrs. Stultz with a silver baby spoon for her recently-arrived daughter. The thimble club met December 22 at the home of Mrs. Lucretia Coates to make a quilt for a needy family.

Officers of Long Beach will be publicly installed January 21. The thimble club will have its regular meeting at the home of Mrs. Gussie Taber, January 14.

KIDDIES MADE HAPPY.

Ramona Parlor No. 109 N.S.G.W. elected officers December 4, Chandos E. Bush being chosen for president and "Jack" Flansburg outside sentinel. December 11, Grand Second Vice-president Justice Emmet Seawell officially visited the Parlor, and in the course of an instructive address highly commended Past President Walter Slosson for his activities. Among other speakers were Junior Past Grand President John T. Newell, District Deputy Albert Cron and Grand Trustee Eldred L. Meyer.

The Christmas dinner December 18 in honor of Charles Gassagne, Walter Slosson and Past Grand President Herman C. Lichtenberger was splendid. The latter, however, was unable to be among those present, having become entangled in a wire fence the unlucky 13th and now being in a hospital. The Christmas tree December 23 was a huge success, and hundreds of kiddies were made happy. An unusually fine program was presented.

Ramona will have no meeting January 8, as the Parlor will join in the installation at San Pedro that date. January 15 has been set aside for initiation. Educational night, to be a monthly feature, will be inaugurated January 22. January 29 the good of the order committee will provide entertainment.

GRAND TRUSTEE INSTALLED.

Ocean Park — Grand Second Vice-president Justice Emmet Seawell paid an official visit to Santa Monica Bay Parlor No. 267 N.S.G.W., December 14, at which time Eldred L. Meyer was installed as Grand Trustee by Junior Past Grand President John T. Newell. Previous to the ceremonies a barbecued lamb supper was served under the supervision of Jack Dailey, Howard Earl and Jack Nelson.

Addresses were delivered by Undersheriff Eugene W. Biscailuz, Justice Seawell, Past Grand President Newell and Grand Trustees Meyer and Samuel M. Shortridge Jr. Officers were elected, Claude Wiseman being selected for president. At the conclusion of the meeting Miss Cordelia Laventhal entertained with several vocal selections.

CHILDREN'S BENEFIT BALL.

The annual ball for the benefit of the homeless children, sponsored by the N.S.G.W. and N.D.G.W. Los Angeles and Orange Counties Joint Committee, is to be held at the Elks Temple February 6. Tickets are one dollar per person. Mrs. Gertrude Tuttle is general chairman of the benefit, Mrs. Ora Evans has charge of the program, and Mrs. Mattie Garra is looking after the prizes.

At the meeting of the joint committee December 4, Santa Monica Bay Parlor No. 245 N.D.G.W. presented a box of baby clothes, made by its sewing club, and a $50 check, and Californiana Parlor No. 247 N.D.G.W. presented a layette and a $50 check. Thus the children's cause, a most worthy one, is assisted. One thousand dollars was forwarded the Central Committee as a donation from all the local N.S.G.W. and N.D.G.W. Parlors.

1932 LICENSE PLATES REQUIRED.

The State Motor Vehicle Department began December 15 distribution of some 2,000,000 1932 auto license plates. After January 15 it will be illegal to drive an auto unless the car owner has obtained, or made application for, the new plates.

Midwinter Fair—A Midwinter Fair is to be held at Susanville, Lassen County, February 12 and 13.

"Don't nurse opportunity too long—take it into active partnership with you at once, lest it leave you for other company."—Exchange.

THE ROMANCE

(Continued from Page 4)

"We all heartily agree with your plans, padre, and we believe that we should honor our saint in just such a way. He has been good to us," remarked one of the priests, and the other members of the band nodded in approval.

Father Dumetz immediately had his soldiers and priests call together all the settlers, and in a very short time some 200 stood before an apostle of Father Junipero Serra. There was a hush among them as they looked into the Christ-like face of their leader.

"You all understand why I have called you together, do you not?" began the padre, as he looked about him. And the nodding of the heads convinced him that these sons and daughters of the valley were approving his action. "Are there any comments or suggestions?" he continued. "You see, there will be two San Joses honoring the good Saint Joseph, and in the years to come there will be much confusion. Too, a mission must be established and also a supply station. Do you all approve of renaming this glorious valley to that of Saint Bernard?"

"Here! Here!" went up a cry of voices. Father Dumetz smiled, and his face took on a new expression of much admiration for those who stood around him. He requested every one to kneel, and raising both arms above his head, with a tone of reverence he offered a prayer of thanksgiving. As he blessed the land and its people, he ended in saying, "I rename this valley of love and life, San Bernardino, in honor of the good Father Saint Bernard of Sienna." Amens were uttered, and the peace-loving folk returned to their chores about the newly-named settlement.

A few days later Father Dumetz held another meeting, of a different nature. Grouped under the widespreading branches of an aged oak, the men of the colony stood before him. He gave them words of cheer and encouragement. He told them of his plans for a supply station and a mission. They became interested and promised their hearty support.

"I have found in looking around me," he continued, "a natural spring or well. There is an unceasing flow of water. It is here that, I feel, should be built a mission or a supply station, as we must think of the future that is to come. We must get the Indians and their chiefs together to help us in the construction of these buildings. They know something about the making of bricks out of clay soil, and they can be taught to use them in erecting livable places, as well as to use the clay for. pottery. These Indian soldiers of mine have already become learned in the ways of mission building and they, in turn, will teach these unchristianized Indians here to do the same. You men must help fell the trees, and do what you see fit. The sooner the station and mission are put into place, the better. We do not want the rain or hot sun to interfere with our important work."

The splendid co-operation obtained by Father Dumetz was shown in the result, two years later. The supply station was first built, and then the mission. Both were erected at the Gauchama Rancho, now known as Bunker Hill, and a few months later, as the building was nearing completion, Father Dumetz and three of his priests fashioned a capilla out of mud, clay soil and straw. This they reverently dedicated to the patron saint of the Valley of San Bernardino. The Gauchama Indians looked to the padre and the capilla as a "good spirit looks to the deeds of its worshipers," and their friendship for the padre was strong.

"It is time for us to return to the San Gabriel station, brothers. Let us prepare for the journey. We can return here when we desire," Father Dumetz told his followers. "But who shall, take care of the mission work, father?" asked one of the priests.

"We have won the admiration and love of these humble Indians, and I am putting the care and trust into the hands of the Indian chief, Hipolito, so be not afraid," said Dumetz in a comforting tone. "He has vowed," continued the padre, "and has faithfully sworn and promised me to care for everything. He understands about the planting of the grain and corn, the caring for the supplies and the superintending of the settlement's difficulties. I have even given him full permission to name this part of the settlement, if he so desires!"

The band of followers then made ready to return to Mission San Gabriel. The Gauchama Indians, under the command of their chief, vowed fullest protection to the community, and with heavy hearts the christianized Indians escorted the mission fathers away from Mission San Bernardino.

Weeks passed, and everything seemed to be prospering. The year had been a good one to the Indians and to the padres, as well as to the White men who had turned the fertile soil to the producing stage. But the Indians were not satisfied with living in an unnamed settlement. Their pride was hurt, and they seemed a little envious of the White man. So, with much ceremony of dances, Indian calls, and a feast of wild game and corn, the settlement was finally named Politana, after the chief. Thus the White man and the Indian appeared to be on friendly terms.

(Continued in February Issue)

"Small is the use of those people who mean well, but who mean well feebly."—Theodore Roosevelt.

MY MESSAGE

To All Native Born Californians

I, DR. FRANK I. GONZALEZ, GRAND PRESIDENT OF THE ORDER OF NATIVE SONS OF THE GOLDEN WEST, DO HEREBY APPEAL TO ALL NATIVE BORN CALIFORNIANS OF THE WHITE MALE RACE BORN WITHIN THE STATE OF CALIFORNIA, OF THE AGE OF EIGHTEEN YEARS AND UPWARD, OF GOOD HEALTH AND CHARACTER, AND WHO BELIEVE IN THE EXISTENCE OF A SUPREME BEING, TO JOIN OUR FRATERNITY AND THEREBY ASSIST IN THE AIMS AND PURPOSES OF THE ORGANIZATION:

To arouse Loyalty and Patriotism for State and for Nation.

To elevate and improve the Manhood upon which the destiny of our country depends.

To encourage interest in all matters and measures relating to the material upbuilding of the State of California.

To assist in the development of the wonderful natural resources of California.

To protect the forests, conserve the waters, improve the rivers and the harbors, and beautify the towns and the cities.

To collect, make known and preserve the romantic history of California.

To restore and preserve all the historic landmarks of the State.

To provide homes for California's homeless children, regardless of race, creed or color.

To keep this State a paradise for the American Citizen by thwarting the organized efforts of all undesirable peoples to control its destiny.

THE ORDER OF NATIVE SONS OF THE GOLDEN WEST IS THE ONLY FRATERNITY IN EXISTENCE WHOSE MEMBERSHIP IS MADE UP EXCLUSIVELY OF WHITE NATIVE BORN AMERICANS.

. . . Builded upon the Foundation Stones of

Friendship
Loyalty
Charity

IT PRESENTS TO THE NATIVE BORN CALIFORNIAN THE MOST PRODUCTIVE FIELD IN WHICH TO SOW HIS ENERGIES, AND IF HE BE A FAITHFUL CULTIVATOR AND DESIRES TO TAKE ADVANTAGE OF THE OPPORTUNITY AFFORDED HIM, HE WILL REAP A RICH HARVEST IN THE KNOWLEDGE THAT HE HAS BEEN FAITHFUL TO CALIFORNIA AND DILIGENT IN PROTECTING ITS WELFARE.

DR. FRANK I. GONZALEZ,
GRAND PRESIDENT N.S.G.W.

The undersigned, having formed a favorable opinion of the Order of Native Sons of the Golden West, desires additional information.

Name ....

Address ....

City or Town..............................

For further information sign the accompanying blank and mail to

GRAND SECRETARY N.S.G.W.,
302 Native Sons Bldg.,
414 Mason St.,
SAN FRANCISCO, California

Grizzly Bear

FEBRUARY — THE ONLY OFFICIAL PUBLICATION OF THE NATIVE SONS AND DAUGHTERS OF THE GOLDEN WEST — 1932

Featuring

GENERAL NEWS OF INTEREST CONCERNING ALL CALIFORNIA, and ORDERS NATIVE SONS and NATIVE DAUGHTERS

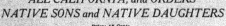

Price: 15 Cents

JOHN SWETT
FATHER OF EDUCATION IN CALIFORNIA

Peter T. Conmy
(Historian Golden Gate Parlor N.S.G.W.)

The accompanying article is by Peter T. Conmy, M.A., historian of Golden Gate Parlor No. 29 N.S.G.W. (San Francisco) who, in sending it to The Grizzly Bear for publication, says: "In his chosen field of endeavor, education, John Swett is regarded as the greatest of early Californians. In the history of American education, he is ranked on equality with Horace Mann and Henry Barnard of the Eastern states. It is lamentable that so little is known about John Swett, because he was a truly great man."—Editor.

JULY 31, 1830, A BOY DESTINED TO BEcome the greatest educational leader California has ever known was born in the old New England town of Pittsfield, New Hampshire. John Swett was of Puritan ancestry, and was educated in the public school of the district and at Pittsfield Academy. Later he entered Russell's Normal School at Reed's Ferry, from which he graduated directly into teaching at the youthful age of seventeen. Between 1847 and 1852 he taught in the schools of Pembroke, New Hampshire, and West Randolph, Massachusetts. Late in 1852 he sailed for California and arrived at San Francisco aboard the good ship "Revere," January 31, 1853, after a voyage of 135 days from Boston.

Lure of the gold fields attracted John Swett, just as it influenced almost every other Pioneer, and, as a result, the first months of this future school leader of California were spent in the mining camps along the Feather River, and not in the classroom. He reported the work was hard and the earnings were inadequate for the amount of energy expended. Very few of the gold miners came out rich. They mined thousands of dollars' worth of gold, but seemed to lose it as fast as they obtained it. Swett was no exception. He, too, came out no richer than he went in. He says, "Thus ended my five months' stay at the mines. I should gladly have remained there longer if I could have found any way of making a living. As it was, I had a small emergency fund carefully strapped around my waist to be used in case of sickness. As I look back on those mining days my only regret is that they did not last longer. They toned up my health and strength and gave me a taste of pioneer life." Swett's period at the mines was not without some productivity, however. He wrote accounts of mining life for the "Boston Cultivator" and penned a very beautiful poem while camping at Morris Ravine, in the Feather River country, titled "'Round the Camp Fire," one stanza of which follows:

"Spread the blankets on the ground,
We must toil again tomorrow;
Labor brings us slumbers sound
No luxurious couch can borrow.
Through the dark topped, sighing pines
Watch the moon 'with white fire laden,'
Fall asleep to dream of mines,
Home, or wife, or child, or maiden."

Happily for the future of the public schools, John Swett was not a very successful miner, and the end of six months found him again in the ranks of education, serving as principal of the old Rincon school in San Francisco, a position he held until his elevation to the state superintendency in 1862. At the time he took over the reins of administration, the Rincon grammar school was a two-teacher institution, located in a house at First and Folsom streets. Later it was moved to Second and Silver streets, where it became, in subsequent decades, the alma mater of thousands of San Franciscans in the old South of Market district. In those days there was no high school in San Francisco and, due to the magnetic personality of John Swett and his very powerful teaching, the Rincon school took the place of such an institution. It is reported that boys ranging in age from sixteen to nineteen were in attendance there, and were coached by Swett for admission to college.

In 1861 came the Civil War, and as there were a large number of Lecompton Democrats, as well as other Southern sympathizers, in California, a very strong attempt was made to prevent the state from supporting the cause of the Union. It so happened that, in 1862, the only office to be filled by a state-wide vote was that of State Superintendent of Public Instruction. Accordingly, both the Lecompton Democrats and the Secessionists advanced candidates—Rev. O. P. Fitzgerald, a Methodist Episcopal clergyman, and General Jonathan D. Stevenson. Both were hostile to President Lincoln, and the election of either would have signified that California was not supporting the Union cause. The Republicans placed no candidate in the field, but joined with the Union party. John Swett was the nominee of that party and, after a hard-fought battle, was swept into office. The late John J. Conmy—the writer's grandfather—wrote the following for his paper, "The Shasta Courier," August 23, 1862: "John Swett should be elected because by education and profession he is fitted for the place, certainly more than a military man or a preacher, and because California is an unconditionally loyal state, and his opponents are mainly disloyal men."

About a half-year before his election, John Swett was united in marriage to Mary Louise Tracy, native of Connecticut, the daughter of the late Judge Frederick Tracy, who had been a distinguished leader of the pioneer San Francisco bar and also of great political prominence. It is interesting to note that just as the schools gave Swett his career as a famous man, so too, they gave the romance which led to his marriage. He met Miss Tracy when, in 1857, at the age of seventeen, she was assigned as a teacher to the Rincon grammar school, of which he was principal. Forty years after this marriage Swett wrote: "Our union was a happy one, cemented by strong friendship, which ended in a deep and abiding love. Though up to this time I had not been fortunate in securing wealth in California, I now won a prize worth more to me than all the gold mines in the state. After a life of joy and sorrow, we are growing old together, with no shadow on the sunlight of our fervent love."

For the five years, 1863 to 1868, John Swett was State Superintendent of Public Instruction, and California has never had a greater official presiding over its public schools. More constructive achievements may be attributed to his administration than to any before or since. The abolition of the rate bill; a state tax of five mills for schools; the publishing of a professional journal, "The California Teacher," for the instructors; establishment of county teachers' institutes; improvement in the method of issuing teachers' certificates, were but a few of the fine accomplishments of the Swett administration.

Following his retirement from the state office in 1868, John Swett again entered the service of the San Francisco schools. From 1868 to 1870 he was, at the same time, principal of the Denman grammar school and the Lincoln evening school; from 1870 to 1873, deputy superintendent of schools; from 1873 to 1876, again prin-

(Continued on Page 23)

GRIZZLY GROWLS

(CLARENCE M. HUNT.)

THE RECONSTRUCTION FINANCE CORporation came into being last month when the Federal Congress passed and President Herbert Hoover signed the bill (H.R. 7360) providing for its creation. "It brings into being a powerful organization with adequate resources," declared the President. "Its purpose is to stop deflation in agriculture and industry and thus to increase employment by the restoration of men to their normal jobs. It is not created for the aid of big industries or big banks. . . . It is created for the support of the smaller banks and financial institutions, . . . to give renewed support to business, industry and agriculture. It should give opportunity to mobilize the gigantic strength of our country for recovery."

The Reconstruction Corporation is to be financed to the extent of $2,000,000,000 by the Federal Government, and its obligations are to be exempted from all taxation, except surtaxes, estate, inheritance and gift taxes. The management is vested in a board of directors, to receive $10,000 each annually. The institutions eligible for loans are federal, state and savings banks, trust companies, building and loan associations, insurance companies, mortgage loan companies, credit unions, federal land banks, joint stock land banks, federal intermediate credit banks, agricultural and livestock credit corporations, interstate steam and electric railways, exporters and farmers. The purpose, as defined by Senator Walcott of Connecticut, is to lift the unliquid collateral of such institutions and substitute cash therefor.

The proponents and sponsors of this legislation claim that it will cure the nation of its depression-ills; that it is the straight and unobstructed path leading direct to that repeatedly-referred-to "corner" around which is prosperity, which has been on vacation and whose prolonged absence has played havoc with the nation's industries. Every loyal American fondly hopes that the prophesies of the measure's proponents are, in due time, fulfilled, and each will honestly aid in their fulfillment.

The Reconstruction Finance Corporation bill received vast majorities in both houses of the Federal Congress. There are not a few, however, in and out of Congress, who believe that the measure is a scheme of the "big boys" to further plunder the American people; that when the time comes for repayment of loans advanced on frozen assets, the dear people will find themselves in the identical role they are now featured in in the foreign-loans tragedy—the sackholder! Here are some publicly-expressed opposing opinions:

"The Corporation we set up here is simply fiction. No one pays any money into it in reality except the Federal Government. . . . If the ordinary businessman gets anything it will be in the form of crumbs from the table surrounded by millionaires who loaned the people's money to foreign countries and to corporations. In some instances, the paper on which it was loaned has gone down to absolute zero. We are not now trying to lock the stable door after the horse has been stolen. We are replacing the horse with some other thing of value and placing that thing of value in the hands of the men who stole the horse."—Senator Norris of Nebraska.

The American people are asked to contribute $2,000,000,000 to help the bankers who are responsible for conditions throughout the world. The bankers want to unload certain securities they hold to the people of the United States through the Reconstruction Finance Corporation. The bill is an "inflationary" measure that will make "the next crash worse than the one we are now in."—Senator Blaine of Wisconsin.

The moneys proposed in the bill are "the merest dole, and you cannot get away from it," but dole to the banks, and not to depositors in them. Not a small businessman nor any farmer will be benefited by the enactment of the bill.—Representative La Guardia of New York.

"This is a scheme for gouging the treasury of the United States. It is a scheme for taking the people's money and giving it to a super-corporation for the sinister purpose of helping a gang of financial looters to cover up their tracks. It is a scheme for giving these financial looters a chance to dispose of evidence which, if brought into the light of day, would cause the doors of our federal penitentiaries to close upon them for a long term of years. After wrecking the business fabric of the country the looters now come forward with the scheme for taking over the remaining property values of the entire United States."—Representative McFadden of Pennsylvania.

There is now before the Federal Congress a bill (H.R. 5869) which, if adopted into law, will exempt alien husbands of American citizens from provisions of the National Immigration Law.

There is grave danger in that bill, and it should, therefore, be squelched! If it becomes a law, every American-born Jap female will have a husband in Japan who will join the mikado's "peaceful invasion" forces in this country.

Remember the "picture bride" menace, by means of which Japan evaded the exclusion law and sent over thousands of its females for breeding purposes? Well, there is suspicion that H.R. 5869 is designed to nullify the exclusion law, for the benefit of Japan.

Two hundred years ago, February 22, 1732, a son was born to Augustine and Mary Washington of Wakefield, Virginia. This year the nation is celebrating the two hundredth anniversary of that son—George Washington, first President of the United States of America.

State Treasurer Charles G. Johnson in a recent public statement remarked: "The continual advance in cost of government has run its course. The roman holiday is over. Economy and retrenchment are imperative if the state is to avert a serious crisis." He estimated more than 594,000 pieces of property will revert to the state, due to inability of owners to pay the taxes thereon. "This is the most serious indictment of the tax burden California has ever known," he declared.

There is nothing whatever to indicate that the "roman holiday"—government squandering of the taxpayers' dollars—is over, and, what is more, there is no likelihood that the holiday will be concluded until and unless the taxpayers unite, without regard for political party affiliations, and make a thorough cleanout of the squanderers.

A Chula Vista garageowner and seven Jap aliens have been indicted by the San Diego County Grand Jury, charged with violating the California Alien Land Law. Ownership of several ranches, including 5,000 acres of fertile land, is involved.

Violations of this law, both by yellow-Japs and white-Japs, are notoriously numerous in nearly every county of the state, but very seldom is an effort made to enforce the law. Yellow-dollars do have a duty-shirking appeal!

A reader of The Grizzly Bear sent in the query, in capital letters, "Why exempt churches from taxation?" There is no good and sufficient reason for so doing. Church organizations are among the wealthiest in the world, and they should be compelled to bear their share of the tax-burden.

Millions of dollars' worth of property in California has been exempted from taxation, but in justice to the citizenry as a whole not a single dollar's worth should be so favored. And, unless the taxpayers look well to their ballots, the tax-exempt list will be materially increased at the May election, for a proposal to that effect will then be submitted to the voters.

Arizona's House of Representatives has unanimously adopted a resolution providing that, where a husband and his wife are both found to be drawing state pay, the employment of one or the other shall be terminated.

That should be the strictly-adhered-to policy in every branch of government and in every private enterprise throughout the nation.

The Berkeley Chamber of Commerce has come out in favor of the quota for Japan, and has an agent in the field endeavoring to get other similar organizations to do likewise. The Berkeley outfit claims that "such action would be a step toward the maintenance of world peace and friendly relations between Pacific powers, and would further commerce between the United States and Japan." The same old bunkum, suggested by Jap agents, that is worked overtime, when the Japs are seeking favors.

To grant the quota to Japan will but hasten the day that this country must pay the full price of its folly in permitting the Japs to plant themselves here—the day that Japan will complete its "peaceful invasion." And that day is not far distant, unless the United States reverses its present course. Events in Mexico, Manchuria, Honolulu and China are handwritings on the wall that should prompt this nation to keep its lamps brightly burning and to be ever, and adequately, prepared.

The Grizzly Bear Magazine

The ALL California Monthly

OWNED, CONTROLLED, PUBLISHED BY GRIZZLY BEAR PUBLISHING CO., (Incorporated)

COMPOSED OF NATIVE SONS.

HERMAN C. LICHTENBERGER, Pres.
JOHN T. NEWELL RAY HOWARD
WM. I. TRAEGER LORENZO F. SOTO
CHAS. R. THOMAS HARRY J. LELANDE
ARTHUR A. SCHMIDT, Vice-Pres.
BOARD OF DIRECTORS

CLARENCE M. HUNT
General Manager and Editor

OFFICIAL ORGAN AND THE ONLY OFFICIAL PUBLICATION OF THE NATIVE SONS AND THE NATIVE DAUGHTERS GOLDEN WEST.

ISSUED FIRST EACH MONTH.
FORMS CLOSE 20th MONTH.
ADVERTISING RATES ON APPLICATION.

SAN FRANCISCO OFFICE:
N.S.G.W. BLDG., 414 MASON ST., RM. 302
(Office Grand Secretary N.S.G.W.)
Telephone: Kearney 1223
SAN FRANCISCO, CALIFORNIA

PUBLICATION OFFICE:
309-15 WILCOX BLDG., 2nd AND SPRING,
Telephone: VAndike 6234
LOS ANGELES, CALIFORNIA

(Entered as second-class matter May 29, 1918, at the Postoffice at Los Angeles, California, under the act of August 24, 1912.)

PUBLISHED REGULARLY SINCE MAY 1907
VOL. L WHOLE NO. 298

The Senate Immigration Committee of the Federal Congress has reported favorably on a bill, by Senator Harris of Georgia, placing Mexico on an immigration quota basis. Reports are that the measure will, in all likelihood, be passed by both houses of the Congress.

The administration temporarily checked Mexican immigration because of the unemployment situation in this country. When business revives, however, jobs will again be offered and given by the special interests to the Mexis in preference to Americans, and they will flock in by the thousands. The quota may lessen the number.

A vast majority of the nationals of Mexico are not of the White race, and not entitled to American citizenship. They should, therefore, be excluded, as are other ineligible-to-citizenship aliens. If, however, the Congress will not exclude them it should restrict, via the quota, their coming. Partial relief from these undesirables is preferable to no relief at all.

"What chance," queries the California Taxpayers Association, "has the property owner of holding his property when he will have to pay at least ten times its assessed valuation to hold it?" And this instance is related:

"A retired businessman of Pennsylvania invested $100,000 in bonds of a San Diego County improvement district, depending on them to furnish him with a steady and reliable income during the last years of his life. The bonds are now in default, and the man faces sickness and old age with his fortune invested in the now-defaulted bonds of this improvement district. The district issued bonds in 1928 in the amount of $292,715.60. The bonds bore interest at 7 percent and were not to be fully retired until 1948. The assessed valuation of the property in the district is $55,470. The bonds issued against this property, together with total interest, amount to $549,638, or nearly ten times the assessed value. The improvement act under which these bonds were issued provides that any delinquency shall be spread the following year against the property in the district. Thus, the man paying his assessment finds himself liable for an ever-increasing amount."

Numerous propertyowners are victims of the special-assessment-district evil, and in many

(Continued on Page 22)

THE ROMANCE OF SAN BERNARDINO

Clara M. Barton

(Continued from January Issue.)

THE YEAR 1812 WAS TERMED THE year of earthquakes. The Indians outside the mission became frightened, as they believed the newlybuilt mission was the whole cause of the eruptions. A fight of life and death began. These Indians hastily made strong and more-dangerous arrows, and those living inside the mission prepared, as best they could, for some protection. War dances began, and loud war whoops rang out. The Indians who did not approve of the building of the mission intended to destroy what was constructed. Their beliefs were very strong. Evil spirits were living within the walls of the station, and they were suffering because of them. They intended to dispose of those evil spirits as soon as possible!

A fire blazed up; arrows, ablaze with red fire, flew into the air and landed dangerously near the mission, setting the brush and projecting stems of the straw ablaze. "What are we going to do?" cried one of the imprisoned Indians. "If we go out now, they will kill us! If we stay in here, we will burn to death!"

Hipolito looked hopelessly around. "The best thing to do now," he said in steady tones, "is to run through the hail of fire and poisoned arrows and escape as best we might. The Indians have more ammunition than we, and have twice as many men. We shall have to let all the supplies go, as there is no way of saving them. Every one dash out, but bend low as you go!" And the faithful Indian chief urged his beloved friends to make haste.

The massacre lasted for several days, and was one of the worst experienced. Many lives were lost, and those who suffered from wounds never fully recovered. Hipolito himself suffered deeply, but silently. His faith in those remaining with him seemed to help him with his heavy burden. With reverent ceremony and words of comfort to those who had lost their loved ones in the affray, Chief Hipolito performed the final rites over the bodies, some of them not recognizable, and with kindly words assisted in placing into shallow graves the remains of the men and women who gave their lives in trying to save that which the mission fathers had left.

EPISODE 3.
THE MISSION OF SAN BERNARDINO.

Events transpiring between 1812 and 1822 are vague, and until 1821 the history of the valley seems to have been at a standstill. However, in 1821 the Gauchama ranchita of Indians asked the padres of San Gabriel to help them establish agriculture and stock-raising farms. "We shall do all we can," remarked one of the priests, "because we are always being attacked by the uneducated Indians who lurk in the shadows of the passes. We have lost too many lives already. This may cease their activities."

In 1822 a priest was sent from San Gabriel to the San Bernardino settlement to establish a mission, and in a very short time had acquired the services of several Indians. Some months later an adobe chapel was erected upon the site where still stands part of the ruins of the old mission.

The Indians were grateful for what was being done for them, and to show their appreciation they appointed a mayor-domo, Casius Garcia. Through him and his officers, a zanja was constructed, and this was the beginning of the raising of large herds of stock and the cultivation of lands.

The mayor-domo looked over his land with pride. "Now, this is something like it," he said. "You people did not know, and will not know, how much admiration I have for you. It is you who have helped make this community something to be proud of, and future generations will always have a warm feeling for those who have gone before. As long as I am your commander, I shall continue to give you as much service as I can."

The colony showed respect for their executive officer by building a zanja "that will have a continuous service." This is now known as Mill Creek Zanja, and its overflow of water has kept the large alder and willow trees ever alive and green.

Romance invaded the mission walls when a tall Indian brave brought to the priest a coy and pretty Indian maiden. "Please, senor," pleaded the Indian boy, "we want to get married. We love one another. I care for her much."

The priest smiled. "And you love him too, little maid?" The Indian girl blushed, nodded and hid her face in the broad shoulder of the boy. "You make her my squaw, senor?"

The priest looked once more at the girl, smiled, and then nodded. "Yes, I shall be glad to. Won't you come into the mission? Do you want me to perform the rites now?" "Yes," remarked the Indian brave. "We were married by the chief of the tribe, but I am christianized and do not like Indian ceremony. My girl, she wants you to marry us in a christian manner."

The form of the ceremony was very simple. But within those walls of adobe two hearts were made happy. And the priests smiled at the couple as they left, hand in hand, for the land of the future. "May the saints bless you both and give you much happiness," said the priest as they disappeared from the shadows of the mission.

Ten years went by, and the land around the mission was producing wealth for its owners. Contentness reigned. A custom was formed in which all the inhabitants took an active part. With the mayor-domo in charge, the men, women and children would gather around a huge bonfire, and old familiar songs rang out into the night air. Some of the voices possessed artistic quality; some did not, but the singers' hearts were in their music.

"Who will be the first to tell the first story? Remember, it must have a moral to it," said the mayor-domo, after all had sung until they could sing no more.

The men looked at one another, and finally one elderly man was seen rising painfully and slowly. He cleared his throat and with a slow drawl told a lengthy story, the moral of which was never related. A weak applause followed the oration. "Guess they didn't like that one so well," the old man muttered disappointedly. He had rehearsed the fable many times, and had hoped to receive some sort of recognition from the mayor-domo.

The second story told brought laughs and tears, and received much favor with the listeners. From then on, numerous stories were related. Too many, in fact, as the children dropped off to sleep in their mothers' arms and the majority of the group began to look weary.

It was quite late when orders were given to retire for the night. "There is much to do in the morning, men, and you must get a good night's rest," said Garcia in parting. Little did he know that more work was to be done than he anticipated!

The morning sun woke the colony, and with it came loud warwhoops of the desert Indians. The men grabbed their crude weapons, and the women loaded themselves with available stones, while the children ran for safety. But the Indians were too many for the mission people. The mission was destroyed, provisions were stolen, and the stock was widely scattered.

"I hope those demons are satisfied!" said Garcia, as the dust of the battle had settled. "It looks like it," said one of the men. "But what are we going to do now? We have lost several men, and nearly all the women are ill from the shock."

"We must not lose heart," returned Garcia. "The best and most substantial thing that we can do is to rebuild at once. We must have a place in which to live again, a place for our provisions and the stock that is left. Too, we must replenish everything that has been salvaged. I hope a priest is sent here to help us."

"Why can't one of us men ride to San Gabriel for help?" suggested one of the settlers. "That would be too long a ride, and we need every man here to help rebuild the mission," replied Garcia.

It was not long, however, until one of the padres was on his way from San Gabriel to the valley. The father had heard about the destruction of the mission, and had become angered about it.

"Something must be done to those evil-doing Indians," said one of the San Gabriel padres. "This has gone entirely too far. Lives have been unnecessarily lost, and the land and stock have been needlessly destroyed. We must see that the San Bernardino Mission is well supplied with proper protection." The padre looked to his fellowmen for a suggestion, but received only an approving nod.

"I shall go to their deliverance," volunteered one of the padres. "God speed you on the way," returned the head padre. So, with the assistance of his fellow priests, the father with the brave heart was on his way to help restore all that was in ruins.

Several days later the priest was supervising the rebuilding of the mission, and in 1832 it was completed and ready for occupancy. The church was constructed of more substantial material, and was 250 feet in length by 125 feet in width, and the walls were three feet thick. The priest insisted on large corrals, and the walls around the enclosure were constructed so as to resist all attacks from savage neighbors. A huge granary of adobe was built near the mission, and the Indians learned, for the first time, how to preserve grain.

In 1834 the settlers found uneasiness and dissatisfaction among the Indians. "Do we have to go through the same things that our fathers did?" asked one of the men of the mayor-domo. "Heaven help us if we do!" exclaimed Garcia in worried tones.

The mission Indians finally revolted, and a messenger was sent to San Gabriel for help. Men and ammunition were scarce, and the women and children were becoming panic-stricken. It was several days, however, before the Indian messenger and a troop from San Gabriel arrived in the mission district. A hard battle was fought between 200 sturdy Indians and a small army of tired men.

As a last resort, Father Estenada was sent for, and arrived in due time with a fresh and larger troop. "So this is what has been happening," he remarked, very much surprised and shocked. "Yes, father," answered the mayor-domo, "and what are we going to do?" "Fight it out!" commanded Father Estenada.

More troops were sent for but, like the others, their ranks were thinned by the poisoned arrows and tomahawks of the Indians. Father Estenada found himself a prisoner, and also discovered that to struggle for freedom meant death. He was robbed of all his belongings, suffered torture from the hands of the Indians who held him, and finally discovered that he was being held for ransom! His first thought was of his people in the mission! Were they in a safe and secluded place, or were they, too, being put to pain by these uncivilized Indians? Little did he know that the Indians had revolted once again, had robbed the church of all its property after committing other indescribable crimes, and then had disappeared into the hills.

With a hard struggle, the padre succeeded in freeing himself of his bonds. He went immediately to the mission, and found it in ruins. A hard lump formed in his throat. A few of the colony settlers were lingering near by, looking down at all that was left of their church, and the feeling of fear was still in their hearts.

"Come, let us leave this beautiful valley, and let the Indian stay with his spoils," said the good padre. "It is no use for us to stay here any longer." And so, with heavy hearts and a feeling of despair, the little band followed Father Estenada back to San Gabriel, where they would remain until activities began anew.

EPISODE 4.
RANCHO DE SAN BERNARDINO.

Time went on. The Spaniards entered the valley and, seeing what had previously been done, decided to continue with its advancement. So, in 1842 a land-grant known as Rancho de San Bernardino was presented by Governor Alvarado to Jose Maria Lugo, Jose Vicente Lugo and Jose Carmen Lugo, sons of the well-known Antonio Lugo. The grant was the first move the governor had made, and was one of the largest grants ever given in California.

"You are now owner of over 37,000 acres, senor, but I believe you will handle the property well," said the governor, as he presented the signed grant to Lugo.

"I shall try and make this territory something to be proud of, governor. I own the San Antonio grant, but my stock has been increasing at such a rate that I decided to take over the Valley of San Bernardino, in order that my sons will have something to work on after I am laid away. That is one reason why I am having the grant made out to my three loyal sons." "You are very wise, and I want to congratulate you and wish you much success in this achievement." Thus the governor bade the senor a kind adios.

Senor Lugo, coming from a long line of blue-blooded Spanish stock, had become known as an expert horseman, a man who kept his word, and one who knew no fear, though he was kind and generous. He had taught his sons how to be just and respectable citizens. It was their love for the community that kept the history of the valley alive, after the death of their father.

"I am going to live in the mission for awhile," remarked Jose Maria to Jose Vicente, as they were looking around the valley. "Splendid idea," replied Vicente. "It ought to be nice and

(Continued on Page 13)

LOS ANGELES
CITY AND COUNTY

ALL ALIENS IN THE EMPLOY OF THE Los Angeles City school district are to be dismissed and the vacancies filled by American citizens, according to instructions recently issued by Superintendent Frank A. Bouelle. "In all instances where American citizenship cannot be fully established, steps should be taken at once to terminate the services of such persons, no matter in what capacity employed," reads the edict of the Los Angeles City Education Board.

That is good news! Action has been long delayed, but it is better late than never. The Education Board should go further, and dispense with the services of married women who have able-bodied husbands. And it should go still further, and prohibit any one person in its employ from filling two or more separate and distinct positions and drawing pay for each position from the taxpayers. If these reforms be brought about, both the community and its public schools will be benefited.

The California state law expressly bars all aliens from the public service, and it is therefore unlawful to employ any person other than an American citizen in state, county, city or township government. There are, however, many such employed by both the County and the City of Los Angeles, as common laborers, so-called "specialists," accountants, etc. There is not a single public-service job but that can be competently filled by some American citizen.

This law should be strictly enforced! Its aboveboard violation or underhand evasion constitutes malfeasance in office on the part of any governing official responsible for its violation or evasion. If the officials themselves will not do their duty, then some citizen or organization interested in the community's welfare and not in the political wellbeing of any individual or clique, should go into court and compel compliance with the law and removal from office of its violator or evader.

There can be no more appropriate time than right now to correct this and the many other faults in government which sorely afflict the body politic and cause heavy demands on the taxpayers. If the officials will not administer government within the law, then the law-abiding citizens should force their retirement from the public service. Although it appears otherwise, no man or woman is beyond the law, provided the majority demand respect for and obedience to the law. Until we do have law obedience, by officials — who should set the example — and other citizens, the clouds will not disappear from the economic skies and the sun of prosperity will not again shine, except, possibly, temporarily.—C.M.H.

COME ON, NATIVES!

Plans are complete for the annual charity ball of the Native Sons and Native Daughters of the Golden West, given under the auspices of a joint committee to aid homeless children. It will be held February 6, in the ballroom of Elks Temple, 607 Parkview street.

President Gertrude Joughin-Tuttle of Californiana Parlor No. 247 N.D.G.W., the general chairman, is being assisted in making the arrangements by an executive committee comprising Irving Baxter, chairman; Grace Norton, vice-chairman; Annie L. Adair, secretary; Hazel Hansen, vice-chairman Grand Parlor N.D.G.W. Extension Order Committee; Gertrude R. Allen, president Los Angeles Parlor No. 124 N.D.G.W.; Mattie Labory-Gara, Clara Hunt, Leila K. Taber, Ora M. Evans, T. Dwight Crittenden, Stanley Dashiell, Clyde Woodworth, Lee Erwin, Chandos Bush and Municipal Judge Leo P. Aggeller.

Chairmen of special committees appointed by Mrs. Tuttle are: Reception, Hazel Hansen; music, Ora M. Evans; floor and dance director, Dwight Crittenden; door prizes, Mattie Labory-Gara; hospitality, Gertrude R. Allen; publicity, Bell Sisson-Maguire.

Mrs. Florence B. Irish will act as master of ceremonies. A popular high-class dance orchestra will supply the music. A surprise feature will be presented in intermission, and many joyous motifs, including the ever-pleasing balloon dance, will be added. The door prizes, which are numerous and attractive, are each worth many times the price of admission, one dollar per person. Ball tickets may be secured through Miss Grace Norton, ATlantic 8648.

Come on, Native Sons and Daughters, let us put this ball over big, and put it in the front ranks, where it belongs! And let it be a coveted distinction to be listed as among those present!—B.S.M.

GOOD TIME TO WEIGH GROWTH.

Wm. M. Horner addressed Los Angeles Parlor No. 124 N.D.G.W. January 20 on "Future Citizens of the World." At its conclusion he answered several questions asked by his listeners. The get-better-acquainted party January 27 at which No. 124 entertained the members of several neighboring Parlors was out of the ordinary and greatly enjoyed by the guests. The last party of the bridge tourney, January 13, drew another large crowd and was most successful. Miss Edna Trombatore directed the affair. January 26 several members accompanied District Deputy Ruth Ruiz to Glendale, where she installed Verdugo Parlor's officers.

"Stock taking time is also a good time to weigh our growth in mental, moral and spiritual values, qualities which no business depression can deprive us of," says President Gertrude Allen.

February 3 Los Angeles will have a pot-luck dinner followed by a business meeting. February 10 will be the start of another bridge tournament, with Ruth Ruiz as chairman of the initial party. February 24 will be given over to a "salamagundi" party, with Miss Dolores Malin as chairman.

SPLENDID CITIZEN PASSES.

California lost a splendid citizen and the Order of Native Sons of the Golden West a highly valued member when W. Joseph Ford passed suddenly away at his Glendale home, January

(Continued on Page 20)

CALIFORNIA HAPPENINGS OF FIFTY YEARS AGO

Thomas R. Jones

(COMPILED EXPRESSLY FOR THE GRIZZLY BEAR.)

FOUR STORMS VISITED CALIFORNIA during February 1882 and dropped 2.40 inches of rain in the Sacramento Valley, making the season's total 10.29 inches. A heavy snowstorm visited California North February 2. While some parts of the state had good crops, there was an apparent failure on the west side of the San Joaquin Valley, and in California South conditions were bad.

Washington's Birthday, February 22, was observed in a patriotic manner, and Flags of the United States of America were prominently displayed everywhere.

Statistics published this month showed that in 1881 California produced 40,000,000 bushels of wheat, 1,410,533 pounds of sugar-beet products, 9,500,000 gallons of wine, and $77,000,000 worth of gold and silver. The population during the year increased 28,987.

The Sunday-closing law continued to agitate various sections of the state. In Modoc County the saloonkeepers unanimously agreed to obey the law. In San Leandro, Alameda County, following acquittal by a jury of the proprietor of the Estudillo house, charged with violating the law, the courtroom crowd made "whoopee."

The Saint Helena, Napa County, Board of Trustees passed an ordinance making the playing of cards, billiards or any other chance game for the drinks a misdemeanor. San Francisco had 2,330 saloons in operation February 1. During the month the police made 759 arrests for drunkenness—nearly one-half the total arrests.

The fifth annual party of Sacramento Parlor No. 3 N.S.G.W. was held in the assembly chamber of the State Capitol February 2. So large was the attendance, the dancers overflowed into the rotunda. Mirrors, to the delight of the fair sex, were extensively used in the decorations. Of the score who arranged the party, John T. Stafford is the sole survivor.

The baldheaded men of Nevada City, Nevada County, gave their first annual grand ball Valentine Day, February 14. The sixty-one shining pates in the grand march were led by Judge A. G. Niles.

NOTED PIONEERS PASS ON.

An Oakland, Alameda County, woman was thrown from a horse and badly injured. This caused a Los Angeles editor to comment: "There is only one safe and easy way for a woman to ride a horse, and that is to do it astride. If the intelligent and cultured women of California had independence enough in their souls they would be seen riding astride."

Three ships arrived from China this month bringing about 2,000 additional Chinks. This gave Dennis Kearney an opportunity to "come back." He organized a dozen Workingmen's ward clubs in San Francisco with the slogan "The Chinese Must Go," and resumed the Sunday sandlot meetings.

L. H. Woodburn, from Muscatine, Iowa, opened a land agency in Los Angeles City to settle colonies of Iowans contemplating coming to California South to reside. From his hometown, seventy families were coming by special train, and he had several more excursions in view.

The twenty-fifth anniversary of the "Sacramento Daily Bee" was celebrated February 4 with a banquet at which prominent editors and other citizens toasted the owner, James McClatchy. The present editor, "C.K.," was an humble listener.

John C. Stader of Sonoma County reported his eighteen-year-old grapevines yielded an average of sixty pounds of grapes to the vine, and he sold the product for $100 a ton.

John Finnell, a rancher, bought in California South at one dollar a head 15,000 sheep, and shipped them by rail to his Tehama County domain. There was no feed for stock in the southland.

Nancy Jane Harris, popularly known in Monterey City as "Aunt Jane," died there February 1. She was a Negress, born in South Carolina in 1784, and was brought to California by her former owner in 1852.

Mike Bryte, who came to California from Ohio in 1849, died at Sacramento City February 3. He established one of the first dairy routes in the Capital City and was once sheriff of Sacramento County.

Juan Foster died at San Diego City February 20, at the age of 67. He landed there in 1836, soon afterward became a Mexican citizen and married into the family of a prominent land-owning don. He once owned the Marguerita Rancho, the largest in California South, and was a leading cattle raiser.

William Gelabert, a native of Spain who came to California with Commodore John Drake Sloat in the United States Navy in 1846 and was one of the party that raised the Flag of the United States of America at Monterey, died at Stockton, San Joaquin County, February 27, aged 60.

TOUCHED BY AN ANGEL.

The passengerless stage from Alturas, Modoc County, while fording the creek near Millville February 24 was upset and carried down stream by the flood. The driver had a narrow escape, and the horses drowned.

The stage from Sonora, Tuolumne County, to Copperopolis was stopped February 3 near Chinese Camp by two masked men, who took $300 from the express box. A week later they were caught in Monterey County.

A 9-year-old girl went into a San Francisco combination corner grocery-saloon and asked the clerk for five cents' worth of tea, explaining the purchase was so small because her mother was ill and had no more money. The clerk being called to attend to the wants of some men at the bar, she sat herself in a chair to await his return, and with the nickel grasped between the thumb and forefinger of her little outstretched hand fell asleep. One of the imbibers finally noticed her, and asked the clerk why she was there. Being informed of the facts, he replaced the nickel with a five-dollar gold piece, bought a nickel's worth of tea which he placed in the sleeping child's other hand, and then wakened her. Gazing in astonishment at her hands, she exclaimed that she had been touched by an angel, and burst into tears of joy.

Dick Fellows, who had robbed seven stages and gotten away with the express boxes in 1881, was captured near the Guadalupe mine in Santa Clara County February 3.

Attorney D. J. Murphy, while making a plea in a San Francisco court for a client, was shot in the throat by Policeman Moroney, who took offense at being called a foreigner. He was rendered speechless for some time.

The Baptist tabernacle in San Jose, Santa Clara County, the largest and finest church structure in that city, burned February 25 with a $20,000 loss.

Bailey's tripe factory in San Francisco's Butchertown burned February 3. The loss was $25,000.

A fire at Colusa City February 1 burned several buildings, causing a $10,000 loss.

The Chinatown of Dutch Flat, Placer County, was partially destroyed by fire February 24. The loss was $20,000.

Winfield Wright's model barn, the largest and best equipped in Sonoma County, burned February 2, causing a $15,000 loss.

MEXI'S INVITATION ACCEPTED.

G. J. Coffee, Butte County sheepman, disposed of his property February 1 and committed suicide. He gave as a reason for the act that he wanted to go to a world where there was no rascality.

Miss Sarah Radcliffe of Farmington, San Joaquin County, had an epileptic fit February 20 and fell into the fireplace. She was fatally burned and the house was destroyed.

John J. Anderson of San Bernardino City was accidentally killed February 19 while drawing his shotgun from a wagon.

John Armstrong of San Francisco was gored to death in Butchertown by a vicious cow February 19.

A 14-year-old girl named Hall accidentally killed her 6-year-old brother with an "unloaded" gun February 6 near Lincoln, Placer County.

A landslide at Cuffey's Cove, Sonoma County, February 13 carried a house into the Russian River. Mrs. Hannah Johnson, her infant and a cook were drowned.

John Adams, halfbreed Mexican, was prospering by stealing horses and cattle in Big Valley, Lassen County. A committee of ranchers sent him word to "vamose," but he refused to do so, and sent them word to come and get him. They did, and February 24 surprised him at his Pit River rendezvous. When they departed, his body was dangling from the limb of an oak tree.

John Day, a farmer, was driving his team along the bank of a canal near Bakersfield, Kern County, February 28. The team became frightened, overturned the wagon into the canal, and Day and the horses were drowned.

The 3-year-old Jenkins lad fell into a tub of hot water while playing at Honcut, Butte County, February 6, and was fatally scalded.

George Bergin, a 17-year-old bellboy at the Baldwin hotel, San Francisco, was crushed to death by an elevator which he attempted to leave while in motion.

William Smithers of Nevada City, Nevada County, went on a spree February 11 and concluded to clean the town of Chinese. After killing one and dangerously wounding another he was taken into custody.

CALIFORNIA GOLD LEADER.

Gold production in the United States durin 1931 totaled 2,365,881 ounces, valued at $48,907,100. Silver production totaled 30,967,61 ounces, valued at $8,980,609.

California led in gold production, 510,23 ounces valued at $10,547,500, and Utah led i silver production, 8,173,203 ounces valued a $2,370,229.

"Slacken Your Gait Where Street Cars Wait is the February slogan of the California Publi Safety Committee in its campaign to lessen th fearful auto death-toll.

PRACTICE RECIPR

DEATH TAKES N. D. PAST GRAND

SANTA ROSA (SONOMA COUNTY)—MISS Minnie Coulter, Past Grand President of the Order of Native Daughters of the Golden West, passed away January 9. She was the daughter of Sterling Coulter, California Pioneer of 1852, and was born at Santa Rosa April 3, 1866. Miss Coulter presided at the Eighth Grand Parlor, in session at Chico, Butte County, June 1894. She was affiliated with Alta Parlor No. 3 (San Francisco).

A TRIBUTE.

(Dr. Mariana Bertola, P.G.P.)

"Death, where is thy sting, where is thy victory?" Life is the hard part; death is a door, portal to a better world. Life is what we make it, and Minnie Coulter made the most of hers. She came of Pioneers. Her father, Sterling Coulter, was of sturdy stock and came to California in 1852; his wife was a fitting mate for so fine a man.

Minnie was one of a large family of children. She was educated in the public schools, and later worked her way through Stanford University, as only an enterprising, determined young woman can do. She attained academic honors, and was especially spoken of as a promising student by Prof. Cubberly of the department of education. Dr. Frederick Burk of the State Teachers College understood her, and appreciated her great worth. She received several fine offers of good positions in the educational world, but her great sense of duty made her remain at home. She was principal of a Santa Rosa school for many years, superintendent of Sonoma County schools for two terms, president of the California Teachers Association and president of the State Council of Education. She brought a fresh outlook to these organizations, giving them renewed vigor.

She was the eighth Grand President of the Order of Native Daughters of the Golden West, a member of the Grand Parlor Board of Relief, and affiliated with Alta Parlor No. 3 (San Francisco).

Her honesty, her integrity, her sincerity inspired her pupils to greater things. She always had a certain sympathy for the pupil who did wrong, because, she said, she was never sure how much the whole system helped him to do wrong. Her understanding reformed many a student who afterward expressed his gratitude for the right kind of a lift. Her sympathy and her genius lighted a torch which was a beacon to many, and they, having lighted their candle at her torch, will carry on in making a better world.

Life is a preparation for better things that await us. Hardship, obstacles to overcome, tasks to accomplish, all make up life. Our behavior toward life is what counts, and goes toward what we may expect in a better world. Friendship, truth, honor, tolerance toward our fellows give us the opportunity to make life a beautiful thing, fitted to be spent in this beautiful world.

Minnie Coulter, the fine mind, the great personality, the understanding heart; Minnie Coulter, the self-sacrificing one; Minnie Coulter, the loving and true friend, has now entered the portals of a broader, greater life, where our Father has prepared us "many mansions." "O Death, where is thy sting, O Death, where is thy victory?"

CONTRIBUTIONS NEEDED TO PURCHASE VALUED HISTORIC LANDMARK.

The General Vallejo Memorial Association has been organized. Its purposes, as set forth in a most interesting illustrated booklet, are: "Proper recognition of General M. G. Vallejo's invaluable and loyal services to California. Securing the Vallejo home place at Sonoma, 'Lachryma Montis,' for a state park or historical landmark."

W. F. Chipman is the president of the association, and on the board of governors are Joseph R. Knowland and Lewis F. Byington, Past Grand Presidents of the Order of Native Sons of the Golden West.

The agreed price for the old Vallejo home and seventeen acres of surrounding land is $17,360, of which amount the California State Park Commission will provide $8,650. The balance must be raised through contributions. The Sonoma Valley Chamber of Commerce will be glad to receive any subscriptions. Send them to Secretary-Manager Wade H. Wilson, Sonoma. The cause is worthy, and the response should be prompt and liberal.

General Mariano Guadalupe Vallejo, of pure Castilian (Spanish) ancestry, was one of the most outstanding characters in California history. He was born at Monterey, this state, July 7, 1808, and died at Sonoma January 18, 1890.—C. M. H.

ROSE TOURNAMENT PRIZE WINNERS.

San Marino won highest honors at Pasadena's annual Tournament of Roses, New Year Day, being represented by a gorgeous work of creative art in flowers and greens depicting the lyre bird.

The theme prize was awarded to Glendale, and the trophy prize to East Pasadena.

Motor Products' Value—The wholesale value of passenger autos produced last year in the United States was $1,175,000,000, and of trucks $260,000,000.

Midwinter Flower Show—Ensenada, San Diego County, will have a National Midwinter Flower Show, February 17-22.

NATIONAL ORANGE SHOW

(E. M. GORE.)

THAT THE 1932 NATIONAL ORANGE Show at San Bernardino, from February 18 to 28—the twenty-second edition of this classic exposition—will be bigger and more spectacular this season than ever before, may be concluded from the advance announcements. The forthcoming show, in addition to being a remarkable exposition of California's hundred-million-dollar orange crop of this year, will also be remarkable, it is declared, from the crowd-drawing standpoints of entertainment and elaborate decoration.

Headlining the citrus fruit arrays, as the "soul" of the show, will be the many elaborate feature displays entered by the cities, towns and counties of California. Holding the stage of decorative splendor, will be a breath-taking motif of Colonial setting, honoring this year's bicentennial of George Washington. And topping the elaborate entertainment, will be constantly changed programs of light opera featuring Perry Askam, noted star of "The Desert Song."

In connection with the inspirational background—a tribute in decorative art to the glorious days of the Revolution—such elements as liberty bells, American eagles, pillared colonial porches, etc., will be wrought into a beautiful ensemble. American flags will be used abundantly. The lighting effects will be marked by gorgeous chandeliers such as hung in Mount Vernon and other rich homes of the period of 1776.

In the feature exhibits, too, this patriotic idea will be borne out. Such features as "Betsy Ross Making the First Flag" or "Washington Crossing the Delaware" will be wrought into elaborate displays, many of them involving motion.

Around the walls of the main show building, and just back of the golden arrays of oranges, lemons and grapefruit—the rack displays of prize fruit—will be a series of colorful mural paintings. These will be reproductions of famous paintings depicting the story of George Washington and America's infancy. "Washington at Valley Forge," "Crossing the Delaware," "At Mount Vernon," and similar pieces of story-telling art will be shown in the form of huge oil paintings upon the walls.

The show, as finally planned, will consist of the following departments: Main show—feature displays, rack displays, stage entertainment. Industrial show—displays of various industrial products, especially of interest to orangegrowers. By-products show—many commercial by-products of the citrus groves, such as perfumes, soaps, cosmetics, marmalade, jams and jellies. Woman's division—exhibit of "home-industry" products created by wives and daughters of California orangegrowers. Boys' and girls' division—display of handiwork by schoolchildren of the "Orange Belt." Educational department—exhibits by State Department of Agriculture, Department of Citrus Education, etc. Carnival division—fun and frolic on the classic "Orange Trail."

The show, it is planned, will have a brilliant opening the evening of February 18. Governor James Rolph Jr. has promised to fly down from the State Capital to open the show formally and deliver, on behalf of California, the address of welcome to visitors. As has been the annual custom, the news-reel operators of the several movie syndicates will sound-photo the feature displays for showing in theaters throughout the world.

All in all, according to General Manager Roy E. Mack, the coming National Orange Show at San Bernardino will be "so much more for the money," that it is conservatively expected record crowds will be drawn.

A BIT O' FARMING and GARDENING

PREPARED EXPRESSLY FOR THE GRIZZLY BEAR BY M. H. ELLIS

FOR THE FIRST TIME IN A NUMBER OF years, California comes out of the winter with a surplus of rainfall. Snow is packed in the mountains to a depth unknown within the memory of most Californians. Every indication is that farmers of the state will start the growing season with the soil holding a miximum of moisture, and that there will be an abundant supply for irrigation during the dry period.

The dry years should have taught the lesson, though, that there should be no waste in the use of water, even when it is plentiful. Hundreds upon hundreds of acres have been rendered sterile through continued over-irrigation without proper drainage. There should be a program of conservation little less strict than that of last year and the years preceding it.

What effect the super-normal rainfall will have on the receding water tables in the districts where pumps are used to supply irrigation will be watched with interest. For several years farmers have had to follow the water down the wells with their pumps; this year it is to be hoped the water will chase the pumps back up the wells to something near, at least, the old level.

And cheerful predictions come with the rains! Droughts and wet years have run in cycles in the past. As we have just ended a long term of sub-normal rainfall, there is pleasant hope in the anticipation of a few years of wet winters to restore conditions to normal.

WATCH ROSE MILDEW.

There is no trouble, perhaps, that bothers city and country gardeners alike with more persistence than rose mildew. In the summer, sulphur dust aids in controlling this fungus, but some lime-sulphur applied right now as spray will account for more than dust in the growing season. Spray while the bushes are dormant, or as nearly so as they get, with lime-sulphur at one to ten strength. Then, when the first new foliage appears, get out the duster. Sulphur dust is better as a preventive than a cure. In spraying, as in dusting, get the under sides of the leaves as well as the more-easily-covered top sides.

PREPARE FOR RED-BERRY.

Growers in all parts of the state have reported trouble in recent years with red-berry in their blackberries. The fruit grows approximately to full size, but does not mature, remaining hard and red. This trouble is caused by a very minute mite, readily controlled through proper measures. Four to eight gallons of lime sulphur in 100 gallons of water, applied when the leaf buds are beginning to open in early spring, usually overcomes the red-berry mite. An additional spray, of five gallons of wettable sulphur to 100 gallons of water, applied during the summer is further insurance. Be prepared to spray when the leaves begin to open this spring.

PLANTING DAHLIA BULBS.

In planting dahlia bulbs, which may be done at any time now in most localities, be sure that every bulb has an eye. Don't, in dividing the bulbs, cut them from the crown. Each tuber should have a small portion of the crown with an eye, or bud, in that portion. If the buds are permitted to swell before the division is made, there need be no difficulty. Be careful in preparing the bed for the bulbs. Rich, sandy loam is best, worked up to a depth of at least a foot; a foot and a half is better. The ground should be well pulverized, and well-rotted cow manure, added after the plants start, will be a potent factor in assuring good blossoms.

GRAFTING SEASON OPENS.

There is no mystery about grafting, as most fruitgrowers know. The work may be done this month or early in March, and by exercising a little care trees may be top-worked without difficulty. The home orchardist can make splendid use of grafting methods. One peach tree, for instance, gives more fruit than can be used at one time. Three or four varieties, grafted to the same root, will furnish a succession of crops. No matter what method of grafting is used, it is necessary only to bring the scion and the wood upon which it is grafted together at an angle so that the cambium layer meets to as great an extent as possible. Tie the graft, protect it with a good wax, and if the work is well done the graft will grow. Roses that are undesirable, fruit trees that do not give the proper crops or that are subject to pests more than other varieties, may be grafted. Of course, some prefer budding. That is a job for the late summer or early fall.

TOBACCO FOR SETTING HENS.

Nicotine sulphate, used on roosts and in the henhouse to protect the laying flock against vermin, also is effective to make hens more comfortable while they are sitting on their eggs. Put a little on the bottom of the nest a day or two before the hen is given her eggs; ten days later put some more in, to continue the protection. Be sure the nicotine sulphate is put under the nest material so that it will not come in contact with the eggs.

ORGANIC AND INORGANIC FERTILIZERS.

With the advent of spring, fertilizers are applied to orchards in varying quantities and of varying qualities. There is danger in using a bulky organic fertilizer at this time of the year, such as cereal straw. Applied now, decomposition takes place during the vigorous growing season and may take so much nitrogen from the soil that the tree will be robbed. Bulky fertilizers of this kind should be used when the tree's nitrogen requirements are at a minimum, from about June to November. Manures with light straw content may be used now, although they are better applied in the fall.

This is, however, just the season of the year when the best use can be made of the commercial, or inorganic, fertilizers, which are quickly available for use by the trees. Study first the needs of the soil; find out what element is needed. Then supply it through some reliable brand of commercial fertilizer. Inorganic fertilizers may be applied at any time now, as soon as the soil is in condition to work. Well chosen and properly applied, such fertilizers will more than pay for themselves; they will increase profits far beyond their costs.

COMBATTING THE CUTWORM.

Where gardens are infested with cutworms, a little precaution before planting will be well repaid. Turn the soil over and let it lie idle for a few weeks while the cutworms are at work. Then, just before planting, a week or so, scatter poisoned bran mash over the soil in the evening. With nothing else to eat, the cutworms will come up at night, feed on the poison, and die. The poisoned mash can be purchased ready made at a supply house, or it can be mixed at home. A good mash of this kind is made by dry-mixing a pound of coarse bran and an ounce of black molasses and enough water to make it crumbly, with the arsenic or other poison added.

NAVEL INFECTIONS OF LAMBS.

Last year serious losses were reported in some sections through an infection acquired by lambs at birth, causing stiffness and swollen joints. This is due to an infection picked up at birth on the navel. The remedy must be applied promptly at birth by taking a wide-mouth bottle of iodine and slipping it over the navel up to the abdominal wall, and leaving it for a few seconds. The treatment marks the lambs, and prevents a number of infections of more or less serious nature.

PRUNING BLIGHTED TREES.

If pear trees were heavily cut back last year in controlling blight, they should have most moderate thinning in pruning. No attempt should be made to restore the balance of the tree this year. The tree will need most of the leaf surface it can develop to store food this season for next year. The pruner should make the rebuilding of the badly-cut-back pear tree a job that extends over three or four years. Trees can be brought back to their original bearing surface if care is taken not to try to do it all at once.

GROWING SWEET CORN.

Sweet corn production in California is growing, and as knowledge of the crop increases its troubles are being solved. Plant as soon as frost danger is over, in rich, well-drained loam. Plenty of water is required. Be sure to keep the suckers out, and the weeds down.

FINISH THE SPRAY CLEANUP.

The dormant season is just about ended. The dormant sprays should have been applied before this time, but it still is not too late to do a lot of good. In many instances the wet weather of the winter months has pretty much precluded any sort of work in orchards. Trees will more than likely have large crops this year. Be sure they are not obliged to feed a host of hungry pests which will weaken them and spoil the quality of their fruit.

LAYERING TO START PLANTS.

Many plants are difficult to start from cuttings. Some of these, the bougainvillea for instance, is rooted in this manner only with extreme care and the loss of most of the cuttings. An easier way to get new plants is by layering. Perhaps the best method is to cut about halfway through the shoot that is to be layered, and by bending gently, open the cut so that a small stick or stone may be inserted to keep the incision open. Then make a little trench in the soil, bend the shoot down and cover it with earth. A wire or hairpin may be used to hold the shoot from being displaced. The shoot should be allowed to remain in the soil for a year. At the end of this time a nicely rooted plant should be found.

"Self-control is only courage in another form."
—Samuel Smiles.

Feminine World's Fads and Fancies

PREPARED ESPECIALLY FOR THE GRIZZLY BEAR BY ANNA STOERMER

SPRING OF 1932 BRINGS SLENDER AND chic silhouettes, tapering from shoulder to ankle. Red, white and blue fabrics have dull, rough surfaces. Milady is to be as becomingly dressed as ever, with the new changes in line, the unusual new shoulder width, and so on.

Hand-knitted weaves are deep ribbed, thick and very swagger. These are mainly white, trimmed with touches of vivid red or the new bright blue, or both. Colorful suede jackets are good, according to the modes displayed, also white gloves, nifty crushed straw berets, grecian sandals and mesh hosiery.

No matter where you are or where you are going, the dresses of wool, suitable for every clime, are indispensable. Whether the weather is hot, cold or dry, a different kind of wool dress may be worn in any of the light shades, as well as the bright shades, and what a cheery accent the bright-colored ones give to the dark coats. You may match these dresses with a light, bright coat, or else plan your individual color contrast.

These dresses are trimmed with tucks in sunburst fashion all around the smart, high neckline, and then the tucking is repeated perpendicularly about the hips. A band, edging the neck, ties in front, as does the narrow band that circles the waist as a belt, and bands draw each full sleeve at the wrist.

Another attractive frock is made of the nubbed lace tweed of woven porous wool. The chic diagonal cross-over effect is achieved by seaming lengthwise to the waistline, then slanting the seam in the other direction. The bodice, slightly bloused, is made more interesting by placing four stunning little buttons, with tiny metal wings and bandings, at the base of the "v" neck. Metal is used again for the prongs and buckle of the leather pull. Loose raglan sleeves are almost bell-shape, and are caught around the wrist by a narrow band with button closings.

To the interested observer, there seems to be a weave and a color for every purpose and every occasion, and more often than not we mistake our woolens for something else. Boucle effects are very much modified and flattened out, as if they were appearing in a variety of weights for a variety of purposes.

That smart and proper silhouette, with its high-fitted waistline, comes naturally with a blouse and skirt. The new blouses are cut that way, and are built high around the neck because fashion says it is the new and smart thing to do. So new in fact, that it is a joy to look at them, and much more joy to wear them.

The most intriguing of the blouses are those for sports wear, chiefly because of the lovely new materials. Of course, crepes and satins are as nice as ever, but the new knits, wools and cottons go with winter suits, making stunning sports costumes. You will see them worn that way a lot this spring and summer.

The frock for afternoon is becoming sophisticated. Many women all but live in the little frock of black satin or crepe-de-chine. They find it fits into almost every scheme, and it confers a charming youthful look on the wearer.

The new satin is called cirol, and is lustrous and supple. It is very popular when trimmed with lace, which should be of the new angel-skin type. This is one of the newest and loveliest of fashion innovations this spring. It is a lace with a soft, smooth surface and exquisite design. It is used for the increasingly popular dinner and evening gowns, as well. It is to be had in almost every color of the rainbow, and the more vivid the hue, it seems, the more striking the effect.

Long gloves are back again. For the ensemble, the eight- and twelve-button kind are shown, with no other radical changes.

Daytime dress lengths will be no longer, just the same number of inches from the floor during the spring and summer. At the moment, the frock with its hemline ten inches from the ground is considered chic.

There will be a variation in the length of costumes for dinner and evening wear, but only according to the ideas of the individual. The ankle-length will be highly popular with the younger girls, while the instep-length will prevail with the more sophisticated. Formal evening gowns will continue to touch the floor.

Spring millinery starts blue, as though that will be the banner color this spring. Straws and felts are shown in bright blues, with shallow crowns, and are worn very much to one side. Piecings, joined by raised seams, are shaped to a joint at the center of the crown.

Generally, right after the new year, the delightful little hats of taffeta, satin or grosgrain ribbon make their welcome reappearance. They pave the way for the first exciting real spring hats. This year, with the vogue for the hat with a mass of closely pressed flowers, they will play a leading role in the spring millinery. Certainly there are always some flower-trimmed hats available, but the new crop of blossoms will bloom under, not upon, the hat.

All sorts of new straw weaves are in the offing, but the good old standbys, such as milan and picot, will be most extensively used, and there will be colorful straws from pastel tones to vivid hues.

Fruit Pack Drops—California's 1931 fruit pack was 12,669,581 cases, the lowest number in five years. The 1930 pack totaled 19,013,400 cases. The highest pack in the five-year period was in 1928, 20,223,024 cases.

Hardware Men To Meet—The eleventh annual convention of the Southern California Retail Hardware Association will be held February 16-20 at Los Angeles City.

Dedication—The California State Building in Los Angeles City, erected at a cost of $2,000,000, is to be dedicated February 18.

Native Daughters of the Golden West

SANTA CRUZ—PAST GRAND PRESIDENT Stella Finkeldey is carrying on most commendably as chairman of the Grand Parlor Veteran Welfare Committee. The following letters, received by her from United States Veteran Hospitals, refer to her activities:

"Closely following your letter of December twelfth have come two packages from you containing the prizes for the very generous number of card parties. We are very, very happy, indeed, to have had you respond so helpfully to our suggestion and we want you to feel that you have our very warmest appreciation for your solution of one of our problems. Not only that, but you have shown such interest and care in carrying out your promise. The packages wrapped so carefully in your colors, and the care taken in arranging the sets of prizes, and the cards written by you, all these will give your parties, 'the Golden West parties,' a really personal touch. We wish that you or some one of your members might be with us to enjoy one of the evenings. After the Christmas rush is over we will write to you and tell you about one of your parties; meanwhile, with all best wishes for the Yuletide, very truly yours, S. H. JAMES, M.D., Medical Officer in Charge, U. S. Veteran Hospital, Tucson, Arizona, December 19, 1931."

(Note—The Grand Parlor Veteran Welfare fund assisted this hospital by supplying seven sets of prizes, five prizes in each set, for seven card parties.—Editor.)

"This will acknowledge your letter of December 17 and the box of California berry shrubs, which are being most effectively used in our decorations. Your kind interest in our hospital is very much appreciated, and I wish to thank you on behalf of the patients as well as the hospital administration. Wishing you the compliments of the season, I am, very truly yours, R. W. BROWNE, Medical Officer in Charge, U. S. Veteran Hospital, Walla Walla, Washington, December 21, 1931."

"The box of nice, hard candies to be used in nut cups for our Christmas trays and tables, arrived on the 17th. The attractive little nut cups of green and red, given to us by the Red Cross Juniors of Pasadena, added quite a festive touch to the trays and tables,—the use of which was made possible by your gift of the candy for filling them. Again please accept the combined thanks of the patients and administration for your assistance in making Christmas as cheery and pleasant as possible in this hospital. Hoping that Christmas brought happiness to the members of your organization, and with all best wishes for the new year, we are, very sincerely yours, MISS FRANCES MAYNARD, Recreational Aide, U. S. Veteran Hospital, Whipple, Arizona, December 28, 1931."

"The two packages containing bridge prizes for parties six and seven sponsored by the Native Daughters of the Golden West reached us safely yesterday. We were most happy to receive these boxes and we wish to take this opportunity to tell you how much pleasure the first two sets of prizes gave the patients and their guests,—so far we have used but the two. Three or four requests were made by prize winners that their thanks be forwarded to you. This service is being greatly appreciated by all, and especially so because it is being offered us with such evident interest and care. Thanking all members of your organization for this co-operation, very truly yours, S. H. JAMES, M.D., Medical Officer in Charge, U. S. Veteran Hospital, Tucson, Arizona, January 16, 1932."

"This will acknowledge receipt of your letter of January 10, 1932, relative to your contribution of eight copies of 'National Geographic' and several copies of the 'Mid-Week Pictorial' which your organization so kindly furnishes yearly for the patients at this hospital. We wish to advise that it will be appreciated if you will continue subscriptions to the same magazines for 1932, and thank you in behalf of the patients. Very truly yours, P. G. LASCHE, Medical Officer in Charge, U. S. Veteran Hospital, Palo Alto, California, January 12, 1932."

"Thank you for your kind letter of Jan. 10, offering us your yearly donation of light-weight wool socks. These have proved very popular with the patients each year, and although we still have several boxes of last year's supply remaining, we would be very happy to have you send us more of them. The many kindnesses which the Native Daughters of the Golden West have extended the patients of this hospital have been deeply appreciated, we assure you, not only by the patients themselves but by the hospital administration as well. Throughout the year we receive many evidences of the deep interest taken by the various Parlors of the Native Daughters in our hospitalized veterans. Sincerest wishes to you and to all Native Daughters of California for the coming year. By direction (Miss) IRMA ANDERSON, Senior Recreational Aide, U. S. Veteran Hospital, Livermore, California, January 12, 1932."

When you purchase goods advertised in The Grizzly Bear, or answer an advertisement in this magazine, please be sure to mention The Grizzly Bear. That's co-operation mutually beneficial.

Delightful Event.

Etna—Eschscholtzia No. 112 gave its annual ball in a hall gay with red bells, evergreens and colored lights. The grand march was led by Miss Dorice Young, president-elect of the Parlor, and Ernest Smith of Etna No. 192 N.S.G.W. Marshal Agnes Calloway and District Deputy L. E. Buchner directed the march.

Since the annual contribution to the homeless children fund is taken from the proceeds of this ball, the Native Daughters were much pleased at having favorable weather, the night of the ball being the only pleasant evening in a very stormy season. As a result, all sections of Scott Valley were represented, and the attendance was all that could be desired. The presence of a number of former residents and young people who had come home from college added greatly to the pleasure of the evening. The music was excellent, a source of enjoyment to the spectators as well as to the dancers. Much credit is due to President Nancy Smith and her committees for the able management that made the affair a most delightful event.

Parlor Planned for Redlands.

San Bernardino—Members of Lugonia No. 241 enjoyed an entertainment January 13 staged by Arrowhead Parlor No. 110 N.S.G.W. A large delegation accompanied District Deputy Eva Mae Bemis to Long Beach, where she installed, January 21, the officers of No. 154. Lugonia's officers, with Gladys Baker as president, were installed January 27. A program of music followed the ceremonies and refreshments were served. The Parlor plans to entertain neighboring Parlors at a dinner in the near-future.

Several members of Lugonia attended a recent gathering at Redlands, at which the institution of a Parlor there was discussed. Organization work is in charge of District Deputy Hazel B. Hansen of Glendale, vice-chairman Grand Parlor Extension of the Order Committee.

Sacramento-Placer District Meet.

Sacramento—Parlors of Sacramento and Placer Counties held a joint district meeting under the direction of Supervising Deputy Bessie Leitch. Among the 300 in attendance were Grand President Evelyn I. Carlson, Grand vice-president Anna Armstrong, Grand Trustees Edna Briggs, Gladys Noce and Florence Boyle, Past Grand Presidents Mary E. Bell, May Boldeman, Dr. Eva Rasmussen, Dr. Louise C. Heilbron and Esther R. Sullivan, Supervising Deputies Bessie Leitch, Ethel Ludwig, Wanda Abeley and Edna Richter, District Deputies Mamie McCormick, Doris Fisher, Nellie Nordstrom, Mae Lucas, Mae Rhodes, Alice Carpenter, Sadie Brainard, Nellie Ramsey, Laura Gay, Alicia Buckley, Mamie Davis, Alice Boldeman, Inna Bloom and Mollye Spaelti.

Two candidates were initiated for Sutter No. 111, the ritual being exemplified by the following: Eva Mordecai (La Bandera No. 110), president; Eva Meyers (Placer No. 138), first vice-president; Margaret Parrish (La Rosa No. 191), second vice-president; Cleora Ritz (Chabolla No. 171), third vice-president; Margaret Wiedeman (Victory No. 216), past president; Lorraine Williams (Sutter No. 111), marshal; Ella Windmiller (Liberty No. 213), inside sentinel; Elizabeth Ryan (Fern No. 123), outside sentinel; Nettie Harry (Coloma No. 212), recording secretary; Florence Berry (Placer No. 138), financial secretary; Alice Artz (Califia No. 22), treasurer; Harriet Hall (Fern No. 123), Frances Wakeman (Liberty No. 213), Phillis Ramsey (Placer No. 138), trustees; Nellie Ramsey (Placer No. 138), junior past president; Elizabeth Walker (Coloma No. 212), senior past president; Emilie Lachmann (Sutter No. 111), pianist. After the meeting dinner was served in the beautifully decorated banquetroom.

Contributes to Unemployed.

Mariposa—Mariposa No. 63, always active in civic affairs, has contributed financially to Mariposa County's general welfare fund for the unemployed. It recently sponsored a successful apron sale for its Loyalty Pledge fund and initiated two candidates.

Supervising Deputy May F. Givens during January attended installations of the four Parlors in her district. At the joint ceremonies of Veritas No. 75 and Yosemite No. 24 N.S.G.W. at Merced City, January 11, she was the principal speaker.

Guests Enthusiastically Welcomed.

San Juan Bautista—The official visit of Grand President Evelyn I. Carlson to Copa de Oro No. 105 and San Juan Bautista No. 179, in joint session here January 6, was a particularly happy event. The pleasures of the evening began at the dinner table, attractively decorated with yellow as the prevailing color. District Deputy Blanche Taix presided, introducing the guests of honor, who were enthusiastically welcomed. A program of community singing, consisting of the "booster" songs of the two Parlors, and toasts by Past Presidents Catherine Nyland and Edna Butterfield, was enjoyed.

At the meeting the officers of San Juan Bautista presented a pleasing picture in evening gowns with corsages of white carnations and ferns, followed by the officers of Copa de Oro, who were designated by corsages of red carnations. Grand officers were presented with corsages of gardenias. A class of four candidates were initiated, two for each Parlor, with President Ellen Murray of San Juan Bautista ably presiding.

Grand President Carlson delivered an inspiring address on the projects of the Order. By her gracious presence, she won the hearts of all present, and was the recipient of gifts from both Parlors. Other grand officers in attendance were Supervising Deputy Rose Rhyner, District Deputy Blanche Taix and Past Grand President Bertha A. Briggs. Visitors were present from Salinas, Santa Cruz, San José and San Francisco. Many unable to be present at the dinner, joined the assemblage for the meeting, and the cosy hall was crowded to capacity.

To Initiate Large Class.

Fullerton—Grace No. 242 had initiation January 8. Among the many guests were District Deputy Ora Evans and President Gertrude Tuttle of Californiana No. 247 (Los Angeles). President Mattie Edwards outlined plans for the term, and Carrie McFadden-Ford and assistants served refreshments. Recent hostesses of the Parlor's sewing circle were President Edwards, Secretary Mary Rothaermel and Lula Forbes.

With Past President Nellie Cline in charge,

the Parlor sponsored a public card party January 22 for the benefit of the Native Daughter Home. Awards were made and refreshments were served. When Grand President Evelyn I. Carlson officially visits February 29, Grace will initiate a large class of candidates. A recent old-fashioned bazaar netted the Parlor treasury a neat sum. Callye Sparkes, a charter member of No. 242, was wedded January 4 to Adolph Blum.

Patriotic Ceremonies for New Citizens.

Oroville—Officers of Gold of Ophir No. 190 and Argonaut No. 8 N.S.G.W. were jointly installed January 6 by District Deputies Cora Hintz and Cyril Macdonald. On behalf of No. 190, gifts and flowers were presented Supervising Deputy Hintz, Past President Jessie Hoover, President Alice Cundy and Mrs. Loretta Ross. Mrs. Romilda Ralph headed a committee which served refreshments at the conclusion of the ceremonies. Mountain greens and pyracantha decorated the lodgeroom and banquetroom.

After twenty-two candidates successfully passed the examination for citizenship January 13, Gold of Ophir had charge of patriotic ceremonies, an honor accorded it for many years. Four fraternal organizations assisted with the program, which included a talk on the "History of Our State" by Grand Trustee Florence Boyle and the presentation of a copy of the "American Creed" to each of the new citizens by President Alice Cundy.

Holiday Cheer.

Vallejo—Vallejo No. 195 and Vallejo No. 77 N.S.G.W. entertained the children of the members at a December 22 Christmas party. A program was presented, Santa Claus distributed presents and candy to all the children, and the enjoyable occasion concluded with dancing. Guilda Keller and Fernan Legoria were the chairmen in charge. Chairman Edith Gutfeld of No. 195's veteran welfare committee visited the Mare Island Hospital and distributed home-made cakes and jams to the tubercular ward patients.

Grand President's Official Itinerary.

San Francisco—During the month of February, Grand President Evelyn I. Carlson will officially visit the following Subordinate Parlors on the dates noted:

3rd—El Carmelo No. 181, Daly City.
4th—Oro Fino No. 9, San Francisco.
6th—Victory No. 216, Courtland.
8th—Marinita No. 198, San Rafael.
9th—Fairfax No. 225, Fairfax.
10th—Gabrielle No. 139, San Francisco.
11th—Encinal No. 156, Alameda.
15th—Mariposa No. 63, Mariposa.
17th—Miocene No. 228, Taft (at 1:30 p.m.).
19th—Fresno No. 187, Fresno.
20th—Madera No. 244, Madera.
24th—San Miguel No. 94, San Miguel (afternoon).
25th—San Luisita No. 108, San Luis Obispo.
26th—El Pinal No. 163, Cambria (afternoon).
29th—Grace No. 242, Fullerton.

Receives Exquisite Gavel.

San Diego—San Diego No. 208 has been presented with an exquisitely hand-carved gavel, made by Mr. Cole, 78-year-old resident of this city. In its making seven different woods typical of this section were used. The handle is of pecan, the head of pear, and there are inlays of black walnut, olive, white thorn, desert thorn and sumac. The presentation was made to President Sarah Miller, for the Parlor, by Evelyn Wurzel.

January Girls Surprised.

Santa Ana—At the January 11 meeting of Santa Ana No. 235, President Marion Crum appointed a committee of eight members on ways and means for each month of the January-July term, to formulate plans for replenishing the treasury. Semi-annual reports were presented by Financial Secretary Rose Ford, Recording Secretary Matilda Lemon and Treasurer Ina Cope.

Members whose birthdays came in January—Mms. Genevieve Hiskey, Hannah Kerr, Ina Cope, Rose Ford, Elizabeth Marsile, Emma Harby and Caroline Alford—were honor-guests at a surprise. Tables decorated in their honor had individual birthday cakes lighted with candles. Secretary Lemon proposed this toast: "Our friends, may we have many of them, and may they be always with us."

The monthly card party was held January 19 at the Balboa home of Mrs. J. A. Grant. Recent meetings of the thimble club were held at the homes of Mms. Myrtle Ellis, Mary Moore and

(Continued on Page 19)

Passing of the California Pioneer

(Confined to Brief Notices of the Demise of Those Men and Women Who Came to California Prior to 1860.)

MRS. THEODORE E. SMITH, NATIVE of Michigan, 85; as an infant, she accompanied her parents to California via Cape Horn in 1848, and shortly thereafter departed for Honolulu, where she remained until 1865; died at San Francisco, survived by seven children. She was a daughter of Asher B. Bates, first judge of California's bankruptcy court.

Thomas R. Carew, native of Australia, 84; since 1850 resident of San Francisco, where he died; nine children survive.

Mrs. Clara Virginia Zane-Gum, native of Ohio, 88; came across the plains in 1852 and settled in Healdsburg, Sonoma County, where she died; three children survive.

James K. P. Clevenger, native of Missouri, 83; came across the plains in 1852 and resided in Sacramento and San Diego Counties; died at Ramona, survived by four children.

Mrs. Nancy Ann Hogan, native of Missouri, 84; crossed the plains in 1852 and settled in Napa City, where she died; three children survive.

John Martin Adamson, native of Utah, 80; came in 1852; died at Lower Lake, Lake County, survived by a wife and three children. For several years he taught school in Mendocino, Lake, Colusa and Shasta Counties, and for twenty-eight years served Lake County as a supervisor.

Mrs. Lydia Garcelon-Steward, native of Maine, 102; came via the Isthmus of Panama in 1853 and for many years resided in Yuba County; died at Redlands, San Bernardino County, survived by three children. She was the widow of Joseph Steward, Pioneer of 1850, to whom she was wedded at Marysville, November 27, 1853.

George A. W. Bailey, native of Wisconsin, 90; crossed the plains in 1853 and resided in the Sacramento valley and San Luis Obispo County; died at San Luis Obispo City, survived by a wife and six children.

Mrs. Almyra A. Williams, native of New York, 89; came across the plains in 1853; died at Red Bluff, Tehama County, survived by two children.

Mrs. Elizabeth H. Meserve, native of Missouri, 87; came across the plains in 1854 and resided in Sacramento, Santa Cruz and Los Angeles Counties; died at Los Angeles City, survived by three children, among them Edwin A. Meserve (Ramona Parlor No. 109 N.S.G.W.) of Los Angeles.

William G. Chiles, born in 1854 while his parents were enroute across the plains, and settled in Napa County; died at Napa City, survived by two children. He was a son of Colonel J. B. Chiles, Pioneer of 1841, who acquired a Mexican grant in Napa County now known as Chiles valley.

Mrs. Esther Ann Halloway, native of Delaware, 92; came in 1854 and resided in Sutter, Butte, Santa Barbara and Los Angeles Counties; died at Long Beach, survived by a daughter, Mrs. Georgia Peirson (Long Beach Parlor No. 154 N.D.G.W.).

Mrs. Annie Marie Cullers, native of Louisiana, 82; came in 1854; died at Tuolumne Town, survived by five children.

Mrs. Martha Monroe-Murgotten, native of Ohio, 83; since 1855 resident San Jose, Santa Clara County, where she died; two sons survive. She was the widow of Alexander P. Murgotten, who for several years published "The Pioneer," a California history magazine.

Benjamin Franklin Campbell, native of Iowa, 82; came across the plains in 1856 and resided in Sonoma and Alameda Counties; died at Berkeley, survived by a wife and three children.

Mrs. Fanny C. Porter, native of Canada, 93; came in 1856; died at Watsonville, Santa Cruz County, survived by a daughter.

Mrs. Lizzie Himes-Dover, native of Missouri, 87; came across the plains in 1856 and resided in Santa Cruz and Alameda Counties; died at Hayward, survived by six children.

John E. Jenner; since 1856 resident San Francisco Bay district; died at Berkeley, Alameda County, survived by a wife and a son.

Mrs. Mary Frances Winters, native of Illinois, 87; since 1858 San Joaquin County resident; died at Stockton, survived by five children.

Mrs. Margaret Whelan-Wosser, native of Ireland, 88; came via the Isthmus of Panama in 1858 and following a residence of ten years in San Francisco settled in Sausalito, Marin County, where she died; surviving are eleven children, among them Thomas J. Wosser (Mount Tamalpais Parlor No. 64 N.S.G.W.) of Sausalito.

William D. Rantz, native of Indiana, 90; came across the plains in 1859 and resided in El Dorado and Lake Counties; died at Lakeport, survived by a wife and eight children.

Mrs. Aroline Nelson-Kemp, native of Massachusetts, 84; since 1859 resident Humboldt County; died at Eureka, survived by six children.

OLD TIMERS PASS

Mrs. Martha Cook-Elledge, native of Missouri, 76; came in 1860; died at Ukiah, Mendocino County, survived by six children.

Mrs. Ellen Beck-Acker, native of Illinois, 87; came in 1860; died at Los Gatos, Santa Clara County, survived by a son. She resided in Alameda County many years.

John J. Hughes, native of New York, 81; since 1861 resident San Francisco, where he died; four children survive.

Mrs. Carrie-Slade Richmond, 75; since 1861 resident Auburn, Placer County, where she died.

Mrs. Mary A. Frichette, native of Massachusetts, 92; came in 1861; died at Sacramento City, survived by four children. She resided many years in Placer County.

Mrs. Catherine Booksin, native of Germany, 82; came in 1862; died at San Jose, Santa Clara County; survived by three children. For many years she resided in Colusa County.

Mrs. Helena Potevin, native of Michigan, 78; came in 1864; died at Bowman, Placer County, survived by a daughter.

Mrs. Mary B. Horton, native of Ohio, 90; since 1865 Inyo County resident; died at Bishop, survived by a daughter.

Mrs. Bridgett McCaffrey, native of Ireland, 83; came in 1865; died at Santa Barbara City, survived by three sons, W. J., H. J. and E. J. McCaffrey (all Santa Barbara Parlor No. 116 N.S.G.W.).

Mrs. Ruth Scribner, native of Iowa, 71; came in 1866; died at Woodland, Yolo County, survived by a husband.

George Bolton, native of Missouri, 83; since 1866 resident Oakland, Alameda County, where he died; a wife and three children survive.

Erastus Sylvester Farnham, native of Michigan, 87; came in 1866; died at Woodland, Yolo County, survived by a wife and six children.

Ernst Emil Lehmann, native of Germany, 83; since 1866 resident San Francisco, where he died; four children survive.

Dr. Harry Clinton Dimock, native of Nova Scotia, 89; came in 1867; died at Lompoc, Santa Barbara County.

Mrs. Jennie Harris-Salisbury, native of Canada, 78; came in 1868; died at Napa City, survived by three children.

Otto Schluer, native of Germany, 85; since 1868 resident Woodland, Yolo County, where he died; a wife and ten children survive.

Mrs. Elizabeth Russell-Wadge, native of England, 87; since 1868 resident Sutter Creek, Amador County, where she died; five children survive.

Peter Tognazzini, native of Switzerland, 79; came in 1868; died at Cambria, San Luis Obispo County, survived by five children.

Mrs. Mary Ann Lennox, native of Scotland, 83; came in 1868; died at Marysville, Yuba County, survived by three children.

Christian Mau, native of Germany, 78; since 1868 resident San Francisco, where he died; a daughter survives.

Mrs. Lumina Barceloux, native of Canada, 89; came in 1869; died at Willows, Glenn County, survived by three children.

Melangthon Engles, native of Denmark, 82; since 1869 Humboldt County resident; died at Eureka, survived by a son.

Mrs. Savilla Loretta Chrisman, native of Vermont, 85; since 1869 San Joaquin County resident; died at Tracy, survived by a son.

Mrs. Sarah Amanda Collier-Taber, native of Tennessee, 88; came in 1869; died at Los Angeles City, survived by seven children, among them Edward R. and Charles R. Taber (both Ramona Parlor No. 109 N.S.G.W.).

George Gregory, native of England, 85; since 1867 resident Placerville, El Dorado County, where he died; a wife and six children survive.

William A. Morris, native of Kentucky, 83; came in 1861; died at Colusa City.

PIONEER NATIVES DEAD

Arcata (Humboldt County)—James Edward Morton, born in this county in 1858, died December 21 survived by a wife and a daughter.

Sacramento City—Mrs. Katherine Ann Keegan, born here in 1855, passed away recently survived by four children.

Eureka (Humboldt County)—John S. Reid, born in Trinity County in 1859, died December 21.

San Francisco—John W. Standley, born in Sonoma County in 1856, died December 23 survived by a wife and five children.

Altadena (Los Angeles County)—Tranquilina Sepulveda, born in this county in 1849, passed away December 24.

San Francisco—John Parker, born in Siskiyou County in 1858, died December 24 survived by a wife and three children.

Grass Valley (Nevada County)—Mrs. Mary Green-Curry, born in this county in 1855, passed away December 25 survived by seven children.

Berkeley (Alameda County)—Leroy J. Cope, born in Sutter County in 1859, died December 25 survived by a wife and three children. For a quarter-century he served Sutter County as treasurer and tax collector.

Roseville (Placer County)—John Henry But-

(Continued on Page 23)

SAN FRANCISCO

HOME DEDICATION ANNIVERSARY.

The third anniversary of the dedication of the N.D.G.W. Home, 555 Baker street, was observed at the Sunday breakfast January 10. Past Grand Presidents Dr. Mariana Bertola and Emma G. Foley were the hostesses. A birthday cake, decorated with United States of America and California State (Bear) Flags and poppies, had this wording: "N.D.G.W. Home. Long life and health to one who made it possible—Dr. Bertola."

Mrs. J. Emmet Hayden gave readings, and the N.D.G.W. Glee Club rendered several selections, the words for one, sung to the tune of "The Gay Caballero," being written especially for the occasion. Speakers included Grand President Evelyn I. Carlson, Past Grand Presidents May C. Boldemann, Margaret G. Hill, Addie L. Mosher and Dr. Louise C. Heilbron. Dr. Bertola was lauded by all for her unselfish interest in the Home. Compliments were given in plenty, and good humor prevailed.

Supervising District Deputy Boldemann presented, in behalf of the San Francisco district, a surprise gift—an end table, purchased with the balance of a $200 donation given at the November 30 district meeting. She promised also, from the same source, a lamp for the reception lounge. Native Daughters were advised they now have an opportunity to show Past Grand President Louise W. Morris that she is fondly remembered, by sending her a shower of friendship cards.

The following Parlors were represented at the dedication anniversary: Native Son—Mount Tamalpais No. 64 and Bret Harte No. 260. Native Daughter—Oro Fino No. 9, Dolores No. 169, Alta No. 3, Golden State No. 50, Orinda No. 56, Twin Peaks No. 185, Keith No. 137, La Estrella No. 89, Buena Vista No. 68, Las Lomas No. 72, Genevieve No. 132, Mission No. 227, Piedmont No. 87, Aloha No. 106, Califia No. 22, San Diego No. 208, Joaquin No. 5, Marinita No. 198 and Santa Cruz No. 26.

"LOBSTERS" FETED.

Stanford Parlor No. 76 N.S.G.W. recently was host to the eight surviving members of the "Lobsters," an organization consisting of those members of the Parlor who served on the 1900 Admission Day committee. The gigantic celebration that year, held in San Francisco, marked the fiftieth anniversary of the admission of California into the Union. It was a huge success, and Stanford's participation was most creditable. When the festivities were brought to a close, the committee returned about two hundred dollars to the Parlor. Some one then remarked: "You lobsters, why did you not keep the money and provide a banquet for yourselves?" The committee, having enjoyed the fruits of true fellowship and being reluctant to separate, then and there decided to organize, taking the name "Lobsters."

Each year since 1900 these "lobsters" have met to talk over old times and relive the great celebration. Now there are but eight of them left, and Stanford fittingly observed the thirty-first anniversary of the organization with an oldtime party. There were songs, speeches, jokes, entertainment, refreshments, smokes and goodfellowship. One of the features of the evening was the exhibition of old programs, relics, pictures and badges, preserved for the Parlor by Historian Charles W. Dechent. The eight survivors are: Amadeo P. Giannini, J. J. McCarthy, John J. Lerman, Wm. D. Hynes, Peter J. Martenstein, Charles D. Steiger, Joseph G. Cox and Charles H. Stanyan.

The hall was decorated with greens entwined with colored electric lights. As each of the "lobsters" entered the hall, he was presented with a specially prepared regalia upon which were printed pictures of lobsters, the name of the member and the date of his entrance into the Parlor. Members of Stanford called for each of the eight, and after the ceremonies returned them to their homes. The feature of the evening's entertainment was the appearance of a huge soup tureen, supported by six members attired as cooks. It was placed before the president and, when opened, a beautiful maiden stepped out and danced for the assemblage. Waldo Postel and Dr. Leo McMahon delighted with comic actions and jokes, and Hal Burmeister entertained with songs and impersonations. Before the festivities were ended each "lobster" was introduced and a few words said about him. A. P. Giannini received highest honors for bringing into Stanford the largest number of new members.

MANY ACTIVITIES PLANNED.

Officers of Alta Parlor No. 3 N.D.G.W. were installed January 12 by District Deputy Annie Franzen, Catherine O'Reilly becoming president. Many activities are planned for her term.

JOINT INSTALLATION.

Officers of Gabrielle Parlor No. 139 N.D.G.W. and Rincon Parlor No. 72 N.S.G.W. were jointly installed January 13 by District Deputies Muriel Sandell and Thos. M. Dillon. Large delegations were present from Twin Peaks Parlor No. 185 N.D.G.W. and Castro Parlor No. 232 N.S.G.W. Refreshments, after the ceremonies, were followed by dancing.

EFFICIENT SERVICE RECOGNIZED.

Golden Gate Parlor No. 158 N.D.G.W. celebrated its twenty-fourth institution anniversary with a banquet, followed by cards, January 20. Past President Anna McQuade was in charge.

Officers of the Parlor were installed by District Deputy Sheehan, Margaret Ramm becoming president. In recognition of efficient service always rendered, the Parlor presented a beautiful emblematic ring to Past President Mary Sullivan.

ANNIVERSARY CELEBRATED.

The twenty-third anniversary of the institution of Dolores Parlor No. 169 N.D.G.W. was celebrated with a banquet, January 12, at which Grand President Evelyn I. Carlson, a member of the Parlor, and District Deputy Agnes McVerry were honored guests. Eighty-three partook of a very enjoyable italian feast, and a delightful evening was spent in dancing. January 27 the officers of Dolores were installed by District Deputy McVerry.

PAST PRESIDENTS INSTALL.

Officers of Past Presidents Association No. 1 N.D.G.W. and San Francisco Assembly No. 1 Past Presidents Association N.S.G.W. were installed at joint ceremonies January 18 by Past President Anna Johnson and Director General James F. Stanley, Minnie F. Dobbin and J. H. Sylvester becoming, respectively, president and governor. Among the speakers were Governor General Louis F. Erb, Past Governor General Arthur J. Cleu and Director General Stanley.

An emblematic pin was presented Anna Johnson by May Rose Barry, and many tokens were presented President Minnie F. Dobbin. Cora Stobing was chairman for the Native Daughters and Walter Stobing for the Native Sons.

THE ROMANCE

(Continued from Page 5)

cool in the summer, and warm in the winter. Too, there seems to be a lot of cultivated soil around the mission."

One year later, 1843, the Lugo brothers found they had lost much stock and provisions through raids of the desert Indians. The problem of subduing these untamed tribes seemed to be almost unsolvable.

"There are a lot of New Mexicans here now. Why can't we trade some of the land to them?" suggested Maria to Vicente. "If they will take it, I will. Possibly, they will help protect our provisions from the Indians. I think I shall interview Lorenza Trujillo. He may want Politana," replied Vicente. The deal was made in a very short time.

"But you must help us to protect our stock and help us to fight the Indians. They are very treacherous at times," said Maria. "You need not worry about that, as I shall be very glad to help you. We are used to fighting the Indian, as we have won many a hard battle with the Utes," replied Trujillo.

(Continued in March issue)

"To inform the minds of the people and to follow their will is the chief duty of those placed at their head."—Thomas Jefferson.

"Remember what Simonides said—that he never repented that he had held his tongue, but often that he had spoken."—Plutarch.

Native Sons of the Golden West

OROVILLE — THE CORNERSTONE OF the Pioneer Memorial Building — a monument that will perpetuate for all time the deeds of Butte County Pioneers and a museum in which will be housed historic relics of the days of old—was laid January 10. The structure, representing a miner's cabin, is being erected by the Butte County Pioneer Memorial Association, composed of members of Argonaut No. 8 and Gold of Ophir No. 190 N.D.G.W.

Florence Boyle, Grand Trustee N.D.G.W., presided and said, "We wish to renew our pledge to the Pioneers who made possible the State of California." The assemblage, led by Alta Baldwin, sang "I Love You, California." Mayor Sam Marks, a member of Argonaut, was the main speaker. He paid a tribute to the Pioneer Mothers and Fathers, and declared, "The erection of this building is as little as we can do to show our appreciation of our Pioneer ancestors whose names will live in history and who gave to the Union the State of California, the land of our birth."

Directors of the building association are Florence D. Boyle, president; Cornelia Lott-Sank, vice-president; F. W. Boyle, secretary; Irene Lund, treasurer; W. H. Hibbard and J. Emory Sutherland. It is expected the building will be ready for dedication at an early date.

Grand Parlor Committee.

Stockton—George D. Avery, as president, heads Stockton No. 7's corps of officers for the January-July term. Grand Trustee Eldred L. Meyer officially visited the Parlor January 18, when a special program was presented.

Stockton has charge of arrangements for the Grand Parlor, which meets here in May, and an elaborate entertainment program is planned. To handle all details, President Avery has appointed the following committee: Ray Friedberger (chairman), W. P. Rothenbush, C. W. Walsh, H. M. Herrmann, Eugene Allison, R. D. Dorcey, W. A. Strong, I. F. Hoult, G. T. Dentoni, Frank Piccordo, W. I. Neeley, R. A. Mitscher, F. R. Fernando and Lawrence Buol.

Services Recognized.

Santa Ana—Officers of Santa Ana No. 265 were installed by District Deputy George McDonald, January 18, Raymond L. Marsile being retained as president. In recognition of his services in the Parlor's upbuilding, No. 265, through Grand Organist Leslie Maloche, presented an emblematic ring to Past President James B. Utt. Entertainment features were presented by the McOwen sisters, and refreshments were served. Several members of Arrowhead No. 110 (San Bernardino) were visitors.

Despite the prevailing depression, Santa Ana is making satisfactory headway and a number of applications for membership have been received.

"Montalvo!" calls to memory the late Senator James D. Phelan, outstanding native Californian long affiliated with Pacific No. 10 (San Francisco). Frequently, in his lifetime, he entertained groups of Natives at his magnificent Santa Clara County estate, Montalvo.—C. M. H.

Ice Carnival for Kiddies' Benefit.

Oakland—The annual benefit for the homeless children sponsored by the Alameda County N.S.G.W. and N.D.G.W. Joint Homeless Children Committee will this year be an ice carnival, to be held at the Oakland Ice Arena, Fourteenth and Grove Streets, February 2. In addition to attractive entertainment features, the program includes a hockey game between Los Angeles and Oakland teams.

The arrangements committee includes Frank Roemer (chairman), Edgar G. Hanson (secretary), Richard M. Hamb, William R. Knowland, John J. Allen, Adrian Hynes, John J. Allen, Jr., James J. Dignan and Ray B. Felton.

Officers Three Parlors Jointly Installed.

Sacramento—Sacramento No. 3, Sunset No. 26 and La Bandera No. 110 N.D.G.W. officers were jointly installed January 14. District Deputies Clyde L. Corcoran, Joseph Lannon and Mamie McCormick officiated, and Joseph L. Hellinge, George Lial and Miss Marion Lund became the respective presidents. Dancing and refreshments followed the ceremonies.

The arrangements committee included: Native Daughters—Grand Trustee Edna B. Briggs (general chairman), Misses Ruth E. Peterson, Hannah Mannerberg, Adrienne Thomas, Helen Filbert, Clara Maurer and Ruth Bachman, Mms. Genevieve Didion and Ethel Miller. Native Sons—George W. Lial, Lawrence Marvin, Theodore Jacka, John Major, Joseph L. Hellinge, Joseph Fitzhenry, Irving Real, J. J. Monteverde, Irving Gibson and Frank R. Didion.

February 11, Sacramento No. 3 will initiate another large class of candidates.

Ritual Team Complimented.

Salinas—Following a turkey dinner, supervised by George McDougall, officers of Santa Lucia No. 97 were installed January 4 by District Deputy John Thompson, E. L. Adcock being retained as president. Plans for the Parlor's annual picnic and other events were discussed. In the course of an address District Deputy Thompson highly complimented No. 97's ritual team which, he said, is one of the best in the state. Cards closed an enjoyable occasion.

Installation Largely Attended.

San Rafael—Officers of Mount Tamalpais No. 64 and Marinita No. 198 N.D.G.W. were jointly installed January 9, Arthur W. Todt and Mrs. Gussie Bannister becoming the respective presidents. The ceremonies were conducted by District Deputies B. J. Brusatori and Mae Shea, who were highly commended by Grand President Evelyn I. Carlson of the Native Daughters for the faultless manner in which they performed their duties.

On behalf of Marinita, gifts were presented Mrs. Carlson, Grand Trustee Ethel Begley, District Deputy Shea, Grand Outside Sentinel Orinda Giannini, Past Grand President Emma G. Foley, President Bannister and Natalie Label, retiring president. For Mount Tamalpais, District Deputy Brusatori presented an emblematic charm to Senior Past President Anthony Faustine.

A delicious repast was served following the ceremonies, and a program contributed by Miss E. Hutto, Eugenie Watson and Helen Morris was followed by dancing. The halls were beautifully decorated for the event, which attracted 268 members of both Orders. Charles Soldavini headed Mount Tamalpais' arrangements committee, and Mrs. Anne Andrade that of Marinita.

Membership Standing Largest Parlors.

San Francisco—Grand Secretary John T. Regan reports the standing of the Subordinate Parlors having a membership of over 400 January 1, 1932, as follows, together with their membership figures January 20, 1932:

Parlor	Jan. 1	Jan. 20	Gain	Loss
Ramona No. 109	1088	1091	3	..
South San Francisco No. 157	822	822	..	..
Castro No. 232	700	700	..	..
Stanford No. 76	614	614	..	..
Arrowhead No. 110	609	611	2	..
Twin Peaks No. 214	585	583	..	2
Stockton No. 7	560	560	..	..
Piedmont No. 120	523	522	..	1
Rincon No. 72	445	445	..	..

To Celebrate Birthday.

Oakland—At public ceremonies January 12, the officers of Claremont No. 240 and Argonaut No. 166 N.D.G.W. were jointly installed by District Deputies Allen G. Norris and Dora Brayton, Fred Buelna and Miss Genevieve Sheehan becoming the respective presidents. Dr. Wm. C. Frietas and Lillian Caton headed the arrangements committee, which presented a very interesting program. Harmon D. Skillin was the principal speaker.

February 9, Claremont will celebrate its twenty-fourth birthday with a class initiation and banquet. It is hoped that arrangements can be made to have Grand Trustee Joseph J. McShane pay his official visit at that time.

Outlook Bright.

San Bernardino—With Lynn Reed as president, officers of Arrowhead No. 110 were installed January 27 by District Deputy Walter E. Hiskey. Refreshments were served. The Parlor closed 1931 with a membership of 609 and assets of $24,064. "New officers full of 'pep' and outlook for 1932 bright," says Recording Secretary Bob Brazelton.

Valentine Dance.

Sonoma—Officers of Sonoma No. 111 were installed January 18 by District Deputy George Peterson, Fred Bulotti becoming president. February 13 the Parlor will have a valentine dance for the benefit of its social fund. Charles E. Bacigalupi, Bud Batto, Tony Barachi, Vic Erlebach and Dave Eraldi are in charge of arrangements.

Anniversary Celebrated.

Santa Clara—Santa Clara No. 100 celebrated its twenty-ninth institution anniversary January 6. A banquet was served, and addresses were made by Past Grand President Thomas Monahan, Grand Treasurer John A. Corotto and District Deputy Phil Blanchard. The arrangements committee included A. Puccinelli, Robert Castro, Thomas Maloney Jr., Frank Sylvia, Fred Dreischmeyer and William Soto.

Oldtimers Take Charge.

Saint Helena—Saint Helena No. 53 had its annual oldtimers night January 11, with Walter Metzner, as president, Dr. Leslie A. Stern, Paul R. Alexander, Martin Anderson, Julius Goodman, J. P. Steckter, William M. Wheeler, George Herdle, E. L. Bonhote, C. Mills, Frank Hoffman, Charles E. Palmer, C. F. Steury, William R. Sheehan and Joseph Vaseoni Sr. in the chairs.

Three charter members—C. Mills, W. R. Sheehan and F. Hoffman—and twenty-one past presidents were among the crowd. Old times were reviewed by the many speakers. Previous to the meeting a turkey dinner, arranged for by Edgar W. Johnson, Lucas Haus and Gilman Clark, was served.

Joint Installation.

Downieville—Officers of Downieville No. 92 and Naomi No. 36 N.D.G.W. were jointly installed January 13, the ceremonies being conducted by J. M. McMahon and Mrs. Neva McMahon. A social time followed and supper was served at midnight.

Three Initiated.

Calistoga—Calistoga No. 86 initiated three candidates January 4, the ritual being exemplified by a team headed by Recording Secretary Louis Carlenzoli as president. A committee was appointed to investigate the proposal to procure a trophy to be contested for by ritual teams of the Napa Valley. Rev. T. J. McKeon, retiring president, in an address summing up the Parlor's accomplishments laid special emphasis on the unity at all times evident among the membership.

Supervisor Heads Parlor.

Oakland—Officers of Piedmont No. 120 were installed jointly with those of Piedmont No. 87 N.D.G.W. January 14, Alameda County Supervisor Walter Melvin Davis becoming president. District Deputy Allen Norris officiated, and Dr. Frederick A. Raulino was chairman of the evening. An entertainment program was followed by dancing.

Benefit Show.

Placerville—Through the co-operation of the Empire theater management, Placerville No. 9 has secured the playhouse for a homeless children benefit show in February.

Past Grand Celebrates Birthday.

Napa — Past Grand President Frank L. Coombs celebrated December 27 his seventy-eighth birthday anniversary at a dinner attended by his children and grandchildren. He is a native of Napa County, and has had a distinguished career in public life.

Tamale Supper.

Ukiah—District Deputy Fred Figone installed the officers of Ukiah No. 71 January 18, Henry Bucknell becoming president. A tamale supper followed the ceremonies.

Past Presidents' Installation.

Oakland—At the joint installation of the officers of East Bay Counties Assembly No. 3 N.S.G.W. Past Presidents and Past Presidents Assembly No. 2 N.D.G.W., F. H. Robson and Mrs. Freida Reichold became, respectively, the governor and the president. Arthur J. Cleu was chairman of the evening, and a group of dancing juveniles presented an hour of pleasing entertainment. Refreshments were served.

Death's Toll.

Bieber (Lassen County)—Henry N. Carlisle, affiliated with Big Valley No. 211, died recently survived by a wife and a daughter.

Hollister (San Benito County) — William Walter Black, charter member and past president of Fremont No. 44, died December 30 survived by a wife, Mrs. Clara L. Black (Copa de Oro No. 105 N.D.G.W.), and a sister-in-law, Past Grand President Bertha A. Briggs. The past quarter-century he attended all the Grand Parlor sessions. He was born at Nevada City, February 15, 1867.

Oroville (Butte County)—George P. Sharkey, charter member Argonaut No. 8, died January 11 survived by a wife and two children. He was a native of Chico, aged 70.

CAMP GROUNDS POPULAR.

The 1,252 designated camp grounds in the eighteen national forests of the California region were used by 1,588,328 campers and picnickers during the 1931 vacation season. The maximum use in any one day was by 68,746 people.

These figures do not include guests at fifteen municipal and county camps maintained by eight cities and two counties, seventy-five camps belonging to clubs and fraternal organizations, and private camps in the California national forests.

Heavy Drop—California's 1931 soil crops brought the producers $317,374,000, a drop, compared with the 1930 revenue, of $82,889,000.

Millions for Highways—During 1931 California spent $42,554,000 for permanent highway improvements.

Official Directory of Parlors of the N. S. G. W.

ALAMEDA COUNTY.

Alameda No. 47, Alameda City—Gus Nelson, Pres.; Robt. H. Cavanaugh, Sec., 1806 Pacific Ave.; Wednesdays, Native Sons Hall, 1406 Park St.

Oakland No. 50, Oakland—A. W. Ainger, Pres.; F. M. Norris, Sec., 4280 Terrace St.; Fridays, Native Sons Hall, 11th and Clay Sts.

Las Positas No. 96, Livermore—R. J. Ruetz, Pres.; John J. Kelly, Sec., P. O. box 341; Thursdays, Foresters Hall.

Eden No. 113, Hayward—Henry L'Ecuyer, Pres.; Stanton R. Soares, Sec., P. O. box 176; 1st and 3rd Wednesdays, Bank Hayward Hall.

Piedmont No. 120, Oakland—Walter M. Davis, Pres.; Charles Morando, Sec., 906 Vermont St.; Thursdays, Native Sons Hall, 11th and Clay Sts.

Wisteria No. 127, Alvarado—Henry May, Pres.; J. M. Scribner, Sec., Livermore; 1st Thursday, I.O.O.F. Hall.

Halcyon No. 146, Alameda City—Charles J. Von-Tagen, Pres.; J. C. Bates, Sec., 2139 Buena Vista Ave.; 1st and 3rd Tuesdays, I.O.O.F. Hall, 2329 Santa Clara Ave.

Brooklyn No. 151, Oakland—Frank B. Perry, Pres.; E. W. Cooney, Sec., 3907 14th Ave.; Wednesdays, Masonic Temple, 8th Ave. and E. 14th St.

Washington No. 169, Centerville—M. B. Silva, Pres.; Allen G. Norris, Sec., P. O. box 31; 2nd and 4th Tuesdays, Hansen Hall.

Athens No. 195, Oakland—Henry G. Kroeckel, Pres.; Harold B. Farley, Sec., 4623 Benevides Ave.; Tuesdays, Native Sons Hall, 11th and Clay Sts.

Berkeley No. 210, Berkeley—S. Levy, Pres.; R. J. Garrett, Sec., 1708 Virginia St.; Tuesdays, Native Sons Hall, 2108 Shattuck Ave.

Estudillo No. 223, San Leandro—Frank V. Pacheco, Pres.; Albert G. Pacheco, Sec., 1736 E. 14th St.; 1st and 3rd Tuesdays, Masonic Temple.

Claremont No. 240, Oakland—Fred Buelna, Pres.; E. N. Thienger, Sec., 839 Hearst Ave., Berkeley; Tuesdays, Veterans Memorial Bldg., 43rd & Salem Sts., Emeryville.

Pleasanton No. 244, Pleasanton—Peter C. Madsen, Pres.; Ernest W. Schween, Sec.; 2nd and 4th Thursdays, I.O.O.F. Hall.

Niles No. 250, Niles—M. L. Fournier, Pres.; C. E. Martenstein, Sec.; 2nd Thursday, I.O.O.F. Hall.

Fruitvale, No. 252, Oakland—Chester B. Abernethy, Pres.; Ray B. Felton, Sec., 1575 Alice St.; Fridays, W.O.W. Hall, 3256 E. 14th St.

AMADOR COUNTY.

Amador No. 17, Sutter Creek—Frank Marre, Pres.; F. J. Payne, Sec.; 1st and 3rd Fridays, Native Sons Hall.

Excelsior No. 31, Jackson—Wm. Daugherty, Pres.; William Going, Sec.; 1st and 3rd Wednesdays, Native Sons Hall, 22 Court St.

Ione No. 33, Ione—Marvin Kidd, Pres.; Josiah H. Saunders, Sec.; 1st and 3rd Wednedays, Native Sons Hall.

Plymouth No. 48, Plymouth—L. E. Houston, Pres.; Thos. D. Davis, Sec.; 1st and 3rd Saturdays, I.O.O.F. Hall.

BUTTE COUNTY.

Argonaut No. 8, Oroville—Fred E. Tegrunde, Pres.; Cyril R. Macdonald, Sec., P. O. box 502; 1st and 3rd Wednesdays, Veterans Memorial Hall.

Chico No. 21, Chico—Marcus Choisser, Pres.; Sam Lindsay Adams, Sec., Sacramento Blvd.; 2nd and 4th Thursdays, Elks Hall.

CALAVERAS COUNTY.

Chispa No. 139, Murphys—John Voitich, Pres.; Antone Malaspina, Sec.; Wednesdays, Native Sons Hall.

COLUSA COUNTY.

Colusa No. 69, Colusa City—Burton L. Smart, Pres.; Phil J. Humburg, Sec., 223 Parkhill St.; Tuesdays, Eagles Hall.

CONTRA COSTA COUNTY.

General Winn No. 32, Antioch—Edmont T. Uren, Pres.; Joel H. Ford, Sec., P. O. box 311; 2nd and 4th Wednesdays, Union Hall.

Mount Diablo No. 101, Martinez—R. P. Anderson, Pres.; G. T. Barkley, Sec.; 1st and 3rd Mondays, I.O.O.F. Hall.

Byron No. 170, Byron—William E. Bunn, Pres.; H. G. Krumland, Sec.; 1st and 3rd Tuesdays, I.O.O.F. Hall.

Carquinez No. 205, Crockett—Thos. Cox, Pres.; Thomas I. Cahalan, Sec.; 1st and 3rd Wednesdays, I.O.O.F. Hall.

Richmond No. 217, Richmond—M. W. Amaral, Pres.; H. D. Mason, Sec.; 11 6th St.; Wednesdays, Redmen Hall, 11th and Neven Ave.

Concord No. 245, Concord—P. M. Soto, Pres.; D. E. Pramberg, Sec., P. O. box 235; 1st Tuesday, I.O.O.F. Hall.

Diamond No. 246, Pittsburg—Victor Ericsson, Pres.; Francis A. Irving, Sec., 248 E. 5th St.; 1st and 3rd Wednesdays, Veterans Memorial Bldg.

GRAND OFFICERS.

John T. Newell........Junior Past Grand President
2666 Benedict, Los Angeles

Dr. Frank I. Gonzalez.............Grand President
Flood Bldg., San Francisco

Seth Millington.............Grand First Vice-pres.
Gridley

Justice Emmet Seawell....Grand Second Vice-pres.
State Bldg., San Francisco

Chas. A. Koenig...........Grand Third Vice-pres.
531 35th Ave., San Francisco

John T. Regan....................Grand Secretary
N.S.G.W. Bldg., 414 Mason St., San Francisco

John A. Corotto....................Grand Treasurer
560 No. 5th St., San Jose

Horace J. Leavitt....................Grand Marshal
Weaverville

W. B. O'Brien................Grand Inside Sentinel
2324 Santa Clara St., Alameda

Gam Hurst ....Grand Outside Sentinel
1400 Financial Center Bldg., Oakland

Leslie Maloche....................Grand Organist
467½ 3rd St., San Bernardino

George H. Barron.................Historiographer
333 12th Ave., San Francisco

GRAND TRUSTEES.

George F. McNoble.......California Bldg., Stockton
Samuel M. Shortridge Jr..................Menlo Park
Jesse H. Miller..712 DeYoung Bldg., San Francisco
Joseph J. McShane..419 Flood Bldg., San Francisco
Frank M. Lane............333 Blackstone, Fresno
John M. Burnett...........................San Jose
Eldred L. Meyer....922 San Vincente, Santa Monica

EL DORADO COUNTY.

Placerville No. 9, Placerville—George M. Smith, Pres.; Duncan Bathurst, Sec., 12 Gilmore St.; 2nd and 4th Tuesdays, Masonic Hall.

Georgetown No. 91, Georgetown—W. H. Breedlove, Pres.; C. F. Irish, Sec.; 2nd and 4th Wednesdays, I.O.O.F. Hall.

FRESNO COUNTY.

Fresno No. 25, Fresno City—A. G. Miller, Pres.; John W. Cappleman, Sec., 1389 Wilson; 2nd and 4th Fridays, W.O.W. Hall, 1354 Van Ness Ave.

Selma No. 107, Selma—Chester E. Shepard, Pres.; E. C. Laughlin, Sec.; 1st Wednesday, American Legion Hall.

HUMBOLDT COUNTY.

Humboldt No. 14, Eureka—Edward J. Quinn, Pres.; Loren M. Nelson, Sec., P. O. Box 195; 2nd and 4th Mondays, Native Sons Hall.

Arcata No. 20, Arcata—George Hale, Pres.; William Peters, Sec., P. O. box 1117; Thursdays, Native Sons Hall.

Ferndale No. 93, Ferndale—O. R. Frame, Pres; C. H. Rasmussen, Sec., R.F.D. 47-A; 1st and 3rd Mondays, K.P. Hall.

KERN COUNTY.

Bakersfield No. 42, Bakersfield—G. E. Taylor, Pres.; Leroy Vandervoort, Sec., Manly Apts.; Wednesdays, Justice Court, City Hall.

LAKE COUNTY.

Lower Lake No. 159, Lower Lake—Harold S. Anderson, Pres.; Albert Kugelman, Sec.; Thursdays, I.O.O.F. Hall.

LASSEN COUNTY.

Honey Lake No. 198, Standish—James C. Meeske, Pres.; N. V. Wemple, Sec., Litchfield; 1st and 3rd Wednesdays, Wrede Hall.

Big Valley No. 211, Bieber—George Bunselmeier, Pres.; A. W. McKenzie, Sec.; 1st and 3rd Wednesdays, I.O.O.F. Hall.

LOS ANGELES COUNTY.

Los Angeles No. 45, Los Angeles City—Lee E. Erwin, Pres.; Richard W. Fryer, Sec., 1629 Champlain Ter.; Thursdays, Merchant Plumbers Hall, 1832 So. Hope.

Ramona No. 109, Los Angeles City—Chandos E. Bush, Pres.; John V. Scott, Sec., Patriotic Hall, 1816 So. Figueroa; Fridays, Patriotic Hall, 1816 So. Figueroa.

Hollywood No. 196, Los Angeles City—Leo Aggeler, Pres.; E. J. Reilly, Sec., 907 W. 2nd St.; Mondays, Hollywood Conservatory Music, 5402 Hollywood Blvd.

Long Beach No. 239, Long Beach—Francis H. Gentry, Pres.; W. W. Brady, Sec., 801 Jergins Trust Bldg.; 2nd and 4th Thursdays, Moose Hall, Elm and Anaheim.

Sepulveda No. 263, San Pedro—Lawrence Powers, Pres.; Frank I. Markey, Sec., 101 W. 7th St.; 2nd and 4th Fridays, Odd Fellows Temple, 10th and Gaffey Sts.

Glendale No. 264, Glendale—Philip D. Molen, Pres.; Abel B. Molen, Sec., 508 So. Belmont St.; 1st and 3rd Tuesdays, Masonic Temple, 234 So. Brand Blvd.

Santa Monica Bay No. 267, Ocean Park—Claude J. Wiseman, Pres.; John J. Smith, Sec., 830 Rialto Ave., Venice; 2nd and 4th Mondays, New Eagle Hall, 2823½ Main St.

Cahuenga No. 268, Reseda—Harold C. Trexler, Pres.; Walter A. Knapp, Sec., 7711 Owensmouth Ave., Canoga Park; first Friday, Alton Hall.

MADERA COUNTY.

Madera No. 130, Madera City—Cornelius Noble, Pres.; T. P. Cosgrave, Sec.; 1st and 3rd Thursdays, First National Bank Bldg.

MARIN COUNTY.

Mount Tamalpais No. 64, San Rafael—Arthur Todt, Pres.; Manual A. Andrade, Sec., 532 Mission Ave.; 1st and 3rd Mondays, Portuguese American Hall.

Sea Point No. 158, Sausalito—Allyn T. Young, Pres.; Manuel Santos, Sec., 6 Glen Drive; 1st and 3rd Wednesdays, Perry Bldg.

Nicasio No. 183, Nicasio—M. T. Farley, Pres.; R. J. Rogers, Sec.; 2nd and 4th Wednesdays, U.A.O.D. Hall.

MENDOCINO COUNTY.

Ukiah No. 71, Ukiah—Albert T. Bechtol, Pres.; Ben Hofman, Sec., P. O. box 473; 1st and 3rd Mondays, I.O.O.F. Hall.

Broderick No. 117, Point Arena—Sam Reinking, Pres.; H. C. Hunter, Sec.; 1st and 3rd Thursdays, Forester Hall.

Alder Glen No. 200, Fort Bragg—Clarence Simpson, Pres.; C. R. Weller, Sec.; 2nd and 4th Fridays, I.O.O.F. Hall.

MERCED COUNTY.

Yosemite No. 24, Merced City—Anthony A. Rodrigues, Pres.; True W. Fowler, Sec., P. O. box 781; 2nd and 4th Mondays, I.O.O.F. Hall.

MONTEREY COUNTY.

Monterey No. 75, Monterey City—John Thomsen, Pres.; T. W. Krieger, Sec., 999 Franklin St.; 1st and 3rd Fridays, Knights Pythias Hall, Main St.

Santa Lucia No. 97, Salinas—E. L. Adcock, Pres.; R. W. Adcock, Sec., Route 2, box 141; Mondays, Native Sons Hall, 32 W. Alisal St.

Gabilan No. 132, Castroville—B. A. McCoy, Pres.; R. H. Martin, Sec., P. O. box 81; 1st and 3rd Thursdays, Native Sons Hall.

NAPA COUNTY.

Saint Helena No. 53, Saint Helena—E. W. Johnson, Pres.; Edw. L. Bonhote, Sec., P. O. box 267; Mondays, Native Sons Hall.

Napa No. 62, Napa City—A. G. Boggs, Pres.; H. J. Hoernle, Sec., 1226 Oak St.; Mondays, Native Sons Hall.

Calistoga No. 86, Calistoga—Frank Mariani, Pres.; Louis Carlenzoli, Sec.; 1st and 3rd Mondays, I.O.O.F. Hall.

NEVADA COUNTY.

Hydraulic No. 56, Nevada City—Spencer G. White, Pres.; Dr. C. W. Chapman, Sec.; Tuesdays, Pythian Castle.

Quartz No. 58, Grass Valley—Allen Joyner, Pres.; H. Ray George, Sec., 151 Conaway Ave.; Mondays, Auditorium Hall.

Donner No. 162, Truckee—J. F. Lichtenberger, Pres.; H. C. Lichtenberger, Sec.; 2nd and 4th Tuesdays, Native Sons Hall.

ORANGE COUNTY.

Santa Ana No. 265, Santa Ana—R. L. Marsile, Pres.; E. F. Marks, Sec., 1124 No. Bristol St.; 1st and 3rd Mondays, K.C. Hall, 4th and French Sts.

PLACER COUNTY.

Auburn No. 59, Auburn—Cosme Vicencio, Pres.; J. G. Walsh, Sec.; 1st and 3rd Fridays, Foresters Hall.

Silver Star No. 63, Lincoln—Ralph Sandstad, Pres.; Barney G. Barry, Sec., P. O. box 72; 3rd Wednesday, I.O.O.F. Hall.

Rocklin No. 233, Roseville—Thomas Elliott, Pres.; M. E. Reed, Sec., 253 W. Duranta; 2nd and 4th Wednesdays, Eagles Hall.

PLUMAS COUNTY.

Quincy No. 131, Quincy—J. D. McLaughlin, Pres.; E. C. Kelsey, Sec.; 2nd Thursday, I.O.O.F. Hall.

Golden Anchor No. 182, La Porte—R. J. McGrath, Pres.; LeRoy J. Post, Sec.; 2nd and 4th Sunday mornings, Native Sons Hall.

Plumas No. 228, Taylorsville—E. E. Sikes, Pres.; George E. Boyden, Sec.; 1st and 3rd Mondays, Native Sons Hall.

SACRAMENTO COUNTY.

Sacramento No. 3, Sacramento City—Joseph Hellinge Jr., Pres.; J. F. Didion, Sec., 1131 "O" St.; Thursdays, Native Sons Bldg., 11th and "J" Sts.

Sunset No. 26, Sacramento City—George W. Lial, Pres.; Edward E. Reese, Sec., County Treasurer Office; Mondays, Native Sons Bldg., 11th and "J" Sts.

Elk Grove No. 41, Elk Grove—Fred Sehlmeyer, Pres.; Walter Martin, Sec.; 2nd and 4th Fridays, Masonic Hall.

Granite No. 83, Folsom—Joe Relvas, Pres.; Frank Showers, Sec.; 2nd and 4th Tuesdays, K.P. Hall.

Courtland No. 106, Courtland—Albert Pyhnan, Pres.; Jos. Green, Sec.; 1st Saturday and 3rd Monday, Native Sons Hall.

Sutter Fort No. 241, Sacramento City—August Lehman, Pres.; C. L. Katzenstein, Sec., P. O. box 914; 2nd and 4th Wednesdays, Native Sons Bldg., 11th and "J" Sts.

Galt No. 243, Galt—John Granadas, Pres.; F. W. Harms, Sec.; 1st and 3rd Mondays, I.O.O.F. Hall.

SAN BENITO COUNTY.

Fremont No. 44, Hollister—Chas. B. Arbeleche, Pres.; J. E. Prendergast Jr., Sec., 1064 Monterey St.; 1st and 3rd Thursdays, Grangers Union Hall.

SAN BERNARDINO COUNTY.

Arrowhead No. 110, San Bernardino City—Lynn A. Reed, Pres.; R. W. Brazelton, Sec., 462 6th St.; Wednesdays, Eagles Hall, 469 4th St.

SAN DIEGO COUNTY.

San Diego No. 108, San Diego City—Gregory A. McHorney, Pres.; A. V. Mayrhofer, Sec., 1572 2nd St.; Wednesdays, K.C. Hall, 4th and Elm Sts.

SAN FRANCISCO CITY AND COUNTY.

California No. 1, San Francisco—Sal Juliano, Pres.; Ellis A. Blackman, Sec., 126 Front St.; Thursdays, Native Sons Bldg., 414 Mason St.

Pacific No. 10, San Francisco—John C. Daly, Pres.; J. Henry Bastein, Sec., 1880 Howard St.; Tuesdays, Native Sons Bldg., 414 Mason St.

Golden Gate No. 29, San Francisco—Thomas I. Schlink, Pres.; Adolph Eberhart, Sec., 183 Carl St.; Mondays, Native Sons Bldg., 414 Mason St.

Mission No. 38, San Francisco—Joseph C. Augustine Jr., Pres.; Thos. J. Stewart, Sec., 1919 Howard St.; Wednesdays, Redmen Hall, 3053 16th St.

San Francisco No. 49, San Francisco—Louis L. Ghiotti, Pres.; David Capurro, Sec., 976 Union St.; Thursdays, Native Sons Bldg., 414 Mason St.

El Dorado No. 52, San Francisco—Eugene Herzog, Pres.; Alfred Vlautin, Sec., 1537 Franklin St.; Thursdays, Native Sons Bldg., 414 Mason St.

Rincon No. 72, San Francisco—Michael J. Joyce, Pres.; John A. Gilmour, Sec., 2069 Golden Gate Ave.; Wednesdays, Native Sons Bldg., 414 Mason St.

Stanford No. 76, San Francisco—Albert W. Groskopf, Pres.; Charles T. O'Kane, Sec., 1111 Pine St.; Tuesdays, Native Sons Bldg., 414 Mason St.

Bay City No. 104, San Francisco—Morris Garren, Pres.; Max E. Licht, Sec., 1831 Fulton St.; 2nd and 4th Wednesdays, Native Sons Bldg., 414 Mason St.

Niantic No. 105, San Francisco—A. Furner, Pres.; J. M. Darcy, Sec., 10 Hoffman Ave.; Wednesdays, Native Sons Bldg., 414 Mason St.

National No. 118, San Francisco—Wayne Burke, Pres.; Martin M. Ratigan, Sec., 1325 Page St., Apt. 6.; Thursdays, 1160 Eddy St.

ATTENTION, SECRETARIES!

THIS DIRECTORY IS PUBLISHED BY AUTHORITY OF THE GRAND PARLOR N.S.G.W., AND ALL NOTICES OF CHANGES MUST BE RECEIVED BY THE GRAND SECRETARY (NOT THE MAGAZINE) ON OR BEFORE THE 20TH OF EACH MONTH TO INSURE CORRECTION IN NEXT ISSUE OF DIRECTORY.

Hesperian No. 137, San Francisco—H. G. Ritter, Pres.; Albert Carlson, Sec., 379 Justin Dr.; Thursdays, Native Sons Bldg., 414 Mason St.
Alcalde No. 154, San Francisco—Conrad Kuhl, Pres.; Harry S. Burke, Sec., 25 Ord St.; 2nd and 4th Wednesdays, Native Sons Bldg., 414 Mason St.
South San Francisco No. 157, San Francisco—Raymond Conroy, Pres.; John T. Regan, Sec., 1489 Newcomb Ave.; Wednesdays, Masonic Bldg., 4705 3rd St.
Sequoia No. 160, San Francisco—Chester Moreno, Pres.; Walter W. Garrett, Sec., 2500 Van Ness Ave.; Mondays, Swedish-American Bldg., 2174 Market St.
Precita No. 187, San Francisco—Elmer F. Sprague, Pres.; Edward Tietjen, Sec., 1367 15th Ave.; Thursdays, Mission Masonic Hall, 2668 Mission St.
Olympus No. 189, San Francisco—Charles Erickson, Pres.; Harvey J. Carty, Sec., 1651 Market St., Apt. 505; 2nd and 4th Tuesdays, Independent Redmen Hall, 3053 16th St.
Presidio No. 194, San Francisco—Geo. R. Schmidt, Pres.; George A. Ducker, Sec., 442 21st Ave.; Mondays, Native Sons Bldg., 414 Mason St.
Marshall No. 202, San Francisco—Arthur Belli, Pres.; Frank Bacigalupi, Sec., 725 Douglas St.; 1st and 3rd Wednesdays, Native Sons Bldg., 414 Mason St.
Dolores No. 208, San Francisco—Daniel Corrigan, Pres.; Eugene O'Donnell, Sec., Mills Bldg.; Tuesdays, Mission Masonic Bldg., 2668 Mission St.
Twin Peaks No. 214, San Francisco—Fred Sooman, Pres.; Thos. Pendergast, Sec., 278 Douglas St.; Wednesdays, Willopi Hall, 4061 24th St.
El Capitan No. 222, San Francisco—Frank Rizzo, Pres.; James Hanna, Sec., 2450 27th Ave.; 1st and 3rd Thursdays, King Soloman Hall, 1739 Fillmore St.
Guadalupe No. 231, San Francisco—George Miles, Pres.; Alvin A. Johnson, Sec., 142 Rousseau St.; Tuesdays, Guadalupe Hall, 4551 Mission St.
Castro No. 232, San Francisco—David A. Simon, Pres.; James H. Hayes, Sec., 4014 18th St.; Tuesdays, Native Sons Bldg., 414 Mason St.
Balboa No. 234, San Francisco—J. LeMer, Pres.; E. W. Boyd, Sec., 45 Carl St.; Thursdays, Maccabee Hall, 5th Ave. and Clement St.
James Lick No. 242, San Francisco—M. G. Mullen, Pres.; Wm. Band, Sec., 2587 22nd Ave.; 1st and 3rd Tuesdays, Redmen Hall, 3053 16th St.
Bret Harte No. 260, San Francisco—J. F. Craig, Pres.; C. J. Eggers, Sec., 194 Prague St.; Tuesdays, West of Twin Peaks Hall, 233 Legion Court.
Utopia No. 270, San Francisco—Joseph Riordan, Pres.; Herbert H. Schneider, Sec., 2455 16th Ave.; Tuesdays, American Hall, 20th and Capp Sts.

SAN JOAQUIN COUNTY.

Stockton No. 7, Stockton—George D. Avery, Pres.; R. D. Dorcey, Sec., P. O. box 388; Mondays, Native Sons Hall.
Lodi No. 18, Lodi—Jerome Solomon, Pres.; Dr. Clyde Bresnan, Sec.; 2nd and 4th Wednesdays, Eagles Hall.
Tracy No. 186, Tracy—R. J. Marraccini, Pres.; R. J. Marraccini, Sec., R.F.D. No. 1, box 217; Thursdays, I.O.O.F. Hall.
Manteca No. 271, Manteca—Louis Ryan, Pres.; Leonard Faria, Sec., R.F.D. No. 1, Lathrop; 1st and 3rd Wednesdays, I.O.O.F. Hall.

SAN LUIS OBISPO COUNTY.

San Miguel No. 150, San Miguel—H. Twisselman, Pres.; George Sonnenberg Jr., Sec.; 1st and 3rd Wednesdays, Fraternal Hall.
Cambria No. 152, Cambria—Roy Cardoza, Pres.; A. S. Gay, Sec.; Wednesdays, Rigdon Hall.

SAN MATEO COUNTY.

Redwood No. 66, Redwood City—Joseph Lodi, Pres.; A. S. Liguori, Sec., P. O. box 212; Thursdays, American Foresters Hall.
Seaside No. 95, Half Moon Bay—William Deeney, Pres.; John G. Gilcrest, Sec.; 2nd and 4th Tuesdays, I.O.O.F. Hall.
Menlo No. 185, Menlo Park—W. H. Wreden, Pres.; F. W. Johnson, Sec., P. O. box 601; Thursdays, Duff & Doyle Hall.
Pebble Beach No. 230, Pescadero—Bernard Cabral, Pres.; E. A. Shaw, Sec.; 2nd and 4th Wednesdays, I.O.O.F. Hall.
El Carmelo No. 256, Daly City—Leonard J. Mohr, Pres.; Andrew P. Murphy, Sec., 931 Hanover St.; 2nd and 4th Wednesdays, Eagles Hall.
Industrial City No. 269, South San Francisco—John C. Hamilton, Pres.; Geo. A. Roll, Sec., P. O. box 237; 2nd and 4th Mondays, Metropolitan Hall.

SANTA BARBARA COUNTY.

Santa Barbara No. 116, Santa Barbara City—C. W. McCormick, Pres.; H. C. Sweetser, Sec., Court House; 1st and 3rd Wednesdays, I.O.O.F. Hall.

SANTA CLARA COUNTY.

San Jose No. 22, San Jose—Joseph Sabatte, Pres.; H. W. McComas, Sec., Suite 7, Porter Bldg.; Mondays, I.O.O.F. Hall.
Santa Clara No. 100, Santa Clara City—John J. Trinajstich, Pres.; Clarence Clevenger, Sec., P. O. box 297; 1st and 3rd Wednesdays, Redmen Hall.
Observatory No. 177, San Jose—Norton J. Mahon, Pres.; A. B. Langford, Sec., Hall Records; Tuesdays, Knights Columbus Hall, 40 No. First St.
Mountain View No. 215, Mountain View—Gilbert F. McCorkle, Pres.; C. A. Antonioli, Sec., 948 California St.; 2nd and 4th Fridays, Mockbee Hall.
Palo Alto No. 216, Palo Alto—John C. Bernal, Pres.; Albert A. Quinn, Sec., 643 High St.; Mondays, Native Sons Bldg., Hamilton Ave. and Emerson St.

SANTA CRUZ COUNTY.

Watsonville No. 65, Watsonville—A. W. Batchelder, Pres.; E. R. Tindall, Sec., 408 East Lake Ave.; 2nd and 4th Tuesdays, I.O.O.F. Hall.
Santa Cruz No. 90, Santa Cruz City—W. H. Mori, Pres.; T. V. Mathews, Sec., 105 Pacheco Ave.; Tuesdays, Native Sons Hall, 117 Pacific Ave.

SHASTA COUNTY.

McCloud No. 149, Redding—Errol Yank, Pres.; Hugh A. Shuffleton, Sec.; 1st and 3rd Thursdays, Moose Hall.

SIERRA COUNTY.

Downieville No. 92, Downieville—J. M. McMahon, Pres.; H. S. Tibbey, Sec.; 2nd and 4th Mondays, I.O.O.F. Hall.
Golden Nugget No. 94, Sierra City—Leonard Thompson Jr., Pres; Arthur R. Pride, Sec.; last Saturday, Masonic Hall.

SISKIYOU COUNTY.

Etna No. 192, Etna—Fred M. Wolford, Pres.; Harvey A. Green, Sec.; 1st and 3rd Wednesdays, I.O.O.F. Hall.
Liberty No. 193, Sawyers Bar—Orrin R. Bigelow, Pres.; John M. Barry, Sec.; 1st and 3rd Saturdays, I.O.O.F. Hall.

N.S.G.W. OFFICIAL DEATH LIST.

Containing the name, the date and the place of birth, the date of death, and the Subordinate Parlor affiliation of deceased members reported to Grand Secretary John T. Regan from December 19, 1931, to January 22, 1932:

Blanchard, Montie Frank; San Francisco, September 15, 1856; November 8, 1931; California No. 1.
Irwin, Fred; Diamond Springs, May 12, 1859; December 16, 1931; Placerville No. 9.
Galleher, Richard F.; Coloma, May 11, 1876; December 17, 1931; Placerville No. 9.
Barrute, Ernest G.; Shingle Springs, January 6, 1863; December 17, 1931; Placerville No. 9.
Faure, Henry E.; Sonoma, February 13, 1862; November 22, 1931; Pacific No. 10.
Lyons, Lloyd M.; San Diego, May 14, 1887; December 23, 1931; Pacific No. 10.

SOLANO COUNTY.

Solano No. 39, Suisun—Karl Koch, Pres.; J. W. Kinlock, Sec.; 1st and 3rd Tuesdays, I.O.O.F. Hall.
Vallejo No. 77, Vallejo—Joseph Clavo, Pres.; Werner B. Hallin, Sec., 912 Carolina; 2nd and 4th Tuesdays, San Pablo Hall.

SONOMA COUNTY.

Petaluma No. 27, Petaluma—George Gells, Pres.; C. F. Fobes, Sec., 114 Prospect St.; 2nd and 4th Mondays, Druid Hall, Gross Bldg., 41 Main St.
Santa Rosa No. 28, Santa Rosa—John Caniff, Pres.; Leland S. Lewis, Sec., Court House; Tuesdays, Native Sons Hall.
Glen Ellen No. 102, Glen Ellen—C. C. Weise, Pres.; Frank Kirch, Sec., Route 3, Santa Rosa; 2nd Monday, N.S.G.W. Hall.
Sonoma No. 111, Sonoma City—Frederick Bulotti, Pres.; L. H. Green, Sec.; 1st and 3rd Mondays, I.O.O.F. Hall.
Sebastopol No. 143, Sebastopol—A. N. Badger, Pres.; F. G. McFarlane, Sec.; 1st and 3rd Fridays, I.O.O.F. Hall.

STANISLAUS COUNTY.

Modesto No. 11, Modesto—Robert H. Hansen, Pres.; C. C. Eastin Jr., Sec., P. O. box 898; 1st and 3rd Wednesdays, I.O.O.F. Hall.
Oakdale No. 142, Oakdale—D W. Tulloch, Pres.; E. T. Gobin, Sec.; 2nd Monday, Legion Hall.
Orestimba No. 247, Crows Landing—Lloyd W. Fink, Pres.; G. W. Fink, Sec.; 1st and 3rd Wednesdays, Community Club Home.

SUTTER COUNTY.

Sutter No. 261, Sutter City—Stanley R. McLean, Pres.; Glen R. Haynes, Sec., Yuba City; 2nd and 4th Mondays, N.D.G.W. Hall.

TRINITY COUNTY.

Mount Bally No. 87, Weaverville—M. F. Kay, Pres.; E. V. Ryan, Sec.; 1st and 3rd Mondays, Native Sons Hall.

TUOLUMNE COUNTY.

Tuolumne No. 144, Sonora—Mathew J. Marshall, Pres.; William M. Harrington, Sec., P. O. box 716; 2nd and 4th Fridays, Knights Columbus Hall.
Columbia No. 258, Columbia—Jos. Cadematori, Pres.; Charles E. Grant, Sec.; 2nd and 4th Thursdays, Native Sons Hall.

VENTURA COUNTY.

Cabrillo No. 114, Ventura City—David Bennett, Pres., 1380 Church St.

YOLO COUNTY.

Woodland No. 30, Woodland—J. L. Aronson, Pres.; E. B. Hayward, Sec.; 1st Thursday, Native Sons Hall.

YUBA COUNTY.

Marysville No. 6, Marysville—John McQuaid, Pres.; Verne Fogarty, Sec., 719 6th St.; 2nd Friday, Foresters Hall.
Rainbow No. 40, Wheatland—W. E. Jones, Pres.; W. A. Bowser, Sec., P. O. box 313; 2nd Thursday, I.O.O.F. Hall.

AFFILIATED ORGANIZATIONS.

Alameda County Extension of the Order Committee, N.S.G.W.—Dr. William C. Freitas, Chmn.; Edgar G. Hansen, Sec., 1260 Russell St., Berkeley; meets 1st and 3rd Mondays, N.S.G.W. Hall, 11th and Clay Sts., Oakland.
Interparlor Committee (Southern District), N.S.G.W. and N.D.G.W.—Burrel D. Neighbours, Chmn.; F. J. Burmester, Sec., 2434 Micheltorena St., Los Angeles; meets 2nd and 4th Fridays, Patriotic Hall, 1816 So. Figueroa St., Los Angeles.
San Francisco Extension of the Order Committee, N.S.G.W.—Harmon D. Skillin, Chmn.; Harold J. Regan, Sec., 414 Mason St., San Francisco; meets 2nd and 4th Fridays, Grizzly Bear Club, 414 Mason St., San Francisco.
San Francisco Assembly No. 1 Past Presidents Association N.S.G.W.—Meets 1st and 3rd Fridays, Native Sons Bldg., 414 Mason St., San Francisco; J. H. Sylvester, Gov., J. F. Stanley, Sec., 1175 O'Farrell St., San Francisco.
East Bay Counties Assembly No. 3 Past Presidents Association N.S.G.W.—Meets 4th Monday, Native Sons Hall, 11th and Clay Sts., Oakland; F. H. Robson, Gov.; Edgar G. Hanson, Sec., 1260 Russell St., Berkeley.
Marin County Assembly No. 5 Past Presidents Association N.S.G.W.—J. S. Rose Jr., Gov.; L. J. Peter, Sec., Peter Bldg., 4th and "C" Sts., San Rafael.
Fred H. Greely Assembly No. 6 Past Presidents Association N.S.G.W.—Meets monthly with different Parlors comprising district; R. L. P. Bigelow, Gov.; Barney Barry, Sec., P. O. box 72, Lincoln.
San Joaquin Assembly No. 7 Past Presidents Association N.S.G.W.—Meets 1st Friday, Native Sons Hall, Stockton; Clyde H. Gregg, Gov.; R. D. Dorcey, Sec., Native Sons Club, Stockton.
Sonoma County Assembly No. 9 Past Presidents Association N.S.G.W.—Meets monthly at different Parlor headquarters in county; Louis Bosch, Gov.; L. S. Lewis, Sec., Court House, Santa Rosa.
General John A. Sutter Assembly No. 10 Past Presidents Association—L. P. Ferron, Gov.; Jas. J. Longshore, Sec., 514 "J" St., Sacramento.
Grizzly Bear Club—Members all Parlors outside San Francisco at all times welcome. Clubrooms top floor Native Sons Bldg., 414 Mason St., San Francisco.
Native Sons and Native Daughters Central Committee on Homeless Children—Main office, 955 Phelan Bldg., San Francisco; Mrs. John W. Stirling, Chmn.; Miss Mary E. Brusie, Sec. Los Angeles branch office, 3924 Sunset Blvd.; Dorothy Schlingman, Sec.

(ADVERTISEMENT.)

Kay, Henry Edwin; Jackson, June 23, 1865; October 18, 1931; Excelsior No. 31.
Murphy, Joseph Patrick; Hollister, February 19, 1876; August 2, 1931; Fremont No. 44.
Black, William Walter; Nevada City, February 15, 1867; December 20, 1931; Fremont No. 44.
Ferrari, Andrew; San Francisco, July 28, 1885; August 16, 1931; San Francisco No. 49.
Segale, William; San Francisco, May 12, 1902; October 21, 1931; San Francisco No. 49.
Thornley, William H.; Sonoma, December 15, 1856; January 5, 1932; San Francisco No. 49.
Backer, Charles; San Francisco, March 21, 1865; January 11, 1932; San Francisco No. 49.
Zeigenfuss, Peter Anton; Mission San Jose, October 26, 1857; December 22, 1931; Oakland No. 50.
Colemann, George; San Francisco, May 14, 1868; December 21, 1931; El Dorado No. 52.
Clemmer, John Francis; San Rafael, March 26, 1895; July 1, 1931; Mount Tamalpais No. 64.
Smith, James J.; San Rafael, August 30, 1884; December 21, 1931; Mount Tamalpais No. 64.
Burnside, Fred Henry; Watsonville, February 9, 1876; January 6, 1932; Watsonville No. 65.
Ottenwalter, S. A.; Modoc, October 19, 1886; December 13, 1931; Colusa No. 69.
Galvin, Edward J.; El Dorado County, February 21, 1865; August 4, 1931; Stanford No. 76.
Westerfeld, Poul C.; San Francisco, August 2, 1876; November 19, 1931; Stanford No. 76.
Barry, Thomas F.; San Francisco, September 24, 1871; December 26, 1931; Stanford No. 76.
Van Weeklen, Martin; Clarksville, March 10, 1864; November 8, 1931; Granite No. 83.
Gilbert, William Franklin; Michigan Bar, August 23, 1856; December 21, 1931; Santa Cruz No. 90.
Dordero, Ralph L.; Santa Barbara, February 5, 1879; December 11, 1931; Santa Barbara No. 116.
Bach, Charles Alfred; San Francisco, October 25, 1872; December 30, 1931; National No. 118.
La Riviere, Ziph; San Andreas, August 28, 1880; August 28, 1931; Chispa No. 139.
Pillsbury, Daniel; El Dorado, December 11, 1863; September 9, 1931; Chispa No. 139.
Gisin, George Clayton; Vendalia, November 28, 1867; January 6, 1932; Cambria No. 152.
Morton, Henrie F.; San Mateo, October 28, 1856; December 31, 1931; Alcalde No. 154.
Rose, Eugene W.; Pope Valley, August 8, 1864; November 18, 1931; Lower Lake No. 159.
Manning, William Edward; San Francisco, October 5, 1906; January 2, 1932; Precita No. 187.
Ness, Jack Kruger; San Francisco, November 1, 1902; August 5, 1931; Marshall No. 202.
Johnson, Edward Lawrence; Sutter Creek, July 7, 1897; January 7, 1932; Dolores No. 208.
Leonard, Jack W.; Redwood City, August 11, 1868; December 24, 1931; Berkeley No. 210.
Mullins, William; San Francisco, October 11, 1890; January 13, 1932; Twin Peaks No. 214.
Ross, Arthur; San Francisco, January 21, 1887; September 29, 1931; Pleasanton No. 244.
McCloskey, Edward B.; Oakland, October 12, 1892; December 31, 1931; Fruitvale No. 252.
Parkhurst, Gordon C.; Los Angeles, November 9, 1893; December 27, 1931; Santa Monica Bay No. 267.

Enjoys The Grizzly.

"I enjoy every copy of The Grizzly Bear, and realize the wonderful good the magazine does for our Orders. Hoping it may live long, and with the best of wishes for a happy and prosperous 1932, very truly yours,

"MARGARET E. WESTON.

"Greenview, January 3."

Imperial Fair—The Imperial Valley Fair is to be held at Imperial, February 9-14.

Poultry Show—The Pacific Coast Poultry Show is billed for Oakland, Alameda County, February 9-17.

Official Directory of Parlors of the N. D. G. W.

ALAMEDA COUNTY.

Angelita No. 32, Livermore—Meets 2nd and 4th Fridays, Foresters Hall; Mrs. Oriena Beck, Rec. Sec., 1109 First St.

Piedmont No. 87, Oakland—Meets Thursdays, Corinthian Hall, Pacific Bldg.; Mrs. Alice E. Miner, Rec. Sec., 421 36th St.

Aloha No. 106, Oakland—Meets Tuesdays, Wigwam Hall, Pacific Bldg.; Gladys I. Farley, Rec. Sec., 4623 Benevides Ave.

Hayward No. 122, Hayward—Meets 1st and 3rd Tuesdays, Bank Hayward Hall, "B" St.; Miss Ruth Gansberger, Rec. Sec., P. O. Box 44, Mount Eden.

Berkeley No. 150, Berkeley—Meets 1st Friday, Masonic Hall; Mrs. Lella B. Baker, Rec. Sec., 915 Contra Costa Ave.

Bear Flag No. 151, Berkeley—Meets 2nd and 4th Wednesdays, Veterans Memorial Bldg., 1931 Center St.; Mrs. Maud Wagner, Rec. Sec., 317 Alcatraz Ave., Oakland.

Encinal No. 156, Alameda—Meets 2nd and 4th Thursdays, N.S.G.W. Hall; Mrs. Laura E. Fisher, Rec. Sec., 1413 Caroline St.

Brooklyn No. 157, East Oakland—Meets Wednesdays, Masonic Temple, 8th Ave. and E. 14th St.; Mrs. Ruth Cooney, Rec. Sec., 3907 14th Ave.

Argonaut No. 166, Oakland—Meets Tuesdays, Klinkner Hall, 59th and San Pablo; Mrs. Ada Spilman, Rec. Sec., 2905 Ellis St., Berkeley.

Bahia Vista No. 167, Oakland—Meets Thursdays, Wigwam Hall, Pacific Bldg.; Mrs. Minnie E. Raper, Rec. Sec., 3449 Helen St.

Fruitvale No. 177, Oakland—Meets Fridays, W.O.W. Hall; Mrs. Agnes M. Grant, Rec. Sec., 1224 30th Ave.

Laura Loma No. 182, Niles—Meets 1st and 3rd Tuesdays, I.O.O.F. Hall; Mrs. Ethel Fournier, Rec. Sec., P. O. Box 515.

El Cereso No. 207, San Leandro—Meets 2nd and 4th Tuesdays, Masonic Hall; Mrs. Mary Tuttle, Rec. Sec., P. O. Box 56.

Pleasanton No. 237, Pleasanton—Meets 1st and 3rd Tuesdays, I.O.O.F. Hall; Mrs. Myrtle Lanini, Rec. Sec.

Betsy Ross No. 238, Centerville—Meets 1st and 3rd Fridays, Anderson Hall; Miss Constance Lucio, Rec. Sec., P. O. Box 187.

AMADOR COUNTY.

Ursula No. 1, Jackson—Meets 2nd and 4th Tuesdays, N.S.G.W. Hall; Mrs. Emma Boarman-Wright, Rec. Sec., 114 Court St.

Chispa No. 40, Ione—Meets 2nd and 4th Fridays, N.S.G.W. Hall; Mrs. Isabel Ashton, Rec. Sec.

Amapola No. 80, Sutter Creek—Meets 2nd and 4th Thursdays, N.S.G.W. Bldg.; Mrs. Hazel M. Marre, Rec. Sec.

Forrest No. 86, Plymouth—Meets 2nd and 4th Tuesdays, I.O.O.F. Hall; Mrs. Marguerite Davis, Rec. Sec.

BUTTE COUNTY.

Annie K. Bidwell No. 168, Chico—Meets 2nd and 4th Thursdays, I.O.O.F. Hall; Mrs. Irene Henry, Rec. Sec., 3015 Woodland Ave.

Gold of Ophir No. 190, Oroville—Meets 1st and 3rd Wednesdays, Memorial Hall; Mrs. Ruth Brown, Rec. Sec., 1265 Leah Court.

CALAVERAS COUNTY.

Ruby No. 46, Murphys—Meets Fridays, N.S.G.W. Hall; Belle Segale, Rec. Sec.

Princess No. 84, Angels Camp—Meets 2nd Wednesday, I.O.O.F. Hall; Emma May, Rec. Sec.

San Andreas No. 113, San Andreas—Meets 1st Friday, Fraternal Hall; Miss Doris Treat, Rec. Sec.

COLUSA COUNTY.

Colusa No. 194, Colusa—Meets 1st and 3rd Mondays, N.S.G.W. Hall; Mrs. Ruby Humburg, 223 Park Hill St.

CONTRA COSTA COUNTY.

Stirling No. 146, Pittsburg—Meets 1st and 3rd Wednesdays, Veteran Memorial Hall; Mrs. Minnie Marcelli, Rec. Sec., 771 E. 12th St.

Richmond No. 147, Richmond—Meets 1st and 3rd Tuesdays, I.O.O.F. Hall, 10th St.; Mrs. Tillie Summers, Rec. Sec., 640 So. 31st St.

Donner No. 193, Byron—Meets 1st and 3rd Wednesdays, I.O.O.F. Hall; Mrs. Anna Pendry, Rec. Sec., P. O. Box 112.

Las Juntas No. 221, Martinez—Meets 1st and 3rd Mondays, Pythias Castle; Mrs. Lola Viera, Rec. Sec., P. O. box 128.

Antioch No. 223, Antioch—Meets 2nd and 4th Tuesdays, I.O.O.F. Hall; Mrs. Estelle Evans, Rec. Sec., 202 E. 5th St., Pittsburg.

Carquinez No. 234, Crockett—Meets 2nd and 4th Wednesdays, I.O.O.F. Hall; Mrs. Cecile Petee, Rec. Sec., 465 Edwards St.

GRAND OFFICERS.

Mrs. Estelle M. Evans........Past Grand President
202 E. Fifth St., Pittsburg

Mrs. Evelyn I. Carlson............Grand President
1965 San Jose Ave., San Francisco

Mrs. Anna M. Armstrong.....Grand Vice-president
Woodland

Mrs. Sallie R. Thaler..............Grand Secretary
555 Baker St., San Francisco

Mrs. Susie K. Christ..............Grand Treasurer
555 Baker St., San Francisco

Mrs. Irma Laird.....................Grand Marshal
Alturas

Mrs. Minna K. Horn.........Grand Inside Sentinel
Etna

Mrs. Orinda G. Giannini.....Grand Outside Sentinel
3142 Filbert St., San Francisco

Mrs. Lola Horgan...................Grand Organist
789 Morse St., San Francisco

GRAND TRUSTEES.

Mrs. Edna Briggs, 1045 Santa Ynez Way, Sacramento
Mrs. Ethel Begley.....1206 Valencia, San Francisco
Mrs. Anna Thuesen....615 38th Ave., San Francisco
Mrs. Gladys Noce ....Sutter Creek
Mrs. Florence Boyle.........................Oroville
Mrs. Florence Schoneman, 1521 5th Ave., Los Angeles
Mrs. Willow Borba.......................Sebastopol

EL DORADO COUNTY.

Marguerite No. 12, Placerville—Meets 1st and 3rd Wednesdays, Masonic Hall; Mrs. Nettie Leonardi, Rec. Sec., 25 Coloma St.

El Dorado No. 186, Georgetown—Meets 2nd and 4th Saturday afternoons, I.O.O.F. Hall; Mrs. Alta L. Douglas, Rec. Sec.

FRESNO COUNTY.

Fresno No. 187, Fresno—Meets Fridays, Pythian Castle, Cor. "R" and Merced Sts.; Mary Aubery, Rec. Sec., 1040 Delphia Ave.

GLENN COUNTY.

Berryessa No. 192, Willows—Meets 1st and 3rd Mondays, I.O.O.F. Hall; Mrs. Leonora Neate, Rec. Sec., 335 No. Lassen St.

HUMBOLDT COUNTY.

Occident No. 28, Eureka—Meets 1st and 3rd Wed-
Rec. Sec., 2309 "B" St.
nesdays, N.S.G.W. Hall; Mrs. Eva L. MacDonald,

Oneonta No. 71, Ferndale—Meets 2nd and 4th Fridays, I.O.O.F. Hall; Mrs. Myra Rumrill, Rec. Sec.

Reichling No. 97, Fortuna—Meets 2nd and 4th Tuesdays, Friendship Hall; Mrs. Grace Swett, Rec. Sec., P. O. Box 328.

KERN COUNTY.

Miocene No. 228, Taft—Meets 1st and 3rd Wednesday afternoons, I.O.O.F. Hall; Mrs. Evalyne Towne, Rec. Sec., P. O. Box 1011.

El Tejon No. 239, Bakersfield—Meets 1st and 3rd Fridays, Castle Hall; Mrs. Grace Dorris, Rec. Sec., 127 Morgan Bldg.

Desert Gold No. 250, Mojave—Meets 2nd and 4th Fridays, I.O.O.F. Hall; Mrs. Mae Coffill, Rec. Sec.

LAKE COUNTY.

Clear Lake No. 135, Middletown—Meets 2nd and 4th Tuesdays, Herrick Hall; Mrs. Retta Reynolds, Rec. Sec., P. O. Box 130.

LASSEN COUNTY.

Nataqua No. 152, Standish—Meets 1st and 3rd Wednesdays, Foresters Hall; Mrs. Olive Bouchard, Rec. Sec.

Mount Lassen No. 215, Bieber—Meets 2nd and 4th Thursdays, I.O.O.F. Hall; Mrs. Angie C. Kenyon, Rec. Sec.

Susanville No. 243, Susanville—Meets 3rd Thursday, I.O.O.F. Hall; Mrs. Georgia Jensen, Rec. Sec., 700 Roop St.

LOS ANGELES COUNTY.

Los Angeles No. 124, Los Angeles—Meets 1st and 3rd Wednesdays, I.O.O.F. Hall, Washington and Oak Sts.; Mrs. Mary K. Corcoran, Rec. Sec., 322 No. Van Ness Ave.

Long Beach No. 154, Long Beach—Meets 1st and 3rd Thursdays, K.P. Hall, 341 Pacific Ave.; Mrs. Alice Waldow, Rec. Sec., 2175 Cedar Ave.

Rudecinda No. 230, San Pedro—Meets 1st and 3rd Fridays, Unity Hall, I.O.O.F. Temple, 10th and Gaffey; Mrs. Carrie E. Northway, Rec. Sec., 561 W. 14th St.

Verdugo No. 240, Glendale—Meets 2nd and 4th Tuesdays, Masonic Temple, 234 So. Brand Blvd.; Miss Etta Fulkerth, Rec. Sec., 526-A No. Orange St.

Santa Monica Bay No. 245, Ocean Park—Meets 1st and 3rd Mondays, New Eagles Hall, 2823½ Main St.; Mrs. Rosalie Hyde, Rec. Sec., 738 Flower St., Venice.

Californiana No. 247, Los Angeles—Meets 2nd and 4th Tuesday afternoons, Hollywood Studio Club, 1215 Lodi Place; Mrs. Inez Sitton, Rec. Sec., 4223 Berenice St.

MADERA COUNTY.

Madera No 244, Madera—Meets 2nd and 4th Thursdays, Masonic Annex; Mrs. Margaret Boyle, Rec. Sec., 225 So. "C" St.

MARIN COUNTY.

Sea Point No. 196, Sausalito—Meets 2nd and 4th Mondays, Perry Hall, 50 Caledonia St.; Mrs. Mary B. Smith, Rec. Sec., 559 Woodward Ave.

Marinita No. 198, San Rafael—Meets 2nd and 4th Mondays, 816 "B" St.; Miss Mollye Y. Spaelti, Rec. Sec., 533 4th St.

Fairfax No. 225, Fairfax—Meets 2nd and 4th Tuesdays, Community Hall; Mrs. Olive A. Greene, Rec. Sec., P. O. Box 277.

Tamelpa No. 231, Mill Valley—Meets 1st and 3rd Tuesdays, I.O.O.F. Hall; Mrs. Delphine M. Todt, Rec. Sec., 400 Grand Ave., San Rafael.

MARIPOSA COUNTY.

Mariposa No. 63, Mariposa—Meets 1st and 3rd Fridays, I.O.O.F. Hall; Mrs. Mamie E. Weston, Rec. Sec.

ATTENTION, SECRETARIES!

THIS DIRECTORY IS PUBLISHED BY AUTHORITY OF THE GRAND PARLOR N.D.G.W., AND ALL NOTICES OF CHANGES MUST BE RECEIVED BY THE GRAND SECRETARY (NOT THE MAGAZINE) ON OR BEFORE THE 20TH OF EACH MONTH TO INSURE CORRECTION IN NEXT PUBLICATION OF DIRECTORY.

MENDOCINO COUNTY.

Fort Bragg No. 210, Fort Bragg—Meets 1st and 3rd Thursdays, I.O.O.F. Hall; Mrs. Ruth W. Fuller, Rec. Sec.

MERCED COUNTY.

Veritas No. 75, Merced—Meets 1st and 3rd Tuesdays, I.O.O.F. Hall; Miss Margaret Thornton, Rec. Sec., 317 18th St.

MODOC COUNTY.

Alturas No. 159, Alturas—Meets 1st Thursday, Alturas Civic Club; Mrs. Irma W. Laird, Rec. Sec.

MONTEREY COUNTY.

Aleli No. 102, Salinas—Meets 2nd and 4th Thursdays, I.O.O.F. Hall; Mrs. Rose Evelyn Rhyner, Rec. Sec., P. O. Box 1274.

Junipero No. 141, Monterey—Meets 1st and 3rd Thursdays, Custom House; Miss Matilda M. Bergschicker, Rec. Sec., 493 Van Buren St.

NAPA COUNTY.

Eschol No. 16, Napa—Meets 2nd and 4th Mondays, N.S.G.W. Hall; Mrs. Ella Ingram, Rec. Sec., 2140 Seminary St.

Calistoga No. 145, Calistoga—Meets 2nd and 4th Mondays, I.O.O.F. Hall; Sadie P. Brooks, Rec. Sec.

La Junta No. 203, Saint Helena—Meets 1st and 3rd Tuesdays, N.S.G.W. Hall; Mrs. Marie Signorelli, Rec. Sec., 1341 Madrona Ave.

NEVADA COUNTY.

Laurel No. 6, Nevada City—Meets 1st and 3rd Wednesdays, I.O.O.F. Hall; Mrs. Nellie E. Clark, Rec. Sec., P. O. Box 212.

Manzanita No. 29, Grass Valley—Meets 1st and 3rd Tuesdays, Auditorium; Mrs. Loraine Keast, Rec. Sec., 123 Race St.

Columbia No. 70, French Corral—Meets Fridays, Farrelley Hall; Mrs. Kate Farrelley-Sullivan, Rec. Sec.

Snow Peak No. 176, Truckee—Meets 2nd and 4th Fridays, I.O.O.F. Hall; Mrs. Henrietta M. Eaton, Rec. Sec., P. O. Box 116.

ORANGE COUNTY.

Santa Ana No. 235, Santa Ana—Meets 2nd and 4th Mondays, K.C. Hall, 4th and French Sts.; Mrs. Matilda S. Lemon, Rec. Sec., 1038 W. Bishop St.

Grace No. 242, Fullerton—Meets 1st and 3rd Thursdays, I.O.O.F. Hall, 116½ E. Commonwealth; Mrs. Mary Rothaermel, Rec. Sec., P. O. Box 235.

PLACER COUNTY.

Placer No. 138, Lincoln—Meets 2nd Wednesday, I.O.O.F. Hall; Miss Carrie Parlin, Rec. Sec.

La Rosa No. 191, Roseville—Meets 1st and 3rd Tuesdays, Eagles Hall; Mrs. Alice Lee West, Rec. Sec., Rocklin.

Auburn No. 233, Auburn—Meets 2nd and 4th Fridays, Foresters Hall; Mrs. Dorothy Reinecke, Rec. Sec., Penryn.

PLUMAS COUNTY.

Plumas Pioneer No. 219, Quincy—Meets 1st and 3rd Mondays, I.O.O.F. Hall; Minnie E. Johnson, Rec. Sec., P. O. Box 243.

SACRAMENTO COUNTY.

Califia No. 22, Sacramento—Meets 2nd and 4th Tuesdays, N.S.G.W. Hall; Miss Lulu Gillis, Rec Sec., 921 8th St.

La Bandera No. 110, Sacramento—Meets 1st and 3rd Fridays, N.S.G.W. Hall; Mrs. Clara Weldon, Rec. Sec., 1310 "O" St.

Sutter No. 111, Sacramento—Meets 1st and 3rd Tuesdays, N.S.G.W. Hall; Mrs. Adele Nix, Rec. Sec., 1238 "S" St.

Fern No. 123, Folsom—Meets 1st and 3rd Tuesdays, K.P. Hall; Mrs. Viola Shumway, Rec. Sec., P. O. Box 48.

Chabolla No. 171, Galt—Meets 2nd and 4th Tuesdays, I.O.O.F. Hall; Mrs. Mary Pritchard, Rec. Sec.

Coloma No. 212, Sacramento—Meets 1st and 3rd Tuesdays, I.O.O.F. Hall, Oak Park; Mrs. Nettie Harry, Rec. Sec., 1217 35th St.

Liberty No. 213, Elk Grove—Meets 2nd and 4th Fridays, I.O.O.F. Hall; Mrs. Frances Wackman, Rec. Sec., P. O. Box 192.

Victory No. 216, Courtland—Meets 1st Saturday and 3rd Monday, N.S.G.W. Hall; Mrs. Agneda Lample, Rec. Sec.

SAN BENITO COUNTY.

Copa de Oro No. 105, Hollister—Meets 2nd and 4th Thursdays, Grangers Union Hall; Mrs. Mollie Daveggio, Rec. Sec., 110 San Benito St.

San Juan Bautista No. 179, San Juan Bautista—Meets 1st Wednesday, Mission Corridor Rooms; Miss Gertrude Breen, Rec. Sec.

SAN BERNARDINO COUNTY.

Lugonia No. 241, San Bernardino—Meets 2nd and 4th Wednesdays, Eagles Hall; Evelyn T. Shaddox, Rec. Sec., 208 Temple St.

Ontario No. 251, Ontario—Meets 1st and 3rd Thursdays, Ontario Hall; Miss Helen Hickman, Rec. Sec., 923 No. Laurel Ave.

SAN DIEGO COUNTY.

San Diego No. 208, San Diego—Meets 2nd and 4th Wednesdays, Directors Room, Chamber Commerce Bldg., 499 W. Broadway; Mrs. Elsie Case, Rec. Sec., 3051 Broadway.

SAN FRANCISCO CITY AND COUNTY.

Minerva No. 2, San Francisco—Meets 1st and 3rd Wednesdays, N.S.G.W. Bldg.; Miss Dorothy Finn, Rec. Sec., 90 Princess St., Sausalito.

Alta No. 3, San Francisco—Meets 2nd and 4th Tuesdays, N.S.G.W. Bldg.; Mrs. Agnese L. Hughes, Rec. Sec., 3980 Sacramento St.

Oro Fino No. 9, San Francisco—Meets 1st and 3rd Thursdays, N.S.G.W. Bldg.; Mrs. Josephine B. Morrisey, Rec. Sec., 4441 20th St.

Golden State No. 50, San Francisco—Meets 1st and 3rd Wednesdays, N.D.G.W. Home; Miss Millie Tietjen, Rec. Sec., 328 Lexington Ave.

Orinda No. 56, San Francisco—Meets 2nd and 4th Fridays, N.D.G.W. Home; Mrs. Anna A. Gruber-Loser, Rec. Sec., 72 Grove Lane, San Anselmo.

Fremont No. 59, San Francisco—Meets 1st and 3rd Tuesdays, N.S.G.W. Bldg.; Miss Hannah Collins, Rec. Sec., 563 Fillmore St.

Buena Vista No. 68, San Francisco—Meets 1st, 3rd and 5th Thursdays, N.D.G.W. Home; Miss Margaret Barrett, Rec. Sec., 3774 20th St.

Las Lomas No. 72, San Francisco—Meets 1st and 3rd Tuesdays, N.D.G.W. Home; Mrs. Marion S. Day, Rec. Sec., 471 Alvarado St.

Yosemite No. 83, San Francisco—Meets 1st and 3rd Tuesdays, American Hall, 20th and Capp Sts.; Miss Mary Bazley, Rec. Sec., 2353 22nd St.

La Estrella No. 89, San Francisco—Meets 2nd and 4th Mondays, N.S.G.W. Bldg.; Miss Birdie Hartman, Rec. Sec., 1018 Jackson St.

Sans Souci No. 96, San Francisco—Meets 2nd and 4th Mondays, N.D.G.W. Home; Mrs. Minnie F. Dobbin, Rec. Sec., 1483 43rd Ave.

Calaveras No. 103, San Francisco—Meets 2nd and 4th Tuesdays, Swedish American Hall, 2174 Market St.; Mrs. Lena Lorsheter, Rec. Sec., 492-C 41st St., Oakland.

Darina No. 114, San Francisco—Meets 1st and 3rd Mondays, N.S.G.W. Bldg.; Miss Adele Walsh, Rec. Sec., 479 Page St.

El Vespero No. 118, San Francisco—Meets 2nd and 4th Tuesdays, Masonic Hall, 4706 3rd St.; Mrs. Nell R. Boege, Rec. Sec., 1626 Kirkwood Ave.

Genevieve No. 132, San Francisco—Meets 1st and 3rd Thursdays, N.S.G.W. Bldg.; Miss Branice Peguillan, Rec. Sec., 2434 16th Ave.

Keith No. 137, San Francisco—Meets 2nd and 4th Thursdays, N.S.G.W. Bldg.; Mrs. Helen T. Mann, Rec. Sec., 575 Pierce St., Apt. 206.

Gabrielle No. 139, San Francisco—Meets 2nd and 4th Wednesdays, N.S.G.W. Bldg.; Mrs. Dorothy Wuesterfeld, Rec. Sec., 1020 Munich St.

Presidio No. 148, San Francisco—Meets 2nd and 4th Tuesdays, N.S.G.W. Bldg.; Mrs. Hattie Gaughran, Rec. Sec., 713 Capp St.

Guadalupe No. 153, San Francisco—Meets 2nd and 4th Mondays, Forester Hall, 170 Valencia St.; Miss May A. McCarthy, Rec. Sec., 336 Elsie St.

Golden Gate No. 158, San Francisco—Meets 2nd and 4th Mondays, N.S.G.W. Bldg.; Mrs. Margaret Ramm, Rec. Sec., 435-A Frederick St.

Dolores No. 169, San Francisco—Meets 2nd and 4th Wednesdays, N.S.G.W. Bldg.; Mrs. Ada Saunders, Rec. Sec., 284 Allison St.

Linda Rosa No. 170, San Francisco—Meets 2nd and 4th Wednesdays, Swedish American Hall, 2174 Market St.; Mrs. Eva P. Tyrrel, Rec. Sec., 2629 Mission St.

Portola No. 172, San Francisco—Meets 1st and 3rd Tuesdays, N.S.G.W. Bldg.; Catherine H. Dolly, Rec. Sec., 4125 23rd St.

Castro No. 178, San Francisco—Meets 1st and 3rd Wednesdays, K.C. Bldg., 150 Golden Gate Ave.; Miss Adeline Sandersfeld, Rec. Sec., 50 Baker St.

Twin Peaks No. 185, San Francisco—Meets 2nd and 4th Fridays, Druids Temple, 44 Page St.; Mrs. Loretta Cameron, Rec. Sec., 3969 Army St.

James Lick No. 220, San Francisco—Meets 1st and 3rd Wednesdays, N.S.G.W. Bldg.; Mrs. Edna Bishop, Rec. Sec., 3841 24th St.

Mission No. 227, San Francisco—Meets 2nd and 4th Fridays, N.S.G.W. Bldg.; Mrs. Ann Dippel, Rec. Sec., 448 Dewey Blvd.

Bret Harte No. 232 San Francisco—Meets 2nd and 4th Tuesdays, Schuberts Hall, 3009 16th St.; Muriele N. Pabst, Rec. Sec., 696 Guerrero St.

La Dorada No. 236, San Francisco—Meets 2nd and 4th Thursdays, N.S.G.W. Hall; Mrs. Theresa R. O'Brien, Rec. Sec., 567 Liberty St.

Balboa No. 249, San Francisco—Meets 1st and 3rd Thursdays, Maccabee Hall, 5th Ave. and Clement St., Jean Moffet, Rec. Sec., 422 Third Ave.

SAN JOAQUIN COUNTY.

Joaquin No. 5, Stockton—Meets 2nd and 4th Tuesdays, N.S.G.W. Hall, 314 E. Main St.; Mrs. Delia Garvin, Rec. Sec., 1122 E. Market St.

El Pescadero No. 82, Tracy—Meets 1st and 3rd Fridays, I.O.O.F. Hall; Mrs. Mary A. Hewitson, Rec. Sec., 215 W. 9th St.

Ivy No. 88, Lodi—Meets 1st and 3rd Wednesdays, Eagles Hall; Mrs. Mae Corson, Rec. Sec., 109 So. School St.

Caliz de Oro No. 206, Stockton—Meets 1st and 3rd Tuesdays, N.S.G.W. Hall, 314 E. Main St.; Mrs. Frances Germain, Rec. Sec., 450 No. Regent.

Phoebe A. Hearst No. 214, Manteca—Meets 2nd and 4th Wednesdays, I.O.O.F. Hall; Mrs. Josie M. Frederick, Rec. Sec., Route A, Box 364, Ripon.

SAN LUIS OBISPO COUNTY.

San Miguel No. 94, San Miguel—Meets 2nd and 4th Wednesday afternoons, Clemon Hall; Mrs. Nellie Wickstrom, Rec. Sec.

San Luisita No. 108, San Luis Obispo—Meets 2nd and 4th Thursdays, W.O.W. Hall; Miss Agnes M. Lee, Rec. Sec., P. O. Box 584.

El Pinal No. 163, Cambria—Meets 2nd, 4th and 5th Tuesdays, N.S.G.W. Hall; Kathryn Luchessa, Rec. Sec.

SAN MATEO COUNTY.

Bonita No. 10, Redwood City—Meets 2nd and 4th Thursdays, I.O.O.F. Hall; Mrs. Dora Wilson, Rec. Sec.; 518 Middlefield Rd.

Vista del Mar No. 155, Halfmoon Bay—Meets 2nd and 4th Thursdays, I.O.O.F. Hall; Mrs. Grace Griffith, Rec. Sec.

Ano Nuevo No. 180, Pescadero—Meets 1st and 3rd Wednesdays, I.O.O.F. Hall; Mrs. Alice Mattei, Rec. Sec.

El Carmelo No. 181, Daly City—Meets 1st and 3rd Wednesdays, Masonic Hall; Mrs. Hattie Kelly, Rec. Sec., 1179 Brunswick St.

Menlo No. 211, Menlo Park—Meets 2nd and 4th Mondays, Masonic Hall; Mrs. Frances E. Maloney, Rec. Sec., P. O. Box 626.

San Bruno No. 246, San Bruno—Meets 2nd and 4th Fridays, N.D. Hall; Mrs. Evelyn Kelly, Rec. Sec., 353 Hazel Ave.

SANTA BARBARA COUNTY.

Reina del Mar No. 126, Santa Barbara—Meets 1st and 3rd Tuesdays, Pythian Castle, 222 W. Carillo St.; Miss Christina Moller, Rec. Sec., 836 Bath St.

SANTA CLARA COUNTY.

San Jose No. 81, San Jose—Meets Thursdays, Catholic Women Center, 5th and San Fernando Sts.; Mrs. Nellie Fleming, Rec. Sec., Catholic Women's Center.

Vendome No. 100, San Jose—Meets Wednesdays, Scottish Rite Hall; Miss Marie Buck, Rec. Sec., 1114 Ellen St.

El Monte No. 205, Mountain View—Meets 2nd and 4th Fridays, Mockbee Hall; Miss Dolores Collett, Rec. Sec., Route 1, Box 677-A, Los Altos.

Palo Alto No. 229, Palo Alto—Meets 1st and 3rd Mondays, N.S.G.W. Hall; Miss Helena G. Hansen, Rec. Sec., 531 Lytton Ave.

SANTA CRUZ COUNTY.

Santa Cruz No. 26, Santa Cruz—Meets Mondays, N.S.G.W. Hall; Mrs. May L. Williamson, Rec. Sec., 170 Walnut Ave.

El Pajaro No. 35, Watsonville—Meets 1st and 3rd Tuesdays, I.O.O.F. Hall; Miss Ruth E. Wilson, Rec. Sec., 16 Laurel St.

SHASTA COUNTY.

Camellia No. 41, Anderson—Meets 1st and 3rd Tuesdays, Masonic Hall; Mrs. Olga E. Welbourn, Rec. Sec.

Lassen View No. 98, Shasta—Meets 2nd Friday, Masonic Hall; Miss Louise Litsch, Rec. Sec.

Hiawatha No. 140, Redding—Meets 2nd and 4th Wednesdays, Moose Hall; Ruth Presleigh, Rec. Sec., Office County Clerk.

SIERRA COUNTY.

Naomi No. 36, Downieville—Meets 2nd and 4th Wednesdays, I.O.O.F. Hall; Mrs. Mary Cook, Rec. Sec.

Imogen No. 134, Sierraville—Meets 2nd and 4th Saturday afternoons, Copren Hall; Mrs. Jennie Copren, Rec. Sec.

SISKIYOU COUNTY.

Eschscholtzia No. 112, Etna—Meets 1st and 3rd Wednesdays, Masonic Hall; Mrs. Bernice E. Smith, Rec. Sec.

Mountain Dawn No. 120, Sawyers Bar—Meets 2nd and last Wednesdays, I.O.O.F. Hall; Miss Edith Dunphy, Rec. Sec.

SOLANO COUNTY.

Vallejo No. 195, Vallejo—Meets 1st and 3rd Wednesdays, K.C. Hall, 820 Marin St.; Mrs. Mary Combs, Rec. Sec., 511 York St.

Mary E. Bell No. 224, Dixon—Meets 2nd and 4th Thursdays, I.O.O.F. Hall; Grace McFadyen, Rec. Sec.

SONOMA COUNTY.

Sonoma No 209, Sonoma—Meets 2nd and 4th Mondays, I.O.O.F. Hall; Mrs. Mae Norrbom, Rec. Sec., R.F.D., Box 171.

Santa Rosa No. 217, Santa Rosa—Meets 1st and 3rd Thursdays, N.S.G.W. Hall; Mrs. Hazel E. Brown, Rec. Sec., 1521 4th St.

Petaluma No. 222, Petaluma—Meets 1st and 3rd Tuesdays, Dania Hall; Mrs. Margaret M. Oeltjen, Rec. Sec., 603 Prospect St.

STANISLAUS COUNTY.

Oakdale No. 125, Oakdale—Meets 1st Monday, I.O.O.F. Hall; Mrs. Lou Reeder, Rec. Sec.

Morada No. 199, Modesto—Meets 2nd and 4th Wednesdays, I.O.O.F. Hall; Mrs. Susan Sullivan, Rec. Sec., 823 10th St.

Eldora No. 248, Turlock—Meets 1st and 3rd Wednesdays, Fraternal Hall; Mrs. Melva Gardner, Rec. Sec., 817 W. Main St.

SUTTER COUNTY.

South Butte No. 226, Sutter—Meets 1st and 3rd Mondays, N.D.G.W. Hall; Mrs. Abbie N. Vagedes, Rec. Sec.

TEHAMA COUNTY.

Berendos No. 23, Red Bluff—Meets 1st and 3rd Tuesdays, W.O.W. Hall, 200 Pine St.; Mrs. Lillie Hammer, Rec. Sec., 636 Jackson St.

TRINITY COUNTY.

Eltapome No. 55, Weaverville—Meets 2nd and 4th Thursdays, N.S.G.W. Hall; Mrs. Lou N. Fetzer, Rec. Sec.

TUOLUMNE COUNTY.

Dardanelle No. 66, Sonora—Meets Fridays, I.O.O.F. Hall; Mrs. Nettie Whitto, Rec. Sec.

Golden Era No. 99, Columbia—Meets 1st and 3rd Thursdays, N.S.G.W. Hall; Miss Irene Punce, Rec. Sec.

Anona No. 164, Jamestown—Meets 2nd and 4th Tuesdays, I.O.O.F. Hall; Mrs. Rosa A. Beckwith, Rec. Sec., P. O. Box 87.

YOLO COUNTY.

Woodland No. 90, Woodland—Meets 2nd and 4th Tuesdays, N.S.G.W. Hall; Mrs. Maude Heaton, Rec. Sec., 153 College St.

YUBA COUNTY.

Marysville No. 162, Marysville—Meets 2nd and 4th Wednesdays, Liberty Hall; Miss Cecelia C. Gomes, Rec. Sec., 701 6th St.

Camp Far West No. 218, Wheatland—Meets 4th Thursday, I.O.O.F. Hall; Mrs. Ethel C. Brock, Rec. Sec., P. O. Box 285.

AFFILIATED ORGANIZATIONS.

General Assembly Past Presidents—Meetings held annually in April at the home-town of Chief President; Miss Josephine Clark, 824 11th St., Oakland, Chief President; Mrs. Anna G. Loser, 72 Grove Lane, San Anselmo, Chief Secretary.

Past Presidents Association No. 1—Meets 1st and 3rd Mondays, N.S.G.W. Bldg., 414 Mason St., San Francisco; Mrs. Margaret Grote-Hill, Pres.; Mrs. May R. Barry, Rec. Sec., 2319 19th Ave., San Francisco.

Past Presidents Association No. 2—Meets 2nd and 4th Mondays, "Wigwam," Pacific Bldg., 16th and Jefferson, Oakland; Francis McGovern, Pres.; Mrs. Elizabeth B. Goodman, Rec. Sec., 134 Juana St., San Leandro.

Past Presidents Association No. 3 (Santa Clara County)—Meets 2nd Tuesday, homes of members; Mrs. Ida Sweeney, Pres.; Amelia S. Hartman, Rec. Sec., 157 Auzerais Ave., San Jose.

Past Presidents Association No. 4 (Sacramento County)—Meets 2nd Monday, Unitarian Hall, 1413 27th St., Sacramento City; Francis Kimball, Pres.; Lily May Tilden, Rec. Sec., 3225 "T" St., Sacramento.

Past Presidents Association No. 5 (Butte County)—Meets 1st Friday, homes of members, Chico and Oroville; Sonora Steadman, Pres; Ruth Brown, Rec. Sec., 1265 Leah Court, Oroville.

Past Presidents Association No. 6 (Nevada County)—Meets 4th Friday, alternately between Nevada City, Odd Fellows Hall, and Grass Valley, Womens Improvement Clubhouse; Anne Conlin, Pres.; Louise Wales, Rec. Sec., 369 Mill St., Grass Valley.

Past Presidents Association No. 7 (Sonoma County)—Meets 1st Thursday, N.S.G.W. Hall, Santa Rosa; Willow Borba, Pres.; Clytie Lewis, Rec. Sec., R.F.D. No. 4, Box 345-A, Santa Rosa.

Past Presidents Association No. 8 (San Joaquin and Stanislaus Counties)—Meets 2nd Thursday, Red Men Hall, Stockton; Mrs. Mattie M. Stein, Pres.; Mrs. Harriet F. Corr, Rec. Sec., 729 E. Sonora St., Stockton.

Native Sons and Native Daughters Central Committee on Homeless Children—Main Office, 955 Phelan Bldg., San Francisco; Mrs. John W. Stirling, Chmn.; Miss Mary E. Brusie, Sec. Los Angeles branch office, 3924 Sunset Blvd.; Dorothy Schlingman, Sec.

(ADVERTISEMENT.)

HOME DONATIONS

San Francisco—Donations for the N.D.G.W. Home since the 1931 (Santa Rosa) Grand Parlor include the following, reported by Past Grand President Emma G. Foley, secretary Grand Parlor N.D.G.W. Home Committee:

Flowers for N.D.G.W. Club breakfasts June 21, August 9, September 13, October 11 and November 8, 1931, large basket flowers, renovating and decorating fernery, Miss Emma Dieckhoff, Aloha Parlor No. 106. Glass punch bowl, six glasses, silver ladle, Mrs. Jennie Morgan, Buena Vista Parlor No. 68. One dozen glasses jelly, one dozen glasses relish, three dozen glasses preserves, one box plums, donations repeated of jam, jelly and meat relish, Mrs. Augusta Huxsol, Piedmont Parlor No. 87. Three books and wicker basket, Past Grand President Dr. Mariana Bertola, Buena Vista Parlor No. 68. Five large glasses apricot jam, one dozen glasses jelly and jam, Mrs. May Noble, Buena Vista Parlor No. 68. One large jar satsuma preserve, one brass bird cage, Past Grand President Emma G. Foley, Orinda Parlor No. 56. Japanese dinner gong, Miss Lela Ewert, Woodland Parlor No. 90. End table, stand for bird cage, Director Laura D. Hawkins, Santa Cruz Parlor No. 26. Water-color picture, Lillie B. Eiselen, Alta Parlor No. 3. Parlor grand piano, Miss Hazel Heyl, Marysville Parlor No. 162, dedicated to the memory of her sister, Violet M. Heyl, organizer of Marysville Parlor. Basket flowers, Grand Trustee Florence Dodson-Schoneman, Rudecinda Parlor No. 230. Twelve sacks almonds, Past Grand President Mamie G. Peyton, Joaquin Parlor No. 5. $100 toward N.D.G.W. Home endowment fund, Rose Alma Reimers, Orinda Parlor No. 56. Throw for parlor grand piano and renovating curtains in diningroom, Mrs. Mae MacDonald, Alta Parlor No. 3. Six books, Mrs. Ella Osburn, Buena Vista Parlor No. 68. Artificial leaves for basket, Past Grand President Addie L. Mosher, Piedmont Parlor No. 87. Box apples, Sonoma Parlor No. 209. Box dish towels and pot holders, Dolores Parlor sewing club. Tong set for fireplace, Mrs. Eleanor Taylor, Eltapome Parlor No. 55. Twelve and one-half pound turkey, bag walnuts, Past Grand President Mary E. Bell, Buena Vista Parlor No. 68. Eight volumes American history, Mrs. Kate Carr. Potted begonia, Mrs. Erickson. End table, Grand President Evelyn I. Carlson, Dolores Parlor No. 169. Two large homemade angel cakes, Miss Birdie Freitag, Eschscholtzia Parlor No. 112. Box fancy cookies, Louis Brown. Large box candy and salted nuts, Past Grand President Genevieve W. Baker, Buena Vista Parlor No. 68. Twenty-one-pound box fancy California fruits and nuts, John Adams, Home janitor. Box assorted candies, Miss Katherine Murphy, Alta Parlor No. 3. End table, district deputies San Francisco district, Past Grand President May C. Boldemann, supervising deputy.

NATIVE DAUGHTER NEWS

(Continued from Page 11)

C. A. Craemer. A new baby daughter recently arrived at the home of Mrs. Hazel Flaherty. Mrs. Genevieve Hiskey has been appointed district deputy for Ontario No. 251, instituted December 19. Mrs. Marguerite Dickinson was general chairman for the recent benefit dinner, which was attended by more than 300.

Raising Grand Parlor Funds.

Merced—Veritas No. 75 is sponsoring monthly dances in Merced and Mariposa Counties to raise funds with which to entertain the Grand Parlor, which meets here in June. A huge grocery basket is also to be disposed of. All the local civic organizations are co-operating with the Parlor in its Grand Parlor endeavors.

San Luis Obispo County Meet.

San Luis Obispo—San Luisita No. 108 entertained January 14 delegates from San Miguel No. 94 and El Pinal No. 163 (Cambria) to the San Luis Obispo County district meeting at an elaborate chicken dinner. Mrs. N. F. Schlicht was in charge. The ritual was exemplified under the direction of Supervising Deputy Hazel Hansen. District Deputies Elsie Loose and Katie Van Gordon were among the many in attendance.

Joint Installations.

Elk Grove—One of the nicest installation parties in many years took place here January 8. It was a joint installation of Liberty No. 213 and Elk Grove No. 41 N.S.G.W. and was followed by a holiday banquet. District Deputies Nellie Nordstrom and Joseph Lannon of Sacramento, with their respective teams, performed the ceremonies, and the perfectness of the work made the occasion a delightful one. Louisa Krull and Ray Hogaboom became the respective presidents. Grand Trustee Edna Briggs and Clyde Corcoran were the marshals for the ceremonies.

Courtland—Officers of Victory No. 216 and Courtland No 106 N.S.G.W. were jointly installed by District Deputies May Lucas and William Pierson, Martha Buckley and Thornton Flyman becoming the respective presidents.

Doings of Past Presidents.

Chico—Past Presidents Association No. 5 was entertained January 8 at the home of Mrs. Mabel K. Richards. Officers were installed, Irene Henry becoming president. Bridge followed the business meeting. February 14 the association will have its annual valentine party at the Butte County Infirmary.

Stockton—Officers of Past Presidents Association No. 8, with Miss Alice McDonald as president, were installed January 14. Among the many who participated in the ceremonies were Past Grand Presidents Carrie Roesch-Durham and Mamie G. Peyton. A program was presented under the supervision of Mrs. Lois Armstrong. At the February 11 meeting of the association several candidates will be initiated.

LOS ANGELES--CITY and COUNTY

LONG BEACH

LOS ANGELES

(Continued from Page 5)

6, survived by a wife and ten children. He was born at Oakland, Alameda County, August 2, 1877.

In early life, "Joe" Ford affiliated with Corona (now Hollywood) Parlor No. 196 N.S.G.W., and a few years ago transferred his membership to Glendale Parlor No. 264. He frequently attended sessions of the Grand Parlor, and during the 1930-31 Grand Parlor year he served the Order as Historiographer. He was a noted attorney, and served the Nation faithfully, in times of war as well as in peace-times.—C.M.H.

DESCENDANT '46 PIONEERS LEADS.

Long Beach—Mrs. Violet Tompkins-Henshilwood, descendant of California Pioneers of 1846, was inducted into the office of president of Long Beach Parlor No. 154 N.D.G.W., January 21, when the officers were installed by District Deputy Eva Mae Bemis. The hall was beautified with wild flowers and birds by Chairman Zella Hodgdon and her committee. Parlors represented included Lugonia, Los Angeles, Rudecinda, San Diego, Verdugo and Woodland.

Addresses were delivered by Grand Trustee Florence Dodson-Schoneman and President Francis Gentry of Long Beach Parlor No. 239 N.S.G.W. Mrs. Kate McFadyen, "mother" of No. 154, presented an emblem to Daisy Hansen, outgoing president. After a program, refreshments and dancing concluded a happy occasion.

The last meeting of Long Beach in 1931 was in honor of the new members received during that year. President Daisy Hansen and District Deputy Clara Fay were hostesses at the banquet. The thimble club's last gathering, at the home of Miss Eleanor Johnson, was in recognition of the birthdays of Mms. Henshilwood and Hansen, sisters by birth.

EDUCATIONAL PROGRAM.

The first meeting in 1932 of Ramona Parlor No. 109 N.S.G.W. was held January 15, when three candidates were initiated. Walter Slosson distributed additional "1932 Bear Club" pins, and Deputy Grand President Ralph I. Harbison spoke on the Order's objectives. The excellent report of the board of trustees was presented by Walter Baskerville. On the Parlor's behalf President Chandos E. Bush presented an emblematic ring to Past President Paul Lombardi.

"Ramona has taken a step to meet the 'universal disturbance'," says Chairman John A. Schwamm of the membership committee. "It offers to its members a way to help themselves as well as the Parlor." Details may be had from him or from Secretary John V. Scott. No. 109's February calendar includes: 12th, initiation. 19th, music and entertainment, followed by refreshments. 26th, educational night.

The officers of Ramona are instituting an educational campaign which will deal with California history, political economy, the Asiatic question and communism. The lectures, to be featured monthly, will start promptly at 8:30 p.m. and will be open to all Native Sons and Native Daughters and their friends. "It is hoped," says the announcement, "that the moral forces of both Orders will, through such educational activities, become mobilized and active and will make themselves felt as a unit in the affairs of California."

Dr. Rockwell D. Hunt, dean of the U.S.C. post-graduate school and a noted authority, will deliver a series of addresses on California history. He will present, in a manner interesting to all, word-pictures such as none but a scholar can depict. For his first talk, to be given February 26, he has chosen as his subject, "California's Historical Heritage."

LISTEN IN ON KTM, FEBRUARY 6.

Ocean Park—Grand Trustee Eldred L. Meyer has arranged with Bert Olbert of radio station KTM to broadcast a program in behalf of the Order of Native Sons February 6 at 7:45 a.m. The program will be mainly devoted to the homeless children work, and in addition to Grand Trustee Meyer, Junior Past Grand President John T. Newell will speak. Miss Cordelia Leventhal of Santa Monica Bay Parlor No. 245 N.D.G.W. will be heard in vocal selections.

Santa Monica Bay Parlor No. 267 N.S.G.W. initiated six candidates December 28 and also elected officers, Claude Wiseman becoming president. Many events are on the Parlor's social calendar for the January-July term, and extra effort will be put forth to increase the membership to at least 200 prior to Grand Parlor. The first class initiation of 1932 is scheduled for February 8.

During January, Grand Trustee Meyer officially visited the following Parlors: 13th, Chispa No. 139, Murphys; 14th, Columbia No. 258; 15th, Tuolumne No. 144, Sonora; 18th, Stockton No. 7; 20th, Modesto No. 11; 21st, Madera No. 130; 22nd, Fresno No. 25; 25th, Yosemite No. 24, Merced; 27th, Lodi No. 18; 28th, Tracy No. 186. Bakersfield No. 42 will be visited February 3.

ENTHUSIASTIC GATHERING.

San Pedro—The largest attended and most enthusiastic gathering of Los Angeles County Native Sons in a long time was that held here January 8 under the auspices of Sepulveda Parlor No. 263, which opened the festivities by serving supper. Following this, the officers of Los Angeles No. 45, Ramona No. 109, Hollywood No. 196, Sepulveda No. 263 and Santa

Monica Bay No. 267 were jointly installed. Lee E. Erwin, Chandos E. Bush, Municipal Judge Leo I. Aggeler, Francis J. Fetzer and Claude Wiseman became the respective presidents. Other Parlors represented in the crowd were Arrowhead No. 110, Santa Barbara No. 116, Glendale No. 264 and Santa Ana No. 265.

District Deputy Burrel D. Neighbors conducted the installation, and was highly commended for the excellence of his work. At the invitation of President Lawrence Powers of Sepulveda, President Victor D. Kremer of Los Angeles presided at the opening ceremonies, and past presidents of Ramona were named as temporary officers for installation. At the conclusion of those ceremonies, the new president of Sepulveda, Fetzer, requested Ramona's new presiding officer, Bush, to conduct the meeting, and his first act was to ask the assemblage to stand in silence for a moment in tribute to the late W. Joseph Ford of Glendale No. 264.

Speakers of the evening included, among many others, District Deputy Neighbors, Grand Trustee Eldred L. Meyer, Judge Walton J. Wood, Leo Youngworth, Judge Henry Willis, James H. Dodson Sr., State Senator Henry E. Carter and President C. W. McCormick of Santa Barbara No. 116. Undersheriff Eugene W. Biscailuz, conducted the good of the order, and he extracted several shekels, for the benefit of the homeless children, from the pockets of those introduced to the gang. For Santa Monica Bay Parlor, Manley Danforth presented a past president emblem to Harry Honn, and Leo Youngworth performed a like service for Sepulveda Parlor, John T. Gower being the recipient.—C.M.H.

SECRETARY GETS ASSISTANT.

At the January 14 meeting of Los Angeles Parlor No. 45 N.S.G.W., Past President Mark W. Hopkins was the recipient of an emblematic watchfob, Andrew M. Stodel making the presentation address. Earl G. Read was named assistant financial secretary to assist Secretary Richard W. Fryer, and President Lee E. Erwin appointed numerous committees to carry on. January 21 the Parlor gave consideration to new bylaws.

Los Angeles' February program, arranged by the good of the order committee, First Vice-president Owen S. Adams chairman, includes: 4th, business, followed by short stories. 11th, musical program arranged by Organist Roger Johnson. 18th, initiation and refreshments. 25th, special entertainment arranged by Anthony Pierce.

STATUE READY FOR PRESENTATION.

Californiana Parlor No. 247 N.D.G.W. is looking forward with eagerness to the months of February and March. During those days thrilling and happy times are in store. Mrs. Ora M. Evans, chairman of the Felipe de Neve statue committee, announces the heroic bronze statue of the founder of Los Angeles has been completed.

It is planned to present the statue to the city during the visit of Grand President Evelyn Carlson, who will be in the south during February and March. She will make her official visit to Californiana March 8. Miss Marion Parks is making a research to find a suitable historical date for presenting the statue, which will occupy the center of the Plaza, the scene of the founding ceremonies. The Grand President is delighted that Californiana will reach the goal for which its members have been striving the past two years. President Gertrude Tuttle hopes to have a large class of candidates for initiation at the time of Mrs. Carlson's visit.

EXCLUSION TAMPERING OPPOSED.

The N.S.G.W. and N.D.G.W. Interparlor Committee January 22 adopted resolutions opposing a bill in the Federal Congress that proposes to exempt the alien husbands of American women from the immigration quota, and directing Chairman Burrel D. Neighbors and Secretary Fred J. Burmester to address a letter to United States Senator Hiram W. Johnson, affiliated with Sunset Parlor No. 26 N.S.G.W. (Sacramento), commending him for the course he is pursuing in the Congress.

Mrs. Mary Noerenberg is chairman of a committee to arrange for a Saint Patrick ball to be given under the auspices of the Interparlor Committee March 17. A committee was also named to arrange for the joint observance of Memorial Day by the local Parlors of Native Sons and Daughters.

COMING, LEAP YEAR BALL.

Glendale—Officers of Verdugo Parlor No. 240 N.D.G.W. were installed January 26 by District

Deputy Ruth Ruiz, Betty Sanders becoming president. District Deputy Hazel Hansen of Verdugo was chairman of the evening, and members of Glendale Parlor No. 264 N.S.G.W. acted as ushers. Grand Trustee Florence Dodson-Schoneman and Past Grand President Grace S. Stoermer were among the many visitors. Entertainment was furnished by Roger Johnson (Los Angeles N.S.), the Goldsbrough sisters, Harry Highsmith, Dave Snell, Bruce Weyman, Misses Zeffie Tilbury and Rambeau, and Mms. Bruce Weyman and Edith Dobson. The Parlor presented an emblematic ring to Past President Rose Bartel, and flowers were presented Past President Kathryn Burke and the grand officers.

Eighteen of the officers and members of Verdugo visited the "baby" Parlor, Ontario No. 251, January 21, and a large delegation went to San Bernardino January 27 to assist in the installation of Lugonia No. 241's officers. Grand President Evelyn I. Carlson will pay her official visit to Verdugo March 8, when a large class of candidates will be initiated.

Verdugo and Glendale No. 264 N.S.G.W. will sponsor a leap year ball the latter part of February. All Parlors will, in due time, be advised by letter of the exact date.

THIMBLE CLUB GREAT ASSET.

San Pedro—Officers of Rudecinda Parlor No. 230 N.D.G.W. were installed by District Deputy Clara Fay January 15, Margaret Kreider becoming president. The hall and tables were beautifully decorated by Carrie Northway, Juanita Brook and Louise Fontes, and refreshments were served by Elizabeth Jorgensen, Mary Doyle and Alice Cottet.

In appreciation for services rendered, the Parlor presented an emblematic ring to Tennie Padilla, retiring president. Claudia Perez, Dorothy Markey and Carrie Northway were recipients of gifts of appreciation, also. The Florencita thimble club is a great asset to the Parlor, having added over $100 to the savings account the past six months.

PERSONAL PARAGRAPHS.

Lee E. Irwin (Los Angeles N.S.) was a recent visitor to San Francisco.

Frank M. Hauser (Ramona N.S.) was a visitor last month to Ogden, Utah.

Mrs. Harriet W. Martin (Los Angeles N.D.) is visiting in Beaumont, her former home.

Mrs. Lilian Carey (Los Angeles N.D.) left January 2 for a three months' tour of Europe.

Monroe Goldstein (Santa Monica Bay N.S.) is temporarily residing in Birmingham, Alabama.

Miss Elsie Hunter (Los Angeles N.D.) was wedded January 1 to Frank Albert Ruiz (Ramona N.S.).

Orva Curtis of Salt Lake City will become the bride of Ernest R. Orfila (Ramona N.S.) February 6.

James O. Cashin (Ramona N.S.), now residing in San Francisco, paid a visit to his old haunts last month.

Dr. William R. Molony (Ramona N.S.) has been elected president of the Los Angeles County Medical Association.

Edward E. Baldwin (Sepulveda N.S.) of San Pedro visited with relatives in Santa Rosa, Sonoma County, last month.

Mrs. Tillie Shearer, mother of Frank D. Shearer (Ramona N.S.), celebrated her eighty-third birthday anniversary last month. She crossed the plains to California in 1852.

Chandos E. Bush (Ramona N.S.) was honor-guest at a banquet-dance January 10, the occasion being his birthday anniversary. It was arranged by Mr. and Mrs. Walter E. Baskerville, Mr. and Mrs. Clarence E. Noerenberg, Mr. and Mrs. Edward R. Taber and Leon J. Leonard.

THE DEATH RECORD.

Frederick S. Hughes, affiliated with Ramona Parlor No. 109 N.S.G.W., died recently. He was born at San Francisco, March 29, 1867.

A. F. Soto, brother of Lorenzo F. Soto (Ramona N.S.), died recently at Concord, Contra Costa County.

Gordon C. Parkhurst, charter member of Santa Monica Bay Parlor No. 267 N.S.G.W., died December 27 at Venice. He was born at Los Angeles, November 9, 1893.

Mrs. Addie E. Appling, wife of Bert C. Appling (Ramona N.S.), passed away January 4.

Mrs. Annie B. Eisen, mother of Percy A. Eisen (Ramona N.S.), passed away January 15.

Mrs. Edna A. Romero, affiliated with Santa Monica Bay Parlor No. 245 N.D.G.W., passed away at Santa Monica January 18, survived by a husband, Phil P. Romero (Santa Monica Bay N.S.).

GRIZZLY GROWLS

(Continued from Page 3)

cases such as the one instanced have just as much chance of saving their holdings as a snowball does of surviving in the lower regions. The law permitting the creation of such districts should be abolished! All the regulations that can possibly be designed to prevent its abuse will not lessen its evils.

Incidentally, is not this law, as generally applied, class legislation and therefore unconstitutional? Why should a few propertyowners in a specified district bear the expense of providing roadways, street lights, etc., for the accommodation of the general public? The state does not create special-assessment districts to improve highways, so why should municipalities create them to improve streets? Propertyowners should, for their own good, provide the means to secure a decision from the United States Supreme Court.

Titled "Economic Oppression," the following—to which we add AMEN!—appeared editorially in the Livingston, Merced County, "Chronicle" of recent date:

"The Dos Palos 'Star' caustically criticises the public record of Senator Hiram W. Johnson as one of 'being against' things, never for things. Well, there is no better way of being for something constructive than to be against things that are destructive. Johnson has been against things that were destructive of human rights. Unfortunately

JOHN SWETT

(Continued from Page 2)

ipal of the Denman grammar school; from 1876 to 1889, principal of the Girls' high school and ormal class; and from 1892 to 1896 superintendent of schools. Following his term as city uperintendent, he did not seek re-election, but etired to his farm in the Alhambra Valley of ontra Costa County. During his active career e wrote some five textbooks, the outstanding f which are "Methods of Teaching" and "School locution." After his retirement he wrote a history of his career in California, titled "Public ducation in California," and also did research ork on the history of New England education. n retirement, he also served on the Contra Costa ounty Board of Education, writing a course of tudy for the schools of that county, and as a rustee of the State Normal School at San Francisco.

As a farmer in retirement, John Swett showed uch of the training of his early youth. He managed his farm to advantage. Hill Girt, as it was alled, was a 185-acre fruit orchard located in the lhambra Valley, near Martinez. He was assisted y his eldest son, Frank. To crown his great areer came the high privilege in 1911 of assisting in the dedication of a school in San Francisco amed in his honor. This was one of his last ublic appearances, and although past eighty he ade an address. In the spring of 1913 the soul f John Swett was called to his Creator, being at e time in the eighty-fourth year of his earthly ilgrimage.

PIONEER NATIVES

(Continued from Page 12)

r, born at Sacramento City in 1852, died December 25.

Folsom (Sacramento County)—Mrs. Helen omes, born in Alameda County in 1856, passed way December 25 survived by four children.

San Jose (Santa Clara County)—Henry Hoover, born here in 1846, died December 27 survived by a daughter. He was a son of Wesley nd Elizabeth (Young) Hoover, California Pioneers of 1846.

Sonora (Tuolumne County)—Andrew J. Shine, orn in this county in 1856, died December 28 urvived by three children.

Selma (Fresno County)—Mrs. Margaret Alexander-Mulligan, born in Sonoma County in 1847, assed away December 30 survived by eight hildren. Her parents, Cyrus and Ruphena (Luerne) Alexander, were, it is said, wedded by aptain John Sutter at Sutter Fort, December 0, 1844.

Visalia (Tulare County)—Henry Calcote, born this county in 1859, died December 31 survived by a wife and four children.

San Francisco—Henrie Fillmore Morton, born San Mateo County in 1856, died December 31 urvived by six children. He was affiliated with lcalde Parlor No. 154 N.S.G.W.

Berkeley (Alameda County)—Hattie Hickan, born in California in 1858, passed away anuary 4.

Sacramento City—Mrs. Susie Cecil, born in anta Clara County in 1856, passed away January 5 survived by a daughter.

San Francisco—William H. Thornley, born Sonoma County in 1856, died January 5 survived by a wife and a son. He was affiliated ith San Francisco Parlor No. 49 N.S.G.W.

Alameda City—Frank Otis, born at San Francisco in 1852, died January 7 survived by a wife nd two sons. He was formerly mayor of Alameda.

Sacramento City—Mrs. Marion Silva, born in acramento County in 1856, passed away January 7 survived by a husband.

San Francisco—Mrs. Jennie Juanita Gonzales-astro, born in Monterey County in 1834, passed way January 8 survived by thirteen children.

Red Bluff (Tehama County)—James Raglan, orn in Shasta County in 1855, died January 9.

Oakland (Alameda County) — Mrs. Belle eefe-Moorshead, born in Tuolumne County in 853, passed away January 9 survived by a aughter.

Palms (Los Angeles County)—John J. Chapan, born in this county in 1856, died January survived by three children, among them rank J. Chapman (Ramona Parlor No. 109 .S.G.W.). His father, Joseph Chapman, is said have been the first American to settle in the cinity of Los Angeles.

Alleghany (Sierra County)—Mrs. Mary Hawns, born at San Francisco in 1856, passed away nuary 11 survived by four children.

Marysville (Yuba County)—F. S. Labadie, born in this county in 1859, died January 12 survived by a wife.

Sacramento City—Mrs. Isabel Miller, born at San Francisco in 1854, passed away January 13 survived by a son.

Placerville (El Dorado County)—Mrs. Alice Pearson, born in this county in 1859, passed away January 18 survived by three children. During the Civil War, she was the "water angel" of Company G, Seventh California Infantry, of which her father, John Balander, was a member.

In Memoriam

JAMES J. SMITH.

Whereas, It has pleased Almighty God to call to his eternal rest our late brother, J. J. Smith; and whereas, Brother Smith was a true and loyal Native Son, a patriotic citizen and a loving husband and father; therefore, be it

Resolved, That Mount Tamalpais Parlor No. 64 N.S.G.W. extends its deepest sympathy to his widow and family in their bereavement; further be it resolved, that a copy of these resolutions be spread upon the minutes of the Parlor, that a copy be sent to the family of our late brother, also a copy to The Grizzly Bear Magazine for publication; also, that the charter of the Parlor be draped for a period of thirty days and that the Parlor stand in silence in respect to his memory.

Respectfully submitted,
C. F. REINDOLLAR,
M. W. LABEL,
LOUIS J. PETER,
Committee on Resolutions.

San Rafael, January 4, 1932.

MARY REYNOLDS.

To the Officers and Members of Plumas Pioneer Parlor No. 219 Native Daughters of the Golden West: Your committee appointed to draft resolutions expressing the sentiments and deep-felt sympathy of the members of our Parlor on the death of Sister Mary Reynolds, respectfully submit the following:

Whereas, It has pleased our Heavenly Father to take from our midst our beloved sister, Mary Reynolds, and to summon her to realms of higher life; and whereas, in her passing our Parlor has lost a most highly esteemed sister, and the community in which she lived a respected and loved citizen; therefore, be it

Resolved, That Plumas Pioneer Parlor extend sincere sympathy to her husband and bereaved relatives; and further be it resolved, that a copy of these resolutions be sent to the family of our sister, that a copy be sent to The Grizzly Bear Magazine for publication, and that a copy be spread upon the minutes of the Parlor.

RHODA THOMPSON,
BERTHA MONCUR,
Committee.

Quincy, January 5, 1932.

ANNA CATHERINE ADAMS.

To the Officers and Members of Eltapome Parlor No. 55 N.D.G.W.—We, your committee appointed to draft resolutions of respect to the memory of our departed sister, Anna Catherine Adams, respectfully submit the following:

Whereas, One of our beloved members, Sister Anna Catherine Adams, has answered the call of our Heavenly Father, with deepest sorrow we bow in humble prayer, realizing our loss is her heavenly gain. While we pay loving tribute to her memory, we are not unmindful of the sympathy we owe her loved ones. Therefore, be it

Resolved, That we extend to her bereaved family, in the loss of a devoted and loving mother, our sincere sympathy; also, that a copy of these resolutions be recorded in the minutes of this Parlor, a copy be sent to the family of our deceased sister, and also to The Grizzly Bear Magazine for publication.

HONORA B. FIELDS,
AGNES H. JUNKANS,
ANNIE W. RYAN,
Committee.

Weaverville, January 8, 1932.

FLORENCE NIGHTINGALE TRUE.

To the Officers and Members of Butte County Association No. 5 Past Presidents of Native Daughters of the Golden West—We, your committee appointed to draft resolutions of respect to the memory of our departed sister, Florence Nightingale True, beg to submit the following:

Whereas, Our beloved sister, Florence Nightingale True, has been called to her heavenly home and this Association has lost an esteemed charter member, the community one of its pioneer citizens, and Annie K. Bidwell Parlor No. 168 N.D.G.W. its organizer; therefore, be it

Resolved, That our charter be draped in her memory, and that this tribute of love be spread upon the minutes of our Association.

ALTA B. BALDWIN,
ALTA D. HENGY,
MAGGIE D. BOWERS.

Oroville, January 8, 1932.

HARRIET HICKMAN.

To the Officers and Members of Piedmont Parlor No. 87 N.D.G.W.—We, your committee appointed to draft resolutions of respect to the memory of our late sister, Harriet Hickman, respectfully submit the following:

Whereas, The Angel of Death has again entered our Parlor and taken from our midst our beloved sister, Harriet Hickman, we deeply feel the loss of her whose kind and genial manner won the love and esteem of all who knew her, but with us there remains the memory of her devotion to our Order, her pride in its achievements and her intense loyalty to its ideals, and we realize the still greater loss of those who were nearest and dearest to her; therefore, be it,

Resolved, That we, the members of Piedmont Parlor No. 87 N.D.G.W., extend our deepest sympathy to her bereaved family and devoted friends; and be it further resolved, that our charter be draped in mourning, that these resolutions be spread upon the minutes of the Parlor, and that a copy be sent to The Grizzly Bear for publication.

EDNA M. HEALEY,
PATRICIA REARDON,
ELLEN MULLER,
Committee.

Oakland, January 14, 1932.

IRENE CASSELMAN.

To the Officers and Members of El Pescadero Parlor No. 82 N.D.G.W.—We, your committee on resolutions, report the following:

Whereas, It has pleased our Heavenly Father to take to our heavenly home our beloved sister and friend, Irene Casselman; and whereas, in view of the loss we have sustained and of the greater loss sustained by those who are nearest and dearest to her, be it

Resolved, That while we bow in humble submission to His will, we are mindful of the vacant chair in our Parlor, and feel that our members are honored to have been associated with one so universally respected; be it further resolved, that we extend our heartfelt sympathy to the bereaved family and commend them for consolation to Him who doeth all things well.

"Let us think of her as a rose that climbs the garden wall and blossoms on the other side." Be it also resolved, that a copy of this resolution be spread upon the minutes of our Parlor, that a copy be sent to The Grizzly Bear Magazine, and that a copy be sent to the family of the departed.

Submitted in P.D.F.A.,
BESSIE JACKSON,
BERTHA McGEE,
Committee.

Tracy, January 15, 1932.

GRACE STANDLEE RICHARDSON.

To the Officers and Members of Californiana Parlor No. 247 N.D.G.W.—We, your committee appointed to draft resolutions of respect to the memory of our late sister, Grace Standlee Richardson, do respectfully submit the following:

Our golden chain of fraternity has been severed, the Angel of Death has entered the portals of our Order and summoned to eternal rest our beloved sister, leaving us to mourn her absence from our midst whose memory we will cherish.

"God is merciful and just!
And so by faith's correcting sight
We bow before His will, and trust
Howe'er they seem, He doeth all things right."

For our sister, the trials, the sorrows and the disappointments that must come in every life, however sheltered, are ended, and she peacefully sleeps. Reverently then would we say, "Thy will be done."

Resolved, That we, the members of Californiana Parlor No. 247 N.D.G.W., extend our sincere sympathy to the sorrowing family; be it further resolved, that a copy of these resolutions be spread upon the minutes of the Parlor, that a copy be forwarded to the family of our deceased sister, and that a copy be sent to The Grizzly Bear Magazine for publication; and be it further resolved, that the Parlor charter be draped in mourning for a period of thirty days.

MILDRED M. DUFFY,
MARGARET ANTHONEY,
OLIVE LOPEZ,
Committee.

Los Angeles, January 16, 1932.

N.D.G.W. OFFICIAL DEATH LIST.

Giving the name, the date of death, and the Subordinate Parlor affiliation of all deceased members as reported to Grand Secretary Sallie R. Thaler from December 18 to January 21:

Eagen, Sarah H.; December 12, 1931; Stirling No. 146.

Sousa, Rebecca; December 8, 1931; Aleli No. 102.

Hunter, Bertha; October 19, 1931; Aleli No. 102.

Stafford, Mary E.; December 6, 1931; Oneonta No. 71.

Philson, Mary G.; December 13, 1931; Joaquin No. 5.

Casselman, Irene M.; December 18, 1931; El Pescadero No. 82.

Minahan, Oraville; December 31, 1931; San Jose No. 81.

Carmichael, Elizabeth; November 24, 1931; Gold of Ophir No. 190.

Grade, Amelia M.; January 3, 1932; Joaquin No. 5.

Eachus, Virginia H.; December 28, 1931; South Butte No. 226.

Manning, Lena P.; January 9, 1932; Castro No. 178.

Mancebo, Julia; December 16, 1931; Sea Point No. 196.

Jones, Miriam; December 31, 1931; Califia No. 22.

Coulter, Minnie; January 9, 1932; Alta No. 3.

"Paradise is here, or nowhere; you must take your joy with you or you will never find it."

MY MESSAGE

To All Native Born Californians

I, DR. FRANK I. GONZALEZ, GRAND PRESIDENT OF THE ORDER OF NATIVE SONS OF THE GOLDEN WEST, DO HEREBY APPEAL TO ALL NATIVE BORN CALIFORNIANS OF THE WHITE MALE RACE BORN WITHIN THE STATE OF CALIFORNIA, OF THE AGE OF EIGHTEEN YEARS AND UPWARD, OF GOOD HEALTH AND CHARACTER, AND WHO BELIEVE IN THE EXISTENCE OF A SUPREME BEING, TO JOIN OUR FRATERNITY AND THEREBY ASSIST IN THE AIMS AND PURPOSES OF THE ORGANIZATION:

To arouse Loyalty and Patriotism for State and for Nation.

To elevate and improve the Manhood upon which the destiny of our country depends.

To encourage interest in all matters and measures relating to the material upbuilding of the State of California.

To assist in the development of the wonderful natural resources of California.

To protect the forests, conserve the waters, improve the rivers and the harbors, and beautify the towns and the cities.

To collect, make known and preserve the romantic history of California.

To restore and preserve all the historic landmarks of the State.

To provide homes for California's homeless children, regardless of race, creed or color.

To keep this State a paradise for the American Citizen by thwarting the organized efforts of all undesirable peoples to control its destiny.

THE ORDER OF NATIVE SONS OF THE GOLDEN WEST IS THE ONLY FRATERNITY IN EXISTENCE WHOSE MEMBERSHIP IS MADE UP EXCLUSIVELY OF WHITE NATIVE BORN AMERICANS.

. . . Builded upon the Foundation Stones of Friendship, Loyalty, Charity

IT PRESENTS TO THE NATIVE BORN CALIFORNIAN THE MOST PRODUCTIVE FIELD IN WHICH TO SOW HIS ENERGIES, AND IF HE BE A FAITHFUL CULTIVATOR AND DESIRES TO TAKE ADVANTAGE OF THE OPPORTUNITY AFFORDED HIM, HE WILL REAP A RICH HARVEST IN THE KNOWLEDGE THAT HE HAS BEEN FAITHFUL TO CALIFORNIA AND DILIGENT IN PROTECTING ITS WELFARE.

DR. FRANK I. GONZALEZ,
GRAND PRESIDENT N.S.G.W.

The undersigned, having formed a favorable opinion of the Order of Native Sons of the Golden West, desires additional information.

Name ....

Address ....

City or Town ....

For further information sign the accompanying blank and mail to

GRAND SECRETARY N.S.G.W.,
302 Native Sons Bldg.,
414 Mason St.,
SAN FRANCISCO, California

Grizzly Bear

MARCH — THE ONLY OFFICIAL PUBLICATION OF THE NATIVE SONS AND DAUGHTERS OF THE GOLDEN WEST — 1932

Featuring

GENERAL NEWS OF INTEREST CONCERNING ALL CALIFORNIA, and ORDERS NATIVE SONS and NATIVE DAUGHTERS

Price: 15 Cents

BOOK REVIEWS

(CLARENCE M. HUNT.)

"LELAND STANFORD."

By George T. Clark; Stanford University Press, Publisher, Stanford University, California; Price, $4.

This book treats of the life and the accomplishments of Leland Stanford, deceased, governor of California during the Civil War, one of the builders of the Central Pacific railroad, and founder of Stanford University in Santa Clara County. It most interestingly presents the life-story of a notable California figure, and in the relating considerable previously unpublished material, dealing with early-day politics, is entwined.

Stanford, born in New York State in 1824, came to California via Nicaragua, arriving at San Francisco aboard the "Independence" July 12, 1852. For three years he operated stores in El Dorado and Placer Counties, selling miners' supplies. In 1855 he went to Sacramento City, his home for many years thereafter, and engaged in general merchandising.

Stanford's first public office in California was as justice of the peace, 1853-4, in the then-thriving mining town of Michigan Bluff, Placer County. In 1861 he was elected governor of the state for a two-year term, 1862-63, and would not consent to be a candidate for re-election. Twice, in 1885 and 1891, he was selected by the State Legislature to represent California in the United States Senate, and he served in that capacity from March 4, 1885, until his death at Palo Alto, June 20, 1893.

Stanford was prominent in the development of California and the West, being one of the organizers at Sacramento City, in 1860, of a company to build a much-needed transcontinental railroad. June 28, 1861, the certificate of incorporation of that company, the Central Pacific Railroad Company of California, was filed with the secretary of state. In 1862 the Federal Government extended aid to the project, actual construction work was begun at Sacramento City, January 8, 1863, and the last spike was driven at Promintory, Utah, May 10, 1869.

In 1884, while traveling abroad, Stanford's only child, Leland Stanford Jr., died at Florence, Italy. In memory of his son, he decided to devote his vast wealth, accumulated in California, to the building and the maintenance of a university, and so, due to his great generosity, Stanford University was founded.

"The crucial test of the character of a rich man is in the use he makes of his wealth," says the author, George T. Clark, director emeritus Stanford University Library. "He may use it to acquire power or for personal aggrandizement, or he may use it to benefit society. Of his great acquired wealth—created wealth—Leland Stanford came to regard himself as trustee, vested with the responsibility of wisely administering it in the interests of society. He could conceive of no higher use for it than of devoting it to an educational purpose and to that end he founded a University which should 'aim to fit men to realize the possibilities of humanity,' in order that the graduates might 'in a measure become missionaries to spread correct ideas of civilization.' That University stands as an enduring monument to the largeness of heart and creative instinct of its Founder, and to his good will toward all mankind."

The book "Leland Stanford" has a bibliography, and is well illustrated. An authentic record of one of the West's noted empire builders, it will be given a hearty welcome by all students and lovers of Californiana.

"FUR TRADE AND EMPIRE."

By Frederick Merk; Harvard University Press, Publisher, Cambridge, Massachusetts.

This volume features the 1824-25 journal of George Simpson, governor of the Hudson's Bay Company territories in America, and as such, director of the economic life of the greater part of what is now the Dominion of Canada and the Pacific Northwest of the United States. It is of varied interest, offering a summary of the industry of half a continent, and containing material for business history as well as for the student of statecraft.

Simpson was born in Scotland, in 1792, and entered the business world as a London clerk in 1809. In 1821 he was a man with a future rather than a past. By 1826 he was governor-in-chief of all the Hudson's Bay Company territories in America. "The Oregon Country, which is the central theme of the document, was in 1824-25 a region in dispute," says the introduc-

GRIZZLY GROWLS

(CLARENCE M. HUNT.)

DISHONESTY, BORN OF DOLLAR-LUST among the few, drove prosperity from this nation and in slipped depression! The economic ills which afflict the whole country are but the offsprings of that dishonesty! Dishonesty rules, and the nation decays!

Dishonesty—which includes deceit, misrepresentation, and any and every act that lacks honesty,—secured a firm foothold in these United States during the world war and then, fostered and encouraged, and in numerous instances practiced, by national leaders in political, business, professional and social life, grew to monstrous proportions. It penetrated every section of the country, and every fibre of the economic system. A national breakdown had, of necessity, to result, for the fiddler always exacts the toll. Now, we are paying for the reign of dishonesty,—the blackest era in the history of this nation—and what a price!

Startling facts revealed in the "Congressional Record" furnish ample substantiation for the statement that international bankers, nationally-known bond dealers and other financially high-powered, but morally low-geared, "leading" citizens have practiced dishonesty so thoroughly and unceasingly that on them should be visited the hatred of the masses, for their acts of dishonesty are mainly responsible for the depression and its accompanying misery. They are openly charged with fleecing the investing public out of billions of dollars, and they are credited with causing most of the small-bank failures. They have not denied the charges, apparently for the reason that they cannot do so successfully.

Is it not queer, then, that so-called depression-relief legislation enacted by the Federal Congress, at the instigation of the national administration, should be so designed as to benefit, first and directly, the identical big interests that, through dishonesty, brought on the depression? A dole, to the extent of two billions of The People's money, has been provided for them, through the Reconstruction Finance Corporation, but the little fellows, a vast majority of whom are at least honest, have been given no direct consideration.

Having launched the Reconstruction Finance Corporation, a campaign was inaugurated to coax out of hiding an estimated $1,300,000,000 supposed to be stored away by the common people. The appeal has merit, but lacks persuasion, in that there is no guarantee that this vast sum, also, will not be hooked by the dishonest favored few. When honesty succeeds dishonesty in the financial-saddle, this money will return to circulation. Until then, its owners are justified in keeping it in their possession.

"What you do speaks so loudly that I cannot hear your words," wrote Emerson. Moratoriums, doles, credit expansions, etc., will not cure the nation's ills. The sainted worshipers of the almighty dollar must be dethroned; they must be cast out of the political and the business life of this country! Honesty must triumph, if the nation is to survive!

The Tehama County Ministerial Association recently adopted this resolution, to be forwarded to the Federal Council of Churches of Christ in America:

"We deplore the indifference and resultant inactivity of the high offices of the Christian Church regarding the Sino-Japanese War. Has the Christian Church no moral indignation? We urge the merciful and most effective method of world boycott against Japan and not military aggression. Above all else the United States of America cannot, under any consideration, agree to the partition of China, and therefore, stands unalterably opposed to any such move. We also condemn the theory and practice of extraterritoriality."

The Federal Council will not be influenced in the least by the resolution, for the manipulators of that organization are pro-Jap through and through. The suggestion of a world boycott against the Japs is an excellent one, just the same, and should be put into effect.

The State Prison Board did a good job when it fixed the term in prison for Gilbert H. Beesemeyer of Los Angeles, who deliberately fleeced hundreds of investors out of millions of dollars, at forty years.

There are other "high-financers" of the Angel City still at large who should also be sojourning at San Quentin or Folsom. They wrecked, for their own financial gain, several institutions into which innocent people poured millions of dollars. They, however, were able to keep the eyes of Justice effectively blindfolded! So, instead of being where they justly belong, they are in the top-crust of the social-pie.

All political barometers indicate Governor James Rolph will, at an early date, call an extra session of the California State Legislature.

Repeal of the Acquisition and Improvement (Mattoon) Act of 1925, which authorizes the creation of special-assessment districts, should be the first thing done at the session. The law is wide open to abuse, and of course the tricksters have taken full advantage of it. As a result, numerous propertyowners have been taxed to their financial ruin. There are other special-assessment laws, too, and all of them should be repealed.

In the meantime, propertyowners in special-assessment districts created for the purpose of improving streets and installing street-lighting systems should unite and take their tax-burden troubles to the courts—the United States Supreme Court, if necessary. There is excellent reason to believe all such improvements, and the tax arising therefrom, would be invalidated on a plea of class legislation. And it certainly is class legislation to compel a few citizens of a

(Continued on Page 23)

MOUNT DIABLO

(JAMES NOBLE HATCH.)

Old Mount Diablo grim and still
Who gave thee that unholy name?
Who would thy merits thus defame
That ne'er hath done us any ill?
O sent'nel grim that hideth there
A guardian of the southern gate
Should not thy name reiterate
Some noble chief's immortal fame?
And yet how little needst thou care
What name mere man may formulate?

As herald of approaching day
Thy brow in crimson splendor shown,
And by thee is the midday known
When o'er thy crest the sun gives stay.
And as the lengthening shadows grow
And day is drawing to a close
The last retreating beam that shows
Rests on thy pinnacle alone,
And then the lingering afterglow
Outlines thy form in calm repose.

And when in through the Golden Gate
The fog comes rolling up the bay
And wraps the foothills all in gray
And all the plains obliterate,
Yet high above this silent sea
Thy noble crest shows still more bright,
Resplendent in the mellow light
That gleams athwart the closing day;
And when deep darkness covers thee
We feel thy presence in the night.

And when the storm-clouds dark as doom
For days have hung their curtains down,
And from the depths with sombre frown
The landscape peers from out the gloom,
Then comes a rift across the skies
And there again thy form appears
As constant as the countless years
That have proclaimed thy fair renown
And therewithal good hopes arise
And Nature dries away her tears.

Old Mount Diablo ages old
That changeth not whate'er betide,
Nor storm nor night can ever hide
Thy pictured presence wreathed in gold,
And when dark gloom beclouds the day
Or taunting shadows fill the night,
The vision of thy sunlight height
Which ever in the thoughts abide,
Chase all the truant fears away
And dire forebodings put to flight.

(This contribution to The Grizzly Bear is from James Noble Hatch of Pasadena, affiliated with Ramona Parlor No. 109 N.S.G.W.—Editor.)

PRESENTATION OF MANY YEARS AGO

HERE IS A MOST INTERESTING article from "The Weekly Alta California" (San Francisco) of March 11, 1876. It was mailed January 5 to The Grizzly Bear by Mrs. Laura J. Frakes-Toman of Nice, Lake County, former Grand Secretary of the Order of Native Daughters of the Golden West. In an accompanying letter, Mrs. Toman says: "Looking through my scrapbook, I came across the enclosed article. I think it would be great to publish it now." The article follows, exactly as originally published:

N.S.G.W.

Meeting of the Native Sons of the Golden West—Presentation of an Elegant Bible.

The Native Sons had a well-attended meeting, notwithstanding the disagreeable weather. Several candidates for membership were elected, and will be initiated next Thursday evening. The Society will join in the procession on the Fourth of July, and have a grand ball in the evening. The Committee has already secured Union Hall for the occasion.

PRESENTATION.

It being announced that a presentation was about to take place, General Winn came into the room and laid upon the altar a large Bible, saying: "Mr. President: I have the honor of representing Messrs. A. L. Bancroft & Co. in presenting to the Society this elegant copy of the Holy Scriptures. In the Old Testament we find the teachings of the Jews, who believe that a Savior will come. In the New Testament we find the teachings of Christians, who believe that the Savior has come. The doctrines of both embrace the moral principle, 'Do unto others as you would have others do unto you.' As your faith is, so you shall be saved.

"Our laws are based upon the Bible; in living up to its teachings we are sure to live in harmonious brotherhood, whether Jew or Christian. In this age of the world every Association of Americans should have a copy of the Scriptures resting upon their altar, to remind the members of their respective duties to God and man. The Bible inspires religious veneration, and directs our attention to things of a Heavenly nature.

"In time, this sacred Book will become a valued relic of this institution, and a memento of the house of Bancroft. In 1856 they commenced business in this city; in 1870 they built their magnificent storehouse on Market Street. There they carry on printing, lithography and engraving. They have a large blank book manufactory and music department; the whole making up one of the largest and most complete publishing establishments in the United States; they employ more than one hundred hands; their skill and energy command our admiration, and furnish an example for all young men to follow.

"As time rolls on we and our successors will respect the teachings of the Bible and learn to love and assist each other. Now, in the name of A. L. Bancroft & Co., I take great pleasure in presenting this splendid Bible to the Native Sons of the Golden West."

Jasper Fishbourne, President, replied by saying: "Brother Winn, we take great pleasure in accepting this sacred work of literature—the Holy Bible. We feel proud of this grand and sacred token of esteem, presented by one of the oldest and largest publishing houses on the Pacific Coast. It shows that we are not only known among ourselves, but appreciated by the public. They would judge us harshly if they did not think us a worthy association of young men. So let us stand as firm as the Rock of Ages, and show to the world what we are and what we will be in future. In conclusion allow me, Brother Winn, to return through you our sincere thanks to Messrs. A. L. Bancroft & Co., and assure them of our gratitude."

The following preamble and resolutions were then unanimously adopted: "Whereas, A. L. Bancroft & Co. have presented to this Society an elegant Bible; therefore Resolved, That we gratefully accept the Holy Book as appropriate to our organization, and will cherish it as a sacred memento of the forethought and generosity of the house of Bancrofts. Resolved, That we sincerely thank Messrs. A. L. Bancroft & Co. for the sacred and elegant present, and that an engrossed copy of these proceedings be signed by the proper officers and presented by the President. Resolved, That this Bible shall be laid upon our altar at every meeting of the Society, and locked up at the hour of adjournment."

The ceremony being ended, it was received with enthusiastic demonstration of peculiar pleasure. The presentation was a great surprise, as none present knew anything about it, except General Winn and the President. Next Sunday at two o'clock their parliamentary school will meet at Anthony's Hall; the ball committee will meet there a half hour before.

The Bible contains all the latest improvements, with a synopsis of each book, and elegantly engraved illustrations; the binding is magnificent. On the outside of it there is an inscription in large gold letters: "A. L. Bancroft & Co. to the Native Sons of the Golden West, San Francisco, March 1st, 1876."

---

with any of the Missions you may tell them we will undertake to import any article they may wish from England." (*The Bonaventura River is the present Sacramento. For years the name was applied in maps of North America to a mythical river of the West which was supposed to flow directly from the interior to the Pacific.)

"Fur Trade and Empire" is one of the Harvard historical studies published under the direction of the department of history from the income of The Henry Warren Torrey Fund. It is edited by Frederick Merk, associate professor of history in Harvard University, who also provides an enlightening introduction.

STATUE OF LOS ANGELES' FOUNDER TO BE PRESENTED CITY BY NATIVE DAUGHTERS

WHILE THE NAME OF FELIPE DE Neve still echoes from the recent celebration in honor of the one hundred and fiftieth anniversary of the founding of the City of Los Angeles, a deferred honor will climax the event when, March 12, a group of California's Native Daughters will unveil and present to the modern metropolis a splendid bronze statue of the man to whom Los Angeles owes its beginning.

For more than two years, Californiana Parlor No. 247 N.D.G.W. has anticipated the coming ceremony as the fulfillment of an idea inspired by love for the city and reverence for the spiritual manner of its founding. Many vicissitudes have attended the work of carrying out the project, which was first suggested by Mrs. Harry Leigh Bentley and Miss Eliza Quinn, at one time members of Californiana's history and landmarks committee.

While enthusiastic and whole-hearted support of the movement has been given by Californiana's members in general, much credit for the successful termination of the project is due to the fidelity, unflagging energy and gentle diplomacy of Mrs. Amos Otis Evans, general chairman of the Felipe de Neve statue project. Many discouraging obstacles have been surmounted, and the quest for a sculptor of renown was most fittingly ended in the selection of Henry Lion, a member of Ramona Parlor No. 109 N.S.G.W. His work has won the recognition of foremost critics, and his figure of De Neve will add enduring luster to his fame.

The site chosen for the placement of the figure is significantly commemorative, being the center of the fountain in the Plaza, at the exact spot where the living De Neve pierced the earth with his sword, at the beginning of the ceremonies attending the city's founding.

Honored by the presence of Grand President Evelyn I. Carlson, the final act in the little drama of Californiana's reverential love for the city and its spiritually minded founder, will begin promptly at 4 o'clock in the afternoon of

MRS. GERTRUDE JOUGHIN TUTTLE.
President Californiana N.D.G.W.

Saturday, March 12. The following program will add to the beauty and the dignity of the ceremony:

The playing of "America," by the R.O.T.C. military band. Chief Lone Star will sound his silver trumpet, Nell Lockwood Josephs answering with Indian calls. A portrayal of Don Felipe de Neve, in costume, reading his original founding proclamation. Unveiling of the statue, with Miss Marion Parks briefly outlining historical highlights of events under the different governments; Mrs. Arthur Wright unfurling the Spanish flag, Mrs. Ysabel del Valle Cram the flag of Mexico, Miss Mary Emily Foy the California (State) Bear Flag, and Mrs. Amos Otis Evans the Flag of the United States of America. Introduction of the sculptor, Henry Lion. Singing of the "Star Spangled Banner." The presentation of the statue to the city, on behalf of Californiana Parlor, by President Gertrude Joughin Tuttle. Acceptance of the gift by the city through Carl B. Wirsching, president Board Public Works and member Los Angeles Parlor No. 45 N.S.G.W. Confirmation of the acceptance by Mayor John C. Porter. Closing address by Grand President

"DON FELIPE DE NEVE
"Founder El Pueblo de Nuestra Senora la Reina de los Angeles. Erected March 12, 1932, in commemoration of the 150th anniversary, by Californiana Parlor No. 247 Native Daughters of the Golden West."

Evelyn I. Carlson, who will pay tribute to the Native Daughters. At the conclusion of the ceremony, a dinner in honor of the Grand President and other distinguished guests will be given.—B.S.M.

FOUNDER and FOUNDING

(OLIVE LOPEZ.)

"Felipe de Neve was one of the few great men of the Spanish regime in California. Eight of the chain of twenty-one missions had been built when, in February 1777, he assumed the governorship of the eight-year-old province of California. He was serving in that capacity when, September 4, 1781, El Pueblo de Nuestra Senora la Reina de Los Angeles was born, one of the few places in the United States founded with forethought and with religious and civil ceremonies.

"King Carlos III of Spain gave his proclamation that three pueblos were to be founded in California, including San Jose and Los Angeles. After Governor Felipe de Neve had received the official document he set the September date for the founding of Los Angeles, on the site of the Indian village called Yang-na, the quiet and happy home of the natives who, in their blissful ignorance, lived naked in the warm sunshine of California. It is probable that they were in the same happy state two centuries before, when Juan Rodriguez Cabrillo, the Christopher Columbus of California, landed at San Pedro to obtain water and found the Indians enjoying a great rabbit drive. The pueblo of Los Angeles was to differ as much from Yang-na as the modern city of today does from the original Spanish settlement. No trace remains of Yang-na nor of the original pueblo founded by De Neve.

"Spain had adopted the plaza plan of laying out a pueblo long used in European colonies. De Neve planned to bring actual settlers to cultivate the soil, to build up the pueblo, and to afford protection to the government and the missions. So he went to the Mission San Gabriel, arriving the day before the date set for the founding. The nine-mile march from the mission was one of pomp and circumstance. It is now like a glamorous dream to look back to that fateful day, a century and a half ago, when Felipe de Neve, the gobernador, rode at the head of the procession upon his milk-white steed, accompanied by his swarthy troopers, brown-robed Franciscan padres, acolytes, eleven settlers with their families, and other inhabitants interested in the unusual ceremonies.

"A plaza had been laid out, and each of the families given a town lot for a home and a farm outside. The proclamation of King Charles was read, the governor and founder, De Neve, made a speech giving his well-thought-out 'regulations' a volley of musketry was fired and a te-deum was sung. Night fell, and the new-born city, wrapped in swaddling clothes, spent its first night in solitary loneliness.

"The roots of Spain are deep and stubborn. Wherever they were planted in the New World they endured. And although El Pueblo la Reina de Los Angeles lay long sleepy and thriftless in the warm sunshine, awaiting its great day, it held on through the years. At last the chrysalis burst and became the great metropolis of today. Not every city in the world has endured 150 years, but the City of Our Lady Queen of the Angels, is as virile as though its youth had just begun. Its splendid past will be as nothing compared with the tremendous future awaiting it. And all honor is due Felipe de Neve, aristocrat of Spain, wise founder and administrator. This city did not 'just happen;' it was deliberately planned.

"De Neve passed away in 1784, the same year that the benevolent presidente of the missions, Father Junipero Serra, went to his reward. The double blow was a terrible one for the young and hesitating province of California, and no pueblo felt the loss of their guiding hands more than Los Angeles. Corporal Vicente Feliz, who took De Neve's place as 'comisionado,' saved the town in its direful straits, his title having been given him by De Neve before his death, while

MRS. AMOS OTIS EVANS.
Chairman De Neve Statue Committee

still thinking of the future of his favorite pueblo.

"The traditions of our Spanish origin still linger and are fondly cherished. Citizens are awakening to the heritage which is theirs. Tradition was born here. The conquistadores swept through this country and established a region of ideals, color and expansive life and culture even while New England was an untrod wilderness. We had haciendas while they had huts; we had ranchos while they had corn patches; we lived while they existed! Long ere the Pilgrims landed in 1620 on the coast of Massachusetts, the Golden West had a well-established civilization. Culture! The mission fathers taught here while Boston was an unkempt, unlettered village.

"In Olvera street, just opposite the spot where Los Angeles began, stands the ancient Avila house, the headquarters of General Stockton. It tells a thrilling tale of the 'days of the dons' and of the culture and traditions of the city 'without a past.' Los Angeles was in existence before England relinquished control over the colonies; in fact, four years before the Boston tea party. Its site was spoken of by Father

(Continued on Page 23)

THE ROMANCE OF SAN BERNARDINO

Clara M. Barton

(Copyrighted, 1931, by the Author.)

(Continued from February Issue.)

JULY 4 BECAME A MEMORABLE DAY FOR the new inhabitants. Word was sent by the Lugos for all the people in the valley to take an active part in flagraising ceremonies in San Gorgonia Pass. Much excitement ensued. The trip to the pass was not as difficult as had been anticipated. As the procession moved upward, with a flagbearer carrying a handwoven American Flag leading the way, the sight was an impressive one. Men, women and children, some horseback and some walking, followed a padre, the Lugos, and the father of the idea, Dan Sexton. National hymns were sung as the group marched onward.

"Got your place picked out to place this here banner?" asked one of the men of Sexton. "Yep. And it's the highest peak in the pass," replied Dan. It was he who suggested placing some sort of a marker, so those coming by the next caravans would know they were nearing a settled grant of extensive land.

It was noon. The small group were tired, but were still carrying on. "We are here!" cried Sexton. "Let us rest a bit before we have our services." The group relaxed somewhat. Several of the men who had been carrying picks and shovels laid them down beside a stake.

"Hey, Dan, what about this stake?" asked one of the men. "Oh, that," replied Sexton, "is the place I want that flag put." And in a short time the men began to dig a cavity in which to set the staff of the flag.

"How's that?" asked Jose Maria Lugo. Dan looked at the excavation, mopped his brow and said, "Couldn't be better." "How soon do you want to begin the rites?" "Now, if Sexton is ready," answered Lugo.

Dan overheard the question and the answer. Turning to the good padre he said, "Father, will you please offer a prayer of thanksgiving?" "Si, senor," answered the padre, and the group, with bowed heads, listened to the resonant and kind voice of the padre. At the conclusion of his short, but beautiful, prayer a loud "Amen!" came from those about him. All eyes then turned to Dan Sexton. "Dan, will you now take charge of the ceremonies?" asked Jose Vicente Lugo.

"Si, senor." And so, with an impressive ritual, the American Flag was hoisted upon its standard, a verse of "The Star-Spangled Banner" was sung, and hats were thrown into the air. Dan Sexton was very happy, and proud! "This flag will be a guiding hand for those who enter this valley. May God lead them safely into this protected abiding place."

The sun was setting behind the mountain peaks and the berloc little band followed the Lugo brothers, the good padre and Dan Sexton back to their homes, still singing in perfect rhythm.

The sun sank behind a tall mountain peak. Dan Sexton, the padre and the three Lugo brothers stood at attention as they faced the flag, waving in the breeze. "The guiding hand of the rancho," said Jose Maria Lugo slowly, and the sun cast its twilight shadows upon the five straight figures as they gave a final salute to the banner fast fading from view.

EPISODE 5.
MILITARISM.

April 1847 was a red-letter month for the settlers of the Spanish grant. The Lugo brothers were becoming more and more concerned. The invasions of the Indians had been many, and tragic. Lives had been lost, and much that was of value had been destroyed.

Jose Carmen Lugo was holding a conference with his men of the mission district. He was becoming discouraged. "Do any one of you know of any way," he asked, "in which to subdue these warring tribes?" "Send for the Mormon battalion!" suggested one. "Not a bad suggestion. But it will take several days before the infantry could receive our dispatch, and this frontier is suffering terribly from these invasions!"

"Senor, I shall go at once, if you desire it," volunteered one of the men. "Yes, and I shall go with him," chimed in another. "No, let's try and find another way out," replied Lugo.

But before the month had passed, a corps of Mormon dragoons had been notified, was enroute to protect the settlers, and orders were given to Colonel A. J. Smith of the United States Infantry to establish a military post in Cajon Pass.

Near the end of the month Colonel Smith and his aides were firmly established at the entrance to the pass. The Indians became afraid of the White man's activities, but the settlers were feeling more at ease. Their property and lives were now secure for the time being.

By the month of June, of the same year, a beautiful romance began to bloom between one of the corporals and a daugher of Jose Maria Lugo. "But I cannot go with you when you go," protested the senorita, as the soldier pleaded for her consent. "I know, darling, but I am not going to return to my infantry. I am going to stay right here, marry you, and be happy." "But how do I know whether you have a wife somewhere else? I must be very careful, you know!" The senorita looked worried, as she had little faith in soldiers.

The young corporal laughed. "If I had a wife, do you think I would be urging you to marry me and keep telling you how much I love you? Do you think I would be here without her? Oh no, she would be here too, if she had to walk!" "Oh!" and the senorita blushed, and hid her face on his shoulder.

Several days later the colonel received orders to return his dragoon to the San Gabriel district. The soldier-lover had not approached his commander concerning his discharge or his intended plans, though he knew full well the colonel was aware of the reason for his numerous evening visits to the valley. Finally, however, the corporal mustered up his courage, and faced his commander with a serious, but frightened, face.

"Well, what can I do for you, young man?" asked Colonel Smith rather sternly. The boy shifted from one foot to the other, swallowed hard, and stammered, "I-I—well—I want to-to get married. I-I want to ask-for an honorable-discharge from the dragoon. I-I- want to stay here. You-you see, I am in love with one of Jose Maria Lugo's daughters, and I just can't leave here. Anyway, I think that I will make a better husband than I am a soldier!"

The colonel burst out laughing. There were tears in his eyes. He slapped the crude table before him with the open palm of his hand. It was several minutes before he could control himself. "So that's it, is it?" he said, after finally controlling himself. "I've been watching you, young man," he continued, "and I knew full well that there was something more than the country you wanted to look at! If you really love her and want to marry her, why there is no reason why you should not do so. Too, your service with this dragoon has been faithful, and you have discharged your duties well. I see no reason why I cannot make arrangements for your honorable discharge."

The young soldier was more than surprised at the commander's attitude toward his plans. Tears rolled down his cheeks, and he threw himself at the feet of the colonel. The commander looked down at the boy, shook his head and said, "Get up, son! I know how it is. I was young once, too, you know, and I, too, fell in love with and married a young Spanish maid. We have lived together, happily, for the last twenty years. I hope you have as much happiness. I shall see that you will receive your honorable discharge and that you have the proper kind of a wedding."

The young soldier arose, but was too overcome to thank the colonel. "Now, sir," continued the officer, "have you seen the girl's father and received his consent?" "No-oo-oo-sir," stammered the boy, "but I intend to, now that I have your permission." "Very well," replied the colonel, "go at once and complete your plans."

Several days later the young corporal had not only received his discharge papers, but had the full consent of Jose Maria Lugo. Until then, he never knew how happy a man could be. And the little senorita was not only as happy, but was spending many busy days completing her wedding costumes.

The wedding day arrived, and the sun never shone more brightly. The birds in the trees sang throughout the ceremony. The old mission was celebrating the first marriage of a Lugo and an American. An abundance of flowers were placed upon the festive table, and the altar in the mission chapel was not only covered with blossoms, but tall tapers burned as they had never burned before!

Prior to the wedding, Spanish music rang out, musicians having come in of their own accord. Laughter and gayety reigned. But as the bridal party approached the altar the air became stilled and an atmosphere of reverence pervaded as the good padre took his place before the happy couple.

Immediately following the ceremony the principals in the event proceeded toward the banquet table. The dragoons lined up, every man raising his shining sword above his head, and with the gaily-costumed senors and senoritas the bridal couple were forced to follow the procession to their respective places at the festive board. The padre waited until every one had been seated, then raised his hand for silence. In tones of deep reverence, he asked the blessings for the future life of the young couple.

"This has been not only one of the happiest days of my life, but a most beautiful one, father," said Jose Maria Lugo. "I never saw the mission look so gay, with its blooming gardens and bright-plumed birds. The costumes here today are of the most brilliant hue. Even your robe looks gayer." "Thank you, senor." "And you presented a most beautiful service."

The following week, the battalion was ordered to return to San Gabriel. With deep regret, and full appreciation for the service the dragoons had given them, the settlers and their padre, with heavy hearts, bade their friend, Colonel A. L. Smith, and his company a sad adios.

EPISODE 6.
LEGIONS.

Within the walls of the old mission sat an Indian chief. He was squatting upon the ground, beneath an oak tree, smoking his long slender pipe of peace and was half dreaming of days gone by. His fast-dimming eyes gazed at the surroundings about him. Near by were a half-dozen Indian and White boys playing one of the Indian games he had taught them some time ago. In the corner of the mission gardens a padre was telling a group of small, interested girls the origin of the flowers.

The old chief sighed, looked at the two groups, and made an incoherent sound. His active life within those walls had now become quiet and serene. His mind had pictured a panorama of the years just passed. How full of activity and gayety they were! Now, he was spending his reclining years in solitude, and love for this younger generation.

The boys had become tired of their play and, seeing the faithful old chief looking forlorn and desolate, held an informal conference among themselves. "Let's have the old chief tell us a story. I'm tired," said the leader of the group. "Let's!" echoed the rest of the playmates, and the small band of companions made their way toward the pensive Indian chief.

The old man looked at the group, smiled and nodded. "Well, well, and what brings my little good friends here?" "Oh, lots! We're tired of running around so much, and we thought that maybe you would tell us a story or something. It would help us with our history lesson," said one of the boys. "We are learning about the Indians now, you know."

"I see, I see," grinned the old chief. "Well, sit down around me and I shall do my best. What do you want me to tell you first?" The boys made themselves comfortable at the feet of the chief. "We don't care," said one, near him.

"Gosh, I do care!" replied the eldest of the group. "I want to learn all about the mountains around here, the story of the Arrowhead and everything. I have a test tomorrow." "I see, I see," nodded the Indian. "And nothing could please me more."

An enthusiastic applause greeted the now-happy Indian. He loved these future citizens, and it was one of his delights to be able to relate to them actual history in an interesting way. He answered no end of questions, and as he held his listeners seemed to live over again the days that had brought hardship and unpleasantness, as well as those that were happier and in harmony.

"Many years ago,' he began, "long before the White man or Spanish people came, and long before I was born, one of my famous ancestors came with a band of warriors. As they rode their spirited and wild horses into the valley, they were amazed at the lay of the land. They saw deer, bear, wild game and many long-horned sheep. My forefather reined in his horse and brought him to a standstill. He shaded his eyes with his hand and scanned the valley. The mountain peaks were alluring. The shadows and the lights were ever changing upon them. These mountains before him were the mountains of mystery, as he knew not what they contained. Here were the slopes of the San Gorgonia, also known as Grayback, San Bernardino, San An-

(Continued on Page 23)

CALIFORNIA HAPPENINGS OF FIFTY YEARS AGO

Thomas R. Jones

(COMPILED EXPRESSLY FOR THE GRIZZLY BEAR.)

THE UNITED STATES SENATE WAS considering, in March 1882, a bill to stop the coming of Chinese. Governor George C. Perkins declared, by proclamation, March 4 a legal holiday and urged the citizens of California to hold demonstrations and to pass resolutions endorsing the bill. Many cities and towns had great non-partisan mass meetings, addressed by leading citizens, and resolutions of endorsement were adopted. This showed the state's citizenry were opposed to the coming of the Chinese. The bill was passed by the Senate, and salutes of one hundred guns were fired in many communities.

A steamer from China arrived at San Francisco March 25 with 1,056 additional Chinks. The captain announced 40,000 more were waiting in Hongkong for steamers to bring them to California. The Federal Congress generously allowed them ninety days in which to get here.

One of the biggest storms that has ever swept over the state began March 13. Three inches of rain fell in California South, four inches in the Sacramento and San Joaquin Valleys and nine inches at Shasta, while the Sierra had a fifteen-foot blanket of snow. Unable to cope with the elements, the Central Pacific railroad was blocked between Dutch Flat, Placer County, and Truckee, Nevada County, for seven days. A snowslide in Lake Canyon, near Bodie, Mono County, buried four miners forty-five feet deep, and their bodies had to remain there until the snow thawed. The rainfall for the season was increased to 13.77 inches, assuring California a bountiful harvest year.

The celebrated "slickens" case of the State of California vs. The Gold Run Hydraulic Company ended with eleven lawyers making arguments for fifty-two hours. The hearing had been in progress fifty-eight days when Judge Temple took the case under advisement, and the daily sessions ceased.

The California Supreme Court, by a four-to-three decision, declared the state's Sunday-closing law constitutional, and then trouble over its enforcement began. The dissenting justices declared the law a violation of the inherent right of the citizen to observe Sunday as he saw fit. Practically every community reported non-observance of the law and a disinterested feeling on the part of the citizenry.

RICH GOLD FIND.

Ione, Amador County, and San Luis Obispo City were the only places reporting general observance of the law. In San Francisco, Police Chief Crowley declared his intention to enforce it, and 540 arrests were made. In Sacramento City, a hundred saloonkeepers were arrested, and demanded jury trials. In Santa Cruz City ten days were consumed in obtaining a jury to try a case involving the law's violation, and it was said every citizen of the township had been summoned. Following a four-day trial the jury disagreed.

The severity of the winter in California South had so damaged the lemon crop that limes were being imported from Mexico.

A shipment of jute seed from Calcutta, India, was distributed to tule-land farmers to experiment in jute growing. There was an enormous demand from graingrowers for jute bags in which to sack their products.

T. Chauvin was granted a franchise to build a street railway in the growing town of Bakersfield, Kern County.

Riverside City had its annual citrus fair commencing March 23. There were 454 exhibitors, and visitors from many places. An incendiary attempt March 25 to set fire to the pavilion caused great excitement.

The stable of the West Oakland, Alameda County, railway burned March 16. Twenty-seven horses were cremated and great quantities of hay and grain were consumed. The financial loss was enormous.

Breuner & Lowery, Shasta County prospecting partners, March 20 discovered near Centerville a seam from which they extracted $2,800 in gold in two days. Another prospector found the seam's extension and in a few hours took out $1,500 in gold. Shasta County was, naturally, greatly excited.

A big deposit of blue gravel, yielding $10 in gold to the pan, was uncovered in the Blue Point mine at Smartsville, Yuba County.

A severe earthquake shock disturbed Santa Cruz, San Benito, Monterey and Merced Counties at 1:45 a.m. of March 6, and Sonoma County was slightly shaken at 8:30 p.m. of the following day.

George F. Baker, State Senator from Santa Clara County and president protem of the Senate, died March 12 at the age of 32. He came to California in 1857.

SQUAWS' WAILS RENT THE AIR.

Henry M. Newhall, who came to the state in 1850 and was in business at San Francisco thirty-one years, died March 14 at Newhall, Los Angeles County. He was the "father" of the town in which he died, and was one of the creators of the San Francisco and San Jose railway.

Dr. W. H. Stone died at San Jose, Santa Clara County, March 23. He came to California from Kentucky in 1849, and amassed a fortune building mining ditches in El Dorado County.

Wm. J. Gau, under an assumed name, wired J. C. Weinberger, Napa Valley viticulturist, to meet him on the arrival of the train at Barrow Station. Following a few moments of conversation, Gau shot and killed Weinberger and then committed suicide.

Nine-year-old Harry Martin of San Francisco, running from a savage dog March 2, fell into Mission Creek and was drowned.

The Vulcan powder works at Stege, Contra Costa County, exploded March 27, and five White men and six Chinamen were blown to pieces.

Willie and Emily, young children of J. D. Franks, found a bottle of strychnine in a bureau drawer near Roseville, Placer County, March 3. They consumed the contents and soon died.

Lakeport, Lake County, was March 10 crowded with visitors desirous of witnessing the execution of Marcus and Jeff, well-known Indian bucks who had killed a White man. The sheriff excluded from the jail yard all but forty Whites and fifty Indian braves. Loud wailing of the squaws outside rent the air as the bucks went stoically to their doom.

M. Van Dyke was killed near Niles, Alameda County, March 26, when his ranch windmill fell upon him.

Ed. West, at Willows, Glenn County, March 7 shot and killed Peter Gallagher, a sportingman who attacked him with a butcherknife.

Mrs. Eliza Andrews, while shopping in San Francisco March 15, was killed by a falling sign.

Mission Cornerstone Laid—The cornerstone of a replica of the original Santa Cruz Mission, founded August 28, 1791, was laid February 14. The structure now under construction is the gift of Mrs. Richard Doyle, in memory of her father, the late Francis J. Sullivan.

California Poetess Honored—The late Ina Coolbrith, California's first poet laureate, has been honored by the United States Geographic Board, which has changed the name of Summit Peak, 8,000-foot mountain of the Sierra Nevada in Sierra County, to Mount Ina Coolbrith.

Feminine World's Fads and Fancies

PREPARED ESPECIALLY FOR THE GRIZZLY BEAR BY ANNA STOERMER

THE WOOL SPORTS FROCK THAT does not boast of a crocheted yoke, or a bit of crochet somewhere or another, is going to feel badly this spring when it sees other frocks. It must have this trimming detail for a contrast with weave to avoid monotony. Then, too, such insets are grand for introducing the color contrast that is so important to almost every type of frock.

The clothes so far shown are simple, smart and neat, with a tailored look that falls very short of being severe. Severe-looking clothes add years to almost every type of woman, while neat clothes, that cleverly avoid frills yet remain feminine are the very essence of youth. Now that this is understood, it seems to be the reason that the mode refrains from any radical change in the new season's styles.

Novel little touches are introduced that really indicate the newness and, at the same time, create a smart touch to even the simplest garment. This season's clothes are in keeping with the times, and are incredibly cheerful. Color has long been recognized as an important factor for cheerfulness and inspired endeavor.

Spring fashions are nothing, if not exacting. Bust, waist and hips must be so moulded that the figure presents one rythmic curve of loveliness. Gone forever is the straight-line flat chest, so-called "boyish type." New fabrics and new trimmings are combined in an extensive collection of garments never before equaled for beauty.

Lines are more than ever important, and the element of comfort is a part of every model. Building the perfect foundation for today's costume has been an inspired proceeding on the part of corset designers and creators. We are slow to accept restraining garments of any kind, after years of freedom, but boned corsets are coming back, so we are on the road to figure beauty. Probably in another year the boned corset will be an accomplished fact. Be that as it may, even now the boned foundation garment is a factor to be reckoned with.

One of the new "step-ins" features the miracle "two-way" stretch elastic that hugs the figure like a second skin, and, when combined with satin, absolutely will not ride up. This will please those who give attention to their personal appearance.

With the new silhouette, new lingerie is quite important, so especially apropos would be lingerie of silken weave whether plain or befrilled with lace. No single undergarment ever has been devised which lends to the feminine form so much of suavity as does the bias slip made from pliant silk and cut to conform to the lines of the figure. This cannot be neglected by the woman who cares. As the season advances and she is wearing the more filmy fabrics of spring and summer, these slips will be found more than ever pleasing. The inventor of this bias conformity is sure to be among the blessed.

Lace and net dresses are creations of charm. Traveling is probably our reason for the rush on lace. Women have learned that it is just about crush and wrinkle proof. Economy is responsible, too, for the wide popularity of lace gowns. Think of buying a dress in February that will keep right on being smart and appropriate through the summer. That is worth anyone's consideration. Besides the practical reasons, there is that never-to-be-forgotten fact that lace is very dainty and more flattering than anything most women could wear.

We have the floral patterns of suede lace, like the muchly-talked-of "angel skin." These are made with the bolero jacket, the little puffed sleeves and the cunning full skirt. The cowl collar neck and the plaited taffeta sash finish these dresses. Laces come in all bright colors, and will be grand for formal affairs all summer.

New spring neckwear has arrived, and how spring-like it appears. Women have been waiting for this lingerie neckwear to brighten their winter frocks. Collars, cuffs and vestees may be worn on different outfits. New lingerie-trimmed dresses have come into fashion, and these collar and cuff sets are beautifully finished on the inner edge without the customary banding. This eliminates a lot of time in keeping them fresh looking. A little tacking, a brooch, or better still a clip-pin, will hold them in place. It's a marvelous idea.

The woman who would be well dressed must not only choose her garments with care, but must select the proper jewelry, whether her choice be for the simple or the ornate. Her taste may be fully satisfied through the vast array of costume jewelry shown in the shops. Not only the color scheme of her costume may be fully carried out in jewelry, but she may choose her most favored material in ornaments.

Simply wearing clips and bracelets has become one of the smart fads at present. A clip is worn especially well if the same touch is repeated in a bracelet, buckle or buttons, but clips and bracelets do not always match. It is fun to combine them individually.

Have you seen those wood and composition clips to match bracelets? Some are of mother-of-pearl. These will be good for spring. Genuine and semi-precious gems are available in necklaces, bracelets, earrings, brooches and rings. Many designs are of metals, chromium and antique silver.

Huge Melon—California motorists paid the state $6,668,062 in license fees last year. The huge melon has been cut, one-half the sum going to the State Highways Division, and the balance being divided among the counties on a motor-vehicle registration basis. Los Angeles County, with 861,004 vehicles, got the lion's share, $1,362,240.

Magnificent Edifice Opened—The new $1,300,000 Civic Auditorium of Pasadena, Los Angeles County, was formally opened February 15.

LOS ANGELES
CITY AND COUNTY

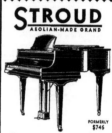

PROPERTYOWNERS OF LOS ANGELES, at last aroused by the ever-growing tax-burden, have become indignant and are organizing to bring about needed reductions. When conditions were normal and dollars were plentiful and easy to get, they worried not over government affairs, paid the tariff exacted and went joyfully on their several ways. Now, when conditions are anything but normal and coin of the realm is a near-curiosity, they are looking into the conduct of public business. The depression, therefore, may in the long run prove to be a blessing! That depends on whether or not the influences that rule with an outstretched hand can change the taxpayers' course. Let's hope not, for Los Angeles, City and County, needs a governmental cleaning, and now's the appointed time!

There are numerous loopholes through which millions of the public's dollars run incessantly to waste, in that the taxpayers get naught in return, except the pleasure of digging up for special and regular tax levies. Some of these loopholes are plainly evident, such as the employment of unneeded and incompetent help. There are departments, if what is commonly rumored be correct, in which employes are so numerous in number their time is mostly occupied in endeavoring to create the impression that their services are required. As to the incompetents whose errors cost the taxpayers thousands upon thousands of dollars, there is a sufficiency of evidence in the record. The powers-that-be, of course, are interested in the quantity, not the quality, of public employes.

Then there are the unseen, but very costly, loopholes. They are numerous, and vast quantities of tax-dollars are necessary to keep them functioning properly. One such is the pension system. Through its operation employes of the city retire on pension and then get on the county payroll, or vice versa. The system is wrong, and operates contrary to the common good. Clean the city and the county pensioners off the payrolls and make places for citizens who receive no compensation from any source. And then there are the special-assessment loopholes. They conceal plenty of the "niggers" that formerly were found in woodpiles. And they're high-priced "niggers," too!

Yes, sir, the propertyowners should now effectively plug up the governmental loopholes! Not just for the depression-day, but permanently; not for their individual benefit, but for the general good.—C.M.H.

SAINT PATRICK DANCE.

The Interparlor N.S.G.W. and N.D.G.W. Committee will sponsor a Saint Patrick day dance at Merchant Plumbers Hall, 1832 South Hope street, March 17. All Natives and their friends are invited. Mrs. Mary Noerenberg has charge of the arrangements.

The committee at its February 12 meeting passed a resolution opposing the proposed change of name of Pasadena avenue to North Figueroa street. A resolution was also adopted calling on the mayor and the chairman of the board of supervisors to furnish a detailed list of all aliens on the payrolls of Los Angeles City and County.

TREE PLANTING.

The get acquainted party of Los Angeles Parlor No. 124 N.D.G.W. was a grand success. A fine program was presented by Helen Sideres, Clara Bird, Louise Graeser, Sophia Stewart and others. Dancing, games and refreshments were also enjoyed. Washington's Birthday, February 22, a tree was planted in Elysian Park. President Gertrude Allen presided at the ceremonies.

The "salamagundi" party of February 24, under the chairmanship of Miss Dolores Malin and Mrs. Mary McAnany, was most enjoyable. Out-of-the-ordinary entertainment was provided and home-made refreshments were served. Invited guests included members of the three local Native Son Parlors—Los Angeles No. 45, Ramona No. 109 and Hollywood No. 196.

President Allen and her assistants—Misses Grace Norton, Grace Du Casse, Dolores Malin, Evelyn Howell, Sali Joseph and Grace Kerns—have completed arrangements for the official visit of Grand President Evelyn I. Carlson to Los Angeles, March 2, when a 6:30 supper and a class initiation will be featured. Other events on the Parlor's March schedule are: 9th, card party, second in the bridge tournament; 16th, address by City Mother Elizabeth Fiske; 30th, baked ham dinner, in charge of Misses Flora Holy and Edna Holcomb.

PROTESTS FORT'S NEGLECT.

February 12, Ramona Parlor No. 109 N.S.G.W. initiated a class of candidates, among them being Judge Arthur Crum. Past President Walter Slosson distributed additional "1932 Bear Club" pins. A resolution, introduced by Arthur R. Hinton, protesting to the Federal Government against the neglect of Fort McArthur, San Pedro, was adopted. In recognition of Abraham Lincoln's birthday anniversary Inside Sentinel Henry V. Harris read an appropriate selection, and among the speakers were Judges Thomas P. White and Lucius P. Green.

The bicentennial of George Washington was observed February 19. President Chandos E. Bush introduced the speakers, J. F. T. O'Connor, whose eloquent remarks were listened to with great interest, and Norbert Savay. Refreshments, prepared by Charles Gassagne and Homer Chappelle, followed the program. At an open meeting February 26 Dr. Rockwell D. Hunt delivered the first of a series of talks on California history. The drum and bugle corps has weekly rehearsals and is making good progress.

Ramona's March calendar includes: 11th, initiation and presentation "1932 Bear Club" pins. 18th, nomination delegates to the Stockton Grand Parlor, followed at 9:15 by entertainment features to be presented by members of Californiana Parlor No. 247 N.D.G.W. and refreshments. 25th, second California history address by Dr. Rockwell D. Hunt; open to the members' families, also eligibles.

BLACKEST SPOT.

Officers of Californiana Parlor No. 247 N.D.G.W. were installed by Past Grand President Grace S. Stoermer, Mrs. Gertrude Tuttle being retained as president. Following the ceremonies the officers entertained at a delightful bridge party. Dainty refreshments were

When you purchase goods advertised in The Grizzly Bear, or answer an advertisement in this magazine, please be sure to mention The Grizzly Bear. That's co-operation mutually beneficial.

served. The second meeting of each month is now devoted to a social function after a brief meeting. February 23 Mrs. Charles Jacobsen was the chairman.

February 9, Mrs. Leland Atherton Irish, program chairman, introduced Coroner Frank Nance, who designated Los Angeles as "the blackest spot in the United States for automobile accidents." Captain Roberts and his crew, from the ambulance and first-aid department of the Los Angeles City receiving hospital, demonstrated in a most efficient and thrilling manner the workings of their equipment in cases of asphyxiation, broken limbs, etc.

LARGE TURNOUT.

Hollywood Parlor No. 196 N.S.G.W. initiated several candidates February 29. This was Past President Henry G. Bodkin night and there was a large turnout. A membership campaign is making good progress. The Parlor's March calendar includes: 14th, refreshments; 21st, initiation; 28th, nomination Stockton Grand Parlor delegates, also refreshments.

MAYOR COMES INTO FOLD.

Ocean Park—Santa Monica Bay Parlor No. 267 N.S.G.W. initiated a class of nine candidates March 8, among them being Mayor William H. Carter. District Deputy Harry Honn presided, and among the speakers was Grand Trustee Eldred L. Meyer.

The Parlor is making fine progress, and another class of candidates will be initiated during March. Arrangements are being made for an informal dinner dance, date to be announced later, and for Santa Monica Bay's annual fiesta and barbecue, which will probably be May Day.

RECORD CROWD.

San Pedro—February 11, Florencita thimble club of Rudecinda Parlor No. 230 N.D.G.W. had a tamale dinner at the home of Lucia Guzman, who was assisted by Viviana Meteljan. A record crowd attended. Helen Trujillo had charge of a card party February 29.

March 4, Grand President Evelyn I. Carlson will officially visit the Parlor, and great preparations are being made for her coming. March 8 a dinner, in charge of First Vice-president Claudia Perez, will be given, and a card party will be held later on in the month.

LEAP YEAR BALL A SUCCESS.

Glendale—Glendale Parlor No. 264 N.S.G.W. and Verdugo Parlor No. 240 N.D.G.W. united in giving a leap-year ball February 20. An unusually large crowd of merrymakers were in attendance and enjoyed the hospitality of the Parlors. Several attractive prizes were awarded, and refreshments were served. Harvey Gillett and Nan Hutchinson, chairmen of the arrangements committee were showered with congratulations on the success of the affair. Another dance will be given in the near-future.

Glendale Parlor is rejoicing because it is to have the services of District Deputy Harry T. Honn as an organizer commencing March 15. He will be given every assistance, and it is expected that he will round up at least twenty-five eligibles. "It looks like a big year for Glendale," says Secretary A. B. Molen.

TAXES VERY BURDENSOME.

Calling attention to the fact that Los Angeles County is at present heavily burdened with governmental indebtedness of more than $700,000,000, which amounts to approximately 25 percent of the assessed value of all real estate and improvements in the county, or about $320 per capita, the Los Angeles County division of the California Taxpayers Association passed a resolution urging that no new bond issues for flood-control purposes be considered until such time as the economic affairs of the community are clarified. [Why specify flood-control bonds? Additional bonds, at this time, for any purpose should be opposed.—Editor.]

It was further pointed out that present taxes are proving very burdensome, as is evidenced by the increasing delinquencies of 4.27 percent in 1928, 5.60 percent in 1929 and 6.61 percent in 1930 for the City of Los Angeles.

TO BEAUTIFY VACANT LOT.

Ocean Park—Officers of Santa Monica Bay Parlor No. 245 N.D.G.W. were installed by District Deputy Flora Holy, Katherine Conterno becoming president. Vocal solos by Cordelia Laventhal and Clayton Brandt were enjoyed. Rosalie Hyde and committee served delicious refreshments in the banquetroom, beautifully decorated with huge baskets of poinsettias. Mary Meyer, retiring president, was, on behalf of the Parlor, presented with an emblematic ring by Past Presi-

(Continued on Page 21)

Native Daughters of th

"TO THE OFFICERS AND MEMBERS of the Subordinate Parlors, Native Daughters of the Golden West—Dear Sisters: Soon the Bells of Easter-tide will ring out and the waiting world will again welcome the glad tidings, 'Christ has risen.'

"Easter and Springtime are the high-tide of the year, and no matter how barren the past may have been, it is enough now that the leaves are green and the lilies are in bloom, because God wills it so.

"When we contemplate the great mysteries of life, our hearts are filled with gratitude, for we may well ask, 'For what purpose did the infinite Creator give existence to this majestic monument of His great power? For what purpose did He create the earth and heavens with all their unnumbered hosts?' Was it not that He might communicate happiness to all?

"We are told we should not slight this wondrous world, with its fruits and flowers. For the prospect of everlasting life and the perfect justice yet to come should cheer and comfort every heart.

"Let us never forget the tragic story of the betrayal and torture of our Lord—of the tomb and the glorious awakening. For that supreme sacrifice was the fulfillment of the sublime promise to mankind.

"For God so loved the World that He gave His only begotten Son that we may be redeemed, and freed of our sadness. He has taught us to be generous; to give, and not to count the cost; to toil, and not to seek for rest; to labor, and not to seek reward. So let us, as true Native Daughters, exemplify all these in our every-day contacts.

"Let us rejoice this Easter morn and sing with the Saints, and with all our hearts pay tribute, in never-ending joy, to our dearest King.

"With loving Easter greetings to each and every member of our organization and the wish that your lives will be filled with peace and happiness, I am,

"Sincerely and affectionately yours in P.D.F.A.,
"EVELYN I. CARLSON,
"Grand President,
"Native Daughters Golden West.
"San Francisco, February 20, 1932."

Jams and Jellies for Vets.

Santa Cruz—District Deputy Pearl N. Reid installed the officers of Santa Cruz No. 26, Miss Lillian E. Smith becoming president. Short talks were given by Past President Verel VanGorder, President Smith, Past Grand President Stella Finkeldey and District Deputy Reid. Miss Finkeldey and Mrs. Reid were presented with boquets of daffodils, and Mrs. Myrtle Richey was the recipient of a past president emblem.

Solicitation was begun among the members for homemade jams and jellies, to be sent disabled veterans. Mrs. Edith K. Dodge has charge of this project of the Parlor, and each year several dozen glasses are sent a veterans hospital. Preceding the meeting a dinner was enjoyed, golden daffodils and purple heather adorning the tables. The dinner committee was composed of Mms. Luene Jensen (chairman), Ethel McFadden, Laura Griffin, and Miss Mamie Cassidy.

Anniversary Celebrated.

Oakland—Piedmont No. 87 celebrated its thirty-sixth institution anniversary with a banquet at which the honored guests were President Rose Martinelli, Past President Kathleen Dombrink, Past Grand President Addie L. Mosher and the charter members. A baked ham dinner was prepared by Chairman Gertrude Noe and a committee consisting of Josephine Collins, Dorothy Davis, Loretta Monahan, Patricia Reardon, Edna Healey, Margaret Thomas, Ella Mullen, Marcella O'Connell, Grace Searing, Hazel Fraizer and Augusta Huxsol. A Saint Patrick party is planned for March, with Mrs. Edna Healey as chairman.

Officers Give Hearts to Grand President.

San Rafael—Despite a severe storm, 135 members of Marinita No. 198 and guests were present to greet Grand President Evelyn I. Carlson on the occasion of her official visit February 8. Other grand officers in attendance were Grand Organist Lola Horgan, Grand Trustees Ethel Begley and Willow Borba, Grand Outside Sentinel Orinda Giannini, Grand Secretary Sallie R. Thaler, Past Grand Presidents Amy McAvoy, Estelle Evans, Mary E. Bell, Dr. Louise C. Heilbron, Addie L. Mosher and Emma G. Foley, District Deputy Mae Shea and fourteen additional deputies. Six candidates were initiated, the ritual work being done perfectly by the officers of the Parlor.

As February was valentine month, the decorations throughout were in red and white, cupids, bows and darts being used. Cupid, portrayed by Esther Trudgett, was in the center of the room, holding a large floral heart of red carnations and freshias, pierced with a dart. Each officer of Marinita, carrying a bow, dart and paper heart, marched by cupid and placed her heart on the dart held by cupid who, after having received all, presented the entire heart and floral offering to Grand President Carlson while Antoinette Hecht sang "Let Us Call You Sweetheart." A delegation from Mount Tamalpais No. 64 N.S.G.W.—Bob Brusatori, Monroe Label and Arthur Todt—appeared and presented Mrs. Carlson with a beautiful boquet of red roses. Organist Eugenie Watson and her partner, Mrs. Eugene Klentz, favored with tap dancing. The Grand President held the complete attention of the assemblage with her beautiful and interesting remarks, after which all the grand officers were presented with gifts.

The Parlor had on display one of the baby layettes which it sends monthly to the Homeless Children Central Committee. This particular one contained nineteen pairs of shoes, besides many other dainty things. At the close of the meeting a tempting hot supper was served in the beautifully decorated banquetroom. It had little attraction, however, for those who, earlier in the evening at the San Anselmo home of Past Grand President Emma G. Foley, had partaken of a delicious turkey supper cooked and served by that perfect chef. Grand Trustee Ethel Begley, a member of Marinita, had entire charge of the wonderful meeting and her assistants co-operated a hundred percent.

Membership Contest Interesting.

San Bernardino—With the lodgeroom decorated with a profusion of flowers, officers of Lugonia No. 241 were installed by District Deputy Hazel Hansen, assisted by a corps of officers from Verdugo No. 240 (Glendale). Gladys Case-Baker, the new president, is a charter member of the Parlor. The costumes of the officers-elect were adorned by arm corsages of sweetpeas, and the installation rites were inspiring. A trio composed of Trustees Grace English, Marguerite Bell and Lily Mae Tompkins sang the ode. Following installation enticing refreshments were served.

February 10 a pot-luck supper was served, with members of Ontario No. 251 and Verdugo No. 240 as guests. Comic valentines were found at each place, and old popular songs were sung following the dinner. The meeting of the Parlor followed, one candidate being initiated. The membership contest is interesting, and each team is striving hard. The losing team is to fete the winners. The contest ends March 1. Past President Frances Wixom recently was wedded to Ernest Wynkoop, and is now residing in Los Angeles. The Parlor presented her with a set of silver salad forks. Extensive plans are being formulated for the official visit of Grand President Evelyn I. Carlson to Lugonia, March 9. On that occasion a class of candidates will be initiated.

Wants Home Mortgage Burned.

Calistoga—The official visit of Grand President Evelyn I. Carlson, January 25, was a gala occasion for Calistoga No. 145. A turkey supper was served at gorgeously decorated tables. Mrs. Katie Butler was chairman of the general arrangements committee, and Miss Edith Cavagnaro headed the decorating committee. Four candidates were initiated, and the Parlor's new officers, headed by President Berenice Martin, exemplified the ritual in a splendid manner.

Grand President Carlson's delightful and instructive message noted advancement of the Order's projects. She stressed the necessity of securing funds to meet the Loyalty Pledge, and expressed a fond hope that the Home mortgage poem entitled "You." Refreshments concluded a happy occasion.

Valentine Party.

Hayward—Officers of Hayward No. 122 and Eden No. 113 N.S.G.W. were installed by District Deputies Marion White and Frank Perry, Florence Hills and Henry L'Ecuyer becoming the respective presidents. Following the ceremonies numerous presentations were made. A theater party for the benefit of the homeless children netted over forty dollars.

Hayward Parlor had a valentine party February 16. The arrangements committee included Mazie Moura, Aldine Pennycott, Dorothy Bruns and Willma Gottberg.

Fund Raising Dinner a Success.

San Juan Bautista—To raise funds for San Juan Bautista No. 179's contribution to the social welfare department which is caring for the unemployed in San Benito County, the Parlor sponsored a ravioli dinner, which was a financial and social success. Mrs. Frank Avilla was the general chairman.

District Deputies Meet.

Redwood City—With Mrs. Alice Lane presiding, the yearly district deputies' meeting, called by Supervising Deputy Renee Mathias, was held January 30. Dinner was served, and a program was presented by Mms. C. Lindquist, H. Chase, G. Anderson and M. Righetti. Among the many visitors were Grand President Evelyn I. Carlson, Grand Secretary Sallie R. Thaler and Past Grand President Dr. Louise C. Heilbron.

Officers of Bonita No. 10 were installed January 28 by District Deputy Alice Lane, Mrs. Alice Johnson becoming president. Past President Margaret Rice was presented with an emblematic pin. A letter from the U. S. Veterans Hospital at Palo Alto thanked the Parlor's hospital committee—Mms. J. Drathman, A. DeRosa and I. Thompson—for interest taken in the veterans.

Grand President's Official Itinerary.

San Francisco—During the month of March, Grand President Evelyn I. Carlson will officially visit the following Subordinate Parlors on the dates noted:

1st—Reina del Mar No. 126, Santa Barbara.
2nd—Los Angeles No. 124, Los Angeles.
3rd—Long Beach No. 154, Long Beach.
4th—Rudecinda No. 230, San Pedro.
5th—San Diego No. 208, San Diego.
7th—Santa Monica No. 245, Ocean Park.
8th—Californiana No. 247, Los Angeles, afternoon; Verdugo No. 240, Glendale, night.
9th—Lugonia No. 241, San Bernardino.
10th—Ontario No. 251, Ontario.
11th—Desert Gold No. 250, Mojave.
14th—Santa Ana No. 235, Santa Ana.
16th—Ivy No. 88, Lodi.
22nd—Chabolla No. 171, Galt.
28th—Guadalupe No. 153, San Francisco.
29th—Portola No. 172, San Francisco.
30th—Stirling No. 146, Pittsburg.
31st—Balboa No. 249, San Francisco.

Cold Fails To Keep Card Players Away.

Petaluma—Officers of Petaluma No. 222 were installed by District Deputy Mae Rose Barry, Elizabeth Dillon being seated as president. February 2 a program of activities for the year was outlined. A public card party followed the meeting, and a large crowd attended despite the cold weather. February 16 a program in memory of George Washington was featured. Pearl Lopez was in charge. Refreshments were served at flower-bedecked tables.

Secretary Margaret Oeltjen, who has been confined to a San Francisco hospital, is much improved and will soon be back at her desk. She is greatly missed, and everyone wishes her a speedy recovery.

Victory Over the Top.

Courtland—Victory No. 216 received an official visit February 6 from Grand President Evelyn I. Carlson. Other visitors included Past Grand Presidents Mary E. Bell, the "mother" of Victory, Dr. Eva R. Rasmussen and Dr. Louise C. Heilbron, Supervising Deputies Bessie Leitch and Ethel Ludwig, District Deputies May Lucas, May Rhodes, Alice Carpenter, Nellie Nordstrom, Mamie McCormick, Sadie Brainard, Alicia Buckley and Doris Fisher, and delegations from the eight Sacramento County Parlors. Four candidates were initiated.

Grand President Carlson gave an instructive talk, following which President Martha Buckley presented her with a valentine containing a check for $113.50, which puts Victory in the Loyalty Pledge over-the-top column. On behalf of the Parlor, Marshal Marie Goodman presented

(Continued on Page 19)

SAN FRANCISCO

COMMEMORATING THE EIGHTY-fourth anniversary of the discovery of gold by James W. Marshall at Coloma, El Dorado County, a largely attended banquet was held in San Francisco, January 23. Included in the number present were members of the Order of Native Sons, the Society of California Pioneers and the California Historical Association.

Past Grand President Lewis F. Byington, who some years ago inaugurated the observance of this most important historic event, presided as toastmaster. Speakers included Grand President Dr. Frank I. Gonzalez, Governor James Rolph Jr., Mayor Angelo J. Rossi of San Francisco, Mayor Fred Morcom of Oakland, Past Grand President Joseph R. Knowland, Grand Trustee George F. McNoble, Past Grand President Fletcher A. Cutler, Grand First Vice-president Seth Millington, Junior Past Grand President John T. Newell, Grand Trustee John M. Burnett, Alfred Cleary and E. A. Wiltsee. A splendid program of singing was presented by Uda Waldrop, Austin Sperry and Chas. Bulotti.

Other Native Sons in attendance were Grand Third Vice-president Chas. A. Koenig, Grand Secretary John T. Regan, Grand Treasurer John A. Corotto, Grand Inside Sentinel W. B. O'Brien, Grand Outside Sentinel Gam Hurst, Historiographer George H. Barron, Grand Trustees Samuel M. Shortridge Jr., Jesse H. Miller, Joseph J. McShane, Frank M. Lane and Eldred L. Meyer, Past Grand Presidents Clarence E. Jarvis, William P. Caubu, James F. Hoey, William J. Hayes, Edward J. Lynch, James A. Wilson and Charles L. Dodge.

VALENTINE DAY AT N.D. HOME.

Valentine day, February 14, was celebrated at the Native Daughter Home by 115 members and their friends who attended the monthly breakfast. The decorations of red carnations, candles and hearts added to the warm glow of friendship that was manifest. Past Grand President Pearl Lamb extended greetings, Grand Secretary Sallie R. Thaler offered prayer, and a delightful program was presented.

Past Grand Lamb complimented the members of the Order on work accomplished, Grand President Evelyn I. Carlson greeted the guests in her usual gracious way and pledged her support at all times, Past Grand President Dr. Mariana Bertola spoke on the activities within the Home, Past Grand President Dr. Louise C. Heilbron, originator of the Loyalty Pledge, was warmly greeted. Master Frank McCormick entertained by sweet singing and gave a tap dance, and a play entitled "Two Tables of Bridge" was presented by the following: Ann Dippel (director), Rose McDonald, Ida Mesquite, Adelaide Cocetts, May Marchant, Isabelle Wilson, Pearl Anderson, Florence Ohler, Lena Wall. The hostesses, Past Grand Lamb and Grand Secretary Thaler, extended sincere thanks to all for assistance in making the breakfast a success. Visitors were present from San Rafael, Sacramento, Martinez, San Jose, Berkeley, Oakland.

TO HONOR N.S. GRAND PRESIDENT.

Under the auspices of the San Francisco N.S.G.W. Extension of the Order Committee, the twenty-eight local Parlors will hold a joint class initiation April 2 in honor of Grand President Dr. Frank I. Gonzalez. There is much enthusiasm, and a successful campaign is assured.

Harmon D. Skillin (Castro No. 232), chairman of the committee, has appointed the following to make arrangements: Harry Romick (Castro No. 232), Martin Huber (Mission No. 38), Joseph Rose (Marshall No. 202), Grand Third Vice-president Chas. A. Koenig and Grand Secretary John T. Regan.

A committee headed by James F. Stanley (Stanford No. 76) will select the initiatory officers, by competition, from the present officers of the San Francisco Parlors. To stimulate interest in the membership drive several trophies will be awarded.

GRAND PRESIDENT N.D. VISITS.

Oro Fino Parlor No. 9 N.D.G.W. received an official visit from Grand President Evelyn I. Carlson February 4. Other visitors were Grand Trustees Gladys Noce, Ethel Begley and Anna Thuesen, Grand Organist Lola Horgan, Past Grand Presidents Mae Boldemann and Margaret Hill, and District Deputy Georgia Nelson.

Grand President Carlson gave an interesting address on the work of the Order, and the other grand officers also gave interesting talks. There was a good attendance, many Parlors being represented. Marshal Edith Rankin sang a solo complimenting the Grand President. The room was artistically decorated with evergreens by an efficient committee under the chairmanship of Beulah Balangero, and refreshments were served by the same committee.

WASHINGTON PARTY.

Genevieve Parlor No. 132 N.D.G.W. had a Washington party February 18. Eugenia Mahely was the goddess of liberty, and entertainment was provided by Lillian Ryan Weisel and Organist Lillian Troy. Refreshments were served at tables decorated in red, white and blue. Elsie Doty was in charge of the evening.

The Parlor is planning a very elaborate affair for Saint Patrick night. The arrangements committee is headed by Katherine Barron. A membership committee has been appointed and a large class of candidates will be initiated at an early date.

OFFICERS INSTALLED.

Officers of Castro Parlor No. 178 N.D.G.W. were publicly installed by District Deputy Myrtle Ross. Both the installing and the installed officers were in full evening dress, making a very effective ensemble. Lavinia Wegener, the new president, promised a very active term and asked the hearty co-operation of officers and members in making it a success.

In appreciation for services rendered, the Parlor presented the retiring past president, Josephine Matison, with a beautiful watch. Many other gifts were presented, the president receiving a goodly share. Castro's February good of the order committee arranged an entertainment in tribute to the bicentennial of George Washington.

"Cutting In Is a Senseless Sin," is the March slogan of the California Public Safety Committee in its campaign to lessen the fearful auto death-toll.

In Memoriam

GEORGIE A. RANDOLPH.
Past President of Encinal Parlor No. 156 N.D.G.W.

We, your committee appointed to draft resolutions of respect to the memory of our departed past president, Sister Georgie A. Randolph, submit the following:

Whereas, The Almighty, in His infinite wisdom, has seen fit to call to the Heavenly Parlor on High our beloved sister, Georgie A. Randolph, thus taking from us one of our most devoted and loyal members—a faithful and true friend. We feel our loss is measureless; that by her death a place has been left vacant in Encinal Parlor which will be hard to refill; and hard though it be, we resign ourselves with the memory of an honorable life just ended, and we feel sure that already she rests amid the rewards she earned while on earth. "None knew her but to love her, none named her but to praise."

Resolved, That in the passing of our beloved sister, the Parlor has lost an honored member, and the Order a true and loyal Native Daughter, and the family a loving and devoted mother. Resolved, that our deepest sympathy be extended to her sorrowing family. May the chain of golden memories lessen their sorrow; may God comfort and bless those near and dear to her. Furthermore, be it resolved, that a page of the records of the Parlor be dedicated to her memory, and that our charter be draped for thirty days, and that this tribute of affection to her memory be sent to the bereaved family and a copy to The Grizzly Bear Magazine.

"There is no death; the sun goes down
To rise again on brighter shores.
And safe in Heaven's jeweled crown
She will shine forever more."

Sincerely and fraternally in P.D.F.A.,
IRENE ROSE,
MARY ORCHISON.

Alameda, February 17, 1932.

Passing of the California Pioneer

(Confined to Brief Notices of the Demise of Those Men and Women Who Came to California Prior to 1860.)

MRS. CAROLINE BALDWIN, NATIVE of Illinois, 89; came across the plains to California in 1850 with her parents, Mr. and Mrs. Levi Carey, and in 1864 settled in the Suisun Valley; died near Fairfield, Solano County, survived by three children.

Mrs. Harmonia Jones, native of Louisiana, 85; came via the Isthmus of Panama in 1852; died at Sacramento City, survived by two children.

Mrs. Sarah Jane Hodge-McLean, native of England, 91; came in 1850 and settled in Nevada County; died at Oakland, Alameda County, survived by a daughter.

Mrs. Rhoda Jane Harter, native of New York, 101, came via Panama in 1851; died at San Francisco.

Garrett J. Young, native of Missouri, 88; came in 1852 and settled in El Dorado County; died at San Francisco, survived by a daughter.

Henry A. Ward, native of Illinois, 97; came in 1852; died at San Diego City.

Mrs. Cloie Talbot-McGuire, 83; came across the plains in 1852 and settled in Sonoma County; died near Sebastopol, survived by three children.

Heber C. Parks, 84; came in 1853 and resided in San Bernardino and Riverside Counties; died at West Riverside, survived by a wife and five children.

Mrs. Estella Huntley-Hall, native of Illinois, 83; came across the plains in 1853 and resided in Amador and Stanislaus Counties; died at Modesto, survived by five children.

William Gann, 88; since 1853 San Joaquin County resident; died at Stockton.

Mrs. Elizabeth Robson-Farnsworth, born in Utah in 1853 while her parents were enroute across the plain to California; settled in El Dorado County; died at Georgetown, survived by a daughter. In honor of this Pioneer Mother, members of El Dorado Parlor No. 186 N.D.G.W. (Georgetown) attended her funeral.

Eugene P. Foster, native of Illinois, 83; came across the plains in 1854; died at Ventura City, survived by a wife and four daughters. He donated Foster Park to Ventura County, and made many other valuable gifts to the city and the county.

Mrs. Lucia Louisa Camp-Early, native of Iowa, 79; came in 1854; died at Manteca, San Joaquin County, survived by a husband and two children.

Carlin S. Kinman, native of Illinois, 85; came across the plains in 1854 and settled in Humboldt County; died at Table Bluff, survived by a wife and a daughter.

Mrs. Jane Mathews, native of Pennsylvania, 83; came in 1855; died at Oakland, Alameda County, survived by five children.

William B. Lillard, native of Missouri, 93; came across the plains in 1859; died at Goleta, Santa Barbara County, survived by seven children.

Mrs. Elvira Gentry Tennyson, native of Missouri, 80; came in 1856 and long resided in Lake County; died at Sacramento City, survived by three children.

OLD TIMERS PASS

Edward Harris, native of England, 87; since 1860 resident San Francisco, where he died; a daughter survives.

Miss Ann Aylette Brooke Wright, native of Mississippi, 78; since 1860 resident San Francisco, where she died.

Richard Johnson, native of Kentucky, 84; came in 1861; died at Oroville, Butte County.

Mrs. Mary Jane Coon-Richardson, native of Illinois, 77; since 1861 Butte County resident; died near Chico, survived by four children.

Giovanni Baptista Raffetto, native of Italy, 87; came in 1862; died at Ventura City, survived by a wife and seven children.

Mrs. Felice Silva, native of Mexico, 93; came in 1862; died at Atwater, Merced County, survived by a daughter.

Mrs. Sarah Houser-Blanchard, native of Pennsylvania, 82; came in 1862; died at Covina, Los Angeles County, survived by six children. For many years she resided in San Joaquin County.

Chris. C. Weisenburger, native of Illinois, 83; came in 1863; died at Watsonville, Santa Cruz County, survived by two children.

Hugo Mansfeldt, native of Germany, 87; came in 1863; died at San Francisco, survived by a daughter.

Mrs. Eunice Cilley-Proper, native of Maine, 86; since 1863 resident Sutter County; died near O'Banion Corners, survived by two children.

James A. Robinson, native of Missouri, 87; came in 1864; died at Stockton, San Joaquin County, survived by a wife and four children. He long resided in Amador County.

Miss Margaret Swope, native of Missouri, 76; since 1864 Santa Clara County resident; died at Santa Clara City.

Frank Luneman, native of Missouri, 87; came in 1865; died at San Francisco, survived by a wife and eight children. He long resided in El Dorado County.

Mrs. Clara Belle Anderson, native of Missouri, 77; since 1865 resident Davis, Yolo County, where she died; a daughter survives.

Nathaniel Leggett Dryden, native of Missouri, 86; came in 1867; died at Cottonwood, San Benito County, survived by a son.

Mrs. Anna A. Leal, native of Azores Islands, 79; came in 1867; died at San Leandro, Alameda County, survived by eight children, among them Mrs. Anna L. Burr (Aloha Parlor No. 106 N.D.G.W.).

James N. Byer, native of Denmark, 81; since 1867 resident Sacramento City, where he died; six children survive.

Mrs. Maria Monnoher-Mattatall, native of Ireland, 78; since 1868 resident Colusa City, where she died; five children survive.

Mrs. Cora Wayland-Kennedy, native of Missouri, 79; since 1868 resident Chico, Butte County, where she died; two sons survive.

Wellington H. Parsons, native of West Virginia, 71; since 1869 Monterey County resident; died near Gonzales, survived by a wife and three children.

Mrs. Marie Probst, native of Germany, 81; since 1869 resident Alameda City, where she died; five children survive.

Mrs. Mary Maxfield-Sheldon, native of New Hampshire, 91; came in 1868; died at Madera City, survived by two sons. She long resided in San Diego County.

Mrs. W. B. Stone, native of Connecticut, 75; came in 1866; died at Los Angeles City, survived by a husband and three children. She long resided in Napa County.

Mrs. Louise Davis, native of Missouri, 75; since 1865 Sutter County resident; died at Live Oak, survived by three children.

Lewis Manford Bish, native of Missouri, 86; came in 1864; died at Richmond, Contra Costa County, survived by a wife and two sons.

Otto von Geldern, native of Germany, 79; came in 1864; died at San Francisco, survived by a wife and three sons.

Mrs. Amanda Spencer-Sanders, native of Michigan, 70; came in 1866; died at Chico, Butte County, survived by a husband and a daughter.

Miles Peerman Lane, native of Missouri, 73; came in 1863; died at Santa Barbara City, survived by a wife and a son.

Mrs. Louisa A. Beardsley, native of Missouri, 87; came in 1861; died at Bakersfield, Kern County, survived by three children.

PIONEER NATIVES DEAD

Placerville (El Dorado County) — Frederick H. Kloepfer, born in this county in 1857, died recently.

Merced City—Martin Zamora, born in Mariposa County in 1855, died recently survived by a wife.

Spanish Flat (El Dorado County)—John William Roelke, born in this county in 1854, died January 19 survived by a wife.

Cedarville (Modoc County)—Joseph F. Allenwood, born in Yuba County in 1857, died January 19 survived by a wife and two children.

Napa City—Mrs. Annie Ware-Swett, born in Sacramento County in 1855, passed away January 20 survived by five daughters.

Williams (Colusa County)—Erastus N. Kimball, born in Yuba County in 1853, died January 25 survived by two children.

San Francisco — William J. Kennedy, born here in 1858, died January 25 survived by a daughter.

San Francisco — Cornelius Harrington, born here in 1858, died January 26 survived by a wife.

Merced City—Dower K. Stoddard, born in Calaveras County in 1858, died January 27 survived by a wife and four children. He was a charter member of Yosemite Parlor No. 24 N.S.G.W., and for years was most active in the affairs of the Order and the Parlor and was a delegate to several Grand Parlors. He was one of the first stagedrivers between Merced and the Yosemite Valley.

Fort Bragg (Mendocino County)—Mrs. Louise Devereux, born in this county in 1857, passed away January 27 survived by five children.

Penngrove (Sonoma County)—Mrs. Mary Ann Bannon-Thomsen, born at San Francisco in 1856, passed away January 28.

Sacramento City—Mrs. Alice Kelly-Johnston, born in California in 1856, passed away January 29 survived by two daughters.

Santa Cruz City—Mrs. Ida Reynolds, born in Sutter County in 1857, passed away January 30 survived by two daughters.

San Francisco—Mrs. Mary A. Napthaly, born here in 1854, passed away January 30. She was a charter member of Alta Parlor No. 3 N.D.G.W.

San Francisco—Miss Agnes McCreery, born here in 1857, passed away February 1. She was affiliated with Alta Parlor No. 3 N.D.G.W.

Auburn (Placer County)—Charles H. Wubbena, born in El Dorado County in 1857, died February 5.

Santa Monica City—Mrs. Beth Sadie Sparkes-Keller, born in Sonoma County in 1858, passed away February 5 survived by three daughters. She was a charter member of Santa Monica Bay Parlor No. 245 N.D.G.W.

(Continued on Page 17)

When you purchase goods advertised in The Grizzly Bear, or answer an advertisement in this magazine, please be sure to mention The Grizzly Bear. That's co-operation mutually beneficial.

Native Sons of the Golden West

THE FIFTY-FIFTH GRAND PARLOR will convene at Stockton May 16, with Grand President Dr. Frank I. Gonzalez presiding. The regulations of the Order specify that Subordinate Parlors shall nominate their delegates the last meeting in March, and elect the first meeting in April. The Grand Parlor will, according to present plans, be in session three days, closing May 19.

Stockton No. 7 is making arrangements for the gathering, the details being handled by the following general committee: Ray Friedberger (chairman), R. D. Dorcey (secretary), Harry M. Herrmann (treasurer), W. P. Rothenbush, Ivan Hoult, Eugene Allison, George D. Avery, C. W. Walsh, Law T. Freitas, Frank Piccardo, W. I. Neeley, Ralph Mitscher, F. R. Fernando, W. A. Strong and L. Buol.

The entertainment program as outlined includes: Reception, Sunday evening, May 15; class initiation, Monday evening; auto trip to Calaveras Big Trees, Tuesday, followed by banquet in the evening; grand ball, Wednesday evening. Special events for the visiting womenfolks are being arranged by Joaquin No. 5 and Caliz de Oro No. 205 N.D.G.W. As a feature of the all-day auto trip Tuesday, Chispa No. 139 (Murphys) will provide a barbecue.

Interest in candidates for Grand Parlor office grows as the date for the meeting nears. Unless past custom be disregarded, which is not likely, the following will be advanced without opposition: Grand First Vice-president Seth Millington to Grand President, Grand Second Vice-president Justice Emmet Seawell to Grand First Vice-president, and Grand Third Vice-president Chas. A. Koenig to Grand Second Vice-president. The Grizzly Bear has communicated with all present officeholders and rumored candidates, and from replies received passes along this information:

Grand Secretary John T. Regan (South San Francisco No. 157) and Grand Treasurer John A. Corotto (San Jose No. 22) will be candidates to succeed themselves.

Rumors are plentiful that there will be at least a half-dozen aspirants for the Grand Third Vice-presidency. One of them, however, Grand Trustee George F. McNoble, has, for personal reasons only, eliminated himself. Two have cast their hats into the ring: J. Hartley Russell (Stanford No. 76) and Harmon D. Skillin (Castro No. 232), both of San Francisco.

Seven Grand Trustees will be chosen. To date, the candidates are: Charles H. Spengemann (Hesperian No. 137) of San Francisco; Samuel M. Shortridge Jr. (Menlo No. 185) of Menlo Park, incumbent; Eldred L. Meyer (Santa Monica Bay No. 267) of Santa Monica, incumbent.

William A. Reuter (Sepulveda No. 263) of San Pedro will be a candidate for Grand Outside Sentinel.

Rumor has it, too, that Eureka will be proposed as the meeting-place for the 1933 Grand Parlor, and Sacramento as the place for holding this year's Admission Day, September 9, celebration.—C.M.H.

TO THE OFFICERS AND MEMBERS OF THE ORDER OF NATIVE SONS—Dear Sirs and Brothers:

At this time I wish to publicly announce that I will not aspire to any further official promotion in our Order. I am compelled to take this step owing to pressure of my personal affairs which will require my undivided attention in the future.

I visited the seventeen Parlors assigned to me and have found them all in a fair condition of prosperity—some better off and some worse off.

At this time I also wish to thank my many friends and well-wishers for the assistance they have given me in the past and have promised me in the future in the way of fraternal promotion in the Order.

In conclusion I wish to say that Stockton Parlor No. 7 intends to give the Grand Parlor a warm welcome and an all-around good time when they visit us in May, 1932.

Very sincerely and fraternally yours,

GEO. F. McNOBLE, Grand Trustee.

Stockton, February 16, 1932.

Flags Presented Courts.

Eureka—Humboldt No. 14, Arcata No. 20 and Ferndale No. 93 presented United States of America and California State (Bear) Flags to the two departments of the Humboldt County Superior Court. A. W. McDonald and Loren M. Nelson made the presentations on behalf of the Parlors, and Judges Harry W. Falk and Thomas H. Selvage accepted the flags.

At a meeting here February 8 of Humboldt County Past Presidents Association an initiatory team was named, composed of Dewey Danielsen, R. E. Byard, R. A. Timmons, J. V. McDonald, A. W. McDonald, C. H. Rasmussen, Len Yocom, R. C. Jacobsen, R. H. Flowers and T. C. Vreeland. March 7 the association will meet at Ferndale.

Natives at Orange Classic.

San Bernardino—Arrowhead No. 110 and Lugonia No. 241 N.D.G.W. had their day at the Twenty-second National Orange Show February 24, when Natives from all the southland gathered to view and participate in the classic. Following supper in the show's restaurant, entertainment features, under the supervision of Leslie D. Case, were presented in the main auditorium.

Louis Wolff was chairman of the general arrangements committee and Henry B. Peake had charge of the refreshments. The hand of welcome was extended by a reception committee which included Police Judge Donald E. Van-Luven (chairman), Benjamin Harrison, Supervisor John Andreson Jr., Grand Organist Leslie Maloche, George J. Maloche, Jerome B. Kavanaugh, Robert W. Brazelton, William Starke, Joseph E. Rich and President Lynn A. Reed.

Anniversary Celebrated.

Oakland—February 9, Claremont No. 240 celebrated its twenty-fourth institution anniversary with a class initiation and banquet. This was also the occasion of the official visit of Grand Trustee Joseph M. McShane. A large number of members of the Order on both sides of the bay were present to extend good wishes to the Parlor for the future and to congratulate the members on achievements of the past. Charter Member Al Fink and Richard M. Hamb of Piedmont No. 120 gave interesting talks on the history of the Parlor.

February 13 the Parlor had a valentine dance which proved a very successful affair, both socially and financially. Ernest Dossa and his committee worked hard, and their efforts were not in vain, as the receipts of the evening were far beyond expectations. The members of Claremont contributed very generously to the ice carnival held at the Oakland Ice Arena for the benefit of the homeless children. The house was filled to capacity, and indications are the committee of arrangements will be able to turn over to the Central Committee a very substantial fund as Alameda County's share for carrying on the kiddies' work.

"Old Guards" and "Kids" at Work.

Calistoga—Calistoga No. 86 has well under way a campaign for members. Two rival teams are at work, the "old guards" and the "kids." J. C. Siemsen and E. E. Light are directing the former, and Henry Pocai and Louis Carlenzoli the latter. The losing team must provide a feast for the entire membership of the Parlor.

The contest is going over big. It will close March 21, when the officers, headed by President Frank Mariani, will initiate those brought into the fold. Several of the grand officers will be guests of Calistoga at that time.

Splendid Service Recognized.

San Diego—The entertainment committee of San Diego No. 108—R. E. Mahony, Burt W. Pauter and Marshall V. Cruze—gave the membership a big time February 3, when a program of music and dancing was presented. March 2 the committee will present boxing bouts and snappy musical numbers, to be followed by refreshments.

At its recent meeting in Berkeley, the California State Historical Association gave recognition to the splendid service of Deputy Grand President Albert V. Mayhrofer, who successfully directed the restoration of Mission San Diego de Alcala, by electing him vice-president.

Joint Installations.

Saint Helena—Saint Helena No. 53 and La Junta No. 203 N.D.G.W. officers were jointly installed by District Deputies William R. Johnson and Zueletta Bellani, Edgar W. Johnson and Inez Costantini becoming the respective presidents. Walter Metzner was master of ceremonies and, with Mrs. Paul R. Alexander at the piano, led the community singing. Dainty refreshments were served. February 13 the Parlors gave their annual dance for the benefit of the homeless children.

Ferndale—Officers of Ferndale No. 93 and Oneonta No. 71 were jointly installed by District Deputies C. H. Rasmussen and Louise Hagen, O. R. Frame and Pearl Robinson becoming the respective presidents. On behalf of Ferndale, Henry Giacomini presented a past president emblem to Lee Diedricksen, and on behalf of Oneonta, Mrs. Hattie Roberts presented gifts to Mrs. Annie Fulton and District Deputy Hagen. Whist was followed by a fine supper.

Daughters Entertained.

Plymouth—Amador No. 17 entertained Amapola No. 80 N.D.G.W. at a delightful supper. Chester Gannon gave an interesting talk on the life of Joaquin Murietta, and there were brief addresses by Past Grand President Clarence E. Jarvis, Grand Trustee Gladys E. Noce, District Deputy Marguerite Davis and District Deputy Thomas Davis. Old-time dances were greatly enjoyed.

Three Initiated.

Santa Ana—Three candidates were initiated by Santa Ana No. 265 February 15, the work being conferred by the officers of the Parlor. This was the first result of a campaign for an increase of membership and to kill "old man depression." Following the initiation a tamale supper was enjoyed.

Unique Contest Under Way.

San Rafael—A big class of candidates was initiated February 15 by Mount Tamalpais No. 64. Visitors from Sea Point No. 158 (Sausalito), Nicasio No. 198 and other Parlors around the bay were in attendance. The ceremonies were conducted by the regular officers, who were highly praised for the impressive and efficient manner in which the ritual was exemplified.

The Parlor is conducting a rather unique membership contest between the regular officers, the past presidents and the "scrubs" or independent team, the losers to prepare and serve a banquet for the winners at the conclusion of the contest. Recording Secretary Manuel Andrade, captain of the "scrub" team, says he has a big surprise in store for his opponents. Monroe Label, captain of the past president team, declares he is confident of the outcome, and President A. W. Todt, captain of the regulars, is bursting with pride because his team has led the contest so far, all the initiates being brought in by that aggregation.

A banquet followed the initiation and a number of pleasing vocal and instrumental selections were rendered. Frank Kelly, who for several years enjoyed the proud distinction of being the only officer of Hibernian extraction in the Parlor, is organizing the musical talent in Mount Tamalpais. He is confident that his plan will contribute much to the success of the meetings, as many of the boys are most enthusiastic over the idea.

Membership Standing Largest Parlors.

San Francisco—Grand Secretary John T. Regan reports the standing of the Subordinate Parlors having a membership of over 400 January 1, 1932, as follows, together with their membership figures February 19, 1932:

Parlor	Jan. 1	Feb. 19	Gain	Loss
Ramona No. 109	1088	1093	5	..
South San Francisco No. 157	822	821	..	1
Castro No. 232	700	700	..	..
Arrowhead No. 110	609	612	3	..
Stanford No. 76	614	609	..	5
Twin Peaks No. 214	585	574	..	11
Stockton No. 7	549	549	..	..
Piedmont No. 120	523	520	..	3
Rincon No. 72	448	446	..	2

Three Generations Present.

Palo Alto—Three generations of the Decker family were at the meeting of Palo Alto No. 216, January 26, when C. C. Decker Jr. was initiated. He is a grandson of Past Grand President Dr. Charles W. Decker (California No. 1) and a son of C. C. Decker Sr., past president No. 216. Officers of Palto Alto were installed by District Deputy A. S. Liguori, J. C. Bernal becoming president.

Annual Turkey Feast.

Fort Bragg—Following the annual turkey feast of Alder Glen No. 200, which was largely attended, officers were installed by District Deputy Ralph Todd, C. N. Simpson becoming president. At the close of the ceremonies the crowd were entertained by three boxing bouts.

Order's Work Extolled.

Folsom—Grand First Vice-president Seth Millingtou officially visited Granite No. 83 January 26 and delivered an address on the history of California, in the course of which he extolled the work of the Order. District Deputy Clyde Corcoran installed the Parlor's officers, J. M. Relvas becoming president. A banquet followed the meeting.

Novel Event.

Pleasanton—With husband and wife acting as installing officers, brother and sister were installed as presidents, respectively, of Pleasanton No. 244 and Pleasanton No. 237 N.D.G.W. District Deputy Frank Perry and wife, District Deputy Evelyn Perry, formally inducted Wm. Busch as president of No. 244 and his sister, Helena Busch, as president of No. 237. Visitors from sixteen Parlors and many townfolk attended the public ceremonies, after which a dance was held and refreshments were served. In attendance were Grand Secretary Sallie R. Thaler and Grand Outside Sentinel Gam Hurst.

Hall Association Elects Officers.

Sacramento—At the annual meeting of the stockholders of the Native Sons Hall Association of Sacramento, Assemblyman Percy G. West was re-elected secretary—for the twenty-fifth consecutive time. Other officers and directors chosen are: John J. Monteverde, president; Charles A. Root, vice-president; Henry Wittpen, treasurer; Irving D. Gibson, J. Frank Didion, Elwood F. Mier, Hugh B. Bradford, J. C. Boyd, M. F. Trebilcox and Roy C. Cothrin, directors.

Official Directory of Parlors of

ALAMEDA COUNTY.

Alameda No. 47, Alameda City—Gus Nelson, Pres.; Robt. H. Cavanaugh, Sec., 1806 Pacific Ave.; Wednesdays, Native Sons Hall, 1406 Park St.

Oakland No. 50, Oakland—A. W. Ainger, Pres.; F. M. Norris, Sec., 4280 Terrace St.; Fridays, Native Sons Hall, 11th and Clay Sts.

Las Positas No. 96, Livermore—R. J. Ruetz, Pres.; John J. Kelly, Sec., P. O. box 341; Thursdays, Foresters Hall.

Eden No. 113, Hayward—Henry L'Ecuyer, Pres.; Stanton R. Soares, Sec., P. O. box 176; 2nd and 4th Tuesdays, Memorial Hall, Main St.

Piedmont No. 120, Oakland—Walter M. Davis, Pres.; Charles Morando, Sec., 906 Vermont St.; Thursdays, Native Sons Hall, 11th and Clay Sts.

Wisteria No. 127, Alvarado—Henry May, Pres.; J. M. Scribner, Sec., Livermore; 1st Thursday, I.O.O.F. Hall.

Halcyon No. 146, Alameda City—Charles J. VonTagen, Pres.; J. C. Bates, Sec., 2139 Buena Vista Ave.; 1st and 3rd Tuesdays, I.O.O.F. Hall, 2329 Santa Clara Ave.

Brooklyn No. 151, Oakland—Frank B. Perry, Pres.; E. W. Cooney, Sec., 3907 14th Ave.; Wednesdays, Masonic Temple, 8th Ave. and E. 14th St.

Washington No. 169, Centerville—M. B. Silva, Pres.; Allen G. Norris, Sec., P. O. box 31; 2nd and 4th Tuesdays, Hansen Hall.

Athens No. 195, Oakland—Henry G. Kroeckel, Pres.; Harold B. Farley, Sec., 4623 Benevides Ave.; Tuesdays, Native Sons Hall, 11th and Clay Sts.

Berkeley No. 210, Berkeley—S. Levy, Pres.; R. J. Garrett, Sec., 1708 Virginia St.; Tuesdays, Native Sons Hall, 2108 Shattuck Ave.

Estudillo No. 223, San Leandro—Frank V. Pacheco, Pres.; Albert G. Pacheco, Sec., 1736 E. 14th St.; 1st and 3rd Tuesdays, Masonic Temple.

Claremont No. 240, Oakland—Fred Bueina, Pres.; E. N. Thienger, Sec., 839 Hearst Ave., Berkeley; Tuesdays, Veterans Memorial Bldg., 43rd & Salem Sts., Emeryville.

Pleasanton No. 244, Pleasanton—Peter C. Madsen, Pres.; Ernest W. Schween, Sec.; 2nd and 4th Thursdays, I.O.O.F. Hall.

Niles No. 250, Niles—M. L. Fournier, Pres.; C. E. Martenstein, Sec.; 2nd Thursday, I.O.O.F. Hall.

Fruitvale, No. 252, Oakland—Chester B. Abernethy, Pres.; Ray B. Felton, Sec., 1575 Alice St.; Fridays, W.O.W. Hall, 3256 E. 14th St.

AMADOR COUNTY.

Amador No. 17, Sutter Creek—Frank Marre, Pres.; F. J. Payne, Sec.; 1st and 3rd Fridays, Native Sons Hall.

Excelsior No. 31, Jackson—Wm. Daugherty, Pres.; William Going, Sec.; 1st and 3rd Wednesdays, Native Sons Hall, 22 Court St.

Ione No. 33, Ione—Marvin Kidd, Pres.; Josiah H. Saunders, Sec.; 1st and 3rd Wednedays, Native Sons Hall.

Plymouth No. 48, Plymouth—L. E. Houston, Pres.; Thos. D. Davis, Sec.; 1st and 3rd Saturdays, I.O.O.F. Hall.

BUTTE COUNTY.

Argonaut No. 8, Oroville—Fred E. Tegrunde, Pres.; Cyril R. Macdonald, Sec., P. O. box 502; 1st and 3rd Wednesdays, Veterans Memorial Hall.

Chico No. 21, Chico—Marcus Choisser, Pres.; Sam Lindsay Adams, Sec., Sacramento Blvd.; 2nd and 4th Thursdays, Elks Hall.

CALAVERAS COUNTY.

Chispa No. 139, Murphys—John Voitich, Pres.; Antone Malaspina, Sec.; Wednesdays, Native Sons Hall.

COLUSA COUNTY.

Colusa No. 69, Colusa City—Burton L. Smart, Pres.; Phil J. Humburg, Sec., 223 Parkhill St.; Tuesdays, Eagles Hall.

CONTRA COSTA COUNTY.

General Winn No. 32, Antioch—Edmont T. Uren, Pres.; Joel H. Ford, Sec., P. O. box 311; 2nd and 4th Wednesdays, Union Hall.

Mount Diablo No. 101, Martinez—R. P. Anderson, Pres.; G. T. Barkley, Sec.; 1st and 3rd Mondays, I.O.O.F. Hall.

Byron No. 170, Byron—William E. Bunn, Pres.; H. G. Krumland, Sec.; 1st and 3rd Tuesdays, I.O.O.F. Hall.

Carquinez No. 205, Crockett—Thos. Cox, Pres.; Thomas I. Cahalan, Sec.; 1st and 3rd Wednesdays, I.O.O.F. Hall.

Richmond No. 217, Richmond—M. W. Amaral, Pres.; H. D. Mason, Sec.; 11 6th St.; Wednesdays, Redmen Hall, 11th and Neven Ave.

Concord No. 245, Concord—P. M. Soto, Pres.; D. E. Pramberg, Sec., P. O. box 235; 1st Tuesday, I.O.O.F. Hall.

Diamond No. 246, Pittsburg—Victor Ericasoh, Pres.; Francis A. Irving, Sec., 248 E. 5th St.; 1st and 3rd Wednesdays, Veterans Memorial Bldg.

GRAND OFFICERS.

John T. Newell........Junior Past Grand President
2388 Benedict, Los Angeles

Dr. Frank I. Gonzalez............Grand President
Flood Bldg., San Francisco

Seth Millington.............Grand First Vice-pres.
Gridley

Justice Emmet Seawell....Grand Second Vice-pres.
State Bldg., San Francisco

Chas. A. Koenig...........Grand Third Vice-pres.
531 35th Ave., San Francisco

John T. Regan.....................Grand Secretary
N.S.G.W. Bldg., 414 Mason St., San Francisco

John A. Corotto..................Grand Treasurer
560 No. 5th St., San Jose

Horace J. Leavitt...................Grand Marshal
Weaverville

W. B. O'Brien...............Grand Inside Sentinel
2324 Santa Clara St., Alameda

Gam Hurst ....Grand Outside Sentinel
1400 Financial Center Bldg., Oakland

Leslie Maloche...................Grand Organist
467½ 3rd St., San Bernardino

George H. Barron.................Historiographer
333 12th Ave., San Francisco

GRAND TRUSTEES.

George F. McNoble......California Bldg., Stockton
Samuel M. Shortridge Jr...............Menlo Park
Jesse H. Miller..712 DeYoung Bldg., San Francisco
Joseph J. McShane..419 Flood Bldg., San Francisco
Frank M. Lane............333 Blackstone, Fresno
John M. Burnett..........................San Jose
Eldred L. Meyer....922 San Vincente, Santa Monica

EL DORADO COUNTY.

Placerville No. 9, Placerville—George M. Smith, Pres.; Duncan Bathurst, Sec., 12 Gilmore St.; 2nd and 4th Tuesdays, Masonic Hall.

Georgetown No. 91, Georgetown—W. H. Breedlove, Pres.; C. F. Irish, Sec.; 2nd and 4th Wednesdays, I.O.O.F. Hall.

FRESNO COUNTY.

Fresno No. 25, Fresno City—A. G. Miller, Pres.; John W. Cappleman, Sec., 1389 Wilson; 2nd and 4th Fridays, W.O.W. Hall, 1354 Van Ness Ave.

Selma No. 107, Selma—Chester E. Shepard, Pres.; E. C. Laughlin, Sec.; 1st and 3rd Wednesdays, American Legion Hall.

HUMBOLDT COUNTY.

Humboldt No. 14, Eureka—Edward J. Quinn, Pres.; Loren M. Nelson, Sec, P. O. Box 195; 2nd and 4th Mondays, Native Sons Hall.

Arcata No. 20, Arcata—George Hale, Pres.; William Peters, Sec., P. O. box 1117; Thursdays, Native Sons Hall.

Ferndale No. 93, Ferndale—O. R. Frame, Pres; C. H. Rasmussen, Sec. R.F.D. 47-A; 1st and 3rd Mondays, K.P. Hall.

KERN COUNTY.

Bakersfield No. 42, Bakersfield—G. E. Taylor, Pres.; Leroy Vandervoort, Sec., Manly Apts.; Wednesdays, Justice Court, City Hall.

LAKE COUNTY.

Lower Lake No. 159, Lower Lake—Harold S. Anderson, Pres.; Albert Kugelman, Sec.; Thursdays, I.O.O.F. Hall.

LASSEN COUNTY.

Honey Lake No. 198, Standish—James C. Meeske, Pres.; N. V. Wemple, Sec., Litchfield; 1st and 3rd Wednesdays, Wrede Hall.

Big Valley No. 211, Bieber—George Bunselmeier, Pres.; A. W. McKenzie, Sec.; 1st and 3rd Wednesdays, I.O.O.F. Hall.

LOS ANGELES COUNTY.

Los Angeles No. 45, Los Angeles City—Lee E. Erwin, Pres.; Richard W. Fryer, Sec., 1629 Champlain Ter.; Thursdays, Merchant Plumbers Hall, 1832 So. Hope.

Ramona No. 109, Los Angeles City—Chandos E. Bush, Pres.; John V. Scott, Sec., Patriotic Hall, 1816 So. Figueroa; Fridays, Patriotic Hall, 1816 So. Figueroa.

Hollywood No. 196, Los Angeles City—Leo Aggeler, Pres.; E. J. Reilly, Sec., 907 W. 2nd St.; Mondays, Hollywood Conservatory Music, 5402 Hollywood Blvd.

Long Beach No. 239, Long Beach—Francis H. Gentry, Pres.; W. W. Brady, Sec., 801 Jergins Trust Bldg.; 2nd and 4th Thursdays, Moose Hall, Elm and Anaheim.

Sepulveda No. 263, San Pedro—Francis G. Fetzer, Pres.; Frank I. Markey, Sec., 101 W. 7th St.; 2nd and 4th Fridays, Odd Fellows Temple, 10th and Gaffey Sts.

Glendale No. 264, Glendale—Philip D. Molen, Pres.; Abel B. Molen, Sec., 508 So. Belmont St.; 1st and 3rd Tuesdays, Masonic Temple, 234 So. Brand Blvd.

Santa Monica Bay No. 267, Ocean Park—Claude J. Wiseman, Pres.; John J. Smith, Sec., 830 Rialto Ave., Venice; 2nd and 4th Mondays, New Eagle Hall, 2823½ Main St.

Cahuenga No. 268, Reseda—Harold C. Trexler, Pres.; Walter A. Knapp, Sec., 7711 Owensmouth Ave., Canoga Park; first Friday, Alton Hall.

MADERA COUNTY.

Madera No. 130, Madera City—Cornelius Noble, Pres.; T. P. Cosgrave, Sec.; 1st and 3rd Thursdays, First National Bank Bldg.

MARIN COUNTY.

Mount Tamalpais No. 64, San Rafael—Arthur Todt, Pres.; Manual A. Andrade, Sec., 532 Mission Ave.; 1st and 3rd Mondays, Portuguese American Hall.

Sea Point No. 158, Sausalito—Allyn T. Young, Pres.; Manuel Santos, Sec., 6 Glen Drive; 1st and 3rd Wednesdays, Perry Bldg.

Nicasio No. 183, Nicasio—M. T. Farley, Pres.; R. J. Rogers, Sec.; 2nd and 4th Wednesdays, U.A.O.D. Hall.

MENDOCINO COUNTY.

Ukiah No. 71, Ukiah—Henry Bucknell, Pres.; Ben Hofman, Sec., P. O. box 472; 1st and 3rd Mondays, I.O.O.F. Hall.

ATTENTION, SECRETARIES!

THIS DIRECTORY IS PUBLISHED BY AUTHORITY OF THE GRAND PARLOR N.S.G.W., AND ALL NOTICES OF CHANGES MUST BE RECEIVED BY THE GRAND SECRETARY (NOT THE MAGAZINE) ON OR BEFORE THE 20TH OF EACH MONTH TO INSURE CORRECTION IN NEXT ISSUE OF DIRECTORY.

sperian No. 137, San Francisco—H. G. Ritter, Pres.; Albert Carlson, Sec., 379 Justin Dr.; Thursdays, Native Sons Bldg., 414 Mason St.
calde No. 154, San Francisco—Conrad Kuhl, Pres.; Harry S. Burke, Sec., 25 Ord St.; 2nd and 4th Wednesdays, Native Sons Bldg., 414 Mason St.
uth San Francisco No. 157, San Francisco—Raymond Conroy, Pres.; John T. Regan, Sec., 1439 Newcomb Ave.; Wednesdays, Masonic Bldg., 4705 3rd St.
quoia No. 160, San Francisco—Chester Moreno, Pres.; Walter W. Garrett, Sec., 2500 Van Ness Ave.; Mondays, Swedish-American Bldg., 2174 Market St.
ecita No. 187, San Francisco—Elmer F. Sprague, Pres.; Edward Tietjen, Sec., 1367 15th Ave.; Thursdays, Mission Masonic Hall, 2668 Mission St.
ympus No. 189, San Francisco—Charles Erickson, Pres.; Harvey J. Carty, Sec., 1651 Market St., Apt. 505; 2nd and 4th Tuesdays, Independent Redmen Hall, 3053 16th St.
esidio No. 194, San Francisco—Geo. R. Schmidt, Pres.; George A. Ducker, Sec., 442 21st Ave.; Mondays, Native Sons Bldg., 414 Mason St.
arshall No. 202, San Francisco—Arthur Belli, Pres.; Frank Bacigalupi, Sec., 725 Douglas St.; 1st and 3rd Wednesdays, Native Sons Bldg., 414 Mason St.
olores No. 208, San Francisco—Daniel Corrigan, Pres.; Eugene O'Donnell, Sec., Mills Bldg.; Tuesdays, Mission Masonic Bldg., 2668 Mission St.
win Peaks No. 214, San Francisco—Fred Sooman, Pres.; Thos. Pendergast, Sec., 278 Douglas St.; Wednesdays, Willopi Hall, 4061 24th St.
l Capitan No. 222, San Francisco—Frank Rizzo, Pres.; James Hanna, Sec., 2450 27th Ave.; 1st and 3rd Thursdays, King Soloman Hall, 1739 Fillmore St.
uadalupe No. 231, San Francisco—George Miles, Pres.; Alvin A. Johnson, Sec., 142 Rousseau St.; Tuesdays, Guadalupe Hall, 4551 Mission St.
astro No. 232, San Francisco—David A. Simon, Pres.; James H. Hayes, Sec., 4014 18th St.; Tuesdays, Native Sons Bldg., 414 Mason St.
albon No. 234, San Francisco—J. LeMer, Pres.; E. W. Boyd, Sec., 45 Carl St.; Thursdays, Maccabee Hall, 5th Ave. and Clement St.
ames Lick No. 242, San Francisco—M. G. Muller, Pres.; Wm. Band, Sec., 2587 22nd Ave.; 1st and 3rd Wednesdays, Redmen Hall, 3052 16th St.
ret Harte No. 260, San Francisco—J. F. Craig, Pres.; C. J. Eggers, Sec., 194 Prague St.; Tuesdays, West of Twin Peaks Hall, 233 Legion Court.
topia No. 270, San Francisco—Joseph Riordan, Pres.; Herbert H. Schneider, Sec., 2455 16th Ave.; Tuesdays, American Hall, 20th and Capp Sts.

SAN JOAQUIN COUNTY.

ockton No. 7, Stockton—George D. Avery, Pres.; R. D. Dorcey, Sec., P. O. box 388; Mondays, Native Sons Hall.
odi No. 18, Lodi—Jerome Solomon, Pres.; Dr. Clyde Bresnan, Sec.; 2nd and 4th Wednesdays, Eagles Hall.
racy No. 186, Tracy—R. J. Marraccini, Pres.; R. J. Marraccini, Sec., R.F.D. No. 1, box 217; Thursdays, I.O.O.F. Hall.
anteca No. 271, Manteca—Louis Ryan, Pres.; Leonard Faria, Sec., R.F.D. No. 1, Lathrop; 1st and 3rd Wednesdays, I.O.O.F. Hall.

SAN LUIS OBISPO COUNTY.

an Miguel No. 150, San Miguel—H. Twisselman, Pres.; George Sonnenberg Jr., Sec.; 1st and 3rd Wednesdays, Fraternal Hall.
ambria No. 152, Cambria—Roy Cardoza, Pres.; A. S. Gay, Sec.; Wednesdays, Rigdon Hall.

SAN MATEO COUNTY.

edwood No. 66, Redwood City—Joseph Lodi, Pres.; A. S. Liguori, Sec., P. O. box 212; Thursdays, American Foresters Hall.
easide No. 95, Half Moon Bay—William Deeney, Pres.; John G. Gilcrest, Sec.; 2nd and 4th Tuesdays, I.O.O.F. Hall.
enlo No. 185, Menlo Park—W. H. Wreden, Pres.; F. W. Johnson, Sec., P. O. box 601; Thursdays, Duff & Doyle Hall.
ebble Beach No. 230, Pescadero—Bernard Cabral, Pres.; E. A. Shaw, Sec.; 2nd and 4th Wednesdays, I.O.O.F. Hall.
l Carmelo No. 256, Daly City—Leonard J. Mohr, Pres.; Andrew P. Murphy, Sec., 931 Hanover St.; 2nd and 4th Wednesdays, Eagles Hall.
ndustrial City No. 269, South San Francisco—John C. Hamilton, Pres.; Geo. A. Roll, Sec., P. O. box 237; 2nd and 4th Mondays, Metropolitan Hall.

SANTA BARBARA COUNTY.

anta Barbara No. 116, Santa Barbara City—C. W. McCormick, Pres.; H. C. Sweetser, Sec., Court House; 1st and 3rd Wednesdays, I.O.O.F. Hall.

SANTA CLARA COUNTY.

an Jose No. 22, San Jose—Joseph Sabatte, Pres.; H. W. McComas, Sec., Suite 7, Porter Bldg.; Mondays, I.O.O.F. Hall.
anta Clara No. 100, Santa Clara City—John J. Trinajstich, Pres.; Clarence Clevenger, Sec., P. O. box 297; 1st and 3rd Wednesdays, Redmen Hall.
bservatory No. 177, San Jose—Norton J. Mahon, Pres.; A. B. Langford, Sec., Hall Records; Tuesdays, Knights Columbus Hall, 40 No. First St.
ountain View No. 215, Mountain View—Gilbert F. McCorkle, Pres.; C. A. Antonioli, Sec., 948 California St.; 2nd and 4th Fridays, Mockbee Hall.
alo Alto No. 216, Palo Alto—John C. Bernal, Pres.; Albert A. Quinn, Sec., 643 High St.; Mondays, Native Sons Bldg., Hamilton Ave. and Emerson St.

SANTA CRUZ COUNTY.

atsonville No. 65, Watsonville—A. W. Batchelder, Pres.; E. R. Tindall, Sec., 408 East Lake Ave.; 2nd and 4th Tuesdays, I.O.O.F. Hall.
anta Cruz No. 90, Santa Cruz City—W. H. Mori, Pres.; T. V. Mathews, Sec., 105 Pacheco Ave.; Tuesdays, Native Sons Hall, 117 Pacific Ave.

SHASTA COUNTY.

cCloud No. 149, Redding—Errol Yank, Pres.; Hugh A. Shuffleton, Sec.; 1st and 3rd Thursdays, Moose Hall.

SIERRA COUNTY.

ownieville No. 92, Downieville—J. M. McMahon, Pres.; H. S. Tibbey, Sec.; 2nd and 4th Mondays, I.O.O.F. Hall.
olden Nugget No. 94, Sierra City—Leonard Thompson Jr., Pres; Arthur R. Pride, Sec.; last Saturday, Masonic Hall.

SISKIYOU COUNTY.

tna No. 192, Etna—Fred M. Wolford, Pres.; Harvey A. Green, Sec.; 1st and 3rd Wednesdays, I.O.O.F. Hall.
iberty No. 193, Sawyers Bar—Orrin R. Bigelow, Pres.; John M. Barry, Sec.; 1st and 3rd Saturdays, I.O.O.F. Hall.

N.S.G.W. OFFICIAL DEATH LIST.

Containing the name, the date and the place of birth, the date of death, and the Subordinate Parlor affiliation of deceased members reported to Grand Secretary John T. Regan from January 22, 1932, to February 19, 1932:

Ryan, Henry Patrick; Sacramento, February 23, 1873; January 30, 1932; Sacramento No. 3.
Kerrick, J. W.; San Joaquin County, October 17, 1868; August 28, 1931; Stockton No. 7.
Eaton, M. D.; San Joaquin County, April 30, 1862; September 28, 1931; Stockton No. 7.
Foreman, Chas.; Waterloo, February 22, 1871; November 16, 1931; Stockton No. 7.
Wyatt, H. S.; Stockton, November 2, 1869; December 28, 1931; Stockton No. 7.
Stoddard, Dower Kenneth; Angels Camp, September 29, 1858; January 27, 1932; Yosemite No. 24.
Paul, John Henry; Sacramento, January 3, 1859; January 25, 1932; Golden Gate No. 29.
Miller, George E.; San Francisco, July 2, 1865; January 29, 1932; El Dorado No. 52.
Schmidt, Walter Joseph; San Francisco, September 20, 1892; January 29, 1932; Rincon No. 72.
Collins, Albert; Danville, February 22, 1883; February 7, 1932; Rincon No. 72.
Taylor, James Edward; Weaverville, August 15, 1872; August 3, 1931; Mount Bally No. 87.
Dominici, George David; Lewiston, October 27, 1891; December 27, 1931; Mount Bally No. 87.
Ruberr, Frederick William; San Francisco, August 24, 1877; January 7, 1932; Mount Bally No. 87.
Altmayer, Berthold; San Francisco, March 2, 1868; February 4, 1932; Bay City No. 104.
Liggett, Theo. Robert; San Francisco, January 15, 1897; July 23, 1931; Niantic No. 105.
Finnegan, James Patrick; San Francisco, May 28, 1898; December 1, 1931; Niantic No. 105.
Pogue, Howard A.; San Francisco, September 2, 1870; January 5, 1932; Niantic No. 105.
Detels, Henry; San Francisco, January 27, 1877; January 18, 1932; Brooklyn No. 151.
Cashen, John T.; San Francisco, December 21, 1870; December 26, 1931; Alcalde No. 154.
Langiel, Julius; San Francisco, April 5, 1907; January 5, 1932; South San Francisco No. 157.
Killimede, Aloysuis James; San Francisco, October 9, 1884; January 16, 1932; South San Francisco No. 157.
Bar, Harry; San Francisco, July 20, 1878; January 16, 1932; South San Francisco No. 157.
Friese, Albert Max; San Francisco, June 7, 1887; January 30, 1932; Sequoia No. 160.
Hughes, Thomas James; San Francisco, December 16, 1875; January 29, 1932; Precita No. 187.
Cullen, Richard; San Francisco, March 10, 1874; January 21, 1932; Olympus No. 189.
Landers, Henry M.; Grass Valley, July 30, 1882; January 24, 1932; Presidio No. 194.
Stephenson, Forster George; Oakland, January 4, 1886; February 1, 1932; Athens No. 195.
Wendt, Herman; San Francisco, January 25, 1888; January 25, 1932; Twin Peaks No. 214.
Bex, Charles Lawrence; Mission San Jose, February 8, 1891; January 13, 1932; Estudillo No. 223.

SOLANO COUNTY.

Solano No. 39, Suisun—Karl Koch, Pres.; J. W. Kinlock, Sec.; 1st and 3rd Tuesdays, I.O.O.F. Hall.
Vallejo No. 77, Vallejo—Joseph Clavo, Pres.; Werner B. Hallin, Sec., 912 Carolina; 2nd and 4th Tuesdays, San Pablo Hall.

SONOMA COUNTY.

Petaluma No. 27, Petaluma—George Gells, Pres.; C. F. Fobes, Sec., 114 Prospect St.; 2nd and 4th Mondays, Druid Hall, Gross Bldg., 41 Main St.
Santa Rosa No. 28, Santa Rosa—John Caniff, Pres.; Leland S. Lewis, Sec., Court House; Tuesdays, Native Sons Hall.
Glen Ellen No. 102, Glen Ellen—C. C. Weise, Pres.; Frank Kirch, Sec., Route 3, Santa Rosa; 2nd Monday, N.S.G.W. Hall.
Sonoma No. 111, Sonoma City—Frederick Bulotti, Pres.; L. H. Green, Sec.; 1st and 3rd Mondays, I.O.O.F. Hall.
Sebastopol No. 143, Sebastopol—A. N. Badger, Pres.; F. G. McFarlane, Sec.; 1st and 3rd Fridays, I.O.O.F. Hall.

STANISLAUS COUNTY.

Modesto No. 11, Modesto—Robert H. Hansen, Pres.; C. C. Eastin Jr., Sec., P. O. box 898; 1st and 3rd Wednesdays, I.O.O.F. Hall.
Oakdale No. 142, Oakdale—D W. Tulloch, Pres.; E. T. Gobin, Sec.; 2nd Monday, Legion Hall.
Orestimba No. 247, Crows Landing—Lloyd W. Fink, Pres.; G. W. Fink, Sec.; 1st and 3rd Wednesdays, Community Club Home.

SUTTER COUNTY.

Sutter No. 261, Sutter City—Stanley R. McLean, Pres.; Glen R. Haynes, Sec., Yuba City; 2nd and 4th Mondays, N.D.G.W. Hall.

TRINITY COUNTY.

Mount Bally No. 87, Weaverville—M. F. Kay, Pres.; E. V. Ryan, Sec.; 1st and 3rd Mondays, Native Sons Hall.

TUOLUMNE COUNTY.

Tuolumne No. 144, Sonora—Mathew J. Marshall, Pres.; William M. Harrington, Sec., P. O. box 716; 2nd and 4th Fridays, Knights Columbus Hall.
Columbia No. 258, Columbia—Jos. Cadematori, Pres.; Charles E. Grant, Sec.; 2nd and 4th Thursdays, Native Sons Hall.

VENTURA COUNTY.

Cabrillo No. 114, Ventura City—David Bennett, Pres., 1380 Church St.

YOLO COUNTY.

Woodland No. 30, Woodland—J. L. Aronson, Pres.; E. B. Hayward, Sec.; 1st Thursday, Native Sons Hall.

YUBA COUNTY.

Marysville No. 6, Marysville—John McQuaid, Pres.; Verne Fogarty, Sec., 719 6th St.; 2nd Friday, Foresters Hall.
Rainbow No. 40, Wheatland—W. E. Jones, Pres.; W. A. Bowser, Sec., P. O. box 313; 2nd Thursday, I.O.O.F. Hall.

AFFILIATED ORGANIZATIONS.

Alameda County Extension of the Order Committee, N.S.G.W.—Dr. William C. Freitas, Chmn.; Edgar G. Hansen, Sec., 1260 Russell St., Berkeley; meets 1st and 3rd Mondays, N.S.G.W. Hall, 11th and Clay Sts., Oakland.
Interparlor Committee (Southern District), N.S.G.W. and N.D.G.W.—Burrel D. Neighbours, Chmn.; F. J. Burmester, Sec., 2434 Micheltorena St., Los Angeles; meets 2nd and 4th Fridays, Patriotic Hall, 1816 So. Figueroa St., Los Angeles.
San Francisco Extension of the Order Committee, N.S.G.W.—Harmon D. Skillin, Chmn.; Harold J. Regan, Sec., 414 Mason St., San Francisco; meets 2nd and 4th Fridays, Grizzly Bear Club, 414 Mason St., San Francisco.
San Francisco Assembly No. 1 Past Presidents Association N.S.G.W.—Meets 1st and 3rd Fridays, Native Sons Bldg., 414 Mason St., San Francisco; J. H. Sylvester, Gov., J. F. Stanley, Sec., 1175 O'Farrell St., San Francisco.
East Bay Counties Assembly No. 3 Past Presidents Association N.S.G.W.—Meets 4th Monday, Native Sons Hall, 11th and Clay Sts., Oakland; F. H. Robson, Gov.; Edgar G. Hanson, Sec., 1260 Russell St., Berkeley.
Marin County Assembly No. 5 Past Presidents Association N.S.G.W.—J. S. Rose Jr., Gov.; L. J. Peter, Sec., Peter Bldg., 4th and "C" Sts., San Rafael.
Fred H. Greely Assembly No. 6 Past Presidents Association N.S.G.W.—Meets monthly with different Parlors comprising district; R. L. P. Bigelow, Gov.; Barney Barry, Sec., P. O. box 72, Lincoln.
San Joaquin Assembly No. 7 Past Presidents Association N.S.G.W.—Meets 1st Friday, Native Sons Hall, Stockton; Clyde H. Gregg, Gov.; R. D. Dorcey, Sec., Native Sons Club, Stockton.
Sonoma County Assembly No. 9 Past Presidents Association N.S.G.W.—Meets monthly at different Parlor headquarters in county; Louis Bosch, Gov.; L. S. Lewis, Sec., Court House, Santa Rosa.
General John A. Sutter Assembly No. 10 Past Presidents Association—C. C. Wachman, Gov.; Jas. J. Longshore, Sec., 514 "J" St., Sacramento.
Grizzly Bear Club—Members all Parlors outside San Francisco at all times welcome. Clubrooms top floor Native Sons Bldg., 414 Mason St., San Francisco.
Native Sons and Native Daughters Central Committee on Homeless Children—Main office, 955 Phelan Bldg., San Francisco; Mrs. John W. Stirling, Chmn.; Miss Mary E. Brusie, Sec. Los Angeles branch office, 3924 Sunset Blvd.; Dorothy Schlingman, Sec.

(ADVERTISEMENT.)

PIONEER NATIVES

(Continued from Page 13)

Soulsbyville (Tuolumne County)—John H. West, born in this county in 1859, died February 5 survived by a wife and four children. He was affiliated with Tuolumne Parlor No. 144 N.S.G.W. (Sonora).

San Jose (Santa Clara County)—James Layton, born in California in 1859, died February 6 survived by a daughter.

San Francisco—Mrs. Sarah Belasco-Mayer, born here in 1856, passed away February 8 survived by a daughter.

Chico (Butte County)—Mrs. Ada A. Preston, born in Tehama County in 1857, passed away February 9 survived by a husband and a daughter.

Downieville (Sierra County)—Lewis C. Clark, born at San Francisco in 1857, died February 10 survived by three children.

Alameda City—Mrs. Sophie Louise Schroeder, born at San Francisco in 1857, passed away February 10 survived by a husband and five children. She was affiliated with Keith Parlor No. 137 N.D.G.W. (San Francisco).

Sacramento City—Charles Edward Humes, born in California in 1857, died February 11 survived by a wife.

Downieville (Sierra County)—William Burns, born in this county in 1859, died February 12.

San Francisco—Mrs. Margaret Collins, born here in 1855, passed away February 12 survived by a son.

Etna (Siskiyou County)—Mrs. Mary A. Walker, born in this county in 1858, passed away February 15 survived by a husband and three children.

Gilroy (Santa Clara County)—Policronio Escolastico Guadalupe Anzar, born in San Benito County in 1851, died February 15 survived by a wife and ten children.

San Francisco—John Francis Corriea, born in Alameda County in 1859, died February 15 survived by a wife and two children. He was affiliated with Alcalde Parlor No. 154 N.S.G.W.

Cranmore (Sutter County)—George Correll, born in Sierra County in 1855, died February 16.

Oakland (Alameda County)—Eugene Hampton Folsom, born at San Francisco in 1859, died February 16 survived by a wife and a daughter. He was affiliated with California Parlor No. 1 N.S.G.W. (San Francisco).

Dixon (Solano County)—Mrs. Rebecca McCune-Silver, born in this county in 1855, passed away February 18 survived by a daughter.

New Low—Auto production in the United States last year fell to an all-time low of 2,389,730 units. The output in 1930 totaled 3,355,986, and in 1922, 2,544,000.

Anniversary Celebration—Jackson, Amador County, celebrated its eighty-third anniversary, February 6, with a leap-year ball.

Official Directory of Parlors of the N. D. G. W.

ALAMEDA COUNTY.

Angelita No. 32, Livermore—Meets 2nd and 4th Fridays, Foresters Hall; Mrs. Myrtle I. Johnson, Rec. Sec.

Piedmont No. 87, Oakland—Meets Thursdays, Corinthian Hall, Pacific Bldg.; Mrs. Alice E. Miner, Rec. Sec., 421 36th St.

Aloha No. 106, Oakland—Meets Tuesdays, Wigwam Hall, Pacific Bldg.; Gladys I. Farley, Rec. Sec., 4623 Benevides Ave.

Hayward No. 122, Hayward—Meets 1st and 3rd Tuesdays, Veterans Memorial Bldg., Main St.; Miss Ruth Gansberger, Rec. Sec., P. O. Box 44, Mount Eden.

Berkeley No. 150, Berkeley—Meets 1st and 3rd Fridays, Masonic Hall; Mrs. Lelia B. Baker, Rec. Sec., 915 Contra Costa Ave.

Bear Flag No. 151, Berkeley—Meets 2nd and 4th Wednesdays, Veterans Memorial Bldg., 1931 Center St.; Mrs. Maud Wagner, Rec. Sec., 317 Alcatraz Ave., Oakland.

Encinal No. 156, Alameda—Meets 2nd and 4th Thursdays, N.S.G.W. Hall; Mrs. Laura E. Fisher, Rec. Sec., 1413 Caroline St.

Brooklyn No. 157, East Oakland—Meets Wednesdays, Masonic Temple, 8th Ave. and E. 14th St.; Mrs. Ruth Cooney, Rec. Sec., 3907 14th Ave.

Argonaut No. 166, Oakland—Meets Tuesdays, Klinkner Hall, 59th and San Pablo; Mrs. Ada Spilman, Rec. Sec., 2905 Ellis St., Berkeley.

Bahia Vista No. 167, Oakland—Meets Thursdays, Wigwam Hall, Pacific Bldg.; Mrs. Minnie R. Raper, Rec. Sec., 3449 Helen St.

Fruitvale No. 177, Oakland—Meets Fridays, W.O.W. Hall; Mrs. Agnes M. Grant, Rec. Sec., 1224 30th Ave.

Laura Loma No. 182, Niles—Meets 1st and 3rd Tuesdays, I.O.O.F. Hall; Mrs. Ethel Fournier, Rec. Sec., P. O. Box 515.

El Cereso No. 207, San Leandro—Meets 2nd and 4th Tuesdays, Masonic Hall; Mrs. Mary Tuttle, Rec. Sec., P. O. Box 56.

Pleasanton No. 237, Pleasanton—Meets 1st Tuesday, I.O.O.F. Hall; Mrs. Myrtle Lanini, Rec. Sec.

Betsy Ross No. 238, Centerville—Meets 1st and 3rd Fridays, Anderson Hall; Miss Constance Lucio, Rec. Sec., P. O. Box 187.

AMADOR COUNTY.

Ursula No. 1, Jackson—Meets 2nd and 4th Tuesdays, N.S.G.W. Hall; Mrs. Emma Boarman-Wright, Rec. Sec., 114 Court St.

Chispa No. 40, Ione—Meets 2nd and 4th Fridays, N.S.G.W. Hall; Mrs. Isabel Ashton, Rec. Sec.

Amapola No. 80, Sutter Creek—Meets 2nd and 4th Thursdays, N.S.G.W. Bldg.; Mrs. Hazel M. Marre, Rec. Sec.

Forrest No. 86, Plymouth—Meets 2nd and 4th Tuesdays, I.O.O.F. Hall; Mrs. Marguerite Davis, Rec. Sec.

BUTTE COUNTY.

Annie K. Bidwell No. 168, Chico—Meets 2nd and 4th Thursdays, I.O.O.F. Hall; Mrs. Irene Henry, Rec. Sec., 3015 Woodland Ave.

Gold of Ophir No. 190, Oroville—Meets 1st and 3rd Wednesdays, Memorial Hall; Mrs. Ruth Brown, Rec. Sec., 1265 Leah Court.

CALAVERAS COUNTY.

Ruby No. 46, Murphys—Meets 4th Friday, N.S.G.W. Hall; Belle Segale, Rec. Sec.

Princess No. 84, Angels Camp—Meets 2nd and 4th Wednesdays, I.O.O.F. Hall; Grace Mills, Rec. Sec.

San Andreas No. 113, San Andreas—Meets 1st Friday, Fraternal Hall; Miss Doris Treat, Rec. Sec.

COLUSA COUNTY.

Colusa No. 194, Colusa—Meets 1st and 3rd Mondays, Eagles Hall; Miss Kate Busch, Rec. Sec., 350 Market St.

CONTRA COSTA COUNTY.

Stirling No. 146, Pittsburg—Meets 1st and 3rd Wednesdays, Veteran Memorial Hall; Mrs. Minnie Marcelli, Rec. Sec., 771 E. 12th St.

Richmond No. 147, Richmond—Meets 1st and 3rd Tuesdays, I.O.O.F. Hall, 10th St.; Mrs. Tillie Summers, Rec. Sec., 640 So. 31st St.

Donner No. 193, Byron—Meets 1st and 3rd Wednesdays, I.O.O.F. Hall; Mrs. Anna Pendry, Rec. Sec., P. O. Box 112.

Las Juntas No. 221, Martinez—Meets 1st and 3rd Mondays, Pythian Castle; Mrs. Lola O. Viera, Rec. Sec., 305 Arreba St.

Antioch No. 223, Antioch—Meets 2nd and 4th Tuesdays, I.O.O.F. Hall; Mrs. Estelle Evans, Rec. Sec., 202 E. 5th St., Pittsburg.

Carquinez No. 234, Crockett—Meets 2nd and 4th Wednesdays, I.O.O.F. Hall; Mrs. Cecile Petee, Rec. Sec., 465 Edwards St.

GRAND OFFICERS.

Mrs. Estelle M. Evans........Past Grand President
202 E. Fifth St., Pittsburg

Mrs. Evelyn I. Carlson............Grand President
1965 San Jose Ave., San Francisco

Mrs. Anna M. Armstrong.....Grand Vice-president
Woodland

Mrs. Sallie R. Thaler...............Grand Secretary
555 Baker St., San Francisco

Mrs. Susie K. Christ...............Grand Treasurer
555 Baker St., San Francisco

Mrs. Irma Laird.......................Grand Marshal
Alturas

Mrs. Minna K. Horn.........Grand Inside Sentinel
Etna

Mrs. Orinda G. Giannini.....Grand Outside Sentinel
2142 Filbert St., San Francisco

Mrs. Lola Horgan...................Grand Organist
789 Morse St., San Francisco

GRAND TRUSTEES.

Mrs. Edna Briggs, 1045 Santa Ynez Way, Sacramento
Mrs. Ethel Begley.....1206 Valencia, San Francisco
Mrs. Anna Thuesen....615 38th Ave., San Francisco
Mrs. Gladys Noce ....Sutter Creek
Mrs. Florence Boyle..........................Oroville
Mrs. Florence Schoneman, 1521 5th Ave., Los Angeles
Mrs. Willow Borba.......................Sebastopol

EL DORADO COUNTY.

Marguerite No. 12, Placerville—Meets 1st and 3rd Wednesdays, Masonic Hall; Mrs. Nettie Leonardi, Rec. Sec., 25 Coloma St.

El Dorado No. 186, Georgetown—Meets 2nd and 4th Saturday afternoons, I.O.O.F. Hall; Mrs. Alta L. Douglas, Rec. Sec.

FRESNO COUNTY.

Fresno No. 187, Fresno—Meets 2nd and 4th Fridays, Pythian Castle, Cor. "R" and Merced Sts.; Mary Aubery, Rec. Sec., 1040 Delphia Ave.

GLENN COUNTY.

Berryessa No. 192, Willows—Meets 1st and 3rd Mondays, I.O.O.F. Hall; Mrs. Leonora Neate, Rec. Sec., 338 No. Lassen St.

HUMBOLDT COUNTY.

Occident No. 28, Eureka—Meets 1st and 3rd Wed-
Rec. Sec., 2309 "B" St.
nesdays, N.S.G.W. Hall; Mrs. Eva L. MacDonald,

Oneonta No. 71, Ferndale—Meets 2nd and 4th Fridays, I.O.O.F. Hall; Mrs. Myra Rumrill, Rec. Sec.

Reichling No. 97, Fortuna—Meets 1st and 3rd Tuesdays, Friendship Hall; Mrs. Grace Swett, Rec. Sec., P. O. Box 328.

KERN COUNTY.

Miocene No. 228, Taft—Meets 1st and 3rd Wednesday afternoons, I.O.O.F. Hall; Mrs. Evalyne Towne, Rec. Sec., P. O. Box 1011.

El Tejon No. 239, Bakersfield—Meets 1st and 3rd Fridays, Eagles Hall, 1714 "G" St.; Miss Mayme Efird, Rec. Sec., 2117 Chester Ave.

Desert Gold No. 250, Mojave—Meets 2nd and 4th Fridays, I.O.O.F. Hall; Mrs. Mae Coffill, Rec. Sec.

LAKE COUNTY.

Clear Lake No. 135, Middletown—Meets 2nd and 4th Tuesdays, Herrick Hall; Mrs. Alma E. Snow, Rec. Sec.

LASSEN COUNTY.

Nataqua No. 152, Standish—Meets 1st and 3rd Wednesdays, Foresters Hall; Mrs. Mayda Elledge, Rec. Sec.

Mount Lassen No. 215, Bieber—Meets 2nd and 4th Thursdays, I.O.O.F. Hall; Mrs. Angie C. Kenyon, Rec. Sec.

Susanville No. 243, Susanville—Meets 3rd Thursday, I.O.O.F. Hall; Mrs. Georgia Jensen, Rec. Sec., 700 Roop St.

LOS ANGELES COUNTY.

Los Angeles No. 124, Los Angeles—Meets 1st and 3rd Wednesdays, I.O.O.F. Hall, Washington and Oak Sts.; Mrs. Mary K. Corcoran, Rec. Sec., 322 No. Van Ness Ave.

Long Beach No. 154, Long Beach—Meets 1st and 3rd Thursdays, K.P. Hall, 341 Pacific Ave.; Mrs. Bertha Hitt, Rec. Sec., 5355 Lime Ave.

Rudecinda No. 230, San Pedro—Meets 1st and 3rd Fridays, Unity Hall, I.O.O.F. Temple, 10th and Gaffey; Mrs. Carrie E. Northway, Rec. Sec., 561 W. 14th St.

Verdugo No. 240, Glendale—Meets 2nd and 4th Tuesdays, Masonic Temple, 234 So. Brand Blvd.; Miss Etta Fulkerth, Rec. Sec., 526-A No. Orange St.

Santa Monica Bay No. 245, Ocean Park—Meets 1st and 3rd Mondays, New Eagles Hall, 2823½ Main St.; Mrs. Rosalie Hyde, Rec. Sec., 738 Flower St., Venice.

Californiana No. 247, Los Angeles—Meets 2nd and 4th Tuesday afternoons, Hollywood Studio Club, 1215 Lodi Place; Mrs. Inez Sitton, Rec. Sec., 4223 Berenice St.

MADERA COUNTY.

Madera No 244 Madera—Meets 2nd and 4th Thursdays, Masonic Annex; Mrs. Margaret C. Boyle, Rec. Sec., 111 No. "B" St.

MARIN COUNTY.

Sea Point No. 196, Sausalito—Meets 2nd and 4th Mondays, Perry Hall, 60 Caledonia St.; Mrs. Mary B. Smith, Rec. Sec., 559 Woodward Ave.

Marinita No. 198, San Rafael—Meets 2nd and 4th Mondays, 316 "B" St.; Miss Mollye Y. Spaelti, Rec. Sec., 539 4th St.

Fairfax No. 225, Fairfax—Meets 2nd and 4th Tuesdays, Community Hall; Mrs. Olive A. Greene, Rec. Sec., P. O. Box 277.

Tamelpa No. 231, Mill Valley—Meets 1st and 2nd Tuesdays, I.O.O.F. Hall; Mrs. Delphine M. Todt, Rec. Sec., 400 Grand Ave., San Rafael.

MARIPOSA COUNTY.

Mariposa No. 63, Mariposa—Meets 1st and 3rd Fridays, I.O.O.F. Hall; Mrs. Mamie E. Weston, Rec. Sec.

ATTENTION, SECRETARIES!

THIS DIRECTORY IS PUBLISHED BY AUTHORITY OF THE GRAND PARLOR N.D.G.W., AND ALL NOTICES OF CHANGES MUST BE RECEIVED BY THE GRAND SECRETARY (NOT THE MAGAZINE) ON OR BEFORE THE 20TH OF EACH MONTH TO INSURE CORRECTION IN NEXT PUBLICATION OF DIRECTORY.

MENDOCINO COUNTY.

Fort Bragg No. 210, Fort Bragg—Meets 1st and 3rd Thursdays, I.O.O.F. Hall; Mrs. Ruth W. Fuller, Rec. Sec.

MERCED COUNTY.

Veritas No. 75, Merced—Meets 1st and 3rd Tuesdays, I.O.O.F. Hall; Miss Margaret Thornton, Rec. Sec., 317 18th St.

MODOC COUNTY.

Alturas No. 159, Alturas—Meets 1st Thursday, Alturas Civic Club; Mrs. Irma W. Laird, Rec. Sec.

MONTEREY COUNTY.

Aleli No. 102, Salinas—Meets 2nd and 4th Thursdays, Knights Pythias Hall; Miss Rose Rhyner, Rec. Sec., 420 Soledad St.

Junipero No. 141, Monterey—Meets 2nd and 4th Fridays, Pythian Hall; Miss Matilda M. Bergschicker, Rec. Sec., 498 Van Buren St.

NAPA COUNTY.

Eschol No. 16, Napa—Meets 2nd and 4th Mondays, N.S.G.W. Hall; Mrs. Ella Ingram, Rec. Sec., 2140 Seminary St.

Calistoga No. 145, Calistoga—Meets 2nd and 4th Mondays, I.O.O.F. Hall; Sadie P. Brooks, Rec. Sec.

La Junta No. 203, Saint Helena—Meets 1st and 3rd Tuesdays, N.S.G.W. Hall; Mrs. Marie Signorelli, Rec. Sec., 1341 Madrona Ave.

NEVADA COUNTY.

Laurel No. 6, Nevada City—Meets 1st and 3rd Wednesdays, I.O.O.F. Hall; Mrs. Nellie E. Clark, Rec. Sec., P. O. Box 212.

Manzanita No. 29, Grass Valley—Meets 1st and 3rd Tuesdays, Auditorium; Mrs. Loraine Keast, Rec. Sec., 123 Race St.

Columbia No. 70, French Corral—Meets Fridays, Farrelley Hall; Mrs. Kate Farrelley-Sullivan, Rec. Sec.

Snow Peak No. 176, Truckee—Meets 1st Monday, I.O.O.F. Hall; Mrs. Henrietta M. Eaton, Rec. Sec., P. O. Box 116.

ORANGE COUNTY.

Santa Ana No. 235, Santa Ana—Meets 2nd and 4th Mondays, K.C. Hall, 4th and French Sts.; Mrs. Matilda S. Lemon, Rec. Sec., 1038 W. Bishop St.

Grace No. 242, Fullerton—Meets 1st and 3rd Thursdays, I.O.O.F. Hall, 116½ E. Commonwealth; Mrs. Mary Rothnermel, Rec. Sec., P. O. Box 235.

PLACER COUNTY.

Placer No. 138, Lincoln—Meets 2nd Wednesday, I.O.O.F. Hall; Miss Carrie Parlin, Rec. Sec.

La Rosa No. 191, Roseville—Meets 1st and 3rd Tuesdays, Eagles Hall; Mrs. Alice Lee West, Rec. Sec., Rocklin.

Auburn No. 233, Auburn—Meets 2nd and 4th Fridays, Foresters Hall; Mrs. Dorothy Reinecke, Rec. Sec., Penryn.

PLUMAS COUNTY.

Plumas Pioneer No. 219, Quincy—Meets 1st and 3rd Mondays, I.O.O.F. Hall; Minnie E. Johnson, Rec. Sec., P. O. Box 243.

SACRAMENTO COUNTY.

Califia No. 22, Sacramento—Meets 2nd and 4th Tuesdays, N.S.G.W. Hall; Miss Lulu Gillis, Rec. Sec., 921 8th St.

La Bandera No. 110, Sacramento—Meets 1st and 3rd Fridays, N.S.G.W. Hall; Mrs. Clara Weldon, Rec. Sec., 1310 "O" St.

Sutter No. 111, Sacramento—Meets 1st and 3rd Tuesdays, N.S.G.W. Hall; Mrs. Adele Nix, Rec. Sec., 1238 "S" St.

Fern No. 123, Folsom—Meets 1st and 3rd Tuesdays, K.P. Hall; Mrs. Viola Shumway, Rec. Sec., P. O. Box 48.

Chabolla No. 171, Galt—Meets 2nd and 4th Tuesdays, I.O.O.F. Hall; Mrs. Mary Pritchard, Rec. Sec.

Coloma No. 212, Sacramento—Meets 1st and 3rd Tuesdays, I.O.O.F. Hall, Oak Park; Mrs. Nettie Harry, Rec. Sec., 1217 35th St.

Liberty No. 213, Elk Grove—Meets 2nd and 4th Fridays, I.O.O.F. Hall; Mrs. Frances Wackman, Rec. Sec., P. O. Box 192.

Victory No. 216, Courtland—Meets 1st Saturday and 3rd Monday, N.S.G.W. Hall; Mrs. Agneda Lample, Rec. Sec.

SAN BENITO COUNTY.

Copa de Oro No. 105, Hollister—Meets 2nd and 4th Thursdays, Grangers Union Hall; Mrs. Mollie Daveggio, Rec. Sec., 110 San Benito St.

San Juan Bautista No. 179, San Juan Bautista—Meets 1st Wednesday, Mission Corridor Rooms; Miss Gertrude Breen, Rec. Sec.

SAN BERNARDINO COUNTY.

Lugonia No. 241, San Bernardino—Meets 2nd and 4th Wednesdays, Eagles Hall; Grace McHenry, Rec. Sec., Base Line and Central, Highland.

Ontario No. 251, Ontario—Meets 2nd and 4th Thursdays, Ontario Hotel; Miss Helen Hickman, Rec. Sec., 923 No. Laurel Ave.

SAN DIEGO COUNTY.

San Diego No. 208, San Diego—Meets 2nd and 4th Wednesdays, Directors Room, Chamber Commerce Bldg., 499 W. Broadway; Mrs. Elsie Case, Rec. Sec., 3051 Broadway.

SAN FRANCISCO CITY AND COUNTY.

Minerva No. 2, San Francisco—Meets 1st and 3rd Wednesdays, N.S.G.W. Bldg.; Miss Dorothy Finn, Rec. Sec., 90 Princess St., Sausalito.

Alta No. 3, San Francisco—Meets 2nd and 4th Tuesdays, N.S.G.W. Bldg.; Mrs. Agnese L. Hughes, Rec. Sec., 3980 Sacramento St.

Oro Fino No. 9, San Francisco—Meets 1st and 3rd Thursdays, N.S.G.W. Bldg.; Mrs. Josephine B. Morrisey, Rec. Sec., 4441 20th St.

Golden State No. 50, San Francisco—Meets 1st and 3rd Wednesdays, N.D.G.W. Home; Miss Millie Tietjen, Rec. Sec., 328 Lexington Ave.

Orinda No. 56, San Francisco—Meets 2nd and 4th Fridays, N.D.G.W. Home; Mrs. Anna A. Gruber-Loser, Rec. Sec., 72 Grove Lane, San Anselmo.

Fremont No. 59, San Francisco—Meets 1st and 3rd Tuesdays, N.S.G.W. Bldg.; Miss Hannah Collins, Rec. Sec., 563 Fillmore St.

Buena Vista No. 68, San Francisco—Meets 1st, 3rd and 5th Thursdays, N.D.G.W. Home; Miss Margaret Barrett, Rec. Sec., 3774 20th St.

Las Lomas No. 72, San Francisco—Meets 1st and 3rd Tuesdays, N.D.G.W. Home; Mrs. Marion S. Day, Rec. Sec., 471 Alvarado St.

Yosemite No. 83, San Francisco—Meets 1st and 3rd Tuesdays, American Hall, 20th and Capp Sts.; Miss Mary Monahan, Rec. Sec., 237 Noe St.

La Estrella No. 89, San Francisco—Meets 2nd and 4th Mondays, N.S.G.W. Bldg.; Miss Birdie Hartman, Rec. Sec., 1018 Jackson St.

Sans Souci No. 96, San Francisco—Meets 2nd and 4th Mondays, N.D.G.W. Home; Mrs. Minnie F. Dobbin, Rec. Sec., 1483 43rd Ave.

Calaveras No. 103, San Francisco—Meets 2nd and 4th Tuesdays, Swedish American Hall, 2174 Market St.; Mrs. Lena Lorsheter, Rec. Sec., 492-C 41st St., Oakland.

Darina No. 114, San Francisco—Meets 1st and 3rd Mondays, N.S.G.W. Bldg.; Miss Adele Walsh, Rec. Sec., 479 Page St.

El Vespero No. 118, San Francisco—Meets 2nd and 4th Tuesdays, Masonic Hall, 4705 3rd St.; Mrs. Nell R. Boege, Rec. Sec., 1526 Kirkwood Ave.

Genevieve No. 132, San Francisco—Meets 1st and 3rd Thursdays, N.S.G.W. Bldg.; Miss Branice Peguillan, Rec. Sec., 2434 16th Ave.

Keith No. 137, San Francisco—Meets 2nd and 4th Thursdays, N.S.G.W. Bldg.; Mrs. Helen T. Mann, Rec. Sec., 575 Pierce St., Apt. 206.

Gabrielle No. 139, San Francisco—Meets 2nd and 4th Wednesdays, N.S.G.W. Bldg.; Mrs. Dorothy Wuesterfeld, Rec. Sec., 1020 Munich St.

Presidio No. 148, San Francisco—Meets 2nd and 4th Tuesdays, N.S.G.W. Bldg.; Mrs. Hattie Gaughran, Rec. Sec., 713 Capp St.

Guadalupe No. 153, San Francisco—Meets 2nd and 4th Mondays, Forester Hall, 170 Valencia St.; Miss May A. McCarthy, Rec. Sec., 336 Elsie St.

Golden Gate No. 158, San Francisco—Meets 2nd and 4th Mondays, N.S.G.W. Bldg.; Miss Mary Sullivan, Rec. Sec., 33 Cuvier St.

Dolores No. 169, San Francisco—Meets 2nd and 4th Wednesdays, N.S.G.W. Bldg.; Mrs. Ada Saunders, Rec. Sec., 284 Allison St.

Linda Rosa No. 170, San Francisco—Meets 2nd and 4th Wednesdays, Swedish American Hall, 2174 Market St.; Mrs. Eva P. Tyrrel, Rec. Sec., 2629 Mission St.

Portola No. 172, San Francisco—Meets 1st and 3rd Tuesdays, N.S.G.W. Bldg.; Catherine H. Dolly, Rec. Sec., 4125 23rd St.

Castro No. 178, San Francisco—Meets 1st and 3rd Wednesdays, K.C. Bldg., 150 Golden Gate Ave.; Miss Adeline Sandersfeld, Rec. Sec., 50 Baker St.

Twin Peaks No. 185, San Francisco—Meets 2nd and 4th Fridays, Druids Temple, 44 Page St.; Mrs. Loretta Cameron, Rec. Sec., 3969 Army St.

James Lick No. 220, San Francisco—Meets 1st and 3rd Wednesdays, N.S.G.W. Bldg.; Mrs. Edna Bishop, Rec. Sec., 3841 24th St.

Mission No. 227, San Francisco—Meets 2nd and 4th Fridays, N.S.G.W. Bldg.; Mrs. Ann Dippel, Rec. Sec., 448 Dewey Blvd.

Bret Harte No. 232 San Francisco—Meets 2nd and 4th Tuesdays, Aloha Hall, 3009 16th St.; Muriele N. Pabst, Rec. Sec., 696 Guerrero St.

La Dorada No. 236, San Francisco—Meets 2nd and 4th Thursdays, N.S.G.W. Hall; Mrs. Theresa R. O'Brien, Rec. Sec., 567 Liberty St.

Balboa No. 249, San Francisco—Meets 1st and 3rd Thursdays, Maccabee Hall, 5th Ave. and Clement St., Jean Moffet, Rec. Sec., 6633 California St.

SAN JOAQUIN COUNTY.

Joaquin No. 5, Stockton—Meets 2nd and 4th Tuesdays, N.S.G.W. Hall, 314 E. Main St.; Mrs. Della Garvin, Rec. Sec., 1122 E. Market St.

El Pescadero No. 82, Tracy—Meets 1st and 3rd Fridays, I.O.O.F. Hall; Mrs. Mary A. Hewitson, Rec. Sec., 215 W. 9th St.

Ivy No. 88, Lodi—Meets 1st and 3rd Wednesdays, Eagles Hall; Mrs. Mae Corson, Rec. Sec., 109 So. School St.

Caliz de Oro No. 206, Stockton—Meets 1st and 3rd Tuesdays, N.S.G.W. Hall, 314 E. Main St.; Mrs. Frances Germain, Rec. Sec., 450 No. Regent.

Phoebe A. Hearst No. 214, Manteca—Meets 2nd and 4th Wednesdays, I.O.O.F. Hall; Mrs. Josie M. Frederick, Rec. Sec., Route A, Box 364, Ripon.

SAN LUIS OBISPO COUNTY.

San Miguel No. 94, San Miguel—Meets 2nd and 4th Wednesday afternoons, Clemon Hall; Mrs. Nellie Wickstrom, Rec. Sec.

San Luisita No. 108, San Luis Obispo—Meets 2nd and 4th Thursdays, W.O.W. Hall; Miss Agnes M. Lee, Rec. Sec., P. O. Box 584.

El Pinal No. 163, Cambria—Meets 2nd, 4th and 5th Tuesdays, N.S.G.W. Hall; Kathryn Luchessa, Rec. Sec.

SAN MATEO COUNTY.

Bonita No. 10, Redwood City—Meets 2nd and 4th Thursdays, I.O.O.F. Hall; Mrs. Dora Wilson, Rec. Sec., 518 Middlefield Rd.

Vista del Mar No. 155, Halfmoon Bay—Meets 2nd and 4th Thursdays, I.O.O.F. Hall; Mrs. Grace Griffith, Rec. Sec.

Ano Nuevo No. 180, Pescadero—Meets 1st and 3rd Wednesdays, I.O.O.F. Hall; Mrs. Alice Mattei, Rec. Sec.

El Carmelo No. 181, Daly City—Meets 1st and 3rd Wednesdays, Masonic Hall; Mrs. Hattie Kelly, Rec. Sec., 1179 Brunswick St.

Menlo No. 211, Menlo Park—Meets 2nd and 4th Mondays, Masonic Hall; Mrs. Frances E. Maloney, Rec. Sec., P. O. Box 626.

San Bruno No. 246, San Bruno—Meets 2nd and 4th Fridays, N.D. Hall; Mildred Foley, Rec. Sec., 217 Miller Ave., South San Francisco.

SANTA BARBARA COUNTY.

Reina del Mar No. 126, Santa Barbara—Meets 1st and 3rd Tuesdays, Pythian Castle, 222 W. Carillo St.; Miss Christina Moller, Rec. Sec., 836 Bath St.

SANTA CLARA COUNTY.

San Jose No. 81, San Jose—Meets Thursdays, Catholic Women Center, 5th and San Fernando Sts.; Mrs. Nellie Fleming, Rec. Sec., Catholic Women's Center.

Vendome No. 100, San Jose—Meets Wednesdays, Old Scottish Rite Temple; Miss Marie Buck, Rec. Sec., 1414 Ellen St.

El Monte No. 205, Mountain View—Meets 2nd and 4th Fridays, American Legion Hall; Miss Mary Ann Rokovich, Rec. Sec., R.F.D. No. 1, Box 412, State Highway.

Palo Alto No. 229, Palo Alto—Meets 1st and 2nd Mondays, N.S.G.W. Hall; Miss Helena G. Hansen, Rec. Sec., 531 Lytton Ave.

SANTA CRUZ COUNTY.

Santa Cruz No. 26, Santa Cruz—Meets Mondays, N.S.G.W. Hall; Mrs. May L. Williamson, Rec. Sec., 170 Walnut Ave.

El Pajaro No. 35, Watsonville—Meets 1st and 3rd Tuesdays, I.O.O.F. Hall; Miss Ruth E. Wilson, Rec. Sec., 16 Laurel St.

SHASTA COUNTY.

Camellia No. 41, Anderson—Meets 1st and 3rd Tuesdays, Masonic Hall; Mrs. Olga E. Welbourn, Rec. Sec.

Lassen View No. 98, Shasta—Meets 2nd Friday, Masonic Hall; Miss Louise Litsch, Rec. Sec.

N.D.G.W. OFFICIAL DEATH LIST.

Giving the name, the date of death, and the Subordinate Parlor affiliation of all deceased members as reported to Grand Secretary Sallie R. Thaler from January 21 to February 18:

Coy, Virginia Arze; September 5, 1931; Desert Gold No. 250.

Richardson, Grace S.; November 24, 1931; Californiana No. 247.

McIver, Mary; December 25, 1931; Las Lomas No. 72.

Williams, Irene P.; January 7, 1932; Reina del Mar No. 126.

Kimball, Rebecca M.; January 17, 1932; Minerva No. 2.

Carrick, Mamie C.; January 17, 1932; Golden State No. 50.

Schmidt, Elizabeth D.; January 11, 1932; Mission No. 227.

Hickman, Marie H.; January 4, 1932; Piedmont No. 87.

Mahoney, Margaret; December 7, 1931; Oro Fino No. 9.

Ortega, Josephine; February 1, 1932; La Dorado No. 236.

Dickinson, Ida M.; January 27, 1932; Plumas Pioneer No. 219.

Peterson, Hilda; February 2, 1932; Gabrielle No. 139.

Gille, Katherine; February 1, 1932; Linda Rosa No. 170.

McCreery, Agnes; February 1, 1932; Alta No. 3.

Napthaly, Mary; January 31, 1932; Alta No. 3.

Braska, Margaret; January 31, 1932; Golden Gate No. 158.

Brown, Louisa; February 7, 1932; El Cereso No. 207.

Hiawatha No. 140, Redding—Meets 2nd and 4th Wednesdays, Moose Hall; Ruth Presleigh, Rec. Sec., Office County Clerk.

SIERRA COUNTY.

Naomi No. 36, Downieville—Meets 2nd and 4th Wednesdays, I.O.O.F. Hall; Mrs. Mary Cook, Rec. Sec.

Imogen No. 134, Sierraville—Meets 2nd and 4th Saturday afternoons, Copren Hall; Mrs. Jennie Copren, Rec. Sec.

SISKIYOU COUNTY.

Eschscholtzia No. 112, Etna—Meets 1st and 3rd Wednesdays, Masonic Hall; Mrs. Bernice E. Smith, Rec. Sec.

Mountain Dawn No. 120, Sawyers Bar—Meets 2nd and last Wednesdays, I.O.O.F. Hall; Miss Edith Dunphy, Rec. Sec.

SOLANO COUNTY.

Vallejo No. 195, Vallejo—Meets 1st and 3rd Wednesdays, K.C. Hall, 820 Marin St.; Mrs. Mary Combs, Rec. Sec., 511 York St.

Mary E. Bell No. 224, Dixon—Meets 2nd and 4th Thursdays, I.O.O.F. Hall; Grace McFadyen, Rec. Sec.

SONOMA COUNTY.

Sonoma No. 209, Sonoma—Meets 2nd and 4th Mondays, I.O.O.F. Hall; Mrs. Mae Norrbom, Rec. Sec., R.F.D., Box 171.

Santa Rosa No. 217, Santa Rosa—Meets 1st and 3rd Thursdays, N.S.G.W. Hall; Mrs. Hazel E. Brown, Rec. Sec., 1521 4th St.

Petaluma No. 222, Petaluma—Meets 1st and 3rd Tuesdays, Dania Hall; Mrs. Margaret M. Oeltjen, Rec. Sec., 503 Prospect St.

STANISLAUS COUNTY.

Oakdale No. 125, Oakdale—Meets 1st Monday, I.O.O.F. Hall; Mrs. Lou Reeder, Rec. Sec.

Morada No. 199, Modesto—Meets 2nd and 4th Wednesdays, I.O.O.F. Hall; Mrs. Susan Sullivan, Rec. Sec., 823 10th St.

Eldora No. 248, Turlock—Meets 1st and 3rd Wednesdays, Fraternal Hall; Effie Lund, Rec. Sec., 624 Minaret Ave.

SUTTER COUNTY.

South Butte No. 226, Sutter—Meets 1st and 3rd Mondays, N.D.G.W. Hall; Mrs. Abbie N. Vagedes, Rec. Sec.

TEHAMA COUNTY.

Berendos No. 23, Red Bluff—Meets 1st and 3rd Tuesdays, W.O.W. Hall, 200 Pine St.; Mrs. Lillie Hammer, Rec. Sec., 636 Jackson St.

TRINITY COUNTY.

Eltapome No. 55, Weaverville—Meets 2nd and 4th Thursdays, N.S.G.W. Hall; Mrs. Lou N. Fetzer, Rec. Sec.

TUOLUMNE COUNTY.

Dardanelle No. 66, Sonora—Meets Fridays, I.O.O.F. Hall; Mrs. Nettie Whitto, Rec. Sec.

Golden Era No. 99, Columbia—Meets 1st and 3rd Thursdays, N.S.G.W. Hall; Miss Irene Ponce, Rec. Sec.

Anona No. 164, Jamestown—Meets 2nd and 4th Tuesdays, I.O.O.F. Hall; Mrs. Rosa A. Beckwith, Rec. Sec., P. O. Box 87.

YOLO COUNTY.

Woodland No. 90, Woodland—Meets 2nd and 4th Tuesdays, N.S.G.W. Hall; Mrs. Maude Heaton, Rec. Sec., 153 College St.

YUBA COUNTY.

Marysville No. 162, Marysville—Meets 2nd and 4th Wednesdays, Liberty Hall; Miss Cecelia C. Gomes, Rec. Sec., 701 6th St.

Camp Far West No. 218, Wheatland—Meets 3rd Tuesday, I.O.O.F. Hall; Mrs. Ethel C. Brock, Rec. Sec., P. O. Box 285.

AFFILIATED ORGANIZATIONS.

General Assembly Past Presidents—Meetings held annually in April at the home-town of Chief President; Miss Josephine Clark, 824 11th St., Oakland, Chief President; Mrs. Anna G. Loser, 72 Grove Lane, San Anselmo, Chief Secretary.

Past Presidents Association No. 1—Meets 1st and 3rd Mondays, N.S.G.W. Bldg., 414 Mason St., San Francisco; Mrs. Minnie F. Dobbin, Pres.; Mrs. May R. Barry, Rec. Sec., 2319 19th Ave., San Francisco.

Past Presidents Association No. 2—Meets 2nd and 4th Mondays, "Wigwam," Pacific Bldg., 16th and Jefferson, Oakland; Frieda Reichhold, Pres.; Mrs. Elizabeth B. Goodman, Rec. Sec., 134 Juana Ave., San Leandro.

Past Presidents Association No. 3 (Santa Clara County)—Meets 2nd Tuesday, homes of members; Mrs. Ida Sweeney, Pres.; Amelia S. Hartman, Rec. Sec., 157 Auzerais Ave., San Jose.

Past Presidents Association No. 4 (Sacramento County)—Meets 2nd Monday, Unitarian Hall, 1413 27th St., Sacramento City; Francis Kimball, Pres.; Lily May Tilden, Rec. Sec., 3225 "T" St., Sacramento.

Past Presidents Association No. 5 (Butte County)—Meets 1st Friday, homes of members, Chico and Oroville; Sonora Steadman, Pres; Ruth Brown, Rec. Sec., 1265 Leah Court, Oroville.

Past Presidents Association No. 6 (Nevada County)—Meets 4th Friday, alternately between Nevada City, Pythian Castle, and Grass Valley, Edna Sampson's home; Margaret V. Nolan, Pres.; Vere Hansen, Rec. Sec., R.F.D. No. 2, Box 41-C, Grass Valley.

Past Presidents Association No. 7 (Sonoma County)—Meets 1st Thursday, N.S.G.W. Hall, Santa Rosa; Willow Borba, Pres.; Clytie Lewis, Rec. Sec., R.F.D. No. 4, Box 345-A, Santa Rosa.

Past Presidents Association No. 8 (San Joaquin and Stanislaus Counties)—Meets 2nd Thursday, Red Men Hall, Stockton; Mrs. Mattie M. Stein, Pres.; Mrs. Harriet F. Corr, Rec. Sec., 729 E. Sonora St., Stockton.

Native Sons and Native Daughters Central Committee on Homeless Children—Main Office, 955 Phelan Bldg., San Francisco; Mrs. John W. Stirling, Chmn.; Miss Mary E. Brusie, Sec. Los Angeles branch office, 3924 Sunset Blvd.; Dorothy Schlingman, Sec.

(ADVERTISEMENT.)

NATIVE DAUGHTER NEWS

(Continued from Page 11)

Mrs. Carlson with a gift of china. The meeting-room was attractively decorated with liveoak boughs.

Following the meeting the assemblage joined Courtland No. 106—which was entertaining Grand First Vice-president Seth Millington and Grand Marshal Horace J. Leavitt—at a banquet. The tables were adorned with small trees, valentines and nutcups. Joseph Berry was the toastmaster, Henry Ehrhardt entertained with songs, and the grand officers of both Orders responded to toasts. Victory Parlor's arrangements for the evening were perfected by these committees: Decorations—Alicia Buckley (chairman), Doris Fisher, Ethel Schiller. Refreshments—Marie Goodman (chairman), Clara Herringer, Clarice Ring, Martha Buckley.

Surprise Handkerchief Shower.

Santa Ana—Mrs. Wm. West, chairman veteran welfare committee Santa Ana No. 235, reported February 8 that seventy-five glasses of marmalade had been distributed to the boys at the San Fernando hospital. Mrs. Lillian Gant was elected to the board of trustees vacancy. Arrangements for the official visit of Grand President Evelyn I. Carlson March 14 were given consideration. At refreshments, President Marion Crum was presented with a candle-lighted cake and a boquet of violets in recognition of her anniversary.

The Parlor's thimble club met February 17 at the home of Mrs. Walter Hiskey. The day was her birthday, and she was surprised with a handkerchief shower. Mrs. Gertrude Carter was complimented by a shower of mysterious lovely things. At a recent meeting of the club at Mrs. Raymond Ross' home a quilt, to be disposed of in the near-future for relief work, was finished.

Anniversary Celebrated.

Oakland—February 25 Aloha No. 106 celebrated its thirty-fourth anniversary with a party at the home of Past President Florence McLean. Grand Secretary Sallie R. Thaler, chairman, and her social committee planned an evening of entertainment, dancing, cards and a late supper, with decorations in honor of George Washington.

The regular monthly whist, under the chairmanship of Past President Maud Mitchell, was held February 27 at the home of Grand Secretary Thaler. A Saint Patrick dance, under the chairmanship of Third Vice-president Caroline Schulze, will be given March 15. The decorations will be most attractive.

Winners Feted.

Oroville—A valentine party February 3 feted the winning group in the recent membership drive of Gold of Ophir No. 190. There were several visitors, and three candidates were initiated. In the banquetroom, where the tables were elaborately decorated with valentine favors, Mrs. Hattie Clark, captain of the winning side, was presented with a gift.

Addresses were made by Grand Trustee Florence Boyle, Mrs. Jeannie Murray and Mrs. Cornelia Sank. The committee in charge for the evening included Mms. Lois Tegrunde, Addie Roderick, Florence Boyle, Rosa Crum and Anna Bernhard.

Ripley Out-rippled.

Alturas—Alturas No. 159 had a dinner to commemorate the twenty-fourth institution anniversary of the Parlor, January 18. The artistic decorations were symbolic of California. Six charter members and the past presidents had places of honor at the festive board. Past President Dorothy Gloster out-rippled Ripley in a pictorial believe-it-or-not presentation of youthful photos of the past and present officers of No. 159. Grand Marshal Irma Laird, Past Grand President Catherine E. Gloster and Past President Bertie Auble responded to toasts, and Master Wilbur Fountain, in cowboy attire, entertained with songs.

A business session of the Parlor followed the dinner, and Supervising Deputy Dorothy Gloster installed the officers. Chairman Mildred Boyd reported the Christmas ball a social and financial success. Donations to several worthy projects were authorized. February 5 a valentine party, with dancing and cards, was largely attended.

Novel Presentation Gift Basket.

Alameda—Grand President Evelyn I. Carlson paid an official visit to Encinal No. 156 February 11. Among the other visitors were Past Grand Presidents Estelle Evans and Addie Mosher, Grand Secretary Sallie R. Thaler, Grand Organist Lola Horgan and her glee club, Grand Outside Sentinel Orinda Giannini, Deputy Grand Presidents Irma Murray and Augusta Huxsol. The hall and banquetroom were beautifully decorated.

Grand President Carlson spoke interestingly of the Order's projects and stressed the importance of the homeless children work and the Loyalty Pledge. She was handed a check for $65 toward Encinal's pledge, and on behalf of the Parlor a basket of gifts was presented to her by Sallie Harmola, attired as George Washington, Muriel Jarret, attired as Abraham Lincoln, and George Harmola and Jack Lavaggetto, attired as Negro boys. Gifts were also presented Past Grand Evans and District Deputy Murray, and all the other grand officers received corsages. Refreshments were served at the close of the meeting. Irene Rose was chairman of the evening.

Ferns for Vets' Easter.

Santa Cruz—Past Grand President Stella Finkeldey, chairman Grand Parlor Veteran Welfare Committee, has received word from Miss Bertha C. Lovell, field director American Red Cross, Letterman General Hospital, San Francisco, expressing the wish that the custom of sending potted ferns for Easter be carried out this year, and twenty-two will be sent, to be distributed to the various wards. She is also in receipt of the following letter:

"This will acknowledge receipt of your letter of February 7, 1932, concerning magazines that have been supplied this hospital by the Native Daughters of the Golden West during the past years. We have consulted our librarian and learn that it would be deeply appreciated by the patients here if instead of the 'Red Book' this year, 'Time' and 'Mid Week Pictorial' be substituted. The balance of the list as submitted by you is most satisfactory to our patients, and we thank you heartily on their behalf for your continued interest. Very truly yours, D. C. FARNSWORTH, medical officer in charge, Veterans Administration Hospital, San Fernando, California."

Entertainment Increases Attendance.

Fullerton—Grace No. 242 enjoyed sociables with games and refreshments after the February meetings. President Mattie Edwards insists on entertainment after every meeting and as a result the attendance has increased. Past President Helen Edwards opened her home for a public card party February 16, and a nice sum was realized for the Parlor's Loyalty Pledge fund.

Grace's sewing club had an all-day meeting at the home of President Edwards February 25. It was her birthday, and she was surprised with a shower. Callye Sparkes-Blum, recent bride, was the recipient of a silver gift from the Parlor February 15, when members called on her to wish her happiness. The Parlor plans to plant a tree in commemoration of the birth of the nation's first president, George Washington.

Goodly Sum Netted.

Elk Grove—A jamboree under the direction of Mrs. Laura Coons was given January 22 for the benefit of the Loyalty Pledge fund of Liberty No. 213. A fine program was presented, and about $65 was netted. In appreciation, the Parlor entertained Mrs. Coons and her assistants at a chicken dinner February 12.

Poppies Aid Homeless.

Modesto—Morada No. 199 and Modesto No. 11 N.S.G.W. had joint installation of officers, with District Deputies Effie Prothero and C. R. Gill officiating. A fine program was presented and addresses were made by Supervising Deputy Katherine Kopf and Mrs. Mae Givens. The Parlors had their joint monthly whist in February, nearly 300 being in attendance. The proceeds of these parties go to general relief work.

Morada's members met at the homes of Mrs. Phillpa Kerr and Mrs. Chas. Blaine February 12 and 19 and made poppies which were sold publicly the 27th for the benefit of the homeless children.

Past Presidents Honored.

San Jose—Vendome No. 100 honored its past presidents at an old-fashioned party February 17. Hazel Haub was in charge and directed a half-hour of minstrelsy. Mrs. Clara Gairaud presented a patriotic tableau, "Betsy Ross." In the diningroom a jolly time was had, and addresses were made by President Imogene Thompson, Marshal Anita Moore and Past President Alice Kady.

Installations.

Placerville—Officers of Marguerite No. 12 and Placerville No. 9 N.S.G.W. were jointly installed by District Deputies Nora Gray and Joseph Scherrer, Annie Jaeger and George M. Smith becoming the respective presidents. A short musical program was followed by a banquet. Appropriate gifts were presented Past President Bessie Waldron and District Deputy Gray by Marguerite.

Lodi—Ivy No. 88's officers were installed by District Deputy Alice McDonald, Elfleda Landback becoming president. The hall and tables were artistically decorated by Thirsa Hunt, Margaret Roberts and Mary Meehl, who were also the refreshment committee. The retiring president, Sarah J. Elwood, was presented with an emblematic pin, and District Deputy McDonald was presented with a gift.

Woodland—Officers of Woodland No. 90 have been installed, Ruth Hickey being the new president. Grand Vice-president Anna Armstrong and Past Grand President Mary E. Bell were among the many in attendance. A dinner followed the ceremonies.

San Luis Obispo—Officers of San Luisita No. 108 were installed February 11 by District Deputy Elsie Loose, Ida Miossi becoming president. Large delegations from San Miguel No. 94 and El Pinal No. 163 (Cambria) were present at the meeting, which closed with a delicious banquet.

Dixon—Officers of Mary E. Bell No. 224 were installed by District Deputy Wanda Abele February 4, Lena Nickum becoming president. Three candidates were initiated. Among the many visitors were Grand Vice-president Anna Mixon-Armstrong, Supervising Deputy Edna Richter, Past Grand Presidents Mary E. Bell and Dr. Louise C. Heilbron. A midnight supper was served at a table cleverly decorated by Mrs. Grace McFadyen in a color scheme of pink and green. February 6 the Parlor had a food sale for the benefit of the homeless children.

Past Presidents' Doings.

Santa Clara—Past Presidents Association No. 3 had an enjoyable meeting at the home of Secretary Mary G. Newton February 16. Three candidates were received. Mrs. Clara Gairaud conducted a program commemorating the birthdays of Edison, Lincoln and Washington.

Oroville—Butte County Past Presidents Association No. 5 was entertained February 5 at the home of Mrs. J. J. LaVoy. February 14 the association sponsored the annual party at the Buttee County Infirmary, the program honoring George Washington, Abraham Lincoln and Saint Valentine.

Grass Valley—Officers of Nevada County Past President Association No. 6 were installed at Nevada City by Miss Annie Conlin, Margaret V. Nolan becoming president. Cards and refreshments followed the ceremonies. Members made aprons for the women at the Nevada County Hospital and presented them during an entertainment given at the institution. The recipients were delighted.

In Memoriam

ELIZABETH SCHMITT.

To the Officers and Members of Mission Parlor No. 227 N.D.G.W.:

Whereas, Almighty God, in His infinite wisdom, has seen fit to call our dearly beloved sister, Elizabeth Schmitt, into the great Heavenly Parlor above. We hold in fond memory her cheerful smile, her loving ways and her happy disposition. So suddenly she has been taken from us but, "Dear sister you are not forgotten. Though you are no more, still in memory you are with us, as you always were before." Therefore, be it

Resolved, That we extend to her bereaved family our deepest sympathy. It is our earnest prayer that God, in His infinite mercy, assuage their deep grief and send peace into their hearts. We here record our tribute of love and affection for one whose kindly ways endeared her to all who knew

LOS ANGELES--CITY and COUNTY

LOS ANGELES

(Continued from Page 9)

dent Anna Pierce. In keeping with the plan to beautify Los Angeles and vicinity for the Olympic games, the Parlor will seed a vacant lot to California poppies.

Following the February 15 meeting Rose vaili and Amelia Stryker as hostesses served a tamale supper. Plans were completed for the official visit of Grand President Evelyn I. Carlson, March 7. A membership campaign is under way and applications are being received from many young women. The Parlor has adopted a Native Son veteran at the Sawtelle National Soldiers Home, and he expresses appreciation for the attentions shown him in beautiful letters. At a recent meeting of Santa Monica Bay's sewing club Virginia, the 9-year-old daughter of Marie Barnes, spoke a little piece.

ANNIVERSARY CELEBRATED.

Long Beach—Long Beach Parlor No. 154 N.D.G.W. celebrated its twenty-fifth institution anniversary February 4, the banquetroom being charmingly decorated for the occasion. Charter Member Kate McFadyen, the first president, related the growth of the Parlor, and interesting events were told by Charter Members Eleanor Martin, Mabel Emery and Ella Ware.

February 18 No. 154 observed the Washington Bicentennial, a program being contributed by Hattie Ketcherside, Clara Fay and Daisy Hansen. In a contest dealing with the life of Washington, Mrs. Fay answered correctly most of the fourteen questions asked by Mrs. McFadyen and was awarded a prize. Grand President Evelyn I. Carlson will officially visit the Parlor March 3. Zella L. Hodgdon and Daisy Hansen are in charge of a plunkett dinner to be held April 7. The next meeting of the thimble club will be at the home of Fannie McPherson.

PAST PRESIDENTS HONORED.

San Pedro—Past presidents night was observed by Sepulveda Parlor No. 263 N.S.G.W. February 26. The program was in charge of President Francis G. Fetzer, and the fish dinner was supervised by David Main and Paul Zirkel. Past President William A. Reuter presided, and among those honored were Roman D. Sepulveda, charter senior past president, and James H. Dodson Sr., charter junior past president. Past President Earl LeMoine of Los Angeles Parlor No. 45 recently gave the Parlor an illustrated talk on California.

PERSONAL PARAGRAPHS.

A native daughter arrived at the home of Paul Lombardi February 10.

Mrs. Rita Machado (Santa Monica Bay N.D.) is the mother of a native daughter.

A native son has arrived at the home of Thomas D. Mott Jr. (Ramona N.S.).

J. Karl Lobdell (Ramona N.S.) departed last month on a pleasure trip through the Panama Canal.

George R. Tomb (Los Angeles N.S.) last month visited his old Marysville, Yuba County, haunts.

Mrs. Fannie Prather (Los Angeles N.D.) was a visitor last month to Stockton, San Joaquin County.

Stanley A. Wheeler and William J. Maggio (both Sepulveda N.S.) of San Pedro were recent visitors to San Francisco.

Miss Antice Ross was wedded to Fred J. Burmester (Los Angeles N.S.) February 11. They are residing at San Bernardino City.

Miss Cordelia Laventhal (Santa Monica Bay N.D) was a visitor last month to San Bernardino, where she sang at the National Orange Show.

Mrs. Evelyn I. Carlson (Grand President N.D.) was the luncheon guest February 29 of Mms. Amos Otis Evans and Leland Atherton Irish (both Californiana N.D.) and Hazel Hansen (Glendale N.D.).

THE DEATH RECORD.

Mrs. Clara K. Lucas, mother of Corliss B. Lucas (Ramona N.S.), passed away January 25 at the age of 61.

Frank Duncan Dewar, father of Donald C. Dewar (Ramona N.S.), died January 29.

Edward J. Valencia, son of Antonio Valencia (Santa Monica Bay N.S.) and Mary Valencia (Santa Monica Bay N.D.), died February 4 at the age of 26.

Mrs. Louise Brown, affiliated with El Cereso Parlor No. 207 N.D.G.W. (San Leandro), passed away February 7 at the age of 71. Four children survive.

William E. Stoermer, father of Miss Grace S. Stoermer (Past Grand President N.D.), died February 10. He was born at Los Angeles in 1862.

Mrs. Frances E. Bullard, mother of John A. Bullard (Ramona N.S.), passed away February 12 at the age of 69. She was a daughter of Theodore A. Schmidt, one of the founders, in 1856, of Anaheim, Orange County, where she was born. She was a charter member of the long-defunct Felicidad Parlor No. 52 N.D.G.W. (Anaheim).

Mrs. Alice M. Maxwell, mother of William H. Maxwell (Ramona N.S.), passed away February 15.

Mrs. Roxie Alma Pollard, affiliated with Los Angeles Parlor No. 124 N.D.G.W., passed away at Orange February 16 at the age of 66. A husband and four children survive.

In Memoriam

W. JOSEPH FORD.

Whereas, It has pleased Almighty God to call to his eternal rest our late brother, W. Joseph Ford; and whereas, Brother Ford was a true and loyal Native Son, a patriotic citizen, an active member of the bar, a loving husband and generous father; therefore, be it

Resolved, That Glendale Parlor No. 264 N.S.G.W. extends its deepest sympathy to his widow and family in thier bereavement; further be it resolved, that a copy of these resolutions be spread upon the minutes of the Parlor, that a copy be sent to the family of our later brother, also a copy to The Grizzly Bear Magazine for publication; also, that the charter of the Parlor be draped for a period of thirty days and that the Parlor stand in silence in respect to his memory.

Respectfully submitted,
A. K. BOECKMANN,
CLINTON E. SKINNER,
Committee.

Glendale, February 5, 1932.

Registrations Gain—California's fee-paid auto registrations last year totaled 2,107,275, an increase of 7,982 over the 1930 total of 2,099,293.

A BIT O' FARMING and GARDENING

PREPARED EXPRESSLY FOR THE GRIZZLY BEAR BY M. H. ELLIS

THERE'S MORE TO A VEGETABLE garden than a backache. True, you may get the backache, but you will get more. You will get health and strength as you use those muscles which should be used; muscles of the stomach walls will be soothed, and the exercise of gardening will reduce flesh that inactivity brings without welcome. More than this, a garden will reduce the family food bill, it will provide an abundant supply of fresh, high quality vegetables in season, it will furnish a supply for canning against the winter's needs, it furnishes food for substitution for more expensive foods, it provides for a more healthful diet, and, if you are interested, it gives you a chance to see how well you can produce and win prizes in the fall neighborhood or county fairs.

In most parts of California there has not been much winter gardening; spring work may be a little late. If it is, all right, don't rush things. Let the soil get dry enough to be really workable before you start operations. But as soon as it is, go to it! Turn up the earth, preferably turning under some barnyard manure at the same time, and let the weeds sprout. Then cultivate so as to kill the weeds and prepare a good seedbed. If commercial fertilizer is the only kind available, use it; it's good if it is the right kind. But be sure your garden gets something to make humus every year.

While exercise is all right, don't make any harder work of gardening than is necessary. In planning to plant, watch the distance between rows so that a wheel hoe or small push cultivator can be used. If a hoe is to be the implement, be sure you give plenty of room for its use. If the soil is dry enough, all the hardy vegetables should be planted at once; the more tender ones may follow as frost danger passes.

WATCH THE CUTWORM.

One of the toughest customers around the garden is the cutworm. It attacks vegetables as willingly as flowers, but it shows little preference. So, get after him early and stay after him late. Use a poison bran mash, which may be made as follows: dry mix a pound of bran and an ounce of calcium arsenate, then add a cup of black molasses and enough water to make it crumbly. This should be sprinkled on the ground in the evening; about three days will find the cutworms a minus quantity. Don't forget it is poison, though; children and chickens should be kept away from it.

DUSTING FOR GARDEN PESTS.

Whether to spray or dust for garden pests, such as the ever-present aphis, is a problem some gardeners have difficulty in answering. Either method is good, if the proper material is used and a thorough coverage is secured. Dust, however, has some advantages. Nicotine dust floats through the air and as soon as it reaches the aphis, it dies. Aphis usually are found where there is an oily appearance of the growth; that is the secretion of the insects. Sprays may be shed by the oil, but dust will stick tight. As aphis are sucking insects, they cannot be poisoned; a contact spray or dust must be used to kill them. Nicotine dust will be found effective, but if there is no dusting apparatus available and there is a spray outfit, use spray, for it has controlled aphis for many a year.

MILDEW OF ROSES.

Mildew of roses is an ever-present problem, one of the most vexatious and persistent with which the flower lover has to contend. It is worse on some varieties than others; this varies with districts. But granted it comes every year, the thing to do now is to apply lime-sulphur spray. Then keep after the mildew with finely ground sulphur dusted at frequent intervals. If the dust is fine and well applied, there should be little trouble with mildew. A help will be to irrigate the roses in the morning or as early in the day as possible; avoid evening irrigation, particularly with sprinklers. Let the rosebush go to bed as dry as possible.

GRAFTING PEACH TREES.

If any grafting is to be done on peach trees, this is the time to do it. Be sure the cuts are clean and smooth and that the cambium layers of the tree to be topworked and the scion are in touch; this is important. Any kind of graft will do, but be sure the cambium layers match. Use a good sealing wax and there should be no difficulty in working over trees to new tops or to new kinds of fruits, as far as that is concerned. For the back-yard gardener, grafting is a profitable hobby, for a single tree may carry enough varieties of different fruiting times to keep the table supplied all season.

PLENTY OF SOIL MOISTURE.

There's plenty of moisture in the soil as the state goes into the growing season. As a result, two mistakes are likely to follow. First, that there is enough to last all season and no irrigation—or very little—is necessary. Second, that the time for irrigation is at hand, and since the water is available, it might as well be used. The truth is, that irigation may not be as necessary as last year, but it may be necessary regardless. The soil auger is the only sure test. Don't pour water on land that has all it can hold; don't let crops suffer because there was an unusual amount of rainfall last winter. Get the auger or soil tube, and find out the needs beneath the surface, and be guided accordingly.

SPRING RENOVATION OF ALFALFA.

There has grown up in the state quite a tendency for renovation, or working up, of alfalfa fields in the spring. Under certain conditions this may be a good practice, may even be necessary; but until the grower is sure it is necessary, or a good practice at least, he should not tear into his alfalfa with a disk or spring-tooth harrow, just to be in style. If the land is hard and foul with weeds, perhaps after the first cutting it will be a good plan to run through the field with a disc harrow. But don't do too strenuous a job.

COCCIDIOSIS SEASON AGAIN.

Every spring when baby chicks start growing up into egg-producing pullets there are terrific losses from coccidiosis. The prevention is more simple than the cure. Be sure the premises are clean. See that the litter is not foul. Give the young birds plenty of air. Keep everything clean. And feed dried skim milk in the mash. If nothing but mash is fed, it should be twenty-five percent dried milk; if scratch is fed, the percentage should be forty. The cure is similar to the prevention. Dried milk should be added to the diet at once. The brooder floor should be thoroughly cleaned three times a day and the litter must be kept dry. The mash with dried milk addition should be fed not less than two weeks. When birds become affected, isolate them at once, of course.

WATCH FOR FROST.

The winter just past has been an unusually wet and cold season. There is abundant snow in the mountains for irigation, but there has been a continued chill in the air which may mean late frosts. The careful and cautious grower will have his heaters placed in the orchard when the blossoms are at the danger period. It costs about $10 an acre to have the equipment ready to save the crop; about one crop in five usually is seriously damaged by frost in districts where frost hits. In 1929 one orchard, saved by heating when neighboring trees bore no crop, returned $900 an acre. It paid. So be sure the heaters are ready, that fuel is available, that the thermometers are in good shape and that the warning service, whether by radio, mail or otherwise, is working and working infallibly.

MEASLES IN GRAPES.

This month is the time to spray for grape measles. Three pounds of sodium arsenate to fifty gallons of water, applied not later than the last week in March, should give a satisfactory control of this trouble.

CHICKWEED IN LAWNS.

Chickweed is likely to appear in any lawn, particularly where there is shade and plenty of moisture. If the weed is not allowed to go to seed, a drying out of the grass may kill it, as it is not at all resistant to dry weather conditions. However, if the seed is in the soil, this method of extermination will not be satisfactory. In that event, the chickweed patches might be dug out and the places re-sodded with good lawn. Iron sulphate will kill chickweed, also it will make desirable grasses look pretty sick. They will recover, though, while the weed will not. But if there are chickweed seeds this method will not be satisfactory. Repeated rakings and prevention of seed maturing will, in time, effect a cure.

APPLYING LAWN FERTILIZER.

The use of well-rotted barnyard manure is one of the best means of supplying plant food for the lawn; commercial fertilizers, however will do the job well, and many prefer to use them because the appearance of the lawn is not marred and there is no other inconvenience from the prepared fertilizers. They may be sown dry raked with a split bamboo lawn rake and then soaked in with water, or they may be dissolved in water and sprinkled on the grass. A sprinkling can is an easy means of applying the dissolved fertilizers. Follow directions in using fertilizers, so that the grass may not be burned. Most persons like to use grass catchers, and leave the lawn spic and span. If the grass is cut before it gets too long, however, a better practice is to let the clippings fall and rake them into the grass. Lime may be necessary once a year if this is done.

Memorial to Washington—The $75,000,000 bridge across San Francisco Bay to connect San Francisco and Oakland will be named the George Washington Memorial Bridge.

"Our deeds shall travel with us from afar and what we have been makes us what we are."

FOUNDER'S STATUE

(Continued from Page 4)

Crespi of the Portola expedition on August 1, 1769, as 'having all the requisites for a large settlement.' The siege of Yorktown was at its hight when the good chronicler's recommendation was acted on by Governor Felipe de Neve, and El Pueblo de Nuestra Senora la Reina de Los Angeles de Portiuncula was founded. Los Angeles was a half-century old when the first locomotive was built in the United States, and New York had just replaced gas with electric lights on Broadway when the city had celebrated its centennial.

"Felipe de Neve's burial place is as yet unknown. He died in Mexico. He was the son of Felipe de Neve y Noguera and Maria Perea y Padilla of Seville, Spain. The sword, carried by the founder of Los Angeles at the time he was governor of California, is now in the possession of his family, of which Jose Maria Blanco de Quintana y de Neve of Madrid is a descendant in the collateral line, as De Neve was unmarried. The silver hilt is engraved with motifs derived from the De Neve escutcheon or coat-of-arms. The coat-of-arms, painted upon linen cloth, was found among De Neve's papers after his death and was sent to his sister in Seville. The military devices on the escutcheon, which was granted in 1610 to Jusepe de Neve, are evidences of the martial leanings of members of the family."

GRIZZLY GROWLS

(Continued from Page 3)

community to pay for public improvements for the benefit, pleasure and convenience of all the citizens!

In Shanghai, the Japanese government called out its reserves—Jap civilians residing there and engaging in various pursuits.

Every Jap in this country, whether an American citizen by birth or a native of Japan, is also a reservist of the Rising Sun. And don't forget that, when the call comes from his worshiped mikado, he will respond!

Governor Gifford Pinchot of Pennsylvania delivered at Springfield, Illinois, February 11, a most timely address on "Lincoln and Today," the occasion being the observance of the one hundred and third anniversary of the birth of Abraham Lincoln. He said:

"Never since he led it through the greatest crisis in its history has our country needed the Lincoln kind of leadership so desperately as now, when millions are in the deepest distress and tens of millions in great trouble. As Lincoln understood liberty, this Nation is not free today. How can men be free and equal when multimillionaires grow and multiply while millions go hungry and cold? How can the Nation be free when the policies of its government are dictated by a handful of the overrich? . . . How can the Nation be free when its leaders put business ahead of human welfare—when they rank money higher than men?

"Prosperity-bred 'tyrants'—the word is Lincoln's—are over us today. And they have brought upon the people the suffering that goes with tyranny, which is another name for government by autocrats, or plutocrats, or international bankers or public utilities, or any other control without the consent of the governed. . . . It is not the form of our government that the people need to change, it is the substance. Under the ancient form, a usurpation has grown up that is far more dangerous than any foreign invasion—a usurpation based on cunning, not on force, but all the harder to overcome on that account.

"What our government is being used for today is not the greatest good of the greatest number, but the greatest wealth of the smaller number. The magnates who control it are seeking through that control the utmost concentration of wealth and power in the hands of the smallest possible number. Their gain is the people's loss. God knows they are succeeding in their evil purpose.

"Let the people use the power that is theirs by every right, and return this government to the rule of the people. Let them ask for nothing that was not demanded in the Declaration and established in the Constitution. Let them ask for nothing that is not American to the core. But let them free themselves and their children from the chains of special privilege and concentrated wealth. Let us have majority rule once more in the United States."

The poem which follows was, according to the "Amador Ledger" of Jackson, recited in the Sutter Creek, Amador County, high school in 1861 by Mrs. Frances Dolores Williams, a Sutter Creek Pioneer who will be eighty years of age April 2:

Disturb not his slumbers; let Washington sleep
'Neath the boughs of the willow that over him weep.
His arm is unnerved, but his deeds remain bright
As the stars in the day, vaulted at night.

Oh, wake not the hero; his battles are o'er;
Let him rest undisturbed on Potomac's fair shore.
On the river's green border, so flowery drest,
With the hearts he loved fondly, let Washington rest.

Awake not his slumbers; tread lightly around.
'Tis the grave of a freeman, 'tis Liberty's mound.
Thy name is immortal, our freedom ye won,
Brave sire of Columbia, our own Washington.

Oh, wake not the hero, his battles are o'er;
Let him calmly rest on his dear native shore,
While the stars and stripes of our country shall wave
O'er the land that can boast of a Washington grave.

THE ROMANCE

(Continued from Page 5)

tonio and the majestic San Jacinto. Here were the mighty chains of the West; here were the natural passes into the valley. Over to the northeast, stood a mountain of intricacy. It rose 2,000 feet above him. He saw the long streak of a ravine pointing downward, and spurring his horse with his bare heel he rode hard and fast away from his tribe and toward the scar in the side of the mountain.

(Continued in April Issue)

CALIFORNIA'S 1931 MINERAL PRODUCTION CONSIDERABLY BELOW 1930 VALUE.

The total value of the mineral production of California for 1931 is conservatively estimated by the State Division of Mines, under the direction of State Mineralogist Walter W. Bradley, to have been $220,290,000. As there are more than fifty mineral substances on California's commercial list, it is impracticable at this date to give definite figures on all the more-important items.

The estimated total of $220,290,000 is a decrease of approximately $145,314,000 from the value of 1930 production. Gold is the only major mineral substance whose output showed an increased value over the previous year. Petroleum registered the largest decrease, with lesser decreases shown by cement, natural gas, metals, structural materials, industrial materials and salines. The value of the crude oil output was approximately 46 percent less, with a decrease of about 39,000,000 barrels in quantity from 1930.

Receipts of bullion showed an increase in the gold yield of about $1,250,000, compared with 1930, this being due to increased production in the principal lode mines, and to the large number of small placer operators, due to unemployment in other industries. The output from the dredges showed little change. Silver and copper showed large decreases in both quantity and value, while lead showed an increased quantity with a decreased value. The quicksilver output was approximately the same, but having a decreased value. The structural group showed a decrease of about 35 percent, as did building permits in fifty-three California cities. Both the industrial and saline groups showed likewise large decreases in value.

A BIT OF HISTORY

The Grizzly Bear received the following from Mrs. Josephine Mohr-Schlichtman of Bethany, San Joaquin County, the wife of Claus Schlichtman, who came to California from Pennsylvania in 1866:

I am a constant reader of The Grizzly Bear, and never miss the pages "Fifty Years Ago in California" and "Passing of the California Pioneer," and often come across names of oldtimers my father knew well.

My father, John Mohr, born June 27, 1834, in Germany, came to San Francisco in 1852 via the Isthmus of Panama, being seven weeks on a sailing vessel from Hamburg to New York. He passed on July 12, 1916, aged 82 years. He went in the cattle and tanning business, and later engaged in farming. He and his brother, Henry Mohr,—who came to California four times in the 1840s before he stayed here—ran a sailing boat between San Francisco and Mohr's Landing, on the San Joaquin River.

Mohr's Landing was about three-quarters of a mile northeast of what is now Bethany. Bethany was at first called Mohr Station. John Mohr deeded land as a gift to the Southern Pacific, with the understanding that it would put a station there. The name was afterward changed to Bethany, on account of there being other Moore's Stations, and railroad men, not being particular about spelling, confused the freight.

When they ran the boat from San Francisco to Mohr's Landing, they brought all the lumber and fencings—fencing was no small article then—for use there and in all the surrounding country for the first buildings and farm houses. Also sold groceries from the boat, before stores got started.

The first post office in this part of San Joaquin County was at Mohr's Landing. The first school was also there; in 1877 it was moved, and called the Lammenville school. Mrs. Baldwin was one of the first teachers. At Mohr's Landing was the Pioneer hotel, Steamboat saloon, blacksmith shops and grocery stores. Many families came to live there, also hundreds of unmarried men. Of the families, I remember the Hewsons, Servos, Allens, Mourinaus, Henesseys, Masseys, McLaughlins, Cline, Hay and many others.

John Mohr in 1868 married Marie Panz, a native of Germany, at the time a nurse in the Marine Hospital, San Francisco. She came to California in 1866. Their oldest daughter was born on Telegraph Hill in San Francisco. John Mohr saw the San Francisco Vigilantes hang ruffians and bandits from the end of a scantling put out of an upperstory window. After that, your life was safe for a while after dark.

The last elk was shot near Mohr's Landing. Antelope, deer, beaver and badger were still plentiful. Grizzly bears came down from the mountains in May and June to eat wild blackberries, growing plentifully along the river bank Horsethieves were hung to the nearest tree.

This was all long before Tracy, Ellis, Midway, Byron, Brentwood and other railroad towns were thought of. All the grain and produce from the Livermore Valley was brought by team through Altamont Canyon to Mohr's Landing, and shipped by boat to San Francisco and other points. There were also very large grain warehouses at Mohr's Landing, and a wharf. Fish were so plentiful my father caught two tons in one night. Sturgeon, perch, black and striped bass were most abundant. Catfish were imported later, as were carp. Salmon weighed thirty pounds, sometimes.

JOHN C. FREMONT

(BETTY L. WHITSELL.)

More than a pathfinder,
More than explorer, too,
With restless breast
He pierced the calm of centuries as
He trekked the West.
Surveyor, engineer with
Kit Carson as a guide,
They blazed the way.
Planted the Bear Flag at Sonoma—
Heroic day!

And once near San Juan
With sixty men, defied
The brave Castro
And there on highest peak
The Flag did show.
He christened Golden Gate,
Became a senator and
Almost president.
A life of strange vicissitudes
For Greatness meant.

And some there are who blame
And drag him in the mire,
Brave Pioneer,
But Californians honor him,
His name revere.
His trails are highways now,
All lighted up and down,
Wondrous to see,
And every light is tribute bright to
His memory.

(This contribution to The Grizzly Bear is from Betty L. Whitsell of Burlingame, San Mateo County.—Editor.)

"And He from the mighty doubter the great believer makes."—Gilder.

MY MESSAGE

To All Native Born Californians

I, DR. FRANK I. GONZALEZ, GRAND PRESIDENT OF THE ORDER OF NATIVE SONS OF THE GOLDEN WEST, DO HEREBY APPEAL TO ALL NATIVE BORN CALIFORNIANS OF THE WHITE MALE RACE BORN WITHIN THE STATE OF CALIFORNIA, OF THE AGE OF EIGHTEEN YEARS AND UPWARD, OF GOOD HEALTH AND CHARACTER, AND WHO BELIEVE IN THE EXISTENCE OF A SUPREME BEING, TO JOIN OUR FRATERNITY AND THEREBY ASSIST IN THE AIMS AND PURPOSES OF THE ORGANIZATION:

To arouse Loyalty and Patriotism for State and for Nation.

To elevate and improve the Manhood upon which the destiny of our country depends.

To encourage interest in all matters and measures relating to the material upbuilding of the State of California.

To assist in the development of the wonderful natural resources of California.

To protect the forests, conserve the waters, improve the rivers and the harbors, and beautify the towns and the cities.

To collect, make known and preserve the romantic history of California.

To restore and preserve all the historic landmarks of the State.

To provide homes for California's homeless children, regardless of race, creed or color.

To keep this State a paradise for the American Citizen by thwarting the organized efforts of all undesirable peoples to control its destiny.

THE ORDER OF NATIVE SONS OF THE GOLDEN WEST IS THE ONLY FRATERNITY IN EXISTENCE WHOSE MEMBERSHIP IS MADE UP EXCLUSIVELY OF WHITE NATIVE BORN AMERICANS.

. . . Builded upon the Foundation Stones of

Friendship
Loyalty
Charity

IT PRESENTS TO THE NATIVE BORN CALIFORNIAN THE MOST PRODUCTIVE FIELD IN WHICH TO SOW HIS ENERGIES, AND IF HE BE A FAITHFUL CULTIVATOR AND DESIRES TO TAKE ADVANTAGE OF THE OPPORTUNITY AFFORDED HIM, HE WILL REAP A RICH HARVEST IN THE KNOWLEDGE THAT HE HAS BEEN FAITHFUL TO CALIFORNIA AND DILIGENT IN PROTECTING ITS WELFARE.

DR. FRANK I. GONZALEZ,
GRAND PRESIDENT N.S.G.W.

The undersigned, having formed a favorable opinion of the Order of Native Sons of the Golden West, desires additional information.

Name ....

Address ....

City or Town..............................

For further information sign the accompanying blank and mail to

GRAND SECRETARY N.S.G.W.,
302 Native Sons Bldg.,
414 Mason St.,
SAN FRANCISCO, California

Grizzly Bear

APRIL — THE ONLY OFFICIAL PUBLICATION OF THE NATIVE SONS AND DAUGHTERS OF THE GOLDEN WEST — 1932

Featuring

GENERAL NEWS OF INTEREST CONCERNING ALL CALIFORNIA, and ORDERS NATIVE SONS and NATIVE DAUGHTERS

Price: 15 Cents

GRIZZLY GROWLS

(CLARENCE M. HUNT.)

CRIME—DISHONESTY—IS THE MASter today in these United States, and the people are its slaves! Naturally, the country is thoroughly depressed, for prosperity cannot abide amid dishonest surroundings. Either the root of the depression-sore must be reached, by casting out of government and business the dishonest, or the lifeblood of the nation will be completely sapped. Apparently, the slaves must rise in their might and do the casting, if it is to be done!

The Federal Congress has been in session since December. Other than to pass, at the urge of the national administration, legislation for the financial relief of the kings of dishonesty, what has been accomplished? Nothing! The common people—the slaves of today—have been given no consideration.

The country has an overabundance of almighty-dollar legislation. What it requires, is legislation that will eliminate the fraud, the inflated-credit, the deflation and the numerous other pests propagated by the dishonest. The successful farmer controls the pests that afflict his holdings. This nation, if it is to survive, must do likewise.

"How may we reduce our traffic accidents," will be the principal theme at a meeting of interested agencies to be held during May at Santa Cruz City.

Not by gabfest resolutions, but by prison sentences! Like the national prohibition law, the state auto law is a huge joke, because it is not fearlessly and impartially enforced. Thousands of people have been killed by drunken auto drivers. How many of those murderers have been prosecuted for that offense, and how many who have been brought to trial at all and proven guilty have been adequately punished?

Occasionally an "unknown" is apprehended, and then Justice moves swiftly. But in most cases, the offender is not of the "goat" class, and so the charge is reduced to "reckless driving." If convicted, he or she is placed on probation or given a nonsensical sentence that makes a mockery of the law. Particularly so, if the offending one be a "goodlooker"—for not all the drunken auto drivers are of the male persuasion—or of the "prominents."

The auto clubs and other traffic agencies must direct their campaign against overly-sympathetic and easily-influenced judges and other law-enforcement officials, if they are actually desirous of lessening the number of traffic accidents.

Representative LaGuardia of New York declared in the Federal House of Representatives: "The big bankers at the time they were selling their own securities on an inflated value knew that they were selling them at an inflated value, and any man who obtains money under misrepresentation—call it what you want in parliamentary language, . . . he is nothing but an ordinary thief and ought to be in jail. . . . Yes, I would hang a banker who stole from the people."

Not only the "big bankers," but numerous other dishonest financiers who brought about the depression should be in jail. True, there would be a considerable thinning of the ranks of the nation's "leaders" but the country would be supremely benefited. There is no possibility, however, of the national administration attempting to jail those birds. On the contrary, they are being aided financially by the government and thereby being encouraged to continue their dishonorable courses—to continue their legalized thievery.

"Things never were rottener than they are in the United States today," said E. Clemons Horst in a recent Sacramento address, "and some sweet day I hope The People will rise up and kick the churches out of politics."

Hasten that sweet day! It will come when, and not until, the law exempting church property from taxation be repealed. There may be a few churches which respect and obey that exemption-law, but the majority of them violate or evade its provisions.

Here is a bit of good news, from Glendale, Los Angeles County, which received no mention in the daily press: A Jap having the fruit concession in a large public market remarked that any Jap was better than six White men. A White butcher, hearing the remark, cleared his counter in one jump, and soon eight of Japan's "peaceful invasion army" were down and out. Three cheers for that Glendale butcher. May his kind increase!

Births in California last year totaled 81,533, a decrease, compared with 1930, of 2,829. Of the 1931 total, 12,886 were Mexis and 2,040 Japs—an addition of 14,926 objectionables to the state's population.

Public-school education cost the California taxpayers the enormous sum of $153,168,453 during 1931. That bill could, and should, be materially reduced by eliminating the many education-fads which provide high-salaried positions for "specialists" and other favorites of the politicians.

In the course of an address at Philadelphia, Pennsylvania, Vice-president Curtis said: "Today there are in our midst men of alien thought and race who would sow the seeds of discord and disunion among us; who would overthrow our cherished ideals and traditions. We must rid our beloved country of all such, and all alien criminals, and of all alien racketeers."

Why limit the ridding to aliens? This country has also a considerable number of dangerous citizens, many of them in high positions. They cannot be deported, but they can be dethroned.

Frank E. Elkins went from Beverly Hills, Los Angeles County, to Sonoma City to reside and, according to the "Index Tribune" of the latter place, was "glad to get away from the terrible conditions in the south . . . from the political graft," etc.

It was neither nice nor loyal of him to make such a public statement, although everyone knows that political graft and other rotten conditions afflict the City and the County of Los Angeles. Truly, the record is terrible!

There were 1,345 bank failures in the United States during 1930 and 2,298 in 1931. Not a few of them resulted from crooked management. In Canada, it is said, there has been not a single bank failure in years. Business conditions have been, and are, no worse in this country than in Canada.

That country, however, punishes criminally and ostracises socially the wreckers of financial institutions, whereas in the United States they are, as a rule, placed on probation and hoisted to the top of the social-ladder. If thievery be encouraged, robbery must be anticipated.

Rev. Clarence Reed, from the pulpit of the First Unitarian Church in Oakland, termed Japan "an international outlaw and a nation that should be treated as such," and declared "The communications of the Japanese foreign office and its diplomats contain hollow promises and are tainted with insincerity. . . . A treaty with Japan today has neither meaning nor sanctity. It is only a scrap of paper."

Japan is the same today as it has always been—a scheming nation, not to be trusted. It is encouraging to note, however, that the yellow bandages are gradually dropping from American eyes.

April 8 has been designated "bird day." What new racketeer stunt have the "big birds" ready for launching?

Finance Director Vandegrift denies the payroll increase in the State Government will be $11,000,000, but admits a $5,000,000 boost. At this time, no salary increase is justified, but the political-ball must be kept rolling even though the taxpayers be overburdened. The cost of government in California is outrageously high, and going higher. Something, other than talk, should be done to force a reduction.

"It is a sad commentary on American civilization and government when an aggrieved person is obliged to appeal to criminals rather than officers of the law," said United States Senator Steiwer of Oregon, commenting on the kidnaping of the Lindbergh boy.

Indeed it is! But what otherwise could be expected in a country where law is in the gutter? Some good may come from this diabolical crime; the masses may become aroused and put an end to the criminal-reign.

THE DESERT DAY

(E. E. KNAPP.)

In the desert when it's summer, with the sky as clear as glass
The hot sun hangs above you like a globe of molten brass;
The heat waves make the hill tops in the distance seem afloat,
And the breeze that stirs is burning like from a furnace throat.

You see enchanted cities rising from the sandy wastes,
With streets and avenues so wide, with verdure all embraced;
In the distance there are visions of lakes so cool and pure
That are only heat mirages, the desert siren's lure.

Like a dancing Dervish driven mad you'll see dust devils twirl
With columns made of yellow dust across the wastes they whirl;
The vultures hang suspended, moving neither tail nor wing,
Waiting patiently and soaring, watching for some dying thing.

The heat pours down increasing on the desert waste so hot,
That you wonder if this is the place they say that God forgot;
In rocky shade you seek to rest as you plod towards your goal,
And you thank the God above you when you reach the water hole.

(This contribution to The Grizzly Bear is from E. E. Knapp of Los Angeles City.—Editor.)

The Grizzly Bear Magazine
The ALL California Monthly
OWNED, CONTROLLED, PUBLISHED BY GRIZZLY BEAR PUBLISHING CO., (Incorporated)
COMPOSED OF NATIVE SONS.
HERMAN C. LICHTENBERGER, Pres.
JOHN T. NEWELL RAY HOWARD
WM. I. TRAEGER LORENZO F. SOTO
CHAS. R. THOMAS HARRY J. LELANDE
ARTHUR A. SCHMIDT, Vice-Pres.
BOARD OF DIRECTORS
CLARENCE M. HUNT
General Manager and Editor
OFFICIAL ORGAN AND THE ONLY OFFICIAL PUBLICATION OF THE NATIVE SONS AND THE NATIVE DAUGHTERS GOLDEN WEST.
ISSUED FIRST EACH MONTH.
FORMS CLOSE 20th MONTH.
ADVERTISING RATES ON APPLICATION.
SAN FRANCISCO OFFICE:
N.S.G.W. BLDG., 414 MASON ST., RM. 302
(Office Grand Secretary N.S.G.W.)
Telephone: Kearney 1223
SAN FRANCISCO, CALIFORNIA
PUBLICATION OFFICE:
309-15 WILCOX BLDG., 2nd AND SPRING,
Telephone: VAndike 6234
LOS ANGELES, CALIFORNIA
(Entered as second-class matter May 29, 1918, at the Postoffice at Los Angeles, California, under the act of August 24, 1912.)
PUBLISHED REGULARLY SINCE MAY 1907
VOL. L WHOLE NO. 300

MANY MAKE PILGRIMAGE TO NOTED FLAG RAISING SITE.

San Juan Bautista (San Benito County)—More than a thousand persons, among them many Native Sons and Daughters, made the annual pilgrimage March 6 to Fremont Peak, to commemorate the first raising of the Flag of the United States of America over California soil.

George Abbe was master of ceremonies, and the speakers included Fielding A. Hodges, Rose Rhyner, E. J. Leach and George H. Moore. Boy Scouts of America from Alameda and San Benito Counties participated in the program, and buglers from the Hollister American Legion sounded the call to the colors.

Public School Week—The thirteenth annual observance of Public School Week will commence April 25.

"Happiness does not consist in things, but in thoughts."—Booth.

THE ROMANCE OF SAN BERNARDINO

Clara M. Barton

(Continued from March Issue.)

"'THAT MARK IS POINTING TO SOMEthing,' he said to himself as he neared his destination. When he came to it, he stopped, looked around, and saw before him a running stream. Sliding off of his horse, he worked his way to it through the underbrush. He knelt and let his fingers lightly touch the singing stream. He was surprised to find that the water was hot! You know, young men, some of my tribe are very superstitious and the young warrior at once believed that some good spirit had led him to this plentiful water. He marked the spot with a rock and dashed back to his men. With excited tones, he told them what he had found.

"'We must take possession of that place at once! It has healing waters, that stream!' exclaimed the young chief." "And did he take possession of it?" asked the youngest boy. "Certainly," continued the chief. "He then decided to make upon that mountain a lasting sear that would show itself for many miles. He pulled from his sheath of many arrows the longest, strongest and largest matras, carefully adjusted it in his colorful bow, drew it toward him with a strong, steady arm and then took careful aim, letting the arrow fly into the air and straight into the mountain side. There it remained! The point of the arrow was down, and this was the marking of the hot water spring! Some tribes believe that the mark of the arrowhead was caused by two gods having a terrible combat. One, in his madness, hurled his burning arrowhead from the sky and it settled itself in the side of that mountain, but my father's father was the one who told me of my forefather letting his arrow fly into the mountain. I have climbed its heights and have found two kinds of growth, a light and a dark, which might have been caused by the burning arrow."

"How large is the arrowhead, Chief Bill?" asked the boy nearest him. "That is hard to say, son," he replied. "But I can truthfully say that it is a quarter of a mile in length, 550 feet in width and it covers about seven and one-half acres. You can see for yourself how large it is when you are up to it. Too, if you will look at your flint arrowhead you will see that the two are very much alike. Whatever power made my ancestor do as he did is something not yet explained. But the mark has brought many people to its healing waters."

The old chief stopped to refill his pipe. The small group had now become under the spell of the story teller. Many questions were on the lips of all the youngsters, but no one wanted to interrupt this spell. It was all too wonderful!

"Old Bill, we have all wondered what the name San Bernardino means," said one of the boys after Chief Bill had relit his pipe. He grunted. "Well," he drawled, "you know that this valley was named after the good Saint Bernard. But the word in our language means 'bold as a bear.'" "How funny!" laughed one of the boys, "but why that name?"

"According to my father," continued the chief, "nature was bold as a bear when she laid out a valley like this. She was bold as a bear in building the mountains around here as she did. Our gods were also bold to let her do such a thing. My tribes believe and think that any unseen hand is bold that goes forth to the extent of putting fertile soil and letting the water flow where it is of the most use."

"Tell some more about the names of the mountains around here," said one of the boys who had crawled nearer the chief. "Well, let me see," he answered. "We are sitting in a protected place. Around us are four ranges of majestically built pieces of nature's work. To the east, the sun rises over Sierra de Yuciape and it sets behind Arroyo de Cajon, which name means a valley shaped like a box or a chest. If you will look closely, you too will see that the Pass has the shape like a box. That is why it is not a hardship to come into the valley. The mountain peak of Serroto Solo, meaning hill being alone, joins that of the Arroyo de Cajon. Look to the south and you see a colorful and well-built range of Lomeras, which means a ridge of hills or mountains. The mountain of the Arrowhead is directly to the north of us, and right beside it is the range of the El Faldo de Sierras, which my forefathers named 'The Brow of the Mountains.' It is well named, as you can see how smooth and flat it is on top. Its shape is like that of a brow."

"But where does San Gorgonia gets its name?" asked one of the youngsters. "I forgot that, young man, and I thank you for reminding me of it. Because of the bareness of the top and because much snow is found and very little vegetation grows on its peak, the name San Gorgonia means 'Gray Back.' The soil is always gray, even after the snow has melted! All of these peaks tower over 5,000 feet and many of them are 11,000 feet!"

"Oh!" exclaimed a chorus of young voices. "Yes, my dear friends," continued their story teller. "And if you climb upon those peaks, you can see a wonderful country. The pine and fir trees whisper their greetings to you and tell you of their beautiful life up there, and the many kinds of mountain birds always give you a warm welcome with their glad songs."

"Chief Bill, tell us about that stream of water running near here. It is always warm," said one of the older boys. "That," said the chief, "is a stream of water that comes from a warm creek in the mountains. It is a vein or an arm of the hot water springs in the Arrowhead region. It is there where your grandparents washed their clothes and made their coffee. This is the water in which they bathed. My forefathers told me that the devil became angry at some of his people and when he saw them bathing their bodies in this stream he poured a boiling solution into it, thus scalding the bathers. From then on, the creek and its adjoining stream have always been warm. The devil's solution had never become cooled!"

The sun had begun to sink behind the mighty Arroyo de Cajon. The old Indian chief was becoming weary. The boys were reluctant to leave, but seeing that their friend was becoming tired, the leader of the small band arose from his sitting position, nodded to the others, who were watching him, and they did likewise.

"Well, I guess we had better go home now, Chief Bill," said the leader. "We thank you a lot for that history lesson. We sure enjoyed it, didn't we, boys?" And there was a loud whoop in approval.

"I am glad that you enjoyed it and I hope that what I have told you will be of some benefit to you as you grow up. Any time that you want to know anything more about what is around you, just come to me, and I shall be glad to tell you what I know. Good night, boys." "Good night, Chief Bill," and the small group wended their way back into the mission for the vesper services.

The old chief arose painfully and slowly, took his pipe from his mouth, looked to the west, raised one arm above his head, and as he peered reverently into the dying shadows he said in slow tones, "The great God of Peace be ever upon this land!"

EPISODE 7.
MORMONISM.

In the early part of March 1852 a company was formed at the request of Brigham Young in Salt Lake City, Utah. "You people must travel slowly, but carefully, to California, through the Cajon Pass. I hear that the roads are very good now," Young told them. "You must cultivate the soil, grow grapes, cotton, olives, wheat and corn. You must help the padres who are already there to select suitable locations for the mail routes. I appoint Amasa M. Lyman and Charles Rich as your leaders, as they are capable to lead you through unpassable territory with safety. They can name the members of their own caravans, if they wish."

A few weeks later Lyman and Rich had formed three divisions. The first, under the direction of Rich himself, was piloted by Captain Jefferson Hunt. Caravan number two was under the supervision of Lyman, and was led by Captain Seeley. The third wagon train was under the leadership of the good Captain Andrew Lytle. The journey was hard and difficult, but the caravans treked onward, and it was Captain Seeley who led his wagon train into the pass June 11 of the same year (1852).

"Are we the first ones here?" asked a member of the train. 'It looks like it," answered the captain. "What a marvelous group of trees! Look at the valley below us. We surely could not have picked out a better place!"

"That looks like God's country," said one of the women. "It is," replied Captain Seeley, and he gave orders to make camp under the large sycamore trees.

June 20th the other two wagon trains arrived and made camp in the Cajon Canyon. They were tired, as they had had to combat early summer storms. Many of the roads had been washed out, and the mud was soft and slippery.

"Well, we're here," remarked Rich. "Where is my good friend Lyman?" "Over on the other side of the canyon," answered one of the wagon drivers. "Oh, I see him!" exclaimed Rich, and he proceeded to wave to the other members of the caravan.

"You know, I felt sorry for Brigham Young the day we left," said one of the women. "You did? Why?" asked Captain Hunt. "When he saw us leaving, he looked dejected and forlorn. He expected only twenty of us to come, but instead the whole community got excited and now, as far as I can make out, there are five hundred of us!" "Poor old Brigham," sighed another feminine member of the troupe. "He couldn't even tell us goodbye, as all were too excited to listen to farewells."

It took several days before the captain and his leaders were able to mount their horses and ride into the valley. Several weeks had passed before the final decision was made to purchase the grant of San Bernardino Rancho from the Lugos.

"We have looked all over the valley and I feel that the best move we can make is to settle a colony right here in San Bernardino. There is an abundance of feed for stock and the land looks as if it would be well worth cultivating. Some of my people are seriously thinking of building homes right here now!" said Lyman. "I'm ready to put the deal through, if you are, Brother Lyman," said Rich.

And so, in the early spring of 1852, the deed of San Bernardino was purchased for the sum of $77,000. Immediately following the buying of the rancho, and when everything looked prosperous, the Indians began to make things look uncomfortable for the peaceful colonists. Both Lyman and Rich decided that something should be done at once, so a messenger was sent posthaste to the coast, where a troop of United States volunteers were stationed.

"Captain Bean, we need help!" exclaimed the messenger. "Our people are in distress!" "I shall go at once!" and the captain ordered his men together and they followed the rider back to the valley.

"Here you are, the first wagon train to enter this great valley of San Bernardino, and you have met obstacles without fear," said the captain as he was holding a conference with Rich. "Yes, I guess you are right. But what are we to do to overcome these hostile tribes?" asked Rich.

Captain Bean looked around him, pondered a bit and then replied, "I would advise you to build a fort and stockades, and to take every precaution against these raids. It will take some time before these Indian tribes are tamed."

Two months passed, and the fort was constructed by the colonists. Two stockades were built, and the houses of adobe and logs were erected inside. Houses which had been built prior to the erection of the fort were moved within the enclosure. The houses were as one continuous room, with partitions separating the walls. The principal entrance to the fort was built on the east side and the gates were made to swing outward. Two additional gateways were provided, on the west and the north sides. The houses were set back from the gateways to protect them from fire. In the center of the fort ran Warm Creek, and the water was used for all purposes. Plans for small wells were made in case of emergency. One of the wagon drivers made a suggestion to use the wagon beds with canvas covers for sleeping apartments, and the idea turned out to be more than anticipated. Over 100 families lived within the walls of the fort, and the men were trained to take any necessary steps to protect their property.

(Continued in May Issue)

GOLD SITE MARKER.

Auburn (Placer County)—A marker designating the spot in this city where gold was first discovered in Placer County was unveiled with fitting ceremonies February 27. The discovery was made by Claude Chana and party in May 1848.

"Watch Signs, Avoid Fines," is the April slogan of the California Public Safety Committee in its campaign to lessen the fearful auto deathtoll.

Physicians' Meet—The sixteenth annual meeting of the American College of Physicians will be held at San Francisco, April 4-8.

"Out of the shadow of night, the world rolls into light."—Longfellow.

A BIT O' FARMING and GARDENING

PREPARED EXPRESSLY FOR THE GRIZZLY BEAR BY M. H. ELLIS

THAT THE FARMER HAS AT LAST turned serious attention to the economics of agriculture, is indicated this year by meetings, institutes and conferences that are being held on the various phases of this subject. Where meetings formerly were held to discuss production matters, these are overshadowed now by marketing, cost accounting and similar angles of economics. The Giannini Foundation for Agricultural Economics at the University of California pioneered this work after its necessity was shown by the Agricultural Extension Service; the State Department of Agriculture is active in this regard; farm advisors are emphasizing it at every turn, co-operative marketing organizations are hard at work showing their members the various means by which profits can be increased after production problems for the year are solved.

Of course, marketing is at the head of the list. Co-operative marketing is being urged by all governmental agencies. And where a co-operative marketing association operates on strictly business lines, feeds the markets carefully so there is no over-supply, does its business cheaply and well, it is bound to be the most profitable means for the farmer to dispose of his crop. But it must operate as efficiently and cheaply as do private concerns, if it hopes to get and hold business. There are no dividends to be paid, save to the farmers themselves, and in just that measure the farmer may expect added profits, with some increase due to advertising and careful spread of the produce on the markets.

It is safe to say that this year's crop will be the highest in quality, the best in pack, and the most carefully distributed that California ever has placed on the markets of the United States and the world.

APHIS ALWAYS PRESENT.

Always in the garden is the aphis. Black leaf forty, mixed according to directions on the bottle, used as a spray, will give good results; so also will nicotine dust. An even better control agent is pyrethrum, to which a little soap has been added. This is easy to use, harmless to the plants and non-poisonous to humans. It is an almost sure-shot killer when it comes into contact with the plant lice or other insects. Used as a spray or injected into hills and along runs, it gives also a good control of ants. Ants and aphis usually go together; the control of both will be beneficial to the control of either.

CANKERWORMS ON TREES.

When the little green worms about an inch long begin to hang from the trees by strands of web, the annual invasion of the cankerworm is on. The females lay their eggs in the trees during the fall or spring, and the larvae descend on the webs. As the females cannot fly, they have to crawl up the trunks, so that bands of tanglefoot will prevent their ascent. If the tanglefoot has been neglected and the worms are already in evidence, spray the limbs and twigs with pyrethrum.

PLANTING CHRYSANTHEMUMS.

Chrysanthemums may be planted at any time now, and up to the middle of June. The ground should be thoroughly prepared, well worked up with rotted dairy manure and bone meal or wood ashes. Plant in rows two feet apart and from nine to twelve inches apart in the rows. Or if but one blossom to the stalk is wanted, they may be planted as close together as six inches in the row. Plant so that when the earth is firmed about them there will be a small depression to hold water. Keep the plants moist until well established; after that, irrigation in furrows every two weeks will be sufficient if enough water is applied to penetrate the soil to the depth of the roots. Cultivate to keep out all weeds that compete for water and plant food. Later treatment will depend upon the kind of flowers wanted. For large blossoms, pinch off all buds but the one to be developed. Cluster chrysanthemums need not be budded back so closely. If the plants are put out early and give indication of coming into blossom before the desired time, prune them back.

MASH AN ALL-YEAR DIET.

Mash should be fed all the year round, unless for some reason it is desired to give the laying flock a rest. In that case lighten up on the mash and increase the grain. Perhaps a little more mash and a little less grain should be fed in the summer than in the winter, but see that it is before the hens at all times in the hoppers. If the mash should be discontinued suddenly, the hens likely would be thrown into a molt and production would be much reduced.

THIN DECIDUOUS FRUIT EARLY.

In deciduous fruit, one of the main features of quality is the size. To secure size, the tree must not be allowed to carry more fruits than it can properly size up. Reducing the number of fruits on the tree will increase the size of those left and will not result in smaller tonnage. Peaches should be thinned before they reach the size of the end of the thumb, and should be spaced from four to six inches apart. Apricots may be thinned with less care, but the number of fruits left must be such that they will attain good size. The main thing in thinning is to get the job done before the pits develop and the vitality of the tree is drained.

BEANS FOR THE HOME GARDEN.

Beans for the home garden may be planted now, and two varieties should be sowed. One of the early bush varieties should be used for the first crop, and a pole bean for later use. Both may be planted at the same time, as the bush beans will be through by the time the later varieties are ready to supply the table. Bush bean rows should be about two and a half feet apart, with seed dropped about four inches apart. Pole beans should be planted in hills about three and a half feet apart with three or four plants to the hill. A stake about five feet in hight should be provided before the climbing stems appear. Irrigate frequently to keep the plants growing and to secure tender, stringless pods.

MELON PRODUCTION.

Nothing in the garden is more appreciated than the melon. From the home garden alone can the vine-ripened fruit be picked with its full flavor. Those who have experienced the half-green fruit often offered at stores will appreciate the incomparable quality of the home-grown melon. Cantaloupes require rich soil, as do casabas, persian melons, honey dews, santa claus melon, etc. Seed should be planted as soon as the danger of frost is over, unless the gardener is willing to undertake to protect them on nights when the temperature bids fair to go below the danger point. About ten or twelve seeds should be placed in a hill, and the plants thinned to two or three of the strongest when the fourth leaves appear. It is best to prepare beds six or seven feet in width, with the irrigation furrows between. The vines are trained away from the ditches. The seed should be planted on the southern or western edge of the bed. The other melons develop more slowly and do not become edible until late summer or fall. Until the fruit is well started, the plants should be dusted frequently with hydrated lime and arsenate, because of the spotted and striped cucumber beetles.

WATCH GRAPE MILDEW.

It is just about time to start the fight against grape mildew; if the battle does not begin on time there will be poor control and poor quality of fruit. When the shoots are from six to eight inches long the first dusting should be done; the second when they are from fifteen to eighteen inches in length; the third when they are from two to three feet. Pay no attention to blossoming. The sulphur should be finely ground and should be applied with a good blower so that a film of dust is left on the leaves, both on the upper and lower surfaces. Throwing handfuls of sulphur into the vines does no good.

SOW BUGS IN THE GARDEN.

Sow bugs are a perennial pest that come with the advent of spring and garden truck. They like sweet feed, so a mixture of one part paris green and five parts of brownsugar will aid in their control. Place the material in pans or on boards in the garden or the strawberry patch. Cover with boards, for the bugs will not work in the open. If the ground is quite damp, sugar will not be satisfactory in the bait mixture; use a pound of bran and enough water to make it crumbly when mixed with the ounce of paris green.

Feminine World's Fads and Fancies

PREPARED ESPECIALLY FOR THE GRIZZLY BEAR BY ANNA STOERMER

TAKING THE CUE FROM THE GREAT out-of-doors and borrowing inspiration from nature's own palette, the shops are giving us the spring atmosphere. With so much loveliness offered, the feminine world can settle down to a really serious consideration of spring fashions, now that they are set before us. Variety, however, is tempered with good judgment.

Each costume seems designed for a specific purpose, or purposes. The silhouette has been simplified, with the result that one notes fewer peplums, frills and flounces.

Lines still point the way to smartness, not only the lines of the model, but the diagonal lines of various woolens and the lines formed by the ever-smart pintucking. Novelties are conspicuous by their absence, as also are freak clothes. Instead, we have smart suits and frocks. We are chic, rather than elegant, these days,—an infinitely better idea.

She will be very trim and jaunty, as neat as a pin, a bit gay and spirited, with deft touches of accenting color, crisp and dainty in every detail. That is, miss summer of nineteen thirty-two, according to fashion experts, who base their predictions upon what the styles are foreshadowing.

Smartness is everywhere in the jauntily tilted hats, in the sleek lines of evening gowns, in the trim neatness of sport outfits, and in the "just enough" accent of vivid color in shoes, hosiery, jewelry, coats, purses, suits, blouses and everything else.

Every little dress will have a jacket all its own. Or, if milady be clever, the tiny, perky coats and dresses will be combined in a dozen different relationships.

Those circular skirts which were so difficult to manage in last summer's breezes have been subdued into modified flares and pleats. Twelve inches from the ground is an average length, with longer for evening and perhaps a little shorter for sports wear.

Hats are uniform in only one point—they are not worn straight. Berets are numerous, sailors are "right." The flat-brimmed sailor hat would never recognize its own descendants, with perky brim twists and frisky angles. Flowers are used, not in quantity but in neat little clusters.

Shoes have gone sandal. They are cut and perforated in every conceivable way, and many are made of fabrics.

Fashion is young this season. Someone once said, "a woman is as young as her choice of clothes." However, that does not mean that good taste must not always play an important part in one's selection. It means simply that any woman may prolong her youth and enhance her charm through her clothes and, of course, the spring fashion helps this project with young colors and materials.

Prints gay and youthful are reappearing in new colorful arrangements. They are smaller in pattern than before and, if anything, daintier. White backgrounds with dainty pastel color combinations are popular, with blue leading the pageant of color in a hundred shades.

One pretty frock was displayed in blue of three shades. The frock itself was designed high-waisted, with a dainty georgette bodice attached to the skirt and trimmed with narrow lace. There was a little bolero jacket with sleeves to complete the picture.

Another frock, showing cape sleeves, was embroidered in white, which created a chic, finished effect. There was a sash of white and red, and a red band on the white shark-skin straw hat added the last touch of jauntiness.

This spring and summer seem to commend light colors, and for that reason fashion has compromised, the result being a combination of light and dark which is both striking and smart. Blue and black, brown and gold, red, white and blue are only a few of the myriad combinations suggested.

Chiffon or crepe roma combined with lace is another fetching idea of fashion. A charming example of this is a dinner gown of black crepe roma with a yoke of that new heaven-blue and a lace jacket of the same shade of blue. Blue accessories are to be worn with this costume.

The young business girl will like the new spring suits. For example, one of the six-buttoned, double-breasted models of wool crepe or jersey, with a white cotton mesh blouse and a bright-hued scarf. This, combined with a cute hat and pretty slippers, well assures her of being dressed in good taste for almost any daytime occasion. For more important occasions one can be "dressed up" by adding a fur scarf, a knot of flowers, a piece of costume jewelry or a more elaborate blouse.

Gloves have become very important. Combinations for general spring wear are black and navy blue with white, eggshell and beige and black with touches of silver. These same combinations obtained in bags and shoes find great favor. Some of the newest gloves for evening wear are elbow length of hand-made silk filet, hand-embroidered from the back of the hand to the elbow. A lacy edge is worked into the top of the glove in filet stitch. Daytime gloves are of kid in black and white with stitching of white. The ribbing on the back of the hand is done in heavy white twist. The gauntlet wri-' of the white kid is open on the outer edge and laced across the opening with a black silk cord.

Knitted garments have great vogue this season. At least, fashion is knitted conscious. Not

(Continued on Page 7)

CALIFORNIA HAPPENINGS OF FIFTY YEARS AGO

Thomas R. Jones

(COMPILED EXPRESSLY FOR THE GRIZZLY BEAR.)

APRIL 4, 1882, PRESIDENT CHESTER A. Arthur vetoed the anti-Chinese bill passed by the Federal Congress, giving as his reasons that it was ambiguous and violated a section of the treaty with China. His action caused widespread dissatisfaction in California, and in several localities he was burned in effigy by indignant citizens. Popular clamor was stilled by a report that Senator J. F. Miller had introduced a new bill—eliminating the objectionable features found by the President in the one vetoed—and that it would be quickly rushed through to a finish. The veto again brought the San Francisco sandlot crowd and Dennis Kearney into the limelight.

Anticipating Chinese immigration would eventually be restricted by the United States, vessels were greatly in demand at China ports to bring a horde of the celestials to California while the coming was good, and tramp steamships were being sent there for the human cargoes. Five vessels, with more than 3,000 Chinks, arrived in the state during April.

An anti-Chinese convention held at San Francisco April 24 was attended by 124 delegates from labor and other organizations. G. R. Wilson was made the chairman. Out of it evolved the League of Freedom, which materialized and consolidated anti-Chinese sentiment.

April weather was beneficial to the state. A three-day norther which started the 15th was followed by nine days of showers. The month's rainfall was 1.99 inches.

On account of a feed shortage, Lankershim and Van Nuys, Los Angeles County sheepmen, sold to John Finnell of Tehama County in 1881 12,000 sheep at $1 a head. He drove 9,000 of them north, and left the remainder on the southern range. During April the price of sheep advanced to $2.50 a head, and Lankershim and Van Nuys bought back the 3,000 for $7,500.

Gulls were laying eggs and nesting on an island in Mono Lake. In one afternoon a party of hunters gathered 600 of the eggs.

Immense flocks of Baltimore orioles arrived in Santa Barbara and adjacent counties. They later moved to other localities.

General W. T. Sherman of Civil War fame came to California with a party April 19 and proceeded to the Yosemite Valley.

There was a big mining excitement in Nevada County. A deposit of auriferous gravel had been found in a buried channel at Mooney Flat, and many locations of acreage were being made.

The State Immigration Society, with headquarters at San Francisco, began its existence by sending to Eastern communities advertising matter inviting people there to settle in California. A Scotchman was in charge, and he was the representative of a colony of fifty families that were coming to the state from the Highlands. They desired to go into the dairy business, and he was looking for suitable lands and localities for them.

A four-story flourmill and several other buildings were destroyed by fire at Stockton, San Joaquin County, April 2. Estimated loss, $250,000.

The San Jose, Santa Clara County, residence of John Britt burned April 30. His wife, unable to escape, was cremated.

A coterie of Sacramento Parlor No. 3 N.S.G.W. members went to a picnic near Roseville, Placer County, April 26 in a tallyho drawn by four white horses. For headgear, they wore "plug" hats, and each was accompanied by a selected Native Daughter.

Nathan Barbour, a farmer in Suisun Valley, Solano County, since 1846, died there April 1.

J. C. Palmer, who came to California in 1849 and with other capitalists established the first bank in San Francisco, died at Oakland, Alameda County.

Garrett W. Ryckman, a Pioneer of 1849, died at San Francisco April 2 at the age of 87.

W. B. C. Brown, who came from Kentucky in 1851, died at Sacramento City April 2. He once was clerk of Sacramento County and comptroller of California.

Isaac Lankershim, who came in 1854, died at Los Angeles City April 10 at the age of 63.

James Spencer, since 1849 a Nevada County miner, died near Colfax, Placer County, April 19, aged 64.

What was claimed to be the biggest locomotive in the world, constructed in the Southern Pacific Shops at Sacramento City, was given a trial run April 16. It weighed sixty-one and one-half tons, and while it was then considered a monster, it was but a pigmy alongside locomotives now in use. It was later named "El Gubernador," and operated over the Tehachapi.

An Indian who threatened to kill a Colusa County farmer residing on Stony Creek was taken by a mob from the custody of a constable April 24 and hanged.

J. G. Van Mater of Oroville, Butte County, was attacked by a swarm of bees April 27. One stung him in the mouth, and in a few minutes he died from suffocation.

George Canmer and Thomas McGeeny went for a boat ride on the Sacramento River April 30 and both were drowned.

Alfred Den was thrown from a horse at Santa Barbara City April 19. His foot caught in the stirrup and he was dragged to death.

Charles J. Kohler fell five stories down a San Francisco elevator shaft April 7 and was killed.

The three-months-old son of Wm. Allen, residing near Fresno City, was smothered to death April 16 by a house-cat which coiled across the infant's mouth and nose while asleep in his cradle.

A Russian named Raten shot at a man on a Sacramento City street April 10 and darted into an alley in an endeavor to escape. He was intercepted by ex-Sheriff James Lansing, whom he mortally wounded with a pistol shot. A mob of 3,000 gathered, intending to taken Raten from the jail and lynch him. The police force of twelve men being powerless, a company of state militia was called and dispersed the angry mob.

Three-year-old Elsie Mattern, waiting for a picnic train April 26 at Oakland, Alameda County, slipped away from her mother, rushed upon the track as the train approached and was crushed to death by the engine.

Thomas Nurse and Wm. Kerkland, farmers of Ione Valley, Amador County, got into a stock-trespassing quarrel April 6, and Kerkland killed Nurse.

At the Derbec mine in Bloomfield, Nevada County, the retortroom had twice been robbed of amalgam, so a trap-gun was set. April 19 it was touched off, and one Chinaman was killed and another was wounded.

FEMININE FANCIES

(Continued from Page 6)

just old-fashion knitted, but fancily minded in criss-crossings, basket weaves, drop stitches, ribbings and so on. A two-piece knitted sports frock in a sort of nile green has a skirt woven diagonally with smart insets in which the weave runs in opposite directions. In the blouse, the shoulder line achieves that new, wide effect, and there is a soft rolled scarf of green and white. A neat knitted belt and puffed sleeves banded a little above the wrists complete a swagger effect.

Accessories displayed include a soft, white, draped beret with tabs of heavy ribbon over the right ear, black and white sandals and heavy white gauntlets. Brick red and navy blue pajamas are made of wool jersey for beach wear. Practical garments are made of sturdy fabrics. Belts are of navy blue patent leather, trimmed with ball buttons in red lacquer. Coats are made of cotton eponge, with large kimono sleeves.

Chiffon is making a strong come-back, both plain and lame weaves being used. There are also many who like the satin that has a new twist, especially when it is black. Ice blue satin is the newest, and tremendously popular.

Picnic Day—The annual picnic of the University of California Branch College of Agriculture will be held at Davis, Yolo County, April 16.

LOS ANGELES CITY AND COUNTY

LOS ANGELES' LATEST HIGH-FINANCE scandal—a judgeship for a suit—involves more "prominent" citizens, including judges of the Superior Court. It is, in reality, but another act in the local investment-tragedy which has robbed thousands of innocent investors of billions of dollars. The "Holy [wholly rotten] City" has, through the manipulations of higherups, in the past few years made rapid progress toward a ranking position as a community where finance-gangsters rule and an invested-dollar is unsafe. One "investment" scheme after another has blown up, and no hardened guntotter had a thing to do with any of the wreckings. They were designed and executed by well-known home-town boys who are lavish spenders—of other people's honest earnings. Receivers for the defunct schemes must eat, and judges who pass on receivership fees must have fine clothes and be entertained with booze-and-female parties—even if mulcted investors must pay the additional freight.

Now, while the latest scandal has front-page publicity, promises galore of cleanups and cleanouts are passed along to the public, but, judging from the past record, nothing will, eventually, be done, and naturally no good will result from the expose. Having adequately proven their fitness, the involved ones will, in due time, be numbered among the local social-elect. Rumors via the grapevine are that judges other than those publicized were in on the elaborate "garden of eden" apartment-houses parties for payment of which the investors are out. Will they, also, be exposed, or are they too prominent? Along the "street" it is commonly stated that graft prevails generally in local receiverships. Will there be an investigation of the conduct of all receiverships, past and present? Horrors, no!

Governmentally, politically, and as an investment field, conditions in the "chemically pure" City of the Angels are notoriously rotten! They shine and stink in the moonlight and in the sunlight. And they are not going to improve unless the honest and decent citizens, vastly in the majority, make a thorough and impartial cleanup. The authorities can not or will not, for one reason or another, function as they should. The majority should organize and get on the job right now, and in some manner rid the community of the crooked minority. History repeats itself, and so it would seem that a vigilance committee, of the calibre of one which operated here effectively in the past, would be a blessing now. Something must be done, that's certain, if Los Angeles is to first come back, and then advance. A real newspaper, fearing no one and free of all entangling alliances, would do a world of good—and how Los Angeles does need such a news vendor!—C.M.H.

LOS ANGELES' FOUNDING SITE.

"Editor Grizzly Bear: March 12 a statue was placed at the Plaza. It was related that there was the spot where Governor Felipe de Neve stuck the point of his sword into the ground and this was the center of the founding of the Pueblo de Los Angeles. That is not correct, and is misleading to those who know nothing of past events. Future generations will believe it to be true, but it is not.

"The real spot where Governor Felipe de Neve stuck the point of his sword is in the center of what is now the block bounded by Sunset boulevard, Bellevue, New High and North Spring streets.

"CHAS. J. PRUDHOMME,
"Ramona Parlor N.S.G.W."

"FRIENDSHIP A HEAVENLY GIFT."

Los Angeles Parlor No. 124 N.D.G.W. was officially visited by Grand President Evelyn I. Carlson March 2. Supper preceded the meeting, Grace Norton and an able committee being in charge. The exquisite table decorations, arranged by Grace Ducasse, Rose Lathrop and Evelyn Howell, carried out the pansy motif. A large crowd assembled in the meetingroom, tastefully adorned with flowers and ferns. The officers' march was very pretty, the white evening gowns being brightened by colorful pansy corsages. Eight candidates were initiated.

The Grand President gave a wonderful talk on the projects of the Order, and she highly complimented President Gertrude Allen and the Parlor and stated that, to date, No. 124 stood first in the number of initiates during her term. In conclusion, she said: "Friendship is a beautiful and heavenly gift, and so needed by us all. In creating fraternal love and harmony, life is sweet for a friendship we've made. Love and true friendship mean, oh, so much to each and every one of us." Addresses were also made by Founder Lilly O. R. Dyer, Past Grand Grace S. Stoermer, Grand Trustee Florence Schoneman, District Deputy Catherine Ross, and Secretary Annie L. Adair of the Los Angeles homeless children committee. Louise Graeser played "On To California," composed by her for the Olympiad, and Sophia Stewart sang the refrain. Delicious refreshments terminated the delightful occasion.

The March 13 card party was largely attended. As a souvenir each guest received a small potted cactus plant. Ann Schiebush and Margaret Carter were in charge. March 16, City Mother Elizabeth Fisk spoke interestingly on the work of the mothers' bureau. The baked ham dinner of March 30 was served by Flora Holy, Edna Holcombe and Mary McAnany. The following went to San Diego to attend the official meeting there: President Gertrude Allen, Olinda Kirby, Ann Schiebusch, Sophia Stewart, Mattie Gara and Evelyn Howell.

Los Angeles' April calendar includes: 13th, monthly card party; 15th and 16th, rummage sale; 20th, nomination Merced Grand Parlor delegates; 27th, thirty-first institution anniversary celebration. Plans are under way for a family picnic May 1.—M.K.C.

CO-OPERATION THE SLOGAN.

Twenty-four members of Los Angeles Parlor No. 45 N.S.G.W., among them fourteen past presidents and Past Grand John T. Newell, gathered at the home of Howard Bentley March 21 and selected "co-operation" as the slogan in an organized campaign to push the Parlor and the Order in the south ahead. Charles W. Lyon offered some good suggestions. Refreshments were served by Mms. H. Bentley, R. W. Fryer and E. H. LeMoine.

A ritual team of the following past presidents was selected: Ray LeMoine, senior past president; Earl H. LeMoine, junior past president; Ronald Ross, president; Sidney B. Witkowski, first vice-president; Richard W. Fryer, second vice-president; Howard G. Bentley, third vice-president; Lewie W. Smith, marshal; Walter Fisher, inside sentinel; Roger Johnson, organist. The team will visit other Parlors and not only assist in the initiatory work, but will do everything possible to stimulate interest generally.

April 21, Los Angeles will sponsor an old-time "doings" to which all Natives and eligibles will be welcome. A buffet supper at 7 p. m. will be followed by a show of real talent under the auspices of "Sid" Witkowski and Charles Lloyd. "Don't miss this," is the warning of the co-operators. "Come along and have a good time as in days of yore." April 7 the Parlor will elect delegates to the Stockton Grand Parlor.

DELIGHTFUL PRE-EASTER BREAKFAST.

Members of Californiana Parlor No. 247 N.D.G.W. are delighted to behold their statue of Felipe de Neve, founder of the city, which became a reality March 12. Now that that project, which was the outstanding work of the Parlor for more than two years, is an accomplished fact, attention will be turned to other worthwhile things. The presence of Grand President Evelyn I. Carlson was second in importance to the presentation. She made an address at the ceremonies, paying high tribute to Californiana and expressing the hope that other organizations would emulate the example by presenting historical statuary.

Mrs. Carlson paid her official visit to the Parlor March 8 and was the honoree at a delightful pre-Easter breakfast, attended by 105 members and visiting friends. Most harmonious and lovely decorations were arranged by Mrs. Edith Adams and committee. An excellent program followed, the program chairman, Mrs. Leland Atherton Irish, presenting Mrs. Charles W. Roadman, Mrs. Pearl Cole McMullan, Miss McKinley and Mrs. John W. Hunt. Three candidates were initiated.

The Grand President, in the course of her remarks, commended Californiana for its outstanding accomplishments. She gave the greatest praise to President Gertrude Tuttle, mentioning the fact she had present five aunts who take an active part in Native Daughter work. On the Parlor's behalf, Mrs. Irish presented Mrs. Carlson with a luncheon set. Other speakers were Grand Trustee Florence Schoneman, Past Grand Grace S. Stoermer and District Deputy Marguerite Dickinson. March 22, Mrs. William Behm was hostess at a card party which proved successful, both socially and financially.—O.L.

HOUSE WARMING.

Hollywood Parlor No. 196 N.S.G.W. is now housed in the I.O.O.F. building at 1089 North Oxford avenue, corner Santa Monica boulevard, one block east of Western avenue. A monster house-warming is being arranged for April 11 by a committee including Henry G. Bodkin (chairman), Bernard Hiss, Lucien Griffin, C. L. Patterson and Martin Meza.

All members of the Order are cordially invited, and also eligibles, as the meeting will be open. Excellent entertainment is promised, and refreshments will be served. April 4 the Parlor will elect delegates to the Stockton Grand Parlor, and initiation will be held April 25. Hollywood is steadily increasing its membership, as it has a result-getting committee at work.

INTERPARLOR DANCE.

There was a goodly attendance at the Interparlor N.S.G.W. and N.D.G.W. Committee's Saint Patrick dance March 17. Past Grands Herman C. Lichtenberger and Grace S. Stoermer were the guests of honor. Musical numbers were contributed by Emmet and Winston Flood, Julie Kellar and Louise Glaeser. Hostesses and hosts included Mary Noerenberg (chairman), Beulah VanLuven, Grace Norton, Past Grand John T. Newell, Harry Honn and Grand Trustee Eldred L. Meyer.

GLENDALE DANCE, APRIL 2.

Glendale—Verdugo Parlor No. 240 N.D.G.W. entertained Grand President Evelyn I. Carlson at a banquet. Decorations were springtime flowers and favors. Several candidates were initiated at the meeting which followed. Other guests were Founder Lilly O. R. Dyer, Grand Trustee Florence Schoneman, Past Grand Grace S. Stoermer, and Miss Marvel Thomas, organizer of the Parlor.

March 22 sixty members and their families enjoyed a wonderful potluck dinner served by

(Continued on Page 22)

Native Daughters of the Golden West

MERCED CITY WILL BE THE MEETing-place of the Forty-sixth Grand Parlor of the Order of Native Daughters of the Golden West. It will convene Monday, June 20, and the constitution prescribes that it shall continue in session for not more than four days. Grand President Evelyn I. Carlson (Dolores No. 169) of San Francisco will preside throughout the Merced deliberations, and in all probability will be succeeded by Vice-president Anna M. Armstrong (Woodland No. 90) of Woodland.

Veritas No. 75 has charge of arrangements for the gathering, and a general committee headed by Hazel Laverty is attending to the details. May F. Givens (Mariposa No. 63) is chairman of the entertainment subcommittee which plans an interesting program.

The Grizzly Bear sought information as to their intentions from all prospective Grand Parlor office candidates, and passes along that received to press-time. Subordinate Parlors must elect their delegates the first meeting in May, and some prospectives are waiting to see what happens then:

Grand Secretary—Sallie R. Thaler (Aloha No. 106) of Oakland, incumbent.

Grand Marshal—Sadie Winn-Brainard (Califia No. 22) of Sacramento; Grand Trustee Gladys E. Noce (Amapola No. 80) of Sutter Creek; May F. Givens (Mariposa No. 63) of Cathay.

Grand Outside Sentinel—Elvena Woodard (Vallejo No. 195) of Vallejo; Hazel B. Hansen (Verdugo No. 240) of Glendale.

Grand Trustees (seven to be selected)—Edna B. Briggs (La Bandera No. 110) of Sacramento, incumbent; Florence D. Boyle (Gold of Ophir No. 190) of Oroville, incumbent; Florence D. Schoneman (Rudecinda No. 230) of San Pedro, incumbent.

Not even a rumor has reached The Grizzly Bear regarding the 1933 Grand Parlor meeting-place. The place to be fixed by the N.S.G.W. Grand Parlor for holding this year's Admission Day, September 9, celebration will, presumably, be endorsed by the Merced Grand Parlor.—C.M.H.

Twenty-second Birthday.

Pescadero—Ano Nuevo No. 180 celebrated its twenty-second birthday at Moss Beach. President Mamie Dias presided as toastmistress and presented the following charter members: Ida M. Mesquite, who organized the Parlor and was its charter president, Margaret Dias, Frances H. Moore, Eva Montivaldo, Lizzie Frey, Rose Bennett, Rose Francis, Lillian Woodhams, Susie Mattei and Margaret Goularti. Vocal selections were rendered by Flora Steele, and Harriet Williamson and Margaret H. Dias played several duets on the piano and saxaphone. Three generations were present—Francis H. Moore, her daughter Louise M. Williamson and her granddaughter Harriet.

Recently the Parlor initiated a large class of candidates, among them Mrs. Esther Armas Brown, born at Santa Cruz City in 1854.

Inspiring Address.

San Bernardino—Lugonia No. 241 had the pleasure March 9 of welcoming Grand President Evelyn I. Carlson and many visitors. In the afternoon there was an informal tea at Redlands, sponsored by those interested in the formation of a parlor there. A reception and dinner followed in the evening at San Bernardino. The unique tables decorations, arranged by First Vice-president Nola Fogler, were of eucalyptus bark, narcissus and greens. A four-piece girl orchestra furnished music.

At the Parlor meeting President Gladys Case Baker introduced the guests, among them Past Grand Dr. Louise C. Heilbron, Grand Trustee Florence Schoneman, organizer of Lugonia, Mrs. Omar Brainard, Helen Anderson and District Deputy Hazel Hansen. Eight candidates were initiated, and following the ceremonies Marshal Evelyn Shaddox and Organist Marguarite McKenzie, accompanied by Secretary Grace McHenry, sang "The Sweetest Story Ever Told."

Grand President Carlson gave an inspiring address, in the course of which she complimented Lugonia on its accomplishments and commended Miss Clara Barton for her history story, "The Romance of San Bernardino," appearing serially in The Grizzly Bear. Mrs. Carlson was presented with gifts of china, flowers and oranges, and the other grand officers were presented with hoquets. The meetingroom was attractively decorated with baskets of colorful spring flowers, including the California poppy, by Clara Barton and committee.

Contributes to Landmark Purchase.

Alturas—At the Alturas Civic Club's annual luncheon Past Grand Dr. Louise C. Heilbron was the guest speaker, Grand Marshal Irma W. Laird chairman of the general arrangements committee and Past Grand Catherine E. Gloster toastmistress. Supervising Deputy Dorothy Gloser gave the opening address, and of the hostesses that presided over the twelve tables, each suggesting a month of the year, six were officers or past presidents of the Parlor. The following day Dr. Heilbron spoke before the Alturas Rotary Club.

March 3 Alturas authorized a cash donation toward the purchase of the historic Vallejo home in Sonoma County, and the purchase of tickets for Mount Lassen No. 215's Loyalty Pledge benefit. Several applications for membership were received. Many invited guests enjoyed bridge and refreshments after the business session. Members of the Parlor are planning a box of baby clothes for the homeless children.

Anniversary Observed.

Fort Bragg—March 3 marked the sixteenth anniversary of Fort Bragg No. 210. District Deputy Edna Kunzler was guest of honor and gave a reading on the flags of California. Delicious refreshments were served. A birthday cake with candles and decorations which called attention to Saint Patrick day made the tables very attractive.

Mms. Ruth Roberts and Mae Johnson entertained the sewing club March 18 at the former's home.

Entertaining Affair.

San Luis Obispo—San Luisita No. 108 entertained Grand President Evelyn I. Carlson. The hall was beautifully decorated with California poppies and fern, while the decorations of the banquetroom, where refreshments were served later in the evening, carried out the same motif with poppies, candles and greenery. An interesting address was given by the Grand President, and other speeches made up an entertaining affair. A group of local members accompanied Mrs. Carlson on her visit to Cambria.

Tune in, Folks.

San Jose—Supervising Deputy Clara Gairaud, a member of the Grand Parlor Publicity Committee, announces a Loyalty Pledge broadcast over K.Q.W. (San Jose) Saturday evening, April 16, 8 to 8:30. Past Grand Dr. Louise C. Heilbron, chairman of the Grand Parlor Loyalty Pledge Committee, will be heard in a five-minute talk from the Sacramento studio of K.Q.W. Mrs. Gairaud has arranged a program of talent. Be sure to tune in.

Old-fashioned Dance.

Santa Rosa—Santa Rosa No. 217 had an old-fashioned dance March 17 and it was largely attended and greatly enjoyed. Joe Avellar received a handsome quilt made by the Poppy club. The committee for the dance included Katherine Branstetter, Pearl Brucker, Jimella Cook and President Carrie Avellar. The Parlor will be represented by a float in the Santa Rosa rose festival during May.

Community Spirit Manifested.

Hollister—Committees of Copa de Oro No. 105 have carried out most successfully a series of highly entertaining social sessions. At an enjoyable leap year party unattached members were given valuable tips on "how to propose" and the best means of capturing husbands in 1932. Appetizing refreshments were served from a charmingly decorated tea table, where Hilda Thompson and Edna Hansen presided at the teapots.

March 10 the members "went irish," with games commemorative of Erin's patron saint. The Parlor has manifested its community spirit by donations to the San Benito County unemployment fund and the San Juan Plaza Preservation League.

Tree Dedicated to Washington.

Georgetown—March 7 El Dorado No. 186, under the direction of President Hattie E. Presby, planted a gigantea sequoia at the home of a charter member, Elizabeth Murdock. The tree was dedicated to the memory of the nation's first President, George Washington, whose two hundredth birthday is being observed in all communities this year. An appropriate program relating to Arbor Day was given, after which delicious refreshments were served.

Forfeit Paid.

San Rafael—In real old Erin fashion, sixty-five members of Marinita No. 198 enjoyed a delicious cornedbeef dinner March 14. The occasion was the outcome of the recent attendance contest. Frances Soldavini was captain of the losing team and she and her company paid their forfeit in this delightful manner. The banquetroom was decorated in the Saint Patrick motif. Guests of honor were Supervising Deputy Emma G. Foley and District Deputy Mae Shea. A large amount of food was left over, so Captain Soldavini notified the police department, and it was taken to the headquarters of the unemployed, called "The Jungles," where it was received with great delight.

Antoinette Hecht was chairman of a card party March 28, held to increase the homeless children fund. A basket of groceries was disposed of. The Parlor has subscribed to the Vallejo memorial fund.

General Assembly To Meet.

Oakland—The annual convention of the Past Presidents General Assembly will be held here April 8 and 9. Association No. 2 has charge of the arrangements, and Emilie Clifford is the general chairwoman. The program includes: 8th—reception and registration. 9th—luncheon 12:30 p.m., meeting and election 2 p.m., banquet 6:30 p.m. Elaborate entertainment features will be presented by a committee headed by Helen Cleu, among them an automobile tour of the bay cities.

To Plant Tree in Pioneers' Memory.

Vallejo—Vallejo No. 295 observed its twentieth institution anniversary, celebrated the bicentennial of George Washington, and honored two of its charter members, Mms. Jennie Ostello and Mary Claus. The many in attendance at the big party made a spectacular appearance in costumes of the past. The banquetroom, where an elaborate supper was served, was beautifully decorated in patriotic colors. The committee in charge included Anna Johnson (chairman), Kathryn Moutoux, Mabel Thompson, Clara Berg, Julia Hill, Eugenia Wachlin, Juliet Bliss, Guilda Keller and Mayme Donnelly.

The Parlor plans, with the co-operation of Vallejo No. 77 N.S.G.W., to plant a tree in the new Memorial Park, atop Vallejo Hights, in honor of the Pioneers of Solano County.

Card Parties at Homes.

Merced—President Helen Krutosik has planned many social events for Veritas No. 75. Among them, each member of the Parlor is sponsoring a card party at her home. An immense grocery box is to be disposed of at a public card party April 5.

"You Try It."

Standish—Nataqua No. 152 has adopted a plan to get out the stay-at-homes: two captains were appointed, both choosing an equal number of members, and each team endeavoring to get out the most members. At the closing of the contest the losers are to fete the winners. The plan is creating great interest in Nataqua as well as in Honey Lake No. 198 N.S.G.W., and March 2 more than fifty members of the Parlors enjoyed refreshments together. "You try it!"

The Parlor's homeless children committee made and disposed of a beautiful silk quilt for the benefit of the kiddies.

Grand President's Official Itinerary.

San Francisco—During the month of April, Grand President Evelyn I. Carlson will officially visit the following Subordinate Parlors on the dates noted:

1st—Betsy Ross No. 238, Centerville.
2nd—Calida No. 22, La Bandera No. 110, Sutter No. 111, Coloma No. 212, jointly at Sacramento.
5th—Caliz de Oro No. 206, Stockton.
6th—Donner No. 193, Byron.
8th—El Monte No. 205, Mountain View.
12th—Forrest No. 86, Plymouth, afternoon; Ursula No. 1, Jackson, evening.
13th—Princess No. 84 (Angels Camp), Ruby No. 46 (Murphys), San Andreas No. 113, jointly at Angels Camp.
14th—Amapola No. 80, Sutter Creek.
15th—Chispa No. 40, Ione.
18th—Colus No. 194, Colusa.
19th—South Butte No. 226 (Sutter), Marysville No. 162, Camp Far West No. 218 (Wheatland), jointly at Sutter.
20th—Gold of Ophir No. 190, Oroville.
22nd—Auburn No. 233, Auburn.
23rd—Annie K. Bidwell No. 168, Chico.
25th—Sea Point No. 196, Sausalito.
26th—Joaquin No. 5, Stockton.
27th—Phoebe A. Hearst No. 214, Manteca.
28th—Mary E. Bell No. 224, Dixon.

Newlyweds Showered.

Sutter—South Butte No. 226 and Sutter No. 261 N.S.G.W. sponsored a surprise shower for Mr. and Mrs. (Necia Vagedes) Henry Correll, officers of the Parlors who were recently wedded. Sixty-two friends of the couple were in attendance, and they were the recipients of many gifts. The refreshments table was attractively decorated, the centerpiece being a white cake ornamented with red hearts.

The Parlors had a carnival March 16, and they soon will have a tree planting ceremony in honor of the bicentennial of George Washington.

Bronze Marker Dedicated.

San Diego—The official visit of Grand President Evelyn I. Carlson to San Diego No. 208 March 5 was the occasion for a charming dinner party. A song, written in honor of and dedicated to Mrs. Carlson, was sung by the past presidents club. For the attractive table decorations, carrying out the Washington bicentennial idea, credit is due Martha Klindt.

Following the dinner was the meeting. Through the efforts of Edith Barngrover and committee the room had been made into a veritable garden of spring flowers. Several visitors were in attendance. Grand President Carlson gave a most interesting address, and was presented with a linen tea set. Sophia Stewart sang "I Love You, California," during the initiation ceremony and later favored with other songs. Light refreshments were served.

March 6, District Deputy Hazel B. Hansen entertained the grand officers at luncheon. In the afternoon a bronze marker was dedicated at Punta de los Muertos in memory of Spanish sailors buried there. The speakers, Grand President Carlson, Grand Trustee Florence D. Schoneman and N.S.G.W. Deputy Grand President Edward H. Dowell were introduced by Past Grand Dr. Louise C. Heilbron. The plaque, presented

(Continued on Page 15)

SAN FRANCISCO

HONORING GRAND PRESIDENT DR. Frank I. Gonzalez (Pacific No. 10), the San Francisco Native Son Parlors will conduct a joint class initiation in the auditorium of Native Son Building, 414 Mason street, the evening of Saturday, April 2. Invitations have been extended all adjacent Parlors, and many past and present grand officers will attend. The arrangements committee is headed by Harry Romick (Castro No. 232).

The ritual will be exemplified by the following picked team, selected by a committee headed by Jas. F. Stanley (Stanford No. 76): H. J. Ritter (Hesperian No. 137), senior past president; Joseph Tinney (Rincon No. 72), junior past president; David Simon (Castro No. 232), president; Otto Elvander (South San Francisco No. 157), first vice-president; Matthew Brady (South San Francisco No. 157), second vice-president; Peter Macarini (South San Francisco No. 157), third vice-president; Joseph Sugrowe (Pacific No. 10), marshal; John Schimelpfenig (Castro No. 232), inside sentinel; C. George Cuthbertson (Castro No. 232), organist.

CONTRA COSTA DAY AT N.D. HOME.

March 13 was Contra Costa day at the N.D. Home Sunday breakfast, and Past Grands Amy V. McAvoy and Estelle M. Evans were the hostesses. District Attorney James F. Hoey, N.S.G.W. Past Grand, was the speaker. Decorations were in keeping with the Saint Patrick theme. Visitors included Past Grands Addie L. Mosher, Dr. Mariana Bertola, Margaret G. Hill and Emma G. Foley, Grand Organist Lola Horgan, Grand Outside Sentinel Orinda Giannini and N.S.G.W. Past Grand Charles Dodge.

NATIVE DAUGHTER PARLOR DOINGS.

Minerva No. 2 celebrated its forty-fifth birthday March 10 at a banquet. Chairman Marie McDonough extended a welcome and President Gertrude McDonough gave an interesting address. A letter, expressing regret at inability to be present, was read from Founder Lily O. R. Dyer, who instituted the Parlor March 10, 1887. A delightful program was followed by dancing.

Alta No. 3 celebrated its forty-fifth birthday March 12 at a banquet under the chairmanship of Mary Conner. The artistically decorated tables commemorated the Washington bicentennial, and the favors were unique. A program of music, dancing and bridge followed the feast. Among the many in attendance were President Catherine O'Reilly, Grand Trustee Annie C. Thuesen, Past Grand Margaret G. Hill and District Deputy Annie Franzen.

Orinda No. 56 had a baby shower for the benefit of the homeless children March 11, and a generous supply of clothes and shoes resulted. The Parlor is particularly interested in child welfare work and has adopted the children in the tubercular wards of the San Francisco hospital; every holiday they are remembered with candy and gifts. Orinda members born in January and February were entertained at a birthday party the latter part of February, and those born in March were entertained March 25; gifts were presented them on both occasions. First Vice-president Marie Stewart-McGrath, a recent bride, was given a surprise shower at the home of Outside Sentinel Mary Miner. Second Vice-president Emma McClure is the proud mother of a native son, born March 14.

The bicentennial of George Washington was the motif for another El Vespero No. 118 sociable. The drill team had charge, and under the leadership of Captain Mary Casey presented a play, "Making Our Flag." Games were followed by a typical early-day american dinner, served at tables beautifully and patriotically decorated. The merrymakers of the Parlor are sponsoring their second annual entertainment and dance, to be held April 2. Anne Godfrey is chairman. The proceeds will be added to No. 118's Loyalty Pledge fund.

Genevieve No. 132 had a Saint Patrick party March 17. Chairman Belle Foley was assisted by a very active committee. The refreshments tables were decorated in Ireland's national colors, green, white and gold. Enjoyable entertainment was provided by the Genevieve choral club, Betty Marquis, Rena Taube, Evelyn Dewight, Lillian Troy, Agnes Deasy, Nora Scheffilin, the Genevieve merrymakers, Rose Regan and the youngsters.

Keith No. 137 celebrated its anniversary at a leap year dinner-dance. District Deputy Alice Boldemann and President Ethel Porter were guests of honor; the latter was presented with a gift by the Parlor. The committee in charge included Helen Mann, Ella Miller, Gertrude LaFortune, Vera Pander, Frances Blaettler, Hilma Rechter, Sallie Sullivan and Gladys Cruise. Washington's birthday was observed with appropriate songs and readings.

Members of Gabrielle No. 139 have donated to the Central Homeless Children Committee a most wonderful layette, containing duplicates of everything a baby wears. The dresses and slips are hand-embroidered in pink and blue. An accompanying card wishes the fortunate recipient health, wealth, happiness and a long and useful life of contentment.

Saint Patrick day was appropriately and enjoyably observed by Presidio No. 148 March 8. The refreshments committee served "jigg's favorite dish."

Linda Rosa No. 170 observed its twenty-third anniversary March 17. The Saint Patrick motif prevailed. Songs, recitations and cards provided entertainment. A miscellaneous shower was given Mrs. Frank Mallet, bride of a few weeks, last month.

NATIVE SON PARLOR DOINGS.

March 7 Golden Gate No. 29 initiated Frederick Thompson and Adolph Eberhart Jr. The latter is a son of Adolph Eberhart, forty-six years a member of the Parlor, forty-three years a past presiedent, forty-two years recording secretary and forty years secretary San Francisco Native Sons Hall Association; he is the dean of all secretaries, in point of service. A record number of No. 29's members were in attendance, and a very large number of visitors. Historian Peter Conmy presided during good of the order, and addresses were made by Grand President Dr. Frank I. Gonzalez, Past Grands Lewis F. Byington and James A. Wilson, Grand Third Vice-president Chas. A. Koenig, Grand Outside Sentinel Gam Hurst, Judge George W. Schonfeld, William J. Wynn and Adolph Eberhart Sr. A buffet supper followed the enjoyable meeting. In attendance were delegations from California, Pacific, San Francisco, Mission, El Dorado, Rincon, Stanford, South San Francisco, Precita, Olympus, El Capitan, Claremont, Piedmont, Niantic, Presidio, Castro, Hesperian and. Balboa Parlors.

With President Eugene Herzog presiding, El Dorado No. 52 initiated Alfred J. Clary, chief San Francisco administrative officer, and Public Works Director William H. Worden. Splendid addresses were delivered by Grand President Dr. Frank I. Gonzalez, District Deputy Robert Donohue and Peter B. Conmy. Among the many in attendance were Mayor Angelo Rossi and Speaker Edgar Levy of the State Assembly. Refreshments closed a very pleasant evening.

March 16 South San Francisco No. 157 honored the bicentennial of George Washington and Saint Patrick day. More than 200 partook of the "corned and" banquet. Past Grand Judge Fletcher A. Cutler was the principal speaker, his theme being the lives of George Washington and Saint Patrick; it was a masterful oration which drew forth tumultuous applause. Other speakers were Harmon D. Skillin, Hubert J. Caveney, District Deputy Thomas Dillon, Judge George W. Schonfeld, Ed. Allen, Sal Juliano, Ellis Blackman and Harry Rommick. Entertainment was provided by Lionel Smith, Carl Prignitz, Ed. Keating, Lloyd Dornell, George Nilan, Tom Keating, George Kendall and George Cerles.

Twin Peaks No. 214 remembered Saint Patrick's birthday at a bounteous dinner March 16. The table and room were attractively decorated with shamrocks and the flags of the United

(Continued on Page 19)

Passing of the California Pioneer

(Confined to Brief Notices of the Demise of Those Men and Women Who Came to California Prior to 1860.)

JULES A. AURADOU, NATIVE OF FRANCE, 99; came to California in 1849 and mined in Placer County, farmed in Sonoma County and engaged in business in San Francisco; died at the latter city, survived by two sons. He was the oldest senior member of the Society of California Pioneers (San Francisco) and the sole survivor of the first group of Frenchmen to settle in this state. Quoting from an interview Dr. Henry duR. Phelan had with him at San Francisco in 1929:

"During the year 1848, the news of the discovery of gold in California reached France and inflamed the imagination of the people. The revolution and labor troubles had left thousands of men without employment. Emigration to California appeared to many as the solution of their difficulties. Auradou and his father joined the first group of French emigrants bound for California, and sailed from Havre in April 1849 on the three-masted French ship 'Meuse,' an old whaler of 500 tons. This vessel could accommodate thirty-four passengers, among whom there were no women. Besides the passengers, the 'Meuse' carried a cargo of provisions for California. While rounding Cape Horn the vessel ran into a storm which cost the lives of three sailors, who were washed overboard. Life preservers, boxes and crates were thrown to them, to no avail. The 'Meuse' reached San Francisco September 14, 1849, after a voyage of 173 days. After discharging her passengers and cargo she sailed for China and returned to France. As she was nearing Havre she was lost, with all on board, save the cabinboy and the captain, who became insane."

Mrs. Sarah Jane Lindsay-Bates, native of Indiana, 89; came across the plains in 1850, arriving at Union, now Arcata, Humboldt County, where she died, July 17 of that year; nine children survive. A delegation from Arcata Parlor No. 20 N.S.G.W. attended the obsequies of this Pioneer Mother.

William H. Throp, native of Alabama, 88; came across the plains in 1852; died at Fresno City, survived by a daughter. He was the builder of Fresno's first flourmill.

Mrs. Addie M. Turner, native of Michigan, 87; came across the plains in 1852; died at Alameda City, survived by three children. She was a former resident of Jackson, Amador County.

Louis Keser, 85; came in 1852; died at Santa Paula, Ventura County, survived by a wife and a daughter.

Mrs. Elizabeth Gardner-McDonald, native of Iowa, 80; came across the plains in 1853; died at Fortuna, Humboldt County. For some time she resided in Sonoma County.

John D. Ackerman, native of Massachusetts, 80; came via the Isthmus of Panama in 1854; died at Oakland, Alameda County, survived by six daughters.

Mrs. Mary Ann Godfrey, native of England, 87; came across the plains in 1854 and settled in Yuba County; died near Camptonville, survived by three children.

Mrs. Harriet Talmadge-Northrup, native of Illinois, 79; came across the plains in 1854; died at San Jose, Santa Clara County, survived by a husband and two children.

Oscar E. Jacobs, born in 1854 while his parents were enroute across the plains to California, died near Zamora, Yolo County; five children survive.

Mrs. Emma Sperry-Carlon, native of Wisconsin, 83; since 1855 San Joaquin County resident; died at Manteca, survived by two children.

Mrs. Mary Belle George, born in 1855 while her parents were enroute across the plains to California, died at Colusa City; three sons survive. For many years she resided in El Dorado County.

Mrs. Mary Schyff-Heap; came in 1856 and resided in San Bernardino and Riverside Counties; died at Riverside City, survived by four children.

George Merenca Furman, native of New York, 92; since 1856 resident Shasta County; died at Redding. He built and operated the county's first flourmill, at Millville.

Mrs. Annie Murphy, native of Missouri, 78; came across the plains in 1856 and settled in Amador County; died at Aukum, El Dorado County, survived by seven children.

Captain Jens Hansen, native of Denmark, 96; came in 1856; died at Redwood City, San Mateo County, survived by a wife and four children.

Mrs. Matilda Angeline Loncor-Sanders, native of Illinois, 79; came in 1859; died at Nuestro, Sutter County, survived by two daughters.

John Hoesch, native of Kentucky, 83; came in 1859; died at Sacramento City, survived by two daughters.

William Darby, native of Ohio, 74; came in 1859 and resided in Solano, San Benito and Stanislaus Counties; died at Modesto, survived by a wife and a son.

John Alexander Koon, native of New York, 87; came in 1859; died at Salyer, Trinity County, survived by four children.

Alexander Gibbons, native of Ireland, 96; came around Cape Horn in 1852 and settled in San Francisco, where he died; five children survive, among them David D. Gibbons (Sequoia Parlor No. 160 N.S.G.W.) of San Francisco.

John R. Page, native of Arkansas, 82; came across the plains in 1857 and resided in Tehama, Sacramento, Placer and El Dorado Counties; died at El Dorado Town, survived by a daughter.

E. L. Coonrod, native of Ohio, 94; came in 1859; died at Little Shasta, Siskiyou County, survived by four children.

OLD TIMERS PASS

(Brief Notices of the Demise of Men and Women who came to California in the '60s.)

Mrs. Carrie Carey-Baldwin, native of New York, 89; came in 1860; died near Rockville, Solano County, survived by three children.

Mrs. Mary Moreland-Anderson, native of Ireland, 89; came in 1861; died at Santa Cruz City, survived by two children.

Fred Bateman Ellsworth, native of England, 90; came in 1862; died at Baker Ranch, Placer County, survived by three children.

Mrs. Mary Hull-Hooper, native of Illinois, 87; came in 1862; died at Holmes, Glenn County, survived by four children.

George Williamson Sr., native of New York, 78; since 1863 El Dorado County resident; died at Placerville, survived by a wife and three sons.

Mrs. Marie Robertson, native of France, 84; came in 1863; died at Oroville, Butte County, survived by a son.

Mrs. Virginia Black-Brokaw, native of Illinois, 77; came in 1863; died at Auburn, Placer County, survived by four children.

Mrs. Katharina Koerner, native of Germany, 87; since 1863 resident San Francisco, where she died; a son survives.

O. B. Hubbell, native of Michigan, 69; came in 1864; died at Van Nuys, Los Angeles County, survived by a wife and a son. He resided many years in Marin and Sonoma Counties.

Mrs. Susan Frances Miller-Hendricks, native of Iowa, 75; came in 1864; died at Yankee Hill, Butte County, survived by a daughter.

Mrs. Mary Dickinson, native of Ireland, 91; came in 1864; died at Michigan Bar, Sacramento County, survived by four children.

Mrs. Katerine McClay-Robinson, native of Scotland, 87; came in 1865; died at Oakland, Alameda County, survived by five daughters. For many years she resided in Santa Clara County.

John H. Simonson, native of Germany, 82; came in 1866; died at Merced City, survived by a wife and a son. He had served Merced County as assessor.

Mrs. Carmolita Cassulio, native of Peru, 80; since 1869 resident Los Angeles City, where she died; six children survive.

L. A. Chester, native of Indiana, 77; came in 1864; died at Chowchilla, Madera County, survived by three daughters. He long resided in Mariposa County.

PIONEER NATIVES DEAD

Galen W. Morrill, born in El Dorado County in 1856, died at Coloma February 20 survived by a wife and a son. He was a charter member of Sacramento Parlor No. 3 N.S.G.W.

George C. Anthony, born in Butte County in 1857, died at Marysville, Yuba County, February 20 survived by six children.

Miss Kate Cole, born at San Francisco in 1855, died at Berkeley, Alameda County, February 20.

Bernard McDonald, born in Shasta County in 1857, died at San Francisco February 21 survived by a wife and eight children. He was affiliated with Mount Bally Parlor No. 87 N.S.G.W. (Weaverville).

Mrs. Hattie Garfield-Heisley, born at Sacramento City in 1853, died at Pacific Grove, Monterey County, February 21 survived by a son.

Mrs. Sarah Webber-McCoy, born in Alameda County in 1854, died February 21 at San Francisco survived by two children.

Mrs. Adeline Dickey-Pearce, born in Los Angeles County in 1856, died February 23 at Long Beach. She was a member of Long Beach Parlor No. 154 N.D.G.W., with which her surviving daughters, Julia Arborn and Lena Hansen, are affiliated.

Alonzo F. Tynan, born in Amador County in 1854, died February 23 at Salinas, Monterey County, survived by a son.

Louis Bonaparte Tully, born in Santa Clara County in 1851, died February 27 at King City, Monterey County, survived by two children.

Claude Terrell Rouner Sr., born in El Dorado County in 1855, died February 28 at Pittsburg, Contra Costa County, survived by seven children. He was affiliated with Quartz Parlor No. 58 N.S.G.W. (Grass Valley).

Sister Mary Ignatius Driscoll, born in Solano County in 1858, died February 28 at Benicia.

Mrs. Armandina Sobranes-Vallejo, born in Monterey County in 1856, died February 29 at Napa City.

Mrs. Mary G. Walsh, born in Trinity County in 1858, died March 1 at Oakland, Alameda County, survived by three children.

Myron L. Crafts, born at San Francisco in 1855, died March 2 at Berkeley, Alameda County, survived by a son.

James C. Brown, born in Nevada County in 1855, died March 4 at San Francisco survived by a wife and eight children.

Charles Sherman Ruggles, born at San Fran-

(Continued on Page 21)

Official Directory of Parlors of

ALAMEDA COUNTY.

Angelita No. 82, Livermore—Meets 2nd and 4th Fridays, Foresters Hall; Mrs. Myrtle I. Johnson, Rec. Sec.

Piedmont No. 87, Oakland—Meets Thursdays, Corinthian Hall, Pacific Bldg.; Mrs. Alice E. Miner, Rec. Sec., 421 36th St.

Aloha No. 106, Oakland—Meets Tuesdays, Wigwam Hall, Pacific Bldg.; Gladys I. Farley, Rec. Sec., 4623 Benevides Ave.

Hayward No. 122, Hayward—Meets 1st and 3rd Tuesdays, Veterans Memorial Bldg., Main St.; Miss Ruth Gansberger, Rec. Sec., P. O. box 44, Mount Eden.

Berkeley No. 150, Berkeley—Meets 1st and 3rd Fridays, Masonic Hall; Mrs. Lelia B. Baker, Rec. Sec., 915 Contra Costa Ave.

Bear Flag No. 151, Berkeley—Meets 2nd and 4th Wednesdays, Veterans Memorial Bldg., 1931 Center St.; Mrs. Maud Wagner, Rec. Sec., 317 Alcatraz Ave., Oakland.

Encinal No. 156, Alameda—Meets 2nd and 4th Thursdays, N.S.G.W. Hall; Mrs. Laura E. Fisher, Rec. Sec., 1413 Caroline St.

Brooklyn No. 157, East Oakland—Meets Wednesdays, Masonic Temple, 8th Ave. and E. 14th St.; Mrs. Ruth Cooney, Rec. Sec., 3907 14th Ave.

Argonaut No. 166, Oakland—Meets Tuesdays, Klinkner Hall, 59th and San Pablo; Mrs. Ada Spilman, Rec. Sec., 2905 Ellis St., Berkeley.

Bahia Vista No. 167, Oakland—Meets Thursdays, Wigwam Hall, Pacific Bldg.; Mrs. Minnie E. Raper, Rec. Sec., 3449 Helen St.

Fruitvale No. 177, Oakland—Meets Fridays, W.O.W. Hall; Mrs. Agnes M. Grant, Rec. Sec., 1224 30th Ave.

Laura Loma No. 182, Niles—Meets 1st and 3rd Tuesdays, I.O.O.F. Hall; Mrs. Ethel Fournier, Rec. Sec., P. O. box 515.

El Cereso No. 207, San Leandro—Meets 2nd and 4th Tuesdays, Masonic Hall; Mrs. Mary Tuttle, Rec. Sec., P. O. box 56.

Pleasanton No. 237, Pleasanton—Meets 1st Tuesday, I.O.O.F. Hall; Mrs. Myrtle Lanini, Rec. Sec.

Betsy Ross No. 238, Centerville—Meets 1st and 3rd Fridays, Anderson Hall; Miss Constance Lucio, Rec. Sec., P. O. box 187.

AMADOR COUNTY.

Ursula No. 1, Jackson—Meets 2nd and 4th Tuesdays, N.S.G.W. Hall; Mrs. Emma Boarman-Wright, Rec. Sec., 114 Court St.

Chispa No. 40, Ione—Meets 2nd and 4th Fridays, N.S.G.W. Hall; Mrs. Isabel Ashton, Rec. Sec.

Amapola No. 80, Sutter Creek—Meets 2nd and 4th Thursdays, N.S.G.W. Bldg.; Mrs. Hazel M. Marre, Rec. Sec.

Forrest No. 86, Plymouth—Meets 2nd and 4th Tuesdays, I.O.O.F. Hall; Mrs. Marguerite Davis, Rec. Sec.

BUTTE COUNTY.

Annie K. Bidwell No. 168, Chico—Meets 2nd and 4th Thursdays, I.O.O.F. Hall; Mrs. Irene Henry, Rec. Sec., 3015 Woodland Ave.

Gold of Ophir No. 190, Oroville—Meets 1st and 3rd Wednesdays, Memorial Hall; Mrs. Ruth Brown, Rec. Sec., 1265 Leah Court.

CALAVERAS COUNTY.

Ruby No. 46, Murphys—Meets 4th Friday, N.S.G.W. Hall; Belle Segale, Rec. Sec.

Princess No. 84, Angels Camp—Meets 2nd and 4th Wednesdays, I.O.O.F. Hall; Grace Mills, Rec. Sec.

San Andreas No. 113, San Andreas—Meets 1st Friday, Fraternal Hall; Miss Doris Treat, Rec. Sec.

COLUSA COUNTY.

Colus No. 194, Colusa—Meets 1st and 3rd Mondays, Eagles Hall; Miss Kate Busch, Rec. Sec., 350 Market St.

CONTRA COSTA COUNTY.

Stirling No. 146, Pittsburg—Meets 1st and 3rd Wednesdays, Veteran Memorial Hall; Mrs. Minnie Marcelli, Rec. Sec., 771 E. 12th St.

Richmond No. 147, Richmond—Meets 1st and 3rd Tuesdays, I.O.O.F. Hall, 10th St.; Mrs. Tillie Summers, Rec. Sec., 640 So. 31st St.

Donner No. 193, Byron—Meets 1st and 3rd Wednesdays, I.O.O.F. Hall; Mrs. Anna Pendry, Rec. Sec., P. O. box 112.

Las Juntas No. 221, Martinez—Meets 1st and 3rd Mondays, Pythian Castle; Mrs. Lola O. Viera, Rec. Sec., 305 Arreba St.

Antioch No. 223, Antioch—Meets 2nd and 4th Tuesdays, I.O.O.F. Hall; Mrs. Estelle Evans, Rec. Sec., 202 E. 5th St., Pittsburg.

Carquinez No. 234, Crockett—Meets 2nd and 4th Wednesdays, I.O.O.F. Hall; Mrs. Cecile Petee, Rec. Sec., 465 Edwards St.

EL DORADO COUNTY.

Marguerite No. 12, Placerville—Meets 1st and 3rd Wednesdays, Masonic Hall; Mrs. Nettie Leonardi, Rec. Sec., 25 Coloma St.

El Dorado No. 186, Georgetown—Meets 2nd and 4th Saturday afternoons, I.O.O.F. Hall; Mrs. Alta L. Douglas, Rec. Sec.

FRESNO COUNTY.

Fresno No. 187, Fresno—Meets 2nd and 4th Fridays, Pythian Castle, Cor. "R" and Merced Sts.; Mary Aubery, Rec. Sec., 1040 Delphia Ave.

GRAND OFFICERS

Mrs. Estelle M. Evans..........Past Grand President
202 E. Fifth St., Pittsburg

Mrs. Evelyn I. Carlson..........Grand President
1965 San Jose Ave., San Francisco

Mrs. Anna M. Armstrong..........Grand Vice-president
Woodland

Mrs. Sallie R. Thaler..........Grand Secretary
555 Baker St., San Francisco

Mrs. Susie K. Christ..........Grand Treasurer
555 Baker St., San Francisco

Mrs. Irma Laird..........Grand Marshal
Alturas

Mrs. Minna K. Horn..........Grand Inside Sentinel
Etna

Mrs. Orinda G. Giannini..........Grand Outside Sentinel
2142 Filbert St., San Francisco

Mrs. Lola Horgan..........Grand Organist
789 Morse St., San Francisco

GRAND TRUSTEES

Mrs. Edna Briggs..........1045 Santa Ynez Way, Sacramento
Mrs. Ethel Begley..........1206 Valencia, San Francisco
Mrs. Anna Thuesen..........615 38th Ave., San Francisco
Mrs. Gladys Noce..........Sutter Creek
Mrs. Florence Boyle..........Oroville
Mrs. Florence Schoneman..........1521 5th Ave., Los Angeles
Mrs. Willow Borba..........Sebastopol

GLENN COUNTY.

Berryessa No. 192, Willows—Meets 1st and 3rd Mondays, I.O.O.F. Hall; Mrs. Leonora Neate, Rec. Sec., 338 No. Lassen St.

HUMBOLDT COUNTY.

Occident No. 28, Eureka—Meets 1st and 3rd Wednesdays, N.S.G.W. Hall; Mrs. Eva L. MacDonald, Rec. Sec., 2309 "B" St.

Oneonta No. 71, Ferndale—Meets 2nd and 4th Fridays, I.O.O.F. Hall; Mrs. Myra Rumrill, Rec. Sec.

Reichling No. 97, Fortuna—Meets 1st and 3rd Tuesdays, Friendship Hall; Mrs. Grace Swett, Rec. Sec., P. O. box 328.

KERN COUNTY.

Miocene No. 228, Taft—Meets 1st and 3rd Wednesday afternoons, I.O.O.F. Hall; Mrs. Evalyne Towne, Rec. Sec., P. O. box 1011.

El Tejon No. 239, Bakersfield—Meets 1st and 3rd Fridays, Eagles Hall, 1714 "G" St.; Miss Mayme Efird, Rec. Sec., 2117 Chester Ave.

Desert Gold No. 250, Mojave—Meets 2nd and 4th Fridays, I.O.O.F. Hall; Mrs. Mae Coffill, Rec. Sec.

LAKE COUNTY.

Clear Lake No. 135, Middletown—Meets 2nd and 4th Tuesdays, Herrick Hall; Mrs. Alma E. Snow, Rec. Sec.

LASSEN COUNTY.

Nataqua No. 152, Standish—Meets 1st and 3rd Wednesdays, Foresters Hall; Mrs. Mayda Elledge, Rec. Sec.

Mount Lassen No. 215, Bieber—Meets 2nd and 4th Thursdays, I.O.O.F. Hall; Mrs. Angie C. Kenyon, Rec. Sec.

Susanville No. 243, Susanville—Meets 3rd Thursday, I.O.O.F. Hall; Mrs. Georgia Jensen, Rec. Sec., 700 Roop St.

LOS ANGELES COUNTY.

Los Angeles No. 124, Los Angeles—Meets 1st and 3rd Wednesdays, I.O.O.F. Hall, Washington and Oak Sts.; Mrs. Mary K. Corcoran, Rec. Sec., 322 No. Van Ness Ave.

Long Beach No. 154, Long Beach—Meets 1st and 3rd Thursdays, K.P. Hall, 341 Pacific Ave.; Mrs. Bertha Hitt, Rec. Sec., 5355 Lime Ave.

Rudecinda No. 230, San Pedro—Meets 1st and 3rd Fridays, Unity Hall, I.O.O.F. Temple, 10th and Gaffey; Mrs. Carrie E. Northway, Rec. Sec., 561 W. 14th St.

Verdugo No. 240, Glendale—Meets 2nd and 4th Tuesdays, Masonic Temple, 234 So. Brand Blvd.; Miss Etta Fulkerth, Rec. Sec., 526-A No. Orange St.

Santa Monica Bay No. 245, Ocean Park—Meets 1st and 3rd Mondays, New Eagles Hall, 2823½ Main St.; Mrs. Rosalie Hyde, Rec. Sec., 738 Flower St., Venice.

Californiana No. 247, Los Angeles—Meets 2nd and 4th Tuesday afternoons, Hollywood Studio Club, 1215 Lodi Place; Mrs. Inez Sitton, Rec. Sec., 4223 Berenice St.

MADERA COUNTY.

Madera No. 244, Madera—Meets 2nd and 4th Thursdays, Masonic Annex; Mrs. Margaret C. Boyle, Rec. Sec., 111 No. "B" St.

MARIN COUNTY.

Sea Point No. 196, Sausalito—Meets 2nd and 4th Mondays, Perry Hall, 50 Caledonia St.; Mrs. Mary B. Smith, Rec. Sec., 559 Woodward Ave.

Marinita No. 198, San Rafael—Meets 2nd and 4th Mondays, 316 "B" St.; Miss Mollye Y. Spaelti, Rec. Sec., 539 4th St.

Fairfax No. 225, Fairfax—Meets 2nd and 4th Tuesdays, Community Hall; Mrs. Olive A. Greene, Rec. Sec., P. O. box 277.

Tamelpa No. 231, Mill Valley—Meets 1st and 2nd Tuesdays, I.O.O.F. Hall; Mrs. Delphine M. Todt, Rec. Sec., 400 Grand Ave., San Rafael.

MARIPOSA COUNTY.

Mariposa No. 63, Mariposa—Meets 1st and 3rd Fridays, I.O.O.F. Hall; Mrs. Mamie E. Weston, Rec. Sec.

MENDOCINO COUNTY.

Fort Bragg No. 210, Fort Bragg—Meets 1st and 3rd Thursdays, I.O.O.F. Hall; Mrs. Ruth W. Fuller, Rec. Sec.

MERCED COUNTY.

Veritas No. 75, Merced—Meets 1st and 3rd Tuesdays, I.O.O.F. Hall; Miss Margaret Thornton, Rec. Sec., 317 18th St.

MODOC COUNTY.

Alturas No. 159, Alturas—Meets 1st Thursday, Alturas Civic Club; Mrs. Irma W. Laird, Rec. Sec.

MONTEREY COUNTY.

Aleli No. 102, Salinas—Meets 2nd and 4th Thursdays, Knights Pythias Hall; Miss Rose Rhyner, Rec. Sec., 420 Soledad St.

Junipero No. 141, Monterey—Meets 2nd and 4th Fridays, Pythian Hall; Miss Matilda M. Bergschicker, Rec. Sec., 498 Van Buren St.

NAPA COUNTY.

Eschol No. 16, Napa—Meets 2nd and 4th Mondays, N.S.G.W. Hall; Mrs. Ella Ingram, Rec. Sec., 2140 Seminary St.

Calistoga No. 145, Calistoga—Meets 2nd and 4th Mondays, I.O.O.F. Hall; Sadie P. Brooks, Rec. Sec.

La Junta No. 203, Saint Helena—Meets 1st and 3rd Tuesdays, N.S.G.W. Hall; Mrs. Marie Signorelli, Rec. Sec., 1341 Madrona Ave.

ATTENTION, SECRETARIES!

THIS DIRECTORY IS PUBLISHED BY AUTHORITY OF THE GRAND PARLOR N.D.G.W., AND ALL NOTICES OF CHANGES MUST BE RECEIVED BY THE GRAND SECRETARY (NOT THE MAGAZINE) ON OR BEFORE THE 20TH OF EACH MONTH TO INSURE CORRECTION IN NEXT PUBLICATION OF DIRECTORY.

Portola No. 172, San Francisco—Meets 1st and 3rd Tuesdays, N.S.G.W. Bldg.; Catherine H. Dolly, Rec. Sec., 4125 23rd St.
Castro No. 178, San Francisco—Meets 1st and 3rd Wednesdays, K.C. Bldg., 150 Golden Gate Ave.; Miss Adeline Sandersfeld, Rec Sec., 50 Baker St.
Twin Peaks No. 185, San Francisco—Meets 2nd and 4th Fridays, Druids Temple, 44 Page St.; Mrs. Loretta Cameron, Rec. Sec., 3969 Army St.
James Lick No. 220, San Francisco—Meets 1st and 3rd Wednesdays, N.S.G.W. Bldg.; Mrs. Edna Bishop, Rec. Sec., 3841 24th St.
Mission No. 227, San Francisco—Meets 2nd and 4th Fridays, N.S.G.W. Bldg.; Mrs. Ann Dippel, Rec. Sec., 448 Dewey Blvd.
Bret Harte No. 232, San Francisco—Meets 2nd and 4th Tuesdays, Aloha Hall, 3009 16th St.; Hildur E. Eggers, Rec. Sec., 194 Prague St.
La Dorada No. 236, San Francisco—Meets 2nd and 4th Thursdays, N.S.G.W. Hall; Mrs. Theresa R. O'Brien, Rec. Sec., 567 Liberty St.
Balboa No. 249, San Francisco—Meets 1st and 3rd Thursdays, Maccabee Hall, 5th Ave. and Clement St.; Jean Moffet, Rec. Sec., 6633 California St.

SAN JOAQUIN COUNTY.

Joaquin No. 5, Stockton—Meets 2nd and 4th Tuesdays, N.S.G.W. Hall, 314 E. Main St.; Mrs. Della Garvin, Rec. Sec., 1122 E. Market St.
El Pescadero No. 82, Tracy—Meets 1st and 3rd Fridays, I.O.O.F. Hall; Mrs. Mary A. Hewitson, Rec. Sec., 215 W. 9th St.
Ivy No. 88, Lodi—Meets 1st and 3rd Wednesdays, Eagles Hall; Mrs. Mae Corson, Rec. Sec., 109 So. School St.
Calla de Oro No. 206, Stockton—Meets 1st and 3rd Tuesdays, N.S.G.W. Hall, 314 E. Main St.; Mrs. Frances Germain, Rec. Sec., 450 No. Regent.
Phoebe A. Hearst No. 214, Manteca—Meets 2nd and 4th Wednesdays, I.O.O.F. Hall; Mrs. Josie M. Frederick, Rec. Sec., Route A, Box 364, Ripon.

SAN LUIS OBISPO COUNTY.

San Miguel No. 94, San Miguel—Meets 2nd and 4th Wednesday afternoons, Clemou Hall; Mrs. Nellie Wickstrom, Rec. Sec.
San Luisita No. 108, San Luis Obispo—Meets 2nd and 4th Thursdays, W.O.W. Hall; Miss Agnes M. Lee, Rec. Sec., P. O. box 584.
El Pinal No. 163, Cambria—Meets 2nd, 4th and 5th Tuesdays, N.S.G.W. Hall; Kathryn Luchessa, Rec. Sec.

SAN MATEO COUNTY.

Bonita No. 10, Redwood City—Meets 2nd and 4th Thursdays, I.O.O.F. Hall; Mrs. Dora Wilson, Rec. Sec., 518 Middlefield Rd.
Vista del Mar No. 155, Halfmoon Bay—Meets 2nd and 4th Thursdays, I.O.O.F. Hall; Mrs. Grace Griffith, Rec. Sec.
Ano Nuevo No. 180, Pescadero—Meets 1st and 3rd Wednesdays, I.O.O.F. Hall; Mrs. Alice Mattei, Rec. Sec.
El Carmelo No. 181, Daly City—Meets 1st and 3rd Wednesdays, Masonic Hall; Mrs. Hattie Kelly, Rec. Sec., 1179 Brunswick St.
Menlo No. 211, Menlo Park—Meets 2nd and 4th Mondays, Masonic Hall; Mrs. Frances E. Maloney, Rec. Sec., P. O. box 626.
San Bruno No. 246, San Bruno—Meets 2nd and 4th Fridays, American Legion Hall; Miss Mildred Foley, Rec. Sec., 217 Miller Ave., South San Francisco.

SANTA BARBARA COUNTY.

Reina del Mar No. 126, Santa Barbara—Meets 1st and 3rd Tuesdays, Pythian Castle, 222 W. Carillo St.; Miss Christina Moller, Rec. Sec., 836 Bath St.

SANTA CLARA COUNTY.

San Jose No. 81, San Jose—Meets Thursdays, Catholic Women Center, 5th and San Fernando Sts.; Mrs. Nellie Fleming, Rec. Sec., Catholic Women Center.
Vendome No. 100, San Jose—Meets Wednesdays, Old Scottish Rite Temple; Miss Marie Buck, Rec. Sec., 1414 Ellen St.
El Monte No. 205, Mountain View—Meets 2nd and 4th Fridays, American Legion Hall; Miss Mary Ann Rokovich, Rec. Sec., R.F.D. No. 1, box 412, State Highway.
Palo Alto No. 229, Palo Alto—Meets 1st and 2nd Mondays, N.S.G.W. Hall; Miss Helena G. Hansen, Rec. Sec., 531 Lytton Ave.

SANTA CRUZ COUNTY.

Santa Cruz No. 26, Santa Cruz—Meets Mondays, N.S.G.W. Hall; Mrs. May L. Williamson, Rec. Sec., 170 Walnut Ave.
El Pajaro No. 35, Watsonville—Meets 1st and 3rd Tuesdays, I.O.O.F. Hall; Miss Ruth E. Wilson, Rec. Sec., 16 Laurel St.

SHASTA COUNTY.

Camellia No. 41, Anderson—Meets 1st and 3rd Tuesdays, Masonic Hall; Mrs. Olga E. Welbourn, Rec. Sec.
Lassen View No. 98, Shasta—Meets 2nd Friday, Masonic Hall; Miss Louise Litsch, Rec. Sec.
Hiawatha No. 140, Redding—Meets 2nd and 4th Wednesdays, Moose Hall; Ruth Presleigh, Rec. Sec., Office County Clerk.

SIERRA COUNTY.

Naomi No. 36, Downieville—Meets 2nd and 4th Wednesdays, I.O.O.F. Hall; Mrs. Mary Cook, Rec. Sec.
Imogen No. 134, Sierraville—Meets 2nd and 4th Saturday afternoons, Copren Hall; Mrs. Jennie Copren, Rec. Sec.

SISKIYOU COUNTY.

Eschscholtzia No. 112, Etna—Meets 1st and 3rd Wednesdays, Masonic Hall; Mrs. Bernice E. Smith, Rec. Sec.
Mountain Dawn No. 120, Sawyers Bar—Meets 2nd and last Wednesdays, I.O.O.F. Hall; Miss Edith Dunphy, Rec. Sec.

SOLANO COUNTY.

Vallejo No. 195, Vallejo—Meets 1st and 3rd Wednesdays, K.C. Hall, 820 Marin St.; Mrs. Mary Combs, Rec. Sec., 511 York St.
Mary E. Bell No. 224, Dixon—Meets 2nd and 4th Thursdays, I.O.O.F. Hall; Grace McFadyen, Rec. Sec.

SONOMA COUNTY.

Sonoma No. 209, Sonoma—Meets 2nd and 4th Mondays, I.O.O.F. Hall; Mrs. Mae Norrbom, Rec. Sec., R.F.D., box 171.
Santa Rosa No. 217, Santa Rosa—Meets 1st and 3rd Thursdays, N.S.G.W. Hall; Mrs. Hazel E. Brown, Rec. Sec., 1521 4th St.
Petaluma No. 222, Petaluma—Meets 1st and 3rd Tuesdays, Dania Hall; Mrs. Margaret M. Oeltjen, Rec. Sec., 503 Prospect St.

STANISLAUS COUNTY.

Oakdale No. 125, Oakdale—Meets 1st Monday, I.O.O.F. Hall; Mrs. Lou Reeder, Rec. Sec.
Morada No. 199, Modesto—Meets 2nd and 4th Wednesdays, I.O.O.F. Hall; Mrs. Susan Sullivan, Rec. Sec., 823 10th St.
Eldora No. 248, Turlock—Meets 1st and 3rd Wednesdays, Fraternal Hall; Effie Lund, Rec. Sec., 624 Minaret Ave.

SUTTER COUNTY.

South Butte No. 226, Sutter—Meets 1st and 3rd Mondays, N.D.G.W. Hall; Mrs. Abbie N. Vagedes, Rec. Sec.

TEHAMA COUNTY.

Berendos No. 23, Red Bluff—Meets 1st and 3rd Tuesdays, W.O.W. Hall, 200 Pine St.; Mrs. Lillie Hammer, Rec. Sec., 636 Jackson St.

TRINITY COUNTY.

Eltapome No. 55, Weaverville—Meets 2nd and 4th Thursdays, N.S.G.W. Hall; Mrs. Lou N. Fetzer, Rec. Sec.

TUOLUMNE COUNTY.

Dardanelle No. 66, Sonora—Meets Fridays, I.O.O.F. Hall; Mrs. Nettie Whitto, Rec. Sec.
Golden Era No. 99, Columbia—Meets 1st and 3rd Thursdays, N.S.G.W. Hall; Miss Irene Ponce, Rec. Sec.
Anona No. 164, Jamestown—Meets 2nd and 4th Tuesdays, I.O.O.F. Hall; Mrs. Rosa A. Beckwith, Rec. Sec., P. O. box 87.

YOLO COUNTY.

Woodland No. 90, Woodland—Meets 2nd and 4th Tuesdays, N.S.G.W. Hall; Mrs. Maude Heaton, Rec. Sec., 153 College St.

YUBA COUNTY.

Marysville No. 162, Marysville—Meets 2nd and 4th Wednesdays, Liberty Hall; Miss Cecelia C. Gomes, Rec. Sec., 701 6th St.
Camp Far West No. 218, Wheatland—Meets 3rd Tuesday, I.O.O.F. Hall; Mrs. Ethel C. Brock, Rec. Sec., P. O. box 283.

AFFILIATED ORGANIZATIONS.

General Assembly Past Presidents—Meetings held annually in April at the home-town of Chief President; Miss Josephine Clark, 824 11th St., Oakland, Chief President; Mrs. Anna G. Loser, 72 Grove Lane, San Anselmo, Chief Secretary.
Past Presidents Association No. 1—Meets 1st and 3rd Mondays, N.S.G.W. Bldg., 414 Mason St., San Francisco; Mrs. Minnie F. Dobbin, Pres.; Mrs. May R. Barry, Rec. Sec., 2319 19th Ave., San Francisco.
Past Presidents Association No. 2—Meets 2nd and 4th Mondays, "Wigwam," Pacific Bldg., 16th and Jefferson, Oakland; Frieda Reichhold, Pres.; Mrs. Elizabeth B. Goodman, Rec. Sec., 134 Juana Ave., San Leandro.
Past Presidents Association No. 3 (Santa Clara County)—Meets 2nd Tuesday, homes of members; Mrs. Clara Briggs, Pres.; Mrs. Mary G. Newton, Rec. Sec., 1070 Jackson St., Santa Clara.
Past Presidents Association No. 4 (Sacramento County)—Meets 2nd Monday, Unitarian Hall, 1413 27th St., Sacramento City; Viola Gennoe, Pres.; Lily May Tilden, Rec. Sec., 3225 "T" St., Sacramento.
Past Presidents Association No. 5 (Butte County)—Meets 1st Friday, homes of members, Chico and Oroville; Sonora Steadman, Pres.; Ruth Brown, Rec. Sec., 1265 Leah Court, Oroville.
Past Presidents Association No. 6 (Nevada County)—Meets 4th Friday, alternately between Nevada City, Pythian Castle, and Grass Valley, Edna Sampson's home; Margaret V. Nolan, Pres.; Vere Hansen, Rec. Sec., R.F.D. No. 2, box 41-C, Grass Valley.
Past Presidents Association No. 7 (Sonoma County)—Meets 1st Thursday, N.S.G.W. Hall, Santa Rosa; Willow Borba, Pres.; Clytie Lewis, Rec. Sec., R.F.D. No. 4, box 345-A, Santa Rosa.
Past Presidents Association No. 8 (San Joaquin and Stanislaus Counties)—Meets 2nd Thursday, Red Men Hall, Stockton; Mrs. Lois Armstrong, Pres.; Mrs. Harriet F. Corr, Rec. Sec., 729 E. Sonora St., Stockton.
Native Sons and Native Daughters Central Committee on Homeless Children—Main Office, 955 Phelan Bldg., San Francisco; Mrs. John W. Stirling, Chmn.; Miss Mary E. Brusie, Sec. Los Angeles branch office, 3924 Sunset Blvd.; Dorothy Schlingman, Sec.

(ADVERTISEMENT.)

N.D.G.W. OFFICIAL DEATH LIST.

Giving the name, the date of death, and the Subordinate Parlor affiliation of all deceased members as reported to Grand Secretary Sallie R. Thaler from February 18 to March 18, 1932:

Keller, Sarah Brady; January 24, 1932; Presidio No. 148.
Gallagher, Isabel K.; February 17, 1932; Castro No. 178.
Belden, Edith M.; February 14, 1932; Presidio No. 148.
Bush, Mary A.; February 7, 1932; Minerva No. 2.
Randolph, Georgie A.; January 31, 1932; Encinal No. 156.
Santini, Clelia Maraini; February 3, 1932; La Rosa No. 191.
Butler, Ida Elliott; February 27, 1932; La Bandera No. 110.
Schroeder, Sophie; February 10, 1932; Keith No. 137.
Bickmore, Alice G.; February 27, 1932; Veritas No. 75.
Fogarty, Malvena Dahlberg; February 25, 1932; Columbia No. 70.

NATIVE DAUGHTER NEWS

(Continued from Page 11)

by Sadie Winn-Brainard of Sacramento, was accepted by President Sarah R. Miller. Sophie Stewart of Los Angeles added to the charm of the occasion by rendering several songs in her beautiful contralto voice. The afternoon concluded with a tea at the home of Alice H. Damarus, at which members of San Diego were hostesses to guests from the north.

Three Initiated.

Cambria—El Pinal No. 163 enjoyed a visit from Grand President Evelyn Carlson. The meeting was preceded by a luncheon, prepared by Mrs. George Steiner at her home. There were twelve visitors, and three candidates were initiated. The hall was beautifully decorated with spring flowers, a large bowl of poppies being placed before the president's station. The Grand President gave a very interesting talk on the work of the Order, and there were brief remarks from Miss Agnes Lee, Mms. Loose, Hill and Lauritson.

Children Guests.

Chico—Annie K. Bidwell No. 168 had a party for the children of its members. Games were played and the guests presented a program. Refreshments were served at a table beautifully decorated in red, white and blue. Miss Alice Herman and Mrs. Olive Pearl had charge of the games, Mrs. Cora Hintz announced the program, Miss Icel Snyder was program chairman, and the following made up the refreshments committee: Mms. Lois Heberle, Ethel Estes, Ila Cole, June Wright, Josephine Alexander.

Aged Songbook Given School.

San Jose—Vendome No. 100 observed Arbor Day by joining with the P.T.A. of the Herbert Hoover junior high school and planting four trees, one of which was dedicated by Miss Tillie Brohaska to the California Pioneers. William H. Laurence, 95-year-old Pioneer, told how the Pioneers served in the Civil War, and Supervising Deputy Clara Gairaud read Goldsboy's gem, "The Pioneer," published in the August 1921 Grizzly Bear. Mrs. Rosalie Andrews presented an aged family songbook to the school in memory of her father, Coleman Younger, founder of the Santa Clara County Pioneer Society.

Afternoon card parties for charitable purposes were sponsored during March by Mms. Faye Withycombe, Sue Mattei, Clara Gairaud, Julia Waddington and Grace Maggini. Evening social chairmen were Miss Dorothy Salas and Mrs. Alice Kady. March 16 an enjoyable skit, "Two Tables of Bridge," was presented and Irish music was enjoyed. Mrs. Stella Baggs directed the games. Mms. Julia Waddington, Emma Nelson and Clara Gairaud were recent hostesses to the Vendome past presidents club. Dainty baby quilts are being made for the homeless children by the club.

Poppy Sale Aids Children.

Bakersfield—A sale of more than a thousand golden poppies by El Tejon No. 239 netted a goodly sum for the homeless children. March 11 fifteen members accompanied Supervising Deputy Grace Davis to Desert Gold No. 250 (Mojave) to greet the Grand President on her official visit to that Parlor. March 13 a large group gathered at Kern County Park for Arbor Day exercises. Two flowering peach trees were planted. March 16 the second of a series of card parties was held at the home of Alice Phillips. A large crowd was in attendance. Tallies, score cards, etc., carried out the Saint Patrick motif.

Sons Are Supper Guests.

Oroville—Gold of Ophir No. 190 was entertained March 2 by Mms. Luretta Ross and Evelyn Joslyn, who interestingly recounted the early-day history of their pioneer families. After the meeting members of Argonaut No. 8 N.S.G.W. were guests at a tamale supper. An effective setting of violets and pink stock was arranged by President Alice Cundy and vice-presidents Rosa Crum, Hattie Clark and Pearl Damon. Grand President Evelyn I. Carlson will be the Parlor's guest April 20.

Arbor Day Program.

Placerville—Members of Marguerite No. 12 met at the home of Nettie Wentworth for their annual Arbor Day program. Mary Swansborough was the honor-guest, and a crepe myrtle tree was dedicated to her memory. Participating in the program were Jane McCusker, Nora Gray, Ida Bailey, Agnes Schipp and President Annie Jaeger. Delicious refreshments were served by Mrs. Wentworth following the exercises.

Projects Explained.

Mariposa—On the occasion of her official visit to Mariposa No. 63, Grand President Evelyn I. Carlson in a pleasing and instructive manner explained the Order's projects. She was presented with a beautiful picture of Yosemite by Trustee Grace Trabucco, acting for the Parlor. A delicious banquet was served at tables decorated in red, white and yellow. Among the many in attendance were Supervising Deputy May F. Givens and District Deputy Eugenia Kahl.

Several Hundred at Card Party.

Modesto—Members of Morada No. 199 enjoyed a "kid's party." All were dressed in appropriate costumes, and games and cards were played. Ethel Mathiasen headed the committee in charge. The Parlor had its annual poppy day and sold poppies for the benefit of the homeless children. Mrs. Emma Smith entertained the sewing club at her home March 18.

Morada and Modesto No. 11 N.S.G.W. had their joint monthly card party March 16, and several hundred were in attendance. Refreshments were served and dancing was enjoyed.

"One of the Girls."

Santa Ana—Santa No. 235 had a very large attendance March 14, the occasion being the official visit of Grand President Evelyn I. Carlson. Thanks to the energy of First Vice-president Mildred Gray, the banquet tables were beautifully decorated with Easter lilies and graceful plants. Two candidates were initiated.

"Grand President Carlson, in the course of her instructive address on the Order's projects," says Recording Secretary Matilda Lemon, "won the hearts of her listeners with her charming, winsome manner. She was not only our Grand President, but one of the girls." Mrs. Carlson

(Concluded on Page 19)

Native Sons of the Golden West

SACRAMENTO—SACRAMENTO NO. 3, the second oldest Parlor in the Order, was instituted March 22, 1878. The fifty-fourth anniversary was celebrated with a banquet and highjinks, March 31, attended by grand officers and numerous other visitors. Irving D. Gibson was master of ceremonies, and following the feast the Parlor convened and the stations were filled by the older past presidents. The oldtimers maintaining a continuous membership of a half-century and more in No. 3 were presented with life memberships. The anniversary festivities were in charge of the following committee: June Longshore (chairman), Thomas W. McAuliffe, Frank Didion, Ervin Beale and John Major.

Some time ago, Treasurer Robert D. Finnie was appointed on the Parlor's goodwill committee. He had special greeting cards designed and sends one to each couple having a golden wedding anniversary and to each individual of 85 years and upward that come to his attention. These cards go not only to natives of the state but to others, and in return many letters of appreciation, expressing goodwill toward the Parlor and the Order, are received.

H. L. Drennon has been appointed chairman of Sacramento's committee to arrange for the joint annual outing of the Parlors of San Joaquin and Sacramento Counties. President Joe Hellinge Jr. heads a committee that is arranging for a dance jointly with La Bandera No. 110 N.D.G.W. April 29. The Parlor had a Saint Patrick night March 17, Archibald Mull Jr. delivering an address and Irish ballads being sung.

Joseph P. Lennon, Thomas W. McAuliffe and Arthur J. Delano had charge of the arrangements.

Opposes Wage Reductions.

San Diego—Over historic Fort Stockton, on the crest of Presidio Hill, the national colors are again flying, San Diego No. 108 having presented a new flag and halyard. March 10 the Parlor approved a resolution, presented by Edward H. Dowell, Gregory McHorney and Deputy Grand President Albert V. Mayrhofer, opposing reduction in the wages of government employes.

The objection is based on the contention that any such reduction would be reflected in the wages paid employes of private concerns. Buying power is decreased proportionately with wage reductions, the Parlor contends.

Golden Anniversary.

Stockton—Over 600 members of the Order attended the celebration of Stockton No. 7's fiftieth (golden) institution anniversary March 14. They came from all parts of the state. Entertainment features were presented, and Warren Atherton, the master of ceremonies, introduced the following speakers: Grand President Dr. Frank I. Gonzalez, Grand Secretary John T. Regan, Grand Trustee George F. McNoble, Superior Judge J. F. Pullen, R. J. Marraccini, Dr. George F. Pache, J. Solomon, Judge George Steele, Joseph Cross, J. L. Whiting, G. Wakeman, A. L. Levinsky, George Catts and Frank Rose.

Following dinner the oldtimers presided at the Parlor meeting, Past Grand President Hubert R. McNoble assuming the presidency. Reports on arrangements for the Grand Parlor, to be held here in May, were received with applause.

Membership Standing Largest Parlors.

San Francisco—Grand Secretary John T. Regan reports the standing of the Subordinate Parlors having a membership of over 400 January 1, 1932, as follows, together with their membership figures March 19, 1932:

Parlor	Jan. 1	Mch. 19	Gain	Loss
Ramona No. 109	1088	1087	....	1
South San Francisco No. 157	822	818	....	4
Castro No. 232	700	700	....	....
Arrowhead No. 110	609	613	4	....
Stanford No. 76	614	610	....	4
Twin Peaks No. 214	585	573	....	12
Stockton No. 7	549	549	....	....
Piedmont No. 120	523	520	....	3
Rincon No. 72	448	444	....	4

Interparlor Visits Beneficial.

Oakland—Claremont No. 240 was host March 22 to the past presidents and oldtimers at a get-together smoker. Members of East Bay Counties Past Presidents Assembly were also guests. A class of candidates were initiated, and a tasty repast was followed by whist. No. 240 is looking forward to a dance which will probably be sponsored by the drum corps, one of its live units.

Several members of Claremont recently visited Golden Gate No. 29 (San Francisco), and March 29 a delegation called on Athens No. 195 (Oakland). For some time a monthly visit has been paid to some Parlor in the bay area, and the Claremonters are positive that the visits are for the Order's general good, as they cre goodfellowship.

Increased Membership—More Delegates.

Santa Rosa—Santa Rosa No. 28 celebrated forty-eighth institution anniversary by initiat March 12 a large class of candidates. The rit was faultlessly exemplified by a team fr Mount Tamalpais No. 64 (San Rafael), and t Parlor's drum corps headed a parade thro the streets previous to the meeting. Many ot visitors were in attendance, from San Francis Petaluma, Sonoma and Sebastopol. A sump ous banquet followed the ceremonies, and c gratulatory addresses were delivered by pr inent members of the Order.

Santa Rosa was instituted through the effo of Dr. Charles W. Decker, now a Past Gra President. Its two remaining charter membe Thomas J. Hutchinson and William Irwin, w present at the anniversary festivities. Dur the past few months the Parlor has so increa its membership that it will be represented four delegates at the Stockton Grand Parlor.

Santa Rosa City will have a rose carnival M 5, 6 and 7, and the Parlor has entered the c test for a cup to be awarded for the best dec ated vacant lot. The property, through the forts of the members, has been planted to lawn. In the center is a large bear, made flowers, with the initials N.S.G.W.

Membership Campaign Launched.

Santa Ana—A membership campaign was augurated by Santa Ana No. 265 March 7. Th teams, captained by Carl Schroeder, Harry F ton and Alvin Selvidge, were named. Points to be allowed for initiates, reinstatements a collections delinquent dues. At the conclusi of the contest, which is to run six weeks, t winning team will be guests of the two los teams at a banquet. March 21 a program a refreshments were enjoyed.

State Flag Presented Legion.

Monterey—Monterey No. 75 presented a Ca fornia State (Bear) Flag to Monterey Penins Post No. 41 American Legion March 10. Co mander Ken Lyman welcomed the Natives, Pr ident John Thomsen made the presentation dress and Past Commander W. A. Irvine sponded. First Vice-president James W. M lington sang "I Love You, California." Oth in the visiting delegation from the Parlor w Charter Member Grant Towle and Financial S retary W. E. Parker.

Past Presidents Exemplify Ritual.

San Bernardino—Arrowhead No. 110 ent tained the members of Lugonia No. 241 N.D.G. at a dinner, March 9, which was followed b program and dancing. March 23 was initiati and the ritual was exemplified by Past Pre dents Bill Jasper, Donald E. VanLuven, Les G. King, J. J. Cadd, Leslie Maloche, Harry Lo George J. MacDonald, Ben Harrison and Jose E. Rich.

The Parlor has a building committee co posed of Harry M. Rouse (chairman), Will Sh Jerry Doyle, O. W. Seccombe, J. A. Gregory, H. Hayden, Elmer Hoein, D. B. Livingston John Hansen. A visit to San Diego No. 108 on Arrowhead's April program.

Complimented for Increase.

Watsonville—Grand Trustee Jesse H. Mil officially visited Watsonville No. 65 March and was greeted by a large attendance of membership. He complimented the Parlor its membership increase. Joseph Katen, acc plished pianist welcomed as a new member, f ored with several selections. During the so hour interesting talks were made by Presid A. W. Batchelder and others.

Talk of Absorbing Interest.

San Rafael—March 15 several members Mount Tamalpais No. 64 and Sea Point No. (Sausalito) accepted an invitation from Cas No. 232 (San Francisco). Among the featu on a splendid program were vocal and ins mental music, legerdemain, boxing bouts and address. Captain Chas. Dullen delivered a of absorbing interest on the crime of kidr ing, dealing with cases of great importance relating incidents in connection therewith

THE GRIZZLY BEAR
IS REGULARLY ON SALE:
SAN FRANCISCO:
N.S.G.W. Bldg., 414 Mason St., Room 302.
OAKLAND:
Fred M. DeWitt, 620 14th St.
LOS ANGELES:
315 Wilcox Bldg., Second and Spring.

which the public is not generally cognizant. There have been no serious cases of kidnaping in California, he stated. In San Francisco there were two cases attracting considerable attention, but the motive in neither was gain; no ransom was demanded and the culprit was eventually caught and punished. A delicious repast was served at the conclusion of the entertainment. Harmon D. Skillin presided at the festivities.

March 21, was "Kelly's Irish Night" at Mount Tamalpais. Frank Kelly, master of ceremonies, planned the menu of cornbeef, cabbage and weak tea, and the program of vocal and instrumental music. It was one of those never-to-be-forgotten events in the annals of No. 64.

Eighteen Initiated.

Manteca—Manteca No. 271 initiated a class of eighteen candidates rounded up by Deputy Grand President Al Lobree. The ritual was exemplified by the Parlor officers headed by President Louis Ryan. Among the many in attendance were Grand President Dr. Frank I. Gonzalez, Grand Secretary John T. Regan, and delegations from Stockton No. 7, Modesto No. 11 and Tracy No. 186. A splendid supper, served by members of Phoebe A. Hearst No. 214 N.D.G.W., was followed by dancing. Manteca plans to sponsor an orchestra.

Much Enthusiasm.

Castroville—Deputy Grand President John Thomsen installed the officers of Gabilan No. 132, B. A. McCoy becoming president. Previous to the ceremonies there was a largely attended banquet. Several fine addresses were listened to, and there was much enthusiasm.

Civic Endeavor.

Placerville—Placerville No. 9 is sponsoring a dance for April 16, the proceeds to go toward completion of the community swimming pool. The Parlor's band and basketball team were guests of Placerville at an entertainment and banquet. Hearty applause greeted the band, which rendered several selections, and for its excellent showing the basketball team was given a hearty vote of thanks.

Anniversary Celebrated.

Oakland—Piedmont No. 120 celebrated its forty-fifth institution anniversary March 10. Among the honor-guests was Grand President Dr. Frank I. Gonzalez. Superior Judge Lincoln S. Church was the principal speaker of the evening. Three charter members, G. D. McHugh, J. B. Donnelly and H. P. Brown, were in attendance.

Important Matters Discussed.

Courtland—Members of General John A. Sutter Past Presidents Assembly were guests of Courtland No. 106 March 21. Many important matters were discussed, among them the date of the next joint class initiation of the Sacramento County Parlors, the marking of historic landmarks and the P.P.A. General Assembly.

Golden Gaters Visitors.

Pleasanton—Pleasanton No. 244 received an official visit from Grand Third Vice-president Chas. A. Koenig, who was accompanied by a delegation from Golden Gate No. 29 (San Francisco). The grand officer spoke on the Order's activities, and other speakers were Past President Peter C. Madsen and Recording Secretary Ernest W. Schween of No. 244. A banquet terminated the meeting. The committee in charge for the evening included John Busch, Will Busch, John S. Silva, Ernest W. Schween, Tony Rabello Jr. and George Trimingham.

Record-Breaking Class.

Calistoga—The largest class of candidates ever initiated in the Napa Valley became members of Calistoga No. 86, March 21. In honor of the Parlor's sole surviving charter member, the initiates were referred to as "The C. E. Butler Class." There was a very large attendance, among the visitors being Grand President Dr. Frank I. Gonzalez, Grand Secretary John T. Regan and Grand Trustee Joseph J. McShane. The Parlor entertained royally. Details of the memorable event will appear in The Grizzly Bear for May.

Marin Show—The eighth annual Marin County Flower Show will be held at Mill Valley, April 20.

Spring Show—Sacramento City will have its annual Spring Flower Show, April 30-May 1.

Gala Week of Flowers—Riverside City will have its annual La Fiesta Floral, April 11-16.

Official Directory of Parlors of the N. S. G. W.

GRAND OFFICERS.

John T. Newell.................Junior Past Grand President
2666 Benedict, Los Angeles
Dr. Frank I. Gonzales.................Grand President
Flood Bldg., San Francisco
Seth Millington.................Grand First Vice-pres.
Gridley
Justice Emmet Seawell.................Grand Second Vice-pres.
State Bldg., San Francisco
Chas. A. Koenig.................Grand Third Vice-pres.
531 35th Ave., San Francisco
John T. Regan.................Grand Secretary
N.S.G.W. Bldg., 414 Mason St., San Francisco
John A. Corotto.................Grand Treasurer
560 No. 5th St., San Jose
Horace J. Leavitt.................Grand Marshal
Weaverville
W. B. O'Brien.................Grand Inside Sentinel
2324 Santa Clara St., Alameda
Gam Hurst.................Grand Outside Sentinel
1400 Financial Center Bldg., Oakland
Leslie Maloche.................Grand Organist
467½ 3rd St., San Bernardino
George H. Barron.................Historiographer
333 12th Ave., San Francisco

GRAND TRUSTEES

George F. McNoble.................California Bldg., Stockton
Samuel M. Shortridge Jr.................Menlo Park
Jesse H. Miller.................712 DeYoung Bldg., San Francisco
Joseph J. McShane.................419 Flood Bldg., San Francisco
Frank M. Lane.................333 Blackstone, Fresno
John M. Barnett.................San Jose
Eldred L. Meyer.................922 San Vincente, Santa Monica

ALAMEDA COUNTY.

Alameda No. 47, Alameda City—Gus Nelson, Pres.; Robt. H. Cavanaugh, Sec., 1806 Pacific Ave.; Wednesdays, Native Sons Hall, 1406 Park St.
Oakland No. 50, Oakland—A. W. Ainger, Pres.; F. M. Norris, Sec., 4280 Terrace St.; Fridays, Native Sons Hall, 11th and Clay Sts.
Las Positas No. 96, Livermore—R. J. Ruetz, Pres.; John J. Kelly, Sec., P. O. box 341; Thursdays, Foresters Hall.
Eden No. 113, Hayward—Henry L'Ecuyer, Pres.; Stanton R. Soares, Sec., P. O. box 176; 2nd and 4th Tuesdays, Memorial Hall, Main St.
Piedmont No. 120, Oakland—Walter M. Davis, Pres.; Charles Morando, Sec., 906 Vermont St.; Thursdays, Native Sons Hall, 11th and Clay Sts.
Wisteria No. 127, Alvarado—Henry May, Pres.; J. M. Scribner, Sec., Livermore; 1st Thursday, I.O.O.F. Hall.
Halcyon No. 146, Alameda City—Charles J. Von Tagen, Pres.; J. C. Bates, Sec., 2139 Buena Vista Ave.; 1st and 3rd Tuesdays, I.O.O.F. Hall, 2329 Santa Clara Ave.
Brooklyn No. 151, Oakland—Frank B. Perry, Pres.; E. W. Cooney, Sec., 3907 14th Ave.; Wednesdays, Masonic Temple, 8th Ave. and E. 14th St.
Washington No. 169, Centerville—M. B. Silva, Pres.; Allen G. Norris, Sec., P. O. box 31; 2nd and 4th Tuesdays, Hansen Hall.
Athens No. 195, Oakland—Henry G. Kroeckel, Pres.; Harold B. Farley, Sec., 4623 Benevides Ave.; Tuesdays, Native Sons Hall, 11th and Clay Sts.
Berkeley No. 210, Berkeley—S. Levy, Pres.; R. J. Garrett, Sec., 1708 Virginia St.; Tuesdays, Native Sons Hall, 2108 Shattuck Ave.
Estudillo No. 223, San Leandro—Frank V. Pacheco, Pres.; Albert G. Pacheco, Sec., 1736 E. 14th St.; 1st and 3rd Tuesdays, U.P.E.C. Hall.
Claremont No. 240, Oakland—Fred Buelna, Pres.; E. N. Thienger, Sec., 839 Hearst Ave., Berkeley; Tuesdays, Veterans Memorial Bldg., 43rd & Salem Sts., Emeryville.
Pleasanton No. 244, Pleasanton—Peter C. Madsen, Pres.; Ernest W. Schween, Sec.; 2nd and 4th Thursdays, I.O.O.F. Hall.
Niles No. 250, Niles—M. L. Fournier, Pres.; C. E. Martenstein, Sec.; 2nd Thursday, I.O.O.F. Hall.
Fruitvale No. 252, Oakland—Chester B. Abernethy, Pres.; Ray B. Felton, Sec., 1575 Alice St.; Fridays, W.O.W. Hall, 3256 E. 14th St.

AMADOR COUNTY.

Amador No. 17, Sutter Creek—Frank Marre, Pres.; F. J. Payne, Sec.; 1st and 3rd Fridays, Native Sons Hall.
Excelsior No. 31, Jackson—Wm. Daugherty, Pres.; William Going, Sec.; 1st and 3rd Wednesdays, Native Sons Hall, 22 Court St.
Ione No. 33, Ione—Marvin Kidd, Pres.; Josiah H. Saunders, Sec.; 1st and 3rd Wednesdays, Native Sons Hall.
Plymouth No. 48, Plymouth—L. E. Houston, Pres.; Thos. D. Davis, Sec.; 1st and 3rd Saturdays, I.O.O.F. Hall.

BUTTE COUNTY.

Argonaut No. 8, Oroville—Fred E. Tegrunde, Pres.; Cyril R. Macdonald, Sec., P. O. box 502; 1st and 3rd Wednesdays, Veterans Memorial Hall.
Chico No. 21, Chico—Marcus Choisser, Pres.; Sam Lindsay Adams, Sec., Sacramento Blvd.; 2nd and 4th Thursdays, Elks Hall.

CALAVERAS COUNTY.

Chispa No. 139, Murphys—John Voitich, Pres.; Antone Malaspina, Sec.; Wednesdays, Native Sons Hall.

COLUSA COUNTY.

Colusa No. 69, Colusa City—Burton L. Smart, Pres.; Phil J. Humburg, Sec., 223 Parkhill St.; Tuesdays, Eagles Hall.

CONTRA COSTA COUNTY.

General Winn No. 32, Antioch—Edmont T. Uren, Pres.; Joel H. Ford, Sec., P. O. box 311; 2nd and 4th Wednesdays, Union Hall.
Mount Diablo No. 101, Martinez—R. P. Anderson, Pres.; G. T. Barkley, Sec.; 1st and 3rd Mondays, I.O.O.F. Hall.
Byron No. 170, Byron—William E. Bunn, Pres.; H. G. Krumland, Sec.; 1st and 3rd Tuesdays, I.O.O.F. Hall.
Carquinez No. 205, Crockett—Thos. Cox, Pres.; Thomas L. Cahalan, Sec.; 1st and 3rd Wednesdays, I.O.O.F. Hall.
Richmond No. 217, Richmond—M. W. Amaral, Pres.; H. D. Mason, Sec., 11 6th St.; Wednesdays, Redmen Hall, 11th and Nevan Ave.
Concord No. 245, Concord—P. M. Soto, Pres.; D. E. Pramberg, Sec., P. O. box 235; 1st Tuesday, I.O.O.F. Hall.
Diamond No. 246, Pittsburg—Victor Ericsson, Pres.; Francis A. Irving, Sec., 248 E. 5th St.; 1st and 3rd Wednesdays, Veterans Memorial Bldg.

EL DORADO COUNTY.

Placerville No. 9, Placerville—George M. Smith, Pres.; Duncan Bathurst, Sec., 12 Gilmore St.; 2nd and 4th Tuesdays, Masonic Hall.
Georgetown No. 91, Georgetown—W. H. Breedlove, Pres.; C. F. Irish, Sec.; 2nd and 4th Wednesdays, I.O.O.F. Hall.

FRESNO COUNTY.

Fresno No. 25, Fresno City—A. G. Miller, Pres.; John W. Cappleman, Sec., 1389 Wilson; 2nd and 4th Fridays, W.O.W. Hall, 1354 Van Ness Ave.
Selma No. 107, Selma—Chester E. Shepard, Pres.; E. C. Laughlin, Sec.; 1st and 3rd Wednesdays, American Legion Hall.

HUMBOLDT COUNTY.

Humboldt No. 14, Eureka—Edward J. Quinn, Pres.; Loren M. Nelson, Sec., P.O. box 195; 2nd and 4th Mondays, Native Sons Hall.
Arcata No. 20, Arcata—George Hale, Pres.; William Peters, Sec., P. O. box 1117; Thursdays, Native Sons Hall.
Ferndale No. 93, Ferndale—O. R. Frame, Pres.; C. H. Rasmussen, Sec., R.F.D., 47-A; 1st and 3rd Mondays, K.P. Hall.

KERN COUNTY.

Bakersfield No. 42, Bakersfield—O. E. Taylor, Pres.; Leroy Vandervoort, Sec., Manly Apts.; Wednesdays, Justice Court, City Hall.

LAKE COUNTY.

Lower Lake No. 159, Lower Lake—Harold S. Anderson, Pres.; Albert Kugelman, Sec.; Thursdays, I.O.O.F. Hall.

LASSEN COUNTY.

Honey Lake No. 198, Standish—James C. Meeske, Pres.; N. V. Wemple, Sec., Litchfield; 1st and 3rd Wednesdays, Wrede Hall.
Big Valley No. 211, Bieber—George Bunselmeier, Pres.; A. W. McKenzie, Sec.; 1st and 3rd Wednesdays, I.O.O.F. Hall.

LOS ANGELES COUNTY.

Los Angeles No. 45, Los Angeles City—Lee E. Erwin, Pres.; Richard W. Fryer, Sec., 1629 Champlain Ter.; Thursdays, Merchant Plumbers Hall, 1832 So. Hope.
Ramona No. 109, Los Angeles City—Chandos E. Bush, Pres.; John V. Scott, Sec., Patriotic Hall, 1816 So. Figueroa; Fridays, Patriotic Hall, 1816 So. Figueroa.
Hollywood No. 196, Los Angeles City—Leo Aggeler, Pres.; E. J. Reilly, Sec., 907 W. 2nd St.; Mondays, 1089 No. Oxford Ave.
Long Beach No. 239, Long Beach—Francis H. Gentry, Pres.; W. W. Brady, Sec., 801 Jergins Trust Bldg.; 2nd and 4th Thursdays, Moose Hall, Elm and Anaheim.
Sepulveda No. 263, San Pedro—Francis G. Fetzer, Pres.; Frank I. Markey, Sec., 101 W. 7th St.; 2nd and 4th Fridays, Odd Fellows Temple, 10th and Gaffey Sts.
Glendale No. 264, Glendale—Philip D. Molen, Pres.; Abel B. Molen, Sec., 508 So. Belmont St.; 1st and 3rd Tuesdays, Masonic Temple, 234 So. Brand Blvd.
Santa Monica Bay No. 267, Ocean Park—Claude J. Wiseman, Pres.; John J. Smith, Sec., 830 Rialto Ave., Venice; 2nd and 4th Mondays, New Eagle Hall, 2823½ Main St.
Cahuenga No. 268, Reseda—Harold C. Trexler, Pres.; Carrol S. Driscoll, Sec., P.O. box 25, Chatsworth; first Friday, Alton Hall.

MADERA COUNTY.

Madera No. 130, Madera City—Cornelius Noble, Pres.; T. P. Cosgrave, Sec.; 1st and 3rd Thursdays, First National Bank Bldg.

MARIN COUNTY.

Mount Tamalpais No. 64, San Rafael—Arthur Todt, Pres.; Manual A. Andrade, Sec., 532 Mission Ave.; 1st and 3rd Mondays, Portuguese American Hall.
Sea Point No. 158, Sausalito—Allyn T. Young, Pres.; Manuel Santos, Sec., 6 Glen Drive; 1st and 3rd Wednesdays, Perry Bldg.
Nicasio No. 183, Nicasio—M. T. Farley, Pres.; R. J. Rogers, Sec.; 2nd and 4th Wednesdays, U.A.O.D. Hall.

MENDOCINO COUNTY.

Ukiah No. 71, Ukiah—Henry Bucknell, Pres.; Ben Hofman, Sec., P. O. box 473; 1st and 3rd Mondays, I.O.O.F. Hall.
Broderick No. 117, Point Arena—Sam Reinking, Pres.; H. C. Hunter, Sec.; 1st and 3rd Thursdays, Forester Hall.
Alder Glen No. 200, Fort Bragg—Clarence Simpson, Pres.; C. R. Weller, Sec.; 2nd and 4th Fridays, I.O.O.F. Hall.

MERCED COUNTY.

Yosemite No. 24, Merced City—Anthony A. Rodrigues, Pres.; True W. Fowler, Sec., P. O. box 781; 2nd and 4th Mondays, I.O.O.F. Hall.

MONTEREY COUNTY.

Monterey No. 75, Monterey City—John Thomsen, Pres.; T. W. Krieger, Sec., 999 Franklin St.; 1st and 3rd Fridays, Knights Pythias Hall, Main St.
Santa Lucia No. 97, Salinas—E. L. Adcock, Pres.; R. W. Adcock, Sec., Route 2, box 141; Mondays, Native Sons Hall, 32 W. Alisal St.
Gabilan No. 132, Castroville—B. A. McCoy, Pres.; R. H. Martin, Sec., P. O. box 81; 1st and 3rd Thursdays, Native Sons Hall.

NAPA COUNTY.

Saint Helena No. 53, Saint Helena—E. W. Johnson, Pres.; Edw. L. Bonhote, Sec., P. O. box 267; Mondays, Native Sons Hall.
Napa No. 62, Napa City—A. G. Boggs, Pres.; H. J. Hoernle, Sec., 1226 Oak St.; Mondays, Native Sons Hall.
Calistoga No. 86, Calistoga—Frank Mariani, Pres.; Louis Carlenzoli, Sec.; 1st and 3rd Mondays, I.O.O.F. Hall.

ATTENTION, SECRETARIES!

THIS DIRECTORY IS PUBLISHED BY AUTHORITY OF THE GRAND PARLOR N.S.G.W., AND ALL NOTICES OF CHANGES MUST BE RECEIVED BY THE GRAND SECRETARY (NOT THE MAGAZINE) ON OR BEFORE THE 20TH OF EACH MONTH TO INSURE CORRECTION IN NEXT ISSUE OF DIRECTORY.

NEVADA COUNTY.

Hydraulic No. 56, Nevada City—Spencer G. White, Pres.; Dr. C. W. Chapman, Sec.; Tuesdays, Pythian Castle.
Quartz No. 58, Grass Valley—Allen Joyner, Pres.; H. Ray George, Sec., 151 Conaway Ave.; Mondays, Auditorium Hall.
Donner No. 162, Truckee—J. F. Lichtenberger, Pres.; H. C. Lichtenberger, Sec.; 2nd and 4th Tuesdays, Native Sons Hall.

ORANGE COUNTY.

Santa Ana No. 265, Santa Ana—R. L. Marsile, Pres.; E. F. Marks, Sec., 1124 No. Bristol St.; 1st and 3rd Mondays, K.C. Hall, 4th and French Sts.

PLACER COUNTY.

Auburn No. 59, Auburn—Cosme Vicencio, Pres.; J. G. Walsh, Sec.; 1st and 3rd Fridays, Foresters Hall.
Silver Star No. 63, Lincoln—Ralph Sandstad, Pres.; Barney G. Barry, Sec., P. O. box 72; 3rd Wednesday, I.O.O.F. Hall.
Rocklin No. 233, Roseville—Thomas Elliott, Pres.; M. E. Reed, Sec., 253 W. Duranta; 2nd and 4th Wednesdays, Eagles Hall.

PLUMAS COUNTY.

Quincy No. 131, Quincy—J. D. McLaughlin, Pres.; E. C. Kelsey, Sec.; 2nd Thursday, I.O.O.F. Hall.
Golden Anchor No. 182, La Porte—R. J. McGrath, Pres.; LeRoy J. Post, Sec.; 2nd and 4th Sunday mornings, Native Sons Hall.
Plumas No. 228, Taylorsville—E. E. Sikes, Pres.; George E. Boyden, Sec.; 1st and 3rd Mondays, Native Sons Hall.

SACRAMENTO COUNTY.

Sacramento No. 3, Sacramento City—Joseph Hellinge Jr., Pres.; J. F. Didion, Sec., 1131 "O" St.; Thursdays, Native Sons Bldg., 11th and "J" Sts.
Sunset No. 26, Sacramento City—George W. Lial, Pres.; Edward E. Reese, Sec., County Treasurer Office; Mondays, Native Sons Bldg., 11th and "J" Sts.
Elk Grove No. 41, Elk Grove—Fred Sehlmeyer, Pres.; Walter Martin, Sec.; 2nd and 4th Fridays, Masonic Hall.
Granite No. 83, Folsom—Joe Relvas, Pres.; Frank Showers, Sec.; 2nd and 4th Tuesdays, K.P. Hall.
Courtland No. 106, Courtland—Albert Pyhnan, Pres.; Jos. Green, Sec.; 1st Saturday and 3rd Monday, Native Sons Hall.
Sutter Fort No. 241, Sacramento City—August Lehman, Pres.; C. L. Katzenstein, Sec., P. O. box 914; 2nd and 4th Wednesdays, Native Sons Bldg., 11th and "J" Sts.
Galt No. 243, Galt—John Granadas, Pres.; F. W. Harms, Sec.; 1st and 3rd Mondays, I.O.O.F. Hall.

SAN BENITO COUNTY.

Fremont No. 44, Hollister—Chas. B. Arbeloche, Pres.; J. E. Prendergast Jr., Sec., 1064 Monterey St.; 1st and 3rd Thursdays, Grangers Union Hall.

SAN BERNARDINO COUNTY.

Arrowhead No. 110, San Bernardino City—Lynn A. Reed, Pres.; R. W. Brazelton, Sec., 462 6th St.; Wednesdays, Eagles Hall, 469 4th St.

SAN DIEGO COUNTY.

San Diego No. 108, San Diego City—Gregory A. McHorney, Pres.; A. V. Mayrhofer, Sec., 1572 2nd St.; Wednesdays, K.C. Hall, 4th and Elm Sts.

SAN FRANCISCO CITY AND COUNTY.

California No. 1, San Francisco—Sal Juliano, Pres.; Ellis A. Blackman, Sec., 126 Front St.; Thursdays, Native Sons Bldg., 414 Mason St.
Pacific No. 10, San Francisco—John C. Daly, Pres.; J. Henry Bastein, Sec., 1880 Howard St.; Tuesdays, Native Sons Bldg., 414 Mason St.
Golden Gate No. 29, San Francisco—Thomas I. Schlink, Pres.; Adolph Eberhart, Sec., 183 Carl St.; Mondays, Native Sons Bldg., 414 Mason St.
Mission No. 38, San Francisco—Joseph C. Augustine Jr., Pres.; Thos. J. Stewart, Sec., 1919 Howard St.; Wednesdays, Redmen Hall, 3053 16th St.
San Francisco No. 49, San Francisco—Louis L. Ghiotti, Pres.; David Capurro, Sec., 978 Union St.; Thursdays, Native Sons Bldg., 414 Mason St.
El Dorado No. 52, San Francisco—Eugene Herzog, Pres.; Alfred Vlautin, Sec., 1537 Franklin St.; Thursdays, Native Sons Bldg., 414 Mason St.
Rincon No. 72, San Francisco—Michael J. Joyce, Pres.; John A. Gilmour, Sec., 2069 Golden Gate Ave.; Wednesdays, Native Sons Bldg., 414 Mason St.
Stanford No. 76, San Francisco—Albert W. Groskopf, Pres.; Charles T. O'Kane, Sec., 1111 Pine St.; Tuesdays, Native Sons Bldg., 414 Mason St.
Bay City No. 104, San Francisco—Morris Garren, Pres.; Max E. Licht, Sec., 1831 Fulton St.; 2nd and 4th Wednesdays, Native Sons Bldg., 414 Mason St.
Niantic No. 105, San Francisco—A. Furner, Pres.; J. M. Darcy, Sec., 10 Hoffman Ave.; Wednesdays, Native Sons Bldg., 414 Mason St.
National No. 118, San Francisco—Wayne Burke, Pres.; Martin M. Ratigan, Sec., 1325 Page St., Apt. 6; Thursdays, 1160 Eddy St.
Hesperian No. 137, San Francisco—H. G. Ritter, Pres.; Albert Carlson, Sec., 879 Justin Dr.; Thursdays, Native Sons Bldg., 414 Mason St.
Alcalde No. 154, San Francisco—Conrad Kuhl, Pres.; Harry S. Burke, Sec., 25 Ord St.; 2nd and 4th Wednesdays, Native Sons Bldg., 414 Mason St.
South San Francisco No. 157, San Francisco—Raymond Conroy, Pres.; John T. Regan, Sec., 1489 Newcomb Ave.; Wednesdays, Masonic Bldg., 4705 3rd St.
Sequoia No. 160, San Francisco—Chester Moreno, Pres.; Walter W. Garrett, Sec., 2500 Van Ness Ave.; Mondays, Swedish-American Bldg., 2174 Market St.
Precita No. 187, San Francisco—Elmer F. Sprague, Pres.; Edward Tietjen, Sec., 1307 15th Ave.; Thursdays, Mission Masonic Hall, 2668 Mission St.
Olympus No. 189, San Francisco—Charles Erickson, Pres.; Harvey J. Carty, Sec., 1651 Market St., Apt. 505; 2nd and 4th Tuesdays, Independent Redmen Hall, 3053 16th St.
Presidio No. 194, San Francisco—Geo. R. Schmidt, Pres.; George A. Ducker, Sec., 442 21st Ave.; Mondays, Native Sons Bldg., 414 Mason St.
Marshall No. 202, San Francisco—Arthur Belli, Pres.; Frank Bacigalupi, Sec., 725 Douglas St.; 1st and 3rd Wednesdays, Native Sons Bldg., 414 Mason St.
Dolores No. 208, San Francisco—Daniel Corrigan, Pres.; Eugene O'Donnell, Sec., Mills Bldg.; Tuesdays, Mission Masonic Bldg., 2668 Mission St.
Twin Peaks No. 214, San Francisco—Fred Sooman, Pres.; Thos. Pendergast, Sec., 278 Douglas St.; Wednesdays, Willopi Hall, 4061 24th St.
El Capitan No. 222, San Francisco—Frank Rizzo, Pres.; James Hanna, Sec., 2450 27th Ave.; 1st and 3rd Thursdays, King Soloman Hall, 1739 Fillmore St.
Guadalupe No. 231, San Francisco—George Miles, Pres.; Alvin A. Johnson, Sec., 142 Rousseau St.; Tuesdays, Guadalupe Hall, 4551 Mission St.
Castro No. 232, San Francisco—David A. Simon, Pres.; James H. Hayes, Sec., 4014 18th St.; Tuesdays, Native Sons Bldg., 414 Mason St.

Balboa No. 234, San Francisco—J. LeMor, Pres.; E. W. Boyd, Sec., 45 Carl St.; Thursdays, Maccabee Hall, 5th Ave. and Clement St.
James Lick No. 242, San Francisco—M. G. Muller, Pres.; Wm. Dand, Sec., 2587 22nd Ave.; 1st and 3rd Wednesdays, Redmen Hall, 3052 16th St.
Bret Harte No. 260, San Francisco—J. F. Craig, Pres.; C. J. Eggers, Sec., 194 Prague St.; Tuesdays, West of Twin Peaks Hall, 233 Legion Court.
Utopia No. 270, San Francisco—Joseph Riordan, Pres.; Herbert H. Schneider, Sec., 2455 16th Ave.; Tuesdays, American Hall, 20th and Capp Sts.

SAN JOAQUIN COUNTY.

Stockton No. 7, Stockton—George D. Avery, Pres.; R. D. Dorcey, Sec., P. O. box 388; Mondays, Native Sons Hall.
Lodi No. 18, Lodi—Jerome Solomon, Pres.; Dr. Clyde Bresnan, Sec.; 2nd and 4th Wednesdays, Eagles Hall.
Tracy No. 186, Tracy—R. J. Marraccini, Pres.; R. J. Marraccini, Sec., R.F.D. No. 1, box 217; Thursdays, I.O.O.F. Hall.
Manteca No. 271, Manteca—Louis Ryan, Pres.; Leonard Faria, Sec., R.F.D. No. 1, Lathrop; 1st and 3rd Wednesdays, I.O.O.F. Hall.

SAN LUIS OBISPO COUNTY.

San Miguel No. 150, San Miguel—H. Twisselman, Pres.; George Sonnenberg Jr., Sec.; 1st and 3rd Wednesdays, Fraternal Hall.
Cambria No. 152, Cambria—Roy Cardoza, Pres.; A. S. Gay, Sec.; Wednesdays, Rigdon Hall.

SAN MATEO COUNTY.

Redwood No. 66, Redwood City—Joseph Lodi, Pres.; A. S. Liguori, Sec., P. O. box 212; Thursdays, American Foresters Hall.
Seaside No. 95, Half Moon Bay—William Deeney, Pres.; John G. Gilcrest, Sec.; 2nd and 4th Tuesdays, I.O.O.F. Hall.
Menlo No. 185, Menlo Park—W. H. Wreden, Pres.; F. W. Johnson, Sec., P. O. box 601; Thursdays, Duff & Doyle Hall.
Pebble Beach No. 230, Pescadero—Bernard Cabral, Pres.; E. A. Shaw, Sec.; 2nd and 4th Wednesdays, I.O.O.F. Hall.
El Carmelo No. 256, Daly City—Leonard J. Mohr, Pres.; Andrew P. Murphy, Sec., 931 Hanover St.; 2nd and 4th Wednesdays, Eagles Hall.
Industrial City No. 269, South San Francisco—John C. Hamilton, Pres.; Geo. A. Roll, Sec., P. O. box 237; 2nd and 4th Mondays, Metropolitan Hall.

SANTA BARBARA COUNTY.

Santa Barbara No. 116, Santa Barbara City—C. W. McCormick, Pres.; H. C. Sweetser, Sec., Court House; 1st and 3rd Wednesdays, I.O.O.F. Hall.

SANTA CLARA COUNTY.

San Jose No. 22, San Jose—Joseph Sabatte, Pres.; H. W. McComas, Sec., Suite 7, Porter Bldg.; Mondays, I.O.O.F. Hall.
Santa Clara No. 100, Santa Clara City—John J. Trinajstich, Pres.; Clarence Clevenger, Sec., P. O. box 297; 2nd and 4th Wednesdays, Redmen Hall.
Observatory No. 177, San Jose—Norton J. Mahon, Pres.; A. B. Langford, Sec., Hall Records; Tuesdays, Knights Columbus Hall, 40 No. First St.
Mountain View No. 215, Mountain View—Gilbert F. McCorkle, Pres.; C. A. Antonioli, Sec., 948 California St.; 2nd and 4th Fridays, Mockbee Hall.
Palo Alto No. 216, Palo Alto—John C. Bernal, Pres.; Albert A. Quinn, Sec., 548 High St.; Mondays, Native Sons Bldg., Hamilton Ave. and Emerson St.

SANTA CRUZ COUNTY.

Watsonville No. 65, Watsonville—A. W. Batchelder, Pres.; E. R. Tindall, Sec., 408 East Lake Ave.; 2nd and 4th Tuesdays, I.O.O.F. Hall.
Santa Cruz No. 90, Santa Cruz City—W. H. Mori, Pres.; T. V. Mathews, Sec., 105 Pacheco Ave.; Tuesdays, Native Sons Hall, 117 Pacific Ave.

SHASTA COUNTY.

McCloud No. 149, Redding—Errol Yank, Pres.; Hugh A. Shuffleton, Sec.; 1st and 3rd Thursdays, Moose Hall.

SIERRA COUNTY.

Downieville No. 92, Downieville—J. M. McMahon, Pres.; H. S. Tibbey, Sec.; 2nd and 4th Mondays, I.O.O.F. Hall.
Golden Nugget No. 94, Sierra City—Leonard Thompson Jr., Pres.; Arthur R. Pride, Sec.; last Saturday, Masonic Hall.

SISKIYOU COUNTY.

Etna No. 192, Etna—Fred M. Wolford, Pres.; Harvey A. Green, Sec.; 1st and 3rd Wednesdays, I.O.O.F. Hall.
Liberty No. 193, Sawyers Bar—Orrin R. Bigelow, Pres.; John M. Barry, Sec.; 1st and 3rd Saturdays, I.O.O.F. Hall.

SOLANO COUNTY.

Solano No. 39, Suisun—Karl Koch, Pres.; J. W. Kinlock, Sec.; 1st and 3rd Tuesdays, I.O.O.F. Hall.
Vallejo No. 77, Vallejo—Joseph Clavo, Pres.; Werner B. Hallin, Sec., 912 Carolina; 2nd and 4th Tuesdays, San Pablo Hall.

SONOMA COUNTY.

Petaluma No. 27, Petaluma—George Geils, Pres.; C. F. Fobes, Sec., 114 Prospect St.; 2nd and 4th Mondays, Druid Hall, Gross Bldg., 41 Main St.
Santa Rosa No. 28, Santa Rosa—John Caniff, Pres.; Leland S. Lewis, Sec., Court House; Tuesdays, Native Sons Hall.
Glen Ellen No. 102, Glen Ellen—C. C. Weise, Pres.; Frank Kirch, Sec., Route 3, Santa Rosa; 2nd Monday, N.S.G.W. Hall.
Sonoma No. 111, Sonoma City—Frederick Bulotti, Pres.; L. H. Green, Sec.; 1st and 3rd Mondays, I.O.O.F. Hall.
Sebastopol No. 143, Sebastopol—A. N. Badger, Pres.; F. G. McFarlane, Sec.; 1st and 3rd Fridays, I.O.O.F. Hall.

STANISLAUS COUNTY.

Modesto No. 11, Modesto—Robert H. Hansen, Pres.; C. C. Eastin Jr., Sec., P. O. box 898; 1st and 3rd Wednesdays, I.O.O.F. Hall.
Oakdale No. 142, Oakdale—D. W. Tulloch, Pres.; E. T. Gobin, Sec.; 2nd Monday, Legion Hall.
Orestimba No. 247, Crows Landing—Lloyd W. Fink, Pres.; G. W. Fink, Sec.; 1st and 3rd Wednesdays, Community Club Home.

SUTTER COUNTY.

Sutter No. 261, Sutter City—Stanley R. McLean, Pres.; Glen R. Haynes, Sec., Yuba City; 2nd and 4th Mondays, N.D.G.W. Hall.

TRINITY COUNTY.

Mount Bally No. 87, Weaverville—M. F. Kay, Pres.; E. V. Ryan, Sec.; 1st and 3rd Mondays, Native Sons Hall.

TUOLUMNE COUNTY.

Tuolumne No. 144, Sonora—Mathew J. Marshall, Pres.; William M. Harrington, Sec., P. O. box 715; 2nd and 4th Fridays, Knights Columbus Hall.
Columbia No. 258, Columbia—Jos. Cadematori, Pres.; Charles F. Grant, Sec.; 2nd and 4th Thursdays, Native Sons Hall.

VENTURA COUNTY.

Cabrillo No. 114, Ventura City—David Bennett, Pres., 1380 Church St.

YOLO COUNTY.

Woodland No. 30, Woodland—J. L. Aronson, Pres.; E. B. Hayward, Sec.; 1st Thursday, Native Sons Hall.

YUBA COUNTY.

Marysville No. 6, Marysville—John McQuaid, Pres.; Verne Fogarty, Sec., 719 6th St.; 2nd Friday, Foresters Hall.
Rainbow No. 40, Wheatland—W. E. Jones, Pres.; W. A. Bowser, Sec., P. O. box 313; 2nd Thursday, I.O.O.F. Hall.

AFFILIATED ORGANIZATIONS.

San Francisco Extension of the Order Committee, N.S.G.W.—Harmon D. Skillin, Chmn.; Harold J. Regan, Sec., 414 Mason St., San Francisco; meets 2nd and 4th Fridays, Grizzly Bear Club, 414 Mason St., San Francisco.
Alameda County Extension of the Order Committee, N.S.G.W.—Dr. William C. Freitas, Chmn.; Edgar G. Hansen, Sec., 1260 Russell St., Berkeley; meets 1st and 3rd Mondays, N.S.G.W. Hall, 11th and Clay Sts., Oakland.
Interparlor Committee (Southern District), N.S.G.W. and N.D.G.W.—Burrel D. Neighbours, Chmn.; F. J. Burmester, Sec., P. O. box 42, Colton; meets 2nd and 4th Fridays, Patriotic Hall, 1816 So. Figueroa St., Los Angeles.
San Francisco Assembly No. 1 Past Presidents Association N.S.G.W.—Meets 1st and 3rd Fridays, Native Sons Bldg., 414 Mason St., San Francisco; J. H. Sylvester, Gov.; J. F. Stanley, Sec., 1175 O'Farrell St., San Francisco.
East Bay Counties Assembly No. 3 Past Presidents Association N.S.G.W.—Meets 4th Monday, Native Sons Hall, 11th and Clay Sts., Oakland; F. H. Robson, Gov.; Edgar G. Hansen, Sec., 1260 Russell St., Berkeley.
Marin County Assembly No. 5 Past Presidents Association N.S.G.W.—J. S. Rose Jr., Gov.; L. J. Peter, Sec., Peter Bldg., 4th and ''C'' Sts., San Rafael.
Fred H. Greeley Assembly No. 6 Past Presidents Association N.S.G.W.—Meets monthly with different Parlors comprising district; R. L. P. Bigelow, Gov.; Barney Barry, Sec., P. O. box 72, Lincoln.
San Joaquin Assembly No. 7 Past Presidents Association N.S.G.W.—Meets 1st Friday, Native Sons Hall, Stockton; Clyde H. Gregg, Gov.; R. D. Dorcey, Sec., Native Sons Club, Stockton.
Sonoma County Assembly No. 9 Past President Association N.S.G.W.—Meets monthly at different Parlor headquarters in county; Louis Bosch, Gov.; L. S. Lewis, Sec., Court House, Santa Rosa.
General John A. Sutter Assembly No. 10 Past Presidents Association—C. C. Wachman, Gov.; Jas. J. Longshore, Sec., 514 ''J'' St., Sacramento.
Grizzly Bear Club—Members all Parlors outside San Francisco at all times welcome. Clubrooms top floor Native Sons Bldg., 414 Mason St., San Francisco.
Native Sons and Native Daughters Central Committee on Homeless Children—Main office, 955 Phelan Bldg., San Francisco; Mrs. John W. Stirling, Chmn.; Miss Mary E. Brusie, Sec. Los Angeles branch office, 3924 Sunset Blvd.; Dorothy Schlingman, Sec.

(ADVERTISEMENT.)

N.S.G.W. OFFICIAL DEATH LIST.

Containing the name, the date and the place of birth, the date of death, and the Subordinate Parlor affiliation of deceased members reported to Grand Secretary John T. Regan from February 19, 1932, to March 19, 1932:

Scouler, Benjamin; San Francisco, May 15, 1861; February 14, 1932; California No. 1.
Folsom, Eugene Hampton; San Francisco, September 12, 1858; February 16, 1932; California No. 1.
Cothran, Abraham Lincoln; Tomales Bay, June 12, 1866; February 23, 1932; San Jose No. 22.
Bellow, John Francis; San Jose, December 19, 1873; March 7, 1932; San Jose No. 22.
Nye, Frederick Dwight; San Francisco, September 18, 1870; January 15, 1932; Mission No. 38.
Silk, Michael J.; San Francisco, March 29, 1870; March 2, 1932; El Dorado No. 52.
Clinch, Willis A.; Uniontown, April 16, 1862; February 10, 1932; Quartz No. 58.
Rouner, Claude Terrell; Coloma, January 6, 1885; February 28, 1932; Quartz No. 58.
McDonald, Bernard; Shasta, September 16, 1857; February 22, 1932; Mount Bally No. 87.
Benson, Willard Benjamin; San Bernardino, May 20, 1873; February 18, 1932; Arrowhead No. 110.
Schade, Frederick C.; San Francisco, September 24, 1870; February 3, 1932; National No. 118.
Porter, George W.; Sacramento, August 23, 1860; February 12, 1932; Alcalde No. 154.
Corries, John Francis; Hayward, May 16, 1859; February 15, 1932; Alcalde No. 154.
Squires, Fred Russell Sr.; San Francisco, September 21, 1870; March 11, 1932; South San Francisco No. 157.
Vogt, Henry C.; Woodland, November 3, 1874; February 22, 1932; Sea Point No. 158.
Mallon, Thomas J.; San Francisco, August 24, 1868; February 13, 1932; Precita No. 187.
McGovern, Thomas H.; San Francisco, December 10, 1864; February 26, 1932; Presidio No. 194.
Costa, David; San Francisco, April 14, 1868; February 28, 1932; Mountain View No. 215.
Shaw, John Elias; Pescadero, October 5, 1877; February 14, 1932; Pebble Beach No. 230.

WIFE WELL-KNOWN N.S. PASSES.

Stockton (San Joaquin County)—Mrs. Lily P. Neumiller, wife of County Treasurer William C. Neumiller (Stockton Parlor No. 7 N.S.G.W.), passed away February 24. She was a native of Sonoma County, aged 57. In addition to her husband, two children survive.

NATIVE DAUGHTER NEWS

(Continued from Page 15)

highly commended President Marion Crum and all the Parlor's officers, as well as District Deputy Hazel Hansen. Other speakers were Founder Lily O. Reichling-Dyer, Past Grand Grace S. Stoermer, Grand Trustee Florence D. Schoneman, District Deputy Hansen, Bertha Hitt, Santa Ana's organizer, and Kate McFadyen. The Grand President was the recipient of two lovely gifts, one from the Parlor and the other, a box of avocados, from Mr. and Mrs. Walter Hiskey. Among the visitors were District Deputies Fay, Towne, Hazel Hansen, Evans, Dickinson and Hiskey. Through Mrs. Walter Moore, chairman, the Parlor recently presented five baskets to needy families.

Secretary Returns to Post.

Petaluma—There was a large attendance, including several eligibles, at the March 1 meeting of Petaluma No. 222, presided over by President Elizabeth Dillon. Cards furnished entertainment and a raviola dinner was greatly enjoyed. Edna Meadows, in charge, was assisted by Sisters Jennings, McCarter, Marra, Marzolf and Miner. Mrs. Gladys Cheda is the happy mother of twins, a son and a daughter; the Parlor presents spoons to all babies.

Recording Secretary Margaret Oeltjen, after a serious illness, was back at her desk March 16, to the delight of all. A Saint Patrick program was presented, followed by cards, and refreshments were served at tables bedecked in green. Past President Mary Garzoli, soon to become a bride, was given a surprise and presented with a silver gift. Valora Matthews, who planned the evening's doings, was assisted by Sisters Moreda, Olsen and Pedrotti. The Parlor's drill team will give a public card party April 5.

Many Visitors.

Lodi—Grand President Evelyn I. Carlson officially visited Ivy No. 88 March 16, a dinner preceding the meeting. There were many visitors, including Past Grands Mattie M. Stein, Carrie R. Durham and Mamie G. Peyton, and Grand Trustee Edna Briggs. A program was given and Mrs. Carlson was presented with a gift. Refreshments were served in the banquetroom, decorated with Saint Patrick motifs.

Founder Special Honor Guest.

Fullerton—Grand President Evelyn I. Carlson paid her first visit to Parlors of the southland when she visited Grace No. 242 February 29. Dinner preceded the meeting; appointments throughout had a California motif, featuring golden poppies and candles. Following the feast the ritual was exemplified under the leadership of President Mattie Edwards. A class of candidates were initiated, three among them being direct descendants of the Yorba family.

Reports of all Parlor activities were given, and members were commended for their work. A gift of silver was presented to the Grand President, and beautiful corsages, made by President Edwards, were presented the visiting grand officers. Past Grand Grace S. Stoermer, Grand Trustee Florence D. Schoneman, District Deputy Ora Evans and delegations from seven southland Parlors were present. A very special guest of honor was Founder Lily O. Dyer, and the Parlor was very happy to be her hostess. Nellie Cline presented a brief program. President Edwards sponsored a public waffle breakfast March 19 for the benefit of the Loyalty Pledge.

Past Presidents Doings.

Oakland—Association No. 2 had a reception March 28 in honor of Miss Josephine Clark, president General Assembly. Harriet Emerson, in charge, was assisted by all members affiliated with Piedmont No. 87

Chico—Association No. 5 was entertained by Mrs. Marie Picanco at her home March 4. A card party, the proceeds of which will purchase a brick in the Pioneer Memorial Relics building in Oroville, was held March 12 at the Oroville home of Grand Trustee Florence D. Boyle.

Santa Rosa—Association No. 7 and escorts enjoyed a delicious italian dinner March 23. Cards followed the feast. Ruby Berger had charge of the entertainment.

Stockton—Association No. 8 was officially visited by Chief President Josephine Clark, who was presented with a gift by Mrs. E. R. Peyton. Four candidates were initiated, bringing the membership to ninety-five.

SAN FRANCISCO

(Continued from Page 12)

States of America, California and Ireland by Leo Pelt and committee. Speakers included Charles J. Powers, Edward P. McAuliffe, Supervisor James B. McSheehy and Grand Trustee Joseph J. McShane. Al Sandell of Twin Peaks has had wonderful success the past two years in handling amateur boxing contests. Under his direction the Parlor is now recognized as the leading organization in athletics.

James Lick No. 242 celebrated its one thousandth night in Redmen hall. Grand Third Vice-president Chas. A. Koenig gave an instructive talk. Officers were installed by District Deputy Tom Dillon, Lawrence Muller becoming president. There were many visitors, and refreshments were served.

Bret Harte No. 260 was officially visited March 15 by Grand Third Vice-president Chas. A. Koenig, who told of the Order's aims and purposes, commended the Parlor officers for their ritual efforts and praised the members for attendance at meetings. Bret Harte initiates candidates at almost every meeting. Its drum corps will give a dance during April.

STOCKTON N. S. GRAND PARLOR

ARRANGEMENTS BEING MADE BY Stockton Parlor No. 7 N.S.G.W. for the Fifty-fifth Native Son Grand Parlor which will be in session at the San Joaquin County government-seat May 16-19 are progressing most satisfactorily under the supervision of a committee, appointed by the Parlor: Ray Friedberger (chairman), R. D. Dorcey (secretary), Harry M. Herrmann (treasurer), W. P. Rothenbush, Ivan Hoult, Eugene Allison, George D. Avery, C. W. Walsh, Law T. Freitas, Frank Piccardo, W. I. Neely, Ralph Mitscher, F. R. Fernando, W. A. Strong and L. Buol. Subcommittees, in charge of various details, have these chairmen: transportation, W. A. Strong; banquet, Harry M. Herrmann; housing, W. I. Neeley; grand ball, W. P. Rothenbush; music, Ivan Hoult; entertainment, Law T. Freitas; printing, L. Buol; registration, R. D. Dorcey; night jinks, Frank Piccardo; badges, F. R. Fernando; reception, Eugene Allison and Ralph Mitscher; decorations, C. W. Walsh.

Grand President Dr. Frank I. Gonzalez, who will preside during the Grand Parlor, and Grand Secretary John T. Regan were in Stockton last month and gave official approval to the plans outlined by the arrangements committee. Business sessions will be held Monday, Wednesday and Thursday, in the Civic Memorial Auditorium.

Tuesday will be given over to a trip to the Calaveras Big Tree Grove, where a barbecue will be served by Chispa Parlor No. 139 (Murphys). The Calaveras Chamber of Commerce, the San Andreas Progressive Club and the Angels Booster Club will co-operate to make this outing a notable one. Other events on the entertainment program include a reception, a banquet, a high-jinks and a grand ball. Special events for the visiting womenfolks are being arranged by Joaquin No. 5 and Caliz de Oro No. 205 N.D.G.W. Indications are that there will be a great many visitors in Stockton for the Grand Parlor, and they will be adequately cared for and thoroughly entertained.

The constitution of the Grand Parlor prescribes that Subordinate Parlors must elect dele-

...cates the first meeting night in April. So, several rumored candidates for office are withholding definite announcement of their intentions. The Grizzly Bear, again last month, communicated with all prospective candidates, and from replies received announces these:

Grand President—Seth Millington (Colusa No. 69) of Gridley.

Grand First Vice-president—Justice Emmet Seawell (Santa Rosa No. 28) of Santa Rosa.

Grand Second Vice-president—Chas. A. Koenig (Golden Gate No. 29) of San Francisco.

Grand Third Vice-president—J. Hartley Russell (Stanford No. 76) of San Francisco; Harmon D. Skillin (Castro No. 232) of San Francisco.

Grand Secretary—John T. Regan (South San Francisco No. 157) of San Francisco, incumbent.

Grand Treasurer—John A. Corotto (San Jose No. 22) of San Jose, incumbent.

Grand Outside Sentinel—William A. Reuter (Sepulveda No. 263) of San Pedro.

Grand Trustees (seven to be chosen)—Jesse H. Miller (California No. 1) of San Francisco, incumbent; Grand Marshal Horace J. Leavitt (Mount Bally No. 87) of Weaverville; Charles H. Spengemann (Hesperian No. 137) of San Francisco; Samuel M. Shortridge Jr. (Menlo No. 185) of Menlo Park, incumbent; Joseph J. McShane (Twin Peaks No. 214) of San Francisco, incumbent; Eldred L. Meyer (San Monica Bay No. 267) of Santa Monica, incumbent.

Grand President Dr. Frank I. Gonzalez (Pacific No. 10) of San Francisco will automatically become the Junior Past Grand President, and John T. Newell (Los Angeles No. 45) of Los Angeles City, now the Junior Past, will retire from the Board of Grand Officers. Grand Trustee Frank M. Lane (Fresno No. 25) of Fresno City will not be a candidates for office.—C.M.H.

PIONEER NATIVES

(Continued from Page 13)

...cisco in 1859, died March 5 at Los Angeles City survived by two sons.

William R. Windsor, born in Solano County in 1854, died March 5 at Oakland, Alameda County, survived by a daughter.

Samuel H. McPherson, born in Tuolumne County in 1856, died March 6 at Stockton, San Joaquin County. He was a charter member of Pacific Parlor No. 10 N.S.G.W. (San Francisco).

Richard Edward Breceda, born in Siskiyou County in 1858, died March 6 at Yreka.

Mrs. Mary E. Curry, born in Sacramento County in 1858, died March 6 at Sacramento City survived by two sons. She was affiliated with Fern Parlor No. 123 N.D.G.W. (Folsom).

Mrs. Nettie Stone-Easterbrook, born at San Francisco in 1854, died March 7 at Oakland, Alameda County.

Mrs. Mary L. Wirt, born at San Francisco in 1857, died March 7 at Santa Rosa, Sonoma County, survived by two children.

James Francis Coonan, born at San Francisco in 1856, died March 8 at Eureka, Humboldt County, survived by a wife and two children.

John Henry Grohl, born in Tuolumne County in 1859, died March 9 near Keystone survived by a wife and three children. He was affiliated with Tuolumne Parlor No. 144 N.S.G.W. (Sonora).

Mrs. Eva Brown-Wiggins, born in Humboldt County in 1857, died March 9 at Rio Dell survived by a son.

Julius Myron Alexander, born in Sonoma County in 1858, died March 9 at Healdsburg. He was a writer of ability and an expert on Indian lore.

Mrs. Maria Cutter, born in Sonoma County in 1857, died March 10 at San Francisco survived by two children. She was a daughter of General Mariano G. Vallejo.

Mrs. Elizabeth Hilliard-Dunn, born in El Dorado County in 1852, died at Santa Cruz City March 11 survived by four children. She was affiliated with Plumas Pioneer Parlor No. 219 N.D.G.W. (Quincy).

Mrs. Elizabeth Johnson-Tupper, born in Merced County in 1859, died at Fresno City March 14 survived by seven children.

John Daniel Cunningham, born in San Bernardino County in 1855, died at Sacramento City March 14 survived by three children.

In Memoriam

MARY HORGAN.

To the Officers and Members of Mission Parlor No. 227 N.D.G.W.—Again our Golden Chain of Fraternity has been severed by the angel of death, who has entered the portals of our Parlor for the second time within a month.

Whereas, It has pleased our Heavenly Father to call our dearly beloved sister, Mary Horgan, to our Eternal Parlor above, let us think of her as a rose that climbs the garden wall and blossoms on the other side. We shall hold in fond memory her cheerful smile, her loving ways and her jolly disposition.

Not dead to those who loved her
Not lost, but gone before;
She lives with us in memory
And will for ever more.

The trials, the sorrows and the disappointments that must come in every life, however sheltered, are ended and our sister peacefully sleeps. Reverently then would we say, "Thy will be done." We hereby record our tribute of love and affection for one whose kindly ways endeared her to all her sisters.

Resolved, That we extend to her bereaved family our sincere sympathy. It is our earnest prayer that God, in His infinite mercy, assuage their deep grief and send peace into their hearts. Be it further resolved, that our charter be draped in mourning in due respect for our late sister; that a copy of these resolutions be spread in full upon our minutes; that a copy be sent to her family, and that a copy be sent to The Grizzly Bear Magazine for publication.

Sincerely and Fraternally in P.D.F.A.,

ANN DIPPEL,
INUE MAYER,
MAME CUNEO,
Committee.

San Francisco, February 23, 1932.

JOHN ELIAS SHAW SR.

Whereas, Almighty God, in His infinite wisdom, has called to the Heavenly Parlor on High our esteemed and beloved brother, John Elias Shaw Sr.; and whereas, Pebble Beach Parlor No. 230 N.S.G.W. has lost a true and loyal member, his son and daughters a devoted father, his brothers and sisters an effectionate brother, and California one of her sons; therefore

Resolved, That the sympathy of the Parlor be extended the bereaved members of the family, and that the charter of the Parlor be draped in mourning for a period of thirty days; and be it further resolved, that a copy of these resolutions be sent his son, daughters, brothers and sisters; that a copy be spread in full upon the minutes of the Parlor, and also that a copy of these resolutions be published in The Grizzly Bear Magazine.

Done in Friendship, Loyalty and Charity this 24th day of February, 1932.

M. R. MATTEI,
JAS. A. MOORE,
C. S. MATTEI,
F. G. WILLIAMSON,
M. BENNETT,
Committee.

Pescadero, California.

ROXIE BRYANT POLLARD.

The Angel of Death has entered the portals of Los Angeles Parlor No. 124 N.D.G.W. and removed from our midst our beloved member, Roxie Bryant Pollard.

Whereas, In her passing, the Parlor has lost a very loyal Native Daughter, therefore be it

Resolved, That we extend our sympathy to her bereaved family; and further be it resolved, that our charter be draped in mourning, that these resolutions be recorded on our minutes, and that copies be sent to the bereaved family, and to The Grizzly Bear for publication.

MARY K. CORCORAN,
ANNIE L. ADAIR,
EDITH B. SCHALLMO,
Committee.

Los Angeles, March 4, 1932.

VIRGINIA EACHUS.

South Butte Parlor No. 226 N.D.G.W. has made the following resolution in memoriam of the late Virginia Eachus:

Whereas, The Dark Angel has visited us and called our beloved sister, Virginia Eachus, therefore be it

Resolved, That we, the members of South Butte Parlor No. 226 N.D.G.W., while realizing the Lord doeth all things well, yet feel the loss of our co-worker to be irreparable both to the Parlor and to the community; be it further resolved, that we extend to the husband, family and friends our profound sympathy and heartfelt prayers that they may have strength in this great affliction; and be it further resolved, that we will ever hold in tender remembrance the memory of our dear sister and the pleasant hours spent together.

ANTHALENA McPHERRIN,
ANNA L. McLEAN,
MYRTIE HAYNES,
Committee.

Sutter City, March 5, 1932.

ALICE BICKMORE.

Whereas, Our Heavenly Father, in His infinite wisdom, has called from our midst our beloved sister, Alice Bickmore; in her passing a place in Veritas Parlor No. 75 N.D.G.W. has been made vacant, and we will greatly miss her bright and cheery presence.

Resolved, That our heartfelt sympathy be extended to the bereaved relatives, and may their grief be lessened by the memory of devotion and courage of the departed. "She has passed from this earth and its sorrow into the glad light of tomorrow." Resolved, that these resolutions be spread upon the minutes of the Parlor, that a copy be sent to the husband and the son, and one to The Grizzly Bear.

HELEN KRUTOSIK,
MARIAN PULCIPER,
MARGARET THORNTON,
Committee.

Merced, March 9, 1932.

MARGARET BROSKA.

To the Officers and Members of Golden Gate Parlor No. 158 N.D.G.W.—We, your committee appointed to draft resolutions expressing the sentiments and deep-felt sympathy of the members of our Parlor on the death of Sister Margaret Broska, respectively submit the following:

Whereas, It has pleased our Heavenly Father to take from our midst our beloved sister, Margaret Broska; whereas, in her passing our Parlor has lost a most highly esteemed sister and a greater loss has been sustained by those who are nearest and dearest to her, be it

Resolved, That while we bow in humble submission to His will, we are mindful of the vacant chair in our Parlor and feel that our members are honored to have been associated with one so kind and faithful; be it further resolved, that we extend our heartfelt sympathy to the bereaved family and commend them for consolation to Him who doeth all things well; that a copy of these resolutions be spread on the minutes of our Parlor, that a copy be sent to The Grizzly Bear Magazine and that a copy be sent to the family of our deceased sister.

SOPHIE SIEBE,
CLAIRE LINDSEY,
Committee.

San Francisco, March 14, 1932.

MARTIN JOHANSEN.

To the Officers and Members of Mount Tamalpais Parlor No. 64 N.S.G.W.:

Whereas, It has pleased the Supreme Ruler to call from his sphere of usefulness to his eternal rest our well-beloved brother, Martin Johansen; and whereas, Brother Johansen was a kind and loving brother, son, husband and father, and a good neighbor whose passing is profoundly and sincerely mourned, who had endeared himself to all who knew him because of his readiness to respond at all times to the cry of distress and to the moan of the heart stricken, and because of his unselfish devotion to the principles of democracy and to those of this great Order. Therefore, be it

Resolved, That this Parlor extend its most heartfelt sympathy to his bereaved family in their hour of sorrow; and be it further resolved, that this Parlor stand in silence in respect to his memory, that the charter of the Parlor be draped for a period of thirty days, and that a copy of the resolutions be spread upon the minutes, a copy be forwarded to the family and a copy be sent to The Grizzly Bear Magazine for publication.

Respectfully submitted in Friendship, Loyalty and Charity.

C. F. REINDOLLAR,
HAROLD J. HALEY,
M. W. LABEL,
LOUIS J. PETER,
Committee.

San Rafael, March 16, 1932.

Auditorium Dedication—The new $3,000,000 auditorium of Long Beach, Los Angeles County, was dedicated March 7.

Flower Show—Redlands, San Bernardino County, will have a Spring Flower Show, April 14 and 15.

"There's a divinity that shapes our ends, rough-hew them how we will."—Shakespeare.

LOS ANGELES--CITY and COUNTY

LOS ANGELES

(Continued from Page 9)

Vera Carlson (chairman), Etta Fulkerth, Berenice Bickerdike and Margaret Donlan. A patriotic program followed, and the traveling flag was introduced. A card party was held March 16 at the home of Margaret Donlan, and the afternoon was enjoyed under the blossom-laden trees in the garden.

The next big event will be a dance, to be held jointly by Verdugo Parlor and Glendale Parlor No. 264 N.S.G.W. April 2 at Glen Arden Club, 357 West Arden, Glendale. All Natives and their friends are invited, and they are assured a wonderful time.

PAST GRANDS HONOR GUESTS.

Ocean Park—Santa Monica Bay Parlor No. 267 N.S.G.W. featured a Past Grands night March 28, Herman C. Lichtenberger, Sheriff William I. Traeger and John T. Newell being the honor-guests. At the same time, it was host to Troupe 10, Boy Scouts of America, which it sponsors. Dinner at 6:30 was followed by an interesting program and the initiation of a large class of candidates. There was a large outpouring of members of the Parlor and visitors. In addition to the guests of honor, Grand Trustee Eldred L. Meyer was among the speakers.

April 8, Santa Monica Bay will have its annual dinner-dance at the Monte Carlo cafe of Harry O'Day in Culver City. May 8 has been selected as the date for the Parlor's annual barbecue and outing.

PLUNKETT DINNER AT LONG BEACH.

Long Beach—Long Beach Parlor No. 154 N.D.G.W. entertained Grand President Evelyn I. Carlson at a dinner, following which five candidates were initiated. Other honor-guests were Grand Trustee Florence Schoneman, Past Grand Grace S. Stoermer and District Deputy Eva Mae Bemis.

The Parlor had two decorated cars in the fraternal day parade, one of the features of the week's celebration incident to the dedication of Long Beach's new municipal auditorium. March 12, on behalf of the Parlor, President Violet T. Henshilwood presented a California State (Bear) Flag to the city, Mayor Asa Fickling accepting the gift. The California thimble club met March 10 at the home of Mary Stultz and after a noontime luncheon worked on pillow tops.

Long Beach will give a plunkett dinner at 6:30 p. m. of April 7 at Knights Pythias hall, 339 Pacific avenue. Zella L. Hodgedon is the chairman and Daisy T. Hansen the assistant chairman. Everybody invited.

PACK THE HALL—BECOME INFORMED.

There was a large attendance at the March 18 open meeting of Ramona Parlor No. 109 N.S.G.W. and a pleasing program was presented by Marion Parks, Marybelle Chapman, Mabel Straube, Jack Lewis, Dwight Crittenden and Edward LeVitt. Refreshments, prepared by "Chef" Charles Gassagne and assistants, followed in the clubrooms. At the meeting preceding the opening of the doors, Past Grand Herman C. Lichtenberger was authorized to raise a fund to purchase for the Parlor the Pio Pico collection of early-day relics. A start was made in the arrangements for No. 109's anniversary celebration in June.

During April, Dr. Rockwell D. Hunt will continue his enlightening talks on the state's early history; the 15th, his subject will be "Arcadian California," and for the 29th, "The Acquisition of California by the United States." All Natives and their friends are welcome to hear these addresses by an authority on history, and the hall should be packed. Other events on Ramona's April calendar are: 1st, election Stockton Grand Parlor delegates; 8th, initiation; 22nd, entertainment provided by the Parlor's troop of Boy Scouts of America, followed by refreshments.

DE NEVE STATUE PRESENTED.

With Grand President Evelyn I. Carlson and members of Californiana Parlor No. 247 N.D.G.W. alone taking part, the unveiling and presentation of the bronze statue of Governor Don Felipe de Neve, founder of Los Angeles, gift to the city of that Parlor, was completed with a simple and impressive ceremony March 12. Throngs assembled around the pool in the Plaza, itself dedicated to De Neve fifty-nine years ago, from the midst of which the statu rises on its boulder pedestal. In the huma background of the event the continuity of Cali fornia's long and changeful history was strik ingly shown. The program was carried out a detailed in The Grizzly Bear for March.

The colorful unveiling, with its accompani ment of spanish and military music, and i which the Spanish, the Mexican, the Californi and the United States of America flags were suc cessively raised from over the statue, was con ducted by Mrs. Arthur Wright, Mrs. Louis Bout tier, Miss Mary E. Foy and Mrs. A. O. Evans chairman of the committee, all of whom wer gowned in period costumes. Also costumed i the old California mode, Miss Marion Park spoke on the historical significance of each fla as it was lifted. First monument of its kin erected in honor of the civil founder of a Cali fornia city, the bronze statue has been highl praised since the unveiling.

Official presentation on behalf of the Parlo was made by Mrs. Ralph Tuttle, president. Sub

COMMUNITY STANDING APPARENT

(EVELYN JOYCE EBY.)

Santa Barbara—Reina del Mar Parlor No. 126 N.D.G.W. was honored March 1 by an official visit from Grand President Evelyn I. Carlson. Colonial costumes and the colorful shawls and lacy mantillas of early Spanish-California mingled at the banquet. The occasion also marked the thirty-first anniversary of the Parlor, it having been instituted in 1901. Signifying the close relationship which Reina del Mar has with civic affairs, honored guests included Mayor Harvey T. Nielson, Fred Schauer, chairman of the local Washington bicentennial committee, and representatives of organizations with which the Parlor has been closely associated in civic, welfare and historical work. These included:

Mrs. W. B. Metcalf, founder regent Santa Barbara chapter D.A.R.; Miss Eleanor Fay, regent LaCumbre chapter D.A.R.; Miss Verita Slaughter, regent Santa Barbara chapter D.A.R.; Mrs. Fred Jackson, regent Mission Canyon chapter D.A.R.; Mrs. Elmer H. Whittaker, president Daughters American Colonists; Rev. Lawrence Mutter, O.F.M., guardian of the old mission; Samuel Stanwood, president Old Spanish Days organization; Miss Elizabeth Mason, secretary history committee Old Spanish Days; Mrs. Francis Price, Santa Barbara County Council Social Agencies; Mrs. Jane Carroll Byrd; Mrs. Nancy Winch Emery, Santa Barbara milk fund; Miss D. Regina Moorhead, executive secretary East Side Social Center; Miss Elizabeth Cudahy; Mrs. Edward Page, president Santa Barbara County Federation Women's Clubs; Mrs. James Thompson, president Santa Barbara Woman's Club; Mrs. J. Edwin McBride, president American Legion Auxiliary; Mrs. S. H. Elliott, president Admiral Bacon Camp Auxiliary, United Spanish War Veterans; A. C. Dinsmore, N.S.G.W. district deputy grand president; Wesley McCormick, president Santa Barbara Parlor N.S.G.W.; Harry C. Sweetser, secretary Santa Barbara Parlor N.S.G.W.

MEMBERS PAST PRESIDENT UNIT REINA DEL MAR PARLOR N.D.G.W., SANTA BARBARA.

Reading left to right: Lower row—Mrs. William Vick, Miss Marian Arroqui, Mrs. Fred Acres, Mrs. George McCrea, Miss Lydia Scudelari, Mrs. Frank Sifford. Second row—Miss Vivian Cavett, Mrs. Donald Eby, Mrs. A. C. Warren, Mrs. Paul Miller, Miss Dorothy Graham. Third row—Mrs. John Mitchell, Mrs. Jack Vercota, Mrs. Clarence Longmire, Mrs. Paul Yule, Mrs. Wesley McCormick. Fourth row—Mrs. Wm. Quinn, Miss Ida Dardi, Miss Anna E. McCaughey, Mrs. Martin Coen, Mrs. Patrick Henry. Back row—Mrs. F. L. Birabent, Mrs. H. A. Spreitz, Mrs. Mamie Harrison, Miss Vera Pacheco, Mrs. Amelia Myers, Mrs. A. E. Platz, Miss Edna Sharpe, Mrs. L. V. Brady, Mrs. J. A. Callis.

The presence of these visitors testified to the standing of the Parlor in the community, where it has worked steadily for the progress of the city. Reina del Mar is proud that its efforts have been so well understood in Santa Barbara, efforts which have resulted in an organization of activities that has prevented overlapping of effort with a consequent extension of results in all departments of work.

The theme of the banquet was the Washington bicentennial, and the California State (Bear) Flag and the flags of Spain and Mexico were mingled with the Flag of the United States of America in the decorations. Members of the Parlor's board of officers were gowned in colonial costumes with wide hoop-skirts, powdered wigs and curls; some wore the old-time bonnets. Members of the board are:

Past president, Mrs. A. C. Warren; president, Mrs. George McCrea; first vice-president, Mrs. Amelia Acres; second vice-president, Miss Marion Arroqui; third vice-president, Mrs. Jack Ross, recording secretary, Mrs. Paul Yule; financial secretary, Mrs. Paul Miller; treasurer, Miss Anna E. McCaughey! marshal, Mrs. Martin Coen; inside sentinel, Miss Ida Dardi; outside sentinel, Mrs. Clarence Longmire; organist, Mrs. Patrick Henry; trustees, Mrs. Donald Eby, Mrs. Wesley McCormick, Mrs. Jack Vercota; junior past president, Mrs. Wm. Quinn; senior past president, Mrs. John Mitchell.

Washington's heritage to this generation is one of devotion to country, Past Grand Dr. Mariana Bertola said in her address on "The Halo of Washington's Day as Reflected Upon Our Own." "The outstanding characteristic of Washington was his work for the amelioration of the conditions in the colonies. His first and last thoughts were for his country and its people, and California's heritage from Washington is its splendid welfare work." Dr. Bertola emphasized the importance of the family in the world effort for peace, and also discussed Washington as a human being—a character of greatness, honesty and courage. "He shared with his men what they endured, and that is the reason for his greatness." Dr. Bertola paid tribute to the work of Reina del Mar in welfare and constructive patriotic effort, and added a tribute to Miss Anna E. McCaughey, who has a statewide reputation for child welfare activities. Miss McCaughey was given an ovation by the assemblage when introduced at the opening of the program. Mrs. A. C. Warren, who presided at the banquet, introduced Dr. Bertola and cited her work in child welfare and women's clubs, and also told of her part in placing the nation's flag in the ritual of the Order of Native Daughters.

Grand President Carlson spoke briefly on the gratitude which the state owes the Pioneers and the allegiance the state and nation gives to Washington, who was himself a great pioneer. Mayor Nielson had a brief word of tribute for the work of Reina del Mar, and Fred Schauer praised its efforts in marking historic spots. Dr. Charles E. Deuel, rector Trinity Episcopal Church, gave the invocation.

Miss Vera Pacheco arranged a program which included songs by Mrs. Daisy Prideaux of Ursula Parlor No. 1 (Jackson), accompanied by Miss Emma Lou Kurtz; harp selections by Mrs. Florence Lyans, vocal selections by the Parlor chorus with Mrs. Ruth Henry at the piano, dancing by Mrs. Theressa Janssens, and vocal duets by Misses Angelina Aliverti and Vera Pacheco. Souvenir copies of "The Club," containing the annual reports of the Parlor, were given as favors. Mrs. Evelyn Eby is the editor, and Mrs. Anita Nichols made the illustrations. Accompanying the Grand President were Grand Trustee Florence Dodson-Schoneman and Supervising Deputy Hazel B. Hansen. Also honored at the speakers' table were District Deputy Jane Vick and Past Grand Cora B. Sifford. Following the banquet the ritual was exemplified under the direction of the following committee:

District Deputy Jane Vick (chairman), Mms. George McCrea (president), Martin Coen, John D. Ross, Patrick Henry, Laurence V. Brady, Clarence Longmire, and Miss Estelle Myers. These twenty-four past presidents of Reina del Mar, headed by Miss Anna McCaughey, had charge of the event: Mms. Amelia Myers, J. A. Callis, Emma Dale, F. L. Birabent, Jack Fanning, G. G. Leslie, L. V. Brady, U. Dardi, Alex Lord, Flora Stewart, C. F. Myers, Wm. Wilson, Wm. Vick, A. E. Plaz, H. A. Spreitz, Mamie Harrison, Wm. Belt, Wm. Quinn, John Mitchell, A. C. Warren; Misses Elisa Bottiani, Edna Sharpe, Vera Pacheco.

---

sequently a banquet was held at which Mrs. Leland Atherton Irish, a chater member of Californiana, presided. There, Mrs. Evans was presented with a lei of gardenias, in appreciation for her devoted efforts, over a period of two years, to bring the plan of the Felipe de Neve statue to fulfillment.

PERSONAL PARAGRAPHS.

Louis Sentous Jr. (Ramona N.S.) is enjoying an extended Mediterranean tour.

A native son arrived at the home of William Hortenstine (Hollywood N.S.) March 13.

William J. Hunsaker (Ramona N.S.) has been selected to head the Los Angeles Bar Association.

Andrew M. Stodel (Los Angeles N.S.) was a visitor last month to Sacramento and San Francisco.

William H. Arellanes (Ramona N.S.) is now residing in the old mining town of Forest Hill, Placer County.

Mrs. Lilly O. Reichling-Dyer (Founder N.D.G.W.) of Jackson, Amador County, is a temporary resident.

Mrs. Evelyn Eby (Reina del Mar N.D.) of Santa Barbara attended last month the De Neve statue dedication.

Judge and Mrs. J. J. Trabucco (Yosemite N.S. and Mariposa N.D., respectively,) of Mariposa were among last month's visitors.

Miss Mary E. Bruise (Argonaut N.D.) of Berkeley, in charge of the Natives' homeless children endeavor, was a visitor last month.

Gloria K. Keeney and Anthony J. Pierce (Los Angeles N.S.) have announced their engagement, the wedding to be June 16.

Miss Alice H. Dougherty (Angelita N.D.) of Oakland, recently appointed to the State Education Board, was a visitor last month.

THE DEATH RECORD.

Thomas Ralph Garnier, father of Ralph L. Garnier (Ramona N.S.), died February 22. He was a native of Virginia, aged 90.

Mrs. Margaret J. Farmer, mother of Bert L. and Daniel W. Farmer (Los Angeles N.S.), passed away March 2.

John Estess, father of Lilian Estess-Schultz (Los Angeles N.D.), died March 5.

Mrs. Priscilla H. Pendegast, mother of Lyle Pendegast (Ramona N.S.), passed away March 7.

Alois Arnet, father of Edwin L. Arnet (Ramona N.S.), died March 11.

George Wade, husband of Aleta Wade (Los Angeles N.D.), died March 13.

Industrial Exposition—The fifth annual Miniature Industrial Exposition is to be held at Los Angeles City, April 13 and 14.

The California Congress of Parents and Teachers will have its annual convention at Fresno City, April 24-28.

Garden Show—The third annual Spring Garden Show of Alameda County will be held at Oakland, April 21-24.

"If thou wouldst conquer thy weakness, thou must never gratify it. No man is compelled to evil; his consent only makes it his. It is no sin to be tempted, but to be overcome."—William Penn.

MY MESSAGE

To All Native Born Californians

I, DR. FRANK I. GONZALEZ, GRAND PRESIDENT OF THE ORDER OF NATIVE SONS OF THE GOLDEN WEST, DO HEREBY APPEAL TO ALL NATIVE BORN CALIFORNIANS OF THE WHITE MALE RACE BORN WITHIN THE STATE OF CALIFORNIA, OF THE AGE OF EIGHTEEN YEARS AND UPWARD, OF GOOD HEALTH AND CHARACTER, AND WHO BELIEVE IN THE EXISTENCE OF A SUPREME BEING, TO JOIN OUR FRATERNITY AND THEREBY ASSIST IN THE AIMS AND PURPOSES OF THE ORGANIZATION:

To arouse Loyalty and Patriotism for State and for Nation.

To elevate and improve the Manhood upon which the destiny of our country depends.

To encourage interest in all matters and measures relating to the material upbuilding of the State of California.

To assist in the development of the wonderful natural resources of California.

To protect the forests, conserve the waters, improve the rivers and the harbors, and beautify the towns and the cities.

To collect, make known and preserve the romantic history of California.

To restore and preserve all the historic landmarks of the State.

To provide homes for California's homeless children, regardless of race, creed or color.

To keep this State a paradise for the American Citizen by thwarting the organized efforts of all undesirable peoples to control its destiny.

THE ORDER OF NATIVE SONS OF THE GOLDEN WEST IS THE ONLY FRATERNITY IN EXISTENCE WHOSE MEMBERSHIP IS MADE UP EXCLUSIVELY OF WHITE NATIVE BORN AMERICANS.

. . . Builded upon the Foundation Stones of

Friendship
Loyalty
Charity

IT PRESENTS TO THE NATIVE BORN CALIFORNIAN THE MOST PRODUCTIVE FIELD IN WHICH TO SOW HIS ENERGIES, AND IF HE BE A FAITHFUL CULTIVATOR AND DESIRES TO TAKE ADVANTAGE OF THE OPPORTUNITY AFFORDED HIM, HE WILL REAP A RICH HARVEST IN THE KNOWLEDGE THAT HE HAS BEEN FAITHFUL TO CALIFORNIA AND DILIGENT IN PROTECTING ITS WELFARE.

DR. FRANK I. GONZALEZ,
GRAND PRESIDENT N.S.G.W.

The undersigned, having formed a favorable opinion of the Order of Native Sons of the Golden West, desires additional information.

Name..........

Address..........

City or Town..........

For further information sign the accompanying blank and mail to

GRAND SECRETARY N.S.G.W.,
302 Native Sons Bldg.,
414 Mason St.,
SAN FRANCISCO, California

Grizzly Bear

MAY — THE ONLY OFFICIAL PUBLICATION OF THE NATIVE SONS AND DAUGHTERS OF THE GOLDEN WEST — 1932

SCENES IN AND ABOUT STOCKTON, SAN JOAQUIN COUNTY, CALIFORNIA.
Dredgers lying in the stream off Rough and Ready Island in the construction of Stockton's $6,000,000 deep water channel (upper left). Louis Terah Haggin Memorial Art Gallery and Pioneer Historical Museum (upper right). Gnarled boughs of Stockton oaks outlined against the winter sky (lower left). Conservatory of Music on College of Pacific Campus (lower right).

TWENTY-FIFTH ANNIVERSARY NUMBER

Featuring

NATIVE SONS 55th GRAND PARLOR

STOCKTON AND ALL CALIFORNIA

Price: 15 Cents

Birthday Celebration — Oakland, Alameda County, will celebrate its eightieth birthday anniversary, May 1-8.

The Grizzly Bear Magazine
The ALL California Monthly
OWNED, CONTROLLED, PUBLISHED BY GRIZZLY BEAR PUBLISHING CO., (Incorporated)
COMPOSED OF NATIVE SONS.
HERMAN C. LICHTENBERGER, Pres.
JOHN T. NEWELL RAY HOWARD
WM. I. TRAEGER LORENZO F. SOTO
CHAS. R. THOMAS HARRY J. LELANDE
ARTHUR A. SCHMIDT, Vice-Pres.
BOARD OF DIRECTORS

CLARENCE M. HUNT
General Manager and Editor

OFFICIAL ORGAN AND THE ONLY OFFICIAL PUBLICATION OF THE NATIVE SONS AND THE NATIVE DAUGHTERS GOLDEN WEST.

ISSUED FIRST EACH MONTH.
FORMS CLOSE 20th MONTH.
ADVERTISING RATES ON APPLICATION.

SAN FRANCISCO OFFICE:
N.S.G.W. BLDG., 414 MASON ST., RM. 302
(Office Grand Secretary N.S.G.W.)
Telephone: Kearney 1223
SAN FRANCISCO, CALIFORNIA

PUBLICATION OFFICE:
309-15 WILCOX BLDG., 2nd AND SPRING,
Telephone: VAndike 6234
LOS ANGELES, CALIFORNIA

(Entered as second-class matter May 29, 1918, at the Postoffice at Los Angeles, California, under the act of August 24, 1912.)
PUBLISHED REGULARLY SINCE MAY 1907
VOL. LI WHOLE NO. 301

NATIVE SONS' AIMS AND DESIRES

PURE, UNSELFISH AND PATRIOTIC

Dr. Frank I. Gonzalez

(GRAND PRESIDENT.)

DR. FRANK I. GONZALEZ OF SAN FRANCISCO, GRAND PRESIDENT OF THE ORDER OF NATIVE SONS OF THE GOLDEN WEST.

"THE FIFTY-FIFTH SESSION OF THE Grand Parlor of the Order of the Native Sons of the Golden West will convene at Stockton, a typical city of California resting upon a foundation built by the toil and the grit of the Pioneers, and carried to its present commanding position in the commercial, the industrial and the agricultural life of California by patriotic and representative citizens. It occupies a unique position, in that it enjoys sea-water transportation which presages a great future for it in trade and commerce, and it stands at the entrance of the great agricultural San Joaquin Valley, contributing to the greatness of the State.

"Five hundred delegates, representing every section of the State, will be the guests of the City of Stockton, far famed for its hospitality and the warmth of its greeting. These Native Sons are coming with pleasant anticipation of the week they will remain in the city and its environs, and by their presence and their action they will truly represent the great Order to which they cling with filial piety. The committee on entertainment of Stockton Parlor No. 7 has arranged for a one-day visit to the old Mother Lode, where sites will be revisited that will bring vividly to the minds of the delegates the story of the men and the women of the days of '49 to whom the Order of Native Sons of the Golden West is dedicated.

"This Order was founded in 1875, at a time when historian, poet and romancer were portraying in history, song and story the journey of the countless thousands who trekked across the continent and made the trip across the Isthmus and around the Horn, all striving to reach the goal of their ambition, for their talisman was 'gold,' and it is that epoch in the history of California that is appealing, and will forever live in the minds of all Native Sons who seek to perpetuate its history and immortalize the men and the women of that day.

"California has a wonderful history, and any organization that has for its purpose its perpetuation, not merely as a cold narrative of facts, but as a history that analyzes and emphasizes each succeeding event which marked an important forward movement in the advance of civilization, is to be commended as engaged in a laudable purpose.

"The youth of the Atlantic Coast are told again and again at their mothers' knees, in the schoolroom and in their later years the story of the Pilgrim Fathers, the Puritans, the Knickerbockers, the Cavaliers, the Quakers, the Revolutionary heroes. Their attention is directed to the great landmarks from Concord Bridge to Yorktown, and they are taught to revere buildings from the old State House at Philadelphia to the Capitol at Washington as landmarks standing out prominently in the history of the settlement and the development of the colonies that afterwards were merged into states.

"When these events were in the making, scenes were being enacted in California whose importance are now emphasized as inspiring patriotism, loyalty and love of country. Where can there be found greater lessons of daring and courage, and indomitable will that impelled the navigators of old, in their primitive boats, to sail the unknown seas until finally they effected landings along our own coast?—Cabrillo at San Diego, Vizcaino at Monterey, and Ferraio at Mendocino. They were the Pioneers making clear the pathway for those who were to follow.

"And when the first mission was planted upon the soil of California, there were planted also the seeds of Christianity that were to spread the gospel of kindness and of sympathy in an endeavor to better the conditions of human beings. From San Diego to Sonoma the Franciscan missions extended as a challenge to all invaders, and they held California until such time that it could be delivered to a people better equipped to hold and preserve it.

"We live again amid the scenes enacted in the old Town of Monterey, the center of Mexican administration, where all the charm of an ideal life prevailed; where homes were open to all, and hospitality was spread with a lavish and free hand. It was colorful, musical and fascinating, and is woven into the history of our State, giving it a dash of vivid colors.

"The flinging of a new flag across the Western sky by Fremont interjected into the placid life of the State a thrill and an adventure that survive to the present day, and led to the adoption of the Bear Flag as the State emblem. The coming of Admiral Sloat to Monterey and the hoisting of the Stars and Stripes proclaimed the very climax of an advance in civilization that commenced at Plymouth Rock.

"When James W. Marshall discovered gold, as if by a magic wand, he summoned to California the greatest migration of human souls that the world had ever witnessed. It was an event that shaped the destiny of the American people, definitely established the western boundary line of the United States, and forever intrenched the American people as the arbiters of affairs in the Western Hemisphere.

"The red-shirted men of the Sierra, in quest of the gold that was to establish the financial prestige of the United States among the nations of the world, have written a chapter in the history of our State illuminated by their fraternity, their mutual sympathy, and their helpfulness towards each other. They gave to the world a rare exhibition of united brotherhood, immortalized in song and story.

"Toil-worn hands of men who met beneath the oaks at Monterey wrote the Constitution of a free state that gained the admission of California as the thirty-first state of the Union, at a time when the turning-point towards the preservation of the Union was in the balance.

"And then came a new people, with new hopes and ambitions, and they caused the transition of the State to a land of incomparable beauty—the fruitful groves of the Southland, the great valleys of San Joaquin, Sacramento, Napa and Sonoma, with their clinging vines, golden harvests and budding orchards. The great Sierra, passing through a second golden era, yields hydro-electric power which is communicated to each community and is a consequent blessing to mankind.

"Today we behold, and reverently pay homage to, a great imperial State, almost boundless in extent, with every variety of climate and resource. And it is because of all these things that the members of the Order of the Native Sons of the Golden West, thrilled with a just and a generous pride, delight to recount each and every event; to visit and to assist in restoring each and every landmark; to write the history of the State through the medium of trained historians at the University of California, that the world may have an authentic account of all that has been enacted within the confines of the State of California; to visit the schools throughout the State, and enjoin upon the students love and veneration for the men and the women who, in every period of California's development, held the highest ideals of American citizenship; to foster a love of home, a love of country and loyalty to the flag, thus dedicating ourselves to a higher and a better life and, in some measure, manifesting a deep sense of gratitude for the wonderful heritage that has been handed to us to enjoy, to bless and to preserve.

"Such is the Order of the Native Sons of the Golden West. Such are its members' aims and desires—pure, unselfish and patriotic. To California and its material progress, we dedicate this session of the Grand Parlor of our beloved Order, and to the citizens of Stockton we extend a cordial greeting as we come to you as sons of a common mother—California."

PUBLISHER'S NOTICE.

The Grand Parlor N.S.G.W. not concluding its deliberations until May 19, and it being advisable to have the proceedings appear in the next (June) issue of The Grizzly Bear, the June number may be delayed in making its appearance. Forms for the regular departments of the June number will, however, close at the usual time, so news contributors and advertisers should be guided accordingly.

"Power dwells with cheerfulness; hope puts us in a working mood, while despair is no muse and untunes the working power."—Emerson.

"Great deeds cannot die; they with the sun and moon renew their light forever, blessing those that look on them."—Tennyson.

STOCKTON, AN INLAND SEAPORT, A HERITAGE OF THE PIONEER

Inez Henderson Pond

(Acting Publicity Secretary, Stockton Chamber of Commerce.)

AMBITION AND INITIATIVE OF THE early California Pioneer, Captain Charles M. Weber, in his desire to further the interests of the Americans and annex the land northeast of San Francisco, San Pablo and Suisun Bays and the San Joaquin River to the Union of States, brought into being the City of Stockton.

Romance and adventure, hardship and pestilence marked the birth of the tiny pueblo, known for a time by the euphonious name of Tuleburgh, chief settlement in the Vale de los Tules, now the Valley of the San Joaquin. The cat-tails which fluttered over the landscape to mark the course of the numerous tributaries of the rugged river suggested the title to the German, Weber. Later, after his friendship with Commodore Robert Stockton had been cemented in the struggles of the Mexican war, the name of the trading-post on his "Rancho del Campo de los Francesses" was changed to honor the American leader. Today, Stockton is one old city whose fortunes are woven in the struggle to bring California under the sheltering aegis of the United States that bears a good Anglo-Saxon name. Most of the pioneer cities whose histories measure in length with that of Stockton show the fingerprint of the Spaniard in their title.

AERIAL VIEW OF STOCKTON,
PIONEER CITY AT GATEWAY OF SAN JOAQUIN VALLEY.

Struggling down the snow-tipped Sierra, Captain Charles Weber, native of Homburg, Bavaria, a member of the famed Bidwell-Bartelson party, first saw the broad valley of the San Joaquin in the latter part of October 1841. To eyes anticipating a land of orange groves and smiling vineyards, fired by tales of earlier immigrants who had visited the southern mission settlements, the land in its brown and mauve autumn garments seemed almost desolate. Distant Coast Range hills beckoned as but another barrier to the land of their desires. After a short rest at the hacienda of Dr. John Marsh at the foot of Mount Diablo, Weber and a small group of friends visited the banks of the San Joaquin and met a party of sturdy voyageurs of the Hudson's Bay Company, whose agents had been trapping and hunting along the many streams in that vicinity since 1828. Their cache at French Camp, five miles south of Stockton, marks the farthest point south to which those intrepid French-Canadians penetrated.

From them, Weber learned of the broad navigable channel which followed to the sea and offered constant communication with the struggling settlement of Yerba Buena, nestled against the hills which guarded the Golden Gate. He was told of the broad plains with their lush grasses for the feeding of great herds of cattle, of the streams stocked with fish and of the innumerable elk, antelope and deer that offered ample food supply. Mysteries of tide and currents of the waterways that spread like a silver seine over the valley were revealed to him.

Later, at the establishment of the German-Swiss, John Sutter, were unfolded the plans of the Americans, who grew restless under the happy-go-lucky regime of the fun-loving Mexicano, to found a new lone star state similar to that of Texas, or else subdivide Alta California along a line northeast of the San Francisco, San Pablo and Suisun Bays and annex it to the growing Oregon region. With these intrepid Americans, Captain Weber determined to cast in his fortunes. In 1843, when the time came to petition for a grant of eleven square leagues through his San Jose partner, Guillermo Gulnac, he chose to establish his rancho in the land east of the San Joaquin and thereby within the confines of the new state visioned by the eager Americans. It also lay in that nomán's land conceded to the Indians by the arcadian dwellers along the coast, suffering periodically from the depredations of those cattle-stealing redmen.

The pueblo of his dreams in the midst of the "Rancho del Campo de los Francesses" was long in materializing. Guillermo Gulnac, his son, Juan, Peter Lassen, for whom the volcanic peak in northern California is named, and several vaqueros took a band of cattle into the territory after Micheltorena granted the request for land on January 18, 1843. Houses of the native oak which are dominant in the plains about Stockton were built and thatched with convenient tules. In July 1844, James Williams and several families also went onto the rancho and built their humble shelters, constructed corrals for their horses and cattle and planted peach seeds and fruit sprouts.

The call to arms by Micheltorena against the fiery Castro interrupted this pastoral idyl, and the settlers who held title to their lands through grace of the Mexican governor fell into march against that Californian whose cause was dear to their hearts. At the conclusion of hostilities, Williams and his friends went back to the rancho beyond the San Joaquin to take up their burden of tilling the soil.

A new peril threatened them. On his return from a visit to the pueblo of San Jose, David Kelsey, who dwelt in a cabin near French Camp, came down with the dread smallpox. His wife and young daughter took the sufferer to the rancho store at Stockton for treatment, and the amateur doctor was so efficient the patient showed immediately the tell-tale eruption. Thereupon all fled to the shelter of the settlement at San Jose, leaving the Kelsey family to shift for themselves. Only a kindly cowherder remained to administer to the sick wife and child on the death of Kelsey in the fall of 1845. The disease spread to the Indians and the terrified natives watched their warriors, their squaws and their children fall as though marked by the hand of a malignant spirit. To avenge the loss of their tribesmen they descended upon the settlement and found only Thomas Lindsay in his cabin at Lindsay Point, site of the City Hall today, left to watch over the cattle roaming on the Weber rancho. Lindsay was killed and most of the cattle driven off to the hills by the Indians, serene in their confidence they had appeased their gods.

The war with Mexico followed, and at the conclusion of hostilities Captain Charles M. Weber, who had thrown himself heart and soul into the cause of the Americans, even suffering capture and probable internment in prison in Mexico except for his escape near Los Angeles, took up in earnest the settlement of his grant along the San Joaquin.

As the tiny village of Stockton was gaining strength after the infusion of new interest and capital, the cry of "gold" sounded by the messenger from Sutter's Fort enroute to the pueblo at San Jose in March 1848, left the settlement depopulated once more. The settlers abandoned all thought of building homes and gardens and deserted to the mines. Other eager miners, however, stumbled upon the humble outpost with its store started by Joe Buzzell, and almost over night a town of tents arose on the level plains. Day by day boatloads of fortune-seekers were landed upon the banks of the Stockton channel, and flags of every land flew from the masts of vessels whose crews sang in every language as they unloaded boxes and bales of goods for the mines.

Stockton grew in spite of itself, and the broad San Joaquin served as the main highway between San Francisco and the interior. Pack trains, creaking freighters laden with goods for the mines in the foothills and swaying stages filled with passengers wore roads to serve the Southern mines. The city, which served so long as the outfitting post for the region to the east, has maintained its prestige as the marketing center for an ever-increasing area for many decades. The enormous wagons with mules to drag them through the mud of winter and the dust of summer have given way to steam and electric railways which tap a growing district. Highways of smooth concrete spread out from the city like the spokes of a wheel to tie in with the three transcontinental railroads and communication by water. Heavy trucks speed the transportation of San Joaquin Valley products.

Modern initiative has secured federal and state aid to amplify Stockton's investment of $3,000,000 to improve existing waterways and construct a channel 26 feet deep and 450 feet wide on the surface and 100 feet wide on the bed of the channel to connect Stockton with deep water at Suisun Bay. A total of $6,000,000 is now being expended on dredging and construction of port facilities. Dredging of the turning basin, just west of historic Mormon Channel, has been completed and the contract for the building of an open dock and covered transit-sheds has been let. Building of the belt-line railway to serve the industrial area and the wharves along the deep-water channel is also under way.

The City of Stockton is building the first unit of the public belt-line railroad as far as the San Joaquin River. The railroads will build a bridge across the river and a line to serve the industrial area of Rough and Ready Island along the deep-water channel. A representative of each of the transcontinental carriers and one from the city will administer the belt-line road, which will insure from the very start that all factories in the industrial district will be saved switching charges and have equal access to water and rail service of all railroads.

Services of an expert in port development and construction have been secured. Colonel B. C. Allin, a recognized authority in port management who is known best perhaps for his success in the upbuilding of the Houston, Texas, harbor, and is called on frequently as a consultant in port plans both in the United States and abroad, is directing the building of Stockton's inland seaport. With an authority on transportation problems at the helm, Stockton is assured of getting off on the right foot in its development plans and eliminating many of the mistakes other municipalities have learned by experience and at great cost.

Stockton has enjoyed the balance-wheel of water transportation for many decades, and will

only take again the prestige it once held as a port of call for ocean-going vessels. Gold which animated the tiny pueblo in its infancy and made certain its steady growth proved also a check, as the silt from the intensive development of the mineral resources of the Mother Lode gradually filled up the bed of the San Joaquin River and its tributaries.

Millions have been expended by the United States and the City of Stockton in dredging and maintaining the channel to a depth of nine feet to secure the movement of ships of light draft. On completion of the present deep-water channel, 85 percent of the shipping entering the Golden Gate may proceed ninety miles inland to unload their cargoes upon Stockton wharves and pick up the thousands of tons of goods produced in the Sacramento and the San Joaquin valleys for coastal and intercoastal trade.

Savings of $900,000 in freight costs on 1,000,000 tons of products available for movement on the channel, rapidly nearing completion, was the impetus behind the co-operation of the United States Government in developing the inland waterway. The producer of the Pacific Coast, facing the longest haul and the highest freight charges for his farm goods of any agricultural community in the Union, is eager to grab at any saving in shipping costs, no matter how small. Railways and motorized vehicles, enjoying a practically floor-level haul in the interior valleys of the state, and having no ferry or bridge tolls or severe mountain grades, have been enabled to give shippers of the San Joaquin-Sacramento basin most attractive rates on goods destined for Stockton.

In the geographic center of the interior of California, Stockton today serves as the mar-

GROVE OF SEQUOIA GIGANTEA,
CALAVERAS BIG TREES.

keting and distributing center for a long list of natural resources. Timber in the foothills and along the slopes of the Sierra Nevada gravitates to this city for rèmanufacture into countless commodities. Pencil slats made in Stockton are shipped now from this city for refinishing in factories of the Atlantic Coast and Germany. Nitrates from South America are brought to this city for making into fertilizers to be shipped from here to growers of the central valleys. Industry of the interior community has progressed along lines of its agricultural development.

Just as irrigation has brought about the necessity for special pumps, local industry has improved types that are sought today by farmers of South America and other foreign lands. Reclamation of a vast acreage of extremely fertile fields has resulted in the invention by local iron mills of machinery that has proved so efficient it has found call from foreign nations, and states beyond the Rockies.

Wool grown in the counties of the San Joaquin Valley finds its way to Stockton for treatment, and shipping to industrial centers of the Atlantic. Wool handled by local firms moves directly from shearing pens to this city by rail and truck, and the future holds important developments in shipping by boat. This city now handles about 3,000,000 out of the 15,000,000 pounds produced in the San Joaquin Valley. San Francisco today exports about 40,000,000 pounds of wool shorn on the Pacific Slope, and one of the interesting problems of the future will be the campaign to teach Western producers to utilize the shorter haul to Stoctkon with its consequent saving in time and expense of handling.

Products from the canneries, field and orchard originating near at home will serve to swell the export business out of this city when the new inland harbor is ready to welcome ocean-going shipping at the close of 1932.

Proximity of over one thousand miles of inland waterways to Stockton has brought about the growth of several boat-building plants along the channel. Steamers which are the pride of the river have left the ways in this city. Launches and barges which ply the countless streams serving the islands of the Delta, with their fabulous crops of onions, potatoes, corn, celery and asparagus, are made in this city. Pleasure cruisers that have become a byword among the boatmen of the nation also are manufactured in this city. Speed boats, racing craft, commodious cruisers and yachts, which are recognized for their fine workmanship wherever boating enthusiasts gather, go slipping into the water from the hands of local boat-builders.

While Stockton is a pioneer city, it has developed along orderly lines through the foresight of its founder, Captain Weber. Laid out in the checkerboard fashion by its planner, Major R. P. Hammond, father of the world-famous mining engineer, John Hays Hammond, the broad streets are proving their utility under modern traffic conditions.

The downtown court house square and the central plaza, after the fashion of old world Spanish cities, is an individual feature of the inland city. Parks scattered throughout the city through the generosity of the founder are a boon to children and a green oasis during the heat of summer. Trees planted along the highways form a green arch to temper the warmth of the valley sun, and the home gardens which surround the cozy Stockton residences are gay with color around the seasons. Stockton is essentially a home city, conservative as older communities are wont to be and just as comfortable and tolerant as only Western towns can be.

(Continued on Page 12)

"ANGELS CAN DO NO MORE!"

Mary E. Brusie

(Secretary N.S.G.W. and N.D.G.W. Central Homeless Children Committee.)

"THE GRIZZLY BEAR MAGAZINE, ALways generous in granting space to the homeless children's work, expects an article for the Native Sons Grand Parlor edition. What special part of the work would you suggest that I write up this year?" asked the secretary of the Native Sons and Native Daughters Central Committee on Homeless Children of a dear friend and member of the Order of Native Daughters. "I do not know which of the many angles of the committee's work involving various individuals would be of greatest interest to the members," she responded, "but I do suggest that you avoid stressing 'depression.' Forget that the Parlors are $2,707.22 behind last year's contribution, and $3,444.40 less than the year before; never mind that your Central Committee feels pessimistic concerning the year ahead, with increasing demands and decreasing revenue, and that we are starting another year with only sufficient funds to carry the work for six months. Write whatever comes into your poor, dull pate, but don't mention 'hard times'."

As a matter of fact, those who are engaged in the work have had a great deal to be grateful for during the past year, and know that the Parlors have made an extra effort to do their best against great odds. "Angels can do no more!"

Many children with their blood-parents have not fared as well as the homeless children who have been under the care and protection provided by the Native Sons and Native Daughters until the permanent home could be selected for them. One hundred ninety-four foster-homes have received children during this year; 180 different children have been placed. Since August 1910, when the work began, the total number of homes secured is 4,528, 4,031 children were placed and 497 re-placed.

The children have gone into their new homes in the best physical condition, because of scientific care and correct feeding, and, thanks to the Native Daughters, they have gone dressed in the sweetest and daintiest of clothes which never fail to call forth an expression of appreciation from the foster-mothers. The children of own parents have profited, too, by the lavish contribution of clothing from the Native Daughters—children whose parents have faced the need of placing them for adoption because of inability to provide for them.

The group of happy children pictured here are but twenty of the 4,031 children in our foster-homes. The following histories, only touched on, may be fitted to whichever child one chooses. Only the foster-parents who might read this page and find a familiar face will know which story refers to their child.

N.S.G.W. N.D.G.W.
Just a few of the 4,031 children placed in homes through the Native Sons and Native Daughters Central Committee on Homeless Children.
When you help the children, you help the future citizens of California!

One little new-born baby girl was found in a gasoline station by the owner early one cold December morning, wrapped in newspapers and an old gray blanket. No name, no date of birth, no means of identifying or tracing the cowardly culprits who resorted to this fiendish method of ignoring their responsibility. The Native Daughters of the community were appealed to, and through court decree the baby was legally transferred to the Central Committee and placed in a receiving-home. After a few months of sadly-needed care the little foundling was chosen by a good man and woman of refinement, with hearts full of love, who had a lucrative business and owned their own home. They knew she needed them, and they realized her lack of history might not appeal to many individuals who demand a child with antecedents of rare perfection. That was six years ago. Now, this little doorstep baby is a bright, healthy, attractive child and a constant joy and credit to those who love her.

A mother and father, convinced that life held no further happiness for them together, decided to part. They placed their boy to board in a home of their selection, paid the board for two months, went their separate ways and promptly forgot all further obligation. All efforts to trace the parents proving unsuccessful, after two years the boy was declared an abandoned child and freed from the control of his parents. A physician and his wife are quite convinced that a child of their own never could have quite equaled this little adopted lad whose parents had failed him.

A mother died in the hospital when her baby was ten days old. The baby lived three weeks. Six other children were at home. The father, without a job, no money to pay rent and no one on whom to call, was a helpless individual who all through the years had depended on a frail, little woman. Two little brothers were ideally placed in a good home.

One little fellow had prayed to Saint Anthony for a baby sister since he could lisp a prayer. He went to the hospital to visit his mother, who was ill, and a nurse, knowing of his longing for a baby sister, took him to the nursery to see all the babies there. He could not play with them, much to his dismay, but he looked through the glass at all of the beds, with a baby in each one, and when he returned to his mother's room he said: "Mother, I am not going to pray to Saint Anthony any more for a baby sister. Miss S— is the one to go to." The Native Sons and Native Daughters Central Committee on Homeless Children later found a sister for him. His joy has never waned, and his unselfishness in sharing is something which own brothers and sisters might well emulate.

A reporter of a San Francisco paper telephoned that he was sending a young girl with a baby to the office, 959 Phelan building, San Francisco, as she wanted to give her baby boy for adoption. The mother came in, a wholesome, bright-appearing girl, neatly dressed, no makeup, carrying in her arms a beautiful baby of eight months. She told her story of having lost both parents by death and of her inability to get the father of the baby to assume any of the financial burden. She lamented having to part with her boy, but she knew of no way to meet $30 a month for board, because she was without a position and had no one to keep her baby while she looked for one. The baby was sadly in need of clean clothes, so he was washed and dressed in the prettiest things that could be found, and there were many to choose from. We told the mother to meet us at the hospital the following morning for a physical examination of herself and baby, and that the worker would then take them to a home where the baby would be boarded until she found work. She said she could remain for the night at the address she had given, and left with her face wreathed in smiles, and the workers equally rejoiced that a way could be provided for the mother to keep her lovely boy.

The next morning the mother failed to keep her appointment and the worker found she had left the given address with her baby about 8 o'clock the evening before to "hitch-hike," she said, to San Diego. Perhaps she went to San Diego, but she did not take her boy, leaving him, instead, upon the steps of a lovely home in one of the best residential districts with this note: "Give my baby to the woman in the Phelan building in the Native Sons and Native Daughters office." A description of her was broadcast but she never was apprehended. Later, it was found that her elderly mother and father, respectable and hard-working had tried to prevail on their daughter to remain at home and care for her baby and the home, as the parents were both working in an effort to meet the payments on their home and thus avoid losing it. It was impossible for the grandparents to keep the baby, consequently putting him where he would be wanted seemed the wisest solution.

About others of the little ones pictured here we might tell the story of lack of watchfulness and restraint on the part of natural parents who allow their boy or girl to go dashing about at all times of day or night in automobiles, to obtain their view of life, or build up their standard from gallery seats in the movie theater. Some parents know nothing of the tragedy of a little one's advent into the world. Other parents know the truth, and bemoan the outraged girlhood and callous boyhood, but are too proud to face the world and keep the baby with his own.

Now that we have observed for twenty-two years hundreds of little ones develop into straightforward, law-abiding youths, we are convinced that a real chance in life seems assured for the adopted children, protected as they are by the vigilance and the understanding of foster fathers and mothers, who know all about the in-

(Continued on Page 25)

Native Sons of the Golden West

SANTA BARBARA—SANTA BARBARA No. 116 will soon be able to continue its highway beautification program inaugurated during the term of George A. Black as president. District Deputy A. C. Dinsmore and First vice-president Philip Bradley recently visited Cambria No. 152, whose members assisted in securing a quantity of Monterey seedling pines. Judge A. S. Gay and M. L. Mayfield, past presidents of Cambria, effected an arrangement with the Phelan estate permitting the Native Sons to take these seedlings from property of the estate. "There have been cases of vandalism by tourists, so that owners of stands of these pines do not generally permit them to be disturbed," says District Deputy Dinsmore, "and we are gratified that the Phelan estate made an exception in our instance, thereby furthering our planting program."

Cambria Parlor had a banquet in honor of the two visitors from Santa Barbara and President Roy Cardoza formally presented the trees. First vice-president Nick Storm was the toastmaster. The trees are being propagated at a nursery until certain they will thrive in the changed location. Meanwhile, No. 116 will seek a permit from the California State Highway Commission to plant them along the highway at Ortega Hill.

Santa Barbara's hew million-dollar Eastside junior high school will be completed for the fall term. The Santa Barbara Board of Education, following a conference with a committee—A. C. Dinsmore and Clifford F. Rizor—from No. 116, delegated to the Native Sons authority to dedicate the structure. Santa Barbara's delegates to the Grand Parlor will confer with the grand officers at Stockton on plans for the dedication, which should be held in September or October.

Board Grand Officers Meets.

San Francisco—The Board of Grand Officers met April 2. In attendance were Grand President Dr. Frank I. Gonzalez, who presided, Junior Past Grand John T. Newell, Grand First vice Seth Millington, Grand Second vice Justice Emmet Seawell, Grand Secretary John T. Regan, Grand Trustees George F. McNoble, Samuel M. Shortridge Jr., Jesse H. Miller, Joseph J. McShane, Frank M. Lane, John M. Burnett and Eldred L. Meyer. Past Grand Thomas Monahan was a visitor.

Motions prevailed that the Grand Secretary prepare a brief form upon which district deputies shall report to the Grand President; limiting the reports of visiting grand officers to one thousand words each; providing that the Grand First vice and the Grand Secretary shall check all reports.

A letter was ordered sent Albert v. Mayrhofer and San Diego No. 108, commending them for splendid service rendered in the restoration of San Diego de Alcala Mission. The Board will submit to the Stockton Grand Parlor resolutions which, on adoption, will give official recognition by the Order to that great accomplishment.

Considerable other business of a routine nature was transacted, and the Board adjourned to the call of the Grand President.

Enviable Record.

Calistoga—As briefly remarked in the April Grizzly Bear, Calistoga No. 86 made an enviable record March 21, when it initiated a class of sixty-eight candidates, the largest percentage class ever initiated by any Parlor at any time, the membership of the Parlor going from 98 to 166. There were numerous visitors, including Grand President Dr. Frank I. Gonzalez, Past Grand Charles L. Dodge, Grand Secretary John T. Regan, Grand Third vice-president Chas. A. Koenig, Grand Trustee Joseph J. McShane and representatives from all surrounding Parlors.

The ritual was most impressively exemplified by Calistoga's prize team of past presidents: L. Carlenzoli, president; Felix Salmina, first vice; Henry Pocai, second vice; Edmund Molinari, third vice; Frederick Heitz, marshal; Theodore Tamagni, inside sentinel; Frank Pocai, senior past; Lionel Saviez, junior past. The class was known as the Charles E. Butler class, in honor of the sole surviving charter member of No. 86. A pleasing feature was the presentation of a past president emblem to Rev. Thomas J. McKeon, Past President Frank Pocai making the presentation address in behalf of the Parlor.

In rounding up this record class of candidates, Calistoga's membership was divided into two teams, the "Old Guard" and the "Young Guard." The youngsters were successful by a few point and so, carrying out the agreement, the old timers treated them to a dinner at Kenny's farm April 11. Following the sumptuous outdoo feast, there was a program of enthusiastic ad dresses. Rev. McKeon was the toastmaster, an the speakers included Grand President Gonzalez Nathan F. Coombs, Felix Salmina, Grand Thir Vice-president Koenig, Past Grand Dodge, Gran Secretary Regan, Harmon D. Skillin and Mayo Andrew Rocca. A group led by Earle E. Brook interspersed the talks with vocal and instrumen tal selections. Grand Trustees Samuel M. Short ridge Jr., Jesse H. Miller and Joseph J. McShan were among the many in attendance. Again Calistoga's "Old Guard" made history in cele brating their defeat by the "Young Guard."

[Calistoga is a small community, in popula tion, in Napa County. What has been accom plished by Calistoga Parlor, without any "out side" assistance, can be duplicated by every Par lor of the Order, in large and small communities if the members of the several Parlors unite, an labor, to that end. NOW is the appointed time California needs a large increase in the numer ical strength of the Order. Let every Parlo respond to California's call for action!—Editor.

Standingroom Only.

San Diego—Standingroom only was availabl at San Diego No. 108 April 6, when Arrowhea No. 110 (San Bernardino) paid a call. Amon the numerous visitors were President Lynn A Reed, Grand Organist Leslie Maloche and Judg Donald E. VanLuven of Arrowhead, District Dep uty Walter E. Hiskey of Santa Ana No. 265, Ed L. Head of Stanford No. 76 (San Francisco) an Tallant Tubbs of Presidio No. 194 (San Fran cisco). The party lasted until well after mid night. Hill billies furnished music, and thre three-round bouts were refereed by Judge Eu gene Daney.

The committee of arrangements for the oc casion included Wilbur Kelley, Martin J. Span gler, Burt W. Pauter, E. U. Emery, M. V. Cruz President Gregory McHorney, John P. Murph and Deputy Grand President Albert V. Mayr hofer.

Anniversary Celebrated.

Sacramento—Sutter Fort No. 241 celebrate its twenty-fourth institution anniversary with banquet and entertainment. Past President D D. L. Durst presided, and Grand Trustee Samu M. Shortridge Jr. was the honor-guest and prin cipal speaker.

While here, Grand Trustee Shortridge wa also entertained at a dinner at the home of Al bert W. Katzenstein, a member of the Parlo The tables were decorated with California pop pies and the placecards were miniature hu dancers.

Membership Standing Largest Parlors.

San Francisco—Grand Secretary John T. Re gan reports the standing of the Subordinate Par lors having a membership of over 400 Januar 1, 1932, as follows, together with their member ship figures April 19, 1932:

Parlor	Jan. 1	April 19	Gain	Lo
Ramona No. 109	1088	1083	....	
South San Francisco No. 157	822	816	....	
Castro No. 282	700	700	....	
Arrowhead No. 110	609	615	6	
Stanford No. 76	614	610	....	
Twin Peaks No. 214	585	569	....	
Stockton No. 7	549	549	....	
Piedmont No. 120	528	519	....	
Rincon No. 72	448	442	....	

Historic Flag Loaned Library.

Oakland—Claremont No. 240 will place in th Golden Gate Library a Flag of the United Stat of America, the property of the Parlor, whic saw service during the world war. In 1918 request from Captain Darrow of Company A Eighteenth Engineers, for a flag appeared in th local press. Harry Burns brought the matter Claremont's attention and the Parlor offered loan its silk parade flag, with the understandin that, if it survived the perils of the war, it woul be returned. At the war's close Captain Darro personally returned the flag and the treasure keepsake is now to be loaned the library for ex hibition to the public.

April 19, Claremont was host to Argonaut N 166 N.D.G.W. at a greatly enjoyed whist part and entertainment.

"Black Shirt" Fete.

Stockton—Stockton No. 7's annual "black shirt" night, sponsored by members of Italian descent, drew an attendance of over 300 April 11. Speakers included Frank Lane, Ralph Lane, Dr. S. W. R. Langdon, Past Grand Hubert R. McNoble, Grand Trustee George F. McNoble, Guard C. Darrah, George Steele, Ray Friedberger and Raymond S. Miller.

Louis F. Dentoni was chairman of the program committee and Frank Piccardo headed the committee of arrangements.

Bricks for Memorial Hall.

Oroville—Names of members of Argonaut No. 8, one of the oldest Parlors, will appear upon bronze plaques as wellwishers of Pioneer Memorial Relics Hall, soon to be dedicated. The Parlor has arranged for bricks in their honor, and also for a brick in its own name. The building is being erected by the local Native Daughters and Native Sons and will house a most interesting and valuable collection of early-day relics and historical data.

Observance Memorial Day Mandatory.

San Francisco—The Grand Parlor Printing and Supplies Committee—Fred H. Nickelson (chairman), Percy A. Marchant and W. G. Maison—April 15 communicated with the Subordinate Parlors, directing their attention to that section of the constitution which makes it mandatory for the Parlors to, in either of the two suggested methods, observe Memorial Day, May 30. The letter should be given prompt consideration.

Solano Pioneers Honored.

Vallejo—In honor of the Pioneer Fathers and Mothers of Solano County, Vallejo No. 77 and Vallejo No. 195 N.D.G.W. dedicated April 3 a tree and a bench in this city's new Memorial Park on Vallejo Hights. Five counties may be viewed from this vantage point, and a magnificent view of Mount Tamalpais is one of the many impressive sights.

Joseph E. Clavo was master of ceremonies, and addresses were delivered by Grand Presidents Evelyn I. Carlson and Dr. Frank I. Gonzalez. "Today we look upon California as one of the most beautiful spots in the entire universe," concluded Mrs. Carlson in telling of modern improvements. Supervisor Andrew Sheveland accepted the gifts. The junior high school brass quartet played "The Star Spangled Banner," and Al. St. John sang "I Love You, California." The committee in charge of the dedication included Elvena Woodard (chairman), Joseph E. Clavo, Carrie Congrave, Grace Birchmore and John Combs.

Will Endeavor to Stop Japs.

Santa Ana—Santa Ana No. 265 entertained April 18 a large delegation from Sepulveda No. 263 (San Pedro) headed by "Bill" Reuter. During the evening there was a heated discussion regarding the Jap and Philipino situation in this locality and Ivan Harper was named chairman of a committee which will endeavor to stop the spread of Jap-controlled produce marketing.

It was decided to feature May 29 a barbecue, at a place to be later announced. Dr. C. E. Price heads the arrangements committee. As a result of the membership campaign now in force, many applications for membership are being received by the Parlor.

May Day Outing.

Sacramento—The annual outing of the Sacramento and San Joaquin Parlors of Native Sons and Daughters will be held May 1, May Day, at Elk Grove. The committee announces everything in readiness. The feature of the day will be a baseball game between the Native Daughters of Sacramento and Courtland.

Visiting Grand Officer Pleased.

San Rafael—Grand Trustee John M. Burnett, accompanied by Past Grand Thomas Monahan and Harmon D. Skillin, officially visited Mount Tamalpais No. 64 April 18. Following initiation Grand Trustee Burnett praised the ritual officers, and expressed a great deal of satisfaction with the officers' reports.

The Parlor, he said, is one of the most active in the Order, showing a gain in membership and being in a sound financial condition. This, he said, is due not only to the activities of the membership, but also to the evident prosperous conditions prevailing in this locality, Marin County having suffered less than many other communities in California North from the depression.

Among other speakers were Harmon D. Skillin, Past Grand Monahan, County Coroner J. Ray Keaton and County Treasurer Chas. Red-

(Continued on Page 19)

When you purchase goods advertised in The Grizzly Bear, or answer an advertisement in this magazine, please be sure to mention The Grizzly Bear. That's co-operation mutually beneficial.

STOCKTON

(Continued from Page 7)

Generous allowance always has been made for the schools, and the Stockton department of education ranks at the top of the nation's best. From kindergarten to post-graduate courses for the high school, equipment is the most modern and the finest. Domestic science and the manual arts receive recognition not only in the grade schools, but in vocational courses in the high school and a special trade school for those of grammar-school age. Through the co-operation of factory managers a coordinated system of school and trade training under actual working conditions has been worked out. With the establishment of the College of the Pacific in Stockton additional educational opportunities have been added. One of the oldest institutions of higher learning in the state, the local college has brought much of value to community life. Stockton itself enjoys the stimulus of youthful activity of a college town, and the cultural assets of lectures, concerts and plays given on the campus.

In listing the cultural advantages of Stockton, one must include the Louis Terah Haggin Memorial Art Gallery and Pioneer Historical Museum. Erected through the generosity of Mrs. Robert McKee of New York as a tribute to her Pioneer Father, the lifetime collection of Haggin, noted art connoisseur, has been made available to the public. Through the activity of the San Joaquin Historical Society, many descendants of early residents of the county have given to the fund that has made possible the building itself and its ever-growing collection of historical relics.

In the south hall and that on the ground floor are housed countless interesting mementos of pioneer life. Fine porcelain and silverware, brought around the Horn or across the plains in a prairie schooner to grace the new homes in the West, are displayed by the side of humble kitchen utensils that knew service in farm and mining camp. Old-fashioned wedding finery, fine bits of home-spun, silken quilts with a bit of history in every scrap, dolls of long ago and childish playthings may be seen. A quaint old perambulator of the vintage of 1860, fire-engines that were the pride of Stockton's early-day volunteer fire department, miniatures of early residents, firearms, pieces of old harness that checked the pace of the patient oxen, and innumerable other relics may be viewed. To the historian as well as the casual sightseer, much of interest may be studied in that collection with its hint of the romance of a more adventurous era.

To the student of early California history every road leading out of Stockton has its bit of story to tell. Highways that were the despair of the Pioneer, when the adobe took on the slick consistency of clay under winter rains, are smooth as glass today. Express stages were wont to boast of making the trip to Sonora, Tuolumne County, in eleven hours, and in this modern era the motorist leaves town at a comfortable hour, visits Sonora, historic Jamestown, Columbia and Tuttletown, haunt of Mark Twain and his pals, the "Gillis boys," and is whisked across the Stanislaus to Melones, Carson Hill and Angels Camp, quaint old towns built by the Argonauts. On the way home he may idle through San Andreas, government seat of Calaveras County, and visit Double Springs, site of the old seat of county government, and be whirled through Lockeford, founded by a group of New England settlers who set out from Boston in 1849 and built a town that still holds true to the traditions of its founders. By evenfall, he will be back in Stockton.

While Stockton is proud of its background of the old, and cherishes the roots nourished by the toil of its Pioneer merchants and builders, it looks to the future with supreme confidence. With the advent of ocean-going shipping another era of progress is imminent, and Stockton citizens are bending every effort to make a success of the project that has been close to their hearts for many years. Construction of facilities to handle expected cargoes is now under way, and Stockton is determined to offer service to shippers throughout the interior of the state that will assure the growth of its harbor.

OAKS OF SAN JOAQUIN

(JAMES R. O'FARRELL.)

All green and grey they stand today the fields of wheat between
To link us with the golden past, the Oaks of San Joaquin.
The mattock and the spade are still, the scars they made grow green
And the Argonauts are sleeping 'neath the Oaks of San Joaquin.

But nightly when the stars grow dim and fogs lie thick and cold
They come again with sluice and pan to dig and delve for gold.
They revel and they live again the lawless days of yore.
They strip Earth's garments from her breast, to loot her golden store.

Their covered wagons stand again beneath a sheltering tree,
Their tents and tattered garments flaunt the night wind from the sea
And oxen with their yokes unslung lie down, 'mid grasses green
Where moonbeams fleck the checkered shade from the Oaks of San Joaquin.

From Sutter's Buttes to Monterey to sate a hunger keen
They ply their unrequited task unhallowed and unseen,
But when the first faint streaks of dawn above the hills are seen
They sink into the shadows of the Oaks of San Joaquin.

Padre and Don alike are gone from sunburned hill and plain
But shadows of the oaks abide to lure them back again
And when the sheep lie sheltered now where cooling shadows lean
Perhaps the padres pray again for the souls of San Joaquin.

Though Commerce craves their sturdy trunks to line her ships of steel
No hand has fashioned forth a mast, no adz has shaped a keel,
No axe has left its sordid mark nor fire has dimmed their green,
For guardian angels watch above the Oaks of San Joaquin.

The giant trees with roots outspread still fling their streamers gay
To grant again a trysting place to the Loves of Yesterday,
And Loves that dream in endless sleep, by mortal eyes unseen
Again a blessed tryst may keep 'neath the Oaks of San Joaquin.

Before the Cross was lifted up on Mission San Jose
The savage stalked with stealthy tread between these trunks so grey,
And still they stand to bless the land, make glad the fertile scene,
Where Peace and Plenty lie beneath the Oaks of San Joaquin.

(This poem came to The Grizzly Bear from Anna Enos of San Leandro, Alameda County.—Editor.)

Livermore Rodeo—Livermore, Alameda County, will present its annual Rodeo, May 14 and 15.

Know your home-state, California! Learn of its past history and of its present-day development by reading regularly The Grizzly Bear. $1.50 for one year (12 issues). Subscribe now.

CALIFORNIA HAPPENINGS OF FIFTY YEARS AGO

Thomas R. Jones

(COMPILED EXPRESSLY FOR THE GRIZZLY BEAR.)

PRESIDENT CHESTER A. ARTHUR signed May 8, 1882, the anti-Chinese bill, introduced by Senator J. F. Miller, and passed by the United States Congress. There was great rejoicing throughout California, and in a number of communities salutes of a hundred guns were fired. The measure was not to go into effect until August, and in the meantime the Chinese continued to come as fast as ships could be obtained to transport them.

During May, five ships, with 4,000 Chinks, arrived. On the "Altenower" were many cases of smallpox. The "Straitmore," with a registered capacity of 814, had 1,130 aboard. Its owners had to pay a fine of $50 for each of the excess 316, the total amounting to $15,800, but as they received $45 for each Chinaman landed they were out but $5 a head.

The Woman's Protective League was organized May 18 at San Francisco. Its object was to induce housewives to dispense with Chinese servants and give employment to White women.

May was a disastrous month for growing crops. A norther started the 5th and blew for three days, spreading disaster throughout the grainfields. A frost the 17th did great damage to vineyards, orchards and vegetable gardens.

May, too, was the great picnic month of the year, and numerous outdoor gatherings were held May Day. The largest, at Woodward's Gardens in San Francisco, was attended by 24,000, including 15,000 schoolchildren.

A picnic at Hock Farm, Sutter County, attended by the sons of toil, developed into an enthusiastic anti-debris meeting.

Veterans of the Mexican War, members of the Grand Army of the Republic and two companies of the California National Guard gathered near Stockton, San Joaquin County, for a joint three-day encampment May 10.

The Pacific Coast Railroad Company was incorporated to build an eighty-mile narrow-gauge railway connecting with the San Luis Obispo and Santa Maria Valley line. William Norris was the promoter.

Leland Stanford, Charles Crocker and other capitalists incorporated a company, with $500,000 capital, to build and operate a cable street-railway in San Francisco.

G. W. Funk of the Pacific Coast Land Bureau secured options on large acreages in San Luis Obispo County. From Kansas, 500 families were coming to settle there.

A Napa County genius applied for a patent on a device to make night-driving safe. It consisted of an electric light attached to a horse's forehead above the eyes. "Juice" was supplied by wires from a battery in the vehicle.

An oak tree, seven and one-third feet in diameter at its base, felled at Newville, Colusa County, was cut into 400 seven-foot posts and 75 cords of stovewood. The product netted $230.

A cave discovered near Buena Vista, Yolo County, was found to be inhabited by spiders, many of them as large as canary birds.

A new theater, with a seating capacity of 1,500, was opened May 10 at Stockton, San Joaquin County.

There was a boom in Napa Valley real estate, and many owners refused to sell at any price. A 200-acre vineyard, sold May 1 for $17,000, was re-sold May 20 for $24,000.

A vein of bituminous coal was discovered at Point Loma, San Diego County.

Piute squaws found rich placer diggings near Bodie, Mono County, and were accumulating wealth from the finds.

Cultivating a vineyard near Middle Bar, Amador County, the plow exposed a seam of gold quartz from which a fortune was being extracted.

A lode of ore, ninety percent iron, was found at Sheep Ranch, Calaveras County. It was 300 feet wide and was traced for two miles.

At Moore Flat, Nevada County, an eighty-five-pound quartz boulder was found May 21. It was oval in shape, and was encircled by an inch-wide gold band. It was valued at $2,000.

District Attorney M. C. Berry of Sutter County went to Dutch Flat, Placer County, to serve injunction papers on the Hickey hydraulic mine. While on the property, he was thoroughly drenched, a giant monitor being "accidentally" turned his way.

Claude Chana, a member of the first party that set out to relieve the ill-fated Donner Party, died May 24. He came to California from France in 1846 and located a domain on Bear River, near what is now Wheatland, Yuba County. At one time he was rated as worth $100,000, but he died a poor man.

Francis B. Murdock, who came from Maryland in 1850 and established a newspaper in 1853, died May 18 at San Jose, Santa Clara County, aged 77.

The fifteenth annual convention of the State Sundayschool Association was held at Stockton, San Joaquin County. The two hundred delegates, from nearly every county of the state, represented 41,418 scholars.

Five hundred fishermen were, it was estimated, engaged in seining salmon in Carquinez Straits.

Mrs. J. D. Hamill of Oakland, Alameda County, May 18 gave birth to a child, and two days later she gave birth to two more children. She was now the mother of ten children.

A church and two saloons were burned at Sierra City, Sierra County, May 5, and the same day fire destroyed Krug's store at Centerville, Alameda County, with a $15,000 loss.

A portion of the business section of Davisville, Yolo County, burned May 10, causing a $30,000 loss, and May 16 Garber's store in Garberville, Humboldt County, was destroyed, the loss being $25,000.

May 9 an incendiary set fire to a Chico, Butte County, planingmill, which was burned. The embers started another fire, a half-mile away, and six dwellings, with barns and outbuildings, were destroyed; loss, $30,000.

(Continued on Page 21)

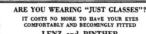

Native Daughters of the Golden West

OAKLAND—THE TENTH ANNUAL SESSION of the Past Presidents General Assembly was held April 9, with Chief President Josephine Clark presiding. Among the many in attendance were Grand President Evelyn I. Carlson, Junior Past Grand President Estelle M. Evans, Grand Trustees Edna Briggs, Ethel Begley and Willow Borba, Grand Treasurer Susie K. Christ, Grand Outside Sentinel Orinda Giannini, Founder Leah Magner-Williams of the Past Presidents Association, Past Chief Presidents Winnie Buckingham, Anna G. Loser, Josephine Schmidt, Susie K. Christ, Millie Tietjen and Lily May Tilden.

Association No. 2, the hostess, spared no effort to please the delegates. Chairman Emilie J. Clifford of the general arrangements committee was assisted by the following chairmen of sub-committees: Winnie Buckingham, Helen R. Cleu, Freda Reichhold, Helen Ring, Elizabeth B. Goodman, Frances McGovern, May C. Ward and Minnie Noyes.

Past Grand Emma G. Foley and Jennie Brown, being original officers of the first assembly, were made permanent members of the General Association. San Francisco was selected as the meeting-place for the 1933 session; Association No. 1 will be hostess. Officers were selected as follows:

MRS. LEAH MAGNER-WILLIAMS,
Founder Past Presidents Association.

Cora Stobing, chief president; Josephine Clark, junior past chief president; Emilie J. Clifford, chief vice-president; Winifred Halter, chief marshal; Anna G. Loser, chief secretary; Emma G. Foley, chief treasurer; Antha Locklin, chief organist; Margaret Grote-Hill, chief inside sentinel; Elizabeth B. Goodman, chief outside sentinel; Mamie Davis, Willow Borba, Mattie M. Stein, Edna D. Sampson and Julia Waddington, directors.

Past Presidents Association No. 1 (San Francisco) was instituted by the Founder, Mrs. Leah Magner-Williams, July 1, 1904. There are now eight associations, with a membership of 675, which make up the General Assembly. The purposes of the organization are: "To further the interests and wellbeing of the Order of N.D.G.W.; to encourage members of Subordinate Parlors in the work of the Order and to bring about a higher understanding and appreciation of the objects, purposes and aims of the N.D.G.W.; to cultivate and encourage sociability and fraternity among the members throughout the state, and generally, to foster and enlarge upon the work of the Order and to be an incentive to members to pass through the chairs."

Tree Plantings.

Fullerton—In recognition of the George Washington bicentennial, Grace No. 242 planted two trees April 2—a liveoak at Hillcrest Park, Fullerton, and a California redwood at the Placentia schoolgrounds. The history and landmarks committee, Carrie McFadden-Ford chairman, presented the following program: Salute to The Flag; "George Washington's Prayer," Carrie Ford; "The George Washington Bicentennial," Carrie Sheppard; "Trees and Tree Planting," Kate Hill; clarionet solo, "Trees," Roy Hill; dedication of trees, President Mattie Edwards.

Past President Mary Rothaermel sponsored a public card party April 28 for the benefit of the Loyalty Fund. Hostesses for all-day April meetings of the Parlor's homeless children sewing circle were Lena Wagner and Kate Hill.

"A Day in School."

Etna—A public hijinks was given April 8 by Eschscholtzia No. 112 for the benefit of its Loyalty Pledge fund. An infinite variety of costumes caused much amusement. Prizes were awarded Mrs. Leland Smith, garbed as an old-fashion lady, and Mrs. Lester Calloway, impersonating a dude.

The program opened with an exhortation by "Deacon Jones," none other than District Deputy Lettie Lewis. Then followed vocal and instrumental selections by Elvira Wilson, Helen Lewis, Virginia Horn, Olive and Esther Buchner and Marjorie Anne Derham. A one-act play, "A Day in School," concluded the program. Grand Inside Sentinel Minna K. Horn was the very cross teacher, and the unruly pupils included Sadie Buchner, Clara Farr, Dorice Young, Lottie Tucker, Bernice Smith, Eleanora Dannenbrink, Evelyn Pitman and District Deputy Ada Wilson. Dancing and refreshments terminated the happy affair.

Past Presidents Honor Guests.

Oakland—Piedmont No. 87 had forty of its past presidents as guests of honor April 14. A delightful program, under the direction of Chairman Dorothy Davis, was presented, including vocal numbers by Edwin Healey, son of Edna Healey, a member of the Parlor. Bridge and whist were followed by a sumptuous banquet.

Kern District Meet.

Bakersfield—At the call of Supervising Deputy Grace S. Dorris, the Kern County Parlors—Miocene No. 228, El Tejon No. 239, Desert Gold No. 250—had a district meeting April 15. The lodgeroom was decorated with baskets of lovely orange blossoms. District Deputy May Givens was instructor of the evening and highly commended the officers of El Tejon. Two candidates were initiated, plans were made for Past President Mary B. Hampson to present a California State (Bear) Flag to the Jefferson grammar school during educational week, and a committee was appointed to arrange a Mothers Day program, the Pioneer Mothers of Kern County to be special guests. Among the numerous presentations was that of an emblematic pin to Past President Mayme Towne.

Preceding the meeting a banquet was served, the tables being beautifully decorated with roses. Short talks were given by District Deputies Miranda Seright and Evalyn Towne, President George Taylor of Bakersfield No. 42 N.S.G.W., Deputy Grand President Al Lobree and Principal H. A. Spindt of the Kern County union high school. Entertainment numbers were contributed by Wimmer Cooper, American Legion Auxiliary, Margaret Carlisle, Ila Kirk and Margaret Stramler.

In arranging for this wonderful gathering Supervising Deputy Dorris was assisted by Florence Hinderliter, Mayme Towne, Jewell Wade, Jennie Dennis, Mary Hampson, Catherine Dodenhoff, Edith Swett, Ernestine Edwards and Anna Scott. May 25 the newly-formed past presidents club of El Tejon will sponsor a card party.

Silver Tea.

San Bernardino—Lugonia No. 241 had a card party for the benefit of the homeless children April 13. Hand-embroidered pillowslips were disposed of and refreshments were served. Plans for an old-fashion southern ham dinner, in charge of Nola Fogler, were made.

Six candidates were initiated April 27, and the social hour at the conclusion of the ceremonies was in charge of Edith Wilson, captain of the losing team in the recent membership campaign. The history and landmarks committee of the Parlor sponsored a silver tea at the home of Chairman Clara Barton, April 30. An interesting program was presented and refresh ments were served.

HOME BEAUTIFUL

(DR. MARIANA BERTOLA, P.G.P., Chairman Grand Parlor Home Committee.)

A STORY OF THE HOME, YOU ASK Why, the story of the Home is glor ious, it is an epic! The struggles, th heartaches, the overcoming of ob stacles, the enthusiasm engendered the loyalty that has sprung into flame the achievement of a big thing actually built i stone and steel, and the spirit of Home fire burning constitute a saga to light the souls o young and old!

The foundation story has been written man times; this will be the fireside story. It ha long been a standing joke that a large body o women cannot live together peacefully. O course, that is a joke. Women are like the brothers. The fireside at the Home is invitin to peace, and comfort. Our older women ther find it especially peaceful. It is good, when ill to have kind ministering hands attend to one and it is good for the spirit to know that other take an interest in one!

Our beautiful Home has been selected by sev eral young women as the scene of their wed dings. There seems to be something "catching" about it, as rumor has it that several others ar about to take the important step. It may b the atmosphere of the Home life that turns one thought to a home of her own.

We are feeling the depression as well as every body else, but the fact remains that we have fe vacancies. Our second-Sunday-of-the-month breakfast at 9 a. m. is always a success. A memory book has been bought and the name of all contributing in honor of dear ones passe away will be entered therein. We desire t make this volume worthy of being handed dow to posterity, and so the leaves are to be illum inated.

It is not quite three years since we started t pay off a $60,000 mortgage on the Home. Th response throughout the Order has been so won derful that the mortgage today is $9,300. Ever Native Daughter, in the years to come, wants t be able to say, "I had a share in the building o the Home." So, come on, with goodwill an enthusiasm, and join us!

State's History Portrayed.

Stockton—Grand President Evelyn I. Carlso officially visited Caliz de Oro No. 206, April and among the honored guests was Past Gran May C. Boldemann, who instituted the Parlo Dinner preceded the meeting, over which Mr Roscoe Platt, president, presided. Grand Pres dent Carlson was the recipient of a gift, the pr sentation of which was arranged by Miss R berta Foley. Stages of the history of Californ were portrayed by Lura Day, Buelah Gratta Katherine Wilde, Clarice Cook and Mrs. La rence Johnson.

During the evening plans were formulated f the spring informal dance, May 7. Mrs. La rence Johnson is the general chairman.

To Initiate Large Class.

Petaluma—Petaluma No. 222 had a ca party April 5 for the benefit of its drill tea Captain Anne Dickson had charge of the ca playing. April 19 several more applicatio were received, and in the near-future a lar class of candidates will be initiated by Preside Elizabeth Dillon and her corps of officers. Fo lowing the meeting cards were played, Nell Pometta and Anne Dickson being in charge, an dainty refreshments were served by Edna Mea ows and Pearl Lopez.

Sonoma County Past Presidents Associati No. 7 met in Petaluma April 13 at the home President Mastrup. Delegates to the Gener Assembly reported, interesting programs we outlined and refreshments were served.

Tells of Early-Day Life.

Oroville—At the April 6 meeting of Gold Ophir No. 190, Laura Kloss told of the earl day life of her mother's people in Californ Alta B. Baldwin was named chairman of t Parlor's committee to serve on the national ed cational program. A committee composed

Mms. Arena Keith (chairman), E. Steadman, Lauretta Ross and George Sollars served refreshments at tables decorated in seasonable flowers.

Mms. Frank O'Brien, Walter Brown and Frank Mekellos were hostesses April 1 to Butte County Past Presidents Association No. 5 at the former's home. Gifts were presented Mms. Frank Boyle, Alvin Bills and Lauretta Ross.

Marker for Landmark.

Alturas—Alturas No. 159 had a delightful social April 7, ten tables of bridge players making merry. Refreshments were served. A class of candidates will be initiated May 5.

A bronze marker, the gift of Sadie Winn-Brainard, is soon to be dedicated by the Parlor at Chimney Rock, one of a group of pyramids near Alturas about which cluster Indian legends. It is a landmark of the old military trail leading from Fort Bidwell, Modoc County, to Yreka, Siskiyou County. The marker will be dedicated to the memory of all Modoc County Pioneers.

Benefit Quilt Ready for Disposal.

Santa Ana—At the April 11 meeting of Santa Ana No. 235 the benefit quilt was reported as finished and ready for disposal. Clara Gerken was awarded the prize in a selling contest for the benefit of the Parlor's veteran welfare work. Mae West, chairman veteran welfare committee, was a recent visitor to San Fernando Hospital, taking the boys several boxes of easter candy, and also visited a veteran at the Sawtelle National Soldiers Home. In observance of national educational week a speaker addressed the Parlor April 25 on an appropriate subject.

Aprilfool Banquet.

Colusa—Colus No. 194 had an aprilfool banquet April 5. The table was adorned with cheeseweeds and large hoquets of yellow mustard in coffee cans. Placecards were funnypapers pictures, and paper towels were used as napkins. Four kerosene lamps provided the only light. Thimbles, buttons, safetypins and a ring were baked in the cakes, and the lucky finders of the "trinkets" were rewarded with prizes.

Grand President Evelyn I. Carlson paid her official visit to the Parlor April 18. A banquet preceded the meeting at which twelve candidates were initiated.

Grand President's Official Itinerary.

San Francisco—During the month of May, Grand President Evelyn I. Carlson will officially visit the following Subordinate Parlors on the dates noted:

2nd—Berryessa No. 192, Willows.
4th—Occident No. 28, Eureka; Oneonta No. 71, Ferndale; Reichling No. 97, Fortuna; jointly at Ferndale.
5th—Fort Bragg No. 210, Fort Bragg.
9th—Golden Gate No. 158, San Francisco.
10th—Antioch No. 223, Antioch.
12th—Pleasanton No. 237, Pleasanton.
13th—San Bruno No. 246, San Bruno.
14th—Napa, Lake and Solano Counties district meeting at Saint Helena.
19th—Genevieve No. 132, San Francisco.
21st—Clear Lake No. 135, Middletown.
23rd—Calaveras No. 103, San Francisco.
24th—Aloha No. 106, Oakland.
26th—La Dorado No. 236, San Francisco.
27th—Liberty No. 213, Elk Grove.
31st—Tamelpa No. 231, Mill Valley.

Officers Congratulated.

Sutter Creek—Amapola No. 80 received an official visit from Grand President Evelyn I. Carlson April 14. A dinner in her honor preceded the meeting, at which 100 members of the Order were present, including fifteen grand officers and representatives of twenty-one Parlors. Following the dinner a program was presented. During the evening garments made by the Parlor members for the homeless children were displayed. The ritual was exemplified by the officers of No. 80, with President Harriet Clemens presiding.

Grand President Carlson gave an interesting address, commending the officers for their perfect work and congratulating the Parlor for having completed its Loyalty Pledge. On the Parlor's behalf Grand Trustee Gladys E. Noce presented a gift of china to Mrs. Carlson, and gifts and flowers were presented to Founder Lilly O. Dyer, Junior Past Grand Estelle M. Evans, Grand Vice-president Anna M. Armstrong, Grand Trustees Ethel Begley, Willow Borba, Edna Briggs, Anna Thuesen and Gladys Noce, Grand Outside Sentinel Orinda Giannini, Past Grands Ella Caminetti, Emma Foley and Dr. Eva Rasmussen, Supervising Deputy Emma Wright and District Deputy Margaret Davis.

Past Presidents Birthday Hostesses.

San Diego—The seventeenth birthday anniversary of San Diego No. 208 was celebrated April 13, with the past presidents as hostesses.

(Continued on Page 23)

Feminine World's Fads and Fancies

PREPARED ESPECIALLY FOR THE GRIZZLY BEAR BY ANNA STOERMER

SILK ENSEMBLES ARE IMPORTANT FOR the early summer, so treat yourself to at least one suit this season. Never have suits been quite so winsome and wearable. We have veered away from the strictly tailor-made. The short coat is kinder to the wearer than the long fitted coat which adds years. The short jacket is jaunty and has a dashing air. A navy blue of heavy rough tussah may be worn with a blouse or guimpe of white or beige with stripes in red and blue.

Even the sports clothes follow the straight and narrow path when it comes to the silhouette. Provision is made for comfort in walking by godets so placed that the slim line of the skirt is not materially widened.

The tailored note of the more dressy mode is cleverly blended into the general scheme without altering the theme of neatness. Elegance is not in fashion, and we prefer to be neat and youthful to achieve chic. One must dwell constantly on the youthful aspect of the mode. Women seek youth not through girlish frocks or models meant for their daughters, but through frocks that, by virtue of their cut, line and detail, create a neat, trig and lithe line with an absence of all but the most essential details.

The military note that sounds through the new collections means that buttons, many buttons, must be worn, for what is a uniform without bright buttons embellishing it? Double-breasted as well as diagonal closings must all be marked by buttons. New coats, especially the unfurred models, are tremendously smart, trig and youthful. One is made of a loosely woven woolen material with a diagonal, wide, raised rib and features the military motif and buttons. The double-breasted closing has three nickel buttons at each side and two at the cuffs. Flaring triangular pockets are attached to each side of the front panel.

All of us want slim figures—natural, or achieved through much sacrifice and care. So we want frocks to set off the form to best advantage.

For some reason, more mystery and romance seem to attach to the springtime brides, not that their prospects for "living happily ever after" are any better, but merely the season itself. No lovelier time of year could be found. With summer days just ahead, bridal wardrobes can be so much more comprehensive. By virtue of priority, white satin is the first choice. As a matter of fact, there is no worthy substitute for the gown of bridal satin, the all-enveloping tulle veil and the symbolic orange blossoms. The bride's choice of costume may rest on an enchanting afternoon frock of blush pink lace with matching jacket, pastel chiffon, or any one of the smart sheers. If the ceremony is due to take place in an out-of-doors setting during the warmer months, then lovely nets, organdies, swisses, or any of the exquisite cotton weaves that have fashionable approval, may be used.

Summer styles struck an economical note, being easily adaptable to silk, wool, crepes and cotton. The latter, once lowly, is now used for everything from evening wraps to bathing suits. Many smart women have met the new season half-way by being forehanded in assembling a cool, comfortable and tubable wardrobe. The vogue for meshes goes merrily on with lace batistes. Skirts are trig and trim, gored, pleated or slightly flared. Higher waistlines prevail, and sleeves are either omitted entirely or are very brief. They exhibit a number of lacy patterns in eyelet embroidery, and go in for self-fabric or self-color. Batiste pleatings, contrasting velvet ribbon bows in tub frock collections are the smart details that have received attention. Bias cuts, extended shoulders, fichus, capelets and many, many buttons, cords and twills are very much in the fabric picture. Piques are used to fashion some of the loveliest costumes. Jacket frocks are as much in evidence here as in the various other ranges. Linens are fulfilling their early season promise.

Each spring much charm and flattery can be, and are, packed into a wisp of straw with a perky bow or an artfully placed cluster of flowers. The new hats are simply grand. Every model is most wearable, and all are youthful, even to other than the very young woman. On every head we see rakish hats tilted over one ear, while the opposite side of the head is sometimes almost entirely exposed. Say what you will about this fashion, there can be no gainsaying its youthful and gay appeal. These hats must have expertly placed trimming to accentuate their lines and must never be over-trimmed. Ribbon is being used in plain bands and shirred fancy loops and rosettes. When flowers are used it is usually to the extent of one or two gardenias. Hats and frocks must match.

Not in many a day have style designers been in such perfect accord regarding what constitutes costume chic. Accessories add so much, we are enjoying many novelties. No sooner do we acquire one article of apparel than we become aware of its inability to function alone. One thing calls for another, and many others sound like extravagance, but really are not, as in most cases they are interchangeable.

Blue is enjoying a period of social prominence as a costume color. In the blue range we have flax, midnight, nassau, colonial and the good old navy, not to mention various other shades. Brown or russet accessories are deemed a bit smarter, though we have a wide range of blue ones. Brown is also indicated as the ideal accessory color. With beige, the tricolor theme has been the subject of unlimited variation. Sports accessories have been largely responsible for the increasing popularity of red, white and blue scarfs, which constitutes style news of first importance. This applies, also, to formal as well as street and sports clothes. A scarf is not always what it started out to be. It may turn itself into a draped collar and sash end, or make a dashing belt.

Olympic Timber Toppers

THE timber toppers are training for the big Olympic meet and each hopes for stardom.

The great majority of us, however, are more concerned in topping the present financial "repression".

To the thrifty, the monthly saving by riding the street car instead of the automobile to work and back—to shop and back—is quite a big item.

Help yourself go over the top by using the street car for your business car.

Los Angeles Railway

CATALINA
ISLAND
It's not too early to plan your summer vacation at Catalina. Early reservations are suggested. New low rates on accommodations this summer. Write for folder.
Steamer leaves Catalina Terminal, foot of Avalon Blvd., Wilmington, 10 a.m. daily. Delightful two hour trip. Also two or more hydroplane flights daily leaving Catalina Terminal, Wilmington, morning and afternoon. Less than 20 minutes to the Island! Tickets and reservations:
Catalina Terminal, Wilmington Phone 1431
Catalina Ticket Office P. E. Bldg., 6th & Main Sts., Los Angeles Phone MAdison 1151
W
CATALINA
IN ALL THE WORLD NO TRIP LIKE THIS

LEGALIZED MONOPOLY

30-Cent Gasoline

MORE MEN Out of Work

—That's what **OIL CONTROL** (Proposition No. 1) will mean to the people of California if approved by the voters at the election of May 3.

It is the **SHARKey** bill, this Proposition No. 1, which attempted to masquerade as "Oil Conservation" until detected by the California State Court of Appeal and given its proper title of **OIL CONTROL.**

Surely the people of California cannot be bamboozled into voting for such a measure.

Kill legalized monopoly by voting **NO** on **OIL CONTROL** (Proposition No. 1) at the primary election on May 3.

INDEPENDENT ASSOCIATION OPPOSED TO MONOPOLY

and

INDEPENDENT PETROLEUM ASSOCIATION OF CALIFORNIA

900 Spring Arcade Bldg., Los Angeles
405 Montgomery Street, San Francisco
409 34th Street, Oakland

WARNING! STOP, LOOK, LISTEN! Great sums of money are now being spent, and far greater sums will be spent by the Major Oil Corporations in every conceivable form of propaganda before election day in the attempt to put over the SHARKey bill. Millions for monopoly! Fat salaried executives do not care how they spend their stockholders' money to play their own cunning game. The best guess is that the people of California will not be fooled no matter how great the flood of paid advertising, paid speakers, radio and propaganda! Vote to kill legalized monopoly by voting NO on OIL CONTROL (PROPOSITION NO. 1) on MAY 3.

FIFTY-FIFTH N.S.G.W. GRAND PARLOR

(CLARENCE M. HUNT.)

THE FIFTY-FIFTH GRAND PARLOR OF the Order of Native Sons of the Golden West will convene at Stockton, San Joaquin County, Monday, May 16, at 10:30 a. m. Grand President Dr. Frank I. Gonzalez (Pacific No. 10) of San Francisco will preside, and at the close of the deliberations he will automatically become the Junior Past Grand President.

The Grand Parlor sessions will be held in the Civic Memorial Auditorium, in the Civic Center, Monday, Wednesday and Thursday. Any member of the Order is privileged to attend. Stockton also entertained the Grand Parlor in 1921, the Forty-fourth session being held there, with the then Grand President, James F. Hoey (Mount Diablo No. 101) of Martinez presiding. It was at that session that John T. Regan (South San Francisco No. 157) of San Francisco was elected to the important office of Grand Secretary, which he has ever since admirably filled.

The reports of the grand officers and the Grand Parlor committees to the five hundred delegates representing the one hundred and fifty-five Subordinate Parlors will set forth the progress made by the Order during 1931 and will, in all likelihood, contain important recommendations for future action. That of Grand Secretary Regan will detail the condition of the Subordinate Parlors. Those of 450 and more members, with their assets, include:

	Members	Assets
Ramona No. 109	1088	$41,498.24
South San Francisco No. 157	822	47,661.39
Castro No. 232	700	12,582.29
Stanford No. 76	614	24,711.46
Arrowhead No. 110	609	24,064.86
Twin Peaks No. 214	585	9,257.55
Stockton No. 7	549	49,319.99
Piedmont No. 120	523	21,230.57

Others, with assets of $20,000 and more, together with their membership-figures, are:

	Members	Assets
San Jose No. 22	358	$59,972.01
Sacramento No. 3	366	44,408.64
Pacific No. 10	397	42,192.65
Presidio No. 194	382	35,769.30
Amador No. 17	144	33,237.76
Santa Lucia No. 97	46	33,049.02
Placerville No. 9	282	31,778.79
Napa No. 62	329	30,058.86
Observatory No. 177	196	29,043.87
Redwood No. 66	183	28,169.89
Sunset No. 26	305	23,058.18
California No. 1	372	22,704.76
Eden No. 113	104	22,231.18
Excelsior No. 31	127	20,577.11

From these figures, it will be noted that Ramona No. 109 (Los Angeles) continues its lead as the largest, numerically, in the Order, and that San Jose No. 22 remains the wealthiest, financially. Santa Lucia No. 97 (Salinas) has the greatest percapita wealth.

At the close of 1931, Subordinate Parlors had total convertible assets of $1,283,974.29, including $304,623.53 cash on hand. Their 1931 receipts totaled $368,373.40, and their disbursements $358,452.14. They paid benefits totaling $115,559.56 to 1,724 members.

During 1931 the Subordinate Parlors presented United States of America and California State (Bear) Flags to the following schools, Grand President Gonzalez and the Board of Grand Officers officiating at all the ceremonies: San Jose No. 22, Peter H. Burnett junior high school; Fremont No. 44 (Hollister), San Benito junior college; Redwood No. 66 (Redwood City), Peninsula Avenue grammar school; Ferndale No. 93, The Island school; Santa Lucia No. 97 (Salinas), El Sausal school; Sea Point No. 158 (Sausalito), The Park school; Lower Lake No. 159, Upper Lake union grammar school; Observatory No. 177 (San Jose), Herbert Hoover junior high school; Estudillo No. 223 (San Leandro), McKinley school; Bret Harte No. 260 (San Francisco), Farragut school.

If there be any fact-foundation for the numerous rumors that are floating about, considerable legislation, some of it destructive in nature, will be presented at the Stockton Grand Parlor. Sure, there will most likely be the usual quantity of resolutions, also, dealing with almost every conceivable subject—of concern to the Order and otherwise. The quality ones will be given due consideration, and the remainder will possibly, as they certainly should, be wastebasketed without consideration.

CANDIDATES FOR OFFICE.

"Oldman rumor" persistently declares there will be presented at Stockton surprise candidates for most of the Grand Parlor elective offices. Every effort has been made to secure definite declarations of intentions from many of the prospective "darkhorses." A couple have repudiated the rumors, while others, most prominently mentioned, if they responded at all to the query, gave evasive answers. The following list of candidates is compiled from authentic information received direct by the Grizzly Bear:

Grand President—Grand First Vice-president Seth Millington (Colusa No. 69) of Gridley.

Grand First Vice-president—Grand Second Vice-president Justice Emmet Seawell (Santa Rosa No. 28) of Santa Rosa.

Grand Second Vice-president—Grand Third Vice-president Chas. A. Koenig (Golden Gate No. 29) of San Francisco.

Grand Third Vice-president—J. Hartley Russell (Stanford No. 76) of San Francisco; Harmon D. Skillin (Castro No. 232) of San Francisco.

Grand Secretary—John T. Regan (South San Francisco No. 157) of San Francisco, incumbent.

PAST GRAND PRESIDENTS AND MEETING PLACES GRAND PARLOR, N.S.G.W.

Elected		Presided	Session Held
		1878	San Francisco
1878	Wm. G. Hawkett*	1879	San Francisco
1879	Jasper Fishbourne*	1880	Sacramento
1880	Frank J. Higgins*	1881	Oakland & S. F.
1881	Henry Clay Chipman*	1882	Sacramento
1882	John H. Grady*	1883	San Francisco
1883	A. F. Jones*	1884	Marysville
1884	John A. Steinbach*	1885	San Jose
1885	Fred H. Greely	1886	Woodland
1886	Chas. W. Decker	1887	Nevada City
1887	C. H. Garroutte*	1888	Fresno
1888	M. A. Dorn*	1889	San Rafael
1889	Frank D. Ryan*	1890	Chico
1890	Wm. H. Miller*	1891	Santa Rosa
1891	R. M. Fitzgerald	1892	Los Angeles
1892	Thos. Flint Jr.	1893	Sacramento
1893	John T. Greany*	1894	Eureka
1894	Jo D. Sproul*	1895	Oakland
1895	Frank H. Dunne	1896	San Luis Obispo
1896	Henry C. Gesford	1897	Redwood City
1897	George D. Clark	1898	Nevada City
1898	Wm. M. Conley	1899	Salinas City
1899	Frank Mattison*	1900	Oroville
1900	R. C. Rust*	1901	Santa Barbara
1901	Frank L. Coombs	1902	Santa Cruz
1902	Lewis F. Byington	1903	Bakersfield
1903	H. R. McNoble	1904	Vallejo
1904	Chas. E. McLaughlin	1905	Monterey
1905	Jas L. Gallagher†	1906	Ventura
1906	Walter D. Wagner	1907	Napa
1907	M. T. Dooling*	1908	Yosemite
1908	C. M. Belshaw*	1909	Marysville
1909	Jos. R. Knowland	1910	Lake Tahoe
1910	Daniel A. Ryan	1911	Santa Cruz
1911	H. C. Lichtenberger	1912	Fresno
1912	Clarence E. Jarvis	1913	Oroville
1913	Thomas Monahan	1914	Los Angeles
1914	Louis H. Mooser†	1915	San Francisco
1915	John F. Davis*	1916	Modesto
1916	Bismarck Bruck*	1917	Redding
1917	Jo V. Snyder*	1918	Truckee
1918	Wm. F. Toomey*	1919	Yosemite
1919	Wm. P. Canbu	1920	San Diego
1920	James F. Hoey	1921	Stockton
1921	William I. Traeger	1922	Oakland
1922	Harry G. Williams	1923	Santa Barbara
1923	William J. Hayes	1924	Sacramento
1924	Edward J. Lynch	1925	San Bernardino
1925	Fletcher A. Cutler	1926	Santa Rosa
1926	Hilliard E. Welch	1927	San Pedro
1927	Charles A. Thompson	1928	Redding
1928	James A. Wilson	1929	San Francisco
1929	Charles L. Dodge	1930	Merced
1930	John T. Newell	1931	Monterey
1931	Frank I. Gonzalez		

*Deceased.
†Connection with Order severed.

Grand Treasurer—John A. Corotto (San Jose No. 22) of San Jose, incumbent.

Grand Marshal—Grand Inside Sentinel W. B. O'Brien (Alameda No. 47) of Alameda City.

Grand Inside Sentinel—Grand Outside Sentinel Gam Hurst (Piedmont No. 120) of Oakland.

Grand Outside Sentinel—William A. Reuter (Sepulveda No. 263) of San Pedro.

Grand Trustees (seven to be selected)—Jesse H. Miller (California No. 1) of San Francisco, incumbent; Henry S. Lyon (Placerville No. 9) of Placerville; John M. Burnett (San Jose No. 22) of San Jose; Grand Marshal Horace J. Leavitt (Mount Bally No. 87) of Weaverville; Charles H. Spengemann (Hesperian No. 137) of San Francisco; Samuel M. Shortridge Jr. (Menlo No. 185) of Menlo Park, incumbent; Joseph J. McShane (Twin Peaks No. 214) of San Francisco, incumbent; Eldred L. Meyer (Santa Monica Bay No. 267) of Santa Monica, incumbent.

The Grand Organist and the Historiographer, additional grand officers, will be appointed by the incoming Grand President.

There is a possibility that the Humboldt County Parlors will invite the next (1933) Grand Parlor to meet in Eureka, and Auburn No. 59 may seek the honor in behalf of Auburn, Placer County.

Latest advices from Sacramento are that the Capital City Parlors are desirous of having this year's Admission Day, September 9, there, "but there remain a couple of hurdles to get over" before a final decision is reached. If those obstacles are satisfactorily negotiated, Sacramento will ask for the celebration.

GRAND PARLOR COMPOSITION.

The Stockton Grand Parlor will be made up of the following:

Grand Officers—John T. Newell, Junior Past Grand President; Dr. Frank I. Gonzalez, Grand President; Seth Millington, Grand First Vice-president; Justice Emmet Seawell, Grand Second Vice-president; Chas. A. Koenig, Grand Third Vice-president; John T. Regan, Grand Secretary; John A. Corotto, Grand Treasurer; Horace J. Leavitt, Grand Marshal; W. B. O'Brien, Grand Inside Sentinel; Gam Hurst, Grand Outside Sentinel; Leslie Maloche, Grand Organist; George H. Barron, Historiographer; George F. McNoble, Samuel M. Shortridge Jr., Jesse H. Miller, Joseph J. McShane, Frank M. Lane, John M. Burnett, Eldred L. Meyer, Grand Trustees.

Senior Past Grand Presidents—Fred H. Greely, Dr. Charles W. Decker, Robert M. Fitzgerald, Senator Thomas Flint Jr., Judge Frank H. Dunne, Judge Henry C. Gesford, George D. Clark, Judge William M. Conley, Frank L. Coombs, Lewis F. Byington, Judge Hubert R. McNoble, Judge Charles E. McLaughlin, Walter D. Wagner, Joseph R. Knowland, Daniel A. Ryan, Herman C. Lichtenberger, Clarence E. Jarvis, Thomas Monahan, William P. Caubu, James F. Hoey, William I. Traeger, Harry G. Williams, William J. Hayes, Edward J. Lynch, Judge Fletcher A. Cutler, Hilliard E. Welch, Judge Charles A. Thompson, James A. Wilson, Charles L. Dodge.

Finance Committee—John S. Ramsay, Harry W. Gaetjen, Joseph Rose.

Board Appeals—Harmon D. Skillin, Edwin A. Meserve, Frank M. Buckley, John Andreson, Frank A. Biedermann.

Board Control—John J. Monteverde, William C. Neumiller, Walter Bammann.

Transportation-Mileage Committee—James L. Foley, P. L. Schlesinger, Alfred Vlautin.

Subordinate Parlor Delegates—The list is complete, insofar as Parlors reported, as requested, to The Grizzly Bear to the time of going to press. Delegates of Parlors which failed to send names direct to The Grizzly Bear are not included:

California No. 1—Ellis A. Blackman, Albert Franzen, B. J. Hanlon, Wm. H. James, A. Nishkian.

Sacramento No. 3—John Major, June Longshore, J. Hellinge Jr., Irving D. Gibson, T. W. McAuliffe.

Marysville No. 6—T. J. O'Brien, A. W. Graves.

Stockton No. 7—Fred G. Krumb, George D. Avery, Ray Friedberger, W. P. Rothenbush, Fred E. Potter, W. I. Neeley.

Argonaut No. 8—Cyril R. MacDonald, Frank H. O'Brien.

Placerville No. 9—Henry S. Lyon, Louis Mocettini, Joseph Scherrer, George M. Smith.

Pacific No. 10—Thomas M. Foley, Harry Alexander, Wilbur B. Doyle, Charles R. Boden, Thomas G. Wyatt.

Modesto No. 11—C. D. Blaine, C. W. Gill.

Humboldt No. 14—Leland Bresbears, Henry Sundfors, Leonard Boulester.

Amador No. 17—John H. Williams, D. V. Ramazzotti.

Arcata No. 20—George Hale, I. C. Flechenstein.

San Jose No. 22—Lawrence F. Hart, B. T. LeGue, Charles Petersen, James W. Craig, Clifford L. Kelley.

Yosemite No. 24—Thomas V. Bell, Edward Bickmore.

Fresno No. 25—George Haines, A. G. Miller.

Sunset No. 26—Edward E. Reese, C. P. Gannon, A. J. Nicoletti, C. L. Corcoran.

Petaluma No. 27—John Murphy, George Petersen.

Santa Rosa No. 28—Wesley Colgan, James Brucker, George Eckman.

Golden Gate No. 29—Thomas C. Conmy, David Wilson, Henry C. Lunsmann, Albert F. Moore.

Woodland No. 30—J. L. Aronson.

Excelsior No. 31—Andrew L. Pierovich, Wm. Going.

General Winn No. 32—R. R. Veale, J. P. Mulhare.

Ione No. 33—Richard Barnett, George J. Yager.

Mission No. 38—Thomas J. Stewart, Edward Grady, William A. Wilkie, George Leahy.

Elk Grove No. 41—Walter Martin, C. C. Wackman.

Los Angeles No. 45—Earl H. LeMoine, Albert W. Metz, Roger M. Johnson.

Alameda No. 47—H. L. Sousa, Joseph H. Peterson, Gus Nelson.

Plymouth No. 48—Waldo A. Barney, George A. Upton.

San Francisco No. 49—George Batchelor, David Oapurro, John H. Nelson, Frank Marini.

Oakland No. 50—Dr. J. A. Plunkett, Elwood Fitzgerald, A. W. Ainger.

El Dorado No. 52—Robert Donohue, Paul Rockwitz, Ed Williams.

Saint Helena No. 53—Lowell Palmer, Frank Harrison.

Hydraulic No. 56—Dr. C. W. Chapman, R. L. P. Bigelow, E. J. Baker.

Quartz No. 58—Allen Joyner, H. Ray George, Robert Kohler.

Auburn No. 59—P. W. Smith, Chas. H. Slade.
Napa No. 62—A. G. Boggs, W. R. Johnson, Harold McCormick, F. C. Cuthbertson.
Mount Tamalpais No. 64—Arthur W. Todt, Walter Mazza, Monroe Label, B. J. Brusatori.
Watsonville No. 65—Matt J. McGowan, A. W. Batchelder.
RedWood No. 66—A. S. Ligtiori, C. M. Junker, H. W. Amphlett.
Colusa No. 69—Fred P. Muttersbach, Phil J. Humburg.
Rincon No. 72—William J. Wynn, John A. Gilmour, Rudolph Marquard, Chris. Kearse, Vincent Jones.
Ukiah No. 71—Harold J. Zimmerman.
Monterey No. 75—James W. Millington.
Stanford No. 76—J. Hartley Russell, Theo. Schmidt, Hubert J. Caveney, Arthur T. Poheim, Chas. T. O'Kane, Fred E. Wissing, Joseph I. McNamara.
Vallejo No. 77—George Weniger, Joseph Clavo.
Calistoga No. 86—Louis Carlenzoli, Felix W. Salmina, Edmund Molinari.
Mount Bally No. 87—R. L. Marshall, M. F. Kay.
Santa Cruz No. 90—Willett Ware, W. S. Rodgers, J. H. Aram.
Downieville No. 92—August Costa, Antone Lavezzola.
Ferndale No. 93—James J. Niebur, Chas. R. Kistner.
Las Positas No. 96—R. J. Ruetz, Wm. Medau.
Santa Clara No. 100—Alfred P. Cunha, Wm. Joe Brown, Theodore C. Venegas.
Mount Diablo No. 101—A. P. Wright, J. A. Schweinitzer.
Glen Ellen No. 102—Louis Pagani.
Bay City No. 104—Dr. Irving S. Zeimer, Thomas R. Hamilton.
Niantic No. 105—Joseph B. Keenan, John J. Hare.
Courtland No. 106—W. H. Thisby, Joe Berry.
San Diego No. 108—Albert V. Mayrhofer, Edward H. DoWell.
Ramona No. 109—W. E. Baskerville, Irving Baxter, Wm. J. Bright, Chandos E. Bush, Jos. P. Coyle, L. J. Flansburg, Chas. J. Gassagne, Burrel D. Neighbours, B. Rey Schauer, Walter M. Slosson, Chas. E. Straube, Leo V. Youngworth.
Arrowhead No. 110—Lynn Reed, Ben Harrison, Hiram More, Lamar McGarvey, Donald E. VanLuven, Gordon Lee, Henry B. Peake.
Sonoma No. 111—Ray F. Tynan, Victor H. Erlebach.
Eden No. 113—Stanton R. Soares, Frank B. Leonard.
Santa Barbara No. 116—A. C. Dinsmore, Paul G. Sweetser, E. O. Ayala.
Broderick No. 117—H. C. Hunter, Harry Byers.
National No. 118—Arthur H. Frank, E. J. Wren.
Piedmont No. 120—Richard M. Hamb, Frank P. Smith, Andrew Costelli, Walter M. Davis, Adrien M. Hynes, George T. Prytz.
Quincy No. 131—W. J. Miller.
Gabilan No. 132—B. A. McCoy.
Hesperian No 137—C. H. Spengemann, H. G. Ritter, W. H. Burke.
Tuolumne No. 144—Ed. L. Gorgas, A. J. Sylva.
Halcyon No. 146—J. C. Bates, Wm. F. Knowland.
McCloud No. 149—Melvin Zeis, Jess Burdick.
Brooklyn No. 151—Frank C. Merritt.
Cambria No. 152—Richard Valci, Efrom Genardini.
Alcalde No. 154—Joseph L. Costa, Louis F. Erb, Nicholas J. Murphy.
South San Francisco No. 157—Fred H. Nickelson, Lloyd J. Doering, James W. Brady, H. F. Zimmerman, Edwin J. Regan, Raymond Conroy, Robert Hoare, John W. Danz, Frank McWilliams.
Sea Point No. 158—J. S. Rosa, C. Antecivich, F. Pasquinucci.
Sequoia No. 160—James L. Vizzard, Valdimar S. Hornung, Henry Scheper.
Washington No. 169—J. D. Norris, Thos. Silva.
Byron No. 170—Ray R. Houston, W. W. Hoffman.
Observatory No. 177—N. J. Mahon, J. E. Cook, W. L. Gerrans Jr.
Nicasio No. 183—Chas. A. Redding.
Menlo No. 185—D. E. O'Keefe, B. G. Larricou.
Precita No. 187—Ed. H. Weber, J. W. Smith, Lloyd Cosgrove.
Olympus No. 189—Harvey J. Carty, Martin Bewden.
Etna No. 192—Fred J. Meamber, Dean P. Kist.
Presidio No. 194—James P. Murphy, Paul Pasquet, Albert Schmidt, Henry Storti, Tallant Tubbs.
Athens No. 195—Allan W. Sunkler, Henry E. Uebner, Henry G. Kroeckel Jr.
Hollywood No. 196—Henry G. Bodkin, Leo Aggeler, Edgar W. Black.
Alder Glen No. 200—Fred Dodge, Leonard Stone, T. J. Simpson.
Marshall No. 202—John D. Sweeney, Arthur Belli.
Carquinez No. 205—A. H. Rogers, Thomas I. Cahalan.
Berkeley No. 210—Harry Corbett, Ed Lambert.
Twin Peaks No. 214—James McSheehy, James Karuza, George Langly, Patrick Gould, Edwin Strei, Fred Kockler, James Kinane.
Mountain View No. 215—Herbert Spencer Jr., William Spiering.
Palo Alto No. 216—Fred J. Simpson, William H. Adams.
El Capitan No. 222—John G. Schroder.
Estudillo No. 223—Albert G. Pacheco.
Plumas No. 228—D. R. Herring.
Pebble Beach No. 230—Wm. F. Rose.
Guadalupe No. 231—Percy A. Marchant, Richard A. Matli, Milton Lawler, Dennis Nolan.
Castro No. 232—Jas. H. Hayes, Ray Williamson, A. C. Bock, A. D. Lobree, Harry Romick, Thos. M. Dillon, Ernest W. Perry, Frank B. Foss.
Claremont No. 240—F. H. Robson, E. Dossa, R. Burke.
James Lick No. 242—M. G. Muller, T. J. Bowen.
Galt No. 243—J. L. McEnerney.
Pleasanton No. 244—Peter C. Madsen.
Fruitvale No. 252—Edward T. Schnarr, Arthur J. E. Cleu, Ray B. Felton, Edw. D. Hensley.
El Carmelo No. 256—Anthony Parmaisano, Herman Christen.
Bret Harte No. 260—C. E. Lillie, E. J. Allen.
Sutter No. 261—John Colford.
Sepulveda No. 263—William A. Reuter, Harry Fairall, E. E. Baldwin.
Glendale No. 264—Phil D. Molen, Clinton Skinner.
Santa Ana No. 265—W. E. Hiskey, Leo Young.
Santa Monica Bay No. 267—Phil P. Romero, Harry T. Honn, George W. Burnett.
Utopia No. 270—T. J. O'Leary, Geo. Linn.
Manteca No. 271—Joseph A. Wilson, Chas. N. Howell Jr.

WANTS LAND LAW PERFECTED.

Petaluma (Sonoma County)—Petaluma Parlor No. 27 N.S.G.W. adopted April 11 the following resolutions, which will be introduced by its delegates at the Stockton Grand Parlor:

"Whereas, The appeal to the Supreme Court of the State of California of the so-called 'Fujita case,' by the Sonoma County District Attorney, which case involved the question of escheat of lands purchased by minor children of one A. P. Fujita, Japanese, by fraud, has been lost by Sonoma County as of March 1, 1932; and

"Whereas, After years of faithful work by the Sonoma County District Attorney, it is with deep disappointment that we realize this decision will further open avenues of acquisition of California lands by questionable subterfuge and deceitful evasion of the intent of the law, written into the statutes to prevent acquisition of such lands by nationals ineligible to our citizenship; it is

"Resolved, By this [Grand Parlor] of the Native Sons of the Golden West, that our State Attorney General, together with any other capable legal ability, be called upon, before the meeting of the next Legislature, to prepare amendment or change in said Land Law which will fully correct beyond question the flimsy and disgracefully widespread evasion of the law now prevalent in our state."

CALIFORNIA'S NATIONAL FOREST CAMP-GROUNDS HAVE COLORFUL NAMES.

Visitors to the 1,252 campgrounds in the eighteen national forests of California will find that the Federal Forest Service has preserved the names given those spots by the pioneers and the forty-niners. Among many camp names suggestive of frontier days are Bacon Rind, Bear Heaven, Dog Town, Graveyard, Hell Creek, Hog Pen Springs, Hobo Hot Springs, Murderers Bar, Pie Canyon, Poison Meadow, Toad Wells and Whiskey Creek.

Why such names were applied to the beauty spots of the national forests where now the summer visitors find recreation and rest, is usually unknown. Once given, these designations have remained to record some forgotten incident in the early history of California.

FORMER EL DORADO N.S. OFFICIAL DEAD.

Placerville (El Dorado County)—Abe Darlington, for sixteen years district attorney of this county, where he was born sixty-four years ago, died April 20 survived by a wife and two children. He was affiliated with Placerville Parlor No. 9 N.S.G.W., and frequently represented it at the Grand Parlor.

Music Festival—With schools of Marin, Sonoma, Napa and Mendocino Counties participating, the annual Music Festival will be held at San Rafael, May 6.

Fiddletown Celebration—Historic Fiddletown, now Oleta, Amador County, will celebrate May 7 its eighty-third birthday.

Lake's Flower Show—The annual Lake County Flower Show will be held at Lakeport, May 7.

Rose Festival—Santa Rosa, Sonoma County, will revive its annual Rose Festival, May 5-8.

Raisin Classic—Fresno City will stage its annual Raisin Festival, May 14.

Regatta—Stockton, San Joaquin County, will stage its sixth annual regatta, May 28-30.

SUTTER'S FORT

(At Sacramento, California.)

(BETTY L. WHITSELL.)

All glorified today
With planted shrubs and trees
And grass clipped short
It stands, like some great giant tomb,
This Sutter's Fort.
Such sacred quietness
All blessed in its decline
Once strong retreat,
For bands of restless pioneers,
A manor-seat.

Behind adobe walls
The Swiss John Sutter lived in
Authority.

STOCKTON N.S.G.W. PROGRAM

(CLARENCE M. HUNT.)

STOCKTON PARLOR NO. 7 N.S.G.W. HAS charge of the arrangements for and the entertainment of the Fifty-fifth Grand Parlor, and "old seven," the home-Parlor of Past Grand President Hubert R. McNoble, can be relied on to adequately care for the needs of its guests and to provide ample entertainment for them. Here is the program:

May 15 (Sunday)—Registration opens at noon at the headquarters, Stockton Hotel, East Weber avenue. In the evening, open house at N.S.G.W. Hall, Main and San Joaquin streets; entertainment and dancing.

May 16 (Monday)—All-day Grand Parlor session in the Civic Memorial Auditorium. For the womenfolks, lunch at the Stockton Golf and Country Club, followed by a visit to the Pioneer Museum, the state hospital and other local places of interest. In the evening, class initiation, in the Civic Auditorium; the officers of Stockton Parlor No. 7 will exemplify the ritual. For the ladies, a card party at N.S.G.W. Hall.

May 17 (Tuesday)—All-day trip to the Calaveras Big Trees; the auto caravan will leave Stockton at 8:30 a. m., and lunch will be served at the grove under the supervision of Chispa Parlor No. 139 (Murphys). In the evening, Grand Parlor banquet; Grand Trustee George F. McNoble will be the toastmaster, and the speakers will include Mayor Angelo J. Rossi of San Francisco, Edwin A. Meserve and Past Grand President Lewis F. Byington. For the womenfolks, a theater party.

May 18 (Wednesday)—All-day Grand Parlor session. The womenfolks will be taken for an auto ride along the Sacramento River, returning for lunch, served under the auspices of Ivy Parlor No. 88 N.D.G.W. (Lodi), at the Lodi Ladies Improvement Club. In the evening, the grand ball, in the Civic Auditorium, which will be preceded by a drill by members of Joaquin Parlor No. 5 N.D.G.W., commencing promptly at nine o'clock. Governor James Rolph Jr. will be in attendance. Floor Director W. P. Rothenbush will be assisted by the following floor managers, all members of Stockton Parlor No. 7: Ray Dorcey, Harry Herrmann, Fred Fernando, Laurence Buol, Irvin Neeley, W. A. Strong, Clarence Walsh, Alden Carey, Alex. Tschierschky, Fred Krumb, John Fisher, Joel Beck Jr., John Gallagher, Ben Waller, George Witherow, Arthur Libhart, George Avery, Ray Lamb and Glenn Kennedy.

May 19 (Thursday)—All-day Grand Parlor session, concluding with installation of the newly-elected grand officers.

The general committee of Stockton Parlor No. 7 that is handling all the details includes: Ray Friedberger (chairman), Walter P. Rothenbush (vice-chairman), Ray D. Dorcey (secretary), Harry M. Herrmann (treasurer), Ivan Hoult, Eugene Allison, George D. Avery, C. W. Walsh, Law T. Freitas, Frank Piccardo, W. I. Neely, Ralph Mitscher, F. R. Fernando, W. A. Strong and L. Buol.

Subcommittee chairmen are: W. A. Strong (transportation), H. M. Herrmann (banquet), W. I. Neeley (housing), W. P. Rothenbush (grand ball), I. F. Hoult (music), L. T. Freitas (banquet entertainment), L. Buol (printing), R. D. Dorcey (registration), F. Piccardo (jinks), F. R. Fernando (badges), R. A. Mitscher and E. Allison (reception), C. W. Walsh (decorations), G. D. Avery (publicity).

Past Grand President Hubert R. McNoble, Warren A. Atherton and George A. Dietz compose the committee arranging for the Calaveras Big Trees outing. At the grove, characteristic Calaveras County hospitality will be dispensed by a committee composed of D. Fricat, C. T. Mills, G. H. Treat, D. W. Brice and H. Bardin. The San Andreas band will furnish music, and there will be some speakers. On the return trip places of historic interest will be visited, including Mercer Cave (Murphys), Moaning Cave (Vallecito), Double Springs, San Andreas and Angels Camp.

Stockton's Native Daughters have a joint committee assisting in arranging for the entertainment of the womenfolks: Joaquin Parlor No. 5—Vera Johnson, Nan Drais, Grace Bessac, Matty Porter, Katherine Wilson and Margaret Paxton. Caliz de Oro Parlor No. 206—Clarice Cook, Mura Day, Christine Neeley, Cathryn Wilde and Florence Carlson.

THE HOST PARLOR.

Stockton Parlor No. 7 was instituted March 12, 1881, by the then Grand President, Frank Higgins, now deceased. Three of the original fifteen charter members are still affiliated with the Parlor—Leroy S. Atwood, Ralph P. Lane and Frank E. Lane. In 1883, according to the "History of Stockton Parlor," the "prosperity and zeal of the Parlor attracting the attention of the Grand Parlor, Stockton was selected for the holding by the Order at large of the first general celebration of the anniversary of Admission Day. Curtis H. Lindley of this Parlor was elected Grand Marshal, and under his excellent management the celebration was made a grand success and an event in the history of the Order."

The Parlor moved into its present home, where it maintains lodge and club rooms, January 1, 1920. It has always taken an active interest in affairs of the Order and has joined heartily in all worthwhile civic undertakings,

RAY FRIEDBERGER,
Chairman General Committee.

HARRY HERRMANN,
Treasurer General Committee.

RAY DORCEY,
Secretary General Committee.
—Logan Photos, Stockton.

just recently making substantial donations to the Pioneer Museum and the kiddies' swimming pool at the Bret Harte preventorium. The present officers of Stockton Parlor are:

George D. Avery, president; Eugene Allison, junior past president; John D. Gallagher, first vice-president; Ben Waller, second vice-president; George Witherow, third vice-president; Ray D. Dorcey, recording secretary; Joel V. Beck Jr., financial secretary; George E. Catts, treasurer; Fred G. Krumb, marshal; R. A. Reid, W. I. Neeley, J. A. Fisher, trustees; M. O. Woods, inside sentinel; J. B. Sacco, outside sentinel; Glenn Kennedy, pianist; Drs. R. R. Hammond, L. M. Haight, S. W. R. Langdon, W. P. J. Lynch, G. J. Vischi, surgeons.

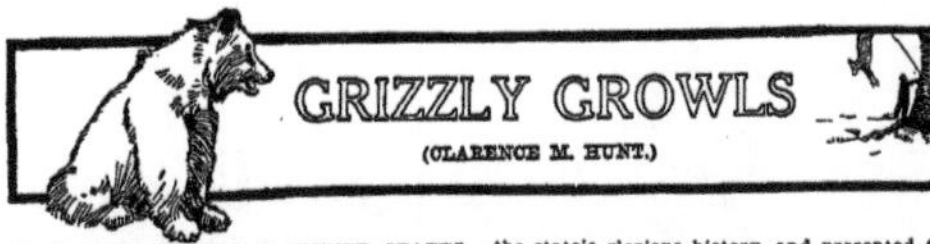

GRIZZLY GROWLS

(CLARENCE M. HUNT.)

SPEAKING BEFORE A UNITED STATES Senate committee the other day, Matthew Woll of the American Federation of Labor said, "Is it that we want revolution in this country? The remarkable thing to me is, that labor has been so calm, so conservative during the depression. But let that condition continue and I'll not venture to say what labor shall do."

Many men conversant with national conditions have hinted that a revolution is coming in this country unless the National Government legislates to relieve the masses. Dollar-relief has been extended the "financially-depressed" higherup moneykings who, through dishonest but within-the-law tactics brought on the depression, but naught but propaganda has been passed out to those in dire need—the common people.

Truly, unless there be an awakening and a change of policy in Washington, serious times, not that long-promised prosperity, are just around the corner!

Rear Admiral Yates Stirling of the United States Navy recently declared: "The large number of aliens in the Hawaiian Islands is a matter of grave concern to our National Government, and years of study by civilian, military and naval authorities of the probable attitude of certain island-born Orientals has led to the conclusion that but doubtful reliance can be placed upon their loyalty to the United States in event of war with an Oriental power." There is no doubt, whatever, that every Jap, irrespective of where he may have been born or where he may be hibernating, would be loyal first, last and always to Japan.

Representative Yamashiro, a Jap member of the Hawaiian Legislature, said the Admiral's doubts "give me a pain in my neck." It would be a glorious thing, indeed, if all the Japs in the United States and its possessions would become so generally afflicted with pain-in-the-neck that they would hasten to Japan for relief and permanent residence. This nation would be greatly relieved, and benefited, by the exodus.

In a decision rendered April 19, the California Supreme Court declared constitutional the state's public works alien employment act passed by the last Legislature.

That's fine! Now, the Order of Native Sons of the Golden West should "go to the bat" and see that the law is strictly and impartially enforced. The law itself is of no value, unless put into effect. Its enforcement will help mightily to clarify labor conditions in this state, and make it possible for a White citizen to secure employment.

This (May) issue is the three hundred and first number of The Grizzly Bear, the magazine having been published continuously since May 1907—a quarter-century. The Grizzly Bear has not achieved perfection—far from it. It has, however, in addition to publicizing the Orders of Native Sons and Native Daughters, featured the state's glorious history, and presented facts on important public questions for the enlightenment and the guidance of its readers. It has played no favorites, and has been influenced neither by the almightiness nor the lowliness of any individual or combination of individuals.

There is suspicion that the monkeywrench which gummed the machinery of the Los Angeles receivership-racket was the loaning of money to a couple of so-called men of the Gospel. Was someone "influenced" to pull that "boner?" Had not those gents been prominently mentioned, would the dailies have "spilled the beans?"

Reports "along the street" have it that the receivership-racket has been in vogue in Los Angeles for several years. Why not go back, say, five years, have a thorough and honest investigation, and see what and who can be uncovered?

There is an increasing demand for submission of the prohibition question to a national referendum, and it should be complied with. Then, if the majority vote to retain the law, the skyscraping hotel, as well as the cellar, speakeasies should be forced to respect it. The law can be enforced, if the powers-that-be choose to enforce it.

Motor-vehicle traffic deaths in California last year totaled 2,591—216 per month. In 1930, 2,384—198 per month. The slaughter goes on, and most of it is accomplished by drunken auto drivers. Every day this heading appears over a newspaper article: "Drunken Driver Given Probation." That accounts for the mounting death-figures, and there will be no lessening in the number of slaughtered until judges fearlessly and impartially enforce the traffic law and suspend the probation-practice.

A report to the United States Senate, April 4, on the social, economic and law-enforcement conditions in the Hawaiian Islands said: "We found a condition of inefficiency in the administration of justice which, in effect, constituted an invitation to the commission of crime."

The identical condition exists throughout the United States mainland, too,—inefficiency plus dishonesty. Administration of justice? It is to laugh! Justice is not possible of administration in a country which has enthroned dishonesty. First, get rid of the crooks—the dishonest in the governmental, the business, the professional and the social life of the nation—and then justice will prevail.

Registration in California's fifty-eight counties for the May 3 presidential primary totals 2,377,710, Los Angeles County alone being credited with 1,040,644 registered voters. The combined southern counties—Santa Barbara, Ventura, San Bernardino, Orange, Riverside, San Diego, Imperial, Kern, Inyo and Los Angeles—have a total registration of 1,367,673—more than one-half the state's total.

For the good of the nation and the state,—for your own good—get out and vote. Don't be a ballotbox slacker! Do your own thinking. Don't be misled by propaganda that fills the air and the daily press. Let your conscience be your only guide, and vote right!

June 16 has been proclaimed "California Farm Products Day." Why not a day for the relief of the suffering farmer who produces those products?

Influences in Washington are endeavoring to have the Federal Congress put off action on a bill, reported unanimously by the House Committee on Immigration, that further reduces the number of aliens admissible under existing quotas and applies quotas to all countries whose nationals are now admissible free of quotas. The pretext is advanced that, as few foreigners are coming in, the legislation is not necessary. The pretext is an insult to American intelligence!

Experience proves the legislation is necessary. Cheap alien labor, hired on arrival and fired when convenient, is always a heavy burden on the taxpayers. The country, and particularly California, is overloaded with that class of labor in flush-times, in order that certain interests may have cheap, newly-imported workers for their requirements, and then the balance of the taxbearers must, via the public-charity course, lug the burden along when those laborers are discharged. A leaky roof should be repaired when it is not raining! Now is the time to enact this needed relief measure, known as House Bill No. 10602.

Millions of dollars to help meet the national treasury deficit could be harvested if the Federal Government would eliminate from the income-tax law the provision exempting employes of The People from payment of the tax. There is no reason whatever, except political, why all such, elective or appointive, should not pay the tax. They are regularly well paid, are not bowed down with dollar-raising worries and have the protection of government. Why should they, or any other class of citizens, be exempt?

Anent the agitation for bonus payments now by the Federal Government to war veterans, Willard Straight Post, New York, last month made public this telegram, sent to the national commander of the American Legion:

"We demand discontinuance of Washington lobby and all attempts to coerce Congress to vote additional billions and special privileges which will thereby degrade patriotism of war service, imperil government finances, gouge taxpayers and make the word 'veteran' synonymous with panhandler and grafter."

"Undoubtedly, 'Grizzly Growls' in April strikes home to many a heart," says a Los Angeles reader of The Grizzly Bear, and she then asks, "Are none of us to escape the heavy hand of the money power?" In answer, these words of Gerald Massey:

"O men, bowed down with labor,
O women, young, yet old,
O hearts, oppressed in the toilers' breast,
And crushed with the power of gold;
Keep on, with your weary struggle,
Against triumphant might;
No question is ever settled
Until it is settled right."

What the country needs most, is fewer damphool laws and more equity—correction of the many deficiencies in sane laws.

The California Council on Oriental Relations, composed of yellow-dollar worshipers, has agents in the field advocating the quota for Orientals. Keep your eye on that outfit!

The United States Supreme Court April 11 rendered a decision of vast importance to California investors who lost heavily through the wrecking—from the inside, by crooked officials,—of many financial enterprises.

The court holds that creditors have valid claims against the directors and the stockholders of all such concerns existent prior to the repeal,

(Continued on Supplement 8)

DORMIDERA

(MINNA McGARVEY.)

The early Californians
In their soft, poetic tongue,
Gave a name to our golden poppy,
Lovely as ever sung.

All day it paints the valleys
And the hills with leafy gold,
But at darkening hint of sundown,
Dreaming, the petals fold.

Sweet sleepy-head of flowers
When the slanting shadows creep!
Called, caressingly, Dormidera,
"Drowsy One" curled in sleep.

(This contribution to The Grizzly Bear is from Mrs. Minna McGarvey of Los Angeles City.—Editor.)

THINK THIS OVER!

The order of Native Sons of the Golden West is, we believe, with the exception of the Order of Native Daughters of the Golden West, the only organization that limits membership exclusively to NATIVE-BORN AMERICANS.

Knowing the serious conditions in this country today, this fact alone should impel every Native Son of California to immediately SEEK AFFILIATION with that American-born and American-operated institution, the man-power and wealth of which are pledged to the protection of American institutions in times of peace as well as in times of war.

THE ROMANCE OF SAN BERNARDINO

Clara M. Barton

(Continued from April Issue.)

"LISTEN, YOU MEN," DEMANDED CAPtain Jefferson Hunt, "you must take my advice. I want at least 150 able-bodied men who are capable of performing a good service, know how to handle a gun and are not afraid to fight, to help me organize a military company. The object is to be prepared to squelch the anger of the Indians. Uncle Grief, our respected colored man, has a large tin horn and has promised to use it as a bugle for giving signals. Are you in favor of the action?" "Aye, aye, sir!" answered a half-hundred voices. Captain Hunt smiled. "You fellows sound like a bunch of sailors on a heavy sea!"

Though elaborate preparations had been made, the Indians made no attack, much to the disappointment of some of the colonists, who had hoped to experience the thrill of an Indian onslaught. For one year the colonists lived happily within the walls of the fort. Then Lyman and Rich decided to make some improvements. The fort was taken down, bit by bit, and the logs, adobe bricks and other building materials were used for the construction of stores, houses and barns.

"It is too bad to destroy such a pretentious fort, but I feel that we need have no more fear of the enemy, and it would be unwise to let the fort material decay and become useless," remarked Rich, and the men all agreed.

Bishop Tenny, an active member of the Lyman caravan, located in the old mission building, and he, with several others of the Lyman and Rich wagon trains, constructed a serviceable irrigation ditch, named Tenny ditch. "The water must come from the Mill Creek zanja," said Tenny, "as that creek seems to have the most water at this time of year." "Yes," remarked Lyman, "and too, this ought to be the foundation of the water system for future generations."

Captain Hunt was delegated to command men of the colony who were to build a road up West Twin Creek Canyon, now known as Waterman Canyon, in order to reach the timber lands. A few months later Captain Hunt was supervising the construction of three sawmills. These supplied the lumber for the Mormons' houses. During the latter part of 1852 a large flourmill was built, and this was the producing center of flour for many years.

When the Mormon colonists received the grant of San Bernardino from the Lugos in 1852, the property was in Los Angeles County, and in 1853 Captain Hunt was delegated by Lyman and Rich to represent Los Angeles County in the State Legislature.

"The settlement of San Bernardino is a thriving one, but we are so far away from the county seat that many of the people want the county divided. We desire to be in a county of our own," Captain Hunt told the legislators. Soon afterward the separation was made, the county being divided and the boundaries marked and approved.

"This county is now the largest in the world," said Rich. "Yes?" asked a doubting Los Angeles County representative. "Certainly," answered the captain. "We are owning 23,472 square miles, 200 miles from east to west and 150 miles from north to south. We should be in line with the best overland routes."

Early in 1853 the Mormons decided that since San Bernardino was separated from Los Angeles, it was time to lay out a lasting settlement. Plans were drawn, but none seemed suitable. "Let's get H. G. Sherwood here from Salt Lake. He can help us, as he laid out Salt Lake," said Rich.

Sherwood was soon drawing the plat of the town. Because of its location, the situations of the buildings and the size and shape of the cultivated lands, the town was laid out in a most perfect square. It was one mile square, containing eight acres, and was laid out in blocks with wide streets running at right angles. Both Lyman and Rich looked at this new sight with pride. They had conquered the winter rains, and the settlement itself was already attracting members of other wagon trains.

The first public building to be erected was the Council House, constructed by Lyman and Rich. It was used as a general office of all Mormon interests, both religious and secular. It boasted of one room below and one above, and a wicker fence surrounded it. But as the ground settled the walls began to crack and the interior became badly damaged. Braces were set against the walls and every precaution was taken to avert damage from weather conditions.

"Father, we simply must have a house to live in. I'm tired of the condition we are now in," said Mrs. Lyman number one, and the other four wives nodded in approval. "I'm sorry, and I shall do all I can to relieve your situation," replied Lyman. Soon afterward he and his five loyal wives were comfortably domiciled in the first two-story adobe house. Happiness once more reigned for his family.

But his pride and joy was a young son, born to his wife Priscilla. He was the first White child born in the valley, and was duly named Lorenzo Snow Lyman. Priscilla and the boy had the privilege of residing in their choice of the house which, for the convenience of the other wives, had been partitioned into various rooms known as apartments. The kitchen and diningroom, however, were together. The wives disapproved of the arrangement, so remained in their own apartments. The house had no windows, but the sun-rays came through a skylight. Lyman had worked out his plans and had the place built beside that of the Council House. The home was soon destroyed by fire.

Charles Rich looked at his partner, Amasa Lyman, with envious eyes. "Mind if I build a house like yours for my family?" asked Rich. "Why not, brother?" answered Lyman. In time Rich had his three wives comfortably settled in a four-room house and the occupants were more than satisfied with the arrangements.

"It will soon be the Fourth of July, Charley, do you realize that?" said Lyman to Rich as they were overlooking their settlement. "How time does fly!" answered Rich. "What are we going to do to celebrate it, brother Amasa?" "We ought to get some one to help us. I wonder if John Brown Senior can handle it." "Don't see why he couldn't," and the two men strode over to the Council House to interview Brown.

After listening to the plans of both men, Brown agreed to accept the responsibility and proceeded to go to Fort Tejon to secure the American Flag from the platoon stationed there. On his return a platform was built of logs, and a huge pole was made from an arm of a large cedar-pine tree. Extensive preparations were made, and soon everyone was prepared to celebrate the first Fourth of July in the settlement of San Bernardino.

The Mormons soon discovered a controversy in which they were playing a prominent part. The Gentiles were arriving! Because these newcomers did not understand the religion of the Mormons, considerable hard feeling grew out of the existing conditions.

"We must curtail these people's feelings at once!" said Rich. "We cannot let our lives and their lives become a disagreeable affair, while we are all together. We must live in harmony." "There is Ambrose Hunt, Brother Charles," said Amasa Lyman. "Why cannot we have Hunt buy from us some of our land? It seems to be the only solution for this disturbance." "I don't think the elders will allow it, but it will do no harm to ask them."

The feeling between the two parties had now become so strong a small battle raged, but with no casualties. Jerome Bensom, once an active member of the Mormons, left the church and decided to attend to some of the affairs of the other side. He was said to be the direct cause of the miniature uprising between the Mormons and the Independents. However, a fort was built southeast of the town and named after him.

The character of the Mormons, who were largely responsible for the laying out of the city and the county, was peaceful, industrious, sincere and earnest, and they were loyal to their beliefs. Their hearty co-operation with every undertaking was in strong contrast to the attitude of the shiftless and prejudiced people. In the six years they had been living in the settlement, prior to their recall to Salt Lake, they had constructed two schoolrooms, the Council House, several store buildings, a flourmill, three sawmills, irrigation ditches and good dirt roads, and had developed domestic water. They had brought a large portion of the 36,000 acres under cultivation. Lyman and Rich worked hard, and were successful in establishing a pony route and stageline between San Bernardino and Los Angeles. The Mormons proved that small farms were profitable, and the Gentiles soon became convinced that the Mormons had paved the way for something that was soon to develop into a new territory.

Jefferson Hunt has been called the pioneer of the Mormon settlement and the father of San Bernardino County. He was captain of the Mormon battalion, and had made two trips from Salt Lake to Southern California. It was he who guided the Mormon colonists into the valley and gave worthwhile advice to Lyman and Rich in their construction of the colony. He took a very prominent part in the building of the fort and was the leader of their military organization. Under his capable direction the road through Waterman Canyon to the timber district was constructed, and he was the owner of the first sawmill. Soon after his arrival in the valley, Hunt was successful in securing a contract from the county to carry mail from Los Angeles to

(Continued on Supplement 8)

"THE OLD RANCHER" BRINGS EARLY-DAY THRILLS INTO CALIFORNIA HOMES.

Of particular interest to all Native Sons and Daughters is the new series of radio programs, "Historical Southern California," being presented by the Pacific Electric Railway and Motor Transit Stages of Los Angeles. These programs, formerly broadcast at 6:45 p.m. Thursdays and 7:30 p. m. Sundays, are now presented Tuesdays and Fridays from 8:30 to 9 p. m.

"Historical Southern California" consists of dramatic re-enactments, in music and story, of the most exciting and important episodes in the history of Southern California. Actual occurrences are used as the basis for the dramas, so that in everything except actual dialogue, of which there remains no record, the episodes are entirely accurate historically. Dialogue is written by Dick Creedon.

"THE OLD RANCHER."

To set the stage for the action and provide transition from scene to scene, the stories are presented as reminiscences of "The Old Rancher," a role played by Harold DeBray, a native of Monrovia, California, who knows and loves the southland and its romantic history. It is said that in all his years of stage experience, DeBray has never played a role for which he was more ideally suited than "The Old Rancher."

The endeavor of the sponsors is to combine genuine entertainment with historical value. Among the subjects already treated are the founding of Los Angeles, Pasadena and San Bernardino, the landing of Joseph Chapman, the first California gold discovery (in Placerita Canyon), the Warner vs. Chapo legal case, the Irving affair, and others. Whenever a story is logically connected with a present-day community, either through geographical locale or subject matter, the broadcast is dedicated to that city.

Programs are under the joint direction of Paul Rickenbacker and Seymour Hastings, representing the sponsors. The entire KHJ staff is employed, including Raymond Paige and his orchestra, Elvia Allman, Vera Van, George Gramlich, Robert Swan, Charles Forsythe, Lindsay McHarrie and other artists as required. The sponsors of the programs welcome suggestions and constructive criticism from Native Sons and Daughters, and urge all members to tune in each Tuesday and Friday night at 8:30.

GRIZZLY GROWLS

(Continued from Supplement 6)

in November 1930, of Section 1, Article XII of the California State Constitution. In other words, the repeal was not retroactive. Perhaps, therefore, some of the many millions lost by innocent investors may be recovered.

Here's good news: An announcement of the Federal Labor Department women's bureau says married women are not employed as new teachers in 77 percent of 1,500 American city school systems. All of California's cities should be included among the number.

Only 37 percent of the cities permit single women teachers to continue teaching after marriage, while more than one-half of the remaining 63 percent require the teachers to resign at once if they marry. Get the married women with able-bodied husbands out of the schools and other endeavors and there will be fewer childless homes, fewer delinquent minors and fewer divorces.

Declaring "concentrated wealth" has resulted from "control of government" exercised by the nation's richest men, Governor Gifford Pinchot of Pennsylvania declared in a recent Cleveland, Ohio, address that he has faith that the American people, "who have the power to set things right but do not use it," are getting ready to act. They should waste no more valuable time getting ready, but act now!

In the United States Senate last month, Senator William E. Borah of Idaho gave figures showing that Great Britain's armament outlay last year was $678,000,000, France's $517,000,000 and Italy's $348,000,000. "From these," he declared, "it is plain that Europe is more completely armed than she has been at any time since the armistice with Germany was signed." And yet, a moratorium on behalf of those countries was forced through the Federal Congress by the national administration—at the expense, as usual, of the American taxpayers.

Senator Hiram W. Johnson of California, speaking on the budget, made reference to that moratorium and read a recent statement by a New York financier,—one of the "big boys"—advocating cancellation of those foreign governments' debts to this nation in order that their debts to private interests here might be paid. Senator Johnson said:

"Talk of the terrific fix we are in! Tell us we cannot balance the budget! And then in the very beginning of the year, when the thing is obvious and known, give $250,000,000 to Europe that is paid to international bankers on short-term credit. And get ready, as I believe those who are in control of us are getting ready, to give another moratorium of $275,000,000 in the middle of this year,—$520,000,000 in all. April 5, Britain paid $200,000,000 on the big loan received previously from American bankers. It was repaid before it came due. Repaid to whom? Why, repaid of course to our masters, [a nationally known banking concern]. What we forget in all this talk of debt cancellation and reduction is that every penny lost in the process has to be made up by American taxpayers. Every dollar of it. Remember that!"

According to a report of the state controller, the bonded debt of the state, the county and the municipal governments of California totaled, at the close of the June 30, 1931, fiscal year, $876,278,331—$154.35 percapita. This is an increase over the previous fiscal year of $35,971,965. During the past ten years, while property values have increased but 89 percent, the bonded debt has advanced 172 percent.

It is about time the people of California stopped mortgaging the state's future! Any and every bond proposition submitted should be swatted by the taxpayers, until complete recovery from the spending orgy promoted by interests which wax rich from bond issues.

Big financial institutions apparently are using the Reconstruction Finance Corporation Act to take money from the Federal Treasury to pay off their own loans, declared United States Senator Arthur Capper of Kansas in a radio broadcast April 5. "It seems to me," he said, "that the Congress has been deceived and the country has been betrayed by powerful banking interests working through the Reconstruction Finance Corporation." His suspicions are probably well founded, for the "powerful banking interests" have had much experience along those lines.

Senator Capper referred particularly to the "loan" made the Missouri Pacific railroad, and continued: "The Reconstruction Finance Corporation reached into the Federal Treasury and gave these [three financial institutions which he named] banking firms dollars worth at least 30 percent more in purchasing power than the dollars they had lent the Missouri Pacific in the first place. This in addition to the interest they received on the loans."

From February 2 to April 19 the Reconstruction Finance Corporation authorized loans aggregating $370,437,802 to 1,757 institutions; in the same period, repayments totaled $11,384,263. The Corporation is authorized to loan $2,000,000,000—of The People's money. As security, it accepts the paper of the borrowers, mostly "big financial institutions." What percentage of the loans will be repaid, dollar for dollar, in coin of the realm? Is the way being paved for yet another moratorium, distant from three to five years, to further relieve the masters, the international bankers, and further distress the slaves, the common people?

BOOK REVIEWS

(CLARENCE M. HUNT.)

"THE VISIT OF THE 'RURIK' TO SAN FRANCISCO IN 1816."

By August C. Mahr; Stanford University Press, Publisher, Stanford University, California; Price, $1.50 Paper, $2.00 Cloth.

This highly interesting publication deals with the visit of the little Russian brig, "Rurik," in the Bay of San Francisco, from October 2 to November 1 of 1816. The vessel was in command of Lieutenant Otto von Kotzebue, and Adelbert von Chamisso, familiar to the lover of German romantic literature and to the student of botanical taxonomy, was the "naturalist of the expedition." The voyage of the "Rurik" was a scientific expedition with the double purpose of exploring certain parts of the South Sea and of investigating the possibility of a northeast passage through Bering Strait into the Arctic Sea and thence into the Atlantic.

Author Mahr, professor of German at the Ohio State University, aptly describes the work: "This book is intended for everybody interested in the past of California in general and that of the city of San Francisco in particular. The reader will find it to be a collective travel-diary, containing the impressions which a group of intelligent travelers received from a visit to the Spanish mission and military post of San Francisco in the year 1816. Moreover, it embodies the results of their scientific investigation of the region visited and includes the various documents which their Spanish hosts considered advisable to file in the California archives with regard to the foreign guests. In order to facilitate the use of the book, a new English translation or a previously printed one has been added to each contribution originally written in German, French, Spanish, or Latin."

The volume has several most valuable illustrations, reproductions from the lithographs made for Louis Choris' "Voyage Pittoresque Autour du Monde," Paris, 1822. The frontispiece, "Eschscholtzia Californica," is a reproduction of the first picture ever drawn of a California poppy; the original accompanied Chamisso's first description of that flower in "Horae Physicae Berolinenses," Bonnae, 1820. Then there is a "View of the Presidio of San Francisco in 1816," and also a drawing of "Ursus Griseus," the grizzly bear of North America.

"THE MISSION OF SAN ANTONIO DE PADUA"

By Frances Rand Smith; Stanford University Press, Publisher, Stanford University, California; Price $3.50.

San Antonio de Padua, near Jolon, Monterey County, is the third oldest in the chain of California's Franciscan missions; it was founded July 14, 1771. The book reviews early explorations in the region, the establishment of the mission, its change of location and its subsequent history. For the first time, the mission's distinctive type of architecture and its system of irrigation are analyzed. The legend of an Indian woman, Agueda, is also presented. The book is extensively illustrated.

THE ROMANCE

(Continued from Supplement 7)

Salt Lake, and this soon led to other important mail contracts throughout the state.

Captain Hunt was born in Kentucky in 1805 and was married to Miss Celia Mount in 1853. Both were baptised into the Mormon church soon after their marriage. When the Mormon battalion was organized, Hunt and his two sons, Gilbert and Marshall, were among the first to enlist and they soon became active in military activities in the Mormon city. This led them to the rancho of San Bernardino, and soon afterward they bought much stock and land from the Lugos.

Captain Jefferson Hunt was a man of strong character and very sincere in his beliefs. He was fitted to be a leader, because of his level-headedness, clear-sightedness and strong will. He filled a large place in the early and the late history of San Bernardino. He died at Oxford, Idaho, in the spring of 1866. Mrs. Hunt survived him, but passed away in 1897 at the home of her daughter. Captain Hunt had eleven children. Eighty-nine grandchildren, one hundred forty-nine great-grandchildren and seventy-nine great-great-grandchildren are his descendants.

It was through Captain Jefferson Hunt's civic activities and pride in the valley that wagon trains from the other states were attracted, and it was through his efforts that San Bernardino had its streets named after the Pioneers and the mother Mormon city. The foundation of the city, laid by him, is a solid one.

(Continued in JUNE Issue)

Subscription Order Blank

For Your Convenience

Grizzly Bear Magazine,
309-15 Wilcox Bldg.,
206 South Spring St.,
Los Angeles, California.

For the enclosed remittance of $1.50 enter my subscription to The Grizzly Bear Magazine for one year.

Name..............................

Street Address..............................

City or Town..............................

Passing of the California Pioneer

(Confined to Brief Notices of the Demise of Those Men and Women Who Came to California Prior to 1860.)

MRS. LEUTITIA LARISSA KILGORE-Beckley, native of Iowa, 83; with her parents crossed the plains to California in 1850 and practically ever since had resided in Colusa County; died at Grimes, survived by three sons.

Mrs. Priscilla Hale-Pendegast, native of Missouri, 82; with her parents, the late Jesse and Sarah A. Clark, crossed the plains in 1852; died at Los Angeles City, her home for thirty-seven years, survived by two sons, Lyle (Ramona Parlor No. 109 N.S.G.W.) and Ernest Pendegast.

Mrs. Sarah Jane Theobald-Macy, native of Missouri, 83; crossed the plains in 1852 and settled in Sacramento County; died at Sacramento City, survived by four children.

Charles Harris, native of Illinois, 83; came in 1852; died at San Francisco. He was an old-time printer, and for several years published the "Mariposa Gazette" and the "Merced Weekly Star."

Mrs. Lucy Poor-Hoxsie, native of Ohio, 85; came in 1852 and settled in Sacramento County; died at Mormon Island, survived by two sons.

Mrs. Mary Jane Cravens, native of New York; crossed the plains in 1852 and settled in Placer County; died at Sacramento City, survived by a daughter.

Joseph Marion Moore, native of Arkansas, 80; crossed the plains in 1853 and long resided in Butte County; died at Magalia, survived by a wife and six children.

Mrs. Emma Harris-Dill, native of Wisconsin, 81; crossed the plains in 1853 and resided in El Dorado and San Joaquin Counties; died near Clements, survived by six children.

Mrs. Edna Ladd-Kingsley, native of New York, 89; came across the plains in 1853; died at San Francisco, survived by four children. Her father, the late Harvey C. Ladd, built in 1855 the Point Loma lighthouse, off San Diego.

Mrs. Margaret Chandler, born in 1854 while her parents were enroute across the plains, died at San Diego City; she long resided in Humboldt and San Mateo Counties.

Junior Baker Booth, 89; came via the Isthmus of Panama in 1854 and long resided in Stanislaus and Tuolumne Counties; died at Uplands, San Bernardino County, survived by five children.

Mrs. Mary McGhee-Lessley, born in 1854 while her parents were enroute across the plains, died at Oakland, Alameda County; eleven children survive. She resided many years in Amador County.

Mrs. Hannah Young-Larson, native of Maine, 100; came via Cape Horn in 1858; died at Santa Cruz City, survived by six children.

Albert J. Look, native of Michigan, 83; came in 1857 and for a half-century resided in Humboldt County; died at Bell, Los Angeles County, survived by four children.

Allen A. Curtis, native of Iowa, 78; came in 1857; died at Thompson Flat, Butte County, survived by four children.

Mrs. Margaret Fortna-Hicok, native of Missouri, 73; as a three-months-old babe came via the Isthmus of Panama in 1859; died at Colusa City, survived by two children.

James McGlynn, native of Ireland, 91; came in 1858; died at San Jose, Santa Clara County, survived by a wife and eight children.

George E. Lewis, native of Kentucky, 75; came across the plains in 1859 and resided for some time in Yuba County; died at Lompoc, Santa Barbara County, survived by a wife and live children.

John Holt, native of England, 93; came in 1858 and settled in Placer County; died at Roseville.

William Jaspar Ford, native of Missouri, 90; came in 1859; died at San Leandro, Alameda County, survived by a wife and six children. He long resided in Yolo and Colusa Counties.

Fred N. Beal, native of Massachusetts, 74; since 1859 a resident of Calaveras County; died at Paloma, survived by a wife and a daughter.

OLD TIMERS PASS

(Brief Notices of the Demise of Men and Women who came to California in the '60s.)

Frank D. Kollenberg, native of Illinois, 77; came in 1860; died at Visalia, Tulare County, survived by two children.

Mrs. Mary Catherine Smith, native of Wisconsin, 83; came in 1860; died at Stillwater, Shasta County, survived by six children.

Ellsworth Benton Jolley, native of Ohio, 87; came in 1861; died at Merced City, survived by a daughter. For many years he operated a chain of freight wagons in the Mother Lode section.

H. J. Klenzendorf, native of Germany, 85; came in 1862 and settled in Yuba County; died at Nevada City, survived by a wife and two sons.

John Alexander, native of Kentucky, 91; since 1863 Solano County resident; died at Fairfield, survived by a son.

Thomas Derby, native of New York, 89; since 1864 Santa Clara County resident; died at San Jose, survived by two sons.

Mrs. Emma K. Allardt, native of Ohio, 87; came in 1865; died at Oakland, Alameda County, survived by a daughter.

Richard Murphy, native of Ireland, 88; came in 1865; died at Fresno City.

Mrs. Caroline Struckmeyer-Dibble, native of Germany; since 1865 resident San Francisco, where she died; a daughter survives.

Andrew Joughin, native of Illinois, 75; since 1866 resident Los Angeles City, where he died; a wife and a daughter survive.

John W. Wells, native of Illinois, 87; since 1867 Sacramento County resident; died at Sacramento City, survived by seven children.

Mrs. Mary Pitman-Sergeant, native of Florida, 72; came in 1867; died at Monrovia, Los Angeles County, survived by a husband and two sons.

Mrs. Meta Kroenke, native of Germany, 87; came in 1867; died at Saint Helena, Napa County, survived by five children.

Mrs. Mary Elizabeth Shields, native of Illinois, 81; came in 1867 and resided in Glenn and Butte Counties; died at Glenn Town, survived by five children.

Dr. Robert Fulton Winchester, native of Maine, 86; came in 1868; died at Santa Barbara City.

Mrs. Sarah Frances Worthington, native of Texas, 72; since 1868 resident Los Angeles City, where she died; a husband survives.

Philip Morse, native of Maine, 87; since 1869 resident San Diego City, where he died; a wife and a son survive.

Mrs. Nancy Mains-Elworthy, native of Maine; came in 1869 and long resided in Sacramento City; died at Berkeley, Alameda County, survived by five children.

George Alexander Minaker, native of Canada, 80; since 1869 Contra Costa County resident; died at Pittsburg, survived by a wife and four children.

Mrs. Lois Acelia Knapp-Perry, native of New York, 75; came in 1868; died at Corte Madera, Marin County, survived by a husband and a daughter.

George M. Francis, native of Michigan, 87; came in 1869; died at Napa City, survived by a son. For many years he edited the "Napa Register."

John E. Edwards, native of Australia, 69; came in 1864; died at Lemoore, Kings County.

PIONEER NATIVES DEAD

(Brief Notices of the Demise of Men and Women born in California Prior to 1860.)

John White, born in Del Norte County in 1858, died recently at Crescent City survived by three children.

Mrs. Mary Tackett-Meany, born in Tuolumne County in 1857, died at Merced City recently survived by a son.

Edwin A. Light, born in Humboldt County in 1850, died at Arcata March 18 survived by a wife and three daughters.

Alexander Peter Martel, born in El Dorado County in 1854, died at Palo Alto, Santa Clara County, March 19 survived by a wife and two children. He was affiliated with Quartz Parlor No. 58 N.S.G.W. (Grass Valley).

Frank W. Lowden, born in Trinity County in 1859, died at Hayfork March 19 survived by three children.

Frank E. Brigham, born at San Francisco in 1857, died at Oakland, Alameda County, March 22 survived by a wife and three children.

James M. Morrison, born in Yuba County in 1857, died at Sacramento City March 22 survived by a wife and three children.

Mrs. Amanda Babcock-Shelton, born in Sonoma County in 1856, died in Potter Valley, Siskiyou County, March 23 survived by six children.

William H. Blakely, born in Amador County in 1857, died at Ione March 23 survived by a wife and three children.

Mrs. Marie Carmen Bejar-Peters, born at Los Angeles City in 1850, died at Santa Barbara City March 24 survived by seven children.

Frank K. Millington, born at Alameda City in 1855, died there March 24 survived by a wife and a daughter.

Mrs. Laura Wells-Lorensen, born in Sonoma County in 1859, died at Hayward, Alameda County, March 24 survived by a husband.

Edward H. Hamilton, born at San Jose, Santa Clara County, in 1859, died at San Francisco March 25. He was one of the state's best-known newspapermen.

Mrs. Jessie Penwell-Pond, born in Napa County in 1859, died near Calistoga March 29 survived by a husband and three children.

Martin A. Schellhouse, born in Placer County in 1858, died March 29 at Roseville.

Mrs. Millie Scott-Biven, born at San Francisco in 1855, died at Oakland, Alameda County, March 30 survived by four children.

George Aschenauer, born in Sacramento County in 1857, died at Marysville, British Columbia, March 31.

Thomas J. Shay, born in Los Angeles County in 1857, died at San Bernardino City March 31 survived by a wife and six children. He

(Continued on Page 20)

Official Directory of Parlors of the N. S. G. W

ALAMEDA COUNTY.

Alameda No. 47, Alameda City—Gus Nelson, Pres.; Robt. H. Cavanaugh, Sec., 1806 Pacific Ave.; Wednesdays, Native Sons Hall, 1406 Park St.

Oakland No. 50, Oakland—A. W. Ainger, Pres.; F. M. Norris, Sec., 4280 Terrace St.; Fridays, Native Sons Hall, 11th and Clay Sts.

Las Positas No. 96, Livermore—R. J. Ruetz, Pres.; John J. Kelly, Sec., P. O. box 341; Thursdays, Foresters Hall.

Eden No. 113, Hayward—Henry L'Ecuyer, Pres.; Stanton R. Soares, Sec., P. O. box 176; 2nd and 4th Tuesdays, Memorial Hall, Main St.

Piedmont No. 120, Oakland—Walter M. Davis, Pres.; Charles Morando, Sec., 906 Vermont St.; Thursdays, Native Sons Hall, 11th and Clay Sts.

Wisteria No. 127, Alvarado—Henry May, Pres.; J. M. Scribner, Sec., Livermore; 1st Thursday, I.O.O.F. Hall.

Halcyon No. 146, Alameda City—Charles J. Von Tagen, Pres.; J. C. Bates, Sec., 2139 Buena Vista Ave.; 1st and 3rd Tuesdays, I.O.O.F. Hall, 2329 Santa Clara Ave.

Brooklyn No. 151, Oakland—Frank B. Perry, Pres.; E. W. Cooney, Sec., 3907 14th Ave.; Wednesdays, Masonic Temple, 8th Ave. and E. 14th St.

Washington No. 169, Centerville—M. B. Silva, Pres.; Allen G. Norris, Sec., P. O. box 31; 2nd and 4th Tuesdays, Hansen Hall.

Athens No. 195, Oakland—Henry G. Kroeckel, Pres.; Harold B. Farley, Sec., 4623 Benevides Ave.; Tuesdays, Native Sons Hall, 11th and Clay Sts.

Berkeley No. 210, Berkeley—S. Levy, Pres.; R. J. Garrett, Sec., 1708 Virginia St.; Tuesdays, Native Sons Hall, 2108 Shattuck Ave.

Estudillo No. 223, San Leandro—Frank V. Pacheco, Pres.; Albert G. Pacheco, Sec., 1736 E. 14th St.; 1st and 3rd Tuesdays, U.P.E.C. Hall.

Claremont No. 240, Oakland—Fred Buelna, Pres.; E. N. Thienger, Sec., 839 Hearst Ave., Berkeley; Tuesdays, Veterans Memorial Bldg., 43rd & Salem Sts., Emeryville.

Pleasanton No. 244, Pleasanton—Peter C. Madsen, Pres.; Ernest W. Schween, Sec.; 2nd and 4th Thursdays, I.O.O.F. Hall.

Niles No. 250, Niles—M. L. Fournier, Pres.; C. E. Martenstein, Sec.; 2nd Thursday, I.O.O.F. Hall.

Fruitvale No. 252, Oakland—Chester B. Abernethy, Pres.; Ray B. Felton, Sec., 1575 Alice St.; Fridays, W.O.W. Hall, 3256 E. 14th St.

AMADOR COUNTY.

Amador No. 17, Sutter Creek—Frank Marre, Pres.; F. J. Payne, Sec.; 1st and 3rd Fridays, Native Sons Hall.

Excelsior No. 31, Jackson—Wm. Daugherty, Pres.; William Going, Sec.; 1st and 3rd Wednesdays, Native Sons Hall, 22 Court St.

Ione No. 33, Ione—Marvin Kidd, Pres.; Josiah H. Saunders, Sec.; 1st and 3rd Wednesdays, Native Sons Hall.

Plymouth No. 48, Plymouth—L. E. Houston, Pres.; Thos. D. Davis, Sec.; 1st and 3rd Saturdays, I.O.O.F. Hall.

BUTTE COUNTY.

Argonaut No. 8, Oroville—Thomas R. Cole, Pres.; Cyril R. Macdonald, Sec., P. O. box 502; 1st and 3rd Wednesdays, Veterans Memorial Hall.

Chico No. 21, Chico—Marcus Choisser, Pres.; Sam Lindsay Adams, Sec., Sacramento Blvd.; 2nd and 4th Thursdays, Elks Hall.

CALAVERAS COUNTY.

Chispa No. 139, Murphys—John Voitich, Pres.; Antone Malaspina, Sec.; Wednesdays, Native Sons Hall.

COLUSA COUNTY.

Colusa No. 69, Colusa City—Burton L. Smart, Pres.; Phil J. Humburg, Sec., 223 Parkhill St.; Tuesdays, Eagles Hall.

CONTRA COSTA COUNTY.

General Winn No. 32, Antioch—Edmont T. Uren, Pres.; Joel H. Ford, Sec., P. O. box 311; 2nd and 4th Wednesdays, Union Hall.

Mount Diablo No. 101, Martinez—R. P. Anderson, Pres.; G. T. Barkley, Sec.; 1st and 3rd Mondays, I.O.O.F. Hall.

Byron No. 170, Byron—William E. Bunn, Pres.; H. G. Krumland, Sec.; 1st and 3rd Tuesdays, I.O.O.F. Hall.

Carquinez No. 205, Crockett—Thos. Cox, Pres.; Thomas I. Cahalan, Sec.; 1st and 3rd Wednesdays, I.O.O.F. Hall.

Richmond No. 217, Richmond—M. W. Amaral, Pres.; H. D. Mason, Sec., 11 6th St.; Wednesdays, Redmen Hall, 11th and Nevan Ave.

Concord No. 245, Concord—P. M. Soto, Pres.; D. E. Pramberg, Sec., P. O. box 235; 1st Tuesday, I.O.O.F. Hall.

Diamond No. 246, Pittsburg—Victor Ericsson, Pres.; Francis A. Irving, Sec., 248 E. 5th St.; 1st and 3rd Wednesdays, Veterans Memorial Bldg.

EL DORADO COUNTY.

Placerville No. 9, Placerville—George M. Smith, Pres.; Duncan Bathurst, Sec., 12 Gilmore St.; 2nd and 4th Tuesdays, Masonic Hall.

Georgetown No. 91, Georgetown—W. H. Breedlove, Pres.; C. F. Irish, Sec.; 2nd and 4th Wednesdays, I.O.O.F. Hall.

FRESNO COUNTY.

Fresno No. 25, Fresno City—A. G. Miller, Pres.; John W. Cappleman, Sec., 1389 Wilson; 2nd and 4th Fridays, W.O.W. Hall, 1354 Van Ness Ave.

Selma No. 107, Selma—Chester E. Shepard, Pres.; E. C. Laughlin, Sec.; 1st and 3rd Wednesdays, American Legion Hall.

GRAND OFFICERS.

John T. Newell.................Junior Past Grand President
2666 Benedict, Los Angeles

Dr. Frank I. Gonzalez.................Grand President
Flood Bldg., San Francisco

Seth Millington.................Grand First Vice-pres.
Gridley

Justice Emmet Seawell.................Grand Second Vice-pres.
State Bldg., San Francisco

Chas. A. Koenig.................Grand Third Vice-pres.
531 35th Ave., San Francisco

John T. Regan.................Grand Secretary
N.S.G.W. Bldg., 414 Mason St., San Francisco

John A. Corotto.................Grand Treasurer
560 No. 5th St., San Jose

Horace J. Leavitt.................Grand Marshal
Weaverville

W. B. O'Brien.................Grand Inside Sentinel
2324 Santa Clara St., Alameda

Gam Hurst.................Grand Outside Sentinel
1400 Financial Center Bldg., Oakland

Leslie Maloche.................Grand Organist
467½ 3rd St., San Bernardino

George H. Barron.................Historiographer
333 12th Ave., San Francisco

GRAND TRUSTEES

George F. McNoble.................California Bldg., Stockton
Samuel M. Shortridge Jr.................Menlo Park
Jesse H. Miller.................712 DeYoung Bldg., San Francisco
Joseph J. McShane.................419 Flood Bldg., San Francisco
Frank M. Lane.................333 Blackstone, Fresno
John M. Burnett.................San Jose
Eldred L. Meyer.................922 San Vincente, Santa Monica

HUMBOLDT COUNTY.

Humboldt No. 14, Eureka—Edward J. Quinn, Pres.; Loren M. Nelson, Sec., P.O. box 195; 2nd and 4th Mondays, Native Sons Hall.

Arcata No. 20, Arcata—George Hale, Pres.; William Peters, Sec., P. O. box 1117; Thursdays, Native Sons Hall.

Ferndale No. 93, Ferndale—O. R. Frame, Pres.; C. H. Rasmussen, Sec., R.F.D., 47-A; 1st and 3rd Mondays, K.P. Hall.

KERN COUNTY.

Bakersfield No. 42, Bakersfield—G. E. Taylor, Pres.; Leroy Vandervoort, Sec., Manly Apts.; Wednesdays, Justice Court, City Hall.

LAKE COUNTY.

Lower Lake No. 159, Lower Lake—Harold S. Anderson, Pres.; Albert Kugelman, Sec.; Thursdays, I.O.O.F. Hall.

LASSEN COUNTY.

Honey Lake No. 198, Standish—James C. Meeske, Pres.; N. V. Wemple, Sec., Litchfield; 1st and 3rd Wednesdays, Wrede Hall.

Big Valley No. 211, Bieber—George Bunselmeier, Pres.; A. W. McKenzie, Sec.; 1st and 3rd Wednesdays, I.O.O.F. Hall.

LOS ANGELES COUNTY.

Los Angeles No. 45, Los Angeles City—Lee E. Erwin, Pres.; Richard W. Fryer, Sec., 1629 Champlain Ter.; Thursdays, Merchant Plumbers Hall, 1832 So. Hope.

Ramona No. 109, Los Angeles City—Chandos E. Bush, Pres.; John V. Scott, Sec., Patriotic Hall, 1816 So. Figueroa; Fridays, Patriotic Hall, 1816 So. Figueroa.

Hollywood No. 196, Los Angeles City—Leo Aggeler, Pres.; E. J. Reilly, Sec., 907 W. 2nd St.; Mondays, 1089 No. Oxford Ave.

Long Beach No. 239, Long Beach—Francis H. Gentry, Pres.; W. W. Brady, Sec., 801 Jergins Trust Bldg.; 2nd and 4th Thursdays, Moose Hall, Elm and Anaheim.

Sepulveda No. 263, San Pedro—Francis G. Fetzer, Pres.; Frank I. Markey, Sec., 101 W. 7th St.; 2nd and 4th Fridays, Odd Fellows Temple, 10th and Gaffey Sts.

Glendale No. 264, Glendale—Philip D. Molen, Pres.; Abel B. Molen, Sec., 508 So. Belmont St.; 1st and 3rd Tuesdays, Masonic Temple, 224 So. Brand Blvd.

Santa Monica Bay No. 267, Ocean Park—Claude J. Wiseman, Pres.; John J. Smith, Sec., 830 Rialto Ave., Venice; 2nd and 4th Mondays, New Eagle Hall, 2823½ Main St.

Cabuenga No. 268, Reseda—Harold C. Trexler, Pres.; Carrol S. Driscoll, Sec., P.O. box 25, Chatsworth; first Friday, Alton Hall.

MADERA COUNTY.

Madera No. 130, Madera City—Cornelius Noble, Pres.; T. P. Cosgrave, Sec.; 1st and 3rd Thursdays, First National Bank Bldg.

MARIN COUNTY.

Mount Tamalpais No. 64, San Rafael—Arthur Todt, Pres.; Manual A. Andrade, Sec., 532 Mission Ave.; 1st and 3rd Mondays, Portuguese American Hall.

Sea Point No. 158, Sausalito—Allyn T. Young, Pres.; Manuel Santos, Sec., 6 Glen Drive; 1st and 3rd Wednesdays, Perry Bldg.

Nicasio No. 183, Nicasio—M. T. Farley, Pres.; R. J. Rogers, Sec.; 2nd and 4th Wednesdays, U.A.O.D. Hall.

MENDOCINO COUNTY.

Ukiah No. 71, Ukiah—Henry Bucknell, Pres.; Ben Hofman, Sec., P. O. box 473; 1st and 3rd Mondays, I.O.O.F. Hall.

Broderick No. 117, Point Arena—Sam Reinking, Pres.; H. C. Hunter, Sec.; 1st and 3rd Thursdays, Forester Hall.

Alder Glen No. 200, Fort Bragg—Clarence Simpson, Pres.; C. R. Weller, Sec.; 2nd and 4th Fridays, I.O.O.F. Hall.

MERCED COUNTY.

Yosemite No. 24, Merced City—Anthony A. Rodrigues, Pres.; True W. Fowler, Sec., P. O. box 781; 2nd and 4th Mondays, I.O.O.F. Hall.

MONTEREY COUNTY.

Monterey No. 75, Monterey City—John Thomsen, Pres.; T. W. Krieger, Sec., 999 Franklin St.; 1st and 3rd Fridays, Knights Pythias Hall, Main St.

Santa Lucia No. 97, Salinas—E. L. Adcock, Pres.; R. W. Adcock, Sec., Route 2, box 141; Mondays, Native Sons Hall, 22 W. Alisal St.

Gabilan No. 132, Castroville—B. A. McCoy, Pres.; R. H. Martin, Sec., P. O. box 81; 1st and 3rd Thursdays, Native Sons Hall.

NAPA COUNTY.

Saint Helena No. 53, Saint Helena—E. W. Johnson, Pres.; Edw. L. Bonhote, Sec., P. O. box 267; Mondays, Native Sons Hall.

Napa No. 62, Napa City—A. G. Boggs, Pres.; H. J. Hoernle, Sec., 1226 Oak St.; Mondays, Native Sons Hall.

Calistoga No. 86, Calistoga—Frank Mariani, Pres.; Louis Carlenzoli, Sec.; 1st and 3rd Mondays, I.O.O.F. Hall.

ATTENTION, SECRETARIES!

THIS DIRECTORY IS PUBLISHED BY AUTHORITY OF THE GRAND PARLOR N.S.G.W., AND ALL NOTICES OF CHANGES MUST BE RECEIVED BY THE GRAND SECRETARY (NOT THE MAGAZINE) ON OR BEFORE THE 20TH OF EACH MONTH TO INSURE CORRECTION IN NEXT ISSUE OF DIRECTORY.

NEVADA COUNTY.

Hydraulic No. 56, Nevada City—Spencer G. White, Pres Dr. C. W. Chapman, Sec.; Tuesdays, Pythian Castle.

Quartz No. 58, Grass Valley—Allen Joyner, Pres.; H. R George, Sec., 151 Conaway Ave.; Mondays, Auditoriu Hall.

Donner No. 162, Truckee—J. F. Lichtenberger, Pres.; 1 C. Lichtenberger, Sec.; 2nd and 4th Tuesdays, Nati Sons Hall.

ORANGE COUNTY.

Santa Ana No. 265, Santa Ana—R. L. Marsile, Pres.; E. Marks, Sec., 1124 No. Bristol St.; 1st and 3rd Monday K.C. Hall, 4th and French Sts.

PLACER COUNTY.

Auburn No. 59, Auburn—Cosme Vicencio, Pres.; J. (Walsh, Sec.; 1st and 3rd Fridays, Foresters Hall.

Silver Star No. 63, Lincoln—Ralph Sandstad, Pres.; Ba ney G. Barry, Sec., P. O. box 72; 3rd Wednesda I.O.O.F. Hall.

Rocklin No. 233, Roseville—Thomas Elliott, Pres.; M. 1 Reed, Sec., 253 W. Duranta; 2nd and 4th Wednesday Eagles Hall.

PLUMAS COUNTY.

Quincy No. 131, Quincy—J. D. McLaughlin, Pres.; E. (Kelsey, Sec.; 2nd Thursday, I.O.O.F. Hall.

Golden Anchor No. 182, La Porte—R. J. McGrath, Pres LeRoy J. Post, Sec.; 2nd and 4th Sunday morning Native Sons Hall.

Plumas No. 228, Taylorsville—E. E. Sikes, Pres.; Geor E. Boyden, Sec.; 1st and 3rd Mondays, Native Sons Hal

SACRAMENTO COUNTY.

Sacramento No. 3, Sacramento City—Joseph Hellinge Jr Pres.; J. F. Didion, Sec., 1131 "O" St.; Thursdays, Na tive Sons Bldg., 11th and "J" Sts.

Sunset No. 26, Sacramento City—George W. Lial, Pres. Edward E. Reese, Sec., County Treasurer Office; Mo days, Native Sons Bldg., 11th and "J" Sts.

Elk Grove No. 41, Elk Grove—Fred Schlmeyer, Pres. Walter Martin, Sec.; 2nd and 4th Fridays, Masonic Hal

Granite No. 83, Folsom—Joe Relvas, Pres.; Frank Shower Sec.; 2nd and 4th Tuesdays, K.P. Hall.

Courtland No. 106, Courtland—Thornton Pylman, Pres. Jos. Green, Sec.; 1st Saturday and 3rd Monday, Nativ Sons Hall.

Sutter Fort No. 241, Sacramento City—August Lehma Pres.; C. L. Katzenstein, Sec., P. O. box 914; 2nd an 4th Wednesdays, Native Sons Bldg., 11th and "J" St

Galt No. 243, Galt—John Granadas, Pres.; F. W. Harm Sec.; 1st and 3rd Mondays, I.O.O.F. Hall.

SAN BENITO COUNTY.

Fremont No. 44, Hollister—Chas. B. Arbeleche, Pres.; E. Prendergast Jr., Sec., 1064 Monterey St.; 1st and 3r Thursdays, Grangers Union Hall.

SAN BERNARDINO COUNTY.

Arrowhead No. 110, San Bernardino City—Lynn A. Ree Pres.; R. W. Brazelton, Sec., 462 6th St.; Wednesday Eagles Hall, 469 4th St.

SAN DIEGO COUNTY.

San Diego No. 108, San Diego City—Gregory A. McHorney Pres.; A. V. Mayrhofer, Sec., 1572 2nd St.; Wednesday K.C. Hall, 4th and Elm Sts.

SAN FRANCISCO CITY AND COUNTY.

California No. 1, San Francisco—Sal Juliano, Pres.; Elli A. Blackman, Sec., 126 Front St.; Thursdays, Nativ Sons Bldg., 414 Mason St.

Pacific No. 10, San Francisco—John C. Daly, Pres.; J Henry Bastein, Sec., 1880 Howard St.; Tuesdays, Nativ Sons Bldg., 414 Mason St.

Golden Gate No. 29, San Francisco—Thomas I. Schlink Pres.; Adolph Eberhart, Sec., 183 Carl St.; Monday Native Sons Bldg., 414 Mason St.

Mission No. 38, San Francisco—Joseph O. Augustine Jr Pres.; Thos. J. Stewart, Sec., 1919 Howard St.; Wednes days, Redmen Hall, 3053 16th St.

San Francisco No. 49, San Francisco—Louis L. Ghiotti Pres.; David Capurro, Sec., 976 Union St.; Thursdays Native Sons Bldg., 414 Mason St.

El Dorado No. 52, San Francisco—Eugene Herzog, Pres. Alfred Vlautin, Sec., 1537 Franklin St.; Thursdays, Na tive Sons Bldg., 414 Mason St.

Rincon No. 72, San Francisco—Michael J. Joyce, Pres. John A. Gilmour, Sec., 2069 Golden Gate Ave.; Wednes days, Native Sons Bldg., 414 Mason St.

Stanford No. 76, San Francisco—Albert W. Groskopf, Pres. Charles T. O'Kane, Sec., 1111 Pine St.; Tuesdays, Na tive Sons Bldg., 414 Mason St.

Bay City No. 104, San Francisco—Morris Garren, Pres. Max E. Licht, Sec., 1831 Fulton St.; 2nd and 4t Wednesdays, Native Sons Bldg., 414 Mason St.

Niantic No. 105, San Francisco—A. Furner, Pres.; J. M Darcy, Sec., 10 Hoffman Ave.; Wednesdays, Native Son Bldg., 414 Mason St.

National No. 118, San Francisco—Wayne Burke, Pres. Martin M. Ratigan, Sec., 1325 Page St., Apt. 6; Thurs days, 1160 Eddy St.

Hesperian No. 137, San Francisco—H. G. Ritter, Pres. Albert Carlson, Sec., 379 Justin Dr.; Thursdays, Nativ Sons Bldg., 414 Mason St.

Alcalde No. 154, San Francisco—Conrad Kuhl, Pres.; Harr S. Burke, Sec., 25 Ord St.; 2nd and 4th Wednesdays Native Sons Bldg., 414 Mason St.

South San Francisco No. 157, San Francisco—Raymon Conroy, Pres.; John T. Regan, Sec., 1489 Newcomb Ave. Wednesdays, Masonic Bldg., 4705 3rd St.

Sequoia No. 160, San Francisco—Chester Moreno, Pres. Walter W. Garrett, Sec., 2500 Van Ness Ave.; Mondays Swedish-American Bldg., 2174 Market St.

Precita No. 187, San Francisco—Elmer F. Sprague, Pres. Edward Tietjen, Sec., 1367 15th Ave.; Thursdays, Mis sion Masonic Hall, 2668 Mission St.

Olympus No. 189, San Francisco—Charles Erickson, Pres. Harvey J. Carty, Sec., 1651 Market St., Apt. 505; 2n and 4th Tuesdays, Independent Redmen Hall, 3053 16t St.

Presidio No. 194, San Francisco—Geo. R. Schmidt, Pres. George A. Ducker, Sec., 442 21st Ave.; Mondays, Nativ Sons Bldg., 414 Mason St.

Marshall No. 202, San Francisco—Arthur Belli, Pres. Frank Bacigalupi, Sec., 725 Douglas St.; 1st and 3r Wednesdays, Native Sons Bldg., 414 Mason St.

Dolores No. 208, San Francisco—Daniel Corrigan, Pres. Eugene O'Donnell, Sec., Mills Bldg.; Tuesdays, Missio Masonic Bldg., 2668 Mission St.

Twin Peaks No. 214, San Francisco—Fred Sooman, Pres. Thos. Pendergast, Sec., 278 Douglas St.; Wednesdays Willopi Hall, 4061 24th St.

El Capitan No. 222, San Francisco—Frank Rizzo, Pres. James Hanna, Sec., 2450 27th Ave.; 1st and 3rd Thurs days, King Soloman Hall, 1739 Fillmore St.

Guadalupe No. 231, San Francisco—George Miles, Pres. Alvin A. Johnson, Sec., 142 Rousseau St.; Tuesdays Guadalupe Hall, 4551 Mission St.

Castro No. 232, San Francisco—David A. Simon, Pres. James H. Hayes, Sec., 4014 18th St.; Tuesdays, Nativ Sons Bldg., 414 Mason St.

Balboa No. 234, San Francisco—J. LeMer, Pres.; E. W. Boyd, Sec., 45 Carl St.; Thursdays, Maccabee Hall, 5th Ave. and Clement St.
James Lick No. 242, San Francisco—M. G. Muller, Pres.; Wm. Band, Sec., 2587 22nd Ave.; 1st and 3rd Wednesdays, Rodmen Hall, 3052 16th St.
Bret Harte No. 260, San Francisco—J. F. Craig, Pres.; C. J. Eggers, Sec., 194 Prague St.; Tuesdays, West of Twin Peaks Hall, 283 Legion Court.
Utopia No. 270, San Francisco—Joseph Riordan, Pres.; Herbert H. Schneider, Sec., 2455 16th Ave.; Tuesdays, American Hall, 20th and Capp Sts.

SAN JOAQUIN COUNTY.

Stockton No. 7, Stockton—George D. Avery, Pres.; R. D. Dorcey, Sec., P. O. box 388; Mondays, Native Sons Hall.
Lodi No. 18, Lodi—Jerome Solomon, Pres.; Dr. Clyde Bresnan, Sec.; 2nd and 4th Wednesdays, Eagles Hall.
Tracy No. 186, Tracy—R. J. Marraccini, Pres.; R. J. Marraccini, Sec., R.F.D. No. 1, box 217; Thursdays, I.O.O.F. Hall.
Manteca No. 271, Manteca—Louis Ryan, Pres.; Leonard Faria, Sec., R.F.D. No. 1, Lathrop; 1st and 3rd Wednesdays, I.O.O.F. Hall.

SAN LUIS OBISPO COUNTY.

San Miguel No. 150, San Miguel—H. Twisselman, Pres.; George Sonnenberg Jr., Sec.; 1st and 3rd Wednesdays, Fraternal Hall.
Cambria No. 152, Cambria—Roy Cardoza, Pres.; A. S. Gay, Sec.; Wednesdays, Rigdon Hall.

SAN MATEO COUNTY.

Redwood No. 66, Redwood City—Joseph Lodi, Pres.; A. S. Liguori, Sec., P. O. box 212; Thursdays, American Foresters Hall.
Seaside No. 95, Half Moon Bay—William Deeney, Pres.; John G. Gilcrest, Sec.; 2nd and 4th Tuesdays, I.O.O.F. Hall.
Menlo No. 185, Menlo Park—W. H. Wreden, Pres.; F. W. Johnson, Sec., P. O. box 601; Thursdays, Duff & Doyle Hall.
Pebble Beach No. 230, Pescadero—Bernard Cabral, Pres.; E. A. Shaw, Sec.; 2nd and 4th Wednesdays, I.O.O.F. Hall.
El Carmelo No. 256, Daly City—Leonard J. Mohr, Pres.; Andrew P. Murphy, Sec., 931 Hanover St.; 2nd and 4th Wednesdays, Eagles Hall.
Industrial City No. 269, South San Francisco—John C. Hamilton, Pres.; Geo. A. Roll, Sec., P. O. box 237; 2nd and 4th Mondays, Metropolitan Hall.

SANTA BARBARA COUNTY.

Santa Barbara No. 116, Santa Barbara City—C. W. McCormick, Pres.; H. C. Sweetser, Sec., Court House; 1st and 3rd Wednesdays, I.O.O.F. Hall.

SANTA CLARA COUNTY.

San Jose No. 22, San Jose—Joseph Sabatte, Pres.; H. W. McComas, Sec., Suite 7, Porter Bldg.; Mondays, I.O.O.F. Hall.
Santa Clara No. 100, Santa Clara City—John J. Trinajstich, Pres.; Clarence Clevenger, Sec., P. O. box 297; 2nd and 4th Wednesdays, Redmen Hall.
Observatory No. 177, San Jose—Norton J. Mahon, Pres.; A. B. Langford, Sec., Hall Records; Tuesdays, Knights Columbus Hall, 40 No. First St.
Mountain View No. 215, Mountain View—Gilbert F. McCorkle, Pres.; C. A. Antonioli, Sec., 948 California St.; 2nd and 4th Fridays, Mockbee Hall.
Palo Alto No. 216, Palo Alto—John C. Bernal, Pres.; Albert A. Quinn, Sec., 643 High St.; Mondays, Native Sons Bldg., Hamilton Ave. and Emerson St.

SANTA CRUZ COUNTY.

Watsonville No. 65, Watsonville—A. W. Batchelder, Pres.; E. R. Tindall, Sec., 408 East Lake Ave.; 2nd and 4th Tuesdays, I.O.O.F. Hall.
Santa Cruz No. 90, Santa Cruz City—W. H. Mori, Pres.; T. V. Mathews, Sec., 105 Pacheco Ave.; Tuesdays, Native Sons Hall, 117 Pacific Ave.

SHASTA COUNTY.

McCloud No. 149, Redding—Errol Yank, Pres.; Hugh A. Shuffleton, Sec.; 1st and 3rd Thursdays, Moose Hall.

SIERRA COUNTY.

Downieville No. 92, Downieville—J. M. McMahon, Pres.; H. S. Tibbey, Sec.; 2nd and 4th Mondays, I.O.O.F. Hall.
Golden Nugget No. 94, Sierra City—Leonard Thompson Jr., Pres.; Arthur R. Pride, Sec.; last Saturday, Masonic Hall.

SISKIYOU COUNTY.

Etna No. 192, Etna—Fred M. Wolford, Pres.; Harvey A. Green, Sec.; 1st and 3rd Wednesdays, I.O.O.F. Hall.
Liberty No. 193, Sawyers Bar—Orrin R. Bigelow, Pres.; John M. Barry, Sec.; 1st and 3rd Saturdays, I.O.O.F. Hall.

SOLANO COUNTY.

Solano No. 39, Suisun—Karl Koch, Pres.; J. W. Kinlock, Sec.; 1st and 3rd Tuesdays, I.O.O.F. Hall.
Vallejo No. 77, Vallejo—Joseph Ciavo, Pres.; Werner B. Hallin, Sec., 912 Carolina; 2nd and 4th Tuesdays, San Pablo Hall.

SONOMA COUNTY.

Petaluma No. 27, Petaluma—George Gelis, Pres.; C. F. Fobes, Sec., 114 Prospect St.; 2nd and 4th Mondays, Druid Hall, Gross Bldg., 41 Main St.
Santa Rosa No. 28, Santa Rosa—John Caniff, Pres.; Leland S. Lewis, Sec., Court House; Tuesdays, Native Sons Hall.
Glen Ellen No. 102, Glen Ellen—C. C. Weise, Pres.; Frank Kirch, Sec., Route 3, Santa Rosa; 2nd Monday, N.S.G.W. Hall.
Sonoma No. 111, Sonoma City—Frederick Bulotti, Pres.; L. H. Green, Sec.; 1st and 3rd Mondays, I.O.O.F. Hall.
Sebastopol No. 143, Sebastopol—A. N. Badger, Pres.; F. G. McFarlane, Sec.; 1st and 3rd Fridays, I.O.O.F. Hall.

STANISLAUS COUNTY.

Modesto No. 11, Modesto—Robert H. Hansen, Pres.; C. C. Eastin Jr., Sec., P. O. box 898; 1st and 3rd Wednesdays, I.O.O.F. Hall.
Oakdale No. 142, Oakdale—D. W. Tulloch, Pres.; E. T. Gobin, Sec.; 2nd Monday, Legion Hall.
Orestimba No. 247, Crows Landing—Lloyd W. Fink, Pres.; G. W. Fink, Sec.; 1st and 3rd Wednesdays, Community Club Home.

SUTTER COUNTY.

Sutter No. 261, Sutter City—Stanley R. McLean, Pres.; Glen R. Haynes, Sec., Yuba City; 2nd and 4th Mondays, N.D.G.W. Hall.

TRINITY COUNTY.

Mount Bally No. 87, Weaverville—M. F. Kay, Pres.; E. V. Ryan, Sec.; 1st and 3rd Mondays, Native Sons Hall.

TUOLUMNE COUNTY.

Tuolumne No. 144, Sonora—Mathew J. Marshall, Pres.; William M. Harrington, Sec., P. O. box 715; 2nd and 4th Fridays, Knights Columbus Hall.
Columbia No. 258, Columbia—Jos. Cadematori, Pres.; Charles E. Grant, Sec.; 2nd and 4th Thursdays, Native Sons Hall.

VENTURA COUNTY.

Cabrillo No. 114, Ventura City—David Bennett, Pres., 1380 Church St.

YOLO COUNTY.

Woodland No. 30, Woodland—J. L. Aronson, Pres.; E. B. Hayward, Sec.; 1st Thursday, Native Sons Hall.

YUBA COUNTY.

Marysville No. 6, Marysville—John McQuaid, Pres.; Verne Fogarty, Sec., 719 5th St.; 2nd Friday, Foresters Hall.
Rainbow No. 40, Wheatland—W. E. Jones, Pres.; W. A. Bowser, Sec., P. O. box 313; 2nd Thursday, I.O.O.F. Hall.

AFFILIATED ORGANIZATIONS.

San Francisco Extension of the Order Committee, N.S.G.W.—Harmon D. Skillin, Chmn.; Harold J. Regan, Sec., 414 Mason St., San Francisco; meets 2nd and 4th Fridays, Grizzly Bear Club, 414 Mason St., San Francisco.
Alameda County Extension of the Order Committee, N.S.G.W.—Edward T. Schnarr, Chmn.; Frank Roemer, Sec., 3297 Morcom Ave., Oakland; meets 1st and 3rd Mondays, N.S.G.W. Hall, 11th and Clay Sts., Oakland.
Interparlor Committee (Southern District), N.S.G.W. and N.D.G.W.—Burrel D. Neighbours, Chmn.; F. J. Burmester, Sec., P. O. box 42, Colton; meets 2nd and 4th Fridays, Patriotic Hall, 1816 So. Figueroa St., Los Angeles.
San Francisco Assembly No. 1 Past Presidents Association N.S.G.W.—Meets 1st and 3rd Fridays, Native Sons Bldg., 414 Mason St., San Francisco; J. H. Sylvester, Gov.; J. F. Stanley, Sec., 1175 O'Farrell St., San Francisco.
East Bay Counties Assembly No. 3 Past Presidents Association N.S.G.W.—Meets 4th Monday, Native Sons Hall, 11th and Clay Sts., Oakland; F. H. Robson, Gov.; Edgar G. Hanson, Sec., 1260 Russell St., Berkeley.
Marin County Assembly No. 5 Past Presidents Association N.S.G.W.—J. S. Rose Jr., Gov.; L. J. Peter, Sec., Peter Bldg., 4th and "C" Sts., San Rafael.
Fred H. Greeley Assembly No. 6 Past Presidents Association N.S.G.W.—Meets monthly with different Parlors comprising district; R. L. P. Bigelow, Gov.; Barney Barry, Sec., P. O. box 72, Lincoln.
San Joaquin Assembly No. 7 Past Presidents Association N.S.G.W.—Meets 1st Friday, Native Sons Hall, Stockton; Clyde H. Gregg, Gov.; R. D. Dorcey, Sec., Native Sons Club, Stockton.
Sonoma County Assembly No. 9 Past President Association N.S.G.W.—Meets monthly at different Parlor headquarters in county; Louis Bosch, Gov.; L. S. Lewis, Sec., Court House, Santa Rosa.
General John A. Sutter Assembly No. 10 Past Presidents Association—C. C. Wachman, Gov.; Jas. J. Longshore, Sec., 514 "J" St., Sacramento.
Grizzly Bear Club—Members all Parlors outside San Francisco at all times welcome. Clubrooms top floor Native Sons Bldg., 414 Mason St., San Francisco.
Native Sons and Native Daughters Central Committee on Homeless Children—Main office, 955 Phelan Bldg., San Francisco; Mrs. John W. Stirling, Chmn.; Miss Mary E. Brusie, Sec. Los Angeles branch office, 3924 Sunset Blvd.; Dorothy Schlingman, Sec.

(ADVERTISEMENT.)

NATIVE SON NEWS

(Continued from Page 11)

ding. The latter paid a most eloquent tribute to his friend, Past Grand Monahan, and sang the praises of Nicasio, the geographical center of Marin County, and Nicasio No. 183, "the wealthiest Parlor, percapita, of any in the Order."

Looking Ahead.

Sacramento—That Sacramento No. 3 may be well represented at Admission Day, September 9, celebrations, a uniform committee was named to devise ways and means of providing funds to assist in outfitting the members. The first effort of the committee—Lew Wallace (chairman), E. Beall, A. Nicolosi, J. Major, J. Fitzhenry, H. Drennon, R. Cothrin, J. Longshore and F. Didion—was a dance April 22 at Native Sons Auditorium. A nine-piece orchestra provided "hot music to drive dull care away."

Past Presidents Active.

Oakland—Several members of East Bay Counties Assembly No. 3 Past Presidents, headed by Governor F. H. Robson, journeyed April 16 to Sonoma to participate in the joint meeting of the Sonoma and the Marin Counties Assemblies. A large delegation, headed by Governor Louis Erb, was also present from San Francisco Assembly No. 1, whose officers exemplified the ritual for the benefit of a class of candidates. A tasty repast was served by Sonoma Assembly, and at the invitation of Toastmaster Erb addresses were made by Grand Trustee Samuel M. Shortridge Jr., Harmon D. Skillin, J. Hartley Russell, Charles H. Spengemann, Director General J. F. Stanley and Past Governor General Virgil Orengo.

East Bay initiated several candidates March 28, and another large class will be presented June 23. A class initiation is being arranged for among the Parlors of Contra Costa County, which is in the jurisdiction of Assembly No. 3.

Many Visitors.

Ukiah—Grand Trustee John M. Burnett paid an official visit to Ukiah No. 71, April 1. Past Grand President Thomas Monahan and several members of Santa Rosa No. 28 and Broderick No. 117 (Point Arena) were also visitors. One candidate was initiated, and at the conclusion of the meeting a banquet was served, and several enthusiastic addresses were delivered.

Chief Justice Weds.

Berkeley—Mrs. Lucile M. Scoonover and Chief Justice William H. Waste of the California Supreme Court, affiliated with Berkeley No. 210, were wedded April 16. Following a honeymoon auto tour of the southland they will reside here.

N.S.G.W. OFFICIAL DEATH LIST.

Containing the name, the date and the place of birth, the date of death, and the Subordinate Parlor affiliation of deceased members reported to Grand Secretary John T. Regan from March 19, 1932, to April 19, 1932:

Langfeld, Joseph Louis; San Francisco, December 6, 1869; March 29, 1932; California No. 1.
McQuaid, John M.; Smartville, April 17, 1870; March 29, 1932; Marysville No. 6.
Lagomarsino, Joseph; Volcano, May 2, 1868; March 30, 1932; Amador No. 17.
Flanders, Roy; Wallace, May 20, 1878; March 15, 1932; Lodi No. 18.
Martel, Alexander P.; Hangtown, February 12, 1854; March 19, 1932; Quartz No. 58.
Gill, Arthur G.; Badger Hill, June 10, 1871; April 3, 1932; Quartz No. 58.
Johansen, Martin; San Francisco; March 11, 1932; Mount Tamalpais No. 64.
Brown, John; San Francisco, March 25, 1860; April 6, 1932; Rincon No. 72.
Cooley, John Sherman; Healdsburg, May 23, 1860; March 21, 1932; Calistoga No. 86.
Evey, David Douglas; Calistoga, May 29, 1864; March 28, 1932; Calistoga No. 86.
Miller, William Egbert; Sierraville, April 4, 1873; April 8, 1932; Downieville No. 92.
Newbauer, Julian Herman; San Francisco, October 22, 1869; April 13, 1932; Bay City No. 104.
Bilderbeck, Charles; Los Angeles, March 7, 1864; March 26, 1932; Ramona No. 109.
Hillard, Robert Cushing; San Francisco, May 3, 1892; March 30, 1932; Ramona No. 109.
Kuhrts, George Jacob; Los Angeles, January 12, 1867; April 1, 1932; Ramona No. 109.
Hanes, John Vernon; San Jacinto, August 9, 1889; April 11, 1932; Ramona No. 109.
Shay, Thomas T.; El Monte, March 10, 1857; March 30, 1932; Arrowhead No. 110.
Collins, William; San Francisco, April 16, 1878; April 10, 1932; Piedmont No. 120.
Loomis, Ed.; Santa Barbara, January 5, 1874; March 25, 1932; Hesperian No. 137.
Scharetg, Walter; San Francisco, January 28, 1878; March 1, 1932; South San Francisco No. 157.
Johnson, Fred; San Francisco, April 6, 1888; March 30, 1932; South San Francisco No. 157.
Wentworth, Charles; San Francisco, September 23, 1871; April 1, 1932; South San Francisco No. 157.
Scott, John A.; San Francisco, May 23, 1870; April 24, 1932; Presidio No. 194.

In Memoriam

SARAH SCOTT.

Whereas, It has pleased Almighty God, in His infinite wisdom, to call from this earthly sphere our beloved sister, Sarah Scott; and whereas, Sister Sarah Scott was a charter member of Stirling Parlor No. 146 N.D.G.W., It is eminently fitting that we should place on record our heartfelt sympathy for her bereaved family; therefore, be it

Resolved, That we, the members of Stirling Parlor No. 146, extend to the bereaved family our deepest sympathy in this, their hour of sorrow; and be it further resolved, that these resolutions be spread upon the minutes of this Parlor, that a copy be sent to the family of our departed sister, and that a copy be forwarded to The Grizzly Bear.

Yours in P.D.F.A.,

VERA LAEDERICH,
ETHEL SCHMALHOLZ,
ANNA FRAIM,
Committee.

By order of Secretary, Minnie N. Marcelli.
Pittsburg, December 21, 1931.

ELIZABETH HILLARD DUNN.

To the Officers and Members of Plumas Pioneer Parlor No. 219 N.D.G.W.—We, your committee appointed to draft resolutions of love and respect in memory of our departed sister, do submit the following;

Once again we bow to the will of Almighty God, who has seen fit to claim His own from amongst our membership and taken to His heavenly home our esteemed sister, pioneer and highly respected citizen of Plumas County, Elizabeth Hillard Dunn; therefore, be it

Resolved, That the sympathy of the Parlor be extended to the bereaved family; and our charter be draped in mourning for a period of thirty days; and a copy of these resolutions be sent to the family of the deceased; and that a copy be spread upon the minutes of this Parlor.

BIRDENA SWINGLE,
RHODA A. THOMPSON,
Committee.

Quincy, April 4, 1932.

EDITH M. BERNARD.

To the Officers and Members of Santa Monica Bay Parlor No. 245 Native Daughters of the Golden West: Again, the Angel of Death has entered the portals of our Parlor and our Heavenly Father, in His infinite wisdom, has called from our midst our beloved sister, Edith M. Bernard,

Resolved, That we extend to her bereaved family our deepest sympathy. It is our earnest prayer that God, in His mercy, assuage their deep grief and send peace to their hearts, for She is not dead to those who love her; not lost, but gone before. She lives with us in memory, and will forever more. We shall hold in fond memory her cheerful smile, her loving ways and always helping hand. Be it further resolved, that our charter be draped for thirty days and a copy of this resolution be spread upon the minutes, a copy sent to the bereaved family and a copy sent to The Grizzly Bear for publication.

Respectfully submitted in Friendship, Loyalty and Charity.

ANNA D. PIERCE,
MARY MEYER,
KATHERINE WORSHAM,
Committee.

Santa Monica, April 10, 1932.

Plant Fair—The Southern California Garden Club will have a Plant Fair at Van Nuys, Los Angeles County, May 5-7.

MOTHER PARLOR COMMEMORATES FOUNDING OF THE N.D.G.W. ORDER

(EMMA BOARMAN WRIGHT,
Recording Secretary Ursula No. 1.)

JACKSON (AMADOR COUNTY)—THE AFternoon of April 12, Ursula Parlor No. 1 N.D.G.W. with impressive ceremonies unveiled and dedicated a bronze plaque at the Dayton building on Main street, Jackson, to commemorate the founding of the Order of Native Daughters of the Golden West on that spot, September 11, 1886.

On that day, almost forty-five years ago, twenty-four California-born young ladies assembled in the reading-room of the Old Pioneer Hall in the basement of this building, in response to a call issued by Miss Lilly O. Reichling. When Miss Reichling revealed the object of the meeting, her purpose met an enthusiastic response, and thirteen of the young women signed the memorandum which dedicated their efforts to the task before them. This precious document is now preserved by Ursula Parlor in safe-deposit, and is the original protocol of association of the Order.

The commemorative ceremonies were in charge of a committee consisting of the resident charter members of Ursula Parlor, and elaborate preparations were made. Consent of Howard Dayton, the owner of the building, had been eagerly given, and the bronze tablet, cast by L. de Rome of Oakland, was in place and draped with the American Flag. Traffic was suspended during the hours of the ceremony, and a large assembly gathered to hear the exercises. Distinguished visitors present included Mrs. Lilly O. Reichling-Dyer, the Founder; Grand President Evelyn I. Carlson, Grand Vice-president Anna Mixon-Armstrong, Past Grand Presidents Estelle M. Evans, Esther Sullivan, Dr. Louise C. Heilbron, Mary E. Bell and Ella E. Caminetti, Grand Trustees Gladys Noce and Edna Briggs. Letters and telegrams of regret were received from all other grand officers, and from the grand officers of the Native Sons.

The ceremonies opened with selections by the Ladies' Band of Jackson, after which Miss Margaret Molfino, president of Ursula Parlor, welcomed the assemblage and introduced the chairman of the day, Mrs. Emma Boarman Wright, a charter member of the Mother Parlor, and supervising district deputy grand president. Mrs. Wright spoke briefly of the first historic gathering in the little basement-room, and of the momentous outcome of that meeting; of the great Order which sprung from that small beginning, and of the magnificent accomplishments of the Order. In happy phrases she welcomed and introduced the speakers on the program, rendering tribute to each, in order.

Mrs. Evelyn I. Carlson, Grand President, reviewed the civic work of the Order, and spoke of its many projects; she extended her congratulations to Ursula Parlor upon its commemoration of this historic event in the Order's life. "Dreaming" was rendered by a trio consisting of Mrs. Henrietta Eudey, Mrs. Leah Peters and Miss Frances Schacht, with Mrs. Alex. Gibson at the piano.

Mrs. Gladys Noce, Grand Trustee, offered a moving tribute to the Worthy Founder, Mrs. Lilly O. Reichling-Dyer, whose inspired genius has set a light to guide the feet of thousands along the path of service. Mrs. Estelle M. Evans, Past Grand President, sang "Trees," accompanied by Miss Frances Schacht at the piano. Mrs. Evans' effort was highly appreciated, and she responded to an encore.

Andrew Perovich of Excelsior Parlor No. 31 N.S.G.W. on behalf of that Order expressed the sympathetic appreciation of the Native Sons, praised the worthy service of commemorative marking, and proffered the co-operation of that organization in every effort to preserve and mark the historic spots of our commonwealth.

The tablet then was dedicated by Mrs. Henrietta O'Neill, a charter member of Ursula Parlor, in a highly impressive and dramatic address. At the conclusion of her remarks, she stepped to the tablet and, assisted by the Worthy Founder, Mrs. Dyer, drew aside the emblem that veiled the plaque.

The Founder then briefly sketched the events of that historic day in September 1886, and told some of the events and impulses that led up to the meeting, the problems that confronted the little group of pioneering women, and the trials and vicissitudes of their early struggles. Music by the Ladies' Band, "Auld Lang Syne" by the audience, and a brief introduction of the notable guests assembled closed this very interesting and noteworthy observance.

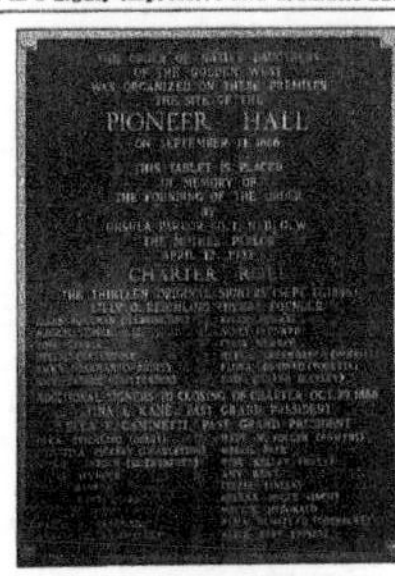

THE BRONZE PLAQUE.
—Pierce Photo, Jackson.

CHARTER MEMBERS THE MOTHER PARLOR.
Seated, left to right—Emma B. Wright, Nellie Fontenrose, P.G.P. Ella E. Caminetti, Flora D. Podesta, Founder Lilly O. R. Dyer, Rose G. Carley, Henrietta G. O'Neill. Standing, left to right—Margaret Stasal, Mellie Peck, Rose Stasal.
—Pierce Photo, Jackson.

A facsimile of the tablet is shown in the accompanying illustration. Here is shown the full charter-roll of the Mother Parlor,—the thirty-three original members of the Order.

Of the thirteen original signers September 11, 1886, seven are still members of the Order, and all of these were present at the dedicatory ceremonies. Two others are still living, but no longer are members of the Order. One of these, Miss Margaret Stasal, was also present at this re-union; the other, Mrs. Ellen Boarman Harrington of Berkeley, was not able to be present.

In addition to the thirteen original signatories, twenty others signed the roster prior to the closing of the charter, October 29, 1886. Of these, only four remain who are members of the Order, and two of these, Past Grand President Ella E. Caminetti and Miss Mellie Peck, were present at the meeting.

Out of the total charter list of thirty-three, eleven are still living and affiliated with the Order; all of these were present at Jackson, April 12, with the exception of two. Eleven charter members have passed away, and eleven have severed their relations with the Order.

This enumeration is of great historic importance, for these charter members of Ursula Parlor No. 1 will ever stand as the pioneers of this great Order. The listing is of additional importance from the fact that, in all probability, never again will so large a number of the charter-roll be assembled together in reunion.

Of the eleven charter members who still survive and retain their membership in the Order, the nine here named were present and appear in the photo accompanying this narrative. They are: Lilly O. R. Dyer, the Founder; Rose Stasal, Nellie Fontenrose, Emma Boarman Wright, Hettie G. O'Neill, Flora Podesta, Rose G. Carley, Ella E. Caminetti, Past Grand President, and Mellie Peek. The two who were absent are Mary Folger Bowers of Retsil, Wash., and Annie Fullen Magee of Mare Island. The photo also shows Miss Margaret Stasal, the first recording secretary of Ursula Parlor; Miss Stasal is no longer affiliated with the Order.

PIONEER NATIVES

(Continued from Page 17)

was affiliated with Arrowhead Parlor No. 110 N.S.G.W. and represented that Parlor at many Grand Parlors.

Milton Albert Glover, born in Butte County in 1856, died at Magalia April 1 survived by a wife and three sons.

Mrs. Izilla Hester McDaniel Holbrook, born in Glenn County in 1853, died at Willows April 3 survived by a husband and four children.

Mrs. Susan Malone, born in El Dorado County in 1856, died at Fairoaks, Sacramento County, April 5 survived by a daughter. She was a daughter of the late James Hale, California Pioneer of '49.

Newell Cate, born in Sutter County in 1858, died at Auburn, Placer County, April 6.

John Williams, born at Napa City in 1858, died there April 6.

Mrs. Emma Frances Novay-Huling, born in Nevada County in 1854, died at Grass Valley April 9 survived by a husband.

Mrs. Mary Minges-Netz-Parsons, born at Stockton, San Joaquin County, in 1851, died there April 12.

Mrs. Ida Jackson, born in Placer County in 1855, died at Sacramento City April 13 survived by a husband and a daughter.

Hawley H. Smith, born in Lake County in 1856, died April 14 at Calistoga, Napa County. He was affiliated with Calistoga Parlor No. 86 N.S.G.W.

Mrs. Nellie Hanford-Furman, born in Amador County in 1856, died at Los Angeles City April 14 survived by a husband and a son.

James Edward Walsh, born at San Francisco in 1859, died there April 15 survived by a wife.

Dr. Arthur W. Scott, born at San Francisco in 1856, died there April 15 survived by a wife and a daughter. He was president of the Mechanics Institute.

In Memoriam

EMMA RAMOS.
Initiated July 6, 1913; died March 25, 1932.

We, your committee appointed to draft resolutions of respect to the memory of our departed sister, Emma Ramos, submit the following:

Again the Angel of Death has entered our Parlor, and taken from our midst our beloved sister, Emma Ramos. We tenderly condole with her bereaved family in this, their hour of trial and affliction, and commend them for consolation to Him who doeth all things well. Let us not think of her as dead, but of having preceded us to that golden shore where she now dwells as one of the daughters of that better land, and where she waits to welcome us as we, too, pass through that golden gate. By her death her family has been deprived of a loving and devoted mother and Encinal Parlor No. 156 N.D.G.W. a sister whose noble character and kind disposition endeared her to all.

Resolved, That our deep sympathy be extended to her sorrowing family; may God bless those near and dear to her. Furthermore, be it resolved, that a page of our records be dedicated to her memory, that our charter be draped for thirty days, and that this tribute of affection to her memory be sent to the bereaved family and a copy to The Grizzly Bear Magazine.

Sincerely and fraternally, in P.D.F.A.,
IRENE ROSE,
MARTHA E. DUNLEAVY,
LAURA E. FISHER,
Alameda, April 18, 1932. Committee.

FIFTY YEARS AGO

(Continued from Page 18)

Near Orland, Glenn County, the home of Briggs Flack was destroyed by fire May 17. His wife, her 12-year-old sister and a baby were fatally burned.

The town of Willows, Glenn County, excepting two fireproof buildings, went up in smoke May 30. The estimated loss was $300,000.

The overland stage from Oregon State was stopped May 24 fourteen miles north of Redding, Shasta County, by robbers who took the express box but did not disturb the passengers.

The stage for Chico, Butte County, was held up at Deadman Hill by two men and a boy, all masked. The three passengers were relieved of their money and jewelry.

Mrs. French and her two children, in a buggy, were May 8 crossing the San Joaquin River via ferryboat at Grayson. The horses backed the buggy off the ferry and all were drowned.

Mrs. A. D. Kemp, while visiting a soapstone mine near Hollister, San Benito County, was caved upon and killed May 8.

Matches in the pocket of Robert Pringle, an Oakland, Alameda County, lad, ignited and set his clothes afire, and he was fatally burned.

Twelve-year-old Edwin Stevens of Grass Valley, Nevada County, was instantly killed May 16 by the accidental discharge of a gun.

Two miners, Clendenning and Record, having no money with which to pay the toll to cross a bridge over the Yuba River near Bloomfield, attempted to swim the stream. The former was drowned.

Joseph Cullen, an oldtimer of Hollister, San Benito County, was killed May 15 by the accidental discharge of a rifle.

John R. and James G. Troy, brothers employed as pressmen in San Francisco, started home, intoxicated, May 2. They quarreled, both drew pocketknives and James was killed.

SON OF NOTED CALIFORNIA PIONEER RESTS IN NEVADA COUNTY CEMETERY.

Alphonse Sutter, son of General John A. Sutter, lies buried in the Pine Grove cemetery at Nevada City, Nevada County. His grave will be among those to be decorated by the Native Sons on Memorial Day, May 30. The "Morning Union," in a story on famous graves in the cemetery, says:

"On the western slope of the hill rests Alphonse Sutter, son of General John A. Sutter. The young man was born in Switzerland and followed his father to this state in 1856. He was appointed aide to Governor Bigler with the rank of colonel. During the maneuvers of the notorious Walker at Nicaragua, he raised a company and went south to assist. There he contracted the dreaded consumption and returned for the benefit of his health. It was a vain hope. He passed on in 1863, leaving a wife and one son.

"His grave is encircled by an iron fence and stone coping and is marked by a simple marble shaft, all due to the energy and financial aid of Hydraulic Parlor No. 56, N.S.G.W. [Nevada City], which annually pays tribute to his memory."

Frog Jump—Angels, Calaveras County, will stage its annual international Frog Jumping Classic, May 14 and 15.

Medico Meet—The California Medical Association will have its annual convention May 2-5 at Pasadena, Los Angeles County.

STATEMENT OF THE OWNERSHIP, MANAGEMENT, CIRCULATION, ETC.,

Required by Act of Congress of August 24, 1912.

of The Grizzly Bear (Insert title of publication.) published Monthly (State frequency of issue.)

at Los Angeles, California, (Name of post office and State where publication is entered.) for April 1, 1932 (State whether for April 1 or October 1.)

State of California }
County of Los Angeles } ss.

Before me, a Notary Public in and for the State and County aforesaid, personally appeared Clarence M. Hunt who, having been duly sworn according to law, deposes and says that he is the Managing Editor (State whether editor, publisher, business manager or owner.) of the Grizzly Bear Magazine (Insert title of publication.) and that the following is, to the best of his knowledge and belief, a true statement of the ownership, management (and if a daily paper, the circulation), etc., of the aforesaid publication for the date shown in the above caption, required by the Act of August 24, 1912, embodied in section 411, Postal Laws and Regulations, printed on the reverse side of this form, to-wit:

1. That the names and addresses of the publisher, editor, managing editor, and business managers are:

NAME OF—		POST-OFFICE ADDRESS
Publisher,	Grizzly Bear Publishing Co. (Inc.)	Los Angeles, Calif.
Managing Editor,	Clarence M. Hunt	Los Angeles, Calif.

2. That the owner is: (If owned by a corporation, its name and address must be stated and also immediately thereunder the names and addresses of stockholders owning or holding one per cent or more of total amount of stock. If not owned by a corporation, the names and addresses of the individual owners must be given. If owned by a firm, company, or other unincorporated concern, its name and address, as well as those of each individual member, must be given.)
The Grizzly Bear Publishing Co., a Corporation, is the owner. 1259 shares of the 7500 authorized shares of stock have been sold. Names all stockholders, and amount stock held by each, attached hereto.

3. That the known bondholders, mortgagees, and other security holders owning or holding 1 per cent or more of total amount of bonds, mortgages, or other securities are: (If there are none, so state.)
None

4. That the two paragraphs next above, giving the names of the owners, stockholders, and security holders, if any, contain not only the list of stockholders and security holders as they appear upon the books of the company, but also, in cases where the stockholder or security holder appears upon the books of the company as trustee or in any other fiduciary relation, the name of the person or corporation for whom such trustee is acting, is given; also that the said two paragraphs contain statements embracing affiant's full knowledge and belief as to the circumstances and conditions under which stockholders and security holders who do not appear upon the books of the company as trustees, hold stock and securities in a capacity other than that of a bonafide owner; and this affiant has no reason to believe that any other person, association, or corporation has any interest direct or indirect in the said stocks, bonds, or other securities than as so stated by him.

5. That the average number of copies of each issue of this publication sold or distributed, through the mails or otherwise, to paid subscribers during the six months preceding the date shown above is————(This information is required from daily publications only.)

CLARENCE M. HUNT,
Managing Editor.

Sworn to and subscribed before me this 30th day of March, 1932.

HARRY J. LELANDE,
[Seal] Notary Public in and for the County of Los Angeles, State of California.
(My commission expires Feb. 18th, 1936)

STOCKHOLDERS OF THE GRIZZLY BEAR PUBLISHING COMPANY (Inc.)

Following is the list of ALL of the stockholders of the Grizzly Bear Publishing Company, Incorporated, as shown by the Stock Ledger, March 30, 1932:

W. Joseph Ford, 257
Harry J. Lelande, Los Angeles, 24
Warren R. Porter, Watsonville, 10
W. H. Marie, Santa Barbara, 10
C. J. Brown, Los Angeles, 10
C. M. Belshaw, San Francisco, 20
George L. Chanler, Los Angeles, 10
J. N. O. Rech, Los Angeles, 10
J. R. Knowland, Oakland, 15
I. B. Dockweiler, Los Angeles, 15
E. A. Meserve, Los Angeles, 25
W. T. Craig, Los Angeles, 10
Ramona Parlor, N.S.G.W., Los Angeles, 122
M. T. Dooling, Hollister, 5
Corona Parlor, N.S.G.W., Los Angeles, 10
Thomas Monahan, San Jose, 10
Andrew Mocker, San Francisco, 5
Daniel A. Ryan, San Francisco, 10
James D. Phelan, San Francisco, 20
Los Angeles Parlor, N.S.G.W., Los Angeles, 10
Frank H. Dunne, San Francisco, 5
J. Emmett Hayden, San Francisco, 10
W. S. Kingsbury, Sacramento, 10
W. W. Shannon, San Francisco, 5
E. A. Forbes, Marysville, 5
H. C. Lichtenberger, Los Angeles, 12
Frank Hauser, Los Angeles, 10
F. W. Young, Los Angeles, 5
Calvert Wilson, Los Angeles, 2
J. M. Hanley, San Francisco, 1
D. J. Wren, San Francisco, 5
Oakland Parlor, N.S.G.W., Oakland, 25
J. C. Griffin, Merced, 1
Sacramento Parlor, N.S.G.W., Sacramento, 15
Pacific Parlor, N.S.G.W., San Francisco, 10
Napa Parlor, N.S.G.W., Napa, 10
Mt. Tamalpais Parlor, N.S.G.W., San Rafael, 5
Athens Parlor, N.S.G.W., Oakland, 15
Raymond H. Kilborn, San Francisco, 2
Leland E. Kilborn, San Francisco, 3
Benjamin L. McKinley, San Francisco, 1
Sunset Parlor, N.S.G.W., Sacramento, 10
Chico Parlor, N.S.G.W., Chico, 5
Placerville Parlor, N.S.G.W., Placerville, 10
J. B. Amestoy, Los Angeles, 35
F. J. Talamantes, Los Angeles, 5
W. J. Variel, Los Angeles, 2
W. B. Metcalf, Santa Barbara, 3
A. Goux, Santa Barbara, 2
E. M. Buckius, Los Angeles, 10
P. A. Blair, Los Angeles, 1
W. D. Wagner, San Bernardino, 15
A. A. Schmidt, Los Angeles, 10
P. F. Johnson, Los Angeles, 1
J. D. Smith, Los Angeles, 3
J. B. Masselin, Los Angeles, 1
Wm. Rudolph, Los Angeles, 1
M. G. Jones, Los Angeles, 5
E. M. Lazard, Los Angeles, 2
E. J. Dillon, Los Angeles, 1
Hugh Glassell, Los Angeles, 10
C. Heinzman, Los Angeles, 2
Florence O. Sharp, 11
J. M. Carson, Los Angeles, 5
J. M. Allen, Los Angeles, 5
M. J. Aquirre, Los Angeles, 5
R. C. Monte, Los Angeles, 1
E. H. Hall, Holtville, 1
H. H. Hall, Holtville, 1
E. Zobelein, Los Angeles, 1
Aubry Austin, Los Angeles, 5
Hydraulic Parlor, N.S.G.W., Nevada City, 10
G. A. Burns, Sacramento, 5
Yosemite Parlor, N.S.G.W., Merced, 2
Excelsior Parlor, N.S.G.W., Jackson, 5
F. A. Stephenson, Los Angeles, 10
E. B. Lovie, Los Angeles, 1
San Francisco Parlor, N.S.G.W., San Francisco, 5
W. F. Bryant, Los Angeles, 25
J. M. Hickey, San Francisco, 1
J. E. O'Connell, San Francisco, 3
J. E. Rigney, San Francisco, 1
Golden Gate Parlor, N.S.G.W., San Francisco, 3
Sequoia Parlor, N.S.G.W., San Francisco, 1
Les Henry, Los Angeles, 2
E. O. Edgerton, Los Angeles, 30
Alcalde Parlor, N.S.G.W., San Francisco, 5
George Beebe, Los Angeles, 3
Fletcher Ford, Los Angeles, 15
Ray Howard, Los Angeles, 5
Santa Barbara Parlor, N.S.G.W., Santa Barbara, 10
Fred Eaton, Los Angeles, 2
John T. Newell, Los Angeles, 8
Clarence Jarvis, Sutter Creek, 5
W. A. Hobson, Ventura, 3
Amador Parlor, N.S.G.W., Sutter Creek, 10
John F. Davis, San Francisco, 5
Clarence M. Hunt, Los Angeles, 20
Grant Jackson, Los Angeles, 20
L. H. Valentine, Los Angeles, 3
J. P. Kiefer, Los Angeles, 10
John Castera, Los Angeles, 5
F. J. Palomares, Los Angeles, 1
W. J. McCaffery, Santa Barbara, 2
A. F. Jones, Oroville, 2
San Jose Parlor, N.S.G.W., San Jose, 5
Byron Parlor, N.S.G.W., Byron, 2
Gen. Winn Parlor, N.S.G.W., Antioch, 2
Alameda Parlor, N.S.G.W., Alameda, 1
Georgetown Parlor, N.S.G.W., Georgetown, 5
Precita Parlor, N.S.G.W., San Francisco, 5
Alder Glen Parlor, N.S.G.W., Fort Bragg, 1
Fruitvale Parlor, N.S.G.W., Fruitvale, 1
Quartz Parlor, N.S.G.W., Grass Valley, 5
Selma Parlor, N.S.G.W., Selma, 1
Carquinez Parlor, N.S.G.W., Crockett, 1
H. G. W. Dinkelspiel, San Francisco, 1
Homeless Children's Agency, San Francisco, 1
Bay City Parlor, N.S.G.W., San Francisco, 2
Chas. R. Thomas, Los Angeles, 2
J. D. Hunter, Los Angeles, 3
Daisy E. L. Eckstrom, 10
Irving Baxter, Los Angeles, 5
Harry G. Folsom, Los Angeles, 1
Mrs. Maria Gibson, San Francisco, 10
Stanford Parlor, N.S.G.W., San Francisco, 5
L. F. Soto, Los Angeles, 5
Chas. Stansbury, Los Angeles, 10
Jo V. Snyder, Nevada City, 3
Lon S. McCoy, Los Angeles, 1
William I. Traeger, Los Angeles, 1

Official Directory of Parlors of the N. D. G. W.

ALAMEDA COUNTY.

Angelita No. 32, Livermore—Meets 2nd and 4th Fridays, Foresters Hall; Mrs. Myrtle I. Johnson, Rec. Sec.
Piedmont No. 87, Oakland—Meets Thursdays, Corinthian Hall, Pacific Bldg.; Mrs. Alice E. Miner, Rec. Sec., 421 35th St.
Aloha No. 106, Oakland—Meets Tuesdays, Wigwam Hall, Pacific Bldg.; Gladys I. Farley, Rec. Sec., 4623 Benevides Ave.
Hayward No. 122, Hayward—Meets 1st and 3rd Tuesdays, Veterans Memorial Bldg., Main St.; Miss Ruth Gansberger, Rec. Sec., P. O. box 44, Mount Eden.
Berkeley No. 150, Berkeley—Meets 1st and 3rd Fridays, Masonic Hall; Mrs. Lelia B. Baker, Rec. Sec., 915 Contra Costa Ave.
Bear Flag No. 151, Berkeley—Meets 2nd and 4th Wednesdays, Veterans MemorialyBldg., 1931 Center St.; Mrs. Maud Wagner, Rec. Sec., 317 Alcatraz Ave., Oakland.
Encinal No. 156, Alameda—Meets 2nd and 4th Thursdays, N.S.G.W. Hall; Mrs. Laura E. Fisher, Rec. Sec., 1413 Caroline St.
Brooklyn No. 157, East Oakland—Meets Wednesdays, Masonic Temple, 8th Ave. and E. 14th St.; Mrs. Ruth Cooney, Rec. Sec., 3907 14th Ave.
Argonaut No. 166, Oakland—Meets Tuesdays, Klinkner Hall, 59th and San Pablo; Mrs. Ada Spilman, Rec. Sec., 2905 Ellis St., Berkeley.
Bahia Vista No. 167, Oakland—Meets Thursdays, Wigwam Hall, Pacific Bldg.; Mrs. Minnie E. Raper, Rec. Sec., 3449 Helen St.
Fruitvale No. 177, Oakland—Meets Fridays, W.O.W. Hall; Mrs. Agnes M. Grant, Rec. Sec., 1224 30th Ave.
Laura Loma No. 182, Niles—Meets 1st and 3rd Tuesdays, I.O.O.F. Hall; Mrs. Ethel Fournier, Rec. Sec., P. O. box 515.
El Cereso No. 207, San Leandro—Meets 2nd and 4th Tuesdays, Masonic Hall; Mrs. Mary Tuttle, Rec. Sec., P. O. box 56.
Pleasanton No. 237, Pleasanton—Meets 1st Tuesday. I.O.O.F. Hall; Mrs. Myrtle Lanini, Rec. Sec.
Betsy Ross No. 238, Centerville—Meets 1st and 3rd Fridays, Anderson Hall; Miss Constance Lucio, Rec. Sec., P. O. box 187.

AMADOR COUNTY.

Ursula No. 1, Jackson—Meets 2nd and 4th Tuesdays, N.S.G.W. Hall; Mrs. Emma Boarman-Wright, Rec. Sec., 114 Court St.
Chispa No. 40, Ione—Meets 2nd and 4th Fridays, N.S.G.W. Hall; Mrs. Isabel Ashton, Rec. Sec.
Amapola No. 80, Sutter Creek—Meets 2nd and 4th Thursdays, N.S.G.W. Bldg.; Mrs. Hazel M. Marre, Rec. Sec.
Forrest No. 86, Plymouth—Meets 2nd and 4th Tuesdays, I.O.O.F. Hall; Mrs. Marguerite Davis, Rec. Sec.

BUTTE COUNTY.

Annie K. Bidwell No. 168, Chico—Meets 2nd and 4th Thursdays, I.O.O.F. Hall; Mrs. Irene Henry, Rec. Sec., 3015 Woodland Ave.
Gold of Ophir No. 190, Oroville—Meets 1st and 3rd Wednesdays, Memorial Hall; Mrs. Ruth Brown, Rec. Sec., 1265 Leah Court.

CALAVERAS COUNTY.

Ruby No. 46, Murphys—Meets 4th Friday, N.S.G.W. Hall; Belle Segale, Rec. Sec.
Princess No. 84, Angels Camp—Meets 2nd and 4th Wednesdays, I.O.O.F. Hall; Grace Mills, Rec. Sec.
San Andreas No. 113, San Andreas—Meets 1st Friday, Fraternal Hall; Miss Doris Treat, Rec. Sec.

COLUSA COUNTY.

Colus No. 194, Colusa—Meets 1st and 3rd Mondays, Eagles Hall; Miss Kate Busch, Rec. Sec., 350 Market St.

CONTRA COSTA COUNTY.

Stirling No. 146, Pittsburg—Meets 1st and 3rd Wednesdays, Veteran Memorial Hall; Mrs. Minnie Marcelli, Rec. Sec., 771 E. 12th St.
Richmond No. 147, Richmond—Meets 1st and 3rd Tuesdays, I.O.O.F. Hall, 10th St.; Mrs. Tillie Summers, Rec. Sec., 640 So. 31st St.
Donner No. 193, Byron—Meets 1st and 3rd Wednesdays, I.O.O.F. Hall; Mrs. Anna Pendry, Rec. Sec., P. O. box 112.
Las Juntas No. 221, Martinez—Meets 1st and 3rd Mondays, Pythian Castle; Mrs. Lola O. Viera, Rec. Sec., 305 Arreba St.
Antioch No. 223, Antioch—Meets 2nd and 4th Tuesdays, I.O.O.F. Hall; Mrs. Estelle Evans, Rec. Sec., 202 E. 5th St., Pittsburg.
Carquinez No. 234, Crockett—Meets 2nd and 4th Wednesdays, I.O.O.F. Hall; Mrs. Cecile Petee, Rec. Sec., 465 Edwards St.

EL DORADO COUNTY.

Marguerite No. 12, Placerville—Meets 1st and 3rd Wednesdays, Masonic Hall; Mrs. Nettie Leonardi, Rec. Sec., 25 Coloma St.
El Dorado No. 186, Georgetown—Meets 2nd and 4th Saturday afternoons, I.O.O.F. Hall; Mrs. Alta L. Douglas, Rec. Sec.

FRESNO COUNTY.

Fresno No. 187, Fresno—Meets 2nd and 4th Fridays, Pythian Castle, Cor. "R" and Merced Sts.; Mary Aubery, Rec. Sec., 1040 Delphia Ave.

GRAND OFFICERS

Mrs. Estelle M. Evans........Past Grand President
202 E. Fifth St., Pittsburg
Mrs. Evelyn I. Carlson........Grand President
1965 San Jose Ave., San Francisco
Mrs. Anna M. Armstrong........Grand Vice-president
Woodland
Mrs. Sallie R. Thaler........Grand Secretary
555 Baker St., San Francisco
Mrs. Susie K. Christ........Grand Treasurer
555 Baker St., San Francisco
Mrs. Irma Laird........Grand Marshal
Alturas
Mrs. Minna K. Horn........Grand Inside Sentinel
Etna
Mrs. Orinda G. Giannini........Grand Outside Sentinel
2142 Filbert St., San Francisco
Mrs. Lola Horgan........Grand Organist
789 Morse St., San Francisco

GRAND TRUSTEES

Mrs. Edna Briggs........1045 Santa Ynez Way, Sacramento
Mrs. Ethel Begley........233 Prospect Ave., San Francisco
Mrs. Anna Thuesen........615 38th Ave., San Francisco
Mrs. Gladys Noce........Sutter Creek
Mrs. Florence Boyle........Oroville
Mrs. Florence Schoneman........1521 5th Ave., Los Angeles
Mrs. Willow Borba........Sebastopol

GLENN COUNTY.

Berryessa No. 192, Willows—Meets 1st and 3rd Mondays, I.O.O.F. Hall; Mrs. Leonora Neate, Rec. Sec., 338 No. Lassen St.

HUMBOLDT COUNTY.

Occident No. 28, Eureka—Meets 1st and 3rd Wednesdays, N.S.G.W. Hall; Mrs. Eva L. MacDonald, Rec. Sec., 2309 "B" St.
Oneonta No. 71, Ferndale—Meets 2nd and 4th Fridays, I.O.O.F. Hall; Mrs. Myra Rumrill, Rec. Sec.
Reichling No. 97, Fortuna—Meets 1st and 3rd Tuesdays, Friendship Hall; Mrs. Grace Swett, Rec. Sec., P. O. box 328.

KERN COUNTY.

Miocene No. 228, Taft—Meets 1st and 3rd Wednesday afternoons, I.O.O.F. Hall; Mrs. Evalyne Towne, Rec. Sec., P. O. box 1011.
El Tejon No. 239, Bakersfield—Meets 1st and 3rd Fridays, Eagles Hall, 1714 "G" St.; Mrs. Grace S. Dorris, Rec. Sec., 127 Morgan Bldg.
Desert Gold No. 250, Mojave—Meets 2nd and 4th Fridays, I.O.O.F. Hall; Mrs. Mae Cohill, Rec. Sec.

LAKE COUNTY.

Clear Lake No. 135, Middletown—Meets 2nd and 4th Tuesdays, Herrick Hall; Mrs. Alma E. Snow, Rec. Sec.

LASSEN COUNTY.

Nataqua No. 152, Standish—Meets 1st and 3rd Wednesdays, Foresters Hall; Mrs. Mayda Elledge, Rec. Sec.
Mount Lassen No. 215, Bieber—Meets 2nd and 4th Thursdays, I.O.O.F. Hall; Mrs. Angie C. Kenyon, Rec. Sec.
Susanville No. 243, Susanville—Meets 3rd Thursday, I.O.O.F. Hall; Mrs. Georgie Jensen, Rec. Sec., 700 Roop St.

LOS ANGELES COUNTY.

Los Angeles No. 124, Los Angeles—Meets 1st and 3rd Wednesdays, I.O.O.F. Hall, Washington and Oak Sts.; Mrs. Mary K. Corcoran, Rec. Sec., 322 No. Van Ness Ave.
Long Beach No. 154, Long Beach—Meets 1st and 3rd Thursdays, K.P. Hall, 341 Pacific Ave.; Mrs. Bertha Hitt, Rec. Sec., 5355 Lime Ave.
Rudecinda No. 230, San Pedro—Meets 1st and 3rd Fridays, Unity Hall, I.O.O.F. Temple, 10th and Gaffey; Mrs. Carrie E. Northway, Rec. Sec., 561 W. 14th St.
Verdugo No. 240, Glendale—Meets 2nd and 4th Tuesdays, Masonic Temple, 234 So. Brand Blvd.; Miss Etta Fulkerth, Rec. Sec., 526-A No. Orange St.
Santa Monica Bay No. 245, Ocean Park—Meets 1st and 3rd Mondays, New Eagles Hall, 2823½ Main St.; Mrs. Rosalie Hyde, Rec. Sec., 738 Flower St., Venice.
Californiana No. 247, Los Angeles—Meets 2nd and 4th Tuesday afternoons, Hollywood Studio Club, 1215 Lodi Place; Mrs. Inez Sitton, Rec. Sec., 4223 Berenice St.

MADERA COUNTY.

Madera No. 244, Madera—Meets 2nd and 4th Thursdays, Masonic Annex; Mrs. Margaret C. Boyle, Rec. Sec., 111 No. "B" St.

MARIN COUNTY.

Sea Point No. 196, Sausalito—Meets 2nd and 4th Mondays, Perry Hall, 50 Caledonia St.; Mrs. Mary B. Smith, Rec. Sec., 559 Woodward Ave.
Marinita No. 198, San Rafael—Meets 2nd and 4th Mondays, 316 "B" St.; Miss Mollye Y. Spaelti, Rec. Sec., 539 4th St.
Fairfax No. 225, Fairfax—Meets 2nd and 4th Tuesdays, Community Hall; Mrs. Olive A. Greene, Rec. Sec., P. O. box 277.
Tamelpa No. 231, Mill Valley—Meets 1st and 2nd Tuesdays, I.O.O.F. Hall; Mrs. Delphine M. Todt, Rec. Sec., 400 Grand Ave., San Rafael.

MARIPOSA COUNTY.

Mariposa No. 63, Mariposa—Meets 1st and 3rd Fridays, I.O.O.F. Hall; Mrs. Mamie E. Weston, Rec. Sec.

MENDOCINO COUNTY.

Fort Bragg No. 210, Fort Bragg—Meets 1st and 3rd Thursdays, I.O.O.F. Hall; Mrs. Ruth W. Fuller, Rec. Sec.

MERCED COUNTY.

Veritas No. 75, Merced—Meets 1st and 3rd Tuesdays, I.O.O.F. Hall; Miss Margaret Thornton, Rec. Sec., 317 18th St.

MODOC COUNTY.

Alturas No. 159, Alturas—Meets 1st Thursday, Alturas Civic Club; Mrs. Irma W. Laird, Rec. Sec.

MONTEREY COUNTY.

Aleli No. 102, Salinas—Meets 2nd and 4th Thursdays, Knights Pythias Hall; Miss Rose Rhyner, Rec. Sec., 420 Soledad St.
Junipero No. 141, Monterey—Meets 2nd and 4th Fridays, Pythian Hall; Miss Matilda M. Bergschicker, Rec. Sec., 498 Van Buren St.

NAPA COUNTY.

Eschol No. 16, Napa—Meets 2nd and 4th Mondays, N.S.G.W. Hall; Mrs. Ella Ingram, Rec. Sec., 2140 Seminary St.
Calistoga No. 145, Calistoga—Meets 2nd and 4th Mondays, I.O.O.F. Hall; Sadie P. Brooks, Rec. Sec.
La Junta No. 203, Saint Helena—Meets 1st and 3rd Tuesdays, N.S.G.W. Hall; Mrs. Marie Signorelli, Rec. Sec., 1341 Madrona Ave.

ATTENTION, SECRETARIES!

THIS DIRECTORY IS PUBLISHED BY AUTHORITY OF THE GRAND PARLOR N.D.G.W., AND ALL NOTICES OF CHANGES MUST BE RECEIVED BY THE GRAND SECRETARY (NOT THE MAGAZINE) ON OR BEFORE THE 20TH OF EACH MONTH TO INSURE CORRECTION IN NEXT PUBLICATION OF DIRECTORY.

NEVADA COUNTY.

Laurel No. 6, Nevada City—Meets 1st and 3rd Wednesdays, I.O.O.F. Hall; Mrs. Nellie E. Clark, Rec. Sec., P. O. box 212.
Manzanita No. 29, Grass Valley—Meets 1st and 3rd Tuesdays, Auditorium; Mrs. Loraine Keast, Rec. Sec., 12[illegible] Race St.
Columbia No. 70, French Corral—Meets Fridays, Farrelley Hall; Mrs. Kate Farrelley-Sullivan, Rec. Sec.
Snow Peak No. 176, Truckee—Meets 1st Monday, I.O.O.F. Hall; Mrs. Henrietta M. Eaton, Rec. Sec., P. O. box 116

ORANGE COUNTY.

Santa Ana No. 235, Santa Ana—Meets 2nd and 4th Mondays, K.C. Hall, 4th and French Sts.; Mrs. Matilda S. Lemon, Rec. Sec., 1038 W. Bishop St.
Grace No. 242, Fullerton—Meets 1st and 3rd Thursdays, I.O.O.F. Hall, 116½ E. Commonwealth; Mrs. Mary Rothaermel, Rec. Sec., P. O. box 235.

PLACER COUNTY.

Placer No. 138, Lincoln—Meets 2nd Wednesday, I.O.O.F. Hall; Miss Carrie Parlin, Rec. Sec.
La Rosa No. 191, Roseville—Meets 1st and 3rd Tuesdays, Eagles Hall; Mrs. Alice Lee West, Rec. Sec., Rocklin.
Auburn No. 233, Auburn—Meets 2nd and 4th Fridays, Foresters Hall; Mrs. Dorothy Reinecke, Rec. Sec., Penryn.

PLUMAS COUNTY.

Plumas Pioneer No. 219, Quincy—Meets 1st and 3rd Mondays, I.O.O.F. Hall; Minnie E. Johnson, Rec. Sec., P. O. box 243.

SACRAMENTO COUNTY.

Califia No. 22, Sacramento—Meets 2nd and 4th Tuesdays, N.S.G.W. Hall; Miss Lulu Gillis, Rec. Sec., 921 8th St.
La Bandera No. 110, Sacramento—Meets 1st and 3rd Fridays, N.S.G.W. Hall; Mrs. Clara Weldon, Rec. Sec., 1310 "O" St.
Sutter No. 111, Sacramento—Meets 1st and 3rd Tuesdays, N.S.G.W. Hall; Mrs. Adele Nix, Rec. Sec., 1238 "S" St.
Fern No. 123, Folsom—Meets 1st and 3rd Tuesdays, K.P. Hall; Mrs. Viola Shumway, Rec. Sec., P. O. box 48.
Chabolla No. 171, Galt—Meets 2nd and 4th Tuesdays, I.O.O.F. Hall; Mrs. Mary Pritchard, Rec. Sec.
Coloma No. 212, Sacramento—Meets 1st and 3rd Tuesdays, I.O.O.F. Hall, Oak Park; Mrs. Nettie Harry, Rec. Sec., 1217 35th St.
Liberty No. 213, Elk Grove—Meets 2nd and 4th Fridays, I.O.O.F. Hall; Mrs. Frances Wackman, Rec. Sec., P. O. box 192.
Victory No. 216, Courtland—Meets 1st Saturday and 3rd Monday, N.S.G.W. Hall; Mrs. Agneda Lample, Rec. Sec.

SAN BENITO COUNTY.

Copa de Oro No. 105, Hollister—Meets 2nd and 4th Thursdays, Grangers Union Hall; Mrs. Mollie Daveggio, Rec. Sec., 110 San Benito St.
San Juan Bautista No. 179, San Juan Bautista—Meets 1st Wednesday, Mission Corridor Rooms; Miss Gertrude Breen, Rec. Sec.

SAN BEARNARDINO COUNTY.

Lugonia No. 241, San Bernardino—Meets 2nd and 4th Wednesdays, Eagles Hall; Grace McHenry, Rec. Sec., Base Line and Central, Highland.
Ontario No. 251, Ontario—Meets 2nd and 4th Thursdays, Ontario Hotel; Miss Helen Hickman, Rec. Sec., 923 No. Laurel Ave.

SAN DIEGO COUNTY.

San Diego No. 208, San Diego—Meets 2nd and 4th Wednesdays, Directors Room, Chamber Commerce Bldg., 499 W. Broadway; Mrs. Elsie Case, Rec. Sec., 3051 Broadway.

SAN FRANCISCO CITY AND COUNTY.

Minerva No. 2, San Francisco—Meets 1st and 3rd Wednesdays, N.S.G.W. Bldg.; Miss Dorothy Finn, Rec. Sec., 90 Princess St., Sausalito.
Alta No. 3, San Francisco—Meets 2nd and 4th Tuesdays, N.S.G.W. Bldg.; Mrs. Agnese L. Hughes, Rec. Sec., 3980 Sacramento St.
Oro Fino No. 9, San Francisco—Meets 1st and 3rd Thursdays, N.S.G.W. Bldg.; Mrs. Josephine B. Morrisey, Rec. Sec., 4441 20th St.
Golden State No. 50, San Francisco—Meets 1st and 3rd Wednesdays, N.D.G.W. Home; Miss Millie Tietjen, Rec. Sec., 328 Lexington Ave.
Orinda No. 56, San Francisco—Meets 2nd and 4th Fridays, N.D.G.W. Home; Mrs. Anna A. Gruber-Loser, Rec. Sec., 72 Grove Lane, San Anselmo.
Fremont No. 59, San Francisco—Meets 1st and 3rd Tuesdays, N.S.G.W. Bldg.; Miss Hannah Collins, Rec. Sec., 617 Fillmore St.
Buena Vista No. 68, San Francisco—Meets 1st, 3rd and 5th Thursdays, N.D.G.W. Home; Miss Margaret Barrett, Rec. Sec., 3774 20th St.
Las Lomas No. 72, San Francisco—Meets 1st and 3rd Tuesdays, N.D.G.W. Home; Mrs. Marion S. Day, Rec. Sec., 471 Alvarado St.
Yosemite No. 83, San Francisco—Meets 1st and 3rd Tuesdays, American Hall, 20th and Capp Sts.; Miss Mary Monahan, Rec. Sec., 237 Noe St.
La Estrella No. 89, San Francisco—Meets 2nd and 4th Mondays, N.S.G.W. Bldg.; Miss Birdie Hartman, Rec. Sec., 1018 Jackson St.
Sans Souci No. 96, San Francisco—Meets 2nd and 4th Mondays, N.D.G.W. Home; Mrs. Minnie F. Dobbin, Rec. Sec., 1483 43rd Ave.
Calaveras No. 103, San Francisco—Meets 2nd and 4th Tuesdays, Swedish American Hall, 2174 Market St.; Mrs. Lena Lorsheter, Rec. ec., 492-C 41st St., Oakland.
Darina No. 114, San Francisco—Meets 1st and 3rd Mondays, N.S.G.W. Bldg.; Miss Adele Walsh, Rec. Sec., 479 Page St.
El Vespero No. 118, San Francisco—Meets 2nd and 4th Tuesdays, Masonic Hall, 4705 3rd St.; Mrs. Nell R. Boege, Rec. Sec., 1526 Kirkwood Ave.
Genevieve No. 132, San Francisco—Meets 1st and 3rd Thursdays, N.S.G.W. Bldg.; Miss Branice Peguillan, Rec. Sec., 2434 16th Ave.
Keith No. 137, San Francisco—Meets 2nd and 4th Thursdays, N.S.G.W. Bldg.; Mrs. Helen T. Mann, Rec. Sec., 575 Pierce St., Apt. 206.
Gabrielle No. 139, San Francisco—Meets 2nd and 4th Wednesdays, N.S.G.W. Bldg.; Mrs. Dorothy Wuesterfeld, Rec. Sec., 1020 Munich St.
Presidio No. 148, San Francisco—Meets 2nd and 4th Tuesdays, N.S.G.W. Bldg.; Mrs. Hattie Gaughran, Rec. Sec., 713 Capp St.
Guadalupe No. 153, San Francisco—Meets 2nd and 4th Mondays, Forester Hall, 170 Valencia St.; Miss May A. McCarthy, Rec. Sec., 336 Elsie St.
Golden Gate No. 158, San Francisco—Meets 2nd and 4th Mondays, N.S.G.W. Bldg.; Mrs. Mary Sullivan, Rec. Sec., 33 Cuvier St.
Dolores No. 169, San Francisco—Meets 2nd and 4th Wednesdays, N.S.G.W. Bldg.; Mrs. Ada Saunders, Rec. Sec., 284 Allison St.
Linda Rosa No. 170, San Francisco—Meets 2nd and 4th Wednesdays, Swedish American Hall, 2174 Market St.; Mrs. Eva P. Tyrrel, Rec. Sec., 2529 Mission St.

ortola No. 172, San Francisco—Meets 1st and 3rd Tuesdays, N.S.G.W. Bldg.; Catherine H. Dolly, Rec. Sec., 4125 23rd St.
astro No. 178, San Francisco—Meets 1st and 3rd Wednesdays, K.C. Bldg., 150 Golden Gate Ave.; Miss Adeline Sandersfeld, Rec Sec., 50 Baker St.
win Peaks No. 185, San Francisco—Meets 2nd and 4th Fridays, Druids Temple, 44 Page St.; Mrs. Loretta Cameron, Rec. Sec., 3969 Army St.
ames Lick No. 220, San Francisco—Meets 1st and 3rd Wednesdays, N.S.G.W. Bldg.; Mrs. Edna Bishop, Rec. Sec., 3841 24th St.
Iission No. 227, San Francisco—Meets 2nd and 4th Fridays, N.S.G.W. Bldg.; Mrs. Ann Dippel, Rec. Sec., 448 Dewey Blvd.
ret Harte No. 232, San Francisco—Meets 2nd and 4th Tuesdays, Aloha Hall, 3009 16th St.; Hildur E. Eggers, Rec. Sec., 194 Prague St.
a Dorada No. 236, San Francisco—Meets 2nd and 4th Thursdays, N.S.G.W. Hall; Mrs. Theresa R. O'Brien, Rec. Sec., 567 Liberty St.
albon No. 249, San Francisco—Meets 1st and 3rd Thursdays, Maccabee Hall, 5th Ave. and Clement St.; Jean Moffet, Rec. Sec., 5633 California St.

SAN JOAQUIN COUNTY.

oaquin No. 5, Stockton—Meets 2nd and 4th Tuesdays, N.S.G.W. Hall, 314 E. Main St.; Mrs. Della Garvin, Rec. Sec., 1122 E. Market St.
El Pescadero No. 82, Tracy—Meets 1st and 3rd Fridays, I.O.O.F. Hall; Mrs. Mary A. Hewitson, Rec. Sec., 215 W. 9th St.
y No. 88, Lodi—Meets 1st and 3rd Wednesdays, Eagles Hall; Mrs. Mae Corson, Rec. Sec., 109 So. School St.
alis de Oro No. 206, Stockton—Meets 1st and 3rd Tuesdays, N.S.G.W. Hall, 314 E. Main St.; Mrs. Frances Germain, Rec. Sec., 450 No. Regent.
Phoebe A. Hearst No. 214, Manteca—Meets 2nd and 4th Wednesdays, I.O.O.F. Hall; Mrs. Josie M. Frederick, Rec. Sec., Route A, Box 364, Ripon.

SAN LUIS OBISPO COUNTY.

San Miguel No. 94, San Miguel—Meets 2nd and 4th Wednesday afternoons, Clemon Hall; Mrs. Nellie Wickstrom, Rec. Sec.
San Luisita No. 108, San Luis Obispo—Meets 2nd and 4th Thursdays, W.O.W. Hall; Miss Agnes M. Lee, Rec. Sec., P. O. box 584.
El Pinal No. 163, Cambria—Meets 2nd, 4th and 5th Tuesdays, N.S.G.W. Hall; Kathryn Luchessa, Rec. Sec.

SAN MATEO COUNTY.

Bonita No. 10, Redwood City—Meets 2nd and 4th Thursdays, I.O.O.F. Hall; Mrs. Dora Wilson, Rec. Sec., 518 Middlefield Rd.
Vista del Mar No. 155, Halfmoon Bay—Meets 2nd and 4th Thursdays, I.O.O.F. Hall; Mrs. Grace Griffith, Rec. Sec.
Ano Nuevo No. 180, Pescadero—Meets 1st and 3rd Wednesdays, I.O.O.F. Hall; Mrs. Alice Mattei, Rec. Sec.
El Carmelo No. 181, Daly City—Meets 1st and 3rd Wednesdays, Masonic Hall; Mrs. Hattie Kelly, Rec. Sec., 1179 Brunswick St.
Menlo No. 211, Menlo Park—Meets 2nd and 4th Mondays, Masonic Hall; Mrs. Frances E. Malouey, Rec. Sec., P. O. box 626.
San Bruno No. 246, San Bruno—Meets 2nd and 4th Fridays, American Legion Hall; Miss Mildred Foley, Rec. Sec., 217 Miller Ave., South San Francisco.

SANTA BARBARA COUNTY.

Reina del Mar No. 126, Santa Barbara—Meets 1st and 3rd Tuesdays, Pythian Castle, 222 W. Carillo St.; Miss Christina Moller, Rec. Sec., 836 Bath St.

SANTA CLARA COUNTY.

San Jose No. 81, San Jose—Meets Thursdays, Catholic Women Center, 5th and San Fernando Sts.; Mrs. Nellie Fleming, Rec. Sec., Catholic Women Center.
Vendome No. 100, San Jose—Meets Wednesdays, Old Scottish Rite Temple; Miss Marie Buck, Rec. Sec., 1414 Ellen St.
El Monte No. 205, Mountain View—Meets 2nd and 4th Fridays, American Legion Hall; Miss Mary Ann Rokovich, Rec. Sec., R.F.D. No. 1, box 412, State Highway.
Palo Alto No. 229, Palo Alto—Meets 1st and 2nd Mondays, N.S.G.W. Hall; Miss Helena G. Hansen, Rec. Sec., 531 Lytton Ave.

SANTA CRUZ COUNTY.

Santa Cruz No. 26, Santa Cruz—Meets Mondays, N.S.G.W. Hall; Mrs. May L. Williamson, Rec. Sec., 170 Walnut Ave.
El Pajaro No. 35, Watsonville—Meets 1st and 3rd Tuesdays, I.O.O.F. Hall; Miss Ruth E. Wilson, Rec. Sec., 16 Laurel St.

SHASTA COUNTY.

Camellia No. 41, Anderson—Meets 1st and 3rd Tuesdays, Masonic Hall; Mrs. Olga E. Welbourn, Rec. Sec.
Lassen View No. 98, Shasta—Meets 2nd Friday, Masonic Hall; Miss Louise Litsch, Rec. Sec.
Hiawatha No. 140, Redding—Meets 2nd and 4th Wednesdays, Moose Hall; Ruth Presleigh, Rec. Sec., Office County Clerk.

SIERRA COUNTY.

Naomi No. 36, Downieville—Meets 2nd and 4th Wednesdays, I.O.O.F. Hall; Louise C. Dubuque, Rec. Sec.
Imogen No. 134, Sierraville—Meets 2nd and 4th Saturday afternoons, Copren Hall; Mrs. Jennie Copren, Rec. Sec.

SISKIYOU COUNTY.

Eschscholtzia No. 112, Etna—Meets 1st and 3rd Wednesdays, Masonic Hall; Mrs. Bernice E. Smith, Rec. Sec.
Mountain Dawn No. 120, Sawyers Bar—Meets 2nd and last Wednesdays, I.O.O.F. Hall; Miss Edith Dunphy, Rec. Sec.

SOLANO COUNTY.

Vallejo No. 195, Vallejo—Meets 1st and 3rd Wednesdays, K.C. Hall, 820 Marin St.; Mrs. Mary Combs, Rec. Sec., 511 York St.
Mary E. Bell No. 224, Dixon—Meets 2nd and 4th Thursdays, I.O.O.F. Hall; Grace McFadyen, Rec. Sec.

SONOMA COUNTY.

Sonoma No. 209, Sonoma—Meets 2nd and 4th Mondays, I.O.O.F. Hall; Mrs. Mae Norrbom, Rec. Sec., R.F.D., box 171.
Santa Rosa No. 217, Santa Rosa—Meets 1st and 3rd Thursdays, N.S.G.W. Hall; Mrs. Hazel E. Brown, Rec. Sec., 1521 4th St.
Petaluma No. 222, Petaluma—Meets 1st and 3rd Tuesdays, Dania Hall; Mrs. Margaret M. Oeltjen, Rec. Sec., 502 Prospect St.

STANISLAUS COUNTY.

Oakdale No. 125, Oakdale—Meets 1st Monday, I.O.O.F. Hall; Mrs. Lou Reeder, Rec. Sec.
Morada No. 199, Modesto—Meets 2nd and 4th Wednesdays, I.O.O.F. Hall; Mrs. Susan Sullivan, Rec. Sec., 823 10th St.
Eldora No. 248, Turlock—Meets 1st and 3rd Wednesdays, Fraternal Hall; Effie Lund, Rec. Sec., 624 Minaret Ave.

SUTTER COUNTY.

South Butte No. 226, Sutter—Meets 1st and 3rd Mondays, N.D.G.W. Hall; Mrs. Abbie N. Vagedes, Rec. Sec.

TEHAMA COUNTY.

Berendos No. 23, Red Bluff—Meets 1st and 3rd Tuesdays, W.O.W. Hall, 200 Pine St.; Mrs. Lillie Hammer, Rec. Sec., 636 Jackson St.

TRINITY COUNTY.

Eltapome No. 55, Weaverville—Meets 2nd and 4th Thursdays, N.S.G.W. Hall; Mrs. Lou N. Fetzer, Rec. Sec.

N.D.G.W. HIGHLY COMMENDED FOR VETERAN WELFARE ENDEAVOR.

Past Grand President Stella Finkeldey, chairman Grand Parlor N.D.G.W. Veterans Welfare Committee, received the following letters, which testify to the splendid work being done by the Native Daughters:

"We wish to thank you for the twenty packages of razor blades which we received March 1. The gift will be greatly appreciated by the patients here, as it is something that is a constant necessity.—MRS. LAURA MACMILLAN, Field Director U. S. Marine Hospital, Mare Island."

"We received your letter of March 19, and are pleased to know that you have so generously put in an order for candy for this hospital at Easter time. The patients will greatly enjoy this treat.—MRS. LAURA MACMILLAN, Field Director U. S. Marine Hospital, Mare Island."

"Could you have seen our wards Easter morning, you would realize how much the beautiful ferns, sent by the members of your Order, meant not only to the patients, but to all who saw them. The Recreation Hall also was beautified by your gift, and these lovely ferns formed its principal ornament when a picture of the room was taken on Sunday evening just after the services. These pictures were taken by order of the War Department, and we hope very much we may have one to show you on your next visit to the hospital. On behalf of the patients please accept our most sincere appreciation, and also that of Fred Barrier, who was delighted to receive the little plant you were so thoughtful to send him—you should see the pleasure he has taken in it.—MISS BERTHA C. LOVELL, Field Director, MISS WILLIE L. HATCH, Recreation Worker Letterman General Hospital U.S.A., San Francisco."

"The small candies and the 300 chocolate rabbits for our Easter tables and trays arrived in good time and in good condition. The amount of small candies sent was ample for nicely filling our nut cups, and the chocolate rabbits made such a nice additional tray favor. We want to express to you our sincere thanks and warm appreciation for again making possible the use of the gay little cups sent to us by the Pasadena Red Cross Juniors. The nut cups were beautifully made and in exquisite pastel shades. Our chief dietitian and her assistants asked that their thanks be included with ours as they are always more than delighted at being able to give such a festive, decorative touch to their tables and trays. We want you to know that we truly appreciate your remembrance of us at the different holiday seasons. With best of wishes to you and to the Order of the Native Daughters of the Golden West, (MISS) FRANCES MAYNARD, Senior Recreational Aide Veterans Administration, Whipple, Arizona."

"Your card of March 25 and the box arrived the same day, that is, last Saturday. This is certainly a wonderful shipment of socks; and even more coming! The Native Daughters of the Golden West are indeed kind to us, and you may be sure the patients are going to be given much pleasure and comfort from the warmth these lovely socks will provide. The light weight style is very popular with them this time of year and during the fall. In behalf of our hospitalized veterans, the hospital administration wishes to extend to the Native Daughters of the Golden West our sincere thanks for the socks and to express our appreciation of the deep interest which your organization takes in the welfare of our sick people.—(MISS) IRMA ANDERSON, Senior Recreational Aide Veterans Administration Hospital, Livermore, California."

N.D.G.W. OFFICIAL DEATH LIST.

Giving, the name, the date of death, and the Subordinate Parlor affiliation of all deceased members as reported to Grand Secretary Sallie R. Thaler from March 18 to April 19, 1932:

TUOLUMNE COUNTY.

Dardanelle No. 66, Sonora—Meets Fridays, I.O.O.F. Hall; Mrs. Nettie Whitto, Rec. Sec.
Golden Era No. 99, Columbia—Meets 1st and 3rd Thursdays, N.S.G.W. Hall; Miss Irene Ponce, Rec. Sec.
Anona No. 164, Jamestown—Meets 2nd and 4th Tuesdays, I.O.O.F. Hall; Mrs. Rosa A. Beckwith, Rec. Sec., P. O. box 87.

YOLO COUNTY.

Woodland No. 90, Woodland—Meets 2nd and 4th Tuesdays, N.S.G.W. Hall; Mrs. Maude Heaton, Rec. Sec., 153 College St.

YUBA COUNTY.

Marysville No. 162, Marysville—Meets 2nd and 4th Wednesdays, Liberty Hall; Miss Cecelia C. Gomes, Rec. Sec., 701 6th St.
Camp Far West No. 218, Wheatland—Meets 3rd Tuesday, I.O.O.F. Hall; Mrs. Ethel C. Brock, Rec. Sec., P. O. box 285.

AFFILIATED ORGANIZATIONS.

General Assembly Past Presidents—Meetings held annually in April at the home-town of Chief President; Mrs. Cora Stobing, 1739 San Jose Ave., San Francisco, Chief President; Mrs. Anna G. Loser, 72 Grove Lane, San Anselmo, Chief Secretary.
Past Presidents Association No. 1—Meets 1st and 3rd Mondays, N.S.G.W. Bldg., 414 Mason St., San Francisco; Mrs. Minnie F. Dobbin, Pres.; Mrs. May R. Barry, Rec. Sec., 2319 19th Ave., San Francisco.
Past Presidents Association No. 2—Meets 2nd and 4th Mondays, "Wigwam," Pacific Bldg., 16th and Jefferson, Oakland; Frieda Reichhold, Pres.; Mrs. Elizabeth B. Goodman, Rec. Sec., 134 Juana Ave., San Leandro.
Past Presidents Association No. 3 (Santa Clara County)—Meets 2nd Tuesday, homes of members; Mrs. Clara Briggs, Pres.; Mrs. Mary G. Newton, Rec. Sec., 1070 Jackson St., Santa Clara.
Past Presidents Association No. 4 (Sacramento County)—Meets 2nd Monday, Unitarian Hall, 1413 27th St., Sacramento City; Viola Gennoe, Pres.; Lily May Tilden, Rec. Sec., 3225 "T" St., Sacramento.
Past Presidents Association No. 5 (Butte County)—Meets 1st Friday, homes of members, Chico and Oroville; Sonora Steadman, Pres.; Ruth Brown, Rec. Sec., 1265 Leah Court, Oroville.
Past Presidents Association No. 6 (Nevada County)—Meets 4th Friday, alternately between Nevada City, Pythian Castle, and Grass Valley, Edna Sampson's home; Margaret V. Nolan, Pres.; Vere Hansen, Rec. Sec., R.F.D. No. 2, box 41-C, Grass Valley.
Past Presidents Association No. 7 (Sonoma County)—Meets 1st Thursday, N.S.G.W. Hall, Santa Rosa; Willow Borba, Pres.; Clytie Lewis, Rec. Sec., R.F.D. No. 4, box 345-A, Santa Rosa.
Past Presidents Association No. 8 (San Joaquin and Stanislaus Counties)—Meets 2nd Thursday, Red Men Hall, Stockton; Mrs. Lois Armstrong, Pres.; Mrs. Harriet F. Corr, Rec. Sec., 729 E. Sonora St., Stockton.
Native Sons and Native Daughters Central Committee on Homeless Children—Main Office, 955 Phelan Bldg., San Francisco; Mrs. John W. Stirling, Chmn.; Miss Mary E. Brusie, Sec. Los Angeles branch office, 3924 Sunset Blvd.; Dorothy Schlingman, Sec.

(ADVERTISEMENT.)

Riley, Kate; January 1, 1932; Chispa No. 40.
Driscoll, Minnie; March 7, 1932; Keith No. 137.
Dunn, Elizabeth H.; March 11, 1932; Plumas Pioneer No. 219.
Horgan, Mary; February 12, 1932; Mission No. 227.
Pollard, Rozie B.; February 6, 1932; Los Angeles No. 124.
Curry, Mary E.; March 6, 1932; Fern No. 123.
Chick, Alice Huse; January 24, 1932; Reina del Mar No. 126.
Graham, Rose; March 17, 1932; Alta No. 3.
Flint, Elizabeth A. Smith; March 10, 1932; San Juan Bautista No. 179.
McNamara, Mary L.; February 25, 1932; Columbia No. 70.
Walsh, Ethel L.; March 25, 1932; Las Lomas No. 72.
Brennan, Agnes; March 28, 1932; Keith No. 137.

NATIVE DAUGHTER NEWS

(Continued from Page 15)

They filled the various stations and also served a collation, including a beautifully decorated birthday cake. A program was presented by Pearl Simpson, Evelyn Wurzell, Irma A. Heilbron, Martha Klindt and Ann Wood. Gifts were presented Supervising Deputy Ann Wood and President Sarah Miller. The second of a series of three card parties was held April 27.

Members of San Diego's past presidents club were entertained by Ann Wood and Martha Klindt at the former's Imperial Beach cottage. A dozen appetites, sharpened by the drive around the bay, did full justice to a delicious and bountiful italian dinner. The next meeting of the club will be at the home of Mrs. Sofia Sharpe.

Shower for Bride.

Oakland—A surprise bridal shower was given by Aloha No. 106 April 5 in honor of District Deputy Mildred Brandt-Erwin, and she received many lovely gifts. Refreshments were served. A very successful whist party was held at the home of Past President Jennie Peterson.

The social committee, under the chairmanship of Grand Secretary Sallie R. Thaler, is actively planning for the official visit of Grand President Evelyn I. Carlson to the Parlor, May 24. Educational week and the birthday of Oakland will be observed at one of the first meetings in May.

Twelve Initiated.

Modesto—The initiation of twelve candidates by Morada No. 199 April 13 was witnessed by a large assemblage. President Eleanor Lewis presided. The hall, decorated with spring flowers by Pearl Gordon and a committee, resembled a real flower garden. Refreshments, in charge of Emma Smith, were served at tables decorated in pastel shades. Among those in attendance were Supervising Deputy Irene Kopf, Effie Prothero and May Givens. Jointly with Modesto No. 11 N.S.G.W., the Parlor had a public whist party April 20. Dancing followed the play and refreshments were served.

A party for those members of Morada whose birthdays come in January, February and March was held March 24. Games were played and refreshments, including a large cake lighted with green candles, were served. A gift was presented each guest.

District Meeting To Be Held.

Napa—Eschol No. 16 entertained twenty-five members of La Junta No. 203 (Saint Helena) April 11. Games were played, and a banquet was served under the supervision of Caroline Boggs. A district meeting is to be held at Saint Helena May 14, with Napa, Lake and Solano Counties Parlors participating. Supervising Deputy Elvena Woodard is in charge.

Card Party.

Crockett—Carquinez No. 234 had a card party April 6 at which several tables of whist and bridge were in operation. The Parlor will give other parties every two or three months.

Mission Sesquicentennial—Ventura City celebrated April 3 the one hundred and fiftieth anniversary of the founding, March 31, 1782, of the Mission San Buenaventura.

Women's Gathering—The California Federation of Women's Clubs will meet in annual convention at Los Angeles City, May 4-6.

Fiesta—San Jose, Santa Clara County, will have its annual Fiesta de las Roses, May 19-21.

A BIT O' FARMING and GARDENING

PREPARED EXPRESSLY FOR THE GRIZZLY BEAR BY M. H. ELLIS

WITH THE FEDERAL FARM BOARD, the University of California through its Giannini Foundation of Agricultural Economics, and the State Department of Agriculture all co-operating in an effort to solve the marketing problem for the farmers of the state, some progress should be made. Indeed, it is but fair to say that some progress already has been made and that indications point to better conditions in the distribution and sale of the specialty crops of California.

There is heard, still, the demand that the farmer be given a price for his produce that will pay costs of production plus a fair margin of profit. Much as this is to be desired, it is impossible of attainment, as often has been pointed out by those who have made a real study of the situation. People will pay just so much for foodstuffs of a certain kind; when the price gets beyond what they are willing to pay, they will substitute something else, even though it be less desirable. The solution of the problem is not in an attempt of this kind. Rather, it is in the production and distribution, together with an efficient sales organization.

Production must be curtailed to the point where the product can be marketed at a profit, or new markets must be opened up and old ones stimulated to take greater supplies. Even then, only what the consumers will take at a price fair to the farmer can be produced on an economically sound basis. Curtailment of production, particularly in tree crops, is in the hands of the producer. He does not have to pull out orchards, necessarily; he can thin down the crop on the trees. This, of course, will take the concerted action of every farmer, not a few. But the problem of the farmers cannot be solved until they are a unit in any action they may take. Nothing less than full co-operation can satisfactorily save the situation. Such action will succeed where legislation has failed; its weakness is the weakness of human nature, the greed of some individuals to profit at the expense of others.

BUDDING AND GRAFTING WALNUTS.

Whether it is best to graft or to bud walnuts will not be settled here. If the owner desires to start work now, he may do so by budding at almost any time during the summer, and then grafting in the spring where the buds do not take. In budding now use dormant buds taken from mature trees where they have failed to push out early, or from cold-storage scions cut last winter.

FOR BETTER ROSES.

The rose bush likes a soil rich in humus and nitrogen. So see that the soil is built up the year round. These means, combined, would make an almost ideal combination: manure in the fall, bone meal in the winter, wood ashes at either time, and a good commercial fertilizer in the spring. Incidentally, don't wet the foliage of roses in the late afternoon or evening unless additional trouble, from mildew, is desired. If mildew appears, either dusting with finely ground sulphur, or spraying with the proper oil emulsion, will control it. The oil also will control the aphis.

BERRY THINNING OF GRAPES.

Thinning grapes on the vine is a subject too long to be intelligently discussed here, but it is a practice that under the right conditions will pay big results to the vineyardist. The thinning is done by snipping out clusters here and there from the bunch. Usually the yield in pounds is greater and the quality better.

FLOWERS TO PLANT IN MAY.

There are dozens of flowers that may be started this month, and while many of them are kinds that the ordinary gardener does not know, there are plenty of the old reliables that should be remembered this month. In no other state, it is safe to say, is such diversity of blossom possible as in California.

GROWING THE HYDRANGEA.

One evergreen shrub that is popular in California is the hydrangea, which thrives everywhere it is given protection from the too-hot sun, and where it gets plenty of moisture. One thing that tends to its popularity, aside from the beauty of the shrub and its masses of blossom, is that there are no serious pests or diseases to attack it. The hydrangea asks little but shade and water. The difference in color of the blossoms is caused by the condition of the soil. An acid soil usually gives blue flowers where an alkaline soil will give pink, from the same variety.

CARROTS EASY TO GROW.

Since the value of vegetables in the diet has become an important topic, no one vegetable has grown more in popularity than the carrot, palatable and easy to grow. Carrots may be obtained from the garden in most parts of the state at any time of the year. The soil should be well pulverized before the seed is planted, and if there is a tendency to crust, the surface should be kept damp so that the plants may come through.

GARDEN CULTIVATION.

Cultivation in the garden has two primary purposes: to keep the weeds down and to preserve the surface of the soil from baking and cracking. Further than this, there is no need for cultivation; constant stirring of the soil does no good; indeed, by turning the soil over and exposing to the sun, it may be damaged. Weeds rob the soil of moisture and plant food; kill them while they are small.

In irrigating the garden, it is better to water along the rows by running furrows than to use overhead sprinkling. Many foliage diseases result from the wetting of the leaves of the plants; often these can be avoided by furrow irrigation. Irrigation should not be frequent, but it should be thorough.

WRY NECK IN HENS.

Lack of exercise and eating of over-stimulating feeds may result in wry neck of hens. This is manifested by the hens holding their heads back and looking up. When the trouble appears, feed a mash with a large proportion of bran, and plenty of greens. Epsom salts, one pound to 125 hens, also will help. Those affected may well be taken from the flock and given a teaspoonful of castor oil each. Sometimes wry neck is a chronic stage of coccidiosis. In this event, use the same control, and feed plenty of milk, either dry or liquid.

WATCH THE WEEDS.

Weeds are water wasters. While it is true there is some water taken from the soil by evaporation, most of it goes out through the leaves or plants by transpiration. Consequently, every weed that grows in the field or orchard or garden is wasting water that in irrigated districts costs money. Be sure that cultivation is frequent and thorough enough to kill the weeds. Cultivation beyond that point is a waste of time.

PRUNING FOR EARLY CANTALOUPES.

While it is a practice not generally followed, the pinching back of cantaloupe vines when they are five or six joints in length is held by many growers to force early production. Pinch the tips or cut them off at this stage and the melons will be from a week to ten days earlier, is the claim made by those who have tried this plan. If the melons were not fed with a well-rotted manure fertilizer before planting, it will be a good thing to give them a side dressing of complete fertilizer, about 5-10-5. Soak it in with the irrigation water; how much good it will do will depend upon the fertility of the soil. Melons are strong feeders and need to be given added plant food in most soils.

FEEDING THE WEANED COLT.

A colt after leaving its mother's side should be given feed rich in protein, calcium and phosphorus. Good pasture is the main thing, preferably blue grass if it is available. For concentrates use wheat bran, cottonseed meal, soybeans and cowpeas—all rich in protein. Alfalfa and barley will do, but oats are better. Milk is not necessary, once the colt has been weaned. Most important of all, however, is the pasture, nature's own feed for the young and growing horse.

BIRDS IN THE GARDEN.

The only real method to prevent bird damage to garden crops, particularly while they are young, is to screen them so that the birds can not get at them. Scarecrows and strings festooned with strips of paper or white cloth are of doubtful value. Spraying with nicotine sulphate may give good results, but this is not by any means certain. As the plants attain size, the danger from birds becomes less.

MERCED N.D.G.W. GRAND PARLOR

VERITAS PARLOR NO. 75 IS ARRANGing for the meeting of the Forty-sixth Grand Parlor of the Order of Native Daughters of the Golden West in Merced City, June 20-24. Grand President Evelyn I. Carlson (Dolores No. 169) of an Francisco will preside, and at the session's ose will automatically become the Junior Past rand President.

A large general committee of Veritas has outned, and submitted to the Grand President for pproval, an attractive entertainment program, nd is attending to all the many other details. azel Laverty is chairman of the general comittee, and Eugenia Kahl is the vice-chairman. he several subcommittees are headed by the llowing: Pauline Zirker (reception), Helen rutosik (finance), Mildred Heinzen (publicity), lay F. Givens (entertainment), Zelphia Thomas decorations), Margaret Thornton (registration nd reservations), Mary Vanden Heuval (housng), Alma Fowler (badges), Fleurette Levy printing), Marion Pulcifer (transportation), ucille Cunningham (dance), Lena Guild punch), Sylvia Rose (refreshments).

While some additional candidates for Grand arlor offices made their intentions known durg April, there are several prospectives who ill not definitely declare themselves until the ubordinate Parlors choose their delegates durg May. Rumors are numerous about the San rancisco Bay that every office will have two or ore contestants. The Grizzly Bear has atmpted to get the lowdown and the highup on e office situation, and from reliable informaon received to presstime presents this lineup:

Grand President—Grand Vice-president Anna lixon-Armstrong (Woodland No. 90) of Woodand.

Grand Vice-president—Grand Marshal Irma . Laird (Alturas No. 159) of Alturas.

Grand Secretary—Sallie R. Thaler (Aloha No. 06) of Oakland, incumbent.

Grand Treasurer—Susie K. Christ (Yosemite o. 83) of San Francisco, incumbent.

Grand Marshal—Sadie Winn-Brainard (Califia o. 22) of Sacramento; Grand Trustee Gladys . Noce (Amapola No. 80) of Sutter Creek; lay F. Givens (Mariposa No. 63) of Cathay.

Grand Inside Sentinel—Grand Outside Sentinel Orinda Gunther-Giannini (Orinda No. 56) of San Francisco.

Grand Outside Sentinel—Elvena Woodard (Vallejo No. 195) of Vallejo; Hazel B. Hansen (Verdugo No. 240) of Glendale.

Grand Trustees (seven to be selected)—Anna Thuesen (Alta No. 3) of San Francisco, incumbent; Edna B. Briggs (La Bandera No. 110) of Sacramento, incumbent; Jane Vick (Reina del Mar No. 126) of Santa Barbara; Alice M. Lane (Castro No. 178) of San Francisco; Florence D. Boyle (Gold of Ophir No. 190) of Oroville, incumbent; Ethel S. Begley (Marinita No. 198) of San Rafael, incumbent; Willow Borba (Santa Rosa No. 217) of Sebastopol, incumbent; Florence D. Schoneman (Rudecinda No. 230) of San Pedro, incumbent.

Still, not even a whisper regarding the probable meeting-place of the 1933 Grand Parlor. The June Grizzly Bear will give all the Merced Grand Parlor news that can be gathered from dependable sources.—C.M.H.

LIFE OF NOTED CALIFORNIA PIONEER DEPICTED IN HISTORICAL PAGEANT.

Williams (Colusa County)—A pageant depicting the life of one of California's noted Pioneers, Dr. Robert B. Semple, was featured here April 22. His remains are interred in the local cemetery, and above the grave is a moss-covered marble slab inscribed "Robert Semple, died October 25, 1854, aged 48 years, 8 months, 22 days." The proceeds of the pageant will be used to mark his grave with a bronze monument.

Dr. Semple, a native of Kentucky, arrived at Sutter Fort (Sacramento) Christmas Day of 1845. He was a member of the Bear Flag Party which, June 14, 1846, raised the California Republic Flag at Sonoma. At Monterey, August 15, 1846, he issued the state's first newspaper, "The Californian," which in May 1847 was moved to Yerba Buena (San Francisco) and later sold to the "California Star." In 1847 he located the site of the present City of Colusa.

He also laid out the present City of Benicia, Solano County, and constructed and operated the first ferry across Carquinez Straits. He also organized the state's first mail service: April 19, 1849, two soldiers on horseback left San Francisco and San Diego, met half-way, exchanged mail sacks and returned to their starting points.

Dr. Semple was the president of California's First Constitutional Convention, which assembled at Monterey, September 1, 1849. He died at Williams, October 25, 1854.

[Dr. Semple was the father of Mrs. Mary E. Turman, affiliated with the long-since-defunct Lydia Parlor No. 15 N.D.G.W. (Colusa City), and she was the elective Past Grand President of a portion of the First and all of Second Grand Parlors, during the time that Tina L. Kane presided as Grand President.—Editor.]

"ANGELS CAN DO NO MORE!"

(Continued from Page 8)

dependence of "flaming youth" and stand eager and equipped to give the necessary firm but quiet handling, and are able to exert the truest moral and religious influence.

This making of a worthwhile citizen is what keeps this project of the Native Sons and the Native Daughters a sacred one, in times of war or peace, tranquillity or despondency, prosperity or depression.

CONDITION OF FINANCES.

The Native Sons and Native Daughters Central Homeless Children Committee's financial statement for the year April 1, 1931, to March 31, 1932, gives the total operating receipts as $20,893.85, $14,137.98 of which amount came from Native Son and Native Daughter sources, $402.85 from friends, $893.90 from interest and dividends, $5,555.57 from board refunds. The year's operating expenses totaled $29,999.24. The operating deficit for the year was $9,105.39.

Bequests totaling $15,750 were received, from the estates of Senator James D. Phelan $10,000, Charles VanDamme $5,000, Max Wagner $250, Dora Washburn $500. These offset the operating deficit, and made the actual cash gain for the year $6,444.61. The Central Committee's available cash March 31, 1932, was $15,012.56.

MOTHER N.S. GRAND SECRETARY DEAD.

San Francisco—Mrs. Mary Regan, mother of John T. Regan (South San Francisco Parlor No. 157), Grand Secretary N.S.G.W., passed away March 27. She was a native of Ireland, aged 87, and had resided here since 1872.

Bret Harte Pageant—Columbia, Tuolumne County, will have its second annual Bret Harte Pageant, May 27-29.

SAN FRANCISCO

"THE HOUNDS"

(PETER T. CONMY,
Historian Golden Gate Parlor N.S.G.W.)

THE DISCOVERY OF GOLD IN CALIFORNIA in 1849 gave impetus to people all over the world to migrate to the valleys and the foothills of the Sacramento and the San Joaquin and to the Sierra Nevada in search of gold. In every popular migration two classes of people are represented, the upright and the evil. The California gold rush was no exception. A great many bad people came here in 1848, 1849 and 1850—the scum of society from the underworld of Eastern cities and from ports of Europe.

The old saying, "birds of a feather flock together," is proved by the quick and startling manner in which undesirables in San Francisco in 1848 found companionship in each other. They organized under the name of "Regulators," professed to be a political organization. To further disguise their real motives, the "Regulators" called their meeting-place "Tammany Hall," which indicated a political club, such as the famous Tammany organization of New York, was being maintained. The "Regulators" were not interested in the civic welfare of the young city, however. They were banded for lawlessness and crime. In the absence of a well-organized government it was a relatively easy matter for a band of ruffians to "get by" with almost any type of illegal adventure upon which they might embark. Foreigners, especially the Spanish and the Mexicans, were made the objects of raids and maraudings of the "Regulators," who came to be known by another name which truly fit them, "The Hounds." Night after night the unfortunate foreign residents were robbed, beaten, wounded, and frequently murdered by "The Hounds."

San Francisco was not alone the sufferer, but the nearby settlements of the east bay were also attacked under the guise of protecting Americans from the foreigners. Regarding "The Hounds," Soule wrote in 1854: "To such a daring extent were matters carried that the body, proud of their strength and numbers, attempted a sort of military display, and on Sundays armed with bludgeons and loaded revolvers, paraded the streets in open daylight, with drum and fife playing and banners flying. It was in the dead of night, however, that their outrages were done. Then they would march to the tents of known Chilenos and tearing them down, rob and spoil the contents of value, and shamefully mistreat and even murder the inmates."

Things went from bad to worse. In one of their attacks a foreigner accidentally killed an innocent American whom he thought to be a "Hound." This caused "The Hounds" to do more violent wrongs than ever. June 15, 1849, they perpetrated a most savage and cruel attack in the broad daylight of a Sunday afternoon. This was the beginning of the end. The next day saw the upright men of the community seeking retribution and an end of lawlessness and strife. At the behest of Captain Bezer Simmons and Samuel Brannan, Alcalde Leavenworth called a mass meeting of citizens in Portsmouth Square. Funds were subscribed to aid the mistreated foreigners and 230 men present volunteered, and were commissioned, as special constables by the alcalde.

In anticipation of the establishment of a state government, a sheriff was elected in the person of J. J. Ellis. The wrongdoers were speedily apprehended and jailed on board the U. S. frigate "Warren," at anchor in the bay. A district attorney was elected, and also judges. A grand jury was empanelled and brought indictments against "The Hounds." The exact charges were, "conspiracy, riot, robbery, and assault with intent to kill." At the ensuing trial a verdict of guilty was returned. The leaders were sentenced to ten years in whatever prison the governor of California might select. The less-important members of the gang were given lighter sentences. However, the sentences were never executed. This was due to the absence of a state government and to the corrupt politics of the times. The desired result was achieved; that is, "The Hounds" as a factor in San Francisco life ceased to exist. The strong arm of righteousness had asserted itself. Lawlessness arose again, however, and in 1851 and in 1856 it was necessary to organize Vigilance Committees.

HISTORIC LANDMARK.

San Francisco is rich in a historic past but woefully lacking in the presence of landmarks of that past. This is due to the fact that between 1849 and 1851 some six great fires swept away various portions of the young and growing city. Most of what survived was, in turn, lost. This is due to the great fire and earthquake of 1906. In the large downtown district of the city there is hardly a structure that can be called a landmark now. The old church next door to Native Sons Building was one until replaced by the present structure. Temple Emmanuel was also a historic building until it gave way to the marvelous building known as "450 Sutter."

At California street and Grant avenue there is, however, a building standing whose walls were erected nearly eighty years ago—old St. Mary's Church. July 7, 1853, the cornerstone of that church was laid by Archbishop Alemany. It was to be the cathedral of the archdiocese of San Francisco. The interior was gutted by the 1906 fire, but was rebuilt within the original walls. As far as can be ascertained this is, therefore, the oldest structure in the downtown section of San Francisco.

ENTHUSIASTIC MEETING.

After an absence of six weeks from San Francisco, Grand President Evelyn I. Carlson was greeted by more than 250 Native Daughters at her official visit to Guadalupe No. 153 March 28. Preceding the meeting a dinner was served at which the Grand President, District Deputy Katherine Keating and President Florence Pyne were honor-guests. The tables were tastefully decorated in keeping with the Easter season. Other grand officers present were Grand Outside Sentinel Orinda Giannini, Grand Organist Lola Horgan, Grand Trustees Ethel Begley and Willow Borba, and Past Grand Margaret Hill. While the Grand President was being escorted to her seat of honor Kathleen Keenan sang "We Love You," and as each grand officer was being escorted she was presented with a small gift. Two candidates were initiated, and the officers exemplified the ritual in a very creditable manner; the Parlor has initiated twenty-five candidates this year.

Guadalupe takes a lively interest in all the projects of the Order, and on this occasion showed its interest in the Home by presenting the Grand President with a check for $175 toward the Loyalty Pledge. A beautiful layette, consisting of about 200 dainty articles for the homeless children, was on display. A letter from Letterman Hospital thanked the Parlor for the delightful Easter party. A token in appreciation of splendid work and long service on the veterans committee was presented Organist Carmel Parenti.

Grand President Carlson, in her usual interesting manner, delivered an inspiring address on the progress and the projects of the Order and thanked Guadalupe for the splendid reception given to her. A gift of china was presented her as a remembrance of the very happy evening. Following the meeting dainty refreshments were served. Much credit is due May Marchant and her committees who were responsible for the success of the affair.

NATIVE DAUGHTER DOINGS.

Alta Parlor No. 3 plans a benefit bridge-whist party at the Home, May 6. May L. MacDonald, the chairman, is being assisted by Grand Trustee Annie C. Thuesen, Catherine O'Reilly, Elizabeth F. Douglas, Angeline Vest and Claire Bolman.

Buena Vista Parlor No. 68 celebrated its forıth anniversary April 14 at a sumptuous din-r, the table decorations for which were carried t in the national colors. Inspirational ad-esses were given by Mrs. Angelo J. Rossi, An-tte Abbott Adams, Past Grand Dr. Mariana ›rtola, Grand Organist Lola Horgan and Presi-nt L. Chamberlain. A unique program was esented in commemoration of George Wash-gton, those participating including Elenia Ben-tt, Dorothy Rathjens, Grand Organist Horgan, ary Gramney, Kittie Schmidt, Hulda Mackin-sh, Florence Bartlett, Margaret Mitchell, Sarah errepont, Golda Minton, Helen Kennerley, Em-Bean, Margaret Barrett. The committee re-onsible for the pleasing affair included Mary amney (chairman), I. Leroi, J. Packer, A. ader, E. Wilson.

La Estrella Parlor No. 89 spent a delightful ening at a layette shower. Many lovely gar-ents were received and the complete outfit ıen given Miss Brusie will add much to the mfort of many little homeless children.

The entertainment and dance given April 2 the Merrymakers of El Vespero Parlor No. 8 for the benefit of the Loyalty Pledge was a g financial and social success. President Anne odfrey, chairman of arrangements, was assisted Marguerite Kemme, Agnes Ryan, Mary Mac-gno, Columbina Zullo, Mary Casey, Evelyn mmens. A play, "A Night in Roseland," ar-nged and directed by Ruby D. Bried and Mary accagno, was presented, with Claire Bolman at e piano. The cast included Ruby D. Bried, nne Godfrey, Marguerite Kemme, Mary Casey, orence Johnson, Agnes Ryan, Mary Maccagno, sephine Paravagno, Irene Lapphaille, Jane apachet, Columbina Zullo, Loretta Winter, ladys Casey, Isabel Casey, Marie Lassallette, aita Schmidt, Helen Reddy, Josephine Buffa, dia Rahn, Mary Delagnes, Esther Walsh, Jean ındini. Dancing followed the entertainment.

Gabriel Parlor No. 139 gave a very successful hist-bridge party March 27, the receipts being lded to the Loyalty Pledge which is fast near-g its quota. Many nice prizes were distrib-ed, after which coffee and cake were served.

Under the capable chairmanship of Nan J. elly the meetingroom of Portola No. 172 was ansformed into an easter garden when the arlor entertained, March 29, Grand President velyn I. Carlson on her official visit. Over 350 ere present to extend greetings, among them rand Trustees Ethel Begley, Anna Thuesen and illow Borba, Past Grands Emma Foley, Mar-ıret Hill, Dr. Louise Heilbron and Mae Himes-oonan, Grand Inside Sentinel Orinda Giannini ıd Grand Organist Lola Horgan. Two candi-ıtes were initiated. Christine Brougham pre-ded, and Grand President Carlson highly com-imented the officers for their splendid exempli-ation of the ritual. The San Francisco glee ub, organized by District Deputy Agnes Curry, tertained during the evening, Grand Organist organ acting as accompanist.

NATIVE SON DOINGS.

Twin Peaks Parlor No. 214 entertained April 3 in honor of its delegates to the Stockton rand Parlor. There were entertainment fea-ıres and refreshments in abundance. The even-g's feature was the address of Grand Trustee Joseph J. McShane, who told of visits to the Parlors in his district. He stated that, with few exceptions, they showed strong gains, both numerically and financially, and he particularly praised the splendid example set by Calistoga No. 86.

The drum corps of Bret Harte No. 260 is making fine progress and will soon be ready for appearance in public. To provide uniform funds the Parlor sponsored a dance April 23. The horseshoe team is being led to victory by Brother Allen. The neighborhood whist games are proving popular in the Ingleside district. They are held the first Tuesday of each month in American Legion Hall.

In Memoriam

SHE HAS PASSED, BUT MEMORY LINGERS.

"It was with sad and heavy hearts, indeed, that the members of Buena Vista Parlor No. 68 N.D.G.W. assembled to bid our last farewell to Sister Nellie Rader. For over thirty years Mrs. Rader has been a member of the Native Daughters of the Golden West and has ever been an inspiration of sterling womanhood to those who knew her. Our heartfelt sympathy is extended to those of her immediate family.

"And now that she has left us,
We'll miss those kindly smiles,
We'll miss that ever-welcome hand
That shortened lonely miles.
For a friendship such as her's will last,
And memory's hand will scroll
Her worth on golden pages
Of our Pioneer Honor roll.
And there's a golden gate that's wide,
Where eternity is sweet,
Where we shall see her smiling face
And outstretched hand to greet.
Let's hold her as our guiding star,
And tread the path she trod,
And trust when we hear our bugle call,
Like her, we'll be with God."

MARGARET BARRETT, Secretary.

San Francisco, April 16, 1932.

PIONEER MEMORIAL RELICS BUILDING TO BE DEDICATED.

Oroville (Butte County)—At the invitation of the Butte County Pioneer Memorial Association, composed principally of members of Argonaut Parlor No. 8 N.S.G.W. and Gold of Ophir No. 190 N.D.G.W., the N.S.G.W. grand officers, headed by Grand President Dr. Frank I. Gonzalez, will dedicate May 12 the Pioneer Memorial Relics building. There will be a parade, and all Parlors of both Orders have been invited to participate.

SIERRA COUNTY N.S. OFFICIAL DEAD.

Downieville—Supervisor W. E. Miller, affiliated with Downieville Parlor No. 92 N.S.G.W., died April 7 at his Nevada County ranch. He was born in Sierra County April 4, 1873, and is survived by a wife and two daughters.

"Stop and Go When Signs Say So," is the May slogan of the California Public Safety Committee in its campaign to lessen the fearful auto death-toll.

LOS ANGELES CITY AND COUNTY

UNIVERSITY SOUTHERN CALIFORNIA FEATURES CALIFORNIA HISTORY

(ROCKWELL D. HUNT, Ph.D.,
Dean of the Graduate School of the
University of Southern California.)

EVEN A CURSORY PERUSAL OF THE records leaves no doubt concerning the interest in promoting the study of California and Western American history taken by the University of Southern California. No group of citizens will be more ready to recognize in this a valuable service to the larger community and a contribution to the welfare of the state than the Native Sons and the Native Daughters of the Golden West.

On coming to the University of Southern California in 1908, the writer, having already lectured at Stanford University and the University of the Pacific, immediately introduced a course in Pacific Slope history, described as follows: "Special lecture course, with special reference to California. Primarily for advanced college students and teachers. One hour throughout the year." This course, popular from the beginning, was later expanded to two units throughout the year. In 1921-22 courses in Latin-American colonies and Latin-American republics were added by Doctor William H. Teeter, who had enjoyed extensive residence in South America.

In 1923, Rolland A. Vandegrift, now State Finance Director, was brought to the University to give special emphasis to California and Latin-American history. Having been a Native Sons Travelling Fellow in the University of California, he possessed high qualifications for the position. Not only did he take over the course in Pacific Slope history but, with the writer of this, he organized a seminar for graduate students who already had a background for research work.

When Professor Vandegrift left the University to take up other work in 1925, Doctor Owen C. Coy was secured to assume charge of the rapidly developing classes in Pacific Slope history. He added a full year course in the history of the West, and became director of the graduate seminar in Pacific Slope history, as well as the undergraduate course in California history. Doctor Coy is well known throughout the state as Manager of the State Historical Association, a coordinating body supported by public funds. An author of note in this particular field, as well as a popular teacher and lecturer, he is devoting himself with marked success to the development and promotion of the study of California history. He is regarded as one of the foremost authorities on the gold days and the development of the American state.

In 1927-28, Doctor George Hammond was added to the University faculty. He is recognized as one of the most capable of the many students of Professor H. E. Bolton of the University of California. He at once took over the classes in Latin-American history, his special field, and added a course in the history of Mexico. Later he organized a graduate seminar in Latin-American history. Doctor Hammond is the founder of the Quivera Society, which publishes important documents in the early Latin-American field, and is a productive and very enthusiastic scholar.

Enough has been said to indicate that the University of Southern California is very much alive to the interests of the rich field of California history, and the thorough cultivation of this field. It should be added that in the magnificent new Edward L. Doheny Junior Memorial Library, now rapidly approaching completion, ample provision has been made for giving California history the prominent place it deserves. The librarian, Miss Charlotte Brown, has omitted nothing making for the complete equipment of this important department. Taking everything into consideration, it is gratifying to be able to report to the Native Sons and the Native Daughters of the Golden West that the University of Southern California has made commendable progress and undoubtedly will continue to expand its work in the history of California and the Southwest,—a field of endeavor at once so attractive in itself and so dear to the entire membership of both Orders.

"ON TO CALIFORNIA."

What could be more fitting for the great recognition California has received in being awarded the tenth Olympiad, soon to be held in Los Angeles, than an Olympic song composed by a Native Daughter? No song has been more favorably received than "On To California," which overflows with rhythm and melody. It was an instant success.

The composer, Louise Graeser, is a member of Los Angeles Parlor No. 124 N.D.G.W. She presented "On To California" to the Parlor, which

LOUISE GRAESER.
—Sheehan Photo.

has had it published. All the receipts from its sale go to the Parlor. Buy a copy, at twenty-five cents, from Composer Graeser (PLeasant 7882), Sophie Stewart (ORegon 6369), who has sung "On To California" on numerous occasions recently, or President Gertrude Allen (CApitol

When you purchase goods advertised in The Grizzly Bear, or answer an advertisement in this magazine, please be sure to mention The Grizzly Bear. That's co-operation mutually beneficial.

4327), who urges: "Be a booster for everything done by a Californian! So, let a copy of this delightful song be on every piano. Sing it, whistle it, hum it, and, above all, buy it."

TO FEAST ON RABBITS.

It looked like old times around the meeting-place of Los Angeles Parlor No. 45 N.S.G.W. April 21, when all the local Parlors were well represented and several of No. 45's oldtimers put in an appearance. The attractions were a buffet supper and entertainment, both of which were greatly enjoyed by the big crowd. Sidney B. Witkowski and Charles Lloyd were in charge, and among their many assistants were Albert Metz, District Deputy Al Cron, Walter Fisher, Harold Linden, Marshal Anthony Pierce and First Vice-president Owen S. Adams. Incidentally, the date was also the birthday anniversary of Junior Past Grand President John T. Newell.

May 12, Los Angeles will have initiation, and on the 19th an open meeting. May 26 a rabbit feast will be the attraction, the rabbits to be supplied by Leslie Packard. A ritual team of past presidents has been organized by Lewie W. Smith. Many members of the Parlor plan to visit Stockton during the Grand Parlor session.

PRE-OLYMPIC SUPPER-DANCE.

Chairman Ora Evans of the Felipe de Neve statue committee of Californiana Parlor No. 247 N.D.G.W. was honored by a pretty surprise, April 5, carried out at the luncheon table. At her plate was a lovely flower basket with ferns, and at each place was a beautiful rosebud. Filing around the table and paying tribute to Mrs. Evans for her efforts, the members arranged the rosebuds artistically in the basket, which was then presented to her. A program, arranged by Trustee Flora Jacobson, presented Irene Roselle in a monologue and Olive Lopez. At the April 19 meeting, Second Vice-president Ysabel Gait was hostess at a delightful bridge tea at which a number of prospective members were guests. Homemade marmalade and the needlework of a large sewing circle made lovely table trophies.

Headed by President Gertrude Joughin-Tuttle, a large committee had a jolly potluck dinner at the home of Mrs. Edward A. Tabor April 21 and decided that, instead of the rose-and-gold spring ball, Californiana will give a pre-Olympic supper-dance May 21. Bridge will be provided for those who do not care to trip the light fantastic. Many features, including a number of surprise events, are planned for the entertainment of guests. It is hoped to stage the event in the University of Southern California gymnasium, but definite announcement of the place will be later announced.

BUILDING EMPIRE OF THE PACIFIC.

There was a large attendance at the April 1 meeting of Ramona Parlor No. 109 N.S.G.W., the occasion being a welcome home to Frank A. Duggan, recently returned from New York City. Many of the former Sierra Madreites were out. Among the speakers were Past Grand Presidents Herman C. Lichtenberger and William I. Traeger, Ray Howard, Percy Eisen, Charles Easton and Dr. George C. Sabichi. With First Vice-president Adams presiding, a class of candidates were initiated April 8. Addresses were made by Judge Walton Wood, Ernest Orfila and Isham Adams, the latter speaking for the class. Dr. Rockwell D. Hunt continued his interesting talks on California history April 15 and 29.

May 6, Grand President Dr. Frank I. Gonzalez will visit Ramona. May 20, President Chandos Bush will speak on "The Immigration Question." May 27, officers will be nominated at a short business session, after which Dr. Hunt will speak on "Building the Empire of the Pacific." All-comers will be welcome to hear the talk, and they will benefit by doing so.

ANNIVERSARY OBSERVED.

President Gertrude Allen closed her April message to the members of Los Angeles Parlor No. 124 N.D.G.W. with: "We need women with courage to tackle the hardest thing, with feet that climb and hands that cling and hearts that never forget to sing; with spirits that help when others are down, that know how to scatter the darkest frown, that love their neighbors and love their town." There was a large crowd at the April 13 card party and everyone had a good time; Miss Edith Strain had charge.

A class of eight candidates were initiated April 20. Several of the members had an enjoyable outing April 17 at the Wrightwood mountain home of Mary McAnany. The Parlor's institution anniversary was observed April 27. It was a big night, commencing with a potluck supper and concluding with "some" program. The sewing circle met April 4 at the home of

LOS ANGELES--CITY and COUNTY

Adeline Waite, and May 2 will assemble at the home of Mattie Gara.

Los Angeles' May program includes: May Day picnic, the 1st, at Sycamore Grove; election delegates to Merced Grand Parlor, the 4th; card party, one of the bridge tourney, the 11th; nomination officers for July-December term, the 18th. The 25th will be a social night of a nature to be later announced.

TO INITIATE LARGE CLASS.

An immense crowd attended the housewarming of the new home of Hollywood No. 196 N.S.G.W. April 11 and all were profuse in their praise of the commodious and uptodate quarters. Grand Trustee Eldred L. Meyer headed a large delegation of Santa Monica Bay No. 267 members, and all the other county Parlors were well represented.

President Leo Aggeler welcomed the guests and introduced as the master of ceremonies Henry G. Bodkin. Among the many speakers were John Costello, J. E. McCurdy, Superior Judges Walton Wood, Joseph Sproul and Reuben Schmidt. Several entertainment features were presented and well received, and refreshments were served. The overcoat went to J. Hartley Russell (Stanford No. 76) of San Francisco.

May 2, Hollywood will initiate a large class of candidates in honor of Judge Joseph P. Sproul. The committee in charge of arrangements includes Lucien Griffin, R. L. Patterson, Fred Youell, Martin Meza, Harold Thomas and Ed Black. Officers for the July-December term will be nominated May 23. No meeting May 30, account of Decoration Day.

DANCE AT GLENDALE, MAY 7.

Glendale—To assist in beautifying Glendale for the Olympics, Verdugo Parlor No. 240 N.D.G.W. will plant a lot on Brand boulevard. Four candidates were initiated April 26, and in observance of educational week G. A. Wheatley addressed the Parlor.

A card party was held April 8 at the home of President Betty Sanders, the hostesses being Mayme Kirri, Berenice Bickerdike and Florence Pratt. Bridge and five hundred were played, high scores going to Carol Payne and Mildred Leach. The next card party will be held at the home of Dorothy Ravn.

The May dance of Verdugo and Glendale N.S.G.W. will be held the 7th at the Masonic Temple, 234 South Brand boulevard. Nan Hutchinson and Harvey Gillette head the committee. All Natives and their friends are invited, and a splendid time is assured.

FIESTA AND BARBECUE MAY 8.

Ocean Park—All arrangements have been completed by Santa Monica Bay Parlor No. 267 N.S.G.W. for its second annual fiesta and barbecue, to be held May 8 in Santa Monica Canyon. Arrows will point the way to the scene of the festivities. The grounds will open at 10 a. m., a barbecue supervised by Jack Dailey and Jack Nelson will be served at noon, and dancing will begin at 2 p. m. Many attractions will be provided in the way of entertainment, and awards will be made for the most original early-day costumes. Members of Santa Monica Bay Parlor No. 245 N.D.G.W. will participate.

Grand President Dr. Frank I. Gonzalez will attend the fiesta and the following evening, May 9, will visit No. 267. In his honor, a large class of candidates will be initiated, Santa Monica Bay having invited all the Parlors in San Bernardino, Orange and Los Angeles Counties to bring in their candidates for the occasion and they have agreed to do so. Headed by Dr. Leland Clark and accompanied by Grand Trustee Eldred L. Meyer, big delegations of Santa Monica Bay members visited all the neighboring Parlors during the past month, including Arrowhead No. 110 at San Bernardino and Sepulveda No. 263 at San Pedro. The dinner-dance at the cafe of Harry O'Day in Culver City April 8 was well attended. Junior Past Grand President and Mrs. Newell were honor-guests, and Mrs. Domenic Conterno went away with a handsome doll presented by Mrs. O'Day.

PLAQUE WILL HONOR NOTED PIONEER.

Long Beach—In honor of the late Mrs. Eliza Donner-Houghton, Long Beach Parlor No. 154 N.D.G.W. will dedicate a plaque, provided by Sadie Winn-Brainard (Califia No. 22) of Sacranento, at 2 p. m. of May 12 at Houghton Park. Mrs. Houghton was a member of the Reed-Donner Party, captained by her father, George Donner, which came overland to California in 1846. She was the author of "The Expedition of the Donner Party," written at the Houghton home, now the site of Houghton Park, a portion of which was given Long Beach by the family. The plaque will be presented by President Violet T. Henshilwood. Miss Eliza Houghton, a member of the Parlor, will be a guest of honor and give an address. At noon of this day the mothers and members will be entertained at a covered-dish luncheon, in charge of District Deputy Clara Fay, at the clubhouse.

The dinner-and-card party of April 7, First Vice-president Zella Hodgedon chairman, was a social and financial success. A social gathering, with cards, was March 30 enjoyed at the home of Kate McFadyen. The thimble club met April 14 at the home of Daisy T. Hansen. At a recent meeting of the Parlor the bedspread made and donated by Lois McDonald was awarded Mrs. . Cutting.

May 5, Long Beach will have a card party. The committee in charge is Eleanor Johnson (chairman), Charlotte Wharton and Mary Stultz. A cooked food sale at the municipal market is planned for May 7. Alice Waldow is the chairman.

BOXING AND WRESTLING PROMISED.

Glendale—Glendale Parlor No. 264 N.S.G.W. is looking forward to a boxing and wrestling event which Leslie Schellbach promises in the near-future. The monthly dances being held jointly with the Native Daughters are great successes, due in no small measure to the energetic efforts of Chairman Harvey Gillette and President Phillip Molen. The Parlor will be at the May 9 meeting of Santa Monica Bay No. 267 a hundred percent, and will have several candidates for initiation.

MANY SOCIAL AFFAIRS.

San Pedro—Rudecinda Parlor No. 230 N.D.G.W. has planned many social affairs for the near-future. April 26 a card party was held, and April 28 the Florencita thimble club, an auxiliary of the Parlor, sponsored a spanish lunch. A get-together meeting with Sepulveda No. 263 N.S.G.W. was held April 29. Music by an eighty-piece boys' band was the feature.

BIG CROWD AT DANCE.

San Pedro—Eight hundred persons attended the annual spring ball given April 2 by Sepulveda Parlor No. 263 N.S.G.W. John P. Paradieu was general chairman of the committee in charge. April 18 some thirty members of the Parlor, led by District Deputy Edward E. Baldwin, President Francis G. Fetzer and Past President William A. Reuter, paid a visit to Santa Ana No. 265.

PERSONAL PARAGRAPHS.

Thurmond Clarke (Ramona N.S.) has been appointed a municipal judge.

J. Hartley Russell (Stanford N.S.) of San Francisco was a visitor last month.

Miss Annie Schiebusch (Los Angeles N.D.) was a recent visitor to Bakersfield.

Ella and Dahlia Vucovich (Los Angeles N.D.) were recent visitors to San Francisco.

A native son arrived at the home of Julius O. Leuschner (Los Angeles N.S.) April 1.

Charles J. Blumenthal (Los Angeles N.S.) has taken up his residence in San Francisco.

Leo V. Youngworth (Ramona N.S.) was a visitor last month to Lincoln, Placer County.

Eldred L. Meyer (Grand Trustee N.S.) was a visitor to Sacramento the latter part of March.

Visitors last month to San Francisco included Sheriff William I. Traeger (Past Grand President N.S.), Richard W. Fryer (Los Angeles N.S.) and Joseph P. Coyle (Ramona N.S.).

Miss Kathryn Dodd (Long Beach N.D.) was wedded to Ivan Bradley at the Long Beach home of her parents, Mr. and Mrs. C. B. Dodd, March 16. The couple are residing in Long Beach.

THE DEATH RECORD.

Charles Bilderback, affiliated with Ramona Parlor No. 109 N.S.G.W., died March 26. He was born at Los Angeles, March 7, 1864.

Robert Cushing Hillard, affiliated with Ramona Parlor No. 109 N.S.G.W., died March 30 survived by a wife and two children. He was born at San Francisco, May 3, 1892.

George Jacob Kuhrts, affiliated with Ramona Parlor No. 109 N.S.G.W., died April 1 survived by a wife and three children. He was the president and manager of the Los Angeles Railway Company.

Evelyn Anna Elser, daughter of William H. Elser (Ramona N.S.), passed away April 2.

John Vernon Hanes, affiliated with Ramona Parlor No. 109 N.S.G.W., died April 11 survived by a wife and two sons. He was born at San Jacinto, Riverside County, August 9, 1889.

Mrs. Annie Donahue-Sullivan, mother of James L. Sullivan (Sepulveda N.S.) of Wilmington, passed away April 18 at Solvang, Santa Barbara County.

Mrs. Sallie Chapin-Collins, mother of Mrs. Lucretia Coates (Long Beach N.D.), passed away April 20 at San Fernando. She was a native of Alabama, aged 86, and settled in Los Angeles County in 1870.

RANGE HORSE

(N. H. DUNNING.)

He comes athirst, in country strange to him,
And yet he finds the water-hole. He drinks
With gladdened heart! And all unconsciously
Gives silent thanks throughout thirst-slaked hours.
Say what men will, we yet must sternly ask,
How did he know? We pray that Power within
Still guides him safely through the unknown ways.

SITE FIRST RELIGIOUS SERVICES IN CALIFORNIA TO BE MARKED.

Following out the movement in California to mark places of historical interest, the Federal War Department has been requested by Representative Phil D. Swing to set aside a plot of ground on Ballast Point, Fort Rosecrans Military Reservation, San Diego, upon which to erect a suitable monument marking the place where the first religious services were held by White men in this state. In the year 1602 Vizcaino, sailing up the Pacific coast from Mexico, entered San Diego Harbor, landing at Ballast Point, where religious devotions were offered to God for the safety of the expedition.

The California State Historical Society, the Native Sons of the Golden West and others have appealed to Representative Swing to secure the necessary permission to place a two-ton native granite boulder upon the site, with a suitable bronze plate describing the historical importance of the spot. No objection is anticipated from the War Department.

HIBISCUS IN CALIFORNIA.

The growing popularity of the hibiscus has led to the planting of varieties not suited to the climate, with discouraging results. In the districts where frost is likely to occur, the hibiscus syriacus or althea should be used. This is hardy, but has not been given a great deal of attention, although it comes in a wide range of colors from red and crimson to white. The Chinese bibiscus, or hibiscus rosa-sinensis, is seen often in the frost-free areas of the southern parts of the state and is listed by most nurserymen. It requires ample heat as well as freedom from killing frosts.

Huge Expenditures—The Federal Government estimates $1,353,000,000 will be spent during 1932 for public road and bridge construction and maintenance.

Pier Dedication—San Diego City dedicated its new million-dollar pier March 25.

In Memoriam

ADELINE PEARCE.

Whereas, Almighty God, in His infinite wisdom, has called from our midst one of our Pioneer Mothers and a member of Long Beach Parlor No. 154 N.D.G.W., Adeline Pearce; and whereas, we feel we have lost a loyal and true member and the daughters a loving mother; therefore, be it

Resolved, That we extend our sincere sympathy to the family, and may these words offer them consolation: "She has passed from this earth and its sorrows to the bright lights of tomorrow." She was privileged to see our beloved California grow to the great State which it is today. Resolved, that these resolutions be spread upon the minutes of the Parlor, a copy be sent the family, and one to The Grizzly Bear.

KATE McFADYEN,
ELNORA MARTIN,
MABEL EMERY,
Committee.

Long Beach, April 22, 1932.

MY MESSAGE

To All Native Born Californians

I, DR. FRANK I. GONZALEZ, GRAND PRESIDENT OF THE ORDER OF NATIVE SONS OF THE GOLDEN WEST, DO HEREBY APPEAL TO ALL NATIVE BORN CALIFORNIANS OF THE WHITE MALE RACE BORN WITHIN THE STATE OF CALIFORNIA, OF THE AGE OF EIGHTEEN YEARS AND UPWARD, OF GOOD HEALTH AND CHARACTER, AND WHO BELIEVE IN THE EXISTENCE OF A SUPREME BEING, TO JOIN OUR FRATERNITY AND THEREBY ASSIST IN THE AIMS AND PURPOSES OF THE ORGANIZATION:

To arouse Loyalty and Patriotism for State and for Nation.

To elevate and improve the Manhood upon which the destiny of our country depends.

To encourage interest in all matters and measures relating to the material upbuilding of the State of California.

To assist in the development of the wonderful natural resources of California.

To protect the forests, conserve the waters, improve the rivers and the harbors, and beautify the towns and the cities.

To collect, make known and preserve the romantic history of California.

To restore and preserve all the historic landmarks of the State.

To provide homes for California's homeless children, regardless of race, creed or color.

To keep this State a paradise for the American Citizen by thwarting the organized efforts of all undesirable peoples to control its destiny.

THE ORDER OF NATIVE SONS OF THE GOLDEN WEST IS THE ONLY FRATERNITY IN EXISTENCE WHOSE MEMBERSHIP IS MADE UP EXCLUSIVELY OF WHITE NATIVE BORN AMERICANS.

. . . Builded upon the Foundation Stones of **Friendship Loyalty Charity**

IT PRESENTS TO THE NATIVE BORN CALIFORNIAN THE MOST PRODUCTIVE FIELD IN WHICH TO SOW HIS ENERGIES, AND IF HE BE A FAITHFUL CULTIVATOR AND DESIRES TO TAKE ADVANTAGE OF THE OPPORTUNITY AFFORDED HIM, HE WILL REAP A RICH HARVEST IN THE KNOWLEDGE THAT HE HAS BEEN FAITHFUL TO CALIFORNIA AND DILIGENT IN PROTECTING ITS WELFARE.

DR. FRANK I. GONZALEZ,
GRAND PRESIDENT N.S.G.W.

The undersigned, having formed a favorable opinion of the Order of Native Sons of the Golden West, desires additional information.

Name..

Address..

City or Town..

For further information sign the accompanying blank and mail to

GRAND SECRETARY N.S.G.W.,
302 Native Sons Bldg.,
414 Mason St.,
SAN FRANCISCO, California

Grizzly Bear

JUNE — THE ONLY OFFICIAL PUBLICATION OF THE NATIVE SONS AND DAUGHTERS OF THE GOLDEN WEST — 1932

Featuring

GENERAL NEWS OF INTEREST CONCERNING ALL CALIFORNIA, and ORDERS NATIVE SONS and NATIVE DAUGHTERS

Price: 15 Cents

GRIZZLY GROWLS

(CLARENCE M. HUNT.)

The Federal Congress has been in session a half-year and, other than to glut the record with messages from the national administration and mouthings by the fire-eaters and the spellbinders, nothing has been done to get at the root of the depression, which expands while the Congress and the administration bicker. Proposed legislation to encourage a return to normalcy has been confined exclusively to the dollar—the almighty god of the powers-that-be.

Dishonesty—petty and otherwise, in high and in low places,—is the root of all of the nation's economic ills! It is the cancer, resultant from dollar-worship, that is gnawing away the very vitals of this country and hastening its doom. Has one single effort been made at Washington or other government-centers to curb dishonesty? NO! For the reason that dishonesty has too closely linked crooks and government. No attempt has been made to provide legislation to curb the activities of the dishonest; there has been not even a suggestion to do so. But legislation has been both suggested and adopted to relieve the dishonest who brought on the depression.

Conditions in this country are a colossal shame! A nation of unexcelled resources rapidly going to decay, simply because the masses, who are honest generally, have permitted a dishonest minority to usurp control, in government, in business and in all other lines of endeavor. Arise in your might, Americans, and repossess that which is yours, through the ballotbox and through complete ostracization of the dishonest! Until honesty is again enthroned in these United States of America, there positively can be no lasting return to normalcy!

Taxpayers of California should be on the lookout for more bond issues which, according to grapevine reports, are in the making for submission to the voters. Of course, the big talk will be the unemployed, in whose name many financial deals have already been slipped over—for the benefit of those who wax richer from bond issues. Swat, decisively, any and all proposed bond issues!

George Washington was the first President of the United States! May 9 the Federal State Department issued an announcement that he was, "not only actually and really but also in the most strict legal sense as well," despite claims that John Hanson or Thomas McKean were first presidents.

Hanson was "President of the United States in Congress assembled," and not the "President of the United States of America." McKean was elected to succeed Samuel Huntington, to preside over the Continental Congress, before the ratification of the Articles of Confederation.

A writer in a national magazine opines that the reason the United States is in such a precarious situation today is because American credit has been lavishly extended foreign nations. He says: "The burden of Europe's private debts to this country is now greater than the burden of the war debt, and the war debt, with arrears of interest, is greater today than it was the day peace was signed."

More than $20,000,000,000 of American capital, public and private, has been "invested" in foreign countries since the United States decided to enter the world war—decided to sacrifice thousands upon thousands of precious American lives to protect the investments of crooked financiers. As the writer well concludes, had that vast sum been used in the United States in productive enterprises of even doubtful value or in building projects in the great cities, this country would at least have the improvements and the betterments thus made, but now it has only scraps of paper. And he might have also concluded that there is excellent ground for suspicion that, in time, such of those scraps of paper as were in possession of the financial highboys when the big jam came will be found in the strongbox of the Federal Reconstruction Finance Corporation as security for liberal loans. And then will be slipped over another moratorium, also at the expense of the honest masses.

"There are many firms that are following a short-sighted policy of unnecessary retrenchment in advertising," said a recent speaker at the San Francisco Exchange Club. The firm that believes it can save money, even in these times, by stopping its advertising is in the same category as the fellow who thinks he can save time by stopping the clock. Advertising is a necessity, not a luxury, and the wise firm, organization and individual recognizes it as such and acts accordingly.

(Continued on Page 33)

The Grizzly Bear Magazine

The ALL California Monthly

OWNED, CONTROLLED, PUBLISHED BY GRIZZLY BEAR PUBLISHING CO., (Incorporated)

COMPOSED OF NATIVE SONS.

HERMAN C. LICHTENBERGER, Pres.
JOHN T. NEWELL RAY HOWARD
WM. I. TRAEGER LORENZO F. SOTO
CHAS. R. THOMAS HARRY J. LELANDE
ARTHUR A. SCHMIDT, Vice-Pres.
BOARD OF DIRECTORS

CLARENCE M. HUNT
General Manager and Editor

OFFICIAL ORGAN AND THE ONLY OFFICIAL PUBLICATION OF THE NATIVE SONS AND THE NATIVE DAUGHTERS GOLDEN WEST.

ISSUED FIRST EACH MONTH.
FORMS CLOSE 20th MONTH.
ADVERTISING RATES ON APPLICATION.

SAN FRANCISCO OFFICE:
N.S.G.W. BLDG., 414 MASON ST., RM. 302
(Office Grand Secretary N.S.G.W.)
Telephone: Kearney 1223
SAN FRANCISCO, CALIFORNIA

PUBLICATION OFFICE:
309-15 WILCOX BLDG., 2nd AND SPRING,
Telephone: VAndike 6234
LOS ANGELES, CALIFORNIA

(Entered as second-class matter May 29, 1918, at the Postoffice at Los Angeles, California, under the act of August 24, 1912.)

PUBLISHED REGULARLY SINCE MAY 1907

VOL. LI WHOLE NO. 302

ORDER OF NATIVE DAUGHTERS HAS JUSTIFIED ITSELF IN EYES OF WORLD

Evelyn I. Carlson

(GRAND PRESIDENT.)

"THE FORTY-SIXTH ANNUAL GRAND Parlor of the Order of Native Daughters of the Golden West will convene June 20 in the City of Merced, the gateway to California's glorious Yosemite National Park, famous the world over for its natural and unsurpassed scenic wonders.

"While I am happy to close my year's work and to report the Order in a substantial condition, financially and numerically, there is sadness within my heart that I must sever my contacts, as the presiding officer, with the members of our organization, whose many kindnesses and warmth of greetings have made this the happiest year of my life.

"I am truly grateful for the opportunity given me by my sisters to serve as the Grand President and to traverse, in my official capacity, the length and the breadth of California, the most productive and enchanting wonderland of all the world. It has been the most instructive and inspiring lesson of my life, and the principles upon which our Order was founded—'Love of Home, Devotion to our Flag, Veneration to the Pioneers, and Abiding Faith in the existence of God'—have been more indelibly impressed upon my mind.

"Our beloved Pioneers taught us the lessons of fortitude and fidelity, openly displayed throughout the organization's existence and lending, in great measure, toward our success.

"In reviewing my work as Grand President—the personal inspection of one hundred sixty-three Subordinate Parlors and the institution of Ontario Parlor No. 251, which bids fair to be an active unit of our Order,—I wish to mention, briefly, the year's results.

HOMELESS CHILDREN.

"One of the most worthy projects of our Order is the placing of homeless children in suitable homes, a service carried on, jointly with the Order of Native Sons, for twenty-two years. The Subordinate Parlors in every section have given loyal support, and contributed willingly and generously of their time and money, but during these trying days and the curtailment of expenses in every avenue, the homeless children cause has been affected. While we have been fortunate in carrying on this worthy project for so many years, I would ask that each and every Parlor make a special effort during the coming year to double its contribution, so that we may continue with this most important endeavor.

"To our state secretary, Miss Mary E. Brusie, and the Central Committee we are indeed indebted beyond expression for the years of loyal and efficient service rendered, a service that has no equal. Personal thanks are herewith expressed to the Native Daughter Parlors which, through their sewing clubs, have contributed this year more garments for the children than any previous record discloses.

MEMBERSHIP.

"As a constructive, fraternal and humane organization, the Order of Native Daughters, as well as the Order of Native Sons, has justified itself in the eyes of the world for welfare work of various kinds, and the emergencies that have arisen in these times of stress have not found our organization wanting.

"It seems easy to give from one's store of abundance when times are good and the world is prosperous with happy, contented people, but it requires a generous, self-sacrificing spirit to divide, in times of uncertainty, one's small savings and worldly goods with others less fortunate. And so, because of the loving fraternal consideration manifested toward our members by the Parlors, we have prevented, as it were, a great many of our sisters leaving our fraternity by extending to them a helping hand, with the assurance that their dues would be provided for them in one way or another.

"Up to the present writing, an increase of four hundred forty-seven members has been noted during the year, which should be most gratifying to all.

PUBLICITY.

"Publicity is of the greatest importance to any organization, and is as necessary for the success of a fraternity as for a commercial enterprise. And so, we should constantly keep our activities before the public through the mediums of our local newspapers, to whom we are indebted, as well as to Clarence Hunt, editor of The Grizzly Bear Magazine, who has co-operated so well with our Parlors as well as with the Grand President.

"Radio stations K.Q.W. (San Jose), K.T.A.B. (Oakland) and K.G.O. (San Francisco) have been most generous with their facilities, thereby giving us the opportunity of contacting many sections that otherwise would have been impossible for us to reach.

NATIVE DAUGHTER HOME.

"Another project dear to every heart is the Native Daughter Home, at 555 Baker street, San Francisco, one of the finest of its kind in the country. The work in behalf of the Home has been one of love, and the efforts of Past Grand President Dr. Mariana Bertola, as chairman, and the efficient Home Committee are recognized and appreciated by every member of our Order. For, though the Home is but three years old, the mortgage of $60,000 which rested upon it at the time of its completion, has been reduced to $7,900. A wonderful accomplishment, and such a tribute to all Native Daughters!

" 'For here's the joy we've worked for,
Here's the scene we've longed to see—
Ours—a Home—all mirth and gladness,
Where our members like to be.'

MRS. EVELYN I. CARLSON OF SAN FRANCISCO, GRAND PRESIDENT N.D.G.W.

SCHOLARSHIPS.

"The scholarships that we maintain at the University of California at Berkeley, the University of California at Los Angeles, and Mills College in Oakland offer to the members of our Order opportunity to enlarge their intellectual sphere.

"Many people go through life without having their nature opened up to any great extent. Perhaps this has been caused by lack of opportunity —they have been unable to get in an ambitious state of mind; so, for this reason, the Native Daughters of the Golden West offer these scholarships—through competitive examinations—to those young students of our fraternity who have ambition and wish to make the most of their time and talents.

"A certain director of education has said: 'Those who, in youth, achieve the invincible armor—Education—are prepared for the conquest of life.'

VETERAN WELFARE.

"Veteran welfare work has been steadily going on, and the Subordinate Parlors are to be commended most highly for the splendid interest they have displayed in the veterans in the Army and the Navy hospitals of California, Washington and Arizona—particularly so, during the past year.

"The little luxuries we supply, such as candies, cigarettes, fruits, magazines and other numerous gifts, bring sunshine and consolation to the heroes who have been placed in the hospitals in an effort to restore their health and to mend their broken limbs. This is a labor of love and gratitude, and that the men appreciate the attention is evidenced in many ways.

HISTORY AND LANDMARKS.

"History and landmarks committees in the Subordinate Parlors are constantly on the lookout for historical spots to be marked and landmarks to be restored. There is still much to be done in this regard, and those who labor for the preservation of all that is colorful and interesting in California are to be congratulated.

"The Pioneer Fathers and Mothers spent their lives making of this great State a home for happy people. Every hour of their time was filled with a desire to serve the State and the communities in which they lived. Therefore we, as native Californians, should, by our conduct in life, prove that we are living in full power for good, and uphold the traditions of our beloved State.

REDWOOD GROVE.

"Another project which we have manifested interest in, is the conservation of our state redwood groves, for we have given much time, thought and money to the acquisition of forty-six acres of majestic redwood trees in Humboldt County, known as the 'Redwood Memorial Grove' and dedicated to the Pioneers of California. One thing that remains for us to do, and should be cared for at the earliest possible moment, is the placing of a bronze plaque, as a marker, upon the boulder in the grove provided for that purpose, so that the passing traveler may know of our pride in our State and its vast resources.

ANOTHER PAGE.

"Thus another page is added to the history of our organization, and it is with gratitude in my heart to the members of our Order for their faithful service that I rapidly approach the close of my year's activities as Grand President. I ask the full co-operation of everyone in behalf of my very worthy successor, Anna Mixon-Armstrong, who will automatically carry on the duties of this important office.

"Fraternal societies, like all other worldly institutions, are no greater than the men and the women who constitute their membership. And so, the Order of Native Daughters of the Golden West has achieved success because of the great number of unselfish women who have retained their membership therein under all conditions and who have done and are doing their part, in various ways, to make our Order an admirable and an admired one."

AIMS AND OBJECTS
of the
ORDER OF NATIVE DAUGHTERS OF THE GOLDEN WEST

To cultivate state pride.
To aid state development.
To advance state progress.
To promote the study of California history.
To preserve California's landmarks, relics and traditions.
To honor and keep in memory California's Pioneers.
To stimulate and inspire patriotism.
To assist in the work of americanization.
To encourage higher education for women, as evidenced by the Order's liberal college scholarship.
To guarantee social enjoyment, mental improvement and mutual benefit to members.
To care, conjointly with the Order of Native Sons of the Golden West, for the orphaned children of California, of whatever class, color or creed, by placing them in permanent homes through legal adoption proceedings, thus engaging in the most humanitarian of public welfare work, that of improving the future citizenship of the state.

If YOU were born in California and believe in these principles, you should be a member of the Order of Native Daughters of the Golden West.

Electricians' Gathering—The Pacific Coast Electrical Association will have its annual convention at Pasadena, Los Angeles County, June 14-17.

46th NATIVE DAUGHTER GRAND PARLOR

(CLARENCE M. HUNT.)

MONDAY, JUNE 20, THE FORTY-sixth annual Grand Parlor of the Order of Native Daughters of the Golden West will convene at Merced City for a four-day session. Grand President Evelyn I. Carlson, affiliated with Dolores Parlor No. 169 (San Francisco), will preside throughout the deliberations, and at their conclusion will automatically become the junior past grand president. The sessions of the Grand Parlor will be held daily, commencing at 9 a. m., in the American Legion Hall. The nomination of grand officers is set for Tuesday morning, the election for Wednesday morning, and the installation for Thursday evening.

The closing Grand Parlor year has been an exceptionally successful one for the Order, considering general conditions. There has been a membership net gain of approximately five hundred, and a Parlor, Ontario No. 251, was instituted at Ontario, San Bernardino County. Before the convening of the Merced session another parlor will be instituted in San Francisco, and other parlors are well on the road to institution.

The finances are in splendid condition. The mortgage on the Home in San Francisco has been materially reduced, and it is not beyond the realm of possibility that, by adjournment of the Merced Grand Parlor, the mortgage will be paid in full. In the financing of the Home and other projects, the Native Daughters have, by thorough co-operation, accomplished near-miracles. They are successful, as an organized group, because they deserve success. They labor indefatigably to that end.

According to information received direct by The Grizzly Bear from the Subordinate Parlors of the Order, Joaquin No. 5 (Stockton) continues to hold the lead as numerically the strongest Parlor, having a membership of 282. Other Parlors with a membership in excess of 200 are: Los Angeles No. 124, 252; Twin Peaks No. 185 (San Francisco), 230; Woodland No. 90, 215; Sutter No. 111 (Sacramento), 212; Marguerite No. 12 (Placerville), 206; Castro No. 178 (San Francisco), 203.

GRAND PARLORS OF THE PAST, AND GRAND PRESIDENTS PRESIDING.

1	July 1887,	San Francisco	Tina L. Kane*
2	July 1888,	Stockton	Tina L. Kane*
3	June 1889,	San Francisco	Louise Watson-Morris
4	June 1890,	Santa Rosa	Carrie Roesch-Durham
5	June 1891,	Santa Cruz	Mollie B. Johnson*
6	June 1892,	Sacramento	Clara K. Wittenmyer*
7	June 1893,	Watsonville	Mae B. Wilkin
8	June 1894,	Chico	Minnie Coulter*
9	June 1895,	Grass Valley	Dr. Elizabeth A. Spencer
10	June 1896,	Napa	Dr. Mariana Bertola
11	June 1897,	Sonora	Mary E. Tillman*
12	June 1898,	Woodland	Belle W. Conrad*
13	June 1899,	Stockton	Lena Hilke-Mills
14	June 1900,	Jackson	Cora B. Sifford
15	June 1901,	Sacramento	Ema Gett*
16	June 1902,	San Francisco	Genevieve Watson-Baker
17	June 1903,	Red Bluff	Eliza D. Keith
18	June 1904,	Pacific Grove	Stella Finkeldey
19	June 1905,	San Jose	Ella E. Caminetti
20	June 1906,	Salinas	Ariana W. Stirling
21	July 1907,	Watsonville	Dr. Eva R. Rasmussen
22	June 1908,	Lodi	Emma Gruber-Foley
23	June 1909,	Del Monte	Anna L. Monroe
24	June 1910,	Santa Barbara	Emma Lou Humphrey
25	June 1911,	Santa Cruz	Mamie G. Peyton
26	June 1912,	San Francisco	Anna F. Lacy*
27	June 1913,	Tallac	Olive Bedford-Matlock
28	June 1914,	Oakland	Alison F. Watt
29	June 1915,	San Francisco	May C. Boldemann
30	June 1916,	Fresno	Margaret Grote-Hill
31	June 1917,	Del Monte	Mamie P. Carmichael
32	June 1918,	Santa Cruz	Grace S. Stoermer
33	June 1919,	Berkeley	Addie L. Mosher
34	June 1920,	San Jose	Mary E. Bell
35	June 1921,	San Francisco	Bertha A. Briggs
36	June 1922,	San Rafael	Dr. Victory A. Derrick
37	June 1923,	Stockton	Mattie M. Stein
38	June 1924,	Santa Cruz	Amy V. McAvoy
39	June 1925,	Placerville	Catherine E. Gloster
40	June 1926,	Sacramento	Sue J. Irwin
41	June 1927,	Modesto	Pearl Lamb
42	June 1928,	San Francisco	Mae Himes-Noonan
43	June 1929,	Santa Cruz	Dr. Louise C. Heilbron
44	June 1930,	Oakland	Esther R. Sullivan
45	June 1931,	Santa Rosa	Estelle M. Evans

*Deceased.

RESOLUTIONS TO BE PROPOSED.

Several resolutions will come before the Grand Parlor for consideration. The Grizzly Bear has been advised of the following:

By Bonita Parlor No. 10 (Redwood City), providing "that the Subordinate Parlor president, by virtue of her office, be delegate number one to the Grand Parlor from each Parlor."

By Los Angeles Parlor No. 124, stipulating that each Subordinate Parlor shall be entitled to one Grand Parlor delegate at large, and one additional delegate for each seventy-five members.

By Clear Lake Parlor No. 135 (Middletown), asking relief for California Indians at the hands of the Federal Government.

By San Diego Parlor No. 208, seeking an appropriation of $139 from the Grand Parlor for the San Diego de Alcala Mission restoration fund. If made, the total contributed by the Native Daughters to this endeavor will reach $500.

By Rudecinda Parlor No. 230 (San Pedro), petitioning the Grand Parlor to allow "the Subordinate Parlors to pledge daughters, sisters, relatives and friends of members from the age of twelve to the Parlors," and "that this organization be known as the Bear Cubs of Native Daughterism."

CANDIDATES FOR OFFICE.

By communicating with all the Subordinate Parlors and the many "rumored" candidates, The Grizzly Bear is enabled to announce the candidacies of several aspirants for Grand Parlor office honors. The list is complete, insofar as definite information has been received, but it is not complete if gossip be founded on fact. For, there are whisperings that every elective office, excepting the grand presidency, will have two, or more, seekers. Be that as it may, here is the authentic "dope" received by The Grizzly Bear:

Grand President—Grand Vice-president Anna Mixon-Armstrong (Woodland No. 90) of Woodland.

Grand Vice-president—Grand Marshal Irma W. Laird (Alturas No. 159) of Alturas.

Grand Secretary—Sallie R. Thaler (Aloha No. 106) of Oakland, incumbent.

Grand Treasurer—Susie K. Christ (Yosemite No. 83) of San Francisco, incumbent.

Grand Marshal—Sadie Winn-Brainard (Califia No. 22) of Sacramento; Grand Trustee Gladys E. Noce (Amapola No. 80) of Sutter Creek; May F. Givens (Mariposa No. 63) of Cathay.

Grand Inside Sentinel—Grand Outside Sentinel Orinda Gunther-Giannini (Orinda No. 56) of San Francisco.

Grand Outside Sentinel—Elvena Woodard (Vallejo No. 195) of Vallejo; Hazel B. Hansen (Verdugo No. 240) of Glendale.

Grand Organist—Clara Gairaud (Vendome o. 100) of San Jose.

Grand Trustees (seven to be selected)—Anna huesen (Alta No. 3) of San Francisco, incument; Edna B. Briggs (La Bandera No. 110) of acramento, incumbent; Jane Vick (Reina del lar No. 126) of Santa Barbara; May A. McCarny (Guadalupe No. 153) of San Francisco; lice M. Lane (Castro No. 178) of San Fransco; Alice Mathias (El Carmelo No. 181) of an Francisco; Florence D. Boyle (Gold of Ophir o. 190) of Oroville, incumbent; Ethel S. Begley (Marinita No. 198) of San Francisco, incumbent; Willow Borba (Santa Rosa No. 217) of Sebastopol, incumbent; Evalyn G. Towne (Miocene No. 228) of Taft; Florence D. Schoneman (Rudecinda No. 230) of San Pedro, incumbent.

No "bids" have been advanced, so far as The Grizzly Bear has information, for next year's Grand Parlor. Perhaps the Native Daughters will designate a place for the holding of this year's Admission Day, September 9, state-wide celebration; the Native Sons failed to do so at their Grand Parlor last month.

ENTERTAINMENT.

Entertainment for the Grand Parlor is in charge of Veritas Parlor No. 75 (Merced). The program includes: Sunday, June 19, reception 9 p. m. Monday, reception 8 p. m. Tuesday, grand ball 9 p. m. Wednesday, exemplification ritual 8 p. m. Thursday, theater party 2:30 p. m. Friday, trip to Yosemite.

GRAND PARLOR MAKEUP.

Any member of the Order is privileged to attend the Grand Parlor. Those entitled to a vote, however, include:

Grand Officers—Mrs. Estelle M. Evans, Past Grand President; Mrs. Evelyn I. Carlson, Grand President; Mrs. Anna M. Armstrong, Grand Vice-president; Mrs. Sallie R. Thaler, Grand Secretary; Mrs. Susie K. Christ, Grand Treasurer; Mrs. Irma Laird, Grand Marshal; Mrs. Minna K. Horn, Grand Inside Sentinel; Mrs. Orinda G. Giannini, Grand Outside Sentinel; Mrs. Lolo Horgan, Grand Organist; Mrs. Edna Briggs, Mrs. Ethel Begley, Mrs. Anna Thuesen, Mrs. Gladys Noce, Mrs. Florence Boyle, Mrs. Florence Schoneman, Mrs. Willow Borba, Grand Trustees.

Founder of the Order—Lily O. Reichling-Dyer (Ursula No. 1).

Past Grand Presidents—Louise Watson-Morris (Buena Vista No. 68), Carrie Roesch-Durham (Joaquin No. 5), Mae B. Wilkin (Santa Cruz No. 26), Dr. Elizabeth A. Spencer (Buena Vista No. 68), Dr. Mariana Bertola (Buena Vista No. 68), Cora B. Sifford (Reina del Mar No. 126), Genevieve Watson-Baker (Buena Vista No. 68), Eliza D. Keith (Alta No. 3), Stella Finkeldey (Santa Cruz No. 26), Ella E. Caminetti (Ursula No. 1), Ariana W. Stirling (Aleli No. 102), Dr. Eva R. Rasmussen (Coloma No. 212), Emma Gruber-Foley (Orinda No. 56), Anna L. Monroe (Oneonta No. 71), Emma Lou Humphrey (Ivy No. 88), Mamie G. Peyton (Joaquin No. 5), Olive Bedford-Matlock (Camellia No. 41), Alison F. Watt (Manzanita No. 29), May C. Boldemann (La Estrella No. 89), Margaret Grote-Hill (Alta No. 3), Mamie Pierce-Carmichael (Vendome No. 100), Grace S. Stoermer (Los Angeles No. 124), Addie L. Mosher (Piedmont No. 87), Mary E. Bell (Buena Vista No. 68), Bertha A. Briggs (Copa de Oro No. 105), Dr. Victory A. Derrick (Aloha No. 106), Mattie M. Stein (Ivy No. 88), Amy V. McAvoy (Stirling No. 146), Catherine E. Gloster (Alturas No. 159), Sue J. Irwin (Berkeley No. 150), Pearl Lamb (El Pescadero No. 82), Mae Himes-Noonan (Portola No. 172), Dr. Louise C. Heilbron (San Diego No. 208), Esther R. Sullivan (Marysville No. 162).

Permanent Members—Grace S. Williams (Alta No. 3), Lizzie Winkley-Pfenninger (Alta No. 3), Josie Hofmeister-Pratt (Marguerite No. 12), Kate Even-Stewart (Eschol No. 16), Mary Hutchings (Buena Vista No. 68), members First Grand Parlor (1887) retaining continuous membership in the Order. Georgia Watson-Cotter-Ryan (Buena Vista No. 68), Laura J. Frakes-Toman (Amapola No. 80), Alice H. Dougherty (Angelita No. 32), former Grand Secretaries.

Ex-officio Members—Mary E. Brusie (Argonaut No. 166), Annie L. Adair (Los Angeles No. 124), secretary and assistant secretary, respectively, of the N.S.G.W. and N.D.G.W. Central Committee on Homeless Children.

Subordinate Parlor Delegates—The list is complete, insofar as Parlors reported, as requested, to The Grizzly Bear up to the time of going to press. Delegates of Parlors not supplying the required information are not listed here:

Ursula No. 1—Henrietta G. O'Neill, Margaret C. Molfino, Lucy L. Lorenson, Jennie Hewitt.

Minerva No. 2—Miss Gertrude McDonough, Mrs. Lena Wall.

Alta No. 3—Catherine O'Reilly, May McDonald, Claire Bolman, Agnes Hayes.

Joaquin No. 5—Mms. Vera Johnson, Emma Starin, Elizabeth Baker, Marion Stormes, Olive Hawley, Grace Bessac.

Laurel No. 6—Marguerite Clarke, Delia Walsh, Mary Martin, Annie Scheemer.

Oro Fino No. 9—Margaret J. Smith, Dollie Bradley.

Bonita No. 10—Mms. Alice Johnson, Ida Thompson, Mamie Glennan.

Marguerite No. 12—Mms. Dora Wood, Ethel Van Vleck, Bertha Reeg, Nettie Leonardi, Miss Jane McCusker.

Eschol No. 16—Mms. Bertha Vidy, Ruby Brien.

Califia No. 22—Mms. Sadie Winn-Brainard, Ella Lambert, Lena Convan.

Berendos No. 23—Mrs. Clara McKenna.

Santa Cruz No. 26—Lillian E. Smith, Melba McKenna, Margaret M. Martin.

Manzanita No. 29—Grace Eva, Anna Rowe, Bernice Deward, Annie Coulin.

Angelita No. 32—Mms. Mary Callaghan, Minnie Cragholm.

El Pajaro No. 35—Dora Zmudowski, Matilda Ruhland, Ruth Wilson.

Naomi No. 36—Genevieve T. Quinn.

Chispa No. 40—Ida Allen, Laten Dooley.

Ruby No. 46—Mrs. Evalyn Stephens.

(Continued on Page 21)

Mission Pageant—The annual Mission San Juan Bautista Pageant will be held at San Juan Bautista, San Benito County, June 26.

"Still closer knit in friendship's ties each passing year."—Burns.

CALIFORNIA HAPPENINGS OF FIFTY YEARS AGO

Thomas R. Jones

(COMPILED EXPRESSLY FOR THE GRIZZLY BEAR.)

JUNE 1882 WAS A DEMOCRATIC CONVENTION month in California, and nearly every county of the state held a convention to nominate county officeseekers and to select delegates to the state convention, which met at San Jose, Santa Clara County, June 20. John Boggs of Colusa County was made chairman, and on the fourteenth ballot General George Stoneman of Los Angeles defeated George Hearst of San Francisco for the nomination for governor. The convention was anti-Chinese and anti-Sunday-closing law, and straddled the debris question. The warhorses sniffed victory, as the state had gone Democratic in 1880 and the Republican party was blamed for the many economic ills affecting the state.

Judge Jackson Temple rendered his decision June 12 in the celebrated debris case of the State of California vs. the Gold Run, Placer County, hydraulic mine. It was lengthy, and nailed down the lid upon the hydraulic mines' coffin, consequently the lowlands were jubilant and the highlands depressed. The decision was to be appealed, it was announced. The trial consumed fifty-eight days, and it was estimated the eleven attorneys engaged in the combat were paid $100,000 in fees.

The annual session of the N.S.G.W. Grand Parlor was held in Sacramento City, commencing June 7, nine Subordinate Parlors being represented by forty delegates. John H. Grady of San Francisco, recently deceased, was elected Grand President. Sacramento Parlor No. 3 was host at a banquet at which John T. Stafford was the toastmaster and Ed. F. Cohn's quartet entertained with songs. A grand ball June 10 was an entertainment feature.

Five ships arrived from China ports during the month, bringing 5,000 additional Chinamen to add to the state's Mongolian horde.

An earthquake felt from Sonoma County down to Santa Cruz County occurred at 5:40 a. m. of June 27.

An artesian well being sunk near Tulare City, June 1, at a depth of 324 feet, struck a flow of water claimed to be the largest yet found in the state: It was estimated at 1,500,000 gallons a day.

Fire June 20 on an Oakland, Alameda County, pier destroyed several ships and freight cars, causing a $100,000 loss.

A. Smith's tinshop at Sierraville, Sierra County, burned June 26 and in attempting to save valuable papers he lost his life.

The Day hotel at Sucker Flat burned June 24, causing a loss of $5,000.

June 21 a whirlwind passed over a portion of Merced, blowing down several buildings and starting a number of fires.

San Francisco's school census showed: Whites, 27,852 boys, 27,073 girls; Negroes, 119 boys, 83 girls; Chinese, 273. Sacramento City's school census showed: Whites, 2,390 boys, 2,503 girls; Negroes, 35 boys, 42 girls.

A masked man stopped the stage a half-mile north of Redding, Shasta County, June 26 and demanded the express box. As it was fastened to the bed of the stage his request could not be complied with, so he vamoosed.

Dent Young and Billy Murray, oldtime Shasta County prospectors, June 3 found a quartz seam along Flat Creek that yielded in one day thirteen ounces of gold worth $234.

The steamer "Escambia," loaded with a $90,000 wheat cargo, sailed June 19 through the Golden Gate for Europe. About five miles out it capsized and sunk. Twenty-one of its crew of twenty-five were drowned.

The State Immigration Association had 10,000 copies of a "boost" pamphlet printed in English and German for distribution throughout the world, except in China, to induce immigration to California.

A combination of ten of the state's flourmills were monthly making up a cargo of 20,000 barrels of flour, which was being sent to Europe, where it was being disposed of at good profit.

R. Nadeau this month commenced the erection of a theater at First and Spring streets, Los Angeles City.

R. E. Houghton prosecuted Editor Maude of the "Kern County Press" for criminal libel, and lost. June 1 the citizens of Bakersfield burned Houghton in effigy on the main street.

A red-and-blue halo around the sun was observed June 13. It created much excitement, and many considered it a bad omen.

George Wiggins of Red Bluff, Tehama County, got married June 1 and went on a prolonged spree, which ended with his drowning in an attempt to recover his hat, which had blown into a stream.

A train derailment June 17 near Glenwood, Santa Cruz County, claimed the life of Fireman John McNamara.

June 25 six young people went for a sail on San Francisco Bay. The boat capsized, and Ida, George and Christina Redfield, aged, respectively, 19, 16 and 12 years, were drowned.

Charlie Hutchins and Johnny Averill were drowned June 17 while bathing in a Los Angeles City zanja.

At Napa City in March, Dolores Garcia shot M. L. Stillwagon. Recovering from the wound, Stillwagon met Garcia on the street June 24 and shot and killed him.

"Boney" Jewell, a Negro character of Sacramento City, June 4 went on a spree, became obstreperous and landed in jail. In the police court, asked to offer a defense, he said: "I've risen and low'r'd de curtin of de Metpolitn theata from de first perform on de leventh day of August '56 until de fourth of June, near twenty-six yeahs, and I've risen wi' Booth, McCullough, Shakespeare and oder brudders and sisterns. Sunday de job quits me and I gets drunk. Jedge, does yo blame me?" The judge did not.

Silas Woodford, Siskiyou County Pioneer, committed suicide in a cave near Callahan.

Robert McGregor, Cherokee, Butte County, miner, was caved upon and killed June 6.

J. Taylor and J. A. Peterson, miners from th Calico district, had breakfast together in Sa Bernardino City June 8 and got into a quarre Taylor drew a revolver and killed Peterson, an then committed suicide.

James Weston, one of a picnic party, wa drowned June 6 while bathing off Angel Islan

FIRST NATIVE CALIFORNIA DAUGHTER BORN OF AMERICAN PARENTS

"The lady who enjoys the distinction of bein the first native California daughter, born o American parents, is Mrs. Mary Semple Turma of Colusa. She was born at Benicia, Solan County, on the 22nd of November, 1848. She i the daughter of Dr. Robert Semple, who came t California in 1845, and who married Mis Frances Ann Cooper in 1847, this wedding bein the first one celebrated in California in whic both contracting parties were Americans.

"In 1846 Dr. Semple started the first new paper ever published in California. It was calle 'The Californian' and was published in Mon terey. Dr. Semple was also President of th first Constitutional Convention ever held in thi state, and helped to frame the old Constitutio Mrs. Turman is not at all ashamed of her ag but is proud of the distinction."

(The above, which came to The Grizzly Bea from Founder Lilly O. Reichling-Dyer of th Order of Native Daughters of the Golden Wes appeared in the "Record-Union" of Sacrament City of June 14, 1892, in connection with pu licity concerning the Order. Founder Dyer say Mrs. Mary Semple-Turman was elected Pa Grand President of the Order when the Fir Grand Parlor was organized in 1887.—Editor.

Passing of the California Pioneer

(Confined to Brief Notices of the Demise of Those Men and Women Who Came to California Prior to 1860.)

OSCAR ALLEN HENLEY, NATIVE OF Missouri, 85; with his parents, crossed the plains to California in 1849 and settled in Sacramento City, where he died; four children survive. His father, the late Arch Henley, was an early-day Sacramento judge.

Mrs. Penelope Ward-Rodgers, native of Arkansas, 84; came across the plains in 1852; died at Le Grand, Merced County, survived by a son.

Mrs. John Stanley, native of Indiana, 80; with her father, the late George Miller, came in 1853 and resided in Colusa and Solano Counties; died at Fairfield, survived by three children.

Mrs. Johanna Botypka-Sheldon, native of Australia, 88; came across the plains in 1854 and settled in Solano County; died at Fairfield, survived by a son.

Mrs. Frances Marion-Kelley-Price, native of Missouri, 100; came across the plains in 1854 and resided in Yolo and Glenn Counties; died at Orland, survived by six children.

Mrs. Maryette Parrish-Keir, native of Iowa, 4; crossed the plains in 1858 and settled in San Bernardino City, where she died; six children survive. She was a member of the San Bernardino Society of California Pioneers.

Edward M. Phelps, native of Missouri, 79; came across the plains in 1859 and settled in Sacramento City, where he died.

Mrs. Catherine O'Donnell, native of Iowa, 74; came via the Isthmus of Panama in 1859 and resided in Nevada and San Benito Counties; died at Hollister, survived by four children. She was a sister of the late Federal Judge Maurice T. Dooling, Past Grand President N.S.G.W.

Mrs. Mary Thomas-Langstroth, native of Missouri, 78; came across the plains in 1859 and resided in Trinity, Alameda and Stanislaus Counties; died at Riverbank, survived by a son.

Mrs. Alicia Lupton, native of Georgia, 82; came via the Isthmus of Panama in 1852; died at San Jose, Santa Clara County, survived by four sons.

John Hunter, native of Iowa, 86; came in 1859; died near Salinas, Monterey County, survived by a wife and two daughters.

Mrs. Caroline Brown, native of Illinois, 79; came across the plains in 1858 and resided in Lassen and Shasta Counties; died at Hat Creek, survived by five children.

Jefferson Asbury Walker, native of Missouri, 6; came in 1856 and resided in Los Angeles and Butte Counties; died at Chico, survived by a wife and three sons.

Mrs. Julia Logan-Inlow, native of Missouri, 3; came in 1854; died at Sacramento City, survived by five children.

Mrs. Emma Jane Blair-Valk, 83; came across the plains in 1853 and resided in Stanislaus and San Joaquin Counties; died at Farmington, survived by a husband and a son.

Colonel William Edwards, native of England, 0; came in 1853 and resided in Sacramento and San Francisco Cities; died at the latter place, survived by a wife and two children.

Richard A. Davis, native of Wisconsin, 84; came across the plains in 1850 and long resided in Placer County; died at San Francisco, survived by a wife and a daughter.

Mrs. Christine Boulanger-Daray, native of Alsace-Lorraine, 90; came via the Isthmus of Panama in 1849; died at Sacramento City, survived by a daughter.

OLD TIMERS PASS

(Brief Notices of the Demise of Men and Women who came to California in the '60s.)

Mrs. Mary Hutchinson, native of Iowa, 73; since 1861 resident San Joaquin County; died at Ripon, survived by a husband and three children.

G. R. Morgan, 83; since 1861 resident San Leandro, Alameda County, where he died; a wife and three daughters survive.

Mrs. Sarah E. Castello, native of Ohio, 89; since 1862 Sacramento County resident; died at Elk Grove, survived by six children.

Dr. Thomas Filben, native of Massachusetts, 75; came in 1862; died at San Francisco, survived by four children. For several years he filled Methodist Church pastorates in various California North cities.

Henry E. Quigley, native of Illinois, 74; came in 1862; died at Sacramento City, survived by seven children. He long resided in Sierra County, and for thirty-three years was clerk of that county.

John Charles Wilson, native of Pennsylvania, 83; came in 1863; died at Davis, Yolo County.

Mrs. Sarah E. Creason, native of Missouri, 85; came in 1864; died at Knights Landing, Yolo County, survived by a daughter.

James Ornbaum, native of Iowa, 72; came in 1866; died at West Sacramento, Sacramento County, survived by a wife and a son. He long resided in Mendocino County.

Mrs. Elizabeth Henry, native of Ohio, 89; since 1866 resident Chico, Butte County, where she died; a daughter survives.

Mrs. Ida Ricker-Alvord, native of Iowa, 78; came in 1866; died at Bakersfield, Kern County, survived by four sons. She resided many years in Ventura County.

Evan Sneed Barley, 93; came in 1867; died at Red Bluff, Tehama County, survived by four children.

Mrs. Mary O'Brien, native of Ireland, 95; since 1868 resident San Francisco, where she died; two children survive.

Mrs. Emelie Melville, native of Pennsylvania, 80; came in 1868; died at San Francisco, survived by a daughter. She was a noted earlyday actress.

Peter Olohan, native of Wisconsin, 72; came in 1866; died near San Mateo City, survived by a wife. He resided many years in San Louis Obispo County.

Mrs. Abbe Chase-Wright, native of Vermont, 88; came in 1865 and resided in Sierra and Nevada Counties; died at Grass Valley.

Mrs. Phoebe Hartman-Carlile, native of Iowa, 92; came in 1862 and long resided in Tulare City; died at Stockton, San Joaquin County, survived by three children.

John Thomas Elam, native of Missouri, 79; came in 1862 and resided in San Joaquin and Sacramento Counties; died at Elk Grove, survived by three sons.

PIONEER NATIVES DEAD

(Brief Notices of the Demise of Men and Women born in California Prior to 1860.)

John Fisher Ames, born in Sonoma County in 1859, died recently at Santa Rosa. He was affiliated with Sebastopol Parlor No. 143 N.S.G.W.

Frank Douglas, born in Shasta County in 1854, died recently at Salinas, Monterey County.

Mrs. Louise Derrick, born in Santa Clara County in 1855, died at Napa City April 19 survived by seven children.

Mrs. Emma Scott-Linscott, born at Santa Cruz City in 1852, died there April 22 survived by six children, among them Mrs. May Williamson and Miss Anna Linscott (Santa Cruz Parlor No. 26 N.D.G.W.).

George William Dornin, born in Nevada County in 1855, died at Inverness, Marin County, April 23 survived by a daughter.

George J. Pilliken, born in Sacramento County in 1858, died at Sacramento City April 24 survived by a wife and five children.

Mrs. Isabella Castro, born in Santa Clara County in 1848, died at Santa Cruz City April 27 survived by a husband and nine children.

Mrs. Hattie Wiggins-Byers, born in Los Angeles County in 1858, died at Arroyo Grande, San Luis Obispo County, April 28 survived by a husband and two daughters.

William Clark LaValla, born in Humboldt County in 1852, died April 30 at Woodland, Yolo County, survived by five children.

Mrs. Cora Petty-Gleason, born in Stanislaus County in 1857, died at Fresno City May 2 survived by eight children.

Lou J. Bosenberg, born at Sacramento City in 1854, died May 2 at Winnemucca, Nevada State, survived by a daughter. He was a plains rider of the old days.

William Martin Van Dyke, born in Humboldt County in 1858, died May 3 at Pasadena, Los Angeles County, survived by three children, among them Douglas Van Dyke (Ramona Parlor No. 109 N.S.G.W.).

Mrs. Susannah Priscilla Hothersall-Clave, born in Nevada County in 1858, died May 8 at Oakland, Alameda County, survived by five children.

William P. Pratt, born in El Dorado County in 1857, died May 8 at Eureka, Humboldt County, survived by a wife and a daughter.

Mrs. Elizabeth Goodwin-Walker, born at San Francisco in 1859, died there May 11.

Joseph Frey, born at Santa Cruz City in 1854, died there May 11 survived by four children.

Mrs. Annie Malone, born at San Jose, Santa Clara County, in 1854, died May 14 at San Francisco survived by a daughter. She was a daughter of Captain Thomas Fallon, who served under General John C. Fremont.

Robert Owen Pierce, born at San Francisco in 1857, died at Vallejo, Solano County, May 14 survived by four sons.

Mrs. Mary Reed-Stewart, born in Colusa County in 1859, died May 17 at Oakland, Alameda County, survived by four daughters. She was the widow of Nat Stewart, for twenty-three years sheriff of Santa Barbara County.

Henry H. Behrens, born in Nevada County in 1858, died at Napa City May 18 survived by a wife and five children. He was a charter member of Napa Parlor No. 62 N.S.G.W.

Jacob Bernhardt, born in Sierra County in 1857, died May 18 at San Francisco. He was affiliated with Downieville Parlor No. 92 N.S.G.W.

"Drive With Care if Children Are There," is the June slogan of the California Public Safety Committee in its campaign to lessen the fearful auto death-toll.

PROCEEDINGS FIFTY-FIFTH N. S. GRAND PARLOR

(CLARENCE M. HUNT.)

THE FIFTY-FIFTH GRAND PARLOR OF the Order of Native Sons of the Golden West was in session at Stockton, San Joaquin County, May 16, 18 and 19. Due to the unavoidable absence of Grand President Dr. Frank I. Gonzalez, Grand First vice-president Seth Millington presided. He was advanced to the Grand Presidency, and following his installation, just preceding adjournment, he requested the co-operation of the entire membership of the Order.

The Fifty-fifth was a resolution Grand Parlor, seventy-two resolves being introduced. For a time, when some of those dealing with finances were under consideration, the debate indicated lasting antagonisms would be created. But, due to skillful navigating of the stormy waters by the Acting Grand President, the "battles" ended with all forces safely and happily anchored in the harbor of harmony. A synopsis of what transpired follows:

REPORTS.

The activities of the Order, recorded in the reports of the grand officers, have heretofore been given publicity in The Grizzly Bear.

The report of Grand Treasurer John A. Corotto showed a cash balance in the treasury March 31, 1932, of $54,064.16, $16,752.87 of the amount being in the general fund.

The report of the Butano Forest Preservation Committee, O. H. Foster (Santa Cruz No. 26) chairman, said "The outlook for the preservation of this magnificent forest of virgin redwoods is brighter than ever before."

The report of the "Lone Grave" Committee, Dr. C. W. Chapman (Hydraulic No. 56) chairman, stated "a sentiment exists which justifies a tribute being established at the spot [seven miles east of Nevada City, Nevada County,] in the name of the N.S.G.W. and N.D.G.W. and the people of the State of California."

The report of the State of the Order Committee regretted "the tragic accident which made it impossible for Grand President Dr. Frank I. Gonzalez to preside. . . . Before meeting with the accident he had done a tremendous amount of work in visiting the Subordinate Parlors and attending dedications and public functions, both of an official and a semiofficial character. Few Grand Presidents worked as industriously and as sincerely for the upbuilding of the Order during a most strenuous period as did Grand President Gonzalez."

LAW CHANGES.

The following changes in the governing laws were made, the abbreviations "G.P.C." and "S.P.C." referring, respectively, to the Grand Parlor Constitution and the Constitution for Subordinate Parlors:

Art. VI, Sec. 12, Art. X, Sec. 2 and Art. XI, Sec. 9 G.P.C. all amended by eliminating reference to withholding the semiannual password from a Parlor delinquent in Grand Parlor payments.

Art. VI, Sec. 14 G.P.C. amended to provide that members of the visiting Board shall "visit those Parlors in the district closest to their respective homes. . . . But no grand officer shall visit the same district twice in the same year."

Art. VIII, Sec. 3 G.P.C. amended to provide for appointment of "A Committee on Education, of five members," and Art. IX G.P.C. amended to provide a new section, No. 20, defining the duties of said committee.

Art. XI, Sec. 8 G.P.C. amended by entirely new wording defining how "Members of a suspended, extinct or dissolved Parlor, and suspended members thereof, may, after such suspension, extinction or dissolution, apply for membership in any Parlor."

Art. VII Sec. 5 S.P.C. amended by entirely new wording defining how "A member suspended for the non-payment of dues may be reinstated to membership in the Order."

Several suggested changes in the Ritual were referred to the 1933 Grand Parlor for consideration.

The application-for-membership blank was amended to include these additional queries: "Have you ever been a member of the Order? If so, in what Parlor."

LEGISLATION ENACTED.

Appropriation for the traveling history fellowship at the University of California was eliminated.

Grass Valley, Nevada County, was selected as the meeting-place of the Fifty-sixth (1933) Grand Parlor.

A Forestry and Conservation Committee of five members, to be appointed by the Grand President, was authorized.

The grand officers were requested to "give full publicity in the Advanced Reports of all of the major activities of the preceding twelve months."

Santa Rosa, Sonoma County, was "designated as the place for the state-wide celebration of California's Admission Day, September 9, 1933." [No place was designated for this year's statewide celebration.—Editor.]

The usual appropriation for publishing the "Official Directory of Parlors of the N.S.G.W." in The Grizzly Bear, the official publication of the Order, was continued.

A budget totaling $29,625 was approved, and the percapita tax was fixed at $1.10,—the lowest in many years—payable in quarterly installments, commencing June 1, of 30c, 30c, 25c and 25c. Included in the budget are these appropriations: Organization work $4,500, landmarks work $500, mileage Stockton session $2,500, Grand Secretary salary $4,500 and salaries assistants in his office $3,900.

A suggested plan for districting the state for organization work in the Order's behalf was referred to the incoming Board of Grand Officers.

Eight Subordinate Parlors were, for good and sufficient reasons, relieved of their indebtedness to the Grand Parlor for fines, percapita, etc.

RESOLUTIONS APPROVED.

Expressing "regrets at the inability of Grand President Dr. Frank I. Gonzalez to be present and preside," and also expressing "best wishes for his speedy recovery and also the recovery of Mrs. Gonzalez."

Endorsing "the National Education Week movement of the National Education Association as a proper exercise for the Parlors of this Order to sponsor."

Petitioning "the Congress of the United States to submit the 'Repeal of the 18th Amendment to the Constitution of the United States of America' to the popular vote of the citizens of the respec tive States."

Favoring "increasing rather than decreasin the obligation of Citizenship and our power c National Defense."

Petitioning the Federal Senate "to amend th Naval Appropriation Bill by deleting from it th provision limiting the rank of Naval Reserv officers on permanent active duty to Lieutenan thereby preserving for California and the natio the present standard of Naval Reserve ade quacy."

Requesting "the Park Commission of th State of California to provide from State fund an appropriation for the restoration and prese vation of the Pio Pico homestead landmark nea Whittier, Los Angeles County.

Expressing "deep appreciation to Albert V Mayrhofer [San Diego Parlor No. 208] for hi successful efforts to completely restore San Di ego de Alcala Mission, rededicated Septembe 13, 1931."

Petitioning California's representatives in th Federal Congress "to do all in their power t maintain the salaries of Government employe in their present status."

Extending "to all Native Sons of the Golde West . . . a most hearty and cordial invitatio

SETH MILLINGTON OF GRIDLEY, GRAND PRESIDENT OF THE ORDER OF NATIVE SONS OF THE GOLDEN WEST.

to attend the" Tenth Olympiad, to be held a Los Angeles City from July 20 to August 15 1932.

Endorsing and supporting "the 'Back to Good Times Movement," and to "assist in carrying it forward to complete success."

Extending thanks to all those who contributed to the success of the session and provided entertainment for the members of the Grand Parlor.

Thanking Grand First Vice-president Seth Millington, "acting Grand President, for the able impartial and masterful manner in which he presided over the deliberations."

RESOLUTIONS REFERRED.

A resolution calling for appointment of a committee "to devise ways and means of discouraging the employment of Filipinos in all lines of industry," was referred to the California Joint Immigration Committee, with which the Order is identified.

Resolutions, calling on the State Legislature to amend the California Alien Land Law so as to "fully correct beyond question the flimsy and disgracefully widespread evasion of the law now prevalent in our State," and petitioning "the proper State authorities to amend the Fish and Game Laws of the State of California, to forbid the issuance of fishing permits to aliens ineligible to citizenship," were referred to the incoming Board of Grand Officers.

GRAND OFFICERS-ELECT.

At the election for grand officers May 19, 383 ballots were cast, and the following were selected:

Grand President, Seth Millington (Colusa No. 69).

Grand First Vice-president, Justice Emmet Seawell (Santa Rosa No. 28).

Grand Second Vice-president, Chas. A. Koenig (Golden Gate No. 29).

Grand Third Vice-president, Harmon D. Skillin (Castro No. 232).

Grand Secretary, John T. Regan (South San Francisco No. 157).

Grand Treasurer, John A. Corotto (San Jose No. 22).

Grand Marshal, W. B. O'Brien (Alameda No. 47).

Grand Inside Sentinel, Gam Hurst (Piedmont No. 120).

Grand Outside Sentinel, William A. Reuter (Sepulveda No. 263).

Grand Trustees (in order of vote received), Jesse H. Miller (California No. 1), Eldred L. Meyer (Santa Monica Bay No. 267), John M. Burnett (San Jose No. 22), Henry S. Lyon (Placerville No. 9), Joseph J. McShane (Twin Peaks No. 214), Horace J. Leavitt (Mount Bally No. 87) and Charles H. Spengemann (Hesperian No. 137).

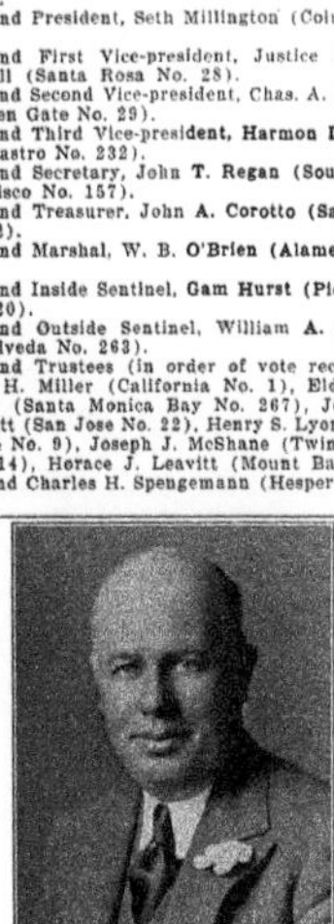

HARMON D. SKILLIN,
Elected Grand Third Vice-president.

They, with a proxy for Dr. Frank I. Gonzalez (Pacific No. 10), who automatically became the Junior Past Grand President, were installed by Past Grand John T. Newell, who was assisted by Past Grands Charles L. Dodge and William J. Hayes, and Clarence M. Hunt (Sacramento No. 3). Grand President Millington, following his installation, completed the Board of Grand Officers by the appointment of:

Leslie Maloche (Arrowhead No. 110) as Grand Organist.

Chester F. Gannon (Sunset No. 26) as Historiographer.

MEMORIAL SERVICES.

Services in memory of members of the Order who departed during the year were held the afternoon of May 16. Junior Past Grand President John T. Newell presided, and eulogies were delivered by Grand Trustee Jesse H. Miller, Henry S. Lyon (Placerville No. 9), Harmon D. Skillin (Castro No. 232), Past Grand Daniel A. Ryan and H. W. Amphlett (Redwood No. 66). Vocal selections were rendered by Grand Inside Sentinel W. B. O'Brien, accompanied by Grand Organist Leslie Maloche.

NOTES OF THE SESSION.

As an expression of sympathy for Colonel and Mrs. Charles A. Lindbergh, the Grand Parlor stood at attention for a moment just before the noon recess the opening day.

Dr. Herbert Eugene Bolton, head of the history department of the University of California, addressed the Grand Parlor May 16 on the accomplishments of the traveling history fellows.

Grand President Evelyn I. Carlson extended May 18 greetings on behalf of the Order of Native Daughters. Her enlightening remarks were applauded. She was accompanied by Grand Secretary Sallie R. Thaler, Junior Past Grand President Estelle M. Evans, Past Grand President Mamie G. Peyton and Carmelita Luhr (Aloha Parlor No. 106).

The outstanding feature of the session—at least, that is the writer's opinion,—was the unexpected—the talk May 19 of Rev. Thomas J. McKeon (Calistoga Parlor No. 86) who, contrary to his will, was prevailed on to address the Grand Parlor. He spoke from the heart, in plain language understood by all, and his admonitions contained much wholesome food for honest and unbiased thought. Too bad, for the Order's good, the whole membership of the Order were not assembled to hear him.

Past Grand Hubert R. McNoble entertained the Past Grands at supper at his home May 18. Dr. Charles W. Decker, elected Grand President in 1886, was among those assembled. After the feast the annual confab was on, and John T. Newell was welcomed as the "baby" member of the Past Grand Presidents Association.

The entertainment program, arranged by Stockton Parlor No. 7, was carried out as published in The Grizzly Bear for May.

PROSPECT OF GROWTH

SETH MILLINGTON, AFFILIATED WITH Colusa Parlor No. 69 and a resident of Gridley, Butte County, became the Grand President of the Order of Native Sons of the Golden West May 19. At the urgent solicitation of the editor of The Grizzly Bear, on his return home from the Stockton Grand Parlor he prepared this statement, setting forth his idea of the Order and its prospect of growth. It should be read and thoroughly digested by every Native Son, for it contains most excellent suggestions—suggestions which, if put into effect, assure the growth and the permanency of the Order:

"The Order of Native Sons of the Golden West, like all other fraternal societies, has reached the point where the ordinary appeals to eligible candidates do not bring about the old reaction. There is no question that the sun of the fraternal society has passed its zenith, and only those which have some special appeal, such as religion or love of country, are going to survive. Our Order is in the latter class, and the appeal that we make is not limited to the platitudes that are the stock-in-trade of the ordinary fraternal society, but goes deeper and makes its appeal to the love of the native land.

"It has been my thought for many years that it was a mistake for the Native Sons of the Golden West ever to have entered upon the field of the secret society. The only justification for our existence is as a patriotic historic society, and the idea of secret signs and passwords is irreconcilable with that thought.

"It is my belief that the Order of the Native Sons of the Golden West will enter upon a great period of growth and prosperity just as soon as we abandon all of the secrecy, symbols, mummery and so-called mysticism of the fraternal society and come out into the open for what we really are and for what we have always been, an honorary historic society dedicated to the preservation of the beautiful and romantic history of California, to the marking with appropriate monuments of the spots where deeds of pioneer historic interest took place, to the preservation of the written record so the future generations may read and know.

"These thoughts are in full consonance with all the ideals of the Order and involve nothing more than the abandonment of all symbolic work, secret signs and passwords. It is my further thought that it might be appropriate to retain these signs, symbols and words, not as active parts of our procedure, but as a memory of the period in our existence when they were actually used. I further believe that the passwords should be retained, to be used on the infrequent occasion when it might be desired to make our meeting secret. I can see no objection to the open meeting for the ordinary transaction of business or initiations, although this, of course, would involve material changes in the oath, particularly eliminating the pledges of secrecy.

"With this statement of my idea of the Order and its prospect of growth, I am going to call upon the members to demonstrate that the pioneer spirit that developed this empire has not been lost in their sons, and that in this period of economic stress we can carry on the work of the Order and develop its influence by deeds, actions, and the enlarging of the membership.

"The Order came into existence largely by reason of the belief of its founder that the sons of California were the ones upon whom the duty of preserving the history of California would fall without burden and would confer a pleasure on them. That we have pursued this course for fifty-eight years with few deviations is shown by the achievements of the Order. From one end of the state to the other historic spots are marked with monuments, ancient structures of dons, padres and forty-niners have been reconstructed and preserved, largely through our efforts and almost always at our instigation.

"I am not overlooking the homeless children movement and the remarkable success in placing homeless children in childless homes that this Order has carried on for twenty-five years, nor the assistance that has accrued to the members through payment of sick benefits, and the host of other things that the Order has stood for and still stands for, but I regard all of these latter as side issues to the main purpose. Any Order with the charity to do so and the industry to carry it out could provide for homeless children. Dozens of fraternal societies provide sickness and disability benefits and death payments, and while any Order could dedicate itself to the proposition of preserving California's history, such an attempt would be an usurpation of the field that is ours as a birthright and this birthright is too dear to us to for one moment permit its neglect or allow anyone else to encroach upon the field of our endeavor.

"I want to assure the members of the Order that, while I have the above views of the future of the Order, and what it stands for, I do not propose to institute any radical changes, but at the next Grand Parlor, with the help of those who feel the same as I do, to propose such changes as are in line with the origin and destiny of the Order. I also believe that our ritual has too little reference to the period of the padres or of Spain and Mexico, and as a consequence does not reflect at all the pioneer period of the southland. There can be no question that the American period is the one with which we have the closest connection, being that of our own forebears, but it is equally true that the first civilization on the Pacific Coast was established by the Spanish discoverers and explorers. They made the original discoveries and the first explorations over a century before the first American crossed the Sierra. That period deserves a place in our work far greater than it now receives, and inasmuch as that period represents the pioneering of the south, I believe that the south would be drawn closer to the Order by enlarging on the activities that gave it the opportunity to be the wonderland that it is today.

"The work of dedicating public buildings will go on this year, probably to a greater extent than the last few years, as this activity places the Order before the public eye and is one of the opportunities to interest eligible Californians.

"I believe that the Grand Parlor which has just closed was a constructive one. There can be no question that the members came there more earnestly and sincerely desiring to do something constructive for the Order than has been true of many Grand Parlors, and demonstrated a strength of opinion in their own thoughts that was only equaled by the tolerance in considering the views of those opposed. And there is no question, in my mind, that we all returned to our homes firmly convinced that great strides had been made, and equally convinced that those who did not agree on details were just as sincere in their efforts.

"It is idle to talk of achieving anything without having that basic strength which large membership gives. Fifty thousand speak with twice the volume of twenty-five thousand, and provide double the means of carrying out the activities.

"The last thing in my desires would be to see the Order crowded with members who do not appreciate what it stands for, and I would very much prefer to see it stand still than to put on intensive drives to sign anyone who would put his name on an application blank. But there are literally thousands of native Californians eligible to join the Order who appreciate the beauties and the glories of their state and would contribute to its advancement if the agency be presented to them. Those are the kind of members that I would like to see in, and they exist by the thousands, unapproached and unsolicited, only waiting for the opportunity to become members. The reaching of that class, with the assistance of the members who want the Order to advance, will be my goal."

Native Daughters of th

OROVILLE—MAY 12 SAW THE REALization of a dream of twenty years, when Gold of Ophir No. 190 and Argonaut No. 8 N.S.G.W. dedicated their "forty-niner stone cabin" in which will be preserved the history and earlyday relics of the Golden State. Hundreds gathered to hear the program, arranged by the board of directors of the Butte County Pioneer Memorial Association, which is composed solely of members of the Parlors.

Cyril Macdonald was chairman of the day and Alta Baldwin led the community singing. Grand Trustee Florence Danforth-Boyle, president of the association's board of directors, told how the $10,000 project was financed. The histories of Gold of Ophir and Argonaut were related, respectively, by Irene Lund and George F. Jones Grand Marshal Irma Laird told of the objects and accomplishments of the Order of Native Daughters, and Grand First Vice-president Seth Millington spoke for the Order of Native Sons. Past Grand Dr. Eva R. Rasmussen paid tribute to the Pioneers, and Grand Second Vice-president Justice Emmet Seawell, the main speaker of the day, gave an inspiring historical discourse.

The building was dedicated by the Native Sons, those participating being Grand First vice Millington, Grand Secretary John T. Regan, Grand Second vice Seawell, Grand Third vice Chas. A. Koenig and Past Grand Fred H. Greely. Governor James Rolph Jr. was also in attendance. Grand President Evelyn I. Carlson, unable to be present, sent this telegram: "Deeply regret my absence. May your influence always be beneficial to your community. Congratulations to the Native Daughters and Native Sons of Oroville."

The building is unique in design. It is constructed of native Butte County rock and will stand for centuries. Two large bronze plaques adorn the walls. One is an honor-roll of Pioneers and the other contains the names of well-wishers. For each name on the two rolls a "memorial brick" has been purchased. Officers and directors of the Butte County Pioneer Memorial Association are: Florence D. Boyle, president; Frank W. Boyle, secretary; Irene E. Lund, treasurer; W. H. Hibbard, Anna Bernhard and J. Emory Sutherland.

Begin the Day in Happy Spirit.

San Bruno—San Bruno No. 246 and visiting members from San Francisco, Santa Clara and San Mateo Counties welcomed Grand President Evelyn I. Carlson on her official visit May 13. The meeting-hall was prettily decorated with roses and multi-colored sweetpeas, and the pastel arrangement of the opening march was made uniform by colorful corsages of pansies.

In her address, the Grand President commended the officers and members of San Bruno on their splendid accomplishments. In conclusion she said: "Those of us who begin our day in a happy spirit with the will to do our work as best we can, will lay down to rest at the end of that day satisfied and happy—our work well done." Addresses were also made by Past Grand Mae Himes Noonan, founder of San Bruno; Grand Trustee Willow Borba, Supervising Deputy Clara Gairaud and District Deputy Hattie Kelley. Gifts were presented Mrs. Carlson and District Deputy Kelley by President Dolores Gilcrest. Delightful refreshments terminated this enjoyable occasion, leaving in the heart of San Bruno the memory of a most beloved Grand President whose kindliness and sweet sincerity endear her to the heart of every Native Daughter. The decorations and refreshments were under the direction of Edythe Knoles.—E.A.F.

Dual Birthday Party.

San Bernardino—Lugonia No. 241 had a dual birthday party May 11, celebrating the fifth institution anniversary of the Parlor and the birthday of Grand Trustee Florence Dodson-Schoneman, founder of Lugonia. The supper tables were beautifully decorated in spring flowers, and there were two birthday cakes; one, decorated in pink, was presented the "mother" of Lugonia, and the other, decorated in yellow, was presented the Parlor. Social Chairman Nola Fogler had charge of the dinner and the table arrangements.

At the meeting which followed the feast Mrs. Schoneman gave a splendid address, and plans were completed by the history and landmarks committee for marking the site of San Bernardino's first public building. Cards and a social hour concluded the evening. May 25 five candidates were initiated.

To Restore Landmark.

Susanville—In recognition of the Washington bicentennial, Susanville No. 243 planted at the "Old Fort" an evergreen tree which was dedicated to Lassen County Pioneers. Zella Mae Arnold, great-granddaughter of Governor Isaac Roop, builder of the fort in 1854, assisted President Maybelle Long in the ceremonies. The local Natives plan to restore this most important landmark in Lassen County for the housing of earlyday relics.

District Deputy Erma Gibson Haley, accompanied by thirty members of Nataqua No. 152 (Standish), visited Susanville April 19 and entertained the latter with a clever drama which made a decided hit. Refreshments completed a most enjoyable evening.

Outstanding Event.

Colusa—The official visit of Grand President Evelyn I. Carlson to Colus No. 194 was an outstanding event in local fraternal circles. Other grand officers attending were Grand Vice-president Anna Armstrong, Grand Trustees Florence Boyle and Edna Briggs, Past Grands Esther Sullivan and Dr. Louise Heilbron, District Deputy Vivian Hastings and Supervising Deputy Mary Meade. Twelve candidates were initiated and there were numerous presentations.

Previous to the meeting the visitors were guests at a largely attended banquet at which President Marjorie Buck presided. Speakers included Grand President Carlson, President Burton Smart of Colusa No. 69 N.S.G.W. and Governor Phil J. Humburg Jr. of Fred H. Greely N.S.G.W. Past Presidents Assembly. The drum corps of Colusa N.S.G.W., directed by P. J. Cook, also attended.

Mothers Entertained.

Salinas—Aleli No. 102 initiated two candidates May 12. Bridge followed, directed by Mrs. Paul Brindero, and refreshments were served at tables decorated with pink and blue flowers. May 26 the mothers were entertained. A musical program was directed by Mrs. Brindero, and a banquet was served by a committee headed by Mrs. Tillie Fry.

"Baby's" First Party.

Ontario—Ontario No. 251, the "baby" Parlor, had its first public social affair, a benefit card supper, April 21. Roses and sweetpeas were used in the decorations, and a tempting light supper was served. The committee in charge included Mms. John Baxter (chairman), Lemuel Graves, Irvin Kremer, Hubert Lucas.

The birthday anniversaries of Mms. Adele Serio Frankish and Dorothea Drew Lucas, members of the Parlor, were the motif for an enjoyable affair at the home of the former. Each was presented with a gift. District Deputy Genevieve Hiskey was a guest. Mrs. Frankish is the president of Ontario.

Grand President's Official Itinerary.

San Francisco—During the month of June, Grand President Evelyn I. Carlson will officially visit the following Subordinate Parlors on the dates noted:

6th—Snow Peak No. 176, Truckee.
7th—Fern No. 123, Folsom.
11th—Dolores No. 169, San Francisco.

Scott Valley Pioneers Reminisce.

Etna—Eschscholtzia No. 112 had the pleasure of entertaining the older mothers of Scott Valley on Mothers Day. The program, arranged by District Deputy Ada Wilson, consisted of vocal numbers by Dolores McCrary, Lois Custer and Elvira Wilson, readings by Laura Chadbourne, Gladys Young and Laura Greene, and a minuet danced by Harriet Holzhauser, Rae Smith, Alma Quigley and Velma Smith. The accompanists were Ada Wilson, Eleanor Campbell, Evelyn Pitman and Grand Inside Sentinel Minna K. Horn. At the close of the program refreshments were served at tables attractively decorated by

The "Loyalty Cook Book," prepared by Grand Trustee Willow Borba and sponsored by the Parlor, will soon be ready for distribution. It contains over a thousand recipes, many of them favorites of Native Daughters throughout the state. Funds realized from the book's sale will go toward Santa Rosa's Loyalty Pledge for the Home.

Gorgeous Decorations.

Chico — Elaborate entertainment honored Grand President Evelyn I. Carlson when she officially visited Annie K. Bidwell No. 168. Gorgeous decorations, in which quantities of flowers and greenery were used, were a feature. Three candidates were initiated. An attractive program was directed by Olive Pearl, several presentations were made, and refreshments were served under the supervision of Josephine Alexander. Among the many visitors were Grand Trustees Edna Briggs and Florence Boyle, Past Grands Dr. Louise Heilbron and Esther Sullivan, Supervising Deputy Cora Hintz, District Deputies Edna Brown, Alice Bass and Mary Meade.

The Parlor has voted to co-operate in requesting eating places of the state to advertise California products during the Olympic games.

Treasury Enriched.

Sierraville—A bicentennial affair given by Imogen No. 134 was greatly enjoyed by many. A play, "Eaglesfeather," short playlets and a flag drill made up the program. The drill seemed to be of special interest to the audience. Dancing and refreshments followed. The returns from this affair added a large sum to the Parlor treasury. A party was later given by the members of Imogen in honor of those who helped prepare for the bicentennial. Modern and old-fashion dances were featured, and refreshments were served.

Interesting Letter From Veteran.

Stockton—Caliz de Oro No. 206 sponsored a spring dance May 7, the proceeds going to the homeless children fund. At the May 3 meeting a very interesting letter from George Samuelson, a world war veteran in the U. S. Veterans Hospital at Livermore adopted by the Parlor, was read. A committee was named to arrange for an evening bridge party at the home of Henrietta Quevillon. The evening concluded with games and light refreshments arranged for by the social committee.

Charming Party for Brides.

Bakersfield—Paying honor to Pioneer Mothers of California and Kern County, El Tejon No. 239 sponsored a delightful party at Jastro Park May 15. Mrs. Ralph Sanders, chairman of the arrangements committee, welcomed the guests, an interesting program was presented and refreshments were served.

May 20 the Parlor initiated four candidates, and had a charming party for the recent brides—Jean Helling-Landes, Margaret Stockton-Lavelle, Mayme Efird-Towne, Bessie Wible-Walker—and two members who will be June brides—Margaret Stramler, Juanita Avery. Each was presented with a gift. A country-store card party, directed by the past presidents, was held May 25, and the handmade quilt donated by President Gladys Cooper was awarded.

State Flag Given Library.

Fullerton—April 25, Grace No. 242 presented a California State (Bear) Flag to the Placentia Public Library, the program being in charge of the history and landmarks committee, Carrie Ford chairman. Nellie Cline gave the history of the flag, and the presentation was made by President Mattie Edwards. Lucanna McFadden, chairman of the library board of trustees, accepted the flag. Within the next few weeks the Parlor will place a marker on the site of Portola's camp, near Brea.

The sewing circle of No. 242 spent a busy day May 13 with Erna Watts, hostess. Lucanna McFadden May 20 sponsored a public card party; it was a lovely affair, and netted a nice sum for the Loyalty Pledge. May 27 was pioneer and oldtimers day; Grace was hostess at the Ebell clubhouse, furnishing a noonday luncheon, which was followed by a program and visiting. It was a very enjoyable occasion.

Kitchen Shower for Bride.

Alturas—Alturas No. 159 was hostess May 5 to a delegation from Mount Lassen No. 215 (Bieber). After the business session husbands and "boy friends" joined the party and bridge was enjoyed. Refreshments were served and then Eleanor Walls Asher, the Parlor's latest bride, was given a kitchen shower. Alturas is planting a memory garden in the Civic Club grounds.

The Parlor recently sent a box of beautiful "adoption clothes" to the Central Homeless Children Committee. A delegation from Alturas visited Mount Lassen No. 215 May 26, and June 1 Susanville No. 243 and Nataqua No. 152 (Standish) will be visited.

Teacher-Members Honored.

Marysville—Marysville No. 162 has participated monthly in historical programs featuring Washington's bicentennial. Educational week was observed with a program to which Gertrude Cable, E. Lunney Ryan, Agnes W. Meade and Past Grand Esther Sullivan contributed interesting addresses. Grand Marshal Irma Laird was a May 11 visitor.

(Continued on Page 19)

Feminine World's Fads and Fancies

PREPARED ESPECIALLY FOR THE GRIZZLY BEAR BY ANNA STOERMER

FIGURE-MOLDING IS CHIC FOR SUMmertime in foundation garments. New styles have made their appearance and new fabrics and new trimmings combine in a variety of models never equaled for beauty. This season has brought with it many subtle changes in the smart silhouette, and modern corsetry recognizes all these tendencies and gives us the correct foundation garment for each and every one. The aim is not so much to change the figure, as to mold it—to revive, as far as possible, youthful lines by controlling the diaphragm and lifting the bust.

Conspicuous among the newer style trends in the new corsetry are: high-waisted, accentuated bust lines in girdles and brassieres, and combinations even in models for the full figure, backless evening combinations for all; new fastenings, including covered slide metal fasteners; short lacings at side or back to give nipped-in effect; two-way stretch elastic in every type of one-piece garment as well as girdles. Unquestionably the greatest improvement made in corsetry has to do with the two-way elastic feature. It gives greater resiliency and durability, stays in place on the body, assuring perfect figure-control, and carries with it the assurance of non-shrinkage after washing.

Then we have the new garments that are described as something between lingerie and corset types, due to the fact that more and more women are wearing their foundation garments next to the body and call for materials that can be laundered as readily as lingerie.

The new modes give the blouse and skirt a high fashion rank. No one is above being economical these days, yet every woman should hesitate before sacrificing her chic for the sake of a few pennies. A wise way to economize is to make one's own, and continue to have a wardrobe made up of the newest and smartest styles. One skirt and several blouses in different colors and materials will provide several entire changes. Skirts are straighter, with fullness placed low, have slim hiplines, sensible and becoming lengths. Jackets are shorter, high, and trim of waist. There are broad-shoulder, hip-length types, nipped in at the waist.

A new evening jacket is high necked and collarless, with enormous sleeves. Molded bustlines through surplice closings, criss-cross collars, drapery, directoire types are new for evening.

Some of the highlights of the new mode are: higher waists through wide belts, cuffs above the belt on skirts, skirts built up onto the bodice, capes rivaling jackets, cape effects on jackets, coats and frocks for every occasion.

Another concession to "readjustment" days is the use of checked and plaid gingham, pique, wooly looking cottons, printed voiles. All the new cottons have "surface interest"—rough ribbed and crinkly effects in silk and wool, mesh fabrics, stripes and polka dots—and are worn for almost every occasion.

You will become devoted to the scarf, both as a collar and as a separate issue, and combine colors courageously and feel more than pleased with the striking results.

Choosing the new summer weaves is more a matter of "feeling" than seeing, on account of rough-and-ready surfaces. Cotton meshes, lacy woolens and seersucker are a few of the open-work weaves. In nubby surfaces there are tweed and ratine effects. Heavier silks have a decided pebbled surface. Semi-sheer dull crepes are noteworthy in both formal day and night modes.

Again this summer we are leaning to linen as the ideal fabric for warm weather clothes. White and blue continue to be in great favor, being shown for all types of summer things.

Above the waistline you find the new things—draped necklines and bloused sleeves. A ruffled blouse of embroidered batiste has a pleated frill around its wide rever. Pretty collar, cuffs and vestee are made of organdy, which just sits upon the shoulders with its ends looped over and the cuffs tied on. As for the vestee, it will do complimentary things to the suit, made single or double breasted. A bow can be used instead of a blouse under a suit.

The new silk organdie that will be seen everywhere this summer is a little more sophisticated than its cotton sister and will be welcomed for evening wear, as well as for more gala occasions. A frock of printed or silk organdie with simple bodice and long, graceful skirt, worn with a little fitted jacket, will, no doubt, prove to be one of the coming season's successes.

A dress of the smartest of printed silk organdie is plaid, in a bold design of yellow, orange, brown. The skirt reaches to the instep, and is flaring. With the dress is worn a short-fitted jacket of chocolate-colored silk with a collar cut in points, and with points on the cuffs of the very brief sleeves.

Satin is popular for evening frocks, despite the insistance of the mode on frocks of the informal type for evening. Cut and line are very important in the new evening frocks, with seams and empiecements used both as decorative treatment and to define the silhouette. Much satin is being shown here, for the satin gown, when well done, has an air of distinction and can be really regal.

Another very new evening combination is of a lovely glowing shade of ivory satin and pale tobacco-colored satin. The deeper tone is used for facing on the frills and a fitted jacket. The dress has a softly draped bodice, and a diagonal closing edged with a circular cut frill which tapers off at the waistline. All edges of the jacket are bordered with zibeline fur.

There are prints and prints now. In a new kind, the effect is sort of shimmering, like the good old moire silk.

Afternoon slippers are still of the pump style, which is perhaps the only one of all the shoes that has not been cut-out. There are also thin strapped sandals for this type of footwear. Dainty kid and patent open-work shoes make the wearing of special stockings necessary. These are made without reinforced soles or toes and are fragile but better looking.

"True freedom is from within; it can only come by the knowledge of truth."—McKenney.

SAN FRANCISCO

A LARGE GROUP OF NATIVE DAUGHTERS, including grand officers and representatives of twenty-five Subordinate Parlors, attended the Mothers Day breakfast at the Home, May 8. The tables were beautifully decorated with spring flowers. Past Grands Ariana W. Stirling and Dr. Louise C. Heilbron were the hostesses. Past Grand Emma Gruber-Foley presented numerous birthday remembrances to Past Grand Dr. Mariana Bertola.

Tributes to mothers were paid in addresses by Past Grands Stirling and Genevieve Baker, and Grand President Evelyn I. Carlson. Selections were rendered by Ann Godfrey, Katherine McLean and Isabelle Theirbault. Sixteen young members of Coloma Parlor No. 212, captained by Louise Finch, journeyed from Sacramento to stage a May Day drill which won enthusiastic applause.

In honor of her mother, Sadie Winn-Brainard (Califia No. 22), Katherine Jones (Califia No. 22) of Sacramento presented to the Home a beautiful bronze plaque depicting a Pioneer Mother and her babes. Grand Secretary Sallie R. Thaler informed the assemblage that the "Mother" Parlor of the Order of Native Daughters, Ursula No. 1 of Jackson, Amador County, had not forgotten Mothers Day, and had sent to Past Grand Heilbron, the "mother" of the Loyalty Pledge, a check for $280, thus placing Ursula in the hundred-percent list of Parlors.

NATIVE DAUGHTERS DOINGS.

Complimenting the San Francisco Glee Club of seventy-four members and Grand Organist Lola Horgan, Grand President Evelyn I. Carlson gave a bridge luncheon at the Native Daughter Home April 30. Following the lunch, which was served at tables beautifully decorated in orchid and pink, cards were enjoyed and attractive prizes were awarded the lucky players. For the past two years Grand Organist Horgan has personally instructed the members of the glee club, and the splendid musical numbers presented at the many Parlors have added greatly to the pleasure of the Grand President's visits.

Success again crowned the efforts of the card committee of Alta Parlor No. 3 on the occasion of the bridge-whist party May 6. Taxing the auditorium of the beautiful Home building to capacity, the players vied happily for the many attractive prizes. The dutch auction of home-made cakes, conducted by Frank McDonald, was quite spirited and most profitable. The next activity will be a bridge-luncheon June 10. May L. MacDonald, chairman of the committee, is being assisted by Grand Trustee Annie C. Thuesen and the officers of the Parlor. Alta has high hopes of completing its Loyalty Pledge for the 1932 Grand Parlor.

A dinner to celebrate the thirty-sixth anniversary of La Estrella Parlor No. 89 was held May 12 and was attended by many members and their friends, including District Deputy Agnes Ryan. The tables were beautifully decorated with choice seasonal flowers in pastel shades. Interesting talks and games made this a most delightful affair. Much merriment was created by the reading of several telegrams supposed to have been sent by persons in the public eye. June 3 the Parlor will give a card party at the Home. Georgia Thierbach is sponsoring the affair.

Gabrielle Parlor No. 139 had its monthly card party April 27. Members and their families attended, also the members of Rincon Parlor No. 72 N.S.G.W. The card parties are held the fourth Wednesday of each month for the benefit of the Loyalty Pledge. Refreshments are served after the games. May 11 Mothers Day was celebrated in a befitting manner. The members were seated at a large table beautifully decorated with flowers from home gardens.

Mothers of the members of Presidio Parlor No. 148 were the guests of honor of their daughters at a most enjoyable mothers night program May 5. Sadie Romick headed the committee in charge. A program was rendered by the O'Neill sisters, through the courtesy and kindness of Sister McCormick. Bridge and other games were provided for, and every mother and nearly every member went home with gifts and prizes. District Deputy May Noble was in attendance.

Guadalupe Parlor No. 153 celebrated public schools week by presenting April 28 an appropriate program. Miss Mary F. Mooney (Darina No. 114), director of texts and libraries of the San Francisco school department, was the speaker of the evening and chose for her topic "The Place of California History in the School Curriculum." Slides of early California and San Francisco were shown. Musical numbers were rendered by Maude Daley (James Lick No. 220) and Etta Morris (Alta No. 3). A "Toast to the Flag" was given by Maude Daley. The committee in charge of the affair was May McCarthy, Pauline Des Roches and Mary O'Connell.

May 9, Golden Gate Parlor No. 158 entertained Grand President Evelyn I. Carlson, and the large attendance of members indicated their pleasure in being privileged to meet with her. The numerous visitors included several grand officers. The hall and banquetroom were beautified by decorations carrying out the Washington bicentennial motif. The work of all the officers was highly praised by the Grand President. A novel idea was the rendition of an original song of welcome as Mrs. Carlson was escorted to a seat of honor. Refreshments were served at the close of the meeting. Past President Pauline Gaetjen was chairwoman of the evening. May 23, Golden Gate celebrated mothers night.

Past Grand President Dr. Mariana Bertola, chairman of the Grand Parlor Home Committee, was tendered a surprise birthday reception at the May 8 Home breakfast. A shower of birthday greetings evidenced that the beloved Past Grand has a host of friends.

NATIVE SON DOINGS.

In observance of the Washington bicentennial, Stanford Parlor No. 76 sponsored "A Night in '76" May 10. The program included vocal and instrumental music and vaudeville numbers. A. J. Cloud, deputy school superintendent, was the main speaker.

The ninth institution anniversary of Bret Harte Parlor No. 260 was celebrated by a delegation of members attending the leaping-frog classic at Angels Camp, Calaveras County. It was a fitting place to celebrate, the site having been made famous by the Parlor's namesake, Bret Harte, the author. No. 260's drum corps paraded in the main event, and received much favorable comment. Those who participated are enthusiastic in their praise of Angels Camp hospitality.

THE LOST CITY

(SARAH HAMMOND KELLY.)

Towers of ivory, roofs of jade,
Sapphire gate in a wall of gold;
Bright was the city our fair dreams made,
Ere we grew fearful and tired and old.

Riot of color and breath of Spring,
Tulip and pansy and lilac tree,
Petals brushed by a butterfly's wing,
Cooled by a breeze from the silver sea;

Sails of silk by a pearl-white beach,
Shallow stream where the rushes lean,
Purple of grape and rose of peach,
Flash of feathers, crimson and green;

Towers of ivory, roofs of jade,
Crumbled and broken and gray with mold,
Hidden in forests where dim trails fade,
Now we've grown fearful and tired and old.
—University California Chronicle.

Fire Regulations—The United States Forest Service announces that summer fire regulations—for the safety of visitors and the protection of forest, watershed and recreational resources—are now in effect in all the national forests of California.

Many Graduates—The University of California at Berkeley graduated 2,610 students at the May 14 commencement day exercises.

Native Sons of the Golden West

DR. FRANK I. GONZALEZ (PACIFIC No. 10) of San Francisco, Grand President of the Order of Nat|ve Sons of the Golden West, did not, as was his right, preside at the Fifty-fifth Grand Parlor, in session at Stockton last month. Fate denied him that honor, which would have fully recompensed him for the many years of faithful service devoted to the Order. While traveling south to visit Parlors there, he and his wife were severely injured in an auto accident near Santa Barbara, May 4, and they have since been confined in a hospital in that city, where they have been given every attention by Santa Barbara No. 116 members.

At the opening of the Stockton Grand Parlor, Grand First Vice-president Seth Millington, who presided, announced that he had just wired Grand President Gonzalez that next year he would extend him the privilege of opening the Fifty-sixth Grand Parlor. The following telegram was received from Grand President Gonzalez: "My dear brothers, words are inadequate to express the feeling I have in my heart at this time, being denied the privilege, honor and pleasure of presiding at this Grand Parlor. I send congratulations, and best wishes for a most successful session."—C.M.H.

Oratorical Contest.

Elk Grove—A large assemblage gathered at the Elk Grove high school May 16 for the eighteenth annual oratorical contest sponsored by Elk Grove No. 41. One of the rules of the contest is that all the orations must be concerned with California's past history or future development. The judges were Justice Hugh L. Preston, Francis Cochrane (Ramona No. 109) and Mrs. Maud Keltner.

First honors went to Jack Bitzer, whose topic was "California's Human Sequoias," and he was presented the trophy-cup by Miss June Grove, winner of last year's contest. Other contestants, and their subjects, were: Elmarine Latta, "History of the Presbyterian Church;" Mary Veach, "The Beauties and Resources of Yosemite;" Wilma Stewart, "Fremont;" Laverle Elam, "Yosemite;" Nels Evans, "The Vigilantes;" Laverl Carlisle, "The Telegraph in California;" Ruth Taylor, "The Covered Wagon." Each was given a present by President Krull of Liberty No. 213 N.D.G.W.

During the evening the high school band, directed by Earl Nichols, rendered several selections, and Harold Sassman and Lowe Coons were heard in vocal numbers. An interesting feature was the showing of oldtime relics.

Picnic.

Auburn—Auburn No. 59 and Auburn No. 233 N.D.G.W. will give a picnic June 12. Guests will include all residents who came here prior to 1875. The joint committee of arrangements includes: No. 59—E. H. Gum, P. W. Smith, J. G. Walsh and Guy Lukens. No. 233—Mms. Wm. Macy, J. A. Livingston, J. A. Shields and M. Beemis, and Miss Oveta Walsh.

Memorial Services.

Downieville—In recognition of Memorial Day, Downieville No. 92 and Naomi No. 36 N.D.G.W. sponsored memorial services May 29. Following a program the members of the Parlors, joined by the schoolchildren and citizens generally, proceeded to the cemetery, where the graves of departed members, as well as those of soldiers, were decorated.

Barstow Initiation.

San Bernardino—Arrowhead No. 110 had a supper May 25 and then heard the reports of its delegates to the Stockton Grand Parlor. May 28 the Parlor initiated a class of candidates at Barstow. Following the ceremonies, which were conducted by President Lynn A. Reed and his assistant officers, a banquet was served. Arrangements are well under way for Arrowhead's annual roundup, in June. Secretary "Bob" Brazelton was an onlooker at Stockton.

Pioneers Entertained.

Oroville—The fourteenth annual entertainment for the Pioneers given by Argonaut No. 8 and Gold of Ophir No. 190 N.D.G.W. was largely attended. Members of the Parlors in earlyday costumes greeted the guests and President Alice Cundy of No. 190 extended a welcome. Quantities of flowers adorned the banquetroom and the tables. A program was presented by Ramilda Ralph, Betty Boyle, Earl Ward Jr., Harriet Jacoby, Earl Ward Sr., Rosa Crum, Frank O'Brien, Bill Palmer, Addie Roderick, Grand Trustee Florence Boyle, Jim Hedge and Leota Brinkerhoff.

Among the Pioneers, and the years of their arrival in California, were C. L. Duhem 1852, Mrs. Caroline Reagan 1853, Edwin Skinner 1854, Mrs. Jennie LaPoint 1857. Pioneer Natives, and the years of their birth, included Mrs. Romeo Breeden 1849, Mrs. Mary Abbott 1853, B. F. Darby 1854, Miss Fredericka Braden 1854, William Mobley 1855, J. H. Hillman 1856, James Nisbet 1857, Mrs. Estella Russell 1858, Fred Faul 1859. Most of the latter were born, or have lived the greater part of their lives, in Butte County. All the guests, oldtimers and natives, related reminiscences. Mayor Sam Marks gave an interesting talk, and First Vice-president Frank O'Brien of Argonaut bade the guests farewell until the next entertainment for their pleasure.

Enjoys The Grizzly Bear.

The following came to The Grizzly Bear from Assemblyman Percy G. West (Sunset No. 26) of Sacramento: "I inclose my check for a renewal of my subscription to The Grizzly Bear, which I have read for twenty-five years and enjoy very much. 'Happenings of Fifty Years Ago,' by Thomas R. Jones [Sacramento No. 3], itself is well worth the subscription price."

Annual Reunion.

Madera—Madera No. 130 had its annual picnic reunion at the site of the Savage monument, and there was a large attendance of members, their families and friends. County Treasurer William Hughes spoke on the history of Madera County, relating first-hand information, and a baseball game provided recreation. The committee in charge included Kenneth Hughes, Fred Barnett, Cornelius Noble and Joseph Barcroft.

Membership Standing Largest Parlors.

San Francisco—Grand Secretary John T. Regan reports the standing of the Subordinate Parlors having a membership of over 400 January 1, 1932, as follows, together with their membership figures May 20, 1932:

Parlor.	Jan. 1	May 20	Gain	Loss
Ramona No. 109	1088	1085	....	3
South San Francisco No. 157	822	812	....	10
Castro No. 232	700	700	....	....
Stanford No. 76	614	610	....	4
Arrowhead No. 110	609	594	....	15
Twin Peaks No. 214	585	562	....	23
Stockton No. 7	549	549	....	....
Pirdmont No. 120	523	520	....	3
Rincon No. 72	448	441	....	7

Rewarded With "Outpost of Empire."

Pleasanton—In an essay contest sponsored by Pleasanton No. 244, Miss Mildred Sorensen was declared the winner. Her subject was "Thomas Starr King." As a reward, she was presented with "Outpost of Empire," written by Dr. Herbert Eugene Bolton, head of the University of California's history department, and dealing with the history of San Francisco. Miss Blair Logue, second in the contest, was also presented with a California history book.

Anniversary Observed.

Calistoga—Calistoga No. 86 observed its forty-sixth institution anniversary May 2. Past Presidents E. E. Light, A. Cavagnaro, W. D. Tucker, J. C. Siemsen, F. Pocai and A. M. Emerick were in the chairs, the former presiding. The hall was packed, a large delegation from Saint Helena No. 53 being among the crowd. The evening's feature was a talk on "Old Times and Old Timers" by N. F. Coombs (Napa No. 62). A fine supper was served, and instrumental and vocal selections were rendered. It was a memorable night.

The Parlor has appointed a committee to arrange a week-end home-coming for former Calistogans. The townspeople will be asked to cooperate, and it is believed the event can be made a long-to-be-remembered civic day.

Mothers Day Entertainment.

Redwood City—Redwood No. 66 was host May 5 to Bonita No. 10 N.D.G.W., their families and friends at a Mothers Day entertainment. Past Grand Fletcher A. Cutler was the principal speaker, and others who contributed to the program were the firemen's orchestra, L. W. Fowler director, Mr. and Mrs. R. A. Hohberger, Kendall Towne, Adolph Zanetti, Harry and Kenneth Mollenhaer, Mr. and Mrs. H. J. Phillips and Duncan Reynard.

Dancing and cards were provided, and a supper was served. The arrangements committee consisted of Edwin Holmquist (chairman), C. M. Junker, C. Rockwell, S. E. Marcus and L. Lodi.

N.S.G.W. OFFICIAL DEATH LIST.

Containing the name, the date and the place of birth, the date of death, and the Subordinate Parlor affiliation of deceased members reported to Grand Secretary John T. Regan from April 19, 1932, to May 20, 1932:

Duden, Wm. C.; Latrobe, October 14, 1875; March 26 1932; Placerville No. 9.

Darlington, Abe; Placerville, November 7, 1867; April 20, 1932; Placerville No. 9.

Auser, Fred; Petaluma, June 24, 1863; April 4, 1932 Golden Gate No. 29.

Stewart, Kenneth Matheson; San Francisco, November 3 1864; April 12, 1932; Golden Gate No. 29.

Brennan, Edmond Hugh; San Francisco, September 15 1863; April 18, 1932; Golden Gate No. 29.

Davis, Pearl Elbridge; El Dorado, February 23, 1870 January 11, 1932; Bakersfield No. 42.

Shayer, William Henry; San Francisco, December 3 1874; April 10, 1932; Oakland No. 50.

Hanifin, Jeremiah Joseph Jr.; San Francisco, Septembe 21, 1863; April 12, 1932; Oakland No. 50.

Gifford, E. H.; Sacramento, August 12, 1889; April 27 1932; Napa No. 62.

Alteridge, Arthur John; Watsonville, December 26, 1881; May 3, 1932; Watsonville No. 65.
O'Brien, Frank; San Francisco, September 2, 1892; April 17, 1932; Rincon No. 72.
Smith, Hawley Hugh; San Francisco, August 16, 1865; April 11, 1932; Calistoga No. 86.
Bernhardt, Jacob; New York Flat, November 2, 1857; April 18, 1932; Downieville No. 92.
Blair, Paul Loughridge; Los Angeles, February 10, 1879; April 27, 1932; Ramona No. 109.
Botto, John; Vallecita, February 1, 1876; April 22, 1932; Chispa No. 139.
Ames, John Fisher; Sebastopol, December 6, 1859; April 14, 1932; Sebastopol No. 143.
Milly, Emil Francis; San Francisco, May 14, 1880; May 28, 1932; South San Francisco No. 157.
Franklin, George; San Francisco, November 24, 1900; April 29, 1932; South San Francisco No. 157.
Partridge, Dr. Harry; Susanville, January 14, 1874; April 24, 1932; Precita No. 187.
Severance, Walter Benjamin; Navarro, August 28, 1868; April 14, 1932; Alder Glen No. 200.
O'Leary, James P.; San Francisco, March 11, 1875; April 16, 1932; Dolores No. 208.
McDonald, George Duncan; San Francisco, August 10, 1867; April 17, 1932; Guadalupe No. 231.

N.S. FORMER JUSTICE PASSES.

San Francisco—Judge Frank M. Angellotti, former Chief Justice of the California Supreme Court, died May 23 survived by a wife and a daughter. He was a native of Marin County, affiliated with Mount Tamalpais Parlor No. 64 N.S.G.W. (San Rafael) and frequently represented the Parlor in the Grand Parlor.

EXPERIMENTAL FOREST ESTABLISHED.

The Swayne Mountain experimental forest, the first to be established in California by the Federal Agricultural Department forest service, has been set aside in the Lassen National Forest. The 6,000 acres will be used as a laboratory for forestry experiments and research. Later on, one or more portions will be selected and designated as "natural forests" and will be left unmolested for the purpose of scientific study.

Auto Output Declined—World auto output in 1931, including trucks and buses, totaled 3,042,069, which is 1,084,401 units less than the 1930 output, according to an announcement of the Federal Commerce Department.

Bicentennial Quarter—As a feature of the nation-wide George Washington bicentennial, the Federal Treasury Department will issue a new George Washington quarter-dollar.

Visalia Rodeo—Visalia, Tulare County, will stage a rodeo June 3-5.

In Memoriam

FRANCES E. WESTOVER.

Whereas, The Almighty God, in His infinite wisdom, has seen fit to take from our midst a dear sister and friend, Sister Frances Westover;

Resolved, That Stirling Parlor No. 146 N.D.G.W. extends through this committee its sincere sympathy to the bereaved husband, Mr. W. E. Westover, and other members of the family; be it further resolved, that a copy of this letter be sent to the husband, one to the local paper, one be spread upon the minutes of this Parlor, and a copy be forwarded to The Grizzly Bear.

Yours in P.D.F.A.,

MARGARET M. DELP,
VERA LAEDERICH,
ADA ERICSSON,
Committee.

Pittsburg, May 5, 1932.

JOHN FISHER AMES.

Whereas, It has pleased our Heavenly Father, in His divine wisdom, to remove from our midst and associations our highly esteemed and beloved brother, John Fisher Ames; and whereas, in the passing of Brother Ames, Sebastopol Parlor No. 143 N.S.G.W. mourns the loss of one of its loyal and faithful members, one who ever held seriously those cardinal virtues of our Order. Therefore, be it

Resolved, That while we will miss our departed brother, nevertheless the memory of his associations will ever remain fresh in our memory, and that we extend the hand of sympathy to the bereaved family in this, their hour of sorrow; and be it further resolved, that these resolutions be spread in full upon the minutes of this meeting, and that a copy be sent to the family of our departed brother, and ha a copy be sent to The Grizzly Bear Magazine for publication.

W. S. BORBA,
F. G. McFARLANE,
H. B. SCUDDER,
J. P. KELLY,
Committee.

Sebastopol, May 6, 1932.

ANNIE FENNON.

After a life of devotion to family and friends, it has been the wish of He who knoweth all things best to take to that heavenly home our beloved sister, Annie Fennon.

The services of Annie Fennon to Angelita Parlor No. 32 N.D.G.W. are a bright spot in our history; the passing of our sister is a loss to the community in which she lived, and to our Parlor. And it is hereby resolved, that her beautiful character, filled with good deeds and kindly thoughts, will always live in our memories.

"Sleep on, dear heart, such lives as thine
Have not been lived in vain,
But shed an influence rare, divine,
On lives that here remain."

ANNIE McDONALD,
AGNES REUSS,
KATIE JENSEN,
Committee.

Livermore, May 17, 1932.

LOS ANGELES
CITY AND COUNTY

THROUGH THE EFFORTS OF A COMmittee appointed by Ramona Parlor No. 109 N.S.G.W., the attention of Governor James Rolph Jr. has been called to the condition of the Pico mansion at Whittier, and the restoration of the famous Pico blue ash tree at the doorway of the landmark has recently been completed under the direction of D. G. Milbrath of the State Department of Agriculture. The big spreading tree, planted in 1830, has undergone extensive pruning and surgery estimated to prolong its life far beyond the century mark. Steps have also been taken to perpetuate the tree by guarding young sprouts to supplant the parent, though this will not be necessary now for many years.

The Pico mansion, home of the last Mexican governor of California and at one time a thirty-room adobe house, was the scene of many tradition-making festivities. The ash tree, a splendid spectacle for the tourist, unusual in size and beauty as well as in historical associations, guards the entrance to the historic house.

All Natives and other lovers of California are interested in such historic old places as the Pico mansion, and there are but a few of these old adobes left. Attention must be given this one soon, as the building is crumbling. It has been the property of the State of California for eighteen years.—J. Harvey McCarthy.

'LET'S ALL BE PEPTOMISTS.

The Olympiad song, "On To California," dedicated to Los Angeles Parlor No. 124 N.D.G.W. by the composer, Louise Graeser, and being sung at numerous functions by Sophia Stewart, has been most favorably received. Copies may be obtained from any member of the Parlor. No. 124 had many visitors May 4, including President Betty Saunders (Verdugo No. 240), Grand Trustee Florence Schoneman and Past Grand President Margaret Grote-Hill. Jennie Raymond proposed organization of a swimming class, and Irene Eden and Peggy Ambler spoke on the opening of the Olympic swimming-pool. The card party May 11, Olinda Kirby chairman, was largely attended.

"A pessimist," says President Gertrude Allen, "is one who sits down and says 'It can't be done.' An optimist says 'Everything is wonderful and it can be done,' then he sits down and waits for someone to do it. The peptomist says 'It can be done,' then he rolls up his sleeves and does it. Let's all be peptomists!" Los Angeles' June calendar includes: 1st, election officers. 8th, card party, last of bridge tournament. 15th, initiation. 22nd, no meeting account Grand Parlor. 29th, all nations dinner dance—a novel idea; sports or informal dress for the occasion; excellent food served by Edna Holcomb.

ANNIVERSARY STAG BARBECUE.

Ramona Parlor No. 109 N.S.G.W. has made great preparations for a stag barbecue to be held June 12 at Glen Oaks, Glendale, in recognition of its forty-fifth institution anniversary. Walter Slosson, in charge, will have the assistance of Ray Rehart, Charles Gassagne, John Stahl, the Drouet "gang" and Fred Staebler. Plenty of sports, food galore and other attractions are promised. All Native Sons are invited, but reservations must be made in advance through Secretary John V. Scott.

June 3 the Parlor will elect officers for the July-December term, June 10 will be initiation night, and June 17 President Chandos Bush will give his delayed talk on "Immigration." June 7, through the kindness of J. Harvey McCarthy, Superior Judge Ruben S. Schmidt will present United States of America and California State (Bear) Flags to the Carthay Center high school.

ANNIVERSARY LUNCHEON.

One of the most interesting meetings of the year for Californiana Parlor No. 247 N.D.G.W. was that of May 17. A sort of reciprocity luncheon was enjoyed with the members of the executive board of the Euterpe Opera Reading Club, of which two members of the Parlor, President Gertrude Tuttle and Mrs. Ora E. Evans, are officers. A delightful program was provided by Chairman Florence Irish, who also belongs to Euterpe, numbers being contributed by Harriet Ware and Mary Teitsworth. Chairman Lela Tabor of the homeless children committee was authorized to keep an album of babies under her supervision.

In recognition of the Parlor's birthday anniversary a bridge luncheon was held May 26 at the home of Mrs. Earl Osborn. Mrs. Matilda J. Murdock was general chairman of arrangements, Mrs. Wilfred L. Chapman directed the program, and President Tuttle headed the guest hostesses.

BANQUET, TO CELEBRATE ANNIVERSARY.

The annual banquet of Hollywood Parlor No. 196 N.S.G.W., in celebration of its institution anniversary, will be held June 6. Governor James Rolph Jr. will be the guest of honor, and a fine entertainment program has been arranged. Invitations have been sent the grand officers and prominent persons throughout the state. Reservations, at two dollars per plate, must be made with Bernard G. Hiss, chairman of the arrangements committee, 622 Hollingsworth building, Sixth and Hill streets. Other members of the committee are Lucien Griffin, Martin Maza, C. L. Patterson, Fred Youell, Jack Gorman, Everett Beesley, James E. Kirby, Henry G. Bodkin and Municipal Judge Leo Aggeler.

The initiation May 2 by Hollywood of the Superior Judge Joseph P. Sproul class of candidates drew a large crowd. Henry G. Bodkin presided during good of the order, and among the speakers were Grand Trustee Eldred L. Meyer, District Deputy Al Cron, Les Shellback, J. E. McCurdy, Philip D. Molen and Judge Sproul. John J. Ford, son of the lately deceased W. Joseph Ford, spoke for the initiates, six in number. Refreshments were served at the meeting's close.

SYMPHONIES UNDER THE STARS.

The opening of Hollywood Bowl's eleventh annual season of "symphonies under the stars" has been set for July 5. The concerts will run continuously for eight weeks and will close August 26, according to Glenn M. Tindall, manager of the bowl. Every effort will be made, says the management, to make the season the greatest in bowl history.

DANCE AT GLENDALE JUNE 11.

Glendale—The dance May 7 given jointly by Verdugo Parlor No. 240 N.D.G.W. and Glendale

Parlor No. 264 N.S.G.W. was most successful, 110 couples having a splendid time. The next dance will be given June 11 at Masonic Temple, 234 South Brand boulevard, under the supervision of the same capable joint committee headed by Nan Hutchinson and Harvey Gillett.

District Deputy Ruth Ruiz visited Verdugo May 10, and at the meeting's close refreshments were served at the home of First Vice-president Vera Carlson. In keeping with the Olympics beautification project, the Parlor is planting a lot on Brand boulevard.

HUGE SUCCESS.

Ocean Park—The class initiation May 9 sponsored by Santa Monica Bay Parlor No. 267 N.S.G.W. in honor of Grand President Dr. Frank I. Gonzalez, who could not attend because of an auto accident that overtook him enroute, was a huge success. There was a very large crowd, every Parlor in the southland being well represented, Santa Barbara Parlor No. 116 sending an extra-large delegation. All present attached their signatures to a greetings-parchment which was delivered to Grand President Gonzalez.

Nineteen candidates were initiated, they being supplied by Ramona No. 109, Santa Barbara No. 116, Sepulveda No. 263, Glendale No. 264, Santa Ana No. 265 and Santa Monica Bay No. 267. The ritual was most creditably exemplified by No. 267's officers, with Claude J. Wiseman as president and J. E. McCurdy as marshal, and at the conclusion of the ceremonies Past Grand William I. Traeger delivered a splendid address for the benefit of the initiates. Among the many other speakers were Past Grand Herman C. Lichtenberger, Grand Trustee Eldred L. Meyer, Grand Organist Leslie Maloche, District Deputies A. C. Dinsmore, Al Cron, Edward E. Baldwin and Walter E. Hiskey. At the meeting's conclusion refreshments were served and an entertainment program was presented.

PLAQUE HONORING PIONEER DEDICATED.

Long Beach—The annual observance of Mothers Day by Long Beach Parlor No. 154 N.D.G.W. at Houghton Park May 12 was largely attended. Luncheon was served on artistically decorated tables by a committee consisting of District Deputy Clara Fay (chairman), President Violet T. Henshilwood, Past President Daisy T. Hansen and First Vice-president Zella L. Hodgedon. A sincere welcome was extended the mother-guests by Charter President Kate McFadyen. A program was presented.

After the luncheon the bronze plaque in honor of Mrs. Eliza Donner-Houghton, referred to in The Grizzly Bear for May, was dedicated. The inscription reads: "In memory of Eliza Donner Houghton, member of Donner Party 1846. Dedicated May 12, 1932, by Long Beach Parlor No. 154 N.D.G.W." The plaque is a gift to the Parlor from Sadie Winn-Brainard (Califia No. 22) of Sacramento. Speakers included President Hensilwood, who presented the plaque, Miss Eliza Houghton, Grand Trustee Florence D. Schoneman, and Park Superintendent Peter Mohrbacker, who accepted the gift.

Long Beach's card party May 5, with Eleanor Johnson in charge, was greatly enjoyed, and the cooked-food sale May 7, Alice Waldow chairman, netted a neat sum. Recent meetings of the Parlor's thimble club have been held at the homes of Kate McFadyen, Daisy T. Hansen and Genevieve Dalton.

TO ROUND UP ELIGIBLES.

San Pedro—During June and July Rudecinda Parlor No. 230 N.D.G.W. will round up eligibles and hopes to add many to its membership-roll. A noontime tamale dinner was served at the Y.W.C.A. May 24, and in June, at the same time and place, an enchilada feast will be served.

WORTHY, BUT POOR, FAMILY ADOPTED.

Ocean Park—Santa Monica Bay Parlor No. 245 N.D.G.W. celebrated May 2 its fourth institution anniversary, and all but eighteen of its entire membership were in attendance. District Deputy Flora Holy and the senior past presidents were guests of honor. Active in arranging for the party were Charter President Rosalie F. Hyde, Past Presidents Reta Smith, Mary Stevens, Joey Denton, Anna Pierce and Mary Meyer, and Treasurer Hazel McCreary.

Chairman Marie Barnes of the homeless children committee announced a benefit card party, the afternoon of June 6 at Fuller Hall. A very interesting program was presented under the direction of Hazel McCreary during public-school week. The Parlor has adopted a worthy, but poor, family; milk is provided for the children, and from time to time showers of food and clothing are held. A new feature in No. 245 is the birthday card, sent each member on her

(Continued on Page 23)

Official Directory of Parlors of the N. D. G. W.

ALAMEDA COUNTY.

Angelita No. 32, Livermore—Meets 2nd and 4th Fridays, Foresters Hall; Mrs. Myrtle I. Johnson, Rec. Sec.

Piedmont No. 87, Oakland—Meets Thursdays, Corinthian Hall, Pacific Bldg.; Mrs. Alice E. Miner, Rec. Sec., 421 36th St.

Aloha No. 106, Oakland—Meets Tuesdays, Wigwam Hall, Pacific Bldg.; Gladys I. Farley, Rec. Sec., 4623 Benevides Ave.

Hayward No. 122, Hayward—Meets 1st and 3rd Tuesdays, Veterans Memorial Bldg., Main St.; Miss Ruth Gansberger, Rec. Sec., P. O. box 44, Mount Eden.

Berkeley No. 150, Berkeley—Meets 1st and 3rd Fridays, Masonic Hall; Mrs. Lelia B. Baker, Rec. Sec., 915 Contra Costa Ave.

Bear Flag No. 151, Berkeley—Meets 2nd and 4th Wednesdays, Veterans Memorial Bldg., 1931 Center St.; Mrs. Maud Wagner, Rec. Sec., 317 Alcatraz Ave., Oakland.

Encinal No. 156, Alameda—Meets 2nd and 4th Thursdays, N.S.G.W. Hall; Mrs. Laura E. Fisher, Rec. Sec., 1413 Caroline St.

Brooklyn No. 157, East Oakland—Meets Wednesdays, Masonic Temple, 8th Ave. and E. 14th St.; Mrs. Ruth Cooney, Rec. Sec., 3907 14th Ave.

Argonaut No. 166, Oakland—Meets Tuesdays, Klinkner Hall, 59th and San Pablo; Mrs. Ada Spilman, Rec. Sec., 2905 Ellis St., Berkeley.

Bahia Vista No. 167, Oakland—Meets Thursdays, Wigwam Hall, Pacific Bldg.; Mrs. Minnie E. Raper, Rec. Sec., 3449 Helen St.

Fruitvale No. 177, Oakland—Meets Fridays, W.O.W. Hall; Mrs. Agnes M. Grant, Rec. Sec., 1224 30th Ave.

Laura Loma No. 182, Niles—Meets 1st and 3rd Tuesdays, I.O.O.F. Hall; Mrs. Ethel Fournier, Rec. Sec., P. O. box 515.

El Cereso No. 207, San Leandro—Meets 2nd and 4th Tuesdays, Masonic Hall; Mrs. Mary Tuttle, Rec. Sec., P. O. box 56.

Pleasanton No. 237, Pleasanton—Meets 1st Tuesday, I.O.O.F. Hall; Mrs. Myrtle Lanini, Rec. Sec.

Betsy Ross No. 238, Centerville—Meets 1st and 3rd Fridays, Anderson Hall; Miss Constance Lucio, Rec. Sec., P. O. box 187.

AMADOR COUNTY.

Ursula No. 1, Jackson—Meets 2nd and 4th Tuesdays, N.S.G.W. Hall; Mrs. Emma Boarman-Wright, Rec. Sec., 114 Court St.

Chispa No. 40, Ione—Meets 2nd and 4th Fridays, N.S.G.W. Hall; Mrs. Isabel Ashton, Rec. Sec.

Amapola No. 80, Sutter Creek—Meets 2nd and 4th Thursdays, N.S.G.W. Bldg.; Mrs. Hazel M. Marre, Rec. Sec.

Forrest No. 86, Plymouth—Meets 2nd and 4th Tuesdays, I.O.O.F. Hall; Mrs. Marguerite Davis, Rec. Sec.

BUTTE COUNTY.

Annie K. Bidwell No. 168, Chico—Meets 2nd and 4th Thursdays, I.O.O.F. Hall; Mrs. Irene Henry, Rec. Sec., 3015 Woodland Ave.

Gold of Ophir No. 190, Oroville—Meets 1st and 3rd Wednesdays, Memorial Hall; Mrs. Ruth Brown, Rec. Sec., 1265 Leah Court.

CALAVERAS COUNTY.

Ruby No. 46, Murphys—Meets 4th Friday, N.S.G.W. Hall; Belle Segale, Rec. Sec.

Princess No. 84, Angels Camp—Meets 2nd and 4th Wednesdays, I.O.O.F. Hall; Grace Mills, Rec. Sec.

San Andreas No. 113, San Andreas—Meets 1st Friday, Fraternal Hall; Miss Doris Treat, Rec. Sec.

COLUSA COUNTY.

Colus No. 194, Colusa—Meets 1st and 3rd Mondays, Eagles Hall; Miss Kate Busch, Rec. Sec., 850 Market St.

CONTRA COSTA COUNTY.

Stirling No. 146, Pittsburg—Meets 1st and 3rd Wednesdays, Veteran Memorial Hall; Mrs. Minnie Marcelli, Rec. Sec., 771 E. 12th St.

Richmond No. 147, Richmond—Meets 1st and 3rd Tuesdays, I.O.O.F. Hall, 10th St.; Mrs. Tillie Summers, Rec. Sec., 640 So. 31st St.

Donner No. 193, Byron—Meets 1st and 3rd Wednesdays, I.O.O.F. Hall; Mrs. Anna Pendry, Rec. Sec., P. O. box 112.

Las Juntas No. 221, Martinez—Meets 1st and 3rd Mondays, Pythian Castle; Mrs. Lola O. Viera, Rec. Sec., 305 Arreba St.

Antioch No. 223, Antioch—Meets 2nd and 4th Tuesdays, I.O.O.F. Hall; Mrs. Estelle Evans, Rec. Sec., 202 E. 5th St., Pittsburg.

Carquinez No. 234, Crockett—Meets 2nd and 4th Wednesdays, I.O.O.F. Hall; Mrs. Cecile Petes, Rec. Sec., 465 Edwards St.

EL DORADO COUNTY.

Marguerite No. 12, Placerville—Meets 1st and 3rd Wednesdays, Masonic Hall; Mrs. Nettie Leonardi, Rec. Sec., 25 Coloma St.

El Dorado No. 186, Georgetown—Meets 2nd and 4th Saturday afternoons, I.O.O.F. Hall; Mrs. Alta L. Douglas, Rec. Sec.

FRESNO COUNTY.

Fresno No. 187, Fresno—Meets 2nd and 4th Fridays, Pythian Castle, Cor. "R" and Merced Sts.; Mary Aubery, Rec. Sec., 1040 Delphia Ave.

GRAND OFFICERS

Mrs. Estelle M. Evans..........Past Grand President
202 E. Fifth St., Pittsburg

Mrs. Evelyn I. Carlson..........Grand President
1965 San Jose Ave., San Francisco

Mrs. Anna M. Armstrong..........Grand Vice-president
Woodland

Mrs. Sallie R. Thaler..........Grand Secretary
555 Baker St., San Francisco

Mrs. Susie K. Christ..........Grand Treasurer
555 Baker St., San Francisco

Mrs. Irma Laird..........Grand Marshal
Alturas

Mrs. Minna K. Horn..........Grand Inside Sentinel
Etna

Mrs. Orinda G. Giannini..........Grand Outside Sentinel
2142 Filbert St., San Francisco

Mrs. Lola Horgan..........Grand Organist
789 Morse St., San Francisco

GRAND TRUSTEES

Mrs. Edna Briggs..........1045 Santa Ynez Way, Sacramento
Mrs. Ethel Begley..........233 Prospect Ave., San Francisco
Mrs. Anna Thuesen..........615 38th Ave., San Francisco
Mrs. Gladys Noce..........Sutter Creek
Mrs. Florence Boyle..........Oroville
Mrs. Florence Schoneman..........1521 5th Ave., Los Angeles
Mrs. Willow Borba..........Sebastopol

GLENN COUNTY.

Berryessa No. 192, Willows—Meets 1st and 3rd Mondays, I.O.O.F. Hall; Mrs. Leonora Neate, Rec. Sec., 338 No. Lassen St.

HUMBOLDT COUNTY.

Occident No. 28, Eureka—Meets 1st and 3rd Wednesdays, N.S.G.W. Hall; Mrs. Eva L. MacDonald, Rec. Sec., 2309 "B" St.

Oneonta No. 71, Ferndale—Meets 2nd and 4th Fridays, I.O.O.F. Hall; Mrs. Myra Rumrill, Rec. Sec.

Reichling No. 97, Fortuna—Meets 1st and 3rd Tuesdays, Friendshi Hall; Mrs. Grace Swett, Rec. Sec., P. O. box 328. p

KERN COUNTY.

Miocene No. 228, Taft—Meets 1st and 3rd Wednesday afternoons, I.O.O.F. Hall; Mrs. Evalyn G. Towne, Rec. Sec., P. O. box 1011.

El Tejon No. 239, Bakersfield—Meets 1st and 3rd Fridays, Eagles Hall, 1714 "G" St.; Mrs. Grace S. Dorris, Rec. Sec., 127 Morgan Bldg.

Desert Gold No. 250, Mojave—Meets 2nd and 4th Fridays, I.O.O.F. Hall; Mrs. Mae Cohill, Rec. Sec.

LAKE COUNTY.

Clear Lake No. 135, Middletown—Meets 2nd and 4th Tuesdays, Herrick Hall; Mrs. Alma E. Snow, Rec. Sec.

LASSEN COUNTY.

Nataqua No. 152, Standish—Meets 1st and 3rd Wednesdays, Foresters Hall; Mrs. Mayda Elledge, Rec. Sec.

Mount Lassen No. 215, Bieber—Meets 2nd and 4th Thursdays, I.O.O.F. Hall; Mrs. Angie C. Kenyon, Rec. Sec.

Susanville No. 243, Susanville—Meets 3rd Thursday, I.O.O.F. Hall; Mrs. Georgia Jensen, Rec. Sec., 700 Roop St.

LOS ANGELES COUNTY.

Los Angeles No. 124, Los Angeles—Meets 1st and 3rd Wednesdays, I.O.O.F. Hall, Washington and Oak Sts.; Mrs. Mary K. Corcoran, Rec. Sec., 322 No. Van Ness Ave.

Long Beach No. 154, Long Beach—Meets 1st and 3rd Thursdays, K.P. Hall, 341 Pacific Ave.; Mrs. Bertha Hitt, Rec. Sec., 5355 Lime Ave.

Rudecinda No. 230, San Pedro—Meets 1st and 3rd Fridays, Unity Hall, I.O.O.F. Temple, 10th and Gaffey; Mrs. Carrie E. Northway, Rec. Sec., 561 W. 14th St.

Verdugo No. 240, Glendale—Meets 2nd and 4th Tuesdays, Masonic Temple, 234 So. Brand Blvd.; Miss Etta Fulkerth, Rec. Sec., 526-A No. Orange St.

Santa Monica Bay No. 245, Ocean Park—Meets 1st and 3rd Mondays, New Eagles Hall, 2823½ Main St.; Mrs. Rosalie Hyde, Rec. Sec., 738 Flower St., Venice.

Californiana No. 247, Los Angeles—Meets 2nd and 4th Tuesday afternoons, Hollywood Studio Club, 1215 Lodi Place; Mrs. Inez Sitton, Rec. Sec., 4223 Berenice St.

MADERA COUNTY.

Madera No. 244, Madera—Meets 2nd and 4th Thursdays, Masonic Annex; Mrs. Margaret C. Boyle, Rec. Sec., 111 No. "B" St.

MARIN COUNTY.

Sea Point No. 196, Sausalito—Meets 2nd and 4th Mondays, Perry Hall, 50 Caledonia St.; Mrs. Mary B. Smith, Rec. Sec., 559 Woodward Ave.

Marinita No. 198, San Rafael—Meets 2nd and 4th Mondays, 316 "B" St.; Miss Mollye Y. Spaelti, Rec. Sec., 539 4th St.

Fairfax No. 225, Fairfax—Meets 2nd and 4th Tuesdays, Community Hall; Mrs. Olive A. Greene, Rec. Sec., P. O. box 277.

Tamelpa No. 231, Mill Valley—Meets 1st and 2nd Tuesdays, I.O.O.F. Hall; Mrs. Delphine M. Todt, Rec. Sec., 400 Grand Ave., San Rafael.

MARIPOSA COUNTY.

Mariposa No. 63, Mariposa—Meets 1st and 3rd Fridays, I.O.O.F. Hall; Mrs. Mamie E. Weston, Rec. Sec.

MENDOCINO COUNTY.

Fort Bragg No. 210, Fort Bragg—Meets 1st and 3rd Thursdays, I.O.O.F. Hall; Mrs. Ruth W. Fuller, Rec. Sec.

MERCED COUNTY.

Veritas No. 75, Merced—Meets 1st and 3rd Tuesdays, I.O.O.F. Hall; Miss Margaret Thornton, Rec. Sec., 317 18th St.

MODOC COUNTY.

Alturas No. 159, Alturas—Meets 1st Thursday, Alturas Civic Club; Mrs. Irma W. Laird, Rec. Sec.

MONTEREY COUNTY.

Aleli No. 102, Salinas—Meets 2nd and 4th Thursdays, Knights Pythias Hall; Miss Rose Rhyner, Rec. Sec., 420 Soledad St.

Junipero No. 141, Monterey—Meets 2nd and 4th Fridays, Pythian Hall; Miss Matilda M. Bergschicker, Rec. Sec., 498 Van Buren St.

NAPA COUNTY.

Eschol No. 16, Napa—Meets 2nd and 4th Mondays, N.S.G.W. Hall; Mrs. Ella Ingram, Rec. Sec., 2140 Seminary St.

Calistoga No. 145, Calistoga—Meets 2nd and 4th Mondays, I.O.O.F. Hall; Sadie P. Brooks, Rec. Sec.

La Junta No. 203, Saint Helena—Meets 1st and 3rd Tuesdays, N.S.G.W. Hall; Mrs. Marie Signorelli, Rec. Sec., 1341 Madrona Ave.

ATTENTION, SECRETARIES!

THIS DIRECTORY IS PUBLISHED BY AUTHORITY OF THE GRAND PARLOR N.D.G.W., AND ALL NOTICES OF CHANGES MUST BE RECEIVED BY THE GRAND SECRETARY (NOT THE MAGAZINE) ON OR BEFORE THE 20TH OF EACH MONTH TO INSURE CORRECTION IN NEXT PUBLICATION OF DIRECTORY.

NEVADA COUNTY.

Laurel No. 6, Nevada City—Meets 1st and 3rd Wednesdays, I.O.O.F. Hall; Mrs. Nellie E. Clark, Rec. Sec., P. O. box 212.

Manzanita No. 29, Grass Valley—Meets 1st and 3rd Tuesdays, Auditorium; Mrs. Loraine Keast, Rec. Sec., 123 Race St.

Columbia No. 70, French Corral—Meets Fridays, Farrelley Hall; Mrs. Kate Farrelley-Sullivan, Rec. Sec.

Snow Peak No. 176, Truckee—Meets 1st Monday, I.O.O.F. Hall; Mrs. Henrietta M. Eaton, Rec. Sec., P. O. box 116.

ORANGE COUNTY.

Santa Ana No. 235, Santa Ana—Meets 2nd and 4th Mondays, K.C. Hall, 4th and French Sts.; Mrs. Matilda S. Lemon, Rec. Sec., 928 W. Fairview.

Grace No. 242, Fullerton—Meets 1st and 3rd Thursdays, I.O.O.F. Hall, 116½ E. Commonwealth; Mrs. Mary Rothaermel, Rec. Sec., P. O. box 285.

PLACER COUNTY.

Placer No. 138, Lincoln—Meets 2nd Wednesday, I.O.O.F. Hall; Miss Carrie Parlin, Rec. Sec.

La Rosa No. 191, Roseville—Meets 1st and 3rd Tuesdays, Eagles Hall; Mrs. Alice Lee West, Rec. Sec., Rocklin.

Auburn No. 233, Auburn—Meets 2nd and 4th Fridays, Foresters Hall; Mrs. Dorothy Reinecke, Rec. Sec., Penryn.

PLUMAS COUNTY.

Plumas Pioneer No. 219, Quincy—Meets 1st and 3rd Mondays, I.O.O.F. Hall; Minnie E. Johnson, Rec. Sec., P. O. box 243.

SACRAMENTO COUNTY.

Califia No. 22, Sacramento—Meets 2nd and 4th Tuesdays, N.S.G.W. Hall; Miss Lulu Gillis, Rec. Sec., 921 8th St.

La Bandera No. 110, Sacramento—Meets 1st and 3rd Fridays, N.S.G.W. Hall; Mrs. Clara Weldon, Rec. Sec., 1310 "O" St.

Sutter No. 111, Sacramento—Meets 1st and 3rd Tuesdays, N.S.G.W. Hall; Mrs. Adele Nix, Rec. Sec., 1238 "S" St.

Fern No. 123, Folsom—Meets 1st and 3rd Tuesdays, K.P. Hall; Mrs. Viola Shumway, Rec. Sec., P. O. box 48.

Chabolla No. 171, Galt—Meets 2nd and 4th Tuesdays, I.O.O.F. Hall; Mrs. Mary Pritchard, Rec. Sec.

Coloma No. 212, Sacramento—Meets 1st and 3rd Tuesdays, I.O.O.F. Hall, Oak Park; Mrs. Nettie Harry, Rec. Sec., 1317 35th St.

Liberty No. 213, Elk Grove—Meets 2nd and 4th Fridays, I.O.O.F. Hall; Mrs. Frances Wackman, Rec. Sec., P. O. box 192.

Victory No. 216, Courtland—Meets 1st Saturday and 3rd Monday, N.S.G.W. Hall; Mrs. Agneda Lample, Rec. Sec.

SAN BENITO COUNTY.

Copa de Oro No. 105, Hollister—Meets 2nd and 4th Thursdays, Grangers Union Hall; Mrs. Mollie Daveggio, Rec. Sec., 110 San Benito St.

San Juan Bautista No. 179, San Juan Bautista—Meets 1st Wednesday, Mission Corridor Rooms; Miss Gertrude Breen, Rec. Sec.

SAN BEARNARDINO COUNTY.

Lugonia No. 241, San Bernardino—Meets 2nd and 4th Wednesdays, Eagles Hall; Grace McHenry, Rec. Sec., Base Line and Central, Highland.

Ontario No. 251, Ontario—Meets 2nd and 4th Thursdays, Ontario Hotel; Miss Helen Hickman, Rec. Sec., 923 No. Laurel Ave.

SAN DIEGO COUNTY.

San Diego No. 208, San Diego—Meets 2nd and 4th Wednesdays, Directors Room, Chamber Commerce Bldg., 499 W. Broadway; Mrs. Elsie Case, Rec. Sec., 3051 Broadway.

SAN FRANCISCO CITY AND COUNTY.

Minerva No. 2, San Francisco—Meets 1st and 3rd Wednesdays, N.S.G.W. Bldg.; Miss Dorothy Finn, Rec. Sec., 90 Princess St., Sausalito.

Alta No. 3, San Francisco—Meets 2nd and 4th Tuesdays, N.S.G.W. Bldg.; Mrs. Agnese L. Hughes, Rec. Sec., 3980 Sacramento St.

Oro Fino No. 9, San Francisco—Meets 1st and 3rd Thursdays, N.S.G.W. Bldg.; Mrs. Josephine B. Morrisey, Rec. Sec., 4441 20th St.

Golden State No. 50, San Francisco—Meets 1st and 3rd Wednesdays, N.D.G.W. Home; Miss Millie Tietjen, Rec. Sec., 328 Lexington Ave.

Orinda No. 56, San Francisco—Meets 2nd and 4th Fridays, N.D.G.W. Home; Mrs. Anna A. Gruber-Loser, Rec. Sec., 72 Grove Lane, San Anselmo.

Fremont No. 59, San Francisco—Meets 1st and 3rd Tuesdays, N.S.G.W. Bldg.; Miss Hannah Collins, Rec. Sec., 617 Fillmore St.

Buena Vista No. 68, San Francisco—Meets 1st, 3rd and 5th Thursdays, N.D.G.W. Home; Miss Margaret Barrett, Rec. Sec., 3774 20th St.

Las Lomas No. 72, San Francisco—Meets 1st and 3rd Tuesdays, N.D.G.W. Home; Mrs. Marion S. Day, Rec. Sec., 471 Alvarado St.

Yosemite No. 83, San Francisco—Meets 1st and 3rd Tuesdays, American Hall, 20th and Capp Sts.; Miss Mary Monahan, Rec. Sec., 237 Noe St.

La Estrella No. 89, San Francisco—Meets 2nd and 4th Mondays, N.S.G.W. Bldg.; Miss Birdie Hartman, Rec. Sec., 1018 Jackson St.

Sans Souci No. 96, San Francisco—Meets 2nd and 4th Mondays, N.D.G.W. Home; Mrs. Minnie F. Dobbin, Rec. Sec., 1483 43rd Ave.

Calaveras No. 103, San Francisco—Meets 2nd and 4th Tuesdays, Swedish American Hall, 2174 Market St.; Mrs. Lena Lorsheter, Rec. Sec., 492-C 41st St., Oakland.

Darina No. 114, San Francisco—Meets 1st and 3rd Mondays, N.S.G.W. Bldg.; Miss Adele Walsh, Rec. Sec., 479 Page St.

El Vespero No. 118, San Francisco—Meets 2nd and 4th Tuesdays, Masonic Hall, 4705 3rd St.; Mrs. Nell R. Boege, Rec. Sec., 1526 Kirkwood Ave.

Genevieve No. 132, San Francisco—Meets 1st and 3rd Thursdays, N.S.G.W. Bldg.; Miss Branice Peguillan, Rec. Sec., 2434 16th Ave.

Keith No. 137, San Francisco—Meets 2nd and 4th Thursdays, N.S.G.W. Bldg.; Mrs. Helen T. Mann, Rec. Sec., 575 Pierce St., Apt. 206.

Gabrielle No. 139, San Francisco—Meets 2nd and 4th Wednesdays, N.S.G.W. Bldg.; Mrs. Dorothy Wuesterfeld, Rec. Sec., 1020 Munich St.

Presidio No. 148, San Francisco—Meets 2nd and 4th Tuesdays, N.S.G.W. Bldg.; Mrs. Hattie Gaughran, Rec. Sec., 713 Capp St.

Guadalupe No. 153, San Francisco—Meets 2nd and 4th Mondays, Forester Hall, 170 Valencia St.; Miss May A. McCarthy, Rec. Sec., 336 Elsie St.

Golden Gate No. 158, San Francisco—Meets 2nd and 4th Mondays, N.S.G.W. Bldg.; Mrs. Mary Sullivan, Rec. Sec., 83 Cuvier St.

Dolores No. 169, San Francisco—Meets 2nd and 4th Wednesdays, N.S.G.W. Bldg.; Mrs. Ada Saunders, Rec. Sec., 284 Allison St.

Linda Rosa No. 170, San Francisco—Meets 2nd and 4th Wednesdays, Swedish American Hall, 2174 Market St.; Mrs. Eva P. Tyrrel, Rec. Sec., 2629 Mission St.

Portola No. 172, San Francisco—Meets 1st and 3rd Tuesdays, N.S.G.W. Bldg.; Catherine H. Dolly, Rec. Sec., 4125 23rd St.
Castro No. 178, San Francisco—Meets 1st and 3rd Wednesdays, K.C. Bldg., 150 Golden Gate Ave.; Miss Adeline Sandersfeld, Rec Sec., 50 Baker St.
Twin Peaks No. 185, San Francisco—Meets 2nd and 4th Fridays, Druids Temple, 44 Page St.; Mrs. Loretta Cameron, Rec. Sec., 3960 Army St.
James Lick No. 220, San Francisco—Meets 1st and 3rd Wednesdays, N.S.G.W. Bldg.; Mrs. Edna Bishop, Rec. Sec., 3841 24th St.
Mission No. 227, San Francisco—Meets 2nd and 4th Fridays, N.S.G.W. Bldg.; Mrs. Ann Dippel, Rec. Sec., 448 Dewey Blvd.
Bret Harte No. 232, San Francisco—Meets 2nd and 4th Tuesdays, Aloha Hall, 3009 16th St.; Hildur E. Eggers, Rec. Sec., 194 Prague St.
La Dorada No. 236, San Francisco—Meets 2nd and 4th Thursdays, N.S.G.W. Hall; Mrs. Theresa R. O'Brien, Rec. Sec., 567 Liberty St.
Balboa No. 249, San Francisco—Meets 1st and 3rd Thursdays, Maccabee Hall, 5th Ave. and Clement St.; Jean Moffet, Rec. Sec., 6633 California St.

SAN JOAQUIN COUNTY.

Joaquin No. 5, Stockton—Meets 2nd and 4th Tuesdays, N.S.G.W. Hall, 314 E. Main St.; Mrs. Della Garvin, Rec. Sec., 1122 E. Market St.
El Pescadero No. 82, Tracy—Meets 1st and 3rd Fridays, I.O.O.F. Hall; Mrs. Mary A. Hewitson, Rec. Sec., 215 W. 9th St.
Ivy No. 88, Lodi—Meets 1st and 3rd Wednesdays, Eagles Hall; Mrs. Mae Corson, Rec. Sec., 109 So. School St.
Caliz de Oro No. 206, Stockton—Meets 1st and 3rd Tuesdays, N.S.G.W. Hall, 314 E. Main St.; Mrs. Frances Germain, Rec. Sec., 450 No. Regent.
Phoebe A. Hearst No. 214, Manteca—Meets 2nd and 4th Wednesdays, I.O.O.F. Hall; Mrs. Josie M. Frederick, Rec. Sec., Route A, Box 304, Ripon.

SAN LUIS OBISPO COUNTY.

San Miguel No. 94, San Miguel—Meets 2nd and 4th Wednesday afternoons, Clemon Hall; Mrs. Nellie Wickstrom, Rec. Sec.
San Luisita No. 108, San Luis Obispo—Meets 2nd and 4th Thursdays, W.O.W. Hall; Miss Agnes M. Lee, Rec. Sec., P. O. box 584.
El Pinal No. 163, Cambria—Meets 2nd, 4th and 5th Tuesdays, N.S.G.W. Hall; Kathryn Luchessa, Rec. Sec.

SAN MATEO COUNTY.

Bonita No. 10, Redwood City—Meets 2nd and 4th Thursdays, I.O.O.F. Hall; Mrs. Dora Wilson, Rec. Sec., 518 Middlefield Rd.
Vista del Mar No. 155, Halfmoon Bay—Meets 2nd and 4th Thursdays, I.O.O.F. Hall; Mrs. Grace Griffith, Rec. Sec.
Ano Nuevo No. 180, Pescadero—Meets 1st and 3rd Wednesdays, I.O.O.F. Hall; Mrs. Alice Mattei, Rec. Sec.
El Carmelo No. 181, Daly City—Meets 1st and 3rd Wednesdays, Masonic Hall; Mrs. Hattie Kelly, Rec. Sec., 1179 Brunswick St.
Menlo No. 211, Menlo Park—Meets 2nd and 4th Mondays, Masonic Hall; Mrs. Frances E. Maloney, Rec. Sec., P. O. box 626.
San Bruno No. 246, San Bruno—Meets 2nd and 4th Fridays, N.D. Hall; Miss Mildred Foley, Rec. Sec., 217 Miller Ave., South San Francisco.

SANTA BARBARA COUNTY.

Reina del Mar No. 126, Santa Barbara—Meets 1st and 3rd Tuesdays, Pythian Castle, 222 W. Carillo St.; Miss Christina Moller, Rec. Sec., 836 Bath St.

SANTA CLARA COUNTY.

San Jose No. 81, San Jose—Meets Thursdays, Catholic Women Center, 5th and San Fernando Sts.; Mrs. Nellie Fleming, Rec. Sec., Catholic Women Center.
Vendome No. 100, San Jose—Meets Wednesdays, Old Scottish Rite Temple; Miss Marie Buck, Rec. Sec., 1414 Ellen St.
El Monte No. 205, Mountain View—Meets 2nd and 4th Fridays, American Legion Hall; Miss Mary Ann Rokovich, Rec. Sec., R.F.D. No. 1, box 412, State Highway.
Palo Alto No. 229, Palo Alto—Meets 1st and 2nd Mondays, N.S.G.W. Hall; Miss Helena G. Hansen, Rec. Sec., 531 Lytton Ave.

SANTA CRUZ COUNTY.

Santa Cruz No. 26, Santa Cruz—Meets Mondays, N.S.G.W. Hall; Mrs. May L. Williamson, Rec. Sec., 170 Walnut Ave.
El Pajaro No. 35, Watsonville—Meets 1st and 3rd Tuesdays, I.O.O.F. Hall; Miss Ruth E. Wilson, Rec. Sec., 16 Laurel St.

SHASTA COUNTY.

Camellia No. 41, Anderson—Meets 1st and 3rd Tuesdays, Masonic Hall; Mrs. Olga E. Welbourn, Rec. Sec.
Lassen View No. 98, Shasta—Meets 2nd Friday, Masonic Hall; Miss Louise Litsch, Rec. Sec.
Hiawatha No. 140, Redding—Meets 2nd and 4th Wednesdays, Moose Hall; Ruth Presleigh, Rec. Sec., Office County Clerk.

SIERRA COUNTY.

Naomi No. 36, Downieville—Meets 2nd and 4th Wednesdays, I.O.O.F. Hall; Louise C. Dubuque, Rec. Sec.
Imogen No. 134, Sierraville—Meets 2nd and 4th Saturday afternoons, Copren Hall; Mrs. Jennie Copren, Rec. Sec.

SISKIYOU COUNTY.

Eschscholtzia No. 112, Etna—Meets 1st and 3rd Wednesdays, Masonic Hall; Mrs. Bernice E. Smith, Rec. Sec.
Mountain Dawn No. 120, Sawyers Bar—Meets 2nd and last Wednesdays, I.O.O.F. Hall; Miss Edith Dunphy, Rec. Sec.

SOLANO COUNTY.

Vallejo No. 195, Vallejo—Meets 1st and 3rd Wednesdays, K.C. Hall, 820 Marin St.; Mrs. Mary Combs, Rec. Sec., 511 York St.
Mary E. Bell No. 224, Dixon—Meets 2nd and 4th Thursdays, I.O.O.F. Hall; Grace McFadyen, Rec. Sec.

SONOMA COUNTY.

Sonoma No. 209, Sonoma—Meets 2nd and 4th Mondays, I.O.O.F. Hall; Mrs. Mae Norrbom, Rec. Sec., R.F.D., box 171.
Santa Rosa No. 217, Santa Rosa—Meets 1st and 3rd Thursdays, N.S.G.W. Hall; Mrs. Hazel E. Brown, Rec. Sec., 1521 4th St.
Petaluma No. 222, Petaluma—Meets 1st and 3rd Tuesdays, Dania Hall; Mrs. Margaret M. Oeltjen, Rec. Sec., 503 Prospect St.

STANISLAUS COUNTY.

Oakdale No. 125, Oakdale—Meets 1st Monday, I.O.O.F. Hall; Mrs. Lou Reeder, Rec. Sec.
Morada No. 199, Modesto—Meets 2nd and 4th Wednesdays, I.O.O.F. Hall; Mrs. Susan Sullivan, Rec. Sec., 823 10th St.
Eldora No. 248, Turlock—Meets 1st and 3rd Wednesdays, Fraternal Hall; Effie Lund, Rec. Sec., 624 Minaret Ave.

SUTTER COUNTY.

South Butte No. 226, Sutter—Meets 1st and 3rd Mondays, N.D.G.W. Hall; Mrs. Abbie N. Vagedes, Rec. Sec.

TEHAMA COUNTY.

Berendos No. 23, Red Bluff—Meets 1st and 3rd Tuesdays, W.O.W. Hall, 200 Pine St.; Mrs. Lillie Hammer, Rec. Sec., 636 Jackson St.

TRINITY COUNTY.

Eltapome No. 55, Weaverville—Meets 2nd and 4th Thursdays, N.S.G.W. Hall; Mrs. Lou N. Fetzer, Rec. Sec.

NATIVE DAUGHTER NEWS

(Continued from Page 11)

May 18 the Parlor had its annual picnic at Hammond Grove in honor of the teacher-members, who have departed for their summer vacations.

Flags for New Citizens.

Vallejo—In the Solano County Superior Court, the americanization committee of Vallejo No. 195 presented April 25 United States of America and California State (Bear) Flags to fifteen candidates for citizenship. Chairman Juliette Bliss made the presentations, and accompanying each state flag was a resume of its history, prepared by her. Judge William T. O'Donnell thanked the Native Daughters for their interest.

May 4 the Parlor had a surprise social in honor of District Deputy Julia Hill, who was presented with a gift of appreciation. Whist and swimming were enjoyed, and refreshments were served.

Tiny Garments Displayed.

Fort Bragg—At a well-attended meeting May 5, Grand President Evelyn I. Carlson officially visited Fort Bragg No. 210. One candidate was initiated. The Grand President spoke interestingly on the Order's work and commended President Elsie Bryans, the other Parlor officers and District Deputy Edna Kunzler.

The first sight that greeted the guests as they entered the diningroom was an attractive display of tiny garments for the homeless children, strikingly arranged. An efficient committee had beautifully decorated the tables with pink roses, and a delicious supper was served. Gifts were presented Mrs. Carlson and District Deputy Kunzler, and words of appreciation from them brought to a close the happy evening.

Annual Mothers Night.

Woodland—Approximately 300 attended the annual mothers night banquet and entertainment of Woodland No. 90 May 5, among them being Grand Vice-president Anna Armstrong, Grand Trustee Edna Briggs, Past Grands Dr. Eva R. Rasmussen and Mary E. Bell. All mothers were presented with flowers. President Ruth Hickey extended a welcome, and Charter Member Harriet Lee was the toastmistress. A group sang "Mothers," a burlesque radio skit was presented, and a "haywire" orchestra furnished music. Miss Nell Proctor led the community singing.

TUOLUMNE COUNTY.

Dardanelle No. 66, Sonora—Meets Fridays, I.O.O.F. Hall; Mrs. Nettie Whitto, Rec. Sec.
Golden Era No. 99, Columbia—Meets 1st and 3rd Thursdays, N.S.G.W. Hall; Miss Irene Ponce, Rec. Sec.
Anona No. 164, Jamestown—Meets 2nd and 4th Tuesdays, I.O.O.F. Hall; Mrs. Rosa A. Beckwith, Rec. Sec., P. O. box 87.

YOLO COUNTY.

Woodland No. 90, Woodland—Meets 2nd and 4th Tuesdays, N.S.G.W. Hall; Mrs. Maude Heaton, Rec. Sec., 153 College St.

YUBA COUNTY.

Marysville No. 162, Marysville—Meets 2nd and 4th Wednesdays, Liberty Hall; Miss Cecelia C. Gomes, Rec. Sec., 701 6th St.
Camp Far West No. 218, Wheatland—Meets 3rd Tuesday, I.O.O.F. Hall; Mrs. Ethel C. Brock, Rec. Sec., P. O. box 285.

AFFILIATED ORGANIZATIONS.

General Assembly Past Presidents—Meetings held annually in April at the home-town of Chief President; Mrs. Cora Stobing, 1739 San Jose Ave., San Francisco, Chief President; Mrs. Anna G. Loser, 72 Grove Lane, San Anselmo, Chief Secretary.
Past Presidents Association No. 1—Meets 1st and 3rd Mondays, N.S.G.W. Bldg., 414 Mason St., San Francisco; Mrs. Minnie F. Dobbin, Pres.; Mrs. May R. Barry, Rec. Sec., 2319 19th Ave., San Francisco.
Past Presidents Association No. 2—Meets 2nd and 4th Mondays, "Wigwam," Pacific Bldg., 16th and Jefferson, Oakland; Frieda Reichhold, Pres.; Mrs. Elizabeth B. Goodman, Rec. Sec., 134 Juana Ave., San Leandro.
Past Presidents Association No. 3 (Santa Clara County)—Meets 2nd Tuesday, homes of members; Mrs. Clara Briggs, Pres.; Mrs. Mary G. Newton, Rec. Sec., 1070 Jackson St., Santa Clara.
Past Presidents Association No. 4 (Sacramento County)—Meets 2nd Monday, Unitarian Hall, 1413 27th St., Sacramento City; Viola Gennoe, Pres.; Lily May Tilden, Rec. Sec., 3225 "T" St., Sacramento.
Past Presidents Association No. 5 (Butte County)—Meets 1st Friday, homes of members, Chico and Oroville; Sonora Steadman, Pres.; Ruth Brown, Rec. Sec., 1265 Leab Court, Oroville.
Past Presidents Association No. 6 (Nevada County)—Meets 4th Friday, alternately between Nevada City, Pythian Castle, and Grass Valley, Edna Sampson's home; Margaret V. Nolan, Pres.; Vere Hansen, Rec. Sec., R.F.D. No. 2, box 41-C, Grass Valley.
Past Presidents Association No. 7 (Sonoma County)—Meets 1st Thursday, N.S.G.W. Hall, Santa Rosa; Willow Borba, Pres.; Clytie Lewis, Rec. Sec., R.F.D. No. 4, box 345-A, Santa Rosa.
Past Presidents Association No. 8 (San Joaquin and Stanislaus Counties)—Meets 2nd Thursday, Red Men Hall, Stockton; Mrs. Lois Armstrong, Pres.; Mrs. Harriet F. Corr, Rec. Sec., 729 E. Sonora St., Stockton.
Native Sons and Native Daughters Central Committee on Homeless Children—Main Office, 955 Phelan Bldg., San Francisco; Mrs. John W. Stirling, Chmn.; Miss Mary K. Brusie, Sec. Los Angeles branch office, 3924 Sunset Blvd.; Dorothy Schlingman, Sec.

(ADVERTISEMENT.)

The Parlor recently had a dance and card party for the benefit of its Home Loyalty Pledge and a substantial sum was realized. Wanda Abele was general chairman.

Family Night.

San Luis Obispo—San Luisita No. 108 had a family night, when members and their families were entertained. Whist was the main attraction. The hall and banquetroom were attractively decorated with flowers, and refreshments were served.

Pupils' Efforts Please.

Sonoma—An excellent Washington bicentennial program was presented May 9 by Sonoma No. 209 and Sonoma No. 111 N.S.G.W. for the pleasure of their members and immediate families. Principal J. F. Prestwood of the Sonoma grammar school gave an interesting address on "The Life of Washington," and pupils of El Verano school, directed by Margaret Corcoran, a member of No. 209, were roundly applauded for their contributions to the program. Refreshments were served. Mrs. Catherine Bulotti was general chairman.

Five Past Grands Guests.

Manteca—Grand President Evelyn I. Carlson officially visited Phoebe A. Hearst No. 214 April 27. There were many visitors, and several candidates were initiated. A program was presented, and the Grand President was the recipient of gifts. California poppies were used in the decorations. Committees in charge were: Refreshment—Eva Gustafson, Margaret Dempsey, Bertha Smith, Pearl Briggs. Program and decorations—Angella Perry, Willa Wilson, Leonia Fulton, Nan Napier, Amelia Rodgers. In attendance were Past Grands Carrie Roesch-Durham, Mamie G. Peyton, Mattie M. Stein, Pearl Lamb and Dr. Louise C. Heilbron.

Arbor Day the Parlor planted trees in honor of Pioneer Lizzie Wolf and two deceased members, Georgia Meredith and Virginia Lyons Paul.

Correction.

"Editor Grizzly Bear: Please correct officers elected at the General Assembly N.D.G.W. Past Presidents in Oakland April 9. I regret having given incorrect list for publication in May issue. —ANNA G. LOSER." The correct list follows:

Junior past chief president, Josephine Clark; chief president, Cora Stobing; chief vice-president, Winifred Halter; chief treasurer, Emma G. Foley; chief secretary, Anna G. Loser; chief marshal, Mary Frances Mitchell; chief organist, Antha Locklin; chief inside sentinel, Margaret Grote-Hill; chief outside sentinel, Emilie J. Clifford; directors, Mamie Davis, Willow Borba, Mattie M. Stein, Edna D. Sampson, Julia Waddington.

N.D.G.W. HOME DONATIONS.

San Francisco—Donations to the N.D.G.W. Home since the list published in The Grizzly Bear for February 1932 include the following: Five dollars, Mrs. Katherine Cobb, Orinda Parlor No. 56. Framed picture Mt. Shasta, Mrs. Elinor Taylor, Eltapome Parlor No. 55. Poster portrait George Washington, Congresswoman Florence Pray Kahn. Birthday cake third anniversary breakfast, dedication home building, P.G.P. Emma G. Foley, Orinda Parlor No. 56. Books, Miss Minnie Spilman, Alta Parlor No. 3. Three potted primrose plants, Miss Mary Rogers, Alta Parlor No. 3. Flowers for N.D.G.W. club breakfasts, Miss Emma Dieckhoff, Aloha Parlor No. 106. Five hundred dollar bequest, Miss Dora Washburn, late member San Andreas Parlor No. 113. Potted tulips, Miss Lela Ewert, Woodland Parlor No. 90. Books, Mrs. Ella Osburn, Buena Vista Parlor No. 68. Large box cauliflower and bag beans, P.G.P. Ariana W. Stirling, Aleli Parlor No. 102. Box fifty-eight books valued at $75, Mrs. Mae Houston, Willows. Eight jars preserves, Mrs. E. Silva, Dolores Parlor No. 169. Flowers for N.D.G.W. club breakfast March 13, P.G.P. Amy McAvoy, Stirling Parlor No. 146. Two lounge pillows, P.G.P. Addie L. Mosher, Piedmont Parlor No. 87. Ten kitchen towels and hot-pot holders, Mrs. Elinor E. Taylor, Eltapome Parlor No. 55. Framed picture monument of Dough Boy, Grove Memory Association, San Francisco. Bronze plaque Pioneer Mother, Mrs. Katherine Jones in honor of her mother, Mrs. Sadie Brainard, Mothers Day, May 8, 1932; both members Califia Parlor No. 22.—P.G.P. EMMA G. FOLEY, secretary Grand Parlor Home Committee, May 9, 1932.

N.D.G.W. OFFICIAL DEATH LIST.

Giving the name, the date of death, and the Subordinate Parlor affiliation of all deceased members as reported to Grand Secretary Sallie R. Thaler from April 19 to May 17, 1932:

Fennon, Annie McCormick; April 7, 1932; Angelita No. 32.
Denahy, Sarah; April 14, 1932; Gabrielle No. 139.
Russell, Evelena V.; April 11, 1932; Sea Point No. 196.
Cooper, Ethel Gray; April 7, 1932; Joaquin No. 5.
Sargent, Lucie; April 17, 1932; Alta No. 3.
Cook, Mary; March 29, 1932; Naomi No. 36.
Rader, Nellie; April 12, 1932; Buena Vista No. 68.
Ramos, Emma E.; March 25, 1932; Encinal No. 156.
Miller, Cassie M. M.; April 10, 1932; Ivy No. 88.
Poncini, Esther; April 1, 1932; Coloma No. 212.
Thomas, Rose; May 3, 1932; El Cereso No. 207.
Dobbas, Helena; April 21, 1932; Auburn No. 233.

Husband N. D. Past Grand Dead.

Red Bluff (Tehama County).—James T. Matlock, husband of Olive Bedford-Matlock, Past Grand President N.D.G.W., died May 11. He was born here November 23, 1876, and was affiliated with McCloud Parlor No. 149 N.S.G.W. (Redding).

Official Directory of Parlors of the N. S. G. W.

ALAMEDA COUNTY.

Alameda No. 47, Alameda City—Gus Nelson, Pres.; Robt. H. Cavanaugh, Sec., 1806 Pacific Ave.; Wednesdays, Native Sons Hall, 1406 Park St.

Oakland No. 50, Oakland—A. W. Ainger, Pres.; F. M. Norris, Sec., 4280 Terrace St.; Fridays, Native Sons Hall, 11th and Clay Sts.

Las Positas No. 96, Livermore—R. J. Ruetz, Pres.; John J. Kelly, Sec., P. O. box 341; Thursdays, Foresters Hall.

Eden No. 113, Hayward—Henry L'Eeuyer, Pres.; Stanton R. Soares, Sec., P. O. box 176; 2nd and 4th Tuesdays, Memorial Hall, Main St.

Piedmont No. 120, Oakland—Walter M. Davis, Pres.; Charles Morando, Sec., 906 Vermont St.; Thursdays, Native Sons Hall, 11th and Clay Sts.

Wisteria No. 127, Alvarado—Henry May, Pres.; J. M. Scribner, Sec., Livermore; 1st Thursday, I.O.O.F. Hall.

Halcyon No. 146, Alameda City—Charles J. Von Tagen, Pres.; J. C. Bates, Sec., 3139 Buena Vista Ave.; 1st and 3rd Tuesdays, I.O.O.F. Hall, 2329 Santa Clara Ave.

Brooklyn No. 151, Oakland—Frank B. Perry, Pres.; E. W. Cooney, Sec., 3907 14th Ave.; Wednesdays, Masonic Temple, 8th Ave. and E. 14th St.

Washington No. 169, Centerville—M. B. Silva, Pres.; Allen G. Norris, Sec., P. O. box 31; 2nd and 4th Tuesdays, Hansen Hall.

Athens No. 195, Oakland—Henry G. Kroeckel, Pres.; Harold B. Farley, Sec., 4623 Benevides Ave.; Tuesdays, Native Sons Hall, 11th and Clay Sts.

Berkeley No. 210, Berkeley—S. Levy, Pres.; R. J. Garrett, Sec., 1708 Virginia St.; Tuesdays, Native Sons Hall, 2108 Shattuck Ave.

Estudillo No. 223, San Leandro—Frank V. Pacheco, Pres.; Albert G. Pacheco, Sec., 1736 E. 14th St.; 1st and 3rd Tuesdays, U.P.E.C. Hall.

Claremont No. 240, Oakland—Fred Buelna, Pres.; E. N. Thienger, Sec., 839 Hearst Ave., Berkeley; Tuesdays, Veterans Memorial Bldg., 43rd & Salem Sts., Emeryville.

Pleasanton No. 244, Pleasanton—Peter C. Madsen, Pres.; Ernest W. Schween, Sec.; 2nd and 4th Thursdays, I.O.O.F. Hall.

Niles No. 250, Niles—M. L. Fournier, Pres.; C. E. Martenstein, Sec.; 2nd Thursday, I.O.O.F. Hall.

Fruitvale No. 252, Oakland—Chester B. Abernethy, Pres.; Ray B. Felton, Sec., 1575 Alice St.; Fridays, W.O.W. Hall, 3256 E. 14th St.

AMADOR COUNTY.

Amador No. 17, Sutter Creek—Frank Marre, Pres.; F. J. Payne, Sec.; 1st and 3rd Fridays, Native Sons Hall.

Excelsior No. 31, Jackson—Wm. Daugherty, Pres.; William Going, Sec.; 1st and 3rd Wednesdays, Native Sons Hall, 22 Court St.

Ione No. 33, Ione—Marvin Kidd, Pres.; Josiah H. Saunders, Sec.; 1st and 3rd Wednesdays, Native Sons Hall.

Plymouth No. 48, Plymouth—L. E. Houston, Pres.; Thos. D. Davis, Sec.; 1st and 3rd Saturdays, I.O.O.F. Hall.

BUTTE COUNTY.

Argonaut No. 8, Oroville—Thomas R. Cole, Pres.; Cyril R. MacDonald, Sec., P. O. box 502; 1st and 3rd Wednesdays, Veterans Memorial Hall.

Chico No. 21, Chico—Marcus Choisser, Pres.; Sam Lindsay Adams, Sec., Sacramento Blvd.; 2nd and 4th Thursdays, Elks Hall.

CALAVERAS COUNTY.

Chispa No. 139, Murphys—John Voitich, Pres.; Antone Malaspina, Sec.; Wednesdays, Native Sons Hall.

COLUSA COUNTY.

Colusa No. 69, Colusa City—Burton L. Smart, Pres.; Phil J. Humburg, Sec., 323 Parkhill St.; Tuesdays, Eagles Hall.

CONTRA COSTA COUNTY.

General Winn No. 32, Antioch—Edmont T. Uren, Pres.; Joel H. Ford, Sec., P. O. box 311; 2nd and 4th Wednesdays, Union Hall.

Mount Diablo No. 101, Martinez—R. P. Anderson, Pres.; G. T. Barkley, Sec.; 1st and 3rd Mondays, I.O.O.F. Hall.

Byron No. 170, Byron—William E. Bunn, Pres.; H. G. Krumland, Sec.; 1st and 3rd Tuesdays, I.O.O.F. Hall.

Carquinez No. 205, Crockett—Thos. Cox, Pres.; Thomas I. Cahalan, Sec.; 1st and 3rd Wednesdays, I.O.O.F. Hall.

Richmond No. 217, Richmond—M. W. Amaral, Pres.; H. D. Mason, Sec., 11 6th St.; Wednesdays, Redmen Hall, 11th and Neven Ave.

Concord No. 245, Concord—P. M. Soto, Pres.; D. E. Pramberg, Sec., P. O. box 235; 1st Tuesday, I.O.O.F. Hall.

Diamond No. 246, Pittsburg—Victor Ericsson, Pres.; Francis A. Irving, Sec., 248 E. 5th St.; 1st and 3rd Wednesdays, Veterans Memorial Bldg.

EL DORADO COUNTY.

Placerville No. 9, Placerville—George M. Smith, Pres.; Duncan Bathurst, Sec., 12 Gilmore St.; 2nd and 4th Tuesdays, Masonic Hall.

Georgetown No. 91, Georgetown—W. H. Breedlove, Pres.; C. F. Irish, Sec.; 2nd and 4th Wednesdays, I.O.O.F. Hall.

FRESNO COUNTY.

Fresno No. 25, Fresno City—A. G. Miller, Pres.; John W. Cappleman, Sec., 1389 Wilson; 2nd and 4th Fridays, W.O.W. Hall, 1354 Van Ness Ave.

Selma No. 107, Selma—Chester E. Shepard, Pres.; E. C. Laughlin, Sec.; 1st and 3rd Wednesdays, American Legion Hall.

GRAND OFFICERS.

Dr. Frank I. Gonzalez........Junior Past Grand President
Flood Bldg., San Francisco

Seth Millington........Grand President
Gridley

Justice Emmet Seawell........Grand First Vice-president
State Bldg., San Francisco

Chas. A. Koenig........Grand Second Vice-president
531 35th Ave., San Francisco

Harmon D. Skillin........Grand Third Vice-president
Mills Bldg., San Francisco

John T. Regan........Grand Secretary
N.S.G.W. Bldg., 414 Mason St., San Francisco

John A. Corotto........Grand Treasurer
560 No. 5th St., San Jose

W. B. O'Brien........Grand Marshal
2324 Santa Clara St., Alameda

Gem Hurst........Grand Inside Sentinel
Financial Center Bldg., Oakland

William A. Reuter........Grand Outside Sentinel
1009 Marine Ave., Wilmington

Leslie Maloche........Grand Organist
467½ 3rd St., San Bernardino

Chester Gannon........Historiographer
613 Capital Ntl. Bank Bldg., Sacramento

GRAND TRUSTEES.

Jesse H. Miller........712 DeYoung Bldg., San Francisco
Eldred L. Meyer........922 San Vicente Blvd., Santa Monica
John M. Burnett........914 Bank Italy Bldg., San Jose
Henry S. Lyon........Placerville
Joseph J. McShane........419 Flood Bldg., San Francisco
Horace J. Leavitt........Weaverville
Chas. H. Spengemann........827 27th Ave., San Francisco

HUMBOLDT COUNTY.

Humboldt No. 14, Eureka—Edward J. Quinn, Pres.; Loren M. Nelson, Sec., P.O. box 195; 2nd and 4th Mondays, Native Sons Hall.

Arcata No. 20, Arcata—George Hale, Pres.; William Peters, Sec., P. O. box 1117; Thursdays, Native Sons Hall.

Ferndale No. 93, Ferndale—O. R. Frame, Pres.; C. H. Rasmussen, Sec., R.F.D., 47-A; 1st and 3rd Mondays, K.P. Hall.

KERN COUNTY.

Bakersfield No. 42, Bakersfield—G. E. Taylor, Pres.; Don S. Simpson, Sec., P.O. Box 924; Wednesdays, Justice Court, City Hall.

LAKE COUNTY.

Lower Lake No. 159, Lower Lake—Harold S. Anderson, Pres.; Albert Kugelman, Sec.; Thursdays, I.O.O.F. Hall.

LASSEN COUNTY.

Honey Lake No. 198, Standish—James C. Meeske, Pres.; N. V. Wemple, Sec., Litchfield; 1st and 3rd Wednesdays, Wrede Hall.

Big Valley No. 211, Bieber—George Bunselmeier, Pres.; A. W. McKenzie, Sec.; 1st and 3rd Wednesdays, I.O.O.F. Hall.

LOS ANGELES COUNTY.

Los Angeles No. 45, Los Angeles City—Lee E. Erwin, Pres.; Richard W. Fryer, Sec., 1629 Champlain Ter.; Thursdays, Merchant Plumbers Hall, 1832 So. Hope.

Ramona No. 109, Los Angeles City—Chandos E. Bush, Pres.; John V. Scott, Sec., Patriotic Hall, 1816 So. Figueroa; Fridays, Patriotic Hall, 1816 So. Figueroa.

Hollywood No. 196, Los Angeles City—Leo Aggeler, Pres.; E. J. Reilly, Sec., 907 W. 2nd St.; Mondays, 1089 No. Oxford Ave.

Long Beach No. 239, Long Beach—Francis H. Gentry, Pres.; W. W. Brady, Sec., 801 Jergins Trust Bldg.; 2nd and 4th Thursdays, Moose Hall, Elm and Anaheim.

Sepulveda No. 263, San Pedro—Francis G. Fetzer, Pres.; Frank I. Markey, Sec., 101 W. 7th St.; 2nd and 4th Fridays, Odd Fellows Temple, 10th and Gaffey Sts.

Glendale No. 264, Glendale—Philip D. Molen, Pres.; Abel B. Molen, Sec., 508 So. Belmont St.; 1st and 3rd Tuesdays, Masonic Temple, 234 So. Brand Blvd.

Santa Monica Bay No. 267, Ocean Park—Claude J. Wiseman, Pres.; John J. Smith, Sec., 830 Rialto Ave., Venice; 2nd and 4th Mondays, New Eagle Hall, 2823½ Main St.

Cahuenga No. 268, Reseda—Harold C. Trexler, Pres.; Carrol S. Driscoll, Sec., P.O. box 25, Chatsworth; first Friday, Alton Hall.

MADERA COUNTY.

Madera No. 130, Madera City—Cornelius Noble, Pres.; T. P. Cosgrave, Sec.; 1st and 3rd Thursdays, First National Bank Bldg.

MARIN COUNTY.

Mount Tamalpais No. 64, San Rafael—Arthur Todt, Pres.; Manual A. Andrade, Sec., 532 Mission Ave.; 1st and 3rd Mondays, Portuguese American Hall.

Sea Point No. 158, Sausalito—Allyn T. Young, Pres.; Manuel Santos, Sec., 6 Glen Drive; 1st and 3rd Wednesdays, Perry Bldg.

Nicasio No. 183, Nicasio—M. T. Farley, Pres.; R. J. Rogers, Sec.; 2nd and 4th Wednesdays, U.A.O.D. Hall.

MENDOCINO COUNTY.

Ukiah No. 71, Ukiah—Henry Bucknell, Pres.; Ben Hofman, Sec., P. O. box 473; 1st and 3rd Mondays, I.O.O.F. Hall.

Broderick No. 117, Point Arena—Sam Reinking, Pres.; H. C. Hunter, Sec.; 1st and 3rd Thursdays, Forester Hall.

Alder Glen No. 200, Fort Bragg—Clarence Simpson, Pres.; C. R. Weller, Sec.; 2nd and 4th Fridays, I.O.O.F. Hall.

MERCED COUNTY.

Yosemite No. 24, Merced City—Anthony A. Rodrigues, Pres.; True W. Fowler, Sec., P. O. box 781; 2nd and 4th Mondays, I.O.O.F. Hall.

MONTEREY COUNTY.

Monterey No. 75, Monterey City—John Thomsen, Pres.; T. W. Krieger, Sec., 999 Franklin St.; 1st and 3rd Fridays, Knights Pythias Hall, Main St.

Santa Lucia No. 97, Salinas—E. L. Adcock, Pres.; R. W. Adcock, Sec., Route 2, box 141; Mondays, Native Sons Hall, 32 W. Alisal St.

Gabilan No. 132, Castroville—B. A. McCoy, Pres.; R. H. Martin, Sec., P. O. box 81; 1st and 3rd Thursdays, Native Sons Hall.

NAPA COUNTY.

Saint Helena No. 53, Saint Helena—E. W. Johnson, Pres.; Edw. L. Bonhote, Sec., P. O. box 267; Mondays, Native Sons Hall.

Napa No. 62, Napa City—A. G. Boggs, Pres.; H. J. Hoernle, Sec., 1226 Oak St.; Mondays, Native Sons Hall.

Calistoga No. 86, Calistoga—Frank Mariani, Pres.; Louis Carlenzoli, Sec.; 1st and 3rd Mondays, I.O.O.F. Hall.

ATTENTION, SECRETARIES!

THIS DIRECTORY IS PUBLISHED BY AUTHORITY OF THE GRAND PARLOR N.S.G.W., AND ALL NOTICES OF CHANGES MUST BE RECEIVED BY THE GRAND SECRETARY (NOT THE MAGAZINE) ON OR BEFORE THE 20TH OF EACH MONTH TO INSURE CORRECTION IN NEXT ISSUE OF DIRECTORY.

NEVADA COUNTY.

Hydraulic No. 56, Nevada City—Spencer G. White, Pres.; Dr. C. W. Chapman, Sec.; Tuesdays, Pythian Castle.

Quartz No. 58, Grass Valley—Allen Joyner, Pres.; H. Ray George, Sec., 151 Conaway Ave.; Mondays, Auditorium Hall.

Donner No. 162, Truckee—J. F. Lichtenberger, Pres.; H. C. Lichtenberger, Sec.; 2nd and 4th Tuesdays, Native Sons Hall.

ORANGE COUNTY.

Santa Ana No. 265, Santa Ana—R. L. Marsile, Pres.; E. F. Marks, Sec., 1124 No. Bristol St.; 1st and 3rd Mondays, K.C. Hall, 4th and French Sts.

PLACER COUNTY.

Auburn No. 59, Auburn—Cosme Vicencio, Pres.; J. G. Walsh, Sec.; 1st and 3rd Fridays, Foresters Hall.

Silver Star No. 63, Lincoln—Ralph Sandstad, Pres.; Barney G. Barry, Sec., P. O. box 72; 3rd Wednesday, I.O.O.F. Hall.

Rocklin No. 233, Roseville—Thomas Elliott, Pres.; M. E. Reed, Sec., 253 W. Duranta; 2nd and 4th Wednesdays, Eagles Hall.

PLUMAS COUNTY.

Quincy No. 131, Quincy—J. D. McLaughlin, Pres.; E. C. Kelsey, Sec.; 2nd Thursday, I.O.O.F. Hall.

Golden Anchor No. 182, La Porte—R. J. McGrath, Pres.; LeRoy J. Post, Sec.; 2nd and 4th Sunday mornings, Native Sons Hall.

Plumas No. 228, Taylorsville—E. E. Sikes, Pres.; George E. Boyden, Sec.; 1st and 3rd Mondays, Native Sons Hall.

SACRAMENTO COUNTY.

Sacramento No. 3, Sacramento City—Joseph Hellinge Jr., Pres.; J. F. Didion, Sec., 1131 "O" St.; Thursdays, Native Sons Bldg., 11th and "J" Sts.

Sunset No. 26, Sacramento City—George W. Lial, Pres.; Edward E. Reese, Sec., County Treasurer Office; Mondays, Native Sons Bldg., 11th and "J" Sts.

Elk Grove No. 41, Elk Grove—Fred Sehlmeyer, Pres.; Walter Martin, Sec.; 2nd and 4th Fridays, Masonic Hall.

Granite No. 83, Folsom—Joe Relvas, Pres.; Frank Showers, Sec.; 2nd and 4th Tuesdays, K.P. Hall.

Courtland No. 106, Courtland—Thornton Pylman, Pres.; Jos. Green, Sec.; 1st Saturday and 3rd Monday, Native Sons Hall.

Sutter Fort No. 241, Sacramento City—August Lehman, Pres.; C. L. Katzenstein, Sec., P. O. box 914; 2nd and 4th Wednesdays, Native Sons Bldg., 11th and "J" Sts.

Galt No. 243, Galt—John Granadas, Pres.; F. W. Harms, Sec.; 1st and 3rd Mondays, I.O.O.F. Hall.

SAN BENITO COUNTY.

Fremont No. 44, Hollister—Chas. B. Arbeleche, Pres.; J. E. Prendergast Jr., Sec., 1064 Monterey St.; 1st and 3rd Thursdays, Grangers Union Hall.

SAN BERNARDINO COUNTY.

Arrowhead No. 110, San Bernardino City—Lynn A. Reed, Pres.; R. W. Brazelton, Sec., 462 6th St.; Wednesdays, Eagles Hall, 469 4th St.

SAN DIEGO COUNTY.

San Diego No. 108, San Diego City—Gregory A. McHorney, Pres.; A. V. Mayrhofer, Sec., 1572 2nd St.; Wednesdays, K.C. Hall, 4th and Elm Sts.

SAN FRANCISCO CITY AND COUNTY.

California No. 1, San Francisco—Sal Juliano, Pres.; Ellis A. Blackman, Sec., 126 Front St.; Thursdays, Native Sons Bldg., 414 Mason St.

Pacific No. 10, San Francisco—John C. Daly, Pres.; J. Henry Bastein, Sec., 1880 Howard St.; Tuesdays, Native Sons Bldg., 414 Mason St.

Golden Gate No. 29, San Francisco—Thomas I. Schlink, Pres.; Adolph Eberhart, Sec., 183 Carl St.; Mondays, Native Sons Bldg., 414 Mason St.

Mission No. 38, San Francisco—Joseph C. Augustine Jr., Pres.; Thos. J. Stewart, Sec., 1919 Howard St.; Wednesdays, Redmen Hall, 3053 16th St.

San Francisco No. 49, San Francisco—Louis L. Ghiotti, Pres.; David Capurro, Sec., 976 Union St.; Thursdays, Native Sons Bldg., 414 Mason St.

El Dorado No. 52, San Francisco—Eugene Herzog, Pres.; Alfred Vlautin, Sec., 1537 Franklin St.; Thursdays, Native Sons Bldg., 414 Mason St.

Rincon No. 72, San Francisco—Michael J. Joyce, Pres.; John A. Gilmour, Sec., 2069 Golden Gate Ave.; Wednesdays, Native Sons Bldg., 414 Mason St.

Stanford No. 76, San Francisco—Albert W. Groskopf, Pres.; Charles T. O'Kane, Sec., 1111 Pine St.; Tuesdays, Native Sons Bldg., 414 Mason St.

Bay City No. 104, San Francisco—Morris Garren, Pres.; Max E. Licht, Sec., 1831 Fulton St.; 2nd and 4th Wednesdays, Native Sons Bldg., 414 Mason St.

Niantic No. 105, San Francisco—A. Furner, Pres.; J. M. Darcy, Sec., 10 Hoffman Ave.; Wednesdays, Native Sons Bldg., 414 Mason St.

National No. 118, San Francisco—Wayne Burke, Pres.; Martin M. Ratigan, Sec., 1325 Page St., Apt. 6; Thursdays, 1160 Eddy St.

Hesperian No. 137, San Francisco—H. G. Ritter, Pres.; Albert Carlson, Sec., 379 Justin Dr.; Thursdays, Native Sons Bldg., 414 Mason St.

Alcalde No. 154, San Francisco—Conrad Kuhl, Pres.; Harry S. Burke, Sec., 25 Ord St.; 2nd and 4th Wednesdays, Native Sons Bldg., 414 Mason St.

South San Francisco No. 157, San Francisco—Raymond Conroy, Pres.; John T. Regan, Sec., 1489 Newcomb Ave.; Wednesdays, Masonic Bldg., 4705 3rd St.

Sequoia No. 160, San Francisco—Chester Moreno, Pres.; Walter W. Garrett, Sec., 2500 Van Ness Ave.; Mondays, Swedish-American Bldg., 2174 Market St.

Precita No. 187, San Francisco—Elmer F. Sprague, Pres.; Edward Tietjen, Sec., 1367 15th Ave.; Thursdays, Mission Masonic Hall, 2668 Mission St.

Olympus No. 189, San Francisco—Charles Erickson, Pres.; Harvey J. Carty, Sec., 1651 Market St., Apt. 505; 2nd and 4th Tuesdays, Independent Redmen Hall, 3053 16th St.

Presidio No. 194, San Francisco—Geo. R. Schmidt, Pres.; George A. Ducker, Sec., 442 21st Ave.; Mondays, Native Sons Bldg., 414 Mason St.

Marshall No. 202, San Francisco—Arthur Belli, Pres.; Frank Bacigalupi, Sec., 725 Douglas St.; 1st and 3rd Wednesdays, Native Sons Bldg., 414 Mason St.

Dolores No. 208, San Francisco—Daniel Corrigan, Pres.; Eugene O'Donnell, Sec., Mills Bldg.; Tuesdays, Mission Masonic Bldg., 2668 Mission St.

Twin Peaks No. 214, San Francisco—Fred Sooman, Pres.; Thos. Pendergast, Sec., 278 Douglas St.; Wednesdays, Willopi Hall, 4061 24th St.

El Capitan No. 222, San Francisco—Frank Rizzo, Pres.; James Hanna, Sec., 2450 27th Ave.; 1st and 3rd Thursdays, King Soloman Hall, 1739 Fillmore St.

Guadalupe No. 231, San Francisco—George Miles, Pres.; Alvin A. Johnson, Sec., 142 Rousseau St.; Tuesdays, Guadalupe Hall, 4551 Mission St.

Castro No. 232, San Francisco—David A. Simon, Pres.; James H. Hayes, Sec., 4014 18th St.; Tuesdays, Native Sons Bldg., 414 Mason St.

alboa No. 234, San Francisco—J. LeMer, Pres.; E. W. Boyd, Sec., 45 Carl St.; Thursdays, Maccabee Hall, 5th Ave. and Clement St.
ames Lick No. 242, San Francisco—M. G. Muller, Pres.; Wm. Band, Sec., 2587 22nd Ave.; 1st and 3rd Wednesdays, Redmen Hall, 3053 16th St.
ret Harte No. 260, San Francisco—J. F. Craig, Pres.; C. J. Eggers, Sec., 194 Prague St.; Tuesdays, West of Twin Peaks Hall, 233 Legion Court.
topia No. 270, San Francisco—Joseph Riordan, Pres.; Herbert H. Schneider, Sec., 2455 16th Ave.; Tuesdays, American Hall, 20th and Capp Sts.

SAN JOAQUIN COUNTY.

tockton No. 7, Stockton—George D. Avery, Pres.; R. D. Dorcey, Sec., P. O. box 388; Mondays, Native Sons Hall.
odi No. 18, Lodi—Jerome Solomon, Pres.; Dr. Clyde Bresnan, Sec.; 2nd and 4th Wednesdays, Eagles Hall.
racy No. 186, Tracy—R. J. Marraccini, Pres.; R. J. Marraccini, Sec., R.F.D. No. 1, box 217; Thursdays, I.O.O.F. Hall.
anteca No. 271, Manteca—Louis Ryan, Pres.; Leonard Faria, Sec., R.F.D. No. 1, Lathrop; 1st and 3rd Wednesdays, I.O.O.F. Hall.

SAN LUIS OBISPO COUNTY.

an Miguel No. 150, San Miguel—H. Twisselman, Pres.; George Sonnenberg Jr., Sec.; 1st and 3rd Wednesdays, Fraternal Hall.
ambria No. 152, Cambria—Roy Cardoza, Pres.; A. S. Gay, Sec.; Wednesdays, Rigdon Hall.

SAN MATEO COUNTY.

edwood No. 66, Redwood City—Joseph Lodi, Pres.; A. S. Liguori, Sec., P. O. box 212; Thursdays, American Foresters Hall.
easide No. 95, Half Moon Bay—William Deeney, Pres.; John G. Gilcrest, Sec.; 2nd and 4th Tuesdays, I.O.O.F. Hall.
enlo No. 185, Menlo Park—W. H. Wreden, Pres.; F. W. Johnson, Sec., P. O. box 601; Thursdays, Duff & Doyle Hall.
ebble Beach No. 230, Pescadero—Bernard Cabral, Pres.; E. A. Shaw, Sec.; 2nd and 4th Wednesdays, I.O.O.F. Hall.
l Carmelo No. 256, Daly City—Edward Eliasen, Pres.; Walter L. Murphy, Sec., 931 Hanover St.; 2nd and 4th Wednesdays, Eagles Hall.
ndustrial City No. 269, South San Francisco—John C. Hamilton, Pres.; Geo. A. Roll, Sec., P. O. box 237; 2nd and 4th Mondays, Metropolitan Hall.

SANTA BARBARA COUNTY.

anta Barbara No. 116, Santa Barbara City—C. W. McCormick, Pres.; H. C. Sweetser, Sec., Court House; 1st and 3rd Wednesdays, I.O.O.F. Hall.

SANTA CLARA COUNTY.

an Jose No. 22, San Jose—Joseph Sabatte, Pres.; H. W. McComas, Sec., Suite 7, Porter Bldg.; Mondays, I.O.O.F. Hall.
anta Clara No. 100, Santa Clara City—John J. Trinajstich, Pres.; Clarence Clevenger, Sec., P. O. box 297; Wednesdays, Redmen Hall.
bservatory No. 177, San Jose—Norton J. Mahon, Pres.; A. B. Langford, Sec., Hall Records; Tuesdays, Knights Columbus Hall, 40 No. First St.
ountain View No. 215, Mountain View—Gilbert F. McCorkle, Pres.; C. A. Antonioli, Sec., 948 California St.; 2nd and 4th Fridays, Mockbee Hall.
alo Alto No. 216, Palo Alto—John C. Bernal, Pres.; Albert A. Quinn, Sec., 643 High St.; Mondays, Native Sons Bldg., Hamilton Ave. and Emerson St.

SANTA CRUZ COUNTY.

Watsonville No. 65, Watsonville—A. W. Batchelder, Pres.; E. R. Tindall, Sec., R.F.D. No. 5, Box 313; 2nd and 4th Tuesdays, I.O.O.F. Hall.
anta Cruz No. 90, Santa Cruz City—W. H. Mori, Pres.; T. V. Mathews, Sec., 105 Pacheco Ave.; Tuesdays, Native Sons Hall, 117 Pacific Ave.

SHASTA COUNTY.

McCloud No. 149, Redding—Errol Yank, Pres.; Hugh A. Shuffleton, Sec.; 1st and 3rd Thursdays, Moose Hall.

SIERRA COUNTY.

Downieville No. 92, Downieville—J. M. McMahon, Pres.; H. S. Tibbey, Sec.; 2nd and 4th Mondays, I.O.O.F. Hall.
Golden Nugget No. 94, Sierra City—Leonard Thompson Jr., Pres.; Arthur R. Pride, Sec.; last Saturday, Masonic Hall.

SISKIYOU COUNTY.

Etna No. 192, Etna—Fred M. Wolford, Pres.; Harvey A. Green, Sec.; 1st and 3rd Wednesdays, I.O.O.F. Hall.
Liberty No. 193, Sawyers Bar—Orrin R. Bigelow, Pres.; John M. Barry, Sec.; 1st and 3rd Saturdays, I.O.O.F. Hall.

SOLANO COUNTY.

Solano No. 39, Suisun—Karl Koch, Pres.; J. W. Kinlock, Sec.; 1st and 3rd Tuesdays, I.O.O.F. Hall.
Vallejo No. 77, Vallejo—Joseph Clavo, Pres.; Werner B. Hallin, Sec., 912 Carolina; 2nd and 4th Tuesdays, San Pablo Hall.

SONOMA COUNTY.

Petaluma No. 27, Petaluma—George Gells, Pres.; C. F. Fobes, Sec., 114 Prospect St.; 2nd and 4th Mondays, Druid Hall, Gross Bldg., 41 Main St.
Santa Rosa No. 28, Santa Rosa—John Caniff, Pres.; Leland S. Lewis, Sec., Court House; Tuesdays, Native Sons Hall.
Glen Ellen No. 102, Glen Ellen—C. C. Weise, Pres.; Frank Kirch, Sec., Route 3, Santa Rosa; 2nd Monday, N.S.G.W. Hall.
Sonoma No. 111, Sonoma City—Frederick Bulotti, Pres.; L. H. Green, Sec.; 1st and 3rd Mondays, I.O.O.F. Hall.
Sebastopol No. 143, Sebastopol—A. N. Badger, Pres.; F. G. McFarlane, Sec.; 1st and 3rd Fridays, I.O.O.F. Hall.

STANISLAUS COUNTY.

Modesto No. 11, Modesto—Robert H. Hansen, Pres.; C. C. Eastin Jr., Sec., P. O. box 898; 1st and 3rd Wednesdays, I.O.O.F. Hall.
Oakdale No. 142, Oakdale—D. W. Tulloch, Pres.; E. T. Gobin, Sec.; 2nd Monday, Legion Hall.
Orestimba No. 247, Crows Landing—Lloyd W. Fink, Pres.; G. W. Fink, Sec.; 1st and 3rd Wednesdays, Community Club Home.

SUTTER COUNTY.

Sutter No. 261, Sutter City—Stanley R. McLean, Pres.; Glen R. Haynes, Sec., Yuba City; 2nd and 4th Mondays, N.D.G.W. Hall.

TRINITY COUNTY.

Mount Bally No. 87, Weaverville—M. P. Kay, Pres.; E. V. Ryan, Sec.; 1st and 3rd Mondays, Native Sons Hall.

TUOLUMNE COUNTY.

Tuolumne No. 144, Sonora—Mathew J. Marshall, Pres.; William M. Harrington, Sec., P. O. box 715; 2nd and 4th Fridays, Knights Columbus Hall.
Columbia No. 258, Columbia—Jos. Cadematori, Pres.; Charles E. Grant, Sec.; 2nd and 4th Thursdays, Native Sons Hall.

VENTURA COUNTY.

Cabrillo No. 114, Ventura City—David Bennett, Pres., 1380 Church St.

YOLO COUNTY.

Woodland No. 30, Woodland—J. L. Aronson, Pres.; E. B. Hayward, Sec.; 1st Thursday, Native Sons Hall.

YUBA COUNTY.

Marysville No. 6, Marysville—John McQuaid, Pres.; Verne Fogarty, Sec., 719 6th St.; 2nd Friday, Foresters Hall.

TO DEDICATE SCHOOL.

Saint Helena (Napa County)—The N.S.G.W. grand officers, headed by Grand President Seth Millington, will dedicate a public school here June 10, at 2 p. m.

N. D. DELEGATES

(Continued from Page 5)

Golden State No. 50—Millie Tietjen, Catherine Tietjen, Mary McGovern.

Orinda No. 56—Mms. Gladys Bennett, Mae Shea, Anna G. Loser.

Fremont No. 59—Kathryn McGrath, Ella Tait.

Dardanelle No. 66—Mary E. Gorgas, Marie Marsh.

Buena Vista No. 68—Florence Bartlett, Helen Kennerley, Mary Growney, Dorothy Rathjens.

Oneonta No. 71—Mms. Myra Rumrill, Emma Holbrook.

Las Lomas No. 72—Emily Ryan, Mary E. Waters.

Veritas No. 75—Helen Krutosik, Marie Sorensen.

Amapola No. 80—Harriett Clemens, Maria Fontenrose, Pauline Quirolo.

San Jose No. 81—Elsie Fisher, Julia Domenici, Mary Frances Mitchell, Augusta Singleton.

El Pescadero No. 82—Mrs. Mary A. Hewitson, Misses Frances Huck, Florence Steinmetz.

Yosemite No. 83—Marguerite Nelson, Lucille Kimbark, Mary H. Monahan.

Princess No. 84—Mrs. Addie Minard.

Forrest No. 86—Marguerite Davis, Sophia Hodges.

Piedmont No. 87—Rose Martinelli, Josephine Collins, Josephine Clark, Ella Mullins.

Ivy No. 88—Elizabeth Adams, Thirsa Hunt.

La Estrella No. 89—Mrs. Marie Seifert.

Woodland No. 90—Mms. Edna Richter, Ruth Hickey, Gladys Evans, Nelle Hebener, Miss Florice Linnell.

San Miguel No. 94—Louisa Davis.

Sans Souci No. 96—Mms. Camile Bowman, Tessie Pearce.

Reichling No. 97—Mrs. Lotta Smith.

Lassen View No. 98—Mrs. Retta Rust.

Vendome No. 100—Imogene Thompson, Clara Gairaud, Marie Buck, Martha Waddington.

Aleli No. 102—Mms. Mary McElheran, Gladys Dodd, Louise Hatton.

Calaveras No. 103—Agnes McVerry.

Copa de Oro No. 105—Edna Butterfield, Elma Chandler, Else Schou.

Aloha No. 106—Irene Madden, Thelma Rogers, Caroline Schulze.

San Luisita No. 108—Mms. Virginia Kenyon, Mae Umbertis.

La Bandera No. 110—Mms. Lucy Roberts, Eva Mordecai, Mae Sydenstricker, Miss Helen Kennedy.

Sutter No. 111—Mms. Lillie Heinreich, Ida Merwin, Emilie Lachman, Loraine Williams, Miss Maybelle Tuggle.

Eschscholtzia No. 112—Margaret E. Weston, Sadie Buckner.

San Andreas No. 113—Zaida Hertzig, Doris Treat.

Darina No. 114—Miss Elise Barth, Mrs. Pearl Young.

El Vespero No. 118—Miss Anne Godfrey, Mms. Agnes Ryan, Nell R. Boege.

Hayward No. 122—Mrs. Florence B. Hills, Miss Ruth M. Gansberger.

Los Angeles No. 124—Gertrude R. Allen, Mary K. Corcoran, Grace T. Haven, Mattie L. Gara, Dolores Malin, Olinda Kerby.

Oakdale No. 125—Mrs. Lou McLeod.

Reina del Mar No. 126—Mms. Christina McCrea, Jane Vick, Evelyn Eby.

Genevieve No. 132—Misses Rena Taube, Lillian Troy, Mms. Lillian Ryan, Elvira Desmond.

Imogen No. 134—Margaret A. Copren.

Clear Lake No. 135—Mrs. Geneva Abercrombie.

Placer No. 138—Laura Goy, Florence Gray.

Gabrielle No. 139—Mms. Ruth Koehler, Bessie Gordon, Miss Gertrude Mallen.

Hiawatha No. 140—Cecelia Anthony, Olive Shultes.

Junipero No. 141—Matilda Bergschicker.

Calistoga No. 145—Berenice Martin, Myrtle Siemsen.

Stirling No. 146—Mary Hulihan, Ada Ericeson.

Richmond No. 147—Gertrude Spierach.

Presidio No. 148—Sadie Romick, Claire Clark, Emilie Clifford, Anna Johnson.

Nataqua No. 152—Lela Fitch, Erma Haley.

Guadalupe No. 153—May McCarthy, May Marchant, Pauline Des Roches.

Long Beach No. 154—Violet T. Henshilwood, Zella Hodgedon.

Vista del Mar No. 155—Elizabeth Olney.

Encinal No. 156—Laura Fisher, May Orchinson.

Brooklyn No. 157—Lillian Smith, Maybelle Lewis.

Golden Gate No. 158—Mms. Margaret Ramm, Annie Franzen, Miss Bessie Ducray.

Alturas No. 159—Mms. Erma Elliott, Mildred Smith.

Marysville No. 162—Doris McKiernan, Cecilia Gomes.

El Pinal No. 163—Mrs. Kathryn Lucheasa.

Anona No. 164—May D. Lightner, Lillian Richards.

Argonaut No. 166—Mms. Lillian Caton, Louise Kehoe.

Bahia Vista No. 167—Miss Bernice Westphal, Mrs. Helen Connell.

Annie K. Bidwell No. 168—Laura Anderson, Hattie Jackson, Edna Boyd.

Dolores No. 169—Emma O'Meara, Elizabeth Both, Amelia Silva.

Linda Rosa No. 170—Mms. Margaretha McGowan, Helen J. O'Connell.

Chabolla No. 171—Georgia Fugazi.

Portola No. 172—Agnes M. Curry, Nan Kelly, Catharine H. Dolly.

Fruitvale No. 177—Alice Miller, Elvira Ragon.

Castro No. 178—Mae E. Waring, Alice Lane, Margaret Kaye, Margaret Griffith, Georgia Nelson.

San Juan Bautista No. 179—Mrs. Catherine Breen-Nyland.

Ano Nuevo No. 180—Ida M. Mesquite.

El Carmelo No. 181—Miss Alice Mathias, Mms. Christine Hume, Hattie Kelly.

Laura Loma No. 182—Mrs. Ethel Fournier.

Twin Peaks No. 185—Loretta M. Cameron, Eugenie Schwarz, Gladys McCarthy, Alice Johnson, Eleanor Walsh.

El Dorado No. 186—Flossie Francis, Alta L. Douglas.

Fresno No. 187—Edith Duncan, Iva Babcock.

Gold of Ophir No. 190—Alice Cundy, Rosa Crum, Anna Bernhard.

La Rosa No. 191—Mrs. Catherine Warnsley, Miss Beryl Sprague.

Berryessa No. 192—Mms. Minnie Mapes, Vera Litster.

Donner No. 193—Mrs. Edna H. Hill.

Colus No. 194—Mrs. Katie Bond.

Vallejo No. 195—Elvena Woodard, Edith Gutfeld.

Sea Point No. 196—Minnie Carreiro, Lillian Azevedo.

Marinita No. 198—Gussie Banister, Mollye Y. Spaelti, Josephine Bergin, Antoinette Hecht.

Morada No. 199—Paula Petersen, Katherine Kopf, Rhoda Jenkinson.

La Junta No. 203—Clara Herdle, Celeste Thorsen.

Caliz de Oro No. 206—Mrs. Lottie Hahn, Miss Clarice Cook.

El Cereso No. 207—Miss Florence Andrade, Mms. Delores Chavez, Olinda Kardoza.

San Diego No. 208—Mms. Isabel Young, Marie James.

Sonoma No. 209—Josephine Andreux.

Fort Bragg No. 210—Mrs. Elsie H. Bryans.

Menlo No. 211—Catherine Derry.

Coloma No. 212—Aleen Thompson, Marie Christy, Gertrude Keehner.

Liberty No. 213—Mms. Louisa Krull, Clara Windmiller.

Phoebe A. Hearst No. 214—Mrs. Nan Napier, Miss Clara Fagundes.

Mount Lassen No. 215—Rubie B. Thompson.

Victory No. 216—Mrs. Marie Goodman.

Santa Rosa No. 217—Ann Beach, Gladys Simoni.

Camp Far West No. 218—Elva Hicks.

Plumas Pioneer No. 219—Minnie E. Johnson, Helen Hall.

James Lick No. 220—Edna Bishop, Lyda Wood.

Las Juntas No. 221—Edna Garretty, Francis Upton.

Petaluma No. 222—Elizabeth Dillon, Ellen Sebesta.

Antioch No. 223—Edythe Easton, Marguerite Peters.

Mary E. Bell No. 224—Mms. Lena Nickum, Emma Lewis.

Fairfax No. 225—Mms. Myrtle DiVita, Louise Johnson.

South Butte No. 226—Mrs. Authalena McPherrin.

Mission No. 227—Inga Meyer, Adelaide Coutts, Ann S. Dippel.

Miocene No. 228—Evalyn G. Towne.

Palo Alto No. 229—Helena G. Hansen.

Rudecinda No. 230—Carrie E. Northway, Louise Fontes.

Tamelpa No. 231—Mrs. Delphine M. Todt.

Carquinez No. 234—Mary Lucey.

Santa Ana No. 235—Mms. Marion Crum, Mae West.

Betsy Ross No. 238—Lucy Day.

El Tejon No. 239—Misses Margaret Stramler, Sadie Clendenen.

Verdugo No. 240—Hazel B. Hansen, Vera Carlson.

Lugonia No. 241—Mary Johnson, Nola Fogler, Grace McHenry.

Susanville No. 243—Mrs. Burla Fulton.

Madera No. 244—Lois M. Roach.

Santa Monica Bay No. 245—Amada Machado.

San Bruno No. 246—Edythe Knoles.

Californiana No. 247—Gertrude J. Tuttle, Ernestine Alyward, Olive Lopez, Hortense Steinike.

Eldora No. 248—Marguerite Johnson.

Balboa No. 249—Marcella Bray, Jean Moffett.

Ontario No. 251—Mrs. Adele Frankish.

Rainbow No. 40, Wheatland—W. E. Jones, Pres.; W. A. Bowser, Sec., P. O. box 818; 2nd Thursday, I.O.O.F. Hall.

AFFILIATED ORGANIZATIONS.

San Francisco Extension of the Order Committee, N.S.G.W.—Harmon D. Skillin, Chmn.; Harold J. Regan, Sec., 414 Mason St., San Francisco; meets 2nd and 4th Fridays, Grizzly Bear Club, 414 Mason St., San Francisco.
Alameda County Extension of the Order Committee, N.S.G.W.—Edward T. Schnarr, Chmn.; Frank Roemer, Sec., 3297 Morcom Ave., Oakland; meets 1st and 3rd Mondays, N.S.G.W. Hall, 11th and Clay Sts., Oakland.
Interparlor Committee (Southern District), N.S.G.W. and N.D.G.W.—Burrel D. Neighbours, Chmn.; F. J. Burmester, Sec., P. O. box 42, Colton; meets 2nd and 4th Fridays, Patriotic Hall, 1816 So. Figueroa St., Los Angeles.
San Francisco Assembly No. 1 Past Presidents Association N.S.G.W.—Meets 1st and 3rd Fridays, Native Sons Bldg., 414 Mason St., San Francisco; J. H. Sylvester, Gov.; J. F. Stanley, Sec., 1175 O'Farrell St., San Francisco.
East Bay Counties Assembly No. 3 Past Presidents Association N.S.G.W.—Meets 4th Monday, Native Sons Hall, 11th and Clay Sts., Oakland; Felix Robison, Gov.; Edgar G. Hanson, Sec., 1260 Russell St., Berkeley.
Marin County Assembly No. 5 Past Presidents Association N.S.G.W.—J. S. Rose Jr., Gov.; L. J. Peter, Sec., Peter Bldg., 4th and "C" Sts., San Rafael.
Fred H. Greeley Assembly No. 6 Past Presidents Association N.S.G.W.—Meets monthly with different Parlors comprising district; R. L. P. Bigelow, Gov.; Barney Barry, Sec., P. O. box 72, Lincoln.
San Joaquin Assembly No. 7 Past Presidents Association N.S.G.W.—Meets 1st Friday, Native Sons Hall, Stockton; Clyde H. Gregg, Gov.; R. D. Dorcey, Sec., Native Sons Club, Stockton.
Sonoma County Assembly No. 9 Past President Association N.S.G.W.—Meets monthly at different Parlor headquarters in county; Louis Bosch, Gov.; L. S. Lewis, Sec., Court House, Santa Rosa.
General John A. Sutter Assembly No. 10 Past Presidents Association—C. C. Wachman, Gov.; Jas. J. Longshore, Sec., 514 "J" St., Sacramento.
Grizzly Bear Club—Members all Parlors outside San Francisco at all times welcome. Clubrooms top floor Native Sons Bldg., 414 Mason St., San Francisco.
Native Sons and Native Daughters Central Committee on Homeless Children—Main office, 955 Phelan Bldg., San Francisco; Mrs. John W. Stirling, Chmn.; Miss Mary E. Brusie, Sec. Los Angeles branch office, 3924 Sunset Blvd.; Dorothy Schlingman, Sec.

(ADVERTISEMENT.)

U. C. SUMMER SESSIONS AS USUAL.

Through misunderstanding, many harbor the erroneous belief that the University of California has abandoned the 1932 summer sessions. The sessions will be, as usual, conducted by the university on both the Berkeley and the Los Angeles campuses, both opening June 27.

Stanislaus First—Last year, Stanislaus County ranked first as the butter-producing section of California, its production totaling 7,337,522 pounds. Fresno County ranked second and Humboldt County third.

Big Trees—There are 17,000 Big Trees in California, according to the Federal Interior Department, 8,772 of them being in the Sequoia National Park.

Bankers' Meet—The American Institute of Banking will have a nation-wide meeting at Los Angeles City, June 7-11.

Endeavorers' Meet—The California Christian Endeavor will meet in annual convention at Visalia, Tulare County, June 23-26.

Water Bonds—May 3, San Francisco voted $6,500,000 bonds for continuing its Hetch Hetchy water project.

THE ROMANCE OF SAN BERNARDINO

Clara M. Barton

(Continued from May Issue.)

EPISODE 8.

PIONEERS.

THE SAN BERNARDINO SOCIETY OF California Pioneers received its organization papers from the county January 21, 1888. Signers of the document were John Brown Sr., John Brown Jr., J. W. Waters, George Lord, S. P. Waite, G. W. Suttenfield, H. M. Willis, N. G. Gill, W. F. Holcomb, R. T. Roberts and De LaM. Woodward.

Listen, my dears, while I relate
About the founders of this great State.
It was the year of forty-nine
That these brave folk, each one sublime,
Decided to invade the big gold rush
Which created excitement in a hush.

So with oxen team of old
This little band became quite bold.
Their trials were many, and hardships, too,
Were all endured by these brave few.
They had their joys and also their griefs,
But still they held the same beliefs.

And now we find from mount to sea
A wonderful valley for you and me.
And all the world with envious eyes
Looks to this State of Paradise.
We've found our happiness and our wealth.
Good cheer, too, to bring us health.

Oh Pioneer great, oh Pioneer wise,
In you, the founder's wisdom lies!
'Twas you who paved the way so great
And gave to us our Golden State.
So let's not forget the ones so dear,
Our noble people, our own Pioneer!

These Pioneers of San Bernardino City and County met with obstacles, great and small. They faced danger from the Indians; trudged through the burning sands of the desert and over rugged mountains; met disasters with a smile, and their courage was tested under a severe strain. The Pioneers started the work that was carried on from the eighteenth to the twentieth century. It was they who laid the foundation upon which to build the present structure. They had no fear, their word was as good as their bond. The early Pioneers were people of great endurance, and they adopted the customs and laws of the country. They were trusted and respected by the native Californians, and held offices as advisors. Large trains of wagons were brought into the valley by these men and women who had come before. Stories of bear fighting were related, and experiences endured were never forgotten.

The Pioneers cultivated social virtues and have preserved that portion of the history of San Bernardino with which they have been associated. They have joined in all undertakings for the advancement of the community, and they have demonstrated that they are bound by ties of brotherhood.

The Pioneers were responsible for the city's incorporation in 1854, and its disincorporation March 6, 1863. There was a reason for the latter, and in 1869 the problem was solved and San Bernardino was re-incorporated as a town. The first official act of the settlers during the year 1853 was to appoint a man to handle the incoming and outgoing mail arriving by pony express or by stage. The United States Government had not established an authorized postoffice, as the mail had been so light there was no need for one. The Pioneers took it upon themselves to elect a mail distributor, and D. M. Thomas, who was at that time appointed judge, was selected to attend to all postal affairs. His "office" was in the Council House, but he distributed mail from his hat in front of the fort, and he continued so to do until recalled to Salt Lake with the rest of the Mormons. He drew no salary, and distributed the mail once a month.

After Thomas resigned the Pioneers became uneasy. "Now what?" asked one of the settlers. "We must have someone to attend to all of our mail." It was not long before the second postmaster was selected. Being the first and only doctor, and having the first drug store, Dr. Ben Barton was selected, and from 1857 to 1860 he served. During his term as postmaster the United States Government began to take an interest in the city's affairs and Dr. Barton was officially recognized by Washington, thus making him the first government postmaster. He had previously built an adobe building in which he had his office and drug store, and he fitted out a corner of the store which he thought would be suitable for the distribution of the mail. Because of this and because the postal activities were carried on under roof, Dr. Barton was officially recognized by the United States Government as postmaster and received a small compensation.

The mail was received once a month by horseback until the stagecoaches were firmly established, when it was delivered once a week. At the postoffice, names were called, and all unclaimed mail was put into a box for further investigation by the latecomers. Following Dr. Barton's term as postmaster the name of Dr. Peacock was forwarded to Washington with a recommendation from the settlers, and he, too, was officially appointed. From then on, Washington continued the service established by the Pioneers.

Dr. Barton came with his small family to California in 1854 and made his first home in El Monte, where two sons were born. He did not tarry there long and followed the wagon trains to San Bernardino. On arrival, he recognized the many advantages. With his family he established himself in the mission and remained there during the building of the three-story brick house by the Indians. As the family grew, a daughter was born within the walls of the mission. Assisted by his sons, he planted the first vineyard and orange orchard. This revived interest in cultivation of the soil, and soon advanced strides were made.

San Bernardino was expanding. The Pioneers wasted neither time nor energy, and constructed three large stores, stocked with goods. These were owned by Meyerstein, Calisher and Ancker. It was not long, however, before seventeen more stores were built. A livery stable, the only one of its kind and owned by Brazelton, was opened and the business was a prosperous one. This idea of a stable inspired a saddler, who opened a harness repair shop, and thus Foy became the first dealer of leather in the town and he was kept busy. Then a hotel, built by Starke, was erected, and was well occupied and the center of all social activities. In 1859 a group of amateurs formed a dramatic club, the San Bernardino Dramatic Association, and they produced plays that created much amusement.

The Pioneers did not stop here, however. Soon a group of writers and editors banded together and June 16, 1860, the first newspaper, christened the "San Bernardino Herald," appeared under the capable management of Judson J. Ames. A rival newspaper came into the field in 1862, but died a natural death; it was called the "San Bernardino Patriot." In 1861 J. S. Waite became editor of the "Herald." In 1858 the first Union Sundayschool and Church was organized, at the request of those who did not embrace the Mormon religion.

The first school was held in a brush structure constructed by the Mormons in the fort and was taught by Rupert Lee. The Pioneers objected strenuously to this, and erected a tent in which school and church services were held. Shortly thereafter a large building of brick and adobe was erected for those purposes. Here the first schoolbell was hung, and when, in 1871, a two-story brick building was erected, the bell was moved with appropriate ceremonies. This was the beginning of a well-established school system throughout the valley. William Stout was the first superintendent and principal of all the schools. The San Bernardino Collegiate School, the first private school in the county, was opened August 25, 1862, by Captain J. C. Allsop.

The first established church of San Bernardino was that of Saint Paul's Methodist Church South, and it is the pioneer church of the county. Here, in 1858, all denominations came to worship under the ministry of Rev. Burns, but it was Father Glover who kept up the strength and fervor of this little church. The first step in establishing a Protestant church was taken by Miss Ellen Pratt, who organized a Sundayschool in a private home. The First Methodist Church was organized in 1867, and Rev. L. M. Leihy was appointed pastor in charge; he, in turn, appointed Rev. Adam Bland as his successor. Dr. J. C. Peacock presented the church with a lot and at his own expense fitted up a small chapel. A Congregational Church was erected in 1864, and M. H. Crafts induced the officials of that denomination to send Rev. J. A. Johnson to fill the pulpit. A Baptist Church was then organized by Dr. Ben Barton, Rev. I. C. Curtis, Mr. and Mrs. Shackleford, Mrs. Huldah Johnson, Ezra Kerfoot and John Culberston. A Catholic Church, "Little Church of Aqua Mansa," came into being in the early '50s with Father Peter Birmingham in charge.

The outstanding organization which has done so much for the San Bernardino Pioneers is Arrowhead Parlor No. 110 of the Order of Native Sons of the Golden West. The Order seeks to establish in the hearts of all sons of California pride of nativity and love of birthplace. Its origin is patriotic, and its purpose is to perpetuate in memory the days and the deeds of the Pioneers. Arrowhead Parlor was organized by a true son of a Pioneer, Dan D. Rich, who was elected its first president and who navigated the Parlor through many hard storms. Lugonia Parlor No. 241 is the third Parlor of the Order of Native Daughters of the Golden West to be organized in San Bernardino. Florence Dodson Schoneman was its founder, and Lois Aldridge Johnson was its charter president. It is most active in preserving the landmarks and the history of the early days.

(Continued in JULY Issue)

APPOINTMENTS

Gridley (Butte County)—Seth Millington, N.S.G.W. Grand President, has announced the following Grand Parlor appointments. Other committeemen, and also district deputy grand presidents, will be named by him next month:

Finance Committee—Harry W. Gaetjen (Golden Gate No. 29), Joseph Rose (Marshall No. 202), James L. Foley (Twin Peaks No. 214).

Board Appeals—Irving D. Gibson (Sacramento No. 3), Ben Harrison (Arrowhead No. 110), R. M. Hamb (Piedmont No. 120), Alfred H. McKnew (San Francisco No. 49), Samuel M. Shortridge Jr. (Menlo No. 185).

Board Control—W. C. Neumiller (Stockton No. 7), Walter Bammann (Pacific No. 10), J. Hartley Russell (Stanford No. 76).

Publicity Committee—William Knowland (Halcyon No. 146), A. V. Mayrhofer (San Diego No. 108), Arthur Poheim (Stanford No. 76).

Printing and Supplies Committee—Fred H. Nickelson (South San Francisco No. 157), John G. Schroder (El Capitan No. 222), W. H. Maison (Castro No. 232).

History Committee—Wm. J. Hayes (P.G.P.), William P. Caubu (P.G.P.), Hilliard E. Welch (P.G.P.), Wm. I. Traeger (P.G.P.), Frank Merrit (Brooklyn No. 151).

Historic Landmarks Committee—Joseph R. Knowland (P.G.P.), Lewis F. Byington (P.G.P.), Fred H. Greely (P.G.P.), H. C. Lichtenberger (P.G.P.), J. Harvey McCarthy (Ramona No. 109).

Homeless Children Committee—Earl Warren (Fruitvale No. 252), I. H. Reuter (Yosemite No. 24), Fletcher A. Cutler (P.G.P.).

Laws of Subordinates—Thomas M. Foley (Pacific No. 10), Joseph I. McNamara (Stanford No. 76), Louis F. Erb (Alcalde No. 154).

Transportation and Mileage Committee—Joseph Berry (Courtland No. 106), P. L. Schlesinger (Balboa No. 234), Percy Marchant (Guadalupe No. 231).

Admission Day Observance—Edward E. Reese (Sunset No. 26), Wm. G. Muntz (Estudillo No. 223), Harry Romick (Castro No. 232), Henry G. Bodkin (Hollywood No. 196), Ray B. Felton (Fruitvale No. 252).

Athletics Committee—Al Sandell (Twin Peaks No. 214), R. J. Garrett (Berkeley No. 210), L. Alva Werner (Golden Gate No. 29), Wesley Colgan (Santa Rosa No. 28), Arthur J. Cleu (Fruitvale No. 252).

Lone Grave Monument—Dr. C. W. Chapman (Hydraulic No. 56), L. T. Sinnott (Marysville No. 6), H. Ray George (Quartz No. 58).

Butano Forest Preservation Committee—Oscar A. Foster (Santa Cruz No. 90), H. W. Amphlett (Redwood No. 66), Edwin A. Meserve (Ramona No. 109), W. A. Gilkey (Los Angeles No. 45), E. A. Shaw (Pebble Beach No. 230).

Headed "Advice on Taxation," the following by H. A. Goetsch of Wadena, Minn., appeared in the "Congressional Record" recently:

Tax the people, tax with care,
To help the multimillionaire.
Tax the farmer, tax his fowl,
Tax the dog, and tax his howl.
Tax the hen and tax her egg
And let the bloomin' mudsill beg.
Tax the pig and tax his squeal,
Tax his boots, run down at heel;
Tax his horses, tax his lands,
Tax the blisters on his hands.
Tax his plow and tax his clothes,
Tax the rag that wipes his nose;
Tax his house and tax his bed,
Tax the bald spot on his head.
Tax the ox, and tax the ass,
Tax his "Henry," tax the gas;
Tax the road that he must pass,
And make him travel o'er the grass.
Tax his cow, and tax his calf,
Tax him if he dares to laugh;
He is just a common man,
So tax the cuss just all you can.
Tax the laborer—be discreet—
Tax him walking on the street,
Tax his bread and tax his meat;
Tax the shoes clear off his feet.
Tax the payroll, tax the sale,
Tax his hard-earned paper kale;
Tax his pipe and tax his smoke—
Teach him government is no joke.
Tax their coffins—tax their shrouds,
Tax their souls beyond the clouds.
Tax the farmer, tax his flocks;
Tax the servants, tax their socks.
Tax the living, tax the dead;
Tax the unborn, ere they're fed.
Tax the water, tax the air—
Tax the sunlight if you dare.
Tax them all, and tax them well,
Tax them to the gates of hell!
But close your eyes so you can't see
The coupon-clipper go tax free.

Planning Conference—A National City Planning Conference will be held June 13-16 at Hollywood, Los Angeles County.

River Pageant—Healdsburg, Sonoma County will hold its annual Russian River Pageant Fiesta, June 17-19.

LOS ANGELES--CITY and COUNTY

CLASSIFIED DIRECTORY LOS ANGELES NATIVE SONS

ATTORNEYS-AT-LAW.

J. A. ADAIR. J. A. ADAIR JR.
516-19 Fay Bldg., Third and Hill.
Office: MAdison 1141 —Phones— Res.: GLadstone 5042.

HENRY G. BODKIN. V. P. LUCAS.
Chester Williams Bldg., 215 W. 5th St.
Phone: MUtual 3151.

DAVID H. CLARK.
215 West Fifth St.
Phone: MUtual 8406.

WM. J. HUNSAKER.
458 So. Spring St., Room 1130.
Phone: TRinity 6656.

EDWIN A. MESERVE. SHIRLEY E. MESERVE.
555 So. Flower St.
Phone: TRinity 6161.

THOS. B. REED.
548 South Spring St.
Phone: VAndike 0687.

DENTIST.

ROBERT J. GREGG, D.D.S.
5801 South Figueroa St.
Phone: THornwall 3690.
Hours 9 to 5, and by appointment.

DETECTIVE SERVICE.

LOUIS A. DUNI.
523 Washington Bldg., 311½ So. Spring.
Phone: TUcker 3013.

PHYSICIAN AND SURGEON.

WILBUR B. PARKER, M.D.
11th Floor Brack Shops, 527 W. 7th St.
Phone: TRinity 5739.
Practice Limited to Urology.

LOS ANGELES

(Continued from Page 13)

birthday; Third Vice-president Burke is chairman.

Secretary Rosalie F. Hyde of Santa Monica Bay submitted a poem in the Los Angeles Breakfast Club's Olympics verse contest. There were 1,500 contributors, and she received honorable mention. Her verse, entitled "California's Greeting," follows:

"A welcome wide as our sunlit skies
To those who come from other lands,
To match their talents with our own,
And forge the links of golden bands
Of Friendships hitherto unknown.
Our glory in the Olympic games,
Our glory in the famous names
Of those who come so brave and bold,
Shall be the theme of songs of praise
When tales of the Olympiad are told."

PERSONAL PARAGRAPHS.

Owen S. Adams (Los Angeles N.S.) was a visitor last month to San Francisco.

Joe Romero (Ramona N.S.) celebrated May 3 his fifty-sixth wedding anniversary.

Miss Ella Vucovich (Los Angeles N.D.) was wedded May 15 to William Steinbeck.

Mrs. Margaret Grote-Hill (N.D. Past Grand) of San Francisco was a visitor last month.

Miss Mabel R. Haines became the bride of Oliver P. Morton (Ramona N.S.) last month.

Mrs. Minnie Sauder (Long Beach N.D.) of Long Beach was recently wedded to Lenord Kofahl.

A native daughter arrived May 7 at the home of Stanley A. Wheeler (Sepulveda N.S.) of San Pedro.

Miss Irene Whitney (Los Angeles N.D.), at Ventura City, April 30, became the bride of Clinton Collins.

Superior Judge J. J. Trabucco (Yosemite N.S.) and wife (Mariposa N.D.) of Mariposa Town are visitors.

Louis J. Peter (Mount Tamalpais N.S.) of San Rafael paid a short visit last month to his birthplace, Los Angeles.

Dr. William R. Molony (Ramona N.S.) has been appointed a member of the State Board of Medical Examiners.

Edward Schallmo (Ramona N.S.) and wife (Los Angeles N.D.) last month visited their daughter, Mrs. Adelaide Hickman (Los Angeles N.D.) in San Francisco.

A native daughter arrived April 29 at the home of Horace R. Martin (Ramona N.S.) of Huntington Park. This is the third grandchild of Sheriff William I. Traeger (N.S. Past Grand).

THE DEATH RECORD.

Samuel B. Eason, father of Bert Eason (Hollywood N.S.), died April 20.

Paul Loughridge Blair, affiliated with Ramona Parlor No. 109 N.S.G.W., died April 25 survived by a wife. He was born at Los Angeles, February 19, 1879.

Mrs. Elizabeth G. Chatterton, mother of George C. Chatterton (Ramona N.S.), died April 26.

Mrs. Margaret Stoll, mother of Adolph G. Stoll (Ramona N.S.), died May 6.

Lyle Pendegast, former Los Angeles police chief affiliated with Ramona Parlor No. 109 N.S.G.W., died May 25 survived by a wife. He was born at Woodland, Yolo County, December 30, 1870.

Ukiah Rodeo—Ukiah, Mendocino County, will stage the annual Ukiah Valley Rodeo, June 10, 11 and 12.

GRIZZLY GROWLS

(Continued from Page 2)

The Federal Congress has been for some time attempting to balance the budget but, lacking a balance of reasoning power, little progress has been made.

Every person knows the National Government must meet its obligations, and every person appears to want to saddle the necessary taxburden on the other fellow. The only fair, honest and equable tax for the present emergency is the general sales tax. The Congress should levy that, and then adjourn.

Several papers of the state last month, in giving publicity to the N.S.G.W. Grand Parlor, said, "The annual contribution toward publication of The Grizzly Bear Magazine was suspended." THAT IS NOT A FACT! The usual appropriation for the magazine was made, although resolutions to suspend it were considered. It is likely those not overly friendly toward The Grizzly Bear gave the resolutions to the press before final action had been taken thereon, with the deliberate intent to injure the magazine.

Wherever one goes, the main topic of conversation is prohibition,—blamed for all the nation's economic ills—which shows the effectiveness of well-directed and adequately-financed propaganda. Prohibition has faults aplenty,—due mostly, however, to faulty administration of the law,—but is not responsible for this nation's sad plight.

Prohibition is a minor issue, and the booze-or-no-booze discussion, when questions of paramount importance should have consideration, are nauseating. The prohibition propaganda is, in fact, but a smoke-screen to divert attention from nationwide corruption, incubated by those in high positions and protected and nursed by governmental agencies. Forget prohibition, for the time being, and labor to eliminate dishonest officials from public office and private enterprise.

For the August primary, 2,377,710 California citizens were registered, and 1,383,236 performed their main duty as citizens by casting their ballots. The remainder, 994,474, probably are so thoroughly disgusted with the rottenness in government they would not exercise their voting privilege. Unawares, perhaps, they thus aided the political gangsters, for the latter thrive because of the apathy of the average citizen. Good government cannot be expected without good citizenship, and the first requisite of good citizenship is to vote always, for the right.

Los Angeles, always to the forefront with the biggest, the best and the largest in all lines, not excepting financial sharpsters, recently added to its wealth-of-fame two "renowned" Fish-ermen. Frank hooked $492,590 from the AMCo investment-lake and Brother Ray landed $180,553. Both are now sojourning in San Quentin, but they will soon be back among the "prominents," for "de dollah am shure" a loud and efficient speaker in these days of enthroned crookedness.

The AMCo lake went dry, the same as many other of Los Angeles' numerous investment enterprises. It has been conservatively estimated investing-suckers put into them around a billion dollars. What will they get out? Experience only, for, after the promoters, the receivers, the attorneys and the judiciary get theirs, nothing else remains. The chemically-pure city certainly has established a fine record as an investment center!

In the Federal House of Representatives, May 13, the chaplain, asking comfort for Colonel and Mrs. Lindbergh, whose baby boy was found murdered, prayed the Eternal God to "Cleanse the arteries of our whole country where breed and

(Concluded on Page 24)

A BIT O' FARMING and GARDENING

PREPARED EXPRESSLY FOR THE GRIZZLY BEAR BY M. H. ELLIS

WHILE THE CORNER AROUND which prosperity is supposed to lurk continues to be somewhat obscure, there are indications that agriculture may be on the upgrade, that a turning point will be reached this year. The so-called "bottom" of the depression has been theoretically reached several times; actually, it seems to be in sight. Whatever conditions may be on farms, in the final analysis the soil always can be depended upon to yield a livelihood. Food can be secured from the soil; it does not grow in the city pavements.

The last census figures showed there are 45,000 farms in California on which there is not a cent of mortgaged indebtedness. Nearly half the farming area of the state is free from debt, despite the rigors of the economic situation. No other industry can show a like statement. And while this year does not give promise of being one of unusual profit for the farmer, it is not to be one which will show abnormal losses,—that is, losses heavier than have been taken in other recent years.

Production problems have not been solved as yet; there are many of them to be worked out. But agriculture has advanced farther along production lines than with marketing. Hence the stress now is laid on the economic situation, and with all agencies co-operating indications are that there will be progress recorded this year. Nevertheless, the prosperity of agriculture must accompany that of the nation;. when buying power returns the farmer will sell his goods at a profit. But better marketing conditions will aid and hasten this, by affording better distribution and quality for the consumer.

HUMUS IN THE SOIL.

Much has been said and written about humus in the soil. A questioner asks how to get it there. Well, any organic matter turned under the surface and left to decompose will add to the humus. Weeds, plowed or spaded under, will add humus; so, too, will manure; lawn clippings will help. Anything that grows or has grown in the field or garden can be turned under, with profit to the condition of the soil as regards humus. Cover crops are turned under for this purpose. in part. Addition of humus to the soil will increase its tilth, or condition, will stop baking and packing, will aid in retention of moisture, and will increase the productivity of the soil. Plow or spade under all weeds, discarded plants, lawn clippings, straw, manure and other organic matter whenever it is available.

SEEDS AND BULBS FOR JUNE.

Most of the flowers with small seeds should be planted in flats for transplanting; many of the larger seeded kinds will do better if thus started before being placed in the beds where they are to bloom. This month (June) there still are many flowers that may be started for late blooming. For planting in flats, this includes english daisy, calendula, cockscomb, cornflower, cineraria, coreopsis, cosmos, sweet william, foxglove, candytuft, stock, forgetmenot, petunia, phlox and tufted pansy. Zinnias and marigolds may be planted in beds, if desired, but no time will be lost in using flats and more and stronger plants usually will develop. Most of these flowers could be transplanted from flats to the garden now, if started earlier; there are many kinds of flowers that can be planted at almost any time.

It is getting late for bulbs and roots, but there still are some that may be planted. Cannas, dahlias, gladiola, tuberoses, german iris, cinnamon vine and madeira vine still will do well, although this is just about the latest that they can be put into the ground with any hope of success in most places. Too, a great deal depends upon the locality; some places in the state where the weather is far ahead of the average cannot be depended upon to give good results even now. On the other hand, in the mountain districts there still is much time, save that the season will end early in the fall. The grower must take the climatic conditions of his locality into consideration, for recommendations can be given only for the average conditions in the valleys.

THE VEGETABLE GARDEN.

As the earlier vegetables in the garden are used and space left by them becomes available, plant with some other kind that will go ahead under summer weather conditions and make a crop. In California, it is possible to plant some kind of vegetable every month in the year. Beets, carrots, peas, radishes and turnips may be planted in the coast counties at any time. In the interior valleys there are some months in the winter when soil and temperature conditions are such that these will not make satisfactory growth, but generally speaking there always can be vegetables in the garden save in the colder districts of the foothills and mountains. Sweet corn may be planted anywhere this month, in addition to the vegetables named, and tomato plants may be set out in the home garden with prospects for success in producing late fruits.

TO CONTROL SLUGS.

While snails may be controlled by the use of a poison bait, slugs ordinarily must have different treatment. One part of calcium arsenate, mixed dry with 15 parts of wheat bran and lightly moistened will usually do away with snails, if spread around where they feed. Carc must be used so that domestic animals and birds do not get the bait. With slugs, a spray made of half a pound of ordinary alum dissolved in a gallon of hot water, then cooled, will be effective. It must, however, be applied at night when the slugs are active so that it will reach them. The treatment should be repeated at intervals of two or three weeks.

SUMMER CITRUS FERTILIZATION.

Organic matter, such as bulky manure, may be applied to citrus groves this month or next, if convenient. Some groves will be found to be showing a tinge of yellow in the foliage. Ordinarily this is caused by a lack of nitrogen, although in some cases it may be due to the presence of toxic salts or over-irrigation. Where it is due to a lack of nitrogen, the application of manure will not handle the situation and the organic fertilizer must decompose before it becomes available. Use, rather, a quickly available commercial nitrogenous fertilizer. Formerly it was the practice to apply commercial fertilizer in a large dose in the spring; a better plan is to distribute the application over the year with perhaps the heaviest dosage in the spring.

GRIZZLY GROWLS

(Continued from Page 23)

swarm the filth and the crime of our national household." May that prayer be speedily answered!

Representative Britten of Illinois, before the House Committee on territories the other day, expressed the opinion that if the homes of Japs in Hawaii were searched "you would find numerous plans for the destruction of our docks." Probably, also, if the Japs' places of worship, etc., in the mainland, particularly California, were searched other plans, and also arms, to aid Japan in its invasion schemes, would be found. And yet, the howl continues to decrease the personnel and the efficiency of this country's army and navy. If nothing else will, a Jap bombardment should, eventually, awaken the pro-Japs and other pacifists.

Unemployment reserves, as a sort of insurance against bad times, are being advocated by those who oppose applying the quota to Mexicans and other objectionable aliens and cutting down European quotas. When the demand is good, this class of employers hire foreign laborers in flocks fresh from the docks, and then, when the demand slackens, they promptly dump the foreigners on the communities to feed, house and clothe. Such a reserve has been building up in this country for several years, and as a result thousands, yes millions, of White American laborers are today without employment.

Fire insurance is a good thing, too, but does not prevent loss due to poor construction, and unemployment reserves cannot lessen the loss that necessarily results from unsound national and business policies. A bill is before the Federal Congress cutting down European quotas and extending the quota to immigration from Mexico and Canada. The United States Chamber of Commerce, always active in behalf of the big interests, is opposing the bill. Native and other real Californians should request, NOW, of this state's representatives in both houses of the Congress, that they support the bill, and thus assist in preventing the organized few from again getting the better of the unorganized many.

Grizzly Bear

JULY — THE ONLY OFFICIAL PUBLICATION OF THE NATIVE SONS AND DAUGHTERS OF THE GOLDEN WEST — 1932

Featuring

GENERAL NEWS OF INTEREST CONCERNING ALL CALIFORNIA, and ORDERS NATIVE SONS and NATIVE DAUGHTERS

Price: 15 Cents

BOOK REVIEWS

(CLARENCE M. HUNT.)

"ONE HUNDRED YEARS IN YOSEMITE."

By Carl Parcher Russell; Stanford University Press, Publisher, Stanford University, California; Price, $3.50.

This romantic story of early human affairs in the central Sierra Nevada is most interesting and enlightening. A work that will add value and charm to any collection of Californiana, it presents authentic information concerning events and people conspicuously linked with the early history of American California, particularly the Sierra country, which embraces Yosemite. It centers attention on the discovery of the world-famed valley by White men. It is liberally illustrated.

The author, Carl Parcher Russell, field naturalist, United States National Park Service, declares in the foreword, "It is the purpose of this book to preserve and disseminate the authentic story of the discovery and development of the wondrous Yosemite region," and he is deserving of unstinted commendation for succeeding, excellently. "Much has been published on the history of Yosemite, but the data are scattered through more than one hundred publications, and even the published material is incomplete and disconnected. Here the published information has been organized, checked, and enriched with authentic data which have not previously appeared in print." He concludes with a plea for the proper preservation of much valuable history material which unquestionably reposes, unthought of, in the libraries (and attics) of innumerable homes in the West.

Reliable knowledge of the Sierra Nevada and the first inkling of the existence of Yosemite Valley resulted, according to the author, from an expedition, made in 1833, led by Joseph Reddeford Walker, a frontiersman. Walker's tombstone, in Martinez, Contra Costa County, bears the inscription, "Camped at Yosemite Nov. 13, 1833." In 1839 Zenas Leonard, clerk of the Walker party, published a narrative of their experiences, and this is declared to be the first authentic printed reference to the Yosemite region. James D. Savage is credited with being the most conspicuous figure in early Yosemite history.

An outstanding feature of "One Hundred Years in Yosemite" is the appendix, which includes nine historic documents, and a chronological outline of the history of the Yosemite region. Among the documents is the muster roll of the famed Mariposa Battalion—"Muster Roll of a Volunteer Battalion under the command of Major James D. Savage, mustered into the service of the State of California by James Burney, Sheriff of Mariposa, persuant to an order from his excellency, the Governor of the State of California, bearing date January 24, 1851, at Aqua Frio, February 10, 1851: James D. Savage, Major; M. B. Lewis, Adjutant; A. Brunston, Sergeant; Robert E. Russell, Sergeant-Major; Francis Laumiester, Quartermaster and Commissary; Theodore Wilson, Quartermaster Sergeant; Vincent Haylix, Guide."

The Grizzly Bear Magazine

The ALL California Monthly

OWNED, CONTROLLED, PUBLISHED BY GRIZZLY BEAR PUBLISHING CO., (Incorporated)

COMPOSED OF NATIVE SONS.

HERMAN C. LICHTENBERGER, Pres.
JOHN T. NEWELL RAY HOWARD
WM. I. TRAEGER LORENZO F. SOTO
CHAS. R. THOMAS HARRY J. LELANDE
ARTHUR A. SCHMIDT, Vice-Pres.
BOARD OF DIRECTORS

CLARENCE M. HUNT
General Manager and Editor

OFFICIAL ORGAN AND THE ONLY OFFICIAL PUBLICATION OF THE NATIVE SONS AND THE NATIVE DAUGHTERS GOLDEN WEST.

ISSUED FIRST EACH MONTH.
FORMS CLOSE 20th MONTH.
ADVERTISING RATES ON APPLICATION.

SAN FRANCISCO OFFICE:
N.S.G.W. BLDG., 414 MASON ST., RM. 302
(Office Grand Secretary N.S.G.W.)
Telephone: Kearney 1223
SAN FRANCISCO, CALIFORNIA

PUBLICATION OFFICE:
309-15 WILCOX BLDG., 2nd AND SPRING,
Telephone: VAndike 6234
LOS ANGELES, CALIFORNIA

(Entered as second-class matter May 29, 1918, at the Postoffice at Los Angeles, California, under the act of August 24, 1912.)

PUBLISHED REGULARLY SINCE MAY 1907

VOL. LI WHOLE NO. 308

In Memoriam

DR. VICTORY A. DERRICK, P.G.P.
JENNIE GOLDSWORTHY.

To the Members of Aloha Parlor No. 106 Native Daughters of the Golden West:

Whereas, Our Heavenly Father has taken unto Himself two beloved members of Aloha Parlor No. 106, we bow our heads in humble resignation. The vacancy caused by the loss of our adored Past Grand President, Victory A. Derrick, and of our devoted sister, Jennie Goldsworthy, will never be filled.

The sweet character of our darling Past Grand President, Victory A. Derrick, will always stand out as a great beacon that will lead us to higher and nobler things. The happy memories of Sister Jennie Goldsworthy will always remind us of the "sunshine of her smile." Therefore, be it

Resolved, That the members of Aloha Parlor No. 106 extend our deepest sympathy to the daughters of Past Grand President Victory A. Derrick and to the husband and daughters of Past Grand President Victory A. Derrick and to the husband and daughters of Sister Jennie Goldsworthy. They are in our thoughts as we pay a lasting tribute to the two sisters who have answered their final rollcall.

As Victory A. Derrick and Jennie Goldsworthy gave love and happiness during their lives, may Almighty God bestow His unceasing love upon them. Victory A. Derrick and Jennie Goldsworthy, our love is wrapped with you in the cradle of the grave.

Be it further resolved, that a copy of these resolutions be spread upon the minutes, that a copy be sent to their bereaved relatives and that a copy be sent to The Grizzly Bear Magazine.

SALLIE R. THALER,
GLADYS I. FARLEY,
GRACE DUPONT,
Committee.

Oakland, June 27, 1932.

GRIZZLY GROWLS

(CLARENCE M. HUNT.)

THE SIGN OF THE CROSS HAS, IN these United States of America, been superseded by the sign of the almighty dollar. From a God-fearing, honesty-loving nation, we have degenerated into a dollar-worshiping, dishonesty-idolizing people. Material wealth, regardless of how obtained, is today the measuring-rod of a man's worth as a citizen; moral wealth is scoffed at and frowned upon.

What we are pleased to term the "economic depression" is but the natural result of the moral decay which has penetrated every section of the country and every avenue of activity, not excepting government. As a nation, we are, in reality, but paying the inevitable price for shattering the high standards established by the founders of this republic, and for discarding the Ten Commandments as the rule of life.

Believe it or not, lasting prosperity cannot be purchased with gold, simply because the metal is emblazoned, deceptively in this year of our Lord 1932, "In God We Trust." The idols of dishonesty that have been set up in the temple of government must first be torn down and cast out, and we must, as a people, cease to worship at the dollar-throne. Honesty—right thinking, right living,—must be enthroned, or the tottering temple will become but a mass of ruins.

The frankest and most sensible comment, on the attempt to force the Federal Congress to pass the bonus bill, that has come to our attention appeared editorially in the San Francisco "Chronicle" under the caption "Let Demagogues Answer Their Bonus Army Dupes." The House of Representatives passed the bill, but it was defeated in the Senate. California voters should check the vote in both branches of the Congress on that vicious measure and ballot accordingly in November. Quoting from the editorial:

"The House knew the bonus gun was not loaded. So, in the hope of impressing veteran votes for next November, the House theatrically pointed the pistol at the heart of the Nation and pulled the trigger. Nothing—and the House knew it would be so—happened, since the Senate accepted the responsibility of safeguarding the country which the House had refused. . . . But what of the poor fellows of the bonus army, deceived by demagogue politicians and newspapers into believing a pot of bonus gold lay ready for them in Washington if they would march on the Capital and overawe Congress into handing it over?

"It is a damnable thing these demagogues have done to the bonus marchers and a damnable thing they would have done to the country had they succeeded in their design to blackjack Congress by an organized display of force. The individual veterans who marched did not, it may be assumed, understand the real meaning of their demonstration. . . . Had this demonstration succeeded it would have set a vicious and ruinous precedent. It would have opened an era in which national legislation would have ceased to be a deliberative function and votes in Congress would have recorded merely the will of whatever mob gathered outside the Capitol to demand tribute. . . . When the truth dawns on the misguided men of the bonus army they will turn their indignation upon those who so grossly deceived them and sent them on the hardships of what from the very nature of things was from the first only a fool's errand."

"There is need of revising the banking laws so as to place our banking structure on a sounder basis generally for all concerned," declares a plank in the Republican presidential campaign platform. The need is most apparent, for the inside record of this country's bigboy bankers which has been uncovered the past few months stinks like a dead mackerel rotting in the moonlight.

But, is there any possibility that the rotten conditions will be righted or that an attempt, even, will be made to correct them? The "prominent international bankers" of this nation have been proven to be bankers in name only; in practice, they are ordinary gamblers and high-powered thieves, operating within and protected by the laws of the country. The national administration and the Congress know the ruin these so-called "bankers" have wrought. No attempt, however, has been made to punish them or to curb their activities. Instead, they have been handed millions of The People's money to aid them to "carry on."

Opposing proposal to shift public-school support entirely to the state, the finance director of California is quoted as having said, "This is no time for tax revolution. It is a time for drastic economy all along the line."

How come the state administration is just now so interested in drastic economy? The depression has been depressing for some time, yet just recently salaries of state employes have been materially increased. Does the finance director imply that any legislation which would lessen the taxpayers' burden would be revolutionary? If so, then on with the revolution, for too long have the propertyowners of this state been legally robbed.

Samuel J. Hume of the "California Council on Oriental Relations," a pro-Jap organization looking longingly at yellow-dollars, is addressing various organizations in California in an endeavor to create sentiment favorable to placing Japan on a quota basis. When he cannot get an audience, he attempts to get his Jap propaganda over via letter. His argument, based on the overworked, in behalf of the Japs, theme, "Good-will is contingent upon a nice consideration of such things as pride, national honor and the like," concludes with the assurance that, if the immigration-door is opened, the Japs will spend more of their money in California.

The answer to his pleadings is, are the people of this state desirous of sacrificing this White man's paradise for a few Jap-dollars? Granting the quota means an increased influx of ineligible-to-citizenship and undesirable Asiatic aliens. We have the Exclusion Law, but through numerous evasions for which they are noted, the Japs continue to come in, and in no small numbers. Given the quota, they will come in droves, to increase the force of reservists of Japan in this country, ready to act when the opportune time comes—and it is coming soon!

Japan is not worrying about the quota, from the numerical viewpoint. The underlying motive of the agitation for it is to inveigle this country into acknowledging racial equality. That is what Japan wants most, and when that is conceded it will make other demands, among them the naturalization privilege for its nationals. Japan's "peaceful invasion" program is far reaching, but "what is a century in the life of a nation?" Advocates of the quota for Japan are aiding materially in the accomplishment of the "peaceful invasion."

California's attorney-general has ruled that rubber-stamp signatures of county officials are legal. It is well, for a great percentage of those "servants of the people" are, in reality, the agents of, and officiate in accord with the dictates of, political groups concerned only with their own welfare. The ruling, therefore, is consistent, at least.

In Whittier, Los Angeles County, the State of California owns a noted landmark, the Pico mansion. Aside from its historical and sentimental value, it is of commercial worth, in that it attracts many tourists and other visitors.

For eighteen years this property has been in possession of the state but, according to report, not a single penny has ever been expended for its upkeep, although the attention of the authorities is repeatedly being called to the need for repairs. Unless something is done NOW, this landmark will likely collapse the coming winter!

A news item, appearing in the "Lompoc Record" of June 10, is called to the attention of the California attorney-general and the Santa Barbara County district attorney. The transaction appears to be a violation of the Alien Land Law, and if so the parties should be prosecuted. There have been numerous similar transactions in Santa Barbara County, but no prosecutions. In fact, the Alien Land Law is openly violated in practically every county of the state, and seldom is an attempt made to enforce the law—another reason for putting into office those who will enforce and respect the law. Here's the item:

"Signing of a four-year lease on the 90-acre Bissinger property in the lower valley took place this week, George Nishimura being the lessee, it was reported. Under the reported terms of the lease, Nishimura will pay yearly rent of $30 per acre, and will install a water well and pipelines preliminary to the production of vegetable crops."

In an address on the conditions existant in this nation, and which seriously threaten its stability, Dr. Arthur A. Briggs of Los Angeles rightfully declared: "Our present crisis is as much a moral as a financial one and we can solve our difficulties only by the re-establishment of those kinds of life which are compatible with the qualities of true and honorable character in individual men and women, as well as in our social organizations."

"The Republican party has always stood and stands today for obedience to and enforcement of the law as the very foundation of orderly government and civilization. There can be no national security otherwise." So humorous is that plank in the Republican platform, one would imagine Will Rogers wrote it for his joke-column. A plank equally as humorous will undoubtedly appear in the Democratic platform.

Instead of enforcing the law, "as they find it enacted by the people," a vast majority of the public officials, Republicans and Democrats alike, are breakers of the law. That is why "national security" has been destructively undermined.

The greatest need of this country today is for The People to ignore the old-line parties' platforms, overflowing with buncomb designed solely to deceive them, and have a thorough house-cleaning. Begin in the garret—the national branch—and continue through to the cellar—the township branch—of government, and get rid of the overload of dishonest, incompetent, and law-breaking public officials, both Republicans and Democrats. November's the time! If there be a will to do, a way will be presented! An independent, fearless, honest, law-respecting, uncontrolled statesman is wanted as a leader! Oh, my!

"The recent disclosures made before the Senate investigating committee regarding deals in the stock of" some nationally advertised corporations, says the "Sacramento Bee" editorially,

(Continued on Page 4)

SHORES OF TAHOE

(JAMES NOBLE HATCH.)

Know you the shores of Tahoe
  Where giants grim and old
In rank and file innumerable
  Their ceaseless vigils hold?
Where fairies frolic all unseen
  On the needle-carpet deep
When darkness draws the curtains down
  And all is hushed in sleep?

Deep cradled 'mongst the mountains
  The waters rest tonight,
A snow-white mist the counterpane
  The stars a bed-time light;
And bordering the coverlid
  Scarce moving in the breeze,
The shadows of the night hang down
  In lace-like draperies.

Rare fragrance born of darkness
  Comes through the whispering pines
And wakens thoughts that long have slept
  In memory's deep confines;
Sweet melodies of ancient lore
  Strange gladsome prophesies
All mingle in the mystic night
  In silent symphonies.

And out across the placid lake
  The brilliant stars still gleam
That sang together gladsomely,
  As writ in ancient theme;
The same strange mystic pictures
  That through the ages old
In every region, land and clime
  Their wondrous tales have told.

So in the bord'ring shadows
  Amongst the friendly trees,
I visit with the peaceful night
  And learn its mysteries;
Those symphonies of silence,
  Those pictures time-extolled,
With voices ear hath ne'er discerned
  Their mystic tales unfold.

(This contribution to The Grizzly Bear is from James Noble Hatch of Pasadena, a member of Ramona Parlor No. 109 N.S.G.W.—EDITOR.)

XTH OLYMPIAD

FLAGS OF FIFTY NATIONS WILL FLUTter from the ramparts of Olympic Stadium, in Los Angeles, when President Herbert Hoover, speaking before a mixed multitude, proclaims open the games of the Xth Oympiad the afternoon of July 30. Two thousand athletes, representing the athletic prowess of every important country, will be in the line of march during the spectacular parade of nations. This will be the greatest representation ever seen at an Olympic celebration.

In keeping with the ancient Greek custom, the 1932 Olympic celebration will open with a dazzling flare of pageantry. A fanfare of trumpets will be heard, cannon will crash out the salute, the Olympic flag will rise slowly on the central mast, and a torch will blaze forth atop the massive peristyle. At the last crack of the cannon, thousands of homing pigeons will be freed to wing their way to their homes hundreds of miles away.

During the succeeding sixteen days and nights of the celebration, competitions will be held in fourteen branches of sport, namely, track and field athletics, boxing, wrestling, weight lifting, fencing, field hockey, cycling, modern pentathlon, yachting, swimming and diving, gymnastics, rowing, equestrian sports and shooting. Fine arts exhibits will also be held during the entire period of the games.

Preparations for this world event, the greatest international amateur sports celebration in history, have been under way for nearly ten years. The most elaborate plans ever made for an Olympic festival have been completed. In anticipation of the huge throngs that will overrun Los Angeles during the games, nine monster stadiums, auditoriums and water courses have been equipped with seating facilities for more than 400,000 spectators. In addition, an Olympic village has been built for the special use of the athletes, their trainers and managers. It is modern in every detail, and consists of 550 two-room houses.

The hub of the Olympic games will be Olympic Stadium, the largest structure of its kind ever built, having a reserved seating capacity of 105,000. In this great coliseum will be held the opening and closing ceremonies, track and field events, field hockey finals, gymnastics, finals of the equestrian sports, the national demonstration game of American football and the international demonstration of lacrosse.

The football game will be between a team selected from the graduating seniors of California, Stanford and Southern California, and a similar team from Yale, Harvard and Princeton. The lacrosse tournament will be between Canada, Great Britain and the United States, with the unofficial world's championship title at stake. The field hockey tournament will be featured by the world-famous team from India, which will defend the title won at Amsterdam.

Preliminaries in the equestrian events will be held at the Riviera Country Club, on the outskirts of Santa Monica, while at Long Beach Marine Stadium will be held the rowing races. This stadium has been described by rowing experts as one of the finest in the world. The yacht races will be staged at Los Angeles Harbor, off Point Firmin. At Pasadena Rose Bowl will be held the track cycling events, and at the University of California at Los Angeles the preliminaries in the field hockey tournament. The shooting events will be held at the rifle range in Elysian Park.

Nations that will participate in the games of the Xth Olympiad include: Argentine, Australia, Austria, Belgium, Bolivia, Brazil, Bulgaria, Canada, Chile, Colombia, Costa Rica, Cuba, Czechoslovakia, Denmark, Egypt, Estonia, Finland, France, Great Britain, Germany, Greece, Guatemala, Haiti, Holland, Hungary, India, Ireland, Italy, Japan, Latvia, Lithuania, Luxembourg, Mexico, Monaco, New Zealand, Norway, Peru, Philippine Islands, Poland, Portugal, Rhodesia, Roumania, Spain, Sweden, Switzerland, Turkey, Union of South Africa, United States of America, Uruguay, Yugoslavia.

INDIANS FIND FRIENDS

SOME NATIVE SONS, VISITING RECENTly at Pala Mission, had called to their attention the condition of the Indians on the reservations in San Diego County. It was claimed they were in great want, and that their plight was distressing. Believing the cause a worthy one, Ramona Parlor No. 109 N.S.G.W. of Los Angeles appointed an Indian relief committee—Past Grand President Herman C. Lichtenberger, J. Harvey McCarthy, James P. Sex and Bernard Murray—to investigate and, if the condition of the Indians was found to be as represented, to make every endeavor to secure relief for these wards from the Federal Government. The committee made a thorough investigation and found conditions among the Indians even worse than originally reported.

Since January the Federal Government has also been investigating, but to date there have been no results, other than reports, and the 2,000 Indians in California South have not been relieved to any appreciable extent. The housing conditions are terrible, in many instances the Indians living in huts, the sides of which are flattened tin cans; the floors are of dirt. The Indians have little or no covering, and their principal articles of food are ground squirrels and acorns.

There appears to be a great misunderstanding as to what the Federal Government is supposed to do for these Mission Indians. "If ever a people needed and deserved the help of the White man, the Indians of Southern California are that people," wrote a San Diegan to Ramona Parlor's committee, which has been in telegraphic communication with Washington and will make every effort to bring about a humane and satisfactory adjustment of the terrible conditions.

June 3, this telegram was sent to Senator Hiram W. Johnson: "Indians at Pala Mission, San Diego County, California, starving, living on ground squirrels and acorns. Understand Government has made apprppriation for Indians. Why no help in sight? . . . Delay means death of many children and older Indians. Please come to rescue." Senator Johnson immediately responded: "Answering yours, views set forth therein presented to Bureau Indian Affairs, recommending that needed relief be extended Indians."

June 4, the committee received from the Federal Interior Department a wire requesting a checkup with welfare workers, among them Margaret Watkins of the State Department of Social Welfare, and advising "assignment Red Cross flour authorized distributed San Diego Indians." The committee conferred, as requested, with Miss Watkins and June 10 sent this message to the Interior Department:

"Miss Watkins is long on Indian reports but short on methods to relieve hungry Indians. Red Cross distributed June third fifty-pound sack flour, which arrived April twenty-second, each family. Urgently recommend furnishing supplies consisting flour, beans and bacon at once to all Indians on reservations in San Diego County. Our investigation satisfies us Indians need help more than government investigation. Please get quick action!"

And so, the poor Indians, who have been consistently and thoroughly robbed and buffeted about from place to place for lo, these many, many years, have found friends, in their hour of direst distress, among the Native Sons of the Golden West.—C.M.H.

GRIZZLY GROWLS

(Continued from Page 3)

"may well cause the general public to wonder what chance the legitimate investor in common stocks has for his money. Apparently in many cases he has no chance at all. . . .

"There is a great deal of talk about the need for 'confidence' on the part of the public. How can the public have any confidence in the face of deals like" those which have been exposed? "How can it have any confidence when it knows that its money when invested in the common stock of a business enterprise is likely at any time to be wiped out by the speculative activities of the very men who head the enterprise and are morally responsible for the safety of the investment?"

The family payroll racket has been quite popular among members of the Federal Congress. Senator Brookhart of Iowa, for one, had, it was discovered, two sons, a daughter and two brothers on the government payroll. Just recently, Brookhart lost out in the primary. Other states would do well to follow Iowa's lead.

Several well-known citizens of the country are climbing upon the Eighteenth-Amendment-repeal bandwagon, and naturally the repeal forces are delighted. Those people have not really changed their view on the liquor question, but are concerned about their pocketbooks. Just as soon as the Federal revenue-raising bill became a law they came out "forninst" prohibition. Their taxes will be considerably increased, and they imagine that if liquor be restored, sufficient tax-revenue will come from that source to make possible repeal of the special-tax act. Some people's minds, and also their hearts, are governed and regulated by their pocketbooks!

As heretofore remarked, the liquor propaganda that is flooding the country and glutting the parties-bound press is but a smokescreen to hide the corruption that exists generally. It is a case of the small minority making a big noise. Prohibition is of minor importance! Hours are devoted to that, however, but momentous questions are given not a moment's consideration. Little wonder this country is in such a sad plight!

AWAKE, NATIVE SONS

Chester F. Gannon

(HISTORIOGRAPHER N.S.G.W.)

OUR ORDER IS FAILING IN THE VERY mission for which it was founded: To perpetuate and preserve the glories and traditions of California's past. The reason is obvious. We are not centralizing our efforts to that end. Ours is a small Order, and we can only do one line of work, and do it well. We cannot divide our energies.

Unless this generation suitably marks historical places, the coming generation will have no knowledge of their whereabouts. The drifting years have already obliterated many of the historical spots in our state which should have been marked.

The site of Fremont's camp, for instance, where he waited in the shadows of Sutter's Fort for a few days just preceding the raising of the Bear Flag at Sonoma, is lost forever. In his biography Fremont wrote concerning this particular period, "I returned to my old camp site near Sutter's Fort and awaited developments." No living man can tell us even the proximate location of that camp site. Past Grand Lewis F. Byington can testify to the difficulty of placing the monuments at the site of the Broderick-Terry duel.

The "National Geographic," under date of May 1932, gives in picture and prose a history of the State of Ohio. In this article are the preserved landmarks of that state. From an examination of the article it would appear that Ohio is far ahead of California in this work and, as far as writer knows, Ohio has no organization similar to the Native Sons. For instance, the home of the founder and father of Ohio, General Rufus Putman, is preserved within a building. The old structure is completely enclosed for preservation within a costly, modern structure. We have shown no such fealty to California's past.

True, some of the missions have been restored, and a little headway has been made in putting suitable markers at different spots, but there are hundreds of unmarked spots in California which, as the trend now goes, will never be marked. If the restoration of Sutter's Fort had not taken place when it did, it is doubtful if today such a big work would have been undertaken. At that time, the Native Sons were loyal to their trust, and since that time they have wandered away to other endeavors.

In Sacramento, the Daughters of the American Revolution have, with bronze tablets, marked the terminal of the Pony Express and the grave of Alexander Hamilton's son, who died there in the early '50s. A bank has, by a bronze marker, marked one of its early offices where millions of dollars' worth of gold dust poured through the door. Thus, other organizations have marked these sites and places while we have done little. There are a few temporary wooden markers on historical spots in Sacramento which must either be replaced soon or they will be destroyed by the elements or human vandals. Sacramento is only one spot in a state filled with traditions to preserve.

So I say, awake, Californians to your fraternal destiny! Let us do our historical work, and when that is completed we can divert our energies into other channels.

—"MARK OUR LANDMARKS"—

"A sculptor wields the chisel, and the stricken marble grows to beauty."—Bryant.

OLD SPANISH DAYS FIESTA AT SANTA BARBARA

Clifford F. Rizor

(Chairman of Publicity, Santa Barbara Parlor N.S.G.W.)

AUGUST 18, SANTA BARBARA CITY will once more don fiesta garb to celebrate its ninth annual "Old Spanish Days," and revive the custom and manner of the days when Spain ruled California. It is, in essence, a vast costume drama, performed with the blue mountains and the Spanish architecture of Santa Barbara as a backdrop, in which thousands of actors, the good people of the community, take part.

The romancer and historian tell of the glamour and romance of California in the pastoral days, but here in Santa Barbara, during this colorful fiesta, they live again. In the moving panorama of parade and pageant a glimpse is once more afforded of the days "before the Gringos came," when the Conestoga wagon and the crack of the stage driver's whip were sight and sound of an alien world, a new world fast encroaching upon the gentler graces and slower tempo of the old. Hubert Howe Bancroft, premier historian of California, speaks of the Spanish period as being the golden age, and defines the spirit of the time in these words: "Never before or since was there a spot in America where life was a long, happy holiday, where there was less labor, less care or trouble, such as the old time golden age under Cronos or Saturn, the gathering of nature's fruits being the chief burden of life, and death coming without decay, like a gentle sleep."

So it is the intent of the "Old Spanish Days" Committee to recreate, for a few short days, the life and atmosphere and historic background of the old romantic age. As the social life of old Santa Barbara centered about the historic mission, so the activities of the fiesta are ushered in with appropriate ceremonies at that famous old church.

The historic parade is one of the most brilliant and colorful pageants in the world. All of the various phases are as historically authentic as possible, and the costumes and equipments are designed only after the most painstaking research, to accurately portray the time they are intended to represent. One may see Cabrillo, with his ship's company; Viscaino, who gave Santa Barbara its name, in company with his sailors and men-at-arms; Bouchard, the pirate of black deeds and ill repute; Portola, accompanied by the illustrious Junipero Serra, the one following the path of conquest, the other the high calling of his faith. The equestrian division is worth traveling miles to see, more than a thousand of California's finest horses appearing. Marching to the strains of that famous old song of the covered-wagon days, "Oh Susanna," appear a group wearing the blue uniform of the pre-Civil War era, the vanguard of Captain Fremont's troops, marching into Santa Barbara just as they did so many years ago. They are followed by stagecoaches, oxcarts, covered wagons, tallyhos and all manner of horse-drawn equipment used in the early days of Santa Barbara.

The pageant, "Romantic California," is another magnificent feature of "Old Spanish Days." Written and directed by Charles E. Pressley and performed nightly in Peabody Stadium, it is a vivid portrayal of life in old Santa Barbara, full of music and gaiety and the carefree spirit of the time. The various episodes of Santa Barbara's history make an unbroken panorama.

The grand officers of the Order of Native Sons of the Golden West will be Santa Barbara's guests during "Old Spanish Days," and as a feature of the program will dedeicate the city's new million-dollar Eastside junior high school. Reina del Mar Parlor No. 126 N.D.G.W. is cooperating with the Native Sons in arranging for the dedication, as well as in plans for participation in other events of the fiesta.

OLD SPANISH DAYS 1931 PARADE ENTRIES.
COURT HOUSE TOWER (center left). SANTA BARBARA MISSION (lower left).

The Ruiz-Botello pageant, enacted in the sunken gardens of the Santa Barbara County Court House, is a beautiful music and dancing sequence in which many descendants of pioneer families take part. Director Maclovio A. Botello is an old-time member of Santa Barbara Parlor No. 116 N.S.G.W. No "Old Spanish Days" program is complete without this famous group of dancers. As midnight of the last day of the fiesta approaches troubadours and serenaders go about the streets strumming guitars and singing "Adios, adios, amores." It is a beautiful gesture of farewell to the many friends and visitors in Santa Barbara.

Upon a wall of the supervisors' room in the Santa Barbara County Court House appear these words, "Felicidad y pesos." It seems, even in the old Spanish days, that happiness and dollars were the two essential elements; yet it was evidently possible to achieve happiness without the possession of great wealth. Everything moved in the easy manner of the time, unhurried and carefree. For us, in the modern commercial scheme, it is hard to realize that "manana por la manana" was then the rule of life. Yet it is possible to see, in "Old Spanish Days," how one might forget cares, enter into the joyous spirit of the dance, and while away the hours of day into night.

And so, Santa Barbara extends an invitation to all to be present during this fiesta. To all Native Sons and Native Daughters she says, "Put on your Spanish costume and help us celebrate." To the world she says, "There is no other celebration like 'Old Spanish Days.' The greater part of all entertainment is free. It is for all the people of California and for all the world. Come and enjoy it!"

GRAVE CALIFORNIA PIONEER HERO MARKED WITH TABLET.

Elk Grove (Sacramento County)—At rites sponsored by Liberty Parlor No. 213 N.D.G.W., a bronze plaque was May 29 unveiled above the grave of John P. Rhoads at Slough House. The plaque, presented by Mrs. Sadie Winn-Brainard of Califia Parlor No. 22 N.D.G.W. (Sacramento), reads: "In memory of John P. Rhoads, who carried Naomi Pike from Donner Lake over forty miles of snow down to Sutter's Fort. Dedicated May 29, 1932, by Liberty Parlor No. 213 N.D.G.W."

Guy Foulks presided, Mrs. Brainard presented the plaque, and it was accepted by President Louisa Krull of Liberty Parlor. The Elk Grove high school orchestra, directed by Earle Nicholls, rendered selections, and community singing was led by Carol Latson. Pic Rhoads, son of John P. Rhoads, related the history of his hero-father.

The main address was delivered by Miss Esther R. Sullivan, Past Grand President N.D.G.W. She spoke interestingly of the California Pioneers, with particular reference to Mrs. Naomi Pike-Schenck—now 89 years of age and residing at The Dalles, Oregon State,—the 3-year-old member of the Reed-Donner Party who was carried to safety across the Sierra snows by John P. Rhoads in 1847.

[The Reed-Donner Party tragedy has heretofore been fully related in The Grizzly Bear. Among the original members of that party were 19-year-old Mrs. Harriet F. Pike, her husband and two children. Her husband was killed enroute. Mrs. Pike was one of the "Forlorn Hope" that left Donner Lake to seek relief for the party December 16, 1846; they reached Johnson's Ranch January 17, 1847. John P. Rhoads, a member of the first relief, promised Mrs. Pike he would bring out her children, and he returned with Naomi, her infant daughter having perished while she was seeking relief. At Sutter Fort, in 1847, Mrs. Pike was wedded to M. C. Nye, and for some time the family resided near Marysville, Yuba County, at that time known as Nye's Ranch. John P. Rhoads was not a member of the Reed-Donner Party. He was born in Kentucky, October 5, 1815, and arrived in California in 1846. He first settled near what is now Wheatland, Yuba County, and later went to the Slough House district of Sacramento County, where he died December 20, 1866.—Editor.]

Know your home-state, California! Learn of its past history and of its present-day development by reading regularly The Grizzly Bear. $1.50 for one year (12 issues). Subscribe now.

Native Sons of the Golden West

SAN FRANCISCO—THE BOARD OF Grand Officers met June 4, in attendance being Grand President Seth Millington, who presided, Grand First Vice Justice Emmet Seawell, Grand Second Vice Chas. A. Koenig, Grand Third Vice Harmon D. Skillin, Grand Secretary John T. Regan, Grand Trustees Jesse H. Miller, Eldred L. Meyer, John M. Burnett, Henry S. Lyon, Joseph J. McShane, Horace J. Leavitt and Charles H. Spengemann. Much routine business was transacted.

Letters of appreciation for the resolutions, pertaining to the naval appropriation bill of the Fèderal Congress, adopted at the Stockton Grand Parlor were received from Rear Admiral T. J. Senn, Rear Admiral W. C. Colé and F. B. Upham, chief of the Navy Department's navigation bureau.

It was ordered that the funds bequeathed the Grand Parlor by the late Senator James D. Phelan (Pacific No. 10) be left in the banks in which now deposited.

Joseph B. Keenan (Niantic No. 105) and Grand Second Vice Koenig were nominated for election as directors of the San Francisco Hall Association, to represent the Grand Parlor's holdings therein.

At the request of Castro No. 232 (San Francisco), a letter of thanks was ordered sent W. K. Kellogg for his gift of a 700-acre Orange County ranch and Arabian horses, together with a maintenance fund, to the people of California and the University of California.

The petition of James Lick No. 242 (San Francisco) to consolidate with Castro No. 232 (San Francisco) was favorably considered, and Grand President Millington authorized the consolidation.

Following the Stockton Grand Parlor, Grand President Millington communicated with members of the Order in various cities regarding the selection of a place for the holding of this year's Admission Day, September 9, celebration. As a result, Thomas M. Foley (Pacific No. 10) urged that San Francisco be selected. It being necessary to consult the Parlors of that city, a motion prevailed that full power to act in the matter be delegated to the Grand President. At a meeting June 10 of the San Francisco Extension of the Order Committee, the suggestion was received favorably, and therefore the statewide celebration will be held in San Francisco.

Grand President Millington, in accordance with a resolution adopted at the Stockton Grand Parlor, assigned the Subordinate Parlor visiting districts as follows:

No. 1, Grand Trustee Eldred L. Meyer—Bakersfield No. 42, Los Angeles No. 45, San Diego No. 108, Ramona No. 109, Arrowhead No. 110, Santa Barbara No. 116, Hollywood No. 196, Long Beach No. 239, Sepulveda No. 263, Glendale No. 264, Santa Ana No. 265, Cahuenga No. 268.

No. 2, Grand Trustee John M. Burnett—Mission No. 38, Fremont No. 44, Watsonville No. 65, Monterey No. 75, Santa Cruz No. 90, Santa Lucia No. 97, Santa Clara No. 100, Gabilan No. 132, San Miguel No. 150, Observatory No. 177, Menlo No. 185, Mountain View No. 215, Palo Alto No. 216, Pleasanton No. 244, Niles No. 250.

No. 3, Grand First Vice Justice Emmet Seawell—Sacramento No. 3, Sunset No. 26, Elk Grove No. 41, Alameda No. 47, Las Positas No. 96, Eden No. 113, Piedmont No. 120, Halcyon No. 146, Brooklyn No. 151, Cambria No. 152, Carquinez No. 205, Berkeley No. 210, Claremont No. 240, Sutter Fort No. 241, Fruitvale No. 252, Santa Monica Bay No. 267.

No. 4, Grand Second Vice Chas. A. Koenig—Stockton No. 7, Solano No. 39, El Dorado No. 52, Napa No. 62, Bay City No. 104, Courtland No. 106, Alcalde No. 154, Nicasio No. 183, Tracy No. 186, Athens No. 195, El Capitan No. 222, Estudillo No. 223, Guadalupe No. 231, Balboa No. 234, El Carmelo No. 256.

No. 5, Grand Third Vice Harmon D. Skillin—California No. 1, Lodi No. 18, Yosemite No. 24, Fresno No. 25, San Francisco No. 49, Oakland No. 50, Mount Tamalpais No. 64, Stanford No. 76, Calistoga No. 86, Niantic No. 105, Selma No. 107, Madera No. 130, Lower Lake No. 159, Dolores No. 208, Galt No. 243, Diamond No. 246.

No. 6, Grand Trustee Jesse H. Miller—Pacific No. 10, Modesto No. 11, Golden Gate No. 29, Saint Helena No. 53, National No. 118, Chispa No. 139, Sebastopol No. 143, Tuolumne No. 144, South San Francisco No. 157, Byron No. 170, Orestimba No. 247, Columbia No. 258, Bret Harte No. 260, Utopia No. 270, Manteca No. 271.

No. 7, Grand Trustee Joseph J. McShane—San Jose No. 22, General Winn No. 32, Redwood No. 66, Ukiah No. 71, Seaside No. 95, Mount Diablo No. 101, Broderick No. 117, Hesperian No. 137, Sequoia No. 160, Olympus No. 189, Alder Glen No. 200, Marshall No. 202, Pebble Beach No. 230, Castro No. 232, Industrial City No. 269.

No. 8, Grand Trustee Charles H. Spengemann—Petaluma No. 27, Santa Rosa No. 28, Woodland No. 30, Rincon No. 72, Vallejo No. 77, Glen Ellen No. 102, Sonoma No. 111, Wisteria No. 127, Oakdale No. 142, Sea Point No. 158, Washington No. 169, Precita No. 187, Presidio No. 194, Twin Peaks No. 214.

No. 9, Grand Trustee Henry S. Lyon—Amador No. 17, Excelsior No. 31, Ione No. 38, Plymouth No. 48, Hydraulic No. 56, Quartz No. 58, Auburn No. 59, Silver Star No. 63, Granite No. 83, Mount Bally No. 87, Georgetown No. 91, Downieville No. 92, Golden Nugget No. 94, Honey Lake No. 198, Rocklin No. 233.

No. 10, Grand Trustee Horace J. Leavitt—Marysville No. 6, Argonaut No. 8, Placerville No. 9, Humboldt No. 14, Arcata No. 20, Chico No. 21, Rainbow No. 40, Colusa No. 69, Ferndale No. 93, Quincy No. 131, McCloud No. 149, Etna No. 192, Big Valley No. 211, Plumas No. 228, Sutter No. 261.

Special—Cabrillo No. 114, Donner No. 162, Golden Anchor No. 182, Liberty No. 193, Richmond No. 217, Concord No. 245.

The Board of Grand Trustees organized by the election of Jesse H. Miller as chairman, and Eldred L. Meyer as secretary.

School Dedicated.

Saint Helena—Under the auspices of Saint Helena No. 53 and in the presence of an assemblage of 700, the grand officers June 10 dedicated the new Saint Helena union high school. A splendid program was presented. President Paul R. Alexander of the board of school trustees extended greetings, and addresses were delivered by Grand President Seth Millington and Grand Third Vice Harmon D. Skillin.

The dedicatory ceremonies were conducted by Grand President Millington, Past Grand Charles L. Dodge, Grand Second Vice Chas. A. Koenig, Grand Third Vice Skillin, Grand Trustee Joseph J. McShane and Grand Secretary John T. Regan. As this was graduation day at the school, the Grand President was accorded the honor of presenting diplomas to the graduates, who were introduced by Principal T. B. Street.

Oldtimers Given Badges.

Auburn—A large number of oldtimers, former or present residents of Placer County, were guests June 12 of Auburn No. 59 and Auburn No. 233 N.D.G.W. at a picnic. Sheriff Elmer Gum and Mayor Jack Walsh had charge of the luncheon, and Mildred Macy and Herbert Merrow headed the committee that arranged the program. P. W. Smith was the toastmaster, and the principal speaker was Past Grand Dr. Louise C. Heilbron, who said "We must see that no pioneer heroes are left unknown."

Miss Onetta Walsh presented badges to J. W. Burner of Auburn and Mrs. F. A. Stone of Oakland, the oldest man and woman in attendance. Burner, a Placer County resident since 1891, was born June 12, 1847, in Sacramento County, the son of A. Burner, who came to California aboard a sailing vessel in 1844. Mrs. Stone, born in Connecticut in 1848, arrived in Placer County with her parents, Mr. and Mrs. C. L. Slade, in 1856, and resided continuously in Auburn until 1913.

Drum Corps Captain Surprised.

San Rafael—Officers of Mount Tamalpais No. 64 were elected June 6, Monroe E. Petersen being selected for president. Installation will be held jointly with Marinita No. 198 N.D.G.W. The forty-seventh institution anniversary of the Parlor was celebrated June 20 with an entertainment and banquet following the initiation of a large class of candidates. This initiation concluded the membership contest between the present officers, the past presidents and the "scrubs."

Manuel A. Andrade recently retired as the captain of Mount Tamalpais' drum and bugle corps, and on behalf of the members of the corps was presented, by Drum Major M. E. Soares, with a beautifully engraved emblematic gold ring. Captain Andrade was tireless in devotion to the interests of the corps which, in its comparatively brief career, has won many trophies and received much praise for its efficiency. He was so completely surprised by the gift of appreciation that he was actually speechless. Jas. Foster succeeds him as captain of the corps.

Hears of "Conditions of the Day."

San Bernardino—Tamar McGarvey was elected president of Arrowhead No. 110 June 1. State Senator Tallant Tubbs of Presidio No. 194 (San Francisco) addressed the Parlor on "Conditions of the Day" June 8. A basket picnic at Sylvan Park, Redlands, June 15 was arranged for by a committee composed of Grand Organist Leslie Maloche (chairman), Gordon Lee, Henry Peake, John Andreson Jr., Robert Reeder, Walter Harris, Jerry Doyle, T. J. Sawyer, Ralph Frederickson and Fred Kramer.

June 18 the Parlor had its fifth annual steak supper at Doyle's ranch. June 29 several candidates were initiated, and final arrangements were made for the annual Fourth of July barbecue.

Sonoma Outing.

Sonoma—Sonoma No. 111 and Sonoma No. 209 N.D.G.W. will hold their annual barbecue and dance July 17. An entertainment feature will be a baseball game between the team of Castro No. 232 (San Francisco) and the local club. Charles Bacigalupi and Emily Providenty head the Parlors' arrangements committees.

Eight candidates were initiated by Sonoma No. 111, June 20, the ritual being exemplified by a team from Fruitvale No. 252 (Oakland). A banquet followed the ceremonies.

Marker Dedicated.

Redding—A marker—a copper plate embedded in a five-ton boulder—to designate the site, two miles north of Anderson, where the old California-Oregon trail deviated from the present highway, was dedicated May 23 by McCloud No. 149 and Hiawatha No. 140 N.D.G.W. The site was deeded to McCloud by Mr. and Mrs. Grover E. Oaks.

Benefit Draws Large Crowd.

Monterey—A large crowd attended the card party and dance given jointly by Monterey No. 75 and Junipero No. 141 N.D.G.W. for the benefit of the homeless children. W. W. Rodehaver was chairman of the general arrangements committee.

Calistoga Home-coming.

Calistoga—Calistoga No. 86 is sponsoring a home-coming celebration for the latter part of September. All former residents will be requested to attend, and a program is being arranged for their entertainment. Plans are also under way for a ritual contest, between the "old guard" and the "kids" of the Parlor, to be held in the fall.

Membership Standing Largest Parlors.

San Francisco—Grand Secretary John T. Regan reports the standing of the Subordinate Parlors having a membership of over 400 January 1, 1932, as follows, together with their membership figures June 15, 1932:

Parlor.	Jan. 1	June 15	Gain	Loss
Ramona No. 109	1088	1082	....	6
South San Francisco No. 157	822	808	....	14
Castro No. 232	700	716	16	....
Stanford No. 76	614	608	....	6
Arrowhead No. 110	609	595	....	14
Twin Peaks No. 214	585	558	....	27
Stockton No. 7	549	549	....	....
Piedmont No. 120	523	521	....	2
Rincon No. 72	448	439	....	9

Parlor To Be Instituted.

Los Banos—Through the efforts of Deputy Grand President Al Lobree, a parlor is to be instituted here by Grand President Seth Millington July 9, and indications now are that there will be at least seventy charter members. Robt.

Pucinelli will be president, L. E. Sarbo recording secretary and Frank Pimental financial secretary. The people of the town generally are giving every encouragement, and this promises to become a large and influential unit of the Order.

This is going to be a big night in Los Banos, according to Deputy Grand President Lobree, who urges all Parlors to be represented and to bring along their drum corps. The townspeople are donating liberally the necessaries for a feast, so there will be plenty to eat. Stockton No. 7 will exemplify the ritual.

Plaque Presented County.

Placerville—A George Washington memorial plaque, presented to El Dorado County by Placerville No. 9 and Marguerite No. 12 N.D.G.W. in recognition of the bicentennial, was unveiled in the lobby of the county court house June 15. Grand Trustee Henry S. Lyon presided, Grand President Seth Millington made the presentation address, and Judge George H. Thompson accepted the gift on the county's behalf. A program of entertainment followed.

Placerville had an informal reception for Grand Trustee Lyon May 24, and on the Parlor's behalf President George M. Smith presented him with a token of esteem. Lyon, who is district attorney of El Dorado County, responded fittingly.

Flag Day Observed.

San Diego—San Diego No. 108 sponsored a unique program at the plaza in Old Town in observance of Flag Day, June 14. The flags of three nations—Spain, Mexico and the United States of America—and also that of the State of California were raised as the national airs of each country were played by the marine band. Deputy Grand President Albert V. Mayrhofer was chairman of the day, and appropriate addresses were delivered by Colonel D. C. Collier, Armando C. Amador, Judge Eugene Daney Jr. and Mayor John F. Forward Jr.

June 10, also at the Old Town plaza, the San Diegans placed the thirty-second of a series of markers indicating the many historic sites throughout San Diego City. The marker reads: "Plaza San Diego Viejo: established as the first Mexican Pueblo in California, 1834. Taken by American Forces under Capt. Ezekiel Merritt late in November, 1846, when the Mexican flag was cut down by Senora Maria Antonia Machado de Selvas and the American flag raised and nailed to the flag pole under enemy fire by Albert B. Smith.' Speakers included Edward Bernard, George W. Marston, David Millan, D. W. Campbell and Albert V. Mayrhofer.

Chain Demon Fire!

San Francisco—The Grand Parlor Forestry and Conservation Committee, Southard M. Modry secretary, has directed a letter to all Subordinate Parlors requesting them to co-operate with the United States Forest Service and the State Division of Forestry in the campaign to reduce forest fire losses. It is urged that open meetings, devoted entirely to the cause, be held, and that county boards of supervisors be petitioned to adopt a suggested uniform fire ordinance.

All members of the Order are urged to assist in the attempt to "Chain Demon Fire! Do your bit to protect and conserve our natural resources, particularly our forests and wild life."

River Excursion.

Sacramento—Sacramento No. 3 sponsored a Sacramento River excursion the night of June 18 and it was greatly enjoyed by a large crowd. The arrangements committee included Jos. Fitzhenry (chairman), June Longshore, Lew Wallace, Irving Beale, Frank Didion, John Majors, Angie Nicolosi, Billy Nesbitt, Marshall Crabb, Carter Pressey, Joe Hellinge Jr., A. M. Mull Jr.

Officers of the Parlor will be installed jointly with those of La Bandera No. 110 N.D.G.W. the early part of July. Jos. Fitzhenry, president-elect of No. 3, will be the chairman of the evening.

Oldtime Picnic.

Oakland—Members of Claremont No. 240 and Argonaut No. 166 N.D.G.W., their families and friends gathered at Valente Park in Contra Costa County for a real oldtime picnic June 21. A baseball game, races and dancing furnished amusement. Officers of Claremont, with Louis Cambet as president, will be installed early in July by District Deputy Victor Raible. The Parlor is looking forward to a successful term.

Entertained With Songs.

Santa Ana—Santa Ana No. 265 was delightfully entertained with a program of songs June 20 by three San Jacinto young women—Marion

(Continued on Page 11)

CALIFORNIA HAPPENINGS OF FIFTY YEARS AGO

Thomas R. Jones

(COMPILED EXPRESSLY FOR THE GRIZZLY BEAR.)

JULY 4, 1882, THE ONE HUNDRED AND sixth anniversary of the signing of the Declaration of Independence of the United States of America was patriotically celebrated throughout California with parades and elaborate displays of fireworks. The weather was extremely hot, thermometers in shaded spots of the valleys going above 100 degrees. The Fourth coming on a Tuesday, a four-day holiday, beginning Saturday, the 1st, was observed generally.

In the parade at Sacramento City, fifty-four members of the Society of California Pioneers, in hacks placarded "The '49ers," were followed by a delegation, afoot, from Sacramento Parlor No. 3 N.S.G.W.

Fred M. Dickerson, firing a salute at Saint Helena, Napa County, had one hand blown away, and James Saultry, a guard at San Quentin, lost both hands while firing the sunrise salute. Rev. F. G. M. Fenn of California Parlor No. 1 N.S.G.W. (San Francisco) delivered the Fourth oration at Cloverdale, Sonoma County; in the evening he went bathing in the Russian River and was drowned.

A cloudburst July 1 in Tejon Canyon caused a fifteen-minute flood which wrought great damage. An Indian rancheria was swept away by a twenty-five-foot-high wall of water and many of the Indians were drowned.

Beginning July 20, Siskiyou County had a series of destructive thunder storms during which eight inches of rain fell. Growing crops were severely damaged.

The season's wheat crop was now estimated at 29,000,000 centals valued, at prevailing prices, at $50,000,000. There were 3,249,000 acres in grain. The yield was larger than in 1880, but smaller than in 1881.

A reunion of the survivors of the ship "Pharsalie," which arrived at San Francisco July 23, 1849, was held. But eight responded to the call.

To build a high school at Auburn, Placer County, Jo Hamilton headed the subscription list with a lot and $500 in cash.

Seven ships arrived this month from Chinese ports, bringing 5,473 more Chinamen to swell the horde coming to California before the restriction act could be put into effect.

A convention of hydraulic miners at Nevada City July 22 was attended by 175 delegates. Resolutions were passed favoring the construction of debris restraining dams on the Yuba River and other streams, and preparations were made to fight the farmers in the courts.

Ten business houses of Smartsville, Yuba County, burned July 17 and one citizen lost his life; the monetary loss was $20,000. Fresno City had a fire July 24 that consumed thirty-five buildings, causing a $300,000 loss.

The Colusa House, built in Colusa City in 1851, was partially destroyed by fire July 28; loss $6,000. The Olive Branch Hotel at Berkeley, Alameda County, burned July 6; loss $7,000.

At Nevada City July 25 thè dwelling of J. H. Boardman was burned and his sons, Edward and Carter, aged, respectively, 8 and 6, were cremated while asleep.

At San Jose, Santa Clara County, July 6 fire destroyed the Lick Mills, built in 1855, partially of mahogany, by the Pioneer philanthropist James Lick. The loss was estimated at $100,000

The vaults at Carmel Mission, Monterey County, containing the remains of Padre Junipero Serra and three other priests were opened July 3 and the coffins were identified. The plate stated Padre Serra died August 28, 1784. Above his coffin was that of Father Julian Lopez, who died in 1803. The coffins, made of redwood, were in an excellent state of preservation. That of Padre Serra was not opened nor removed.

John Sullivan, who came overland to California in 1844, was employed at Sutter fort (Sacramento) in 1846, and in 1850 went to San Francisco, where he invested in real estate and accumulated a fortune, died at the latter place July 30.

In boring a well at Cloverdale, Sonoma County, the auger, at a depth of forty feet, went through a white pine log. Six feet further down the auger contacted a tree, standing upright, and the boring ceased.

July 13 two attempts were made to rob the La Porte, Sierra County, and Marysville, Yuba County, stage. In the morning, near Strawberry Valley, the express guard, G. M. Hackett, responded with a volley of buckshot to a masked man's command to halt; the robber returned the fire and ran away. In the afternoon, near Forbestown, the stage was again commanded to halt, and the guard and the robber fired simultaneously; the latter again escaped.

A pavilion constructed atop Telegraph Hill, San Francisco, was thrown open July 4 and the cable streetcar line began operation. The pavilion, circular in shape, was surrounded by a balcony from which visitors had a grand view.

John Ballou and his son had an altercation July 7 with a Chinaman in Visalia, Tulare County. The Chink drew a pistol and killed Ballou, the father of fifteen children. The lad then procured a knife and ended the murderer's existence.

J. B. Kaiser of Antioch, Contra Costa County, became insanely jealous. July 11 he shot and dangerously wounded his wife and a young man in his employ, and then drowned himself.

An Italian gardener near Oroville, Butte County, became weary of having his garden raided repeatedly and set a watch. The night of July 2 he shot and killed a Chinaman.

George Gift, aged 18, was killed near Calistoga, Napa County, July 12 by the accidental discharge of his shotgun.

L. B. Tucker, at Grimes, Colusa County, went blind in January, and July 28 cut his throat and died. He was the third brother to commit suicide.

Wm. K. McClintlock, aged 18, attempting to ford the Klamath River in Siskiyou County, was thrown from his horse and drowned July 20.

Hiram Mariner, a sawmill employe, was accidentally killed July 5 near Nevada City.

Frank L. Griswold, aged 17, fell from a load of hay in Yolo County July 5 and his head was crushed under a wheel of the wagon.

OLD DESERTED HOUSE

(JEANETTE NORLAND.)

What can be more mournful
Than an old deserted house,
With its shutters and its doorways all awry
Its ceilings full of cobwebs
And its floors all thick with dust.
It somehow makes you want to sit and cry.

Yet here, in years gone by,
A young husband brought his bride,
And here they raised a group of girls and boys.
But sickness took its toll,
Things went from bad to worse;
And grim despair sapped all their hopes and joys.

And so the place is left
To revert to Mother Earth.
For, when loving hands remove their tender care,
All the ravages of time—
All the agents of decay,
Cooperate to leave a ruin there.

(This contribution to The Grizzly Bear is from Jeanette Norland of Los Angeles City.—Editor.)

"When sorrows come, they come not single spies, but in battalions."—Shakespeare.

Passing of the California Pioneer

(Confined to Brief Notices of the Demise of Those Men and Women Who Came to California Prior to 1860.)

MRS. NANCY AUBERY-HELLYER, native of Missouri, 100; crossed the plains to California in 1850 and after three years' residence in El Dorado County settled in Santa Clara County; died at Los Gatos, survived by three children. She was reputed to have been the first White woman to settle in the Edenvale district of the Santa Clara Valley.

James Tweedy, 88; came across the plains in 1852; died at Los Angeles City.

Mrs. Rhoda McAlister, native of Ohio, 89; came in 1853 and in 1860 settled in Humboldt County; died at Waddington, survived by four children.

Mrs. Ellen Neary-Nolan, native of Ireland, 98; came via Cape Horn in 1855 and in 1860 settled in Santa Cruz City, where she died; a daughter survives.

Father John M. Cassin, native of New York, 85; came in 1856; died at Santa Rosa, Sonoma County, where for forty-two years he was connected with Saint Rose's church, which he built.

Mrs. Mary Parlee Ross-Welch, native of Arkansas, 85; came across the plains in 1857 and settled in Shasta County; died at Anderson, survived by five children.

Mrs. Annie Landers-Walton, native of Pennsylvania, 74; since 1859 Tuolumne County resident; died at Sonora, survived by a husband.

Charles M. Dougherty, native of Mississippi; came across the plains in 1850 and resided in Sacramento and Alameda Counties; died at Dublin, survived by two children.

Mrs. Eliza Woodworth-Wilson, native of Ohio, 89; came across the plains in 1853 and settled in Sonoma County; died at San Francisco, survived by two sons.

Mrs. Nancy Johnson-Greeley, native of Quebec, 91; came via the Isthmus of Panama in 1854 and settled in El Dorado County; died near Placerville, survived by two children.

Mrs. Mary Jane Goodin, native of Missouri, 89; came across the plains in 1856 and for many years resided in Colusa County; died at Bellflower, Los Angeles County, survived by four children.

Mrs. Gatsy Rebecca Bailey-Robertson, native of South Carolina, 79; came across the plains in 1857 and resided in Stanislaus and Tulare Counties; died at Visalia, survived by a husband.

Charles R. Nauert, native of New York, 91; came in 1857 and the following year settled in Alvarado, Alameda County, where he died; five children survive.

Amzi V. Bush, native of Ohio, 81; came in 1859; died at Davis, Yolo County, survived by five children.

OLD TIMERS PASS

(Brief Notices of the Demise of Men and Women who came to California in the '60s.)

Mrs. Nancy Olilah Moon-Witcher, native of Iowa, 78; came in 1860; died at Salinas, Monterey County.

Cassius Warren Crawford, 78; came in 1860; died at Pacific Grove, Monterey County, survived by three children. For many years he farmed in Fresno County.

Mrs. Lillie Newton-Lockie, native of Oregon, 72; since 1861 Suisun Valley resident; died at Fairfield, Solano County, survived by a son.

Maxmillian William Muller, native of Iowa, 72; came in 1861; died at Red Bluff, Tehama County, survived by four children.

Mrs. Jennie Taylor-Waterman, native of Pennsylvania, 82; since 1861 resident Santa Cruz City, where she died; four children survive.

Mrs. Matilda Ann Collins-Fowler, native of Missouri, 75; came in 1862; died at Porterville, Tulare County, survived by two children. For some time she resided in Stanislaus County.

Mrs. Jennie Miller-Simpson, native of Iowa, 78; came in 1863; died in Scotts Valley, Lake County, survived by three children.

James K. Polk Rader, native of Arkansas, 87; came in 1864; died at Chino, San Bernardino County, survived by a daughter, Lilly McDonald (Ontario Parlor No. 251 N.D.G.W.).

William Casper Heffelfinger, native of Louisiana, 75; since 1864 Shasta County resident; died at Redding, survived by three children.

Mrs. Rachel Jane Dickson, native of Vermont, 90; came in 1865; died at San Rafael, Marin County, survived by four children.

Charles W. Lucas, native of Iowa, 77; came in 1865; died at Weimar, Placer County.

Mrs. Melvina Josephine Jory-Gilstrap, native of Illinois, 70; came in 1866; died at San Luis Obispo City, survived by a husband and two sons. For many years she resided in Yuba County.

Albert W. Hook, native of Maine, 76; came in 1866; died at Balboa, Orange County, survived by a wife and two sons.

Mrs. Elizabeth Claraty, native of Pennsylvania, 85; came in 1868; died at San Francisco, survived by five children.

Selwyn L. Shaw, native of Vermont, 83; since 1868 resident Ventura City, where he died; four children survive.

Mrs. Astoria Campbell-Makinney, native of Iowa, 87; came in 1867 and following a residence of six years in El Dorado County settled in Santa Cruz City, where she died; two children survive.

Mrs. Eldora Goings-Rannels, native of Iowa, 70; came in 1863; died at Corning, Tehama County, survived by eight children.

Mrs. Nancy Bonham-Jackson, native of Illinois, 75; came in 1864 and long resided in Napa County; died at Oakland, Alameda County, survived by six daughters.

Mrs. Jennie Spillman-Foster, native of Michigan, 80; came in 1865 and long resided in Yuba County; died at Fontana, San Bernardino County, survived by six children.

Mrs. Agnes McCullough, native of New Brunswick, 90; came in 1865 and resided in Humboldt and Kern Counties until 1887, when she took up her residence in Los Angeles City, where she died; a son, W. B. McCullough (Humboldt Parlor No. 14 N.S.G.W.) of Los Angeles, survives.

"It is only by labor that thought can be made healthy, and only by thought that labor can be made happy; and the two cannot be separated with impunity."—Ruskin.

PIONEER NATIVES DEAD

(Brief Notices of the Demise of Men and Women born in California Prior to 1860.)

Francisco Soto, born in Santa Cruz County in 1857, died May 21 at Santa Cruz City survived by a son.

Miss Josephine M. Robinson, born in Yolo County in 1859, died May 23 near Winters.

Mrs. Mary Lawley-Patten, born in Napa County in 1855, died May 24 at Mount Saint Helena survived by a son.

Charles C. Crane, born in Marin County in 1856, died May 25 at San Francisco survived by two children.

William Henry Toland, born in Butte County in 1856, died May 25 at Oroville survived by a son.

Frank Joseph Solinsky, born in Tuolumne County in 1857, died May 28 at Merced City survived by a wife and three sons.

Mrs. Sarah Ann Sharpe, born in Placer County in 1855, died May 28 at San Carlos, San Mateo County, survived by four daughters.

Judge Henry Victor Alvarado, born in Alameda County in 1857, died May 30 at Richmond, Contra Costa County, survived by a wife and two daughters. He was a son of Juan Bautista Alvarado, Mexican governor of California, 1836-1842. At the time of his death he was superior judge of Contra Costa County and had previously served that county as district attorney.

Edward F. Gartland, born in Shasta County in 1857, died May 30 at San Francisco.

Mrs. Samantha Frame-Farrell, born in El Dorado County in 1850, died May 30 at Berkeley, Alameda County, survived by four children.

Mrs. Mary L. Harper, born in Santa Clara County in 1856, died May 31 at Alameda City survived by seven children.

Mrs. Mary Crone-Hern, born at Sacramento City in 1855, died there June 2 survived by a husband and three children.

James J. Dolan, born in San Mateo County in 1858, died June 4 at Vallejo, Solano County, survived by a wife.

Mrs. Carrie Vanderhoof, born at Sonora, Tuolumne County, in 1858, died there June 5 survived by a husband and five children. She was affiliated with Dardanelle Parlor No. 66 N.D.G.W.

Louis Narvaez, born at San Jose, Santa Clara County, in 1858, died there June 5 survived by five children. He was a descendant of Augustine Narvaez, who settled in the Santa Clara Valley in 1792.

Mrs. Julia Barbour-Collins, born in Solano County in 1857, died June 6 at Tracy, San Joaquin County, survived by two sons.

Mrs. Fannie S. Sinsheimer, born at Sacramento City in 1855, died June 6 at San Francisco survived by two children.

Mrs. Louise Granger-Hays, born at Los Angeles City in 1851, died June 7 at Sacramento City survived by four children. She was a daughter of Judge Lewis Cass Granger, California Pioneer of 1847, an early-day jurist and legislator.

(Continued on Page 15)

Native Daughters of the Golden West

DR. VICTORY A. DERRICK, PAST Grand President, passed away May 31 at her Oakland home. She was born at Chinese Camp, Tuolumne County, in 1871, and was affiliated with Aloha Parlor No. 106 (Oakland). In 1893 she graduated from the University of California Medical School, and until just recently was most active in Native Daughter affairs. Surviving are two daughters—Mrs. Charles K. Gamble of Melbourne, Australia, and Mrs. James de St. Maurice of Oakland (Aloha N.D.).

Dr. Derrick was chosen Grand President at the Thirty-fifth (San Francisco 1921) Grand Parlor, and presided at the Thirty-sixth (San Rafael 1922) session. A woman of keen judgment and pleasing personality, a staunch friend always, and exemplifying as well as expounding the precepts of the Order, she numbered her admirers by the thousands. Through her passing, the Native Daughters suffered a distinct loss.—C.M.H.

Cook Book for Home Benefit.

The Grizzly Bear for June referred to the "Loyalty Cook Book," now on sale; prepared by Grand Trustee Willow Borba, and incorrectly stated funds realized from its sale will go towards the Loyalty Pledge of Santa Rosa No. 217. In a letter dated June 3, Mrs. Borba called attention to the error and said:

"The 'LOYALTY COOK BOOK' SALE is not to pay the Santa Rosa pledge, as you have stated. It is TO PAY THE LOYALTY PLEDGE OF ALL PARLORS. ALL FUNDS ARE TO BE GIVEN TO THE HOME, TO PAY THE BALANCE DUE ON THE MORTGAGE. I am working to lift the mortgage from the Native Daughter Home."

Pioneers Not Forgotten.

Colusa—Colusa No. 194 dedicated May 30 a bronze plaque, donated by Mrs. Sadie Winn-Brainard (Califia No. 22), in memory of Colonel Charles D. Semple, founder of this city. When he landed here in 1850 the site was inhabited by 10,000 Indians of several different tribes, the Colus tribe, from which the city derived its name, being the most powerful. Colonel Semple's remains rest in the Colusa cemetery.

Addresses were delivered by Past Grand Esther R. Sullivan, Margaret Davison and Mrs. Brainard. A Pioneer Mother, Mrs. Geo. White, presented to the committee in charge a beautiful boquet for the grave. All neighboring Parlors were well represented at the ceremonies.

The assemblage then proceeded to the new Will S. Green Park, where a marker was placed upon a cedar tree in memory of Joseph Warren Hilsee, Mrs. Brainard's grandfather, who was buried in Colusa in 1870. His daughter, Mrs. Winn, now 84 years of age, gave a very interesting account of the Hilsees' journey to California.

Site First Public Building Marked.

San Bernardino—Lugonia No. 241 sponsored a Loyalty Pledge benefit card party, which was a complete success, June 7. Twenty-two tables were reserved, and delicious refreshments were served. The committee in charge included Rhoda Smith (general chairman), Mary Johnson, Lois Poling, Clara Barton, Eva Bemis, Daisy Davenport, Nola Fogler, Ada McInerney and Marjorie Beck. June 8 officers were elected, Nola Fogler, being chosen president, and June 16 the Parlor members were picnic guests of Arrowhead No. 110 N.S.G.W.

June 25, Lugonia marked with appropriate ceremonies the site of the Council House, San Bernardino's first public building. Following the marking the Pioneers were entertained at their log cabin and they were presented with a California State (Bear) Flag.

Enthusiastic Anniversary.

Petaluma—Petaluma No. 222 had a most enthusiastic meeting June 7, the occasion being its tenth institution anniversary. It was termed "Mae Rose Berry night," in honor of the district deputy, who was the honor-guest. She was presented with a gift, the presentation being made by Elsie Deloca, for the Parlor. Among the many visitors were Past Grand Emma Foley and Grand Trustee Willow Borba.

At tables beautifully decorated with flowers a sumptuous dinner was served by a committee composed of Florence Anderson, Pearl Lopus, Josephine Tagliaferri, Julia Perolini, Edna Meadows, Margaret Oeltjen, Ida Morra, Annie Dickson and Ella Sebesta. Following this, six candidates were initiated, President Elizabeth Dillon presiding at the ceremonies. Officers for the July-December term were elected, Pearl Lopus being chosen president.

"Shabby Affair."

Hollister—The "poverty party" staged by Copa de Oro No. 105 was quite a "shabby affair," but a howling success. In the "parade of the needy," Hilda Thompson was awarded a bag of potatoes for a strikingly shabby appearance, and Edith Chandler won a can of beans for a realistic portrayal of a beggar at work. A bread line was formed and good old mulligan stew, bread, coffee and "sinkers" were doled out in regular style.

Faithful Service Appreciated.

San Diego—Recognition of education week was shown by San Diego No. 208 and San Diego No. 108 N.S.G.W. by participation in a program at the Southwest junior high school at Nestor, at which time a California State (Bear) Flag was given the school by the Parlors, the presentation speech being delivered by Judge Eugene Daney Jr.

At a recent meeting of the past presidents club of No. 208 at the home of Miss Marion S. Stough, Mrs. Elsie Case was received as an honorary member, as a reward for her long and faithful service as secretary of that Parlor. Mrs. Pearl Adams Simpson was hostess at the June meeting.

Wonderful Talk.

Elk Grove—Fifteen Parlors were represented at the official visit of Grand President Evelyn I. Carlson to Liberty No. 213 May 27. Visiting grand officers were Grand Trustee Edna Briggs, Past Grands Mary E. Bell, Mattie M. Stein and Dr. Louise C. Heilbron, Supervising Deputy Bessie Leitch and District Deputy Nellie Nordstrom.

Mrs. Carlson gave a wonderful talk and, on the Parlor's behalf, was presented with a gift by President Louise Krull. A program was rendered by Robert Krull, Beatrice Colton, Muriel Blodgett and Juanita Lovdal, and delicious refreshments were served.

Depression Party.

San Rafael—Many members and guests gathered June 13 to celebrate the twentieth anniversary of Marinita No. 198 at a depression party. A hard-times parade was held, and prizes were awarded those who best carried out the idea in their costumes. Much amusement was caused by imposing fines on those sitting on the side lines. Several dancing and vocal numbers were greatly enjoyed, after which all retired to the banquetroom, which showed no hard times. The hall was decorated in bicentennial colors; a huge birthday cake adorned the center table and tasty refreshments were served.

Guests of the evening were Past Grand Emma G. Foley, the "mother" of Marinita, District Deputy Mae Shea, Grand Trustee Ethel Begley and four charter members: Ann Spinney, Lillian Whitmore, Myra Murphy and Ann Andrade. Each was presented with a dainty corsage and favored with remarks.

New Baby in Family.

San Francisco—Utopia No. 252, organized by Alice Cummins, was instituted June 3 with forty charter members by Grand President Evelyn I. Carlson, who was assisted by Past Grand Estelle M. Evans, Grand Secretary Sallie R. Thaler, Grand Trustees Ethel Begley, Anna Thuesen and Willow Borba, Grand Outside Sentinel Orinda Giannini, Senior Past Grands Margaret G. Hill and Amy V. McAvoy. Grand President Carlson addressed the members of the "baby Parlor" and presented a silver-mounted gavel. The Grand Parlor presented United States of America and California State (Bear) Flags.

Officers of Utopia include: Alice Cummins, president; Madelyn Collins, past president; Rose Burke, first vice; May Sullivan, second vice; Phyllis Burke, third vice; Lelia Little, recording secretary; Mary Pitterson, financial secretary; Esther Cooper, treasurer; Edna Higgins, marshal; Mary Fitzgerald, inside sentinel; Ursula Lawless, Lillian Boulanger, Lottie Benson, trustees.

Historic Site Marked.

Fullerton—One hundred and fifty Pioneers and their descendants were guests of Grace No. 242 at the annual reunion for oldtimers. Luncheon was followed by a program. Among the speakers were President Mattie Edwards, Thos. McFadden, Mrs. J. E. Pleasants and Past President Nellie Cline. The Parlor celebrated its fifth institution anniversary with a family picnic June 3 at Irvine Park. June 16 Past President Carrie Ford sponsored a public dinner, which was followed by a program of moving pictures and a lecture on South America by John Tuffree.

To mark the site where Gaspar de Portola camped, Grace June 18 dedicated in Brea Canyon a six-foot shaft bearing an appropriately worded bronze plaque, the latter being contributed by Sadie Winn-Brainard (Califia No. 22) of Sacramento. Mrs. Carrie McFadden-Ford, chairman of the Parlor's history and landmarks committee, presided, and the speakers included Dr. John Ball, Assemblyman Fred Craig, Mrs. W. W. Blackmer, Mrs. Nellie Cline and President Mattie Edwards. June 23 the sewing club had an all-day session at the home of Rena Johnson.

Tree Dedicated to Pioneer.

Stockton—Joaquin No. 5 had a bicentennial tree planting in Victory Park and dedicated a sequoia to James A. Turner, only living member of the San Joaquin branch of the California Pioneers, who will be 102 years of age August 6. Past Grand President Carrie Roesch-Durham gave the introductory remarks, and three charter members—Clara Stier, Hannah Gray and Mrs. Durham, conducted the ceremonies. Mrs. Minnie Logan, a daughter of Turner, accepted the tree.

Contributing appropriate numbers to the program were Mrs. John W. Gealey, Miss Josephine Licay, Mrs. George Finkbohner, Mrs. Hattie A. Ward and Miss Roberta Foley.

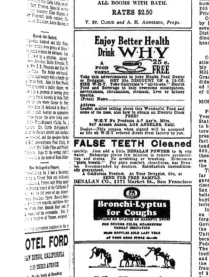

Successful Card Party.

Ontario—A most delightful and successful card party was held June 6 under the auspices of the sewing branch of Ontario No. 251. The decorations, flowers of every hue, were beautiful. Thirty tables were in operation, the players coming from all surrounding communities and as far distant as Los Angeles. A delightful musical program was given by Mrs. Lois Johnson, accompanied by Mrs. V. B. Anderson. Refreshments were served by Mms. Adele Frankish and Eva Mendelson.

NATIVE SON NEWS

(Continued from Page 7)

Johansen, Ione Johansen and Blanche Gaskill—who are to be heard over a Los Angeles radio station. A palatable repast, prepared by H. C. Kellogg and committee, followed. A goodly number enjoyed the barbecue sponsored by No. 265 and Santa Ana No. 235 N.D.G.W. Dr. C. E. Price was the general chairman.

Officers of Santa Ana will be installed July 18 by District Deputy George MacDonald. July 6 several members of the Parlor will accompany District Deputy Raymond Marsile to San Bernardino, where he will install the officers of Arrowhead No. 110.

Historic Site for Initiation.

Camptonville—The annual outdoor class initiation of Fred H. Greely Past Presidents Assembly No. 6 was held June 26 at historic Galena Hill, on the road to Downieville, where Past Grand President Fred H. Greely was born. Candidates were furnished by the Parlors represented in the association, and delegations from all of them attended the function.

MOST FAMOUS CALIFORNIA LAND CLAIM DECLARED FRAUD.

February 5, 1853, a Mexican named Jose Yves Limantour appeared before the United States Land Commission with papers purporting to be grants of land to him by Governor Micheltorena in 1843. He said the reason for his not presenting the claims previously was due to the fact that he had been too busy heretofore to attend to his California properties. In all, some 600,000 acres in California were claimed under these grants, including practically all the northern half of San Francisco County, the islands of the bay, and the Farallones.

The Land Commission rejected the claims, so far as the outside lands were concerned, but gave its confirmation to the claims to San Francisco. This immediately caused a land panic in San Francisco. Many citizens who were led to believe that Limantour had a valid title began buying the lands back from him. In all, he collected some $300,000.

In the meantime, Henry Halleck, an authority on Spanish titles, pronounced the documents forgeries. There were lawyers, too, who said Governor Micheltorena could not have deeded the government lands in this manner. The United States Government took up the matter, because under the claim the Presidio and other Federal properties had been given to Limantour. The famous geologist, George Davidson, examined the documents for the Federal Government and agreed that they were spurious. Finally, the United States Court pronounced the papers fraudulent. Limantour was arrested, gave bail of $30,000, and left the state. This is the most famous of all the land cases arising in California.—PETER T. CONMY, historian Golden Gate Parlor No. 29 N.S.G.W.

"Complain as little as possible of the wrongs done you; for, commonly speaking, he who complains sins, because self-love always makes us believe the injuries done to us greater than they really are."—Francis de Sales.

"Wait When Wigwags Warn," is the July slogan of the California Public Safety Committee in its campaign to lessen the fearful auto death-toll.

Rodeo—Salinas, Monterey County, will have its annual California Rodeo, July 20-24.

PROCEEDINGS FORTY-SIXTH N. D. GRAND PARLOR

(CLARENCE M. HUNT.)

MRS. ANNA MIXON-ARMSTRONG OF Woodland, Yolo County, affiliated with Woodland Parlor No. 90, is now the Grand President of the Order of Native Daughters of the Golden West, having been installed as such just preceding the close of the Forty-sixth Grand Parlor, in session at Merced City June 20, 21, 22 and 23. Following her induction into office, Grand President Armstrong addressed the assemblage as follows:

"Tonight is one of great moment to the members of my Parlor and to me—an occasion that brings happiness, joy and appreciation. The honor you have conferred in elevating me to the highest office within the power of the Order, Grand President of the Native Daughters of the Golden West, brings forcibly to my mind and heart the loyal support and steadfast devotion you have manifested in behalf of my Parlor and myself. Words are inadequate to express my emotion as I accept your fraternal gift.

"The pulse of fraternity is organized endeavor, stability of purpose, endurance and foresight. With your assistance and the Divine Master's guidance, I trust my term of office will prove my worth and justify your confidence in me. My fullest appreciation must be shown in my endeavor to carry on the responsibilities which have been laid upon me. In that effort, I pledge my full energy.

"I would ask that each delegate carry back to her Parlor an enthusiasm that will reflect and inspire an added activity of its entire membership. The very fact that you were chosen to represent your fellow-members at this Grand session sets you apart as a leader in your community. Upon you, therefore, devolves a responsibility of leadership which I urge each one of you to embrace.

"If I may use the very expressive word, 'pep' up your Parlor. Encourage each member to have a real part in a fraternal revival that will carry the banner of our Order to the front of all fraternal organizations. If you do that, the Native Daughters of the Golden West will become a greater and ever-increasing factor in fraternal and community life, and we will draw to ourselves hosts of worthwhile women who will welcome the opportunity of having part in maintaining the pioneer traditions to which we are pledged.

"The promulgation of the tenets of our Order is a duty every Native Daughter bears. It should also be considered a privilege.

"It is my ardent hope that we may see a material advance in our work for the homeless children during the year; that the Subordinate Parlors and individual members will interest themselves in planning activities whereby money may be raised for carrying on this work of benevolence and love.

"Let us justify the trust that was placed into our keeping by Fairfax Wheelan and his associates by putting forth greater efforts and achieving greater results, so that the home placing of homeless children may continue to grow in magnitude.

"This is my first word to you as your Grand President. Will you do these things for our Order and for me? I am confident you will not fail in these important services!"

WHAT TRANSPIRED

Grand President Evelyn I. Carlson, affiliated with Dolores Parlor No. 169 (San Francisco), presided throughout the deliberations of the Forty-sixth Grand Parlor. The reports of grand officers and committees dealt mostly with accomplishments of the Order which heretofore have been recorded in The Grizzly Bear, so no reference is here made to them. A synopsis of what otherwise transpired at the Grand Parlor follows:

In keeping with the George Washington bicentennial, the grand officers appeared at the opening session in attractive colonial costumes.

"How indifferent, many times, we become towards our organization!" said Grand President Carlson in her report to the Grand Parlor. "If we would pause, while hurrying through life, and consider the great benefits of our Order and its wonderful teachings and ideals, we would realize how much it means to us whom God has permitted to be born in this glorious paradise. The organization of Native Daughters of the Golden West has been recognized as a fraternity of real accomplishments of the things worthwhile, and has brought us to the pinnacle of wonderful achievements. The influence of our work, I am sure, will ever remain as a monument of unified effort of wisdom and love." During the stewardship of Mrs. Carlson the membership showed a net increase of 447 and two new parlors were instituted.

MRS. ANNA MIXON-ARMSTRONG,
GRAND PRESIDENT N.D.G.W.

The report of Grand Secretary Sallie R. Thaler gave a detailed account of the numerous transactions of that most important office. During the Grand Parlor year 138 members passed away and death benefits totaling $9,227 were paid.

Grand Treasurer Susie K. Christ reported the cash balances in the several Grand Parlor funds June 1, 1932, as follows: general, $18,447.02; trust, $10,116.60; death benefit, $2,971.68; Mills College scholarship, $988.73; university scholarship, $598.71; redwood memorial grove, $895.86; Home savings, $5,427.43.

Millie Tietjen, assistant treasurer Home Committee, reported the cash balances June 1, 1932: $5,087.10 savings account, $2,848.88 general fund, $831.90 furnishing fund, $794.11 endowment fund. The Home receipts for the Grand Parlor year totaled $20,036.35 and the disbursements $18,277.38. Loyalty Pledge receipts were $9,284.40, and $9,306.27 was paid on the mortgage.

IN MEMORIAM.

Shortly after the convening of the Grand Parlor the following resolution, presented by Past Grands Dr. Mariana Bertola, Margaret Grote-Hill and May C. Boldemann, was adopted by rising vote:

"To the memory of P.G.P. Minnie Coulter, Grand President of 1894, and P.G.P. Dr. Victory A. Derrick, Grand President of 1922, who passed away this year. Whereas, we appreciate and glory in the past work for the Order which they have given, be it

"Resolved, That we express our sympathy to the respective families of the deceased, and also our love and recognition of the lives of these two splendid women, each in her own way contributing to the welfare of her community. They are not lost to us; their work and their affectionate friendship will always be with us. 'Death is the chilliness that precedes the dawn; we shudder for a moment, then awake in the broad sunshine of the other life.'"

At the close of Monday's session, Grand President Carlson declared the Grand Parlor would recess in loving memory of Past Grands Coulter and Derrick.

LEGISLATION ENACTED.

The following changes in the governing laws were authorized, the abbreviations "C.G.P." and "C.S.P." referring, respectively, to the Constitution Grand Parlor and the Constitution Subordinate Parlors:

Art. V, Sec. 3 C.G.P., amended by adding, "The candidates for Grand Parlor offices who have no opposition shall be elected by acclamation and their names omitted from the ballot."

Art. VI, Sec. 3 C.G.P., amended by eliminating from the prescribed duties of the Grand Secretary, "and to drape the Grand Parlor Flag for thirty days."

Art. IX, Sec. 11 C.G.P., amended by substituting for the provision referring to financial support of the Committee on Children's Agency, "it . . . shall be supported by such funds as may be raised or voted by the respective Parlors."

Art XI, Sec. 1 C.G.P., amended to provide, "not fewer than thirty qualified persons" must make written application to work as a Subordinate Parlor.

Art. II, Sec. 2 C.S.P., amended by substituting for the provision relating to office eligibility, "Any member in good standing may be eligible to hold office, providing she has been a member of the Parlor six months; under extenuating circumstances the six-month membership period may be waived."

Art. IV, Sec. 7 C.S.P., amended to read, "The Recording Secretary, Financial Secretary, Treasurer and Trustees shall not be permitted to hold more than one office at any one time."

The Order of Business for Subordinate Parlors was amended to read: "No. 15, Report of Sick or Disabled Members. No. 16, Report of Visiting Committee. No. 17, Ordering Drafts for Benefits."

Several changes were made in the Ritual, which was considerably shortened and simplified. The report of the Ritual Committee was so favorably received that the members thereof were, on motion, given a rising vote of thanks.

The title "district deputy grand president" was changed to "deputy grand president."

It was ordered: That no meetings, whether open or closed, be held on Sundays. That members, to be elected delegates to Grand Parlor, attend at least two-thirds of their Parlor meetings during the year. That an applicant who desires to receive the benefits of the Home be a member of the Order at least ten years. That all recording secretaries be compelled to send registered letters notifying members of their suspension. That recording secretaries forward membership cards not later than the 10th of each month.

To encourage new Parlors, it was ordered that those newly instituted "receive a complete set of banners and regalias complimentary from the Grand Parlor, and that those Parlors instituted during the last two years be allowed some credit on their account."

BUSINESS TRANSACTED.

Alameda County was selected as the place of meeting for the Forty-seventh (1933) Grand Parlor.

It was ordered that the mortgage on the Home be liquidated at this time, the necessary sum to be drawn from the Home's reserve funds.

It was ordered that the $10,000 willed to the Grand Parlor by the late Senator James D. Phelan (Pacific No. 10 N.S.G.W.) "be held and maintained in trust by the Grand Parlor, to be used as specified by the will of Senator Phelan."

A resolution was adopted, requesting the State Park Commission to set aside the Donner Lake, Nevada County, area as a state park.

San Francisco was endorsed as the place for holding this year's Admission Day, September 9, celebration, and the Subordinate Parlors were urged to co-operate therein.

A budget of $14,914 was approved, and to provide that amount a percapita tax of one dollar was levied. In addition, a fifty-cent percapita assessment for the Home was voted.

The granting of charters to Ontario Parlor No. 251 and Utopia Parlor No. 252 (San Francisco) was ratified.

One hundred and fifty dollars was contributed to the Mission San Diego restoration fund, and fifty dollars to San Juan Capistrano Mission.

The incoming Grand President was directed to appoint a committee to supervise completion of the Pioneer Redwood Memorial Grove marker.

The Grizzly Bear Magazine was re-endorsed as the official organ of the Order, and financial provision was made for the publication therein of the official directory of Subordinate Parlors.

A resolution was adopted extending thanks to various organizations and individuals who contributed to the entertainment and the pleasure of the Grand Parlor.

Subordinate Parlors so requiring were given an additional year's time in which to complete their Loyalty Pledge payments. And it was ordered that all receipts from the Loyalty Pledge and the cook books be sent direct to Past Grand Emma G. Foley, secretary Home Committee.

To cut down the expense incident to the printing of the "Grand Parlor Proceedings," it was ordered that reports be simplified, and that the directory of Subordinate Parlors be eliminated.

A resolution prevailed, directing that a letter

be sent the Federal Interior Department's Indian field service asking relief for California Indians, and requesting each individual Parlor to write California's senators and congressmen in the Federal Congress urging their support. "As natives of the State of California, let us give this our earnest consideration," as conditions are deplorable.

GRAND OFFICERS-ELECT.

At the election for grand officers June 22, 382 ballots were cast, and the following were selected:

Grand President, Anna Mixon-Armstrong (Woodland No. 90).

Grand Vice-president, Irma W. Laird (Alturas No. 159).

Grand Secretary, Sallie R. Thaler (Aloha No. 106).

Grand Treasurer, Susie K. Christ (Yosemite No. 83).

Grand Marshal, Gladys E. Noce (Amapola No. 80).

MRS. GLADYS E. NOCE,
GRAND MARSHAL-ELECT.

Grand Inside Sentinel, Orinda Gunther-Giannini (Orinda No. 56).

Grand Outside Sentinel, Hazel B. Hansen (Verdugo No. 240).

Grand Organist, Clara A. Gairaud (Vendome No. 100).

Grand Trustees (in order of vote received), Florence D. Boyle (Gold of Ophir No. 190); Edna B. Briggs (La Bandera No. 110); Anna Thuesen (Alta No. 3); Ethel S. Begley (Marinita No. 198); Minna Kane-Horn (Eschscholtzia No. 112); Jane Vick (Reina del Mar No. 126); Willow Borba (Santa Rosa No. 217).

They, with Evelyn I. Carlson (Dolores No. 169), who automatically became the Past Grand President, were installed by Past Grand Estelle M. Evans, who was assisted by Past Grand Amy V. McAvoy, Sadie Winn-Brainard (Califia No. 22) and Elvena Woodard (Vallejo No. 195).

PUBLICITY.

Past Grand Bertha A. Briggs, chairman Publicity Committee, reported in detail the publicity efforts of the Subordinate Parlors. "The publicity group have, in every way possible, broadcasted to the world a clearer and broader knowledge of our Order's contribution to state and to country. . . . We have tried to do our part in remodeling material thought in accordance with the highest specifications of the spirit. . . . Individual workers have been most diligent in rendering a needful service of the very highest type, locally and in joint development of the entire Order.

"The Grizzly Bear, our official publication, has been exceedingly helpful to our cause throughout the year by the generous allotment of space to stories of our activities. . . . This valuable publication should be encouraged by our contributions to its columns and generously assisted by our subscriptions. While contributing to our local press, we should not overlook the vital fact that each and every member of our Order should be a reader of and a subscriber to this distinctively Californian magazine, so definitely devoted to the advancement of California and all things Californian."

NOTES OF THE SESSION.

Past Grand Carrie Roesch-Durham (Joaquin No. 5), who has the distinction of having attended every Grand Parlor, again headed the credentials committee. She instituted Veritas No. 75, the hostess Parlor.

Past Grand Dr. Mariana Bertola tendered her resignation as permanent chairman of the Home Committee, but because of her devotion to the Home and years of service to the Order the Grand Parlor refused to accept the resignation.

The Order's scholarship at the University of California at Berkeley for the 1932-33 year was again awarded Winona Laverty (Veritas No. 75). Scholarships at Mills College and the University of California at Los Angeles will be awarded later.

The Election Board was composed of Past Grands Emma Lou Humphrey, Pearl Lamb and Mamie G. Peyton, Mollye Y. Spaciti (Marinita No. 198) and Gertrude Tuttle (Californiana No. 247). Past Grand Ariana W. Stirling was the official timekeeper for nominating speeches.

Greetings on behalf of the Order of Native Sons of the Golden West were extended by Grand President Seth Millington, who was accompanied by Grand First Vice Chas. A. Koenig, Grand Secretary John T. Regan and Past Grand Charles L. Dodge.

Miss Mary E. Brusie (Argonaut No. 166), secretary N.S.G.W. and N.D.G.W. Central Homeless Children Committee, delighted the Grand Parlor with a report, unusual in presentation and clearness of detail, on the splendid accomplishments of the committee. She was assisted by a group of happy children and their mothers. She also had on exhibition a bountiful supply of artistic and useful children's garments, prepared by willing workers and contributed by various Subordinate Parlors.

Past Grand Dr. Louise C. Heilbron, originator of the Loyalty Pledge, reported thirty-eight Subordinate Parlors had paid their pledges in full, and that the balance on the Home mortgage had been reduced to $4,400. During the session an additional $765.85 was turned in to the Loyalty Pledge Committee.

At the ball Tuesday night the grand march was led by Grand President Evelyn I. Carlson and Governor James Rolph Jr. Prior to the dance the drill team of Joaquin Parlor No. 5 (Stockton) entertained, and the excellent maneuvers were highly commended. Members of the team wore dainty gowns of orange with green slippers and carried garlands of California poppies.

Following the exemplification of the ritual Wednesday night, Past President Association No. 1 of San Francisco presented a historical pageant, directed by Grand Trustee Ethel S. Begley.

Numerous presentations were made during the session, including an emblematic ring to Grand President Evelyn I. Carlson by the Grand Parlor, Past Grand May C. Boldemann making the presentation address.

Grand Trustee Willow Borba reported on the cook book compiled by her from recipes sent in by members of the Order, and stated that each Subordinate Parlor would be allowed one dollar for every book disposed of, the amount to be credited to the Parlor's Loyalty Pledge.

PAST GRANDS' ANNUAL FEAST.

With Dr. Mariana Bertola as hostess, the Past Grand Presidents had their annual reunion dinner Tuesday evening. The George Washington bicentennial was the motif of the happy occasion. Those assembled appeared in colonial dress, each impersonating some outstanding character of Washington's time, as follows:

Dr. Bertola, Martha Washington; Carrie Roesch-Durham, George Washington; Cora B. Sifford, Abigail Adams; Ariana W. Stirling, Miss Harriet Lane; Dr. Eva Rasmussen, Rev. Jos. Thaxton; Emma Lou Humphrey, Mrs. Alexander Hamilton; Mamie G. Peyton, Mrs. John Quincy Adams; Mamie Pierce-Carmichael, Sally Fairfax; Mary E. Bell, Betsy Ross; Bertha A. Briggs, Dorothy Quincy Hancock; Mattie M. Stein, Thomas Jefferson; Amy V. McAvoy, Emma Willard; Catherine E. Gloster, Mary Washington; Dr. Louise C. Heilbron, Dolly Madison; Esther R. Sullivan, Betty Washington Lewis; Emma Gruber-Foley, May C. Boldemann, Margaret Grote-Hill, Addie L. Mosher, Pearl Lamb, Alison F. Watt, Grace S. Stoermer, colonial dames.

Estelle M. Evans, appropriately gowned and equipped, was welcomed as the baby member of the college of Past Grands and initiated in usual form. Olive Bedford-Matlock was reelected president, and Bertha A. Briggs was retained as secretary. May C. Boldemann was chosen hostess for 1933.

ONE

(EVA BRAZIER.)

Beauty and Truth share one abode, I know;
It is a fallacy that Truth is plain;
As beautiful as mountains tipped with snow,
So loveliness adorns the Truth's domain.
To worship Beauty is not heresy;
As light comes with the Dawn, so does Truth
shine
Through moments of exalted ecstacy,
With pristine clarity at Beauty's shrine.
Truth wears no varnish, but incomparably
'Tis clothed upon with Beauty's light and shade;
It is not theirs the heart of Truth to see,
Who with fine scorn have Beauty's spirit flayed.
Beauty and Truth are one in Light and Power
As is the rose the seed and blossomed flower.

—University California Chronicle.

CALIFORNIA HISTORY AUTHORITY AWARDED GOLD MEDAL FOR BOOK.

San Francisco—Dr. Herbert Eugene Bolton, head of the University of California history department, was June 9 awarded a gold medal by the Commonwealth Club of California for his "Outpost of Empire," designated the "finest book by a California author published in 1931." Forty-six books were entered by authors of the state in competition.

"Outpost of Empire" is based on early California history and was pieced together from translations made by Dr. Bolton of the original diaries and correspondence of Juan Bautista de Anza and the friars who accompanied him, in opening the road from Sonora, Mexico, to California in 1774.

Inventions Exposition—A Western States Inventions and Industrial Exposition is to be held July 17-24 at Long Beach, Los Angeles County.

"The kiss of the sun for pardon, the song of the birds for mirth; you are nearer God's heaven in a garden than anywhere else on earth."

Official Directory of Parlors of the N. D. G. W.

ALAMEDA COUNTY.

Angelita No. 32, Livermore—Meets 2nd and 4th Fridays, Foresters Hall; Mrs. Myrtle I. Johnson, Rec. Sec.

Piedmont No. 87, Oakland—Meets Thursdays, Corinthian Hall, Pacific Bldg.; Mrs. Alice E. Miner, Rec. Sec., 421 36th St.

Aloha No. 106, Oakland—Meets Tuesdays, Wigwam Hall, Pacific Bldg.; Gladys I. Farley, Rec. Sec., 4623 Benevides Ave.

Hayward No. 122, Hayward—Meets 1st and 3rd Tuesdays, Veterans Memorial Bldg., Main St.; Miss Ruth Gansberger, Rec. Sec., P. O. box 44, Mount Eden.

Berkeley No. 150, Berkeley—Meets 1st and 3rd Fridays, Masonic Hall; Mrs. Lelia B. Baker, Rec. Sec., 915 Contra Costa Ave.

Bear Flag No. 151, Berkeley—Meets 2nd and 4th Wednesdays, Veterans Memorial Bldg., 1931 Center St.; Mrs. Maud Wagner, Rec. Sec., 317 Alcatraz Ave., Oakland.

Encinal No. 156, Alameda—Meets 2nd and 4th Thursdays, N.S.G.W. Hall; Mrs. Laura E. Fisher, Rec. Sec., 1413 Caroline St.

Brooklyn No. 157, East Oakland—Meets Wednesdays, Masonic Temple, 8th Ave. and E. 14th St.; Mrs. Ruth Cooney, Rec. Sec., 3907 14th Ave.

Argonaut No. 166, Oakland—Meets Tuesdays, Klinkner Hall, 59th and San Pablo; Mrs. Ada Spilman, Rec. Sec., 2905 Ellis St., Berkeley.

Bahia Vista No. 167, Oakland—Meets Thursdays, Wigwam Hall, Pacific Bldg.; Mrs. Minnie E. Raper, Rec. Sec., 3449 Helen St.

Fruitvale No. 177, Oakland—Meets Fridays, W.O.W. Hall; Mrs. Agnes M. Grant, Rec. Sec., 1224 30th Ave.

Laura Loma No. 182, Niles—Meets 1st and 3rd Tuesdays, I.O.O.F. Hall; Mrs. Ethel Fournier, Rec. Sec., P. O. box 515.

El Cereso No. 207, San Leandro—Meets 2nd and 4th Tuesdays, Masonic Hall; Mrs. Mary Tuttle, Rec. Sec., P. O. box 56.

Pleasanton No. 237, Pleasanton—Meets 1st Tuesday, I.O.O.F. Hall; Mrs. Myrtle Lanini, Rec. Sec.

Betsy Ross No. 238, Centerville—Meets 1st and 3rd Fridays, Anderson Hall; Miss Constance Lucio, Rec. Sec., P. O. box 187.

AMADOR COUNTY.

Ursula No. 1, Jackson—Meets 2nd and 4th Tuesdays, N.S.G.W. Hall; Mrs. Emma Boarman-Wright, Rec. Sec., 114 Court St.

Chispa No. 40, Ione—Meets 2nd and 4th Fridays, N.S.G.W. Hall; Mrs. Isabel Ashton, Rec. Sec.

Amapola No. 80, Sutter Creek—Meets 2nd and 4th Thursdays, N.S.G.W. Bldg.; Mrs. Hazel M. Marre, Rec. Sec.

Forrest No. 86, Plymouth—Meets 2nd and 4th Tuesdays, I.O.O.F. Hall; Mrs. Marguerite Davis, Rec. Sec.

BUTTE COUNTY.

Annie K. Bidwell No. 168, Chico—Meets 2nd and 4th Thursdays, I.O.O.F. Hall; Mrs. Irene Henry, Rec. Sec., 3015 Woodland Ave.

Gold of Ophir No. 190, Oroville—Meets 1st and 3rd Wednesdays, Memorial Hall; Mrs. Ruth Brown, Rec. Sec., 1265 Leah Court.

CALAVERAS COUNTY.

Ruby No. 46, Murphys—Meets 4th Friday, N.S.G.W. Hall; Belle Segale, Rec. Sec.

Princess No. 84, Angels Camp—Meets 2nd and 4th Wednesdays, I.O.O.F. Hall; Grace Mills, Rec. Sec.

San Andreas No. 113, San Andreas—Meets 1st Friday, Fraternal Hall; Miss Doris Treat, Rec. Sec.

COLUSA COUNTY.

Colus No. 194, Colusa—Meets 1st and 3rd Mondays, Eagles Hall; Miss Kate Busch, Rec. Sec., 350 Market St.

CONTRA COSTA COUNTY.

Stirling No. 146, Pittsburg—Meets 1st and 3rd Wednesdays, Veteran Memorial Hall; Mrs. Minnie Marcelli, Rec. Sec., 771 E. 12th St.

Richmond No. 147, Richmond—Meets 1st and 3rd Tuesdays, I.O.O.F. Hall, 10th St.; Mrs. Tillie Summers, Rec. Sec., 640 So. 31st St.

Donner No. 193, Byron—Meets 1st and 3rd Wednesdays, I.O.O.F. Hall; Mrs. Anna Pendry, Rec. Sec., P. O. box 112.

Las Juntas No. 221, Martinez—Meets 1st and 3rd Mondays, Pythian Castle; Mrs. Lola O. Viera, Rec. Sec., 305 Arreba St.

Antioch No. 223, Antioch—Meets 2nd and 4th Tuesdays, I.O.O.F. Hall; Mrs. Estelle Evans, Rec. Sec., 202 E. 5th St., Pittsburg.

Carquinez No. 234, Crockett—Meets 2nd and 4th Wednesdays, I.O.O.F. Hall; Mrs. Cecile Petee, Rec. Sec., 465 Edwards St.

EL DORADO COUNTY.

Marguerite No. 12, Placerville—Meets 1st and 3rd Wednesdays, Masonic Hall; Mrs. Nettie Leonardi, Rec. Sec., 25 Coloma St.

El Dorado No. 186, Georgetown—Meets 2nd and 4th Saturday afternoons, I.O.O.F. Hall; Mrs. Alta L. Douglas, Rec. Sec.

FRESNO COUNTY.

Fresno No. 187, Fresno—Meets 2nd and 4th Fridays, Pythian Castle, Cor. "R" and Merced Sts.; Mary Aubery, Rec. Sec., 1040 Delphia Ave.

GRAND OFFICERS.

Mrs. Evelyn I. Carlson............Past Grand President
1965 San Jose Ave., San Francisco

Mrs. Anna M. Armstrong............Grand President
Woodland

Mrs. Irma Laird............Grand Vice-president
Alturas

Mrs. Sallie R. Thaler............Grand Secretary
555 Baker St., San Francisco

Mrs. Susie K. Christ............Grand Treasurer
555 Baker St., San Francisco

Mrs. Gladys Noce............Grand Marshal
Sutter Creek

Mrs. Orinda G. Giannini............Grand Inside Sentinel
2142 Filbert St., San Francisco

Mrs. Hazel B. Hansen............Grand Outside Sentinel
501 Griswold St., Glendale

Mrs. Clara Gairaud............Grand Organist
134 Locust St., San Jose

GRAND TRUSTEES.

Mrs. Florence Boyle............Oroville
Mrs. Edna Briggs............1045 Santa Ynez Way, Sacramento
Mrs. Anna Thuesen............615 38th Ave., San Francisco
Mrs. Ethel Begley............233 Prospect Ave., San Francisco
Mrs. Minna K. Horn............Etna
Mrs. Jane Vick............418 Bath St., Santa Barbara
Mrs. Willow Borba............Sebastopol

GLENN COUNTY.

Berryessa No. 192, Willows—Meets 1st and 3rd Mondays, I.O.O.F. Hall; Mrs. Leonora Neate, Rec. Sec., 338 No. Lassen St.

HUMBOLDT COUNTY.

Occident No. 28, Eureka—Meets 1st and 3rd Wednesdays, N.S.G.W. Hall; Mrs. Eva L. MacDonald, Rec. Sec., 2309 "B" St.

Oneonta No. 71, Ferndale—Meets 2nd and 4th Fridays, I.O.O.F. Hall; Mrs. Myra Rumrill, Rec. Sec.

Reichling No. 97, Fortuna—Meets 1st and 3rd Tuesdays, Friendship Hall; Mrs. Grace Swett, Rec. Sec., P. O. box 328.

KERN COUNTY.

Miocene No. 228, Taft—Meets 1st and 3rd Wednesday afternoons, I.O.O.F. Hall; Mrs. Evalyn G. Towne, Rec. Sec., P. O. box 1011.

El Tejon No. 239, Bakersfield—Meets 1st and 3rd Fridays, Eagles Hall, 1714 "G" St.; Mrs. Grace S. Dorris, Rec. Sec., 127 Morgan Bldg.

Desert Gold No. 250, Mojave—Meets 2nd and 4th Fridays, I.O.O.F. Hall; Mrs. Mae Coffill, Rec. Sec.

LAKE COUNTY.

Clear Lake No. 135, Middletown—Meets 2nd and 4th Tuesdays, Herrick Hall; Mrs. Alma E. Snow, Rec. Sec.

LASSEN COUNTY.

Nataqua No. 152, Standish—Meets 1st and 3rd Wednesdays, Foresters Hall; Mrs. Mayda Elledge, Rec. Sec.

Mount Lassen No. 215, Bieber—Meets 2nd and 4th Thursdays, I.O.O.F. Hall; Mrs. Angie C. Kenyon, Rec. Sec.

Susanville No. 243, Susanville—Meets 3rd Thursday, I.O.O.F. Hall; Mrs. Georgia Jensen, Rec. Sec., 700 Roop St.

LOS ANGELES COUNTY.

Los Angeles No. 124, Los Angeles—Meets 1st and 3rd Wednesdays, I.O.O.F. Hall, Washington and Oak Sts.; Mrs. Mary K. Corcoran, Rec. Sec., 322 No. Van Ness Ave.

Long Beach No. 154, Long Beach—Meets 1st and 3rd Thursdays, K.P. Hall, 341 Pacific Ave.; Mrs. Bertha Hitt, Rec. Sec., 5355 Lime Ave.

Rudecinda No. 230, San Pedro—Meets 1st and 3rd Fridays, Unity Hall, I.O.O.F. Temple, 10th and Gaffey; Mrs. Carrie E. Northway, Rec. Sec., 561 W. 14th St.

Verdugo No. 240, Glendale—Meets 2nd and 4th Tuesdays, Masonic Temple, 234 So. Brand Blvd.; Miss Etta Fulkerth, Rec. Sec., 526-A No. Orange St.

Santa Monica Bay No. 245, Ocean Park—Meets 1st and 3rd Mondays, New Eagles Hall, 2823½ Main St.; Mrs. Rosalie Hyde, Rec. Sec., 738 Flower St., Venice.

Californiana No. 247, Los Angeles—Meets 2nd and 4th Tuesday afternoons, Hollywood Studio Club, 1215 Lodi Place; Mrs. Inez Sitton, Rec. Sec., 4228 Berenice St.

MADERA COUNTY.

Madera No. 244, Madera—Meets 2nd and 4th Thursdays, Masonic Annex; Mrs. Margaret O. Boyle, Rec. Sec., 111 No. "B" St.

MARIN COUNTY.

Sea Point No. 196, Sausalito—Meets 2nd and 4th Mondays, Perry Hall, 50 Caledonia St.; Mrs. Mary B. Smith, Rec. Sec., 559 Woodward Ave.

Marinita No. 198, San Rafael—Meets 2nd and 4th Mondays, 816 "B" St.; Miss Mollye Y. Spaelti, Rec. Sec., 539 4th St.

Fairfax No. 225, Fairfax—Meets 2nd and 4th Tuesdays, Community Hall; Mrs. Olive A. Greene, Rec. Sec., P. O. box 277.

Tamelpa No. 231, Mill Valley—Meets 1st and 2nd Tuesdays, I.O.O.F. Hall; Mrs. Delphine M. Todt, Rec. Sec., 400 Grand Ave., San Rafael.

MARIPOSA COUNTY.

Mariposa No. 63, Mariposa—Meets 1st and 3rd Fridays, I.O.O.F. Hall; Mrs. Mamie E. Weston, Rec. Sec.

MENDOCINO COUNTY.

Fort Bragg No. 210, Fort Bragg—Meets 1st and 3rd Thursdays, I.O.O.F. Hall; Mrs. Ruth W. Fuller, Rec. Sec.

MERCED COUNTY.

Veritas No. 75, Merced—Meets 1st and 3rd Tuesdays, I.O.O.F. Hall; Miss Margaret Thornton, Rec. Sec., 317 18th St.

MODOC COUNTY.

Alturas No. 159, Alturas—Meets 1st Thursday, Alturas Civic Club; Mrs. Irma W. Laird, Rec. Sec.

MONTEREY COUNTY.

Aleli No. 102, Salinas—Meets 2nd and 4th Thursdays, Knights Pythias Hall; Miss Rose Rhyner, Rec. Sec., 420 Soledad St.

Junipero No. 141, Monterey—Meets 2nd and 4th Fridays, Pythian Hall; Miss Matilda M. Bergschicker, Rec. Sec., 498 Van Buren St.

NAPA COUNTY.

Eschol No. 16, Napa—Meets 2nd and 4th Mondays, N.S.G.W. Hall; Mrs. Ella Ingram, Rec. Sec., 2140 Seminary St.

Calistoga No. 145, Calistoga—Meets 2nd and 4th Mondays, I.O.O.F. Hall; Sadie P. Brooks, Rec. Sec.

La Junta No. 203, Saint Helena—Meets 1st and 3rd Tuesdays, N.S.G.W. Hall; Mrs. Marie Signorelli, Rec. Sec., 1341 Madrona Ave.

ATTENTION, SECRETARIES!

THIS DIRECTORY IS PUBLISHED BY AUTHORITY OF THE GRAND PARLOR N.D.G.W., AND ALL NOTICES OF CHANGES MUST BE RECEIVED BY THE GRAND SECRETARY (NOT THE MAGAZINE) ON OR BEFORE THE 20TH OF EACH MONTH TO INSURE CORRECTION IN NEXT PUBLICATION OF DIRECTORY.

NEVADA COUNTY.

Laurel No. 6, Nevada City—Meets 1st and 3rd Wednesdays, I.O.O.F. Hall; Mrs. Nellie E. Clark, Rec. Sec., P. O. box 312.

Manzanita No. 29, Grass Valley—Meets 1st and 3rd Tuesdays, Auditorium; Mrs. Loraine Keast, Rec. Sec., 12[illegible] Race St.

Columbia No. 70, French Corral—Meets Fridays, Farrelley Hall; Mrs. Kate Farrelley-Sullivan, Rec. Sec.

Snow Peak No. 176, Truckee—Meets 1st Monday, I.O.O.F. Hall; Mrs. Henrietta M. Eaton, Rec. Sec., P. O. box 116.

ORANGE COUNTY.

Santa Ana No. 235, Santa Ana—Meets 2nd and 4th Mondays, K.C. Hall, 4th and French Sts.; Mrs. Matilda S. Lemon, Rec. Sec., 928 W. Fairview.

Grace No. 242, Fullerton—Meets 1st and 3rd Thursdays, I.O.O.F. Hall, 116½ E. Commonwealth; Mrs. Mary Rothaermel, Rec. Sec., P. O. box 236.

PLACER COUNTY.

Placer No. 138, Lincoln—Meets 2nd Wednesday, I.O.O.F. Hall; Miss Carrie Parlin, Rec. Sec.

La Rosa No. 191, Roseville—Meets 1st and 3rd Tuesdays, Eagles Hall; Mrs. Alice Lee West, Rec. Sec., Rocklin.

Auburn No. 233, Auburn—Meets 2nd and 4th Fridays, Foresters Hall; Mrs. Dorothy Reinecke, Rec. Sec., Penryn.

PLUMAS COUNTY.

Plumas Pioneer No. 219, Quincy—Meets 1st and 3rd Mondays, I.O.O.F. Hall; Minnie E. Johnson, Rec. Sec., P. O. box 243.

SACRAMENTO COUNTY.

Califia No. 22, Sacramento—Meets 2nd and 4th Tuesdays, N.S.G.W. Hall; Miss Lulu Gillis, Rec. Sec., 921 8th St.

La Bandera No. 110, Sacramento—Meets 1st and 3rd Fridays, N.S.G.W. Hall; Mrs. Clara Weldon, Rec. Sec., 1310 "O" St.

Sutter No. 111, Sacramento—Meets 1st and 3rd Tuesdays, N.S.G.W. Hall; Mrs. Adele Nix, Rec. Sec., 1238 "S" St.

Fern No. 123, Folsom—Meets 1st and 3rd Tuesdays, K.P. Hall; Mrs. Viola Shumway, Rec. Sec., P. O. box 48.

Chabolla No. 171, Galt—Meets 2nd and 4th Tuesdays, I.O.O.F. Hall; Mrs. Mary Pritchard, Rec. Sec.

Coloma No. 212, Sacramento—Meets 1st and 3rd Tuesdays, I.O.O.F. Hall, Oak Park; Mrs. Nettie Harry, Rec. Sec., 1217 35th St.

Liberty No. 213, Elk Grove—Meets 2nd and 4th Fridays, I.O.O.F. Hall; Mrs. Frances Wackman, Rec. Sec., P. O. box 192.

Victory No. 216, Courtland—Meets 1st Saturday and 3rd Monday, N.S.G.W. Hall; Mrs. Agneda Lample, Rec. Sec.

SAN BENITO COUNTY.

Copa de Oro No. 105, Hollister—Meets 2nd and 4th Thursdays, Grangers Union Hall; Mrs. Mollie Daveggio, Rec. Sec., 110 San Benito St.

San Juan Bautista No. 179, San Juan Bautista—Meets 1st Wednesday, Mission Corridor Rooms; Miss Gertrude Breen, Rec. Sec.

SAN BEARNARDINO COUNTY.

Lugonia No. 241, San Bernardino—Meets 2nd and 4th Wednesdays, Eagles Hall; Grace McHenry, Rec. Sec., Base Line and Central, Highland.

Ontario No. 251, Ontario—Meets 2nd and 4th Thursdays, Ontario Hotel; Miss Helen Hickman, Rec. Sec., 923 No. Laurel Ave.

SAN DIEGO COUNTY.

San Diego No. 208, San Diego—Meets 2nd and 4th Wednesdays, Directors Room, Chamber Commerce Bldg., 499 W. Broadway; Mrs. Elsie Case, Rec. Sec., 3051 Broadway.

SAN FRANCISCO CITY AND COUNTY.

Minerva No. 2, San Francisco—Meets 1st and 3rd Wednesdays, N.S.G.W. Bldg.; Miss Dorothy Finn, Rec. Sec., 90 Princess St., Sausalito.

Alta No. 3, San Francisco—Meets 2nd and 4th Tuesdays, N.S.G.W. Bldg.; Mrs. Agnese L. Hughes, Rec. Sec., 3980 Sacramento St.

Oro Fino No. 9, San Francisco—Meets 1st and 3rd Thursdays, N.S.G.W. Bldg.; Mrs. Josephine B. Morrissey, Rec. Sec., 4441 20th St.

Golden State No. 50, San Francisco—Meets 1st and 3rd Wednesdays, N.D.G.W. Home; Miss Millie Tietjen, Rec. Sec., 328 Lexington Ave.

Orinda No. 56, San Francisco—Meets 2nd and 4th Fridays, N.D.G.W. Home; Mrs. Anna A. Gruber-Loser, Rec. Sec., 72 Grove Lane, San Anselmo.

Fremont No. 59, San Francisco—Meets 1st and 3rd Tuesdays, N.S.G.W. Bldg.; Miss Hannah Collins, Rec. Sec., 617 Fillmore St.

Buena Vista No. 68, San Francisco—Meets 1st, 3rd and 5th Thursdays, N.D.G.W. Home; Miss Margaret Barrett, Rec. Sec., 3774 20th St.

Las Lomas No. 72, San Francisco—Meets 1st and 3rd Tuesdays, N.D.G.W. Home; Mrs. Marion S. Day, Rec. Sec., 471 Alvarado St.

Yosemite No. 83, San Francisco—Meets 1st and 3rd Tuesdays, American Hall, 20th and Capp Sts.; Miss Mary Monahan, Rec. Sec., 237 Noe St.

La Estrella No. 89, San Francisco—Meets 2nd and 4th Mondays, N.S.G.W. Bldg.; Miss Birdie Hartman, Rec. Sec., 1018 Jackson St.

Sans Souci No. 96, San Francisco—Meets 2nd and 4th Mondays, N.D.G.W. Home; Mrs. Minnie F. Dobbin, Rec. Sec., 1483 43rd Ave.

Calaveras No. 103, San Francisco—Meets 2nd and 4th Tuesdays, Swedish American Hall, 2174 Market St.; Mrs. Lena Lorsheter, Rec. Sec., 492-C 41st St., Oakland.

Darina No. 114, San Francisco—Meets 1st and 3rd Mondays, N.S.G.W. Bldg.; Miss Adele Walsh, Rec. Sec., 479 Page St.

El Vespero No. 118, San Francisco—Meets 2nd and 4th Tuesdays, Masonic Hall, 4705 3rd St.; Mrs. Nell B. Boege, Rec. Sec., 1626 Kirkwood Ave.

Genevieve No. 132, San Francisco—Meets 1st and 3rd Thursdays, N.S.G.W. Bldg.; Miss Branice Peguillan, Rec. Sec., 2434 16th Ave.

Keith No. 137, San Francisco—Meets 2nd and 4th Thursdays, N.S.G.W. Bldg.; Mrs. Helen T. Mann, Rec. Sec., 575 Pierce St., Apt. 206.

Gabrielle No. 139, San Francisco—Meets 2nd and 4th Wednesdays, N.S.G.W. Bldg.; Mrs. Dorothy Wuesterfeld, Rec. Sec., 1020 Munich St.

Presidio No. 148, San Francisco—Meets 2nd and 4th Tuesdays, N.S.G.W. Bldg.; Mrs. Hattie Gaughran, Rec. Sec., 713 Capp St.

Guadalupe No. 153, San Francisco—Meets 2nd and 4th Mondays, Forester Hall, 170 Valencia St.; Miss May A. McCarthy, Rec. Sec., 336 Elsie St.

Golden Gate No. 158, San Francisco—Meets 2nd and 4th Mondays, N.S.G.W. Bldg.; Mrs. Mary Sullivan, Rec. Sec., 33 Cuvier St.

Dolores No. 169, San Francisco—Meets 2nd and 4th Wednesdays, N.S.G.W. Bldg.; Mrs. Ada Saunders, Rec. Sec., 284 Allison St.

Linda Rosa No. 170, San Francisco—Meets 2nd and 4th Wednesdays, Swedish American Hall, 2174 Market St.; Mrs. Eva P. Tyrrel, Rec. Sec., 2629 Mission St.

Portola No. 172, San Francisco—Meets 1st and 3rd Tuesdays, N.S.G.W. Bldg.; Catherine H. Dolly, Rec. Sec., 4125 23rd St.
Castro No. 178, San Francisco—Meets 1st and 3rd Wednesdays, K.O. Bldg., 150 Golden Gate Ave.; Miss Adeline Sandersfeld, Rec Sec., 50 Baker St.
Twin Peaks No. 185, San Francisco—Meets 2nd and 4th Fridays, Druids Temple, 44 Page St.; Mrs. Loretta Cameron, Rec. Sec., 3969 Army St.
James Lick No. 220, San Francisco—Meets 1st and 3rd Wednesdays, N.S.G.W. Bldg.; Mrs. Edna Bishop, Rec. Sec., 3841 24th St.
Mission No. 227, San Francisco—Meets 2nd and 4th Fridays, N.S.G.W. Bldg.; Mrs. Ann Dippel, Rec. Sec., 448 Dewey Blvd.
Bret Harte No. 232, San Francisco—Meets 2nd and 4th Tuesdays, Aloha Hall, 3009 16th St.; Hildur E. Eggers, Rec. Sec., 194 Prague St.
La Dorada No. 236, San Francisco—Meets 2nd and 4th Thursdays, N.S.G.W. Hall; Mrs. Theresa K. O'Brien, Rec. Sec., 567 Liberty St.
Balboa No. 249, San Francisco—Meets 1st and 3rd Thursdays, Maccabee Hall, 5th Ave. and Clement St.; Jean Moffet, Rec. Sec., 6033 California St.
Utopia No. 252, San Francisco—Meets 2nd and 4th Tuesdays, American Hall, 20th and Capp Sts.; Lelia Little, Rec. Sec.

SAN JOAQUIN COUNTY.

Joaquin No. 5, Stockton—Meets 2nd and 4th Tuesdays, N.S.G.W. Hall, 314 E. Main St.; Mrs. Della Garvin, Rec. Sec., 1122 E. Market St.
El Pescadero No. 82, Tracy—Meets 1st and 3rd Fridays, I.O.O.F. Hall; Mrs. Mary A. Hewitson, Rec. Sec., 215 W. 9th St.
Ivy No. 88, Lodi—Meets 1st and 3rd Wednesdays, Eagles Hall; Mrs. Mae Corson, Rec. Sec., 109 So. School St.
Dalia de Oro No. 206, Stockton—Meets 1st and 3rd Tuesdays, N.S.G.W. Hall, 314 E. Main St.; Mrs. Frances Germain, Rec. Sec., 450 No. Regent.
Phoebe A. Hearst No. 214, Manteca—Meets 2nd and 4th Wednesdays, I.O.O.F. Hall; Mrs. Josie M. Frederick, Rec. Sec., Route A, Box 864, Ripon.

SAN LUIS OBISPO COUNTY.

San Miguel No. 94, San Miguel—Meets 2nd and 4th Wednesday afternoons, Clemon Hall; Mrs. Nellie Wickstrom, Rec. Sec.
San Luisita No. 108, San Luis Obispo—Meets 2nd and 4th Thursdays, W.O.W. Hall; Miss Agnes M. Lee, Rec. Sec., P. O. box 584.
El Pinal No. 163, Cambria—Meets 2nd, 4th and 5th Tuesdays, N.S.G.W. Hall; Kathryn Luchessa, Rec. Sec.

SAN MATEO COUNTY.

Bonita No. 10, Redwood City—Meets 2nd and 4th Thursdays, I.O.O.F. Hall; Mrs. Dora Wilson, Rec. Sec., 518 Middlefield Rd.
Vista del Mar No. 155, Halfmoon Bay—Meets 2nd and 4th Thursdays, I.O.O.F. Hall; Mrs. Grace Griffith, Rec. Sec.
Ano Nuevo No. 180, Pescadero—Meets 1st and 3rd Wednesdays, I.O.O.F. Hall; Mrs. Alice Mattei, Rec. Sec.
El Carmelo No. 181, Daly City—Meets 1st and 3rd Wednesdays, Masonic Hall; Mrs. Hattie Kelly, Rec. Sec., 1179 Brunswick St.
Menlo No. 211, Menlo Park—Meets 2nd and 4th Mondays, Masonic Hall; Mrs. Frances E. Maloney, Rec. Sec., P. O. box 626.
San Bruno No. 246, San Bruno—Meets 2nd and 4th Fridays, N.D. Hall; Miss Mildred Foley, Rec. Sec., 217 Miller Ave., South San Francisco.

SANTA BARBARA COUNTY.

Reina del Mar No. 126, Santa Barbara—Meets 1st and 3rd Tuesdays, Pythian Castle, 222 W. Carillo St.; Miss Christina Moller, Rec. Sec., 836 Bath St.

SANTA CLARA COUNTY.

San Jose No. 81, San Jose—Meets Thursdays, Catholic Women Center, 5th and San Fernando Sts.; Mrs. Nellie Fleming, Rec. Sec., Catholic Women Center.
Vendome No. 100, San Jose—Meets Wednesdays, Old Scottish Rite Temple; Miss Marie Buck, Rec. Sec., 1414 Ellen St.
El Monte No. 205, Mountain View—Meets 2nd and 4th Fridays, American Legion Hall; Miss Mary Ann Rokovich, Rec. Sec., R.F.D. No. 1, box 412, State Highway.
Palo Alto No. 229, Palo Alto—Meets 1st and 2nd Mondays, N.S.G.W. Hall; Miss Helena G. Hansen, Rec. Sec., 531 Lytton Ave.

SANTA CRUZ COUNTY.

Santa Cruz No. 26, Santa Cruz—Meets Mondays, N.S.G.W. Hall; Mrs. May L. Williamson, Rec. Sec., 170 Walnut Ave.
El Pajaro No. 35, Watsonville—Meets 1st and 3rd Tuesdays, I.O.O.F. Hall; Miss Ruth E. Wilson, Rec. Sec., 16 Laurel St.

SHASTA COUNTY.

Camellia No. 41, Anderson—Meets 1st and 3rd Tuesdays, Masonic Hall; Mrs. Olga E. Welbourn, Rec. Sec.
Lassen View No. 98, Shasta—Meets 2nd Friday, Masonic Hall; Miss Louise Litsch, Rec. Sec.
Hiawatha No. 140, Redding—Meets 2nd and 4th Wednesdays, Moose Hall; Ruth Presleigh, Rec. Sec., Office County Clerk.

SIERRA COUNTY.

Naomi No. 36, Downieville—Meets 2nd and 4th Wednesdays, I.O.O.F. Hall; Louise O. Dubuque, Rec. Sec.
Imogen No. 134, Sierraville—Meets 2nd and 4th Saturday afternoons, Copren Hall; Mrs. Jennie Copren, Rec. Sec.

SISKIYOU COUNTY.

Eschscholtzia No. 112, Etna—Meets 1st and 3rd Wednesdays, Masonic Hall; Mrs. Bernice E. Smith, Rec. Sec.
Mountain Dawn No. 120, Sawyers Bar—Meets 2nd and last Wednesdays, I.O.O.F. Hall; Miss Edith Dunphy, Rec. Sec.

SOLANO COUNTY.

Vallejo No. 195, Vallejo—Meets 1st and 3rd Wednesdays, K.C. Hall, 820 Marin St.; Mrs. Mary Combs, Rec. Sec., 511 York St.
Mary E. Bell No. 224, Dixon—Meets 2nd and 4th Thursdays, I.O.O.F. Hall; Grace McFadyen, Rec. Sec.

SONOMA COUNTY.

Sonoma No. 209, Sonoma—Meets 2nd and 4th Mondays, I.O.O.F. Hall; Mrs. Mae Norrbom, Rec. Sec., R.F.D., box 171.
Santa Rosa No. 217, Santa Rosa—Meets 1st and 3rd Thursdays, N.S.G.W. Hall; Mrs. Hazel E. Brown, Rec. Sec., 1521 4th St.
Petaluma No. 222, Petaluma—Meets 1st and 3rd Tuesdays, Dania Hall; Mrs. Margaret M. Oeltjen, Rec. Sec., 503 Prospect St.

STANISLAUS COUNTY.

Oakdale No. 125, Oakdale—Meets 1st Monday, I.O.O.F. Hall; Mrs. Lou Reeder, Rec. Sec.
Morada No. 199, Modesto—Meets 2nd and 4th Wednesdays, I.O.O.F. Hall; Mrs. Susan Sullivan, Rec. Sec., 823 10th St.
Eldora No. 248, Turlock—Meets 1st and 3rd Wednesdays, Fraternal Hall; Effie Lund, Rec. Sec., 624 Minaret Ave.

SUTTER COUNTY.

South Butte No. 226, Sutter—Meets 1st and 3rd Mondays, N.D.G.W. Hall; Mrs. Abbie N. Vagedes, Rec. Sec.

TEHAMA COUNTY.

Berendos No. 23, Red Bluff—Meets 1st and 3rd Tuesdays, W.O.W. Hall, 200 Pine St.; Mrs. Lillie Hammer, Rec. Sec., 536 Jackson St.

PIONEER NATIVES

(Continued from Page 9)

Mrs. Ionia Fourts-Moon, born in Placer County in 1854, died June 10 at Piedmont, Alameda County, survived by two daughters.

John C. Elwell, born in Ventura County in 1853, died June 11 at Santa Paula survived by five children.

Mrs. Agustia Romero-Lopez, born in Monterey County in 1843, died June 13 at Hollister, San Benito County.

John Ysunza, born in Alameda County in 1858, died June 13 at Berkeley survived by a widow and six children. He was a son of John Ysunza, California Pioneer of 1847.

Mrs. Emilie Berson, born at San Francisco in 1852, died June 15 at Palo Alto, Santa Clara County, survived by a husband and three children.

Mrs. Mary Duffy-Bathurst, born in El Dorado County in 1856, died June 21 at Represa, Sacramento County, survived by six children.

N.D.G.W. OFFICIAL DEATH LIST.

Giving the name, the date of death, and the Subordinate Parlor affiliation of all deceased members as reported to Grand Secretary Sallie R. Thaler from May 17 to June 18, 1932:

Goldsworthy, Jennie H.; May 30, 1932; Aloha No. 106.
Derrick, Victory A. Dr.; May 31, 1932; Aloha No. 106.
Burns, Inez Croci; May 1, 1932; Sea Point No. 196.
Davilla, Kitty; May 25, 1932; El Pescadero No. 82.
Murray, Belle; May 27; Annie K. Bidwell No. 168.
Lambert, Matilda; June 2, 1932; Gabrielle No. 139.
Vanderhoof, Carrie; June 5, 1932; Dardanelle No. 66.
Westover, Frances D.; April 27, 1932; Stirling No. 146.
Currington, Emma M.; April 15, 1932; Fairfax No. 225.

N.S.G.W. OFFICIAL DEATH LIST.

Containing the name, the date and the place of birth, the date of death, and the Subordinate Parlor affiliation of deceased members reported to Grand Secretary John T. Regan from May 20, 1932, to June 15, 1932:

Cayle, James Daniel; Sacramento, August 25, 1859; June 4, 1932; Sunset No. 26.
Bennett, Charles; Los Angeles, July 19, 1863; June 8, 1932; Los Angeles No. 45.
Behrens, Henry H.; Nevada City, February 17, 1858; May 17, 1932; Napa No. 62.
Conlon, Frank Joseph; San Francisco, 1870; May 19, 1932; Rincon No. 72.
Monahan, Frank J.; San Francisco, April 8, 1872; May 21, 1932; Rincon No. 72.
Williamson, John M.; San Francisco, June 20, 1861; April 2, 1932; Stanford No. 76.
Russell, Philip; San Francisco, May 13, 1891; May 24, 1932; Stanford No. 76.
Pierce, Robert Owen; Vallejo, July 20, 1860; May 14, 1932; Vallejo No. 77.
Schumaker, Albert Conard; San Francisco, May 6, 1893; May 4, 1932; Courtland No. 106.
Pendegast, Lyle; Woodland, December 30, 1870; May 25, 1932; Ramona No. 109.
Whitcher, Arthur Hamilton; Oakland, December 20, 1862; May 18, 1932; Arrowhead No. 110.
Woods, Jesse H.; San Leandro, May 3, 1872; May 13, 1932; Piedmont No. 120.
Ingersoll, George O.; San Francisco, February 16, 1880; May 13, 1932; Athens No. 195.
Fallon, James R.; San Francisco, October 11, 1887; February 8, 1932; Castro No. 232.
Crotty, George Raymond; San Francisco, February 23, 1896; March 9, 1932; Castro No. 232.
Keenan, Arthur J.; San Francisco, June 13, 1890; March 11, 1932; Castro No. 232.
Bettman, Alfred; San Francisco, June 24, 1868; March 13, 1932; Castro No. 232.

TRINITY COUNTY.

Eltapome No. 55, Weaverville—Meets 2nd and 4th Thursdays, N.S.G.W. Hall; Mrs. Lou N. Fetzer, Rec. Sec.

TUOLUMNE COUNTY.

Dardanelle No. 66, Sonora—Meets Fridays, I.O.O.F. Hall; Mrs. Nettie Whitto, Rec. Sec.
Golden Era No. 99, Columbia—Meets 1st and 3rd Thursdays, N.S.G.W. Hall; Miss Irene Ponce, Rec. Sec.
Anona No. 164, Jamestown—Meets 2nd and 4th Tuesdays, I.O.O.F. Hall; Mrs. Rosa A. Beckwith, Rec. Sec., P. O. box 87.

YOLO COUNTY.

Woodland No. 90, Woodland—Meets 2nd and 4th Tuesdays, N.S.G.W. Hall; Mrs. Maude Heaton, Rec. Sec., 153 College St.

YUBA COUNTY.

Marysville No. 162, Marysville—Meets 2nd and 4th Wednesdays, Liberty Hall; Miss Cecelia C. Gomes, Rec. Sec., 701 6th St.
Camp Far West No. 218, Wheatland—Meets 3rd Tuesday, I.O.O.F. Hall; Mrs. Ethel C. Brock, Rec. Sec., P. O. box 285.

AFFILIATED ORGANIZATIONS.

General Assembly Past Presidents—Meetings held annually in April at the home-town of Chief President; Mrs. Cora Stebing, 1739 San Jose Ave., San Francisco, Chief President; Mrs. Anna G. Loser, 72 Grove Lane, San Anselmo, Chief Secretary.
Past Presidents Association No. 1—Meets 1st and 3rd Mondays, N.S.G.W. Bldg., 414 Mason St., San Francisco; Mrs. Minnie F. Dobbin, Pres.; Mrs. May R. Barry, Rec. Sec., 2319 19th Ave., San Francisco.
Past Presidents Association No. 2—Meets 2nd and 4th Mondays, "Wigwam," Pacific Bldg., 16th and Jefferson, Oakland; Frieda Reichhold, Pres.; Mrs. Elizabeth B. Goodman, Rec. Sec., 134 Juana Ave., San Leandro.
Past Presidents Association No. 3 (Santa Clara County)—Meets 2nd Tuesday, homes of members; Mrs. Clara Briggs, Pres.; Mrs. Mary G. Newton, Rec. Sec., 1070 Jackson St., Santa Clara.
Past Presidents Association No. 4 (Sacramento County)—Meets 2nd Monday, Unitarian Hall, 1413 27th St., Sacramento City; Viola Gennoe, Pres.; Lily May Tilden, Rec. Sec., 3225 "T" St., Sacramento.
Past Presidents Association No. 5 (Butte County)—Meets 1st Friday, homes of members, Chico and Oroville; Sonora Steadman, Pres.; Ruth Brown, Rec. Sec., 1265 Leab Court, Oroville.
Past Presidents Association No. 6 (Nevada County)—Meets 4th Friday, alternately between Nevada City, Pythian Castle, and Grass Valley, Edna Sampson's home; Margaret V. Nolan, Pres.; Vere Hansen, Rec. Sec., R.F.D. No. 2, box 41-C, Grass Valley.
Past Presidents Association No. 7 (Sonoma County)—Meets 1st Thursday, N.S.G.W. Hall, Santa Rosa; Willow Borba, Pres.; Clytie Lewis, Rec. Sec., R.F.D. No. 4, box 345-A, Santa Rosa.
Past Presidents Association No. 8 (San Joaquin and Stanislaus Counties)—Meets 2nd Thursday, Red Men Hall, Stockton; Mrs. Lois Armstrong, Pres.; Mrs. Harriet F. Corr, Rec. Sec., 729 E. Sonora St., Stockton.
Native Sons and Native Daughters Central Committee on Homeless Children—Main Office, 955 Phelan Bldg., San Francisco; Mrs. John W. Stirling, Chmn.; Miss Mary E. Brusie, Sec. Los Angeles branch office, 3924 Sunset Blvd.; Dorothy Schlingman, Sec.

(ADVERTISEMENT.)

In Memoriam

JUSTICE FRANK MARION ANGELLOTTI.

Whereas, It has pleased the Supreme Ruler to summon from his sphere of usefulness to the Grand Parlor on High our well-beloved brother, Frank Marion Angellotti; and whereas, Mount Tamalpais Parlor No. 64 N.S.G.W. has lost a loyal member, our Order a staunch supporter, his country a patriotic citizen and the bar one of its most brilliant members.

As District Attorney, Superior Judge, Associate Justice and Chief Justice of the State of his nativity, he was just, courageous, upright, painstaking, considerate, ever courteous, kindly and charitable toward the faults of others. He never neglected or betrayed a client; he enjoyed the confidence of his fellow-citizens to the utmost; a strong partisan, he enjoyed the friendship, respect and support of his political opponents, and he was repeatedly returned to the high offices he so ably and so faithfully filled as long as he was willing to accept them, and it was with deep and genuine regret that his fellow-citizens learned that he no longer sought public office. As son, brother, husband and father, he was kind, loving and devoted; a devout Christian, a leader in civic affairs, he always labored for the advancement and progress of his community and for the uplift of humanity. Therefore, be it

Resolved, That this Parlor tender to his bereaved family our sincerest sympathies and that we humbly pray that the Merciful Father shall comfort them in this, their dark hour of sorrow; and be it further resolved, that the charter of this Parlor be draped for a period of thirty days; that the Parlor stand in silence following the reading of these resolutions in respect to his memory; that a copy of these resolutions be forwarded to the family of our late brother; that a copy of these resolutions be spread upon the minutes of the Parlor, and that a copy be forwarded to The Grizzly Bear Magazine for publication.

HAROLD J. HALEY,
C. G. REINDOLLAR,
LOUIS J. PETER,
ARTHUR W. TODT,
MONROE W. LABEL,
Committee on Resolutions.

San Rafael, June 7, 1932.

MARY E. MATHEWSON.

To the Officers and Members of Bahia Vista Parlor No. 167 N.D.G.W.—We, your committee appointed to draft resolutions to the memory of our departed sister, Mary E. Mathewson, respectfully submit the following:

Whereas, Almighty God, in His infinite wisdom, has called to the Heavenly Parlor on High our esteemed and beloved sister, Mary E. Mathewson; and whereas, Bahia Vista Parlor has lost a true and loyal member, her husband a devoted wife and companion, her four sons and daughter a lovable mother, and her brother an affectionate sister;

Resolved, That the sympathy of the Parlor be extended to the bereaved members of the family and that the charter of the Parlor be draped in mourning for a period of thirty days; that a copy of these resolutions be sent to the family, and that a copy be spread in full upon the minutes of the Parlor; also, that a copy of the resolutions be published in The Grizzly Bear Magazine.

LOUISE McDOUGALL,
LOTTIE BISCHOFF,
DORA BRAYTON,
Committee.

Oakland, June 10, 1932.

MRS. CARRIE A. VANDERHOOF.

To the Officers and Members of Dardanelle Parlor No. 66 N.D.G.W.—We, your committee appointed to draft resolutions of condolence and respect to the memory of our departed sister, Mrs. Carrie A. Vanderhoof, respectfully submit the following:

Resolved, That in the death of Sister Vanderhoof, Dardanelle Parlor suffers the loss of a member worthy of the highest respect and esteem. We shall miss her deeds of kindness and sisterly love. And whereas, the "Portals of Eternal Pearl" opened to remove from our midst our beloved sister, Carrie A. Vanderhoof, we grieve and condole with those bereft. Yet they must find consolation in this thought:

"Forever from the Hand that takes
One blessing from us, others fall.
And soon or late, our Father makes
His perfect recompense to all."

Resolved, That the charter of Dardanelle Parlor be draped in mourning for a period of thirty days; that a copy of these resolutions be spread on the minutes of the Parlor, and that a copy be sent to the family of the deceased sister and one to The Grizzly Bear Magazine for publication.

Respectfully submitted,
HANNAH M. DOYLE,
NETTIE WHITTO,
ELIZABETH WRIGHT,
Committee.

Sonora, June 20, 1932.

Junior Boosters—The United States Junior Chamber of Commerce will meet in convention at Pasadena, Los Angeles County, July 20-24.

Recreation Congress—An International Recreation Congress is to be held at Los Angeles City, July 23-29.

"You do ill if you praise, and still worse if you reprove in a matter you do not understand." —Da Vinci.

SAN FRANCISCO

THIS YEAR'S STATEWIDE ADMISSION Day, September 9, celebration under the auspices of the Order of Native Sons of the Golden West will be held at San Francisco. That was decided by the San Francisco N.S.G.W. Extension of the Order Committee June 10, when Grand President Seth Millington was requested to designate San Francisco as the celebration city, and he did so. The Native Daughters will, as heretofore, join wholeheartedly in the festivities.

September 9, also, the American Legion will dedicate San Francisco's $5,500,000 Memorial building, and the Legion and the Natives will co-operate in fittingly observing Admission Day.

The Extension of the Order Committee elected the following officers: Grand Trustee Joseph J. McShane (Twin Peaks Parlor No. 214), chairman; Lloyd L. Doering (South San Francisco Parlor No. 157), vice-chairman; Harold J. Regan (South San Francisco Parlor No. 157), secretary; Grand Second Vice-president Chas. A. Koenig (Golden Gate Parlor No. 29), treasurer; Virgil Orengo (Rincon Parlor No. 72), sergeant-at-arms.

NATIVE DAUGHTER DOINGS.

Officers of Alta Parlor No. 3 were elected June 14, May L. MacDonald being chosen president.

At tables beautifully decorated with pink roses, Fremont Parlor No. 59 had a delightful dinner June 2. A musical program followed, under the direction of Mrs. May Dwyer. Participants included Mms. A. Groome, Kathryn McGrath, Ella Tait, Anita Johnson, May Grantley, Essie Gill, Etta O'Shea, Ella Hurd, and Miss Louise Adami.

In observance of mothers night, El Vespero Parlor No. 118 entertained twenty mothers with the playlet "Why Mothers Grow Gray." In the cast were Edna Farrell, Evelyn Simmens, Kate Paganucci, Helen Reddy, Irene Lapphaile and Renee Lozahic. Specialty numbers were given by President Anne Godfrey, Isabelle Casey, Ruby Bried. June 1 the Parlor celebrated its thirty-second institution anniversary at a banquet, the honor-guests being District Deputy Mae Marchant and Charter Members Nell R. Boege, organizer of El Vespero, Lillian Biggs, Anne Walsh, Mary Jordan, Mary Mahoney. The tables were decorated in bicentennial colors and the favors were martha washington dolls. New and fascinating games were played. Chairman Evelyn Simmens and her committee were highly praised for the very enjoyable affair they had arranged. The semi-annual whist June 14 was a success, financially and socially; Jane Lapachet was in charge.

The official visit of Grand President Evelyn I. Carlson to Genevieve Parlor No. 132 was an inspiring occasion. Among the many other visitors were Past Grands Genevieve Baker, after whom the Parlor was named, Dr. Mariana Bertola, Margaret Hill and Emma Foley, Grand Organist Lola Horgan, Grand Trustees Ethel Begley and Anna Thuesen, and Supervising Deputy Mae Boldemann. The hall was beautifully decorated with greens and flags, and an electrically lighted portrait of George Washington added much to its attractiveness. Numerous presentations were made, including $300 for the Loyalty Pledge fund from No. 132. Selections were rendered by the San Francisco and the Genevieve glee clubs. Grand President Carlson highly complimented President Rena Taube and her corps of competent officers, and spoke interestingly of the Order's projects. Refreshments were served at the meeting's conclusion.

The card party of Gabrielle Parlor No. 139 was enjoyed by a large number of members and their friends. The anniversary banquet was held June 7. The entertainment program was arranged by President Ruth Koehler, who put on an amusing play.

In observance of mothers night, the officers of Golden Gate Parlor No. 158 presented the play, "Let Mary Do It." Following the show the guests were escorted to the banquetroom, where the table was ladened with goodies. Each mother was presented with a beautiful handkerchief and hand-made sachet. Anita Werner had charge of the wonderful affair. In recognition of Flag Day, the past presidents were entertained June 13. At the beautifully decorated festive board the honor-guests were seated in rotation according to their terms of service. Each received a souvenir of the occasion.

An outstanding event was the official visit of Grand President Evelyn I. Carlson to her home-Parlor, Dolores No. 169, June 11. Dinner preceded the meeting, which was attended by an immense crowd, including visitors from all sections of the state. Native Sons auditorium, where the meeting was held, was gorgeously decorated. Mrs. Carlson was presented with an exquisite wrist watch. The entire arrangements for the homecoming were under the capable supervision of Ida Corrigan, who had the assistance of the Parlor's entire membership. At the supper served at the meeting's conclusion members of Dolores Parlor No. 208 N.S.G.W. poured the coffee.

Mae Waring was in charge of the entertainment for the mothers of the members of Castro Parlor No. 178. A program was presented by the N.D.G.W. glee club, Jacqueline Hogan, Rudie Swall, Barbara Latz, Jean Clare Mook, Venise Vaughn, Ruby Bried, Frances Dougherty and Al. Cirimelli. Refreshments were served.

Mrs. Amelia Silva of Dolores No. 169 N.D.G.W. entertained Grand President Evelyn I. Carlson at a delightful bridge luncheon at the Native Daughter Home June 2. The tables were decorated with choice flowers and attractive prizes were awarded. Guests included Grand Secretary Sallie R. Thaler, Past Grand Mae C. Boldemann, District Deputy Agnes McVerry, Erna Lazarus, Edna Gunther, Hazel Nelson, Mae Godfrey, Emma O'Meara, Millie Ghirardelli, Clara Casella, Lorayne Starner.

RECEPTION FOR OFFICIAL.

Castro Parlor No. 232 N.S.G.W. had a reception June 14 in honor of its past president, Harmon D. Skillin, elected Grand Third Vice-president at the Stockton Grand Parlor. Over three hundred attended to pay their respects, including delegations from all the bay region; Municipal Judge Leo Aggeler and Bernard Hiss (Hollywood Parlor No. 196); J. Hartley Russell (Stanford Parlor No. 76), Richard M. Hamb (Piedmont Parlor No. 120) and Alfred H. McKnew (San Francisco Parlor No. 49), former grand trustees; Sheriff Richard R. Veale (General Winn Parlor No. 32); James A. Wilson and Charles L. Dodge, Past Grands.

The grand officers in attendance included Grand President Seth Millington, Grand Second Vice Chas. A. Koenig, Grand Secretary John T. Regan, Grand Inside Sentinel Gam Hurst, Grand Trustees Jesse H. Miller, Joseph J. McShane and Charles H. Spengemann. An excellent entertainment program was presented, brief addresses were made and refreshments were served.

KEEP AFTER THE WEEDS.

Weeds have no place on the farm or in the garden. They rob the other plants of water, food, air and sunlight—all necessary for their proper development. There never has been a time when the farmers of the state have been so "weed conscious" as at present. Control of weeds, rather than an ineffectual attempt to eradicate them, has been made the basis of a program throughout California. In the home garden the control of weeds is simpler. But there is a tendency, as the season advances, to neglect work with the hoe and cultivator. See that weeds are kept out; each one removed means there will be less trouble next year. Control of weeds conserves moisture, saves plant food for the crops that should grow and adds to the sightliness of the garden.

Feminine World's Fads and Fancies

PREPARED ESPECIALLY FOR THE GRIZZLY BEAR BY ANNA STOERMER

A FLARE FOR COMBINING UNUSUAL colors, a penchant for wide swank girdles, a knack of adding just the vivid and vital touch of color to make a dashing effect—these are the things that have won a place in the hall of e and the smart shops. Let us review a few hem: One is made in the two-color theme, y with yellow, and red scarf to match. re's a two-piece sports dress in a waffle ive which has an interesting angora scarf elbow-length sleeves; a two-piece jersey h a satin vest and a wide girdle belt. An ependence-blue dress of sheer wool, but taild smartly, has great wine-red buttons as a or splash to fasten it.

n more formal things we dye the lace to ich the fabric exactly. For our Sunday-best ss of nile-green we use big pearl buttons that k like eardrops. "Stardust" is the name of a evening dress of heaven-blue, glistening h rhinestones. Another, more or less deiding on whether or not the jacket is worn, dress of pale yellow mousseline-de-soie with ash and bow of burnt-orange taffeta to match tiny bolero jacket with romantic puffed ves which tops it.

Pink and blue together offer one of the newest l loveliest of color notes as the summer sea- opens. An evening dress of orchid pink nbines chiffon and cartwheel lace, with the e in the skirt and sleeves in a beautifully cifful design. It is suggested that it be worn h turquoise accessories—turquoise shoes and jewels. Apple-green is another happy color to choose for wear with pink.

The tucked chiffon dress in dark colors with a collar of white satin is a favorite for the moment. Wine-red, in the popular soft woolens, crepes and prints, is a decidedly new fashion note. In the prints the white background with dark red dots, stripes, checks or other designs is very smart. This shade is also effectively combined with the new dust-pink.

The waffle-pleated scarf has entered the mode in scarf styles. The smart, flat, but higher, necklines characterize the new summer blouses in the popular new silks, rayon and cotton materials. For the white jacket-suit the print blouse in dots, checks or stripes is particularly favored.

Summer things can be as smartly and as chicly tailored as winter things. The new and fascinating styles prove that. The tailored sports things in washable materials are cool, serviceable and appropriate for a land where the sun is warm and the nights balmy.

It is a question that you must decide for yourself—whether you will join the "dotted" brigade or go in for stripes. Both are going strong. For business days and after-business informalities, there are flag stripes, candy stripes, sailor stripes, pin stripes, zigzag stripes, and so on, endlessly.

The knitted fashions have firmly entrenched themselves in feminine favor. Individuality is the keynote of the new collections. Even the design and fabric are "breezy," not to mention the mental stimulation derived from the lovely colors and subtle color harmonies. Boucle, angora and jersey are all represented in innumerable weaves and weights, with meshes and lacy weaves well in the lead.

"A scarf for every neck," would seem to be the slogan for this summer. Small ones are best—in any fabric, pattern and color scheme which look well with the rest of the costume. They should be worn tight around the throat, and are most chic if tied a little to one side. A hand-knitted scarf, with rows of three or four colors, is very smart, and so easy to make. Bangle bracelets are the smartest accessories to wear with sports clothes of all types.

A little less than nothing, is the answer to what's what in bathing suits this year. The so-called swim suit has a skirt knitted all in one—either a complete skirt or just an apron effect in front. Both types go in for a lot of intricate strappings, halter necks, suspender backs, and the like, to keep things where they should be, and still give the sun every chance. Sapphire and royal blue are most popular this year. White is still used a lot.

The day of so-called "modern art" in bathing-suit decoration is gone. Now, all the color contrast comes in the straps. Lime-yellow makes a clever suit, which has a lace weave to the straps and around the waist, making it look somewhat like a brassiere model. Nickknacks to go with slacks are halter sweaters, like those halter scarfs, except that they are knitted, striped and slip on over the head. The scarfs are adjustable, with metal clips. Other accessories are ballyhoo interlaced beach sandals and little bellhop jackets that match or contrast. Slacks themselves are of botany flannel, pique, jersey or corduroy, and are tailored navy-fashion—stylishly voluminous with metal buttons or zippers as trims.

During the outdoor season a smart sports costume "goes" everywhere except on the most formal occasion. So we're being practical as well as economical, and concentrating largely on simple tailored things.

With a long period of play-days just ahead for the little ones, mothers will be enthusiastic over the wide variety of styles offered. The grown-up fashion trends are apparent in all juvenile collections. Tailored styles vie with empire and waistline models, surpliced, ruffled and sashed. Color contrast is used effectively, and appliqued motifs, scallops, fine tuckings, pleatings, seamings, pockets, belts, embroidered motifs and buttons are useful and ornamental. Children's bathing suits are gay, brief affairs that leave the major portion of the body exposed to the health-giving rays of the summer sun. Swagger nautical togs are the most exciting of beach fashions for boys and girls. Slacks and pajamas in bicentennial colors are high favorites.

Apple Show—Sebastopol, Sonoma County, will stage its annual Gravenstein Apple Show, August 2-7.

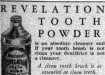

Official Directory of Parlors of

ALAMEDA COUNTY.

Alameda No. 47, Alameda City—Perry F. Badgley, Pres.; Robt. H. Cavanaugh, Sec., 1806 Pacific Ave.; Wednesdays, Native Sons Hall, 1406 Park St.
Oakland No. 50, Oakland—R. L. Engell, Pres.; F. M. Norris, Sec., 4280 Terrace St.; Fridays, Native Sons Hall, 11th and Clay Sts.
Las Positas No. 96, Livermore—Dr. Donald M. Fraser, Pres.; John J. Kelly, Sec., P. O. box 341; Thursdays, Foresters Hall.
Eden No. 113, Hayward—Henry L'Ecuyer, Pres.; Stanton R. Soares, Sec., P. O. box 176; 2nd and 4th Tuesdays, Memorial Hall, Main St.
Piedmont No. 120, Oakland—Frank Smith, Pres.; Charles Morando, Sec., 906 Vermont St.; Thursdays, Native Sons Hall, 11th and Clay Sts.
Wisteria No. 127, Alvarado—Henry May, Pres.; J. M. Scribner, Sec., Livermore; 1st Thursday, I.O.O.F. Hall.
Halcyon No. 146, Alameda City—Charles J. Von Tagen, Pres.; J. C. Bates, Sec., 2139 Buena Vista Ave.; 1st and 3rd Tuesdays, I.O.O.F. Hall, 2329 Santa Clara Ave.
Brooklyn No. 151, Oakland—Frank B. Perry, Pres.; E. W. Cooney, Sec., 3907 14th Ave.; Wednesdays, Masonic Temple, 8th Ave. and E. 14th St.
Washington No. 169, Centerville—M. B. Silva, Pres.; Allen G. Norris, Sec., P. O. box 31; 2nd and 4th Tuesdays, Hansen Hall.
Athens No. 195, Oakland—Elmer L. Bullock, Pres.; Harold B. Farley, Sec., 4623 Benevides Ave.; Tuesdays, Native Sons Hall, 11th and Clay Sts.
Berkeley No. 210, Berkeley—F. M. McGrath, Pres.; R. J. Garrett, Sec., 1708 Virginia St.; Tuesdays, Native Sons Hall, 2108 Shattuck Ave.
Estudillo No. 223, San Leandro—Frank V. Pacheco, Pres.; Albert G. Pacheco, Sec., 1736 E. 14th St.; 1st and 3rd Tuesdays, U.P.E.C. Hall.
Claremont No. 240, Oakland—Fred Buelna, Pres.; E. N. Thienger, Sec., 839 Hearst Ave., Berkeley; Tuesdays, Veterans Memorial Bldg., 43rd & Salem Sts., Emeryville.
Pleasanton No. 244, Pleasanton—Peter C. Madsen, Pres.; Ernest W. Schween, Sec.; 2nd and 4th Thursdays, I.O.O.F. Hall.
Niles No. 250, Niles—M. L. Fournier, Pres.; C. E. Martenstein, Sec.; 2nd Thursday, I.O.O.F. Hall.
Fruitvale No. 252, Oakland—William J. Keating Jr., Pres.; Ray B. Felton, Sec., 1575 Alice St.; Fridays, W.O.W. Hall, 3256 E. 14th St.

AMADOR COUNTY.

Amador No. 17, Sutter Creek—Frank Marre, Pres.; F. J. Payne, Sec.; 1st and 3rd Fridays, Native Sons Hall.
Excelsior No. 31, Jackson—Wm. Daugherty, Pres.; William Going, Sec.; 1st and 3rd Wednesdays, Native Sons Hall, 22 Court St.
Ione No. 33, Ione—Marvin Kidd, Pres.; Josiah H. Saunders, Sec.; 1st and 3rd Wednesdays, Native Sons Hall.
Plymouth No. 48, Plymouth—L. E. Houston, Pres.; Thos. D. Davis, Sec.; 1st and 3rd Saturdays, I.O.O.F. Hall.

BUTTE COUNTY.

Argonaut No. 8, Oroville—Thomas R. Cole, Pres.; Cyril R. Macdonald, Sec., P. O. box 502; 1st and 3rd Wednesdays, Veterans Memorial Hall.
Chico No. 21, Chico—Marcus Choisser, Pres.; Sam Lindsay Adams, Sec., Sacramento Blvd.; 2nd and 4th Thursdays, Elks Hall.

CALAVERAS COUNTY.

Chispa No. 139, Murphys—Maynard Segale, Pres.; Antone Malaspina, Sec.; Wednesdays, Native Sons Hall.

COLUSA COUNTY.

Colusa No. 69, Colusa City—Burton L. Smart, Pres.; Phil J. Humburg, Sec., 223 Parkhill St.; Tuesdays, Eagles Hall.

CONTRA COSTA COUNTY.

General Winn No. 32, Antioch—Edmont T. Uren, Pres.; Joel H. Ford, Sec., P. O. box 311; 2nd and 4th Wednesdays, Union Hall.
Mount Diablo No. 101, Martinez—R. P. Anderson, Pres.; G. T. Barkley, Sec.; 1st and 3rd Mondays, I.O.O.F. Hall.
Byron No. 170, Byron—William E. Bunn, Pres.; H. G. Krumland, Sec.; 1st and 3rd Tuesdays, I.O.O.F. Hall.
Carquinez No. 205, Crockett—Thos. Cox, Pres.; Thomas I. Cahalan, Sec.; 1st and 3rd Wednesdays, I.O.O.F. Hall.
Richmond No. 217, Richmond—M. W. Amaral, Pres.; H. D. Mason, Sec., 11 6th St.; Wednesdays, Redmen Hall, 11th and Nevan Ave.
Concord No. 245, Concord—P. M. Soto, Pres.; D. E. Pramberg, Sec., P. O. box 235; 1st Tuesday, I.O.O.F. Hall.
Diamond No. 246, Pittsburg—Victor Ericsson, Pres.; Francis A. Irving, Sec., 248 E. 5th St.; 1st and 3rd Wednesdays, Veterans Memorial Bldg.

EL DORADO COUNTY.

Placerville No. 9, Placerville—George M. Smith, Pres.; Duncan Bathurst, Sec., 12 Gilmore St.; 2nd and 4th Tuesdays, Masonic Hall.
Georgetown No. 91, Georgetown—W. H. Breedlove, Pres.; C. F. Irish, Sec.; 2nd and 4th Wednesdays, I.O.O.F. Hall.

FRESNO COUNTY.

Fresno No. 25, Fresno City—A. G. Miller, Pres.; John W. Cappleman, Sec., 1889 Wilson; 2nd and 4th Fridays, W.O.W. Hall, 1354 Van Ness Ave.

GRAND OFFICERS.

Dr. Frank I. Gonzalez..............Junior Past Grand President
Flood Bldg., San Francisco
Seth Millington..............................Grand President
Gridley
Justice Emmet SeaWell..............Grand First Vice-president
State Bldg., San Francisco
Chas. A. Koenig..................Grand Second Vice-president
531 35th Ave., San Francisco
Harmon D. Skillin.................Grand Third Vice-president
Mills Bldg., San Francisco
John T. Regan...............................Grand Secretary
N.S.G.W. Bldg., 414 Mason St., San Francisco
John A. Corotto.............................Grand Treasurer
560 No. 5th St., San Jose
W. B. O'Brien.................................Grand Marshal
2324 Santa Clara St., Alameda
Gam Hurst,...........................Grand Inside Sentinel
Financial Center Bldg., Oakland
William A. Reuter...................Grand Outside Sentinel
1009 Marine Ave., Wilmington
Leslie Maloche...............................Grand Organist
467½ 3rd St., San Bernardino
Chester Gannon.............................Historiographer
613 Capital Ntl. Bank Bldg., Sacramento

GRAND TRUSTEES.

Jesse H. Miller...............712 DeYoung Bldg., San Francisco
Eldred L. Meyer.........922 San Vicente Blvd., Santa Monica
John M. Burnett................914 Bank Italy Bldg., San Jose
Henry S. Lyon..Placerville
Joseph J. McShane...............419 Flood Bldg., San Francisco
Horace J. Leavitt....................................Weaverville
Chas. H. Spengemann.............827 27th Ave., San Francisco

Selma No. 107, Selma—Chester E. Shepard, Pres.; E. C. Laughlin, Sec.; 1st and 3rd Wednesdays, American Legion Hall.

HUMBOLDT COUNTY.

Humboldt No. 14, Eureka—Edward J. Quinn, Pres.; Loren M. Nelson, Sec., P.O. box 195; 2nd and 4th Mondays, Native Sons Hall.
Arcata No. 20, Arcata—I. C. Fleckenstein, Pres.; William Peters, Sec., P. O. box 1117; Thursdays, Native Sons Hall.
Ferndale No. 93, Ferndale—Elwood Pries, Pres.; C. H. Rasmussen, Sec., R.F.D., 47-A; 1st and 3rd Mondays, K.P. Hall.

KERN COUNTY.

Bakersfield No. 42, Bakersfield—G. E. Taylor, Pres.; Don S. Simpson, Sec., P.O. Box 924; Wednesdays, Justice Court, City Hall.

LAKE COUNTY.

Lower Lake No. 159, Lower Lake—Harold S. Anderson, Pres.; Albert Kugelman, Sec.; Thursdays, I.O.O.F. Hall.

LASSEN COUNTY.

Honey Lake No. 198, Standish—James C. Meeske, Pres.; N. V. Wemple, Sec., Litchfield; 1st and 3rd Wednesdays, Wrede Hall.
Big Valley No. 211, Bieber—George Bunselmeier, Pres.; A. W. McKenzie, Sec.; 1st and 3rd Wednesdays, I.O.O.F. Hall.

LOS ANGELES COUNTY.

Los Angeles No. 45, Los Angeles City—Owen S. Adams, Pres.; Richard W. Fryer, Sec., 1629 Champlain Ter.; Thursdays, Merchant Plumbers Hall, 1832 So. Hope.
Ramona No. 109, Los Angeles City—James M. Watson, Pres.; John V. Scott, Sec., Patriotic Hall, 1816 So. Figueroa; Fridays, Patriotic Hall, 1816 So. Figueroa.
Hollywood No. 196, Los Angeles City—Leo Aggeler, Pres.; E. J. Reilly, Sec., 907 W. 2nd St.; Mondays, 1089 No. Oxford Ave.
Long Beach No. 239, Long Beach—Francis H. Gentry, Pres.; W. W. Brady, Sec., 801 Jergins Trust Bldg.; 2nd and 4th Thursdays, Moose Hall, Elm and Anaheim.
Sepulveda No. 263, San Pedro—Francis G. Fetzer, Pres.; Frank I. Markey, Sec., 101 W. 7th St.; 2nd and 4th Fridays, Odd Fellows Temple, 10th and Gaffey Sts.
Glendale No. 264, Glendale—Philip D. Molen, Pres.; Abel B. Molen, Sec., 508 So. Belmont St.; 1st and 3rd Tuesdays, Masonic Temple, 234 So. Brand Blvd.
Santa Monica Bay No. 267, Ocean Park—Orrin G. Welch, Pres.; John J. Smith, Sec., 830 Rialto Ave., Venice; 2nd and 4th Mondays, New Eagle Hall, 2823½ Main St.
Cahuenga No. 268, Reseda—Harold C. Trexler, Pres.; Carrol S. Driscoll, Sec., P.O. box 25, Chatsworth; first Friday, Alton Hall.

MADERA COUNTY.

Madera No. 130, Madera City—Cornelius Noble, Pres.; T. P. Cosgrave, Sec.; 1st and 3rd Thursdays, First National Bank Bldg.

MARIN COUNTY.

Mount Tamalpais No. 64, San Rafael—M. E. Peterson, Pres.; Manual A. Andrade, Sec., 532 Mission Ave.; 1st and 3rd Mondays, Portuguese American Hall.
Sea Point No. 158, Sausalito—A. H. Bettencourt, Pres.; Manuel Santos, Sec., 6 Glen Drive; 1st and 3rd Wednesdays, Perry Bldg.
Nicasio No. 183, Nicasio—M. T. Farley, Pres.; R. J. Rogers, Sec.; 2nd and 4th Wednesdays, U.A.O.D. Hall.

MENDOCINO COUNTY.

Ukiah No. 71, Ukiah—Henry Bucknell, Pres.; Ben Hofman, Sec., P. O. box 473; 1st and 3rd Mondays, I.O.O.F. Hall.
Broderick No. 117, Point Arena—Sam Reinking, Pres.; H. C. Hunter, Sec.; 1st and 3rd Thursdays, Forester Hall.
Alder Glen No. 200, Fort Bragg—H. M. Bohn, Pres.; C. R. Weller, Sec.; 2nd and 4th Fridays, I.O.O.F. Hall.

MERCED COUNTY.

Yosemite No. 24, Merced City—John J. Thronton, Pres.; True W. Fowler, Sec., P. O. box 781; 2nd and 4th Mondays, I.O.O.F. Hall.

MONTEREY COUNTY.

Monterey No. 75, Monterey City—John Thomsen, Pres.; T. W. Krieger, Sec., 999 Franklin St.; 1st and 3rd Fridays, Knights Pythias Hall, Main St.
Santa Lucia No. 97, Salinas—E. L. Adcock, Pres.; R. W. Adcock, Sec., Route 2, box 141; Mondays, Native Sons Hall, 32 W. Alisal St.
Gabilan No. 132, Castroville—B. A. McCoy, Pres.; R. H. Martin, Sec., P. O. box 81; 1st and 3rd Thursdays, Native Sons Hall.

NAPA COUNTY.

Saint Helena No. 53, Saint Helena—E. W. Johnson, Pres.; Edw. L. Bonhote, Sec., P. O. box 267; Mondays, Native Sons Hall.
Napa No. 62, Napa City—R. O. Akers, Pres.; H. J. Hoernle, Sec., 1226 Oak St.; Mondays, Native Sons Hall.

ATTENTION, SECRETARIES!

THIS DIRECTORY IS PUBLISHED BY AUTHORITY OF THE GRAND PARLOR N.S.G.W., AND ALL NOTICES OF CHANGES MUST BE RECEIVED BY THE GRAND SECRETARY (NOT THE MAGAZINE) ON OR BEFORE THE 20TH OF EACH MONTH TO INSURE CORRECTION IN NEXT ISSUE OF DIRECTORY.

James H. Hayes, Sec., 4014 18th St.; Tuesdays, Native Sons Bldg., 414 Mason St.

alboa No. 234, San Francisco—J. LeMer, Pres.; E. W. Boyd, Sec., 45 Carl St.; Thursdays, Maccabee Hall, 5th Ave. and Clement St.

ret Harte No. 260, San Francisco—J. F. Craig, Pres.; O. J. Eggers, Sec., 194 Prague St.; Tuesdays, West of Twin Peaks Hall, 233 Legion Court.

topia No. 270, San Francisco—George Walters, Pres.; Herbert H. Schneider, Sec., 2455 19th Ave.; Tuesdays, American Hall, 20th and Capp Sts.

SAN JOAQUIN COUNTY.

tockton No. 7, Stockton—John D. Gallagher, Pres.; R. D. Dorcey, Sec., P. O. box 388; Mondays, Native Sons Hall.

odi No. 18, Lodi—Jerome Solomon, Pres.; Dr. Clyde Bresnan, Sec.; 2nd and 4th Wednesdays, Eagles Hall.

racy No. 186, Tracy—R. J. Marraccini, Pres.; R. J. Marraccini, Sec., R.F.D. No. 1, box 217; Thursdays, I.O.O.F. Hall.

anteca No. 271, Manteca—Louis Ryan, Pres.; Leonard Faria, Sec., R.F.D. No. 1, Lathrop; 1st and 3rd Wednesdays, I.O.O.F. Hall.

SAN LUIS OBISPO COUNTY.

an Miguel No. 150, San Miguel—H. Twisselman, Pres.; George Sonnenberg Jr., Sec.; 1st and 3rd Wednesdays, Fraternal Hall.

ambria No. 152, Cambria—Roy Cardoza, Pres.; A. S. Gay, Sec.; Wednesdays, Rigdon Hall.

SAN MATEO COUNTY.

edwood No. 66, Redwood City—Joseph Lodi, Pres.; A. S. Liguori, Sec., P. O. box 212; Thursdays, American Foresters Hall.

easide No. 95, Half Moon Bay—William Deeney, Pres.; John G. Gilcrest, Sec.; 2nd and 4th Tuesdays, I.O.O.F. Hall.

enlo No. 185, Menlo Park—C. T. Maloney, Pres.; F. W. Johnson, Sec., P. O. box 601; Thursdays, Masonic Hall.

ebble Beach No. 230, Pescadero—Harold Souza, Pres.; E. A. Shaw, Sec.; 2nd and 4th Wednesdays, I.O.O.F. Hall.

l Carmelo No. 256, Daly City—Edward Eliasen, Pres.; Walter L. Murphy, Sec., 931 Hanover St.; 2nd and 4th Wednesdays, Eagles Hall.

dustrial City No. 269, South San Francisco—John C. Hamilton, Pres.; Geo. A. Roll, Sec., P. O. box 237; 2nd and 4th Mondays, Metropolitan Hall.

SANTA BARBARA COUNTY.

anta Barbara No. 116, Santa Barbara City—C. W. McCormick, Pres.; H. C. Sweetser, Sec., Court House; 1st and 3rd Wednesdays, I.O.O.F. Hall.

SANTA CLARA COUNTY.

an Jose No. 22, San Jose—Joseph Sabatte, Pres.; H. W. McComas, Sec., Suite 7, Porter Bldg.; Mondays, I.O.O.F. Hall.

anta Clara No. 100, Santa Clara City—John J. Trinajstich, Pres.; Clarence Clevenger, Sec., P. O. box 297; Wednesdays, Redmen Hall.

bservatory No. 177, San Jose—William L. Gerrans, Pres.; A. B. Langford, Sec., Hall Records; Tuesdays, Knights Columbus Hall, 40 No. First St.

ountain View No. 215, Mountain View—Gilbert F. McCorkle, Pres.; C. A. Antonioli, Sec., 301 Castro St.; 2nd and 4th Wednesdays, Mockbee Hall.

alo Alto No. 216, Palo Alto—John C. Bernal, Pres.; Albert A. Quinn, Sec., 643 High St.; Mondays, Native Sons Bldg., Hamilton Ave. and Emerson St.

SANTA CRUZ COUNTY.

atsonville No. 65, Watsonville—A. W. Batchelder, Pres.; R. R. Tindall, Sec., R.F.D. No. 5, Box 313; 2nd and 4th Tuesdays, I.O.O.F. Hall.

anta Cruz No. 90, Santa Cruz City—W. H. Mori, Pres.; T. V. Mathews, Sec., 105 Pacheco Ave.; Tuesdays, Native Sons Hall, 117 Pacific Ave.

SHASTA COUNTY.

cCloud No. 149, Redding—Errol Yank, Pres.; Hugh A. Shuffleton, Sec.; 1st and 3rd Thursdays, Moose Hall.

SIERRA COUNTY.

ownieville No. 92, Downieville—Frank H. Turner, Pres.; H. S. Tibbey, Sec.; 2nd and 4th Mondays, I.O.O.F. Hall.

olden Nugget No. 94, Sierra City—Elmer Thompson, Pres.; Arthur R. Pride, Sec.; last Saturday, Masonic Hall.

SISKIYOU COUNTY.

na No. 192, Etna—Fred M. Wolford, Pres.; Harvey A. Green, Sec.; 1st and 3rd Wednesdays, I.O.O.F. Hall.

berty No. 193, Sawyers Bar—Orrin R. Bigelow, Pres.; John M. Barry, Sec.; 1st and 3rd Saturdays, I.O.O.F. Hall.

SOLANO COUNTY.

lano No. 39, Suisun—Karl Koch, Pres.; J. W. Kinlock, Sec.; 1st and 3rd Tuesdays, I.O.O.F. Hall.

llejo No. 77, Vallejo—Joseph Clavo, Pres.; Werner B. Hallin, Sec., 912 Carolina; 2nd and 4th Tuesdays, San Pablo Hall.

SONOMA COUNTY.

taluma No. 27, Petaluma—George Geils, Pres.; C. F. Fobes, Sec., 114 Prospect St.; 2nd and 4th Mondays, Druid Hall, Gross Bldg., 41 Main St.

nta Rosa No. 28, Santa Rosa—Wesley Beach, Pres.; Leland S. Lewis, Sec., Court House; Mondays, Native Sons Hall.

en Ellen No. 102, Glen Ellen—C. C. Weise, Pres.; Frank Kirch, Sec., Route 3, Santa Rosa; 2nd Monday, N.S.G.W. Hall.

noma No. 111, Sonoma City—Joseph Andrieux, Pres.; L. H. Green, Sec.; 1st and 3rd Mondays, I.O.O.F. Hall.

bastopol No. 143, Sebastopol—O. A. McChristian, Pres.; F. G. McFarlane, Sec.; 1st and 3rd Fridays, I.O.O.F. Hall.

STANISLAUS COUNTY.

odesto No. 11, Modesto—Robert H. Hansen, Pres.; C. C. Eastin Jr., Sec., P. O. box 898; 1st and 3rd Wednesdays, I.O.O.F. Hall.

kdale No. 142, Oakdale—D. W. Tulloch, Pres.; E. T. Gobin, Sec.; 2nd Monday, Legion Hall.

estimba No. 247, Crows Landing—Lloyd W. Fink, Pres.; G. W. Fink, Sec.; 1st and 3rd Wednesdays, Community Club Home.

SUTTER COUNTY.

tter No. 261, Sutter City—Stanley R. McLean, Pres.; Glen R. Haynes, Sec., Yuba City; 2nd and 4th Mondays, N.D.G.W. Hall.

TRINITY COUNTY.

unt Bally No. 87, Weaverville—M. F. Kay, Pres.; E. V. Ryan, Sec.; 1st and 3rd Mondays, Native Sons Hall.

TUOLUMNE COUNTY.

olumne No. 144, Sonora—Mathew J. Marshall, Pres.; William M. Harrington, Sec., P. O. box 715; 2nd and 4th Fridays, Knights Columbus Hall.

lumbia No. 258, Columbia—Jos. Cadematori, Pres.; Charles E. Grant, Sec.; 2nd and 4th Thursdays, Native Sons Hall.

VENTURA COUNTY.

brillo No. 114, Ventura City—David Bennett, Pres., 1380 Church St.

YOLO COUNTY.

odland No. 30, Woodland—J. L. Aronson, Pres.; E. B. Hayward, Sec.; 1st Thursday, Native Sons Hall.

YUBA COUNTY.

rysville No. 6, Marysville—Ray C. Burris, Pres.; Verne Fogarty, Sec., 719 6th St.; 2nd Friday, Foresters Hall.

inbow No. 40, Wheatland—F. M. Beilby, Pres.; W. A. Bowser, Sec., P. O. box 313; 2nd Thursday, I.O.O.F. Hall.

GRAND PRESIDENT'S ASSISTANTS

GRIDLEY—IN ADDITION TO THOSE announced in The Grizzly Bear for June, Grand President Seth Millington has made the following appointments of committeemen, district deputies and deputy grand presidents for the 1932-33 N.S.G.W. Grand Parlor year:

COMMITTEES.

Ritual—Burrel D. Neighbours (Ramona No. 109), Thomas J. McKeon (Calistoga No. 86), Chandos E. Bush (Ramona No. 109), James F. Stanley (Stanford No. 76), Frank M. Buckley (National No. 118).

Employment—First District, Joseph B. Keenan (Niantic No. 105), Herman Zimmerman (South San Francisco No. 157), William H. James (California No. 1). Second District, Leonard Stone (Alder Glen No. 200), Thomas D. Davis (Plymouth No. 48), Thomas McAuliffe (Sacramento No. 3). Third District, Eugene W. Biscailuz (Santa Monica Bay No. 267), H. C. Sweetser (Santa Barbara No. 116), Earl Hus LeMoine (Los Angeles No. 45).

State Board Relief—D. D. Gibbons (Sequoia No. 160), R. M. Hamb (Piedmont No. 120), John J. Ryan (South San Francisco No. 157), Felix Robson (Claremont No. 240), Jesse M. Waterman (Observatory No. 177), Thomas J. Bowen (James Lick No. 242), Al Cron (Los Angeles No. 45), Ralph I. Harbison (Ramona No. 109), C. H. Rasmussen (Ferndale No. 93).

Education—Peter T. Conmy (Golden Gate No. 29), Charles R. Boden (Pacific No. 10), A. J. Cloud (Stanford No. 76), George F. McNoble (Stockton No. 7), Henry G. Bodkin (Hollywood No. 196).

Forestry and Conservation—R. L. P. Bigelow (Hydraulic No. 56), Southard M. Modry (Bret Harte No. 260), Carl O. Gerhardy (Alder Glen No. 200), Joseph P. Sproul (Hollywood No. 196), John Andreson Jr. (Arrowhead No. 110).

DISTRICT DEPUTY GRAND PRESIDENTS.

No. 1, Liberty No. 193—John M. Barry (Liberty No. 193).

No. 2, Etna No. 192—L. E. Buchner (Etna No. 192).

No. 3, McCloud No. 149—Arthur M. Dean (McCloud No. 149).

No. 4, Mount Bally No. 87—R. L. Marshall (Mount Bally No. 87).

No. 5, Humboldt No. 14, Arcata No. 20, Ferndale No. 93—J. B. Tilley (Arcata No. 20).

No. 6, Ukiah No. 71—Joseph R. Figone (Ukiah No. 71).

No. 7, Broderick No. 117, Alder Glen No. 200—Ralph W. Todd (Alder Glen No. 200).

No. 8, Honey Lake No. 198—Zehnor Johnson (Honey Lake No. 198).

No. 9, Big Valley No. 211—Ben Dunscimeier (Big Valley No. 211).

No. 10, Quincy No. 131, Golden Anchor No. 182, Plumas No. 228—J. D. McLaughlin (Quincy No. 131).

No. 11, Colusa No. 69, Sutter No. 261—Elton C. Fitch (Colusa No. 69).

No. 12, Downieville No. 92, Golden Nugget No. 94—J. M. McMahon (Downieville No. 92).

No. 13, Hydraulic No. 56, Quartz No. 58, Auburn No. 59—Wendel F. Roble (Auburn No. 59).

No. 14, Donner No. 162—M. J. McGwinn (Donner No. 162).

No. 15, Marysville No. 6, Argonaut No. 8, Chico No. 21—C. R. MacDonald (Argonaut No. 8).

No. 16, Rainbow No. 40, Silver Star No. 63, Rocklin No. 233—H. A. Schroeder (Silver Star No. 63).

No. 17, Petaluma No. 27, Sebastopol No. 143—R. J. Brusatori (Mount Tamalpais No. 64).

No. 18, Glen Ellen No. 102, Sonoma No. 111—L. S. Lewis (Santa Rosa No. 28).

No. 19, Santa Rosa No. 28—Louis Busch (Sonoma No. 111).

No. 20, Mount Tamalpais No. 64, Sea Point No. 158, Nicasio No. 183—Joseph S. Rosa (Sea Point No. 158).

No. 21, Mount Diablo No. 101, Byron No. 170, Carquinez No. 205—J. J. Meaney (Carquinez No. 205).

No. 22, General Winn No. 32, Richmond No. 217, Concord No. 245, Diamond No. 246—W. A. Clement (Diamond No. 246).

No. 23, Saint Helena No. 53, Napa No. 62, Calistoga No. 86, Lower Lake No. 159—Lucien SaViez (Calistoga No. 86).

No. 24, Solano No. 39, Vallejo No. 77—Melvin F. Brooks (Vallejo No. 77).

No. 25, Sunset No. 26, Elk Grove No. 41, Galt No. 243—W. H. Thisby (Courtland No. 106).

No. 26, Woodland No. 30, Granite No. 83, Sutter Fort No. 241—Joseph Lannon (Sacramento No. 3).

No. 27, Sacramento No. 3, Courtland No. 106—Clyde L. Corcoran (Sunset No. 26).

No. 28, Placerville No. 9, Georgetown No. 91—George Smith (Placerville No. 9).

No. 29, Amador No. 17, Excelsior No. 31, Ione No. 33, Plymouth No. 48—Thomas D. Davis (Plymouth No. 48).

No. 30, Chispa No. 139—Milton Stevens (Chispa No. 139).

No. 31, Tuolumne No. 144, Columbia No. 258—Rowan Hardin (Tuolumne No. 144).

No. 32, Stockton No. 7, Tracy No. 186—Walter Solomon (Lodi No. 18).

No. 33, Lodi No. 18, Oakdale No. 142, Manteca No. 271—Lawrence Buol (Stockton No. 7).

No. 34, Alameda No. 47, Halcyon No. 146—Allen O. Norris (Washington No. 169).

No. 35, Oakland No. 50, Eden No. 113—Frank B. Perry (Brooklyn No. 151).

No. 36, Washington No. 169, Pleasanton No. 244—Albert O. Pacheco (Estudillo No. 223).

No. 37, Brooklyn No. 151, Fruitvale No. 252—Ernest Schweeu (Pleasanton No. 244).

No. 38, Las Positas No. 96, Piedmont No. 120—Elwood Fitzgerald (Oakland No. 50).

No. 39, Berkeley No. 210, Claremont No. 240—Victor A. Raible (Piedmont No. 120).

No. 40, Athens No. 195, Estudillo No. 223—Joseph F. Ehrhart (Fruitvale No. 252).

No. 41, Wisteria No. 127, Niles No. 250—Henry E. Uebner (Athens No. 195).

No. 42, San Jose No. 22, Mountain View No. 215—Jesse M. Waterman (Observatory No. 177).

No. 43, Santa Clara No. 100, Observatory No. 177, Menlo No. 185—P. F. Blanchard (Menlo No. 185).

No. 44, Redwood No. 66, Palo Alto No. 216—A. S. Liguori (Redwood No. 66).

No. 45, Seaside No. 95, Pebble Beach No. 230—M. R. Mattei (Pebble Beach No. 230).

No. 46, Fremont No. 44, Watsonville No. 65, Santa Cruz No. 90—Arnold R. Baldwin (Santa Cruz No. 90).

No. 47, Monterey No. 75, Santa Lucia No. 97, Gabilan No. 132—John R. Thomsen (Monterey No. 75).

No. 48, San Miguel No. 150—Henry Twisselman (San Miguel No. 150).

No. 49, Cambria No. 152—A. S. Gay (Cambria No. 152).

No. 50, Modesto No. 11, Yosemite No. 24, Orestimba No. 247—Charles W. Gill (Modesto No. 11).

No. 51, Fresno No. 25, Selma No. 107, Madera No. 130—George Haines (Fresno No. 25).

No. 52, Bakersfield No. 42—Frank M. Lane (Fresno No. 25).

No. 53, Cabrillo No. 114, Santa Barbara No. 116—A. C. Dinsmore (Santa Barbara No. 116).

No. 54, Los Angeles No. 45, Cahuenga No. 268—Walter E. Baskerville (Ramona No. 109).

No. 55, Ramona No. 109, Hollywood No. 196—Howard Bentley (Los Angeles No. 45).

No. 56, Sepulveda No. 263, Glendale No. 264—Harry T. Honn (Santa Monica Bay No. 267).

No. 57, Long Beach No. 239, Santa Monica Bay No. 267—E. E. Baldwin (Sepulveda No. 263).

No. 58, Santa Ana No. 265—George J. MacDonald (Arrowhead No. 110).

No. 59, Arrowhead No. 110—Ray Marsile (Santa Ana No. 265).

No. 60, San Diego No. 108—Edward H. Dowell (San Diego No. 108).

No. 61, Pacific No. 10, El Dorado No. 52, Industrial City No. 269—Lloyd J. Doering (South San Francisco No. 157).

No. 62, Mission No. 38, Utopia No. 270—Fred A. Hornblower (Rincon No. 72).

No. 63, San Francisco No. 49, Dolores No. 208—Dr. William R. Vizzard (Sequoia No. 160).

No. 64, California No. 1, Stanford No. 76—Robert Donohue (El Dorado No. 52).

No. 65, South San Francisco No. 157, Precita No. 187—Walter T. Podd (Presidio No. 194).

No. 66, Bay City No. 104, Sequoia No. 160—Harry Alexander (Pacific No. 10).

No. 67, Hesperian No. 137, Twin Peaks No. 214—Thomas M. Dillon (Castro No. 232).

No. 68, Marshall No. 202, Castro No. 232—Gustave E. Ritter (Hesperian No. 137).

No. 69, Presidio No. 194, Balboa No. 234—Theo Schmidt (Stanford No. 76).

No. 70, Golden Gate No. 29, Rincon No. 72—Paul Conniff (Pacific No. 10).

No. 71, National No. 118, Alcalde No. 154—Hubert J. Caveney (Stanford No. 76).

No. 72, Niantic No. 105, Guadalupe No. 231—J. W. Smith (Precita No. 187).

No. 73, El Capitan No. 222, Olympus No. 189—Howard Stewart (Mission No. 38).

No. 74, El Carmelo No. 256, Bret Harte No. 260—Ferdinand Hauck (Alcalde No. 154).

DEPUTY GRAND PRESIDENTS AT LARGE.

Fred Ehlers (California No. 1), Clarence M. Hunt (Sacramento No. 3), L. T. Sinnott (Marysville No. 6), Walter Rothenbush (Stockton No. 7), W. H. Hibbard (Argonaut No. 8), Walton E. Holmes (Sunset No. 26), Al Cron (Los Angeles No. 45), Alfred Vlautin (El Dorado No. 52), Joseph Tinney (Rincon No. 72), I. M. Peckham (Stanford No. 76), C. E. Newton (Santa Clara No. 100), A. V. Mayrhofer (San Diego No. 108), Donald E. VanLueven (Arrowhead No. 110), Walter Melvin Davis (Piedmont No. 120), Frank Roemer (Piedmont No. 120), R. J. Marraccini (Tracy No. 186), James B. McSheehy (Twin Peaks No. 214), Al Lobree (Castro No. 232), Walter Hiskey (Santa Ana No. 265), John T. Regan (Grand Secretary).

AFFILIATED ORGANIZATIONS.

San Francisco Extension of the Order Committee, N.S.G.W.—Harmon D. Skillin, Chmn.; Harold J. Regan, Sec., 414 Mason St., San Francisco; meets 2nd and 4th Fridays, Grizzly Bear Club, 414 Mason St., San Francisco.

Alameda County Extension of the Order Committee, N.S.G.W.—Edward T. Schnarr, Chmn.; Frank Roemer, Sec., 3297 Morcom Ave., Oakland; meets 1st and 3rd Mondays, N.S.G.W. Hall, 11th and Clay Sts., Oakland.

Interparlor Committee (Southern District), N.S.G.W. and N.D.G.W.—Burrel D. Neighbours, Chmn.; F. J. Burmester, Sec., P. O. box 43, Colton; meets 2nd and 4th Fridays, Patriotic Hall, 1816 So. Figueroa St., Los Angeles.

San Francisco Assembly No. 1 Past Presidents Association N.S.G.W.—Meets 1st and 3rd Fridays, Native Sons Bldg., 414 Mason St., San Francisco; J. H. Sylvester, Gov.; J. F. Stanley, Sec., 1175 O'Farrell St., San Francisco.

East Bay Counties Assembly No. 3 Past Presidents Association N.S.G.W.—Meets 4th Monday, Native Sons Hall, 11th and Clay Sts., Oakland; Felix Robison, Gov.; Edgar G. Hanson, Sec., 1260 Russell St., Berkeley.

Marin County Assembly No. 5 Past Presidents Association N.S.G.W.—J. S. Rose Jr., Gov.; L. J. Peter, Sec., Peter Bldg., 4th and "C" Sts., San Rafael.

Fred H. Greeley Assembly No. 6 Past Presidents Association N.S.G.W.—Meets monthly with different Parlors comprising district; R. L. P. Bigelow, Gov.; Barney Barry, Sec., P. O. box 72, Lincoln.

San Joaquin Assembly No. 7 Past Presidents Association N.S.G.W.—Meets 1st Friday, Native Sons Hall, Stockton; Clyde H. Gregg, Gov.; R. D. Dorcey, Sec., Native Sons Club, Stockton.

Sonoma County Assembly No. 9 Past President Association N.S.G.W.—Meets monthly at different Parlor headquarters in county; Louis Bosch, Gov.; L. S. Lewis, Sec., Court House, Santa Rosa.

General John A. Sutter Assembly No. 10 Past Presidents Association—C. C. Wachman, Gov.; Jas. J. Longshore, Sec., 514 "J" St., Sacramento.

Grizzly Bear Club—Members all Parlors outside San Francisco at all times welcome. Clubrooms top floor Native Sons Bldg., 414 Mason St., San Francisco.

Native Sons and Native Daughters Central Committee on Homeless Children—Main office, 955 Phelan Bldg., San Francisco; Mrs. John W. Stirling, Chmn.; Miss Mary E. Brusie, Sec. Los Angeles branch office, 3924 Sunset Blvd.; Dorothy Schlingman, Sec.

(ADVERTISEMENT.)

Olympic Stamps—In honor of the Olympic games at Los Angeles City, the Federal Government has issued two special stamps, a three-cent of violet color and a five-cent of blue.

Historic Name Revived—Oleta, in Amador County, has, by order of the Federal Postoffice Department, had its name changed to the original title, Fiddletown.

LOS ANGELES
CITY AND COUNTY

HOLLYWOOD BOWL'S ELEVENTH ANnual season of "Symphonies Under the Stars" will open Tuesday evening, July 5, in the great amphitheater. Dr. Alfred Hertz, "father of the bowl," has been chosen to conduct the first program, and Bowl officials announce the occasion will be one of the events of the Olympic year concert series. Preparations for the special events to be presented with the orchestra during the eight-week summer season have been under way for several weeks, and with the completion recently of the list of ballet producers to be represented, and the addition of two noted soloists' names, but few details of the ambitious plans for the season remain to be arranged.

A highlight of the first week's concerts will be the appearance July 8 of the 300-voice Los Angeles civic chorus, singing "Hiawatha's Wedding Feast," by Coleridge-Taylor, with Sir Hamilton Harty, who will follow Hertz in the conductor's stand, directing. Bowl officials announced that Adolph Bolm and Jose Torres y Fernandez, the latter the producer of the brilliant Spanish ballet for La Fiesta last year, have been engaged to present the third and fourth dance spectacles this season. Theodore Kosloff and Ernest Belcher will do the others. Cyrena Van Gordon, beautiful contralto of the Chicago civic opera, and Paul Althouse, tenor of the Chicago and Metropolitan operas, also have been engaged as solcists. Others include Richard Bonelli, Alfred Wallenstein, Bianca Saroya, Dimitri Onofrei and Ruggiero Ricci.

FLAGS PRESENTED SCHOOL.

Carthay Center elementary school was June 7 presented with United States of America and California State (Bear) Flags by Ramona Parlor No. 109 N.S.G.W., through the generosity of J. Harvey McCarthy. Past Grand President Herman C. Lichtenberger briefly outlined the aims and purposes of the Order and told of its interest in educational matters. Superior Judge Ruben Schmidt delivered the presentation address, and the children gave a musical interpretation of "California Under Four Flags."

There was a large gathering of parents, teachers and pupils, among them Mrs. McGraw, principal of the school; Mrs. Frances Day, president of the association; Mrs. Mary B. Murray, supervisor California history department Los Angeles City schools; Mrs. John S. McGroarty. Flags were presented the Carthay Center school when dedicated in 1925; it then had 19 pupils, now it has 960.

MOTHER INITIATES DAUGHTER.

At the final initiation of her term as president of Los Angeles Parlor No. 124 N.D.G.W., Mrs. Gertrude R. Allen had the distinctive honor June 15 of initiating her daughter, Miss Lois Barbara Allen, and six other candidates. Since she was 5 years of age, Miss Lois has attended the Parlor meetings, but always patiently waiting in the anteroom, and developed into an ardent supporter of the Order. Including this class, Mrs. Allen initiated a total of seventy-three during her term. She will be succeeded by Mrs. Mattie Gara.

The card party of June 8 was largely attended; in charge were Ruth Ruiz, Margaret Carter, Edith Strain and Olinda Kerby. June 8 the sewing club met at the home of Grace T. Haven, who provided a delightful luncheon. The all-nations dinner dance June 29 was a very splendid affair. The menu was in charge of Edna Holcomb, and how it was enjoyed! Several

MISS LOIS BARBARA ALLEN.

"stars" were among the many who thoroughly appreciated the occasion. Irene Whitney-Collins and Ella Vucovich-Steinbeck, recent brides of the Parlor, were given a shower June 15; Irene Eden and Leonie Clos were in charge.

Los Angeles' July program includes: Report Grand Parlor delegates, 6th. Monthly card party, 13th, Mrs. Ruth Traeger hostess. Public installation officers, 27th. President Allen's June message was: "You may travel, no matter how fast or far; you cannot escape it, wherever you are; some duty awaits you, some good you should do—there is something the world is expecting of you."

ANNIVERSARY BANQUET.

The thirty-sixth anniversary banquet of Hollywood Parlor No. 196 N.S.G.W. was a most enjoyable occasion and largely attended. Governor James Rolph Jr. was the guest of honor. Many prominent in civic, political and governmental affairs, as well as noted athletes were introduced. A most excellent program of entertainment features was presented under the supervision of Mrs. Leland Atherton-Irish.

George Breslin was the toastmaster, and kept the crowd in good humor with his well-directed witticisms. Among the many speakers were Municipal Judge Leo Aggeler, president of Hollywood, Bernard G. Hiss, Henry G. Bodkin, Leo Youngworth, Mrs. Irish, Governor Rolph, and H. M. Gurney, Henri Didot, Dr. Gustav Struve and Ryan A. Grut, consuls, respectively, of England, France, Germany and Denmark.

July 25, Hollywood will initiate a class of candidates in honor of Grand President Seth Millington, and at the same time will introduce features honoring recent initiates. Refreshments will be served. The Parlor plans to materially increase its membership the next six months.

BIRTHDAY PARTY NETS GOODLY SUM.

Ernestine Aylward will head the new corps of

officers of Californiana Parlor No. 247 N.D.G.W., having been selected at the election held June 14. The luncheon speaker was District Attorney Buron Fitts, who was introduced by Mrs. Florence Irish, program chairman. "He spoke plainly about the condition of affairs, especially about gangsters, eighty-seven of the worst from the East having made Los Angeles their mecca at one time. Things were made so hot for them, however, that they have departed."

The fourth birthday party of the Parlor, a beautiful affair held in the lovely home of Mrs. Earl Osborn, netted a substantial sum for the treasury of Californiana. A vote of thanks was extended Mrs. Osborn and her sister, Mrs. Matilda Murdock.

JOINT N.S. INSTALLATION AT GLENDALE.

Officers of the Los Angeles County Native Son Parlors will be jointly installed at public ceremonies in Masonic Temple, 234 South Brand boulevard, Glendale, July 6. Arrangements are in charge of Glendale Parlor No. 264. Supper, for which advance reservations must be made, will precede the ceremonies, which will be open to all Natives and their friends.

BRIDES RECEIVE GIFTS.

Long Beach—District Deputy Eva Mae Bemis and Miss Lois Poling visited Long Beach Parlor No. 154 N.D.G.W. June 2, and the Parlor presented the former with a silver gift, President Violet T. Henshilwood delivering the presentation address. A party honoring all members who had birthdays the first six months of 1932 followed the meeting. Second Vice-president Eleanor Johnson had charge of arrangements.

June 16 one candidate was initiated, and two recent brides, Mms. Katheryn Dodd-Bradley and Minnie Kofahl, were presented with gifts, the presentation addresses being made by Past Presidents Daisy T. Hansen and Lucretia Coates. A dinner and card party June 30 was in charge of District Deputy Clara Fay and Mrs. Leola Temby.

Recent meetings of the thimble club have been held at the hall. The quilt, the cover for which was made and donated by Mrs. Fannie Baker, has been finished and will be disposed of July 7. Mrs. Kate McFadyen, "mother" of the Parlor, who has been quite ill, is very much improved. Headed by Mrs. Zella L. Hodgedon as president, the newly elected officers of Long Beach will be installed July 21.

WATERMELON FEAST.

The July calendar for Ramona Parlor No. 109 N.S.G.W. includes: 8th, brief entertainment and watermelon feast. 15th, class initiation. 22nd, Superior Judge B. Rey Schauer will have charge of a program. 29th, Walter Slosson promises entertainment by a mystifying magician.

Ramona's anniversary barbecue June 12 was well attended and everybody had a good time. June 10 four candidates were initiated. Dr. James M. Watson, the incoming president, will introduce several novel entertainment features during his term.

"OH, BLESSED MISSION!"

The following came to The Grizzly Bear from Lewie W. Smith of Los Angeles Parlor No. 45 N.S.G.W. with the statement: "Enclosed is a bit of poetry written by one of the schoolgirls of Highland Park. Her teacher thought it good enough to publish." Evelynne Judd, aged 14, a student at the Luther Burbank Junior high school, is the schoolgirl referred to:

"See you decaying structure
Towering in the moonlight
Dark against the starry sky—
A tragic yet majestic sight.
That building is a mission—
A refuge of the forgotten padres who
Yet live in glory in the great beyond;
Whose wonderful work reached not a few,
But many ignorant neophytes who
Were not ready to grasp knowledge
With eager hands,
But slowly seeking in exchange
The love and care the fathers gave them.
The sloping fields and fruited lands
Resound their praises with
Rumblings of waves on ocean sands.
A wonderful country, this land of ours,
All made possible by mightier powers
Than mine.
Oh, blessed mission!"

N. S. OFFICIAL HONORED.

Ocean Park—Santa Monica Bay Parlor No. 245 N.D.G.W. had a very successful dance party June 17 in honor of Eldred L. Meyer, Grand Trustee N.S.G.W. Second Vice-president Katherine Worsham was the hostess. In keeping with the pioneer celebration, the guests came in costume, and for the most typical prizes were awarded Elizabeth Valencia and Elmer Barnes. The affair proved so delightful it has been decided to hold a dance each month.

The June 6 card party, featuring the Olympic motif, was well attended; Marie Barnes was hos-

LOS ANGELES--CITY and COUNTY

tess. The Parlor had an entry in the pioneer parade June 24 and will be represented in the Independence Day parade. Officers for the July-December term will be installed July 18.

ATHLETIC SHOW AT GLENDALE.

Glendale—Glendale Parlor No. 264 N.S.G.W. had one of the finest showings in the June 7 parade, sponsored by this city, honoring Governor James Rolph Jr. Clinton Skinner was chief of staff. July 13 the Parlor will feature another wrestling and boxing program at Glen Arden Club, 357 West Arden. Les Schellback, in charge, is being aided by President Phil Molen, Harvey Gillette and Secretary A. B. Molen. A great athletic show is promised.

N. S. OFFICIAL POPULAR.

San Pedro—Past President William A. Reuter of Sepulveda Parlor No. 263 N.S.G.W., elected Grand Outside Sentinel at the Stockton Grand Parlor, was honor-guest at a barbecued dinner June 15 in Sepulveda Grove. Members and their ladies to the number of 150 were in attendance, indicating the popularity of "Bill." Burrel D. Neighbours was the guest speaker, and Harry E. Fairall had charge of the arrangements.

PERSONAL PARAGRAPHS.

Mrs. Vivian Wickser (Los Angeles N.D.) is the mother of a native son.

Robert E. Dunn (Ramona N.S.) was a visitor last month to San Francisco.

A native son arrived June 6 at the home of Norbert Palomares (Ramona N.S.).

Mrs. Lillian Carey (Los Angeles N.D.) has returned from a journey around the world.

Miss Rose J. Renaud and Captain Frank D. Shearer (Ramona N.S.) were recently wedded.

Miss Grace S. Stoermer (Past Grand President N.D.) was a visitor last month to Eastern cities.

Elizabeth Sanders and Vera Carlson (Verdugo N.D.) of Glendale were visitors to San Francisco last month.

Miss Edith Strain (Los Angeles N.D.) recently enjoyed a vacation in Humboldt County and Yosemite Valley.

Mrs. Marie McFadyen-Monroe (Long Beach N.D.) of Pendleton, Oregon, is spending the summer in Long Beach.

Charles Giegerich (Sepulveda N.S.) and family of San Pedro have returned from a vacation in the northern part of the state.

Miss Aileen Corsman and Frank E. Baxter (Ramona N.S.) were recently wedded at Salt Lake, Utah. The groom's father, Irving Baxter (Ramona N.S.) was present at the ceremonies. The couple will reside at Mariposa.

Dr. Harold J. Stonier (Ramona N.S.) of New York City, national educational director American Institute Banking, has been designated one of the United States' twelve official delegates to an international commercial education congress to be held this month in London, England.

THE DEATH RECORD.

Charles Bennett, affiliated with Los Angeles Parlor No. 45 N.S.G.W., died June 8 survived by a wife. He was born at Los Angeles, July 19, 1863. He was the Parlor's oldest past president.

Miss Margaret Holleran, sister of Drs. James F. and Walter M. Holleran (Hollywood N.S.), passed away June 9.

George Robert Emmet Milligan, affiliated with Ramona Parlor 109 N.S.G.W., died June 10 survived by a wife. He was born at Angels Camp, Calaveras County, June 22, 1864, and was a charter member of the long-defunct Tulare Parlor No. 48 N.S.G.W.

Archie V. Howard, affiliated with Santa Monica Bay Parlor No. 267 N.S.G.W., died June 19 at Sacramento City, as the result of an auto accident. Surviving is a wife. He was a native of Santa Monica, aged 43.

Anthony Joseph Pierce, affiliated with Los Angeles Parlor No, 45 N.S.G.W., was drowned June 19 while swimming in Merced County. June 16, at Riverside City, he was wedded to Mrs. Gloryne A. Keeney, and they were on their honeymoon when tragedy intervened. "Tony" was born at Los Angeles City, July 5, 1898.

KEEP ON KEEPIN' ON.

If the day looks kinder gloomy
 And your chances kinder slim,
If the situation's puzzlin'
 And the prospect's awful grim;
If perplexities keep pressin'
 Till hope is nearly gone,
Just bristle up and grit your teeth
 And keep on keepin' on.

Frettin' never wins a fight
 And fumin' never pays;
There ain't no use in broodin'
 In these pessimistic ways;
Smile just kinder cheerfully
 Though hope is nearly gone,
And bristle up and grit your teeth
 And keep on keepin' on.

There ain't no use in growlin'
 And grumblin' all the time,
When music's ringing everywhere
 And everything's a rhyme.
Just keep on smilin' cheerfully
 If hope is nearly gone,
And bristle up and grit your teeth
 And keep on keepin' on.

—Exchange.

Know your home-state, California! Learn its past history and of its present-day develo ment by reading regularly The Grizzly Be $1.50 for one year (12 issues). Subscribe no

THE ROMANCE OF SAN BERNARDINO

Clara M. Barton

(Copyrighted, 1931, by the Author.)

(Continued from June Issue)

THE SAN BERNARDINO PIONEER SOciety is composed of citizens who came to the valley in 1850 and 1860. It became an active society April 26, 1853, and was made up of men who shared in the harrowing events of early days and were responsible for the building up of the City of San Bernardino. The society has taken an active part in all civic affairs. It was the first to make a move toward the construction of the county court house, the federal building and the first public park, and it was the Pioneer Society which made daring and successful moves to preserve the historical sites of the valley. At the first election of officers George Lord was made president. Vice-presidents were John Brown Sr., David Seeley, James W. Waters, William F. Holcomb and N. P. Earp. Henry M. Willis acted as corresponding secretary, John Brown Jr. as recording secretary, B. B. Harris as treasurer, and G. Gill as marshal.

THE GOLDEN LAND.

We've entered now the Golden State,
Where warmest welcomes for us wait;
The land where corn and oil and wine
Are free and plenty as sunshine.

Oh Golden Land, proud Golden Land,
We hail our welcome, and our hand
Is given now with right good will
To those who greet us, for we still
Remember that in forty-nine
We had no oil, nor corn, nor wine.

San Bernardino leads the van
With fruits delicious, and we can
But tell them what our hearts now feel
And wish them joy, long life and weal.

The ladies and the children sweet
Who gladden us with smiles and greet
The Veterans of forty-nine,
For them we ask for bliss divine.

God bless the ties that henceforth bind
Old Argonauts, and may we find
This happy hour, in all our Years,
The pleasantest for Pioneers.

So let us all, while gathered here
Each Saturday throughout the year,
In memory our friends enshrine
Who gave us corn, and oil, and wine.

This ode was composed by B. F. Whittemore aboard the excursion train when coming into the valley April 17, 1890, and the melody is "Beulah Land." A custom of the society is to clasp the hand of a visitor as the song is being sung—a custom which will ever linger in the minds of those who have been cordially received as guests by the Pioneers. So, the noble and courageous Pioneer is never forgotten or forsaken.

EPISODE 9.
THE FIRST ADMINISTRATION.

A few short years had passed and the settlers, as well as those who had been born and raised in the city, realized this now-thriving settlement was in position to form its own charter and to have its own government.

"We can't go on this way," said one of the active businessmen. "Every township has its own way of self government, so why shouldn't we? We have enough citizens who are taking an active part in all of our plans and I fully believe that we can accomplish more, if we have a purpose to work for. It would mean advancement and independence."

July 30, 1904, a few citizens who were keeping the town machinery in order elected a board of trustees, which would receive from the state special permission to hold an election. The qualified electors then chose the following highly respected and capable citizens, who were ordered to prepare a charter to be submitted to the voters of the city: John Andreson Sr., H. M. Barton, I. R. Brunn, J. W. Catick, M. L. Cook, G. M. Cooley, Frank Daly, J. J. Hanford, W. S. Hooper, A. G. Kendall, James Murray, L. D. Houghton, Joseph Ingersoll, W. M. Parker, Horace C. Rolph.

They constituted the organized Board of Trustees. The state gave them ninety days in which to prepare the charter, and January 30, 1905, it was heartily approved by both houses of the Legislature. The activities did not stop here, however, and plans for forming a complete city government were formulated. Several of the old residents, who could not see the importance and necessity of so doing, became antagonistic. Several weeks were required to win them over! The new charter provided for a mayor, common council, water commission, city planning, fire, police and other departments.

Hiram Merritt Barton, a charter member of Arrowhead Parlor No. 110 N.S.G.W. and a former member of the State Legislature, was elected mayor by a large majority. He appointed Walter A. Shay chief of police and found in him a man of capability, always fair and square. To take full charge of the fire department, Albert A. Glatz, whose past experience in handling the fire situation won approval from the citizens of San Bernardino, was named.

Mayor Barton's movements were closely watched, and his suggestions as to future advancement won much favor with the public. It was his custom to interview the councilmen and the heads of the various departments before each council meeting and get their opinions of the various ordinances to be drawn up, and thus he overcame complications that were bound to arise. By the time his administration was completed, in 1907, he had to his credit necessary ordinances that were being enforced. The cooperation received from employes of the city departments revealed to him that his efforts in constructing a solid foundation upon which a thriving city was building were not given in vain.

The first move made by Mayor Barton was to build a fire hall, to house all the fire apparatus and be fitted throughout with comforts for the firemen who were to live there. This was the first step necessary toward the building up of a substantial fire department, but Mayor Barton found many objections to conquer. He succeeded, however, in not only erecting the splendid fire hall, but other city buildings as well.

The charter and original ordinances are still in effect, and the foundation constructed in 1905 is still supporting the San Bernardino City government.

(Concluded in August Issue)

"Life is an opportunity for service; not as little as we dare, but as much as we can."—B. F. Westcott.

"Nature, exerting an unwearied power, forms, opens, and gives scent to every flower."—Cowper.

HORNED TOBACCO WORM.

A large green worm that appears on tomato plants, known as the horned tobacco worm, will do real damage both to foliage and fruit unless prompt control measures are taken. Where it first appears, handpicking may control it. Where there is a larger patch, or a field, and the infestation is heavy, then spraying or dusting must be used for control. If dusting is preferred, use five parts of air-slaked lime and one part of powdered arsenate of lead. For a spray, use two ounces of powdered arsenate of lead, two ounces of laundry soap and three gallons of water.

TOMATOES AND IRRIGATION.

Be careful of the irrigation when tomatoes begin to set their fruit. Give the plants plenty of water up to the blossoming period, but when it is time for the tomatoes to set, let up on irrigation. Otherwise there will be difficulty in getting early fruits; they will drop. After the tomatoes have set, the water may be applied again. Of course, the plants should not be allowed to get to the wilting stage because of lack of soil moisture, but the ground should not be kept too wet when the blossoms appear.

Grizzly Bear

AUGUST — THE ONLY OFFICIAL PUBLICATION OF THE NATIVE SONS AND DAUGHTERS OF THE GOLDEN WEST — 1932

Featuring

GENERAL NEWS OF INTEREST CONCERNING ALL CALIFORNIA, and ORDERS NATIVE SONS and NATIVE DAUGHTERS

Price: 15 Cents

GRIZZLY GROWLS

(CLARENCE M. HUNT.)

THE FIRST SESSION OF THE SEVENTY-second Federal Congress terminated July 16, and just prior to adjournment passed what is generally referred to as the "relief bill," but officially titled "Emergency Relief and Construction Act of 1932." The measure has since been approved by President Herbert Hoover. Its main features are: $300,000,000 to be made available for "direct" relief of the destitute; $1,500,000,000 for loans through the Reconstruction Finance Corporation for self-liquidating projects, and $322,224,000 for a public works program.

This measure is linked with the Reconstruction Finance Corporation Act, the "pet" legislation of the national administration which has been vigorously condemned, and as vigorously extolled, by members of the Congress and others. So, whether any but the highboys—the thieving bankers and their like who brought on the bountiful depression—will be directly benefited by the "relief" bill is problematical. The great obstacle in the way of the bill's final passage was the amendment providing that all loans of the R.F.C. shall be made public. The national administration strenuously opposed that provision, but it is in the bill as passed and approved, and the bill also contains this provision:

"Sec. 207. No loan or advance shall be approved under this section or under the Reconstruction Finance Corporation Act, directly or indirectly, to any financial institution any officer or director of which is a member of the board of directors of the Reconstruction Finance Corporation or has been such a member within the twelve months preceding the approval of the loan or advance."

That section was undoubtedly added following the nationwide clamor after the making known of the fact that former Vice-president Charles G. Dawes had, shortly after his voluntary retirement as president of the R.F.C., borrowed $80,000,000 from the Corporation in the interest of his Chicago bank. Commenting on the Dawes borrow, the "Tri-County Labor News" said:

"Eighty million dollars is by odds the largest single loan made by the Reconstruction Finance Corporation; nor is that the chief item of surprise. The Corporation is a Government institution. It has not a dollar of cash or credit except as these are provided by the people of the United States. Mr. Dawes was the first president of this concern. His eulogists described him at the time as a superman who had put aside his own affairs so he might 'serve' his country. When he resigned a few weeks ago he modestly admitted that he had finished the job and that prosperity was on the way. . . . Now it appears that 'Hell an' Maria's' principal accomplishment in connection with the R. F. C. was to borrow $80,000,000 for his own bank. Whether the deal was arranged before or after he resigned as head of the institution is not clear. All we know is that he got the money, plenty of it, and now proudly proclaims that his bank is 'impregnable.' Of course it is 'impregnable.' Any bank may be rendered 'impregnable' if its chief is turned loose among Uncle Sam's billions and permitted to help himself."

Congressman William C. Lankford of Georgia, speaking in the House of Representatives July 7 on the "relief" bill, commented thusly:

"Much has been said about this being a superbanking bill and the Reconstruction Finance Corporation being a superbanking institution. To my mind there is no doubt about this question. The only problem is whether or not this superbanking institution shall be operated for the benefit of the big corporations of the country or shall be operated for the benefit of the whole people. . . . Why not make these loans directly to the individual citizen rather than lending it to the large corporations on the theory that part of the money will eventually inure to the benefit of the ordinary private citizen! . . .

"You can not bring back to life a dead, decaying body by the engrafting of a little live skin. You can not take the Reconstruction Finance Corporation, set up by the monopolistic interests of the country, owned by Wall Street international bankers, operated for the immensely rich, and officered by those who look at everything from the standpoint of the capitalist, and make that corporation an agency of service for the common people by feebly and gently suggesting that its officers may, if entirely satisfactory to them, make an occasional loan to some wealthy individual who is able to hire lawyers and comply with all the red tape that would be required of him by those who do not want to loan any amount to any individual. . . . . Big corporation men, like Dawes, are able to get $80,000,000 at a clip, probably in the midst of a bacchanalian feast of mirth and hilarious glee. It is so easy for those that have millions upon top of millions to get more."

Some information regarding the R.F.C. is not amiss at this time. Its second quarterly report, made public July 8, sets forth that from February 2 to June 30 loans totaling $1,054,814,486 were authorized to 4,196 borrowers—$642,789,313 to banks and trust companies, and $213,882,724 to railroads. The greatest number of loans in any single state was in Illinois, where 307 institutions, including 274 banks, were accommodated. Loans in California totaled 99. The report lists 10 employes of the Corporation receiving $1,000 or more monthly, and an additional 112 employes receiving more than $400 monthly.

There is a deficit in California State Government funds; just how much, no one appears to know definitely, but there are rumors it reaches high up into the millions. Records of the controller's office reveal that the present administration spent during the 1931-32 fiscal year $24,770,930 more than was expended during the previous fiscal year. And that enormous increase with conditions as they are, and have been for some time past! The state attorney-general remarks,

"The cost of government, national, state, county and municipal, has rapidly increased in the last few years. Charges everywhere are made that the increase far exceeds the advantageous result achieved, and, so far as I know, no one has disputed the correctness of this charge."

No one has disputed, because the charge is indisputable.

"Though the present stifling depression broke early in 1929," continues the attorney-general, "no effort to cut governmental extravagances or to reduce the cost of government was made until the surpluses were completely exhausted and deficits occurred."

Not only has no effort been made to reduce the cost of government, but it has actually been increased by materially boosting the salaries of favored state employes. The suggestion that the highest salary paid to any state officer shall be $5,000 per annum should be enacted into law.

August 30 will be primary election day. Carefully consider the reputations and the qualifications of each of the record-breaking number of candidates for public offices, and then vote for those who, in your own judgment, will best serve the masses, not the classes.

The near-intolerable conditions existant throughout this nation are the direct result of the failure of the majority to perform their chief duty as American citizens—their neglect of the ballot-box. The minority govern, because the majority have been slackers. Are you satisfied with conditions? If not, express your dissatisfaction at the polls!

One hundred and twenty-one immigration bills were introduced at the recent session of the Federal Congress. Eight became laws and the others go over to the December session for consideration. Of those adopted, two, of particular interest to California, are not so good:

Public Law 248, recognizes as American citizens at birth native women of the Hawaiian Islands who lost citizenship by reason of marriage to aliens. More voting wives of ineligible-to-citizenship husbands.

Public Law 277, provides that if an alien husband married a citizen wife prior to July 1, 1932, the alien husband is given a non-quota status, but if the marriage was on or after July 1, 1932, the alien is given first preference within the immigration quota. Opens the immigration door for more Japs and other undesirables.

"Unless American civilization is made moral, it will become unsafe," said Rev. John Snape, addressing the Northern Baptist Convention at San Francisco. "We must enforce our laws or confess that our form of government is a failure." Had the church, all denominations, devoted more time and energy to expounding the Gospel and less to politics and associated activities the moral-cancer would not have had such a spread.

An excellent suggestion comes from Superior Judge Harry B. Miller of Chicago, who urges that the marriage and divorce laws be federal rather than state. The conflicts between enactments of the various states destroy the sanctity of marriage and its social benefits. He urges that:

"Persons mentally or physically unfit be barred from marriage. Men divorced from wives with minor children be barred from remarriage until their obligation to the children has ceased or permanent arrangements for their support made. The regulations surrounding marriage be strengthened and that marriages and divorces both be made less easy."

The purchasing power of the dollar, estimates the Federal Labor Department, is now fifty percent greater than in 1929. As dollars are, with most people, about seventy-five percent fewer than in 1929, where's the cheer in their increased purchasing power? More dollars, in possession of more people, is the crying need.

The Grizzly Bear Magazine

The ALL California Monthly

OWNED, CONTROLLED, PUBLISHED BY GRIZZLY BEAR PUBLISHING CO., (Incorporated)

COMPOSED OF NATIVE SONS.

HERMAN C. LICHTENBERGER, Pres.
JOHN T. NEWELL RAY HOWARD
WM. I. TRAEGER LORENZO F. SOTO
CHAS. R. THOMAS HARRY J. LELANDE
ARTHUR A. SCHMIDT, Vice-Pres.
BOARD OF DIRECTORS

CLARENCE M. HUNT
General Manager and Editor

OFFICIAL ORGAN AND THE ONLY OFFICIAL PUBLICATION OF THE NATIVE SONS AND THE NATIVE DAUGHTERS GOLDEN WEST.

ISSUED FIRST EACH MONTH.
FORMS CLOSE 20th MONTH.
ADVERTISING RATES ON APPLICATION.

SAN FRANCISCO OFFICE:
N.S.G.W. BLDG., 414 MASON ST., RM. 302
(Office Grand Secretary N.S.G.W.)
Telephone: Kearney 1223
SAN FRANCISCO, CALIFORNIA

PUBLICATION OFFICE:
309-15 WILCOX BLDG., 2nd AND SPRING,
Telephone: VAndike 6234
LOS ANGELES, CALIFORNIA

(Entered as second-class matter May 29, 1918, at the Postoffice at Los Angeles, California, under the act of August 24, 1912.)

PUBLISHED REGULARLY SINCE MAY 1907
VOL. LI WHOLE NO. 304

California's chief executive has in mind the calling of a special session of the State Legislature to initiate a statewide water plan, the initial step in which would be to ask the voters to authorize a $160,000,000 bond issue "to finance the first unit of the water plan." The cost of the succeeding units has not been made known, but would be more than plenty. The chief executive probably will change his mind, but if he does not and the proposal goes to vote, the propertyowners of the state, already over their heads in taxes due to too-generous bond voting and other causes, should swamp the suggested water, and any and all other, bonds with negative votes. Commenting on this water scheme, the "Manteca Bulletin," published in one of California's richest agricultural sections, said editorially:

"The suggestion that the State of California might secure a hundred million dollars for the proposed statewide water program, is about the only reason we can see for a revival of the measure. We always seem to have an idea that because some other tax-producing source underwrites an expenditure, that in the last analysis we don't pay the bill. But it's always the man at the bottom of the heap that pays the taxes, whether he thinks he does or not.

"California has about as much need for the proposed statewide water program at present, as the City of San Francisco has for a second Hetch Hetchy project. But because we think there is some easy money in sight we all want to grab it. California has a long ways to go before it can show the need for more irrigation. First, we must find a market for what we produce—then we must demonstrate that more lands can be farmed to a profit."

Several factories, particularly in Eastern states, have been employing additional help since the adjournment of the Federal Congress, and some newspapers express the belief business was waiting for the national lawmakers to quit before starting "the climb toward renewed prosperity."

That may be true, but more likely it is the often-staged pre-election "full dinner pail" "stunt," put on at the command of the powers-that-be to attract votes. Anyway, more people are being employed.

Seldom does a writer receive commendation for effort put forth solely to enlighten readers on important public questions which should be the concern of all. Exceptions follow:

"I have read with much interest your several 'Grizzly Growls' in The Grizzly Bear of July 1932. The first is especially opportune; I have said somewhat the same, but not in the emphatic and clear way in which you have. . . . The second 'growl' regarding the bonus situation, the third

(Continued on Page 24)

THE ROMANCE OF SAN BERNARDINO

Clara M. Barton

(Continued from July Issue)

EPISODE 10.
FAIRS.

WHILE THE EASTERN STATES were having their country fairs, San Bernardino was holding its street fair. This was a yearly event looked forward to by all who took an active part in community affairs. The fair was held in the spring of the year, when the products of the soil were at their best.

A queen was chosen by popular vote and the prime minister was appointed by the executive committee in charge of all arrangements. During the few days of the fair's activities the reigning queen was at her place upon a flower-bedecked throne. From this regal place, her majesty viewed the parades. Before her passed gaily-decorated buggies, wagons, horses, tricycles, bicycles and other conveyances; those who preferred to walk did so, in costume.

A scant five years ended street-fair activities, as the citizens found themselves preparing to pay homage to the hundredth birthday of their natal city. From May 17 to 21, 1910, there was a celebration in which every person in the city took some active part. As a link in the chain of missions, on May 20, 1810, a branch of San Gabriel was established one mile south of the center of San Bernardino, and directly in front of it was the main highway that led to all missions, El Camino Real. A little chapel was built, surrounded by the beautiful Valley of San Bernardino.

The first steps toward honoring the birth of the city were taken by the San Bernardino Pioneer Society and Arrowhead Parlor No. 110 N.S.G.W. Their plans met with widespread approbation and soon the matter was placed in the hands of committees from all parts of the valley. Vast changes had taken place during the expanse of a hundred years.

The celebration opened with a historical pageant. As for a queen, the city elected by popular vote an "indian princess," Miss Lena Johnson, and her entry before her people was from the center of a large century plant. As it slowly opened, she gracefully stepped out and bowed in recognition to the greetings given her. Her chief was James McGregor, and her court consisted of indian maids and braves. The city also appointed spanish rulers, in the persons of Miss Rose Aguirre, who was honored as the "spanish guevendora," and her escort, a "spanish guevendor," W. M. Parker. With their attendants, they had special places beside those of the indian tribe upon the stage from which the numerous events were witnessed.

The centennial celebration was the closing chapter for street fairs of any kind, and the beginning of a new life of activities. March 6, 1911, the curtain went up on a new type of entertainment, and a display was presented for the approval of the citizens of the valley. It was then that the dreams of Harry M. Perkins were realized. On this day, the First National Orange Show was held. William W. Brison, at that time president of the San Bernardino Chamber of Commerce, was, by virtue of that office, president of the show. Because of his successful achievements with the centennial, Ralph E. Swing was appointed general chairman.

The first orange exposition was held in a small tent, and the exhibits of citrus seemed quite a novelty to the many visitors who came from other parts of the valley. Finding only citrus were to be displayed by the men, and that no effort was to be made to educate visitors in the use of the fruits, Mrs. Thomas Hadden got a group of women together and the now-popular and educational byproducts department was originated.

This first show was the firm foundation upon which the now-famous National Orange Show was built. Each succeeding year brings more enthusiasts and exhibitors. Sweepstakes in the form of silver cups and cash are presented, and ribbons are issued as special prizes. For several years the show was housed in a tent, but now has a home of its own, the largest exposition building on the Pacific Coast. The San Bernardino Orange Show has become a substantial and permanent institution. Much credit for its success is due Royal H. Mack, who for many years has stood at the helm.

California is noted for three annual events, the Tournament of Roses at Pasadena every January first, the San Bernardino National Orange Show the latter part of every February, and the "Mission Play" at San Gabriel. These have become known all over the world, and their stories never weaken.

EPISODE 11.
ADVANCEMENT.

One enters the San Bernardino Valley by Kendall drive. From its peak may be viewed a prosperous and peaceful territory outlined by evergreen trees—a panorama of the ideal homesite. At night the lights of the valley are like brilliant gems, and the tourist receives a fairyland impression. Too, the newcomer finds the valley is ideally located. Leaving the sunshine and the orange groves, and climbing via the high-gear road, the visitor later finds himself up on the mountain peaks, amid snow.

Ambition and self-confidence have been the direct cause of the rapid strides taken by the citizens of the valley during the twentieth century. Readjustments had to be made. Historic landmarks, that should have been protected, have been razed to make way for the progress of the city; old trees, planted by the loving hands of the Pioneer, have also felt the cruel blow of the axe.

San Bernardino has not been at a standstill, and with a population of 38,000 has accomplished much. It has a residential section that is an outstanding feature, and to encourage the beautifying of homes the Chamber of Commerce sponsors home-garden contests. A silver cup is given during the Yuletide season for the most beautiful living decorated evergreen tree by Mrs. H. M. Barton, who is active in civic affairs of the city. Citizens of the city have extended their homesites to the foothills, and citizens of the valley look up to them with pride. The business section has modern and pretentious buildings that are monuments to the men and the women who constructed them.

In the center of Lugo Park stands a towering and substantial building sponsored by all civic heads and erected by the taxpayers. Previously, there stood a wooden frame building, but a tongue of fire lapped it to the ground. Though the military unit had housed its ammunition within the flimsy structure, and lost it, the destruction of the building made way for another step in the advancement of the city. The Municipal Auditorium was many months in the making, and accommodates several thousand people.

West of the Auditorium stands a delightful and charming log cabin, erected by those directly responsible for the building of the city. It is the home of the Pioneers, built of hand-hewed logs. No nail mars or scars those logs, and all early-day treasures are housed and guarded therein. In this three-room building the Pioneers meet every Saturday, rain or shine. It is here they come to pay undying tribute to the men and the women who so courageously built a splendid community.

The Pioneers and those born and raised in the city have seen many drastic and startling changes. There are modern electric cars to replace the once-popular horse cars; the huge new San Bernardino County Court House, ever surrounded by spacious and blooming gardens; the old rundown parks have been made anew, and even the unsightly washes of sand and debris have been converted into charming parks; new schools have replaced the old, and a junior college, surrounded by spacious lawns, has been recently constructed in which children of the less-fortunate may obtain some advantages. The most important industry of the city is the Santa Fe shops.

Opposite Lugo Park stands a homey looking building known as the Woman's Club. The American Legion building is an asset to the city. Uncle Sam has taken an active interest in the advancement of the city and has erected a Federal building at the cost of $350,000.

Fraternal and patriotic organizations are numerous, and many own their own buildings. But two organizations, however, are striving to preserve the landmarks and history of the San Bernardino Valley—Arrowhead Parlor No. 110 N.S.G.W. and Lugonia Parlor No. 241 N.D.G.W. Through them, much has been done. Their interest in civic affairs is evidenced by their accomplishments. Though both Parlors meet in rented quarters, plans are being made to be in a home of their own in the very near future.

And so, in keeping with loyalty and the upbuilding of the City of San Bernardino, we find that the efforts given in the beginning prove that no one shirked his duties. Those carrying on in the twentieth century are continuing the work their ancestors began. From a barren desert to a garden of paradise, the co-operation, the aims and the ideals of all concerned have been vividly shown. Thus continue the links in the chain of success, and San Bernardino has won for itself a warm and respected reputation as to its manner of homage.

HISTORIC PLACES ARE PLAQUED

BRENTWOOD (CONTRA COSTA COUNTY)—Donner Parlor No. 193 N.D.G.W. (Byron), assisted by Byron Parlor No. 170 N.S.G.W., unveiled and dedicated June 26 at the entrance to the Dr. John Marsh home, familiarly known as the "Stone House," a bronze plaque presented by Mrs. Sadie Winn-Brainard of Califia Parlor No. 22 N.D.G.W. (Sacramento), a granddaughter of General Andrew Maver Winn, Founder of the Order of Native Sons of the Golden West. The plaque is inscribed: "In memory of John and Abbie Marsh, pioneers; he was the first doctor in California; born 1799, arrived 1836, murdered September 24, 1856; Abbie Marsh died August, 1855; builders of the Stone House; dedicated by Donner Parlor N.D.G.W., 1932."

Richard R. Veale, charter member of General Winn Parlor No. 32 N.S.G.W. (Antioch) and sheriff of Contra Costa County, was the master of ceremonies, and among the many in attendance was the 71-year-old granddaughter of Dr. Marsh, Miss Sarah Marsh. Vocal selections were rendered by Mrs. Estelle M. Evans, Past Grand President N.D.G.W., accompanied by Miss Frances Diffin, and a quintet,—Mrs. Clara Houston, Ray Houston, William Anderson, Miss Gwendolyn Richardson and Leslie Richardson—accompanied by Thelma Richardson. Speakers included Past Grand President Amy V. McAvoy and Supervising Deputy Edna Hill of the Native Daughters; Past Grand President James F. Hoey and State Senator Will R. Sharkey of the Native Sons; State Finance Director Rolland A. Vandegrift, State Assemblyman R. P. Easley, A. F. Bray and C. W. St. John. The Liberty union high school band of Brentwood favored with selections. The committee of Donner Parlor in charge of the ceremonies included Mms. Edna Hill (chairman), Virginia Boltzen, Mabel Peterson and President Josephine Pimentel.

John Marsh, one of the greatest of early American adventurers, was an outstanding Pioneer of Contra Costa County. Born in 1799, he graduated from Harvard University, and came to California in 1836, arriving at the Pueblo of Los Angeles. Here he registered as a physician and was accepted as such on the strength of his Latin-worded diploma from Harvard, as no one could be found to translate it. Thus he became California's first doctor, and rendered splendid services. His practice took him from Monterey to Sutter's Fort.

Early in 1837 Dr. Marsh bought a vast ranch, located in the shadows of Mount Diablo and extending from the base of the mountain to the banks of the San Joaquin River, nine miles distant; it was known as the Los Medanos Rancho. He soon became the wealthiest man in California, both in gold and cattle. He was a leader in a plan to unite California and Oregon—he to become president or governor—but a fued between Governor Alvarado and General Micheltorena prevented its consummation. He also participated in the struggles of the California Republic.

For almost twenty years, he lived in an adobe house located back of the present "Stone House." With the advent of a daughter, Alice, born to his wife, Abbie, Dr. Marsh's dreams had come true—he had wealth, an accomplished wife, and a child. Now, for a home, the finest in California. Joyously he and Abbie planned every detail of the magnificent edifice, which still stands as a monument to their memory. The bricks of which it is made were burnt on the place and the ornamentation of freestone was quarried on the property. But their hopes were unrequited. Abbie died in August 1855, almost a year before the completion of the house. September 24, 1856, enroute by horse and buggy to Martinez, Dr. Marsh was waylaid by vaqueros, seeking revenge, and murdered just outside the town.

MEMORIAL FOUNTAIN MARKS SITE CALIFORNIA'S FIFTH STATE FAIR.

Marysville (Yuba County)—Marysville Parlor No. 162 N.D.G.W. dedicated July 4 in Cortez Square a fountain, erected in memory of the women and men who founded the city, in 1850. The fountain stands upon the site of the pavilion which housed California's Fifth State Fair, in

858. The exhibitors at that exposition, it is aid, included General John A. Sutter, outstanding Pioneer; General John Bidwell, founder of Chico, Butte County; Peter Lassen, for whom Lassen County and Lassen National Park are amed; Kit Carson, famous guide.

The fountain bears a bronze plaque embellished with a covered wagon and inscribed as ollows: "Dedicated to the memory of the Pioneer Men and Women of Marysville. Erected by Marysville Parlor No. 162 Native Daughters of he Golden West July 4, 1932."

Mrs. Gertrude Cable presided, and among the peakers were Councilman Leo J. Smith; Past irand President Fred H. Greely of the Native ons; Past Grand Presidents Dr. Louise C. Heilron and Esther R. Sullivan, and Grand Secreary Sallie R. Thaler of the Native Daughters. n the course of her remarks Miss Sullivan said: "Sutter's New Helvetia grant from the Mexican government covered territory now embraced in Sacramento and Sutter Counties and portions of Placer, Yuba and Colusa Counties. He called the Marysville portion of it New Mecklenburg, but the settlement, starting with two adobe buildings at the foot of what is now 'D' street, was better known as Nye's Ranch, then Yubaville, until Mary Murphy Covillaud's name was given it in 1850."

MONUMENT MARKS SITE SAN BERNARDINO'S FIRST PUBLIC BUILDING.

San Bernardino City—The site of this city's first public building is now designated by a monument, erected by Lugonia Parlor No. 241 N.D.G.W., which was dedicated June 25. A plaque has the following inscription: "In memory of Charles C. Rich and Amasa M. Lyman, builders of the Council House, 1852. First school, church and later court house of this county. Dedicated by Lugonia Parlor No. 241, Native Daughters of the Golden West. June 25, 1932."

Miss Clara M. Barton, chairman of the Parlor's landmarks committee, presided at the ceremonies. Rev. Golder I. Lawrence delivered an invocation, and the dedicatory address was delivered by Dr. Richard R. Lyman of Salt Lake City, grandson of one of San Bernardino's founders. President Gladys Case Baker of Lugonia made the presentation address, which was responded to by Supervisor C. E. Grier. President George W. Beattie of the San Bernardino Historical Society recounted the history of the city and the county. Miss Naomi Rich of Riverside City, a granddaughter of Charles C. Rich, was among the many in attendance.

Following the ceremonies the Native Daughters entertained at the log cabin in Pioneer Park. President C. J. Daley of the San Bernardino Pioneer Society extended a welcome. Associated with Miss Barton in arranging the day's program were Laura Clark, Daisy Davenport, Catherine McIntosh and Gladys Case Baker.

SIERRA COUNTY MUSEUM DEDICATED.

Downieville (Sierra County) — Downieville Parlor No. 92 N.S.G.W. and Naomi Parlor No. 36 N.D.G.W. dedicated July 4 the Sierra County Museum, in which will be housed, under control of the Parlors, early-day relics. The dedicatory address was delivered by District Attorney J. M. McMahon. Mr. and Mrs. William Lloyd presented a Flag of the United States of America.

The building, made entirely of stone, was presented to Downieville by the heirs of J. M. B. Meroux, Sierra County Pioneer. It is one of the oldest structures in the northern section of the state, and is believed to have been erected in 1852. It has survived three disastrous fires.

July 14 the Parlors placed upon the Sierra County court house a plaque reading: "The erection of this Building commenced April 18, 1854. Completed May 6, 1855. David G. Webber, builder."

Gas Tax—With the addition of the new Federal Government tax, motorists of the United States are now paying gasoline taxes at the rate of approximately $2,000,000 a day.

Assessors' Meet—The annual convention of the California County Assessors Association will be held at Al Tahoe, Nevada County, August 22-24.

Native Sons of the Golden West

WHO WAS "ROBERT SEMPLE"? IF you had read carefully The Grizzly Bear for May 1932 you would know. Refer to page 25 of that issue and you will find this, which answers the question: Dr. Robert B. Semple was one of California's noted Pioneers. A native of Kentucky, he arrived at Sutter Fort (Sacramento) Christmas Day of 1845. He was a member of the Bear Flag Party which, June 14, 1846, raised the California Republic Flag at Sonoma. At Monterey, August 15, 1846, he issued the state's first newspaper, "The Californian," which in May 1847 was moved to Yerba Buena (San Francisco) and later sold to the "California Star." In 1847 he located the site of the present City of Colusa. He also laid out the present City of Benicia, Solano County, and constructed and operated the first ferry across Carquinez Straits. He also organized the state's first mail service; April 19, 1849, two soldiers on horseback left San Francisco and San Diego, met half-way, exchanged mail sacks and returned to their starting points. Dr. Semple was the president of California's First Constitutional Convention, which assembled at Monterey, September 1, 1849. He died at Williams, Colusa County, October 25, 1854.—Editor.

Good News.

Members of the Order will be delighted to learn that Junior Past Grand President Dr. Frank I. Gonzalez and his wife, who were seriously injured in an auto accident near Santa Barbara last May, left the hospital for their San Francisco home July 4. Mrs. Gonzalez is still troubled with a broken shoulder bone, but is improving, and Dr. Gonzales expects to resume his practice August 1. He plans, also, to be at Santa Barbara for the school dedication August 19.

Would Promote Athletics.

The Grand Parlor Athletic Committee—Al. Sandell (chairman), R. J. Garrett, L. Alva Werner, Wesley Colgan and Arthur J. Cleu—will meet early in September to discuss the advisability of promoting athletics throughout the Order.

A questionnaire has been sent all Subordinate Parlors, and they are requested to fill it out and return not later than September 1 to Chairman Al. Sandell, 830 Market street, San Francisco. This should have prompt attention.

Busy in the Field.

Deputy Grand President Al Lobree, engaged in field work for the Grand Parlor, was in Madera City last month and reports a large class of candidates will be initiated for Madera No. 130 by the officers of Fresno No. 25. From Madera, he will proceed to Hanford, Visalia and Tulare City, where he hopes to institute new parlors.

Parlor Instituted.

Los Banos—Los Banos No. 206 was instituted July 9 by Grand President Seth Millington, who was assisted by Grand Secretary John T. Regan, Grand Trustee Joseph J. McShane and Deputy Grand President Al Lobree. The ritual was exemplified by a team from Stockton No. 7 composed of George D. Avery, president; C. W. Walsh, senior past; L. Buol, junior past; J. D. Gallagher, first vice; Ben J. Waller, second vice; George Witherow, third vice; W. A. Strong, marshal; R. A. Mitscher, assistant marshal; M. O. Woods, inside sentinel; J. B. Sacco, outside sentinel; Glenn Kennedy, pianist.

Officers of Los Banos were installed by Deputy Laurence Buol as follows: Robert L. Puccinelli, president; Joseph A. Enos, junior past; Manuel J. DeParsia, first vice; Daniel L. Pedrone, second vice; John L. Pasmore, third vice; Louis Edw. Sarbo, recording secretary; Frank Pimentel, financial secretary; George L. Hoke, treasurer; Frank Damberasio, marshal; Daniel J. Galatio, inside sentinel; Joseph Celano, outside sentinel; Paul L. Negra, Ralph Newsome, James Wm. Ives, trustees. Modesto No. 11 presented the "baby" with a seal of the State of California.

Anniversary Observed.

San Bernardino—Officers of Arrowhead No. 110, with F. L. McGarvey as president, were installed July 13 by Deputy Ray Marsile. The Parlor's forty-fifth institution anniversary was observed July 20 with a short program in honor of the three remaining charter members, Albert Burcham, Emory Tyler and Joe Rich.

The Arrowheaders and many visitors had one big night at the Parlor's clubhouse at Crestline July 23. A feast of barbecued steak was followed by the initiation of several candidates. The officers appeared in "wild west" costumes for the occasion. An Admission Day observance committee has been appointed, composed of Ben Harrison (chairman), Lyman A. Reed, M. G. Hale and Grand Organist Leslie Maloche.

Will Be in Line.

Santa Rosa—Santa Rosa No. 28 will be represented in the Admission Day parade at San Francisco, and a committee composed of Wesley Colgan (chairman), Frank Berger, Jim Brucker, Dr. W. C. Shipley and Secretary Leland S. Lewis has been appointed to make the arrangements. President Wesley Beach headed a delegation that July 23 paid a visit to Mount Tamalpais No. 64 at San Rafael.

Membership Standing Largest Parlors.

San Francisco—Grand Secretary John T. Regan reports the standing of the Subordinate Parlors having a membership of over 400 January 1, 1932, as follows, together with their membership figures July 20, 1932:

Parlor.	Jan. 1	July 20	Gain	Loss
Ramona No. 109	1088	1083	....	5
South San Francisco No. 157	822	808	....	14
Castro No. 232	700	716	16	....
Stanford No. 76	614	606	....	8
Arrowhead No. 110	609	584	....	25
Stockton No. 7	549	563	14	....
Twin Peaks No. 214	585	550	....	35
Piedmont No. 120	523	520	....	3
Rincon No. 72	448	436	....	12

Five Parlors Install Jointly.

Sacramento—Officers of Sacramento No. 3 and Sunset No. 26, and La Bandera No. 110, Sutter No. 111 and Coloma No. 212 N.D.G.W. were jointly installed at Native Son Hall July 15. Joseph Drennon, Clyde Corcoran, Doris Fisher, Esther Mulligan and Mary Lucas were the officiating deputies, and Joseph Fitzhenry, L. W. Marvin, Miss Helen Kennedy, Mrs. Ida Merwin and Miss Marie Christie became the respective presidents.

Grand Trustee Edna B. Briggs was chairman of the general arrangements committee, and she was assisted by a large number of co-workers from all five Parlors. Dancing followed the ceremonies, which were largely attended, and refreshments were served.

Purchases Home.

Plymouth—Plymouth No. 48, through a committee composed of H. Jameson, O. Harrell and E. Hodges, has completed arrangements for the purchase of its own home, the former clubhouse of the Plymouth Gold Mines. The property is being renovated and improved, and will make a cosy meetingplace for the Parlor.

Historic Fort Ross Attracts.

Sebastopol—An Independence Day celebration supervised by Sebastopol No. 143 at historic Fort Ross, built by Russian settlers in 1812, attracted a large crowd. W. S. Borba was master of ceremonies. State Assemblyman Hubert Scudder officiated at the dedication of a marker placed at the settlement by the Redwood Empire Association. State Senator Herbert Slater was the speaker of the day.

SANTA BARBARA SCHOOL DEDICATION

CLIFFORD F. RIZOR
(Chairman of Publicity,
Santa Barbara Parlor N.S.G.W.)

THE OLD SPANISH DAYS FIESTA AT Santa Barbara will open August 18. At least ten of the grand officers of the Order of Native Sons of the Golden West, and possibly several grand officers of the Orders of Native Daughters will be Santa Barbara's guests during the celebration. On the second day of the fiesta the Native Son grand officers will dedicate Santa Barbara's new Eastside junior high school. This structure, representing an investment in land, building and equipment of nearly one million dollars, marks the completion of a twelve-year program of intensive building and improvement in the school system of Santa Barbara.

In the years since 1920 Santa Barbara, like many other cities of California, has grown rapidly. As a consequence, the enrollment in its schools here during that period has increased 200 percent, necessitating a constant expansion of school facilities and teaching staff to properly meet the demand. Paul E. Stewart, superintendent of schools for Santa Barbara, stated in a recent talk that it has been necessary to rebuild and modernize the entire school system, for the reason that until 1920 the schools were housed in old wooden buildings built previous to 1904. The erection of the new junior high school is significant as marking Santa Barbara's complete transition from the "red schoolhouse" era, and gives adequate facilities to what is now one of the highest accredited school systems in California.

Thus it comes about that when Grand President Seth Millington, with his co-worker, Grand First Vice-president Justice Emmet Seawell, make their dedicatory addresses on behalf of the Native Sons, they will signalize not only the completion of a fine new building, but a renewed and modernized educational scheme, infused with new life and ambitions.

The four city blocks which form the campus of this new school were once swamp land. Scientific filling and drainage have changed them from an intolerable eyesore and made them into a very desirable community asset. The potential value of surrounding property has thus been considerably increased.

The building itself is of Spanish architecture from designs furnished by the school architect W. H. Weeks, who has designed many fine school buildings, some of which have been dedicated by the Native Sons in other cities. He has provided a recess for the dedicatory plaque in the floor of the front entrance to the building, so that the entire ceremony of dedication, including the laying of the plaque, may be witnessed from the area fronting on the entrance. This permits of the entire program being held out-of-doors.

The committee of Santa Barbara Parlor No. 116 N.S.G.W. on dedications has enlisted the support of the newspapers, womens clubs, parent-teacher organizations and other civic bodies with the purpose of securing a large attendance at the dedication. The committee is working to secure an outpouring of at least 1,500 people at the ceremony.

Special transportation rates to Santa Barbara from all points in California will be in effect during Old Spanish Days week. This will afford an opportunity to all residents of the state to witness the fiesta at a very nominal cost. Santa Barbara promises an entertainment, and a vacation experience, unique and satisfying.

Determined To Increase Visits.

San Rafael—Officers of Mount Tamalpais No. 64 and Marinita No. 198 N.D.G.W. were jointly installed July 23 by Deputies J. S. Rosa Jr. and Mrs. A. W. Todt, Monroe E. Petersen and Lena Mazza becoming the respective presidents. Charles Soldavini Jr. and Antionette Hecht had charge of the decorations and entertainment. Many visitors were in attendance and the evening proved most enjoyable.

Deputy Monroe Label has installed the officers of Petaluma No. 27 and Sebastopol No. 143. An enthusiastic member of Mount Tamalpais, he is making determined efforts to increase fraternal visits between the Sonoma and the Marin County Parlors through an interparlor committee.

July 13 officers of Marin County Past Presidents Assembly No. 5 were installed by Director-general James F. Stanley, Charles Soldavini Jr. succeeding J. S. Rosa Jr. as governor. Governor-general Louis F. Erb and Trustee-general Adolph Gudehus spoke most encouragingly of the outlook for the past presidents association. A sumptuous repast was served at the close of the meeting.

Former Grand Officer Dead.

Stockton—Edward Van Vranken, former Grand Trustee, died July 3 at Vallejo, Solano County, survived by a wife and two children. He was affiliated with Stockton No. 7, and had served San Joaquin County as district attorney and supervisor.

N.S.G.W. OFFICIAL DEATH LIST.

Containing the name, the date and the place of birth, the date of death, and the Subordinate Parlor affiliation of deceased members reported to Grand Secretary John T. Regan from June 15, 1932, to July 20, 1932:

Morrell, George W.; Diamond Springs, February 2, 1856; February 21, 1932; Sacramento No. 3.
Quintaro, William F.; West Point, October 16, 1873; March 27, 1932; Sacramento No. 3.
Mulleney, Manuel; Grass Valley, January 30, 1863; April 18, 1932; Sacramento No. 3.
Denegri, Anton; San Francisco, June 5, 1873; April 22, 1932; Stockton No. 7.
Sanquenetti, D. A.; Lathrop, April 20, 1885; April 25, 1932; Stockton No. 7.
Fox, Henry C.; San Andreas, April 3, 1860; May 14, 1932; Stockton No. 7.
Scott, Chester A.; Ione, December 14, 1884; May 18, 1932; Stockton No. 7.
Marsh, Clyde Charles; Diamond Springs, October 24, 1888; June 23, 1932; Placerville No. 9.
McPherson, Samuel H.; Tuolumne, November 19, 1856; March 6, 1932; Pacific No. 10.
Swift, James F.; Sacramento, January 6, 1860; May 7, 1932; Pacific No. 10.
Coffe, Louis Elias; San Jose, June 24, 1862; May 6, 1932; San Jose No. 22.
Parker, George W.; Petaluma, July 4, 1866; February 6, 1932; Petaluma No. 27.
Ratto, Ernest; Jeuse Marie, December 28, 1868; May 1, 1932; Golden Gate No. 29.
Delano, Frank M.; Morsville, May 8, 1858; May 25, 1932; Mission No. 38.
Pierce, Anthony Joseph; Los Angeles, July 5, 1898; June 19, 1932; Los Angeles No. 45.
Haines, Martin Leopold; Madison, April 10, 1867; June 29, 1932; Los Angeles No. 45.
Lachman, Adolph B.; Los Angeles, September 8, 1867; July 5, 1932; Los Angeles No. 45.
Gee, Henry Gilbert; El Dorado, February 13, 1890; June 23, 1932; Plymouth No. 48.
Koning, Max J.; San Francisco, October 25, 1858; April 5, 1932; El Dorado No. 52.
Angellotti, Frank M.; San Rafael, October 29, 1861; May 23, 1932; Mount Tamalpais No. 64.
Shermantine, John F.; Santa Clara, January 17, 1854; June 9, 1932; Redwood No. 66.
Romero, Jose; Old San Diego, May 15, 1853; June 30, 1932; Ramona No. 109.
Duhring, Fred. Thomas; Sonoma, September 2, 1862; January 21, 1932; Sonoma No. 111.
Enfield, Joseph Louis; Sonoma, July 3, 1885; June 14, 1932; Sonoma No. 111.
Powell, Henry Jr.; Birchville, August 13, 1869; March 18, 1932; Eden No. 113.
Reitz, William; Sonora, March 27, 1874; June 15, 1932; National No. 118.
West, John H.; Soulsbyville, July 3, 1859; February 3, 1932; Tuolumne No. 144.
Grohl, John H.; Keystone, December 20, 1860; May 15, 1932; Tuolumne No. 144.
Mattock, James Thompson; Red Bluff, November 23, 1876; May 16, 1932; McCloud No. 149.
Nedderman, Roy N.; Oakland, July 17, 1891; June 13, 1932; Brooklyn No. 151.
Mayer, Fred C.; San Francisco, February 10, 1872; May 28, 1932; South San Francisco No. 157.
Erickson, Victor; San Francisco, February 14, 1870; July 7, 1932; South San Francisco No. 157.
Rannells, Warren Bert; San Joaquin, October 31, 1871; July 14, 1932; Lower Lake No. 159.
Richards, John Evan; San Jose, July 7, 1856; June 25, 1932; Observatory No. 177.
Brown, Victor Forrest; Saratoga, January 2, 1894; June 28, 1932; Observatory No. 177.
Smith, Mathias Frederick; Etna, March 9, 1872; June 28, 1932; Etna No. 192.
Gibney, George Patrick; Merced, February 6, 1880; July 8, 1932; Alder Glen No. 200.
Fahrenholz, Arthur; San Francisco, November 26, 1875; June 20, 1932; Twin Peaks No. 214.
Ford, W. Joseph; Oakland, August 2, 1877; January 5, 1932; Glendale No. 264.
Howard, Archie Valentine; Santa Monica, February 14, 1888; June 19, 1932; Santa Monica Bay No. 267.

"Your Half of the Road Is Not in the Middle," is the August slogan of the California Public Safety Committee in its campaign to lessen the constantly increasing auto death-toll.

LOS ANGELES
CITY AND COUNTY

NUMEROUS NOTORIOUSLY OBNOXious political rackets have been propagated in Los Angeles, but what appears to be the outstanding one was the just-recent indictment of a superior court judge by the grand jury. Here are the facts, as revealed in the public press from time to time: A "receivership racket" was uncovered some months ago and the grand jury proceeded to investigate. Just prior to its discharge from duty, the grand jury returned a bribery indictment against a judge of the superior court who is a candidate for re-election at the August primary; the indictment was voted on the unsupported testimony of one man. The grand jury did not indict the man who claimed to have accepted the "bribe" from the indicted judge, nor did it indict three superior court judges who are not August primary candidates for re-election, but who have been linked with the receivership racket and against whom the Bar Association is sponsoring a recall.

That indictment, irrespective of the innocence or the guilt of the accused and in view of the facts above set forth, stinks to high heaven! It has every earmark of a political racket, and further lessens faith in judicial uprightness. If the truth has been made public, but one conclusion can be drawn from that indictment: the political gangsters have wedged their way into the grand jury precincts. There should be a thorough and competent investigation, by the Bar Association preferably, of the local grand jury system, to ascertain if the members of that body are selected in full accord with the statute or if they are handpicked directly or indirectly by and at the suggestion of those in and those out of public office who do not want their careers investigated by an inquisitorial body whose members play no favorites and are beyond reach.

Los Angeles is overburdened with financial, political and other gangsters, and they prey unmercifully on the decent element of the citizenry; that is the main reason why taxes are so burdensome. Justice is continuously outraged! The great majority of the citizenry, who are honest and lawabiding, should awake to this situation and clean out the gangsters and their agents by electing to public office citizens of unquestioned integrity who will not only respect and obey the laws of the land themselves but will administer those laws impartially and fearlessly.

Unless there be a cleanup of the rotten conditions, the Angel(ess) City cannot possibly regain its place in the sun of safe communities—safe for investment, safe for honest endeavor, and safe as a homeplace. Begin the cleaning-out at the August 30 primary! The ballot-box, if used with care and after due consideration of existant conditions, is the weapon that will rout the gangsters!—C.M.H.

COME OUT, NATIVE SONS!

Seth Millington of Gridley, Butte County, Grand President of the Order of Native Sons of the Golden West, will arrive in Los Angeles August 5. He wants to discuss affairs of the Order with members of all the southland Parlors, and to make that possible arrangements have been made for a joint meeting the night of August 5 on the fourth floor of Patriotic Hall, 1816 South Figueroa street. Every Native Son who can possibly do so, should attend that meeting.

In honor of the Grand President, a noonday luncheon August 6 has been arranged for by Grand Trustee Eldred L. Meyer, and the following day he will be the guest of Santa Monica Bay Parlor No. 267 at a barbecue in Santa Monica Canyon.

August 8, Grand President Millington will visit Hollywood Parlor No. 196, and the following night he will be at the meeting of Glendale Parlor No. 264. Classes of candidates will be initiated on both these occasions.

SPECIAL BOWL EVENTS.

Three of the most important special events planned for the Olympic year series of Symphonies Under the Stars in the Hollywood Bowl will be presented early in August.

Tuesday, the 2nd, the pageant, "California Welcomes the World," will be given as a part of the regular Bowl program. More than 2,000 persons will take part in this spectacle, including representatives of every foreign nation participating in the games.

The next concert under the warm summer skies will be "International Night," Thursday, the 4th, with Alfred Wallenstein, world-famous cellist, making his Bowl debut as conductor. It will be his only appearance in the conductor's stand, although he will be heard later in the season as soloist with the orchestra.

The following night, Friday, the 5th, will bring the Bowl's third choral production, Verdi's "Requiem," sung by the Los Angeles Civic Chorus, with an all-star cast in the solo parts. Bernardino Molinari, conductor of the Augusteum Symphony of Rome, will direct the orchestra in all of these programs except Wallenstein's.

SPLENDID AFFAIR.

A most noteworthy function in Native Son circles was the public installation of the officers of seven Parlors at Glendale, July 6, under the auspices of Glendale Parlor No. 264. A tasty supper, prepared and served by the Glendale Native Daughters and Native Sons, preceded the ceremonies. The Glendale Fire Department orchestra, directed by H. T. Mundon, furnished music. Earl LeMoine was the toastmaster, and introduced numerous personages. Some 300 were in attendance, Santa Barbara Parlor No. 116 sending a large delegation in "Old Spanish Days" costumes.

President Phil D. Molen of Glendale Parlor presided at the installation ceremonies, and introduced Superior Judge B. Rey Shauer as master of ceremonies. Mayor Frank P. Taggart of Glendale extended a welcome, and among the other speakers were Past Grand Presidents Herman C. Lichtenberger, William I. Traeger and John T. Newell, Grand Trustee Eldred L. Meyer, Grand Outside Sentinel William I. Reuter, Leo V. Youngworth and Harry C. Sweetser. Under Sheriff Eugene W. Biscailuz successfully and painlessly conducted the good of the order. Others in attendance were Deputy Grand President Al Cron, and District Deputies A. C. Dinsmore, H. G. Bentley, E. E. Baldwin, Ray Marsile and W. E. Baskerville. Organ selections were rendered by Mrs. Hazel K. Skinner, and Mrs. Thelma A. Leaton was heard in two vocal selections.

Burrel D. Neighbours, chairman Grand Parlor Ritual Committee, most impressively delivered the installation charges, and Grand Organist Leslie Maloche presided at the piano. Presidents of the Parlors whose officers were installed include: Owen S. Adams, Los Angeles No. 45; Dr. James M. Watson, Ramona No. 109; W. C. McCormick, Santa Barbara No. 116; Kenneth Case, Hollywood No. 196; Joseph A. Pia, Sepulveda No. 263; Leslie Schellbach, Glendale No. 264; Orin Welch, Santa Monica Bay No. 267. Glendale Parlor's arrangements committee for the event included: Phil D. Molen (general chairman), Clinton E. Skinner (chairman installation), Leslie Schellbach (chairman banquet), Louis G. Verdugo (chairman supplies), Leslie Henderson, Albert Boeckman, Abel R. Molen, Walter Kent, Harold R. Bowen, Harvey T. Gillette, Carl Stahl and Loring Kent.—C.M.H.

ADMISSION DAY OBSERVANCE.

The Native Sons and the Native Daughters of Los Angeles County have organized a committee to arrange for the observance of Admission Day, eptember 9. Burrel D. Neighbours, Ramona 'arlor No. 109 N.S.G.W., was elected chairman; drs. Mary Noorenberg, Californians Parlor No. 47 N.D.G.W., vice-chairman; Fred J. Burmeser, Los Angeles Parlor No. 45 N.S.G.W., secreary; Frank Frank, Los Angeles Parlor No. 45 N.S.G.W., treasurer.

At a meeting July 22 the committee decided o sponsor a brief program, to be followed by a lance. Clinton Skinner, Mrs. Gertrude Allen, 'ast Grand President John T. Newell and Grand 'rustee Eldred L. Meyer were appointed a comnittee to make the necessary arrangements, and hey were authorized to select co-workers. The ffair will be held in the ballroom of the I.O.O.F. uilding, Oak and Washington streets.

HAND-MADE FLAG PRESENTED.

Officers of Los Angeles Parlor No. 124 N.D.G.W. were publicly installed by Deputy Rita mith July 27, Mrs. Mattie Garn becoming presilent. The hall was prettily decorated and there ras a large attendance of members and friends. splendid program was presented, including an ddress by Sheriff William I. Traeger, Past rand President N.S.G.W., and short talks by 'ast Grand Grace S. Stoermer, Mary Foye and Marion Parks. The swimming class is making ne progress. A letter of thanks has been sent Bert Harwell, Yosemite Valley naturalist, for ourtesies extended the Parlor's delegates to the rand Parlor. Ruth Traeger was hostess for he July 13 card party, which was well attended.

Mrs. Estelle Hard has presented the Parlor vith a hand-crocheted and framed Flag of the Jnited States of America. The gift, the work f the donor, was accompanied by a card incribed: "Greetings to you all in honor of our ountry's flag, the dear old red, white and blue. 'his friendly greeting will convey sincere reembrances to you all. July 4, 1932." The dinner of all nations" was a wonderful success, ocially, financially and gastronomically. Quite few Olympic stars gave brief talks.

August 10, Los Angeles will have another of ts popular monthly card parties; Effie Walters nd Katharine Sens are the hostesses. August 4 a beach party, including swimming, will be eatured.

OUTDOOR FESTIVAL AT SANTA MONICA.

Ocean Park—Santa Monica Bay Parlor No. 267 N.S.G.W. is staging an outdoor festival in honor of Grand President Seth Millington, August 7, in Santa Monica Canyon, foot of Seventh street, Santa Monica. All members of the Order and of the Native Daughters, as well as their families and friends, will be welcome. An admission fee of 75c for adults and 25c for children will be charged.

The grounds will open at 10:30 a. m., and the festivities will continue into the evening. From noon until 2 p.m. an old-time California barbecue will be served, and "plenty" good music

(Continued on Page 16)

Native Daughters of the Golden West

WOODLAND — GRAND PRESIDENT Anna Mixon-Armstrong was tendered a reception by her home-Parlor, Woodland No. 90, on her return from the Merced Grand Parlor. President Ruth Hickey welcomed Mrs. Armstrong, and in the course of her response she expressed appreciation for the efforts put forth by the Parlor to advance her to the highest position in the gift of the Order. Miss Henrietta Toothaker sang "Dawning," and then presented Mrs. Armstrong with a huge basket of beautiful flowers. Others on the program were Maida Jean Stephens, Ross Baldwin, Frank Mixon and Stacy Armstrong. A banquet was served under the direction of Leia Ewert.

One of the first official acts of Grand President Armstrong was to present to Rowena Norton, superintendent Yolo County schools, a California State (Bear) Flag to be displayed in her office.

Youth Must Assume Leadership.

Santa Barbara—The July 5 meeting of Reina del Mar No. 126 was in honor of Grand Trustee Jane Vick. A program, arranged by Mrs. John D. Ross, Mrs. George McCrea, the president, and Supervising Deputy Anna McCaughey, included an address by Clark Kerr of the Society of Friends on "The Economic Aspects of Peace and What It Means to Youth." He said:

"The youth of the world, and particularly in our own country, must be prepared to assume leadership. Study of international economics is fundamental in this preparation. I make a plea for consideration of the future. It is up to the younger leaders, now being developed, to perfect the machinery for arbitration which is only in a rudimentary stage." A round table discussion followed the address.

Planning for Official Visit.

Oakland—Officers of Piedmont No. 87 and Piedmont No. 120 N.S.G.W. were jointly installed July 7 by Deputies Edna Healey and Elwood Fitzgerald, Mrs. Josephine Collins and Frank Patrick Smith becoming the respective presidents. Past president emblems were presented Mrs. Kathleen Dombrink and Andrew Costello by Grand Secretary Sallie R. Thaler and Grand Inside Sentinel Gam Hurst. Past Grand President Sue J. Irwin was among the visitors. Chairmen of the evening were Mrs. Edna M. Healey and Thomas J. Healey. Dancing concluded the ceremonies.

Piedmont No. 87 is making extensive plans for the official visit, the first in Alameda County, of Grand President Anna Mixon-Armstrong August 4. Chairman Edna M. Healey is being assisted by Gretta Murden, Alice Ollson, Dorothy Davis, Ella Mullen, Margaret Thomas, Augusta Huxsol, Jennie L. Jordan, Kate Ford, Grace Searing, Dorothy Hadlen, Marcella O'Connell, May Meade and Rose Martinelli.

Two Initiated.

Oroville—Gold of Ophir No. 190 initiated two candidates and installed officers July 6. Deputy Annie Skelly officiated and Rosa Crum became the president. Numerous presentations were made, including an emblematic pin to Past President Jessie Hoover and flowers to Grand Trustee Florence Boyle. Following the meeting refreshments were served on the veranda at Memorial Hall.

Gold of Ophir has recessed until September 7, at which time a program in recognition of Admission Day will be presented.

Thimble Club Recesses.

Santa Ana—Officers of Santa Ana No. 235 were installed July 25 by Deputy Eva Bemis, Mrs. Mildred Gray becoming president. The ways and means committee, headed by Mrs. Muriel Bray, is very busy with a newspaper contest. Mms. Marion Crum, Genevieve Hiskey and Matilda Lemon attended last month meetings of the Los Angeles committee that is arranging for the observance of Admission Day, September 9. No. 235 joined Santa Ana No. 265 N.S.G.W. in a picnic at Irvine Park which proved very enjoyable and profitable. The membership drive which closed recently resulted in a tie, but both sides will serve a potluck dinner in celebration.

Santa Ana's thimble club has had sessions recently at the homes of Olive Witt, Lillian Gant, Olive Seba and Marion Crum. At the latter gathering, July 14, Mrs. Crum, the retiring president of the Parlor, was presented with a basket of flowers as a token of the club's love and appreciation. Meetings of the club will be resumed in September. Past President Mary Moore, seriously ill at Modesto, has returned to Santa Ana much improved in health. Miss Emma Hadley of Newport Beach, a member of the Parlor, recently became Mrs. Emma Crawford.

Reception for Grand Trustee.

San Rafael—There was a large attendance at the July 11 meeting of Marinita No. 198. Visitors included Deputy Delphine Todt, Mms. Walker, Gandolfo and Label, and a delegation from Fairfax No. 225. After the usual business was completed all were invited to the banquetroom by Catherine Kelly, chairman of the evening's festivities,

An informal reception was there held for Grand Trustee Ethel Begley, this being her third year on the Board of Grand Parlor Trustees. The hall was artistically decorated in bicentennial colors and huge vases of gladiolas. An immense cake was on the table at Mrs. Begley's place, and she was presented with a gift. All visitors favored with interesting and complimentary remarks. Tasty refreshments were served.

Order's Projects Explained.

Alturas—During the Independence Day celebration and roundup Alturas No. 159 had charge of the parade, and the organizations to which units were assigned gave splendid co-operation. The Parlor entered a float, which was awarded first prize by the Roundup Association. Grand Vice-president Irma W. Laird was a guest speaker before the Rotary Club and explained the Order's outstanding projects.

S. D. Evans of Roseburg, Oregon, in appreciation for services rendered has presented the Parlor with a gavel set made of native Oregon maple. During recent roadmaking activities hereabouts some prehistoric stone weapons and implements were unearthed, and they have been placed in the Native Daughter Museum.

Doing Creditable Work.

San Diego—San Diego No. 208 participated in the three-day Independence Day celebration here by the entrance in the July 4 parade of a very beautiful float depicting a California flower garden. Three of the Parlor's charming members adorned the float, Misses Floribel Barngrover, Alice Damarus and Iris Kalben. A reception to the Grand Parlor delegates followed the meeting of July 13.

The evening of July 18 Mrs. Edith Barngrover threw open her attractive home for a card party to aid the Parlor treasury. The Indian welfare committee of No. 208, under the chairmanship of Mrs. Doris Hoffner, has been doing creditable work, having sent out numerous donations of clothing and food.

Grand President's Official Itinerary.

Woodland—During the month of August Grand President Anna Mixon-Armstrong will officially visit the following Subordinate Parlors on the dates noted:

1st—Santa Cruz No. 26, Santa Cruz.
2nd—El Pajaro No. 35, Watsonville.
3rd—Vendome No. 100, San Jose.
4th—Piedmont No. 87, Oakland.
8th—La Estrella No. 89, San Francisco.
11th—Aleli No. 102, Salinas.
12th—Junipero No. 141, Monterey.
16th—Petaluma No. 222, Petaluma.
17th—Vallejo No. 195, Vallejo.
18th—Santa Rosa No. 217, Santa Rosa.
22nd—Sonoma No. 209, Sonoma.
25th—Encinal No. 156, Alameda.
26th—Twin Peaks No. 185, San Francisco.

Joint Installation.

Oakland—Officers of Aloha No. 106 and Athens No. 195 N.S.G.W. were jointly installed July 12. Deputies Irma Murray and Joseph Ehrhart officiated, and Thelma D. Rogers and E. L. Bullock became the respective presidents. On Aloha's behalf, Grand Secretary Sallie R. Thaler presented an emblematic jewel to Past President Martha Watson. Dancing followed the installation ceremonies, and refreshments were served.

To Honor Pioneers.

Chico—Officers of Annie K. Bidwell No. 16 were installed July 12 by Deputy Anna Barnard, Laura Anderson becoming president. Past President Frances Snider and Deputy Barnard were presented with gifts. Visitors included Grand Trustee Florence Boyle, Deputies Annie Skelley and Ruth Brown. Refreshments were served.

Members of the Parlor enjoyed an all-day picnic July 10. Plans are under way for honoring the Pioneers of the community Admission Day, September 9, with a bicentennial program.

President Entertains.

Fullerton—President Mattie Edwards of Grace No. 242 presided at the last business session of her year July 7. After the meeting she and her daughter entertained the Parlor members at a bridge party and served a late supper at a beautifully decorated table. President Edwards presented her officers with gold hand-painted sugar-and-creamer sets, which she designed and painted, and each guest was given a pastel felt colonial dame needlebook. On behalf of the officers Past President Nellie Cline presented Mrs. Edwards with a large floral basket.

The newly-elected officers of the Parlor were installed July 21 by Deputy Mary Noorenberg, Lena Aspden becoming president. Visitors included a large delegation from Californiana No. 247 (Los Angeles).

Cook Book for Reward.

San Jose—Vendome No. 100 held a reception in honor of Grand Organist Clara A. Gairaud. A "stunt" program under the leadership of Mrs. Veronica Lind was thoroughly enjoyed. A banquet closed the festivities, during which Mrs. Gairaud was given a shower of gifts and flowers, the Parlor's token being a beautiful evening bag. Mrs. Gairaud is president of the Santa Clara County Music Teachers Association. Vendome is making elaborate preparations to receive Grand President Anna M. Armstrong on her official visit August 3.

Grand Organist Gairaud is sending out a challenge to any member of the Order (Vendome and San Jose Parlors excepted) to guess the initial "A" of her name. The first correct answer received by October 1 will be rewarded with one of Grand Trustee Willow Borba's 3,000-recipe "Loyalty Pledge Cook Books."

Encouraging Reports.

Santa Rosa—A joint public installation of the officers of Santa Rosa No. 217 and Santa Rosa No. 28 N.S.G.W. was held July 7, and there was a large attendance of visitors and members. No. 217 anticipates a pleasant evening August 18, when Grand President Anna M. Armstrong officially visits.

There are very encouraging reports on the "Loyalty Cook Book," sponsored by Grand Trustee Willow Borba. Members of the Order are finding ready sale for it, and they have the satisfaction of having the purchasers well pleased with their investment.

Birthday Party.

Modesto—Thirteen members who had recent birthdays were honored by Morada No. 199. The guests sat at a table adorned with beautiful boquets and a huge lighted birthday cake, and each was presented a lovely gift. With Deputy Ethel Mathiasen presiding, officers of Morada were installed July 27 jointly with those of Modesto No. 11 N.S.G.W.

Benefit Card Party.

San Bernardino—Lugonia No. 241 had as guests July 13 Grand Outside Sentinel Hazel Hansen, who gave a delightful talk, and a group from Ontario No. 251. July 19 a benefit card party was held in the home gardens of Mary Johnson, incoming first vice-president. Prizes were awarded and refreshments were served.

Successful Whist.

Mountain View—El Monte No. 205 and Mountain View No. 215 N.S.G.W. July 13 gave a joint whist party, which was very successful.

Past Presidents Doings.

Oakland—Association No. 2 entertained in honor of Frances McGovern, retiring president. An enjoyable program was followed by dainty refreshments. Many beautiful gifts were presented the honor-guest by Chairwoman Josephine Clark. At joint ceremonies July 25, officers of No. 2 and Past Presidents Assembly No. 3 N.S.G.W. were installed, Emma Haggerty becoming president of the former. C. Bartlett headed a large committee in charge of the social program, and an emblematic pin was presented Frances McGovern.

San Jose—Association No. 3 had a very happy meeting July 12, when a potluck dinner was served. The hall was beautifully decorated. Officers were installed by Miss Elsie Fisher, Mrs. Amelia Hartman becoming president.

Chico—Association No. 5 installed officers July 1 at the home of Margaret Hudspeth, Marie Picanco becoming president. Plans for the annual picnic August 5 were outlined. Mae Belle Bills and Irene Henry are in charge of arrangements. Cards followed the meeting.

N.D.G.W. OFFICIAL DEATH LIST.

Giving the name, the date of death, and the Subordinate Parlor affiliation of all deceased members as reported to Grand Secretary Sallie R. Thaler from June 18 to July 18, 1932:

Stockwell, Amelia I.; May 21, 1932; Joaquin No. 5.

Sellinger, Annie F.; May 29, 1932; Califia No. 22.

Curtis, Nellie; June 20, 1932; Junipero No. 141.

"Men are neither suddenly rich nor suddenly good."—Libanius.

In Memoriam

KITTY DAVILLA.

Whereas, It has pleased Almighty God to again visit El Pescadero Parlor No. 82 N.D.G.W. and call to the Grand Parlor on High our beloved sister, Kitty DaVilla; and whereas, our Parlor feels keenly the loss of one who, for many years, was a loyal and faithful member, therefore, be it

Resolved, That while we mourn her removal from our midst, we bow in humble submission to the will of Him who doeth all things well.

"Her work on earth is done,
In Heaven just begun.
And may she greet each one of us
At the setting of our sun."

Be it further resolved, that we extend to the bereaved husband our sincere and heartfelt sympathy; that he be sent a copy of these resolutions, that a copy be published in The Grizzly Bear Magazine, and that a copy be spread upon the minutes of our Parlor.

Respectfully submitted in P.D.F.A.,
BERTHA M. McGEE,
EMMA J. FRERICHS,
Committee.

Tracy, July 6, 1932.

Feminine World's Fads and Fancies

PREPARED ESPECIALLY FOR THE GRIZZLY BEAR BY ANNA STOERMER

TIME WAS, WHEN SUMMER MEANT light colored clothes for nearly every occasion, if one hoped to look cool on a warm day. And the theory was all very lovely, but the difficulty became apparent shortly after one started out, trying to return looking enviably clean. Today, the mention of sheer white does not necessarily conjure a picture of wispy materials that fluff and billow by visions of ruffles and frills. The new fabric is something of a paradox. While it is thin and cool, it is heavy enough to tailor beautifully and trims with interesting detail.

A sheer suit, in dark color plus a bit of crisp white organdy, is most comfortable, fresh looking and cool. With the Olympics at hand, and every day crowded full, the dark sheer is a blessing undisguised. The dark light-weight ensemble meets the demand for all occasions. It has a reserve that is most becoming, especially for the larger woman. It is well known that dark colors minimize one's size.

The small checked, conventional pattern in white and blue, brown and beige, or black and white, dotted or checked, is lovely. The next time you go in search of just one costume, ask for a tailored sheer with touches of white, and wear this costume with white cotton gloves, white purse and a white hat. You will then be attired correctly for the warm days.

Prints are a little like organdies—never quite out of fashion. Attractive summer sports frocks have narrow stripes running so as to define the lines of the silhouette. Some are made of white briella, a suede-finished jersey fabric of the dull acele which follows the vogue for chalky suede finish.

Knit fabrics are being shown in piques, drop-stitch effects and a variety of fancy cords. For summer golf, heather-checked costumes are made in new versions of rustic eponge in either rayon or cotton.

Woven checks are not only very modern and attractive, but practical as well. Pin pleats in the back, and large military bellows pockets are useful style features. In the front of the waist, and in the front and in the back of the skirt are more pin pleats. Self-colored belts are held by tiny buckles.

Just about the very smartest color combination for the summer months, and certainly one of the most effective, is white with touches of red. One of the most popular types is that which is not really a sports frock, nor yet for afternoon attire, but rather, one that may be worn all day.

A white crepe-de-chine of good quality is trimmed with a red shiny-leather belt, red buttons and a red kid bow. Reds that are bright and light adorn this year's most successful clothes for beach, casino and club wear. There is, of course, more red and white than any other combination.

One of the new serge weaves is slightly softer than the old-fashioned serge, yet not soft enough to be classed as a tweed. One outfit has a skirt which gets its fullness through four pleats that begin below the yoke line, a straight well-fitted jacket and a blouse of red-and-white striped crepe-de-chine. The blouse is cut along the shoulders and at the throat on the same lines as the jacket. There is a cravat scarf of white crepe, edged with the striped silk.

Cotton dresses and suits are still being favored, gingham along with the others. Cottons are more fascinating than ever. A checked gingham coat is combined with a pique dress. Clever gingham blouses accompany the tailored suit of linen. Pique is by far the most popular for active sports wear. A striped linen vest has lapels, and is buttoned down the front. This is just the thing when a change is wanted from sweaters.

It is no secret that cotton, for summer evening frocks, has proved to be altogether charming and picturesque. When it is tucked and ruffled, or when it has the utter restraint of pique, it is perfect for a summer night of gaiety. The little chiffon is likely to look quite limp beside it. From the tennis jumper to the eyelet frock and the mousseline evening gown, cotton is the word!

Thrift continues to be not only a virtue, but also a smart fashion, making the dollars go as far as possible on the road to style. One good dress may serve in place of three, by change of accessories such as coats and guimpes. Black crepe evening frocks have removable guimpes and scarfs. A smart scarf is tied at the back and, when loosened, it may be flung about the shoulders.

Today, silk is more or less common; that is, common in its universal use. But satin remains to carry on tradition. White, ivory and ice-blue satins, and those with the faintest suggestion of a rose tint are being pressed into gorgeous services, and this is just a hint which will be elaborated on later.

Of course, the summer nets, laces and organdies are still good. The lace gown is popular; that is, when the lines are long and willowy. It can be tailored and still be an evening frock, and may be worn for dinner or afternoon affairs with a little bolero with loose, short sleeves and a tie that knots carelessly in front. When the bolero is removed, you are ready for the formal affair.

It takes an expert to tell an evening dress from a pair of pajamas these days. Clothes made for sunshine and those made to shine under night lights are pretty much alike. Heavy

(Continued on Page 13)

Passing of the California Pioneer

(Confined to Brief Notices of the Demise of Those Men and Women Who Came to California Prior to 1860.)

MRS. EMMA SULLIVAN, NATIVE OF Australia, 92; came to California in 1850 and resided in San Francisco, Sacramento and Marin Counties; died at Belvedere, survived by four daughters. She is said to have witnessed California's First State Fair, at San Francisco in 1854.

William Jardine Clayton, native of New South Wales, 96; came in 1850 and resided in Napa and Lake Counties; died near Lakeport.

Lucian Villinger, native of Pennsylvania, 88; came via Cape Horn in 1850 and three years later settled in San Joaquin County; died at Stockton.

Mrs. Loverne Shaw-White, native of Illinois, 83; came in 1851 and resided in Santa Clara and Napa Counties; died near Saint Helena, survived by five children.

Giuseppe Gagliardo, native of Italy, 93; came via the Isthmus of Panama in 1851 and resided in Tuolumne, Calaveras and Mariposa Counties; died at Hornitos, survived by two daughters.

Timothy J. Crowley, native of Massachusetts, 85; came in 1851 and resided in Sacramento and San Francisco Cities; died at the latter place, survived by a daughter.

Mrs. Anna L. Rawson, native of New York, 83; came across the plains in 1852; died at Arcadia, Los Angeles County, survived by four children. For many years she resided in San Francisco City and Contra Costa County.

James Beavers, native of Ohio, 90; came across the plains in 1852 and resided in Sonoma and San Luis Obispo Counties; died at San Luis Obispo City.

George Willard Kahl, native of Missouri, 82; came across the plains in 1853 and settled in Tuolumne County; died at Rawhide, survived by fourteen children.

Emery Maxwell Long, native of Ohio, 85; came in 1853 and resided in El Dorado, Alameda and Napa Counties; died at Suisun, Solano County, survived by three children.

Mrs. Jennie Wheat-Gillam, native of Iowa, 80; came across the plains in 1853 and settled in Calaveras County; died at Double Springs, survived by three children.

John D. Bushnell, native of New York, 79; came via the Isthmus of Panama in 1855; died near Sebastopol, Sonoma County, survived by a daughter. His father, the late Amasa Bushnell, is said to have been the first to grow hops on the Pacific Coast.

Mrs. Frances Jane Louise Jasper-Washburn, native of Missouri, 77; came across the plains in 1857 and resided many years in Tulare County; died at Watsonville, Santa Cruz County, survived by seven children.

Mrs. Mary Ann Penter, native of Iowa, 83; came in 1856 and resided in El Dorado and Calaveras Counties; died at Angels Camp, survived by a husband and a daughter.

Miss Jennie McCormick, native of Michigan, 82; since 1856 Alameda County resident; died near Newark.

Mrs. Lydia Ann Mitchell-Richardson, native of Oregon; since 1854 resident Siskiyou County; died at Etna, survived by a husband and nine children.

Jerome Miller, native of Oregon, 78; came in 1855; died at Sonora, Tuolumne County, survived by a wife and a son.

Mrs. Johanna Margarete Hansen, native of Denmark, 83; since 1856 a resident of Redwood City, San Mateo County, where she died; four children survive.

Thomas Clark, born in 1856 while his parents were enroute to California via Cape Horn, died near Hanford, Kings County.

Mrs. Mary Ann Alford-Belieu Sr., native of Arkansas, 77; came across the plains in 1857 and resided in Shasta, Butte and Glenn Counties; died at Willows, survived by a husband and five children.

Mrs. Mary Kean, native of Ohio, 83; since 1857 a resident of Napa County; died at Napa City, survived by three children.

Harry K. Day, native of Pennsylvania, 80; came via the Isthmus of Panama in 1858 and resided in Santa Clara, San Benito and San Diego Counties; died at De Luz.

Senator William Winnie Kellogg, native of Massachusetts, 95; came via the Isthmus of Panama in 1858 and the following year settled in Plumas County; died at Quincy, survived by a wife and a son. He had served the county as assessor and also as a member of the State Assembly and the State Senate. At the funeral ceremonies Judge Charles E. McLaughlin of Sacramento, Past Grand President N.S.G.W., paid tribute to the deceased.

OLD TIMERS PASS

(Brief Notices of the Demise of Men and Women who came to California in the '60s.)

George Dennis Lee, native of Canada, 87; came in 1860; died at Quincy, Plumas County.

Lewis S. Black, native of Missouri, 76; came in 1861; died near Cloverdale, Sonoma County, survived by a wife and a son.

William Henry Castner, native of Maine, 76; came in 1861 and resided in Solano and Napa Counties; died at Napa City, survived by a wife and seven children.

A. M. Eaton, native of Missouri, 80; came in 1862; died at Oakland, Alameda County, survived by a wife and four children. For many years he resided in Yolo County.

James N. Block Sr., native of Missouri, 92; came in 1862; died at San Francisco, survived by a wife and two daughters. He served three terms as tax collector of San Francisco.

Rev. James M. Newell, native of West Virginia, 91; came in 1863; died at Los Angeles City, survived by three children. His first pasforate as a Presbyterian minister was at Placerville, El Dorado County.

James John Peterson, native of Denmark, 85; since 1864 Shasta County resident; died at Redding, survived by two children.

Mrs. Mary Kaufman Borchard, native of Minnesota, 79; since 1864 Ventura County resident; died near Oxnard, survived by nine children.

Francis Marion Cole, native of Missouri, 76; came in 1864; died at Calistoga, Napa County, survived by a wife and four children.

Mrs. Elizabeth Kersey, 72; since 1865 resident Kern County; died at Bakersfield, survived by four children.

William Herbison, native of Canada, 89; came in 1865; died near Cordelia, Solano County, survived by three daughters.

Mrs. Anna A. Pitman, native of New York, 88; came in 1866; died at Berkeley, Alameda County.

Dr. Max V. Kempe, native of Germany, 77; came in 1866; died at Oakland, Alameda County, survived by a wife.

Lawrence English, native of New York, 79; came in 1867; died at Sacramento City.

Thomas Lean Plummer, native of England, 82; came in 1869; died at Grass Valley, Nevada County, survived by six children.

Mrs. Mary Odermatt-Hafner, native of Switzerland, 81; came in 1865; died at Sacramento City, survived by six children.

Mrs. Elizabeth Read-Shattuck, came in 1866, died at Hermosa Beach, Los Angeles County.

FEMININE FANCIES

(Continued from Page 12)

crepes and silks are being worn at many of the hotels and clubs.

Following the general trend, the lighter and less-sophisticated fabrics are used for young girls' fashions. A pale pink organidie has rayon checks in the same color. With this, several colorful accessories are worn: a bodice with trimmings of rayon flowers in shades of pink, a necklace of pink beads and shoes of pink rayon crepe-de-chine.

Collar and cuffs are made of pleated organdie, featuring an ornament in bright blue pyralin and chromium-plated metal. The belt and handbag are of the same shade of blue.

A frock for the little one, when playing at any out-of-door place, is made of yellow and white shantung, with pleated skirt and yoke of white. It has no sleeves, and a low back for comfort. An embroidered monogram adds a smart touch of decoration.

Population Grows—The Federal Census Bureau estimates the population of California, as of July 1, 1932, at 5,947,000, an increase of 269,749 since the April 1930 census. California's growth is the greatest of all the states of the nation.

State Fair—California's annual State Fair will be featured at Sacramento City, September 3-10.

Official Directory of Parlors of the N. D. G. W.

ALAMEDA COUNTY.

Angelita No. 32, Livermore—Meets 2nd and 4th Fridays, Foresters Hall; Mrs. Myrtle I. Johnson, Rec. Sec., P.O. box 258.

Piedmont No. 87, Oakland—Meets Thursdays, Corinthian Hall, Pacific Bldg.; Mrs. Alice E. Miner, Rec. Sec., 421 36th St.

Aloha No. 106, Oakland—Meets Tuesdays, Wigwam Hall, Pacific Bldg.; Mrs. Lurine Martin, Rec. Sec., 2815 Wallace St., Berkeley.

Hayward No. 122, Hayward—Meets 1st and 3rd Tuesdays, Veterans Memorial Bldg., Main St.; Miss Ruth Gansberger, Rec. Sec., P. O. box 44, Mount Eden.

Berkeley No. 150, Berkeley—Meets 2nd and 4th Wednesdays, Masonic Hall; Mrs. Lelia B. Baker, Rec. Sec., 915 Contra Costa Ave.

Bear Flag No. 151, Berkeley—Meets 2nd and 4th Wednesdays, Veterans Memorial Bldg., 1931 Center St.; Mrs. Maud Wagner, Rec. Sec., 317 Alcatraz Ave., Oakland.

Encinal No. 156, Alameda—Meets 2nd and 4th Thursdays, N.S.G.W. Hall; Mrs. Laura E. Fisher, Rec. Sec., 1413 Caroline St.

Brooklyn No. 157, East Oakland—Meets Wednesdays, Masonic Temple, 8th Ave. and E. 14th St.; Mrs. Ruth Cooney, Rec. Sec., 3907 14th Ave.

Argonaut No. 166, Oakland—Meets Tuesdays, Klinkner Hall, 59th and San Pablo; Mrs. Ada Spilman, Rec. Sec., 3905 Ellis St., Berkeley.

Bahia Vista No. 167, Oakland—Meets Thursdays, Wigwam Hall, Pacific Bldg.; Mrs. Minnie E. Raper, Rec. Sec., 3449 Helen St.

Fruitvale No. 177, Oakland—Meets Fridays, W.O.W. Hall; May E. Barthold, Rec. Sec., 3832 Santa Rita St.

Laurel Loma No. 182, Niles—Meets 1st and 3rd Tuesdays, I.O.O.F. Hall; Mrs. Ethel Fournier, Rec. Sec., P. O. box 515.

El Cereso No. 207, San Leandro—Meets 2nd and 4th Tuesdays, Masonic Hall; Mrs. Mary Tuttle, Rec. Sec., P. O. box 56.

Pleasanton No. 237, Pleasanton—Meets 1st Tuesday, I.O.O.F. Hall; Mrs. Myrtle Lanini, Rec. Sec.

Betsy Ross No. 238, Centerville—Meets 1st and 3rd Fridays, Anderson Hall; Miss Constance Lucio, Rec. Sec., P. O. box 187.

AMADOR COUNTY.

Ursula No. 1, Jackson—Meets 2nd and 4th Tuesdays, N.S.G.W. Hall; Mrs. Emma Boarman-Wright, Rec. Sec., 114 Court St.

Chispa No. 40, Ione—Meets 2nd and 4th Fridays, N.S.G.W. Hall; Mrs. Isabel Ashton, Rec. Sec.

Amapola No. 80, Sutter Creek—Meets 2nd and 4th Thursdays, N.S.G.W. Bldg.; Mrs. Hazel M. Marre, Rec. Sec.

Forrest No. 86, Plymouth—Meets 2nd and 4th Tuesdays, I.O.O.F. Hall; Mrs. Marguerite Davis, Rec. Sec.

BUTTE COUNTY.

Annie K. Bidwell No. 168, Chico—Meets 2nd and 4th Thursdays, I.O.O.F. Hall; Mrs Irene Henry, Rec. Sec., 3015 Woodland Ave.

Gold of Ophir No. 190, Oroville—Meets 1st and 3rd Wednesdays, Memorial Hall; Mrs. Ruth Brown, Rec. Sec., 1265 Leah Court.

CALAVERAS COUNTY.

Ruby No. 46, Murphys—Meets 4th Friday, N.S.G.W. Hall; Belle Segale, Rec. Sec.

Princess No. 84, Angels Camp—Meets 2nd and 4th Wednesdays, I.O.O.F. Hall; Mrs. Grace M. Mills, Rec. Sec., P.O. box 313.

San Andreas No. 113, San Andreas—Meets 1st Friday, Fraternal Hall; Miss Doris Treat, Rec. Sec.

COLUSA COUNTY.

Colus No. 194, Colusa—Meets 1st and 3rd Mondays, Eagles Hall; Miss Kate Busch, Rec. Sec., 350 Market St.

CONTRA COSTA COUNTY.

Stirling No. 146, Pittsburg—Meets 1st and 3rd Wednesdays, Veteran Memorial Hall; Mrs. Leslie Clement, Rec. Sec., 468 E. Santa Fe.

Richmond No. 147, Richmond—Meets 1st and 3rd Tuesdays, I.O.O.F. Hall, 10th St.; Mrs. Tillie Summers, Rec. Sec., 640 So. 31st St.

Donner No. 193, Byron—Meets 1st and 3rd Wednesdays, I.O.O.F. Hall; Mrs. Anna Pendry, Rec. Sec., P. O. box 112.

Las Juntas No. 221, Martinez—Meets 1st and 3rd Mondays, Pythian Castle; Mrs. Lola O. Viera, Rec. Sec., 305 Arreba St.

Antioch No. 223, Antioch—Meets 2nd and 4th Tuesdays, I.O.O.F. Hall; Mrs. Estelle Evans, Rec. Sec., 202 E. 5th St., Pittsburg.

Carquinez No. 234, Crockett—Meets 2nd Wednesday, I.O.O.F. Hall; Mrs. Cecile Petee, Rec. Sec., 465 Edwards St.

EL DORADO COUNTY.

Marguerite No. 12, Placerville—Meets 1st and 3rd Wednesdays, Masonic Hall; Mrs. Nettie Leonardi, Rec. Sec., 25 Coloma St.

El Dorado No. 186, Georgetown—Meets 2nd and 4th Saturday afternoons, I.O.O.F. Hall; Mrs. Alta L. Douglas, Rec. Sec.

FRESNO COUNTY.

Fresno No. 187, Fresno—Meets 2nd and 4th Fridays, Pythian Castle, Cor. "R" and Merced Sts.; Mary Aubery, Rec. Sec., 1040 Delphia Ave.

GRAND OFFICERS.

Mrs. Evelyn I. Carlson..........Past Grand President
1965 San Jose Ave., San Francisco

Mrs. Anna M. Armstrong..........Grand President
Woodland

Mrs. Irma Laird..........Grand Vice-president
Alturas

Mrs. Sallie R. Thaler..........Grand Secretary
555 Baker St., San Francisco

Mrs. Susie K. Christ..........Grand Treasurer
555 Baker St., San Francisco

Mrs. Gladys Noce..........Grand Marshal
Sutter Creek

Mrs. Orinda G. Giannini..........Grand Inside Sentinel
2142 Filbert St., San Francisco

Mrs. Hazel B. Hansen..........Grand Outside Sentinel
501 Griswold St., Glendale

Mrs. Clara Gairaud..........Grand Organist
124 Locust St., San Jose

GRAND TRUSTEES.

Mrs. Florence Boyle..........Oroville
Mrs. Edna Briggs..........1045 Santa Ynez Way, Sacramento
Mrs. Anna Thuesen..........615 38th Ave., San Francisco
Mrs. Ethel Begley..........233 Prospect Ave., San Francisco
Mrs. Minna K. Horn..........Etna
Mrs. Jane Vick..........418 Bath St., Santa Barbara
Mrs. Willow Borba..........Sebastopol

GLENN COUNTY.

Berryessa No. 192, Willows—Meets 1st and 3rd Mondays, I.O.O.F. Hall; Mrs. Leonora Neate, Rec. Sec., 338 No. Lassen St.

HUMBOLDT COUNTY.

Occident No. 28, Eureka—Meets 1st and 3rd Wednesdays, N.S.G.W Hall; Mrs. Eva L. MacDonald, Rec. Sec., 2309 "B" St.

Oneonta No. 71, Ferndale—Meets 2nd and 4th Fridays, I.O.O.F. Hall; Mrs. Myra Rumrill, Rec. Sec., P.O. box 142.

Reichling No. 97, Fortuna—Meets 1st and 3rd Tuesdays, Friendship Hall; Mrs. Grace Swett, Rec. Sec., P. O. box 328.

KERN COUNTY.

Miocene No. 228, Taft—Meets 1st and 3rd Wednesday afternoons, I.O.O.F. Hall; Mrs. Evalyn G. Towne, Rec. Sec., P. O. box 1011.

El Tejon No. 239, Bakersfield—Meets 1st and 3rd Fridays, Eagles Hall, 1714 "G" St.; Mary B. Hampson, Rec. Sec., 908 Quincy St.

Desert Gold No. 250, Mojave—Meets 2nd and 4th Fridays, I.O.O.F. Hall; Rein H. Everett, Rec. Sec., P.O. box 83.

LAKE COUNTY.

Clear Lake No. 135, Middletown—Meets 2nd and 4th Tuesdays, Herrick Hall; Mrs. Alma E. Snow, Rec. Sec.

LASSEN COUNTY.

Nataqua No. 152, Standish—Meets 1st and 3rd Wednesdays, Foresters Hall; Mrs. Mayda Elledge, Rec. Sec.

Mount Lassen No. 215, Bieber—Meets 2nd and 4th Thursdays, I.O.O.F. Hall; Mrs. Angie C. Kenyon, Rec. Sec.

Susanville No. 243, Susanville—Meets 3rd Thursday, I.O.O.F. Hall; Mrs. Georgia Jensen, Rec. Sec., 700 Roop St.

LOS ANGELES COUNTY.

Los Angeles No. 124, Los Angeles—Meets 1st and 3rd Wednesdays, I.O.O.F. Hall, Washington and Oak Sts.; Mrs. Mary K. Corcoran, Rec. Sec., 322 No. Van Ness Ave.

Long Beach No. 154, Long Beach—Meets 1st and 3rd Thursdays, K.P. Hall, 341 Pacific Ave.; Mrs. Bertha Hitt, Rec. Sec., 5355 Lime Ave.

Rudecinda No. 230, San Pedro—Meets 1st and 3rd Fridays, Unity Hall, I.O.O.F. Temple, 10th and Gaffey; Letitia Sarciaux, Rec. Sec., 483 16th St.

Verdugo No. 240, Glendale—Meets 2nd and 4th Tuesdays, Masonic Temple, 234 So. Brand Blvd.; Miss Etta Fulkerth, Rec. Sec., 526 No. Orange St.

Santa Monica Bay No. 245, Ocean Park—Meets 1st and 3rd Mondays, New Eagles Hall, 2823½ Main St.; Mrs. Rosalie Hyde, Rec. Sec., 738 Flower St., Venice.

Californiana No. 247, Los Angeles—Meets 2nd and 4th Tuesday afternoons, Hollywood Studio Club, 1215 Lodi Place; Mrs. Inez Sitton, Rec. Sec., 4223 Berenice St.

MADERA COUNTY.

Madera No. 244, Madera—Meets 2nd and 4th Thursdays, Masonic Annex; Mrs. Margaret C. Boyle, Rec. Sec., 111 No. "B" St.

MARIN COUNTY.

Sea Point No. 196, Sausalito—Meets 2nd and 4th Mondays, Perry Hall, 50 Caledonia St.; Mrs. Mary B. Smith, Rec. Sec., 559 Woodward Ave.

Marinita No. 198, San Rafael—Meets 2nd and 4th Mondays, 316 "B" St.; Miss Mollye Y. Spaelti, Rec. Sec., 539 4th St.

Fairfax No. 225, Fairfax—Meets 2nd and 4th Tuesdays, Community Hall; Mrs. Olive A. Greene, Rec. Sec., P. O. box 277.

Tamelpa No. 231, Mill Valley—Meets 1st and 2nd Tuesdays, I.O.O.F. Hall; Mrs. Delphine M. Todt, Rec. Sec., 400 Grand Ave., San Rafael.

MARIPOSA COUNTY.

Mariposa No. 63, Mariposa—Meets 1st and 3rd Fridays, I.O.O.F. Hall; Elizabeth E. Johnson, Rec. Sec.

MENDOCINO COUNTY.

Fort Bragg No. 210, Fort Bragg—Meets 1st and 3rd Thursdays, I.O.O.F. Hall; Mrs. Ruth W. Fuller, Rec. Sec.

MERCED COUNTY.

Veritas No. 75, Merced—Meets 1st and 3rd Tuesdays, I.O.O.F. Hall; Miss Margaret Thornton, Rec. Sec., 317 18th St.

MODOC COUNTY.

Alturas No. 159, Alturas—Meets 1st Thursday, Alturas Civic Club; Mrs. Irma W. Laird, Rec. Sec.

MONTEREY COUNTY.

Aleli No. 102, Salinas—Meets 2nd and 4th Thursdays, Pythian Hall; Miss Rose Rhyner, Rec. Sec., 420 Soledad St.

Junipero No. 141, Monterey—Meets 2nd and 4th Fridays, K. of P. Hall, Main St.; Miss Matilda M. Bergschicker, Rec. Sec., 498 Van Buren St.

NAPA COUNTY.

Eschol No. 16, Napa—Meets 2nd and 4th Mondays, N.S.G.W. Hall; Mrs. Ella Ingram, Rec. Sec., 2140 Seminary St.

Calistoga No. 145, Calistoga—Meets 2nd and 4th Mondays, I.O.O.F. Hall; Sadie P. Brooks, Rec. Sec.

La Junta No. 203, Saint Helena—Meets 1st and 3rd Tuesdays, N.S.G.W. Hall; Mrs. Marie Signorelli, Rec. Sec., 1341 Madrona Ave.

ATTENTION, SECRETARIES!

THIS DIRECTORY IS PUBLISHED BY AUTHORITY OF THE GRAND PARLOR N.D.G.W., AND ALL NOTICES OF CHANGES MUST BE RECEIVED BY THE GRAND SECRETARY (NOT THE MAGAZINE) ON OR BEFORE THE 20TH OF EACH MONTH TO INSURE CORRECTION IN NEXT PUBLICATION OF DIRECTORY.

NEVADA COUNTY.

Laurel No. 6, Nevada City—Meets 1st and 3rd Wednesdays, I.O.O.F. Hall; Mrs. Nellie E. Clark, Rec. Sec., P. O. box 212.

Manzanita No. 29, Grass Valley—Meets 1st and 3rd Tuesdays, Auditorium; Mrs. Loraine Keast, Rec. Sec., 123 Race St.

Columbia No. 70, French Corral—Meets Fridays, Farrelley Hall; Mrs. Kate Farrelley-Sullivan, Rec. Sec.

Snow Peak No. 176, Truckee—Meets 1st Monday, I.O.O.F. Hall; Mrs. Henrietta M. Eaton, Rec. Sec., P. O. box 116.

ORANGE COUNTY.

Santa Ana No. 235, Santa Ana—Meets 2nd and 4th Mondays, K.C. Hall, 4th and French Sts.; Mrs. Matilda S. Lemon, Rec. Sec., 928 W. Fairview.

Grace No. 242, Fullerton—Meets 1st and 3rd Thursdays, I.O.O.F. Hall, 116½ E. Commonwealth; Mrs. Mary Rothaermel, Rec. Sec., P. O. box 235.

PLACER COUNTY.

Placer No. 138, Lincoln—Meets 2nd Wednesday, I.O.O.F. Hall; Miss Carrie Parlin, Rec. Sec.

La Rosa No. 191, Roseville—Meets 1st and 3rd Tuesdays, Eagles Hall; Mrs. Alice Lee West, Rec. Sec., Rocklin.

Auburn No. 233, Auburn—Meets 2nd and 4th Fridays, Foresters Hall; Mrs. Elsie Patrick, Rec. Sec.

PLUMAS COUNTY.

Plumas Pioneer No. 219, Quincy—Meets 1st and 3rd Mondays, I.O.O.F. Hall; Minnie E. Johnson, Rec. Sec., P. O. box 243.

SACRAMENTO COUNTY.

Califia No. 22, Sacramento—Meets 2nd and 4th Tuesdays, N.S.G.W. Hall; Miss Lulu Gillis, Rec. Sec., 921 8th St.

La Bandera No. 110, Sacramento—Meets 1st and 3rd Fridays, N.S.G.W. Hall; Mrs. Clara Weldon, Rec. Sec., 1310 "O" St.

Sutter No. 111, Sacramento—Meets 1st and 3rd Tuesdays, N.S.G.W. Hall; Mrs. Adele Nix, Rec. Sec., 1238 "S" St.

Fern No. 123, Folsom—Meets 1st and 3rd Tuesdays, K.P. Hall; Mrs. Viola Shumway, Rec. Sec., P. O. box 48.

Chabolla No. 171, Galt—Meets 2nd and 4th Tuesdays, I.O.O.F. Hall; Mrs. Mary Pritchard, Rec. Sec.

Coloma No. 212, Sacramento—Meets 1st and 3rd Tuesdays, I.O.O.F. Hall, Oak Park; Mrs. Nettie Harry, Rec. Sec., 1217 35th St.

Liberty No. 213, Elk Grove—Meets 2nd and 4th Fridays, I.O.O.F. Hall; Mrs. Frances Wackman, Rec. Sec., P. O. box 192.

Victory No. 216, Courtland—Meets 1st Saturday and 3rd Monday, N.S.G.W. Hall; Mrs. Agneda Lample, Rec. Sec.

SAN BENITO COUNTY.

Copa de Oro No. 105, Hollister—Meets 2nd and 4th Thursdays, Grangers Union Hall; Mrs. Mollie Daveggio, Rec. Sec., 110 San Benito St.

San Juan Bautista No. 179, San Juan Bautista—Meets 1st Wednesday, Mission Corridor Rooms; Miss Gertrude Breen, Rec. Sec.

SAN BERNARDINO COUNTY.

Lugonia No. 241, San Bernardino—Meets 2nd and 4th Wednesdays, Eagles Hall; Miss Lois Poling, Rec. Sec., 1098 Waterman Ave.

Ontario No. 251, Ontario—Meets 2nd Thursday, Ontario Hotel; Miss Helen Hickman, Rec. Sec., 923 No. Laurel Ave.

SAN DIEGO COUNTY.

San Diego No. 208, San Diego—Meets 2nd and 4th Wednesdays, Directors Room, Chamber Commerce Bldg., 49[illegible] W. Broadway; Mrs. Elsie Case, Rec. Sec., 3051 Broadway.

SAN FRANCISCO CITY AND COUNTY.

Minerva No. 2, San Francisco—Meets 1st and 3rd Wednesdays, N.S.G.W. Bldg.; Miss Dorothy Finn, Rec. Sec., 9[illegible] Princess St., Sausalito.

Alta No. 3, San Francisco—Meets 2nd and 4th Tuesdays, N.S.G.W. Bldg.; Mrs. Agnese L. Hughes, Rec. Sec., 395[illegible] Sacramento St.

Oro Fino No. 9, San Francisco—Meets 1st and 3rd Thursdays, N.S.G.W. Bldg.; Mrs. Josephine B. Morrisey, Rec. Sec., 4441 20th St.

Golden State No. 50, San Francisco—Meets 1st and 3rd Wednesdays, N.D.G.W. Home; Miss Millie Tietjen, Rec. Sec., 328 Lexington Ave.

Orinda No. 56, San Francisco—Meets 2nd, 4th and 5th Fridays, N.D.G.W. Home; Mrs. Anna A. Gruber-Loser, Rec. Sec., 72 Grove Lane, San Anselmo.

Fremont No. 59, San Francisco—Meets 1st and 3rd Tuesdays, N.S.G.W. Bldg.; Miss Hannah Collins, Rec. Sec., 617 Fillmore St.

Buena Vista No. 68, San Francisco—Meets 1st, 3rd and 5th Thursdays, N.D.G.W. Home; Miss Margaret Barrett, Rec. Sec., 2774 20th St.

Las Lomas No. 72, San Francisco—Meets 1st and 3rd Tuesdays, N.D.G.W. Home; Mrs. Marion S. Day, Rec. Sec., 469 Noe St.

Yosemite No. 83, San Francisco—Meets 1st and 3rd Tuesdays, American Hall, 20th and Capp Sts.; Miss Mar[illegible] Monahan, Rec. Sec., 237 Noe St.

La Estrella No. 89, San Francisco—Meets 2nd and 4th Mondays, N.S.G.W. Bldg.; Miss Birdie Hartman, Rec. Sec., 1018 Jackson St.

Sans Souci No. 96, San Francisco—Meets 2nd and 4th Mondays, N.D.G.W. Home; Mrs. Minnie F. Dobbin, Rec. Sec., 1483 43rd Ave.

Calaveras No. 103, San Francisco—Meets 2nd and 4th Tuesdays, Swedish American Hall, 2174 Market St.; Mary L. Krogh, Rec. Sec., 4235 Cabrillo St.

Darina No. 114, San Francisco—Meets 1st and 3rd Mondays, N.S.G.W. Bldg.; Miss Adele Walsh, Rec. Sec., 47 Page St.

El Vespero No. 118, San Francisco—Meets 2nd and 4th Tuesdays, Masonic Hall, 4705 3rd St.; Mrs. Nell K[illegible] Boege, Rec. Sec., 1526 Kirkwood Ave.

Genevieve No. 132, San Francisco—Meets 1st and 3rd Thursdays, N.S.G.W. Bldg.; Miss Branice Peguillan, Rec. Sec., 2434 16th Ave.

Keith No. 137, San Francisco—Meets 2nd and 4th Thursdays, N.S.G.W. Bldg.; Mrs. Helen T. Mann, Rec. Sec., 575 Pierce St., Apt. 206.

Gabrielle No. 139, San Francisco—Meets 2nd and 4th Wednesdays, N.S.G.W. Bldg.; Mrs. Dorothy Wuesterfeld, Rec. Sec., 1020 Munich St.

Presidio No. 148, San Francisco—Meets 2nd and 4th Tuesdays, N.S.G.W. Bldg.; Mrs. Hattie Gaughran, Rec. Sec., 713 Capp St.

Guadalupe No. 153, San Francisco—Meets 2nd and 4th Mondays, Forester Hall, 170 Valencia St.; Miss May [illegible] McCarthy, Rec. Sec., 336 Elsie St.

Golden Gate No. 158, San Francisco—Meets 2nd and 4th Mondays, N.S.G.W. Bldg.; Mrs. Mary Sullivan, Rec. Sec., 33 Cuvier St.

Dolores No. 169, San Francisco—Meets 2nd and 4th Wednesdays, N.S.G.W. Bldg.; Mrs. Ada Saunders, Rec. Sec., 284 Allison St.

Linda Rosa No. 170, San Francisco—Meets 2nd and 4th Wednesdays, Swedish American Hall, 2174 Market St.; Mrs. Eva P. Tyrrel, Rec. Sec., 2629 Mission St.

Portola No. 172, San Francisco—Meets 1st and 3rd Tuesdays, N.S.G.W. Bldg.; Catherine H. Dolly, Rec. Sec., 4125 23rd St.
Castro No. 178, San Francisco—Meets 1st and 3rd Wednesdays, K.C. Bldg., 150 Golden Gate Ave.; Miss Adeline Sandersfeld, Rec Sec., 50 Baker St.
Twin Peaks No. 185, San Francisco—Meets 2nd and 4th Fridays, Druids Temple, 44 Page St.; Mrs. Loretta Cameron, Rec. Sec., 3969 Army St.
James Lick No. 220, San Francisco—Meets 1st and 3rd Wednesdays, N.S.G.W. Bldg.; Mrs. Edna Bishop, Rec. Sec., 3841 24th St.
Mission No. 227, San Francisco—Meets 2nd and 4th Fridays, N.S.G.W. Bldg.; Mrs. Ann Dippel, Rec. Sec., 448 Dewey Blvd.
Bret Harte No. 232, San Francisco—Meets 2nd and 4th Tuesdays, Aloha Hall, 3009 16th St.; Hildur E. Eggers, Rec. Sec., 194 Prague St.
La Dorada No. 236, San Francisco—Meets 2nd and 4th Thursdays, N.S.G.W. Hall; Mrs. Theresa R. O'Brien, Rec. Sec., 567 Liberty St.
Balboa No. 249, San Francisco—Meets 2nd and 4th Thursdays, Maccabee Hall, 5th Ave. and Clement St.; Jean Moffet, Rec. Sec., 6633 California St.
Utopia No. 252, San Francisco—Meets 2nd and 4th Tuesdays, American Hall, 20th and Capp Sts.; Miss Lelia M. Little, Rec. Sec., 892 Noe St.

SAN JOAQUIN COUNTY.

Joaquin No. 5, Stockton—Meets 2nd and 4th Tuesdays, N.S.G.W. Hall, 314 E. Main St.; Mrs. Della Garvin, Rec. Sec., 1122 E. Market St.
El Pescadero No. 82, Tracy—Meets 1st and 3rd Fridays, I.O.O.F. Hall; Mrs. Mary A. Hewitson, Rec. Sec., 122 Walnut St.
Ivy No. 88, Lodi—Meets 1st and 3rd Wednesdays, Eagles Hall; Mrs. Mae Corson, Rec. Sec., 109 So. School St.
Caliz de Oro No. 206, Stockton—Meets 1st and 3rd Tuesdays, N.S.G.W. Hall, 314 E. Main St.; Mrs. Frances Germain, Rec. Sec., 450 No. Regent.
Phoebe A. Hearst No. 214, Manteca—Meets 2nd and 4th Wednesdays, I.O.O.F. Hall; Mrs. Josie M. Frederick, Rec. Sec., Route A, Box 364, Ripon.

SAN LUIS OBISPO COUNTY.

San Miguel No. 94, San Miguel—Meets 2nd and 4th Wednesday afternoons, Clemon Hall; Mrs. Nellie Wickstrom, Rec. Sec.
San Luisita No. 108, San Luis Obispo—Meets 2nd and 4th Thursdays, W.O.W. Hall; Miss Agnes M. Lee, Rec. Sec., P. O. box 584.
El Pinal No. 163, Cambria—Meets 2nd, 4th and 5th Tuesdays, N.S.G.W. Hall; Kathryn Luchessa, Rec. Sec.

SAN MATEO COUNTY.

Bonita No. 10, Redwood City—Meets 2nd and 4th Thursdays, I.O.O.F. Hall; Mrs. Dora Wilson, Rec. Sec., 518 Middlefield Rd.
Vista del Mar No. 155, Halfmoon Bay—Meets 2nd and 4th Thursdays, I.O.O.F. Hall; Elizabeth Olney, Rec. Sec.
Ano Nuevo No. 180, Pescadero—Meets 1st and 3rd Wednesdays, I.O.O.F. Hall; Mrs. Alice Mattei, Rec. Sec.
El Carmelo No. 181, Daly City—Meets 1st and 3rd Wednesdays, Masonic Hall; Mrs. Hattie Kelly, Rec. Sec., 1179 Brunswick St.
Menlo No. 211, Menlo Park—Meets 2nd and 4th Mondays, Masonic Hall; Mrs. Frances E. Maloney, Rec. Sec., P. O. box 626.
San Bruno No. 246, San Bruno—Meets 2nd and 4th Fridays, Legion Hall; Miss Mildred Foley, Rec. Sec., 217 Miller Ave., South San Francisco.

SANTA BARBARA COUNTY.

Reina del Mar No. 126, Santa Barbara—Meets 1st and 3rd Tuesdays, Pythian Castle, 222 W. Carillo St.; Mrs. Dorothy Yule, Rec. Sec., P.O. box 670.

SANTA CLARA COUNTY.

San Jose No. 81, San Jose—Meets Thursdays, Catholic Women Center, 5th and San Fernando Sts.; Mrs. Nellie Fleming, Rec. Sec., Catholic Women Center.
Vendome No. 100, San Jose—Meets Wednesdays, Old Scottish Rite Temple; Miss Marie Buck, Rec. Sec., 245 Hawthorne St.
El Monte No. 205, Mountain View—Meets 2nd and 4th Fridays, American Legion Hall; Miss Mary Ann Rokovich, Rec. Sec., P.O. box 422-B.
Palo Alto No. 229, Palo Alto—Meets 1st and 2nd Mondays, N.S.G.W. Hall; Miss Helena G. Hansen, Rec. Sec., 531 Lytton Ave.

SANTA CRUZ COUNTY.

Santa Cruz No. 26, Santa Cruz—Meets Mondays, N.S.G.W. Hall; Mrs. May L. Williamson, Rec. Sec., 170 Walnut Ave.
El Pajaro No. 35, Watsonville—Meets 1st and 3rd Tuesdays, I.O.O.F. Hall; Miss Ruth E. Wilson, Rec. Sec., 16 Laurel St.

SHASTA COUNTY.

Camellia No. 41, Anderson—Meets 1st and 3rd Tuesdays, Masonic Hall; Mrs. Olga E. Welbourn, Rec. Sec.
Lassen View No. 98, Shasta—Meets 2nd Friday, Masonic Hall; Miss Louise Litsch, Rec. Sec.
Hiawatha No. 140, Redding—Meets 2nd and 4th Wednesdays, Moose Hall; Ruth Presleigh, Rec. Sec., Office County Clerk.

SIERRA COUNTY.

Naomi No. 36, Downieville—Meets 2nd and 4th Wednesdays, I.O.O.F. Hall; Louise C. Dubuque, Rec. Sec.
Imogen No. 134, Sierraville—Meets 2nd and 4th Saturday afternoons, Copren Hall; Mrs. Jennie Copren, Rec. Sec.

SISKIYOU COUNTY.

Eschscholtzia No. 112, Etna—Meets 1st and 3rd Wednesdays, Masonic Hall; Mrs. Bernice E. Smith, Rec. Sec.
Mountain Dawn No. 120, Sawyers Bar—Meets 2nd and last Wednesdays, I.O.O.F. Hall; Miss Edith Dunphy, Rec. Sec.

SOLANO COUNTY.

Vallejo No. 195, Vallejo—Meets 1st and 3rd Wednesdays, K.C. Hall, 820 Marin St.; Mrs. Mary Combs, Rec. Sec., 511 York St.
Mary E. Bell No. 224, Dixon—Meets 2nd and 4th Thursdays, I.O.O.F. Hall; Grace McFadyen, Rec. Sec.

SONOMA COUNTY.

Sonoma No. 209, Sonoma—Meets 2nd and 4th Mondays, I.O.O.F. Hall; Mrs. Mae Norrbom, Rec. Sec., R.F.D., box 171.
Santa Rosa No. 217, Santa Rosa—Meets 1st and 3rd Thursdays, N.S.G.W. Hall; Mrs. Hazel E. Brown, Rec. Sec., 1521 4th St.
Petaluma No. 222, Petaluma—Meets 1st and 3rd Tuesdays, Dania Hall; Mrs. Margaret M. Oeltjen, Rec. Sec., 503 Prospect St.

STANISLAUS COUNTY.

Oakdale No. 125, Oakdale—Meets 1st Monday, I.O.O.F. Hall; Mrs. Lou Reeder, Rec. Sec.
Morada No. 199, Modesto—Meets 2nd and 4th Wednesdays, I.O.O.F. Hall; Mrs. Susan Sullivan, Rec. Sec., 823 10th St.
Eldora No. 248, Turlock—Meets 1st and 3rd Wednesdays, Fraternal Hall; Effie Lund, Rec. Sec., 624 Minaret Ave.

SUTTER COUNTY.

South Butte No. 226, Sutter—Meets 1st and 3rd Mondays, N.D.G.W. Hall; Mrs. Abbie N. Vagedes, Rec. Sec.

TEHAMA COUNTY.

Berendos No. 23, Red Bluff—Meets 1st and 3rd Tuesdays, W.O.W. Hall, 200 Pine St.; Mrs. Lillie Hammer, Rec. Sec., 636 Jackson St.

TRINITY COUNTY.

Eltapome No. 55, Weaverville—Meets 2nd and 4th Thursdays, N.S.G.W. Hall; Mrs. Lou N. Fetzer, Rec. Sec.

TUOLUMNE COUNTY.

Dardanelle No. 66, Sonora—Meets Fridays, I.O.O.F. Hall; Mrs. Nettie Whitto, Rec. Sec.
Golden Era No. 99, Columbia—Meets 1st and 3rd Thursdays, N.S.G.W. Hall; Miss Irene Ponce, Rec. Sec.
Anona No. 164, Jamestown—Meets 2nd and 4th Tuesdays, I.O.O.F. Hall; Nellie Hope, Rec. Sec.

YOLO COUNTY.

Woodland No. 90, Woodland—Meets 2nd and 4th Tuesdays, N.S.G.W. Hall; Mrs. Maude Heaton, Rec. Sec., 153 College St.

YUBA COUNTY.

Marysville No. 162, Marysville—Meets 2nd and 4th Wednesdays, Liberty Hall; Miss Cecelia C. Gomes, Rec. Sec., 701 6th St.
Camp Far West No. 218, Wheatland—Meets 3rd Tuesday, I.O.O.F. Hall; Mrs. Ethel C. Brock, Rec. Sec., P. O. box 285.

AFFILIATED ORGANIZATIONS.

General Assembly Past Presidents—Meetings held annually in April at the home-town of Chief President; Mrs. Cora Stobing, 1739 San Jose Ave., San Francisco, Chief President; Mrs. Anna G. Loser, 72 Grove Lane, San Anselmo, Chief Secretary.
Past Presidents Association No. 1—Meets 1st and 3rd Mondays, N.S.G.W. Bldg., 414 Mason St., San Francisco; Mrs. Minnie F. Dobbin, Pres.; Mrs. May R. Barry, Rec. Sec., 2319 19th Ave., San Francisco.
Past Presidents Association No. 2—Meets 2nd and 4th Mondays, "Wigwam," Pacific Bldg., 16th and Jefferson, Oakland; Emma Haggerty, Pres.; Mrs. Elizabeth B. Goodman, Rec. Sec., 134 Juana Ave., San Leandro.
Past Presidents Association No. 3 (Santa Clara County)—Meets 2nd Tuesday, homes of members; Mrs. Amelia Hartman, Pres.; Mrs. Mary G. Newton, Rec. Sec., 1070 Jackson St., Santa Clara.
Past Presidents Association No. 4 (Sacramento County)—Meets 2nd Monday, Unitarian Hall, 1413 27th St., Sacramento City; Viola Gennoe, Pres.; Lily May Tilden, Rec. Sec., 3225 "T" St., Sacramento.
Past Presidents Association No. 5 (Butte County)—Meets 1st Friday, homes of members, Chico and Oroville; Marie Picanco, Pres.; Ruth Brown, Rec. Sec., 1265 Leah Court, Oroville.
Past Presidents Association No. 6 (Nevada County)—Meets 4th Friday, alternately between Nevada City, Pythian Castle, and Grass Valley, Edna Sampson's home; Margaret V. Nolan, Pres.; Vere Hansen, Rec. Sec., R.F.D. No. 2, box 41-C, Grass Valley.
Past Presidents Association No. 7 (Sonoma County)—Meets 1st Thursday, N.S.G.W. Hall, Santa Rosa; Willow Borba, Pres.; Clytie Lewis, Rec. Sec., R.F.D. No. 4, box 345-A, Santa Rosa.
Past Presidents Association No. 8 (San Joaquin and Stanislaus Counties)—Meets 2nd Thursday, Red Men Hall, Stockton; Mrs. Lois Armstrong, Pres.; Mrs. Harriet F. Corr, Rec. Sec., 729 E. Sonora St., Stockton.
Native Sons and Native Daughters Central Committee on Homeless Children—Main Office, 955 Phelan Bldg., San Francisco; Mrs. John W. Stirling, Chmn.; Miss Mary E. Brusie, Sec. Los Angeles branch office, 3924 Sunset Blvd.; Dorothy Schlingman, Sec.

(ADVERTISEMENT.)

GRAND PRESIDENT NAMES ASSISTANTS

WOODLAND (YOLO COUNTY)—MRS. Anna Mixon-Armstrong, Grand President of the Order of Native Daughters of the Golden West, announces the following appointments of standing and special committees, and supervising and district deputies for the 1932-33 Grand Parlor year:

STANDING COMMITTEES.

Finance—Ariana Stirling (P.G.P.), Emma L. Humphrey (P.G.P.), Sue J. Irwin (P.G.P.).

Appeals and Grievances—Grace S. Stoermer (P.G.P.), Mamie Peyton (P.G.P.), Mary E. Bell (P.G.P.), Mattie M. Stein (P.G.P.), Lucy Roberts (La Bandera No. 110).

Petitions—Dr. Eva R. Rasmussen (P.G.P.), Margaret Grote-Hill (P.G.P.), Amy McAvoy (P.G.P.).

State of the Order—Sue J. Irwin (P.G.P.), Cora B. Sifford (P.G.P.), Grace S. Stoermer (P.G.P.), Edna Richter (Woodland No. 90), Olive B. Matlock (P.G.P.).

Credentials—Carrie Roesch-Durham (P.G.P.), Pearl Lamb (P.G.P.), Gladys Evans (Woodland No. 90).

Legislation—Emma L. Humphrey P.G.P.), Olive B. Matlock (P.G.P.), Louise Hattau (Aleli No. 102), Eliza D. Kieth (P.G.P., Maude Heaton (Woodland No. 90).

Ritual—Bertha A. Briggs (P.G.P.), Alda Nelson (Berkeley No. 150), Mae C. Boldeman (P.G.P.), Estelle Evans (P.G.P.), Ruth Gansberger (Hayward No. 122).

Printing and Supplies—Addie L. Mosher (P.G.P.), Laura Fisher (Encinal No. 156), Ella Tate (Fremont No. 59).

Laws and Supervision—Irma W. Laird (G.V.P.), Dr. Eva Rasmussen (P.G.P.), Edna Boyd (Annie K. Bidwell No. 168), Katherine Gloster (P.G.P.), Florence Gray (Placer No. 138).

Transportation—Emma G. Foley (P.G.P.), Sallie R. Thaler (G.S.), Mae Himes-Noonan (P.G.P.).

California History and Landmarks—Esther R. Sullivan (P.G.P.), Frieda Gapp (Colus No. 194), Henrietta O'Neill (Ursula No. 1), Sadie Brainard (Califia No. 22), Nelle Hebener (Woodland No. 90), Helen Hall (Plumas Pioneer No. 219), Jane McCosker (Marguerite No. 12), Mary Gorgas (Dardanelle No. 66), Mary Weston (Mariposa No. 63), Marguerite Davis (Forrest No. 86), Nellie Ramsey (Placer No. 138), Grace T. Haven (Los Angeles No. 124), Leonore Neate (Berryessa No. 192), Margaret Ramm (Golden Gate No. 158), May Mead (Piedmont No. 87), Doris Treat (San Andreas No. 113), Jennie Copren (Imogen No. 134).

N.D.G.W. Home—Dr. Mariana Bertola (P.G.P.), Sue J. Irwin (P.G.P.), Genevieve Watson-Baker (P.G.P.), Emma G. Foley (P.G.P.), Jennie Greene (Buena Vista No. 68), Millie Tietjen (Golden State No. 50), Mary E. Bell (P.G.P.), Minnie F. Dobbin (Sans Souci No. 96), Elizabeth Douglas (Alta No. 3), Carrie R. Durham (P.G.P.), Dr. Louise C. Heilbron (P.G.P.), Pearl Lamb (P.G.P.), Addie L. Mosher (P.G.P.), Mamie G. Peyton (P.G.P.), Ariana W. Stirling (P.G.P.), Grace S. Stoermer (P.G.P.), Sallie R. Thaler (G.S.), Estelle Evans (P.G.P.), Amy McAvoy (P.G.P.), Alice Lane (Castro No. 178), Evelyn I. Carlson (P.G.P.), Agnes Curry (Portola No. 172), Anna M. Armstrong (G.P.).

SPECIAL COMMITTEES.

Education—Edna Richter (Woodland No. 90), Gertrude LaFortune (Keith No. 137), Agnes Meade (Marysville No. 162), Eliza D. Keith (P.G.P.), Hattie Roberts (Oneonta No. 71).

Americanization—Dr. Louise C. Heilbron (P.G.P.), May Huston (Berryessa No. 192), Ada Spillman (Argonaut No. 166), Ruth McDonald (Twin Peaks No. 185), Ella Leght (Calistoga No. 145), Ella Ingram (Eschol No. 16), Martha Klubescheidt (La Junta No. 203), Thelma Rogers (Aloha No. 106).

Pioneer Roster and Relics—Mamie P. Carmichael (P.G.P.), Mamie Davis (Coloma No. 212), Kate McFadyen (Long Beach No. 154), Ruth Hickey (Woodland No. 90), and one member selected by the president of each Subordinate Parlor.

Extension of the Order—Sue J. Irwin (P.G.P.), all supervising district deputy grand presidents and all district deputy grand presidents.

Board of Control—Anna M. Armstrong (G.P.), Ariana W. Stirling (P.G.P.), Anna Thuesen (G.T.), Daisy Hansen (Long Beach No. 154), Marguerite Sullivan (Alta No. 3).

Mills College Scholarship—Dr. Mariana Bertola (P.G.P.), Alison F. Watt (P.G.P.), Dora Zmudowski (El Pajaro No. 35), Genevieve Watson-Baker (P.G.P.), Harriet Cate (Twin Peaks No. 185).

University Scholarships—Dorothy Doyle Dimmler (Berkeley No. 150), Marvel Thomas (Los Angeles No. 124), Olive B. Matlock (P.G.P.).

Redwood Memorial Marker—Sallie R. Thaler (G.S.), Mildred Irwin (Berkeley No. 150), Hattie Roberts (Oneonta No. 71), Eva L. MacDonald (Occident No. 28), Anna M. Armstrong (G.P.).

Publicity—Bertha A. Briggs (P.G.P.), Olive Lopez (Californiana No. 247), Evelyn Eby (Reina del Mar No. 126), Edith Kelly (Califia No. 22), Irma Murray (Aloha No. 106), Isobel Granville (Minerva No. 2), Estelle M. Evans (P.G.P.), and publicity chairman each Subordinate Parlor.

Veterans Welfare—Stella Finkeldey (P.G.P.), Augusta Huxsol (Piedmont No. 87), Ann McDonald (Angelita No. 32), Gertrude Tuttle (Californiana No. 247), Dora Brayton (Bahia Vista No. 167).

SUPERVISING AND DISTRICT DEPUTIES.

District No. 1, Del Norte, Humboldt, Mendocino Counties—Hattie E. Roberts, supervising deputy. Fort Bragg No. 210, Edna Kunzler (Fort Bragg No. 210). Occident No. 28, Oneonta No. 71, Reichling No. 97, Myra Rumrill (Oneonta No. 71).

District No. 2, Siskiyou County—Margaret E. Weston, supervising deputy. Eschscholtzia No. 112, Clara Farr (Eschscholtzia No. 112). Mountain Dawn No. 120, Lettie Lewis (Mountain Dawn No. 120).

District No. 3, Trinity, Shasta, Tehama Counties—Edna Saygrover, supervising deputy. Berendos No. 23, Eltapome No. 55, Lassen View No. 98, Olive Endicott (Hiawatha No. 140). Camellia No. 41, Hiawatha No. 140, Elsie Juhay (Berendos No. 23).

District No. 4, Modoc, Lassen Counties—Dorothy Gloster, supervising deputy. Susanville No. 243, Nataqua No. 152, appointment pending. Mount Lassen No. 215, Alturas No. 159, Mildred Boyd (Alturas No. 159).

District No. 5, Butte, Yuba, Colusa Counties—Cecilia C. Gomes, supervising deputy. Marysville No. 162, Elva Hicks (Camp Far West No. 218). Camp Far West No. 218, Tessie Putman (South Butte No. 226). South Butte No. 226, Elsie Schofield (Marysville No. 162). Colus No. 194, Eunice McAvoy (Berryessa No. 192).

District No. 6, Plumas, Sutter, Glenn Counties—Ruth Brown, supervising deputy. Annie K. Bidwell No. 168, Anna Bernhard (Gold of Ophir No. 190). Berryessa No. 192, Margaret Davison (Colus No. 194). Gold of Ophir No. 190, Annie S. Kelly (Annie K. Bidwell No. 168). Plumas Pioneer No. 219, Minnie E. Johnson (Plumas Pioneer No. 219).

District No. 7, Yolo, Solano (part) Counties—Edna Richter, supervising deputy. Woodland No. 90, Lena Nickum (Mary E. Bell No. 224). Mary E. Bell No. 224, Maude Heaton (Woodland No. 90).

District No. 8, Sonoma County—Hazel E. Brown, supervising deputy. Sonoma No. 209, Mary Vogt (Orinda No. 56). Petaluma No. 222, Mae Rose Barry (Mission No. 227). Santa Rosa No. 217, Gertrude Groskopf (Sonoma No. 209).

District No. 9, Marin County—Hazel E. Brown, supervising deputy. Marinita No. 198, Delphine M. Todt (Tamelpa No. 231). Fairfax No. 225, Mary B. Smith (Sea Point No. 196). Tamelpa No. 231, Irene Griffin (Marinita No. 198). Sea Point No. 196, Anna Loser (Orinda No. 56).

District No. 10, Napa, Lake, Solano (part) Counties—Wilma Mitchell, supervising deputy. Vallejo No. 195, Emma McGlumphy (Eschol No. 16). Clear Lake No. 135, Calistoga No. 145, La Junta No. 203, Sadie Brooks (Calistoga No. 145). Eschol No. 16, Elvena Woodard (Vallejo No. 195).

District No. 11, Sierra, Nevada (part) Counties—P.G.P. Emma Lou Humphrey, supervising deputy. Naomi No. 36, Rosa Merrill (Imogen No. 134). Snow Peak No. 176, Lotta Bryant (Snow Peak No. 176). Imogen No. 134, Neva McMahon (Ivy No. 88).

District No. 12, Nevada County—P.G.P. Alison F. Watt, supervising deputy. Columbia No. 70, Beatrice George (Manzanita No. 29). Laurel No. 6, Melita Hutchison (Manzanita No. 29). Manzanita No. 29, Adeline O'Connor (Laurel No. 6).

District No. 13, Placer County—Sadie W. Brainard, supervising deputy. Auburn No. 233, Elizabeth Livingston (Auburn No. 233). La Rosa No. 191, Placer No. 138, Laura Goy (Placer No. 138).

District No. 14, El Dorado County—Agnes Schiff, supervising deputy. El Dorado No. 186, Marguerite No. 12, Hattie Presby (El Dorado No. 186).

District No. 15, Sacramento County—Bessie Leitch, supervising deputy. Liberty No. 213, Sophie Monteverde (La Bandera No. 110). Chabolla No. 171, Lillie Tilden (Sutter No. 111). Victory No. 216, Gertrude Kuhner (Coloma No. 212). Fern No. 123, Anna Kloss (Liberty No. 213). Califia No. 22, Alice Wright (Chabolla No. 171). Coloma No. 212, Mary Lucas (Fern No. 123). La Bandera No. 110, Doris Fisher (Victory No. 216). Sutter No. 111, Esther Mulligan.

District No. 16, Amador, Calaveras Counties—Emma Boarman Wright, supervising deputy. Amapola No. 80, Forrest No. 86, Harriet Clemens (Amapola No. 80). Chispa No. 40, Ursula No. 1, Margaret Molfino (Ursula No. 1). Ruby No. 46, Princess No. 84, San Andreas No. 113, Ruth G. Lemuse (Princess No. 84).

District No. 17, Contra Costa (part) County—Myra Rademacher, supervising deputy. Stirling No. 146, Edna Garrety (Las Juntas No. 221). Donner No. 193, Edith Easton (Antioch No. 223). Las Juntas No. 221, Ada Ericsson (Stirling No. 146). Antioch No. 223, Josephine Pimentel (Donner No. 193).

District No. 18, San Francisco County—Alice Lane, supervising deputy. Minerva No. 2, Ida Mesquite (Ano Nuevo No. 180). Alta No. 3, May McCarthy (Guadalupe No. 153). Oro Fino No. 9, Gertrude La Fortune (Keith No. 137). Golden State No. 50, Emma O'Meara (Dolores No. 169). Orinda No. 56, Mae Waring (Castro No. 178) Fremont No. 59, Lena Wall (Minerva No. 2). Buena Vista

(Continued on Page 19)

LOS ANGELES--CITY and COUNTY

LOS ANGELES

(Continued from Page 9)

will be provided for dancing. Other features in the way of entertainment will be presented.

Grand Trustee Eldred L. Meyer, Dr. A. B. Mayhew, Manly Danforth and Judge Joseph Call compose a reception committee, and the following will look after the festival details: President Orin Welch, Outside Sentinel Hector Baida, First vice-president Arthur Leonard, Arthur Giroux, Dr. Robert Eshelman, Ernest Reyes, Elden Price, Harper Ledbetter, Harry Dailey, Edward Grom, Clayton Brent, Jack Dailey, Harry Prager, Douglas McCreery, Elton Gripp, Dr. Leland Clark, Bert Bair, Secretary John Smith and Henry Levy.

FINE RECORD.

Impressive ceremonies marked the open installation of officers of Californiana Parlor No. 247 N.D.G.W., July 20. The hall was decorated beautifully with large baskets of vari-colored blossoms, and with the attractive costumes of visiting officers and officers-elect the scene presented was inspiring. Deputy Mattie Edwards installed the officers, including Mrs. Milo D. Aylward as president. Reports showed that Californiana made a fine record in civic and philanthropic affairs during the term of President Gertrude Tuttle.

Organist Wilfred Chapman presented the program, which included musical and dance numbers. Honor-guests were Past Grand Grace S. Stoermer, Florence Dodson-Schoneman and Grand Outside Sentinel Hazel B. Hansen. Gifts were presented Mary Noerenberg, junior past president, and Gertrude Tuttle, retiring president, and floral offerings were presented the grand officers, President Aylward and Mrs. Charles Decker, first vice-president. Mrs. Edith Adams, hospitality chairman, and committee served cooling refreshments at the close of the evening to the company of 200, which included large delegations from Grace Parlor No. 242 (Fullerton) and Los Angeles Parlor No. 124. July 12, Mrs. Leland Atherton-Irish presented Raymond Yauqua, tenor, and Richard Cardos, pianist, in a fine program. July 26 the Parlor adjourned to September 27 for vacation. August 9, Californiana will hold "open house" for Olympic visitors, all Natives and friends.

Mrs. Ida Potts McKenzie of Californiana sponsored a delightful bridge tea at the Uplifters ranch July 9 for the benefit of the California Olympic hostess fund. She was ably assisted by her daughters, Mms. George Horgan and Paul Gilbert, and Mms. Mary Noerenberg, Adelina Waite, Josephine Stewart and Mary Skinner. Past Grand Grace S. Stoermer, hostess for California, introduced Mrs. Arthur Wright, head of Olympic hostesses. Musical numbers were presented by Mrs. Josephine Stewart, who sang "To California," Olympic song composed by Mrs. Louise Glaeser, and Mrs. Mary Skinner. Two hundred guests were in attendance, and the function was a complete social as well as financial success.

GLENDALE EXTENDS INVITATION.

Glendale—The boxing bouts featured by Glendale Parlor No. 264 N.S.G.W. July 20 drew a large crowd. President Leslie Schellbach was in charge. Junior Past President Phil D. Molen wishes to thank all those who in any way cooperated with the Parlor during his term as president.

Grand President Seth Millington will be the guest of Glendale, August 9, and an invitation to all members of the Order to be present is extended. The ritual will be exemplified, and any Parlor having candidates is requested to bring them in for initiation.

CARD PARTY AT OCEAN PARK.

Ocean Park—Santa Monica Bay Parlor No. 245 N.D.G.W. is holding monthly dances at the Rendezvous; Katherine Worsham was chairman for July 22. Rosalie F. Hyde served on the committee that arranged for the dedication of the California State building in Los Angeles July 29. Eight members of the Parlor will each day during the Olympics serve at the registration headquarters. Santa Monica Bay will have a card party August 29, at which time a patchwork quilt will be disposed of.

PROFESSOR NELEH MYSTIFIES.

Ramona Parlor No. 109 N.S.G.W. has adopted the policy of one open meeting each month for the members, their families and friends. Th of July 22 was in charge of Past Presidents W ter M. Slosson and B. Rey Schauer, and the who failed to attend missed a real treat. T program opened with a piano selection by C ganist A. Trembley of Saint Vincent church, f

lowed by vocal selections by a trio—Glen LeVitt, John Robinson and Marco Linero—and an enlightening talk on "Military Preparedness" by Lieutenant John Oliver of the 977th Anti-Aircraft Service.

Then came the evening's surprise—Professor C. Neleh, magician of the age, better known as Charles Hubbard Smith, a member of Ramona. He certainly mystified his audience, holding them spellbound for two hours. Most magicians specialize in some particular phase of the art, but Neleh is finished in Occidental, Oriental, Hindu and Egyptian magic, and for good measure he has other big feats. In a short time Neleh will tour the state.

George Reeves Schmidt, a son of Superior Judge Ruben S. Schmidt, was initiated into membership in Ramona July 15. Homer J. Chapelle has been made curator of the Parlor's historical relics collection at Exposition Park Museum, succeeding Charles J. Prudhomme. August 5, following the Grand President Millington meeting, Ramona will serve refreshments in the clubroom; August 12, the ritual will be exemplified; August 26, a hijinks and smoker will be featured.

PERSONAL PARAGRAPHS.

Superior Judge John L. Fleming (Ramona N.S.) is a grandpa.

Ernest W. Parsons (Ramona N.S.) is visiting in Eastern states.

Marvel Thomas (Los Angeles N.D.) is attending a university in Mexico City.

Anita Santo (Los Angeles N.D.) and husband enjoyed a vacation in Yosemite.

A native son arrived at the home of James Bernardino (Hollywood N.S.) recently.

A seven-and-one-half-pound native son arrived at the home of Everist C. Teel (Ramona N.S.).

Lucy Dudley, Susan Kennedy and Loretta Donahue (Los Angeles N.D.) were recent visitors to San Francisco.

Miss Leota LeHew of Kansas City became the bride June 30 of Clarence S. Hunt (Ramona N.S.). The honeymoon was spent in Yosemite.

Jeanne Clos (Los Angeles N.D.) recently enjoyed a visit to Alaska, and Leonie Clos (Los Angeles N.D.) departed July 3 on a Panama Canal voyage.

J. H. Brenner (Hollywood N.S.) and wife of San Francisco were visitors last month. Brenner resided for many years in Los Angeles, where he was prominent in musical circles.

Police Chief Clarence E. Webb (Santa Monica Bay N.S.) of Santa Monica and wife departed July 15 for a visit with their daughter, Mrs. Rudy Valle, in Maine and New York.

THE DEATH RECORD.

Mrs. Christina McDonald-McNeil, mother of William A., Lawrence G., Andrew M. and Joseph A. McNeil (Ramona N.S.), passed away July 25. She was a native of Nova Scotia, aged 65.

Martin Leopold Haines, affiliated with Los Angeles Parlor No. 45 N.S.G.W., died July 29 survived by a wife and two sons. He was born at Madison, Yolo County, April 10, 1887.

Jose Romero, affiliated with Ramona Parlor No. 109 N.S.G.W., died June 30 survived by a wife and four children. He was born at Old San Diego, May 15, 1853.

Adolph B. Lachman, affiliated with Los Angeles Parlor No. 45 N.S.G.W., died July 5. He was born at Los Angeles City, September 8, 1867.

Will H. Willis, brother of Fred A. Willis (Ramona N.S.), died July 9.

John C. Gatti, stepfather of Mrs. Mary Meyer (Santa Monica Bay N.D.) and Dominic and John Conterno (Santa Monica Bay N.S.), died July 21 at Santa Monica.

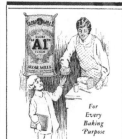

Official Directory of Parlors of the N. S. G. W

ALAMEDA COUNTY.

Alameda No. 47, Alameda City—Perry F. Badgley, Pres.; Robt. H. Cavanaugh, Sec., 1806 Pacific Ave.; Wednesdays, Native Sons Hall, 1406 Park St.

Oakland No. 50, Oakland—R. L. Engell, Pres.; F. M. Norris, Sec., 5595 Taft Ave.; Fridays, Native Sons Hall, 11th and Clay Sts.

Las Positas No. 96, Livermore—Dr. Donald M. Fraser, Pres.; John J. Kelly, Sec., P. O. box 841; Thursdays, Foresters Hall.

Eden No. 113, Hayward—Henry L'Ecuyer, Pres.; Stanton R. Soares, Sec., P. O. box 176; 2nd and 4th Tuesdays, Memorial Hall, Main St.

Piedmont No. 120, Oakland—Frank Smith, Pres.; Charles Morando, Sec., 908 Vermont St.; Thursdays, Native Sons Hall, 11th and Clay Sts.

Wisteria No. 127, Alvarado—Henry May, Pres.; J. M. Scribner, Sec., Livermore; 1st Thursday, I.O.O.F. Hall.

Halcyon No. 146, Alameda City—S. Chesley Anderson, Pres.; J. C. Bates, Sec., 2139 Buena Vista Ave.; 1st and 3rd Tuesdays, I.O.O.F. Hall, 2329 Santa Clara Ave.

Brooklyn No. 151, Oakland—Frank B. Perry, Pres.; E. W. Cooney, Sec., 3907 14th Ave.; Wednesdays, Masonic Temple, 8th Ave. and E. 14th St.

Washington, No. 169, Centerville—M. D. Silva, Pres.; Allen G. Norris, Sec., P. O. box 31; 2nd and 4th Tuesdays, Hansen Hall.

Athens No. 195, Oakland—Elmer L. Bullock, Pres.; Harold B. Farley, Sec., 4623 Benevides Ave.; Tuesdays, Native Sons Hall, 11th and Clay Sts.

Berkeley No. 210, Berkeley—F. M. McGrath, Pres.; R. J. Garrett, Sec., 1708 Virginia St.; Tuesdays, Native Sons Hall, 2108 Shattuck Ave.

Estudillo No. 223, San Leandro—Frank V. Pacheco, Pres.; Albert G. Pacheco, Sec., 1736 E. 14th St.; 1st and 3rd Tuesdays, U.P.E.C. Hall.

Claremont No. 240, Oakland—Louis F. Cambet, Pres.; E. N. Thienger, Sec., 839 Hearst Ave., Berkeley; Tuesdays, Veterans Memorial Bldg., 43rd & Salem Sts., Emeryville.

Pleasanton No. 244, Pleasanton—Peter C. Madsen, Pres.; Ernest W. Schween, Sec.; 2nd and 4th Thursdays, I.O.O.F. Hall.

Niles No. 250, Niles—M. L. Fournier, Pres.; C. E. Martenstein, Sec.; 2nd Thursday, I.O.O.F. Hall.

Fruitvale No. 252, Oakland—William J. Keating Jr., Pres.; Ray B. Felton, Sec., 1575 Alice St.; Fridays, W.O.W. Hall, 3256 E. 14th St.

AMADOR COUNTY.

Amador No. 17, Sutter Creek—Frank Marre, Pres.; F. J. Payne, Sec.; 1st and 3rd Fridays, Native Sons Hall.

Excelsior No. 31, Jackson—Wm. Daugherty, Pres.; William Going, Sec.; 1st and 3rd Wednesdays, Native Sons Hall, 22 Court St.

Ione No. 33, Ione—Marvin Kidd, Pres.; Josiah H. Saunders, Sec.; 1st and 3rd Wednesdays, Native Sons Hall.

Plymouth No. 48, Plymouth—John J. Upton, Pres.; Thos. D. Davis, Sec.; 1st and 3rd Saturdays, I.O.O.F. Hall.

BUTTE COUNTY.

Argonaut No. 8, Oroville—Thomas R. Cole, Pres.; Cyril R. Macdonald, Sec., P. O. box 502; 1st and 3rd Wednesdays, Veterans Memorial Hall.

Chico No. 21, Chico—Marcus Choisser, Pres.; Sam Lindsay Adams, Sec., Sacramento Blvd.; 2nd and 4th Thursdays, Elks Hall.

CALAVERAS COUNTY.

Chispa No. 139, Murphys—Maynard Segale, Pres.; Antone Malaspina, Sec.; Wednesdays, Native Sons Hall.

COLUSA COUNTY.

Colusa No. 69, Colusa City—Burton L. Smart, Pres.; Phil J. Humburg, Sec., 223 Parkhill St.; Tuesdays, Eagles Hall.

CONTRA COSTA COUNTY.

General Winn No. 32, Antioch—Edmont T. Uren, Pres.; Joel H. Ford, Sec., P. O. box 811; 2nd and 4th Wednesdays, Union Hall.

Mount Diablo No. 101, Martinez—R. P. Anderson, Pres.; G. T. Barkley, Sec.; 1st and 3rd Mondays, I.O.O.F. Hall.

Byron No. 170, Byron—William E. Bunn, Pres.; H. G. Krumland, Sec.; 1st and 3rd Tuesdays, I.O.O.F. Hall.

Carquinez No. 205, Crockett—Thos. Cox, Pres.; Thomas I. Cahalan, Sec.; 1st and 3rd Wednesdays, I.O.O.F. Hall.

Richmond No. 217, Richmond—M. W. Amaral, Pres.; H. D. Mason, Sec., 11 ,6th St.; Wednesdays, Redmen Hall, 11th and Neven Ave.

Concord No. 245, Concord—P. M. Soto, Pres.; D. E. Framberg, Sec., P. O. box 235; 1st Tuesday, I.O.O.F. Hall.

Diamond No. 246, Pittsburg—Victor Ericsson, Pres.; Francis A. Irving, Sec., 248 E. 5th St.; 1st and 3rd Wednesdays, Veterans Memorial Bldg.

EL DORADO COUNTY.

Placerville No. 9, Placerville—Chas. C. Cook, Pres.; Clyde C. Berriman, Sec., Wood St.; 2nd and 4th Tuesdays, Masonic Hall.

Georgetown No. 91, Georgetown—W. H. Breedlove, Pres.; C. F. Irish, Sec.; 2nd and 4th Wednesdays, I.O.O.F. Hall.

FRESNO COUNTY.

Fresno No. 25, Fresno City—Oliver M. Akers, Pres.; W. C. Guard, Sec., 5060 Belmont; 2nd and 4th Fridays, W.O.W. Hall, 1354 Van Ness Ave.

GRAND OFFICERS.

Dr. Frank I. Gonzalez..........Junior Past Grand President
Flood Bldg., San Francisco

Seth Millington..........Grand President
Gridley

Justice Emmet Seawell..........Grand First Vice-president
State Bldg., San Francisco

Chas. A. Koenig..........Grand Second Vice-president
381 35th Ave., San Francisco

Harmon D. Skillin..........Grand Third Vice-president
Mills Bldg., San Francisco

John T. Regan..........Grand Secretary
N.S.G.W. Bldg., 414 Mason St., San Francisco

John A. Corotto..........Grand Treasurer
560 No. 5th St., San Jose

W. B. O'Brien..........Grand Marshal
2324 Santa Clara St., Alameda

Gam Hurst..........Grand Inside Sentinel
Financial Center Bldg., Oakland

William A. Reuter..........Grand Outside Sentinel
1009 Marine Ave., Wilmington

Leslie Maloche..........Grand Organist
467½ 3rd St., San Bernardino

Chester Gannon..........Historiographer
613 Capital Ntl. Bank Bldg., Sacramento

GRAND TRUSTEES.

Jesse H. Miller..........712 DeYoung Bldg., San Francisco
Eldred L. Meyer..........922 San Vicente Blvd., Santa Monica
John M. Burnett..........914 Bank Italy Bldg., San Jose
Henry S. Lyon..........Placerville
Joseph J. McShane..........419 Flood Bldg., San Francisco
Horace J. Leavitt..........Weaverville
Chas. H. Spengemann..........827 27th Ave., San Francisco

Selma No. 107, Selma—Chester E. Shepard, Pres.; E. C. Laughlin, Sec.; 1st and 3rd Wednesdays, American Legion Hall.

HUMBOLDT COUNTY.

Humboldt No. 14, Eureka—Henry Sundfors, Pres.; Loren M. Nelson, Sec., P.O. box 195; 2nd Monday, Native Sons Hall.

Arcata No. 20, Arcata—I. C. Fleckenstein, Pres.; William Peters, Sec., P. O. box 1117; Thursdays, Native Sons Hall.

Ferndale No. 93, Ferndale—Elwood Pries, Pres.; C. H. Rasmussen, Sec., R.F.D., 47-A; 1st and 3rd Mondays, K.P. Hall.

KERN COUNTY.

Bakersfield No. 42, Bakersfield—Ralph C. Hinderliter, Pres.; Henry A. Bannister, Sec., 610 "F" St.; 2nd and 4th Fridays, Justice Court, City Hall.

LAKE COUNTY.

Lower Lake No. 159, Lower Lake—Harold S. Anderson, Pres.; Albert Kugelman, Sec.; Thursdays, I.O.O.F. Hall.

LASSEN COUNTY.

Honey Lake No. 198, Standish—James C. Meeske, Pres.; N. V. Wemple, Sec., Litchfield; 1st and 3rd Wednesdays, Wrede Hall.

Big Valley No. 211, Bieber—George Bunselmeier, Pres.; A. W. McKenzie, Sec.; 1st and 3rd Wednesdays, I.O.O.F. Hall.

LOS ANGELES COUNTY.

Los Angeles No. 45, Los Angeles City—Owen S. Adams, Pres.; Richard W. Fryer, Sec., 1629 Champlain Ter.; Thursdays, Merchant Plumbers Hall, 1832 So. Hope.

Ramona No. 109, Los Angeles City—James M. Watson, Pres.; John V. Scott, Sec., Patriotic Hall, 1816 So. Figueroa; Fridays, Patriotic Hall, 1816 So. Figueroa.

Hollywood No. 196, Los Angeles City—Kenneth A. Case, Pres.; E. J. Reilly, Sec., Olive View; Mondays, 1089 No. Oxford Ave.

Long Beach No. 239, Long Beach—Francis H. Gentry, Pres.; W. W. Brady, Sec., 801 Jergins Trust Bldg.; 2nd and 4th Thursdays, Moose Hall, Elm and Anaheim.

Sepulveda No. 263, San Pedro—Joseph Pla, Pres.; Harry Fairall, Sec., 1925 Pacific Ave.; 2nd and 4th Fridays, Odd Fellows Temple, 10th and Gaffey Sts.

Glendale No. 264, Glendale—Leslie F. Schellback, Pres.; Abel B. Molen, Sec., 508 So. Belmont St.; 1st and 3rd Tuesdays, Masonic Temple, 234 So. Brand Blvd.

Santa Monica Bay No. 267, Ocean Park—Orrin G. Welch, Pres.; John J. Smith, Sec., 830 Rialto Ave., Venice; 2nd and 4th Mondays, New Eagle Hall, 2823½ Main St.

Cahuenga No. 268, Reseda—Harold C. Traxler, Pres.; Carrol S. Driscoll, Sec., P.O. box 25, Chatsworth; first Friday, Alton Hall.

MADERA COUNTY.

Madera No. 130, Madera City—Cornelius Noble, Pres.; T. P. Cosgrave, Sec.; 1st and 3rd Thursdays, First National Bank Bldg.

MARIN COUNTY.

Mount Tamalpais No. 64, San Rafael—M. E. Peterson, Pres.; Manual A. Andrade, Sec., 532 Mission Ave.; 1st and 3rd Mondays, Portuguese American Hall.

Sea Point No. 158, Sausalito—A. H. Bettencourt, Pres.; Manuel Santos, Sec., 6 Glen Drive; 1st and 3rd Wednesdays, Perry Bldg.

Nicasio No. 183, Nicasio—M. T. Farley, Pres.; R. J. Rogers, Sec.; 2nd and 4th Wednesdays, U.A.O.D. Hall.

MENDOCINO COUNTY.

Ukiah No. 71, Ukiah—Henry Bucknell, Pres.; Ben Hofman, Sec., P. O. box 473; 1st and 3rd Mondays, I.O.O.F. Hall.

Broderick No. 117, Point Arena—A. L. McCallum, Pres.; C. J. Buchanan, Sec.; 1st and 3rd Thursdays, Forester Hall.

Alder Glen No. 200, Fort Bragg—H. M. Bohn, Pres.; C. R. Weller, Sec.; 2nd and 4th Fridays, I.O.O.F. Hall.

MERCED COUNTY.

Yosemite No. 24, Merced City—John J. Thronton, Pres.; True W. Fowler, Sec., P. O. box 781; 2nd and 4th Mondays, I.O.O.F. Hall.

MONTEREY COUNTY.

Monterey No. 75, Monterey City—James Millington, Pres.; T. W. Krieger, Sec., 999 Franklin St.; 1st and 3rd Fridays, Knights Pythias Hall, Main St.

Santa Lucia No. 97, Salinas—Roy Martella, Pres.; R. W. Adcock, Sec., Route 2, box 180; Mondays, Native Sons Hall, 33 W. Alisal St.

Gabilan No. 132, Castroville—B. A. McCoy, Pres.; R. H. Martin, Sec., P. O. box 81; 1st and 3rd Thursdays, Native Sons Hall.

NAPA COUNTY.

Saint Helena No. 53, Saint Helena—Lucas Haus, Pres.; Edw. L. Bonhote, Sec., P. O. box 267; Mondays, Native Sons Hall.

Napa No. 62, Napa City—R. O. Akers, Pres.; H. J. Hoernle, Sec., 1226 Oak St.; Mondays, Native Sons Hall.

ATTENTION, SECRETARIES!

THIS DIRECTORY IS PUBLISHED BY AUTHORITY OF THE GRAND PARLOR N.S.G.W., AND ALL NOTICES OF CHANGES MUST BE RECEIVED BY THE GRAND SECRETARY (NOT THE MAGAZINE) ON OR BEFORE THE 20TH OF EACH MONTH TO INSURE CORRECTION IN NEXT ISSUE OF DIRECTORY.

Calistoga No. 86, Calistoga—Edmund Molinari, Pres.; Lou Carlenzoli, Sec.; 1st and 3rd Mondays, I.O.O.F. Hall.

NEVADA COUNTY.

Hydraulic No. 56, Nevada City—Arthur W. Davis, Pres Dr. C. W. Chapman, Sec.; Tuesdays, Pythian Castle.

Quartz No. 58, Grass Valley—Robert Kohler, Pres.; H. R. George, Sec., 151 Conaway Ave.; Mondays, Auditoriu Hall.

Donner No. 162, Truckee—J. F. Lichtenberger, Pres.; J C. Lichtenberger, Sec.; 2nd and 4th Tuesdays, Nati Sons Hall.

ORANGE COUNTY.

Santa Ana No. 265, Santa Ana—Amos Huntzinger, Pres E. F. Marks, Sec., 1124 No. Bristol St.; 1st and 3 Mondays, K.C. Hall, 4th and French Sts.

PLACER COUNTY.

Auburn No. 59, Auburn—Iris Garcia, Pres.; J. G. Wals Sec.; 1st and 3rd Fridays, Foresters Hall.

Silver Star No. 63, Lincoln—L. J. Browning, Pres.; Ba ney G. Barry, Sec., P. O. box 72; 3rd Wednesda I.O.O.F. Hall.

Rocklin No. 233, Roseville—Wm. La Due, Pres.; M. Reed, Sec., 253 W. Duranta; 2nd and 4th Wednesday Eagles Hall.

PLUMAS COUNTY.

Quincy No. 131, Quincy—J. D. McLaughlin, Pres.; E. Kelsey, Sec.; 2nd Thursday, I.O.O.F. Hall.

Golden Anchor No. 182, La Porte—R. J. McGrath, Pres LeRoy J. Post, Sec.; 2nd and 4th Sunday morning Native Sons Hall.

Plumas No. 228, Taylorsville—E. E. Sikes, Pres.; Geor E. Boyden, Sec.; 1st and 3rd Mondays, Native Sons Ha

SACRAMENTO COUNTY.

Sacramento No. 3, Sacramento City—J. G. Fitzhen Pres.; J. F. Didion, Sec., 1131 "O" St.; Thursdays, N tive Sons Bldg., 11th and "J" Sts.

Sunset No. 26, Sacramento City—L. W. Marvin, Pres Edward E. Reese, Sec., County Treasurer Office; Mo days, Native Sons Bldg., 11th and "J" Sts.

Elk Grove No. 41, Elk Grove—Fred Sehlmeyer, Pres Walter Martin, Sec.; 2nd and 4th Fridays, Masonic Ha

Granite No. 83, Folsom—Joe Relvas, Pres.; Frank Showe Sec.; 2nd and 4th Tuesdays, K.P. Hall.

Courtland No. 106, Courtland—Thornton Pylman, Pres Jos. Green, Sec.; 1st Saturday and 3rd Monday, Nati Sons Hall.

Sutter Fort No. 241, Sacramento City—Ed. T. Goyn Pres.; C. L. Katzenstein, Sec., P. O. box 914; 2nd an 4th Wednesdays, Native Sons Bldg., 11th and "J" St

Galt No. 243, Galt—John Granadas, Pres.; F. W. Harm Sec.; 1st and 3rd Mondays, I.O.O.F. Hall.

SAN BENITO COUNTY.

Fremont No. 44, Hollister—S. Churchill, Pres.; J. Prendergast Jr., Sec., 1064 Monterey St.; 1st and 3 Thursdays, Grangers Union Hall.

SAN BERNARDINO COUNTY.

Arrowhead No. 110, San Bernardino City—F. L. McGarve Pres.; R. W. Brazelton, Sec., 462 6th St.; Wednesday Eagles Hall, 469 4th St.

SAN DIEGO COUNTY.

San Diego No. 108, San Diego City—Martin J. Spangle Pres.; A. V. Mayrhofer, Sec., 1572 2nd St.; Wednesday K.C. Hall, 4th and Elm Sts.

SAN FRANCISCO CITY AND COUNTY.

California No. 1, San Francisco—Joseph Lawlor, Pres.; Ell A. Blackman, Sec., 1248-A Divisadero St.; Thursday Native Sons Bldg., 414 Mason St.

Pacific No. 10, San Francisco—Walter Mohrdick, Pres.; Henry Bastein, Sec., 426 City Hall; Tuesdays, Nati Sons Bldg., 414 Mason St.

Golden Gate No. 29, San Francisco—Thomas I. Schlia Pres.; Adolph Eberhart, Sec., 183 Carl St.; Monday Native Sons Bldg., 414 Mason St.

Mission No. 38, San Francisco—George Leahy, Pres.; Tho J. Stewart, Sec., 1919 Howard St.; Wednesdays, Redme Hall, 3053 16th St.

San Francisco No. 49, San Francisco—Charles Miller, Pres David Capurro, Sec., 976 Union St.; Thursdays, Nati Sons Bldg., 414 Mason St.

El Dorado No. 52, San Francisco—Edward Victor, Pres Alfred Vlautin, Sec., 1537 Franklin St.; Thursdays, N tive Sons Bldg., 414 Mason St.

Rincon No. 72, San Francisco—Frank D. Sericano, Pres John A. Gilmour, Sec., 2069 Golden Gate Ave.; Wedne days, Native Sons Bldg., 414 Mason St.

Stanford No. 76, San Francisco—Dr. Vincent V. Hardema Pres.; Charles T. O'Kane, Sec., 1111 Pine St.; Tuesday Native Sons Bldg., 414 Mason St.

Bay City No. 104, San Francisco—Morris Garren, Pres Max E. Licht, Sec., 1831 Fulton St.; 2nd and 4t Wednesdays, Native Sons Bldg., 414 Mason St.

Niantic No. 105, San Francisco—A. Furner, Pres.; J. M Darcy, Sec., 10 Hoffman Ave.; Wednesdays, Native So Bldg., 414 Mason St.

National No. 118, San Francisco—Wayne Burke, Pres Martin M. Ratigan, Sec., 1325 Page St., Apt. 6; Thur days, 1160 Eddy St.

Hesperian No. 137, San Francisco—C. McLaughlin, Pres Albert Carlson, Sec., 379 Justin Dr.; Thursdays, Nati Sons Bldg., 414 Mason St.

Alcalde No. 154, San Francisco—Charles Kurpinsky, Pres Harry S. Burke, Sec., 25 Ord St.; 2nd and 4th Wedne days, Native Sons Bldg., 414 Mason St.

South San Francisco No. 157, San Francisco—Otto A. E vander, Pres.; John T. Regan, Sec., 1489 Newcomb Ave Wednesdays, Masonic Bldg., 4705 3rd St.

Sequoia No. 160, San Francisco—Harry Grover, Pres Walter W. Garrett, Sec., 2500 Van Ness Ave.; Monday Swedish-American Bldg., 2174 Market St.

Precita No. 187, San Francisco—Lloyd J. Cosgrove, Pres Edward Tietjen, Sec., 1367 15th Ave.; Thursdays, Mi sion Masonic Hall, 2668 Mission St.

Olympus No. 189, San Francisco—Henry H. McGowa Pres.; Harvey J. Carty, Sec., 1651 Market St., Apt. 505 2nd and 4th Tuesdays, Independent Redmen Hall, 305 16th St.

Presidio No. 194, San Francisco—Lester Figone, Pres George A. Ducker, Sec., 442 21st Ave.; Mondays, Nati Sons Bldg., 414 Mason St.

Marshall No. 202, San Francisco—Alexander Jean, Pres Frank Bacigalupi, Sec., 725 Douglas St.; 1st and 3r Wednesdays, Native Sons Bldg., 414 Mason St.

Dolores No. 208, San Francisco—James F. Vahey, Pres Eugene O'Donnell, Sec., Mills Bldg.; Tuesdays, Missio Masonic Bldg., 2668 Mission St.

Twin Peaks No. 214, San Francisco—Clifford Roberts, Pres Thos. Pendergast, Sec., 278 Douglas St.; Wednesday Willopi Hall, 4061 24th St

El Capitan No. 222, San Francisco—Frank Rizzo, Pres James Hanna, Sec., 2450 27th Ave.; 1st and 3rd Thur days, King Soloman Hall, 1789 Fillmore St.

Guadalupe No. 231, San Francisco—Roy Tenafeldt, Pres Alvin A. Johnson, Sec., 142 Rousseau St.; Tuesday Guadalupe Hall, 4551 Mission St.

Castro No. 232, San Francisco—Ralph Willis, Pres

James H. Hayes, Sec., 4014 18th St.; Tuesdays, Native Sons Bldg., 414 Mason St.
alboa No. 234, San Francisco—George Schroth, Pres.; E. W. Boyd, Sec., 437 Cherry St.; Thursdays, Maccabee Hall, 5th Ave. and Clement St.
ret Harte No. 260, San Francisco—Chas. E. Lillie, Pres.; A. W. McElhatton, Sec., 103 Holloway Ave.; Tuesdays, West of Twin Peaks Hall, 233 Legion Court.
topia No. 270, San Francisco—George Walters, Pres.; Herbert H. Schneider, Sec., 2455 16th Ave.; Tuesdays, American Hall, 20th and Capp Sts.

SAN JOAQUIN COUNTY.

tockton No. 7, Stockton—John D. Gallagher, Pres.; R. D. Dorcey, Sec., P. O. box 388; Mondays, Native Sons Hall.
odi No. 18, Lodi—Jerome Solomon, Pres.; Dr. Clyde Bresnan, Sec.; 2nd and 4th Wednesdays, Eagles Hall.
racy No. 186, Tracy—C. S. Seina, Pres.; R. J. Marraccini, Sec., R.F.D. No. 1, box 217; Thursdays, I.O.O.F. Hall.
anteca No. 271, Manteca—Chas. N. Howell Jr., Pres.; Leonard Farin, Sec., R.F.D., box 75, Lathrop; 1st and 3rd Wednesdays, I.O.O.F. Hall.

SAN LUIS OBISPO COUNTY.

an Miguel No. 150, San Miguel—H. Twisselman, Pres.; Otto Kuehl, Sec., Paso Robles; 1st and 3rd Wednesdays, Fraternal Hall.
ambria No. 152, Cambria—J. M. Soto, Pres.; A. S. Gay, Sec.; Wednesdays, Rigdon Hall.

SAN MATEO COUNTY.

edwood No. 66, Redwood City—Frank Deluchi, Pres.; A. S. Liguori, Sec., P. O. box 212; Thursdays, American Foresters Hall.
easide No. 95, Half Moon Bay—Andrew F. Gilcrest, Pres.; John G. Gilcrest, Sec.; 2nd and 4th Tuesdays, I.O.O.F. Hall.
enlo No. 185, Menlo Park—C. T. Maloney, Pres.; F. W. Johnson, Sec., P. O. box 601; Thursdays, Masonic Hall.
ebble Beach No. 230, Pescadero—Harold Souza, Pres.; E. A. Shaw, Sec.; 2nd and 4th Wednesdays, I.O.O.F. Hall.
l Carmelo No. 256, Daly City—Theodore A. Clemens, Pres.; Ernest L. Micco, Sec., 639 Morse St., San Francisco; 2nd and 4th Wednesdays, Eagles Hall.
ndustrial City No. 269, South San Francisco—John C. Hamilton, Pres.; Geo. A. Roll, Sec., P. O. box 237; 2nd and 4th Mondays, Metropolitan Hall.

SANTA BARBARA COUNTY.

anta Barbara No. 116, Santa Barbara City—C. W. McCormick, Pres.; H. C. Sweetser, Sec., Court House; 1st and 3rd Wednesdays, I.O.O.F. Hall.

SANTA CLARA COUNTY.

an Jose No. 22, San Jose—Joseph Sabatte, Pres.; H. W. McComas, Sec., Suite 7, Porter Bldg.; Mondays, I.O.O.F. Hall.
anta Clara No. 100, Santa Clara City—John J. Trinajstich, Pres.; Clarence Clevenger, Sec., P. O. box 297; Wednesdays, Redmen Hall.
bservatory No. 177, San Jose—William L. Gerrans, Pres.; A. B. Langford, Sec., Hall Records; Tuesdays, Knights Columbus Hall, 40 No. First St.
ountain View No. 215, Mountain View—Gilbert F. McCorkle, Pres.; C. A. Antonioli, Sec., 301 Castro St.; 2nd and 4th Wednesdays, Mockbee Hall.
alo Alto No. 216, Palo Alto—John C. Bernal, Pres.; Albert A. Quinn, Sec., 643 High St.; Mondays, Native Sons Bldg., Hamilton Ave. and Emerson St.

SANTA CRUZ COUNTY.

Watsonville No. 65, Watsonville—Fred R. Baese, Pres.; E. R. Tindall, Sec., R.F.D. No. 5, Box 313; 2nd and 4th Tuesdays, I.O.O.F. Hall.
anta Cruz No. 90, Santa Cruz City—Horace Burkett, Pres.; T. V. Mathews, Sec., 105 Pacheco Ave.; Fridays, Native Sons Hall, 117 Pacific Ave.

SHASTA COUNTY.

cCloud No. 149, Redding—A. E. Welbourn, Pres.; Hugh A. Shuffleton, Sec.; 1st and 3rd Thursdays, Moose Hall.

SIERRA COUNTY.

ownieville No. 92, Downieville—Frank H. Turner, Pres.; H. S. Tibbey, Sec.; 2nd and 4th Mondays, I.O.O.F. Hall.
olden Nugget No. 94, Sierra City—Elmer Thompson, Pres.; Arthur R. Pride, Sec.; last Saturday, Masonic Hall.

SISKIYOU COUNTY.

tna No. 192, Etna—Frank B. Quigley, Pres.; Harvey A. Green, Sec.; 1st and 3rd Wednesdays, I.O.O.F. Hall.
iberty No. 193, Sawyers Bar—Orrin R. Bigelow, Pres.; John M. Barry, Sec.; 1st and 3rd Saturdays, I.O.O.F. Hall.

SOLANO COUNTY.

olano No. 39, Suisun—Karl Koch, Pres.; J. W. Kinlock, Sec.; 1st and 3rd Tuesdays, I.O.O.F. Hall.
allejo No. 77, Vallejo—Joseph Clavo, Pres.; Werner B. Hallin, Sec., 912 Carolina; 2nd and 4th Tuesdays, San Pablo Hall.

SONOMA COUNTY.

etaluma No. 27, Petaluma—Fred G. Ilg, Pres.; C. F. Fobes, Sec., 114 Prospect St.; 2nd and 4th Mondays, Druid Hall, Gross Bldg., 41 Main St.
anta Rosa No. 28, Santa Rosa—Wesley Beach, Pres.; Leland S. Lewis, Sec., Court House; Mondays, Native Sons Hall.
len Ellen No. 102, Glen Ellen—Tony Cereghino, Pres.; Frank Kirch, Sec., Route 3, Santa Rosa; 2nd Monday, N.S.G.W. Hall.
onoma No. 111, Sonoma City—Joseph Andrieux, Pres.; L. H. Green, Sec.; 1st and 3rd Mondays, I.O.O.F. Hall.
ebastopol No. 143, Sebastopol—O. A. McChristian, Pres.; F. G. McFarlane, Sec.; 1st and 3rd Fridays, I.O.O.F. Hall.

STANISLAUS COUNTY.

odesto No. 11, Modesto—Chas. D. Blaine, Pres.; C. C. Eastin Jr., Sec., P. O. box 898; 1st and 3rd Wednesdays, I.O.O.F. Hall.
akdale No. 142, Oakdale—D. W. Tulloch, Pres.; E. T. Gobin, Sec.; 2nd and 4th Mondays, Legion Hall.
restimba No. 247, Crows Landing—Lloyd W. Fink, Pres.; G. W. Fink, Sec.; 1st and 3rd Wednesdays, Community Club Home.

SUTTER COUNTY.

utter No. 261, Sutter City—Albert Thomasen, Pres.; Glen R. Haynes, Sec., R.F.D. No. 2, Yuba City; 2nd and 4th Mondays, N.D.G.W. Hall.

TRINITY COUNTY.

ount Hally No. 87, Weaverville—R. L. Marshall, Pres.; E. V. Ryan, Sec.; 1st and 3rd Mondays, Native Sons Hall.

TUOLUMNE COUNTY.

uolumne No. 144, Sonora—Mathew J. Marshall, Pres.; William M. Harrington, Sec., P. O. box 715; 2nd and 4th Fridays, Knights Columbus Hall.
olumbia No. 258, Columbia—Jos. Cadematori, Pres.; Charles E. Grant, Sec.; 2nd and 4th Thursdays, Native Sons Hall.

VENTURA COUNTY.

abrillo No. 114, Ventura City—David Bennett, Pres., 1380 Church St.

YOLO COUNTY.

Woodland No. 30, Woodland—J. L. Aronson, Pres.; E. B. Hayward, Sec.; 1st Thursday, Native Sons Hall.

YUBA COUNTY.

Marysville No. 6, Marysville—Ray C. Burris, Pres.; Verne Fogarty, Sec., 719 6th St.; 2nd Friday, Foresters Hall.
Rainbow No. 40, Wheatland—F. M. Beilby, Pres.; W. A. Bowser, Sec., P. O. box 318; 2nd Thursday, I.O.O.F. Hall.

N.D. ASSISTANTS

(Continued from Page 15)

No. 68, Lola Horgan (La Estrella No. 89). Las Lomas No. 72, Pearl Wedde (Bret Harte No. 232). Yosemite No. 83, Margaret Grant (Alta No. 3). La Estrella No. 89, Agnes Ryan (El Vespero No. 118). San Souci No. 96, Margaret Barrett (Buena Vista No. 68). Calaveras No. 103, Mary Hayes (Sans Souci No. 96). Darina No. 114, Mazie Roderick (Oro Fino No. 9). El Vespero No. 118, appointment pending. Genevieve No. 132, Agnes Curry (Portola No. 172). Keith No. 137, Helen McMahon (Yosemite No. 83). Gabrielle No. 139, Merle Sandell (Twin Peaks No. 185). Presidio No. 148, Ann Dippel (Mission No. 227). Guadalupe No. 153, Nora Scheflin (Genevieve No. 132). Golden Gate No. 158, Maude Daly (James Lick No. 220). Dolores No. 169, Agnes McVerry (Calaveras No. 103). Linda Rosa No. 170, Jewel Strei (Presidio No. 148). Portola No. 172, Helen Mann (Keith No. 137). Castro No. 178, Myrtle Ross (Dolores No. 169). Twin Peaks No. 185, Elizabeth Muller (Golden State No. 50). James Lick No. 220, Loretta Cameron (Twin Peaks No. 185). Mission No. 227, Claire Lindsay (Golden Gate No. 158). Bret Harte No. 232, Helen Sprung (Gabrielle No. 139). La Dorado No. 236, Adele Walsh (Darina No. 114). Balboa No. 249, Nan Kelly (Portola No. 172). Utopia No. 252, Evelyn I. Carlson (Dolores No. 169).

District No. 19, Alameda, Contra Costa (part) Counties—Mildred Irwin, supervising deputy. Angelita No. 32, Olinda Kardoza (El Cereso No. 207). Aloha No. 106, Ellen Hitch (Berkeley No. 150). Argonaut No. 166, Elsie Haven (Bear Flag No. 151). Berkeley No. 150, Martha Watson (Aloha No. 106). Betsy Ross No. 238, Ella Freites (Argonaut No. 166). Laura Loma No. 182, Pauline Cleu (Fruitvale No. 177). Piedmont No. 87, Thelma Schonick (Bear Flag No. 151). Encinal No. 156, Kathryn B. Walde (Hayward No. 122). Bear Flag No. 151, Lurine Martin (Aloha No. 106). Brooklyn No. 157, Marion White (Piedmont No. 87). Bahia Vista No. 167, Kathleen Dombrink (Piedmont No. 87). Fruitvale No. 177, Anna Quinn (Bahia Vista No. 167). El Cereso No. 207, Matilda Enos (Betsy Ross No. 238). Hayward No. 122, Ann Mello (Fruitvale No. 122). Pleasanton No. 237, Anna Lewis (El Cereso No. 207). Richmond No. 147, Rosaline Correia (Argonaut No. 166). Carquinez No. 234, Grace Curry (Richmond No. 147).

District No. 20, San Joaquin County—Grace Bessac, supervising deputy. Joaquin No. 5, Frances Huck (El Pescadero No. 82). Caliz de Oro No. 206, Josephine Bianchi (Phoebe A. Hearst No. 214). El Pescadero No. 82, Henrietta Quevillcon (Caliz de Oro No. 206). Ivy No. 88, Catherine Tully (Joaquin No. 5). Phoebe A. Hearst No. 214, Eva Meyers (Ivy No. 88).

District No. 21, Stanislaus, Tuolumne Counties—Katherine Kopf, supervising deputy. Eldora No. 248, Morada No. 199, Ethel Mathiasen. Oakdale No. 125, Alice Dorrah (Oakdale No. 125). Anona No. 164, Dardanelle No. 66, Golden Era No. 99, Threse B. Eckel (Golden Era No. 99).

District No. 22, Merced, Fresno, Madera, Mariposa Counties—May F. Givens, supervising deputy. Mariposa No. 63, Christine James (Mariposa No. 63). Veritas No. 75, Hazel Laverty (Veritas No. 75). Fresno No. 187, Lois M. Roach (Madera No. 244). Madera No. 244, Frances Oliver (Fresno No. 187).

District No. 23, San Mateo County—Rena Mathias, supervising deputy. Bonita No. 10, Alice Mathias (El Carmelo No. 181). Menlo No. 211, Ida Pfaff (El Monte No. 205). Vista del Mar No. 155, Alice Mattei (Ano Nuevo No. 180). Ano Nuevo No. 180, Alta Macaulay (Santa Cruz No. 26). El Carmelo No. 181, Laura Bartels (Menlo No. 211). San Bruno No. 246, Mary Junker (Bonita No. 10).

District No. 24, Santa Clara County—Catherine Nelson, supervising deputy. San Jose No. 81, Faye Withycombe (Vendome No. 100). Vendome No. 100, Elsie Fisher (San Jose No. 81). El Monte No. 205, Genevieve M. Commerford (Palo Alto No. 229). Palo Alto No. 229, Marie Buck (Vendome No. 100).

District No. 25, San Benito, Santa Cruz, Monterey Counties—Rose Rhyner, supervising deputy. Santa Cruz No. 26, El Pajaro No. 35, Thelma Wishardt (El Pajaro No. 35). Aleli No. 102, Copa de Oro No. 105, San Juan Bautista No. 179, Junipero No. 141, Edna Butterfield (Copa de Oro No. 105).

District No. 26, Kern County—Minnie B. Heath, supervising deputy. El Tejon No. 239, Miocene No. 228, Grace S. Dorris (El Tejon No. 239). Desert Gold No. 250, Jennie Dennis (El Tejon No. 239).

District No. 27, San Luis Obispo County—Katie G. Vangordon, supervising deputy. San Miguel No. 94, San Luisita No. 108, El Pinal No. 163, Julia Bell (San Luisita No. 108).

District No. 28, Santa Barbara County—Anna McCaughey, supervising deputy. Reina del Mar No. 126, Vera Pacheco (Reina del Mar No. 126).

District No. 29, San Diego, Imperial Counties Ann Wood, supervising deputy. San Diego No. 208, Carrie E Northway (Rudecinda No. 230).

District No. 30, Los Angeles County—P.G.P. Grace S Stoermer, supervising deputy. Los Angeles No. 124, Rita Smith (Santa Monica Bay No. 245). Long Beach No. 154, Nellie Cline (Grace No. 242). Rudecinda No. 230, Kate McFadyen (Long Beach No. 154). Verdugo No. 240, Gertrude Allen (Los Angeles No. 124). Santa Monica Bay No. 245, Violet T. Henshilwood (Long Beach No. 154). Californiana No. 247, Mattie Edwards (Grace No. 242).

District No. 31, San Bernardino, Orange, Riverside Counties—Florence D. Schoneman, supervising deputy. Santa Ana No. 235, Eva Bemis (Lugonia No. 241). Lugonia No. 241, Marion Crum (Santa Ana No. 235). Grace No. 242, Mary Noerenberg (Californiana No. 247). Ontario No. 251, Ella Madden (Verdugo No. 240).

PIONEER NATIVES DEAD

(Brief Notices of the Demise of Men and Women born in California Prior to 1860.)

Dr. B. F. Clarke, born in Yolo County in 1854, died June 23 at San Jose, Santa Clara County, survived by a wife and a daughter.

Justice John E. Richards, born at San Jose, Santa Clara County, July 7, 1856, died there June 25 survived by a wife. He was affiliated with Observatory Parlor No. 177 N.S.G.W. From 1907 to 1913 he was superior judge of Santa Clara County, and in 1924 was elevated to the State Supreme Court. He was also an author as well as lecturer of note.

Mrs. Frances Jane Cornish, born in Tuolumne County in 1854, died at Grass Valley, Nevada County, June 27 survived by three children.

Amel Nelson, born in Tuolumne County in 1858, died at Sonora June 30 survived by three children.

Mrs. Elizabeth Lewis-Cranmer, born in Mariposa County in 1854, died near Sanger, Fresno County, July 1 survived by four children.

Mrs. Margaret Rutherford, born in Shasta County in 1858, died near Bella Vista July 2 survived by a husband and five sons.

George P. Johnson, born in El Dorado County in 1855, died July 4 at Auburn, Placer County. He was affiliated with Auburn Parlor No. 59 N.S.G.W.

Bird Harris, born in Orange County in 1853, died July 6 at Decoto, Alameda County. He was a son of William Britton and Amanda (Jordan) Harris, California Pioneers of 1849.

Charles F. Walter, born in Calaveras County in 1854, died July 13 at San Andreas survived by a wife and a daughter.

William Leakey, born in El Dorado County in 1858, died July 13 at Placerville.

Milton Honey, born in Tuolumne County in 1858, died at Sacramento City July 16 survived by a wife and two children.

In Memoriam

SAIDE MAE HALCOMB.

"Not in anger, not in wrath
The Reaper came that day,
'Twas an Angel visited the earth
And took the flower away."

Be comforted, ye loved ones who weep,
She lives with God; she is just asleep.

Green be her memory in the Parlor's heart,
She loved so well, through her true life's span;
Blessed be her rest who acted well her part,
Who honor'd God in doing good with all her heart.

Whereas, We, the members of Eltapome Parlor No. 55 N.D.G.W., have learned with deep sorrow and regret that God has seen fit to remove from this life our dear and beloved sister, Saide Mae Halcomb. Therefore, be it

Resolved, That it is but a just tribute to the memory of the departed to say that in her removal from this earth and our midst we mourn for one who was beloved by all; be it further resolved, that we sincerely sympathize with the bereaved families on the dispensation with which it has pleased a Divine Providence to afflict them; be it further resolved, that these resolutions be spread upon the minutes of this Parlor, that a copy of the same be presented to the bereaved families, and that a copy be sent to The Grizzly Bear for publication.

And like a bell, with solemn sweet vibrations,
We hear the Voice of God say "Peace."

Sweet be her rest and gentle be her sleeping;
God's way is best; she is in His keeping.

CAROLINE E. SMITH,
MARGARET C. TRIMBLE,
ADELENE HANOVER,
Committee.

Weaverville, July 16, 1932.

CALIFORNIA HAPPENINGS OF FIFTY YEARS AGO

Thomas R. Jones

(COMPILED EXPRESSLY FOR THE GRIZZLY BEAR.)

AUGUST 1882 WAS POLITICAL CONVENTION month in California. Every county had a gathering of Republicans to name delegates to the state convention and to select nominees for county offices. The state convention, held at Sacramento City August 30, was a harmonious gathering. The adopted platform was anti-Chinese and anti-railroad, and for a fair-and-square Sunday law, but dodged the debris question. Among the nominees were M. M. Estee of San Francisco for governor, A. R. Conklin of Yolo County for lieutenant-governor and F. A. Pedlar of Yolo County for secretary of state.

The Federal Government Chinese restriction act went into effect August 1. From January 1 to that date 27,105 Chinks arrived in California and 4,141 departed for their homeland, adding 22,964 to the state's Oriental population in that period. A few more arrived after August 1 but were not allowed to land, and the influx of the undesirables practically ceased.

Although it was claimed the Coolies were displacing White men, there was a scarcity of the latter to harvest the crops, and so Sacramento Valley farmers were, in many instances, compelled to hire the Chinese. The labor-shortage trouble, however, apparently was not due to lack of White help but to an overabundance of booze emporiums.

The Stockton, San Joaquin County, "Independent" published the following: "Our city was, as is usual at this season, crowded with ranch hands on Sunday who came into town to have theit weekly drunk and spend their earnings." A farmer near Chico, Butte County, drove into that town Sunday night with his header wagon and searched out the saloon where his harvest hands were rendezvousing. He carried out seven, "two full for resistance," loaded them into the wagon and hauled them back to his farm.

Wild blackberries were growing in immense acreage in Mendocino County and bushels of them were being gathered by families, many of which came from points forty miles distant.

An artesian well bored on Washington street, San Francisco, struck at a depth of 115 feet a flow of 6,000 gallons of water an hour.

J. B. Rame, a Santa Ana, Orange County, hop-grower, sold his crop in New York City for $16,000, and cleared $11,000.

A company was formed at Oakland, Alameda County, to manufacture belting from sheep intestines. It was turning out belting fifty-five feet long and of light weight, said to be more durable than leather.

August 10 was the hottest day recorded for several years. At Red Bluff, Tehama County, the thermometer went up to 105 degrees, and at Fresno City it mounted to 110.

Hollister, San Benito County, and adjacent towns were severely shaken by earthquake at 12:21 a. m. of August 7.

A brilliant meteor flashed across the heavens at 2 a. m. of August 9. It illuminated the Sacramento Valley as bright as day and left a tail of light behind that glowed for several minutes.

The G.A.R. of California South had a week's reunion at Santa Monica, Los Angeles County, beginning August 8. The veterans camped along the beach and paraded daily.

The state school fund was apportioned this month. There were 215,522 schoolchildren in California, and for their education $334,659 was distributed to the several counties.

The First Artillery Regiment N.G.C., consisting of companies from Sacramento City, Woodland, Yolo County, Nevada City, Nevada County, and Camptonville, Yuba County, went by steamboat to San Rafael, Marin County, August 20 for a week's encampment.

B. B. Redding, Pioneer of 1850 and secretary of state in 1862, died at San Francisco August 21 at the age of 58. He introduced several varieties of fish, including the rainbow trout, into California waters.

Ygnacio Miramontez died at Searsville, San Mateo County, August 29. He was born there in 1811 and was the owner of El Corta Rancho.

The last spike of the California Southern Railroad was driven August 15 at Colton, San Bernardino County, and the first passenger train ran that day from San Diego City to that town, where a celebration was held.

The hydraulic mines around Smartsville were shut down August 15 in compliance with an injunction issued out of the Yuba County court. They were valued at $3,000,000 and supported a population of 2,000. In twenty years, $20,000,000 worth of gold had been washed out by these mines.

Tunneling into a mountain at the Morning Star drift mine in Iowa Hill, Placer County, an ancient river bed, 400 feet wide and of unknown length, was found. The gravel was "lousy" with gold.

The Eagle Gulch mine in Plumas County struck a seam from which was chiseled a piece of gold weighing thirteen pounds and worth $2,700. In one day over ten thousand dollars' worth of gold was extracted from the seam.

Los Angeles was greatly excited over the report of rich placers being found in San Gabriel Canyon, and rainbow chasers were rushing through Azusa by the hundreds. Twenty-one thousand dollars' worth of gold dust was said to have been brought out and sold August 25.

The "Anti-Debris Guards," an organization of a hundred Sacramento City youths, was formed this month with Tom Fox as president and Joe Wiseman as captain. What the guards were to do was not divulged, but they were uniformed and began drilling.

The Hardy powder works near Vallejo, Solano County, exploded August 11, and Superintendent A. H. Hall, George Edgecomb and Fergus McArdle were killed.

Fires during August caused heavy losse among them: Lemoore, Kings County, ten buil ings the 6th, $50,000; Suisun, Solano Count hotel the 7th, $10,000; Courtland, Sacramen County, salmon cannery the 5th, $12,000; Pla erville, El Dorado County, foundry the 15 $20,000; sawmill near Dutch Flat, Placer Cou ty, the 15th, $25,000; South San Francisco c barns the 28th, $25,000; Sacramento Cit cracker bakery the 30th, $25,000.

Red Bluff, Tehama County, had a disastro fire August 13, nearly all its business hous and a number of residences being destroye The loss was estimated at $500,000. The pla of the Sierra Flume and Lumber Company ne that city burned August 29, causing a $200,00 loss.

John Farrell, known as "Jack of Clubs," in fight with Charles Michel at San Francisco A gust 21, hit him a heavy blow that broke h neck.

Shadrick Jones, Chico, Butte County, farme was murdered August 5 by his son-in-law, Jam Parker.

Ernest Baldwin, 5-year-old son of the trea urer of San Benito County, fell off a wagon Hollister August 6 and was killed.

Sol Heslem and Sam Brooks got into a quarr at Columbia, Tuolumne County, August 10 an the latter was killed.

A cavein August 9 at the Moore Flat, Nevad County, hydraulic mine buried and killed fo Chinamen.

S. C. Stevens, Colusa City attorney, went the home of Ashford Christian August 27 to co lect a fee. A fight ensued and Stevens w kicked to death.

Wm. M. Dair, a miner, fell 350 feet down th shaft of the Red Cloud mine at Bodie, Mon County, August 15 and was killed.

NATIONAL FOREST'S NAME CHANGED.

By presidential proclamation of July 12, th California National Forest will now be known the Mendocino National Forest. The purpose the change of name is to avoid the confusio resulting from a national forest having the sam name as the state in which it is located. Th national forest is located in the Coast Range parts of six different counties.

The name Mendocino was selected as the mo euphonious as well as the most appropriate hi torically because it is the oldest in the enti California coast region. Cabrillo, the Spanis explorer, named a prominent cape Mendocino 1543 in honor of his patron, Antonio de Me doza, then governor of New Spain, now Mexic

SEVENTY-NINTH MILESTONE.

Berkeley (Alameda County)—Berkele reaches its seventy-ninth milestone this mont August. The Chamber of Commerce has disco ered that the first building around which th city grew was a combined hotel and store erect by Captain William J. Bowen in the fall of 185 The first postoffice was established in 1872.

The oldest structure within the Berkeley li its is the adobe of Jose Domingo Peralta, co structed in 1841.

NATURAL AREA DEDICATED.

The United States Forest Service announc the dedication of the Indiana Summit Natur Area, a tract of 1,000 acres set aside to preser for posterity a typical virgin forest of Jeffr pine. This natural area is located on the slop of Bald Mountain at an elevation of 8,000 fe and six miles south of Mono Lake in the In National Forest. No lumbering has ever be done on the area and none will hereafter be a lowed.

Petroleum Decline—Final figures issued Ju 15 by the Federal Commerce Department Bure of Mines discloses the nation's 1931 crude production was 851,081,000 barrels, a decline 5 percent from 1930. The value dropped $550,630,000, the lowest since 1917.

Promising Future—Gold production is no one of the most prosperous industries in th United States, according to the Federal Interi Department Geological Survey, and has a pro ising future. There is a steady increase in go production and decreasing costs are stimulati the introduction of better machinery and met ods of mining.

Santa Barbara Fair—August 13 is the da for the annual Santa Barbara County Fair Santa Maria.

Melon Festival—Turlock, Stanislaus Count will have a Melon Festival, August 15-21.

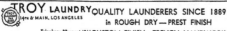

"MARK OUR LANDMARKS"

FORGOTTEN HERO

Chester F. Gannon

(HISTORIOGRAPHER N.S.G.W.)

N THE CITY CEMETERY AT SACRAMENTO is a grave surmounted by a ten-foot marble shaft. On one side is the chiseled face of a man, on another side is engraved, "Presented by the People of the State of California."

Despite that tribute from a young state, to-y that grave is forgotten, and the man whose mains lie interred therein is scarcely given a ssing thought by the present generation who ss that way.

Yet, in that grave in the State Plot of former ficials of the State of California, lie the re-ains of a hero. That hero was William I. erguson. At the time of his death he was a ate Senator from Sacramento County. Many ecoration Days have come and gone since the terment in 1858, and the people of that gener-ion have passed on. No friend or admirer to-y lays a floral offering to the memory of the an whose mortal remains have practically gone ck to nature.

The very lack of them shows that no matter w noble, brave and honorable a man may have en, yet the passing years quickly submerge his rsonality into the unnumbered legion of dead. It is the duty of the Native Sons to keep alive e traditions of the past and the memories of ose men and women who contributed so much the glory of California's pioneer days.

There was no nobler or finer type of Pioneer an Ferguson. Born in Pennsylvania, he grew in Illinois and became a lawyer. He filled any public offices with distinction and was a rsonal friend of Abraham Lincoln. In 1853 left the City of Springfield, Illinois, and came Sacramento and immediately became inter-ted in politics and law. A fervid orator, he came one of the leading spokesmen against avery and thereby incurred the wrath of the avery party in California. The pro-slavery fac-n was strong, and contained many influential d reckless men. To speak one's mind in ref-ence to slavery was almost to invite one's own ath. However, Ferguson had the courage of s convictions, and spoke often and eloquently ainst human bondage. Another young man by the name of George Penn Johnston, likewise interested in politics, Southern born, an attorney-at-law and an advocate of slavery, quarreled with Ferguson in a saloon in San Francisco.

When one desires to quarrel with another, it

is easy to attain that end. Johnston forced the quarrel over a slight jocular statement of Ferguson's. He challenged Ferguson to a duel. Angel Island, in San Francisco Bay, on August 21, 1858, was the scene and date of that so-called "field of honor."

In the exchange of shots Ferguson fell, mortally wounded, but lived for three weeks thereafter. His courage on his deathbed was an example of genuine stability and great fortitude. He forgave his antagonist and asked that his friends do likewise. One of his last requests was that his personal friend, Edward D. Baker, who had likewise come to California from Illinois, would deliver his funeral oration. This was his last request as he entered the operating room to have his leg amputated. He never spoke after the ether was applied. He died in his thirty-second year.

He had all the qualities which spell success. He was amiable, kind, intelligent, courageous. He was liked by all who knew him, and a brilliant future was assured had he lived.

Baker delivered the eulogy over his body as it lay in the Senate Chamber at Sacramento on the 16th day of September, 1858. Then the body was interred, and the monument hereinbefore referred to was erected. It is doubtful if there is another monument in California to a public official with a similar inscription thereon. At his bier, the great Baker said:

"I have perhaps known him longer than anybody here. I have known him, more particularly in his early youth, perhaps better than any one here assembled. I have watched the bud, the blow, the fruit, and lastly the untimely decay; and while I desire to speak of him as he himself would wish to be spoken of; while I do not mean that personal friendship shall warp my judgment or lead me to say as his friend anything unduly in his praise, so also, on the other hand, shall I say nothing against him or others that is unjust or unkind . . . .

"The gentleman whose remains you are about to consign to his last resting-place until the trump of the Archangel shall sound, was a native of the State of Pennsylvania. I knew his father well; a respectable, worthy, honest man; a mechanic by pursuit, intelligent, self-reliant, and in every respect honorable. The young man was ambitious from his boyhood. He sought the profession of the law, not merely for itself, but as an opening that would lead to what he considered were higher and more noble positions . . . .

"In conclusion, I would remark that I have no words sufficient to express my own personal regret. I have lost a warm personal friend. I may find others, but I shall not be able to find friends that I have loved in other years. I shall not often find those to whom I can, as I could to him, talk of the old familiar times and the lessons I taught him in early life—of the virtues and example of his parents—of his mother's, his poor afflicted mother's affection and love—of his old contests—his old hopes, so often broken. I shall not often find friends like these, nor can the breach which death has made be so easily repaired."

Except for the grave, there is nothing in the City of Sacramento to show where this man lived for five years. There is nothing to show the building in which he died or where he had his office. No marker points out to the passerby of this age where the footsteps of Ferguson once trod.

It is our bounden duty to keep alive the memory, the virtues, the nobility of such men as William I. Ferguson. We can do it, by placing suitable markers on the spots which once knew them when they ran quick with life.

—"MARK OUR LANDMARKS"—

"Some" Tree—The Governor Stoneman tree, a sequoia in the South Calaveras grove in the Stanislaus National Forest of California, contains enough lumber to build twenty five-room bungalows—179,000 board feet. The larger limbs are six feet in diameter.

Old Spanish Days—Santa Barbara City will again present its noted Old Spanish Days Fiesta, August 18-20.

"When love and skill work together, expect a masterpiece."—Ruskin.

Know your home-state, California! Learn of i[ts] past history and of its present-day development b[y] reading regularly The Grizzly Bear. $1.50 for o[ne] year (12 issues). Subscribe now.

SAN FRANCISCO

THE ORDERS OF NATIVE SONS AND Native Daughters of the Golden West, and the Society of California Pioneers are working together to obtain the right to erect, atop Telegraph Hill, San Francisco, a monument to the California Pio-ieers. A counter plan is afoot to place there a olt memorial shaft, using therefor funds left y the late Mrs. Colt "to beautify San Francis-o." Voicing disapproval of the Colt-shaft plan, ie following resolution has been adopted by ie Telegraph Hill Memorial Committee—Lewis . Byington (chairman), John T. Regan, James . Wilson, Joseph R. Knowland, William F. umphreys, Angelo J. Rossi, John H. Nelson, has. A. Koenig, William J. Fitzgerald, Mrs. velyn I. Carlson and Mrs. Sallie R. Thaler:

"Whereas, Telegraph Hill, known as Loma Alta by the d Spanish explorers, is one of the most prominent land-arks in San Francisco and closely associated with the panish navigators of the Pacific Ocean, the discovery of ld in California and the early Pioneers who were the unders and builders of San Francisco, and around it also ew up the first commercial settlement on San Francisco y, known as Yerba Buena; and

"Whereas, The Native Sons of the Golden West and the ciety of California Pioneers were the first to suggest the ection of a monument on this splendid site, to commem-ate the heroic deeds of the Pioneer Fathers and Mothers California and their patriotic labors in bringing Cali-rnia into the Union; and

"Whereas, These Orders and their members were the st to subscribe funds for the erection of a monument to e Pioneers on this site, to the amount of thirty thousand llars, and stand ready to secure additional subscriptions r a much larger amount, believing that all citizens inter-ted in the history of California should have an oppor-nity of aiding in the erection of such an appropriate emorial; now, therefore, be it

"Resolved, That we, the Native Sons of the Golden West d the Native Daughters of the Golden West, hereby re-est the members of the Park Commission and the Art ommission of San Francisco to labor to the end that any onument erected on historic Telegraph Hill shall be of ch hight and artistic design as shall attract the attention d the admiration of all our citizens and of all travelers no visit our shores, and that said monument shall be erect-; to the memory of the Pioneer Men and Women of the est and be known as the Monument to the Pioneers of alifornia."

Past Grand President Lewis F. Byington pro-oses that the $30,000 already pledged by the ioneers and Native Sons, together with the 25,000 bequest of the late Senator James D. helan, be included with the Colt sum to erect suitable monument.

TO BURN HOME MORTGAGE.

At the breakfast Sunday, August 14, the Na-ve Daughters will burn the Home mortgage, hich has been paid in full. The property, at 55 Baker street, is now free of debt. Past rand Genevieve Watson-Baker and Mrs. Jennie reene, senior members of the Board of Relief, ill act as hostesses.

The Grand Parlor Home Committee has osen the following officers: Past Grand Dr. ariana Bertola, chairman; Past Grand Gene-eve Watson-Baker, first vice-chairman; Miss lizabeth F. Douglas, second vice-chairman; ast Grand Emma Gruber-Foley, secretary; Mrs. Jennie Greene, treasurer; Miss Millie Tietjen, assistant treasurer.

Know your home-state, California! Learn of s past history and of its present-day develop-ent by reading regularly The Grizzly Bear. 1.50 for one year (12 issues). Subscribe now.

PLANNING FOR ADMISSION DAY.

Plans for the state-wide Admission Day, September 9, celebration in San Francisco under the auspices of the N.S.G.W. Extension of the Order Committee, are progressing. The Native Daughters are co-operating, and many of the local Parlors will appear in the parade in colonial costumes, in commemoration of the Washington bicentennial. The parade will be held the morning of Admission Day, and in the evening a grand ball will be held. Other entertainment features are being arranged for.

Grand Trustee Joseph J. McShane, chairman Extension of the Order Committee, has appointed committees to handle the various details, the chairmen of which are: Joseph Rose (Marshall No. 202), finance; Arthur Poheim (Stanford No. 76), ways and means; Harry W. Gaetjen (Golden Gate No. 29), parade; Jesse H. Miller (Grand Trustee), Admission Day observance; Harmon D. Skillin (Grand Third Vice-president), accommodations; P. L. Schlesinger (Balboa No. 234), music; Frank Foss (Castro No. 232), publicity; Percy Marchant (Guadalupe No. 231), transportation; Ivo Monte (Stanford No. 76), grand ball; Lloyd J. Doering (N.S.G.W.) and Agnes Curry (N.D.G.W.), reception.

NATIVE DAUGHTER DOINGS.

Officers of Gabrielle Parlor No. 139 and Rincon Parlor No. 72 N.S.G.W. were jointly installed July 13, Carmelita Dieterichsen and Frank Sericano becoming the respective presidents. A large crowd witnessed the ceremonies, which were followed by dancing and refreshments.

Castro Parlor No. 178 observed its twenty-second institution anniversary July 6 at a banquet. The tables were decorated with flowers of bicentennial colors, red, white and yellow, and the favors were of the same hues. Supervising deputy Alice Lane and Deputy Myrtle Ross were honor-guests. After the feast the officers were installed, Ella Teeling becoming president. She was the recipient of many gifts, and Past President Mae Waring was presented with a hand-embroidered tablecloth in recognition of faithful services rendered the Parlor.

Past Grand President Dr. Mariana Bertola has, at the invitation of the executive committee of the General Federation of Womens Clubs, become the vice-chairman of public welfare for that organization. Her work for the establishment of children's and maternity wards in county hospitals, known as the "California Plan," has been duplicated in other states and won national recognition.

NATIVE SON DOINGS.

Officers of Stanford Parlor No. 76 were installed July 9 by Deputy Robert B. Donohue, Dr. Vincent V. Hardeman becoming president. Municipal Judge George J. Steiger was master of ceremonies, and Superior Judge James G. Conlan greeted the new officers.

South San Francisco Parlor No. 157 will hold a picnic at Menlo Park, August 21.

Castro Parlor No. 232 July 5 absorbed James Lick Parlor No. 242.

Grand Third Vice-president Harmon D. Skillin and family returned July 13 from a vacation trip to Alaska.

Grand Second Vice-president Chas. A. Koenig and family, Grand Secretary John T. Regan and family, and Joseph Rose (Marshall No. 202) and wife have been vacationing together along the Redwood highway.

JOINT N.S. INSTALLATION.

Fort Bragg (Mendocino County)—At a joint meeting of Broderick Parlor No. 117 and Alder Glen Parlor No. 200 N.S.G.W., July 22, officers were installed by Deputy Ralph W. Todd, A. L. McCollum and Harold Bohn becoming the respective presidents. A banquet followed the ceremonies.

Alder Glen Parlor, in observance of Admission Day, will sponsor a dance September 3 and a committee has been appointed to make arrangements.

In Memoriam

KATIE BROME.

Whereas, The Almighty God, in His infinite wisdom, has seen fit to take from our midst a dear sister and friend, Katie Brome; and whereas, in the passing of Sister Brome, Coloma Parlor No. 212 N.D.G.W. mourns the loss of one of its loyal and faithful members; and it is hereby

Resolved, That her beautiful character, filled with good deeds and kindly thoughts, will live always in our memory; be it further resolved, that these resolutions be spread on the minutes of our Parlor, that a copy be sent to the family of our departed sister, and a copy to The Grizzly Bear Magazine.

GERTRUDE KEHNER,
NETTIE HARRY,
EVA R. RASMUSSEN,
Committee.

Sacramento, July 22, 1932.

Autos Decline—Fee-paid registrations for all types of auto vehicles in California for the half-year ended June 30 totaled 1,962,360, a decrease of 33,805, compared with the 1931 total. The heaviest loss was recorded in pleasure cars, which totaled 1,805,819, and 748,170 of them were credited to Los Angeles County.

San Joaquin Fair—The annual San Joaquin County Fair will be held August 22-28 at Stockton.

BANDIT RAID OF EARLY DAYS

(CHARLES F. EMERY.)

NESTLED AMONG THE OLD GRANITE mountains along and north of the Mexican border in San Diego County, is a chain of valleys named by Indians and Mexicans Jacumba, Milquatay (now Campo), Mattaquequat (now Cameron Valley), Morena (now Morena Lake), Los Alamos (now Buckman Springs Valley), La Posta, Laguna, Valle de los Pinos (Pine Valley), Cuyamaca, Quatay (now Descanso). The elevations vary from 2,000 to 6,000 feet.

Shortly after the Civil War a number of families from the Southern states, the majority from Texas, came overland, passing through the hot and dreary deserts of Arizona and New Mexico, and the Colorado Desert, now the Imperial Valley. When they arrived in the lower valleys next to the border, among the green meadows and groves of large oak trees, willows and manzanita, general settlements were established and homesteads were built on government land.

At the lower end of Milquatay Valley a little town was started by two brothers, Silas and Luman Gaskill, and named Campo. They were Western Pioneers, bear and deer hunters, and both were dead shots with firearms. Tiring of wild life, they came to Campo and started a general merchandise store, hotel, flourmill and blacksmith shop, and did a thriving business for many years.

One fine day six Mexican bandits, heavily armed, rode into the town from Mexico, prepared to rob the store and the town. Luman was the storekeeper and the millkeeper, and Silas was the blacksmith. Three of the bandits went into the store and opened fire on Luman, who fell behind the counter, shot through the upper part of a lung. The other three went into the blacksmith shop to kill Silas, but he saw them coming and dodged, receiving only a flesh wound in the arm. He immediately jumped behind the door and grabbed his old shotgun loaded with buckshot, and killed one of the bandits and wounded another.

Silas then ran across an orchard to a dwelling house to get more guns. In the meantime, all of the bandits in the store came out to shoot at Silas, firing at him as he ran to the house. It was reached safely, however, and, with his three-barreled rifle, he dropped one and wounded another bandit. The other two ran to their horses, but during the fight outside Luman had crawled out of the store and gone over to the hotel to get his rifle. As the two bandits were riding away he opened fire and hit one of them in the neck. It was reported the man was later found dead near Jacumba Valley.

News of the raid soon spread throughout the settlement, and that night a number of cowboys took the two wounded bandits and hung them to a large oak tree near the site of the new hotel. Thus ended a raid wherein two brave Americans dispatched five out of six Mexican bandits without any help.

At that time the military telegraph lines passed through Campo, from San Diego to Arizona. A young man who was stationed there was continually bragging to the cowboys about his new patented gun. But as Luman crawled under the store to get to the hotel he found the young fellow hiding there, without the gun. Luman and Silas both recovered from their wounds and lived to a ripe old age.

These valleys proved to be too cold and too frosty for farming, also too far away from the markets, so most of the early settlers sold out to the cattlemen and moved away. Now, the San Diego and Arizona railroad passes through the Campo Valley. A paved boulevard winds through the hills and valleys, and many beautiful resorts nestle among the large oaks and pines.

(This story came to The Grizzly Bear from Charles F. Emery of Point Loma, San Diego County, with this notation: "I was born at Woodland, Yolo County, August 6, 1857, and enjoy reading The Grizzly Bear." Emery is affiliated with San Diego Parlor No. 108 N.S.G.W.—Editor.)

Subscription Order Blank

For Your Convenience

Grizzly Bear Magazine,
309-15 Wilcox Bldg.,
206 South Spring St.,
Los Angeles, California.

For the enclosed remittance of $1.50 enter my subscription to The Grizzly Bear Magazine for one year.

Name...

Street Address...

City or Town...

GRIZZLY GROWLS

(Continued from Page 3)

re banking laws, and the next to the last re enforcement of law are fine and timely. Only wish every man and woman in California, and for that matter in the nation, could read your editorials, and then, if they would only think them over, what a difference in voting there would be. We are too prone to follow demagogic sayings. . . . . More power to you, and more readers!"—OSCAR W. LORD, Eureka.

"Just read your fine 'growl,' 'The Sign of the Cross,' in July issue. I congratulate you. Yes, there is only one cause to which can be justly charged the depression—man's dollar godism, greed! Continue your good work."—FRED E. POTTER, Stockton.

"We are appreciative of your good advice on voting. All too often voters have gone to the polls with little thought,—but a lot of advice from doubtful friends(!)—dropped in their ballots, and let it go at that. This year it may be different! Sincere best wishes for your work."—NELLIE H. DUNNING, Los Angeles.

"Was very glad to see in The Grizzly Bear for July 1932 your 'growl' referring to the initiative amendment [shifting public-school support to the state] which is to be presented at the November election. This is the first definite step taken in several years for protection of the real-estate taxpayer. If it is favored by the voters it will, in turn, spread the tax base and will result in a real and general demand for economy in governmental activities. This proposed amendment to the State Constitution, if passed, will be one of the best moves for the return of prosperity on this coast, as it will no doubt result in a building program which will, in some measure, relieve the unemployment situation."—EDWARD C. HALL, San Diego.

An example of present-day contempt for the law and the right was recently presented at Santa Cruz City. A councilman, charged with accepting a bribe, admitted the charge and offered no defense. The jury disagreed, and he was discharged. He must have known his townsmen!

"Strange that there should be a famine when there is an abundance of everything! Would it not be better," queries Philip Reilly in the "Free Press" of Oakland, "instead of stopping the growing of fruit and the plowing up of every third row of cotton and the killing of every third cow, that we eliminate every third corrupt politician and every third corrupt judge and give us instead honest men who can give this country an honest government?" Far better, by far. But why limit the eliminating to the "thirds?" Make it unanimous, and then conditions may improve.

The Federal Government's internal revenue collections fell from $2,428,228,754 for the 1930-31 fiscal year to $1,557,729,042 for the 1931-32 fiscal year. Every source of revenue showed a decreased tax yield, excepting grape brandy, and cigaret papers and tubes. And the "corner" is not yet in sight.

HILL FOLK

(LORI PETRI.)

I thought of greeting people who had sucked
The sturdy sap of pines into their veins,
Had dyed their dreams in mountain dawns, and
plucked
A silver speech from lisping forest rains.

I thought to find the fair fruits of a pact
Between mankind and mountain, sire and so[n]
But battle was the blunt and bitter fact,
And always, everywhere, the hills had won.

The redwood roots had fattened on their fles[h]
Till it was withered bark on knotted boles.
The leaping streams had left a tangled mesh
Of broken drift and dark silt in their souls.
The wide-armed winds had whipped their brit[tle]
words
To earth, like shattered leaves or crumpled bir[ds]
—University California Chronicle.

"While it is illuminating to see how enviro[n]ment molds men, it is absolutely essential th[at] men regard themselves as molders of their e[n]vironment."—Lippman.

"How idle a boast, after all, is the immortali[ty] of a name!"—Irving.

Grizzly Bear

SEPTEMBER — THE ONLY OFFICIAL PUBLICATION OF THE NATIVE SONS AND DAUGHTERS OF THE GOLDEN WEST — 1932

ADMISSION DAY (September 9) ANNUAL, Featuring

GENERAL NEWS OF INTEREST CONCERNING ALL CALIFORNIA, and ORDERS NATIVE SONS and NATIVE DAUGHTERS

Price: 15 Cents

"What hath been written shall remain, nor be erased nor written o'er again. The future only remains for thee; take heed, and ponder well what that shall be."

The Grizzly Bear Magazine

The ALL California Monthly

OWNED, CONTROLLED, PUBLISHED BY
GRIZZLY BEAR PUBLISHING CO.,
(Incorporated)
COMPOSED OF NATIVE SONS.
HERMAN C. LICHTENBERGER, Pres.
JOHN T. NEWELL RAY HOWARD
WM. I. TRAEGER LORENZO F. SOTO
CHAS. R. THOMAS HARRY J. LELANDE
ARTHUR A. SCHMIDT, Vice-Pres.
BOARD OF DIRECTORS

CLARENCE M. HUNT
General Manager and Editor

OFFICIAL ORGAN AND THE
ONLY OFFICIAL PUBLICATION OF
THE NATIVE SONS AND THE
NATIVE DAUGHTERS GOLDEN WEST.

ISSUED FIRST EACH MONTH.
FORMS CLOSE 20th MONTH.
ADVERTISING RATES ON APPLICATION.

SAN FRANCISCO OFFICE:
N.S.G.W. BLDG., 414 MASON ST., RM. 302
(Office Grand Secretary N.S.G.W.)
Telephone: Kearney 1223
SAN FRANCISCO, CALIFORNIA

PUBLICATION OFFICE:
309-15 WILCOX BLDG., 2nd AND SPRING,
Telephone: VAndike 6234
LOS ANGELES, CALIFORNIA

(Entered as second-class matter May 29, 1918, at the Postoffice at Los Angeles, California, under the act of August 24, 1912.)

PUBLISHED REGULARLY SINCE MAY 1907
VOL. LI WHOLE NO. 305

GRIZZLY GROWLS

(CLARENCE M. HUNT.)

SEPTEMBER 9, 1850, MILLARD FILLmore, President of the United States of America, attached his signature to "An Act for the Admission of California into the Union," passed by the Senate and the House of Representatives during the first ssion of the Thirty-first Congress, and Califrnia became one of the Sisterhood of States. nd so, Friday, September 9, 1932, will be the ghty-second anniversary of that momentous vent in the history of the State of California.

In California, the date, September 9, is known, nd in the state statutes is referred to, as Adission Day. In 1888, the State Legislature deared the day one of holiday, when all public hools and all offices under state jurisdiction ust close. It is a day when, in memory of ose sturdy American Pioneers who made posble the California of today, every place of busiess should close and every building should be lorned with the Flag of the United States of merica and the California (State) Bear Flag. the history of California, Admission Day ocpies a like position to that of Independence ay in the history of these United States. It is sociated, exclusively, with the American era in e romantic and resourceful history of Califora, and not with either the Spanish or the Mexan eras. In any and every observance of the y true to history, the American Pioneers—eir customs, songs and dances—alone will be atured.

Referring to the Eighteenth Amendment to e Constitution of the United States, the Presient, in his address of acceptance of re-nominaon, said: "There has been a spread of disreect not only for this law, but for all laws, rave dangers of practical nullification of the onstitution, a degeneration in municipal govnment and an increase in subsidized crime and olence." He also said he "cannot consent to e continuation of this regime," and so, he vors giving the states the right to deal with e liquor problem, but contends there shall be return to the saloon system.

He neglected to say the "spread of disrespect" mainly the result of public officials violating eir oaths of office and openly ignoring the ighteenth Amendment, and, what is indeed sad, carefully avoided citing the manifold good ohibition has accomplished! The contention at there shall be no return of the saloon is aught but pre-election propaganda, for, when e Federal Government grants to the states the ght to regulate the liquor traffic, the states one will stipulate how, when and where liquor ay be dispensed, if at all, within their several oundaries!

The President practically expresses the opinn, therefore, that, because there "is in large ctions an increasing illegal traffic in liquor," e Federal Government should not choose to mpel respect for and compliance with the Conitution, but that the Constitution should be nended to satisfy those who disrespect the onstitution and defy the Government. Ye ds! where is this nation drifting? Had Abraam Lincoln been of that opinion, slavery would day be within the law in these United States America!

California has an enormous deficit, and so, llars are monthly rebated by state employes ceiving small paychecks and pennies by those ceiving larger ones. Yes, sir! To be consisnt and help clear away the red, every departent operates at a minimum of expense; in fact, penurious. And how! As proof, here's the st-sheet of furnishings for the executive offices the state building just recently opened in Los ngeles. The data, from the office of the state ntroller, was accompanied by this notation: Pursuant to your letter of August 5th I am enosing herewith such items of expense as are operly to be allocated to the furnishing and uipment of the Governor's Office in the State uilding at Los Angeles."

One 18x32 Oriental rug, $1,615; 3 pairs blue lvet drapes, $325; Georgian walnut desk, 50; Georgian walnut swivel chair (upholered in silk and velvet), $170; two arm chairs ame), $306; oak hand-carved cabinet, $200; ecial oak hand-carved flagholder, $85; hand-carved walnut table, $132; waste basket, $17; solid walnut secretary's chair (silk and velvet upholstered), $22.75; walnut arm chair (same), $192.60; wall cabinet serving table, $51.40; davenport (down back and cushions), $192.80; club chair (same), $94.40; coffee table, $35; porcelain enamel refrigerator, $150. Total, a mere $4,138.95.

California paid the bill, of course,—from tax funds. Commendably conservative, is it not, considering that the treasury is in the red and that thousands of citizens are unable to pay their taxes! Oh, yes, there's the bathroom, also, attached to those executive offices. The partitions and the plumbing just had to be changed, and suitable knickknacks had to be installed. While the state controller could give no definite figures, other reliable sources report this "extra" cost the taxpayers an additional small sum—$4,350.

Arthur Evans, writing from Kansas City, Missouri, to the San Francisco "Chronicle" anent investigation of the Federal Farm Board by a congressional committee, said: "As to farm relief, it appeared from the evidence that the farmer has been relieved of nearly everything but his shirt." That was written July 25. By now, the dirt-farmer should have been successfully separated from his shirt.

According to the Federal Census Director, the 1930 census showed California had 251,252 homemakers gainfully employed away from home. A homemaker is defined as that woman member of the family who is responsible for the care of the home and family. Does not that lamentable record account, in no small measure, for the constantly increasing number of divorces and juvenile delinquents, and the decreasing number of small-home owners and births? And, too, there is no denying the fact that those gainfully-employed homemakers keep thousands of able-bodied men, anxious to work, out of employment.

SAN FRANCISCO

(BETTY L. WHITSELL.)

Once Yerba Buena Cove
A city built of tents
In forty-eight
A wind-blown mass of canvas huts
Conglomerate.
Quite lost in fog and sand
Yet fluttering with hope
And mad desire—
A cactus budding into bloom
Thorny attire.

Chaparral, sage-brush
A wilderness of hills
Dense fogs at night
Queer sounds of foreign emigrants
In wretched plight.
Amazing, tattered town
Where conquering youth had come
With stoic eye
To work or scheme for glorious gold
In camps near by.

Commanding was the site
A natural harbor there
For ships to freight
Six hundred vessels that first year
Through Golden Gate.
Saloons, resorts, black crime
Grew with the shabby tents
A hideous dream
Until the Vigilantes formed
And held supreme.

Advancing with the years
Strong rock replaced the tents
Quite permanent
Important industries grew
And government.
Today metropolis
Surprising, beautiful stands
All bathed in light
The cactus flower is in full bloom
Tis man's delight.

(This contribution to The Grizzly Bear is from Betty L. Whitsell of Burlingame, San Mateo County.)

American rubber-shoe manufacturers are howling because the Japs are dumping rubber shoes in this country at a price less than the cost of production here, and, of course, they now want protection from the Federal Government. For once, more power to the Japs!

The manufacturers of this nation have, as a rule, opposed California every inch of the way in its campaign against the Japs. When their pocketbooks are affected, however, the yellow-film is removed from their eyes. Eventually, this nation will have a belly full—not a full dinner pail—of Japs, and the sooner the better.

The Governor of New York, writing recently in a magazine, criticises the President of the United States because the American public have been fleeced out of billions of dollars, and says: "These three forms of scandalously unsound speculation [watered stocks, unsound foreign loans, fake investments] could and should have been instantly suppressed by straightforward comment from Washington."

Most of the scandalously unsound speculation originates in New York State, where the financial highboys habitat and have their offices. Has Albany done anything to suppress the speculation or to control the operators? Criticism of the national by the Empire State administration is, in this instance and under existing conditions, a case of the pot calling the kettle black!

Charged with participation in a lottery, several officials of a nation-wide fraternal order have been indicted. The complained-of racket has been in unhindered operation for many moons, and it has been carried on through the United States mails.

How come the Government just now has discovered its operation, and why were the officials of another nation-wide fraternal order, which just recently most successfully conducted a similar lottery, not included in the indictment?

During the first six months of this year, there were 808 bank suspensions, involving a total of $524,354,000 in deposits, in the United States. In Canada, there was one bank failure in 1923, and none since. Draw your own conclusions.

The soldier-bonus agitation is waxing quite warm, and it appears the facts are ignored by those demanding immediate payment. In 1924, the Federal Congress authorized the issuance to World War veterans of adjusted service or "bonus" certificates, dated January 1, 1925, and payable January 1, 1945, or at death of the holder.

The demand for payment now, is being made twelve-and-more years before the certificates mature. And demand is made also that payment be on the basis of the face value, rather than the present value, of the certificates. The demand is unjust and unreasonable.

The revival of gold mining in California by jobless prospectors has made a new demand upon the Federal Power Commission, says a statement issued by the commission August 7. Placer deposits along the rivers in the old Gold Belt commonly come within the boundaries of power-site reservations, which makes action by the commission a necessary preliminary to the granting of mineral location or entry by the General Land Office.

Inasmuch as generally the use of the withdrawn land for power development cannot be expected in the near-future, and the proposed mining of these gold-bearing gravels is planned for the present season, there is no conflict between the two uses. On this basis, the commission can make a finding that will permit the gold-mining operation to begin without delay with full protection of the future value of the same area for power development.

An area of 620 acres of placer lands was thus recently restored to mineral entry by the commission, and another 110 acres will be acted upon this month. The localities mentioned in the orders restoring these lands to mineral entry—Yuba River and American River—bring to mind the stories of pioneer mining days.

Under the terms of the emergency relief and regular appropriation bills passed by the last Federal Congress, $3,584,615 will be spent during the 1932-33 fiscal year in the national forests of California for the construction and improvement of forest highways, roads, trails, bridges and fire prevention projects, according to report of S. B. Show, chief of the California Region, United States Forest Service. This is the largest sum ever received in one year by the local forest service for such work, and will furnish employment for large numbers of men.

"The United States Forest Service," says Show, "welcomes the opportunity to give sub-

(Continued on Page 21)

CALIFORNIA'S STATE FAIR

THE $10,000,000 CALIFORNIA STATE Fair show, opening in Sacramento City September 3 and continuing through the 10th, with its fifteen centers of interest will surpass in interest any three-ring circus that ever appeared, according to Secretary-Manager Charles W. Paine, who announces that more than half the counties of the state will exhibit their products. Last year 350,000 passed through the turnstiles, an all-time record for the eight-day show, and this year's mark is expected to exceed even that record.

Directors of the fourteen departments report entries in larger number than ever before. The displays of livestock, horticultural and agricultural products will be of high class this year because of the banner year on the farms.

The national classic, the California horse show, heads the list of entertainment features in many ways. Thousands annually jam the huge arena each evening to see the thoroughbreds go through their paces and strive to carry off prizes aggregating $22,240.

The main Horticultural Building will house the county exhibits and many commercial displays. Ten counties will be awarded trophies for the best county and feature exhibits, and Director D. Eyman Huff of Orange, in charge of this department, believes the class this year will be of such excellence as to exceed those of previous years.

Twenty-five thousand square feet of floor space will be devoted to displays of farm equipment, implements and machinery, housed in the modern Machinery Building. Thomas E. Anderson of Calexico is director in charge.

Educational exhibits and displays will be entered by pupils from 1,000 California schools, and Director Ellis Franklin of Colfax predicts that the class of work shown by the youngsters will be higher than ever.

The best horse racing in twenty-five years is forecast by Manager Paine, a veteran fair official, with harness and running horses competing each afternoon for purses aggregating $34,000. There will be thirty-nine races, with two added stake races.

California artists will exhibit their paintings and drawings in the Womens Building for prizes totaling $1,350. These exhibits will be by invitation only. Housewives will be interested in the domestic arts and science displays, for which hundreds of prizes are offered. These will consist of articles made on the sewing machine, embroidery and kindred displays, and food.

Showing last year for the first time in the new building, the poultry and rabbit show, directed by Harold J. McCurry of Sacramento, scored one of the biggest successes. Satisfaction with the new, well-lighted quarters was so pronounced that he expects the show quarters to be overcrowded at this year's exposition.

An opportunity to view $2,000,000 worth of livestock at a glance, in a vista through the new Livestock Pavilions, will be afforded the visitors. Blooded horses and cattle, sheep and swine always attract major attention at the State Fair. Premiums and prizes for this department total nearly $40,000. Fred H. Bixby of Long Beach is director in charge.

The Sacramento Valley Retail Grocers Association has taken 15,000 square feet of space to display food products of the state and the valley. Everything which enters into the production and manufacture of food will be shown in this department.

Spectacular circus acts and features have been engaged by Secretary Paine and will be shown in front of the grandstand every afternoon and evening. Each evening, also, there will be a display of fireworks, many set pieces carrying out the idea of the Washington bicentennial. Concerts, dancing and vaudeville, in addition to "Midway" attractions, provide an extensive amusement program.

Boxing bouts, wrestling matches and a "rolleo" will add to the fun for those who enjoy sports of an athletic nature. The "rolleo" is a new feature this year and consists of log-rolling contests and stunts on wood balls and blocks in a huge plunge in front of the grandstand. Pete Hooper and Sam Harris, world champions, will challenge allcomers in log-rolling contests.

A huge farmer's picnic, to which Will Rogers has been invited as the special guest of Governor James Rolph, is expected to draw 50,000 farmers and their lunch baskets of fried chicken.

Popular features again this year will be the spelling contests for elementary and high school students and adults. The winner of the latter contest, which is open to all, will be eligible to contest in the national contest at the Chicago world's fair in 1933.

A contest for the honor of representing California at the Chicago fair as "Miss California" will be staged. The event is open to any girl or woman in California who has sufficient knowledge of the state, and the attractive personality necessary to successfully meet the public as California's official representative. Entries should visit their local chamber of commerce or grange, or write direct to Miss California Committee, State Fair Grounds, Sacramento, California.

INTERESTED IN STATE'S YOUTH

PETER T. CONMY

(Chairman N.S.G.W. Education Committee.)

AT THE 1932 GRAND PARLOR OF THE Order of Native Sons of the Golden West legislation was enacted committing the organization to an interest in public education in California. For many years back the National Education Association has been holding an annual observance of education, the second week of November, and asking patriotic and fraternal societies to hold suitable programs. In response to that movement Golden Gate Parlor No. 29 of San Francisco last year sponsored a program of education. Encouraged by the response, the Parlor's delegates presented two resolutions to the Grand Parlor and both were accepted. One endorsed the observance of National Education Week, and the other provided for establishment of a Grand Parlor Committee on Education, the duties of which are to encourage and supervise the holding of education week programs by Subordinate Parlors, to study educational affairs in the state and to report to the Grand Parlor on the state of public education in California.

The Order of Native Sons of the Golden West was founded to perpetuate the history and the traditions of the Pioneers; to remind future generations of the valor and virtue of the men and the women of long ago; to promote patriotism, love of country and good citizenship. An order with the broad foundation of the Native Sons, a society that is so linked with the destiny of California, must of its very nature be interested in the youth of the state. The schoolboy of today will be the applicant for admission to the fraternity tomorrow. More important than that, the child of today will be the citizen of tomorrow. Citizenship depends on training, and on guidance. In the days of our fathers, training and guidance were given in abundance in the homes, planted in all corners of the state by the Pioneers.

Today, the breakdown of the home,—especially in the cities, where there are numerous distractions interfering with the training that children should receive from their parents,—leaves thousands of the younger generation with no source of wholesome guidance, save that which they receive in school. The school is no longer an institution where the "three Rs" are taught. It has transcended the aims and the purposes of the "little red schoolhouse." It is today an institution entrusted with the imparting of the rudiments of knowledge, with the training of good citizenship, and with the stimulation of morality. To thousands of children, it takes the place of the old-fashioned home. Although lamentable, it is none the less true, that thousands of boys and girls who come from broken homes receive their only thought of higher things in the school.

For all of these reasons, the school of today is a tremendously important institution. It is an institution that, like the Order of Native Sons, is very closely linked to the welfare of California. We who guard California's past are also interested in her future, and therefore the Grand Parlor is attempting to direct the minds of the brethren toward solicitation for the welfare of the schools. Until the home is re-established upon a secure footing, we must look to the school as the leading social institution.

Today, the schools of California are facing a crisis. On the one hand, they are being asked to extend their activities, to do more and more for the people. On the other hand, there are those who begrudge them sufficiency of money to meet ever-increasing costs. There are also those who are fostering the expansion of the school, and those who would restrict its operations to the three fundamental subjects, reading, writing and arithmetic. There are those who would remove children with criminal tendencies, and those who believe that it would be better to let these misfits remain among the other children, to outgrow their viciousnes There are many conflicting opinions about t control and the management of our schools which we, as Native Sons of the Golden We and guardians of California's historic destin should be greatly interested.

To this end and purpose, the Grand Parl Committee on Education [Peter T. Conm Charles R. Boden, A. J. Cloud, George F. M Noble and Henry G. Bodkin] asks all Subord nate Parlors to hold, during the second week November, a celebration in honor of Nation Education Week. It is suggested that they e list the co-operation of the local Native Daug ter Parlor, and that they secure, as far as th are able to do so, musical talent from the schoo themselves. The committee will gladly furni information as to the type of speaker suitab to the occasion. It asks all members of t Order to lend their hearty co-operation to th movement for the welfare of the public school the boys and the girls of California.

DEDICATION SANTA BARBARA JUNIOR HIGH SCHOOL MEMORABLE OCCASIO

Santa Barbara—Under the auspices of San Barbara Parlor No. 116 N.S.G.W., the officers the Grand Parlor dedicated September 19 th city's splendid new junior high school. An e cellent program, arranged by the Parlor's de cation committee, District Deputy A. C. Din more and Clifford F. Rizor, was presented the commodious school auditorium, which w filled to capacity. Officers and members of San Barbara and Reina del Mar Parlor No. 1 N.D.G.W. were present in force, and acted as reception committee. Seated upon the platfor were men and women prominently identifi with the civic and fraternal life of Californi Queen City.

C. Wesley McCormick, president Santa Ba bara Parlor, presided, and the program includ an invocation by Rev. Tom B. Clark; vocal sele tions by the B.P.O.E. Glee Club, Dr. Harry Ha cock director, the Aeolians,—Roderick V. Jac son, W. Lloyd Taylor, Leslie B. Jackson, Wilfr Woodburn—Ruth E. Rizor accompanist, a Mrs. Lois Aldridge Johnson (Lugonia Parlor N 241 N.D.G.W.), accompanied by Leslie A. M loche (Grand Organist N.S.G.W.); addresses Dr. P. C. Means, president Education Boar Harvey T. Nielson, mayor Santa Barbara, Pa E. Stewart, superintendent city schools, Mrs. R. Stow, president Parent-Teacher Associatio Justice Emmet Seawell, Grand First Vice-pre dent N.S.G.W., and Seth Millington, Grand Pr ident N.S.G.W.

The dedicatory ceremonies were conducted Grand President Millington, who was assist by Junior Past Grand President Dr. Frank Gonzalez, Grand First Vice-president Seawe Grand Second Vice-president Chas. A. Koen Grand Third Vice-president Harmon D. Skil and Grand Secretary John T. Regan. Others attendance were Grand Treasurer John A. C otto and Grand Trustee Eldred L. Meyer of t Native Sons, Grand Trustee Jane Vick, Superv ing Deputy Anna E. McCaughey and Depu Vera Pacheco of the Native Daughters.

Following the dedication, Reina del Mar Pa lor N.D.G.W. was hostess at a most delightful i formal luncheon, enjoyed by some one hundre Mrs. Fred Acres, acting president, preside Father Victor offered a blessing, various perso ages were introduced and some made brief r marks, and pleasing vocal numbers were re dered. Santa Barbara's renowned Old Spani Days Fiesta, in which the Natives of that ci had a most prominent part, was in progre Following the historical parade of the previo day they sponsored a reception in honor of t old families and visitors. Mrs. A. C. Warr and Paul C. Sweetser, chairmen, respectively, the history committee of Reina del Mar a Santa Barbara Parlors, were in charge.—C.M.

COUNTIES' EXPOSITIONS.

Expositions featuring the resources of sever California counties will be held during Septe ber, as follows:

Fresno County Fair at Fresno City, 13th 18th.

Shasta County Fair at Shasta Town, 16th 19th.

Los Angeles County Fair at Pomona, 16th 25th.

Lassen County Fair at Susanville, 17th a 18th.

Glenn County Fair at Orland, 19th to 24th.

Tulare County Fair at Tulare City, 20th 24th.

Kern County Fair at Bakersfield, 21st to 25t

San Diego County Fair at San Diego City, 27 to October 1.

Monterey County Fair at Monterey City, 29 to October 2.

SAN FRANCISCO

SAN FRANCISCO INVITES YOU

SAN FRANCISCO'S NATIVE SONS AND Native Daughters, aided by the citizens generally, have arranged an elaborate program for the statewide Admission Day Fiesta, Friday, September 9, in celebration of the eighty-second anniversary of California's admittance to the Union. The arrangements have been made by a committee officered by the following: Joseph J. McShane, general chairman; Lloyd J. Doering and Mrs. Agnes Curry, vice-chairmen; Harold J. Regan, secretary; Catharine H. Dolly, assistant secretary; Chas. A. Koenig, treasurer; Virgil Orengo, sergeant-at-arms. Honorary chairmen include Angelo J. Rossi, Mayor of San Francisco; Seth Millington, Grand President N.S.G.W., and Mrs. Anna Mixon Armstrongo, Grand President N.D.G.W. San Francisco invites you to join in the festivities.

THE PROGRAM.

The main event on the program is the Admission Day parade, at 10:30 a. m., detailed otherwheres in this number of The Grizzly Bear. Grandstands along the line of march provide 18,000 reserved seats, selling at fifty cents each. Reservations may be made at the office of the Grand Secretary N.S.G.W., 414 Mason street.

At 2 p.m., the $5,000,000 War Memorial Building, Van Ness avenue and Fulton street, will be dedicated by the San Francisco War Memorial Trustees.

At 8 p.m., a grand ball and pageant, free to all, will be held in the Civic Auditorium. During the first hour of the evening a fashion show and girl review will be featured.

JOSEPH J. McSHANE, Grand Trustee N.S.G.W., Chairman Admission Day Committee.

To arouse interest in Admission Day and California history, Lewis F. Byington, Past Grand President N.S.G.W., has been broadcasting weekly, over NBC stations, a series of talks on "Romantic California." The evening of September 8, a script of California's history, interspersed with appropriate vocal and instrumental music, will be broadcast over the same stations.

"OPEN HOUSE" HOSPITALITY.

The evening of September 8 and throughout the afternoon and evening of Admission Day, Native Son and Native Daughter Parlors will maintain headquarters where dancing and entertainment will prevail for the enjoyment of all. One of the chief delights of an Admission Day celebration is to visit these "open houses," where true California hospitality holds sway. The list of headquarters follows:

Alameda County N.S.G.W. and N.D.G.W. Parlors—Knights Columbus Hall, 150 Golden Gate avenue.

California Parlor No. 1 N.S.G.W.—Native Sons Building, 414 Mason street.

Pacific Parlor No. 10 N.S.G.W.—Bellevue Hotel, Geary and Taylor streets.

Golden Gate Parlor No. 29 N.S.G.W.—Scottish Rite Hall, Van Ness avenue and Sutter street.

El Dorado Parlor No. 52 N.S.G.W.—Native Sons Building, 414 Mason street.

Stanford Parlor No. 76 N.S.G.W.—Fairmount Hotel.

Niantic Parlor No. 105 N.S.G.W.—Native Sons Building, 414 Mason street.

Hesperian Parlor No. 137 N.S.G.W.—Native Sons Building, 414 Mason street.

South San Francisco Parlor No. 157 N.S.G.W.—Eagles Hall, 273 Golden Gate avenue.

Marshall Parlor No. 202 N.S.G.W.—Native Sons Building, 414 Mason street.

Guadalupe Parlor No. 231 N.S.G.W.—Y.M.I. Hall, 50 Oak street.

(Continued on Page 22)

CALIFORNIA HAPPENINGS OF FIFTY YEARS AGO

Thomas R. Jones

(COMPILED EXPRESSLY FOR THE GRIZZLY BEAR.)

ADMISSION DAY, SEPTEMBER 9, 1882, the thirty-second anniversary of California's admittance to statehood, was declared by proclamation of Governor George C. Perkins a legal holiday, and observed generally as such. At Sacramento City, the Society of California Pioneers and Sacramento Parlor No. 3 N.S.G.W. had a joint picnic at which I. N. Hoag of the Pioneers and Charles N. Post of the Natives delivered addresses, and Ed. F. Cohn and his Golden West quartet sang.

The San Francisco Society of California Pioneers had a picnic-barbecue, with orations and dancing, at San Rafael, Marin County. The Native Son Parlors of San Francisco and Alameda County joined forces at a largely attended picnic in Scheutzen Park, Alameda. M. A. Dorn was the orator. A number of minor celebrations were held in other places by Pioneers and Natives.

September was a political cleanup month, parties which had not completed nominations for county offices, and citizens whose isms had not been satisfactorily considered by the two dominant parties, holding conventions. The Greenbackers and the Prohibitionists met in San Francisco and put in the field state tickets headed, respectively, by T. J. McQuiddy of Mussel Slough fame and Dr. R. H. McDonald of "vinegar bitters" fame for governor. The farmers of the lowlands, incensed because neither of the major parties even mentioned "slickens" in their platforms, called a state convention, but the net results of the four-day gabfest were an anti-debris resolution and a $2.50 assessment levied on each of the many who attended.

The Republicans of San Francisco split, and each faction, one dubbed the "Duffers" and the other the "Bluffers," held a municipal convention. J. B. Campbell, Republican nominee for Sierra County sheriff, while on his campaign tour got into an argument at Randolph with Citizen Stubbs who, to terminate the words-battle, drew a pistol and killed Campbell. Wm. Whadden, Republican candidate for Alameda County sheriff, died suddenly September 10.

The annual California State Fair opened at Sacramento City September 11. Racing was the main attraction. Rain fell the fifth day of the exposition and reduced the attendance. The receipts were $17,097. The fair drew to the Capital City so many touts, gamblers, etc., who expected to make dishonest dollars, that the police force of a dozen men gave up the effort to have a "closed town," and vice was first endured and then embraced.

Other September fairs, all well attended and successful, were: Sonoma County, at Petaluma, 1st; Northern District, at Chico, Butte County, 4th; Golden Gate, at Oakland, Alameda County, 4th; San Joaquin Valley, at Stockton, 19th; Plumas County, at Greenville, 19th; Lake County, at Lakeport, 27th.

The 135,000-acre Foster rancho in south Los Angeles County and north San Diego County was bought by Daniel Murphy and O. Livermore of Santa Clara County for $500,000.

Fourteen steamboats were plying the Sacramento River, hauling the wheat crop to Port Costa, Contra Costa County; they handled an average of 100,000 sacks a week. Dr. Glenn harvested 400,000 centals of wheat valued at $640,000 on his Colusa County domain.

Statistics showed there were forty-four distilleries in Los Angeles County handling grapes. They made 200,000 gallons of brandy annually and paid a tax of $190,000 to the Federal Government.

Philander Bell, San Diego County homesteader, in his affidavit before the land commissioner stated he was the father of thirty-two children. Although a widower, he was willing to again marry and increase his brood.

The first was the hottest September day on record—140 degrees in the sun of the valleys. The first rain of the season came September 15, the precipitation being .61 of an inch.

Samuel Hoover, Cosumnes River rancher, September 8 drove through the streets of Sacramento City with his crop of hops loaded upon four wagons drawn by twelve belled mules. Atop the bales of each wagon was a ten-gallon keg of beer, and above that the Flag of the United States of America. He had sold his 30,000 pounds of hops at fifty cents per pound and was more than $10,000 ahead on the venture.

A boom in mining stocks started suddenly September 1 in California street, San Francisco, and the list advanced more than a hundred percent for several days. Finally the inevitable break came, and the rainbow chasers were sad.

The gold mining excitement in San Gabriel Canyon, Los Angeles County, continued and the influx of prospectors increased.

The committee to select the site for a state-owned soldiers home reported a 900-acre tract of land about nine miles from Napa City had been secured.

A lone highwayman September 17 held up the stage from Oregon State near Redding, Shasta County. He carried away three sacks of U.S. mail.

Mrs. Yuidora Forster, a sister of Pio Pico, former governor, died at Los Angeles City September 18, aged 71.

Lee On Law, grand master of California Chinese Masons, died September 16 at San Francisco. His funeral procession, over two miles in length and headed by a sixty-piece brass band was viewed by thousands as it passed up Market street.

William Clark, a Scotchman and pioneer Nevada County miner, was found dead near You Bet. In 1849 he set out afoot from Pike County, Missouri, trundling a wheelbarrow, which contained his effects. It took him two years to make the trip to California, and it is said he walked every inch of the way.

September was another month of disastrous fires. Great losses resulted from forest and brush blazes in Sacramento, Siskiyou, San Mateo, Lake and Alameda Counties. Other conflagrations, with monetary losses, included:

Red Bluff, Tehama County, several stores and residences, $20,000; Chico, Butte County, hotel and several houses, $50,000; Port Costa, Contra Costa County, tannery, $15,000; Merced City, hotel and several houses, $20,000; Columbia, Tuolumne County, Chinese theater and other buildings, $10,000; Clipper Gap, Placer County, smelting works, $150,000; San Francisco, several buildings, $110,000; Sacramento City, Chinatown structures, $20,000; Susanville, Lassen County, fifty-seven buildings, $200,000; Gridley, Butte County, seven buildings, $10,000.

A. J. Hughett came to California in February, located in Farmington, San Joaquin County, and then sent for his fiancee, Miss Sarah Kelly, to come from Montgomery County, Missouri, and become his wife. She arrived at Sacramento City September 19 and was met at the depot by Hughett, who insisted they go to Farmington for the ceremony, but she insisted it be performed there and then. The dispute continued until Miss Kelly hired a hack, drove to the courthouse to procure a marriage license, and returned with a peace justice. She then hustled A. J. into the depot waitingroom and, in the presence of a gaping crowd of idlers, the knot was tied.

Derailment of a South Coast railroad train near San Leandro, Alameda County, September 11 took the lives of Fireman Driscoll and Brakeman Daley.

Claude Raus, 12 years of age, was September 11 dragged to his death through the streets of Santa Barbara City by a runaway horse.

Ten-year-old Ira Wilder was killed near Grass Valley, Nevada County, September 28 by the accidental discharge of a shotgun.

Assistant Fire Chief Wm. Brady of San Francisco was killed September 20 while driving to a fire.

At Tehachapi, Kern County, Wm. Fickert entered the store of Henry Pauli September 30 to buy a pair of boots. Not liking the quality offered, he killed Pauli.

James W. Sharon, a prospector, started to hike across the desert from Calico, San Bernardino County, to Kern County, September 20. A few days later his body was found, he having perished from thirst.

Robert Patterson, 9 years of age, September 26 fell 200 feet down Telegraph Hill, San Francisco, and was killed.

W. L. Williams, a '49er formerly of Marysville, Yuba County, but now a San Diego City businessman, was accidentally killed in his flour mill there September 27.

Grandeur Unexcelled—Mountain grandeur is available for equestrians and hikers with the opening of the trail to Mount Whitney, 14,49[illegible] feet in elevation, highest peak in continental United States.

Floral Exhibit—The third annual exhibit of the Dahlia and Floral Society of Long Beach, Los Angeles County, will be held September [illegible] and 9, in the Municipal Auditorium.

"The best portion of a good man's life: his little nameless, unremembered acts of kindness and of love."—Wordsworth.

"MARK OUR LANDMARKS"

A SECOND MESSAGE TO GARCIA

Chester F. Gannon

(HISTORIOGRAPHER N.S.G.W.)

ELBERT HUBBARD IMMORTALIZED Lieutenant Rowan's exploit in the Spanish-American War when the lieutenant carried a message to General Garcia of the Cuban forces. Had no literary man like Elbert Hubbard taken note of the exploit and publicised it by an article entitled "A Message to Garcia," Rowan's feat would have merely been one of many performed by Americans in the Spanish-American War.

It was similar literary publicity which immortalized the fighting ability and valor of the Marines in the World War. Their exploits were given publicity by competent literary men. Infantry organizations, which accomplished just as much in the way of service and valor, are practically unknown today to the American people. All on account of a lack of publicity.

There was no publicity man in California in the year 1846. Therefore a performance equal, even superior, to that of Lieutenant Rowan appears to have passed unnoticed through the passing years. In the case of Rowan, whether or not he had found Garcia, perhaps would have made little difference in history.

However, the case the writer wishes to call attention to was that of the exploit in 1846 of Lieutenant Archibald Gillespie of the Marine Corps. This young naval officer left Monterey to deliver a message to John C. Fremont "somewhere in the Sacramento Valley." Gillespie had never been in the West before. He had only a vague idea that Fremont was somewhere in the broad Sacramento Valley. His was a mission from the War Department at Washington to deliver a message to Fremont "somewhere in the Sacramento Valley."

With this scant information he set out in an unknown country beset by known and unknown dangers to deliver messages to Fremont. In addition to the written communication Gillespie carried, he had memorized verbal instructions to Fremont, and in substance and effect the verbal instructions were these:

"The time has come. England must not get a foothold. We must be first. Act discreetly but positively." In other words, Fremont was given semi-official instructions to seize California for the United States—if the opportunity presented itself. Not being at war with Mexico, official Washington did not want to commit an overt act with that country, and adroitly hit upon the scheme of having Fremont return to Sacramento, watch, and await developments.

This he did. The rest is history, but standing out in the background of that historical event is the exploit of this young marine officer, traveling his lonely way from Monterey up into Oregon and finding the object of his search, Captain John C. Fremont. Let Fremont, in his own biography, relate the circumstances of Gillespie's entrance into his camp:

"How fate pursues a man! Thinking and ruminating over these things, I was standing alone by my camp-fire, enjoying its warmth, for the night air of early spring is chill under the shadows of the high mountains. Suddenly my ear caught the faint sound of horses' feet, and while I was watching and listening as the sounds, so strange hereabout, came nearer, there emerged from the darkness—into the circle of the firelight—two horsemen, riding slowly as though horse and man were fatigued by long traveling. In the foremost I recognized the familiar face of Neal, with a companion whom I also knew. They had ridden nearly a hundred miles in the last two days, having been sent forward by a United States officer who was on my trail with despatches for me; but Neal doubted if he would get through. After their horses had been turned into the band and they were seated by my fire, refreshing themselves with good coffee while more solid food was being prepared, Neal told me his story. The officer who was trying to overtake me was named Gillespie. He had been sent to California by the Government and had letters for delivery to me. Neal knew the great danger from Indians in this country, and his party becoming alarmed and my trail being fresh, Mr. Gillespie had sent forward Neal and Sigler upon their best horses to overtake me and inform me of his situation. They had left him on the morning of the day before, and in the two days had ridden nearly a hundred miles, and this last day had severely tried the strength of their horses. When they parted from him they had not reached the lake, and for greater safety had not kept my trail quite to the outlet, but crossed to the right bank of the river, striking my trail again on the lake shore. They had discovered Indians on my trail after they had left Gillespie, and on the upper part of the lake the Indians had tried to cut them off, and they had escaped only by the speed and strength of their horses, which Neal had brought from his own rancho. He said that in his opinion I could not reach Gillespie in time to save him, as he had with him only three men and was traveling slow." Early the next morning, Gillespie came through in safety with his important messages.

Lieutenant Archibald Gillespie can rightfully claim a place in California history. He kept the faith. He ran the course. He performed his mission.

Has any recognition ever been accorded this young officer? As far as the writer knows, his name is historically unrecorded. A monument might well have been erected near Klamath Lake, Oregon, where Fremont and Gillespie met, for there history was made. Had Gillespie not reached Fremont, he, Fremont, who was then on his way into Oregon, would undoubtedly have proceeded on eastward to Washington, and what fate would have befallen California only conjecture can touch. The name of Gillespie is another pioneer name which should be saved to California history by a monument or similar recognition.

"MARK OUR LANDMARKS"

"I hold the maxim no less applicable to public than private affairs, that honesty is always the best policy."—George Washington.

ADMISSION DAY PARADE

THE ADMISSION DAY, SEPTEMBER 9, parade in San Francisco, honoring the eighty-second anniversary of California's statehood, promises to equal in colorfulness and splendor similar pageants of the past. It is being held under the auspices of the Order of Native Sons of the Golden West, and will be directed by Grand Marshal W. Bernard O'Brien. Numerous Parlors of Native Sons and Native Daughters from all quarters of the state will participate, with their bands, drill teams, drum corps, etc. Many ingenious floats will add to the attractiveness of the display.

The parade will start at 10:30 a.m. sharp from the Ferry building, Market street and the Embarcadero, and proceed west on Market to Fulton street, along Fulton to Hyde street, south on Hyde to Grove street, west on Grove to Larkin street, north on Larkin to McAllister street, west on McAllister to Polk street, and south on Polk to Hayes street, where it will disband. A reviewing stand will be on Polk street, directly in front of the entrance to the City Hall. The makeup of the parade follows:

ADVANCE.

Mounted police. Police Chief William J. Quinn of San Francisco. San Francisco police band. San Francisco police drum corps. Platoon San Francisco policemen.

Grand Marshal W. Bernard O'Brien. Chief of Staff James L. Foley. Chief Aide Arthur J. Cleu. Director General J. Hartley Russell. Adjutant Ray B. Felton.

Aides de Camp: Emmet Hayden, R. R. Veale, Jos H. Kreig, William J. Bright, R. L. P. Bigelow, Lawrence Hart, Wm. F. Knowland, A. V. Fisher, June Longshore, John S. Ramsay, R. M. Hamb, Harry Romick, Geo. Scharetg, Julian Dresser.

Aides to Grand Marshal: Frank B. Foss, Jefferson Peyser, Frank Seamas, H. L. Sonsa, Philip Carey, Jessie H. Peterson, A. W. Graves, Thomas E. Wait, Laura Fisher, Irene Rose, Geo. J. Hans, Harry G. Williams, Jos. H. Peterson, Gus Nelson, Geo. Leydecker, Ralph A. Wait, Margaret Davies, Sue Irwin, Carmelita Luhr, Agusta Huxol, May Mead.

Autos containing: Grand President Seth Millington and other N.S.G.W. grand officers. Past Grand Presidents N.S.G.W. Grand President Anna Mixon Armstrong and other N.D.G.W. grand officers. Past Grand Presidents N.D.G.W. Past Presidents Association No. 1 N.D.G.W. James Rolph Jr., Governor of California. Angelo J. Rossi, Mayor of San Francisco. United States Senator Samuel M. Shortridge. Congresswoman Florence P. Kahn. Congressman Richard J. Welch. Officers San Francisco 1932 Admission Day Committee: Grand Trustee Joseph J. McShane, chairman; Mrs. Agnes Curry, Lloyd J. Doering, vice-chairmen; Harold J. Regan, secretary; Grand Second Vice-president Chas. A. Koenig, treasurer. Arthur T. Poheim, chairman ways and means committee. Harry W. Gaetjen, chairman parade committee. San Francisco Board Supervisors. Society California Pioneers. Ladies Auxiliary of Society Pioneers. Daughters California Pioneers. Association Pioneer Women California.

Thirtieth United States Infantry, Colonel Chas. Stone commanding. Naval Reserve, Lieutenant-Commander W. C. Tooge commanding. National Guard. California Grays, Captain Seth L. Butler commanding.

Charles J. Brennan, chief engineer San Francisco Fire Department. Platoon San Francisco firemen. Members Veteran Fire Association.

Float, birthday cake.

FIRST DIVISION.

Marshal, Elwood Fitzgerald. Aides, Vincent Hahn, Allan W. Sunkler, Judge Allen G. Norris, Helen Ring, Evelyn Palmer, Sallie Harmola. Board Supervisors Alameda County. Mayor Fred N. Morcom and other city officials of Oakland. Alameda County Parade Committee: Edward T. Schnarr (chairman), Arthur Ainger, V. L. Denlis, Mae Mead, Frank Smith, Sallie R. Thaler, Ray Burke.

W. BERNARD O'BRIEN,
Grand Marshal N.S.G.W.

Alameda County float. Oakland boys band.

Alameda No. 47 N.S. drum corps. Alameda No. 47 N.S. Halcyon No. 146 N.S. drill team. Encinal No. 156 N.D. drill team. Oakland No. 50 N.S. drum corps. Oakland No. 50 N.S. Bahia Vista No. 167 N.D. Eden No. 113 N.S. Hayward No. 122 N.D. Brooklyn No. 151 N.S. drum corps. Brooklyn No. 151 N.S. Brooklyn No. 157 N.D. Washington No. 169 N.S. Betsey Ross No. 238 N.D. Athens No. 195 N.S. Aloha No. 106 N.D. Berkeley No. 210 N.S. Bear Flag No. 151 N.D. drum corps. Bear Flag No. 151 N.D. Berkeley No. 150 N.D. Past Presidents Association No. 2 N.D. East Bay Counties Past Presidents Assembly No. 3 N.S.

SECOND DIVISION.

Marshal, Frank Roemer. Aides, Dr. J. A. Plunket, Walter Hayes, Felix Robinson, Lillian Caton, Maude Wagner, Mrs. Cardoza.

City of Oakland float.

Piedmont No. 120 N.S. band. Piedmont No. 120 N.S. drum corps. Piedmont No. 120 N.S. Piedmont No. 87 N.D. Estudillo No. 223 N.S. El Cereso No. 207 N.D. Claremont No. 240 N.S. drum corps. Claremont No. 240 N.S. Argonaut No. 166 N.D. drill team. Argonaut No. 166 N.D. Fruitvale No. 252 N.S. drum corps. Fruitvale No. 252 N.S. Fruitvale No. 177 N.D. drill team. Fruitvale No. 177 N.D. Angelita No. 32 N.D. Wisteria No. 127 N.S. Pleasanton No. 244 N.S. Pleasanton No. 237 N.D. Niles No. 250 N.S. Laura Loma No. 182 N.D.

THIRD DIVISION.

Band. San Jose No. 22 N.S. San Jose No. 81 N.D. Vendome No. 100 N.D. Observatory No. 177 N.S. Santa Clara No. 100 N.S. Float. Menlo No. 185 N.S. Menlo No. 211 N.D. El Carmelo No. 256 N.S. drum corps. El Carmelo No. 256 N.S. El Carmelo No. 181 N.D. El Carmelo No. 181 N.D. drill team.

FOURTH DIVISION.

Band. Stockton No. 7 N.S. Joaquin No. 5 N.D. Lodi No. 18 N.S. Ivy No. 88 N.D. Mount Tamalpais No. 64 N.S. drum corps. Mount Tamalpais No. 64 N.S. Marinita No. 198 N.D. drill team. Marinita No. 198 N.D. Tamelpa No. 231 N.D. drum corps. Tamelpa No. 231 N.D. La Bandera No. 110 N.D. drill team. La Bandera No. 110 N.D. Sea Point No. 158 N.S. drum corps. Sea Point No. 158 N.S. Sea Point No. 196 N.D.

FIFTH DIVISION.

Marshal, Wesley Colgan.

Napa No. 62 N.S. drum corps. Napa No. 62 N.S. Eschol No. 16 N.D. Santa Rosa No. 28 N.S. Santa Rosa No. 217 N.D. Float. Petaluma No. 27 N.S. Petaluma No. 222 N.D. drill team. Petaluma No. 222 N.D. Glen Ellen No. 102 N.S. Sonoma No. 111 N.S. Sonoma No. 209 N.D. Sebastopol No. 143 N.S.

SIXTH DIVISION.

Marshal, Walter Bammann. Aides, Bertha Edler, Ann Dippel, Helen T. Mann.

San Francisco municipal band. San Francisco parade committee. San Francisco float.

(Continued on Page 22)

LOS ANGELES CITY AND COUNTY

"THERE IS NO SUBSTITUTE FOR MEMBERSHIP"

SETH MILLINGTON OF GRIDLEY, BUTTE County, Grand President of the Order of Native Sons of the Golden West, spent several days in Los Angeles last month talking over affairs of the Order with members in the southland interested in its welfare. The initial gathering was in the nature of a reception, under the auspices of Ramona Parlor No. 109, Friday, August 5.

The Grand President outlined his plans for the Order's advancement. They include, among others, a new ritual, and removal from the governing laws of obstacles which keep out a vast number who desire to be in. He believes the founders intended the Order should be a history society, and he favors its operation as such. He stressed the undeniable assertion, "There is no substitute for membership!" His forceful address won hearty applause, and approval of his suggestions was voiced by Past Grand President John T. Newell, Senator R. F. DelValle, Grand Trustee Eldred L. Meyer, William J. Hunsaker, Frank Adams and other speakers. Among the large number in attendance were Past Grand President William I. Traeger, Grand Organist Leslie Maloche, District Deputies Albert Cron, Walter Baskerville, Edwin Baldwin, Howard Bentley and Walter Hiskey, Grand Outside Sentinel William I. Reuter and Chairman Burrel D. Neighbours of the Grand Parlor Ritual Committee.

Saturday, Grand President Millington was guest at a luncheon. An unusual gathering, in that representatives were there from every southland Parlor—Santa Barbara No. 116, Los Angeles No. 45, Ramona No. 109, Hollywood No. 196, Sepulveda No. 263, Glendale No. 264, Long Beach No. 239, Santa Monica Bay No. 267, Santa Ana No. 265, Arrowhead No. 110 and San Diego No. 208. A wonderful opportunity for constructive discussion! The following day he was honor-guest of Santa Monica Bay Parlor No. 267 at a California barbecue.

Monday, the Grand President visited Hollywood Parlor No. 196. Several candidates were initiated. Henry G. Bodkin welcomed him, and there were brief addresses by Bernard G. Hiss, Municipal Judge Leo I. Aggeler, Grand Trustee Eldred L. Meyer and others. The following night Glendale No. 264 was visited, and the Grand President spoke most interestingly on California history. The ritual was impressively exemplified by Glendale's officers, and there was a general discussion of various matters.

As a result of Grand President Millington's visit, the Los Angeles County Native Sons have organized for a membership campaign. Grand Trustee Eldred L. Meyer is the executive head. Clinton E. Skinner has been engaged as fieldman, and may be reached by phoning VAndike 6891. The plan is to stage a monster class initiation and demonstration December 3. It is necessary, in order to achieve desired results, that the membership of the Parlors be at least doubled. And it can be done, if every member will, as he should, co-operate, for a more fertile field in which to cultivate Native Sonism nowhere exists. There are thousands upon thousands of most desirable eligibles, waiting for an invitation to affiliate. Every Native Son should be an invitation bearer!

SETH MILLINGTON,
Grand President N.S.G.W.

Remember, "There is no substitute for membership." Enroll now, Native Sons, in this campaign, for the good of the Order and the glory of California!—C.M.H.

ADMISSION DAY OBSERVANCE.

Admission Day, September 9, will be observed locally with a dance, under the auspices of the Native Sons and Native Daughters, in the Chateau ballroom of I.O.O.F. building, Oak and Washington streets. While admission will be by invitation, all Natives, their families and friends will be welcome. Good music has been provided for, and a program in keeping with the occasion will be presented during the dance intermission.

Mrs. Gertrude Allen, Past Grand President John T. Newell, Clinton E. Skinner and Grand Trustee Eldred L. Meyer constitute the committee of arrangements. Invitations of admission may be procured from the secretary of any Native Son or Native Daughter Parlor.

ATTRACTIVE SOCIAL CALENDAR.

Miss Margaret Search gave a splendid talk on "Social Welfare" at the August 17 meeting of Los Angeles Parlor No. 124 N.D.G.W. Deputy Rita Smith was among the many visitors. Dolores Malin, in charge of history and landmarks for the Parlor, is doing fine work. The swimming club, headed by Irene Eden, meets every Monday evening. The sewing club met August 23 at the home of Mrs. D. Vuccovich. The beach party of August 24, staged in Santa Monica Canyon, was a wonderful success. Jennie Raymond, Irene Eden and Peggy Ambler were "mermaids" at the Olympic pool dedication. President Mattie Gara is promoting a building fund.

Los Angeles' September calendar includes: 7th, initiation. 14th, monthly card party; committee in charge, Irene Eden (chairman), Charlotte Gherke, Virginia Bell, Carmel Bregante, Edith Strain, Jennie Gilmer, Jean Clos. 21st, potluck dinner 6 o'clock, followed by an exhibition of desert slides by Kathryn Ronan at 8:15. 24th, noon luncheon, followed by cards, at the home of Ruth Traeger, 677 South Lorraine; menfolks, as well as womenfolks, welcome; Sophia Stewart chairman. During October the Parlor will have a rummage sale, the proceeds to be applied to homeless children work.

(Continued on Page 20)

Native Sons of the Golden West

"TO THE OFFICERS AND MEMBERS of all Parlors of the Native Sons of the Golden West — Dear Sirs and Brothers: The City of San Francisco has been designated as the city in which the Native Sons of the Golden West will celebrate Admission Day. The Parlors of that city have arranged a magnificent celebration in which the natal day of our State will be properly presented not only to Native Californians, but to all who will be in that city on September 9. The Veterans' Memorial Building in San Francisco is being dedicated during that week and San Francisco will be the host to a great number of people from the East at that time in addition to those attracted by our Day.

"Our Order has complete charge of the Admission Day activities and nothing remains undone excepting the attendance of the members of the Parlors outside of the host city. This letter is sent to express my hope that all members of the Order who can possibly attend will be present in San Francisco to participate in the parade and other features incidental to the celebration of the day. It is the one day when our Order is presented to the public and the one day when we have an opportunity to make a public demonstration of our respect to the Pioneers who laid the foundation for this empire that we now enjoy.

"May I again express my hope that every Native Son who can possibly be there will attend the celebration in San Francisco, participate in the parade, and incidentally have the opportunity of seeing the Order in its annual display of historic floats and exhibits that again bring to our minds the fact that our forebears crossed the continent in order to establish the great State of California on the shores of the Pacific?

"Sincerely and Fraternally yours,
"SETH MILLINGTON,
"Grand President N.S.G.W.
"Gridley, August 6, 1932."

Observe Admission Day.

The Grand Parlor Admission Day Observance Committee—Edward E. Reese (chairman), William G. Muntz, Harry Romick, Eugene H. O'Donnell and Ray B. Felton—sent a letter to all Subordinate Parlors, August 10, urging them to promote a more general observance of Admission Day, September 9, in their respective localities by appointment of an observance committee. In conclusion, the letter states:

"The Grand Parlor general celebration will be at San Francisco this year, and every Parlor that can, should participate in this event. If that is not possible, then do everything you can to foster local observance and celebrate fittingly in your own locality. When our duty is done as it should be, the celebration of Admission Day will truly commemorate the birth of our State and keep alive the memory of the Pioneer Men and Women who made its beginning possible."

Alameda Enthusiastic.

Oakland—The Alameda County September Ninth Committee, made up of representatives from every Native Son and Native Daughter Parlor in the county, with Ray B. Felton (Fruitvale No. 252) as chairman, has about completed arrangements for Alameda's participation in the San Francisco Admission Day festivities. This year, probably for the first time in the Order's history, the county will have the place of honor in the parade, marching directly back of Grand Marshal W. Bernard O'Brien (Alameda No. 47). All the Parlors will have large marching units, and their bands, drum corps and drill teams will accompany. Claremont No. 240 will have an exceptionally big turnout, and its recently reorganized drum corps will appear in snappy new uniforms.

Grand Trustee Joseph McShane, chairman of the San Francisco committee, paid a visit to the Alameda County contingent and highly praised them for enthusiastic co-operation. Grand Secretary Sally R. Thaler gave an interesting talk, in the course of which she specially commended the Native Daughters for their wonderful support. September 2 the Booster Committee, under the direction of Grand Inside Sentinel Gam Hurst, will broadcast a program over station K.R.E. Competent speakers will outline the Admission Day program, several vocal selections will be rendered, and the band of Piedmont No. 120 will be heard. The Alameda County Parlors will jointly maintain headquarters the afternoon and evening of September 9 at Knights Columbus Hall, 150 Golden Gate avenue, San Francisco. All Natives and their friends will be cordially welcomed.

Community Club Co-operates.

Ferndale—Ralph Jacobsen, representing Ferndale No. 93, appeared before the Community Club and requested its co-operation in having the business houses close Admission Day, September 9. The club voted its support. The Parlor is sponsoring a program in the high school auditorium and athletic events on the school grounds in observance of the day.

To Re-institute Old Parlor.

Visalia—Through the efforts of Deputy Grand President Al Lobree, Visalia No. 19, for several years defunct, will be re-instituted the early part of September by Grand President Seth Millington. Gareth W. Houk has been selected for president, and C. H. Wenn for secretary.

Past President Gets Ring.

Santa Ana—Raymond L. Marsile was the recipient of a past president ring at the August 1 meeting of Santa Ana No. 265. The presentation, on behalf of the Parlor, was made by District Deputy Walter E. Hiskey. August 15 a repast of icecream and cake was enjoyed after a brief meeting. Several members of the Parlor attended last month the meetings in Los Angeles at which Grand President Seth Millington appeared. Claude E. Agard has taken up his residence in Santa Barbara City.

Membership Standing Largest Parlors.

San Francisco—Grand Secretary John T. Regan reports the standing of the Subordinate Parlors having a membership of over 400 January 1, 1932, as follows, together with their membership figures August 20, 1932:

Parlor.	Jan. 1	Aug. 20	Gain	Loss
Ramona No. 109	1088	1085	....	3
South San Francisco No. 157	822	809	....	13
Castro No. 232	700	716	16	....
Stanford No. 76	614	605	....	9
Arrowhead No. 110	609	583	....	26
Stockton No. 7	549	563	14	....
Twin Peaks No. 214	585	539	....	46
Piedmont No. 120	523	521	....	2
Rincon No. 72	448	434	....	14

Would Revive Fiesta Spirit.

San Rafael—District Deputy Monroe W. Label of Mount Tamalpais No. 64 accompanied Grand Trustee Charles H. Spengemann on his official visits last month to Santa Rosa, Petaluma and Sea Point Parlors. He is a strong believer in interparlor activities as a means of promoting increased membership and interest in the Order. Deputy Label is also interested in reviving the spirit of the old Spanish fiesta days, and hopes to secure the Parlor's co-operation in a movement, now on foot, to bring back the recollection of the city's colorful and romantic history. San Rafael is one of California's oldest towns. The mission, established here in 1817, was one of the last to be erected by the padres. Though the landmark long since disappeared, the spirit of the romantic days still lingers.

Mount Tamalpais' Admission Day committee has made extensive preparations for the Parlor's participation in the San Francisco festivities. An attractive uniform has been selected, and headquarters have been secured. Immediately after the parade the marchers will gather around the festive board.

Initiation at Sutter Fort.

Sacramento—Members of Sacramento No. 3 will appear in the San Francisco Admission Day parade in attractive uniforms. June Longshore is chairman of arrangements. Plans for the initiation of a large class of candidates at historic Sutter Fort October 1 are well under way. President Joseph Fitzhenry announces a movement is on foot to form a joint dancing club for the winter season.

Secretary Passes Suddenly.

San Jose—Henry William McComas, for thirty years the recording secretary of San Jose No. 22, died suddenly July 28 near Agnew. He was born here September 25, 1871, and for twelve years was chairman of the local N.S.G.W. and N.D.G.W. joint homeless children committee. At the August 15 meeting the Parlor elected Joseph Lawrence to fill the vacancy.

August 22, San Jose initiated a class of candidates, President Arthur Davison officiating. The Admission Day celebration committee includes B. T. LeGue, James Craig, Cliff Kelly, J. R. Sabatte, Charles Baldissini and Lawrence Hart.

Benefit Dance.

Monterey—Officers of Monterey No. 75 were installed by District Deputy John Thomsen, James W. Millington becoming president. L. P. Chavoya, an oldtime member, gave an interesting account of the Parlor's earlyday activities. A benefit dance will be given Admission Day, September 9, the arrangements being in charge of a committee composed of Dr. A. J. Hart (chairman), F. W. Hellam and E. H. Raymond.

Big Night at Crestline.

San Bernardino—Initiation in Arrowhead No. 110 August 10 was followed by a watermelon "feed." August 27 was another big night at the Parlor's Crestline clubhouse. A steak supper was served and then a class of candidates were initiated. A large delegation of Arrowheaders, led by President F. L. McGarvey and including Grand Organist Leslie Maloche, attended the reception to Grand President Seth Millington in Los Angeles August 5.

Charles Doyle, one of the mainstays of No. 110, died July 27, and the young daughter of Ben Harrison, former grand trustee, passed away August 4.

Infant Grows.

Los Banos—Los Banos No. 206, instituted in July, now has a membership of more than fifty, according to President R. L. Puccinelli. A class of sixteen candidates were recently initiated, the ritual being exemplified by the officers of Modesto No. 11. A banquet concluded the ceremonies.

Baseball Team Going Strong.

Santa Rosa—Sonoma County's Native Son and Native Daughter Parlors will march in the San Francisco Admission Day parade, headed by the drum and bugle corps of Napa No. 62. Wes Colgan, George Gilman and James Bertino made the arrangements.

Grand Trustee Charles H. Spengemann officially visited Santa Rosa No. 28 August 22, when four candidates were initiated. Twenty members of the Parlor paid a visit to Sonoma No. 111 August 15. Santa Rosa's baseball team is still going strong, having been defeated but once this season. A few dates are still open, and if any N.S. team wants a game get in touch with Wes Colgan, First and Main streets.

To Initiate Large Class.

Modesto—"Early Government in California"

as the subject of an address delivered by Myron Mole at the August 17 meeting of Modesto No. 11, at which President Charles D. Blaine presided. District Deputy L. E. Bither and a delegation of No. 11 members perfected plans to officiate at the installation of officers of Yosemite No. 24 (Merced).

September 21, Modesto will initiate a large class of candidates. Plans are under way for celebrating the Parlor's birthday November 2.

PIONEER NATIVES DEAD

(Brief Notices of the Demise of Men and Women born in California Prior to 1860.)

Miss Louisa Meckel, born in Trinity County in 1859, died July 19.

Mrs. Iza Vista Ellis-Ledyard, born at San Francisco in 1854, died July 22 at Sunol, Alameda County, survived by a son.

Pinckney Jackson Hensley, born in Calaveras County in 1855, died July 23 at Madera City.

Mrs. Mary Tierney-Schmidt, born in Humboldt County in 1859, died July 23 at Eureka survived by six children.

John A. Bartow, born in Humboldt County in 1856, died July 23 at Willits, Mendocino County, survived by a wife and ten children.

Mrs. Mary Murphy-O'Connell, born at San Francisco in 1859, died July 23 at Mountain View, Santa Clara County, survived by three children. She was a daughter of Daniel C. Murphy, an officer in the regiment of Colonel Stevenson which came to California in 1846.

Abraham Diaz, born in Santa Clara County in 1859, died July 23 at Lone Pine, Inyo County, survived by a wife and four daughters.

William N. Coyle, born in Sacramento County in 1858, died July 24 at Petaluma, Sonoma County, survived by a wife and a son.

Mrs. Dela Gregson-Baker, born in Sonoma County in 1859, died July 25 at Los Angeles City survived by four children. She was a daughter of James and Eliza Gregson, said to have arrived at Sutter Fort in 1845.

Dr. Samuel H. Crow, born in Lake County in 1856, died July 25 at Martinez, Contra Costa County, survived by three children. He was well known in Lassen County, where he spent most of his life.

Mrs. Mollie Gordon-Arbuckle, born in Santa Clara County in 1858, died July 31 at Santa Clara City survived by four children. She was a daughter of Benjamin and Mary Gordon, who crossed the plains in 1846 and the following year located at San Jose.

James Joseph Flaherty, born at San Francisco in 1859, died August 1 at Huntington Park, Los Angeles County, survived by a wife and four children.

Michael Nelis, born in Sacramento County in 1859, died August 1 at Sacramento City survived by a wife.

Mrs. Amparo Cecelia Olivas, born in Santa Barbara County in 1852, died August 2 at Ventura City survived by four children.

John C. Daly, born in Contra Costa County in 1856, died August 4 at Napa City survived by a wife and three children.

Austin Kramer, born in Sutter County in 1859, died August 4 near Knights Landing survived by a wife and nine children.

Harry Wake, born in Marin County in 1855, died August 6 at San Francisco survived by four children.

Mrs. Arcadia Alvarado-Rivera, born at Los Angeles in 1843, died there August 7 survived by four children, among them Mrs. Lucy Malin (Los Angeles Parlor No. 124 N.D.G.W.) and Adolfo G. Rivera (Ramona Parlor No. 109 N.S.G.W.). She was a descendant of the Alvarados and the Lugos, among California's earliest Pioneers.

Isaac Joel Ingram, born in Sonoma County in 1854, died August 8 at Gonzales, Monterey County, survived by a wife and two children.

Charles D. Sweitzer, born in Contra Costa County in 1859, died August 9 at Napa City. He was affiliated with Napa Parlor No. 62 N.S.G.W.

Alfred P. Bruce, born in Butte County in 1856, died August 9 at Chico survived by a wife and six children.

Mrs. Louisa Daegner-Volkman, born in Tuolumne County in 1855, died August 14 at San Francisco survived by a husband and two children.

Mariano Pacheco, born in Santa Barbara County in 1852, died August 14 at San Luis Obispo City survived by three daughters. He was a nephew of Romualdo Pacheco, former governor of California.

Mrs. Mary Marsh-Hulbert, born in Placer County in 1855, died August 15 at Sacramento City survived by three children.

Otto Rubel, born in Yuba County in 1859, died August 16 at Marysville.

"Obey the Rule—Slow Past a School," is the September slogan of the California Public Safety Committee in its campaign to lessen the constantly increasing auto death-toll.

Flower Festival—The eighth annual California Flower Festival will be held at San Leandro, Alameda County, September 16-18.

Feminine World's Fads and Fancies

PREPARED ESPECIALLY FOR THE GRIZZLY BEAR BY ANNA STOERMER

CLOSE-FITTING HATS FOR FALL HAVE an international flare. The spanish sailor, the tricorne, the tiny turban, the close-fitting cloche and the small hats with varied brims are all worn far down over the right eye. Bows and a great many feather effects for trimmings are being shown. The skull-shaped and beret crowns are favored, with many folded, shirred, tucked and stitched effects.

Felts, new crepe-like wools, velour cloth and some dull silks are used in daytime hats. Velvets will lead for evening, with shirred transparent velvet and chenille favored. Soileil felt, satin and a number of feathered turbans are shown for formal wear. Black is the predominating color, with brown and red shading from a deep wine tone to a brilliant orange. The flippant veil is expected to find extreme favor with the new models.

Little by little the new fall clothes are making their way. Better be turning over in your mind which of the alluring models will suit your needs. Some of the newest are informal afternoon dresses, the kinds one wears very often and which are frequently hard to find.

Waistlines have been hoisted to two inches below the bust. Coats and dresses are cut on a diagonal line. Skirts are nine to ten inches from the floor.

New coats feature removable collars and bibs, making it possible to wear them with many costumes. The coats are generally belted, and are made of heavy diagonal-ribbed wools.

Velvet and velveteens and short fur wraps of astrakan and broadtail will be much in evidence, worn hip length. If you are in quest of a wrap that is smart, yet inexpensive, remember, first of all, that quality will be one of the distinguishing marks of the season. The little fur collarette that ties in front, of stenciled lapin, galyak or persian lamb, will add richness to an otherwise plain dress.

Maybe you will be interested in choosing a street outfit of navy with touches of red, a particularly smart and becoming style for almost any wearer. The material used is triple-sheer chiffon. The jacket is extremely smart, with short cape sleeves. Gauntlet gloves are worn with this outfit.

For the early fall formal gowns we will have fringe, and plenty of it. Velvet girdles for evening will be much worn in matching colors.

It is very smart to build up the shoulders of the formal frock with crestlike ruffles, ribbon bands or, what is newer still, huge velvet flowers.

Bordeaux red on a pink dress is very attractive. Artificial flowers are sweetpeas, flat climbing roses and gardenias.

Beige, an afternoon and evening color, is staging a comeback. It was deserted the last few seasons in favor of the brighter hues. Beige and wine-red are most popular to start the early fall season. Beige is worn under brown or green coats for formal suits. This year's beige is not in the wishy-washy tones of the past. The smart new beiges have a dash of yellow in their makeup, or perhaps they verge on light greenish tones. These are the tints which combine best with the dark green and warm browns of the coats that are being worn for afternoon, and they are most flattering. Blue is probably second only to beige as a favorite among afternoon colors.

Again we have fagoting. This time, in a chalky blue pastel frock. The skirt is perfectly plain, with diagonal lines of fagoting. The same idea is carried out on the smart coat, with capelet sleeves.

Furs will add a note of luxury to fall fashions. The new furs are beautifully supple. Many look like lustrous fabrics. Flat furs are by far the most widely used. Even in furs, we find the predominance of wide shoulders, interesting collars and intricate sleeve treatments. Caracul, galyak and leopard make lovely sports coats.

Very new is the three-quarters-length swagger coat, flaring from the shoulders, with full sleeves. It has a smart air. The intriguing little fur capes and capelets, the tricky scarfs and the throws of various descriptions will produce most becoming effects in their quaint, fascinating ways.

It is well to keep in mind that a small amount of fine fur is worth many times its chic value. A large quantity of cheap fur is not a necessity, and unless fur lays claim to quality one who wears it is likely to be judged as not having good taste. With the longing in a woman's heart to make herself look lovelier, to imagine herself in luxury, furs continue to be as intriguing and as flattering as ever. This season's furs are so much less expensive, we can all cherish the hope of actual possession.

The good old summertime is flying by, and school days approach. Sometimes the very little girl has her mind made up as to what she wants for school togs, and we find all the smart fall styles in school wear for misses, juniors and the wee tots. There are the swagger suits and jumper types. The fabrics are checked, diagonal and herringbone wools. Cotton tweeds, printed and striped cottons, and printed crepes are made exactly like mother's.

Misses' apparels are very swagger, made of beige wool in jacket suits or two-piece frocks. Blouses with suspenders are worn with pleated

(Continued on Page 13)

Passing of the California Pioneer

(Confined to Brief Notices of the Demise of Those Men and Women Who Came to California Prior to 1870.)

)HN BROWN JR., NATIVE OF COLOrado, 84; crossed the plains to California in 1849 and since 1852 had resided in San Bernardino County; died at San Bernardino City; among the surviving relatives are a daughter, Mrs. Neil Wiggett, and a r, Mrs. Sylvia Davenport (both Lugonia or No. 241 N.D.G.W.); he was one of the nizers and for forty-four years the secretary he San Bernardino Pioneer Society. Deed was the son of John Brown Sr., Rocky ntain explorer, hunter and trapper, born in achusetts in 1817; the junior was born in a abin on the bank of Greenhorn Creek, in the itory of New Mexico, now Colorado, October 847; in 1849 the Brown family joined a car- California-bound, and arrived at Sutter September 15 of that year.

rs. Elizabeth Muncey, 88; came in 1851 and ded for many years in Nevada County; died Los Angeles City, survived by three daugh-.

homas Atkinson, native of Indiana, 93; sed the plains in 1852 and resided in El ado and Mendocino Counties; died at Covelo.

)omingo Ghirardelli, native of Peru, 83; since 2 resident San Francisco, where he died; a and three children survive.

'rank M. Pense, native of Arkansas, 82; came 852 and until 1917 resided in Amador Coun- died at Santa Cruz City survived by two chiln.

:rwin Frost, native of Wisconsin, 82; came 853 and long resided in Santa Clara County; d at San Francisco, survived by a wife and sons.

Irs. Emma F. Reeves, native of Ohio, 82; e across the plains in 1855; died at South adena, Los Angeles County.

Villiam C. Penter, native of Arkansas, 79; e across the plains in 1856 and long resided El Dorado County; died at Angels Camp, Calaas County, survived by two children.

Frederick Moody Sterling, native of Canada, ; came in 1858; died at Los Angeles City.

Mrs. Adelaide Isabella Wallace, native of Missippi, 91; came in 1859 and long resided in lo County; died at Durham, Butte County. rvived by four children.

Mrs. Harriet Alwilda Mayo-Coleman, native of ine, 102; since 1859 resident San Francisco y district; died at Berkeley, Alameda County.

Mrs. Mary Luella Griffiths-Whiting, native of va, 74; crossed the plains in 1860 and long ided in Nevada County; died at Richmond, ntra Costa County, survived by a daughter.

WESTWARD, HO!

(A. L. SMITH.)

In days of old, in the quest for gold
A one-way course was run,
And the wagon train, over hill and plain,
Went West with the setting sun.
There was never a state, be it small or great,
That didn't feed that line;
California skies filled the whole world's eyes
In the days of forty-nine.

As everyone knows, when the question rose
If the Union was supreme,
And the North and South, at the cannon's mouth,
Prepared to defend their dream,
All eyes turned west,—California's test
Of her love for the flag had come;
To her final man, she led the van
In the days of sixty-one.

Now that wheels are clog'd and brains are fog'd,
Again does our nation turn
To the Western door, where Faith once more
Has caused Hope's fire to burn.
When the years have fled and depression's dead
In the pages of history,
They'll tell what was done, by the Native Son,
In thirty-two and three.

(The above came to The Grizzly Bear from A. L. Smith, affiliated with Argonaut Parlor No. 8 N.S.G.W. (Oroville), who now resides at Brookville, Pennsylvania. Accompanying was this note: "Contributed to our magazine with best wishes by the strolling minstrel of California."—Editor.)

W. H. Lippincott, native of Illinois, 80; since 1860 resident Yolo County; died at Woodland, survived by a daughter.

Mrs. Nancy Newton-Malchi, native of Oregon, 74; came in 1861 and long resided in Solano County; died at San Anselmo, Marin County, survived by three daughters.

Mrs. Rachel A. Hills, native of Ohio, 95; came across the plains in 1862 and long resided in Riverside County; died at La Canada, Los Angeles County, survived by a daughter.

Mrs. Lucy Draper-Harlan, native of Ohio, 79; came across the plains in 1862 and settled in Fresno County; died at Laton, survived by four children.

Mrs. Abbie Hayden, native of Ireland, 94; came via the Isthmus of Panama in 1862; died at Sacramento City, survived by a son.

Mrs. Frances E. Ryder, native of Maine, 89; came via the Isthmus of Panama in 1865 and resided in Alameda and Placer Counties; died at Loomis.

Tom Scott Sr., native of Scotland, 81; came via the Isthmus of Panama in 1867; died at Sacramento City, survived by a wife and five children.

Mrs. Josephine Kueny-Bowman, native of Missouri, 85; since 1867 Shasta County resident; died at Cottonwood, survived by six children.

Mrs. Ida May Pratt, native of Ohio, 84; came in 1869 and long resided in Amador County; died at Sacramento City, survived by three children.

Mrs. Clotilde Maria Ventre-Abbott, native of Tahiti, 87; came in 1850 and resided some time in Sacramento City; for sixty years she made her home in Los Angeles County; died at Artesia, survived by a son.

Charles Hurt, native of Missouri, 82; came across the plains in 1852 and resided in Lake and Mendocino Counties; died at Covelo, survived by a wife and twelve children.

Mrs. Emma Fisher-Dopkins, native of Indiana, 82; came across the plains in 1852 and resided in Sacramento and Yolo Counties; died at Woodland, survived by two children.

Mrs. Amelia Neik, native of Germany, 91; came in 1864 and resided a half-century in Colusa County; died at Oakland, Alameda County.

Right Rev. Monsignor Michael D. Connolly, native of Ireland, 81; came in 1869; died at San Francisco.

Mrs. Bertha Germeshausen, native of Germany, 86; since 1868 Yolo County resident; died near Woodland, survived by four children.

Harry Quinn, native of Ireland, 89; since 1868 Kern County resident; died near Delano, survived by a wife and seven children, among them Supervisor John R. Quinn (Los Angeles Parlor No. 45 N.S.G.W.) of Los Angeles.

Mrs. Eliza Mason-Dewar, native of England, 97; came in 1862; died at Berkeley, Alameda County, survived by a daughter.

Mrs. Anna Elizabeth Richards-Weymouth, native of Wisconsin, 86; crossed the plains in 1861 and long resided in El Dorado County; died at Sacramento City, survived by three children.

George W. Gries, native of Ohio, 75; came via the Isthmus of Panama in 1860 and resided in Butte and Humboldt Counties; died at Ferndale, survived by six children.

Mrs. Heralda Rissman, native of Missouri, 89; came across the plains in 1859; died at Pepperwood, Humboldt County, survived by seven children.

Mrs. Sarah Heintzen, native of Missouri, 91; came in 1857 and resided in Sierra, Yolo and Sacramento Counties; died at Sacramento City, survived by two daughters.

FEMININE FANCIES

(Continued from Page 12)

skirts, top coats and scarf collars. Pockets are fur trimmed.

If one could list the requirements of each girl who is to start on her school adventure, it would be easier to arrange for accessories to vary their frocks. A plaid scarf and different belts would effect one change. A bolero and a small fur neckpiece would be the second, and for the third, a military cape would change the entire effect of affairs.

The younger girl isn't quite satisfied with mother's conservative choice of a frock with leanings toward handwork and daintiness, rather than showiness. One of printed crepe should satisfy. This has a yoke extending over the shoulders, which carries out the popular wide-shoulder effect, and clever little puffed sleeves and pleats on both sides. Fagoting marks the yokeline and pipings of blue add a touch of decoration. A bit or trimming often makes the smallest of clothes the smartest. One can find excellent quality, now priced most inexpensively.

"We ought either to be silent or speak things better than silence."—Pythagoras.

Native Daughters of the Golden West

"TO THE SUBORDINATE PARLORS, Native Daughters of the Golden West—Dear Sisters: Eighty-two years ago on the coming ninth of September California sprang full-fledged into Statehood. This was made possible by the energy and the constructive genius of those hardy Pioneers who blazed the way across the continent, on a journey where they were beset with danger and hardship rarely overcome by men. This natal day of ours is set aside by the law of the State as a legal holiday, during which men and women, irrespective of their nativity, join in celebration of the accomplishments of the Pioneers who wrought so well and so lastingly.

"In equal co-operation with the Native Sons, our Order has a peculiar and loving interest in this event. We are pledged to bear the banner of State progress which has passed to us by our forebears. Make every effort to participate in the State celebration at San Francisco. If, for any reason, you are not able to do so, make some preparation to fittingly observe Admission Day in your respective localities by honoring the Pioneer Fathers and Mothers of this Western Empire.

"Let us nurture the Pioneer Spirit and hold high the lamp which has continually lighted the way down the space of time as our glorious State has progressed year by year. Thus shall we meet the full responsibility we have laid upon our shoulders and, in a measure, pay our debt of love to the Pioneers for their heroism, their devotion to duty and their undying loyalty to country.

"Sincerely yours in P.D.F.A.,
"ANNA MIXON ARMSTRONG,
"Grand President N.D.G.W.
"Woodland, August 20, 1932."

Bride Showered.

Alturas—At the August 4 meeting of Alturas No. 159 the Parlor's latest bride, Dorothy Dean Anklin, was the recipient of a kitchen shower. Many responded to Dorothy Gloster's appeal for a hundred percent fulfillment of Loyalty Pledges. The suggestion for a benefit bridge, during the autumn, to supplement the fund received enthusiastic approval. President Erma Elliott desires to make completion of the fund the outstanding project of her term.

Plans were laid and committees were appointed to take charge of the pioneer reception Admission Day, September 9, and the reception of Grand President Anna Mixon Armstrong September 21.

New Ritual Exemplified.

Santa Cruz—Santa Cruz No. 26 was honored August 1 by the first official visit of Grand President Anna Mixon Armstrong. A potluck supper, planned by Pearl Reid, Leona Geyer, Grace Reynolds and Elsie Sayre, was served. Other guests included Grand Secretary Sallie R. Thaler, Grand Organist Clara Gairaud, Past Grand Bertha A. Briggs, several deputies and supervising district deputies, and delegations from many Parlors. The July birthdays of members of the Parlor were observed, a birthday cake with lighted candles being a feature. Following the supper a program of dances was much enjoyed. Flowers on the tables and in the meetinghall were in the colors of the Order.

The new ritual was beautifully exemplified at the meeting, presided over by President Melba E. McKenna. Mrs. Armstrong's talk was unusually inspiring, and she told of the happy memories she will always carry of her first official visit. She and the other grand officers received gifts, and Past President Verel van Gorder was given an emblematic pin. The evening was a very happy one for the members of Santa Cruz.

Grand Marshal Honor-guest.

Sutter Creek—More than a hundred members of the Amador County Parlors were present by invitation at the meeting of Amapola No. 80 at which Grand Marshal Gladys Noce was honor-guest. Officers were installed by Deputy Harriett Clemens, Miss Marea Fontenrose becoming president. A past president emblem was presented Deputy Clemens, and Grand Marshal Noce was the recipient of a basket of beautiful flowers.

A feature of the evening was a program at which members of Amador No. 17 N.S.G.W. were guests: Vocal solo, "Amapola," Mrs. Riandi; remarks, Grand Marshal Noce, Past Grand Ella Caminetti, Supervising Deputy Emma B. Wright, Deputy Clemens and President Fontenrose. Refreshments followed the program.

Given Rising Vote Thanks.

Santa Ana—At the August 8 meeting of Santa Ana No. 235, with the new president, Mildred Gray, presiding, Chairman Muriel Bray and her ways and means committee were given a rising vote of thanks for bringing in a very neat sum of money from a newspaper contest. Both teams which tied in a recent membership contest provided a covered-dish dinner August 22. A public benefit card party August 29 was well attended.

Large Class Initiated.

Vallejo—On behalf of Vallejo No. 195, President Mabel Thompson welcomed Grand President Anna Mixon Armstrong on her official visit August 17 and presented her with a gift of silver. Flowers were used effectively by Mabel Thompson, Nellie Reilly, Carrie Congrave and Anna Johnson in the decorations. A large class of candidates were initiated, and there were many visitors.

Interesting talks were given by Grand President Armstrong, Grand Secretary Sallie R. Thaler, Past Grands Amy V. McAvoy, Dr. Louise C. Heilbron and Estelle M. Evans, Supervising Deputy Wilma Mitchell, Deputies Emma McGlumphy and Elvena Woodard. The meeting closed with an elaborate banquet, in charge of Julia Hill, Minerva Gold, Guilda Keller, Clara Berg, Anita McKenzie, Helen Segoria, Celia Barskey and Florence Metcalf.

OUR PIONEERS

(SULENE M. COWAN.)

Time has hung a vivid painting,
Westward Bound, The Pioneers!
'Tis a priceless gift remaining,
Treasured still thru all the years.

Mighty painters, ease forsaking,
Formed this picture on the plains;
It was matchless in the making,
We, their children, share the gains.

'Tis an old and oft-told story
Heard by fireside's evening glow;
Let us live again and glory
In these tales of long ago.

From the wind-swept eastern shoreline,
From the cities by the sea,
From the valleys and the highline
Came the sires of you and me.

On the far and dim horizon,
A mere thread on distant plain,
Moved a civilization westward,
Sheltered in a wagon train.

Long and sinuous line slow moving,
Winding, climbing, creeping on,
Trackless wastes, the desert's vastness—
Moving westward each new dawn.

Mountains steep with rugged ranges,
Rivers that were torrents, crossed,
These they conquered, dared all dangers,—
Had they faltered, all was lost.

Often thru the long night watches
Came the Red men, bringing fear;
Terror reigned, and desolation
Left its mark of grief and tear.

Can we feel the mother's courage
Guarding helpless children's bed
In the calm and silent magic
Of the quiet stars o'erhead!

Drab and dusty canopies
For hearts so brave and strong,
Yet 'neath those canvas cov'rings
A new nation's soul was born.

We may search thru history's pages
Deeds of courage and of fame,
There are none in all the ages
Braver than our sires can claim.

They will live on in our memory
Down the fleeting years of time;
Courage, faith, and souls undaunted
Fill this masterpiece sublime!

(This tribute to the California Pioneers, written by Sulene M. Cowan, affiliated with Califia Parlor No. 22 N.D.G.W. (Sacramento), came to The Grizzly Bear from Past Grand President Dr. Louise C. Heilbron with a request that it be published in the Admission Day number.—Editor.)

Entertains Camp Fire Girls.

Calistoga—Calistoga No. 145 entertained the Camp Fire Girls August 8, and the guests had a royal time. The program, consisting of music, recitations, drills, games and dancing, was followed by a watermelon feast. In charge of the affair was a committee composed of Susie Tamagni, Lillie Decker, Irma Howard, Bretta Lundell, Evelyn Tamagni and Corina Fallieri.

Officers of the Parlor were installed July 25 by Deputy Sadie Brooks, Bretta Lundell becoming president. There was a splendid attendance, and the hall was beautifully decorated. Past President Berenice Martin was the recipient of an emblematic pin and gifts were presented Deputy Brooks, Supervising Deputy Wilma Mitchell. The affair was a complete success, due to the energetic efforts of the several committees in charge.

Anticipate Happy Evening.

Berkeley—President Mary Briglia has appointed committees to carry out planned activities of Berkeley No. 151. August 10 Berkeley No. 210 N.S.G.W. was entertained, August 24 a class of candidates were initiated, and a happy evening is anticipated when Grand President Anna Mixon Armstrong officially visits Septem-

...r 28. The Parlor, headed by its drum corps, will be in the September 9 parade in San Francisco honoring California's birthday.

Notable Decorations.

San Jose—Vendome No. 100 royally received Grand President Anna Mixon Armstrong August ... Dinner was served at 6:45. The guest table was notable for the historical decoration, the work of William H. Haub (San Jose No. 22 N.S.G.W.). It consisted of raised gold letters of the Parlor's name and number in the center ... covered-wagon train was depicted on its way to a tradingpost, with Uncle Sam's postoffice. Old Glory waved over the building, and a pony express rider stood at the door. President Imogene Thompson presided as hostess.

The meeting attracted a very large attendance, representatives from twenty-one Parlors being present. The Grand President was accompanied by Grand Secretary Sallie R. Thaler, Grand Inside Sentinel Orinda G. Giannini, Grand Organist Clara Gairaud, Past Grand Bertha Adele Briggs, Supervising Deputies Kathryn Nelson, Alice Lane and Rose Rhyner. Seven deputies were also present. Two candidates were initiated. The meeting featured two stately drills by Vendome members; during one, Grand President Armstrong was presented with the Parlor's gift of silver. Many flower presentations were made, and refreshments were served. The favors were unique reproductions of wide-open California poppies; in the heart of each was a picture of the Grand President. The committee chairmen for the evening were: Mrs. Alice Kady, reception; Mrs. Ella Graham, decorations; Mrs. Julia Waddington, refreshments; Mrs. Hazel Haub, accommodations. Installation was held August ...0, with Miss Elsie Fisher officiating. Miss Marna Waddington is the new president. A social hour and banquet followed the ceremonies.

Anniversary Celebrated.

Napa—The forty-fifth institution anniversary of Eschol No. 16 was celebrated with a reception to the remaining five charter members. Gifts were presented to each, and also to Past President Emma Glumphy and Deputy Elvena Woodward. A delightful entertainment was presented and there were talks by many visitors. Miss Eleanor Simpkins is the Parlor's new president.

Past President Honored.

San Bernardino—Lugonia No. 241 had an important meeting August 24, when President Nola Fogler appointed committees to carry on various activities. One candidate was initiated. Past President Lois Aldridge Johnson has been selected to direct the community singing at the next Grand Parlor. Grand Outside Sentinel Hazel B. Hansen was a recent visitor.

August 17 members of Lugonia joined those of Arrowhead No. 110 N.S.G.W. at a basket picnic. Swimming and various games were the attractions.

MORTGAGE BURNING CEREMONY AT NATIVE DAUGHTER HOME.

San Francisco—The Native Daughters met August 14 at their Home, 555 Baker street, to burn the mortgage. The ceremonies, written by Past Grand Dr. Mariana Bertola, chairman Grand Parlor Home Committee, were well carried out at the altar as follows: Procession—Chairman Bertola, as the Flag Grand President, carrying the flag; Past Grand Dr. Louise C. Heilbron, light bearer; Grand President Anna M. Armstrong, Grand Trustee Anna Thuesen; the hostess, Past Grand Genevieve Baker; the home committee, Past Grand Emma Foley, secretary, Millie Tietjen, treasurer, Past Grands Mary Bell, Evelyn Carlson and Carrie Durham, Grand Secretary Sallie R. Thaler, Agnes Curry, Alice Lane, Elizabeth Douglass; Past Grands Eliza Keith, Margaret Hill and Mattie Stein, Grand Treasurer Susie Christ, Grand Inside Sentinel Orinda Giannini.

The ceremony—Grand President Armstrong, Grand Trustee Thuesen and Past Grand Heilbron advance to the altar. Dr. Heilbron: "Worthy Grand President, I present to you this light." (Hands over candle.) Mrs. Armstrong: "I accept it as symbolic of the spirit of our Order, and I hold it for you, Worthy Grand Trustee, that you may use it to burn the mortgage." (Holds the candle over the bowl.) Mrs. Thuesen: "Sisters of our Order, it is with pleasure, and at the same time with a feeling of solemnity, that I burn this mortgage." (Touches the document to the candle held by the Grand President and the ashes fall into the bowl.) The glee club then sang "How Firm a Foundation."

Annette A. Adams congratulated the Order, saying the achievement was not only for the Order of Native Daughters but for the honor of all women in the world in their power of advancement. Judge Fletcher A. Cutler, Past Grand N.S.G.W., spoke most eloquently on the Home and what it has done, and on what the Orders of Native Sons and Native Daughters can do for the state. Chairman Bertola spoke of Past Grand Pearl Lamb, in whose Grand Parlor was passed the resolution to build the Home. Also, of Mrs. Estelle Evans, Mrs. Evelyn Carlson and Miss Esther Sullivan who, as Grand Presidents, had done a big work for the Home, and of the valiant Board of Trustees—Estelle Evans, Marvel Thomas, Evelyn Carlson, Irma Laird, May Givens, Eldora McCarty and Vida Vollers—who had the courage to go forward with arrangements for the mortgage.

Past Grand Baker, as hostess, closed the meeting in her usual pleasing manner, reminding those assembled that considerate affection for one another made for happiness, and progress for the Order. Beautiful flowers, contributed by Judge Cutler, Mms. Dieckoff, Baker and Foley, adorned the lounge, the auditorium and the diningroom. Parlors represented were: Californiana, Los Angeles, the first to pay its Loyalty Pledge; Orinda, Buena Vista, Alta, Gabrielle, Mission, Dolores, Golden State, Minerva, Yosemite, La Estrella, Twin Peaks, Castro, El Vespero, all San Francisco; Laurel, Nevada City; Califia, Sacramento; El Carmelo, Daly City; Woodland; Piedmont and Aloha, Oakland; Ivy, Lodi; Joaquin, Stockton; San Diego; Santa Cruz.

Grand President's Official Itinerary.

Woodland—During the month of September, Grand President Anna Mixon-Armstrong will officially visit the following Subordinate Parlors on the dates noted:

2nd—San Andreas No. 113, San Andreas; Ruby No. 46, Murphys; Princess No. 84, Angels Camp; jointly at Murphys.

7th—Ano Nuevo No. 80, Pescadero.

13th—Dardanelle No. 66, Sonora; Golden Era No. 99, Columbia; Anona No. 164, Jamestown; jointly at Jamestown.

14th—Morada No. 199, Modesto.

15th—Oro Fino No. 9, San Francisco.

17th—Naomi No. 36, Downieville; Imogen No. 134, Sierraville; jointly at Downieville, afternoon.

19th—Plumas Pioneer No. 219, Quincy.

20th—Susanville No. 243, Susanville; Nataqua No. 152, Standish; jointly at Susanville.

21st—Alturas No. 159, Alturas.

22nd—Mount Lassen No. 215, Bieber.

(Continued on Page 17)

Official Directory of Parlors of the N. D. G. W.

ALAMEDA COUNTY.

Angelita No. 32, Livermore—Meets 2nd and 4th Fridays, Foresters Hall; Mrs. Myrtle I. Johnson, Rec. Sec., P.O. box 253.
Piedmont No. 87, Oakland—Meets Thursdays, Corinthien Hall, Pacific Bldg.; Mrs. Alice E. Miner, Rec. Sec., 421 35th St.
Aloha No. 106, Oakland—Meets Tuesdays, Wigwam Hall, Pacific Bldg.; Mrs. Lurine Martin, Rec. Sec., 2815 Wallace St., Berkeley.
Hayward No. 122, Hayward—Meets 1st and 3rd Tuesdays, Veterans Memorial Bldg., Main St.; Miss Ruth Gansberger, Rec. Sec., P. O. box 44, Mount Eden.
Berkeley No. 150, Berkeley—Meets 2nd and 4th Wednesdays, Masonic Hall; Mrs. Lelia B. Baker, Rec. Sec., 915 Contra Costa Ave.
Bear Flag No. 151, Berkeley—Meets 2nd and 4th Wednesdays, Veterans Memorial Bldg., 1931 Center St.; Mrs. Maud Wagner, Rec. Sec., 317 Alcatraz Ave., Oakland.
Encinal No. 156, Alameda—Meets 2nd and 4th Thursdays, N.S.G.W. Hall; Mrs. Laura E. Fisher, Rec. Sec., 1413 Caroline St.
Brooklyn No. 157, East Oakland—Meets Wednesdays, Masonic Temple, 8th Ave. and E. 14th St.; Mrs. Ruth Cooney, Rec. Sec., 3907 14th Ave.
Argonaut No. 166, Oakland—Meets Tuesdays, Klinkner Hall, 59th and San Pablo; Mrs. Ada Spilman, Rec. Sec., 2905 Ellis St., Berkeley.
Bahia Vista No. 167, Oakland—Meets Thursdays, Wigwam Hall, Pacific Bldg.; Mrs. Minnie E. Raper, Rec. Sec., 3449 Helen St.
Fruitvale No. 177, Oakland—Meets Fridays, W.O.W. Hall; May E. Barthold, Rec. Sec., 3832 Santa Rita St.
Laura Loma No. 182, Niles—Meets 1st and 3rd Tuesdays, I.O.O.F. Hall; Mrs. Ethel Fournier, Rec. Sec., P. O. box 515.
El Cereso No. 207, San Leandro—Meets 2nd and 4th Tuesdays, Masonic Hall; Mrs. Mary Tuttle, Rec. Sec., P. O. box 56.
Pleasanton No. 237, Pleasanton—Meets 1st Tuesday, I.O.O.F. Hall; Mrs. Myrtle Lanini, Rec. Sec.
Betsy Ross No. 238, Centerville—Meets 1st and 3rd Fridays, Anderson Hall; Miss Constance Lucio, Rec. Sec., P. O. box 187.

AMADOR COUNTY.

Urania No. 1, Jackson—Meets 2nd and 4th Tuesdays, N.S.G.W. Hall; Mrs. Emma Boarman-Wright, Rec. Sec., 114 Court St.
Chispa No. 40, Ione—Meets 2nd and 4th Fridays, N.S.G.W. Hall; Mrs. Isabel Ashton, Rec. Sec.
Amapola No. 80, Sutter Creek—Meets 2nd and 4th Thursdays, N.S.G.W. Bldg.; Mrs. Hazel M. Marre, Rec. Sec.
Forrest No. 86, Plymouth—Meets 2nd and 4th Tuesdays, I.O.O.F. Hall; Mrs. Marguerite Davis, Rec. Sec.

BUTTE COUNTY.

Annie K. Bidwell No. 168, Chico—Meets 2nd and 4th Thursdays, I.O.O.F. Hall; Mrs Irene Henry, Rec. Sec., 3015 Woodland Ave.
Gold of Ophir No. 190, Oroville—Meets 1st and 3rd Wednesdays, Memorial Hall; Mrs. Ruth Brown, Rec. Sec., 1265 Leah Court.

CALAVERAS COUNTY.

Ruby No. 46, Murphys—Meets 4th Friday, N.S.G.W. Hall; Belle Segale, Rec. Sec.
Princess No. 84, Angels Camp—Meets 2nd and 4th Wednesdays, I.O.O.F. Hall; Mrs. Grace M. Mills, Rec. Sec., P.O. box 313.
San Andreas No. 113, San Andreas—Meets 1st Friday, Fraternal Hall; Miss Doris Treat, Rec. Sec.

COLUSA COUNTY.

Colus No. 194, Colusa—Meets 1st and 3rd Mondays, Eagles Hall; Miss Kate Busch, Rec. Sec., 350 Market St.

CONTRA COSTA COUNTY.

Stirling No. 146, Pittsburg—Meets 1st and 3rd Wednesdays, Veteran Memorial Hall; Mrs. Leslie Clement, Rec. Sec., 468 E. Santa Fe.
Richmond No. 147, Richmond—Meets 1st and 3rd Tuesdays, I.O.O.F. Hall, 10th St.; Grace Curry, Rec. Sec., 1134 Ohio St.
Donner No. 193, Byron—Meets 1st and 3rd Wednesdays, I.O.O.F. Hall; Mrs. Anna Pendry, Rec. Sec., P. O. box 112.
Las Juntas No. 221, Martinez—Meets 1st and 3rd Mondays, Pythian Castle; Mrs. Lola O. Viera, Rec. Sec., 805 Arreba St.
Antioch No. 223, Antioch—Meets 2nd and 4th Tuesdays, I.O.O.F. Hall; Mrs. Estelle Evans, Rec. Sec., 202 E. 5th St., Pittsburg.
Carquinez No. 234, Crockett—Meets 2nd Wednesday, I.O.O.F. Hall; Mrs. Cecile Petee, Rec. Sec., 465 Edwards St.

EL DORADO COUNTY.

Marguerite No. 12, Placerville—Meets 1st and 3rd Wednesdays, Masonic Hall; Mrs. Nettie Leonardi, Rec. Sec., 25 Coloma St.
El Dorado No. 186, Georgetown—Meets 2nd and 4th Saturday afternoons, I.O.O.F. Hall; Mrs. Alta L. Douglas, Rec. Sec.

FRESNO COUNTY.

Fresno No. 187, Fresno—Meets 2nd and 4th Fridays, Pythian Castle, Cor. "R" and Merced Sts.; Mary Aubery, Rec. Sec., 1040 Delphia Ave.

GRAND OFFICERS.

Mrs. Evelyn I. Carlson....................Past Grand President
1965 San Jose Ave., San Francisco
Mrs. Anna M. Armstrong....................Grand President
Woodland
Mrs. Irma Laird....................Grand Vice-president
Alturas
Mrs. Sallie R. Thaler....................Grand Secretary
555 Baker St., San Francisco
Mrs. Susie K. Christ....................Grand Treasurer
555 Baker St., San Francisco
Mrs. Gladys Noce....................Grand Marshal
Sutter Creek
Mrs. Orinda G. Giannini....................Grand Inside Sentinel
2142 Filbert St., San Francisco
Mrs. Hazel B. Hansen....................Grand Outside Sentinel
501 Griswold St., Glendale
Mrs. Clara Gairaud....................Grand Organist
134 Locust St., San Jose

GRAND TRUSTEES.

Mrs. Florence Boyle....................Oroville
Mrs. Edna Briggs..........1045 Santa Ynez Way, Sacramento
Mrs. Anna Thuesen..........615 38th Ave., San Francisco
Mrs. Ethel Begley..........233 Prospect Ave., San Francisco
Mrs. Minna K. Horn....................Etna
Mrs. Jane Vick..........418 Bath St., Santa Barbara
Mrs. Willow Borba....................Sebastopol

GLENN COUNTY.

Berryessa No. 192, Willows—Meets 1st and 3rd Mondays, I.O.O.F. Hall; Mrs. Leonora Neate, Rec. Sec., 338 No. Lassen St.

HUMBOLDT COUNTY.

Occident No. 28, Eureka—Meets 1st and 3rd Wednesdays, N.S.G.W Hall; Mrs. Eva L. MacDonald, Rec. Sec., 2309 "B" St.
Oneonta No. 71, Ferndale—Meets 2nd and 4th Fridays, I.O.O.F. Hall; Mrs. Myra Rumrill, Rec. Sec., P.O. box 142.
Reichling No. 97, Fortuna—Meets 1st and 3rd Tuesdays, Friendship Hall; Mrs. Grace Swett, Rec. Sec., P. O. box 328.

KERN COUNTY.

Miocene No. 228, Taft—Meets 1st and 3rd Wednesday afternoons, I.O.O.F. Hall; Mrs. Evalyn G. Towne, Rec. Sec., P. O. box 1011.
El Tejon No. 239, Bakersfield—Meets 1st and 3rd Fridays, Eagles Hall, 1714 "G" St.; Mary B. Hampson, Rec. Sec., 908 Quincy St.
Desert Gold No. 250, Mojave—Meets 2nd and 4th Fridays, I.O.O.F. Hall; Rein H. Everett, Rec. Sec., P.O. box 83.

LAKE COUNTY.

Clear Lake No. 135, Middletown—Meets 2nd and 4th Tuesdays, Herrick Hall; Mrs. Alma E. Snow, Rec. Sec.

LASSEN COUNTY.

Nataqua No. 152, Standish—Meets 1st and 3rd Wednesdays, Foresters Hall; Mrs. Mayda Elledge, Rec. Sec.
Mount Lassen No. 215, Bieber—Meets 2nd and 4th Thursdays, I.O.O.F. Hall; Mrs. Angie C. Kenyon, Rec. Sec.
Susanville No. 243, Susanville—Meets 3rd Thursday, I.O.O.F. Hall; Mildred Hardy, Rec. Sec., P.O. box 425.

LOS ANGELES COUNTY.

Los Angeles No. 124, Los Angeles—Meets 1st and 3rd Wednesdays, I.O.O.F. Hall, Washington and Oak Sts.; Mrs. Mary K. Corcoran, Rec. Sec., 322 No. Van Ness Ave.
Long Beach No. 154, Long Beach—Meets 1st and 3rd Thursdays, K.P. Hall, 341 Pacific Ave.; Mrs. Bertha Hitt, Rec. Sec., 5355 Lime Ave.
Rudecinda No. 230, San Pedro—Meets 1st and 3rd Fridays, Unity Hall, I.O.O.F. Temple, 10th and Gaffey; Letitia Sarciaux, Rec. Sec., 483 16th St.
Verdugo No. 240, Glendale—Meets 2nd and 4th Tuesdays, Masonic Temple, 234 So. Brand Blvd.; Miss Etta Fulkerth, Rec. Sec., 526 No. Orange St.
Santa Monica Bay No. 245, Ocean Park—Meets 1st and 3rd Mondays, New Eagles Hall, 2823½ Main St.; Mrs. Rosalie Hyde, Rec. Sec., 738 Flower St., Venice.
Californiana No. 247, Los Angeles—Meets 2nd and 4th Tuesday afternoons, Hollywood Studio Club, 1215 Lodi Place; Mrs. Inez Sitton, Rec. Sec., 4223 Berenice St.

MADERA COUNTY.

Madera No. 244, Madera—Meets 2nd and 4th Thursdays, Masonic Annex; Mrs. Margaret C. Boyle, Rec. Sec., 111 No. "B" St.

MARIN COUNTY.

Sea Point No. 196, Sausalito—Meets 2nd and 4th Mondays, Perry Hall, 50 Caledonia St.; Mrs. Mary B. Smith, Rec. Sec., 559 Woodward Ave.
Marinita No. 198, San Rafael—Meets 2nd and 4th Mondays, 816 "B" St.; Miss Mollye Y. Spaelti, Rec. Sec., 539 4th St.
Fairfax No. 225, Fairfax—Meets 2nd and 4th Tuesdays, Community Hall; Mrs. Olive A. Greene, Rec. Sec., P. O. box 277.
Tamelpa No. 231, Mill Valley—Meets 1st and 2nd Tuesdays, I.O.O.F. Hall; Mrs. Delphine M. Todt, Rec. Sec., 400 Grand Ave., San Rafael.

MARIPOSA COUNTY.

Mariposa No. 63, Mariposa—Meets 1st and 3rd Fridays, I.O.O.F. Hall; Elizabeth E. Johnson, Rec. Sec.

MENDOCINO COUNTY.

Fort Bragg No. 210, Fort Bragg—Meets 1st and 3rd Thursdays, I.O.O.F. Hall; Mrs. Ruth W. Fuller, Rec. Sec.

MERCED COUNTY.

Veritas No. 75, Merced—Meets 1st and 3rd Tuesdays, I.O.O.F. Hall; Miss Margaret Thornton, Rec. Sec., 317 18th St.

MODOC COUNTY.

Alturas No. 159, Alturas—Meets 1st Thursday, Alturas Civic Club; Mrs. Irma W. Laird, Rec. Sec.

MONTEREY COUNTY.

Aleli No. 102, Salinas—Meets 2nd and 4th Thursdays, Pythian Hall; Miss Rose Rhyner, Rec. Sec., 420 Soledad St.
Junipero No. 141, Monterey—Meets 2nd and 4th Fridays, K. of P. Hall, Main St.; Miss Matilda M. Bergschicker, Rec. Sec., 498 Van Buren St.

NAPA COUNTY.

Eschol No. 16, Napa—Meets 2nd and 4th Mondays, N.S.G.W. Hall; Mrs. Ella Ingram, Rec. Sec., 2140 Seminary St.
Calistoga No. 145, Calistoga—Meets 2nd and 4th Mondays, I.O.O.F. Hall; Sadie P. Brooks, Rec. Sec.
La Junta No. 203, Saint Helena—Meets 1st and 3rd Tuesdays, N.S.G.W. Hall; Mrs. Marie Signorelli, Rec. Sec., 1341 Madrona Ave.

ATTENTION, SECRETARIES!

THIS DIRECTORY IS PUBLISHED BY AUTHORITY OF THE GRAND PARLOR N.D.G.W., AND ALL NOTICES OF CHANGES MUST BE RECEIVED BY THE GRAND SECRETARY (NOT THE MAGAZINE) ON OR BEFORE THE 20TH OF EACH MONTH TO INSURE CORRECTION IN NEXT PUBLICATION OF DIRECTORY.

NEVADA COUNTY.

Laurel No. 6, Nevada City—Meets 1st and 3rd Wednesda[ys], I.O.O.F. Hall; Mrs. Nellie E. Clark, Rec. Sec., P. [O.] box 212.
Manzanita No. 29, Grass Valley—Meets 1st and 3rd Tu[es]days, Auditorium; Mrs. Loraine Keast, Rec. Sec., 1[...] Race St.
Columbia No. 70, French Corral—Meets Fridays, Farrell Hall; Mrs. Kate Farrelley-Sullivan, Rec. Sec.
Snow Peak No. 176, Truckee—Meets 1st Monday, I.O.O.[F.] Hall; Mrs. Henrietta M. Eaton, Rec. Sec., P. O. box 11[...]

ORANGE COUNTY.

Santa Ana No. 235, Santa Ana—Meets 2nd and 4th Mo[n]days, K.C. Hall, 4th and French Sts.; Mrs. Matilda Lemon, Rec. Sec., 928 W. Fairview.
Grace No. 242, Fullerton—Meets 1st and 3rd Thursda[ys], I.O.O.F. Hall, 116½ E. Commonwealth; Mrs. Ma[...] Rothaermel, Rec. Sec., P. O. box 285.

PLACER COUNTY.

Placer No. 138, Lincoln—Meets 2nd Wednesday, I.O.O.[F.] Hall; Miss Carrie Parlin, Rec. Sec.
La Rosa No. 191, Roseville—Meets 1st and 3rd Tuesda[ys], Eagles Hall; Mrs. Alice Lee West, Rec. Sec., Rocklin.
Auburn No. 233, Auburn—Meets 2nd and 4th Fridays, Fo[r]esters Hall; Mrs. Elsie Patrick, Rec. Sec.

PLUMAS COUNTY.

Plumas Pioneer No. 219, Quincy—Meets 1st and 3rd Mo[n]days, I.O.O.F. Hall; Minnie E. Johnson, Rec. Sec., P. [O.] box 243.

SACRAMENTO COUNTY.

Califia No. 22, Sacramento—Meets 2nd and 4th Tuesda[ys], N.S.G.W. Hall; Miss Lulu Gillis, Rec. Sec., 921 8th [St.]
La Bandera No. 110, Sacramento—Meets 1st and 3rd F[ri]days, N.S.G.W. Hall; Mrs. Clara Weldon, Rec. Sec., 13[...] "O" St.
Sutter No. 111, Sacramento—Meets 1st and 3rd Tuesda[ys], N.S.G.W. Hall; Mrs. Adele Nix, Rec. Sec., 1238 "S" [St.]
Fern No. 123, Folsom—Meets 1st and 3rd Tuesdays, K. [...] Hall; Mrs. Viola Shumway, Rec. Sec., P. O. box 48.
Chabolla No. 171, Galt—Meets 2nd and 4th Tuesday[s], I.O.O.F. Hall; Mrs. Mary Pritchard, Rec. Sec.
Coloma No. 212, Sacramento—Meets 1st and 3rd Tuesday[s], I.O.O.F. Hall, Oak Park; Mrs. Nettie Harry, Rec. Se[c.], 1217 35th St.
Liberty No. 213, Elk Grove—Meets 2nd and 4th Friday[s], I.O.O.F. Hall; Mrs. Frances Wackman, Rec. Sec., P. [O.] box 192.
Victory No. 216, Courtland—Meets 1st Saturday and 3rd Monday, N.S.G.W. Hall; Mrs. Agneda Lample, Rec. Se[c.]

SAN BENITO COUNTY.

Copa de Oro No. 105, Hollister—Meets 2nd and 4th Thursdays, Grangers Union Hall; Mrs. Mollie Davegg[...], Rec. Sec., 110 San Benito St.
San Juan Bautista No. 179, San Juan Bautista—Meets 1[...] Wednesday, Mission Corridor Rooms; Miss Gertru[de] Breen, Rec. Sec.

SAN BERNARDINO COUNTY.

Lugonia No. 241, San Bernardino—Meets 2nd and 4[th] Wednesdays, Eagles Hall; Miss Lois Poling, Rec. Se[c.], 1098 Waterman Ave.
Ontario No. 251, Ontario—Meets 2nd and 4th Thursday[s], Ontario Hotel; Miss Helen Hickman, Rec. Sec., 923 N[...] Laurel Ave.

SAN DIEGO COUNTY.

San Diego No. 208, San Diego—Meets 2nd and 4th We[d]nesdays, Directors Room, Chamber Commerce Bldg., 4[...] W. Broadway; Mrs. Elsie Case, Rec. Sec., 3051 Broadwa[y]

SAN FRANCISCO CITY AND COUNTY.

Minerva No. 2, San Francisco—Meets 1st and 3rd Wedne[s]days, N.S.G.W. Bldg.; Miss Dorothy Finn, Rec. Sec., [...] Princess St., Sausalito.
Alta No. 3, San Francisco—Meets 2nd and 4th Tuesday[s], N.S.G.W. Bldg.; Mrs. Agnese L. Hughes, Rec. Sec., 39[...] Sacramento St.
Oro Fino No. 9, San Francisco—Meets 1st and 3rd Thur[s]days, N.S.G.W. Bldg.; Mrs. Josephine B. Morrisey, Re[c.] Sec., 4441 20th St.
Golden State No. 50, San Francisco—Meets 1st and 3[rd] Wednesdays, N.D.G.W. Home; Miss Millie Tietjen, Re[c.] Sec., 328 Lexington Ave.
Orinda No. 56, San Francisco—Meets 2nd, 4th and 5th Fr[i]days, N.D.G.W. Home; Mrs. Anna A. Gruber-Loser, Re[c.] Sec., 72 Grove Lane, San Anselmo.
Fremont No. 59, San Francisco—Meets 1st and 3rd Tue[s]days, N.S.G.W. Bldg.; Miss Hannah Collins, Rec. Sec[.], 617 Fillmore St.
Buena Vista No. 68, San Francisco—Meets 1st, 3rd an[d] 5th Thursdays, N.D.G.W. Home; Miss Margaret Barret[t], Rec. Sec., 3774 20th St.
Las Lomas No. 72, San Francisco—Meets 1st and 3rd Tue[s]days, N.D.G.W. Home; Mrs. Marion S. Day, Rec. Sec[.], 469 Noe St.
Yosemite No. 83, San Francisco—Meets 1st and 3rd Tue[s]days, American Hall, 20th and Capp Sts.; Miss Mar[...] Monahan, Rec. Sec., 237 Noe St.
La Estrella No. 89, San Francisco—Meets 2nd and 4t[h] Mondays, N.S.G.W. Bldg.; Miss Birdie Hartman, Re[c.] Sec., 1018 Jackson St.
Sans Souci No. 96, San Francisco—Meets 2nd and 4th Mo[n]days, N.D.G.W. Home; Mrs. Minnie F. Dobbin, Rec. Sec[.], 1483 43rd Ave.
Calaveras No. 103, San Francisco—Meets 2nd and 4t[h] Tuesdays, Swedish American Hall, 2174 Market St. Mary L. Krogh, Rec. Sec., 4285 Cabrillo St.
Darina No. 114, San Francisco—Meets 1st and 3rd Mo[n]days, N.S.G.W. Bldg.; Miss Adele Walsh, Rec. Sec., 47[...] Page St.
El Vespero No. 118, San Francisco—Meets 2nd and 4t[h] Tuesdays, Masonic Hall, 4705 3rd St.; Mrs. Nell [...] Boege, Rec. Sec., 1526 Kirkwood Ave.
Genevieve No. 132, San Francisco—Meets 1st and 3r[d] Thursdays, N.S.G.W. Bldg.; Miss Branice Peguillan, Re[c.] Sec., 2434 16th Ave.
Keith No. 137, San Francisco—Meets 2nd and 4th Thur[s]days, N.S.G.W. Bldg.; Mrs. Helen T. Mann, Rec. Sec[.], 575 Pierce St., Apt. 206.
Gabrielle No. 139, San Francisco—Meets 2nd and 4t[h] Wednesdays, N.S.G.W. Bldg.; Mrs. Dorothy Wuesterfel[d], Rec. Sec., 1020 Munich St.
Presidio No. 148, San Francisco—Meets 2nd and 4th Tue[s]days, N.S.G.W. Bldg.; Mrs. Hattie Gaughran, Rec. Sec[.], 713 Capp St.
Guadalupe No. 153, San Francisco—Meets 2nd and 4t[h] Mondays, Forester Hall, 170 Valencia St.; Miss May [...] McCarthy, Rec. Sec., 336 Elsie St.
Golden Gate No. 158, San Francisco—Meets 2nd and 4t[h] Mondays, N.S.G.W. Bldg.; Mrs. Mary Sullivan, Rec. Sec[.], 83 Cuvier St.
Dolores No. 169, San Francisco—Meets 2nd and 4th We[d]nesdays, N.S.G.W. Bldg.; Mrs. Ada Saunders, Rec. Sec[.], 284 Allison St.
Linda Rosa No. 170, San Francisco—Meets 2nd and 4t[h] Wednesdays, Swedish American Hall, 2174 Market St. Mrs. Eva P. Tyrrel, Rec. Sec., 2629 Mission St.

ortola No. 173, San Francisco—Meets 1st and 3rd Tuesdays, N.S.G.W. Bldg.; Catherine H. Dolly, Rec. Sec., 4125 23rd St.
astro No. 178, San Francisco—Meets 1st and 3rd Wednesdays, K.C. Bldg., 150 Golden Gate Ave.; Miss Adeline Sandersfeld, Rec Sec., 50 Baker St.
win Peaks No. 185, San Francisco—Meets 2nd and 4th Fridays, Druids Temple, 44 Page St.; Mrs. Loretta Cameron, Rec. Sec., 3969 Army St.
ames Lick No. 220, San Francisco—Meets 1st and 3rd Wednesdays, N.S.G.W. Bldg.; Mrs. Edna Bishop, Rec. Sec., 3841 24th St.
lission No. 227, San Francisco—Meets 2nd and 4th Fridays, N.S.G.W. Bldg.; Mrs. Ann Dippel, Rec. Sec., 448 Dewey Blvd.
ret Harte No. 232, San Francisco—Meets 2nd and 4th Tuesdays, Aloha Hall, 3009 16th St.; Pearl Wedde, Rec. Sec., 225 7th Ave.
a Dorada No. 236, San Francisco—Meets 2nd and 4th Thursdays, N.S.G.W. Hall; Mrs. Theresa R. O'Brien, Rec. Sec., 567 Liberty St.
alboa No. 249, San Francisco—Meets 2nd and 4th Thursdays, Maccabees Hall, 5th Ave. and Clement St.; Jean Moffet, Rec. Sec., 6633 California St.
topia No. 252, San Francisco—Meets 2nd and 4th Tuesdays, American Hall, 20th and Capp Sts.; Miss Lelia M. Little, Rec. Sec., 892 Noe St.

SAN JOAQUIN COUNTY.

oaquin No. 5, Stockton—Meets 2nd and 4th Tuesdays, N.S.G.W. Hall, 314 E. Main St.; Mrs. Della Garvin, Rec. Sec., 1122 E. Market St.
l Pescadero No. 82, Tracy—Meets 1st and 3rd Fridays, I.O.O.F. Hall; Mrs. Mary A. Hewitson, Rec. Sec., 122 Walnut St.
vy No. 88, Lodi—Meets 1st and 3rd Wednesdays, Eagles Hall; Mrs. Mae Corson, Rec. Sec., 109 So. School St.
alle de Oro No. 206, Stockton—Meets 1st and 3rd Tuesdays, N.S.G.W. Hall, 314 E. Main St.; Mrs. Frances Germain, Rec. Sec., 450 No. Regent.
hoebe A. Hearst No. 214, Manteca—Meets 2nd and 4th Wednesdays, I.O.O.F. Hall; Mrs. Josie M. Frederick, Rec. Sec., Route A, Box 864, Ripon.

SAN LUIS OBISPO COUNTY.

an Miguel No. 94, San Miguel—Meets 2nd and 4th Wednesday afternoons, Clemon Hall; Mrs. Nellie Wickstrom, Rec. Sec.
an Luisita No. 108, San Luis Obispo—Meets 2nd and 4th Thursdays, W.O.W. Hall; Miss Agnes M. Lee, Rec. Sec., P. O. box 584.
l Pinal No. 163, Cambria—Meets 2nd, 4th and 5th Tuesdays, N.S.G.W. Hall; Kathryn Luchessa, Rec. Sec.

SAN MATEO COUNTY.

onita No. 10, Redwood City—Meets 2nd and 4th Thursdays, I.O.O.F. Hall; Mrs. Dora Wilson, Rec. Sec., 518 Middlefield Rd.
ista del Mar No. 155, Halfmoon Bay—Meets 2nd and 4th Thursdays, I.O.O.F. Hall; Elizabeth Olney, Rec. Sec.
no Nuevo No. 180, Pescadero—Meets 1st and 3rd Wednesdays, I.O.O.F. Hall; Mrs. Alice Mattei, Rec. Sec.
l Carmelo No. 181, Daly City—Meets 1st and 3rd Wednesdays, Masonic Hall; Mrs. Hattie Kelly, Rec. Sec., 1179 Brunswick St.
enlo No. 211, Menlo Park—Meets 2nd and 4th Mondays, Masonic Hall; Mrs. Frances E. Maloney, Rec. Sec., P. O. box 626.
an Bruno No. 246, San Bruno—Meets 2nd and 4th Fridays, Legion Hall; Miss Mildred Foley, Rec. Sec., 217 Miller Ave., South San Francisco.

SANTA BARBARA COUNTY.

eina del Mar No. 126, Santa Barbara—Meets 1st and 3rd Tuesdays, Pythian Castle, 222 W. Carillo St.; Mrs. Dorothy Yule, Rec. Sec., P.O. box 670.

SANTA CLARA COUNTY.

an Jose No. 81, San Jose—Meets Thursdays, Catholic Women Center, 5th and San Fernando Sts.; Mrs. Nellie Fleming, Rec. Sec., Catholic Women Center.
endome No. 100, San Jose—Meets Wednesdays, Old Scottish Rite Temple; Miss Marie Buck, Rec. Sec., 245 Hawthorne St.
l Monte No. 205, Mountain View—Meets 2nd and 4th Fridays, American Legion Hall; Miss Mary Ann Rokovich, Rec. Sec., P.O. box 422-B.
alo Alto No. 229, Palo Alto—Meets 1st and 2nd Mondays, N.S.G.W. Hall; Miss Helena G. Hansen, Rec. Sec., 531 Lytton Ave.

SANTA CRUZ COUNTY.

anta Cruz No. 26, Santa Cruz—Meets Mondays, N.S.G.W. Hall; Mrs. May L. Williamson, Rec. Sec., 170 Walnut Ave.
l Pajaro No. 35, Watsonville—Meets 1st and 3rd Tuesdays, I.O.O.F. Hall; Miss Ruth E. Wilson, Rec. Sec., 16 Laurel St.

SHASTA COUNTY.

amellia No. 41, Anderson—Meets 1st and 3rd Tuesdays, Masonic Hall; Mrs. Olga E. Welbourn, Rec. Sec.
assen View No. 98, Shasta—Meets 2nd Friday, Masonic Hall; Miss Louise Litsch, Rec. Sec.
iawatha No. 140, Redding—Meets 2nd and 4th Wednesdays, Moose Hall; Ruth Presleigh, Rec. Sec., Office County Clerk.

SIERRA COUNTY.

aomi No. 36, Downieville—Meets 2nd and 4th Wednesdays, I.O.O.F. Hall; Louise C. Dubuque, Rec. Sec.
mogen No. 134, Sierraville—Meets 2nd and 4th Saturday afternoons, Copren Hall; Mrs. Jennie Copren, Rec. Sec.

SISKIYOU COUNTY.

schscholtzia No. 112, Etna—Meets 1st and 3rd Wednesdays, Masonic Hall; Mrs. Bernice E. Smith, Rec. Sec.
ountain Dawn No. 120, Sawyers Bar—Meets 2nd and last Wednesdays, I.O.O.F. Hall; Miss Edith Dunphy, Rec. Sec.

SOLANO COUNTY.

allejo No. 195, Vallejo—Meets 1st and 3rd Wednesdays, K.C. Hall, 820 Marin St.; Mrs. Mary Combs, Rec. Sec., 511 York St.
ary E. Bell No. 224, Dixon—Meets 2nd and 4th Thursdays, I.O.O.F. Hall; Grace McFadyen, Rec. Sec.

SONOMA COUNTY.

onoma No. 209, Sonoma—Meets 2nd and 4th Mondays, I.O.O.F. Hall; Mrs. Mae Norrbom, Rec. Sec., R.F.D., box 171.
anta Rosa No. 217, Santa Rosa—Meets 1st and 3rd Thursdays, N.S.G.W. Hall; Mrs. Hazel E. Brown, Rec. Sec., 1521 4th St.
etaluma No. 222, Petaluma—Meets 1st and 3rd Tuesdays, Dania Hall; Mrs. Margaret M. Oeltjen, Rec. Sec., 503 Prospect St.

STANISLAUS COUNTY.

akdale No. 125, Oakdale—Meets 1st Monday, I.O.O.F. Hall; Mrs. Lou Reeder, Rec. Sec.
orada No. 199, Modesto—Meets 2nd and 4th Wednesdays, I.O.O.F. Hall; Mrs. Susan Sullivan, Rec. Sec., 823 10th St.
ldora No. 248, Turlock—Meets 1st and 3rd Wednesdays, Fraternal Hall; Effie Lund, Rec. Sec., 624 Minaret Ave.

SUTTER COUNTY.

outh Butte No. 226, Sutter—Meets 1st and 3rd Mondays, N.D.G.W. Hall; Mrs. Abbie N. Varedes, Rec. Sec.

TEHAMA COUNTY.

erendos No. 23, Red Bluff—Meets 1st and 3rd Tuesdays, W.O.W. Hall, 200 Pine St.; Mrs. Lillie Hammer, Rec. Sec., 636 Jackson St.

TRINITY COUNTY.

Eltapome No. 55, Weaverville—Meets 2nd and 4th Thursdays, N.S.G.W. Hall; Mrs. Lou N. Fetzer, Rec. Sec.

TUOLUMNE COUNTY.

Dardanelle No. 66, Sonora—Meets Fridays, I.O.O.F. Hall; Mrs. Nettie Whitto, Rec. Sec.
Golden Era No. 99, Columbia—Meets 1st and 3rd Thursdays, N.S.G.W. Hall; Miss Irene Ponce, Rec. Sec.
Anona No. 164, Jamestown—Meets 2nd and 4th Tuesdays, I.O.O.F. Hall; Nellie Hope, Rec. Sec.

YOLO COUNTY.

Woodland No. 90, Woodland—Meets 2nd and 4th Tuesdays, N.S.G.W. Hall; Mrs. Maude Heaton, Rec. Sec., 153 College St.

YUBA COUNTY.

Marysville No. 162, Marysville—Meets 2nd and 4th Wednesdays, Liberty Hall; Miss Cecelia C. Gomes, Rec. Sec., 701 6th St.
Camp Far West No. 218, Wheatland—Meets 3rd Tuesday, I.O.O.F. Hall; Mrs. Ethel C. Brock, Rec. Sec., P. O. box 285.

AFFILIATED ORGANIZATIONS.

General Assembly Past Presidents—Meetings held annually in April at the home-town of Chief President; Mrs. Cora Stobing, 1739 San Jose Ave., San Francisco, Chief President; Mrs. Anna G. Loser, 72 Grove Lane, San Anselmo, Chief Secretary.
Past Presidents Association No. 1—Meets 1st and 3rd Mondays, N.S.G.W. Bldg., 414 Mason St., San Francisco; Mrs. Minnie F. Dobbin, Pres.; Mrs. May R. Barry, Rec. Sec., 2319 19th Ave., San Francisco.
Past Presidents Association No. 2—Meets 2nd and 4th Mondays, "Wigwam," Pacific Bldg., 16th and Jefferson, Oakland; Emma Haggerty, Pres.; Mrs. Elizabeth B. Goodman, Rec. Sec., 184 Juana Ave., San Leandro.
Past Presidents Association No. 3 (Santa Clara County)—Meets 2nd Tuesday, homes of members; Mrs. Amelia Hartman, Pres.; Mrs. Mary G. Newton, Rec. Sec., 1070 Jackson St., Santa Clara.
Past Presidents Association No. 4 (Sacramento County)—Meets 2nd Monday, Unitarian Hall, 1413 27th St., Sacramento City; Viola Gennoe, Pres.; Lily May Tilden, Rec. Sec., 3225 "T" St., Sacramento.
Past Presidents Association No. 5 (Butte County)—Meets 1st Friday, homes of members, Chico and Oroville; Marie Picanco, Pres.; Ruth Brown, Rec. Sec., 1265 Leah Court, Oroville.
Past Presidents Association No. 6 (Nevada County)—Meets 4th Friday, alternately between Nevada City, Pythian Castle, and Grass Valley, Edna Sampson's home; Margaret V. Nolan, Pres.; Vere Hansen, Rec. Sec., R.F.D. No. 2, box 41-C, Grass Valley.
Past Presidents Association No. 7 (Sonoma County)—Meets 1st Thursday, N.S.G.W. Hall, Santa Rosa; Willow Borba, Pres.; Clytie Lewis, Rec. Sec., R.F.D. No. 4, box 345-A, Santa Rosa.
Past Presidents Association No. 8 (San Joaquin and Stanislaus Counties)—Meets 2nd Thursday, Red Men Hall, Stockton; Mrs. Lois Armstrong, Pres.; Mrs. Harriet F. Corr, Rec. Sec., 729 E. Sonora St., Stockton.
Native Sons and Native Daughters Central Committee on Homeless Children—Main Office, 955 Phelan Bldg., San Francisco; Mrs. John W. Stirling, Chmn.; Miss Mary E. Brusie, Sec. Los Angeles branch office, 3924 Sunset Blvd.; Dorothy Schlingman, Sec.

(ADVERTISEMENT.)

NATIVE DAUGHTER NEWS

(Continued from Page 15)

23rd—Eschscholtzia No. 112, Etna; Mountain Dawn No. 120, Sawyers Bar; jointly at Etna.
27th—Presidio No. 148, San Francisco.
28th—Bear Flag No. 151, Berkeley.
30th—San Francisco district meeting.

Seven Initiated.

Petaluma—Grand President Anna Mixon Armstrong officially visited Petaluma No. 222 August 16, and was accompanied by a large delegation from her home-Parlor, Woodland No. 90. Golden blossoms were used profusely in decorating the meetingroom and the banquethall. Seven candidates were initiated, and the perfect rendition of the ritual reflected much credit on the officers and the drillteam. Gifts were presented various grand officers, and speechmaking and merriment prevailed at an elaborate banquet.

Among the large number assembled were Grand Trustee Willow Borba, Past Grands Emma G. Foley, Amy v. McAvoy and Estelle M. Evans, Supervising Deputy Hazel Brown, Deputies Gertrude Grauskopf and Mae Rose Barry, and delegations from many surrounding Parlors.

Awarded Scholarship.

Saint Helena—Miss Phyllis Thompson of La Junta No. 203 has been awarded a Grand Parlor scholarship at Mills College. Her mother, Mrs. O. C. Thompson, and her grandmother, Mrs. C. E. Palmer, are also affiliated with the Parlor.

Installation Functions.

Jackson—Officers of Ursula No. 1 were installed by Deputy Margaret Molfino, Lucy Lorenson becoming president. Two candidates were initiated, and a past president emblem was presented to Deputy Molfino. Among the many in attendance were Grand Marshal Gladys E. Noce, Past Grand Ella E. Caminetti, Supervising Deputy Emma B. Wright and Deputy Harriett Clemens.

Eureka—Officers of Occident No. 28 were installed by Deputy Myra Rumrill, Mary McPherson becoming president. The hall was a gorgeous bower of summer flowers, with yellow blooms predominating. Supervising Deputy Hattie Roberts was among the many present. Whist was played and refreshments were served. Sadie Barry, Anna Fulton and Louise Hogan had charge of the decorations, and Stella Locke, Elma Long, Margaret McNeil, Lola McDonald and Ione McCarthy constituted the entertainment committee.

San Jose—Officers of San Jose No. 81 were installed by Deputy Fay Wythecomb, Miss Iola Shannon becoming president. The attendance was large. Refreshments were served at prettily decorated tables, and lovely gifts were presented Elva Dee, Deputy Wythecomb, President Shannon, Supervising Deputy Kathryn Nelson, Deputy Elsie Fisher and Ruby King. Julia Domenici was the recipient of a past president emblem. The Parlor will participate in the San Francisco Admission Day parade. Afternoon card parties are held fortnightly, and the monthly card parties continue interesting features. Much grief is felt over the tragic death of Mrs. Anna Dougherty, instantly killed in an auto accident August 9.

Lodi—Officers of Ivy No. 88 were installed by Deputy Catherine Tully, Thirsa E. Hunt becoming president. Two candidates were initiated, many interesting addresses were made and refreshments were served. Among those present were Past Grands Carrie Roesch-Durham, Mamie G. Peyton and Mattie M. Stein.

Oakdale—Officers of Oakdale No. 125 were installed by Deputy Alice Dorroh, Theresa Panetto becoming president. Summer flowers decorated the lodgeroom. Gifts were presented Supervising Deputy Katherine Kopf, Eva Fogarty and Deputy Dorroh. Refreshments were served by Mms. Jessie Acker, Hattie Hover and Esther Marty.

Sausalito—Officers of Sea Point No. 196 were installed by Deputy Anna Loser, Lillian Azavedo becoming president. Visitors included Past Grand Emma G. Foley, Grand Inside Sentinel Orinda Giannini and representatives of several Parlors. Refreshments were served at prettily decorated tables. The committee in charge of the affair—Emma Young, Helen Wetzler, Helen Sullivan, Alice McGowan and Mary B. Smith—was given many compliments.

San Diego—Officers of San Diego No. 208 were installed by Deputy Carrie Northway, Isabel Young becoming president. All officers carried arm boquets of gladioli and fern, and the hall was a bower of flowers. Gifts were presented retiring and incoming officers, Deputy Northway and Nellie Cline (Grace No. 242), who for three years served the Parlor as deputy.

Fullerton—Officers of Grace No. 242 were installed by Deputy Mary Noerenberg, Lena Aspden becoming president. Many guests, among them Past Grand Grace S. Stoermer, were in attendance. Mattie Edwards, retiring president, was the recipient of an emblematic pin, and in appreciation for generous service rendered Ora

(Concluded on Page 19)

In Memoriam

ANGIE BONES.

Whereas, Our Heavenly Father has seen fit to enter our Parlor and take from our midst, to the Grand Parlor above, our honored and beloved sister, Angie Bones; whereas, in view of the loss we have sustained and of the greater loss sustained by those who were nearest and dearest to her, be it

Resolved, That though we bow in humble submission to the divine will, we deeply feel our loss in being deprived of her presence and loving friendship, and may the memory of her noble life be an inspiration and help to us for all time.

"And at home, in the beautiful hills of God,
By the valley of rest so fair,
Some day, some time, when our work is done,
With joy we shall meet her there."

To the bereaved family we extend our loving and heartfelt sympathy, and commend them for consolation to Him who doeth all things well. Resolved, that the charter of our Parlor be draped for a period of thirty days; that copies of these resolutions be sent to the family of our late sister; that a copy be sent to The Grizzly Bear, and that a copy be spread upon the minutes of El Dorado Parlor No. 186 N.D.G.W.

ALTA L. DOUGLAS,
ELLA C. STANTON,
IRENE M. IRISH,
Committee.

Georgetown, July 23, 1932.

MARY BATHURST.

To the Officers and Members of Marguerite Parlor No. 12 N.D.G.W.—We, your committee appointed to draft resolutions of love and respect in memory of our departed sister, Mary Bathurst, do submit the following:

Once again we bow to the will of Almighty God, who has seen fit to claim His own from amongst our membership and taken to His Heavenly Home our esteemed sister and Pioneer. The vacancy caused by the loss of our devoted sister will never be filled. Not dead to those who loved her, not lost but gone before, she lives with us in memory, and will for evermore.

Resolved, That we extend to her bereaved family our heartfelt sympathy, and commend them for consolation to Him who doeth all things well; and be it further resolved, that a copy of these resolutions be sent to the family and a copy be spread upon the minutes.

Respectfully submitted in P.D.F.A.,
ESTHER E. DUGAN,
LILLA M. ZEISS,
BERTHA REEG.
Committee.

Placerville, July 25, 1932.

Official Directory of Parlors of the N. S. G. W.

ALAMEDA COUNTY.

Alameda No. 47, Alameda City—Perry F. Badgley, Pres.; Robt. H. Cavanaugh, Sec., 1806 Pacific Ave.; Wednesdays, Native Sons Hall, 1406 Park St.
Oakland No. 50, Oakland—R. L. Engell, Pres.; F. M. Norris, Sec., 5595 Taft Ave.; Fridays, Native Sons Hall, 11th and Clay Sts.
Las Positas No. 96, Livermore—Dr. Donald M. Fraser, Pres.; John J. Kelly, Sec., P. O. box 341; Thursdays, Foresters Hall.
Eden No. 113, Hayward—Henry L'Ecuyer, Pres.; Stanton R. Soares, Sec., P. O. box 176; 2nd and 4th Tuesdays, Memorial Hall, Main St.
Piedmont No. 120, Oakland—Frank Smith, Pres.; Charles Morando, Sec., 906 Vermont St.; Thursdays, Native Sons Hall, 11th and Clay Sts.
Wisteria No. 127, Alvarado—Henry May, Pres.; J. M. Scribner, Sec., Livermore; 1st Thursday, I.O.O.F. Hall.
Halcyon No. 146, Alameda City—S. Chesley Anderson, Pres.; J. C. Bates, Sec., 2139 Buena Vista Ave.; 1st and 3rd Tuesdays, I.O.O.F. Hall, 2329 Santa Clara Ave.
Brooklyn No. 151, Oakland—Frank B. Perry, Pres.; E. W. Cooney, Sec., 3907 14th Ave.; Wednesdays, Masonic Temple, 8th Ave. and E. 14th St.
Washington, No. 169, Centerville—M. D. Silva, Pres.; Allen G. Norris, Sec., P. O. box 31; 2nd and 4th Tuesdays, Hansen Hall.
Athens No. 195, Oakland—Elmer L. Bullock, Pres.; Harold B. Farley, Sec., 4623 Benevides Ave.; Tuesdays, Native Sons Hall, 11th and Clay Sts.
Berkeley No. 210, Berkeley—F. M. McGrath, Pres.; R. J. Garrett, Sec., 1708 Virginia St.; Tuesdays, Native Sons Hall, 2108 Shattuck Ave.
Estudillo No. 223, San Leandro—Frank V. Pacheco, Pres.; Albert G. Pacheco, Sec., 1736 E. 14th St.; 1st and 3rd Tuesdays, U.P.E.C. Hall.
Claremont No. 240, Oakland—Louis F. Cambet, Pres.; E. N. Thienger, Sec., 839 Hearst Ave., Berkeley; Tuesdays, Veterans Memorial Bldg., 43rd & Salem Sts., Emeryville.
Pleasanton No. 244, Pleasanton—Peter C. Madsen, Pres.; Ernest W. Schween, Sec.; 2nd and 4th Thursdays, I.O.O.F. Hall.
Niles No. 250, Niles—M. L. Fournier, Pres.; C. E. Martenstein, Sec.; 2nd Thursday, I.O.O.F. Hall.
Fruitvale No. 252, Oakland—William J. Keating Jr., Pres.; Ray B. Felton, Sec., 1575 Alice St.; Fridays, W.O.W. Hall, 3256 E. 14th St.

AMADOR COUNTY.

Amador No. 17, Sutter Creek—Frank Marre, Pres.; F. J. Payne, Sec.; 1st and 3rd Fridays, Native Sons Hall.
Excelsior No. 31, Jackson—Wm. Daugherty, Pres.; William Geing, Sec.; 1st and 3rd Wednesdays, Native Sons Hall, 22 Court St.
Ione No. 33, Ione—Marvin Kidd, Pres.; Josiah H. Saunders, Sec.; 1st and 3rd Wednesdays, Native Sons Hall.
Plymouth No. 48, Plymouth—John J. Upton, Pres.; Thos. D. Davis, Sec.; 1st and 3rd Saturdays, I.O.O.F. Hall.

BUTTE COUNTY.

Argonaut No. 8, Oroville—George N. Westwood, Pres.; Cyril R. Macdonald, Sec., P. O. box 502; 1st and 3rd Wednesdays, Veterans Memorial Hall.
Chico No. 21, Chico—Marcus Choisser, Pres.; Sam Lindsay Adams, Sec., Sacramento Blvd.; 2nd and 4th Thursdays, Elks Hall.

CALAVERAS COUNTY.

Chispa No. 139, Murphys—Maynard Segale, Pres.; Antone Malaspina, Sec.; Wednesdays, Native Sons Hall.

COLUSA COUNTY.

Colusa No. 69, Colusa City—Percy J. Cooke, Pres.; Phil J. Humburg, Sec., 223 Parkhill St.; Tuesdays, Eagles Hall.

CONTRA COSTA COUNTY.

General Winn No. 32, Antioch—Edmont T. Uren, Pres.; Joel H. Ford, Sec., P. O. box 311; 2nd and 4th Wednesdays, Union Hall.
Mount Diablo No. 101, Martinez—R. P. Anderson, Pres.; G. T. Barkley, Sec.; 1st and 3rd Mondays, I.O.O.F. Hall.
Byron No. 170, Byron—William E. Bunn, Pres.; H. G. Krumland, Sec.; 1st and 3rd Tuesdays, I.O.O.F. Hall.
Carquinez No. 205, Crockett—Thos. Cox, Pres.; Thomas I. Cahalan, Sec.; 1st and 3rd Wednesdays, I.O.O.F. Hall.
Richmond No. 217, Richmond—M. W. Amaral, Pres.; H. D. Mason, Sec., 11 6th St.; Wednesdays, Redmen Hall, 11th and Nevan Ave.
Concord No. 245, Concord—P. M. Soto, Pres.; D. E. Pramberg, Sec., P. O. box 235; 1st Tuesday, I.O.O.F. Hall.
Diamond No. 246, Pittsburg—Victor Ericsson, Pres.; Francis A. Irving, Sec., 248 E. 5th St.; 1st and 3rd Wednesdays, Veterans Memorial Bldg.

EL DORADO COUNTY.

Placerville No. 9, Placerville—Chas. C. Cook, Pres.; Clyde R. Berriman, Sec., Wood St.; 2nd and 4th Tuesdays, Masonic Hall.
Georgetown No. 91, Georgetown—W. H. Breedlove, Pres.; C. F. Irish, Sec.; 2nd and 4th Wednesdays, I.O.O.F. Hall.

FRESNO COUNTY.

Fresno No. 25, Fresno City—Oliver M. Akers, Pres.; W. C. Guard, Sec., 5060 Belmont; 2nd and 4th Fridays, W.O.W. Hall, 1354 Van Ness Ave.

GRAND OFFICERS.

Dr. Frank I. Gonzalez..........Junior Past Grand President
Flood Bldg., San Francisco
Seth Millington..........Grand President
Gridley
Justice Emmet Seawell..........Grand First Vice-president
State Bldg., San Francisco
Chas. A. Koenig..........Grand Second Vice-president
531 35th Ave., San Francisco
Harmon D. Skillin..........Grand Third Vice-president
Mills Bldg., San Francisco
John T. Regan..........Grand Secretary
N.S.G.W. Bldg., 414 Mason St., San Francisco
John A. Corotto..........Grand Treasurer
560 No. 5th St., San Jose
W. B. O'Brien..........Grand Marshal
2324 Santa Clara St., Alameda
Gam Hurst..........Grand Inside Sentinel
Financial Center Bldg., Oakland
William A. Reuter..........Grand Outside Sentinel
1009 Marine Ave., Wilmington
Leslie Maloche..........Grand Organist
467½ 3rd St., San Bernardino
Chester Gannon.......... Historiographer
618 Capital Ntl. Bank Bldg., Sacramento

GRAND TRUSTEES.

Jesse H. Miller..........712 DeYoung Bldg., San Francisco
Eldred L. Meyer..........922 San Vicente Blvd., Santa Monica
John M. Burnett..........914 Bank Italy Bldg., San Jose
Henry S. Lyon..........Placerville
Joseph J. McShane..........419 Flood Bldg., San Francisco
Horace J. Leavitt..........Weaverville
Chas. H. Spengemann..........827 27th Ave., San Francisco

Selma No. 107, Selma—Chester E. Shepard, Pres.; E. C. Laughlin, Sec.; 1st and 3rd Wednesdays, American Legion Hall.

HUMBOLDT COUNTY.

Humboldt No. 14, Eureka—Henry Sundfors, Pres.; Loren M. Nelson, Sec., P.O. box 195; 2nd Monday, Native Sons Hall.
Arcata No. 20, Arcata—I. C. Fleckenstein, Pres.; William Peters, Sec., P. O. box 1117; Thursdays, Native Sons Hall.
Ferndale No. 93, Ferndale—Elwood Pries, Pres.; C. H. Rasmussen, Sec., R.F.D., 47-A; 1st and 3rd Mondays, K.P. Hall.

KERN COUNTY.

Bakersfield No. 42, Bakersfield—Ralph C. Hinderliter, Pres.; Henry A. Bannister, Sec., 610 "F" St.; 2nd and 4th Fridays, Justice Court, City Hall.

LAKE COUNTY.

Lower Lake No. 159, Lower Lake—Harold S. Anderson, Pres.; Albert Kugelman, Sec.; Thursdays, I.O.O.F. Hall.

LASSEN COUNTY.

Honey Lake No. 198, Standish—James C. Meeske, Pres.; N. V. Wemple, Sec., Litchfield; 1st and 3rd Wednesdays, Wrede Hall.
Big Valley No. 211, Bieber—George Bunselmeier, Pres.; A. W. McKenzie, Sec.; 1st and 3rd Wednesdays, I.O.O.F. Hall.

LOS ANGELES COUNTY.

Los Angeles No. 45, Los Angeles City—Owen S. Adams, Pres.; Richard W. Fryer, Sec., 1629 Champlain Ter.; Thursdays, Merchant Plumbers Hall, 1832 So. Hope.
Ramona No. 109, Los Angeles City—James M. Watson, Pres.; John V. Scott, Sec., Patriotic Hall, 1816 So. Figueroa; Fridays, Patriotic Hall, 1816 So. Figueroa.
Hollywood No. 196, Los Angeles City—Kenneth A. Case, Pres.; E. J. Reilly, Sec., Olive View; Mondays, 1089 No. Oxford Ave.
Long Beach No. 239, Long Beach—Francis H. Gentry, Pres.; W. W. Brady, Sec., 801 Jergins Trust Bldg.; 2nd and 4th Thursdays, Moose Hall, Elm and Anaheim.
Sepulveda No. 263, San Pedro—Joseph Pia, Pres.; Harry Fairall, Sec., 1925 Pacific Ave.; 2nd and 4th Fridays, Odd Fellows Temple, 10th and Gaffey Sts.
Glendale No. 264, Glendale—Leslie F. Schellback, Pres.; Abel B. Molen, Sec., 508 So. Belmont St.; 1st and 3rd Tuesdays, Masonic Temple, 234 So. Brand Blvd.
Santa Monica Bay No. 267, Ocean Park—Orrin G. Welch, Pres.; John J. Smith, Sec., 830 Rialto Ave., Venice; 2nd and 4th Mondays, New Eagle Hall, 2823¼ Main St.
Cahuenga No. 268, Reseda—Harold C. Trexler, Pres.; Carrol S. Driscoll, Sec., P.O. box 25, Chatsworth; first Friday, Aiton Hall.

MADERA COUNTY.

Madera No. 130, Madera City—Cornelius Noble, Pres.; T. P. Cosgrave, Sec.; 1st and 3rd Thursdays, First National Bank Bldg.

MARIN COUNTY.

Mount Tamalpais No. 64, San Rafael—M. E. Peterson, Pres.; Manual A. Andrade, Sec., 532 Mission Ave.; 1st and 3rd Mondays, Portuguese American Hall.
Sea Point No. 158, Sausalito—A. H. Bettencourt, Pres.; Manuel Santos, Sec., 6 Glen Drive; 1st and 3rd Wednesdays, Perry Bldg.
Nicasio No. 183, Nicasio—M. T. Farley, Pres.; R. J. Rogers, Sec.; 2nd and 4th Wednesdays, U.A.O.D. Hall.

MENDOCINO COUNTY.

Ukiah No. 71, Ukiah—Henry Bucknell, Pres.; Ben Hofman, Sec., P. O. box 473; 1st and 3rd Mondays, I.O.O.F. Hall.
Broderick No. 117, Point Arena—A. L. McCallum, Pres.; C. J. Buchanan, Sec.; 1st and 3rd Thursdays, Forester Hall.
Alder Glen No. 200, Fort Bragg—H. M. Bohn, Pres.; C. R. Weller, Sec.; 2nd and 4th Fridays, I.O.O.F. Hall.

MERCED COUNTY.

Yosemite No. 24, Merced City—John J. Thronton, Pres.; True W. Fowler, Sec., P. O. box 781; 2nd and 4th Mondays, I.O.O.F. Hall.
Los Banos No. 206, Los Banos—Robert L. Puccinelli, Pres.; L. E. Sarbo, Sec., R.F.D., box 21; 2nd and 4th Wednesdays, Eagles Hall.

MONTEREY COUNTY.

Monterey No. 75, Monterey City—James Millington, Pres.; T. W. Krieger, Sec., 999 Franklin St.; 1st and 3rd Fridays, Knights Pythias Hall, Main St.
Santa Lucia No. 97, Salinas—Roy Martella, Pres.; R. W. Adcock, Sec., Route 2, box 180; Mondays, Native Sons Hall, 32 W. Alisal St.
Gabilan No. 132, Castroville—B. A. McCoy, Pres.; R. H. Martin, Sec., P. O. box 81; 1st and 3rd Thursdays, Native Sons Hall.

NAPA COUNTY.

Saint Helena No. 53, Saint Helena—Lucas Haus, Pres.; Edw. L. Bonhote, Sec., P. O. box 267; Mondays, Native Sons Hall.
Napa No. 62, Napa City—R. O. Akers, Pres.; H. J. Hoernle, Sec., 1226 Oak St.; Mondays, Native Sons Hall.
Calistoga No. 86, Calistoga—Edmund Molinari, Pres.; Louis Carlenzoli, Sec.; 1st and 3rd Mondays, I.O.O.F. Hall.

NEVADA COUNTY.

Hydraulic No. 56, Nevada City—Arthur W. Davis, Pres.; Dr. C. W. Chapman, Sec.; Tuesdays, Pythian Castle.
Quartz No. 58, Grass Valley—Robert Kohler, Pres.; H. Ray George, Sec., 151 Conaway Ave.; Mondays, Auditorium Hall.
Donner No. 162, Truckee—J. F. Lichtenberger, Pres.; H. C. Lichtenberger, Sec.; 2nd and 4th Tuesdays, Native Sons Hall.

ORANGE COUNTY.

Santa Ana No. 265, Santa Ana—Amos Huntzinger, Pres.; E. F. Marks, Sec., 1124 No. Bristol St.; 1st and 3rd Mondays, K.C. Hall, 4th and French Sts.

PLACER COUNTY.

Auburn No. 59, Auburn—Iris Garcia, Pres.; J. G. Walsh, Sec.; 1st and 3rd Fridays, Foresters Hall.
Silver Star No. 63, Lincoln—L. F. Browning, Pres.; Barney G. Barry, Sec., P. O. box 72; 3rd Wednesday, I.O.O.F. Hall.
Rocklin No. 233, Roseville—Wm. La Due, Pres.; M. E. Reed, Sec., 253 W. Duranta; 2nd and 4th Wednesdays, Eagles Hall.

PLUMAS COUNTY.

Quincy No. 131, Quincy—J. D. McLaughlin, Pres.; E. C. Kelsey, Sec.; 2nd Thursday, I.O.O.F. Hall.
Golden Anchor No. 182, La Porte—R. J. McGrath, Pres.; LeRoy J. Post, Sec.; 2nd and 4th Sunday mornings, Native Sons Hall.
Plumas No. 228, Taylorsville—E. E. Sikes, Pres.; George E. Boyden, Sec.; 1st and 3rd Mondays, Native Sons Hall.

SACRAMENTO COUNTY.

Sacramento No. 3, Sacramento City—J. G. Fitzhenry, Pres.; J. F. Didion, Sec., 1131 "O" St.; Thursdays, Native Sons Bldg., 11th and "J" Sts.
Sunset No. 26, Sacramento City—L. W. Marvin, Pres.; Edward E. Reese, Sec., County Treasurer Office; Mondays, Native Sons Bldg., 11th and "J" Sts.
Elk Grove No. 41, Elk Grove—Fred Sehlmeyer, Pres.; Walter Martin, Sec.; 2nd and 4th Fridays, Masonic Hall.
Granite No. 83, Folsom—Joe Reivas, Pres.; Frank Showers, Sec.; 2nd and 4th Tuesdays, K.P. Hall.
Courtland No. 106, Courtland—Thornton Pylman, Pres.; Jos. Green, Sec.; 1st Saturday and 3rd Monday, Native Sons Hall.
Sutter Fort No. 241, Sacramento City—Ed. T. Goyne, Pres.; C. L. Katzenstein, Sec., P. O. box 914; 2nd and 4th Wednesdays, Native Sons Bldg., 11th and "J" Sts.
Galt No. 243, Galt—John Granadas, Pres.; F. W. Harms, Sec.; 1st and 3rd Mondays, I.O.O.F. Hall.

SAN BENITO COUNTY.

Fremont No. 44, Hollister—S. Churchill, Pres.; J. E. Prendergast Jr., Sec., 1064 Monterey St.; 1st and 3rd Thursdays, Grangers Union Hall.

SAN BERNARDINO COUNTY.

Arrowhead No. 110, San Bernardino City—F. L. McGarvey, Pres.; R. W. Brazelton, Sec., 462 6th St.; Wednesdays, Eagles Hall, 469 4th St.

SAN DIEGO COUNTY.

San Diego No. 108, San Diego City—Martin J. Spangler, Pres.; A. V. Mayrhofer, Sec., 1572 2nd St.; Wednesdays, K.C. Hall, 4th and Elm Sts.

SAN FRANCISCO CITY AND COUNTY.

California No. 1, San Francisco—Joseph Lawlor, Pres.; Ellis A. Blackman, Sec., 1248-A Divisadero St.; Thursdays, Native Sons Bldg., 414 Mason St.
Pacific No. 10, San Francisco—Walter Mohrdick, Pres.; J. Henry Bastein, Sec., 426 City Hall; Tuesdays, Native Sons Bldg., 414 Mason St.
Golden Gate No. 29, San Francisco—Thomas I. Schlink, Pres.; Adolph Eberhart, Sec., 188 Carl St.; Mondays, Native Sons Bldg., 414 Mason St.
Mission No. 38, San Francisco—George Leahy, Pres.; Thos. J. Stewart, Sec., 1919 Howard St.; Wednesdays, Redmen Hall, 3053 16th St.
San Francisco No. 49, San Francisco—Charles Miller, Pres.; David Capurro, Sec., 976 Union St.; Thursdays, Native Sons Bldg., 414 Mason St.
El Dorado No. 52, San Francisco—Edward Victor, Pres.; Alfred Viautin, Sec., 1537 Franklin St.; Thursdays, Native Sons Bldg., 414 Mason St.
Rincon No. 72, San Francisco—Frank D. Sericano, Pres.; John A. Gilmour, Sec., 2069 Golden Gate Ave.; Wednesdays, Native Sons Bldg., 414 Mason St.
Stanford No. 76, San Francisco—Dr. Vincent V. Hardeman, Pres.; Charles T. O'Kane, Sec., 1111 Pine St.; Tuesdays, Native Sons Bldg., 414 Mason St.
Bay City No. 104, San Francisco—Morris Garren, Pres.; Max E. Licht, Sec., 1831 Fulton St.; 2nd and 4th Wednesdays, Native Sons Bldg., 414 Mason St.
Niantic No. 105, San Francisco—A. Furner, Pres.; J. M. Darcy, Sec., 10 Hoffman Ave.; Wednesdays, Native Sons Bldg., 414 Mason St.
National No. 118, San Francisco—Wayne Burke, Pres.; Martin M. Ratigan, Sec., 1325 Page St., Apt. 6; Thursdays, 1160 Eddy St.
Hesperian No. 137, San Francisco—C. McLaughlin, Pres.; Albert Carlson, Sec., 379 Justin Dr.; Thursdays, Native Sons Bldg., 414 Mason St.
Alcalde No. 154, San Francisco—Charles Kurpinsky, Pres.; Harry S. Burke, Sec., 25 Ord St.; 2nd and 4th Wednesdays, Native Sons Bldg., 414 Mason St.
South San Francisco No. 157, San Francisco—Otto A. Elvander, Pres.; John T. Regan, Sec., 1489 Newcomb Ave.; Wednesdays, Masonic Bldg., 4705 3rd St.
Sequoia No. 160, San Francisco—Harry Grover, Pres.; Walter W. Garrett, Sec., 2500 Van Ness Ave.; Mondays, Swedish-American Bldg., 2174 Market St.
Precita No. 187, San Francisco—Lloyd J. Cosgrove, Pres.; Edward Tietjen, Sec., 1367 15th Ave.; Thursdays, Mission Masonic Hall, 2668 Mission St.
Olympus No. 189, San Francisco—Henry H. McGowan, Pres.; Harvey J. Carty, Sec., 1651 Market St., Apt. 505; 2nd and 4th Tuesdays, Independent Redmen Hall, 3053 16th St.
Presidio No. 194, San Francisco—Lester Figone, Pres.; George A. Ducker, Sec., 442 21st Ave.; Mondays, Native Sons Bldg., 414 Mason St.
Marshall No. 202, San Francisco—Alexander Jean, Pres.; Frank Bacigalupi, Sec., 725 Douglas St.; 1st and 3rd Wednesdays, Native Sons Bldg., 414 Mason St.
Dolores No. 208, San Francisco—James F. Vahey, Pres.; Eugene O'Donnell, Sec., Mills Bldg.; Tuesdays, Mission Masonic Bldg., 2668 Mission St.
Twin Peaks No. 214, San Francisco—Clifford Roberts, Pres.; Thos. Pendergast, Sec., 278 Douglas St.; Wednesdays, Willopi Hall, 4061 24th St.
El Capitan No. 222, San Francisco—Frank Rizzo, Pres.; James Hanna, Sec., 2450 27th Ave.; 1st and 3rd Thursdays, King Soloman Hall, 1739 Fillmore St.

ATTENTION, SECRETARIES!

THIS DIRECTORY IS PUBLISHED BY AUTHORITY OF THE GRAND PARLOR N.S.G.W., AND ALL NOTICES OF CHANGES MUST BE RECEIVED BY THE GRAND SECRETARY (NOT THE MAGAZINE) ON OR BEFORE THE 20TH OF EACH MONTH TO INSURE CORRECTION IN NEXT ISSUE OF DIRECTORY.

Guadalupe No. 231, San Francisco—Roy Tensfeldt, Pres.; Alvin A. Johnson, Sec., 142 Rousseau St.; Tuesdays, Guadalupe Hall, 4551 Mission St.
Castro No. 232, San Francisco—Ralph Willis, Pres.; James H. Hayes, Sec., 4014 18th St.; Tuesdays, Native Sons Bldg., 414 Mason St.
Balboa No. 234, San Francisco—George Schroth, Pres.; E. W. Boyd, Sec., 437 Cherry St.; Thursdays, Maccabee Hall, 5th Ave. and Clement St.
Bret Harte No. 260, San Francisco—Chas. E. Lillie, Pres.; A. W. McElhatton, Sec., 103 Holloway Ave.; Tuesdays, West of Twin Peaks Hall, 233 Legion Court.
Utopia No. 270, San Francisco—George Walters, Pres.; Herbert H. Schneider, Sec., 2455 16th Ave.; Tuesdays, American Hall, 20th and Capp Sts.

SAN JOAQUIN COUNTY.

Stockton No. 7, Stockton—John D. Gallagher, Pres.; R. D. Dorcey, Sec., P. O. box 388; Mondays, Native Sons Hall.
Lodi No. 18, Lodi—Jerome Solomon, Pres.; Dr. Clyde Brennan, Sec.; 2nd and 4th Wednesdays, Eagles Hall.
Tracy No. 186, Tracy—C. S. Selna, Pres.; R. J. Marraccini, Sec., R.F.D. No. 1, box 217; Thursdays, I.O.O.F. Hall.
Manteca No. 271, Manteca—Chas. N. Howell Jr., Pres.; Leonard Faria, Sec., R.F.D., box 75, Lathrop; 1st and 3rd Wednesdays, I.O.O.F. Hall.

SAN LUIS OBISPO COUNTY.

San Miguel No. 150, San Miguel—H. Twisselman, Pres.; Otto Kuchl, Sec., Paso Robles; 1st and 3rd Wednesdays, Fraternal Hall.
Cambria No. 152, Cambria—J. M. Soto, Pres.; A. S. Gay, Sec.; Wednesdays, Rigdon Hall.

SAN MATEO COUNTY.

Redwood No. 66, Redwood City—Frank Deluchi, Pres.; A. S. Liguori, Sec., P. O. box 212; Thursdays, American Foresters Hall.
Seaside No. 95, Half Moon Bay—Andrew F. Gilcrest, Pres.; John G. Gilcrest, Sec.; 2nd and 4th Tuesdays, I.O.O.F. Hall.
Menlo No. 185, Menlo Park—C. T. Maloney, Pres.; F. W. Johnson, Sec., P. O. box 601; Thursdays, Masonic Hall.
Pebble Beach No. 230, Pescadero—Harold Souza, Pres.; E. A. Shaw, Sec.; 2nd and 4th Wednesdays, I.O.O.F. Hall.
El Carmelo No. 256, Daly City—Theodore A. Clemens, Pres.; Ernest L. Micco, Sec., 639 Morse St., San Francisco; 2nd and 4th Wednesdays, Eagles Hall.
Industrial City No. 269, South San Francisco—John C. Hamilton, Pres.; Geo. A. Roll, Sec., P. O. box 237; 2nd and 4th Mondays, Metropolitan Hall.

SANTA BARBARA COUNTY.

Santa Barbara No. 116, Santa Barbara City—C. W. McCormick, Pres.; H. C. Sweetser, Sec., Court House; 1st and 3rd Wednesdays, I.O.O.F. Hall.

SANTA CLARA COUNTY.

San Jose No. 22, San Jose—Joseph Sabatte, Pres.; Joseph Lawrence, Sec., 1095 No. First St.; Mondays, I.O.O.F. Hall.
Santa Clara No. 100, Santa Clara City—John J. Trinajstich, Pres.; Clarence Clevenger, Sec., P. O. box 297; Wednesdays, Redmen Hall.
Observatory No. 177, San Jose—William L. Gerrans, Pres.; A. B. Langford, Sec., Hall Records; Tuesdays, Knights Columbus Hall, 40 No. First St.
Mountain View No. 215, Mountain View—Gilbert F. McCorkle, Pres.; C. A. Antonioli, Sec., 301 Castro St.; 2nd and 4th Wednesdays, Mockbee Hall.
Palo Alto No. 216, Palo Alto—John C. Bernal, Pres.; Albert A. Quinn, Sec., 643 High St.; Mondays, Native Sons Bldg., Hamilton Ave. and Emerson St.

SANTA CRUZ COUNTY.

Watsonville No. 65, Watsonville—Fred R. Baese, Pres.; E. R. Tindall, Sec., R.F.D. No. 5, Box 313; 2nd and 4th Tuesdays, I.O.O.F. Hall.
Santa Cruz No. 90, Santa Cruz City—Horace Burkett, Pres.; T. V. Mathews, Sec., 105 Pacheco Ave.; Fridays, Native Sons Hall, 117 Pacific Ave.

SHASTA COUNTY.

McCloud No. 149, Redding—A. E. Welbourn, Pres.; Hugh A. Shuffleton, Sec.; 1st and 3rd Thursdays, Moose Hall.

SIERRA COUNTY.

Downieville No. 92, Downieville—Frank H. Turner, Pres.; H. S. Tibbey, Sec.; 2nd and 4th Mondays, I.O.O.F. Hall.
Golden Nugget No. 94, Sierra City—Elmer Thompson, Pres.; Arthur R. Pride, Sec.; 1st and 3rd Wednesdays, Masonic Hall.

SISKIYOU COUNTY.

Etna No. 192, Etna—Frank B. Quigley, Pres.; Harvey A. Green, Sec.; 1st and 3rd Wednesdays, I.O.O.F. Hall.
Liberty No. 193, Sawyers Bar—Orrin R. Bigelow, Pres.; John M. Barry, Sec.; 1st and 3rd Saturdays, I.O.O.F. Hall.

SOLANO COUNTY.

Solano No. 39, Suisun—Karl Koch, Pres.; J. W. Kinlock, Sec.; 1st and 3rd Tuesdays, I.O.O.F. Hall.
Vallejo No. 77, Vallejo—Joseph Clavo, Pres.; Werner B. Hallin, Sec., 912 Carolina; 2nd and 4th Tuesdays, San Pablo Hall.

SONOMA COUNTY.

Petaluma No. 27, Petaluma—Fred G. Ilg, Pres.; C. F. Fobes, Sec., 114 Prospect St.; 2nd and 4th Mondays, Druid Hall, Gross Bldg., 41 Main St.
Santa Rosa No. 28, Santa Rosa—Wesley Beach, Pres.; Leland S. Lewis, Sec., Court House; Mondays, Native Sons Hall.
Glen Ellen No. 102, Glen Ellen—Tony Cereghino, Pres.; Frank Kirch, Sec., Route 3, Santa Rosa; 2nd Monday, N.S.G.W. Hall.
Sonoma No. 111, Sonoma City—Joseph Andrieux, Pres.; L. H. Green, Sec.; 1st and 3rd Mondays, I.O.O.F. Hall.
Sebastopol No. 143, Sebastopol—O. A. McChristian, Pres.; F. G. McFarlane, Sec.; 1st and 3rd Fridays, I.O.O.F. Hall.

STANISLAUS COUNTY.

Modesto No. 11, Modesto—Chas. D. Blaine, Pres.; C. C. Eastin Jr., Sec., P. O. box 898; 1st and 3rd Wednesdays, I.O.O.F. Hall.
Oakdale No. 142, Oakdale—D. W. Tulloch, Pres.; E. T. Gobin, Sec.; 2nd and 4th Mondays, Legion Hall.
Orestimba No. 247, Crows Landing—Lloyd W. Fink, Pres.; G. W. Fink, Sec.; 1st and 3rd Wednesdays, Community Club Home.

SUTTER COUNTY.

Sutter No. 261, Sutter City—Albert Thomassen, Pres.; Glen R. Haynes, Sec., R.F.D. No. 2, Yuba City; 2nd and 4th Mondays, N.D.G.W. Hall.

TRINITY COUNTY.

Mount Bally No. 87, Weaverville—R. L. Marshall, Pres.; E. V. Ryan, Sec.; 1st and 3rd Mondays, Native Sons Hall.

TUOLUMNE COUNTY.

Tuolumne No. 144, Sonora—Mathew J. Marshall, Pres.; William M. Harrington, Sec., P. O. box 715; 2nd and 4th Fridays, Knights Columbus Hall.
Columbia No. 258, Columbia—Jos. Cadematori, Pres.; Charles E. Grant, Sec.; 2nd and 4th Thursdays, Native Sons Hall.

VENTURA COUNTY.

Cabrillo No. 114, Ventura City—David Bennett, Pres., 1880 Church St.

YOLO COUNTY.

Woodland No. 30, Woodland—J. L. Aronson, Pres.; E. B. Hayward, Sec.; 1st Thursday, Native Sons Hall.

YUBA COUNTY.

Marysville No. 6, Marysville—Ray C. Burris, Pres.; Verne Fogarty, Sec., 719 6th St.; 2nd Friday, Foresters Hall.
Rainbow No. 40, Wheatland—F. M. Beilby, Pres.; W. A. Bowser, Sec., P. O. box 313; 2nd Thursday, I.O.O.F. Hall.

AFFILIATED ORGANIZATIONS.

San Francisco Extension of the Order Committee, N.S.G.W.—Joseph J. McShane, Chmn.; Harold J. Regan, Sec., 414 Mason St., San Francisco; meets 2nd and 4th Fridays, Grizzly Bear Club, 414 Mason St., San Francisco.
Alameda County Extension of the Order Committee, N.S.G.W.—Edward T. Schnarr, Chmn.; Frank Roemer, Sec., 3297 Morcom Ave., Oakland; meets 1st and 3rd Mondays, N.S.G.W. Hall, 11th and Clay Sts., Oakland.
Interparlor Committee (Southern District), N.S.G.W. and N.D.G.W.—Burrel D. Neighbours, Chmn.; F. J. Burmester, Sec., P. O. box 42, Colton; meets 2nd and 4th Fridays, Patriotic Hall, 1816 So. Figueroa St., Los Angeles.
San Francisco Assembly No. 1 Past Presidents Association N.S.G.W.—Meets 1st and 3rd Fridays, Native Sons Bldg., 414 Mason St., San Francisco; J. H. Sylvester, Gov.; J. F. Stanley, Sec., 1175 O'Farrell St., San Francisco.
East Bay Counties Assembly No. 3 Past Presidents Association N.S.G.W.—Meets 4th Monday, Native Sons Hall, 11th and Clay Sts., Oakland; Felix Robison, Gov.; Edgar G. Hanson, Sec., 1260 Russell St., Berkeley.
Marin County Assembly No. 5 Past Presidents Association N.S.G.W.—J. S. Rose Jr., Gov.; L. J. Peter, Sec., Peter Bldg., 4th and "C" Sts., San Rafael.
Fred H. Greeley Assembly No. 6 Past Presidents Association N.S.G.W.—Meets monthly with different Parlors comprising district; R. L. P. Bigelow, Gov.; Barney Barry, Sec., P. O. box 72, Lincoln.
San Joaquin Assembly No. 7 Past Presidents Association N.S.G.W.—Meets 1st Friday, Native Sons Hall, Stockton; Clyde H. Gregg, Gov.; R. D. Dorcey, Sec., Native Sons Club, Stockton.
Sonoma County Assembly No. 9 Past President Association N.S.G.W.—Meets monthly at different Parlor headquarters in county; Louis Bosch, Gov.; L. S. Lewis, Sec., Court House, Santa Rosa.
General John A. Sutter Assembly No. 10 Past Presidents Association—C. C. Wachman, Gov.; Jas. J. Longshore, Sec., 514 "J" St., Sacramento.
Grizzly Bear Club—Members all Parlors outside San Francisco at all times welcome. Clubrooms top floor Native Sons Bldg., 414 Mason St., San Francisco.
Native Sons and Native Daughters Central Committee on Homeless Children—Main office, 955 Phelan Bldg., San Francisco; Mrs. John W. Stirling, Chmn.; Miss Mary E. Brusie, Sec. Los Angeles branch office, 3924 Sunset Blvd.; Dorothy Schlingman, Sec.

(ADVERTISEMENT.)

N.S.G.W. OFFICIAL DEATH LIST.

Containing the name, the date and the place of birth, the date of death, and the Subordinate Parlor affiliation of deceased members reported to Grand Secretary John T. Regan from July 20, 1932, to August 20, 1932:

Bodinnar, James; Amador City, May 26, 1880; July 15, 1932; Amador No. 17.
Ebeling, William Henry; San Francisco, May 25, 1865; July 15, 1932; San Jose No. 22.
McComas, Henry William; San Jose, September 25, 1871; July 28, 1932; San Jose No. 22.
Strohl, Louis; San Francisco, January 22, 1869; August 1, 1932; San Francisco No. 49.
McKibbon, David; San Francisco, March 22, 1863; July 20, 1932; El Dorado No. 52.
Meeker, Edward; Howland Flat, December 4, 1870; July 24, 1932; Quartz No. 58.
Sweitzer, C. D.; Martinez, February 12, 1859; August 9, 1932; Napa No. 62.
Gunther, Charles Augustus; San Francisco, May 21, 1873; July 25, 1932; Watsonville No. 65.
Henry, Edward; Watsonville, March 29, 1860; August 8, 1932; Watsonville No. 65.
Graus, Carl Theodore; San Francisco, April 29, 1870; January 11, 1932; Stanford No. 76.
Bancroft, Walter Gardner; Clipper Gap, August 13, 1878; February 6, 1932; Santa Cruz No. 90.
Niehur, James John; Ferndale, August 16, 1872; July 16, 1932; Ferndale No. 93.
Samuels, Jacob; San Francisco, June 16, 1867; July 17, 1932; Bay City No. 104.
Doyle, Charles Michel; San Bernardino, October 27, 1891; July 27, 1932; Arrowhead No. 110.
Daley, Charlie P.; Ventura, June 21, 1884; June 10, 1932; Cabrillo No. 114.
Lux, Frank August; Sacramento, February 24, 1872; June 28, 1932; Olympus No. 189.
Marks, Abe; Healdsburg, June 12, 1879; July 31, 1932; Presidio No. 194.
Walsh, Clarence; Greenwood, January 13, 1899; August 3, 1932; Alder Glen No. 200.

N.D.G.W. OFFICIAL DEATH LIST.

Giving the name, the date of death, and the Subordinate Parlor affiliation of all deceased members as reported to Grand Secretary Sallie R. Thaler from July 18, 1932, to August 18, 1932:

Doyle, Isabelle F.; June 26; Linda Rosa No. 170.
Woodall, Annie; July 1; Sans Souci No. 96.
Brome, Katie I.; July 3; Coloma No. 212.
Greiner, Eliza Jane; June 28; Aunona No. 164.
Spohn, Ruth Tornblom; July 12; Aloha No. 106.
Read, Carrie B.; July 16; Junipero No. 141.
Hughes, Mary A.; July 10; Marguerite No. 12.
Amick, Susie M.; July 9; Chispa No. 40.
Bathurst, Mary Duffy; June 21; Marguerite No. 12.
Crowley, Mary K.; July 29; Guadalupe No. 153.
Foster, Theresa M.; July 29; Santa Cruz No. 26.
Carlile, Catherine; July 14; Marinita No. 198.

NATIVE DAUGHTER NEWS

(Continued from Page 17)

Edwards was presented with a gift. Refreshments were served. Activities of the Parlor will be resumed September 15, when a 6:30 dinner will be served by Dora Trendle and associates, losers in a recent membership contest.

Ontario—Officers of Ontario No. 251 were installed by Past President Genevieve Hiskey (Santa Ana No. 235), Mrs. Ethel Baxter becoming president. During the ceremonies Mrs. Lois Johnson favored with several vocal numbers. Mrs. Adele Frankish, retiring president, was the recipient of a beautiful emblematic pin, and in appreciation for services rendered Mrs. Hiskey was presented with a silver set. Flowers were presented Grand Outside Sentinel Hazel B. Hansen, organizer of the Parlor, President Betty Saunders of Verdugo No. 240 and President Mattie Edwards of Grace No. 242. Many visitors were in attendance. Cards followed the installation, and the evening concluded with the serving of a bountiful spanish supper prepared by a committee headed by Beatrice Herzberg. Flowers in abundance and of every hue were used in decorating the meetingroom and the banquetroom.

Joint Installations.

Placerville—Officers of Marguerite No. 12 and Placerville No. 9 N.S.G.W. were jointly installed by Supervising Deputy Agnes Schiff and District Deputy George M. Smith, Miss Monica McCusker and Charles C. Cook becoming the respective presidents. Past president emblems were presented Frances Hancock and Louis Mocettini. Refreshments were served and a movie entertainment was presented.

Menlo Park—Officers of Menlo No. 211 and Menlo No. 185 N.S.G.W. were jointly installed by Deputies Ida Pfaff and Phil Blanchard. Deputy Pfaff was presented with a gift, and a banquet was followed by old-fashioned dancing. Both Parlors will march in the San Francisco Admission Day parade.

Bakersfield—Officers of El Tejon No. 239 and Bakersfield No. 42 N.S.G.W. were jointly installed by Deputy Jennie Dennis and Frank M. Lane, Mrs. Gladys Cooper and George Taylor becoming the respective presidents. Refreshments were served, and during the social hour Lane discoursed on California history. Among the visitors were Supervising Deputy Minnie B. Heath and Deputy Grand President Al Lobree.

Past Presidents Doings.

Association No. 3 is doing much charitable work through its welfare committee, Mrs. Claire Borchers chairman. A card party, with Mrs. Dora Dunn as chairman, is billed for September 13, and plans are being formulated to entertain Association No. 2 in October. Grand Organist Clara Gairaud and Mrs. Julia Waddington were seriously injured in an auto accident August 15.

Chico—Association No. 5 had its annual outdoor party August 5. Swimming, the main entertainment feature, was followed by a supper.

Bar Meet—The Fifth annual meeting of the California State Bar Association will be held at Coronado, San Diego County, September 29 to October 1.

Rodeo and Stock Show—Merced City will feature a rodeo and stock show, September 17 and 18.

Grape Day—Escondido, San Diego County, will have its annual Grape Day celebration, September 9, which also is Admission Day.

In Memoriam

SUSIE AMICK.

"Sunset and evening star,
And one clear call for me,
And may there be no moaning of the bar,
When I put out to sea;

Twilight and evening bell,
And after that the dark,
And may there be no sadness of farewell
When I embark;

For tho' from out our bourne of Time and Place,
The flood may bear me far,
I hope to see my Pilot face to face
When I have crost the bar."

Again our Golden Chain of Fraternity has been severed by the angel of death, who once more has entered the portals of Chispa Parlor No. 40 N.D.G.W.

Whereas, It has pleased our Heavenly Father to call our dearly beloved sister, Susie Amick, to the Eternal Parlor above, let us always cherish the fond memory of her noble character, her loving ways and kindly deeds.

Not dead to those who loved her,
Not lost, but gone before;
She lives with us in memory,
And will for ever more.

The trials, the sorrows and disappointments that must enter every life, however sheltered, are ended and our sister peacefully sleeps. Reverently then would we say, "Thy will be done." We now record our tribute of love and affection to one whose thoughtfulness endeared her to all.

Resolved, That we extend to her bereaved family our sincere sympathy. It is our earnest prayer that God, in His infinite mercy, assuage their deep grief and send peace into their hearts. Be it further resolved, that our charter be draped in mourning in due respect for our late sister; that a copy be sent to her family, and one to The Grizzly Bear Magazine for publication.

EDITH L. CAMPBELL,
ESTHER M. GEBHARDT,
IDA ALLEN,
Committee.

Ione, August 17, 1932.

LOS ANGELES--CITY and COUNTY

LOS ANGELES

(Continued from Page 9)

BENEFIT FOR WORTHY CAUSE.

Los Angeles Parlor No. 45 N.S.G.W. will stage a '49 camp at the Malibu ranch of William D. Newell, September 24 and 25. The charge is one dollar. This is a benefit, for the relief of needy members and their families, and the response should be liberal. A rousing good time is assured. Tickets, and information as to how to reach the scene of action, may be procured from any member of the committee of arrangements: Leslie A. Packard (chairman), Earl H. LeMoine, Howard G. Bentley, Past Grand President John T. Newell, Charles E. Lloyd and Walter Fisher.

THIMBLE CLUB HAS PARK SESSION.

Long Beach—Officers of Long Beach Parlor No. 154 N.D.G.W. were installed August 4 by Deputy Nellie Cline, Zella L. Hodgedon becoming president. Officers-elect and acting grand officers wore corsages of gladioli. Gifts were presented Violet T. Henshilwood, retiring president, and Daisy T. Hansen, retiring past president, and a corsage was given Kate McFadyen, "mother" of the Parlor. A musical program was presented by Chairman Claudia Miller. Eight Parlors were represented among the guests.

Long Beach's thimble club had an allday session at Bixby Park August 11, with Chairman Lucretia Coates presiding. August 18 a card party was held, with Eleanor Johnson as chairman.

TRAVELOGUE MOVIE.

Ramona Parlor No. 109 N.S.G.W. will initiate a class of candidates September 16. Following a brief business session September 23 an address on "Fencing and Duelling" will be given. Those who witnessed the fencing and pistol-shooting contests during the Olympics should be interested. A light lunch will be served. September 30 an interesting and instructive travelogue movie will be the entertainment feature.

BEAR FLAG GIVEN STATE BUILDING.

Glendale—For use in the assemblyroom of the state building in Los Angeles, Verdugo Parlor No. 240 N.D.G.W. August 9 presented to California a 6x10-foot State (Bear) Flag. President Elizabeth Sanders introduced Grand Outside Sentinel Hazel B. Hansen, who made the presentation address, which was responded to by Governor James Rolph. That evening, Grand President Seth Millington visited Glendale Parlor No. 264 N.S.G.W., and President Sanders, on behalf of Verdugo, presented him with a gift.

Officers of the Parlor were installed by Deputy Gertrude Allen July 27, and there was a large attendance. Miss Ruth Ruiz, former deputy, was given a surprise shower, and a banquet was served. August 12, Verdugo sponsored an evening beach party at Castle Rock.

OFFICIAL TO VISIT.

The September 12 meeting of Hollywood Parlor No. 196 N.S.G.W. will be in honor of Grand First Vice-president Emmet Seawell, justice of the California Supreme Court, who will be a visitor. A large class of candidates will be initiated, a program of entertainment will be presented and refreshments will be served. September 5 being Labor Day, the Parlor will hold no meeting.

DELEGATION FOR S. F. CELEBRATION.

At the August 12 meeting of the Interparlor N.S.G.W. and N.D.G.W. Committee, a committee—Grand Trustee Eldred L. Meyer, Grand Outside Sentinel William I. Reuter, William J. Bright and Clinton E. Skinner of the Native Sons, and Mms. Olinda Kerby, Hazel Clinger, Mary Meyer and Walter Hiskey of the Native Daughters—was appointed to endeavor to arrange for participation of a Los Angeles County delegation in the San Francisco Admission Day parade. Any Native desiring to make the trip should get in touch with Grand Trustee Eldred Meyer.

The Interparlor Committee also voted to sponsor in November a suitable program in observance of National Education Week.

HAS "MISS SAN PEDRO" CANDIDATE.

San Pedro—Through the Chamber of Commerce, four local organizations are sponsoring a candidate to represent San Pedro at the California State Fair in Sacramento. The one selling the most theater tickets will have its candidate sent as "Miss San Pedro" to the fair. Rudecinda Parlor No. 230 N.D.G.W. is sponsoring Miss Thelma Ross, and the members are working hard to win success for her.

The Parlor's Florencita thimble club is growing, and accomplishing more, each meeting. The members are now engaged in embroidering, in preparation for the Christmas holidays.

THANKSGIVING APPEAL.

The N.S.G.W. and N.D.G.W. Homeless Children Committee elected officers August 5, the following being selected: Irving Baxter, chairman; Miss Grace Norton, vice-chairman; Mrs. Annie L. Adair, secretary; Mrs. Calista Stefan, treasurer. There was a large attendance, Lugonia Parlor No. 241 N.D.G.W. and Arrowhead Parlor No. 110 N.S.G.W. of San Bernardino being well represented.

A Thanksgiving letter will be sent in November by the committee to the membership of the Orders, appealing for funds for carrying on this splendid work in behalf of homeless children of all races, colors and creeds.

SURPRISE VISITOR.

Ocean Park—Santa Monica Bay Parlor No. 267 N.S.G.W. had a surprise, but most welcome, visitor August 22, Grand President Seth Millington. He stressed the necessity for increased membership, and was assured that the Parlor will make a good showing during his term. Grand Trustee Eldred L. Meyer outlined the Admission Day plans, and Arthur Giroux, wreathed in smiles, announced that he is a granddaddy. Other speakers were Secretary John Smith, Howard Bentley, Roger Johnson and Dr. Harry L. Coffman.

The Parlor now has an orchestra, and has under way the organization of a glee club and an athletic team. During August four new names were added to the membership roll, the candidates being initiated at Hollywood and Glendale. The outing in Santa Monica Canyon August 7 was a complete success.

PRESENTATIONS.

San Pedro—The State (Bear) Flag of California now flies from the "Aldoran," new cruising yacht of Bernard B. Lippman of Sepulveda Parlor No. 263 N.S.G.W. Presentation of the banner was carried out with ceremony August 5, at the time when the yachtsman had a number of Natives aboard to witness opening events in the Olympic sailing regatta off Point Fermin. Past President Clyde H. Foot made the presentation address, and following a gracious word of acceptance, Captain Lippman hoisted the California flag to the same breeze that was sending racing sloops of eleven nations through the waters of historic San Pedro Channel.

A silver plaque, properly inscribed, was presented the giant tank steamer "California" in Los Angeles Harbor August 13. It was attached to a framed silk flag of the State of California which had previously been placed in the officers' quarters of the ship by Sepulveda. Grand Outside Sentinel William A. Reuter and Past President John T. Gower presented the plaque, which was accepted by Captain A. H. Atkins and Chief Engineer Clarence Petersen. State Senator Henry E. Carter was the guest-speaker at the Parlor August 12. Frank I. Markey, who retired as secretary of No. 263 after five years of faithful service, was presented with an emblematic ring; Harry E. Fairall is his successor. Members of Sepulveda plan a dance at Cabrillo Beach the evening of September 3.

OPPORTUNITY TO HELP DESERVING LAD.

If you know of a farm or ranch where a 17-year-old boy might find work, notify Scoutmaster Robert E. Dunn or Secretary John V. Scott of Ramona Parlor No. 109 N.S.G.W. The lad is a Boy Scout of America. Recently his mother was burned seriously, leaving him homeless. He has been unable to find a steady position. He has had a good deal of experience with stock and farm products.

PERSONAL PARAGRAPHS.

Ed. F. Cohn (Sacramento N.S.) is now residing at 804 Strand, Redondo Beach.

Mrs. Susan Kennedy (Los Angeles N.D.) is visiting in San Francisco and Grass Valley.

Mrs. Adelaide Hickman (Los Angeles N.D.) of San Francisco is visiting her mother, Mrs. Edith B. Schallmo.

Mrs. Ramona Block-Thoroughgood (Los Angeles N.D.) departed August 20 on a visit to British Columbia.

Leon J. Leonard (Ramona N.S.) is seeking the precious, and elusive, metal, gold, near Weaverville, Trinity County.

Mrs. Margaret Carter (Los Angeles N.D.) enjoyed a vacation at Lake Tahoe and other places of interest in the northern part of the state.

Native Son visitors last month included: Joseph J. McShane (Grand Trustee) of San Francisco, Barney G. Barry (Silver Star) of Lincoln.

Miss Cornelia Niles (Californiana N.D.) was guest-artist at the history pageant featured in Santa Barbara's Old Spanish Days Fiesta last month.

Miss Virginia Bird, daughter of Mrs. Clara Bird (Los Angeles N.D.), was wedded August 17 to C. Wagner Johnston. The couple will reside in Newark, New Jersey.

Mrs. Rosalie F. Hyde (Santa Monica Bay N.D.), accompanied by her daughter, Dorothy, visited last month in San Francisco, where Mrs. Hyde resided for many years.

A native daughter arrived August 1 at the Beverly Hills home of John A. Bullard (Ramona N.S.) and wife (Los Angeles N.D.)—the third grandchild of Clarence M. Hunt (Sacramento N.S.).

Native Daughter visitors last month included: Mrs. Bertha A. Briggs (Past Grand) of Hollister, Mrs. Grace Bessac (Joaquin) of Stockton, Mrs. Ariana W. Stirling (Past Grand) of Berkeley.

THE DEATH RECORD.

Charles Augustus Gunther, affiliated with Watsonville Parlor No. 65 N.S.G.W., died July 25 survived by three children. He was born at San Francisco, May 21, 1873.

Mrs. Angele Taix, mother of Marius Taix (Ramona N.S.), died July 29.

Joseph Spear, father of Dr. Edgar and Erwin Spear (both Los Angeles N.S.), died August 1 at the age of 72.

Mrs. Juana Espelet, mother of Domingo Pilaria (Ramona N.S.), died August 14.

Mrs. Mary McDowell, mother of Alfred A. McDowell (Ramona N.S.), died August 22.

Mrs. Isabelle Norton, mother of Miss Grace J. Norton and Mrs. Lloyd A. Duncan (both Los Angeles N.D.), Thomas J. and Walter W. Norton (both Ramona N.S.), died August 23. She was a native of Illinois, aged 67.

James Albert Ford, father of Fletcher Ford (Ramona N.S.), died August 23. He was a native of Ohio, aged 89, and came to California in 1869; for many years he resided in Sierra and San Luis Obispo Counties, where he was well known as an educator and publisher.

GOOD NEWS.

Readers of The Grizzly Bear will be pleased to hear that Fred Miller, builder of the beautiful Carthay Circle theater, Los Angeles, has again re-leased this famous showplace of the Golden West and re-established old policies of the cream of super motion-picture productions, surrounded with elaborate shows, including colorful prologues, and a great concert orchestra.

Carthay Circle is known to thousands of Native Sons and Native Daughters by reason of its fascinating historical atmosphere, perpetuating the great pioneer episodes of California by a series of especially commissioned oil paintings executed by noted Western painters. Many relics of the '49ers, as well as statues erected in its beautiful parks, keep fresh the memory of stalwart figures in the early history of California.

GRIZZLY GROWLS

(Continued from Page 3)

stantial aid to those who are out of work. We are also planning to continue our co-operation with the California Unemployment Commission in the establishment of labor camps in or near the national forests as was done last winter."

"In the interest of a clean judicial system," says the "News" of Van Nuys, Los Angeles County, "the Los Angeles Bar Association is sponsoring the recall of three [superior court] judges. Jurists who accept gifts of clothing or permit other people to pay their bills, cannot ethically pass judgment on the weaknesses of their fellowmen."

Why single out jurists? They are not, by a jugfull, the only public officials who carry on likewise. In the interest of impartial, quick and genuine justice, any and every public official who accepts a gratuity of any nature from any source should be removed from office!

President Henry J. Haas of the American Bankers Association suggested in a recent address better qualifications for those engaged in the banking business. Consider these: first and foremost, they should be honest financiers, not dishonest gamblers; and they should be compelled to engage exclusively in the banking business, not flimflam schemes.

SIERRA COUNTY GOLD MINING.

The Alleghany district, in the southern part of Sierra County, has been a producer of gold since the earliest days of gold mining in California, says the Federal Interior Department's Geological Survey. The district differs from other gold-quartz districts of the state in that nearly all the production, which has probably exceeded $20,000,000 from the lode mines only, has been derived from small shoots of very high-grade ore. A distinctly favorable view is taken of the outlook for lode mining in the future.

CLASSIFIED DIRECTORY
LOS ANGELES NATIVE SONS

ATTORNEYS-AT-LAW.

J. A. ADAIR. J. A. ADAIR JR.
516-19 Fay Bldg., Third and Hill.
Office: MAdison 1141 —Phones— Res.: GLadstone 5042.

HENRY G. BODKIN. V. P. LUCAS.
Chester Williams Bldg., 215 W. 5th St.
Phone: MUtual 3151.

DAVID H. CLARK.
215 West Fifth St.
Phone: MUtual 8406.

WM. J. HUNSAKER.
458 So. Spring St., Room 1130.
Phone: TRinity 6656.

EDWIN A. MESERVE. SHIRLEY E. MESERVE.
555 So. Flower St.
Phone: TRinity 6161.

THOS. B. REED.
548 South Spring St.
Phone: VAndike 0687.

DENTIST.

ROBERT J. GREGG, D.D.S.
5801 South Figueroa St.
Phone: THornwall 3590.
Hours 9 to 5, and by appointment.

DETECTIVE SERVICE.

LOUIS A. DUNI.
523 Washington Bldg., 311½ So. Spring.
Phone: TUcker 3913.

PHYSICIAN AND SURGEON.

WILBUR B. PARKER, M.D.
11th Floor Brack Shops, 527 W. 7th St.
Phone: TRinity 5739.
Practice Limited to Urology.

SAN FRANCISCO

(Continued from Page 5)

Castro Parlor No. 232 N.S.G.W.—N.S.G.W. Hall, 430 Mason street.

Balboa Parlor No. 234 N.S.G.W.—Maccabee Hall, Fifth avenue and Clement street.

Utopia Parlor No. 270 N.S.G.W.—Native Sons Building, 414 Mason street.

COMMITTEEMEN.

Numerous subcommittees, appointed by Chairman McShane of the general committee, have for weeks been diligently at work perfecting the details for the 1932 Admission Day celebration. They include the following:

FINANCE—Joseph Rose (chairman), John T. Regan, Harry W. Gaetjen, Thomas Foley, John Ramsay.

WAYS AND MEANS—Arthur Poheim (chairman), John T. Regan, Chas. A. Koenig, James L. Foley, Louis F. Erb.

PARADE—Harry W. Gaetjen (chairman), Geo. W. Schonfeld, Walter Bammann, Herbert De la Rosa, Nicholas Murphy, Percy Marchant, Helen Mann, Adeline Taxeira, Bertha Edler, Kittie Mullaney, Abbie Groom.

ADMISSION DAY OBSERVANCE—Jesse H. Miller (chairman), John T. Regan, Arthur Poheim, Mildred Hoehn, Nora Scheflin.

ACCOMMODATIONS—Harmon D. Skillin (chairman), Gustave E. Ritter, Chas. M. Craig, Otto A. Elvander, George F. Barry, Gertrude McDonough, Emily Murphy, Mary Casey, Mrs. E. Tietjen.

MUSIC—P. L. Schlesinger (chairman), Louis Erb, Eugene Herzog, Wm. H. James, John Sweeney, Edw. Wren, Claire Bohman, Alice Johnson, Ann Godfrey, Sadie Romick, Gertrude Drews.

PUBLICITY—Frank Foss (chairman), V. V. Hardeman, F. M. Buckley, Martin Huber, Robt. Donohue, Peter Conmy, Josephine Morrisey, Ethel Reading, Florence Pyne, Hildur Eggers, Lena Wall.

TRANSPORTATION—Percy Marchant (chairman), John F. Craig, P. L. Schlesinger, John Schroder, Fannie Moore, Hilda Fuchs, Flora Justus, Hazel Croswind, A. Fauss, Theresa Nolen.

COSTUMES—Millie Rock, Olive Tyndall, Florence Stayart, Alice Cummins, Theresa O'Brien.

GRAND BALL—Ivo R. Monti (chairman), Harry Romick, Walter Bammann, Geo. Stocker, Harry Alexander, John W. Smith, Raymond Conroy, Elvira Desmond, Ella Teeling, Dorothy Raymond, H. Driscoll, A. Jebe, Frank Biedermann, Frank M. Buckley, Louis Erb.

RECEPTION—N.S.G.W: Lloyd J. Doering (chairman), I. M. Peckham, George Batchelor, Alfred Vlautin, W. H. Burke. N.D.G.W: Agnes Ourry (chairman), Catherine Dolly, Helen Mann, Marcella Bray, Edna Brilliant, Ethel Deneri, Gertrude LaFortune, Ann Dippel.

NATIVE DAUGHTER DOINGS.

President May L. McDonald of Alta Parlor No. 3 has launched a program of exceptional interest. August 27 the semi-annual card party was held at the Home. Elaborate plans are being made to honor Mms. Isabel Pomeroy and Otilia McLaughlin on the occasion of thier golden wedding anniversaries. In the late fall a tour will be made through a bakery to observe the intricacies of the baking art. Four candidates were recently initiated.

Officers of Keith Parlor No. 137 were installed August 11 by Deputy Helen McMahon, Gladys Cruiss becoming president. The ceremonies were followed by dancing, entertainment features and refreshments.

Presidio Parlor No. 148's officers were publicly installed August 9 by Deputy Anna Dibble, with Elba Mascarella as president. The drill team participated in the ceremonies, which were followed by dancing and refreshments. There was a large attendance.

Officers of Golden Gate Parlor No. 158 were publicly installed by Deputy Maud Daly, Helen Lewis being elevated to the presidency. On the Parlor's behalf Past President Sophie Siebe presented an electric clock to Junior Past President Bessie Ducray. Entertainment was provided by Sara Ella Bennett and Lorraine Young. Ice-cream and cake concluded the pleasant occasion.

Members of Linda Rosa Parlor No. 170 met August 10 in compliment to Gertrude LaFortune, former deputy who showed the Parlor many kindnesses and was untiring in efforts to assist in every possible manner. The evening was pleasantly spent. Delicious refreshments were served at beautifully decorated tables.

NATIVE SON DOINGS.

Stanford Parlor No. 76 has embarked on a new era in fraternal history. During the term of President Dr. Vincent H. Hardeman the Parlor is endeavoring to carry out a program which will surpass all past records. It includes hikes, whist parties, boxing matches, past presidents night, dinner dances, theater parties, Christmas tree, etc. In addition, a membership drive is under way, and meeting with great success. The Parlor will hold an elaborate ball the night of Admission Day.

Officers of Twin Peaks Parlor No. 214 and Twin Peaks Parlor No. 185 N.D.G.W. were jointly installed by District Deputy Thomas Dillon and Deputy Elizabeth Mueller, Cliff Roberts and Alice Johnson becoming the respective presidents. More than 300 guests assembled in the large auditorium, beautifully decorated with flags. Past president emblems were presented Grand Trustee Joseph J. McShane and Gladys

In Memoriam

RUTH SPOHN.

To the Officers and Members of Aloha Parlor No. 106 N.D.G.W.—Again the Angel of Death has entered our Parlor, and taken from our midst our beloved sister, Ruth Spohn. We tenderly condole with her bereaved family in this, their hour of trial and affliction, and commend them for consolation to Him who dorth all things well. Let us not think of her as dead, but of having preceded us to the Golden Shore where she now dwells as one of the daughters of that better land, and where she waits to welcome us as we, too, pass through the Golden Gate. By her death, the members of Aloha Parlor No. 106 N.D.G.W. have been deprived of a loving and devoted sister, whose noble character and kind disposition endeared her to all.

Resolved, That our deep sympathy be extended to her sorrowing family; may God bless those that are near and dear to her. Furthermore be it resolved, that our charter be draped for thirty days, that a copy of this resolution be spread upon the minutes, that copies be sent to the bereaved family, and that a copy be sent to The Grizzly Bear for publication.

Sincerely and fraternally in P.D.F.A.,

GRACE DUPONT.

Oakland, August 18, 1932.

MILTON L. MAYFIELD.

To the Officers and Members of Cambria Parlor No. 152 N.S.G.W.:

Whereas, It has pleased the Supreme Ruler to call from his sphere of usefulness to his eternal rest our well-beloved brother, Milton L. Mayfield; and whereas, Brother Mayfield was a kind and good neighbor, a charter member of this Parlor, and a useful member of the society in which he moved; one whose passing is sincerely mourned, who had endeared himself to all who knew him, because of his readiness to respond at all times to the cry of distress, and because of his unselfish devotion to the principles of this Order; therefore, be it

Reolved, That this Parlor stand in silence in respect to his memory, that its charter be draped for a period of thirty days, that a copy of these resolutions be spread upon the minutes, that a copy be forwarded to each of his heirs, and that a copy be sent to The Grizzly Bear for publication.

Respectfully submitted in Friendship, Loyalty and Charity,

A. S. GAY,
GEO. W. GILLESPIE,
J. F. STEWART,
Committee.

Cambria, August 26, 1932.

Dahlia Festival—Bellflower, Los Angeles County, will stage its annual Dahlia Festival, September 23 and 24.

"It is not so much the width of your field of usefulness as the quality of your care for it, that tells in the harvest."—Exchange.

"You can never have a greater or a less dominion than that over yourself."—Leonardo da Vinci.

Admission Day!

FRIDAY, SEPTEMBER 9, 1932

The Eighty-second Anniversary of California's Recognition as One of the Sovereign Commonwealths of the United States

A LEGAL HOLIDAY!

Native and Adopted Sons and Daughters Give Due Recognition to This Important Date in the Romantic and Resourceful History of the State of California

Close Your Places of Business!

Display the California State (Bear) Flag!

Join in Admission Day Festivities!

Grand Parlor, Native Sons of the Golden West.

Grizzly Bear

OCTOBER THE ONLY OFFICIAL PUBLICATION OF THE NATIVE SONS AND DAUGHTERS OF THE GOLDEN WEST 1932

Featuring

GENERAL NEWS OF INTEREST CONCERNING ALL CALIFORNIA, and ORDERS NATIVE SONS and NATIVE DAUGHTERS

Price: 15 Cents

GRIZZLY GROWLS

(CLARENCE M. HUNT.)

DELEGATES TO THE NATIONAL CONvention of the American Legion, in Portland, Oregon, much to the disappointment of hordes of the organization's best friends, both within and without the Legion, passed by an overwhelming majority vote a resolution demanding full payment now by the Federal Government of the adjusted compensation (bonus) certificates, not due for more than twelve years. This question, prominently before the people of this country for some time, has, therefore, progressed to a very serious stage, for the government is not in a financial position to meet the demand, even if acceded to by the Congress. As remarked last month, the demand is unjust and unreasonable!

This question is of such vital importance to the Nation's wellbeing, voters should give it the most careful consideration. It has become a paramount issue in the national election campaign. Following the convention's action, United States Senator William E. Borah of Idaho, one of the nation's outstanding citizens, recognized internationally as a sound and conservative thinker, declared: "I am sorry the Legion thought it expedient and just to pass the resolution for the payment of the bonus at this time. I am sure it would have been far more satisfactory to the Legion hereafter if they had taken into consideration the condition of the country and awaited its recovery to some extent at least before acting.

"When 10,000,000 men and women face the winter without work; when homes are being lost and farms are being abandoned because of taxes and debts; when it is a very serious question of how the Government is going to get through the winter with its terrific load to carry, it would have been far better for the standing and reputation of the Legion if it had postponed action.

"If the Congress is made up of men worthy to represent a great people in an hour of trouble, it will respectfully, but firmly, say that the taxpayers of this country are carrying all the burden they can carry at this time and that these veterans must share the common load with the people and wait.

"But Congress ought not to be compelled to bear the brunt of this affair alone. Both political parties are now out asking the taxpayers for their votes. Now is the time the taxpayers can pass their resolution by their votes and protect their homes and their businesses."

President Herbert Hoover has steadfastly opposed payment now of this not-due bonus. He has been severely condemned by some, whereas he should be applauded by all for his courage. He has demonstrated in this instance that he has the "guts" to do that which he believes to be right, and for the best interest of the majority. He is a candidate for re-election to the presidency, and despite the fact that he knew that he would be further displeasing the powerful bonus advocates, he issued, during the Legion convention, a frank statement which should be digested by every voter. Quoting therefrom: "It is due to the country and to the veterans that there should be no misunderstanding of my position upon payment of the face value of the adjusted service certificates prior to maturity. . . . I have consistently opposed it. In public interest I must continue to oppose it. I have the duty not alone to see that justice and a sympathetic attitude is taken by this Nation toward the 4,000,000 veterans and their families, but also to exert myself for justice to the other 21,000,000 families to whom consummation of this proposal at this time would be a calamity.

"Cash payment of face value of certificates today would require an appropriation from the Treasury of about $2,300,000,000. No matter how or in what form the payment to the veterans is imposed, it will come out of all these families, but, of more importance, it will indefinitely set back any hope of recovery for employment, agriculture or business and will impose infinite distress upon the whole country.

"We owe justice and generosity to the men who have served under our Flag. Our people have tried to discharge that obligation. Regular expenditures on account of the veterans already constitute nearly a billion a year, or almost one-fourth of our whole Federal budget. Every right-thinking man has the deepest sympathy for the veteran suffering from disability, for those out of work or for veterans on farms struggling with the adversities of the depression. . . . But there are many million others in the same circumstances. They, too, must be entitled to consideration. Their employment and their farm recovery, as well as that of the veterans, can be secured only by the restoration of the normal economic life of the Nation. . . . Anything that stands in the way must be opposed. The welfare of the Nation as a whole must take precedence over the demands of any particular group.

"I do not believe that the veterans generally really understand the adjusted service certificate law (so-called bonus law) which was proposed by themselves. In its simplest terms that law provides that an annual sum of about $112,000,000 is to be paid into a fund which, with compound interest, is calculated to amount to a total of $3,500,000,000, the face value of certificates to be distributed in 1945. Approximately $1,300,000,000 has been paid into this fund. Under the law of last year authorizing loans up to 50 percent of the face amount of the certificates, if we take into consideration loans made through the veterans' life insurance fund which will have to be repaid, all this accumulated sum and more has already been distributed. If the Government distributed to the veterans the $112,000,000 annually from now on it would represent the Government's obligation. If these sums be kept in the fund the Government adds compound interest on each installment and gives a life insurance right.

"By paying the adjusted service certificates at their 1945 face value now the Government would not only be paying all remaining thirteen annual installments in advance, but would be paying the compound interest upon them in advance. This would, I am advised, add about $2,250,000,000 to the amount which the people of the United States, acting through Congress, undertook to pay when they gave the certificates.

"No such sum is available. It cannot be raised by adding to the crushing burden of taxes which drain every family budget in our country today and weigh heavily on business struggling in the midst of depression. It cannot be borrowed without impairment of the credit of the National Government and thus destroy that confidence upon which our whole system depends. It is unthinkable that the Government of the United States should resort to the printing press and the issuance of fiat currency as provided in the bill which passed the House at the last session of Congress. . . .

"Such an act of moral bankruptcy would depreciate and might ultimately destroy the value of every dollar in the United States. It would cause the collapse of all confidence in our Government and would bring widespread ruin to the entire country and to every one of our citizens. Daniel Webster, 100 years ago, stated: 'He who tampers with the currency robs labor of its bread. He panders, indeed, to greedy capital, which is keen sighted, and may shift for itself; but he beggars labor, which is honest, unsuspecting and too busy with the present to calculate for the future. The prosperity of the working classes lives, moves and has its being in established credit, and a steady medium of payment.' And the experience of every government in the world since that day has confirmed Webster's statement.

"Let us not forget that while we have lost much in this depression, we still have much more to lose. And our whole future may be said to depend upon early recovery. . . . . The proposal to levy over $2,000,000,000 and to pay it to a particular group constitutes a fatal threat to the entire program of recovery to the success of which all must look for their wellbeing, security and happiness. In my judgment the enactment of any such proposal into legislation would be a deadly blow at the welfare of the Nation."

Speaking in the House of Representatives, July 6, on the bonus, Representative William A. Ayres of Kansas said, "I am not finding fault with those of the World War veterans who are making their demand at this time for the cash payment of their adjusted-compensation certificates, even though they are not due until 1945. I believe they have been misinformed. They have been misguided, used, and misused. They have been badly advised. No language of my own could as effectively demonstrate this as that used by a World War veteran Congressman, Representative Simmons, of Nebraska, who said:

" 'Demagogues on the floor of this House and elsewhere have repeatedly told the veteran he is not being well treated; that the Government owes him money; and that he should have it. Here are the figures, authenticated, based on facts, that our Government now is doing more for its veterans than all of the nations named in that list combined. Gentlemen, when you go back to your veterans and to your taxpayers, take these figures with you. Tell them the facts of the loyalty, the generosity, and the fairness of your Government and mine toward the veteran. Then, again, may I say to my comrades among the veterans, as I did briefly yesterday, that this table ought to tell the veterans themselves to stop in their demands upon the Treasury. When the taxpayers of the country find out the sums that Congress has paid and the amount that is being incessantly and constantly demanded by minority groups within the veterans, and by those nonveterans who curry political favor from veterans, the situation may develop in this country again that developed following the Revolutionary and Civil Wars, when the Nation demanded and secured a purging of

(Continued on Page 24)

RISING TIDE

(DELMAR H. WILLIAMS.)

I'm settled in a peaceful spot—
I'm basking on the sand
To watch the tide that upward creeps
On old Pacific's strand.
Between the weaker waves that start
From out the halting sea,
By mighty combers sent, the foam
Is coming nearer me.

And even so the rising power
Of upward climbing men.
For it must backward fall before
It surges forth again.
The bravest souls retreat to crush
The fear of ages down
Before they make the bold advance
That earns a just renown.

(This contribution to The Grizzly Bear is from Delmar H. Williams of San Francisco, well known California poet.—Editor.)

The Grizzly Bear Magazine
The ALL California Monthly
OWNED, CONTROLLED, PUBLISHED BY
GRIZZLY BEAR PUBLISHING CO.,
(Incorporated)
COMPOSED OF NATIVE SONS.
HERMAN C. LICHTENBERGER, Pres.
JOHN T. NEWELL RAY HOWARD
WM. I. TRAEGER LORENZO F. SOTO
CHAS. R. THOMAS HARRY J. LELANDE
ARTHUR A. SCHMIDT, Vice-Pres.
BOARD OF DIRECTORS

CLARENCE M. HUNT
General Manager and Editor

OFFICIAL ORGAN AND THE
ONLY OFFICIAL PUBLICATION OF
THE NATIVE SONS AND THE
NATIVE DAUGHTERS GOLDEN WEST.

ISSUED FIRST EACH MONTH.
FORMS CLOSE 20th MONTH.
ADVERTISING RATES ON APPLICATION.

SAN FRANCISCO OFFICE:
N.S.G.W. BLDG., 414 MASON ST., RM. 302
(Office Grand Secretary N.S.G.W.)
Telephone: Kearney 1223
SAN FRANCISCO, CALIFORNIA

PUBLICATION OFFICE:
309-15 WILCOX BLDG., 2nd AND SPRING,
Telephone: VAndike 6234
LOS ANGELES, CALIFORNIA

(Entered as second-class matter May 29, 1918, at the Postoffice at Los Angeles, California, under the act of August 24, 1912.)

PUBLISHED REGULARLY SINCE MAY 1907
VOL. LI WHOLE NO. 306

CALEB DEVINE'S RETRIBUTION

Frances Fairchild

FOLLOWING THE ROUTE OF THE PIONEERS of 1849, east from Auburn or west from Placerville a distance of about an hour's ride, the traveler comes upon one of the prettiest towns in the mountains—Georgetown, El Dorado County. Like all her sister towns founded at that time, it was started and settled by men of all nationalities and creeds—intelligent, ignorant, influential in their native spheres, but swung loose from former habits, home memories, sentiments of morality. Outlaws and gamblers were trying their luck in a new land and all were plunging feverishly into the whirling tide that swept before and about them to delve for fabulous riches in the mines. Some wished to forget their past, others were just at the beginning of a career which seemed to have a golden outlook.

At this early period of history the nucleus of the present town was built in Georgetown Canyon, south of the main and business street of today, the dwellings and business houses in close proximity on either side of the sloping hills. Near the center of the town loomed the famous "Round Tent," looking like a huge circus canvas, and such a place as Placerville boasted of in the "Hangtown" days where the mixed element of humanity was wont to congregate, gamble, steal from each other, fight, and glean their wealth at any hazard. There was always someone in these tents from sunrise until sunset and from then until another day dawned for new adventure.

At the time the following tragedy was enacted there was not a house of worship or even a school for the boys and girls. The former ran about bareheaded and barefooted; the girls were more closely guarded by their mothers to keep them from hearing profanity and seeing an element of lawlessness which was rampant at most any time. Every house had its firearms polished and ready for use in case of a surprise at any moment, for who could tell at what time a drunken revel might end in bloodshed? This was a new country, peopled by classes from all walks of life.

There was gold aplenty then—on the banks of the clear streams, under the flowers and rocks and ferns; all that was needed was persistence of the quest. Shrubbery that cast reflections in the clear pools and crystal streams had roots fastened in pockets of the golden ore.

The primeval forests had not been subjected to the woodman's ax—the songs of the wild birds as they sat on the swaying branches of the trees echoed triumphantly through dells and canyons. The meadows and sloping hillsides were carpeted with hues of green and delicate tints of wild flowers, their perfume permeating the balmy spring air. The woodpeckers hammered the bark on the tree trunks, happy in their native element. Some of the wandering hunters were inspired by the voiceless stillness and the beauty of nature—others passed through the glades unheeding.

Among the inhabitants of this frontier town in 1850 were Caleb Devine and his wife, Mary. They came from the State of New York via the Isthmus of Panama. Their principal reason for leaving the East was that Caleb wished to begin life anew in a country of different environment. He was a sailor—an English sea captain and a deserter from the English army. Gray-headed, short, thick-set, broad-shouldered, and with piercing black eyes that twinkled from under long, shaggy eyebrows, one would turn about to look at him a second time. Like many a man who is his worst enemy, he loved old John Barleycorn. His wife, in hopes of reforming him, left her only child, a daughter, in the East while they sought refuge in this new land. The move proved a good one for a time. It had been a year now since Caleb had tasted the luring beverage. In the meantime he worked hard and steadily and accumulated quite a "stake." Seemingly they were a devoted and loving couple. Many there were who would sit in the waning light of the evening's glow beside his cottage door and listen to Caleb spin yarns of the land and briny deep as all old sailors love to do.

Mrs. Devine was just the opposite of her husband—gentle, refined, dignified, reserved, and always thoughtful for those about her and shrinking from the coarse and rude. In her deep blue eyes gleamed the spirit of "long ago." It may have been something from the deepest recesses of her soul, beyond the reach of the great action-throbbing hand of the present, which enveloped her; it may have been a memory standing sentinel to guard the gate through which a shadowy spirit might come again; it may have been love, for love outlives memory and lends a delucive rose-tint to life; it may have been that she sensed the coming of the unbidden guest with prophetic finger pointing to the portals of some distant star. At any rate, her inmost thoughts were stamped upon her sensitive features.

In the corner of their modest diningroom stood the firearms. Caleb had many of these, loaded and ready for action—one a double-barrelled shotgun. Of course, every one had these wicked harbingers, but to Mary Devine they were ill-omened; she never let her gaze fall upon them without a convulsive shiver. For, hadn't Caleb threatened her at times when filled with liquor?

There came a day when Caleb was feeling unusually genial. He entertained his friends within the portals of the "Round Tent" with story after story of the briny deep, interwoven with hair-breadth 'scapes—blood and thunder.

At last the loungers became fed up on salt-water tales, and Jim Davis proposed a game of cards. Within less time than it would take to tell it, stools were drawn up to the rude table, and the stakes, amounting to several thousand dollars, were piled in the center.

The tent was filled with dense tobacco smoke and each one in the crowd showed the excitement aroused by Caleb's bloodthirsty narratives. The game was in progress. Caleb was calm, fascinated, fixed to the spot. All the money he had with him was on that pile and it looked good to him.

"O, if I can only rake that into my jeans," he said to himself. He had been lucky at times; why not now? The thought fascinated him.

Among the gamblers was a tall, swarthy-looking individual with shifting, coal-black eyes, a long nose, firm thin lips, slick black hair. His hands were small, with long tapering fingers. During Caleb's story telling he sat studying each of the men. When Jim Davis said cards, his expression changed to one of furtive expectancy, and he lost no time in drawing his stool up to the table. He was cool; uninterested, seemingly.

The cards were dealt and the ones he held absorbed him. They played in silence and it was soon observed he was winning the game with amazing rapidity. His fellow players began to realize he was an old hand at the business and they might lose their all. Betting ran high and Caleb played like a madman. At length the pile of money was turned over to the stranger; he had played calmly. The expression of his face had not changed since the game began.

Caleb was not satisfied with the finish and wanted to play another game. He searched his pockets for more money, but they were empty. The moustached stranger sauntered to the bar and ordered liquor for the crowd. The glasses tinkled.

"Devine, old shipmate, have one with us to the luck of the 'Round Tent.' Your wife has you on parole in this new country, I am told, but have a nip with us for better times later on."

Caleb looked upon it, longed for it, but shook his grizzled head. "No, no, I've made a solemn promise to the missus, never agin."

The stranger put his hand on Caleb's should[e] and said: "Why let a woman rule you? Yo[u] are old enough to do as you please. She wi[ll] never be the wiser."

At this, the stranger picked up the glass an[d] pressed it upon him. "Drink, drink, old sal[t]. Drink to Californy and her gold." Caleb too[k] it with trembling fingers, with misgivings crow[d]ing his consciousness, and drained the content[s].

"Just that much—no more—a little will n[ot] hurt you—just this one—Mary will never know," the tempter whispered. "Then, never again," his consciousness replied. That one cup was th[e] forerunner of many more. The promises h[e] made were broken, forgotten. That night Mar[y] watched beside the sotted man, while the odo[r] of his breath, laden with the poisoned stil[l] worm's fumes, filled the air about her.

From that time on the tempter lay coiled b[y] the wayside. Caleb's mastery over self was los[t] and he would go on protracted sprees, to th[e] terror of his wife and the neighborhood. Whe[n] sober, he was kind and considerate—a devote[d] mate—a desirable neighbor. At such times h[e] would implore Mary to keep the firearms out o[f] sight, as he was irresponsible when drinking. Then his one possessive thought was to kill hi[s] wife. After that first drink out West, he san[k] deeper and deeper into the slough of dissipation. He was nearing the end of the trail. For month[s] he had not threatened Mary. She became les[s] wary.

Late one balmy June night the report of [a] gun was heard. The first impression was o[f] trouble at the "Round Tent." Few paid hee[d] to it. The denizens of night life were soon scurrying about telling the startling news: "Cale[b] Devine had shot his wife!" He had demande[d] money several times during the evening. Sh[e] had refused. He threatened her. Knowing hi[s] insane desires she poured water in the gun barrels to prevent discharge, but had neglected on[e] of the barrels of the double-barrelled gun. Lat[e] at night he again demanded money. Again sh[e] refused. He became infuriated and grabbed th[e] gun. Mary quickly extinguished the candlelight, ran into the woodshed, closed the door an[d] stepped to one side. Caleb pointed the gun t[o] the spot where he saw his wife disappear an[d] pulled the trigger. The one good charge wen[t] through the door casing, striking Mary Devin[e] between the shoulders and passing through th[e] chest. The bullet was so close to the skin th[e] doctor had no trouble in taking it out with hi[s] penknife. Ready hands seized Caleb. The[y] hurried him to the "Round Tent," where he wa[s] tied hand and foot.

In the early morning Mary, in her suffering—the life blood oozing from her chest—called shrilly for Caleb to come. Her wailing cr[y] pierced his dazed senses. It seemed to sobe[r] him; he gazed at his hands and feet, demanding to know "Where he was, what he had done."

"You shot your wife," they answered wit[h] oaths. "It can't be so, it can't be so," h[e] groaned. "Mary, my dear, come, tell me the[y] lie—lie—lie. Tell me you are safe—that thi[s] is an ugly dream—that I have lost my senses. O, I wouldn't kill her, I'd die for her, my swee[t] lassie."

"Yes, you have done just that cowardly thing. You do not deserve pity, and be sure you don'[t] ask for it or we will take you to the nearest tree and hang you now." "O, God! Take me to her; let me go," he shrieked. He became palsied—his lips bloodless. His entreaty was so pitifu[l] they took him to her bedside, placed him in [a] chair and took the rawhide from his wrists.

Kindly hands were administering to Mrs. Devine's suffering. Gently they raised her and placed her in poor old Caleb's arms, so that her snowy head could rest upon his heaving breast. As long as strength lasted she talked and prayed to him while her almost lifeless fingers tried to caress his rugged visage. They talked of the days when first they met—of their early married life—of the daughter so far away—of the strength of their love that brought them to California. And she gave him many fond messages to carry to their only child.

"No, no, dear one, I shall never see our sweet Joan. Don't you know that I, too, shall soon be with you in a better land? They will lose no time to hang me as soon as you are sleeping." "I have left a message for them not to harm you. O, they will not, they will not," she gasped.

And while they bade each other a last earthly farewell, men surrounded the house ready to grab him the moment Mary Devine had closed her eyes in death, and mete out to him the punishment he so richly deserved. Mary's voice grew fainter and fainter; her fluttering gasps were no longer intelligible. Soon after, those in

(Continued on Page 28)

HERE LET ME STAY

(ETHEL BRODT WILSON.)

I wander in my garden of hills
As a child wanders in a garden of flowers.
My nostrils quiver to their scent,
Their touch is upon my heart.
Their color is a narcotic
That quiets my rebellious longing
And brings forgetfulness—
From my heart the years slip away.

I would not change the mountain-roofs
For shelter of a town—
Let me stay
An humble tenant
Where I have wakened
To hear the orioles singing
Along the rim of morning,
The stars and moon still shining.

I have learned the beauty of the mountains,
And their rhythm,
I have seen them from the mists of dawn
Emerging—
They move me and leave me shaken.
Here my soul has had preparation for immortality,
Here is the blue of eternity—
Here let me stay.

—University California Chronicle.

CALIFORNIA HAPPENINGS OF FIFTY YEARS AGO

Thomas R. Jones

(COMPILED EXPRESSLY FOR THE GRIZZLY BEAR.)

AT THE CLOSE OF OCTOBER 1882 THE political situation in California was badly mixed. In fact, so many complications had arisen, wagering on the result of the November election was considered inadvisable by the wiseacres. Both the Republican and the Democratic candidates for governor were winemakers. While Estes made speeches, he did not satisfy the discontented; Stoneman made no speeches, and no one knew where he stood on controversial issues.

With delegates from twenty-eight counties in attendance, a Farmers Anti-monopoly party convention was held at Stockton, San Joaquin County, October 7. Attempting to name a ticket for the guidance of farmers, by the selection of candidates from among Republican and Democratic nominees, the gathering disbanded in a rumpus, as a majority of the delegates proved to be extreme partisans.

The Negro voters, disgruntled because they had not received political recognition by the major parties, had a state convention October 21, attended by 250 delegates. It split in two when, by a small majority, the Democratic ticket was endorsed.

The split in the Republican party in San Francisco over the municipal ticket was bridged through the efforts of party leaders, and the "Duffers" and the "Bluffers" united forces. This union was followed by the coming into being of the "Taxpayers," and so, another opposition ticket entered the field.

"Unusual" weather, for a fortnight, ushered in October. Rain began falling the 1st and continued at intervals to the 16th, the precipitation totaling 2.59 inches. There was a heavy frost the 4th. The "oldest inhabitant" had no recollection of a parallel season. The inclement weather did no good. In fact, it damaged the grape and the grain crops to the extent of many thousands of dollars.

The Los Angeles County Fair opened October 17 at Los Angeles City. Prominent among the exhibits were 200 varieties of grapes, and a large array of bottled wines and brandies. The Siskiyou County Fair opened at Yreka, October 11.

The apple crop of the Llewelling orchard at San Lorenzo, Alameda County, was sold at a dollar a box and shipped to China.

At Sacramento, October 17, 700 bales of hops were sold for $85,000, and they went to England. Owing to a short crop in Europe, buyers had boosted the price for California-grown hops to more than fifty cents a pound. In consequence, state brewers raised the price of lager beer to eight dollars for a ten-gallon keg.

In Mendocino County, so many schoolchildren went to work picking hopes at seventy-five cents a day the public schools in several districts were closed until the season ended.

During the spring months of 1882, 4,600,000 grape vines were set out in Los Angeles County, which now had a total of 13,370,000 vines. Plans were being made to plant a few million additional vines in 1883.

The San Francisco Board of Trade, at a meeting October 21, passed a resolution urging the Federal Congress to build a Nicaragua canal.

A disastrous forest fire swept down Mission Canyon, Santa Barbara County, October 16, destroying seven farmhouses, a schoolhouse, several barns and other property, and causing a $50,000 loss. Other conflagrations during the month were:

Star brewery, Eureka, Humboldt County, 1st, $15,000 loss; Kelly & Co. paint store, San Francisco, 4th, $20,000 loss; J. Riley's farmhouse and buildings near Chico, Butte County, 4th, $10,000 loss; Hoen winery, Windsor, Sonoma County, 4th, $50,000 loss; armory hall and several businesshouses at Woodland, Yolo County, 18th, $25,000 loss; Livermore, Alameda County, flourmill, 17th, $20,000 loss; several business blocks at Truckee, Nevada County, 27th, $100,000 loss.

Two 13-year-old lads were arrested for committing a highway robbery near Wheatland, Yuba County, October 1. Armed with four revolvers, they stopped a Chinaman. When he saw a gun directed toward him from every point of the compass, the Chink dropped upon his knees and handed over seven dollars.

Deer, grouse and quail were so plentiful in the Sierra foothills the lumberjacks of mills in Placer and Nevada Counties notified their employers that unless beef and pork were served them at meals, in place of so much wild game, they would quit.

Los Angeles County was shaken by an earthquake at 3 a. m. of October 8, and Mendocino County had a shake at 7:12 p. m. of October 31.

The Bald Mountain mine at Forest City, Sierra County, October 10 unearthed a six-pound gold nugget worth $1,300.

The North Bloomfield, Nevada County, hydraulic mine cleaned up its sluices after a twenty-day run. The gold dust, weighing 450 pounds, was valued at $115,000.

A call was issued for a convention of dairymen to meet November 1 at Santa Cruz City to form a protective organization against the manufacture and the sale of oleomargarine.

Frank Ledden, aged 17, and another lad, skylarking with shotguns near Alviso, Santa Clara County, October 8, was accidentally killed.

N. Lauridsen, attempting to lasso an infuriated bull on Wood Island, was gored to death.

Bright N. Noll, aged 18, was thrown from a horse at Bakersfield, Kern County, and killed.

George Crandall, a miner at Dogtown, Nevada County, at a ball October 26 was married to Miss Mary Atkins of Nimshew. After dancing all night he took the bride to her home in a buggy. Returning with the rig to Dogtown, he fell asleep, the team went over an embankment, and he was killed.

Charles Addington of Auburn, Placer County, early in the summer bought a bunch of bananas in which he found an egg. He placed it in a dish, which was covered and put in a cupboard. This month he accidentally uncovered the dish and found in it a three-inch-long live alligator.

October 21, the San Francisco police arrested seventy-seven intoxicated persons, among them nine females, for minor law infractions. Most of them were unable to navigate.

Fourteen-year-old Willie Keen, as sharp as his name, boarded an east-bound train at Sacramento City, October 16, with a New York ticket. A policeman, suspicioning him, took him in charge and a search of his clothing produced $2,885, which he acknowledged picking up the previous day on a west-bound train. Willie was taken to Oakland, Alameda County, where he was identified as the lad who had relieved a peddlar of his horse and wagonload of watermelons.

BOOK REVIEWS

(CLARENCE M. HUNT.)

"HISTORIC SPOTS IN CALIFORNIA"— THE SOUTHERN COUNTIES.

By Hero Eugene and Ethel Grace Rensch; Stanford University Press, Stanford University, California, Publisher; Price, $2.50.

This work, sponsored by the California State Conference of the National Society, Daughters of the American Revolution, is the first of a series calling attention to historic spots in California, the southern counties being featured. "The purpose," as set forth in the preface, "is threefold: to create interest in the local history of California among its citizens, both juvenile and adult: to make knowledge of the historic spots of the different localities available, . . . and to arouse a statewide interest in the preservation of those vanishing historic landmarks which still survive." Truly, a most commendable purpose!

An introduction, by Dr. Robert G. Cleland of Occidental College, Los Angeles, summarizes the history of California to the completion of the first transcontinental railway, in 1869. "On this voyage [1542] Juan Rodriguez Cabrillo and his companion, [Bartolome] Ferrelo, in two tiny ships, the 'San Salvador' and the 'Victoria,' sailed the full length of the California coast and for the first time made known to Europeans the characteristics and vast extent of the land which stretched away to the north above the peninsula of Lower California," he says. "The leader of the first overland expedition to California [1826] was Jedediah Strong Smith, . . . one of the greatest explorers in the annals of Western America, an outstanding contributor to the history of California and the true pathfinder of the Sierra. . . . The formal transfer [by Mexico] of the territory [California] to the United States did not take place until the Treaty of Guadalupe Hidalgo on February 2, 1848."

"With the coming of the railways," concludes Dr. Cleland, "California entered upon its present-day development. . . . Looking on toward the future one's imagination is scarcely bold enough to visualize the destiny which awaits California. Looking to the past one sees a history, fascinating, romantic, inseparably a part of the great drama of international affairs and of the development of the United States, made inspiring by the heroic figures which move across its pages, and touched everywhere by elements of true greatness. To identify and preserve the landmarks where so many of the stirring episodes of this history occurred is assuredly to render a notable service to the state." A notable service, indeed, which has been for many years faithfully rendered by the tirders of Native Sons and Native Daughters of the Golden West!

In describing several of the most important historic spots in Imperial, Inyo, Los Angeles, Mono, Orange, Riverside, San Diego, San Bernardino, Santa Barbara and Ventura Counties much authentic historical data is presented. Practically all of the data has been heretofore presented in The Grizzly Bear during its quarter-century-and-more of publication. Referring to Imperial County, the authors say: "Probably the first White man to touch California soil was Hernando de Alarcon," who "reached the mouth of the Colorado River on August 17 or 18 [1540]. . . . 'It can hardly be doubted that he landed at various times on the California side of the river'." Quoting further from "Historic Spots in California":

In San Diego County, "Padre Junipero Serra, on July 16, [1769], . . . founded Mision San Diego de Alcala, mother of the Alta California missions." Referring to Santa Barbara County, "The land expedition from Mision San Diego to Monterey Bay, under direct command of Gaspar de Portola, left San Diego on July 14, 1769. . . . On August 18, Portola reached a very large native town on the site of the modern city of Santa Barbara." "As early as 1772, Pedro Fages traversed the region of the Cajon Pass," in San Bernardino County, "while on his way north into the San Joaquin Valley." In Riverside County is "San Carlos Pass, the first inland gateway to the coast of California, discovered by Captain Juan Bautista de Anza in 1774 on the first continuous overland journey into the state."

"The first Spanish grant made in Alta California was the great Rancho San Rafael,"— comprising 36,000 acres in Los Angeles County now the sites of Glendale, Eagle Rock and other modern towns—"granted to Jose Maria Verdugo on October 20, 1784." In Ventura County "is one of the most famous adobes in California. Located on Rancho Camulos, . . . and famous as the setting for part of . . . 'Ramona'." In Orange County is "Anaheim. . . . one of the oldest colony experiments in the state, started in 1857 by some Germans, chiefly from San Francisco." Aurora, the first county seat of Mono County, in 1864 was found to be in Nevada State, so Bridgeport became the government-seat. "Monoville," in that county, "the first settlement of any consequence east of the Sierra and south of Lake Tahoe, was different from the majority of mining camps in that it 'left no notable record of crime'." Inyo County "contains within its borders a more varied topography [Mount Whitney and Death Valley] than any other equal territory on this continent, probably than any other in the world."

"Historic Spots in California" is most interesting, throughout. It should be possessed, and its contents digested, by every lover of California. Its sponsors are deserving of unstinted commendation.

"LEATHER DOLLARS."

By Ana Begue Packman; The Times-Mirror Press, Los Angeles, Publisher; Price, $1.00.

This is a collection, quoting the author, of "The simple stories of the neighboring ranchos and rancheros of El Pueblo de Los Angeles, told me by my grandaunt and my mother: folktales, legends, songs, customs and the intimacies of a Hispano-California household, handed down throughout the generations. My grandaunt, Estefana Reyes Olivera, daughter of Spanish founders, was born in 1836; . . . My mother, Louisa Reyes Alaniz, was born on February 17, 1854. Both were born in El Pueblo de Nuestra Senora La Reina de Los Angeles." A small book that affords much enjoyment.

Bankers To Meet—The tenth annual convention of the Association of Bank Women will be held at Los Angeles City, October 3-5, in conjunction with the annual conclave of the American Bankers Association.

"Let us have a government by which our lives, liberties and properties will be secured."—George Washington.

EARLY HISTORY OF MARYSVILLE

Esther R. Sullivan

(Past Grand President N.D.G.W.)

"How cruelly sweet are the echoes that start,
When memory plays an old tune on the heart."

ONE OF THE PRIMAL OBJECTS OF the Order of Native Daughters of the Golden West is to perpetuate in memory the glorious deeds of the pioneer men and women of California. So today, Marysville Parlor No. 162 is very happy to participate in placing this tablet in this historic park in memory of the pioneer men and women who made Marysville possible.

John A. Sutter, the pioneer of pioneers, secured a grant of land from the Mexican governor in 1839. It included parts of Sacramento and Placer Counties, the valley portion of Yuba County, all of Sutter County, and a small portion of Colusa County.

Theodore Cordua obtained in 1842 from Sutter a lease of the land on which Marysville is located. Cordua erected at the foot of "D" street an adobe building which was later used as a trading post. Captain Sutter called the new settlement New Mecklenburg. This name was never popular, so the names Yuba River, Nye's Ranch and Yubaville were given to this settlement.

In 1846, Charley Covillaud and Michael Nye arrived and secured employment from Cordua. During the spring of 1847, the Murphy family, survivors of the Donner Party, came to the new settlement on the Yuba River. The family consisted of William G. Murphy, one of our honored pioneers; a sister, Mrs. Foster; her husband, William Foster; another sister, Mrs. Pike, and her 3-year-old daughter, Naomi, and an unmarried sister, Mary Murphy.

During 1847, Covillaud became a partner of Cordua. Another adobe building was erected at the foot of "D" street. One building was used as a lodginghouse and the other as a boardinghouse. In 1848, Foster became a member of the firm, which was known as Nye, Foster & Covillaud. Covillaud married Mary Murphy, and Nye married Mrs. Pike.

After the discovery of gold, Yubaville became a thriving settlement. When the great influx of goldseekers came to California in 1849, Stockton, Sacramento and Marysville were the important towns for access to the mines. They were easily contacted by river boats. Forty thousand men stayed in Marysville overnight on their way to the mines. They could secure a place to sleep, but had to provide their blankets.

Stephen J. Field arrived in January 1850. He was a welcome addition, for his services as a lawyer were needed. Covillaud had purchased the land which previously had been leased, and was selling lots. Field immediately began preparing deeds for the purchasers. After three days' residence here an election was held and Field was elected alcalde. Shortly thereafter he called the people of the vicinity into conference to discuss many necessary details for the development of the new town.

It was decided that Yubaville was too similar to Yuba City, so Rev. Wadsworth proposed calling the new town Marysville, in honor of Mrs. Mary Murphy-Covillaud, the wife of Charley Covillaud and a survivor of the ill-fated Donner Party. The new name met with the approval of all present. Mrs. Covillaud was loved for her many acts of kindness. Covillaud many times reported at his home that a young man was ill at the lodginghouse; Mrs. Covillaud immediately went to see him and, if necessary, stayed and nursed him back to health; if financial aid was needed for him to resume his journey to the mines, she gave that assistance. So the name Marysville was given in honor of a woman whose beauty of character and deeds of kindness made the way easier for those far from home and friends.

Stephen J. Field wrote the city charter adopted in 1850. S. M. Miles was elected the first mayor. His grave in the old City Cemetery is appropriately marked.

All the business houses fronted on the Yuba River, as all freight was delivered by boats. In 1850 the U. S. Hotel, a canvas structure, was on the east side of "D" street, between First and Second streets. The City Hotel, another canvas structure, was at First and "D" streets. All resident tents were scattered between Second street and the river. Old drygoods and grocery boxes were sold for two and three dollars. When torn apart, they formed excellent floors for the canvas tents.

In the state superintendent of public instruction's first report, in 1852, Marysville is reported as having thirty pupils, taught by Tyler Thatcher and wife. D. A. Stone became principal of the Marysville school in 1854, and served until 1868; he later became deputy city school superintendent of San Francisco. The "B" street school building was erected in 1858. The Convent of Notre Dame was built in 1856, and opened for pupils as soon as completed.

Father Peter Magganotta began the erection of the first Catholic church in September 1852 on the site of the present parochial residence. The cornerstone of St. Joseph's church was laid September 10, 1855, by Archbishop J. S. Alemany. Covillaud gave the land where St. Joseph's church and the College of Notre Dame are located. The cornerstone for St. John's Episcopal church was laid in 1854; it is the oldest Episcopalian church in Northern California, and is admired for its architectural beauty and simplicity of interior decoration. The Presbyterian Church was erected in 1861; it is a beautiful edifice in English Gothic, built after the mode of the fourteenth century, and is considered one of the beauty spots of Marysville.

The lack of roads in the mountains made packing by mules a necessity. In 1852, 100 packmules left here daily for the mines. W. H. Parks, another prominent pioneer who represented this vicinity in the State Legislature, ran a pack train to Foster's Bar. He proposed the name of Downieville for that thriving mountain settlement. Later wagons were employed in transporting supplies to the mines. Over 400 of them were used in freighting out of Marysville. Pack animals, and teams that pulled the wagons, totaled about 6,000, a great number to be fed and cared for in a small settlement. The California Stage Company was located on "B" street, between First and Second streets, the site of the old woolen mills. The company had a capitalization of $1,000,000. It carried passengers from Sacramento to Portland, and from Marysville to the various mining districts.

The prominent members of the bar associated with Stephen J. Field were Judge I. S. Belcher, William Belcher, Gabriel Sweezy and Charles DeLong. The latter became Minister to Japan. Field spent many years as a chief justice of the Supreme Court in Washington.

In this park in which we are assembled, known as Cortez Square, the State Agricultural Society erected a pavilion in 1858. The building was in the form of a cross, and surmounting the center of the roof was a large glass dome. French doors and windows were on every side. The Fifth State Fair was held here in 1858. It began August 23 and continued for five days. Among the exhibitors were Sutter, Bidwell, Lassen and Kit Carson. The latter had an interesting collection of relics and souvenirs of his eventful career. The building was later destroyed by fire.

Many excellent pioneer women came to Marysville. Through their influence followed the church and the school, to prepare for our future citizens. "The pioneer mother went forth with courage as her loadstone, with love as her guide, with a song on her lips, and a lantern in her hand to light the way for future generations."

To these pioneer men and women of Marysville we owe a debt of gratitude for their courage, their self-sacrifices, and their great vision in creating the possibilities which are the realities of today. "We love the dear old pioneers who made us what we are, and gave to us our glorious State, the Nation's brightest star."

(This is the address delivered at Marysville, Yuba County, by Miss Esther R. Sullivan, Past Grand President N.D.G.W., at the dedication of the fountain erected in memory of the men and women who founded that city. An account of the dedication appeared in The Grizzly Bear for August 1932.—Editor.)

THE LETTER BOX

Comments on subjects of general interest and importance received from readers of The Grizzly Bear.

SPIRIT OF OUTLAWRY MILITATES AGAINST DEMOCRATIC GOVERNMENT.

Editor Grizzly Bear—Let me express my appreciation of the "Grizzly Growl" on the Eighteenth Amendment, which appears in the first column of your September issue. You are quite right in the suggestion that the Federal Government is under solemn obligation to "compel respect for and compliance with our Constitution," and that it is no part of this obligation to seek to amend the Constitution merely to satisfy those who defy the Government and hold it in disrespect.

The amendments to our Federal Constitution, being part and parcel of the Constitution itself, must be secure and safe from the clamor of noisy minorities. It is a plain dictate of good citizenship that those who hold the law in cor tempt shall themselves be answerable to th law; theirs is the spirit of outlawry, a spirit tha militates against democratic government an tends to breed anarchy.

The way to see the Eighteenth Amendmer more perfectly enforced is clear—that is, for th people to refuse absolutely to participate in th liquor traffic, which means that they shall ab stain from alcoholic drink. If all the men wh have been lifting up their voices in complair about the non-enforcement of the prohibitio laws would themselves consistently practice per sonal prohibition, there would be no prohibitio problem, and the nation would be vastly bett off. Incidentally, the "spread of disrespect" o account of the Eighteenth Amendment woul immediately disappear from the land.

I am as thoroughly opposed to the liquor tra fic in the United States as I was when strivin for the enactment of the Eighteenth Amend ment, and for the same reasons. I believe th Amendment to be sound and salutary; and conceive it to be my duty as well as my privileg as a citizen to obey and uphold it with all goo citizens, to "promote the general welfare and s cure the blessings of Liberty to ourselves an our posterity."

ROCKWELL D. HUNT.

Los Angeles, September 2, 1932.

CONDITION MUST BE CHANGED, OTHERWISE DIRE RESULTS FOLLOW

Editor Grizzly Bear—I am one of the "Nativ Sons," born at Indian Diggings, El Dorado Coun ty, in 1856, so you see I am one of the veteran

My personal history does not matter, but wish to offer a word of praise for the "Grizzl Growls" that you are publishing in the mag zine. I hope you will continue till the Nativ Sons of California are aroused to their respons bilities and impressed with the duty of correc ing many of the evils that congest state, count and city government, to say nothing of th nation.

The evils all center around too numerou functions of government that do not benefit th people in general, or at least are not necessar These are in the form of commissions, bureau and useless individual appointees at a tremen dous public expense.

If the condition cannot be changed or im proved, I really believe that the final result wi be the abandonment of private property and drift into a form of socialism, or else the estab lishment of a dictator as Italy was forced to d in order to prevent socialism.

G. A. RICHARDSON.

Sacramento, September 4, 1932.

GOD BE WITH US.

Editor Grizzly Bear—It's hoped that ever voter in California saw "Grizzly Growls" of Au gust '32 and will profit. A good slogan for th coming election would be: we and all the voter are going to the right place, at the right tim and we are voting according to the will of Go

For God, and not Wall street, banks or mone is ruler of this country and every other countr God be with us when we go to the polls to vot —to lead, guide, direct and protect us now.

NELLIE H. DUNNING.

Los Angeles, August 14, 1932.

ANAHEIM FOUNDED BY GERMANS TO SUPPLY WINE SHORTAGE

Anaheim, Orange County, was originall founded in 1858—by fifty German settlers wh came to California during the gold rush—as co-operative project for the cultivation of win grapes. Such is the story told by Hallock F Raup in a booklet entitled "The German Colon zation of Anaheim." Two names for the colon were proposed, "Anaheim"—home on the Sant Ana—and "Anagua," and the former won out b a single vote. From Juan Pacifico Ordivera owner of Rancho de los Coyotes, about 1,00 acres were purchased at $2 per acre.

Raup says the idea of establishing Anahei apparently arose from San Francisco's need fo an augmented wine supply in the '50s. Lack o harmony dissolved the co-operative organizatio in September 1859, and each of the sharehol ers was given twenty acres and a business lot o Main street. The Germans, however, continue their efforts, and the wine output increased an nually from 75,000 gallons in 1861 to 1,250 000 gallons in 1884. The size of the townshi was also increased, to 3,200 acres. The chang from grape growing to citrus culture starte about 1884, following an epidemic of some vin disease which killed off the vineyards and threa ened the Anaheim colony with economic disaste

Depression—The whole world is moaning an groaning under the terrific weight of its sel wrought folly.—Jeanette Nourland.

WILL STRENGTHEN FAITH

AT SUNRISE THE MORNING OF SUNDAY, September 11, Grand President Anna Mixon Armstrong of the Order of Native Daughters of the Golden West and Grand President Seth Millington of the Order of Native Sons of the Golden West moved earth atop Mount Davidson, in the City of San Francisco, thereby participating in an event destined to hold forth particular significance in the history not only of California, but also of both illustrious Orders. Upon this spot, the highest in the city, 938 feet above sea level, there is to be erected a giant structure, designated as the "Sunrise Easter Cross," one hundred feet in hight, its top to stand 1,038 feet above the heaving surface of the Pacific, and to remain for all time as an emblem and shrine for the adherents of all Christian religions.

Originally, The Cross was left as a heritage to mankind by The Savior of civilization. For more than two thousand years it has beckoned humans on towards the achievement of better things through the medium of its inspiration, to emulate the example of The Christ, and wherever there has been an advance of civilization, there The Cross has been planted. The vanguard of civilization came here through the Spaniards, and as the padres conquered the wilderness and inculcated the doctrines of their church in the heart of the Indian they established in each spot the emblem of faith—The Cross.

James G. Decatur was inspired to construct the first cross upon Mount Davidson, and the first sunrise Easter service was held there in 1923. He rallied many friends and associates to support the project, and the San Francisco district immediately adopted the cross and services as an institution. The first cross was a wooden one, forty feet in hight; it was replaced by another, eighty feet high. Unknown persons proceeded to burn the second structure, as they did the one that followed, the latter being seventy feet high.

Decatur, Clarence F. Pratt and the local group of San Franciscans who were interested then decided to have a permanent cross built with materials that would endure and which could not be destroyed. This time it will be made of concrete and steel. The grand officers of both the Native Sons and Native Daughters graciously agreed not only that the new and permanent cross should be constructed, but also gladly cooperated, and the result was that when ground was broken it was done under their auspices.

The hard rock and earth were loosened by Grand President Millington, who wielded a pick. Grand President Armstrong plied a shovel. The first earth removed was placed in a metal box held by Decatur, and it will be placed in the cornerstone, together with other important souvenirs and documents, in the not-distant future.

The sunrise dedicatory speech was delivered by Lewis F. Byington, Past Grand President N.S.G.W. Other prominent officers of the two Orders present and participating included: Junior Past Grand President Dr. Frank I. Gonzalez, Grand Secretary John T. Regan, Grand Third Vice-president Harmon D. Skillin, Grand Second Vice-president Chas. A. Koenig, Grand Trustees Jesse H. Miller, Horace J. Leavitt, Joseph J. McShane and Charles H. Spengemann of the Native Sons; Grand Trustee Ethel Begley and Grand Inside Sentinel Orinda Giannini of the Native Daughters. In their addresses they stressed what this, the highest cross in the world, stands for and will accomplish.

"It is fitting," said Grand President Millington, "that we should today initiate an event which will add greater honor to our Order in the great city located on the peninsula between the great Pacific and San Francisco Bay. We shall be happy when it shall be completed and the eyes of the millions may daily note this pure-white emblem pointing upward as a true inspiration of truth and faith."

"This cross will strengthen our faith in God," commented Grand President Armstrong. "It will strengthen church attendance. Next spring there may be 100,000 pilgrims of faith attending the Easter service here at sunrise, and there will be millions listening in as the services are broadcast over the radio. This cross will be the greatest of its kind in the world, and will serve to remind us that from the high places have come the dearest precepts of religion. Here, then, in San Francisco, this wonder city, we, the Daughters of the Golden West, feel a pride in offering our small help in dedicating another shrine which will lift the minds of women and men from worrying about material things to those consoling reflections which tend to sooth troubled minds. May the gleam from the lights of this cross remind us that the brotherhood of man is a religious tenent." At the conclusion of the ground-breaking ceremony the grand officers of the Orders, together with members of the Sunrise Easter Service Committee, were breakfast guests of Ernest Drury.

Left to right—DR. FRANK I. GONZALEZ, Junior Past Grand N.S.; JESSE H. MILLER, Grand Trustee N.S.; SETH MILLINGTON, Grand President N.S.; MRS. ANNA M. ARMSTRONG, Grand President N.D.; LEWIS F. BYINGTON, Past Grand N.S.; HORACE J. LEAVITT, Grand Trustee N.S.; JOSEPH J. McSHANE, Grand Trustee N.S.; JOHN T. REGAN, Grand Secretary N.S.; HARMON D. SKILLIN, Grand Third Vice N.S.; MRS. ORINDA G. GIANNINI, Grand Inside Sentinel N.D.; MRS. ETHEL BEGLEY, Grand Trustee N.D.; CHAS. A. KOENIG, Grand Second Vice N.S.; CHARLES H. SPENGEMANN, Grand Trustee N.S.

PASTORAL

(GERTRUDE MOORE.)

So cool, so quietly it came,
Like a river flowing,
I only knew that love was here
And it would not be going.

So sure, so even was his step,
So quietly he came,
I looked up once and saw him there
And Heaven was his name.

He didn't speak; I didn't smile;
The day was all around us;
We sat among the singing flowers
And gentle beauty found us.

—University California Chronicle.

CENTURY-OLD PEAR TREES PRODUCE.

Pear trees 126 years old are bearing fruit in an orchard at Mission San Juan Bautista, San Benito County. Evidently, says Dr. W. P. Tufts of the University of California pomology division, these pears were planted by the padres during the mission days of California, for they are growing in orchards at several other missions. The variety is similar to some that are grown today, but is identical with none of the present-day pears.

"Virtue, even in an enemy, is respected by generous minds."—Baker.

TARNISHED GOLD

Ruth Parle

"And my knife shall never rust from the want of blood!"

THE SHADOWS OF APPROACHING twilight were playing hide and seek behind huge moss-covered rocks. How long had those rocks been there? Parts of them were now blasted away, making a site for a thriving town, "the gem of the Southern mines," and its ever-increasing populous.

Saturday night always brought the people to the hight of excitement, it seemed; there was invariably a murder, holdup, robbery, street brawl, or something. The Fandango House on one side of the street—with the men in high heels, front shirts ruffled, lace in their sleeves, wide-brimmed hats with ball fringes dangling, and sash at the waist—was a center of attraction.

Down the street, on the other side, lived old Dr. Sharno and his pet lion. Fun the women had when that pet went for a walk. And then, there was old Mr. Ghen, who rented the barracks and lived there with "French Mary," she who went out riding mounted upon a gay nag, with a long sweeping black skirt habit and a white plume in her hat.

The tumult hightened as the throng of over 15,000 men crowded the streets and stores to sell their gold dust. Saturday night the successful miner made merry, while the unlucky one drowned his sorrows in wine. Even down in Chinatown and in the Chinese theatre there was much noise to make the evening hideous. Even on rainy nights this town could not be stopped.

A native village was an adjunct of the town —Diggers they were called—and John Cook, a White man with a squaw wife, took charge of the place, very dirty with many dogs and fleas. These Indians turned out enmasse after a rain, each armed with a goose quill, and patiently gathered the gold particles left in the street.

On this particular night everything was in commotion. It seemed to have been a prosperous week for everyone. Strangers were going in and out of the old town continuously. Over by the Broadway House stood a dark young man who had come into the town at noon. His sombrero, slouched down over his forehead, failed to hide entirely the sparkling Spanish eyes and the handsome face. His zarrape, of bright colors, swung over his shoulder, betrayed his fatherland. He had been wandering up and down the crooked streets with an air which told of nobility and wealth. He was a true caballero, and a vaquero too. "I saw him ride in, 'twas in the heat of the day, and that lad rode with never a thought about it. Strange, he was; his quietness got on my nerves. You know, those were the days when men walked around with their hands upon their holsters. If this muchacho had not been Don Murietta, many a man would have walked past him with an eye to their guns."

The night had worn on midst the noises and colors of the pioneer town, and lights were going out, one by one, as the early hours of the morning came on. The streets were practically deserted as Old Tom, the only representative of the government and the man who weighed all men's gold, walked on his way home after closing the postoffice. Yes, the old town is wealthy tonight, mused the old fellow; he had weighed $20,000 worth of gold since seven o'clock that morning. Quite a day's work!

Thus he walked along, but suddenly stopped. Was someone calling him? He looked around; no, no one was there. Tom was not a nervous fellow, but he actually jumped a little when he heard someone call his name softly. Turning, he saw no one. Too much work for his nerves that day, he consoled himself as he continued on his way. By this time the full summer moon hid behind a cloud, and as things darkened he again heard his name whispered softly. This time he turned not around: in his back he felt the hard iron of a revolver. The voice asked for the key to the office, but Old Tom was not a coward, and he turned on his man. A look of surprise, then full recognition, came over his face.

The neighbors came running out as they heard the report of a revolver. Old Tom was lying upon his face in the street, a pool of blood on the ground. Someone had worked fast and thoroughly. The next day Tom was laid away in the old churchyard on the hill. As the old keeper went, so the keepings; they found the rusty iron box open and empty.

As days went on the puzzle grew deeper, and finally folks began to shake their grey heads and sigh. Saturday night had come again, and the streets had barely a soul in them. A few drank their wine and felt gay. But a man makes not merry when his life blood is gone; his gold is his life blood.

All week Don Murietta—that was the dark stranger of the previous week who had now become quite the favorite of the town—had been lazying in the hot summer sun. The belles of the town were often favored by the presence of the dark-clad Spaniard. He was liberal with his gold, and many a man became his friend over the bar.

The ground had barely hardened on the grave of Old Tom when, in the cool of the evening, shots disturbed the quietude. With the first outbreak men came running to the old Fandango, where the shots had evidently originated. The lamps were out, all except one, which had come blazing to the dance floor from its hanging wire attached to the ceiling. The dancers had rushed to the door, while men fought with fists and chairs or tables, which they flung at any onrushing assailant. The oil from the old lamps ran in streams over the floor, leaving tongues of flame in all directions. The dried wood burned quickly, and flames broke out everywhere. Other fallen lamps brought blazes of brilliant red to dark corners, betraying terrified faces of occupants of the doomed place. Buildings caught fire, one by one, and soon most of the town was ablaze. Men with leaking buckets ran to the scene of disaster, finding to their greatest dismay that all their effort was of no avail.

In every pioneer town there was a place much favored in time of war, but much terrifying in time of fire, the ammunition house. If those snaky tongues of fire were to make their lightning-like way to that horrible spot the town would be no more—years of endless toil vanishing to bits of wood scattered here and there, and the site, perhaps, a giant hole left as an only landmark.

In one last desperate attempt at saving the pot of Midas gold all horses and wagons available had been loaded with ammunition, which was then conveyed to a place outside the range of fire. The smoke was so dense one could not see. The horses were blindfolded and driven through the street to safety. That white heat scorched the hair from their hides, but the ammunition went through. Don Murietta, at the head of these horses, raced them through for fear the flying sparks might light the ammunition. Time and again he ran fearlessly into a flaming house, bringing out in his arms an unconscious girl or her mother.

It was during this fury of excitement that Dr. Sharno's lion broke loose. Its yellow body could be seen flying at the back of some man or showing its fangs to some fainting woman. It was crazed by the flames and ran through the streets at lightning speed. In the center of the roadway lay French Mary, prostrate. The onrushing lion stopped short as it came upon her. It would have been a work of but a few minutes had not the dashing caballero leaned down from his horse and picked up the fainting woman. Murietta showed all his skill as he worked that night fighting against the fire-god. A fire is bad enough, without having a crazed pet lion running loose, so the jungle beast was a good target for the vaquero's good marksmanship.

Jim, the new man in Old Tom's place, had rushed up into the blanket of flames toward the Mill Bank. The people had lost their money, and they would not lose it again, if he could help it. As he rounded the corner of a wall he heard the pound of a hammer upon iron. Had someone beat him to it? He would sneak up on the intruder and see if it be friend or enemy. The hammering ceased as he entered the building. A black shadow moved swiftly out of sight. There was the iron box, open. He clenched his fists as he stood over the empty box. What was this? A black glove lay beside the iron container. He leaned over to pick it up. Soft footsteps came from behind. It must be the crackling of the flames close by. Was someone calling him? He was sure he heard his name called softly this time. There was someone behind him! He clenched the glove in his hand. The owner of that glove was near. Yes, he saw the initials, and he knew them. He reached for his gun. He had his man. He turned around and drew his weapon. His face showed surprise, then recognition, as he slumped to the floor, the unfired gun clutched limply in his dead fingers.

As the first stray ray of sun pierced through dawn's grey mantel and the wavering spirals of smoke wound their way up from the ruins, homeless wanderers could be seen searching the ruins of the part of the town which had been burned. They came to the bank, which had fortunately been untouched by the flames. They looked through the windows of broken glass, and started back with amazement. Was that a fallen fixture? The door was open, and the men thronged in. On closer investigation they found Jim lying upon his face, a bullet hole in his heart.

Their gold was gone again! Would that golden gem dazzle for them once more in this apparently God-forsaken town? There were two new graves on the hillside now, and people concluded that the last straw had been pulled. Every eye searched for the burglar-murderer.

One day the town felt the thrill of excitement once again. A horseman had ridden in, telling the town that a gang of thieves and cut-throats were hiding in the hills. He told of their leader, a blood-thirsty young man whose adventures were now spreading like wildfire over Northern and Central California. "And who do ye think he be?" asked one excited miner of the breathless messenger.

"Wal, this is the story from what I've gathered on my way up heer. I heerd that you folks was havin' some trouble with a gold bug. He was born in Sonora, Mexico, of a wealthy family. And he was edjicated, too. 'Magine a edjicated man turnin' cut-throat—wal that's what he done. Edjication never did nobody no good.

"Wal, enyhow, his older brother, Carlos, goes up in ter California and gits married and sech. Wal, up comes some horse stealing and, as usual, a Mexican hangs fer it. Meanwhile this heer gang leader, he was a good feller then, he comes huntin' fer his brother. On his way up heer he falls in love with Carmen, a black-eyed senorita, and they marries. Enyway, when they finds out that Carlos is dead they moves up ter Hangtown, where he staked a claim. Them miners up thar is awful upish and they orders him ta git. He won't do it, and they revolt and kill Carmen."

The men had now walked with the storyteller to the old hotel. There he told them of how, out of the torture of nightmare, the boy awoke a bitter enemy of all men and vowing that revenge would be his until the last bit of strength had faded from his being. Thus he went, wandering over the hills, to strange places, becoming at the age of nineteen a man-beast terror bandit of California.

Months and years passed while Mexican outcasts, riff-raff of the mining camps, joined the boy-terror. His band grew from a few to hundreds. Here his word was law; he was respected by them all. He was a tyrant in his rule. In a virgin canyon just east of Pachecho Pass the gang built their camp. There were three lieutenants, Rinaldo Felix, the brother of Carmen, Joaquin Valenzuela, and a wild beast named Manuel Garcia who, having lost a finger, was called "Jack Three Fingers."

Through campaigns of horror went the gentle eyed boy-leader, yet wielding always his bloody knife. He appeared in a thousand different disguises—once a monk, again a gambler, but always a good sport. He killed in fair battles, but he struck quickly and accurately, giving his opposer hardly a chance.

As the messenger finished his tale a long hearty laugh rang out over the group of silent listening men. "And what is hees name, senor?" laughed the joyful Murietta, one of the most earnest listeners. "Joaquin Murietta," replied the messenger, pronouncing each syllable slowly and looking Murietta full in the eye.

Murietta, stepping back a few feet, drew from his sash belt a blood-stained knife. Flinging his arm high over his head, he cried: "I have given my word, my knife shall never rust from the want of blood!" With that, the man leaped upon his horse and rode, as he had ridden in, like lightning away down the old crooked streets to the hills.

Joaquin Murietta rode over the hill at sunset, was shot down on the hill at sunset, went "out west" at sunset. From east to west, north to south, Joaquin Murietta rode, the blood on his knife never dry. Many Pioneers felt the heartless revenge of the most sorrowful, yet the most terrible, outlaw in the history of California.

CAPTIVE AMONG THE INDIANS

Peter T. Conmy

(Historian Golden Gate Parlor N.S.G.W.)

AUGUST 10, 1850, A PARTY OF IMMIgrants set out from Independence, Missouri, to settle in lands between the mouth of the Colorado River and the Gila River. Among the groups of settlers in the party was a family by the name of Oatman, consisting of the father, the mother and five minor children. The oldest of the children was Lorenzo, a boy 16 years of age; the next in line of age was Olive, aged 15; the others were of more tender years, the youngest being but 2. This party, like many other immigrant parties of the time, had hard luck in crossing the continent. In this particular case storms, lack of funds and quarrels between the various factions weakened the morale and as a consequence many of the families dropped out along the route.

At the end of the first six months but three families, the Wilders, the Kellys and the Oatmans, remained. February 16, 1851, these three families, worn out by winter travel, arrived at the Indian village of Pimole in eastern New Mexico. During the trip the party had been menaced by the Apaches, who preyed on them along the route. Other Indians were friendly to the White people, and were deadly enemies of the Apaches. Consequently the party found green pastures of rest and welcome at Pimole. The Wilders and the Kellys decided to remain there indefinitely.

Oatman deemed it best to move on to Fort Yuma, 190 miles distant and in California, just across the Colorado River. Accordingly, the Oatman family pressed on, alone. They had the usual immigrant, or Conestoga, wagon, two yoke of cows and one yoke of oxen. March 18 they reached the waters of the Gila River and camped upon a sandbar island in the middle of the stream. The next day they completed their crossing of the Gila, and also removed everything from the wagon in order to get it over a hill beyond. The belongings were carried up the hill by hand and again placed in the wagon.

The family then decided to rest during the remainder of the day and to proceed during the moonlight of the night. At dusk, as they were preparing to move on, a group of Indians approached and simulated friendliness. They even went so far as to smoke the pipe of peace with Oatman. After this they gathered in council at one side and suddenly let out war whoops and brandished clubs which had been concealed under their buckskins. They killed all except three. Lorenzo, the 16-year-old boy, was hit on the head and left for dead. Mary Ann, aged 7, and Olive, aged 15, were not attacked but taken prisoners. After raiding the provisions the Indians took the two girls and returned east to their own habitation.

Lorenzo Oatman regained consciousness after many hours. He wandered in the wilderness for several days and was attacked by wolves. Finally he was met by two Indians from Pimole who took him in charge and cared for him until they met the Wilders, who were now pressing west. Wilder visited the scene of the massacre and reported he was able to identify the body of each member of the family, save Olive and Mary Ann. This confirmed Lorenzo's suspicion that they had been taken captives, for in his delirium he had heard the cries of his sisters as the Indians were leading them away. Lorenzo came on to California. He worked in San Francisco and in the mining region for three years, but his thoughts were constantly of his sisters. In 1854 he moved to Los Angeles, in order to keep in touch with doings in the Fort Yuma region.

In the meantime, the girls had been taken eastward by their cruel captors, to the home of the tribe. They were put to work under the women of the tribe who, in customary Indian fashion, did all of the work. At first the Apaches were harsh to the girls, but after a time became lenient. In the fall of 1851 Indians from the Mojave region of California visited the Apaches and in the transactions that followed the two girls were sold to them. Then followed a trying journey of 350 miles into California, where they took up their abode among the Mojave tribe. The winter of 1851-52 was a severe one, even in the mild climate of the Mojave district of California. Worn out from constant exposure, shocked from the terrible sight of the massacre of her family the year before, without the proper nourishment that a child of 8 must have, Mary Ann sickened and died in the early spring of 1852. Her last words were, "I am willing to die. Oh, I shall be so better off there."

Lorenzo Oatman caused investigations to be made. Word came that there was a White girl captive among the Mojaves and that there had been two of them, but that one had died. Spurred on with this information, the Government of the United States became interested and finally, in 1856, Olive Oatman was found by a friendly Indian and, through his strategy, was released by the chief who owned her. Then fol-

(Continued on Page 17)

Feminine World's Fads and Fancies

PREPARED ESPECIALLY FOR THE GRIZZLY BEAR BY ANNA STOERMER

GONE ARE THE DAYS WHEN THE spell of that magic label, "imported creation," suffices to force unbecoming freaks of fashion upon the American women. Good taste and independence of thought are triumphing now, as er before, in the selection of feminine ward-es. The women of this country realize, at , that ugly or impractical fashions need not accepted blindly, merely because they are nsored by foreign designers.

Unless all fashion signs fail, we are about to bark upon an era of victorian elegance of es, the like of which has not been seen in ny a day. The victorian influence extends oughout the length and breadth of the mode. Fashion interest is centered in the bodice of autumn coat. Collar, sleeves and shoulder ails become important. The variety achieved collars is remarkable. They are high, wide, uminous and adjustable.

The cape is by far the most important style te. Capes and capelets appearing in both furs d fabrics on a large proportion of coat types worn fastened at center-front, center-back over the left shoulder by buttons, buckles or appy forms. In most cases they are detach-le.

The winter ensemble is less likely to be a ess-and-coat combination than an alliance of suit and coat. Suits do not, in these cases, ke the place of dresses. One of the smartest sembles is a striking purple wool suit with a et and scarf of louis blue and a slightly low-ed waistline. A coat of black and white rodier material boasts of a cravat in place of the customary fur at the throat.

The tweed suit-dress follows classic double-breasted lines, with variations in the belt, which does not cross the front, and double lapels on the collar. There is also a noticeable absence of belts on the more dressy coat models. Other distinguishing features are the increased luxury of the fabrics and the regal use of furs.

Gray is prophesied as one of the outstanding color fashions. It appears in many variations, such as putty, dove breast, asbestos, pumice-stone, slate and oxford. One of the interesting phases of this new color range is in its combination with other colors, such as chocolate brown, yellow, orange, dark and light reds, navy blue, black, and all pastels and dark rich flower colors.

Knitted fabrics in two of the darker variations of gray are used to make a coat-dress and topcoat which may be worn together. The coat is made of coarser weave than the dress, but both are of a stout quality which will stand the rigors of travel and general knockabout wear. The dress has raglan shoulders, and the coat has classic sleeves and shoulder lines. Both are fastened at the front in a side V-fastening marked with your initials. Both make clever use of a cravat scarf in brilliant shades of orange and yellow.

Another frock, of black rough crepe, rather long and yet of the approved street length, is made with well-fitting skirt lines, broken at the knees with insets of tiny pleats. The feature, however, is a scarf collar of heavy ivory satin, its widely-spread ends fastened with ornaments. Long sleeves are finished at the wrists with narrow bands of white satin, fastened with brilliant buttons. Capelets over the shoulders follow the mode for wide shoulder effects. A tiny black turban is worn at a smart tip-tilted angle and decorated by a still smaller veil. Black suede oxfords and purse, white gloves and a silver fox fur complete this very attractive costume.

One could go on indefinitely talking about the new lovely and unusual fashions, but one has to see for herself to appreciate them, since shopping or even "window shopping" is not satisfactory by remote control.

Elegance is the keynote of the evening, and is expressed in luxurious fabrics. Fur is used as trimming. Feathers, beads and sequins embellish many beaded boleros and strike a new note in formal fashions.

Velvet holds first place. Transpartent and chiffon are closely followed by the new satins, crinkled crepes, lames, lace and taffeta. Some of the two-fabric combinations are chic in satin and velvet. Velvet is used as trimmings. Quaint shoulder capes are made of the velvet in darker tones. A burgundy velvet dress has a bodice top of printed lame.

The new shoulder cape of velvet, trimmed with fur, is just big enough to cover the shoulders and ties like a scarf at the front. It is adorable, and just enough wrap for dashing from theater or hotel entrance to the waiting car, or to wear indoors when a shoulder wrap is needed.

Taffeta, faille and other silk fabrics that rustle and swish may possibly be one of the big winter fashions. At present the rustling silks are used in one form or another, such as sash trimmings, dresses to be worn under autumn coats, slips under lace dresses, entire dresses, matching jackets, and petticoats under lace-and-net dresses with unhemmed pinked edges that are reminders of fashions of the late '90s.

The change that has come over women's clothes within the last few seasons is tangible proof of the fact that, in general, they are growing more and more practical, more comfortable, and more economical in price, without losing any of their smartness.

Fur trimmings are much in evidence, not only on suits and coats, but on dresses as well. Strips of black astrakan are incrusted into wool dresses in the little stripes and squares that formerly were made of satin. There probably is more of a variety of furs used on clothes this year than ever before, but there is no parade of heavy fox bands. Gray astrakan, with white and gray squirrel and shaved lamb, are used most for dress trimmings. Bands of fur placed high on the sleeves serve two purposes: to add to the wide-shouldered line and to effect a narrowing hip. This also makes the suit more formal.

The newest evening wrap is a classic cape.

(Continued on Page 21)

Native Sons of the Golden West

SAN FRANCISCO—WITH GRAND PRESIDENT Seth Millington presiding, the Board of Grand Officers met September 10. Others in attendance were Junior Past Grand President Dr. Frank I. Gonzalez, Grand First Vice-president Justice Emmet Seawell, Grand Second Vice-president Chas. A. Koenig, Grand Third Vice-president Harmon D. Skillin, Grand Secretary John T. Regan, Grand Trustees Jesse H. Miller, Eldred L. Meyer, John M. Burnett, Joseph J. McShane, Horace J. Leavitt and Charles H. Spengemann.

The Riverside Commerce Chamber, in a letter to Past Grand William I. Traeger requested that the next Grand Parlor be held in that city. The Grand Secretary was directed to advise the Riverside organization that Grass Valley, Nevada County, had previously been selected as the 1933 meeting place.

It was ordered that Resolution No. 39—concerning Filipino employment—submitted to the Stockton Grand Parlor and referred to the California Joint Immigration Committee, be given further consideration.

To save Subordinate Parlors a considerable increase in the cost of surety bonds for their officers, "Condition No. 3" in the schedule bond was ordered eliminated; it provides: "The surety shall be liable for loss by reason of any officer or officers hereunder making unauthorized advances to delinquent members for dues or assessments, causing a shortage in the accounts of officer or officers."

Charters were ordered granted Visalia No. 19 and Alturas No. 134, now in course of formation, "providing that the petitions received in the office of the Grand Secretary shall have fifty or more names attached to each."

Los Banos No. 206, recently instituted, having initiated more than fifty charter members, was voted a supplies credit of $150.

On motion Grand President Millington, a vote of thanks was given Grand Trustee McShane, the chairman, and other members of the San Francisco Admission Day Celebration Committee for making possible the wonderful celebration held September 9.

Following the transaction of much additional business of a routine nature the Board adjourned, late in the afternoon, to the call of the Grand President.

Deputy Grand President Busy.

Deputy Grand President Al Lobree spent three days in Suisun, Solano County, last month and signed up several candidates for Solano No. 39. They will be initiated October 4 by the officers of Napa No. 62.

September 15, Deputy Lobree returned to Visalia, Tulare County, and completed the charter list for a new parlor there, having over fifty signatures. The parlor will be instituted by Grand President Seth Millington some time this month (October), according to reports, and the ritual will be exemplified by officers of Fresno No. 25 and Bakersfield No. 42.

September 20, Deputy Lobree departed for Alturas, Modoc County, where he hopes to secure a sufficient number of charter petitioners to warrant the institution of a parlor in the near-future.

Married Men Outrun Single Boys.

Ferndale—Ferndale No. 93 sponsored an Admission Day program at the Ferndale high school which was largely attended. Dr. Joseph Hindley was chairman of the day. The Sea Scouts and the Boy Scouts presented the colors; Raymond Grinsell, accompanied at the piano by Ross Ring, sang "California, the Land of My Dreams," and "I Love You, California;" John Lund gave a splendid talk on "The Early History of California."

The assemblage then adjourned to the high school track, where many interesting sports events were held. In a 440-yard relay race the married men outran the single boys; John Trigg was the star performer, taking up so much room the other runners were forced from the track. In a fast game of Olympic baseball the Native Sons defeated the Community Club by a 26-to-6 score. Ferndale's Admission Day committee was composed of Ralph C. Jacobsen (chairman), V. O. Givins, E. H. Lanini, Dr. J. N. D. Hindley and O. A. Bartlett.

"Day of Reminiscing."

Santa Barbara—Many oldtimers assembled September 9 at Rockwood, in Mission Canyon, as guests of Santa Barbara No. 116 and Reina del Mar No. 126 N.D.G.W. at the seventh annual "day of reminiscing." Weston E. Learned presided at the co-ordinated Admission Day and Washington bicentennial program, and Fred H. Schauer was the main speaker. Vocal selections were rendered by Mrs. Daisy L. Prideaux, and there were brief addresses by Mrs. George McCrea and Wesley McCormick, president, respectively of Reina del Mar and Santa Barbara, and Supervising Deputy Anna E. McCaughey.

County Surveyor Owen O'Neill was master of ceremonies for the informal hour, following the program, during which the oldtimers were called on for reminiscences. Light refreshments were served. In the evening the Native Daughters were hostesses at their annual Admission Day ball.

Anniversary Banquet.

Menlo Park—Menlo No. 185 celebrated its fortieth institution anniversary at a banquet September 17. Among the many in attendance were three charter members, Past President Jas. Anderson, President D. E. O'Keefe and Outside Sentinel Billy Casey. C. T. Maloney presided, and introduced as the toastmaster Mayor Harry Weeden. Inspiring talks were given by Grand Second Vice-president Chas. A. Koenig, Grand Secretary John T. Regan, Grand Trustees John M. Burnett and Joseph J. McShane, and District Deputy Phil Blanchard. A most enjoyable evening concluded with all joining in singing "I Love You, California."

Membership Standing Largest Parlors.

San Francisco—Grand Secretary John T. Regan reports the standing of the Subordinate Parlors having a membership of over 400 January 1, 1932, as follows, together with their membership figures September 20, 1932:

Parlor.	Jan. 1	Sept. 20	Gain	Loss
Ramona No. 109	1088	1085	....	3
South San Francisco No. 157	822	808	....	14
Castro No. 232	700	797	97	....
Stanford No. 76	614	609	....	5
Arrowhead No. 110	609	583	....	26
Stockton No. 7	549	563	14	....
Twin Peaks No. 214	585	538	....	47
Piedmont No. 120	523	523	....	....
Rincon No. 72	448	436	....	12

Ritual Contest.

San Rafael—All the Marin County Parlors made big showings in the San Francisco Admission Day parade. Notwithstanding the excessive heat, the drum and bugle corps of Mount Tamalpais performed splendidly and carried away first prize. Marinita No. 198 N.D.G.W. turned out with its newly-organized drill corps, in brilliant cossack uniforms, and made a fine appearance. Tamelpa No. 231 N.D.G.W. (Mill Valley), with its drum corps, helped put Marin on the map. No. 64 maintained headquarters, where folks of the county were hospitably entertained after the parade.

District Deputy Monroe Label, who is promoting interparlor visits and ritual contests because he believes they promote a necessary fraternal spirit among members, accompanied Grand Trustee Charles H. Spengemann on his official visit to Petaluma No. 27, September 26. October 19, Mount Tamalpais will conduct a class initiation, and the Sonoma County Parlors have been invited to attend. Deputy Label declares this will be another red-letter night in No. 64 history.

The ritual officers of Mount Tamalpais have accepted a challenge to a ritual contest from National No. 118 (San Francisco), to be held in San Francisco, probably some time in November. The San Rafael boys have earned quite a reputation for faultless ritual work and a number of Parlors have contemplated issuing challenges, but this is the first received. Many grand officers look with a great deal of favor on these contests, as a means of stimulating interest in Parlor activities.—L.J.P.

Historic Site Setting for Initiation.

Sacramento—General John A. Sutter Past Presidents Assembly No. 10 will hold its annual outdoor Sacramento County class initiation at historic Sutter Fort, October 1. Candidates for all the Subordinate Parlors of the county will be presented, and the past presidents perpetual membership trophy will be awarded the Parlor having the most initiates.

The past presidents will exemplify the ritual and the ceremonies will be witnessed by Grand President Seth Millington and most of the grand officers. The noteworthy occasion promises to attract a large number of Native Sons from the Sacramento Valley.

Historic Bear Flag Presented.

Modesto—A short talk on the wanderings of Stanislaus County's government seat was given by Past President L. E. Bither at the September 7 meeting of Modesto No. 11. The speaker's source of information was "Stories of Stanislaus," by Sol P. Elias, a member of the Parlor. First Vice-president Benjamin Munson presided.

A California State (Bear) Flag with a historical background floated September 9 from the mast atop Modesto's meetingplace. It is one of the flags used in the California building at the Columbia World's Fair in Chicago in 1893. J. M. Cross presented it to the Parlor, and it was accepted by President Charles D. Blaine. The flag was flown here for the first time Admission Day, and will be displayed on special occasions.

"Krazy" Party for Children Benefit.

Fort Bragg—In recognition of Labor Day and Admission Day, Alder Glen No. 200 sponsored a dance September 3 and a large crowd attended. Officers of Alder Glen and Broderick No. 117 (Point Arena) were jointly installed here by District Deputy Ralph Todd. A fine banquet was enjoyed after the meeting.

Alder Glen has appointed a committee of five to put on, in conjunction with Fort Bragg No. 210 N.D.G.W., a "krazy" party for the benefit of the homeless children some time in October.

Admission Day Party.

San Bernardino—In observance of the eighty-second anniversary of California's admission to statehood Arrowhead No. 110 had an Admission Day party at its Crestline clubhouse September 9. A steak supper was followed by dancing and speechmaking. Members of Lugonia No. 241 N.D.G.W. were among the many in attendance. The arrangements committee included Leslie Case (chairman), Henry Peake, John Andreson Jr., Eugene W. Lee, Ed Poppett, Gordon Lee, Hal Davies, Don VanLeuven, Jean Ward, Lamar McGarvey, Grand Organist Leslie Maloche, Walter Harris, John Cadd, Lynn Reed, Jeff Sawyer, Ralph Frederickson.

September 21 several candidates were initiated, the ceremonies being followed by a buffet lunch and entertainment.

Drum Corps' Initial Appearance.

Sausalito—Sea Point No. 158 and Sea Point No. 196 N.D.G.W. were well represented in the San Francisco Admission Day parade. Police

(Continued on Page 19)

"MARK OUR LANDMARKS"

Chester F. Gannon
(HISTORIOGRAPHER N.S.G.W.)

"MARK OUR LANDMARKS"

"THE PATHS OF GLORY"

THE BONES OF THE GREAT EDWARD D. Baker lie in a forgotten and forsaken grave! In life, was there ever a more talented, brilliant man than Baker? What a many-sided man he was! What heights did he reach! Had he lived in the golden age of oratory he would have spoken from the same platform with the peerless Demosthenes and the immortal Cicero.

America, with the possible exception of Webster and Ingersoll, has had none before or since his time to compare with him. The few brilliant flashes of Patrick Henry pale before his flood of word pictures and heart-stirring flashes. Lawyer, statesman, orator, soldier. What a gamut of human emotion did he run! And to crown a life of talented endeavor, he died at the head of Union forces in one of the first engagements of the Civil War.

Why has he never received the tribute from posterity which is his? Why is his grave neglected and his name practically unhonored? Why is not his bust in California's Hall of Fame at Washington, D. C.? Why was that of a lesser light, Thomas Starr King, given the honor? These are but a few of the unanswered questions for the Native Sons to ponder over and remedy some of their shortcomings.

During the past Admission Day celebration your historian journeyed to Laurel Hill Cemetery (formerly Lone Mountain) in San Francisco. A sign at the gateway denotes it a "Pioneer Cemetery." The main purpose of the trip was to visit the graves of Broderick and Baker. It was not difficult to find the grave of Broderick. Although forgotten, also, yet another generation of men, long gone, erected over his heroic bones a pile of granite which readily points out his bier to the passerby.

But the grave of Baker has no such marker. Search did not reveal its site, and finally a caretaker was appealed to. He led the way to a spot which had been passed without a thought that one so noble could be lying in such humble surroundings. When the guide did point out the simple monument, and the weed-grown plot where no hand has been raised for years to arrest the erosions of the elements and Time itself, then the utter abandonment of California greatness became unhappily apparent. Among the weeds were two empty bottles, long since drained of the "cup that clears of past regrets and future fears."

Over the grave of Baker and the bier of Broderick should float the Bear Flag of the State for which they gave so much. That flag would be a tribute to the past. It would direct admirers to these shrines. A small flagpole would serve the purpose, and in fair weather the flags, at a small expense, could be thrown to the breeze.

A few hundred dollars would remedy the defects and plant shrubs and lawn. If the Grand Parlor cannot do it, then some progressive San Francisco Parlor like Twin Peaks, Castro or Pacific could go out with a few tools and a few dollars and do the work. However, it should be done, and done at once, by some agency or the Native Sons admit that their interests are mostly contemporary and that our allegiance to the Past only secondary, if at all.

Your historian believes that our obligation is to the Pioneers first, and that that duty must never cease until we have fully paid that obligation, and then present-day endeavors may encompass our efforts and our fraternal life. This is the purpose of our fraternal existence, as I view our Fraternity.

Why not a memorial at the graves aforesaid? They are close together. Why not assemble

(Concluded on Page 19)

LOS ANGELES
CITY AND COUNTY

FOR SOME TIME, PRIOR TO AUGUST 30, the local daily papers devoted much space to informing taxbearers that, because of great reductions being made in the cost of government by governing officials of Los Angeles, city and county, the tax rate for 1932-33 would be materially reduced. That was being brought about, so it was said, by cutting out needless expenditures, reducing personnel and salaries, etc., etc. The publicity was pre-primary propaganda!

The promised tax-reducing program has not been carried out, for the total tax will not be lowered! On the contrary, it has been raised, considerably! But election day in November is ahead, and so, to ease the tax situation, the clique now contend the actual amount of tax to be paid will be lessened, through reduction in assessment. The "prominent boys' probably will have to pay less taxes on their holdings, but it is a near-safe bet ordinary householders will this year pay equally as much, if not more, than last year. Tax bills should be presented prior to election dates!

It is very doubtful if the numbers on the taxpayers' payrolls and the salaries of public officials, elective and appointive, have actually been reduced to any appreciable extent. Certainly, the services of hundreds could be dispensed with and the pay of thousands considerably decreased without in the least endangering governmental "efficiency." Of course, to do that would seriously affect the power and the influence of "the courthouse, the city hall, the departments and the bureaus gangs," whose watchword is "perpetuation in office." Other millions could be saved by rectifying the "family racket," whereby husband and wife, and in some instances the whole damn family, suck at the public teat; by eliminating the part-time-service vogue, particularly in the courts, with full-time pay; by ceasing to purchase and to operate with tax funds autos for the personal use and pleasure of public employes and their families; by directing less attention to and spending less money on Mexican cholos and other non-citizens, while thousands of White citizens and their families are in tax-distress; by doing away with fads and frills carried on, mainly for the benefit of Mexican cholos and their like, in the guise of education; by abolishing numerous other notoriously unsound tax-gormandizing customs which result in a stupendous waste of public funds!

Both the assessed value and the tax rate should come down, and the ballotbox, if resorted to by the tax-suffering majority, will force them down. Public officials of today are, as a rule, afflicted with "spenditis," an uncontrollable desire to be extremely lavish in the expenditure of other people's money. The services of all so afflicted should be dispensed with! The Realty Board, which has been waging a battle for tax reduction, could render no better service to Los Angeles than to head a movement to clean up the local governmental-swamp, via the recall. Let it be a thorough cleanup, too, by including the city and the county systems. Now's the time!—C.M.H.

ADMISSION DAY OBSERVED.

There was a large attendance at the Admission Day celebration arranged by a joint committee of Native Sons and Native Daughters, with Mrs. Gertrude Allen as chairman. Dancing was the main entertainment feature, and during an intermission a program was presented.

Superior Judge B. Rey Schauer spoke on "California's Admission to Statehood." He recalled to the minds of his hearers numerous historic anecdotes concerning the early history of the state, and referred to the courage and ambition that have always characterized the people of California. Mrs. Sophia Stewart sang "To California," a composition of Mrs. Louise Graeser, who accompanied at the piano, and the Edward LeVitt trio rendered several vocal numbers.

STORY ENMESHED IN FLAG'S FOLDS.

A beautiful flag of the immortal colors, the red, the white and the blue, was presented as a gift to Los Angeles Parlor No. 124 N.D.G.W. by two most earnest members, Mrs. Edith Shallmo and her daughter, Mrs. Adelaide Hickman. Numerous were the expressions of delight by the members as this large flag was unfurled. There is quite a history to this well-appreciated gift, the following story being enmeshed in its folds:

Among the many splendid American youths who enlisted in the World War was a fine, manly young fellow named Joseph Rogon. Handsome of face and form was he, and joyous of disposition, with a merry twinkle in his Irish blue eyes. Bravely he left his Eastern home and loving parents, to go to "No Man's Land" to fight, under the Stars and Stripes, to make this world safe for women and little children. Courageously he went "over the top," and won his medal for valor. But alas! the poisonous gas thrown by the enemy came his way and this splendid specimen of young manhood came home a victim of gassed lungs. His parents had passed on during his absence, and the lonely, sick lad was without any kin.

Uncle Sam thought to benefit him, and to try, if possible, to restore his health. So he was sent to our beloved California to recuperate, and become the splendid man that God intended him to be. With his slender pension he secured a modest room, and he boarded with his kindly landlady; among the neighbors were Mms. Shallmo and Hickman, who took a deep interest in the lonely afflicted soldier. They made him welcome in their home, and cooked dainty meals to tempt his appetite. How grateful was he for all these wonderful attentions, kindnesses and comforts.

This lonely soldier lad loved a home atmosphere, and he became very happy. How he loved our wonderful California, with its sunshine, fruits and flowers, and its beauty of sea and mountain. He longed to grow strong and well under its azure skies. His new friends did all in their power to help him, but alas! it was not his fate to have good health again, so he went to the U. S. Veteran Hospital at San Fernando, and Mms. Shallmo and Hickman took the keenest interest in making his room there cheerful and bright. Deeply this lonely soldier appreciated these two good Daughters of California who did so much for his comfort.

There shortly came a day when Joseph Rogon answered his final roll-call, and his soul went forth to greet the Great Commander in his heavenly home. They laid his brave body away with military honors, and as the final taps sounded the commanding officer presented the flag that adorned the casket of this splendid soldier to Mrs. Hickman. So, in memory of Joseph Rogon, this Flag of the United States of America was presented to Los Angeles Parlor. It will float over the new clubhouse, when the roseate dream of the Parlor becomes a reality.—A.L.A.

RESPOND TO THE DUTY CALL!

To aid in bringing to a successful conclusion, December 3, a membership campaign inaugu-

When you purchase goods advertised in The Grizzly Bear, or answer an advertisement in this magazine, please be sure to mention The Grizzly Bear. That's co-operation mutually beneficial.

Know your home-state, California! Learn of its past history and of its present-day development by reading regularly The Grizzly Bear. $1.50 for one year (12 issues). Subscribe now.

rated by Grand President Seth Millington, the Native Sons of Los Angeles County have formed a central committee composed of representatives from all the Parlors. Bernard J. Hiss of Hollywood No. 196 is the chairman, Clinton E. Skinner of Glendale No. 264 secretary, and Walter E. Baskerville of Ramona No. 109 treasurer.

The committee was organized mainly to get the individual Native Sons into action, for "There is no substitute for membership." Accordingly, its meetings will be held with the several Parlors. Los Angeles No. 45 was visited September 15, and Santa Monica Bay No. 267 September 26. Reports were to the effect that new parlors will be instituted in the southwest section of Los Angeles City and at Compton, and that many applications are being secured for the Parlors now in existence.

"It is our aim and hope to initiate a thousand members before the campaign ends," says Grand Trustee Eldred L. Meyer. "And that can be done, if every Native Son will do his duty."

PIONEER NATIVE AFFILIATES.

Long Beach—Long Beach Parlor No. 154 N.D.G.W. had an all-day picnic in Bixby Park September 9. Mrs. Lucretia Coates was chairman of arrangements. This picnic, in observance of Admission Day, has been a custom with the Parlor for many years.

Mrs. Alice Lyall Borden affiliated with No. 154 September 15. She was born at Hangtown, now Placerville, El Dorado County, in 1857, and related some very interesting family history.

DANCE AT GLENDALE.

Glendale—The officers of Glendale Parlor No. 264 N.S.G.W., assisted by Ralph I. Harbison (Ramona No. 109) as third vice-president and Roger Johnson (Los Angeles No. 45) as organist, September 20 initiated two candidates. All the neighboring Parlors were well represented, Hollywood No. 196 having a big delegation. Among the speakers were District Deputies Walter E. Baskerville, Edward E. Baldwin and Howard E. Bentley, Grand Outside Sentinel William A. Reuter, Lee Owen, Ralph Harbison, Alfred Boeckman and Clinton E. Skinner. The Parlor has appointed committees to promote athletics and other activities. After the meeting refreshments, prepared by members of Verdugo Parlor No. 240 N.D.G.W., were served, and the girls were given three rousing cheers.

During October, Glendale and Verdugo will resume their monthly dances. Last season these proved most popular, and the committee promises the same excellent music for the new series. Patrons are assured a good time at these dances. The initial dance will be held at Masonic Hall, Saturday, October 22.

OCTOBER BIRTHDAY PARTY.

Some forty past presidents of Ramona Parlor No. 109 N.S.G.W. met September 16 and outlined a campaign of activity to promote the wellbeing of the Parlor. Organization was perfected by the election of Walter Baskerville as the chairman, and Seth Williams as the secretary. During October Past Grand President Herman C. Lichtenberger will entertain all the past presidents of No. 109 at his South Pasadena home.

September 23 the Parlor featured an instructive debate on the trust-deed initiative measure which will be presented to the voters in November. The speakers, Marion P. Betty and George A. Schneider, were introduced by Abbott C. Bernay. September 30, Captain Tommy Lafthouse and his motorcycle police entertained the Parlor.

Ramona's October program includes: 14th, initiation. 21st, birthday party for all members born in October; at 6:30 a tamale supper will be served. 28th, a speaker on a subject of national importance will be presented by Outside Sentinel Clarence S. Hunt.

HALLOWE'EN DANCE.

Los Angeles Parlor No. 124 N.D.G.W. initiated two candidates September 7, when President Mattie Gara and her corps of officers exemplified the new ritual for the first time. Splendid talks were given by Lucy Malin, Annie L. Adair, Dolores Malin, Ann Schiebusch, Flora Holy, Gertrude Allen and Marvel Thomas. The opening party, September 14, in a bridge tourney drew a large crowd. Irene Eden, the chairman, was assisted by Charlotte Gehrke, Virginia

(Continued on Page 22)

Native Daughters of the Golden West

SAN ANDREAS—THE HISTORIC MOUNTAIN town of Murphys was the setting for a representative gathering of the members of Calaveras County Parlors—Ruby No. 46 (Murphys), Princess No. 84 (Angels Camp), San Andreas No. 113—to welcome Grand President Anna Mixon Armstrong on her official visit September 2. Presidents Evalyn Stephens of Ruby, the hostess Parlor, presided in a capable manner, and the ritual was commendably exemplified in sections by officers of the three Parlors.

In her address, Grand President Armstrong expressed appreciation for the hearty welcome accorded, making her first trip into the Mother Lode interesting and memorable. She complimented the officers on their sincere endeavors and accomplishments for the benefit of the Order, and brought an inspiring message for co-operation in the worthy projects sponsored by the organization. Deputy Lemue responded briefly on behalf of the Calaveras County Parlors, and Mrs. L. A. Mills of Stockton delighted with three recitations. A banquet, prepared by Mrs. Belle Segale of Ruby was served at tables in "U" formation. Decorations were boquets of flowers from the Mercer garden, surrounded by candles in colors of the Order.

Sons Guests at Admission Day Program.

Salinas—Aleli No. 102 celebrated Admission Day with an appropriate program September 8. Members of Santa Lucia No. 97 (Salinas) and Gabilan No. 132 (Castroville) N.S.G.W., and friends and relatives of the members of Aleli made up the audience. The program follows: Solo, "I Love You, California," Mrs. Sam Black, assisted by her daughter, Bertha, as "California;" talk, "Admission Day," Mrs. J. T. Riley; modeling early-day California costumes, Miss Doris Tavernetti; Mrs. Addie Fowler, aged 87, talked of her life as a girl in the mining towns of California; solo, "California Lullaby," Miss Etta Juhler; Mrs. Nathan Clark sketched recollections of her arrival in California in 1850; Senator C. C. Baker sang "Asleep in the Deep;" the Native Daughter glee club sang "When Honey Sings an Old-time Song;" Mrs. Frances Leidig, accompanied by Mrs. Alice Lingley, sang a group of Spanish songs; Mrs. Mabel Baker told of early Salinas, when twelve houses constituted the town; the glee club sang "Out Where the West Begins;" chorus, "America," assembly.

The entertainment committee was composed of Miss Rose Rhyner, Mrs. W. J. Larkin, Mrs. William Hatton. Refreshments were served at prettily decorated tables by a committee headed by Mrs. R. Paulsen. Dancing concluded the evening's entertainment.

Children Present Play.

Byron—Admission Day was commemorated by Donner No. 193 with a special program September 7. A children's play, "California, Bit by Bit," was given, in which the following, all children of members of the Parlor, took part: Oliver Richardson, Charlotte and Georgia Peterson, Thelma and Barbara Reynolds, Virginia, Donald and Henry Boltzen, Harold Houston. During the play Trustee Clara Houston sang several songs, accompanied by Organist Mae Lewis. Stories of interesting occurrences in early California history were related: Past President Josephine Pimentel told of the early legends of Mount Diablo; Marshal Ruby Lawrence, the duel between Broderick and Terry; First Vice-president Virginia Boltzen, the history of James Lick; Trustee Edna Hill, the discovery and naming of Yosemite Valley. A piano solo was rendered by Miss Josephine Pimentel. Ice cream, made by Third Vice-president Evelyn Christenson, was served at the conclusion of the program.

President Entertains at Home.

Modesto—Grand President Anna Mixon Armstrong officially visited Morada No. 199 September 14. One hundred members of the Order were in attendance, including Past Grand Dr. Louise C. Heilbron, Supervising Deputies Mae Givens and Katherine Kopf, Deputies Alice Dorroh, Hazel Laverty and Ethel Mathiasen, and delegations from Woodland, Sacramento, Oakdale, Merced, Manteca, Turlock and Sonora. Spanish decorations were featured in the meetingroom. Three candidates were initiated.

Mrs. Armstrong delivered an inspiring address and paid high tribute to the floor work of the Parlor officials. Past Grand Heilbron announced a plaque would be placed at the Home October 9. Refreshments followed the meeting, the tables being adorned with autumn leaves and horns-of-plenty filled with fruit. Members of Morada were guests of President Violet Vierra at her home September 23; Lillian Stammerjohan was joint hostess. All members having birthdays in July, August and September were special guests of the Parlor September 28.

Plans are under way for the first of a series of whist parties to be given jointly by No. 199 and Modesto No. 11 N.S.G.W. October 19. Several members of Morada plan to attend the Sunday breakfast at the Home, San Francisco, October 9.

Dinner Marks Close of Recess.

Hollister—Copa de Oro No. 105 marked the close of the usual summer recess with a potluck dinner September 8. The tables were prettily decorated with baskets of seasonal fruits, golden-hued blossoms, autumn foliage, and Bear Flags commemorative of Admission Day. Myrtle Palmtag sang "I Love You, California," and led in community singing. Dee Briggs gave a short talk on "Historic Landmarks of San Benito County," and Past Grand Bertha A. Briggs outlined events immediately preceding California's admission into the Union.

At the close of the dinner, Deputy Edna Butterfield installed officers. Gifts and flowers were presented to the retiring president, Elma Chandler, the newly-installed president, Rose Guilhamet, and Deputy Butterfield. Interesting talks were given by Catherine Hooton, Dee Briggs, Mrs. Butterfield and Past Grand Briggs. President Alma Nyland of San Juan Bautista No. 179 built a pyramid of yellow blooms with a tribute to each installed officer. Plans were formulated for the annual district meeting and the usual benefit for the homeless kiddies. Both dinner and meeting were decided social successes.

"California Becomes a State."

Oroville—The September 7 meeting of Gold of Ophir No. 190 was in a floral-bower setting arranged by Mms. J. H. Bowers, Anna Bernhard and Alta B. Baldwin. In recognition of Admission Day a program, including a pageant, "California Becomes a State," was presented. Those participating were Grand Trustee Florence Boyle, Evelyn Joslyn, Pauline Ware, Alta Baldwin, Edith Reece Westwood, Alma Crum, Rachel Martin, Elza Wirth, Georgia Karageris, Betty Gould, Alice Frazier, Helen Fletcher, Cyril Macdonald, George Tegrunde, June Scott, Will Hibbard, Corinne Gregory, Betty Boyle, Hazel Scott, Jake Bump, Gordon Nisbet, Frank Boyle, Romilda Ralph, Eleanor Ross, Mae Mitchell. Refreshments, in charge of Anna Bernhard, Mary Woodall, Emma Danforth, Florence Boyle and Margaret Gilbert, were served at tables carrying out a color scheme of red, white and blue.

Open house was maintained at Relics Hall the afternoon of Admission Day, September 9, and scores of local and out-of-town people visited and enjoyed inspecting the numerous relics. Committees from Gold of Ophir and Argonaut No. 8 N.S.G.W. extended a welcome to all and served light refreshments. Since the building was formally opened May 12, more than nine hundred people have visited the hall.

Past Presidents Showered.

San Bernardino—Members of Lugonia No. 241 were entertained with a supper and card party at the Crestline mountain home of Lucy Meecham August 31. September 4 the Parlor assisted Mrs. Laura Clark, charter member, and her husband in celebrating their sixtieth wedding anniversary. An informal reception was held and refreshments were served.

September 14 a miscellaneous shower was given Past President Lily Tompkins-McKray, a recent bride, and a baby shower was given Past President Frances Wixom-Wynkoop of Los Angeles. One candidate was initiated. Special guests were Deputy Marion Crumm and Mrs. Walter Hiskey of Santa Ana. Plans for a miniature carnival for October were discussed; Miss Clara Barton is the chairman.

History Reviewed.

Sonoma—Sonoma No. 209 welcomed Grand President Anna Armstrong August 22. A dinner, attended by sixty-two guests, including many grand officers, was served. With Josephine Andrieux presiding, four candidates were initiated, and much praise was bestowed on the officers for the splendid manner in which they exemplified the ritual. Mrs. Armstrong discoursed on the history of Sonoma and California, and held the assemblage at close attention.

Refreshments concluded the meeting. Adorning the center of the table was a large birthday cake with seventeen lighted candles, signifying the seventeenth institution anniversary of the Parlor. Huge boquets of beautiful flowers resembled an old-fashioned garden. The committee in charge included Gertrude Groskopf, Dorothy Bosch, Carola Picetti and Wanda Kearney.

Admission Day Program.

Ferndale—In observance of Admission Day, the following program was presented at the September 9 meeting of Oneonta No. 71: Reading, "Discovery of Gold in California," Verna Peers; piano solo, "Country Gardens," Lillie Petersen; vocal solo, "Going Back to California," Bernice Mills, accompanied by Emma Becker; reading, "Mother's Wedding," Annie Blanks; reading, "General Vallejo and the Bear Flag," Hattie Roberts; vocal solo, "My California Home," Grace LeMar, accompanied by Miss Becker; reading, "California, Golden Empire," Myra Rumrill; piano solo, "Meditation," Emma Becker; address, "The Flag," Lena Kausen.

Scholarship Winner Surprised.

Saint Helena—Miss Phyllis Thompson of La Junta No. 243 was awarded the N.D.G.W. scholarship at Mills College, and to assist in furnishing her room there the Parlor tendered her a surprise shower. After delightful refreshments Mrs. John A. Mitchell presented her with a box containing many useful articles. The appropriate table decorations included a miniature college, and a birthday cake in recognition of No. 203's nineteenth institution anniversary.

Miss Edna Thompson and her niece, Miss Phyllis Thompson, were honor-guests at a surprise party at the former's home in celebration of their birthday anniversaries. Dutch whist was played, tempting refreshments were served and the Misses Thompson were presented with many gifts. Those who enjoyed the delightful evening were: Mms. Lowell Palmer, N. Thorsen, L. Critser, A. B. Johnson, D. Thorson, W. Arighi; Misses Minnie Caughey, Elise Metzner, Louise and Martha Klubeschidt, Marion Senter, Gretchen and Juanita Groff, June Samuels, Mary Jane Twichell, Nancy Harrington, Carol Woodworth, Ruth Thompson.

Versatility Proven.

Richmond—California day was fittingly celebrated at the September 6 meeting of the Richmond Lions. Dr. C. R. Blake presided. Past Grand Estelle M. Evans, as speaker and soloist, proved her versatility by delivering a most interesting talk on the history of California and the rendition of two vocal solos. President Maud Arnold of Richmond No. 147 was also a guest of the occasion.

Grand President's Official Itinerary.

Woodland—During the month of October, Grand President Anna Mixon-Armstrong will officially visit the following Subordinate Parlors on the dates noted:

3rd—Berryessa No. 192, Willows.
4th—La Rosa No. 191, Roseville.
5th—Gold of Ophir No. 190, Oroville.
6th—Camellia No. 41, Anderson; Lassen View No. 98, Shasta; Hiawatha No. 140, Redding; Berendos No. 23, Red Bluff; jointly at Red Bluff.
7th—Eltapome No. 55, Weaverville.
10th—Eschol No. 16, Napa.
11th—Bret Harte No. 232, San Francisco.
12th—Carquinez No. 234, Crockett.
13th—Bonita No. 10, Redwood City.
17th—Las Juntas No. 221, Martinez.
18th—La Junta No. 203, Saint Helena.
19th—Castro No. 178, San Francisco.
21st—El Pescadero No. 82, Tracy.
24th—Calistoga No. 145, Calistoga.
26th—Linda Rosa No. 170, San Francisco.
27th—Bahia Vista No. 167, Oakland.
28th—Mission No. 227, San Francisco.

Evolution American Dance.

Alturas—The annual dinner of Alturas No. 159 in honor of Modoc County Pioneers September 9 was a most enjoyable social event, and more than eighty guests were entertained. Grand Vice-president Irma Laird delivered an eloquent welcome address, and other speakers were Pioneer J. E. Niles, Past Grand Catherine E. Gloster and President Erma Elliott. Miss Elizabeth Gloster rendered a group of memory songs. An original drama, "The Evolution of the American Dance," was presented.

Miss Dorothy Gloster was the reader, and Mrs. Eva Williams and Miss Catherine Gloster were aristocratic colonial dames of old Virginia. Through the agencies of a love apple, a rabbit foot and a magic potion their little black slave girl cast a spell over them, after which they viewed the dances of the past and the present. Groups of members and friends interpreted the various dances, beginning with the minuet and concluding with most exaggerated versions of dances of today. Mrs. Irene Cummings, violinist, and Mrs. Irma Laird, pianist, provided the musical background for the skit.

Grand President Anna Mixon Armstrong officially visited the Parlor September 21, and in the afternoon dedicated to the memory of the Modoc County Pioneers at Chimney Rock, near Alturas, a bronze marker donated by Mrs. Sadie Winn Brainard (Califia No. 22). That the pupils might attend the ceremonies, the public schools were closed.

Drill Team Makes Hit.

Petaluma—There was a large attendance at the September 6 meeting of Petaluma No. 222, President Pearl Lopus presiding. Following the transaction of much business a public card party was held under the auspices of the drill team, Captain Annie Dickson presiding. As usual, the team made a big hit in the San Francisco Admission Day parade.

A sociable for members and friends was featured September 20. Elsie DeLoca and Elmira DeCarli had charge of the entertainment.

State Flag Given School.

Woodland—Officers of Woodland No. 90 were installed by Deputy Maude Heaton, Mrs. Florice White becoming president. Among the many in attendance were Grand President Anna M. Armstrong and Past Grand Dr. Louise C. Heilbron. Addresses were delivered and refreshments were served. October 1, as a benefit for the Home, the Parlor will have its annual dance and card party at the Yolo Fliers Club. The arrangements committee includes Ruth Hickey (chairman), Nellie Hebner, Henrietta Toothaker, Hilda Richie, Leona Sachs and Ramona Roth.

September 6, on behalf of No. 90, Grand President Armstrong presented the Monument school with a California State (Bear) Flag. Edna

(Continued on Page 17)

Official Directory of Parlors of

GRAND OFFICERS.

Mrs. Evelyn I. Carlson......Past Grand President
1965 San Jose Ave., San Francisco
Mrs. Anna M. Armstrong......Grand President
Woodland
Mrs. Irma Laird......Grand Vice-president
Alturas
Mrs. Sallie R. Thaler......Grand Secretary
555 Baker St., San Francisco
Mrs. Susie K. Christ......Grand Treasurer
555 Baker St., San Francisco
Mrs. Gladys Noce......Grand Marshal
Sutter Creek
Mrs. Orinda G. Giannini......Grand Inside Sentinel
2142 Filbert St., San Francisco
Mrs. Hazel B. Hansen......Grand Outside Sentinel
501 Griswold St., Glendale
Mrs. Clara Gairaud......Grand Organist
134 Locust St., San Jose

GRAND TRUSTEES.

Mrs. Florence Boyle......Oroville
Mrs. Edna Briggs......1045 Santa Ynez Way, Sacramento
Mrs. Anna Thuesen......615 38th Ave., San Francisco
Mrs. Ethel Begley......233 Prospect Ave., San Francisco
Mrs. Minna K. Horn......Etna
Mrs. Jane Vick......418 Bath St., Santa Barbara
Mrs. Willow Borba......380 So. Main St., Sebastopol

ALAMEDA COUNTY.

Angelita No. 32, Livermore—Meets 2nd and 4th Fridays, Foresters Hall; Mrs. Myrtle I. Johnson, Rec. Sec., P.O. box 253.

Piedmont No. 87, Oakland—Meets Thursdays, Corinthian Hall, Pacific Bldg.; Mrs. Alice E. Miner, Rec. Sec., 421 58th St.

Aloha No. 106, Oakland—Meets Tuesdays, Wigwam Hall, Pacific Bldg.; Mrs. Lurine Martin, Rec. Sec., 2815 Wallace St., Berkeley.

Hayward No. 122, Hayward—Meets 1st and 3rd Tuesdays, Veterans Memorial Bldg., Main St.; Miss Ruth Gansberger, Rec. Sec., P. O. box 44, Mount Eden.

Berkeley No. 150, Berkeley—Meets 2nd and 4th Wednesdays, Masonic Hall; Mrs. Lelia B. Baker, Rec. Sec., 915 Contra Costa Ave.

Bear Flag No. 151, Berkeley—Meets 2nd and 4th Wednesdays, Veterans Memorial Bldg., 1931 Center St.; Mrs. Maud Wagner, Rec. Sec., 317 Alcatraz Ave., Oakland.

Encinal No. 156, Alameda—Meets 2nd and 4th Wednesdays, Veterans Memorial Bldg., Central Ave. and Walnut St.; Mrs. Laura E. Fisher, Rec. Sec., 1413 Caroline St.

Brooklyn No. 157, East Oakland—Meets 2nd and 4th Wednesdays, Masonic Temple, 8th Ave. and E. 14th St.; Mrs. Ruth Cooney, Rec. Sec., 3907 14th Ave.

Argonaut No. 166, Oakland—Meets Tuesdays, Klinkner Hall, 59th and San Pablo; Mrs. Ada Spilman, Rec. Sec., 2905 Ellis St., Berkeley.

Bahia Vista No. 167, Oakland—Meets Thursdays, Wigwam Hall, Pacific Bldg.; Mrs. Minnie E. Raper, Rec. Sec., 3449 Helen St.

Fruitvale No. 177, Oakland—Meets Fridays, W.O.W. Hall; May E. Barthold, Rec. Sec., 3832 Santa Rita St.

Laura Loma No. 182, Niles—Meets 1st and 3rd Tuesdays, I.O.O.F. Hall; Mrs. Ethel Fournier, Rec. Sec., P. O. box 515.

El Cereso No. 207, San Leandro—Meets 2nd and 4th Tuesdays, Masonic Hall; Mrs. Mary Tuttle, Rec. Sec., P. O. box 56.

Pleasanton No. 237, Pleasanton—Meets 1st Tuesday, I.O.O.F. Hall; Mrs. Myrtle Lanini, Rec. Sec.

Betsy Ross No. 238, Centerville—Meets 1st and 3rd Fridays, Anderson Hall; Miss Constance Lucio, Rec. Sec., P. O. box 187.

AMADOR COUNTY.

Ursula No. 1, Jackson—Meets 2nd and 4th Tuesdays, N.S.G.W. Hall; Mrs. Emma Boarman-Wright, Rec. Sec., 114 Court St.

Chispa No. 40, Ione—Meets 2nd and 4th Fridays, N.S.G.W. Hall; Mrs. Isabel Ashton, Rec. Sec.

Amapola No. 80, Sutter Creek—Meets 2nd and 4th Thursdays, N.S.G.W. Bldg.; Mrs. Hazel M. Marre, Rec. Sec.

Forrest No. 86, Plymouth—Meets 2nd and 4th Tuesdays, I.O.O.F. Hall; Mrs. Marguerite Davis, Rec. Sec.

BUTTE COUNTY.

Annie K. Bidwell No. 168, Chico—Meets 2nd and 4th Thursdays, I.O.O.F. Hall; Mrs Irene Henry, Rec. Sec., 3015 Woodland Ave.

Gold of Ophir No. 190, Oroville—Meets 1st and 3rd Wednesdays, Memorial Hall; Mrs. Ruth Brown, Rec. Sec., 1265 Leah Court.

CALAVERAS COUNTY.

Ruby No. 46, Murphys—Meets 4th Friday, N.S.G.W. Hall; Belle Segale, Rec. Sec.

Princess No. 84, Angels Camp—Meets 2nd and 4th Wednesdays, I.O.O.F. Hall; Mrs. Grace M. Mills, Rec. Sec., P.O. box 313.

San Andreas No. 113, San Andreas—Meets 1st Friday, Fraternal Hall; Miss Doris Treat, Rec. Sec.

COLUSA COUNTY.

Colus No. 194, Colusa—Meets 1st and 3rd Mondays, Eagles Hall; Miss Kate Busch, Rec. Sec., 350 Market St.

CONTRA COSTA COUNTY.

Stirling No. 146, Pittsburg—Meets 1st and 3rd Wednesdays, Veteran Memorial Hall; Mrs. Leslie Clement, Rec. Sec., 468 E. Santa Fe.

Richmond No. 147, Richmond—Meets 1st and 3rd Tuesdays, I.O.O.F. Hall, 10th St.; Grace Curry, Rec. Sec., 1134 Ohio St.

Donner No. 193, Byron—Meets 1st and 3rd Wednesdays, I.O.O.F. Hall; Mrs. Anna Pendry, Rec. Sec., P. O. box 112.

Las Juntas No. 221, Martinez—Meets 1st and 3rd Mondays, Pythian Castle; Mrs. Lois O. Viera, Rec. Sec., 305 Arreba St.

Antioch No. 223, Antioch—Meets 2nd and 4th Tuesdays, I.O.O.F. Hall; Mrs. Estelle Evans, Rec. Sec., 202 E. 5th St., Pittsburg.

Carquinez No. 234, Crockett—Meets 2nd and 4th Wednesdays, I.O.O.F. Hall; Mrs. Cecile Peters, Rec. Sec., 465 Edwards St.

EL DORADO COUNTY.

Marguerite No. 12, Placerville—Meets 1st and 3rd Wednesdays, Masonic Hall; Mrs. Nettie Leonardi, Rec. Sec., 25 Coloma St.

El Dorado No. 186, Georgetown—Meets 2nd and 4th Saturday afternoons, I.O.O.F. Hall; Mrs. Alta L. Douglas, Rec. Sec.

FRESNO COUNTY.

Fresno No. 187, Fresno—Meets 2nd and 4th Fridays, Pythian Castle, Cor. "R" and Merced Sts.; Mary Aubery, Rec. Sec., 1040 Delphia Ave.

GLENN COUNTY.

Berryessa No. 192, Willows—Meets 1st and 3rd Mondays, I.O.O.F. Hall; Mrs. Leonora Neate, Rec. Sec., 338 No. Lassen St.

HUMBOLDT COUNTY.

Occident No. 28, Eureka—Meets 1st and 3rd Wednesdays, N.S.G.W Hall; Mrs. Eva L. MacDonald, Rec. Sec., 2309 "B" St.

Oneonta No. 71, Ferndale—Meets 2nd and 4th Fridays, I.O.O.F. Hall; Mrs. Myra Rumrill, Rec. Sec., P.O. box 142.

Reichling No. 97, Fortuna—Meets 1st and 3rd Tuesdays, Friendship Hall; Mrs. Grace Swett, Rec. Sec., P. O. box 328.

KERN COUNTY.

Miocene No. 228, Taft—Meets 1st and 3rd Wednesday afternoons, I.O.O.F. Hall; Mrs. Evalyn G. Towne, Rec. Sec., P. O. box 1011.

El Tejon No. 239, Bakersfield—Meets 1st and 3rd Fridays, Eagles Hall, 1714 "G" St.; Mary B. Hampson, Rec. Sec., 908 Quincy St.

Desert Gold No. 250, Mojave—Meets 2nd and 4th Fridays, I.O.O.F. Hall; Rein H. Everett, Rec. Sec., P.O. box 83.

LAKE COUNTY.

Clear Lake No. 135, Middletown—Meets 2nd and 4th Tuesdays, Herrick Hall; Mrs. Alma E. Snow, Rec. Sec.

LASSEN COUNTY.

Nataqua No. 152, Standish—Meets 1st and 3rd Wednesdays, Foresters Hall; Mrs. Mayda Elledge, Rec. Sec.

Mount Lassen No. 215, Bieber—Meets 2nd and 4th Thursdays, I.O.O.F. Hall; Mrs. Angie C. Kenyon, Rec. Sec.

Susanville No. 243, Susanville—Meets 3rd Thursday, I.O.O.F. Hall; Mildred Hardy, Rec. Sec., P.O. box 425.

LOS ANGELES COUNTY.

Los Angeles No. 124, Los Angeles—Meets 1st and 3rd Wednesdays, I.O.O.F. Hall, Washington and Oak Sts.; Mrs. Mary K. Corcoran, Rec. Sec., 322 No. Van Ness Ave.

Long Beach No. 154, Long Beach—Meets 1st and 3rd Thursdays, K.P. Hall, 341 Pacific Ave.; Mrs. Bertha Hitt, Rec. Sec., 5355 Lime Ave.

Rudecinda No. 230, San Pedro—Meets 1st and 3rd Fridays, Unity Hall, I.O.O.F. Temple, 10th and Gaffey; Letitia Sarciaux, Rec. Sec., 483 16th St.

Verdugo No. 240, Glendale—Meets 2nd and 4th Tuesdays, Masonic Temple, 234 So. Brand Blvd.; Miss Etta Fulkerth, Rec. Sec., 526 No. Orange St.

Santa Monica Bay No. 245, Ocean Park—Meets 1st and 3rd Mondays, New Eagles Hall, 2823½ Main St.; Mrs. Rosalie Hyde, Rec. Sec., 738 Flower St., Venice.

Californiana No. 247, Los Angeles—Meets 2nd and 4th Tuesday afternoons, Hollywood Studio Club, 1215 Lodi Place; Mrs. Inez Sitton, Rec. Sec., 4223 Berenice St.

MADERA COUNTY.

Madera No. 244, Madera—Meets 2nd and 4th Thursdays, Masonic Annex; Mrs. Margaret C. Boyle, Rec. Sec., 111 No. "B" St.

MARIN COUNTY.

Sea Point No. 196, Sausalito—Meets 2nd and 4th Mondays, Perry Hall, 50 Caledonia St.; Mrs. Mary B. Smith, Rec. Sec., 559 Woodward Ave.

Marinita No. 198, San Rafael—Meets 2nd and 4th Mondays, 316 "B" St.; Miss Mollye Y. Spaelti, Rec. Sec., 539 4th St.

Fairfax No. 225, Fairfax—Meets 2nd and 4th Tuesdays, Community Hall; Mrs. Olive A. Greene, Rec. Sec., P. O. box 277.

Tamelpa No. 231, Mill Valley—Meets 1st and 2nd Tuesdays, I.O.O.F. Hall; Mrs. Delphine M. Todt, Rec. Sec., 400 Grand Ave., San Rafael.

MARIPOSA COUNTY.

Mariposa No. 63, Mariposa—Meets 1st and 3rd Fridays, I.O.O.F. Hall; Elizabeth E. Johnson, Rec. Sec.

MENDOCINO COUNTY.

Fort Bragg No. 210, Fort Bragg—Meets 1st and 3rd Thursdays, I.O.O.F. Hall; Mrs. Ruth W. Fuller, Rec. Sec.

MERCED COUNTY.

Veritas No. 75, Merced—Meets 1st and 3rd Tuesdays, I.O.O.F. Hall; Miss Margaret Thornton, Rec. Sec., 317 18th St.

MODOC COUNTY.

Alturas No. 159, Alturas—Meets 1st Thursday, Alturas Civic Club; Mrs. Irma W. Laird, Rec. Sec.

MONTEREY COUNTY.

Aleli No. 102, Salinas—Meets 2nd and 4th Thursdays, Pythian Hall; Miss Rose Rhyner, Rec. Sec., 420 Soledad St.

Junipero No. 141, Monterey—Meets 2nd and 4th Fridays, K. of P. Hall, Main St.; Miss Matilda M. Bergschicker, Rec. Sec., 498 Van Buren St.

NAPA COUNTY.

Eschol No. 16, Napa—Meets 2nd and 4th Mondays, N.S.G.W. Hall; Mrs. Ella Ingram, Rec. Sec., 2140 Seminary St.

Calistoga No. 145, Calistoga—Meets 2nd and 4th Mondays, I.O.O.F. Hall; Sadie P. Brooks, Rec. Sec.

La Junta No. 203, Saint Helena—Meets 1st and 3rd Tuesdays, N.S.G.W. Hall; Mrs. Marie Signorelli, Rec. Sec., 1341 Madrona Ave.

ATTENTION, SECRETARIES!

THIS DIRECTORY IS PUBLISHED BY AUTHORITY OF THE GRAND PARLOR N.D.G.W., AND ALL NOTICES OF CHANGES MUST BE RECEIVED BY THE GRAND SECRETARY (NOT THE MAGAZINE) ON OR BEFORE THE 20TH OF EACH MONTH TO INSURE CORRECTION IN NEXT PUBLICATION OF DIRECTORY.

ortola No. 172, San Francisco—Meets 1st and 3rd Tuesdays, N.S.G.W. Bldg.; Catherine H. Dolly, Rec. Sec., 4125 23rd St.
astro No. 178, San Francisco—Meets 1st and 3rd Wednesdays, K.C. Bldg., 150 Golden Gate Ave.; Miss Adeline Sandersfeld, Rec Sec., 50 Baker St.
win Peaks No. 185, San Francisco—Meets 2nd and 4th Fridays, Druids Temple, 44 Page St.; Mrs. Loretta Cameron, Rec. Sec., 3069 Army St.
ames Lick No. 220, San Francisco—Meets 1st and 3rd Wednesdays, N.S.G.W. Bldg.; Mrs. Edna Bishop, Rec. Sec., 3841 24th St.
ission No. 227, San Francisco—Meets 2nd and 4th Fridays, N.S.G.W. Bldg.; Mrs. Ann Dippel, Rec. Sec., 448 Dewey Blvd.
ret Harte No. 232, San Francisco—Meets 2nd and 4th Tuesdays, Aloha Hall, 3009 16th St.; Pearl Wedde, Rec. Sec., 225 7th Ave.
a Dorada No. 236, San Francisco—Meets 2nd and 4th Thursdays, N.S.G.W. Hall; Mrs. Theresa R. O'Brien, Rec. Sec., 567 Liberty St.
alboa No. 249, San Francisco—Meets 2nd and 4th Thursdays, Maccabees Hall, 5th Ave. and Clement St.; Jean Moffet, Rec. Sec., 6633 California St.
topia No. 252, San Francisco—Meets 2nd and 4th Tuesdays, American Hall, 20th and Capp Sts.; Miss Lelia M. Little, Rec. Sec., 4450 20th St.

SAN JOAQUIN COUNTY.

oaquin No. 5, Stockton—Meets 2nd and 4th Tuesdays, N.S.G.W. Hall, 314 E. Main St.; Mrs. Della Garvin, Rec. Sec., 1122 E. Market St.
l Pescadero No. 82, Tracy—Meets 1st and 3rd Fridays, I.O.O.F. Hall; Mrs. Mary A. Hewitson, Rec. Sec., 123 Walnut St.
ry No. 88, Lodi—Meets 1st and 3rd Wednesdays, Eagles Hall; Mrs. Mae Corson, Rec. Sec., 109 So. School St.
alis de Oro No. 206, Stockton—Meets 1st and 3rd Tuesdays, N.S.G.W. Hall, 314 E. Main St.; Mrs. Frances Germain, Rec. Sec., 450 No. Regent.
hoebe A. Hearst No. 214, Manteca—Meets 2nd and 4th Wednesdays, I.O.O.F. Hall; Mrs. Josie M. Frederick, Rec. Sec., Route A, Box 864, Ripon.

SAN LUIS OBISPO COUNTY.

an Miguel No. 94, San Miguel—Meets 2nd and 4th Wednesday afternoons, Clemon Hall; Mrs. Nellie Wickstrom, Rec. Sec.
an Luisita No. 108, San Luis Obispo—Meets 2nd and 4th Thursdays, W.O.W. Hall; Miss Agnes M. Lee, Rec. Sec., P. O. box 584.
l Pinal No. 163, Cambria—Meets 2nd, 4th and 5th Tuesdays, N.S.G.W. Hall; Kathryn Luchessa, Rec. Sec.

SAN MATEO COUNTY.

onita No. 10, Redwood City—Meets 2nd and 4th Thursdays, I.O.O.F. Hall; Mrs. Dora Wilson, Rec. Sec., 518 Middlefield Rd.
ista del Mar No. 155, Halfmoon Bay—Meets 2nd and 4th Thursdays, I.O.O.F. Hall; Elizabeth Olney, Rec. Sec.
no Nuevo No. 180, Pescadero—Meets 1st and 3rd Wednesdays, I.O.O.F. Hall; Mrs. Alice Mattei, Rec. Sec.
l Carmelo No. 181, Daly City—Meets 1st and 3rd Wednesdays, Masonic Hall; Mrs. Hattie Kelly, Rec. Sec., 1179 Brunswick St.
enlo No. 211, Menlo Park—Meets 2nd and 4th Mondays, Masonic Hall; Mrs. Frances E. Maloney, Rec. Sec., P. O. box 626.
an Bruno No. 246, San Bruno—Meets 2nd and 4th Fridays, Legion Hall; Miss Mildred Foley, Rec. Sec., 217 Miller Ave., South San Francisco.

SANTA BARBARA COUNTY.

eina del Mar No. 126, Santa Barbara—Meets 1st and 3rd Tuesdays, Pythian Castle, 222 W. Carillo St.; Mrs. Dorothy Yule, Rec. Sec., P.O. box 670.

SANTA CLARA COUNTY.

an Jose No. 81, San Jose—Meets Thursdays, Catholic Women Center, 5th and San Fernando Sts.; Mrs. Nellie Fleming, Rec. Sec., Catholic Women Center.
endome No. 100, San Jose—Meets Wednesdays, Old Scottish Rite Temple; Miss Marie Buck, Rec. Sec., 245 Hawthorne St.
l Monte No. 205, Mountain View—Meets 2nd and 4th Fridays, American Legion Hall; Miss Mary Ann Rokovich, Rec. Sec., P.O. box 422-B.
alo Alto No. 229, Palo Alto—Meets 1st and 2nd Mondays, N.S.G.W. Hall; Miss Helena G. Hansen, Rec. Sec., 531 Lytton Ave.

SANTA CRUZ COUNTY.

anta Cruz No. 26, Santa Cruz—Meets Mondays, N.S.G.W. Hall; Mrs. May L. Williamson, Rec. Sec., 170 Walnut Ave.
l Pajaro No. 35, Watsonville—Meets 1st and 3rd Tuesdays, I.O.O.F. Hall; Miss Ruth E. Wilson, Rec. Sec., 16 Laurel St.

SHASTA COUNTY.

amellia No. 41, Anderson—Meets 1st and 3rd Tuesdays, Masonic Hall; Mrs. Olga E. Welbourn, Rec. Sec.
assen View No. 98, Shasta—Meets 2nd Friday, Masonic Hall; Miss Louise Litsch, Rec. Sec.
iawatha No. 140, Redding—Meets 2nd and 4th Wednesdays, Moose Hall; Ruth Presleigh, Rec. Sec., Office County Clerk.

SIERRA COUNTY.

aomi No. 36, Downieville—Meets 2nd and 4th Wednesdays, I.O.O.F. Hall; Louise C. Dubuque, Rec. Sec.
mogen No. 134, Sierraville—Meets 2nd and 4th Saturday afternoons, Copren Hall; Mrs. Jennie Copren, Rec. Sec.

SISKIYOU COUNTY.

schscholtzia No. 112, Etna—Meets 1st and 3rd Wednesdays, Masonic Hall; Mrs. Bernice E. Smith, Rec. Sec.
ountain Dawn No. 120, Sawyers Bar—Meets 2nd and last Wednesdays, I.O.O.F. Hall; Miss Edith Dunphy, Rec. Sec.

SOLANO COUNTY.

allejo No. 195, Vallejo—Meets 1st and 3rd Wednesdays, K.C. Hall, 820 Marin St.; Mrs. Mary Combs, Rec. Sec., 511 York St.
Mary E. Bell No. 224, Dixon—Meets 2nd and 4th Thursdays, I.O.O.F. Hall; Grace McFadyen, Rec. Sec.

SONOMA COUNTY.

onoma No. 209, Sonoma—Meets 2nd and 4th Mondays, I.O.O.F. Hall; Mrs. Mae Norrbom, Rec. Sec., R.F.D., box 171.
anta Rosa No. 217, Santa Rosa—Meets 1st and 3rd Thursdays, N.S.G.W. Hall; Mrs. Hazel E. Brown, Rec. Sec., 1521 4th St.
Petaluma No. 222, Petaluma—Meets 1st and 3rd Tuesdays, Dania Hall; Mrs. Margaret M. Oeltjen, Rec. Sec., 503 Prospect St.

STANISLAUS COUNTY.

akdale No. 125, Oakdale—Meets 1st Monday, I.O.O.F. Hall; Mrs. Lou Reeder, Rec. Sec.
orada No. 199, Modesto—Meets 2nd and 4th Wednesdays, I.O.O.F. Hall; Mrs. Susan Sullivan, Rec. Sec., 823 10th St.
ldora No. 248, Turlock—Meets 1st and 3rd Wednesdays, Fraternal Hall; Effie Lund, Rec. Sec., 624 Minaret Ave.

SUTTER COUNTY.

South Butte No. 226, Sutter—Meets 1st and 3rd Mondays, N.D.G.W. Hall; Mrs. Abbie N. Vagedes, Rec. Sec.

TEHAMA COUNTY.

erendos No. 23, Red Bluff—Meets 1st and 3rd Tuesdays, W.O.W. Hall, 200 Pine St.; Mrs. Lillie Hagquet, Rec. Sec., 636 Jackson St.

NATIVE DAUGHTER NEWS

(Continued from Page 15)

Richter and Wanda Allok accompanied Mrs. Armstrong.

Pioneer Day Observed.

Sutter City—Officers of South Butte No. 226 were installed by Deputy Elsie Schofield, Mrs. Wilhelmina Beecroft becoming president. Numerous presentations were made, including an emblematic pin to Past President Anthalena McPherrin. Past Grand Esther R. Sullivan was among the visitors. The hall and banquetroom were artistically decorated, and delicious refreshments were served.

Admission Day, September 9, South Butte joined with Marysville No. 162, Colus No. 194 (Colusa) and Camp Far West No. 218 (Wheatland) in observing pioneer day in Cortez Square, Marysville. Mrs. Gertrude Cable presided, and refreshments were provided by Marysville No. 6 N.S.G.W.

Tri Counties Annual Meet.

Santa Cruz—The six Parlors of Monterey, Santa Cruz and San Benito Counties will hold their annual district meeting and overnite party October 1 and 2 at Happy Valley, near Santa Cruz. Saturday evening a Washington bicentennial dinner will be served. Short talks on six periods of Washington's life will be given by the presidents of the participating Parlors, and community singing will feature songs that Washington knew.

A pageant, "Pioneer California History," will follow the supper, each Parlor presenting a feature, as follows: "The Raising of the Bear Flag," Copa de Oro No. 105 (Hollister); "The Legend of the Sherman Rose," Junipero No. 141 (Monterey); "The Discovery of Gold," Santa Cruz No. 26; "The Donner Party," San Juan Bautista No. 179; "The Vigilantes," El Pajaro No. 35 (Watsonville); "Driving the Last Spike," Aleli No. 102 (Salinas). Sunday will be given over to a paper chase, nature talks, hiking, swimming, etc.

Pioneers Honored.

Chico—Honoring eighty Pioneers of this district, Annie K. Bidwell No. 168 gave a Washington bicentennial program September 9. On the stage were a large portrait of George Washington and United States of America and California State (Bear) Flags. An interesting program included musical selections and a paper on "The Mother of George Washington." At the festive board the guests were entertained with songs and guitar selections. President Laura Anderson headed the entertainment committee.

Quaint County Seat Visited.

Sierraville—September 17, sixteen members of Imogen No. 134 motored to the quaint Sierra County government-seat, Downieville, to hold a joint meeting with Naomi No. 36 in honor of Grand President Anna Mixon Armstrong. Naomi opened the meeting and exemplified the ritual, while Imogen exemplified the balloting. After a chicken supper the members retired to the lodgeroom and finished the work. Inspiring talks were given by the Grand President, Past Grand Emma Humphrey and Deputies McMahon and Merrill. It was a meeting that will long be remembered. Other visitors were Mrs. Miller of Woodland and Mrs. Sadie Brainard of Sacramento.

Past Presidents Doings.

Oroville—Association No. 5 met at the home of Mrs. H. A. Baldwin September 2. Flags and boquets of beautiful flowers were used in the decorations. Mms. Elice LaVoy, Verna Parker and Mae Belle Bills were appointed a committee to arrange for the annual banquet, to be held in November.

Petaluma—Association No. 7 met at the home of President Violet Mastrup September 13 and there was a large attendance. Following the transaction of much business there was an enjoyable social time, and refreshments were served at flower-bedecked tables. At the next meeting, October 11, several new members will be received.

TRINITY COUNTY.

Eltapome No. 55, Weaverville—Meets 2nd and 4th Thursdays, N.S.G.W. Hall; Mrs. Lou N. Fetzer, Rec. Sec.

TUOLUMNE COUNTY.

Dardanelle No. 66, Sonora—Meets Fridays, I.O.O.F. Hall; Mrs. Nettie Whitto, Rec. Sec.
Golden Era No. 99, Columbia—Meets 1st and 3rd Thursdays, N.S.G.W. Hall; Miss Irene Ponce, Rec. Sec.
Anona No. 164, Jamestown—Meets 2nd and 4th Tuesdays, I.O.O.F. Hall; Nellie Hope, Rec. Sec.

YOLO COUNTY.

Woodland No. 90, Woodland—Meets 2nd and 4th Tuesdays, N.S.G.W. Hall; Mrs. Maude Heaton, Rec. Sec., 153 College St.

YUBA COUNTY.

Marysville No. 162, Marysville—Meets 2nd and 4th Wednesdays, Liberty Hall; Miss Cecelia C. Gomes, Rec. Sec., 701 6th St.
Camp Far West No. 218, Wheatland—Meets 3rd Tuesday, I.O.O.F. Hall; Mrs. Ethel C. Brock, Rec. Sec., P. O. box 285.

AFFILIATED ORGANIZATIONS.

General Assembly Past Presidents—Meetings held annually in April at the home-town of Chief President; Mrs. Cora Stobing, 1739 San Jose Ave., San Francisco, Chief President; Mrs. Anna G. Loser, 72 Grove Lane, San Anselmo, Chief Secretary.
Past Presidents Association No. 1—Meets 1st and 3rd Mondays, N.S.G.W. Bldg., 414 Mason St., San Francisco; Mrs. Minnie F. Dobbin, Pres.; Mrs. May R. Barry, Rec. Sec., 2319 19th Ave., San Francisco.
Past Presidents Association No. 2—Meets 2nd and 4th Mondays, "Wigwam," Pacific Bldg., 16th and Jefferson, Oakland; Emma Haggerty, Pres.; Mrs. Elizabeth B. Goodman, Rec. Sec., 184 Juana Ave., San Leandro.
Past Presidents Association No. 3 (Santa Clara County)—Meets 2nd Tuesday, homes of members; Mrs. Amelia Hartman, Pres.; Mrs. Mary G. Newton, Rec. Sec., 1070 Jackson St., Santa Clara.
Past Presidents Association No. 4 (Sacramento County)—Meets 2nd Monday, Unitarian Hall, 1413 27th St., Sacramento City; Viola Gennoe, Pres.; Lily May Tilden, Rec. Sec., 3225 "T" St., Sacramento.
Past Presidents Association No. 5 (Butte County)—Meets 1st Friday, homes of members, Chico and Oroville; Marie Picanco, Pres.; Ruth Brown, Rec. Sec., 1265 Leah Court, Oroville.
Past Presidents Association No. 6 (Nevada County)—Meets 4th Friday, alternately between Nevada City, Pythian Castle, and Grass Valley, Edna Sampson's home; Margaret V. Nolan, Pres.; Vere Hansen, Rec. Sec., R.F.D. No. 2, box 41-C, Grass Valley.
Past Presidents Association No. 7 (Sonoma County)—Meets 1st Thursday, Violet Mastrup home, 622 5th St., Petaluma; Willow Borba, Pres.; Elizabeth Dillon, Rec. Sec., Petaluma.
Past Presidents Association No. 8 (San Joaquin and Stanislaus Counties)—Meets 2nd Thursday, Red Men' Hall, Stockton; Mrs. Lois Armstrong, Pres.; Mrs. Harriet F. Corr, Rec. Sec., 729 E. Sonora St., Stockton.
Native Sons and Native Daughters Central Committee on Homeless Children—Main Office, 955 Phelan Bldg., San Francisco; Mrs. John W. Stirling, Chmn.; Miss Mary E. Brusie, Sec. Los Angeles Branch office, 3924 Sunset Blvd.; Dorothy Schlingman, Sec.

(ADVERTISEMENT.)

N.D.G.W. OFFICIAL DEATH LIST.

Giving the name, the date of death, and the Subordinate Parlor affiliation of all deceased members as reported to Grand Secretary Sallie R. Thaler from August 18, 1932, to September 20, 1932:

Wackford, Nellie I.; August 8; Coloma No. 212.
Laskey, Theresa H.; August 5; Woodland No. 90.
McCann, Annie E.; August 8; Mary E. Bell No. 224.
Woods, Mary L.; August 8; Califia No. 22.
Mackintosh, Stella; August 17; Buena Vista No. 68.
Ryan, Ella B.; August 9; Califia No. 22.
Plum, Alice E.; August 31; Sutter No. 111.
Hoy, Jessie A.; August 16; Alturas No. 159.
Halcomb, Sadie May; July 7; Eltapome No. 55.
Boulon, Nonie; August 24; Alta No. 3.
Maynard, Mattie; September 11; Marguerite No. 12.

In Memoriam

NELLIE WACKFORD.

Whereas, The Angel of Death has again entered our Parlor and has called to the Great Beyond our dear friend and sister, Nellie Wackford,

Resolved, That by her death Coloma Parlor No. 212 N.D.G.W. has lost a loving and devoted sister, whose noble character and kind disposition endeared her to all; be it further resolved, that Coloma Parlor extend its sincere sympathy to the bereaved son and other members of the family, and that these resolutions be spread on the minutes of the Parlor, and a copy sent to the family of the deceased sister, and one to The Grizzly Bear Magazine for publication.

NETTIE HARRY,
GERTRUDE KEEHNER,
MAMIE DAVIS,
Committee.

Sacramento, September 6, 1932.

CAPTIVE

(Continued from Page 8)

lowed the meeting with her brother and her removal to Oregon. The Oatman girls remained hopeful during their captivity. "It was our custom," says Olive, "to go by ourselves and commit ourselves to God in faithful prayer every day, and this we would do after we had laid our weary frames to rest on our sand bed, if no other opportunity offered."

The Mojave Indians, among whom Olive Oatman spent five years as a captive, belong to that larger group of Indians known by the anthropological name Shoshoneans. They are generally called the Colorado River tribes. Luckily for Mary Ann and Olive Oatman, these Indians lacked many of the barbarous traits of other tribes. On the death of little Mary Ann, the regular procedure would have been to cremate the body. The chief's wife interceded, however, and secured permission for Olive to inter her sister's remains. The Mojaves were an agricultural people. They wore few clothes at any time, and none in summer. Unlike the other tribes of California, the Colorado River Indians were good warriors. They were darker skinned than most California Indians and represent a branch of Aztec civilization.

Redwood Convention—The twelfth annual convention of the Redwood Empire Association will be held October 14 and 15 at Eureka, Humboldt County.

Official Directory of Parlors of the N. S. G. W.

ALAMEDA COUNTY.

Alameda No. 47, Alameda City—Perry F. Badgley, Pres.; Robt. H. Cavanaugh, Sec., 1806 Pacific Ave.; Wednesdays, Native Sons Hall, 1406 Park St.

Oakland No. 50, Oakland—R. L. Engell, Pres.; F. M. Norris, Sec., 5595 Taft Ave.; Fridays, Native Sons Hall, 11th and Clay Sts.

Las Positas No. 96, Livermore—Dr. Donald M. Fraser, Pres.; John J. Kelly, Sec., P. O. box 341; Thursdays, Foresters Hall.

Eden No. 113, Hayward—Henry L'Ecuyer, Pres.; Stanton R. Soares, Sec., P. O. box 176; 2nd and 4th Tuesdays, Memorial Hall, Main St.

Piedmont No. 120, Oakland—Frank Smith, Pres.; Charles Morando, Sec., 906 Vermont St.; Thursdays, Native Sons Hall, 11th and Clay Sts.

Wisteria No. 127, Alvarado—Henry May, Pres.; J. M. Scribner, Sec., Livermore; 1st Thursday, I.O.O.F. Hall.

Halcyon No. 146, Alameda City—S. Chesley Anderson, Pres.; J. C. Bates, Sec., 2139 Buena Vista Ave.; 1st and 3rd Tuesdays, I.O.O.F. Hall, 2329 Santa Clara Ave.

Brooklyn No. 151, Oakland—Frank B. Perry, Pres.; E. W. Cooney, Sec., 3907 14th Ave.; Wednesdays, Masonic Temple, 8th Ave. and E. 14th St.

Washington, No. 169, Centerville—M. D. Silva, Pres.; Allen G. Norris, Sec., P. O. box 31; 2nd and 4th Tuesdays, Hansen Hall.

Athens No. 195, Oakland—Elmer L. Bullock, Pres.; Harold B. Farley, Sec., 4623 Benevides Ave.; Tuesdays, Native Sons Hall, 11th and Clay Sts.

Berkeley No. 210, Berkeley—F. M. McGrath, Pres.; R. J. Garrett, Sec., 1708 Virginia St.; Tuesdays, Native Sons Hall, 2108 Shattuck Ave.

Estudillo No. 223, San Leandro—Frank V. Pacheco, Pres.; Albert G. Pacheco, Sec., 1736 E. 14th St.; 1st and 3rd Tuesdays, U.P.E.C. Hall.

Claremont No. 240, Oakland—Louis F. Cambet, Pres.; E. N. Thienger, Sec., 839 Hearst Ave., Berkeley; Tuesdays, Veterans Memorial Bldg., 43rd & Salem Sts., Emeryville.

Pleasanton No. 244, Pleasanton—Peter C. Madsen, Pres.; Ernest W. Schween, Sec.; 2nd and 4th Thursdays, I.O.O.F. Hall.

Niles No. 250, Niles—M. L. Fournier, Pres.; C. E. Martenstein, Sec.; 2nd Thursday, I.O.O.F. Hall.

Fruitvale No. 252, Oakland—William J. Keating Jr., Pres.; Ray B. Felton, Sec., 1575 Alice St.; Fridays, W.O.W. Hall, 3256 E. 14th St.

AMADOR COUNTY.

Amador No. 17, Sutter Creek—Frank Marra, Pres.; F. J. Payne, Sec.; 1st and 3rd Fridays, Native Sons Hall.

Excelsior No. 31, Jackson—Wm. Daugherty, Pres.; William Going, Sec.; 1st and 3rd Wednesdays, Native Sons Hall, 22 Court St.

Ione No. 33, Ione—Marvin Kidd, Pres.; Josiah H. Saunders, Sec.; 1st and 3rd Wednesdays, Native Sons Hall.

Plymouth No. 48, Plymouth—John J. Upton, Pres.; Thos. D. Davis, Sec.; 1st and 3rd Saturdays, I.O.O.F. Hall.

BUTTE COUNTY.

Argonaut No. 8, Oroville—George N. Westwood, Pres.; Cyril R. Macdonald, Sec.; P. O. box 502; 1st and 3rd Wednesdays, Veterans Memorial Hall.

Chico No. 21, Chico—Marcus Choiaser, Pres.; Sam Lindsay Adams, Sec., Sacramento Blvd.; 2nd and 4th Thursdays, Elks Hall.

CALAVERAS COUNTY.

Chispa No. 139, Murphys—Maynard Segale, Pres.; Antone Malaspina, Sec.; Wednesdays, Native Sons Hall.

COLUSA COUNTY.

Colusa No. 69, Colusa City—Percy J. Cooke, Pres.; Phil J. Humburg, Sec., 223 Parkhill St.; Tuesdays, Eagles Hall.

CONTRA COSTA COUNTY.

General Winn No. 32, Antioch—Edmont T. Uren, Pres.; Joel H. Ford, Sec., P. O. box 311; 2nd and 4th Wednesdays, Union Hall.

Mount Diablo No. 101, Martinez—R. P. Anderson, Pres.; G. T. Barkley, Sec.; 1st and 3rd Mondays, I.O.O.F. Hall.

Byron No. 170, Byron—William E. Bunn, Pres.; H. G. Krumland, Sec.; 1st and 3rd Tuesdays, I.O.O.F. Hall.

Carquinez No. 205, Crockett—Thos. Cox, Pres.; Thomas I. Cahalan, Sec.; 1st and 3rd Wednesdays, I.O.O.F. Hall.

Richmond No. 217, Richmond—M. W. Amaral, Pres.; H. D. Mason, Sec., 11 6th St.; Wednesdays, Redmen Hall, 11th and Nevan Ave.

Concord No. 245, Concord—P. M. Soto, Pres.; D. E. Pramberg, Sec., P. O. box 235; 1st Tuesday, I.O.O.F. Hall.

Diamond No. 246, Pittsburg—Victor Ericsson, Pres.; Francis A. Irving, Sec., 248 E. 5th St.; 1st and 3rd Wednesdays, Veterans Memorial Bldg.

EL DORADO COUNTY.

Placerville No. 9, Placerville—Chas. C. Cook, Pres.; Clyde R. Berriman, Sec., Wood St.; 2nd and 4th Tuesdays, Masonic Hall.

Georgetown No. 91, Georgetown—W. H. Breedlove, Pres.; C. F. Irish, Sec.; 2nd and 4th Wednesdays, I.O.O.F. Hall.

FRESNO COUNTY.

Fresno No. 25, Fresno City—Oliver M. Akers, Pres.; W. C. Guard, Sec., 5060 Belmont; 1st and 3rd Fridays, Pythian Castle, Cor. "R" and Merced Sts.

Selma No. 107, Selma—Chester E. Shepard, Pres.; E. C. Laughlin, Sec.; 1st and 3rd Wednesdays, American Legion Hall.

GRAND OFFICERS.

Dr. Frank I. Gonzalez.............Junior Past Grand President
Flood Bldg., San Francisco

Seth Millington.............Grand President
Gridley

Justice Emmet Seawell.............Grand First Vice-president
State Bldg., San Francisco

Chas. A. Koenig.............Grand Second Vice-president
331 35th Ave., San Francisco

Harmon D. Skillin.............Grand Third Vice-president
Mills Bldg., San Francisco

John T. Regan.............Grand Secretary
N.S.G.W. Bldg., 414 Mason St., San Francisco

John A. Corotto.............Grand Treasurer
560 No. 5th St., San Jose

W. B. O'Brien.............Grand Marshal
2324 Santa Clara St., Alameda

Gam Hurst.............Grand Inside Sentinel
Financial Center Bldg., Oakland

William A. Reuter.............Grand Outside Sentinel
1009 Marine Ave., Wilmington

Leslie Maloche.............Grand Organist
467½ 3rd St., San Bernardino

Chester Gannon.............Historiographer
613 Capital Ntl. Bank Bldg., Sacramento

GRAND TRUSTEES.

Jesse H. Miller.............712 DeYoung Bldg., San Francisco
Eldred L. Meyer.............922 San Vicente Blvd., Santa Monica
John M. Burnett.............914 Bank Italy Bldg., San Jose
Henry S. Lyon.............Placerville
Joseph J. McShane.............419 Flood Bldg., San Francisco
Horace J. Leavitt.............Weaverville
Chas. H. Spengemann.............827 27th Ave., San Francisco

HUMBOLDT COUNTY.

Humboldt No. 14, Eureka—Henry Sundfors, Pres.; Loren M. Nelson, Sec., P.O. box 195; 2nd Monday, Native Sons Hall.

Arcata No. 20, Arcata—I. C. Fleckenstein, Pres.; William Peters, Sec., P. O. box 1117; Thursdays, Native Sons Hall.

Ferndale No. 93, Ferndale—Elwood Pries, Pres.; C. H. Rasmussen, Sec., R.F.D., 47-A; 1st and 3rd Mondays, K.P. Hall.

KERN COUNTY.

Bakersfield No. 42, Bakersfield—George Taylor, Pres.; Henry A. Bannister, Sec., care Bank of America; 2nd and 4th Fridays, Justice Court, City Hall.

LAKE COUNTY.

Lower Lake No. 159, Lower Lake—Harold S. Anderson, Pres.; Albert Kugelman, Sec.; Thursdays, I.O.O.F. Hall.

LASSEN COUNTY.

Honey Lake No. 198, Standish—James C. Meeske, Pres.; N. V. Wemple, Sec., Litchfield; 1st and 3rd Wednesdays, Wrede Hall.

Big Valley No. 211, Bieber—George Bunselmeier, Pres.; A. W. McKenzie, Sec.; 1st and 3rd Wednesdays, I.O.O.F. Hall.

LOS ANGELES COUNTY.

Los Angeles No. 45, Los Angeles City—Owen S. Adams, Pres.; Richard W. Fryer, Sec., 1629 Champlain Ter.; Thursdays, Merchant Plumbers Hall, 1832 So. Hope.

Ramona No. 109, Los Angeles City—James M. Watson, Pres.; John V. Scott, Sec., Patriotic Hall, 1816 So. Figueroa; Fridays, Patriotic Hall, 1816 So. Figueroa.

Hollywood No. 196, Los Angeles City—Kenneth A. Case, Pres.; E. J. Reilly, Sec., Olive View; Mondays, 1089 No. Oxford Ave.

Long Beach No. 239, Long Beach—Francis H. Gentry, Pres.; W. W. Brady, Sec., 801 Jergins Trust Bldg.; 2nd and 4th Thursdays, Moose Hall, Elm and Anaheim.

Sepulveda No. 263, San Pedro—Joseph Pia, Pres.; Harry Fairall, Sec., 1925 Pacific Ave.; 2nd and 4th Fridays, Redman Hall, 543 Shepherd St., Point Firmin.

Glendale No. 264, Glendale—Leslie F. Schellback, Pres.; Abel B. Molen, Sec., 508 So. Belmont St.; 1st and 3rd Tuesdays, Masonic Temple, 234 So. Brand Blvd.

Santa Monica Bay No. 267, Ocean Park—Orrin G. Welch, Pres.; John J. Smith, Sec., 830 Rialto Ave., Venice; 2nd and 4th Mondays, New Eagle Hall, 2823½ Main St.

Cahuenga No. 268, Reseda—Harold C. Trexler, Pres.; Carrol S. Driscoll, Sec., P.O. box 25, Chatsworth; first Friday, Alton Hall.

MADERA COUNTY.

Madera No. 130, Madera City—Cornelius Noble, Pres.; T. P. Cosgrave, Sec.; 1st and 3rd Thursdays, First National Bank Bldg.

MARIN COUNTY.

Mount Tamalpais No. 64, San Rafael—M. E. Peterson, Pres.; Manual A. Andrade, Sec., 532 Mission Ave.; 1st and 3rd Mondays, Portuguese American Hall.

Sea Point No. 158, Sausalito—A. H. Bettencourt, Pres.; Manuel Santos, Sec., 6 Glen Drive; 1st and 3rd Wednesdays, Perry Bldg.

Nicasio No. 183, Nicasio—M. T. Farley, Pres.; R. J. Rogers, Sec.; 2nd and 4th Wednesdays, U.A.O.D. Hall.

MENDOCINO COUNTY.

Ukiah No. 71, Ukiah—Henry Bucknell, Pres.; Ben Hofman, Sec., P. O. box 473; 1st and 3rd Mondays, I.O.O.F. Hall.

Broderick No. 117, Point Arena—A. L. McCallum, Pres.; C. J. Buchanan, Sec.; 1st and 3rd Thursdays, Forester Hall.

Alder Glen No. 200, Fort Bragg—H. M. Bohn, Pres.; C. R. Weller, Sec.; 2nd and 4th Fridays, I.O.O.F. Hall.

MERCED COUNTY.

Yosemite No. 24, Merced City—John J. Thronton, Pres.; True W. Fowler, Sec., P. O. box 781; 2nd and 4th Mondays, I.O.O.F. Hall.

Los Banos No. 206, Los Banos—Robert L. Puccinelli, Pres.; L. E. Sarbo, Sec., R.F.D., box 21; 2nd and 4th Wednesdays, Eagles Hall.

MONTEREY COUNTY.

Monterey No. 75, Monterey City—James Millington, Pres.; T. W. Krieger, Sec., 999 Franklin St.; 1st and 3rd Fridays, Knights Pythias Hall, Main St.

Santa Lucia No. 97, Salinas—Roy Martella, Pres.; R. W. Adcock, Sec., Route 2, box 180; Mondays, Native Sons Hall, 32 W. Alisal St.

Gabilan No. 132, Castroville—B. A. McCoy, Pres.; R. H. Martin, Sec., P. O. box 81; 1st and 3rd Thursdays, Native Sons Hall.

NAPA COUNTY.

Saint Helena No. 53, Saint Helena—Lucas Haus, Pres.; Edw. L. Bonhote, Sec., P. O. box 267; Mondays, Nati Sons Hall.

Napa No. 62, Napa City—R. O. Akers, Pres.; H. Hoernle, Sec., 1226 Oak St.; Mondays, Native Sons Ha

Calistoga No. 86, Calistoga—Edmund Molinari, Pres.; Lou Carlenzoli, Sec.; 1st and 3rd Mondays, I.O.O.F. Hall.

NEVADA COUNTY.

Hydraulic No. 56, Nevada City—Arthur W. Davis, Pres Dr. C. W. Chapman, Sec.; Tuesdays, Pythian Castle.

Quartz No. 58, Grass Valley—Robert Kohler, Pres.; H. R. George, Sec., 151 Conaway Ave.; Mondays, Auditoriu Hall.

Donner No. 162, Truckee—J. F. Lichtenberger, Pres.; C. Lichtenberger, Sec.; 2nd and 4th Tuesdays, Nati Sons Hall.

ORANGE COUNTY.

Santa Ana No. 265, Santa Ana—Amos Huntzinger, Pres E. F. Marks, Sec., 1124 No. Bristol St.; 1st and 3 Mondays, K.C. Hall, 4th and French Sts.

PLACER COUNTY.

Auburn No. 59, Auburn—Iris Garcia, Pres.; J. G. Wals Sec.; 1st and 3rd Fridays, Foresters Hall.

Silver Star No. 63, Lincoln—L. F. Browning, Pres.; Ba ney G. Barry, Sec., P. O. box 72; 3rd Wednesda I.O.O.F. Hall.

Rocklin No. 233, Roseville—Wm. La Due, Pres.; M. Reed, Sec., 253 W. Duranta; 2nd and 4th Wednesday Eagles Hall.

PLUMAS COUNTY.

Quincy No. 131, Quincy—J. D. McLaughlin, Pres.; E. Kelsey, Sec.; 2nd Thursday, I.O.O.F. Hall.

Golden Anchor No. 182, La Porte—R. J. McGrath, Pres LeRoy J. Post, Sec.; 2nd and 4th Sunday morning Native Sons Hall.

Plumas No. 228, Taylorsville—E. E. Sikes, Pres.; Geor E. Boyden, Sec.; 1st and 3rd Mondays, Native Sons Ha

SACRAMENTO COUNTY.

Sacramento No. 3, Sacramento City—J. G. Fitzhenr Pres.; J. F. Didion, Sec., 1213 "O" St.; Thursdays, N tive Sons Bldg., 11th and "J" Sts.

Sunset No. 26, Sacramento City—L. W. Marvin, Pres Edward E. Reese, Sec., County Treasurer Office; Mo days, Native Sons Bldg., 11th and "J" Sts.

Elk Grove No. 41, Elk Grove—Fred Schimeyer, Pres Walter Martin, Sec.; 2nd and 4th Fridays, Masonic Ha

Granite No. 83, Folsom—Joe Relvas, Pres.; Frank Showe Sec.; 2nd and 4th Tuesdays, K.P. Hall.

Courtland No. 106, Courtland—Thornton Pylman, Pres Jos. Green, Sec.; 1st Saturday and 3rd Monday, Nati Sons Hall.

Sutter Fort No. 241, Sacramento City—Ed. T. Goyn Pres.; C. L. Katzenstein, Sec., P. O. box 914; 2nd a 4th Wednesdays, Native Sons Bldg., 11th and "J" S

Galt No. 243, Galt—John Granadas, Pres.; F. W. Harm Sec.; 1st and 3rd Mondays, I.O.O.F. Hall.

SAN BENITO COUNTY.

Fremont No. 44, Hollister—S. Churchill, Pres.; J. Prendergast Jr., Sec., 1064 Monterey St.; 1st and 3 Thursdays, Grangers Union Hall.

SAN BERNARDINO COUNTY.

Arrowhead No. 110, San Bernardino City—F. L. McGarve Pres.; R. W. Brazelton, Sec., 462 6th St.; Wednesday Eagles Hall, 469 4th St.

SAN DIEGO COUNTY.

San Diego No. 108, San Diego City—Martin J. Spangl Pres.; A. V. Mayrhofer, Sec., 1572 2nd St.; Wednesday K.C. Hall, 4th and Elm Sts.

SAN FRANCISCO CITY AND COUNTY.

California No. 1, San Francisco—Joseph Lawlor, Pres.; Ell A. Blackman, Sec., 1248-A Divisadero St.; Thursday Native Sons Bldg., 414 Mason St.

Pacific No. 10, San Francisco—Walter Mohrdick, Pres.; Henry Bastein, Sec., 426 City Hall; Tuesdays, Nati Sons Bldg., 414 Mason St.

Golden Gate No. 29, San Francisco—Thomas I. Schlis Pres.; Adolph Eberhart, Sec., 183 Carl St.; Monday Native Sons Bldg., 414 Mason St.

Mission No. 38, San Francisco—George Leahy, Pres.; The J. Stewart, Sec., 1919 Howard St.; Wednesdays, Redm Hall, 3053 16th St.

San Francisco No. 49, San Francisco—Charles Miller, Pres David Capurro, Sec., 976 Union St.; Thursdays, Nati Sons Bldg., 414 Mason St.

El Dorado No. 52, San Francisco—Edward Victor, Pres Alfred Vlautin, Sec., 1537 Franklin St.; Thursdays, N tive Sons Bldg., 414 Mason St.

Rincon No. 72, San Francisco—Frank D. Sericano, Pres John A. Gilmour, Sec., 2069 Golden Gate Ave.; Wedne days, Native Sons Bldg., 414 Mason St.

Stanford No. 76, San Francisco—Dr. Vincent V. Hardema Pres.; Charles T. O'Kane, Sec., 1111 Pine St.; Tuesday Native Sons Bldg., 414 Mason St.

Bay City No. 104, San Francisco—Morris Garren, Pres Max E. Licht, Sec., 1881 Fulton St.; 2nd and 4 Wednesdays, Native Sons Bldg., 414 Mason St.

Niantic No. 105, San Francisco—A. Furner, Pres.; J. Darcy, Sec., 10 Hoffman Ave.; Wednesdays, Native So Bldg., 414 Mason St.

National No. 118, San Francisco—Wayne Burke, Pres Martin M. Ratigan, Sec., 1325 Page St., Apt. 6; Thur days, 1160 Eddy St.

Hesperian No. 137, San Francisco—C. McLaughlin, Pres Albert Carlson, Sec., 879 Justin Dr.; Thursdays, Nati Sons Bldg., 414 Mason St.

Alcalde No. 154, San Francisco—Charles Kurpinsky, Pres Harry S. Burke, Sec., 25 Ord St.; 2nd and 4th Wedne days, Native Sons Bldg., 414 Mason St.

South San Francisco No. 157, San Francisco—Otto A. E vander, Pres.; John T. Regan, Sec., 1489 Newcomb Ave Wednesdays, Masonic Bldg., 4705 3rd St.

Sequoia No. 160, San Francisco—Harry Grover, Pres Walter W. Garrett, Sec., 2500 Van Ness Ave.; Monday Swedish-American Bldg., 2174 Market St.

Precita No. 187, San Francisco—Lloyd J. Cosgrove, Pres Edward Tietjen, Sec., 1367 15th Ave.; Thursdays, Mi sion Masonic Hall, 2668 Mission St.

Olympus No. 189, San Francisco—Henry H. McGowa Pres.; Harvey J. Carty, Sec., 1651 Market St., Apt. 50 2nd and 4th Tuesdays, Independent Redmen Hall, 305 16th St.

Presidio No. 194, San Francisco—Lester Figone, Pres George A. Ducker, Sec., 442 21st Ave.; Mondays, Nativ Sons Bldg., 414 Mason St.

Marshall No. 202, San Francisco—Alexander Jean, Pres Frank Bacigalupi, Sec., 725 Douglas St.; 1st and 3 Wednesdays, Native Sons Bldg., 414 Mason St.

Dolores No. 208, San Francisco—James F. Vahey, Pres Eugene O'Donnell, Sec., Mills Bldg.; Tuesdays, Missio Masonic Bldg., 2668 Mission St.

Twin Peaks No. 214, San Francisco—Clifford Roberts, Pres Thos. Pendergast, Sec., 278 Douglas St.; Wednesday Willopi Hall, 4061 24th St

El Capitan No. 222, San Francisco—Frank Rizzo, Pres James Hanna, Sec., 2450 27th Ave.; 1st and 3rd Thur days, King Soloman Hall, 1739 Fillmore St.

ATTENTION, SECRETARIES!

THIS DIRECTORY IS PUBLISHED BY AUTHORITY OF THE GRAND PARLOR N.S.G.W., AND ALL NOTICES OF CHANGES MUST BE RECEIVED BY THE GRAND SECRETARY (NOT THE MAGAZINE) ON OR BEFORE THE 20TH OF EACH MONTH TO INSURE CORRECTION IN NEXT ISSUE OF DIRECTORY.

Guadalupe No. 231, San Francisco—Roy Tensfeldt, Pres.; Alvin A. Johnson, Sec., 142 Rousseau St.; Tuesdays, Guadalupe Hall, 4551 Mission St.
Castro No. 232, San Francisco—Ralph Willis, Pres.; James H. Hayes, Sec., 4014 18th St.; Tuesdays, Native Sons Bldg., 414 Mason St.
Balboa No. 234, San Francisco—George Schroth, Pres.; E. W. Boyd, Sec., 437 Cherry St.; Thursdays, Maccabee Hall, 5th Ave. and Clement St.
Bret Harte No. 260, San Francisco—Chas. E. Lillie, Pres.; A. W. McElhatton, Sec., 103 Holloway Ave.; Tuesdays, West of Twin Peaks Hall, 233 Legion Court.
Utopia No. 270, San Francisco—George Walters, Pres.; Herbert H. Schneider, Sec., 2455 16th Ave.; Tuesdays, American Hall, 20th and Capp Sts.

SAN JOAQUIN COUNTY.

Stockton No. 7, Stockton—John D. Gallagher, Pres.; R. D. Dorcey, Sec., P. O. box 388; Mondays, Native Sons Hall.
Lodi No. 18, Lodi—Jerome Solomon, Pres.; Dr. Clyde Brennan, Sec.; 2nd and 4th Wednesdays, Eagles Hall.
Tracy No. 186, Tracy—C. S. Selna, Pres.; R. J. Marraccini, Sec., R.F.D. No. 1, box 217; Thursdays, I.O.O.F. Hall.
Manteca No. 271, Manteca—Chas. N. Howell Jr., Pres.; Leonard Farin, Sec., R.F.D., box 75, Lathrop; 1st and 3rd Wednesdays, I.O.O.F. Hall.

SAN LUIS OBISPO COUNTY.

San Miguel No. 150, San Miguel—H. Twisselman, Pres.; Otto Kuehl, Sec., Paso Robles; 1st and 3rd Wednesdays, Fraternal Hall.
Cambria No. 152, Cambria—J. M. Soto, Pres.; A. S. Gay, Sec.; Wednesdays, Rigdon Hall.

SAN MATEO COUNTY.

Redwood No. 66, Redwood City—Frank Deluchi, Pres.; A. S. Liguori, Sec., P. O. box 212; Thursdays, American Foresters Hall.
Seaside No. 95, Half Moon Bay—Andrew F. Gilcrest, Pres.; John G. Gilcrest, Sec.; 2nd and 4th Tuesdays, I.O.O.F. Hall.
Menlo No. 185, Menlo Park—C. T. Maloney, Pres.; F. W. Johnson, Sec., P. O. box 601; Thursdays, Masonic Hall.
Pebble Beach No. 230, Pescadero—Harold Souza, Pres.; E. A. Shaw, Sec.; 2nd and 4th Wednesdays, I.O.O.F. Hall.
El Carmelo No. 256, Daly City—Theodore A. Clemens, Pres.; Ernest L. Micco, Sec., 639 Morse St., San Francisco; 2nd and 4th Wednesdays, Eagles Hall.
Industrial City No. 269, South San Francisco—John C. Hamilton, Pres.; Geo. A. Roll, Sec., P. O. box 237; 2nd and 4th Mondays, Metropolitan Hall.

SANTA BARBARA COUNTY.

Santa Barbara No. 116, Santa Barbara City—C. W. McCormick, Pres.; H. C. Sweetser, Sec., Court House; 1st and 3rd Wednesdays, I.O.O.F. Hall.

SANTA CLARA COUNTY.

San Jose No. 22, San Jose—Joseph Sabatte, Pres.; Joseph Lawrence, Sec., 1095 No. First St.; Mondays, I.O.O.F. Hall.
Santa Clara No. 100, Santa Clara City—C. A. Castro, Pres.; Clarence Clevenger, Sec., P. O. box 297; Wednesdays, Redmen Hall.
Observatory No. 177, San Jose—William L. Gerrans, Pres.; A. B. Langford, Sec., Hall Records; Tuesdays, Knights Columbus Hall, 40 No. First St.
Mountain View No. 215, Mountain View—Gilbert F. McCorkle, Pres.; C. A. Antonioli, Sec., 301 Castro St.; 2nd and 4th Wednesdays, Mockbee Hall.
Palo Alto No. 216, Palo Alto—John C. Bernal, Pres.; Albert A. Quinn, Sec., 643 High St.; Mondays, Native Sons Bldg., Hamilton Ave. and Emerson St.

SANTA CRUZ COUNTY.

Watsonville No. 65, Watsonville—Fred R. Baese, Pres.; E. R. Tindall, Sec., R.F.D. No. 5, Box 313; 2nd and 4th Tuesdays, I.O.O.F. Hall.
Santa Cruz No. 90, Santa Cruz City—Horace Burkett, Pres.; T. V. Mathews, Sec., 105 Pacheco Ave.; Fridays, Native Sons Hall, 117 Pacific Ave.

SHASTA COUNTY.

McCloud No. 149, Redding—A. E. Welbourn, Pres.; Hugh A. Shuffleton, Sec.; 1st and 3rd Thursdays, Moose Hall.

SIERRA COUNTY.

Downieville No. 92, Downieville—Frank H. Turner, Pres.; H. S. Tibbey, Sec.; 2nd and 4th Mondays, I.O.O.F. Hall.
Golden Nugget No. 94, Sierra City—Elmer Thompson, Pres.; Arthur R. Pride, Sec.; 1st and 3rd Wednesdays, Masonic Hall.

SISKIYOU COUNTY.

Etna No. 192, Etna—Frank B. Quigley, Pres.; Harvey A. Green, Sec.; 1st and 3rd Wednesdays, I.O.O.F. Hall.
Liberty No. 193, Sawyers Bar—Orrin R. Bigelow, Pres.; John M. Barry, Sec.; 1st and 3rd Saturdays, I.O.O.F. Hall.

SOLANO COUNTY.

Solano No. 39, Suisun—Karl Koch, Pres.; J. W. Kinlock, Sec.; 1st and 3rd Tuesdays, I.O.O.F. Hall.
Vallejo No. 77, Vallejo—Joseph Clavo, Pres.; Werner B. Hallin, Sec., 912 Carolina; 2nd and 4th Tuesdays, San Pablo Hall.

SONOMA COUNTY.

Petaluma No. 27, Petaluma—Fred G. Ilg, Pres.; C. F. Fobes, Sec., 114 Prospect St.; 2nd and 4th Mondays, Druid Hall, Gross Bldg., 41 Main St.
Santa Rosa No. 28, Santa Rosa—Wesley Beach, Pres.; Leland S. Lewis, Sec., Court House; Mondays, Native Sons Hall.
Glen Ellen No. 102, Glen Ellen—Tony Cereghino, Pres.; Frank Kirch, Sec., Route 3, Santa Rosa; 2nd Monday, N.S.G.W. Hall.
Sonoma No. 111, Sonoma City—Joseph Andrieux, Pres.; L. H. Green, Sec.; 1st and 3rd Mondays, I.O.O.F. Hall.
Sebastopol No. 143, Sebastopol—O. A. McChristian, Pres.; F. G. McFarlane, Sec.; 1st and 3rd Fridays, I.O.O.F. Hall.

STANISLAUS COUNTY.

Modesto No. 11, Modesto—Chas. D. Blaine, Pres.; C. C. Eastin Jr., Sec., P. O. box 898; 1st and 3rd Wednesdays, I.O.O.F. Hall.
Oakdale No. 142, Oakdale—D. W. Tulloch, Pres.; E. T. Gobin, Sec.; 2nd and 4th Mondays, Legion Hall.
Orestimba No. 247, Crows Landing—Lloyd W. Fink, Pres.; G. W. Fink, Sec.; 1st and 3rd Wednesdays, Community Club Home.

SUTTER COUNTY.

Sutter No. 261, Sutter City—Albert Thomasen, Pres.; Glen R. Haynes, Sec., R.F.D. No. 2, Yuba City; 2nd and 4th Mondays, N.D.G.W. Hall.

TRINITY COUNTY.

Mount Bally No. 87, Weaverville—R. L. Marshall, Pres.; E. V. Ryan, Sec.; 1st and 3rd Mondays, Native Sons Hall.

TUOLUMNE COUNTY.

Tuolumne No. 144, Sonora—Mathew J. Marshall, Pres.; William M. Harrington, Sec., P. O. box 715; 2nd and 4th Fridays, Knights Columbus Hall.
Columbia No. 258, Columbia—Jos. Cadematori, Pres.; Charles E. Grant, Sec.; 2nd and 4th Thursdays, Native Sons Hall.

VENTURA COUNTY.

Cabrillo No. 114, Ventura City—David Bennett, Pres., 1380 Church St.

YOLO COUNTY.

Woodland No. 30, Woodland—J. L. Aronson, Pres.; R. G. Lawson, Sec.; 1st Thursday, Native Sons Hall.

PATHS OF GLORY

(Continued from Page 11)

there and have Lewis Byington or Fletcher Cutler speak of the dead in a way that the new generation will not forget the greatness and the glories of the Pioneer Past?

Time has not dimmed that scene at the old American Theatre in San Francisco when the great Baker, on his way, as Senator, from Oregon to Washington, visited the city he loved and, to an overflowing audience,—when the war clouds of the Civil War hung dark and ominous, when the tomtoms of war were in the air, and when the roar of artillery, the crash of musketry and the shock and the recoil of armed bodies could already be heard by those who understood,—said:

"We are a city set on a hill. Our light cannot be hid. As for me, I dare not, I will not, be false to freedom! [Applause] Where in youth my feet were planted, there my manhood and my age shall march. I will walk beneath her banner. I will glory in her strength. I have seen her, in history, struck down on a hundred chosen fields of battle. I have seen her friends fly from her; I have seen them bind her to the stake; I have seen them give her ashes to the winds, regathering them that they might scatter them yet more widely. But when they turned to exult, I have seen her again meet them face to face, clad in complete steel, and brandishing in her strong right hand a flaming sword red with insufferable light! [vehement cheering] And I take courage. The Genius of America will at last lead her sons to freedom! [Great applause]"

NATIVE SON NEWS

(Continued from Page 10)

Chief Manuel Menotti led the local contingent. The drum corps of No. 158 made its initial public appearance on this occasion, under the leadership of Drummajor Clarence D. Rosa.

General Assembly P.P.A. To Meet.

Sacramento—The General Assembly of the Past Presidents Association will hold its annual session in Native Sons Building Saturday, October 15, at 2:30 p.m. Governor General Louis F. Erb of San Francisco Assembly No. 1 will preside, and in all likelihood will be succeeded by Lieutenant-governor General J. J. Longshore of General John A. Sutter Assembly No. 10 (Sacramento). Legislation will be proposed to strengthen the organization and to advance the interests of the parent Order.

Relief Bonds—San Francisco voters August 30 authorized a $6,500,000 bond issue for the relief of financially distressed citizens of that city.

"But if we hope for that we see not, then do we with patience wait for it."—Bible.

YUBA COUNTY.

Marysville No. 6, Marysville—Ray C. Burris, Pres.; Verne Fogarty, Sec., 719 6th St.; 2nd Friday, Foresters Hall.
Rainbow No. 40, Wheatland—F. M. Beilby, Pres.; W. A. Bowser, Sec., P. O. box 313; 2nd Thursday, I.O.O.F. Hall.

AFFILIATED ORGANIZATIONS.

San Francisco Extension of the Order Committee, N.S.G.W.—Joseph J. McShane, Chmn.; Harold J. Regan, Sec., 414 Mason St., San Francisco; meets 2nd and 4th Fridays, Grizzly Bear Club, 414 Mason St., San Francisco.
Alameda County Extension of the Order Committee, N.S.G.W.—Edward T. Schnarr, Chmn.; Frank Roemer, Sec., 3297 Morcom Ave., Oakland; meets 1st and 3rd Mondays, N.S.G.W. Hall, 11th and Clay Sts., Oakland.
Interparlor Committee (Southern District), N.S.G.W. and N.D.G.W.—Burrel D. Neighbours, Chmn.; F. J. Burmester, Sec., P. O. box 42, Colton; meets 2nd and 4th Fridays, Patriotic Hall, 1816 So. Figueroa St., Los Angeles.
San Francisco Assembly No. 1 Past Presidents Association N.S.G.W.—Meets 1st and 3rd Fridays, Native Sons Bldg., 414 Mason St., San Francisco; Jos. E. Tracy, Gov.; J. F. Stanley, Sec., 1175 O'Farrell St., San Francisco.
East Bay Counties Assembly No. 3 Past Presidents Association N.S.G.W.—Meets 4th Monday, Native Sons Hall, 11th and Clay Sts., Oakland; Felix Robison, Gov.; Edgar G. Hanson, Sec., 1260 Russell St., Berkeley.
Marin County Assembly No. 5 Past Presidents Association N.S.G.W.—J. S. Rose Jr., Gov.; L. J. Peter, Sec., Peter Bldg., 4th and "C" Sts., San Rafael.
Fred H. Greeley Assembly No. 6 Past Presidents Association N.S.G.W.—Meets monthly with different Parlors comprising district; R. L. P. Bigelow, Gov.; Barney Barry, Sec., P. O. box 72, Lincoln.
San Joaquin Assembly No. 7 Past Presidents Association N.S.G.W.—Meets 1st Friday, Native Sons Hall, Stockton; Clyde H. Gregg, Gov.; R. D. Dorcey, Sec., Native Sons Club, Stockton.
Sonoma County Assembly No. 9 Past President Association N.S.G.W.—Meets monthly at different Parlor headquarters in county; Louis Bosch, Gov.; L. S. Lewis, Sec., Court House, Santa Rosa.
General John A. Sutter Assembly No. 10 Past Presidents Association—C. C. Wachman, Gov.; Jas. J. Longshore, Sec., 514 "J" St., Sacramento.
Grizzly Bear Club—Members all Parlors outside San Francisco at all times welcome. Clubrooms top floor Native Sons Bldg., 414 Mason St., San Francisco.
Native Sons and Native Daughters Central Committee on Homeless Children—Main office, 955 Phelan Bldg., San Francisco; Mrs. John W. Stirling, Chmn.; Miss Mary E. Brusie, Sec. Los Angeles branch office, 3924 Sunset Blvd.; Dorothy Schlingman, Sec.

(ADVERTISEMENT.)

In Memoriam

HENRY W. McCOMAS.

The undersigned, constituting a Committee appointed by San Jose Parlor No. 22 of the Native Sons of the Golden West for the purpose of drafting resolutions of respect to the memory of our deceased brother, Henry W. McComas, beg leave to report as follows:

That Henry W. McComas was born in Santa Clara County in the year 1871 of parents who were early settlers of California, they having come to this state from the Eastern seaboard by way of the Isthmus of Panama in the year 1861. For a time he served the County of Santa Clara in the capacity of Deputy County Treasurer; later studied law in the offices of F. E. Spencer and D. W. Burchard, and was admitted to the bar in 1895. From the time of his admission to the bar until his death, he was continuously engaged in the practice of the law before the courts of California, maintaining his office in San Jose, and his career at the bar has been one of success and has been marked by such high character and nobility of purpose that never during his long professional career has there been the slightest stain or blemish against his name.

He was active in community and patriotic affairs, having been one of the organizers of Company "H" of the National Guard, which company entered the service of the United States during our war with Spain in 1898. During the World War he also gave of his time and energy to the service of his country in the capacity of County Chairman of the Four Minute Men of Santa Clara County.

He was also a most active and loyal member of the Order of Native Sons of the Golden West. Joining Palo Alto Parlor No. 82 on August 22, 1898, he became its recording and financial secretary in 1900 and served continuously in that capacity until Palo Alto, whose name in the meantime had been changed to Garden City Parlor, was merged with San Jose Parlor No. 22 in the year 1922, when he became the Recording Secretary of the consolidated Parlor and served in that capacity until the date of his death.

He also served the Parlor and the Order as Chairman of San Jose Native Sons and Daughters Joint Homeless Children Committee for the last twelve years, and in his zealous and untiring work as chairman of that committee he was responsible for placing many homeless children in childless homes in this vicinity. Now, therefore, we respectfully submit the following resolution:

Resolved, That this Parlor sincerely deplores and regrets the loss of our brother, Henry W. McComas; be it further resolved, that this resolution and testimonial be spread upon the minutes of this Parlor and that a copy thereof be transmitted by the Secretary of this Parlor, under the seal thereof, to each of the three sisters of Henry W. McComas, and to The Grizzly Bear.

JOHN M. BURNETT,
JOHN R. SULLIVAN,
CHAS. M. BALDASINI.

The foregoing resolution was regularly adopted by San Jose Parlor No. 22 N.S.G.W. on August 15, 1932. Attest: ARTHUR DAVISON, President; JOSEPH LAWRENCE, Secretary.

Whereas, In the wisdom of our Heavenly Father, the father of Charles D. Blaine, president of Modesto Parlor No. 11 N.S.G.W., has been called to his eternal rest, therefore, be it

Resolved, That the members of Modesto Parlor No. 11 Native Sons of the Golden West extend their most heartfelt sympathy to our president, Charles D. Blaine, and his family in this, their sad hour of bereavement, and sincerely pray that their sorrow may be tempered in the thought that God, in His infinite mercy, knows best; and be it further resolved, that this resolution be spread upon the minutes of the Parlor in respect to Brother Blaine, and that a copy thereof be sent to him.

The foregoing is a copy of a resolution adopted by Modesto Parlor No. 11 N.S.G.W. at their regular meeting September 7, 1932. Attest: C. C. EASTIN, Recording Secretary.

N.S.G.W. OFFICIAL DEATH LIST.

Containing the name, the date and the place of birth, the date of death, and the Subordinate Parlor affiliation of deceased members reported to Grand Secretary John T. Regan from August 20, 1932, to September 20, 1932:

Pratt, Neal; Amador City, December 26, 1876; August 21, 1932; Amador No. 17.
Cuneo, Rinaldo; San Francisco, June 15, 1875; August 19, 1932; San Francisco No. 49.
Cuneo, Frank; San Francisco, August 8, 1886; September 15, 1932; San Francisco No. 49.
Kenneally, Charles Francis; Stockton, August 9, 1864; September 6, 1932; Rincon No. 72.
Cordano, Joseph; Los Angeles, September 13, 1891; September 16, 1932; Ramona No. 109.
Poullain, Robert Joseph; Marysville, February 4, 1885; August 29, 1932; Sonoma No. 111.
Boucher, Thomas P.; San Francisco, July 23, 1855; August 17, 1932; Piedmont No. 120.
Agrella, Manuel Lewis; Oakland, June 12, 1891; August 12, 1932; Brooklyn No. 151.
Mayfield, Milton L.; Sebastopol, September 3, 1862; August 20, 1932; Cambria No. 152.
Boyle, Edward Francis; San Francisco, December 31, 1902; September 5, 1932; South San Francisco No. 157.
Hanson, Henry Christian; San Francisco, September 27, 1904; August 25, 1932; Sequoia No. 160.
Stackler, Eugene; San Francisco, June 28, 1878; August 30, 1932; Athens No. 195.
Glover, Robert; San Francisco, February 28, 1896; August 28, 1932; Dolores No. 208.
Soto, Presentation Marcus; Concord, November 21, 1860; September 20, 1932; Concord No. 245.
Dunn, Charles; Concord, October 14, 1867; July 29, 1932; Concord No. 245.

"Swear by the blood of the Revolution never to violate in the least particular the laws of the country, and never to tolerate their violation by others."—Abraham Lincoln.

SAN FRANCISCO

SAN FRANCISCO'S NATIVE SONS AND Native Daughters staged a wonderful Admission Day program September 9 in celebration of the eighty-second anniversary of California's becoming one, the thirty-first, of the sovereign states of the United States of America. Old Sol was there in breezeless splendor, so there was a hot time in the old town, weatherically speaking. Arrangements for the celebration were made by a joint committee chairmaned by Joseph J. McShane, Grand Trustee N.S.G.W. The program, as presented in detail in The Grizzly Bear for September 1932, was admirably carried out, and there was not a single incident that could cause unfavorable comment. A perfect day, from every viewpoint.

The morning parade, in which thousands of Native Sons and Native Daughters appeared, was most colorful, and won hearty plaudits from the immense viewing throngs. Every participating Parlor is deserving of commendation for the splendid showing made. Of the "outside" delegations, those of Alameda and Marin Counties are deserving of special mention. San Francisco's Natives, as always no matter where the Admission Day celebration is held, were in line in large numbers. Winners of parade awards were:

Best decorated float, City of Oakland; best decorated Native Son or Native Daughter float, Alta Parlor No. 3 N.D.G.W. (San Francisco); best Native Son playing and marching drum corps with field music, Mount Tamalpais Parlor No. 64 (San Rafael); best Native Daughter drill team, Presidio Parlor No. 148 (San Francisco); best appearing Native Daughter marching unit, Joaquin Parlor No. 5 (Stockton); best appearing Native Son marching unit, Guadalupe Parlor No. 231 (San Francisco); largest marching Native Daughter unit, Twin Peaks Parlor No. 185 (San Francisco); largest marching Native Son unit, South San Francisco Parlor No. 157 (San Francisco); best Native Daughter drum corps, Tamelpa Parlor No. 231 (Mill Valley); best Native Son drum corps only, California Parlor No. 1 (San Francisco); best decorated auto, Mission Parlor No. 227 N.D.G.W. (San Francisco); Native Son or Native Daughter drum corps receiving least points in competition, Claremont Parlor No. 240 N.S.G.W. (Oakland).

Twenty thousand people crowded into the Civic Auditorium in the evening for the grand ball and prosperity pageant. Wilhelmina von Bremen, selected as the Admission Day queen, was there, and music was supplied by the San Francisco Municipal Orchestra. A fashion revue held the attention of the assemblage for more than an hour. Brief addresses were made by Governor James Rolph; Mrs. Anna Mixon-Armstrong, Grand President N.D.G.W.; Seth Millington, Grand President N.S.G.W., and Joseph J. McShane, Grand Trustee N.S.G.W. Captain Hugh Barrett Dobbs was the master of ceremonies. Ivo R. Monti was chairman of the committee which arranged this excellent feature of the celebration.—C.M.H.

BALL FOR CHILDREN BENEFIT.

The San Francisco N.S.G.W. and N.D.G.W. Homeless Children Committee has been organized to conduct a costume ball in the Civic Auditorium, Thanksgiving Eve, November 23. Officers of the committee are: James L. Foley, Twin Peaks Parlor No. 214 N.S.G.W., chairman; Kittie Mullaney, Dolores Parlor No. 169 N.D.G.W., vice-chairman; Edna Urmy, Buena Vista Parlor No. 68 N.D.G.W., recording secretary; Bertha Mauser, Keith Parlor No. 137 N.D.G.W., financial secretary; Chas. A. Koenig, Golden Gate Parlor No. 29 N.S.G.W., treasurer; P. L. Schlessinger, Balboa Parlor No. 234 N.S.G.W., sergeant-at-arms.

Proceeds of the ball will be used to carry on the splendid work of the Native Sons and Native Daughters in behalf of California's homeless children—a most worthy endeavor deserving of wholehearted support and encouragement.

NATIVE DAUGHTER DOINGS.

An event of unusual interest was the celebration by Alta Parlor No. 3 of the golden wedding anniversaries of Mms. Isabel Pomeroy and Otille McLaughlin. A mock wedding ceremony was arranged by President May L. MacDonald, Mrs. Mary Warren acting as the minister. Each bride was the recipient of a sandwich tray ornamented in gold, the gift of the Parlor. Supper followed the ceremony, and the evening of rejoicing concluded with the rendition of songs, Mrs. Sadie Blake presiding at the piano. The committee in charge of the barn dance to be held October 8 is working hard to make it an outstanding social and financial success; Mrs. Agnes Hughes is the chairman.

Orinda Parlor No. 56 had a reception and dance in honor of Grand Inside Sentinel Orinda Giannini, who was escorted into the hall by Past Grand Emma Foley and presented with a silver gift. Deputy Mae Waring was among the many in attendance. Dancing helped to make the evening a wonderful success. September 23, all members born in September were given a birthday party and presented with gifts by the Parlor.

Genevieve Parlor No. 132 has planned a monster whist for the benefit of the Home Loyalty Pledge fund October 18. Miss Rena Taube is chairman of the arrangements committee, which is working hard to make the affair a huge success. The Parlor has outlined many activities for the fall and winter months.

Miss Vera Pander, whose marriage to Charles Thompson took place in September, was tendered a shower August 25 by Keith Parlor No. 137. A mock marriage was the entertainment feature. Refreshments were served at tables decorated in pastel shades, and around the festive board best wishes for health, wealth and prosperity were extended.

Dolores Parlor No. 169 set aside September 14 as "german night." The following, in costume, sang appropriate songs that added to the evening's entertainment: Ida Carrigan (chairman), Betty Both, Mae Baumeister, Evelyn Carlson, Mary Elb, Alma Hall, Kittie Mullaney, Emma O'Meara, Myrtle Ross, Rose Spaelti. Ann Dippel was the schoolteacher and kept everyone laughing. Past Grand Mae C. Boldemann was among the guests. German food was served at beautifully decorated tables. Plans are under way for a monster whist party October 27; Past Grand Evelyn I. Carlson is the chairman.

Castro Parlor No. 178 is featuring a series of whist luncheons, and they are proving very successful. Alice Lane was the August hostess and Mae Warring the September hostess. The Parlor is making a monthly donation toward the support of a homeless child at the Aid Society; Margaret Lou Shirk is the lucky baby chosen.

San Francisco Past Presidents Association No. 1 had an enjoyable banquet August 29, ninety members attending. Instructive and entertaining talks added zest to the evening's entertainment.

POETRY TRIED ON POOR DRIVERS.

The following parody on Joyce Kilmer's poem, "Trees," author unknown, is a new line of attack on careless auto drivers:

"I think that I shall never see
Along the road an unscraped tree
With bark intact, and painted white,
That no car ever hit at night.
For every tree that's near the road
Has caused some auto to be towed.
Sideswiping trees is done a lot
By drivers who are not so hot.
God gave them eyes so they could see
Yet any fool can hit a tree."

Millions for Schools—For the fiscal year ending June 30, 1933, California apportioned September 12 to the several counties for public schools \$19,796,785.56—\$16,774,498.78 to elementary schools, \$1,620,165.45 to high schools and \$1,402,121.33 to junior colleges.

Grape Festival—Kentfield, Marin County, will have its twenty-ninth annual Grape Festival, October 8.

"The most hopeless idleness is that most smoothed with excellent plans."—Bagehot.

Passing of the California Pioneer

(Confined to Brief Notices of the Demise of Those Men and Women Who Came to California Prior to 1870.)

MRS. MARY SPEAR-MARKWELL, NAtive of Oregon, 83; with her parents crossed the plains to California in 1851 and resided in Napa, Sacramento and Los Angeles Counties; died at Saint Helena, survived by a daughter. She was a granddaughter of Rev. Asa White, Pioneer of 1849, who erected in San Francisco the first Methodist church.

Mrs. Susan J. Wood, native of Missouri, 84; with her parents, William N. and Sarah J. Seawell, crossed the plains in 1852 and resided in Napa, Sonoma and Alameda Counties; died at Healdsburg, survived by two children and a brother, Justice Emmet Seawell of the California Supreme Court, Grand First Vice-president N.S.G.W. Deceased was a true type of early California womanhood; she did her full part in every duty of life, and left behind a memory that will be always cherished by those who knew her.

William G. Smith, native of Missouri, 82; came across the plains in 1852; died at Santa Clara City.

Mrs. Margaret Harrison-Kloppenburg, native of Illinois, 96; crossed the plains in 1852; died at Sacramento City, survived by a daughter.

Mrs. Hanna Mary Stewart-Smith, native of Missouri, 86; crossed the plains in 1852 and for many years resided in Sonoma County; died at San Francisco, survived by three sons.

Mrs. Rebecca Byrn, 92; since 1852 Alameda County resident; died at Oakland, survived by three children.

Louis Sturla, native of Italy, 94; came around Cape Horn in 1852 and long resided in Calaveras and Tuolumne Counties; died at San Francisco, survived by a daughter.

Mrs. Permelia Davidson, native of Missouri, 82; came across the plains in 1852 and resided in Sonoma and Mendocino Counties; died at Willits, survived by three children.

Mrs. Hattie L. Laurensen, native of New York, 84; came in 1852; died in Suisun Valley, Solano County.

Mrs. Mary Haskell, native of England, 88; came via the Isthmus of Panama in 1852 and long resided in Humboldt County; died at Oakland, Alameda County, survived by five children.

Eli Megonigil, native of Missouri, 91; crossed the plains in 1852 and settled in Yolo County; died at Woodland.

Mrs. Laura Sample, native of Kentucky, 89; crossed the plains in 1852 and resided in El Dorado and Stanislaus Counties; died at Denair, survived by a husband and a daughter.

Mrs. Elvesta Lucas-Sayles, native of Illinois, 82; crossed the plains in 1852 and resided in El Dorado and Sacramento Counties; died at Sacramento City.

J. P. Glenn, native of Missouri, 87; came across the plains in 1853 and settled in Sutter County; died at Sacramento City, survived by five children.

Mrs. Sarah Strain-Swift, native of Ireland, 88; came across the plains in 1853 and long resided in Yuba County; died at Oakland, Alameda County, survived by a daughter.

Mrs. Mary E. Fletcher, native of Pennsylvania, 80; since 1854 resident Vallejo, Solano County, where she died; ten children survive.

William J. Dutton, native of Maine, 85; since 1855 resident San Francisco, where he died; four children survive.

Mrs. Emma Marhoffer-Harper, native of Ohio, 80; since 1856 resident Del Norte County; died at Crescent City.

Thomas Jefferson Stewart, 91; came across the plains in 1856 and resided in San Mateo, Sonoma and Mendocino Counties; died at Bridgeport, survived by a daughter.

Michael Early, native of Ireland, 90; came via the Isthmus of Panama in 1857 and settled in San Joaquin County; died at Escalon, survived by two children.

Byard Davidson, native of Nova Scotia, 81; came via the Isthmus of Panama in 1858 and resided in Marin County for several years; died at Lompoc, Santa Barbara County, survived by four children.

Mrs. Lucille Rose Huscroft, native of Missouri, 86; came in 1859 and resided in Trinity, Yolo, San Mateo, Napa and Alameda Counties; died at Berkeley, survived by two daughters.

James Kiernan, native of New York, 79; since 1859 resident Siskiyou County; died at Yreka, survived by three children.

Mrs. Lillian Clark, native of Scotland, 90; came in 1860; died at Berkeley, Alameda County, survived by ten children.

Mrs. Martha Woolridge-Charlton, 74; since 1861 resident Humboldt County; died at Loleta, survived by three children.

Joseph H. Andrews, 83; came via the Isthmus of Panama in 1863 and resided in Marin and Contra Costa Counties; died at Oakland, Alameda County, survived by a wife and three children.

Mrs. Mary Elizabeth Stillwell, native of New Jersey, 72; came across the plains in 1863 and resided many years in Santa Clara County; died at Los Angeles City, survived by a husband and two daughters.

Frank Grimes, native of New York, 71; since 1863 resident San Francisco, where he died; a wife and six children survive.

Mrs. Ella Farnham, native of Indiana, 78; since 1864 resident Yolo County; died at Woodland, survived by six children.

Obadiah Gobel, native of North Carolina, 91; came across the plains in 1864 and resided in Amador and Colusa Counties; died at Maxwell, survived by eight children.

Mrs. Mary Garrett-Freeman, native of New York, 91; came across the plains in 1864 and resided many years in Yuba County; died at Santa Cruz City.

Mrs. Sabina Handley-Mulhern, native of New York, 86; since 1864 resident Santa Cruz City, where she died; eight children survive.

William Crocker, native of England, 73; since 1865 resident San Francisco, where he died; a wife and a daughter survive.

Peter DeMartini, native of Italy, 96; came in 1865; died at Sonora, Tuolumne County.

Mrs. Rebecca Ohm, native of Germany, 86; since 1866 resident San Joaquin County; died at Vernalis, survived by six children.

Amos L. Bowsher, native of Ohio, 93; came in 1866; died at Sacramento City, survived by two daughters.

Mrs. Margherita Toroni, native of Switzerland, 90; came in 1866 and resided sixty-two years in Sonoma Valley; died at Sonoma City, survived by three daughters.

Mrs. Amanda Blunkall, 86; came across the plains in 1866; died at Oakland, Alameda County, survived by four children.

Mrs. Mary Jane Hunt, native of New York, 88; came via the Isthmus of Panama in 1868; died at Chico, Butte County, survived by five children.

William Joseph Michell, native of England, 84; since 1867 resident Grass Valley, Nevada County, where he died; two children survive.

Mrs. Annie Banz-Mitscher, native of Maryland, 71; came via the Isthmus of Panama in 1868; died at Stockton, San Joaquin County, survived by a husband and six children.

Mrs. Mary Hollenbeak, native of Illinois, 79; came in 1868; died at McArthur, Shasta County, survived by three children.

Mrs. Margaret B. Fleming, native of Scotland, 79; crossed the plains in 1868 and settled in Amador County; died near Jackson, survived by ten children.

Reuben Eldred LeMoin, native of Illinois, 74; settled in Contra Costa County in 1869; died at Berkeley, Alameda County, survived by a wife and three children.

Mrs. Anna Consiglieri, native of Italy, 86; since 1869 resident Sacramento City, where she died; three daughters survive.

Mrs. Johanna Silvey, native of Azores Islands, 80; since 1869 resident Benicia, Solano County, where she died; a son survives.

FEMININE FANCIES

(Continued from Page 9)

Not one held closely about the hip, but which flares and has an added shoulder cape of the same material and a little upstanding collar finished at the front with two cut-steel buttons. This new kind of wrap is made for purely practical reasons. Its length is such as to keep a frock from being crushed, and it lacks the heaviness of a long wrap. Its ample width is designed with full-puffed sleeves and frequent ruffles and flares, with this year's evening dresses in mind.

"Adjust Your Brake for Safety's Sake," is the October slogan of the California Public Safety Committee in its campaign to lessen the constantly increasing auto death-toll.

LOS ANGELES--CITY and COUNTY

LOS ANGELES

(Continued from Page 13)

Bell, Edith Strain, Jean Clos, Carmel Brigante and Jennie Gilmer.

The potluck dinner September 21 was well attended and justice was done the tempting viands prepared by the members. Following the feast Miss Kathryn Ronan entertained with an illustrated talk on "The Desert." September 28 a reception was tendered returned travelers—Mrs. Lillian Carey, Mrs. Ramona Thoroughgood, Misses Leona and Jean Clos, Mrs. Grace Haven. All gave interesting accounts of their travels. Mrs. Mary McAnany was chairman of the evening. Delicious refreshments were served. "Mermaids" Irene Eden and Jennie Raymond want more recruits for the life-saving class. The bridge luncheon September 24 at the home of Mrs. Ruth Traeger was largely attended, and netted a goodly sum for the Parlor's clubhouse fund. Among those members who assisted Hostess Traeger were Sophia Stewart, Dolores Malin, Sali Joseph, Florence Nolte, Effie Walters, Emma Kaiser and Peggy Ambler.

The Parlor's program for October includes: 12th, card party, Mrs. Olinda Kerby chairman; 15th, beach party at the Hermosa home of Mrs. Elizabeth Jones; 21st and 22nd, rummage sale for the benefit of the homeless children fund; 26th, Hallowe'en dance.

COUNCILMEN LOOK OUT FOR SELVES.

The Los Angeles City Council has voted to further burden the November ballot by presenting twenty proposed charter amendments for consideration by the electorate. It is outrageous that these propositions should be submitted at a presidential election, and at a time when several state legislative propositions will be presented. The California election law should be amended to prohibit submission of local questions at a general election.

The Council voted down submission of a proposal to decrease the salaries of councilmen, but it will submit one to increase the term of councilmanic office from two to four years. The former would certainly have been approved, and the latter should be rejected.—C.M.H.

TO HAVE EDUCATIONAL PROGRAM.

San Pedro—Sepulveda Parlor No. 263 N.S.G.W. is now meeting in a new home, the Redman building at historic Point Fermin. The Parlor will observe national educational week in November, President Joseph A. Pia having appointed a committee, composed of Past Presidents John T. Gower, Stanley A. Wheeler and Vincent E. Hopkins, to arrange a suitable program.

WELFARE WORK BENEFIT.

Ocean Park—Santa Monica Bay Parlor No. 267 N.S.G.W. is sponsoring a night at the Culver City Kennel Club Friday, October 7. The Interparlor N.S.G.W. and N.D.G.W. Committee has endorsed the project, and all the Parlors of both Orders in Los Angeles, Orange and San Bernardino Counties will benefit. Tickets are forty cents each, and through the generosity of the club the Parlors will retain the entire amount of their ticket sales for welfare work. Among the many patrons and patronesses are Messrs. and Mesdames Freeman, Nesa, Conterno, Burke, Sunquist, Pierce, Noerenberg, Chappman, Meyer, Tuttle, Newell, Price, McCurdy, Badia, McCreery, Koster.

The Parlor had a rousing good meeting September 26, the occasion being the official visit of Grand First Vice-president Justice Emmet Seawell. Every nearby Parlor was largely represented, and there was enthusiasm aplenty. Three candidates were initiated. In welcoming the visitor, Municipal Judge Joseph L. Call said, "We have with us tonight in Brother Seawell one whose name, fame, and deeds of accomplishment have reached from one end of the state to the other."

Justice Seawell delivered a delightful address, which thoroughly impressed his auditors; he pointed out that the Order is deserving of the best effort of every affiliate, and urged united action for increased membership. Among the many other speakers were Grand Trustee Eldred L. Meyer, Dr. George Sabichi, Grand Outside Sentinel William Reuter, Municipal Judge Leo Aggeler, Bernard J. Hiss, Clinton E. Skinner and Past Grand President John T. Newell. Pleasing entertainment numbers were presented by Santa Monica's own, refreshments were served, and Undersheriff Eugene W. Biscailuz, the modern Jesse James, relieved many of their spare change, and through his successful extracting the charity fund of No. 267 was considerably enriched.

PERSONAL PARAGRAPHS.

Owen S. Adams (Los Angeles N.S.) visited Sequoia National Park last month.

Al Lobree (Castro N.S.) of San Francisco was a visitor the latter part of August.

Mrs. Jennie Elliott (Los Angeles N.D.) and husband vacationed in Washington State.

Frank I. Beers (Los Angeles N.S.) has taken up his residence in Oil City, Pennsylvania.

Miss Emma Kaiser (Los Angeles N.D.) vacationed a couple of weeks in San Francisco.

Miss Grace S. Stoermer (Past Grand President N.D.) has returned from a trip to Yosemite.

Mrs. Leonora Ashman (Los Angeles N.D.) and husband are visiting in Saint Louis, Missouri.

Sheriff William I. Traeger (Past Grand President N.S.) was a visitor to Sacramento City last month.

Mrs. Hazel Scheide became the bride of Lee E. Erwin (Los Angeles N.S.) at Santa Ana September 19. They will reside in Los Angeles.

Mrs. Evelyn Troutwein (Los Angeles N.D.) and husband has returned from a motor visit to West Virginia, New York, and Washington, D. C.

Miss Evelyne Farnsworth of Santa Ana and Francis A. Cochran (Ramona N.S.) were wedded September 7 at Riverside City. They will reside in Sacramento City.

Mrs. Marie McFadyen-Monroe (Long Beach N.D.), who had been visiting with relatives in Long Beach during the summer, has returned with her two sons to her home in Pendleton, Oregon.

THE DEATH RECORD.

Mrs. Marie Rambaud, mother of Mrs. Mathilde Besson (Los Angeles N.D.), died August 24.

George O. Vail, father of Grove Vail (Ramona N.S.), died August 27.

Mrs. Silmonena Pirri, mother of Angelo Pir (Ramona N.S.), died September 7.

Joseph Cordano, affiliated with Ramona Pa lor No. 109 N.S.G.W., died September 16. H was born at Los Angeles, September 13, 189 Among the surviving relatives is a brothe Frank Cordano (Ramona N.S.).

Mrs. Elizabeth S. Lovie, mother of Edward Lovie (Hollywood N.S.), died September 17.

CLASSIFIED DIRECTORY
LOS ANGELES NATIVE SONS

ATTORNEYS-AT-LAW.

J. A. ADAIR. J. A. ADAIR J
516-19 Fay Bldg., Third and Hill.
Office: MAdison 1141 —Phones— Res.: GLadstone 504

HENRY G. BODKIN. V. P. LUCA
Chester Williams Bldg., 215 W. 5th St.
Phone: MUtual 3151.

DAVID H. CLARK.
215 West Fifth St.
Phone: MUtual 8406.

WM. J. HUNSAKER.
458 So. Spring St., Room 1130.
Phone: TRinity 6666.

EDWIN A. MESERVE. SHIRLEY E. MESERV
555 So. Flower St.
Phone: TRinity 6161.

THOS. B. REED.
548 South Spring St.
Phone: VAndike 0687.

DENTIST.

ROBERT J. GREGG, D.D.S.
5801 South Figueroa St.
Phone: THornwall 3690.
Hours 9 to 5, and by appointment.

DETECTIVE SERVICE.

LOUIS A. DUNI.
523 Washington Bldg., 311½ So. Spring.
Phone: TUcker 3013.

ORDER NATIVE SONS LOSES TWO MOST PROMINENT MEMBERS.

Just as the final pages of this issue of The Grizzly Bear were being printed, this sad news was received:

Dr. Charles W. Decker of Palo Alto, Santa Clara County, Past Grand President, died September 25. He was born at Sutterville, Sacramento County, in 1855, and was affiliated with California Parlor No. 1 (San Francisco).

William J. Hayes of Oakland, Alameda County, Past Grand President, died September 27. He was born at Havilah, Kern County, in 1885, and was affiliated with Berkeley Parlor No. 210.

PIONEER NATIVES DEAD

(Brief Notices of the Demise of Men and Women born in California Prior to 1860.)

Mrs. Columbia Ellen Rupley-Holliday, born in El Dorado County in 1858, died August 23 at Placerville survived by two children.

Mrs. Noonie Briggs-Boulon, born in Sonoma County in 1853, died August 24 at Vallejo, Solano County. She was affiliated with Alta Parlor No. 3 N.D.G.W. (San Francisco).

Mrs. Katherine T. Casey, born in Sacramento County in 1858, died August 24 at Sacramento City survived by a husband and five children.

Ephraim Porter Gann, born in El Dorado County in 1852, died August 24 at Lakeport, Lake County, survived by a wife and three children.

Frank Daniel, born at San Francisco in 1856, died there August 26.

Dr. James L. Mayon, born in Yuba County in 1858, died August 27 at Santa Cruz City survived by a wife and four daughters.

Mrs. Martha Louise Richmond, born in Sonoma County in 1857, died August 29 at Mendocino Town survived by four children.

Isaac Steindler, born in El Dorado County in 1854, died August 29 at San Francisco survived by a son.

Mrs. Susie Churchman, born in Sonoma County in 1856, died August 30 at Santa Cruz City survived by two daughters.

Solomon Ury, born at San Leandro, Alameda County, in 1857, died there September 1 survived by a wife and four daughters.

George Gawn Murdock, born in Sutter County in 1856, died September 1 at Upper Lake, Lake County, survived by a wife.

Arthur Hill, born in San Joaquin County in 1857, died September 2 at Merced City.

John L. Allen, born in Calaveras County in 1855, died September 13 at Bakersfield, Kern County, survived by nine children.

Mrs. Georgiana Hartmann-Scherrer, born at San Jose, Santa Clara County, in 1856, died there September 14.

Mrs. Isabel Poile-Thompson, born in Santa Cruz County in 1847, died September 18 at Santa Cruz City survived by two daughters.

Mrs. Mary Emma Cameron-Martin, born in Sonoma County in 1851, died September 18 at San Francisco survived by two daughters.

Sister Mary Genevieve Kane, born at Vallejo, Solano County, in 1859, died there September 19.

Mrs. Mary E. Cook-Piratsky, born at San Francisco in 1855, died September 19 at Watsonville, Santa Cruz County, survived by a husband and a daughter.

"God plants us, and waters, and weeds us, and gives the increase; and so God is our gardener."—Donne.

RETRIBUTION

(Continued from Page 4)

the adjoining room heard Caleb crooning to the lifeless body between fits of violent sobbing.

The mob was not informed of her passing until she was dressed for burial and her erring husband had pressed his bloodless lips to those of his lost and loved one. Dry-eyed he left the room and when surrounded by the swaying mob he asked no clemency. Some there were in the pulsing throng who would have stayed the hands of the hangmen, but the odds were against him. They placed him on a mule which was led to the crest of the hill beyond. A large and suitable tree was selected. The noose was adjusted to Caleb's neck, the other end thrown over a stout oak limb. They asked him if he had anything to say. He replied:

"No, only that I be laid beside my dear wife." "That cannot be, old man. You are unfit to lie beside the one you so unjustly slew. We will dig your grave beneath this great oak limb, and may God have mercy on your wicked soul." At the last word the mule was given a sharp lash, which freed him of his burden. Caleb swung into eternity.

Judge Lynch did not deem it necessary for trial and jury, and summary proceedings were considered justifiable by the type of men who peopled California in 1849.

At the same time that Caleb was being hanged, Mary Devine's friends were laying her in her long and narrow resting place on a sunny hillslope. It is told by early Pioneers that the oak died soon after Caleb was buried there. The elements bleached the limbs of the tree and many of those white arms were lifted heavenward as though in supplication for the old sailor's murderous deeds.

MILLIONS FOR FEDERAL PROJECTS.

The Federal War Department announced September 13 allotments of funds provided for under the Emergency Relief and Construction Act of 1932 for flood control and river and harbor projects in various parts of the country totaling in all $41,577,260. California allotments include:

San Joaquin River, $133,000; Petaluma Creek, $166,500; San Diego Harbor, $134,000; Los Angeles and Long Beach Harbors, $700,000.

Values Decrease—Assessed values of California property for 1932 decreased $1,316,965,641, compared with 1931, this year's total being $8,081,944,342.

Yosemite Acreage Increased—Wawona Basin and an area of timber land totaling more than 9,000 acres have been added to Yosemite National Park.

No Registration Depression—The total registration of students at the University of California for the 1931-32 year, 25,150, exceeded the 1930-31 registration by 579.

Forest Funds—The Federal Agricultural Department allotted September 20 to thirty-three states and territories with national forests their shares of receipts from the forests in the last fiscal year. California receives $209,165.53.

Bicentennial Stamps Discontinued—The Federal Postoffice Department announces that manufacture of the George Washington bicentennial stamps will be discontinued October 1. Approximately 7,000,000,000 of them had been printed up to September 1.

THINK THIS OVER!

The order of Native Sons of the Golden West is, we believe, with the exception of the Order of Native Daughters of the Golden West, the only organization that limits membership exclusively to NATIVE-BORN AMERICANS.

Knowing the serious conditions in this country today, this fact alone should impel every Native Son of California to immediately SEEK AFFILIATION with that American-born and American-operated institution, the man-power and wealth of which are pledged to the protection of American institutions in times of peace as well as in times of war.

GRIZZLY GROWLS

(Continued from Page 3)

the pension rolls. Gentlemen, study those figures before you vote.' "

The figures referred to show that in the World War, Germany, France, Great Britain, Italy and Canada, combined, had a total of 34,244,636 men mobilized; 16,563,907 died or were wounded. The combined annual relief bills of these five nations is $891,190,360. The United states, alone, had 4,355,000 men mobilized; 360,300 died or were wounded. The annual veterans' relief bill of the United States, alone, is $860,000,000—but $31,000,000 less than the five nations, combined, expend for the relief of 12,000,000 more men.

There is a growing public sentiment that something must be done to curb the expenditures of the Federal Government veteran bureau. This, because of facts, coming into the light, which cause suspicion that the undeserving are getting a considerable portion of relief funds, and that extravagance, favoritism and graft are not conspicuous by their absence. The veteran bureau now gets approximately twenty-five cents of every dollar paid into the federal treasury. The cost-tide continues to rise, too, and unless checked the financial stability of the country will be seriously jeopardized. For instance, forces in the Civil War were about half those in the World War. Pension payments account of the Civil War, reaching the peak in 1923, fifty-eight years after that war, totaled $238,000,000. Payments to World War veterans in 1932, but fourteen years after that war, reached $650,000,000.

Speaking at Boston, Massachusetts, Rear-Admiral William S. Simms, retired, of the United States Navy said: "The Spanish-American War lasted exactly 114 days, and although less than 400 were killed and less than 5,000 died of wounds and disease, yet more than 227,000 out of the 280,000 who served are now drawing government pensions. The cost this year for Spanish-American War pensions is $119,000,000." He described this pension system, according to press dispatches, as a "steal of the nastiest kind and an outrage to the American taxpayer."

The American Medical Association, through Willam C. Woodard, makes this public protest: "The medical profession cries as loudly as any other group of citizens for the liberal treatment of all persons suffering from disabilities incurred in military service and of the widows and orphans of those who have died or may hereafter die because of such disabilities. . . . What the medical profession complains of, however, is the treatment at public expense of veterans who are suffering from disabilities not incurred in military service and having no relation to such service. Patriotism and national honor call for no such gratuity."

Roger Burlingame, a World War veteran, in his book, "Peace Veterans," warns: "We cannot shut our ears to the word that is whispered and finally will be spoken aloud among the people as we go by; the new word, the new harsh word 'racket.' The word and the accusation will not be altogether just. As the storm grows, the hatred of every man who wore a uniform will be profoundly unjust. We must not wait, we the veterans. We must rise in defense of our own honor as well as in the defense of our country in its new emergency. We must admit our fault and take the lead against its consequences."

Indignation was aroused, and justly so, in Los Angeles when it was discovered that A. I. Lasker, one of the several "Angel City" prominents sent up for robbing innocent investors, had been given his liberty by the State Parole Board. He had served but twenty-five months of a fifteen-to-twenty-year sentence. The excuse for releasing him was, that he "was suffering from pernicious anemia and must be released or die."

Queer, isn't it, how all the higherup crooks become physically afflicted, after they have been convicted? Apparently they know "gwanadie" is the password to freedom! How long before Beesemeyer, the Fishes, Ferguson, etc., etc., will be released? Not a single one of those crooked financiers is deserving of pity. If prison confinement means certain death, they should be confined, for they have wrecked the lives, aye, caused the deaths, of numerous honest, hard-working people. Lasker's parole should be revoked, and he and all of his kind should be compelled to serve the maximum sentences prescribed by the trial judges.

The State Legislature should amend the statutes so that no person convicted of a felony may benefit from the parole and the indeterminate-sentence provisions. The trial judge, being the best qualified to do so, should fix the maximum period of confinement. Let that be done, and California will have less crime and fewer criminals.

Rev. Dr. Jones I. Corrigan of the Catholic Church, speaking of the divorce evil, in the course of a radio address said: "It possesses the appetite that grows with what it feeds on. . . . Public opinion has not been sufficiently aroused to take a stand against divorce. . . . The time has come to face the facts and destroy this national cancer. . . . By our divorce laws and by pandering to divorce, we have poisoned the public mind not alone by suggesting evil, but by suggesting a plausible excuse for it."

He may well have summed up his excellent discourse by stating that marriage in this country has, because of insane interpretations of divergent regulatory statutes, degenerated into legalized prostitution.

Red Cross officials of Salina, Kansas, have decreed that persons who have autos will have to surrender their license tags before they can receive further aid. Welfare authorities throughout California should follow this lead. A person owning or operating an auto is not justly entitled to be aided at public expense—at the expense of numbers of taxpayers who, because they cannot honestly afford to do so, do not own or operate a car. Another form of waste of public funds that should be stopped.

Speaking in San Francisco anent existing court procedure, Federal Judge William B. Sheppard of Florida is quoted thusly: "It is so clumsy that perpetrators of heinous crimes manage, with the aid of racketeering lawyers, to slip through the fingers of the law and go free, or obtain light sentences or fines when they should be severely punished." Perhaps this accounts for crime being the outstanding profession of the nation, as well as for its practicers sittin' pretty atop the social pie.

Continuing, he said, "There is no determination on the part of the Government to enforce it [the prohibition law], nor any real prosecution of those who violate it." Isn't it so?

State Controller Ray L. Riley has served notice he will not approve any salary increase during the next twelve months, unless compelled to do so by the courts. It appears that, although the state administration is preaching economy to relieve the deficit, some forty employes, probably on the specially-favored payroll, were given increases, but the state controller refused to pay the advances. Hurrah for Riley! May his kind increase in public office!

Dr. Nicholas Murray Butler of Columbia University is, according to press dispatches, for unconditional repeal of the Eighteenth Amendment to the Federal Constitution, and he must think it is coming, for he is reported to have a plan for state liquor control modeled after the Quebec act.

Which recalls the frequently advanced argument that repeal will produce liquor-tax revenue to balance the national budget. In ten years, Quebec collected $68,032,472 in liquor revenue, but to produce it the enormous sum of $589,944,914 was expended for liquor. What price, liquor revenue!

Another "investment" scandal, the Insull Industries, is being publicized, and again the nation's "giants of finance" are linked with within-the-law thievery. These blowups are of almost daily occurrence, but not a single "highboy" has had his wings clipped.

Captioned "Japan's Words Disproved Again by Japanese Deeds," the San Francisco "Chronicle" said editorially September 6: "Japan is now the only nation on earth the solemn word of honor of whose government is unanimously disbelieved by every other government." Shades of the mikado!—and from the heretofore decidedly pro-Jap "Chronicle." As that government, so its nationals in this country. Their protestations of friendliness are not sincere, as time will prove.

The "jokiest" joke of the open season: Director Amos Woodcock of the Federal Prohibition Bureau, addressing a W.C.T.U. convention at Seattle, Washington—"There is practically no open sale of intoxicating liquor in the United States." Andy wasn't there to complete the picture, either.

"By keeping silence when we ought to speak, men may be lost. By speaking when we ought to keep silence, we waste our words. The wise man is careful to do neither."—Confucius.

Grizzly Bear

NOVEMBER — THE ONLY OFFICIAL PUBLICATION OF THE NATIVE SONS AND DAUGHTERS OF THE GOLDEN WEST — 1932

Featuring

GENERAL NEWS OF INTEREST CONCERNING ALL CALIFORNIA, and ORDERS NATIVE SONS and NATIVE DAUGHTERS

Price: 15 Cents

GRIZZLY GROWLS

(CLARENCE M. HUNT.)

ANNUALLY, STATE CONTROLLER RAY L. Riley presents for the information of the general public figure-facts of the assessed value of property in, and the indebtedness of, each of California's fifty-eight counties. The figures in the 1932 statement are startling! Propertyowners should give them serious consideration, for they clearly indicate that, unless prompt and decisive action be taken by the taxbearers to stop governmental extravagance and waste, bankruptcy must come to every holder of realty.

Bear in mind that these figures do not refer to the state government administration which, with enormously lessened revenue, has not decreased the operating cost. In fact, although facing a deficit reaching into the millions, salaries and other operating costs have been increased and the numbers on the payrolls have not been lessened.

Nor do the figures include the bonded indebtedness of the incorporated municipalities within the several counties. The outstanding bonded debt of the fifty-five municipalities in Los Angeles County alone, December 31, 1931, was $233,711,669. Taxpayers in nearly every other county have proportionately as heavy bond burdens to carry.

But never forget that, irrespective of the claims of promoters and politicians otherwise, every cent of indebtedness—whether resulting from bond issues or operation—of state, county, municipality and township governments is a first lien against every parcel of real estate. Here are some figures from Riley's statement:

Grand total 1932 assessed value all taxable property in California, $8,498,447,651. A decrease, compared with the 1931 value ($9,402,188,441) of $903,740,790, and, compared with the 1930 value ($10,203,866,630), a decrease of $1,705,418,979. Thus, in the two-year period since the presence of the depression was generally recognized, except by California's overnumerous governing authorities, the assessed value of all property in the state has decreased $1,705,418,979, and the opinion is ventured that the actual, or sale, value has decreased double that stupendous sum.

Total 1932 indebtedness of all the counties, $209,725,819. An increase, compared with the 1931 total ($201,724,158) of $8,001,661, and, compared with the 1930 total ($188,866,324), an increase of $20,859,495. So, in the same two-year period while property values have been skyrocketing downward at the rate of close to a billion dollars a year, the indebtedness, resulting mostly from reckless spending, has skyrocketed upward close to twenty-one million dollars. That—loading more debt on falling value—is the governmental efficiency so extensively propagandaed; the efficiency which has caused, and is causing, thousands of propertyowners to abandon their holdings. Here are more comparative figures:

Value real estate—$3,265,550,724 (1932), $3,786,492,171 (1931), $3,867,173,026 (1930). Value real estate improvements—$2,023,307,157 (1932), $2,191,885,304 (1931), $2,143,372,981 (1930). Value personal property—$749,543,070 (1932), $764,220,678 (1931), $962,028,425 (1930). Money—$2,473,208 (1932), $2,762,926 (1931), $2,591,679 (1930). Solvent credits—$411,439,873 (1932), $358,227,892 (1931), $499,841,574 (1930). Stocks, bonds, notes, etc.—$710,098,960 (1932), $874,496,002 (1931), $1,334,481,852 (1930).

From the just-above figures note that the 1932 assessed value of real estate and improvements is $5,288,857,881; the 1930 total was $6,010,546,007—a reduction in two years of $721,688,126. The 1932 assessed value of personal property, money, solvent credits, stocks, bonds, notes, etc., is $1,873,555,111; the 1930 total was $2,798,943,530—a reduction in two years of $925,392,419. Realty, representing approximately sixty-two percent of the tax-producing holdings, gets a reduction of but $721,688,126, while the other holdings are reduced $925,392,419. It is plainly evident, therefore, that realty is discriminated against—shamefully and ruinfully tax burdened!

Note, too, that the 1932 assessed value of stocks, bonds, notes, etc., is $710,098,960; the 1930 total was $1,334,481,852. The two-year decrease, $624,382,892, multiplied by five, gives a conservative estimate, about three billion dollars, of the amount crooked bankers, financiers and promoters of California, thieving without molestation by the authorities, have deliberately and knowingly stolen from honest, hard-working residents of the state. A few of the bigboys have been "goated," and prosecuted at enormous expense to the taxpayers. When convicted, they are, or in all likelihood will be, turned loose, either by the trial magistrate or the state authorities,—to resume preying on the unsuspecting public.

Really, the whole system of government has become a huge farce, and the propertyowners are paying dearly for a continuous performance of the comedy of waste, extravagance, inefficiency, ad infinitum ad nauseum. And just so long as they sit and stand idly by, the farce will be uninterruptedly continued, at no lessening of the cost. Returning to the state controller's statement:

Total value of property [nonoperative and operative] as returned by county assessors—$8,224,150,764 (1932), $9,085,717,507 (1931), $9,868,881,785 (1930); a two-year decrease of $1,644,731,021.

Value of railroads as assessed by State Board Equalization—$274,296,887 (1932), $316,470,934 (1931), $334,984,845; a two-year decrease of $60,687,958.

Los Angeles continues as the richest tax-assessed county in the state. Its 1932 grand total, $3,559,159,860, is, however, $955,102,108 less than the 1930 total of $4,514,261,968. The peak-year in this county was 1929, when the assessment totaled $4,522,926,824. The county's indebtedness has, in the two-year period, increased $527,601, from $9,952,188 in 1930 to $10,479,789 in 1932. The county's 1932 tax rate is $1.532 (inside) and $1.672 (outside); the 1930 rate was $1.369 (inside) and $1.619 (outside). This tax rate is for the county's general expenses, and does not include numerous assessment-district special taxes. The Los Angeles City 1932 rate is considerably above four dollars per $100 valuation, for the city had, D cember 31, 1931, an outstanding bonded debt $168,511,961, and the taxpayers must dig u $30,000 a day to pay interest charges on th sum. The county has 1,291,924 acres of a sessed land. Nearly 42 percent of the who state's taxable property is in this one county.

San Francisco, the only combined city-an county subdivision of California, is the next rich est. Its 1932 grand total assessment, $1,433 788,594, is $308,671,149 less than the 1930 tot of $1,742,459,743. San Francisco's peak-asses ment year was 1930. Its indebtedness has i creased $24,176,300 in two years, from $137 729,400 in 1930 to $161,906,200 in 1932. Th year's tax rate, $3.96, is eight cents less tha the 1930 rate of $4.04. San Francisco has bu 29,888 acres of assessed land.

These two are the only California counties i the ten-figure, billion-dollar, assessment clas In the nine-figure class are the following cou ties, with their grand total assessments for 193 1931 and 1930:

Alameda—$538,046,157 (1932), $587,867 173 (1931), $602,733,625 (1930); two-year d crease, $64,687,468.

San Diego—$216,027,076 (1932), $253,647 549 (1931), $278,043,620 (1930); two-year d crease, $62,016,544.

Fresno—$195,265,571 (1932), $204,589,21 (1931), $211,437,014 (1930); two-year d crease, $16,171,443.

Kern—$191,660,550 (1932), $216,814,42 (1931), $221,391,937 (1930); two-year d crease, $29,731,387.

Orange—$178,047,055 (1932), $187,226,04 (1931), $206,832,045 (1930); two-year d crease, $28,784,990.

Sacramento—$174,182,694 (1932), $176 771,004 (1931), $178,394,240 (1930); two year decrease, $4,211,546.

Santa Clara—$141,619,660 (1932), $145 812,454 (1931), $146,760,202 (1930); two year decrease, $5,140,542.

Santa Barbara—$133,092,558 (1932), $156 940,051 (1931), $160,908,377 (1930); two year decrease, $27,815,819.

San Bernardino—$129,662,460 (1932), $136 033,314 (1931), $140,025,917 (1930); two year decrease, $10,363,457.

San Joaquin—$125,390,519 (1932), $134 198,792 (1931), $149,870,943 (1930); two-yea decrease, $15,672,151.

Contra Costa—$105,771,626 (1932), $112 641,523 (1931), $116,053,724 (1930); two-yea decrease, $10,282,098.

Ventura County's 1932 total assessment i $88,568,979; in 1931 it was $119,181,867 an in 1930, $124,720,684; a two-year decrease o $36,151,705.

But three of the state's fifty-eight countie show an increased grand total assessment in th two-year period: Amador—$8,794,432 (1932) $8,575,305 (1930); increase, $219,127. King —$48,150,472 (1932), $44,248,847 (1930); in crease, $3,901,625. Mono—$6,674,265 (1932) $6,624,202 (1930); increase, $50,063.

Alpine County, with 50,707 acres of assesse land, stands alone in the six-figure grand-tota class. In the two-year period its assessment ha decreased $106,935, from $901,059 (1930) t $794,124 (1932).

Kern County has the largest number of acre of assessed land, 3,829,498. San Bernardin County is next, with 2,730,145, and then Fresn County, with 2,178,000.

The following counties are free of debt: Amador, Calaveras, Humboldt, Inyo, Madera, Mariposa, Mono, Nevada, Placer, Shasta, Sierra, Siskiyou, Trinity, Tuolumne and Yuba.

Three counties—Alpine, Del Norte and Lake—have no railroads. In but nineteen countie could the assessors find money for assessment The people of Alpine, Del Norte, Marin, Mono Plumas and Trinity evidently are wondrous wise for no stocks and bonds are assessed in those counties. Trinity County has the highest tax rate, $4 per hundred, and Kings County has the lowest, $1.45 (inside) and $1.75 (outside).

A new organization, dubbed "California Council on Oriental Relations," was publicly announced last month in San Francisco. Its purpose is to bring about a change in the Federal Immigration Act, so that more Japs and other ineligible-to-citizenship and undesirable aliens may come into this country via the quota. President Robert G. Sproul of the University of California heads the outfit, a byproduct of the deceptively-titled "California State Chamber of Commerce" which, although operated by big interests for their special benefit, is financed largely by public tax-funds donated by boards of supervisors. Taxpayers of every county should unite, and deal this "State Chamber" a death-blow by compelling their supervisors to with-

(Continued on Page 24)

The Grizzly Bear Magazine

The ALL California Monthly

OWNED, CONTROLLED, PUBLISHED BY GRIZZLY BEAR PUBLISHING CO., (Incorporated)

COMPOSED OF NATIVE SONS.

HERMAN C. LICHTENBERGER, Pres.
JOHN T. NEWELL RAY HOWARD
WM. I. TRAEGER LORENZO F. SOTO
CHAS. R. THOMAS HARRY J. LELANDE
ARTHUR A. SCHMIDT, Vice-Pres.
BOARD OF DIRECTORS

CLARENCE M. HUNT
General Manager and Editor

OFFICIAL ORGAN AND THE ONLY OFFICIAL PUBLICATION OF THE NATIVE SONS AND THE NATIVE DAUGHTERS GOLDEN WEST.

ISSUED FIRST EACH MONTH.
FORMS CLOSE 20th MONTH.
ADVERTISING RATES ON APPLICATION.

SAN FRANCISCO OFFICE:
N.S.G.W. BLDG., 414 MASON ST., RM. 302
(Office Grand Secretary N.S.G.W.)
Telephone: Kearney 1223
SAN FRANCISCO, CALIFORNIA

PUBLICATION OFFICE:
309-15 WILCOX BLDG., 2nd AND SPRING,
Telephone: VAndike 6234
LOS ANGELES, CALIFORNIA

(Entered as second-class matter May 29, 1918, at the Postoffice at Los Angeles, California, under the act of August 24, 1912.)

PUBLISHED REGULARLY SINCE MAY 1907
VOL. LII WHOLE NO. 307

PUBLIC GOOD MUST BE PARAMOUNT TO EVERY PRIVATE CONSIDERATION.

Regardless of how involved the present presidential campaign now drawing to a close may have become, with Republicans voting Democrat and Democrats voting Republican, it cannot rival the campaign of 1800, when the Federal Congress was called on to settle the fight, and the leader of the opposing political party was, for all practical purposes, the man who chose the president, declared Professor E. I. McCormac of the University of California history department in the course of an address on famous presidential campaigns.

Because the founders of the country had not visualized the formation of political parties, he explained, the method of election was to have the presidential electors vote for two candidates. The candidate receiving the greatest number of votes would be president, and the second candidate would be vice-president. In 1800, however, the Federalist and the Republican parties had developed. The latter party was in the majority, and voted solidly for its two candidates, Jefferson and Burr. In other words, somebody had to decide which one should be president and which one should be vice-president.

Alexander Hamilton, leader of the opposition Federalists, was a bitter enemy of Jefferson, yet he succeeded in swinging the congressional vote to Jefferson, rather than Burr, because he believed that Jefferson was more honest and more capable.

In a letter to a friend, Hamilton said: "If there be a man in the world I ought to hate, it is Jefferson—but public good must be paramount to every private consideration." He disliked Jefferson, but admitted his honesty and patriotism, whereas Burr, he said, "has no principle, public or private; would be bound by no agreement; will listen to no monitor but his ambition; and for this purpose will use the worst part of the community as a ladder to climb to permanent power, and an instrument to crush the better part. He is sanguine enough to hope everything, daring enough to attempt anything; wicked enough to scruple nothing. From the elevation of such a man may heaven preserve the country." So, Hamilton fought for his enemy.

"Great powers and natural gifts do not bring privileges to their possessor so much as they bring duties."—Beecher.

PIONEER NATIVES DEAD

(Brief Notices of the Demise of Men and Women born in California Prior to 1860.)

John S. Hayden, born in the Sacramento Valley in 1851, died recently near Stewarts Point, Sonoma County, survived by two children.

Nathan E. Stone, born in Los Angeles County in 1856, died September 16 at Fillmore, Ventura County. His surviving 94-year-old mother, Mrs. Mahala Asbell-Stone, crossed the plains in 1848.

Mrs. Mary Ellis-Bowerman, born in Colusa County in 1859, died September 18 at Olympia, Washington State, survived by two daughters.

George N. Martin, born in Santa Clara County in 1858, died September 18 at Berkeley, Alameda County, survived by a wife and four daughters.

Mrs. Matilda Shaver, born in San Joaquin County in 1852, died September 21 at San Francisco survived by two sons.

Mrs. Clara Aymes, born in Calaveras County in 1848, died September 22 at Los Angeles City survived by a daughter.

Mrs. Sarah Johnson-Leake, born in Sonoma County in 1859, died September 22 at Willows, Glenn County, survived by two sons. She was affiliated with Berryessa Parlor No. 192 N.D.G.W.

Mrs. Margaret Brownlee-Durbin, born in Solano County in 1857, died September 24 near Napa City survived by a husband and a son.

Mrs. Mary Tyler-Simmons, born in San Mateo County in 1854, died September 24 at San Jose, Santa Clara County, survived by a husband.

Mrs. Elizabeth Venable-Albright, born in Contra Costa County in 1856, died September 26 at Los Angeles City survived by two children.

Mrs. Helen Buzzell-Reed, born at Sutter Fort (now Sacramento City) in 1845, died September 26 at Hillsboro, San Mateo County, survived by a daughter. She was affiliated with Alta Parlor No. 3 N.D.G.W. (San Francisco), and is said to have been the first child born to American parents in the Sacramento Valley. Her father, Joseph Buzzell, a Pioneer of the early '40s, in 1845 served in the California Battalion under Captain John C. Fremont.

Mrs. Hattie Baruch-Olcovich, born in Mariposa County in 1857, died October 1 at San Francisco survived by two children.

Jared Harrison Darrow, born in Tuolumne County in 1856, died October 3 at Santa Cruz City survived by a wife and two daughters.

E. Lee Crafts, born in Sierra County in 1859, died October 3 at Alleghany.

Edward C. Williams, born in Monterey County in 1856, died October 5 at Santa Cruz City survived by a wife and three children. He was a grandson of James Watson, Pioneer of 1830, and Mariana Escamilla-Watson, descendant of one of the early Monterey County families.

Mrs. Gracias Palamantes-Machado, born in Los Angeles County in 1833, died October 5 at Los Angeles City survived by three children. She was a daughter of Tomas Palamantes who, with the Machado family, at one time owned the 147,000-acre Ballona grant, the center of which is now Culver City.

Mrs. Alice Jane Harris-Lear, born in Yolo County in 1854, died October 5 at Colusa City survived by two sons.

Mrs. Victoria Kaiser, born at Greenwood, El Dorado County, in 1852, died there October 5 survived by five children.

Mrs. Susie Clow, born in Sacramento County in 1856, died October 7 at Santa Cruz City survived by a son.

Mrs. Clotilda Bernero, born in Glenn County in 1859, died October 9 at Jackson Gate, Amador County, survived by seven children.

Frank Happersberger, born in Placer County in 1858, died October 10 at San Anselmo, Marin County, survived by two sons. He was a sculptor of note, among his works being the Garfield and the Lick monuments in San Francisco.

Mrs. Olive Shaw-Parlow, born in El Dorado County in 1854, died October 10 at Sacramento City. She was a daughter of John Shaw, Pioneer of 1849.

Gus Valencia, born in Santa Clara County in 1835, died October 11 near San Rafael, Marin County.

George F. Baldwin, born in Shasta County in 1859, died October 13 near Lonoak, San Benito County, survived by a wife.

Louis J. Harrison, born in San Francisco in 1858, died October 16 at Los Angeles City survived by a wife and five children.

Mrs. Annie Buchler-Hughes, born in El Dorado County in 1857, died October 17 at Georgetown survived by a husband and five children.

Charles E. Durgan, born in Tuolumne County in 1859, died October 17 at Jamestown.

Rodeo—Bakersfield, Kern County, will stage its first annual rodeo, November 12 and 13.

CALIFORNIA HAPPENINGS OF FIFTY YEARS AGO

Thomas R. Jones

(COMPILED EXPRESSLY FOR THE GRIZZLY BEAR.)

CALIFORNIA'S QUADRENNIAL STATE election was held November 7, 1882, and it was a Democratic landslide. Few Republicans secured even a look-in at the ballot-box. General George M. Stoneman, Democratic nominee for Goveruor, received 90,694 votes, and Morris M. Estee, the Republican nominee, 67,175. The Democrats elected the state's entire congressional delegation of six. Among the successful ones was "Jim" Budd of Stockton, San Joaquin County, who made a celebrated buckboard campaign and defeated the heretofore invincible Republican warhorse, Frank Page. The State Legislature, also, became overwhelmingly Democratic.

Thanksgiving Day was November 30. With a wet winter in view, and plenty of rain to satisfy the wants of the miners, the farmers and the livestock men, an optimistic feeling prevailed and everybody celebrated. The godly attended church services, while the others had sporting events, dinners, grand balls, etc. Drink emporiums gave their numerous patrons a free roast-turkey lunch. Times were never better in California.

Wheat, selling for $1.70 and barley for $1.40 a cental, and hay for $16 a ton, made the farmers a good profit, and the hopraisers, disposing of their crops at a dollar a pound, were getting rich. Dressed turkey retailed at 20c, prime roast beef 9c, mutton 4c and pork 6c a pound. Chickens were 50c each, and butter 35c a pound. California-layed eggs brought 50c a dozen, while those from Iowa retailed at 35c. To supply the demand, potatoes had to be brought from Salt Lake City, and were selling at one cent a pound.

November was a month of freakish weather. Rain, beginning on the 1st, continued for a week, and a chilling norther came along on the 11th. A fortnight of frosty mornings followed, with the thermometer going below zero at Truckee, Nevada County, and as low as 22 degrees in the valleys. The month's rainfall of 3.22 inches brought the season's total up to 7.42 inches.

A brilliant aurora borealis, shooting red beams of light from the North Pole to the zenith, appeared the night of November 15. It was of fan shape, and with its streaks of red lined with blue was described as one of the most dazzling ever seen. At the same time, the savants at Berkeley, Alameda County, announced three large sun spots, visible through smoked glasses. So, the eyes of California's citizens were trained heavenward.

During the month, sixty-nine vessels arrived at San Francisco. Seventeen from Australia and five from British Columbia were ladened with coal, six from Honolulu had cargoes of sugar, three from Peru brought nitrates for the manufacture of powder, and three from the South Sea Islands had cargoes of oranges.

General John Bidwell donated to the California Immigration Association, for exhibition purposes, nineteen varieties of wheat and a pumpkin three and one-third feet in circumference grown in Butte County.

Santa Cruz County dairymen organized a protective association to fight the sale of oleomargarine, popularly known as "bull butter." Their lead was being followed by butter producers of other counties, for the sale of the substitute, "ole," at about half the price that genuine butter could be marketed, was affecting the dairymen of the state financially.

The first carload of apples to be shipped out of California by rail went from Shingle Springs, El Dorado County, November 13, destined for Denver, Colorado.

H. F. Buckley of Merced County had a sixty-one-acre hop yard. He sold the yield for $26,000, making a $21,000 profit. H. Wittenbrock of Sacramento County had sold his hop crop for $85,000. Had he held it until this month, November, he would have received an additional $50,000.

The stage from Cloverdale, Sonoma County, to Lakeport, Lake County, was stopped four miles from the former place by a lone man who took away the expressbox and the mailbags.

The Nevada Hydraulic Company at New York Flat, Nevada County, made its final cleanup and sent the product, $22,000 worth of golddust, to Marysville, Yuba County. Six men, armed with sawed-off shotguns, guarded the treasure.

Mr. and Mrs. Frederick Cox and Mr. and Mrs. C. W. Clark, who were married at a double wedding ceremony Thanksgiving Day, November 29, 1857, celebrated at Sacramento City November 29 their silver wedding anniversaries. Hundreds of the oldtimers of California North attended the grand social event. Cox and Clark, as young men, formed a partnership in the early '50s and made millions from land and livestock investments. Mrs. Cox and Mrs. Clark subsequently became widows and, strange to relate, both died several years ago on the same day.

T. Lundy arrived from London with a proposition from a company of English promoters to supply San Francisco and other cities with water drawn from the Blue Lakes in Alpine County and other Sierra ponds. It was proposed to use the Mokelumne River for a canal to the foothills. The promoters had purchased the land they intended to use.

The Judson Manufacturing Company of Emeryville, Alameda County, turned out November 15 the first lot of tacks produced in California. One hundred and fifty men were employed, and the product was being shipped to foreign countries.

Fires during November caused heavy financial losses: Schambacher tannery, Watsonville, Santa Cruz County, 2nd, $20,000; several buildings, Santa Cruz City, 7th, $10,000; Lyman House, Point Arena, Mendocino County, 10th, $15,000; palatial residence, Samuel M. Wilson, San Francisco, 16th, $100,000; block business houses, Wilmington, Los Angeles County, 13th, $50,000; Fry's shinglemill, near Eureka, Humboldt County, 15th, $30,000; Golden Eagle livery stable, Sacramento City, 28th, $40,000.

A building erected at the corner of Sacramento and Webster streets, San Francisco, was dedicated November 4 and christened Cooper Institute. Built by Dr. L. C. Lane, it opened as a medical college November 16 with a faculty c sixteen prominent physicians. It is now know as Stanford Medical School, an adjunct of Star ford University.

E. Pickett, popularly known as the politics "stormy petrel" and nicknamed "The Philosc pher," died at Merced City November 17. H arrived at Sutter Fort in 1844, and was the firs White man tried for homicide in California. H shot a man in selfdefense and was tried for th deed at the Fort. He became famous as a per renial issuer of pamphlets discussing politica topics of the times, and one day occupied th seat of a supreme court judge, claiming he ha as much right to usurp it as the judge, who, h claimed, had not been legally chosen. Charge with contempt of court, he languished in jai many weeks before being freed.

John W. Simonton, publisher of the San Fran cisco "Call" and "Bulletin," died in Napa Valle November 2 at the age of 60. He came to Cali fornia in 1850 and a few days after arriving be came a publisher.

H. N. Nutting, who had served four terms a district attorney of San Mateo County, was No vember 30 standing upon the sidewalk at Red wood City, waiting for a funeral procession t pass, when he dropped dead.

R. F. Wilson of Lemoore, Kings County, wa accidentally killed November 11 while firing a anvil salute in celebration of the Democratic vic tory at the polls.

W. S. Reed of Oakland, Alameda County, wa drowned in San Francisco Bay November 5, th waves of a ferryboat capsizing the boat in whic he was sailing.

James, 6-year-old son of District Attorney E J. Edwards of Tulare County, was accidentall killed November 5 while on a hunting trip wit his father.

James B. Smith, a fisherman living near Sant Ana, Orange County, November 2 killed his 14 year-old son by cutting his throat. He claime to have received a message from the Lord to d so, and his wife corroborated the claim. He ha called at the postoffice thrice during the previou week, saying he was expecting a message fro the Lord, but not receiving it there, it must hav reached him by some other route. Smith was firm believer in the Bible, and in defense of hi act cited the experience of Abraham.

A passenger train struck the rear of a freigh near Davis, Yolo County, November 19 and th caboose caught fire. Brakeman William Haggett was burned to death.

The 3-year-old son of P. Ryan of Smartsville Yuba County, while throwing chips November 28 into a mining ditch to watch them float away, fell in and was drowned.

Three children of a San Francisco citizen named Sullivan died of ptomaine poisoning after eating of a mess of fish.

George J. Reek and James E. Anderson had a shooting affray November 4 at Eureka, Humboldt County, and the latter was fatally wounded.

"This country, with its institutions, belongs to the people who inhabit it. Whenever they shall grow weary of the existing Government, they can exercise their constitutional right of amending it or their revolutionary right to dismember or overthrow it."—Abraham Lincoln.

Household Show—The Southern California Retail Grocers Association will stage its eighth annual Food and Household Show at Los Angeles City, November 13-19.

ANOTHER EPIC

SAN FRANCISCO—SUNDAY, OCTOBER 9, marked another epic in the history of the Order of Native Daughters of the Golden West Home. Two hundred and fifty reservations were made, and an equal number could not be accommodated. Carrying out the Washington bicentennial theme, the tables were beautifully decorated in red, white and blue, and each grand officer was presented with a corsage of those colors. Past Grand Presidents Dr. Louise C. Heilbron and Mary E. Bell were the hostesses and provided an entertaining and instructive program.

Dr. Heilbron, originator of the Loyalty Pledge, by means of which the entire mortgage on the Home was liquidated in three years' time, presented a beautiful solid bronze plaque, 29x31, bearing the names of all Subordinate Parlors which have paid in full their pledges. In presenting the plaque she said, "I ask you to accept this plaque in the name of the Native Daughters of the Golden West." In speaking of the work accomplished by the three Grand Presidents succeeding her,—Esther Sullivan, Estelle Evans and Evelyn Carlson—Dr. Heilbron remarked that it was singular their names began with "E," typifying energy, efficiency and enthusiasm, and she told the part each had played in the liquidation of the mortgage.

Past Grand President Dr. Mariana Bertola, chairman Grand Parlor Home Committee, in the absence of Grand President Anna Mixon Armstrong accepted the plaque, and spoke of the wonderful results accomplished by the Subordinate Parlors in contributing the amount necessary to pay the mortgage. Congresswoman Florence Kahn spoke on the work accomplished at the last session of the Federal Congress. Past Grands Sullivan, Evans and Carlson complimented Past Grand Heilbron for the thought of the Loyalty Pledge.

The plaque, unveiled by Emma Boarman Wright and Henrietta O'Neill, charter members Ursula No. 1, the "mother" Parlor, is adorned with a laurel wreath and inscribed as follows: "Honor Roll Subordinate Parlors Native Daughters of the Golden West whose contributions of Loyalty Pledges made possible our Worthy Achievement—the Native Daughter Home. Cornerstone laid by Grand Parlor, 1928. Building dedicated, Jan. 12, 1929. Mortgage canceled, Grand Parlor 1932. 1929 Californiana. 1930 Marysville, Palo Alto, Camp Far West, Imogen, Buena Vista, Anna K. Bidwell, Golden State, Mary E. Bell. 1931 California, South Butte, Clear Lake, Orinda, Marinita, Vallejo, Presidio, Dolores, La Bandera, Ano Nuevo, La Estrella, Antioch, Copa de Oro, Victory. 1932 Liberty, Ursula, La Junta, Alta, Miocene, Woodland, Sea Point, Amapola, James Lick, Marguerite, Eshcol, Oakdale, Fairfax, Morada, Mission, Golden Gate, Castro, Tamelpa, Colus, El Dorado."

DR. LOUISE C. HEILBRON,
Originator the Loyalty Pledge.

The San Francisco N.D.G.W. glee club rendered several selections, and as the representative of each Parlor that has paid its Loyalty Pledge was introduced, girls of the club, in colonial costumes, presented each with a boquet of red, white and blue flowers. Past Grand Estelle M. Evans charmed everyone with her wonderful voice, rendering "Trees," "Estralita" and "Sweet Mystery of Life." The following Subordinate Parlors responded to rollcall: Copa de Oro No. 105 (Hollister), Dolores No. 169 (San Francisco), Califia No. 22 (Sacramento), Sutter No. 111 (Sacramento), Ursula No. 1 (Jackson), Morada No. 199 (Modesto), La Junta No. 203 (Saint Helena), Golden Gate No. 158 (San Francisco), Alta No. 3 (San Francisco), Marguerite No. 12 (Placerville), Castro No. 178 (San Francisco), Eshcol No. 16 (Napa), Oakdale No. 125 (Oakdale), Orinda No. 56 (San Francisco), Miocene No. 228 (Taft), Fairfax No. 225 (Fairfax), El Dorado No. 186 (Georgetown), Colus No. 194 (Colusa), Woodland No. 90 (Woodland), Reina del Mar No. 126 (Santa Barbara), Santa Cruz No. 26 (Santa Cruz), El Pescadero No. 82 (Tracy), Marysville No. 162 (Marysville), Camp Far West No. 218 (Wheatland), Annie K. Bidwell No. 168 (Chico), Palo Alto No. 229 (Palo Alto), Golden State No. 50 (San Francisco), Imogen No. 134 (Sierraville), Buena Vista No. 68 (San Francisco), Mary E. Bell No. 224 (Dixon), Marinita No. 198 (San Rafael), Ano Neuvo No. 180 (Pescadero), South Butte No. 226 (Sutter), Vallejo No. 195 (Vallejo), Minerva No. 2 (San Francisco), Stirling No. 146 (Pittsburg), Antioch No. 223 (Antioch).

Wild Life Conserved—Wild life in California is conserved in thirty-two state game reserves, covering a total area of more than 2,000,000 acres, within the national forests of the state.

Dairy Show—The annual Pacific Slope Dairy Show will be held at Oakland, Alameda County, November 12-18.

CROSSED THE BAR --- GONE AHEAD

TWO SPLENDID SPECIMENS OF NAtive-Californian manhood greatly admired within the Order of Native Sons of the Golden West—Past Grand Presidents Dr. Charles William Decker and William Joseph Hayes—crossed the bar to the other shore the latter part of last month, as briefly chronicled in The Grizzly Bear for October 1932.

PAST GRAND DECKER

Dr. Charles William Decker was born at Sutterville, Sacramento County, March 31, 1855, and died at Palo Alto, Santa Clara County, September 25, 1932, survived by two children. He affiliated with California Parlor No. 1 (San Francisco), August 23, 1877. At the Sixth Grand Parlor (San Francisco 1883) he was elected Grand Treasurer, at the Seventh Grand Parlor (Marysville 1884) Grand Lecturer, at the Eighth Grand Parlor (San Jose 1885) Grand Vice-president, at the Ninth Grand Parlor (Woodland 1886) Grand President, at the Tenth Grand Parlor (Nevada City 1887) Past Grand President. Excepting the Seventeenth, Nineteenth and Twenty-second, he attended every Grand Parlor from the Sixth to and including the Fifty-fifth.

During the term of Dr. Decker as Grand President, these Subordinate Parlors were instituted: Sierra No. 85, now defunct, at Forest Hill, Placer County; McLane, now Calistoga, No. 86 at Calistoga, Napa County; Mount Bally No. 87 at Weaverville, Trinity County; Golden Star No. 88, now defunct, at Rohnerville, Humboldt County; Benicia No. 89, now defunct, at Benicia, Solano County; Santa Cruz No. 90 at Santa Cruz City; Georgetown No. 91 at Georgetown, El Dorado County; Downieville No. 92 at Downieville, Sierra County; Ferndale No. 93 at Ferndale, Humboldt County; Golden Nugget No. 94 at Sierra City, Sierra County; Seaside No. 95 at Halfmoon Bay, San Mateo County; Las Positas No. 96 at Livermore, Alameda County; Santa Lucia No. 97 at Salinas, Monterey County; Meridian No. 98, now defunct, at Nord, Butte County; Lassen No. 99, now defunct, at Susanville, Lassen County; Mount Diablo No. 101 at Martinez, Contra Costa County; Glen Ellen No. 102 at Glen Ellen, Sonoma County; Silver Tip No. 103, now defunct, at Vacaville, Solano County; Bay City No. 104 at San Francisco; Niantic No. 105 at San Francisco. Of the twenty Parlors instituted, he personally conducted twelve of the ceremonies. He instituted a greater number of Parlors than any Grand President.

At funeral services for Past Grand President Decker conducted in Native Sons Building, San Francisco, Past Grand President Lewis F. Byington spoke as follows:

"One for whom the brothers of this fraternity have long held a tender and high affection and regard in the maturity of his years has reached the end of life's journey. It is fitting that the final word of tribute due him should be spoken within this building dedicated to the patriotic work of the sons of California. Love of California, its history and traditions, and veneration for the early pioneers of the West, was the dominant characteristic in the life of Past Grand President Charles W. Decker. He often expressed the wish that when he passed away the ceremonies attending his funeral should be held in this building, the home of the fraternity, with the brothers gathered round whose friendship he so deeply cherished, and that the ceremonies should be conducted by the Past Grand Presidents with whom he had been associated, in close ties of affection, for many years.

"Brother Decker was born in Sutterville, Sacramento County, March 31, 1855, and died at Palo Alto, September 25th. The more than seventy-seven years of his life spanned the period reaching almost back to the time of the discovery of gold by Marshal, on through the years of our state's matchless growth and to her present unrivalled supremacy in the Union; from the days of the slow ox team crossing the prairies to those of the aeroplane circling the earth.

"When he was a boy his parents conducted a hotel in Sacramento, and he well remembered the miners from the mountains, who stopped there, entrusting their buckskin bags of gold to his mother, as depositary, and many, when departing, presented her with a golden nugget from their store. The memory of those days was cherished in his heart and when the fraternity of the Native Sons of the Golden West was organized in 1875, to perpetuate the memory of the men and events of the 'days of '49,' he was among the first to enroll. No more loyal son of California had his name upon the roster. He was inspired by the aims and purposes of the fraternity; he loved his country and his state.

"In 1886, at Woodland, he was elected Grand President of the Order. During his administration he was untiring in his zeal for building up and strengthening the organization. At his own expense, he visited every section of the state where he thought a Parlor could be instituted and, as a result, 21 new Parlors were brought into the fraternity. An unprecedented increase. In years devoted to his profession, he was one of the oldest practitioners of dentistry in the state and by vote of the people had served San Francisco as a member of the Board of Education.

"No patriotic celebration, under the auspices of the Order, has been held in which he was not a participant and he attended practically every session of the Grand Parlor since its organiza-

DR. CHARLES WILLIAM DECKER.

WILLIAM JOSEPH HAYES.

tion. Neither the demands of business nor the infirmities of age could keep him away. I well remember when in 1931 Past Grands Ryan, Cutler and myself called upon him at Palo Alto on our way to the Grand Parlor at Merced, and found him ill and under orders from his physicians not to travel, he insisted on accompanying us, and, when seated in the automobile and on his way to greet his brothers, the ills and cares of life seemed to drop from his shoulders and joy filled his heart. Presented to the delegates at the session as one of our oldest and best tried members, and greeted with the heartiest of applause, tears filled his eyes and emotion choked his utterance.

"At the recent state celebration of Admission Day in San Francisco, weakened by illness, it was impossible for him to be present; but he was not forgotten by the loyal members of the fraternity for his old time friend, Brother Richard Veale of General Winn Parlor, veteran sheriff of Contra Costa County, moved by kindly and brotherly impulse, had in the parade an automobile beautifully decorated with flowers in remembrance of Charley Decker and bearing, prominently displayed, a large framed photograph of our Past Grand President. He often recalled, in fond and loving remembrance, those with whom he had worked in the early days of the Order and who, as the companions of his youth and manhood, were ever cherished.

"We leave him today to his silent rest in the bosom of the state he loved so well. Life has been made brighter for all of us who have enjoyed his companionship and shared with him the pleasures which come to those who dwell on California's soil, and as at last, in answer to the final summons, he moves on to the silent realm beyond the stars, I see him turn and cast one loving, lingering look at the hills of his native land and smile farewell to the friends here left behind."

PAST GRAND HAYES

William Joseph Hayes was born at Havilah, Kern County, December 25, 1885, and died at Oakland, Alameda County, September 27, 1932, survived by a wife and four children. He affiliated with Berkeley Parlor No. 210, June [illegible] 1909. His first Grand Parlor was the Thirty-fourth (Santa Cruz 1911). At the Thirty-eighth (San Francisco 1915) Grand Parlor he was elected Grand Trustee, and was re-elected at the Thirty-ninth (Modesto 1916), the Fortieth (Redding 1917) and the Forty-second (Yosemite Valley 1919) Grand Parlors. At the Forty-third (San Diego 1920) Grand Parlor he was elected Grand Third Vice-president, at the Forty-fourth (Stockton 1921) Grand Parlor, Grand Second Vice-president, at the Forty-fifth (Oakland 1922) Grand Parlor, Grand First Vice-president and at the Forty-sixth (Santa Barbara 1923) Grand Parlor, Grand President. For many years he was a member of the Grand Parlor History Committee, at the time of his passing being chairman thereof.

Past Grand President Lewis F. Byington speaking at the funeral services for Past Grand Hayes, said:

"In response to the request of the Grand Officers of our fraternity and of those who were near and dear to Past Grand President William J. Hayes, I rise to pay a just tribute to those gentle qualities of mind and heart which earned for him the friendship of all who knew him, and to his sterling character of manhood which commanded the highest admiration of those in every walk of life.

"In passing along the varied course of life with its trials and tribulations, its joys and triumphs, it is the extreme good fortune of many of us to meet at times a fellow-traveler whose kindly soul, gentle ways and nobility of character draw us to him in bonds of friendship which time can never sever. Such a friend and brother was William J. Hayes and at the shrine of friendship we are mourners today.

"Yesterday we bore to his eternal rest one of the oldest Past Grand Presidents of our fraternity, Dr. Decker; one whose years had reached almost four score and whose long and honorable service had brought to him the respect and love of his associates. Today we stand by the side of one who was stricken down at the high noon of vigorous manhood and whose honorable career and success in life we believed had just begun.

"Past Grand President Hayes was born in [Kern] County on Christmas Day, 1885. As a boy he was keen in the pursuit of knowledge and by his individual efforts acquired a liberal education and was graduated from the University of California. He thereafter zealously and successfully followed the profession of the law and held positions of honor and trust in the community. Deeply interested in the history of California and in the patriotic work of the Native Sons of the Golden West he joined Berkeley Parlor in 1909, and in 1923, at Santa Barbara was elected Grand President of the Order. He was a zealous member, spreading the influence of the fraternity and ever teaching its patriotic and historical purposes, while his companionable ways and fine personality tied all with whom he came in contact to him in bonds of friendship. He was a loving and kind husband, a tender and affectionate father, a patriotic and a loyal man, a generous, faithful and lovable friend. From our association with him springs no feeling other than fond regret at his passing and the most tender of recollections. Our grief at parting from him is not unmixed with pride. He has left to his loved wife and children the heritage of an honored name and the memory of kind acts and noble deeds.

"We realize more than ever on occasions like this that it is alloted to all men to die. Surrounded by family and friends, with health and strength and in a land of the beauty and wealth of California, life is indeed pleasant and joyful [illegible]

HEALTH CONSERVATION GOES WITH RED CROSS RELIEF

INTERPRETING THE MAGNITUDE OF THE unemployment problem as "a national disaster," the American Red Cross is courageously facing the issue, relying upon the support of the devoted legions whose membership dues make possible her program of humanitarian service to enable her to carry on.

The demands of the coming winter from our millions of unemployed constitute a definite obligation on the part of those blessed with jobs. Last year, through its local chapters, the Red Cross aided 337,000 families in the unemployment category, representing some 3,000,000 individuals; 76,000 families in 130 coal mining counties were also aided.

In addition to this form of rehabilitation, the Greatest Mother gave succor to the victims of sixty disasters, within the confines of Continental United States, affecting thirty-one states. These figures include 242,824 persons in the northwest areas affected by drought and insect plagues; 13,000 victims of tornado in the southeastern states, and 53,000 flood sufferers in Mississippi and Louisiana.

Concomitantly with these outstanding items the normal activities of the organization to ex-service men and their dependents, public health projects and other services were carried on. During the winter months alone the cases of 400,000 ex-service men were handled by the American Red Cross. Many of these cases necessitated hours of tedious detail, and correspondence with dozens of other chapters in the search for corroborative data and witnesses whose supporting affidavits were indispensable in substantiating claims for disability compensation. Information on new legislation and the Federal Government provisions both for active-service men and veterans of all wars and of peace-time service, is relayed to the chapters by Red Cross national headquarters. Thus chapters are enabled at all times to supply veterans with up-to-minute data as to their rights and to assist them in proper presentation of their state and federal claims.

To meet the encroachments of disease and malnutrition, always rife in periods of distress and financial stringency, an army of 750 Red Cross nurses has given nursing and maternity care, often constituting the sole relief agency to be found in rural communities. They are giving post-partum care and bedside nursing to families unable to pay for them, safeguarding the rising generation from disease by inspecting schoolchildren, urging parents to have physical defects, thus discovered, corrected at Red Cross and other welfare clinics, immunizing them against communicable diseases by vaccination and inoculation, and in other ways carrying on health education programs.

In twenty-three states where the long drought of 1930-31 had reduced millions of our fellow-citizens to abject want, the immediate succor in the form of food and clothing supplied by the Red Cross was later supplemented by the distribution of more than 300,000 packages of garden seed—enough to cover 100,000 acres. Each package weighed about five pounds and contained a score of varieties of the best tested seed, sufficient to give each recipient from one-quarter to one-half acre of vegetables.

Side by side with the seed distribution was carried on a countrywide canning project, with every housewife urged to can the surplus harvest for winter needs. Whenever instruction was needed in homes unused to this form of conservation, the Red Cross led the way in setting up local centers where experts of the United States Department of Agriculture and the Red Cross nutrition service gave daily demonstrations in canning fruits and vegetables.

In at least two-thirds of the chapters which make up the nationwide network of the American Red Cross, together with some 1,200 branches, unemployment problems are now being met. Hand in hand with distribution of the necessities of life have gone job campaigns and stimulation of public works, in order that the social menace of the soup kitchen might be obviated.

When, on March 7, 1932, the Federal Congress appropriated 40,000,000 bushels of wheat and authorized the American Red Cross to distribute it, requests poured in from more than 2,000 of the 3,600 chapters comprising the Red Cross membership at large. Every state in the Union was represented by these applications for relief. By August 20, the "Red Cross wheat" had replenished the larders of 3,387,156 families, representing some 15,000,000 individuals.

Subsequently the voting by the Congress of 500,000 bales of government-owned cotton for similar relief again made the American Red Cross the disburser of the donation. In thousands of Red Cross workrooms all over the land Red Cross volunteers are assembling, as in the days of the World War, to sew for their fellow-countrymen. It is estimated that 90,000 workers will be required for the task of making into garments the textiles into which the raw cotton is being manufactured. Nor will this gigantic contribution be sufficient to fill the demands of the destitute. As during the two previous winters, the flow of garments, new and reconditioned, from other sources must be continued.

From the membership dues pledged at the annual Roll Call between Armistice Day and Thanksgiving Day, the Red Cross derives the funds to finance these humanitarian projects. Don't neglect to enroll as a member!

At the blaze of high noon, or when the shadows of evening are stretched out, or when the mountain peaks put on the glory of the rising sun,' to the one who loves nature and can be inspired by all this, life is indeed a joy. But, as has been said, it is not man's to keep, for the Master camps on his trail and the night will come when the waxing and waning moon will look for him in vain. But a man's honor is his to keep. And when a good man passes to that land beyond our earthly vision his honor, and his character springing therefrom, should live on forever. The blessed gift of memory is given to man with which to recall the tender words, the loving smile, the noble deeds of those we cherished and have lost.

"And so it was with our brother William J. Hayes. He walked in the path of rectitude, he loved his God, he honored his country, he cherished his family and friends, he kept his honor bright. And these will go on forever as a heritage to his children and a fond memory to those who associated with him in fraternal and business life."

MARKED

FOLSOM (SACRAMENTO COUNTY)—UNder the auspices of Fern Parlor No. 123 N.D.G.W., the historic Wells-Fargo building here was marked with a bronze plaque September 25. President Mary H. Curry presided, and the Folsom high school band, directed by Charles W. Ball, contributed musical numbers. Speakers were Grand President Anna Mixon Armstrong and Past Grand President Esther R. Sullivan. The plaque was unveiled by Mrs. Sadie Winn-Brainard, whose grandfather, General Andrew Maver Winn, founded the Order of Native Sons of the Golden West. It is embellished with a covered wagon on its westward journey, and is inscribed: "Early Day Assay Office and Home of Wells Fargo and Co., 1860. Marker placed by Fern Parlor No. 123, Native Daughters Golden West, September 25, 1932." Grand President Armstrong's address follows, in full:

"Scattered up and down the State of California, in vale and mountain, by stream and along roadside, are located many ancient structures that enter into song and story, and around which is written much of the tradition, the romance and the history of our state.

"Outstanding among these, of course, are the old adobe missions—silent expressions of the devotion of godly men who planted the seeds of modern civilization in this golden west. Then we would, no doubt, name these old places along the Mother Lode, where foregathered John Marshall, Mark Twain, Bret Harte, Joaquin Miller and other famed oldtimers, and from which came much of the enchanting legend of the West. Nor would we forget the old buildings of Monterey, whence came the first laws governing our state, nor that focal point, Fort Sutter, from which radiated most of the early activity of this portion of California. All of these have an enduring place in our history.

"But there are other buildings of ancient origin that may claim our attention, built for commercial purposes but which the glamour of the time has surrounded with a sort of glory that intrigues our minds. You folks of Folsom have such a building, erected almost three-quarters of a century ago. It became the financial center of a wide expanse of country and the activities emanating from it had much to do with the material well-being of your early residents.

"Imagine with me, if you will, what transpired around this old Wells-Fargo building. We see from its vicinity the sturdy prospector lading, either himself or his burro, with pan and rocker, pick and shovel, heading for mountain or stream or gulch in quest of gold—and still more gold. We see him, thousands of him, returning successful; we see him seek these doors; we see him produce his pack—and we see the yellow gleaming metal poured upon the delicately adjusted balances to determine its worth. Maybe some of you have had that very experience.

"It is said that California saved the Union, back in the days of the Civil War, by the wealth of gold which she poured into the nation's lap. This building was erected in 1860, just prior to the beginning of that war. Who knows, how shall we tell, how much of that stream of gold flowed through these doors? Who can tell just how much of a part Folsom had in preserving a nation from disruption? At any rate, this building is worthy of preservation, and worthy of this memorial plaque, and as Grand President of the Native Daughters of the Golden West it is a sincere pleasure to join with my sisters of Fern Parlor of Folsom in marking this as an historic spot in California, the Golden State." At the conclusion of the ceremonies Fern Parlor entertained at luncheon, the guests, in addition to those participating in the program, including Grand Trustee Edna Briggs and Past Grand Presidents Dr. Eva R. Rasmussen and Dr. Louise C. Heilbron.

HISTORIC SAN BERNARDINO COUNTY SITE DESIGNATED BY MONUMENT.

Upland (San Bernardino County)—At the foot of Red Hill, near the intersection of Foothill boulevard and San Bernardino road, Ontario Parlor No. 251 N.D.G.W. erected a California Bear monument with bronze marker, which was unveiled October 12. The work was done under the supervision of the Parlor's history and landmarks section, Mrs. Frank Van Fleet chairman. A delightful prologue dealt in pageant form with the early history of the Indians, the Spanish and the covered wagon.

(Concluded on Page 18)

SAN FRANCISCO

MOST WORTHY CAUSE DESERVES MOST GENEROUS RESPONSE FROM ALL.

The San Francisco N.S.G.W. and N.D.G.W. Joint Committee for Homeless Children, a statewide child welfare organization, is perfecting plans for a costume ball to be held at Exposition Auditorium, Thanksgiving Eve, Wednesday, November 23. The funds raised will be contributed to the central committee of the Order to carry on the work of caring, and providing homes with the proper environment, for hundreds of waifs.

This committee had its inception in 1909 and has taken care of more than thirty-five hundred little orphans and abandoned children of California. It knows no race, no creed, no color, no birthplace, and its activities embrace welfare work among all needy children, whether native or adopted Californians. Due to the fact that it is statewide in character, it receives no financial assistance from local community chests or charitable organizations. A nominal admission fee of 50 cents is charged, to assist this worthy cause.

Commencing at 8 o'clock there will be a competitive drill by Native Daughter Parlors, also a contest for Native Son and Native Daughter drum corps, and at 9 o'clock the costume ball. Following are the officers: James L. Foley, Twin Peaks Parlor No. 214, chairman; Kittie Mullaney, Dolores Parlor No. 169, vice-chairman; Edna A. Urmy, Buena Vista Parlor No. 68, secretary; Bertha Mauser, Keith Parlor No. 137, financial secretary; Chas. A. Koenig, Golden Gate Parlor No. 29, treasurer.

DISTRICT MEETING.

September 30 was a wonderful evening for the local Native Daughters, because it was the district meeting of San Francisco County, and the new ritual was exemplified by the deputies under the supervision of Alice M. Lane of Castro Parlor. A large gathering, representing forty-six Parlors, assembled to welcome the Grand President to "Anna Mixon Armstrong Parlor No. 1932." The artistic decorations were symbolic of state and country.

The officers were gowned in beautiful evening attire, and as they entered in the opening march each carried a staff decorated with flowers in pastel shades; they formed a line across the hall, and at a given signal turned the staffs and spelled the words "We welcome our Anna" in silver lettering. Marshal Gertrude LaFortune presented the Grand President with a boquet of roses while the San Francisco N.D.G.W. glee club sang a welcome song. The ritual was exemplified by the following deputies: Loretta Cameron, Emma O'Meara, Gertrude LaFortune, Nora Schefflin, Lola Horgan, Merle Sandell, Mazie Roderick, Maud Daley, Helen Sprung, Nan J. Kelly, Mae Waring, Agnes M. Curry, Lena Wall, Mary Hayes, Adele Walsh, Pearl Wedde, Ida Mesquite. Assistants to the marshal were Deputies May McCarthy, Margaret Grant, Agnes Ryan, Margaret Barrett, Emily Ryan, Helen McMahon, Anna Dippell, Jewel Strei, Helen T. Mann, Myrtle Ross, Elizabeth Muller, Claire Lindsey.

Ann Godfrey read a brief history of the glee club and introduced the members, Director Lola Horgan and Organizer Agnes Curry. A very inspiring address was delivered by Grand President Armstrong. "To a Wild Rose" was rendered by the glee club. Remarks by Past Grands Evelyn Carlson, Eliza Keith, Margaret Hill, Emma G. Foley and May Boldeman, Grand Vice-president Irma Laird, Grand Marshal Gladys Noce, Grand Secretary Sallie Thaler, Grand Inside Sentinel Orinda Giannini, Grand Trustees Florence Boyle, Ethel Begley and Anna Thuesen, and Supervising Deputy Rene Mathias completed a very happy and interesting evening.

NATIVE DAUGHTER DOINGS.

President May L. MacDonald of Alta Parlor No. 3 has launched a program of activities and each month finds a new and novel feature introduced. During October there was the sport dance, which afforded an evening of pleasure for the members as well as being the means of increasing the funds of the Parlor; Mrs. Agnese L. Hughes was chairman of the delightful affair. October 25 was social night, the success of which was due to Mrs. Angeline Vest, an energetic worker. November 1, with Mrs. May L. MacDonald chairman and Mrs. Catherine O'Reilly subchairman, a benefit bridge-whist will be given; this will be an outstanding event of the winter.

September 22, Keith Parlor No. 137 tendered Past President Gertrude LaFortune a reception. The evening was spent with various members and friends, after which all retired to the banquethall and partook of refreshments. The guest of honor was the recipient of a gift presented by President Gladys Cruise. October 13, Miss Lorraine MacCauley, a member of Keith, was given a miscellaneous shower previous to her marriage to Francis Klein. She received many gifts. Her marriage took place at Mission Dolores, October 16.

Dolores Parlor No. 169 held a delightful Hallowe'en costume party October 12. Many games were played. Chairman Ida Carrigan was dressed as Hot-Cha and gave interpretations of South Sea Islands dances. Hazel Nelson danced a spring dance, while Juanita Blanchfield favored with piano selections. A spanish supper was served at tables decorated with Hallowe'en favors. Agnes McVerry was the honored guest. Plans are now being made to organize a drill team in the Parlor. At the district meeting three candidates were initiated for Dolores.

Grand President Anna M. Armstrong paid her official visit to Castro Parlor No. 178 October 19. A banquet preceding the meeting was presided over by Supervising Deputy Alice M. Lane. A large percentage of the membership was present to greet the Grand President who, in the course of her remarks, paid high tribute to the floorwork of the Parlor officials. Refreshments were served in the banquethall, where Hallowe'en was the motif for the decorations. A monster whist party is being planned for the benefit of the Parlor's relief fund; Paula Hizinger is chairman of the committee, which is working hard to make the affair a huge success.

The San Francisco N.D.G.W. glee club recently met at the home of Mrs. Lola Horgan for reorganization. Members of the club, under the direction of Mrs. Horgan, have endeavored to perfect themselves in order to assist or take entire charge of musical features of official visits, breakfasts, etc. Officers are Lola Horgan of La Estrella Parlor, director; Ruby D. Bried of El Vespero Parlor, secretary; Claire Bolman of Alta Parlor, treasurer; Anne Godfrey of El Vespero Parlor, publicity chairman. September 24, at the home of Ethel Browning, one of the members, a delightful party was given by the club; Mrs. Agnes M. Curry, organizer, was the guest of honor.

NATIVE SON DOINGS.

November 4, the Extension of the Order Committee will feature an educational program in the rooms of the Grizzly Bear Club. Arrangements are being made for the annual basketball league. The committee has taken an option on headquarters in Santa Rosa for next year's Admission Day, September 9, celebration.

The monthly whist parties of Hesperian Parlor No. 137 are proving quite successful. They are held the first Thursday of each month, with Jim O'Rourke as chairman. A wonderful time is promised those who attend November 3. There will be sixteen hands, with an entertainment feature between every fourth hand. Refreshments will be served after the play, and from then until midnight dancing will be in order, Hesperian orchestra furnishing the music.

In Memoriam

ISABELLE L. CUDDY.

To the Officers and Members of Bahia Vista Parlor No. 167 N.D.G.W.—We, your committee appointed to draft resolutions to the memory of our departed sister, Isabelle L. Cuddy, respectfully submit the following:

Whereas, Almighty God, in His infinite wisdom, has called to the Heavenly Parlor on High our esteemed and beloved sister, Isabelle L. Cuddy, a charter member of our Parlor; and whereas, Bahia Vista Parlor has lost a loyal member, her sister and two brothers a devoted and affectionate sister, and her many acquaintances a true friend. To know her was to love her.

Resolved, That the sympathy of the Parlor be extended to the bereaved sister and brothers, and that the charter of the Parlor be draped in mourning for a period of thirty days; that a copy of these resolutions be sent to the family; that a copy be spread in full upon the minutes of the Parlor, and that a copy be published in The Grizzly Bear Magazine.

LOUISE McDOUGALL,
ANNA QUINN,
ANNA YTTING,
Committee.

Oakland, October 13, 1932.

Potential Vote—Slightly more than 70,000,000 persons in the United States will be of voting age on election day, November 8, according to an estimate of the Federal Commerce Department census bureau.

CLASSIFIED DIRECTORY
SAN FRANCISCO NATIVE SONS

ATTORNEYS-AT-LAW.

LEWIS F. BYINGTON.
Balboa Bldg., 593 Market St.
Phone: SUtter 4949.

WILLIAM P. CAUBU.
607-615 Claus Spreckels Bldg., 703 Market St.
Phone: SUtter 25.

FLETCHER A. CUTLER.
1217 Russ Bldg., 235 Montgomery St.
Phone: SUtter 3430.

EDWARD J. LYNCH.
Mills Bldg., 220 Montgomery St.
Phone: DOuglas 1282.

JESSE H. MILLER.
712 DeYoung Bldg., Market & Kearny.
Phone: DOuglas 1953.

DENTISTS.

FRANK I. GONZALEZ, D.D.S.
Dentist. Pyorrhea Treatment and Prevention.
1116-1118 Flood Bldg., 870 Market St.
Office: SUtter 5286—Phones—Res.: BAyview 1300.

OPTOMETRIST.

L. A. WERNER.
915 Howard Bldg., 209 Post St.
Phone: EXbrook 3915.

Feminine World's Fads and Fancies

PREPARED ESPECIALLY FOR THE GRIZZLY BEAR BY ANNA STOERMER

THE NEW ENSEMBLES ARE JUST AS easy to make as frocks. You will practically live in an ensemble this winter. A three-quarters or a seven-eighths length garment is the coat news of the season. Matching frocks or suits are smartest ensembles. With these, "short-ɡ" coats are stunning. The jacket costume is ıvorite and, of course, you have heard about hip-length jackets.

'elvet heads the list, both for entire suits and :hes of trimming. Velveteen is popular, too, so are plaids and ribbed woolens. Crinkled /et and velvet lace are highlights of the new ıals.

lack velvet is smartest for princess or puffed-ıve frocks. You will double the chic of any :k this season if you remember that two fab-ı and two colors are twice as smart as one. › new combinations are wool with velvet, ɔoth with crinkled silks, velvet lace with in, or satin alone in black with white, gray emerald green.

We cannot decide which we like better, the ıic or princess frock, so smart women are aring both, and looking perfectly stunning. grand example is the princess, looking its regal best in dull black satin with the shiny side used for trimming. The tunic, of course, will be in very rough crinkle crepe—and do not forget to use fur trimming.

Remember whether you are going with or without a collar this winter, the neckline must be high. It will be becoming, and you will, if you are clever, measure your style by the width of your sleeves.

Lace trimmings are used on velvet, and fur trimmings are used on everything. New scarfs, buttons and fur are details that are different. Tailored lines call for diagonal seamings, slashes here and there, and accented points with buttons.

For business or general wear, here are some good starts for the smartest, most inexpensive winter wardrobe you have ever had. You will need one of the new slim coats in beige or brown, and you can wear this over all the newest frocks in colors such as green, wine, bright red and blue.

You should have two or three sheer woolen frocks for general daytime wear, not to mention a few heavy rough crepes for more-important afternoon engagements. In choosing them, remember that broad cape-collars, bows, puffed sleeves, grouped buttons and checks are fashion details with a future.

It is no problem for the mature woman to dress smartly this season, the new silhouette being so slim and graceful of line. Choose velvet, sheer woolens and any of the crinkly silks, and don't forget fabric contrast is necessary.

The most important of all frocks is dull, creamy-white velvet for the bride; mossy, uncut or novelty crinkled velvet for her attendant, and deep, rich lyons velvet for mother. These will be smart long after the wedding, and may be worn to parties later.

With a few new blouses and skirts you may have many changes—and remember, skirts should be slender. High necklines and fancy sleeves are very new and very chic. Satin yokes or collars and cuffs are worn on woolen dresses. Black is smartest, then deep rich brown, red, green and purplish blue. Checks, stripes and new color contrasts make the young mode gay.

For the well-dressed juniors, one of the very attractive models which the fall has introduced is the jumper suit or frock. Simple in style, it is becoming, not only for girls of the younger age, but also for older girls. They may be made to resemble a two-piece suit, with the double-breasted effect. Made of your favorite color, the guimpe is of plaid georgette. The effective color combinations are red, orange and brown. The younger set wear wool and favor swagger plaids. Every smart junior knows that a generous supply of pretty underthings and gay pajamas are most important items in her wardrobe.

Charming gift suggestions are being offered at this time at all the shops, and the gift that is appreciated most is that which has your own fine needlework to add to its charm and value. Handmade lingerie, pajamas, lacy bed jackets, dainty boudoir pillows, guest towels and many novelties are to be had in great varieties. The shops are bulging now with new ideas.

For the little ones, we have the circus pets. Make them cuddly and well stuffed. You may buy the printed patterns and make them up of novelty materials. Horses and dogs of every description, elephants and, of course, dolls, large and small. The time is slipping by quickly, and the holiday rush will be with us before we realize.

With winter, comes the revival of the cape. Perhaps it should not be called a revival, for the new capes are not much like any that we have seen for a long time. They are new, if any fashion can really be called new. There are capes of all varieties: sturdy, all-weather affairs of tweed; frilled little things that just cover the shoulders and are made of velvet or soft fur; jacket-length and dress-length capes.

One of the most successful capes is finger-tip length, of black velvet, trimmed with ermine or mink. The collar wraps closely around the throat, with the outside end tucked into an immense buttonhole just below the throatline. The cape swings free from the shoulders, and the arm slits are trimmed with fur, forming a comfortable cuff.

Top coats are tailored, with slim lines. Sleeves are elaborate, and collars are flattering. A collar that frames the face becomingly is the making of the whole coat. There are no belts for dressy coats. Loose, swagger lines hang straight from the shoulders, and smart scarf collar and pockets are used.

Building Dams—A dam-building program under way in California South, alleviating needs for water conservation and unemployment relief, will add about 387,000 acre-feet in water storage in that section at an approximate cost of $31,-904,000.

November—A month to garner in and store away, what summer grew against a winter day. —Jeanette Nourland.

"Our grand business undoubtedly is, not to see what lies dimly at a distance, but to do what lies clearly at hand."—Carlyle.

Native Sons of the Golden West

TO ALL SUBORDINATE PARLORS NATIVE Sons of the Golden West—Greetings: At the last session of the Grand Parlor legislation was enacted endorsing the observance of National Education Week as a suitable exercise for the Subordinate Parlors of this Order, and establishing a Grand Parlor committee, one of the duties of which is to encourage Subordinate Parlors to hold such National Education Week programs.

The week of November 6 to 12 is National Education Week, and I hereby recommend the same for optional observance by all Subordinate Parlors. While it is an entirely optional matter whether or not a Parlor, or groups of Parlors, shall hold any Education Week program, I would strongly urge all Parlors to avail themselves of the opportunity to do so.

Education is a very important matter and a field of activity in which our Order should be vitally interested. If we can educate our members to the needs of the schools, and they in turn as citizens will strive for what is necessary and good and wholesome in the schools, we may look toward the coming generation with high prospects.

Our Order, dedicated as it is to the perpetuation of the memories of the Pioneers of long ago, must see to it that California history is included in the course of study of both elementary and secondary schools. We must insist that courage, valor, honesty and truth, virtues so characteristic of the Pioneers, are instilled into our children. We must ever stand for the proper support of the schools, giving to the children of the state the best possible education, on the assumption and with the hope that our schools will graduate good citizens for the years that are to come. . . . I would suggest that Parlors contemplating the presentation of flags to educational institutions do so during National Education Week.

I therefore, in accordance with the national plan, endorse November 6 to 12, 1932, National Education Week for optional observance by all Subordinate Parlors, and I strongly urge all Parlors, either individually or in groups, either in closed or open meeting, to conduct a program in which thoughts on educational matters are presented by appropriate speakers.

Respectfully submitted in F. L. & C.,

SETH MILLINGTON,
Grand President, N.S.G.W.

Gridley, October 10, 1932.

To All Subordinate Parlors Native Sons of the Golden West—Dear Sirs and Brothers:. Please be advised that the grand officers, headed by Grand President Seth Millington, will dedicate the Jefferson grammar school at Redwood City, San Mateo County, Sunday, November 6, at 2 o'clock p. m. All members and their friends are invited to attend. The date selected is the opening of Education Week, and a special program of music and singing will be rendered.

Sincerely and fraternally yours,

JOHN T. REGAN,
Grand Secretary, N.S.G.W.

San Francisco, October 11, 1932.

State Flag for Customs Building.

San Diego—Grand Trustee Eldred L. Meyer officially visited San Diego No. 108 September 28. There was a large attendance and much enthusiasm. Three candidates were initiated, and they were addressed by District Deputy Edward H. Dowell. Other speakers were Grand Trustee Meyer, Grand First Vice-president Justice Emmet Seawell, Frank C. Merritt (Brooklyn No. 151) and Ed. L. Head (Stanford No. 76). An excellent entertainment program and a buffet supper concluded the meeting.

The following day the Parlor, with the consent of the United States Treasury Department, presented a California State (Bear) Flag to federal customs and immigration officials at the San Ysidro port of entry. Deputy Grand President Albert V. Mayrhofer presided, and Judge Eugene Daney Jr. made the presentation address. The flag was accepted by William H. Ellison, collector of customs in the district. When the customs and immigration building is completed at the border, this flag will be placed on the flagstaff, along with the Flag of the United States of America. Brief remarks were also made by Grand First Vice-president Seawell, Grand Trustee Meyer and Martin J. Spangler, president San Diego Parlor.

Back in the Fold.

Visalia—Visalia No. 19, reorganized through the efforts of Deputy Grand President Al Lobree, was instituted October 1 by Grand Second Vice-president Chas. A. Koenig, Grand Third Vice-president Harmon D. Skillin and Grand Secretary John T. Regan. Twenty-one of the fifty-nine charter signers appeared for initiation, and the ritual was exemplified by a team from Fresno No. 25. October 25 additional candidates, to bring the charter membership in the new Parlor to well above the fifty-mark, will, it is promised, be initiated.

Historic Setting for Initiation.

Sacramento—Under the auspices of General John A. Sutter Past Presidents Assembly No. 10, the ritual was exemplified outofdoors at historic Sutter Fort, October 1. Twenty-five candidates were presented for initiation into Sacramento No. 3, Sunset No. 26, Elk Grove No. 41, Courtland No. 106 and Sutter Fort No. 241. Members of the Order from all parts of the Sacramento Valley were in attendance. The ritual team was made up of the following past presidents: J. J. Longshore, president; Irving D. Gibson, junior past; A. W. Katzenstein, senior past; L. P. Ferron, first vice; Roy C. Cothrin, second vice; G. E. Pressey, third vice; C. L. Corcoran, marshal; A. J. Frank, inside sentinel.

At the conclusion of the ceremonies, which were most impressive, refreshments were served. Addresses were made by Grand President Seth Millington, Historiographer Chester F. Gannon and Irving D. Gibson, former grand trustee.

Eight Initiated.

Hayward—Eden No. 113 honored its veteran members at an oldtimers banquet October 12. Three of the five remaining charter members were in attendance, Neal McConaghy, John E. Geary and James D. Smalley. Frank B. Leonard was the toastmaster, and Grand First Vice-president Justice Emmet Seawell was the principal speaker. He reviewed the work of the California Constitutional Convention of 1849, and said that although free public education was just making headway in the oldest of the Eastern states, this young Western state provided for it in its first constitution. The convention also barred slavery, despite the controversy then agitating the other states, and the young state adopted a code of mining law since patterned after by many Western states.

Following the banquet, the Parlor met in regular session and eight candidates were initiated by a team of Alameda County district deputies including Frank Smith, W. Dombrink, Frank B. Perry, E. Fitzgerald, T. Palmer, Grand Inside Sentinel Gam Hurst, Edward Schnarr, Richard Hamb and R. Nielson. After these ceremonies addresses were made by President Henry L'Ecuyer, Grand Secretary John T. Regan and Charter Member Neal McConaghy.

Early Preparations.

Grass Valley—Quartz No. 58 and Hydraulic No. 56 (Nevada City) are already perfecting plans for the Grand Parlor which meets in this city in May 1933. Among the entertainment features decided on is a trip to the many historic places in Nevada and Sierra Counties.

Large delegations of both Parlors visited Downieville No. 92, October 10, and that Parlor voted its co-operation by agreeing to serve an outdoor lunch to the caravan in Downieville. At Sierra City, which will be visited also, Golden Nugget No. 94 will provide some sort of entertainment, probably a dance.

Oldtimers Have Inning.

Watsonville—Oldtimers night at Watsonville No. 65 brought out a big crowd, including a delegation of fifty from Santa Cruz No. 90. The festivities opened with a delicious ham dinner, served by Jim Rowe. Entertainment was provided by Anthony Vyeda, Horace Burkett and Allen Dudley.

Following the program, the Parlor session was called to order by President Fred Baese, who turned the meeting over to the oldtimers, with "Veteran" Matt McGowan as chairman. Early experiences in the Order were related by the long-standing members, including W. G. Ryason, a charter member of Watsonville. The committee in charge of the enjoyable occasion included A. T. Enos (chairman), C. H. Close, Charles Scrivani and James Giacoma.

Charter Signers Disappoint.

Alturas—Alturas No. 134 was to have been re-instituted here October 8, thirty-nine having signed the charter petition circulated by Deputy Grand President Al Lobree. Grand President Seth Millington was on hand to officiate, and to exemplify the ritual Fred H. Greely Past Presidents Assembly sent a delegation which included Past Grand President Fred H. Greely, Barney G. Barry, Harry Schroeder, Ray C. Burris, Elton C. Fitch, John P. Colford and J. H. Hamill. Big Valley No. 211 (Bieber) was also well represented.

For some reason, but nine of the charter-petition signers put in an appearance, and so Grand President Millington called a meeting of Big Valley and the nine became, temporarily, members of that Parlor. Deputy Grand President Lobree says another initiation will be held December 1, and he expresses the belief that at that time a sufficient number will be initiated to institute the proposed parlor in Alturas.

Past Presidents Elect.

Santa Rosa—Sonoma County Past Presidents Assembly No. 9 elected officers October 6, and they were installed by Frank Harrison, as follows: P. A. R. Gambini, Santa Rosa, governor; E. L. Mangin, Petaluma, junior past; A. K. Kerner, Sonoma, first vice; Henry Thomas, Sebastopol, second vice; R. A. Pauli, Sonoma, third vice; A. N. Badger, Sebastopol, marshal; L. S. Lewis, Santa Rosa, secretary; George Peterson, Petaluma, treasurer; W. S. Borba, Sebastopol, L. H. Green, Sonoma, W. A. Andrews, Santa Rosa, Trustees; O. A. McChristian, inside sentinel; Henry Ronsheimer, Petaluma, outside sentinel.

To Visit Neighbor in Adjoining County.

Weaverville—The officers of Mount Bally No. 87 will journey to Redding November 3 and exemplify the ritual for McCloud No. 149. Several candidates for both Parlors will be initiated, and many members of Mount Bally will accompany the officers.

Know your home-state, California! Learn of s past history and of its present-day developent by reading regularly The Grizzly Bear. 1.50 for one year (12 issues). Subscribe now.

THE GRIZZLY BEAR
IS REGULARLY ON SALE:
SAN FRANCISCO:
N.S.G.W. Bldg., 414 Mason St., Room 302.
OAKLAND:
Fred M. DeWitt, 620 14th St.
LOS ANGELES:
315 Wilcox Bldg., Second and Spring.

Pessimistic Remarks Refuted.

San Rafael—Delegations from twenty-one Parlors were guests of Mount Tamalpais No. 64. The visitors, led by the drum corps of Hesperian No. 137 (San Francisco), Sea Point No. 158 (Sausalito) and No. 64, marched through the principal streets to Native Sons Hall where, in the presence of more than 200 members, a large class of candidates were initiated, the ritual being exemplified by Mount Tamalpais' officers.

In the course of a spirited address, Grand Third Vice-president Harmon D. Skillin called attention to pessimistic remarks, which were refuted by increased membership, despite the depression; he told the initiates to be proud of the emblem presented them, and to take an active interest in affairs of the Order. Grand Secretary John T. Regan made a stirring appeal for the preservation of California history, and asked his hearers to vigorously oppose any and every attempt to discontinue the observance of Admission Day, September 9. Warden James B. Holohan (Watsonville No. 65) of San Quentin State Prison recalled adoption by the State Legislature of a bill, presented by himself, designating the Bear Flag as the official flag of the State of California; February 1911 the bill was signed by the then Governor, now United States Senator, Hiram W. Johnson (Sunset No. 26). Grand Trustee Charles H. Spengemann expressed pride and pleasure at seeing delegations from every Parlor in his visitation district.

At the banquet, a real old-fashion italian dinner, a pair of North Beach serenaders sang and played Italian and Spanish folksongs. The orchestra of Sea Point Parlor rendered selections, Mrs. Antoinette Hecht favored with vocal numbers, and Eugenia Watson & Co. entertained with tap dances. Mount Tamalpais has accepted a challenge to a ritual contest with National No. 118 in Native Sons Building, San Francisco, November 3. Marinita No. 198 N.D.G.W. and Mount Tamalpais plan a series of joint social events for the benefit of the homeless children.

First of Mission Talks.

Calistoga—With President E. Molinari presiding, Calistoga No. 86 had a largely attended and peppy meeting October 3. Father T. J. McKeon gave an illustrated talk on San Fernando Mission. This was the first of a series of talks on the California missions to be given during the winter months.

Membership Standing Largest Parlors.

San Francisco—Grand Secretary John T. Regan reports the standing of the Subordinate Parlors having a membership of over 400 January 1, 1932, as follows, together with their membership figures October 20, 1932:

Parlor.	Jan. 1	Oct. 20	Gain	Loss
Ramona No. 109	1088	1087	....	1
South San Francisco No. 157	822	808	....	14
Castro No. 232	700	797	97	....
Stanford No. 76	614	609	....	5
Arrowhead No. 110	609	582	....	27
Stockton No. 7	549	563	14	....
Twin Peaks No. 214	585	531	....	54
Piedmont No. 120	523	523	....	....
Rincon No. 72	448	435	....	13

Many Places Represented.

Wheatland—The October meeting of Fred H. Greely Past Presidents Assembly No. 6, held here the 15th, was largely attended by members from Oroville, Lincoln, Roseville, Marysville, Grass Valley, Nevada City and Sutter City. Fred N. Beilby of Rainbow No. 40 was the toastmaster at the banquet, and among the speakers were Past Grand President Fred H. Greely, Barney Barry, Frank Meyer, Harry Schroeder, Dr. C. W. Chapman, R. L. P. Bigelow, Edward Baker, Bert Reed, William Tregaillis, A. W. Graves and William E. Bowser.

Progress Commended.

Sausalito—Grand Trustee Charles H. Spengemann officially visited Sea Point No. 158. He was accompanied by the drum and bugle corps of his home Parlor, Hesperian No. 137 (San Francisco), and the visitors were met by the drum corps of Sea Point. The united forces then paraded to the meetingplace. Four candidates were initiated, and No. 158's progress was highly commended by the Grand Trustee. Refreshments were served, and there was a program of music and speechmaking.

Newsy Paragraphs.

Grand President Seth Millington has appointed Past Grand President Edward J. Lynch of San Francisco chairman of the Grand Parlor History Committee, to succeed Past Grand President William J. Hayes, lately deceased.

Deputy Grand President Al Lobree advises The Grizzly Bear that since the last (October) issue he has been working in Modoc and Lassen

(Continued on Page 13)

Official Directory of Parlors of the N. S. G. W.

ALAMEDA COUNTY.

Alameda No. 47, Alameda City—Perry F. Badgley, Pres.; Robt. H. Cavanaugh, Sec., 1808 Pacific Ave.; Wednesdays, Native Sons Hall, 1405 Park St.
Oakland No. 50, Oakland—R. L. Engell, Pres.; F. M. Norris, Sec., 5595 Taft Ave.; Fridays, Native Sons Hall, 11th and Clay Sts.
Las Positas No. 96, Livermore—Dr. Donald M. Fraser, Pres.; John J. Kelly, Sec., P. O. box 341; Thursdays, Foresters Hall.
Eden No. 113, Hayward—Henry L'Ecu er, Pres.; Stanton R. Soares, Sec., P. O. box 176; 2ndyand 4th Tuesdays, Memorial Hall, Main St.
Piedmont No. 120, Oakland—Frank Smith, Pres.; Charles Morando, Sec., 906 Vermont St.; Thursdays, Native Sons Hall, 11th and Clay Sts.
Wisteria No. 127, Alvarado—Henry May, Pres.; J. M. Scribner, Sec., Livermore; 1st Thursday, I.O.O.F. Hall.
Halcyon No. 146, Alameda City—S. Chesley Anderson, Pres.; J. C. Bales, Sec., 2139 Buena Vista Ave.; 1st and 3rd Tuesdays, I.O.O.F. Hall, 2329 Santa Clara Ave.
Brooklyn No. 151' Oakland—Frank B. Perry, Pres.; E. W. Cooney, Sec., 3907 14th Ave.; Wednesdays, Masonic Temple, 8th Ave. and E. 14th St.
Washington, No. 169, Centerville—M. D. Silva, Pres.; Allen G. Norris, Sec., P. O. box 91; 2nd and 4th Tuesdays, Hansen Hall.
Athens No. 195, Oakland—Elmer L. Bullock, Pres.; Harold B. Farley, Sec., 4623 Benevides Ave.; Tuesdays, Native Sons Hall, 11th and Clay Sts.
Berkeley No. 210, Berkeley—F. M. McGrath, Pres.; R. J. Garrett, Sec., 1708 Virginia St.; Tuesdays, Native Sons Hall, 2108 Shattuck Ave.
Estudillo No. 223, San Leandro—Frank V. Pacheco, Pres.; Albert G. Pacheco, Sec., 1736 E. 14th St.; 1st and 3rd Tuesdays, U.P.E.C. Hall.
Claremont No. 240, Oakland—Louis F. Cambet, Pres.; E. N. Thienger, Sec., 839 Hearst Ave., Berkeley; Tuesdays, Veterans Memorial Bldg., 43rd & Salem Sts., Emeryville.
Pleasanton No. 244, Pleasanton—Peter C. Madsen, Pres.; Ernest W. Schween, Sec.; 2nd and 4th Thursdays, I.O.O.F. Hall.
Niles No. 250, Niles—M. L. Fournier, Pres.; C. E. Martenstein, Sec.; 2nd Thursday, I.O.O.F. Hall.
Fruitvale No. 252, Oakland—William J. Keating Jr., Pres.; Ray B. Felton, Sec., 1575 Alice St.; Fridays, W.O.W. Hall, 3256 E. 14th St.

AMADOR COUNTY.

Amador No. 17, Sutter Creek—Frank Marre, Pres.; F. J. Payne, Sec.; 1st and 3rd Fridays, Native Sons Hall.
Excelsior No. 31, Jackson—Wm. Daugherty, Pres.; William Going, Sec.; 1st and 3rd Wednesdays, Native Sons Hall, 22 Court St.
Ione No. 33, Ione—Marvin Kidd, Pres.; Josiah H. Saunders, Sec.; 1st and 3rd Wednesdays, Native Sons Hall.
Plymouth No. 48, Plymouth—John J. Upton, Pres.; Thos. D. Davis, Sec.; 1st and 3rd Saturdays, I.O.O.F. Hall.

BUTTE COUNTY.

Argonaut No. 8, Oroville—George N. Westwood, Pres.; Cyril R. Macdonald, Sec., P. O. box 502; 1st and 3rd Wednesdays, Veterans Memorial Hall.
Chico No. 21, Chico—Marcus Choisser, Pres.; Sam Lindsay Adams, Sec., Sacramento Blvd.; 2nd and 4th Thursdays, Elks Hall.

CALAVERAS COUNTY.

Chispa No. 139, Murphys—Maynard Segale, Pres.; Antone Malaspina, Sec.; Wednesdays, Native Sons Hall.

COLUSA COUNTY.

Colusa No. 69, Colusa City—Percy J. Cooke, Pres.; Phil J. Humburg, Sec., 223 Parkhill St.; Tuesdays, Eagles Hall.

CONTRA COSTA COUNTY.

General Winn No. 32, Antioch—Edmont T. Uren, Pres.; Joel H. Ford, Sec., P. O. box 311; 2nd and 4th Wednesdays, Union Hall.
Mount Diablo No. 101, Martinez—R. P. Anderson, Pres.; G. T. Barkley, Sec.; 1st and 3rd Mondays, I.O.O.F. Hall.
Byron No. 170, Byron—William E. Bunn, Pres.; H. G. Krumland, Sec.; 1st and 3rd Tuesdays, I.O.O.F. Hall.
Carquinez No. 205, Crockett—Thos. Cox, Pres.; Thomas I. Cahalan, Sec.; 1st and 3rd Wednesdays, I.O.O.F. Hall
Richmond No. 217, Richmond—M. W. Amaral, Pres.; H. D. Mason, Sec., 11 6th St.; Wednesdays, Redmen Hall, 11th and Nevan Ave.
Concord No. 245, Concord—P. M. Soto, Pres.; D. E. Pramberg, Sec., P. O. box 235; 1st Tuesday, I.O.O.F. Hall.
Diamond No. 246, Pittsburg—Victor Ericsson, Pres.; Francis A. Irving, Sec., 248 E. 5th St.; 1st and 3rd Wednesdays, Veterans Memorial Bldg.

EL DORADO COUNTY.

Placerville No. 9, Placerville—Chas. C. Cook, Pres.; Clyde R. Berriman, Sec., Wood St.; 2nd and 4th Tuesdays, Masonic Hall.
Georgetown No. 91, Georgetown—W. H. Breedlove, Pres.; C. F. Irish, Sec.; 2nd and 4th Wednesdays, I.O.O.F. Hall.

FRESNO COUNTY.

Fresno No. 25, Fresno City—Oliver M. Akers, Pres.; W. C. Guard, Sec., 5060 Belmont; 1st and 3rd Fridays, Pythian Castle, Cor. "R" and Merced Sts.

GRAND OFFICERS.

Dr. Frank I. Gonzalez..............Junior Past Grand President
Flood Bldg., San Francisco
Seth Millington..............Grand President
Gridley
Justice Emmet Seawell..............Grand First Vice-president
State Bldg., San Francisco
Chas. A. Koenig..............Grand Second Vice-president
531 35th Ave., San Francisco
Harmon D. Skillin..............Grand Third Vice-president
Mills Bldg., San Francisco
John T. Regan..............Grand Secretary
N.S.G.W. Bldg., 414 Mason St., San Francisco
John A. Corotto..............Grand Treasurer
560 No. 5th St., San Jose
W. B. O'Brien..............Grand Marshal
2324 Santa Clara St., Alameda
Gam Hurst..............Grand Inside Sentinel
Financial Center Bldg., Oakland
William A. Reuter..............Grand Outside Sentinel
1009 Marine Ave., Wilmington
Leslie Maloche..............Grand Organist
1611 No. Hudson Ave., Los Angeles
Chester Gannon.............. Historiographer
613 Capital Ntl. Bank Bldg., Sacramento

GRAND TRUSTEES.

Jesse H. Miller..............712 DeYoung Bldg., San Francisco
Eldred L. Meyer..........922 San Vicente Blvd., Santa Monica
John M. Burnett..............914 Bank Italy Bldg., San Jose
Henry S. Lyon..............Placerville
Joseph J. McShane..............419 Flood Bldg., San Francisco
Horace J. Leavitt..............Weaverville
Chas. H. Spengemann..............827 27th Ave., San Francisco

Selma No. 107, Selma—Chester E. Shepard, Pres.; E. C. Laughlin, Sec.; 1st and 3rd Wednesdays, American Legion Hall.

HUMBOLDT COUNTY.

Humboldt No. 14, Eureka—Henry Sundfors, Pres.; Loren M. Nelson, Sec., P.O. box 195; 2nd Monday, Native Sons Hall.
Arcata No. 20, Arcata—I. C. Fleckenstein, Pres.; William Peters, Sec., P. O. box 1117; Thursdays, Native Sons Hall.
Ferndale No. 93, Ferndale—Elwood Pries, Pres.; C. H. Rasmussen, Sec., R.F.D., 47-A; 1st and 3rd Mondays, K.P. Hall.

KERN COUNTY.

Bakersfield No. 42, Bakersfield—George Taylor, Pres.; Henry A. Bannister, Sec., care Bank of America; 2nd and 4th Fridays, Justice Court, City Hall.

LAKE COUNTY.

Lower Lake No. 159, Lower Lake—Harold S. Anderson, Pres.; Albert Kugelman, Sec.; Thursdays, I.O.O.F. Hall.

LASSEN COUNTY.

Honey Lake No. 198, Standish—James C. Meeske, Pres.; N. V. Wemple, Sec., Litchfield; 1st and 3rd Wednesdays, Wrede Hall.
Big Valley No. 211, Bieber—George Bunselmeier, Pres.; A. W. McKenzie, Sec.; 1st and 3rd Wednesdays, I.O.O.F. Hall.

LOS ANGELES COUNTY.

Los Angeles No. 45, Los Angeles City—Owen S. Adams, Pres.; Richard W. Fryer, Sec., 1629 Champlain Ter.; Thursdays, Merchant Plumbers Hall, 1832 So. Hope.
Ramona No. 109, Los Angeles City—James M. Watson, Pres.; John V. Scott, Sec., Patriotic Hall, 1816 So. Figueroa; Fridays, Patriotic Hall, 1816 So. Figueroa.
Hollywood No. 196, Los Angeles City—Kenneth A. Case, Pres.; E. J. Reilly, Sec., Olive View; Mondays, 1089 No. Oxford Ave.
Long Beach No. 239, Long Beach—Francis H. Gentry, Pres.; W. W. Brady, Sec., 801 Jergins Trust Bldg.; 2nd and 4th Thursdays, Moose Hall, Elm and Anaheim.
Sepulveda No. 263, San Pedro—Joseph Pia, Pres.; Harry Fairall, Sec., 1925 Pacific Ave.; 1st and 3rd Fridays, Redman Hall, 543 Shepherd St., Point Firmin.
Glendale No. 264, Glendale—Leslie F. Schellback, Pres.; Abel B. Molen, Sec., 508 So. Belmont St.; 1st and 3rd Tuesdays, Masonic Temple, 234 So. Brand Blvd.
Santa Monica Bay 267, Santa Monica—Orrin G. Welch, Pres.; John J. Smith, Sec., 830 Rialto Ave., Venice; 1st and 3rd Wednesdays, Odd Fellows Hall, 1431 Third St.
Cahuenga No. 268, Reseda—Harold C. Trexler, Pres.; Carrol S. Driscoll, Sec., P.O. box 25, Chatsworth; first Friday, Alton Hall.

MADERA COUNTY.

Madera No. 130, Madera City—Cornelius Noble, Pres.; T. P. Cosgrave, Sec.; 1st and 3rd Thursdays, First National Bank Bldg.

MARIN COUNTY.

Mount Tamalpais No. 64, San Rafael—M. E. Peterson, Pres.; Manual A. Andrade, Sec., 532 Mission Ave.; 1st and 3rd Mondays, Portuguese American Hall.
Sea Point No. 158, Sausalito—A. H. Bettencourt, Pres.; Manuel Santos, Sec., 6 Glen Drive; 1st and 3rd Wednesdays, Perry Bldg.
Nicasio No. 183, Nicasio—M. T. Farley, Pres.; R. J. Rogers, Sec.; 2nd and 4th Wednesdays, U.A.O.D. Hall.

MENDOCINO COUNTY.

Ukiah No. 71, Ukiah—Henry Bucknell, Pres.; Ben Hofman, Sec., P. O. box 473; 1st and 3rd Mondays, I.O.O.F. Hall.
Broderick No. 117, Point Arena—A. L. McCallum, Pres.; C. J. Buchanan, Sec.; 1st and 3rd Thursdays, Forester Hall.
Alder Glen No. 200, Fort Bragg—H. M. Bohn, Pres.; C. R. Weller, Sec.; 2nd and 4th Fridays, I.O.O.F. Hall.

MERCED COUNTY.

Yosemite No. 24, Merced City—John J. Thronton, Pres.; True W. Fowler, Sec., P. O. box 781; 2nd and 4th Mondays, I.O.O.F. Hall.
Los Banos No. 206, Los Banos—Robert L. Puccinelli, Pres.; L. E. Sarbo, Sec., R.F.D., box 21; 2nd and 4th Wednesdays, Eagles Hall.

MONTEREY COUNTY.

Monterey No. 75, Monterey City—James Millington, Pres.; T. W. Krieger, Sec., 999 Franklin St.; 1st and 3rd Fridays, Knights Pythias Hall, Main St.
Santa Lucia No. 97, Salinas—Roy Martella, Pres.; R. W. Adcock, Sec., Route 2, box 180; Mondays, Native Sons Hall, 32 W. Alisal St.
Gabilan No. 132, Castroville—B. A. McCoy, Pres.; R. H. Martin, Sec., P. O. box 81; 1st and 3rd Thursdays, Native Sons Hall.

NAPA COUNTY.

Saint Helena No. 53, Saint Helena—Lucas Haus, Pres.;

ATTENTION, SECRETARIES!

THIS DIRECTORY IS PUBLISHED BY AUTHORITY OF THE GRAND PARLOR N.S.G.W., AND ALL NOTICES OF CHANGES MUST BE RECEIVED BY THE GRAND SECRETARY (NOT THE MAGAZINE) ON OR BEFORE THE 20TH OF EACH MONTH TO INSURE CORRECTION IN NEXT ISSUE OF DIRECTORY.

Edw. L. Bonhote, Sec., P. O. box 267; Mondays, Nati[ve] Sons Hall.
Napa No. 62, Napa City—R. O. Akers, Pres.; H. Hoernle, Sec., 1226 Oak St.; Mondays, Native Sons Ha[ll].
Calistoga No. 86, Calistoga—Edmund Molinari, Pres.; Lo[u] Carlenzoli, Sec.; 1st and 3rd Mondays, I.O.O.F. Hall.

NEVADA COUNTY.

Hydraulic No. 56, Nevada City—Arthur W. Davis, Pres[.]; Dr. C. W. Chapman, Sec.; Tuesdays, Pythian Castle.
Quartz No. 58, Grass Valley—Robert Kohler, Pres.; H. B. George, Sec., 151 Conaway Ave.; Mondays, Auditori[um] Hall.
Donner No. 162, Truckee—J. F. Lichtenberger, Pres.; C. Lichtenberger, Sec.; 2nd and 4th Tuesdays, Nati[ve] Sons Hall.

ORANGE COUNTY.

Santa Ana No. 265, Santa Ana—Amos Huntzinger, Pre[s.]; E. F. Marks, Sec., 1124 No. Bristol St.; 1st and 3rd Mondays, K.C. Hall, 4th and French Sts.

PLACER COUNTY.

Auburn No. 59, Auburn—Iris Garcia, Pres.; J. G. Wal[...] Sec.; 1st and 3rd Fridays, Foresters Hall.
Silver Star No. 63, Lincoln—L. F. Browning, Pres.; B[...]ney G. Barry, Sec., P. O. box 72; 3rd Wednesda[y], I.O.O.F. Hall.
Rocklin No. 233, Roseville—Wm. La Due, Pres.; M. Reed, Sec., 253 W. Duranta; 2nd and 4th Wednesday[s], Eagles Hall.

PLUMAS COUNTY.

Quincy No. 131, Quincy—J. D. McLaughlin, Pres.; E. Kelsey, Sec.; 2nd Thursday, I.O.O.F. Hall.
Golden Anchor No. 182, La Porte—R. J. McGrath, Pre[s.]; LeRoy J. Post, Sec.; 2nd and 4th Sunday morning[s], Native Sons Hall.
Plumas No. 228, Taylorsville—E. E. Sikes, Pres.; Geo[rge] E. Boyden, Sec.; 1st and 3rd Mondays, Native Sons Ha[ll].

SACRAMENTO COUNTY.

Sacramento No. 3, Sacramento City—J. G. Fitzhen[...] Pres.; J. F. Didion, Sec., 1213 "O" St.; Thursdays, Na[...]tive Sons Bldg., 11th and "J" Sts.
Sunset No. 26, Sacramento City—L. W. Marvin, Pres[.]; Edward E. Reese, Sec., County Treasurer Office; Mo[n]days, Native Sons Bldg., 11th and "J" Sts.
Elk Grove No. 41, Elk Grove—Robert Carr, Pres.; Wal[...] Martin, Sec.; 2nd and 4th Fridays, Masonic Hall.
Granite No. 83, Folsom—Joe Relvas, Pres.; Frank Shower[...] Sec.; 2nd and 4th Tuesdays, K.P. Hall.
Courtland No. 106, Courtland—Thornton Pylman, Pre[s.]; Jos. Green, Sec.; 1st Saturday and 3rd Monday, Nati[ve] Sons Hall.
Sutter Fort No. 241, Sacramento City—Ed. T. Guys[...] Pres.; C. L. Katzenstein, Sec., P. O. box 914; 2nd an[d] 4th Wednesdays, Native Sons Bldg., 11th and "J" St[s].
Galt No. 243, Galt—John Granadas, Pres.; F. W. Harm[...] Sec.; 1st and 3rd Mondays, I.O.O.F. Hall.

SAN BENITO COUNTY.

Fremont No. 44, Hollister—S. Churchill, Pres.; J. [...] Prendergast Jr., Sec., 1064 Monterey St.; 1st and 3r[d] Thursdays, Grangers Union Hall.

SAN BERNARDINO COUNTY.

Arrowhead No. 110, San Bernardino City—F. L. McGarve[y], Pres.; R. W. Brazelton, Sec., 462 6th St.; Wednesday[s], Eagles Hall, 469 4th St.

SAN DIEGO COUNTY.

San Diego No. 108, San Diego City—Martin J. Spangle[r], Pres.; A. V. Mayrhofer, Sec., 1572 2nd St.; Wednesday[s], K.C. Hall, 4th and Elm Sts.

SAN FRANCISCO CITY AND COUNTY.

California No. 1, San Francisco—Joseph Lawler, Pres.; Eli[...] A. Blackman, Sec., 1248-A Divisadero St.; Thursday[s], Native Sons Bldg., 414 Mason St.
Pacific No. 10, San Francisco—Walter Mohrdick, Pres.; Henry Bastein, Sec., 426 City Hall; Tuesdays, Nati[ve] Sons Bldg., 414 Mason St.
Golden Gate No. 29, San Francisco—Thomas I. Schlin[...] Pres.; Adolph Eberhart, Sec., 183 Carl St.; Monday[s], Native Sons Bldg., 414 Mason St.
Mission No. 38, San Francisco—George Leahy, Pres.; Tho[s.] J. Stewart, Sec., 1919 Howard St.; Wednesdays, Redme[n] Hall, 3053 16th St.
San Francisco No. 49, San Francisco—Charles Miller, Pres[.]; David Capurro, Sec., 975 Union St.; Thursdays, Nati[ve] Sons Bldg., 414 Mason St.
El Dorado No. 52, San Francisco—Edward Victor, Pres.; Alfred Vlautin, Sec., 1537 Franklin St.; Thursdays, Na[...]tive Sons Bldg., 414 Mason St.
Rincon No. 72, San Francisco—Frank D. Sericano, Pres.; John A. Gilmour, Sec., 2069 Golden Gate Ave.; Wedne[s]days, Native Sons Bldg., 414 Mason St.
Stanford No. 76, San Francisco—Dr. Vincent V. Hardeman[,] Pres.; Charles T. O'Kane, Sec., 1111 Pine St.; Tuesday[s], Native Sons Bldg., 414 Mason St.
Bay City No. 104, San Francisco—Morris Garren, Pres.; Max E. Licht, Sec., 1831 Fulton St.; 2nd and 4th Wednesdays, Native Sons Bldg., 414 Mason St.
Niantic No. 105, San Francisco—A. Furner, Pres.; J. M. Darcy, Sec., 10 Hoffman Ave.; Wednesdays, Native So[ns] Bldg., 414 Mason St.
National No. 118, San Francisco—Wayne Burke, Pres.; Martin M. Ratigan, Sec., 1325 Page St., Apt. 6; Thurs[days], 1160 Eddy St.
Hesperian No. 137, San Francisco—C. McLaughlin, Pres.; Albert Carlson, Sec., 379 Justin Dr.; Thursdays, Nativ[e] Sons Bldg., 414 Mason St.
Alcalde No. 154, San Francisco—Charles Kurpinsky, Pres.; Harry S. Burke, Sec., 25 Ord St.; 2nd and 4th Wednes[days], Native Sons Bldg., 414 Mason St.
South San Francisco No. 157, San Francisco—Otto A. El[...]vander, Pres.; John T. Regan, Sec., 1489 Newcomb Ave.; Wednesdays, Masonic Bldg., 4705 3rd St.
Sequoia No. 160, San Francisco—Harry Grover, Pres.; Walter W. Garrett, Sec., 2500 Van Ness Ave.; Mondays, Swedish-American Bldg., 2174 Market St.
Precita No. 187, San Francisco—Lloyd J. Cosgrove, Pres.; Edward Tietjen, Sec., 1367 15th Ave.; Thursdays, Mission Masonic Hall, 2668 Mission St.
Olympus No. 189, San Francisco—Henry H. McGowan[,] Pres.; Harvey J. Carty, Sec., 1651 Market St., Apt. 505; 2nd and 4th Tuesdays, Independent Redmen Hall, 305[...] 16th St.
Presidio No. 194, San Francisco—Lester Figone, Pres.; George A. Ducker, Sec., 442 21st Ave.; Mondays, Native Sons Bldg., 414 Mason St.
Marshall No. 202, San Francisco—Alexander Jean, Pres.; Frank Bacigalupi, Sec., 725 Douglas St.; 1st and 3rd Wednesdays, Native Sons Bldg., 414 Mason St.
Dolores No. 208, San Francisco—James F. Vahey, Pres.; Eugene O'Donnell, Sec., Mills Bldg.; Tuesdays, Mission Masonic Bldg., 2668 Mission St.
Twin Peaks No. 214, San Francisco—Clifford Roberts, Pres.; Thos. Pendergast, Sec., 278 Douglas St.; Wednesdays, Willopi Hall, 4061 24th St.
El Capitan No. 222, San Francisco—Frank Rizzo, Pres.; James Hanna, Sec., 2450 27th Ave.; 1st and 3rd Thurs[days], King Soloman Hall, 1739 Fillmore St.

uadalupe No. 231, San Francisco—Roy Tensfeldt, Pres.; Alvin A. Johnson, Sec., 142 Rousseau St.; Tuesdays, Guadalupe Hall, 4551 Mission St.
astro No. 232, San Francisco—Ralph Willis, Pres.; James H. Hayes, Sec., 4014 18th St.; Tuesdays, Native Sons Bldg., 414 Mason St.
alboa No. 234, San Francisco—George Schroth, Pres.; E. W. Boyd, Sec., 437 Cherry St.; Thursdays, Maccabee Hall, 5th Ave. and Clement St.
ret Harte No. 260, San Francisco—Chas. E. Lillie, Pres.; A. W. McElhatton, Sec., 103 Holloway Ave.; Tuesdays, West of Twin Peaks Hall, 233 Legion Court.
topia No. 270, San Francisco—George Walters, Pres.; Herbert H. Schneider, Sec., 2455 16th Ave.; Tuesdays, American Hall, 20th and Capp Sts.

SAN JOAQUIN COUNTY.

tockton No. 7, Stockton—John D. Gallagher, Pres.; R. D. Dorcey, Sec., P. O. box 388; Mondays, Native Sons Hall.
odi No. 18, Lodi—Jerome Solomon, Pres.; Dr. Clyde Bresnan, Sec.; 2nd and 4th Wednesdays, Eagles Hall.
racy No. 186, Tracy—C. S. Selna, Pres.; R. J. Marraccini, Sec., R.F.D. No. 1, box 217; Thursdays, I.O.O.F. Hall.
anteca No. 271, Manteca—Chas. N. Howell Jr., Pres.; Leonard Faria, Sec., R.F.D., box 75, Lathrop; 1st and 3rd Wednesdays, I.O.O.F. Hall.

SAN LUIS OBISPO COUNTY.

an Miguel No. 150, San Miguel—H. Twisselman, Pres.; Otto Kuchi, Sec., Paso Robles; 1st and 3rd Wednesdays, Fraternal Hall.
ambria No. 152, Cambria—J. M. Soto, Pres.; A. S. Gay, Sec.; Wednesdays, Rigdon Hall.

SAN MATEO COUNTY.

edwood No. 66, Redwood City—Frank Deluchi, Pres.; A. S. Liguori, Sec., P. O. box 212; Thursdays, American Foresters Hall.
easide No. 95, Half Moon Bay—Andrew F. Gilcrest, Pres.; John G. Gilcrest, Sec.; 2nd and 4th Tuesdays, I.O.O.F. Hall.
enlo No. 185, Menlo Park—C. T. Maloney, Pres.; F. W. Johnson, Sec., P. O. box 601; Thursdays, Masonic Hall.
ebble Beach No. 230, Pescadero—Harold Souza, Pres.; E. A. Shaw, Sec.; 2nd and 4th Wednesdays, I.O.O.F. Hall.
l Carmelo No. 256, Daly City—Theodore A. Clemens, Pres.; Ernest L. Micco, Sec., 639 Morse St., San Francisco; 2nd and 4th Wednesdays, Eagles Hall.
ndustrial City No. 269, South San Francisco—John C. Hamilton, Pres.; Geo. A. Roll, Sec., P. O. box 237; 2nd and 4th Mondays, Metropolitan Hall.

SANTA BARBARA COUNTY.

anta Barbara No. 116, Santa Barbara City—C. W. McCormick, Pres.; H. C. Sweetser, Sec., Court House; 1st and 3rd Wednesdays, I.O.O.F. Hall.

SANTA CLARA COUNTY.

an Jose No. 22, San Jose—Joseph Sabatte, Pres.; Joseph Lawrence, Sec., 1095 No. First St.; Mondays, I.O.O.F. Hall.
anta Clara No. 100, Santa Clara City—C. A. Castro, Pres.; Clarence Clevenger, Sec., P. O. box 297; Wednesdays, Redmen Hall.
bservatory No. 177, San Jose—William L. Gerrans, Pres.; A. B. Langford, Sec., Hall Records; Tuesdays, Knights Columbus Hall, 40 No. First St.
ountain View No. 215, Mountain View—Gilbert F. McCorkle, Pres.; C. A. Antonioli, Sec., 301 Castro St.; 2nd and 4th Wednesdays, Mockbee Hall.
alo Alto No. 216, Palo Alto—John C. Bernal, Pres.; Albert A. Quinn, Sec., 643 High St.; Mondays, Native Sons Bldg., Hamilton Ave. and Emerson St.

SANTA CRUZ COUNTY.

atsonville No. 65, Watsonville—Fred R. Baese, Pres.; E. R. Tindall, Sec., R.F.D. No. 5, Box 313; 2nd and 4th Tuesdays, I.O.O.F. Hall.
anta Cruz No. 90, Santa Cruz City—Horace Burkett, Pres.; T. V. Mathews, Sec., 105 Pacheco Ave.; Fridays, Native Sons Hall, 117 Pacific Ave.

SHASTA COUNTY.

cCloud No. 149, Redding—A. E. Welbourn, Pres.; Hugh A. Shuffleton, Sec.; 1st and 3rd Thursdays, Moose Hall.

SIERRA COUNTY.

ownieville No. 92, Downieville—Frank H. Turner, Pres.; H. S. Tibbey, Sec.; 2nd and 4th Mondays, I.O.O.F. Hall.
olden Nugget No. 94, Sierra City—Elmer Thompson, Pres.; Arthur R. Pride, Sec.; 1st and 3rd Wednesdays, Masonic Hall.

SISKIYOU COUNTY.

tna No. 192, Etna—Frank B. Quigley, Pres.; Harvey A. Green, Sec.; 1st and 3rd Wednesdays, I.O.O.F. Hall.
iberty No. 193, Sawyers Bar—Orrin R. Bigelow, Pres.; John M. Barry, Sec.; 1st and 3rd Saturdays, I.O.O.F. Hall.

SOLANO COUNTY.

olano No. 39, Suisun—Karl Koch, Pres.; J. W. Kinlock, Sec.; 1st and 3rd Tuesdays, I.O.O.F. Hall.
allejo No. 77, Vallejo—Joseph Clavo, Pres.; Werner B. Hallin, Sec., 912 Carolina; 2nd and 4th Tuesdays, San Pablo Hall.

SONOMA COUNTY.

etaluma No. 27, Petaluma—Fred G. Ilg, Pres.; C. F. Fobes, Sec., 114 Prospect St.; 2nd and 4th Mondays, Druid Hall, Gross Bldg., 41 Main St.
anta Rosa No. 28, Santa Rosa—Wesley Beach, Pres.; Leland S. Lewis, Sec., Court House; Mondays, Native Sons Hall.
len Ellen No. 102, Glen Ellen—Tony Cereghino, Pres.; Frank Kirch, Sec., Route 3, Santa Rosa; 2nd Monday, N.S.G.W. Hall.
onoma No. 111, Sonoma City—Joseph Andrieux, Pres.; L. H. Green, Sec.; 1st and 3rd Mondays, I.O.O.F. Hall.
ebastopol No. 143, Sebastopol—O. A. McChristian, Pres.; F. G. McFarlane, Sec.; 1st and 3rd Fridays, I.O.O.F. Hall.

STANISLAUS COUNTY.

odesto No. 11, Modesto—Chas. D. Blaine, Pres.; C. C. Eastin Jr., Sec., P. O. box 898; 1st and 3rd Wednesdays, I.O.O.F. Hall.
akdale No. 142, Oakdale—D. W. Tulloch, Pres.; E. T. Gobin, Sec.; 2nd and 4th Mondays, Legion Hall.
restimba No. 247, Crows Landing—Lloyd W. Fink, Pres.; G. W. Fink, Sec.; 1st and 3rd Wednesdays, Community Club Home.

SUTTER COUNTY.

utter No. 261, Sutter City—Albert Thomsen, Pres.; Glen R. Haynes, Sec., R.F.D. No. 2, Yuba City; 2nd and 4th Mondays, N.D.G.W. Hall.

TRINITY COUNTY.

ount Bally No. 87, Weaverville—R. L. Marshall, Pres.; E. V. Ryan, Sec.; 1st and 3rd Mondays, Native Sons Hall.

TUOLUMNE COUNTY.

uolumne No. 144, Sonora—Mathew J. Marshall, Pres.; William M. Harrington, Sec., P. O. box 715; 2nd and 4th Fridays, Knights Columbus Hall.
olumbia No. 258, Columbia—Jos. Cadematori, Pres.; Charles E. Grant, Sec.; 2nd and 4th Thursdays, Native Sons Hall.

VENTURA COUNTY.

abrillo No. 114, Ventura City—David Bennett, Pres., 1380 Church St.

YOLO COUNTY.

oodland No. 30, Woodland—J. L. Aronson, Pres.; R. G. Lawson, Sec.; 1st Thursday, Native Sons Hall.

NATIVE SON NEWS

(Continued from Page 11)

Counties, also in Richmond, Contra Costa County. In the latter place he hopes to have a class ready for initiation into Richmond No. 147. While driving in Modoc County, Lobree got stuck in the mud and had to be towed out by two Native Daughters—Mrs. Jessie Madison, superintendent of schools, and Miss Emily Rothlin.

Deputy Grand President Clinton E. Skinner, working in Los Angeles County, reports a new parlor, to be known as University, ready for institution in Los Angeles City, and that a parlor will also be instituted at Compton in the very near future.

The Oakland Pioneer Society gave a testimonial dinner September 28 to Past Grand President Harry G. Williams, city auditor and president of the Merchants Exchange. Judge Lincoln Church presided, and spoke on early days.

Well Known Native Sons Pass On.

Elk Grove (Sacramento County)—Perley Kilbourne Bradford, affiliated with Elk Grove No. 41 and a former county supervisor, died October 1 survived by a wife and three children. He was born at Bruceville, Sacramento County, July 8, 1872, and was a delegate to many Grand Parlors.

Napa City—Henry H. Thompson, affiliated with Napa No. 62 and for more than thirty years clerk of this city, died October 10 survived by a wife and three children. He was born at San Francisco, January 26, 1866.

N.S.G.W. OFFICIAL DEATH LIST.

Containing the name, the date and the place of birth, the date of death, and the Subordinate Parlor affiliation of deceased members reported to Grand Secretary John T. Regan from September 20, 1932, to October 20, 1932:

Decker, Charles William; Sutterville, March 31, 1855; September 25, 1932; California No. 1.
Greer, Walter William; Sacramento, September 5, 1865; October 6, 1932; Sunset No. 26.
Owens, Henry Franklin; Lincoln, November 28, 1882; October 14, 1932; Sunset No. 26.
Bradford, Perley K.; Bruceville, July 8, 1872; October 1, 1932; Elk Grove No. 41.
Burch, Louis Frederick; Napa, May 20, 1892; October 2, 1932; Napa No. 62.
Thompson, Henry H.; San Francisco, January 26, 1866; October 10, 1932; Napa No. 62.
Hogue, Joseph Maurice; San Francisco, August 14, 1889; September 17, 1932; Rincon No. 72.
Kelsey, Van Rensselaer; Los Angeles, June 30, 1890; October 13, 1932; Ramona No. 109.
Sackett, Robert Gordon; Bellflower, February 27, 1902; September 23, 1932; Santa Barbara No. 116.
Schullerts, Bernard T.; San Francisco, October 25, 1878; October 8, 1932; Piedmont No. 120.
McLean, Charles H.; San Francisco, May 13, 1864; October 9, 1932; Piedmont No. 120.
Osslin, Walter; El Dorado, September 11, 1871; September 5, 1932; Chispa No. 139.
Falltrick, Richard; Vallejo, April 25, 1881; August 23, 1932; Donner No. 162.
Ludwig, Henry Peter; Tracy, October 11, 1870; September 22, 1932; Tracy No. 187.
Olson, John Elfred; San Francisco, February 13, 1891; September 21, 1932; Precita No. 187.

YUBA COUNTY.

Marysville No. 6, Marysville—Ray C. Burris, Pres.; Verne Fogarty, Sec., 719 6th St.; 2nd Friday, Foresters Hall.
Rainbow No. 40, Wheatland—F. M. Beilby, Pres.; W. A. Bowser, Sec., P. O. box 313; 2nd Thursday, I.O.O.F. Hall.

AFFILIATED ORGANIZATIONS.

San Francisco Extension of the Order Committee, N.S.G.W.—Joseph J. McShane, Chmn.; Harold J. Regan, Sec., 414 Mason St., San Francisco; meets 2nd and 4th Fridays, Grizzly Bear Club, 414 Mason St., San Francisco.
Alameda County Extension of the Order Committee, N.S.G.W.—Edward T. Schnarr, Chmn.; Frank Roemer, Sec., 3297 Morcom Ave., Oakland; meets 1st and 3rd Mondays, N.S.G.W. Hall, 11th and Clay Sts., Oakland.
Interparlor Committee (Southern District), N.S.G.W. and N.D.G.W.—Burrel D. Neighbours, Chmn.; F. J. Burmester, Sec., P. O. box 42, Colton; meets 2nd and 4th Fridays, Patriotic Hall, 1816 So. Figueroa St., Los Angeles.
San Francisco Assembly No. 1 Past Presidents Association N.S.G.W.—Meets 1st and 3rd Fridays, Native Sons Bldg., 414 Mason St., San Francisco; Jos. E. Tracy, Gov.; J. F. Stanley, Sec., 1175 O'Farrell St., San Francisco.
East Bay Counties Assembly No. 3 Past Presidents Association N.S.G.W.—Meets 4th Monday, Native Sons Hall, 11th and Clay Sts., Oakland; Felix Robison, Gov.; Edgar G. Hanson, Sec., 1260 Russell St., Berkeley.
Marin County Assembly No. 5 Past Presidents Association N.S.G.W.—J. S. Rose Jr., Gov.; L. J. Peter, Sec., Peter Bldg., 4th and "C" Sts., San Rafael.
Fred H. Greeley Assembly No. 6 Past Presidents Association N.S.G.W.—Meets monthly with different Parlors comprising district; R. L. P. Bigelow, Gov.; Barney Barry, Sec., P. O. box 72, Lincoln.
San Joaquin Assembly No. 7 Past Presidents Association N.S.G.W.—Meets 1st Friday, Native Sons Hall, Stockton; Clyde H. Gregg, Gov.; R. D. Dorcey, Sec., Native Sons Club, Stockton.
Sonoma County Assembly No. 9 Past President Association N.S.G.W.—Meets monthly at different Parlor headquarters in county; Louis Bosch, Gov.; L. S. Lewis, Sec., Court House, Santa Rosa.
General John A. Sutter Assembly No. 10 Past Presidents Association—C. C. Wachman, Gov.; Jas. J. Longshore, Sec., 514 "J" St., Sacramento.
Grizzly Bear Club—Members all Parlors outside San Francisco at all times welcome. Clubrooms top floor Native Sons Bldg., 414 Mason St., San Francisco.
Native Sons and Native Daughters Central Committee on Homeless Children—Main office, 955 Phelan Bldg., San Francisco; Mrs. John W. Stirling, Chmn.; Miss Mary E. Brusie, Sec. Los Angeles branch office, 3924 Sunset Blvd.; Dorothy Schlingman, Sec.

(ADVERTISEMENT.)

NATIVE SON PAST PRESIDENTS HAVE GENERAL ASSEMBLY MEETING.

The twelfth annual General Assembly of the N.S.G.W. Past Presidents Association was in session the afternoon of October 15 with Governor General Louis F. Erb presiding. Assemblies represented included San Francisco No. 1, East Bay No. 3, Marin County No. 5, Fred H. Greely No. 6, San Joaquin No. 7, Sonoma No. 9, General John A. Sutter No. 10, Napa-Solano No. 11. Also in attendance were the following N.S.G.W. grand officers: Grand President Seth Millington, Grand Second Vice-president Chas. A. Koenig and Grand Third Vice-president Harmon D. Skillin.

Much routine business was transacted, and many resolutions were presented, but none of any great importance were adopted. Oakland was selected as the meetingplace of the Thirteenth (1933) session. Public Works Director Earl Lee Kelly extended greetings on behalf of Governor James Rolph Jr. Officers were elected, as follows:

J. J. Longshore, Sacramento, governor general; Louis F. Erb, San Francisco, past governor general; Frank Roemer, Oakland, lieutenant-governor general; James F. Stanley, San Francisco, director general; John T. Regan, San Francisco, secretary-treasurer general; Frank Harrison, Saint Helena, marshal general; Frank Wilhelm, San Francisco, guard general; Hubert J. Caveney, San Francisco, sentinel general; Monroe Label, San Rafael, R. L. P. Bigelow, Nevada City, Wesley A. Strong, Stockton, trustees.

Memorial services were held in honor of Dr. Charles W. Decker and William J. Hayes, Past Grand Presidents N.S.G.W., and Henry Faure, Past Governor General P.P.A. Eulogies were delivered, respectively, by Grand President Millington, Grand Third Vice Skillin and Grand Second Vice Koenig. Officers of the General Assembly were installed by Past Governor General Ray B. Felton, assisted by Edward Schnarr, acting marshal general.

In the evening a banquet was held, Irving D. Gibson acting as toastmaster, and the speakers including Grand President Millington, Grand Vices Koenig and Skillin, Grand Secretary John T. Regan, Grand Trustee Charles A. Spengemann, Governor General Longshore, Past Governor General Erb. Fred Kane and Joseph Tracy entertained with songs, and W. A. Strong displayed moving pictures of the 1932 N.S.G.W. Grand Parlor.

Purcell, John F.; Oakland, December 25, 1865; September 25, 1932; Presidio No. 194.
Harris, Rause Bird; San Juan, August 31, 1851; July 6, 1932; Alder Glen No. 200.
Hayes, William J.; Havilah, December 25, 1885; September 26, 1932; Berkeley No. 210.
Devine, Thomas; San Francisco, April 11, 1870; September 28, 1932; Twin Peaks No. 214.
Mason, Henry D.; Plainsburg, November 28, 1872; September 2, 1932; Richmond No. 217.
Haynes, James Louis; Sutter, October 11, 1879; September 20, 1932; Sutter No. 261.

DEATH REMOVES SON PIONEERS.

San Bernardino—Walter J. Tompkins, 61, native, and the son of Pioneer settlers of this city, passed away September 27. He leaves a widow, Lulu Alexander Tompkins (Lugonia Parlor No. 251 N.D.G.W.), six sons and daughters, among them Walter Tompkins (Arrowhead Parlor No. 110 N.S.G.W.) and Lily May McKray (Lugonia No. 241), also two granddaughters and six brothers and sisters, among the latter being Henry Tompkins (Arrowhead No. 110), Daisy T. Hansen and Violet T. Henshilwood (both Long Beach Parlor No. 154 N.D.G.W.).

In Memoriam

RITA GILLERAN SCHOENENBERGER.

We, your committee appointed to draft a testimonial of respect to the memory of Sister Rita Gilleran Schoenenberger, respectfully submit the following:

Again our golden chain has been broken, and it is with deep sorrow we bow in humble submission to the will of our Heavenly Father, who has called from our midst our beloved and highly esteemed member, Rita Gilleran Schoenenberger.

By her untimely passing, San Jose Parlor No. 81 Native Daughters of the Golden West has lost a faithful member, and her family a devoted mother and wife, and a loving daughter and sister.

To these, we extend our heartfelt sympathy, and commend them to a Higher Power for consolation in their grief. We ask that a copy of this testimonial be spread upon the minutes of the Parlor, that a copy be sent to the family, and one to The Grizzly Bear for publication.

CLAIRE BORCHERS,
CLARA BRIGGS,
ELSIE M. FISHER,
Committee.

San Jose, September 22, 1932.

Child Parley—A California conference on child health and protection will be held at San Francisco, November 11 and 12.

Native Daughters of the Golden West

SAN DIEGO—The first of the fall card parties given by San Diego No. 208 was for the benefit of the homeless children and was satisfactorily successful, in that the desired amount was raised. Monthly card parties for the benefit of the general fund of the Parlor will be continued until the holidays. Deputy Carrie E. Northway was a visitor October 12, when one candidate was admitted to membership. Miss Elva Crowley read a number of original poems and Miss Marion S. Stough gave a short sketch of the life and character of Columbus. The Columbus Day idea was also cleverly carried out in the refreshments. Chairmen of committees in charge of arrangements for the occasion were Mms. Marie James and Mabel H. Burgert.

The past presidents club met October 17 at the home of Mrs. Mabel Burgert and made comprehensive plans for the winter's work. At the next meeting, November 16, at the home of Mrs. Elsie Case, the study of the constitution will be begun under the leadership of Miss Elsie Frank. A few days ago a sudden heavy storm following a long wet season swept away the small, frail dam, dating from the early days of San Diego, across the old Switzer Canyon, a spot well known and well beloved in this locality. There has recently been talk of erecting a "bigger and better" dam in its place, which would create a beautiful lake in Balboa Park. All of which inspired the following from the pen of Miss Elva Crowley of No. 208:

Breathing to the city
Its inspiration true,
Balboa Park seeks ardently
Another day and you.
When each and all that heed
The beauty lingering there
Will feel her further need
And hear her tranquil prayer:
"A lake with mirrored trees
Close to the canyon's rim
And mossy banks and lees
Along a sunlit stream,
Which murmurs to enchant
As it flows along,
Winking ever at
All the hurrying throng.
Down thru the hills it goes
Beneath a bridge of stone;
Its secrets it unfolds
To a morning world of tone.
Then covers with its sands
Hopes of a world at work,
Till evening, homeward, wends
Man, its thoughts to dream,
As of a book."

Notable Occasion.

Oroville—Grand President Anna Mixon Armstrong paid an official visit to Gold of Ophir No. 190 October 5. Numerous other visitors were in attendance, including Grand Trustees Edna Briggs and Florence Boyle, Past Grand Presidents Dr. Eva R. Rasmussen and Esther R. Sullivan, Supervising Deputies Ruth Brown and Sadie Brainard, and Deputies Annie Skelly and Anna Bernhard. A turkey dinner preceded the meeting, which was held in Memorial Hall, gorgeously adorned with potted plants and autumn flowers. The new ritual was impressively exemplified, Miss Alma Crum, daughter of President Rosa Crum, affiliating with the Parlor. Mrs. Armstrong spoke of the Order's projects and lauded the Oroville Native Daughters and Native Sons for erecting the Pioneer Memorial Relics Building and placing therein valuable relics.

Grand President Armstrong is postmistress at Woodland, and so, Addie Roderick, attired as a mail carrier, delivered packages of gifts to her and the other grand officers. From Argonaut No. 8 N.S.G.W., Mrs. Armstrong received a boquet of beautiful carnations. During the evening numerous addresses were made, and as a concluding feature an italian supper was served. Committees responsible for the success of the notable occasion included: Decorations—Dorothy Meader, Lauretta Ross, Frances O'Brien, Anna Bernhard, Alma Ghianda. Supper—Alice Frazier, Mattie Lund, Irene Lund, Freda Cole, Alice Tewers. Reception—President Rosa Crum, Grand Trustee Florence Boyle, Flora Sutherland, Addie Roderick, Hazel Scott.

Gold Nuggets for Placecards.

Sierraville—October 1, Imogen No. 134 was hostess at a pioneer dinner at which "Grandma" Emma Perry was guest of honor. She is the oldest woman in Sierra County, being 91 years of age. Eight other Pioneers were present: Mms. Sarah Webber, L. L. Blatchley, Ida A. Joy, Etta Small, O. N. Webber, Emma Nichols, Harry Pearce and Dillon, all of Sierraville.

A plate dinner was served, after which Deputy McMahon gave a very interesting talk. Several Pioneers related earlyday experiences and "Grandma" Perry recited a poem in keeping with the occasion. The table decorations were original and unique, the theme being the old immigrant trail—two immigrant wagons, drawn by oxen, making their way through sagebrush and trees, while in the distance were buffalo and deer. The placecards were in the form of gold nuggets. At the close of the day the immigrant wagons and ox teams were presented to the two oldest guests, "Grandma" Perry and Mrs. Sarah Webber.

Surprise.

Hayward—Hayward No. 122 had a surprise October 4 for Fire Chief and Mrs. Manuel G. Riggs, and many members of Eden No. 113 N.S.G.W. joined in the festivities. Mrs. Riggs, nee Miss Zelda Chisholm, has for more than twenty years been financial secretary of No. 122. Miss Lena Harder played the wedding march and the assemblage proceeded to the banquet-room, elaborately decorated in red. Small fire hats were the placecards. A miscellaneous shower of gifts were presented the honor-guests.

President Florence Hill presided at the festive board, and among the speakers were Mr. and Mrs. Riggs, John Dobbel, Deputy Anna Mello and Mrs. Marion White. The affair was arranged by Mms. Ruth Stromberg, Kathryn Walde and Mrs. Ella Knudsen, and Miss Ruth Gansberger. Whist was played.

Able Work Praised.

Etna—At a joint meeting, Eschscholtzia No. 112 and Mountain Dawn No. 120 (Sawyers Bar) welcomed Grand President Anna M. Armstrong on her official visit. She was accompanied by Supervising Deputy Sadie Brainard of Sacramento and Mrs. Estelle Miller of Woodland. Others present were Grand Trustee Minna K. Horn, Supervising Deputy Margaret E. Weston and Deputy Clara Farr. The lodgeroom was effectively decorated with baskets of dahlias, zinnias and asters. Two candidates were initi ated, one for each of the Parlors.

In a most inspiring address, Mrs. Armstron spoke of her projects for the year, and expresse pleasure in the able work of President Anit Tucker and her corps of officers, who had exem plified the ritual in a very efficient and impres sive manner. At the conclusion of the cere monies delicious refreshments were served a tables attractively decorated with flowers an candles. Piano selections by Miss Margaret Pit man and an informal program of songs an stories by other members brought the pleasann evening to a close. Mms. Armstrong, Brainard Miller and Weston were guests of Grand Truste Horn during their stay in Etna.

Visit Pony Express Museum.

San Bernardino—October was an active mont for Lugonia No. 241, all committees working t replenish the treasury. The 9th, with Chairma Clara Barton of the history and landmarks com mittee as guide, several members drove to Pas dena, where they were guests of W. Parker Lyo sole owner of the Pony Express Museum. A interesting day was spent, and the party ha lunch in the barroom. The 12th, announcemen was made that President Nola Fogler ha changed her name to Mrs. Clifford Noyes, Se tember 30, at Las Vegas, Nevada. Followin the meeting, many of the members drove to Or tario to attend the dedication ceremonies of th marking of the historical station, a pagean dance and card party, all sponsored by Ontari No. 251.

The 22nd, under the supervision of First Vic president Mary Johnson, a benefit luncheon an card party were given. The 26th, the histor and landmarks committee sponsored a miniatu carnival, opened to the public. Concessions i cluded a museum of pioneer relics and an a tique shop. Dancing was in order, and the Pa lor members appeared in historical costumes.

Hawaiian Party.

Sacramento—An elaborate hawaiian part was given by Califia No. 22, the decorations entertainment and refreshments carrying ou the theme in perfect detail. Leis and crown of flowers were presented the grand officers an district deputies at a ceremony in the lodge room, and as the guests entered the banquet room they were given leis. The committee i charge wore costumes of grass skirts, leis an flower wreaths. The ritual was exemplified b a select team under the direction of Mrs. J. G Leitch, supervising deputy. Hawaiian dance were given by Miss Dorothy Brown in costum and songs of the islands were sung by Misse Winifred Fisher and Thelma Chappell, and Mr Evangeline Baker. Guests of the occasion in cluded members of the Sacramento, Stockton Elk Grove, Courtland, Galt and Folsom Parlor

Mrs. Henry Jones planned the evening, wit Mrs. J. G. Leitch as the general chairman. Sub committees included: Decorations—Misse Oneida and Zitka Wilhelm; Mms. Edward Kenn and Alma Craze. Refreshments—Mms. Henr Jones, J. G. Leitch, J. E. Sullivan, Geo. Art Iora Maltby, Alma Craze, Edward Kenny an Hazel Leitch; Misses Oneida Wilhelm, Vivia Hall, Minnie Hopley, Nellie Hopley, Zitka Wil helm and Amy Turner.

Native Sons Banquet Guests.

Quincy—Grand President Anna Mixon Arm strong officially visited Plumas No. 219 Septem ber 19. She was accompanied by Sadie Brainar and Estelle Miller. District Deputy Minnie Johnson was in attendance. Two candidate were initiated, the ritual being exemplified in highly creditable manner. The hall was beaut fully decorated with a profusion of fall flower

At a bounteous banquet members of Quinc No. 131 N.S.G.W. were guests. Mrs. Len Droege was toastmistress, and Grand Presiden Armstrong delivered an inspiring and instru tive address. Other speakers were J. D. Mc Laughlin, Mrs. Brainard, M. McIntosh and Wil son Hogan. Mrs. Thelma Erickson read a poem and Helen Hall entertained with accordion se lections.

Decided Success.

Hollister—October 1 the Parlors of Sant Cruz, Monterey and San Benito Counties hel their annual district meeting at Happy Valley. Representatives of all the Parlors were present, with guests from San Jose, San Francisco and Oakland. The opening function was the Washington bicentennial dinner, with eighty-five seated at the charmingly decorated tables. At the speakers' table were thirteen candles, to represent the thirteen original colonies. A revolving picture of George Washington occupied a place of honor. Martha Washington, in the person of Supervising Deputy Rose Rhyner, was hostess, and famous women of Washington's period, attired in quaint colonial dress, were introduced by Past Grand Bertha A. Briggs. Grand Secretary Sallie R. Thaler, Deputy Edna Butterfield and Supervising Deputy Alice Lane were among the speakers. The program for the outing was carried out as presented in detail in The Grizzly Bear for October. The entire affair was declared a decided success, and many were surprised to discover "unexpected talent (?)" among the performers.

Old Folks Guests.

Willows—Grand President Anna Mixon Armstrong officially visited Berryessa No. 192 October 3. Other visitors included District Deputy Margaret Davison and delegations from Woodland No. 90 and Colus No. 194. Talks were given by Mrs. Armstrong, District Deputy Davison and Edna Richter, and Henrietta Toothaker gave a reading. The lodgeroom was beautifully decorated, and a delicious supper preceded the meeting.

Glenn County oldtimers were guests of the Parlor September 26. They talked over the past, and were served a delicious dinner at tables decorated in yellow and white. Mrs. E. P. Mapes, president of the Parlor, extended a welcome, and Mrs. Jack Knight spoke on "Early California." Entertainment was furnished by an orchestra directed by L. A. McArthur; Misses Vivian and Frances Turman, Eileen McArthur; Mms. Harry Schnurbusch, J. A. McDonald, A. G. Jansen, L. E. Tuttle; Messrs. J. A. Cogswell, Bennie and Eddie Freeman, Karl Kob. For the old folks to dance, Mrs. Laura Cummins played quadrilles.

Pioneers Reception Guests.

Middletown—Clear Lake No. 135 had its annual reception for the Pioneers, and each of the guests was given a California (State) Bear Flag. The hall was beautifully decorated with flags, ferns and late-autumn flowers. Special guests were Supervising Deputy Wilma Mitchell, Deputy Sadie Brooks and Mrs. Ella Parker, charter president of the Parlor, which was instituted in 1902. President Geneva Abercrombie welcomed the guests.

Participants in a most enjoyable program, which opened with a well-executed drill by sixteen members of No. 135 in white uniforms, included Mms. Clara Hunt, Merle Bohn, Leslie Simonsen, Sadie Brooks, Belle Farmer, Maurice Pape, Retta Reynolds and Florence 'Elliott; Frances Herman, Leroy Elliott, Gladys Brooks, Madeline Simonsen. Dainty refreshments were served, and speeches were made by the Pioneers and others.

Grand President's Official Itinerary.

Woodland—During the month of November, Grand President Anna Mixon-Armstrong will officially visit the following Subordinate Parlors on the dates noted:

1st—Richmond No. 147, Richmond.
2nd—Marguerite No. 12, Placerville.
3rd—Buena Vista No. 68, San Francisco.
5th—Victory No. 216, Courtland.
8th—Chabolla No. 171, Galt.
10th—Keith No. 137, San Francisco.
14th—Sea Point No. 196, Sausalito.
15th—Manzanita No. 29, Grass Valley.
16th—Columbia No. 70, French Corral, afternoon; Laurel No. 6, Nevada City, evening.
22nd—El Cereso No. 207, San Leandro.
26th—Woodland No. 90, Woodland.
28th—Guadalupe No. 153, San Francisco.
29th—Fremont No. 59, San Francisco.

Spectacular Drill.

Martinez—The official visit of Grand President Anna Mixon Armstrong to Las Juntas No. 221 October 17 was a most pleasurable occasion. Numerous other visitors were in attendance, among them being Past Grands Amy V. McAvoy, Dr. Louise C. Heilbron and Estelle M. Evans, and Supervising Deputy Myra Rademaker. Two candidates were initiated.

The Parlor's drillteam, composed of twelve young women with Nina Keefe as captain, put on a most spectacular drill. A banquet, at which members of Mount Diablo No. 101 N.S.G.W. were guests, was served by Phoenia Kane, Adah

(Continued on Page 17)

Official Directory of Parlors of the N. D. G. W

GRAND OFFICERS.

Mrs. Evelyn I. Carlson..........Past Grand President
281 E. Tuscaloosa Ave., Atherton
Mrs. Anna M. Armstrong..........Grand President
Woodland
Mrs. Irma Laird..........Grand Vice-president
Alturas
Mrs. Sallie R. Thaler..........Grand Secretary
555 Baker St., San Francisco
Mrs. Susie K. Christ..........Grand Treasurer
555 Baker St., San Francisco
Mrs. Gladys Noce..........Grand Marshal
Sutter Creek
Mrs. Orinda G. Giannini..........Grand Inside Sentinel
2142 Filbert St., San Francisco
Mrs. Hazel B. Hansen..........Grand Outside Sentinel
501 Griswold St., Glendale
Mrs. Clara Gairaud..........Grand Organist
134 Locust St., San Jose

GRAND TRUSTEES.

Mrs. Florence Boyle..........Oroville
Mrs. Edna Briggs..........1045 Santa Ynez Way, Sacramento
Mrs. Anna Thuesen..........615 38th Ave., San Francisco
Mrs. Ethel Begley..........233 Prospect Ave., San Francisco
Mrs. Minna K. Horn..........Etna
Mrs. Jane Vick..........418 Bath St., Santa Barbara
Mrs. Willow Borba..........330 So. Main St., Sebastopol

ALAMEDA COUNTY.

Angelita No. 32, Livermore—Meets 2nd and 4th Fridays, Foresters Hall; Mrs. Myrtle I. Johnson, Rec. Sec., P.O. box 253.
Piedmont No. 87, Oakland—Meets Thursdays, Corinthian Hall, Pacific Bldg.; Mrs. Alice E. Miner, Rec. Sec., 421 36th St.
Aloha No. 106, Oakland—Meets Tuesdays, Wigwam Hall, Pacific Bldg.; Mrs. Lurine Martin, Rec. Sec., 2815 Wallace St., Berkeley.
Hayward No. 122, Hayward—Meets 1st and 3rd Tuesdays, Veterans Memorial Bldg., Main St.; Miss Ruth Gansberger, Rec. Sec., P. O. box 44, Mount Eden.
Berkeley No. 150, Berkeley—Meets 2nd and 4th Wednesdays, Masonic Hall; Mrs. Lelia B. Baker, Rec. Sec., 915 Contra Costa Ave.
Bear Flag No. 151, Berkeley—Meets 2nd and 4th Wednesdays, Veterans Memorial Bldg., 1931 Center St.; Mrs. Maud Wagner, Rec. Sec., 317 Alcatraz Ave., Oakland.
Encinal No. 156, Alameda—Meets 2nd and 4th Wednesdays, Veterans Memorial Bldg., Central Ave. and Walnut St.; Mrs. Laura E. Fisher, Rec. Sec., 1413 Caroline St.
Brooklyn No. 157, East Oakland—Meets 2nd and 4th Wednesdays, Masonic Temple, 8th Ave. and E. 14th St.; Mrs. Ruth Cooney, Rec. Sec., 3907 14th Ave.
Argonaut No. 166, Oakland—Meets Tuesdays, Klinkner Hall, 59th and San Pablo; Mrs. Ada Spilman, Rec. Sec., 2905 Ellis St., Berkeley.
Bahia Vista No. 167, Oakland—Meets Thursdays, Wigwam Hall, Pacific Bldg.; Mrs. Minnie E. Raper, Rec. Sec., 3449 Helen St.
Fruitvale No. 177, Oakland—Meets Fridays, W.O.W. Hall; May E. Barthold, Rec. Sec., 3832 Santa Rita St.
Laura Loma No. 182, Niles—Meets 1st and 3rd Tuesdays, I.O.O.F. Hall; Mrs. Ethel Fournier, Rec. Sec., P. O. box 515.
El Cereso No. 207, San Leandro—Meets 2nd and 4th Tuesdays, Masonic Hall; Mrs. Mary Tuttle, Rec. Sec., P. O. box 56.
Pleasanton No. 237, Pleasanton—Meets 1st Tuesday, I.O.O.F. Hall; Mrs. Myrtle Lanini, Rec. Sec.
Betsy Ross No. 238, Centerville—Meets 1st and 3rd Fridays, Anderson Hall; Miss Constance Lucio, Rec. Sec., P. O. box 187.

AMADOR COUNTY.

Ursula No. 1, Jackson—Meets 2nd and 4th Tuesdays, N.S.G.W. Hall; Mrs. Emma Boarman-Wright, Rec. Sec., 114 Court St.
Chispa No. 40, Ione—Meets 2nd and 4th Fridays, N.S.G.W. Hall; Mrs. Isabel Ashton, Rec. Sec.
Amapola No. 80, Sutter Creek—Meets 2nd and 4th Thursdays, N.S.G.W. Bldg.; Mrs. Hazel M. Marre, Rec. Sec.
Forrest No. 86, Plymouth—Meets 2nd and 4th Tuesdays, I.O.O.F. Hall; Mrs. Marguerite Davis, Rec. Sec.

BUTTE COUNTY.

Annie K. Bidwell No. 168, Chico—Meets 2nd and 4th Thursdays, I.O.O.F. Hall; Mrs Irene Henry, Rec. Sec., 3015 Woodland Ave.
Gold of Ophir No. 190, Oroville—Meets 1st and 3rd Wednesdays, Memorial Hall; Mrs. Ruth Brown, Rec. Sec., 1265 Leah Court.

CALAVERAS COUNTY.

Ruby No. 46, Murphys—Meets 4th Friday, N.S.G.W. Hall; Belle Segale, Rec. Sec.
Princess No. 84, Angels Camp—Meets 2nd and 4th Wednesdays, I.O.O.F. Hall; Mrs. Grace M. Mills, Rec. Sec., P.O. box 313.
San Andreas No. 113, San Andreas—Meets 1st Friday, Fraternal Hall; Miss Doris Treat, Rec. Sec.

COLUSA COUNTY.

Colus No. 194, Colusa—Meets 1st and 3rd Mondays, Eagles Hall; Miss Kate Busch, Rec. Sec., 350 Market St.

CONTRA COSTA COUNTY.

Stirling No. 146, Pittsburg—Meets 1st and 3rd Wednesdays, Veteran Memorial Hall; Mrs. Leslie Clement, Rec. Sec., 468 E. Santa Fe.
Richmond No. 147, Richmond—Meets 1st and 3rd Tuesdays, I.O.O.F. Hall, 10th St.; Grace Curry, Rec. Sec., 1134 Ohio St.
Donner No. 193, Byron—Meets 1st and 3rd Wednesdays, I.O.O.F. Hall; Mrs. Anna Pendry, Rec. Sec., P. O. box 112.
Las Juntas No. 221, Martinez—Meets 1st and 3rd Mondays, Pythian Castle; Mrs. Lola O. Viera, Rec. Sec., 305 Arreba St.
Antioch No. 223, Antioch—Meets 2nd and 4th Tuesdays, I.O.O.F. Hall; Mrs. Estelle Evans, Rec. Sec., 202 E. 5th St., Pittsburg.
Carquinez No. 234, Crockett—Meets 2nd and 4th Wednesdays, I.O.O.F. Hall; Mrs. Cecile Petee, Rec. Sec., 465 Edwards St.

EL DORADO COUNTY.

Marguerite No. 12, Placerville—Meets 1st and 3rd Wednesdays, Masonic Hall; Mrs. Nettie Leonardi, Rec. Sec., 25 Coloma St.
El Dorado No. 186, Georgetown—Meets 2nd and 4th Saturday afternoons, I.O.O.F. Hall; Mrs. Alta L. Douglas, Rec. Sec.

FRESNO COUNTY.

Fresno No. 187, Fresno—Meets 2nd and 4th Fridays, Pythian Castle, Cor. "R" and Merced Sts.; Mary Aubery, Rec. Sec., 1040 Delphia Ave.

GLENN COUNTY.

Berryessa No. 192, Willows—Meets 1st and 3rd Mondays, I.O.O.F. Hall; Mrs. Leonora Neate, Rec. Sec., 338 No. Lassen St.

HUMBOLDT COUNTY.

Occident No. 28, Eureka—Meets 1st and 3rd Wednesdays, N.S.G.W Hall; Mrs. Eva L. MacDonald, Rec. Sec., 2809 "B" St.
Oneonta No. 71, Ferndale—Meets 2nd and 4th Fridays, I.O.O.F. Hall; Mrs. Myra Rumrill, Rec. Sec., P.O. box 142.
Reichling No. 97, Fortuna—Meets 1st and 3rd Tuesdays, Friendship Hall; Mrs. Grace Swett, Rec. Sec., P. O. box 328.

KERN COUNTY.

Miocene No. 228, Taft—Meets 1st and 3rd Wednesday afternoons, I.O.O.F. Hall; Mrs. Evalyn G. Towne, Rec. Sec., P. O. box 1011.
El Tejon No. 239, Bakersfield—Meets 1st and 3rd Fridays, Eagles Hall, 1714 "G" St.; Mary B. Hampson, Rec. Sec., 908 Quincy St.
Desert Gold No. 250, Mojave—Meets 2nd and 4th Fridays, I.O.O.F. Hall; Rein H. Everett, Rec. Sec., P.O. box 83.

LAKE COUNTY.

Clear Lake No. 135, Middletown—Meets 2nd and 4th Tuesdays, Herrick Hall; Mrs. Alma E. Snow, Rec. Sec.

LASSEN COUNTY.

Nataqua No. 152, Standish—Meets 1st and 3rd Wednesdays, Foresters Hall; Mrs. Mayda Elledge, Rec. Sec.
Mount Lassen No. 215, Bieber—Meets 2nd and 4th Thursdays, I.O.O.F. Hall; Mrs. Angie C. Kenyon, Rec. Sec.
Susanville No. 243, Susanville—Meets 3rd Thursday, I.O.O.F. Hall; Mildred Hardy, Rec. Sec., P.O. box 425.

LOS ANGELES COUNTY.

Los Angeles No. 124, Los Angeles—Meets 1st and 3rd Wednesdays, I.O.O.F. Hall, Washington and Oak Sts.; Mrs. Mary K. Corcoran, Rec. Sec., 322 No. Van Ness Ave.
Long Beach No. 154, Long Beach—Meets 1st and 3rd Thursdays, K.P. Hall, 341 Pacific Ave.; Mrs. Bertha Hitt, Rec. Sec., 5355 Lime Ave.
Rudecinda No. 230, San Pedro—Meets 2nd and 4th Thursdays, Unity Hall, I.O.O.F. Temple, 10th and Gaffey; Letitia Sarciaux, Rec. Sec., 483 16th St.
Verdugo No. 240, Glendale—Meets 2nd and 4th Tuesdays, Masonic Temple, 234 So. Brand Blvd.; Miss Etta Fulkerth, Rec. Sec., 526 No. Orange St.
Santa Monica Bay No. 245, Santa Monica—Meets 2nd and 4th Wednesdays, Odd Fellows Hall, 1431 Third St.; Mrs. Rosalie Hyde, Rec. Sec., 738 Flower St., Venice.
Californiana No. 247, Los Angeles—Meets 2nd and 4th Tuesday afternoons, Hollywood Studio Club, 1215 Lodi Place; Mrs. Inez Sitton, Rec. Sec., 4228 Berenice St.

MADERA COUNTY.

Madera No. 244, Madera—Meets 2nd and 4th Thursdays, Masonic Annex; Mrs. Margaret C. Boyle, Rec. Sec., 111 No. "B" St.

MARIN COUNTY.

Sea Point No. 196, Sausalito—Meets 2nd and 4th Mondays, Perry Hall, 50 Caledonia St.; Mrs. Mary B. Smith, Rec. Sec., 559 Woodward Ave.
Marinita No. 198, San Rafael—Meets 2nd and 4th Mondays, 316 "B" St.; Miss Mollye Y. Spaelti, Rec. Sec., 539 4th St.
Fairfax No. 225, Fairfax—Meets 2nd and 4th Tuesdays, Community Hall; Mrs. Marguerite Geary, Rec. Sec.
Tamelpa No. 231, Mill Valley—Meets 1st and 2nd Tuesdays, I.O.O.F. Hall; Mrs. Delphine M. Todt, Rec. Sec., 400 Grand Ave., San Rafael.

MARIPOSA COUNTY.

Mariposa No. 63, Mariposa—Meets 1st and 3rd Fridays, I.O.O.F. Hall; Elizabeth E. Johnson, Rec. Sec.

MENDOCINO COUNTY.

Fort Bragg No. 210, Fort Bragg—Meets 1st and 3rd Thursdays, I.O.O.F. Hall; Mrs. Ruth W. Fuller, Rec. Sec.

MERCED COUNTY.

Veritas No. 75, Merced—Meets 1st and 3rd Tuesdays, I.O.O.F. Hall; Miss Margaret Thornton, Rec. Sec., 817 18th St.

MODOC COUNTY.

Alturas No. 159, Alturas—Meets 1st Thursday, Alturas Civic Club; Mrs. Irma W. Laird, Rec. Sec.

MONTEREY COUNTY.

Aleli No. 102, Salinas—Meets 2nd and 4th Thursdays, Pythian Hall; Miss Rose Rhyner, Rec. Sec., 420 Soledad St.
Junipero No. 141, Monterey—Meets 2nd and 4th Fridays, K. of P. Hall, Main St.; Miss Matilda M. Bergschicker, Rec. Sec., 498 Van Buren St.

NAPA COUNTY.

Eshcol No. 16, Napa—Meets 2nd and 4th Mondays, N.S.G.W. Hall; Mrs. Ella Ingram, Rec. Sec., 2140 Seminary St.
Calistoga No. 145, Calistoga—Meets 2nd and 4th Mondays, I.O.O.F. Hall; Sadie P. Brooks, Rec. Sec.
La Junta No. 203, Saint Helena—Meets 1st and 3rd Tuesdays, N.S.G.W. Hall; Mrs. Marie Signorelli, Rec. Sec., 1341 Madrona Ave.

NEVADA COUNTY.

Laurel No. 6, Nevada City—Meets 1st and 3rd Wednesday I.O.O.F. Hall; Mrs. Nellie E. Clark, Rec. Sec., P. (box 212.
Manzanita No. 29, Grass Valley—Meets 1st and 3rd Tue days, Auditorium; Mrs. Loraine Keast, Rec. Sec., 12 Race St.
Columbia No. 70, French Corral—Meets Fridays, Farrelle Hall; Mrs. Kate Farrelley-Sullivan, Rec. Sec.
Snow Peak No. 176, Truckee—Meets 1st Monday, I.O.O. Hall; Mrs. Henrietta M. Eaton, Rec. Sec., P. O. box 11

ORANGE COUNTY.

Santa Ana No. 235, Santa Ana—Meets 2nd and 4th Mo days, K.C. Hall, 4th and French Sts.; Mrs. Matilda Lemon, Rec. Sec., 1628 W. 8th St.
Grace No. 242, Fullerton—Meets 1st and 3rd Thursday I.O.O.F. Hall, 115½ E. Commonwealth; Mrs. Ma Rothaermel, Rec. Sec., P. O. box 235.

PLACER COUNTY.

Placer No. 138, Lincoln—Meets 2nd Wednesday, I.O.O. Hall; Miss Carrie Parlin, Rec. Sec.
La Rosa No. 191, Roseville—Meets 1st and 3rd Tuesday Eagles Hall; Mrs. Alice Lee West, Rec. Sec., Rocklin.
Auburn No. 233, Auburn—Meets 2nd and 4th Fridays, Fo esters Hall; Mrs. Elsie Patrick, Rec. Sec.

PLUMAS COUNTY.

Plumas Pioneer No. 219, Quincy—Meets 1st and 3rd Mo days, I.O.O.F. Hall; Minnie E. Johnson, Rec. Sec., P. (box 243.

SACRAMENTO COUNTY.

Califia No. 22, Sacramento—Meets 2nd and 4th Tuesday N.S.G.W. Hall; Miss Lulu Gillis, Rec. Sec., 921 8th S
La Bandera No. 110, Sacramento—Meets 1st and 3rd Fr days, N.S.G.W. Hall; Mrs. Clara Weldon, Rec. Sec., 131 "O" St.
Sutter No. 111, Sacramento—Meets 1st and 3rd Tuesday N.S.G.W. Hall; Mrs. Adele Nix, Rec. Sec., 1238 "S" S
Fern No. 123, Folsom—Meets 1st and 3rd Tuesdays, K. Hall; Mrs. Viola Shumway, Rec. Sec., P. O. box 48.
Chabolla No. 171, Galt—Meets 2nd and 4th Tuesday I.O.O.F. Hall; Mrs. Mary Pritchard, Rec. Sec.
Coloma No. 212, Sacramento—Meets 1st and 3rd Tuesday I.O.O.F. Hall, Oak Park; Mrs. Nettie Harry, Rec. Se 1217 35th St.
Liberty No. 213, Elk Grove—Meets 2nd and 4th Friday I.O.O.F. Hall; Mrs. Frances Wackman, Rec. Sec., P. (box 192.
Victory No. 216, Courtland—Meets 1st Saturday and 3 Monday, N.S.G.W. Hall; Mrs. Agneda Lampie, Rec. Se

SAN BENITO COUNTY.

Copa de Oro No. 105, Hollister—Meets 2nd and 4 Thursdays, Grangers Union Hall; Mrs. Mollie Davegg Rec. Sec., 110 San Benito St.
San Juan Bautista No. 179, San Juan Bautista—Meets 1 Wednesday, Mission Corridor Rooms; Miss Gertru Breen, Rec. Sec.

SAN BERNARDINO COUNTY.

Lugonia No. 241, San Bernardino—Meets 2nd and 4 Wednesdays, Eagles Hall; Miss Lois Poling, Rec. Se 1098 Waterman Ave.
Ontario No. 251, Ontario—Meets 2nd and 4th Thursday Ontario Hotel; Miss Helen Hickman, Rec. Sec., 923 N Laurel Ave.

SAN DIEGO COUNTY.

San Diego No. 208, San Diego—Meets 2nd and 4th We nesdays, Directors Room, Chamber Commerce Bldg., 4 W. Broadway; Mrs. Elsie Case, Rec. Sec., 3051 Broadwa

SAN FRANCISCO CITY AND COUNTY.

Minerva No. 2, San Francisco—Meets 1st and 3rd Wedne days, N.S.G.W. Bldg.; Miss Dorothy Finn, Rec. Sec., Princess St., Sausalito.
Alta No. 3, San Francisco—Meets 2nd and 4th Tuesday N.S.G.W. Bldg.; Mrs. Agnese L. Hughes, Rec. Sec., 39 Sacramento St.
Oro Fino No. 9, San Francisco—Meets 1st and 3rd Thu days, N.S.G.W. Bldg.; Mrs. Josephine B. Morrisey, Re Sec., 4441 20th St.
Golden State No. 50, San Francisco—Meets 1st and 3 Wednesdays, N.D.G.W. Home; Miss Millie Tietjen, Re Sec., 328 Lexington Ave.
Orinda No. 56, San Francisco—Meets 2nd, 4th and 5th F days, N.D.G.W. Home; Mrs. Anna A. Gruber-Loser, Re Sec., 72 Grove Lane, San Anselmo.
Fremont No. 59, San Francisco—Meets 1st and 3rd Tue days, N.S.G.W. Bldg.; Miss Hannah Collins, Rec. Se 617 Fillmore St.
Buena Vista No. 68, San Francisco—Meets 1st, 3rd a 5th Thursdays, N.D.G.W. Home; Miss Margaret Barre Rec. Sec., 3774 20th St.
Las Lomas No. 72, San Francisco—Meets 1st and 3rd Tu days, N.D.G.W. Home; Mrs. Marion S. Day, Rec. Se 469 Noe St.
Yosemite No. 83, San Francisco—Meets 1st and 3rd Tu days, American Hall, 20th and Capp Sts.; Miss Ma Monahan, Rec. Sec., 237 Noe St.
La Estrella No. 89, San Francisco—Meets 2nd and 4 Mondays, N.S.G.W. Bldg.; Miss Birdie Hartman, Re Sec., 1018 Jackson St.
Sans Souci No. 96, San Francisco—Meets 2nd and 4th Mo days, N.D.G.W. Home; Mrs. Minnie F. Dobbin, Rec. Se 1483 43rd Ave.
Calaveras No. 103, San Francisco—Meets 2nd and 4 Tuesdays, Swedish American Hall, 2174 Market S Mary L. Krogh, Rec. Sec., 4235 Cabrillo St.
Darina No. 114, San Francisco—Meets 1st and 3rd Mo days, N.S.G.W. Bldg.; Miss Adele Walsh, Rec. Sec., 4 Page St.
El Vespero No. 118, San Francisco—Meets 2nd and 4 Tuesdays, Masonic Hall, 4705 3rd St.; Mrs. Nell Boege, Rec. Sec., 1526 Kirkwood Ave.
Genevieve No. 132, San Francisco—Meets 1st and 3 Thursdays, N.S.G.W. Bldg.; Miss Branice Peguillan, Re Sec., 2434 16th Ave.
Keith No. 137, San Francisco—Meets 2nd and 4th Thu days, N.S.G.W. Bldg.; Mrs. Helen T. Mann, Rec. Se 575 Pierce St., Apt. 206.
Gabrielle No. 139, San Francisco—Meets 2nd and 4 Wednesdays, N.S.G.W. Bldg.; Mrs. Dorothy Wuesterfe Rec. Sec., 1020 Munich St.
Presidio No. 148, San Francisco—Meets 2nd and 4th Tu days, N.S.G.W. Bldg.; Mrs. Hattie Gaughran, Rec. Se 713 Capp St.
Guadalupe No. 153, San Francisco—Meets 2nd and 4 Mondays, Forester Hall, 170 Valencia St.; Miss May McCarthy, Rec. Sec., 336 Elsie St.
Golden Gate No. 158, San Francisco—Meets 2nd and 4 Mondays, N.S.G.W. Bldg.; Mrs. Mary Sullivan, Rec. Se 33 Cuvier St.
Dolores No. 169, San Francisco—Meets 2nd and 4th W nesdays, N.S.G.W. Bldg.; Mrs. Ada Saunders, Rec. Se 284 Allison St.
Linda Rosa No. 170, San Francisco—Meets 2nd and 4 Wednesdays, Swedish American Hall, 2174 Market S Mrs. Eva P. Tyrrel, Rec. Sec., 2629 Mission St.

ATTENTION, SECRETARIES!

THIS DIRECTORY IS PUBLISHED BY AUTHORITY OF THE GRAND PARLOR N.D.G.W., AND ALL NOTICES OF CHANGES MUST BE RECEIVED BY THE GRAND SECRETARY (NOT THE MAGAZINE) ON OR BEFORE THE 20TH OF EACH MONTH TO INSURE CORRECTION IN NEXT PUBLICATION OF DIRECTORY.

ortola No. 172, San Francisco—Meets 1st and 3rd Tuesdays, N.S.G.W. Bldg.; Catherine H. Dolly, Rec. Sec., 4125 23rd St.
astro No. 178, San Francisco—Meets 1st and 3rd Wednesdays, K.C. Bldg., 150 Golden Gate Ave.; Miss Adeline Sandersfeld, Rec Sec., 50 Baker St.
win Peaks No. 185, San Francisco—Meets 2nd and 4th Fridays, Druids Temple, 44 Page St.; Mrs. Loretta Cameron, Rec. Sec., 3909 Army St.
ames Lick No. 220, San Francisco—Meets 1st and 3rd Wednesdays, N.S.G.W. Bldg.; Mrs. Edna Bishop, Rec. Sec., 3841 24th St.
ission No. 227, San Francisco—Meets 2nd and 4th Fridays, N.S.G.W. Bldg.; Mrs. Ann Dippel, Rec. Sec., 448 Dewey Blvd.
ret Harte No. 233, San Francisco—Meets 2nd and 4th Tuesdays, Aloha Hall, 3009 16th St.; Pearl Weddo, Rec. Sec., 225 7th Ave.
a Dorada No. 236, San Francisco—Meets 2nd and 4th Thursdays, N.S.G.W. Hall; Mrs. Theresa R. O'Brien, Rec. Sec., 567 Liberty St.
alboa No. 249, San Francisco—Meets 2nd and 4th Thursdays, Maccabee Hall, 5th Ave. and Clement St.; Miss Jean Moffet, Rec. Sec., 476 26th Ave.
topia No. 252, San Francisco—Meets 2nd and 4th Tuesdays, American Hall, 20th and Capp Sts.; Miss Lelia M. Little, Rec. Sec., 4450 20th St.

SAN JOAQUIN COUNTY.

oaquin No. 5, Stockton—Meets 2nd and 4th Tuesdays, N.S.G.W. Hall, 314 E. Main St.; Mrs. Della Garvin, Rec. Sec., 1122 E. Market St.
l Pescadero No. 82, Tracy—Meets 1st and 3rd Fridays, I.O.O.F. Hall; Mrs. Mary A. Hewitson, Rec. Sec., 122 Walnut St.
ry No. 88, Lodi—Meets 1st and 3rd Wednesdays, Eagles Hall; Mrs. Mae Oorson, Rec. Sec., 109 So. School St.
alls de Oro No. 206, Stockton—Meets 1st and 3rd Tuesdays, N.S.G.W. Hall, 314 E. Main St.; Mrs. Frances Germain, Rec. Sec., 450 No. Regent.
hoebe A. Hearst No. 214, Manteca—Meets 2nd and 4th Wednesdays, I.O.O.F. Hall; Mrs. Josie M. Frederick, Rec. Sec., Route A, Box 364, Ripon.

SAN LUIS OBISPO COUNTY.

an Miguel No. 94, San Miguel—Meets 2nd and 4th Wednesday afternoons, Clemon Hall; Mrs. Nellie Wickstrom, Rec. Sec.
an Luisita No. 108, San Luis Obispo—Meets 2nd and 4th Thursdays, W.O.W. Hall; Miss Agnes M. Lee, Rec. Sec., P. O. box 584.
l Pinal No. 163, Cambria—Meets 2nd, 4th and 5th Tuesdays, N.S.G.W. Hall; Kathryn Luchessa, Rec. Sec.

SAN MATEO COUNTY.

onita No. 10, Redwood City—Meets 2nd and 4th Thursdays, I.O.O.F. Hall; Mrs. Dora Wilson, Rec. Sec., 518 Middlefield Rd.
ista del Mar No. 155, Halfmoon Bay—Meets 2nd and 4th Thursdays, I.O.O.F. Hall; Elizabeth Olney, Rec. Sec.
no Nuevo No. 180, Pescadero—Meets 1st and 3rd Wednesdays, I.O.O.F. Hall; Mrs. Alice Mattei, Rec. Sec.
l Carmelo No. 181, Daly City—Meets 1st and 3rd Wednesdays, Masonic Hall; Mrs. Hattie Kelly, Rec. Sec., 1179 Brunswick St.
enlo No. 211, Menlo Park—Meets 2nd and 4th Mondays, Masonic Hall; Mrs. Frances E. Maloney, Rec. Sec., P. O. box 626.
an Bruno No. 246, San Bruno—Meets 2nd and 4th Fridays, Legion Hall; Miss Mildred Foley, Rec. Sec., 217 Miller Ave., South San Francisco.

SANTA BARBARA COUNTY.

eina del Mar No. 126, Santa Barbara—Meets 1st and 3rd Tuesdays, Pythian Castle, 222 W. Carillo St.; Mrs. Dorothy Yule, Rec. Sec., P.O. box 670.

SANTA CLARA COUNTY.

an Jose No. 81, San Jose—Meets Thursdays, Catholic Women Center, 5th and San Fernando Sts.; Mrs. Nellie Fleming, Rec. Sec., Catholic Women Center.
endome No. 100, San Jose—Meets Wednesdays, Old Scottish Rite Temple; Miss Marie Buck, Rec. Sec., 245 Hawthorne St.
l Monte No. 205, Mountain View—Meets 2nd and 4th Fridays, American Legion Hall; Miss Mary Ann Rokovich, Rec. Sec., P.O. box 422-B.
alo Alto No. 229, Palo Alto—Meets 1st and 2nd Mondays, N.S.G.W. Hall; Miss Helena G. Hansen, Rec. Sec., 531 Lytton Ave.

SANTA CRUZ COUNTY.

anta Cruz No. 26, Santa Cruz—Meets Mondays, N.S.G.W. Hall; Mrs. May L. Williamson, Rec. Sec., 170 Walnut Ave.
l Pajaro No. 35, Watsonville—Meets 1st and 3rd Tuesdays, I.O.O.F. Hall; Miss Ruth E. Wilson, Rec. Sec., 16 Laurel St.

SHASTA COUNTY.

amellia No. 41, Anderson—Meets 1st and 3rd Tuesdays, Masonic Hall; Mrs. Olga E. Welbourn, Rec. Sec.
assen View No. 98, Shasta—Meets 2nd Friday, Masonic Hall; Miss Louise Litsch, Rec. Sec.
iawatha No. 140, Redding—Meets 2nd and 4th Wednesdays, Moose Hall; Ruth Presleigh, Rec. Sec., Office County Clerk.

SIERRA COUNTY.

aomi No. 36, Downieville—Meets 2nd and 4th Wednesdays, I.O.O.F. Hall; Louise C. Dubuque, Rec. Sec.
negen No. 134, Sierraville—Meets 2nd and 4th Saturday afternoons, Copren Hall; Mrs. Jennie Copren, Rec. Sec.

SISKIYOU COUNTY.

schscholtzia No. 112, Etna—Meets 1st and 3rd Wednesdays, Masonic Hall; Mrs. Bernice E. Smith, Rec. Sec.
ountain Dawn No. 120, Sawyers Bar—Meets 2nd and last Wednesdays, I.O.O.F. Hall; Miss Edith Dunphy, Rec. Sec.

SOLANO COUNTY.

allejo No. 195, Vallejo—Meets 1st and 3rd Wednesdays, K.C. Hall, 820 Marin St.; Mrs. Mary Combs, Rec. Sec., 511 York St.
ary E. Bell No. 224, Dixon—Meets 2nd and 4th Thursdays, I.O.O.F. Hall; Grace McFadyen, Rec. Sec.

SONOMA COUNTY.

onoma No. 209, Sonoma—Meets 2nd and 4th Mondays, I.O.O.F. Hall; Mrs. Mae Norrbom, Rec. Sec., R.F.D., box 171.
anta Rosa No. 217, Santa Rosa—Meets 1st and 3rd Thursdays, N.S.G.W. Hall; Mrs. Clytie L. Lewis, Rec. Sec., R.F.D. No. 4, Box 345-A.
etaluma No. 222, Petaluma—Meets 1st and 3rd Tuesdays, Dania Hall; Mrs. Margaret M. Oeltjen, Rec. Sec., 503 Prospect St.

STANISLAUS COUNTY.

akdale No. 125, Oakdale—Meets 1st Monday, I.O.O.F. Hall; Mrs. Lou Reeder, Rec. Sec.
orada No. 199, Modesto—Meets 2nd and 4th Wednesdays, I.O.O.F. Hall; Mrs. Susan Sullivan, Rec. Sec., 823 10th St.
ldora No. 248, Turlock—Meets 1st and 3rd Wednesdays, Fraternal Hall; Effie Lund, Rec. Sec., 624 Minaret Ave.

SUTTER COUNTY.

outh Butte No. 226, Sutter—Meets 1st and 3rd Mondays, N.D.G.W. Hall; Mrs. Abbie N. Varedes, Rec. Sec.

TEHAMA COUNTY.

erendos No. 23, Red Bluff—Meets 1st and 3rd Tuesdays, W.O.W. Hall, 200 Pine St.; Mrs. Lillie Hammer, Rec. Sec., 636 Jackson St.

TRINITY COUNTY.

Eltapome No. 55, Weaverville—Meets 2nd and 4th Thursdays, N.S.G.W. Hall; Mrs. Lou N. Fetzer, Rec. Sec.

TUOLUMNE COUNTY.

Dardanelle No. 66, Sonora—Meets Fridays, I.O.O.F. Hall; Mrs. Nettie Whitto, Rec. Sec.
Golden Era No. 99, Columbia—Meets 1st and 3rd Thursdays, N.S.G.W. Hall; Miss Irene Ponce, Rec. Sec.
Anona No. 164, Jamestown—Meets 2nd and 4th Tuesdays, I.O.O.F. Hall; Nellie Hope, Rec. Sec.

YOLO COUNTY.

Woodland No. 90, Woodland—Meets 2nd and 4th Tuesdays, N.S.G.W. Hall; Mrs. Maude Heaton, Rec. Sec., 153 College St.

YUBA COUNTY.

Marysville No. 162, Marysville—Meets 2nd and 4th Wednesdays, Liberty Hall; Miss Cecelia C. Gomes, Rec. Sec., 701 6th St.
Camp Far West No. 218, Wheatland—Meets 3rd Tuesday, I.O.O.F. Hall; Mrs. Ethel C. Brock, Rec. Sec., P. O. box 285.

AFFILIATED ORGANIZATIONS.

General Assembly Past Presidents—Meetings held annually in April at the home-town of Chief President; Mrs. Cora Stobing, 1739 San Jose Ave., San Francisco, Chief President; Mrs. Anna G. Loser, 72 Grove Lane, San Anselmo, Chief Secretary.
Past Presidents Association No. 1—Meets 1st and 3rd Mondays, N.S.G.W. Bldg., 414 Mason St., San Francisco; Mrs. Minnie F. Dobbin, Pres.; Mrs. May R. Barry, Rec. Sec., 2319 19th Ave., San Francisco.
Past Presidents Association No. 2—Meets 2nd and 4th Mondays, "Wigwam," Pacific Bldg., 16th and Jefferson, Oakland; Emma Haggerty, Pres.; Mrs. Elizabeth B. Goodman, Rec. Sec., 134 Juana Ave., San Leandro.
Past Presidents Association No. 3 (Santa Clara County)—Meets 2nd Tuesday, homes of members; Mrs. Amelia Hartman, Pres.; Mrs. Mary G. Newton, Rec. Sec., 1070 Jackson St., Santa Clara.
Past Presidents Association No. 4 (Sacramento County)—Meets 2nd Monday, N.S.G.W. Hall, 11th and "J" Sts., Sacramento City; Edna Briggs, Pres.; Lily May Tilden, Rec. Sec., 3225 "T" St., Sacramento.
Past Presidents Association No. 5 (Butte County)—Meets 1st Friday, homes of members, Chico and Oroville; Marie Picanco, Pres.; Ruth Brown, Rec. Sec., 1265 Leah Court, Oroville.
Past Presidents Association No. 6 (Nevada County)—Meets 4th Friday, alternately between Nevada City, Pythian Castle, and Grass Valley, Edna Sampson's home; Margaret V. Nolan, Pres.; Vere Hansen, Rec. Sec., R.F.D. No. 2, box 41-C, Grass Valley.
Past Presidents Association No. 7 (Sonoma County)—Meets 1st Thursday, Violet Mastrup home, 622 5th St., Petaluma; Willow Borba, Pres.; Elizabeth Dillon, Rec. Sec., Petaluma.
Past Presidents Association No. 8 (San Joaquin and Stanislaus Counties)—Meets 2nd Thursday, Red Men Hall, Stockton; Mrs. Lois Armstrong, Pres.; Mrs. Harriet F. Corr, Rec. Sec., 729 E. Sonora St., Stockton.
Native Sons and Native Daughters Central Committee on Homeless Children—Main Office, 955 Phelan Bldg., San Francisco; Mrs. John W. Stirling, Chmn.; Miss Mary E. Brusie, Sec. Los Angeles branch office, 3924 Sunset Blvd.; Dorothy Schlingman, Sec.

(ADVERTISEMENT.)

NATIVE DAUGHTER NEWS

(Continued from Page 15)

Johnston, Cecilia Rogers, Georgia Doss, Nellie Nicholson, Ethel Claeys and Gertrude King.

President Is Hostess.

Sacramento—President Ida Merwin of Sutter No. 111 honored her officers at her home in Clarksburg. An elaborate dinner was followed by bridge. In attendance were Mms. Lorraine Williams, Audrey Brown, Lavinia Blakeley, Edna Mooney, Adele Nix, Lottie Patterson, Helene Islip, Lily Hinrich and Emilie Lachmann; Misses Ethel Riley, Margaret Nix, Lorene Patterson, Maybelle Tuggle, Thelma Toft and Lily Tilden.

The Parlor had past presidents night October 11. After an enjoyable program all retired to the banquetroom, where refreshments were served. A large number of past presidents were seated at a center table, where each of the honored guests found a potted plant at her place. Mrs. Lavinia Bennetts was in charge of the evening. Deputy Esther Mulligan and Past Grand Dr. Louise Heilbron attended.

Novel Experience.

Alturas—A novel experience awaited Grand President Anna Mixon Armstrong when she officially visited Alturas No. 159 in the heart of "the cow country." Typifying the hospitality of the range, a "buckaroo" dinner was served to the distinguished officer and her companion, Mrs. Sadie Winn-Brainard of Califia No. 22 (Sacramento). In cowboy attire, Grand Vice-president Irma Laird presided as foreman of "the Alturas outfit," and with her cowboy entertainers, Rachel Asher, Irene Cummings, Lelah and Mildred Boyd, presented excellent musical numbers. Past Grand Catherine Gloster and Supervising Deputy Dorothy Gloster also contributed to the program. A business session followed the banquet. All present evinced deep interest in and appreciation of the splendid message brought by the Grand President, who took occasion to compliment the Parlor for the good work it is doing in carrying on the projects of the Order, as well as contributing its quota to the civic welfare of its own community.

At the October 6 meeting Grand Vice-president Irma Laird and Elizabeth Callaghan reported on their visit to the district meeting of the San Francisco Parlors and the Home. The museum committee reported the promise of relics from Pioneers. October 8, Grand President Seth Millington and a group of Sacramento Valley past presidents were in Alturas to re-institute Alturas No. 134. Following the meeting a committee of Native Daughters served refreshments.

Pleasurable Program.

Saint Helena—Over a hundred enthusiastic Native Daughters participated in a district meeting, with La Junta No. 203 as hostess. The affair was arranged as a get-together meeting to give the members in the district an opportunity to become better acquainted, and was the first of a series which, it is hoped, will be continued. All participating Parlors had large delegations—Eshcol No. 16 (Napa), Vallejo No. 195, Calistoga No. 145, Clear Lake No. 135 (Middletown) and La Junta. The regular meeting of No. 203 was held, and these special guests were escorted to places of honor: Mrs. W. Mitchell, supervising deputy, Mms. Sadie Brooks, Elvina Woodward and Emma McGlunphy, deputies. The ritualistic and other phases of Parlor work were executed by La Junta for the pleasure of the visitors. The guests of honor each said a few words, which revealed enthusiasm for the get-together plan.

The Parlor meeting was adojurned and an interesting program followed. The Calistoga girls put on a pretty drill. Mrs. Mitchell led community singing, while the Napa girls were preparing for a humorous skit, "The Human Ford;" after a few flat tires they finally got started. A "Half Hour's Pleasure at the Beach," a reading by Mrs. Farmer, followed, then Mms. Waldeck and M. Alexander sang two lovely songs, "Neopolitan Nights" and "California Lullaby." After this pleasurable program refreshments were served in the banquet hall, where autumn leaves and huge baskets of fruit formed the table decorations.

Wedded at Mission.

Modesto—Morada No. 199 and Modesto No. 11 N.S.G.W. held the first of a series of whist parties October 19. Guests were seated at forty-five tables. Dancing and refreshments followed the card playing. Robert Hansen was master of ceremonies. The next party will be given November 9.

Morada's sewing club met at the home of Mrs. Lena Browder October 22, at which time garments were made for a family of eight which the Parlor is caring for. Mrs. Ethel Gardner was chairman of a costume party October 26. All members not in Hallowe'en costume paid a penalty. Deputy Ethel Mathiasen was married in the Santa Barbara Mission October 19 to Frank Enos of Modesto.

Past Presidents Doings.

Oakland—Association No. 2 celebrated its twenty-first anniversary with a carnival and dinner dance October 8. Guests were Emma Haggerty, Frieda Reichhold, Jennie Brown, Leah Williams. Elizabeth Goodman and committee had charge of the affair, and the humorous program and games were in charge of A. Silva, A. Hofmeister, E. Hall, M. Ward.

San Jose—Association No. 3 entertained Alameda County past presidents October 11. The feature was the report of the welfare committee, Claire Borchers chairman. A Hallowe'n sociable was enjoyed. The arrangements committee included Clara Briggs, Fay Withycombe, Claire Borchers, Elizabeth Hayes, President Amelia Hartman.

Oroville—Mary Woodall, Margaret Gilbert and Emma Logan jointly entertained Association No. 5 October 7 at the home of the former. Three candidates were initiated. Bridge was played. In observance of the Association's fifth anniversary a dinner will be held November 3 in Oroville.

(Additional N.D.G.W. News on Page 19)

N.D.G.W. OFFICIAL DEATH LIST.

Giving the name, the date of death, and the Subordinate Parlor affiliation of all deceased members as reported to Grand Secretary Sallie R. Thaler from September 20, 1932, to October 18, 1932:

Leake, Sarah Johnson; September 22; Berryessa No. 192.

Reed, Helen; September 26; Alta No. 3.

Schonenberger, Rita G.; September 11; San Jose No. 81.

Bremer, Martha Duston; September 13; Sutter No. 111.

"Lights That Blind Are Most Unkind," is the November slogan of the California Public Safety Committee in its campaign to lessen the constantly increasing auto death-toll.

Birthday Celebration—Santa Cruz City, October 8, celebrated the one hundred and sixty-third anniversary of its beginning.

Passing of the California Pioneer

(Confined to Brief Notices of the Demise of Those Men and Women Who Came to California Prior to 1870.)

MRS. MARY ISABELLA CARSON, native of Indiana, 95; with her parents, Mr. and Mrs. Consider Mitchell, crossed the plains to California, arriving at Stockton, San Joaquin County, in November 1850; died near Stockton, survived by seven children. She was the widow of William McK. Carson, for sixteen years supervisor of San Joaquin County.

Mrs. Ellen Cecelia Egan-Glover, native of Louisiana, 82; came in 1852; died at Benicia, Solano County, her home for seventy-eight years, survived by three children.

Mrs. Lavina McClain, native of Ohio, 81; came via the Isthmus of Panama in 1853 and resided in San Francisco, and Alameda, Napa and Stanislaus Counties; died at Oakland.

E. DeWitt, native of Kentucky, 89; came across the plains in 1855 and resided in Yuba and Tulare Counties; died at Long Beach, Los Angeles County, survived by five children.

Mrs. Sarah Martha Hunt, native of Missouri, 84; since 1855 resident Shasta County; died at Millville, survived by four children.

Mrs. Dorothea Morales, native of Mexico, 87; since 1855 resident Calaveras County; died at Melones, survived by ten children.

Mrs. Helen Miller-Eby, native of Illinois, 88; came across the plains in 1856 and long resided in Tehama County; died at Sacramento City, survived by three daughters. She was the widow of Jackson Eby, for many years Tehama County assessor.

Mrs. Emma Elphina Cooper-Bentley, native of Illinois, 78; came in 1856 and settled in Yolo County; died at Winters, survived by two children.

Albert J. Ismert, native of New York, 86; came in 1856 and settled in Nevada County; died near Grass Valley, survived by three sons.

Thomas Lawson Barry, native of Missouri, 86; came across the plains in 1857 and resided in Napa, Los Angeles and Humboldt Counties; died at Eel Rock, survived by three children.

William J. Lovelady, native of Arkansas, 77; crossed the plains in 1857 and resided in Nevada and Colusa Counties; died at Lodoga.

Mrs. Sophie Christinia Hall, native of Pennsylvania, 89; came across the plains in 1858 and for fifty-nine years resided in Shasta County; died at Wengler, survived by three children.

Benjamin F. Dailey, native of New York, 88; came across the plains in 1860 and eight years later settled in Tulare County; died near Exeter, survived by a wife and four children.

Mrs. Henrietta Dorothea Boce-Hibbard, native of Germany, 94; came via the Isthmus of Panama in 1860 and resided in Solano and Lake Counties; died at Vallejo, survived by three daughters.

Mrs. Mary Catherine Lynch, native of Ireland, 90; since 1860 Butte County resident; died at Gridley, survived by six children.

Thomas B. Roy, native of Vermont, 91; came in 1861 and the following year settled in Marin County; died at San Geronimo, survived by a wife and a son.

Thomas William O'Brien, native of Massachusetts, 100; in 1861 arrived via the Isthmus of Panama in San Francisco, where he died; seven children survive.

William Henry McGregor, native of Illinois, 84; came in 1862; died at Camino, El Dorado County, survived by five children. He served in Company A of the California Militia during the Civil War.

Mrs. Elizabeth Herrington-Stevens, native of Iowa, 73; came across the plains in 1863 and resided in Sonoma and Marin Counties; died at San Rafael, survived by a husband and a son.

John Henry Palmer, native of Massachusetts, 83; came in 1863 and resided in Yuba and Butte Counties; died at Gridley, survived by two children.

Mrs. Maria DeBernardi-Cola, native of Switzerland, 82; came in 1863 and long resided in El Dorado County; died at Sacramento City, survived by five children.

George W. Cousins, native of Maine, 72; since 1864 resident Humboldt County; died at Eureka, survived by a wife and two sons. He served eight years as clerk of Humboldt County and two terms as mayor of Eureka.

Mrs. Ellen Wilson-Hemphill, native of England, 90; came via the Isthmus of Panama in 1865 and resided many years in Santa Clara County; died at Berkeley, Alameda County, survived by four children.

Harry Roberts, native of England, 86; came in 1865; died at Ventura City, survived by a wife and seven children.

Mrs. Dina Sheela, native of Canada, 72; came in 1867 and resided in Kings, Tulare and Fresno Counties; died at Oakland, Alameda County, survived by six children.

Dr. Page Brown, native of Missouri, 77; came in 1867 and resided in San Francisco, Santa Cruz and Los Angeles Cities; died at the latter place, survived by a wife and a son.

Mrs. Rachael Jost, native of England, 86; since 1867 resident Sacramento City, where she died; two children survive.

Anton Vaccarezza, native of Italy, 88; came in 1868; died at Hollister, San Benito County, survived by a wife and four children.

Mrs. Charles Tomlinson-Taylor, native of Nova Scotia, 79; came in 1868 and settled in Eureka, Humboldt County; died at San Francisco, survived by two children.

Mrs. Clarinda Rowley LaSalle, native of Illinois, 84; came in 1868 and shortly thereafter settled in Santa Barbara County; died at Lompoc, survived by three children.

Mrs. Caroline S. Seamans, native of South Carolina, 92; since 1869 resident Vallejo, Solano County, where she died; two daughters survive.

Chresten Nicholaisen, native of Denmark, 82; since 1869 resident Hayward, Alameda County, where he died; two children survive.

Mrs. Sydnie M. Baker, native of Virginia, 88; came in 1862; died at Chico, Butte County, survived by two sons.

James Turner, native of Ohio, 102; came in 1850 and settled in San Joaquin County; died near Turner Station, survived by six children. He was the sole surviving member of the San Joaquin County Pioneer Society.

Mrs. Yetta Alexander, native of Texas, 97; came in 1849 and resided in Sacramento and San Francisco Cities; died at the latter place, survived by a daughter.

MARKED

(Continued from Page 7)

Mrs. John W. Baxter, president of Ontario presided at the impressive ceremonies, and the speakers included Mrs. Florence Dodson-Schoneman, Judge Benjamin F. Warmer and Grand Outside Sentinel Hazel B. Hansen. The monument is inscribed: "In memory of the California Pioneers. Bear Gulch, the Home of Osos. In 1779, Father Font camped here on his way to Monterey. Dedicated by Ontario Parlor, No. 251, Native Daughters of the Golden West, October 12, 1932."

CHIMNEY ROCK DEDICATION RECALLS PROGRESS SINCE COVERED WAGON DAYS

Alturas (Modoc County)—Under the auspices of Alturas Parlor No. 159 N.D.G.W., Grand President Anna Mixon Armstrong dedicated September 21 a bronze plaque on Chimney Rock. Here in 1871, Thos. Denson, the second settler in Pit River Valley, chiseled out a fireplace for his earlyday home. Mrs. Sadie Winn-Brainard unveiled the plaque. Others on the program were Rev. Schwabenland, President Erma Elliott, Rev. O'Driscoll, Grand Vice-president Irma Laird, Dorothy Gloster, Past Grand President Catherine Gloster, Fred Cronemiller, Clifford Harter and Judge E. C. Bonner. The Alturas high school band furnished music.

This pyramid-shaped rock stands beside the Yellowstone railway cutoff. The Alturas-Lakeview train was held between Alturas and Chimney Rock until the completion of the ceremonies. Then, as the long train moved slowly away, to the large crowd of citizens assembled came the realization of the great progress made since the Pioneers toiled westward in covered wagons.

Gas Funds Divided—California apportioned October 17 between the counties and the State Highways Division $9,811,881.94 gasoline taxes collected during the quarter ended September 30. The counties got $3,270,627.32 and the highway division $6,541,254.62. Of the fifty-eight counties, Los Angeles received the largest divvy, $1,325,883.58.

Armistice Day—Armistice Day, November 11 will be observed generally throughout California.

NATIVE DAUGHTER NEWS

Napa—Grand President Anna M. Armstrong visited Eshcol No. 16 October 10. A turkey dinner preceding the meeting was attended by sixty-one. The hall was beautifully decorated, and two candidates were initiated. Mrs. Armstrong was presented with a silver dish, and other grand officers were presented with flowers. Past Grand Estelle Evans sang several solos, and the Grand President gave a very inspiring talk on the projects sponsored by the Order. Visitors were present from all Parlors in the district. Eshcol is planning its annual card party for the benefit of the homeless children during November.

Merced—Veritas No. 75 had a reception October 11 in honor of Supervising Deputy May S. Givens, who is now residing in this city. Mrs. Lennie Crawford delivered a welcome address, and musical numbers were given by Miss Marian Pulcifer, and Mms. Grace Leonard and Alma Fowler. Following cards, refreshments were served in the banquetroom, decorated in the Hallowe'en motif, by a committe comprising Mms. Mary vanden Heuvel (chairman), Lennie Crawford, Alma Fowler, Hazel Laverty, Mayme Reuter, Zelphia Thomas, and Miss Marian Pulcifer.

Woodland—Grand President Anna Mixon Armstrong, in the course of a charming address, presented a California State (Bear) Flag to the C. F. Dingle grammar school September 29. Seventh and eighth grades pupils staged a program, and Miss Henrietta Toothaker of Woodland No. 90 sang "California Is Calling Me."

Oakland—October 11, Aloha No. 106 entertained members and guests with a country fair. The social committee, under the able guidance of Past President Gladys Farley, had charge of booths containing candy, cakes, cookies, pies, jellies, jams, handkies, aprons, doughnuts, hotdogs and coffee. A "haywire orchestry" provided music for the two-cent dance, and fortunetellers were in evidence. The various booths were attractively decorated with all colors of crepe paper, serpentine and comical signs. Plans are being made by Chairman Caroline Schulze and committee for a theater party November 15.

San Andreas—San Andreas No. 113 entertained the menfolks October 15 at a delightful social. A series of games, arranged by President Zaida Hertzig, Oleta Meyer and Myrtle Schwoerer, were played, and an excellent supper was served by Grace Tiscornia, Bessie Serra and Gertrude Leonard. Hallowe'en was the theme of the evening.

Crockett—October 12, Grand President Anna M. Armstrong made her official visit to Carquinez No. 234. Delegations from Woodland, San Diego, Aloha, Antioch, Stirling, Piedmont, Richmond, Chispa and Santa Rosa Parlors, Past Grand Presidents Dr. Louise C. Heilbron and Estelle Evans, Grand Secretary Sallie R. Thaler, Grand Trustee Willow Borba, Supervising Deputy Myra Rademaker and Deputy Grace Curry were present. One candidate was initiated. A short program was given by Arthur Franges, Miss Doris Franges and Arlene Smith. Arthur and Doris Franges are children of Mrs. Lucile Franges, a member of No. 234. The Parlor plans a food sale some time in November.

Fullerton—Grace No. 242 resumed activities when the losing side in a recent membership contest served a chicken dinner. Cards followed, and a social time was enjoyed. Past President Carrie Ford entertained September 29 the homeless children sewing club at an all-day meeting. The next meeting of the club will be at the Los Angeles home of Deputy Mary Noerenberg. This will also be an all-day affair, and one to which members are looking forward. The regular meetings in October were well attended, with Past Presidents Mary Rothaermel and Nellie Cline sponsoring the social hours. Plans are being formed for numerous Parlor activities.

Madera—Mae S. Givens, supervising deputy of Fresno, Madera, Merced and Mariposa Counties, called a meeting of the deputies of the Parlors in those counties at the home of Lois Roach of Madera No. 244. Instructions from the Grand President were read and noted. Plans were discussed for a district meeting in Madera, April 6.

Ontario—Ontario No. 251 had a Hallowe'en party October 27 in honor of Mrs. Frank Van Fleet, largely responsible for the building of the bear monument. Guests were Grand Outside Sentinel Hazel Hansen, Mrs. Florence Schonemann, Deputy Ella Madden, Mrs. Muriel Bray and Mrs. D. Pope. Cards were played and refreshments were served. Esther Kremer, Vada Austin and Dorthea Lucas constituted the committee in charge.

STATEMENT OF THE OWNERSHIP, MANAGEMENT, CIRCULATION, ETC.,

Required by Act of Congress of August 24, 1912.

of The Grizzly Bear (Insert title of publication.) published Monthly (State frequency of issue.)

at Los Angeles, California, (Name of post office and State where publication is entered.) for October 1, 1932 (State whether for April 1 or October 1.)

State of California }
County of Los Angeles } ss.

Before me, a Notary Public in and for the State and County aforesaid, personally appeared Clarence M. Hunt who, having been duly sworn according to law, deposes and says that he is the Managing Editor (State whether editor, publisher, business manager or owner.) of the Grizzly Bear Magazine (Insert title of publication.) and that the following is, to the best of his knowledge and belief, a true statement of the ownership, management (and if a daily paper, the circulation), etc., of the aforesaid publication for the date shown in the above caption, required by the Act of August 24, 1912, embodied in section 411, Postal Laws and Regulations, printed on the reverse side of this form, to-wit:

1. That the names and addresses of the publisher, editor, managing editor, and business managers are:

NAME OF—	POST-OFFICE ADDRESS
Publisher, Grizzly Bear Publishing Co. (Inc.)	Los Angeles, Calif.
Managing Editor, Clarence M. Hunt	Los Angeles, Calif.

2. That the owner is: (If owned by a corporation, its name and address must be stated and also immediately thereunder the names and addresses of stockholders owning or holding one per cent or more of total amount of stock. If not owned by a corporation, the names and addresses of the individual owners must be given. If owned by a firm, company, or other unincorporated concern, its name and address, as well as those of each individual member, must be given.)

The Grizzly Bear Publishing Co., a Corporation, is the owner. 1259 shares of the 7500 authorized shares of stock have been sold. Names all stockholders, and amount stock held by each, attached hereto.

3. That the known bondholders, mortgagees, and other security holders owning or holding 1 per cent or more of total amount of bonds, mortgages, or other securities are: (If there are none, so state.)

None

4. That the two paragraphs next above, giving the names of the owners, stockholders, and security holders, if any, contain not only the list of stockholders and security holders as they appear upon the books of the company, but also, in cases where the stockholder or security holder appears upon the books of the company as trustee or in any other fiduciary relation, the name of the person or corporation for whom such trustee is acting, is given; also that the said two paragraphs contain statements embracing affiant's full knowledge and belief as to the circumstances and conditions under which stockholders and security holders who do not appear upon the books of the company as trustees, hold stock and securities in a capacity other than that of a bonafide owner; and this affiant has no reason to believe that any other person, association, or corporation has any interest direct or indirect in the said stocks, bonds, or other securities than as so stated by him.

5. That the average number of copies of each issue of this publication sold or distributed, through the mails or otherwise, to paid subscribers during the six months preceding the date shown above is——(This information is required from daily publications only.)

CLARENCE M. HUNT,
Managing Editor.

Sworn to and subscribed before me this 30th day of September, 1932.

HARRY J. LELANDE,
[Seal] Notary Public in and for the County of Los Angeles, State of California.
(My commission expires Feb. 18th, 1936)

STOCKHOLDERS OF THE GRIZZLY BEAR PUBLISHING COMPANY (Inc.)

Following is the list of ALL of the stockholders of the Grizzly Bear Publishing Company, Incorporated, as shown by the Stock Ledger, September 30, 1932:

W. Joseph Ford, 257
Harry J. Lelande, Los Angeles, 24
Warren R. Porter, Watsonville, 10
W. H. Maris, Santa Barbara, 10
C. J. Brown, Los Angeles, 10
C. M. Belshaw, San Francisco, 20
George L. Chanler, Los Angeles, 10
J. N. O. Rech, Los Angeles, 10
J. R. Knowland, Oakland, 15
I. B. Dockweiler, Los Angeles, 15
E. A. Meserve, Los Angeles, 25
W. T. Craig, Los Angeles, 10
Ramona Parlor, N.S.G.W., Los Angeles, 122
M. T. Dooling, Hollister, 5
Corona Parlor, N.S.G.W., Los Angeles, 10
Thomas Monahan, San Jose, 10
Andrew Mocker, San Francisco, 5
Daniel A. Ryan, San Francisco, 10
James D. Phelan, San Francisco, 20
Los Angeles Parlor, N.S.G.W., Los Angeles, 10
Frank H. Dunne, San Francisco, 5
J. Emmett Hayden, San Francisco, 10
W. S. Kingsbury, Sacramento, 10
W. W. Shannon, San Francisco, 5
E. A. Forbes, Marysville, 5
H. C. Lichtenberger, Los Angeles, 12
Frank Hausel, Los Angeles, 10
F. W. Young, Los Angeles, 5
Calvert Wilson, Los Angeles, 2
J. M. Hanley, San Francisco, 1
D. J. Wren, San Francisco, 5
Oakland Parlor, N.S.G.W., Oakland, 25
J. C. Griffin, Merced, 1
Sacramento Parlor, N.S.G.W., Sacramento, 15
Pacific Parlor, N.S.G.W., San Francisco, 10
Napa Parlor, N.S.G.W., Napa, 10
Mt. Tamalpais Parlor, N.S.G.W., San Rafael, 5
Athens Parlor, N.S.G.W., Oakland, 15
Raymond H. Kilborn, San Francisco, 2
Leland E. Kilborn, San Francisco, 3
Benjamin L. McKinley, San Francisco, 1
Sunset Parlor, N.S.G.W., Sacramento, 10
Chico Parlor, N.S.G.W., Chico, 5
Placerville Parlor, N.S.G.W., Placerville, 10
J. B. Amestoy, Los Angeles, 35
F. J. Talamantes, Los Angeles, 5
W. J. Variel, Los Angeles, 2
W. B. Metcalf, Santa Barbara, 2
A. Goux, Santa Barbara, 2
E. M. Buckius, Los Angeles, 10
P. A. Blair, Los Angeles, 1
W. D. Wagner, San Bernardino, 15
A. A. Schmidt, Los Angeles, 10
P. F. Johnson, Los Angeles, 1
J. D. Smith, Los Angeles, 3
J. B. Masselin, Los Angeles, 1
Wm. Rudolph, Los Angeles, 1
M. G. Jones, Los Angeles, 5
E. M. Lazard, Los Angeles, 2
E. J. Dillon, Los Angeles, 1
Hugh Glassell, Los Angeles, 10
C. Heinzman, Los Angeles, 2
Florence C. Sharp, 11
J. M. Carson, Los Angeles, 5
J. M. Allen, Los Angeles, 5
M. J. Aquirre, Los Angeles, 5
R. C. Monte, Los Angeles, 1
E. H. Hall, Holtville, 1
H. H. Hall, Holtville, 1
E. Zobelein, Los Angeles, 1
Aubry Austin, Los Angeles, 5
Hydraulic Parlor, N.S.G.W., Nevada City, 10
G. A. Burns, Sacramento, 5
Yosemite Parlor, N.S.G.W., Merced, 2
Excelsior Parlor, N.S.G.W., Jackson, 5
F. A. Stephenson, Los Angeles, 10
E. B. Lovie, Los Angeles, 1
San Francisco Parlor, N.S.G.W., San Francisco, 5
W. F. Bryant, Los Angeles, 25
J. M. Hickey, San Francisco, 1
J. E. O'Connell, San Francisco, 3
J. E. Rigney, San Francisco, 1
Golden Gate Parlor, N.S.G.W., San Francisco, 3
Sequoia Parlor, N.S.G.W., San Francisco, 1
Lee Henry, Los Angeles, 2
E. O. Edgerton, Los Angeles, 30
Alcalde Parlor, N.S.G.W., San Francisco, 5
George Beebe, Los Angeles, 3
Fletcher Ford, Los Angeles, 15
Ray Howard, Los Angeles, 5
Santa Barbara Parlor, N.S.G.W., Santa Barbara, 10
Fred Eaton, Los Angeles, 2
John T. Newell, Los Angeles, 6
Clarence Jarvis, Sutter Creek, 5
W. A. Hobson, Ventura, 3
Amador Parlor, N.S.G.W., Sutter Creek, 10
John F. Davis, San Francisco, 5
Clarence M. Hunt, Los Angeles, 20
Grant Jackson, Los Angeles, 20
L. H. Valentine, Los Angeles, 3
J. P. Kiefer, Los Angeles, 10
John Castera, Los Angeles, 5
F. J. Palomares, Los Angeles, 1
W. J. McCaffery, Santa Barbara, 2
A. F. Jones, Oroville, 2
San Jose Parlor, N.S.G.W., San Jose, 5
Byron Parlor, N.S.G.W., Byron, 2
Gen. Winn Parlor, N.S.G.W., Antioch, 2
Alameda Parlor, N.S.G.W., Alameda, 1
Georgetown Parlor, N.S.G.W., Georgetown, 5
Precita Parlor, N.S.G.W., San Francisco, 5
Alder Glen Parlor, N.S.G.W., Fort Bragg, 1
Fruitvale Parlor, N.S.G.W., Fruitvale, 1
Quartz Parlor, N.S.G.W., Grass Valley, 5
Selma Parlor, N.S.G.W., Selma, 1
Carquinez Parlor, N.S.G.W., Crockett, 1
H. G. W. Dinkelspiel, San Francisco, 1
Homeless Children's Agency, San Francisco, 1
Bay City Parlor, N.S.G.W., San Francisco, 2
Chas. R. Thomas, Los Angeles, 2
J. D. Hunter, Los Angeles, 3
Daisy E. L. Eckstrom, 10
Irving Baxter, Los Angeles, 5
Harry G. Folsom, Los Angeles, 1
Mrs. Maria Gibson, San Francisco, 10
Stanford Parlor, N.S.G.W., San Francisco, 5
L. F. Soto, Los Angeles, 5
Chas. Stansbury, Los Angeles, 10
Jo V. Snyder, Nevada City, 2
Lon S. McCoy, Los Angeles, 1
William I. Traeger, Los Angeles, 1

LOS ANGELES CITY AND COUNTY

UNIVERSITY PARLOR NO. 272 OF THE Order of Native Sons of the Golden West, organized through the efforts of Deputy Grand President Clinton E. Skinner, Lucien A. Griffin, Martin Meza and Leslie Patterson, was instituted October 25 with forty-one members. Some two hundred members from all the neighboring Parlors assembled to witness the ceremonies and to cheer the new Parlor on its way.

Past Grand President John T. Newell officiated at the institution ceremonies, and was assisted by Grand Trustee Eldred L. Meyer, acting as junior past grand president; Owen S. Adams, as grand marshal; Deputy Grand President Clarence M. Hunt, as grand secretary; Grand Organist Leslie Maloche, as grand inside sentinel, and Grand Outside Sentinel William A. Reuter.

The initiatory ritual was exemplified by the following: Orrin C. Welch, president; Harry T. Honn, senior past; Claude J. Wiseman, junior past; Arthur L. Leonard, first vice; Eldred L. Meyer, second vice; Walter Odemar, third vice; Dr. Leland W. Clark, marshal; John J. Smith, secretary; Municipal Judge Joseph L. Call, treasurer; Dr. Robert C. Eshelman, inside sentinel; Ernest Reyes, outside sentinel; George W. Burnett, Eldèn W. Price, trustees; Maurice Macurda, pianist, and Joel A. Bair violinist. All are affiliated with Santa Monica Bay Parlor No. 267 except Walter Odemar, who is third vice-president of Ramona Parlor No. 109.

The officers of University Parlor were installed by District Deputy Ralph I. Harbison, who was assisted by the following, acting as temporary officers: Frank Adams, District Deputy Al Cron, Dr. J. M. Watson, District Deputy Howard Bentley, Orrin Welch, Walter Odemar, Walter Slosson, District Deputy Edward Baldwin, District Deputy Walter Hiskey, Edward Grom, Claude Wiseman, Harry Honn and Arthur Leonard. University's officers include:

Bernard G. Hiss, president; Dr. Phillip Miller, charter senior past; James English, charter junior past; Maynard Garrison, first vice; Dr. George Woods, second vice; Dr. James Encell, third vice; Leslie Patterson, marshal; Howard F. Babb, inside sentinel; William J. Quast, outside sentinel; Martin DeFazio, recording secretary; John McLaughlin, financial secretary; Lucien A. Griffin, treasurer; Glenn Duvall, Martin Meza, Dr. Herbert Root, trustees. The Parlor will meet every Tuesday night, at Palestine Masonic Hall, northeast corner Figueroa street and Forty-first place.

Municipal Judge Leo I. Aggeler conducted the good of the order, and the speakers were President Bernard Hiss of University Parlor, Superior Judge B. Rey Schauer, Past Grand John T. Newell, Leo V. Youngworth, Grand Trustee Eldred Meyer and Harold T. Power (Auburn No. 59) who, as a lad, marched in the 1875 Independence Day parade in San Francisco out of which originated the Order of the Native Sons. Presentations to University Parlor were made as follows: President Owen Adams, for Los Angeles Parlor No. 45, the Holy Bible; President Dr. James Watson, for Ramona Parlor No. 109, map of California; District Deputy Edward Baldwin, for Sepulveda Parlor No. 263 (San Pedro), United States of America and California State (Bear) Flags; President Leslie Shellbach, for Glendale Parlor No. 264, gavel; President Orrin Welch, for Santa Monica Bay Parlor No. 267, altar flag. Past Grand President William I. Traeger was in attendance for the institution ceremonies, and many congratulatory messages were received, including one from President Mattie Labory-Gara of Los Angeles Parlor No. 124 N.D.G.W.—C.M.H.

A PERFECT DAY.

Hospitality reigned supreme, October 15, at the beautiful South Pasadena home of Herman C. Lichtenberger, Past Grand President N.S.G.W., when he and his good wife entertained the past presidents of Ramona Parlor No. 109 N.S.G.W. and a number of "outsiders." A delicious supper, including home-barbecued beef, was served in the outofdoors, and during the afternoon and evening there was much speechifying, mostly of a reminiscent nature. It was a perfect day, from every viewpoint, spent amid ideal surroundings with princess and prince of hostess and host. Those privileged to enjoy the occasion included:

Frank Adams, Fred Batser, Walter Baskerville, Irving Baxter, George Beebe, Charles Bright, Charles Brittain, Chandos Bush, William Calderwood, James Coffey, Senator Henry Carter, William Coffey, Joseph Coyle, Dwight Crittenden, Senator Reginaldo DelValle, Major John Diss, Isidore B. Dockweiler, Louis Duni, William Durm, Frank Duggan, Percy Eisen, Harry Folsom, Fletcher Ford, R. P. Fontana, Dr. Robert Gregg, Judge Lucius Green, G. M. Guzman, Ralph Harbison, Perry Harris, Martin Hauser, Ray Howard, William Hunsaker, Clarence S. Hunt, Clarence M. Hunt, Paul Kiefer, Julius Krause, Louis Lamy, Bernard Lee, David Lee, Leon Leonard, Harry Lelande, Paul Lombardi, Lon McCoy, Edwin Meserve, Eldred Meyer, John Newell, Ernest Orfila, Julius Plath, Sol Rehart,

Know your home-state, California! Learn of its past history and of its present-day development by reading regularly The Grizzly Bear. $1.50 for one year (12 issues). Subscribe now.

Adolfo Rivera, Judge Louis Russill, Ray Russill, Dr. George Sabichi, John Scott, Clinton Skinner, Walter Slosson, Fred Stephenson, Charles Straube, Deacon Taggart, Charles Thomas, Robert Todd, Sheriff William I. Traeger, Frank Turner, Frank Tyrell, William J. Variel, Dr. James Watson, Jared Wenger, Seth S. Williams, Calvert Wilson, Leo Youngworth, and Mayor B. A. Garlinghouse of South Pasadena.—C.M.H.

PLAN ROSE ARBOR FOR GROVE.

The October 12 card party of Los Angeles Parlor No. 124 N.D.G.W., supervised by Chairman Olinda Kerby and an able committee, was a wonderful success, forty-eight tables being in operation. The party at the Manhattan Beach home of Mrs. Elizabeth Jones was most enjoyable. President Mattie Gara was in charge. The Hallowe'en party, Doris Malin hostess, was a splendid success, the affair being in every way appropriate to the season.

Sunday, October 23, the Parlor featured a breakfast in the memorial grove at Griffith Park, and ample justice was done the delicious viands served by Mrs. Mary McAnany and Miss Edna Holcomb. This is the grove set aside for the Natives, and No. 124 plans to erect a rose arbor to honor the Pioneer Mothers of the Parlor.

Mrs. Harriet W. Martin represents Los Angeles on the Christmas remembrance committee for the National Soldiers Home at Sawtelle. She gave a splendid report of the activities of the committee, which plans to remember 7,000 veterans at Christmas time, and made a liberal donation to the fund in the name of the Parlor. The sewing club met during October at the home of Mrs. Sophia Stewart and made baby bags and sheets for the homeless children; the hostess served delicious refreshments to the busy workers. The Parlor is planning much Christmas work.

Los Angeles' November calendar has these dates: 2nd, initiation; 9th, monthly card party, one of the bridge tournament; 16th, potluck dinner preceding the meeting, and an address on a timely topic. The 19th, the sewing club meets at the home of Mrs. Lucy and Miss Dolores Malin.

ANNIVERSARY PARTY.

Los Angeles Parlor No. 45 N.S.G.W. will have an oldtimers night November 3, with past presidents in the chairs. The old boys will provide the entertainment. The Parlor will celebrate its institution anniversary November 17, and the womenfolks will be welcome. Supper will be served, a program will be presented, and dancing will conclude the festivities. First Vice-president Leslie Packard heads the arrangements committee. November 24 being Thanksgiving Day, the Parlor will have no meeting that night.

NATIONAL PARTIES.

Californiana Parlor No. 247 N.D.G.W. has planned a series of "national" parties to follow the last meeting of each month. October 25 was spanish day; chairman Olive Waite Lopez was assisted by Mrs. Edith Harmon Adams. Hostesses were Hortense Chapman Steinike, Arcadia Bandini Gaffey, Ysabel del Valle Cram, Isabel Cram Marquard, Marguerite Moore O'Neill, Ida Bacigalupi Chappell, Marybelle Chapman, Stella Gonzales Connor, Martina Yorba Pelanconi, Rosa Yorba Locke, Pauline Bodrero, Marianne Etchemendy, Madeline Etchemendy, Maria Lopez Lowther, Teresa L. Troconiz, Guadalupe Estudillo Wright, Lisita Pico Williamson, Aurelia Castruccio Weber, Teresa S. Bouttier, Teresa Toro Brockway, Eloisa Mitchell Cadd, Ysabel Mitchell Golt, Carmen Troconiz Holliday, Rosa Santa Cruz Logan, Dolores Machado Barrow, Petra Pelanconi Hartwick, Ynez del Valle Kirby, Florence Steinike, Amenaida R. Moore, Juanita Sands Flores, Constance Rimpau Seals, Rhea Rimpau Sparling. A collection of historic gowns, shawls and other articles of the days of the Spanish, owned by Ysabel del Valle Cram, was shown, and Isabel Lopez Fages exhibited an ancient hand organ with colorful dancing figures. Marybelle Chapman delighted with a group of ancient Spanish folksongs, recently discovered and set to music by Gertrude Ross, well-known composer. Typical awards for bridge and sewing were made and appropriate refreshments were served.

Mrs. Amos Otis Evans, program chairman, presented Anna McConnell Beckley, member of

LOS ANGELES--CITY and COUNTY

the Parlor and art authority, in a lecture on "The Treasures of Russia," October 11, following a delightful and well-attended luncheon at which Harry J. McClean gave an enlightening talk on "The Ethics of the Judiciary." Mrs. Evans is exerting every effort to present programs of interest. Past President Gertrude Tuttle announces a bridge breakfast for November 17. The committee, of which she is chairman, is actively engaged with arrangements for the elaborate affair, which will include a fashion show. Deputy Mattie Edwards was a visitor at both October meetings. A silver spoon has been presented to the new daughter of Mrs. Elizabeth Seymour. Hortense Steinike reports progress in the membership drive.

INSIDE PARK-WRECKING FACTS.

Ramona Parlor No. 109 N.S.G.W. heard from Paul Robinson, October 21, the inside facts, regarding the attempt of interests who want to enhance the value of their realty holdings, to put a roadway across, and thereby wreck as a public outing ground, Westlake Park. The speaker's declaration, that neither a bridge nor a dirt fill should be permitted, was vociferously applauded. Professor Day of Occidental College presented first-hand information of conditions in Russia, October 28.

Ramona has inaugurated a series of monthly birthday parties. The October boys were guests the 21st, and there was a very large attendance. October 7, Past Grands Herman C. Lichtenberger and William I. Traeger were speakers. Initiation was held October 14, among the candidates being Vincenzo Pometti, a musician of note who brought up a thirty-piece orchestra and, preceding the ceremonies, entertained with delightful music. September 30, Captain Tommy Lofthouse, assisted by a squad of motorcycle police, provided splendid entertainment, the numbers coming largely from Paris Inn talent. Chairman Ralph Harbison of the membership committee reports good progress, and Captain "Bill" Bright is promoting a band, a bugle corps and an orchestra for No. 109.

Ramona's November program includes: 4th, initiation, and discussion by competent speakers of proposed city charter amendments; 18th, birthday party, with supper at 6:30 and entertainment by Ramona Troop Boy Scouts; 25th, nomination officers January-July term.

HALLOWE'EN PARTY.

Long Beach—Mrs. Clara Fay of Long Beach Parlor No. 154 N.D.G.W. entertained the Natives and their friends at her home September 30; bunco was the evening's diversion. Deputy Nellie Cline visited the Parlor October 6.

A very successful cooked-food sale was held October 13; Gertrude Riddle, chairman, was assisted by Alice Waldow and President Eleonor Johnson. Members of Long Beach Parlor No. 239 N.S.G.W. were invited guests at a most enjoyable Hallowe'en party October 20. The committee in charge included Claudia Miller (chairman), Leola Temby and Alice Waldow.

MEETING WITH SUCCESS.

Hollywood Parlor No. 196 N.S.G.W. has at work an energetic membership committee, headed by John J. Ford, which is meeting with success. November 14 a class of candidates will be initiated. Officers for the new term will be nominated November 28.

RECEPTION FOR N.D. GRAND OFFICER.

Glendale—Verdugo Parlor No. 240 N.D.G.W. had an "advanced officers" night October 11, with First Vice-president Vera Carlson presiding. President Betty Sanders was absent on vacation—deer hunting at Buckhorn Flats. For her new native daughter, Sandra Claire Wilson, Mrs. Evelyn Wilson was presented a baby spoon. A potluck dinner, in charge of Mrs. Ruby Eubank, was held at the home of Mrs. Arline Newel. Food sales October 15 and 29 were great successes. A card party, with Mrs. Margaret Donlan as chairman, was held October 25.

Preparations are well advanced for a reception, sponsored by Verdugo Parlor, in honor of Grand Outside Sentinel Hazel B. Hansen, to be held November 15 in Masonic Temple. All Natives and their escorts are invited. A program and dance will follow the reception.

PERSONAL PARAGRAPHS.

William F. Reilly (Ramona N.S.) has gone to San Francisco to reside.

Mrs. Estella Haid (Los Angeles N.D.) was a visitor to San Francisco last month.

Mrs. Mabel Martin (Los Angeles N.D.) was a visitor last month to Oakland.

Miss Lou Fessler and George H. Francis (Ramona N.S.) were wedded October 13.

Leslie Maloche (Grand Organist N.S.) of San Bernardino is now domiciled in Hollywood.

Paul Robinson (Ramona N.S.) and wife (Los Angeles N.D.) were visitors last month to San Francisco.

Harold T. Power (Auburn N.S.), for many years active in Placer County affairs, is now residing in Glendale.

Miss Irene G. Eden (Los Angeles N.D.) became the bride of Sinclair Aubrey, October 22. Mrs. Jennie Raymond was matron of honor.

THE DEATH RECORD.

J. O. Metz, brother of Al Metz (Los Angeles N.S.), died October 3 at Santa Ana. He was born at Compton, in 1870.

Van Rensselaer Kelsey, affiliated with Ramona Parlor No. 109 N.S.G.W., died October 13, survived by a wife and three sons. He was born at Los Angeles, June 30, 1890.

Mrs. Ella Hayward, wife of Hubert T. Hayward (Santa Monica Bay N.S.), died October 16.

Mrs. Gertrude Blumenthal, wife of Charles J. Blumenthal (Los Angeles N.S.), died October 20 at San Francisco.

GOOD WELFARE WORK.

Santa Monica—Santa Monica Bay Parlor No. 245 N.D.G.W. had as guests October 17 delegations from Long Beach Parlor No. 154, headed by Deputy Lucretia Coats, and Verdugo Parlor No. 240 (Glendale), headed by Grand Outside Sentinel Hazel B. Hansen. Trustee Myrtle Baden and Grace Abila were the hostesses. Chairman Marie Barnes told of plans for the card party, October 31, for the benefit of the homeless children.

A dance October 14 was an enjoyable affair. The Parlor is looking after the needs of a worthy family, providing, among other things, two quarts of milk daily. Chairman Rosalie Hyde of the veteran welfare committee visited the National Soldiers Home at Sawtelle and presented, from the Parlor, a check for Christmas cheer.

anta Monica Bay has changed its meetingplace Odd Fellows Hall, 1431 Third street, Santa onica, where it meets the second and fourth ednesdays.

PROMOTING ATHLETICS.

Glendale—Grand Trustee Eldred L. Meyer ficially visited Glendale Parlor No. 264 .S.G.W. October 4, and there was a large at-ndance, including visitors from all the Los An-les County Parlors, to greet him. Three can-idates were initiated. Ted Verdugo presented artistically designed map of California to the arlor. Among the many speakers, in addition Grand Trustee Meyer, were Past Grand John Newell, Grand Outside Sentinel William Reu-r and Harold T. Power (Auburn No. 59). lendale is very active, and has committees pro-oting athletics, etc. At the conclusion of the eeting refreshments were served by members Verdugo Parlor No. 240 N.D.G.W.

NEW HOME.

Santa Monica—Commencing November 2, nta Monica Bay Parlor No. 267 N.S.G.W. will meet the first and third Wednesdays in Odd Fellows Hall, 1431 Third street. A housewarming will be a near-future attraction, and plans are being made for the famous annual lobster supper. Members of No. 267, in force, made visits during October to neighboring Parlors.

PUT YOUR THANKS IN GIVING.

The Los Angeles N.S.G.W. and N.D.G.W. Homeless Children Committee has sent out a letter, signed by Chairman Irving Baxter, asking for a Thanksgiving offering toward the homeless children work, which receives nothing from the community chest. All Natives and their loyal friends should respond liberally, for this year the need is far greater than heretofore.

For twenty-two years the placing of homeless children in childless homes has been carried on by the Native Sons and Daughters, and as a result the hearts of thousands of abandoned little children and foster-parents have been mutually gladdened. There is no more worthy charity than this. Thanksgiving Day approaches. Send an offering to Mrs. Calista de Soto-Stefan, treasurer of the joint committee, 400½ West Seventy-eighth street.—C.M.H.

GRIZZLY GROWLS

(Continued from Page 2)

draw all financial support. If not inclined to do so, take steps to force action.

"Big business," which has put numberless obstacles in the way of keeping the Japs and their like out of this country, is now appealing to Washington for help; the pocketbooks have become affected, hence the howl. The Japs are dumping their products into this country, where they are sold at prices far below the cost of manufacture here. The highboys are agreeable to permitting the Japs, but not their products, to flood this country. Consistent, are they not! Looks like a hookup between quota and dumping—another "gentlemen's agreement," whereby the white-Japs would swing ajar the immigration-gates, if the yellow-Japs will cease dumping their products. In the meantime, perhaps it would be a good idea to purchase Jap-made, in preference to American-made, goods, for in no way other than via the pocketbook is it possible to reach "big business."

A considerable quantity of political-smoke, generated in the Capital City, has been stenching the state. The California State Grange, evidently suspicioning, as do numerous citizens, that there must be some fire where there is so much smoke, at its annual meeting in Fresno City adopted this resolution:

"Whereas, The condition of the state government is such as to require investigation and a disclosure of the facts to the rural taxpayers of California; be it, therefore, resolved, that we, the California State Grange, in regular session assembled, do urge and petition that an investigation into the affairs of the state administration be made by a committee of the State Senate, and that, guided by the findings of this committee, the State Legislature take such action as it deems wise and necessary."

Recalling that "Prosperity is just around the corner," an editor inquires, "Are we prepared for prosperity?" No! Dishonesty brought on the depression, and no attempt has been made to legislate against the practice and there have been no prosecutions of the nationally-infamous dishonest. So when, and if, prosperity comes from around the corner dishonesty will continue the vogue and the dishonest, only, will prosper, at the expense of the honest. Until honesty, from top to bottom in government and in every walk of life, be again enthroned in this country and the dishonest minority be cast to the swine, we will not be prepared for the return of real prosperity—the prosperity of the masses.

November 8 will be election day. The first and foremost duty of every man and woman privileged to be an American citizen is to vote. Think first, with your own God-endowed brains, and carefully consider the qualities of the candidates. Things accomplished should have a far greater appeal than things promised, and particularly so when some pre-election promises are not possible of human accomplishment. Vote, and let your conscience, not prejudice or partyism, be your guide!

Apparently, a new racket has come into being—the bankruptcy. Chain-store outfits, whose admitted assets exceed liabilities, are going into receivership. The purpose is to repudiate leases, through cancelation, for a receiver has the powers of a czar. The scheme includes the formation of a company with a new name, but controlled by the manipulators of the "bankrupt" company, to re-lease, if possible, property at greatly reduced rentals. In other words, the chain-store racketeers are using the federal bankruptcy law—which, by the way, was declared by Federal Judge Sheppard to be a national disgrace—to legally repudiate just obligations. In flush times they sought out and leased all available storerooms, to prevent competition. Now that the dollars flow not so lavishly into their coffers, they want to get from under, and are using the bankruptcy court to accomplish that purpose.

As long suspicioned, the state administration, through its finance director, publicly admitted in San Francisco that California has a $40,000,000 deficit. The director said, "There is only one way to reduce governmental expenditures. That is to spend less." Nothing new in the contention and conclusion; both are as old as the hills. Sanely and efficiently managed corporations have been spending less for two and more years. But what has the State of California, one of the nation's biggest corporations, been doing? Spending more!

Federal Attorney-general Mitchell, addressing the American Bar Association in Washington, D. C., said, "It is an affront to decent citizens for convicted persons to go at large for such periods—one to three years—before their cases are finally disposed of. These conditions should not exist." How about those convicted of felonies being at large, on parole, after their cases have been finally disposed of by the courts? Should that condition exist? Does not its existence encourage crookedness, particularly on the part of those adequately supplied with influence and coin of the realm?

The State Appellate Court has rendered a decision to the effect that dual public-school positions, once established, cannot be abolished. The law which permits the establishment of dual positions should be abolished, in the interest of economy and the thousands of competent, unemployed teachers.

Incidentally, the State Legislature should materially lessen the public-school costs by eliminating the too-numerous fads and frills, provided to create jobs. In 1915, California spent $35,717,000 on education; by 1930, the cost had jumped up to $171,110,000—an increase of 379.1 percent in total cost and 151.6 percent in percapita cost. A material jumping downward of the cost is required, in the interest of the taxpayers. Addressing a state convention of school superintendents in San Francisco, Benjamin Macomber truthfully said:

"The schools and school managements are being severely criticized on the point of taxation. There is substantial basis for the complaint. Every enterprise has been forced to draw in its horns. The two that so far have cut down their operations least are the political enterprise and the school enterprise. There is a revolt against taxes to keep up the political enterprise on its old flush-time scale.

"People are beginning, and very loudly, to classify the schools with the political enterprise. This is not, in my opinion, altogether fair. Yet it has some ground. The teachers have the strength of their organizations. This is a dangerous time for them to use their strength in any way that will lead people to classify them definitely as one of the minorities organized for loot."

CO-OPERATION ASKED, THAT DESERVING UNEMPLOYED WHITES MAY HAVE WORK.

A San Franciscan received a letter from Anna Brown, secretary Laundry Workers Union No. 26 of San Francisco, and sent it to The Grizzly Bear with the suggestion that it be published in this magazine. Here it is:

"The great problem facing us today is to create work for our deserving unemployed who are, through no fault of their own, thrown into enforced idleness, brought about by the most devastating depression in the history of this country.

"The continuation of this depression, now i[n] its third year, has well-nigh exhausted the limited resources of thousands of our people, whos[e] means of livelihood have been swept away. Tax-ation and private contributions are severel[y] strained to meet this crisis.

"There are ways and means to ameliorate, t[o] some extent, this distressing situation. Take fo[r] instance the white laundry industry. In norma[l] times this industry gave employment, at remun-erative wages, to thousands of our citizens. To-day the white plants have, through necessity greatly reduced their working forces and hav[e] been forced to place those still employed on [a] part-time basis.

"Many of these men and women could be re-employed, and made self-supporting if our Whit[e] people who patronize Oriental laundries under-stood the situation and gave their preference o[f] their patronage to the white laundry industry.

"The standards of living of the Oriental an[d] Occidental races, diametrically are at varianc[e]. The Oriental has a system of frugality, inherite[d] from ancestral privations, that is not adaptabl[e] to Caucasian ideals. However, the proverbia[l] thrift of the Asiatic in our midst stands him i[n] good stead during the present economic depres-sion. His accumulated resources place him in [a] superior position to the White man to face th[e] present industrial disruption.

"We seek your co-operation in this crisis. Re-member that the white laundries have a servic[e] to meet every requirement of the family bud-get."

"Government is free to the people under [it] when the laws rule and the people are a part[y] to those laws; and all the rest is tyranny, olig-archy, and confusion."—William Penn.

Grizzly Bear

ECEMBER — THE ONLY OFFICIAL PUBLICATION OF THE NATIVE SONS AND DAUGHTERS OF THE GOLDEN WEST — 1932

Merry Christmas

Featuring

GENERAL NEWS OF INTEREST CONCERNING ALL CALIFORNIA, and ORDERS NATIVE SONS and NATIVE DAUGHTERS

Price: 15 Cents

THE LETTER BOX

Comments on subjects of general interest and importance received from readers of The Grizzly Bear.

TWO WRONGS NEVER DID AND NEVER WILL MAKE A RIGHT.

Editor Grizzly Bear—Just finished reading the "Growl" concerning what happened at the national [American Legion] convention in Portland regarding the so-called "bonus." . . . I am fortunate to have a job, but God knows plenty have not. Remember, fourteen years ago it was said nothing will be too good when you come back. Here is an editorial written by a mere comrade that will answer your article.

B. R. NORTHRUP,
Navy Post No. 278
American Legion
Dept. of California.

Los Angeles, October 3, 1932.

The editorial referred to, by Henry L. Marshall, commander of Covina Post, American Legion, and captioned "A Simple Solution," appeared in "The American Legion Weekly Bulletin" of October 1, 1932. It follows, in full:

"Just to keep the record straight, we would like to remind the country and the world that the world war veteran did not start the war, nor did he participate in the councils that approved Liberty loans, afterwards reloaned to the Allies, nor in huge bonuses to railroad corporations and other groups just after the war.

"The world war veteran did not pile up the great debt that now takes eighty cents of every dollar the taxpayers disgorge to the federal governments here and abroad. He went to war cheerfully when told to go, but without any enthusiasm for war, either then, or now.

"The church ritual intones that 'We have left undone those things which we ought to have done, and have done those things which we ought not to have done, and there is no health in us . . . the burden is intolerable.'

"The sin of the war—this last one, and others—is an intolerable burden, but the culpability falls upon all, and with less force upon the soldier in the war than anyone. He didn't start it. He stopped it.

"Just now it seems popular to brand the veteran as a treasury raider, it somehow having been worked around that he is responsible for this expensive aftermath of war; to name him at this late day as unpatriotic, placing a price on patriotism. Two wrongs do not, of course, make a right. The returned soldier should not attempt to put a dollar premium on his service, even though this was done with gusto and with complete unanimity of action by the railroads, all other corporations and every group that supplied food and munitions for the war at cost plus—and, O, my God, what a cost!

"It is said that if the world war veteran is paid his bonus now instead of in 1945, he will pitch it away in riotous living, and will be broke in a very short space of time. Assuming that he will squander it—which we do not admit—what did the railroads and other corporations and the munitions groups do with their adjusted compensations paid by the government in 1919 and 1920? They are all broke now, and asking the government for more.

"Why didn't the government defer these corporation adjusted compensations until 1945? If it had done so, perhaps there still might be something remaining in the United States treasury.

"The solution of the whole problem is simple. If you don't want soldiers to become expensive during and after a war—don't start a war."

PIONEER MOTHER'S EXPERIENCES.

Editor Grizzly Bear—You may be interested to hear of my early California life? I was born in Lee County, Illinois, in 1849. Came to California in 1852. We were six months enroute. My father, Frank D. Swartwont, died of heart trouble and was buried in blankets by the side of the road, in sight of Fort Laramie. Mother was only twenty-two years of age and had never been away from her mother. But there was no going back, so, after two weeks' rest at Salt Lake, we came on. As she was doing some washing in a little creek, an old man, perhaps a Mormon, proposed to her. At that time she had not shed a tear, but she soon drove him away.

There were only three women in the train and they were not very friendly, fearing that she had no money. But she was plentifully supplied, and on arrival sold the horses and, with the money, bought a lot and built a house on one of the main streets of Hangtown, now Placerville. As there were so many miners and desperadoes, she married Samuel W. Huff, who was a widower. He was a kind stepfather.

I could tell you of the gold I have picked up—did not save it—and the fires, bad people, singing schools and my very happy life. I married in 1866. Have four children, two boys and two girls, all married but one, who is a semi-invalid.

(Continued on Page 21)

GRIZZLY GROWLS

(CLARENCE M. HUNT.)

FROM ARTHUR L. SMITH, AFFILIATED with Argonaut Parlor No. 8 N.S.G.W. of Oroville, but for some time a resident of Brookville, Pennsylvania, The Grizzly Bear editor November 4 received the following, titled "Washington or Tokio?":

"In the O. A. MacIntyre column of the Hearst papers of Sunday, October 30, appeared this highly interesting statement:

" 'Recently I told of a New York photographer who refused to take pictures of Chinese and Japanese. His reason was not racial, but due to the skin coloring for his type of photography. Not a Chinese has written me, but a flood of viciously insulting letters come from Japanese. Typical of all is this—which incidentally has been turned over to Uncle Sam:

" ' "Tell that stupid photographer that he will soon be taking photographs of us Japanese by imperial orders. The supremacy of the so-called Yellow Race is around the corner. America will be taking orders from Tokio in 10 years. We who are valets, house servants and the like occupy our posts but we are finding out things that will aid our country when the Great Day comes. We have brought China to her knees and America is next. We have only contempt for America!' "

"The famous columnist made no comment other than that I have mentioned, and passed on to another subject. Yet he left unsaid a great volume of speculation for the United States, and confirmation of California views. For years we have been considered alarmists in our preaching of the dangerous yellow peril. Champions—yellow whites—have not been wanting, to rise to the defense of the 'little brown brothers from far Nippon,' even in our own state [California]. Some are sentimentalists, some are dreamers and some are traitors. Yellow skins have been made to look very beautiful when covered by 'yellow backs,' and the tide of race tolerance has never lacked bombastic orators.

"But, just as the writer of this note to MacIntyre has pointed out, we have had deeds, not words, to base our contentions on. The rape of China is still fresh in the mind of every normal person in these United States. The echoes of the cannon at Shanghai still pulse in the air, the smoke of the conflict that raged through Manchuria is only beginning to settle, and the graves of the Chapai area have yet to sprout their first blade of grass—'AND AMERICA IS NEXT!'

"What caused the cessation of war in China? It was not the League of Nations. They met in solemn conclave and threatened the Japanese with a strict boycott of produced articles. But the government at Tokio sent back word that such an act would be considered as an open declaration of hostilities, and the various governments, fearing secret treaties and underground alliances, withdrew.

"What caused the cessation of war in China? It was not the Peace Conference at The Hague. All that these gentlemen and ladies managed to evoke from Japan was a typical Oriental 'No sabe.' There wasn't any war in China; war had never been declared; Japan was having a mere 'military maneuver,' and if any Chinese citizens managed to get in the way and were subsequently shot it was an entirely regretted, but totally unforeseen, calamity.

"What caused the cessation of war in China? As I recall the words of that dynamic newsreeler, Floyd Gibbons, they ran something like this: 'China has stopped calling for help. She has opened up in an effort to save herself. From behind every tree, from behind every bush, over every rise of ground and from every cellar and river bank come the roll of rifle fire and the rattle of machine guns.'

"China saved herself! China was only partly prepared, but she became tired of Japan's 'military maneuver' and decided that she would have a 'field day' herself. Fortunately for her, she decided to operate in the same section of China where the yellow boys from Nippon were having such a good time. But her delay cost her a big slice of Manchuria. PREPAREDNESS WOULD HAVE SAVED MANCHURIA!

"It is possible that Japan has 'only contempt for America,' but she has a wholesome respect for the nearest state of the Union [California], and her reluctance to hold a 'military maneuver' on the soil of California has been partly due to the knowledge that such an operation must take place in the area watched over by those to whom, under certain conditions, a counter 'military maneuver' would be highly interesting. As Mexico has often boasted that she could whip the entire United States if it wasn't for Texas, just so has Japan felt that she could invade the United States were it not necessary first to cross that country whose citizens handle a rifle with the deadly precision and accuracy of Kentucky mountaineers.

"But 'ten years' will bring a change. There is poison gas, there are airplanes, there are machine guns and highly dangerous explosives that push individual bravery into the background. If the American Government doesn't want the tragic error of Manchuria to be reenacted with all the ferocious defense of the Alamo she had better begin to forge better locks for her Western door.

"Do I believe the letter? Does any Native Son disbelieve it? It tells the truth, as we have seen and warned of for a long time; it tells the truth with the open candor that we may expect from a drunken or an angry man; it tells the truth, as our country will realize, let us hope, before it is too late.

"I am not preaching war, but preparedness. The only way that we can keep the Golden State from getting her name off the skins of her inhabitants, rather than her fruit, sunshine and mineral products, is for Uncle Sam to forget a lot of his petty troubles and make ready to receive and properly entertain Oriental 'military maneuvers' on the Western seaboard. Of course, the writer of the letter was wrong to 'let the cat out of the bag' so soon, and has probably either committed harikari by now or had matihari committed on him. But either way, let us take a little lesson from the anger evoked by a photographer who did not care to photograph 'yellow skins'."

And it came to pass, that wickedness was everywhere enthroned throughout the Nation, and that depression, with consequent unemployment and misery, hung like a pall o'er the land. Ominous dissention-clouds gathered, peals of political-thunder resounded, and then came the deluge—of November eighth ballots. Long-eared jackasses, heeding the "Forgotten Man" warning, sought safety in such large numbers in the government-ark, but few elephants could find refuge therein, and they perished, politically, in large numbers.

And behold, when the ballot-flood had subsided, atop the government-seat perched, undisturbed by the ferocity of the mighty storm, the eagle, proclaiming: cease worship of the dollar-sign; cleanse the Nation, and all that therein is, of dishonesty; give heed to the needs of the masses; cast out from the temples of government and of business the traitorous high priests; observe these commandments, that prosperity may return and that all may be well with this land that floweth with milk and honey.

The Fiftieth California Legislature convenes at Sacramento City Monday, January 2, 1933. Ordinarily, when New Year Day comes on a Sunday the following day is observed as a holiday. The California Constitution, however, requires the State Legislature to meet "the first Monday after the first of the year." The Fiftieth will be the eighth Legislature to meet January 2, the other sessions being in 1854, 1860, 1893, 1899, 1905, 1911 and 1918. The 1854 session convened at Benicia, Solano County, but removed to Sacramento March 1.

The George Washington Bicentennial celebration officially closed Thanksgiving Day, November 24, when more than 75,000 churches held appropriate ceremonies. During the nine-month celebration more than one million separate programs in commemoration of the Nation's founder were featured in all parts of the world—the greatest tribute ever paid to a national hero.

The Federal Interstate Commerce Commission disclaims any right under the law to regulate practices of radio-broadcasting stations. That being so, the Federal Congress should provide the right. Broadcasters, like newspaper and periodical publishers, are dispensers of advertising. The competition is unfair, however, broadcasters not being affected by regulations governing publishers. For instance, broadcasters extensively advertise lotteries, which right is denied publishers by the Federal Postal Department, and as a result advertisers featuring chance schemes choose the radio. In the interest of honest competition, either the numerous restrictions governing publishers should be removed, or they should be applied in their entirety to broadcasters. The best interest of the general public unquestionably would be served by the latter course.

A recent press dispatch quoted Murray W. Garsson, special assistant to the Federal Secretary of Labor, as stating: "A preliminary survey shows Hollywood is flooded with alien actors whose permits have long since expired or who came here illegally." There are also numerous actresses in the same category. All should be deported, and the cost of operating the state judiciary materially lessened thereby. As a

(Continued on Page 24)

I SAW GOD WASH THE WORLD

(WILLIAM L. STIDGER.)

I saw God wash the world last night
With His sweet showers on high;
And then when morning came
I saw Him hang it out to dry.

He washed each tiny blade of grass,
And every trembling tree;
He flung His showers against the hills
And swept the billowy sea.

The white rose is a cleaner white,
The red rose is more red,
Since God washed every fragrant face
And put them all to bed.

There's not a bird, there's not a bee
That wings along the way,
But is a cleaner bird and bee
Than it was yesterday.

I saw God wash the world last night;
Ah, would He had washed me
As clean of all my dust and dirt
As that old white birch tree.

—Benicia Herald-New Era.

The Grizzly Bear Magazine

The ALL California Monthly

OWNED, CONTROLLED, PUBLISHED BY GRIZZLY BEAR PUBLISHING CO., (Incorporated)

COMPOSED OF NATIVE SONS.

HERMAN C. LICHTENBERGER, Pres.
JOHN T. NEWELL RAY HOWARD
WM. I. TRAEGER LORENZO F. SOTO
CHAS. R. THOMAS HARRY J. LELANDE
ARTHUR A. SCHMIDT, Vice-Pres.
BOARD OF DIRECTORS

CLARENCE M. HUNT
General Manager and Editor

OFFICIAL ORGAN AND THE ONLY OFFICIAL PUBLICATION OF THE NATIVE SONS AND THE NATIVE DAUGHTERS GOLDEN WEST.

ISSUED FIRST EACH MONTH.
FORMS CLOSE 20th MONTH.
ADVERTISING RATES ON APPLICATION.

SAN FRANCISCO OFFICE:
N.S.G.W. BLDG., 414 MASON ST., RM. 302
(Office Grand Secretary N.S.G.W.)
Telephone: Kearney 1223
SAN FRANCISCO, CALIFORNIA

PUBLICATION OFFICE:
309-15 WILCOX BLDG., 2nd AND SPRING,
Telephone: VAndike 6234
LOS ANGELES, CALIFORNIA

(Entered as second-class matter May 29, 1918, at the Postoffice at Los Angeles, California, under the act of August 24, 1912.)

PUBLISHED REGULARLY SINCE MAY 1907
VOL. LII WHOLE NO. 308

CALIFORNIA'S ROMANTIC

Lewis F. Byington
(PAST GRAND PRESIDENT N.S.G.W.)

Prior to the 1932 Admission Day, September 9, celebration in San Francisco, Lewis F. Byington of that city, Past Grand President of the Order of Native Sons of the Golden West, broadcast a series of six addresses on California. They were most favorably received, and requests came from all quarters of the state for copies of the talks. So, The Grizzly Bear suggested to Byington that the addresses be published in this magazine and, always willing to co-operate, he consented. The first of the series is here presented; the others will appear in succeeding issues.—Editor.

THE HISTORY OF CALIFORNIA IS A romantic and an appealing history. California's sons and daughters have enrolled themselves into fraternities to perpetuate the memory of those early pioneers who brought civilization to the West and laid the foundation of our state. The citizens of California are also most patriotic and loyal to the nation. Inspired by this feeling of patriotism, the Legislature of California has provided that the annual recurrence of the date of her admission into the Union, which took place September 9, 1850, should be a legal holiday throughout the state, known as Admission Day, and should be fittingly celebrated. Preliminary to this year's celebration, I have been requested to deliver a series of addresses on the romantic history and on some of the most interesting events of our state's forward march. Let us, as an introductory, sketch the important periods in the civilization and development of California:

LEGENDARY PERIOD.

In the Spanish romance known as "Las Sergas de Esplandian" (The Deeds of Esplandian), written by Montalvo and published about 1498, shortly after Columbus discovered America, the author tells of an island "lying at the right hand," as you sail toward the Indies, and near the Terrestrial Paradise, named "California." "The island everywhere abounded with gold and precious stones." It was inhabited exclusively by women, who lived in the manner of Amazons. They were robust of body, with strong and passionate hearts and great virtues. There ruled over the island of California a queen of majestic proportions, and in the very vigor of her womanhood. Her name was Califia. She was a great warrior, and her armor and weapons were all of gold and adorned with precious stones. Cortez, when he discovered Lower California, in 1535, thought it was an island, and believed that it lay "at the right hand of the Indies," and it was quite natural that he should give it the name of the mythical island, "California," referred to in the popular romance of that day.

THE INDIAN PERIOD.

The prehistoric settlers of California were the Indians, who for centuries prior to the voyage of Columbus to the west in search of the Indies had their homes along this coast. Whether they came from Asia by way of the Aleutian islands and Alaska, or from the Pacific isles, or across some prehistoric continent lying where the Pacific now stretches, neither tradition nor history informs us.

Before the padres came, the trees and the brush were their only shelter, save in the case of a tribe along the Santa Barbara channel, more civilized than the others, who lived in thatched huts. Their raiment was an apron of tule grass; their faces, necks and breasts were tattooed, and the only art they practiced was weaving baskets.

It was the missionary fathers who afterwards taught these rude tribes the arts of peace, gathered them in settlements, trained them to sing and to play on musical instruments, to cultivate the fields and to tend the herds, and to build from adobe bricks and timbers the twenty-one beautiful missions which stretched from San Diego to Sonoma.

THE NAVIGATORS.

The foot of no White man pressed the soil of California until the arrival of the navigators.

California, in the days of the early navigators, was the most distant land on earth from the center of White civilization. To reach it from Europe required a hazardous voyage around South America, or a much longer voyage around Africa and beyond Asia. Little can we appreciate today the daring and hardihood of those adventurous navigators who sailed their small wooden boats over unknown seas.

As one writer expressed it: "They were true pioneers. They gambled with luck. Life to them was a glorious adventure. And all the suffering, the thirst and the hunger and the pain, were forgotten when their eyes beheld the dim outline of a new coast or the placid waters of an ocean that had lain undiscovered since the beginning of time."

One of the bold navigators of that early day was Juan Rodriguez Cabrillo, a Portuguese sailing under the flag of Spain, who in 1542, just fifty years after Columbus had sighted the New World, braved the dangers of an uncharted sea and sailed up the coast of California. He was searching for a waterway that would shorten the sailing distance from Spain to India. What he found was the wonderland of California. He entered the port of San Diego, and he and his crew were the first White men to land on our coast. He passed the bay, afterwards known as San Francisco, but did not see it.

A third of a century later, 1579, the intrepid Englishman, Sir Francis Drake, sailed the "Golden Hind" into the waters of the great Pacific and found his way to the California coast. He named the land New Albion and claimed it for Queen Elizabeth. All that now remains to commemorate that eventful voyage are Drake's Bay to the north of San Francisco, and the Prayer Book Cross in Golden Gate Park. Although the navigator Cabrillo sailed past the Golden Gate in 1542, it was not until 233 years later that the first vessel entered the port. All others passed without noticing it. In 1775, Juan Manuel Ayala, lieutenant in the Spanish navy, was commanded to sail from Mexico and explore San Francisco Bay, which prior thereto had been seen only from the land. On the evening of August 5, 1775, Ayala, on his ship, the "San Carlos," entered through the Golden Gate. His vessel was the first to enter that harbor and open it to the commerce of the world.

THE MISSION PERIOD.

No military conquest marked the acquisition of California by Spain. In this respect California stands unique among lands taken from native tribes. The Spaniards came, not with the sword, but with the prayer-book and the cross. The California missions brought the native tribes from barbarism to civilization peacefully, without bloodshed.

In 1769, while yet the American colonies on the Atlantic were a part of Great Britain, Gaspar de Portola, the brave and able governor of Lower California, led the pioneer expedition into the land that is now our Golden State. He planted the banner of Castile and Leon on the crescent shore of the harbor of Monterey, established the military posts and the presidios, and discovered the world-famed San Francisco Bay.

While Portola represented the military arm of Spain, the zealous and saintly Junipero Serra, who accompanied him, was the civilizing influence that established permanent settlements here and paved the way for the future growth of California. With never ending patience, unabating zeal and ceaseless effort, he planted mission after mission along the coast of California from San Diego to San Francisco, linked them together by El Camino Real (the king's highway), and brought within their spiritual influence the heathen natives of this western land. The missions which remain of the twenty-one stretching from San Diego to Sonoma should be preserved and treasured as landmarks representative of the earliest civilization brought to this coast. To Portola and Serra, California owes a debt of everlasting gratitude.

Bells of the Past, whose long forgotten music
 Still fills the wide expanse,
Tingeing the sober twilight of the present
 With color of romance!

Before me rise the dome-shaped Mission towers,
 The white Presidio;
The swart commander in his leathern jerkin,
 The priest in stole of snow.

O solemn bells! whose consecrated masses
 Recall the faith of old;
O tinkling bells! that lulled with twilight music
 The spiritual fold!

Your voices break and falter in the darkness,—
 Break, falter and are still;
And veiled and mystic, like the Host descending,
 The sun sinks from the hill.

THE SPANISH PERIOD.

It may be said that California owes its foundation to the Spanish era. It was during that period that it had its boundaries defined, its harbors explored and surveyed, and its civilization established; the sweet-sounding names given to its mountains, rivers and towns come from Spain. The period following the arrival of the Spaniard was a period of romance filled with the spirit of a carefree people. They had here a land of scenic beauty and enchanting climate, a land gorgeous with flowers and rich with plenty, where lived a happy, peaceful and contented race, "the world forgetting and by the world

Christmas Trees

MINNA McGARVEY.

In ev'ry clime are Christmas trees. Some decked with drifted snow
And hung with crystal pendants, until each branch bends low;
As frosted plumes they glitter, in beautiful array,
A row of faithful sentries, to greet the Christmas Day.

Beneath the trees the drifting flakes bank high and feather-light,
Above, the skies are leaden, one Star shines all the night;
No ripple of a river, the snow-bird's chirp is shrill,
The lonely trees are silent and keep their vigil, still.

Then out along a western shore, a far-flung sunny land,
Between the blue Sierras and the ocean's silver strand,
The circling breezes wander mid trees in starry bloom
Till all the air is laden with heavenly perfume.

The pepper in its lacy garb, with gems of ruby hue,
The whisp'ring eucalyptus, outlined against the blue,
The flowery acacia, the waving palm spread wide,
Their rustling music mingle with bells at Christmastide.

Some smile beneath an azure sky, some stand where winds blow chill,
God's solace to all mankind, and stationed at His will.
Oh, all the trees are lovely, north, south, or east or west,
Wherever trees are growing, that is a land God-blest.

ILL DESTROY E ONLY LOGICAL ARRIER AGAINST .P INVASION

HE GRAND PARLOR OF THE ORDER of Native Sons of the Golden West for many years has been prominent in the demand for a general law that would bar the immigration gates to further entrance of unassimilable Asiatic races. three other state organizations, represent- egion, Labor and Grange, it organized the ornia Joint Immigration Committee to aid curing such a law, and since the passage of in 1924 the Joint Committee has been tained to defend the law against repeated k on the part of various interests—sec- l, class and group—more concerned in self- ose or advantage than in the nation's future re. Its efforts in that direction have been assisted during the past few years by the American Coalition of Patriotic Societies. offices in New York and Washington, com- l of over ninety affiliated bodies, including ons and Daughters of the American Revo- n, Veterans of Foreign Wars, R.O.T.C. As- tion, Disabled American Veterans, Amer- War Mothers, various immigration restric- leagues, etc. The organizations referred to titute a remarkable aggregation of bodies idely differing membership and purpose, but nited in this matter in unselfish protection e Nation's interest.

OPPONENTS IN CALIFORNIA.

ithin the past year there has been organized California Council on Oriental Relations for avowed purpose of securing immigration a for Japan and thereby repealing the sec- of the Immigration Act of 1924 which bars those ineligible to American citizenship as igrants for permanent settlement. The proposed would necessitate the abandon- t for all time of the principle recognized in present law. The organization named has e public announcement of its intent to de- p a public sentiment in California favorable ts purpose and then approach the Federal gress with a demand for the necessary leg- tion. For many months past it has prose- d the first of its two objectives by the pre- ation of its views before service and other s throughout the state through Samuel J. ne, its executive secretary. The announced nbership of the California Council is as fol- s:

ugh S. Jewett, Bakersfield; Robert G. Sproul, keley; Warren N. Woodson, Corning; S. ker Frisselle, Fresno; Major M. J. Dillman, coln; Harry Chandler, Los Angeles; Clinton Miller, Los Angeles; R. B. von KleinSmid, Angeles; Halsey H. Dunning, Marysville; elia H. Reinhardt, Mills College; Allen Grif- Monterey; Brother Z. Leo, Moraga; Rabbi lolph I. Coffee, Oakland; Justus F. Craemer, nge; Almon E. Roth, Palo Alto; Allen P. nols, Pomona; Dudley V. Saeltzer, Redding; nk Miller, Riverside; Fred W. Kiesel, Sacra- to; Frederick J. Koster, San Francisco; lace M. Alexander, San Francisco; Edward Richmond, San Jose; C. C. Teague, Santa la; Ernest L. Finley, Santa Rosa; Col. Fred Robson, Vina; James M. Burke, Visalia; Rob- H. Hudson, Watsonville.

n the list will be found, so far as known, the e of no one who has insisted that immigra- shall be so controlled as to guarantee a enry qualified and disposed to maintain erican standards rather than that it shall be sed as to promote present profit or interests ection, class or group. All those named are oubtedly earnest and sincere in urging their t of view; a few, in absence of intimate wledge of the history and present conditions he problem, regard quota as a harmless con- ion to a friendly nation; many are prom- t in connection with such interests as plan- on and commercial enterprises of Hawaii, e land and orchard holdings in California, mbers of commerce—United States, Califor- State, and local—and enterprises whose its depend, or are believed to depend, in e part upon a practically unrestricted supply cheap labor; or groups anxious to placate ign nations by special concessions on the ory that trade conditions will be benefited eby; some have connection with religious international organizations committed to theory of subordination of national interest. he activities of organizations and interests rred to and individuals representing them, before the public, before civic and business bodies and before committees of the Congress, in opposing measures which would permanently close the gates to introduction of cheap alien labor and safeguard the character of our future citizenship, have been pronounced and continuous.

THE EXCLUSION MEASURE.

The California Council on Oriental Relations and Hume are in error in claiming that the 1924 exclusion measure was passed without due consideration and because of resentment induced by the Hanihara "grave consequences" letter. In 1920, and before, California demanded a measure excluding further entrance of Japanese, whose number in continental United States had trebled under operation of the "gentlemen's agreement," although President Roosevelt advised the California Legislature in 1909 that if increase of Japanese population followed operation of the agreement exclusion would be resorted to. Other Asiatic immigration had been stopped. The Federal Council of the Churches of Christ in America was urging adoption of "quota for Japan," and hearings were held thereon by the House Immigration Committee in 1919 and 1921 in Washington, D. C., and in 1920 in California, Oregon and Washington.

The national organizations of the American Legion, American Federation of Labor and the Grange, urged by their California state bodies, demanded a general uniform law which would keep out all the Asiatic races ineligible to American citizenship. The California Joint Immigration Committee presented the case to the Senate Immigration Committee in March 1924, the plan suggested being to enact a simple exclusion provision applicable to all the ineligible colored races and taking the place not only of the "gentlemen's agreement," but also of the Chinese Exclusion Act and the "barred zone" provision of the 1917 act.

QUOTA PLAN REJECTED.

The Senate Immigration Committee first declined to grant a hearing, saying it had decided to concede quota to Japan. After the first two days' presentation of facts, however, the committee acknowledged that it could not, in fairness to the United States, under any conditions concede quota, and consideration was then given to four other plans proposed—a straight Japanese exclusion act, a new "gentlemen's agreement," a treaty, and exclusion of all ineligibles. Full presentation of the case for quota was made on behalf of the Federal Council of Churches by Sidney Gulick. The general exclusion plan was endorsed as the only one which met the requirements of the case. A week or ten days before the Hanihara letter appeared, a poll of the Senate members, made by Senator Pat Harrison of Mississippi and ex-Senator James D. Phelan of California, showed that two-thirds thereof approved the findings of the Senate committee favoring exclusion. The House of Representatives had always been conceded as overwhelmingly for exclusion.

ORIGINAL INTENT NULLIFIED.

Various interests and influences forced certain modifications in the bill which changed the scope of the exclusion measure by (1) retaining in operation the Chinese Exclusion Act and the Barred Zone Act, (2) excepting from provisions of the bill the Filipinos, who are ineligible to citizenship, and (3) throwing the gates wide open to all Mexicans, some millions of whom, as Indians, are also ineligible to citizenship. It was thus made to appear that the Japanese were singled out by a discriminatory piece of legislation, and they have been naturally resentful.

Reasons which were conclusive in 1924 as to adoption of the exclusion measure have since been reinforced by added experience and present conditions. The California Council on Oriental Relations, however, instead of urging a correction of the blunders of 1924 by so modifying the law as to adhere to the non-discriminatory plan of the projectors, demands now that the law be, in effect, repealed by making eligible for entrance as immigrants all those who, under the principle approved, are expressly declared ineligible.

ITS PLAN WOULD DESTROY FOR ALL TIME THE ONLY LOGICAL, NON-DISCRIMINATORY BARRIER THUS FAR SUGGESTED TO PREVENT PEACEFUL INVASION OF UNASSIMILABLE ASIATICS UNDER ANY AND ALL POSSIBLE FUTURE CONDITIONS.

Change in Auto License Date—A change in the opening date for renewal of motor vehicle licenses for 1933 from December 15 to January 3 is announced by the State Motor Vehicle Department.

Knowledge—The more a person learns about HOW to live, the greater the desire to keep on living.—Jeanette Nourland.

Native Sons of the Golden West

MODESTO—AN ELABORATE PROGRAM was presented at the institution anniversary party of Modesto No. 11 November 2. Grand President Seth Millington spoke on "The Aims and Objects of the Order," Grand Secretary John T. Regan on "The Order's Work in Caring for Homeless Children" and Grand Trustee Jesse H. Miller on "Activities of the Parlors." Other speakers were Grand Second Vice-president Chas. A. Koenig, Grand Treasurer John A. Corotto, and Charles Swan, George Stoddard, George Nelson and Joe Kelly of No. 11. First Vice-president B. E. Munson presided, and among the 125 in attendance were visitors from Merced, Manteca, Stockton and Los Banos.

During the banquet an orchestra directed by Harold Macomber furnished music. Vocal selections were given by Betty Morris, Rose Hyslop, Dona Smith, Nancy McFee, Kenneth Steiger; violin selections by George Hatfield, Arthur Clinkenbeard, Gus Hewitt; dance numbers by Myrne Hawkins, Robert Robertson, Sam Zeff. The arrangements committee included C. E. Tucker (chairman), Mark Wilson, B. C. Hawkins, Harvey Wright, George Ingle, George Hansen, Arthur Crabb, B. E. Munson, C. C. Eastin, L. E. Bither, Robert Hansen.

Six Initiated.

Redding—McCloud No. 149 and Mount Bally No. 87 (Weaverville) had a joint meeting here November 3. Among the many in attendance were Grand President Seth Millington, Grand Trustees Henry S. Lyons and Horace J. Leavitt, and thirty-five members of Mount Bally. The occasion was the official visit of Grand Trustee Lyons to the two Parlors.

At the conclusion of supper, officers of No. 87 exemplified the ritual, three candidates being presented for each Parlor. Interesting talks were delivered by the grand officers, and Edwin Regan (South San Francisco No. 157) complimented Mount Bally's officers for their ritual work. A return get-together of the Parlors is planned for Weaverville in the near-future.

Notable Historic Site Marked.

San Diego—Murphy Canyon road, which places San Diego Mission on El Camino Real, was dedicated November 5. Albert V. Mayrhofer of San Diego No. 108 presided at the ceremonies, and the speakers included Assemblymen Ed. L. Head and George Bowers, Supervisor Edgar Hastings, George Kerrigan, W. J. Saunders and C. H. Harris.

Commemorating celebration of the first mass in California 330 years ago, a marker was November 12 unveiled at Ballast Point, the site where Father Antonio, a Carmelite priest, first raised the Cross of Christianity. Native Sons were represented by District Deputy Edward H. Dowell and Albert V. Mayrhofer, who delivered addresses. The marker is inscribed:

"This boulder, erected Nov. 12, 1932, by Court San Diego de Alcala No. 1099 of the Catholic Daughters of America to commemorate the first holy mass celebrated in California, Nov. 12, 1602, upon the arrival on this site of Sebastian Vizcaino, who named the port of San Diego in honor of the feast of Senor San Diego de Alcala and who was accompanied by three Carmelite friars, Fray Andres de la Asuncion, Fray Antonio de la Asension and Fray Tomas de Aquino."

Christmas Greeting

"To all Members of the Order of Native Sons of the Golden West—Dear Sirs and Brothers: It is only a brief time before the Christmas Season will be on us. Ordinarily a period of happiness and rejoicing, in these times of terrible economic distress Christmas will mean little more than a date on the calendar to many.

"Out here in California, however, even the conditions of the time have fallen with comparative lightness. Although we are feeling the depression with other parts of the country, it is not affecting us as it is other sections. Although we cannot ignore the fact that poverty and distress are in our midst, we can be thankful that the mild and beneficent climate of California prevents the acute suffering of the East. Although labor is not employed to the extent that gives satisfactory living, nevertheless we have the means to carry into another year even though in a lesser degree.

"I want to extend my Christmas Greetings to all members of the Order, and to wish them a happy and successful New Year, hoping that the turning of the page of the calendar will issue in a happier time than the last few years have been.

"I want to thank the brothers for the magnificent courage with which they have maintained the Order during the past year, and I need only look at the roll of membership to know that the spirit of the Forty-niner still exists in his descendants.

"My best greetings are sent to the members of the Order for the Holiday Season, and I cannot restrain from saying that I congratulate them on living in California, with its warmth and sunshine, with many advantages and helpful climate, in these days when the hand of nature has helped us where the hand of man has failed.

"Sincerely and fraternally yours,
"SETH MILLINGTON,
"Grand President N.S.G.W.
"Gridley, November 7, 1932."

School Dedicated.

Redwood City—Under the auspices of Redwood No. 66, the grand officers November 6 dedicated the $66,000 Jefferson school in the presence of a large number of parents and others. John W. Poole, president of the Board of Trustees, presided, and the speakers were Mayor W. J. Dusel, Roy W. Cloud, superintendent San Mateo County schools, Jewett Abbott, Grand First Vice-president Justice Emmet Seawell and Grand President Seth Millington.

To Assist Santa.

Livermore—Las Positas No. 96 is arranging for its annual Christmas tree, December 19, for Livermore Valley children who might otherwise be overlooked by Santa Claus. The general arrangements committee includes R. J. Rue (chairman), Carl G. Clarke and John Rose, and sub-committee chairmen are J. J. Kelly, H. Wente, J. M. Beazell, Peter Reuss, L. A. McVicar, William Medau and J. M. Baughman.

Grand Trustee Visitor.

Fort Bragg—Alder Glen No. 210 received an official visit October 28 from Grand Trustee Joseph J. McShane, who was accompanied by James L. Foley of Twin Peaks No. 214 (San Francisco) and James Bruchner of Santa Rosa No. 28. All gave enjoyable talks. November Grand Trustee McShane officially visited Broderick No. 117 (Point Arena), and a large delegation from Alder Glen attended. Banquet concluded both meetings.

The annual "krazy party" given jointly by Alder Glen and Fort Bragg No. 210 N.D.G.W. netted $50 for the homeless children.

To Establish Museum.

Santa Barbara—Plans for the establishment of a museum of particular interest to students of Santa Barbara County history have been announced by Paul Sweetser, chairman of the history committee of Santa Barbara No. 116. The supervisors have set aside a room for the purpose in the tower of the county court house. Letters, documents, relics and other articles of historical significance will be preserved.

Membership Standing Largest Parlors.

San Francisco—Grand Secretary John T. Regan reports the standing of the Subordinate Parlors having a membership of over 400 January 1, 1932, as follows, together with their membership figures November 19, 1932:

Parlor	Jan. 1	Nov. 19	Gain	Lo
Ramona No. 109	1088	1082	....	
South San Francisco No. 157	822	811	....	
Castro No. 232	700	782	82	
Stanford No. 76	614	598	....	
Arrowhead No. 110	609	579	....	
Stockton No. 7	549	563	14	
Twin Peaks No. 214	585	527	....	
Piedmont No. 120	523	524	1	
Rincon No. 72	448	431	....	

Ritual Contests Have Value.

San Rafael—Officers of Mount Tamalpais No. 64 were losers by a narrow margin in a ritual contest with National No. 118 (San Francisco) November 3. The contest was judged by a committee headed by Jas. Stanley of San Francisco Past Presidents Assembly. Following the contest all repaired to the social quarters of National, where refreshments were served and talks on the Order were made by prominent members. Tentative arrangements are being made for a return contest, some time in February, in San Rafael.

All speakers agreed these contests are of inestimable value to the Parlors, both from the standpoint of promoting interest and attendance and also in maintaining a high standard of ritualistic perfection, thus insuring a proper impression and appreciation of the beauty of the work and of the aims and purposes of the Order and in securing the co-operation of the candidates in carrying on the work of the Order.

Winter Night Stag.

San Bernardino—Arrowhead No. 110 presented a National Education Week program November 9; Ben Harrison was in charge. The first winter Saturday night stag was held at the Parlor's Crestline clubhouse November 1. A class of candidates were initiated November 16. A large crowd, including members of Lugonia No. 241 N.D.G.W., attended the Thanksgiving party November 23. A turkey dinner was followed by entertainment and dancing. Henry Peake headed the committee in charge.

Christmas Gift Suggestion—Gige a year's subscription to The Grizzly Bear, the only ALL California publication. Costs but $1.50.

Generous.

Ferndale—Recording Secretary Chris. H. Rasmussen of Ferndale No. 93, prominent Humboldt County dairyman, donated to the American Red Cross, for distribution to the unemployed, three and one-half acres of high-grade table carrots.

Pioneers Entertained.

Placerville—Placerville No. 9 and Marguerite No. 12 N.D.G.W. October 23 had their annual dinner for the Pioneers, forty of whom were present. Presidents Charles Cook and Monica McCusker extended greetings, solos were rendered by Amos Fuller and Nettie Leonardi, and dance numbers were given by Bernice Baumhoff, Colin Clayton and Jamie Ball. Pioneers related their early-day experiences. Ethel Van Vleck was chairman of the dinner and Lilla Zeisz of the decorations.

Grand Trustee Horace J. Leavitt will officially visit Placerville Parlor December 2.

Ready for Official's Visit.

Calistoga—With President Edmund Molinari presiding, Calistoga No. 86 had a fine meeting November 7, when elaborate plans were made for the official visit December 5 of Grand Third Vice-president Harmon D. Skillin. Among the features will be the initiation of a class of candidates by the Parlor's splendid ritual team. The recent benefit given jointly by No. 86 and Calistoga No. 145 N.D.G.W. netted the goodly sum of $115 for the homeless children.

Thanksgiving Ball.

Bieber—Big Valley No. 211 and Mount Lassen No. 215 N.D.G.W. sponsored a Thanksgiving ball November 24. At midnight a turkey supper was served. The proceeds went to the homeless children fund.

November 10, Mount Lassen had the first of a series of bridge-whist parties to be given through the winter. The committee in charge was Amye Mitchell, Marie Walsh and Nettie McKenzie.

CORNERSTONE LAYING.

The grand officers, headed by Grand President Seth Millington, will lay the cornerstone of the new junior high school at Vallejo, Solano County, Sunday, December 11.

LESS RAIN AND SNOW FORECAST.

California and the Pacific Coast area are due for less rain and snow this winter than was recorded during last winter, according to a forecast issued October 17 by Dr. George F. McEwen, oceanographer, and Dr. A. F. Gorton, meteorologist, of the U. C. Scripps Institution of Oceanography, at La Jolla, San Diego County.

The two predict the precipitation this winter will be from two to three inches greater than the average precipitation for the past sixteen years. The forecast is based on study of surface temperatures of inshore ocean water, of sun spots and of various cycles that apparently indicate the volume of precipitation.

N.S.G.W. OFFICIAL DEATH LIST.

Containing the name, the date and the place of birth, the date of death, and the Subordinate Parlor affiliation of deceased members reported to Grand Secretary John T. Regan from October 20, 1932, to November 19, 1932:

Dyer, Richard William; San Francisco, June 21, 1862; October 19, 1932; California No. 1.

Mariani, Albert; San Francisco, May 16, 1886; October 19, 1932; San Francisco No. 49.

Mansfield, J. M.; Napa, January 9, 1867; October 24, 1932; Napa No. 62.

Lommel, Clarence A.; San Rafael, October 29, 1902; November 11, 1932; Napa No. 62.

Trautvetter, Andrew C.; San Francisco, April 11, 1866; August 17, 1932; Stanford No. 76.

Guenley, William F.; San Francisco, August 1, 1894; August 29, 1932; Stanford No. 76.

Siemsen, John William; Napa, March 21, 1874; October 30, 1932; Calistoga No. 86.

Williams, Manuel; Douglas City, April 24, 1870; October 15, 1932; Mount Bally No. 87.

Bernal, Dennis Filbert; Pleasanton, April 8, 1856; November 2, 1932; Las Positas No. 96.

Beyer, Chester Hansen; Livermore, October 10, 1898; November 4, 1932; Las Positas No. 96.

Vejar, Rudolph Goss; Los Angeles, May 2, 1891; November 12, 1932; Ramona No. 109.

Case, John Marion; San Bernardino, April 24, 1863; October 15, 1932; Arrowhead No. 110.

Mathis, Hiram Alonzo; San Bernardino, November 27, 1882; October 15, 1932; Arrowhead No. 110.

Parker, Thomas B.; San Francisco, January 1, 1860; October 23, 1932; Presidio No. 194.

Gary, Charles; Sacramento, April 1, 1861; October 28, 1932; Twin Peaks No. 214.

Kerrigan, John Joseph; San Francisco, September 7, 1869; July 19, 1932; Castro No. 232.

Ferrant, Henry Victor; San Jose, July 10, 1892; August 30, 1932; Castro No. 232.

Sjostedt, George Eric; Eureka, July 29, 1913; September 5, 1932; Castro No. 232.

Bush, John L.; San Francisco, May 23, 1878; October 1, 1932; Castro No. 232.

Durgan, Charles Edwin; Stent, May 6, 1859; October 18, 1932; Columbia No. 258.

Know your home-state, California! Learn of its past history and of its present-day development by reading regularly The Grizzly Bear. $1.50 for one year (12 issues). Subscribe now.

CALIFORNIA HAPPENINGS OF FIFTY YEARS AGO

Thomas R. Jones

(COMPILED EXPRESSLY FOR THE GRIZZLY BEAR.)

CHRISTMAS DAY, DECEMBER 25, 1882, came on a Monday. The churches and the communities had their Christmas trees and other festivities on Saturday. With balmy days, an optimistic spirit and everybody employed, the holiday time was of exceptionally good cheer, and citizens of California spent their money freely.

But mild storms passed over the state during the month. One inch of rain fell, making the total for the season 7.15 inches.

Venus crossed the sun December 6, and the transit, which began at 11:40 a.m., was viewed, through smoked glasses, by the state's entire population. The official time, computed by the savants, was nineteen minutes and forty seconds. Venus will not transit again until the year 2004.

V. V. Mann, Democrat, and J. B. Russell, Republican, ran for treasurer of Placer County at the November election, and the result was a tie vote. At a run-off election December 12, Mann won by 218 majority.

Los Angeles City had an election December 4, and Captain Thom was elected mayor, defeating Lieutenant-governor John Mansfield.

Dairymen of the state met at San Francisco December 12 and organized an association to fight the introduction of oleomargarine as a butter substitute. A committee was named to secure legislation tabooing "bull butter" at the 1883 State Legislature.

California produced this year 43,000,000 pounds of wool, valued at $5,000,000.

Napa County produced 2,644,000 gallons of wine during the season. There were sixty-one wine cellars in that county.

The State Viticultural Association was advised that Californians were going into the wine-grape industry so extensively there would soon be an overproduction.

Lumber mills at Truckee, Nevada County, reported a successful season, which ended this month. They had cut 46,000,000 board-feet of lumber and had disposed of over $700,000 worth of the product.

Petaluma, Sonoma County, was now becoming the world's egg basket. To the San Francisco market alone, it was sending weekly 9,000 dozen henfruit.

Dr. E. T. Barnette purchased a ranch near Los Gatos, Santa Clara County, and tunneled into a hill to find a water supply. He struck a deposit of ninety-percent-pure sulphur, worth a fortune.

Gas in Los Angeles City was being supplied at $4 per one thousand feet. The rate is now 75 cents.

Austin Roberts, head of the San Jose, Santa Clara County, gas company, went insane worrying over the illumination of that city with electricity.

Etiwanda, a new mining town at the foot of the Cucamonga Range in San Bernardino County, was the first California South community to be illuminated with electric lights. It had its initial lighting up December 4.

Jose de Maria Amador, a 106-year-old "youngster," took his first ride on a railroad train December 18, going from Watsonville, Santa Cruz County, to Gilroy, Santa Clara County. He was born at San Francisco in 1776.

Henry Yantes, a Negro slave emancipated by his owner in 1847, crossed the plains in 1849 and settled in Sacramento City, where he started a laundry. With his earnings, he purchased the freedom of his wife and three children, held in bondage in Missouri. He died at the Capital City December 1 at the age of 82.

Mrs. E. J. C. Kewen died at San Francisco Christmas Day. She was a daughter of Dr. T. J. White, speaker of the Assembly at the first session of the California Legislature. In 1850 she was wedded to Colonel E. J. C. Kewen of Los Angeles, who at one time owned most of the acreage now occupied by Pasadena.

Ben Levy, who went to Alaska to take possession of that territory for the United States Government and at New Archangel pulled down the flag of Russia and in its stead raised the Stars and Stripes, died at San Francisco December 8.

On Indian Creek, near Happy Camp, Del Norte County, a gold nugget weighing twelve and a half ounces and worth $2,750 was found December 5.

Bread & Taylor, hydraulicing at Smartville, Yuba County, had their sluices robbed the night of December 12 by a gang of Chinamen, who carried away $1,500 worth of gold dust.

At Scott Bar, Nevada County, George W. Smith purchased a building used by Wells-Fargo. He removed the floor, panned the dirt underneath and recovered gold dust worth $600.

During December the United States Mint a[t] San Francisco coined $2,240,000 in twenty-dollar gold pieces and 600,000 silver dollars.

The Berry & Evans warehouse, with 2,00[0] tons of hay, burned at San Jose, Santa Clar[a] County, December 4, causing a $25,000 loss. Fire in San Leandro, Alameda County, destroyed McDuffie's livery stable; four valuable horses were cremated, and the loss was $10,000. Buildings on the farm of Jos. Sliger, near Gridley, Butte County, with eleven horses and quantities of hay and equipment, burned December 20 causing a $25,000 loss.

Fire at Fresno City December 9 destroyed seven buildings, including the post and the Wells-Fargo offices; the loss was $20,000. The warehouse and wine cellar of Draghicervich & Co. at Santa Clara City burned December 18; 40,000 gallons of wine was destroyed, and the loss was $50,000.

At a statewide teachers convention in San Francisco December 28, Governor George C. Stoneman, in the course of an address, advocated free text books for the public schools.

A Modoc County Methodist minister had one of his two horses stolen, and the congregation gathered and prayed for the thief's penitence and the horse's return. While they prayed, the thief returned and stole the other horse.

Alex Girvin and Catherine Daly were married in 1832. At an event in elite social circles, they celebrated at San Francisco December 4 their golden wedding anniversary.

C. A. Harriman and A. J. Chase had a twenty-seven-hour pedestrian match at Nevada City, Nevada County, December 15. The former won, scoring 117¾ miles in twenty-five hours. Harriman then challenged twenty of the city's best sprinters, for a twenty-mile run, each contestant to run a mile. The race was run December 21, and Harriman was victorious, covering the distance in two hours and forty minutes.

The Sacramento Valley Coursing Club had a meet on the plains near the Capital City December 1. Numerous fans and fleet greyhounds assembled, and the hares were plentiful and nimble.

Sierra Valley ranchers December 10 killed a prairie schooner load of jack rabbits and too[k] them to Virginia City, Nevada State, where the[y] sold for a dollar each.

ROMANTIC HISTORY

(Continued from Page 4)

Buena, the name of which was soon after changed to San Francisco. In honor of Captain Montgomery, the street then running along the water front was thereafter called Montgomery, and the plaza was called Portsmouth to commemorate his ship. From San Francisco Lieutenant Revere carried the American Flag to Sonoma and it there replaced the Bear Flag, being greeted with the loyal cheers of the Bear Flag Party. The Bear Flag, now the State Flag of California, is preserved as an historic emblem.

THE PERIOD OF GOLD DISCOVERY.

There is no more important date in the history of California than January 24, 1848, which marks the discovery of gold by James W. Marshall, an event which set the whole civilized world on fire with excitement. Marshall was employed by General John A. Sutter, of Sutter's Fort, at Sacramento, to erect a sawmill on the South Fork of the American River near what is now Coloma. The millrace had been built and the water turned in to carry the loose dirt away and the water then shut off, leaving the bedrock exposed. As Marshall walked along the millrace in the morning, he noticed some bright golden particles lying upon the rock. As he picked them up, his heart leaped with excitement at the thought that they might be gold. That they were gold was quickly verified.

To every farm, mill, workshop and city of America, to every region of the whole world, the news of the discovery of gold in California spread. The Argonauts came by land and sea, and over desert and mountain. No such days as these were ever known before, nor shall the like of them be known again. Gold had been discovered near the mission of San Fernando as early as 1843, but the placers from which the gold came were not extensively worked and news of the discovery did not spread.

In the "days of '49" the brave, the dauntless, the men of great hope and vision, with strong arm and clear head, relying upon individual exertion and native ability to conquer all hardships and dangers and build a nation, came here from every land. And side by side with the men of those days stood the Pioneer Mother, facing the perils of the forest, the heat of the desert, the snows of the mountain, and the un[told] perils and tribulations by land and sea. Truly may it be said, "God sifted a whole natio[n] to send seed over here into the wilderness."

AGRICULTURE AND COMMERCE.

It is said that California has twenty millio[n] acres of irrigable land. In early days much o[f] her area was made up of vast ranches, ove[r] which immense herds and droves of cattle an[d] sheep ranged. With the coming of the Amer[ican], the plow was set to the broad fields of th[e] Sacramento and San Joaquin Valleys and thou[sands] of acres of wheat and barley ripened an[d] made the plains golden in the summertime. These crops were, however, uncertain, dependin[g] upon the fall of rain in the wet season. N[o] other state, however, had as great an availabl[e] supply of water for irrigation purposes as ha[d] California. It needed but to be stored in th[e] mountains and the supply drawn upon as re[quired], both for irrigation and electric powe[r] purposes. The engineering skill of America wa[s] called into action, vast storage reservoirs wer[e] built, and immense irrigation systems construc[ted]. At the touch of living water, deserts blos[somed].

Valleys, once deserts, now smile with untol[d] wealth. The orange groves of the South an[d] North, the splendid orchards of all our valley[s], the broad fields of alfalfa, the dairy farms o[n] every hand, have sprung into being within th[e] last few years from the life-giving waters of ou[r] mountains, and not millions, but hundreds o[f] millions of dollars have been poured into th[e] channels of trade from the farms of California. Power enough to turn all the wheels of th[e] myriad industries of the nation are stored in th[e] snows and waters of the Sierra, and $1,800,000,000 in gold has come from our mines. California's oil fields add $275,000,000 annually to th[e] wealth of the nation.

Truly should the citizens of California b[e] proud of their splendid heritage.

"Never Lose Sight of the Pedestrian's Right" is the December slogan of the California Publi[c] Safety Committee in its campaign to lessen th[e] constantly increasing auto death-toll.

Christmas Gift Suggestion—Give a year's subscription to The Grizzly Bear, the only ALL California publication. Costs but $1.50.

HELP FIGHT TUBERCULOSIS

BUY CHRISTMAS SEALS

(KENDALL EMERSON, M.D., Managing Director, National Tuberculosis Association.)

THE APPEARANCE OF THE CHEERY little Christmas seals on Thanksgiving Day marked the beginning of the second quarter-century of the organized fight against tuberculosis in the United States. The design this year shows a little boy and girl, dressed in the costume of the Middle Ages, standing in the snow and lustily singing a carol in the warm red glow of a near-by window.

It is expected that during the campaign many persons will ask, "What are they singing?" The answer may very well be, "A hymn of thanks for the protection Christmas seals have given in the past, and a plea for the continuance of that protection." The picture is especially appropriate because a large proportion of the funds raised by the sale of these seals is used by tuberculosis associations throughout the United States for discovering the disease among children and guarding them from it.

Why do children need such protection, and how is it accomplished? It is a surprise to most people to learn that tuberculosis is one of the greatest causes of death among infants under one year of age, and that many children are so seriously infected they break down with the active disease during the "teen" age.

It took thousands of tests and reports to develop the safeguards that now ward off this insidious disease from children. One doctor supervised the X-raying of thousands upon thousands of children and spent many years analyzing the carefully-kept photos and records of each case. Other physicians made test after test upon children with a substance called tuberculin, which reveals years before the active disease flares up whether tubercle bacilli exist in a child's body. In such cases preventive treatment can be undertaken immediately. Careful observations have shown the effect of sunlight, diet and sleep on the growing child and their effect upon the treatment of tuberculosis.

The research committee of the National Tuberculosis Association searches tirelessly for a cure for the disease, as well as making intensive efforts to improve existing means of discovery and treatment. The outstanding feat of this group to date has been the development of a new pure tuberculin, which assures greatly increased accuracy in testing children for infection. This committee also has devoted itself to the improvement of X-ray technique and X-ray materials, and noteworthy progress and contributions to this science have been made both in the methods of taking the photographs and in the materials used in their manufacture.

And so, bit by bit, our modern knowledge about tuberculosis has been pieced together. Those facts, as they concern children, are as follows:

The majority of the entire population of the United States have tubercle bacilli in their bodies, even though all do not break down with the disease. These bacilli may invade the body during childhood and even infancy. The tuberculin test will show whether or not a child has been infected with the bacilli.

A child who has the bacilli in his body may have a condition known as the "childhood type of tuberculosis," which is often shown by the X-ray as darker shadows in the glands between the lungs, or in the lungs themselves. This, of course, is not the active disease, but it is a warning that the "seeds" of the disease are present and that the child is in danger of breaking down with active tuberculosis if his health is not carefully watched.

To keep children healthy, they should not be permitted to come into contact with a person who has tuberculosis. They should at all times be given proper amounts of sleep, day-time rest periods, good food, and play in sunshine and fresh air.

These facts point the way for the work and programs of many tuberculosis associations. Some provide free tuberculin tests, and X-rays if needed, for all schoolchildren. Others maintain a preventorium to which children who have the childhood type of tuberculosis may be sent free for treatment. Still other associations maintain free summer camps to which children who are underweight and generally under par are sent to be built up physically and thus aided to fight off tuberculosis.

So it is that the design of the little Christmas seal is appropriate. The singing children are both hymning their thanks and making a plea. And that plea is directed at you, because it is you who buy and use Christmas seals and thus make it possible to protect all children from tuberculosis—the disease that kills more persons between the ages of 15 and 45 than any other disease. Be a liberal purchaser of 1932 Christmas seals.

SERVICE

(EDGAR A. GUEST.)

I have no wealth of gold to give away,
But I can pledge to worthy causes these:
I'll give my strength, my days and hours of ease,
My finest thought and courage when I may,
And take some deed accomplished for my pay.
I cannot offer much in silver fees,
But I can serve when richer people pay,
And with my presence fill some vacancies.
There are some things beyond the gift of gold.
Some joys life needs which are not bought or
sold,
A richer treasure's needed now and then;
The high occasion often calls for men.
Some for release from service give their pelf,
But he gives most who freely gives himself.

"Happiness grows at our own firesides, and is not to be picked in strangers' gardens."—Gerrold.

Official Directory of Parlors of the N. S. G. W.

ALAMEDA COUNTY.

Alameda No. 47, Alameda City—Perry F. Badgley, Pres.; Robt. H. Cavanaugh, Sec., 1806 Pacific Ave.; Wednesdays, Native Sons Hall, 1406 Park St.
Oakland No. 50, Oakland—R. L. Engell, Pres.; F. M. Norris, Sec., 5595 Taft Ave.; Fridays, Native Sons Hall, 11th and Clay Sts.
Las Positas No. 96, Livermore—Dr. Donald M. Fraser, Pres.; John J. Kelly, Sec., P. O. box 341; Thursdays, Foresters Hall.
Eden No. 113, Hayward—Henry L'Ecu er, Pres.; Stanton R. Soares, Sec., P. O. box 176; 2nd and 4th Tuesdays, Memorial Hall, Main St.
Piedmont No. 120, Oakland—Frank Smith, Pres.; Charles Morando, Sec., 906 Vermont St.; Thursdays, Native Sons Hall, 11th and Clay Sts.
Wisteria No. 127, Alvarado—Henry May, Pres.; J. M. Scribner, Sec., Livermore; 1st Thursday, I.O.O.F. Hall.
Halcyon No. 146, Alameda City—S. Chesley Anderson, Pres.; J. C. Bates, Sec., 2139 Buena Vista Ave.; 1st and 3rd Tuesdays, I.O.O.F. Hall, 2329 Santa Clara Ave.
Brooklyn No. 151, Oakland—Frank B. Perry, Pres.; E. W. Cooney, Sec., 3907 14th Ave.; Wednesdays, Masonic Temple, 8th Ave. and E. 14th St.
Washington, No. 169, Centerville—M. D. Silva, Pres.; Allen G. Norris, Sec., P. O. box 31; 2nd and 4th Tuesdays, Hansen Hall.
Athens No. 195, Oakland—Elmer L. Bullock, Pres.; Harold B. Farley, Sec., 4623 Benevides Ave.; Tuesdays, Native Sons Hall, 11th and Clay Sts.
Berkeley No. 210, Berkeley—F. M. McGrath, Pres.; R. J. Garrett, Sec., 1708 Virginia St.; Tuesdays, Native Sons Hall, 2108 Shattuck Ave.
Estudillo No. 223, San Leandro—Frank V. Pacheco, Pres.; Albert G. Pacheco, Sec., 1736 E. 14th St.; 1st and 3rd Tuesdays, U.P.E.C. Hall.
Claremont No. 240, Oakland—Louis F. Cambet, Pres.; E. N. Thienger, Sec., 839 Hearst Ave., Berkeley; Tuesdays, Veterans Memorial Bldg., 43rd & Salem Sts., Emeryville.
Pleasanton No. 244, Pleasanton—Peter C. Madsen, Pres.; Ernest W. Schween, Sec.; 2nd and 4th Thursdays, I.O.O.F. Hall.
Niles No. 250, Niles—M. L. Fournier, Pres.; C. E. Martenstein, Sec.; 2nd Thursday, I.O.O.F. Hall.
Fruitvale No. 252, Oakland—William J. Keating Jr., Pres.; Ray B. Felton, Sec., 1575 Alice St.; Fridays, W.O.W. Hall, 3256 E. 14th St.

AMADOR COUNTY.

Amador No. 17, Sutter Creek—Frank Marre, Pres.; F. J. Payne, Sec.; 1st and 3rd Fridays, Native Sons Hall.
Excelsior No. 31, Jackson—Wm. Daugherty, Pres.; William Going, Sec.; 1st and 3rd Wednesdays, Native Sons Hall, 22 Court St.
Ione No. 33, Ione—Marvin Kidd, Pres.; Josiah H. Saunders, Sec.; 1st and 3rd Wednesdays, Native Sons Hall.
Plymouth No. 48, Plymouth—John J. Upton, Pres.; Thos. D. Davis, Sec.; 1st and 3rd Saturdays, N.S.G.W. Hall.

BUTTE COUNTY.

Argonaut No. 8, Oroville—George N. Westwood, Pres.; Cyril R. Macdonald, Sec., P. O. box 502; 1st and 3rd Wednesdays, Veterans Memorial Hall.
Chico No. 21, Chico—Marcus Choisser, Pres.; Sam Lindsay Adams, Sec., Sacramento Blvd.; 2nd and 4th Thursdays, Elks Hall.

CALAVERAS COUNTY.

Chispa No. 139, Murphys—Maynard Segale, Pres.; Antone Malaspina, Sec.; Wednesdays, Native Sons Hall.

COLUSA COUNTY.

Colusa No. 69, Colusa City—Percy J. Cooke, Pres.; Phil J. Humburg, Sec., 223 Parkhill St.; Tuesdays, Eagles Hall.

CONTRA COSTA COUNTY.

General Winn No. 32, Antioch—Edmont T. Uren, Pres.; Joel H. Ford, Sec., P. O. box 311; 2nd and 4th Wednesdays, Union Hall.
Mount Diablo No. 101, Martinez—R. P. Anderson, Pres.; G. T. Barkley, Sec.; 1st and 3rd Mondays, I.O.O.F. Hall.
Byron No. 170, Byron—William E. Bunn, Pres.; H. G. Krumland, Sec.; 1st and 3rd Tuesdays, I.O.O.F. Hall.
Carquinez No. 205, Crockett—Thos. Cox, Pres.; Thomas I. Cahalan, Sec.; 1st and 3rd Wednesdays, I.O.O.F. Hall.
Richmond No. 217, Richmond—M. W. Amaral, Pres.; Lloyd N. Mason, Sec., 11 6th St.; Wednesdays, Redmen Hall, 11th and Nevan Ave.
Concord No. 245, Concord—P. M. Soto, Pres.; D. E. Pramberg, Sec., P. O. box 235; 1st Tuesday, I.O.O.F. Hall.
Diamond No. 246, Pittsburg—Victor Ericsson, Pres.; Francis A. Irving, Sec., 248 E. 5th St.; 1st and 3rd Wednesdays, Veterans Memorial Bldg.

EL DORADO COUNTY.

Placerville No. 9, Placerville—Chas. C. Cook, Pres.; Clyde R. Berriman, Sec., Wood St.; 2nd and 4th Tuesdays, Masonic Hall.
Georgetown No. 91, Georgetown—W. H. Breedlove, Pres.; O. F. Irish, Sec.; 2nd and 4th Wednesdays, I.O.O.F. Hall.

FRESNO COUNTY.

Fresno No. 25, Fresno City—Oliver M. Akers, Pres.; W. C. Guard, Sec., 5060 Belmont; 1st and 3rd Fridays, Pythian Castle, Cor. "R" and Merced Sts.

GRAND OFFICERS.

Dr. Frank I. Gonzalez..........Junior Past Grand President
Flood Bldg., San Francisco
Seth Millington..........Grand President
Gridley
Justice Emmet Seawell..........Grand First Vice-President
State Bldg., San Francisco
Chas. A. Koenig..........Grand Second Vice-president
531 35th Ave., San Francisco
Harmon D. Skillin..........Grand Third Vice-president
Mills Bldg., San Francisco
John T. Regan..........Grand Secretary
N.S.G.W. Bldg., 414 Mason St., San Francisco
John A. Corotto..........Grand Treasurer
560 No. 5th St., San Jose
W. B. O'Brien..........Grand Marshal
2324 Santa Clara St., Alameda
Gam Hurst..........Grand Inside Sentinel
Financial Center Bldg., Oakland
William A. Reuter..........Grand Outside Sentinel
1009 Marine Ave., Wilmington
Leslie Maloche..........Grand Organist
1611 No. Hudson Ave., Los Angeles
Chester Gannon.......... Historiographer
613 Capital Ntl. Bank Bldg., Sacramento

GRAND TRUSTEES.

Jesse H. Miller..........712 DeYoung Bldg., San Francisco
Eldred L. Meyer..........922 San Vicente Blvd., Santa Monica
John M. Burnett..........914 Bank Italy Bldg., San Jose
Henry S. Lyon..........Placerville
Joseph J. McShane..........419 Flood Bldg., San Francisco
Horace J. Leavitt..........Weaverville
Chas. H. Spengemann..........827 27th Ave., San Francisco

Selma No. 107, Selma—Chester E. Shepard, Pres.; E. C. Laughlin, Sec.; 1st Wednesday, American Legion Hall.

HUMBOLDT COUNTY.

Humboldt No. 14, Eureka—Henry Sundfors, Pres.; Loren M. Nelson, Sec., P.O. box 195; 2nd and 4th Mondays, Native Sons Hall.
Arcata No. 20, Arcata—I. C. Fleckenstein, Pres.; William Peters, Sec., P. O. box 1117; Thursdays, Native Sons Hall.
Ferndale No. 93, Ferndale—Elwood Pries, Pres.; C. H. Rasmussen, Sec., R.F.D., 47-A; 1st and 3rd Mondays, K.P. Hall.

KERN COUNTY.

Bakersfield No. 42, Bakersfield—George Taylor, Pres.; Henry A. Bannister, Sec., care Bank of America; 2nd and 4th Fridays, Justice Court, City Hall.

LAKE COUNTY.

Lower Lake No. 159, Lower Lake—Harold S. Anderson, Pres.; Albert Kugelman, Sec.; Thursdays, I.O.O.F. Hall.

LASSEN COUNTY.

Honey Lake No. 198, Standish—James C. Meeske, Pres.; N. V. Wemple, Sec., Litchfield; 1st and 3rd Wednesdays, Wrede Hall.
Big Valley No. 211, Bieber—George Bunselmeier, Pres.; A. W. McKenzie, Sec.; 1st and 3rd Wednesdays, I.O.O.F. Hall.

LOS ANGELES COUNTY.

Los Angeles No. 45, Los Angeles City—Owen S. Adams, Pres.; Richard W. Fryer, Sec., 1629 Champlain Ter.; Thursdays, Merchant Plumbers Hall, 1832 So. Hope.
Ramona No. 109, Los Angeles City—James M. Watson, Pres.; John V. Scott, Sec., Patriotic Hall, 1816 So. Figueroa; Fridays, Patriotic Hall, 1816 So. Figueroa.
Hollywood No. 196, Los Angeles City—Kenneth A. Case, Pres.; E. J. Reilly, Sec., Olive View; Mondays, 1089 No. Oxford Ave.
Long Beach No. 239, Long Beach—Francis H. Gentry, Pres.; W. W. Brady, Sec., 801 Jergins Trust Bldg.; 2nd and 4th Thursdays, Moose Hall, Elm and Anaheim.
Sepulveda No. 263, San Pedro—Joseph Pia, Pres.; Harry Fairall, Sec., 1925 Pacific Ave.; 1st and 3rd Fridays, Redman Hall, 543 Shepherd St., Point Firmin.
Glendale No. 264, Glendale—Leslie F. Schellback, Pres.; Abel B. Molen, Sec., 508 So. Belmont St.; 1st and 3rd Tuesdays, Masonic Temple, 234 So. Brand Blvd.
Santa Monica Bay 267, Santa Monica—Orrin G. Welch, Pres.; John J. Smith, Sec., 830 Rialto Ave., Venice; 1st and 3rd Wednesdays, Odd Fellows Hall, 1431 Third St.
Cahuenga No. 268, Reseda—Harold C. Trexler, Pres.; Carrol S. Driscoll, Sec., P.O. box 25, Chatsworth; first Friday, Alton Hall.
University No. 272, Los Angeles—Bernard G. Hiss, Pres.; Martin DeFazio, Sec., 845 W. 53rd St.; Tuesdays, 471 W. 41st Place.

MADERA COUNTY.

Madera No. 130, Madera City—Cornelius Noble, Pres.; T. P. Cosgrave, Sec.; 1st and 3rd Thursdays, First National Bank Bldg.

MARIN COUNTY.

Mount Tamalpais No. 64, San Rafael—M. E. Peterson, Pres.; Manual A. Andrade, Sec., 532 Mission Ave.; 1st and 3rd Mondays, Portuguese American Hall.
Sea Point No. 158, Sausalito—A. H. Bettencourt, Pres.; Manuel Santos, Sec., 6 Glen Drive; 1st and 3rd Wednesdays, Perry Bldg.
Nicasio No. 183, Nicasio—M. T. Farley, Pres.; R. J. Rogers, Sec.; 2nd and 4th Wednesdays, U.A.O.D. Hall.

MENDOCINO COUNTY.

Ukiah No. 71, Ukiah—Henry Bucknell, Pres.; Ben Hofman, Sec., P. O. box 473; 1st and 3rd Mondays, I.O.O.F. Hall.
Broderick No. 117, Point Arena—A. L. McCallum, Pres.; C. J. Buchanan, Sec.; 1st and 3rd Thursdays, Forester Hall.
Alder Glen No. 200, Fort Bragg—H. M. Bohn, Pres.; C. R. Weller, Sec.; 2nd and 4th Fridays, I.O.O.F. Hall.

MERCED COUNTY.

Yosemite No. 24, Merced City—John J. Thronton, Pres.; True W. Fowler, Sec., P. O. box 781; 2nd and 4th Mondays, I.O.O.F. Hall.
Los Banos No. 206, Los Banos—Robert L. Puccinelli, Pres.; L. E. Sarbo, Sec., R.F.D., box 21; 2nd and 4th Wednesdays, Eagles Hall.

MONTEREY COUNTY.

Monterey No. 75, Monterey City—James Millington, Pres.; T. W. Krieger, Sec., 999 Franklin St.; 1st and 3rd Fridays, Knights Pythias Hall, Main St.
Santa Lucia No. 97, Salinas—Roy Martella, Pres.; R. W. Adcock, Sec., Route 2, box 180; Mondays, Native Sons Hall, 32 W. Alisal St.
Gabilan No. 132, Castroville—B. A. McCoy, Pres.; R. H. Martin, Sec., P. O. box 81; 1st and 3rd Thursdays, Native Sons Hall.

ATTENTION, SECRETARIES!

THIS DIRECTORY IS PUBLISHED BY AUTHORITY OF THE GRAND PARLOR N.S.G.W., AND ALL NOTICES OF CHANGES MUST BE RECEIVED BY THE GRAND SECRETARY (NOT THE MAGAZINE) ON OR BEFORE THE 20TH OF EACH MONTH TO INSURE CORRECTION IN NEXT ISSUE OF DIRECTORY.

NAPA COUNTY.

Saint Helena No. 53, Saint Helena—Lucas Haus, Pres.; Edw. L. Bonhote, Sec., P. O. box 267; Mondays, Native Sons Hall.
Napa No. 62, Napa City—R. O. Akers, Pres.; H. J. Hoernle, Sec., 1226 Oak St.; Mondays, Native Sons Hall.
Calistoga No. 86, Calistoga—Edmund Molinari, Pres.; Louis Carlenzoli, Sec.; 1st and 3rd Mondays, I.O.O.F. Hall.

NEVADA COUNTY.

Hydraulic No. 56, Nevada City—Arthur W. Davis, Pres.; Dr. C. W. Chapman, Sec.; Tuesdays, Pythian Castle.
Quartz No. 58, Grass Valley—Robert Kohler, Pres.; H. Ray George, Sec., 151 Conaway Ave.; Mondays, Auditorium Hall.
Donner No. 162, Truckee—J. F. Lichtenberger, Pres.; H. C. Lichtenberger, Sec.; 2nd and 4th Tuesdays, Native Sons Hall.

ORANGE COUNTY.

Santa Ana No. 265, Santa Ana—Amos Huntzinger, Pres.; E. F. Marks, Sec., 1124 No. Bristol St.; 1st and 3rd Mondays, K.C. Hall, 4th and French Sts.

PLACER COUNTY.

Auburn No. 59, Auburn—Iris Garcia, Pres.; J. G. Walsh, Sec.; 1st and 3rd Fridays, Foresters Hall.
Silver Star No. 63, Lincoln—L. F. Browning, Pres.; Barney G. Barry, Sec., P. O. box 72; 3rd Wednesday, I.O.O.F. Hall.
Rocklin No. 233, Roseville—Wm. La Due, Pres.; M. E. Reed, Sec., 253 W. Duranta; 2nd and 4th Wednesdays, Eagles Hall.

PLUMAS COUNTY.

Quincy No. 131, Quincy—J. D. McLaughlin, Pres.; E. C. Kelsey, Sec.; 2nd Thursday, I.O.O.F. Hall.
Golden Anchor No. 182, La Porte—R. J. McGrath, Pres.; LeRoy J. Post, Sec.; 2nd and 4th Sunday mornings, Native Sons Hall.
Plumas No. 228, Taylorsville—E. E. Sikes, Pres.; George E. Boyden, Sec.; 1st and 3rd Mondays, Native Sons Hall.

SACRAMENTO COUNTY.

Sacramento No. 3, Sacramento City—J. G. Fitzhenry, Pres.; J. F. Didion, Sec., 1213 "O" St.; Thursdays, Native Sons Bldg., 11th and "J" Sts.
Sunset No. 26, Sacramento City—L. W. Marvin, Pres.; Edward E. Reese, Sec., County Treasurer Office; Mondays, Native Sons Bldg., 11th and "J" Sts.
Elk Grove No. 41, Elk Grove—Robert Carr, Pres.; Walter Martin, Sec.; 2nd and 4th Fridays, Masonic Hall.
Granite No. 83, Folsom—Joe Relvas, Pres.; Frank Showers, Sec.; 2nd and 4th Tuesdays, K.P. Hall.
Courtland No. 106, Courtland—Thornton Pylman, Pres.; Jos. Green, Sec.; 1st Saturday and 3rd Monday, Native Sons Hall.
Sutter Fort No. 241, Sacramento City—Ed. T. Goyne, Pres.; C. L. Katzenstein, Sec., P. O. box 914; 2nd and 4th Wednesdays, Native Sons Bldg., 11th and "J" Sts.
Galt No. 243, Galt—John Granadas, Pres.; F. W. Harms, Sec.; 1st and 3rd Mondays, I.O.O.F. Hall.

SAN BENITO COUNTY.

Fremont No. 44, Hollister—S. Churchill, Pres.; J. E. Prendergast Jr., Sec., 1064 Monterey St.; 1st and 3rd Thursdays, Grangers Union Hall.

SAN BERNARDINO COUNTY.

Arrowhead No. 110, San Bernardino City—F. L. McGarvey, Pres.; R. W. Brazelton, Sec., 462 6th St.; Wednesdays, Eagles Hall, 469 4th St.

SAN DIEGO COUNTY.

San Diego No. 108, San Diego City—Martin J. Spangler, Pres.; A. V. Mayrhofer, Sec., 1572 2nd St.; Wednesdays, K.C. Hall, 4th and Elm Sts.

SAN FRANCISCO CITY AND COUNTY.

California No. 1, San Francisco—Joseph Lawlor, Pres.; Ellis A. Blackman, Sec., 1248-A Divisadero St.; Thursdays, Native Sons Bldg., 414 Mason St.
Pacific No. 10, San Francisco—Walter Mohrdick, Pres.; J. Henry Bastein, Sec., 426 City Hall; Tuesdays, Native Sons Bldg., 414 Mason St.
Golden Gate No. 29, San Francisco—Thomas I. Schlink, Pres.; Adolph Eberhart, Sec., 183 Carl St.; Mondays, Native Sons Bldg., 414 Mason St.
Mission No. 38, San Francisco—George Leahy, Pres.; Thos. J. Stewart, Sec., 1919 Howard St.; Wednesdays, Redmen Hall, 3053 16th St.
San Francisco No. 49, San Francisco—Charles Miller, Pres.; David Capurro, Sec., 976 Union St.; Thursdays, Native Sons Bldg., 414 Mason St.
El Dorado No. 52, San Francisco—Edward Victor, Pres.; Alfred Vlautin, Sec., 1537 Franklin St.; Thursdays, Native Sons Bldg., 414 Mason St.
Rincon No. 72, San Francisco—Frank D. Sericano, Pres.; John A. Gilmour, Sec., 2069 Golden Gate Ave.; Wednesdays, Native Sons Bldg., 414 Mason St.
Stanford No. 76, San Francisco—Dr. Vincent V. Hardeman, Pres.; Charles T. O'Kane, Sec., 1111 Pine St.; Tuesdays, Native Sons Bldg., 414 Mason St.
Bay City No. 104, San Francisco—Morris Garren, Pres.; Max E. Licht, Sec., 1831 Fulton St.; 2nd and 4th Wednesdays, Native Sons Bldg., 414 Mason St.
Niantic No. 105, San Francisco—A. Furner, Pres.; J. M. Darcy, Sec., 10 Hoffman Ave.; Wednesdays, Native Sons Bldg., 414 Mason St.
National No. 118, San Francisco—Wayne Burke, Pres.; Martin M. Ratigan, Sec., 1325 Page St., Apt. 6; Thursdays, 1160 Eddy St.
Hesperian No. 137, San Francisco—C. McLaughlin, Pres.; Albert Carlson, Sec., 379 Justin Dr.; Thursdays, Native Sons Bldg., 414 Mason St.
Alcalde No. 154, San Francisco—Charles Kurpinsky, Pres.; Harry S. Burke, Sec., 25 Ord St.; 2nd and 4th Wednesdays, Native Sons Bldg., 414 Mason St.
South San Francisco No. 157, San Francisco—Otto A. Elvander, Pres.; John T. Regan, Sec., 1489 Newcomb Ave.; Wednesdays, Masonic Bldg., 4705 3rd St.
Sequoia No. 160, San Francisco—Harry Grover, Pres.; Walter W. Garrett, Sec., 2500 Van Ness Ave.; Mondays, Swedish-American Bldg., 2174 Market St.
Precita No. 187, San Francisco—Lloyd J. Cosgrove, Pres.; Edward Tietjen, Sec., 1367 15th Ave.; Thursdays, Mission Masonic Hall, 2668 Mission St.
Olympus No. 189, San Francisco—Henry H. McGowan, Pres.; Harvey J. Carty, Sec., 1651 Market St., Apt. 505; 2nd and 4th Tuesdays, Independent Redmen Hall, 3053 16th St.
Presidio No. 194, San Francisco—Lester Figone, Pres.; George A. Ducker, Sec., 442 21st Ave.; Mondays, Native Sons Bldg., 414 Mason St.
Marshall No. 202, San Francisco—Alexander Jean, Pres.; Frank Bacigalupi, Sec., 725 Douglas St.; 1st and 3rd Wednesdays, Native Sons Bldg., 414 Mason St.
Dolores No. 208, San Francisco—James F. Vahey, Pres.; Edward P. Webb, Sec., 2801 Sacramento St.; Tuesdays, Mission Masonic Bldg., 2668 Mission St.
Twin Peaks No. 214, San Francisco—Clifford Roberts, Pres.; Thos. Pendergast, Sec., 278 Douglas St.; Wednesdays, Willopi Hall, 4061 24th St.

El Capitan No. 222, San Francisco—Frank Rizzo, Pres.; James Hanna, Sec., 2450 27th Ave.; 1st and 3rd Thursdays, King Solomon Hall, 1739 Fillmore St.
Guadalupe No. 231, San Francisco—Roy Tensfeldt, Pres.; Alvin A. Johnson, Sec., 142 Rousseau St.; Tuesdays, Guadalupe Hall, 4551 Mission St.
Castro No. 232, San Francisco—Ralph Willis, Pres.; James H. Hayes, Sec., 4014 18th St.; Tuesdays, Native Sons Bldg., 414 Mason St.
Balboa No. 234, San Francisco—George Schroth, Pres.; E. W. Boyd, Sec., 437 Cherry St.; Thursdays, Maccabee Hall, 5th Ave. and Clement St.
Bret Harte No. 260, San Francisco—Chas. E. Lillie, Pres.; A. W. McElhatton, Sec., 103 Holloway Ave.; Tuesdays, West of Twin Peaks Hall, 233 Legion Court.
Utopia No. 270, San Francisco—George Walters, Pres.; Herbert H. Schneider, Sec., 2455 16th Ave.; Tuesdays, American Hall, 20th and Capp Sts.

SAN JOAQUIN COUNTY.

Stockton No. 7, Stockton—John D. Gallagher, Pres.; R. D. Dorcey, Sec., P. O. box 388; Mondays, Native Sons Hall.
Lodi No. 18, Lodi—Jerome Solomon, Pres.; Dr. Clyde Bresnan, Sec.; 2nd and 4th Wednesdays, Eagles Hall.
Tracy No. 186, Tracy—C. S. Seina, Pres.; R. J. Marraccini, Sec., R.F.D. No. 1, box 217; Thursdays, I.O.O.F. Hall.
Manteca No. 271, Manteca—Chas. N. Howell Jr., Pres.; Leonard Faria, Sec., R.F.D., box 75, Lathrop; 1st and 3rd Wednesdays, I.O.O.F. Hall.

SAN LUIS OBISPO COUNTY.

San Miguel No. 150, San Miguel—H. Twisselman, Pres.; Otto Kuehl, Sec., Paso Robles; 1st and 3rd Wednesdays, Fraternal Hall.
Cambria No. 152, Cambria—J. M. Soto, Pres.; A. S. Gay, Sec.; Wednesdays, Rigdon Hall.

SAN MATEO COUNTY.

Redwood No. 66, Redwood City—Frank Deluchi, Pres.; A. S. Liguori, Sec., P. O. box 212; Thursdays, American Foresters Hall.
Seaside No. 95, Half Moon Bay—Andrew F. Gilcrest, Pres.; John G. Gilcrest, Sec.; 2nd and 4th Tuesdays, I.O.O.F. Hall.
Menlo No. 185, Menlo Park—C. T. Maloney, Pres.; F. W. Johnson, Sec., P. O. box 601; Thursdays, Masonic Hall.
Pebble Beach No. 230, Pescadero—Harold Souza, Pres.; E. A. Shaw, Sec.; 2nd and 4th Wednesdays, I.O.O.F. Hall.
El Carmelo No. 256, Daly City—Theodore A. Clemens, Pres.; Ernest L. Micco, Sec., 639 Morse St., San Francisco; 2nd and 4th Wednesdays, Eagles Hall.
Industrial City No. 269, South San Francisco—John C. Hamilton, Pres.; Geo. A. Roll, Sec., P. O. box 237; 2nd and 4th Mondays, Metropolitan Hall.

SANTA BARBARA COUNTY.

Santa Barbara No. 116, Santa Barbara City—C. W. McCormick, Pres.; H. C. Sweetser, Sec., Court House; 1st and 3rd Wednesdays, I.O.O.F. Hall.

SANTA CLARA COUNTY.

San Jose No. 22, San Jose—Joseph Sabatte, Pres.; Joseph Lawrence, Sec., 1095 No. First St.; Mondays, I.O.O.F. Hall.
Santa Clara No. 100, Santa Clara City—C. A. Castro, Pres.; Clarence Clevenger, Sec., P. O. box 297; Wednesdays, Redmen Hall.
Observatory No. 177, San Jose—William L. Gerrans, Pres.; A. R. Langford, Sec., Hall Records; Tuesdays, Knights Columbus Hall, 40 No. First St.
Mountain View No. 215, Mountain View—Gilbert F. McCorkle, Pres.; C. A. Antonioli, Sec., 301 Castro St.; 2nd and 4th Wednesdays, Mockbee Hall.
Palo Alto No. 216, Palo Alto—John C. Bernal, Pres.; Albert A. Quinn, Sec., 643 High St.; Mondays, Native Sons Bldg., Hamilton Ave. and Emerson St.

SANTA CRUZ COUNTY.

Watsonville No. 65, Watsonville—Fred R. Baese, Pres.; E. R. Tindall, Sec., R.F.D. No. 5, Box 313; 2nd and 4th Tuesdays, I.O.O.F. Hall.
Santa Cruz No. 90, Santa Cruz City—Horace Burkett, Pres.; T. V. Mathews, Sec., 105 Pacheco Ave.; Fridays, Native Sons Hall, 117 Pacific Ave.

SHASTA COUNTY.

McCloud No. 149, Redding—A. E. Welbourn, Pres.; Hugh A. Shuffleton, Sec.; 1st and 3rd Thursdays, Moose Hall.

SIERRA COUNTY.

Downieville No. 92, Downieville—Frank H. Turner, Pres.; H. S. Tibbey, Sec.; 2nd and 4th Mondays, I.O.O.F. Hall.
Golden Nugget No. 94, Sierra City—Elmer Thompson, Pres.; Arthur R. Pride, Sec.; 1st and 3rd Wednesdays, Masonic Hall.

SISKIYOU COUNTY.

Etna No. 192, Etna—Frank B. Quigley, Pres.; Harvey A. Green, Sec.; 1st and 3rd Wednesdays, I.O.O.F. Hall.
Liberty No. 193, Sawyers Bar—Orrin R. Bigelow, Pres.; John M. Barry, Sec.; 1st and 3rd Saturdays, I.O.O.F. Hall.

SOLANO COUNTY.

Solano No. 39, Suisun—Karl Koch, Pres.; J. W. Kinlock, Sec.; 1st and 3rd Tuesdays, I.O.O.F. Hall.
Vallejo No. 77, Vallejo—Joseph Clavo, Pres.; Werner B. Hallin, Sec., 912 Carolina; 2nd and 4th Tuesdays, San Pablo Hall.

SONOMA COUNTY.

Petaluma No. 27, Petaluma—Fred G. Ilg, Pres.; C. F. Fobes, Sec., 114 Prospect St.; 2nd and 4th Mondays, Druid Hall, Gross Bldg., 41 Main St.
Santa Rosa No. 28, Santa Rosa—Wesley Beach, Pres.; Leland S. Lewis, Sec., Court House; Mondays, Native Sons Hall.
Glen Ellen No. 102, Glen Ellen—Tony Cereghino, Pres.; Frank Kirch, Sec., Route 3, Santa Rosa; 2nd Monday, N.S.G.W. Hall.
Sonoma No. 111, Sonoma City—Joseph Andrieux, Pres.; L. H. Green, Sec.; 1st and 3rd Mondays, I.O.O.F. Hall.
Sebastopol No. 143, Sebastopol—O. A. McChristian, Pres.; F. G. McFarlane, Sec.; 1st and 3rd Fridays, I.O.O.F. Hall.

STANISLAUS COUNTY.

Modesto No. 11, Modesto—Chas. D. Blaine, Pres.; C. C. Eastin Jr., Sec., P. O. box 898; 1st and 3rd Wednesdays, I.O.O.F. Hall.
Oakdale No. 142, Oakdale—D. W. Tulloch, Pres.; E. T. Gobin, Sec.; 2nd and 4th Mondays, Legion Hall.
Orestimba No. 247, Crows Landing—Lloyd W. Fink, Pres.; G. W. Fink, Sec.; 1st and 3rd Wednesdays, Community Club Home.

SUTTER COUNTY.

Sutter No. 261, Sutter City—Albert Thomasen, Pres.; Glen R. Haynes, Sec., R.F.D. No. 2, Yuba City; 2nd and 4th Mondays, N.D.G.W. Hall.

TRINITY COUNTY.

Mount Bally No. 87, Weaverville—R. L. Marshall, Pres.; E. V. Ryan, Sec.; 1st and 3rd Mondays, Native Sons Hall.

TULARE COUNTY.

Visalia No. 19, Visalia—G. W. Houk, Pres.; C. H. Wenn, Sec.

TUOLUMNE COUNTY.

Tuolumne No. 144, Sonora—Mathew J. Marshall, Pres.; William M. Harrington, Sec., P. O. box 715; 2nd and 4th Fridays, Knights Columbus Hall.
Columbia No. 258, Columbia—Jos. Cadematori, Pres.; Charles E. Grant, Sec.; 2nd and 4th Thursdays, Native Sons Hall.

VENTURA COUNTY.

Cabrillo No. 114, Ventura City—David Bennett, Pres., 1380 Church St.

YOLO COUNTY.

Woodland No. 30, Woodland—J. L. Aronson, Pres.; R. G. Lawson, Sec.; 1st Thursday, Native Sons Hall.

YUBA COUNTY.

Marysville No. 6, Marysville—Ray C. Burris, Pres.; Verne Fogarty, Sec., 719 6th St.; 2nd Friday, Foresters Hall.
Rainbow No. 40, Wheatland—F. M. Beilby, Pres.; W. A. Bowser, Sec., P. O. box 313; 2nd Thursday, I.O.O.F. Hall.

AFFILIATED ORGANIZATIONS.

San Francisco Extension of the Order Committee, N.S.G.W.—Joseph J. McShane, Chmn.; Harold J. Regan, Sec., 414 Mason St., San Francisco; meets 2nd and 4th Fridays, Grizzly Bear Club, 414 Mason St., San Francisco.
Alameda County Extension of the Order Committee, N.S.G.W.—Edward T. Schnarr, Chmn.; Frank Roemer, Sec., 3297 Morcom Ave., Oakland; meets 1st and 3rd Mondays, N.S.G.W. Hall, 11th and Clay Sts., Oakland.
Interparlor Committee (Southern District), N.S.G.W. and N.D.G.W.—Burrel D. Neighbours, Chmn.; F. J. Burmester, Sec., P. O. box 42, Colton; meets 2nd and 4th Fridays, Patriotic Hall, 1816 So. Figueroa St., Los Angeles.
San Francisco Assembly No. 1 Past Presidents Association N.S.G.W.—Meets 1st and 3rd Fridays, Native Sons Bldg., 414 Mason St., San Francisco; Jos. E. Tracy, Gov.; J. F. Stanley, Sec., 1175 O'Farrell St., San Francisco.
East Bay Counties Assembly No. 3 Past Presidents Association N.S.G.W.—Meets 4th Monday, Native Sons Hall, 11th and Clay Sts., Oakland; Felix Robison, Gov.; Edgar G. Hanson, Sec., 1260 Russell St., Berkeley.
Marin County Assembly No. 5 Past Presidents Association N.S.G.W.—J. S. Rose Jr., Gov.; L. J. Peter, Sec., Peter Bldg., 4th and "C" Sts., San Rafael.
Fred H. Greeley Assembly No. 6 Past Presidents Association N.S.G.W.—Meets monthly with different Parlors comprising district; R. L. P. Bigelow, Gov.; Barney Barry, Sec., P. O. box 72, Lincoln.
San Joaquin Assembly No. 7 Past Presidents Association N.S.G.W.—Meets 1st Friday, Native Sons Hall, Stockton; Clyde H. Gregg, Gov.; R. D. Dorcey, Sec., Native Sons Club, Stockton.
Sonoma County Assembly No. 9 Past President Association N.S.G.W.—Meets monthly at different Parlor headquarters in county; Louis Bosch, Gov.; L. S. Lewis, Sec., Court House, Santa Rosa.
General John A. Sutter Assembly No. 10 Past Presidents Association—C. C. Wachman, Gov.; Jas. J. Longshore, Sec., 514 "J" St., Sacramento.
Grizzly Bear Club—Members all Parlors outside San Francisco at all times welcome. Clubrooms top floor Native Sons Bldg., 414 Mason St., San Francisco.
Native Sons and Native Daughters Central Committee on Homeless Children—Main office, 955 Phelan Bldg., San Francisco; Mrs. John W. Stirling, Chmn.; Miss Mary E. Brusie, Sec. Los Angeles branch office, 3924 Sunset Blvd.; Dorothy Schlineman, Sec.

(ADVERTISEMENT.)

"MARK OUR LANDMARKS"

Chester F. Gannon

(HISTORIOGRAPHER N.S.G.W.)

"MARK OUR LANDMARKS"

FORGOTTEN GRAVE

IN MAY OF 1933 THE GRAND PARLOR OF the Order of Native Sons of the Golden West will convene at Grass Valley, Nevada County. There the delegates will participate in the usual light deliberations of a Grand Parlor and spend considerable of their time in play and fraternization, a worthy object of every gathering where men commingle for a few days each year and leave behind them their business and, perhaps, their domestic, cares.

But when they convene in the old California mining town of Grass Valley, on every side will be the footprints of the '49ers. There is scarcely a section of California more replete with the romance, the chivalry and the history of the days agone than this present California town, situated midway between the high Sierra and the lowly Valley of the Sacramento.

Your historian has called attention in the past, and will continue to call attention in the future, to the almost absolute neglect of Native Sons to perpetuate and glorify the days of the pioneer either with monument or with ceremony. Too busy are we in following the paths designated by those who never found in their breasts the real purpose of our Order. May your historian call to your attention another glaring dereliction of duty, and trust as he calls it to your attention that the same will be rectified before the year of 1933 has waned.

In a half-abandoned cemetery just outside of Grass Valley is the grave of John Rollin Ridge, a remarkable man, half Cherokee Indian, whose writings of a half-century ago showed the spark and fire of genius. Ridge came to California when the state was young. He arrived in 1850, at the age of 23, and immediately his pen flowed with poetry and prose, and he became one of the foremost literary lights in California. He served here and there as an editor, operated a number of newspapers on the Pacific Coast, and dipped into politics. It is not his pioneer activities which the writer desires to dwell upon, but rather the genius of a man forgotten. He published a book called "John R. Ridge's Poems," and prose which he wrote still stands out as perhaps the best treatise on the subject when Ridge wrote a biography of Joaquin Murietta, the bandit. Space does not permit the tracing of his lineage from a full-blooded Indian prince and a Puritan mother to his final restingplace in Grass Valley.

A year ago the writer visited the old cemetery with Raymond Clinch of Quartz Parlor No. 58 and in an area of perhaps two or three hundred square feet Clinch pointed rather vaguely thereabouts and said, "Somewhere in that spot is Ridge's grave. There is only one woman who can definitely point it out, and she is well past eighty." Therefore, is it not time that we should arise to our fraternal destiny and rescue him, and dozens of other characters and spots, from the oblivion in which the drifting years relegate them?

Should the man who wrote the following words be forgotten and unnamed among the Pioneers whose names and deeds we should revere? Has anything finer been written of Mount Shasta, our natural, beautiful landmark, than that which Ridge, with his prophetic vision, in about 1856 wrote of that northern landmark. His peroration to Mount Shasta is regarded by many as his masterpiece. This is but a snatch of the poem, but it gives a splendid idea of the magic in his pen and the poetry in his soul:

"And well I ween in after years how,
In the middle of his furrowed track the plowman,
In some sultry hour, will pause and, wiping
From his brow the dusty sweat, with reverence
Gaze upon that hoary peak. The herdsman
Oft will rein his charger in the plain and drink
Into his inmost soul the calm sublimity;
And little children, playing on the green, shall
Cease their sport, and, turning to that mountain
Old, shall of their mother ask: 'Who made it?'
And she shall answer—'God!'"

In Memoriam

WILLIAM J. HAYES, P.G.P.

"Whereas, Our Heavenly Father has recently seen fit to take from our midst an honored and loyal member of the Order of the Native Sons of the Golden West and an honored and respected Past Grand President of the Order, in the passing of William J. Hayes; and whereas, all members of our Order deeply appreciate the loss we have sustained in losing such a tireless worker and such an honored member of our Order; yet, whereas, we bow to the will of the Supreme Power in His omnipotent wisdom, in His taking our brother to the great undiscovered country where he may still be of greater service than to us; now, therefore, be it

Resolved, That the Extension of the Order Committee of the Native Sons of the Golden West hereby extends to the family of our late brother, William J. Hayes, our deepest sincere sympathy in the loss of a devoted husband and worthy father; and be it further resolved, that a copy of these resolutions be spread upon the minutes of the Extension of the Order Committee of the N.S.G.W., that a copy be sent to the family of our late departed brother, and that a copy also be sent to The Grizzly Bear Publishing Company, to be printed in The Grizzly Bear Magazine.

RAY B. FELTON,
L. L. STEELE,
T. A. FITZGERALD,
L. J. STIRLING,
R. M. HAMB,
Committee.

Oakland, November 7, 1932.

MARTHA J. O'BRIEN.

To the Officers and Members of Piedmont Parlor No. 87 N.D.G.W.—We, your committee appointed to draft resolutions of respect to the memory of our departed sister, Martha J. O'Brien, respectfully submit the following:

Whereas, After a life of devotion to her five sons and many friends, our Heavenly Father has seen fit to call our beloved sister, Martha J. O'Brien, home, to enjoy the eternal reward she so richly deserves; and whereas, Piedmont Parlor No. 87 N.D.G.W. has suffered the great loss of a true and loyal member; therefore, be it

Resolved, That it is but a just tribute to the memory of the departed to say, that in regretting her removal from our midst we mourn for one who was in every way worthy of our respect, and that we extend the hand of sympathy to the bereaved family in this, their hour of trial; be it further resolved, that a copy of these resolutions be sent to the family of our departed sister, that a copy be spread in full upon the minutes of this Parlor, and that a copy be sent to The Grizzly Bear for publication.

JOSEPHINE CLARK,
NELL REALY MOORE,
MARY RING,
Condolence Committee.

Oakland, November 17, 1932.

The West—Beauty, tranquility, health and prosperity are what the West has to offer the world.—Jeanette Nourland.

LOS ANGELES CITY AND COUNTY

SATURDAY EVENING, DECEMBER 3, THE southland Parlors of Native Sons will initiate a class of candidates in honor of Grand President Seth Millington, the ceremonies to be held at Elks Temple, 607 South Park View. The ritual will be exemplified by the following: Charles E. Young (Ramona No. 109), senior past; Judge Leo Aggeler (Hollywood No. 196), junior past; Orrin G. Welch (Santa Monica Bay No. 267), president; Patrick Doran (Sepulveda No. 263), first vice; Roger M. Johnson (Los Angeles No. 45), second vice; John B. Martin Jr. (Sepulveda No. 263), third vice; Henry V. Harris (Ramona No. 109), marshal; Clinton E. Skinner (Glendale No. 264), inside sentinel; William Quast (University No. 272), outside sentinel; Grand Organist Leslie Maloche (Arrowhead No. 110), organist.

Arrangements for the initiation have been under way since August 15, when a joint committee, with Bernard G. Hiss as chairman, was organized to conduct a membership campaign. To assist the Parlors, Grand President Millington appointed Clinton E. Skinner as fieldman. As a result of the campaign, University Parlor No. 272 has been instituted, another parlor is in prospect for Compton, and a large number of candidates will, it is promised, be presented for initiation by all the southland Parlors December 3. Following the initiatory ceremonies, Grand Trustee Eldred L. Meyer will welcome the grand officers, many of whom are expected to be in attendance, and will introduce Grand President Millington, who will address the assemblage.

Preceding the initiatory ceremonies will be a 6:30 supper at Elks Temple, to which all Native Daughters and Native Sons, together with their escorts, are invited. Tickets, at one dollar per plate, may be secured from the secretary of any Parlor. While the Sons are in secret session for the initiation the womenfolks will be entertained at cards. Grand President Millington arrived November 28, and that evening paid a visit to Santa Ana Parlor No. 265. The 29th he visited University Parlor No. 272, and the 30th, Arrowhead Parlor No. 110 at San Bernardino. December 1 he will visit Los Angeles Parlor No. 45, and December 2, Sepulveda Parlor No. 263 at San Pedro. "There is no substitute for membership!" Remember that, and have your candidates ready for initiation December 3.—C.M.H.

DELIGHTFUL AFFAIR.

Glendale—A most delightful affair, largely attended by Native Daughters and Native Sons from Santa Barbara to San Diego as well as numerous other admiring friends, was the reception sponsored by Verdugo Parlor No. 240 N.D.G.W. in honor of Grand Outside Sentinel Hazel Bruschi-Hansen, a past president of the Parlor, November 15. President Betty Sanders presided, and in the receiving line were the following past presidents and officers of Verdugo: Ida N. Gilman, Clytell Hewitt, Doria Phillips, Ella Mae Madden, Beulah VanLeuven, Kathryn Burke, Vera Carlson, Sarah Burleson, Margaret Donlon, Ruby Eubank, Etta Fulkerth, Ada Steele, Myrtize Tregea, Bernice Binkerdyke, Edith Dobson, Gussie Anderson, Nan Hutcheson, Mayme Kerrie, Dorothy Ravin.

Among the guests were the following Native Daughters: Founder Lilly O. Reichling-Dyer, Past Grand Grace S. Stoermer, Grand Trustee

MRS. HAZEL B. HANSEN.

Jane Vick, Deputy Grand Presidents Nettie Edwards, Nellie Cline, Lucretia Coates, Gertrude Allen, Marion Crum, Mary Noerenberg. And these Native Sons: Grand Trustee Eldred L. Meyer, Deputy Grand President Clinton E. Skinner, District Deputies Walter Hiskey, Raymond Marsile, Walter Baskerville.

Mrs. Hansen was showered with beautiful floral remembrances; Mitzi Chandler, accompanied by May Jordan Arbenz, entertained with dance numbers, and dainty refreshments were served. Dancing was the evening's diversion. Sarah Burleson was program chairman; Ruby Eubank, Myrtize Tregea and Ada Steele looked after the decorations and the refreshments, and Vera Carlson, Nan Hutcheson and Ione Gillette had charge of the music.

EDUCATION WEEK PROGRAM.

Santa Monica—Santa Monica Bay Parlor No. 267 N.S.G.W., assisted by Santa Monica Bay Parlor No. 245 N.D.G.W., featured a National Education Week program November 9. Some two hundred were in attendance. President Orrin G. Welch called the assemblage to order and introduced as chairman of the evening Past President Harold Barden.

Grand Trustee Eldred L. Meyer spoke on "Native Sons History Fellowships," Dr. George Sabichl on "Early Schools of Los Angeles," Miss Mary Foye on "Present Day Method of Teaching," Dr. O. R. Hull, professor of education U.S.C., on "Constitutions," and Geoffrey Morgan on "The Community Chest." Entertainment was furnished by a ukelele band of ten small boys, and Clayton Brendt, accompanied by Elizabeth Marles, rendered vocal selections. The arrangements committee included Harold Barden (chairman), J. Howard Blanchard and Dyke C. Freeman, all senior past presidents of No. 267.

PROMOTING CLUBHOUSE.

Los Angeles Parlor No. 124 N.D.G.W. initiated five candidates November 2. Grand Outside Sentinel Hazel B. Hansen was a visitor. A donation was ordered sent the Grand Parlor Veteran Welfare Committee, and Chairman Dolores Malin gave a splendid report for the Parlor's history and landmarks committee. The November 9 card party under the direction of Mrs. Effie Walters was a complete success and delicious refreshments were served. The potluck dinner November 16 was greatly enjoyed. Secretary Mary K. Corcoran remembered the November "birthdayites" with a decorated tower cake and Miss Kathryn Ronan sent a box of Death Valley dates. At the meeting following the dinner Mrs. Annie L. Adair gave a fine talk on the homeless children work, and a donation of $15 was sent the local joint committee. The Parlor sewing club spent a pleasant afternoon November 19 at the home of Mrs. Lucy and Miss Dolores Malin. Thanksgiving baskets were distributed to several needy families.

Los Angeles' December calendar includes: 7th, initiation and shower of groceries for Christmas baskets; 14th, monthly card party, Miss Leonie Clos chairman; 21st, Christmas party for members, Mrs. Gertrude Allen in charge. President Mattie Labory-Gara is promoting a clubhouse for the Parlor and is meeting with much encouragement.

FORTY-EIGHTH BIRTHDAY.

Los Angeles Parlor No. 45 N.S.G.W. had an oldtimers night November 3 and there was a large attendance. With George Perdue presiding, the following past presidents filled the several stations: Howard Bentley, Ray LeMoine, Andrew Stodel, Victor Kremer, Mark Hopkins, Al Cron, Earl LeMoine, Richard Fryer, Al Metz, John T. Newell, Walter Fisher and Sid Witkowski. There was a lot of fun, which enriched the charity box, and heart-reaching talks by Henry Brodek, Past Grand John Newell and George Perdue. "Outside" speakers were Grand Trustee Eldred L. Meyer, District Deputy Walter Baskerville, President Bernard Hiss of University No. 272 and Deputy Grand President Clinton Skinner.

November 17, the Parlor observed its forty-eighth institution anniversary at a family gathering which opened with an excellent home-cooked supper. Vocal selections were rendered by Sybilla Moore, Jack Lewis and Mabel Straube, and music for dancing was furnished by Roger Johnson, Jack Lewis and Charles Straube. Sid Witkowski was in charge, and among his assistants were President Owen Adams, Walter Fisher, Mike Botello, Al Cron, Al Metz and Howard Bentley.

Los Angeles' main December event will be a Christmas tree party, December 22, to which the children of the members are especially invited. Santa Claus will be there, and from a gayly-decorated tree will distribute presents and goodies to all the kiddies. First Vice-president Leslie Packard heads the arrangements committee. Earl LeMoine is still very active with his illustrated California talks; November 18 he addressed Sepulveda Parlor No. 263 (San Pedro). The past presidents of the Parlor have organized a proficient ritual team and will gladly respond to a call from any Parlor.

BUSY SEWING.

Long Beach—Long Beach Parlor No. 154 N.D.G.W. had a card party November 3 with Lois McDougall as chairman. The thimble club, Lucretia Coates chairman, had an all-day meeting at the home of Secretary Bertha Hitt November 10 and finished blocks for a quilt. Gertrude Riddle, social chairman, called a special sewing session November 10 and considerable

(Continued on Page 20)

Know your home-state, California! Learn of its past history and of its present-day development by reading regularly The Grizzly Bear. $1.50 for one year (12 issues). Subscribe now.

Native Daughters of the Golden West

GRASS VALLEY—THE THIRD ANNUAL celebration of Gold Discovery Day drew a large crowd to the quartz-gold marker site on Gold Hill October 30. E. K. Smart presided, and greetings were extended by President Bernice Deward of Manzanita No. 29. The principal speaker, Past Grand Esther R. Sullivan, chairman Grand Parlor History Committee, classed George Knight, reputed discoverer of gold quartz in California, as among the small group of men and women who contributed great things to the fame and the wealth of the state.

Past Grand Alison F. Watt's address overflowed with highlights of local history, and Past Grand Dr. Louise C. Heilbron paid tribute to the California Pioneers. Barbara Foote gave a poetic reading, Mrs. L. Talbot gave a vocal solo and a band led by Harold George rendered several selections.

Marked Enthusiasm.

Saint Helena—La Junta No. 203 looks forward eagerly to the annual official visit of the grand president, but this year the enthusiasm was even more marked than usual, for the reason that Mrs. Anna Mixon Armstrong was born and spent most of her youth in this city. She was the guest of La Junta October 18. The festivities started with a delicious turkey dinner. The table decorations were in autumn style, with huge palm branches forming arches over the tables, and autumn leaves and fruits being artistically arranged thereon. At the Parlor meeting delegations were present from Calistoga, Napa, Vallejo, Woodland and Golden Gate, and guests included Supervising Deputy Wilma Mitchell and Deputies Sadie Brooks, Emma McGlumphy and Elvina Woodard. Mrs. Doris Filtz presided, and one candidate was initiated.

Mrs. Armstrong gave a splendid address, expressing joy at visiting her hometown and meeting old friends, and outlining the projects of the Order. Mms. F. Waldeck and M. Alexander sang "California Lullaby," and on the Parlor's behalf Marshal Emma Navone presented the Grand President with a set of silver spoons concealed in an old-fashion boquet of flowers. Then, as a pleasant surprise, came a huge basket of flowers from Saint Helena No. 53 N.S.G.W. Each deputy grand president was presented with a block print of the historic Bale mill. The evening, one of the most enjoyable ever held by La Junta, will long be remembered. A splendid fraternal feeling prevailed. The committee arranging the details included Mms. Murial Vasconi, Agnes Street, Lois Gifford, Mildred Griffeth, Elmina Bafigo, Effie Baber; Misses Regina Ghirenghelli, Gretchen Graff, Zulletta Bellani.

Christmas Greeting

"Christmas! When all the world celebrates; when family ties are strengthened and more firmly welded; when fraternal love glows brighter; when compassion and helpfulness for the unfortunate become more acutely expressive; when all mankind feels the urge for mutual comradeship; the season when we really take stock of our finer human qualities.

"That gladsome day will soon be with us. Let each Native Daughter find a means of full expression of all those sentiments which tend to brighten the lives of relative, of friend and of neighbor. By a full exercise of such a sentiment our own lives will reflect in greater peace and happiness.

"At this season I wish to express my deepest appreciation to every Native Daughter in making my term of office thus far the great pleasure it has been to me.

"I wish every Parlor would have a 'Christmas Party' and that from it will grow deeper, purer love and esteem between individuals as well as greater consecration to the principles of our Order. Then will we have a miracle of true consciousness that cannot be surpassed.

"I wish each and every one of you a very, very, Happy Christmas, and express a hope that your dearest wishes may be fully realized.

"May God's blessing rest upon all of us this Christmas Season. Sincerely and fraternally yours in P.D.F.A.,

"ANNA MIXON ARMSTRONG,
"Grand President N.D.G.W.
"Woodland, November 7, 1932."

Pioneers Given Flags.

San Bernardino—October 22 Mms. Thelma Nett, Evelyn Shaddox and Marjorie Beck, and Misses Eva Bemis and Marguerite McKenzie were hostesses at a miscellaneous shower for President Nola Fogler-Noyes at the home of Miss Bemis in Rialto. Many lovely articles were presented the bride for her home. The miniature carnival October 26 was a success. An orchestra of stringed instruments played by children made quite a sensation.

At appropriate ceremonies November 5 the Parlor presented the San Bernardino Pioneer Society with United States of America and California State (Bear) Flags. Katherine McIntosh presided, Lois A. Johnson sang "I Love You, California," Gladys Baker gave the benediction and President Noyes made the presentation address, to which Vice-president Matt Eaton of the Pioneers responded. November 9 National Educational Week was observed, with First Vice-president Mary Johnson in charge. City Nurse Dorothea K. Stewart commended the Parlor for its interest in supplying milk to tubercular children and for co-operating with her in her undertakings.

Outstanding Musical Event.

Salinas—Aleli No. 102 and Santa Lucia No. 97 N.S.G.W. presented Frances Nason Leidig, dramatic soprano, in a concert program for the benefit of the homeless children in the Civic Club Auditorium. The affair was an outstanding musical event in the history of the town, and the local Parlors were highly commended for their sponsorship. Frances Nason Leidig is a descendant of early Spanish California and has grown up in the atmosphere of Spanish music, of which she is a notable interpreter.

Silver Anniversary.

Alameda—Encinal No. 156 celebrated its silver institution anniversary October 26. The tables were beautifully decorated in pastel shades, with sprays of silver leaves and autumn flowers. Hand-painted placecards, banded in silver, were presented the guests of honor, and the favors were tulip-shaped baskets mounted upon silver leaves. Charter President Irene Rose was the toastmistress, and at the speakers' table were President Mary Orchison, President Perry Badgley of Alameda No. 47 N.S.G.W., Grand Secretary Sallie R. Thaler, Past Grand Addie L. Mosher, Grand Marshal W. B. O'Brien of the Native Sons and Mrs. O'Brien, Lola Horgan, A. V. Fisher, Dice Peterson, Deputy Catherine Waldie. Charter members in attendance included Laura E. Fisher, Loretta DuFosse, Sarah Hulse, Dora McMaster, Reta Roberts, Alice Brown.

The drill team of Encinal presented a skit, "The Old Fashioned Girl and the Girl of Today," the participants being Mary Orchison, Fanny Holod, Margaret Larabee, Marguerite Davies, Elvira Davies, Muriel Jarratt, Elsie Flogel, Virginia Davies, Lou Flogel, Ursula Klauman. Captain Soila Harmola was the director. Musical numbers were rendered by Mrs. Geo. Hagy, W. B. O'Brien and Lola Horgan.

Silver gifts were presented Miss Irene Rose, Mrs. Laura E. Fisher and Miss Lorretta DuFosse, who have held office continuously since the institution of the Parlor in 1907. Dancing concluded a most enjoyable occasion. The committee in charge included Irene Rose (chairwoman), Laura Fisher, Loretta DuFosse, Barbara Rose, Fanny Holod, Evans Dunleavy, Elvira Davies, Myrtle Wilson, Emily Jack, Alice Matter, Gertrude Connor, Agnes Reid, Soila Harmola, May Lundstead, Muriel Jarratt.

Grand President's Official Itinerary.

Woodland—During the month of December, Grand President Anna Mixon-Armstrong will officially visit the following Subordinate Parlors on the dates noted:

1st—San Jose No. 81, San Jose.
6th—Ursula No. 1, Jackson.
7th—Forrest No. 86, Plymouth.
8th—Amapola No. 80, Sutter Creek.
9th—Chispa No. 40, Ione.
12th—Menlo No. 211, Menlo Park.
13th—Alta No. 3, San Francisco.
14th—Placer No. 138, Lincoln.

Bicentennial Program.

Oroville—Gold of Ophir No. 190 had a program in observance of the George Washington Bicentennial November 2. A living picture portraying A. M. Willard's "Spirit of '76" was presented by Mrs. Margaret Gilbert, Grand Trustee Florence Boyle and Mrs. Romilda Ralph. Talks on "George Washington" and "Betsy Ross" were given, respectively, by Mrs. Alta B. Baldwin and Miss Irene Lund, both in colonial costumes. Accompanied by Mrs. Claire McKinsey, Mrs. Ralph sang "Love's Old Sweet Song."

Students of the Bird-street school were enlightened on California and Butte County history when Grand Trustee Boyle addressed them. October 28, 259 of the pupils visited the Natives' relics building and were told the stories connected with the various articles on exhibition.

Carnival Dance Nets Neat Sum.

Cambria—A committee of El Pinal No. 163 comprising Katheryn Luchessa, Myrtle Warren, Ethel Mathison and Irma Thorndyke entertained at a Hallowe'en costume party. The decorations, in keeping with the "spook" season, presented a colorful scene. After hours of merriment a grand march was held and costume awards were made to Mms. Maud Ioppini, L. Gamboni, Verna Soto, Katie Van Gorden, Porte, Anabel Kester and Maud Thorndyke. Mrs. F. Lowell, Mrs. Geo. Soto and Alta Thorndyke were the judges.

The Parlor gave a carnival dance November 5. A large crowd attended and a neat sum was realized. A pedro party was sponsored November 8 and ten tables were in operation. The proceeds helped to replenish El Pinal's treasury.

Message an Inspiration.

Calistoga—Calistoga No. 145 had a very large attendance October 24, the occasion being the official visit of Grand President Anna Mixon Armstrong. Other guests were from La Junta, Clear Lake, Woodland, Bahia Vista and Califia Parlors. A turkey dinner, served at tables decorated with autumn leaves and baskets of fruit, preceded the meeting. As the Parlor officers entered the lodgeroom each was presented by President Bretta Lundell with a corsage, as were also the five candidates initiated by a splendid corps of officers.

The Grand President's message, dealing with the Order's projects, was an inspiration: without service and love these projects could not go on, she said, and she stressed the needs of the homeless children. Gifts were presented Mrs. Armstrong, Supervising Deputy Wilma Mitchell, Deputy Sadie Brooks and President Lundell, the presentation addresses being made by Past President Bernice Martin and Marshal Audriena Lercari. A drill was executed, and Edith Cavagnaro was complimented on the team's finished work. During the evening Irma Howard favored with vocal selections.

Living Poppy Graces Float.

Fullerton—In the Orange County Armistice Day parade, Grace No. 242 entered a beautiful float which was awarded first prize. Hundreds of California poppies and garlands of smilax decorated the car, and the grizzly bear, carrying the United States of America and the California

(State) Bear Flags, was a prominent feature. Dainty little Viola Watts, attired in yellow silk and holding a yellow parasol, was a living poppy. Lena Aspden, president of the Parlor, and Christine McFarland, committee chairman, rode in the car.

Grace celebrated family night November 17 when, under the direction of Past President Helen Anderson, dinner was served the members and their families. Deputy Mary Noerenberg and Florence Dodson Schoneman were guests of honor. Cards and a social time followed the feast. The homeless children sewing circle of the Parlor had an all-day meeting, with pot-luck luncheon, at the home of Secretary Mary Rothaermel November 29.

Drill Team Makes Big Hit.

Petaluma—Petaluma No. 222 had a most enjoyable social evening October 18. The younger members danced, and the older ones played cards. Delicious homemade refreshments were served. With President Pearl Lopus presiding, three candidates were initiated November 1. Plans were perfected for a November 5 public food sale, which realized a goodly sum, and several card parties.

The drill team participated in the Sonoma County Armistice Day celebration at Healdsburg and, as usual, made a big hit. November 14 a large delegation of Petaluma's members went to Sausalito to attend the official visit of Grand President Armstrong to Sea Point No. 196. Edna Mead was chairman of a turkey whist November 15. A large crowd contributed to the big success.

NATIVE DAUGHTER ACTIVITIES.

Placerville—Grand President Anna Mixon Armstrong paid her official visit to Marguerite No. 12 November 2. More than one hundred were in attendance, including Grand Marshal Gladys Noce, Grand Trustee Edna Briggs, Past Grand Dr. Louise C. Heilbron and representatives of twelve Parlors. On the Parlor's behalf Lilla Zeiz presented a gift to Mrs. Armstrong who, in responding, spoke briefly of the Order's projects. Eight candidates were initiated and a short program followed the ceremonies.

Santa Cruz—Santa Cruz No. 26 had a supper October 31 honoring members whose birthdays occurred in September and October. A realistic ghost greeted members on their arrival at the darkened hall entrance, and the Hallowe'en motif was used in the table decorations. Helen Miller, accompanied by Pearl Reid, sang "The Goblins." The Parlor meeting was held in the

(Continued on Page 19)

Passing of the California Pioneer

(Confined to Brief Notices of the Demise of Those Men and Women Who Came to California Prior to 1870.)

CHARLES HENRY (HANK) HAWN, native of Illinois, 92; crossed the plains to California in 1850 and resided in various places, among them Sacramento, Los Angeles and Fresno Cities; died at the latter place, survived by a wife and seven children.

Mrs. Arsinoe Bloom-Taylor, native of Iowa, 88; came across the plains in 1850 and resided in El Dorado and Sacramento Counties; died at Sacramento City, survived by two sons.

Mrs. Katherine Mullins-Ridgway, native of Louisiana, 82; came in 1851 and long resided in Mariposa County; died at Petaluma, Sonoma County, survived by three children, among them Mrs. J. J. Trabucco (Mariposa No. 63 N.D.G.W.).

Captain Thomas Patrick Whitelaw, native of Scotland, 86; came in 1852; died at San Francisco, survived by a daughter.

Mrs. Frances Blodgett-Eilerman, native of Illinois, 85; came across the plains in 1852 and long resided in Yuba and Butte Counties; died at Santa Cruz City, survived by a son.

Thomas Jackson Byrd, native of Georgia, 97; came across the plains in 1852 and resided in El Dorado and Yuba Counties; died at the Masonic Home, Decoto, Alameda County.

Mrs. Emily Rose Crouch, native of Indiana, 83; came across the plains in 1853 and long resided in Alameda County; died at Long Beach, Los Angeles County, survived by two daughters.

Frank Evan Hughes, native of Maine, 80; came in 1853 and resided many years in El Dorado County; died at Oakland, Alameda County, survived by five children.

George E. Wilds, native of Massachusetts, 80; came via the Isthmus of Panama in 1854; died at Lakeport, Lake County, survived by a wife and five sons.

Henry Jameson, native of Illinois, 83; came across the plains in 1854 and resided in Napa, Solano and Glenn Counties; died near Willows, survived by a wife.

Mrs. Annie Finley-Fitch, native of Alabama, 86; came in 1855 and settled in Placer County; died at Alameda City, survived by five children.

Lynn A. Finney, native of Missouri, 87; came across the plains in 1857 and resided seventy-one years in Stanislaus County; died near Salida, survived by a wife and six children.

James Milton Howell, native of Missouri, 90; came across the plains in 1859 and resided in Amador and Tehama Counties; died at Red Bluff, survived by a wife and five children.

Mrs. Ann Caroline Gover, native of Kentucky, 89; crossed the plains in 1860 and long resided in Shasta County; died at Merced City, survived by four children.

Mrs. Polly Morris, native of Ohio, 78; crossed the plains in 1861 and resided in Solano and Yolo Counties; died at Woodland, survived by a daughter.

Lorenzo Dow Cleghorn, natice of Iowa, 80; came in 1861 and two years later settled in San Bernardino County; died at Highland.

Mrs. Hattie Munch, native of New York, 85; crossed the plains in 1861; died near Solvang, Santa Barbara County, survived by a son.

Clarence W. Shaw, native of Missouri, 72; came in 1863 and six years later settled in Lassen County; died at Susanville, survived by a wife.

Mrs. Gloria Rose, native of Azores Islands, 95; since 1863 resident Alameda County; died at Centerville, survived by seven children.

William James Costar, native of Iowa, 72; came in 1863; died at Chico, Butte County, survived by a wife and four children. At one time he was a member of the State Assembly.

Mrs. Susan Fox-Whitten, native of Missouri, 80; since 1868 Butte County resident; died at Chico, survived by a husband and six sons.

Edward Anthony Preuss, native of Louisiana, 85; since 1864 resident Los Angeles City, where he died; a son survives.

Mrs. Louesa Jewett-Crites, native of Vermont, 99; came via the Isthmus of Panama in 1866 and settled in Kern County; died at Bakersfield, survived by three sons.

Webster Thomas Simonds, native of Canada, 87; came in 1867; died at Fort Bragg, Mendocino County, survived by a wife and three children.

Peter Hamilton, native of Canada, 91; since 1867 resident Rio Vista, Solano County, where he died; six children survive.

Mrs. Annie Wicks, native of England; came in 1867 and long resided in Nevada County; died at Sacramento City, survived by a husband and three children.

Marcus E. E. Von Dollen, native of Germany, 91; came in 1868 and resided in San Luis Obispo and Contra Costa Counties; died at Richmond, survived by three children.

Mrs. Maggie Kerr-McRae, native of Canada, 76; came in 1868; died at Roseville, Placer County, survived by four children.

George Warren Fletcher, native of Massachusetts, 78; came in 1869; died at Los Molinos, Tehama County, survived by a wife and five children.

Oliver George Bainbridge, native of Iowa, 82; came across the plains in 1859 and settled in Butte County; died at Upham.

Mrs. Harriet Johnson, native of Wisconsin, 90; came via the Isthmus of Panama in 1852 and resided in Santa Clara, San Benito and Monterey Counties; died at Saratoga, survived by five children.

Mrs. Margaret Kennedy-Welch, native of Ireland, 84; since 1867 a resident of Sacramento City, where she died; two sons survive.

Antone Williams, native of Massachusetts, 71; came in 1865 and long resided in Trinity County; died at Stockton, San Joaquin County, survived by two children.

Mrs. Marie Annie Dunham-Albee, native of Iowa, 72; crossed the plains in 1861 and resided in Shasta and Humboldt Counties; died at Fortuna, survived by a husband and four daughters.

Mrs. Flora Cooley, 88; crossed the plains in 1860 and resided in Amador and San Joaquin Counties; died at Stockton, survived by five children.

Mrs. J. W. Heath, 79; crossed the plains in 1857 and settled in Sacramento County; died at Michigan Bar, survived by five children.

Mrs. Agnes Cornelia Wicks-Baudouin, native of Maryland, 82; came in 1857 and resided in Nevada, Yuba and Monterey Counties; died at Pacific Grove, survived by a daughter.

Derrett Oliver Harrelson, native of Wisconsin, 92; came in 1859 and resided many years in San Joaquin and Tulare Counties; died at San Francisco, survived by two sons. At one time he served Stockton as police chief.

Mrs. Susan Owens-Howell, native of Missouri, 76; came in 1862 and resided in Tehama and Alameda Counties; died at Red Bluff, survived by a husband.

Daniel Goodwin, native of Vermont, 86; came via the Isthmus of Panama in 1867; died at Modesto, Stanislaus County, survived by a wife and four children.

ISOLATED SURVIVORS INDICATE STATE'S FOREST AREAS DECREASING IN SIZE

In the days of '49, when the mud flats of San Francisco Bay extended to Montgomery street and Los Angeles was a pueblo, the pine forests of the Sierra Nevada and the douglas fir forests of the Coast Range clothed the mountains and foothills in a much wider belt than they do today, according to A. E. Wieslander of the California forest experiment station of the United States Forest Service. Logging, grazing and particularly forest fires are the chief factors which have converted the old commercial forests to what are now comparatively worthless lands and have created a land management problem of large proportions in California.

In El Dorado County alone, the ponderosa pine forests have retreated ten miles up the mountain slopes, leaving a strip of 162,000 acres entirely deforested and an even larger area thinly stocked with second-growth trees. The land, capable of producing a forest stand of 37,000 board-feet of lumber per acre, is now mostly covered with half-scrub woodland, worthless for timber and too dense or too brushy for good grazing.

Isolated survivors of the original forest, scattered groups of second growth and such names as Sawmill Flat, Sawmill Creek and Shingle Springs, occurring in what are now treeless areas, indicate that they were once in forested territory. This theory is confirmed by old records which prove that from 1850 to 1870 many sawmills supplied lumber to the placer mines in the central Sierra region.

World Affairs Institute—The tenth annual session of the Institute of International Relations will be held at Riverside City, December 11-16.

Feminine World's Fads and Fancies

PREPARED ESPECIALLY FOR THE GRIZZLY BEAR BY ANNA STOERMER

CHRISTMAS GREETINGS! SANTA'S drama of dolls and toys is in progress, and gift-shopping has begun in earnest! Shops are gloriously ready and overflowing with every conceivable type of gift, and the greatly lowered prices that prevail on all Christmas merchandise offer an added incentive to more buying. The Yuletide spirit is manifesting itself in a myriad of ways.

Dolls, no less than toys, each year grow more lifelike and take on more of the human qualities. Educational and instructive toys are those known as developmental toys—those that increase the child's physical or mental skill or knowledge. There is a growing tendency, too, for toys exactly timed to the child's age and stage of development, and a goodly number of interesting games for both old and young provide diverting home entertainment.

Music in the home is a major consideration at holiday time. Discriminating giftseekers will find radios of every style and size, including excellent little models that require a small investment; sideshows, with professional entertainers 'n everything hold youthful audiences spellbound. A "calico circus" is the theme which one of the large toy shops features. A tent provides the circus atmosphere, the comical clown dispenses fun aplenty, and the kiddies are further delighted by the antics of the human pony.

Christmas linens solve countless gift problems quickly and happily for those who would choose something practical and decorative. Never have prices on quality linens been so low, from the most elaborate hand-embroidered and hand-drawn banquet sets to the simple hand-embroidered guest towels. And the linens, whether for table, bedroom or bathroom, were never lovelier, never more appropriate for their individual uses, or more suited to the individual type of home. They reflect the tempo of our lives, and harmonize with all the other smart furnishings.

Collections of fine china, exquisite glassware, sterling silver and lifetime plate offer suggestions without end for gifts both useful and good to look on. In the limitless assortments from which to choose are many that have come from lands across the sea, and many more from American marts—all bespeaking the faith and the confidence of the time-honored tradition of Christmas and the perpetuation of the Yuletide spirit in heart and home.

With the calendar already crowded with coming events, the problem of a formal wardrobe is one that demands immediate attention. The new elegance is achieved by means of luxurious fabrics and much elaboration of detail. The feminine form is glorified anew, and not in many years have styles offered such opportunities for expressing good taste. Fabrics of rough surface have had considerable success. The new pebble-weave satin seems likely to be popular during the winter season. The need for an attractive business dress is one which offers a problem—it must be neat and simple, yet possess a chic smartness.

With such a wide range of coat fashions to choose from, and all at reasonable prices, there are, of course, some very luxurious models. But for a coat that must do duty for more than one season, it is wise to select a simpler style and one not markedly ultra.

Elegance and individuality distinguish themselves in a variety of original ways that are nothing, if not "different" from the coats of other years. They are chiefly remarkable for slimness of lines. Collar, sleeve and shoulder details are increasingly important. Waistlines are moulded. Closings are definitely to the side, with buttons or adjustable ties placed slightly higher than last year.

Fine furs are lavishly applied in all manner of standing, convertible, swirling and shawl collars, not to mention all-fur or fur-trimmed capes and capelets. Speaking of fur, circular separate collars of mink or ermine are the final word in chic. They give a smartness and sophistication to the simplest wool or silk frock, or they may be worn with untrimmed coats.

The autumn and winter gloves are something to conjure with. They are so cleverly keyed to the varied wardrobe requirements that there is a different glove for every costume. They run the gamut from sports to formal evening types, and emphasize glace kidskin, suede, pigskin, the new velvets and various other kinds and fabrics. Pigskin is the very smartest glove one can wear with suits, woolen dresses, tailored or sports costumes, and shirred velvet is the high novelty for evening.

Color combinations are an important factor this season. All-black or all-brown costumes are worn with light-colored furs, hat and gloves. There are, in general, two types of color plans: one, a repetition of double colors, such as tweed coat in multicolor, with hat, gloves and bag which repeat two or three of the tweed colors; or, solid-color dress, coat or suit, with contrasting accents in shoes, hat and bag. Brilliant velvets and satins are the favorites, and shining bright-colored fabrics are the evening vogue.

Cire satins, and silk weaves that have a touch of gold thread here and there in their textures are great favorites. The gowns are simply made, to allow the brilliance of the fabric full play under artificial lights. They are worn with glittering jewels, and if flowers are permitted they are those with waxy, shiny leaves.

Evening clothes, like the occasions they grace, must be brilliant. Somber colors and dull fabrics by day, but night lights must shine on bright hues and vivid materials.

So far, this is a red winter. Bright reds,

(Continued on Page 21)

Official Directory of Parlors of the N. D. G. W

ALAMEDA COUNTY.

Angelita No. 32, Livermore—Meets 2nd and 4th Fridays, Foresters Hall; Mrs. Myrtle I. Johnson, Rec. Sec., P.O. box 253.

Piedmont No. 87, Oakland—Meets Thursdays, Corinthian Hall, Pacific Bldg.; Mrs. Alice E. Miner, Rec. Sec., 421 36th St.

Aloha No. 106, Oakland—Meets Tuesdays, Wigwam Hall, Pacific Bldg.; Mrs. Lurine Martin, Rec. Sec., 2815 Wallace St., Berkeley.

Hayward No. 122, Hayward—Meets 1st and 3rd Tuesdays, Veterans Memorial Bldg., Main St.; Miss Ruth Gansberger, Rec. Sec., P. O. box 44, Mount Eden.

Berkeley No. 150, Berkeley—Meets 2nd and 4th Wednesdays, Masonic Hall; Mrs. Lelia B. Baker, Rec. Sec., 915 Contra Costa Ave.

Bear Flag No. 151, Berkeley—Meets 2nd and 4th Wednesdays, Veterans Memorial Bldg., 1931 Center St.; Mrs. Maud Wagner, Rec. Sec., 317 Alcatraz Ave., Oakland.

Encinal No. 156, Alameda—Meets 2nd and 4th Wednesdays, Veterans Memorial Bldg., Central Ave. and Walnut St.; Mrs. Laura E. Fisher, Rec. Sec., 1418 Caroline St.

Brooklyn No. 157, East Oakland—Meets 2nd and 4th Wednesdays, Masonic Temple, 8th Ave. and E. 14th St.; Mrs. Ruth Cooney, Rec. Sec., 3907 14th Ave.

Argonaut No. 166, Oakland—Meets Tuesdays, Klinkner Hall, 59th and San Pablo; Mrs. Ada Spilman, Rec. Sec., 2905 Ellis St., Berkeley.

Bahia Vista No. 167, Oakland—Meets Thursdays, Wigwam Hall, Pacific Bldg.; Mrs. Minnie E. Raper, Rec. Sec., 3449 Helen St.

Fruitvale No. 177, Oakland—Meets Fridays, W.O.W. Hall; May E. Barthold, Rec. Sec., 3832 Santa Rita St.

Laura Loma No. 182, Niles—Meets 1st and 3rd Tuesdays, I.O.O.F. Hall; Mrs. Ethel Fournier, Rec. Sec., P. O. box 515.

El Cereso No. 207, San Leandro—Meets 2nd and 4th Tuesdays, Masonic Hall; Mrs. Mary Tuttle, Rec. Sec., P. O. box 56.

Pleasanton No. 237, Pleasanton—Meets 1st Tuesday, I.O.O.F. Hall; Mrs. Myrtle Lanini, Rec. Sec.

Betsy Ross No. 238, Centerville—Meets 1st and 3rd Fridays, Anderson Hall; Miss Constance Lucio, Rec. Sec., P. O. box 187.

AMADOR COUNTY.

Ursula No. 1, Jackson—Meets 2nd and 4th Tuesdays, N.S.G.W. Hall; Mrs. Emma Boarman-Wright, Rec. Sec., 114 Court St.

Chispa No. 40, Ione—Meets 2nd and 4th Fridays, N.S.G.W. Hall; Mrs. Isabel Ashton, Rec. Sec.

Amapola No. 80, Sutter Creek—Meets 2nd and 4th Thursdays, N.S.G.W. Bldg.; Mrs. Hazel M. Marre, Rec. Sec.

Forrest No. 86, Plymouth—Meets 2nd and 4th Tuesdays, I.O.O.F. Hall; Mrs. Marguerite Davis, Rec. Sec.

BUTTE COUNTY.

Annie K. Bidwell No. 168, Chico—Meets 2nd and 4th Thursdays, I.O.O.F. Hall; Mrs Irene Henry, Rec. Sec., 3015 Woodland Ave.

Gold of Ophir No. 190, Oroville—Meets 1st and 3rd Wednesdays, Memorial Hall; Mrs. Ruth Brown, Rec. Sec., 1365 Leah Court.

CALAVERAS COUNTY.

Ruby No. 46, Murphys—Meets 4th Friday, N.S.G.W. Hall; Belle Segale, Rec. Sec.

Princess No. 84, Angels Camp—Meets 2nd and 4th Wednesdays, I.O.O.F. Hall; Mrs. Grace M. Mills, Rec. Sec., P.O. box 313.

San Andreas No. 113, San Andreas—Meets 1st Friday, Fraternal Hall; Miss Doris Treat, Rec. Sec.

COLUSA COUNTY.

Colus No. 194, Colusa—Meets 1st and 3rd Mondays, Eagles Hall; Miss Kate Busch, Rec. Sec., 350 Market St.

CONTRA COSTA COUNTY.

Stirling No. 146, Pittsburg—Meets 1st and 3rd Wednesdays, Veteran Memorial Hall; Mrs. Leslie Clement, Rec. Sec., 468 E. Santa Fe.

Richmond No. 147, Richmond—Meets 1st and 3rd Tuesdays, I.O.O.F. Hall, 10th St.; Grace Curry, Rec. Sec., 1134 Ohio St.

Donner No. 193, Byron—Meets 1st and 3rd Wednesdays, I.O.O.F. Hall; Mrs. Anna Pendry, Rec. Sec., P. O. box 112.

Las Juntas No. 221, Martinez—Meets 1st and 3rd Mondays, Pythian Castle; Mrs. Lola O. Viera, Rec. Sec., R.F.D. No. 1.

Antioch No. 223, Antioch—Meets 2nd and 4th Tuesdays, I.O.O.F. Hall; Mrs. Estelle Evans, Rec. Sec., 202 E. 5th St., Pittsburg.

Carquinez No. 234, Crockett—Meets 2nd and 4th Wednesdays, I.O.O.F. Hall; Mrs. Cecile Petee, Rec. Sec., 465 Edwards St.

EL DORADO COUNTY.

Marguerite No. 12, Placerville—Meets 1st and 3rd Wednesdays, Masonic Hall; Mrs. Nettie Leonardi, Rec. Sec., 25 Coloma St.

El Dorado No. 186, Georgetown—Meets 2nd and 4th Saturday afternoons, I.O.O.F. Hall; Mrs. Alta L. Douglas, Rec. Sec.

FRESNO COUNTY.

Fresno No. 187, Fresno—Meets 2nd and 4th Fridays, Pythian Castle, Cor. "R" and Merced Sts.; Mary Aubery, Rec. Sec., 1040 Delphia Ave.

GRAND OFFICERS.

Mrs. Evelyn I. Carlson........Past Grand President
281 E. Tuscaloosa Ave., Atherton

Mrs. Anna M. Armstrong........Grand President
Woodland

Mrs. Irma Laird........Grand Vice-president
Alturas

Mrs. Sallie R. Thaler........Grand Secretary
555 Baker St., San Francisco

Mrs. Susie K. Christ........Grand Treasurer
555 Baker St., San Francisco

Mrs. Gladys Noce........Grand Marshal
Sutter Creek

Mrs. Orinda G. Giannini........Grand Inside Sentinel
2142 Filbert St., San Francisco

Mrs. Hazel B. Hansen........Grand Outside Sentinel
501 Griswold St., Glendale

Mrs. Clara Gairaud........Grand Organist
134 Locust St., San Jose

GRAND TRUSTEES.

Mrs. Florence Boyle........Oroville
Mrs. Edna Briggs........1045 Santa Ynez Way, Sacramento
Mrs. Anna Thuesen........615 38th Ave., San Francisco
Mrs. Ethel Begley........233 Prospect Ave., San Francisco
Mrs. Minna K. Horn........Etna
Mrs. Jane Vick........418 Bath St., Santa Barbara
Mrs. Willow Borba........330 So. Main St., Sebastopol

GLENN COUNTY.

Berryessa No. 192, Willows—Meets 1st and 3rd Mondays, I.O.O.F. Hall; Mrs. Leonora Neate, Rec. Sec., 338 No. Lassen St.

HUMBOLDT COUNTY.

Occident No. 28, Eureka—Meets 1st and 3rd Wednesdays, N.S.G.W Hall; Mrs. Eva L. MacDonald, Rec. Sec., 2309 "B" St.

Oneonta No. 71, Ferndale—Meets 2nd and 4th Fridays, I.O.O.F. Hall; Mrs. Myra Rumrill, Rec. Sec., P.O. box 142.

Reichling No. 97, Fortuna—Meets 1st and 3rd Tuesdays, Friendship Hall; Mrs. Grace Swett, Rec. Sec., P. O. box 328.

KERN COUNTY.

Miocene No. 228, Taft—Meets 1st and 3rd Wednesday afternoons, I.O.O.F. Hall; Mrs. Evalyn G. Towne, Rec. Sec., P. O. box 1011.

El Tejon No. 239, Bakersfield—Meets 1st and 3rd Fridays, Eagles Hall, 1714 "G" St.; Mary B. Hampson, Rec. Sec., 908 Quincy St.

Desert Gold No. 250, Mojave—Meets 2nd and 4th Fridays, I.O.O.F. Hall; Rein H. Everett, Rec. Sec., P.O. box 83.

LAKE COUNTY.

Clear Lake No. 135, Middletown—Meets 2nd and 4th Tuesdays, Herrick Hall, Mrs. Alma E. Snow, Rec. Sec.

LASSEN COUNTY.

Nataqua No. 152, Standish—Meets 1st and 3rd Wednesdays, Foresters Hall; Mrs. Mayda Elledge, Rec. Sec.

Mount Lassen No. 215, Bieber—Meets 2nd and 4th Thursdays, I.O.O.F. Hall; Mrs. Angie C. Kenyon, Rec. Sec.

Susanville No. 243, Susanville—Meets 3rd Thursday, I.O.O.F. Hall; Mildred Hardy, Rec. Sec., P.O. box 425.

LOS ANGELES COUNTY.

Los Angeles No. 124, Los Angeles—Meets 1st and 3rd Wednesdays, I.O.O.F. Hall, Washington and Oak Sts.; Mrs. Mary K. Corcoran, Rec. Sec., 322 No. Van Ness Ave.

Long Beach No. 154, Long Beach—Meets 1st and 3rd Thursdays, K.P. Hall, 341 Pacific Ave.; Mrs. Bertha Hitt, Rec. Sec., 5355 Lime Ave.

Rudecinda No. 230, San Pedro—Meets 2nd and 4th Thursdays, Unity Hall, I.O.O.F. Temple, 10th and Gaffey; Letitia Sarciaux, Rec. Sec., 483 16th St.

Verdugo No. 240, Glendale—Meets 2nd and 4th Tuesdays, Masonic Temple, 234 So. Brand Blvd.; Miss Etta Fulkerth, Rec. Sec., 526 No. Orange St.

Santa Monica Bay No. 245, Santa Monica—Meets 2nd and 4th Wednesdays, Odd Fellows Hall, 1431 Third St.; Mrs. Rosalie Hyde, Rec. Sec., 738 Flower St., Venice.

Californiana No. 247, Los Angeles—Meets 2nd and 4th Tuesday afternoons, Hollywood Studio Club, 1215 Lodi Place; Mrs. Inez Sitton, Rec. Sec., 4223 Berenice St.

MADERA COUNTY.

Madera No. 244, Madera—Meets 2nd and 4th Thursdays, Masonic Annex; Mrs. Margaret C. Boyle, Rec. Sec., 111 No. "B" St.

MARIN COUNTY.

Sea Point No. 196, Sausalito—Meets 2nd and 4th Mondays, Perry Hall, 50 Caledonia St.; Mrs. Mary B. Smith, Rec. Sec., 559 Woodward Ave.

Marinita No. 198, San Rafael—Meets 2nd and 4th Mondays, 316 "B" St.; Miss Mollye Y. Spaelti, Rec. Sec., 539 4th St.

Fairfax No. 225, Fairfax—Meets 2nd and 4th Tuesdays, Community Hall; Mrs. Marguerite Geary, Rec. Sec.

Tamelpa No. 231, Mill Valley—Meets 1st and 2nd Tuesdays, I.O.O.F. Hall; Mrs. Delphine M. Todt, Rec. Sec., 400 Grand Ave., San Rafael.

MARIPOSA COUNTY.

Mariposa No. 63, Mariposa—Meets 1st and 3rd Fridays, I.O.O.F. Hall; Elizabeth E. Johnson, Rec. Sec.

MENDOCINO COUNTY.

Fort Bragg No. 210, Fort Bragg—Meets 1st and 3rd Thursdays, I.O.O.F. Hall; Mrs. Ruth W. Fuller, Rec. Sec.

MERCED COUNTY.

Veritas No. 75, Merced—Meets 1st and 3rd Tuesdays, I.O.O.F. Hall; Miss Margaret Thornton, Rec. Sec., 317 18th St.

MODOC COUNTY.

Alturas No. 159, Alturas—Meets 1st Thursday, Alturas Civic Club; Mrs. Irma W. Laird, Rec. Sec.

MONTEREY COUNTY.

Aleli No. 102, Salinas—Meets 2nd and 4th Thursdays, Pythian Hall; Miss Rose Rhyner, Rec. Sec., 420 Soledad St.

Junipero No. 141, Monterey—Meets 2nd and 4th Fridays, K. of P. Hall, Main St.; Miss Matilda M. Bergschicker, Rec. Sec., 498 Van Buren St.

NAPA COUNTY.

Eshcol No. 16, Napa—Meets 2nd and 4th Mondays, N.S.G.W. Hall; Mrs. Ella Ingram, Rec. Sec., 3140 Seminary St.

Calistoga No. 145, Calistoga—Meets 2nd and 4th Mondays, I.O.O.F. Hall; Sadie P. Brooks, Rec. Sec.

La Junta No. 203, Saint Helena—Meets 1st and 3rd Tuesdays, N.S.G.W. Hall; Mrs. Marie Signorelli, Rec. Sec., 1341 Madrona Ave.

ATTENTION, SECRETARIES!

THIS DIRECTORY IS PUBLISHED BY AUTHORITY OF THE GRAND PARLOR N.D.G.W., AND ALL NOTICES OF CHANGES MUST BE RECEIVED BY THE GRAND SECRETARY (NOT THE MAGAZINE) ON OR BEFORE THE 20TH OF EACH MONTH TO INSURE CORRECTION IN NEXT PUBLICATION OF DIRECTORY.

NEVADA COUNTY.

Laurel No. 6, Nevada City—Meets 1st and 3rd Wednesday I.O.O.F. Hall; Mrs. Nellie E. Clark, Rec. Sec., P. box 212.

Manzanita No. 29, Grass Valley—Meets 1st and 3rd Tue days, Auditorium; Mrs. Loraine Keast, Rec. Sec., 1 Race St.

Columbia No. 70, French Corral—Meets Fridays, Farrell Hall; Mrs. Kate Farrelley-Sullivan, Rec. Sec.

Snow Peak No. 176, Truckee—Meets 1st Monday, I.O.O. Hall; Mrs. Henrietta M. Eaton, Rec. Sec., P. O. box 11

ORANGE COUNTY.

Santa Ana No. 235, Santa Ana—Meets 2nd and 4th Mo days, K.C. Hall, 4th and French Sts.; Mrs. Matilda Lemon, Rec. Sec., 1628 W. 8th St.

Grace No. 242, Fullerton—Meets 1st and 3rd Thursday I.O.O.F. Hall, 116½ E. Commonwealth; Mrs. Ma Rothsermel, Rec. Sec., P. O. box 235.

PLACER COUNTY.

Placer No. 138, Lincoln—Meets 2nd Wednesday, I.O.O. Hall; Miss Carrie Parlin, Rec. Sec.

La Rosa No. 191, Roseville—Meets 1st and 3rd Tuesday Eagles Hall; Mrs. Alice Lee West, Rec. Sec., Rocklin.

Auburn No. 233, Auburn—Meets 2nd and 4th Fridays, Fo esters Hall; Mrs. Elsie Patrick, Rec. Sec.

PLUMAS COUNTY.

Plumas Pioneer No. 219, Quincy—Meets 1st and 3rd Mo days, I.O.O.F. Hall; Minnie E. Johnson, Rec. Sec., P. box 243.

SACRAMENTO COUNTY.

Califia No. 22, Sacramento—Meets 2nd and 4th Tuesday N.S.G.W. Hall; Miss Lulu Gillis, Rec. Sec., 921 8th S

La Bandera No. 110, Sacramento—Meets 1st and 3rd F days, N.S.G.W. Hall; Mrs. Clara Weldon, Rec. Sec., 13 "O" St.

Sutter No. 111, Sacramento—Meets 1st and 3rd Tuesday N.S.G.W. Hall; Mrs. Adele Nix, Rec. Sec., 1238 "S"

Fern No. 123, Folsom—Meets 1st and 3rd Tuesdays, K. Hall; Mrs. Viola Shumway, Rec. Sec., P. O. box 48.

Chabolla No. 171, Galt—Meets 2nd and 4th Tuesday I.O.O.F. Hall; Mrs. Mary Pritchard, Rec. Sec.

Coloma No. 212, Sacramento—Meets 1st and 3rd Tuesday I.O.O.F. Hall, Oak Park; Mrs. Nettie Harry, Rec. Se 1217 35th St.

Liberty No. 213, Elk Grove—Meets 2nd and 4th Friday I.O.O.F. Hall; Mrs. Frances Wackman, Rec. Sec., P. box 192.

Victory No. 216, Courtland—Meets 1st Saturday and 3 Monday, N.S.G.W. Hall; Mrs. Agneda Lample, Rec. Se

SAN BENITO COUNTY.

Copa de Oro No. 105, Hollister—Meets 2nd and 4 Thursdays, Grangers Union Hall; Mrs. Mollie Davegg Rec. Sec., 110 San Benito St.

San Juan Bautista No. 179, San Juan Bautista—Meets 1 Wednesday, Mission Corridor Rooms; Miss Gertru Breen, Rec. Sec.

SAN BERNARDINO COUNTY.

Lugonia No. 241, San Bernardino—Meets 2nd and 4 Wednesdays, Eagles Hall; Miss Lois Poling, Rec. Se 1098 Waterman Ave.

Ontario No. 251, Ontario—Meets 2nd and 4th Thursday Ontario Hotel; Miss Helen Hickman, Rec. Sec., 923 N Laurel Ave.

SAN DIEGO COUNTY.

San Diego No. 208, San Diego—Meets 2nd and 4th We nesdays, Directors Room, Chamber Commerce Bldg., 4 W. Broadway; Mrs. Elsie Case, Rec. Sec., 3051 Broadwa

SAN FRANCISCO CITY AND COUNTY.

Minerva No. 2, San Francisco—Meets 1st and 3rd Wedne days, N.S.G.W. Bldg.; Miss Dorothy Finn, Rec. Sec., Princess St., Sausalito.

Alta No. 3, San Francisco—Meets 2nd and 4th Tuesday N.S.G.W. Bldg.; Mrs. Agnese L. Hughes, Rec. Sec., 39 Sacramento St.

Oro Fino No. 9, San Francisco—Meets 1st and 3rd Thur days, N.S.G.W. Bldg.; Mrs. Josephine B. Morrisey, Re Sec., 4441 20th St.

Golden State No. 50, San Francisco—Meets 1st and 3 Wednesdays, N.D.G.W. Home; Miss Millie Tietjen, Re Sec., 328 Lexington Ave.

Orinda No. 56, San Francisco—Meets 2nd, 4th and 5th F days, N.D.G.W. Home; Mrs. Anna A. Gruber-Loser, Re Sec., 72 Grove Lane, San Anselmo.

Fremont No. 59, San Francisco—Meets 1st and 3rd Tue days, N.S.G.W. Bldg.; Miss Hannah Collins, Rec. Se 617 Fillmore St.

Buena Vista No. 68, San Francisco—Meets 1st, 3rd a 5th Thursdays, N.D.G.W. Home; Miss Margaret Barre Rec. Sec., 3774 20th St.

Las Lomas No. 72, San Francisco—Meets 1st and 3rd Tue days, N.D.G.W. Home; Mrs. Marion S. Day, Rec. Se 459 Noe St.

Yosemite No. 83, San Francisco—Meets 1st and 3rd Tue days, American Hall, 20th and Capp Sts.; Miss Ma Monahan, Rec. Sec., 237 Noe St.

La Estrella No. 89, San Francisco—Meets 2nd and 4 Mondays, N.S.G.W. Bldg.; Miss Birdie Hartman, Re Sec., 1018 Jackson St.

Sans Souci No. 96, San Francisco—Meets 2nd and 4th Mo days, N.D.G.W. Home; Mrs. Minnie F. Dobbin, Rec. Se 1483 43rd Ave.

Calaveras No. 103, San Francisco—Meets 2nd and 4 Tuesdays, Swedish American Hall, 2174 Market S Mary L. Krogh, Rec. Sec., 4235 Cabrillo St.

Darina No. 114, San Francisco—Meets 1st and 3rd Mo days, N.S.G.W. Bldg.; Miss Adele Walsh, Rec. Sec., 4 Page St.

El Vespero No. 118, San Francisco—Meets 2nd and 4 Tuesdays, Masonic Hall, 4705 3rd St.; Mrs. Nell Boege, Rec. Sec., 1526 Kirkwood Ave.

Genevieve No. 132, San Francisco—Meets 1st and 3 Thursdays, N.S.G.W. Bldg.; Miss Branice Peguillan, Re Sec., 2434 16th Ave.

Keith No. 137, San Francisco—Meets 2nd and 4th Thur days, N.S.G.W. Bldg.; Mrs. Helen T. Mann, Rec. Se 575 Pierce St., Apt. 206.

Gabrielle No. 139, San Francisco—Meets 2nd and 4 Wednesdays, N.S.G.W. Bldg.; Mrs. Dorothy Wuesterfe Rec. Sec., 1020 Munich St.

Presidio No. 148, San Francisco—Meets 2nd and 4th Tu days, N.S.G.W. Bldg.; Mrs. Hattie Gaughran, Rec. Se 713 Capp St.

Guadalupe No. 153, San Francisco—Meets 2nd and 4 Mondays, Forester Hall, 170 Valencia St.; Miss May McCarthy, Rec. Sec., 336 Elsie St.

Golden Gate No. 158, San Francisco—Meets 2nd and 4 Mondays, N.S.G.W. Bldg.; Mrs. Mary Sullivan, Rec. Se 33 Cuvier St.

Dolores No. 169, San Francisco—Meets 2nd and 4th We nesdays, N.S.G.W. Bldg.; Mrs. Ada Saunders, Rec. Se 284 Allison St.

Linda Rosa No. 170, San Francisco—Meets 2nd and 4 Wednesdays, Swedish American Hall, 2174 Market St Mrs. Eva P. Tyrrel, Rec. Sec., 2629 Mission St.

Portola No. 172, San Francisco—Meets 1st and 3rd Tuesdays, N.S.G.W. Bldg.; Catherine H. Dolly, Rec. Sec., 4125 23rd St.
Castro No. 178, San Francisco—Meets 1st and 3rd Wednesdays, K.C. Bldg., 150 Golden Gate Ave.; Miss Adeline Sandersfeld, Rec Sec., 50 Baker St.
Twin Peaks No. 185, San Francisco—Meets 2nd and 4th Fridays, Druids Temple, 44 Page St.; Mrs. Loretta Cameron, Rec. Sec., 3969 Army St.
James Lick No. 220, San Francisco—Meets 1st and 3rd Wednesdays, N.S.G.W. Bldg.; Mrs. Edna Bishop, Rec. Sec., 3841 24th St
Mission No. 227, San Francisco—Meets 2nd and 4th Fridays, N.S.G.W. Bldg.; Mrs. Ann Dippel, Rec. Sec., 448 Dewey Blvd.
Bret Harte No. 232, San Francisco—Meets 2nd and 4th Tuesdays, Aloha Hall, 3009 16th St.; Pearl Wedde, Rec. Sec., 225 7th Ave.
La Dorada No 236, San Francisco—Meets 2nd and 4th Thursdays, N.S.G.W. Hall; Mrs. Theresa R. O'Brien, Rec. Sec., 567 Liberty St.
Balboa No. 249, San Francisco—Meets 2nd and 4th Thursdays, Maccabee Hall, 5th Ave. and Clement St.; Miss Jean Moffet, Rec. Sec., 476 26th Ave.
Utopia No. 252, San Francisco—Meets 2nd and 4th Tuesdays, American Hall, 20th and Capp Sts.; Miss Lelia M. Little, Rec. Sec., 4450 20th St.

SAN JOAQUIN COUNTY.

Joaquin No. 5, Stockton—Meets 2nd and 4th Tuesdays, N.S.G.W. Hall, 314 E. Main St.; Mrs. Della Garvin, Rec. Sec., 1122 E. Market St.
El Pescadero No. 82, Tracy—Meets 1st and 3rd Fridays, I.O.O.F. Hall; Mrs. Mary A. Hewitson, Rec. Sec., 122 Walnut St.
Ivy No. 88, Lodi—Meets 1st and 3rd Wednesdays, Eagles Hall; Mrs. Mae Corson, Rec. Sec., 109 So. School St.
Calls de Oro No. 206, Stockton—Meets 1st and 3rd Tuesdays, N.S.G.W. Hall, 314 E. Main St.; Mrs. Frances Germain, Rec. Sec., 450 No. Regent.
Phoebe A. Hearst No. 214, Manteca—Meets 2nd and 4th Wednesdays, I.O.O.F. Hall; Mrs. Josie M. Frederick, Rec. Sec., Route A, Box 364, Ripon.

SAN LUIS OBISPO COUNTY.

San Miguel No. 94, San Miguel—Meets 2nd and 4th Wednesday afternoons, Clemon Hall; Mrs. Nellie Wickstrom, Rec. Sec.
San Luisita No. 108, San Luis Obispo—Meets 2nd and 4th Thursdays, W.O.W. Hall; Miss Agnes M. Lee, Rec. Sec., P. O. box 584.
El Pinal No. 163, Cambria—Meets 2nd, 4th and 5th Tuesdays, N.S.G.W. Hall; Kathryn LuChessa, Rec. Sec.

SAN MATEO COUNTY.

Bonita No. 10, Redwood City—Meets 2nd and 4th Thursdays, I.O.O.F. Hall; Mrs. Dora Wilson, Rec. Sec., 518 Middlefield Rd.
Vista del Mar No. 155, Halfmoon Bay—Meets 2nd and 4th Thursdays, I.O.O.F. Hall; Elizabeth Olney, Rec. Sec.
Ano Nuevo No. 180, Pescadero—Meets 1st and 3rd Wednesdays, I.O.O.F. Hall; Mrs. Alice Mattel, Rec. Sec.
El Carmelo No. 181, Daly City—Meets 1st and 3rd Wednesdays, Masonic Hall; Mrs. Hattie Kelly, Rec. Sec., 1179 Brunswick St.
Menlo No. 211, Menlo Park—Meets 2nd and 4th Mondays, Masonic Hall; Mrs. Frances E. Maloney, Rec. Sec., P. O. box 626.
San Bruno No. 246, San Bruno—Meets 2nd and 4th Fridays, Legion Hall; Miss Mildred Foley, Rec. Sec., 217 Miller Ave., South San Francisco.

SANTA BARBARA COUNTY.

Reina del Mar No. 126, Santa Barbara—Meets 1st and 3rd Tuesdays, Pythian Castle, 222 W. Carillo St.; Mrs. Dorothy Yule, Rec. Sec., P.O. box 670.

SANTA CLARA COUNTY.

San Jose No. 81, San Jose—Meets Thursdays, Catholic Women Center, 5th and San Fernando Sts.; Mrs. Nellie Fleming, Rec. Sec., Catholic Women Center.
Vendome No. 100, San Jose—Meets Wednesdays, Old Scottish Rite Temple; Miss Marie Buck, Rec. Sec., 245 Hawthorne St.
El Monte No. 205, Mountain View—Meets 2nd and 4th Fridays, American Legion Hall; Miss Mary Ann Rokovich, Rec. Sec., P.O. box 422-B.
Palo Alto No. 229, Palo Alto—Meets 1st and 2nd Mondays, N.S.G.W. Hall; Miss Helena G. Hansen, Rec. Sec., 531 Lytton Ave.

SANTA CRUZ COUNTY.

Santa Cruz No. 26, Santa Cruz—Meets Mondays, N.S.G.W. Hall; Mrs. May L. Williamson, Rec. Sec., 170 Walnut Ave.
El Pajaro No. 35, Watsonville—Meets 1st and 3rd Tuesdays, I.O.O.F. Hall; Miss Ruth E. Wilson, Rec. Sec., 16 Laurel St.

SHASTA COUNTY.

Camellia No. 41, Anderson—Meets 1st and 3rd Tuesdays, Masonic Hall; Mrs. Olga E. Welbourn, Rec. Sec.
Lassen View No. 98, Shasta—Meets 2nd Friday, Masonic Hall; Miss Louise Litsch, Rec. Sec.
Hiawatha No. 140, Redding—Meets 2nd and 4th Wednesdays, Moose Hall; Ruth Presleigh, Rec. Sec., Office County Clerk.

SIERRA COUNTY.

Naomi No. 36, Downieville—Meets 2nd and 4th Wednesdays, I.O.O.F. Hall; Louise C. Dubuque, Rec. Sec.
Imogen No. 134, Sierraville—Meets 2nd and 4th Saturday afternoons, Copren Hall; Mrs. Jennie Copren, Rec. Sec.

SISKIYOU COUNTY.

Eschscholtzia No. 112, Etna—Meets 1st and 3rd Wednesdays, Masonic Hall; Mrs. Bernice E. Smith, Rec. Sec.
Mountain Dawn No. 120, Sawyers Bar—Meets 2nd and last Wednesdays, I.O.O.F. Hall; Miss Edith Dunphy, Rec. Sec.

SOLANO COUNTY.

Vallejo No. 195, Vallejo—Meets 1st and 3rd Wednesdays, K.C. Hall, 820 Marin St.; Mrs. Mary Combs, Rec. Sec., 511 York St.
Mary E. Bell No. 224, Dixon—Meets 2nd and 4th Thursdays, I.O.O.F. Hall; Grace McFadyen, Rec. Sec.

SONOMA COUNTY.

Sonoma No. 209, Sonoma—Meets 2nd and 4th Mondays, I.O.O.F. Hall; Mrs. Mae Norrbom, Rec. Sec., R.F.D., box 171.
Santa Rosa No. 217, Santa Rosa—Meets 1st and 3rd Thursdays, N.S.G.W. Hall; Mrs. Clytie L. Lewis, Rec. Sec., R.F.D. No. 4, Box 345-A.
Petaluma No. 222, Petaluma—Meets 1st and 3rd Tuesdays, Dania Hall; Mrs. Margaret M. Oeltjen, Rec. Sec., 503 Prospect St.

STANISLAUS COUNTY.

Oakdale No. 125, Oakdale—Meets 1st Monday, I.O.O.F. Hall; Mrs. Lou Reeder, Rec. Sec.
Morada No. 199, Modesto—Meets 2nd and 4th Wednesdays, I.O.O.F. Hall; Mrs. Susan Sullivan, Rec. Sec., 823 10th St.
Eldora No. 248, Turlock—Meets 1st and 3rd Mondays, Masonic Temple; Effie Lund, Rec. Sec., 624 Minaret Ave.

SUTTER COUNTY.

South Butte No. 226, Sutter—Meets 1st and 3rd Mondays, N.D.G.W. Hall; Mrs. Abbie N. Vagedes, Rec. Sec.

TEHAMA COUNTY.

Berendos No. 23, Red Bluff—Meets 1st and 3rd Tuesdays, W.O.W. Hall, 200 Pine St.; Mrs. Lillie Hammer, Rec. Sec., 636 Jackson St.

TRINITY COUNTY.

Eltapome No. 55, Weaverville—Meets 2nd and 4th Thursdays, N.S.G.W. Hall; Mrs. Lou N. Fetzer, Rec. Sec.

TUOLUMNE COUNTY.

Dardanelle No. 66, Sonora—Meets Fridays, I.O.O.F. Hall; Mrs. Nettie Whitto, Rec. Sec.
Golden Era No. 99, Columbia—Meets 1st and 3rd Thursdays, N.S.G.W. Hall; Miss Irene Ponce, Rec. Sec.
Anona No. 164, Jamestown—Meets 2nd and 4th Tuesdays, I.O.O.F. Hall; Nellie Hope, Rec. Sec.

YOLO COUNTY.

Woodland No. 90, Woodland—Meets 2nd and 4th Tuesdays, N.S.G.W. Hall; Mrs. Maude Heaton, Rec. Sec., 153 College St.

YUBA COUNTY.

Marysville No. 162, Marysville—Meets 2nd and 4th Wednesdays, Liberty Hall; Miss Cecelia C. Gomes, Rec. Sec., 701 6th St.
Camp Far West No. 218, Wheatland—Meets 3rd Tuesday, I.O.O.F. Hall; Mrs. Ethel C. Brock, Rec. Sec., P. O. box 285.

AFFILIATED ORGANIZATIONS.

General Assembly Past Presidents—Meetings held annually in April at the home-town of Chief President; Mrs. Cora Stobing, 1739 San Jose Ave., San Francisco, Chief President; Mrs. Anna G. Loser, 72 Grove Lane, San Anselmo, Chief Secretary.
Past Presidents Association No. 1—Meets 1st and 3rd Mondays, N.S.G.W. Bldg., 414 Mason St., San Francisco; Mrs. Minnie F. Dobbin, Pres.; Mrs. May R. Barry, Rec. Sec., 2319 19th Ave., San Francisco.
Past Presidents Association No. 2—Meets 2nd and 4th Mondays, "Wigwam," Pacific Bldg., 16th and Jefferson, Oakland; Emma Haggerty, Pres.; Mrs. Elizabeth B. Goodman, Rec. Sec., 134 Juana Ave., San Leandro.
Past Presidents Association No. 3 (Santa Clara County)—Meets 2nd Tuesday, homes of members; Mrs. Amelia Hartman, Pres.; Mrs. Mary G. Newton, Rec. Sec., 1070 Jackson St., Santa Clara.
Past Presidents Association No. 4 (Sacramento County)—Meets 2nd Monday, N.S.G.W. Hall, 11th and "J" Sts., Sacramento City; Edna Briggs, Pres.; Lily May Tilden, Rec. Sec., 3225 "T" St., Sacramento.
Past Presidents Association No. 5 (Butte County)—Meets 1st Friday, homes of members, Chico and Oroville; Marie Picanco, Pres.; Ruth Brown, Rec. Sec., 1265 Leah Court, Oroville.
Past Presidents Association No. 6 (Nevada County)—Meets 4th Friday, alternately between Nevada City, Pythian Castle, and Grass Valley, Edna Sampson's home; Margaret V. Nolan, Pres.; Vere Hansen, Rec. Sec., R.F.D. No. 2, box 41-C, Grass Valley.
Past Presidents Association No. 7 (Sonoma County)—Meets 2nd Tuesday, Violet Mastrup home, 622 5th St., Petaluma; Viola Mastrup, Pres.; Elizabeth Dillon, Rec. Sec., Petaluma.
Past Presidents Association No. 8 (San Joaquin and Stanislaus Counties)—Meets 2nd Thursday, Red Men Hall, Stockton; Mrs. Lois Armstrong, Pres.; Mrs. Harriet F. Corr, Rec. Sec., 729 E. Sonora St., Stockton.
Native Sons and Native Daughters Central Committee on Homeless Children—Main Office, 955 Phelan Bldg., San Francisco; Mrs. John W. Stirling, Chmn.; Miss Mary E. Brusie, Sec. Los Angeles branch office, 3924 Sunset Blvd.; Dorothy Schlingman, Sec.

(ADVERTISEMENT.)

NATIVE DAUGHTER NEWS

(Continued from Page 15)

lodgeroom, beautified with baskets of autumn flowers. Two candidates were initiated. Supervising Deputy Rose Rhyner and a delegation from Aleli No. 102 (Salinas) were guests. A feature was an account of her recent visit to Europe by Past Grand Stella Finkeldey. The lodgeroom was decorated by Myrtle Richey, Marjorie Dellamonica and Mary Gregory, while those in charge of the supper and table decorations were Pearl Reid, Elsie Sayre, Grace Reynolds, Florence McCormick, Mamie Cavanagh and Alberta McCormick.

Richmond—November 1, Grand President Anna Mixon Armstrong paid her official visit to Richmond No. 147. Other guests were Grand Secretary Sallie R. Thaler, Past Grand President Dr. Louise C. Heilbron, Deputy Rosaline Correa and delegations from Fruitvale, Argonaut, Piedmont, Berkeley, Carquinez, San Diego, Woodland and Aloha Parlors. Three candidates were initiated, among them Mrs. Harriet Diercks and Miss Maud E. Muller, respectively the mother and the daughters of Mrs. Mary Muller, already a member, and thus giving the Parlor the membership of three generations of one family.

Hollister—Copa de Oro No. 105 added a new member to its roster November 10 and after the ceremonies, ably conducted, a social hour commemorated Armistice Day. The Parlor and Fremont No. 44 N.S.G.W. had their annual benefit for the homeless children November 27 and it was a social and a financial success.

Berkeley—Bear Flag No. 151 will give a dance and entertainment December 10. The talent will consist entirely of Natives from the various Alameda County Parlors.

Galt—Chabolla No. 171 was officially visited by Grand President Anna Mixon Armstrong November 8. Other visitors were Grand Trustee Edna Briggs, Supervising Deputy Bessie Leitch, Deputy Lily Tilden, Past Grands Dr. Eva R. Rasmussen and Dr. Louise C. Heilbron, and representatives of Coloma, La Bandera, Sutter, Califia, Victory and Woodland Parlors. Flags and flowers decorated the lodgeroom, and the banquet tables were adorned with nuggets, picks and shovels. Each honored guest was presented with a miniature ox-drawn covered wagon. One candidate was initiated, and the new ritual was beautifully exemplified by the Parlor's corps of officers headed by President Elberta Carpenter.

Vallejo—Vallejo No. 195 had a party in honor of Mrs. Mary Combs, for fifteen years recording secretary. On the Parlor's behalf President Mabel Thompson presented to her a radio lamp. Following initiation of a class of candidates a program was presented, and a banquet was served by a committee headed by Mrs. Julia Hill. Mrs. Anna Johnson was chairman of a card party November 2.

Santa Ana—Deputy Eva Bemis visited Santa Ana No. 235 November 14 and favored with an instructive talk; one candidate was initiated. Chairman Muriel Bray of the ways and means committee reported a neat sum from a recent dance. Chairman Genevieve Hiskey told of the joint entry of No. 235 and Santa Ana No. 265 N.S.G.W. in the Fullerton Armistice Day parade —a float depicting the pioneers, with children costumed for that period. The thimble club had an all-day meeting with Rose Ford.

Ontario—Ontario No. 251, under the direction of President Ethel Baxter, entered a float in the Armistice Day parade and won first prize in the historical division. Yellow chrysanthemums were used to decorate the car, while bronze-colored ones composed the initials N.D.G.W.

Berkeley—Past Grand Ariana W. Stirling, affiliated with Aleli No. 102 (Salinas), accompanied by her husband and daughter, departed November 16 on a trip to the Orient. They will be away most of the winter.

N.D.G.W. OFFICIAL DEATH LIST.

Giving the name, the date of death, and the Subordinate Parlor affiliation of all deceased members as reported to Grand Secretary Sallie R. Thaler from October 18, 1932, to November 18, 1932:

Piratsky, Mary Ann; September 19; El Pajaro No. 35.
Tuggle, Maybelle; October 11; Sutter No. 111.
Knightly, Angeline; October 14; Hayward No. 122.
Shaver, Nettie C.; October 10; Bonita No. 10.
O'Brien, Martha; October 27; Piedmont No. 87.
Cuddy, Isabel L.; October 4; Bahia Vista No. 167.
Gambini, Alta C.; October 21; Santa Rosa No. 217.
Toner, Libbie N.; October 27; San Jose No. 81.
Yaeger, Mary B.; November 5; Marguerite No. 12.

In Memoriam

MABEL TUGGLE.

Whereas, Almighty God, in His infinite wisdom, has called from our midst a member of the Native Daughters of the Golden West, Mabel Tuggle; and whereas, we feel we have lost a loyal member of this Order and a true friend; now, therefore, be it

Resolved, That we, the members of Gold of Ophir Parlor No. 190 N.D.G.W., extend our sincere sympathy to her mother and other members of the family, and to Sutter Parlor No. 111 N.D.G.W. of Sacramento, in their bereavement; be it further resolved, that a copy of these resolutions be spread upon the minutes of the Parlor, that a copy be sent to the family, that a copy be sent to Sutter Parlor No. 111, and a copy to The Grizzly Bear Magazine, in respect to her memory.

Respectfully submitted,
FLORENCE DANFORTH-BOYLE,
ALICE CUNDY,
VERNA PARKER,
Committee.

Oroville, October 19, 1932.

IDA C. CHILDRESS.

Having been appointed a Committee to draft resolutions to the memory of our late sister, Ida C. Childress, we respectfully submit the following:

Whereas, In the passing of Sister Childress, El Dorado Parlor No. 186 N.D.G.W. has lost another charter member, loyal to the last, those to whom she was nearest, a true friend; she has passed from this earth and its sorrows into the light of the Great Beyond; she has gained that for which the rest of us are striving. In drafting these resolutions of respect we are performing the last tribute in our power for an honored and revered sister.

Resolved, That our Charter be draped in mourning, and that a copy of these resolutions be sent to The Grizzly Bear for publication, and that a copy be spread upon the minutes.

"May the California winds blow lightly,
May the California sun shine brightly,
May the California rain fall lightly
Where sleeps our sister dear."

Respectfully submitted in P.D.F.A.,
IRENE M. IRISH,
ELLA C. STANTON,
BEATRICE S. LUCE,
Committee.

Georgetown, November 16, 1932.

NETTIE SHAVER.

To the family of the late Nettie Shaver—The following resolution has been adopted by Bonita Parlor No. 10 Native Daughters of the Golden West:

The Angel of Death has entered the portals of Bonita Parlor No. 10 N.D.G.W. and taken from our midst our Sister Nettie Shaver. She was a loyal Native Daughter and loved California with a true and tender love. Our Order has lost a faithful member. Therefore, be it

Resolved, That our charter be draped in mourning, that a copy of these resolutions be sent to her bereaved family and published in the "Redwood City Standard," and that a copy be sent The Grizzly Bear Magazine for publication.

"May the California winds blow lightly,
May the California sun shine brightly,
May the California rain fall softly—
Where sleeps our Sister dear."

Respectfully submitted in P.D.F.A.,
DORA WILSON,
MAMIE GLENNAN,
IDA THOMPSON,
Committee.

Redwood City, November 1, 1932.

LOS ANGELES--CITY and COUNTY

When you purchase goods advertised in The Grizzly Bear, or answer an advertisement in this magazine, please be sure to mention The Grizzly Bear. That's co-operation mutually beneficial.

LOS ANGELES

(Continued from Page 13)

work for the Red Cross was accomplished. One candidate was initiated November 20.

INTENSIVE MEMBERSHIP DRIVE.

Under the supervision of Municipal Judge Leo I. Aggeler, Hollywood Parlor No. 196 N.S.G.W. has inaugurated an intensive membership drive which, it is believed, will produce excellent results early in the new year. December 5 officers for the January-July term will be elected, and there will be no meetings December 26 or January 2, those dates being legal holidays.

FIRST SOCIAL FUNCTION.

University Parlor No. 272 N.S.G.W. will stage its first social function, a dance, at Palestine Masonic Temple, 471 West Forty-first place, December 2. The committee in charge includes John McLaughlin (chairman), Martin DeFazio, Dr. J. H. Encell, Walter Hartwell, Thomas P. Riley, Howard Babb, Gennaro Berardino. The Parlor has a committee promoting athletics, and an orchestra and a quartet are being organized.

ANNUAL CHRISTMAS PARTY.

Californiana Parlor No. 247 N.D.G.W. will initiate a class of five candidates December 13, among them Mrs. Mattie Lee Porter, the wife of Mayor John C. Porter. That is the date also for the annual Christmas party and homeless children benefit. A bazar will be featured, including a grabbag and cooked-food sale. Mrs. Edward Tabor is in charge.

Mrs. Amos Otis Evans, program chairman, presented a delightful opera reading of "Rigoletto" November 8, with Blanche Pilmer and Raymond Yanqua in the title roles. Richard Cardos was at the piano, and Mrs. Charles W. Roadman was the reader. November 22, the hospitality committee sold delicious cooked food, donated by the members, netting a goodly sum for the Parlor treasury. Refreshments were served. Deputy Mattie B. Edwards and Miss Gladys Edwards were among the visitors.

PARTY FOR "DECEMBERITES."

There was an extra-large attendance at the November 18 meeting of Ramona Parlor No. 109 N.S.G.W., when the November boys were guests of honor. Among the speakers were Charles O. Brittain, Charles Gassagne and Past Grand Herman Lichtenberger. Walter Slosson made the first presentation of 1933 "Bear Club" pins. Chairman Ralph Harbison gave a progress report for the membership committee. The Caballeros of Ramona will have a benefit dance January 21; tickets a quarter each. Charles Straube is promoting an unusual birthday party for the Parlor at Catalina next year.

Ramona's December program includes: 2nd, election officers; 9th, initiation; 16th, birthday party for the "Decemberites," all members of the Parlor being invited to join in; 30th, old-year-out-new-year-in jinks.

PERSONAL PARAGRAPHS.

Andrew M. Stodel (Los Angeles N.S.) made another trip to Eastern cities last month.

Leslie Patterson (University N.S.) departed last month for New York City on business.

James F. Hoey (Past Grand N.S.) of Martinez, district attorney Contra Costa County, was a visitor last month.

Miss Grace J. Norton, Mrs. Lucille Duncan and Mrs. Mildred Ripling (all Los Angeles N.D.) were recent visitors to Ensenada.

Sheriff William I. Traeger (Past Grand N.S.) and wife (Los Angeles N.D.) were visitors last month to the San Francisco Bay district.

Mrs. Hazel B. Hansen (Grand Outside Sentinel N.D.) went to Woodland November 26 to attend the official visit of Grand President Anna Mixon Armstron to her home-Parlor, Woodland No. 90.

THE DEATH RECORD.

Mrs. Johanna Schepp, mother of Phillip Schepp (Los Angeles N.S.), died recently. She was a native of Kentucky, came to California in 1872, and for many years resided in Sacramento City.

Alonzo William Lopez, son of Mrs. Olive Lopez (Californiana N.D.), died at Monrovia November 2. He was a native of Orange County, aged 32.

Henry W. Edelman, brother of Dr. D. W. Edelman (Hollywood N.S.), died November 4.

Rudolph Goss Vejar, affiliated with Ramona Parlor No. 109 N.S.G.W., died November 12. He was born in Los Angeles May 2, 1894.

Mrs. Harriett Burch, mother of Samuel F. Arthur (Ramona N.S.), died November 20.

George Henry Carson, affiliated with Ramona Parlor No. 109 N.S.G.W., died November 20. He was born in Los Angeles County, October 26, 1865. November 17 his wife, Mrs. Ellen Carson, passed away.

PIONEER NATIVES DEAD

(Brief Notices of the Demise of Men and Women born in California Prior to 1860.)

Miss Effie Josephine Newell, born in San Francisco in 1859, died October 23 at Sacramento City.

Rev. Peter Alphonse Riley, born in San Francisco in 1855, died at Oakland, Alameda County, October 24.

George Waitstel Hastings, born in Sacramento County in 1859, died at Sacramento City October 25. He was a son of Daniel Hastings who, with his brother, Lansford W. Hastings, crossed the plains in 1843 and established "Hastings Cutoff," over which many Pioneers came to California.

John W. Heath, born in Trinity County in 1849, died at Bakersfield, Kern County, October 26 survived by a wife. He was at one time coroner of Trinity County.

John Stanford Hemenway, born in Sacramento City in 1855, died there October 26 survived by two children.

Charles V. Reche, born in Santa Clara County in 1854, died at Fall Brook, San Diego County, October 29.

Mrs. Cornelia E. Caine, born in San Francisco in 1855, died there October 30 survived by a husband.

Abraham Bernstein, born in Sacramento City in 1855, died at San Francisco October 31 survived by a wife.

George W. Covey, born in Sonoma County in 1857, died at Forestville November 2 survived by a daughter. His parents, Mr. and Mrs. Uriah Covey, were among Sonoma's earliest settlers.

Mrs. Frances Ellen Scranton-Wilson, born in Lake County in 1857, died near Middletown November 2 survived by two daughters.

Dennis Filbert Bernal, born in Alameda County in 1856, died at Livermore November 2 survived by a wife and four children. He was affiliated with Las Positas Parlor No. 96 N.S.G.W.

Mrs. Isabelle Wood, born at Sacramento City in 1855, died November 4 at King City, Monterey County, survived by four children.

Oscar Kleine, born in Sacramento City in 1859, died at Chico, Butte County, November 4 survived by a wife and three daughters.

William N. Lamphrey, born in San Francisco in 1856, died at Sacramento City November 6 survived by a wife. He was affiliated with Sacramento Parlor No. 3 N.S.G.W.

Edwin Smith, born in Nevada City, Nevada County, in 1856, died there November 7 survived by four children.

Mrs. Alice Bradford-Wetmore, born in Tuolumne County in 1853, died at Napa City November 10.

William Pond Cantelow, born in Napa County in 1856, died at Sacramento City November 12 survived by a wife and a daughter.

Mrs. Nellie Moore-Ridge, born in Nevada County in 1859, died November 12 at San Anselmo, Marin County, survived by two daughters.

Eldorado Driscoll, born in El Dorado County in 1855, died at Lodi, San Joaquin County, November 13.

Frank Dana, born in San Luis Obispo County in 1842, died at Los Angeles City November 14. He was a son of Captain William G. Dana, grantee of one of the original Spanish land grants in San Luis Obispo County.

Mrs. Cecelia Griffin-Clark, born in Humboldt County in 1853, died November 14 at Eureka survived by a husband and four children.

Mrs. Mary Wade-Bradley, born in Santa Clara County in 1851, died November 15 at San Jose survived by a daughter.

Mrs. Mary P. A. Bourne, born in Marin County in 1845, died November 16 at Bolinas survived by six children.

Thomas Motherwell, born in Trinity County in 1856, died November 18 at Weaverville.

FEMININE FANCIES

(Continued from Page 17)

scarlets and vermillions, grape and wine reds, burgundies, are the colors that repeat themselves everywhere. It was expected that bright colors would fall into the discard, but red remains among the current favorites, and will always remain as an accessory color. Red hats, scarfs and bags, and even shoes, are popular favorites. Dark red woolen in coarse weave, run through in striped lines with coarse white thread and cut on the bias, makes a handsome tailored dress or suit, to be worn with plain red hat, bag and shoes.

THE LETTER BOX

(Continued from Page 2)

My eldest daughter, Mrs. P. McPhee, lives in Vancouver, B. C. The other three live here: Archer T. and Frank D. Shearer, and Mrs. Rena Mathews—all God-fearing, respectable people. No drinking in the family. I was obliged to care for them at an early age; learned telegraphy; was agent for the Santa Fe Railway for six years at Mentone, California, and surely had many books to keep. I do not wish to brag, but I always had work. I wrote in the San Bernardino County recorder's office for one and a half years until I took the Mentone office.

Now, at eighty-three years and over, I am well cared for and have many friends. Belong to the W.R.C. and the P.T.A., where I held offices until illness kept me at home. I ride out, but neuritis has been my oppressor—all but my right hand. I think I write pretty well, even at that.

MRS. TILLIE SHEARER.

Used to call myself Halley Sarpy Mahala Swartwont.

Los Angeles, 1932.

"WEAVERVILLE."

Editor Grizzly Bear—I am inclosing a piece of poetry recently published in the "Weekly Trinity Journal" here, and wish you would publish same in The Grizzly Bear when you have the space. . . . You'll probably remember me ten years back as secretary of Mount Bally Parlor No. 87 N.S.G.W. . . . Moved away from here to Richmond, Contra Costa County, eight years ago, but returned to "God's country" last year. I am now news editor of the "Journal." Best wishes.

HARRY H. NOONAN.

Weaverville, September, 1932.

The poem, entitled "Weaverville," follows. It was composed by Mrs. Betty L. Whitsell of Burlingame, San Mateo County, who recently visited Weaverville and was so enthused over the town the poem was the result:

No town in all this state
Is quaint as Weaverville.
For there it lies,
An active little mining town,
That time defies.
High up where Nature makes
Great walls with mountain peaks,
Men found new ways
To cross the summits and the streams
In early days.

In eighteen-fifty-one,
They went with horse and gun
To Weaverville.
And pack-trains brought supplies to men,
With many a thrill.
And there it is today,
A mining-camp unchanged,
With iron doors,
And spiral stairways leading up
For troubadours.

A Chinese temple, too,
Stands with its ancient gods.
It reeks incense,
And old and faded are its walls
Without pretence.
Four Chinese stores remain,
With deep cement-made walls.
These stand so bold
And strangely seem symbolical,
Of spirits old.

Oh, yes, I say again
No place in this whole State
Is just as quaint and still.
Old Father Time with arms outstretched,
Left Weaverville.

SUFFERED, THAT OTHERS MIGHT ENJOY

(ALICE LYALL-BORDEN.)

THERE IS SOMETHING ABOUT THE words "Native Sons and Native Daughters" that suggests pioneering. The present generation can only guess, by reading the history of the earlier days, at the hardships endured by the old Pioneers. The unreliability of obtaining the few items of provisions which they did not raise, and the Isolation from the rest of the world, did not daunt their spirit of adventure.

My father, Ambrose Lyall, was born in South Carolina in 1824 and was filled with that indomitable spirit of adventure which actuated all the early settlers. He left home when a boy and landed in Missouri in 1842. My mother, Martha Davis, was born in 1827 and they were married in 1843 and raised a family of ten children.

In 1849 my father came to California. His stay must have been short the first time, because he returned to Missouri and took my mother and their two children back. After organizing a train of about fifty people, they started across the plains by way of the never-to-be-forgotten covered wagon and ox team, and arrived here in 1853 and settled near Marysville. My eldest sister, who now lives in the northern part of the state, is, I presume, the oldest covered-wagon baby living today. She was born in Nevada before my parents reached the California line. They lived in Marysville for a time and then went to Hangtown, where I was born in 1857.

By this time, ox teams had been discarded, and they used horses with the same old covered wagon. In 1860 my parents moved to Fresno County, on Kings River. Up and down this river was a land grant handed down from Mexico. It was about twenty-five miles long and several miles wide. No one seemed to know who the owners were. Every few miles on this land were houses; some were log houses and some were built of clapboards. Those coming in could live in these houses as long as they wanted to. These people were called "squatters." In one of these houses we "squatted."

My first recollection was of the '62 flood. We kept a boat, as the older children had to cross the river to go to school, a little red schoolhouse where eight or ten children attended. During this flood, we stayed in the house until the water became knee-deep, when my father took the boat, put the family in it and started out to find higher ground. After finding a place to camp, we found that our cows, horses and sheep had already gone to the plains to higher ground. As soon as the water went down so that we could travel, we started back to Marysville. We were gone a year and then returned to the same old place.

I remember the old spinning wheel. My mother spun yarn and knitted stockings and socks for the whole family. I remember the old crane in the old fireplace where the old kettles hung to do our cooking, and the old dutch ovens to bake our bread. Up and down Kings River was very rich bottom land that would raise anything. It seems truly, that "necessity is the mother of invention." My mother would cut corn from the cob and dry it; also the old field corn made delicious hominy. We would gather

(Continued on Page 24)

Rose Tournament—The annual Tournament of Roses parade and the East-West football game at Pasadena, Los Angeles County, will be held Monday, January 2, 1933, instead of January 1, as heretofore.

"The gentleman is a man of truth, lord of his own actions, and expressing that lordship in his behaviour."—Emerson.

"Who can be more gorgeously and splendidly apparalled than the flowers of the field?"—Sharp.

SAN FRANCISCO

SELECTED FROM MORE THAN 800 PHOTOGRAPHS submitted in response to the California trees photographic competition, seven winners of cash prizes have been announced by the California Conservation Committee of The Garden Club of America and the Save-the-Redwoods League, joint sponsors of the contest, which was launched in June and entries for which closed September 7.

The prizewinners, in order of preference, are: Edward Weston of Carmel, "Joshua Tree, Mojave Desert;" Alma R. Lavenson of Oakland, "Snow Blossoms;" A. Kono of Los Angeles, "Eucalyptus;" Ansel Easton Adams of San Francisco, "Sugar Pine;" Victor S. Matson of South Pasadena, "Desert Vista;" Albert Barrows of San Francisco, "Live Oak Arabesque;" Willard VanDyke of Piedmont, "Detail of Madrone."

AMERICAN-BORN JAPS DEVELOP HERE FRICTION-CREATING COLONIES.

"Discontinue all immigration and develop a homogenous people, an American race," declared Chairman Paul Stinchfield of the immigration section of the Commonwealth Club, San Francisco, in an address at the club's Oriental immigration dinner November 10.

He reported the section flatly opposes granting an immigration quota to all Asiatic countries, and favors retention of the present naturalization law which disqualifies Asiatics from citizenship. Tracing the history of Oriental immigration to the United States, Stinchfield stated the two major reasons for opposition to Asiatic immigration seem to have been the inability of American labor to compete with cheap Oriental labor, and the self-evident unassimilability of Asiatics.

"All the opposition to Asiatic immigration we have heard," he said, "has been based not on prejudice or lack of international sympathy, but on ineradicable racial and cultural differences. Both sides seem agreed as to the undesirability of Asiatic immigration.

"Japanese in America, even though American born, develop foreign colonies which lead to friction and misunderstanding. Such conditions are not desirable. It would be equally undesirable for large colonies of Americans to settle in Japan for permanent residence."

EDUCATION WEEK PROGRAM.

The N.S.G.W. Grand Parlor Education Committee, Peter T. Conmy chairman, November 4 presented a National Education Week program in the auditorium of Native Son Building. The principal speakers were Father Lornegan, president University of San Francisco, and Miss Eliza D. Keith, Past Grand President N.D.G.W.

NATIVE DAUGHTER DOINGS.

Minerva Parlor No. 2 had a post-Hallowe'en party November 2, and the members were rivals for costume honors. The festive board was a galaxy of orange and black, and groaned under its burden of tempting delicacies. Mrs. Croter, sole remaining charter member, was honor-guest and spoke of the days of old. Deputy Ida Mesquite favored with kind words, and musical numbers concluded the program. Visitors were present from Genevieve No. 132 and Gabrielle No. 139. The Parlor will have its annual Christmas tree party December 16 and Santa Claus promises to be there.

A luncheon, followed by bridge and whist, will be given by Alta Parlor No. 3 December 8; Mrs. Mary Schultz is the chairman. Grand President Anna Mixon-Armstrong will officially visit the Parlor in December; Grand Trustee Annie C. Thuesen heads the arrangements committee. The annual Christmas "jinks," December 27, will conclude a series of activities sponsored by President May L. MacDonald.

El Vespero Parlor No. 118 had a Hollowe'en party October 25 which was a great success. Many members appeared in costume, and a lovely banquet was served. The drill team members, under the leadership of Mary Casey, were hostesses. A whist party was given November 22; Jane Lapachet was the chairwoman.

Genevieve Parlor No. 132 had a delightful Hallowe'en party November 3, all members being in costume and each contributing a song or a dance to the evening's enjoyment. An enchilada supper was served at appropriately decorated tables. May Keane was chairman of the arrangements committee, and Deputy Agnes Curry was the guest of honor. The recent benefit whist was a great success. A dinner November 14 was in charge of Hannah Toohig.

Keith Parlor No. 137 was officially visited by Grand President Anna Mixon-Armstrong November 10. Dinner preceded the meeting. In observance of Armistice Day the lodgeroom was decorated in red, white and blue. Past President Gertrude LaFortune presided. Among those present were Junior Past Grand Evelyn I. Carlson, Grand Trustees Ethel Begley and Anna Thuesen, Grand Inside Sentinel Orinda Giannini, Past Grands Mae Himes Noonan, May C. Boldemann, Mary E. Bell, Dr. Mariana Bertola, Margaret Grote Hill and Eliza D. Keith, Supervising Deputy Alice Lane. The Parlor presented gifts to all, and each responded with enjoyable remarks.

The Hallowe'en party held by Gabrielle No. 139 provided an enjoyable evening for the many in attendance. Full credit went to First Vice-president Ranzulo and committee for the startling decorations—ghosts, black cats and witches. Refreshments were served.

Golden Gate Parlor No. 158 had a Hollowe'en party October 24 at which many original and beautiful costumes were worn. A whist party October 31 netted a nice sum for the treasury. In honor of her anniversary, a birthday-card shower was tendered Past President Margret Ramm November 14.

Members of Dolores Parlor No. 169 visited Letterman Hospital October 30 and served home-made cakes, candy, oranges and cigarets to the veterans, to each of whom was also given a Hallowe'en favor carrying out the holiday spirit. Magazines were distributed and greatly appreciated. Betty Both, as hostess, was assisted by Rose Spaelti and Emma O'Meara. The Parlor's drill team met November 15 for its first instruction and Josephine Doray, who originated the team, was selected for captain.

Castro Parlor No. 178 gave a surprise baby shower to Mrs. Georgia Nelson, and among the many beautiful gifts was a bank book showing a deposit of $24, which the little stranger will have to start the life journey. Each officer contributed a dollar, and eight dollars was added by various members. A benefit whist was held November 17, the proceeds being the nucleus for the Parlor's relief fund. Mrs. Paula Hilzinger was the chairman. The affair was most successful, $58.17 being turned into the relief fund and $19.38 going into the Parlor treasury.

N.D. PAST PRESIDENTS WILL PROVIDE CHRISTMAS CHEER FOR ORPHANS

Sacramento—Chief President Cora Stobing of the N.D.G.W. Past Presidents Association officially visited Association No. 4 November 14. Armistice Day and Thanksgiving Day were fea

TASKMASTER

(F. ELLENORE PRINCE.)

To live as bravely as the pioneers
And win, nor quarter seek from first to last;
To look with steady eye to coming years
And carve a future empire unsurpassed;
To live with head uplifted to the skies,
Nor gather plunder, stoop to greed nor lust;
To heed the hope in little children's eyes,
Nor let my emblem tarnish in the dust;
To live with all mankind in brotherhood,
And smile my way with unquenched faith of youth;
To fight for right and seek the common good;
To pray for guidance and to search for truth.
The God of Nations only this will ask;
So let it ever be my sovereign task.

(Editor's Note—This is the prizewinner in a poem contest, sponsored by the "San Francisco Chronicle," which produced many verses of merit.)

PRACTICE RECI

tured in the decorations; each of the many guests received a small turkey as a favor. Past Grand Dr. Eva R. Rasmussen was the general chairman, Miss Mae E. Lucas had charge of the program, and Mrs. Sophie Monteverde was head of the banquet committee.

The Sacramento Association is planning its annual Christmas dinner for twenty-five girls from the Sacramento Orphanage. Mrs. Hazel Leitch is the general chairman, and Mrs. Anne Tilden will select the gifts for the tree. On the birthday of each of these girls she is presented by the Association with a cake and a remembrance.

OUTDOOR CHRISTMAS TREES FOR EVERY CALIFORNIA HOME AND CITY.

All California is preparing again to say "Merry Christmas" to the rest of the world with thousands of outdoor Christmas trees. On front lawns, in city parks and schoolyards, and along the highways trees will gleam with cheer, and do much toward replacing depression and fear with confidence.

Sponsored by the Outdoor Christmas Tree Association of California, the cause of the living tree has won such public favor it is expected there will be more than 100,000 decorated outdoor trees and shrubs in California this year.

The Outdoor Christmas Tree Association of California was started in 1927. This year it has as its twin slogans "An Outdoor Christmas Tree for Every California Home" and "A Mile of Outdoor Christmas Trees for Every California City."

COMMENDABLE ENDEAVOR.

Santa Rosa—Santa Rosa Parlor No. 217 N.D.G.W. had its annual benefit for the homeless children November 18. A drill team has been organized and will soon be ready to appear in public. Instead of the annual Christmas party, this year the Parlor will prepare boxes of holiday goodies for needy families. For the benefit of undernourished children, a milk fund has been created.

FISH POND CREATES MERRIMENT.

Sierraville—Imogen Parlor No. 134 N.D.G.W. had its annual fish pond, and the big crowd present got a lot of merriment fishing. Refreshments were served, and dancing continued until midnight. November 12 twenty members of Naomi Parlor No. 36 came over from Downieville to enjoy Imogen's armistice and colonial program. Deputy Grand President Neva McMahon gave an address. A splendid banquet closed the affair.

In Memoriam

ALTA COLE GAMBINI.

Whereas, The Angel of Death has again entered our Parlor and has called to the Great Beyond our dear friend and sister, Alta Cole Gambini,

Resolved, That by her death, Santa Rosa Parlor No. 217 N.D.G.W. has lost a loving and devoted sister, whose noble character and kind disposition endeared her to all; be it further resolved, that Santa Rosa Parlor extend its sincere sympathy to the bereaved husband and sons and other members of the family, and that these resolutions be spread upon the minutes of the Parlor; that a copy be sent to the family of the deceased sister, and one to The Grizzly Bear Magazine for publication.

LONIE E. ALLEGRINI,
CLYTIE L. LEWIS,
KATHRYN BRANSTETTER,
Committee.

Santa Rosa, November 16, 1932.

STATE HIGHWAY COMMISSION MARKS SITE SHASTA'S FIRST GOLD DISCOVERY.

At the northwest end of the new highway bridge across Clear Creek, on the Pacific highway three miles south of Redding, Shasta County, says "California Highways and Public Works" for October 1932, is a bronze tablet, mounted upon a native boulder, placed there by the California Highway Commission to tell the traveler that on this historic stream the most northern gold discovery in California was made by Major P. B. Reading in the early spring of 1848. The site of the discovery is five miles up the creek at Reading's Bar, marked by a wooden sign. At the top of the tablet is depicted Mount Shasta and the California grizzly bear, the official emblem of the Shasta Historical Society. The inscription reads: "In 1848 gold was first discovered on this creek by Major Pierson Barton Reading, Early California Pioneer. Erected by the California Highway Commission, 1931—Dedicated May 23, 1932."

Major Reading entered California via the Pit River gateway and arrived at Sutter's Fort November 10, 1843, and in December 1844 secured from Governor Micheltorena the northernmost land grant in California, comprising more than 26,000 acres extending along the Sacramento River from Salt Creek to the mouth of Cottonwood Creek. When Marshall made the discovery of gold at Coloma, El Dorado County, Major Reading was among the first to visit the scene and, noting the soil was the same, he was satisfied there was gold near his ranch. Returning home he and his Indians washed out the first gold on a bar at the mouth of the canyon of Clear Creek in March 1848. He employed 150 Indians and squaws and took out as much as fifty-two ounces in a day.

UNDERSEA MOUNTAIN DISCOVERED.

A submarine mountain one mile in hight, about sixty nautical miles southwest of the Golden Gate and the same distance westward from Santa Cruz, was recently discovered by the survey ship "Guide," according to a Federal Coast and Geodetic Survey announcement.

This undersea mountain, like all outstanding differences in the configuration of the ocean floor, furnishes another guide to the mariner whose vessel is equipped with echo depth-sounding equipment, in fixing his position when out of sight of land.

"Give not that which is holy unto the dogs, neither cast your pearls before swine."—Bible.

GRIZZLY GROWLS

(Continued from Page 3)

matter of fact, this country has an overabundance of bad actors and actresses, aliens and otherwise, and all of them are not harbored in Hollywood, either.

United States Senator William E. Borah of Idaho, chairman Senator Foreign Relations Committee, declared November 10: "Our program has consisted of levying taxes and lending the credit of the government to a limited number of individuals. The event on November 8 was a political revolution. And there will be a more serious revolution than that if taxes continue to increase and the expenditures of the government continue to enlarge. At a time when millions of our people are saving their pennies to keep soul and body together, we are talking about levying a [sales] tax which will take that penny." Taxes must be reduced, that's a certainty, and a material reduction would come with the elimination of governmental extravagance and political graft.

Dr. Julius Klein, assistant secretary Federal Commerce Department, declared in an address: "It surely should be plain by now that every retailer has got to fish for business—and fish skillfully and resolutely. . . . Shrewd, forceful, truthful, persistent advertising is especially necessary at this time." Good advice, that not only retailers, but all others who have something to sell, should heed.

State Finance Director Rolland Vandegrift declares that "No one should be permitted to vote on bonds that incumber real property unless he pays a property tax." An excellent suggestion which the coming State Legislature should enact into legislation. The voters who pay no property tax have been instrumental in saddling onto the propertyowners of California a bonded indebtedness of some $875,000,000—more than enough!

Ruling that a wife's earnings are community property, a Shasta County judge has ordered a married schoolteacher to pay thirty dollars a month from her salary to her husband's former wife for the support of two minor children. A learned judge!

The Wright Act having been decisively repealed, California's Governor plans to release from the state's prisons and jails all those convicted of liquor-law violations. 'At a boy, Governor! The highup financial and kindred felons are freed without the necessity of financing an initiative, so the lowdown bootleggers and associates who spent thousands to "educate" the voters should be rewarded for their effort and success.

What worries now, is the fact that the statutes against gambling, narcotics and prostitution continue to operate "contrary to Constitution-guaranteed freedom of individual action." Will not some one, please, finance and promote initiatives against those laws, that Californians may enjoy perfect liberty?

Pasadena has joined the increasing ranks of communities and firms which are dispensing with the services of married women with able-bodied husbands. It has decreed: "(1.) No married women will be employed by any city department in the future unless they are supporting a family. (2.) All women employees who marry must resign their positions within six months. (3.) All married women now employed by the city must resign within six months unless their husbands are unemployed." The weeding out of all such from the state, the counties, the cities and the townships governments, as well as from all other lines of endeavor, will, to a large degree, solve the rottenness sorely afflicting the social structure.

Yassah! Topsigned by Ira Mack, the October 28 "Calistogan" of Calistoga, Napa County, had a front-page article, headed "Smooth Political Opportunist Raising All Sorts of Dust To Cover Own Acts," which began thusly:

"The fat tax-eaters now gathered at the California feed-troughs in Sacramento, Los Angeles and San Francisco are raising all the dust they possibly can to obscure the sharp eyes of those who are coming, finally, to see that somehow they are being literally robbed out of hand by a state administration that is eating regularly and at the most expensive places, while the rank and file of taxpayers of California are having an awful time to meet small grocery bills, or to gather cash to buy at bargain, cash prices, barely enough to get by with, and then only by tightening the belt considerably. Meanwhile, if anyone thinks that Vandegrift, Rolph and family, including its insurance agency members, are not eating out and in style, they are not trailing the state limousines or the state fly-car. Anyway, the governor is never at home, but is fed by the generosity of would-be boosters or appointees; hence, he is not worrying about how the taxpayers are eating, if at all."

Considerable has been published about the Los Angeles County Board of Supervisors reducing personnel and salary costs. As heretofore remarked, the assertion was propaganda, for political purposes. Here are the figures, just revealed: In 1929 the salary costs for the county were $17,569,082; in 1930 they increased to $19,481,826; in 1931 they went up to $20,874,553; this year, 1932, they total $21,820,999. Where does the muchly-heralded reduction come in?

SUFFERED

(Continued from Page 21)

wild blackberries and elderberries and dry them for the winter.

In 1865, my father bought his first land. We moved just across the river, into Tulare County. At this time, land was thrown open for preemption and sold by the government for twenty-five cents an acre. My father had lots of sheep, and wool was high. He had twelve mule teams running from Visalia to Stockton, hauling all kinds of merchandise; he also hauled lumber out of the mountains. But when, in 1871, the Southern Pacific built its first railroad through the country, the teaming business was stopped. Many people were moving in and taking up land. My father also bought up every piece of land he could get. A canal was taken out of the upper Kings River and the people began farming. The farmers and stockmen fought for a few years

over the "No Fence Law." Finally, the law was passed, which prevented open stock raising. Eventually, my father sold his land and went to Arizona and became a wealthy man, having gone into the cattle business. Yet, if he had kept his land in California for fifteen years longer and done nothing else, he would have been almost a millionaire; for that part of the country settled up very fast and land increased in value by leaps and bounds, and today is one of the most flourishing parts of the state.

I must have inherited that pioneer spirit of wanderlust, or whatever it might be called, for although I never left the state until I was thirty years of age, yet after that I traveled across the continent, lived awhile in the South and then in the East, but always longing to come back to my native state, which I did about twenty-five years ago, as I found nothing half so good.

I desire, by these few words, to pay homage to the memory of our beloved Pioneers, with their stout hearts and courageous spirits. How little the people of today, old or young, know what the Pioneers went through with to help build our beloved state to what it is today. They truly suffered, that others might enjoy.

(The above came to The Grizzly Bear, under date of November 15, 1932, from Mrs. Alice L. Borden of Long Beach, who affiliated with Long Beach Parlor No. 154 N.D.G.W. September 15. She says: "I am inclosing a little story of pioneer days as I found them."—Editor.)

"Work well done invests the doer with a certain authority."—Emerson.

Grizzly Bear

JANUARY — THE ONLY OFFICIAL PUBLICATION OF THE NATIVE SONS AND DAUGHTERS OF THE GOLDEN WEST — 1933

Featuring

GENERAL NEWS OF INTEREST CONCERNING ALL CALIFORNIA, and ORDERS NATIVE SONS and NATIVE DAUGHTERS

Price: 15 Cents

SITE CALIFORNIA'S FIRST PROTESTANT CHURCH MARKED

AT BENICIA, SOLANO COUNTY, NOVEMBER 27 the site of the first Protestant church building in California was marked with a plaque which reads: "First Protestant Church in California. On April 15th, 1849, Rev. Sylvester Woodbridge organized a Presbyterian Church in Benicia. On the property now used as a park the first Protestant Church was erected. The church was abandoned in 1871."

Rev. Sylvester Woodbridge arrived in California in February 1849. Like many others, he believed that Benicia, originally known as Francisco, was to be the metropolis of California. Capitalists of San Francisco transferred their interests to the place and induced him to accompany them, promising him land for a college. April 15, 1849, in a school building, he organized the church. An interesting feature of the marker dedication was the reading of excerpts from the diary of Harvey Havey Hyde Jr., who was in Benicia in 1849:

"July 22nd, 1849—This Sabbath is another fine day, just warm enough to be comfortable. I have been here just a fortnight and a greater part of the time it is cool enough to wear an overcoat, and even when hard at work. There are scarcely any clouds and no rain, yet the N. N. W. winds blow steady this season of the year.

"This place has been built up within six months. A very wealthy man by the name of Vallejo (proun. Valahho) sold the land for the sum of $1.00. He owns all the land from here to Sonoma, and as far in width up the river (Sacramento), and as soon as people settle here more thickly they will buy from him. I now see about a dozen houses, a few stores, one gambling shop, one or two restaurants. It seems to be as good a place as could be found, being at the head of San Pablo Bay, which empties into San Francisco Bay. Ships can come and unload up to the very banks with but little expense. Seven miles from here the Government is building a Navy Yard and is now building three buildings, dwellings for the officers. Their progress is slow, for everything is so scarce or hard to get.

"This Sabbath day, August 19th, there is a man by the name of Rev. Dr. Woodbridge, who teaches school week days and preaches Sundays. His text today was from Joshua, 'As for me and my house, we will serve the Lord.' He clearly proved the existence of a deity by many good illustrations, and very applicable, for which he has a peculiar taste. He spoke of the affection which God has for His chilren, the same which a parent has for his child. He does not use notes, but spoke from the Bible as fast as his tongue could give utterance. These meetings were held in an out building belonging to Mr. Cooper. The shed adjoins a yard where are his cows and calves, which are noisy when the evening meetings are held. He had an audience of 66, very orderly and attentive. We have just finished a building for the town (18x32) in which he will preach after this. Took the job for $3800 and on which we realized $20 a day."

"WHAT MAN HATH DONE, MAN CAN DO"

(ELLA STERLING MIGHELS.)

"I MIGHT NEVER HAVE KNOWN THE story of William Gwin, if I had not met him when I was a little girl of ten, with another girl, when going down my father's toll road in Aurora Esmeralda, Nevada. We were wandering along heedlessly, just like children, when all at once came down the road a span of oxen driven by a very fair young man on his way out to Bodie, the next town. We asked him for a ride, but he was not willing, as he said we should only be going further away from home. But we insisted and got on via the back wheels, and there we were!

"But he kept saying, 'You will have to get off pretty soon, for I'm not going to let you go along with me—your mother would not be pleased.' So, true to his word, he made the oxen stop, and made us get off. He told us we were far away from home by now, and to hurry back before it got any darker. And as he insisted on it, we knew we had to mind him.

"When we reached home, I saw my mother standing at the door, waving her arms. So we hurried up, and she told us the papers were full of a terrible case in Boston, where a young boy and his sister were killed on Boston Common. As we had just come from the East, and as I had been taken to Boston Common to see it, I knew what she was talking about. So I told her how the young man who was driving the oxen had made us get off and go home to our parents, because he said it would soon be dark. She agreed at once it was nice of him to send us home, that our men in Aurora were good men and not like the brutes on Boston Common whose names, by the way, were never revealed. I had the shivers for several days just thinking of it.

"Later on I met the young man, who came back from Bodie, and thanked him for making us go home. And my mother approved of him. I think I never saw a more blonde-looking young man than he. He tried to look grown up and so wore a full beard, though only twenty-one. At first he drove an oxteam, but after-

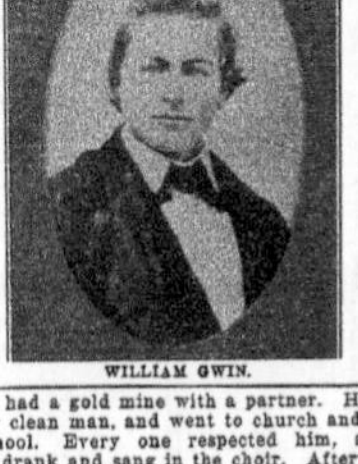

WILLIAM GWIN.

wards had a gold mine with a partner. He was a very clean man, and went to church and Sunday-school. Every one respected him, as he never drank and sang in the choir. Afterwards they got up a temperance society, with the choir to help them out. And everybody liked him and thought well of him. It seems once he had had a milk wagon, down in the civilized world when first he came to California, and went to the Methodist college in Santa Clara, which he attended for a while. And he always meant to go back there. I think it was a wonderful story he told me, of how he learned to read. I never

(Continued on Page 19)

GRIZZLY GROWLS

(CLARENCE M. HUNT.)

WELL, ANOTHER YEAR HAS passed, and although there were, during the last six months of thirty-two, spasmodic indications of improving business conditions, the "beautiful" depression continues, in full force and glory, as thirty-three makes its advent. Millions are unemployed, a sad condition, in a land of plenty. What the future will bring, no human knows; what the past brought, is a matter of history.

Dishonesty is undeniably the chief underlying cause of the depression that has reigned supreme for three years. Dishonesty, embracing wrongdoing of every degree, is the economic-cancer eating at the vitals of these United States and seriously threatening the very life of the nation. Its tentacles have spread, unhampered, into every walk of life—government, business, profession, church, school, civic, club, and even fraternal.

And it is a most remarkable—a non-understandable—fact that, in this so-called Christian country, no attempt whatever has been made to curb, if not cure, that cancer, and to thereby rout the depression. Sorry to say, even the church and the school have been found wanting in a time of direst need, and have allied themselves with the agencies, including government, that are appealing to and depending solely on the dollar to restore the nation's health.

All the monetary-wealth of the world will not, can not, cure the depression-cancer! But honesty, in all dealings, practiced by the government and by the citizenry generally, will rout the depression and assure lasting prosperity! The Golden Rule, rather than the dollar-sign, must be the guide! Oh, for a Moses of unimpeachable moral worth to administer to the nation's ills—to marshal the forces of Right, and to lead this magnificent country to its rightful place in the sun!

The devastating tide of dishonesty in which this nation now flounders came in with the World War, when the United States was thrown into that fracas ostensibly to "make the world safe for democracy," but, in reality, to make abroad-investments safe for the financial-swine with which this country has long been, and is today, over-cursed. Uninterrupted, either by moral or governmental forces, the dishonesty-tide, sweeping aside all barriers to its destructive progress, has wrought inestimable havoc, and is fast carrying this government of democracy to complete engulfment.

The Federal Congress grasps at straws, such as booze, to turn the tide—a pitiable exhibition of brainless endeavor! No one is suffering for want of beer, wine, or any other liquor, but millions are suffering for want of food, for need of employment. And certainly all governmental officials, including members of the Congress and others who have sworn to uphold the Constitution, are procuring and consuming all the booze they want—many of them far more than they need. And this Constitution-violating of public officials is decidedly a contributing cause, of no small import, to the growth of the dishonesty-cancer and to the continuance of the depression. The need for men in public office whose vision of the nation's and of the people's needs is unobstructed by a booze-barrel was never more paramount! Intelligence with integrity and truth by the leaders, is the greatest need today of these United States!

Unless checked, civic complacency will result in social disaster, declared Dr. F. W. Hart of the University of California at a recent meeting of the Oakland, Berkeley and Alameda Realty Boards. "One does not need to go to Chicago to find this same civic complacency," said he. "It is everywhere in this Nation. Unless citizens generally arouse themselves from their civic lethargy, the situation found in Chicago today will be nation-wide. Popular government will have fallen the victim of its own hand."

The local property tax is universally condemned by competent authorities. By experts on taxation, it has been called the worst tax known in the civilized world. "This tax fails to place a proper share of the burden of taxation upon the large amounts of intangible wealth and income which modern economic organization has created. It cannot be effectively administered, even under favorable conditions, and otherwise fails to meet the requirements of a sound tax."

California's three-ring circus, the State Legislature with its senate, assembly and lobby, opens at Sacramento January 2 for an indefinite run. The booted ringmaster will be an added attraction, in his aerial glory. From all accounts, it's going to be the greatest show ever.

Among the thrilling stunts will be the budget-balancing act—converting the general fund's red-ink balance of some twelve million dollars into a black-ink balance. It is hoped the lawmakers will not become so mystified by that act as to countenance the foisting of additional insane laws on a long-suffering citizenry, and the piling up of additional appropriations to care for needy politicians and to promote pet schemes of a favored few.

Senator Hiram W. Johnson of California will endeavor to have the Federal Congress adopt legislation, proposed by him, that would bar from the American market bonds and other obligations of a foreign government which has defaulted on obligations to the government or the investors of the United States. Any person offering such foreign paper for sale would be subject to a five-year prison sentence or a maximum fine of $10,000.

The measure should become a law! The fine-provision should be eliminated, however, for this country is overrun with financial "wizards" who will gladly contribute ten thousand, repeatedly, to the federal coffers for the privilege of mulcting honest and unsuspecting investors.

Severely, but justly, criticising Governor Rolph for pardoning numerous Wright Act violators, State Senator Ralph E. Swing of San Bernardino issued the following public statement December 20: "The Governor proceeded on the theory that they were simply violators of the Wright Act, in that they had disbursed intoxicating liquor in violation of that act, and that act having been repealed, the pardon was justified. If he were correct in this assumption, he would perhaps have reason for justifying their release.

"Unfortunately for the Governor's position, however, most of these persons, while convicted under the Wright Act, were in fact guilty of the heinous offense of manufacturing and disbursing to our unsuspecting youth, constituting the hope of posterity, a dirty, filthy and poisonous substitute for intoxicating liquor, which has affected, both mentally and physically, this upcoming generation to an undeterminable degree and has developed in them a disrespect for constituted authority and for the laws of our land. For such an offense no penalty is too severe, nor can any pardon eradicate the stigma nor convert them into law-abiding citizens."

The southern branch of the California State Teachers Association, meeting last month in Los Angeles City, got quite "het up" over reports that determined efforts are to be made to materially lower the cost of education. A resolution was adopted recommending a "firm adherence to and support of the present standard"—of taxation for so-called educational purposes—"that the ideals of American democracy may be maintained."

No thinking citizen desires that the "ideals of American democracy" as exemplified today shall be maintained; they are a threatening disgrace to the Union, and should be forsaken. If education claims credit for them, then education should be discouraged, rather than encouraged. In any event, the school-tax must be lowered, and it can be substantially reduced by eliminating numerous fads, reducing personnel, etc.

Donaldson Thorburn, speaking before the San Francisco Center on prohibition, quoted a prominent bootlegger as saying: "Women folk will not be satisfied with light wines and beers, repeal or no repeal. The ladies want whisky highballs first, cocktails second, gin fizzes third, and beer and wine not at all." Is not that the real situation as regards all the booze-howlers, irrespective of sex? The quoted bootlegger, however, must have been referring to women, not ladies.

"Something Is Wrong Here," is the heading of a Van Nuys "News" editorial referring to the pardoning, by Governor Rolph, of Fayette Marble, son of a wealthy South Pasadena family, convicted of running down and killing three persons with his auto. Young Marble was sentenced to from one to ten years, and served ninety days in jail. Something is decidedly wrong! Little wonder the killing of people by drunk and irresponsible auto drivers has become a favorite pastime among the "select."

(Continued on Page 6)

IN THEE WE TRUST

(FRED G. EAST.)

Oh, Lord of Nations, power supreme,
  Who guidest every sun and star
Enthroned above the cosmic scheme,
  We look to Thee, so near, yet far.
Through war and famine, greed and lust,
  Lord God on High, in Thee we trust!

Storm tossed and battered though we be,
  Our barque of Destiny sails on
Through many a rough and treacherous sea
  In staunch and steadfast union.
Toward the sun our prow is thrust,
  Lord God on High, in Thee we trust!

That flag of Liberty unfurled
  At Valley Forge and many a field,
O'er land and sea its challenge hurled;
  Though battered sore we cannot yield,
And, blindly struggling in the dust,
  Lord God on High, in Thee we trust!

We stagger onward; see the light
  Which brightly glows beyond the mist
To guide us through the years aright;
  E'en though the path may ever twist
We cannot fail for Thou art just—
  Lord God on High, in Thee we trust!

Oh, Lord of Nations, this our theme,
  We bow before Thy throne of grace;
Give us the vision, God supreme,
  Preserve our strength and pride of race,
Sustain us 'gainst each blow and thrust
  Because, Lord God, in Thee we trust!

(This is another of the many splendid poems submitted in a contest recently sponsored by the "San Francisco Chronicle."—Editor.)

The Grizzly Bear Magazine
The ALL California Monthly
OWNED, CONTROLLED, PUBLISHED BY GRIZZLY BEAR PUBLISHING CO., (Incorporated)
COMPOSED OF NATIVE SONS.
HERMAN C. LICHTENBERGER, Pres.
JOHN T. NEWELL RAY HOWARD
WM. I. TRAEGER LORENZO F. SOTO
CHAS. R. THOMAS HARRY J. LELANDE
ARTHUR A. SCHMIDT, Vice-Pres.
BOARD OF DIRECTORS
CLARENCE M. HUNT
General Manager and Editor
OFFICIAL ORGAN AND THE ONLY OFFICIAL PUBLICATION OF THE NATIVE SONS AND THE NATIVE DAUGHTERS GOLDEN WEST.
ISSUED FIRST EACH MONTH.
FORMS CLOSE 20th MONTH.
ADVERTISING RATES ON APPLICATION.
SAN FRANCISCO OFFICE:
N.S.G.W. BLDG., 414 MASON ST., RM. 302
(Office Grand Secretary N.S.G.W.)
Telephone: Kearney 1223
SAN FRANCISCO, CALIFORNIA
PUBLICATION OFFICE:
309-15 WILCOX BLDG., 2nd AND SPRING,
Telephone: VAndike 6234
LOS ANGELES, CALIFORNIA
(Entered as second-class matter May 29, 1918, at the Postoffice at Los Angeles, California, under the act of August 24, 1912.)
PUBLISHED REGULARLY SINCE MAY 1907
VOL. LII WHOLE NO. 309

CALIFORNIA'S ROMANTIC HISTORY

Lewis F. Byington

(PAST GRAND PRESIDENT N.S.G.W.)

(*Continuing the series of California history talks commenced in The Grizzly Bear for December 1932.*)

THE MISSIONS

NOTHING SHOULD APPEAL MORE strongly to all Californians than the unique, romantic and interesting history of our state. In no way can that history be more eloquently told than by preserving the structures reared by those who brought civilization to, and established permanent settlements in, the West.

Pride in the history and traditions of a state is what tends to make loyal men and women, and to elevate and ennoble citizenship. A movement was started several years ago to restore the missions, those beautiful structures, rich with the traditions of a century past, and which are the oldest monuments, architecturally, in the state. If permitted to fall into ruin much that would serve to throw a flood of light upon the achievements and the noble work of the earliest Pioneers on this coast is lost forever. Every man who appreciates beauty or is charmed by romance should labor for their preservation.

For countless years before the missionary fathers built the twenty-one missions of California, this land had been peopled by Indians. The race remained in darkness, devoid of science, art or agricultural advancement. The missionaries brought civilization, and established permanent settlements. The Franciscan friars were the first Pioneers of the West.

How much that word "pioneer" signifies—it embodies the development of the nation. It speaks to us of dangers, tribulations and hardships. It was the pioneer spirit which led those who founded California over barren deserts and rugged mountains, overcoming every peril and danger. It has planted the fig tree, the vine and the olive where the sagebrush grew and the manzanita blossomed. It has builded cities and homes, and dotted our bays with the messengers of commerce.

The colonization of California followed the discovery of America by Christopher Columbus. The lure of gold, the expansion of empire, was the impelling motive that caused Spain to send her ships ever westward. Within twenty years after the landing of Columbus, the Spanish explorers had reached Mexico and entered the barbors of South America. Within fifty years the flag of Spain had been carried across Mexico to the Pacific Ocean, and ships were being fitted out for the exploration of the Pacific Coast. Cabrillo sailed up the coast in 1542, Sir Francis Drake, with the English flag, in 1579, and ships of other nations in the years following. Spain claimed California by right of discovery, but for over two hundred years no attempt was made to establish permanent settlements. Russia was pressing down from the north, and eventually reached Mount St. Helena, Bodega Bay and Fort Ross. The ships of England and France had sailed along the coast, and California presented an inviting field for conquest. Spain wakened to the fact that permanent settlements must be established to forestall acquisition by other nations, and she determined to colonize the country and christianize the Indians.

Had Russia or England controlled California when gold was discovered, the territory would not have been acquired by the United States, for we had no reason to go to war with them. The war with Mexico, the successor of Spain to this territory, resulted in bringing California under the "Stars and Stripes."

Spain, having awakened to the necessity of colonizing and protecting the territory, Jose de Galvez, governor general, selected Junipero Serra, a Franciscan monk, to take charge of the spiritual part of the expedition, and Don Gaspar Portola to head the military division. They were authorized to established three missions—one at San Diego, one at Monterey, and one in between these, to be called San Buenaventura. The pious and kindly Serra, in accepting the labor of civilizing California, said to Galvez: "Every colony that has heretofore been brought under the dominion of Spain and under its banner, has been brought by the power of the sword, let me bring to Spain this new land of California by the power of the cross."

At San Diego, July 16, 1769, Father Serra founded his first mission. Here a presidio was also established. Then Portola, anxious to carry out orders to hasten north and prevent the feared invasion by Russia, England or France, marched in search of Monterey Bay as described by the navigators. Unknowingly, he passed that bay, and his sergeant, Ortega, unexpectedly ran upon the Golden Gate and discovered the great harbor extending far inland and which, in honor of St. Francis, was named the Bay of San Francisco.

The failure of Portola to locate Monterey Bay led to another effort in 1770, when Serra himself raised the cross there and established his second mission, San Carlos Monterey, afterwards removed to Carmel. Carmel was Serra's own particular mission until his death in 1784. It was for years the first in importance, being the residence of the Father President, and because of its nearness to, only five miles to Monterey, the capital of California, where lived the Spanish governors. The original plan was to establish the mission at Monterey, where a chapel was built in 1770, but the rich lands of the Carmel Valley offered a more favorable field for the welfare and the moral training of the Indians, and the mission was moved to that pleasant valley in 1771. It was there he taught the natives the arts of peace, the virtue of christian charity, and the loving greeting to stranger and friend of Amár á Diós,—love God—which became a kindly salutation used by the Spaniards of California. His co-worker, Padre Palou, on returning from dinner one day to Serra's humble cell, found him lying peacefully with closed eyes, stretched on the rough boards which served as his couch, in the quiet sleep of eternity, and beneath him the half of a blanket. The other half he had given away.

Portola established at Monterey the second presidio, and proclaimed Monterey the capital of Upper California. After the establishment of the Carmel Mission, Serra set forth to found the third mission. He traveled south from Monterey along the Salinas River some seventy-five miles and reached a beautiful valley with wide-spreading oak trees and well-watered fruitful soil, and there on July 14, 1771, established the Mission San Antonio de Padua, now off the beaten path and much neglected, except for the work of preservation done by the Native Sons several years ago, but in the past one of the most famous of all the missions and renowned for the great number of Indian converts and the wonderful horses, cattle and sheep bred there.

This led up to the founding of the fourth mission, further south, and later to the establishment of the first settlement at what is now Los Angeles. The mission was to be called San Gabriel Arcangel. Two Franciscan fathers, Somera and Cambon, with a number of soldiers, left San Diego and marched northward until they came to a wide valley extending eastward to the Sierra Madre Mountains and with a splendid stream flowing through it. On September 8, 1771, a site was selected, a cross erected, and the Mission San Gabriel established. It was the first mission in what is now the County of Los Angeles, and grew so rapidly and became so prosperous that it was referred to as "The Queen of the Missions." Thousands of sheep, cattle and horses fed in the fertile valley, and vineyards and orchards covered the plains and hillsides. The little town of San Gabriel is one of the most interesting and, after San Diego, the oldest town in southern California.

It was from San Gabriel Mission that Felipe de Neve, Spanish Governor of California, with soldiers, missionary fathers and Indians, started forth and, proceeding some ten miles toward the sea, made the first permanent settlement which has become the City of Los Angeles. Governor de Neve started from the Spanish capital, Monterey, marched to San Gabriel, and from the mission to a point near the Los Angeles River, then known by the name "Porciuncula," where the ceremonies of founding a Spanish pueblo, or town, were conducted. A cross was raised, muskets were discharged by the soldiers, choruses were sung and ground was broken. The original name given to the pueblo was "Pueblo El Rio de Nuestra Senora La Reina de Los Angeles de Porciuncula," (The Town of the River of Our Lady, Queen of the Angels of Porciuncula). The shortened name Los Angeles literally means "The Angels." The date of the order of Governor de Neve for the foundation was September 7, 1781. The famous old Plaza church was built a few years later, but was not one of California's twenty-one missions.

In rapid succession, Serra founded the Missions San Antonio de Padua, July 14, 1771; San Gabriel, September 8, 1771; San Luis Obispo, September 1, 1772; San Francisco de Asis, October 9, 1776; San Juan Capistrano, November 1, 1776; Santa Clara, January 18, 1777, and San Buenaventura, March 31, 1782. This zealous and saintly leader of men and founder of California died at Carmel, August 28, 1784; and near the spot where he landed on the beach at historic Monterey, Mrs. Leland Stanford has reared to his memory a beautiful monument bearing the inscription: "In Memory of Father Junipero Serra, a Philanthropist seeking the welfare of the Humblest, a Hero daring and ready to sacrifice himself for the Good of his Fellow Beings, a Faithful Servant of his Master."

The work of founding the other twelve missions, Santa Barbara, in 1786, La Purisima Concepcion, La Soledad, Santa Cruz, San Jose (Alameda County), San Juan Bautista, San Fernando, San Luis Rey, Santa Ynez, San Rafael, and the last at Sonoma, August 25, 1823, was carried on by his followers. Serra and his brother friars had devoted some fifty years to building missions and spreading religion and civilization along the coast. Nearly all were located along the coast line, a day's journey on horseback apart, and connected by a road called El Camino Real,—The King's Highway—stretching some five hundred miles from San Diego to Mission Dolores, at San Francisco.

There were no hotels in those days in California. Every home was open to the traveler, and the master of the hacienda would meet the stranger at the threshold and bowing low say: "Enter, senor, the home is yours." Money was given to the guest on his departure, and a fresh horse to carry him on his way. It is said that Father Serra and his followers scattered mustard seed along the highway, for thus they had a trail ever bordered by yellow blossoms, shoulder high, and so the traveler might readily find his way.

For the protection of the missions and the settlers, the Spaniards established four presidios in California, at San Diego, Monterey, San Francisco and Santa Barbara.

The Spanish friars selected the most beautiful spots in California upon which to plant their settlements. The matchless beauty of San Diego, of San Gabriel, of Santa Barbara, of Monterey, of the Santa Clara Valley and of Sonoma appeals to all who visit them. Hills and mountains and sea lend a romantic charm to the landscape. The architectural beauty of the missions is today reflected in many of our schools and rural homes.

The mission at San Francisco, established in 1776, was the sixth mission founded in California, and located beside a small stream, fed by a spring, on the eastern slope of "Los Pechos de la Choca," now known as "Twin Peaks." This stream flowed down about the line of Eighteenth street and emptied into a lagoon called "La Laguna de los Dolores," and the Mission San Francisco de Asis came to be called the "Mission Dolores."

In that day there was no San Francisco, and the Spanish presidio was several miles north of the mission. At first there were only mission and presidio. Then grew up the village of Yerba Buena at the cove, which came up to Montgomery street, some three miles from the mission. Today a great American city stretches from mission to presidio. The quaint old mission, with its quiet churchyard, is at Sixteenth and Dolores, a beautiful and interesting reminder of the old Spanish days; but the lagoon, or lake, from which the mission derived its name has disappeared.

For three-quarters of a century local history centered around the old mission, and then came the mad rush for gold, in the days of '49, and quiet Yerba Buena became restless San Francisco. But historic memories still cling to the mission. There, in 1791, the beautiful Concepcion Arguello, immortalized in verse by Bret Harte, was christened. On the headstones in the mission cemetery may still be read the names of many who assisted in making local history, including Don Luis Antonio Arguello, Concepcion's brother, the first governor of California under Mexican rule. Mission Dolores is still a beautiful and a holy shrine, within whose walls and churchyard the traveler may breathe again the quiet air of that peaceful and romantic time "before the Gringo came."

The friars, with civilizing influence, gathered around them the Indians, and instructed them in the arts of trade and peace. In a few years fields of golden grain covered the lowlands, and the purpled hillsides smiled with the vine, the olive and the fig tree. Thousands of sheep and cattle grazed in the meadows and some thirty thousand hitherto untutored savages tended the herds and flocks, worked at the anvil and carpenter's bench, ploughed the fields, raised their voices in festival songs, or knelt humbly in prayer to the Great Father of All. From sav-

A FORTIFIED ADOBE

(RALPH LeROY MILLIKEN.)

WHEN THE ABORIGINES WHOM we call Indians first began roaming over the Pacific Coast they naturally selected as their places of abode the most desirable locations in the whole country. A sheltered spot beside a never-failing spring, like that on the San Luis Gonzaga Rancho, surrounded by timber and in a region abounding in game, was without doubt occupied as a rancheria by the Indians from the very earliest times.

Lieutenant Moraga when making an expedition from Mission San Juan Bautista in 1806 to the Tulare Plains traveled through what is now known as the Pacheco Pass. September 22 he camped over night at this Indian rancheria. It had already been discovered by some still-earlier Mexican expedition and named the San Luis Gonzaga.

It is at this spring that there still stands an old adobe house. It is so old that its origin is unknown. Who built the house, nor when, nobody knows. Old Mexicans whose knowledge of the country dates back to the stories their fathers told them remember hearing that in 1836 the adobe was already an old house.

The distinctive feature of this old adobe is the port holes in the walls. They are on all sides of the building and are just large enough to poke the muzzle of a musket through. It is very plain that this old building, with its walls two feet thick, was a fortress as well as a dwelling. The building is all in one room, and is sixteen feet wide inside and forty-two feet long. It sets north and south across the Pass. The chimney is on the south end. There are three windows on the west side, and one on the north. On the east side are two doors and two windows. The port holes are on each side of the windows and are five feet above the floor, which is of dirt. The foundations of the building are pieces of sandstone rock. The spring that attracted the attention of the Indians and later caused the Mexicans to select this spot for the location of their guardian of the Pass is only a few feet north of the old building.

The Pacheco Pass has been an avenue of travel since the beginning of history in California. The Mexican explorers in their efforts to reach the vast unexplored regions of the present San Joaquin Valley soon found their way over the mountains by way of this Pass. The Tulare Indians, in turn, when once they had learned that there were newcomers on the west side of the mountains with large bands of horses, were just as anxious to visit the mission settlements. They missed no opportunities in making raids to drive off as many horses as possible, not for the use that Mexicans made of horses but for the purpose of holding great feasts of horse flesh on the Tulare Plains.

It was to hold back these roving Tulare Indians and prevent their making inroads on the mission stock that the Mexican governors made grants of large tracts of land to Don Francesco Pacheco and other outstanding persons on condition that their ranches should take the brunt of these raids and that they should hold back the Tulares from the mission settlements. There

HISTORIC MERCED COUNTY ADOBE.

is no doubt but that this old adobe with its port holes in the sides of the building was built with that very purpose in view.

Today the Indians are gone. What once was the farthest outpost of Mexican civilization is now only an empty building on the highway leading from the coast region over into the great San Joaquin Valley. A never-ending stream of travel flows past the door night and day.

The first road over the Pacheco Pass was begun in 1855 by a ruddy-complected young man from Virginia by the name of Andrew D. Firebaugh. His forefathers were Pennsylvania Dutch, and his name was originally Fierbaugh. At the outbreak of the Mexican War he was down in Texas and promptly enlisted in the First Texas Mounted Riflemen. Later he came to California, and when the Mariposa Battalion was organized he was right on hand and helped to discover the Yosemite Valley. In 1854 he established a ferry and trading post on the San Joaquin River that is still known by his name, Firebaugh.

In the early fifties some cattlemen by the name of Murphy Brothers, who lived in San Jose, used to have great difficulty in driving their stock across the mountains to the summer pasture around Tulare Lake. They urged Firebaugh to build a toll road over the Pacheco Pass. Firebaugh went at the task with his usual vigor, but the undertaking was more difficult than he anticipated and it was not until 1857 that he succeeded in finishing the road. In many places the old original road is still plainly visible. It followed for the most part the bed of the streams. Over the summit, it followed the top of the ridge. The ruins of the toll house itself are still to be seen in the bed of the creek about two miles west of the summit.

Hardly had Firebaugh got his road finished when the Butterfield Overland Stage Company began, in 1858, running its stages from San Francisco to St. Louis, Missouri. They used Firebaugh's toll road in getting over the Pacheco Pass. The San Luis Gonzaga Rancho became one of the stage stations and here the passengers, after leaving San Francisco before daylight, arrived the same day in time for their supper. In 1860 the telegraph line between Los Angeles and San Francisco was built and passed within a stone's throw of the old adobe.

The overland stages ran only a little over a year through the Pacheco Pass and then were routed by way of Placerville. But the old adobe at the San Luis Gonzaga Rancho was not to be deserted by travelers, for in 1863 Henry Miller began buying up the Santa Rita Grant on the San Joaquin River and from that time on for twenty-five years his bands of cattle, sheep and hogs for the San Francisco market were driven in ever-increasing numbers over the Pass on their way to Butchertown.

In 1878 the toll road was abandoned and a new road built by the counties of Santa Clara and Merced. This was called the "New Grade," and was considered a marvelous road in its day. But the unforseen is always happening on the Pacheco Pass. With the coming of the automobile, the once-famous "New Grade" was soon intolerable and in 1923 the state built the present highway over the Pass.

The old adobe that has stood for a hundred years and has seen all these marks of progress is in itself falling into ruin. Those in charge of the old building are apparently indifferent to its fate. The roof leaks, the windows are gone, and the walls are beginning to crumble in places. The newly-organized Parlor of Native Sons at Los Banos [Los Banos No. 206] took notice of the building's dire needs to the extent of patching up a gap in the chimney. In doing so the workmen tore off part of one of the door casings to make a form for the concrete! A few years ago the Merced Parlor of Native Sons [Yosemite No. 24] discovered that this was the oldest building in Merced County and erected an elaborate plaque beside the south wall.

The future will blame us if we let the present fall into ruins. This old landmark could be preserved for another hundred years. It needs repairs to the roof. An adobe melts very rapidly when once the roof is left to decay. The walls should be plastered. The foundations should be supported in places with cement. It needs new windows and doors. With a little help this fortified old dwelling could again look forth defiantly on those who travel the Pass, whether they come on horseback as of old, in automobiles as at present, or look down from airships floating overhead in the future.

---

ages they were changed into gentle and kindly men and women. When Serra passed on, he left behind picturesque buildings to take the place of huts of mud and reeds; he left gardens and orchards, vineyards, grain fields, flocks and herds, and civilization to replace barbarism. He left behind a new California and a new spirit in the hearts of men. Our poet, George Sterling, has said of him:

"O spirit pure,
Who in an age of infamy and gold
Saw souls alone."

The glory of the missions lasted some sixty-three years; when Mexico revolted from Spain, many of the missions remaining loyal to the old country, the government began their secularization and, appropriating their lands, the Indians and friars scattered, and the mission languished. The Native Sons Landmarks Committee and other historical societies of late have done much to restore their beauty. The Spanish names given to the missions commemorate illustrious saints, and, soft and musical, appeal to the ear. As Dr. Charles Gayley, in one of his poems, has said:

"To name them is to pray;
For their names fulfill the chorus
Of a thousand saints that o'er us
Swing their censers night and day."

There is a legend referred to in the writings of Bret Harte which foretold the passing of the flags of Spain and Mexico and the coming of a new race bearing the "Stars and Stripes." The story runs that before the Gringo came, a Spanish priest left the mission and bent his steps toward a neighboring mountain, since known as Mt. Diablo. From its commanding summit, he could view for miles the surrounding hills and valleys and with the zeal which characterized these humble friars, seek, perhaps, a favorable spot where a new mission, a shrine or a cross might be planted to lead the savage to christianity and civilization. Having reached the top, he turned and gazed over mountain, plain and valley and to the ocean beyond, but in a few minutes was surprised to see, seated on a rock near him, an elderly hidalgo, dressed in the garb of a century before and wearing a plumed hat, and whom he surmised to be his satanic majesty.

The hidalgo sought to convince the holy man that all his work for the redemption of these lands would come to naught, and the missions fall to ruin, but the zealous soul would not believe this and saw a future, in imagination, more glorious than the past. The hidalgo said, "Look then to the west," and waved his plumed hat toward the ocean. The fog was seen to melt from canyon, hill and forest, and the landscape, beautiful and green, opened clear to the ocean. The padre gazed, and he beheld defiling from ravine and canyon long cavalcades of horsemen and cavaliers, with the royal banners of Spain glistening in the sunlight above them. They were all marching to the sea, where stately vessels awaited to bear them from the shore. "Behold," said the hidalgo, "the departing footsteps of gallant knight and priest from Aragon and Castile. Behold the fading glory of Spain. This land shall be lost to her forever." The venerable priest raised his hand in benediction and exclaimed, "Farewell, ye gallant cavaliers and Christian gentlemen. Farewell, Nunez de Balboa, Cabrillo and ye saintly missionaries of God."

"Now turn to the east," the hidalgo said. The father looked far to the distant snow-capped Sierra and, through the passes and down the mountain sides, beheld advancing a myriad host of strange, fair-haired and stalwart men and women, and at their head floated a banner, new to him, flashing in the golden sunlight, with brilliant stripes of red and white and in a field of blue the stars of heaven. "Behold," said the hidalgo, "the future rulers of this fair land. The flag which shall be known o'er land and sea throughout the West."

And even as this legend foretold, so has it come to pass. The Pioneers came and they founded here a great American state, and they gave to it the beautiful Spanish name "California," and they preserved and cherished the traditions of Spanish cavalier and missionary padre, and retained the soft Castilian names of Santa Barbara, Los Angeles, Santa Maria, Santa Ynez, San Gabriel, Santa Rosa and San Francisco, all closely associated with what we now call home and country.

CALIFORNIA HAPPENINGS OF FIFTY YEARS AGO

Thomas R. Jones

(COMPILED EXPRESSLY FOR THE GRIZZLY BEAR.)

NEW YEAR DAY, MONDAY, JANUARY 1, 1883, dawned with California covered by a mantle of snow. A snowstorm lasting several hours prevailed New Year Eve and deposited from three to six inches of "the beautiful" over the state. San Francisco had a snowfall of five inches, and sleighs with tinkling bells appeared on Market street. Eighteen eighty-two went out with tooting horns, exploding firecrackers and a bombardment of snowflakes. In the valley towns, for the first time within a decade, citizens enjoyed the pastime of snowballing. Weather savants searched the records of the past for similar seasons, but could find none.

While New Year Day was one of frequent showers, prominent dames throughout the state continued the time-honored custom of keeping "open house," and felicitous greetings were exchanged.

January 1, a shower of mud covered Fresno City and adjacent farms with a coating of gray sandy material. At Bakersfield, Kern County, there was a dense sandstorm, said to be the worst ever experienced there; the drifts so obstructed the railroad line trains ceased operating. At Los Angeles City, .60 of an inch of rain fell.

A norther prevailed January 5 throughout California North and did much damage to shipping in San Francisco Bay. It also blew down the seventy-foot-high "spite" fence of Charles Crocker, on Nob Hill, San Francisco, to the great delight of other residents of that district.

The rainfall for the month was 2.82 inches, bringing the season's total to 10.47 inches. There were seventeen frosty nights, and in the valleys the thermometers went down to 22 degrees.

The stock market was still in a torpid state, and the extremely low selling prices of mining stocks indicated the public's opinion of their worth.

January 10, General George A. Stoneman was inaugurated Governor of California, and the Democrats replaced the Republicans in control of the state government. The Senate, with thirty-one Democrats and nine Republicans, organized by electing Senator R. F. DelValle of Los Angeles president-protem. The Assembly, with sixty Democrats and nineteen Republicans, elected Assemblyman H. M. LaRue of Sacramento speaker. The Senate, being in an economical frame of mind, did not select a chaplain, so no prayers were uttered in its behalf.

The quadrennial inauguration ball, sponsored by the citizens of Sacramento, was held in the State Capitol January 16. Mayor John Q. Brown was chairman of the arrangements committee. Governor Stoneman and Mrs. George C. Perkins led the grand march, in which several hundred citizens from all parts of the state joined. Supper was served, and champagne flowed freely.

Statistics showed it had cost $5,384,891 to run the state government during 1882. That the assessed value of property in the state was: real estate, $318,860,810; improvements, $115,218,911; personal property, $140,180,978; railroad property, $31,820,680; money, $19,597,500; total valuation of all taxable property, $658,601,059. The rate of state taxation was 62½ cents on the $100 of valuation.

During 1882 the United States Mint at San Francisco turned out 9,250,000 silver dollars, 1,170,000 five-dollar gold pieces, 2,880,000 ten-dollar gold pieces and 24,175,000 twenty-dollar gold pieces, all minted from Pacific Coast precious metals.

Internal revenue collections by the Federal Government in California during 1882 from liquors and tobaccos totaled $3,891,757.

From July 1, 1882, to January 1, 1883, one hundred seventy-three vessels ladened with California-grown grain cleared through the Golden Gate for foreign countries.

M. P. Kay, deputy clerk of Alameda County, was this month found to be a defaulter. Over $20,000 was missing, and his many political friends were greatly shocked.

A south-bound Southern Pacific passenger train stopped January 25 at Tehachapi, Kern County, and the engine was cut off to take on a coal supply. Robbers, it was claimed, attempted to drop the train down the grade a short distance. Out of control, the cars rushed down the track several miles until finally ditched. Fire resulted, and several sleepers were burned. Twenty-one passengers were killed outright, among them Mrs. Downey, the wife of ex-Governor J. G. Downey, who was burned to death. Five of the killed were never identified.

A large tin ledge was this month uncovered in San Diego County.

In Fine Gold Gulch, Fresno County, a seam of decomposed quartz was found which, for over sixty feet, paid $200 a foot in gold.

A quartz ledge was discovered near Windwhistle, Sonoma County, which assayed $600 a ton in silver.

A four-foot-wide copper vein, portions of it nearly pure metal, was discovered near Garden Valley, El Dorado County.

Nichols & Reem, mining near Grass Valley, Nevada County, discovered a pocket that, the first day, yielded $670 in gold nuggets.

Alameda County was reported to be feeding its county jail prisoners at a cost of five cents a meal.

Fire January 23 destroyed twenty-five buildings in the Chinatown of Truckee, Nevada County. The thermometer being five degrees below zero, icicles were more plentiful than the water supply. The loss was $30,000. The same day, four business houses at Hanford, Kings County, burned, with a heavy loss.

The main conservatory building of San Francisco's Golden Gate Park was destroyed by fire January 5.

Seven saloons and five business houses in Tehama City burned January 15, with a $20,000 loss. Susanville, Lassen County, had a disastrous fire January 20. A loss of $20,000 resulted from the burning of several business houses in Biggs, Butte County, January 23.

Simon Sweet & Co., wholesale produce merchants in San Francisco since the '50s, went into bankruptcy this month on account of having been systematically robbed of over $100,000 by a trusted bookkeeper.

Sixty-one persons arrived from Denver, Colorado, by railroad train January 18, to settle in San Diego County.

Smallpox broke out in the Red Bluff jail. The news becoming known, not a single "wearie willie" could be found rendezvousing in Tehama County.

Fresno City was illuminated by gas for the first night January 23, and the event was duly celebrated.

John LaPorte, who arrived in Monterey City in 1849, died there January 7.

Major Henry Hancock, who came to California South in 1847, died at San Monica, Los Angeles County, January 9.

H. P. Osborne, one of the organizers and first presidents of the Sacramento Association of California Pioneers, membership in which was limited to those arriving in the state prior to January 1, 1850, died at the Capital City January 9.

Mrs. Selma Wilder, claimed to be the first White child born in Grass Valley, Nevada County, died January 14. Her maiden name was Selma Rice.

Judge R. C. Clark, who came from Kentucky in 1853, died at Sacramento City January 27, aged 68. From 1861 to the day of his death he was a judge of Sacramento County.

Henry L. Langley, whose name was a household one in San Francisco, he being from the '50s publisher of that city's directory, died there January 29.

"Lucky" Baldwin was again a press headliner, on account of another of his amours. January 4 Miss Fanny Baldwin—said to be his cousin and to have been employed as schoolteacher at his Santa Anita rancho in Los Angeles County—after a discussion with him in the lobby of the Baldwin hotel in San Francisco, drew a gun and fired, the bullet wounding him in the arm. Miss Fanny claimed "Lucky" had reneged.

An explosion of nitro-glycerine January 18 at the acid works near San Pablo, Contra Costa County, blew three employes to pieces.

A cave-in January 18 at the McCullum mine near Nevada City suffocated Bradford Woodward. A similar accident at the Indian Spring mine near Magalia, Butte County, January 10 crushed to death Ed. Perkins and John Ferrin.

John E. Dever and Charles Schaffer of Vallejo, Solano County, went duck hunting January 3. They were found dead in their boat the next morning, having frozen to death during the night.

An explosion January 21 at a giant-powder works near Berkeley, Alameda County, resulted in Foreman Kompff and twenty-nine Chinamen being blown to pieces.

Four Chinamen attempted to rob the sluices of the Malakoff mine near North Bloomfield, Nevada County, the night of January 26. The watchman fired, and killed one.

J. L. Smith, who killed his son at Santa Ana, Orange County, in obedience, so he claimed, to the Lord's command, was convicted of murder and sentenced to life imprisonment. Enroute January 6 to San Quentin, he jumped from the moving train near Caliente, Kern County, had a leg cut off, and died a few days later.

GRIZZLY GROWLS

(Continued from Page 3)

Voicing opposition to the proposal for the Federal Government to grant an immigration quota to Japan and other Asiatic nations, V. S. McClatchy, executive secretary of the California Joint Immigration Committee, addressing the San Francisco Commonwealth Club said: "Such a quota would repeal the only logical, non-discriminatory barrier we have against the possibility of a future invasion of unassimilable Asiatics."

He reminded his hearers that Japan would not be satisfied with being granted only a limited quota, but would demand one equal to that of leading European nations. "Concede the Japanese the right to enter on the same basis as the Europeans and they would in time demand a number of immigrants equal to that permitted any other first-class power. We would have no logical ground for refusal."

That there is no great scarcity of dollars in this country, but a growing feeling of distrust, is evidenced by the record of the postal savings system, "in a year of unparalleled financial disturbance." For the fiscal year ended June 30, 1932, the deposits totaled $784,820,623,—more than double the amount on deposit with the Federal Government at the end of the previous fiscal year—and the number of depositors increased one hundred percent, to 1,545,190. By the end of November 1932, the deposits had mounted to $881,054,718. Pretty good argument for government-guaranteed bank deposits!

Because some ten percent of the 17,000 officials and employes of California failed to cooperate in the voluntary salary-reduction plan to balance the budget, the state has abandoned that plan. The modest-salaried employes "came through" all right, but the high-salaried babies refused to co-operate.

Reliable information received by The Grizzly Bear says the judges of the state,—supreme, appellate and superior—excepting those of the superior court in San Francisco, refused to contribute, anticipating the State Legislature will reduce their salaries. The lawmaking body should not disappoint the judges, and should also prune the salaries of numerous other overpaid officials and employes.

Every property owner knows that realty in California is taxed to a near-confiscation degree, and something must be done to lessen the burden. A just procedure, with that in view, would be for the State Legislature to proceed to repeal the damphool legislation excluding certain properties, including churches, from taxation.

In Los Angeles County alone the non-taxable property has an assessed valuation of $80,842,620. Every parcel of property and every individual should bear its and his fair share of the tax-burden. In flush times the voters, unthinkingly, committed many errors. Now is the opportune time to wipe out the tax-exemption and numerous other legalized evils.

California's Governor, so press dispatches say, will again, for 1933, assign the "R" series of automobile license plates to a select list of his friends. Efficient and honest government plays no favorites! The State Legislature should deal a death-blow to the Governor's "R"-oyal family.

Auto License Time—The 1933 auto license renewal period is shorter than in former years. It opens January 3 and ends at midnight of January 31.

Bumper Crop—The San Fernando Valley section of Los Angeles County is this season harvesting the largest lettuce crop in its history.

"Duty—Duty should never be considered an unpleasant task, but a privilege to be enjoyed." —Jeanette Nourland.

"Ever learning, and never able to come to the knowledge of the truth."—Bible.

OMPTON PARLOR NO. 273 OF THE Order of Native Sons of the Golden West, organized under the supervision of Deputy Grand President Clinton E. Skinner, was formally instituted December 8 with a charter membership hirty-one. The institution ceremonies were lucted by the following, representing Sepul- No. 263 (San Pedro), Santa Monica Bay 267, Glendale No. 264 and Ramona No. 109 Angeles) Parlors, as acting grand officers: h I. Harbison, junior past grand; District uty Edward E. Baldwin, grand president; ick Doran, grand first vice; Walter D. Rich- , grand second vice; Dr. L. W. Clarke, grand d vice; Grand Outside Sentinel William A. ter, grand marshal; George Fontes, grand de sentinel; Arthur R. Leonard, grand out- sentinel; Clinton E. Skinner, grand secre- ; Fred Staebler, grand organist.

fficers of Compton Parlor were then installed Ralph I. Harbison as follows: Dr. "Larry" Cowan, president; Donn R. Crockett, charter or past president; Ray W. Hecock, first vice- ident; Clarence R. Hann, second vice-presi- t; Dr. Morgan S. Ralls, third vice-president; liam Don Castillo, recording secretary; Ern- Spurlock, financial secretary; Roy Lee Otis ms, treasurer; Raymond C. "Tay" Brown, shal; Hector Hecock, inside sentinel; Frank Hawkins, outside sentinel; Alfred R. Brown, er L. Knight, Loyal F. Simmons, trustees.

Parlor plans the initiation of several addi- al candidates during January. It meets the ond and fourth Tuesdays at Mayo Hall, 231½ t Compton boulevard, in the City of Compton.

AST PRESIDENTS DIRECT ACTIVITIES.

ong Beach—The December activities of Long ch Parlor No. 154 N.D.G.W. were in charge the past presidents. The 1st, a mock-turkey ner was enjoyed. Grain troughs were the ors, and huge paper turkeys graced the table. nior Past President Daisy Hansen was the irman. Deputy Nellie Cline spoke on the der, Past President Violet T. Henshilwood re an interesting reading of early transporta- n in Long Beach, and Miss Eliza Houghton re a vivid account of her experiences in South rican jungles.

The 15th, the members were served a real- key dinner and were entertained with a play- . The following past presidents were respon- le for the success of the occasion: Mms. ra Fay (chairman), Daisy Hansen, Violet nshilwood, Lillian Lassiter, Fannie McPher- , Kate McFadyen, Lottie Wharton, Bertha t, Rosa Faust, Lucretia Coats and Carrie Northway (Ruderinda Parlor No. 230); E. Mabel Emery, Ellen Rogers and Rose Ford. Mrs. Flora Elder, for twelve years financial secretary, was presented with an emblematic pin. Under the direction of Mrs. Lucretia Coats, the thimble club recently completed a very pretty quilt. Officers of the Parlor will be publicly installed by Deputy Nellie Cline January 5. All Natives are invited.

THIRTY-EIGHT INITIATED.

The supper and initiation held December 3 in honor of Grand President Seth Millington of the Native Sons attracted a goodly number and proved a very enjoyable occasion. Several Native Daughters, among them Founder Lily O. R. Dyer, Past Grand President Grace S. Stoermer and Grand Outside Sentinel Hazel B. Hansen, were in attendance at the dinner.

At the ritual ceremonies, thirty-eight candidates were initiated—twenty-six for Compton Parlor No. 273, five for Santa Monica Bay Parlor No. 267, three for Ramona Parlor No. 109, and two each for Los Angeles Parlor No. 45 and Hollywood Parlor No. 196. Bernard Hiss was chairman of the evening. Among the speakers following initiation were Past Grand Presidents Herman C. Lichtenberger, William I. Traeger and John T. Newell, Grand Trustee Eldred L. Meyer, Grand Outside Sentinel William A. Reuter, Earl LeMoine, Sheriff Eugene W. Biscailuz and Grand President Millington. Every southland Parlor from San Diego to Santa Barbara was represented.

DINNER AND BRIDGE PARTY.

Santa Monica—Santa Monica Bay Parlor No. 245 N.D.G.W. elected officers December 14, Amada Machado being chosen president. Public installation ceremonies will be held January 11, with Deputy Lucretia Coats officiating. A shower of canned goods for the day nursery was held, and it was voted to continue furnishing a needy family with two quarts of milk daily. Myrtle Barden was hostess for the evening.

The Parlor's ways and means committee announces a dinner and bridge party for January 28; tickets 35 cents. A large delegation of members were guests December 10 of Dr. and Mrs. George Sabichi and Harold Barden at the Whittier State School. Following luncheon the boys provided entertainment.

CHILDREN GUESTS.

The Christmas party sponsored by Los Angeles Parlor No. 45 N.S.G.W. December 22 was a great success. Many less-fortunate children were guests. From a beautiful Christmas tree they were given gifts and candy, and bountiful refreshments were served. The grownups, also, were well entertained. President Owen S. Adams was the Santa Claus, and Sidney B. Witkowski headed the arrangements committee.

Past Grand President John T. Newell has resigned as treasurer of the Parlor and been succeeded by Frank Frank. Grand President Seth Millington paid a visit to the Parlor December 1 and there was a large crowd out to greet him.

OLDTIMERS NIGHT.

Hollywood Parlor No. 196 N.S.G.W. elected officers December 5 and for the third time Henry G. Bodkin was selected as president. He plans many activities for the Parlor, including a membership campaign. The officers-elect will be installed January 16, and refreshments will be served.

January 30 has been set aside by Hollywood as "oldtimers night," and members who were active in the distant past will preside as chair officers. All Native Sons are extended an invitation by President-elect Bodkin to be on hand.

STATE FLAG PRESENTED COUNCIL.

Glendale—Mrs. Vera Carlson will head the new corps of officers of Verdugo Parlor No. 240 N.D.G.W., being elected president December 13. A Christmas party was held December 20 for the children of the members of No. 240, those of Glendale Parlor No. 264 N.S.G.W. and the Scouts of Troop No. 3. Harvey Gillett showed three reels of movies, and short addresses were made by J. Marion Wright and H. E. Cleveland. Santa Claus distributed gifts and candy.

December 22 Verdugo, through President Betty Sanders, presented a California State

(Continued on Page 18)

Native Sons of the Golden West

VALLEJO—UNDER THE AUSPICES OF Vallejo No. 77, the cornerstone of the General Mariana Guadalupe Vallejo junior high school was laid by the grand officers December 11. Russell F. O'Hara, president Education Board, was chairman of the day, Rev. W. L. Gaston delivered an invocation, and Rev. Louie Naselli a benediction. Several selections were rendered by the junior high school band. Addresses were delivered by Grand President Seth Millington, Past Grand Joseph R. Knowland, William J. Tormey (Vallejo No. 77) and Past Grand Dr. Louise C. Heilbron of the Native Daughters.

Assisting Grand President Millington in the cornerstone laying ceremonies were Grand Second Vice-president Chas. A. Koenig, Grand Third Vice-president Harmon D. Skillin, Grand Secretary John T. Regan, Past Grands Joseph R. Knowland and Charles L. Dodge. Among the articles deposited in the cornerstone box by School Directors Mrs. Elon A. Mitchell and Samuel J. Knight Sr. were copies of Vallejo Parlor's bylaws, the Grand Parlor Constitution and The Grizzly Bear for December 1932.

Jurist Honored.

Weaverville—Mount Bally No. 87 was host to a large gathering of Natives and friends December 15, when Judge James W. Bartlett, a charter member and former grand trustee, was guest of honor. After thirty years of service to Trinity County as superior judge, Judge Bartlett is voluntarily retiring January 1.

President R. L. Marshall presided, and the speakers included Grand Trustee Horace J. Leavitt, Mrs. Elizabeth H. Gehm, Edwin J. Regan (South San Francisco No. 157), C. A. Paulsen and Judge Bartlett. Musical selections were rendered by Misses Ida Koop, Pauline Clark, Alaire Beckstrum and Vivian Bennett. Refreshments concluded the program, and then card playing was in order.

Historical Association's Annual Meet.

San Diego—Deputy Grand President Albert V. Mayrhofer of San Diego No. 108 was accorded the honor of presiding at the annual meeting of the California State Historical Association in Los Angeles, December 28. The meeting was held on the campus of the University of Southern California, and a feature was a tour of the magnificent Doheny Memorial Library, where speakers recounted recent activities in California history. Dr. Owen C. Coy, director of the association, made a report for 1932, and there was a conference pertaining to the various fields of activity for the promotion and the preservation of California history.

December 4, Grand President Seth Millington debated with Samuel Hume the question of "Quota for Japan" before the San Diego Open Forum. Some six hundred people displayed much interest in the subject. The rules of the Forum forbid applause until a speaker has concluded, but so frequently were the Grand President's remarks cheered the chairman of the evening found it necessary to call the assemblage to order.

District Athletics Urged.

San Francisco—The Grand Parlor Athletic Committee—Al. Sandell, Alva Werner, R. J. Garrett, Wesley Colgan and Arthur Cleu—has concluded that, owing to the uncertainty of conditions generally, it is not advisable to promote state-wide athletics competition on a large scale at present. The state was divided into nine sections, and the Subordinate Parlors in each have been requested to organize an athletics committee to conduct tournaments.

Answers to questionnaires revealed the fact that the following sports, in the order listed, are the most popular with Subordinate Parlors: basketball, baseball, indoor horseshoes, bowling, indoor baseball and golf. "By starting local activities this season," advises the Grand Parlor committee, "it will be easier to organize competition for state championships next year."

Gala Night.

Calistoga—December 5 was a gala night in the annals of Calistoga No. 86, the occasion being the official visit of Grand Third Vice-president Harmon D. Skillin. Among the large crowd were visitors from all sections of Lake, Sonoma and Napa Counties. President Angelo Molinari presided, and the ritual was impressively exemplified by the Parlor's splendid ritual team.

Grand Third Vice Skillin discoursed on "Friendship," and Grand Second Vice Chas. A. Koenig spoke on "Immigration Restriction of Asiatics." Grand Trustee Joseph J. McShane created a lot of fun by his remarks, and Grand Trustee Charles H. Spengemann said "if all Parlors had the spirit of Calistoga it would be well with the Order." C. E. Butler of No. 86 told what the Order means to him, and there were many other speakers. Bounteous refreshments concluded the festivities.

Annual Masquerade Great Success.

Antioch—The forty-eighth annual masquerade of General Winn No. 32 was a most colorful affair and largely attended. There were many very clever costumes, and prizes were awarded the following: Miss Elnora Elliott and B. R. Garrow, best dressed, representing, respectfully, an old-fashioned girl and a spanish don; Miss Aileen Peters and Harry Hobbs, most original; Mrs. W. A. Christiansen and Frank Baer, best sustained characters. The grand march, directed by Charles Hornback and F. J. Biglow, was led by Mr. and Mrs. B. R. Garrow.

Public Whist Draws.

Salinas—An unusually large crowd attended the public whist party of Santa Lucia No. 97. Following cards, an hour was given to dancing, and refreshments were served. As a special feature Mrs. Frances Leidig rendered several vocal selections. The party was held under th supervision of E. Dougherty, Everall Adcock John Souza and George McDougall.

Benefit for Homeless Children.

Ferndale—Ferndale No. 93 and Oneonta No 71 N.D.G.W. had an entertainment and danc December 2 for the benefit of the homeless chil dren, and it was an enjoyable affair and ver successful. N. J. Lund gave a short talk, and comic skit was presented by the high schoo students, directed by E. J. Clabby. Musica numbers were rendered by R. A. Grinsell, Mme Grace Rusk and Bernice Mills, Misses Mari Goff, Gertrude Hartley and Leona Simms, an Hazel Christensen and Hazel Hogan appeare in dance numbers.

Noted Peace Officer Passes.

San Rafael—Mount Tamalpais No. 64 electe officers for the January-July term December 5 Arthur B. Hecht being chosen as president. Ex tensive arrangements for installation are bein made by a committee.

Hugh I. McCurdy, a member of the Parlor died suddenly December 12, survived by a wif and two daughters. He was born at Bolinas Marin County, in 1877. He was one of the mos widely-known peace officers in California. Hi kindly and humane treatment of the down-and outers of the genus hobo was well known an favorably commented on throughout the Sa Francisco Bay region. He had secured a shel ter, jocularly known as "Stumble Bums' Roost," on the outskirts of San Rafael, where wanderer are cared for and provided with work wherewit to earn enough to eke out a scanty living unti such time as they are ready to move on. As result of this policy, the wandering guests o San Rafael seldom cause any annoyance. It ha been said that word is passed that weary willie sojourning in San Rafael must behave, or tak the consequences from their own companions.

Grand President Visitor.

San Bernardino—Arrowhead No. 110 had a its guest of honor November 30 Grand Presiden Seth Millington, who spoke on the Order's ac complishments and future plans. Many othe visitors were in attendance, among them Gran Trustee Eldred L. Meyer, Deputy Grand Presi dent Walter Hiskey, District Deputy Ray Marsil and President Bernard Hiss of University No 272 (Los Angeles). The present officers of th Parlor, headed by President F. L. McGarvey were re-elected for another term.

December 1, Grand President Millington ad dressed the San Bernardino Lions Club, bein introduced by Ben Harrison. Arrowhead i making great preparations for a winter week end party at its Crestline clubhouse in San Ber nardino Mountains, January 28. All Native Son are extended an invitation to join in the festiv ities.

Membership Standing Largest Parlors.

San Francisco—Grand Secretary John T. Re gan reports the standing of the Subordinate Par lors having a membership of over 400 Januar 1, 1932, as follows, together with their member ship figures December 20, 1932:

Parlor	Jan. 1	Dec. 20	Gain	Lo
Ramona No. 109	1088	1041	....	4
South San Francisco No. 157	822	807	....	1
Castro No. 232	700	784	84	..
Stanford No. 76	614	598	....	1
Arrowhead No. 110	609	579	....	3
Stockton No. 7	549	563	14	..
Twin Peaks No. 214	585	526	....	5
Piedmont No. 120	523	526	3	..
Rincon No. 72	448	430	....	1

Christmas Party.

Modesto—Modesto No. 11 elected officers De cember 21, Charles D. Blaine being retained a president for another term. December 14 th Parlor, with Morada No. 199 N.D.G.W., spon sored a card party for the benefit of the home less children. Robert Benson and Mrs. Ethe Enos were in charge. The Parlors also joine forces for a Christmas party.

Interparlor Gatherings.

Sebastopol—Representatives of Sonoma, Ma rin and Napa Counties Parlors, meeting here arranged to hold monthly interparlor gather ings. The January meeting will be held i Napa, the February meeting in Sausalito an the March meeting in Santa Rosa. District Dep

(Continued on Page 17)

"MARK OUR LANDMARKS"

Chester F. Gannon

(HISTORIOGRAPHER N.S.G.W.)

"MARK OUR LANDMARKS"

THE HOLIDAYS OF FREMONT

BOOM! BOOM! BOOM! THE DISCHARGE of a lone howitzer reverberates on the bank of an unnamed lake. Fremont and his small band are encamped to celebrate the Christmas Day of 1843. Their location is an uncertain place in northern Nevada or eastern Oregon.

Fremont, with his chief lieutenant, Kit Carson, is pressing south from the Columbia River into Nevada, looking for the Buenaventura River. Adown it they expect to float into the Bay of San Francisco. Like a mythical search of centuries ago, the Pathfinder and his redoubtable followers are questing the unfindable. They have yet to learn that between the Bay of San Francisco and the Great Basin of Nevada a lofty chain of mountains rears its pinnacles skyward and that no river can penetrate their vastness and loftiness.

Yet, the year is 1843. The rough maps of the day in possession of Fremont plainly show this river flowing from Nevada into the Bay of San Francisco. Carson is no more aware of the maps' errors than his chief. So, into barren Nevada the troop of thirty men search, and search in vain. They encounter hardships and suffering, but Fate still seals the supreme test that she has in store for them.

As Fremont rested on the 25th of December, 1843, he records the day and its significance in his faithfully written diary. Let him comment on the 25th of December in his own words:

"We were roused on Christmas morning, by a discharge from the small arms and howitzer, with which our people saluted the day; and the name of which we bestowed on the lake. It was the first time, perhaps, in this remote and desolate region, in which it had been so commemorated.

"Always, on days of religious or national commemoration, our voyageurs expect some unusual allowance; and, having nothing else, I gave to them each a little brandy (which was carefully guarded as one of the most useful articles a traveller can carry) with some coffee and sugar, which here, where every eatable was a luxury, was sufficient to make them a feast. The day was sunny and warm, and resuming our journey, we crossed some slight dividing grounds into a similar basin, walled in on the right by a lofty mountain ridge. The plainly beaten trail still continued, and occasionally we passed camping grounds of the Indians, which indicated to me that we were on one of the great thoroughfares of the country.

"In the afternoon I attempted to travel in a more eastern direction; but after a few laborious miles was beaten back into the basin by an impassable country. There were fresh Indian tracks about the Valley, and last night a horse was stolen. We encamped on the Valley bottom, where there was some cream-like water in pounds, colored by a clay soil and frozen over."

So southward after his lonely observance of our most popular holiday—spent two thousand miles from his bride of less than two years—he again charters his way and soon arrives at Pyramid Lake, Nevada. At this time he gave the lake its name. Then on southward again and a cheerless New Year Eve came with the passing days but still no view of the Buenaventura River. The arid, dry, rocky character of the mountain, the cold weather and limited food are taking their toll from Fremont and his men. Was it any wonder that on this night, in the loneliness of barren Nevada, his thoughts turned toward his compatriots miles away, celebrating the advent of the new year and the death of the old one in the normal way which civilized beings through the years have observed the departure and advent of time?

Surrounded by physical discomforts and the loneliness which must have been his, he made this entry in his never failing diary:

"After an hour's ride this morning our hopes were once more destroyed. The Valley opened out, and before us again lay one of the dry basins. After some search, we discovered a high water outlet, which brought us in a few miles, and by a descent of several hundred feet, into another long broad basin, in which we found the bed of a stream, and obtained sufficient water by cutting the ice. The grass on the bottoms was salt and unpalatable.

"Here we concluded the year 1843, and our new year's eve was rather a gloomy one. The result of our journey began to be very uncertain; the country was singularly unfavorable to travel; the grasses being frequently of a very unwholesome character, and the hoofs of our animals were so worn and cut by the rocks, that many of them were lame, and could scarcely be got along."

On the 18th of January, 1844, Fremont finally determined that his maps showing the Buenaventura River were incorrect, and wrote:

"And I determined to cross the Sierra Nevadas into the valley of the Sacramento whenever a practical pass could be found. My decision was heard with joy by the people, and diffused new life throughout the camp."

Had Fremont and his men known of the horrors ahead of them, they would have received the news of his decision with horror and foreboding. The date is the 18th of January, 1844. It is the middle of winter. The Sierras are snow-covered. In the year 1844 there was not even a summer trail across them. And now the trackless mountains are covered with many feet of snow, and into this snow trap plunged Fremont and his men. It might be asked why Carson did not advise against it. The truth is, that Carson was as unfamiliar with this section of the West as Fremont. Carson had only been to California once, fifteen years before, and had reached San Francisco and had gone back the southern route. Is it any wonder that they started on what today might be termed the impossible? And, once in, there was no turning back. Their hardships and suffering from cold, hunger and fatigue form a heroic chapter in pioneer history. They endured thirteen-below-zero weather, they ate their mules and had to finally consume their pet dog. Mule soup keeps their brave hearts beating.

Then, on March 7, they reach the Sacramento Valley and Sutter's Fort. I doubt if human beings ever went through forty-eight days of such suffering. Starving, frozen and exhausted, they were met by Captain Sutter, and Fremont ever faithfully records the meeting as follows:

"In a few miles were met a short distance from the fort by Captain Sutter himself. He gave us a most frank and cordial reception, conducted us immediately to his residence and under his hospitable roof we had a night of rest, enjoyment and refreshment which none but ourselves could appreciate."

Fremont, who was to play such an important part in the great drama of California, thus entered the territory his name was to be so closely associated with. Remember that California is at this time Mexican domain.

It was not until his third expedition that he wrote his history of accomplishment and forever determined that California should not be either Mexican or British, but part of the Union.

Without his presence near Sutter Fort it is possible that the Bear Flag Party would never

(Continued on Page 17)

Native Daughters of the Golden West

QUINOY—A MONUMENT NOW STANDS at the foot of the steepest pitch on the old emigrant road over which the mining man of the early '50s and his family traveled between Johnsville and Gibsonville—at the foot of grand old Eureka Peak. It is an old arastra stone—a perfectly round slab of granite from one of the earliest Jamison Creek quartz-crushing mills. Upon it is fastened a bronze plaque reading: "The Emigrant Trail, 1850. Marysville, Jamison City. Tablet set in stone from early day arastra used in Jamison Creek. Erected and dedicated by Plumas Pioneer Parlor No. 219 N.D.G.W. and Quincy Parlor No. 131 N.S.G.W."

President Lena Droege of Plumas Pioneer welcomed the crowd at the dedicatory ceremonies. Mrs. Violet Mori introduced the speakers, who included: Mrs. Verbenia Hall, "Tribute to the First Pioneers;" E. C. Kelsey, Plumas County treasurer, "Early Trails and Roads;" J. D. McLaughlin, "The Mining Industry;" M. C. Kerr, "Preservation of Early History."

West of Johnsville, at the Split Rock from which the arastra stones were cut, a second marker was dedicated. Mrs. Birdenia Swingle read a poem descriptive of early-day Johnsville, and Miss Sally Hardgrave told some of her early memories and referred to Messrs. Kerr, McLaughlin and Kelsey as "mere boys who didn't know what it was all about."

AIMS AND OBJECTS
of the
ORDER OF NATIVE DAUGHTERS
OF THE GOLDEN WEST

To cultivate state pride.

To aid state development.

To advance state progress.

To promote the study of California history.

To preserve California's landmarks, relics and traditions.

To honor and keep in memory California's Pioneers.

To stimulate and inspire patriotism.

To assist in the work of americanization.

To encourage higher education for women, as evidenced by the Order's liberal college scholarship.

To guarantee social enjoyment, mental improvement and mutual benefit to members.

To care, conjointly with the Order of Native Sons of the Golden West, for the orphaned children of California, of whatever class, color or creed, by placing them in permanent homes through legal adoption proceedings, thus engaging in the most humanitarian of public welfare work, that of improving the future citizenship of the state.

If YOU were born in California and believe in these principles, you should be a member of the Order of Native Daughters of the Golden West.

Greet N. S. Grand President.

Santa Ana—Grand Outside Sentinel Hazel B. Hansen, Supervising Deputy Florence D. Schoneman and President Mattie Edwards of Grace No. 242 (Fullerton) were among the November 28 visitors to Santa Ana No. 235. During the evening members and visitors joined with Santa Ana No. 265 N.S.G.W., which was entertaining Grand President Seth Millington. Numerous addresses were made, Miss Marion Parks speaking of the history of early California, and telling the origin of the names of many of the state's cities, towns, etc.

December 19, Santa Ana No. 235 celebrated its seventh institution anniversary. A card party was recently held at the home of Olive Seba, and the evening was most enjoyable.

Grand President Visits Home Parlor.

Woodland—Grand President Anna Mixon Armstrong officially visited her home-Parlor, Woodland No. 90, November 26. President Florice White presided at the banquet preceding the meeting, and among the speakers were Le R. Pierce, Tax Collector Robert Woods and Sheriff James W. Monroe. Three charter members—Lulu Shelton, Harriett Lee and Mattie Zimmermann—were in attendance.

Some 300 members of the Order—including Junior Past Grand Evelyn I. Carlson, Grand Secretary Sallie R. Thaler, Grand Trustees Edna Briggs, Florence Boyle, Anna Thuesen and Ethel Begley, Grand Marshal Gladys Noce, Grand Inside Sentinel Orinda Giannini, Grand Outside Sentinel Hazel Hansen, Past Grands Sue J. Irwin, Mary E. Bell, Dr. Eva R. Rasmussen, May C. Boldemann and Dr. Louise C. Heilbron, and Deputy Barbara Bell—were in attendance at the Parlor meeting. Four candidates were initiated. Mrs. Armstrong was the recipient of many gifts, including one from the Parlor, presented by Miss Lela Ewert. Edna Richter was chairman of the committee of arrangements for the notable affair.

Old Folks Not Forgotten.

Alturas—Beautiful Christmas decorations radiated the spirit of festivity at the December 1 meeting of Alturas No. 159. After the business meeting friends joined the members and eighteen tables of bridge were in operation. Delicious refreshments were served. As usual, a basket of Christmas cheer was sent the old people in the Modoc County Hospital.

A committee from Alturas was successful in securing the high school auditorium for the Parlor's annual Christmas ball—the first time in history a fraternal organization or club has been privileged to give a public ball there. From the proceeds of this event Alturas provides funds for the homeless children cause and for all of its many local charitable activities.

Installation To Be Public.

Crockett—Carquinez No. 234 had a surprise Christmas party for the members December 14. There was a beautifully decorated tree, and Santa Claus distributed presents. Officers were elected, Mrs. Lucille Franges becoming president. Installation will be held January 25, and will be public. December 28 the Parlor had a whist party and refreshments were served.

Old Sacramento Plaza Marked.

Sacramento—A marker commemorating the historic City Plaza, between Ninth and Tenth, I and J streets, the first park given to the City of Sacramento by Captain John A. Sutter in 1850, has been dedicated by Califia No. 22. The marker is mounted upon a large granite boulder on the Tenth-street side of the park, between two towering trees. It carries a replica of a covered wagon, a reminder of the important role the plaza has played in Sacramento's life.

The park once was a pony-express center, and a hay market once graced the outer of the two walks on J street. And, of course, it was a popular rendezvous on Sundays and holidays when public band concerts constituted an important part of the people's entertainment. Many Sacramentans also recall the City Plaza as a favorite "sparking" place for young bloods and their girl friends.

The dedicatory program featured an address by Past Grand Esther Sullivan, chairman Grand Parlor History and Landmarks Committee. Grand President Anna M. Armstrong also spoke, and unveiled the tablet, and Mayor C. H. S. Bidwell made the address of acceptance on behalf of the city. Mrs. Sadie Brainard was i charge of arrangements.

Grand President's Official Itinerary.

Woodland—During the month of January Grand President Anna Mixon Armstrong wil officially visit the following Subordinate Parlor on the dates noted:

3rd—Laura Loma No. 162, Niles.
4th—Minerva No. 2, San Francisco.
10th—Califia No. 22, Sacramento.
13th—Orinda No. 56, San Francisco.
16th—Colus No. 194, Colusa.
17th—Fern No. 123, Folsom.
18th—Ivy No. 88, Lodi.
24th—El Vespero No. 118, San Francisco.
27th—Auburn No. 233, Auburn.
31st—Las Lomas No. 72, San Francisco.

Big Sisters To Unfortunates.

San Bernardino—Lugonia No. 241 had Christmas party for twenty unfortunate childre December 21. A huge tree, loaded with gift candy and bright decorations, was the main at traction. Santa Claus was there to greet th youngsters, games were played and refresh ments were served. First Vice-president Mar Johnson had charge of the arrangements, an members of the Parlor were "big sisters" to th guests. Officers of Lugonia were installed De cember 28 by Deputy Marion Crum of Santa Ana

Amador County Products Featured.

Sutter Creek—Grand President Anna Mixo Armstrong officially visited Amapola No. 80 De cember 8, when one candidate was initiated. program was presented and then Santa Clau (Theresa Cuneo) appeared, and from a larg Christmas tree, gorgeously decorated, distrib uted gifts to Mrs. Armstrong, Grand Marsha Gladys Noce, Grand Trustee Edna Briggs, Su pervising Deputy Emma Wright, Deputies Har riett Clemens and Margaret Molfino, Sadi Brainard, Henrietta O'Neill, and President Mace Fontenrose of Amapola. The recipients re sponded in words of thanks, and the Gran President spoke highly of the ritualistic work o the Parlor officers. A banquet concluded th festivities, the centerpiece of the table being horn of plenty with Amador County-grow fruits and nuts. The favors were replicas of th centerpiece. Harriett Clemens arranged th decorations.

Amapola is working diligently for the homeless children fund under the able chairmanship of Grand Marshal Noce; it plans to adopt one of the babies for the six-week period, according to the plan of the Central Committee. The Parlor is also selling Loyalty Pledge cook books, and having the amount realized credited to the pledge of Forrest No. 86 (Plymouth).

Proud of Living Christmas Tree.

Petaluma—The card party and dance sponsored by Petaluma No. 222 December 6 for the benefit of the homeless children was a great success. Mrs. Elizabeth Dillon had charge of the cards, and Mrs. Julia Perolini supervised the dance. Members have been liberal purchasers of Christmas seals.

The Parlor had its annual Christmas party December 20. Petaluma is very proud of the living Christmas tree which it planted three years ago in Hill Plaza. It was lighted for the first time this year and was a big holiday attraction.

Charter Members Honored.

Byron—The remaining charter members of Donner No. 193—Elizabeth Plumley, Maud Plumley, Grace Krumland and Clara Houston—were honored at a recent dinner. A turkey whist drew a large crowd and everyone had a good time. Officers for the January-July term were elected December 7, Virginia Boltzen being selected for president.

In conjunction with Byron No. 170 N.S.G.W., Donner sponsored a Christmas party December 16 for the needy children of the community and the Parlors' members. An appropriate program was presented and gifts, candy and fruits were distributed.

Dainty Foods Bring Good Returns.

Mountain View—El Monte No. 205 had a very successful food sale for the benefit of the homeless children. A goodly supply of dainty foods attracted many purchasers, making it possible for the Parlor to send a check for a substantial sum to the Central Committee.

Two Initiated.

Menlo Park—Menlo No. 211 entertained December 12 in honor of Grand President Anna Mixon Armstrong, who was accompanied by Junior Past Grand Evelyn I. Carlson and Grand Trustee Edna Briggs. Two candidates were initiated. The banquet table was decorated in holiday effect, with a miniature Christmas tree, Santa and his reindeer. Gifts were presented Grand President Armstrong, Supervising Deputy Rena Mathais, Deputy Ida Pfaff and President Velma Ewers.

N.D.G.W. OFFICIAL DEATH LIST.

Giving the name, the date of death, and the Subordinate Parlor affiliation of all deceased members as reported to Grand Secretary Sallie R. Thaler from November 18, 1932, to December 17, 1932:

Childress, Ida; October 12; El Dorado No. 186.
McNulty, Bernita E.; November 20; Gabrielle No. 139.
Fisher, Ethel I.; November 13; Santa Cruz No. 26.
Litsch, Varena D. Miles; November 1; Lassen View No. 98.
Evans, Nellie Maude; November 22; Eltapome No. 55.
Obradovich, Olga; November 29; Amapola No. 80.
Farnum, Mattie Shoemaker; October 31; Manzanita No. 29.
Peyton, Sarah E. Ford; November 26; Amapola No. 80.

CALIFORNIA GOVERNOR OF '60s WILL BE REMEMBERED BY STATE UNIVERSITY.

In memory of the man who signed the organic act creating the University of California, March 23, 1868, the University of California will establish a Henry Huntley Haight scholarship in the school of jurisprudence.

Haight was elected Governor of California in 1867. In his inaugural address, December 5 of that year, he said: "The reformation of our present defective state prison system and the organization of a state university are objects of great public importance, the attainment of which I should be glad to facilitate in any way within my power."

Before coming to California in January 1850, Haight was editor of a Free Soil newspaper in St. Louis, and was an ardent critic of slavery. His father, Fletcher M. Haight, came to California in 1854, and was later appointed district judge for the southern district of California by President Abraham Lincoln.

"Time—Time is but the fleeting zephyr of the wind that ever blows; whence it cometh, whence it goeth, no one tells, for no one knows."—Jeanette Nourland.

National Orange Show—San Bernardino City is arranging for its annual classic, the National Orange Show, February 16-26.

Official Directory of Parlors of the N. D. G. W.

GRAND OFFICERS.

Mrs. Evelyn I. Carlson........................Past Grand President
281 E. Tuscaloosa Ave., Atherton

Mrs. Anna M. Armstrong........................Grand President
Woodland

Mrs. Irma Laird........................Grand Vice-president
Alturas

Mrs. Sallie R. Thaler........................Grand Secretary
555 Baker St., San Francisco

Mrs. Susie K. Christ........................Grand Treasurer
555 Baker St., San Francisco

Mrs. Gladys Noce........................Grand Marshal
Sutter Creek

Mrs. Orinda G. Giannini........................Grand Inside Sentinel
2142 Filbert St., San Francisco

Mrs. Hazel B. Hansen........................Grand Outside Sentinel
501 Griswold St., Glendale

Mrs. Clara Gairaud........................Grand Organist
134 Locust St., San Jose

GRAND TRUSTEES.

Mrs. Florence Boyle........................Oroville
Mrs. Edna Briggs............1045 Santa Ynez Way, Sacramento
Mrs. Anna Thuesen..................615 38th Ave., San Francisco
Mrs. Ethel Begley..............233 Prospect Ave., San Francisco
Mrs. Minna K. Horn........................Etna
Mrs. Jane Vick..................418 Bath St., Santa Barbara
Mrs. Willow Borba..................330 So. Main St., Sebastopol

ALAMEDA COUNTY.

Angelita No. 32, Livermore—Meets 2nd and 4th Fridays, Foresters Hall; Mrs. Myrtle I. Johnson, Rec. Sec., P.O. box 253.

Piedmont No. 87, Oakland—Meets Thursdays, Corinthian Hall, Pacific Bldg.; Miss Helen Ring, Rec. Sec., 822 11th St.

Aloha No. 106, Oakland—Meets Tuesdays, Wigwam Hall, Pacific Bldg.; Mrs. Lurine Martin, Rec. Sec., 2815 Wallace St., Berkeley.

Hayward No. 122, Hayward—Meets 1st and 3rd Tuesdays, Veterans Memorial Bldg., Main St.; Miss Ruth Gansberger, Rec. Sec., P. O. box 44, Mount Eden.

Berkeley No. 150, Berkeley—Meets 2nd and 4th Wednesdays, Masonic Hall; Mrs. Lelia B. Baker, Rec. Sec., 915 Contra Costa Ave.

Bear Flag No. 151, Berkeley—Meets 2nd and 4th Wednesdays, Veterans Memorial Bldg., 1931 Center St.; Mrs. Maud Wagner, Rec. Sec., 317 Alcatraz Ave., Oakland.

Encinal No. 156, Alameda—Meets 2nd and 4th Wednesdays, Veterans Memorial Bldg., Central Ave. and Walnut St.; Mrs. Laura E. Fisher, Rec. Sec., 1413 Caroline St.

Brooklyn No. 157, East Oakland—Meets 2nd and 4th Wednesdays, Masonic Temple, 8th Ave. and E. 14th St.; Mrs. Ruth Cooney, Rec. Sec., 3907 14th Ave.

Argonaut No. 166, Oakland—Meets Tuesdays, Klinkner Hall, 59th and San Pablo; Mrs. Ada Spilman, Rec. Sec., 2905 Ellis St., Berkeley.

Bahia Vista No. 167, Oakland—Meets Thursdays, Wigwam Hall, Pacific Bldg.; Mrs. Minnie E. Raper, Rec. Sec., 3449 Helen St.

Fruitvale No. 177, Oakland—Meets Fridays, W.O.W. Hall; May E. Barthold, Rec. Sec., 3882 Santa Rita St.

Laurel Loma No. 182, Niles—Meets 1st and 3rd Tuesdays, I.O.O.F. Hall; Mrs. Ethel Fournier, Rec. Sec., P. O. box 515.

El Cereso No. 207, San Leandro—Meets 2nd and 4th Tuesdays, Masonic Hall; Mrs. Mary Tuttle, Rec. Sec., P. O. box 56.

Pleasanton No. 237, Pleasanton—Meets 1st Tuesday, I.O.O.F. Hall; Mrs. Myrtle Lanini, Rec. Sec.

Betsy Rose No. 238, Centerville—Meets 1st and 3rd Fridays, Anderson Hall; Miss Constance Lucio, Rec. Sec., P. O. box 187.

AMADOR COUNTY.

Ursula No. 1, Jackson—Meets 2nd and 4th Tuesdays, N.S.G.W. Hall; Mrs. Emma Boarman-Wright, Rec. Sec., 114 Court St.

Chispa No. 40, Ione—Meets 2nd and 4th Fridays, N.S.G.W. Hall; Mrs. Isabel Ashton, Rec. Sec.

Amapola No. 80, Sutter Creek—Meets 2nd and 4th Thursdays, N.S.G.W. Bldg.; Mrs. Hazel M. Marre, Rec. Sec.

Forrest No. 86, Plymouth—Meets 2nd and 4th Tuesdays, I.O.O.F. Hall; Mrs. Marguerite Davis, Rec. Sec.

BUTTE COUNTY.

Annie K. Bidwell No. 168, Chico—Meets 2nd and 4th Thursdays, I.O.O.F. Hall; Mrs Irene Henry, Rec. Sec., 3015 Woodland Ave.

Gold of Ophir No. 190, Oroville—Meets 1st and 3rd Wednesdays, Memorial Hall; Mrs. Ruth Brown, Rec. Sec., 1365 Leah Court.

CALAVERAS COUNTY.

Ruby No. 46, Murphys—Meets 4th Friday, N.S.G.W. Hall; Belle Segale, Rec. Sec.

Princess No. 84, Angels Camp—Meets 2nd and 4th Wednesdays, I.O.O.F. Hall; Mrs. Grace M. Mills, Rec. Sec., P.O. box 313.

San Andreas No. 113, San Andreas—Meets 1st Friday, Fraternal Hall; Miss Doris Treat, Rec. Sec.

COLUSA COUNTY.

Colus No. 194, Colusa—Meets 1st and 3rd Mondays, Eagles Hall; Miss Kate Busch, Rec. Sec., 350 Market St.

CONTRA COSTA COUNTY.

Stirling No. 146, Pittsburg—Meets 1st and 3rd Wednesdays, Veteran Memorial Hall; Mrs. Leslie Clement, Rec. Sec., 468 E. Santa Fe.

Richmond No. 147, Richmond—Meets 1st and 3rd Tuesdays, I.O.O.F. Hall, 10th St.; Grace Curry, Rec. Sec., 1134 Ohio St.

Donner No. 193, Byron—Meets 1st and 3rd Wednesdays, I.O.O.F. Hall; Mrs. Anna Pendry, Rec. Sec., P. O. box 112.

Las Juntas No. 221, Martinez—Meets 1st and 3rd Mondays, Pythian Castle; Mrs. Lola O. Viera, Rec. Sec., R.F.D. No. 1.

Antioch No. 223, Antioch—Meets 2nd and 4th Tuesdays, I.O.O.F. Hall; Mrs. Estelle Evans, Rec. Sec., 202 E. 5th St., Pittsburg.

Carquinez No. 234, Crockett—Meets 2nd and 4th Wednesdays, I.O.O.F. Hall; Mrs. Cecile Petee, Rec. Sec., 465 Edwards St.

EL DORADO COUNTY.

Marguerite No. 12, Placerville—Meets 1st and 3rd Wednesdays, Masonic Hall; Mrs. Nettie Leonardi, Rec. Sec., 25 Coloma St.

El Dorado No. 186, Georgetown—Meets 2nd and 4th Saturday afternoons, I.O.O.F. Hall; Mrs. Alta L. Douglas, Rec. Sec.

FRESNO COUNTY.

Fresno No. 187, Fresno—Meets 2nd and 4th Fridays, Pythian Castle, Cor. "R" and Merced Sts.; Mary Aubery, Rec. Sec., 1040 Delphia Ave.

GLENN COUNTY.

Berryessa No. 192, Willows—Meets 1st and 3rd Mondays, I.O.O.F. Hall; Mrs. Leonora Neate, Rec. Sec., 338 No. Lassen St.

HUMBOLDT COUNTY.

Occident No. 28, Eureka—Meets 1st and 3rd Wednesdays, N.S.G.W. Hall; Mrs. Eva L. MacDonald, Rec. Sec., 2309 "B" St.

Oneonta No. 71, Ferndale—Meets 2nd and 4th Fridays, I.O.O.F. Hall; Mrs. Myra Rumrill, Rec. Sec., P.O. box 142.

Reichling No. 97, Fortuna—Meets 1st and 3rd Tuesdays, Friendship Hall; Mrs. Grace Swett, Rec. Sec., P. O. box 328.

KERN COUNTY.

Miocene No. 228, Taft—Meets 1st and 3rd Wednesday afternoons, I.O.O.F. Hall; Mrs. Evalyn G. Towne, Rec. Sec., P. O. box 1011.

El Tejon No. 239, Bakersfield—Meets 1st and 3rd Fridays, Eagles Hall, 1714 "G" St.; Mary B. Hampson, Rec. Sec., 908 Quincy St.

Desert Gold No. 250, Mojave—Meets 2nd and 4th Fridays, I.O.O.F. Hall; Rein H. Everett, Rec. Sec., P.O. box 83.

LAKE COUNTY.

Clear Lake No. 135, Middletown—Meets 2nd and 4th Tuesdays, Herrick Hall; Mrs. Alma E. Snow, Rec. Sec.

LASSEN COUNTY.

Nataqua No. 152, Standish—Meets 1st and 3rd Wednesdays, Foresters Hall; Mrs. Mayda Elledge, Rec. Sec.

Mount Lassen No. 215, Bieber—Meets 2nd and 4th Thursdays, I.O.O.F. Hall; Mrs. Angie O. Kenyon, Rec. Sec.

Susanville No. 243, Susanville—Meets 3rd Thursday, I.O.O.F. Hall; Mildred Hardy, Rec. Sec., P.O. box 425.

LOS ANGELES COUNTY.

Los Angeles No. 124, Los Angeles—Meets 1st and 3rd Wednesdays, I.O.O.F. Hall, Washington and Oak Sts.; Mrs. Mary K. Corcoran, Rec. Sec., 322 No. Van Ness Ave.

Long Beach No. 154, Long Beach—Meets 1st and 3rd Thursdays, K.P. Hall, 341 Pacific Ave.; Mrs. Bertha Hitt, Rec. Sec., 5355 Lime Ave.

Rudecinda No. 230, San Pedro—Meets 2nd and 4th Thursdays, Unity Hall, I.O.O.F. Temple, 10th and Gaffey; Letitia Sarciaux, Rec. Sec., 483 16th St.

Verdugo No. 240, Glendale—Meets 2nd and 4th Tuesdays, Masonic Temple, 234 So. Brand Blvd.; Miss Etta Fulkerth, Rec. Sec., 526 No. Orange St.

Santa Monica Bay No. 245, Santa Monica—Meets 2nd and 4th Wednesdays, Odd Fellows Hall, 1431 Third St.; Mrs. Rosalie Hyde, Rec. Sec., 738 Flower St., Venice.

Californiana No. 247, Los Angeles—Meets 2nd and 4th Tuesday afternoons, Hollywood Studio Club, 1215 Lodi Place; Mrs. Inez Sitton, Rec. Sec., 4223 Berenice St.

MADERA COUNTY.

Madera No. 244, Madera—Meets 2nd and 4th Thursdays, Masonic Annex; Mrs. Margaret C. Boyle, Rec. Sec., 111 No. "B" St.

MARIN COUNTY.

Sea Point No. 196, Sausalito—Meets 2nd and 4th Mondays, Perry Hall, 50 Caledonia St.; Mrs. Mary B. Smith, Rec. Sec., 15 Rose Court Lane.

Marinita No. 198, San Rafael—Meets 2nd and 4th Mondays, 316 "B" St.; Miss Mollye Y. Spaelti, Rec. Sec., 539 4th St.

Fairfax No. 225, Fairfax—Meets 2nd and 4th Tuesdays, Community Hall; Mrs. Marguerite Geary, Rec. Sec.

Tamelpa No. 231, Mill Valley—Meets 1st and 2nd Tuesdays, I.O.O.F. Hall; Mrs. Delphine M. Todt, Rec. Sec., 400 Grand Ave., San Rafael.

MARIPOSA COUNTY.

Mariposa No. 63, Mariposa—Meets 1st and 3rd Fridays, I.O.O.F. Hall; Elizabeth E. Johnson, Rec. Sec.

MENDOCINO COUNTY.

Fort Bragg No. 210, Fort Bragg—Meets 1st and 3rd Thursdays, I.O.O.F. Hall; Mrs. Ruth W. Fuller, Rec. Sec.

MERCED COUNTY.

Veritas No. 75, Merced—Meets 1st and 3rd Tuesdays, I.O.O.F. Hall; Miss Margaret Thornton, Rec. Sec., 317 18th St.

MODOC COUNTY.

Alturas No. 159, Alturas—Meets 1st Thursday, Alturas Civic Club; Mrs. Irma W. Laird, Rec. Sec.

MONTEREY COUNTY.

Aleli No. 102, Salinas—Meets 2nd and 4th Thursdays, Pythian Hall; Miss Rose Rhyner, Rec. Sec., 420 Soledad St.

Junipero No. 141, Monterey—Meets 2nd and 4th Fridays, K. of P. Hall, Main St.; Miss Matilda M. Bergschicker, Rec. Sec., 498 Van Buren St.

NAPA COUNTY.

Eshcol No. 16, Napa—Meets 2nd and 4th Mondays, N.S.G.W. Hall; Mrs. Ella Ingram, Rec. Sec., 2140 Seminary St.

Calistoga No. 145, Calistoga—Meets 2nd and 4th Mondays, I.O.O.F. Hall; Sadie P. Brooks, Rec. Sec.

La Junta No. 203, Saint Helena—Meets 1st and 3rd Tuesdays, N.S.G.W. Hall; Mrs. Marie Signorelli, Rec. Sec., 1341 Madrona Ave.

NEVADA COUNTY.

Laurel No. 6, Nevada City—Meets 1st and 3rd Wednesdays, I.O.O.F. Hall; Mrs. Nellie E. Clark, Rec. Sec., P. O box 212.

Manzanita No. 29, Grass Valley—Meets 1st and 3rd Tuesdays, Auditorium; Mrs. Loraine Keast, Rec. Sec., 123 Race St.

Columbia No. 70, French Corral—Meets Fridays, Farrelley Hall; Mrs. Kate Farrelley-Sullivan, Rec. Sec.

Snow Peak No. 176, Truckee—Meets 1st Monday, I.O.O.F. Hall; Mrs. Henrietta M. Eaton, Rec. Sec., P. O. box 116.

ORANGE COUNTY.

Santa Ana No. 235, Santa Ana—Meets 2nd and 4th Mondays, K.C. Hall, 4th and French Sts.; Mrs. Matilda S. Lemon, Rec. Sec., 1528 W. 8th St.

Grace No. 242, Fullerton—Meets 1st and 3rd Thursdays, I.O.O.F. Hall, 116½ E. Commonwealth; Mrs. Mary Rothaermel, Rec. Sec., P. O. box 235.

PLACER COUNTY.

Placer No. 138, Lincoln—Meets 2nd Wednesday, I.O.O.F. Hall; Miss Carrie Parlin, Rec. Sec.

La Rosa No. 191, Roseville—Meets 1st and 3rd Tuesdays, Eagles Hall; Mrs. Alice Lee West, Rec. Sec., Rocklin.

Auburn No. 233, Auburn—Meets 2nd and 4th Fridays, Foresters Hall; Mrs. Elsie Patrick, Rec. Sec.

PLUMAS COUNTY.

Plumas Pioneer No. 219, Quincy—Meets 1st and 3rd Mondays, I.O.O.F. Hall; Minnie E. Johnson, Rec. Sec., P. O. box 243.

SACRAMENTO COUNTY.

Califia No. 22, Sacramento—Meets 2nd and 4th Tuesdays, N.S.G.W. Hall; Miss Lulu Gillis, Rec. Sec., 921 8th St.

La Bandera No. 110, Sacramento—Meets 1st and 3rd Fridays, N.S.G.W. Hall; Mrs. Clara Weldon, Rec. Sec., 1310 "O" St.

Sutter No. 111, Sacramento—Meets 1st and 3rd Tuesdays, N.S.G.W. Hall; Mrs. Adele Nix, Rec. Sec., 1238 "S" St.

Fern No. 123, Folsom—Meets 1st and 3rd Tuesdays, K.P. Hall; Mrs. Viola Shumway, Rec. Sec., P. O. box 48.

Chabolla No. 171, Galt—Meets 2nd and 4th Tuesdays, I.O.O.F. Hall; Mrs. Mary Pritchard, Rec. Sec.

Coloma No. 212, Sacramento—Meets 1st and 3rd Tuesdays, I.O.O.F. Hall, Oak Park; Mrs. Nettie Harry, Rec. Sec., 1217 35th St.

Liberty No. 213, Elk Grove—Meets 2nd and 4th Fridays, I.O.O.F. Hall; Mrs. Frances Wackman, Rec. Sec., P. O. box 192.

Victory No. 216, Courtland—Meets 1st Saturday and 3rd Monday, N.S.G.W. Hall; Mrs. Agneda Lampie, Rec. Sec.

SAN BENITO COUNTY.

Copa de Oro No. 105, Hollister—Meets 2nd and 4th Thursdays, Grangers Union Hall; Mrs. Mollie Daveggio, Rec. Sec., 110 San Benito St.

San Juan Bautista No. 179, San Juan Bautista—Meets 1st Wednesday, Mission Corridor Rooms; Miss Gertrude Breen, Rec. Sec.

SAN BERNARDINO COUNTY.

Lugonia No. 241, San Bernardino—Meets 2nd and 4th Wednesdays, Eagles Hall; Miss Lois Poling, Rec. Sec., 1098 Waterman Ave.

Ontario No. 251, Ontario—Meets 2nd and 4th Thursdays, Ontario Hotel; Miss Helen Hickman, Rec. Sec., 928 No. Laurel Ave.

SAN DIEGO COUNTY.

San Diego No. 208, San Diego—Meets 2nd and 4th Wednesdays, Directors Room, Chamber Commerce Bldg., 499 W. Broadway; Mrs. Elsie Case, Rec. Sec., 3051 Broadway.

SAN FRANCISCO CITY AND COUNTY.

Minerva No. 2, San Francisco—Meets 1st and 3rd Wednesdays, N.S.G.W. Bldg.; Miss Dorothy Finn, Rec. Sec., 90 Princess St., Sausalito.

Alta No. 3, San Francisco—Meets 2nd and 4th Tuesdays, N.S.G.W. Bldg.; Mrs. Agnese L. Hughes, Rec. Sec., 3980 Sacramento St.

Oro Fino No. 9, San Francisco—Meets 1st and 3rd Thursdays, N.S.G.W. Bldg.; Mrs. Josephine B. Morrisey, Rec. Sec., 4441 20th St.

Golden State No. 50, San Francisco—Meets 1st and 3rd Wednesdays, N.D.G.W. Home; Miss Millie Tietjen, Rec. Sec., 328 Lexington Ave.

Orinda No. 56, San Francisco—Meets 2nd, 4th and 5th Fridays, N.D.G.W. Home; Mrs. Anna A. Gruber-Loser, Rec. Sec., 72 Grove Lane, San Anselmo.

Fremont No. 59, San Francisco—Meets 1st and 3rd Tuesdays, N.S.G.W. Bldg.; Miss Hannah Collins, Rec. Sec., 617 Fillmore St.

Buena Vista No. 68, San Francisco—Meets 1st, 3rd and 5th Thursdays, N.D.G.W. Home; Miss Margaret Barrett, Rec. Sec., 3774 20th St.

Las Lomas No. 72, San Francisco—Meets 1st and 3rd Tuesdays, N.D.G.W. Home; Mrs. Marion S. Day, Rec. Sec., 469 Noe St.

Yosemite No. 83, San Francisco—Meets 1st and 3rd Tuesdays, American Hall, 20th and Capp Sts.; Miss Mary Monahan, Rec. Sec., 237 Noe St.

La Estrella No. 89, San Francisco—Meets 2nd and 4th Mondays, N.S.G.W. Bldg.; Miss Birdie Hartman, Rec. Sec., 1018 Jackson St.

Sans Souci No. 96, San Francisco—Meets 2nd and 4th Mondays, N.D.G.W. Home; Mrs. Minnie F. Dobbin, Rec. Sec., 1483 43rd Ave.

Calaveras No. 103, San Francisco—Meets 2nd and 4th Tuesdays, Swedish American Hall, 2174 Market St.; Mary L. Krogh, Rec. Sec., 4235 Cabrillo St.

Darina No. 114, San Francisco—Meets 1st and 3rd Mondays, N.S.G.W. Bldg.; Miss Adele Walsh, Rec. Sec., 479 Page St.

El Vespero No. 118, San Francisco—Meets 2nd and 4th Tuesdays, Masonic Hall, 4705 3rd St.; Mrs. Nell R. Boege, Rec. Sec., 1526 Kirkwood Ave.

Genevieve No. 132, San Francisco—Meets 1st and 3rd Thursdays, N.S.G.W. Bldg.; Miss Branice Peguillan, Rec. Sec., 2434 16th Ave.

Keith No. 137, San Francisco—Meets 2nd and 4th Thursdays, N.S.G.W. Bldg.; Mrs. Helen T. Mann, Rec. Sec., 575 Pierce St., Apt. 206.

Gabrielle No. 139, San Francisco—Meets 2nd and 4th Wednesdays, N.S.G.W. Bldg.; Mrs. Dorothy Wuesterfeld, Rec. Sec., 1020 Munich St.

Presidio No. 148, San Francisco—Meets 2nd and 4th Tuesdays, N.S.G.W. Bldg.; Mrs. Hattie Gaughran, Rec. Sec., 713 Capp St.

Guadalupe No. 153, San Francisco—Meets 2nd and 4th Mondays, Forester Hall, 170 Valencia St.; Miss May A. McCarthy, Rec. Sec., 336 Elsie St.

Golden Gate No. 158, San Francisco—Meets 2nd and 4th Mondays, N.S.G.W. Bldg.; Mrs. Mary Sullivan, Rec. Sec., 88 Cuvier St.

Dolores No. 169, San Francisco—Meets 2nd and 4th Wednesdays, N.S.G.W. Bldg.; Mrs. Ada Saunders, Rec. Sec., 284 Allison St.

Linda Rosa No. 170, San Francisco—Meets 2nd and 4th Wednesdays, Swedish American Hall, 2174 Market St.; Mrs. Eva P. Tyrrel, Rec. Sec., 2629 Mission St.

ATTENTION, SECRETARIES!

THIS DIRECTORY IS PUBLISHED BY AUTHORITY OF THE GRAND PARLOR N.D.G.W., AND ALL NOTICES OF CHANGES MUST BE RECEIVED BY THE GRAND SECRETARY (NOT THE MAGAZINE) ON OR BEFORE THE 20TH OF EACH MONTH TO INSURE CORRECTION IN NEXT PUBLICATION OF DIRECTORY.

Portola No. 172, San Francisco—Meets 1st and 3rd Tuesdays, N.S.G.W. Bldg.; Catherine H. Dolly, Rec. Sec., 4125 23rd St.
Castro No. 178, San Francisco—Meets 1st and 3rd Wednesdays, K.C. Bldg., 150 Golden Gate Ave.; Miss Adeline Sandersfeld, Rec Sec., 50 Baker St.
Twin Peaks No. 185, San Francisco—Meets 2nd and 4th Fridays, Druids Temple, 44 Page St.; Mrs. Loretta Cameron, Rec. Sec., 3969 Army St.
James Lick No. 220, San Francisco—Meets 1st and 3rd Wednesdays, N.S.G.W. Bldg.; Mrs. Edna Bishop, Rec. Sec., 3841 24th St.
Mission No. 227, San Francisco—Meets 2nd and 4th Fridays, N.S.G.W. Bldg.; Mrs. Ann Dippel, Rec. Sec., 448 Dewey Blvd.
Bret Harte No. 232, San Francisco—Meets 2nd and 4th Tuesdays, Aloha Hall, 3009 16th St.; Pearl Wedde, Rec. Sec., 225 7th Ave.
La Dorada No. 236, San Francisco—Meets 2nd and 4th Thursdays, N.S.G.W. Hall; Mrs. Theresa R. O'Brien, Rec. Sec., 567 Liberty St.
Balboa No. 249, San Francisco—Meets 2nd and 4th Thursdays, Maccabee Hall, 5th Ave. and Clement St.; Miss Jean Moffet, Rec. Sec., 476 26th Ave.
Utopia No. 252, San Francisco—Meets 2nd and 4th Tuesdays, American Hall, 20th and Capp Sts.; Miss Lelia M. Little, Rec. Sec., 4450 20th St.

SAN JOAQUIN COUNTY.

Joaquin No. 5, Stockton—Meets 2nd and 4th Tuesdays, N.S.G.W. Hall, 314 E. Main St.; Mrs. Della Garvin, Rec. Sec., 1122 E. Market St.
El Pescadero No. 82, Tracy—Meets 1st and 3rd Fridays, I.O.O.F. Hall; Mrs. Mary A. Hewitson, Rec. Sec., 122 Walnut St.
Ivy No. 88, Lodi—Meets 1st and 3rd Wednesdays, Eagles Hall; Mrs. Mae Corson, Rec. Sec., 109 So. School St.
Calle de Oro No. 206, Stockton—Meets 1st and 3rd Tuesdays, N.S.G.W. Hall, 314 E. Main St.; Mrs. Frances Germain, Rec. Sec., 450 No. Regent.
Phoebe A. Hearst No. 214, Manteca—Meets 2nd and 4th Wednesdays, I.O.O.F. Hall; Mrs. Josie M. Frederick, Rec. Sec., Route A, Box 364, Ripon.

SAN LUIS OBISPO COUNTY.

San Miguel No. 94, San Miguel—Meets 2nd and 4th Wednesday afternoons, Clemon Hall; Mrs. Nellie Wickstrom, Rec. Sec.
San Luisita No. 108, San Luis Obispo—Meets 2nd and 4th Thursdays, W.O.W. Hall; Miss Agnes M. Lee, Rec. Sec., P. O. box 584.
El Pinal No. 163, Cambria—Meets 2nd, 4th and 5th Tuesdays, N.S.G.W. Hall; Kathryn Luchessa, Rec. Sec.

SAN MATEO COUNTY.

Bonita No. 10, Redwood City—Meets 2nd and 4th Thursdays, I.O.O.F. Hall; Mrs. Dora Wilson, Rec. Sec., 518 Middlefield Rd.
Vista del Mar No. 155, Halfmoon Bay—Meets 2nd and 4th Thursdays, I.O.O.F. Hall; Elizabeth Olney, Rec. Sec.
Ano Nuevo No. 180, Pescadero—Meets 1st and 3rd Wednesdays, I.O.O.F. Hall; Mrs. Alice Mattei, Rec. Sec.
El Carmelo No. 181, Daly City—Meets 1st and 3rd Wednesdays, Masonic Hall; Mrs. Hattie Kelly, Rec. Sec., 1179 Brunswick St.
Menlo No. 211, Menlo Park—Meets 2nd and 4th Mondays, Masonic Hall; Mrs. Frances E. Maloney, Rec. Sec., P. O. box 626.
San Bruno No. 246, San Bruno—Meets 2nd and 4th Fridays, Legion Hall; Miss Mildred Foley, Rec. Sec., 217 Miller Ave., South San Francisco.

SANTA BARBARA COUNTY.

Reina del Mar No. 126, Santa Barbara—Meets 1st and 3rd Tuesdays, Pythian Castle, 222 W. Carillo St.; Mrs. Dorothy Yule, Rec. Sec., P.O. box 670.

SANTA CLARA COUNTY.

San Jose No. 81, San Jose—Meets Thursdays, Catholic Women Center, 5th and San Fernando Sts.; Mrs. Nellie Fleming, Rec. Sec., Catholic Women Center.
Vendome No. 100, San Jose—Meets Wednesdays, Old Scottish Rite Temple; Miss Marie Buck, Rec. Sec., 245 Hawthorne St.
El Monte No. 205, Mountain View—Meets 2nd and 4th Fridays, American Legion Hall; Miss Mary Ann Rokovich, Rec. Sec., P.O. box 422-B.
Palo Alto No. 229, Palo Alto—Meets 1st and 2nd Mondays, N.S.G.W. Hall; Miss Helena G. Hansen, Rec. Sec., 531 Lytton Ave.

SANTA CRUZ COUNTY.

Santa Cruz No. 26, Santa Cruz—Meets Mondays, N.S.G.W. Hall; Mrs. May L. Williamson, Rec. Sec., 170 Walnut Ave.
El Pajaro No. 35, Watsonville—Meets 1st and 3rd Tuesdays, I.O.O.F. Hall; Miss Ruth E. Wilson, Rec. Sec., 16 Laurel St.

SHASTA COUNTY.

Camellia No. 41, Anderson—Meets 1st and 3rd Tuesdays, Masonic Hall; Mrs. Olga E. Welbourn, Rec. Sec.
Lassen View No. 98, Shasta—Meets 2nd Friday, Masonic Hall; Miss Louise Litsch, Rec. Sec.
Hiawatha No. 140, Redding—Meets 2nd and 4th Wednesdays, Moose Hall; Ruth Presleigh, Rec. Sec., Office County Clerk.

SIERRA COUNTY.

Naomi No. 36, Downieville—Meets 2nd and 4th Wednesdays, I.O.O.F. Hall; Louise C. Dubuque, Rec. Sec.
Imogen No. 134, Sierraville—Meets 2nd and 4th Saturday afternoons, Copren Hall; Mrs. Jennie Copren, Rec. Sec.

SISKIYOU COUNTY.

Eschscholtzia No. 112, Etna—Meets 1st and 3rd Wednesdays, Masonic Hall; Mrs. Bernice E. Smith, Rec. Sec.
Mountain Dawn No. 120, Sawyers Bar—Meets 2nd and last Wednesdays, I.O.O.F. Hall; Miss Edith Dunphy, Rec. Sec.

SOLANO COUNTY.

Vallejo No. 195, Vallejo—Meets 1st and 3rd Wednesdays, K.C. Hall, 820 Marin St.; Mrs. Mary Combs, Rec. Sec., 511 York St.
Mary E. Bell No. 224, Dixon—Meets 2nd and 4th Thursdays, I.O.O.F. Hall; Grace McFadyen, Rec. Sec.

SONOMA COUNTY.

Sonoma No. 209, Sonoma—Meets 2nd and 4th Mondays, I.O.O.F. Hall; Mrs. Mae Norrbom, Rec. Sec., R.F.D., box 171.
Santa Rosa No. 217, Santa Rosa—Meets 1st and 3rd Thursdays, N.S.G.W. Hall; Mrs. Clytie L. Lewis, Rec. Sec., R.F.D. No. 4, Box 345-A.
Petaluma No. 222, Petaluma—Meets 1st and 3rd Tuesdays, Dania Hall; Mrs. Margaret M. Oeltjen, Rec. Sec., 503 Prospect St.

STANISLAUS COUNTY.

Oakdale No. 125, Oakdale—Meets 1st Monday, I.O.O.F. Hall; Mrs. Lou Reeder, Rec. Sec.
Morada No. 199, Modesto—Meets 2nd and 4th Wednesdays, I.O.O.F. Hall; Mrs. Susan Sullivan, Rec. Sec., 823 10th St.
Eldora No. 248, Turlock—Meets 1st and 3rd Mondays, Masonic Temple; Effie Lund, Rec. Sec., 624 Minaret Ave.

SUTTER COUNTY.

South Butte No. 226, Sutter—Meets 1st and 3rd Mondays, N.D.G.W. Hall; Mrs. Abbie N. Vagedes, Rec. Sec.

TEHAMA COUNTY.

Berendos No. 23, Red Bluff—Meets 1st and 3rd Tuesdays, W.O.W. Hall, 200 Pine St.; Mrs. Lillie Hammer, Rec. Sec., 636 Jackson St.

TRINITY COUNTY.

Eltapome No. 55, Weaverville—Meets 2nd and 4th Thursdays, N.S.G.W. Hall; Mrs. Lou N. Fetzer, Rec. Sec.

TUOLUMNE COUNTY.

Dardanelle No. 66, Sonora—Meets Fridays, I.O.O.F. Hall; Mrs. Nettie Whitto, Rec. Sec.
Golden Era No. 99, Columbia—Meets 1st and 3rd Thursdays, N.S.G.W. Hall; Miss Irene Ponce, Rec. Sec.
Anona No. 164, Jamestown—Meets 2nd and 4th Tuesdays, I.O.O.F. Hall; Nellie Hope, Rec. Sec.

YOLO COUNTY.

Woodland No. 90, Woodland—Meets 2nd and 4th Tuesdays, N.S.G.W. Hall; Mrs. Maude Heaton, Rec. Sec., 153 College St.

YUBA COUNTY.

Marysville No. 162, Marysville—Meets 2nd and 4th Wednesdays, Liberty Hall; Miss Cecelia C. Gomes, Rec. Sec., 701 8th St.
Camp Far West No. 218, Wheatland—Meets 3rd Tuesday, I.O.O.F. Hall; Mrs. Ethel C. Brock, Rec. Sec., P. O. box 285.

AFFILIATED ORGANIZATIONS.

General Assembly Past Presidents—Meetings held annually in April at the home-town of Chief President; Mrs. Cora Stobing, 1739 San Jose Ave., San Francisco, Chief President; Mrs. Anna G. Loser, 72 Grove Lane, San Anselmo, Chief Secretary.
Past Presidents Association No. 1—Meets 1st and 3rd Mondays, N.S.G.W. Bldg., 414 Mason St., San Francisco; Mrs. Minnie F. Dobbin, Pres.; Mrs. May R. Barry, Rec. Sec., 2319 19th Ave., San Francisco.
Past Presidents Association No. 2—Meets 2nd and 4th Mondays, "Wigwam," Pacific Bldg., 16th and Jefferson, Oakland; Emma Haggerty, Pres.; Mrs. Elizabeth B. Goodman, Rec. Sec., 134 Juana Ave., San Leandro.
Past Presidents Association No. 3 (Santa Clara County)—Meets 2nd Tuesday, homes of members; Mrs. Amelia Hartman, Pres.; Mrs. Mary G. Newton, Rec. Sec., 1070 Jackson St., Santa Clara.
Past Presidents Association No. 4 (Sacramento County)—Meets 2nd Monday, N.S.G.W. Hall, 11th and "J" Sts., Sacramento City; Edna Briggs, Pres.; Lily May Tilden, Rec. Sec., 3225 "T" St., Sacramento.
Past Presidents Association No. 5 (Butte County)—Meets 1st Friday, homes of members, Chico and Oroville; Marie Picanco, Pres.; Ruth Brown, Rec. Sec., 1265 Leah Court, Oroville.
Past Presidents Association No. 6 (Nevada County)—Meets 4th Friday, alternately between Nevada City, Pythian Castle, and Grass Valley, Edna Sampson's home; Margaret V. Nolan, Pres.; Vere Hansen, Rec. Sec., R.F.D. No. 2, box 41-C, Grass Valley.
Past Presidents Association No. 7 (Sonoma County)—Meets 2nd Tuesday, Violet Mastrup home, 622 5th St., Petaluma; Viola Mastrup, Pres.; Elizabeth Dillon, Rec. Sec., Petaluma.
Past Presidents Association No. 8 (San Joaquin and Stanislaus Counties)—Meets 2nd Thursday, Red Men Hall, Stockton; Mrs. Lois Armstrong, Pres.; Mrs. Harriet F. Corr, Rec. Sec., 729 E. Sonora St., Stockton.
Native Sons and Native Daughters Central Committee on Homeless Children—Main Office, 955 Phelan Bldg., San Francisco; Mrs. John W. Stirling, Chmn.; Miss Mary E. Brusie, Sec. Los Angeles branch office, 3924 Sunset Blvd.; Dorothy Schlingman, Sec.

(ADVERTISEMENT.)

In Memoriam

EVANGELINE HENSLEY.

To the Officers and Members of Golden Gate Parlor No. 158 N.D.G.W.—We, your committee appointed to draft resolutions of love and respect in memory of our departed sister, Evangeline Hensley, do submit the following:

Whereas, It has pleased our Heavenly Father to call our beloved sister, Evangeline Hensley, to the Eternal Parlor above, let us always cherish the fond memory of her noble character and smiling countenance.

Resolved, That we extend to her bereaved family our sincere sympathy. It is our earnest prayer that God, in His infinite mercy, assuage their deep grief and send peace into their hearts. Be it further resolved, that our charter be draped in mourning, that a copy of these resolutions be sent the parents and husband of our deceased sister, and one to The Grizzly Bear Magazine for publication.

SOPHIE SIEBE,
MARGARET RAMM,
Committee.

San Francisco, November 14, 1932.

HELENA WULBERN.

To the Officers and Members of Bear Flag Parlor No. 151 N.D.G.W.—Whereas, With the Birthday of the Lord drawing nigh and the beginning of a new year approaching, Almighty God has called our loving friend and loyal member, Helena Wulbern, to enter the dawn of a new life in His Eternal Home; and whereas, the work left for our thoughtful sister to do had reached its culmination in her many friendships and generous actions, and will be carried forward by her noble sons and daughters; and whereas, we are not unmindful of the respect within our souls and the responsibility incumbent upon us in so grave and reverent a transition; therefore, be it

Resolved, That Bear Flag Parlor hereby recognizes the spiritual advancement and the physical departure of a willing worker and devoted sister, and with all honor shrouds her vacant chair; and, as a symbol of our love and affection, extends sympathy from our hearts to her grieving family, who greatly mourn her passing; be it further resolved, that a copy of this resolution be presented to the family of our late sister, that this resolution be entered in full in the minutes of the Parlor, and that a copy also be sent to The Grizzly Bear for publication.

MARY BRIGLIA,
MAUD WAGNER,
ELSIE HAVEN,
Committee.

Berkeley, December 7, 1932.

CLEMENCE CHICON.

To the Officers and Members of Argonaut Parlor No. 166 N.D.G.W.—We, your Committee appointed to draft resolutions expressing the sentiments and heartfelt sympathy of the members of the Parlor on the death of our sister, Clemente Chicon, respectfully submit the following:

Whereas, It has pleased our Heavenly Father to take from our midst our beloved charter sister, Clemence Chicon, and to summon her to a higher life; and whereas, in her passing our Parlor has lost a most esteemed sister, and the community in which she lived a most respected and loved citizen; therefore, be it

Resolved, That Argonaut Parlor extend sincere sympathy to the husband and the bereaved family; that a copy of these resolutions be sent to the family of our sister; that a copy be sent to The Grizzly Bear for publication, and that a copy be spread upon the minutes of this Parlor.

MAMIE FONTES, President,
CHRISTINA BARTLETT,
ADA SPILMAN, Secretary.

Oakland, December 17, 1932.

HUGH McCURDY.

God's finger touched him, and he slept. Once more a brother has answered the dread summons. But a few short days ago a brother, in the flower of his manhood, was called with tragic suddenness to stand before his Maker.

A brave, generous, humane, sympathetic officer of the law, a faithful and a loyal Native Son, an honest, upright and patriotic citizen, Hugh McCurdy will ever live in our memories as one who always remembered that we pass this way but once; he was a friend to the friendless, the downtrodden, the broken-spirited; he enforced the law through kindness, rather than through arrogance; he set a noble example; he has not lived in vain.

The lesson he has taught will not be lost. He was a kind and loving husband and father, and with hearts bowed down we humbly beseech our Merciful Father in Heaven to mitigate the grief no poor words of ours can possibly assuage, and to give comfort and consolation to his bereaved family none but He can give. Be it

Resolved, That a copy of this memorial be spread upon the minutes of Mount Tamalpais Parlor No. 64 N.S.G.W.; that a copy be forwarded under the seal of the Parlor to his bereaved relatives; that a copy be published in the official publication of the Order; that the charter be draped for a period of thirty days; and be it further resolved, that the Parlor stand in silence in respect to the memory of our departed brother.

CHARLES F. REINDOLLAR,
HAROLD J. HALEY,
MONROE W. LABEL,
LOUIS J. PETER,
Committee on Resolutions.

San Rafael, December 17, 1932.

MRS. JOSEPHINE JONES FISCHER.

The Angel of Death has again invaded the portals of Los Angeles Parlor No. 124 N.D.G.W. and taken from our midst our well-beloved and faithful Native Daughter, Josephine Jones Fischer. We, your committee, beg leave to submit the following:

Whereas, God, in His infinite wisdom, has called our sister, Josephine Jones Fischer, to her eternal home, therefore, be it

Resolved, Los Angeles Parlor has lost one of her finest members, a lover of her native state, and we extend to her husband and relatives our sincere sympathy; and may He who has bereft them give them strength to bear up under their great affliction; also be it resolved, that a copy of these resolutions be sent to the family, and a copy to The Grizzly Bear Magazine for publication.

ANNIE L. ADAIR,
GRACE T. HAVEN,
EDITH B. SCHALLMO,
Committee.

Los Angeles, December 19, 1932.

THE LETTER BOX

Comments on subjects of general interest and importance received from readers of The Grizzly Bear.

CO-OPERATION APPRECIATED.

Editor Grizzly Bear—Thank you so much for the generous contribution of space which you gave to the American Red Cross in The Grizzly Bear Magazine. In thus aiding us in extending a universal invitation to participate in Red Cross work through individual membership, you made a most substantial contribution to our membership roll call.

Please allow me to express to you in behalf of our national officers and the leaders of our 3,600 Red Cross chapters sincere appreciation for your generous co-operation. Cordially yours,

DOUGLAS GRIESEMER,
National Director of Roll Call.

Washington, D. C., December 1, 1932.

APPRECIATION EXPRESSED.

Editor Grizzly Bear—Thank you very much for your thoughtfulness in sending us a copy of The Grizzly Bear in which you so kindly used some of our Christmas seal material. We wish to take this opportunity of expressing our appreciation for this contribution to our work. Sincerely yours,

A. SCHAEFFER JR.,
Director of Publicity
National Tuberculosis Association.

New York City, December 7, 1932.

A JEST

(N. H. DUNNING.)

He gave the World a friendly nod,
And asked of it a little space
In which to keep the modern pace,
Yet save a speedy fall from grace . . . . .
It only frowned a bit and said,
"Keep off the grass!"

Again he said, "Dear World, how odd
Indeed, I'll chance a little fall . . . . .
If you can make it rational,
The thing I said was just a 'stall'."
The World replied, "Just go ahead,
I'm sure you'll pass!"

(This is from Mrs. Nellie H. Dunning of Los Angeles, a frequent contributor to The Grizzly Bear.—Editor.)

"It is better to do deep thinking on a small problem than thin thinking on a big problem."
—Henry Suzzallo.

Passing of the California Pioneer

(Confined to Brief Notices of the Demise of Those Men and Women Who Came to California Prior to 1870.)

MRS. ANGELINE CHIPMAN-DRIGGERS, native of Illinois, 85; came across the plains to California in 1851 and settled in the San Bernardino Valley; died at San Bernardino City, survived by seven children, among them Mrs. Myrtle Spangler (Lugonia Parlor No. 241 N.D.G.W.). She was a member of the San Bernardino Pioneer Society.

Henry Clay Stevens, native of Missouri, 82; came via the Isthmus of Panama in 1853 and resided in Butte, Ventura and Santa Clara Counties; died at Morgan Hill, survived by a wife and three children.

John Thomas Brown, native of Missouri, 85; crossed the plains in 1853 and most of the time since resided in Visalia, Tulare County; died at Fresno City, survived by two sons.

Mrs. Margaret Ann Gillick, native of Illinois, 83; crossed the plains in 1854 and following a short residence in Siskiyou County settled in Amador County; died at Jackson, survived by twelve children.

Hiram G. Clark, 81; crossed the plains in 1854; died at San Bernardino City, survived by a wife and three children.

Henry Bingham, native of Utah, 78; came in 1856; died at North Los Angeles, Los Angeles County, survived by two sons.

Thomas Hart Cate, native of Missouri, 83; crossed the plains in 1857 and resided in Sutter and Placer Counties; died near Lincoln, survived by a wife and five children.

Morgan Strange Harrington, native of Iowa, 77; came in 1857; died at Redding, Shasta County.

James Benjamin Griffin, native of Missouri, 80; crossed the plains in 1857 and settled in Yolo County; died at Arbuckle, Colusa County, survived by a wife and a son.

James H. Proctor, native of Missouri, 86; crossed the plains in 1852 and long resided in Tehama County; died at Los Angeles City, survived by two daughters.

Mrs. Kate Stewart Brown-Philbrook, native of Maine, 100; came in 1860 and resided many years in Trinity County; died at Oakland, Alameda County, survived by a daughter. She was the widow of John W. Philbrook, Pioneer of 1856, at various times clerk, sheriff and district attorney of Trinity County.

William Henry Gunsolus, native of Canada, 93; came via the Isthmus of Panama in 1860 and resided in Sierra and Amador Counties; died at Sutter Creek, survived by a wife and a daughter.

Mrs. Harriet Goodrich-Ink, native of Michigan, 90; came in 1860 and long resided in Napa County; died at Stockton, San Joaquin County, survived by two children. She was the widow of Theron H. Ink, Pioneer of 1852, for several years Napa County supervisor.

Joseph Dimock, native of Nova Scotia, 93; came across the plains in 1861 and resided in Santa Clara, Santa Barbara and Monterey Counties; died at Salinas, survived by a daughter.

Mrs. Frances M. Cottle, native of Illinois, 87; came in 1862 and resided many years in the Santa Clara Valley; died at Modesto, Stanislaus County, survived by four children.

Joseph E. Jackson, native of Iowa, 80; since 1862 Sacramento County resident; died at Sacramento City, survived by four children.

Mrs. Mary A. Bransford, native of Missouri, 92; since 1864 Sonoma County resident; died at Santa Rosa, survived by six children.

Mrs. Mary Rosilla Stevens-Gray, native of Maine, 76; came via the Isthmus of Panama in 1864 and settled in Mendocino County; died at San Rafael, Marin County, survived by five children.

Royal C. Wight, native of Iowa, 86; crossed the plains in 1865 and resided in Solano and Lake Counties; died near Kelseyville, survived by three children.

William Leal DaRosa, native of Azores Islands, 78; came via the Isthmus of Panama in 1865 and settled in Sacramento City, where he died; three sons survive.

George N. Chittenden, native of Michigan, 86; came in 1865 and for many years resided in Mendocino and Sonoma Counties; died at San Rafael, Marin County, survived by a wife and three children.

Elon L. Warner, native of Illinois, 79; came in 1865 and resided in Sierra and Alameda Counties; died at Oakland, survived by a wife and a son.

Thomas M. Kendrick, native of Connecticut, 84; came in 1865 and most of the time since resided in Tuolumne and Inyo Counties; died at Palo Alto, Santa Clara County. He had served Inyo County as recorder.

Mrs. Eliza Brittingham-Lennon, native of Maryland, 94; came via the Isthmus of Panama in 1867 and two years later settled in Gilroy, Santa Clara County, where she died; three children survive.

Eugene P. Butler, native of Iowa, 78; since 1867 Glenn County resident; died near Elk Creek, survived by a wife and five children.

Mrs. Ignacia Phillips Dutra, native of the Azores Islands, 93; since 1867 San Mateo County resident; died near Halfmoon Bay, survived by five children.

Joseph Serra, native of Italy, 93; since 1867 resident Sutter Creek, Amador County, where he died; two children survive.

William Watson, native of Iowa, 79; came in 1868; died at Willows, Glenn County, survived by a son.

Curtis A. Higgins, native of North Carolina, 86; since 1869 Modoc County resident; died at Adin, survived by a wife and four children.

Mrs. Sarah Jane Gale-Robinson, native of Missouri; crossed the plains in 1855 and in 1862 settled in Healdsburg, Sonoma County, where she died; a daughter survives.

Hugo August Hornlein, native of Wisconsin, 73; came in 1869 and resided many years in Sacramento City; died at San Francisco.

Mrs. Frances A. Reynolds, native of Tennessee, 93; came via the Isthmus of Panama in 1855 and resided many years in the mining counties; dies at Oakland, Alameda County, survived by a daughter.

Richard B. Fentem, native of Missouri, 84; since 1867 San Joaquin Valley resident; died at Gustine, Merced County, survived by a wife and five children.

Mrs. Sarah Jane Happy, native of New York, 88; since 1867 Napa County resident; died at Napa City, survived by two children.

Mrs. Pauline Schad-Robles, native of Switzerland, 84; since 1866 resident Sacramento City, where she died; two children survive.

John Sylvester Upton, native of Illinois, 85; came in 1863; died at Lompoc, Santa Barbara County, survived by six children.

Judge Montgomery L. Short, native of New York, 81; came in 1863; died at Hanford, Kings County, survived by a wife and two children. He was Kings County's first district attorney and for eight years served as superior judge.

Mrs. Mary E. Fimple, native of Illinois, 72; came in 1862; died at Durham, Butte County, survived by eight children.

Louis Peter, native of France, 91; came in 1867 and after a short residence in San Francisco and Los Angeles Cities, settled fifty-seven years ago in San Rafael, Marin County, where he died; surviving are three children, among them Financial Secretary Louis J. Peter (Mount Tamalpais Parlor No. 64 N.S.G.W.).

Mrs. Helen Butler-Littlejohn, native of Ohio, 85; came via the Isthmus of Panama in 1859 and settled in Sutter County; died at Yuba City, survived by nine children.

Mrs. Roseana Kent, native of Ireland, 98; since 1858 resident Sacramento City, where she died; five children survive.

Mrs. Ella Whitmore-Gregory, native of Maine, 80; came in 1857 and settled in Alameda County; died at Livermore, survived by a husband. For years she taught school in Alameda County.

John W. Hinds, native of Tennessee, 93; came via the Isthmus of Panama in 1855 and resided in Nevada, Santa Clara and Alameda Counties; died at Berkeley, survived by a wife and ten children.

Gaston E. Bacon, native of France; since 1884 resident San Francisco, where he died; a wife survives.

Mrs. Irene Birnbaum-Frantz, native of Illinois; crossed the plains in 1852 and settled in Siskiyou County; died at Etna, survived by two daughters.

PIONEER NATIVES DEAD

(Brief Notices of the Demise of Men and Women born in California Prior to 1860.)

Edwin Lewis Meyer, born in Yuba County in 1856, died November 17 at San Francisco survived by a wife. He was a charter member of California Parlor No. 1 N.S.G.W.

Mrs. Julia Richmond-Tower, born at Sacramento City in 1857, died November 20 at San Jose, Santa Clara County, survived by three children.

William H. Keyes, born in Sierra County in 1855, died November 21 at Stockton, San Joaquin County, survived by a wife and two daughters.

Joseph Deighn Redding, born at Sacramento City in 1859, died November 21 at San Francisco survived by a wife. He was world famous as a musician and litterateur.

Mrs. Betty Safford, born in Del Norte County in 1852, died November 25 at Requa, survived by six children.

SAN FRANCISCO

rs. Bertha Meyor-Brown, born at San Fran-) in 1856, died November 25 at Marysville, a County, survived by three children. Most er life was spent in Sierra and Sutter Coun-

Irs. Katie Barry-Blois, born at San Francisco 859, died at Oakland, Alameda County, No-ber 26.

Irs. Lucy Lorenzana-Molares, born in Santa z County in 1857, died November 26 at Ala-la City survived by five children. She came n a family, the Lorenzanas, for 135 years ntified with Santa Cruz County history.

Irs. Sarah Ford-Peyton, born in Amador nty in 1853, died November 26 at Stockton, Joaquin County, survived by three children. was affiliated with Amapola Parlor No. 80 .G.W. (Sutter Creek).

harles B. Overacker, born in Placer County 1853, died November 27 near Niles, Alameda nty, survived by a wife and two children.

Irs. Frances Winship-Ahlf, born in Sutter nty in 1854, died November 27 at Yuba City vived by four children.

Villiam Derrick, born in Sonoma County in 5, died November 28 near Oregon House, ba County.

William A. Swerer, born in Tuolumne County 1859, died November 28 at Sonora.

Richard T. Hauskins, born in San Joaquin nty in 1852, died November 28 at Elk Grove, ramento County, survived by a wife and ee children. He was affiliated with Elk Grove rlor No. 41 N.S.G.W.

Mrs. Carmilla Garcia-Gomez, born in Mon-ey County in 1851, died November 29 at King y.

Mrs. Fannie Groves-Fulton, born in Yuba unty in 1858, died November 29 at Auburn, cer County, survived by three daughters.

Charles Grant Kopp, born in Amador County 1859, died December 1 at Woodland, Yolo unty, survived by a wife and a daughter.

Delphin M. Alvarado, born in Los Angeles unty in 1859, died December 1 at San Ber-rdino City survived by a wife and a son. He s a descendant of the Alvarado family iden-ed with the state's earliest history.

Henry M. Hyde, born in Fresno County in 54, died December 2 at Fresno City survived two daughters. He was a son of Mr. and s. S. S. Hyde, Pioneers of 1850.

Mrs. Elizabeth Bates-Clark, born in Humboldt unty in 1858, died December 2 at Ontario, n Bernardino County, survived by a daughter.

Perry Emerson, born in Sonoma County in 58, died December 4 near Greenfield, Kern unty, survived by two children. He was a son Mr. and Mrs. E. S. Emerson, Pioneers of 1849.

William H. Pyburn, born in Monterey County 1852, died December 4 at San Francisco sur-ed by three children. For fourteen years he ved Monterey County as recorder.

Larkin Green Fowler, born at San Francisco 1854, died December 4 at Lincoln, Placer unty, survived by a wife and seven children. was affiliated with Silver Star Parlor No. 63 S.G.W.

James Ellery, born in Shasta County in 1858, d December 7 at Oakland, Alameda County, rvived by a wife and three daughters.

Anthony Correll, born in Sierra County in 56, died December 8 at Woodland, Yolo Coun-survived by eight children. He resided many ars in Sutter County.

Mrs. Hannah F. Murphy, born at San Francisco in 1857, died December 9 at San Mateo City.

Arizona Charley Meadows, born in Tulare County in 1852, died December 11 at Yuma, Arizona State. He was a son of John Meadows, Tulare County's first coroner, who was killed by Indians in the Tonta Basin massacre.

Mrs. Ella Cushman-Bridgman, born in Tuolumne County in 1857, died December 13 at Oakland, Alameda County.

Thomas J. Dormody, born in El Dorado County in 1857, died December 14 at Placerville survived by a wife and nine children.

Miss Alameda Ballard, born in Solano County in 1857, died December 14 at Oakland, Alameda County.

Timothy Francis Murray, born at French Gulch, Shasta County, in 1858, died there December 16 survived by a wife and a daughter.

Miss Helen Louise Schlieman, born in Yolo County in 1859, died December 17 near Zamora.

BENEFIT BALL A SUCCESS.

The annual ball of the San Francisco N.S.G.W. and N.D.G.W. Parlors for the benefit of the homeless children was a huge success, financially and socially. James L. Foley was chairman of the arrangements committee, Mrs. W. H. Urmy the secretary and Chas. A. Koenig the treasurer. Judge A. J. Fritz was the floor director, and the grand march was led jointly by Governor James Rolph Jr. and Mayor Angelo J. Rossi.

Winners in the drum corps and drill team contests were: Mission Parlor No. 227 N.D.G.W., best N.D. drum corps; Alcalde Parlor No. 154 N.S.G.W., best N.S. drum corps; Mount Tamalpais Parlor No. 64 N.S.G.W. (San Rafael), best N.S. drum and field-music corps; Twin Peaks Parlor No. 185 N.D.G.W., best N.D. drill team.

NATIVE DAUGHTER DOINGS.

The children welfare committe of Orinda Parlor No. 56, under the leadership of Grand Inside Sentinel Orinda Giannini, visited Thanksgiving Day the tubercular wards of the San Francisco Hospital and presented each child with a chocolate football and funny paper. At the birthday party for the November girls, each was presented with a gift; Deputy Mae Waring was the guest of honor. December 9 the Parlor elected officers, Marie McGrath being chosen president. Orinda is looking forward to the official visit of the Grand President January 13.

Genevieve Parlor No. 132 had a delightful Christmas party December 15. Games were played, carols were sung and a delicious supper was served. Miss Hannah Toohig, as Santa Claus, gave each member a gift and candy. Mms. Lillian Ryan and Lillian Weisel arranged the attractive table decorations.

HEADS PROSPERITY DRIVE.

Grand Trustee Joseph J. McShane heads the 1933 prosperity drive of Twin Peaks Parlor No. 214 N.S.G.W. He has prepared a practical system whereby all delinquent members will be given an opportunity to be placed in good standing. The Order and the Parlor will, it is contended, be greatly benefited by his constructive resolution.

STATE'S OLDEST NATIONAL FOREST CELEBRATES FORTIETH ANNIVERSARY.

California's first national forest was created by President Benjamin Harrison December 20, 1892. His proclamation set aside 555,520 acres in Los Angeles County, known as the San Gabriel Timberland Reserve. This area was regarded as valuable for watershed protection by the United States Interior Department's geological survey and by the first California State Forestry Commission appointed by Governor George Stoneman in 1885.

From 1892 until 1897 it remained "reserved" from all forms of use except recreation. In 1908 it was consolidated with the old San Bernardino National Forest under the name of the Angeles, but in 1925 the two areas were again separated and administered as distinct units. Today the Angeles National Forest, with its area of 643,836 acres, is more intensively used for recreation than any other national forest in the United States, and two million persons obtain 80 percent of their water supply from the streams rising from its watersheds. Within its boundaries over one million persons annually find recreation.

Bridge Celebration—San Francisco is planning to celebrate January 15 commencement of construction work on the mammoth Golden Gate bridge.

Auto Show—The seventeenth annual Pacific Automobile Show will be held in the San Francisco Civic Auditorium commencing January 7.

Interest Reawakened—Interest in mining in California has been considerably reawakened, and many old mines are being worked.

Official Directory of Parlors of

ALAMEDA COUNTY.

Alameda No. 47, Alameda City—R. H. Fallmer, Pres.; Robt. H. Cavanaugh, Sec., 1806 Pacific Ave.; Wednesdays, Veterans Memorial Bldg.

Oakland No. 50, Oakland—F. R. Born, Pres.; F. M. Norris, Sec., 5595 Taft Ave.; Fridays, Native Sons Hall, 11th and Clay Sts.

Las Positas No. 96, Livermore—Dr. Donald M. Fraser, Pres.; John J. Kelly, Sec., P. O. box 341; Thursdays, Foresters Hall.

Eden No. 113, Hayward—John Meincke, Pres.; Filbert M. Soares, Sec., 1487 "B" St.; 2nd and 4th Tuesdays, Memorial Hall, Main St.

Piedmont No. 120, Oakland—Stanley Hadlen, Pres.; Charles Morando, Sec., 906 Vermont St.; Thursdays, Native Sons Hall, 11th and Clay Sts.

Wisteria No. 127, Alvarado—Henry May, Pres.; J. M. Scribner, Sec., Livermore; 1st Thursday, I.O.O.F. Hall.

Halcyon No. 146, Alameda City—S. Chesley Anderson, Pres.; J. C. Bates, Sec., 2139 Buena Vista Ave.; 1st and 3rd Tuesdays, I.O.O.F. Hall, 2329 Santa Clara Ave.

Brooklyn No. 151, Oakland—Frank B. Perry, Pres.; E. W. Cooney, Sec., 3907 14th Ave.; Wednesdays, Masonic Temple, 8th Ave. and E. 14th St.

Washington, No. 169, Centerville—M. D. Silva, Pres.; Allen G. Norris, Sec., P. O. box 31; 2nd and 4th Tuesdays, Hansen Hall.

Athens No. 195, Oakland—Milton O. Peterson, Pres.; Harold B. Farley, Sec., 4623 Benevides Ave.; Tuesdays, Native Sons Hall, 11th and Clay Sts.

Berkeley No. 210, Berkeley—F. Gohl, Pres.; R. J. Garrett, Sec., 1708 Virginia St.; Tuesdays, Native Sons Hall, 2108 Shattuck Ave.

Estudillo No. 223, San Leandro—Frank V. Pacheco, Pres.; Albert G. Pacheco, Sec., 1736 E. 14th St.; 1st and 3rd Tuesdays, U.P.E.C. Hall.

Claremont No. 240, Emeryville—Raymond P. Burke, Pres.; E. N. Thienger, Sec., 839 Hearst Ave., Berkeley; Tuesdays, Veterans Memorial Bldg., 43rd and Salem Sts.

Pleasanton No. 244, Pleasanton—Peter C. Madsen, Pres.; Ernest W. Schween, Sec.; 2nd and 4th Thursdays, I.O.O.F. Hall.

Niles No. 250, Niles—M. L. Fournier, Pres.; C. E. Martenstein, Sec.; 2nd Thursday, I.O.O.F. Hall.

Fruitvale No. 252, Oakland—William J. Keating Jr., Pres.; Ray B. Felton, Sec., 1575 Alice St.; Fridays, W.O.W. Hall, 3256 E. 14th St.

AMADOR COUNTY.

Amador No. 17, Sutter Creek—Frank Marre, Pres.; F. J. Payne, Sec.; 1st and 3rd Fridays, Native Sons Hall.

Excelsior No. 31, Jackson—Wm. Daugherty, Pres.; William Going, Sec.; 1st and 3rd Wednesdays, Native Sons Hall, 22 Court St.

Ione No. 33, Ione—Earl Grover, Pres.; Josiah H. Saunders, Sec.; 1st and 3rd Wednesdays, Native Sons Hall.

Plymouth No. 48, Plymouth—Chester G. Johnson, Pres.; Thos. D. Davis, Sec.; 1st and 3rd Saturdays, N.S.G.W. Hall.

BUTTE COUNTY.

Argonaut No. 8, Oroville—George N. Westwood, Pres.; Cyril R. Macdonald, Sec., P. O. box 502; 1st and 3rd Wednesdays, Veterans Memorial Hall.

Chico No. 21, Chico—Marcus Choisser, Pres.; Sam Lindsay Adams, Sec., Sacramento Blvd.; 2nd and 4th Thursdays, Elks Hall.

CALAVERAS COUNTY.

Chispa No. 139, Murphys—Maynard Segale, Pres.; Antone Malaspina, Sec.; Wednesdays, Native Sons Hall.

COLUSA COUNTY.

Colusa No. 69, Colusa City—Percy J. Cooke, Pres.; Phil J. Humburg, Sec., 223 Parkhill St.; Tuesdays, Eagles Hall.

CONTRA COSTA COUNTY.

General Winn No. 32, Antioch—Edmont T. Uren, Pres.; Joel H. Ford, Sec., P. O. box 311; 2nd and 4th Wednesdays, Union Hall.

Mount Diablo No. 101, Martinez—R. P. Anderson, Pres.; G. T. Barkley, Sec.; 1st and 3rd Mondays, I.O.O.F. Hall.

Byron No. 170, Byron—William E. Bunn, Pres.; H. G. Krumland, Sec.; 1st and 3rd Tuesdays, I.O.O.F. Hall.

Carquinez No. 205, Crockett—Thos. Cox, Pres.; Thomas I. Cahalan, Sec.; 1st and 3rd Wednesdays, I.O.O.F. Hall.

Richmond No. 217, Richmond—M. W. Amaral, Pres; Lloyd N. Mason, Sec., 11 6th St.; Wednesdays, Redmen Hall, 11th and Nevan Ave.

Concord No. 245, Concord—P. M. Soto, Pres.; D. E. Pramberg, Sec., P. O. box 235; 1st Tuesday, I.O.O.F. Hall.

Diamond No. 246, Pittsburg—Victor Ericsson, Pres.; Francis A. Irving, Sec., 248 E. 5th St.; 1st and 3rd Wednesdays, Veterans Memorial Bldg.

EL DORADO COUNTY.

Placerville No. 9, Placerville—Chris. C. Orelli, Pres.; Clyde R. Berriman, Sec., Wood St.; 2nd and 4th Tuesdays, Masonic Hall.

Georgetown No. 91, Georgetown—W. H. Breedlove, Pres.; O. F. Irish, Sec.; 2nd and 4th Wednesdays, I.O.O.F. Hall.

FRESNO COUNTY.

Fresno No. 25, Fresno City—Oliver M. Akers, Pres.; W. C. Guard, Sec., R.F.D. No. 2, box 379; 1st and 3rd Fridays, Pythian Castle, Cor. "R" and Merced Sts.

GRAND OFFICERS.

Dr. Frank I. Gonzalez..........Junior Past Grand President
Flood Bldg., San Francisco
Seth Millington..........Grand President
Gridley
Justice Emmet Seawell..........Grand First Vice-president
State Bldg., San Francisco
Chas. A. Koenig..........Grand Second Vice-president
531 35th Ave., San Francisco
Harmon D. Skillin..........Grand Third Vice-president
Mills Bldg., San Francisco
John T. Regan..........Grand Secretary
N.S.G.W. Bldg., 414 Mason St., San Francisco
John A. Corotto..........Grand Treasurer
560 No. 5th St., San Jose
W. B. O'Brien..........Grand Marshal
2324 Santa Clara St., Alameda
Gam Hurst..........Grand Inside Sentinel
Financial Center Bldg., Oakland
William A. Reuter..........Grand Outside Sentinel
1009 Marine Ave., Wilmington
Leslie Maloche..........Grand Organist
1611 No. Hudson Ave., Los Angeles
Chester Gannon.......... Historiographer
613 Capital Ntl. Bank Bldg., Sacramento

GRAND TRUSTEES.

Jesse H. Miller..........712 DeYoung Bldg., San Francisco
Eldred L. Meyer..........922 San Vicente Blvd., Santa Monica
John M. Burnett..........914 Bank Italy Bldg., San Jose
Henry S. Lyon..........Placerville
Joseph J. McShane..........419 Flood Bldg., San Francisco
Horace J. Leavitt..........Weaverville
Chas. H. Spengemann..........827 27th Ave., San Francisco

Selma No. 107, Selma—Chester E. Shepard, Pres.; E. C. Laughlin, Sec.; 1st Wednesday, American Legion Hall.

HUMBOLDT COUNTY.

Humboldt No. 14, Eureka—Henry Sundfors, Pres.; Loren M. Nelson, Sec., P.O. box 195; 2nd and 4th Mondays, Native Sons Hall.

Arcata No. 20, Arcata—F. A. Nicholson, Pres.; William Peters, Sec., P. O. box 1117; Thursdays, Native Sons Hall.

Ferndale No. 93, Ferndale—Hans P. Petersen, Pres.; C. H. Rasmussen, Sec., R.F.D., 47-A; 1st and 3rd Mondays, K.P. Hall.

KERN COUNTY.

Bakersfield No. 42, Bakersfield—George Taylor, Pres.; Henry A. Bannister, Sec., care Bank of America; 2nd and 4th Fridays, Justice Court, City Hall.

LAKE COUNTY.

Lower Lake No. 159, Lower Lake—Harold S. Anderson, Pres.; Albert Kugelman, Sec.; Thursdays, I.O.O.F. Hall.

LASSEN COUNTY.

Honey Lake No. 198, Standish—James C. Meeske, Pres.; N. V. Wemple, Sec., Litchfield; 1st and 3rd Wednesdays, Wrede Hall.

Big Valley No. 211, Bieber—George Bunselmeier, Pres.; A. W. McKenzie, Sec.; 1st and 3rd Wednesdays, I.O.O.F. Hall.

LOS ANGELES COUNTY.

Los Angeles No. 45, Los Angeles City—Leslie A. Packard, Pres.; Richard W. Fryer, Sec., 1629 Champlain Ter.; Thursdays, Merchant Plumbers Hall, 1832 So. Hope.

Ramona No. 109, Los Angeles City—Frank S. Adams, Pres.; John V. Scott, Sec., Patriotic Hall, 1816 So. Figueroa; Fridays, Patriotic Hall, 1816 So. Figueroa.

Hollywood No. 196, Los Angeles City—Henry G. Bodkin, Pres.; E. J. Reilly, Sec., Olive View; Mondays, 1089 No. Oxford Ave.

Long Beach No. 239, Long Beach—Francis H. Gentry, Pres.; W. W. Brady, Sec., 801 Jergins Trust Bldg.; 2nd and 4th Thursdays, Moose Hall, Elm and Anaheim.

Sepulveda No. 263, San Pedro—Patrick H. Doran, Pres.; H. E. Fairall, Sec., 1925 So. Pacific Ave.; 1st and 3rd Fridays, Redman Hall, 543 Shepherd St., Point Firmin.

Glendale No. 264, Glendale—Leslie F. Schellback, Pres.; Abel B. Molen, Sec., 508 So. Belmont St.; 1st and 3rd Tuesdays, Masonic Temple, 234 So. Brand Blvd.

Santa Monica Bay 267, Santa Monica—Arthur R. Leonard, Pres.; John J. Smith, Sec., 830 Rialto Ave., Venice; 1st and 3rd Wednesdays, Odd Fellows Hall, 1431 Third St.

Cahuenga No. 268, Reseda—Harold C. Trexler, Pres.; Carrol S. Driscoll, Sec., P.O. box 25, Chatsworth; first Friday, Alton Hall.

University No. 272, Los Angeles City—Bernard G. Hiss, Pres.; Martin DeFazio, Sec., 845 W. 53rd St.; Tuesdays, 471 W. 41st Place.

Compton No. 273, Compton—Laurence W. Cowan, Pres.; Wm. Don Castillo, Sec., 641 W. Bennett St.; 2nd and 4th Tuesdays, Mayo Hall, 231½ East Compton Blvd.

MADERA COUNTY.

Madera No. 130, Madera City—Cornelius Noble, Pres.; T. P. Cosgrave, Sec.; 1st and 3rd Thursdays, First National Bank Bldg.

MARIN COUNTY.

Mount Tamalpais No. 64, San Rafael—Arthur Hecht, Pres.; Manual A. Andrade, Sec., 532 Mission Ave.; 1st and 3rd Mondays, "B" Street Hall.

Sea Point No. 158, Sausalito—A. H. Bettencourt, Pres.; Manuel Santos, Sec., 6 Glen Drive; 1st and 3rd Wednesdays, Perry Bldg.

Nicasio No. 183, Nicasio—M. T. Farley, Pres.; R. J. Rogers, Sec.; 2nd and 4th Wednesdays, U.A.O.D. Hall.

MENDOCINO COUNTY.

Ukiah No. 71, Ukiah—W. B. Danis, Pres.; Ben Hofman, Sec., P. O. box 473; 1st and 3rd Mondays, I.O.O.F. Hall.

Broderick No. 117, Point Arena—Ivan Lawson, Pres.; C. J. Buchanan, Sec.; 1st and 3rd Thursdays, Forester Hall.

Alder Glen No. 200, Fort Bragg—Thomas Cooney, Pres.; C. R. Weller, Sec.; 2nd and 4th Fridays, I.O.O.F. Hall.

MERCED COUNTY.

Yosemite No. 24, Merced City—John J. Thronton, Pres.; True W. Fowler, Sec., P. O. box 781; 2nd and 4th Mondays, I.O.O.F. Hall.

Los Banos No. 206, Los Banos—Robert L. Puccinelli, Pres.; L. E. Sarbo, Sec., R.F.D., box 21; 2nd and 4th Wednesdays, Eagles Hall.

MONTEREY COUNTY.

Monterey No. 75, Monterey City—James Millington, Pres.; T. W. Krieger, Sec., 999 Franklin St.; 1st and 3rd Fridays, Knights Pythias Hall, Main St.

Santa Lucia No. 97, Salinas—Roy Martella, Pres.; R. W. Adcock, Sec., Route 3, box 180; Mondays, Native Sons Hall, 32 W. Alisal St.

ATTENTION, SECRETARIES!

THIS DIRECTORY IS PUBLISHED BY AUTHORITY OF THE GRAND PARLOR N.S.G.W.; AND ALL NOTICES OF CHANGES MUST BE RECEIVED BY THE GRAND SECRETARY (NOT THE MAGAZINE) ON OR BEFORE THE 20TH OF EACH MONTH TO INSURE CORRECTION IN NEXT ISSUE OF DIRECTORY.

win Peaks No. 214, San Francisco—Clifford Roberts, Pres.; Thos. Pendergast, Sec., 278 Douglas St.; Wednesdays, Willopi Hall, 4061 24th St.
l Capitan No. 222, San Francisco—Frank Rizzo, Pres.; James Hanna, Sec., 2450 27th Ave.; 1st and 3rd Thursdays, King Soloman Hall, 1739 Fillmore St.
uadalupe No. 231, San Francisco—Thomas Wall, Pres.; Alvin A. Johnson, Sec., 142 Rousseau St.; Tuesdays, Guadalupe Hall, 4551 Mission St.
astro No. 232, San Francisco—Roy Lund, Pres.; James H. Hayes, Sec., 4014 18th St.; Tuesdays, Native Sons Bldg., 414 Mason St.
alboa No. 234, San Francisco—George Schroth, Pres.; E. W. Boyd, Sec., 437 Cherry St.; Thursdays, Maccabee Hall, 5th Ave. and Clement St.
ret Harte No. 260, San Francisco—Chas. E. Lillie, Pres.; A. W. McElhatton, Sec., 103 Holloway Ave.; Tuesdays, West of Twin Peaks Hall, 233 Legion Court.
topia No. 270, San Francisco—A. E. Rosenbaum, Pres.; Herbert H. Schneider, Sec., 2455 16th Ave.; Tuesdays, American Hall, 20th and Capp Sts.

SAN JOAQUIN COUNTY.

Stockton No. 7, Stockton—John D. Gallagher, Pres.; R. D. Dorcey, Sec., P. O. box 388; Mondays, Native Sons Hall.
odi No. 18, Lodi—Jerome Solomon, Pres.; Dr. Clyde Brennan, Sec.; 2nd and 4th Wednesdays, Eagles Hall.
racy No. 186, Tracy—C. S. Selna, Pres.; R. J. Marraccini, Sec., R.F.D. No. 1, box 217; Thursdays, I.O.O.F. Hall.
anteca No. 271, Manteca—Chas. N. Howell Jr., Pres.; Leonard Faria, Sec., R.F.D., box 75, Lathrop; 1st and 3rd Wednesdays, I.O.O.F. Hall.

SAN LUIS OBISPO COUNTY.

San Miguel No. 150, San Miguel—H. Twisselman, Pres.; Otto Kuehl, Sec., Paso Robles; 1st and 3rd Wednesdays, Fraternal Hall.
ambria No. 152, Cambria—N. Storni, Pres.; A. S. Gay, Sec.; Wednesdays, Rigdon Hall.

SAN MATEO COUNTY.

edwood No. 66, Redwood City—Frank Deluchi, Pres.; A. S. Liguori, Sec., P. O. box 212; Thursdays, American Foresters Hall.
easide No. 95, Half Moon Bay—Andrew F. Gilcrest, Pres.; John G. Gilcrest, Sec.; 2nd and 4th Tuesdays, I.O.O.F. Hall.
enlo No. 185, Menlo Park—C. T. Maloney, Pres.; F. W. Johnson, Sec., P. O. box 601; Thursdays, Masonic Hall.
ebble Beach No. 230, Pescadero—Earle A. Williamson, Pres.; E. A. Shaw, Sec.; 2nd and 4th Wednesdays, I.O.O.F. Hall.
l Carmelo No. 256, Daly City—Theodore A. Clemens, Pres.; Ernest L. Micco, Sec., 639 Morse St., San Francisco; 2nd and 4th Wednesdays, Eagles Hall.
ndustrial City No. 269, South San Francisco—John C. Hamilton, Pres.; Geo. A. Roll, Sec., P. O. box 237; 2nd and 4th Mondays, Metropolitan Hall.

SANTA BARBARA COUNTY.

anta Barbara No. 116, Santa Barbara City—C. W. McCormick, Pres.; H. C. Sweetser, Sec., Court House; 1st and 3rd Wednesdays, I.O.O.F. Hall.

SANTA CLARA COUNTY.

San Jose No. 22, San Jose—Fred Carmichael, Pres.; Joseph Lawrence, Sec., 1095 No. First St.; Mondays, I.O.O.F. Hall.
anta Clara No. 100, Santa Clara City—C. A. Castro, Pres.; Clarence Clevenger, Sec., P. O. box 297; Wednesdays, Redmen Hall.
bservatory No. 177, San Jose—James J. Flannery, Prse.; A. B. Langford, Sec., Hall Records; Tuesdays, Knights Columbus Hall, 40 No. First St.
ountain View No. 215, Mountain View—Henry A. Schultze, Pres.; C. A. Antonioli, Sec., 301 Castro St.; 2nd and 4th Wednesdays, Mockbee Hall.
Palo Alto No. 216, Palo Alto—John C. Bernal, Pres.; Albert A. Quinn, Sec., 643 High St.; Mondays, Native Sons Bldg., Hamilton Ave. and Emerson St.

SANTA CRUZ COUNTY.

Watsonville No. 65, Watsonville—Fred R. Baese, Pres.; E. R. Tindall, Sec., R.F.D. No. 5, Box 313; 2nd and 4th Tuesdays, I.O.O.F. Hall.
Santa Cruz No. 90, Santa Cruz City—Horace Burkett, Pres.; T. V. Mathews, Sec., 105 Pacheco Ave.; Fridays, Native Sons Hall, 117 Pacific Ave.

SHASTA COUNTY.

McCloud No. 149, Redding—Roy Hawes, Pres.; Hugh A. Shuffleton, Sec.; 1st and 3rd Thursdays, Moose Hall.

SIERRA COUNTY.

Downieville No. 92, Downieville—Frank H. Turner, Pres.; H. S. Tibbey, Sec.; 2nd and 4th Mondays, I.O.O.F. Hall.
Golden Nugget No. 94, Sierra City—Elmer Thompson, Pres.; Arthur R. Pride, Sec.; 1st and 3rd Wednesdays, Masonic Hall.

SISKIYOU COUNTY.

Etna No. 192, Etna—Frank B. Quigley, Pres.; Harvey A. Green, Sec.; 1st and 3rd Wednesdays, I.O.O.F. Hall.
Liberty No. 193, Sawyers Bar—David H. Bobinson, Pres.; John M. Barry, Sec.; 1st and 3rd Saturdays, I.O.O.F. Hall.

SOLANO COUNTY.

Solano No. 39, Suisun—Karl Koch, Pres.; J. W. Kinlock, Sec.; 1st and 3rd Tuesdays, I.O.O.F. Hall.
Vallejo No. 77, Vallejo—Frank J. Heldener, Pres.; Werner B. Hallin, Sec., 912 Carolina; 2nd and 4th Tuesdays, San Pablo Hall.

SONOMA COUNTY.

Petaluma No. 27, Petaluma—Fred G. Ilg, Pres.; C. F. Fobes, Sec., 114 Prospect St.; 2nd and 4th Mondays, Druid Hall, Gross Bldg., 41 Main St.
Santa Rosa No. 28, Santa Rosa—George A. Eckman, Pres.; Leland S. Lewis, Sec., Court House; Mondays, Native Sons Hall.
Glen Ellen No. 102, Glen Ellen—Tony Cereghino, Pres.; Frank Kirch, Sec., Route 3, Santa Rosa; 2nd Monday, N.S.G.W. Hall.
Sonoma No. 111, Sonoma City—Chas. E. Baciglupi, Pres.; L. H. Green, Sec.; 1st and 3rd Mondays, I.O.O.F. Hall.
Sebastopol No. 143, Sebastopol—O. A. McChristian, Pres.; F. G. McFarlane, Sec.; 1st and 3rd Fridays, I.O.O.F. Hall.

STANISLAUS COUNTY.

Modesto No. 11, Modesto—Chas. D. Blaine, Pres.; C. C. Eastin Jr., Sec., P. O. box 898; 1st and 3rd Wednesdays, I.O.O.F. Hall.
Oakdale No. 142, Oakdale—D. W. Tulloch, Pres.; E. T. Gobin, Sec.; 2nd and 4th Mondays, Legion Hall.
Orestimba No. 247, Crows Landing—Lloyd W. Fink, Pres.; G. W. Fink, Sec.; 1st and 3rd Wednesdays, Community Club Home.

SUTTER COUNTY.

Sutter No. 261, Sutter City—Albert Thomasen, Pres.; Glen R. Haynes, Sec., R.F.D. No. 2, Yuba City; 2nd and 4th Mondays, N.D.G.W. Hall.

TRINITY COUNTY.

Mount Bally No. 87, Weaverville—R. L. Marshall, Pres.; E. V. Ryan, Sec.; 1st and 3rd Mondays, Native Sons Hall.

TULARE COUNTY.

Visalia No. 19, Visalia—G. W. Houk, Pres.; C. H. Wenn, Sec.

TUOLUMNE COUNTY.

Tuolumne No. 144, Sonora—Mathew J. Marshall, Pres.; William M. Harrington, Sec., P. O. box 715; 2nd and 4th Fridays, Knights Columbus Hall.

FREMONT HOLIDAYS

(Continued from Page 9)

have been organized and would never have committed its overt act against Mexican rule. Fremont, the Pathfinder, the man unafraid, despite all of his services to his country, had finally settled on his head more unhappy circumstances than perhaps any other figure in American history. Between the jealousies of the Army and the Navy, the attacks by politicians and petty men in Washington, a cloud of calumny was raised which still hangs over the name of this noble American, whose greatest weakness, perhaps, was his independency, his incorruptibility and his refusal to fawn upon the petty politicians of his day.

NATIVE SON NEWS

(Continued from Page 8)

uty Monroe Label and Manuel Soares are active in promoting the interparlor organization.

Dinner Dance.

Menlo Park—Menlo No. 185 and Menlo No. 211 N.D.G.W. had their annual Christmas dinner dance December 15. President C. T. Maloney of No. 185 was the toastmaster, and a feature was the singing of carols. The Parlors are taking an active part in local relief work and made cash donations to help fill the Christmas baskets for the needy.

Past Grand Celebrates Anniversary.

Napa—Past Grand Henry C. Gesford and wife celebrated December 3 their golden wedding anniversary at the San Francisco home of their daughter, Mrs. Maidie Jones. Gesford, seventy-six years of age, was born near Calistoga, Napa County, and his wife is a native of Fairfield, Solano County. For eighteen successive years he was superior judge of Napa County, and also served the county as school superintendent and district attorney, and was for two terms a member of the State Senate.

Publishers To Meet—Newspaper publishers of California will have their forty-fifth annual convention at Marysville, Yuba County, January 19-21.

"To be prepared for war is one of the most effectual means of preserving peace."—George Washington.

"Curses are like young chickens, and still come home to roost."—Bulwer.

Columbia No. 258, Columbia—Jos. Cadematori, Pres.; Charles E. Grant, Sec.; 2nd and 4th Thursdays, Native Sons Hall.

VENTURA COUNTY.

Cabrillo No. 114, Ventura City—David Bennett, Pres., 1380 Church St.

YOLO COUNTY.

Woodland No. 30, Woodland—J. L. Aronson, Pres.; R. G. Lawson, Sec.; 1st Thursday, Native Sons Hall.

YUBA COUNTY.

Marysville No. 6, Marysville—Ray C. Burris, Pres.; Verne Fogarty, Sec., 719 6th St.; 2nd Friday, Foresters Hall.
Rainbow No. 40, Wheatland—F. M. Beilby, Pres.; W. A. Bowser, Sec., P. O. box 313; 2nd Thursday, I.O.O.F. Hall.

AFFILIATED ORGANIZATIONS.

San Francisco Extension of the Order Committee, N.S.G.W.—Joseph J. McShane, Chmn.; Harold J. Regan, Sec., 414 Mason St., San Francisco; meets 2nd and 4th Fridays, Grizzly Bear Club, 414 Mason St., San Francisco.
Alameda County Extension of the Order Committee, N.S.G.W.—Edward T. Schnarr, Chmn.; Frank Roemer, Sec., 3297 Morcom Ave., Oakland; meets 1st and 3rd Mondays, N.S.G.W. Hall, 11th and Clay Sts., Oakland.
Interparlor Committee (Southern District), N.S.G.W. and N.D.G.W.—Burrel D. Neighbours, Chmn.; F. J. Burmester, Sec., P. O. box 42, Colton; meets 2nd and 4th Fridays, Patriotic Hall, 1816 So. Figueroa St., Los Angeles.
San Francisco Assembly No. 1 Past Presidents Association N.S.G.W.—Meets 1st and 3rd Fridays, Native Sons Bldg., 414 Mason St., San Francisco; Jos. E. Tracy, Gov.; J. F. Stanley, Sec., 1175 O'Farrell St., San Francisco.
East Bay Counties Assembly No. 3 Past Presidents Association N.S.G.W.—Meets 4th Monday, Native Sons Hall, 11th and Clay Sts., Oakland; Felix Robison, Gov.; Edgar G. Hanson, Sec., 1260 Russell St., Berkeley.
Marin County Assembly No. 5 Past Presidents Association N.S.G.W.—J. S. Rose Jr., Gov.; L. J. Peter, Sec., Peter Bldg., 4th and "C" Sts., San Rafael.
Fred H. Greeley Assembly No. 6 Past Presidents Association N.S.G.W.—Meets monthly with different Parlors comprising district; R. L. P. Bigelow, Gov.; Barney Barry, Sec., P. O. box 72, Lincoln.
San Joaquin Assembly No. 7 Past Presidents Association N.S.G.W.—Meets 1st Friday, Native Sons Hall, Stockton; Clyde H. Gregg, Gov.; R. D. Dorcey, Sec., Native Sons Club, Stockton.
Sonoma County Assembly No. 9 Past President Association N.S.G.W.—Meets monthly at different Parlor headquarters in county; P. A. R. Gambini, Gov.; L. S. Lewis, Sec., Court House, Santa Rosa.
General John A. Sutter Assembly No. 10 Past Presidents Association—C. C. Wachman, Gov.; Jas. J. Longshore, Sec., 514 "J" St., Sacramento.
Grizzly Bear Club—Members all Parlors outside San Francisco at all times welcome. Clubrooms top floor Native Sons Bldg., 414 Mason St., San Francisco.
Native Sons and Native Daughters Central Committee on Homeless Children—Main office, 955 Phelan Bldg., San Francisco; Mrs. John W. Stirling, Chmn.; Miss Mary E. Brusie, Sec. Los Angeles branch office, 3974 Sunset Blvd.; Dorothy Schlingman, Sec.

(ADVERTISEMENT.)

BOOK REVIEWS

(CLARENCE M. HUNT.)

"ON THE TRAILS OF YESTERDAY."

By Roy W. Cloud; Harr Wagner Publishing Co., San Francisco, Publishers; Price, $2.50.

This work, in simple language, most interestingly recites considerable of the history of California, and makes special reference to some of those most prominent in the making of that history. The story features the American era, opening with the journey of the Wilsey family overland in 1853, and continuing with accounts of their visits to various places of the state. The author has dedicated the book "To my mother and to the other Pioneer Mothers of the West. Overcoming unknown dangers, they builded on the Pacific a mighty commonwealth."

Anyone interested in California history will enjoy "On the Trails of Yesterday," which is extensively illustrated by Ray Bethers. Author Cloud is a member of Redwood Parlor No. 66 N.S.G.W. of Redwood City. He was formerly superintendent of San Mateo County schools, and is now executive secretary of the California Teachers Association.

N.S.G.W. OFFICIAL DEATH LIST.

Containing the name, the date and the place of birth, the date of death, and the Subordinate Parlor affiliation of deceased members reported to Grand Secretary John T. Regan from November 20, 1932, to December 20, 1932:

Meyer, Edwin Lewis; Marysville, June 10, 1855; November 17, 1932; California No. 1.
Abraham, Henry; Weaverville, September 7, 1873; December 14, 1932; California No. 1.
Clark, Wallace G.; Nevada City, May 9, 1880; September 11, 1932; Sacramento No. 3.
Lamphrey, William N.; San Francisco, June 10, 1855; November 6, 1932; Sacramento No. 3.
Maltby, Maynard; Smiths, March 11, 1872; December 11, 1932; Sacramento No. 3.
Kuehler, Frank John; Sacramento, November 20, 1862; December 14, 1932; Sacramento No. 3.
Quirolo, Victor; Sutter Creek, April 16, 1868; November 11, 1932; Amador No. 17.
Stanton, Oscar F.; Linden, April 27, 1873; November 1, 1932; Santa Rosa No. 28.
Toomey, Henry Christopher Jos.; San Francisco, May 29, 1878; November 10, 1932; Golden Gate No. 29.
Davis, David Elmer; Sutter Creek, November 21, 1864; November 25, 1932; Golden Gate No. 29.
Donovan, Robert Joseph; San Francisco, December 29, 1879; July 28, 1932; Mission No. 38.
Barnes, Fred H.; San Francisco, April 25, 1905; October 5, 1932; Mission No. 38.
Schroder, John D.; San Francisco, June 3, 1868; November 18, 1932; El Dorado No. 52.
Lindley, Bayliss Bartlett; Nevada City, March 28, 1901; November 6, 1932; Hydraulic No. 56.
Evans, Walter; Forest, August 3, 1891; November 27, 1932; Hydraulic No. 56.
Wynn, John Edward; San Francisco, August 2, 1864; December 2, 1932; Rincon No. 72.
Carson, George Henry; Los Angeles, October 26, 1863; November 20, 1932; Ramona No. 109.
Cashin, James Owen; Nevada City, October 16, 1865; December 3, 1932; Ramona No. 109.
Heyer, Charles; Alvarado, April 22, 1866; November 18, 1932; Eden No. 113.
Miller, August; Point Arena, March 3, 1865; November 10, 1932; Broderick No. 117.
Wolf, August; San Francisco, February 4, 1874; February 1932; San Miguel No. 150.
Sanchez, Michael D.; Ventura, August 29, 1865; July 1932; San Miguel No. 150.
Davis, Charles; Monterey, February 21, 1864; October 21, 1932; San Miguel No. 150.
Code, George Robert; San Francisco, January 5, 1863; October 19, 1932; South San Francisco No. 157.
Finnocchio, Peter Jerome; San Francisco, January 1, 1880; October 26, 1932; South San Francisco No. 157.
Giblin, Francis; San Francisco, August 2, 1876; December 2, 1932; South San Francisco No. 157.
Naughton, Charles Leremiah; San Francisco, June 24, 1880; November 17, 1932; Sequoia No. 160.
Swanson, John J.; San Francisco, October 11, 1876; December 12, 1932; Presidio No. 194.
Schnieder, Roy Albert; San Francisco, August 10, 1897; December 6, 1932; Twin Peaks No. 214.
Malcolm, Norman E.; Swedes Flat, June 21, 1862; October 31, 1932; Palo Alto No. 216.
Kerr, Ignatius A.; San Francisco, August 1, 1886; November 11, 1932; Castro No. 232.
McGrath, Raymond J.; Redlands, September 15, 1892; November 17, 1932; Glendale No. 264.

THANKSGIVING.

(GEORGE E. PHAIR.)

"I thank Thee, Lord," the workman said,
"For all Thy golden wheat,
Enough to flood the world with bread,
Though I have none to eat.

"I thank Thee for the cotton bales
That tower high in the air
To fend the world from wintry gales
Though I have naught to wear.

"I thank Thee for the whirring wheels
That fashion shoes to wear
Although the stony pavement feels
Unkind when soles are bare.

"I thank Thee for the teeming herds
That graze on grasses sweet
Though statesmen fling me empty words
Instead of good red meat.

"And though the landlord's heart is cold
Against my last appeal,
I thank Thee, Lord, for all the gold
That fills our vaults of steel!"

—Washington Herald, Nov. 1931.

LOS ANGELES--CITY and COUNTY

LOS ANGELES

(Continued from Page 7)

(Bear) Flag to the Glendale City Council. This was the Parlor's third flag presentation for 1932, others going to the Glendale high school and the California State building in Los Angeles. December 27 the Parlor had a birthday party for its November and December members.

STOP SINGING THE BLUES.

Ramona Parlor No. 109 N.S.G.W. had a real old-spirit meeting December 16, and the attendance was big, as in the pre-depression days. Special consideration was given the members born in December and they were honor-guests at a dinner preceding the meeting. Past President Charles G. Young was presented with an emblematic ring, there were many enthusiastic talks, and Past Grand President Herman C. Lichtenberger and Leo V. Youngworth staged an indoor horseshoe match. The Doce Caballeros, a Ramona auxiliary, is sponsoring a dance at Patriotic Hall January 21; 25 cents per person. "Let's stop singing the blues and make this a smashing success," urges Fred Staebler, who will be the floor director.

Scoutmaster Robert Dunn took the Scouts of Troop No. 109 on a hiking trip into the snow-covered mountains the week-end of December 17, and they had a glorious time. The Scouts will distribute baskets to needy families the latter part of January, and members of Ramona are urged to make liberal contributions of canned foods every Friday night including January 27. Ramona wants to start 1932 off with a bang, and so has arranged an affair for January 20 which all Natives and their friends, female and male, are urged to enjoy. Dinner will be served at 6:30, the January boys being guests and all non-members paying the small sum of 25 cents. Following the feast a marvelous program is promised, under the direction of Beulah Belle Smith of Glendale. No charge for the show. Those intending to be at the dinner must notify Secretary John V. Scott not later than January 18. Charles Straube has charge of the affair. January 13 the Parlor will have initiation.

HOSTESS TO NEIGHBORING PARLORS.

Los Angeles Parlor No. 124 N.D.G.W. initiated a class of candidates December 7. Dr. Madeline Verneka, director of the course of study in the public schools, delivered an educational message. Florence Dodson Schoneman praised the history work done by the Parlor, and other speakers were Past Grand President Grace S. Stoermer, Grand Outside Sentinel Hazel Hansen and Deputy Rita Smith. December 21 was a gala night with No. 124—the annual Christmas party under the chairmanship of Gertrude Allen, assisted by the other past presidents. Such fun, presents and "eats!"

The veteran welfare committee of No. 124—Inez O'Shea (chairman), Edna Trombatore, Ann Schiebusch, Evelyn Trautwein, Juanita Porter and Ramona Thoroughgood—visited the National Soldiers Home at Sawtelle Thanksgiving Day and presented lovely, generously filled gift-boxes to the bed-ridden vets. A committee chairmaned by President Mattie Labory-Gara presented numerous Christmas boxes to the deserving. Olinda Kerby and committee are receiving compliments for the Parlor's artistic yearbook.

Los Angeles was hostess at a joint meeting of representatives of Long Bech No. 154, Rudecinda No. 230, Santa Ana No. 235, Verdugo No. 240, Grace No. 242, Santa Monica Bay No. 245 and Californiana No. 247 Parlors, to plan for the official visit of Grand President Anna Mixon Armstrong to the southland from March 7 to 23. The gathering was called by Past Grand President Grace S. Stoermer. Refreshments were served in the tea room, beautifully decorated in Christmas colors, the poinsettia predominating. Delicious home-made refreshments, prepared by Edna Holcomb, were served at tables arranged to form a star. Mrs. Juanita Porter headed the able arrangements committee, and Mrs. Acension Simon furnished music. All enjoyed the wonderful evening. The January calendar for Los Angeles includes: 4th, initiation. 11th, card party, final of the tournament; Olinda Kerby chairman. 18th, potluck dinner, followed by a talk on "Bret Harte's Writings of California" by Dr. Chamberlain. 25th, reception to Congressman-elect and Mrs. William I. Traeger.

SEVEN INITIATED.

University Parlor No. 272 N.S.G.W. added seven additional names to its rolls December 20, the ritual being impressively rendered by a team of present and past officers of Sepulveda Parlor No. 263 (San Pedro) and Arrowhead Parlor No. 110 (San Bernardino), with Francis Fetzer, of the former, as president. Many visitors were in attendance, including a large delegation from Arrowhead, and on that Parlor's behalf President F. L. McGarvey presented University with a seal.

Among the speakers of the evening were Grand Organist Leslie Maloche, Deputy Grand President Walter Hiskey, District Deputy Walter Baskerville, Bob Brazelton, Vincent Hopkins, President Joseph Pia of San Pedro, President Bernard Hiss of University and Judge Donald E. VanLuven. University Parlor had its second monthly dance December 27.

HOUSEWARMING.

Santa Monica—Santa Monica Bay Parlor No. 267 N.S.G.W. and Santa Monica Bay Parlor No. 245 N.D.G.W. had a joint housewarming at their new meetingplace, Odd Fellows Hall, 1431 Third street, December 28. Some 200 guests were entertained. Dancing and cards were provided as entertainment features, and refreshments were served. Arthur R. Leonard and Mrs. Eldred Meyer had charge of arrangements.

Santa Monica N.S.G.W. will hold its annual lobster feast February 1—good news that will be received with delight by all southland Native Sons.

JOINT N.S. INSTALLATION.

Officers of Los Angeles Parlor No. 45, Ramona Parlor No. 109, Santa Monica Bay Parlor No. 267 and University Parlor No. 272 N.S.G.W. will be jointly installed January 10 at public ceremonies to be held at the meetingplace of University Parlor, 471 West Forty-seventh place. The presidents-elect of the Parlors are, respectively, Leslie Packard, Frank Adams, Arthur Leonard and Bernard Hiss.

PERSONAL PARAGRAPHS.

Miss Ann Schiebusch (Los Angeles N.D.) made a flying visit to San Francisco last month.

A native daughter arrived at the home of Oscar Nyland (Ramona N.S.) during November.

Irving Baxter (Ramona N.S.) spent the Thanksgiving holiday in Fresno City, visiting his son.

Mrs. Ralph Tuttle (Californiana N.D.) entertained at supper at her home, for the benefit of the Parlor, December 1.

Miss Julia Larson (Los Angeles N.D.) and William Jeff Morrison were married at the home of her mother in Bakersfield, November 30. They are residing in Santa Ana.

Miss Mildred Connolly and Walter H. Odemar (Ramona N.S.) were wedded November 18, and following a honeymoon in San Francisco and Seattle are residing in Los Angeles.

Robert W. Kenny (Ramona N.S.) has been appointed a superior judge, and Albert Scott (Hollywood N.S.) and George Dockweiler (Ramona N.S.) have been appointed municipal judges.

Eugene W. Biscailuz (Santa Monica Bay N.S.) was appointed sheriff of Los Angeles County by the Board of Supervisors to succeed William I. Traeger (Past Grand President N.S.), elected to Congress.

In recognition of their fifteenth wedding anniversary, Mrs. Clarence E. Noerenberg (Californiana N.D.) and husband were tendered a surprise December 10. It being the crystal anniversary of the couple they were presented with a goodly number of appropriate remembrances following a delightful spanish dinner. Those present included Messrs. and Mms. Walter E. Baskerville, Larry Chapman, Robert Shinn, Edward Tabor, Louis Hansen, Edward Gibbs, Paul P. Lombardi, Stephen Stevenson; Mms. Narcisse de Garnier, Chandos E. Bush; Ursula Silver, Mildred Beckwith, Jeanne Parker, Leon J. Leonard, J. Perry Lewis Jr.

THE DEATH RECORD.

Raymond J. McGrath, former secretary of Glendale Parlor No. 264 N.S.G.W., died November 17. He was born at Redlands, San Bernardino County, September 15, 1892.

Claude L. Friel, brother of Grant Friel (Ramona N.S.), died November 30 at Chicago, Illinois State.

James Owen Cashin, affiliated with Ramona Parlor No. 109 N.S.G.W., died December 3 at San Francisco. He was born at Nevada City, Nevada County, October 16, 1865.

Mrs. Grace Riley, wife of Charles Riley (Hollywood N.S.), died December 8.

Mrs. Mary E. Borden, mother of Perry R. Borden (Ramona N.S.), died December 12.

Mrs. Elizabeth A. Waterman, mother of Herbert R. Waterman (Ramona N.S.), died December 17.

Rosa del Valle, sister of Mrs. Walter B. Cram and Mrs. John R. Kirby (Californiana N.D.), died December 17 at Santa Monica.

Mrs. Josephine Jones Fischer, affiliated with Los Angeles Parlor No. 124 N.D.G.W., died December 18.

Louis P. Waterman, affiliated with Los Angeles Parlor No. 45 N.S.G.W., died at West Los Angeles December 24 survived by a wife and a daughter. He was a native of San Francisco, aged 64, and was chief deputy public administrator of Los Angeles County.

Frank LeGrande Turner, affiliated with Ramona Parlor No. 109 N.S.G.W., died at South Pasadena December 25 survived by a wife. He was a native of Hayward, Alameda County, aged 47, and was a deputy sheriff of Los Angeles County.

WHAT MAN HATH DONE

(Continued from Page 2)

heard that he told it to anyone else. He knew that I sympathized with him.

"I am now seventy-nine and have not seen him since 1868, but think of him as a wonderful man to do so well for his education. Having had a letter from the secretary of the Y.M.C.A. in Sacramento, which is my home-town, who has read my 'Life and Letters of a '49er's Daughter' and seems to understand it, I decided to send this story to The Grizzly Bear. Because, what man hath done, man can do! And we do not need any more 'illiteracy,' if only boys will start out like William Gwin. This is the story that was told to me by him:

"'My father married a baby-doll, and when he died she wanted a good time, so she gave me away to a colored mammy and moved to another town, and I have never seen her since. I worked for my living since I was six years old. I saw the colored boys growing up, and they laughed all the time and danced to funny steps. But I soon made up my mind not to dance or carry on so!

"'Very soon I found out that people must learn to read. By the time I was six years old I nearly went crazy. My colored mammy was good to me, but she could not read, so I worked for a primer with the letters in, but there was no one to teach me. Finally I met in the street a man who was very fair, with bright hair. Some one told him I was making every one wild trying to learn my letters, and he took notice of me. He asked me my name, and it was the same as his own. Pretty soon he found out we were related—he was an uncle of my father. By that time I was ten years old, and he helped me to learn to read. When I was twelve he advised me to join a party going west to California, by being a driver of cattle, and grow up with a new beginning to my life.

"'He helped me to get a start, being a driver of cattle himself. Soon after he died, but I always remembered him because he was a perfect gentleman. I tried to be like him, because he was the only one of my family I ever knew. It was a long time before we got across the many miles to the West, and I studied every spare moment I had. Most of the people along the way could read and write, and some of the women helped me.

"'At last I came to Sacramento and became a helper to a man who sold milk. By this time I was a big, husky boy. However, I still kept on with my books, and one day I learned about the Methodist college in Santa Clara. There was a Catholic college there, also, but I decided to be a Methodist. My uncle had been a Methodist, and I wanted to be like him. So I worked for a man in Santa Clara who helped me so I could work my way through college. I don't remember how long I was there, but I expected to go back, when I came over to Aurora Esmeralda and got a job driving oxen.

"'That was when I saw you that day, and made you go home. And since then I have joined the Methodist church here, and sing in the choir. Some have made fun of me in this town, but I'm going to sell my mine, and go East and marry a schoolteacher so that the little fellows, if there are any, will learn to read at home and know more than their father.'

"I have not seen William Gwin since 1868, but I heard that he had married a schoolteacher and was perfectly happy."

Here is an excerpt from the Sacramento letter referred to by Mrs. Mighels: "What a long, useful life you have led, and think of the great good that you have done. One reason why we are carrying on this Y.M.C.A. work for mountain young people is because the 'church around that Pioneer Mother's knee' seems to have faded away in these modern times, and many of those old church buildings that were built during the days of '49 now stand with broken windows, the yards grown up in weeds, and the buildings going into decay. I find that ninety-seven percent of the boys and girls of high-school age in these mountain counties have no church relationships. They are such a fine group of boys and girls, too, who respond so willingly to any challenge that is given to them.—F. M. Duckles, district secretary Mountain District Y.M.C.A."

(This story came to The Grizzly Bear from Mrs. Ella Sterling Mighels of San Francisco, well known to readers of the magazine. She says: "I knew William Gwin of Virginia in the mines, and was so impressed by his story I gave it in a magic-lantern-slide lecture here in the public schools years ago. I think his wonderful story should be published in The Grizzly Bear because I have been informed there is 'illiteracy up in the northern counties.'"—Editor.)

KATE OBRADOVICH.

It was with sad and heavy hearts that the members of Amapola Parlor No. 80 N.D.G.W. received word of the passing of Sister Kate Obradovich. After a life of devotion to family and friends, it has been the wish of Him who doeth all things well to call our sister home.

Resolved, That we extend to her bereaved family our deepest sympathy.

"Be comforted, ye loved ones who weep,
She lives with God, she is just asleep."

Be it further resolved, that these resolutions be spread upon the minutes of the Parlor, that a copy of the same be presented to the sorrowing family, and that a copy be sent to The Grizzly Bear for publication.

ROSE LAWLOR,
ETHEL J. DANERI,
HILDA ESOLA,
Committee.

Sutter Creek, December 22, 1932.

Auto Show—The twentieth annual Los Angeles Auto Show will open January 7 and continue nine days.

CLASSIFIED DIRECTORY
LOS ANGELES NATIVE SONS

ATTORNEYS-AT-LAW.

HENRY G. BODKIN. V. P. LUCAS.
Chester Williams Bldg., 215 W. 5th St.
Phone: MUtual 3151.

DAVID H. CLARK.
215 West Fifth St.
Phone: MUtual 5406.

WM. J. HUNSAKER.
458 So. Spring St., Room 1130.
Phone: TRinity 6656.

EDWIN A. MESERVE. SHIRLEY E. MESERVE.
555 So. Flower St.
Phone: TRinity 6161.

THOS. B. REED.
548 South Spring St.
Phone: VAndike 0687.

DENTIST.

ROBERT J. GREGG, D.D.S.
5801 South Figueroa St.
Phone: THornwall 3690.
Hours 9 to 5, and by appointment.

DETECTIVE SERVICE.

LOUIS A. DUNI.
523 Washington Bldg., 311½ So. Spring.
Phone: TUcker 3013.

Feminine World's Fads and Fancies

PREPARED ESPECIALLY FOR THE GRIZZLY BEAR BY ANNA STOERMER

WHEN THE RAINY DAYS COME, and come they must, one may note with interest the new designs in wet weather togs. They have improved from heavy practical rubber to cravenet, and now to waterproof tweeds, rubberized crepes and waterproof leather. A stunning new model has nothing of the old style dreary, cloudy-day look. It is made of waterproof tweed in a deep but very dull blue, and is belted. Many models are made of reversible rubberized crepe on one side and ostrich plaid wool on the other side.

Black and blue are the two smartest colors for coats and suits; gray and blue with either dark blue or bright blue. We never have a good thing to say for the dark blue, having for years considered it too middle-aged for words, but if you like it, don't mind, just go ahead and wear it, with the knowledge that it is one of the season's smart shades.

Gray strikes a high note in the fashion world, being shown in varied tones from the soft dove and pearl grays to those with a tint of pink or lavender in their mixtures. It looks so new, so chic and so different, both in lighter and oxford grays. But please don't wear gray stockings or gray gloves with gray outfits. This new popularity has lifted gray into a dominant place. It is being used for every occasion, day and evening, formal and informal, and in every fabric from velvets and crepes to the soft woolens and knitted materials.

A frock of gray rabbit-hair cloth resembling angora in fuzzy texture has the sleeves gathered into deep cuffs, adorned with large white-yarn dots. The waist is plain, is cut with a "V" neck in front, and has a scarf. The frock is belted at the normal waistline, and the skirt is plain except for two kick-plaits at the front widths. This suit is worn with black accessories. The skirt is of average length, well down over the calves.

Most all of the new sports dresses are rough, but loosely woven and light in weight. Beside the various wool textures, the popular materials include chevrons, cords, both fancy and plain jerseys, and knit goods. Everyone will be wearing suits again and the smartest will be tailored, making them becoming to more people. They are plain and quite refreshing, after two seasons of fancier things.

With the new suits we have the adorable sailor hats. Please notice that they are worn straight down over the forehead and turned up at the back. And right here I pause to remark that they must be black, to be worn with gray suits. Brown accessories have been smart with gray, but they must be black this season to be considered smart with gray.

We are going strong just now with old-gold and brown, which is still considered good style. Browns continue to cover the favorite range of colors. They seem almost to have covered the place of the old reliable black. Brown in dark shades is used for afternoon coats and suits, no matter what the fashion costume. They have heavy trimmings of fur, preferably astrakan or fox. Light, soft browns make the sports suits for the younger generation, and browns of all varieties appear in evening dresses and wraps.

Brown lace for evening wear is kept in a solid color scheme, or is trimmed with beige or some bright touch of green or red. Brilliant hues rule in garb for evening. Pale pastel and white evening gowns have yielded their long established prestige to the rich and brilliant tones. Purples dark and light, violet and hyacinth have led the way to the introduction of other deep colors, including fuschia, green, turquoise, blue and red. Vivid nasturtium yellows and browns range from autumn leaf to the rich dark browns.

You may want to select something particularly smart for dinner. Why not choose one of the new taffetas of black, strikingly trimmed with bandings of gold and having a little jacket which, if removed, leaves a decollete evening gown for formal wear? If fashion has a favorite for formal wear, it is perhaps white. So again milady might turn with certainty of chic and charm to white.

A simple, stately gown, looming in its very severity for loveliness, has a perfectly plain skirt rippling at the bottom, and the bodice is a solid mass of sequins in silver, designed with a high straightly crossing line in front and a very low decolletage in the back. The shoulders are draped, and gathered with an ornament of brilliants.

Of course, we have heard a lot about the smartest evening gowns for this winter made of wool crepe. There are practical reasons for this popularity, for those who wear girdles and corset variations find that it is only in the woolen dress that the figure remains smoothly outlined. The weight of the fabric eliminates the breaks in the line of the silhouette that are bound to come, even on the youngest, most girlish figure. Women who consider themselves too full of figure to wear white satin or crepe, find white wool is thoroughly satisfactory.

Greater stress than ever before is centered this season about accessories that complete the smart costume. Never have there been so many different styles of hats, bags and shoes, not to mention costume jewelry, and scarfs of both fur and fabric. Certainly, never before has costume jewelry been so lovely nor so interesting as it is this time of the year. A costume is in no way complete without necklace, earrings, bracelet or some other intriguing decorative fancy. When choosing for formal wear, be restrained in your choice when you cast your eye toward costume jewelry for dinner gowns. For formal afternoon look for the picturesque, but when you seek costume jewelry to wear with sports clothes then let your conscience be your guide. Sports jewelry is exotic, and follows the primitive trend this season.

"To the Elder Brother—My hand goes out to all those who are trying to teach man to THINK and to act on his thoughts."—Jeanette Nourland.

"Deeds are greater than words. . . . We must work because the capacity to work is given to us and if no fruit of our work ever comes to us, so much the greater honor we are entitled to if we work faithfully."—Exchange.

"A word fitly spoken is like apples of gold in baskets of silver."—Bible.

Grizzly Bear

FEBRUARY — THE ONLY OFFICIAL PUBLICATION OF THE NATIVE SONS AND DAUGHTERS OF THE GOLDEN WEST — 1933

Featuring

GENERAL NEWS OF INTEREST CONCERNING ALL CALIFORNIA, and ORDERS NATIVE SONS and NATIVE DAUGHTERS

Price: 15 Cents

"MARK OUR LANDMARKS"

Chester F. Gannon
(HISTORIOGRAPHER N.S.G.W.)

"MARK OUR LANDMARKS"

EDWARD D. BAKER

HERETOFORE, THIS COLUMN HAS adverted to the neglected grave of Edward D. Baker in Laurel Hill Cemetery, San Francisco. Feeling that we are inexcusably and forever neglectful of our fraternal mission, if we do not rescue from oblivion the grave of California's most gifted and heroic Pioneer, this subject is again alluded to.

Were Baker of the ordinary mold of Pioneer, then perhaps the unanswered "call to remembrance" of your Historian would have fulfilled his duty, and he would have passed on to other subjects during his incumbency. But we cannot be faithful to our trust, we cannot be faithful to the past, we cannot call ourselves a fraternity dedicated to history, its men and achievements, unless we perform this duty.

Is Baker neglected because he is little known? Is not his greatness known to all loyal Californians? Perhaps the answer is that it is not and, for that reason, neglect and inattention have played their unhappy parts.

If there was a Californian of the early days who was entitled to the homage, the reverence and the respect of all who followed him, that man was Baker. He far outstrode his contemporaries. His record had been brilliant before he came to this state. Once here, he became California's foremost orator, its greatest criminal lawyer, and its most heroic defender to keep it a free state. A man of handsome exterior, he possessed the spark of genius born once in a generation. It is said of him that only one man in the Congress of the United States was abler on the floor of the Senate than he, and that man was the immortal Daniel Webster. Space does not permit a more comprehensive study of his life at this writing, so his untimely end is only dealt with, and mayhap at some other time a more complete story of Baker may be written.

On the 30th of May, 1854, San Francisco, feeling the need of a suitable burial place for its dead, selected a site called Lone Mountain. Later this name was changed to Laurel Hill, and Laurel Hill it is today. By a singular coincidence, the balmy day selected for its dedication was the 30th of May, a date to become immortal at the close of the Civil War. At the dedication, Baker was at his best, and it is difficult to say just what was his greatest forensic effort. Here is a flash of his mind on that long-forgotten day in May:

> "Here future generations, in long and solemn procession, shall bring warriors who have given their lives for their country; statesmen, remembered by the liberty they helped to create, and the institutions they aided to perfect. Here shall be brought the poet, who buoyant, passed through sea and land, through earth and sky, and vale and river, penetrating the affections and accomplishing the refinement of men. The projector—worn with toil and gray with thought—leaving monuments to his fame and memorials of his greatness. Here, too, shall come to end his life; and, too, the tender maiden, smitten in early blossom; and the little child, the pledge of love, to whose grave the aching heart shall oft repair to weep and pray."

We now pass quickly from the dedication to his untimely death, in his fifty-first year, in one of the first engagements of the Civil War, at Ball's Bluff, Virginia, October 21, 1861. In the face of overwhelming odds, in an untenable position and at the head of his troops, the great Baker fell upon the field of honor.

It is said that President Abraham Lincoln mourned the loss of Colonel Baker more deeply, probably, than any other death caused by the war. Lincoln and Baker had practiced law together in Sangamon County, Illinois, and were warm personal and professional friends. It was Baker who carried the Lincoln banner on the Pacific Coast in the great campaign of 1860 and helped win both Oregon and California as Lincoln states. The peerless orator was at his best when he spoke for Lincoln. No distance was too great to travel, if he could find an audience to talk to of the greatness of the then-little-known-on-the-Pacific-Coast Illinoian who was to achieve immortality.

Baker was a duly commissioned colonel in the Union forces at the time of his death and had been in two wars theretofore, the Black Hawk Indian War and the Mexican War. Lincoln personally attended the commemorative session of the Senate when eulogies of Baker were delivered, for be it not forgotten that Baker laid aside his toga as a Senator to don the service uniform of a colonel of infantry.

The news of Baker's death reached the Pacific Coast in the second message to be sent over the just-completed overland telegraph line. With woe, with sorrow and with uncontrolled grief, the news ran from city to mining camp and to remote habitations throughout California as well as Oregon. Be it remembered that Baker, on account of the strength of the slavery forces in California, failed in his election to Congress.

He was invited, after his defeat, to the State of Oregon, with the promise that, perhaps with his personality and with his rare charm of speech, he could go to Washington as the senator from that new state. Those who conceived the plan, saw it become a reality, and we find Baker retiring from the Senate to the field of honor. Edwin Booth, the actor, was appearing in San Francisco at the time of Baker's death and announced the sorrowful message from the stage. The grief, the gloom, the sorrow were indescribable, and afterwards rage seized the auditors. In several towns disloyalists who expressed gratification at the unhappy news were roughly handled, and in San Francisco several were hanged for a time to street gas posts.

Funeral and commemorative services were held in many cities and mining camps. Oregon and California both put forth their respective claims that the body should repose in its state. The short residence of Baker in Oregon and his far greater work and residence in California were facts presented by the Californians. The committee representing the government and citizens of Oregon, in urging its claim for interment in the soil of that state, promised that the state would erect a suitable monument if Baker were buried there. The contest was earnest, but carried on with faultless taste. Baker's widow finally selected San Francisco as his final resting-place, and at the grave Thomas Starr King delivered the funeral address. At Musi

(Continued on Page 15)

SITUATION SERIOUS—AID A WORTHY CAUSE

Mary E. Brusie

(Secretary N.S.G.W. and N.D.G.W. Central Homeless Children Committee.)

FOR MANY YEARS THE NATIVE Daughters of the Golden West have been providing clothes for the homeless children in care of the N.S.G.W. and N.D.G.W. Central Homeless Children Committee. Every baby has gone to his or her new home dressed in the daintiest and most attractive garments that the Native Daughters could make or buy in different parts of California. Also, the children awaiting placement have been amply provided for. This generosity on the part of the Native Daughters has been favorably commented on by thousands of foster-mothers who have received the first little layettes for their babies, pleased that they were the handiwork of enthusiastic Native Daughters.

Evelyn I. Carlson, during her term as Grand President, was particularly eager to interest an even greater number of Parlors in something tangible, something aside from their collection of funds, necessary as she knew this part of the work to be, and so she stressed the need of clothing as part of her gospel to the Subordinate Parlors. Their response was prompt, and overwhelmingly generous. Never has there been a more beautiful display of baby things than the one of the girls' work during the Grand Parlor session in Merced last June.

Our present Grand President, Anna Mixon Armstrong, realizing the pent-up enthusiasm awaiting expression, suggested that the feeding of the babies be the next undertaking, as sufficient clothes for a year or more had been supplied, and she has advocated the adoption of a baby by each Native Daughter Parlor while the baby is awaiting placement. The six-week period of caring for a child before placement enables the natural-parents to consider more seriously the irrevocableness of their decision. The cost of this six weeks' care is $37.50. Many of the Parlors have undertaken the payment of this sum in specified monthly amounts, thus making the demand on each member less burdensome.

Some interesting sidelights have been the reactions of the members to this message of the Grand President. Alta Parlor No. 3 (San Francisco), for instance, wondered if any one would want to adopt a colored baby, so it took John, a fine little chocolate drop who is looking for a mammy whom he may keep always. Portola Parlor No. 172 (San Francisco) wanted "any needy little fellow." Woodland Parlor No. 90 wanted a girl so it could name her "Anna," after Grand President Armstrong. La Bandera Parlor No. 110 (Sacramento) wanted a girl to name after its Grand Trustee, Edna Briggs. Other Parlors want to name babies after their presidents or, if the majority of the members insist upon a boy, they work in the president's name in some way as a handle. Lovely layettes were sent at Christmas time by Grand Trustee Briggs and James Lick Parlor No. 220 (San Francisco) to the foster-parents, and the Parlors received acknowledgments for the expression of interest in their charity by letters signed, "Baby's mother."

It is the plan of the Central Committee to keep the Parlors informed as to their adopted child's development and progress, and to send them photographs as long as the foster-parents remember the Central Committee, which, bless these foster-parents' hearts, seems always, as the pictures of seventeen- and eighteen-year-old young men and women received by the Central Committee each year bear testimony.

In the face and outstretched hands of a helpless baby there is a direct heart appeal, and if furnished the opportunity to choose a child and keep in touch with him through photographs the interest of the members is intensified and continued success is assured.

The Native Sons have not been appealed to along these lines although, as a matter of fact, a bystander has only to see the twinkle of pleasure in the eyes of a Native Son when he picks up a tiny sunsuit or a small boy's b-v-ds and ejaculates, "Cute as the devil!", to know that he is not altogether indifferent to baby clothes and milk bottles and hungry babies.

Native Daughter Parlors that have adopted babies are: Eschol No. 16, Napa; Oneonta No. 71, Ferndale, sewing club; Veritas No. 75, Merced; Amapola No. 80, Sutter Creek; Woodland No. 90; Calistoga No. 145; Colus No. 194, Colusa; Marinita No. 198, San Rafael; La Junta No. 203, Saint Helena; Caliz de Oro No. 206, Stockton; Phoebe A. Hearst No. 214, Manteca; South Butte No. 226, Sutter; Piedmont No. 87, Argonaut No. 166 and Fruitvale No. 177, Oakland; Alta No. 3, Golden State No. 50, Buena Vista No. 68, Sans Souci No. 96, Keith No. 137, Presidio No. 148, Linda Rosa No. 170, Portola No. 172, Castro No. 178 and James Lick No. 220, San Francisco. Also: Sacramento homeless children sewing club; Past Presidents Association No. 8; Golden Gate Auxiliary, friends of the Order; Past Presidents Association No. 2.

The amounts received to January first for the milk fund, as it is termed, total $198.62.

A circular letter for 1933 sent by the Central Committee to the Parlors not yet contributing to remind them that April first will be here "ere we are aware," states that the number of children placed to January first is 130, making a total of 4,161 different children in homes; that the bank balance amounts to $2,944.80, with a bequest of $12,000 available during the year; that the time is not now to convert securities into cash; that there is at present about seven months' income on hand, we having disbursed $18,024.23 from April 1, 1932, to January 1, 1933. Only one glance at these figures reveals the fact that, unless every Parlor responds generously to the appeal, we shall have difficulty in getting through the next lean year.

The Central Committee is not unmindful of the many members of both Orders who have been hard hit in various ways during the past two years, and realizes that while there has been no waning interest in the homeless children there has been a decided change in the circumstances and conditions of many of the members.

Quoting from the "Contra Costa Gazette," whose article, "Help Natives Help Others," Las Juntas Parlor No. 221 N.D.G.W. and Mount Diablo Parlor No. 101 N.S.G.W. consider was largely instrumental in the success of the benefit enabling them to contribute over $100 to the cause:

"Tomorrow night a benefit card party, the proceeds of which go to the homeless childrens fund of the Orders, will be given at the Woman's club by the Native Daughters and Native Sons of the Golden West.

"It is a benefit affair that deserves the support of all Martinez. The funds are used for a good work that means a great deal to chances many children have to develop into future good citizens of our city, county and state. It is an annual affair that deserves the support of all loyal, true and progressive citizens, and one that will undoubtedly receive that support to help those in need.

"Let's keep on with that work. Let's keep that record of 'Martinez Knows How.' It means something. Not only to our pride in our community, our citizens and the standard of living among them, but to ourselves. All of us will feel a great deal better than we would ordinarily if we know we have done something to help some one else."

In every Parlor there is a leader who would perhaps lend his time and ability toward working out a plan to help his Parlor meet its yearly donation, if the members would importune him to make the effort. The situation is serious, and the members must know it before the eleventh hour!

ALTA No. 3 KEITH No. 137 CALIZ DE ORO No. 206 ARGONAUT No. 166

MISS SACRAMENTO.

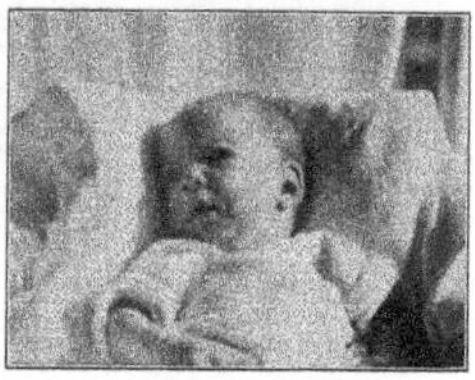

GOLDEN GATE No. 50

STIMULATE CALIFORNIA HISTORY INTEREST VIA THE GRIZZLY BEAR.

Albert V. Mayrhofer, Secretary San Diego Parlor N.S.G.W.—We appreciate the generosity of San Diego Parlor in the past in supplying us with a subscription to The Grizzly Bear and should like very much to have you re-subscribe for it if this is at all possible for you to do.

It is a splendid magazine for stimulating interest in California history. We should regret not being able to circulate it which, I fear, will be the case if you cannot send it to us. The old subscription expired with the October 1932 issue, so if you do re-subscribe for us, will you have the subscription begin with the November 1932 issue? In that way, our file will not be broken. Very truly yours,

ADA M. JONES, Librarian
San Diego High School Library.

San Diego, January 11, 1933.

(San Diego Parlor renewed the subscription. For the very reason cited in this letter, Parlors of Native Sons and Native Daughters should send The Grizzly Bear regularly to all public and school libraries in their several communities.—Editor.)

Dawn—The rosy finger of the dawn opens wide the golden gate through which the shining King of Day rides forth in robes of state.—Jeanette Nourland.

"In the corrupted currents of this world, offence's gilded hand may shove by justice; and oft 'tis seen the wicked prize itself buys out the law."

GRIZZLY GROWLS

(CLARENCE M. HUNT.)

CALIFORNIA IS IN A WOEFUL STATE, financially! The all-wise administration just now admits the truth of the state controller's statement some months ago—that, in place of the bountiful surplus at the end of 1930 there is a deficit of many millions, and that, in all probability, the state will shortly be unable to meet its obligations. Numerous measures, many of them most worthy, have been presented to the State Legislature in the hope of balancing the budget without an increase in taxes.

There is a decided split in the legislative branch of the state government, and there is every likelihood, therefore, that the best of the economy measures—those which would eliminate wasteful extravagances and tend to lessen the rate of taxation—will fail of enactment, unless the taxpayers forcibly impress on their legislators that they will not countenance additional taxes of any nature. Taxes should be lowered, and but for the political racketeers they would be, and, too, the budget would be balanced. If taxes are not lowered, a threatened tax-strike will be justified!

Both the administrative and the legislative wings of the state government are preaching economy, but every department is lobbying to prevent passage of any economy measure directed its way. For instance, the public-schools' cost could be materially lessened, but the education-lobby is spending thousands—probably taken from tax funds—to prevent any curtailment there.

All salaries of more than $3,000 per annum paid wholly or in part by the state should be reduced at least twenty-five percent, and the personnel should be reduced, also. What a fight the administration-lobby will wage to prevent those reductions! An election approaches—may possibly arrive ahead of the scheduled time—and manpower and dollars are most essential in a political campaign.

As heretofore remarked, several excellent bills are before the Legislature and, if enacted, will save the suffering taxpayers millions of dollars and, what is as necessary, deal a knockout blow to the "political racket," largely responsible for California's sad financial plight. Among them are these: abolishment of several unnecessary departments entirely, and of branch departments in San Francisco and Los Angeles; elimination of special attorneys for all of the numerous departments; abolishment of all tax exemptions; prohibiting husband and wife from both holding pay positions with the state or any political subdivision; banning adult education, at public expense, a scheme to extract from the state more dollars for average daily attendance; making it illegal to employ on any public payroll any person already on pension from the state or any political subdivision; reducing the number of superior court judges in Los Angeles to forty, and the number of municipal court judges to twenty-four. The fact-finding committee of the State Senate is deserving of unstinted commendation; it has presented many suggestions worthy of approval.

But, there is grave danger ahead! The Legislature recesses during February, and in the interim every force will be employed by political racketeers and those seeking special favors to assure defeat of needed legislation—legislation that will benefit the majority.

Calvin Coolidge, thirtieth President of the United States, died suddenly at Northampton, Massachusetts, January 5. One of the finest tributes paid to him is this, from "El Nacional" of Mexico City, January 8: "He was a stern thinker, a tireless man of action, a slave to the law and of his given word, firm, incorruptible, simple, disdainful of money. . . . The death of Coolidge is an irreparable loss not only for the United States, but for all humanity."

The Twentieth Amendment to the Constitution of the United States has at last been ratified by thirty-six states, and will become operative October 15. In future, the country will not be burdened and harassed by "lame duck" sessions of the Federal Congress. Each regular session of the Congress will begin January 3 every year, with no fixed adjournment date, and each new president will be inaugurated January 20.

There is growing suspicion that Japan is paving the way to, and fully prepared for, war on this country. "There is no uneasiness concerning our relations with the United States," declared Foreign Minister Uchida in the Japanese Diet the other day. That declaration increases the suspicion, for the Japs always pass out to the public the opposites of their real thoughts and intentions. The record of Japan, at home and abroad, proves that that is true.

For twenty-odd years The Grizzly Bear has contended that, unless the Japs be expelled from the Pacific Coast, Japan would, in time, make a strenuous fight for full possession of this portion of the United States. The Japs have been permitted to remain, and their numbers have increased by thousands. The day when we must pay the terrible price for our folly draweth nigh!

Six officials of Sebastopol, a city in Russia, convicted of grafting, are to be shot. What a thinning-out of public sèrvants would result, if the Russian policy for dealing with dishonesty were enforced in this state and nation! It would hasten the return of honesty, the one thing absolutely necessary to bring about better conditions for the masses.

Humboldt County has joined the growing ranks of charity dispensers refusing to extend aid to any person owning and operating an auto. A person who can afford to own and operate a car is not in such financial distress as to be honestly entitled to relief at public expense. Conditions have produced many charity racketeers. It is incumbent on the state and all its governmental subdivisions to weed them out, that all those honestly in need may be adequately provided for, and at considerably less expense.

A proposal for a one-cent tax on every dollar of all gross income from every source, without exceptions, deductions or any qualifications, has been advanced in the Federal Congress by Representative Griffin of New York as a revenue producer to balance the budget. An excellent suggestion that should be enacted into law! "Such a tax," as the proposer says, would be "a true income tax," because no one would be excepted, not even the horde of office-holders and public employes who are exempt under the present income-tax law.

The state's finance director apparently looks with disfavor on the State Senate investigating committee, for he is quoted as having said, "The Inman investigation reminds me of Nero fiddling while Rome burned." California had been pretty thoroughly burned, financially, prior to the convening of the State Legislature, thanks to the fiddling, queening, frogracing, airplaning, modern Nero, the director's boss.

Dubbing technocracy a myth, Professor Paul D. Converse of the University of Illinois rightly declares woman, and not the machine, is the chief danger of modern civilization. From 1920 to 1930 the number of married women in this country gainfully employed increased from 1,920,000 to 3,071,000. Just another, of many excellent reasons, why working women with able-bodied husbands should be replaced by men with families to support.

According to the report of the State Division of Immigration and Housing for November, the population of 157 inspected labor camps totaled 6,615. Close to one-half of them, 3,210 to be exact, were classed as ineligible-to-citizenship aliens—2,443 Mexis, 619 Filipinos and 148 Japs. These figures are cited as proof of the statement that at least one-half the millions put up by the people of California for depression relief go to undesirable aliens. Were all such aliens deported, there would be fewer unemployed White citizens and the annual charity bill paid by the taxpayers would be substantially decreased.

Declaring liquor propagandists had capitalized the depression condition of dissatisfaction and discouragement to inaugurate a movement against prohibition, Senator Sheppard of Texas delivered in the Federal Senate January 16 a forceful address against repeal of the Eighteenth Amendment. In conclusion, he said:

"Prohibition has made such progress in helping conditions as not only to justify but to demand its continuance. The figures and studies of the Government indicate a decline in liquor consumption from an average of 23 gallons per capita in wet 1914, the last unqualified wet year, with illicit drink included, to an average of 7½ gallons in dry 1930, including illicit drink. Does any one with the good of the country at heart want to return to the former status?

"The claim of increased drinking is due to the fact that happenings among people of station and influence and their satellites are chronicled far and wide, while the doings of the vast bulk of our inhabitants who earn a living with the labor of their hands never come into public notice. What a perversion of reason it is to say that because the prominent few insist on breaking the law and becoming partners with the underworld, drink must be forced upon the masses with its accompanying poverty and degradation."

THE SILENT MAN

(ESTHER CRONE.)

In death he speaks, the world has heard,
This silent man so scarce of word.
A nation bows its head in grief,
To mourn this noble life so brief.
A life that stood so true and strong;
By many blamed, yet seldom wrong.
Such wisdom, too; we count him great,
For he guided well the Ship of State.
Thus time has proved his matchless worth,
As years reveal the work put forth.
His voice no longer greets our ears,
Yet being dead, the nation hears;
Though doubly silent, still the more
He speaketh louder than before.

(The above, dedicated to Calvin Coolidge, recently deceased former President of the United States, is a contribution to The Grizzly Bear from Miss Esther Crone of Los Angeles.—Editor.)

The Grizzly Bear Magazine
The ALL California Monthly
OWNED, CONTROLLED, PUBLISHED BY
GRIZZLY BEAR PUBLISHING CO.,
(Incorporated)
COMPOSED OF NATIVE SONS.
HERMAN C. LICHTENBERGER, Pres.
JOHN T. NEWELL RAY HOWARD
WM. I. TRAEGER LORENZO F. SOTO
CHAS. R. THOMAS HARRY J. LELANDE
ARTHUR A. SCHMIDT, Vice-Pres.
BOARD OF DIRECTORS

CLARENCE M. HUNT
General Manager and Editor

OFFICIAL ORGAN AND THE
ONLY OFFICIAL PUBLICATION OF
THE NATIVE SONS AND THE
NATIVE DAUGHTERS GOLDEN WEST.

ISSUED FIRST EACH MONTH.
FORMS CLOSE 20th MONTH.
ADVERTISING RATES ON APPLICATION.

SAN FRANCISCO OFFICE:
N.S.G.W. BLDG., 414 MASON ST., RM. 302
(Office Grand Secretary N.S.G.W.)
Telephone: Kearney 1223
SAN FRANCISCO, CALIFORNIA

PUBLICATION OFFICE:
309-15 WILCOX BLDG., 2nd AND SPRING,
Telephone: VAndike 6234
LOS ANGELES, CALIFORNIA

(Entered as second-class matter May 29, 1918, at the Postoffice at Los Angeles, California, under the act of August 24, 1912.)
PUBLISHED REGULARLY SINCE MAY 1907
VOL. LII WHOLE NO. 310

THE LETTER BOX

Comments on subjects of general interest and importance received from readers of The Grizzly Bear.

HOUSE NO LONGER HABITABLE, IMPORTANT REPAIRS MUST BE MADE

Editor Grizzly Bear—I have just read your January number of The Grizzly Bear. I find in it many items of interest, but am particularly interested in your column "Grizzly Growls," in which you forcibly discuss the present tragic era and the apparent inability of national lead

(Continued on Page 17)

CALIFORNIA'S ROMANTIC HISTORY

Lewis F. Byington
(PAST GRAND PRESIDENT N.S.G.W.)

(Continuing the series of California history talks commenced in The Grizzly Bear for December 1932.)

EARLY DAYS IN SAN FRANCISCO

WHEN THE GREAT TIDE OF IMMIGRATION swept toward California in the "days of '49," after the discovery of gold by James W. Marshall at Coloma, on the American River, January 24, 1848, the Bay of San Francisco and the city of the same name became known all round the world. Romance and adventure were centered there.

But the site of the Presidio on the bay and the location of the Mission had been selected by the Spaniards some seventy-two years preceding this discovery of gold, and we Californians should be proud of the fact that our city by the Golden Gate was founded the very same year that the United States became a nation, namely, in 1776. In fact, Captain Juan Bautista Anza, in March 1776, over three months before the signing of the Declaration of Independence in Philadelphia, chose the spot where the Presidio should be established and the place where the Mission Church should be erected. There is no more colorful event in the history of the West than the founding of San Francisco on the shores of the bay of St. Francis.

If we pause occasionally to review the history of this city and to absorb something of the sweet spirit of romance which clusters about it and has followed down through the years, it is not surprising that our hearts glow with the retrospect, and our love is renewed with the passing years.

It is a rather remarkable fact that while the Spaniards, in their explorations and voyages to America, were seeking harbors where settlements could be planted, they overlooked entirely the Bay of San Francisco. Cabrillo, the earliest Spanish navigator, passed it by in 1542, when he sailed up the coast. Sir Francis Drake, in 1579, landed at what is now known as Drake's Bay, some twenty-five miles north of San Francisco, remained there a month, explored the surrounding country, called the region New Albion, and never realized that a wonderful harbor lay within a few miles of his anchorage. Had he entered it, the English flag might have flown permanently in that port. Sebastian Viscaino, under orders from Spain, explored and charted the coast from San Diego to British Columbia in 1602, but overlooked the greatest harbor on the Pacific Coast.

For over 225 years vessels of Spain and other nations were passing the port now known as San Francisco, without a single navigator suspecting its existence. The headlands must be deceptive from the ocean. It was eventually discovered by an overland party. Portola and the pious Franciscan friar, Junipero Serra, were directed to establish missions at San Diego and Monterey, and Portola in coming northward overland did not recognize Monterey Bay, and his sergeant, Jose Francisco Ortega, sent forward to explore Point Reyes, unexpectedly came upon the entrance to San Francisco Bay. Serra, the Franciscan, had wished a harbor to bear the name of the patron saint of his order, St. Francis, and when he heard of the discovery he believed the hand of God had conducted the explorers, and he named it San Francisco.

In March 1775, Lieutenant Don Manuel de Ayala, in command of the Spanish boat "San Carlos," was sent north from Mexico to survey the harbor. It took him 110 days to reach the Golden Gate from San Blas. On the evening of August 5, 1775, as night was coming on, the "San Carlos" sailed through the "uncharted narrows, passed its inner portal and opened the Golden Gate to the commerce of the world." It was the first ship to cast anchor in the harbor of San Francisco. Ayala was welcomed by tribes of Indians and remained a month, making a survey of the bay.

It was soon realized by Spain that California could not be colonized by sea, on account of the hardships of the voyage and the length of time consumed. In 1775, a gallant soldier, Captain Anza, the father of San Francisco, was commissioned to lead an overland expedition from Mexico and establish a permanent settlement on the bay. It took him over six months to cross mountains and deserts, with a company of 240 men and women and 825 head of stock. On March 27, 1776, Anza stood at the entrance of the bay, planted a cross above where the fort now stands, and designated the mesa, or table land, where the Presidio now stands, as the location for a new town. Padre Font, his secretary, declared that the port was a marvel of nature, the "port of ports," and prophesied that on this wonderful bay should rise a wonderful city.

The next day Anza explored what is now the Mission and designated the spot where the church should be built. It was near a lagoon, or lake, covering some eight blocks where 17th and 19th streets now cross Valencia and Mission streets. This lake is no longer there, and a stream coming from the hills, now Twin Peaks, but called by the Spaniards Los Pechos de la Choca, has disappeared.

The city did not grow up, however, at the Presidio as contemplated by Anza. Trade and commerce fixed its location. When, in early days, ships entered the harbor they proceeded to a cove which lay below Telegraph Hill, first called Loma Alta—high hill—, and where the waters came up to what is now the corner of Montgomery and Jackson streets. To this sheltered spot came the boats from the missions around the bay with their hides, tallow and produce, which were transferred to the ocean-going vessels bound for other lands. About 1835 a little village sprang up at this cove, and around the Spanish Plaza, which village was known as Yerba Buena. It was two and one-half miles from the Presidio and about the same distance from the Mission.

Most interesting, historically, of the small parks of San Francisco is this old Plaza on Kearny street, between Washington and Clay streets, opposite the Hall of Justice and known as Portsmouth Plaza. The first two houses built by Americans were erected within half a block of the Plaza, near the corner of Clay and Dupont streets. One by Captain Richardson, considered the first inhabitant of San Francisco, erected in 1835, made of ship's canvas supported by redwood poles, and the other, the first frame building in Yerba Buena, erected in 1836 by Jacob Leese, a native of Ohio, who married the sister of General Vallejo. Of course, there are at least two buildings in San Francisco erected prior to this, and made of adobe, namely, the old Mission Church at Dolores and 16th streets, and the officer's club at the upper end of the parade ground at the Presidio. The home of Leese on Dupont street was finished on the 4th day of July, 1836, and resulted in the first celebration of that day in San Francisco, then Yerba Buena, accompanied by the first raising of the American Flag. Here also, in 1838, was born Rosalie Leese, the first White child born in Yerba Buena.

The principal buildings of the little settlement rose around the Plaza. The first hotel—the City Hotel—was erected at the southwest corner of Clay and Kearny. The postoffice was at Pike street, now Waverly place, and Clay street, and in pioneer days a line of men, waiting for mail brought by steamer, stretched across the Plaza and down Washington street. The first custom house was erected on the northwest corner of the Plaza, in 1844, and it served at times as school house, court house and public meeting house. In 1840, Nathan Spear built the first grist mill in California, on Clay near Kearny. The first bank stood at Kearny and Washington, and east of the Plaza was conducted the old El Dorado, the most famous saloon and gambling house in the West, and the well-known Jenny Lind theatre adjoined it.

On July 6, 1846, Commodore Sloat raised the American Flag at Monterey, the Mexican capitol of California, and on July 9, 1846, Captain John Montgomery of the U. S. sloop "Portsmouth," then lying in the bay, landed his marines at the present site of the Bank of Italy, southwest corner Clay and Montgomery streets, and with appropriate ceremonies raised the flag on the Plaza, and proclaimed the occupation of northern California by the United States. Montgomery street then received its name in honor of the American commander, and the Plaza was named Portsmouth in commemoration of his ship.

The first landing place for steamers was at Clark's Point, now the corner of Broadway and Battery streets. William S. Hinckley, who was alcalde in 1844, built a bridge across the neck of the lagoon, at Jackson and Montgomery streets, enabling the citizens to pass to Clark's Point. This was the first street improvement in the town. The original bay shore line in those days extended from the corner of Battery and Market to the corner of Sansome and California, where the Bank of California now stands, and then on to Montgomery and Jackson streets. All the land from Montgomery street to the Ferry has since been filled in.

Afterwards wharves were extended into the bay for landing purposes. One extended from the bay shore between Sacramento and Clay streets, 2,000 feet out into the bay. Here was sufficient depth of water to allow the Pacific Mail steamers to land. When the bay was filled in, the site of Long Wharf became Commercial street.

The first brick building in San Francisco was built by Mellus & Howard, in 1848, on the southwest corner of Clay and Montgomery streets. The finest hotel in those days was the St. Francis, a four-story building, standing at the southwest corner of Clay and Dupont streets, now the center of Chinatown. The sleeping apartments there were the best in California. The Oriental Hotel, an elegantly appointed house built in 1850, stood at the corner of Bush and Battery streets.

The first newspaper published in California appeared in Monterey, August 15, 1846, edited by Walter Colton and Robert Semple, and was called "The Californian.' It was afterwards merged with the "California Star," first published in San Francisco by Sam Brennan, January 9, 1847, and in January 1849 the name was changed to "Alta California."

Near the Plaza the first fire companies organized in San Francisco were located, and the splendid fire department had upon its rolls the names of the leading men who laid the foundations of the city. Six times in the year and a half after the discovery of gold, the wooden city was destroyed by fire, and each time, through the energy of the Pioneers, it was rebuilt. On San Francisco's municipal flag are written the words "Oro En Paz, En Guerra Fierro"—"Gold in peace, iron in war!" And embroidered on said flag is the fabled bird, the Phoenix of mythology, which in its old age gathered fagots around it and with the rapidity of the movements of its wings kindled a fire and was entirely consumed. And from the ashes rose a re-created bird more beautiful and aspiring than the one which had been consumed. A true symbol of the unconquerable spirit of San Francisco!

Around the old Plaza, in the days following the discovery of gold, moved and surged the colorful life of every land, and there mingled people speaking the language of every race. German, Italian, French, Irish, Greek, Mohammedan and Chinese mingled in one restless throng in the mad rush for gold. Those interested in the history of California are deeply indebted to Catherine Coffin Phillips for her lately published book, "Portsmouth Plaza—The Cradle of San Francisco," which tells most interestly and instructively the history of the old Plaza, and it is superbly printed and bound and most beautifully illustrated.

The old town of Yerba Buena lay between Broadway and Sacramento, Montgomery and Powell streets. On January 30, 1847, Washington Bartlet, American alcalde, issued an order changing the name to San Francisco, and this name was later extended to the adjacent territory.

In 1847, the population of San Francisco was estimated at 459. With the discovery of gold, came the great tide of immigration and the complete change in the appearance of the town. Over 700 vessels entered the harbor from April 1, 1849, to the end of the year, and over 40,000 people landed here in 1849. Many vessels were beached and converted into warehouses, stores and lodging houses. One of these was the old vessel "Niantic," on the site of what is now the Niantic building, Sansome street, and on which the Native Sons Historic Landmarks Committee has placed a bronze tablet. Everything that could afford shelter was utilized, from a dry goods box to a tent, or a shanty, lined with bunks. The great human tide which swept through the Golden Gate in the "days of gold" was such as had never been witnessed before in any place.

September 9, 1850, California was admitted as a state. The news of the admission was received with the wildest excitement on the arrival of the mail steamer "Oregon," October 18. Business was suspended and the hills and housetops were covered with people. At night, bonfires blazed on the higher places and rockets were exploded. On October 29, the official celebration took place; there was a great parade

(Continued on Page 8)

Native Sons of the Golden West

WILLOWS (GLENN COUNTY)—Willows No. 255, organized by Deputy Grand President Al Lobree, was instituted with twenty-nine members December 30 by Grand President Seth Millington, assisted by District Deputy Elton C. Fitch (Colusa No. 69) as acting junior past grand president; J. R. Manville (Colusa No. 69) as acting grand secretary, and Ray Burris (Marysville No. 6) as acting grand marshal. The ritual was exemplified by the following team from Fred H. Greely Assembly No. 6 Past Presidents Association:

J. P. Colford (Sutter No. 261), president; Elton C. Fitch (Colusa No. 69), junior past president; William H. Tregallis (Argonaut No. 8), senior past president; Fayette H. Fitch (Colusa No. 69), first vice-president; J. R. Manville (Colusa No. 69), second vice-president; Grand President Seth Millington (Colusa No. 69), third vice-president; Ray Burris (Marysville No. 6), marshal; Thomas F. O'Connor (Marysville No. 6), inside sentinel. Officers of the new Parlor were installed by District Deputy Fitch, as follows:

Ralph W. Camper, president; Lee V. Logan, first vice-president; Daniel H. Terzain, second vice-president; Ralph Smith, third vice-president; Leon Marshall, recording secretary; Robert Nier, financial secretary; Chester J. Spooner, treasurer; Wilfred L. Fox, marshal; Hugh E. Logan, inside sentinel; James H. Locey, outside sentinel; W. C. Danley, J. W. Monroe, E. S. Ball, trustees. Deputy Grand President Lobree was again in Willows from January 19 to 24, and several additional charter signers were initiated.

"A Noble Example."

San Diego—San Diego No. 108 adopted a resolution—prepared by Past President Eugene Daney Jr., District Deputy Edward H. Dowell, President Martin J. Spangler and Deputy Grand President Albert V. Mayrhofer—expressive of sorrow on account of the death, in Los Angeles last month, of William Jefferson Hunsaker (Ramona No. 109), the charter president of No. 108. "We knew his worth not only to San Diego, but to the State of California. His loss has made our hearts heavy. He was a noble example to us all."

On behalf of the Parlor, Deputy Grand President Mayrhofer presented a Flag of the United States of America to the San Diego Historical Society. The flag, which was accepted by President George W. Marston of the society, will be flown at Fort Stockton.

Unusual Record.

San Jose—The good of the order committee of Observatory No. 177 provided a wonderful turkey dinner January 3, and although no notices were sent out a large number of members, including twenty-six past presidents, responded. President William Gerrans, exceedingly popular with the boys of No. 177, presided in his always-genial manner and there were several short, but enthusiastic, talks. An unusual record, considering conditions: during 1932 the Parlor lost not a single member for non-payment of dues.

Several members accompanied District Deputy Alfred C. Hansen to Mountain View January 11 and assisted him in installing the officers of Mountain View No. 215. Observatory has resolved to do big things during 1933, and as a startoff is lining up a number of candidates. James J. Flannery, as president, heads the corps of officers for the January-July term.

Whereas, A group of individuals, styling themselves the "California Council on Oriental Relations," are waging a campaign to have the Federal Government amend the Immigration Act of 1924, so as to extend the immigration quota to Japs and other ineligible-to-citizenship aliens; and whereas, this plan, if successful, would for all time destroy the only logical, non-discriminatory barrier against further peaceful invasion of these United States,—and particularly the Pacific Coast states, including California,—by unassimilable Asiatics and others; therefore, be it

Resolved, That the N.S.G.W. and N.D.G.W. Interparlor Committee of Southern California is unalterably opposed to granting an immigration quota to any and all ineligible-to-citizenship aliens, and to any tampering with the Federal Immigration Act of 1924 which bars all those ineligible to American citizenship as immigrants for permanent settlement; and be it further

Resolved, That the Interparlor Committee condemns, as disloyal and unamerican, the activities for extension of such quota by the "California State Chamber of Commerce," the "United States Chamber of Commerce," the "California Council on Oriental Relations," and certain well-known California individuals who should know that the welfare of California depends on the supremacy of the White race in this state, and not on a temporary flood of yellow-dollars; and be it further resolved, that copies of this resolution be sent to California's Senators and Representatives in the Federal Congress; also, to Senator J. W. McKinley and Assemblyman Charles W. Lyon of the State Legislature, and that the latter be requested to have the State Legislature voice a strong protest to the Federal Congress against any change in the 1924 Immigration Act.

(The above was adopted by the N.S.G.W. and N.D.G.W. Interparlor Committee (Southern District) at a meeting in Los Angeles City January 13. Subordinate Parlors in Los Angeles, Orange and San Bernardino Counties are represented by this committee.—Editor.)

Admission Day Committee Named.

Santa Rosa—Santa Rosa No. 28 January 10 featured its annual turkey dinner, which was attended by more than one hundred. Following the feast two candidates were initiated and officers, with George Eckman as president, were installed by District Deputy Louis Bosch. Plans are under way for a celebration, possibly March 18, of the forty-ninth institution anniversary of No. 28.

To arrange for the celebration of Admission Day, September 9, President Eckman has appointed the following committee: Wes Colgan (chairman), Frank Berger, Dr. W. C. Shipley, Leland S. Lewis and James Brucker. The statewide celebration of California's natal day will most likely be held at Santa Rosa, under the Parlor's auspices.

Oratorical Contest Winner.

Sacramento—The third annual oratorical contest on California history between students of the Sacramento high school, sponsored by Sacramento No. 3, drew a crowd of several hundred to Native Sons Auditorium January 19. The judges were Justice John F. Pullen, Superior Judge Martin Welch and Professor Everett. Archibald M. Mull Jr. was in charge for the Parlor.

Lawrence Schei, whose subject was "Vigilantes of San Francisco," was the winner, and to him Irving D. Gibson presented a cup. Second place went to Edith Jett, whose subject was "The Golden Legend," and third place went to Veryl Dunn, whose subject was "California Vendetta."

The seventy-fifth anniversary of the cornerstone laying of an early-day Sacramento firehouse, Young America No. 6, was celebrated January 3, and the local Natives presented a plaque to mark the site. George A. Burns was the speaker of the day, N.D. Grand President Anna Mixon Armstrong made the presentation address, and among others active at the affair were John T. Stafford, Joseph Fitzhenry and N.D. Grand Trustee Edna Briggs. Henry A. Senf, a member of Sacramento No. 3, has been named Sacramento County Supervisor, to succeed the late Robert E. Callahan. At an early date the N.S. grand officers will lay the cornerstone for one of Sacramento's three new school buildings, the California.

Basketball Team Making Record.

Ukiah—Officers of Ukiah No. 71 were installed January 16 by District Deputy Joseph Figone, W. B. Davis becoming president. A clam chowder supper concluded the ceremonies.

February 4 the Parlor will sponsor a dance for the benefit of its basketball team, which is making a splendid record. Al Bechtol is the team manager. February 10 the basketballers of No. 71 will play the House of David team from Chicago, Illinois, in the Ukiah high school gymnasium.

SUBORDINATE PARLORS BRIEFS.

Stockton—Officers of Stockton No. 7 were installed January 9 by District Deputy Walter Salomon, Ben S. Waller becoming president. Among the many visitors were Deputy Grand President Al Lobree and a delegation from Manteca No. 271 headed by President John F. Mulholand.

Modesto—Modesto No. 11 and Morada No. 199 N.D.G.W. had their monthly card party January 18. Refreshments and dancing followed the play. Robert Benson and Effie Prothero were in charge. January 25 the Parlors' officers were jointly installed by Deputies Laurence Bither and Ethel Enos.

Napa — Past Grand President Frank L. Coombs, affiliated with Napa No. 62, celebrated his birthday anniversary December 27. He was born in Napa County in 1853.

Salinas—With District Deputy John Thomsen presiding, officers of Santa Lucia No. 97 were installed January 16, James Pedroni becoming president. Following a banquet an elaborate entertainment program was presented.

Lower Lake—Lower Lake No. 159 entertained the womenfolks at a whist party January 12. An enchilada supper was served by Pete Bramlette, Max Berlin and Ray Kiggins.

Fort Bragg—At a well attended meeting January 13 officers of Alder Glen No. 200 were installed by District Deputy Ralph Todd, T. D. Cooney becoming president. A turkey supper preceded the meeting and subjects of interest were discussed by several speakers. Cards concluded the enjoyable occasion.

Manteca—A class of candidates rounded up for Manteca No. 271 by Deputy Grand President Al Lobree were initiated January 18, the officers

NATIONAL ORANGE SHOW

(E. M. GORE.)

SIXTY YEARS AGO, THE FIRST NAVEL orange trees were planted in Riverside County, and the National Orange Show at San Bernardino City will celebrate this sixtieth anniversary February 16 to 26. **It was in 1873 that Mrs. L. C. Tibbets** wrote to the Federal Agricultural Department in Washington for samples of the orange tree that produced fruit "without seeds." She received a couple of the trees, and it is from them that the great navel orange industry of today sprung.

Sixty years have gone by, and there are now millions of navel orange trees in California. Many times referred to as the hundred-million-dollar industry, meaning that the citrus crop annually sells for that enormous sum, it is particularly fitting that the National Orange Show should recognize this anniversary.

The great midwinter classic at San Bernardino has for its sole purpose the publicizing and development of the citrus industry in California. It is called the "show window" for the citrus industry. Producing and selling oranges is a serious business, but the ten days of the Orange Show provides the beautiful side of this great fruit industry. In design, in theme and in decoration, the Orange Show expects to convey to the visitor the story of the navel orange.

The National Orange Show is in its twenty-third year. Its 1933 edition promises to excel in beauty and magnitude all former presentations by this organization. It is little wonder that more than a quarter-million persons annually visit the Orange Show. This attendance has kept up year after year, because nowhere else in all the world is there such a beautiful exposition. Visitors for the first time, as they cross the portals of the Orange Show's mammoth exposition building, pause, bewildered, awed, and then exclaim, "isn't it beautiful!" And the designer has worked out a decorative scheme that transforms the big fruit section into a veritable fairyland of beauty. The scene this year is typically Californian—colorful, blazing with lights, resplendent with multicolored flowers, a picture indeed that no artist can paint.

There are a score of gorgeous feature displays, some stationary and others in motion. They are built of lights and fruits and flowers, while overhead there apparently is a reproduction of the magic sky of a perfect California day. Ten million oranges repose in rack displays, the finest fruit grown anywhere in the world. These oranges are on dress parade. Colored wrappers work out designs that are pleasing to look upon, but the real fact remains that these millions of oranges are on display for a serious business. They are entered in competition for the rich cash awards that go to the community or organization for producing well-nigh perfect fruit.

An industrial display with scores of exhibitors, a byproducts department, the Citrus Institute, the Department of Citrus Education, the amusement zone—all go to make up this great midwinter event. And on the stage will be presented the light opera which last year brought admiration from thousands of visitors. The Californians will present not only typical California music and song, but the best numbers from the leading light operas of Victor Herbert, George Gershwin, Zigmund Romberg, Oscar Strauss and many others of equal fame. And the National Orange Show has scored a ten-strike in offering for its musical director Arthur Kay, one of the most celebrated musical directors in America. There will be special days for the Native Sons, the Canadian Society, the American Legion, lodges and fraternal organizations, communities, etc.

It is a far cry from oranges to ice, and "never shall the twain mix," as far as the orange-grower is concerned, but there will be, for the first time, a real ice-skating rink as a feature of the show. Champion ice hockey teams will play during the entire time of the show and, of course, visitors may don the skates and enjoy the pastime themselves. The dates for the National Orange Show are February 16 to 26, and all San Bernardino County extends a welcome.

---

of Stockton No. 7 exemplifying the ritual. Officers of the Parlor were installed January 4 by District Deputy Laurence Buol, John F. Mulholand becoming president.

Deputy Grand President Al Lobree is very active visiting and assisting Subordinate Parlors in various sections. His program for February and March, according to information sent The Grizzly Bear, includes: During February he will be in Fresno, Bakersfield and Visalia, working for Fresno No. 25, Bakersfield No. 42 and Visalia No. 19. All of March will be devoted to Yosemite No. 24 at Merced. In April he may institute a parlor at Turlock, Stanislaus County.

Membership Standing Largest Parlors.

San Francisco—Grand Secretary John T. Regan reports the standing of the Subordinate Parlors having a membership of over 400 January 1, 1933, as follows, together with their membership figures January 20, 1933:

Parlor.	Jan. 1	Jan. 20	Gain	Loss
Ramona No. 109	1033	1032	....	1
South San Francisco No. 157	803	803	....	....
Castro No. 232	784	784	....	....
Stanford No. 76	575	575	....	....
Arrowhead No. 110	573	573	....	....
Stockton No. 7	563	563	....	....
Twin Peaks No. 214	522	518	....	4
Piedmont No. 120	491	492	1	....
Lincoln No. 72	418	418	....	....

Visitors Give Encouragement.

Galt—Members of Galt No. 243 spent a very enjoyable and profitable evening January 16, the occasion being the official visit of Grand Third Vice-president Harmon D. Skillin. He related some of the present troubles of the Order and the Parlors, and spoke encouragingly of the future. He urged his hearers to do their utmost to retain the members the Parlor now has and to secure new ones.

District Deputy W. H. Thisby, accompanied by a delegation from Courtland No. 106, installed Galt's officers, Abel G. Stock becoming president. An unexpected pleasure was the arrival of Deputy Grand President Al Lobree and several members of Manteca No. 271. A social hour was spent around the festive board. The Parlor was greatly cheered by the presence of the visitors and will carry on with renewed interest.

Good Start.

Santa Barbara—Santa Barbara No. 116 has made a good start for 1933, initiating four candidates during January and receiving five additional applications. As a New Year gift, and to aid in the fight against depression, the Parlor presented all its delinquent members with paid-up receipts for dues to January 1, 1933.

Officers of Santa Barbara and Reina del Mar No. 126 N.D.G.W. were jointly installed January 17 at a public function which attracted more than 300. Deputies A. C. Dinsmore and Vera Pacheco presided, and Philip Bradley and Amelia Acres became the respective presidents. Past president pins were presented C. W. McCormick and Mrs. McCrea by Paul Sweetser and Supervising Deputy Anna McCaughey. Arrangements for the successful affair were made by a joint committee composed of Mms. A. C. Warren (general chairman), Dorothy Henslin and Frank Castro; Clifford Rizor, Leland Smith and Frank Castro.

Rich in Service.

Oakland—Officers of Claremont No. 240 and Argonaut No. 166 N.D.G.W. were jointly installed January 17 at public ceremonies, Raymond Burke and Angeline Delucchi becoming the respective presidents. District Deputy Victor Raible officiated for No. 240. Refreshments and dancing followed the ceremonies.

Claremont, instituted February 13, 1908, will celebrate its twenty-fifth anniversary with a class initiation and banquet February 14. It is hoped many of the grand officers and oldtime members of the Parlor will be in attendance. Active in organizing No. 240 were E. F. Garrison (Athens No. 195), former grand trustee lately deceased, and Richard M. Hamb and James J. Dignan (Piedmont No. 120). Among the remaining charter members are Al Finck, original financial secretary, and Milton Mooney, charter second vice-president.

Claremont is rich in history and community service. It is composed of men never too busy to help good causes. It now has over 200 members and has paid more than $10,000 in sick benefits.

Plugging Along.

San Jose—"Old San Jose No. 22 is plugging along at its usual gait and doing its share of the work required of our Order," says Recording Secretary Joseph Lawrence. "In spite of the turbulent economic conditions, it holds its membership close to the 300-mark." An old-

(Continued on Page 11)

CALIFORNIA HAPPENINGS OF FIFTY YEARS AGO

Thomas R. Jones

(COMPILED EXPRESSLY FOR THE GRIZZLY BEAR.)

FEBRUARY 2, 1883, A POLARIZED WAVE swept down the Pacific Coast and coated it with frost. From British Columbia to San Diego came reports of freezing weather. The thermometer at Truckee, Nevada County, went to ten degrees below zero. The Truckee River, frozen stiff, did "not choose to run." Trout incased in the ice could be plainly seen, and fishermen were using axes and picks instead of tackle.

This state of weather lasted a fortnight, and brought to a close the coldest winter California had endured since the '40s. During the cold spell a snowstorm dropped two to four inches of snow over the state as far south as Bakersfield, Kern County. The month's rainfall was 1.10 inches, making 11.57 inches for the season.

At the end of February the State Legislature had been in session fifty-six days and, it was claimed, had not passed a single bill. Most of the state press complained bitterly of the inertia. Some of the editors said the Legislature was the laziest on record, and others claimed it was trying so hard to get Republicans out of and Democrats in to office, and to "cinch" the S. P., nothing else would be done.

At a citizens mass meeting in Tulare City February 28 the assemblyman representing Tulare County in the State Legislature was burned in effigy, because of the record he was making.

A state census showed a total of 216,830 schoolchildren, and $1,585,412 was appropriated to pay for their education.

The 1882 hop yield in California totaled 1,808,500 pounds, Sacramento County producing 1,200,000 pounds. The price had advanced during the harvest season to $1.20 a pound, but was now $1. A large increase in acreage was expected.

George Baker, a Feather River fisherman, captured five beaver near Oroville, Butte County, February 1. Bruno Grundlach killed near San Jose, Santa Clara County, a beautiful bird—an albino hawk; its white plumage was flecked with gold, and it had a bronze-colored tail.

Two Siskiyou County hunters killed 1,000 deer during the season, and sold the skins at 30 cents a pound. Wm. Long, a hunter of the Suisun, Solano County, marshes, was killing geese by the hundreds, rendering the fat and selling it for 80 cents a pound.

Six men from Niles, Alameda County, went hunting February 18. They returned with 700 ducks, 25 geese and 49 snipe.

On the ranch of General J. R. Brierly near San Pedro, Los Angeles County, a petrified clam was picked up atop a hill 660 feet above sea level.

Coyotes, rendezvousing in large packs in the Marysville Buttes, were raiding Sutter County flocks. In one night a sheepman lost thirty-one lambs.

Young women of Salinas, Monterey County, formed a society to abate the cigaret-smoking habit of the town's youths—a cigaret smoker was to be tabooed.

Saint Helena, Napa County, was greatly excited over the arrest of five of its prominent citizens for playing poker in a room of the principal hotel. They were charged with violating the anti-gambling law, and a hot legal battle was in prospect.

Sacramento Parlor No. 3 N.S.G.W. had its sixth annual party February 13. The arrangements committee included Clarence E. Parker, Frank D. Ryan, Robert T. Devlin and John T. Stafford. Notwithstanding a heavy rainstorm, 700 couples appeared in the grand march, many coming from San Francisco and other cities.

In Lake County February 27, George Washington, as black as the ace of spades, was arrested for killing a man in Red Bluff, Tehama County. George had won a jackpot but, before he could rake it in, a discomfitted bettor reached for it, and George "jes hed" to shoot him.

The stage from San Andreas, Calaveras County, to Milton was held up February 23 by a lone man, who retired with the United States mail.

Lodi, San Joaquin County, had an exciting footrace along its main street February 24 between George Harrison of Stockton and Jack Nelson of Hawks Corner. The betting was heavy, and as Nelson came in ahead the Stockton contingent went home broke.

James H. Moore, who came to California in 1849, was shot and killed by F. Bennett in an altercation at Dixon, Solano County, February 4.

John Vogan, Pioneer of 1849 who organized the first stage line running from Sacramento City to Mokelumne Hill, Calaveras County, died at the Capital City February 5 at the age of 61. For several years he was sheriff of Amador County.

Charles Brown who, at the age of 22, arrived in San Francisco in 1829, died there February 10.

J. S. Woods, who came to California from Ohio in 1848, died at Sacramento City February 15. He was at one time sheriff of Sacramento County.

Victor Ustrusano, who arrived in Ventura City in 1828, while going to his home the night of February 16 fell headlong into an irrigation ditch and drowned in six inches of water.

Dr. Hugh J. Glenn, a gubernatorial candidate in 1878 and owner and farmer of a princely domain in Colusa County, was shot and killed by Huron Miller—a bookkeeper discharged for intoxication—at Jacinto, Glenn County, February 17. Dr. Glenn, a native of Virginia, came across the plains in 1849. He became a drover, and frequently brought herds of cattle, horses, mules and sheep overland from the Missouri River to California. In 1867 he began farming operations in Colusa County, and they grew to such an extent that, at the time of his murder, he was tilling 65,000 acres of land and using a thousand mules and several hundred men. He shipped his wheat crop by steamboat from Colusa to Port Costa, Contra Costa County; there it was loaded aboard vessels bound for Liverpool, England, and sold at that port. He did without the services of a middleman, and was considered the wheat baron of the West.

Daniel F. Holbrook, who arrived in Nevada County in 1850, died February 27 at Grass Valley.

The business section of Princeton, Colusa County, burned February 1; loss, $20,000. A Riverside City business block was destroyed by fire February 7, causing a $30,000 loss. Twelve buildings of Fresno City's Chinatown burned February 17; loss, $20,000.

Fire February 16 destroyed ten buildings of the business section of Knights Landing, Yolo County, and caused a $40,000 loss; James Dinwiddie was burned to death. In a Chico, Butte County, fire February 26 twenty-five horses were cremated; the loss was $40,000.

Unsuccessful attempts were made February 18 to burn Red Bluff, Tehama County. Fires were set at several places in the schoolhouse and the county court house.

EARLY DAYS IN S. F.

(Continued from Page 5)

through the streets; thirty-one salutes from large cannon, California being the thirty-first state; orations at Portsmouth Plaza; fireworks; a grand ball in the evening, and rejoicing everywhere. California is indeed a proud and a patriotic state!

It was but a short walk from the Plaza to the restaurants and cafés which made the old city by the Golden Gate famous, such as the Poodle Dog, Pup, Marchand's and others. Mark Twain, Bret Harte, and in the later days Robert Louis Stevenson, strolling through the Plaza or seated in the cafés, from the motley crowd, the ebb and flow of human life, and the tales of adventure by sea and land told by the sailor and the miner, secured the local coloring which made their writings so attractive. Actors, artists and musicians gathered at the tables of the less-pretentious restaurants, where for fifty cents bounteous meals were served, including a bottle of wine and a liberal portion of cognac for your coffee. The color and the romance which clustered around the days of old, the days of gold, may never return, but the memory lingers on.

From the vine-clad hills of France, Spain and Italy came those who gave color to the Latin quarter and brought to mind the lays of Ancient Rome, when the poets sang:

> And in the vats of Luna,
> This year the wine shall foam
> Round the white feet of laughing girls
> Whose sires have marched to Rome.

Up the slopes of Telegraph Hill, known by the Spaniards as Loma Alta, stretched the Latin quarter. As early as 1849 a station was erected on its summit from which could be observed the arrival of incoming vessels, bearing news from the outer world. A tall pole with a movable arm, called a semaphore, signaled the character of the ship to the town below and advised as to whether it was a sailing vessel or a side-wheel steamer of the Pacific Mail. In 1853 a telegraph line, the first in California, connected the hill with Point Lobos and gave notice of the arrival, far out at sea, of vessels from Panama or around the Horn.

In the days of '49 the region from California to Market streets was one of high sand hills covered with scrub oak, but south of Market between First and Second streets, and supplied with a good spring of water, was a small protected valley where about 1,000 tents were set up and the place was known as Happy Valley. Between this and Rincon Hill stretched Pleasant Valley.

On Calhoun street, near the summit of Telegraph Hill, lived for some time America's and the world's greatest actor, Edwin Booth, and his father, Junius Brutus Booth. San Francisco has always cherished the memory and traditions of the stage. Maguire's Opera House, in the early fifties, stood on Washington street near Montgomery. Near the same corner was the Metropolitan Theatre, once called "the most magnificent temple of histrionic art in America." Beginning with 1850, three Jenny Lind Theatres stood on the site of the present Hall of Justice two being destroyed by fire and the last sold in 1852, to San Francisco for a City Hall. Th American Theatre was on Sansome and Halleck streets, the Grand Opera House on Mission, an the California on Bush street. Among the ac tors who played here and were dear to th hearts of San Franciscans were the great trage dians Edwin and Junius Brutus Booth, Joh McCullough, Tom Keene, Lawrence Barrett, Ed win Forrest, Barry Sullivan, John T. Raymon the elder Sothern, Mrs. Judah, Mary Anderso Mrs. John Drew, Annie Pixley, Lotta Crabtre and Emily Melville, and a long line of th world's great opera singers. The moving pi ture shows will never dim the luster or detra from the fame of the great artists whose geniu voices and graceful art won the hearts of o Pioneer Fathers and Mothers. Every lover San Francisco must desire to see reared on th summit of historic Telegraph Hill a lofty an artistic monument to those who most deserve —the Pioneers of California.

Irvin S. Cobb, the versatile and genial Ame ican writer, has said: "If I could start in a over again back at 20 or 25 I should choose f my early abiding place some spot in a hundr mile radius of San Francisco. Half the year should like to spend in the city itself; the oth half on a roaming commission to the verges the desert, or to the glorious hills and mou tains of California. Then when I grew tired rambling, I could go back to that city which, my way of thinking, is of the American cities whatsoever size, the most friendly on prelim nary inspection, and on further acquaintan the most likable—the one which on all coun wears the best and the longest. Los Angel already is, and I reckon always will be, Calif nia's diamond-studded stomacher, but San Fra cisco is the golden poppy blossom in her hair

LOS ANGELES CITY AND COUNTY

THE N.S.G.W. AND N.D.G.W. INTERparlor Committee (Southern District)—Burrel D. Neighbours chairman, Fred J. Burmester secretary—at a largely attended meeting January 13 adopted two resolutions of particular portance at this time. One, anent the prosed Jap quota, appears in full on page 6 of is issue of The Grizzly Bear; the other follows:

Some twenty years ago, the Orders of Native ns and Native Daughters of the Golden West unched a "Buy American" drive, and in their rchasing the members of the Order adhere to at policy. The N.S.G.W. and N.D.G.W. Interrior Committee of Southern California notes th delight the movement, now gaining nationde momentum, in furtherance of the "Buy merican" policy. It is an evidence that the ed sown by the patriotic Orders of California atives is finally producing a desired harvest.

Resolved, That the Interparlor Committee rendorses the "Buy American" campaign, as a eans of returning to employment millions of e nation's now-idle workers. As a matter of nsistency and expediency, however, there ould be linked with the "Buy American," a Employ American" movement, that citizens of is country may be the beneficiaries.

Resolved, That copies of this resolution be nt to the Senate and the Assembly of the Calirnia State Legislature, and that that body be quested to enact legislation which will make mandatory for the State Government and any d all of its several departments to specify in y and all contracts or orders for the purchase supplies, goods or materials of any and every ture, that such supplies, goods or materials ust be manufactured or produced in the United ates of America by citizens of this nation.

A SPLENDID NATIVE SON PASSES.

William Jefferson Hunsaker, an outstanding alifornian,—a stalwart citizen of the highest egree, a barrister of unimpeachable character d a friend, always, in deed,—crossed the great vide January 13. He was born in Contra Costa ounty, September 21, 1855, and received his rly education in the public schools of that unty and San Diego City. For two years he rved San Diego County as district attorney, d he was a former president of the California d the Los Angeles Bar Associations.

"Bill" Hunsaker was a charter member of n Diego Parlor No. 108 N.S.G.W. and its origal president. When he moved to Los Angeles ty to make his home he transferred his memrship to Ramona Parlor No. 109, with which was actively identified to the moment of his

WILLIAM JEFFERSON HUNSAKER.

untimely passing. Surviving are three children—Daniel M. Hunsaker (Ramona No. 109), Mrs. Mary H. Brill and Mrs. Rose H. Steehler.—C.M.H.

GOOD SLOGAN TO EXEMPLIFY.

Santa Monica—Officers of Santa Monica Bay Parlor No. 245 N.D.G.W. were installed at public ceremonies January 11, Amada Machado becoming president. In her inspiring talk she stressed "co-operation and friendship," the Parlor's slogan for the term. Special guests were Grand Outside Sentinel Hazel B. Hansen, Florence Dodson-Schoneman and N.S. Grand Trustee Eldred Meyer. Among the many presentations was that of an emblematic ring to Past President Katherine Conterno. Entertainment was provided by Clayton Brandt and others, and refreshments were served. Myrtle Barden, Hazel McCreary, Helen Burke, Emelia Sunquist and Rosalie F. Hyde were the evening's hostesses.

January 25 an "all american" dinner was followed by bridge; Katherine Worsham headed the committee in charge. The Parlor plans a membership drive, and is making arrangements for a rummage sale, a food sale and a dance. The members are delighted with the new quarters.

FOUR N.S. PARLORS INSTALL JOINTLY.

The meetingplace of University Parlor No. 272 N.S.G.W. was crowded January 10, when the officers of Los Angeles No. 45, Ramona No. 109, Glendale No. 264 and Santa Monica Bay No. 267 Parlors were installed at joint public ceremonies. District Deputy Harry Haun officiated, and Leslie Packard, Frank Adams, Harvey Gillette and Arthur Leonard became the respective presidents. Assisting the deputy were Albert Cron, past president, Ralph Harbison, marshal, Howard Babb, sentinel, Roger Johnson, pianist, and Mrs. Clinton Skinner, organist.

President Bernard Hiss of University presided following the ceremonies, and a program, arranged by Howard Babb, was presented by Carter Wright, Jenny Alice Farrand, Jackie Jean Simpson and Aileen DeFazio. William A. Packard, 89-year-young Civil War veteran, contributed a couple of vocal selections, acting as his own accompanist and delighting the crowd. Brief addresses were made by Grand Outside Sentinel Hazel B. Hansen of the Native Daughters, Grand Trustee Eldred Meyer, Past Grand President John T. Newell, District Deputies Edward Baldwin, Walter Baskerville and Howard Bentley.

VALENTINE DANCE.

Los Angeles Parlor No. 124 N.D.G.W. is sponsoring a semi-formal dance at Odd Fellows Temple, Oak and Washington streets, February 11. The valentine motif will be carried out, and a "snappy" orchestra has been engaged. Marshal Edna Trombatore heads the arrangements committee and is being assisted by the following hostesses: Evelyn Trautwein, Juanita Porter, Louise McNary, Olinda Kerby, Ella Steinbeck, Grace DuCasse, Lillian Mills, Violet Latham.

(Continued on Page 16)

Official Directory of Parlors of the N. S. G. W.

ALAMEDA COUNTY.

Alameda No. 47, Alameda City—R. H. Fallmer, Pres.; Robt. H. Cavanaugh, Sec., 1806 Pacific Ave.; Wednesdays, Veterans Memorial Bldg.

Oakland No. 50, Oakland—F. R. Born, Pres.; F. M. Norris, Sec., 5595 Taft Ave.; Fridays, Native Sons Hall, 11th and Clay Sts.

Las Positas No. 96, Livermore—Dr. Donald M. Fraser, Pres.; John J. Kelly, Sec., P. O. box 341; Thursdays, Foresters Hall.

Eden No. 113, Hayward—John Meincke, Pres.; Filbert M. Soares, Sec., 1437 "B" St.; 2nd and 4th Tuesdays, Memorial Hall, Main St.

Piedmont No. 120, Oakland—Stanley Hadlen, Pres.; Charles Morando, Sec., 906 Vermont St.; Thursdays, Native Sons Hall, 11th and Clay Sts.

Wisteria No. 127, Alvarado—Henry May, Pres.; J. M. Scribner, Sec., Livermore; 1st Thursday, I.O.O.F. Hall.

Halcyon No. 146, Alameda City—S. Chesley Anderson, Pres.; J. C. Bates, Sec., 2189 Buena Vista Ave.; 1st and 3rd Tuesdays, I.O.O.F. Hall, 2329 Santa Clara Ave.

Brooklyn No. 151, Oakland—Frank B. Perry, Pres.; E. W. Cooney, Sec., 3907 14th Ave.; 1st and 3rd Wednesdays, Masonic Temple, 8th Ave. and E. 14th St.

Washington, No. 169, Centerville—M. D. Silva, Pres.; Allen G. Norris, Sec., P. O. box 31; 2nd and 4th Tuesdays, Hansen Hall.

Athens No. 195, Oakland—Milton O. Peterson, Pres.; Harold B. Farley, Sec., 4623 Benevides Ave.; Tuesdays, Native Sons Hall, 11th and Clay Sts.

Berkeley No. 210, Berkeley—F. Gohl, Pres.; R. J. Garrett, Sec., 1708 Virginia St.; Tuesdays, Native Sons Hall, 2108 Shattuck Ave.

Estudillo No. 223, San Leandro—E. E. King, Pres.; Albert G. Pacheco, Sec., 1736 E. 14th St.; 1st and 3rd Tuesdays, U.P.E.C. Hall.

Claremont No. 240, Emeryville—Raymond P. Burke, Pres.; E. N. Thienger, Sec., 839 Hearst Ave., Berkeley; Tuesdays, Veterans Memorial Bldg., 43rd and Salem Sts.

Pleasanton No. 244, Pleasanton—Edward Holzreitu, Pres.; Ernest W. Schween, Sec.; 2nd and 4th Thursdays, I.O.O.F. Hall.

Niles No. 250, Niles—M. L. Fournier, Pres.; C. E. Martenstein, Sec.; 2nd Thursday, I.O.O.F. Hall.

Fruitvale No. 252, Oakland—William J. Keating Jr., Pres.; Ray B. Felton, Sec., 1575 Alice St.; Fridays, W.O.W. Hall, 3256 E. 14th St.

AMADOR COUNTY.

Amador No. 17, Sutter Creek—J. H. Williams, Pres.; F. J. Payne, Sec.; 1st and 3rd Fridays, Native Sons Hall.

Excelsior No. 31, Jackson—Wm. Daugherty, Pres.; William Going, Sec.; 1st and 3rd Wednesdays, Native Sons Hall, 22 Court St.

Ione No. 33, Ione—Earl Grover, Pres.; Josiah H. Saunders, Sec.; 1st and 3rd Wednesdays, Native Sons Hall.

Plymouth No. 48, Plymouth—Chester G. Johnson, Pres.; Thos. D. Davis, Sec.; 1st and 3rd Saturdays, N.S.G.W. Hall.

BUTTE COUNTY.

Argonaut No. 8, Oroville—Frank H. O'Brien, Pres.; Cyril R. Macdonald, Sec., P. O. box 502; 1st and 3rd Wednesdays, Veterans Memorial Hall.

Chico No. 21, Chico—Marcus Choisser, Pres.; Sam Lindsay Adams, Sec., Sacramento Blvd.; 2nd and 4th Thursdays, Elks Hall.

CALAVERAS COUNTY.

Chispa No. 139, Murphys—Maynard Segale, Pres.; Antone Malaspina, Sec.; Wednesdays, Native Sons Hall.

COLUSA COUNTY.

Colusa No. 69, Colusa City—Rotheus A. Gray, Pres.; Phil J. Humburg, Sec., 223 Parkhill St.; Tuesdays, Eagles Hall.

CONTRA COSTA COUNTY.

General Winn No. 32, Antioch—Edmont T. Uren, Pres.; Joel H. Ford, Sec., P. O. box 311; 2nd and 4th Wednesdays, Union Hall.

Mount Diablo No. 101, Martinez—R. P. Anderson, Pres.; G. T. Barkley, Sec.; 1st and 3rd Mondays, I.O.O.F. Hall.

Byron No. 170, Byron—William E. Bunn, Pres.; H. G. Krumland, Sec.; 1st and 3rd Tuesdays, I.O.O.F. Hall.

Carquinez No. 205, Crockett—Thos. Cox, Pres.; Thomas I. Cahalan, Sec.; 1st and 3rd Wednesdays, I.O.O.F. Hall.

Richmond No. 217, Richmond—Frank Weber, Pres.; Lloyd N. Mason, Sec., 11 6th St.; 1st Wednesday, 818 Macdonald Ave.

Concord No. 245, Concord—Chas. H. Gray, Pres.; D. E. Pramberg, Sec., P. O. box 235; 1st Monday, Guy's Parlors.

Diamond No. 246, Pittsburg—Victor Ericsson, Pres.; Francis A. Irving, Sec., 248 E. 5th St.; 1st and 3rd Wednesdays, Veterans Memorial Bldg.

EL DORADO COUNTY.

Placerville No. 9, Placerville—Chris. C. Orelli, Pres.; Clyde R. Berriman, Sec., Wood St.; 2nd and 4th Tuesdays, Masonic Hall.

Georgetown No. 91, Georgetown—George W. Brichler, Pres.; C. F. Irish, Sec.; 2nd and 4th Wednesdays, I.O.O.F. Hall.

FRESNO COUNTY.

Fresno No. 25, Fresno City—Oliver M. Akers, Pres.; W. C. Guard, Sec., R.F.D. No. 2, box 379; 1st and 3rd Fridays, Pythian Castle, Cor. "R" and Merced Sts.

Selma No. 107, Selma—Chester E. Shepard, Pres.; E. C. Laughlin, Sec.; 1st Wednesday, American Legion Hall.

GLENN COUNTY.

Willows No. 255—Ralph W. Camper, Pres.; Leon Marshall, Sec., Westwood St.

HUMBOLDT COUNTY.

Humboldt No. 14, Eureka—Henry Sundfors, Pres.; Loren M. Nelson, Sec., P.O. box 195; 2nd and 4th Mondays, Native Sons Hall.

Arcata No. 20, Arcata—F. A. Nicholson, Pres.; William Peters, Sec., P. O. box 1117; Thursdays, Native Sons Hall.

Ferndale No. 93, Ferndale—Hans P. Petersen, Pres.; C. H. Rasmussen, Sec., R.F.D., 47-A; 1st and 3rd Mondays, K.P. Hall.

KERN COUNTY.

Bakersfield No. 42, Bakersfield—George Taylor, Pres.; Henry A. Bannister, Sec., care Bank of America; 2nd and 4th Fridays, Justice Court, City Hall.

LAKE COUNTY.

Lower Lake No. 159, Lower Lake—Harold S. Anderson, Pres.; Albert Kugelman, Sec.; Thursdays, I.O.O.F. Hall.

LASSEN COUNTY.

Honey Lake No. 198, Standish—Leo T. Davis, Pres.; N. V. Wemple, Sec., Litchfield; 1st and 3rd Wednesdays, Wrede Hall.

Big Valley No. 211, Bieber—Fred Bunselmeier, Pres.; A. W. McKenzie, Sec.; 1st and 3rd Wednesdays, I.O.O.F. Hall.

LOS ANGELES COUNTY.

Los Angeles No. 45, Los Angeles City—Leslie A. Packard, Pres.; Willard F. Allen, Sec., 4955 Los Feliz Blvd.; Thursdays, Merchant Plumbers Hall, 1832 So. Hope.

Ramona No. 109, Los Angeles City—Frank S. Adams, Pres.; John V. Scott, Sec., Patriotic Hall, 1816 So. Figueroa; Fridays, Patriotic Hall, 1816 So. Figueroa.

Hollywood No. 196, Los Angeles City—Henry G. Bodkin, Pres.; E. J. Reilly, Sec., Olive View; Mondays, 1089 No. Oxford Ave.

Long Beach No. 239, Long Beach—Francis H. Gentry, Pres.; W. W. Brady, Sec., 801 Jergins Trust Bldg.; 2nd and 4th Thursdays, Moose Hall, Elm and Anaheim.

Sepulveda No. 263, San Pedro—Patrick H. Doran, Pres.; H. E. Fairall, Sec., 1925 So. Pacific Ave.; 1st and 3rd Fridays, Redman Hall, 543 Shepherd St., Point Firmin.

Glendale No. 264, Glendale—Harvey T. Gillette, Pres.; Abel B. Molen, Sec., 508 So. Belmont St.; 1st and 3rd Tuesdays, Masonic Temple, 234 So. Brand Blvd.

Santa Monica Bay 267, Santa Monica—Arthur R. Leonard, Pres.; John J. Smith, Sec., 830 Rialto Ave., Venice; 1st and 3rd Wednesdays, Odd Fellows Hall, 1431 Third St.

Cahuenga No. 268, Reseda—Harold C. Trexler, Pres.; Carrol S. Driscoll, Sec., P.O. box 25, Chatsworth; first Friday, Alton Hall.

University No. 272, Los Angeles City—Bernard G. Hiss, Pres.; Martin DeFazio, Sec., 845 W. 53rd St.; Tuesdays, 471 W. 41st Place.

Compton No. 273, Compton—Laurence W. Cowan, Pres.; Wm. Don Castillo, Sec., 641 W. Bennett St.; 2nd and 4th Tuesdays, Mayo Hall, 231½ East Compton Blvd.

MADERA COUNTY.

Madera No. 130, Madera City—Cornelius Noble, Pres.; T. P. Cosgrave, Sec.; 1st and 3rd Thursdays, First National Bank Bldg.

MARIN COUNTY.

Mount Tamalpais No. 64, San Rafael—Arthur Hecht, Pres.; Manual A. Andrade, Sec., 532 Mission Ave.; 1st and 3rd Mondays, "B" Street Hall.

Sea Point No. 158, Sausalito—Wm. W. Taylor, Pres.; Manuel Santos, Sec., 6 Glen Drive; 1st and 3rd Wednesdays, Perry Bldg.

Nicasio No. 183, Nicasio—M. T. Farley, Pres.; R. J. Rogers, Sec.; 2nd and 4th Wednesdays, U.A.O.D. Hall.

MENDOCINO COUNTY.

Ukiah No. 71, Ukiah—W. B. Danis, Pres.; Ben Hofman, Sec., P. O. box 478; 1st and 3rd Mondays, I.O.O.F. Hall.

Broderick No. 117, Point Arena—Ivan Lawson, Pres.; C. J. Buchanan, Sec.; 1st and 3rd Thursdays, Forester Hall.

Alder Glen No. 200, Fort Bragg—Thomas Cooney, Pres.; C. R. Weller, Sec.; 2nd and 4th Fridays, I.O.O.F. Hall.

MERCED COUNTY.

Yosemite No. 24, Merced City—John J. Thronton, Pres.; True W. Fowler, Sec., P. O. box 781; 2nd and 4th Mondays, I.O.O.F. Hall.

Los Banos No. 206, Los Banos—Daniel Pedroni, Pres.; L. E. Sarbo, Sec., R.F.D., box 21; 2nd and 4th Wednesdays, Eagles Hall.

MONTEREY COUNTY.

Monterey No. 75, Monterey City—James Millington, Pres.; T. W. Krieger, Sec., 999 Franklin St.; 1st and 3rd Fridays, Knights Pythias Hall, Main St.

Santa Lucia No. 97, Salinas—Roy Martella, Pres.; R. W. Adcock, Sec., Route 2, box 180; Mondays, Native Sons Hall, 32 W. Alisal St.

Gabilan No. 132, Castroville—B. A. McCoy, Pres.; R. H. Martin, Sec., P. O. box 81; 1st and 3rd Thursdays, Native Sons Hall.

NAPA COUNTY.

Saint Helena No. 53, Saint Helena—Gilman Clark, Pres.; Edw. L. Bonhote, Sec., P. O. box 267; Mondays, Native Sons Hall.

Napa No. 62, Napa City—E. L. Miller, Pres.; H. J. Hoernle, Sec., 1226 Oak St.; Mondays, Native Sons Hall.

Calistoga No. 86, Calistoga—Fred Heits, Pres.; Louis Carlenzoli, Sec.; 1st and 3rd Mondays, I.O.O.F. Hall.

NEVADA COUNTY.

Hydraulic No. 56, Nevada City—Verne Gleason, Pres.; Dr. C. W. Chapman, Sec.; Tuesdays, Pythian Castle.

Quartz No. 58, Grass Valley—Robert Kohler, Pres.; H. Ray George, Sec., 151 Conaway Ave.; Mondays, Auditorium Hall.

Donner No. 162, Truckee—J. F. Lichtenberger, Pres.; H. C. Lichtenberger, Sec.; 2nd and 4th Tuesdays, Native Sons Hall.

ORANGE COUNTY.

Santa Ana No. 265, Santa Ana—Amos Huntzinger, Pres.; E. F. Marks, Sec., 1124 No. Bristol St.; 1st and 3rd Mondays, K.C. Hall, 4th and French Sts.

PLACER COUNTY.

Auburn No. 59, Auburn—Hans J. Petersen, Pres.; J. G. Walsh, Sec.; 1st and 3rd Fridays, Foresters Hall.

Silver Star No. 63, Lincoln—Robert P. Davis, Pres.; Barney G. Barry, Sec., P. O. box 72; 3rd Wednesday, I.O.O.F. Hall.

Rocklin No. 233, Roseville—Wm. La Dua, Pres.; M. E. Reed, Sec., 253 W. Duranta; 2nd and 4th Wednesdays, Eagles Hall.

PLUMAS COUNTY.

Quincy No. 131, Quincy—Herbert Hard, Pres.; E. C. Kelsey, Sec.; 2nd Thursday, I.O.O.F. Hall.

Golden Anchor No. 182, La Porte—R. J. McGrath, Pres.; LeRoy J. Post, Sec.; 2nd and 4th Sunday mornings, Native Sons Hall.

Plumas No. 228, Taylorsville—E. E. Sikes, Pres.; George E. Boyden, Sec.; 1st and 3rd Mondays, Native Sons Hall.

SACRAMENTO COUNTY.

Sacramento No. 3, Sacramento City—Parker Kelly, Pres.; J. F. Didion, Sec., 1213 "O" St.; Thursdays, Native Sons Bldg., 11th and "J" Sts.

Sunset No. 26, Sacramento City—Albert Costa, Pres.; Edward E. Reese, Sec., County Treasurer Office; Mondays, Native Sons Bldg., 11th and "J" Sts.

Elk Grove No. 41, Elk Grove—Robert Carr, Pres.; Walter Martin, Sec.; 2nd and 4th Fridays, Masonic Hall.

Granite No. 83, Folsom—Joe Relvas, Pres.; Frank Showers, Sec.; 2nd and 4th Tuesdays, K.P. Hall.

Courtland No. 106, Courtland—N. H. Thisby, Pres.; Jos. Green, Sec.; 1st Saturday and 3rd Monday, Native Sons Hall.

Sutter Fort No. 241, Sacramento City—Ed. T. Goyne, Pres.; C. L. Katzenstein, Sec., P. O. box 914; 2nd and 4th Wednesdays, Native Sons Bldg., 11th and "J" Sts.

Galt No. 243, Galt—Abel G. Stock, Pres.; F. W. Harms, Sec.; 1st and 3rd Mondays, I.O.O.F. Hall.

SAN BENITO COUNTY.

Fremont No. 44, Hollister—S. Churchill, Pres.; J. E. Prendergast Jr., Sec., 1064 Monterey St.; 1st and 3rd Thursdays, Grangers Union Hall.

SAN BERNARDINO COUNTY.

Arrowhead No. 110, San Bernardino City—F. L. McGarvey, Pres.; R. W. Brazelton, Sec., 462 6th St.; Wednesdays, Eagles Hall, 469 4th St.

SAN DIEGO COUNTY.

San Diego No. 108, San Diego City—Martin J. Spangler, Pres.; A. V. Mayrhofer, Sec., 1572 2nd St.; Wednesdays, K.C. Hall, 4th and Elm Sts.

SAN FRANCISCO CITY AND COUNTY.

California No. 1, San Francisco—Joseph Lawlor, Pres.; Ellis A. Blackman, Sec., 1248-A Divisadero St.; Thursdays, Native Sons Bldg., 414 Mason St.

Pacific No. 10, San Francisco—A. L. Anders, Pres.; J. Henry Bastein, Sec., 426 City Hall; Tuesdays, Native Sons Bldg., 414 Mason St.

Golden Gate No. 29, San Francisco—Ernest H. Allen, Pres.; Adolph Eberhart, Sec., 183 Carl St.; Mondays, Native Sons Bldg., 414 Mason St.

Mission No. 38, San Francisco—Martin H. Huber, Pres.; Thos. J. Stewart, Sec., 419 South Van Ness Ave.; Wednesdays, Redmen Hall, 3053 16th St.

San Francisco No. 49, San Francisco—Robert Hallenbarter, Pres.; David Capurro, Sec., 976 Union St.; Thursdays, Native Sons Bldg., 414 Mason St.

El Dorado No. 52, San Francisco—Fred Ageno, Pres.; Alfred Vlautin, Sec., 1537 Franklin St.; Thursdays, Native Sons Bldg., 414 Mason St.

Rincon No. 72, San Francisco—Frank Granzella, Pres.; John A. Gilmour, Sec., 2069 Golden Gate Ave.; Wednesdays, Native Sons Bldg., 414 Mason St.

Stanford No. 76, San Francisco—Charles J. Barry, Pres.; Charles T. O'Kane, Sec., 2900 Scott St.; Tuesdays, Native Sons Bldg., 414 Mason St.

Bay City No. 104, San Francisco—Jacob A. Helbing, Pres.; Max E. Licht, Sec., 1831 Fulton St.; 2nd and 4th Wednesdays, Native Sons Bldg., 414 Mason St.

Niantic No. 105, San Francisco—A. Furner, Pres.; J. M. Darcy, Sec., 10 Hoffman Ave.; Wednesdays, Native Sons Bldg., 414 Mason St.

National No. 118, San Francisco—Walter J. Murphy, Pres.; Martin M. Ratigan, Sec., 1325 Page St., Apt. 6; Thursdays, 1160 Eddy St.

Hesperian No. 137, San Francisco—N. G. Reimers, Pres.; Albert Carlson, Sec., 379 Justin Dr.; Thursdays, Native Sons Bldg., 414 Mason St.

Alcalde No. 154, San Francisco—Robert DeSparr, Pres.; Harry S. Burke, Sec., 25 Ord St.; 2nd and 4th Wednesdays, Native Sons Bldg., 414 Mason St.

South San Francisco No. 157, San Francisco—Mathew Brady, Pres.; John T. Regan, Sec., 1489 Newcomb Ave.; Wednesdays, Masonic Bldg., 4705 3rd St.

Sequoia No. 160, San Francisco—John Lynch, Pres.; Walter W. Garrett, Sec., 2500 Van Ness Ave.; Mondays, Swedish-American Bldg., 2174 Market St.

Precita No. 187, San Francisco—Leland J. Jenkins, Pres.; Edward Tietjen, Sec., 1367 15th Ave.; Thursdays, Mission Masonic Hall, 2668 Mission St.

Olympus No. 189, San Francisco—Henry H. McGowan, Pres.; Harvey J. Carty, Sec., 1651 Market St., Apt. 505; 2nd and 4th Tuesdays, Independent Redmen Hall, 3053 16th St.

Presidio No. 194, San Francisco—Charles Maker, Pres.; George A. Ducker, Sec., 442 21st Ave.; Mondays, Native Sons Bldg., 414 Mason St.

Marshall No. 202, San Francisco—Eugene Biancalona, Pres.; Frank Bacigalupi, Sec., 725 Douglas St.; 1st and 3rd Wednesdays, Native Sons Bldg., 414 Mason St.

ATTENTION, SECRETARIES!

THIS DIRECTORY IS PUBLISHED BY AUTHORITY OF THE GRAND PARLOR N.S.G.W., AND ALL NOTICES OF CHANGES MUST BE RECEIVED BY THE GRAND SECRETARY (NOT THE MAGAZINE) ON OR BEFORE THE 20TH OF EACH MONTH TO INSURE CORRECTION IN NEXT ISSUE OF DIRECTORY.

Dolores No. 208, San Francisco—Henry J. Adami, Pres.; Edward F. Webb, Sec., 2801 Sacramento St.; Tuesdays, Mission Masonic Bldg., 2668 Mission St.

Twin Peaks No. 214, San Francisco—Oswald Storni, Pres.; Thos. Pendergast, Sec., 278 Douglas St.; Wednesdays, Willopi Hall, 4061 24th St.

El Capitan No. 222, San Francisco—John C. Conmy, Pres.; James Hanna, Sec., 2450 27th Ave.; 1st and 3rd Thursdays, King Solomon Hall, 1739 Fillmore St.

Guadalupe No. 231, San Francisco—Thomas Wall, Pres.; Alvin A. Johnson, Sec., 142 Rousseau St.; Tuesdays, Guadalupe Hall, 4551 Mission St.

Castro No. 232, San Francisco—Roy Lund, Pres.; James H. Hayes, Sec., 4014 18th St.; Tuesdays, Native Sons Bldg., 414 Mason St.

Balboa No. 234, San Francisco—George Schroth, Pres.; E. W. Boyd, Sec., 437 Cherry St.; Thursdays, Maccabee Hall, 5th Ave. and Clement St.

Bret Harte No. 260, San Francisco—Louis S. Merrill, Pres.; A. W. McElhatton, Sec., 103 Holloway Ave.; Tuesdays, West of Twin Peaks Hall, 233 Legion Court.

Utopia No. 270, San Francisco—A. E. Rosenbaum, Pres.; Herbert H. Schneider, Sec., 2455 16th Ave.; Tuesdays, American Hall, 20th and Capp Sts.

SAN JOAQUIN COUNTY.

Stockton No. 7, Stockton—Ben S. Waller, Pres.; R. D. Dorcey, Sec., P. O. box 388; Mondays, Native Sons Hall.

Lodi No. 18, Lodi—Jerome Solomon Pres.; Dr. Clyde Bresnan, Sec.; 2nd and 4th Wednesdays, Eagles Hall.

Tracy No. 186, Tracy—C. S. Selna, Pres.; R. J. Marsocini, Sec., R.F.D. No. 1, box 217, Thursdays, I.O.O.F. Hall.

Manteca No. 271, Manteca—John F. Mulholand, Pres.; Leonard Faria, Sec., R.F.D., box 75, Lathrop; 1st and 3rd Wednesdays, I.O.O.F. Hall.

SAN LUIS OBISPO COUNTY.

San Miguel No. 150, San Miguel—H. Twisselman, Pres.; Otto Kuebi, Sec., Paso Robles; 1st and 3rd Wednesdays, Fraternal Hall.

Cambria No. 152, Cambria—N. Storni, Pres.; A. S. Gay, Sec.; Wednesdays, Rigdon Hall.

SAN MATEO COUNTY.

Redwood No. 66, Redwood City—H. E. Holmquist, Pres.; A. S. Liguori, Sec., P. O. box 212; Thursdays, American Foresters Hall.

Seaside No. 95, Half Moon Bay—Melvin Frey, Pres.; John G. Gilcrest, Sec.; 2nd and 4th Tuesdays, I.O.O.F. Hall.

Menlo No. 185, Menlo Park—C. T. Maloney, Pres.; F. W. Johnson, Sec., P. O. box 601; 1st and 3rd Thursdays, Masonic Hall.

Pebble Beach No. 230, Pescadero—Earle A. Williamson, Pres.; E. A. Shaw, Sec.; 2nd and 4th Wednesdays, I.O.O.F. Hall.

El Carmelo No. 256, Daly City—Theodore A. Clemens, Pres.; Ernest L. Micco, Sec., 639 Morse St., San Francisco; 2nd and 4th Wednesdays, Eagles Hall.

Industrial City No. 269, South San Francisco—John C. Hamilton, Pres.; Geo. A. Roll, Sec., P. O. box 237; 2nd and 4th Mondays, Metropolitan Hall.

SANTA BARBARA COUNTY.

Santa Barbara No. 116, Santa Barbara City—C. W. McCormick, Pres.; H. C. Sweetser, Sec., Court House; 1st and 3rd Wednesdays, I.O.O.F. Hall.

SANTA CLARA COUNTY.

San Jose No. 22, San Jose—Fred Carmichael, Pres.; Joseph Lawrence, Sec., 1095 No. First St.; Mondays, I.O.O.F. Hall.

Santa Clara No. 100, Santa Clara City—C. A. Castro, Pres.; Clarence Clevenger, Sec., P. O. box 297; Wednesdays, Redmen Hall.

Observatory No. 177, San Jose—James J. Flannery, Pres.; A. B. Langford, Sec., Hall Records; Tuesdays, Knights Columbus Hall, 40 No. First St.

Mountain View No. 215, Mountain View—Henry A. Schultze, Pres.; C. A. Antonioli, Sec., 301 Castro St.; 2nd and 4th Wednesdays, Mockbee Hall.

Palo Alto No. 216, Palo Alto—John C. Bernal, Pres.; Albert A. Quinn, Sec., 643 High St.; Mondays, Native Sons Bldg., Hamilton Ave. and Emerson St.

SANTA CRUZ COUNTY.

Watsonville No. 65, Watsonville—J. E. Giacoma, Pres.; E. R. Tindall, Sec., R.F.D. No. 5, Box 313; 2nd and 4th Tuesdays, I.O.O.F. Hall.

Santa Cruz No. 90, Santa Cruz City—W. S. Rodgers, Pres.; T. V. Mathews, Sec., 105 Pacheco Ave.; Fridays, Native Sons Hall, 117 Pacific Ave.

SHASTA COUNTY.

McCloud No. 149, Redding—Roy Hawes, Pres.; Hugh A. Shuffleton, Sec.; 1st and 3rd Thursdays, Moose Hall.

SIERRA COUNTY.

Downieville No. 92, Downieville—Frank H. Turner, Pres.; H. S. Tibbey, Sec.; 2nd and 4th Mondays, I.O.O.F. Hall.

Golden Nugget No. 94, Sierra City—Elmer Thompson, Pres.; Arthur R. Pride, Sec.; 1st and 3rd Wednesdays, Masonic Hall.

SISKIYOU COUNTY.

Etna No. 192, Etna—Frank B. Quigley, Pres.; Harvey A. Green, Sec.; 1st and 3rd Wednesdays, I.O.O.F. Hall.

Liberty No. 193, Sawyers Bar—David H. Robinson, Pres.; John M. Barry, Sec.; 1st and 3rd Saturdays, I.O.O.F. Hall.

SOLANO COUNTY.

Solano No. 39, Suisun—John S. Cannon, Pres.; J. W. Kinlock, Sec.; 1st and 3rd Tuesdays, I.O.O.F. Hall.

Vallejo No. 77, Vallejo—Frank J. Heldener, Pres.; Werner B. Hallin, Sec., 912 Carolina; 2nd and 4th Tuesdays, San Pablo Hall.

SONOMA COUNTY.

Petaluma No. 27, Petaluma—Clarence Christiansen, Pres.; C. F. Fobes, Sec., 114 Prospect St.; 2nd and 4th Mondays, Druid Hall, Gross Bldg., 41 Main St.

Santa Rosa No. 28, Santa Rosa—George A. Eckman, Pres.; Leland S. Lewis, Sec., Court House; Mondays, Native Sons Hall.

Glen Ellen No. 102, Glen Ellen—Tony Cereghino, Pres.; Frank Kirch, Sec., Route 3, Santa Rosa; 2nd Monday, N.S.G.W. Hall.

Sonoma No. 111, Sonoma City—Chas. E. Baciglalupi, Pres.; L. H. Green, Sec.; 1st and 3rd Mondays, I.O.O.F. Hall.

Sebastopol No. 143, Sebastopol—O. A. McChristian, Pres.; F. G. McFarlane, Sec.; 1st and 3rd Fridays, I.O.O.F. Hall.

STANISLAUS COUNTY.

Modesto No. 11, Modesto—Chas. D. Blaine, Pres.; C. C. Eastin Jr., Sec., P. O. box 897; 1st and 3rd Wednesdays, I.O.O.F. Hall.

Oakdale No. 142, Oakdale—D. W. Tulloch, Pres.; E. T. Gobin, Sec.; 2nd Monday, Legion Hall.

Orestimba No. 247, Crows Landing—Lloyd W. Fink, Pres.; G. W. Fink, Sec.; 1st and 3rd Wednesdays, Community Club Home.

SUTTER COUNTY.

Sutter No. 261, Sutter City—Henry Correll, Pres.; Glen R. Haynes, Sec., R.F.D. No. 2, Yuba City; 2nd and 4th Mondays, N.D.G.W. Hall.

TRINITY COUNTY.

Mount Bally No. 87, Weaverville—H. W. Day, Pres.; E. V. Ryan, Sec.; 1st and 3rd Mondays, Native Sons Hall.

TULARE COUNTY.

Visalia No. 19, Visalia—G. W. Houk, Pres.; C. H. Wenn, Sec.

TUOLUMNE COUNTY.

Tuolumne No. 144, Sonora—Mathew J. Marshall, Pres.; William M. Harrington, Sec., P. O. box 715; 2nd and 4th Fridays, Knights Columbus Hall.

Columbia No. 258, Columbia—Jos. Cadematori, Pres.; Charles E. Grant, Sec.; 2nd and 4th Thursdays, Native Sons Hall.

VENTURA COUNTY.

Cabrillo No. 114, Ventura City—David Bennett, Pres., 1380 Church St.

YOLO COUNTY.

Woodland No. 30, Woodland—J. L. Aronson, Pres.; R. G. Lawson, Sec.; 1st Thursday, Native Sons Hall.

YUBA COUNTY.

Marysville No. 6, Marysville—A. W. Graves, Pres.; Verne Fogarty, Sec., 719 5th St.; 2nd Friday, Foresters Hall.

Rainbow No. 40, Wheatland—F. M. Beilby, Pres.; W. A. Bowser, Sec., P. O. box 313; 2nd Thursday, I.O.O.F. Hall.

AFFILIATED ORGANIZATIONS.

San Francisco Extension of the Order Committee, N.S.G.W.—Joseph J. McShane, Chmn.; Harold J. Regan, Sec., 414 Mason St., San Francisco; meets 2nd and 4th Fridays, Grizzly Bear Club, 414 Mason St., San Francisco.

Alameda County Extension of the Order Committee, N.S.G.W.—Gam Hurst, Chmn.; Frank Roemer, Sec., 3297 Morcom Ave., Oakland; meets 1st and 3rd Mondays, N.S.G.W. Hall, 11th and Clay Sts., Oakland.

Interparlor Committee (Southern District), N.S.G.W. and N.D.G.W.—Burrel D. Neighbours, Chmn.; F. J. Burmester, Sec., P. O. box 42, Colton; meets 2nd and 4th Fridays, Patriotic Hall, 1816 So. Figueroa St., Los Angeles.

San Francisco Assembly No. 1 Past Presidents Association N.S.G.W.—Meets 1st and 3rd Fridays, Native Sons Bldg., 414 Mason St., San Francisco; Jos. E. Tracy, Gov.; J. F. Stanley, Sec., 1175 O'Farrell St., San Francisco.

East Bay Counties Assembly No. 3 Past Presidents Association N.S.G.W.—Meets 4th Monday, Native Sons Hall, 11th and Clay Sts., Oakland; M. W. Louden, Gov.; Edgar G. Hanson, Sec., 1260 Russell St., Berkeley.

Marin County Assembly No. 5 Past Presidents Association N.S.G.W.—J. S. Rose Jr., Gov.; L. J. Peter, Sec., Peter Bldg., 4th and "C" Sts., San Rafael.

Fred H. Greeley Assembly No. 6 Past Presidents Association N.S.G.W.—Meets monthly with different Parlors comprising district; R. L. P. Bigelow, Gov.; Barney Barry, Sec., P. O. box 72, Lincoln.

San Joaquin Assembly No. 7 Past Presidents Association N.S.G.W.—Meets 1st Friday, Native Sons Hall, Stockton; Clyde H. Gregg, Gov.; R. D. Dorcey, Sec., Native Sons Club, Stockton.

Sonoma County Assembly No. 9 Past President Association N.S.G.W.—Meets monthly at different Parlor headquarters in county; P. A. R. Gambini, Gov.; L. S. Lewis, Sec., Court House, Santa Rosa.

General John A. Sutter Assembly No. 10 Past Presidents Association—C. C. Wachman, Gov.; Jas. J. Longshore, Sec., 514 "J" St., Sacramento.

Grizzly Bear Club—Members all Parlors outside San Francisco at all times welcome. Clubrooms top floor Native Sons Bldg., 414 Mason St., San Francisco.

Native Sons and Native Daughters Central Committee on Homeless Children—Main office, 955 Phelan Bldg., San Francisco; Mrs. John W. Stirling, Chmn.; Miss Mary E. Brusie, Sec. Los Angeles branch office, 3924 Sunset Blvd.; Dorothy Schlingman, Sec.

(ADVERTISEMENT.)

NATIVE SON NEWS

(Continued from Page 7)

time member, Supervisor A. L. Hubbard, recently passed away.

Officers of the Parlor, with Fred A. Carmichael as president, were installed by District Deputy A. C. Hansen January 30.

Popular Grand Officer To Visit.

San Rafael—Mount Tamalpais No. 64 will receive an official visit February 20 from Grand Third Vice-president Harmon D. Skillin, who will, at the invitation of No. 64, be accompanied by a big delegation from Castro No. 232 (San Francisco), of which he is a member. A reception and banquet will be featured, and the occasion promises to be one long remembered, as the Grand Third is immensely popular in the San Francisco Bay region. The Parlor will make an extra effort to secure the attendance of its veteran members.

Officers of Mount Tamalpais were installed, jointly with those of Marinita No. 198 N.D.G.W., January 28 by District Deputy J. S. Rosa, Arthur B. Hecht becoming president. The Parlor has again suffered a sad and serious loss in the death of Dr. R. G. Dufficy, a most successful physician and surgeon who, through his many kindnesses to the sick and afflicted, endeared himself to the whole community.

To Celebrate Anniversary.

Colusa—Colusa No. 69, the home-Parlor of Grand President Seth Millington, plans a big time February 2, when the thirtieth anniversary of its institution will be celebrated. Numerous invitations have been extended, and it is hoped to have present as a guest of honor Past Grand Lewis F. Byington, who instituted Colusa during his term as Grand President. A banquet will be served, there will be many noted speakers, and entertainment features will be provided. In charge of arrangements are Percy J. Cooke, Pihl J. Humburg Jr., R. G. Powers, Ben R. Ragain, Thomas F. Bush, Timothy Sullivan and Elton C. Fitch.

Joint Installations.

Sacramento—Officers of Sacramento No. 3 and Sunset No. 26, and Califia No. 22, La Bandera No. 110, Sutter No. 111 and Coloma No. 212 N.D.G.W. were jointly installed January 12. The new presidents are, respectively, Parker Kelly, Albert J. Costa, Sulene Cowan, Mae K. Sydonstricker, Emilie Lachmann and Amy Sweet. Dancing concluded the ceremonies.

Oroville—Officers of Argonaut No. 8 and Gold of Ophir No. 190 N.D.G.W. were jointly installed January 5. Deputies Cyril Macdonald and Annie Skelly presided, and Frank O'Brien and Hattie Clark became the respective presidents. President O'Brien presided as toastmaster at a banquet spread by No. 8 and there were humorous and historical talks by several.

Santa Cruz—Officers of Santa Cruz No. 90 and Santa Cruz No. 26 N.D.G.W. were jointly installed January 13. Deputies Arnold M. Baldwin and Edna Butterfield presided, and W. S. Rogers and Marjory Brunjas became the respective presidents. Horace Burkett took charge after the ceremonies. There were brief addresses, cards were played, refreshments were served and, in celebration of her birthday anniversary, Miss Melba McKenna presented a beautifully decorated cake. Among the many visitors from Watsonville, Hollister and Salinas were Past Grand Bertha A. Briggs and Supervising Deputy Rose Rhyner of the Native Daughters.

Hayward—Officers of Eden No. 113 and Hayward No. 122 N.D.G.W. were jointly installed January 10 by Deputies Frank Perry and Ann Mello, John A. Meincke and Ella Knudsen becoming the respective presidents. Musical numbers were presented by Carmen Dobbel, Harold Kohen and Anna V. Staley.

N.S.G.W. OFFICIAL DEATH LIST.

Containing the name, the date and the place of birth, the date of death, and the Subordinate Parlor affiliation of deceased members reported to Grand Secretary John T. Regan from December 20, 1932, to January 20, 1933:

McElroy, John Joseph; San Francisco, April 7, 1862; January 4, 1933; California No. 1.

Allen, Fred Dickerhoff; Placerville, September 26, 1870; December 17, 1932; Placerville No. 9.

Campbell, Thomas; San Francisco, January 26, 1862; October 28, 1932; Pacific No. 10.

Borman, Koonie; San Francisco; January 24, 1872; December 14, 1932; Pacific No. 10.

Harvey, Hobbert Courtney; San Francisco, May 29, 1876; July 21, 1932; Fresno No. 25.

Atkins, Frank Sheridan; Sheldon, October 5, 1872; January 12, 1933; Sunset No. 26.

McReynolds, Dennis Hardin; Sebastopol, March 20, 1879; January 2, 1933; Santa Rosa No. 28.

Hatch, Frank B.; Sacramento, October 18, 1859; January 7, 1933; Santa Rosa No. 28.

Briscoe, Fred Smith; Woodland, June 28, 1880; December 28, 1932; Mission No. 38.

Peterson, Emil John; Caspar, February 27, 1877; December 29, 1932; Mission No. 38.

Waterman, Louis Philip; San Francisco, October 2, 1868; December 24, 1932; Los Angeles No. 45.

Mccurdy, Hugh J.; Bolinas, January 28, 1877; December 12, 1932; Mount Tamalpais No. 64.

Dufficy, Rafael G.; San Rafael, November 20, 1885; December 22, 1932; Mount Tamalpais No. 64.

Palmtag, Charles Alvin; Watsonville, November 1, 1872; December 19, 1932; Watsonville No. 65.

Cano, Frank Telespho; Calistoga, January 5, 1882; December 17, 1932; Redwood No. 66.

Peterson, Charles; San Francisco, May 13, 1867; December 8, 1932; Rincon No. 72.

Schord, Mulford H.; San Francisco, June 18, 1876; November 8, 1932; Stanford No. 76.

Irwin, Eugene J.; Oakland, March 3, 1893; December 21, 1932; Stanford No. 76.

Shaen, Samuel; Stockton, August 5, 1857; December 31, 1932; Stanford No. 76.

Haywood, George Payne; Ferndale, November 2, 1875; December 20, 1932; Ferndale No. 93.

Dinsmore, Irving Winfield; Hydesville, August 29, 1866; January 6, 1933; Ferndale No. 93.

Victor, Morris; Livermore, February 6, 1887; December 19, 1932; Las Positas No. 96.

Turner, Frank Legrand; Napa, December 10, 1885; December 25, 1932; Ramona No. 109.

Brown, Daniel Michiel; San Francisco, March 17, 1863; December 23, 1932; Ramona No. 109.

Hunsaker, William Jefferson; Contra Costa, September 21, 1855; January 13, 1933; Ramona No. 109.

Paine, Elsworth Elmer; San Bernardino, August 5, 1897; December 27, 1932; Arrowhead No. 110.

Ellis, George V.; San Francisco, February 13, 1887; November 27, 1932; National No. 118.

Frichette, L. Joseph; San Francisco, August 7, 1870; December 26, 1932; Hesperian No. 137.

Desmond, Dennis; French Gulch, April 7, 1860; March 3, 1932; McCloud No. 149.

O'Donnell, W. J.; Nevada City, July 16, 1857; July 3, 1932; McCloud No. 149.

Holcomb, George Raymond; Redding, September 6, 1907; July 5, 1932; McCloud No. 149.

Lion, Henry Joseph; San Jose, September 21, 1868; December 23, 1932; Observatory No. 177.

Bustillos, Armedio Joseph; Marysville, January 12, 1870; November 5, 1932; Golden Anchor No. 182.

Berger, Robert; San Juan, June 8, 1867; December 12, 1932; Precita No. 187.

Wagner, William; Etna, May 11, 1872; September 3, 1932; Etna No. 192.

Sovy, Clement S.; Etna, June 1, 1909; September 17, 1932; Etna No. 192.

Dunn, James M.; San Francisco, July 4, 1897; January 3, 1933; Presidio No. 194.

Babue, Edward Stephen; Oakland, September 18, 1883; January 9, 1933; Athens No. 195.

Dewitt, Chas. A.; Milford, April 14, 1886; November 5, 1932; Honey Lake No. 198.

Nagle, John; San Francisco, January 12, 1882; December 30, 1932; Twin Peaks No. 214.

Fouchet, Edmond; Sausalito, October 11, 1882; August 30, 1932; Fruitvale No. 252.

"Street Cars Heed, and Slow Your Speed!" is the February slogan of the California Public Safety Committee in its campaign to lessen the constantly increasing auto death-toll.

SAN FRANCISCO

THE TOTAL VALUE OF THE MINERAL production of California for 1932 is conservatively estimated by the State Mines Division, Walter W. Bradley state mineralogist, to have been $209,725,000. As there are more than fifty mineral substances on California's commercial list, it is impracticable at this early date to obtain definite figures on other than the more important items.

The estimated 1932 total is a decrease of approximately $6,239,000 from the 1931 production value of $215,964,420. Petroleum and gold were the only major mineral substances whose 1932 output showed an increased value over the preceding year. Large decreases in values were registered by cement, miscellaneous stone, natural gas, copper, quicksilver, brick, industrial materials and salines.

The value of the 1932 petroleum output, $153,220,000, was approximately 8.5 percent higher than in 1931, although the 1932 quantity, 179,533,000 barrels, showed a decrease of about 8,840,000 barrels compared with 1931.

Gold produced in 1932 had an estimated value of $11,700,000; compared with 1931, this is an increase of about $886,000. Small placer operations, brought about by unemployment, accounted for about $300,000 of that increase. The outputs of the lode mines and the dredges also showed an increase. The 1932 value of other metals was: silver, $141,000; copper, $67,000; lead, $61,000; quicksilver, $325,000.

California Leads Nation.

According to a report of the United States Mint, California led all the states of the Union in 1932 gold production—566,031 ounces valued at $11,700,900. For the whole country the totals were 2,507,587 ounces, $51,836,000 value. Utah led in silver production, 7,815,956 ounces valued at $2,204,099. For the whole country the totals were 24,425,089 ounces, $6,887,875 value.

HISTORIC DAY CELEBRATED.

The annual Gold Discovery Day banquet, under the auspices of the Native Sons of the Golden West, January 24 attracted a large attendance, including members of the Society of California Pioneers, N.S.G.W. grand officers and public officials.

Past Grand President Lewis F. Byington, the "father" of the celebration, was chairman of the arrangements committee. Among the speakers were Governor James Rolph Jr., Mayor Angelo J. Rossi of San Francisco, Mayor Fred N. Morcom of Oakland, and Grand President Seth Millington.

ELABORATE CELEBRATION OF GREAT ENTERPRISE.

San Francisco is making elaborate arrangements to officially celebrate, February 26, ground breaking for the $35,000,000 Golden Gate bridge project. A citizens committee, headed by Supervisor William P. Stanton, is handling the details of what promises to be the greatest celebration ever held in the San Francisco Bay region.

The fete will open with a mammoth parade in which all uniformed units of the Orders of Native Sons and Native Daughters in San Francisco, Alameda, Contra Costa, Marin, Sonoma, Napa, San Mateo and Santa Clara Counties have been invited to, and should, participate. Other spectacular entertainment features will be a regatta, an aerial show, massed band concerts and a public banquet.

The Golden Gate bridge project, one of the most extensive undertaken in California in many a year, will physically link "The City That Knows How" with the counties of the Redwood Empire. The enterprise will give employment to hundreds of men.

NATIVE DAUGHTER PARLORS DOINGS.

Officers of Alta No. 3 were installed January 24 at public ceremonies, Angeline Vest becoming president. Credit for the success of the past term is due the retiring president, May L. MacDonald, who devoted much time and energy to furthering the Order's aims; through her efforts the Parlor has adopted a colored baby boy. The first activity for the new term was a benefit bridge luncheon January 27; Claire Bolman and Elizabeth F. Douglass headed the committee.

Minerva No. 2 was greatly honored by having been the first Parlor in San Francisco officially visited by Grand President Anna Mixon Armstrong in 1933. Present also were Junior Past Grand Evelyn I. Carlson, Grand Trustees Anna C. Thuesen and Ethel Begley, Grand Inside Sentinel Orinda Giannini, Past Grands Dr. Mariana Bertola, Margaret Grote-Hill and May Himes-Noonan, and representatives from fifteen Parlors. Four candidates were initiated, and the Grand President praised highly the exemplification of the ritual. A highlight of the evening was a talk by Past Grand Bertola in which she forcefully impressed the slogan "Buy American." Minerva will adopt a baby for the Central Homeless Children Committee. Officers were installed January 18.

Golden State No. 50's officers were installed January 4 by Deputy Emma O'Meara, I. Milan becoming president. A program, greatly enjoyed, was presented by Hazel Heyl, Virginia Eggles, Pat Buckman, Thelma Tiano, Marie Lotts, Wm. Stellwager, Ray Cate and Hazel Burns.

Golden Gate No. 158 had a shower January 9 for Hazel Cerreli, a recent bride. A mock wedding was followed by the presentation of useful gifts to her. The members also had their annual exchange of gifts, and a great deal of merriment was created. All went home with pleasant memories of a very happy evening. The Parlor entertained the children December 19 at a Christmas party.

Officers of Dolores No. 169 were installed January 11 by Deputy Agnes McVerry, Kittie Mullaney becoming president. Louise Winkler, retiring president, was presented with a china service. January 19 the Parlor celebrated its twenty-fourth institution anniversary at a banquet, and many members enjoyed a delightful evening. Mae Baumeister was chairman of the evening. Members of Dolores paid a visit Christmas Day to Letterman Hospital, served seventeen veterans with home-made delicacies and presented each with a handkerchief.

Officers of Castro No. 178 were publicly installed January 18 by Deputy Myrtle Ross. Despite the inclemency of the weather, a large number of relatives and friends of the members braved the elements to see the enthusiastic young president, Luella Cauvin, enter upon her term. After installation the N.D.G.W. choral club entertained; Ruby Gried's "Autograph Album of the Officers of Castro Parlor," a clever skit, was a scream, displaying quite a bit of histrionic ability. The annual Christmas party, given to the kiddies of members and friends, was a huge success. The boys at Letterman Hospital were not forgotten during the holiday rush, a stocking filled with goodies being given each, and the children in the tubercular wa[illegible] of San Francisco Hospital were given scra[illegible] books, balloons and bags of candy.

CALIFORNIA SKI DATES.

Dates fixed by the directors of the Californ[illegible] Ski Association are: February 8, Truckee, N[illegible]vada County, tournament; February 11-13, sta[illegible] meet at Los Angeles City; February 19, Aubur[illegible] Placer County, Ski Club tournament; Februar[illegible] 26, Mount Lassen Ski Club tournament.

State Employes' Meet—The California Sta[illegible] Employes Association will hold its first annu[illegible] convention at Sacramento City, February 11-1[illegible]

Relief Bonds—Alameda County voters ha[illegible] approved a $3,000,000 bond issue for reli[illegible] work.

"Great works are performed not by strengt[illegible] but by perseverance."—Johnson.

Passing of the California Pioneer

(Confined to Brief Notices of the Demise of Those Men and Women Who Came to California Prior to 1870.)

MRS. AUGUSTA TRIMINGHAM, native of Germany, 91; crossed the plains to California in 1850 and resided in Tuolumne and Alameda Counties; died at Sunol, her home for sixty-five years, survived by seven children.

Emile S. Pitois, native of France, 90; came via the Isthmus of Panama in 1852 and five years later settled in Amador County; died near Jackson, survived by four children.

Harry T. Payne, native of Illinois, 88; came across the plains in 1851; died at Glendale, Los Angeles County. He was well known as a newspaperman and an artist, at one time being city editor of the old "Los Angeles Tribune."

Frank S. Fugitt, native of Missouri, 83; since 1852 Kern County resident; died at Bakersfield, survived by five children.

Mrs. Alice E. Gordon, native of Indiana, 87; came across the plains in 1853 and resided many years in Santa Clara County; died at San Francisco. She was a daughter of John H. Adams, who served in the Mexican War and in 1849 arrived in El Dorado County; as sheriff of Santa Clara County, he won fame for his part in the capture of Tiburcio Vasquez, notorious bandit, and for distinguished service during the troublesome Civil War days.

Mrs. Margaret E. Byrum, native of Missouri, 85; crossed the plains in 1852 and settled in Stanislaus County; died near Salida, survived by five children.

Charles H. Nolte, native of Germany, 96; came via the Isthmus of Panama in 1853 and resided several years in San Francisco; died at Hollister, San Benito County, survived by a wife and four children.

Mrs. Ellen Elizabeth Vincent-Bacon, native of Canada, 89; came via Cape Horn in 1853 and two years later settled at Lockeford, San Joaquin County, where she died; two children survive.

Joseph Wright, native of Iowa, 85; came across the plains in 1853 and resided in Yuba, San Luis Obispo and Los Angeles Counties; died at Canoga Park, survived by four children.

Forrest Foote, native of New York, 80; came in 1856 and resided in Calaveras and San Joaquin Counties; died at Stockton, survived by a wife and six children.

Mrs. Jane Cadd-Smithson, native of Australia, 81; since 1856 San Bernardino County resident; died at San Bernardino City, survived by seven children, among them Mrs. Edward McGarvey (Lugonia Parlor No. 241 N.D.G.W.). She was a member of the San Bernardino Pioneer Society.

Carl Dresel, native of Texas, 81; since 1856 Sonoma County resident; died at Sonoma City, survived by a wife and six children.

George W. Wilson, native of Missouri, 81; came in 1857 and long resided in Mendocino County; died at Compton, Los Angeles County, survived by eight children.

Mrs. Amand M. Flowers, native of Illinois, 89; came in 1858 and resided many years in Trinity County; died at San Francisco, survived by five children. She was the widow of Ellis Flowers, earlyday sheriff of Trinity County.

David Squires, native of Wisconsin, 81; came in 1858 and resided in Yuba, Mendocino and Lake Counties; died near Lakeport, survived by a wife and two daughters.

Mrs. Norma Trout-Fox, native of Ohio, 78; came in 1858 and resided many years in Tuolumne County; died at Alameda City, survived by a daughter. She was the widow of John Trout, former Tuolumne County sheriff.

Mrs. Winnie A. Cliff, native of Kentucky, 88; came across the plains in 1858 and long resided in Yolo County; died at Los Angeles City, survived by two children.

Henry C. Oest, native of New York, 75; since 1859 Placer County resident; died at Roseville, survived by three children.

Mrs. Isabel Rose-Bishop, native of Azores Islands, 93; came in 1859; died near Livermore, Alameda County.

Mrs. Louisa Amelia Lorenz-Boege, native of Chile, 81; since 1859 resident of Anaheim, Orange County, where she died.

Norris D. Dutcher, native of New York, 82; came via Panama in 1860 and settled in Alameda County; died at Livermore, survived by a son.

Frank E. Haile, native of Wisconsin, 75; came via Cape Horn in 1860 and settled in Alameda County; died at Alameda City, survived by a wife and two daughters.

James S. Thompson, native of North Carolina, 83; came in 1860; died at San Leandro, Alameda County.

Mrs. Kate Briggs-Rice, native of Illinois, 76; since 1861 Stanislaus County resident; died at Modesto, survived by a daughter.

William F. Buttie, native of Scotland, 75; came in 1861 and resided in San Francisco City and Monterey County; died near Bradley survived by a wife and two children.

Mrs. Anna Hallowell-Kynock, native of Wisconsin, 80; came via Panama in 1862 and resided in Yuba, Sierra and Butte Counties; died at Chico, survived by four children.

Thomas Rowlands, native of Wales, 88; came in 1862; died at San Francisco, survived by two daughters.

Herman Henry Tegrunde, native of Germany, 99; Butte County resident since 1862; died near Oroville.

Mrs. Naomi Elizabeth Poole, native of Indiana, 88; crossed the plains in 1862 and resided in Yuba and Humboldt Counties; died at Clatsop Plains, Oregon State, survived by six children.

Mrs. Mary Murray, native of New York, 85; came in 1862 and long resided in Mendocino County; died at Berkeley, Alameda County, survived by three children.

M. Levy, native of France, 95; came in 1863 and resided in Solano, Tulare and Fresno Counties; died at Coalinga, survived by five children.

Phillip J. Goumaz, native of Switzerland, 89; came via Nicaragua in 1863 and two years later settled in Lassen County; died at Susanville, survived by a wife and a daughter.

Mrs. Florence Decker-Welch, native of Wisconsin, 81; came across the plains in 1867; died near Smith Flat, El Dorado County, survived by two sons.

Joseph Fabry, native of Germany, 76; came via Panama in 1865 and settled in Monterey County; died at Salinas, survived by a wife and two children.

Mrs. Annie Offe, native of Germany, 75; since 1867 resident Berkeley, Alameda County, where she died; a husband and a daughter survive.

Frank O. George Sr., native of Azores Islands, 92; since 1865 Contra Costa County resident; died at Pacheco, survived by four children.

Cassius F. Boardman, native of Connecticut, 86; came via the Horn in 1866 and resided in Nevada and Yuba Counties; died near Wheatland, survived by six children.

Hiram Jasper Frederick, native of Iowa, 75; came in 1866; died at Red Bluff, Tehama County.

Mrs. Bridget O'Neill, native of Ireland, 86; came in 1867 and resided in Solano and Alameda Counties; died at Oakland, survived by ten children.

J. M. Sharp, native of Ohio, 88; came in 1867; died near Saticoy, Ventura County, survived by a wife and six children.

Mrs. Kathryn English, native of Canada, 88; came in 1867; died near North Columbia, Nevada County, survived by five children.

Hiram Snyder Eicher, native of Pennsylvania, 80; came in 1867; died at Chico, Butte County, survived by a wife and two daughters.

John Alexander Fraser, native of Canada, 83; came in 1867 and the following year settled in Pinole, Contra Costa County, where he died; five children survive.

Miss Anna Head, native of Massachusetts, 75; came in 1868; died at Berkeley, Alameda County.

Mrs. Mary E. Fleming, native of Texas, 79; since 1869 Los Angeles County resident; died at Wilmington, survived by a husband and seven children.

Charles Kechner, native of Germany, 85; since 1869 Placer County resident; died at Roseville, survived by a wife and five children.

Mrs. Sophrona Johnson, native of Texas, 83; came in 1869; died at Los Angeles City, survived by three children.

Elmon Starr Daniels, native of New York, 78; came via Panama in 1862; died at Santa Cruz City, survived by a wife and a daughter.

Mrs. Katherine Frank, native of Germany, 95; came via Panama in 1859 and settled in San Francisco, where she died; four children survive.

George H. Hughes, native of Illinois, 85; came in 1860; died at Red Bluff, Tehama County, survived by four children.

Mrs. Areni Thankful Lewis-Carson, native of Missouri, 79; crossed the plains in 1854; died near Chico, Butte County, survived by three children.

John W. Brown, native of Iowa, 86; crossed the plains in 1853; died at Forestville, Sonoma County.

WILL PERPETUATE PIONEER'S MEMORY.

To be known as the Charles Holbrook Redwood Grove, a 297-acre stand of redwood trees near Garberville, Humboldt County, has been added to the state park system. Holbrook, born in New Hampshire in 1830, came to California in 1850, and died in 1925.

Native Daughters of the Golden West

EVIDENCING THE GOOD WORK BEING done by the Order of Native Daughters of the Golden West in one of its many worthwhile endeavors, there follow letters received by Past Grand Stella Finkeldey of Santa Cruz City, chairman Grand Parlor Veterans Welfare Committee. "I take great pleasure in reporting the response from our Order," writes Miss Finkeldey to The Grizzly Bear. "To date (January 18, 1933,) 135 Subordinate Parlors have responded to the call, and I wish especially to express my appreciation, taking into consideration present conditions of world affairs. The wishes of those in charge of the various hospitals are being carried out as they desire."

"This will acknowledge receipt of one dozen duplicate bridge boards and one dozen decks of playing cards, which have been delivered to our recreational aide. The bridge boards arrived at a most opportune time, as a group of men who have been much interested in starting a duplicate contract tournament had been planning to improvise with ordinary paper envelopes. They will be very pleasantly surprised to have these professional looking boards to use. Will you please extend to your organization our sincere thanks for this manifestation of their interest in our disabled veterans!" Also, "This will acknowledge receipt of your letter and the package containing two dozen decks of playing cards for the use of our patients. The cards are very attractive and will be most welcome to the recreational aide for use in the card contests. Will you please convey our appreciation to all of your members for their thoughtfulness."—United States Veterans Hospital, Walla Walla, Washington.

"We wish to acknowledge receipt of forty pounds of small candies which you sent for the Christmas nut cups, also your letter. Will you please extend to your organization our sincere thanks for their share in making Christmas in this hospital a time of as much cheer and happiness as possible! With all best wishes to you and your organization for the new year."—United States Veterans Hospital, Whipple, Arizona.

"In the rush of Christmas work, reply to your letter has been delayed somewhat. As we still have qiute a good supply of wool socks remaining from the generous quantity sent us last spring by the Native Daughters of the Golden West, it is not believed we shall need any more until next winter. Without first looking over the supply closet and determining our needs, we do not know what to suggest in place of socks. However, there always seems to be needed little extras not provided the patients by the Veterans Administration. May we write you later in regard to this? Meanwhile, many thanks indeed for the kind interest of the Native Daughters in the welfare of our patients."—United States Veterans Hospital, Livermore, California.

"It was a very great pleasure to receive your letter and to learn that even in this year of stress our patients are to be remembered again so generously by your organization. We believe that there is no service that you could render them that would afford the patients more enjoyment than that which you gave them so splendidly last year. The patients seem to get so very much pleasure from the card parties and of course the prizes are the crowning event of the parties. We cannot tell you how happy we all are, patients and staff, that we are to have more 'Native Daughters of the Golden West Parties,' and we do wish that some member of your organization might happen to be here to attend one. With many thanks for your thought of us, and with all best wishes."—United States Veterans Hospital, Tucson, Arizona.

GRAND PRESIDENT'S OFFICIAL ITINERARY.

Woodland—Grand President Anna Mixon Armstrong will, during February and March, visit the following Subordinate Parlors on the dates noted:

FEBRUARY.

1st—El Carmelo No. 81, Daly City.
2nd—Genevieve No. 132, San Francisco.
6th—Oakdale No. 125, Oakdale.
7th—Veritas No. 75, Merced.
8th—Phoebe A. Hearst No. 214, Manteca.
9th—Madera No. 244, Madera.
11th—Mariposa No. 63, Mariposa.
15th—Golden State No. 50, San Francisco.
17th—District meeting, Sonoma.
20th—Darina No. 114, San Francisco.
21st—Hayward No. 122, Hayward.
23rd—Copa de Oro No. 105, Hollister; San Juan Bautista No. 179, San Juan Bautista; jointly at Hollister.
24th—Angelita No. 32, Livermore.
27th—Sans Souci No. 96, San Francisco.
28th—Fairfax No. 225, Fairfax.

MARCH.

1st—Stirling No. 146, Pittsburg.
3rd—El Tejon No. 239, Bakersfield; Miocene No. 228, Taft; jointly at Bakersfield.
7th—Reina del Mar No. 126, Santa Barbara.
8th—Lugonia No. 241, San Bernardino.
9th—Ontario No. 251, Ontario.
10th—Desert Gold No. 250, Mojave.

Pioneer Decorations a Feature.

Sacramento—Grand President Anna Mixon Armstrong officially visited Califia No. 22 January 10, and a banquet at which the pioneer theme was carried out in the decoration was served in her honor. Other guests were Grand Trustees Ethel Begley, Florence Boyle and Edna Briggs, Grand Marshal Gladys Noce, Grand Inside Sentinel Orinda Giannini, Supervising Deputy Bessie Leitch, Deputy Alice Wright, Past Grands Emma G. Foley, Dr. Eva R. Rasmussen, Mary K. Bell and Dr. Louise C. Heilbron. Edith Kelley was general chairman of the evening.

The placecards, made by Katherine Jones, were replicas of Sutter Fort in 1849, and the favors were glass plaques decorated with silhouettes of covered wagons. Grand President Armstrong and the other guests were presented with dolls, dressed in typical '49 style, which were brought into the room in a miniature prairie schooner.

SUBORDINATE PARLORS BRIEFS.

Hollister—Copa de Oro No. 105 January 14 had a jig-saw puzzle night, arranged by Ruby Nyland. Activity games were presided over by Margaret King, and a social hour was spent over the coffee cups. The Parlor's annual Christmas highjinks December 22 was, as usual, a most enjoyable affair. Rachel Maroney was chairman of arrangements. For skill in guessing contests awards were made Past Grand Bertha A. Briggs and Mary Prendergast.

Etna—The Christmas ball, sponsored annually by Eschscholtzia No. 112, was a delightful event, enjoyed by people from all parts of the valley. Miss Florence and Ernest Smith led the grand march. Since the Parlor's annual contribution to the homeless children fund is taken from the proceeds of this ball, members of No. 112 were greatly pleased with the success of the enterprise.

Santa Barbara—Incidental to the resumption of restoration activities at Santa Ynez Mission, Reina del Mar No. 126 held ceremonies there January 22. Marion Parks (Californiana No. 247) was the principal speaker, and Grand Tru tee Jane Vick presented a California Sta (Bear) Flag to the historic landmark.

Saint Helena—Elise Metzner became pre dent of La Junta No. 203 when Deputy Sad Brooks installed the officers January 17. The was a large attendance, including Supervisi Deputy Wilma Mitchell and delegations fro Calistoga and Napa. Several presentations we made, including a past president jewel to In Constantini. Tempting refreshments we served. The Parlor and Saint Helena No. N.S.G.W. will give a dance for the benefit the homeless children February 11.

Santa Ana—The thimble club of Santa Ar No. 235 had an all-day session January 12 the home of Mrs. Eunice Fox. A potluc luncheon was served, and the members worke on a quilt and also on articles for a hamper f the coming spring. The club recently presente the Parlor with eight dozen cups and saucers.

Bakersfield—Officers of El Tejon No. 23 were installed January 6 by Deputy Jennie De nis, Mrs. Georgia Sanders becoming presiden Numerous presentations of flowers were mad Mms. Louise Herod, Mary Baker, Minnie Heath, Etta Borgwardt, Katie Kincer, Mary Hampson and Florence Hinderliter were charge of the evening's arrangemnets.

San Bernardino—With Deputy Genevie Hiskey presiding, officers of Lugonia No. 24 were installed January 25, and two candidate were initiated. Plans were made for a car party. The committee which assisted Arrow head No. 110 N.S.G.W. at the New Year danc reported January 11 that a splendid sum ha been raised for the homeless children.

Ontario—Mrs. Nelson Van Fleet, as president heads the new corps of officers of Ontario No 251 who were installed January 14. Mrs. J. A Baxter, retiring president, entertained her offi cers at her home, which was beautifully decor ated. Following a repast cards were played With Mrs. F. C. Osgood in charge, the Parlo recently entertained fifty children.

Reception for Mothers and Babes.

Bieber—Mount Lassen No. 215 entertaine at a card party December 27. A potluck suppe furnished delicious eatables. A committee composed of Angie Kenyon, Frances Summers and Lucy Jones arranged for the enjoyable evening. A series of card parties are being held; Stella Tyler and Hazel Iverson had charge for January, and Marie Walsh, Bertie Bunselmeier and Lucy Jones will be in charge for February.

A reception was held January 15 at the home of Annye Mitchell in honor of Mrs. L. B. Watts and son, Lou, a N.S. and N.D. Central Committee baby; he is seven months old, very bright and attractive, and is much loved by his foster-parents. Other mothers, members of the Parlor, present with their babies were Grace Bunselmeier, Gladys Steiger and Margaret Garrison. A souvenir silver cup was presented each baby by Past President Nettie McKenzie who, with Angie Kenyon and Marie Walsh, was in charge of arrangements for the affair.

Joyous Greetings Extended.

San Jose—The officers of Vendome No. 100 were hostesses at a bridge-whist party January 4; joyous greetings were extended Grand Organist Clara Gairaud and Susie Bickford when they appeared, as they were severely injured last July in an auto accident. A public whist party January 11 was in charge of Gertrude Musser and Hazel Brett. Deputy Elsie Fisher installed the Parlor's officers January 25, Dorothy Salas becoming president. One hundred little children were guests of the Parlor at a Christmas-tree party December 21. Mrs. Elwin Baker took to the non-compensated veterans at the Palo Alto Veterans Hospital December 24 gifts provided by Vendome and Observatory No. 177 N.S.G.W.

The past presidents club of Vendome had its annual reunion and installation January 12. Retiring President Alice Kady provided the favors, corsage boquets of blue and yellow pansies. Grand Organist Gairaud was the installing officer, and Faye Withycombe is the new president. Dorothy Lorentz of No. 100 has been selected at the State Teachers College as soprano soloist for the oratorio, "Elijah," to be presented there.

Purchases Home.

Chico—Annie K. Bidwell No. 168 has pur- ased the historic Lusk building for a home. ie structure will be remodeled to provide all -to-date accommodations, and a feature will a relics room in which will be securely housed ie Parlor's collection of early-day mementos. dication of the building will be the main ent of the silver anniversary year of No. 168, hich was instituted December 18, 1908. Mrs. F. Hudspeth, a charter member, heads the ilding committee.

Officers of the Parlor were installed January by Deputy Anna Bernard, Edna Boyd becom- g president. Laura Anderson, retiring presi- nt, was the recipient of a gift, and a past esident emblem was presented Francis Snider. committee headed by Lois Heberlie served a male supper. December 22 the Parlor, carry- g out an annual custom, entertained fifty chil- en at a Yuletide party; chairmen of commit- es were Mms. Ralph Girdler, Hubert Estes d Josephine Alexander.

Past and Present Presidents Honored.

Sacramento—La Bandera No. 110 honored its itgoing president, Helen Kennedy, at a party inuary 4. She was the recipient of numerous fts, Grand Trustee Edna Briggs making a pre- ntation on the Parlor's behalf. Past Grands r. Eva R. Rasmussen and Dr. Louise C. Heil- on, Supervising Deputy Bessie Leitch and Dep- ty Doris Fisher were guests. A banquet was rved and entertainment was provided. The rangements committee included Sofia Cec- hettini (chairman), Ethel Miller, Geneva Si- onsen, Mary Pierini, Mae K. Sydenstricker, ucie Roberts, Lottie Cummings, Leah Michell, drienne Thomas, Bernice Roberts.

January 19 the Parlor entertained in honor its new president, Mae K. Sydenstricker, and iss Mary Ghelfi, who was wedded January 29 nd has gone to San Francisco to reside. Past resident Marion Lund was presented with an mblematic pin. Carrying out a plan of the entral Homeless Children Committee, La Ban- era adopted a baby who was named in honor f Grand Trustee Briggs.

Children Lose Friend.

Oakland—Mrs. Mabel C. Hamb, for thirty-two ears affiliated with Piedmont No. 87 and ac- vely identified with the endeavors of the Pa- ent Teachers Association and the N.S.G.W. and .D.G.W. Homeless Children Committee, passed way December 12. She was born here Sep- ember 26, 1878, and her life was spent in Ala- eda and Sonoma Counties.

Mrs. Hamb was the wife of Richard M. Hamb Piedmont No. 120) former N.S.G.W. grand rustee, and the mother of Richard C. Hamb Piedmont No. 120 N.S.G.W.) and Mabel G. leu (Piedmont No. 87 N.D.G.W.). She was a aughter of Joseph and Annie Cannell- Moore, who came to Oakland from Bodie, Mono County, a 1875.

Charter Member Passes.

Modesto—Morada No. 199 observed its twen- ieth anniversary December 28, when members orn in October, November and December were pecial guests. The annual Christmas party was eld at the home of Hattie Hunsacker Decem- er 20; Ethyl Gardner had charge of the re- reshments. The followнig night the Parlor and Modesto No. 11 N.S.G.W. had their annual Yule- ide party for children.

The sewing club of Morada met January 13 t the home of Emma Smith and completed a ayette to be given with other clothing to the eedy. Thirty members accompanied Deputy Ethel Enos to Turlock, where she installed the fficers of Eldora No. 248 January 16. The Parlor mourns the loss of Charter Member Blanche Semple-Moorehead, wife of John B. Moorehead (Modesto No. 11 N.S.G.W.), who passed away January 11.

Red Cross Aided.

Santa Cruz—January 9, Santa Cruz No. 26 honored those members born in December. A cake, made and beautifully decorated by Ethel McFadden, was a supper feature. The arrange- ments committee included Florence L. McCor- mick, Mamie Cavanaugh, Hazel Brass and Al- berta McCormick.

Members of the Parlor have spent several evenings recently sewing for the Red Cross, and as a result many dainty baby garments have been turned over to the local chapter. February 3, Santa Cruz will sponsor a public card party, the proceeds to go to the homeless children fund.

Past Presidents Activities.

San Jose—Association No. 3 installed officers January 10, Augusta Singleton succeeding Amelia Hartman as president. Clara Briggs was presented with a dresser set. Arrange- ments for the evening were in charge of Faye Withycombe, Augusta Singleton and Margaret Gilleran. February 14, Chief President Cora Stobing will pay an official visit. Under the supervision of Claire Borchers, the association is accomplishing a large amount of charitable work.

Sacramento—Officers of Association No. 4 were installed January 7 by Viola Gennoe, Edith Kelley becoming president. Mrs. Gennoe, retir- ing president, wsa presented wtih a gift by Grand Trustee Edna Briggs on the association's behalf. Entertainment was provided and re- freshments were served. Frances Wachman headed the arrangements committee, which in- cluded Annie Almeida, Jessie Borchers, Irma Wonderly, Ruby Durst, Grace Miller, Mae Rhodes, Anne Cox, Mae Colgrove, Elizabeth Ryan, Amy Dal Porte and Eva Mae Mordecai.

EDWARD D. BAKER

(Continued from Page 2)

Hall, where the indoor services were held, the Honorable Edward Stanley, at one time Baker's law partner, delivered the oration. His observ- ances were based on a close personal contact with the departed. This is but a fragment of that notable address:

"He had as much unworldliness as Goldsmith. No love of filthy lucre ever found a resting-place in his heart. For years I have known him well, and part of that time was associated with him in business, and I never heard a pro- fane word or irreverent expression from his lips. He never uttered a word that could impair the celestial comfort of a Christian's hope. . . . I have never known a man in public life whose heart more abounded in generous philanthropy for all mankind."

Thomas Starr King, at the grave, poured out this heartfelt eulogy:

"Yes, warrior and statesman, wise in counsel, graceful and electric as few have been in speech, ardent and vig- orous in debate, but nobler than for all these qualities by the devotion which prompted thee to give more than thy wisdom, more than thy energy and weight in the hall of senatorial discussion, more than the fervor of thy tongue and the fire of thy eagle eye in the assemblies of the people, —even the blood of thy indomitable heart when thy coun- try called with a cry of peril,—we receive thee with tears and pride. We find thee dearer than when thou camest to speak to us in the full tide of life and vigor. Thy wounds through which thy life was poured are not 'dumb mouths,' but eloquent with the intense and perpetual appeal of thy soul. We receive thee to 'reverence and gratitude' as we lay thee gently to thy sleep; and we pledge to thee not only a monument that shall hold thy name, but a memorial in the hearts of a grateful people so long as the Pacific moans near thy resting-place, and a fame eminent among the heroes of the Republic as long as the mountain shall feel the Oregon."

This monthly contribution ends at this point, and as we review the years from the day that King delivered his beautiful thoughts, we search our hearts and find that King's promise of a grateful remembrance by posterity has not been fulfilled. There is not a monument to mark Baker's grave, there is not even respect shown his last resting-place. Perhaps economic condi- tions do not warrant a monument, but we are not so poor as to justify the grave of Califor- nia's greatest being covered with weeds, the simple grave marker to become battered and a coping to become worn and battered by time. A few hundred dollars would rescue the grave from oblivion and demonstrate that we are mindful of our obligations to our past.

Broderick has a beautiful monument over his last resting-place. Referring to the graves of Baker and Broderick, so close to each other, at the funeral, the orator said:

"Let their monuments arise to meet the eye of the ocean-worn exile as he comes near this haven of rest. Let them tell the traveler, as the landscape fades from his sight on leaving our gorgeous land, that 'the paths of glory lead but to the grave'."

What is the answer of the Native Sons? If we are essentially a historical organization, we cannot fail in our duty to that shrine, our first duty of the present day.

LOS ANGELES--CITY and COUNTY

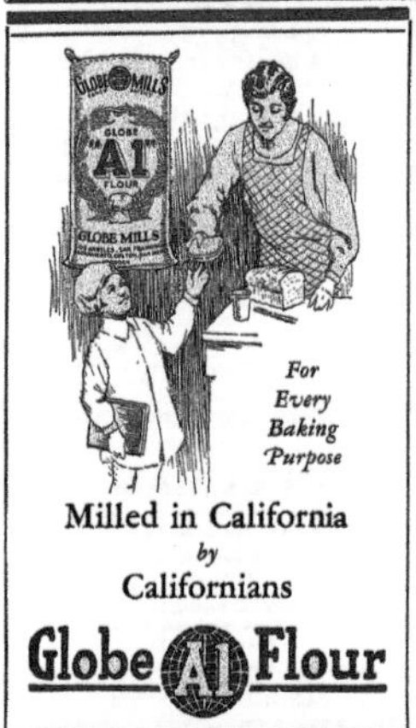

LOS ANGELES

(Continued from Page 9)

Ella Lazzarevich, Anne Schiebusch, Florence Nolte, Peggy Ambler, Thelma Stengel, Erlinda Sepulveda, Mary McAnany, Dolores Malin, Evelyn Howell, Anita Santo, Carmel Brigante and Phyllis Rooke. The admission fee is forty cents per person. All Natives and their friends are extended a cordial invitation, and the committee assures a most enjoyable evening.

MISS EDNA TROMBATORE.

Los Angeles initiated nine candidates January 4 and listened to interesting reports on charitable endeavors and history work by Lucy Malin, Harriet Martin, Dolores Malin and Jennie Raymond. The January 11 card party was most successful. January 15 about forty members, led by President Mattie Labory-Gara, pilgrimaged to the Cota adobe. A pot-luck dinner honoring those born in January preceded the January 18 meeting; Dr. Chamberlain gave a greatly enjoyed talk on "Bret Harte and His Writings." Marshal Edna Trombatore entertained the sewing circle at her home January 7; delicious refreshments were served.

The Parlor's program for February includes: 5th, sewing circle meeting at home of Marvel Thomas; 8th, monthly card party, Evelyn Trautwein in charge; 11th, Valentine dance; 22nd, George Washington party.

ENTHUSIASTIC MEETING.

Compton—Compton Parlor No. 273 N.S.G.W. had a most enthusiastic meeting January 24. All neighboring Parlors were represented among the large number of visitors, big delegations coming from Los Angeles, San Pedro and Santa Monica. Among the speakers were Grand Trustee Eldred Meyer, Grand Outside Sentinel William Reuter, Deputy Grand President Clinton Skinner, District Deputies Edward Baldwin, Harry Hann and Howard Bentley, Past Grand President John Newell and President Laurence Cowan of No. 273.

Seven candidates were initiated, the ritual being most impressively exemplified by a team from Los Angeles Parlor No. 45 with Ray LeMoine as president and the following participating: Earl LeMoine, Lee Erwin, Sidney Witkowski, Roger Johnson, Howard Bentley, Walter Fisher, Clyde Davis and Chester Staley. Due to good-natured "panning" among the visitors, Compton's charity box was considerably enriched, and refreshments ended what one oldtimer declared was the most pleasant evening he had spent at a Native Son meeting in a long time.

SECRETARY RESIGNS.

Los Angeles Parlor No. 45 N.S.G.W. will be officially visited February 23 by Grand Trustee Eldred Meyer. Preceding the meeting a buffet supper will be served. Richard W. Fryer, long the efficient recording secretary of the Parlor, resigned at the close of 1932 and has been succeeded by Willard F. Allen, an oldtime member of the Order, originally affiliated with Chico Parlor No. 21.

"CHINA TODAY," FEBRUARY FEATURE.

Officers of Hollywood Parlor No. 196 N.S.G.W. wtih Henry G. Bodkin as president, were installed by Ralph I. Harbison January 16. Previous to the ceremonies the officers-elect exemplified the ritual and they were highly commended by District Deputy Howard Bentley. There was a goodly attendance, considering the rain downpour, and Bodkin was highly praised for getting into the harness for the third time. Among the several speakers was Grand Trustee Eldred Meyer. The Parlor had an oldtime

ight January 30, and officers of the long-ago resided. A splendid program, arranged for by resident Bodkin, was presented.

The feature attraction on Hollywood's February calendar is an address by Leonard Husar Ramona No. 109), for some time in the Fed-ral Government's diplomatic service in China, n "China Today," scheduled for the 20th. 'hat evening, also, a class of candidates will be nitiated. February 27, Grand Trustee Eldred leyer will pay his official visit.

DANCE AT GLENDALE.

Glendale—Amidst most colorful surroundings, fficers of Verdugo Parlor No. 240 N.D.G.W. vere publicly installed January 23 at impressive eremonies attended by some two hundred. Deputy Gertrude Allen officiated, and Vera Carl-on succeeded to the presidency. A program of nusical selections was presented by Joseph Dis-tay, Dorothy Courtney and Adelia Larson. Among the speakers were Founder Lily O. R. Dyer, Past Grand Grace S. Stoermer and Grand Outside Sentinel Hazel B. Hansen of the Native Daughters, and Grand Trustee Eldred L. Meyer, President Harvey Gillette of Glendale Parlor No. 264, President Arthur Leonard of Santa Monica Bay Parlor No. 267 and District Deputy Harry Hann of the Native Sons. Numerous presenta-tions were made, among them an emblematic ring to Betty Sanders, retiring president.

February 11, Verdugo No. 240 and Glendale No. 264 will give a dance at Masonic Hall, 234 South Brand boulevard, and all Natives and their friends will be welcome. The same good music furnished for the Parlors' past dances will be provided, and an equally good time is guaranteed. Ione and Harvey Gillette are in charge. February 15, at Chevy Chase Country Club, Verdugo will feature a 12:30 bridge luncheon. Margaret Donlan heads the arrangements committee.

MEMBERSHIP RECORD.

Following the initiation of three candidates January 17, University Parlor No. 272 N.S.G.W. presented Roscoe Goodcell, for ten years a resident of China, who delivered an interesting and informative address on "The Awakening of China." The Parlor plans to have a speaker each month on some timely subject. It has what is believed to be a membership-record—five DeFazio brothers, Angelo, Frank, Joe, John and Martin. It is promoting athletics, and its monthly dances are most successful.

VALENTINE BRIDGE-LUNCHEON.

At the January 10 meeting of Californiana Parlor No. 247 N.D.G.W. an enlightening lecture on "Why the Nation Builds California" was delivered by Charles Horworth, who was presented by Chairman Ora Evans of the program committee. Miss Grace Anderson (Grace No. 242) of Fullerton, who succeeds Mrs. Mattie B. Edwards as deputy for the Parlor, was a visitor. Chairman Gertrude Tuttle of the ways and means committee announced a Saint Valentine bridge-luncheon February 16 at the Beverly Hills hotel. As a special feature Mrs. Constance Rimpau-Seals will present a fashion show.

January 24, Mrs. Edith Adams and Miss Lillian Anderson of the hospitality committee sponsored a charming Swedish party. The committee were in costume, and refreshments peculiar to that country were served. Numerous curios of Swedish origin were displayed. Cards provided the afternoon's diversion.

JOINT INSTALLATION.

San Pedro—At joint ceremonies January 6, the officers of Rudecinda Parlor No. 230 N.D.G.W. and Sepulveda Parlor No. 263 N.S.G.W. were installed by Deputies Kate McFadyen and Harry Hann, Carrie Kuhlman and P. H. Doran becoming the respective presidents. The ceremonies were preceded by a supper, served by Sepulveda. Among the many in attendance were Grand Outside Sentinel Hazel Hansen, Grand Trustee Eldred Meyer, Mrs. Florence D. Schoneman and District Deputy Edward Baldwin. An informal dance followed the ceremonies.

MUSICAL TREAT.

Through the courtesy of Beulah Belle Smith, Ramona Parlor No. 109 N.S.G.W. presented January 20 a musical program of exceptional merit—a real treat to those who enjoy high-class music by artists. Vocal selections were rendered by Constance Piper, Dora Bach, Olga Petrova and Layar Samoiloff. Thelma Leggett was the accompanist. Preceding the concert a dinner, largely attended, was served, the boys born in January being honor-guests. First Vice-president Charles Straube was master of ceremonies and there were impromptu remarks from several. Ernest Orilla extended the Parlor's well wishes.

Ramona's February program includes: 10th, initiation. 17th, birthday dinner for the Februaryites; a stag affair, free to all members of the Parlor, at which Judge Dawson and Leonard G. Husar will be the speakers. 24th, official visit of Grand Trustee Meyer and initiation.

N.S. OFFICIAL TO VISIT.

Santa Monica—Santa Monica Bay Parlor No. 267 N.S.G.W initiated four candidates during January. In future, initiation will be featured the third Wednesday of each month, and under the leadership of President Arthur Leonard a large increase in membership is anticipated. The Parlor, through its quartet—Clayton Brandt, Al Toenjes, Edward Curran and Royal Stanton, with Miss Elizabeth Marles accompanist,—and Ernesto Reyes with his Spanish revue, is keeping the Order before the public. They contribute their talents for the good of the cause, and appear at many functions, Native and otherwise.

Grand Trustee Eldred L. Meyer, a member of No. 267, announces the following itinerary to complete his official visits to Parlors: February—7th, University No. 272; 9th, Long Beach No. 239; 10th, Bakersfield No. 42; 15th, Santa Barbara No. 116; 17th, Sepulveda No. 263; 20th, Santa Ana No. 265. March 1, Arrowhead No. 110.

PERSONAL PARAGRAPHS.

Ernest W. Parsons (Ramona N.S.) was a visitor to San Francisco last month.

A native son recently arrived at the home of William John Hamilton (Ramona N.S.).

Miss Mildred Beckwith and Leon J. Leonard (Ramona N.S.) were wedded December 31.

Martin S. Hauser (Ramona N.S.), secretary Master Plumbers Association, is a granddaddy.

United States Marshal Al. Sittel (Ramona N.S.) and wife last month visited several Eastern cities.

Congressman-elect William I. Traeger (Past Grand N.S.) paid a visit last month to Sacramento City.

Carl B. Wirsching (Los Angeles N.S.) has been appointed general manager of the Los Angeles Harbor Department.

THE DEATH RECORD.

Daniel Michiel Brown, affiliated with Ramona Parlor No. 109 N.S.G.W., died December 23, survived by a wife and nine children. He was born at San Francisco, March 17, 1863.

Nedra, the baby daughter of Victor D. Kremer (Los Angeles N.S.), died December 27.

Mrs. Charlotte Campbell-Wharton, affiliated with Long Beach Parlor No. 154 N.D.G.W., died December 28 at Long Beach.

Gus Odemar, father of Walter H. Odemar (Ramona N.S.), died December 28.

Mrs. Lucy Laubersheimer, mother of Daniel H. Laubersheimer (Hollywood N.S.), died January 1 at the age of 82.

Mrs. Delfina Roth, mother of Eugene H. and Raoul A. Roth (Hollywood N.S.), died January 2 at the age of 88. She had resided in Los Angeles since the early '60s.

Mrs. Jennie Longuevan, mother of Joseph B. Longuevan Jr. (Ramona N.S.), died January 7.

Frank C. Carrell, father of Frank R. Carrell (Ramona N.S.), died January 9.

Henry Sloss, affiliated with Hollywood Parlor No. 196 N.S.G.W., died January 12, survived by a wife and a daughter. He was a native of San Francisco, aged 65.

Mrs. Mary Elizabeth Fleming, mother of John L. Fleming (Ramona N.S.), died January 14 at the age of 79. She had resided in Los Angeles County since 1869.

William Knickrehm, father of Allen Knickrehm (Ramona N.S.), died January 15.

Mrs. Frances G. Stoddard, mother of William M. Stoddard (Ramona N.S.), died January 19. She was born in Los Angeles County in 1858.

Curtis E. Kruckeberg, son of Hal S. Kruckeberg (Ramona N.S.), died January 19, and a few hours later Hal's mother, Mrs. Jennie Kruckeberg, a writer and painter of note, passed away.

THE LETTER BOX

(Continued from Page 4)

ers in Congress or in the business world to accurately gage the size and seriousness of the depression, its causes or promising remedies.

I agree with what you say. We are apparently drifting, hoping in some way to muddle through without very much clear seeing or clear thinking, and with an obvious unwillingness to recognize that the house in which we have lived is no longer habitable and cannot be made habitable without some rather radical repairs involving important departures from our past method of living and doing business, which produced the present depression.

Congratulations on your excellent editorial! Sincerely,

PHIL D. SWING, Congressman
Eleventh California District.

Washington, D. C., January 14, 1933.

ORIGINAL NATIVE SON'S PASSING.

Editor Grizzly Bear—Edwin Lewis Meyer [whose death was chronicled in The Grizzly Bear for January 1933] was a charter member of the Native Sons, San Francisco, which body subsequently became California Parlor No. 1 of the Order of Native Sons of the Golden West.

On organization July 11, 1875, the members were given certificates of membership, in the order in which they joined. Meyer's certificate was No. 106. The charter was kept open from the time of organization to March 24, 1876, when 113 members had signed the charter-roll. My certificate is No. 4.

CHARLES H. SMITH.

Avalon, January 5, 1933.

(Smith is a member of Ramona Parlor No. 109 N.S.G.W., Los Angeles. He was born in Contra Costa County, and was the first secretary of the original organization of Native Sons.—Editor.)

FIRST CALIFORNIA GOLD DISCOVERY.

Editor Grizzly Bear—Thought the item herewith may be of interest to the readers of The Grizzly Bear.

EMIL C. MALZ JR.

San Rafael, December 21, 1932.

Here's the item: "When was gold discovered in California? The first well authenticated discovery of gold in California was made near Los Angeles in 1842, six years before a workman named James Marshall discovered gold at John Sutter's mill on the south fork of the American river near Coloma" [El Dorado County].

PIONEER NATIVES DEAD

(Brief Notices of the Demise of Men and Women born in California Prior to 1860.)

William B. Cutler, born in Solano County in 1853, died December 22 at San Jose, Santa Clara County, survived by three children. He was for many years an educator, and was the son of Nathan Cutler, Pioneer of 1849 who served in an early-day State Legislature.

Fred Branch, born in San Luis Obispo County in 1853, died December 23 at Santa Barbara City survived by a wife. He was a son of Francis Ziba Branch, Pioneer of 1831 to whom the Mexican government in 1837 granted the Santa Manuela rancho.

Leonidas Clay Branch, born in Stanislaus County in 1851, died December 29 at Los Angeles City survived by a son. [At one time he was affiliated with Modesto Parlor No. 11 N.S.G.W., and as a representative of that Parlor at the Fifth (Sacramento 1882) Grand Parlor was elected Grand Lecturer, an office long since abolished; later he was identified with the original Visalia Parlor No. 19 N.S.G.W.—Editor.]

Mrs. Francis A. Musick, born in Santa Barbara County in 1857, died December 30 at Crescent City, Del Norte County, survived by five children.

Mrs. Adella Huskey, born at Sacramento City in 1857, died December 31 at Berkeley, Alameda County, survived by two daughters. She was a daughter of H. D. Gosling, Napa County Pioneer of 1845.

J. Q. Buffington, born in Nevada County in 1850, died December 31 at Inglewood, Los Angeles County, survived by a wife and five children.

Samuel Shaen, born in San Joaquin County in 1857, died December 31 at San Francisco survived by a daughter. He was a member of Stanford Parlor No. 76 N.S.G.W. (San Francisco).

Mrs. Emma Hotfilter, born at Sacramento City in 1857, died there January 1. Her brother, William J. Grafmiller, born at Sacramento in 1858, died there January 4. They were children of Andrew Grafmiller, Pioneer of 1850.

James Washington Ogan, born in Santa Clara County in 1857, died January 4 at Carpinteria, Santa Barbara County, survived by four children.

Mrs. Mary Arborn-Guess, born in Riverside County in 1859, died January 7 at Rosemead, Los Angeles County, survived by a husband and two children.

Mrs. Mary Ann Green-Hook, born in San Bernardino County in 1856, died January 8 at Sacramento City survived by two children.

Mrs. Sarah Owsley-Holton, born in Napa County in 1850, died January 8 at Oakland, Alameda County, survived by three children. She is said to have been the first White child born at Calistoga.

Mrs. Soledad Garcia-Yonez, born in Santa Barbara County in 1841, died January 21 at Ventura City.

"Keep doing, keep moving, because still water becomes stagnant."—Frederic B. Acosta.

Official Directory of Parlors of the N. D. G. W.

ALAMEDA COUNTY.

Angelita No. 32, Livermore—Meets 2nd and 4th Fridays, Foresters Hall; Mrs. Myrtle I. Johnson, Rec. Sec., P.O. box 353.

Piedmont No. 87, Oakland—Meets Thursdays, Corinthian Hall, Pacific Bldg.; Miss Helen Ring, Rec. Sec., 822 11th St.

Aloha No. 106, Oakland—Meets Tuesdays, Wigwam Hall, Pacific Bldg.; Mrs. Lurine Martin, Rec. Sec., 2815 Wallace St., Berkeley.

Hayward No. 122, Hayward—Meets 1st and 3rd Tuesdays, Veterans Memorial Bldg., Main St.; Miss Ruth Gansberger, Rec. Sec., P. O. box 44, Mount Eden.

Berkeley No. 150, Berkeley—Meets 2nd and 4th Wednesdays, Masonic Hall; Mrs. Lelia B. Baker, Rec. Sec., 915 Contra Costa Ave.

Bear Flag No. 151, Berkeley—Meets 2nd and 4th Wednesdays, Veterans Memorial Bldg., 1931 Center St.; Mrs. Maud Wagner, Rec. Sec., 317 Alcatraz Ave., Oakland.

Encinal No. 156, Alameda—Meets 2nd and 4th Wednesdays, Veterans Memorial Bldg., Central Ave. and Walnut St.; Mrs. Laura E. Fisher, Rec. Sec., 1413 Caroline St.

Brooklyn No. 157, East Oakland—Meets 2nd and 4th Wednesdays, Masonic Temple, 8th Ave. and E. 14th St.; Mrs. Ruth Cooney, Rec. Sec., 3907 14th Ave.

Argonaut No. 166, Oakland—Meets Tuesdays, Klinkner Hall, 59th and San Pablo; Mrs. Ada Spilman, Rec. Sec., 2905 Ellis St., Berkeley.

Bahia Vista No. 167, Oakland—Meets Thursdays, Wigwam Hall, Pacific Bldg.; Mrs. Minnie E. Raper, Rec. Sec., 3449 Helen St.

Fruitvale No. 177, Oakland—Meets Fridays, W.O.W. Hall; May E. Barthold, Rec. Sec., 3833 Santa Rita St.

Laura Loma No. 182, Niles—Meets 1st and 3rd Tuesdays, I.O.O.F. Hall; Mrs. Ethel Fournier, Rec. Sec., P. O. box 515.

El Cereso No. 207, San Leandro—Meets 2nd and 4th Tuesdays, Masonic Hall; Mrs. Mary Tuttle, Rec. Sec., P. O. box 56.

Pleasanton No. 237, Pleasanton—Meets 1st Tuesday, I.O.O.F. Hall; Mrs. Myrtle Lanini, Rec. Sec.

Betsy Ross No. 238, Centerville—Meets 1st and 3rd Fridays, Anderson Hall; Miss Constance Lucio, Rec. Sec., P. O. box 187.

AMADOR COUNTY.

Ursula No. 1, Jackson—Meets 2nd and 4th Tuesdays, N.S.G.W. Hall; Mrs. Emma Boarman-Wright, Rec. Sec., 114 Court St.

Chispa No. 40, Ione—Meets 2nd and 4th Fridays, N.S.G.W. Hall; Mrs. Isabel Ashton, Rec. Sec.

Amapola No. 80, Sutter Creek—Meets 2nd and 4th Thursdays, N.S.G.W. Bldg.; Mrs. Hazel M. Marre, Rec. Sec.

Forrest No. 86, Plymouth—Meets 2nd and 4th Tuesdays, I.O.O.F. Hall; Mrs. Marguerite Davis, Rec. Sec.

BUTTE COUNTY.

Annie K. Bidwell No. 168, Chico—Meets 2nd and 4th Thursdays, I.O.O.F. Hall; Mrs. Irene Henry, Rec. Sec., 3015 Woodland Ave.

Gold of Ophir No. 190, Oroville—Meets 1st and 3rd Wednesdays, Memorial Hall; Mrs. Ruth Brown, Rec. Sec., 1265 Leah Court.

CALAVERAS COUNTY.

Ruby No. 46, Murphys—Meets 4th Friday, N.S.G.W. Hall; Belle Segale, Rec. Sec.

Princess No. 84, Angels Camp—Meets 2nd and 4th Wednesdays, I.O.O.F. Hall; Mrs. Grace M. Mills, Rec. Sec., P.O. box 313.

San Andreas No. 113, San Andreas—Meets 1st Friday, Fraternal Hall; Miss Doris Treat, Rec. Sec.

COLUSA COUNTY.

Colus No. 194, Colusa—Meets 1st and 3rd Mondays, Eagles Hall; Miss Kate Busch, Rec. Sec., 350 Market St.

CONTRA COSTA COUNTY.

Stirling No. 146, Pittsburg—Meets 1st and 3rd Wednesdays, Veteran Memorial Hall; Mrs. Leslie Clement, Rec. Sec., 468 E. Santa Fe.

Richmond No. 147, Richmond—Meets 1st and 3rd Tuesdays, I.O.O.F. Hall, 10th St.; Grace Curry, Rec. Sec., 932 Ohio Ave.

Donner No. 193, Byron—Meets 1st and 3rd Wednesdays, I.O.O.F. Hall; Mrs. Anna Pendry, Rec. Sec., P. O. box 112.

Las Juntas No. 221, Martinez—Meets 1st and 3rd Mondays, Pythian Castle; Mrs. Lola O. Viera, Rec. Sec., R.F.D. No. 1.

Antioch No. 223, Antioch—Meets 2nd and 4th Tuesdays, I.O.O.F. Hall; Mrs. Estelle Evans, Rec. Sec., 202 E. 5th St., Pittsburg.

Carquinez No. 234, Crockett—Meets 2nd and 4th Wednesdays, I.O.O.F. Hall; Mrs. Cecile Petee, Rec. Sec., 465 Edwards St.

EL DORADO COUNTY.

Marguerite No. 12, Placerville—Meets 1st and 3rd Wednesdays, Masonic Hall; Mrs. Nettie Leonardi, Rec. Sec., 25 Coloma St.

El Dorado No. 186, Georgetown—Meets 2nd and 4th Saturday afternoons, I.O.O.F. Hall; Mrs. Alta L. Douglas, Rec. Sec.

FRESNO COUNTY.

Fresno No. 187, Fresno—Meets 2nd and 4th Fridays, Pythian Castle, Cor. "R" and Merced Sts.; Mary Aubery, Rec. Sec., 1040 Delphia Ave.

GRAND OFFICERS.

Mrs. Evelyn I. Carlson.................Past Grand President
381 E. Tuscaloosa Ave., Atherton

Mrs. Anna M. Armstrong.................Grand President
Woodland

Mrs. Irma Laird.................Grand Vice-president
Alturas

Mrs. Sallie R. Thaler.................Grand Secretary
555 Baker St., San Francisco

Mrs. Susie K. Christ.................Grand Treasurer
555 Baker St., San Francisco

Mrs. Gladys Noce.................Grand Marshal
Sutter Creek

Mrs. Orinda G. Giannini.................Grand Inside Sentinel
2142 Filbert St., San Francisco

Mrs. Hazel B. Hansen.................Grand Outside Sentinel
501 Griswold St., Glendale

Mrs. Clara Gairaud.................Grand Organist
134 Locust St., San Jose

GRAND TRUSTEES.

Mrs. Florence Boyle.................Oroville
Mrs. Edna Briggs.................1045 Santa Ynez Way, Sacramento
Mrs. Anna Thuesen.................615 38th Ave., San Francisco
Mrs. Ethel Begley.................238 Prospect Ave., San Francisco
Mrs. Minna K. Horn.................Etna
Mrs. Jane Vick.................418 Bath St., Santa Barbara
Mrs. Willow Borba.................330 So. Main St., Sebastopol

GLENN COUNTY.

Berryessa No. 192, Willows—Meets 1st and 3rd Mondays, I.O.O.F. Hall; Mrs. Leonora Neate, Rec. Sec., 338 No. Lassen St.

HUMBOLDT COUNTY.

Occident No. 28, Eureka—Meets 1st and 3rd Wednesdays, N.S.G.W. Hall; Mrs. Eva L. MacDonald, Rec. Sec., 2309 "B" St.

Oneonta No. 71, Ferndale—Meets 2nd and 4th Fridays, I.O.O.F. Hall; Mrs. Myra Rumrill, Rec. Sec., P.O. box 142.

Reichling No. 97 Fortuna—Meets 1st and 3rd Tuesdays, Friendship Hall; Mrs. Grace Swett, Rec. Sec., P. O. box 328.

KERN COUNTY.

Miocene No. 228, Taft—Meets 1st and 3rd Wednesday afternoons, I.O.O.F. Hall; Mrs. Evalyn G. Towne, Rec. Sec., P. O. box 1011.

El Tejon No. 239, Bakersfield—Meets 1st and 3rd Fridays, Eagles Hall, 1714 "G" St.; Mary B. Hampson, Rec. Sec., 906 Quincy St.

Desert Gold No. 250, Mojave—Meets 2nd and 4th Fridays, I.O.O.F. Hall; Rein H. Everett, Rec. Sec., P.O. box 83.

LAKE COUNTY.

Clear Lake No. 185, Middletown—Meets 2nd and 4th Tuesdays, Herrick Hall; Mrs. Alma E. Snow, Rec. Sec.

LASSEN COUNTY.

Nataqua No. 152, Standish—Meets 1st and 3rd Wednesdays, Foresters Hall; Mrs. Mayda Elledge, Rec. Sec.

Mount Lassen No. 215, Bieber—Meets 2nd and 4th Thursdays, I.O.O.F. Hall; Mrs. Angie C. Kenyon, Rec. Sec.

Susanville No. 243, Susanville—Meets 3rd Thursday, I.O.O.F. Hall; Mildred Hardy, Rec. Sec., P.O. box 425.

LOS ANGELES COUNTY.

Los Angeles No. 124, Los Angeles—Meets 1st and 3rd Wednesdays, I.O.O.F. Hall, Washington and Oak Sts.; Mrs. Mary K. Corcoran, Rec. Sec., 322 No. Van Ness Ave.

Long Beach No. 154, Long Beach—Meets 1st and 3rd Thursdays, K.P. Hall, 341 Pacific Ave.; Mrs. Bertha Hitt, Rec. Sec., 5355 Lime Ave.

Rudecinda No. 230, San Pedro—Meets 2nd and 4th Thursdays, Unity Hall, I.O.O.F. Temple, 10th and Gaffey; Letitia Sarciaux, Rec. Sec., 1054 W. 24th St.

Verdugo No. 240, Glendale—Meets 2nd and 4th Tuesdays, Masonic Temple, 234 So. Brand Blvd.; Miss Etta Fulkerth, Rec. Sec., 526 No. Orange St.

Santa Monica Bay No. 245, Santa Monica—Meets 2nd and 4th Wednesdays, Odd Fellows Hall, 1431 Third St.; Mrs. Rosalie Hyde, Rec. Sec., 738 Flower St., Venice.

Californiana No. 247, Los Angeles—Meets 2nd and 4th Tuesday afternoons, Hollywood Studio Club, 1215 Lodi Place; Mrs. Inez Sitton, Rec. Sec., 4228 Berenice St.

MADERA COUNTY.

Madera No. 244, Madera—Meets 2nd and 4th Thursdays, Masonic Annex; Mrs. Margaret O. Boyle, Rec. Sec., 111 No. "B" St.

MARIN COUNTY.

Sea Point No. 196, Sausalito—Meets 2nd and 4th Mondays, Perry Hall, 50 Caledonia St.; Mrs. Mary B. Smith, Rec. Sec., 47½ Glen Drive.

Marinita No. 198, San Rafael—Meets 2nd and 4th Mondays, 316 "B" St.; Miss Mollye Y. Spaelti, Rec. Sec., 539 4th St.

Fairfax No. 225, Fairfax—Meets 2nd and 4th Tuesdays, Community Hall; Mrs. Marguerite Geary, Rec. Sec.

Tamelpa No. 231, Mill Valley—Meets 1st and 2nd Tuesdays, I.O.O.F. Hall; Mrs. Delphine M. Todt, Rec. Sec., 400 Grand Ave., San Rafael.

MARIPOSA COUNTY.

Mariposa No. 63, Mariposa—Meets 1st and 3rd Fridays, I.O.O.F. Hall; Elizabeth E. Johnson, Rec. Sec.

MENDOCINO COUNTY.

Fort Bragg No. 210, Fort Bragg—Meets 1st and 3rd Thursdays, I.O.O.F. Hall; Mrs. Ruth W. Fuller, Rec. Sec.

MERCED COUNTY.

Veritas No. 75, Merced—Meets 1st and 3rd Tuesdays, I.O.O.F. Hall; Miss Margaret Thornton, Rec. Sec., 317 18th St.

MODOC COUNTY.

Alturas No. 159, Alturas—Meets 1st Thursday, Alturas Civic Club; Mrs. Irma W. Laird, Rec. Sec.

MONTEREY COUNTY.

Aleli No. 102, Salinas—Meets 2nd and 4th Thursdays, Pythian Hall; Miss Rose Rhyner, Rec. Sec., 420 Soledad St.

Junipero No. 141, Monterey—Meets 2nd and 4th Fridays, K. of P. Hall, Main St.; Miss Matilda M. Bergschicker, Rec. Sec., 498 Van Buren St.

NAPA COUNTY.

Eshcol No. 16, Napa—Meets 2nd and 4th Mondays, N.S.G.W. Hall; Mrs. Ella Ingram, Rec. Sec., 2140 Seminary St.

Calistoga No. 145, Calistoga—Meets 2nd and 4th Mondays, I.O.O.F. Hall; Sadie P. Brooks, Rec. Sec.

La Junta No. 203, Saint Helena—Meets 1st and 3rd Tuesdays, N.S.G.W. Hall; Mrs. Marie Signorelli, Rec. Sec., 1341 Madrona Ave.

ATTENTION, SECRETARIES!

THIS DIRECTORY IS PUBLISHED BY AUTHORITY OF THE GRAND PARLOR N.D.G.W., AND ALL NOTICES OF CHANGES MUST BE RECEIVED BY THE GRAND SECRETARY (NOT THE MAGAZINE) ON OR BEFORE THE 20TH OF EACH MONTH TO INSURE CORRECTION IN NEXT PUBLICATION OF DIRECTORY.

NEVADA COUNTY.

Laurel No. 6, Nevada City—Meets 1st and 3rd Wednesda I.O.O.F. Hall; Mrs. Nellie E. Clark, Rec. Sec., P. box 212.

Manzanita No. 29, Grass Valley—Meets 1st and 3rd Tu days, Auditorium; Mrs. Loraine Keast, Rec. Sec., 1 Race St.

Columbia No. 70, French Corral—Meets Fridays, Farrell Hall; Mrs. Kate Farrelley-Sullivan, Rec. Sec.

Snow Peak No. 176, Truckee—Meets 1st Monday, I.O.O Hall; Mrs. Henrietta M. Eaton, Rec. Sec., P. O. box 1

ORANGE COUNTY.

Santa Ana No. 235, Santa Ana—Meets 2nd and 4th Mo days, K.C. Hall, 4th and French Sts.; Mrs. Matilda Lemon, Rec. Sec., 1628 W. 8th St.

Grace No. 242, Fullerton—Meets 1st and 3rd Thursda I.O.O.F. Hall, 116½ E. Commonwealth; Mrs. Ma Rothaermel, Rec. Sec., P. O. box 235.

PLACER COUNTY.

Placer No. 138, Lincoln—Meets 2nd Wednesday, I.O.O. Hall; Miss Carrie Parlin, Rec. Sec.

La Rosa No. 191, Roseville—Meets 1st and 3rd Tuesda Eagles Hall; Mrs. Alice Lee West, Rec. Sec., Rocklin.

Auburn No. 233, Auburn—Meets 2nd and 4th Fridays, Fo esters Hall; Mrs. Elsie Patrick, Rec. Sec.

PLUMAS COUNTY.

Plumas Pioneer No. 219, Quincy—Meets 1st and 3rd Mo days, I.O.O.F. Hall; Minnie E. Johnson, Rec. Sec., P. box 243.

SACRAMENTO COUNTY.

Califia No. 22, Sacramento—Meets 2nd and 4th Tuesda N.S.G.W. Hall; Miss Lulu Gillis, Rec. Sec., 921 8th

La Bandera No. 110, Sacramento—Meets 1st and 3rd F days, N.S.G.W. Hall; Mrs. Clara Waldon, Rec. Sec., 13 "O" St.

Sutter No. 111, Sacramento—Meets 1st and 3rd Tuesda N.S.G.W. Hall; Mrs. Adele Nix, Rec. Sec., 1238 "S"

Fern No. 123, Folsom—Meets 1st and 3rd Tuesdays, K. Hall; Elizabeth Ryan, Rec. Sec., Represa.

Chabolla No. 171, Galt—Meets 2nd and 4th Tuesday I.O.O.F. Hall; Mrs. Mary Pritchard, Rec. Sec.

Coloma No. 212, Sacramento—Meets 1st and 3rd Tuesday I.O.O.F. Hall, Oak Park; Mrs. Nettie Harry, Rec. Se 1217 35th St.

Liberty No. 213, Elk Grove—Meets 2nd and 4th Friday I.O.O.F. Hall; Mrs. Frances Wackman, Rec. Sec., P. box 192.

Victory No. 216, Courtland—Meets 1st Saturday and 3 Monday, N.S.G.W. Hall; Mrs. Agneda Lample, Rec. Se

SAN BENITO COUNTY.

Copa de Oro No. 105, Hollister—Meets 2nd and 4 Thursdays, Grangers Union Hall; Mrs. Mollie Daveggi Rec. Sec., 110 San Benito St.

San Juan Bautista No. 179, San Juan Bautista—Meets 1 Wednesday, Mission Corridor Rooms; Miss Gertru Breen, Rec. Sec.

SAN BERNARDINO COUNTY.

Lugonia No. 241, San Bernardino—Meets 2nd and 4 Wednesdays, Eagles Hall; Miss Lois Poling, Rec. Se 1098 Waterman Ave.

Ontario No. 251, Ontario—Meets 2nd and 4th Thursday Ontario Hotel; Miss Helen Hickman, Rec. Sec., 923 N Laurel Ave.

SAN DIEGO COUNTY.

San Diego No. 208, San Diego—Meets 2nd and 4th We nesdays, Directors Room, Chamber Commerce Bldg., 49 W. Broadway; Mrs. Elsie Case, Rec. Sec., 3051 Broadwa

SAN FRANCISCO CITY AND COUNTY.

Minerva No. 2, San Francisco—Meets 1st and 3rd Wedne days, N.S.G.W. Bldg.; Miss Dorothy Finn, Rec. Sec., 9 Princess St., Sausalito.

Alta No. 3, San Francisco—Meets 2nd and 4th Tuesday N.S.G.W. Bldg.; Mrs. Agnese L. Hughes, Rec. Sec., 398 Sacramento St.

Oro Fino No. 9, San Francisco—Meets 1st and 3rd Thur days, N.S.G.W. Bldg.; Mrs. Josephine B. Morrissey, Re Sec., 4441 20th St.

Golden State No. 50, San Francisco—Meets 1st and 3r Wednesdays, N.D.G.W. Home; Miss Millie Tietjen, Re Sec., 328 Lexington Ave.

Orinda No. 56, San Francisco—Meets 2nd, 4th and 5th Fr days, N.D.G.W. Home; Mrs. Anna A. Gruber-Loser, Re Sec., 72 Grove Lane, San Anselmo.

Fremont No. 59, San Francisco—Meets 1st and 3rd Tue days, N.S.G.W. Bldg.; Miss Hannah Collins, Rec. Sec 617 Fillmore St.

Buena Vista No. 68, San Francisco—Meets 1st, 3rd an 5th Thursdays, N.D.G.W. Home; Miss Margaret Barrett Rec. Sec., 3774 20th St.

Las Lomas No. 72, San Francisco—Meets 1st and 3rd Tue days, N.D.G.W. Home; Mrs. Marion S. Day, Rec. Sec. 469 Noe St.

Yosemite No. 83, San Francisco—Meets 1st and 3rd Tue days, American Hall, 20th and Capp Sts.; Miss Mar Monahan, Rec. Sec., 237 Noe St.

La Estrella No. 89, San Francisco—Meets 2nd and 4t Mondays, N.S.G.W. Bldg.; Miss Birdie Hartman, Rec Sec., 1018 Jackson St.

Sans Souci No. 96, San Francisco—Meets 2nd and 4th Mon days, N.D.G.W. Home; Mrs. Minnie F. Dobbin, Rec. Sec. 1483 43rd Ave.

Calaveras No. 103, San Francisco—Meets 2nd and 4t Tuesdays, Swedish American Hall, 2174 Market St. Mary L. Krogh, Rec. Sec., 4235 Cabrillo St.

Darina No. 114, San Francisco—Meets 1st and 3rd Mon days, N.S.G.W. Bldg.; Miss Adele Walsh, Rec. Sec., 47 Page St.

El Vespero No. 118, San Francisco—Meets 2nd and 4t Tuesdays, Masonic Hall, 4705 3rd St.; Mrs. Nell E Boege, Rec. Sec., 1526 Kirkwood Ave.

Genevieve No. 132, San Francisco—Meets 1st and 3r Thursdays, N.S.G.W. Bldg.; Miss Branice Peguillan, Rec Sec., 2434 16th Ave.

Keith No. 137, San Francisco—Meets 2nd and 4th Thurs days, N.S.G.W. Bldg.; Mrs. Helen T. Mann, Rec. Sec. 575 Pierce St., Apt. 206.

Gabrielle No. 139, San Francisco—Meets 2nd and 4th Wednesdays, N.S.G.W. Bldg.; Mrs. Dorothy Wuesterfeld, Rec. Sec., 1020 Munich St.

Presidio No. 148, San Francisco—Meets 2nd and 4th Tues days, N.S.G.W. Bldg.; Mrs. Hattie Gaughran, Rec. Sec., 713 Capp St.

Guadalupe No. 153, San Francisco—Meets 2nd and 4th Mondays, Forester Hall, 170 Valencia St.; Miss May A. McCarthy, Rec. Sec., 336 Elsie St.

Golden Gate No. 158, San Francisco—Meets 2nd and 4th Mondays, N.S.G.W. Bldg.; Mrs. Mary Sullivan, Rec. Sec., 33 Cuvier St.

Dolores No. 169, San Francisco—Meets 2nd and 4th Wednesdays, N.S.G.W. Bldg.; Mrs. Ada Saunders, Rec. Sec., 284 Allison St.

Linda Rosa No. 170, San Francisco—Meets 2nd and 4th Wednesdays, Swedish American Hall, 2174 Market St.; Mrs. Eva P. Tyrrel, Rec. Sec., 2629 Mission St.

Portola No. 172, San Francisco—Meets 1st and 3rd Tuesdays, N.S.G.W. Bldg.; Catherine H. Dolly, Rec. Sec., 4125 23rd St.
Castro No. 178, San Francisco—Meets 1st and 3rd Wednesdays, K.O. Bldg., 150 Golden Gate Ave.; Miss Adeline Sandersfeld, Rec Sec., 50 Baker St.
Twin Peaks No. 185, San Francisco—Meets 2nd and 4th Fridays, Druids Temple, 44 Page St.; Mrs. Loretta Cameron, Rec. Sec., 3969 Army St.
James Lick No. 220, San Francisco—Meets 1st and 3rd Wednesdays, N.S.G.W. Bldg.; Mrs. Edna Bishop, Rec. Sec., 3841 24th St.
Mission No. 227, San Francisco—Meets 2nd and 4th Fridays, N.S.G.W. Bldg.; Mrs. Ann Dippel, Rec. Sec., 448 Dewey Blvd.
Bret Harte No. 232, San Francisco—Meets 2nd and 4th Tuesdays, Aloha Hall, 3009 16th St.; Pearl Wedde, Rec. Sec., 225 7th Ave.
La Dorada No. 236, San Francisco—Meets 2nd and 4th Thursdays, N.S.G.W. Hall; Mrs. Theresa R. O'Brien, Rec. Sec., 567 Liberty St.
Balboa No. 249, San Francisco—Meets 2nd and 4th Thursdays, Maccabee Hall, 5th Ave. and Clement St.; Miss Jean Moffet, Rec. Sec., 476 26th Ave.
Utopia No. 252, San Francisco—Meets 2nd and 4th Tuesdays, American Hall, 20th and Capp Sts.; Miss Lelia M. Little, Rec. Sec., 4450 20th St.

SAN JOAQUIN COUNTY.

Joaquin No. 5, Stockton—Meets 2nd and 4th Tuesdays, N.S.G.W. Hall, 314 E. Main St.; Mrs. Della Garvin, Rec. Sec., 1122 E. Market St.
El Pescadero No. 82, Tracy—Meets 1st and 3rd Fridays, I.O.O.F. Hall; Mrs. Mary A. Hewitson, Rec. Sec., 122 Walnut St.
Ivy No. 88, Lodi—Meets 1st and 3rd Wednesdays, Eagles Hall; Mrs. Mae Corson, Rec. Sec., 109 So. School St.
Calla de Oro No. 206, Stockton—Meets 1st and 3rd Tuesdays, N.S.G.W. Hall, 314 E. Main St.; Mrs. Frances Germain, Rec. Sec., 450 No. Regent.
Phoebe A. Hearst No. 214, Manteca—Meets 2nd and 4th Wednesdays, I.O.O.F. Hall; Mrs. Josie M. Frederick, Rec. Sec., Route A, Box 364, Ripon.

SAN LUIS OBISPO COUNTY.

San Miguel No. 94, San Miguel—Meets 2nd and 4th Wednesday afternoons, Clemon Hall; Mrs. Nellie Wickstrom, Rec. Sec.
San Luisita No. 108, San Luis Obispo—Meets 2nd and 4th Thursdays, W.O.W. Hall; Miss Agnes M. Lee, Rec. Sec., P. O. box 586.
El Pinal No. 163, Cambria—Meets 2nd, 4th and 5th Tuesdays, N.S.G.W. Hall; Kathryn Luchessa, Rec. Sec.

SAN MATEO COUNTY.

Bonita No. 10, Redwood City—Meets 2nd and 4th Thursdays, I.O.O.F. Hall; Mrs. Dora Wilson, Rec. Sec., 518 Middlefield Rd.
Vista del Mar No. 155, Halfmoon Bay—Meets 2nd and 4th Thursdays, I.O.O.F. Hall; Elizabeth Olney, Rec. Sec.
Ano Nuevo No. 180, Pescadero—Meets 1st and 3rd Wednesdays, I.O.O.F. Hall; Mrs. Alice Mattei, Rec. Sec.
El Carmelo No. 181, Daly City—Meets 1st and 3rd Wednesdays, Masonic Hall; Mrs. Hattie Kelly, Rec. Sec., 1179 Brunswick St.
Menlo No. 211, Menlo Park—Meets 2nd and 4th Mondays, Masonic Hall; Mrs. Frances E. Maloney, Rec. Sec., P. O. box 626.
San Bruno No. 246, San Bruno—Meets 2nd and 4th Fridays, Legion Hall; Miss Mildred Foley, Rec. Sec., 217 Miller Ave., South San Francisco.

SANTA BARBARA COUNTY.

Reina del Mar No. 126, Santa Barbara—Meets 1st and 3rd Tuesdays, Pythian Castle, 232 W. Carillo St.; Mrs. Dorothy Yule, Rec. Sec., 112 Ocean Ave.

SANTA CLARA COUNTY.

San Jose No. 81, San Jose—Meets Thursdays, Catholic Women Center, 5th and San Fernando Sts.; Mrs. Nellie Fleming, Rec. Sec., Catholic Women Center.
Vendome No. 100, San Jose—Meets Wednesdays, Old Scottish Rite Temple; Miss Marie Buck, Rec. Sec., 245 Hawthorne St.
El Monte No. 205, Mountain View—Meets 2nd and 4th Fridays, American Legion Hall; Miss Elizabeth Spencer, Rec. Sec., 512 Hope St.
Palo Alto No. 229, Palo Alto—Meets 1st and 2nd Mondays, N.S.G.W. Hall; Miss Helena G. Hansen, Rec. Sec., 531 Lytton Ave.

SANTA CRUZ COUNTY.

Santa Cruz No. 26, Santa Cruz—Meets Mondays, N.S.G.W. Hall; Mrs. May L. Williamson, Rec. Sec., 170 Walnut Ave.
El Pajaro No. 35, Watsonville—Meets 1st and 3rd Tuesdays, I.O.O.F. Hall; Miss Ruth E. Wilson, Rec. Sec., 16 Laurel St.

SHASTA COUNTY.

Camellia No. 41, Anderson—Meets 1st and 3rd Tuesdays, Masonic Hall; Mrs. Olga E. Welbourn, Rec. Sec.
Lassen View No. 98, Shasta—Meets 2nd Friday, Masonic Hall; Miss Louise Litsch, Rec. Sec.
Hiawatha No. 140, Redding—Meets 2nd and 4th Wednesdays, Moose Hall; Ruth Presleigh, Rec. Sec., Office County Clerk.

SIERRA COUNTY.

Naomi No. 36, Downieville—Meets 2nd and 4th Wednesdays, I.O.O.F. Hall; Louise C. Dubuque, Rec. Sec.
Imogen No. 134, Sierraville—Meets 2nd and 4th Saturday afternoons, Copren Hall; Mrs. Jennie Copren, Rec. Sec.

SISKIYOU COUNTY.

Eschscholtzia No. 112, Etna—Meets 1st and 3rd Wednesdays, Masonic Hall; Mrs. Bernice E. Smith, Rec. Sec.
Mountain Dawn No. 120, Sawyers Bar—Meets 2nd and last Wednesdays, I.O.O.F. Hall; Miss Edith Dunphy, Rec. Sec.

SOLANO COUNTY.

Vallejo No. 195, Vallejo—Meets 1st and 3rd Wednesdays, K.O. Hall, 820 Marin St.; Mrs. Mary Combs, Rec. Sec., 811 York St.
Mary E. Bell No. 224, Dixon—Meets 2nd and 4th Thursdays, I.O.O.F. Hall; Grace McFadyen, Rec. Sec.

SONOMA COUNTY.

Sonoma No. 209, Sonoma—Meets 2nd and 4th Mondays, I.O.O.F. Hall; Mrs. Mae Norrbom, Rec. Sec., R.F.D., box 171.
Santa Rosa No. 217, Santa Rosa—Meets 1st and 3rd Thursdays, N.S.G.W. Hall; Mrs. Clytie L. Lewis, Rec. Sec., R.F.D. No. 4, Box 345-A.
Petaluma No. 222, Petaluma—Meets 1st and 3rd Tuesdays, Dania Hall; Mrs. Margaret M. Oeltjen, Rec. Sec., 503 Prospect St.

STANISLAUS COUNTY.

Oakdale No. 125, Oakdale—Meets 1st Monday, I.O.O.F. Hall; Mrs. Lou Reeder, Rec. Sec.
Morada No. 199, Modesto—Meets 2nd and 4th Wednesdays, I.O.O.F. Hall; Mrs. Susan Sullivan, Rec. Sec., 828 10th St.
Eldora No. 248, Turlock—Meets 1st and 3rd Mondays, Masonic Temple; Effie Lund, Rec. Sec., 312 Mitchell St.

SUTTER COUNTY.

South Butte No. 226, Sutter—Meets 1st and 3rd Mondays, N.D.G.W. Hall; Mrs. Abbie N. Vagedes, Rec. Sec.

TEHAMA COUNTY.

Berendos No. 23, Red Bluff—Meets 1st and 3rd Tuesdays, W.O.W. Hall, 200 Pine St.; Mrs. Lillie Hammer, Rec. Sec., 636 Jackson St.

In Memoriam

DR. RAFAEL C. DUFFICY.

Again the solemn hour has struck, and another dearly beloved brother of Mount Tamalpais Parlor No. 64 N.S.G.W. has departed this Vale of Tears.

The son of a pioneer family, Dr. Rafael C. Dufficy was true to the principles of this great Order; the community has lost a public-spirited citizen, his family a kind and loving husband and father, and to them we offer that poor consolation within our power to give, and we commend them to the all-wise and loving and merciful Father who has called him to his final rest. He only can console and comfort them in these, their dark hours of sorrow and tribulation. Be it

Resolved, That a copy of this memorial be spread upon the minutes of the Parlor; that a copy be forwarded under the seal of the Parlor to the bereaved relatives; that a copy be published in the official publication of the Order, and that the charter be draped for a period of thirty days; and be it further resolved, that the Parlor stand in silence, in respect to the memory of our departed brother.

C. F. REINDOLLAR,
M. W. LABEL,
HAROLD J. HALEY,
LOUIS J. PETER,
Committee.

San Rafael, December 23, 1932.

MABEL HAMB.

To the Officers and Members of Piedmont Parlor No. 87 N.D.G.W.—We, your committee appointed to draft resolutions of respect to the memory of our late, beloved sister, Mabel Hamb, submit the following:

Whereas, Again the Angel of Death has entered our Parlor and taken from our midst our dearly beloved sister, Mabel Hamb, whose kind and gentle manner won the love and esteem of all who knew her; and whereas, in her passing our Parlor has lost a most highly respected and loyal member, her family a devoted wife and loving mother, the community a citizen who was always ready and willing to help and do for others; therefore, be it

Resolved, That we extend our sincere and heartfelt sympathy to her bereaved family; and further be it resolved, that a copy of these resolutions be sent to the family of our departed sister, that a copy be spread in full upon the minutes of this Parlor, and that a copy be sent to The Grizzly Bear for publication.

Respectfully submitted,
JOSEPHINE COLLINS,
ROSE MARTINELLI,
MAE MEAD,
AUGUSTA HUXSOL.

Oakland, December 29, 1932.

TILLIE BARGMAN.

To the Officers and Members of El Pescadero Parlor No. 82 N.D.G.W.—We, your committee on resolutions in respect to the memory of Sister Tillie Bargman, submit the following: There is another vacant chair in our Parlor, and our heads are bowed in loving memory for our sister who has passed to higher and better things.

Whereas, In view of the loss we have sustained, and of the greater loss sustained by those who were nearest and dearest to her, be it

Resolved, That it is only a tribute to her memory to say that we mourn for one who was in every way worthy of our regard.

Her work here is finished,
Over there it's just begun,
And we know she'll greet each of us
At the setting of the sun.

Be it further resolved, that to the bereaved family we extend our heartfelt sympathy, and commend them for consolation to Him who doeth all things well; resolved, that the charter of our Parlor remain draped for a period of thirty days, that a copy of these resolutions be spread upon the minutes of the Parlor, that a copy be published in The Grizzly Bear Magazine and that a copy be sent to the family of our departed sister.

Sincerely submitted in P.D.F.A.,
BERTHA McGEE,
EMMA FRERICHS,
Committee.

Tracy, January 23, 1933.

LILLIAN ROBINO.

Whereas, Our Heavenly Father has called to His home Sister Lillian Robino, a member of Golden Gate Parlor No. 158 N.D.G.W.; and whereas, in the death of Sister Robino Golden Gate Parlor has lost an honored member, her family a loving sister and a devoted wife and mother; therefore, be it

Resolved, That we extend our sincere sympathy and condolence to the family; that our charter be draped in mourning; that a copy of these resolutions be sent to the family, and that one be sent to The Grizzly Bear Magazine for publication in the current issue.

MARGARET RAMM,
SOPHIE SIEBE,
Committee.

San Francisco, January 14, 1933.

TRINITY COUNTY.

Eltapome No. 55, Weaverville—Meets 2nd and 4th Thursdays, N.S.G.W. Hall; Mrs. Lou N. Fetzer, Rec. Sec.

TUOLUMNE COUNTY.

Dardanelle No. 66, Sonora—Meets Fridays, I.O.O.F. Hall; Mrs. Nettie Whitto, Rec. Sec.
Golden Era No. 99, Columbia—Meets 1st and 3rd Thursdays, N.S.G.W. Hall; Miss Irene Ponce, Rec. Sec.
Anona No. 164, Jamestown—Meets 2nd and 4th Tuesdays, I.O.O.F. Hall; Nellie Hope, Rec. Sec.

YOLO COUNTY.

Woodland No. 90, Woodland—Meets 2nd and 4th Tuesdays, N.S.G.W. Hall; Mrs. Maude Heaton, Rec. Sec., 153 College St.

YUBA COUNTY.

Marysville No. 162, Marysville—Meets 2nd and 4th Wednesdays, Liberty Hall; Miss Cecelia C. Gomes, Rec. Sec., 701 6th St.
Camp Far West No. 218, Wheatland—Meets 3rd Tuesday, I.O.O.F. Hall; Mrs. Ethel C. Brock, Rec. Sec., P. O. box 285.

AFFILIATED ORGANIZATIONS.

General Assembly Past Presidents—Meetings held annually in April at the home-town of Chief President; Mrs. Cora Stobing, 1739 San Jose Ave., San Francisco, Chief President; Mrs. Anna G. Loser, 72 Grove Lane, San Anselmo, Chief Secretary.
Past Presidents Association No. 1—Meets 1st and 3rd Mondays, N.S.G.W. Bldg., 414 Mason St., San Francisco; Mrs. Minnie F. Dobbin, Pres.; Mrs. May R. Barry, Rec. Sec., 2319 19th Ave., San Francisco.
Past Presidents Association No. 2—Meets 2nd and 4th Mondays, "Wigwam," Pacific Bldg., 16th and Jefferson, Oakland; Emma Haggerty, Pres.; Mrs. Elizabeth B. Goodman, Rec. Sec., 184 Juana Ave., San Leandro.
Past Presidents Association No. 3 (Santa Clara County)—Meets 2nd Tuesday, Musicians Hall, 114 E. Santa Clara St., San Jose; Augusta Singleton, Pres.; Clara Briggs, Rec. Sec., 1336 Magnolia Ave., San Jose.
Past Presidents Association No. 4 (Sacramento County)—Meets 2nd Monday, N.S.G.W. Hall, 11th and "J" Sts., Sacramento City; Edna Briggs, Pres.; Lily May Tilden, Rec. Sec., 3225 "T" St., Sacramento.
Past Presidents Association No. 5 (Butte County)—Meets 1st Friday, homes of members, Chico and Oroville; Marie Picanco, Pres.; Ruth Brown, Rec. Sec., 1265 Leah Court, Oroville.
Past Presidents Association No. 6 (Nevada County)—Meets 4th Friday, alternately between Nevada City, Pythian Castle, and Grass Valley, Edna Sampson's home; Margaret V. Nolan, Pres.; Vere Hansen, Rec. Sec., R.F.D. No. 2, box 41-C, Grass Valley.
Past Presidents Association No. 7 (Sonoma County)—Meets 2nd Tuesday, Violet Mastrup home, 622 5th St., Petaluma; Viola Mastrup, Pres.; Elizabeth Dillon, Rec. Sec., Petaluma.
Past Presidents Association No. 8 (San Joaquin and Stanislaus Counties)—Meets 2nd Thursday, Red Men Hall, Stockton; Mrs. Lois Armstrong, Pres.; Mrs. Harriet F. Corr, Rec. Sec., 729 E. Sonora St., Stockton.
Native Sons and Native Daughters Central Committee on Homeless Children—Main Office, 955 Phelan Bldg., San Francisco; Mrs. John W. Stirling, Chmn.; Miss Mary E. Brusie, Sec. Los Angeles branch office, 3924 Sunset Blvd.; Dorothy Schlingman, Sec.

(ADVERTISEMENT.)

GORGEOUS BLOOMS ON PARADE SEEN BY HUNDREDS OF THOUSANDS

The forty-fourth annual Tournament of Roses parade at Pasadena, January 2, was declared by the multitude of onlookers as the most gorgeous ever presented. Fairyland was the theme, and the designs were presented in myriads of exquisite blooms of endless color.

The grand sweepstakes prize went to the City of Glendale for its elaborate "Hanzel and Gretel." The City of Long Beach was awarded the theme prize for "The Peacock," a magnificent presentation; a symphony in white and pink blooms. Other prizewinners were:

Class A (civic bodies)—Los Angeles Chamber Commerce first, "Little Boy Blue;" County of Los Angeles second, "Once in a Blue Moon;" City of San Francisco third, "Six White Swans;" City of Santa Monica special, "Their Breakwater."

Class A-1 (civic bodies)—City of Santa Barbara first, "A Castle in Spain;" City of Pomona second, "The King of Flowers;" City of Inglewood third, "Rainbow Palace;" City of San Jose special, "Fairy Barge;" City of San Bernardino special, "National Orange Show;" City of Santa Ana special, "The Lady of the Silver Moon;" City of Alhambra special, "Peter Rabbit."

Class A-2 (civic bodies)—Santa Catalina Island first, "Magic Isle;" City of Altadena second, "Queen Titania;" City of San Marino third, "Little Miss Muffet;" City of Covina special, "The Rainbow and the Pot of Gold;" City of South Gate special, "A City Built of Flowers."

Other most attractive floats were: "Alice in Wonderland," Pasadena Chamber of Commerce; "Water Babies" and "Mary, Mary, Quite Contrary," City of Pasadena public schools; "Little Bo Peep," Pasadena Junior Chamber of Commerce; "Pasadena Fairyland," Pasadena Park Department; "Dream of Youth," Pasadena Water Department; "Daughter of the Dragon," united service clubs of Pasadena; "Cinderella," Camp Fire Girls; "Jack and the Beanstalk," Boy Scouts of America, Culver City, and "Thumbelisa," Boy Scouts of America, Pasadena.

Citrus Institute—The annual California South Citrus Institute is to be held at Anaheim, Orange County, February 13 and 14.

Tree Giant—The tallest tree on state-owned lands in California is in the North Dyerville Flat State Park, Humboldt County, 364 feet.

Stanislaus Big Producer—The value of the 1932 products of Stanislaus County's farms was $18,253,600.

N.D.G.W. OFFICIAL DEATH LIST.

Giving the name, the date of death, and the Subordinate Parlor affiliation of all deceased members as reported to Grand Secretary Sallie R. Thaler from December 17, 1932, to January 17, 1933:

Chicou, Clemence; November 15; Argonaut No. 166.
Perry, Josephine Ober Reynolds; December 3; Marguerite No. 12.
Kingery, Adelaide Bailey; November 1; San Miguel No. 94.
Fischer, Josephine L. Jones; December 18; Los Angeles No. 124.
Sherwood, Nellie; December 13; Aleli No. 102.
Hamb, Mabel Cannell; December 12; Piedmont No. 87.
Wester, Elizabeth; December 5; Chispa No. 40.
Beauchemin, Rose; December 24; Ursula No. 1.
Smith, Julia; December 9; Alta No. 3.
Wharton, Charlotte Campbell; December 28; Long Beach No. 154.
Feenaty, Grace Roberts; December 28; Oneonta No. 71.
Solari, Anna; December 25; Joaquin No. 5.
Moorehead, Blanche E.; January 11; Morada No. 199.
Roche, Elizabeth Smith; January 2; El Vespero No. 118.
Brunner, Lillie Gingg; December 4; Oneonta No. 71.

Feminine World's Fads and Fancies

PREPARED ESPECIALLY FOR THE GRIZZLY BEAR BY ANNA.STOERMER

SEQUINS AND BEADS, HAVING WON their way back into the winter fashions, promise to be increasingly popular during the spring and the summer months. These sparkling beaded effects, however, will be achieved with a new artistry, one of the most attractive being in attached trimmings, such as capelets, collars, scarfs or sashes.

A delightful evening gown owes much of its allure to bright beads. The frock, of shiny cobbly crepe, is made very simple, with a high waistline and quite a deep decolletage in back. It can be worn for dinner with its separate bolero of black crepe, heavily beaded in silver and white beads. The same bolero may do duty, also, with any other black frock.

Glittering ornaments on dark or neutral backgrounds are good. Metallic and gem-set evening bags are among the new features for evening use. Bright and glittering is the current recipe for smartness in evening clothes. Bright metallic belts are worn on both day and dinner dresses. They are buckled, and fastened in the tailored manner.

Belts, sashes and girdles are shown, of glossy satin or cire. The ribbon is placed flat across the back of the waist, but is twisted into a single knot at the center front. The dress is tunic type, of chiffon, with a scarf-like arrangement which drapes gracefully.

We have some good, early tips on spring clothes. Everyone will be wearing suits again and the smartest will be tailored. Though tailored, they are softly so, therefore more becoming to most people. Woolens amaze and delight by their variety. So lovely are they, so different, they almost challenge the mode fabric. Woolens, silks and cottons all have importance. We are chiefly concerned at the moment with woolens. The new tweeds are most attractive, in broken checks and diagonal stripes. Then we have the sheer and light-weight rabbits hair tweeds, available in a choice of natural and pastel shades, which may be used in connection with tricolored checks in perfect harmony. Plain and novelty jerseys are well represented in the showings of angora, pebbly woolens and crepy woolens.

Black and white effects are the height of chic, and may always be depended on to be both stylish and in good taste whatever the occasion of use. Whether for every-day street wear or for formal evening, black and white combinations are necessary, or at least a popular adjunct to every woman's wardrobe.

A one-piece dress is of bagdad crepe, in black and white. The skirt, of black crepe, follows the long, slender lines that are today's vogue, molded closely to the form at the hips and falling into graceful folds from the knees. The bodice, of snowy white crepe, is most attractive, and is fashioned in combination with the full-black girdle, rather high so as to give the effect of a vest and jacket. The high-pointed girdle ties at the side back, and falls into long black streamers, which are finished at the ends with a fringe of long white silk. The sleeves, of one piece, are fitted close at the wrist, and broaden toward the shoulder to form the upper front of the blouse, and turn back at the neck into a bias fold that makes the collar. With this unusual gown is worn a handsome black caracul neckpiece, fastened with two large buttons.

The blouse and skirt have come into their own again, offering a happy variation from the one-piece frock which has held almost undisputed favor for so long a time. Not only for street wear, but now the skirt and blouse are finding popular favor for dinner wear, and there is every evidence that they will gain greater momentum with the new spring fashions.

It looks like capes and capelets are here to stay, for the current year at least. They will adorn suits and frocks, formal and informal, and are shown in varying lengths and styles for outdoor wraps. Evening coats continue to be of all lengths. Velvet holds a more definite place for the very formal wrap. The long silhouette lines are likewise quite firmly set, for the winter months at least. The full sleeves are effective in producing the broad shoulder lines. An outstanding novel idea is the treatment of the sleeves, which are in one with the back width of the wrap itself.

Many of the new shoes this year have matching colors for frocks. The new spring shoes will borrow their lines and colors from last-minute fashions in frocks and hats. Rounder toes and slightly lower heels will distinguish shoes for morning wear. Oxfords, pumps and strap models are the favorite designs, while kid, reptile and light-weight calf are combined with tweed matching the fabric of the costume. For afternoon, pumps and sandals hold the spotlight. Reptile and suede are displayed for the more informal models.

A brocade sandal for spring and evening wear is woven with gold threads flecked with many colors. Its varied color scheme makes it practical for wear with many frocks. Another for evening wear is of white crepe-de-chine, with collar and heel of gold or silver. New models run higher at the instep, and the counters point well up at the ankles. With formal evening wear, the slender sandals will leave the heels exposed.

The smartest thing for underwear is white, and after that, tea-rose. Ivory and egg-shell are best in satin. They look richer than white in that fabric. Then, just for a change, there are aquamarine, peach, apricot, the palest green, the faintest blue and the most luscious pale beige. Pink is conspicuously absent. The or pink we like for lingerie is tea-rose, a yell pink. All lingerie should be in color sets. one wears a white slip, the panties and brassie should be white also. Sets may be had in rai bow shades, but as long as you wear only o color at a time, you will feel well dressed.

Spring millinery shows a trend toward sma round hats with tilted brims, worn sauci at an angle, some of them almost hiding t right eye and exhibiting the hair freely at t left side. The prevailing colors are black, brov and navy blue, and there are also models gray, hyacinth, flame red and putty bei Feathers, flowers and bright metal orname are used.

Grizzly Bear

MARCH — THE ONLY OFFICIAL PUBLICATION OF THE NATIVE SONS AND DAUGHTERS OF THE GOLDEN WEST — 1933

Featuring

GENERAL NEWS OF INTEREST CONCERNING ALL CALIFORNIA, and ORDERS NATIVE SONS and NATIVE DAUGHTERS

Price: 15 Cents

"MARK OUR LANDMARKS"

Chester F. Gannon

(HISTORIOGRAPHER N.S.G.W.)

"MARK OUR LANDMARKS"

TWO FRIENDS

ABRAHAM LINCOLN! EDWARD D. Baker! What genius, what talent, humanity and Americanism these two names recall. Their lives ran a similar course. From early manhood they lived as contemporaries and friends. Their lives closed in tragedy, one the victim of the assassin's bullet—the other of a rebel shot on the field of the great Civil War.

How little do Californians realize that in Baker was a man as close to Lincoln as any man who lived. The days just closing have heard praise bestowed and the name of Lincoln glorified. But few interested in the history of this state realize that Edward D. Baker's life was inseparably interwoven with the great Emancipator. It is not amiss to recall at this time—and then let the subject-matter rest—the intimate association of these two men.

From 1837 to the date of Baker's death, we find them battling in a common political cause. In the aforesaid year, when Baker, speaking at Springfield to a hostile crowd, was threatened with bodily harm, he saw at his side the tall, lank figure of Lincoln threatening defiance. As he seized a stone water-jug, he exclaimed, "I'll break this over the head of the first man who lays a hand on Baker!" To that far-away date of 1861 when Lincoln attended the Congressional memorial services to Baker the warm and admirable friendship continued.

In 1844, Baker and Lincoln both sought the nomination for Congress in the Springfield district, and Baker won after a contest of honorable rivalry. Lincoln was elected the following term, when Baker declined to contest against him.

In 1860, when Baker was elected as Senator from Oregon and Lincoln had been elected President, upon Baker's arrival in Washington he found there a message from Lincoln inviting him to proceed at once to Springfield to talk over the then-serious situation. Baker left on the first train for Springfield, Illinois, and before the travel stains had been removed from his person there appeared at the window of a relative's home in which he was resting the tall, gaunt figure of the President-elect. It was their first meeting since Baker had left Illinois for his conquest of the Far West. As these two strong men shook hands, Lincoln said, "Hell, Baker, I am glad to see you. I'd rather have had you elected Senator than any man alive." With mock formality, Baker responded, "I was coming soon to call on you, Mr. President." Whereupon Lincoln interrupted with, "None of that between us, Baker."

No other ears than those of the two principals heard what then transpired, but undoubtedly there was spoken at that time conversation which was as momentous and as important as any of that troublesome era.

When Lincoln prepared for his inaugural address at Washington, it was decided that the man to be given the signal honor of the introduction of President Lincoln to the assemblage on that dramatic and momentous occasion would be Baker.

Thus, on the 4th day of March 1861, when the retiring President, James Buchanan, walked arm in arm with Lincoln to the inaugural platform, they were escorted by Senators Foot, Pearce and Baker. While Senator Douglas held Lincoln's hat in a show of respect to the man whose bitter political rival he had been, the melodious voice of Baker rang out over the vast assemblage with these simple words: "Fellow citizens, I introduce to you, Abraham Lincoln, the President of the United States."

With Lincoln in office, the two men had more in common than ever before. Baker had access to the White House at any and all times and hours. He could have received from Lincoln anything within his power to bestow. But days of tragedy soon dawned, and the incomparable Baker was soon on the battlefield where Fate without much ado, decreed that he should be an early sacrifice.

While training his regiment near Washington, Baker frequently had as a visitor to the camp his friend and the President, Abraham Lincoln.

If the immortal Lincoln thought so much of the living Edward D. Baker, is it not just and reasonable that we, the Native Sons who have for years declared for homage and reverence to our honored pioneer dead, do our duty to his memory? THE GRAVE OF EDWARD D. BAKER IS NEGLECTED AND FORGOTTEN IN SAN FRANCISCO.

CITRUS, BRIGHT SPOT IN DISCOURAGING 1932 FARM PICTURE

California's fruit and nut growers had abundant crops during 1932, but owing to adverse conditions, the farmers received for their products "probably an all-time low" price, according to the Federal-State Co-operative Crop Reporting service.

In farm products value, 1929 was California's peak-year, $256,071,000. The 1932 production exceeded that of 1929 by more than 500,000 tons, but the 1932 value, $123,460,000, was $132,611,000 less than in 1929. The citrus industry represented the one bright spot in an otherwise discouraging farm-picture; the value of the orange crop increased from $38,390,000 in 1931 to $46,760,000 in 1932.

The value of the nut and the fruit crops of California for the past six years, as reported by the service, follows: 1927, $254,900,000; 1928, $218,734,000; 1929, $256,071,000; 1930, $179,515,000; 1931, $135,977,000; 1932, $123,460,000. A big decrease during each of the three past, depression, years.

"**Hand Signals Prevent Confusion**" is the March slogan of the California Public Safety Committee in its campaign to lessen the constantly increasing auto death-toll.

Example—Always our reasoning carries us back to the fact that example is the best teacher. —Jeanette Nourland.

"Talent is that which is in a man's power; genius is that in whose power a man is."—Lowell.

CALIFORNIA'S ROMANTIC HISTORY

Lewis F. Byington
(PAST GRAND PRESIDENT N.S.G.W.)
(Continuing the series of California history talks commenced in The Grizzly Bear for December 1932.)

THE BRODERICK-TERRY DUEL

AMONG THE STRIKING INCIDENTS IN the early history of California was the tragic duel between David C. Broderick, a United States Senator, and David S. Terry, Chief Justice of the California Supreme Court. Broderick was born in Washington, D. C., February 4, 1820, the son of a stonecutter who worked as such upon the National Capitol. Before the boy was fourteen years of age the family removed to New York. He grew strong and self-reliant and attached himself to a volunteer fire company. Those were the days in which the fire department was manned by volunteers who not alone fought the fires of that city but nearly everything else, including other firemen. He became foreman of his company at the age of twenty and entered politics. For a while he kept a saloon but never drank liquor, smoked or gambled in his life. At the age of twenty-six he was nominated for Congress, but owing to dissensions in his party was defeated. Shortly thereafter he determined to go to California, and when parting from a friend stated, with his indomitable spirit, that if he ever returned to the East, he would do so as a United States senator from the new and untrammeled State of California. As a boy, with his father, he had seen the United States Senate in session.

Colonel J. D. Stevenson, a friend of young Broderick, had written him: "Come out to California and try this new land, this new El Dorado." He did so and, by way of Panama, reached the Golden Gate in June 1849, at the age of twenty-nine. He at once entered the political activities of San Francisco, and within seven months after his arrival was elected State Senator. A vacancy occurred in the office of lieutenant-governor and at the age of thirty he was chosen by the Senate to the position. He organized the first fire company in San Francisco, Empire No. 1, of which he was foreman, and which took his name after his death.

He was indefatigable as a leader, but somewhat intolerant at times, awakening a spirit of enmity in some quarters, but tied many to him in the strongest bonds of friendship. The Democratic party became Broderick and anti-Broderick. He declared, "My goal is the Senate and I will arrive there if I live." He never avoided a conflict, personal or political, and was fearless in the conflicts of those days, even where weapons were drawn.

At the time he was chosen by the Senate as lieutenant-governor, a member of the Legislature by the name of Moore made an address on the floor of the Assembly reflecting on Broderick. When they afterwards met on the street Broderick resented the attack and Moore drew a revolver and, leveling it at Broderick, threatened his life. The crowd scattered, but Broderick, fearlessly looking into the eyes of Moore, said: "You cowardly assassin, why don't you fire? You dare not, you coward!" The courage of Broderick awed his opponent; Moore hesitated, and the weapon was wrested from his grasp. These were the days in which the Vigilance Committee was organized in San Francisco to suppress crime. Charles Cora was hanged for the killing of United States Marshal Richardson, and James Casey for the killing of James King of William, editor of the "Bulletin."

Broderick first campaigned for election as United States senator in 1855, and although defeated prevented the choice of any other candidate by the Legislature. In the session of 1857, at the age of thirty-seven, he was elected United States Senator. Broderick took his position with those opposed to slavery. In a speech delivered upon the floor of the Senate he spoke of his humble birth, and how he, the son of a poor stonecutter who had worked on the columns of the National Capitol, had by the genius and liberality of our American institutions taken his seat in that same Capitol as the representative of the young but imperial State of California.

Returning to California, factional differences arose within his party, and a quarrel ensued between him and David S. Terry, who came to California from Texas in 1849 and settled in Stockton. Being defeated in 1859 for renomination as justice of the Supreme Court, Terry referred to the faction of his party which opposed him as "the personal chattels of a single individual of whom they are ashamed; they belong heart, soul and breeches to David C. Broderick." These were the words of the chief justice of the state. Reading Terry's address while at the breakfast table in the International Hotel at San Francisco, Broderick, angered at the reference to him, stated that he had once paid $200 a week to support a newspaper to defend Terry while held by the Vigilance Committee, and added that he had stated that Terry was one of the most honest men on the supreme bench, "but now I take it all back." This remark being repeated to Judge Terry, he, by letter, demanded a retraction from Senator Broderick, which was refused, and on September 9, 1859, Terry sent the Senator a written challenge to a duel. The challenge was accepted. They were both men of unquestioned courage, but victims of the so-called code of honor which prevailed at the time. Broderick had for some time believed that his life was in danger through the political animosities of the day. When he was last in New York, he said to a friend who accompanied him to the steamer: "Good bye, you may never see me again."

The duel was fought on the 13th day of September, 1859, in a small valley near the southern end of Lake Merced and near the San Francisco and San Mateo county line. The spot has been since marked by the Landmarks Committee of the Native Sons. The principals had met the day before, but the duel was prevented by the sheriff, and the following morning they took their positions just over the county line. Both Pioneers of 1849, and yet under forty years of age, they had attained the highest positions in the gift of the people. Pistols of the duelling pattern were used, with barrels twelve inches long. It was afterwards found that the hair trigger of one was so light that it would be discharged on a sudden motion. Broderick had never seen the weapon before, and Terry having won the choice, unfortunately, and some declare intentionally, it happened that the pistol with the delicate trigger fell to Broderick. Broderick won the choice for position and stood with his back to the rising sun.

One, in describing the duel, said: "Fronting the ocean, like himself, was California, that California on whose soil he stood and to whose fame and future he had consecrated his hopes, his energy and devotion. With troubled look he turned to the pistol, of a type with which he was not familiar." One of the seconds, Colton, said, "Gentlemen, are you ready?" Terry, who stood cold and unmoved, at once replied, "Ready." Broderick, handling the unfamiliar weapon for a few seconds then answered, "Ready." Colton after a moment's pause said, "Fire—one—two." It had been agreed that the word "three" should be omitted and that the principals should fire between the words "fire—one, two." As "one" was uttered Broderick's pistol was discharged, the bullet striking the earth midway between the opponents. Broderick said, on his death bed, that he did not touch the trigger of the pistol as he raised it. Terry fired at "two," and his bullet entered the right breast of Broderick, who staggered and fell on his left side, the pistol dropping from his nerveless grasp. Terry said to his second, Calhoun Benham, "The wound is not mortal; I hit two inches too far out." Broderick was at once conveyed to the home of Leonidas Haskell at Black Point, Fort Mason, on the west side of Van Ness avenue, near the bay. The house still stands. He was shot Tuesday and died Friday morning, September 15, "in the very morning of his career."

Then followed universal sorrow for the dead. His body was conveyed to the parlors of the Union Hotel, Kearny and Merchant streets, and on Sunday afternoon taken to the Plaza, opposite where, in the presence of thirty thousand men, Colonel E. D. Baker, matchless orator and friend of the deceased, afterwards United States Senator from the State of Oregon and at the same time colonel in the United States Army and later killed at the battle of Ball's Bluff during the Civil War, delivered a memorial address unrivaled in American literature. The closing sentences of his oration I quote as a tribute to Broderick and as illustrative of the ability and character of the men who came to California as Pioneers in the days of '49. He said:

"And now, as the shadows turn toward the east, and we prepare to bear these poor remains to their silent resting place, let us not seek to repress the generous pride which prompts a recital of noble deeds and manly virtues. Senator Broderick rose unaided and alone; he began his career without family or fortune in the face of difficulties; he inherited poverty and obscurity; he died a Senator in Congress, having written his name in the history of the great struggle for the rights of the people against the despotism of organization and the corruption of power. He leaves in the hearts of his friends the tenderest and proudest recollections. He was honest, faithful, earnest, sincere, generous and brave; he felt in all the great crises of his life that he was a leader in the ranks; that it was his high duty to uphold the interests of the masses. When he returned from that fatal field, while the dark wing of the Archangel of Death was casting its shadows upon his brow, his greatest anxiety was as to the performance of his duty. He felt that all his strength and all his life belonged to the cause to which he had devoted them. 'Baker,' said he,—and to me they were his last words,—'Baker, when I was struck I tried to stand firm, but the blow blinded me, and I could not.' I trust it is no shame to my manhood that tears blinded me as he said it. Of his last hour I have no heart to speak. He was the last of his race; there was no kindred hand to smooth his couch or wipe the death damp from his brow; but around the dying bed strong men, the friends of early manhood, the devoted adherents of later life, bowed in grief, 'and lifted up their voices and wept'."

The death of Broderick and the oration of Baker brought an end to dueling in California. The remains of Senator Broderick and Colonel Baker rest in Laurel Hill Cemetery, San Francisco.

Judge Terry himself met a violent death August 15, 1889. While in the railroad diningroom at Lathrop he struck Justice Stephen J. Field of the United States Supreme Court in the face and was thereupon shot and killed by United States Deputy Marshal Nagle. Justice Field and Terry had sat together as judges of the Supreme Court of California in 1858. President Lincoln later appointed Field a justice of the United States Supreme Court. Terry had become attorney for a colorful, headstrong young woman, Sarah Althea Hill, in her suit concerning an alleged contract of marriage with United States Senator William Sharon of Nevada, owner of the Palace Hotel, San Francisco, and later married her.

Judge Field, in the United States Circuit Court, rendered a decision adverse to the client of Terry and she arose in court and upbraided the judge, who ordered her removed, and Terry aided her in forcibly resisting the bailiff. They were both adjudged guilty of contempt and sent to prison. This aroused in Terry bitter hatred for his former associate. Justice Field returned to Washington and the next year, in performance of judicial duties, came to California. He had been told of threats made by Terry. When on the way from Los Angeles to San Francisco Field, accompanied by Nagle, left the train for breakfast at Lathrop. Terry and his wife, it so happened, had boarded the same train at Fresno and also entered the diningroom and took seats. When Sarah Althea saw Field, she returned to the train, but Judge Terry, who was a man over six feet in height and weighed 250 pounds, in a fit of anger arose and, walking over and behind the veneral justice, who was seated, struck him in the face and was thereupon shot and killed by the United States deputy marshal, who testified that Terry, when ordered to stop, made a motion as though to draw a weapon.

LOVE STORY OF CONCEPCION ARGUELLO

Of equal interest to the Broderick-Terry duel is the romantic love story of Concepcion Arguello, which story is connected with the Presidio at San Francisco. Concepcion, in the year 1806, was sixteen years of age, the daughter of the commandante of the Presidio, and the recognized beauty of California. Into the Bay of San Francisco that year sailed Prince Rezanoff, ambassador from the czar of Russia, who came to secure provisions for the settlement in Alaska. He was most hospitably received by the Spaniards, and met and was at once charmed by the fair Concepcion. Being a distinguished and handsome courtier, he deeply impressed the beautiful girl. In time they fell desperately in love and though of different faiths secured the consent of Concepcion's father and the friars to an engagement. The prince sailed for Siberia and Russia to report to the czar, and gave a promise to return soon for his affianced bride. The years passed and no word came to Dona Concepcion who, with unwavering faith in her lover, hoped on through the passing years. Keeping in mind that she, in time, became a nun, let the California poet, Bret Harte, continue the story:

Long beside the deep embrasures, where the brazen cannon are,
Did they wait the promised bridegroom and the answer of the Czar;
Day by day on wall and bastion beat the hollow, empty breeze,
Day by day the sunlight glittered on the vacant, smilin' seas.

(Continued on Page 11)

GRIZZLY GROWLS

(CLARENCE M. HUNT.)

THE FREQUENTLY-REPEATED DECLARATION by the oversigned, that dishonesty is the underlying cause of the numerous ills afflicting this nation and its inhabitants, is daily amply verified by the newspapers, but, for one reason or another, the half is not made public by those dispensers of current events. Quantities of additional facts and figures substantiating the declaration are available in the "Congressional Record." Dishonesty is the source whence flows the depression-stream, growing more turbulent and causing greater havoc!

Dishonesty applies not alone to what are generally regarded as criminal acts of major magnitude. It includes every act not wholly honest: lack of honesty in principle; preaching one thing and practicing its opposite; deceitfulness; faithlessness; violation of a trust, etc. Dishonesty, petty or otherwise, is dishonesty, and any act which is not honest is dishonest. Dishonesty, rampant in government, as well as everywhere else, not excepting religious, educational or fraternal activities, is the guide piloting this nation to eventual doom!

Racketeering is one of the offshoots of dishonesty. And the most pernicious of the bountiful crop of rackets is the political one, fostered by those who thrive on "the hidden things of dishonesty." The political racket accounts for the general disrespect for all law, both God-made and man-made; for open defiance of constituted authority; for the overload of taxation; for the colossal waste of tax-exacted dollars; for the maladministration of public affairs; for the temporary absence of justice. The gangster racket, always featured in the press as a national disgrace, as it is, is but a pigmy, compared with the giant, far-reaching political racket!

Government sets the example, good or bad, for the governed! And government in this country has proven such a prolific field for cultivation by political racketeers, all other fields of endeavor have, naturally, become infested by racketeer-pests. For one such, analyze the financial field, the putridity of which stinks like a dead mackerel rotting in the moonlight. And conditions in this land of plenty,—where honest men by the millions are unemployed, are suffering from want of the necessities of life, and are being dispossessed of their hard-earned, honestly-acquired holdings,—stamp this nation as one controlled by racketeers. And the shame that cries to high heaven is, that no attempt whatever is made to purge the nation of dishonesty, to eliminate the racketeers.

Basically, nothing is wrong with this nation, but everything is radically wrong with the system in vogue! A system which condones, aye, rewards, dishonesty; a system which vaults to hights of prominence and plenty the dishonest few, and crushes to ignominy and want the honest many; a system which so thoroughly disintegrates the foundation that, unless checked, must, as a natural consequence, bring about collapse of the government-structure.

Who, and what, are responsible for existant conditions? That vast majority who have been perfectly content to honestly acquire the things they desire, but who have failed to fulfill their first and chief duty as citizens, in that they have neglected to take an active interest in government. They have, through their passiveness, bartered their heritage—the greatest and the grandest country God's sun ever smiled on—for a few prosperity-sheckels, scattered among "the rabble." As a result of their apathy, a dishonest few have become the dictators of government and of business, the masters of the honest many. The masses can, if they unitedly determine so to do, rectify conditions; they have the power, and the wherewith, to rout the national enemy—the racketeers—by enforcing the dictum, "Nothing is profitable which is dishonest."

All the gold of the world will not, can not, permanently right conditions, except it be coupled with a return of honesty. And honesty will not endure unless, and until, the dishonest be ostracized—be completely excluded from the governmental, the business, the social, the religious, the educational and the fraternal life of this nation. If, as a nation, we choose to worship at the shrine of dishonesty, then we must, uncomplainingly, accept the certain reward, want and degradation. But if, as a people, we are not content with existant conditions, then we must again enthrone honesty and maintain its enthronement.

The above, referring to national conditions, applies as forcibly to California, where the situation is no worse, and decidedly no better, than in any other state. The press has publicized a sufficient number of state happenings to verify the assertion that racketeering is rampant here in government—state, county, city and township—and otherwheres. The political and other racketeers are responsible for the deplorable conditions!

Californians, generally speaking, are patient and long-suffering. They gave the "system" an unobstructed right-of-way, and behold the result. The course must now be changed, in the interest of the masses. The cost of government must be reduced, materially, and injections of honesty will bring it down, without endangering government efficiency. Consider, among other things, the number of high-salaried positions that have been created, during the past two depression years, for the care of favored ones, many relatives, and the increasing of salaries of the "select." Considerable of the talk about the excessive, and always increasing, costs of state government being chargeable to "fixed charges" is "long hooey."

> "I desire so to conduct the affairs of this administration that if, at the end, when I come to lay down the reins of power, I have lost every other friend on earth, I shall at least have one friend left, and that friend shall be down inside of me."—ABRAHAM LINCOLN.

The time has come for a cleanup! And it is incumbent on the State Legislature, now in session, to do the job, speedily and thoroughly, irrespective of the pleadings and the protestations of the political, the education, the public utilities and the numberless other lobbies. Taxes must be lowered, not shifted, and they can be lowered by eliminating "the hidden things of dishonesty." If, for any reason, the Legislature fails in this crisis, then the masses should undertake the task by invoking the recall against those legislators and other public servants who fail in their duty and then assembling a new legislature composed of citizens who, having the welfare of this great state at heart and in mind, can and will serve, faithfully and honestly, the majority, not the minority. Too much time and too many dollars have been wasted in fiddling with dishonesty and incompetency in public affairs. Charges and counter-charges lead nowhere, except to additional taxes. Action, not talk, is what the people of this state demand, and, unless their present attitude be misinterpreted, they will get action!

A statement of the Federal Commerce Department, issued February 11, says the total value of the foreign trade of the United States with the Far East declined some $300,000,000 in 1932, compared with 1931. "During 1932," according to the statement, "Japan bought 28 percent more American raw cotton than in the previous year, but at reduced prices; and trebled her purchase of kerosene oil. Additional purchases included 33 percent more crude petroleum and 16 percent more lead, besides larger quantities of iron and steel-mill products. Sharp declines in both the quantity and value of other important items, however, tended to reduce total United States exports to Japan."

Note that all the increased exports to Japan are absolutely necessary for carrying on war. Couple that fact with Japan's militaristic expansion program, and the highly suspicious actions of Japan's nationals in California, a few of which have been publicly revealed, and watch the "rising sun." Eventually, this country must pay a stupendous cost for its insane folly in permitting the Japs to "peacefully invade" the Pacific Coast and to use the Western states as a breeding-ground for subjects of Japan. History warns that the possessors of the land have in their keeping the destiny of a country, and the Japs possess thousands of the best acres in California.

H. L. Mencken has been investigating public-school costs, and calling education a "hold up," he writes:

> "There was a time when they (these costs) were cheaper, and by billions. In the year of my advent upon these scenes, the 'annus mirabilis' 1880, they (the pedagogues) took but $78,094,687 for flogging the elements into 15,065,767 pupils, which worked out to but little more than $5 per capita per annum. This 'Golden Age' lingered all through the '80s and '90s. Not until 1903 did the bill go beyond a quarter of a billion. In 1914, the year of fate, there were 26,002,153 boys and girls in the schools, and 'making them fit for democracy' cost $555,077,146, or $21.34 a head, four times as much as in 1880, but still within the means of a rich and gallant people.
>
> "But then the pedagogues began to call upon the taxpayer in real earnest, and presently they had him down and were turning his pockets inside out. By 1920 they were taking a billion of his money, by 1926 they had advanced to two billions, and now they are somewhere between three and four billions. In other words, they have increased their demands forty times over in forty-three years—and during the same time they have little more than doubled the number of pupils they teach; in 1933 they have a shade more than 30,000,000. But in 1880 they performed

(Continued on Page 20)

COURAGE

(ELEANOR McCARTHY.)

Courage isn't a brilliant dash,
A daring deed in a moment's flash;
It isn't an instantaneous thing,
Born of despair, with a sudden spring;
It isn't a creature of flickering hope
Or the final tug at a slipping rope;
But it's something deep in the soul of man
That is working always to serve some plan.

Courage isn't the last resort
In the work of life or the game of sport;
It isn't a thing that a man can call
At some future time when he's apt to fall;
If he hasn't it now, he will have it not
When the strain is great and the pace is hot.
For who would strive for a distant goal
Must always have courage within his soul.

Courage was never designed for show;
It isn't a thing that can come and go;
It's written in victory and in defeat
And every trial a man may meet;
It's part of his hours, his days and his years,
Back of his smiles and behind his tears.
Courage is more than a daring deed:
It's the breath of life and a strong man's creed.

(These lines are from a very attractive New Year greeting card received from Miss Anna E. McCaughey of Reina del Mar Parlor No. 126 N.D.G.W., Santa Barbara.—Editor.)

The Grizzly Bear Magazine
The ALL California Monthly
OWNED, CONTROLLED, PUBLISHED BY GRIZZLY BEAR PUBLISHING CO., (Incorporated)
COMPOSED OF NATIVE SONS.
HERMAN C. LICHTENBERGER, Pres.
JOHN T. NEWELL RAY HOWARD
WM. I. TRAEGER LORENZO F. SOTO
CHAS. R. THOMAS HARRY J. LELANDE
ARTHUR A. SCHMIDT, Vice-Pres.
BOARD OF DIRECTORS

CLARENCE M. HUNT
General Manager and Editor

OFFICIAL ORGAN AND THE ONLY OFFICIAL PUBLICATION OF THE NATIVE SONS AND THE NATIVE DAUGHTERS GOLDEN WEST.

ISSUED FIRST EACH MONTH.
FORMS CLOSE 20th MONTH.
ADVERTISING RATES ON APPLICATION.

SAN FRANCISCO OFFICE:
N.S.G.W. BLDG., 414 MASON ST., RM. 302
(Office Grand Secretary N.S.G.W.)
Telephone: Kearney 1223
SAN FRANCISCO, CALIFORNIA

PUBLICATION OFFICE:
309-15 WILCOX BLDG., 2nd AND SPRING,
Telephone: VAndike 6234
LOS ANGELES, CALIFORNIA

(Entered as second-class matter May 29, 1918, at the Postoffice at Los Angeles, California, under the act of August 24, 1912.)
PUBLISHED REGULARLY SINCE MAY 1907
VOL. LII WHOLE NO. 311

CALIFORNIA HAPPENINGS OF FIFTY YEARS AGO

Thomas R. Jones

(COMPILED EXPRESSLY FOR THE GRIZZLY BEAR.)

MARCH 1883 was a freakish weather month in California. A hot, dry north wind prevailed the first fortnight, and for twenty-five days not a cloud floated in the sky. It became so warm, straw hats were donned and coats were shed, and many large corporations began laying off men and otherwise economizing in expectation of a hard-times dry year. Others climbed upon the anxious-seat, fearing deluges and other weather calamities foretold by self-appointed prophets.

Away back in March 1783, Padre Anseleno predicted that a hundred years hence (1883) a flood of mammoth proportions would sweep through Livermore Valley, Alameda County. Led by Bernard Alviso, numerous Mexican families left their homes for quarters atop Cedar Hill and other elevations and awaited the flood that never came. And not one of the many other similar prophesies was fulfilled, either.

A heavy storm came March 26 and dropped from three to five inches of rain in the valleys and six feet of snow in the mountains. The month's rainfall was officially tabulated as 3.70 inches, and the season's total to date 14 inchse. This was below the average, but rain had come at opportune times. So, by the end of the month, the dry-year fear having been dispelled, people again began spending.

Easter Sunday, March 25, was religiously and fashionably observed throughout the state.

The State Legislature adjourned sine die March 10. Some newspapers condemned it for what it did, and others for what it did not. One measure appropriated $80,000 for a pavilion in Sacramento City for State Fair exhibits, the sum to be available when the Capital City contributed an additional $50,000. The city promptly responded and the building was erected at the Fifteenth and N streets corner of State Capital Park. A few years ago the structure was demolished.

The cornerstone of the Chaffey Agricultural College was laid at Ontario, San Bernardino County, March 17.

The U. S. Mint in San Francisco this month received 6,070 pounds of gold dust, worth $1,341,470, and 43,800 pounds of silver—all produced on the Pacific Coast.

Wheat advanced to $2.00 and barley to $1.50 a cental during the month.

Boca, Nevada County, now in the heydey of its business career, was exporting lumber, ice and beer. One company reported shipping 15,000 barrels of beer during 1882.

The Big Bend Tunnel Company, promoted by New York State citizens, was running a tunnel—2 miles long, 8 feet high and 15 feet wide—fourteen miles east of Oroville, Butte County. The purpose was to divert the Feather River from its channel near Big Bend Mountain and allow thirteen miles of it to be mined.

N. P. Vallejo of Sonoma County received from the Mexican government an order for 1,000,000 grapevine cuttings.

Yuba County reported mudhens were devastating the grain fields adjacent to the Feather and the Yuba Rivers.

Coon hunting was providing sport and meat for the residents of Sutter County.

A Nevada City, Nevada County, newspaper reported four breweries and thirty-seven saloons in successful operation there.

San Francisco had a charter election March 4. The total vote was 18,613, and the proposed new charter was defeated by thirty-two votes.

During the month 4,555 people came to the state—673 by sea and 3,882 by rail. Departures totaled 2,388—610 by sea and 1,778 by rail. The population gain was 2,167.

Davis and Drumm built a house at Lompoc, Santa Barbara County, and announced their intention of opening a saloon March 17. A citizens mass meeting was called in front of the building, and the assembled crowd was asked to divide, for and against. The antis were far in the majority, so a committee offered to reimburse the proprietors for money expended. They were given five minutes to consider the offer, but refused to sell. Then followed a crash, for a long rope had been circled around the building and at a given signal several hundred men, women and children tugged at it and the saloon-home became a mass of disorganized lumber. Lompoc had been saloonless for eight years, and evidently intended to so remain.

Two Redding, Shasta County, citizens discovered a gold quartz lode on Olney Gulch. Using a hand mortar to crush the rock, they got a yield of twenty dollars a day.

An artesian well was being bored near Fresno City. At a depth of 320 feet a tree was encountered, and wood, charcoal and nuts were brought to the surface.

A citrus fair opened March 2 at National City, San Diego County. Excursion trains from several cities hauled many people desirous of viewing what was then a novelty.

A fire March 8 in San Jose, Santa Clara County, destroyed a furniture and two box factories, causing a $30,000 loss.

Forest City, Sierra County, March 16 had a disastrous conflagration in which G. Miller, a hotelman, was cremated. Eighty-five buildings were destroyed, forty families lost their homes, and the monetary loss was estimated at $250,000. Much suffering resulted.

A man named McCullom, convicted in Los Angeles City of whipping his mother with a blacksnake, was fined $200.

Mrs. Mariette Judah, oldest actress on the California stage, died March 2 at San Francisco, aged 74. She came to the state in 1853.

John S. Haines, '49er and early-day San Joaquin County sheriff, died March 12 at Stockton.

Adna Hecox, who arrived in Santa Cruz City in 1848 and was the lighthouse keeper for twenty years, died there March 17.

Captain W. S. Moss, a Virginian who came to California in the '50s died at French Camp, San Joaquin County, March 25, aged 85. He was one of the founders of the "San Francisco Examiner," in 1865.

March 25 an immense crowd gathered at the racetrack near Los Angeles City to witness a fifty-mile riding race for a $5,000 wager between Charles Anderson and Jose Figuron. Each rider was allowed to use but ten horses. Anderson won, in one hour and forty-seven minutes, and the Spanish-Mexican contingent returned home broke.

John S. Gay, secretary of the San Francisco Board of Harbor Commissioners, was about $50,000 short in his accounts and levanted. The grand jury indicted him on forty-nine count of embezzlement, and he was subsequently apprehended in Guaymas, Mexico.

A runaway team caused the death of Mrs. J. R. Gries near Ventura City March 8.

Peter Miller, Siskiyou County miner, was thrown into a flame by the bursting of a hydraulic pipe March 17 and drowned.

Pat Hurley, Oroville, Butte County, Pioneer, March 17 sold his land for $1,100 and banked the money. He then bought a butcherknife and went into a livery stable and committed suicide.

I. N. Randolph, who came to California with Stevenson's famous regiment and in 1864 was sheriff of Amador County, ended his life at Sutter Creek March 26.

Long Lim, a highbinder convicted of murdering a fellow Chinaman, was to have been hanged in the San Francisco jail March 2, but committed suicide the previous night.

W. P. Renowden and Archie McIntyre were found murdered on a farm near Lexington, Santa Clara County, March 12. Robbery was the motive, and it was found the deeds had been committed by Jewell and Showers, abetted by Myers, a saloonkeeper. Taken to the San Jose jail, the sheriff announced they could there be viewed by the public March 24. Between 8 a.m. and 4 p.m. more than 5,000 people, actuated by morbid curiosity mostly, visited the jail.

The husband of Mrs. Barnes, in Shasta County, March 20 brought home a shotgun with the announced intention of killing his wife's father. She, however, secured the gun and put friend husband out of the way.

PRESERVATION OF LANDMARK WILL PERPETUATE PIONEER'S MEMORY.

A gift of land December 30 in Santa Barbara County assures preservation of a historic landmark. To be known as the Benjamin Foxen Memorial, the property includes more than an acre of ground at Sisquoc, near Santa Maria, with an old chapel.

During Christmas week of 1846, Benjamin Foxen led John C. Fremont and his troops through rain and storm over the San Marcos Pass into Santa Barbara, traversing the steep mountain barrier for the first time with wagons. As a result, Fremont raised the Flag of the United States of America over Santa Barbara in a bloodless conquest. Had Foxen not aided him by pointing out this new road, Fremont and his battalion probably would have been annihilated in an ambush at Gaviota Pass, the other entrance through the mountains from the north into San Barbara, and at that time thought to be the only one.

Foxen's aid to Fremont circumvented this tragedy and saved the day for Fremont, but it cost the American ranchero dearly. His California contemporaries regarded him as a traitor and made life difficult for him for many years after. He lived a life of isolation on his rancho, Tinaquaic, where he died and was buried.

HISTORY IN THEM THAR NAMES, AND MUSIC ALSO IN FIDDLETOWN.

Amador County has many historic landmarks, among them Fiddletown, settled by gold miners in 1849 and once having a population in excess of a thousand. In 1878 its name was changed to Oleta, but lately there has been a revival of the early-day California spirit, and so July 1, 1932, the town was officially given its original name. Incidentally, Fiddletown was the birthplace of Senator Charles M. Belshaw, deceased, at one time Grand President and for many years a most valued member of the Order of Native Sons of the Golden West.

Like others of the many California mining towns of the glorious gold days of the past, the naming of Fiddletown resulted from a unique local incident. There's history in every one of "them thar" names. In this case, so Amador County history asserts, the first arrivals at Fiddletown were a company of Missourians, all of whom were fiddle artists. While a miner was at work with pick and shovel, his partner, perched upon a nearby rock, entertained him with fiddle-music.

Slavery Revived—"Slavery has been revived in the United States. Within recent years the number of Americans turned slaves has shockingly increased. I refer to those citizens who have had to submit to usury at the hands of some of our lenders, both large and small. Usury is the lending of money at more than the legal rate of interest. . . . It is a national problem very urgently needing solution."—Franklin D. Roosevelt.

Native Cypress Preserved—California has acquired as a state park Point Lobos, embracing the only grove of Monterey cypress remaining intact. The new park is located four miles south of Carmel, Monterey County.

Beautifying Highways—During the past ten years the California State Nursery has planted more than a million trees along state highways.

Native Sons of the Golden West

SAN FRANCISCO—WITH GRAND PRESIdent Seth Millington presiding, the Board of Grand Officers met February 18. Other grand officers in attendance were Grand First Vice-president Justice Emmet Seawell, Grand Second Vice-president Chas. A. Koenig, Grand Third Vice-president Harmon D. Skillin, Grand Secretary John T. Regan, Grand Trustees Jesse H. Miller, Eldred L. Meyer, John M. Burnett, Henry S. Lyon, Joseph J. McShane, Horace J. Leavitt and Charles H. Spengemann. Junior Past Grand Dr. Frank I. Gonzalez, again suffering from the effects of last year's auto accident, was unable to attend and a letter of good wishes was ordered sent him.

Communications pertaining to immigration and ineligible-to-citizenship aliens were received from V. S. McClatchy, executive secretary California Joint Immigration Committee, and the Grand Secretary was ordered: to communicate with the Subordinate Parlors regarding the activities of Samuel J. Hume in behalf of a quota for Japan; to urge members of the State Legislature to adopt the bill forbidding intermarriage of Caucasians and Filipinos; to request California's representatives in the Federal Congress to favorably consider the measure for return of indigent Filipinos to their native islands.

Richard P. Doolan (Hesperian No. 137) requested, in a letter, action in the economic situation, and urged that, if possible, a special Grand Parlor session be held in Sacramento to assist the State Legislature in finding means to alleviate conditions. Every consideration was given the present serious conditions by the Board, but the laws of the Order provide how special sessions may be called, and the regular Grand Parlor meets in the near-future. The Grand Secretary was ordered to so advise Doolan.

Grand Trustee Miller, Grand Third Vice Skillin and Grand Second Vice Koenig were appointed a committee to prepare resolutions of condolence on the passing of Past Grands Dr. Charles W. Decker and William J. Hayes for submission to the Grand Parlor.

It was ordered that Grand Parlor reports of the grand officers be limited to 1,500 words each, and those of district deputies to 250 words.

Visalia No. 19 and University No. 272 (Los Angeles) having, so the Grand Secretary reported, complied with the regulation stipulating that Parlors instituted with fifty or more charter members will be allowed a $150 supplies credit, were voted the allowance. It was also ordered that Compton No. 273 and Willows No. 255 be given a similar credit if their charter rolls are completed within the time allowed by the Grand President.

Assemblyman Ray Williamson (Castro No. 232), Assemblyman Lucius Powers Jr. (Fresno No. 25) and Senator Ray Fellom (Stanford No. 76) were appointed a committee to present Resolution No. 24 1932 Grand Parlor, relating to the conservation of the state's natural resources, to the State Legislature.

Grand Trustees McShane, Burnett, Miller and Meyer, Grand Third Vice Skillin, Grand Second Vice Koenig and Grand First Vice Seawell were appointed a committee to draft and present at the next Board meeting welfare legislation which, if approved by the Board, will be submitted to the Grand Parlor.

Much additional business, of a routine nature, was transacted, and there was discussion on matters pertaining to the welfare of the Order in general. Adjournment was taken to the call of Grand President Millington.

GRASS VALLEY GRAND PARLOR.

The Fifty-sixth Grand Parlor will convene in the City of Grass Valley, Nevada County, Monday, May 15. Arrangements for the gathering are in charge of Quartz No. 58 (Grass Valley) and Hydraulic No. 56 (Nevada City), which have a general committee that knows just what to do and how to do it. The two communities always put things over with a bang, and the 1933 Grand Parlor will prove no exception.

Each Subordinate Parlor must elect its delegates to the Grand Parlor the first meeting-night in April, and at least one week must elapse between nomination and election.

Interest in Grand Parlor office candidates is being aroused, and The Grizzly Bear has communicated with all rumored candidates. From responses received to date, this information is passed on:

Grand Trustee Joseph J. McShane (Twin Peaks No. 214) will be a candidate for Grand Third Vice-president.

John T. Regan (South San Francisco No. 157) will be a candidate for re-election as Grand Secretary.

Henry S. Lyon (Placerville No. 9), Charles H. Spengemann (Hesperian No. 137) and Eldred L. Meyer (Santa Monica Bay No. 267) will be candidates for re-election to the Board of Grand Trustees, composed of seven members.

Unless the unusual happens, these grand officers will be advanced: Grand First Vice Justice Emmet Seawell (Santa Rosa No. 28), to Grand President; Grand Second Vice Chas. A. Koenig (Golden Gate No. 29), to Grand First Vice; Grand Third Vice Harmon D. Skillin (Castro No. 232), to Grand Second Vice. Grand President Seth Millington, who will preside at the Grass Valley session, will automatically become the Junior Past Grand.

Thirtieth Anniversary Celebrated.

Colusa—At a long-to-be remembered function, largely attended, Colusa No. 69 celebrated February 2 the thirtieth anniversary of its institution. The ceremonies opened with a street drill by the Parlor's drum corps, with George Jameson as drum major. P. J. Cooke then led the way to the banquetroom, where Past President R. G. Power presided as toastmaster. During the discussion of the excellent menu entertainment features were presented.

Past Grand President Lewis F. Byington, who was the head of the Order when Colusa was instituted, said he was proud to be the "father" of No. 69. "I was not born in Colusa County, as has been often stated," he continued. "I was born in Sierra County, and came here with my father at the age of eight." He reviewed the history of California, and said it remained for the Native Sons to perpetuate the ideals of the Pioneers. Grand President Seth Millington, affiliated with Colusa, said "that California's old missions should be further restored, and that the Native Sons should confine their efforts to perpetuating historic things and refrain from taking up matters of less importance."

Other speakers were Tim Sullivan, Phil B. Arnold, Secretary Phil Humburg Jr., R. G. Lawson, Superior Judge Ernest Weyand, C. J. Frost, Herman Schroeder, W. C. Stokes Sr., W. G. Davison, Burton Smart and President Rotheus A. Gray, who outlined the projects the Parlor has for the future. The celebration was in charge of a committee composed of Postmaster R. G. Power, Ben R. Ragain, Thomas F. Busch, Tim Sullivan and Elton C. Fitch.

Resources Belong to Citizens.

San Diego—San Diego No. 108 had as honored guests February 15 its past presidents. With President Martin J. Spangler presiding, the officers initiated a class of candidates. Deputy Grand President Albert V. Mayrhofer reported on the Parlor's many activities, civic and historical, and No. 108 went on record as favoring an appropriation by the State Legislature for the support of the California State Historical Association. A program following the business session was in charge of J. P. Murphy, M. V. Cruze, P. Raske, J. Spencer, R. E. Mahony, B. Pauter and J. Navarro.

The following resolution, submitted by District Deputy Edward H. Dowell, Past President Edgar F. Hastings, President Martin J. Spangler, Deputy Grand President Albert V. Mayrhofer and Past President Eugene Daney Jr., has been adopted by the Parlor:

"Whereas, The preservation of our natural resources constitutes one of the objects of the Native Sons of the Golden West; and whereas, the benefits derived from the natural resources of this state should reflect to the citizens of the state; and whereas, the fishing industry constitutes one of the most important occupations along our coast and furnishes employment to numbers of our citizens; and whereas, our citizens are gradually being forced out of the fishing industry and their places being taken by aliens ineligible to citizenship; therefore, be it Resolved, That San Diego Parlor No. 108 Native Sons of the Golden West petition our Senator and Assemblymen to introduce and support such measures as shall prohibit the issuance of fishing licenses to aliens ineligible to citizenship."

"Old Guards" Give "Kids" a Run.

Calistoga—The ritual contest between the "old guard" and the "kids" of Calistoga No. 86 attracted a large crowd from Napa and Lake Counties February 2, and they had the pleasure of listening to and witnessing two splendid exemplifications. Two candidates were initiated. So near-perfect were both teams, the judges—James F. Stanley of the Grand Parlor Ritual Committee, John Schroeder (El Capitan No. 222), Hubert Covey and Arthur Poheim (Stanford No. 76) and Grand Secretary John T. Regan—deliberated for some time before awarding the honors to the "kids," who appeared in duck trousers, dark coats and golden ties.

A picture of McLane Parlor, the original name

WILLIAM B. IDE

WILLIAM BROWN IDE? WELL, HE achieved fame as one of the Bear Flag Party. He arrived in California October 25, 1845. Living on Belden's rancho—now Red Bluff, Tehama County,—an Indian messenger delivered to him an unsigned letter which resulted in his identifying himself with the party which, led by Ezekiel Merritt, started the Bear Flag Revolution at Sonoma, June 14, 1846, and took possession of that Mexican military post. General M. G. Vallejo and others were arrested, and taken by Merritt to Sutter Fort (Sacramento). John Grigsby was elected captain of the garrison of about eighteen left in charge at Sonoma. Prior to his departure, General Vallejo had caused confusion in the Bear Flag ranks by inquiring as to the authority for his arrest. No one appeared to know. Grigsby evidently did not fancy the outlook, for he exclaimed, "Gentlemen, I have been deceived; I cannot go with you; I resign and back out of this scrape."

A crisis had come, and with it the man. William B. Ide, realizing the peril of the moment, in trumpet tones called to the receding men: "I will lay my bones here before I will take upon myself the ignominy of commencing an honorable work and then flee like cowards, like thieves, when no enemy is in sight. In vain will you say you had honorable motives. Who will believe it? Flee this day, and the longest life cannot wear out your disgrace! Choose ye this day what you will be. We are robbers, or we must be conquerors."

With renewed hope, the men gathered about Ide and made him commander-in-chief of the Bear Flag forces—governor of the new-born California Republic. A flag was necessary, so the historic Bear Flag, now the official flag of the State of California, was designed. June 18, Commander-in-Chief William B. Ide issued a proclamation, setting forth the reasons for the Bear Flag revolution. Few, apparently, have read this remarkable document, so it is here presented:

"A proclamation to all persons and citizens of the District of Sonoma, requesting them to remain at peace and follow their rightful occupations without fear of molestation.

"The Commander-in-Chief of the troops assembled at the fortress of Sonoma gives this inviolable pledge to all persons in California, not found under arms, that they shall not be disturbed in their persons, their property or social relation, one with another, by men under his command.

"He also solemnly declares his object to be: First, to defend himself and companions in arms, who were invited to this country by a promise of lands on which to settle themselves and families; who were also promised a Republican Government; when, having arrived in California, they were denied the privilege of buying or renting lands of their friends, who, instead of being allowed to participate in or being protected by a Republican Government, were oppressed by a military despotism; who were even threatened by a proclamation by the chief officers of the aforesaid despotism with extermination if they should not depart out of the country, leaving all their property, arms and beasts of burden; and thus deprived of their means of flight or defense, were to be driven through deserts inhabited by hostile Indians, to certain destruction.

"To overthrow a Government which has seized upon the property of the Missions for its individual aggrandizement; which has ruined and shamefully oppressed the laboring people of California by enormous exactions on goods imported into the country, is the determined purpose of the brave men who are associated under my command.

"I also solemnly declare my object, in the second place, to be to invite all peaceable and good citizens of California who are friendly to the maintenance of good order and equal rights, and I do hereby invite them to repair to my camp at Sonoma without delay to assist us in establishing and perpetuating a Republican Government, which shall secure to all civil and religious liberty; which shall encourage virtue and literature; which shall leave unshackled by fetters, agriculture, commerce and manufactures.

"I further declare that I rely upon the rectitude of our intentions, the favor of Heaven and the bravery of those who are bound and associated with me by the principles of self-preservation, by the love of truth and the hatred of tyranny, for my hopes of success.

"I furthermore declare that I believe that a Government to be prosperous and happy must originate with the people who are friendly to its existence; that the citizens are its guardians, the officers its servants, its glory its reward."

William Brown Ide, a native of Ohio, was a lawyer by profession. Following the Bear Flag incident he was appointed land surveyor for the northern district of California by the Federal Government, and later was elected treasurer and county judge of Colusa County. He died in 1852, at the age of 50.—C.M.H.

of Calistoga, in the 1890 Admission Day celebration in San Francisco, donated by E. E. Light, inspired Charter Member C. E. Butler to reminisce on the early days of the Order.

Living Example Order's Precepts.

Santa Clara—C. E. "Doc" Newton, financial secretary Santa Clara No. 100, passed the fifty-eighth milestone February 7, and is "still going strong." A charter member of the Parlor, he has held every office, and in years past was a familiar figure at Grand Parlor sessions. His wife, Mrs. Mary Newton, and a daughter, Miss Myrtle Newton, are affiliated with the Native Daughters, and a son, C. Elmer Newton, is affiliated with No. 100. "To those who know him," says Recording Secretary Clarence Clevenger of Santa Clara, "he is a living example of friendship, loyalty and charity."

Open-air Initiation in Trinity.

Marysville—At the meeting of Fred H. Greely Assembly of past presidents February 11 it was decided to hold the annual open-air initiation of the assembly near Weaverville, Trinity County, June 4. Mount Bally No. 87 will be the host. A dance will be featured the evening prior to the ceremonies.

Officers of the assembly were installed, Peter J. Delay of Marysville No. 6 becoming governor. Grand Trustee Horace J. Leavitt was initiated, and Grand President Seth Millington was among the speakers. Sutter City was designated as the place for the March meeting of the assembly.

To Celebrate Anniversary.

Santa Rosa—Native Sons of Napa, Sonoma and Marin Counties will gather here March 18 to help Santa Rosa No. 28 celebrate its forty-ninth institution anniversary. Art Janssen is progressing in his efforts to form a drum corps. A large delegation, headed by President George Eckman, visited Mount Tamalpais No. 64 (San Rafael) February 25.

One candidate was initiated January 31, and Chairman Matt Rogina of the baseball committee reported a team is being organized for the coming season. With Chairman George Gilman of the good of the order committee in charge, a banquet was served.

Membership Standing Largest Parlors.

San Francisco—Grand Secretary John T. Regan reports the standing of the Subordinate Parlors having a membership of over 400 January 1, 1933, as follows, together with their membership figures February 20, 1933:

Parlor	Jan. 1	Feb. 20	Gain	Loss
Ramona No. 109	1033	1033	....	....
South San Francisco No. 157	803	803	....	....
Castro No. 232	784	784	....	....
Stanford No. 76	575	575	....	....
Arrowhead No. 110	573	568	....	5
Stockton No. 7	563	563	....	....
Twin Peaks No. 214	522	517	....	5
Piedmont No. 120	491	492	1	....
Rincon No. 72	418	414	....	4

Subordinate Parlors Briefs.

Marysville—Grand Trustee Horace J. Leavitt officially visited Marysville No. 6 and Rainbow No. 40 (Wheatland) in joint session here February 10. Argonaut No. 8 (Oroville) was represented by a delegation of fifteen. Officers of Marysville were installed by District Deputy Cyril R. Macdonald, A. W. Graves becoming president.

Modesto—Charles D. Blaine and Minnie Hogan are the presidents of Modesto No. 11 and Morada No. 199 N.D.G.W., having been installed, along with other officers, at joint ceremonies conducted by Deputies L. E. Bither and Ethel Enos. Brief talks followed the installation.

Auburn—Death has removed three of the old-time active members of Auburn No. 59, George Keehner Walsh, Louis Armbruster and Charles Henry "Guy" Walsh. George Walsh, born here January 29, 1870, and Armbruster, city councilman, born here July 29, 1868, died February 2. "Guy" Walsh, also a native of Auburn, born May 31, 1869, died February 3.

Halfmoon Bay—Grand Trustee Joseph J. McShane paid a visit February 14 to Seaside No. 95. Accompanying him were the officers, the ritual team and a large number of the active members of Twin Peaks No. 214 (San Francisco). In an enlightening address, Grand Trustee McShane related the wonderful progress he has noted in visits to northern and southern Parlors. Other speakers were Frank Matulich, Joseph Tracy, Eddie Doody, Oswald Storm and Edward P. McAuliffe.

Livermore—Morris Victor, very active in the affairs of Las Positas No. 96, died recently. Indicative of his interest in the community's welfare and the less-fortunate, he bequeathed one thousand dollars each to the Presbyterian, the Methodist and the Catholic churches, and one thousand dollars to the N.S.G.W. and N.D.G.W. Central Homeless Children Committee.

Cambria—Officers of Cambria No. 152 were installed by District Deputy Henry Twisselmann, San Luis Obispo County supervisor, N. Storni becoming president. A delicious banquet, prepared by Mrs. George Steiner, followed the ceremonies.

Sonoma—Grand Trustee Charles H. Spengemann officially visited Sonoma No. 111, February 20. A class of candidates were initiated, the ritual being exemplified by the officers of Hesperian No. 137 (San Francisco). A banquet and highjinks, in charge of Emil Andrieux, followed the ceremonies.

(Continued on Page 11)

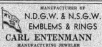

THE GRIZZLY BEAR
IS REGULARLY ON SALE:
SAN FRANCISCO:
N.S.G.W. Bldg., 414 Mason St., Room 302.
OAKLAND:
Fred M. DeWitt, 620 14th St.
LOS ANGELES:
315 Wilcox Bldg., Second and Spring.

Feminine World's Fads and Fancies

PREPARED ESPECIALLY FOR THE GRIZZLY BEAR BY ANNA STÓERMER

SMART WOMEN ARE GOING IN HEAVILY for transformation dresses. These are the frocks which may be taken apart and made into something else. A cape may be worn as a skirt, and a scarf may be wound about one's head as a turban. The newest transformation dresses are designed so that a busy woman who leaves home in the morning may be correctly dressed at each one of her occupations during the day.

The dress which has detachable sleeves is one such device. Without the long, tight sleeve, it is suitable for afternoon bridge, for dining out, or even for the theater. The sleeves may be pulled on and off as easily as a glove. This dress is correct for business or shopping.

There are many designs for women who want to economize in planning, and thus give closer attention to details. Thrifty fashions are often the best for all. Women who are obliged to make little economies in the planning of their clothes often pay more attention to every detail of their costumes.

In the first days of spring, not every woman who would like a between-season coat can afford one. Yet, there is a model which is three things in one. A double coat, warm enough for winter, a furless coat of the between-season type, and a little jacket to be worn over wool dresses.

The first days of spring this season are dedicated, primarily, to comfort. It naturally follows that the new masculine styles should have enthusiastic endorsement. They are particularly adaptable to resort activities, where freedom of movement is the first requirement. Flannel slacks lead the trouser mode, followed by various types of shorts, ankle-tight trows and the new lounge suits, delightfully feminine and at the same time practical. Leisure hours in one's boudoir are made more enjoyable and restful in pajamas, which are smart and comfortable.

For sports wear this spring, there will be real rivalry between the two- and the one-piece suits for popular favor. One thing certain, according to the first models for beach and other recreational centers, they will be colorful and will be modeled along lines that are becoming to youth and maturity alike.

Among the most attractive being shown is a natty one-piece garment of angora lacy-knit material, whose outstanding note is the peasant sleeves of vivid multi-colored stripes. The sleeves are cut raglan style, with the upper part full to the cuff, which is tight fitting. The scarf-collar at the ends carries the same bright color note as the sleeves. The skirt is cut circular, and is generously full at the hem. White shoes with colored stripe and white knitted cap and gloves complete this costume, which is suitable for many informal occasions.

Sweaters amaze one by their versatility, sheer loveliness and color beauty. Coat styles are new, with high-neck versions and turtle-necks in openwork, stripes, plaid, and solid colors. Long and short sleeves are seen in the many types available. They ensemble themselves effectively with straight tailored skirts of flannel, plaid or checked wool.

The new tennis dresses are frankly short, ending just below the knee, and have the bracelet neck, exposing the entire back. Bathing suits and beach clothes are identical, whether for sunshine resorts or bicycling costumes.

Gay and charming, a one-piece bicycle dress is made of yellow flannel, with divided skirt, fitted hipline, deep armholes, two pockets, rever collar and center front closings. If you prefer to ensemble your own bicycle costume, use a white flannel divided skirt with yoke top, and a printed or plaid pique shirt with cap-sleeves and open throat. Red suede belt and gloves are worn to match a knitted red beret, pompon trimmed.

There is much talk about the new square neckline. It is forecasted as one of the big fashion features for spring. It is scheduled to appear in all types of clothes, from active sports garments to formal evening gowns. Many of the newest evening gowns show this new neckline, especially at the back. The style is said to have originated (in its 1933 version) with the bathing suit. Women who wore square-backed bathing suits last summer found that they stayed in place and gave a smart, tailored, trim look to the figure, so they turned to square-back evening clothes. They found them to have an added virtue, a new medium for wearing jewels. Immense clips may be worn at the corners or along the base of a square.

Women who watch carefully for any change in style, often say that it is the evening clothes which first indicate any new trend, such as fullness in skirts, higher-than-usual waistlines, new necklines or new wrap closings. All these appear often in evening dresses and wraps long before they are taken up for daytime wear.

If you have given no serious thought to your wash frock needs for the coming spring and summer, then you are due for some happy surprises. They have so advanced that to attempt to classify them as house dresses is to do them a rank injustice. Since tub frocks elected to step out of their plebeian role and exchange the kitchen for the parlor, they have qualified for all manner of smart daytime needs. Delightful ensemble effects have been achieved in this connection with the new cottons.

Strictly tailored linen suits with contrasting blouses are very much in the picture, and the smart style revival of plaid and checked ginghams is reminiscent of the gay nineties. Wash frocks subscribe to the cape influence, flaunting capes and capelets in variety, thus achieving the necessary shoulder width. They are further used in lieu of sleeves, with flattering effect. Detachable features characterize some models.

Trimming touches also indicate the trend toward more style for less money. They include white organdie collars, sleeves, sashes, frills, pleatings, jabots, bows and buttons. The rayon weaves are hardly distinguishable from silk, and are exquisite in their colorings. They bid fair to enjoy well-merited popularity during the months ahead.

The highlights of the new spring apparels are higher necklines with definite shoulder width, sleeves to elbow or above, normal waistlines, and skirt lengths unchanged. The newer frocks will give an impression of vertical lines. Evening frocks are ankle length for dinner gowns and heel touching for formal wear.

Brown is at the peak of style, with blue in navy or paler shades, beige, gray and pastels following. White, with color accent, is good. Small prints are shown for day use, and floral prints for evening.

Coats and scarfs are popular. Many coats have capes. Sports coats are polo or tailored, and are belted. Furs are detachable. Suits are styled for every figure, and this is a suit season.

Hats will be worn forward, straight or tilted. New styles include the cossack fez, or the bonnet hat with no brim in the back. Large hats are shown for summer with lots of trimming. Hosiery in neutral colors is best. Gray and sun-tan are the most popular.

Shoes are higher, and are cut in front, and the vamps incline to shorter lengths. Colors, materials and trimmings appeal to diversity of tastes. The new shorter vamps have been so treated that the shoe is commodious and comfortable on the inside and appears smaller when viewed from the outside. The new colors are blue, the ever-favorite black, beige varying from medium dark and fawn brown to chaff, and gray. Materials for the season indicate high popularity for white light-weight buckskin, pigskin, lizard or patent leathers. Heels for walking types vary from one and one-fourth inches to two and one-half inches. Semi-dress and afternoon dressy sports heels will be from one to one and three-quarters inches.

National Monument—By proclamation of President Herbert Hoover, Death Valley, California, has been set aside as a national monument.

"There is always a better way to do anything."—Henry Suzzallo.

Passing of the California Pioneer

(Confined to Brief Notices of the Demise of Those Men and Women Who Came to California Prior to 1870.)

MRS. LOUISA JANE STEVINSON, native of Illinois, 93; came to California via the Santa Fe Trail in 1849 and after wintering in San Diego City moved north to the Merced River section, residing in Mariposa and Merced Counties; died at San Francisco. She was a daughter of Isham J. Cox, who established Cox's Ferry on the Merced River; at Quartzburg, December 27, 1855, the year Merced County was organized, she was wedded to Colonel James J. Stevinson.

Mrs. Nancy Moore Wheeler, native of Connecticut, 106; came via Panama in 1851 and resided in Los Angeles City many years; died at San Luis Obispo City. She was the widow of John Wheeler, who arrived in Los Angeles City in 1849 and established the first newspaper there, "The Californian," in 1853.

Carl Van Jenkins, native of Ohio, 93; came via Panama in 1850, landing at San Pedro March 9; died at Los Angeles City. At the outbreak of the Civil War he joined the California battalion which enlisted as the Second Massachusetts Cavalry.

Mrs. Elizabeth Simpson Fugitt-Fuqua, born in Nebraska Territory in 1850 while her parents were enroute to California, died at Stockton, San Joaquin County; two children survive.

David T. Scoggins, native of Tennessee, 83; came across the plains in 1852; died at Lodi, San Joaquin County,survived by a wife and a son.

Mrs. Amelia Dixon-Williams, native of Missouri, 84; crossed the plains in 1852 and settled in Amador County; died at Reno, Nevada State, survived by two children.

Emil R. Freeman, native of Illinois, 81; came in 1853 and resided in Marin, San Luis Obispo and Santa Clara Counties; died at Mountain View, survived by a wife. At one time he was a supervisor of San Luis Obispo County.

Mrs. Mariah Oats-Burgan, native of Missouri, 85; crossed the plains in 1854 and resided in Tulare and San Luis Obispo Counties; died at Arroyo Grande, survived by seven children.

Rev. Leroy B. Hinman, native of Illinois, 83; crossed the plains in 1854 and long resided in Sacramento City; died at Redwood City, San Mateo County, survived by a wife and a son. His father, Rev. J. M. Hinman, was one of California's first Methodist ministers.

Mrs. Jane Pizer-Morgan, native of Missouri, 100; came in 1854 and resided in Santa Cruz and Merced Counties; died at Santa Cruz City, survived by five children. She was the widow of John William Morgan, Pioneer of 1849 who was in Santa Cruz City when, in October 1850, the steamer "Oregon" brought word of California's admission to statehood.

Mrs. Elizabeth Crofton-Lillis, native of Ohio, 82; came via Panama in 1854; died at San Francisco, survived by a daughter.

Emil Bayer, native of Germany, 82; came via Cape Horn in 1856 and settled in Sacramento City, where he died; a wife survives.

Mrs. Isabelle Walton-Lusk, native of Maine, 97; came via Panama in 1856 and resided in Sierra County and Sacramento City; died at the latter place, survived by five children.

Charles Montier Everhart, native of Kentucky, 76; came in 1858 and settled at Gold Run, Placer County, where he died.

Mrs. Caroline Bacigalupi-Paramino, native of New York, 80; came via Panama in 1857 and settled in Amador County; died at Jackson, survived by eight children.

Jackson A. Graves, native of Iowa, 80; came in 1858 and resided in Yuba County, San Francisco and Los Angeles County; died at Alhambra, survived by a wife and three children. He was the author of several books, the latest entitled "California Memories."

Mrs. Doris Pemberton-Lewis, native of Missouri, 91; came via Panama in 1858 and long resided in Tulare County; died at Oakland, Alameda County, survived by four children.

William Harrison Eakle, native of Tennessee, 86; since 1859 Yolo County resident; died near Woodland.

Mrs. Sarah Spence-Fowler, native of England, 90; came via Cape Horn in 1860 and resided in Yolo and Lake Counties; died at Highland, survived by two sons.

Charles Doerr, native of Germany, 93; came via Panama in 1860 and settled in San Jose, Santa Clara County, where he died; two sons survive.

Warren Jones, native of Ohio, 90; came in 1860; died at Eureka, Humboldt County, survived by a wife and seven children.

George Walcom, native of Germany, 91; came via Panama in 1861 and settled in San Francisco, where he died; four children survive.

Harry G. Crafts, native of Michigan, 81; came in 1861 and resided in San Bernardino and Napa Counties; died at Saint Helena, survived by a wife and a son.

Edward B. Williams, native of New York, 81; came in 1862; died at Fillmore, Ventura County, survived by two daughters.

Mrs. Victoria Adams, native of Illinois, 90; crossed the plains in 1862 and for some time resided in Placer County; died at Santa Cruz City, survived by five children.

Mrs. Harriett Elizabeth Ralston-Salisbury, native of Ohio, 84; crossed the plains in 1862 and resided in Siskiyou and Modoc Counties; died at Alturas, survived by four sons.

Mrs. Grace Ann Donnell-Beau, native of Maine, 93; came via Panama in 1862 and settled in Sonoma County; died at Guerneville, survived by four children.

Fernando McIntyre, native of Maine, 86; came via Panama in 1863; died at Willows, Glenn County, survived by a wife and eight children.

Mrs. Colistia Dutton-Fishback, native of Illinois, 75; crossed the plains in 1863; died at Woodland, Yolo County, survived by seven children.

Anton J. de Mello, native of Azores Islands, 98; since 1864 Contra Costa County resident; died at Martinez, survived by four children.

Jay P. Harter, native of Michigan, 74; crossed the plains in 1864 and resided in Yuba, Modoc and Santa Clara Counties; died at San Jose, survived by a wife and four children.

Mrs. Lydia Jane Crane, native of Maine, 84; came via Panama in 1867; died at Oakland, Alameda County.

Thomas P. Lonigan, native of Indiana, 89; came in 1868; died at Lakeport, Lake County, survived by four children.

Mrs. Ella Virginia Porter-Hall, native of Virginia, 81; since 1868 resident Plumas County; died at Quincy, survived by two sons.

Captain William H. Winne, native of New York, 91; since 1868 resident Woodland, Yolo County, where he died.

John Cubbon, native of Isle of Man, 84; came in 1868; died at Santa Ana, Orange County, his home for sixty-three years, survived by three children.

John D. Droge, native of Germany, 93; came in 1868; died at Tracy, San Joaquin County.

E. George Northrup, native of New York, 85; came in 1868; died at San Jose, Santa Clara County, survived by two children.

John Christ, native of Germany, 94; came in 1866 and long resided in San Mateo County; died at Kenwood, Sonoma County, survived by a wife and two children.

Mrs. Catherine Alice Wright, native of Massachusetts, 84; came via Panama in 1864; died at Healdsburg, Sonoma County, survived by three children. She was the widow of Francis Wright, Pioneer of 1849.

George Armstrong, native of Utah, 73; came in 1863; died at San Luis Obispo City; since 1865 he had resided in the Cambria section of San Luis Obispo County.

Mrs. Mary Ann Congdon, 85; came in 1858 and resided in Los Angeles and Orange Counties; died at Santa Ana, survived by eight children.

Mrs. Catherine R. Martin, native of Ireland, 86; came via Panama in 1864 and long resided in Alameda County; died at Pleasanton, survived by two children. She was the widow of William H. Martin, whose father, Dennis Martin, was one of the early settlers in San Mateo County; he located above Searsville, where he opened the first mill and later carried on the first gold mining.

GRAVE OF NOTED PIONEER OF WEST FOUND IN CALIFORNIA GRAVEYARD.

"In the community graveyard at Franklin, Sacramento County," said the "Sacramento Bee" of February 11, "lies almost forgotten the grave of Alexander Willard. He died on March 6, 1865. He was one of the Argonauts, but although the tombstone fails to indicate the fact, and, perhaps, few of his neighbors of the gold-rush days were aware, he knew the West almost a half-century before John Marshall made his momentous discovery on the headwaters of the American River. Willard was a member of the famous Lewis and Clark expedition that paved the way for the conquest of the great Northwest for the United States in the years 1804, 1805 and 1806.

"This discovery, or re-discovery, was announced in San Francisco today by Edward P. Fitzgerald, a biographer. He revealed that he has identified the grave of Alexander Willard, marked by a mossy marble monument in the little cemetery at Franklin, fourteen miles from Sacramento, as that of a member of the intrepid band of thirty-two who, between 1804 and 1806, crossed the continent in one of the greatest explorations ever attempted by the United States Government."

Official Directory of Parlors of

ALAMEDA COUNTY.

Alameda No. 47, Alameda City—R. H. Fallmer, Pres.; Robt. H. Cavanaugh, Sec., 1806 Pacific Ave.; Wednesdays, Veterans Memorial Bldg.

Oakland No. 50, Oakland—F. R. Born, Pres.; F. M. Norris, Sec., 5595 Taft Ave.; Fridays, Native Sons Hall, 11th and Clay Sts.

Las Positas No. 96, Livermore—Dr. Donald M. Fraser, Pres.; John J. Kelly, Sec., P. O. box 341; Thursdays, Foresters Hall.

Eden No. 113, Hayward—John Meincke, Pres.; Filbert M. Soares, Sec., 1437 "B" St.; 2nd and 4th Tuesdays, Memorial Hall, Main St.

Piedmont No. 120, Oakland—Stanley Hadlen, Pres.; Charles Morando, Sec., 906 Vermont St.; Thursdays, Native Sons Hall, 11th and Clay Sts.

Wisteria No. 127, Alvarado—Henry May, Pres.; J. M. Scribner, Sec., Livermore; 1st Thursday, I.O.O.F. Hall.

Halcyon No. 146, Alameda City—S. Chesley Anderson, Pres.; J. C. Bates, Sec., 2139 Buena Vista Ave.; 1st and 3rd Tuesdays, I.O.O.F. Hall, 2329 Santa Clara Ave.

Brooklyn No. 151, Oakland—Frank B. Perry, Pres.; E. W. Cooney, Sec., 3907 14th Ave.; 1st and 3rd Wednesdays, Masonic Temple, 8th Ave. and E. 14th St.

Washington, No. 169, Centerville—M. D. Silva, Pres.; Allen G. Norris, Sec., P. O. box 31; 2nd and 4th Tuesdays, Hansen Hall.

Athens No. 195, Oakland—Milton O. Peterson, Pres.; Harold B. Farley, Sec., 4623 Benevides Ave.; Tuesdays, Native Sons Hall, 11th and Clay Sts.

Berkeley No. 210, Berkeley—F. Gohl, Pres.; R. J. Garrett, Sec., 1708 Virginia St.; Tuesdays, Native Sons Hall, 2108 Shattuck Ave.

Estudillo No. 223, San Leandro—E. E. King, Pres.; Albert G. Pacheco, Sec., 1736 E. 14th St.; 1st and 3rd Tuesdays, U.P.E.C. Hall.

Claremont No. 240, Emeryville—Raymond P. Burke, Pres.; E. N. Thienger, Sec., 839 Hearst Ave., Berkeley; Tuesdays, Veterans Memorial Bldg., 43rd and Salem Sts.

Pleasanton No. 244, Pleasanton—Edward Holzreiter, Pres.; Ernest W. Schween, Sec.; 2nd and 4th Thursdays, I.O.O.F. Hall.

Niles No. 250, Niles—M. L. Fournier, Pres.; O. E. Martenstein, Sec.; 2nd Thursday, I.O.O.F. Hall.

Fruitvale No. 252, Oakland—William J. Keating Jr., Pres.; Ray B. Felton, Sec., 1575 Alice St.; Fridays, W.O.W. Hall, 3256 E. 14th St.

AMADOR COUNTY.

Amador No. 17, Sutter Creek—J. H. Williams, Pres.; F. J. Payne, Sec.; 1st and 3rd Fridays, Native Sons Hall.

Excelsior No. 31, Jackson—Thomas G. Negrich, Pres.; William Going, Sec.; 1st and 3rd Wednesdays, Native Sons Hall, 22 Court St.

Ione No. 33, Ione—Earl Grover, Pres.; Josiah H. Saunders, Sec.; 1st and 3rd Wednesdays, Native Sons Hall.

Plymouth No. 48, Plymouth—Chester G. Johnson, Pres.; Thos. D. Davis, Sec.; 1st and 3rd Saturdays, N.S.G.W. Hall.

BUTTE COUNTY.

Argonaut No. 8, Oroville—Frank H. O'Brien, Pres.; Cyril R. Macdonald, Sec., P. O. box 502; 1st and 3rd Wednesdays, Veterans Memorial Hall.

Chico No. 21, Chico—Marcus Choisser, Pres.; Sam Lindsay Adams, Sec., Sacramento Blvd.; 2nd and 4th Thursdays, Elks Hall.

CALAVERAS COUNTY.

Chispa No. 139, Murphys—Maynard Segale, Pres.; Antone Malaspina, Sec.; Wednesdays, Native Sons Hall.

COLUSA COUNTY.

Colusa No. 69, Colusa City—Rotheus A. Gray, Pres.; Phil J. Humburg, Sec., 223 Parkhill St.; Tuesdays, Eagles Hall.

CONTRA COSTA COUNTY.

General Winn No. 32, Antioch—Edmont T. Uren, Pres.; Joel H. Ford, Sec., P. O. box 311; 2nd and 4th Wednesdays, Union Hall.

Mount Diablo No. 101, Martinez—R. P. Anderson, Pres.; G. T. Barkley, Sec.; 1st and 3rd Mondays, I.O.O.F. Hall.

Byron No. 170, Byron—William E. Bunn, Pres.; H. G. Krumland, Sec.; 1st and 3rd Tuesdays, I.O.O.F. Hall.

Carquinez No. 205, Crockett—Thos. Cox, Pres.; Thomas I. Cahalan, Sec.; 1st and 3rd Wednesdays, I.O.O.F. Hall.

Richmond No. 217, Richmond—Frank Weber, Pres.; Lloyd N. Mason, Sec., 11 6th St.; 1st Wednesday, 818 Macdonald Ave.

Concord No. 245, Concord—Chas. H. Gray, Pres.; D. E. Pramberg, Sec., P. O. box 235; 1st Monday, Guy's Parlors.

Diamond No. 246, Pittsburg—Victor Ericsson, Pres.; Francis A. Irving, Sec., 248 E. 5th St.; 1st and 3rd Wednesdays, Veterans Memorial Bldg.

EL DORADO COUNTY.

Placerville No. 9, Placerville—Chris. C. Orelli, Pres.; Clyde R. Berriman, Sec., Wood St.; 2nd and 4th Tuesdays, Masonic Hall.

Georgetown No. 91, Georgetown—George W. Brichler, Pres.; C. F. Irish, Sec.; 2nd and 4th Wednesdays, I.O.O.F. Hall.

FRESNO COUNTY.

Fresno No. 25, Fresno City—Oliver M. Akers, Pres.; W. C. Guard, Sec., R.F.D. No. 2, box 379; 1st and 3rd Fridays, Pythian Castle, Cor. "R" and Merced Sts.

Selma No. 107, Selma—Chester E. Shepard, Pres.; E. C. Laughlin, Sec.; 1st Wednesday, American Legion Hall.

GLENN COUNTY.

Willows No. 255—Ralph W. Camper, Pres.; Leon Marshall, Sec., P.O. box 747; 2nd and 4th Tuesdays, I.O.O.F. Hall.

HUMBOLDT COUNTY.

Humboldt No. 14, Eureka—Henry Sundfors, Pres.; Loren M. Nelson, Sec., P.O. box 195; 2nd and 4th Mondays, Native Sons Hall.

Arcata No. 20, Arcata—F. A. Nicholson, Pres.; William Peters, Sec., P. O. box 1117; Thursdays, Native Sons Hall.

Ferndale No. 93, Ferndale—Hans P. Petersen, Pres.; C. H. Rasmussen, Sec., R.F.D., 47-A; 1st and 3rd Mondays, Danish Hall.

KERN COUNTY.

Bakersfield No. 42, Bakersfield—George Taylor, Pres.; Henry A. Bannister, Sec., care Bank of America; 2nd and 4th Fridays, Justice Court, City Hall.

LAKE COUNTY.

Lower Lake No. 159, Lower Lake—LeRoy England, Pres.; Albert Kugelman, Sec.; Thursdays, I.O.O.F. Hall.

LASSEN COUNTY.

Honey Lake No. 198, Standish—Leo T. Davis, Pres.; N. V. Wemple, Sec., Litchfield; 1st and 3rd Wednesdays, Wrede Hall.

Big Valley No. 211, Bieber—Fred Bunselmeier, Pres.; A. W. McKenzie, Sec.; 1st and 3rd Wednesdays, I.O.O.F. Hall.

LOS ANGELES COUNTY.

Los Angeles No. 45, Los Angeles City—Leslie A. Packard, Pres.; Willard F. Allen, Sec., 4955 Los Feliz Blvd.; Thursdays, Merchant Plumbers Hall, 1832 So. Hope.

Ramona No. 109, Los Angeles City—Frank S. Adams, Pres.; John V. Scott, Sec., Patriotic Hall, 1816 So. Figueroa; Fridays, Patriotic Hall, 1816 So. Figueroa.

Hollywood No. 196, Los Angeles City—Henry G. Bodkin, Pres.; E. J. Reilly, Sec., Olive View; Mondays, 1089 No. Oxford Ave.

Long Beach No. 239, Long Beach—Francis H. Gentry, Pres.; W. W. Brady, Sec., 801 Jergins Trust Bldg.; Dept. No. 1 Municipal Court, 8th floor Jergins Trust Bldg.

Sepulveda No. 263, San Pedro—Patrick H. Doran, Pres.; H. E. Fairall, Sec., 1925 So. Pacific Ave.; 1st and 3rd Fridays, Redman Hall, 543 Shepherd St., Point Firmin.

Glendale No. 264, Glendale—Harvey T. Gillette, Pres.; Abel B. Molen, Sec., 508 So. Belmont St.; 1st and 3rd Tuesdays, Masonic Temple, 234 So. Brand Blvd.

Santa Monica Bay 267, Santa Monica—Arthur R. Leonard, Pres.; John J. Smith, Sec., 830 Rialto Ave., Venice; 1st and 3rd Wednesdays, Odd Fellows Hall, 1431 Third St.

Cahuenga No. 268, Reseda—Harold C. Trexler, Pres.; Carrol S. Driscoll, Sec., P.O. box 25, Chatsworth; first Friday, Alton Hall.

University No. 272, Los Angeles City—Bernard G. Hiss, Pres.; Martin DeFazio, Sec., 845 W. 53rd St.; Tuesdays, 471 W. 41st Place.

Compton No. 273, Compton—Laurence W. Cowan, Pres.; Wm. Don Castillo, Sec., 641 W. Bennett St.; 2nd and 4th Tuesdays, Mayo Hall, 231½ East Compton Blvd.

MADERA COUNTY.

Madera No. 130, Madera City—Cornelius Noble, Pres.; T. P. Cosgrave, Sec.; 1st and 3rd Thursdays, First National Bank Bldg.

MARIN COUNTY.

Mount Tamalpais No. 64, San Rafael—Arthur Hecht, Pres.; Manuel A. Andrade, Sec., 532 Mission Ave.; 1st and 3rd Mondays, "B" Street Hall.

Sea Point No. 158, Sausalito—Wm. W. Taylor, Pres.; Manuel Santos, Sec., 6 Glen Drive; 1st and 3rd Wednesdays, Perry Bldg.

Nicasio No. 183, Nicasio—M. T. Farley, Pres.; R. J. Rogers, Sec.; 2nd and 4th Wednesdays, U.A.O.D. Hall.

MENDOCINO COUNTY.

Ukiah No. 71, Ukiah—W. B. Danis, Pres.; Ben Hofman, Sec., P. O. box 473; 1st and 3rd Mondays, I.O.O.F. Hall.

Broderick No. 117, Point Arena—Ivan Lawson, Pres.; C. J. Buchanan, Sec.; 1st and 3rd Thursdays, Forester Hall.

Alder Glen No. 200, Fort Bragg—Thomas Cooney, Pres.; C. R. Weller, Sec.; 2nd and 4th Fridays, I.O.O.F. Hall.

MERCED COUNTY.

Yosemite No. 24, Merced City—John J. Thronton, Pres.; True W. Fowler, Sec., P. O. box 781; 2nd and 4th Mondays, I.O.O.F. Hall.

Los Banos No. 206, Los Banos—Daniel Pedroni, Pres.; L. E. Sarbo, Sec., R.F.D., box 21; 2nd and 4th Wednesdays, Eagles Hall.

MONTEREY COUNTY.

Monterey No. 75, Monterey City—James Millington, Pres.; T. W. Krieger, Sec., 999 Franklin St.; 1st and 3rd Fridays, Knights Pythias Hall, Main St.

GRAND OFFICERS.

Dr. Frank I. Gonzalez .... Junior Past Grand President
Flood Bldg., San Francisco

Seth Millington .... Grand President
Gridley

Justice Emmet Seawell .... Grand First Vice-president
State Bldg., San Francisco

Chas. A. Koenig .... Grand Second Vice-president
531 35th Ave., San Francisco

Harmon D. Skillin .... Grand Third Vice-president
Mills Bldg., San Francisco

John T. Regan .... Grand Secretary
N.S.G.W. Bldg., 414 Mason St., San Francisco

John A. Corotto .... Grand Treasurer
560 No. 5th St., San Jose

W. B. O'Brien .... Grand Marshal
2324 Santa Clara St., Alameda

Gem Hurst .... Grand Inside Sentinel
Financial Center Bldg., Oakland

William A. Reuter .... Grand Outside Sentinel
1009 Marine Ave., Wilmington

Leslie Maloche .... Grand Organist
1511 No. Hudson Ave., Los Angeles

Chester Gannon .... Historiographer
613 Capital Ntl. Bank Bldg., Sacramento

GRAND TRUSTEES.

Jesse H. Miller .... 712 DeYoung Bldg., San Francisco
Eldred L. Meyer .... 922 San Vicente Blvd., Santa Monica
John M. Burnett .... 914 Bank Italy Bldg., San Jose
Henry S. Lyon .... Placerville
Joseph J. McShane .... 419 Flood Bldg., San Francisco
Horace J. Leavitt .... Weaverville
Chas. H. Spengemann .... 827 27th Ave., San Francisco

ATTENTION, SECRETARIES!

THIS DIRECTORY IS PUBLISHED BY AUTHORITY OF THE GRAND PARLOR N.S.G.W., AND ALL NOTICES OF CHANGES MUST BE RECEIVED BY THE GRAND SECRETARY (NOT THE MAGAZINE) ON OR BEFORE THE 20TH OF EACH MONTH TO INSURE CORRECTION IN NEXT ISSUE OF DIRECTORY.

Dolores No. 208, San Francisco—Henry J. Adami, Pres.; Edward F. Webb, Sec., 2801 Sacramento St.; 2nd and 4th Tuesdays, Redmen Hall, 3053 16th St.
Twin Peaks No. 214, San Francisco—Oswald Sturm, Pres.; Thos. Pendergast, Sec., 278 Douglas St.; Wednesdays, Willopi Hall, 4061 24th St.
El Capitan No. 222, San Francisco—John O. Conmy, Pres.; James Hanna, Sec., 2450 27th Ave.; 1st and 3rd Thursdays, King Soloman Hall, 1739 Fillmore St.
Guadalupe No. 231, San Francisco—Thomas Wall, Pres.; Alvin A. Johnson, Sec., 142 Rousseau St.; Tuesdays, Guadalupe Hall, 4551 Mission St.
Castro No. 232, San Francisco—Roy Lund, Pres.; James H. Hayes, Sec., 4014 18th St.; Tuesdays, Native Sons Bldg., 414 Mason St.
Balboa No. 234, San Francisco—George Schroth, Pres.; E. W. Boyd, Sec., 437 Cherry St.; Thursdays, Maccabee Hall, 5th Ave. and Clement St.
Bret Harte No. 260, San Francisco—Louis S. Merrill, Pres.; A. W. McElhatton, Sec., 103 Holloway Ave.; Tuesdays, West of Twin Peaks Hall, 233 Legion Court.
Utopia No. 270, San Francisco—A. E. Rosenbaum, Pres.; Herbert H. Schneider, Sec., 2455 16th Ave.; Tuesdays, American Hall, 20th and Capp Sts.

SAN JOAQUIN COUNTY.

Stockton No. 7, Stockton—Ben S. Waller, Pres.; R. D. Dorcey, Sec., P. O. box 388; Mondays, Native Sons Hall.
Lodi No. 18, Lodi—Herbert Osterman, Pres.; Dr. Clyde Brennan, Sec.; 2nd Wednesday, Eagles Hall.
Tracy No. 186, Tracy—C. S. Seina, Pres.; R. J. Marraccini, Sec., R.F.D. No. 1, box 217, Thursdays, I.O.O.F. Hall.
Manteca No. 271, Manteca—John F. Mulholand, Pres.; Leonard Faria, Sec., R.F.D., box 75, Lathrop; 1st and 3rd Wednesdays, I.O.O.F. Hall.

SAN LUIS OBISPO COUNTY.

San Miguel No. 150, San Miguel—H. Twisselman, Pres.; Otto Kuehl, Sec., Paso Robles; 1st and 3rd Wednesdays, Fraternal Hall.
Cambria No. 152, Cambria—N. Storni, Pres.; A. S. Gay, Sec.; Wednesdays, Rigdon Hall.

SAN MATEO COUNTY.

Redwood No. 66, Redwood City—H. E. Holmquist, Pres.; A. S. Lignori, Sec., P. O. box 212; Thursdays, American Foresters Hall.
Seaside No. 95, Half Moon Bay—Melvin Frey, Pres.; John G. Gilcrest, Sec.; 2nd and 4th Tuesdays, I.O.O.F. Hall.
Menlo No. 185, Menlo Park—O. T. Maloney, Pres.; F. W. Johnson, Sec., P. O. box 601; 1st and 3rd Thursdays, Masonic Hall.
Pebble Beach No. 230, Pescadero—Earle A. Williamson, Pres.; E. A. Shaw, Sec.; 2nd and 4th Wednesdays, I.O.O.F. Hall.
El Carmelo No. 256, Daly City—Harry McDonald, Pres.; Ernest L. Micco, Sec., 639 Morse St., San Francisco; 2nd and 4th Wednesdays, Eagles Hall.
Industrial City No. 269, South San Francisco—John C. Hamilton, Pres.; Geo. A. Roll, Sec., P. O. box 237; 2nd and 4th Mondays, Metropolitan Hall.

SANTA BARBARA COUNTY.

Santa Barbara No. 116, Santa Barbara City—Philip Bradley, Pres.; H. C. Sweetser, Sec., Court House; 1st and 3rd Wednesdays, I.O.O.F. Hall.

SANTA CLARA COUNTY.

San Jose No. 22, San Jose—Fred Carmichael, Pres.; Joseph Lawrence, Sec., 1095 No. First St.; Mondays, I.O.O.F. Hall.
Santa Clara No. 100, Santa Clara City—O. A. Castro, Pres.; Clarence Clevenger, Sec., P. O. box 297; Wednesdays, Redmen Hall.
Observatory No. 177, San Jose—James J. Flannery, Prse.; A. B. Langford, Sec., Hall Records; Tuesdays, Knights Columbus Hall, 40 No. First St.
Mountain View No. 215, Mountain View—Henry A. Schultze, Pres.; C. A. Antonioli, Sec., 301 Castro St.; 2nd and 4th Wednesdays, Mockbee Hall.
Palo Alto No. 216, Palo Alto—John C. Bernal, Pres.; Albert A. Quinn, Sec., 643 High St.; Mondays, Native Sons Bldg., Hamilton Ave. and Emerson St.

SANTA CRUZ COUNTY.

Watsonville No. 65, Watsonville—J. E. Giacoma, Pres.; E. R. Tindall, Sec., R.F.D. No. 5, Box 313; 2nd and 4th Tuesdays, I.O.O.F. Hall.
Santa Cruz No. 90, Santa Cruz City—W. S. Rodgers, Pres.; T. V. Mathews, Sec., 105 Pacheco Ave.; Fridays, Native Sons Hall, 117 Pacific Ave.

SHASTA COUNTY.

McCloud No. 149, Redding—Roy Hawes, Pres.; Hugh A. Shuffleton, Sec.; 1st and 3rd Thursdays, Moose Hall.

SIERRA COUNTY.

Downieville No. 92, Downieville—Frank H. Turner, Pres.; H. S. Tibbey, Sec.; 2nd and 4th Mondays, I.O.O.F. Hall.
Golden Nugget No. 94, Sierra City—Elmer Thompson, Pres.; Arthur R. Pride, Sec.; 1st and 3rd Wednesdays, Masonic Hall.

SISKIYOU COUNTY.

Etna No. 192, Etna—Frank B. Quigley, Pres.; Harvey A. Green, Sec.; 1st and 3rd Wednesdays, I.O.O.F. Hall.
Liberty No. 193, Sawyers Bar—David H. Bobinson, Pres.; John M. Barry, Sec.; 1st and 3rd Saturdays, I.O.O.F. Hall.

SOLANO COUNTY.

Solano No. 39, Suisun—John S. Cannon, Pres.; J. W. Kinlock, Sec.; 1st and 3rd Tuesdays, I.O.O.F. Hall.
Vallejo No. 77, Vallejo—Frank J. Heldener, Pres.; Werner B. Hallin, Sec., 912 Carolina; 2nd and 4th Tuesdays, San Pablo Hall.

SONOMA COUNTY.

Petaluma No. 27, Petaluma—Clarence Christiansen, Pres.; C. F. Fobes, Sec., 114 Prospect St.; 2nd and 4th Mondays, Druid Hall, Gross Bldg., 41 Main St.
Santa Rosa No. 28, Santa Rosa—George A. Eckman, Pres.; Leland S. Lewis, Sec., Court House; Mondays, Native Sons Hall.
Glen Ellen No. 102, Glen Ellen—Tony Cereghino, Pres.; Frank Kirch, Sec., Route 3, Santa Rosa; 2nd Monday, N.S.G.W. Hall.
Sonoma No. 111, Sonoma City—Chas. E. Bacigalupi, Pres.; L. H. Green, Sec.; 1st and 3rd Mondays, I.O.O.F. Hall.
Sebastopol No. 143, Sebastopol—O. A. McChristian, Pres.; F. G. McFarlane, Sec.; 1st and 3rd Fridays, I.O.O.F. Hall.

STANISLAUS COUNTY.

Modesto No. 11, Modesto—Chas. D. Blaine, Pres.; C. C. Eastin Jr., Sec., P.O. box 898; 1st and 3rd Wednesdays, I.O.O.F. Hall.
Oakdale No. 142, Oakdale—D. W. Tulloch, Pres.; E. T. Gobin, Sec.; 2nd Monday, Legion Hall.
Orestimba No. 247, Crows Landing—Lloyd W. Fink, Pres.; G. W. Fink, Sec.; 1st and 3rd Wednesdays, Community Club Home.

SUTTER COUNTY.

Sutter No. 261, Sutter City—Henry Correll, Pres.; Glen R. Haynes, Sec., R.F.D. No. 2, Yuba City; 2nd and 4th Mondays, N.D.G.W. Hall.

TRINITY COUNTY.

Mount Bally No. 87, Weaverville—H. W. Day, Pres.; E. V. Ryan, Sec.; 1st and 3rd Mondays, Native Sons Hall.

TULARE COUNTY.

Visalia No. 19, Visalia—G. W. Houk, Pres.; C. H. Wenn, Sec.

NATIVE SON NEWS

(Continued from Page 7)

Manteca—With a ritual team from Stockton No. 7 in charge, Manteca No. 271 initiated three candidates. Among the many visitors was Deputy Grand President Al Lobree. At the conclusion of the ceremonies a committee from Phoebe A. Hearst No. 214 N.D.G.W. served a turkey dinner, and the following members of that Parlor, accompanied by Edward Perry, rendered vocal selections: Gudrun Evenson, Helen Evenson, Jessie Grisham and Dorothy Brown. Dancing followed the feast, music being furnished by Edward Perry, Carl Hill and Lawrence Mendosa.

Joint Installations.

San Rafael—Officers of Mount Tamalpais No. 64 and Marinita No. 198 N.D.G.W. were jointly installed by Deputies J. S. Rosa Jr. and Delphine Todt. Arthur B. Hecht and Mary Zapatini became the presidents and both promised, in the course of inaugural addresses, to keep things humming in their respective Parlors. Presentations were made as follows: to Mrs. Todt, a set of glassware; to Arthur W. Todt, a gold wrist watch engraved with emblems of the Order; to Mrs. Gussie Bannister, an emblematic bracelet. A delicious banquet, at the conclusion of the installation ceremonies, was followed by dancing.

Redwood City—Officers of Redwood No. 66 and Palo Alto No. 216 were jointly installed by Past President Frank Delucchi, H. E. Holmquist and J. C. Bernal becoming the respective presidents. Two candidates were initiated for No. 66. At a banquet concluding the ceremonies several enthusiastic addresses were made.

Georgetown—Officers of Georgetown No. 91 and El Dorado No. 186 N.D.G.W. were jointly installed by Deputies George M. Smith and Hattie E. Presby, George W. Buchler and Georgia Gardner becoming the respective presidents. Owing to the deep snow the attendance was limited in numbers, but those who did "make the grade" enjoyed a splendid turkey banquet at the close of the ceremonies.

Pleasanton—Officers of Pleasanton No. 244 and Pleasanton No. 237 N.D.G.W. were jointly installed, Edward Holzreiter and Julia Crommie becoming the respective presidents. Many visitors were present from Fruitvale No. 252 (Oakland) and El Cereso No. 207 N.D.G.W. (San Leandro). Following the ceremonies refreshments and dancing were in order.

TUOLUMNE COUNTY.

Tuolumne No. 144, Sonora—Mathew J. Marshall, Pres.; William M. Harrington, Sec., P. O. box 715; 2nd and 4th Fridays, Knights Columbus Hall.
Columbia No. 258, Columbia—Jos. Cadematori, Pres.; Charles E. Grant, Sec.; 2nd and 4th Thursdays, Native Sons Hall.

VENTURA COUNTY.

Cabrillo No. 114, Ventura City—David Bennett, Pres., 1380 Church St.

YOLO COUNTY.

Woodland No. 30, Woodland—J. L. Aronson, Pres.; R. G. Lawson, Sec.; 1st Thursday, Native Sons Hall.

YUBA COUNTY.

Marysville No. 6, Marysville—A. W. Graves, Pres.; Verne Fogarty, Sec., 719 6th St.; 2nd Friday, Foresters Hall.
Rainbow No. 40, Wheatland—F. M. Beilby, Pres.; W. A. Bowser, Sec., P. O. box 818; 2nd Thursday, I.O.O.F. Hall.

AFFILIATED ORGANIZATIONS.

San Francisco Extension of the Order Committee, N.S.G.W.—Joseph J. McShane, Chmn.; Harold J. Regan, Sec., 414 Mason St., San Francisco; meets 2nd and 4th Fridays, Grizzly Bear Club, 414 Mason St., San Francisco.
Alameda County Extension of the Order Committee, N.S.G.W.—Gam Hurst, Chmn.; Frank Roemer, Sec., 3297 Morcom Ave., Oakland; meets 1st and 3rd Mondays, N.S.G.W. Hall, 11th and Clay Sts., Oakland.
Interparlor Committee (Southern District), N.S.G.W. and N.D.G.W.—Burrel D. Neighbours, Chmn.; F. J. Burmester, Sec., P. O. box 42, Colton; meets 2nd and 4th Fridays, Patriotic Hall, 1816 So. Figueroa St., Los Angeles.
San Francisco Assembly No. 1 Past Presidents Association N.S.G.W.—Meets 1st and 3rd Fridays, Native Sons Bldg., 414 Mason St., San Francisco; Fred T. Kane, Gov.; J. F. Stanley, Sec., 1175 O'Farrell St., San Francisco.
East Bay Counties Assembly No. 3 Past Presidents Association N.S.G.W.—Meets 4th Monday, Native Sons Hall, 11th and Clay Sts., Oakland; M. W. Louden, Gov.; Edgar G. Hanson, Sec., 1260 Russell St., Berkeley.
Marin County Assembly No. 5 Past Presidents Association N.S.G.W.—J. S. Rose Jr., Gov.; L. J. Peter, Sec., Peter Bldg., 4th and "C" Sts., San Rafael.
Fred H. Greeley Assembly No. 6 Past Presidents Association N.S.G.W.—Meets monthly with different Parlors comprising district; R. L. P. Bigelow, Gov.; Barney Barry, Sec., P. O. box 72, Lincoln.
San Joaquin Assembly No. 7 Past Presidents Association N.S.G.W.—Meets 1st Friday, Native Sons Hall, Stockton; Clyde H. Gregg, Gov.; R. D. Dorcey, Sec., Native Sons Club, Stockton.
Sonoma County Assembly No. 9 Past President Association N.S.G.W.—Meets monthly at different Parlor headquarters in county; P. A. R. Gambini, Gov.; L. S. Lewis, Sec., Court House, Santa Rosa.
General John A. Sutter Assembly No. 10 Past Presidents Association—C. C. Wachman, Gov.; Jas. J. Longshore, Sec., 514 "J" St., Sacramento.
Grizzly Bear Club—Members all Parlors outside San Francisco at all times welcome. Clubrooms top floor Native Sons Bldg., 414 Mason St., San Francisco.
Native Sons and Native Daughters Central Committee on Homeless Children—Main office, 955 Phelan Bldg., San Francisco; Mrs. John W. Stirling, Chmn.; Miss Mary E. Brusie, Sec. Los Angeles branch office, 3924 Sunset Blvd.; Dorothy Schlingman, Sec.

(ADVERTISEMENT.)

Hall Association Elects.

Sacramento—At the annual meeting of the stockholders of the Native Sons Hall Association of Sacramento officers were elected as follows: John J. Monteverde, president; Irving D. Gibson, vice-president; Henry Wittpen, treasurer; Percy G. West, secretary. They, with the following, compose the new board of directors: John F. Didion, Roy C. Cothrin, J. C. Boyd, Hugh B. Bradford, M. F. Treblicox, Bessie Leitch and Edna Briggs.

N.S.G.W. OFFICIAL DEATH LIST.

Containing the name, the date and the place of birth, the date of death, and the Subordinate Parlor affiliation of deceased members reported to Grand Secretary John T. Regan from January 20 to February 20, 1933:

Harris, Joseph; San Francisco, January 2, 1876; January 12, 1933; California No. 1.
Scollin, Joseph Charles; San Francisco, December 9, 1884; January 26, 1933; California No. 1.
Matthias, Louis William; San Francisco, August 13, 1858; January 24, 1933; California No. 1.
McVanner, James; San Rafael, March 13, 1862; January 31, 1933; California No. 1.
Schulz, Edward Gustave; Gilroy, March 16, 1870; February 10, 1933; California No. 1.
Wright, William James; Rocklin, April 5, 1882; January 18, 1933; Sacramento No. 3.
Balkwell, Harry G.; Waterloo, March 20, 1876; July 1, 1932; Stockton No. 7.
VanVankren, Ed; Marysville, July 23, 1876; July 3, 1932; Stockton No. 7.
Ratto, John P.; Stockton, June 24, 1890; August 15, 1932; Stockton No. 7.
VonDetton, Otto; Stockton, December 11, 1871; September 19, 1932; Stockton No. 7.
Conchete, Paul; San Francisco, February 25, 1878; September 26, 1932; Stockotn No. 7.
Haunnong, R. R.; Stockton, May 19, 1874; October 30, 1932; Stockton No. 7.
Wurster, F. W.; Stockton, May 12, 1866; October 10, 1932; Stockton No. 7.
Atwood, A. W.; Stockton, February 19, 1880; October 17, 1932; Stockton No. 7.
Sanguinetti, Louis; Stockton, August 7, 1882; December 9, 1932; Stockton No. 7.
Torre, Joseph John; Stockton, November 19, 1905; December 22, 1932; Stockton No. 7.
Cooiot, August Emanuel; Sacramento, May 9, 1867; January 15, 1933; Sunset No. 26.
Hauskins, Richard T.; Stockton, August 3, 1852; December 9, 1932; Elk Grove No. 41.
Hoffman, Frank C.; San Francisco, June 8, 1865; January 30, 1933; Saint Helena No. 53.
Highstreet, Edward J.; Colusa, November 6, 1893; September 28, 1932; Colusa No. 69.
St. Louis, George G.; Woodland, December 4, 1881; December 27, 1932; Colusa No. 69.
Dillian, Frank Albert; Ione, November 6, 1872; July 8, 1932; Silver Star No. 63.
Fowler, Larkin G.; San Francisco, October 14, 1854; December 4, 1932; Silver Star No. 63.
McLaughlin, George Joseph; San Francisco, July 1, 1873; February 5, 1933; Rincon No. 72.
Imley, Abraham G.; Alameda, October 1, 1866; October, 1932; Santa Cruz No. 90.
Dinsmore, Irving Winfield; Hydesville, August 29, 1866; January 6, 1933; Ferndale No. 93.
Scully, John Edward; San Francisco, March 4, 1872; September 13, 1932; Niantic No. 105.
Bussenius, Robert George; Nevada City, October 2, 1862; October 16, 1932; Ramona No. 109.
Grubbs, James Earl; San Bernardino, June 28, 1908; January 30, 1933; Arrowhead No. 110.
Finley, Theodore Randolph; Santa Rosa, June 3, 1858; January 26, 1933; Santa Barbara No. 116.
Reilly, John Joseph; San Francisco, February 26, 1879; January 10, 1933; Sequoia No. 160.
Kupfer, Edward Herman; San Francisco, June 9, 1888; January 10, 1933; Sequoia No. 160.
Pausman, Henry George; San Francisco, October 9, 1878; January 22, 1933; Sequoia No. 160.
Eddy, Thos. David; Grass Valley, November 25, 1875; February 12, 1933; Sequoia No. 160.
Martin, Samuel; San Jose, December 10, 1869; February 10, 1933; Observatory No. 177.
Sloss, Henry; San Francisco, January 23, 1865; January 13, 1933; Hollywood No. 196.
Riley, John; San Francisco, March 7, 1871; December 23, 1932; Carquinez No. 205.
Callan, Matthew C.; Colma, June 24, 1871; September 26, 1932; Dolores No. 208.
Taaffe, Joseph L.; San Francisco, November 18, 1873; October 12, 1932; Dolores No. 208.
Hearne, Frank; Moores Flat, February 29, 1876; January 24, 1933; Twin Peaks No. 214.
Donohue, Frank; San Francisco, June 10, 1884; January 29, 1933; Twin Peaks No. 214.
Dougherty, Daniel; Jamestown, July 26, 1861; February 1, 1933; Twin Peaks No. 214.

Almond Fete—Oakdale, Stanislaus County, will feature its seventh annual Almond Blossom Festival, March 4 and 5.

"Popular government cannot succeed by following the line of least resistance."—Elihu Root.

SAN FRANCISCO

IN 1930, A MOVEMENT WAS INAUGURATED by a "select" few in California to create public sentiment in favor of granting immigration quota to Japan, on the grounds that it was necessary to promote goodwill and to prevent loss of trade with that nation. In 1931, the California Council on Oriental Relations was organized, and Samuel J. Hume was secured to address service clubs and other organizations in favor of the quota movement and to obtain pledges of support therefor.

In 1932, the Commonwealth Club of California, an outstanding civic organization of San Francisco, undertook, in its usual thorough style, through its immigration section a study of the question, and all of the section's semimonthly meetings for practically a year were devoted to hearing speakers on various phases of the subject and to discussing arguments advanced for and against the proposed quota.

At the club's dinner meeting November 17, 1932, a comprehensive report of the section's work was made, and a final debate was held between Hume, speaking for the quota, and V. S. McClatchy, executive secretary of the California Joint Immigration Committee, in opposition thereto. The California Joint Immigration Committee is an organization established by the California Department of the American Legion, the State Federation of Labor and the Order of Native Sons of the Golden West to secure enactment of a law to exclude from the United States aliens ineligible to American citizenship. Since the passage of the Federal Immigration Law of 1924, which contains such a provision, the committee has been continued, to oppose repeal or any modification of the exclusion measure.

The report and the debate were published in full in "The Commonwealth" of December 20, 1932, copies of which were mailed to each of the club members, largely business and professional men, with a request for careful study thereof and an expression of opinion on certain phases of the problem. The result of that vote, announced by the club, follows:

1—Do you favor granting an immigration quota to Japan? Yes, 364. No, 715. 2—Do you favor granting an immigration quota to Japan exclusive of other Asiatic countries? Yes, 81. No, 959. 3—Do you favor granting an immigration quota to all Asiatic countries? Yes, 279. No, 788. 4—Do you favor repeal of the naturalization law which now disqualifies certain races from United States citizenship? Yes, 194. No, 875.

IMMORTAL LINCOLN INSPIRES.

The February 12 breakfast at the Native Daughter Home, in honor of the birthday anniversary of Abraham Lincoln, was largely attended. Grand Secretary Sallie R. Thaler and Millie Tietjen were the hostesses. The tables were prettily decorated in the national colors, and the attractive placecards had this inscription, most appropriate at this time:

"The American's Creed: I believe in the United States of America as a government of the people, by the people, for the people; whose just powers are derived from the consent of the governed; a democracy in a republic; a sovereign nation of many sovereign states; a perfect union, one and inseparable; established upon those principles of Freedom, Equality, Justice, and Humanity for which American patriots sacrificed their lives and fortunes. I therefore believe it is my duty to my country to love it; to support its Constitution; to obey its laws; to respect its Flag; and to defend it against all enemies."

The main speaker of the occasion was Peter T. Conmy, Golden Gate Parlor No. 29 N.S.G.W., whose subject was "Lincoln, the Westerner." Presenting the immortal Lincoln in an entirely new light, his remarks were inspirational and greatly enjoyed. Past Grand President Dr. Mariana Bertola spoke on "Patriotism," Past Grand President Eliza D. Keith on "Education," Past Grand President Dr. Louise C. Heilbron on "Loyalty," and United States District Attorney I. M. Peckham (Stanford Parlor No. 76 N.S.G.W.) on "Significance of the Day."

NATIVE SONS BRIEFS.

Pacific Parlor No. 10 had its annual dinner dance February 21. The arrangements committee included Harry C. Alexander (chairman), Charles F. Strothoff, Henry Bastein, Walter W. Mohrdick, Frank A. Soracco, Bert D. Paolinelli, Thomas F. Duffy, Joseph Sugrowe, William G. Boyce, Kenneth Wehser and Andy Theusen. Grand Trustee Jesse H. Miller paid an official visit to the Parlor February 28.

Golden Gate Parlor No. 29 was signally honored by the selection of Harry W. Gaetjen as the grand marshal of the big Golden Gate bridge ground-breaking parade February 26.

Twin Peaks Parlor No. 214 received an official visit February 16 from Grand Trustee Charles H. Spengemann. A feature was a ritual contest between the Parlor officers, headed by President Oswald Storm, and a team of past presidents with Frank Matulich as president; the latter won, by five points. Grand Trustee Spengemann paid a tribute to the splendid achievements of Twin Peaks, Grand Trustee Joseph J. McShane spoke on the Golden Gate bridge, and Past President Charles J. Powers discoursed on civic activities. An italian dinner was served at the meeting's close. Members of the Parlor actively assisting throughout the evening, and contributing to the huge success of the occasion, included Augie Sandel, Harry Sandel, Albert Sandel, Eddie Doody, John J. O'Brien, Mel Norton, Thomas McLaughlin, Edward P. McAuliffe, Thomas Pendergast and John Kirrane.

Mrs. Carlotta Musto-Keenan, wife of Joseph B. Keenan (Niantic No. 105), for many years active in the affairs of the Order, passed awya February 14.

NATIVE DAUGHTER BRIEFS.

Forty-six years ago this month (March), Alta Parlor No. 3 came into existence. Reminiscences will be told by many charter members at the anniversary banquet to be held the evening of March 13. The bridge luncheon at the club and the bridge whist at the N.D. Home the eve of Washington's Birthday were social and financial successes.

Grand President Anna Mixon Armstrong paid an official visit to Golden State No. 50 February 15. Dinner preceded the meeting. Among those in attendance were Grand Secretary Sallie Thaler, Grand Trustees Anna Thuesen, Ethel Begley and Willow Borba, Grand Inside Sentinel Orinda Giannini, Past Grands Evelyn Carlson, Margaret Hill, Dr. Mariana Bertola, Genevieve Baker and Eliza Keith, Supervising Deputy Sadie Brainard and Deputy Emma O'Meara.

Orinda Parlor No. 56 received an official visit from Grand President Anna Mixon Armstrong. In recognition of the fact that the Orinda girls, attired to represent the various colleges, won the first group prize at the recent homeless children benefit dance, it was a football meeting, and an immense crowd enjoyed the occasion. Mrs. Armstrong was escorted into the hall by

PRACTICE RECIP

Grand Inside Sentinel Orinda Giannini and presented with a football filled with handkerchiefs. A dinner was served previous to, and a buffet supper following, the meeting. Past Grand Emma Foley was in charge of all arrangements. Officers of the Parlor were installed at public ceremonies by Deputy Mae Waring, Marie McGrath becoming president; dancing followed the installation.

At public ceremonies attended by a host of friends, the officers of Golden Gate No. 158 were installed by Deputy Maud Daily, Wilma Creighton becoming president. Beautiful gifts were presented by Sophie Siebe, "mother" of the Parlor, to Deputy Daily and Margaret Ramm, outgoing past president. After the installation a very fine program, under the direction of Gertrude Mariane, was enjoyed. Golden Gate celebrated its silver anniversary at a banquet which was largely attended, eleven charter members being among the number. Cards, dancing and music were enjoyed, and "Mother" Siebe was presented with a silver basket. Anna McQuade and Flora Justis had charge of the delightful affair.

Officers of Linda Rosa Parlor No. 170 were installed by Deputy Jewel Strei, Gladys P. Huber becoming president. Vocal selections were rendered by Marie Sharkey and Deputy Strei. Refreshments were served.

Castro Parlor No. 178 celebrated its twenty-third institution anniversary at a banquet. Many members enjoyed a most delightful evening. Supervising Deputy Alice Lane and Deputy Myrtle Ross were honored guests. Isabel Thiebaut will be hostess for the next whist party, to be held at her home March 7.

Officers of James Lick Parlor No. 220 were installed by Deputy Lauretta Cameron, Margaret Kane becoming president. Beautiful gifts were presented President Kane, Senior Past Hattie Driscoll and Junior Past Irma Collins. The Parlor has adopted a baby girl and named her Irma Jeanne. February 14 several members visited the various children's wards of San Francisco Hospital and presented scrapbooks, candy and valentines to the little shutins.

Past Presidents Association No. 1 will give a card party March 6 for the benefit of the fund being raised to entertain attendants at the annual convention of the General Association, to be held in San Francisco April 22. Chief President Cora Stobing will officially visit Association No. 1 March 20.

PIONEER NATIVES DEAD

(Brief Notices of the Demise of Men and Women born in California Prior to 1860.)

Augustine P. Omnes, born Santa Cruz County, 1858; died January 18, Santa Cruz City; wife and four children survive. His father, Guy Omnes, arrived prior to 1840.

Alfred McClure, born Alameda County, 1857; died January 19, Los Angeles City; wife and three children survive.

Michael McGinn, born Tuolumne County, 1855; died January 20, Stent.

Captain John Matheson, born San Francisco, 1859; died there January 21; wife and three children survive.

Mrs. Ellen J. Jones, born San Francisco, 1859; died there January 22; daughter survives.

George Douglas Thatcher, born Butte County, 1858; died January 24, near Oroville; son survives.

Louis William Matthias, born San Francisco, 1859; died January 24, Sacramento City; wife and three children survive. Was affiliated with California Parlor No. 1 N.S.G.W. (San Francisco).

Theodore Randolph Finley, born Sonoma County, 1858; died January 26, Santa Barbara City; two sons survive. Was affiliated with Santa Barbara Parlor No. 116 N.S.G.W., twice served the city as mayor, and was at one time member State Assembly.

Edwin Haigh, born Sonoma County, 1857; died January 26, Berkeley, Alameda County. His parents, Mr. and Mrs. John B. Haigh, crossed the plains in 1849.

Mrs. Margaret Keir-Cochran, born San Bernardino City, 1855; died there January 27; three children survive.

Mrs. Mary Elizabeth Ellis-Stone, born San Bernardino County, 1859; died January 27, Santa Cruz City; husband and nine children survive.

Patrick John Moss, born Tuolumne County, 1853; died January 30, Sonora.

Fred C. Rimpau, born Los Angeles City, 1855; died January 31, Anaheim, Orange County.

Mrs. Martha Ellen Owen-Blanchard, born Tuolumne County, 1856; died January 31, Oakland, Alameda County; five children survive. Her parents, Alonzo and Elizabeth Owen, came via Cape Horn in 1849.

Mrs. Martha Grigsby-Lyons, born Napa County, 1856; died February 1, Arcata, Humboldt County; husband and four children survive.

Mrs. Carrie Bertha Ayer-Engle, born Sierra County, 1859; died February 2, Oakland, Alameda County; husband and five children survive.

Mrs. Mary Wootton-Franck, born San Francisco, 1850; died February 4, Los Angeles City; seven children survive.

George Edward Dudley, born Sacramento County, 1853; died February 5, San Francisco.

Mrs. Lily Johnson-Cory, born El Dorado County, 1856; died February 7, San Francisco.

Mrs. Leanna Custer-True, born Napa County, 1859; died February 9, Napa City; husband and son survive. She was a daughter of Mr. and Mrs. John Custer, who crossed the plains in 1845 and settled in Napa County in 1848.

Mrs. Alice Fairlee-Henry, born Yuba County, 1853; died February 9, San Francisco; three daughters survive.

Mrs. Leila E. Lewright, born El Dorado County, 1856; died February 9, Stockton, San Joaquin County; five children survive.

Mrs. May Fish-Abraham, born Nevada County, 1857; died February 10, Mill Valley, Marin County; three children survive.

Charles Spears Brown, born San Francisco, 1856; died there February 11; two children survive.

Captain William B. Swears, born Yuba County, 1858; died February 14, Oakland, Alameda County; wife and two children survive.

Mrs. Clotilda Branch, born San Luis Obispo County, 1859; died February 14, near Arroyo Grande; five children survive.

Mrs. Nettie L. Walton, born San Francisco, 1854; died February 15, Los Angeles City; five children survive.

Mrs. Addie McDonald, born Sierra County, 1855; died February 15, Suisun, Solano County; two daughters survive.

Mrs. Emma Strauch, born Sacramento County, 1855; died February 15, North Sacramento; eight children survive.

Mrs. Bernarda Velarte-Dominguez, born Los Angeles City, 1858; died there February 16; nine children survive. Her father, Apolonia Velarte, arrived in 1845.

William W. Fowler, born Sonoma County, 1858; died February 17, Oakland, Alameda County; wife and three children survive.

LOVE STORY

(Continued from Page 8)

So each year the seasons shifted, wet and warm and drear and dry;
Half a year of clouds and flowers, half a year of dust and sky.

. . . .

Yet she heard the varying message, voiceless to all ears beside;
"He will come," the flowers whispered; "Come no more," the dry hills sighed.

. . . .

Or the small mouth curved and quivered as for some denied caress,
And the fair young brow was knitted in an infantine distress.

. . . .

Forty years on wall and bastion swept the hollow idle breeze,
Since the Russian eagle fluttered from the California seas;
Forty years on wall and bastion wrought its slow but sure decay,
And St. George's cross was lifted in the port of Monterey,
And the citadel was lighted, and the hall was gayly drest,
All to honor Sir George Simpson, famous traveler and guest.

. . . .

Till, the formal speeches ended, and amidst the laugh and wine,
Some one spoke of Concha's lover, heedless of the warning sign.
Quickly then cried Sir George Simpson: "Speak no ill of him, I pray!
He is dead. He died, poor fellow, forty years ago this day,—
"Died while speeding home to Russia, falling from a fractious horse,
Left a sweetheart, too, they tell me. Married, I suppose, of course!
"Lives she yet?" A deathless silence fell on banquet, guests and ball,
And a trembling figure rising fixed the awe-struck gaze of all.
Two black eyes in darkened orbits gleamed beneath the nun's white hood;
Black serge hid the wasted figure, bowed and stricken where it stood.
"Lives she yet?" Sir George repeated. All were hushed as Concha drew
Closer yet her nun's attire. "Senor, pardon, she died, too!"

MISSION TRAILS

(RUTH PARLE.)

Old adobe, grey in the sun,
Sheltering old bronze bells now green
Whose task for long has been done
Of tolling chimes o'er peaceful scene.

Mighty beams of old brown wood
Hold up the roof of red clay tile
Under which the fathers stood,
Teaching the Word with kindly smile.

These are the symbols of the trail,
Remnants of Serra's work so vast,
The paths where soft shod feet have trod;
Let us follow them into the past.

(This poem came to The Grizzly Bear from Miss Ruth Parle of Oakland, who has contributed short stories to the magazine, "Tarnished Gold" appearing in the October 1932 issue.—Editor.)

"Patience serves us against insults precisely as clothes do against cold. . . . Increase your patience under great offenses and they cannot hurt your feelings."—Leonardo da Vinci.

Native Daughters of the Golden West

"IN THE HOPE THAT IT MAY BE OF SOME news value as an indication of what the Native Sons and Daughters may do by concerted effort in their respective communities, and at the suggestion of Grand President Armstrong, I am enclosing herewith a biref article for publication. Very truly yours, NEVA B. McMAHON, D.G.P." This letter, dated Downieville, February 13, was received by The Grizzly Bear. The article, captioned "The Rejuvenation of Naomi No. 36—A resume of events as related by Deputy Grand President Neva B. McMahon on the occasion of the visit of the Grand President," follows:

"May I be permitted a few words on the growth and achievements of Naomi Parlor during the past two years! In 1930, when I became deputy grand president for this Parlor, it had a total membership of twenty-one, two of whom have since passed away. At the close of my second term as deputy, in 1932, the membership was forty-two, a net gain of twenty-one, or 100 percent. During this period the Parlor, acting in conjunction with the Native Sons, accomplished much for the benefit of the community, the most important of which were the mounting and dedication of the cannon at Cannon Point; the dedication of the Sierra County Museum, the celebration of the completion of Yuba Pass national highway, the placing of a plaque on the Sierra County Court House, the presentation of a stand of flags to the superior court, and the restoration of the old gallows.

"The old cannon that had belonged to Company K, Sixth Regiment, California Volunteers, in Downieville during the Civil War had lain unnoticed for many years and finally passed into the possession of Sister Butler and her husband, who generously relinquished their claim to it with the understanding that it wohld be suitably mounted on Cannon Point. This was accomplished, and the dedication was made June 14, 1931, by Neva B. McMahon, chairman of the joint committee.

"The old stone building on upper Main street was deeded to the trustees of the Native Daughters and Native Sons by the heirs of J. M. B. Meroux, one of the pioneers of Downieville, for use as a public museum. A suitable plaque was placed thereon and the building dedicated July 3, 1932, by J. M. McMahon, president Downieville Parlor No. 92 N.S.G.W.

"At the request of the Board of Supervisors of Sierra County, the Native Daughters and Sons, July 17, 1932, conducted a celebration of the completion of Yuba Pass national forest highway. This celebration was held at the Masonic picnic grounds, near the summit of the Sierra, and was attended by federal and state officials and people from many parts of California and Nevada.

"Judge Henry B. Neville, the beloved judge of our superior court and one of the outstanding jurists of California, presented a plaque showing the date of the construction of our court house, and requested the Native Sons and Daughters to place the same with appropriate ceremonies. This was done July 22, 1932, the plaque being placed in position by Past President Antone Lavezzola of Downieville Parlor, Native Sons.

"Following a custom in vogue throughout California, the Native Daughters and Sons of Sierra County, July 23, 1932, presented a stand of flags to the superior court of Sierra County. These flags consist of the National Flag and the Bear Flag, upheld by small bears, and are placed upon the judge's dais. August 20, 1932, a crew of Native Sons re-erected the old gallows—that had not been used for an execution since 1885—upon a site chosen by the joint committee of Native Sons and Daughters.

"Sisters, I have much pleasure, as well as pride, in recounting the achievements of this Parlor, and now that I have retired from official activity in this Parlor and assumed the duties of deputy for Imogen Parlor, may I not express the hope that that Parlor will grow and prosper, and that the two Parlors will work together, hand in hand, for the advancement of our fraternity and the glory of the great State of California!"

New Citizens Given Flags.

Grass Valley—Officers of Manzanita No. 29 and Quartz No. 58 N.S.G.W. were jointly installed by Deputies Adeline O'Connor and John Thomas. A beautiful addition to the ceremonies was the appearance of sixteen members of No. 29 dressed in yellow silk and carrying large boquets of yellow poppies and ferns. They acted as an escort to the officers-elect and executed a very pretty drill. A turkey dinner after the installation was followed by brief talks and community singing. Many Nevada City visitors were in attendance.

Anna Rowe, Annie Conlin, Louise Wales, Lorraine Keast, Grace Eva and Kitty Clemo, representing Manzanita, journeyed through the snow to the Nevada County Court House at Nevada City January 29 to witness the examination of aliens who had applied for citizenship. To the three successful ones they presented United States of America and California State (Bear) Flags. The committee was highly praised by Superior Judge Raglan Tuttle, affiliated with Hydraulic No. 56 N.S.G.W.

GRAND PRESIDENT'S OFFICIAL ITINERARY.

Woodland—Grand President Anna Mixon Armstrong will, during March and April, visit the following Subordinate Parlors on the dates noted:

MARCH.

10th—Desert Gold No. 250, Mojave.
13th—Santa Ana No. 235, Santa Ana.
14th—Californiana No. 247, Los Angeles, afternoon; Verdugo No. 240, Glendale, evening.
15th—Los Angeles No. 124, Los Angeles, and Santa Monica Bay No. 245, Santa Monica, jointly at Los Angeles.
16th—Grace No. 242, Fullerton.
17th—Long Beach No. 154, Long Beach, and Rudecinda No. 230, San Pedro, jointly at Long Beach.
18th—San Diego No. 208, San Diego.
20th—San Luisita No. 108, San Luis Obispo.
21st—El Pinal No. 163, Cambria, afternoon.
22nd—San Miguel No. 94, San Miguel, afternoon.
23rd—Pleasanton No. 237, Pleasanton.
25th—Berkeley No. 150, Berkeley, afternoon.
28th—Argonaut No. 166, Oakland.
29th—Gabrielle No. 139, San Francisco.

APRIL.

3rd—Snow Peak No. 176, Truckee.
4th—Caliz de Oro No. 206, Stockton.
5th—San Joaquin district meeting at Madera.
7th—Fruitvale No. 177, Oakland.
10th—Marinita No. 198, San Rafael.

Message Inspires.

Folsom—On the occasion of the official visit of Grand President Anna Mixon Armstrong to Fern No. 123, visitors were present from Sacramento, Elk Grove, Grass Valley, San Francisco, Oakland and Woodland. Among the number were Grand Trustee Edna Briggs, Supervising Deputies Bessie Leitch and Sadie Brainard, and Deputies Anna Kloss, May Lucas and Gertrude Keehner. One candidate was initiated.

Grand President Armstrong gave an interesting address touching on the work, the ideals and the aims of the Order. She left with the members inspiration for better and more enthusiastic efforts in the Order's behalf. Several presentations were made, and at the meeting's close a supper was served at flower-bedecked tables.

Unique Feature.

Santa Rosa—A unique feature, designed to stimulate attendance and to raise funds, was added to the program of Santa Rosa No. 217 February 2. The members invited their "boy friends" to be guests during the social hour. Box suppers were auctioned, and each purchaser had the privilege of sharing the food with the Native Daughter who had prepared it. Kathryn Branstetter had charge of a program presented by the male chorus of Santa Rosa No. 28 N.S.G.W., Ida Losch, Florence Irwin, Althea Leggett, Georgia Heintz and Ruby Berger.

The Parlor sent a delegation to the district meeting at Sonoma City February 17. It plans a membership drive, with Ann Beach and Ruby Berger as the captains. Ida Losch, as president, heads the corps of officers for the January-July term.

Protests Mispronunciations.

San Bernardino—Lugonia No. 241 had as special guests Ferbuary 8, Grand Outside Sentinel Hazel B. Hansen, Deputy Genevieve Hiskey and President Maude Van Fleet and Past President Ethel Baxter of Ontario No. 251, who brought inspiring messages. Chairman Clara Barton of the press committee reported sending letters to various broadcasting stations regarding the mispronunciation of California place names. On display were a generous supply of canned goods, brought by the members for the unemployed. February 15, a benefit card party at the Colton Womans Club attracted a large crowd. A cake, made by Mrs. H. M. Barton, brought a splendid sum.

February 22 was Natives day at the National Orange Show. Lugonia and Arrowhead No. 110 N.S.G.W. were in charge. A basket supper was served, and a special program was presented.

Pioneer Mother Presented Boquet.

Oakland—Piedmont No. 87 celebrated its anniversary February 16 with a delightful dinner served under the chairmanship of Josephine Collins. An enjoyable evening, with games and entertainment features, followed. In the course of events, Mrs. Raymond Ford (Marcella O'Connell) was presented with a lovely gift from her many friends in the Parlor.

At joint ceremonies, officers of Piedmont No. 87 and Piedmont No. 120 N.S.G.W., with Ella Mullen and Stanley Hadlen as presidents, were installed by Supervising Deputy Mildred Irwin and District Deputy Frank Perry. Mrs. French, the mother of President Mullen, was presented with a boquet; when but a few months old she came to California via Cape Horn and has since resided in this state.

Anniversary Celebrated.

Alturas—Alturas No. 159 celebrated its silver anniversary at a delicious dinner presided over by President Erma Elliott. The charter members and the past officers responded to the call for reminiscences, and each received a gift from the Parlor. Past president emblems were presented Mildred Boyd and Annie Estes. The table centerpiece was a huge "Golden West" cake, made and decorated by Grand Vice-president Irma Laird, and the favors were tiny individual cakes with a single candle atop each.

Officers of the Parlor were installed February 2 by Deputy Mildred Boyd, Mildred Smith becoming president. The "buy american" movement was endorsed. Mrs. Lulu Ferguson (Phoebe A. Hearst No. 214) of Manteca was a viistor.

Keep Actively Engaged.

Merced—Grand President Anna Mixon Armstrong officially visited Veritas No. 75, February 7. Preceding the meeting, at which Zelphia Thomas presided, a delicious turkey dinner was served. In attendance were delegations from all neighboring Parlors, Supervising Deputies May F. Givens and Katherine Kopf, and Deputies Hazel Laverty, Lois Roach, Frances Oliver and Ethel Enos.

Grand President Armstrong gave a most beautiful and inspiring address. She first dealt with the projects of the Parlor, then emphasized the fact that "though it is a difficult time to gain new members, we must keep actively engaged in our work at all times." She said that "though conditions are difficult, they have served a purpose in that they have brought us nearer to one another, to our homes and firesides; they have brought affection." Mrs. Armstrong was presented with a gift, following which Lois Roach sang "I Love You Truly." Refreshments concluded a meeting with lovely memories to cherish.

Joint Installations.

Ferndale—Officers of Oneonta No. 71 and Ferndale No. 93 N.S.G.W. were jointly installed at public ceremonies. Deputies Myra Rumrill and J. B. Tilley officiated, and Anna Jespersen and Hans P. Petersen became the respective presidents. Ferndale was host following the ceremonies. Cards were played and a delicious supper was served. Supervising Deputy Hattie Roberts was among the many in attendance.

Calistoga—Some 160 attended the joint installation ceremonies of Calistoga No. 145 and Calistoga No. 86 N.S.G.W. Deputies Sadie

THE LETTER BOX

Comments on subjects of general interest and importance received from readers of The Grizzly Bear.

From Past Grand President Stella Finkeldey of Santa Cruz, chairman Grand Parlor Veterans Welfare Committee, The Grizzly Bear received this letter, dated February 18: "Enclosed please find copies of letters from the various hospitals in re service given by the Native Daughters of the Golden West. . . . Will you kindly publish the enclosed in March number of the magazine?" The letters follow:

"It is noted that the subscriptions to [several] magazines, donated by the Native Daughters of the Golden West, will expire with the March 1933 numbers. Since all have been greatly enjoyed by the ex-service men and women hospitalized here, it is believed that the Native Daughters of the Golden West may wish to renew the subscriptions to these magazines for another year. We wish to thank you again for your co-operation and interest in the patients undergoing treatment in this hospital. They have derived much pleasure from the above listed contribution of periodicals and join the hospital staff in expressions of appreciation for this generous gift."—Veteran Administration Hospital, San Francisco, California. The requested magazines have been ordered for another year.

"This will acknowledge receipt of your letter relative to the renewal of subscriptions to magazines which your organization has been furnishing for the pleasure of the patients in this hospital. Please be advised that [those specified] will be greatly appreciated. Thanking you for your kindly interest." Veterans Administration Hospital, Palo Alto, California. The requested magazines have been ordered for another year.

"We received your letter in which you have so kindly offered to provide us with Easter candy and razor blades. (Same as last year, S. F.). These articles are most satisfactory and we shall be very happy to have them. At this time we are collecting furnishings for a small recreation room for mental patients. If you have anything which you wish to send, such as a few cushions, table runner, card table covers, ash trays, etc., they would be greatly appreciated. Thank you kindly for your interest in the patients at our hospital. . . . Received the five glass and nine metal ash trays and twenty packages of razor blades. We are indeed grateful for these very useful articles, and wish to thank you most heartily for your interest in our work at this hospital. Expressing appreciation of your helpful cooperation." United States Naval Hospital, Mare Island, California.

"This is in further reference to your communication and my tentative reply. In going over the supply of comfort articles on hand at the present time, there does not seem to be anything in this line of which we are particularly in need. However, there are a number of magazine subscriptions which the librarian reports she would like very much to have for the enjoyment of her readers. If the Native Daughters of California would like to subscribe to any of the above magazines for the patients, it would be a kindness which our hospitalized veterans would greatly appreciate. All of the men and women would benefit from the subscriptions, for all reading material is being continuously circulated throughout the wards."—Veterans Administration Hospital, Livermore, California. The suggested magazines have been subscribed for.

Brooks and Lionel Saviez officiated, and Adele Nolasco and Fred Heitz became the respective presidents. After refreshments dancing was in order, the music being furnished by Edith Cavagnaro, Fred Tedeschi, Leonard J. Moors and Atillio Bagnasco. Among the many visitors were Supervising Deputy Wilna Mitchell and delegations from Saint Helena and Napa.

Subordinate Parlors Doings.

Lodi—Six Parlors were represented when Grand President Anna Mixon Armstrong officially visited Ivy No. 88. Deputy Catherine Tully installed the officers, Verna Weesner becoming president. Theresa E. Hunt, retiring president, was presented with an emblematic pin. The Parlor is holding a series of card parties for the benefit of the homeless children.

Willows—Berryessa No. 192 has set aside the first meeting night of each month to celebrate the birthdays of members occurring during that month. February 6 the January and the February girls were guests.

Byron—Donner No. 193's officers were installed February 4 by Deputy Edith Easton, Virginia Doltzen becoming president. Supervising Deputy Myra Rodemacher and a delegation from Antioch were guests. Past President Josephine Pimental was presented with an emblematic pin by Vera Thomas, the outgoing president. A banquet and social hour concluded the ceremonies. A series of bunco parties being held by the Parlor are creating much fun and interest.

Santa Ana—The thimble club of Santa Ana No. 235 had an all-day gathering at the Anaheim home of Marguerite Cramer. In the evening several attended the card party of Grace No. 242 (Fullerton). The card club met with Deputy Genevieve Hiskey, February 21.

Interesting Group Entertains.

Mojave—Desert Gold No. 250's officers were installed February 10 in a hall aglow with floral decorations and a warm fire. Deputy Jennie Dennis was the installing officer, and among the many visitors were Grand Outside Sentinel Hazel B. Hansen, Supervising Deputy Florence D. Schoneman, President Mattie Labory-Garra of Los Angeles No. 124, and delegations from Kern County Parlors.

An interesting group of friendly guests helped to pass a very pleasant evening. Miss Ramona Crabtree, a teacher, brought from Tehachapi a group of little girls, dressed in orange costumes, who sang California songs and gave a poppy dance; also, ten small boys, who sang. The high school principal spoke on the state's history. Grand Outside Sentinel Hansen told of the aims of the Order, and Supervising Deputy Schoneman emphasized the necessity of keeping California history alive. Junior Past Reni Evertt of Desert Gold was presented with an emblematic pin by Senior Past W. M. Truitt. Delicious refreshments were served at tables decorated with real flowers, a rare thing on the desert.

Cute Costumes at Valentine Party.

Petaluma—Officers of Petaluma No. 222 were installed by Deputy May Rose Barry, Edna Meadows becoming president. February 7 a social time was held and dainty refreshments were served. Zora Tompkins was in charge. A large delegation from the Parlor attended February 17 the Sonoma district meeting.

A Saint Valentine "kid" party February 14 brought out some very cute costumes, many of the members appearing in rompers. Appropriate games were played and home-made refreshments were served. Josie Tagliaferro headed the arrangements committee, which included also Edith Witham, Alma Tilman, Anna Trontelle, Emma Tomosi and Bonnie Ross. February 21 a public card party was featured.

Hear of Indians' Conditions.

San Diego—The monthly card parties of San Diego No. 208 have been most successful, both socially and financially. Other charming affairs given for the benefit of the Parlor were a waffle bake February 8 at the home of Doris Hoffner, and a bridge dinner February 23 at the home of Marie James. The past presidents are rehearsing a program to be presented in April, on the occasion of the Parlor's birthday anniversary. At the February 22 meeting Purl Willis spoke on "Conditions Among the Indians of San Diego County."

At the third anniversary celebration of the Past Presidents Association President Irma Heilbron, Secretary Marion Stough and Treasurer Elsie Frank were re-elected, and Sofia Sharpe was made vice-president. A vase was presented President Heilbron and she, in turn, presented gifts to her assisting officers. The untimely passing of Miss Florence Brewer, well-known educator and member of San Diego Parlor, is mourned; she was born in Contra Costa County, sixty years ago.

Card Party Attracts.

Modesto—At its February 8 meeting, Morada No. 199 voted to adopt a Central Homeless Children Committee baby. Supervising Deputy Katherine Kopf, Deputy Ethel Enos and a number of members went to Oakdale February 6 to attend the official visit of Grand President Anna Mixon Armstrong to Oakdale No. 125. A sociable February 22 was in charge of Rhoda Jenkinson.

At the whist party given jointly February 15 by Morada and Modesto No. 11 N.S.G.W., guests were entertained at forty tables. Emma Smith and Lena Browder had charge of the card playing and dance, and Katherine Kopf and Robert Benson looked after the refreshments. The next card party and dance, scheduled for March 16, will be in charge of Annette Petersen and Robert Benson.

LOS ANGELES
CITY AND COUNTY

THAT LOS ANGELES IS ONE OF THE few American large cities whose origin is traced to a formal founding, in the choosing of a location, "eminently satisfactory for an agricultural colony," is disclosed in a human geography study made by Dr. Ruth E. Baugh, assistant professor of geography, University of California at Los Angeles.

"Analysis of the historical development of present-day cities," she says, "shows that in a majority of cases favorable geographical conditions attracted settlers to places where simple requisites of water, fuel and food supply, or of protection of market facilities were provided. While some cities mark the successive stages of urban growth, other cities have been chosen arbitrarily and settlers directed to occupy them. Such artificially created cities may degenerate if the basic elements for survival and growth are absent."

Los Angeles, according to Dr. Baugh, is one of the rare cases among the great cities of the United States whose origin was prescribed in accordance with conditions viewed necessary for settlement. It was Governor Felipe De Neve who ordered that, "after selecting a spot for a dam and ditch with a view of irrigating the largest possible area of land," a site for the pueblo was to be chosen "on high ground in sight of the sowing lands, but at least 500 feet distant, near the river or main ditch, with sufficient exposure to the north and south winds."

To this site, September 4, 1781, Governor de Neve conducted the forty-six settlers recruited in northern Mexico, and with impressive ceremony formally founded El Pueblo de Nuestra Senora La Reina de Los Angeles, she says. The river still serves the city, contributing from 19 to 20 percent of the total water supply of the state's metropolis, adds Dr. Baugh.

PLAN FOR VISITS N.D. HEAD.

The Native Daughter Parlors in the southern district are eagerly anticipating the official visits of Grand President Anna Mixon Armstrong, scheduled elsewhere in The Grizzly Bear. At a meeting February 1 attended by many officials, attractive features were planned for Mrs. Armstrong's entertainment. Among those present were Past Grand President Grace S. Stoermer, who presided, Grand Outside Sentinel Hazel B. Hansen, Supervising Deputy Florence D. Schoneman, Deputies Gertrude Allen, Lucretia Coates, Carrie Lenhouse-Northway, Genevieve Hiskey, Ellen Mae Madden, Grace Anderson, Rita Smith, Mary Noerenberg, Eva Bemis, Nellie Cline and Kate McFadyen.

When you purchase goods advertised in The Grizzly Bear, or answer an advertisement in this magazine, please be sure to mention The Grizzly Bear. That's co-operation mutually beneficial.

CARAVAN VISITS.

Los Angeles Parlor No. 45 N.S.G.W. had a surprise visitor February 2—Grand Trustee Joseph J. McShane of San Francisco, who discoursed on conditions in the Order. He was welcomed by Past Grand John T. Newell. February 13 a caravan of 45ers, led by First Vicepresident Roger Johnson, paid a visit to Hollywood No. 196 and furnished entertainment there. February 23 the Parlor was officially visited by Grand Trustee Eldred L. Meyer, and preceding the meeting Sid Witkowski and his "gang" served a buffet supper. William Gilkey is doing fine work in behalf of landmarks.

DELIGHTFUL BRIDGE LUNCHEON.

Glendale—President Vera Carlson of Verdugo Parlor No. 240 N.D.G.W. has appointed several committees to carry on the many spring activities. The dance of February 11 held in conjunction with Glendale No. 264 N.S.G.W. was a huge success, more than 200 attending; Ione and Harvey Gillett were in charge. A dinner under the chairmanship of Margaret Donlan preceded the February 14 meeting.

Chevy Chase Country Club was the scene of a delightful bridge luncheon sponsored by the Parlor February 15. The decorations were in the valentine motif, and guests came from Ontario, Fullerton and Los Angeles. A. D. Orr gave piano numbers and Dorothy Courtney sang. Margaret Donlan was in charge. Following the February 28 meeting lovely refreshments were enjoyed at the home of Ione Gillett; Historian Dorothy Rawn gave an interesting talk. A food sale was held February 25.

March 18, Verdugo and Glendale Parlors will feature a Saint Patrick Day dance at Masonic Temple, 234 South Brand boulevard. Ione Gillett and Albert Boeckman, who are making the arrangements, extend an invitation to all Natives and friends, and President Carlson of No. 240 assures a joyous time.

GALA OCCASION.

Santa Monica—Some three hundred Native Sons, including delegations from every nearby Parlor, attended the annual lobster feast of Santa Monica Bay No. 267, February 1. And what a feast! It was an all-around gala occasion, perfectly handled by President Arthur Leonard and his able assistants. Sheriff Eugene Biscailuz, a Black Bart at extracting funds for charity, directed the good of the order, and between his extractions some excellent entertainment features were presented. Speakers, limited, of the evening were Past Grands Herman C. Lichtenberger, William I. Traeger and John T. Newell, Grand Trustees Joseph J. McShane and Eldred L. Meyer, Grand Outside Sentinel William A. Reuter, District Deputies Howard Bentley, Edwin Baldwin, Walter Baskerville and Harry Honn.

March 1 the Parlor starts a membership drive, which will be in progress to May 1. March 15 will be past presidents night, and there will be special entertainment features and other attractions. Secretary Smith assures "a big night for all."

ANNIVERSARY CELEBRATED.

Long Beach—In a pretty spring setting of ferns and sweetpeas, the officers of Long Beach Parlor No. 154 N.D.G.W., with Miss Eleanor Johnson as president, were publicly installed February 2 by Deputy Nellie Cline. Entertainment was contributed by Marietta Brown, Orville Cooper, Ruth Dwelly and Kermit Holven. Clara Fay, Daisy Hansen, Victoria Thompson and Elnora Martin constituted the refreshments committee, and Lillian Lassiter and Daisy Hansen had charge of the decorations. Among the visitors were a delegation from Grace No. 242 (Fullerton). The thimble club met February 9 at the home of Alice Waldow and completed tying a comfort. A bridge-bunco party was held at Kate McFadyen's home February 11.

A birthday party celebrating the Parlor's twenty-sixth institution anniversary was held February 16. Louise McDougall was the chairman. Several members of Rudecinda No. 230 (San Pedro) were guests. A bridge-luncheon was held February 23 at the home of Lillian Lassiter. A plunkett dinner and card party will be held March 2; Mrs. Lassiter heads the arrangements committee.

DANCE WITH THE CABALLEROS.

Ramona Parlor No. 109 N.S.G.W. initiated three candidates February 16. Deputy Grand President Albert V. Mayrhofer, a visitor, gave a resume of the splendid work being accomplished by San Diego No. 108, and urged co-operation with all organizations and agencies that are in sympathy with the Order's undertakings. Past Grand Herman C. Lichtenberger and Edward Fitzgerald were among the other speakers. Walter Slosson distributed additional "1933 Bear Club" pins.

March 25 the "Doce Caballeros," an auxiliary of the Parlor commendably promoting the best interests of the Order and deserving encouragement, will give another dance at Patriotic Hall. Ralph Harbison assures all who attend a good time. First Vice-president Charles Straube says he has heard it announced that No. 109 will this year celebrate its birthday with a big affair at Catalina.

Ramona's March calendar includes: 10th, initiation. 17th, monthly birthday dinner for those members born in March; all members of the Order and their friends of both sexes invited; Henry Carter will speak on "The Boundaries of the Counties of the State;" reservations must be made with Secretary John Scott not later than March 10. 24th, reception to those members initiated during March of previous years. 31st, nomination of delegates to Grass Valley Grand Parlor.

SPIRIT OF ENDEAVOR PERVADES.

Santa Monica—Kathryn Worsham was chairman of the bridge-dinner given by Santa Monica Bay Parlor No. 245 N.D.G.W. January 25. February 15, Native Sons were guests at a spanish dinner in charge of Elizabeth Valencia. February 18, Helen Burke, Myrtle Barden and Rosalie Hyde of the Parlor's welfare committee visited the National Soldiers Home at Sawtelle and distributed jams, jellies, magazines and jigsaw puzzles. A Washington party, February 22, was in charge of Mary Rittner and Helen Burke.

A spirit of endeavor pervades the Parlor, and planned events include a beach club bridge breakfast, Emelia Sundquist chairman; a patio bridge at the Beverly Hills home of Catherine Conterno; a dance, Myrtle Barden chairman; a benefit bridge at the Elks Club, sponsored by Willette Biscailuz.

THE DEATH RECORD.

Mrs. Gertrude Schilz, mother of Nicholas M. Schilz (Ramona N.S.), died February 4 at the age of 73.

Mrs. Laura Sagar, wife of William S. Sagar (Los Angeles N.S.), died February 16. She was a daughter of John T. Newell (Past Grand President N.S.) and a sister of William G. Newell (Los Angeles N.S.).

Mrs. Mary B. Pico, mother of Mrs. Lisita Pico-Williamson (Californiana N.D.), died February 20.

HOMELESS CHILDREN BENEFIT.

The N.S.G.W. and N.D.G.W. Homeless Children Committee has elected the following officers: Irving Baxter, chairman; Grace Norton, vice-chairman; Annie L. Adair, secretary; Calista Stefan, treasurer; John Gower, financial secretary.

Hazel B. Hansen, N.D. Grand Outside Sentinel, and Eldred L. Meyer, N.S. Grand Trustee, head a joint committee appointed to arrange for the annual homeless children benefit ball, which will be held at the Breakfast Club, April 22. At a preliminary meeting of the joint committee at the home of Mrs. Edward Taber, February 17, several subcommittees were named to look after details.

HEARS OF CHINA.

The "oldtimers nite" of Hollywood Parlor No. 196 N.S.G.W. attracted a large crowd, including a big delegation from University No. 272.

(Continued on Page 20)

CLASSIFIED DIRECTORY
LOS ANGELES NATIVE SONS

ATTORNEYS-AT-LAW.

HENRY G. BODKIN. — V. P. LUCAS.
Chester Williams Bldg., 215 W. 5th St.
Phone: MUtual 3151.

DAVID H. CLARK.
215 West Fifth St.
Phone: MUtual 5406.

EDWIN A. MESERVE. — SHIRLEY E. MESERVE.
555 So. Flower St.
Phone: TRinity 4161.

THOS. B. REED.
548 South Spring St.
Phone: VAndike 0687.

DETECTIVE SERVICE.

LOUIS A. DUNI.
522 Washington Bldg., 311½ So. Spring.
Phone: TUcker 3013.

GENERAL INSURANCE.

THOMAS C. STEPHENS.
208 W. Eighth St., Suite 926.
Phone: TUcker 5543.

RIGHT NOW IS A GOOD TIME
TO BECOME A SUBSCRIBER TO
THE GRIZZLY BEAR
The ALL California Monthly

Official Directory of Parlors of the N. D. G. W.

ALAMEDA COUNTY.

Angelita No. 32, Livermore—Meets 2nd and 4th Fridays, Foresters Hall; Mrs. Myrtle I. Johnson, Rec. Sec., P.O. box 253.

Piedmont No. 87, Oakland—Meets Thursdays, Corinthian Hall, Pacific Bldg.; Miss Helen Ring, Rec. Sec., 822 11th St.

Aloha No. 106, Oakland—Meets Tuesdays, Wigwam Hall, Pacific Bldg.; Mrs. Lurine Martin, Rec. Sec., 2815 Wallace St., Berkeley.

Hayward No. 122, Hayward—Meets 1st and 3rd Tuesdays, Veterans Memorial Bldg., Main St.; Miss Ruth Gansberger, Rec. Sec., P. O. box 44, Mount Eden.

Berkeley No. 150, Berkeley—Meets 2nd Saturday afternoon, Berkeley City Women's Club, 2315 Durant; Mrs. Lelia B. Baker, Rec. Sec., 915 Contra Costa Ave.

Bear Flag No. 151, Berkeley—Meets 2nd and 4th Wednesdays, Veterans Memorial Bldg., 1931 Center St.; Mrs. Maud Wagner, Rec. Sec., 317 Alcatraz Ave., Oakland.

Encinal No. 156, Alameda—Meets 2nd and 4th Wednesdays, Veterans Memorial Bldg., Central Ave. and Walnut St.; Mrs. Laura E. Fisher, Rec. Sec., 1413 Caroline St.

Brooklyn No. 157, East Oakland—Meets 2nd and 4th Wednesdays, Masonic Temple, 8th Ave. and E. 14th St.; Mrs. Ruth Cooney, Rec. Sec., 3907 14th Ave.

Argonaut No. 166, Oakland—Meets Tuesdays, Klinkner Hall, 59th and San Pablo; Mrs. Ada Spilman, Rec. Sec., 2905 Ellis St., Berkeley.

Bahia Vista No. 167, Oakland—Meets Thursdays, Wigwam Hall, Pacific Bldg.; Mrs. Minnie E. Rapar, Rec. Sec., 3449 Helen St.

Fruitvale No. 177, Oakland—Meets Fridays, W.O.W. Hall; May E. Barthold, Rec. Sec., 3832 Santa Rita St.

Laura Loma No. 182, Niles—Meets 1st and 3rd Tuesdays, I.O.O.F. Hall; Mrs. Ethel Fournier, Rec. Sec., P. O. box 515.

El Cereso No. 207, San Leandro—Meets 2nd and 4th Tuesdays, Masonic Hall; Mrs. Mary Tuttle, Rec. Sec., P. O. box 56.

Pleasanton No. 237, Pleasanton—Meets 1st Tuesday. I.O.O.F. Hall; Mrs. Myrtle Lanini, Rec. Sec.

Betsy Ross No. 238, Centerville—Meets 1st and 3rd Fridays, Anderson Hall; Miss Constance Lucio, Rec. Sec., P. O. box 187.

AMADOR COUNTY.

Ursula No. 1, Jackson—Meets 2nd and 4th Tuesdays, N.S.G.W. Hall; Mrs. Emma Boarman-Wright, Rec. Sec., 114 Court St.

Chispa No. 40, Ione—Meets 2nd and 4th Fridays, N.S.G.W. Hall; Mrs. Isabel Ashton, Rec. Sec.

Amapola No. 80, Sutter Creek—Meets 2nd and 4th Thursdays, N.S.G.W. Bldg.; Mrs. Hazel M. Marre, Rec. Sec.

Forrest No. 86, Plymouth—Meets 2nd and 4th Tuesdays, I.O.O.F. Hall; Mrs. Marguerite Davis, Rec. Sec.

BUTTE COUNTY.

Annie K. Bidwell No. 168, Chico—Meets 2nd and 4th Thursdays, I.O.O.F. Hall; Mrs. Irene Henry, Rec. Sec., 3015 Woodland Ave.

Gold of Ophir No. 190, Oroville—Meets 1st and 3rd Wednesdays, Memorial Hall; Mrs. Ruth Brown, Rec. Sec., 1265 Leah Court.

CALAVERAS COUNTY.

Ruby No. 46, Murphys—Meets 4th Friday, N.S.G.W. Hall; Belle Segale, Rec. Sec.

Princess No. 84, Angels Camp—Meets 2nd and 4th Wednesdays, I.O.O.F. Hall; Mrs. Grace M. Mills, Rec. Sec., P.O. box 313.

San Andreas No. 113, San Andreas—Meets 1st Friday, Fraternal Hall; Miss Doris Treat, Rec. Sec.

COLUSA COUNTY.

Colus No. 194, Colusa—Meets 1st and 3rd Mondays, Eagles Hall; Miss Kate Busch, Rec. Sec., 350 Market St.

CONTRA COSTA COUNTY.

Stirling No. 146, Pittsburg—Meets 1st and 3rd Wednesdays, Veteran Memorial Hall; Mrs. Leslie Clement, Rec. Sec., 468 E. Santa Fe.

Richmond No. 147, Richmond—Meets 1st and 3rd Tuesdays, I.O.O.F. Hall, 10th St.; Grace Curry, Rec. Sec., 932 Ohio Ave.

Donner No. 193, Byron—Meets 1st and 3rd Wednesdays, I.O.O.F. Hall; Mrs. Anna Pendry, Rec. Sec., P. O. box 112.

Las Juntas No. 221, Martinez—Meets 1st and 3rd Mondays, Pythian Castle; Mrs. Lola O. Viera, Rec. Sec., R.F.D. No. 1.

Antioch No. 223, Antioch—Meets 2nd and 4th Tuesdays, I.O.O.F. Hall; Mrs. Estelle Evans, Rec. Sec., 202 E. 5th St., Pittsburg.

Carquinez No. 234, Crockett—Meets 2nd and 4th Wednesdays, I.O.O.F. Hall; Mrs. Cecile Petee, Rec. Sec., 465 Edwards St.

EL DORADO COUNTY.

Marguerite No. 12, Placerville—Meets 1st and 3rd Wednesdays, Masonic Hall; Mrs. Nettie Leonardi, Rec. Sec., 25 Coloma St.

El Dorado No. 186, Georgetown—Meets 2nd and 4th Saturday afternoons, I.O.O.F. Hall; Mrs. Alta L. Douglas, Rec. Sec.

FRESNO COUNTY.

Fresno No. 187, Fresno—Meets 2nd and 4th Fridays, Pythian Castle, Cor. "R" and Merced Sts.; Mary Aubery, Rec. Sec., 1040 Delphia Ave.

GRAND OFFICERS.

Mrs. Evelyn I. Carlson..........Past Grand President
281 E. Tuscaloosa Ave., Atherton
Mrs. Anna M. Armstrong..........Grand President
Woodland
Mrs. Irma Laird..........Grand Vice-president
Alturas
Mrs. Sallie R. Thaler..........Grand Secretary
555 Baker St., San Francisco
Mrs. Susie K. Christ..........Grand Treasurer
555 Baker St., San Francisco
Mrs. Gladys Noce..........Grand Marshal
Sutter Creek
Mrs. Orinda G. Giannini..........Grand Inside Sentinel
2142 Filbert St., San Francisco
Mrs. Hazel B. Hansen..........Grand Outside Sentinel
501 Griswold St., Glendale
Mrs. Clara Gairaud..........Grand Organist
134 Locust St., San Jose

GRAND TRUSTEES.

Mrs. Florence Boyle..........Oroville
Mrs. Edna Briggs..........1045 Santa Ynez Way, Sacramento
Mrs. Anna Thuesen..........615 38th Ave., San Francisco
Mrs. Ethel Begley..........233 Prospect Ave., San Francisco
Mrs. Minna K. Horn..........Etna
Mrs. Jane Vick..........418 Bath St., Santa Barbara
Mrs. Willow Borba..........330 So. Main St., Sebastopol

GLENN COUNTY.

Berryessa No. 192, Willows—Meets 1st and 3rd Mondays, I.O.O.F. Hall; Mrs. Leonora Neate, Rec. Sec., 338 No. Lassen St.

HUMBOLDT COUNTY.

Occident No. 28, Eureka—Meets 1st and 3rd Wednesdays, N.S.G.W. Hall; Mrs. Eva L. MacDonald, Rec. Sec., 2309 "B" St.

Oneonta No. 71, Ferndale—Meets 2nd and 4th Fridays, I.O.O.F. Hall; Mrs. Myra Rumrill, Rec. Sec., P.O. box 142.

Reichling No. 97, Fortuna—Meets 1st and 3rd Tuesdays, Friendship Hall; Mrs. Grace Swett, Rec. Sec., P. O. box 328.

KERN COUNTY.

Miocene No. 228, Taft—Meets 1st and 3rd Wednesday afternoons, I.O.O.F. Hall; Mrs. Evalyn G. Towne, Rec. Sec., P. O. box 1011.

El Tejon No. 239, Bakersfield—Meets 1st and 3rd Fridays, Eagles Hall, 1714 "G" St.; Mary B. Hampson, Rec. Sec., 908 Quincy St.

Desert Gold No. 250, Mojave—Meets 2nd and 4th Fridays, I.O.O.F. Hall; Rein H. Everett, Rec. Sec., P.O. box 83.

LAKE COUNTY.

Clear Lake No. 135, Middletown—Meets 2nd and 4th Tuesdays, Herrick Hall; Mrs. Alma E. Snow, Rec. Sec.

LASSEN COUNTY.

Nataqua No. 152, Standish—Meets 1st and 3rd Wednesdays, Foresters Hall; Mrs. Mayda Elledge, Rec. Sec.

Mount Lassen No. 215, Bieber—Meets 2nd and 4th Thursdays, I.O.O.F. Hall; Mrs. Angie C. Kenyon, Rec. Sec.

Susanville No. 243, Susanville—Meets 3rd Thursday, I.O.O.F. Hall; Mildred Hardy, Rec. Sec., P.O. box 425.

LOS ANGELES COUNTY.

Los Angeles No. 124, Los Angeles—Meets 1st and 3rd Wednesdays, I.O.O.F. Hall, Washington and Oak Sts.; Mrs. Mary K. Corcoran, Rec. Sec., 322 No. Van Ness Ave.

Long Beach No. 154, Long Beach—Meets 1st and 3rd Thursdays, K.P. Hall, 341 Pacific Ave.; Mrs. Bertha Hitt, Rec. Sec., 5355 Lime Ave.

Rudecinda No. 230, San Pedro—Meets 2nd and 4th Thursdays, Unity Hall, I.O.O.F. Temple, 10th and Gaffey; Letitia Sarciaux, Rec. Sec., 1054 W. 24th St.

Verdugo No. 240, Glendale—Meets 2nd and 4th Tuesdays, Masonic Temple, 284 So. Brand Blvd.; Miss Etta Fulkerth, Rec. Sec., 526 No. Orange St.

Santa Monica Bay No. 245, Santa Monica—Meets 2nd and 4th Wednesdays, Odd Fellows Hall, 1431 Third St.; Mrs. Rosalie Hyde, Rec. Sec., 738 Flower St., Venice.

Californiana No. 247, Los Angeles—Meets 2nd and 4th Tuesday afternoons, Hollywood Studio Club, 1215 Lodi Place; Mrs. Inez Sitton, Rec. Sec., 4223 Berenice St.

MADERA COUNTY.

Madera No. 244, Madera—Meets 2nd and 4th Thursdays, Masonic Annex; Mrs. Margaret C. Boyle, Rec. Sec., 111 No. "B" St.

MARIN COUNTY.

Sea Point No. 196, Sausalito—Meets 2nd and 4th Mondays, Perry Hall, 50 Caledonia St.; Mrs. Mary B. Smith, Rec. Sec., 47½ Glen Drive.

Marinita No. 198, San Rafael—Meets 2nd and 4th Mondays, 316 "B" St.; Miss Mollye Y. Spaelti, Rec. Sec., 539 4th St.

Fairfax No. 225, Fairfax—Meets 2nd and 4th Tuesdays, Community Hall; Mrs. Marguerite Geary, Rec. Sec.

Tamelpa No. 231, Mill Valley—Meets 1st and 2nd Tuesdays, I.O.O.F. Hall; Mrs. Delphine M. Todt, Rec. Sec., 400 Grand Ave., San Rafael.

MARIPOSA COUNTY.

Mariposa No. 63, Mariposa—Meets 1st and 3rd Fridays, I.O.O.F. Hall; Elizabeth E. Johnson, Rec. Sec.

MENDOCINO COUNTY.

Fort Bragg No. 210, Fort Bragg—Meets 1st and 3rd Thursdays, I.O.O.F. Hall; Mrs. Ruth W. Fuller, Rec. Sec.

MERCED COUNTY.

Veritas No. 75, Merced—Meets 1st and 3rd Tuesdays, I.O.O.F. Hall; Miss Flora Fernandes, Rec. Sec., Parkside Apt.

MODOC COUNTY.

Alturas No. 159, Alturas—Meets 1st Thursday, Alturas Civic Club; Mrs. Irma W. Laird, Rec. Sec.

MONTEREY COUNTY.

Aleli No. 102, Salinas—Meets 2nd and 4th Thursdays, Pythian Hall; Miss Rose Rhyner, Rec. Sec., 420 Soledad St.

Junipero No. 141, Monterey—Meets 2nd and 4th Fridays, K. of P. Hall, Main St.; Miss Matilda M. Bergschicker, Rec. Sec., 498 Van Buren St.

NAPA COUNTY.

Eshcol No. 16, Napa—Meets 2nd and 4th Mondays, N.S.G.W. Hall; Mrs. Ella Ingram, Rec. Sec., 2140 Seminary St.

Calistoga No. 145, Calistoga—Meets 2nd and 4th Mondays, I.O.O.F. Hall; Sadie P. Brooks, Rec. Sec.

La Junta No. 203, Saint Helena—Meets 1st and 3rd Tuesdays, N.S.G.W. Hall; Mrs. Marie Signorelli, Rec. Sec., 1341 Madrona Ave.

ATTENTION, SECRETARIES!

THIS DIRECTORY IS PUBLISHED BY AUTHORITY OF THE GRAND PARLOR N.D.G.W., AND ALL NOTICES OF CHANGES MUST BE RECEIVED BY THE GRAND SECRETARY (NOT THE MAGAZINE) ON OR BEFORE THE 20TH OF EACH MONTH TO INSURE CORRECTION IN NEXT PUBLICATION OF DIRECTORY.

NEVADA COUNTY.

Laurel No. 6, Nevada City—Meets 1st and 3rd Wednesdays, I.O.O.F. Hall; Mrs. Nellie E. Clark, Rec. Sec., 412 Pine St.

Manzanita No. 29, Grass Valley—Meets 1st and 3rd Tuesdays, Auditorium; Mrs. Loraine Keast, Rec. Sec., 128 Race St.

Columbia No. 70, French Corral—Meets Fridays, Farrelley Hall; Mrs. Kate Farrelley-Sullivan, Rec. Sec.

Snow Peak No. 176, Truckee—Meets 1st Monday, I.O.O.F. Hall; Mrs. Henrietta M. Eaton, Rec. Sec., P. O. box 116

ORANGE COUNTY.

Santa Ana No. 235, Santa Ana—Meets 2nd and 4th Mondays, K.C. Hall, 4th and French Sts.; Mrs. Matilda S. Lemon, Rec. Sec., 1628 W. 8th St.

Grace No. 242, Fullerton—Meets 1st and 3rd Thursdays, I.O.O.F. Hall, 116½ E. Commonwealth; Mrs. Mary R. Rothnermel, Rec. Sec., Acacia St. & Commonwealth.

PLACER COUNTY.

Placer No. 138, Lincoln—Meets 2nd Wednesday, I.O.O.F. Hall; Miss Carrie Parlin, Rec. Sec.

La Rosa No. 191, Roseville—Meets 1st and 3rd Tuesdays, Eagles Hall; Mrs. Alice Lee West, Rec. Sec., Rocklin.

Auburn No. 233, Auburn—Meets 2nd and 4th Fridays, Foresters Hall; Mrs. Elsie Patrick, Rec. Sec.

PLUMAS COUNTY.

Plumas Pioneer No. 219, Quincy—Meets 1st and 3rd Mondays, I.O.O.F. Hall; Minnie E. Johnson, Rec. Sec., P. O. box 243.

SACRAMENTO COUNTY.

Califia No. 22, Sacramento—Meets 2nd and 4th Tuesdays, N.S.G.W. Hall; Miss Lulu Gillis, Rec. Sec., 921 8th St.

La Bandera No. 110, Sacramento—Meets 1st and 3rd Fridays, N.S.G.W. Hall; Mrs. Clara Weldon, Rec. Sec., 131[illegible] "O" St.

Sutter No. 111, Sacramento—Meets 1st and 3rd Tuesdays, N.S.G.W. Hall; Mrs. Adele Nix, Rec. Sec., 1238 "S" St.

Fern No. 123, Folsom—Meets 1st and 3rd Tuesdays, K.P. Hall; Elizabeth Ryan, Rec. Sec., Represa.

Chabolla No. 171, Galt—Meets 2nd and 4th Tuesdays, I.O.O.F. Hall; Mrs. Mary Pritchard, Rec. Sec.

Coloma No. 212, Sacramento—Meets 1st and 3rd Tuesdays, I.O.O.F. Hall, Oak Park; Mrs. Nettie Harry, Rec. Sec., 1217 35th St.

Liberty No. 213, Elk Grove—Meets 2nd and 4th Fridays, I.O.O.F. Hall; Mrs. Frances Wackman, Rec. Sec., P. O. box 192.

Victory No. 216, Courtland—Meets 1st Saturday and 3rd Monday, N.S.G.W. Hall; Mrs. Agneda Lample, Rec. Sec.

SAN BENITO COUNTY.

Copa de Oro No. 105, Hollister—Meets 2nd and 4th Thursdays, Grangers Union Hall; Mrs. Mollie Daveggio, Rec. Sec., 110 San Benito St.

San Juan Bautista No. 179, San Juan Bautista—Meets 1st Wednesday, Mission Corridor Rooms; Miss Gertrude Breen, Rec. Sec.

SAN BERNARDINO COUNTY.

Lugonia No. 241, San Bernardino—Meets 2nd and 4th Wednesdays, Eagles Hall; Miss Lois Poling, Rec. Sec., 295 E. 11th St.

Ontario No. 251, Ontario—Meets 2nd and 4th Thursdays, Ontario Hotel; Miss Helen Hickman, Rec. Sec., 923 No. Laurel Ave.

SAN DIEGO COUNTY.

San Diego No. 208, San Diego—Meets 2nd and 4th Wednesdays, Directors Room, Chamber Commerce Bldg., 49[illegible] W. Broadway; Mrs. Elsie Case, Rec. Sec., 3051 Broadway

SAN FRANCISCO CITY AND COUNTY.

Minerva No. 2, San Francisco—Meets 1st and 3rd Wednesdays, N.S.G.W. Bldg.; Miss Dorothy Finn, Rec. Sec., 9[illegible] Princess St., Sausalito.

Alta No. 3, San Francisco—Meets 2nd and 4th Tuesdays, N.S.G.W. Bldg.; Mrs. Aguese L. Hughes, Rec. Sec., 398[illegible] Sacramento St.

Oro Fino No. 9, San Francisco—Meets 1st and 3rd Thursdays, N.S.G.W. Bldg.; Mrs. Josephine B. Morrissey, Rec. Sec., 4441 20th St.

Golden State No. 50, San Francisco—Meets 1st and 3rd Wednesdays, N.D.G.W. Home; Miss Millie Tietjen, Rec. Sec., 328 Lexington Ave.

Orinda No. 56, San Francisco—Meets 2nd, 4th and 5th Fridays, N.D.G.W. Home; Mrs. Anna A. Gruber-Loser, Rec. Sec., 72 Grove Lane, San Anselmo.

Fremont No. 59, San Francisco—Meets 1st and 3rd Tuesdays, N.S.G.W. Bldg.; Miss Hannah Collins, Rec. Sec., 617 Fillmore St.

Buena Vista No. 68, San Francisco—Meets 1st, 3rd and 5th Thursdays, N.D.G.W. Home; Miss Margaret Barrett, Rec. Sec., 3774 20th St.

Las Lomas No. 72, San Francisco—Meets 1st and 3rd Tuesdays, N.D.G.W. Home; Mrs. Marion S. Day, Rec. Sec., 469 Noe St.

Yosemite No. 83, San Francisco—Meets 1st and 3rd Tuesdays, American Hall, 20th and Capp Sts.; Miss Mary Monahan, Rec. Sec., 237 Noe St.

La Estrella No. 89, San Francisco—Meets 2nd and 4th Mondays, N.S.G.W. Bldg.; Miss Birdie Hartman, Rec. Sec., 1018 Jackson St.

Sans Souci No. 96, San Francisco—Meets 2nd and 4th Mondays, N.D.G.W. Home; Mrs. Minnie F. Dobbin, Rec. Sec., 1483 43rd Ave.

Calaveras No. 103, San Francisco—Meets 2nd and 4th Tuesdays, Swedish American Hall, 2174 Market St.; Mary L. Krogh, Rec. Sec., 4235 Cabrillo St.

Darina No. 114, San Francisco—Meets 1st and 3rd Mondays, N.S.G.W. Bldg.; Miss Adele Walsh, Rec. Sec., 47[illegible] Page St.

El Vespero No. 118, San Francisco—Meets 2nd and 4th Tuesdays, Masonic Hall, 4705 3rd St.; Mrs. Nell B. Boege, Rec. Sec., 1526 Kirkwood Ave.

Genevieve No. 132, San Francisco—Meets 1st and 3rd Thursdays, N.S.G.W. Bldg.; Miss Branice Peguillan, Rec. Sec., 2434 16th Ave.

Keith No. 137, San Francisco—Meets 2nd and 4th Thursdays, N.S.G.W. Bldg.; Mrs. Helen T. Mann, Rec. Sec., 575 Pierce St., Apt. 206.

Gabrielle No. 139, San Francisco—Meets 2nd and 4th Wednesdays, N.S.G.W. Bldg.; Mrs. Dorothy Wuesterfeld, Rec. Sec., 1020 Munich St.

Presidio No. 148, San Francisco—Meets 2nd and 4th Tuesdays, N.S.G.W. Bldg.; Mrs. Hattie Gaughran, Rec. Sec., 713 Capp St.

Guadalupe No. 153, San Francisco—Meets 2nd and 4th Mondays, Forester Hall, 170 Valencia St.; Miss May A. McCarthy, Rec. Sec., 336 Elsie St.

Golden Gate No. 158, San Francisco—Meets 2nd and 4th Mondays, N.S.G.W. Bldg.; Mrs. Mary Sullivan, Rec. Sec., 33 Cuvier St.

Dolores No. 169, San Francisco—Meets 2nd and 4th Wednesdays, N.S.G.W. Bldg.; Mrs. Ada Saunders, Rec. Sec., 284 Allison St.

Linda Rosa No. 170, San Francisco—Meets 2nd and 4th Wednesdays, Swedish American Hall, 2174 Market St.; Mrs. Eva P. Tyrrel, Rec. Sec., 2629 Mission St.

Portola No. 172, San Francisco—Meets 1st and 3rd Tuesdays, N.S.G.W. Bldg.; Catherine H. Dolly, Rec. Sec., 4125 23rd St.
Castro No. 178, San Francisco—Meets 1st and 3rd Wednesdays, K.C. Bldg., 150 Golden Gate Ave.; Miss Adeline Sandersfeld, Rec Sec., 50 Baker St.
Twin Peaks No. 185, San Francisco—Meets 2nd and 4th Fridays, Druids Temple, 44 Page St.; Mrs. Loretta Cameron, Rec. Sec., 3969 Army St.
James Lick No. 220, San Francisco—Meets 1st and 3rd Wednesdays, N.S.G.W. Bldg.; Mrs. Edna Bishop, Rec. Sec., 3341 24th St.
Mission No. 227, San Francisco—Meets 2nd and 4th Fridays, N.S.G.W. Bldg.; Mrs. Ann Dippel, Rec. Sec., 448 Dewey Blvd.
Bret Harte No. 232, San Francisco—Meets 2nd and 4th Tuesdays, Aloha Hall, 3009 16th St.; Pearl Wedde, Rec. Sec., 225 7th Ave.
La Dorada No. 236, San Francisco—Meets 2nd and 4th Thursdays, N.S.G.W. Hall; Mrs. Theresa R. O'Brien, Rec. Sec. 567 Liberty St.
Balboa No. 249, San Francisco—Meets 1st and 3rd Thursdays, Knights Columbus Hall, 382 18th Ave.; Miss Jean Moffet, Rec. Sec., 476 26th Ave.
Utopia No. 252, San Francisco—Meets 2nd and 4th Tuesdays, American Hall, 20th and Capp Sts.; Miss Lelia M. Little, Rec. Sec., 4450 20th St.

SAN JOAQUIN COUNTY.

Joaquin No. 5, Stockton—Meets 2nd and 4th Tuesdays, N.S.G.W. Hall, 314 E. Main St.; Mrs. Della Garvin, Rec. Sec., 1122 E. Market St.
El Pescadero No. 82, Tracy—Meets 1st and 3rd Fridays, I.O.O.F. Hall; Mrs. Mary A. Hewitson, Rec. Sec., 122 Walnut St.
Ivy No. 88, Lodi—Meets 1st and 3rd Wednesdays, Eagles Hall; Mrs. Mae Corson, Rec. Sec., 109 So. School St.
Calis de Oro No. 206, Stockton—Meets 1st and 3rd Tuesdays, N.S.G.W. Hall, 314 E. Main St.; Mrs. Frances Germain, Rec. Sec., 450 No. Regent.
Phoebe A. Hearst No. 214, Manteca—Meets 2nd and 4th Wednesdays, I.O.O.F. Hall; Mrs. Josie M. Frederick, Rec. Sec., Route A, Box 364, Ripon.

SAN LUIS OBISPO COUNTY.

San Miguel No. 94, San Miguel—Meets 2nd and 4th Wednesday afternoons, Clemon Hall; Mrs. Nellie Wickstrom, Rec. Sec.
San Luisita No. 108, San Luis Obispo—Meets 2nd and 4th Thursdays, W.O.W. Hall; Miss Agnes M. Lee, Rec. Sec., P. O. box 584.
El Pinal No. 163, Cambria—Meets 2nd, 4th and 5th Tuesdays, N.S.G.W. Hall; Kathryn Luchessa, Rec. Sec.

SAN MATEO COUNTY.

Bonita No. 10, Redwood City—Meets 2nd and 4th Thursdays, I.O.O.F. Hall; Mrs. Dora Wilson, Rec. Sec., 518 Middlefield Rd.
Vista del Mar No. 155, Halfmoon Bay—Meets 2nd and 4th Thursdays, I.O.O.F. Hall; Elizabeth Olney, Rec. Sec.
Ano Nuevo No. 180, Pescadero—Meets 1st and 3rd Wednesdays, I.O.O.F. Hall; Mrs. Alice Mattei, Rec. Sec.
El Carmelo No. 181, Daly City—Meets 1st and 3rd Wednesdays, Masonic Hall; Miss Alice Mathias, Rec. Sec., 2218 26th Ave., San Francisco.
Menlo No. 211, Menlo Park—Meets 2nd and 4th Mondays, Masonic Hall; Mrs. Frances E. Maloney, Rec. Sec., P. O. box 626.
San Bruno No. 246, San Bruno—Meets 2nd and 4th Fridays, Legion Hall; Miss Mildred Foley, Rec. Sec., 217 Miller Ave., South San Francisco.

SANTA BARBARA COUNTY.

Reina del Mar No. 126, Santa Barbara—Meets 1st and 3rd Tuesdays, Pythian Castle, 222 W. Carillo St.; Mrs. Dorothy Yule, Rec. Sec., 112 Ocean Ave.

SANTA CLARA COUNTY.

San Jose No. 81, San Jose—Meets Thursdays, Catholic Women Center, 5th and San Fernando Sts.; Mrs. Nellie Fleming, Rec. Sec., Catholic Women Center.
Vendome No. 100, San Jose—Meets Wednesdays, Old Scottish Rite Temple; Miss Marie Buck, Rec. Sec., 245 Hawthorne St.
El Monte No. 205, Mountain View—Meets 2nd and 4th Fridays, American Legion Hall; Miss Elizabeth Spencer, Rec. Sec., 512 Hope St.
Palo Alto No. 229, Palo Alto—Meets 1st and 2nd Mondays, N.S.G.W. Hall; Miss Helena G. Hansen, Rec. Sec., 531 Lytton Ave.

SANTA CRUZ COUNTY.

Santa Cruz No. 26, Santa Cruz—Meets Mondays, N.S.G.W. Hall; Mrs. May L. Williamson, Rec. Sec., 170 Walnut Ave.
El Pajaro No. 35, Watsonville—Meets 1st and 3rd Tuesdays, I.O.O.F. Hall; Miss Ruth E. Wilson, Rec. Sec., 16 Laurel St.

SHASTA COUNTY.

Camellia No. 41, Anderson—Meets 1st and 3rd Tuesdays, Masonic Hall; Mrs. Olga E. Welbourn, Rec. Sec.
Lassen View No. 98, Shasta—Meets 2nd Friday, Masonic Hall; Miss Louise Litsch, Rec. Sec.
Hiawatha No. 140, Redding—Meets 2nd and 4th Wednesdays, Moose Hall; Ruth Presleigh, Rec. Sec., Office County Clerk.

SIERRA COUNTY.

Naomi No. 36, Downieville—Meets 2nd and 4th Wednesdays, I.O.O.F. Hall; Louise C. Dubuque, Rec. Sec.
Imogen No. 134, Sierraville—Meets 2nd and 4th Saturday afternoons, Copren Hall; Mrs. Jennie Copren, Rec. Sec.

SISKIYOU COUNTY.

Eschscholtzia No. 112, Etna—Meets 1st and 3rd Wednesdays, Masonic Hall; Mrs. Bernice E. Smith, Rec. Sec.
Mountain Dawn No. 120, Sawyers Bar—Meets 2nd and last Wednesdays, I.O.O.F. Hall; Miss Edith Dunphy, Rec. Sec.

SOLANO COUNTY.

Vallejo No. 195, Vallejo—Meets 1st and 3rd Wednesdays, K.C. Hall, 820 Marin St.; Mrs. Mary Combs, Rec. Sec., 511 York St.
Mary E. Bell No. 224, Dixon—Meets 2nd and 4th Thursdays, I.O.O.F. Hall; Mary Young, Rec. Sec.

SONOMA COUNTY.

Sonoma No. 209, Sonoma—Meets 2nd and 4th Mondays, I.O.O.F. Hall; Mrs. Mae Norrbom, Rec. Sec., R.F.D., box 171.
Santa Rosa No. 217, Santa Rosa—Meets 1st and 3rd Thursdays, N.S.G.W. Hall; Mrs. Clytie L. Lewis, Rec. Sec., R.F.D. No. 4, Box 345-A.
Petaluma No. 222, Petaluma—Meets 1st and 3rd Tuesdays, Dania Hall; Mrs. Margaret M. Oeltjen, Rec. Sec., 503 Prospect St.

STANISLAUS COUNTY.

Oakdale No. 125, Oakdale—Meets 1st Monday, I.O.O.F. Hall; Mrs. Lou Reeder, Rec. Sec.
Morada No. 199, Modesto—Meets 2nd and 4th Wednesdays, I.O.O.F. Hall; Mrs. Susan Sullivan, Rec. Sec., 828 10th St.
Eldora No. 248, Turlock—Meets 1st and 3rd Mondays, Masonic Temple; Effie Lund, Rec. Sec., 312 Mitchell St.

SUTTER COUNTY.

South Butte No. 226, Sutter—Meets 1st and 3rd Mondays, N.D.G.W. Hall; Mrs. Abbie N. Vagedes, Rec. Sec.

TEHAMA COUNTY.

Berendos No. 23, Red Bluff—Meets 1st and 3rd Tuesdays, W.O.W. Hall, 200 Pine St.; Mrs. Lillie Hammer, Rec. Sec., 636 Jackson St.

In Memoriam

THOMAS P. BOYD.

Once again Death has invaded our ranks and taken a well-beloved brother. Thomas P. Boyd, a Past President of Mount Tamalpais Parlor No. 64 N.S.G.W. has answered the final call. To those who knew him best, this passing is an irreparable loss. He was one of those splendid characters whom this Parlor has been justly proud to claim as a member, whose affiliation has helped to give it the enviable standing and prestige it has ever enjoyed in this community.

Brother Thomas P. Boyd was a self-made man. Left an orphan at an early age by the passing of his father, a hardy Pioneer, he quickly realized the importance of preparing himself for the serious affairs of life. A good mind, hard work and close application to his studies soon enabled him to reach the highest attainments in his profession.

Self-sacrificing and self-effacing, he sought no political preferment. After serving several terms at the important post of District Attorney of Marin County, with credit to himself and satisfaction to the community, he renounced all further ambition in that direction. Kindly and sympathetic, he devoted much of his time and talents to aiding his less-fortunate fellow-citizens. His loyalty to his clients won him a splendid reputation in his profession.

An ardent believer in the cause of education, he served his community well, sparing neither time nor labor in its advancement. His unwavering devotion to his political principles, prompted by motives of highest patriotism, gained for him the respect and admiration of friend and foe alike. No triumph, however great, made him arrogant; no defeat discouraged him.

A just man, an earnest leader, a kind and loving husband, father, brother and son, we deeply deplore his passing, and we extend to his bereaved family our most sincere sympathy in their dark hour of sorrow. We realize how futile it is for us to attempt to comfort them, and we commend them to the Just and Merciful Father who, in His infinite wisdom, has called our brother to his eternal rest.

Resolved, That a copy of this memorial be spread upon the minutes of the Parlor, that a copy be sent to the bereaved family, and that a copy be sent to The Grizzly Bear Magazine for publication; be it further resolved, that the charter of this Parlor be draped for a period of thirty days, and that the Parlor stand in silence in respect to the memory of our departed brother.

HAROLD J. HALEY,
MONROE W. LABEL,
C. F. REINDOLLAR,
LOUIS J. PETER,
Committee.

San Rafael, February 6, 1933.

MILDRED OBARR WALIZER.

Whereas, Our Heavenly Father has called to His home Sister Mildred Obarr Walizer, a member of Rudecinda Parlor No. 230 N.D.G.W.; and whereas, in the death of Sister Walizer, Rudecinda Parlor has lost an honored member and her family a loving sister; therefore, be it

Resolved, That we extend our sincere sympathy and condolence to the family, and that a copy of this resolution be sent to The Grizzly Bear Magazine for publication in the current issue.

MERCY J. POWERS,
BERNICE W. DRANT,
LETITIA SARCIAUX,
Committee.

San Pedro, February 10, 1933.

TRINITY COUNTY.

Eltapome No. 55, Weaverville—Meets 2nd and 4th Thursdays, N.S.G.W. Hall; Mrs. Lou N. Fetzer, Rec. Sec.

TUOLUMNE COUNTY.

Dardanelle No. 66, Sonora—Meets Fridays, I.O.O.F. Hall; Mrs. Nettie Whitto, Rec. Sec., P.O. box 122.
Golden Era No. 99, Columbia—Meets 1st and 3rd Thursdays, N.S.G.W. Hall; Miss Irene Ponce, Rec. Sec.
Anona No. 164, Jamestown—Meets 2nd and 4th Tuesdays, I.O.O.F. Hall; Nellie Hope, Rec. Sec.

YOLO COUNTY.

Woodland No. 90, Woodland—Meets 2nd and 4th Tuesdays, N.S.G.W. Hall; Mrs. Maude Heaton, Rec. Sec., 153 College St.

YUBA COUNTY.

Marysville No. 162, Marysville—Meets 2nd and 4th Wednesdays, Liberty Hall; Miss Cecelia C. Gomes, Rec. Sec., 701 6th St.
Camp Far West No. 218, Wheatland—Meets 3rd Tuesday, I.O.O.F. Hall; Mrs. Ethel C. Brock, Rec. Sec., P. O. box 285.

AFFILIATED ORGANIZATIONS.

General Assembly Past Presidents—Meetings held annually in April at the home-town of Chief President; Mrs. Cora Stobing, 1739 San Jose Ave., San Francisco, Chief President; Mrs. Anna G. Loser, 72 Grove Lane, San Anselmo, Chief Secretary.
Past Presidents Association No. 1—Meets 1st and 3rd Mondays, N.S.G.W. Bldg., 414 Mason St., San Francisco; Mrs. Alice Ogburn, Pres.; Mrs. Leah M. Williams, Rec. Sec., 956 Pierce St., Apt. 104, San Francisco.
Past Presidents Association No. 2—Meets 2nd and 4th Mondays, "Wigwam," Pacific Bldg., 16th and Jefferson, Oakland; Emma Haggerty, Pres.; Mrs. Elizabeth B. Goodman, Rec. Sec., 134 Juana Ave., San Leandro.
Past Presidents Association No. 3 (Santa Clara County)—Meets 2nd Tuesday, Musicians Hall, 114 E. Santa Clara St., San Jose; Augusta Singleton, Pres.; Clara Briggs, Rec. Sec., 1336 Magnolia Ave., San Jose.
Past Presidents Association No. 4 (Sacramento County)—Meets 2nd Monday, N.S.G.W. Hall, 11th and "J" Sts., Sacramento City; Edna Briggs, Pres.; Lily May Tilden, Rec. Sec., 3225 "T" St., Sacramento.
Past Presidents Association No. 5 (Butte County)—Meets 1st Friday, homes of members, Chico and Oroville; Marie Picanco, Pres.; Ruth Brown, Rec. Sec., 1265 Leah Court, Oroville.
Past Presidents Association No. 6 (Nevada County)—Meets 4th Friday, alternately between Nevada City, Pythian Castle, and Grass Valley, Edna Sampson's home; Margaret V. Nolan, Pres.; Vere Hansen, Rec. Sec., R.F.D. No. 2, box 41-C, Grass Valley.
Past Presidents Association No. 7 (Sonoma County)—Meets 2nd Tuesday, Violet Mastrup home, 622 5th St., Petaluma; Viola Mastrup, Pres.; Elizabeth Dillon, Rec. Sec., Petaluma.
Past Presidents Association No. 8 (San Joaquin and Stanislaus Counties)—Meets 2nd Thursday, Red Men Hall, Stockton; Mrs. Lois Armstrong, Pres.; Mrs. Harriet F. Corr, Rec. Sec., 729 E. Sonora St., Stockton.
Native Sons and Native Daughters Central Committee on Homeless Children—Main Office, 955 Phelan Bldg., San Francisco; Mrs. John W. Stirling, Chmn.; Miss Mary E. Brusie, Sec. Los Angeles branch office, 3924 Sunset Blvd.; Dorothy Schlingman, Sec.

(ADVERTISEMENT.)

HISTORIC BACKGROUND OF "MORGAN TERRITORY" HOME.

The home of Jeremiah Morgan, Pioneer of Contra Costa County and once owner of "Morgan Territory," originally consisting of 40,000 acres, was built eighty years ago. The lumber was hauled by him from the Santa Cruz Mountains by oxen. Pegs were used in place of nails. The house consisted of eight rooms, five on the ground and three on the upper floor.

Jeremiah Morgan came to California in 1849 from Tennessee and settled in Ignacio Valley, Contra Costa County. Later he went back to Tennessee, where he was married. He returned with his bride to his holdings in Ignacio Valley which he sold soon after, in 1852, to take up 40,000 acres near the foot and on the east side of Mount Diablo. This vast acreage came to be known as "Morgan Territory."

Fourteen children were born to Mr. and Mrs. Morgan, ten of them in the historic old home. Jeremiah Morgan died at the age of 85 years. A son, I. N. Morgan, the only one of the fourteen children now living, has always resided in "Morgan Territory," which at the present time consists of but 1,400 acres, instead of 40,000.

(The above came to The Grizzly Bear from Edna Hill of Brentwood, affiliated with Donner Parlor No. 193 N.D.G.W. (Byron). She says: "This item seems to me to be of some historic value. It was given to me by a member of Donner Parlor, a descendant of Morgan, and concerns a very old historical home located near the foot of Mount Diablo. It was burned September 15, 1932. No one seems to have known much of its historical background until very recently."—Editor.)

INA SWANK.

To the Officers and Members of Bahia Vista Parlor No. 167, N.D.G.W.—We, your committee appointed to draft a resolution to the memory of our departed sister, Ina Swank, respectfully submit the following:

Whereas, Almighty God, in His infinite wisdom, has called to the Heavenly Parlor on High our esteemed and beloved sister, Ina Swank; and whereas, Bahia Vista Parlor has lost a loyal member, her husband a devoted wife, and her two daughters and son an affectionate mother;

Resolved, That the sympathy of the Parlor be extended to the bereaved family, that a copy of these resolutions be sent to the family, that a copy be spread in full upon the minutes of the Parlor, and that a copy be published in The Grizzly Bear Magazine.

LOUISE F. McDOUGALL,
HELEN O'CONNELL,
MINNIE E. RAPER,
Committee.

Oakland, February 2, 1933.

CHARLOTTE WHARTON.

To the Officers and Members of Long Beach Parlor No. 154 N.D.G.W.—We, your committee appointed to draft resolutions of respect to the memory of our late, beloved sister, Charlotte Wharton, submit the following:

Whereas, Again the Angel of Death has entered our Parlor and taken from our midst our dearly beloved sister, Charlotte Wharton, whose kind and gentle manner won the love and esteem of all who knew her; and whereas, in her passing our Parlor has lost a most highly respected and faithful member, the community a useful citizen, her husband a devoted wife and her mother a loyal and loving daughter.

Resolved, That we extend our sincere and heartfelt sympathy to her bereaved family; and further be it resolved, that a copy of these resolutions be sent to the husband and also a copy be sent to the loving mother; that a copy in full be spread upon the minutes of this Parlor, and a copy be sent to The Grizzly Bear for publication. In drafting these resolutions of respect we are performing the last tribute in our power for an honored and revered sister.

"May the California winds blow lightly,
May the California sun shine brightly,
May the California rain fall lightly
Where sleeps our Sister dear."

Respectfully submitted in P.D.F.A.,

KATE McFADYEN,
DAISY T. HANSEN,
CLARA HARPER FAY,
Committee.

Long Beach, February 16, 1933.

EDNA KNIGHT.

To the Officers and Members of Piedmont Parlor No. 87 N.D.G.W.—We, your committee appointed to draft resolutions of respect to the memory of our departed sister, Edna Knight, respectfully submit the following:

Once again we bow to the will of Almighty God, Who has seen fit to claim His own from amongst our membership and taken to His heavenly home our beloved sister, Edna Knight; therefore, be it

Resolved, That we extend our sincere and heartfelt sympathy to her bereaved family; and be it further resolved, that a copy of these resolutions be sent to the family of our departed sister, that a copy be spread in full upon the minutes of this Parlor, and that a copy be sent to The Grizzly Bear for publication.

Respectfully submitted,

ROSE MARTINELLI,
ANNIE ROGERS,
AUGUSTA HUNSOL,
Committee.

Oakland, February 16, 1933.

N.D.G.W. OFFICIAL DEATH LIST.

Giving the name, the date of death, and the Subordinate Parlor affiliation of all deceased members as reported to Grand Secretary Sallie R. Thaler from January 17, 1933, to February 18, 1933:

Howard, Aileen Condrin; January 3; Bret Harte No. 232.
Borg-Mann, Tulle Von Rosten; December 8; El Pescadero No. 82.
Swank, Ina R. Gregory; January 25; Bahia Vista No. 167.
Tremelling, Martha; January 16; Alta No. 3.
Gerichten, Anna; February 4; Darina No. 114.
Nicholson, Vina; January 31; Castro No. 178.
Foley, Catherine; February 8; Yosemite No. 83.
Brewer, Florence; January 26; San Diego No. 208.

Midwinter Fair—The Imperial County Midwinter Fair is billed for Imperial, March 4-12.

LOS ANGELES

(Continued from Page 17)

Speakers of the evening were Grand Trustees Joseph J. McShane and Eldred L. Meyer, Grand Outside Sentinel William I. Reuter, Past Grand John T. Newell, Superior Judges Samuel Blake and Joseph Sproul, Municipal Judge Leo Aggeler and President Henry Bodkin. A good program was presented, and refreshments were served.

February 20, Leonard Husar of Ramona No. 109 spoke before the Parlor on "China." He related bits of the early history of that country, and told something of conditions there today. His informative remarks were greatly enjoyed. Among the "strangers" were Henry Ireland, who originated the homeless children penny march several years ago, J. M. Lynch, John Concannon, J. S. Jeffers and W. R. Topham. March 20, Hollywood will initiate a class of candidates.

CLUBHOUSE FUND ENRICHED.

The February 1 meeting of Los Angeles Parlor No. 124 N.D.G.W. was largely attended and most enjoyable. Matters of importance were discussed, among the speakers being Past Grand Grace S. Stoermer, Deputy Rita Smith, Grand Outside Sentinel Hazel B. Hansen, Dolores Malin, Mary McAnany and Deputy Mary Noerenberg. Mrs. Mary and Miss Marvel Thomas entertained the sewing club at their home February 5; delicious refreshments were served.

The valentine party February 11 was very unique and a great success. Due to the untiring efforts of Chairman Edna Trombatore and her assistants a neat sum was raised for the clubhouse fund. The Washington Birthday party February 22, under the chairmanship of Juanita Porter, was thoroughly appreciated. All members having February birthdays were entertained. The "dessert bridge" at the home of Evelyn Howell, February 18, attracted a large crowd.

Los Angeles' March program includes: 8th, monthly card party, Grace Haven chairman; 22nd, get-together meeting; 29th, drill team night. President Mattie Gara says: "Through understanding and co-operation, we will have progress."

UNIVERSITY IN NEW HOME.

University Parlor No. 272 N.S.G.W. has changed its time and place of meeting. Commencing March 8 it will meet Wednesday nights at 1008 West Adams street, and a dinner at 7 p. m. will precede the initial gathering in the new quarters. An outing at Big Pines is scheduled for March 12. Through the courtesy of Bert Rovere, entertainers from the Paris Inn will be featured March 22; Howard Babb will be in charge, and all Natives, including the womenfolks, are invited. President Bernard Hiss announces that Monday nights have been set aside for the Natives at the Olympic Swimming Stadium.

University had a Valentine Day program, under the direction of Howard Babb, February 14. Numbers were presented by Carter Wright, Evelyn McCarthy, Maryjo Beebe, Jackie Jean Simpson, Jennie Alice Farrand, Wallace Weberg, Florence Goodale, Florence Leedom and Margaret Maupin.

BRILLIANT SOCIAL EVENT.

Californiana Parlor No. 247 N.D.G.W. was hostess at a delightful bridge luncheon and fashion show at Beverly Hills, February 18. A valentine motif was carried out, and the function was one of the most successful in the Parlor's history. Gertrude Tuttle and a corps of able assistants carried out the plans. The program vied with bridge in holding the interest of the large number of guests. The funds obtained from this brilliant social event will be used for homeless children and philanthropic activities of Californiana.

GRIZZLY GROWLS

(Continued from Page 4)

their magic at a cost of $5 per pupil, whereas in 1933 they are making off with something close to $100.

"The plain fact is that the public schools have gone on a joy-ride. If they did their work competently in 1914 there is no reason why they shouldn't do it at no more than twice the price today. And if they really need all the money they are now taking, then it must be manifest that they were so ineffective in 1914 that it was scarcely worth while to keep them open at all."

The dastardly attempt on the life of President-elect Franklin D. Roosevelt at Miami, Florida, should hasten closer scrutiny, by United States agents at foreign ports, of aliens desiring to come into this country for permanent or temporary residence. Also, a law should be passed, and rigidly enforced, requiring the registration and fingerprinting of all aliens.

All the undesirables in this country, however, are not of alien birth. We are burdened with a too-considerable number of native production. The latter are not generally referred to as anarchists, communists or what have you, but as "prominents," "international bankers," "business princes," etc. All undesirables, alien and native, are a constant menace and, being such, should be disposed of by deportation or penitentiary confinement.

Monteville Flowers of Pasadena, at a meeting in Sacramento of California taxpayers, suggested that control of government be taken from taxeaters and returned to taxpayers. He conveyed the astounding information, "Los Angeles County's public employes used physical force to break up tax reduction meetings," and declared "this sort of thing shows we must give control of government back to the people who pay."

The "lame duck" Federal Congress accomplished one thing—put the Eighteenth Amendment proposal on the glory-road. Here's something for the statisticians and others to worry over: the Congress devoted approximately three months' valuable time, and millions of dollars that could have provided food and shelter for thousands, in getting the proposal launched; how much time and how many dollars will be expended before the sought-for goal is reached, if it be reached?

State Controller Ray L. Riley has proposed and is advocating a taxation plan which, he contends, will relieve California of possible bankruptcy and reduce the tax burden on common property. It limits state, county and city taxes, reduces the proportion of state government supported by common property taxes to 50 percent, and establishes a gross receipts tax on all forms of corporate income. "The purpose of this plan," says Riley, "is to afford direct relief to real estate."

Bernard M. Baruch, addressing, by invitation, the Federal Senate Finance Committee, asserted that Congress is trifling with disaster. "No nation is living within its income now," he said, "and the money of all is unsound or suspected. That is the defective cause of continued misery, and cure of that is the controlling principle for any council among nations. There is no need for long agenda or complicated plans. The program for both talk and action can be written on a calling card, 'Balance the budgets of the world.'

"We should make one single and invariable dictum and theme of every discourse: Balance budgets. Stop spending money we haven't got. Sacrifice for frugality and revenue. Cut governmental spending—cut it as rations are cut in a siege. Tax—tax everybody for everything. But take hungry men off the world's pavements and let people smile again."

"The moral and spiritual bankruptcy of the modern age, not the depression, is causing the hopeless futility facing most of us today," declared Martin Kiddle of the Oxford Group, in a Los Angeles address. "The crisis we are facing is at least as momentous as the fall of the Roman empire. Sooner or later we must discover that the only way out of it is to . . . . learn from Him [God] that we must get back to the fundamentals of life.

"It is very easy for us to sneak out of the mess some other way. For instance, we might try making good resolutions for the future. But I do not need to remind you that hell is paved with good resolutions. We have to realize today that the world is in the mess it is because the world is like each of us. If we would make the world better, we must begin with ourselves."

William E. Borah, in the United States Senate February 14, declared: "There is already a revolution in this country. There are places where the courts cannot operate, where they are frustrated by sheer force. That has spread from the old State of Pennsylvania to my own State of Idaho. We know what has happened in Nebraska, Minnesota and Iowa. Every farmer in the United States is looking with anxious solicitude toward the Congress to know whether anything is going to be done by March 4. If nothing is done by then, this condition will be accentuated beyond the measure of words to portray."

Several good bills, and some not so good, are before the State Legislature for consideration. Lack of space prevents a listing of all, but a few of the meritorious ones were referred to last month. Another, of the good class, is S.B. No. 178, which will, if enacted, make it possible for county assessors to collect a personal property tax from all auto owners. Twenty percent of them, it is said, now avoid payment and saddle approximately $2,500,000 annually onto those who do pay.

One bill which should not pass is A.B. No. 1528, which provides for the creation of a state license tax commission—of three members to be appointed by the governor for six-year terms—to license manufacturers, purveyors, transporters and sellers of alcoholic beverages. That is dangerous legislation, in that it opens wide the government-door for the entrance of dishonesty! When, and if, the Eighteenth (prohibition) Amendment be repealed, each community, not the state, should have the right to license and to regulate its liquor business.

The Indeterminate Sentence Law should be repealed! It increases in number the miscarriages of justice, is expensive, and is a statutory reflection on the efficiency of the judiciary. The presiding judge, hearing the evidence in a criminal case, should fix the definite penalty for the convicted. If it be desired, however, that the prison board, who do not, under the existing law, hear the evidence, shall fix the definite penalty, then the courts dealing with criminal cases should be abolished, and to the board should be delegated complete jurisdiction in all criminal cases—to hear the evidence and to fix the definite penalty. The indeterminate statute, providing for one of the too-many overlapping or duplicating functions of government, should be repealed, for the common good.

It is most gratifying to note that many of the state's papers, incensed at prevailing conditions, have their guns trained on the system that exists on "the hidden things of dishonesty" and those who profit therefrom. With very few exceptions, they are expressing opinions in mighty plain language. It is well, for if the press unite in battling the system, tranquility will, in time, succeed chaos. Here are some sample hot-shots:

"Why Honeycomb the State? We are for the best plan to relieve taxpayers and it is up to the men we send to Sacramento to determine the surest way to achieve this result. There has been a suggestion giving more powers to boards of supervisors, but judging by the experience of Marin County and Los Angeles County, and the mixup in San Mateo, it is not a very reassuring method of lifting the burden which a lot of enthusiasts, plus many skilled lobbyists, put upon us. Supervisors are not immune to such influences and are no longer the guileless rurals who represented their neighbors and shaved expenditure down to the last nickel. The day of such supervisors passed long ago, and too many now belong to the vast army of sophisticates who puff the cigars of big business and cement friendship with highway contractors."—Editorial "Sonoma Index-Tribune," February 17.

"Well, you poor devil of a businessman and farmer, who can see nothing but ruin ahead, what are you going to do about it? So far you have acted like you didn't have an ounce of gumption, and not enough spunk to bat a mosquito. Are you going on like this? Are you going to continue to be but a human worm in the dust to be set upon by a lot of public leeches who are bleeding you to death! Come, let us have mass meetings. . . . Let us tell our public servants what's what. A well-backed-up recall here and there might clarify the situation and bring decency to some through fear, who have no honor for honor's sake. It is this or ruin. We are rushing down the precipice of financial collapse at a pace that is appalling. And we are doing nothing. Our officials are doing nothing. In God's name, what is wrong with Americans?"—Editorial "Township Register," Niles, Alameda County, February 16.

"In response to an inquiry from a Weaverville, Trinity County, correspondent, regarding the comparative expenditures of the governor's office during the terms of Governors Richardson, Young and Rolph, The Bee prints the following figures obtained from the state controller's office: Governor Richardson, total for four years' administration, $176,018; average yearly expenditure, $44,004. Governor Young, total for four years, $184,140; average yearly expenditure, $46,035. Governor Rolph, total for two years and one month, $188,919; average yearly expenditure, $90,681, or approximately twice that of either Governor Young or Governor Richardson."—Featured news item "Sacramento Bee," February 15.

J. H. Hoepfel, congressman-elect from California, went to the National Capital to look around. He was shocked at the evidence of extravagance, according to the "La Verne Leader" of February 9, which featured a letter from him. Quoting from the letter:

"In the senate office building we find an elegantly conducted beauty shop, which cost the taxpayers a small fortune to construct, while in the same building we find elegant white marble-trimmed baths and a plunge, reported to have cost $200,000, where our ninety-six senators, and perhaps their male secretaries, may bathe to their hearts content before and after a strenuous day's work of sitting idly by. . . . That millions upon millions of our American youth do not even have a galvanized tub today in which to bathe has probably not entered the craniums of the (reported) Wall-street representatives in the senate. Of course, we will disregard the bathhouse attendants paid with funds which come from the American farmer and others who are losing their homes through foreclosure or taxes. . . . Why does the Senate prate about economy, with these conditions so glaring that they must stumble over them daily, unless they are mentally inert and physically blind? Under the vicious patronage system 13-year-old boys are receiving $110 a month as pages, paid from funds derived through taxation from farmers who are forced to sell their cotton and wheat below cost of production."

"To gild refined gold, to paint the lily,
To throw a perfume on the violet,
To smooth the ice, or add another hue
Unto the rainbow, . . .
Is wasteful and ridiculous excess."

Grizzly Bear

APRIL — THE ONLY OFFICIAL PUBLICATION OF THE NATIVE SONS AND DAUGHTERS OF THE GOLDEN WEST — 1933

Featuring

GENERAL NEWS OF INTEREST CONCERNING ALL CALIFORNIA, and ORDERS NATIVE SONS and NATIVE DAUGHTERS

Price: 15 Cents

THE LETTER BOX

Comments on subjects of general interest and importance received from readers of The Grizzly Bear.

DESCENDANT WM. ISAAC TUSTIN, PIONEER OF 1845, SEEKS DATA.

Editor Grizzly Bear—I am a member of Rudecinda Parlor (San Pedro) N.D.G.W. and a subscriber to The Grizzly Bear Magazine. In January 1933 I noticed an article that interests me greatly. It is printed on page 2, is about the first Protestant church in California, and quotes from Harvey Hovey Hyde Jr.'s diary.

It tells about only six houses being in Benicia July 22, 1849, and speaks of the government constructing some buildings there. This interests me, as my grandfather built the first house in Benicia (of adobe) and he contracted and built for the government the barracks there (1847). My grandfather's name was Wm. Isaac Tustin. He was a charter member of California Pioneer Lodge and I have his memorial, drafted by them, and my daughter is assembling the facts from that and from other relatives and hopes to have an article that you might be interested in. When she has it finished, I will gladly send it to you.

Referring to the article printed in the January Grizzly Bear: I wonder if there are any copies of Harvey Hovey Hyde Jr.'s diary printed in book form? Where could I find one, or do you know where the original diary is? The town of Tustin, Orange County, is named for my grandfather's brother.

MRS. MARGARET BIRKENBERG.
Sierra Madre, March 1, 1933.

(The "California Pioneer Lodge" above referred to is the Society of California Pioneers, San Francisco. From Mrs. Birkenberg a copy of the memorial has been received, and it will be published later in The Grizzly Bear.—Editor.)

FIFTY-ONE YEARS AGO—THE GREAT SNOWSTORM OF 1882.

Editor Grizzly Bear—I am sending you a true story of the great storm of 1882. The records show it was the greatest ever known in Southern California, I think. I was alone at our Pine Valley cattle ranch, in the mountains of San Diego County. We were having a very cold northeast wind, and the ground was dry and frozen. In the afternoon great black clouds came rolling in from the southwest, and the snow began to fall very fast.

The next morning I could not get out of the front door, on the west side. Before the storm ended the snow was four feet deep, and in many places great drifts were ten feet deep. I had to dig a path to the barn, to lead the horses and cows to the well for water. It was a week before I could break a trail to another valley, three miles away, where my father and mother lived, and I would go over there most every day for a warm dinner.

In those days, we would buy our food for winter in large wagonloads, and we had lots of flour, sugar, potatoes, beans, dried fruit, bacon, etc., on hand. We did not have canned food then. To pass the lonesome hours, I had a Bible to read, a pack of cards, my violin, and my good old dog, Trusty, to talk to.

In three weeks I started with a large saddlehorse to break a trail to Descanso, six miles distant, to get the mail. About half-way I met two neighbor cattlemen on their way to their ranch, six miles beyond Pine Valley. They had the mail, and stayed all night with me. Next day we broke a trail to their ranch at "Corta Medara." We found many cattle that had perished with cold and fallen into drifts. In one canyon I found nine head dead, in a little flat. They had eaten all the brush they could reach, but they could not get out through the snow. It snowed clear to the ocean that storm.

Tecate, March 8, 1933. C. F. EMERY.

The Grizzly Bear Magazine
The ALL California Monthly
OWNED, CONTROLLED, PUBLISHED BY GRIZZLY BEAR PUBLISHING CO., (Incorporated)
COMPOSED OF NATIVE SONS.
HERMAN C. LICHTENBERGER, Pres.
JOHN T. NEWELL RAY HOWARD
WM. I. TRAEGER LORENZO F. SOTO
CHAS. R. THOMAS HARRY J. LELANDE
ARTHUR A. SCHMIDT, Vice-Pres.
BOARD OF DIRECTORS
CLARENCE M. HUNT
General Manager and Editor
OFFICIAL ORGAN AND THE ONLY OFFICIAL PUBLICATION OF THE NATIVE SONS AND THE NATIVE DAUGHTERS GOLDEN WEST.
ISSUED FIRST EACH MONTH.
FORMS CLOSE 20th MONTH.
ADVERTISING RATES ON APPLICATION.
SAN FRANCISCO OFFICE:
N.S.G.W. BLDG., 414 MASON ST., RM. 302
(Office Grand Secretary N.S.G.W.)
Telephone: Kearney 1223
SAN FRANCISCO, CALIFORNIA
PUBLICATION OFFICE:
309-15 WILCOX BLDG., 2nd AND SPRING,
Telephone: VAndike 6234
LOS ANGELES, CALIFORNIA
(Entered as second-class matter May 29, 1918, at the Postoffice at Los Angeles, California, under the act of August 24, 1912.)
PUBLISHED REGULARLY SINCE MAY 1907
VOL. LII WHOLE NO. 312

DAUGHTER FIRST AMERICAN COUPLE WEDDED IN CALIFORNIA PASSES.

San Luis Obispo—Mrs. Anna Davis, born at Santa Cruz City in 1862, died February 24. She was a daughter of George and Elecia Sumner Davis, who were wedded at Sutter Fort (now Sacramento) July 17, 1843, the ceremony being performed by Captain John A. Sutter.

George Davis crossed the plains in 1838 and was first lieutenant under General John C. Fremont, and his wife, Elecia Sumner, came across the plains in 1842. It is believed theirs was the first marriage of citizens of the United States in California.

Inland Seaport—The six-million-dollar deepwater channel constructed by the Federal Government and Stockton, San Joaquin County, was officially completed January 18. Since then several ocean vessels have visited California's seaport ninety miles inland from the Golden Gate, and regular service between Stockton and Atlantic and Pacific ports will start April 1.

"Though man a thinking being is defined, few use the grand prerogative of Mind."—Jane Taylor.

CALIFORNIA'S ROMANTIC HISTORY

Lewis F. Byington
(PAST GRAND PRESIDENT N.S.G.W.)

(Continuing the series of California history talks commenced in The Grizzly Bear for December 1932.)

DAYS OF GOLD

ONE OF THE MOST COLORFUL PERIods in the history of California, and of all times, was the period following the discovery of gold by James W. Marshall. "It set the whole civilized world on fire with excitement." No such days were ever known before, nor shall a like period be seen again. If gold-fields of equal wealth were discovered in this age, rapid transportation would rob the discovery of the romance of the "days of forty-nine." Railroads, the automobile, the airplane and rapid steamships would bring people to the new "El Dorado" in a few hours, and the treasure of the mines would fall into the hands of organized companies and syndicates. It was the poor man who had his opportunity in the gold rush to California. Never again will we have the romance of the emigrant trail, the slow-moving ox-team, the long sea voyage around Cape Horn or by way of the Isthmus of Panama, the heat of trackless deserts, the storms and snows of the mountains, and the dangers that beset the journey through attacks by Indians or wild animals.

It is not generally known that, prior to the discovery by Marshall, placer mines had been worked in southern California, near the San Fernando Mission, and within two years following this first discovery, in March 1842, some $80,000 had been taken out. But the missionary fathers apparently discouraged mining. They were not in search of wealth, but were seeking to Christianize the Indians. It remained for James W. Marshall, an American, to make the important discovery near what is now Coloma, on the south fork of the American River, January 24, 1848, a discovery which turned the eyes of the world toward California.

General John A. Sutter had been given a large grant of land by the Mexican government, an empire of eleven square leagues, 48,825 acres, and established himself on the present site of the city of Sacramento, in 1839, erecting what is now known as Sutter's Fort. Finding himself in need of lumber to use on his vast estate, he employed Marshall, a millman, to search for a location and directed him to build a sawmill on the American River. Marshall built his mill near Coloma, in El Dorado County. He constructed a mill-race and turned the water of the river in at night to wash away the loose dirt which had been dug during the day, and, having shut the water off in the morning, the bedrock was exposed and he noticed bright golden-colored particles on the rock. His heart leaped with excitement at the thought that they might be gold. His belief was soon verified. Marshall reported his find to Sutter, but Sutter was anxious to complete the mill and also a flour-mill on the American River and he and Marshall agreed to keep the discovery a secret, but the men had picked up other pieces of gold and at once quit work and went to mining. The news of the discovery spread like magic and in a few weeks hundreds were engaged in digging along the river and creek beds.

In July 1848, Colonel Richard B. Mason, under orders from the Federal Government, made a tour of the mining region and in his official report stated that he could not believe at first the accounts of the great wealth of gold in the mountains and could not realize the value of the discovery until he visited the mining district, but that he now had no hesitation in saying that there was more gold in the country drained by the Sacramento and San Joaquin Rivers than would pay the cost of the war with Mexico a hundred times over. In a later letter he stated that if he had said five hundred times over he would be nearer the mark. Colonel Mason's official report to Washington soon reached the world at large and brought the great rush of gold-seekers to California. Mason street in San Francisco is named after him.

San Francisco at first did not credit the reports, but in a short time a number of gold-diggers drifted into the town with bottles, tin cans and buckskin bags filled with golden nuggets, and the well-known Pioneer, Sam Brannan, one day appeared on the Plaza with a bottle of gold dust in one hand and, swinging his hat with the other, yelled: "Gold! Gold! from the American River." The town was at once fired with excitement. Business houses closed their doors, schoolteachers, lawyers and doctors left their offices, sailors deserted their ships, and soldiers the Presidio. By boat up the rivers, by mule and horse and on foot they struck for the mines, fearing that the gold would be gone before each dug his share. By August 1, over 4,000 men were working along the river and in ravines. Ships began to arrive from all quarters of the world, filled with treasure-seekers from every state and land. By November, 600 vessels had entered the harbor and many of these were left at the wharves while passengers and crews hurried to the gold mines. Not alone by sea, but across mountain and desert they came, and it is estimated that in the year 1849 over 42,000 people reached California overland. Thirst, privations, dangers and death could not check the rush, and the stories of adventure by land and sea, told by the Argonauts, were more marvelous than any theretofore recorded.

To reach the gold-producing Sierras from San Francisco the earliest miners first proceeded slowly up the rivers by boat. There were three distributing towns through which the mines were reached, Sacramento, Stockton and Marysville. At the levees of these towns the boats landed and on them the provisions and supplies for the mines were stacked, and from there at first trains of pack-mules, and later wagons and stages, started on their way across the valley, over the foothills and on upward to the mining camps. The gold-producing counties of early days stretched from Mariposa to Sierra, including Nevada, Placer, El Dorado, Tuolumne, Amador and Calaveras. The gold in prehistoric days had been washed down from the higher levels and deposited in the river beds and was found in the large gravel bars along the rivers and in the creeks, gulches and ravines tributary thereto, and in the deep channels of ancient river beds running back into the hills and often covered by lava.

The earliest miners, with pick and shovel, dug the richer gravel from the crevices or seams in the bedrock and washed it out in the gold pan. Later still, they used a rocker, which was more expeditious; and afterwards ground sluices, hundreds of feet long, into which the gravel was shoveled and carried along by a stream of water and the gold sinking to the bottom was held by riffles. When the miner by digging a tunnel followed the ancient river channel back into the mountain it was called "drifting." The gravel in these ancient channels frequently abounded in gold, particularly on the bedrock. In the gradual development of mining operations long ditches and flumes were built from the foothills far up toward the summit of the mountains, where the deep snows of winter conserved the water for spring and summer use. Later on, we had hydraulic mining, by which water under the highest pressure was directed through a nozzle, tearing down high banks and hills and carrying the gravel through large flumes in which the gold was caught. In 1850, on Gold Hill, at Grass Valley, quartz mining was first started, stamp mills being erected to crush the quartz which was found in rocky veins, and after being crushed the gold was separated from the rock by means of mercury or quicksilver.

The discovery of gold in 1848 changed completely the character of California. The Spanish settlers had been engaged entirely in agricultural pursuits and in cattle and stock raising. Care-free and contented, they lived a quiet, happy life, with the least of toil and caring little for outside life. Then came the gold discovery, and the news spread everywhere. The New England farmer left his plough in the furrow, the Southerner his cotton in the field, the laborer turned at once from the work bench, the peasant from the vine-clad hills of Europe, all thrilled with the thought that they might cross the mountains and plains, or sail by sea around the Horn, throw off the bondage of poverty and never-ending toil and, in after years, return from California to the old homestead, rich beyond the dreams of other times. They poured through the Golden Gate,—the Celt, the Saxon, the Teuton, the fair-haired Scandinavian, the Spaniard of South America and the yellow races of the Orient.

As the result of this great influx of people into quiet Spanish San Francisco with its not more than fifty small houses prior thereto, forty thousand landing in 1849, whereas the population had been but a few hundred the year before, there was a magic change in its appearance. The people could not be housed except in tents and shanties lined with bunks. Many houses were made in Boston and shipped to San Francisco in sections. One writer speaks of seventy-five houses imported from China. Though houses sprang up by hundreds over night, they could not begin to hold the thousands who arrived in '49. The streets were unpaved and so deep with mud that in the wintertime horses and wagons were literally swallowed up. General Sherman, who was here in those days, stated he had seen mules stumble and drown in the liquid mud, and had seen a sign erected at Clay and Kearny streets bearing the warning: "This street is impassable, not even jackassable." Streets were filled in with all kinds of material.

One traveler speaks of a sidewalk, near the express office, some 200 feet in length, constructed of a row of large cooking stoves, beyond these a double row of boxes of tobacco, and rolls of wire and sheet lead. Owing to an over-shipment of these materials they were cheaper than lumber, which sold for $600 per thousand. But before the next winter Montgomery and Kearny streets were graded and planked. And within a year good hotels, splendidly-fitted saloons, attractive theaters and places of amusement had been built. But strong, self-reliant, dauntless Americans conquered all difficulties and built a splendid city and state within a few months. The miner was a rollicking, care-free soul. A Pioneer of '53 has handed me the words of a typical song, very popular in early days and sung in every mining camp and towu, written by John Woodard, which goes thus:

Before you now stands Old Tom Moore,
A relic of former days,
A bummer too, they call me now,
But what care I for praise,
For my heart is filled with the days of yore,
And oft do I repine
For the days of old, the days of gold,
The days of '49.

I had comrades then who loved me well,
A jovial, saucy crew,
There were some hard cases I must confess,
Still they were staunch and true.
Who never flinched whate'er the pinch,
Would never fret nor whine,
But like good old bricks, they stood the kicks,
In the days of '49.

There was Racenback Bill who could outroar
A buffalo bull, you bet,
He would roar all night
He would roar all day,
And I believe Bill's roaring yet.
One night he fell in a prospect hole,
Which was a roaring bad design,
For in that hole Bill roared out his soul,
In the days of '49.

There was Monte Pete, I'll ne'er forget,
For the luck that he'd always had,
He'd play all day and he'd play all night,
Or as long as you had a scad,
He'd play you "draw," or ante a slug,
He would go a hatful blind,
But in the game with death Pete lost his breath,
In the days of '49.

There was poor lame Jess, a hard old case,
Who never would repent;
Jess was never known to miss a meal,
Or to ever pay a cent;
But poor old Jess like all the rest,
Did to Death at last resign,
For in his bloom he went up the flume,
In the days of '49.

Of all the comrades I had then,
Not one is left to toast;
They have left me here in my misery,
Like some poor wandering ghost,
And as I go from place to place,
Folks call me a traveling sign,
Saying "Here's Old Tom Moore, a bummer sure,
From the days of '49."

Men of courage and character found their way up the rivers, canyons and ravines of the gold regions. At first the trees were felled, clearings made, and then tents arose. These gave way to the log cabin, and then to pleasant homes. The hills were terraced, and orchards and flowers planted. Wherever a settlement was established, an American schoolhouse was built, and beside it a flagpole cut from a tall pine was placed and the American Flag raised. The miner was, above all, patriotic. Every national holiday was celebrated. The miner's band and the local fire department led the parades through streets decorated with pine trees from the mountainside. And the fair daughters of the mountains and their sturdy partners, to the tunes of the fiddle, danced until the rising sun came peeping over the eastern hills. The hardy miners in their search for gold quickly followed up the canyons and ravines to the very sources of the mountain streams and built their rude log cabins and pitched their camps under the snow-capped peaks of the Sierra Nevadas. Bret Harte caught the romance and spirit of the times when he wrote:

Above the pines the moon was slowly drifting,
The river sang below;
The dim Sierras, far beyond uplifting
Their minarets of snow.

(Continued on Page 19)

GRIZZLY GROWLS

(CLARENCE M. HUNT.)

GLORY BE! THERE HAS BEEN A DEcided change, for the better, since March fourth. While no appreciable upturn in business is yet noticeable, improvement in the tenor of the people is everywhere apparent. Hope and courage have replaced dejection and fear, and out of that replacement must come "happy days." The "corner" has, at least, been sighted, and there is every indication that "old man depression" will, in reasonable time, be routed.

All the credit, for the splendid progress made in getting this country back to normalcy, belongs to Franklin Delano Roosevelt, who became President of the United States of America March 4. Quoting from his inaugural address, a remarkable document, confidence inspiring:

"I am certain that my fellow Americans expect that on my induction into the Presidency I will address them with a candor and a decision which the present situation of our Nation impels. This is preeminently the time to speak the truth, the whole truth, frankly and boldly. Nor need we shrink from honestly facing conditions in our country today. This great Nation will endure as it has endured, will revive and will prosper. So first of all, let me assert my firm belief that the only thing we have to fear is fear itself—nameless, unreasoning, unjustified terror which paralyzes needed efforts to convert retreat into advance. In every dark hour of our national life a leadership of frankness and vigor has met with that understanding and support of the people themselves which is essential to victory. I am convinced that you will again give that support to leadership in these critical days.

"In such a spirit on my part and on yours we face our common difficulties. They concern, thank God, only material things. Values have shrunken to fantastic levels; taxes have risen; our ability to pay has fallen; government of all kinds is faced by serious curtailment of income; the means of exchange are frozen in the currents of trade; the withered leaves of industrial enterprise lie on every side; farmers find no markets for their produce; the savings of many years in thousands of families are gone. More important, a host of unemployed citizens face the grim problem of existence, and an equally great number toil with little return. Only a foolish optimist can deny the dark realities of the moment.

"Yet our distress comes from no failure of substance. We are stricken by no plague of locusts. Compared with the perils which our forefathers conquered because they believed and were not afraid, we have still much to be thankful for. Nature still offers her bounty and human efforts have multiplied it. Plenty is at our doorstep, but a generous use of it languishes in the very sight of the supply. Primarily this is because the rulers of the exchange of mankind's goods have failed, through their own stubbornness and their own incompetence, have admitted their failure, and abdicated. Practices of the unscrupulous money changers stand indicted in the court of public opinion, rejected by the hearts and minds of men.

"True they have tried, but their efforts have been cast in the pattern of an outworn tradition. Faced by failure of credit they have proposed only the lending of more money. Stripped of the lure of profit by which to induce our people to follow their false leadership, they have resorted to exhortations, pleading tearfully for restored confidence. They know only the rules of a generation of self-seekers. They have no vision, and when there is no vision the people perish.

"The money changers have fled from their high seats in the temple of our civilization. We may now restore that temple to the ancient truths. The measure of the restoration lies in the extent to which we apply social values more noble than mere monetary profit. Happiness lies not in the mere possession of money; it lies in the joy of achievement, in the thrill of creative effort. The joy and moral stimulation of work no longer must be forgotten in the mad chase of evanescent profits. These dark days will be worth all they cost us if they teach us that our true destiny is not to be ministered unto, but to minister to ourselves and to our fellow men.

"Recognition of the falsity of material wealth as the standard of success goes hand in hand with the abandonment of the false belief that public office and high political position are to be valued only by the standards of pride of place and personal profit; and there must be an end to a conduct in banking and in business which too often has given to a sacred trust the likeness of callous and selfish wrongdoing. Small wonder that confidence languishes, for it thrives only on honesty, on honor, on the sacredness of obligations, on faithful protection, on unselfish performance; without them it can not live.

"Restoration calls, however, not for changes in ethics alone. This Nation asks for action, and action now. Our greatest primary task is to put people to work. This is no unsolvable problem if we face it wisely and courageously. . . . Hand in hand with this we must frankly recognize the overbalance of population in our industrial centers and, by engaging on a national scale in a redistribution, endeavor to provide a better use of the land for those best fitted for the land. . . . Finally, in our progress toward a resumption of work we require two safeguards against a return of the evils of the old order; there must be a strict supervision of all banking and credits and investments; there must be an end to speculation with other people's money, and there must be provision for an adequate but sound currency. These are the lines of attack.

"If I read the temper of our people correctly, we now realize as we have never realized before our interdependence on each other; that we cannot merely take but we must give as well; that if we are to go forward, we must move as a trained and loyal army willing to sacrifice for the good of a common discipline, because without such discipline no progress is made, no leadership becomes effective. We are, I know, ready and willing to submit our lives and property to such discipline, because it makes possible a leadership which aims at a larger good. This I propose to offer, pledging that the larger purposes will bind upon us all as a sacred obligation with a unity of duty hitherto evoked only in time of armed strife. With this pledge taken, I assume unhesitatingly the leadership of this great army of our people dedicated to a disciplined attack upon our common problems.

"Action in this image and to this end is feasible under the form of government which we have inherited from our ancestors. Our Constitution is so simple and practical that it is possible always to meet extraordinary needs by changes in emphasis and arrangement without loss of essential form. That is why our constitutional system has proved itself the most superbly enduring political mechanism the modern world has produced. It has met every stress of vast expansion of territory, of foreign wars, of bitter internal strife, of world relations. . . . For the trust reposed in me I will return the courage and the devotion that befit the time. I can do no less.

"We face the arduous days that lie before us in the warm courage of national unity; with the clear consciousness of seeking old and precious moral values; with the clean satisfaction that comes from the stern performance of duty by old and young alike. We aim at the assurance of a rounded and permanent national life.

"We do not distrust the future of essential democracy. The people of the United States have not failed. In their need they have regis-

A PRAYER

(HUGH RANDALL ACKLEY.)

God lead us back to simple ways
Of living, as in bygone days,
With Truth and Honor, once again,
The lights that guide the lives of men.

God give each man the saving grace
To mentally exchange his place
With one less fortunate than he,
His duty to more clearly see.

God free men's hearts and minds of greed
And plant, instead, therein the seed
Of Love and Charity again;
Send Christ to dwell on earth with men.

—Exchange.

CALIFORNIA HAPPENINGS OF FIFTY YEARS AGO

Thomas R. Jones

(COMPILED EXPRESSLY FOR THE GRIZZLY BEAR.)

WHILE NO FULLY-DEVELOPED rainstorm visited California during April 1883, showers fell frequently in different parts of the state, and there were no desiccating north winds. While the month's rainfall was but .87 of an inch, it was sufficient to keep the growing crops in good condition, and the state was assured a prosperous year.

April 19 being the centennial anniversary of the day when the king of England recognized the independence of the United States of America, the national flag was flung to the breeze from every California flagpole.

The Grand Parlor of the Order of Native Sons of the Golden West met in sixth annual session at San Francisco April 9 to 12. Major A. F. Jones (Argonaut Parlor No. 8) of Oroville, Butte County, was elected Grand President; Clarence E. Parker (Sacramento Parlor No. 3) of Sacramento, Grand Secretary; C. H. Lindley (Stockton Parlor No. 7) of Stockton, Grand Marshal; M. A. Dorn (Pacific Parlor No. 10) of San Francisco, Grand Lecturer.

The telephone company, lately organized, made an experimental long-distance test April 1. Using a telegraph wire, telephonic communication was had between San Francisco, San Jose and Sacramento, a distance of 190 miles. Communication between operators at those points was perfect, and the fact was hailed with front-page publicity enthusiasm by the daily press.

A. F. Coronel offered for sale in 1880, at $400 an acre, fifty-three acres of his vineyard near Los Angeles City, but could find no purchaser. This year (1883), owing to improved business conditions, he was offered $1,000 an acre for the land, but refused it. Land values in California South were bounding upward, due to increased immigration.

In Calaveras County, a petition signed by a majority of the voters asked the Board of Supervisors to increase saloon licenses to $150 a quarter, that the number of drink emporiums in that county might be materially reduced.

The palatial residence of ex-Senator Milton S. Latham in Menlo Park, San Mateo County, was sold to Mrs. Mark Hopkins for $205,000.

The Rancho Paso de Bartolo of 2,700 acres in Los Angeles County, owned by Pio Pico, was sold to B. Cohn for $62,837.

A special train of two cars, chartered by Henry Villard, made the run from Ogden, Utah State, to Oakland, Alameda County, a distance of 833 miles, in twenty-three hours. This was the fastest time yet made on a Pacific Coast railroad.

A large flourmill, to be run by water power, was built at Smartsville, Yuba County.

A pulpmill established at Towle, Placer County, began operations April 5. The first week it produced ten carloads of pulp, which was shipped to a Stockton, San Joaquin County, papermill.

The Glenn ranch domain in Colusa County had seeded 47,000 acres to wheat. Heavy storms in March saved the seed from dying out, and a bumper crop was now assured.

A shipment of 130,000 sheep was made by railroad from Los Angeles County to Texas State.

An oak tree, eight feet in diameter and twenty-four feet in circumference, was felled in Yuba County. It produced twenty-seven cords of stovewood.

A San Francisco mass meeting of carpenters April 13 decided to put into effect May 1 a nine-hour day. The plumbers followed suit. The eight-hour day came later.

The North Bloomfield hydraulic mine in Nevada County cleaned up, from a two-weeks washing, $16,000 worth of gold dust.

A prospector came into Fresno City and reported finding in the Sierra east of there a quartz ledge, two hundred feet wide and three miles long, speckled with gold. Specimens he exhibited assayed $43 a ton. He named the find "Mother of Gold."

A nickel, circulated only in California, bearing on one side the character "V," with the usual word "cents" omitted, was being plated with goldleaf and passed on the unwary as a five-dollar piece. Chinamen were the most numerous victims. The Federal Government quickly remedied the fault by adding the word "cents."

Charles H. Harriman, champion pedestrian, at Truckee, Nevada County, April 19 walked 121 miles, without a minute's rest, in twenty-nine hours. He won a dollar an hour.

The Lakeport, Lake County, stage was held up by a highwayman near Cloverdale, Sonoma County, April 12. The express box and the mail sacks were carried away by the robber.

The Chinatown of Dutch Flat, Placer County, for the third time in a few years, burned April 17 with a $25,000 loss.

Peter Branstetter's planingmill at Grass Valley, Nevada County, burned April 8, causing a loss of $8,000.

The night of April 19 fire broke out in a Sacramento City K-street restaurant. The brick wall fell and crushed to the floor the roof of an adjoining saloon, filled with musicians and others from a dance, just concluded. Six well-known citizens were killed, and many others were severely injured.

John B. Linn, Pioneer and owner of extensive hydraulic mine properties, died April 9 at Dutch Flat, Placer County.

Thomas H. Hanson, who arrived in Marin County in 1847 from Virginia, died at San Rafael, April 17.

Captain Thomas Blythe, millionaire San Francisco real estate owner, dropped dead April 4. He was believed to be unmarried, but a claimed-to-be wife and about a hundred relatives from distant places came forward to claim kinship and thus share in his valuable estate.

W. C. Fletcher was killed April 10 by a cavein at a mine in Washington, Nevada County.

George Keeny was duck hunting near Rio Vista, Solano County, April 8. An accidental discharge of the shotgun blew off his head.

Henry E. Johnson and James Donnelly got into a quarrel over a trivial matter in a Stockton, San Joaquin County, saloon April 16. Both drew bowie knives and carved each other to death.

A man named McCullough, living at Dayton, Butte County, went to Chico, got drunk, went home and fell in a stupor upon the kitchen floor. Attempting to raise him, his wife burst a bloodvessel and died instantly.

Mrs. Ann Flaherty was decapitated in the Nevada Bank building, San Francisco, April 29, as the result of elevator trouble.

Harry T. Banning and Barney Ashley, lighthouse keepers at Point New Year, San Mateo County, April 9 attempted to convey two friends to the mainland in a boat. The boat capsized and the four men were drowned.

"WHO REMEMBERS EXCITEMENT OF FLOOD WHICH NEVER OCCURRED?"

The above query tops an article in the "Livermore Herald" of March 10, which follows: "Did fear of a flood which never came send Mexican residents of the Livermore Valley to the mountains for safety in March 1883, just fifty years ago? The question has been raised by a statement in the 'California Happenings of Fifty Years Ago' in the March issue of The Grizzly Bear and the inability of The Herald to locate anyone who has first-band or even second-hand knowledge of such an event. . . . Questioning of a number of pioneers who were in Livermore in March 1883, and of other persons who are familiar with the early history of the valley has not located even one who remembers such an occurrence or having heard of it. A number remember the heavy rainfall of the month, the precipitation in Livermore amounting to 3.45 inches according to official records. M. G. Callaghan, Livermore's authority on early California history, seriously doubts that a Padre Anseleno was in California in 1783. He has not encountered such a name in his studies of the history of that period. It would be interesting to learn if there is anyone who has any knowledge of the event described by The Grizzly Bear, and The Herald would be glad to learn if something like that did actually occur or existed only in the mind of some imaginative newspaper writer of the day."

Captioned "No Exodus of Mexicans Here in '83'" the following appeared in the "Herald" of March 17: "There was no exodus of Mexican families to Cedar Mountain in March 1883, for fear of a flood which never came, but prediction of the flood did cause some Mexicans in the Pleasanton district to go to the Sunol hills for fancied safety—this is the information derived from the question asked in The Herald last Friday, prompted by a story in the 'Fifty Years Ago' department of the March Grizzly Bear.

"There is incontrovertible testimony that Cedar Mountain did not harbor any persons seeking refuge from an expected flood. John McGlinchey, veteran stockman, was in charge of a band of sheep belonging to the late Jas. Gallagher on the mountain in March 1883, the time the exodus from the valley was supposed to have occurred, and he did not see even one person there for that reason. Horace Overacker, pioneer of the Mocho district, was residing at his place in the canyon just opposite Cedar Mountain in 1883, and he states that no persons ever camped on it to escape a flood. Neither John Barry, who has a keen memory of events in the early history of the valley, Thos. Green of Dublin, who was also very familiar with the valley at that time, nor J. A. Rochin, another pioneer, have any recollection of any such event.

"However, Mrs. A. J. Young of Oakland, one of the earliest settlers in the valley still living, has a distinct recollection of some Mexican families in the vicinity of Pleasanton going into the hills near Sunol to escape a flood which had been predicted. Geo. K. Taylor, pioneer of the valley and until recently rural mail carrier, was clerk in a grocery store here at that time and remembers that a number of Mexican families purchased extra supplies at that time and said that they were going to the hills, but would not give a reason or say just where they were going. It appears that the story published in The Grizzly Bear was founded on fact, but that the details are not entirely correct.

"Discussion of this event reminded several persons that a number of years later, probably in the early '90s a religious fanatic in Oakland predicted a tidal wave which would destroy the city, and large numbers of persons from that city were so influenced as to dispose of their homes and move into the hills. Thos. Green remembers seeing several hundred camped in the Palomares district between Dublin and Hayward, and Livermore people remember seeing others camped in the mountains south of this valley. The tidal wave failed to materialize, as had the flood of ten years before."

New Peach—A new variety of clingstone peach, the Babcock, has been developed by Professor E. B. Babcock of the University of California.

Range Life—Desert moonlight, glowing campfires, cattle bedding down. Youthful cowpunchers singing of love.—Jeanette Nourland.

"The truth should be kept constantly in mind by every free people desiring to preserve the sanctity and poise indispensable to the permanent success of self government."—Theodore Roosevelt.

Native Sons of the Golden West

ARRANGEMENTS FOR THE FIFTY-SIXTH Grand Parlor, which convenes at Grass Valley, Nevada County, May 15, are progressing under the supervision of Quartz No. 58, the host-Parlor. A general committee, composed of the following, is in charge: Loyle Freeman (chairman), Allen Joyner, James Oliver, Robert Kohler, John R. Thomas, Ralph Vincent and Fred Coombs. Financial success has already been guaranteed by the business houses of Grass Valley.

President Frank J. Rowe and the general committee of Quartz Parlor have appointed the following subcommittees to work out all details: Finance—William Sampson (chairman), Alvon Jones, Earl Bonham, Frank J. Rowe. Transportation—Frank L. Hooper (chairman), Wm. P. Fox, George Hammill, R. L. P. Bigelow, Ed Baker, J. C. Tyrrell. Banquet—Fred Coombs (chairman), Henry Beretta, Allen Joyner. Housing—Native Daughters, and Loyle Freeman, Ralph Vincent. Grand Ball—John R. Thomas (chairman), Joseph Henwood, James Chellew, Stanley Wilcox, George Hammill, Eliza Kilroy, George Neagle. Music—H. Ray George (chairman), Edward F. Burtner, Harold George. Entertainment — Robert Kohler (chairman), William Phillips, Dr. C. W. Chapman, R. L. P. Bigelow, H. Ray George. Reception—Frank Rowe (chairman), George L. Jones, M. J. Brock, Thomas Harris, R. L. P. Bigelow, Dr. C. W. Chapman. Decorations—Edward Burtner (chairman), Lester Whitburn, Charles Beloud. Other committee chairmen include: publicity, H. Ray George; badges and registration, James Oliver; general program, J. C. Tyrrell; special entertainment, M. J. Brock.

"This will be more than just a meeting," writes Robert J. Deward to The Grizzly Bear in Quartz Parlor's behalf, "for Grass Valley is the center of the gold-rush country, and in precincts can still be found much of the glamor and color which made it famous as a mining camp. In spite of the fact that Grass Valley is an old mining town, it has kept pace with the world in progress, and all the conveniences of any modern city will be found there. Set aside May 15 to 18 on your calendar for the journey to Grass Valley and the Fifty-sixth Grand Parlor."

A Sketch of the Entertainment.

First—For those fortunate enough to reach Grass Valley by Sunday noon, May 14, there is a trip to the famous gold mines, a chance to see them producing the yellow metal, and a trip 9,000 feet down into the depths of the earth to see the quartz gold being taken from the veins.

Second — Welcome entertainment Monday night, May 15.

Third—Grand Parlor banquet. Also, a grand ball and, as Sluice Box Ike says, "If yuh ain't never been t' a gran' ball in these yere hills yuh ain't seen nothin' yet!"

Fourth—An all-day tour of the gold country and forgotten mining camps; stalking the trail of the '49er through the famous hydraulic diggings and along the high Sierran streams.

Note—Room reservations may be made through the Grass Valley Chamber of Commerce. State the number of people, number of rooms desired, with or without bath, etc.

Candidates for Grand Parlor Offices.

Grand President Seth Millington (Colusa No. 69) will preside at the Grass Valley Grand Parlor, and at its close will automatically become the Junior Past Grand. There is not a rumor to indicate other than that Grand First Vice Justice Emmet Seawell (Santa Rosa No. 28) will be advanced to Grand President, Grand Second Vice Chas. A. Koenig (Golden Gate No. 29) to Grand First Vice, and Grand Third Vice Harmon D. Skillin (Castro No. 232) to Grand Second Vice. Candidates for other elective offices are:

DEDICATIONS—ATTEND!

At Martinez, Contra Costa County, the Hall of Records will be dedicated Sunday, April 9, at 2 p.m.

At Petaluma, Sonoma County, the new Postoffice will be dedicated Saturday, April 15, at 2 p.m.

Grand President Seth Millington will preside at both ceremonies, and will be assisted by grand officers and past grand presidents. All Natives are especially requested to attend these dedications, which are of a public nature.

Grand Third Vice-president—Grand Trustee seph J. McShane (Twin Peaks No. 214) of n Francisco.

Grand Secretary—John T. Regan (South San ancisco No. 157) of San Francisco, incumbent.

Grand Treasurer—John A. Corotto (San Jose ., 22) of San Jose, incumbent.

Grand Inside Sentinel—Grand Outside Sen- iel William A. Reuter (Sepulveda No. 263) of n Pedro.

Grand Trustees (seven to be chosen)—Jesse Miller (California No. 1) of San Francisco, :umbent; Henry S. Lyon (Placerville No. 9) Placerville, incumbent; Horace J. Leavitt fount Bally No. 87) of Weaverville, incum- nt; Charles H. Spengemann (Hesperian No. 7) of San Francisco, incumbent; Eldred L. eyer (Santa Monica Bay No. 267) of Santa onica, incumbent.

Plentiful rumors of other candidates for va- ous Grand Parlor offices have reached The izzly Bear; in fact, as regards one particular fice they have been persistent, and have orig- ated at several different sources. All rumored ndidates for every office have been communi- ted with. Those only who have supplied defi- te information are listed above. Some pros- ctive candidates are, no doubt, waiting for eir Parlors to select delegates, and as all Sub- dinate Parlors must elect at the first meetings April, there may shortly be several hats, some them new, thrown into the Grand Parlor fice freeforall. The Grizzly Bear for May will ve specially interesting news.—C.M.H.

Forty-ninth Anniversary Celebrated.

Santa Rosa—Native Sons by the hundreds ocked here March 18 to help Santa Rosa No. 3 celebrate its forty-ninth institution anniver- ary. From the Parlors of Marin, Napa, So- oma, Alameda and San Francisco they came in rge delegations, several being accompanied by rum and bugle corps. At 8:30 a parade was rmed and, led by the drum and bugle corps of lount Tamalpais No. 64, paraded the principal reets, gaily decorated and illuminated for the vent. At the Parlor meeting two candidates ere initiated, the officers of the Parlor, headed y President George Eckman, exemplifying the itual in a very efficient manner. This was also he occasion of the official visit of Grand Trustee harles H. Spengemann, who brought with him wenty-five members of Hesperian No. 137 (San rancisco. Other grand officers in the crowd ere Grand Second Vice-president Chas. A. Koe- ig, Grand Third Vice-president Harmon D. Skil- n, Grand Secretary John T. Regan, Grand Trus- ees Joseph J. McShane and Jesse H. Miller, nd Grand Inside Sentinel Gam Hurst.

The principal address of the evening was de- vered by Grand First Vice-president Justice mmet Seawell, a charter member and the first ecording secretary of Santa Rosa. In a resume f the Parlor's history he stated it was orig- ally known as "Western Star," and was insti- ated with thirty-two charter members March 5, 1884, by the late Dr. Charles W. Decker, hen a district deputy and subsequently a Grand resident. He spoke hopefully of the state of he Order, and declared "We are holding our embership better than any other order in alifornia. Despite the present financial strin- ency the prospects for the future are bright, ut the Order can not and must not stand still— t must be progressive." Thomas Hutchinson, nother of the three remaining charter mem- ers, was a participant in the festivities. A umptuous banquet concluded the most enjoy- ble affair.

During the evening attention was called to he fact that Justice Seawell will, in May, be- ome the Grand President of the Order, and it was urged that, in recognition of his fifty years f activity in the Order, all Parlors enthusias- ically endeavor to increase their membership nder his leadership. Representatives of San rancisco and other Parlors pledged 100 percent upport for the Admission Day, September 9, elebration to be held in Santa Rosa.

Olney Pedigo, Wesley Colgan and James Brucker have been named a committee to ar- ange a membership drive for No. 28. Practice eason opened March 19 for the Parlor's base- all team. Matt Rogina, athletic chairman, ex- ects to turn out a fast club.

Cornerstone Federal Building Laid.

Marysville—The cornerstone of this city's 150,000 federal building was laid March 11 by Grand President Seth Millington, assisted by Past Grands Fred H. Greeley and Lewis F. By- ngton, Grand Secretary John T. Regan, and Grand Trustees Joseph J. McShane and Charles H. Spengemann. A crowd of 300 witnessed the eremonies.

Peter J. Delay (Marysville No. 6) was chairman of the day, and addresses were made by Mayor Dan E. Bryant of Marysville, Grand President Millington, Postmaster James M. Cremin of Marysville, Postmaster Harold J. McCurry of Sacramento, Past Grand Greeley, Past Grand Byington, and Past Grands Esther R. Sullivan and Alison F. Watt of the Native Daughters. The Marysville highschool band, directed by F. D. Silver, contributed several selections.

Plan Landmarks' Restoration.

San Diego—San Diego No. 108 had a birthday party March 15 for members born in March. The program was arranged by President Martin J. Spangler, who was assisted by Jack Spencer, Dr. Clinton H. Henderson, Virgil Bruschi Jr., Charles H. Korander, James Navarro, John P. Murphy, Marshall V. Cruze and Burt W. Pauter. District Deputy Edward H. Dowell explained immigration legislation in which the Order is interested.

Deputy Grand President Albert V. Mayrhofer outlined a program for the restoration of two San Diego County landmarks conspicuous in early California history—El Campo Santo and the Butterfield stage station in Vallecitos Valley.

Splendid Talk.

Sonora—Grand Trustee Jesse H. Miller officially visited Tuolumne No. 144 and Columbia No. 258 in joint session here. He gave a splendid talk and in referring to the difficulties of fraternal orders expressed the opinion that "local lodges were the better qualified to shape their own destinies and map out a course to carry on during the present conditions." Other speakers at the enthusiastic meeting were John J. Slattery and Fred Ehlers (California No. 1), President T. M. Wilzinski of Tuolumne and Rowan Hardin. A chicken-pie repast concluded the gathering.

Proud of Basketball Laurels.

Oakland—Claremont No. 240 has a membership committee, headed by George Davis, securing new recruits. Two class initiations have been held, and another large class of candidates will be initiated in the near-future. A benefit whist drew a large crowd and, through the generosity of Harry Burns, a neat sum was realized for the homeless children. The Parlor has voted to send The Grizzly Bear to the Golden Gate Branch Public Library, believing that it will further the aims and objects of the Order in the community. The overseas flag of No. 240 is on display at the library.

Claremont has the honor of being the first Alameda County Parlor to win the basketball trophy in the San Francisco Bay area. After winning the largest percentage of games in the Alameda County tournament the Claremonters clashed with the team of Castro No. 232 (San Francisco) and carried off the laurels by a large majority. A large crowd witnessed the game. No. 240 hopes to have as well-organized a team next season, and to retain the prize it labored so hard to win.

Membership Standing Largest Parlors.

San Francisco—Grand Secretary John T. Regan reports the standing of the Subordinate Parlors having a membership of over 400 January 1, 1933, as follows, together with their membership figures March 20, 1933:

Parlor.	Jan. 1	Mch. 20	Gain	Loss
Ramona No. 109	1032	1033	1	....
South San Francisco No. 157	803	803	....	....
Castro No. 232	764	764	....	....
Stanford No. 76	575	578	3	....
Arrowhead No. 110	573	572	....	1
Stockton No. 7	535	535	....	....
Twin Peaks No. 214	522	517	....	5
Piedmont No. 120	491	490	....	1
Rincon No. 72	418	414	....	4

Large Class Initiated.

Merced—A large class of candidates, rounded up by Deputy Grand President Al Lobree, were added to the membership roll of Yosemite No. 24, March 27. The ritual was exemplified by a team made up of A. B. Gibson (Arrowhead No. 110), president; George H. Medina (Modesto No. 11), second vice; P. A. Dillard, A. E. Daneri, P. R. Murray, P. V. Bell and I. H. Reuter of Yosemite. Modesto No. 11 sent over a large delegation, headed by a committee composed of L. E. Bither (chairman), Carol Downer, Myron Moyle, Guy Allen and M. V. Wilson.

Saint Patrick's Dance.

San Bernardino—There was a big crowd at the March 1 meeting of Arrowhead No. 110, when Grand Trustee Eldred L. Meyer paid his official visit. Officers of Los Angeles No. 45, headed by President Leslie A. Packard, exemplified the ritual, and Past Grand John T. Newell

(Continued on Page 15)

LOS ANGELES
CITY AND COUNTY

THE EVENING OF MARCH 10 A SEvere earthquake shock occurred in Los Angeles and Orange Counties, and caused the loss of several lives and millions of dollars. The Cities of Long Beach, Compton, San Pedro and Santa Ana were the hardest hit, but all other communities, including Los Angeles City, were well shaken. Some grossly exaggerated statements of the catastrophe and, also, some minimizing the havoc wrought, have been published. The Grizzly Bear, therefore, presents "The Facts About the Earthquake" compiled by the Los Angeles Chamber of Commerce, believing them to be conservative:

"At about 5:55 p.m. a temblor that apparently, according to experts, originated in the Pacific Ocean and moved eastwardly, shook southern California. Those communities that were nearest the origin of the quake felt it the most severely. Communication of all kinds was interrupted, and in the ensuing confusion rumor followed rumor in rapid succession. At first it was stated that entire communities were razed. Subsequent check the next morning revealed a very different situation. The appalling loss of life prematurely announced proved to be a great deal less. While the loss of a single life is to be regretted, and no one would minimize the suffering of the 119 who died and the scores of others who were injured to a more or less serious degree, this figure is not enormous compared to the total population of approximately three millions who reside in this area.

"The loss of buildings in some communities was more severe than in others. In nearly every case those buildings which collapsed were ones that had been built for many years or were not modern in their construction.

"One community with an assessed valuation of $165,000,000 and a population of 140,000 sustained a loss estimated at $25,000,000. Other communities received considerable damage to their business districts, which consisted largely of one-story buildings rather poorly constructed. The total amount of damage in the entire area is estimated at not to exceed $45,000,000.

"Work was begun the next day to clear away the debris. The reconstruction program is already well under way. At this writing, March 14, all communities affected have already undertaken a program to reconstruct their buildings not only upon the most modern lines, but also in the modernizing to include provision for beautification. . . . The assessed valuation of these two counties [Los Angeles and Orange] most affected by the shake is approximately three and three-quarters billions, which would equal an actual valuation of over seven billions. The ratio of forty-five millions to seven billions gives an approximation of the amount of physical damage. . . .

"Southern California has not lost its faith or confidence in itself or in its future. With the courage characteristic of this entire community, we are proceeding with our task of rebuilding damaged structures and strengthening others. Business is going on as usual."

The American Red Cross is conducting a drive for funds to aid sufferers in the earthquake zone, particularly small-home owners, who were heavy losers. The cause is most worthy, so contribute liberally!

When you purchase goods advertised in The Grizzly Bear, or answer an advertisement in this magazine, please be sure to mention The Grizzly Bear. That's co-operation mutually beneficial.

NATIVE DAUGHTERS CARRY ON—PRESENT FLAG TO "CONSTITUTION."

Long Beach—Still nervous and a bit pale, the members of Long Beach Parlor No. 154 N.D.G.W. carried on, with the indomitable spirit of their forebears, March 16, escorting Grand President Anna Mixon Armstrong to the United States Frigate "Constitution," where they were most cordially received by Commander Louis J. Gulliver. Passes to proceed through the quake zone were issued by Sheriff Eugene W. Biscailuz.

President Eleanor Johnson introduced Mrs. Armstrong who, on behalf of Long Beach Parlor, presented to the "Constitution" the emblem of the Order—the "California Republic" Flag—attractively framed and appropriately inscribed. She told "the purpose it had served in 1846, when the Pioneers wrested California from the Mexicans and held it until the Flag of the Union replaced it." In accepting the gift, Commander Gulliver paid high tribute to California.

Arrangements for the flag's presentation were made by the history and landmarks committee of Long Beach Parlor—Mms. Ana Begue Packman, Gertrude Riddle and Julie Pedroli. Others in attendance were Grand Outside Sentinel Hazel B. Hansen, Supervising Deputy Florence Dodson Schoneman, Deputy Kate McFadyen, Gladys Neiman (Woodland No. 90), President Mattie Labory-Gara and Teresa Labory-Bouttier (Los Angeles No. 124). Under date of March 17, Mrs. Packman received the following letter:

"I write to thank you for the beautiful flag of the California Republic, presented by the Native Daughters of the Golden West, Long Beach Parlor No. 154. This flag, representing as it does, part of the glorious traditions of the sovereign State of California, will form a much cherished and highly valuable addition to the collection on board 'Old Ironsides.'

"I want also to express my appreciation for your thrilling account of the origin of California as a State of the United States; it made me realize more than ever the fact that those who pioneered into California were of the same caliber as the men of iron who manned this gallant ship in her heyday. Please accept the thanks of the officers and crew for this gift, and for the fine spirit of patriotism which accentuated it. With my deep appreciation, I have the pleasure to remain, very sincerely yours, LOUIS J. GULLIVER, Commander, U. S. Navy, Commanding United States Frigate Constitution."

QUAKE STALLS INITIATION.

Compton—Compton Parlor No. 273 N.S.G.W. had initiation February 28, six candidates being received and the ritual being exemplified by a team from Sepulveda Parlor No. 263 (San Pedro), with President Patrick H. Doran in charge. Grand Outside Sentinel William A. Reuter was among the many visitors.

Another class of candidates was to have been initiated by Compton, with its own ritual team officiating, March 14, but the quake demolished its meetingplace. The Parlor will soon be operating again, however, and it has a "live" membership committee in the field composed of Reid Young (chairman), Dr. Morgan S. Ralls and Secretary William Don Castillo.

HISTORIC SPOT PLAQUED.

At a colorful ceremony March 12, Los Angeles Parlor No. 124 N.D.G.W. marked with a copper plaque—made and donated by Mrs. Lucy and Miss Dolores Malin—one of Los Angeles County's many historic spots, the Rocha adobe, located on Cadillac avenue, Culver City. This old homesite was originally part of one of the early Mexican grants and was deeded to Jose

Rocha November 8, 1872. About one hundred guests were present, with several of the Parlor's members in Spanish costumes.

Past Grand President Grace S. Stoermer was mistress of ceremonies, and a prayer was offered by Archbishop Francisco Orozco Jeminez of Mexico. Miss Marvel Thomas delivered the dedicatory message. The plaque was unveiled by Grand President Anna Mixon Armstrong, and in the name of the Rocha family was accepted by Mrs. Ascension Simon. The ceremonies concluded with the singing of "I Love You, California," led by Mrs. John B. Stewart.

HELP HOLLYWOOD CELEBRATE!

Hollywood Parlor No. 196 N.S.G.W. is making extraordinary arrangements for its institution anniversary party, which will be held Wednesday evening, April 19, at the Hollywood Athletic Club, 6521 Sunset boulevard. Dinner will be served at 7 o'clock. The fee is $1.50 per plate.

This year Hollywood's annual will be a strictly stag affair, "in keeping with the traditional manner of old Corona." The committee in charge—W. L. O'Meara (chairman), John J. Ford and Lee Owen—promises the best of entertainment. President Henry G. Bodkin extends an invitation to all members of the Order to join in and help Hollywood celebrate. April 17, the Parlor will initiate several candidates. "Gene" Murphy, well and favorably known to all Native Sons, has again donned the "harness" and is now the first vice-president of No. 196.

"SWEET ARE ALL THINGS."

March 15, Grand President Anna Mixon Armstrong paid her official visit to Los Angeles Parlor No. 124 and Santa Monica Bay Parlor No. 245 N.D.G.W. in joint session. Owing to the earthquake turmoil, No. 124, the hostess, invited Long Beach Parlor No. 154 and Rudecinda Parlor No. 230 (San Pedro) to participate, and they accepted. Among the many in attendance were representatives of several other Parlors, Founder Lily O. Reichling-Dyer, Past Grand Grace S. Stoermer, Grand Outside Sentinel Hazel B. Hansen and Supervising Deputy Florence Schoneman.

For the meeting, which was preceded by a supper, the hall was adorned with baskets of spring flowers. Eighteen candidates were initiated, thirteen for Los Angeles, three for Santa Monica Bay and two for Long Beach. Grand President Armstrong gave a most inspiring talk on the Order's projects and complimented No. 124 on the letter-perfect rendition of the ritual. Other speakers were Founder Dyer, Past Grand Stoermer, Alice M. Lane (Castro No. 178) of San Francisco, Mrs. Leland Atherton Irish and Deputy Rita Smith. Reports from members of participating Parlors showed activity in all of the Order's projects, and Los Angeles adopted a baby.

A delightful surprise of the evening was the presentation to ever-faithful Annie L. Adair by President Matty Gara of a life membership in Los Angeles Parlor. Grand President Armstrong was the recipient of many gifts, a specially unique one being that of Rudecinda Parlor—a mailbox, designed by Carrie Northway, containing five dollars in currency; Carrie Kuhlman made the presentation address. Home-made refreshments, in charge of Edna Holcomb, concluded a most delightful gathering pervaded by a true fraternal atmosphere.

Los Angeles Parlor's April calendar includes: monthly card party, 12th, Ella Steinbeck chairman; potluck dinner and speaker, 19th; thirty-second birthday party, Jennie Raymond chairman, 26th. President Matty Gara's Easter greetings: "Sweet are all things, when we learn to prize them. Not for their sake, but His who grants them or denies them."

COME, ALL YE NATIVE SONS!

Santa Monica—April 5, Santa Monica Bay Parlor No. 267 N.S.G.W. will inaugurate a series of past presidents nights. The first will honor Sheriff Eugene W. Biscauliz. A large class of candidates will be presented for initiation, and the ritual will be exemplified by the officers of Los Angeles Parlor No. 45. A program of entertainment up to the standard set by No. 267 will be featured, and refreshments will be served. President Art Leonard says, "Come on, all ye Native Sons, and we will make you happy."

APRIL FOOL DANCE, AT GLENDALE.

Glendale—Grand President Anna Mixon Armstrong was honored by Verdugo Par or No. 240 N.D.G.W. at a dinner March 14. ı Miniature orange trees and orange blossoms were the California decorative motif. Other guests were Past Grand Grace S. Stoermer, Supervising Deputy

(Continued on Page 13)

CLASSIFIED DIRECTORY LOS ANGELES NATIVE SONS

ATTORNEYS-AT-LAW.

HENRY G. BODKIN. V. P. LUCAS.
Chester Williams Bldg., 215 W. 5th St.
Phone: MUtual 8151.

DAVID H. CLARK.
215 West Fifth St.
Phone: MUtual 8406.

EDWIN A. MESERVE. SHIRLEY E. MESERVE.
555 So. Flower St.
Phone: TRinity 6161.

THOS. B. REED.
548 South Spring St.
Phone: VAndike 6687.

DETECTIVE SERVICE.

LOUIS A. DUNI.
523 Washington Bldg., 311½ So. Spring.
Phone: TUcker 3911.

GENERAL INSURANCE.

THOMAS C. STEPHENS.
208 W. Eighth St., Suite 926.
Phone: TUcker 5543

Native Daughters of the Golden West

THE FORTY-SEVENTH GRAND PARlor of the Order of Native Daughters of the Golden West convenes Monday, June 19, and "shall continue in session for not more than four days." The meetingplace has not, as yet, been determined. The 1932 (Merced) Grand Parlor voted to hold the 1933 session in Alameda County, and the grand officers will fix the place. Subordinate Parlors are required to elect their delegates—one at large and one additional for each fifty members at the time of election—at the first regular meeting in May.

Grand President Anna Mixon Armstrong (Woodland No. 90) of Woodland will preside at the 1933 Grand Parlor. Grand Vice-president Irma Laird (Alturas No. 159) of Alturas will, unless the usual custom be reversed, be selected to succeed her as head of the Order.

Indications are that there will be a considerable number of candidates for the other Grand Parlors elective offices. The Grizzly Bear has communicated with all "suspicioned" and rumored candidates, and from information received announces these:

Grand Vice-president—Grand Marshal Gladys E. Noce (Amapola No. 80) of Sutter Creek.

Grand Marshal—Grand Trustee Anna Thuesen (Alta No. 3) of San Francisco; Grand Trustee Edna B. Briggs (La Bandera No. 110) of Sacramento.

Grand Inside Sentinel—Grand Outside Sentinel Hazel B. Hansen (Verdugo No. 240) of Glendale.

Grand Outside Sentinel—Alice Mathias (El Carmelo No. 181) of Daly City.

Grand Organist—Clara Gairaud (Vendome No. 100) of San Jose, incumbent.

Grand Trustees (seven to be selected)—Grand Inside Sentinel Orinda G. Giannini (Orinda No. 56) of San Francisco; Minna Kane Horn (Eschscholtzia No. 112) of Etna, incumbent; Alice M. Lane (Castro No. 178) of San Francisco; Florence D. Boyle (Gold of Ophir No. 190) of Oroville, incumbent; Ethel S. Begley (Marinita No. 198) of San Rafael, incumbent.

The Grizzly Bear has additional first-hand information which leads to the conclusion that there will likely be other aspirants for all the Grand Parlor offices, excepting of course the grand presidency and the grand vice-presidency. So, look for future announcements.—C.M.H.

GRAND PRESIDENT'S OFFICIAL ITINERARY.

Woodland—Grand President Anna Mixon Armstrong will, during April and May, visit the following Subordinate Parlors on the dates noted:

APRIL.

5th—Fresno, Madera, Merced and Mariposa Counties district meeting, at Merced.
10th—Marinita No. 198, San Rafael.
11th—Joaquin No. 5, Stockton.
17th—Palo Alto No. 229, Palo Alto.
18th—Yosemite No. 83, San Francisco.
19th—Donner No. 198, Byron.
20th—Balboa No. 249, San Francisco.
21st—Betsy Ross No. 238, Centerville.
22nd—Calaveras and Amador Counties district meeting, at Ione.
24th—Golden Gate No. 158, San Francisco.
25th—Antioch No. 223 (Antioch) and Stirling No. 146 (Pittsburg), jointly at Antioch.
26th—Dolores No. 169, San Francisco.
27th—Mary E. Bell No. 224, Dixon.
29th—Clear Lake No. 135, Middletown.

MAY.

1st—Eldora No. 248, Turlock.
2nd—Portola No. 172, San Francisco.
3rd—James Lick No. 220, San Francisco.
6th—District meeting, Gold of Ophir No. 190 (Oroville), Annie K. Bidwell No. 168 (Chico), Plumas Pioneer No. 219 (Quincy), Berryessa No. 192 (Willows), at Chico.
9th—Utopia No. 252, San Francisco.

Revival of Interest in the Home.

Bakersfield—Grand President Anna Mixon Armstrong officially visited El Tejon No. 239 and Miocene No. 228 (Taft) in joint session here March 3. "More applications to adopt children have been made since the depression than ever before, a fact we ascribe to definite revival of interest in the home," declared Mrs. Armstrong in the course of an address dealing with the Order's worth-while projects.

One candidate was initiated, the ritual being exemplified by the officers of El Tejon, with Georgia Florence Sanders as president. Seven Parlors were represented, and among the visitors were Grand Outside Sentinel Hazel B. Hansen, Supervising Deputies Florence Schoneman and Minnie B. Heath, and Deputy Jennie Dennis. The hall was decorated in spring flowers, and presentations were made. March 12, in recognition of Arbor Day, El Tejon planted trees at Kern County Park. Etta Borgwardt, Grace Dorris and Ernestine Edwards were in charge.

Past Presidents To Meet.

San Francisco—The sixth annual meeting of the Past Presidents General Association will be held April 22 at the N.D.G.W. Home, 555 Baker street, with Chief President Cora Stobing presiding. Other officers are: Lily May Tilden, senior chief president; Josephine Clark, junior chief president; Winifred Halter, vice-president; Mary Frances Mitchell, marshal; Antha Locklin, organist; Anna G. Loser, secretary; Emma G. Foley, treasurer; Margaret Grote Hill, inside sentinel; Emilie J. Clifford, outside sentinel.

Leah M. Williams founded the association, and the past chief presidents include Beda Pacheco, Winnie Buckingham, Anna G. Loser, Josephine Schmidt, Susie K. Christ, Eldora F. McCarty and Millie Tietjen. May R. Barry, Jeunie Brown and Emma G. Foley are permanent members.

Eventful Occasion.

Hollister—Grand President Anna Mixon Armstrong officially visited Copa de Oro No. 105 and San Juan Bautista No. 179 in joint session here February 23. Other visitors were Grand Secretary Sallie R. Thaler, Grand Trustee Anna Thuesen, Grand Organist Clara A. Gairaud, Past Grand Bertha A. Briggs, Supervising Deputy Rose Rhyner and Deputy Edna Butterfield. A potluck dinner and program preceded the meeting.

The eventful occasion marked also the thirty-fourth anniversary of Copa de Oro and the twenty-third of San Juan Bautista. Three candidates were initiated for the former Parlor. Mrs. Armstrong delivered an inspiring address. Numerous presentations were made, among them flower vases to the hostess Parlors by President Gladys Dodd on behalf of Aleli No. 102 (Salinas). The following morning Deputy Butterfield entertained at breakfast in honor of Grand President Armstrong.

March 9, Copa de Oro had a hilarious party in honor of Saint Patrick and initiated one candidate. "Tay" was poured at a table made attractive with refreshments of green. Representatives of Ireland's first families were on hand to engage in appropriate contests.

Eight Redwoods Planted and Dedicated.

San Jose—Vendome No. 100 had a get-together dinner March 8, and some 150 were in attendance. President Dorothy Salas extended greetings, and Past Grand President Thomas Monahan of the Native Sons and President Dorothy Koeber of San Jose No. 81 were the speakers. Mrs. Herbert Stockton was general chairman of the affair. A jolly "Irish night" was held March 5 with Grand Organist Clara Gairaud as chairman. She was assisted by Gertrude Musser, Julia Waddington, Alice Roll, Martha Waddington and Eleanor Thompson. A class of candidates will be initiated during April. The past presidents club of the Parlor met March 7 at the home of Julia Waddington and arranged for the annual Easter treat for the tubercular children at the Preventorium.

Eight redwood trees were planted and dedicated March 12 in the Rose Gardens. John Burnett, Grand Trustee N.S., was the principal speaker. The affair was under the auspices of San Jose No. 22 and Observatory No. 177 N.S.G.W., and San Jose No. 81 and Vendome No. 100 N.D.G.W. Grand Organist Clara Gairaud sends, through The Grizzly Bear, thanks to the hundreds of Natives who sent messages to her expressing hope for her complete recovery from the terrible auto accident of August 12. "I can never thank those members enough for their wonderful kindness," she says. "Thank God, I am myself again."

Sonoma-Marin District Meet.

Sonoma—The annual district meeting of the Sonoma and Marin Counties Parlors attracted some 300, among them Grand President Anna Mixon Armstrong, Grand Secretary Sallie R. Thaler, Grand Trustees Willow Borba, Ethel Begley and Anna Thuesen, Grand Inside Sentinel Orinda Giannini, Past Grands Emma Foley, Margaret Hill and Dr. Louise C. Heilbron, Supervising Deputy Clytie Lewis. Sonoma No. 209 was the hostess. Three candidates were initiated for Santa Rosa No. 217, the ritual being faultlessly rendered by a team headed by Deputy Mary Vogt as president.

Grand President Armstrong gave a fine talk on the California State (Bear) Flag, and made a most impressive appeal for support of the Order's homeless children program. Several presentations were made, and a humorous program was presented by members from San Rafael, Santa Rosa and Fairfax. Refreshments, served under the direction of Gertrude Groskopf, concluded a most delightful gathering.

Benefit Card Party.

Vallejo—With President Mabel Thompson presiding, Vallejo No. 195 initiated three candidates March 15. Among the many in attendance

"MARK OUR LANDMARKS"

Chester F. Gannon

(HISTORIOGRAPHER N.S.G.W.)

"MARK OUR LANDMARKS"

ORATORY FLIGHTS

THE PIONEER ERA WAS NOT ONLY A golden era for material things, but also the Golden Age of Oratory. Then was a time in which the spoken word was triumphant, and he who was preeminent rhetorically was also destined to become preeminent in law, public office and kindred endeavors.

As we survey our oratorical past, we conclude that orators of that era were of a different calibre than popular public speakers of today. A reading of public addresses and orations of the fifties and sixties leaves the reader with one impression—that those orators were academic, that they carefully prepared their addresses, that they were skilled in metaphysics, logic, literature, law, and knew well the wide and lengthy channels of history. Particularly did they have an absolute knowledge of Greek and Roman mythology, and often did they parade their gods and godesses as they were needed to embellish the subject.

As we review California's forensic past, the wonder grows that this state in its babyhood could have been so blessed with such artists of the spoken word. Recently the writer reviewed a book published in San Francisco in 1870. It contains biographical sketches of the coast's prominent citizens from the Mexican era to the year 1869. As one reads, he is astounded that men of such rare ability should be so little known today. It might be added that capable public speakers were plentiful, and one who gained prominence in such a class was capable indeed.

Another thing which marks that era as distinctive is the fact that most of those learned men were not college bred but had a prescribed education but little longer than did Abraham Lincoln. But ambition, that mighty fire which can burn so brightly, spurred them on to do what appears today to be almost the impossible, and proves, as an American recently said, that "education is a matter of desire."

Despite the splendidness of those masterly addresses it is doubtful if present audiences would be responsive and appreciative. The principal reason for doubt is that they were academic and dealt with subjects and references not altogether familiar with a present-day general assemblage. Also, they were lengthy. It must have taken the speakers at least two hours to have concluded their addresses. What gathering would be satisfied today to sit, even in comfortable chairs and amid pleasant surroundings, to hear such lengthy discourses? Cannot you hear the comment "longwinded," "baloney," "applesauce," and kindred expressions which oft greet the spoken word?

One of the foremost speakers of his day was Frank Tilford. Of true pioneer stock, he sprang from ancestors who had driven the Indian tribes from the Mississippi River. At the age of 27, in the year 1849, he turned his face westward and arrived the same year in San Francisco. There he lived the remainder of his days. This is no place to trace his legal and political career. For the purpose of depicting his style—and as this article is written, St. Patrick's Day is being celebrated—it is not amiss to revert back to that other day in San Francisco when, on the 17th of March, 1863, at the Metropolitan Theater he delivered an oration on St. Patrick. This is but a fragment of his utterances:

"On the banks of the Shannon, in the mines of Australia, amid the orange groves of the Tropics, in the ruined cities of the Orient, and under the shade of the primeval forests which fringe the waters of the Mississippi, thousands of eyes will beam with rapture as they behold unfurled to the breeze, and radiant in the bright light of heaven, that symbol of nationality and emblem of freedom, the ancient banner of the 'Harp and Sunburst.' Thousands of generous hearts will throb with exultation, as they recall the glorious memories of the Emerald Isle; memories, musical and immortal as the leaves of the Tooba tree which blooms only in the Garden of Paradise, and 'whose scent is the breath of eternity.' The history of Ireland!—the very words awaken feelings unutterable in the heart of the exile. What intellect can do justice to the theme? As the rainbow is formed by the tears of the clouds and the rays of the sun, so are the annals of Erin colored and varied; now by the tears of sorrow, now by the flashes of wit and sunshine of joy."

Edward J. C. Kewen was another of the array who could indulge in the artistry of words and mould his mental thoughts into expressions of beauty and intelligence. On the 9th of September, 1854, before the Society of California Pioneers at San Francisco, on the occasion of the fourth celebration of California's entry into statehood, this brilliant, self-educated man said:

"In the history of Greece, we are enchanted with the descriptions of consecrated groves; we read with rapture of azure mountains, of flowing plains, of golden isles, and sunny fountains; but beneath this western sky are revealed as splendid attributes of nature as ever attracted the eye of the Grecian in the palmiest period of his country's glory. Ionia never boasted of fairer skies, Italy never rejoiced in a firmament more deeply blue, France never produced the luscious grape in more luxuriance, and never exhibited greener fields or more exuberant gardens; Germany never revealed sublimer forests, and Switzerland grander mountains, nor more romantic scenery than meets the gaze of the wanderer on the Pacific slope. But lovelier than the cerulean of its skies, more to be prized than the estuaries of its coast, sublimer than the undulations of its surface, greater than the exuberance of its products, more magnificent than the sublimity of its mountains, the placidity of its lakes, the abruptness and grandeur of its scenery, is the symmetrical edifice of its republican construction. Virtue and industry form the basis of its morality; shrewdness, wisdom and sagacity the distinguishing features of its mind; simplicity the proof of social excellence, and progress the aim and end of its political aspirations."

Twenty other orators are the equal to the two selected as exemplars. Is it any wonder that we may justly claim that past age as "California's Golden Age of Oratory?"

---

were Supervising Deputy Wilma Mitchell, Deputy Emma McGlumphy, and large delegations from Eschol No. 16 (Napa) and La Junta No. 203 (Saint Helena). Refreshments were served.

The Parlor and Vallejo No. 77 N.S.G.W. had a card party for the benefit of the homeless children March 14. The committee in charge included Anna Johnson (chairman), Elizabeth Bruno, Mabel Thompson, Mary Combs, John Combs, Fermin Segoria, Mike Higuera and Frank J. Holdener.

Message of Inspiration.

San Bernardino — Grand President Anna Mixon Armstrong paid an official visit March 8 to Lugonia No. 241, and was accompanied by Grand Outside Sentinel Hazel Hansen, Supervising Deputy Florence D. Schoneman and Deputy Genevieve Hiskey. Neighboring Parlors were well represented among the visitors. Spring flowers decorated the meetingplace, and three candidates were initiated.

Mrs. Armstrong's message was one of inspiration, encouragement and fellowship. Active in arranging for the occasion were Lois A. Johnson and Clara Barton. March 25, for the benefit of the Parlor, a silver tea was held at the home of Miss Barton, with members of the history and landmarks committee as hostesses.

SUBORDINATE PARLORS DOINGS.

Placerville—Marguerite No. 12 observed Arbor Day at the home of Mrs. Lloyd Hancock. In honor of President Franklin Delano Roosevelt, a birch tree was planted by President Dorian Sutton. A program was presented, games were played and refreshments were served. Ruth Baumhoff, the chairman, was assisted by Annie Jaeger, Agnes Schiff and Eva Shuman.

Lodi—Ivy No. 88 enjoyed cards and refreshments March 15. The Saint Patrick motif prevailed, and Juanita Pope and Sara Elwood were in charge. President Verna Weesner will give a card party April 4, the proceeds to go to the milk fund for the Parlor's adopted baby.

Oakland—Aloha No. 106 observed its thirty-second institution anniversary at a dinner Feb-

(Continued on Page 17)

Passing of the California Pioneer

(Confined to Brief Notices of the Demise of Those Men and Women Who Came to California Prior to 1870.)

WILLIAM A. TRUBODY, NATIVE OF Missouri, 93; with his parents crossed the plains to California and arrived at Sutter Fort (now Sacramento) in 1847; in 1856 he settled in Napa County; died at Napa City, survived by three children. He served three terms as supervisor and three terms as treasurer of Napa County.

Mrs. Charlotte Brians-Foster, native of Missouri, 88; crossed the plains in 1849 and resided in Sonoma, San Luis Obispo and Santa Cruz Counties; died at Watsonville, survived by a son.

Elias G. Compton, native of Missouri, 99; crossed the plains in 1850 and mined in El Dorado County and farmed in Mendocino County; died at Palo Alto, Santa Clara County, survived by a daughter.

Mrs. Mary Catherine Grey Arndt, native of Missouri; crossed the plains in 1850 and settled in Placer County; died at Lincoln, survived by six children.

Mrs. Isabelle Thompson, 93; crossed the plains in 1852; died at Los Angeles City, survived by two daughters.

Mrs. Vera Frances Dillon-Farmer, native of Kentucky, 84; came in 1852 and resided in El Dorado, Los Angeles and Sonoma Counties; died near Skaggs Springs, survived by three children.

Mrs. Mary Cameron-Crowe, native of Louisiana; came in 1852; died at San Francisco.

Mrs. Elizabeth Ann Ram-Howell, native of Kansas, 86; came in 1853; died at Red Bluff, Tehama County, her home for seventy-six years, survived by two daughters.

A. T. Courtright, native of Illinois, 85; came in 1855 and long resided in Amador County; died at Ione, survived by a wife. He was a veteran of the stage and the screen.

John H. Hurd, native of Pennsylvania, 80; came in 1856 and for some time resided in Nevada County; died at San Francisco.

Mrs. Mary G. Harley, native of Massachusetts, 100; came via Cape Horn in 1857 and resided in Yolo, Sacramento and Solano Counties; died at Benicia, survived by three children.

Tulare County.

Mrs. Sarah M. Furniss, 83; came via Panama in 1857 and resided in Placer and Alameda Counties; died at Oakland, survived by two sons.

Mrs. Jeanette Liddell Smith, native of Pennsylvania, 81; came in 1857 and for some time resided in Placer County; died at Sacramento City, survived by three children.

John Stephen Owen, native of Missouri, 83; came in 1859 and resided in Siskiyou, Lassen and Modoc Counties; died at San Jose, Santa Clara County.

Mrs. Lucinda Butler-Cook, native of Pennsylvania, 92; crossed the plains in 1859 and resided in Napa and San Luis Obispo Counties; died at San Luis Obispo City, survived by a daughter.

Mrs. May S. Brown, native of Iowa, 80; crossed the plains in 1860 and resided in San Joaquin and San Benito Counties; died at Santa Cruz City, survived by two children.

Mrs. Susan Beecher Hartwick-Innes, native of New York, 79; came via Panama in 1861, and resided in Santa Clara and Napa Counties; died at Alameda City, survived by two sons.

Mrs. Adeline McCarger-Mutch, 76; crossed the plains in 1861 and settled in Butte County; died at Long Beach, Los Angeles County, survived by two children.

Mrs. Ellen Brown-Loechel, native of Iowa, 79; came in 1861 and resided in Napa and Tulare Counties; died at Woodlake, survived by four children.

Charles Granier, native of Illinois, 72; came across the plains in 1862 and resided in Amador and Butte Counties; died at Oroville.

Wallace Brotherwell McKenney, native of Illinois, 86; came via Cape Horn in 1862 and settled in El Dorado County; died at Lotus, survived by a son.

Mrs. Anna Schilling-Kleine, native of Germany, 85; came via Panama in 1865 and resided many years in Santa Barbara County; died at Berkeley, Alameda County, survived by nine children.

Newton H. Foster, native of Vermont, 84; came via Panama in 1867; died at Los Angeles City, survived by a wife and three children.

Mrs. Lisetta Laux, native of Germany, 89; since 1868 Colusa County resident; died near Colusa City, survived by five children.

Henry Strippel, native of Germany, 91; came in 1868; died at Dixon, Solano County.

Mrs. Maddalena Rossetti, native of Switzerland, 82; came via Panama in 1868 and resided in San Francisco, Santa Barbara and Los Angeles Cities; died at the latter place, survived by six children.

Trovillo H. Trumbo, native of Iowa, 74; since 1868 resident Santa Cruz County; died at Swanton, survived by a wife and two children.

Ernest Gieseke, native of Germany, 83; came via Panama in 1868 and settled in San Joaquin County; died at Tracy, survived by a wife and three children, among them Mrs. Pearl Lamb, Past Grand President N.D.G.W.

Mrs. Catherine Webb, native of England; came in 1869; died at Elk Grove, Sacramento County, survived by three sons.

William P. Russell, native of Indiana, 83; came in 1869 and long resided in Riverside County; died at the Pythian Home, near Santa Rosa, Sonoma County; he was a pioneer in the state's citrus industry.

John Ashurst, native of Missouri, 75; since 1868 resident San Benito County; died near Hollister, survived by a wife and two children.

Manuel V. Brazil, 86; came in 1862; died near Georgetown, El Dorado County, survived by a wife and two children.

Asaph Alexson, native of Wisconsin, 84; came in 1864; died at Hilmar, Merced County, survived by a wife and three children.

Marcus Mullen, native of Maine, 77; since 1859 Tuolumne County resident; died at Sonora, survived by a daughter.

Mrs. Florence Adell Slade-Stone, native of Connecticut, 84; came via Panama in 1858 and settled in Placer County; died at Oakland, Alameda County, survived by six children.

Benjamin Basil Parker, native of Arkansas, 77; since 1857 resident Visalia, Tulare County, where he died; three children survive. He served Tulare County as auditor and sheriff.

Mrs. Persis H. Ainsworth, 97; came across the plains in 1853; died at Orange, Orange County, survived by a son.

PIONEER NATIVES DEAD

(Brief Notices of the Demise of Men and Women born in California Prior to 1860.)

Mrs. Martina Smith-Miles, born Contra Costa County, 1850; died February 16, Gustine, Merced County; two sons survive.

Fred Grotefend, born Shasta County, 1857; died February 18, Yreka, Siskiyou County.

Mrs. Catherine Judge, born Sierra County, 1855; died February 20, Reno, Nevada State; six children survive.

Mrs. Ellen Geraldine Robinson, born Humboldt County, 1857; died February 20, Petrolia; husband and four children survive.

Dr. August L. Vancrom, born San Francisc 1858; died February 24, Yucaipa, San Bernai dino County; wife and three children survive.

Mrs. Minnie Brown, born San Francisc 1858; died February 24, Los Angeles City; hus band and four children survive.

Mrs. Eduarda Branch-Jones, born San Lui Obispo County, 1850; died February 26, Arroy Grande; eight children survive.

Joseph Ray Hunt, born Shasta County, 1854 died February 27, Redding; wife and eight chil dren survive.

Mrs. Joseph Higuera, born Monterey County 1842; died March 1, Paso Robles, San Loui Obispo County; five children survive.

George Sims, born Lake County, 1859; die March 2, Woodland, Yolo County; wife and fou children survive.

Arthur H. Moore, born Placer County, 1854 died March 3, Oakland, Alameda County.

Cerilo Velasco, born Santa Clara County 1854; died March 6, near Watsonville, Sant Cruz County; six children survive.

Mrs. Mary Bunker-Morton, born San Francisc 1854; died there March 8; two sons survive.

Mrs. Alice Moulton-Warner, born San Fran cisco, 1854; died March 9, Piedmont, Alamed County; three children survive.

Mrs. Frances Ramona Padillo-Bernal, bor Santa Clara County, 1835; died March 10, Sa Jose.

Jake Cline, born Amador County, 1858; die March 11, Jackson.

Dennis W. Long, born San Francisco, 1857 died March 12, near Petaluma, Sonoma County three children survive.

William Henry Adams, born Sacramento City 1855; died there March 15; three children sur vive.

Robert Harris Callahan, born Tuolumn County, 1853; died March 16, Copperopolis wife and daughter survive.

James P. Logue, born Butte County, 1859 died March 17, Oroville; wife and two childre survive.

Raymond Morris Locke, born El Dorad County, 1859; died March 18, San Francisco wife and five children survive.

Mrs. Virginia Arnaz-Anguisola, born Sant Clara County, 1849; died March 20, San Fe nando, Los Angeles County.

LOS ANGELES--CITY and COUNTY

LOS ANGELES

(Continued from Page 9)

Florence Schoneman, Deputy Gertrude Allen and Grand Outside Sentinel Hazel Hansen. At the Parlor meeting three candidates were initiated, and Grand President Armstrong spoke on "True Fraternity." Dorothy Courtney sang "The Hand of You," and President Vera Carlson, on Verdugo's behalf, presented a gift to Mrs. Armstrong. Active in arranging for the delightful occasion were Myrteze Tregea, Ada Steele and Margaret Donlan.

Verdugo and Glendale Parlor No. 264 N.S.G.W. will feature an "all fools" dance Saturday evening, April 1, at Masonic Temple, 234 South Brand boulevard. The joint committee promises this will be a bigger and better dance than any previous one. April 11, Verdugo will have a dinner and card party; a magician will be there, too; all for forty cents. Everybody invited. Make reservations by April 9; phone Douglas 7781-R. To aid the Central Homeless Children Committee, Verdugo has adopted a baby.

EARTHQUAKE SHOWS REAL CHARACTER.

A beautiful side of the character of Mrs. Anna Mixon Armstrong, Grand President N.D.G.W., was shown the members of the Order in the southland during her official visits last month. Usually all is joy and gaiety when the distinguished visitor comes, and Parlors vie with one another to make her stay happy and carefree. But this year it was her misfortune, or perhaps good fortune, to be here during the earthquake, and to witness the sufferings of the people in the stricken area. She proved a great comfort, and her sisterly sympathy and womanly understanding will always remain with the people in the southland as a tender memory.

Grand President Armstrong paid her official visit, as scheduled, to Californiana Parlor No. 247, March 14. Luncheon was served, and the bright and cheery appointments helped to dispel the gloom. At the speakers' table with the honor-guest were President Ernestine Aylward; Mrs. Leland Atherton Irish, toastmistress; Mayor and Mrs. John C. Porter; Superior Judges Howell Smith and William Aggeler; Supervising Deputy Florence Schoneman; Mattie B. Edwards and Helen B. Anderson (Grace No. 242); Gladys Nieman (Woodland No. 90), sister of the Grand President; Mary Foy; Francis Hickson, the speaker of the day, who graphically described the "Mission Play of Monterey."

At the Parlor meeting, four candidates were initiated, and Mrs. Armstrong highly complimented Californiana on its activities and accomplishments. On behalf of No. 247, Mrs. Irish presented to her a gift, and a presentation was made by Past President Gertrude Tuttle to Mrs. Edwards, the Parlor's former deputy.—O.L.

DON'T FORGET THE BENEFIT DANCE!

To raise much-needed funds to carry on the homeless children work, the N.S.G.W. and N.D.G.W. Homeless Children Committee is sponsoring a dance Saturday, April 22, at the Breakfast Club. Mrs. Hazel B. Hansen heads the arrangements committee. "Cast your bread upon the waters;"—give this most deserving charity wholehearted support.

BENEFIT FOR BOY SCOUTS.

Ramona Parlor No. 109 N.S.G.W. has initiated several candidates, among them William H. Burroughs, grandson of Past Grand President Herman C. Lichtenberger. Good work in the Parlor's behalf is being done by Scoutmaster Bob Dunn, Fieldman Ralph Harbison, Curator Homer Chapelle and First Vice-president Charles Straube.

Ramona's April calendar includes: 7th, election Grass Valley Grand Parlor delegates. 14th, initiation. 21st, 6:30 dinner, complimentary to the members born in April; entertainment for benefit Ramona Boy Scouts Troop No. 109; dinner "stag," tree for all members of Parlor, public invited to entertainment. 28th, reception for members initiated during April, regardless of the year.

THE DEATH RECORD.

Rudolph Guenther Weyse, brother of Henry G. Weyse (Ramona N.S.), died at Pasadena, February 22.

John Cozzaglio, affiliated with Ramona Parlor N.S.G.W., died February 24. He was born in Sierra County, May 28, 1886.

PERSONAL PARAGRAPHS.

Sheriff Eugene W. Biscailuz (Santa Monica Bay N.S.) has been elected president of the Los Angeles County Peace Officers Association.

Congressman William I. Traeger (Past Grand President N.S.) and wife (Los Angeles N.D.) departed by airplane March 6 for Washington, D. C.

Miss Mary E. Brusie (Argonaut N.D.) of San Francisco, secretary N.S.G.W. and N.D.G.W. Central Homeless Children Committee, was a visitor last month.

GRIZZLY GROWLS

(Continued from Page 4)

by millions and not lessen government efficiency. In the interest of the near-bankrupt taxpayers, its program should have the unanimous support of the legislative and the executive branches of the State Government.

San Francisco is after the "charity racketeers." It appears that some 2,000 of them, with substantial balances in banks, have been "horning in" on funds and commodities collected for the benefit of those actually in need.

"The same sort of investigation ought to be instituted in Los Angeles," suggests a newspaper of that city, "where, in all probability, the same sort of thing has been going on." If half the rumors be true, charity racketeering is, and for a long time has been, a common practice in Los Angeles. It is doubtful, however, if the example of San Francisco will be followed there and the "charity racketeers" exposed, prosecuted, and removed from the enormous aid-list.

The "new-deal" in national affairs is, apparently, going to be a square deal, from the top, as well as from the bottom, of the pack. Instance the arrest of a couple of high-powered "nationally [in]famous financiers." Looks like the sponsors of "the hidden things of dishonesty" are, at last, to be brought to justice.

This is certain: vigorous prosecution of the highboy political, financial and business racketeers will do more to restore confidence than anything else. PROVE to the masses that "Crime [dishonesty] does not pay!", whether committed by the uppercrusters or the lowercrusters of society!

The revelations anent the disposal of worthless foreign bonds to innocent investors are appalling. Should not every individual, irrespective of who or what he be, be prosecuted for using the United States mails to defraud?

The California Garden Club Federation is anxious to have Section 384a of the State Penal Code amended so as to provide protection to any "herb or bulb or flower" similar to that now given "any native tree or shrub, or any fern." There is no good reason why the State Legislature should not provide the asked-for protection.

In last month's "Growls," reference was made to Congressman Hoeppel of California who, according to his published statement, was "shocked at the evidence of extravagance" in the National Capital. Congressman Hoeppel, however,

(Concluded on Page 20)

Official Directory of Parlors of the N. S. G. W.

ALAMEDA COUNTY.

Alameda No. 47, Alameda City—R. H. Fallmer, Pres.; Robt. H. Cavanaugh, Sec., 1806 Pacific Ave.; Wednesdays, Veterans Memorial Bldg.

Oakland No. 50, Oakland—F. R. Born, Pres.; F. M. Norris, Sec., 5595 Taft Ave.; Fridays, Native Sons Hall, 11th and Clay Sts.

Las Positas No. 96, Livermore—Dr. Donald M. Fraser, Pres.; John J. Kelly, Sec., P. O. box 341; Thursdays, Foresters Hall.

Eden No. 113, Hayward—John Meincke, Pres.; Filbert M. Soares, Sec., 1437 "B" St.; 2nd and 4th Tuesdays, Memorial Hall, Main St.

Piedmont No. 120, Oakland—Stanley Hadlen, Pres.; Charles Morando, Sec., 906 Vermont St.; Thursdays, Native Sons Hall, 11th and Clay Sts.

Wisteria No. 127, Alvarado—Henry May, Pres.; J. M. Scribner, Sec., Livermore; 1st Thursday, I.O.O.F. Hall.

Halcyon No. 146, Alameda City—S. Chesley Anderson, Pres.; J. C. Bates, Sec., 2139 Buena Vista Ave.; 1st and 3rd Tuesdays, I.O.O.F. Hall, 2329 Santa Clara Ave.

Brooklyn No. 151, Oakland—Frank B. Perry, Pres.; E. W. Cooney, Sec., 3907 14th Ave.; 1st and 3rd Wednesdays, Masonic Temple, 8th Ave. and E. 14th St.

Washington, No. 169, Centerville—M. D. Silva, Pres.; Allen G. Norris, Sec., P. O. box 31; 2nd and 4th Tuesdays, Hansen Hall.

Athens No. 195, Oakland—Milton O. Peterson, Pres.; Harold B. Farley, Sec., 4628 Benevides Ave.; Tuesdays, Native Sons Hall, 11th and Clay Sts.

Berkeley No. 210, Berkeley—F. Gohl, Pres.; R. J. Garrett, Sec., 1708 Virginia St.; Tuesdays, Native Sons Hall, 2108 Shattuck Ave.

Estudillo No. 223, San Leandro—E. E. King, Pres.; Albert G. Pacheco, Sec., 1786 E. 14th St.; 1st and 3rd Tuesdays, U.P.E.C. Hall.

Claremont No. 240, Emeryville—Raymond P. Burke, Pres.; E. N. Thienger, Sec., 839 Hearst Ave., Berkeley; Tuesdays, Veterans Memorial Bldg., 43rd and Salem Sts.

Pleasanton No. 244, Pleasanton—Edward Holzreiter, Pres.; Ernest W. Schween, Sec.; 2nd and 4th Thursdays, I.O.O.F. Hall.

Niles No. 250, Niles—M. L. Fournier, Pres.; C. E. Martenstein, Sec.; 2nd Thursday, I.O.O.F. Hall.

Fruitvale No. 252, Oakland—William J. Keating Jr., Pres.; Ray B. Felton, Sec., 1575 Alice St.; Fridays, W.O.W. Hall, 3256 E. 14th St.

AMADOR COUNTY.

Amador No. 17, Sutter Creek—J. H. Williams, Pres.; F. J. Payne, Sec.; 1st and 3rd Fridays, Native Sons Hall.

Excelsior No. 31, Jackson—Thomas G. Negrich, Pres.; William Going, Sec.; 1st and 3rd Wednesdays, Native Sons Hall, 22 Court St.

Ione No. 33, Ione—Earl Grover, Pres.; Josiah H. Saunders, Sec.; 1st and 3rd Wednesdays, Native Sons Hall.

Plymouth No. 48, Plymouth—Chester G. Johnson, Pres.; Thos. D. Davis, Sec.; 1st and 3rd Saturdays, N.S.G.W. Hall.

BUTTE COUNTY.

Argonaut No. 8, Oroville—Frank H. O'Brien, Pres.; Cyril R. Macdonald, Sec., P. O. box 502; 1st and 3rd Wednesdays, Veterans Memorial Hall.

Chico No. 21, Chico—Marcus Choisser, Pres.; Sam Lindsay Adams, Sec., Sacramento Blvd.; 2nd and 4th Thursdays, Elks Hall.

CALAVERAS COUNTY.

Chispa No. 139, Murphys—Maynard Segale, Pres.; Antone Malaspina, Sec.; Wednesdays, Native Sons Hall.

COLUSA COUNTY.

Colusa No. 69, Colusa City—Rotheus A. Gray, Pres.; Phil J. Humburg, Sec., 223 Parkhill St.; Tuesdays, Eagles Hall.

CONTRA COSTA COUNTY.

General Winn No. 32, Antioch—Edmont T. Uren, Pres.; Joel H. Ford, Sec., P. O. box 811; 2nd and 4th Wednesdays, Union Hall.

Mount Diablo No. 101, Martinez—R. P. Anderson, Pres.; G. T. Barkley, Sec.; 1st and 3rd Mondays, I.O.O.F. Hall.

Byron No. 170, Byron—William E. Bunn, Pres.; H. G. Krumland, Sec.; 1st and 3rd Tuesdays, I.O.O.F. Hall.

Carquinez No. 205, Crockett—John McManus, Pres.; Thomas R. Cox, Sec., P.O. box 721; 1st and 3rd Wednesdays, I.O.O.F. Hall.

Richmond No. 217, Richmond—Frank Weber, Pres.; Lloyd N. Mason, Sec., 11 6th St.; 1st Wednesday, 818 Macdonald Ave.

Concord No. 245, Concord—Chas. H. Gray, Pres.; D. E. Pramberg, Sec., P. O. box 235; 1st Monday, Guy's Parlors.

Diamond No. 246, Pittsburg—Victor Ericsson, Pres.; Francis A. Irving, Sec., 248 E. 5th St.; 1st and 3rd Wednesdays, Veterans Memorial Bldg.

EL DORADO COUNTY.

Placerville No. 9, Placerville—Chris. C. Orelli, Pres.; Clyde R. Berriman, Sec., Wood St.; 2nd and 4th Tuesdays, Masonic Hall.

Georgetown No. 91, Georgetown—George W. Brichler, Pres.; O. F. Irish, Sec.; 2nd and 4th Wednesdays, I.O.O.F. Hall.

FRESNO COUNTY.

Fresno No. 25, Fresno City—Oliver M. Akers, Pres.; W. O. Guard, Sec., R.F.D. No. 2, box 379; 1st and 3rd Fridays, Pythian Castle, Cor. "R" and Merced Sts.

GRAND OFFICERS.

Dr. Frank I. Gonzalez..........Junior Past Grand President
Flood Bldg., San Francisco

Seth Millington..........Grand President
Gridley

Justice Emmet Seawell..........Grand First Vice-president
State Bldg., San Francisco

Chas. A. Koenig..........Grand Second Vice-president
531 35th Ave., San Francisco

Harmon D. Skillin..........Grand Third Vice-president
Mills Bldg., San Francisco

John T. Regan..........Grand Secretary
N.S.G.W. Bldg., 414 Mason St., San Francisco

John A. Corotto..........Grand Treasurer
560 No. 5th St., San Jose

W. B. O'Brien..........Grand Marshal
2324 Santa Clara St., Alameda

Gam Hurst..........Grand Inside Sentinel
Financial Center Bldg., Oakland

William A. Reuter..........Grand Outside Sentinel
1009 Marine Ave., Wilmington

Leslie Maloche..........Grand Organist
1611 No. Hudson Ave., Los Angeles

Chester Gannon..........Historiographer
613 Capital Ntl. Bank Bldg., Sacramento

GRAND TRUSTEES.

Jesse H. Miller..........712 DeYoung Bldg., San Francisco
Eldred L. Meyer..........922 San Vicente Blvd., Santa Monica
John M. Burnett..........914 Bank Italy Bldg., San Jose
Henry S. Lyon..........Placerville
Joseph J. McShane..........419 Flood Bldg., San Francisco
Horace J. Leavitt..........Weaverville
Chas. H. Spengemann..........827 27th Ave., San Francisco

Selma No. 107, Selma—Chester E. Shepard, Pres.; E. C. Laughlin, Sec.; 1st Wednesday, American Legion Hall.

GLENN COUNTY.

Willows No. 255—Ralph W. Camper, Pres.; Leon Marshall, Sec., P.O. box 747; 2nd and 4th Tuesdays, I.O.O.F. Hall.

HUMBOLDT COUNTY.

Humboldt No. 14, Eureka—Henry Sundfors, Pres.; Loren M. Nelson, Sec., P.O. box 195; 2nd and 4th Mondays, Native Sons Hall.

Arcata No. 20, Arcata—F. A. Nicholson, Pres.; William Peters, Sec., P. O. box 1117; Thursdays, Native Sons Hall.

Ferndale No. 93, Ferndale—Hans P. Petersen, Pres.; C. H. Rasmussen, Sec., R.F.D., 47-A; 1st and 3rd Mondays, Danish Hall.

KERN COUNTY.

Bakersfield No. 42, Bakersfield—George Taylor, Pres.; Henry A. Bannister, Sec., care Bank of America; 2nd and 4th Fridays, Justice Court, City Hall.

LAKE COUNTY.

Lower Lake No. 159, Lower Lake—LeRoy England, Pres.; Albert Kugelman, Sec.; Thursdays, I.O.O.F. Hall.

LASSEN COUNTY.

Honey Lake No. 198, Standish—Leo T. Davis, Pres.; N. V. Wemple, Sec., Litchfield; 1st and 3rd Wednesdays, Wrede Hall.

Big Valley No. 211, Bieber—Fred Bunselmeier, Pres.; A. W. McKenzie, Sec.; 1st and 3rd Wednesdays, I.O.O.F. Hall.

LOS ANGELES COUNTY.

Los Angeles No. 45, Los Angeles City—Leslie A. Packard, Pres.; Willard F. Allen, Sec., 4955 Los Feliz Blvd.; Thursdays, Merchant Plumbers Hall, 1832 So. Hope.

Ramona No. 109, Los Angeles City—Frank S. Adams, Pres.; John V. Scott, Sec., Patriotic Hall, 1816 So. Figueroa; Fridays, Patriotic Hall, 1816 So. Figueroa.

Hollywood No. 196, Los Angeles City—Henry G. Bodkin, Pres.; E. J. Reilly, Sec., Olive View; Mondays, 1089 No. Oxford Ave.

Long Beach No. 239, Long Beach—Francis H. Gentry, Pres.; W. W. Brady, Sec., 801 Jergins Trust Bldg.; Dept. No. 1 Municipal Court, 8th floor Jergins Trust Bldg.

Sepulveda No. 263, San Pedro—Patrick H. Doran, Pres.; H. E. Fairall, Sec., 1925 So. Pacific Ave.; 1st and 3rd Fridays, Redman Hall, 543 Shepherd St., Point Firmin.

Glendale No. 264, Glendale—Harvey T. Gillette, Pres.; Philip D. Molen, Sec., 222 So. Glendale; 1st and 3rd Thursdays, Starr Heights Recreation Bldg., 3246 Community Place.

Santa Monica Bay 267, Santa Monica—Arthur R. Leonard, Pres.; John J. Smith, Sec., 830 Rialto Ave., Venice; 1st and 3rd Wednesdays, Odd Fellows Hall, 1431 Third St.

Cahuenga No. 268, Reseda—Harold C. Trexler, Pres.; Carrol S. Driscoll, Sec., P.O. box 25, Chatsworth; first Friday, Alton Hall.

University No. 272, Los Angeles City—Bernard G. Hiss, Pres.; Martin DeFazio, Sec., 845 W. 53rd St.; Wednesdays, 1008 West Adams St.

Compton No. 273, Compton—Laurence W. Cowan, Pres.; Wm. Don Castillo, Sec., 641 W. Bennett St.; 2nd and 4th Tuesdays, Mayo Hall, 231½ East Compton Blvd.

MADERA COUNTY.

Madera No. 130, Madera City—Cornelius Noble, Pres.; T. P. Cosgrave, Sec.; 1st and 3rd Thursdays, First National Bank Bldg.

MARIN COUNTY.

Mount Tamalpais No. 64, San Rafael—Arthur Hecht, Pres.; Manuel A. Andrade, Sec., 532 Mission Ave.; 1st and 3rd Mondays, "B" Street Hall.

Sea Point No. 158, Sausalito—Wm. W. Taylor, Pres.; Manuel Santos, Sec., 6 Glen Drive; 1st and 3rd Wednesdays, Perry Bldg.

Nicasio No. 183, Nicasio—M. T. Farley, Pres.; R. J. Rogers, Sec.; 2nd and 4th Wednesdays, U.A.O.D. Hall.

MENDOCINO COUNTY.

Ukiah No. 71, Ukiah—W. B. Danis, Pres.; Ben Hofman, Sec., P. O. box 473; 1st and 3rd Mondays, I.O.O.F. Hall.

Broderick No. 117, Point Arena—Ivan Lawson, Pres.; C. J. Buchanan, Sec.; 1st and 3rd Thursdays, Forester Hall.

Alder Glen No. 200, Fort Bragg—Thomas Cooney, Pres.; C. R. Weller, Sec.; 2nd and 4th Fridays, I.O.O.F. Hall.

MERCED COUNTY.

Yosemite No. 24, Merced City—John J. Thronton, Pres.; True W. Fowler, Sec., P. O. box 781; 2nd and 4th Mondays, I.O.O.F. Hall.

Los Banos No. 206, Los Banos—Daniel Pedroni, Pres.; L. E. Sarbo, Sec., R.F.D., box 21; 2nd and 4th Wednesdays, Eagles Hall.

MONTEREY COUNTY.

Monterey No. 75, Monterey City—James Millington, Pres.; T. W. Krieger, Sec., 999 Franklin St.; 1st and 3rd Fridays, Knights Pythias Hall, Main St.

Santa Lucia No. 97, Salinas—Roy Martella, Pres.; R. W. Adcock, Sec., Route 2, box 180; Mondays, Native Sons Hall, 32 W. Alisal St.

Gabilan No. 132, Castroville—B. A. McCoy, Pres.; R. H. Martin, Sec., P. O. box 81; 1st and 3rd Thursdays, Native Sons Hall.

NAPA COUNTY.

Saint Helena No. 53, Saint Helena—Gilman Clark, Pres.; Edw. L. Bonhote, Sec., P. O. box 267; Mondays, Native Sons Hall.

Napa No. 62, Napa City—E. L. Miller, Pres.; H. J. Hoernle, Sec., 1226 Oak St.; Mondays, Native Sons Hall.

Calistoga No. 86, Calistoga—Fred Heitz, Pres.; Louis Carlenzoli, Sec.; 1st and 3rd Mondays, I.O.O.F. Hall.

NEVADA COUNTY.

Hydraulic No. 56, Nevada City—Verne Gleason, Pres.; Dr. C. W. Chapman, Sec.; Tuesdays, Pythian Castle.

Quartz No. 58, Grass Valley—Frank J. Rowe, Pres.; H. Ray George, Sec., 151 Conaway Ave.; Mondays, Auditorium Hall.

Donner No. 162, Truckee—J. F. Lichtenberger, Pres.; H. C. Lichtenberger, Sec.; 2nd and 4th Tuesdays, Native Sons Hall.

ORANGE COUNTY.

Santa Ana No. 265, Santa Ana—Amos Huntzinger, Pres.; E. F. Marks, Sec., 1124 No. Bristol St.; 1st and 3rd Mondays, K.C. Hall, 4th and French Sts.

PLACER COUNTY.

Auburn No. 59, Auburn—Hans J. Petersen, Pres.; J. G. Walsh, Sec.; 1st and 3rd Fridays, Foresters Hall.

Silver Star No. 63, Lincoln—Robert P. Dixon, Pres.; Barney G. Barry, Sec., P. O. box 72; 3rd Wednesday, I.O.O.F. Hall.

Rocklin No. 233, Roseville—Wm. La Due, Pres.; M. E. Reed, Sec., 253 W. Duranta; 2nd and 4th Wednesdays, Eagles Hall.

PLUMAS COUNTY.

Quincy No. 131, Quincy—Herbert Hard, Pres.; E. C. Kelsey, Sec.; 2nd Thursday, I.O.O.F. Hall.

Golden Anchor No. 182, La Porte—R. J. McGrath, Pres.; LeRoy J. Post, Sec.; 2nd and 4th Sunday mornings, Native Sons Hall.

Plumas No. 228, Taylorsville—E. E. Sikes, Pres.; George E. Boyden, Sec.; 1st and 3rd Mondays, Native Sons Hall.

SACRAMENTO COUNTY.

Sacramento No. 3, Sacramento City—Parker Kelly, Pres.; J. F. Didion, Sec., 1213 "O" St.; Thursdays, Native Sons Bldg., 11th and "J" Sts.

Sunset No. 26, Sacramento City—Albert Costa, Pres.; Edward E. Reese, Sec., County Treasurer Office; Mondays, Native Sons Bldg., 11th and "J" Sts.

Elk Grove No. 41, Elk Grove—Robert Carr, Pres.; Walter Martin, Sec.; 2nd and 4th Fridays, Masonic Hall.

Granite No. 83, Folsom—Joe Reivas, Pres.; Frank Showers, Sec.; 2nd and 4th Tuesdays, K.P. Hall.

Courtland No. 106, Courtland—N. H. Thisby, Pres.; Jos. Green, Sec.; 1st Saturday and 3rd Monday, Native Sons Hall.

Sutter Fort No. 241, Sacramento City—Ed. T. Goyne, Pres.; C. L. Katzenstein, Sec., P. O. box 914; 2nd and 4th Wednesdays, Native Sons Bldg., 11th and "J" Sts.

Galt No. 243, Galt—Abel G. Stock, Pres.; F. W. Harms, Sec.; 1st and 3rd Mondays, I.O.O.F. Hall.

SAN BENITO COUNTY.

Fremont No. 44, Hollister—S. Churchill, Pres.; J. E. Prendergast Jr., Sec., 1064 Monterey St.; 1st and 3rd Thursdays, Grangers Union Hall.

SAN BERNARDINO COUNTY.

Arrowhead No. 110, San Bernardino City—F. L. McGarvey, Pres.; R. W. Brazelton, Sec., 462 6th St.; Wednesdays, Eagles Hall, 469 4th St.

SAN DIEGO COUNTY.

San Diego No. 108, San Diego City—Martin J. Spangler, Pres.; A. V. Mayrhofer, Sec., 1572 2nd St.; Wednesdays, K.C. Hall, 4th and Elm Sts.

SAN FRANCISCO CITY AND COUNTY.

California No. 1, San Francisco—Joseph Lawlor, Pres.; Ellis A. Blackman, Sec., 1248-A Divisadero St.; Thursdays, Native Sons Bldg., 414 Mason St.

Pacific No. 10, San Francisco—A. L. Anders, Pres.; J. Henry Bastein, Sec., 426 City Hall; Tuesdays, Native Sons Bldg., 414 Mason St.

Golden Gate No. 29, San Francisco—Ernest H. Allen, Pres.; Adolph Eberhart, Sec., 183 Carl St.; Mondays, Native Sons Bldg., 414 Mason St.

Mission No. 38, San Francisco—Martin H. Huber, Pres.; Thos. J. Stewart, Sec., 419 South Van Ness Ave.; Wednesdays, Redmen Hall, 3053 16th St.

San Francisco No. 49, San Francisco—Robert Hallenbarter, Pres.; David Capurro, Sec., 976 Union St.; Thursdays, Native Sons Bldg., 414 Mason St.

El Dorado No. 52, San Francisco—Fred Ageno, Pres.; Alfred Vlautin, Sec., 1537 Franklin St.; Thursdays, Native Sons Bldg., 414 Mason St.

Rincon No. 72, San Francisco—Frank Granzella, Pres.; John A. Gilmour, Sec., 2069 Golden Gate Ave.; Wednesdays, Native Sons Bldg., 414 Mason St.

Stanford No. 76, San Francisco—Charles J. Barry, Pres.; Charles T. O'Kane, Sec., 2900 Scott St.; Tuesdays, Native Sons Bldg., 414 Mason St.

Bay City No. 104, San Francisco—Jacob A. Helbing, Pres.; Max E. Licht, Sec., 1831 Fulton St.; 2nd and 4th Wednesdays, Native Sons Bldg., 414 Mason St.

Niantic No. 105, San Francisco—A. Furner, Pres.; J. M. Darcy, Sec., 10 Hoffman Ave.; Wednesdays, Native Sons Bldg., 414 Mason St.

National No. 118, San Francisco—Walter J. Murphy, Pres.; Martin M. Ratigan, Sec., 1325 Page St., Apt. 6; Thursdays, 1160 Eddy St.

Hesperian No. 137, San Francisco—N. G. Reimers, Pres.; Albert Carlson, Sec., 379 Justin Dr.; Thursdays, Native Sons Bldg., 414 Mason St.

Alcalde No. 154, San Francisco—Robert DeSparr, Pres.; Harry S. Burke, Sec., 25 Ord St.; 2nd and 4th Wednesdays, Native Sons Bldg., 414 Mason St.

South San Francisco No. 157, San Francisco—Mathew Brady, Pres.; John T. Regan, Sec., 1489 Newcomb Ave.; Wednesdays, Masonic Bldg., 4705 3rd St.

Sequoia No. 160, San Francisco—John Lynch, Pres.; Walter W. Garrett, Sec., 2500 Van Ness Ave.; Mondays, Swedish-American Bldg., 2174 Market St.

Precita No. 187, San Francisco—Leland J. Jenkins, Pres.; Edward Tietjen, Sec., 1367 15th Ave.; Thursdays, Mission Masonic Hall, 2668 Mission St.

Olympus No. 189, San Francisco—Henry H. McGowan, Pres.; Harvey J. Carty, Sec., 1651 Market St., Apt. 505; 2nd and 4th Tuesdays, Independent Redmen Hall, 3053 16th St.

Presidio No. 194, San Francisco—Charles Maker, Pres.; George A. Ducker, Sec., 442 21st Ave.; Mondays, Native Sons Bldg., 414 Mason St.

Marshall No. 202, San Francisco—Eugene Biancalona, Pres.; Frank Bacigalupi, Sec., 725 Douglas St.; 1st and 3rd Wednesdays, Native Sons Bldg., 414 Mason St.

ATTENTION, SECRETARIES!

THIS DIRECTORY IS PUBLISHED BY AUTHORITY OF THE GRAND PARLOR N.S.G.W., AND ALL NOTICES OF CHANGES MUST BE RECEIVED BY THE GRAND SECRETARY (NOT THE MAGAZINE) ON OR BEFORE THE 20TH OF EACH MONTH TO INSURE CORRECTION IN NEXT ISSUE OF DIRECTORY.

Dolores No. 208, San Francisco—Henry J. Adami, Pres.; Edward F. Webb, Sec., 2801 Sacramento St.; 2nd and 4th Tuesdays, Redmen Hall, 3053 16th St.
Twin Peaks No. 214, San Francisco—Oswald Storm, Pres.; Thos. Pendergast, Sec., 278 Douglas St.; Wednesdays, Willopi Hall, 4061 24th St.
El Capitan No. 222, San Francisco—John C. Conmy, Pres.; James Hanna, Sec., 2450 27th Ave.; 1st and 3rd Thursdays, King Soloman Hall, 1739 Fillmore St.
Guadalupe No. 231, San Francisco—Thomas Wall, Pres.; Alvin A. Johnson, Sec., 142 Rousseau St.; Tuesdays, Guadalupe Hall, 4551 Mission St.
Castro No. 232, San Francisco—Roy Lund, Pres.; James H. Hayes, Sec., 4014 18th St.; Tuesdays, Native Sons Bldg., 414 Mason St.
Balboa No. 234, San Francisco—J. E. Killeen, Pres.; E. W. Boyd, Sec., 437 Cherry St.; Thursdays, Maccabee Hall, 5th Ave. and Clement St.
Bret Harte No. 260, San Francisco—Louis S. Merrill, Pres.; A. W. McElhatton, Sec., 103 Holloway Ave.; Tuesdays, West of Twin Peaks Hall, 233 Legion Court.
Utopia No. 270, San Francisco—A. E. Rosenbaum, Pres.; Herbert H. Schneider, Sec., 2455 16th Ave.; Tuesdays, American Hall, 20th and Capp Sts.

SAN JOAQUIN COUNTY.

Stockton No. 7, Stockton—Ben S. Waller, Pres.; R. D. Dorcey, Sec., P. O. box 388; Mondays, Native Sons Hall.
Lodi No. 18, Lodi—Herbert Osterman, Pres.; Dr. Clyde Bresnan, Sec.; 2nd Wednesday, Eagles Hall.
Tracy No. 186, Tracy—O. S. Selna, Pres.; R. J. Marraccini, Sec., R.F.D. No. 1, box 217, Thursdays, I.O.O.F. Hall.
Manteca No. 271, Manteca—John F. Mulholand, Pres.; Leonard Faria, Sec., R.F.D., box 75, Lathrop; 1st and 3rd Wednesdays, I.O.O.F. Hall.

SAN LUIS OBISPO COUNTY.

San Miguel No. 150, San Miguel—H. Twisselman, Pres.; Otto Kuebl, Sec., Paso Robles; 1st and 3rd Wednesdays, Fraternal Hall.
Cambria No. 152, Cambria—N. Storni, Pres.; A. S. Gay, Sec.; Wednesdays, Rigdon Hall.

SAN MATEO COUNTY.

Redwood No. 66, Redwood City—H. E. Holmquist, Pres.; A. S. Liguori, Sec., P. O. box 212; Thursdays, American Foresters Hall.
Seaside No. 95, Half Moon Bay—Melvin Frey, Pres.; John G. Gilcrest, Sec.; 2nd and 4th Tuesdays, I.O.O.F. Hall.
Menlo No. 185, Menlo Park—C. T. Maloney, Pres.; F. W. Johnson, Sec., P. O. box 601; 1st and 3rd Thursdays, Masonic Hall.
Pebble Beach No. 230, Pescadero—Earle A. Williamson, Pres.; E. A. Shaw, Sec.; 2nd and 4th Wednesdays, I.O.O.F. Hall.
El Carmelo No. 256, Daly City—Harry McDonald, Pres.; Ernest L. Micco, Sec., 639 Morse St., San Francisco; 2nd and 4th Wednesdays, Eagles Hall.
Industrial City No. 269, South San Francisco—John C. Hamilton, Pres.; Geo. A. Roll, Sec., P. O. box 237; 2nd and 4th Mondays, Metropolitan Hall.

SANTA BARBARA COUNTY.

Santa Barbara No. 116, Santa Barbara City—Philip Bradley, Pres.; H. C. Sweetser, Sec., Court House; 1st and 3rd Wednesdays, I.O.O.F. Hall.

SANTA CLARA COUNTY.

San Jose No. 22, San Jose—Fred Carmichael, Pres.; Joseph Lawrence, Sec., 1095 No. First St.; Mondays, I.O.O.F. Hall.
Santa Clara No. 100, Santa Clara City—C. A. Castro, Pres.; Clarence Clevenger, Sec., P.O. box 297; 1st and 3rd Wednesdays, Redmen Hall.
Observatory No. 177, San Jose—James J. Flannery, Pres.; A. B. Langford, Sec., Hall Records; Tuesdays, Knights Columbus Hall, 40 No. First St.
Mountain View No. 215, Mountain View—Henry A. Schultze, Pres.; C. A. Antonioli, Sec., 301 Castro St.; 2nd and 4th Wednesdays, Mockbee Hall.
Palo Alto No. 216, Palo Alto—John C. Bernal, Pres.; Albert A. Quinn, Sec., 643 High St.; Mondays, Native Sons Bldg., Hamilton Ave. and Emerson St.

SANTA CRUZ COUNTY.

Watsonville No. 65, Watsonville—J. E. Giacoma, Pres.; E. R. Tindall, Sec., R.F.D. No. 5, Box 313; 2nd and 4th Tuesdays, I.O.O.F. Hall.
Santa Cruz No. 90, Santa Cruz City—W. S. Rodgers, Pres.; T. V. Mathews, Sec., 105 Pacheco Ave.; Fridays, Native Sons Hall, 117 Pacific Ave.

SHASTA COUNTY.

McCloud No. 149, Redding—Roy Hawes, Pres.; Hugh A. Shuffleton, Sec.; 1st and 3rd Thursdays, Moose Hall.

SIERRA COUNTY.

Downieville No. 92, Downieville—Frank H. Turner, Pres.; H. S. Tibbey, Sec.; 2nd and 4th Mondays, I.O.O.F. Hall.
Golden Nugget No. 94, Sierra City—Elmer Thompson, Pres.; Arthur R. Pride, Sec.; 1st and 3rd Wednesdays, Masonic Hall.

SISKIYOU COUNTY.

Etna No. 192, Etna—Frank B. Quigley, Pres.; Harvey A. Green, Sec.; 1st and 3rd Wednesdays, I.O.O.F. Hall.
Liberty No. 193, Sawyers Bar—David H. Robinson, Pres.; John M. Barry, Sec.; 1st and 3rd Saturdays, I.O.O.F. Hall.

SOLANO COUNTY.

Solano No. 39, Suisun—John S. Cannon, Pres.; J. W. Kinlock, Sec.; 1st and 3rd Tuesdays, I.O.O.F. Hall.
Vallejo No. 77, Vallejo—Frank J. Heidener, Pres.; Werner B. Hallin, Sec., 912 Carolina; 2nd and 4th Tuesdays, San Pablo Hall.

SONOMA COUNTY.

Petaluma No. 27, Petaluma—Clarence Christiansen, Pres.; C. F. Fobes, Sec., 114 Prospect St.; 2nd and 4th Mondays, Druid Hall, Gross Bldg., 41 Main St.
Santa Rosa No. 28, Santa Rosa—George A. Eckman, Pres.; Leland S. Lewis, Sec., Court House; Mondays, Native Sons Hall.
Glen Ellen No. 102, Glen Ellen—Tony Cereghino, Pres.; Frank Kirch, Sec., Route 3, Santa Rosa; 2nd Monday, N.S.G.W. Hall.
Sonoma No. 111, Sonoma City—Chas. E. Bacigalupi, Pres.; L. H. Green, Sec.; 1st and 3rd Mondays, I.O.O.F. Hall.
Sebastopol No. 143, Sebastopol—O. A. McChristian, Pres.; F. G. McFarlane, Sec.; 1st and 3rd Fridays, I.O.O.F. Hall.

STANISLAUS COUNTY.

Modesto No. 11, Modesto—Chas. D. Blaine, Pres.; C. C. Eastin Jr., Sec., P.O. box 898; 1st and 3rd Wednesdays, I.O.O.F. Hall.
Oakdale No. 142, Oakdale—D. W. Tulloch, Pres.; E. T. Gobin, Sec.; 2nd Monday, Legion Hall.
Orestimba No. 247, Crows Landing—Lloyd W. Fink, Pres.; G. W. Fink, Sec.; 1st and 3rd Wednesdays, Community Club Home.

SUTTER COUNTY.

Sutter No. 261, Sutter City—Henry Correll, Pres.; Glen R. Haynes, Sec., R.F.D. No. 2, Yuba City; 2nd and 4th Mondays, N.D.G.W. Hall.

TRINITY COUNTY.

Mount Bally No. 87, Weaverville—H. W. Day, Pres.; E. V. Ryan, Sec.; 1st and 3rd Mondays, Native Sons Hall.

TULARE COUNTY.

Visalia No. 19, Visalia—G. W. Houk, Pres.; O. H. Wenn, Sec.; 2nd and 4th Tuesdays, Woodman Hall.

NATIVE SON NEWS

(Continued from Page 7)

was among the speakers. John Andreson Jr., assisted by Jerome Kavanaugh, exhibited March 8 some very interesting moving pictures.

A Saint Patrick's dance March 15 drew a large crowd and everybody had a good time. Another Saturday night celebration was held at the Parlor's Crestline clubhouse March 25. Santa Ana No. 265 was well represented. "Chet Peake" provided a real spanish supper, and the usual good time followed.

Prize Ritual Team Officiates.

San Jose—Grand Trustee Joseph J. McShane officially visited San Jose No. 22, and was accompanied by some twenty-five members of the San Francisco Bay district. Noted among those present were Grand Secretary John T. Regan, Grand Trustee John M. Burnett and Past Grand Thomas Monahan. One candidate was initiated by the prize-winning ritual team of Twin Peaks No. 214 (San Francisco). Following some very fine speeches the crowd adjourned to the banquetroom, where the good of the order committee served a feast of enchiladas.

Open-Air Initiation.

Weaverville—Mount Bally No. 87 is going ahead with arrangements for the meeting here June 3 and 4 of Fred H. Greeley Past Presidents Association. Grand Trustee Horace J. Leavitt is chairman and D. E. Ryan vice-chairman of the committee in charge of details. The tentative program includes:

June 3—Drills by Colusa No. 69 drum corps and Marysville No. 6 bugle corps. Ball game between teams from Sutter No. 261 and Mount Bally. All-night dance. June 4—Open-air initiation, followed by noontime dinner. The occasion is expected to attract a large crowd.

Fifty-second Anniversary.

Stockton—Stockton No. 7 observed its fifty-second institution anniversary March 13 and presented life memberships to the three remaining charter members, Leroy S. Atwood, Frank E. Lane and Ralph P. Lane. The presentation address was made by Grand President Seth Millingtou.

The ceremonies opened with a dinner at which G. M. Steele was master of ceremonies, and concluded with a program of entertainment. The arrangements committee included A. J. Carey (chairman), G. Owings, A. W. Dunning, F. J. Piccardo, L. Javote, G. Umberger and L. Buol.

Subordinate Parlors Briefs.

Modesto—President Charles D. Blaine of Modesto No. 11 has appointed several committees to carry on the affairs of the Parlor, among them: Admission Day observance, C. W. Gill, Arthur Crabb, Hugo McKinley and W. R. Service; athletic, Floyd Allen, Fred Marshall, J. B. Fiscalini, Harry D. Crow and Guy Allen.

Ferndale—Following the initiation of one candidate March 6, Ferndale No. 93 had a card party, nine tables being in operation. At the conclusion of the play a fine clam chowder, prepared by the famous chef, Chas. Kistner, was served.

A new parlor is to be instituted during April at Turlock, Stanislaus County, according to Deputy Grand President Al Lobree, who says this "will complete a chain from Bakersfield to Stockton." During May he expects to go to Yreka, Siskiyou County, to organize a parlor.

PAST GRAND'S WIFE PASSES.

Napa—Mrs. Mollie Caroline Gesford, wife of Judge Henry C. Gesford, Past Grand President N.S.G.W., died March 13 at the age of 75. She was a native of Solano County, the daughter of William and Betsy Anne Bullock, Pioneers of 1850.

N.S.G.W. OFFICIAL DEATH LIST.

Containing the name, the date and the place of birth, the date of death, and the Subordinate Parlor affiliation of deceased members reported to Grand Secretary John T. Regan from February 20 to March 20, 1933:

Greenberg, Lazarus J.; Monterey, March 19, 1867; February 3, 1933; Humboldt No. 14.
Hubbard, Albert Lester; San Jose, May 20, 1872; December 5, 1932; San Jose No. 22.
White, Claud J.; Oleander, December 4, 1897; February 13, 1933; Fresno No. 25.
Hails, Charles Hamilton; Santa Barbara, June 13, 1886; March 6, 1933; Sunset No. 26.
Gaddis, Edward Everett; Zamora, February 25, 1862; May 9, 1932; Woodland No. 30.
Hayward, Edward Babbitt; San Francisco, May 9, 1868; June 21, 1932; Woodland No. 30.
Frye, Eugene; Franklin, January 1, 1861; February 22, 1933; Elk Grove No. 41.
Villamur, Horace Archie; Beckworth; February 19, 1893; March 13, 1933; Watsonville No. 65.
Pilliken, George Joseph; Negro Hill, December 13, 1857; April 23, 1932; Granite No. 83.
Tagtmeier, George Henry; Placerville, August 25, 1866; May 6, 1932; Granite No. 83.
Fowler, William W.; Sonoma, February 17, 1858; February 17, 1933; Calistoga No. 86.
Zane, Elmer C.; Glen Ellen, January 26, 1862; February 14, 1933; Glen Ellen No. 102.
Cozzaglio, John; Sierra City, May 28, 1886; February 24, 1933; Ramona No. 109.
Bouquet, Joseph A.; San Pablo, March 9, 1868; February 9, 1933; Piedmont No. 120.
McClellan, John; San Francisco, October 12, 1864; March 4, 1933; Piedmont No. 120.
Thayer, Herbert A.; San Francisco, August 25, 1878; January 3, 1933; Hesperian No. 137.
Sylva, Joseph; Shaws Flat, February 6, 1870; September 8, 1932; Tuolumne No. 144.
Brown, Edward John; San Francisco, July 2, 1873; February 3, 1933; Brooklyn No. 151.
Broderick, Edward; San Francisco, February 18, 1865; March 4, 1933; Sea Point No. 158.
Wales, George Alfred; Newark, February 2, 1890; July 19, 1932; Washington No. 169.
Ruebold, Alfred F.; San Francisco, October 2, 1877; March 10, 1933; Presidio No. 194.

N.D.G.W. OFFICIAL DEATH LIST.

Giving the name, the date of death, and the Subordinate Parlor affiliation of all deceased members as reported to Grand Secretary Sallie R. Thaler from February 18, 1933, to March 19, 1933:

Jewell, Laura A. Forni; February 8; Marguerite No. 12.
McMurray, Evelyn H.; January 29; Phoebe A. Hearst No. 214.
Felton, Lola; February 1; Alta No. 3.
Kraus, Matilda C.; November 13; Califia No. 22.
Trevellian, Frances; February 17; Darina No. 114.
Knight, Edna Irene D.; January 27; Piedmont No. 87.
Parsons, Mamie; January 25; Laurel No. 6.
Hickey, Jennie Shields; February 25; Sutter No. 111.
Converse, Pauline Canepa; January 24; Fairfax No. 225.
Gable, Jessie Miller; February 14; Oneonta No. 71.
Brunner, Lillie Gingg; December 5; Oneonta No. 71.
Clark, Lucy E. Dickerman; February 19; Forrest No. 86.
Wulbern, Helena; October 27; Bear Flag No. 151.
Tietjen, Elizabeth; March 7; Linda Rosa No. 170.
Nihell, Kate; February 21; Laurel No. 6.
Lee, Lottie Bryan; January 12; Anona No. 164.
Blythe, Eleanor Stamps; February 15; Santa Ana No. 235.
Neumann, Mary; February 12; Palo Alto No. 229.

HISTORIC SITE VISITED.

Hollister (San Benito County)—Commemorating the eighty-seventh anniversary of the raising of the United States of America Flag by General John C. Fremont, fitting ceremonies were held atop Fremont Peak, March 5. Mayor George Abbe of San Juan Bautista was master of ceremonies, and George Moore was the main speaker.

Among the four hundred making the pilgrimage to the historic site were many members of Copa de Oro Parlor No. 105 N.D.G.W. and Fremont Parlor No. 44 N.S.G.W.

TUOLUMNE COUNTY.

Tuolumne No. 144, Sonora—Mathew J. Marshall, Pres.; William M. Harrington, Sec., P. O. box 715; 2nd and 4th Fridays, Knights Columbus Hall.
Columbia No. 258, Columbia—Jos. Cadematori, Pres.; Charles E. Grant, Sec.; 2nd and 4th Thursdays, Native Sons Hall.

VENTURA COUNTY.

Cabrillo No. 114, Ventura City—David Bennett, Pres., 1880 Church St.

YOLO COUNTY.

Woodland No. 30, Woodland—J. L. Aronson, Pres.; R. G. Lawson, Sec.; 1st Thursday, Native Sons Hall.

YUBA COUNTY.

Marysville No. 6, Marysville—A. W. Graves, Pres.; Verne Fogarty, Sec., 719 6th St.; 2nd Friday, Foresters Hall.
Rainbow No. 40, Wheatland—F. M. Beilby, Pres.; W. A. Bowser, Sec., P. O. box 313; 2nd Thursday, I.O.O.F. Hall.

AFFILIATED ORGANIZATIONS.

San Francisco Extension of the Order Committee, N.S.G.W.—Joseph J. McShane, Chmn.; Harold J. Regan, Sec., 414 Mason St., San Francisco; meets 2nd and 4th Fridays, Grizzly Bear Club, 414 Mason St., San Francisco.
Alameda County Extension of the Order Committee, N.S.G.W.—Gam Hurst, Chmn.; Frank Roemer, Sec., 3297 Morcom Ave., Oakland; meets 1st and 3rd Mondays, N.S.G.W. Hall, 11th and Clay Sts., Oakland.
Interparlor Committee (Southern District), N.S.G.W. and N.D.G.W.—Burrel D. Neighbours, Chmn.; F. J. Burmester, Sec., P. O. box 42, Colton; meets 2nd and 4th Fridays, Patriotic Hall, 1816 So. Figueroa St., Los Angeles.
San Francisco Assembly No. 1 Past Presidents Association N.S.G.W.—Meets 1st and 3rd Fridays, Native Sons Bldg., 414 Mason St., San Francisco; Fred T. Kane, Gov.; J. F. Stanley, Sec., 1175 O'Farrell St., San Francisco.
East Bay Counties Assembly No. 3 Past Presidents Association N.S.G.W.—Meets 4th Monday, Native Sons Hall, 11th and Clay Sts., Oakland; M. W. Louden, Gov.; Edgar G. Hanson, Sec., 1260 Russell St., Berkeley.
Marin County Assembly No. 5 Past Presidents Association N.S.G.W.—J. S. Rose Jr., Gov.; L. J. Peter, Sec., Peter Bldg., 4th and "C" Sts., San Rafael.
Fred H. Greeley Assembly No. 6 Past Presidents Association N.S.G.W.—Meets monthly with different Parlors comprising district; R. L. P. Bigelow, Gov.; Barney Barry, Sec., P. O. box 72, Lincoln.
San Joaquin Assembly No. 7 Past Presidents Association N.S.G.W.—Meets 1st Friday, Native Sons Hall, Stockton; Clyde H. Gregg, Gov.; R. D. Dorcey, Sec., Native Sons Club, Stockton.
Sonoma County Assembly No. 9 Past President Association N.S.G.W.—Meets monthly at different Parlor headquarters in county; P. A. R. Gambini, Gov.; L. S. Lewis, Sec., Court House, Santa Rosa.
General John A. Sutter Assembly No. 10 Past Presidents Association—C. O. Wachman, Gov.; Jas. J. Longshore, Sec., 514 "J" St., Sacramento.
Grizzly Bear Club—Members all Parlors outside San Francisco at all times welcome. Clubrooms top floor Native Sons Bldg., 414 Mason St., San Francisco.
Native Sons and Native Daughters Central Committee on Homeless Children—Main office, 955 Phelan Bldg., San Francisco; Mrs. John W. Stirling, Chmn.; Miss Mary E. Brusie, Sec. Los Angeles branch office, 3924 Sunset Blvd.; Dorothy Schlingman, Sec.

(ADVERTISEMENT.)

Official Directory of Parlors of the N. D. G. W.

ALAMEDA COUNTY.

Angelita No. 32, Livermore—Meets 2nd and 4th Fridays, Foresters Hall; Mrs. Myrtle I. Johnson, Rec. Sec., P.O. box 253.

Piedmont No. 87, Oakland—Meets Thursdays, Corinthian Hall, Pacific Bldg.; Miss Helen Ring, Rec. Sec., 822 11th St.

Aloha No. 106, Oakland—Meets Tuesdays, Wigwam Hall, Pacific Bldg.; Mrs. Lurine Martin, Rec. Sec., 2815 Wallace St., Berkeley.

Hayward No. 122, Hayward—Meets 1st and 3rd Tuesdays, Veterans Memorial Bldg., Main St.; Miss Ruth Gansberger, Rec. Sec., P. O. box 44, Mount Eden.

Berkeley No. 150, Berkeley—Meets 2nd Saturday afternoon, Berkeley City Women's Club, 2315 Durant; Mrs. Lelia B. Baker, Rec. Sec., 915 Contra Costa Ave.

Bear Flag No. 151, Berkeley—Meets 2nd and 4th Wednesdays, Veterans Memorial Bldg., 1931 Center St.; Mrs. Maud Wagner, Rec. Sec., 317 Alcatraz Ave., Oakland.

Encinal No. 156, Alameda—Meets 2nd and 4th Wednesdays, Veterans Memorial Bldg., Central Ave. and Walnut St.; Mrs. Laura E. Fisher, Rec. Sec., 1413 Caroline St.

Brooklyn No. 157, East Oakland—Meets 2nd and 4th Wednesdays, Masonic Temple, 8th Ave. and E. 14th St.; Mrs. Ruth Cooney, Rec. Sec., 3907 14th Ave.

Argonaut No. 166, Oakland—Meets Tuesdays, Klinkner Hall, 59th and San Pablo; Mrs. Ada Spilman, Rec. Sec., 2905 Ellis St., Berkeley.

Bahia Vista No. 167, Oakland—Meets 1st and 3rd Thursdays, Wigwam Hall, Pacific Bldg.; Mrs. Minnie E. Raper, Rec. Sec., 3449 Helen St.

Fruitvale No. 177, Oakland—Meets Fridays, W.O.W. Hall; May E. Barthold, Rec. Sec., 3832 Santa Rita St.

Laura Loma No. 182, Niles—Meets 1st and 3rd Tuesdays, I.O.O.F. Hall; Mrs. Ethel Fournier, Rec. Sec., P. O. box 515.

El Cereso No. 207, San Leandro—Meets 2nd and 4th Tuesdays, Masonic Hall; Mrs. Mary Tuttle, Rec. Sec., P. O. box 56.

Pleasanton No. 237, Pleasanton—Meets 1st Tuesday, I.O.O.F. Hall; Mrs. Myrtle Lanini, Rec. Sec.

Betsy Ross No. 238, Centerville—Meets 1st and 3rd Fridays, Anderson Hall; Miss Constance Lucio, Rec. Sec., P. O. box 187.

AMADOR COUNTY.

Ursula No. 1, Jackson—Meets 2nd and 4th Tuesdays, N.S.G.W. Hall; Mrs. Emma Boarman-Wright, Rec. Sec., 114 Court St.

Chispa No. 40, Ione—Meets 2nd and 4th Fridays, N.S.G.W. Hall; Mrs. Isabel Ashton, Rec. Sec.

Amapola No. 80, Sutter Creek—Meets 2nd and 4th Thursdays, N.S.G.W. Bldg.; Mrs. Hazel M. Marre, Rec. Sec.

Forrest No. 86, Plymouth—Meets 2nd and 4th Tuesdays, I.O.O.F. Hall; Mrs. Marguerite Davis, Rec. Sec.

BUTTE COUNTY.

Annie K. Bidwell No. 168, Chico—Meets 2nd and 4th Thursdays, I.O.O.F. Hall; Mrs Irene Henry, Rec. Sec., 3015 Woodland Ave.

Gold of Ophir No. 190, Oroville—Meets 1st and 3rd Wednesdays, Memorial Hall; Mrs. Ruth Brown, Rec. Sec., 1265 Leah Court.

CALAVERAS COUNTY.

Ruby No. 46, Murphys—Meets 4th Friday, N.S.G.W. Hall; Belle Segale, Rec. Sec.

Princess No. 84, Angels Camp—Meets 2nd and 4th Wednesdays, I.O.O.F. Hall; Mrs. Grace M. Mills, Rec. Sec., P.O. box 313.

San Andreas No. 113, San Andreas—Meets 1st Friday, Fraternal Hall; Miss Doris Treat, Rec. Sec.

COLUSA COUNTY.

Colus No. 194, Colusa—Meets 1st and 3rd Mondays, Eagles Hall; Miss Kate Busch, Rec. Sec., 350 Market St.

CONTRA COSTA COUNTY.

Stirling No. 146, Pittsburg—Meets 1st and 3rd Wednesdays, Veteran Memorial Hall; Mrs. Leslie Clement, Rec. Sec., 468 E. Santa Fe.

Richmond No. 147, Richmond—Meets 1st and 3rd Tuesdays, I.O.O.F. Hall, 10th St.; Grace Curry, Rec. Sec., 932 Ohio Ave.

Donner No. 193, Byron—Meets 1st and 3rd Wednesdays, I.O.O.F. Hall; Mrs. Anna Pendry, Rec. Sec., P.O. box 442.

Las Juntas No. 221, Martinez—Meets 1st and 3rd Mondays, Pythian Castle; Mrs. Lola O. Viera, Rec. Sec., R.F.D. No. 1.

Antioch No. 223, Antioch—Meets 2nd and 4th Tuesdays, I.O.O.F. Hall; Mrs. Estelle Evans, Rec. Sec., 202 E. 5th St., Pittsburg.

Carquinez No. 234, Crockett—Meets 2nd and 4th Wednesdays, I.O.O.F. Hall; Mrs. Cecile Petee, Rec. Sec., 465 Edwards St.

EL DORADO COUNTY.

Marguerite No. 12, Placerville—Meets 1st and 3rd Wednesdays, Masonic Hall; Mrs. Nettie Leonardi, Rec. Sec., 25 Coloma St.

El Dorado No. 186, Georgetown—Meets 2nd and 4th Saturday afternoons, I.O.O.F. Hall; Mrs. Alta L. Douglas, Rec. Sec.

FRESNO COUNTY.

Fresno No. 187, Fresno—Meets 2nd and 4th Fridays, Pythian Castle, Cor. "R" and Merced Sts.; Mary Aubery, Rec. Sec., 1040 Delphia Ave.

GRAND OFFICERS.

Mrs. Evelyn I. Carlson........Past Grand President
281 E. Tuscaloosa Ave., Atherton

Mrs. Anna M. Armstrong........Grand President
Woodland

Mrs. Irma Laird........Grand Vice-president
Alturas

Mrs. Sallie R. Thaler........Grand Secretary
555 Baker St., San Francisco

Mrs. Susie K. Christ........Grand Treasurer
555 Baker St., San Francisco

Mrs. Gladys Noce........Grand Marshal
Sutter Creek

Mrs. Orinda G. Giannini........Grand Inside Sentinel
2142 Filbert St., San Francisco

Mrs. Hazel B. Hansen........Grand Outside Sentinel
501 Griswold St., Glendale

Mrs. Clara Gairaud........Grand Organist
134 Locust St., San Jose

GRAND TRUSTEES.

Mrs. Florence Boyle........Oroville
Mrs. Edna Briggs........1045 Santa Ynez Way, Sacramento
Mrs. Anna Thuesen........615 38th Ave., San Francisco
Mrs. Ethel Begley........233 Prospect Ave., San Francisco
Mrs. Minna K. Horn........Etna
Mrs. Jane Vick........418 Bath St., Santa Barbara
Mrs. Willow Borba........330 So. Main St., Sebastopol

GLENN COUNTY.

Berryessa No. 192, Willows—Meets 1st and 3rd Mondays, I.O.O.F. Hall; Mrs. Leonora Neate, Rec. Sec., 338 No. Lassen St.

HUMBOLDT COUNTY.

Occident No. 28, Eureka—Meets 1st and 3rd Wednesdays, N.S.G.W Hall; Mrs. Eva L. MacDonald, Rec. Sec., 2309 "B" St.

Oneonta No. 71, Ferndale—Meets 2nd and 4th Fridays, I.O.O.F. Hall; Mrs. Myra Rumrill, Rec. Sec., P.O. box 142.

Reichling No. 97, Fortuna—Meets 1st and 3rd Tuesdays, Friendship Hall; Mrs. Grace Swett, Rec. Sec., P. O. box 328.

KERN COUNTY.

Miocene No. 228, Taft—Meets 1st and 3rd Wednesday afternoons, I.O.O.F. Hall; Mrs. Evalyn G. Towne, Rec. Sec., P. O. box 1011.

El Tejon No. 239, Bakersfield—Meets 1st and 3rd Fridays, Eagles Hall, 1714 "G" St.; Mary B. Hampson, Rec. Sec., 908 Quincy St.

Desert Gold No. 250, Mojave—Meets 2nd and 4th Fridays, I.O.O.F. Hall; Jane Lucile Waters, Rec. Sec., Tehachapi.

LAKE COUNTY.

Clear Lake No. 135, Middletown—Meets 2nd and 4th Tuesdays, Herrick Hall; Mrs. Alma E. Snow, Rec. Sec.

LASSEN COUNTY.

Nataqua No. 152, Standish—Meets 1st and 3rd Wednesdays, Foresters Hall; Mrs. Mayda Elledge, Rec. Sec.

Mount Lassen No. 215, Bieber—Meets 2nd and 4th Thursdays, I.O.O.F. Hall; Mrs. Angie C. Kenyon, Rec. Sec.

Susanville No. 243, Susanville—Meets 3rd Thursday, I.O.O.F. Hall; Mildred Hardy, Rec. Sec., P.O. box 425.

LOS ANGELES COUNTY.

Los Angeles No. 124, Los Angeles—Meets 1st and 3rd Wednesdays, I.O.O.F. Hall, Washington and Oak Sts.; Mrs. Mary K. Corcoran, Rec. Sec., 322 No. Van Ness Ave.

Long Beach No. 154, Long Beach—Meets 1st and 3rd Thursdays, K.P. Hall, 341 Pacific Ave.; Mrs. Bertha Hitt, Rec. Sec., 5355 Lime Ave.

Rudecinda No. 230, San Pedro—Meets 2nd and 4th Thursdays, Unity Hall, I.O.O.F. Temple, 10th and Gaffey; Letitia Sarciaux, Rec. Sec., 1054 W. 24th St.

Verdugo No. 240, Glendale—Meets 2nd and 4th Tuesdays, Masonic Temple, 234 So. Brand Blvd.; Miss Etta Fulkerth, Rec. Sec., 526 No. Orange St.

Santa Monica Bay No. 245, Santa Monica—Meets 2nd and 4th Wednesdays, Odd Fellows Hall, 1431 Third St.; Mrs. Rosalie Hyde, Rec. Sec., 738 Flower St., Venice.

Californiana No. 247, Los Angeles—Meets 2nd and 4th Tuesday afternoons, Hollywood Studio Club, 1215 Lodi Place; Mrs. Inez Sitton, Rec. Sec., 4223 Berenice St.

MADERA COUNTY.

Madera No. 244, Madera—Meets 2nd and 4th Thursdays, Masonic Annex; Mrs. Margaret O. Boyle, Rec. Sec., 111 No. "B" St.

MARIN COUNTY.

Sea Point No. 196, Sausalito—Meets 2nd and 4th Mondays, Perry Hall, 50 Caledonia St.; Mrs. Mary B. Smith, Rec. Sec., 47½ Glen Drive.

Marinita No. 198, San Rafael—Meets 2nd and 4th Mondays, 316 "B" St.; Miss Mollye Y. Spaeiti, Rec. Sec., 539 4th St.

Fairfax No. 225, Fairfax—Meets 2nd and 4th Tuesdays, Community Hall; Mrs. Marguerite Geary, Rec. Sec.

Tamelpa No. 231, Mill Valley—Meets 1st and 2nd Tuesdays, I.O.O.F. Hall; Mrs. Delphine M. Todt, Rec. Sec., 400 Grand Ave., San Rafael.

MARIPOSA COUNTY.

Mariposa No. 63, Mariposa—Meets 1st and 3rd Fridays, I.O.O.F. Hall; Elizabeth E. Johnson, Rec. Sec.

MENDOCINO COUNTY.

Fort Bragg No. 210, Fort Bragg—Meets 1st and 3rd Thursdays, I.O.O.F. Hall; Mrs. Ruth W. Fuller, Rec. Sec.

MERCED COUNTY.

Veritas No. 75, Merced—Meets 1st and 3rd Tuesdays, I.O.O.F. Hall; Miss Flora Fernandes, Rec. Sec., Parkside Apt.

MODOC COUNTY.

Alturas No. 159, Alturas—Meets 1st Thursday, Alturas Civic Club; Mrs. Irma W. Laird, Rec. Sec.

MONTEREY COUNTY.

Aleli No. 102, Salinas—Meets 2nd and 4th Thursdays, Pythian Hall; Miss Rose Rhyner, Rec. Sec., 420 Soledad St.

Junipero No. 141, Monterey—Meets 2nd and 4th Fridays, K. of P. Hall, Main St.; Miss Matilda M. Bergschicker, Rec. Sec., 498 Van Buren St.

NAPA COUNTY.

Eshcol No. 16, Napa—Meets 2nd and 4th Mondays, N.S.G.W. Hall; Mrs. Ella Ingram, Rec. Sec., 2140 Seminary St.

Calistoga No. 145, Calistoga—Meets 2nd and 4th Mondays, I.O.O.F. Hall; Sadie P. Brooks, Rec. Sec.

La Junta No. 203, Saint Helena—Meets 1st and 3rd Tuesdays, N.S.G.W. Hall; Mrs. Marie Signorelli, Rec. Sec., 1341 Madrona Ave.

ATTENTION, SECRETARIES!

THIS DIRECTORY IS PUBLISHED BY AUTHORITY OF THE GRAND PARLOR N.D.G.W., AND ALL NOTICES OF CHANGES MUST BE RECEIVED BY THE GRAND SECRETARY (NOT THE MAGAZINE) ON OR BEFORE THE 20TH OF EACH MONTH TO INSURE CORRECTION IN NEXT PUBLICATION OF DIRECTORY.

NEVADA COUNTY.

Laurel No. 6, Nevada City—Meets 1st and 3rd Wednesdays, I.O.O.F. Hall; Mrs. Nellie E. Clark, Rec. Sec., 412 Pine St.

Manzanita No. 29, Grass Valley—Meets 1st and 3rd Tuesdays, Auditorium; Mrs. Loraine Keast, Rec. Sec., 123 Race St.

Columbia No. 70, French Corral—Meets Fridays, Farrelley Hall; Mrs. Kate Farrelley-Sullivan, Rec. Sec.

Snow Peak No. 176, Truckee—Meets 1st Monday, I.O.O.F. Hall; Mrs. Henrietta M. Eaton, Rec. Sec., P. O. box 116.

ORANGE COUNTY.

Santa Ana No. 235, Santa Ana—Meets 2nd and 4th Mondays, K.C. Hall, 4th and French Sts.; Mrs. Matilda S. Lemon, Rec. Sec., 1628 W. 8th St.

Grace No. 242, Fullerton—Meets 1st and 3rd Thursdays, I.O.O.F. Hall, 116½ E. Commonwealth; Mrs. Mary R. Rothaermel, Rec. Sec., Acacia St. & Commonwealth.

PLACER COUNTY.

Placer No. 138, Lincoln—Meets 2nd Wednesday, I.O.O.F. Hall; Miss Carrie Parlin, Rec. Sec.

La Rosa No. 191, Roseville—Meets 1st and 3rd Tuesdays, Eagles Hall; Mrs. Alice Lee West, Rec. Sec., Rocklin.

Auburn No. 233, Auburn—Meets 2nd and 4th Fridays, Foresters Hall; Mrs. Elsie Patrick, Rec. Sec.

PLUMAS COUNTY.

Plumas Pioneer No. 219, Quincy—Meets 1st and 3rd Mondays, I.O.O.F. Hall; Minnie E. Johnson, Rec. Sec., P. O. box 243.

SACRAMENTO COUNTY.

Califia No. 22, Sacramento—Meets 2nd and 4th Tuesdays, N.S.G.W. Hall; Miss Lulu Gillis, Rec. Sec., 921 8th St.

La Bandera No. 110, Sacramento—Meets 1st and 3rd Fridays, N.S.G.W. Hall; Mrs. Clara Weldon, Rec. Sec., 1310 "O" St.

Sutter No. 111, Sacramento—Meets 1st and 3rd Tuesdays, N.S.G.W. Hall; Mrs. Adele Nix, Rec. Sec., 1238 "S" St.

Fern No. 123, Folsom—Meets 1st and 3rd Tuesdays, K.P. Hall; Elizabeth Ryan, Rec. Sec., Represa.

Chabolla No. 171, Galt—Meets 2nd and 4th Tuesdays, I.O.O.F. Hall; Mrs. Mary Pritchard, Rec. Sec.

Coloma No. 212, Sacramento—Meets 1st and 3rd Tuesdays, I.O.O.F. Hall, Oak Park; Mrs. Nettie Harry, Rec. Sec., 1217 35th St.

Liberty No. 213, Elk Grove—Meets 2nd and 4th Fridays, I.O.O.F. Hall; Mrs. Frances Wackman, Rec. Sec., P. O. box 192.

Victory No. 216, Courtland—Meets 1st Saturday and 3rd Monday, N.S.G.W. Hall; Mrs. Agneda Lample, Rec. Sec.

SAN BENITO COUNTY.

Copa de Oro No. 105, Hollister—Meets 2nd and 4th Thursdays, Grangers Union Hall; Mrs. Mollie Daveggio, Rec. Sec., 110 San Benito St.

San Juan Bautista No. 179, San Juan Bautista—Meets 1st Wednesday, Mission Corridor Rooms; Miss Gertrude Breen, Rec. Sec.

SAN BERNARDINO COUNTY.

Lugonia No. 241, San Bernardino—Meets 2nd and 4th Wednesdays, Eagles Hall; Miss Lois Poling, Rec. Sec., 295 E. 11th St.

Ontario No. 251, Ontario—Meets 2nd and 4th Thursdays, Ontario Hotel; Miss Helen Hickman, Rec. Sec., 923 No. Laurel Ave.

SAN DIEGO COUNTY.

San Diego No. 208, San Diego—Meets 2nd and 4th Wednesdays, Directors Room, Chamber Commerce Bldg., 419 W. Broadway; Mrs. Elsie Case, Rec. Sec., 3051 Broadway.

SAN FRANCISCO CITY AND COUNTY.

Minerva No. 2, San Francisco—Meets 1st and 3rd Wednesdays, N.S.G.W. Bldg.; Miss Dorothy Finn, Rec. Sec., 90 Princess St., Sausalito.

Alta No. 3, San Francisco—Meets 2nd and 4th Tuesdays, N.S.G.W. Bldg.; Mrs. Agnese L. Hughes, Rec. Sec., 3980 Sacramento St.

Oro Fino No. 9, San Francisco—Meets 1st and 3rd Thursdays, N.S.G.W. Bldg.; Mrs. Josephine B. Morrisey, Rec. Sec., 4441 26th St.

Golden State No. 50, San Francisco—Meets 1st and 3rd Wednesdays, N.D.G.W. Home; Miss Millie Tietjen, Rec. Sec., 328 Lexington Ave.

Orinda No. 56, San Francisco—Meets 2nd, 4th and 5th Fridays, N.D.G.W. Home; Mrs. Anna A. Gruber-Loser, Rec. Sec., 72 Grove Lane, San Anselmo.

Fremont No. 59, San Francisco—Meets 1st and 3rd Tuesdays, N.S.G.W. Bldg.; Miss Hannah Collins, Rec. Sec., 617 Fillmore St.

Buena Vista No. 68, San Francisco—Meets 1st, 3rd and 5th Thursdays, N.D.G.W. Home; Miss Margaret Barrett, Rec. Sec., 3774 20th St.

Las Lomas No. 72, San Francisco—Meets 1st and 3rd Tuesdays, N.D.G.W. Home; Mrs. Marion S. Day, Rec. Sec., 469 Noe St.

Yosemite No. 83, San Francisco—Meets 1st and 3rd Tuesdays, American Hall, 20th and Capp Sts.; Miss Mary Monahan, Rec. Sec., 237 Noe St.

La Estrella No. 89, San Francisco—Meets 2nd and 4th Mondays, N.S.G.W. Bldg.; Miss Birdie Hartman, Rec. Sec., 1018 Jackson St.

Sans Souci No. 96, San Francisco—Meets 2nd and 4th Mondays, N.D.G.W. Home; Mrs. Minnie F. Dobbin, Rec. Sec., 1488 43rd Ave.

Calaveras No. 103, San Francisco—Meets 2nd and 4th Tuesdays, Swedish American Hall, 2174 Market St.; Mary L. Krogh, Rec. Sec., 4235 Cabrillo St.

Darina No. 114, San Francisco—Meets 1st and 3rd Mondays, N.S.G.W. Bldg.; Miss Adele Walsh, Rec. Sec., 479 Page St.

El Vespero No. 118, San Francisco—Meets 2nd and 4th Tuesdays, Masonic Hall, 4705 3rd St.; Mrs. Nell R. Boege, Rec. Sec., 1526 Kirkwood Ave.

Genevieve No. 132, San Francisco—Meets 1st and 3rd Thursdays, N.S.G.W. Bldg.; Miss Branice Peguillan, Rec. Sec., 2434 16th Ave.

Keith No. 137, San Francisco—Meets 2nd and 4th Thursdays, N.S.G.W. Bldg.; Mrs. Helen T. Mann, Rec. Sec., 575 Pierce St., Apt. 206.

Gabrielle No. 139, San Francisco—Meets 2nd and 4th Wednesdays, N.S.G.W. Bldg.; Mrs. Dorothy Wuesterfeld, Rec. Sec., 1020 Munich St.

Presidio No. 148, San Francisco—Meets 2nd and 4th Tuesdays, N.S.G.W. Bldg.; Mrs. Hattie Gaughran, Rec. Sec., 713 Capp St.

Guadalupe No. 153, San Francisco—Meets 2nd and 4th Mondays, Forester Hall, 170 Valencia St.; Miss May A. McCarthy, Rec. Sec., 335 Elsie St.

Golden Gate No. 158, San Francisco—Meets 2nd and 4th Mondays, N.S.G.W. Bldg.; Mrs. Mary Sullivan, Rec. Sec., 33 Cuvier St.

Dolores No. 169, San Francisco—Meets 2nd and 4th Wednesdays, N.S.G.W. Bldg.; Mrs. Ada Saunders, Rec. Sec., 284 Allison St.

Linda Rosa No. 170, San Francisco—Meets 2nd and 4th Wednesdays, Swedish American Hall, 2174 Market St.; Mrs. Eva P. Tyrrel, Rec. Sec., 3629 Mission St.

Portola No. 172, San Francisco—Meets 1st and 3rd Tuesdays, N.S.G.W. Bldg.; Catherine H. Dolly, Rec. Sec., 4125 23rd St.
Castro No. 178, San Francisco—Meets 1st and 3rd Wednesdays, K.C. Bldg., 150 Golden Gate Ave.; Miss Adeline Sandersfeld, Rec Sec., 50 Baker St.
Twin Peaks No. 185, San Francisco—Meets 2nd and 4th Fridays, Druids Temple, 44 Page St.; Mrs. Loretta Cameron, Rec. Sec., 3969 Army St.
James Lick No. 220, San Francisco—Meets 1st and 3rd Wednesdays, N.S.G.W. Bldg.; Mrs. Edna Bishop, Rec. Sec., 3841 24th St.
Mission No. 227, San Francisco—Meets 2nd and 4th Fridays, N.S.G.W. Bldg.; Mrs. Ann Dippel, Rec. Sec., 448 Dewey Blvd.
Bret Harte No. 232, San Francisco—Meets 2nd and 4th Tuesdays, Aloha Hall, 3009 16th St.; Pearl Wedde, Rec. Sec., 225 7th Ave.
La Dorada No. 236, San Francisco—Meets 2nd and 4th Thursdays, N.S.G.W. Hall; Mrs. Theresa R. O'Brien, Rec. Sec., 567 Liberty St.
Balboa No. 249, San Francisco—Meets 1st and 3rd Thursdays, Knights Columbus Hall, 382 18th Ave.; Miss Jean Moffet, Rec. Sec., 476 26th Ave.
Utopia No. 252, San Francisco—Meets 2nd and 4th Tuesdays, American Hall, 20th and Capp Sts.; Miss Lelia M. Little, Rec. Sec., 4450 20th St.

SAN JOAQUIN COUNTY.

Joaquin No. 5, Stockton—Meets 2nd and 4th Tuesdays, N.S.G.W. Hall, 314 E. Main St.; Mrs. Della Garvin, Rec. Sec., 1122 E. Market St.
El Pescadero No. 82, Tracy—Meets 1st and 3rd Fridays, I.O.O.F. Hall; Mrs. Mary A. Hewitson, Rec. Sec., 122 Walnut St.
Ivy No. 88, Lodi—Meets 1st and 3rd Wednesdays, Eagles Hall; Mrs. Mae Corson, Rec. Sec., 109 So. School St.
Calla de Oro No. 206, Stockton—Meets 1st and 3rd Tuesdays, N.S.G.W. Hall, 314 E. Main St.; Mrs. Frances Germain, Rec. Sec., 450 No. Regent.
Phoebe A. Hearst No. 214, Manteca—Meets 2nd and 4th Wednesdays, I.O.O.F. Hall; Mrs. Josie M. Frederick, Rec. Sec., Route A, Box 364, Ripon.

SAN LUIS OBISPO COUNTY.

San Miguel No. 94, San Miguel—Meets 2nd and 4th Wednesday afternoons, Clemon Hall; Mrs. Nellie Wickstrom, Rec. Sec.
San Luisita No. 108, San Luis Obispo—Meets 2nd and 4th Thursdays, W.O.W. Hall; Miss Agnes M. Lee, Rec. Sec., P. O. box 584.
El Pinal No. 163, Cambria—Meets 2nd, 4th and 5th Tuesdays, N.S.G.W. Hall; Kathryn Luchessa, Rec. Sec.

SAN MATEO COUNTY.

Bonita No. 10, Redwood City—Meets 2nd and 4th Thursdays, I.O.O.F. Hall; Mrs. Dora Wilson, Rec. Sec., 518 Middlefield Rd.
Vista del Mar No. 155, Halfmoon Bay—Meets 2nd and 4th Thursdays, I.O.O.F. Hall; Elizabeth Olney, Rec. Sec.
Ano Nuevo No. 180, Pescadero—Meets 1st and 3rd Wednesdays, I.O.O.F. Hall; Mrs. Alice Mattei, Rec. Sec.
El Carmelo No. 181, Daly City—Meets 1st and 3rd Wednesdays, Masonic Hall; Miss Alice Mathias, Rec. Sec., 2218 26th Ave., San Francisco.
Menlo No. 211, Menlo Park—Meets 2nd and 4th Mondays, Masonic Hall; Mrs. Frances E. Maloney, Rec. Sec., P. O. box 626.
San Bruno No. 246, San Bruno—Meets 2nd and 4th Fridays, Legion Hall; Miss Mildred Foley, Rec. Sec., 217 Miller Ave., South San Francisco.

SANTA BARBARA COUNTY.

Reina del Mar No. 126, Santa Barbara—Meets 1st and 3rd Tuesdays, Pythian Castle, 222 W. Carillo St.; Mrs. Dorothy Yule, Rec. Sec., 112 Ocean Ave.

SANTA CLARA COUNTY.

San Jose No. 81, San Jose—Meets Thursdays, Catholic Women Center, 5th and San Fernando Sts.; Mrs. Nellie Fleming, Rec. Sec., Catholic Women Center.
Vendome No. 100, San Jose—Meets Wednesdays, Old Scottish Rite Temple; Miss Marie Buck, Rec. Sec., 245 Hawthorne St.
El Monte No. 205, Mountain View—Meets 2nd and 4th Fridays, American Legion Hall; Miss Elizabeth Spencer, Rec. Sec., 512 Hope St.
Palo Alto No. 229, Palo Alto—Meets 1st and 2nd Mondays, N.S.G.W. Hall; Miss Helena G. Hansen, Rec. Sec., 531 Lytton Ave.

SANTA CRUZ COUNTY.

Santa Cruz No. 26, Santa Cruz—Meets Mondays, N.S.G.W. Hall; Mrs. May L. Williamson, Rec. Sec., 170 Walnut Ave.
El Pajaro No. 35, Watsonville—Meets 1st and 3rd Tuesdays, I.O.O.F. Hall; Miss Ruth E. Wilson, Rec. Sec., 16 Laurel St.

SHASTA COUNTY.

Camellia No. 41, Anderson—Meets 1st and 3rd Tuesdays, Masonic Hall; Mrs. Olga E. Welbourn, Rec. Sec.
Lassen View No. 98, Shasta—Meets 2nd Friday, Masonic Hall; Miss Louise Litsch, Rec. Sec.
Hiawatha No. 140, Redding—Meets 2nd and 4th Wednesdays, Moose Hall; Ruth Presleigh, Rec. Sec., Office County Clerk.

SIERRA COUNTY.

Naomi No. 36, Downieville—Meets 2nd and 4th Wednesdays, I.O.O.F. Hall; Louise C. Dubuque, Rec. Sec.
Imogen No. 134, Sierraville—Meets 2nd and 4th Saturday afternoons, Copren Hall; Mrs. Jennie Copren, Rec. Sec.

SISKIYOU COUNTY.

Eschscholtzia No. 112, Etna—Meets 1st and 3rd Wednesdays, Masonic Hall; Mrs. Bernice E. Smith, Rec. Sec.
Mountain Dawn No. 120, Sawyers Bar—Meets 2nd and last Wednesdays, I.O.O.F. Hall; Miss Edith Dunphy, Rec. Sec.

SOLANO COUNTY.

Vallejo No. 195, Vallejo—Meets 1st and 3rd Wednesdays, K.C. Hall, 820 Marin St.; Mrs. Mary Combs, Rec. Sec., 511 York St.
Mary E. Bell No. 224, Dixon—Meets 2nd and 4th Thursdays, I.O.O.F. Hall; Mary Young, Rec. Sec.

SONOMA COUNTY.

Sonoma No. 209, Sonoma—Meets 2nd and 4th Mondays, I.O.O.F. Hall; Mrs. Mae Norrbom, Rec. Sec., R.F.D., box 171.
Santa Rosa No. 217, Santa Rosa—Meets 1st and 3rd Thursdays, N.S.G.W. Hall; Mrs. Clytie L. Lewis, Rec. Sec., R.F.D. No. 4, Box 345-A.
Petaluma No. 222, Petaluma—Meets 1st and 3rd Tuesdays, Dania Hall; Mrs. Margaret M. Oeltjen, Rec. Sec., 503 Prospect St.

STANISLAUS COUNTY.

Oakdale No. 125, Oakdale—Meets 3rd Monday, McLeod Home; Mrs. Lou Reeder, Rec. Sec.
Morada No. 199, Modesto—Meets 2nd and 4th Wednesdays, I.O.O.F. Hall; Mrs. Susan Sullivan, Rec. Sec., 823 10th St.
Eldora No. 248, Turlock—Meets 1st and 3rd Mondays, Masonic Temple; Effie Lund, Rec. Sec., 312 Mitchell St.

SUTTER COUNTY.

South Butte No. 226, Sutter—Meets 1st and 3rd Mondays, N.D.G.W. Hall; Mrs. Abbie N. Vagedes, Rec. Sec.

TEHAMA COUNTY.

Berendos No. 23, Red Bluff—Meets 1st and 3rd Tuesdays, W.O.W. Hall, 200 Pine St.; Mrs. Lillie Hammer, Rec. Sec., 636 Jackson St.

NATIVE DAUGHTER NEWS

(Continued from Page 11)

ruary 28. The Parlor and Athens No. 195 N.S.G.W. celebrated Saint Valentine Day with a dance and valentine box.

Lincoln—Placer No. 138 celebrated March 8 its thirtieth institution anniversary with a program, cards and refreshments. Charter members in attendance were Carrie Parlin, Florence Berry, Bertha Landis, Emma Jansen, Mabel Ahart, Mary Finney, Kate Temple, Millie Wyatt, Sophie Neville, May Herold and Etta Leavell.

Alturas—One candidate was initiated by Alturas No. 159 March 2, and plans were made for a theater benefit party, with Irene Cummings as chairman. A large party of guests and members paid tribute to "Old Erin" during the social hour following the meeting. Grand Vice-president Irma Laird spent the week of March 19 in San Francisco, where she was a speaker at a luncheon of the presidents' assembly of Federated Clubs, attended a tea given by the League of American Penwomen, of which she is a member, and as honorary state vice-president was at the luncheon of the Republican Women's Club of California.

Daly City—Through the means of a telephone bridge party, El Carmelo No. 181 raised the necessary funds to adopt a homeless child. The baby, a little girl, is to be called "Carmel." Miss Alice Mathias was in charge of the party.

San Rafael—The drill team of Marinita No. 198 had its spring dance March 11. The committee in charge included Ida Sampaulesi, Mary Brusatori and Marguerite Hecht. Entertainment was presented by Florence Carr, Alice Hagan, Helen Kientz, Eugenia Watson, Arthur Perotti and Everett Begley.

Santa Rosa—Santa Rosa No. 217 honored Saint Patrick's Day with a "kids" party March 16. Kathryn Branstetter presented a "special" program, and extra-good "eats" were provided by Ann Beach. President Ida Losch and thirty members of the Parlor attended the district meeting at Sonoma.

Ontario—The sewing branch of Ontario No. 251, under the able management of President Adele Frankish, is accomplishing many things. An all-day meeting was held March 1 at the Cucamonga residence of Effie Van Fleet. A card party after Lent is being planned.

Past Presidents Notes.

San Jose—Association No. 3 continues to increase in membership, and welfare work is an outstanding activity. Alice Roll was social leader at the March 14 meeting, when a very enjoyable hour was passed honoring Saint Patrick. A card party is to be given April 11; President Augusta Singleton heads the arrangements committee.

TRINITY COUNTY.

Eltapome No. 55, Weaverville—Meets 2nd and 4th Thursdays, N.S.G.W. Hall; Mrs. Lou N. Fetzer, Rec. Sec.

TUOLUMNE COUNTY.

Dardanelle No. 66, Sonora—Meets Fridays, I.O.O.F. Hall; Mrs. Nettie Whitto, Rec. Sec., P.O. box 122.
Golden Era No. 99, Columbia—Meets 1st and 3rd Thursdays, N.S.G.W. Hall; Miss Irene Ponce, Rec. Sec.
Anona No. 164, Jamestown—Meets 2nd and 4th Tuesdays, I.O.O.F. Hall; Nellie Hope, Rec. Sec.

YOLO COUNTY.

Woodland No. 90, Woodland—Meets 2nd and 4th Tuesdays, N.S.G.W. Hall; Mrs. Maude Heaton, Rec. Sec., 153 College St.

YUBA COUNTY.

Marysville No. 162, Marysville—Meets 2nd and 4th Wednesdays, Liberty Hall; Miss Cecelia C. Gomes, Rec. Sec., 701 6th St.
Camp Far West No. 218, Wheatland—Meets 3rd Tuesday, I.O.O.F. Hall; Mrs. Ethel C. Brock, Rec. Sec., P. O. box 285.

AFFILIATED ORGANIZATIONS.

General Association Past Presidents—Meetings held annually in April at the home-town of Chief President; Mrs. Cora Stobing, 1739 San Jose Ave., San Francisco, Chief President; Mrs. Anna G. Loser, 72 Grove Lane, San Anselmo, Chief Secretary.
Past Presidents Association No. 1—Meets 1st and 3rd Mondays, N.S.G.W. Bldg., 414 Mason St., San Francisco; Mrs. Alice Ogburn, Pres.; Mrs. Leah M. Williams, Rec. Sec., 956 Pierce St., Apt. 104, San Francisco.
Past Presidents Association No. 2—Meets 2nd and 4th Mondays, "Wigwam," Pacific Bldg., 16th and Jefferson, Oakland; Emma Haggerty, Pres.; Mrs. Elizabeth B. Goodman, Rec. Sec., 134 Juana Ave., San Leandro.
Past Presidents Association No. 3 (Santa Clara County)—Meets 2nd Tuesday, Musicians Hall, 114 E. Santa Clara St., San Jose; Augusta Singleton, Pres.; Clara Briggs, Rec. Sec., 1336 Magnolia Ave., San Jose.
Past Presidents Association No. 4 (Sacramento County)—Meets 2nd Monday, N.S.G.W. Hall, 11th and "J" Sts., Sacramento City; Edith Kelley, Pres.; Lily May Tilden, Rec. Sec., 3225 "T" St., Sacramento.
Past Presidents Association No. 5 (Butte County)—Meets 1st Friday, homes of members, Chico and Oroville; Marie Picanco, Pres.; Ruth Brown, Rec. Sec., 1265 Leah Court, Oroville.
Past Presidents Association No. 6 (Nevada County)—Meets 4th Friday, alternately between Nevada City, Pythian Castle, and Grass Valley, Edna Sampson's home; Margaret V. Nolan, Pres.; Vere Hansen, Rec. Sec., R.F.D. No. 2, box 41-C, Grass Valley.
Past Presidents Association No. 7 (Sonoma County)—Meets 2nd Tuesday, Violet Mastrup home, 622 5th St., Petaluma; Viola Mastrup, Pres.; Elizabeth Dillon, Rec. Sec., Petaluma.
Past Presidents Association No. 8 (San Joaquin and Stanislaus Counties)—Meets 2nd Thursday, Red Men Hall, Stockton; Mrs. Lois Armstrong, Pres.; Mrs. Harriet F. Corr, Rec. Sec., 729 E. Sonora St., Stockton.
Native Sons and Native Daughters Central Committee on Homeless Children—Main Office, 955 Phelan Bldg., San Francisco; Mrs. John W. Stirling, Chmn.; Miss Mary E. Brusie, Sec. Los Angeles branch office, 3924 Sunset Blvd.; Dorothy Schlingman, Sec.

(ADVERTISEMENT.)

DEATH RECALLS EARLY-DAY ROMANCE.

Healdsburg (Sonoma County)—The recent death here of Mrs. Anita Fitch-Grant recalls an early-day California romance in which Josefa Carillo and Captain Henry Fitch were the principals. Owing to religious scruples, they eloped in the early '40s to Valparaiso, where they were wed, and then returned to California. Mrs. Grant was the youngest child of that union. Captain Fitch died in 1849, and the following year the Fitch family moved from Sonoma to Healdsburg. Here, in 1862, Anita was wedded to John D. Grant. She is survived by four children.

Music Conference—The California Western School Music Conference will be held April 10-12 at Oakland, Alameda County.

Livermore Rodeo—May 13 and 14 are the dates selected for this year's rodeo at Livermore, Alameda County.

Wild Flower Show—Niles, Alameda County, will have its sixth annual Wild Flower Show, April 22 and 23.

Flower Show—Sacramento City will have its tenth annual Spring Flower Show, April 20-21.

OH, FOR A LINCOLN NOW.

(GEORGE E. PHAIR.)

His was the hand that broke the iron chain
And raised the burden from a bonded race.
His was the hand predestined to efface
A Nation's guilt and wipe away the stain.
And now across the years he hears again
The cries he strove to make the world forget:
Despairing farmers chained by hopeless debt,
White-collar slaves reduced to want and pain.
Slaves of the bread line standing in the cold
Begging a humble crust of bread to eat,
While granaries are overwhelmed with wheat
And in the banks the coffers burst with gold.
Oh, for a Lincoln now with dauntless hand
To break the golden chain that grips the land!

—Exchange.

"True greatness, if it be anywhere on earth, is in private virtue, removed from the notion of pomp and vanity, confined to a contemplation of itself, and centering on itself."—Dryden.

"When thou camest into the world, all about thee were laughing! So live that when thou goest out of the world all about thee may be weeping!"

In Memoriam

LUCY E. CLARK.

We, your committee appointed to draft resolutions of respect to the memory of our departed sister, Lucy E. Clark, respectfully submit the following:

Another member of Forrest Parlor No. 86 N.D.G.W. has gone from us to join the Heavenly Parlor on High; and while, in all reverence, we submit our minds and hearts to the will of Him who ordereth all things for the best, we mourn our loss and feel the deepest sympathy for the family of our departed sister in their even greater loss. Therefore, be it

Resolved, That, as a mark of our sense of loss, our charter be draped in mourning for a period of thirty days, and these resolutions be spread in full upon the minutes of this Parlor; and, as evidence of our sympathy for our sister's family, a copy of these resolutions be sent to her bereaved husband and a copy sent to The Grizzly Bear for publication.

MARGUERITE DAVIS,
GRACE ROOS,
ELVIRA LEVAGGI.

Plymouth, March 9, 1933.

SAN FRANCISCO

"CALIFORNIA HAPPENINGS OF FIFTY Years Ago," to be found elsewhere in this issue of The Grizzly Bear, refer briefly to the Sixth Grand Parlor of the Order of Native Sons of the Golden West, in session at San Francisco, April 9-12, 1883. The reports submitted disclosed that, as of December 31, 1882, the Order had thirteen Subordinate Parlors, with a total membership of 696. Of that total, 173 were affiliated with California No. 1 (San Francisco), 138 with Sacramento No. 3 and 122 with Pacific No. 10 (San Francisco). At that session, as noted in the "Proceedings":

"The [Legislation] Committee recommended the changing of the word 'Parlor,' wherever found in the Constitution, to the word 'Lodge,' and also changing the words 'Native Sons Golden West' to 'Native Sons of California,' but the minority report . . . , protesting against said changes, was adopted by a large majority."

"The Committee on Petitions reported unfavorably upon the institution of a Parlor at Tombstone [Arizona Territory], which report was adopted, and the Grand Secretary instructed to notify those interested of the action of the Grand Parlor."

Among the officials of the Grand Parlor at that time was the Grand Lecturer. Leonidas Clay Branch, whose death was recorded in The Grizzly Bear for February 1933, was the incumbent. He was affiliated with Modesto No. 11. His report to the Sixth (1883) Grand Parlor concluded with:

"The fires of patriotism are kept burning, and a reverence for the memories of our fathers—the pioneers—exists among the brotherhood. I have on all occasions endeavored to excite them to an emulation of the examples of industry and frugality set us by our sires; . . .

"I find many young men who are anxious to become members, but who are at present excluded on account of their age; and I am satisfied, from my observations, that the membership of the Order would have greatly increased during the past ten months had the maximum age remained at eighteen years; and I earnestly recommend a repeal of the present law, which deprives some of the brightest and most desirable material from membership and fellowship with those who chance to be a few years their seniors. . . . Prevailing everywhere within the sacred precincts of every Parlor there is a profound veneration for the pioneers. Their work is done, ours is but begun.

" 'They need
No statue nor inscription to reveal
Their greatness. It is round them; and the joy
With which their children tread the hallowed ground
That holds their venerated bones, the peace
That smiles on all they fought for, and the wealth
That clothes the land they rescued—these though mute
As feeling ever is when deepest—these
Are monuments more lasting than the fanes
Rear'd to the kings and demi-gods of old.' "

The recommendation of Grand Lecturer Branch concerning age-limit bore fruit, for the law was amended to read: "Candidates [for membership in Subordinate Parlors] must be of the age of eighteen or upwards, but each Subordinate Parlor may fix the limit of age beyond eighteen."—C.M.H.

N.D.G.W. HOME BREAKFAST.

Past Grand President Emma G. Foley and Supervising Deputy Alice M. Lane were hostesses at the N.D.G.W. Home breakfast Sunday, March 12, and in tribute to them members of Orinda No. 56 and Castro No. 178 Parlors attended in numbers. The decorations were in token of Saint Patrick's Day, and each guest was presented with a cake shaped like a frog, with a bit of shamrock in its mouth. Marin County Parlors attended, to carry out the "Marin County Day" designation for the breakfast.

Mrs. Foley presided, and prayer was offered by Mrs. Lane. Postmaster Harry L. Todd spoke on "The Constitution of the United States," and said its adoption was due to the arguments advanced by Benjamin Franklin, and the one-minute and only public address of George Washington. Vocal numbers were rendered by Mildred Gibson and the N.D.G.W. Glee Club. Among the guests introduced were Past Grand Presidents Dr. Mariana Bertola, Dr. Louise C. Heilbron and Evelyn I. Carlson, Grand Trustee Ethel Begley and Grand Inside Sentinel Orinda Giannini. N.D.G.W. Parlors represented included Portola No. 172, Buena Vista No. 68, Genevieve No. 132, Golden State No. 50, Alta No. 3, Dolores No. 169, Twin Peaks No. 185, La Estrella No. 89, San Diego No. 208, Gabrielle No. 139, El Carmelo No. 181, Marinita No. 198, Sea Point No. 196, Castro No. 178 and Orinda No. 56.

OPTIMISTIC SPIRIT CREATED.

Grand Trustee Jesse H. Miller made his official visit to South San Francisco Parlor No. 157 N.S.G.W. March 15. This was also the occasion of the Parlor's annual Saint Patrick's Day banquet. Over two hundred members of the Order were in attendance. Grand Trustee Miller, after listening to the initiatory ceremony by the officers of the Parlor, paid them a very high compliment for the efficient manner in which they rendered the ritual, as well as for the conduct of the business of the Parlor. He made a splendid address on the work the Order is engaged in, and the possibilities for the future. His remarks seemed to leave the spirit of optimism with those assembled—a splendid spirit to create under present conditions.

Addresses were also made by Grand Second Vice-president Chas. A. Koenig, Eugene H. O'Donnell (Dolores No. 208) and George H. Barron (Precita No. 187), the latter speaking on the "Life of Saint Patrick." Community singing was engaged in, and solos were rendered by Carl Prignitz, Bert Cuevas, George Kendall, Jim Williams and Jack Brady. Organist Lionel (Babe) Smith was the accompanist. This annual celebration of Saint Patrick's Day is conducted by members of South San Francisco of German extraction in honor of the descendants of the Irish race. It has been an event in the Parlor for a great many years, and seems to grow in spirit and enthusiasm as the years go on. As additional entertainment, moving pictures were shown of three of the principal football games held on the coast last session. The evening was voted by all a very enjoyable one.

BIRTHDAY BANQUET.

March 9, Minerva Parlor No. 2 N.D.G.W. held its forty-sixth birthday banquet. Among the many present were Mrs. E. Kroder, a charter member, and Deputy Ida Mesquite. During the course of the evening's entertainment a letter of congratulation was received from Founder Lily Reichling-Dyer, with which was enclosed a newspaper clipping of the election of officers in Minerva at the time of its organization. The Parlor is the second oldest of the Order, having been organized and granted a charter in 1887.

DRILL TEAM TO APPEAR PUBLICLY.

March 8, Dolores Parlor No. 169 N.D.G.W. tendered a surprise Saint Patrick's party to Ida Carrigan, who has served as chairman of the social committee for many years. She received a beautiful coffee table from the Parlor, in appreciation of faithful services, and was also the recipient of many other gifts. Dainty refreshments were served at beautifully decorated tables. Junior Past Grand President Evelyn I. Carlson was chairman of the occasion. The same evening, the Parlor voted to adopt a baby boy from the Central Homeless Children Committee. The baby will be named "Carlson," in honor of Past Grand Carlson. Dolores extends sincere greetings to the Parlors of the southland, and wishes them speedy recovery from the recent catastrophe.

The newly-organized drill team of the Parlor meets every week, and within a short time will make its initial public appearance. Josephine Doray has been appointed captain, while Alvina Burkhardt and Helen Lokken serve as lieutenants. Chairman Betty Both of the veterans welfare committee visited the tubercular ward of Letterman Hospital February 26 and served the boys with cigarets and home-made goodies. Each boy was presented a valentine. Rose Spaelti and Juanita Blanchfield were co-hostesses.

GRAND OFFICERS N.S. VISIT.

Stanford Parlor No. 76 N.S.G.W. had an "Irish Night" stag dinner March 14. Ticket distribution was in charge of "representatives of the league of nations": Theo. Schmidt, Arthur Poheim, Frank F. Morris and Harry Kamphoefner. The arrangements committee included Dr. Thos. R. Flinn (chairman), Wm. F. Burke Jr., Hubert J. Caveney, Jos. T. Curley, Elmer B. Dooley, Arthur Finnegan, Wm. J. Flinn, Harry M. Kelly Jr., Michael D. McGill, Dr. Leo J. McMahon, Joseph I. McNamara, Hugh J. McGuire, Thos. J. Moran, Dan Murphy Jr., Martin M. Murphy and Dr. John T. Scully.

Grand Third Vice-president Harmon D. Skillin paid the Parlor an official visit March 7, and Grand First Vice-president Justice Emmet Seawell was a guest speaker March 21. The monthly whist party March 28 was in charge of Frank F. Morris (chairman), President Charles J. Barry and Recording Secretary Charles T. O'Kane. April 22, Stanford will feature a dinner-dance.

LUNCHEON AND CARD PARTY.

Alta Parlor No. 3 N.D.G.W. celebrated its forty-sixth birthday at a banquet March 13. Treasured as souvenirs were the favors, potted cacti. Mrs. Agnese L. Hughes, chairman of the affair, presented a fine vaudeville program, and Grand Trustee Annie C. Thuesen gave an original reading. Among those who enjoyed this delightful anniversary were Deputy May A. McCarthy, Past Grand Presidents Eliza D. Keith and Margaret Grote Hill, and nine charter members.

Members of Alta are now looking forward with interest to a luncheon and card party to be given at the Home, April 27. This will be the first activity of the Parlor after the Lenten season, and success is assured since it is under the chairmanship of Past President May L. McDonald. Tickets are fifty cents.

WHIST PARTIES TO RAISE FUNDS.

Castro Parlor No. 178 N.D.G.W. is giving a series of whist parties to raise funds for the return of a loan. They are well attended, and the response is generous. Mae Edwards will be the April hostess, and the party will be held at her home the 4th of that month.

At the March 15 meeting of the Parlor the married members entertained the unmarried sisters, and a jolly good time prevailed. Muttonleg sleeves and other style fashions of the gay nineties were much in evidence.

DAYS OF GOLD

(Continued from Page 8)

The roaring campfire, with rude humor, painted
The ruddy tints of health
On haggard face and form that drooped and fainted
In the fierce race for wealth.

Their famous camps were, at first, given descriptive names such as Hangtown, Poker Flat, Whisky Diggings, Rich Bar, Brandy City, Fiddle Town, Poverty Flat, Poorman's Gulch, Jimtown and Piety Hill. Never in the history of the world were so many poor men made rich in so short a time. Nuggets worth from $4,000 to $10,000 were often picked up. The celebrated monumental nugget from near Downieville, Sierra County, weighing 141 pounds and 4 ounces, was exhibited at Woodward's Gardens, San Francisco, and smelted brought the owners about $30,000. In 1848, the year of Marshall's discovery, our mines added $5,000,000 in gold to the supply of the world, and in 1853 the record was $65,000,000. The total production of the California gold mines has been over $1,852,000,000. The gold from California saved the nation at the time of the Civil War.

As to the extent and boundaries of a mining claim we have the court opinion ascribed to an early day Downieville justice. A man was building a house on Jersey Flat and before the work had proceeded far was advised not to build as the ground was another's mining claim which he intended to work. The man, nevertheless, continued work on the house and the miner began operations, tearing away the earth near the foundations, which resulted in a lawsuit and the matter of title being brought into court. Attorney Spear argued for the house builder and the justice asked him if his client had not received a warning from the mine owner. This the attorney admitted, but continued arguing for surface rights when the justice jumped to his feet and shouted: "Mr. Spear, what is the use of all this talk? You admitted that your client had a warning, and it is the opinion of this court that a mining claim reaches up to heaven and down to hell. Now, Mr. Spear, if you can't get above or below that, sit down."

Into California, at the time of the discovery of gold, poured all kinds and conditions of men, but the dominant force was the spirit of the American youth, trained to respect the law, strong and self-reliant. There were men of education and legal attainments who, spurred on by the urge of adventure, were the first to pioneer the West. They quickly placed themselves in touch with one another, called public meetings, organized local governments, and framed mining laws and other laws to govern themselves and to control men of violence.

As indicative of the character of the men of those days a political convention was held in Downieville just prior to July 4, 1851, and attended by Stephen J. Field, afterwards justice of the United States Supreme Court; William M. Stewart, afterwards United States Senator from Nevada; Chas. N. Felton, future United States Senator from California, and the magnetic William Walker who, in later years led expeditions into Mexico and Nicaragua and was known as the "Gray-eyed Man of Destiny." The convention was followed by a celebration on July 4, which drew a large crowd from the surrounding country, and a young miner, somewhat intoxicated, attempted to enter the house of an attractive Spanish woman, named Juanita, and she stabbed him in the breast, death resulting. Feeling ran high; a court was hastily organized from the miners, the woman convicted and hanged from the bridge crossing the Yuba River. Field strongly protested against the acts of those who participated. It is the only case of the execution of a woman in California.

A movement has been started, which we hope will be carried forward, to construct through the beautiful and picturesque Sierra Nevada Mountains the Mother Lode highway, from Downieville to Mariposa, and linking together the historic towns and settlements of the mining region of California which tend to preserve the memory of the Pioneer and the recounting of whose deeds of daring thrills the heart.

We, the citizens of California, and the traveler from abroad, should take pleasure in visiting the scenes where the early Pioneers dug the gold from our mountains. They were the bold spirits who carved out the destiny of the great West,—the builders of a state,—the Pioneers of Freedom. One by one they have crossed the last divide. Their claims are no longer worked, —their camps are silent. They have bequeathed to us a golden heritage,—California; and yet, too often the sole monument which stands to commemorate their greatness is a dismantled cabin or crumbling chimney around which the wild vine trails its creeping tendrils. Their dreams were always of the golden future, and the poet Joaquin Miller has thus expressed their hopes and thoughts:

We have worked our claims,
We have spent our gold,
Our barks are astrand on the bars;
We are battered and old
Yet at night we behold
Outcroppings of gold in the stars.
Tho' battered and old
Our hearts are bold,
Ye oft do we repine
For the days of old,
For the days of gold,
For the days of forty-nine.

"Danger Lurks Around Blind Corners," is the April slogan of the California Public Safety Committee in its campaign to lessen the constantly increasing auto death-toll.

Horse Show—The annual San Francisco Horse Show will be held April 19 to 22.

Feminine World's Fads and Fancies

PREPARED ESPECIALLY FOR THE GRIZZLY BEAR BY ANNA STOERMER

THE NEWEST AND SMARTEST THING to wear at the neck of your dark dress is white organdy, in the form of an ascot jabot or in a great big bow tied under the chin. Plain organdy is all right, but seersucker is better, newer, fresher, crisper and more frosty. Women this spring will follow two distinct vogues, one favoring mannish garments, which will dominate daytime wear, and the other, for formal occasions, will follow fashions quite feminine, like those which characterized the day of the Gibson girl.

The introduction of the straight-line tailored and quite-boyish modes, including slacks, for daytime wear and sports, brings the smart swagger coat into popularity again. It is so easy to wear over these stylish garments. A new swagger coat, such as we see today, is made of a broken plaid in brown and white tweed with straight mannish lines. When the coat is of figured material, the dress and accessories should be of monotone pattern, but when the coat features a plain color, the accessories should be gaily contrasted. According to the fashionists carrying this idea in mind, a plain brown stitched hat and monogramed scarf are worn with the plain coat, and shoes and gloves emphasize the brown tone of the garment.

The tendency toward starched or cired finishes in sheer fabrics is definitely a youthful fashion, and one that none but the younger girl or the younger woman should attempt. These new fabrics are a happy substitute for the organdy of other years. Their lightness, without ungainly stiffness, makes them graceful in their airy fullness, and they are admirably suited to winter or summer dancing. The black dress with the flowered shoulders is made of cired chiffon, which is braided to form a sash at the low waistline. The simple bodice has a square neckline in front, and the white flowers, starting high at the shoulders, form a flattering frame for the face. The skirt is full and light.

Next in order, and the newest of the young dance frocks, is the almost-tailored dress. It boasts of long sleeves, and bases its claim to the dance floor on the soft starched chiffon of which it is made. One is made of red, with a high neckline tying in a soft bow under the chin. Cartridge pleats give a fullness to the sleeves, that diminish toward the tightly buttoned wrists. The godets on the skirt are cleverly set to help the sleeves in accenting a slender waistline. Another new idea in white starched mousseline-de-soie, with fine check stripes in black, makes a dress that will find its way into many a youthful wardrobe. The skirt is gracefully full, and short puff sleeves and a wide red suede belt produce an effect that is lovely in its simplicity.

Taffeta rustles into the spring style picture and should be warmly welcomed, if only as a variant to the softly draping and closely clinging fabrics which have held the spotlight for so long a time. Its scope will, of necessity, be limited, but its advent in the mode gives promise of some refreshing interpretations, whether alone or in the role of a contrasting fabric. In the latter connection we have the new cloque taffetas and the embroidered taffetas. Celanese taffeta, in the luscious pastel colorings of the new season, qualifies for enchanting dinner and dance frocks for youthful sophisticates. Organdy over taffeta is reminiscent of the gay nineties. Taffeta, in one form or another, will be much in evidence during this busy month of parties and crowded social calendars.

With the returned popularity of the suit comes the blouse, in many new designs and styles. What woman ever has blouses enough for her suit, no matter how many she possesses? A lovely little affair is made of crepe and net, the latter forming the smart tucked yoke. The color is the very popular beige-gray. Fullness in the sleeves centers around the three folds coming from under the arm of each sleeve. Another dainty one, of triple sheer chiffon, is in a pale pastel pink shade, having especially attractive puff sleeves with shirring and dainty ruffled edges. The model may be worn either as a tuck-in or an over blouse, as can so many of the new spring and summer blouses.

A really good black frock for afternoon or dinner wear is an outlay that more than pays for itself when one finds that she always can present a smart appearance without having to rush out, perhaps, and buy a frock every time a sudden invitation comes along. A black crepe is combined with shirred sheer materials to give a striking effect. Jeweled clips are worn at either side of the square-cut neckline. The sash always gives a soft, flattering touch.

Quite the newest wrap in fashion is the cape, as everyone knows by this time. Just now, the smartest cape of all is made of check material, and is to be worn with a plain wool skirt or a dress of the check color. Capes also are smart as the third piece of a suit. Imagine one in dark oxford gray with a suit of lighter gray.

All women love prints, but they must be small. The material may be rough or ribbed like a silk serge, smooth as the foulard in men's ties, or have a close resemblance to a patterned woolen. They can be gay or gray, and they are combined with almost any fabric. For instance, a three-piece costume combines a dress, jacket and detachable cape. The figured silk makes the top of the dress and decorations. The cape is of blue, with dots in greenish yellow, and is combined with the plain blue wool of the dress. Either jacket or cape may be worn. The dress follows the lines of the cape in its use of the print, with small jabots instead of the large scarf. The collarless jacket buttons high at the neck.

GRIZZLY GROWLS

(Continued from Page 13)

voted against President Roosevelt's economy bill! Also, when an amendment was proposed to the bill in the Senate, to reduce the mileage allowance of senators and representatives, it was voted down, although the allowance is excessive.

Numerous persons, including lawmakers, howl for a reduction in the cost of government, but they want the reducing processes to exclude themselves, their friends and their pet hobbies. That's why it is so difficult to balance government budgets. The substantial lawmaker, national and state, will, in these days of stress, forget lobbies and hobbies and think of the masses. Reduction should be applied all down the line, with not a single exception.

In a scathing denunciation of the New York Stock Exchange, Samuel Untermyer, in Los Angeles March 8, expressed the hope that the Federal Congress will put stock exchanges under government regulation and make them answerable to the courts of law. He said that if the proposed regulatory bill of 1912 had been enacted, "much of the recent scandals, misfortune and misery that have overtaken millions of small investors over the country would have been averted." The bill, he said, was defeated "by the lobby of the black horse cavalry of high finance."

"Of all the anomalous and incongruous evidences," said the famed lawyer, "that ours is not an orderly government of laws but a government of, by and for the favorites of finance and special privilege at the expense of the masses, the fact that in the face of its long history of crimes and misdemeanors the stock exchange continues immune from all legal regulation, restriction and control, is the most conclusive proof. . . . It has been in the past years the one and only known safe, lawful, respectable, crooked confidence game, and one that can be and has been practiced with immunity every day in the year except Sundays and holidays by the most devout of its members."

"But the blood that is unjustly spilt is not again gathered up from the ground by repentance."—Raleigh.

Know your home-state, California! Learn of its past history and of its present-day development by reading regularly The Grizzly Bear. $1.50 for one year (12 issues). Subscribe now.

Grizzly Bear

MAY — THE ONLY OFFICIAL PUBLICATION OF THE NATIVE SONS AND DAUGHTERS OF THE GOLDEN WEST — 1933

GLORIOUS NEVADA COUNTY SCENERY, ADJACENT TO GRASS VALLEY

(For captions see Page 5)

TWENTY-SIXTH ANNIVERSARY NUMBER, FEATURING N.S.G.W. 56TH GRAND PARLOR, GRASS VALLEY AND NEVADA CITY, NEVADA COUNTY, AND DOWNIEVILLE, SIERRA COUNTY.

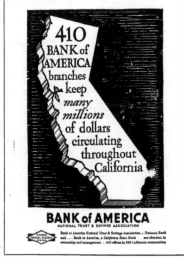

"RECOGNIZE AND WIPE OUT MISTAKES, AND PLAN FOR THE FUTURE"

Seth Millington
(GRAND PRESIDENT N.S.G.W.)

"THE CONVENING OF THE FIFTY-sixth Grand Parlor at Grass Valley, Nevada County, this year will bring to a close almost fifty-eight years of existence of the Order of Native Sons of the Golden West, founded on the 11th day of July, 1875. All of the evidence points to the fact that the altruistic purposes of its founding, and the ideals behind the suggestion that brought it into existence, was California history. While we must concede that there might have been other motives, not so altruistic or so idealistic, that may have rested in the mind of the founder, the only thing that survives today is the purity of the main idea, free from all blemishes, selfishness and self-seeking.

"During the past year, I have become thoroughly convinced that almost without exception the membership of the Order is true to the main thought, and that all of the members recognize our true purpose, and desire to see the historic idea behind the formation of this Order brought to its fullest consummation. The only difficulty, apparently, is the difference of opinion as to how that may be brought about.

"With the thought in mind that the purpose of the organization of the Native Sons of the Golden West is to preserve and perpetuate the beauty and romance of California's golden, colorful history, to preserve the written record that future generations may read and know, to restore the historic landmarks that they might see and appreciate, and to mark the spots with proper monuments where events of historic importance took place, let us consolidate our gains, recognize and wipe out our mistakes, and plan for the future.

"From the day I entered the Order, I never was able to reconcile an honorary historic society with the signs, words and pretended mysticism of a secret fraternity, and after all these years the two are just as irreconcilable as they were in the beginning. We are either an honorary historic society, in which the right to enrollment is a privilege and an honor, or we are a secret fraternity, copied largely from older fraternities, with, of course, our work adjusted to our unique eligibility requirements, and faced with the fact that we have concealed our light under a bushel, or rather behind the closed doors of secret meetings.

"Analyzing the situation, I can see only one reason why this Order originally was instituted as a secret society. In 1875 the secret society in America was at the hey-day of its existence, the social center about which revolved all activities, and in the absence of the modern vehicles of entertainment such as radio, moving pictures, automobiles and a host of other things that afford amusement, the meeting of the secret society easily attracted all of its members, who were physically able to attend, as the almost only outlet for pleasure in a rather drab existence. Consequently, the secret society flourished and the Native Sons, coming into existence at that period, fell into the line that was characteristic of that time and it became a secret society with its ritual; with its initiation ceremonies; with its habiliments, signs and words,—pure mummery, so far as meaning was concerned, and useless surplusage, so far as effect is concerned,—and with secret drapery behind which was concealed the real worth of the society.

"During the last few years, I have been very forcibly impressed with the fact, that is beyond contradiction, that the secret society in this State is rapidly losing ground, most of the societies with a rapidity that is almost devastating. While we have suffered losses, they have been trifling, in comparison with others, and I attribute our maintaining of our strength not to our ritual, not to our secret work, not to our closed doors, but to the fact that we have a background of achievement, of development of historic research work in our State, of preserving the record, of restoring the edifices and the old towns, and of properly marking the historic spots. Five years ago, the Order abandoned the secret signs, and that, in my opinion, was the start in the direction of ultimately clearing the record of surplusage and leaving us what we really are, an honorary historic society, dedicated to the preservation of the memories and glories of our forebears who crossed the continent to give us this magnificent empire, within whose limits can be found every physical feature of the rest of the globe:

"The delta of the Sacramento and San Joaquin, equaling the fertility of the delta of the Nile; the snow-clad granite peaks of the Sierras, rivaling the peaks of the Alps; the harbor of San Francisco, unequaled elsewhere on this earth, where the fleets of the world could be anchored in safety; the beaches of the Southland, with their mellow warmth of air and water, excelling the Riviera; the North coast, with mountains meeting the sea, comparable to the rugged fjord indented coast of Norway; deserts of the Mojave and the Colorado, similar in effect if not in size to the Sahara, but changed by the industry of man to earth's most fertile spot; the lakes of Lake County, as beautiful as the lakes of Scotland; a State with snow-clad Shasta, at the north, looking down the length of the fertile Sacramento and San Joaquin Valleys to the Tehachapi, and beyond to the luxuriant tropical groves of the Southland. Amid these scenes were enacted two of time's finest dramas, each distinctive and each unique.

"When Gaspar DePortola and Father Junipero Serra, in the spring of 1769, wended their way northward along the coastal plain of California, stopping at intervals to designate a site and ultimately to build a Christian mission, another method of occupying and developing a new and raw land and of civilizing the barbarous aborigines began. Twenty-three mission buildings ultimately dotted the Pacific border of the Western continent from San Diego to Sonoma, and from the bell towers of some sounded the chimes before the liberty bell rang in Philadelphia. Without war, without oppression and without malice, these fathers of old, almost unaided by soldiery, developed and made fertile a new land.

"True, they failed in their ultimate aim in raising the California Indian to their own state of civilization, not because of their own lack of effort or ability, but because of the crude human clay from which they tried to mold. Today, many of their old buildings are falling to ruin, and one of the finest historic heritages of California has been squandered by the devastating hand of time. No finer monuments to an era that stands out so distinctive on the pages of history could be found than these old mission buildings. The fortune of birth has placed upon us, as one of our paramount duties, the obligation of seeing that the wastage of wind and weather is stopped and that these old missions are restored, so that not only Californians, but visitors to our State, for all times can see this distinctive architecture, representing a period of a century and half ago that will not again be duplicated.

SETH MILLINGTON, OF GRIDLEY,
GRAND PRESIDENT OF THE ORDER OF NATIVE SONS OF THE GOLDEN WEST.

"We turn from the coastal plain of California, from the gentle tread of the sandaled feet of the Padres and the soft, euphonious tones of the Spanish nomenclature, to the canyons of the Sierras, and there hear, echoing from the granite walls, the harsh clanging of the hobnail boot of the Forty-niners, with the rough but forcible designations of the Anglo-Saxon tongue, contrasting Santa Barbara, Ventura, San Luis Obispo, Monterey, Santa Cruz, San Mateo, Santa Clara and San Francisco of the Spanish tongue with Hangtown, Poker Flat, Murderers Gulch, Shirt Tail Canyon, Rich Bar, Fiddle Town and other descriptive names of the Forty-niners.

"Here in these canyons, for the brief period of the existence of placer mines, lived and mined a hardy race who crossed two thousand miles of mountains and desert, lured by the irresistible call of gold, the marks of their brief, but vigorous, stay in the mother lode country now all but obliterated. Still, up there in the vastness of the Sierras, remain part of Columbia, Downieville, Old Shasta, the old part of Auburn, Nevada City, Placerville, as well as other remnants of the days of the Forty-niners that still may be seen at Rough and Ready, Georgetown and Weaverville. But unless the hand of the vandal is stayed and the consuming effect of fire is stopped and the wear of winter rains and snows is retarded, they will soon be gone.

"No state in America can equal either of these periods in California's history, and yet this organization, brought into existence for the purpose of saving these very things, has been handicapped in the ultimate achievement of its purpose by concealing its altruistic desires behind a cloak of secrecy and the habiliments of a secret society.

"The records show that a man of prominence and ability rarely joins a secret society if he has passed his youth. While most of the big men of California belong to our Order, I think that almost without exception they joined while young. Few men of affairs have either the time or the inclination to go through the initiation ceremony of a secret society, and I am thoroughly convinced that we have lost thousands of men from our Order who would deem it a privilege to join if they could do so without offering themselves for initiation,—for two reasons: First, they may hesitate to give the time. Second, the elaborate words and sounding phrases do not affect the modern man as they did his father. He is not enthralled with beautiful words arranged in sounding, but sometimes meaningless, phrases, but is rather irritated and sometimes disgusted. This last statement is no reflection on our ritual, but is a general statement as to the reaction that many times comes to a candidate who, upon being initiated, feels that he spends hours as the target of empty oratory.

"How much better it would be, so far as practical achievement of our purposes is concerned, to bring in members by subscribing their names to a brief, but carefully worded, pledge of loyalty to the organization; and, for those who appreciate and enjoy the ceremony of initiation, to let them have it. By permitting the enrollment of members without subjecting the candidate to the initiation ceremonies, unless he desires it, I am firmly convinced that thousands of men would apply for membership.

"I believe that our initiatory work should embody a general outline of California's past, so that the candidate upon final acceptance and at the conclusion of the initiatory ceremony should have a good, substantial, general idea of the history of our native State. Whether this will be presented to the Grass Valley Grand Parlor, is at this time problematical. The change has been somewhat revolutionary, and it is questionable whether the proposed new ritual will be in that stage of development that makes me feel justified in asking the members to accept it. I am very doubtful that that will happen.

"Many years ago, the Order went into the insurance business. This is rather a brutal way of stating that we endeavored to assist distressed brothers with sick benefits. That it has not been a success, is demonstrated by the record. I have examined the books of many Subordinate Parlors that have surrendered their charters and, without one single exception, the surrender of the charter was preceded by an epidemic of sickness that exhausted the treasury through sick benefits and prevented, through financial inability, the carrying on of social affairs, with the resulting loss of interest and the eventual disintegration. There is no doubt that many years ago, due to lack of facilities by the ordinary run of insurance companies, that this activity may have had its justification. Today, legal commercial insurance companies will furnish this service fully as cheaply and with greater certainty.

"The fraternal society is presented with another difficulty in the sick benefit administration that does not confront a cold-blooded insurance company, and that is the malingerer. It is no coincidence that the call for sick relief bears a direct relation to the prosperity of the times. A malingerer would get short shift at the hands of an insurance company; sympathy and fraternal relationship place a heavy hand on the effort of the administration of sick benefits by a fraternity. Furthermore, the weekly benefits bear no relation to the dues. One Parlor, for the same monthly dues, may pay three times as much as another. Obviously, one of them must be wrong, and a comparison with insurance rates, based upon the American mortality rate, shows that we pay too much. But the final answer is, that the insurance business bears no relation to a historic society and cannot be reconciled with the thought.

"I fully appreciate the fact, so far as our old members are concerned,—those who joined when sick benefits were payable,—we are probably in somewhat of a contractional relation and, without their consent, they possibly could not be deprived of their rights to sick benefits. Many Parlors are changing their by-laws to have two classes of members, beneficial and non-beneficial. The beneficial members pay, in addition to the regular Parlor dues, such sum as is commensurate with the value of the agreed benefit payment. I believe that we can strengthen our Order by not taking in any more beneficial members, although I am thoroughly committed to the idea of assisting a brother when in need, not because of the cold-blooded wording of a contract, but because of sympathy and love, and then not in a stated sum, but in whatever amount of money is required, within the limitation of the ability of the treasury of the Parlor.

"Some years back the Order, in conjunction with our sister Order, the Native Daughters of the Golden West, instituted the Central Committee of Homeless Children. In my opinion, this is one of the finest and most idealistic activities ever instituted by any society. Without reference to race, color or religion, to accept a homeless child and endeavor to place that child in a home where it can become a useful citizen of the Nation, without hope of reward on the

DESTINY

(BETTY L. WHITSELL.)

The Indian knew the priest
The priest, the ranchero.
A time of prayer.
Warm sunny days and singing nights
Adored and rare!
Before the days of gold
Were consecrated hours
When native trod
Adobe missions, meekly calm,
To worship God.

But shifting tides brought change
And fickle fortune lured
To western lands
A swarm of nationalities
In restless bands.
No time since the Crusades
Had men so thundered on
With dauntless feet.
They came to California
Blind fate to meet.

They came from foreign lands
The Malays, Hindoos, Dutch
Pig-tailed Chinese!
Americans from every state
New wealth to seize.
The young of every race
Adaptable and shrewd.
The good, the bad,
A modern Babylonia
All strangely clad.

In camp they met and lived
Eye met eye, hand met hand
When life was hard,
Heart-hunger coined a sacred word
The soul-word, "Pard."

The Grizzly Bear Magazine

The ALL California Monthly

OWNED, CONTROLLED, PUBLISHED BY GRIZZLY BEAR PUBLISHING CO., (Incorporated)

COMPOSED OF NATIVE SONS.

HERMAN C. LICHTENBERGER, Pres.
JOHN T. NEWELL RAY HOWARD
WM. I. TRAEGER LORENZO F. SOTO
CHAS. R. THOMAS HARRY J. LELANDE
ARTHUR A. SCHMIDT, Vice-Pres.
BOARD OF DIRECTORS

CLARENCE M. HUNT
General Manager and Editor

OFFICIAL ORGAN AND THE ONLY OFFICIAL PUBLICATION OF THE NATIVE SONS AND THE NATIVE DAUGHTERS GOLDEN WEST.

ISSUED FIRST EACH MONTH.
FORMS CLOSE 20th MONTH.
ADVERTISING RATES ON APPLICATION.

SAN FRANCISCO OFFICE:
N.S.G.W. BLDG., 414 MASON ST., RM. 302
(Office Grand Secretary N.S.G.W.)
Telephone: Kearney 1223
SAN FRANCISCO, CALIFORNIA

PUBLICATION OFFICE:
309-15 WILCOX BLDG., 2nd AND SPRING,
Telephone: VAndike 6234
LOS ANGELES, CALIFORNIA

(Entered as second-class matter May 29, 1918, at the Postoffice at Los Angeles, California, under the act of August 24, 1912.)

PUBLISHED REGULARLY SINCE MAY 1907
VOL. LIII (53). WHOLE NO. 313

GRASS VALLEY, LAND OF THE PIONEER, CENTRAL POINT OF THE SIERRA PLAYGROUND

Robert J. Deward

ROAMING BACK OVER THE TRAILS OF the Forty-niner, up through the valley of the Sacramento and into the forested foothills of the Sierra, delegates to the 1933 Grand Parlor of the Order of Native Sons of the Golden West will come nto the city of Grass Valley, Nevada County, he home of Quartz Parlor No. 58, host to the Native Sons of California.

In its setting of pine-clad hills, its air of peace nd detachment, the visitor will soon perceive he atmosphere of this little city hidden away mong the foothills of the Sierra,—the atmoshere of sufficiency unto itself. Perhaps it is an nheritance from those self-sufficient people who rossed the prairies by oxcart, or took the equaly perilous journey around the Horn. The mark eft by the Forty-niner is still there, easily perelved in the crooked, narrow streets sided by eather-beaten brick buildings with their stout ron doors and iron shuttered windows.

Any native son with the history of the gold ush in his mind can visualize a party of laborrs, artisans, merchants and farmers who came nto the little settlement f Boston Ravine in 1849, ollowing the trail to the ot of gold at the end of he rainbow. It had been hard path for many, nd only the few kept heir rich harvests from he creek bottoms. Boson Ravine grew from a nt city to one of log abins and rough-lumber tores, interspersed with n occasional brick building fortified with twooot walls and iron doors nd shutters, not to keep onest people out, but to eep the dross of the elting-pot from leaking . Many fortunes came ut of the creeks, and ngle claims yielded rom $10,000 to $50,000 a comparatively short me.

EARLY SETTLEMENT AND MINING.

From Boston Ravine he settlement spread rther along the bed of Volf Creek, and a new own, Centerville, sprang up. The name of this ettlement was later changed to Grass Valley. While placer and hydraulic mining was still in s infancy around Grass Valley, gold in quartz as discovered on what is now known as Gold ill, the prominence overlooking Boston Ravine. was here that James Knight first discovered old in the white rock, and from his discovery prung one of the richest gold mines of the reon. Shortly after gold in quartz was discoved on this location another discovery was ade on the opposite divide, about a half-mile way. It was on this quartz ledge that the Empre mine was started.

Since 1851 the Empire mine has been runng continuously in that same location and has roduced over $65,000,000 in gold. Today, the roperty is still producing at a profit, and men ave burrowed into the earth to a depth of 000 feet. Miles of tunnels extend in every rection from the main shaft, and in spite of e millions of tons of rock which have been illed for gold there is still an unlimited supy to be mined.

LAW ENFORCEMENT.

With the early growth of Grass Valley, there me an influx of people from all over the naon,—lawyers, doctors, merchants, artisans, iners, clerks, and dregs from the slums of the ties. Government was a problem, but justice, a kind, was meted out swiftly to offenders. roperty and mining laws were strictly enforced, d the basis of all mining law in this country as established in this vicinity. That it was uitable and just, is shown by the fact that it s persisted almost intact to this day. Much the law concerning water rights and water propriation from the streams originated in is region, and local residents still hold water ghts handed down to them by their families, ttlers of the early fifties.

In spite of the fact that measures to enforce the law were drawn up in fairness to everyone, it was a difficult matter, especially in the seventies and eighties, to give much protection to Chinese and Negroes. The former were often robbed and swindled of their earnings, which often ran as high as $1.25 per day, and the Chinese placer miner was often relieved of his dust without much effort being made to recover his property.

While Grass Valley was still full of the wild and woolly miners, and Negroes in the South were still slaves, a Negro came into town astride a white horse. A Negro on the loose was enough to cause a sensation anywhere, but to have one ride sedately into town on a white horse was beyond the comprehension of the miners. They immediately concluded that the horse must have been stolen, because Negroes were not supposed to own horses, much less any other form of property. He was promptly arrested, and given a trial. It took but a few minutes to hear the evidence, and less time to find the Negro guilty of stealing a horse. He maintained that he had purchased the horse in Marysville, which subsequently proved to be true. However, a necktie party was promptly arranged, and the Negro was duly hanged. A doctor happened to be present at the hanging, and examined the Negro after the crime had been expiated. His examination disclosed that the Negro was not dead, but would revive if left alone. Knowing that the man could not be hanged twice for the same crime, the officials promptly got busy and buried the unfortunate wretch before he could revive.

A VIEW OF GRASS VALLEY FROM NEAL STREET HILL.
—Maurice Photo, Grass Valley.

ENTERTAINMENT FEATURES.

But there was the better side to the life of the miner, and in spite of the crudity of his method of living, he did have a variety of entertainment. Lola Montez was acclaimed far and wide by the miners of Grass Valley, and no doubt her entertaining helped to lighten the burden of dreary hours spent on the creek bottoms. Her home still stands on Mill street in Grass Valley, the sole reminder of her palmy days in the roaring mining camp. Lotta Crabtree, another entertainer of those early days, specialized in dancing for the boys, and the story went the rounds that upon occasion the miners filled her dainty slippers with virgin nuggets from the stream beds. She held a warm spot in the hearts of those rough-and-ready miners, and Lotta was at her best when performing for them. Lotta also is reputed to have lived on Mill street, and her residence is now a rooming-house and, curiously enough, for miners.

> **GLORIOUS NEVADA COUNTY SCENERY**
> (Frontispiece)
> (1) ONE OF NEVADA COUNTY'S MANY BEAUTIFUL LAKES—BOWMAN
> (2) A FISHIN' HOLE ON OREGON CREEK
> (3) PASTORAL SCENE NEAR ROUGH AND READY
> (4) WOODLAND SCENE NEAR GRASS VALLEY
> (5) A VIEW OF THE SIERRA NEVADA FROM A HILLTOP NEAR GRASS VALLEY
> (6) A GRASS VALLEY FARM SCENE
> —Photos by Maurice, Grass Valley

ROUGH AND READY VS. NEVADA CITY.

While Grass Valley was still in its infancy, Nevada City, four miles to the north, was the center of life for miners along the Yuba and the various small creeks adjacent to it. But even then it had a rival, and strange as it seems at this time, Rough and Ready, now a ghost town with little left to mark it as a thriving city of the early fifties, was putting in a strong bid for the county seat. It had been settled by people from the Southern states to a great extent, and many of them proved to be highly enterprising individuals. Rivalry between Rough and Ready and Nevada City grew tense during the Civil War days, and upon one occasion a messenger rode into Nevada with the word that the Southerners from Rough and Ready were planning a raid on the county seat and meant to take it in the name of the Confederacy. The rumor spread like wildfire, and in a short time a great body of miners and townspeople were organized and armed, and hasty defenses were thrown up. Streets were barricaded, and the army kept its vigil all night long. The attack did not come that night, as expected, but the defenders were wary.

As the next day wore on and the army grew impatient for the conflict, it was decided to send out scouts to determine the position of the enemy, as well as their number and equipment. Stealing cautiously over the intervening hills and valleys, the scouts were amazed at not seeing the invaders. Pushing on to the hills surrounding Rough and Ready, the scouts still failed to find the hostile forces and finally decided to ride into the town. Everything was peaceable there, and no signs of armed activity could be found. The guides meekly turned around to go back and lift the seige of Nevada City.

As the Civil War progressed without decisiveness on either side, the people of Rough and Ready, strong Southern sympathizers, became more and more disgruntled with the administration of Abraham Lincoln. The climax was reached when those reckless souls decided to take matters in their own hands and secede from the Union. In all formality the Republic of Rough and Ready was established, and so came into being the smallest republic in the history of the world. The republic, however, was short-lived, and died of its own inertia, combined with the lack of interest among unsympathizing communities.

THE "HUNGRY CONVENTION."

The Rough and Ready "revolution" had a close parallel in Grass Valley shortly after the miners along the creeks became more numerous. As there was no agriculture in the county at the time, the whole region was dependent upon the outside for foodstuffs and supplies. Practically all of the merchants had been buying their foodstuffs in San Francisco, and since the existence of the whole populace was more or less of a hand-to-mouth proposition no great reserves of stock were carried. One particularly hard winter, '52-'53, supplies ran perilously low and a good part of the people were on rations. Supplies had been ordered from San Francisco many weeks previously, but had not been delivered. Exorbitant prices had been put upon the little foodstuff remaining. The situation demanded a public meeting, and the citizenry gathered at Beatty's Hotel, on Main street, with the house filled to overflowing with excited miners.

An early-day writer, describing the event, said: "Judge Murphy took the chair, and if he had discharged the office of governor with as much zeal and ability as he did that of the presiding officer of the hungry convention, he deserves the thanks of unborn millions, and probably will get it."

A number of town wags saw the opportunity, and stole the show. Working upon the sympathies of the crude miners, who were always more or less ready to flaunt the gauntlet in the face of the devil, the assemblage agreed to draw up some resolutions, as well as to take foodstuffs away from the soulless speculators who were driving them to starvation. So, "At a meeting of the miners and citizens of Grass Valley, in convention assembled, the following preamble and resolutions were adopted: Whereas, When, in the course of human events, it becomes necessary for a people to protect themselves against want and starvation, when they are at the mercy of soulless speculators, who demand all their earnings for the support of life, we deem it right to act in self-defense, and demand provisions for our need, and at prices which we are able to give. A decent respect for the opinions of the world induces us to give a catalogue of our grievances, in order to show the justice of our cause. Therefore, we declare

"That in consequence of the impassable roads we are short of supplies necessary to the support of human life. That the merchants refuse to sell at reasonable prices. That there are abundant supplies of flour and other necessaries in San Francisco, which soulless speculators, taking advantage of our position, are holding for exorbitant prices, and refuse to sell. Therefore, be it resolved, That appealing to high Heaven for the justice of our cause, we will go to San Francisco and obtain the necessary supplies, 'Peaceably if we can, but forcibly if we must'."

It was a motley army which was hastily recrufted—armed with long toms, picks, shovels and other odd weapons. The "war" was under way. A body of scouts were sent out as an advance guard to lead the way, and after proceeding as far as Rough and Ready, four miles to the south, they came upon a train of wagons mired in the mud and loaded with the long-awaited supplies. The war was forgotten, and the probable demolition of San Francisco averted.

THE PICTURE AFTER THE FIRE OF '51.

As was to be expected, fires proved a great menace to the early-day mining camps, and the flimsy structures were so much tinder when a fire started. Bucket brigades were of no value in combating the flames, and the only recourse was to let a fire burn itself out. Both Grass Valley and Nevada City were wholly or partially destroyed by fire at various times, the first coming in Nevada in 1850, and in Grass Valley in 1851. In spite of these reverses the towns rapidly built up again, and each rebuilding was an improvement. The final result was attained with the construction of fireproof brick buildings.

Writing of Grass Valley in 1851, A. A. Sargent, later a power in state politics, presented a picture which should be impressed upon the mind of the visitor. He related: "The dwellings among the trees, the gentle swelling of the hills, the beautiful broad valleys, and the air of mixed primitiveness and business bustle, all go to make a delightful spot. In addition to all this, the heavy pulsations of the many quartz mills that are laboring tirelessly day and night, save on the Sabbath, give an air of permanence and solidity to the town unlike the many ephemeral, mine-created towns that have arisen, prospered, and become deserted in California within a few years. The improvements taking place in Grass Valley are all of a solid nature: handsome houses are being erected, and stores, with heavy stocks of goods, are being prepared for the coming winter. There are many families already in the town, and more are coming, and when the pleasant, harmonizing influences of female society are more largely added to Grass Valley, the sun will not shine on a more desirable residence.

"The miracles that enterprise can accomplish have no better example than this town. Two or three years ago the echoes of its woods were awakened only by the cry of the wild bird and beast, or of the almost equally wild and degraded Indian. The riches of its ravines first attracted notice, then the treasure locked up in quartz, requiring skill and energy to obtain it. The demand created the supply; and, as the result, powerful machinery is in motion, a permanent town grown up, and the wilderness has changed to a cheerful and crowded haunt of men."

The visitor to Grass Valley today should keep this description of Sargent's in mind, and practically the only changes he will notice are the greater signs of permanence, and the vanishing of the Indians.

FOLLOWING THE LURE OF GOLD.

At the same time the country around Grass Valley was swarming with miners, untold numbers of adventurers were working their way all over the western slopes of the Sierras. All along the North, Middle and South Yuba Rivers men were washing the stream-bed sands in cradles and sluices, and at other places miles of ditches had been constructed to bring water to inaccessable places, that the hillsides might be washed away for the gold in the gravel. Along the San Juan Ridge, at French Corral and North Bloomfield there were great hydraulic mines, with huge monitors gnawing at the earth and washing their silt into the rivers. At the little town of Washington, on the South Yuba River, there were hundreds of miners working in the diggings of Alpha and Omega. On the edge of the Omega diggings the celebrated Emma Nevada was born, her name later becoming known throughout the whole country.

With the coming of the early eighties, the cry against hydraulic mining became so persistent that it was finally banned, and the once-populous villages of the Sierras became the ghost towns of the West. Little remains of French Corral and North San Juan, Washington, Rough and Ready, You Bet and Red Dog. The vanishing of the prosperity and happiness of the people living in contentment in these places might well be called the tragedy of the golden age of the Sierras.

PREDOMINANCE OF QUARTZ MINING.

After George McKnight stubbed his toe on a piece of jutting rock on Gold Hill and subsequently discovered that the rock was heavily

MILL STREET, IN THE BUSINESS SECTION OF GRASS VALLEY.

impregnated with gold, and that the particle came from a quartz ledge, the character of mining changed, to a great extent, around Grass Valley. McKnight's "boot," made in 1850, brought a great rush of miners to follow the trail of the quartz vein. Crude stampmills were set up, and the hillsides became dotted with the "dumps" of mine shafts. Not a great many of the earliest mines succeeded, because the methods of mining were so crude, but as the years passed improvements came, and soon the quartz mines of Grass Valley were the sustenance of the community. After the Empire became a steady producer the North Star, the Idaho-Maryland, Bullion, Pennsylvania and many other lesser properties came into being. The North Star has run almost continuously since 1875, and the Idaho-Maryland has been operating for the past twelve years after a long shut-down period, and is at the present time one of the finest mines in the district. The Bullion, closed since 1917, has again started operations, and with new water-pumping equipment installed, is expected to take its place as a big producer of gold.

WHITE SPOTS OF THE NATION.

While the rest of the nation has been suffering the pangs of depression and nations have been maneuvering to gain control of the world's supply of gold, the demand for the yellow metal has steadily increased, and with the falling prices it became possible to work mines of low-grade ore and make them yield profits. Since 1929, Grass Valley and Nevada City have become more prosperous than at any time since the early days of their history, and new properties have been constantly opening. Men who were released from the copper and silver mines of the Western states have flocked to this area, and great numbers of them have found profitable employment. Once again there came a gold rush to the creeks, but the yield to the average amateur has been very slight, but the life in the open and the ability to sustain themselves has served to keep up their morale and keep them out of the breadlines in the cities.

A GRASS VALLEY RESIDENCE.
—Maurice Photo, Grass Valley.

The great hordes of Chinese who combed over the hydraulic tailings during the seventies, eighties and nineties did not leave a great deal of the yellow metal behind, and with the vanishing of quantities of free gold along the creek beds the Orientals went down into the valleys to farm. Grass Valley and Nevada City, as well as all of the Sierra mining camps, were at one time heavily populated with the Chinese, and in Grass Valley two of the famous old joss houses still stand, preserved with all their relics since the early days.

GRASS VALLEY TODAY.

Changing conditions elsewhere have also changed Grass Valley from a helter-skelter mining camp to a modern city of paved streets, city parks, fine homes and modern schools. The high Sierra at its back door, with lakes and streams and virgin forests, each year becomes more popular with the residents of the crowded metropolitan areas. With fish and game in abundance, the region has become a vacationer's paradise, and has changed many a visitor's dream of retirement to a home among its pine-clad hills.

Aside from the points of interest to the visiter seeking a delve into the throbbing past of the Forty-niner, the city of Grass Valley is the central point of the Sierra playground. But a two-hour drive away is Lake Tahoe, the ideal of the vacationist. Within that driving range are the famous Sierra-Buttes, Lakes Fordyce, Faucherie, Spaulding; the Salmons, Sardines, and a great chain of some twenty other mountain lakes.

To the delegate who does not care to stray, Grass Valley offers the facilities of tennis courts, a golf course, swimming pools, boating, hiking and picnicking. In all of the miles of the country to be traveled, the visitor never gets away from the influences of the lure of gold. The roar of stamp mills, the great gashes left in the earth by the huge hydraulic monitors, the remains of ghost towns, and the prosperity of the whole region all lead back to the precious yellow metal.

GOLD PRODUCTION.

With the mines of Nevada City and Grass Valley combined from the production standpoint, they have yielded hundreds of millions of dollars in gold. The Empire has produced about $65,000,000, the North Star $35,000,000, the Idaho-Maryland $30,000,000, Champion group about $25,000,000, and other smaller producers another $50,000,000. To this huge pile of gold may be added the unknown millions taken out of the hydraulic, gravel and placer mines, estimated in the neighborhood of $100,000,000 to $150,000,000.

Although these mines have been operating since the fifties, engineers estimate that there is still over $400,000,000 left in these hills in placer gold alone! Surely, as the old prospector said, "There's gold in them thar hills."

Much of the vision, courage and tenacity of the miners of the earlier days still exists among the miners of today, for gold mining is still considerable of a gamble, and gold is still where they find it. So the spirit of the Forty-niner still lives among the physical traces of his habitation, among the old mine dumps and deserted shafts which remain as monuments more graphic and enduring than all of the plaques and marble shafts erected in his memory.

Grass Valley is the land of the Pioneer, the original virile type of manhood from which sprung the best in our Golden State today, for only the strong survived and only the courageous stayed. It is to this primitive land that Quartz Parlor invites all Native Sons,—a land with much of its virgin beauty unsullied by the progress of industrialism, its rural life as serene and undisturbed as it has existed through decades past. The spirit of mountain hospitality still prevails. The doctrine of live and let live has stayed with the spirit of the past.

CECIL BRUNER ROSES

(MINNA McGARVEY.)

They climb up to the window
To swing into your room,
There smilingly to greet you
And wave a fairy plume.

Yet if you think to hold them
Forever, or a day,
They airily elude you
And 'round the corner sway.

A breath of necromancy
From never-never land;
And Tinker-Bell is winging
About that kindred band.

They won't grow up! They're elfin;
Of all that lovely clan
In the Kingdom of the Roses
The petaled Peter Pan!

QUARTZ PARLOR HOST TO THE N.S.G.W. GRAND PARLOR

(ROBERT J. DEWARD.)

OVER FORTY-EIGHT YEARS AGO, A group of the young men who were leaders in the civic life of Grass Valley, Nevada County, received a charter from John A. Steinbach, then Grand President of the Order of Native Sons of the Golden West, for Quartz Parlor No. 58. For many weeks prior to receiving the charter, they had worked diligently interesting young men in the Order, and on March 28, 1885, there were thirty-four members present to form the nucleus of the parlor. The "Grass Valley Union" of March 30 said of the meeting:

"After the installation ceremonies a fine banquet was held at the Wisconsin Hotel, where eighty-six of the Sons sat down to partake of the good things spread before them. There was an absence of wines and liquors, which are not permitted by the rules of the Order, but this was no drawback to the good cheer and fellowship of the occasion, as it was a season of real enjoyment to all. J. A. Steinbach, Grand President, did not arrive on the early train, and in consequence a delay of several hours was occasioned until his arrival from Colfax, he having come by overland, so it was near the hour of 1 a.m. before the installation ceremonies were commenced."

FRANK J. ROWE, President.
—Maurice Photo, Grass Valley.

The charter of Quartz Parlor was kept open, and when it was finally closed there were sixty charter members. The first president was Thomas C. Hocking, who passed away just recently at Modesto, Stanislaus County, and the first recording secretary was Robert D. Finnie [now affiliated with Sacramento Parlor No. 3]. Other charter members still living are C. W. Kitts, Charles Othet, John Frank, C. B. Adams, Lucius C. Duval and F. J. Thomas. The Parlor now has a membership of 186.

H. RAY GEORGE, Recording Secretary.
—Maurice Photo, Grass Valley.

Charter Member Othet, in reminiscing states that the first few years of Quartz Parlor were rather trying, with frequent assessments necessary to keep solvent. The heavy drain on finances was occasioned by the fact that the Parlor had to pay for the upkeep of the meeting halls. The first meeting place was in a building which burned in one of Grass Valley's many fires. From there the Parlor went to the old Temperance Hall, but as it was replaced by more modern buildings and more of the elite of the townspeople joined the Parlor, the meeting place was moved to the more modern Lord's Hall, on lower Main street. That, too, grew outmoded, and the next shift was to Wm. George's Hall, still standing on the corner of Auburn and Neal streets. From there the Parlor moved to the present meeting place, the Auditorium Building. Being tired of the constant shiftings of its meeting place, Quartz decided to erect a structure that would be a credit to the town. Not having sufficient funds, it interested other fraternal organizations, and with pooled resources the hall was constructed.

Quartz Parlor occupied an enviable position in the early history of Grass Valley, and provided most of the civic leaders of the day. Practically all of the school buildings in the city were dedicated by the Native Sons, including the new and modern high school. Other public buildings also were dedicated by the Parlor. On one occasion Quartz staged an Admission Day celebration which, for technical detail and impressiveness, has never been equaled in the history of the city.

Of late years the endeavors of Quartz Parlor have been directed toward the perpetuation of the history of early California, and particularly as affecting the gold country. Only last year the Native Sons and Native Daughters of Grass Valley erected a monument to the memory of George McKnight, on the spot where he made the original discovery of quartz gold, and staged an elaborate two-day celebration.

Quartz Parlor has interested itself not only in California history, but also in perpetuating the spirit and patriotism of the Pioneers. Flags have been presented to the schools of the city, and the Parlor still has in its possession a flag presented to it by Mrs. George W. Starr in 1887. Judge George L. Jones is the only member in the history of Quartz Parlor who has served as a grand officer, he having been elected Grand Trustee.

In securing the Grand Parlor for Grass Valley, Quartz Parlor did so with the hopes of being able to impress upon the visiting delegates some of the glamor of California's early history, especially that reflected in the mining camps of the gold rush. It has prepared a program which will interest every Native Son, and arouse in him a feeling of belonging to the land.

The present officers of Quartz Parlor are: Frank J. Rowe, president; Robert Kohler, past president; Frank L. Hooper, first vice-president; John Thomas, second vice-president; Henry Beretta, third vice-president; H. Ray George, recording secretary; W. R. Vincent, financial secretary; Loyle Freeman, treasurer; W. P. Fox, marshal; William Phillips, inside sentinel; Charles Beloud, outside sentinel; James E. Oliver, R. L. Payne, Chester Edwards, trustees.

Quartz Parlor cordially invites every Native Son to Grass Valley for the Grand Parlor, from May 15 to 18, and promises one of the most interesting sessions ever held.

Real Beauty—"Beauty is a virtue. Longing for beauty is not vanity. Only the unworthy pride of beauty and its vulgar exposition is vanity, a contemptible vanity. If we philosophize that the good is the beautiful, then genuine beauty must have a foundation in goodness. . . . Beauty, to my way of thinking, is as essential to human life and happiness as the very air we breathe and the food we eat. This dreary old world needs beauty to enliven it."—Frederic B. Acosta.

Know your home-state, California! Learn of its past history and of its present-day development by reading regularly The Grizzly Bear. $1.50 for one year (12 issues). Subscribe now.

Pets Restricted—National park rules for 1933 prohibit dogs or cats in the areas, except that they may be transported in to and out of parks under leash and on through roads when owners have secured written permission of park superintendents.

Native Sons of the Golden West

MARTINEZ—MORE THAN 5,000 PEOple witnessed the dedication of the Contra Costa County Hall of Records by the Board of Grand Officers April 9. Preceding the ceremony there was a parade, marshaled by Sheriff R. R. Veale (General Winn No. 32) and participated in by many local and county organizations.

With Past Grand James F. Hoey presiding, an extensive program was presented. Supervisor W. J. Buchanan (Diamond No. 246) extended a welcome, and among the speakers were Grand President Seth Millington, State Senator Will R. Sharkey (Mount Diablo No. 101), Past Grands Dr. Mariana Bertola and Estelle M. Evans of the Native Daughters, Past Grand Lewis F. Byington and Supervisor J. N. Long (Richmond No. 217). On behalf of Mount Diablo Parlor, Recording Secretary George T. Barkeley presented the California State (Bear) Flag.

The ceremony of dedication was conducted by Grand President Seth Millington, Past Grands Charles L. Dodge, Lewis F. Byington and James F. Hoey, Grand First Vice-president Justice Emmet Seawell, Grand Second Vice-president Chas. A. Koenig, Grand Third Vice-president Harmon D. Skillin, Grand Secretary John T. Regan, Grand Trustee Charles H. Spengemann and Grand Inside Sentinel Gam Hurst. The committee of Mount Diablo Parlor in charge of the program included A. P. Wright (chairman), George T. Barkley, Past Grand Charles L. Dodge, Joe Schweinitzer and R. Anderson. A feature of the parade was a drill by Las Juntas No. 221 N.D.G.W., accompanied by the American Legion drum corps.

Postoffice Dedicated.

Petaluma—At public ceremonies attended by more than 2,000 this city's new United States Postoffice building was formally dedicated by the Board of Grand Officers April 15. Preceding the ceremony there was a parade, headed by Sheriff Marcus Flohr (Petaluma No. 27) and participated in by Native Sons from all parts of Sonoma County.

President Lewis H. Cromwell of the Petaluma Chamber of Commerce presided during the program, and the dedicatory address was delivered by Grand First Vice-president Justice Emmet Seawell. Other speakers were Grand President Seth Millington and Mayor Will J. Farrell (Petaluma No. 27).

The dedicatory ceremonies were conducted by Grand President Seth Millington, Past Grand Charles L. Dodge, Grand First Vice-president Justice Emmet Seawell, Grand Second Vice-president Chas. A. Koenig, Grand Third Vice-president Harmon D. Skillin, Grand Secretary John T. Regan, Grand Trustees Joseph J. McShane and Charles H. Spengemann. Arrangements for the dedication were made by a committee of Petaluma No. 27 headed by Past President John W. Murphy.

Must Observe Memorial Day.

San Francisco—The Grand Parlor Printing and Supplies Committee—Fred H. Nickelson (chairman), J. G. Schroeder and W. G. Maison—has advised the Subordinate Parlors that it is mandatory for them to observe Memorial Day, May 30, in either of the two ways prescribed by the Grand Parlor Constitution. Arrangements should, the committee urges, be made not later than May 10.

Golden Anniversary Celebrated.

Pescadero—Mr. and Mrs. William A. Moore celebrated their golden wedding anniversary April 9 surrounded by many relatives and friends. Better known as "Uncle Bill," Moore is the son of Mr. and Mrs. Alexander Moore, who crossed the plains to California in 1847. He was born at Santa Cruz City, July 19, 1851, and in 1854 came with his parents to Pescadero, where he has ever since resided. His parents celebrated their golden wedding anniversary in 1897, and his sister and her husband, Mrs. and Mr. Charles Steele Sr., celebrated theirs in 1930. Mrs. Moore, the former Miss Hattie Huff, is 79 years of age.

"Uncle Bill" is a prominent member of Pebble Beach No. 230, and the Parlor presented him with a life membership, and Ano Nuevo No. 180 N.D.G.W. remembered the couple with a golden basket of flowers. Moore is the uncle of Ida Mesquite, Louise Williamson and Harriet Williamson, members of Ano Nuevo. Telegrams of congratulations were received by the golden wedding couple from many relatives and friends. —I.M.M.

Annual Get-Together May 7.

San Diego—At a splendid meeting of San Diego No. 108 April 12, the ritual team of Arrowhead No. 110 (San Bernardino) initiated two candidates for the Parlor. Among the number in attendance were President F. L. McGarvey, Treasurer John Andreson and Judge Donald VanLuven of Arrowhead, and District Deputy Walter Hiskey and Leo Young of Santa Ana No. 265.

April 24, the Parlor presented to San Diego City a California State (Bear) Flag, which stands at the right of the mayor's chair in the councilroom. El Campo Santo, Old Town cemetery, is being restored; the adobe walls will soon be up. The Butterfield stage station in Vallecitos Valley is also to be restored.

May 7, San Diego will have its annual picnic and barbecue in El Monte Park. This is the reunion that brings all the oldtimers and the Natives together. James Murphy will have charge of the barbecue, Marshall Cruze the refreshments, and Bob Mahony the sports.

Twenty-Year Buttons Presented.

Livermore—At an oldtimers night April 13, Las Positas No. 96 presented twenty-year buttons to all who have been affiliated with the Parlor twenty years or more. The list includes:

J. M. Beazell, Roy Beck, C. G. Clarke, N. D. Dutcher Jr., E. T. Ellis, H. T. Holley, H. W. Hupers, C. E. Livermore, Norman McLeod, Clarence B. Mally, Fred M. Mally, Wm. Medau, R. L. Ruetz, M. L. Silva, all of Livermore; A. C. McLeod of San Francisco, Arthur J. St. Clair of Gustine, Jos. A. Guanziroli of Richmond, George H. Jackson of Berkeley. Each year, as others reach their twentieth milestone in the Parlor, they will be given similar tokens.

Balancing the Budget.

Plymouth—As a means to balancing the budget of Plymouth No. 48, members donned workaday clothes April 9 and, armed with axes and saws, spent the day gathering wood to be used in the Parlor's recently acquired home next winter. The timber was donated by Harvey Jameson of Shenandoah Valley, who was also on the wood-gathering job with President Chester Johnson, First Vice-president D. A. Upton, Secretary T. D. Davis, S. K. Davis of Sacramento, an oldtimer, and several others. Another economy day is scheduled for the near-future, for there is plenty of timber to be converted into stovewood.

Nineteen Initiated.

Colusa—Colusa No. 69 initiated a class of nineteen candidates—the largest since its institution in 1903. Grand President Seth Millington, a member of the Parlor, was the honored guest, and spoke on the historical significance of the Order. Other speakers were District Deputy Elton Fitch, Charter Members J. J. O'Rourke, President R. A. Gray, and Warren G. Davison and Everett Bowes of the initiates.

A vote of thanks was given Erwin Burtis, who signed up most of the candidates. Following the ceremonies a chicken pie supper was enjoyed. Arrangements for the successful evening were made by a committee composed of Bill Yopp (chairman), Julius Ferriauolo, Adair Wilson and Glenn Muttersbach.

Membership Standing Largest Parlors.

San Francisco—Grand Secretary John T. Regan reports the standing of the Subordinate Parlors having a membership of over 400 January 1, 1933, as follows, together with their membership figures April 20, 1933:

Parlor.	Jan. 1	Apl. 20	Gain	Loss
Ramona No. 109	1032	1034	2	....
South San Francisco No. 157	803	802	....	1
Castro No. 232	764	766	2	....
Stanford No. 76	575	569	....	6
Arrowhead No. 110	573	566	....	7
Stockton No. 7	535	535	....	....
Twin Peaks No. 214	522	517	....	5
Piedmont No. 120	491	490	....	1
Rincon No. 72	418	408	....	10

Arranging for Big Celebration.

Santa Rosa—Santa Rosa No. 28 is busy working out plans for the Admission Day, September 9, celebration which, it is expected, will be awarded by the Grass Valley Grand Parlor to the City of Roses. An enthusiastic meeting of the general committee, of which Wesley Colgan is chairman, was held April 14. Every Sonoma County Parlor was represented. The line of march was presented by Dr. W. C. Shipley, chairman of the parade committee, and approved. Several San Francisco and Alameda County Parlors have already arranged for headquarters.

Several members of the Parlor attended the reception to Grand President Seth Millington in San Francisco April 28. Santa Rosa's newly organized drum corps, Art Janssen chairman, will make its first public appearance in a parade here May 17, and it will also appear in the Rose Carnival parade May 20.

Twenty-two Initiated.

Merced—Yosemite No. 24 added twenty-two names to its muster roll March 27, the class being rounded up by Deputy Grand President Al Lobree. A. E. Daneri headed the initiatory team. Modesto No. 11 and Los Banos No. 206 were represented by large delegations headed, respectively, by President Charles Blaine and First Vice-president M. Ambrosio.

Addresses were delivered by Grand Second Vice-president Chas. A. Koenig, Grand Secretary John T. Regan, District Deputy L. E. Bither, and President J. J. Thornton of Yosemite. J. C. Cocanour was in charge of the banquet and entertainment which followed the initiatory ceremonies.

Wants 1934 Meet.

Ukiah—Ukiah No. 71 sponsored April 3 at

ENTERTAINMENT PRODUCES GOOD RESULTS

Santa Barbara—Santa Barbara No. 116 during the past few months has been most active in presenting various types of social entertainment for the dual purpose of increasing its numerical strength and attracting members to the regular meetings. The plan has been most successful, the membership having been increased more than twenty-five, with many applications on file, and the attendance at the meetings has increased nearly one hundred percent. "This is interesting news for all Parlors," says District Deputy A. C. Dinsmore, "when one takes into consideration that the past year has been a very hard one for most of us."

The accompanying illustration pictures but one—the Saint Patrick's banquet—of the many very fine affairs put on by Frank Castro and his good of the order committee. First Vice-president James E. Sloan was the master of ceremonies, and was assisted by Percy Johnston. The music was furnished by No. 116's Native Sons boys band, and the decorations were handled by Frank Calderon, A. C. Dinsmore and C. Wesley McCormick. The upper picture shows members of the Parlor at the festive board; the center, the committee that handled the successful affair, and the lower, the band. Santa Barbara has moved to new quarters, in Pythian Castle, one of the city's finest halls.

entertainment by the dancing class of Mrs. Ruth McKenzie. After the program a feast was given the Native Son baseball team and friends. Initiation will be held May 1. The Parlor wants the fifty-seventh (1934) Grand Parlor held in Ukiah, and a letter signed by President W. B. Davis and Secretary Ben Hofman says: "The Ukiah Chamber of Commerce and all civic and municipal bodies are prepared to give us full co-operation to make 1934 an outstanding Grand Parlor session."

Historical Review.

San Jose—The Santa Clara County Pioneer Association had a historical review of Spanish California April 18. President Rosalie Younger Andrews extended a welcome, and Grand Trustee John M. Burnett was master of ceremonies. The speaker of the evening was Past Grand Lewis F. Byington, whose subject was "Important Periods in the History of California." Other speakers were Judge William F. James and Clara Gairaud, Grand Organist N.D.G.W. A one-act play by Lutheria Cunningham, "Rosa de Castilla," brought back remembrances of old Spain in 1776, and "the new home in California" ten years later.

SUBORDINATE PARLORS DOINGS.

Lincoln—Silver Star No. 63 was host April 19 to Fred H. Greely Past Presidents Assembly. Sacramento County past presidents were special guests. Plans for the open-air initiation to be held in June at Weaverville, Trinity County, were advanced.

Watsonville—Watsonville No. 65 was visited April 11 by Grand Trustee John M. Burnett and Past Grand Thomas Monahan, and the members heard interesting discussions by both on affairs of the Order.

Santa Cruz—Grand Trustee John M. Burnett officially visited Santa Cruz No. 90 March 31 and in the course of an address recalled the early history of California. Among the other speakers were Past Grand Thomas Monahan. A number of visitors were present from Watsonville No. 65. Refreshments were served.

Downieville—Downieville No. 92 is sponsoring a dance May 6 to raise funds with which to entertain the Grass Valley Grand Parlor caravan that will pay a visit May 15 to Sierra County and lunch at Downieville.

Santa Clara—George Peter Fallon, a member of Santa Clara No. 100 and head of this city's police department, has completed twenty-two years of fearless devotion to duty with the forces of law and order. Public opinion has placed its approval on his record by retaining him in office.—C.C.

Deputy Grand President Al Lobree, who is engaged in field work for the Grand Parlor, advises The Grizzly Bear that he will institute a parlor at Turlock, Stanislaus County, May 5. He attended a special meeting of Bakersfield No. 42 April 17; the Parlor has a list of 3,500 eligibles, he says, and he expects to have a class for initiation there late in May or in June. April 18, Lobree paid a visit to Visalia No. 19, and the next day was back in Turlock.

"If we work upon marble, it will perish; if we work upon brass, time will efface it; if we rear temples, they will crumble to the dust. But if we work on men's immortal minds, if we imbue them with high principles, with the just fear of God and love of their fellowmen, we engrave on those tablets something which not time can efface and which will brighten to all eternity."—Webster.

Air Base Commissioned—The $5,000,000 air base at Sunnyvale, Santa Clara County, was officially commissioned a part of the United States Navy, April 12.

CALIFORNIA HAPPENINGS OF FIFTY YEARS AGO

Thomas R. Jones

(COMPILED EXPRESSLY FOR THE GRIZZLY BEAR.)

THE PICNIC SEASON WAS IN FULL swing in California during May 1883, and fraternal and social organizations as well as churches in practically every city and town of the state were daily providing outings for their members in the woods, gorgeous with flowers of myriad hues. The May Day picnic at Woodward's Gardens, San Francisco, attracted 20,000 children and 5,000 parents; a feature was the maypole dance, in which 200 girls participated.

May had ten rainy days. The month's precipitation was 2.85 inches, bringing the season's total rainfall to 17.90 inches. This was sufficient to assure a prosperous year for miners and farmers.

There was a migration May 19 of Mexican families into Cantua Canyon, in the Coast Range about fifty miles west of Firebaugh Ferry, on the San Joaquin River. A Mexican ffom Sonora, Mexico, came to the San Joaquin Valley and spread the information that at Joaquin Murietta's old retreat in the Coast Range was a mineral spring, the waters of which had a cure for all bodily ailments, and the superstitious Mexicans believed him.

I. N. Hoag of Yolo County was sent by the Central Pacific Railway to Chicago to encourage immigration from Eastern states to California. He was to deliver lectures and to circulate literature extolling the state's climate and resources. Subsequently, immigration bureaus were also established in London, Berlin and Bordeaux, to induce Europeans to come to California.

Memorial Day, May 30, was given statewide observance under the auspices of various posts of the Grand Army of the Republic.

The California Sportsmen Association had a state convention at Gilroy, Santa Clara County. Twenty-six clubs were represented by 228 delegates. A resolution favoring protection for mallard ducks was given unanimous approval.

Another fifty-mile riding contest was staged at Los Angeles May 15 between Charles Anderson and Carl DePugh. The latter won, in one hour and fifty minutes, the fastest time yet made.

May 1, San Francisco's city and county government went temporarily broke. The April salaries of the police force could not be paid, and members of the fire department had to take half-pay. The gas was shut off from the city's street lights, much to the delight of night prowlers.

Citizens of Sacramento were greatly agitated over a bonded indebtedness of the city amounting to $2,608,000 falling due in 1884. The commissioners had been trying to buy it up at thirty-five cents on the dollar.

Two-thirds of the voters of San Bernardino County presented to the Board of Supervisors a petition asking that saloon licenses be increased to $25 a month, and thereby close ninety percent of the saloons operating in the county.

In Merced County, the Board of Supervisors fixed the saloon license at $45 a month.

The Society of California Pioneers, in Stockton, advanced the claim that Curtis H. Lindley was the first White boy born in Yuba County, and James H. Tam the first in San Joaquin County.

In Colusa County lived a Chinese lawyer who was retained by the Mongolians there to take care of their legal needs.

The salmon run up the Sacramento River was at its maximum. More than 200 boats, manned by over 600 fishermen, were seining in Carquinez Straits, and the canneries were working to capacity.

A Tuolumne County rancher was said to be having a steady income from a skunk ranch. Chinamen were his principal customers.

The new state prison at Folsom, Sacramento County, was being inclosed with a stone wall four feet thick and twenty feet high. Two hundred and ninety-eight prisoners were confined there.

A cable 18,000 feet long and weighing thirty tons was produced in a San Francisco factory for the street railway system of that city.

The 1001 mine in Sierra County was washing gravel that paid an average of three dollars in gold dust to the pan.

A gold nugget weighing ten ounces was picked up on a street in Shasta Town.

Fire May 15 destroyed a block of Maxwell, Colusa County, structures, causing a $15,000 loss.

A portion of the business section of Guerneville, Sonoma County, burned May 23.

The court house, at the corner of Commercial and Main streets, Los Angeles, was partially destroyed by fire May 24. The loss was $7,000.

Four business houses of Suisun, Solano County, burned May 25, with a $25,000 loss.

Samuel R. Throckmorton, Pioneer of '49 and one of the state's largest landowners, died May 28 at the age of 74. He owned a domain in Marin County.

At Los Angeles City, May 19, Charles McAffrey stole a horse, which he sold for two dollars. He got drunk, was arrested, pleaded guilty, was sentenced to two years in San Quentin, and was taken to the prison—all in one day.

The boiler of the ferry steamer "Pilot," enroute from Petaluma, Sonoma County, to San Francisco, exploded May 25 opposite Donahue. Mrs. G. McNear was thrown a thousand feet and killed, as were also the four sons of W. F. Mather, aged from 18 years to 6 months, who were seated on the deck over the boiler. The parents of the children, elsewhere on the boat, were not hurt. Five other people were killed, and several badly injured.

Rains undermined the path up Telegraph Hill, San Francisco, which James Rigney had followed since he established his domicile atop the eminence in 1853. May 14 he fell from the path down a bluff and was killed.

Charles Avat, painting the spire of a San Leandro, Alameda County, church May 8, fell seventy-five feet to his death.

Leon Slusser, well-known Sonoma County citizen, committeed suicide May 12. His wife, being advised of his act, dropped dead.

Charles Hensch, in San Francisco May 13, attempted to prevent his wife being struck by a Baker-street cable car. He rescued her, but was himself killed.

Incensed at a jocose remark made by Robert Elwell, a lookeron at a card game in a Hicksville saloon May 14, the proprietor, McPorter, hit him with a wooden maul and killed him.

Charles Fisher was caught in the flywheel of a San Francisco factory May 31 and whirled to his death.

MEMORIES OF THREE

"MARK OUR LANDMARKS"

Chester F. Gannon

(HISTORIOGRAPHER N.S.G.W.)

"MARK OUR LANDMARKS"

GRASS VALLEY, THE STIRRING MOUNtain town of the '50s where romance, life, wealth and color blended to make its name ring down through the passing years, will feel again the pulse of dead and forgotten days when the Native Sons there assemble the middle of May. Their presence will call from the past the spirits of those who lived there awhile when California was young and then passed on, leaving behind them a heritage of history seldom equaled.

It had been suggested that people whose lives once brightened the Grass Valley of old, be touched upon in this article. It is not possible to go to lengthy discussions of a few whose lives were entwined in the past of a town which still lives progressively, but around whose existence the halo of former greatness still shines bright.

Grass Valley of old knew two women who walked the gilded path of fame to its end. A part of their lives were there lived and, having lived there, will always be associated with that pioneer town. Both of these women were children of the public. One, Lola Montez, a toast of the courts of Europe and particularly of a rather loose king, Louis the First of Bavaria. The other, a simple child whose animation, loveliness and talent established her the toast and joy of rough men, miners, small merchants and others made rough by a rough age in rough communities. The child was Lotta Crabtree, whose twinkling toes, gay voice, pretty face and enthralling personal charm made her the idol of her era and around whose name all the romance and glory of departed days still linger.

In this pioneer town is still pointed out the home once occupied by Lola Montez, and adown the street a short way is the dwelling where Lotta, as a child of six, lived. Lola Montez, born Maria Dolores Gilbert in the county of Limerick, Ireland, on July 3, 1818, was of Irish and Spanish ancestry. Raised in India, the imprint of that country of mysticism and loose morals soon left their imprint on a girl made susceptible by blood and temperament, with a grace of carriage and a beautiful face. It is no wonder that this child of destiny walked the path she trod. It is unbelievable that she could have done otherwise.

Her mother, scenting the possibility of the daughter straying from the normal path, became an ardent matchmaker and soon arranged a match with her 18-year-old daughter and an estimable Englishman, but of the age of 60. This wedding of May and December did not appeal to the impetuous Lola, and her answer was to elope with a young officer, Thomas James, of the Bengal Guards. The hasty marriage soon brought unhappiness to both parties, and Lola was divorced. The reason for the separation was her relations with not one man, but many. Thus we see that, at an early age, she started to tread the primrose path.

Rapidly she flitted from place to place, ensnaring this man and that. Enjoying her existence and setting her cap for bigger and bigger fish in the sea of men, she decides that Louis the First, king of Bavaria, should fall before her wiles and the conquest is not difficult. An enraged country tears her from the side of her king consort and she leaves the country. Then follow more affairs, marriages and still more affairs until the New World beckons and she arrives in New York in 1851. She moves southward to New Orleans and hears the call of the glamorous West, just the place to suit her bubbling nature.

In 1853 she arrived in San Francisco, and after a brief courtship married a newspaperman by the name of Patrick Hull. At the Mission Dolores this strange, exotic woman again plighted her troth at the altar of that sacred edifice. A brief honeymoon to Sacramento by river steamer, and the newlyweds appear in Grass Valley. Biographers are not in accord with how long they lived together as man and wife at Grass Valley, but it is safe to assume that most of her life was spent there without her husband.

Into the roughness and gaiety of this newborn mining town she plunged with all her lightheartedness and exuberance, and soon became its best-known female resident. She built a pretentious home, called it a "castle" and carried out the effect by placing a cupola on an ornamental roof. Little of the original house remains today, but the location is unchanged, and that is something dear to the heart of him who follows the trail of history. Her former career did not seem to be a social detriment. Gay parties, gay men and women there assembled, and hearts that were light reveled in the glow of bright lamps, and romance held its sway although, perchance, sordidness may have crept in now and then. She publicly horsewhipped an editor who had written disparagingly of her; at least Lola thought he had, and her point of view was sufficient to justify such punishment.

As she stepped along the gay pathway of her then happy, if not moderate, life, into her existence came a child who was destined to sing and dance her way into the hearts of the surging mobs of rugged California. Lotta Crabtree's career can scarcely be more than touched. Born in New York of an improvident father and a capable and talented mother, Lotta, with her parents, soon joined the gold rush to California. The family arrived in California, and Crabtree found it just as difficult to make headway here as he had in New York. Mining was too arduous for him, and he seemed to possess talents for no other pursuit or calling. However, as many profligate men, he seemed to be able to give birth to ideas which would put other people to work. He conceived the idea that Grass Valley needed a private boarding house. He wfote to his wife to come to Grass Valley, that a great

(Continued on Page 24)

Official Directory of Parlors of

ALAMEDA COUNTY.

Alameda No. 47, Alameda City—R. H. Fallmer, Pres.; Robt. H. Cavanaugh, Sec., 1806 Pacific Ave.; Wednesdays, Veterans Memorial Bldg.

Oakland No. 50, Oakland—F. R. Born, Pres.; F. M. Norris, Sec., 5595 Taft Ave.; Fridays, Native Sons Hall, 11th and Clay Sts.

Las Positas No. 96, Livermore—Dr. Donald M. Fraser, Pres.; John J. Kelly, Sec., P. O. box 341; Thursdays, Foresters Hall.

Eden No. 113, Hayward—John Meincke, Pres.; Filbert M. Soares, Sec., 1437 "B" St.; 2nd and 4th Tuesdays, Memorial Hall, Main St.

Piedmont No. 120, Oakland—Stanley Hadlen, Pres.; Charles Morando, Sec., 906 Vermont St.; Thursdays, Native Sons Hall, 11th and Clay Sts.

Wisteria No. 127, Alvarado—Henry May, Pres.; J. M. Scribner, Sec., Livermore; 1st Thursday, I.O.O.F. Hall.

Halcyon No. 146, Alameda City—S. Chesley Anderson, Pres.; J. C. Bates, Sec., 2139 Buena Vista Ave.; 1st and 3rd Tuesdays, I.O.O.F. Hall, 2329 Santa Clara Ave.

Brooklyn No. 151, Oakland—Frank B. Perry, Pres.; E. W. Cooney, Sec., 3907 14th Ave.; 1st and 3rd Wednesdays, Masonic Temple, 8th Ave. and E. 14th St.

Washington, No. 169, Centerville—M. D. Silva, Pres.; Allen G. Norris, Sec., P. O. box 81; 2nd and 4th Tuesdays, Hansen Hall.

Athens No. 195, Oakland—Milton O. Peterson, Pres.; Harold B. Farley, Sec., 4623 Benevides Ave.; Tuesdays, Native Sons Hall, 11th and Clay Sts.

Berkeley No. 210, Berkeley—F. Gohl, Pres.; R. J. Garrett, Sec., 1708 Virginia St.; Tuesdays, Native Sons Hall, 2108 Shattuck Ave.

Estudillo No. 223, San Leandro—E. E. King, Pres.; Albert G. Pacheco, Sec., 1736 E. 14th St.; 1st and 3rd Tuesdays, U.P.E.C. Hall.

Claremont No. 240, Emeryville—Raymond P. Burke, Pres.; E. N. Thienger, Sec., 889 Hearst Ave., Berkeley; Tuesdays, Veterans Memorial Bldg., 43rd and Salem Sts.

Pleasanton No. 244, Pleasanton—Edward Holzreiter, Pres.; Ernest W. Schween, Sec.; 2nd and 4th Thursdays, I.O.O.F. Hall.

Niles No. 250, Niles—M. L. Fournier, Pres.; C. E. Martenstein, Sec.; 2nd Thursday, I.O.O.F. Hall.

Fruitvale No. 252, Oakland—Ernest Perry, Pres.; Ray B. Felton, Sec., 1575 Alice St.; Fridays, W.O.W. Hall, 3256 E. 14th St.

AMADOR COUNTY.

Amador No. 17, Sutter Creek—J. H. Williams, Pres.; F. J. Payne, Sec.; 1st and 3rd Fridays, Native Sons Hall.

Excelsior No. 31, Jackson—Thomas G. Negrich, Pres.; William Going, Sec.; 1st and 3rd Wednesdays, Native Sons Hall, 22 Court St.

Ione No. 33, Ione—Earl Grover, Pres.; Josiah H. Saunders, Sec.; 1st and 3rd Wednesdays, Native Sons Hall.

Plymouth No. 48, Plymouth—Chester G. Johnson, Pres.; Thos. D. Davis, Sec.; 1st and 3rd Saturdays, N.S.G.W. Hall.

BUTTE COUNTY.

Argonaut No. 8, Oroville—Frank H. O'Brien, Pres.; Cyril R. Macdonald, Sec., P. O. box 502; 1st and 3rd Wednesdays, Veterans Memorial Hall.

Chico No. 21, Chico—Marcus Choisser, Pres.; Sam Lindsay Adams, Sec., Sacramento Blvd.; 2nd and 4th Thursdays, Elks Hall.

CALAVERAS COUNTY.

Chispa No. 139, Murphys—Maynard Segale, Pres.; Antone Malaspina, Sec.; Wednesdays, Native Sons Hall.

COLUSA COUNTY.

Colusa No. 69, Colusa City—Rotheus A. Gray, Pres.; Phil J. Humburg, Sec., 223 Parkhill St.; Tuesdays, Eagles Hall.

CONTRA COSTA COUNTY.

General Winn No. 32, Antioch—Edmont T. Uren, Pres.; Joel H. Ford, Sec., P. O. box 311; 2nd and 4th Wednesdays, Union Hall.

Mount Diablo No. 101, Martinez—R. P. Anderson, Pres.; G. T. Barkley, Sec.; 1st and 3rd Mondays, I.O.O.F. Hall.

Byron No. 170, Byron—William E. Bunn, Pres.; H. G. Krumland, Sec.; 1st and 3rd Tuesdays, I.O.O.F. Hall.

Carquinez No. 205, Crockett—John McManus, Pres.; Thomas R. Cox, Sec., P.O. box 721; 1st and 3rd Wednesdays, I.O.O.F. Hall.

Richmond No. 217, Richmond—Frank Weber, Pres.; Lloyd N. Mason, Sec., 11 6th St.; 1st Wednesday, 818 Macdonald Ave.

Concord No. 245, Concord—Chas. H. Gray, Pres.; D. E. Pramberg, Sec., P. O. box 235; 1st Monday, Guy's Parlors.

Diamond No. 246, Pittsburg—Victor Ericsson, Pres.; Francis A. Irving, Sec., 248 E. 5th St.; 1st and 3rd Wednesdays, Veterans Memorial Bldg.

EL DOBADO COUNTY.

Placerville No. 9, Placerville—Chris. C. Orelli, Pres.; Clyde R. Berriman, Sec., Wood St.; 2nd and 4th Tuesdays, Masonic Hall.

Georgetown No. 91, Georgetown—George W. Brichler, Pres.; C. F. Irish, Sec.; 2nd and 4th Wednesdays, I.O.O.F. Hall.

FRESNO COUNTY.

Fresno No. 25, Fresno City—Oliver M. Akers, Pres.; W. C. Guard, Sec., R.F.D. No. 2, box 379; 1st and 3rd Fridays, Pythian Castle, Cor. "R" and Merced Sts.

GRAND OFFICERS.

Dr. Frank I. Gonzales..........Junior Past Grand President
Flood Bldg., San Francisco
Seth Millington..........Grand President
Gridley
Justice Emmet SeaWell..........Grand First Vice-president
State Bldg., San Francisco
Chas. A. Koenig..........Grand Second Vice-president
531 35th Ave., San Francisco
Harmon D. Skillin..........Grand Third Vice-president
Mills Bldg., San Francisco
John T. Regan..........Grand Secretary
N.S.G.W. Bldg., 414 Mason St., San Francisco
John A. Corotto..........Grand Treasurer
560 No. 5th St., San Jose
W. B. O'Brien..........Grand Marshal
2324 Santa Clara St., Alameda
Gam Hurst..........Grand Inside Sentinel
Financial Center Bldg., Oakland
William A. Reuter..........Grand Outside Sentinel
1009 Marine Ave., Wilmington
Leslie Maloche..........Grand Organist
1611 No. Hudson Ave., Los Angeles
Chester Gannon.......... Historiographer
613 Capital Ntl. Bank Bldg., Sacramento

GRAND TRUSTEES.

Jesse H. Miller..........712 DeYoung Bldg., San Francisco
Eldred L. Meyer..........922 San Vicente Blvd., Santa Monica
John M. Burnett..........914 Bank Italy Bldg., San Jose
Henry S. Lyon..........Placerville
Joseph J. McShane..........419 Flood Bldg., San Francisco
Horace J. Leavitt..........Weaverville
Chas. H. Spengemann..........827 27th Ave., San Francisco

Selma No. 107, Selma—Chester E. Shepard, Pres.; E. C. Laughlin, Sec.; 1st Wednesday, American Legion Hall.

GLENN COUNTY.

Willows No. 255, Willows—Ralph W. Camper, Pres.; Leon Marshall, Sec., P.O. box 747; 2nd and 4th Tuesdays, I.O.O.F. Hall.

HUMBOLDT COUNTY.

Humboldt No. 14, Eureka—Henry Sundfors, Pres.; Loren M. Nelson, Sec., P.O. box 195; 2nd and 4th Mondays, Native Sons Hall.

Arcata No. 20, Arcata—F. A. Nicholson, Pres.; William Peters, Sec., P. O. box 1117; Thursdays, Native Sons Hall.

Ferndale No. 93, Ferndale—Hans P. Petersen, Pres.; C. H. Rasmussen, Sec., R.F.D., 47-A; 1st and 3rd Mondays, Danish Hall.

KERN COUNTY.

Bakersfield No. 42, Bakersfield—George Taylor, Pres.; Henry A. Bannister, Sec., care Bank of America; 2nd and 4th Fridays, Justice Court, City Hall.

LAKE COUNTY.

Lower Lake No. 159, Lower Lake—LeRoy England, Pres.; Albert Kugelman, Sec.; Thursdays, I.O.O.F. Hall.

LASSEN COUNTY.

Honey Lake No. 198, Standish—Leo T. Davis, Pres.; N. V. Wemple, Sec., Litchfield; 1st and 3rd Wednesdays, Wrede Hall.

Big Valley No. 211, Bieber—Fred Bunselmeier, Pres.; A. W. McKenzie, Sec.; 1st and 3rd Wednesdays, I.O.O.F. Hall.

LOS ANGELES COUNTY.

Los Angeles No. 45, Los Angeles City—Leslie A. Packard, Pres.; Willard F. Allen, Sec., 4955 Los Feliz Blvd.; Thursdays, Merchant Plumbers Hall, 1832 So. Hope.

Ramona No. 109, Los Angeles City—Frank S. Adams, Pres.; John V. Scott, Sec., Patriotic Hall, 1816 So. Figueroa; Fridays, Patriotic Hall, 1816 So. Figueroa.

Hollywood No. 196, Los Angeles City—Henry G. Bodkin, Pres.; E. J. Reilly, Sec., Olive View; Mondays, 1089 No. Oxford Ave.

Long Beach No. 239, Long Beach—Francis H. Gentry, Pres.; W. W. Brady, Sec., 801 Jergins Trust Bldg.; Dept. No. 1 Municipal Court, 8th floor Jergins Trust Bldg.

Sepulveda No. 263, San Pedro—Patrick H. Doran, Pres.; H. E. Fairall, Sec., 1925 So. Pacific Ave.; 1st and 3rd Fridays, Redman Hall, 543 Shepherd St., Point Firmin.

Glendale No. 264, Glendale—Harvey T. Gillette, Pres.; Philip D. Molen, Sec., 222 So. Glendale; 1st and 3td Thursdays, Starr Heights Recreation Bldg., 3246 Community Place.

Santa Monica Bay No. 267, Santa Monica—Arthur R. Leonard, Pres.; John J. Smith, Sec., 830 Rialto Ave., Venice; 1st and 3rd Wednesdays, Odd Fellows Hall, 1431 Third St.

Cahuenga No. 268, Reseda—Harold C. Trexler, Pres.; Carrol S. Driscoll, Sec., P.O. box 25, Chatsworth; first Friday, Alton Hall.

University No. 272, Los Angeles City—Bernard G. Hiss, Pres.; Martin DeFazio, Sec., 845 W. 53rd St.; Wednesdays, 1008 West Adams St.

Compton No. 273, Compton—Laurence W. Cowan, Pres.; Wm. Don Castillo, Sec., 641 W. Bennett St.; 2nd and 4th Tuesdays, Elks Hall, 6172 No. Long Beach Blvd., North Long Beach.

MADERA COUNTY.

Madera No. 130, Madera City—Cornelius Noble, Pres.; T. P. Cosgrave, Sec.; 1st and 3rd Thursdays, First National Bank Bldg.

MARIN COUNTY.

Mount Tamalpais No. 64, San Rafael—Arthur Hecht, Pres.; Manuel A. Andrade, Sec., 532 Mission Ave.; 1st and 3rd Mondays, "B" Street Hall.

Sea Point No. 158, Sausalito—Wm. W. Taylor, Pres.; Manuel Santos, Sec., 6 Glen Drive; 1st and 3rd Wednesdays, Perry Bldg.

Nicasio No. 183, Nicasio—M. T. Farley, Pres.; R. J. Rogers, Sec.; 2nd and 4th Wednesdays, H.A.C.D. Hall.

MENDOCINO COUNTY.

Ukiah No. 71, Ukiah—W. B. Danis, Pres.; Ben Hofman, Sec., P. O. box 473; 1st and 3rd Mondays, I.O.O.F. Hall.

Broderick No. 117, Point Arena—Ivan Lawson, Pres.; C. J. Buchanan, Sec.; 1st and 3rd Thursdays, Forester Hall.

Alder Glen No. 200, Fort Bragg—Thomas Cooney, Pres.; C. R. Weller, Sec.; 2nd and 4th Fridays, I.O.O.F. Hall.

MERCED COUNTY.

Yosemite No. 24, Merced City—John J. Thronton, Pres.; True W. Fowler, Sec., P. O. box 781; 2nd and 4th Mondays, I.O.O.F. Hall.

Los Banos No. 206, Los Banos—Daniel Pedroni, Pres.; L. E. Sarbo, Sec., R.F.D., box 21; 2nd and 4th Wednesdays, Eagles Hall.

ATTENTION, SECRETARIES!

THIS DIRECTORY IS PUBLISHED BY AUTHORITY OF THE GRAND PARLOR N.S.G.W., AND ALL NOTICES OF CHANGES MUST BE RECEIVED BY THE GRAND SECRETARY (NOT THE MAGAZINE) ON OR BEFORE THE 20TH OF EACH MONTH TO INSURE CORRECTION IN NEXT ISSUE OF DIRECTORY.

NATIVE DAUGHTER NEWS

SUBORDINATE PARLORS DOINGS.

Sacramento—Califia No. 22 had an Eastertide party April 11 at which the officers and the committee were dressed as children. There was an egg hunt and a guessing game contest, awards going to Mrs. Alma Craze and Past Grand Dr. Louise C. Heilbron. The refreshment tables, arranged to form a cross, were adorned with wild flowers. Among the decorative features was a Humpty Dumpty, made by Mrs. Mary Jones. The favors, made by Miss Zitka Wilhelm, were handpainted eggshells filled with poppies. In charge of the affair were Misses Oneida and Zitka Wilhelm, Ada Cochrane, Helena Biewener; Mms. Bessie Leitch, Mary Jones, Edna Brackley.

Santa Cruz—Santa Cruz No. 26 observed its forty-fifth anniversary March 20. Jointly with Santa Cruz No. 90 N.S.G.W. a potluck supper was enjoyed at tables decorated in keeping with the Saint Patrick season. Speakers were Past Grand Stella Finkeldey, a charter member of No. 26, and President W. S. Rodgers of No. 90. The pleasant affair was in charge of Mms. Wallace Rihcey, Stanley Tait, Edward O'Donnell, George Pratchner.

Stockton—Grand President Anna Mixon Armstrong paid an official visit April 4 to Caliz de Oro No. 206. At a banquet preceding the meeting the tables were decorated with masses of pansies. One candidate was initiated, the ritual being exemplified by President Clarice Cook and her officers. Visitors included Grand Marshal Gladys Noce, Grand Trustees Anna Thuesen and Edna Briggs, Past Grands Carrie R. Durham, Mamie G. Peyton, Pearl Lamb, May C. Boldemann, Dr. Louise C. Heilbron and Evelyn I. Carlson, Supervising Deputy Grace Bassac, Deputy Josephine Bianchi, and representatives of several Parlors. A novel presentation ceremony, originated by Roberta Foley, was participated in by ten members of the Parlor, and Buelah Grattan and Grace Johnson entertained with dances.

Palo Alto—Palo Alto No. 229 officially received Grand President Anna Mixon Armstrong April 17. Other visitors were Grand Trustee Anna Thuesen, Grand Organist Clara Gairaud, Past Grand Margaret Grote Hill, Supervising Deputy Kathryn Nelson, Deputy Marie Buck. Mrs. Armstrong gave an inspiring address on "Courage." Lovely gifts were presented. Baskets of spring flowers were used in the decorations.

Letters of Appreciation.

From Past Grand President Stella Finkeldey of Santa Cruz, chairman N.D.G.W. Grand Parlor Veterans Welfare Committee, The Grizzly Bear editor received this letter, dated April 18: "Enclosed please find copies of letters of appreciation from four hospitals receiving attention from the Native Daughters of the Golden West. I will thank you very much for placing them in the May number. As these will be the last of my reports on veterans welfare, I wish to thank you for your kindness in giving us space for the year's activity." The letters follow:

"Your letter about magazines has just come. The magazines have been the finest kind of gift for the recreation room. We have regular readers for them, men who will ask for 'the first chance on the new copy.' We are delighted at the prospect of renewal for another year. Please accept our grateful appreciation of the kindness and generosity of the Native Daughters of the Golden West."—American Red Cross, U.S. Naval Hospital, San Diego, California.

"The candy which you sent for Easter arrived in very fine condition and will indeed add to the pleasure of the patients at this hospital. We wish to thank the Native Daughters of the Golden West sincerely for their generosity and for their kindness in donating such a splendid Easter gift."—American Red Cross, U.S. Naval Hospital, Mare Island, California.

"The small hard candies and the chocolate rabbits arrived safely and in good time for Easter. The Red Cross Juniors of Pasadena have sent us some of the most beautiful cups in pastel shades that we have ever had—so we are wonderfully well taken care of for Easter. We send our sincere thanks to the Native Daughters of the Golden West for their very generous Easter remembrance to the ex-service men in this hospital."—Veterans Administration Hospital, Whipple, Arizona.

"Your annual donation of Easter ferns reached us last Friday morning and they are fulfilling their mission in bringing good cheer and happiness to our patients. We kept three for the recreation room, where they are being admired by all who see them, and the rest we sent to the wards where the bed patients as well as the convalescents are enjoying them. On behalf of the administration as well as the patients will you please express our appreciation to the members of the Native Daughters of the Golden West and accept personally our most sincere thanks."—American Red Cross, Letterman General Hospital U.S.A., San Francisco, California.

N.S.G.W. OFFICIAL DEATH LIST.

Containing the name, the date and place of birth, the date of death, and the Subordinate Parlor affiliation of deceased members reported to Grand Secretary John T. Regan from March 20 to April 20, 1933:

Rippon, George J.; Sacramento, September 10, 1871; April 13, 1933; Sacramento No. 3.

Lewis, Harry C.; San Jose, October 12, 1872; March 16, 1933; San Jose No. 22.

Coster, Robert Alfred; Plymouth, July 4, 188-; March 13, 1933; Sunset No. 26.

Look, Wesley Edward; Mountain Ranch, November 2-, 1878; March 20, 1933; Plymouth No. 48.

Cuneo, Paul; San Francisco, date of birth missing; February 27, 1933; San Francisco No. 49.

Damozonio, Louis J.; San Francisco, April 17, 1897; March 20, 1933; San Francisco No. 49.

Casassa, Charles; San Francisco, October 2, 1880; April 6, 1933; San Francisco No. 49.

Schwartz, Carl Bernhardt; Nevada City, April 10, 1875; April 14, 1933; Hydraulic No. 56.

McCabe, Edward; Snow Point, September 10, 1853; April 15, 1933; Watsonville No. 65.

Swift, James Vincent; West Union, January 20, 1862; March 10, 1933; Redwood No. 66.

Carne, Andrew Edward; Alvarado, November 17, 1866; March 27, 1933; Rincon No. 72.

Warren, Frederick C.; San Francisco, September 5, 1870; April 17, 1933; Rincon No. 72.

Tuckey, Athol B.; San Francisco, September 18, 1892; January 9, 1933; Stanford No. 76.

Corey, Charles E.; San Francisco, October 30, 1869; January 19, 1933; Stanford No. 76.

Evans, Alfred J.; San Francisco, March 22, 1864; January 20, 1933; Stanford No. 76.

Glynn, Charles A.; San Francisco, December 13, 1892; January 30, 1933; Stanford No. 76.

Lask, Harry J.; San Francisco, May 22, 1854; January 31, 1933; Stanford No. 76.

Reese, Dell Lewelyn; American Canyon, November 2, 1862; March 11, 1933; Vallejo No. 77.

Martin, William; Glenwood, November 6, 1861; March 19, 1933; Santa Cruz No. 90.

Zane, Elmer C.; Glen Ellen, January 26, 1862; February 14, 1933; Glen Ellen No. 102.

Rosas, Antonio Ignacio; Compton, May 26, 1871; April 1, 1933; Ramona No. 109.

Marks, Jack Earl; Redlands, April 6, 1899; April 11, 1933; Arrowhead No. 110.

Sorensen, Lawrence Thorwald; Dublin, October 19, 1894; February 12, 1933; Eden No. 113.

Toohig, James; San Francisco, March 3, 1885; March 20, 1933; South San Francisco No. 157.

Strittmatter, Walter Francis; Sausalito, March 10, 1890; March 15, 1933; Sea Point No. 158.

Frerichs, George Louis; San Francisco, March 27, 1867; February 8, 1933; Tracy No. 186.

Michaelis, Emil Rudolph; San Francisco, January 1, 1874; April 2, 1933; El Capitan No. 222.

Thurston, Chester; Redwood City, December 8, 1884; February 8, 1933; Castro No. 232.

Edgar, George A.; Vallejo, July 18, 1859; March 13, 1933; Santa Ana No. 265.

"Safety Signals Save Sorrow," is the May slogan of the California Public Safety Committee in its campaign to lessen the constantly increasing auto death-toll.

CALIFORNIA'S ROMANTIC HISTORY
ADMISSION TO THE SISTERHOOD OF STATES

Lewis F. Byington
(PAST GRAND PRESIDENT N.S.G.W.)

(Continuing the series of California history talks commenced in The Grizzly Bear for December 1932.)

AT THE JUNCTION OF MARKET AND Mason streets, in the City of San Francisco, stands an artistic monument, presented to the city by former Mayor James D. Phelan, and commemorating the admission of California into the Union. On the base of that monument is carved the prophetic sentence: "The unity of our Empire hangs on the decision of this day." This prophecy was uttered on the floor of the United States Senate in the year 1850, during the debate preceding the admission of California, and by that farseeing American statesman, Senator William H. Seward, afterwards Secretary of State in the cabinet of President Abraham Lincoln.

Well did Seward glimpse the future of the Nation. Without territorial childhood, California was knocking at the doors of Congress with a constitution in her hand which provided that she should enter as a free and not as a slave state. This would turn the balance of power in the Senate, there having been, theretofore, an equal number of free and slave states. When the war eventually came, which was to determine whether the Union of States should be forever preserved or the ties severed which bound the South to the North, it was the stream of gold from the mines of California, in the days when gold was so much needed, that, more than any other one thing, maintained the credit and preserved the life of the Nation.

The news of the discovery of gold at Coloma, on the American River, January 24, 1848, had spread to all quarters of the globe. Into the harbor of San Francisco had come vessels from every known sea of the world, bearing adventurous spirits bound for the gold fields. Across the prairies, over deserts and mountains, facing innumerable dangers and privations, pressed the long emigrant trains made up of the young, the strong and the daring of every land. There will never be such another march in the history of civilization, or in the progress of the world, as that of these American Pioneers. From the rock-bound coast of the Atlantic, the great valleys of the Ohio and Mississippi, the farms and prairies on the then frontier, and from other lands, ever westward they marched—through forest, over river, across desert and mountain—to the gold mines of California. In less than ten years after the discovery, it is estimated that over $500,000,000 in gold was taken from our mountains.

The early "Argonauts" were not mere adventurers, for among the Pioneers of California were many men of education, of broad vision and constructive minds, and of dauntless spirit; men trained in the ways of a republican form of government, and qualified to organize a free state. And so we find that within two years after the discovery of gold, they met at Monterey, adopted a constitution for the government of a new state, and elected two United States Senators, who at once proceeded to Washington and demanded that California be admitted into the Union. And so, without any probationary period of territorial childhood, on September 9, 1850, she was admitted as a sovereign state. In this respect California was unique among the states of the Union. It is no wonder that the people of this favored land, with her romantic and colorful history, proud of their golden heritage of mountain, valley and stream, should unite in patriotic and joyful celebration on the occasion of September 9, the anniversary of her admission into the Sisterhood of American States.

We have heretofore traced many important events in the colorful history of California leading up to her admission: we have recalled the days of the adventurous navigators, who were the first White men to reach these shores, starting with Juan Rodriguez Cabrillo in 1542, and followed by Sir Francis Drake in 1579, and Sebastian Viscaino in 1603. Then came the immortal pathfinders led by the intrepid and saintly Junipero Serra, his soul filled with unquenchable zeal for the conversion of the Indians, and who, with his followers, established the twenty-one mission of California; beginning with San Diego, in 1769, and ending with Sonoma, in 1823. Again we see Captain Anza, the valiant soldier, sent by orders from Spain to found a permanent settlement on San Francisco Bay, standing at the entrance of the great harbor with the cross uplifted and the standard of Spain unfurled, proclaiming that this was the port of ports and that here should be built the city of St. Francis. There also rises before us the vision of Lieutenant Juan Ayala, of the Spanish navy, on the deck of the "San Carlos," sailing through the uncharted Golden Gate on the evening of August 5, 1775, the first navigator to cast anchor in the San Francisco Bay. Again we see Governor Felipe de Neve leading the way from Mission San Gabriel to found the pueblo of Los Angeles, September 4, 1781.

We have reviewed the romantic period from 1769 to 1822 when Spain ruled California, defined her boundaries and gave the beautiful Spanish names to her counties, rivers and bays. Then followed the period when the American trapper and explorer pressed westward from the valleys of the Ohio and Mississippi. Jedediah Smith, the first American to cross the continent, in 1826; Kit Carson, the famous scout; Colonel John C. Fremont, General John A. Sutter, John Bidwell and hundreds of others who reached here prior to 1846. This was followed by the raising of the Bear Flag at Sonoma June 14, 1846, by a party of Americans who had heard that General Castro, representing the Mexican government, contemplated driving the American settlers from California; but the Americans would not be driven out and, then and there, designed and raised a new flag and declared California to be a republic.

The following month, Commodore John Drake Sloat, in command of the U.S.S. "Savannah" in the Pacific, heard that war had been declared between the United States and Mexico, and having orders from Washington to capture the California ports, in the event of war, landed American marines at Monterey, the Mexican capital, July 7, 1846, and raised the "Stars and Stripes" over the Custom House. California from that time was a part of the United States. The treaty of Guadalupe Hidalgo, ceding California to this country, was concluded February 2, 1848, only nine days after the discovery of gold by Marshall, January 24, and fortunately before news of that discovery had reached the city of Mexico, otherwise the treaty might not have been signed by Mexico. Then came the colorful days of old, the days of gold, the days of '49. when within a few months, from every state of the then American Union, from the countries of Europe, and the Orient and other far-distant lands, had been brought here a population of nearly one hundred thousand to take the place of the few small, scattered communities in the state. All of these events led up to the admission of California into the Union, and were the inspiration for the organization of this American commonwealth.

After the raising of the American Flag by Commodore Sloat at Monterey, military governors were appointed from Washington to control the governmental affairs of California, from the raising of the flag until the establishment of a permanent state government in 1849. These military governors were John Drake Sloat, Robert F. Stockton, John C. Fremont, Stephen W. Kearny, Richard B. Mason, Persifor F. Smith and Bennet Riley.

The people who came here, with the American idea of self government in their hearts, and with ability and courage which challenged the wonder and admiration of the world, determined to create and organize an American state on the shores of the Pacific. The first official act looking to the establishment of a state government was the issuance of a proclamation by Brigadier-General Bennet Riley, the then military governor of the territory, on June 30, 1849, recommending the formation of a state constitution. The election was held August 1, 1849, and the convention met in Colton Hall, in the town of Monterey, September 1, with forty-eight delegates present. It was composed, in most part, of young men in the full vigor of life, many of whom were men of talent, and also of education and refinement.

Bayard Taylor, the writer, who was present during the sessions of this constitutional convention, declared that it was composed of many men of ability who were well versed in the history of representative government, and was a gathering which would have reflected credit upon any of the older states. There were six natives of California in the convention, and men from New York, Maine, Massachusetts, Vermont, Maryland, Virginia, Kentucky, Tennessee and Ohio. Among the native California delegates were General Vallejo, Pablo de la Guerra and Jose Carillo. Among the Americans present, who afterwards became well known, were General Henry W. Halleck; William M. Gwin and John McDougal, later United States Senators; Rodman M. Price, afterwards Governor of New Jersey; Thomas O. Larkin, United States Consul; Edward Gilbert, editor of the "Alta California;" Robert Semple, General John A. Sutter and Francis Lippett.

The convention selected Robert Semple president, and William G. Marcy secretary. It completed its labors October 12, 1849. During the signing of the instrument by the members, General Sutter was called to the chair. When the last signature was attached the event was celebrated by a salute of thirty-one shots from a cannon near by, California being the thirty-first state to enter the Union. As the last shot was heard, old General Sutter leaped to his feet with tears rolling down his cheeks and, waving his arm as though he held a sword, cried out, "That's for California. Thank God, California has come into the Union!" Colton Hall was cleared for a grand ball, which was a great success, and attended by General Riley, military governor, the officers of the Presidios and the well-known people of Monterey and the State.

The constitution was ratified by vote of the people November 13, 1849, and at the same election the officers for the new state were selected, Peter H. Burnett being chosen the first governor of California. Governor Riley issued a proclamation declaring the constitution ratified. A great people had been brought together from every quarter of the globe, with but one idea at first, that of enriching themselves as quickly as possible and then returning to the lands whence they came; but having once seen California, they determined to remain here and, within a year after arriving, drafted a constitution and founded a great American commonwealth, an unprecedented thing in the history of the Nation.

The first State Legislature met at San Jose, December 15, 1849, and at once elected two United States Senators, John C. Fremont and William M. Gwin, who received their credentials and proceeded to Washington and knocked at the door of Congress, demanding admission for California without territorial childhood. They were not seated, however, until the following September 10. Many at first opposed the admission, as it would disturb the balance between free and slave states, and even the great Daniel Webster argued that the lands of the West were barren and unproductive, and the greater portion of the territory a desert and not adapted for statehood.

Congress, however, eventually passed the act admitting California, and on September 9, 1850, the President, Millard Fillmore, signed the act and it became effective as of that date. There was in those days no transcontinental telegraph line, and San Francisco did not receive the news until October 18, 1850, when the mail steamer "Oregon" came in through the Golden Gate gaily bedecked with bunting and bearing a streaming pennant flying from the mast with the words "California Is a State!" The news was received with the wildest excitement and rejoicing. Business was suspended. Ships were decorated. Fires were lit on the summits of the hills, cheering people filled the streets, cannon roared, and the happy citizens met in cafes and at bars to toast in sparkling beakers of champagne the new State of their adoption and love. On October 29, the official celebration was held, when there was a great parade through the street, patriotic songs, the music of bands and orations in the Plaza. In the evening there was a grand ball, fireworks and the discharge of cannon. California has, all down through the years, continued to celebrate her birthday, September 9.

California, at the end of eighty-two years of statehood, celebrates a development unrivaled in the history of the world. No other land has such scenic grandeur, such matchless mountains, lakes and streams, such diversified resources and industries. The products of her mines, her fields and her orchards have added billions of dollars to the wealth of the Nation. The value of the gold alone that has come from her river beds and mountains is $1,852,000,000. The broad-armed bay of San Francisco welcomes the commerce of the world, and from this bay

(Continued on Page 31)

LOS ANGELES
CITY AND COUNTY

DESPITE THE SERIOUS FINANCIAL depression which has brought difficulties not only to industry but to educational institutions as well, the University of Southern California has been able to maintain a high level of work and activities during the current academic year. The student enrollment has held up remarkably well, some departments being even more largely attended than ever before. Nevertheless, it has been necessary to curtail expenses and to proceed as economically as possible.

An unusually large number of students have this year applied for some form of financial assistance, and the University has responded with a generous spirit, thus making it possible for many to continue their studies who otherwise would have felt compelled to leave college. It is this spirit of service, this human touch, that distinguishes the University of Southern California and is so greatly appreciated.

During the year there have been some notable developments, which may be mentioned: The Department of Journalism has been organized into a School of Journalism, headed by Director Roy French. This school is now planning to add a graduate department, which is expected to offer facilities for the regular master of arts degree within the next year or two.

The University has also announced the Junior College program, which will be opened next September under the direction of Dr. Frank C. Touton, vice-president of the University. The program, which will be entirely separate from the regular divisions of the University, will comprise a two-year curriculum of letters, arts and sciences courses selected with special reference to training for general culture and American citizenship.

Curricula of the new University Junior College are provided especially for the following classes of students, all graduates of accredited secondary schools: (1) Those who have a limited time to give to college training. (2) Those who need and wish more than the usual amount of work and guidance in the pursuit of the work of the first two years of the college curriculum. (3) Those who do not meet satisfactorily the requirements of the college divisions of the University. (4) Those who transfer from other collegiate institutions but do not meet the requirements of the college or the university to which they apply.

Southern California is the second university in the United States to establish a Junior College, the University of Minnesota having founded a division last fall. Commenting on the new University Junior College, Dr. Touton issued the following statement: "In establishing the University Junior College as a minor division of the University of Southern California, the administration of the University is continuing and extending the program of instruction and research which was initiated two years ago as an experimental entrance procedure. Through the University Junior College, it is the plan of the University to offer on the University campus a two-year opportunity of study to that considerable group of secondary school graduates who fail to meet fully the stated entrance requirements of the other college divisions of the University.

"Students admitted in the University Junior College will in each case present from their preparatory schools academic and personnel records which indicate scholarly interests and achievements in several courses and fields of effort. Students admitted to the University Junior College will be given opportunity under well planned guidance to develop and demonstrate those traits of character and habits of study which are necessary to college success. The curriculum guarantees basic training for culture and citizenship while the groups of electives offer opportunities for the selection of courses in several fields of student interests."

LONG BEACH TO CELEBRATE.

Long Beach will stage a rehabilitation celebration—"Neptune's Electrical Extravaganza"—Saturday, May 6. As a climax to the day's festivities an illuminated maritime spectacle will be staged in the Long Beach Marine Stadium. The entire day will be given over to demonstrating how Long Beach plans to carry on and put the recent earthquake on the ancient-history list.

The celebration has the endorsement of the Los Angeles and the Long Beach Chambers of Commerce. The Long Beach committee in charge includes Charles H. Tucker (general chairman), Charles S. Henderson (finance chairman), A. A. Miller, Karl Gibbs, Harry Buffum, Graydon Hoffman, Frank H. Church, W. F. Prisk, Lloyd C. Leedom, C. E. Demarest, Jonah Jones Jr., Richard H. Loynes, Paul Peek, Walter Scott and Jack Horner.

LARGE CROWD AT BENEFIT.

The homeless children benefit ball, given April 22 by the N.S.G.W. and N.D.G.W. Homeless Children Committee of Los Angeles and Orange Counties, drew a large crowd to the Breakfast Club and was a complete social success. Mrs. Hazel B. Hanseu, Grand Outside Sentinel N.D.G.W., general chairman, was assisted by a large committee who for weeks worked faithfully in preparation for the affair. During the evening several entertainment features were presented under the guidance of Mrs. Leland Atherton Irish.

ATTEND, ALL YE N.S., THE N.D. BAZAR.

Los Angeles Parlor No. 124 N.D.G.W. has adopted a homeless child, little Diann. Dolores Malin of the history and landmarks committee states that a rose arbor in memory of the Pioneer Mothers is to be built in Griffith Park by the Parlor. The sewing circle met at the home of Mildred Ripling, who served delicious refreshments; Esther Rinne could not attend, but she sent a bundle of lovely little garments, made by her. The April card party under the chairmanship of Ella Steinbeck was a social and financial success. The Parlor's veteran welfare committee took twelve Easter baskets to shutins at the Sawtelle National Soldiers Home.

April 19, President Louise Ward Watkins of the Friday Morning Club gave a talk on "The Founders of the Missions." Prior to the Parlor meeting a potluck dinner was enjoyed. Past

(Continued on Supplement 6)

FIFTY-SIXTH N.S.G.W. GRAND PARLOR

(CLARENCE M. HUNT.)

THE FIFTY-SIXTH GRAND PARLOR OF the Order of Native Sons of the Golden West will convene at Grass Valley, Nevada County, Monday, May 15, at 10:30 a.m. Sessions will be held in the Veterans Memorial Building, South Auburn street, Monday, Tuesday and Thursday. Grand President Seth Millington (Colusa Parlor No. 69) of Gridley, Butte County, will preside throughout the deliberations, and at their close will automatically become the Junior Past Grand President.

This will be the fourth Grand Parlor meeting in Nevada County, the Tenth (1887) and the Twenty-first (1898) sessions having been held at Nevada City, and the Forty-first (1918) at Truckee. Past Grand President Dr. Charles W. Decker, lately deceased, presided in 1887, Past Grand President George D. Clark in 1898, and Past Grand President Jo V. Snyder, now among the honored dead, in 1918.

The reports of the grand officers and the Grand Parlor committees at the Grass Valley session will deal with the Order's activities during 1932. Some most important legislation proposals will, it is believed, be submitted, and there will undoubtedly be the usual flood of resolutions.

The report of Grand Secretary John T. Regan will deal with the condition of the Subordinate Parlors as of December 31, 1932. Those of 450 or more members, with their assets-figures include:

Parlors	Members	Assets
Ramona No. 109	1032	$44,788.02
South San Francisco No. 157	803	44,500.01
Castro No. 232	764	12,221.75
Stanford No. 76	575	24,512.77
Arrowhead No. 110	573	24,930.66
Stockton No. 7	535	48,432.39
Twin Peaks No. 214	522	7,692.28
Piedmont No. 120	491	21,242.18

PAST GRAND PRESIDENTS AND MEETING PLACES GRAND PARLOR, N.S.G.W.

Elected		Presided	Session Held
		1878	San Francisco
1878	Wm. G. Hawkett*	1879	San Francisco
1879	Jasper Fishbourne*	1880	Sacramento
1880	Frank J. Higgins*	1881	Oakland & S. F.
1881	Henry Clay Chipman*	1882	Sacramento
1882	John H. Grady*	1883	San Francisco
1883	A. F. Jones*	1884	Marysville
1884	John A. Steinbach*	1885	San Jose
1885	Fred H. Greely	1886	Woodland
1886	Chas. W. Decker*	1887	Nevada City
1887	C. H. Garroutte*	1888	Fresno
1888	M. A. Dorn*	1889	San Rafael
1889	Frank D. Ryan*	1890	Chico
1890	Wm. H. Miller*	1891	Santa Rosa
1891	R. M. Fitzgerald	1892	Los Angeles
1892	Thos. Flint Jr.	1893	Sacramento
1893	John T. Greany*	1894	Eureka
1894	Jo D. Sproul*	1895	Oakland
1895	Frank H. Dunne	1896	San Luis Obispo
1896	Henry C. Gesford	1897	Redwood City
1897	George D. Clark	1898	Nevada City
1898	Wm. M. Conley	1899	Salinas City
1899	Frank Mattison*	1900	Oroville
1900	R. C. Rust*	1901	Santa Barbara
1901	Frank L. Coombs	1902	Santa Cruz
1902	Lewis F. Byington	1903	Bakersfield
1903	H. R. McNoble	1904	Vallejo
1904	Chas. E. McLaughlin	1905	Monterey
1905	Jas L. Gallagher†	1906	Ventura
1906	Walter D. Wagner	1907	Napa
1907	M. T. Dooling*	1908	Yosemite
1908	C. M. Belshaw*	1909	Marysville
1909	Jos. R. Knowland	1910	Lake Tahoe
1910	Daniel A. Ryan	1911	Santa Cruz
1911	H. C. Lichtenberger	1912	Fresno
1912	Clarence E. Jarvis	1913	Oroville
1913	Thomas Monahan	1914	Los Angeles
1914	Louis H. Mooser†	1915	San Francisco
1915	John F. Davis*	1916	Modesto
1916	Bismarck Bruck*	1917	Redding
1917	Jo V. Snyder*	1918	Truckee
1918	Wm. F. Toomey*	1919	Yosemite
1919	Wm. P. Canbu	1920	San Diego
1920	James F. Hoey	1921	Stockton
1921	William I. Traeger	1922	Oakland
1922	Harry G. Williams	1923	Santa Barbara
1923	William J. Hayes*	1924	Sacramento
1924	Edward J. Lynch	1925	San Bernardino
1925	Fletcher A. Cutler	1926	Santa Rosa
1926	Hilliard E. Welch	1927	San Pedro
1927	Charles A. Thompson	1928	Redding
1928	James A. Wilson	1929	San Francisco
1929	Charles L. Dodge	1930	Merced
1930	John T. Newell	1931	Monterey
1931	Frank I. Gonzales	1932	Stockton
1932	Seth Millington		

*Deceased.
†Connection with Order severed.

Others, with assets of $20,000 or more, together with their membership-figures, are:

Parlors	Members	Assets
San Jose No. 22	305	$67,876.80
Sacramento No. 3	347	44,069.49
Pacific No. 10	378	43,428.56
Presidio No. 194	357	36,006.78
Amador No. 17	140	33,326.02
Santa Lucia No. 97	49	33,129.70
Placerville No. 9	256	31,838.77
Observatory No. 177	193	30,482.69
Napa No. 62	277	29,910.85
Redwood No. 66	170	28,539.14
Sunset No. 26	292	28,212.62
California No. 1	355	22,895.41
Eden No. 113	101	22,199.70
Excelsior No. 31	177	21,199.29

From these figures, it will be noted that Ramona Parlor No. 109 (Los Angeles) continues its lead as the largest, numerically, in the Order, and that San Jose Parlor No. 22 (San Jose) remains the wealthiest, financially. Santa Lucia Parlor No. 97 (Salinas) has the greatest per-capita wealth.

At the close of 1932, the Subordinate Parlors had assets totaling $1,283,758.00, including $288,943.32 cash on hand. Their receipts for 1932 totaled $297,796.92, and their disbursements $315,729.46. They paid benefits totaling $109,294.52 to 1,589 members.

During 1932, the Board of Grand Officers, headed by Grand President Millington, dedicated and laid the cornerstones of many public buildings in various sections of the state. At all these events, the ceremonies were very largely attended, indicating the general public's interest in that phase of the Order's many worthwhile endeavors. During the year, also, the Subordinate Parlors made numerous presentations of United States of America and California State (Bear) Flags.

VETERANS MEMORIAL BUILDING, GRASS VALLEY, where the Grand Parlor will meet, and all other activities, including social, will be centered.
—Maurice Photo, Grass Valley.

CANDIDATES FOR OFFICE.

If there be any fact-foundation for the numerous rumors that are floating about, there will be several surprise candidates for Grand Parlor offices presented at the Grass Valley session. The Grizzly Bear has been on the trail of the "darkhorses;" some have repudiated the rumors, while others, if they responded at all to the query, gave evasive answers. So, there may be, at nomination-hour, some proverbial "darkhued" boys bob up in the office-woodpile. Be that as it may, the following list of candidates is compiled from authentic information received direct by The Grizzly Bear from authoritative sources:

Grand President—Grand First Vice-president Justice Emmet Seawell (Santa Rosa Parlor No. 28) of Santa Rosa.

Grand First Vice-president—Grand Second Vice-president Chas. A. Koenig (Golden Gate Parlor No. 29) of San Francisco.

Grand Second Vice-president—Grand Third Vice-president Harmon D. Skillin (Castro Parlor No. 232) of San Francisco.

Grand Third Vice-president—J. Hartley Russell (Stanford Parlor No. 76) of San Francisco; Grand Trustee Joseph J. McShane (Twin Peaks Parlor No. 214) of San Francisco.

Grand Secretary—John T. Regan (South San Francisco Parlor No. 157) of San Francisco, incumbent.

Grand Treasurer—John A. Corotto (San Jose Parlor No. 22) of San Jose, incumbent.

Grand Marshal—Grand Inside Sentinel Gam Hurst (Piedmont Parlor No. 120) of Oakland.

Grand Inside Sentinel—Grand Outside Sentinel William A. Reuter (Sepulveda Parlor No. 263) of San Pedro.

Grand Outside Sentinel—To date, no candidate announced.

Grand Trustees (seven to be selected)—Jesse H. Miller (California Parlor No. 1) of San Francisco, incumbent; Henry S. Lyon (Placerville Parlor No. 9) of Placerville, incumbent; Thos. M. Foley (Pacific Parlor No. 10) of San Francisco; John M. Burnett (San Jose Parlor No. 22) of San Jose, incumbent; Horace J. Leavitt (Mount Bally Parlor No. 87) of Weaverville, incumbent; Charles H. Spengemann (Hesperian Parlor No. 137) of San Francisco, incumbent; Eldred L. Meyer (Santa Monica Bay Parlor No. 267) of Santa Monica, incumbent.

The Grand Organist and the Historiographer, additional grand officers, will be appointed by the incoming Grand President.

Two cities, Ukiah, Mendocino County, and Santa Cruz, will seek designation as the meeting-place for the Fifty-seventh (1934) Grand Parlor. Their claims will be advanced, respectively, by Ukiah Parlor No. 71 and Santa Cruz Parlor No. 90.

Santa Rosa, Sonoma County, wants this year's Admission Day, September 9, celebration, and Santa Rosa Parlor No. 28 will present the invitation. Last year's (Stockton) Grand Parlor favored the selection of the "City of Roses" in 1933, and it is most likely legislation to that effect will be enacted at Grass Valley.

GRAND PARLOR COMPOSITION.

The Grass Valley Grand Parlor will be made up of the following. Any member of the Order, however, is privileged to attend the sessions, but of course only those here listed are entitled to vote:

Grand Officers—Dr. Frank I. Gonzalez, Junior Past Grand President; Seth Millington, Grand President; Justice Emmet Seawell, Grand First Vice-president; Chas. A. Koenig, Grand Second Vice-president; Harmon D. Skillin, Grand Third Vice-president; John T. Regan, Grand Secretary; John A. Corotto, Grand Treasurer; W. B. O'Brien, Grand Marshal; Gam Hurst, Grand Inside Sentinel; William A. Reuter, Grand Outside Sentinel; Leslie Maloche, Grand Organist; Chester Gannon, Historiographer; Jesse H. Miller, Eldred L. Meyer, John M. Burnett, Henry S. Lyon, Joseph J. McShane, Horace J. Leavitt, Charles H. Spengemann, Grand Trustees.

Senior Past Grand Presidents—Fred H. Greely, Robert M. Fitzgerald, Senator Thomas Flint Jr., Judge Frank H. Dunne, Judge Henry C. Gesford, George D. Clark, Judge William M. Conley, Frank L. Coombs, Lewis F. Byington, Judge Hubert R. McNoble, Judge Charles E. McLaughlin, Walter D. Wagner, Joseph R. Knowland, Daniel A. Ryan, Herman C. Lichtenberger, Clarence E. Jarvis, Thomas Monahan, William P. Caubu, James F. Hoey, William L. Traeger, Harry G. Williams, Edward J. Lynch, Judge Fletcher A. Cutler, Hilliard E. Welch, Judge Charles A. Thompson, James A. Wilson, Charles L. Dodge, John T. Newell.

Finance Committee—Harry W. Gaetjen (chairman), Joseph Rose, James L. Foley.

Board Control—William C. Neumiller (chairman), Walter Bammann, J. Hartley Russell.

Board Appeals—Irving D. Gibson (chairman), Ben Harrison, Richard M. Hamb, Alfred H. McKnew, Samuel M. Shortridge Jr.

Transportation-Mileage Committee—Joseph Berry (chairman), P. L. Schlesinger, Percy Marchant.

Subordinate Parlor Delegates—The list is complete, insofar as Parlors reported, as requested, to The Grizzly Bear to the time of going to press. Delegates of Parlors which failed to send names direct to The Grizzly Bear are not included:

California No. 1—Ellis A. Blackman, Albert Franzen, B. F. Hanlon, Wm. H. James, A. M. Nishkian.

Sacramento No. 3—Robt. D. Finnie, June Longshore, Joseph Fitzhenry, A. Nicolosi.

Marysville No. 6—T. J. O'Brien.

Stockton No. 7—Benj. S. Waller, Laurence Buol, A. J. Carey, A. W. Dunning, W. P. Rothenbush, Geo. F. McNoble.

Placerville No. 9—Joseph Scherrer, George M. Smith, Chas. C. Cook, Chris C. Orelli.

Pacific No. 10—William H. Doidge, Paul Conniff, Thomas M. Foley, Harry Alexander, Wilbur B. Doyle.

Modesto No. 11—Chas. D. Blaine, Chas. W. Gill.

Humboldt No. 14—John Hult, A. W. McDonald, Fay E. Hornung.

Amador No. 17—Walter Hartwick, William R. Liddicoat.

Visalia No. 19—Gareth W. Houk, Frank Bullard.

Arcata No. 20—William Peters, F. A. Nicholson.

San Jose No. 22—Cliff L. Kelley, Barney T. Legue, Lawrence F. Hart, Fred A. Carmichael.

Yosemite No. 24—John J. Thornton, True W. Fowler.

Fresno No. 25—Frank M. Lane, A. G. Miller.

Sunset No. 26—Frank H. Conn, L. W. Marvin, J. J. Monteverde, Edw. E. Reese.

Petaluma No. 27—L. Carpenter, W. Christiansen.

Santa Rosa No. 28—Wesley Colgan, James Brucker.

Golden Gate No. 29—David A. Hughes, Thomas I. Schlink, Henry C. Lunsmann, David Wilson.

Woodland No. 30—W. H. Lawson.

Excelsior No. 31—Thomas G. Negrich, Wm. Going.

Ione No. 33—Earl Grover, Will C. Fithian.

Mission No. 38—Martin H. Huber, William A. Wilkie, Thomas J. Stewart, Otis Pierce Cosbie.

Los Angeles No. 45—Leslie A. Packard, Sid Witkowski, Walter Fisher.

Alameda No. 47—Geo. Leydecker, H. L. Sousa, J. Hanson.

Plymouth No. 48—Chester G. Johnson, D. A. Upton.

San Francisco No. 49—John H. Nelson, David Capurro, Geo. Batchelor, Louis L. Ghiotti.

Oakland No. 50—T. A. Fitzgerald, A. J. Lindquist.

El Dorado No. 52—Robt. Donohue, Alfred F. Viautin, Paul Rockwitz.

Saint Helena No. 53—Lowell Palmer, Frank Harrison.

Hydraulic No. 56—Dr. C. W. Chapman, R. L. P. Bigelow, E. J. Baker.

Quartz No. 58—Robert Kohler, Frank Rowe, John R. Thomas.

Auburn No. 59—Chas. H. Slade, P. W. Smith.

Napa No. 62—Fred Flake, Theo. Freitas, Harry N. Bunce, Milton Talley.

Mount Tamalpais No. 64—Walter Mazza, Chas. Soldavini Jr., Monroe Label.

(Continued on Supplement 8)

Flower Show—The Solano County flower show will be held at Vacaville, May 3 and 4.

Rodeo Classic—Livermore, Alameda County, will stage its annual rodeo May 13 and 14.

Raisin Festival—Fresno City will May 13 stage its annual raisin festival. A pageant will be a feature.

GRAND PARLOR PROGRAM

(CLARENCE M. HUNT.)

QUARTZ PARLOR NO. 58 OF GRASS Valley has completed arrangements for the entertainment of the Fifty-sixth N.S.G.W. Grand Parlor which meets in the little Nevada County city May 15. And what a program! There will not be an idle moment. All of the affairs will be held in the Veterans Memorial Building, South Auburn street. There has been some concern expressed in various quarters about accommodations, but The Grizzly Bear assures that there need be no worry on that score. Grass Valley can accommodate all who choose to visit there during the Grand Parlor and, what is more, Quartz Parlor extends an unlimited invitation.

The festivities begin Sunday, May 14, when a reception committee from the "twin" cities Parlors—Quartz of Grass Valley and Hydraulic of Nevada City—will welcome the arrivals. A special train will arrive from San Francisco some time that evening. The registration headquarters will open that day, too. For those who get to Grass Valley in time, a trip through the gold mines is on this day's program. In the evening there will be an informal reception.

Monday evening will be given over to a formal reception. An outstanding feature will be the Gold Miners Glee Club. The program includes: Orchestra selection, Grass Valley high school orchestra; addresses of welcome, Mayor M. J. Brock for Grass Valley, and Superior Judge Raglan Tuttle for Nevada County; response, Grand President Seth Millington; selection, Miners Glee Club of forty voices; vocal solo, Mrs. Jack Wolff; selection, Grass Valley high school orchestra; vocal solo, Mrs. Gove Celio; selection, Miners Glee Club.

Tuesday evening has been set aside for the grand ball. It will be informal, and visitors will enjoy themselves at a "shindig" such as they have never before attended.

Wednesday will be devoted to an all-day tour of the Yuba River Canyon country, to Downieville and Sierra City, in Sierra County. At the former place, Downieville Parlor No. 92 N.S.G.W. will be host at a lunch in the public square. Some idea of the glories of this trip through God's country may be had from the accompanying brief outline.

Wednesday evening will be the Grand Parlor banquet, and it will be different than the general run. There will be a few talks, and a fine program of musical numbers.

For Thursday night, Quartz Parlor will present some surprise entertainment features for the pleasure of those not in too big a rush to get homeward bound.

QUARTZ PARLOR'S GRAND PARLOR GENERAL COMMITTEE.
Rear, left to right, JOHN R. THOMAS, JAMES OLIVER, FRED COOMBS, ALLEN JOYNER. Front, left to right, FRANK J. ROWE, RALPH VINCENT, LOYLE FREEMAN (chairman), FRANK L. HOOPER.
—Maurice Photo, Grass Valley.

All the affairs above mentioned, except the banquet, are open and free to all visitors, male and female. Members of the Grand Parlor will be Quartz Parlor's guests at the banquet; all other Native Sons may purchase tickets.

Special entertainment features for the womenfolks have been arranged by Manzanita Parlor No. 29 N.D.G.W. of Grass Valley and Laurel Parlor No. 6 N.D.G.W. of Nevada City. They include: Monday afternoon, reception at the Empire Country Club; Tuesday afternoon, drive and picnic in the mountains; Wednesday evening, bridge party at the Elks Club, Main and School streets.

For some weeks, Quartz Parlor has had a large committee busily engaged in arranging the details for the Grand Parlor, and it has had splendid co-operation from the neighbor Parlor, Hydraulic. The general committee of Quartz includes: Loyle Freeman (chairman), John R. Thomas, Fred Coombs, Allen Joyner, Frank J. Rowe, Ralph Vincent, Frank L. Hooper, James Oliver. Subcommittees are composed as follows:

Finance—William Sampson (chairman), Alvon Jones, Earl Bonham, Frank J. Rowe.

Transportation—Frank L. Hooper (chairman), George Hammill, R. L. P. Bigelow, Edward Baker, J. C. Tyrrell.

Banquet—Fred Coombs (chairman), Henry Beretta, Allen Joyner.

Housing—Native Daughters, Loyle Freeman, Ralph Vincent.

Ball—John R. Thomas (chairman), Joseph Henwood, James Chellew, Stanley Wilcox, George Hammill, Elza Kilroy, George Neagle.

Music—H. Ray George (chairman), Edward Burtner, Harold George.

Entertainment—Robert Kohler (chairman), William G. Phillips, Dr. C. W. Chapman, R. L. P. Bigelow, H. Ray George.

Reception—Frank J. Rowe (chairman), Judge George L. Jones, Mayor M. J. Brock, Thomas M. Harris, R. L. P. Bigelow, Dr. C. W. Chapman, J. M. McMahon, August Costa, Anthony Lavezzola, Sheriff Dewey Johnson, Judge H. B. Neville, Miles D. Coughlin, E. J. Kilroy, George Neagle, Judge Raglan Tuttle, Richard Eddy, Chester Scheemer, Vernon Gleason, Carl Tobiassen, William P. Fox, William Sampson, Carrol Thomas, Edward A. Bennetts, Howard Bennetts.

Decorations—Edward Burtner (chairman), Lester Whitburn, Charles Beloud.

General program, James C. Tyrrell; special entertainment, Mayor M. J. Brock; publicity, H. Ray George; registration and badges, James Oliver.

THE TOUR OF GOD'S COUNTRY

(RICHARD L. P. BIGELOW,
Supervisor Tahoe National Forest.)

THE TRIP THAT HAS BEEN PLANNED by Quartz Parlor No. 58 N.S.G.W. for the outing day for the delegates to the Grass Valley Grand Parlor is through a most interesting mining region of California's early-day history, the Yuba River country in Nevada and Sierra Counties. Leaving Grass Valley the morning of May 17, we will follow the Yuba Pass state highway through Nevada City. The South Fork of the Yuba River is the first of the Yubas to cross. It was on this stream that the first hydro-electric power plant in California was operated. It was the old Rome power house, which is situated a few miles above the highway crossing.

About seven miles further we come to the town of North San Juan, situated on the San Juan Ridge, where extensive early-day hydraulic mining was in full blast when the debris law closed down all of the hydraulic mines of the Yubas. San Juan was then a thriving town of some five thousand inhabitants. It is now a small hamlet, a ghost of the former thriving town. The old brick buildings are still standing as relics of the past.

Just after leaving North San Juan, the caravan will enter the Tahoe National Forest and then cross the Middle Yuba River. Here you will note the itinerant "snipers" along the river with their rockers, "long toms" and sluice boxes, trying to make an honest living by mining for gold along the river bars.

This stream and many of the creeks and gulches from here to Sierra City are lined with several thousand of these miners. They come from the crowded cities and towns to get away from paying rent, water, light and fuel bills, and to earn an average of twenty cents a day from these streams where Nature has deposited, in the bedrock crevices and in the gravel, the golden nuggets. They are honest workers, and sometimes one will see father, mother and the children working in the "diggings" to make an honest living during these hard times. Leaving the river you wind up Oregon Creek. The towns of Alleghany and Forest lie at the head of this stream, both old mining towns. But your road does not pass through them.

At the top of the grade lies the town of Camptonville where, many years ago, the Pelton waterwheel was invented. This is another old placer "diggings" town. It will pay you, on your return from Downieville, to take the road into this town and meet Bill Meek, an old Native Son who can tell you more of the romance of the golden days than any man in California. He was driving stages and packtrains to the mining towns of this region long before most of us were born. The town is only a few minutes' drive from the highway, and you will find Bill at the Meek mercantile store. You will also see the monument that honors Pelton, the inventor of the waterwheel, which was dedicated a few years ago by the Masonic Order. It was at Galena Hill, a few miles from Camptonville, just off the highway, that Past Grand President Fred H. Greely was born. You can see the "diggings," across Willow Creek as you go up the highway after passing Camptonville, where Fred's father mined in the early '50s.

(Continued on Supplement 8)

RICHARD L. P. BIGELOW,
Hydraulic Parlor N.S.G.W.
—Maurice Photo, Grass Valley.

GRIZZLY GROWLS

(CLARENCE M. HUNT.)

MANY THINGS OF OUTSTANDING IMportance to every citizen of the United States are daily happening in the National Capital. President Franklin Roosevelt is "on the job," and is not permitting the Federal Congress to loaf. In a few quarters, his proposals, particularly those relating to finances, are condemued, but there is no doubt that the masses have every confidence in his ability to solve the nation's distressing problems, for the benefit of the majority. The President cannot work miracles and, being human, he probably will make mistakes. If he does, however, he will readily acknowledge them, and change the course. He is endeavoring to lead this nation back to normalcy, and the people must aid him by forgetting self and follow, cheerfully, willingly and unitedly, his leadership.

At Sacramento, the State Legislature continues the budget-balancing show. Little, however, has been accomplished, due to the activities of the lobbies. Every one agrees that government cost must come down, but no one wants the pruning directed his way. Numerous wasteful extravagances that could, and unhesitatingly should, be eliminated have been pointed out, but "stalling" is the general policy. There must be drastic reductions, all down the line, and the sooner the legislators recognize that fact and act accordingly, the better for them and the state. If they fail, for any reason, to do extensive pruning without fear or favor, the indications are the taxpayers will seize the shears and perform the task.

The plan now is, for the Legislature to recess until July, and in the interim submit to the voters, probably in June, several measures dealing with revenue and taxation. Among them will be more bond proposals, to which the electorate should give most careful attention, for we are already bond-burdened to a near-confiscatory degree. A measure should, but probably will not, be on the ballot to repeal all enactments exempting churches and other private interests from taxation. That would ease the tax burden on the small-home owner, the backbone of the state and the nation, and would go a long way toward balancing the state government budget.

Some of the legislation passed by the Legislature and already in force, such as the mortgage moratorium and the reduction of the interest rate on building and loan investment certificates, is, it would seem from past court decisions, purely unconstitutional, in that obligations of existing contracts are impaired. This might be termed "bluff" legislation, enacted, however, to relieve existing conditions and to save many institutions and individuals from bankruptcy. If no one calls the "bluff,"—and no one should, for the welfare of all,—the provisions of the legislation will be generally respected. This might be termed unconstitutional, but needful, legislation. Everyone must give—take his losses goodnaturedly—to aid in routing the depression.

A movement is under way in the State Legislature, and gaining supporters, to force the return to Sacramento,—the constitutional seat of state government, the capital of California,—of the many state offices now located in various other cities. It is declared that "The policy of scattering the state government is wrong in principle, decidedly expensive to the taxpayers and a great inconvenience to the public. It is the duty of the Legislature to see that the practice of scatterization of government is abolished." This scatterization of state offices is another of the many government abuses which should be corrected now, for the very excellent reasons cited.

Anent the Jap situation: The "California Council on Oriental Relations," a suspicioned auxiliary of the misnamed "California State Chamber of Commerce," through Samuel Hume is aggressively continuing its activities in favor of repeal of the Federal Exclusion Law and the grant of quota to Japan. Service and civic organizations are being addressed, in an effort to gain their support. Keep your eyes on this outfit, and combat its activities!

Representative Charles Kramer of California has proposed in the Federal Congress legislation to prohibit future entry to the United States of foreign-born children of Jap or Chinese parentage. This proposal was offered as an amendment to a measure now pending before the House Immigration Committee which would permit a mother to transmit her American citizenship to a foreign-born child in the manner now reserved to the father. Kramer proposes to require that both parents be citizens, or of a race eligible to citizenship. Give this measure wholehearted support!

Inspired by a recent decision of the United States Supreme Court upholding the California Alien Land Law in a case appealed from Sonoma County, the district attorney has taken steps to oust alien Japs from agricultural and garden lands in San Diego County. More power to him, and may the district attorney of every county become similarly inspired to do his duty, before it is too late! Incidentally, there are no Japs in Nevada County.

Colonel William Mitchell, testifying recently before the military affairs committee of the House of Representatives, said America's principal defense problems now center on the Pacific Coast. "There is a very virile, strong outfit there seeking mastery of the world," he testified. "I have been around them in Siberia and Manchuria and Japan and I know. They are out on a 'Genghis Khan' expedition, if there ever was one. Of course, we are going to have a conflict with them sooner or later, whether we want to or not. Under the circumstances we are making a tremendous mistake in not developing our air power. Nobody is going to build battleships—they aren't silly enough."

"Gold is the only commodity that has withstood the ravages of the greatest depression the world has ever known," declared State Treasurer Charles Johnson in a recent address. "Production of gold in California created adventure and romance, wealth and prosperity. It provided for and contributed directly and indirectly to building the gigantic empire of the Pacific, lovingly known throughout the world as California. The flow of gold from our mines created a prosperity that knew no bounds. It was a direct benefit to every human endeavor within and beyond the borders of our state. In this period of general depression, why not turn the energy of our thousands of unemployed to reviving the mining industry of California?"

Since 1929, there has been a substantial yearly increase in the world production of gold: $420,000,000 in 1930, $440,000,000 in 1931, and $491,120,000 in 1932.

With his regulations reducing payments to veterans, President Franklin Roosevelt issued the following statement April 1: "In connection with the publication today of the regulations having to do with veterans' benefits, I do not want any veteran to feel that he and his comrades are being singled out to make sacrifices. On the contrary, I want them to know that the regulations issued are but an integral part of our economy program embracing every department and agency of the Government to which every employe is making his or her contribution. I ask them to appreciate that not only does their welfare but also the welfare of every American citizen depend upon the maintenance of the credit of their Government and that they also bear in mind that every citizen in every walk of life is being called upon, directly or otherwise, to share in this."

The proportion of married women among the gainfully employed females in the United States is growing, according to the Women's Bureau. That's one of many reasons why unemployment among males is on the increase. Also, it accounts for the increase in the number of divorce actions, and the decrease in the nation's birth rate. The growth should be stopped, insofar as married women with able-bodied husbands are concerned.

Commemorating the one hundred and fiftieth anniversary of the issuance of the Proclamation of Peace at Newburgh, New York, April 10, 1783,—marking the formal close of the Revolutionary War—a special postage stamp was placed on sale April 19. Of the three-cent denomination, the stamp, printed in purple ink, shows Washington's headquarters at Newburgh, with his flag flying from the staff, and depicts the surrounding mountains and rivers; at the top is "U. S. Postage." A statement of the Federal Postoffice Department contains this information:

"The Hasbrouck House, at Newburgh, which Washington occupied as his headquarters and which is still standing, claims to be among our most cherished and famous Revolutionary shrines. Washington occupied the home from April 1, 1782, to Aug. 19, 1783. It was from this house that he wrote his famous letter of advice to the Governors of the States, and also his reply to Colonel Nicola, disdaining the offer of a crown. The headquarters are often referred to both as the first White House and the Cradle of the Republic. It was here, on April 19, 1783, that General Washington issued the formal Proclamation of Peace with the British and from here that many of the continental troops were disbanded. Martha Washington spent considerable time at the Newburgh headquarters, and helped to receive the distinguished guests and to entertain the Generals and their wives. The headquarters and surrounding park are owned by the State of New York. The official order, issued by General Washington, containing the Proclamation of Peace, reads as follows:

"'Headquarters,
"'Newburgh, April 18, 1783.

"'The Commander-in-Chief orders the cessation of hostilities between the United States of America and the King of Great Britain to be publicly proclaimed tomorrow at 12 o'clock at the new building, and that the proclamation which will be communicated herewith will be read tomorrow evening at the head of every regiment and corps of the Army, after which the chaplain will render thanks to Almighty God for all his mercies, particularly for his overruling the wrath of man to his own glory and causing the rage of war to cease among the Nations.'"

Facts concerning the life of Emma Marwedel have been assembled by Dr. F. H. Swift, professor of education in the University of California. He says she established, at Los Angeles in 1876, the first kindergarten to be conducted in California, and in 1878 and 1879 established in Oakland and Berkeley classes for training kindergartens.

"Emma Marwedel's life," writes Dr. Swift, "was animated by the belief that through the kindergarten, and the extension of Froebelian principles to the home, motherhood, and higher levels of education, lay the path to prevention of crime and regeneration of human society. She thus became one of the most important educational pioneers, not only in the kindergarten

(Continued on Supplement 8)

THE LITTLE THINGS THAT MOTHERS DO

(A. L. SMITH.)

The little things that mothers do—
Their labor that is never through,
Urged by a love that won't expire
In hearts that, it seems, never tire;
The tearing sacrifices made,
The many plans aside they've laid
For us. Yet still their spirit sings,
Content to do these "little things."

The little things that mothers do—
The smiles when tears are breaking through,
The prayers that in the night are said,
The hearts that have in silence bled,
The courage rising o'er shame's tide
That brings them to the culprit's side;
Yes, even hearts of stone it wrings
To contemplate these "little things."

The little things that mothers do—
A broken heart to build anew,
A shattered life to mold again,
The soothing of a soul in pain;
A man, a miracle would ask,
To her 'tis just a mother's task;
But angels halt their speeding wings
To mark what she calls "little things."

The little things that mothers do—
But this, God bless them, isn't true,
And some day, in the courts of heaven,
When from God's hand rewards are given,
A radiant angel, from the throne,
Will fly to where she sits alone;
And the glittering treasure that he brings
She won by doing "little things."

(The above came to The Grizzly Bear from A. L. Smith, a member of Argonaut Parlor No. 8 N.S.G.W., residing in Brookville, Pennsylvania. "California's Wandering Minstrel" says, in an accompanying letter: "Perhaps you can use this poem in May, for Mothers Day. It is one of my own, never before published. I know of no publication where I would rather see it born than in our magazine."—Editor.)

LOS ANGELES--CITY and COUNTY

LOS ANGELES

(Continued from Supplement 1)

Grand Grace S. Stoermer was among the many in attendance. Twelve dollars from the April card party was donated to the American Red Cross for relief work in Long Beach. In observance of its institution anniversary, No. 124 had a truly typical birthday party April 26 under the joint chairmanship of Jennie Raymond and Marvel Thomas. The entertainment was splendid, and the occasion was heartily enjoyed.

Los Angeles' calendar includes: May 10, card party, Peggie Ambler chairman. May 13, sewing club meets at the home of Louise McNary. May 17, initiation; speaker, Supervising Deputy Florence D. Schoneman. May 24, grand bazar, Grace Haven in charge; dancing and all kinds of games; "come, all ye N.S., spend a happy evening and help the N.D." May 30, memorial ceremonies, 10:30 a.m. in the N.S. and N.D. Memorial Park, Western-avenue entrance of Griffith Park. President Mattie Labory Gara extends greeting to all mothers: "The month of May brings to us beautiful flowers; flowers radiate kind thoughts of everlasting friendship."

COMPTON TO INITIATE CLASS.

Compton—Compton Parlor No. 273 N.S.G.W. had its first meeting since the March 10 shock in its new quarters at the Compton Elks Club, 6172 North Long Beach boulevard, North Long Beach, where it will meet regularly, the second and fourth Tuesdays, until such time as a suitable meetingplace is available in Compton. Undaunted by the experience undergone, there was a good attendance of members, and keen interest was shown in the program for building a better and larger Compton. Visitors were present from Sepulveda No. 263 (San Pedro) and Santa Monica Bay No. 267 Parlors, and District Deputy Harry T. Honn was sincerely thanked for services rendered in a great emergency.

May 9, Compton plans to receive a large class of candidates, many of them having been ready for initiation at the time the shock temporarily made meetings of the Parlor impossible. Through Secretary William Don Castillo, No. 273 extends thanks to all Parlors for their interest in its welfare.

BUSY, SEWING FOR THE NEEDY.

Long Beach—Long Beach Parlor No. 154 N.D.G.W. met April 5 at the home of President Eleanor Johnson, where meetings will be held until further notice. A benefit card party was held at the home of Mrs. Lillian Lassiter April 12. The thimble club met April 13 at the home of Mrs. Leola Temby and started another quilt as well as putting clothes in shape for needy children; luncheon was served outofdoors. At the April 20 meeting of the Parlor candidates were initiated, and refreshments were served by a committee made up of Mms. Bertha Hitt, Eleanor Johnson, Gertrude Riddle and Leola Temby.

Writing to The Grizzly Bear in behalf of Long Beach, Mrs. Leola Temby says: "Inclosed find publicity of March. Please excuse our being tardy with this, but the earthquake caused such confusion we neglected many things." Here's the news: March 2, plunkett dinner, Mrs. Lillian Lassiter chairman; bridge and five hundred followed. March 9, thimble club met at the home of Mrs. Kate McFadyen; covered-dish luncheon served, and worn clothes were put in shape for needy children. March 23, thimble club met at home of President Eleanor Johnson and fixed more clothes for the needy; a potluck luncheon was served. March 30, thimble club met at home of Mrs. Alice Waldow and made a comfort for a family in need.

"HARD TIMES" DANCE.

Los Angeles Parlor No. 45 N.S.G.W. is featuring a "hard times" dance at 1832 South Hope street May 11 in honor of its delegates to the Grass Valley Grand Parlor. All Natives and their friends are invited. An eight-piece orchestra will "strut their stuff." The good of the order committee, Roger Johnson chairman, has charge of arrangements. In the near-future, the Parlor will have its annual rabbit feast, President Leslie A. Packard providing the rabbits.

CARD PARTY AT SANTA MONICA.

Santa Monica—Members of Santa Monica Bay Parlor No. 245 N.D.G.W. had a full day of pleasure at the Venice beach home of Mrs. Ruth Davis April 29. A pajama party was staged, with swimming filling the morning hours, then a potluck luncheon, and in the afternoon cards.

The evening of May 12, the Parlor will have a card party at the home of Mrs. Eldred Meyer, 922 San Vicente boulevard, Santa Monica. All Native Sons and Daughters and their friends are invited. Fee, twenty-five cents. The ways and means committee, Hazel T. McCreary chairman, is in charge.

SPIRIT OF OLD DAYS PERVADED.

Hollywood Parlor No. 196 N.S.G.W. had its anniversary banquet at the Hollywood Athletic Club April 19, and many of the oldtimers were among the large number in attendance. The floral decorations were a gift from A. Goldenson. The menu was excellent. Credit for the success of the party goes largely to W. L. O'Meara, chairman of the arrangements committee. The spirit of the old days pervaded, and the party disbanded with three rousing cheers for Hollywood.

President Henry G. Bodkin was master of ceremonies, and the speakers, all of whom had to like a constant bombardment of good-natured interruptions, included Charter Member L. Zinnamon, John Costello, Municipal Judge Joseph Call, Ernest Orfila, Edward B. Lovie (the silver-tongued orator of the evening), Superior Judge Joseph Sproul, Grand Trustee Eldred Meyer, Alfred Sutro, Grand Outside Sentinel "Bill" Reuter, Robert Ford, Judge William S. Baird (a Scotch native), Fred Lovie, John Ford, John Holmes and, last but not least, First Vice-president Gene Murphy. The Germans almost stole the show from the Irish, when Past Grand Herman Lichtenberger and Arthur Schmidt sang a duet.

BENEFIT FOR CHILDREN, AT GLENDALE.

Glendale—Verdugo Parlor No. 240 N.D.G.W. had a most successful baked ham dinner and card party April 11. Margaret Donlan, in charge of the dinner, was assisted by Gussie Anderson, Ione Gillette, Betty Sanders and Maude Molen. Sarah Burleson and Dorothy Ravn had charge of the card playing. President Fae Robinson of the Glendale City Teachers Club addressed the Parlor on "Educational Week" April 25; she was introduced by President Vera Carlson.

Verdugo will have a dessert bridge for the benefit of the homeless children at the Elks Club in Glendale, May 18 at 1 p.m. The price is thirty-five cents. The arrangements committee includes Gussie Anderson, Ada Steele, Sarah Burleson, Myrtize Tregea and Margaret Donlan. Past presidents of the Parlor will entertain at dinner May 9 the members of Verdugo and their mothers. Betty Sanders is the general chairman, and Edith Dobson has arranged a wonderful "mothers nite" program.

PAST PRESIDENTS NIGHTS INAUGURATED.

Santa Monica—The first of a series of monthly past presidents nights was featured April 5 by Santa Monica Bay Parlor No. 267 N.S.G.W. Sheriff Eugene W. Biscailuz was the honor-guest, and President Arthur Leonard extended a welcome to the many in attendance. J. Edward McCurdy directed the program, which included entertainment numbers and brief addresses, among the speakers being Past Grand John T. Newell, Grand Trustee Eldred L. Meyer and Sheriff Biscailuz. A buffet supper was served by "Chefs" Harry Dailey and Harper Ledbetter. Past President Dike C. Freeman will be honored May 3.

ALL SET FOR CATALINA OUTING.

Ramona Parlor No. 109 N.S.G.W. had a rousing good meeting April 7, the occasion being election of Grass Valley Grand Parlor delegates. Among the many who had something to say were Senator Reginaldo Del Valle, Edwin A. Meserve, Ray Northrup, Charles Thomas, Superior Judge Rey Schauer, Paul Lombardi, Leon Leonard, Jack Lewis, Walter Odemar, Walter Baskerville, Past Grands Herman Lichtenberger and John Newell, Leo Youngworth and President Frank Adams. "Let's have more, and bigger elections," remarked Inside Sentinel Clarence S. Hunt.

The stage is all set for Ramona's anniversary

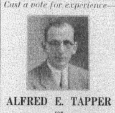

picnic at Catalina, June 11. "All Californians at heart are supposed to be there," says First Vice-president Charles Straube, who is directing the affair. "Something doing every minute of the day. Make reservations with the secretary not later than June 7, for we will not guarantee to accommodate anyone applying for reservation after that date. Better attend to this now, to play safe. Let us make this the outstanding Native Son and Native Daughter event of all time!" May 12, Ramona will have initiation. May 26, monthly birthday dinner, nomination of officers and report Grand Parlor delegates.

PERSONAL PARAGRAPHS.

Arthur T. Poheim (Stanford N.S.) of San Francisco was a visitor last month.

Mrs. Mae Edward (Castro N.D.) of San Francisco was among last month's visitors.

Mrs. Kate McFadyen (Long Beach N.D.) of Long Beach is visiting her daughter, Mrs. Marie Monroe (Long Beach N.D.) at Pendleton, Oregon.

THE DEATH RECORD.

Mrs. Kathleen Steigmaier-Maier, wife of Edward R. Maier (Ramona N.S.), died March 24. Four children, also, survive.

Mrs. Deborah Lyndall, wife of Charles P. Lyndall (Ramona N.S.), died March 26.

Mrs. Elizabeth Poole-Jones, wife of Thomas R. Jones (Sacramento N.S.) of Pasadena, died there March 27. Four children, also, survive. She was a native of New Jersey, aged 71.

Michael T. Herzog, father of Theodore Herzog (Los Angeles N.S.), died March 29.

Antonio Ignacio Rosas, affiliated with Ramona Parlor No. 109 N.S.G.W., died April 1, survived by nine children. He was born at Compton, May 26, 1874.

Wayne Early Jordan, affiliated with Hollywood Parlor No. 196 N.S.G.W., died April 6, survived by a wife and two children. For years he was a member of the district attorney's staff.

Dr. Lucius A. Wright, father of Loyd E. Wright (Ramona N.S.), died April 8.

Mrs. Natalie Vera Burton-Adair, affiliated with Santa Monica Bay Parlor No. 245 N.D.G.W., died April 8, survived by a husband, Aubury Adair (Ramona N.S.) and two children. She was born at Pasadena, October 8, 1903.

William T. Kendrick Sr., father of William T. Kendrick Jr. (Ramona N.S.), died April 10. He was a native of Texas, aged 78.

Jack Fouche Merlo, 5-year-old son of Frank V. Merlo (Ramona N.S.), died April 13.

Alexander P. Cohn, brother of Edward F. Cohn (Sacramento N.S.) of Redondo Beach, died April 16 in Victoria, B. C. He was a native of Sacramento, aged 70.

Bernardo J. Higuera, affiliated with Ramona Parlor No. 109 N.S.G.W., died April 20. He was born at The Palms, Los Angeles County, March 28, 1858.

DELEGATES

(Continued from Supplement 3)

Watsonville No. 65—Julian Colberg, A. T. Enos.
Colusa No. 69—Wm. Yopp, Henry Stinchfield.
Ukiah No. 71—Kenneth Phillips.
Rincon No. 72—John A. Gilmour, William J. Wynn, Frank H. Vivian, Virgil Orengo, Fred T. Kane.
Monterey No. 75—J. E. Freeman, L. P. Chavoya.
Stanford No. 76—H. J. Angelo, Frank A. Biedermann, H. J. Caveney, A. W. Grosskopf, Chas. T. O'Kane, Theo. Schmidt, Fred E. Wirsing.
Vallejo No. 77—Joseph Clavo, George Weniger.
Calistoga No. 86—Louis Carlenzoli, Fred Heitz, Victor Costa.
Mount Bally No. 87—R. L. Marshall, H. W. Day.
Santa Cruz No. 90—C. E. Canfield, Willett Ware, Jas R. Griffin.
Georgetown No. 91—R. C. M. Berriman.
Downieville No. 92—J. M. McMahon, Ross F. Taylor.
Ferndale No. 93—N. John Lund, Andran L. Early.
Golden Nugget No. 94—Elmer Thompson.
Las Positas No. 96—Fred S. Young, C. J. Turner.
Santa Lucia No. 97—Roy Martella.
Santa Clara No. 100—J. J. Trinajstich, Anthony Trigueiro.
Glen Ellen No. 102—Joe Pagani.
Bay City No. 104—Max E. Licht, Jacob Lewis.
Niantic No. 105—Joseph B. Keenan, George E. Bosch.
Courtland No. 106—Raymond Hefringer, C. E. Bunnell.
Selma No. 107—Dan J. Sullivan.
San Diego No. 108—Albert V. Mayrhofer, Ed. F. Cooper.
Ramona No. 109—W. E. Baskerville, Wm. J. Bright, Jos. P. Coyle, Chas. J. Gassagne, Edwin A. Meserve, Burrel D. Neighbours, Geo. C. Sabichi, B. Rey Schauer, Walter M. Slosson, Chas. E. Straube, Leo. V. Youngworth.
Arrowhead No. 110—F. L. McGarvey, R. W. Brazelton, John Andreson Jr., Donald E. VanLuven, Henry B. Peake, Leslie D. Case, J. W. Jasper.
Sonoma No. 111—Jos. T. Keiser, L. H. Green.
Eden No. 113—F. B. Leonard, Fred Hoffer.
Santa Barbara No. 116—Frank H. Castro, C. W. McCormick, A. C. Dinsmore.
Broderick No. 117—Ivan Lawson.
National No. 118—Frank M. Buckley, E. J. Wren.
Piedmont No. 120—Adrien M. Hynes, Frank P. Smith, Frank Roemer, Andrew Costelli, Thomas W. Palmer, James G. Dignan.
Gabilan No. 132—John Rodriguez.
Hesperian No. 137—W. W. Bermingham, G. E. Ritter, W. L. Goldsmith.
Chispa No. 139—John Voitich.
Sebastopol No. 143—W. S. Borba, T. F. Hyland.
Halcyon No. 146—William E. Knowland, J. C. Bates.
McCloud No. 149—A. E. Welbourn, Melvin Zeis.
Cambria No. 152—J. A. Soto.
Alcalde No. 154—Nicholas J. Murphey, Jno. J. McNaughton, Louis F. Erb.
South San Francisco No. 157—Fred H. Nickelson, James W. Brady, George Kendall, Otto Elvander, Raymond Conroy, Robert Hoare, John P. Brady, Frank McWilliams, Henry Delagnes.
Sea Point No. 158—Frank C. Pasquinucci, Clarence D. Rosa.
Lower Lake No. 159—L. H. Fuqua.
Sequoia No. 160—Wm. R. Vizzard, Harry N. Grover.
Washington No. 169—Thos. Silva, Allen G. Norris.
Byron No. 170—John A. Kennedy, Glen Van Horn.
Observatory No. 177—Alfred C. Hansen, Roy S. Field, James J. Flannery.
Menlo No. 185—W. H. Weeden.
Tracy No. 186—Lawerance Sullivan, Joe Payne.
Precita No. 187—Thomas H. Jenkins, Ed. H. Weber, Leland J. Jenkins.
Olympus No. 189—Harvey Joseph Carty, Charles Erickson.
Etna No. 192—Fred M. Wolford, L. E. Buchner.
Presidio No. 194—Albert Schmidt, Henry Storti, Paul Pasquet, James P. Murphy, Chas. Maker.
Athens No. 195—Henry Uebner, Allen Sunkler, Milton Peterson.
Hollywood No. 196—Henry G. Bodkin, Leo Aggeler, John J. Ford.
Honey Lake No. 198—H. C. Davis, James S. Meeske.
Alder Glen No. 200—Fred Dias, F. J. Simpson.
Marshall No. 202—Alex Jean, Arthur Belli.
Carquinez No. 205—Thomas I. Cabalan, Jefferson McNamara.
Los Banos No. 206—D. L. Pedrone, D. E. Bambauer.
Dolores No. 208—Henry Adami, Gus Einselen, Thos. Curtin.
Berkeley No. 210—H. P. Corbett, E. Lambert.
Twin Peaks No. 214—James Karnya, Patrick Gould, Oswald Storm, Clifford Roberts, Edwin Stirl, Geo. Langley.
Palo Alto No. 216—Raymond J. White, John C. Bernal.
El Capitan No. 222—John G. Schroder.
Pebble Beach No. 230—M. R. Mattei.
Guadalupe No. 231—Thomas Wall, Timothy Crowley, Richard Matli, Alvin A. Johnson.
Castro No. 232—Frank B. Foss, A. W. Forsell, Jack Schimmel, T. M. Dillon, J. S. Ramsay, A. D. Lobree, A. C. Bock, R. D. Williamson, W. G. Maison.
Rocklin No. 233—M. E. Reed.
Balboa No. 234—E. W. Boyd, W. F. Schroth.
Claremont No. 240—Felex H. Robson, Raymond P. Burke, Edward Ginochio.
Galt No. 243—J. L. McEnerney.
Pleasanton No. 244—P. Edward Holzreiter.
Niles No. 250—C. E. Martenstein.
Fruitvale No. 252—E. T. Schnarr, E. D. Hensley, D. A. Norris, A. J. Cleu.
Willows No. 255—Ralph Smith.
Bret Harte No. 260—Charles Elmer Lillie.
Sutter No. 261—Stanley McLean.
Sepulveda No. 263—Walter C. Richards, Harry E. Fairall, Lee L. Buckley.
Glendale No. 264—Abel B. Molen, Leslie E. Henderson.
Santa Ana No. 265—Walter R. Gisler, L. A. Young.
Santa Monica Bay No. 267—Eugene W. Biscailuz, George W. Burnett, Harry T. Honn.
Utopia No. 270—T. J. O'Leary, Geo. A. Gillespie.
University No. 272—Ben Hiss, Martin Mesa.
Compton No. 273—Dr. L. W. Cowan, J. Reid Young.

THE TOUR

(Continued from Supplement 4)

At the head of Willow Creek, near Oak Valley, you will have the pleasure of seeing a hydraulic mine operating and the big monitor sluicing down the gravel from an ancient channel. Fred Joubert will welcome you, if you care to climb down the steep banks into the "diggings," and will let you hold the monitor that is sending an "8" stream of water against the gravel bank. This mine has paid big money for many years and is not yet exhausted of its wealth of golden nuggets.

After passing Depot Hill, where Joubert's mine is located, you descend rapidly to the North Fork of the Yuba River. Drive slowly down this grade, so that the occupants of your car can view the gorgeous canyon you are dropping into. Governor James Rolph has named this grade the seasick road to Downieville, so it is advisable to drive slowly, to save trouble in the rear seat. At Indian Valley the State Fish and Game Department operates a fish hatchery which replenishes the streams of Sierra County with the speckled beauties.

For the balance of the trip, you are following up the North Yuba River. Watch for the "snipers" along the river, and the makeshift miners' cabins where families existed during the past winter. Regular '49er miner times here during the past year—with the fights for claims, claim jumping, but no killings in this mining excitement. Shortly you will see Goodyear's Bar, an old-time mining camp of the '50s, now a small

PREPARE FOR GREATER EFFORT

Mary E. Brusic

(Secretary N.S.G.W. and N.D.G.W. Central Homeless Children Committee.)

"WHERE DID YOU COME FROM?" was the greeting of the secretary to a slight, fair-haired, well-groomed young man of twenty-five years as he sat in the office of 959 Phelan building, San Francisco, one April afternoon. The sun came in the window and shone on a human bundle in his arms swathed in a pink Easter-bunny blanket—a blanket, by the way, that was given by a Native Daughter Parlor last June during Grand Parlor time. He smiled in a boyish sort of way as he proudly unwrapped the baby and said:

"This is the boy that my wife and I had decided to give for adoption. I am not working today, so I came in to thank you for the baby's clothes and basket, and bottles which your organization furnished when our baby arrived. I must confess that I hated to meet you, not knowing what you would think of us for wanting to place our baby for adoption. I often think of what you told my wife when she came in to see you before going to the hospital: 'Good foster parents are plentiful, but good, moral blood-parents mean more to a child than anything else in the world. Poverty never hurts anyone, and where there is a will you'll find a way.' We are going to find the way! It will not be easy, for work is scarce. Our parents while good are poor, and cannot help us, but we'll manage, and I want to thank you for your advice and kindness, and for recommending us to the very considerate relief agency. If you have any stray baby buggy around, I'd like it. I make an awful bungle of carrying this boy around and sometimes I have his feet where his head ought to be. You know that our apartment is pretty dark and the baby must have air and all the sunshine we can get for him, and my wife isn't as strong as

WELL STARTED ON GOOD MILK, CONTINUED BY INTELLIGENT FOSTER PARENTS.

she ought to be. Her arms soon tire 'cause he is a 'bouncer.' Now, don't you think that he is a fine little fellow for two months?"

"He is," we agreed, but with the answer came the oft-recurring doubt: Was it wise to persuade the parents to keep him? Is their struggle going to be too great? Would it have been fairer to the boy to have placed him where he could have had a surer prospect in one of the hundreds of outstanding homes? "Hundreds of homes," someone asks, "during these times?" Yes, hundreds of good homes—forty-three applications in October, thirty in November, forty-three in December, fifty-nine in January, one hundred eighteen in February and March, making a total of 478 for the year, and 1,141 applications now on file waiting for children; 10,342 have applied since the beginning of the work.

The conclusion that one reaches after noting the amazing number of applications during times of depression is, that in prosperous times men and women spend their money in traveling to Europe, or Florida, or the beauty spots of California, but now that their incomes have been reduced they are staying at home. They realize as never before that home is a pretty good place, but incomplete without a child, and follow the wife's suggestion: "Let's do what we always have planned to do if no children of our own came to us, adopt one. We can afford it." Eventually one finds that there are compensations in times of financial stress. There seems to come a renewed appreciation of family life and friends, a truer sympathy, and a clearer understanding of what the other fellow is going through, and a keener desire to help.

The young man and his wife and boy referred to constitute but one of the sixty-eight different families who have come to our attention during this year, and whose children we have not accepted for adoption but who have been aided by the Native Sons and Native Daughters Central Committee on Homeless Children. All were experiencing the pinch of poverty, and were panicky when they thought of another mouth to feed and saw as their only solution the giving of their baby for adoption. The Central Committee has been glad to be able to help with temporary

WHAT GOOD MILK FEEDING IN INFANCY WILL DO.

care, and clothing which the Native Daughters and our foster-parents and friends have provided, and has referred the families to relief agencies, which have generously and kindly aided parents when they learned that they were facing separation from their child.

We have placed 168 children during the year, 13 have been replaced, 176 new homes have taken children, making a total of 4,199 children, 510 replacements and 4,709 homes since April 1910.

We are giving for comparison the amounts of the contributions received from the Parlors during the last four years, not with any spirit of criticism. Realizing that everyone has been affected by hard times, the Committee especially appreciates the ability of many of the Parlors to equal their usual contributions while others have exceeded their usual amount. A joint committee of Native Sons and Native Daughters which has aided largely in previous years placed its funds in a bank for safe keeping and was unable to get the money in time for this year's report. Another Native Daughter Parlor sent a check for $37.50 for the milk fund and the bank asked for a receiver before the check was cashed. Your Central Committee is alive to the danger-line, and is giving these figures that "all who read may run" and prepare for a greater effort during the next fiscal year, April 1933 to April 1934, if the work for the homeless children is to be continued.

From 1928 to 1929 the receipts from the Parlors were $16,332.10; 1929 to 1930, $17,474.83; 1930 to 1931, $16,748.75; 1931 to 1932, $14,127.98; 1932 to 1933, $10,929.91, including $879.25 from the Native Daughter milk fund, making $4,198.07 less than last year's contribution, $5,818.84 less than the year before, and $6,544.92 less than in 1930.

The cash receipts from April 1932 to March 31, 1933, totaled $29,560.19, of which amount $10,929.91 came from Native Sons and Native Daughters, $361 from friends, $742.14 from interest and dividends, $4,778.28 from board refunds, and bequests of estates of Aubrey Montgomery $12,508.23 and Henry G. W. Dinkelspiel $250.

The operating expense from April 1932 to March 31, 1933, totaled $27,005.56, leaving available cash in the commercial account $6,226.51, with bequest and interest in savings banks $12,243.54. Our expenses were $2,993.68 less than last year.

We are carrying on the work as economically as possible and with as few workers as consistent with good work. Finding homes for children ranks throughout the universe as the most important work known to social service, demanding judgment, sympathy, tact, loyalty, honest and untiring effort on the part of every worker. The members of the Central Committee recognize their full responsibility for a child's influence and training, and feel that they are accountable to the Orders, to the State of California, and to the mothers and fathers who give, as well as to the mothers and fathers who receive, a child.

The Native Daughter Parlors listed in the February issue of The Grizzly Bear as having followed Grand President Anna Mixon Armstrong's suggestion to adopt a baby are sending their contributions regularly each month. We are listing the Parlors which have paid the $37.50 for the six-weeks care of a baby: Ursula No. 1 (Jackson), Orinda No. 56 (San Francisco), Aloha No. 106 (Oakland), Dolores No. 169 (San Francisco), Castro No. 178 (San Francisco) paid in full and taken a second child, El Carmelo No. 181 (Daly City), Morada No. 199 (Modesto), Plumas Pioneer No. 219 (Quincy) sent check in good faith but the bank has closed, El Tejon No. 239 (Bakersfield), Grand Parlor N.D.G.W. Home Committee, Portola No. 172 (San Francisco), Presidents Assembly of Women's Clubs.

Additional Parlors adopting a baby, and some within a few dollars of paying the full amount for the six weeks, are: Ivy No. 88 (Lodi), Copa de Oro No. 105 (Hollister), La Bandera No. 110 (Sacramento), Mary E. Bell No. 224 (Dixon). San Francisco: Minerva No. 2, Golden State No. 50, Genevieve No. 132, Golden Gate No. 158, Mission No. 227. Alameda County: Hayward

ALL ADOPTED IN ONE COMMUNITY.

No. 122, Brooklyn No. 157, Bahia Vista No. 167, Alameda County Past Presidents Association. Los Angeles and Orange Counties: Los Angeles No. 124, Santa Ana No. 235, Verdugo No. 240, Grace No. 242, Santa Monica Bay No. 245, Californiana No. 247.

Mrs. Rena Mathias of El Carmelo Parlor was instrumental in interesting the Parlors of her district in adopting a baby. The following Parlors and members have contributed toward this fund instead of spending it for a district meeting: Bonita No. 10, Vista del Mar No. 155, Ano Nuevo No. 180, El Carmelo No. 181, Menlo No. 211, San Bruno No. 246, Deputy Mary Junker of Bonita Parlor, Alta McCauley of Ano Nuevo Parlor, Alice Mathias and Rena Mathias of El Carmelo Parlor.

A Native Son or Native Daughter cannot be deaf to the words of commendation from his own communities for the willingness of fraternal organizations to promote and carry on a charitable work in the interest of children. The most indifferent Native Son or Native Daughter must be convinced of the appropriateness of a charity concerned with the future citizens of the state he or she loves. Children are an asset to any community, if given the chance of careful

(Continued on Page 29)

Native Daughters of the Golden West

THE FORTY-SEVENTH GRAND PARLOR of the Order of Native Daughters of the Golden West is to be held at Oakland, Alameda County. The four-day session will convene Monday, June 19. Grand President Anna Mixon Armstrong (Woodland No. 90) of Woodland, Yolo County, will preside throughout the deliberations. Past Grand President Sue J. Irwin and Grand Secretary Sallie R. Thaler are co-chairmen in charge of arrangements for the meeting.

Subordinate Parlors will select their delegates to the Grand Parlor at their first meeting in May. Following the choosing of delegates, quite a few new hats will, according to rumor, appear in the office-ring. There are persistent rumors, many of them from reliable sources, that there will be contests at Oakland for every Grand Parlor office, excepting the grand presidency. The Grizzly Bear endeavors to get first-hand information from candidates, and the following have, in answer to queries directed to them, definitely announced their candidacies to date:

Grand President—Grand Vice-president Irma Laird (Alturas No. 159) of Alturas, Modoc County.

Grand Vice-president—Grand Marshal Gladys E. Noce (Amapola No. 80) of Sutter Creek.

Grand Secretary—Sallie R. Thaler (Aloha No. 106) of Oakland, incumbent.

Grand Treasurer—Susie K. Christ (Yosemite No. 83) of San Francisco, incumbent.

Grand Marshal—Grand Trustee Anna Thuesen (Alta No. 3) of San Francisco; Grand Trustee Edna B. Briggs (La Bandera No. 110) of Sacramento.

Grand Inside Sentinel—Grand Outside Sentinel Hazel B. Hansen (Verdugo No. 240) of Glendale.

Grand Outside Sentinel—Alice Mathias Oldham (El Carmelo No. 181) of Daly City. Miss Mathias, whose candidacy was announced in The Grizzly Bear for April, became a bride April 23.

Grand Organist—Clara Gairaud (Vendome No. 100) of San Jose, incumbent.

Grand Trustees (seven to be selected)—Sadie Winn Brainard (Califia No. 22) of Sacramento; Grand Inside Sentinel Orinda Gunther Giannini (Orinda No. 56) of San Francisco; Minna Kane Horn (Eschscholtzia No. 112) of Etna, incumbent; Jane D. Vick (Reina del Mar No. 126) of Santa Barbara, incumbent; Alice M. Lane (Castro No. 178) of San Francisco; Florence Danforth Boyle (Gold of Ophir No. 190) of Oroville, incumbent; Ethel S. Begley (Marinita No. 198) of San Rafael, incumbent; Willow Borba (Santa Rosa No. 217) of Sebastopol, incumbent.—C.M.H.

GRAND PRESIDENT'S OFFICIAL ITINERARY.

Woodland—Grand President Anna Mixon Armstrong will, during May and June, visit the following Subordinate Parlors on the dates noted:

MAY.

6th—Gold of Ophir No. 190 (Oroville), Berryessa No. 192 (Willows), Annie K. Bidwell No. 168 (Chico), Plumas Pioneer No. 219 (Quincy), district meeting at Oroville.

10th—Marysville No. 162, Marysville; South Butte No. 226, Sutter; Camp Far West No. 218, Wheatland; jointly at Marysville.

11th—Vista del Mar No. 155, Halfmoon Bay.

12th—El Monte No. 205, Mountain View.

17th—Occident No. 28, Eureka; Oneonta No. 71, Ferndale; Reichling No. 97, Fortuna; jointly at Eureka.

18th—Fort Bragg No. 210, Fort Bragg.

19th—San Bruno No. 246, San Bruno.

23rd—Aloha No. 106, Oakland.

25th—Annie K. Bidwell No. 168, Chico.

26th—Liberty No. 213, Elk Grove.

27th—El Dorado No. 186, Georgetown, afternoon.

JUNE.

6th—Tamelpa No. 231, Mill Valley.

"A Ceremony by the River."

Sacramento—Rio Rita No. 253, the latest link in the Native Daughter chain, was instituted April 8 in the presence of 200 members of the Order. It was organized by Supervising Deputy Sadie Winn-Brainard, and is made up of a group of young women all under thirty years of age. The name, meaning "a ceremony by the river," is quite fitting, as the broad, beautiful Sacramento flows by California's Capital City, the "baby's" birthplace.

Grand President Anna Mixon Armstrong, who officiated at the Parlor's institution, was assisted by Grand Secretary Sallie R. Thaler, Grand Marshal Gladys Noce, Grand Trustees Florence Boyle, Edna Briggs and Willow Borba, Past Grands Mary E. Bell, Dr. Eva Rasmussen, Dr. Louise Heilbron and Esther Sullivan, Supervising Deputy Bessie Leitch, and Oneida Wilhelm, Sulene Cowan, Vivian Hall, Maud Cook and Clara Kenny of Califia No. 22. Officers of Rio Rita were installed by Mrs. Brainard, as follows:

Alpha Filcher, president; Evalan Earle, senior past president; Clare Rossi, junior past president; Helen Quick, past president; Alice Fredericks, first vice-president; Virginia Skeele, second vice-president; Claudia Jones, third vice-president; Dorothea Rouke, recording secretary; Edna Seydel, financial secretary; Marian Weber, treasurer; Frances Howe, marshal; Evelyn Stearns, Zelda Hanrahan, Helen King, trustees; Melba Giorgi, inside sentinel; Jeanette Eschleman, outside sentinel; Henrietta Farley, pianist.

Grand President Armstrong gave a fine talk on the Order's projects, and was presented, by the Parlor, with a gift, and numerous other speakers expressed good wishes. To Mrs. Brainard, the organizer, Rio Rita presented a pair of silver candlesticks; her response indicated to the assemblage just how dear the girls are to her. The first act of the Parlor was to adopt a homeless baby boy with the stipulation that he shall be named Winn, in honor of the N.S.G.W

Founder. A committee was named to place a marker at some historic spot, and a subscription was made to the Order's veteran fund, used to make a little happier the lives of the veterans who are in hospitals paying with their sufferings for the country's safety. Concluding a delightful and never-to-be-forgotten evening, punch was served.

Entertainment Established Standard.

Grass Valley—Manzanita No. 29 had its forty-fifth institution anniversary celebration March 21, and what a celebration! Mrs. James Wales and a minstrel troupe of thirty members, in darkface disguise and heterogeneous garb, provided entertainment that established a standard fori merriment. Members of Quartz No. 58 N.S.G.W. were special guests of the evening.

After the show, chicken campstew, apple pie and coffee were served. At the festive board H. Ray George presided as master of ceremonies, and among the speakers were Past Grand Alison F. Watt, Deputy Adaline O'Connor, President Anna Rowe of Manzanita and President Frank Rowe of Quartz. In the minstrel group were Louise Wales, Ethel Veale, Grace Eva, Irene Eldridge, Hazel Veale, Melita Hutchinson, Beatrice George, Sue Harris, Ann Whiting, Bee Deward, Hannibelle Daley, Hilda Sandow, Florence George, Hazel Jenkins, Vashti Schwartz, Ruth Lindwall, Anna Rowe, Lorraine Keast, Sadie Bennetts, Annie Conlin, Esther Fuller, Caroline Hotchkiss, Venita Jones, Ethel Foote, Marie Foote, Inez Hammill, Jean Briggs, Betty Briggs and Dorothy Daley.

Drill Team Featured.

Stockton—Grand President Anna Mixon Armstrong paid an official visit April 11 to Joaquin No. 5 at Native Sons Hall, transformed into a bower of wisteria blossoms. Mrs. J. B. Maguire Jr. presided, and among the many visitors were Past Grands Carrie R. Durham, Mamie G. Peyton, Mattie M. Stein and Pearl Lamb, Grand Trustee Edna Briggs, Supervising Deputy Grace Bessac and Deputy Frances Huck. Many gifts were presented Mrs. Armstrong, and corsages were given all officers.

A feature of the occasion was the appearance of the Parlor's noted drill team, in beruffled gowns of pink over wisteria. The team is composed of Mms. H. H. Drais (captain), C. V. Garvin, L. S. Baker, Ralph Smith, Louis Starin, Otto Kern, Charles Heineman, Charlotte Lent, George Sanguinetti, A. Worth, H. K. Valentine, H. Storms, Leo Johnson, J. E. Wilson, Brem Bessac, T. L. Porter, G. J. Schwall, Leroy Corr, Stephen Paxton; Fern Driscoll, Eva Bona, Constance Storms, Edith Beach, Tillie Bona, Doris Pettagliata. Several intricate drills were charmingly executed, and a program was presented. In charge of arrangements for the occasion were Mms. L. S. Baker (general chairman), H. H. Drais and T. L. Potter (decorations), Leroy Corr (social phases).

Joaquin celebrated its forty-sixth anniversary March 28, with the three remaining charter members as honor guests. A turkey supper was served and a suitable program staged under the chairmanship of Elizabeth Baker and Harriet Corr. In greeting the charter members, President Margaret McGuire said:

"We have assembled tonight to celebrate our forty-sixth anniversary and to pay homage to our three charter members, Miss Hannah Gray, Mrs. Carrie R. Durham and Miss Clara Steir, whom we are very happy to have as our honor guests. To Sister Gray goes the honor of having organized Joaquin Parlor, and in so doing she has not only assembled a group of women who enjoy meeting together in a social way, but she has organized a body of women who are an asset to our community and State; Sister Gray, we congratulate you on your foresight, and hope we may have you as our guiding star for many years to come. You, Sister Durham, might be compared to 'Minerva,' the chosen goddess of our State and Order; with your womanly charms and gracious manners you have been a leading figure in our Parlor; no Native Daughter in the state is loved and respected more than you, and we are proud to claim you as our own. Sister Steir, we are pleased to have you with us; a woman of keen intellect, devoting your time and energy to the educating of our future native daughters and native sons, you are an asset to any organization. These three noble women are the backbone of our Parlor, and fit examples for us to follow. May God bless them, and may we enjoy their company and good influence for many, many years."

Harmony Club Formed.

San Bernardino—Lugonia No. 241 enjoyed a potluck dinner and program April 12. Thelma Nett had charge. The table was decorated with red roses and sweetpeas. A public school educational program was presented by First Vice-president Mary Johnson April 16. Among the visitors was Florence D. Schoneman who, in the afternoon, was guest speaker on the California day program at the Woman's Club. The Parlor assisted on this occasion by exhibiting historic relics.

To arouse interest, the Harmony Club was organized at the home of Katherine McIntosh

(Continued on Page 28)

Passing of the California Pioneer

(Confined to Brief Notices of the Demise of Those Men and Women Who Came to California Prior to 1870.)

FRANCIS DOUD, BORN IN NEW YORK City, June 6, 1849; with his parents came to California via Cape Horn aboard the "Orpheus," landing at San Francisco July 6, 1849; died at Monterey City, his home for many years.

Mrs. Mahala Ashell-Stone, native of Missouri, 95; came across the plains in 1849 and resided in Sutter, Santa Cruz and Ventura Counties; died at Fillmore, survived by three children.

Willow Springs Shearer, born in Wyoming in July 1849, while his parents were enroute across the plains; settled in Sutter County; died at Yuba City, survived by three children.

Mrs. Mary McCreagh, native of Ireland, 100; came in 1849; died at San Francisco.

Mrs. Katherine Lehman, native of Germany, 90; came in 1847 and settled in El Dorado County; died near Georgetown, survived by eight children.

Miss Josephine Fanny Daniels, native of Texas, 84; since 1851 resident San Francisco, where she died.

Mrs. Katherine M. Fry, native of Indiana, 84; came in 1852; died at Oroville, Butte County.

William Henry Pile, native of Pennsylvania, 103; came across the plains in 1852; died at Glencoe, Calaveras County, survived by a daughter.

Mrs. Nancy J. Harris, native of Missouri, 81; came across the plains in 1852 and resided in Ventura and Los Angeles Counties; died at Santa Monica, survived by five children.

William C. Clark, native of Illinois, 104; crossed the plains in 1853 and resided in El Dorado, San Mateo and San Diego Counties; died at San Diego City, survived by two children.

Miss Eleanor Jane Pond, native of Wisconsin, 87; crossed the plains in 1853 and resided in Solano and Napa Counties; died at Napa City.

Simeon Clark Jordan, native of Iowa, 91; came in 1853 and settled in Placer County; died at Iowa Hill, survived by a daughter.

Mrs. W. A. Brinchuhoff, native of Missouri; crossed the plains in 1853; died at San Diego City, survived by two children.

William Francis Howe, native of Massachusetts, 95; came via Cape Horn in 1853; died at San Francisco, survived by two sons.

Mrs. Hannah Prothero Anthony, native of Pennsylvania, 84; came in 1853 and resided in Tuolumne and Stanislaus Counties; died at Denair, survived by three children. A few hours following her passing her husband, **Paul Lyman Anthony**, died at Denair; he was a native of Massachusetts, aged 80, and came in 1855.

Peter Moorhead Robinson, native of Illinois, 80; since 1854 Sacramento County resident; died at Bradshaw Station, survived by five children.

Mrs. Ellen Meyer, native of New York, 83; since 1854 Tuolumne County resident; died at Sonora, survived by two daughters.

William M. Hall, native of Missouri, 83; came across the plains in 1855 and settled in Santa Clara County; died at Los Gatos, survived by a wife and five children.

Mrs. Margaret A. McCormick, native of New York, 78; as a babe, came in 1855 to Los Angeles City, where she died; three children survive.

Mrs. William Donahue, native of Ireland, 91; came via Panama in 1855 and long resided in El Dorado County; died at San Francisco.

Julius Marion Alford, native of Arkansas, 87; came in 1857; died at Red Bluff, Tehama County, survived by five children.

Mrs. M. L. Bonney, native of Switzerland, 90; came via Cape Horn in 1857 and long resided in Nevada County; died at San Francisco, survived by four children.

Thomas H. McArdle, native of Massachusetts, 87; came via Panama in 1856 and settled in Tuolumne County; died at Sonora, survived by a wife and two daughters.

Mrs. Louisa Reubold, native of New York; came via Panama in 1853; died at San Francisco, survived by four children.

Mrs. Maria M. Habler, native of Michigan, 84; came via Panama in 1861 and for some time resided in Nevada County; died at Pittsburg, Contra Costa County, survived by three children.

Mrs. Maria A. Whaland, native of New York, 87; came via Panama in 1861 and resided in Santa Clara and Santa Cruz Counties; died at Santa Cruz City, survived by two children.

E. Pesley, 75; came via Panama in 1862 and settled in Inyo County; died at Glendale, Los Angeles County, survived by a wife and three children.

Mrs. Adelaide Costa, native of Italy, 90; since 1862 resident Sonora, Tuolumne County, where she died; two daughters survive.

Mrs. Cassia Anderson, native of Sweden, 87; came in 1861 and resided in Humboldt and Tuolumne Counties; died at Sonora, survived by five children.

Angelo Basso, native of Italy, 86; came in 1863; died at La Grange, Stanislaus County, survived by a wife and three children.

Harry W. Bodwell, native of Michigan, 73; crossed the plains in 1863 and resided many years in San Francisco; died at Burlingame, San Mateo County, survived by two sons.

Andrew Mason, 98; came in 1863 and resided many years in Colusa County; died at Ogden, Utah State, survived by six children.

Charles Harrison Church, 82; came across the plains in 1864 and resided in Sonoma and Tulare Counties; died at Visalia, survived by a wife and five sons.

Miss Gertrude E. Heckart, native of Iowa, 78; since 1865 Butte County resident; died at Oroville.

Gustave Peterson, native of Sweden, 80; since 1865 resident San Francisco, where he died.

Mrs. Barbara Fabry, native of Germany, 86; since 1866 Monterey County resident; died at Salinas, survived by eight children.

Hubert Daniels, 76; came in 1866 and long resided in Modoc County; died at Winnemucca, Nevada State.

Dewitt Clinton McKinsey, native of Indiana, 75; since 1867 Monterey County resident; died at King City, survived by three sons.

Mrs. Elizabeth Roth, native of Germany, 90; since 1868 Yolo County resident; died at Woodland, survived by five children.

Jacob R. Sachau, native of Germany, 78; since 1868 resident Alameda County; died near Livermore, survived by a wife and seven children.

Henry Booth Old, native of Alabama, 86; since 1868 resident Monterey County; died near Salinas, survived by a wife and three children.

Mrs. Mary Ann Shaw, native of New York, 79; came via Panama in 1869; died at Freshwater, Humboldt County, survived by nine children.

Miss Lilly Norman, native of Illinois, 81; as a babe in arms came via Panama in 1852 and resided in Amador County and San Francisco City many years; died at Napa City.

Mrs. Caroline Tagmeier, native of New York, 86; since 1863 resident Placerville, El Dorado County, where she died.

Mrs. Sophia Ellis-Russell, native of Mississippi, 91; came across the plains in 1857 and resided for some time in Tulare County; died at Hanford, Kings County, survived by a son.

Mrs. Eva Smith-Beck, native of Maine, 86; came via Panama in 1853; died at Oakland, Alameda County, survived by five children.

In Memoriam

MRS. MARY GILDAY GUNDRY.

To the Officers and Members of Orinda Parlor No. 56 N.D.G.W.—We, your committee appointed to draft resolutions expressing the sentiments and heartfelt sympathy of the members of the Parlor on the death of our sister, Mary Gilday Gundry, respectfully submit the following:

Whereas, It has pleased our Heavenly Father to take from our midst our beloved sister, Mary Gilday Gundry, and to summon her to a higher life; and whereas, in her passing our Parlor has lost a loyal member and her family a devoted sister; therefore, be it

Resolved, That Orinda Parlor extend sincere sympathy to the bereaved sister and brother; that a copy of these resolutions be sent to the family of our sister, that a copy be sent to The Grizzly Bear Magazine for publication, and that a copy be spread upon the minutes of this Parlor.

ADELINE TAXEIRA,
MAE SHEA,
EMMA McCLURE,
ANNA G. LOSER.

San Francisco, March 24, 1933.

SARAH T. CLARK.

To the Officers and Members of Forrest Parlor No. 86 N.D.G.W.—We, your committee appointed to draft resolutions to the memory of our departed sister, Sarah T. Clark, respectfully submit the following:

Whereas, In accordance with the plan of our Heavenly Father, the "Silent Messenger" has entered our Parlor and summoned our beloved member, Sister Clark; she has laid down the burdens of life, and entered into rest; may we cherish her deeds and honor her sacred memory.

"Gone from her home and Parlor,
Over the silvery strand,
Out from the shadowy valley
Into the beautiful land."

Resolved, That the sympathy of the Parlor be extended to her bereaved family, and may God, in His tender mercy, give peace and consolation in their sorrowing homes; be it further resolved, that a copy of these resolutions be sent to her family, a copy be spread upon the minutes of the Parlor, and that a copy be sent to The Grizzly Bear for publication.

Respectfully submitted in P.D.F.A.,
LAURA G. WESTON,
SUSIE C. NOE,
SADIE FIPPETT,
Committee.

Plymouth, April 11, 1933.

"I think by far the most important bill in our whole code is that for the diffusion of knowledge among the people. No other sure foundation can be devised for the preservation of freedom and happiness."—Thomas Jefferson.

Feminine World's Fads and Fancies

PREPARED ESPECIALLY FOR THE GRIZZLY BEAR BY ANNA STOERMER

NOT IN MANY SEASONS HAS INDIVIDuality played such an important part in coat fashions as is evidenced in the summer collections. Somewhat to our surprise, we find coats occupying a strategic position in the mode. The square shoulder is, of course, the distinguishing feature of coat fashions in general. We have the leg o'mutton, the melon, the cartridge-pleated top, the Gibson girl, the bicycle sleeve and many more.

Epaulettes, capelets, leis and revers emphasize smart shoulders in spirited new ways. Necklines compete with sleeves for style attention. They are draped, fitted, tied, buttoned and furred in diverse ways.

A large percentage of the more dressy coats subscribe to the vogue for detachable parts, such as capes, collars and scarfs, which add so materially to the chic of the garment. Unless all signs fail, we are due to hear more from the loose, swagger or boxy-type coat within the next few months. It is a type that has much to recommend to women in general, knee-length for the younger set and longer for the more-mature woman. These coats include types that can be worn either belted or swagger.

The new frocks are gay deceivers and, like so many of their predecessors, change their personality to suit the occasion. The dawn-to-dusk double-purpose dresses are more than ever intriguing in their styling, not to mention the beauty of their fabrics and the fineness of finished detail. Gray and beiges are finding favor with smart dressers, and in the case of these neutral shades there is a tendency to introduce laces tinted to match. On the other hand, and by way of striking contrast, we have the dramatic affinity of two colors, such as chocolate brown and chartreuse. Multicolored plaids and stripes, too, frequently ally themselves with soft monotones. It is the exceptional frock that is permitted to follow an independent course.

Every model has a complimentary jacket or cape, for many smart as well as practical purposes. These outfits are apt to be a bit tailored and quite a bit dressy. The jacket is frequently embellished with fur. Fabrics in many new versions have been introduced this season, but the favorite of them all, it would seem, is the organza, which is a sort of organdie presented in a new and slightly changed form. Its crispness is the dominant note of the season's styles, for the tendency is to accentuate one's crisp, chic appearance in every possible form. Orderly, slick styles predominate.

Cotton's popularity is definitely established for morning, afternoon or evening wear. Printed lawns and linens are in evidence everywhere. With the new type of linen, suits are heavier and less "wrinkly" than before, and dark blouses are to be worn with them. Ginghams, prints, flowered chiffons and crepes are still in favor.

Spring coats are practically all lengths, ranging from three-quarters and seven-eighths to the full-dress length. The fox trim is especially good, although many are shown without trimming. The color range runs largely to gray, beige and blue, the latter stressing the new postman or powder blues.

For the resorts, slacks and pajama suits promise to attain greater popularity than ever, and a new garment for the beach has made its appearance in the rubber bathing suit. Corsets and girdles are worn to preserve trimness of figure.

Gloves, of course, are appearing in every and all kinds of materials, matching those of the frock in many instances. Pique, taffeta and organdie are among the new glove fabrics. White hats may be worn with dark dresses or suits, provided there is a touch of white combined in the trimming of the dress. Shoe styles have adopted the rounder toe and lower heel for evening as well as day wear. The new boulevard heel averages from one to one and one-half inches in hight.

Light and heavy weight materials are being combined. For instance, pique blouses have insets of tucked dimity. Silk and cotton are combined. Taffeta jackets are worn over sheer organdie frocks. Rough materials are still good, but there is a tendency toward the smoother fabrics, and the highly lustrous satins are coming in. On the whole, the spring and summer styles allow a wide variety for individual taste and selection. The early shopper indicates a tendency to buy fewer, but better, clothes, favoring one higher priced garment over two of lesser value.

One of the most radical changes is seen in the styles of hats, with a definite trend toward the higher crowns. Slightly wider brims are shown for the smaller hats. A new popularity is promised for the wide-brim hat for dinner or formal afternoon wear. Millinery has gone "high hat;" not in the snobbish sense, of course. Perhaps we might say the additional head-hight gives a balance to the squared shoulders of the mode. Higher trimmings are also sponsored, and flowers, ribbons or feathers break the silhouette. Turned-up or cuff brims and various other subtle millinery trimmings give rise to greater hights of smartness.

Checks may be large or small. They appear in many delightful varieties. They pep one up, after a long winter of monotones. They are nice all by themselves, and even nicer when they are contrasted with a plain material which repeats one of their colors. Plan to wear at least one of the checked or plaided hats with a matching scarf. All the shops have them. Tie the scarf high around the neck, knotting it under the chin or tying it in a bow. Plaid blouses are very doggy, too.

The Padre—His dear old wrinkled face was open as a child's, his wise old eyes gentle and free from guile.—Jeanette Nourland.

"Life is made up of sobs, sniffles and smiles, with sniffles predominating."—O. Henry.

Official Directory of Parlors of the N. D. G. W.

ALAMEDA COUNTY.

Angelita No. 32, Livermore—Meets 2nd and 4th Fridays, Foresters Hall; Mrs. Myrtle I. Johnson, Rec. Sec., P.O. box 253.

Piedmont No. 87, Oakland—Meets Thursdays, Corinthian Hall, Pacific Bldg.; Miss Helen Ring, Rec. Sec., 822 11th St.

Aloha No. 106, Oakland—Meets Tuesdays, Wigwam Hall, Pacific Bldg.; Mrs. Lurine Martin, Rec. Sec., 2815 Wallace St., Berkeley.

Hayward No. 122, Hayward—Meets 1st and 3rd Tuesdays, Veterans Memorial Bldg., Main St.; Miss Ruth Gansberger, Rec. Sec., P. O. box 44, Mount Eden.

Berkeley No. 150, Berkeley—Meets 2nd Saturday afternoon, Berkeley City Women's Club, 2315 Durant; Mrs. Lelia B. Baker, Rec. Sec., 915 Contra Costa Ave.

Bear Flag No. 151, Berkeley—Meets 2nd and 4th Wednesdays, Veterans Memorial Bldg., 1931 Center St.; Mrs. Maud Wagner, Rec. Sec., 817 Alcatraz Ave., Oakland.

Encinal No. 156, Alameda—Meets 2nd and 4th Wednesdays, Veterans Memorial Bldg., Central Ave. and Walnut St.; Mrs. Laura E. Fisher, Rec. Sec., 1413 Caroline St.

Brooklyn No. 157, East Oakland—Meets 2nd and 4th Wednesdays, Masonic Temple, 8th Ave. and E. 14th St.; Mrs. Ruth Cooney, Rec. Sec., 3907 14th Ave.

Argonaut No. 166, Oakland—Meets Tuesdays, Klinkner Hall, 59th and San Pablo; Mrs. Ada Spilman, Rec. Sec., 2905 Ellis St., Berkeley.

Bahia Vista No. 167, Oakland—Meets 1st and 3rd Thursdays, Wigwam Hall, Pacific Bldg.; Mrs. Minnie E. Raper, Rec. Sec., 3449 Helen St.

Fruitvale No. 177, Oakland—Meets Fridays, W.O.W. Hall; May E. Barthold, Rec. Sec., 3832 Santa Rita St.

Laura Loma No. 182, Niles—Meets 1st and 3rd Tuesdays, I.O.O.F. Hall; Mrs. Ethel Fournier, Rec. Sec., P. O. box 515.

El Cereso No. 207, San Leandro—Meets 2nd and 4th Tuesdays, Masonic Hall; Mrs. Mary Tuttle, Rec. Sec., P. O. box 56.

Pleasanton No. 237, Pleasanton—Meets 1st Tuesday, I.O.O.F. Hall; Mrs. Myrtle Lanini, Rec. Sec.

Betsy Ross No. 238, Centerville—Meets 1st and 3rd Fridays, Anderson Hall; Miss Constance Lucio, Rec. Sec., P. O. box 187.

AMADOR COUNTY.

Ursula No. 1, Jackson—Meets 2nd and 4th Tuesdays, N.S.G.W. Hall; Mrs. Emma Boarman-Wright, Rec. Sec., 114 Court St.

Chispa No. 40, Ione—Meets 2nd and 4th Fridays, N.S.G.W. Hall; Mrs. Isabel Ashton, Rec. Sec.

Amapola No. 80, Sutter Creek—Meets 2nd and 4th Thursdays, N.S.G.W. Bldg.; Mrs. Hazel M. Marre, Rec. Sec.

Forrest No. 86, Plymouth—Meets 2nd and 4th Tuesdays, I.O.O.F. Hall; Mrs. Marguerite Davis, Rec. Sec.

BUTTE COUNTY.

Annie K. Bidwell No. 168, Chico—Meets 2nd and 4th Thursdays, I.O.O.F. Hall; Mrs. Irene Henry, Rec. Sec., 3015 Woodland Ave.

Gold of Ophir No. 190, Oroville—Meets 1st and 3rd Wednesdays, Memorial Hall; Mrs. Ruth Brown, Rec. Sec., 1265 Leah Court.

CALAVERAS COUNTY.

Ruby No. 46, Murphys—Meets 4th Friday, N.S.G.W. Hall; Belle Segale, Rec. Sec.

Princess No. 84, Angels Camp—Meets 2nd and 4th Wednesdays, I.O.O.F. Hall; Mrs. Grace M. Mills, Rec. Sec., P.O. box 313.

San Andreas No. 113, San Andreas—Meets 1st Friday, Fraternal Hall; Miss Doris Treat, Rec. Sec.

COLUSA COUNTY.

Colus No. 194, Colusa—Meets 1st and 3rd Mondays, Eagles Hall; Miss Kate Busch, Rec. Sec., 350 Market St.

CONTRA COSTA COUNTY.

Stirling No. 146, Pittsburg—Meets 1st and 3rd Wednesdays, Veteran Memorial Hall; Mrs. Leslie Clement, Rec. Sec., 468 E. Santa Fe.

Richmond No. 147, Richmond—Meets 1st and 3rd Tuesdays, I.O.O.F. Hall, 10th St.; Grace Curry, Rec. Sec., 932 Ohio Ave.

Donner No. 193, Byron—Meets 1st and 3rd Wednesdays, I.O.O.F. Hall; Mrs. Anna Pendry, Rec. Sec., P.O. box 442, Brentwood.

Las Juntas No. 221, Martinez—Meets 1st and 3rd Mondays, Pythian Castle; Mrs. Lola O. Viera, Rec. Sec., R.F.D. No. 1.

Antioch No. 223, Antioch—Meets 2nd and 4th Tuesdays, I.O.O.F. Hall; Mrs. Estelle Evans, Rec. Sec., 202 E. 5th St., Pittsburg.

Carquinez No. 234, Crockett—Meets 2nd and 4th Wednesdays, I.O.O.F. Hall; Mrs. Cecile Petee, Rec. Sec., 465 Edwards St.

EL DORADO COUNTY.

Marguerite No. 12, Placerville—Meets 1st and 3rd Wednesdays, Masonic Hall; Mrs. Nettie Leonardi, Rec. Sec., 25 Coloma St.

El Dorado No. 186, Georgetown—Meets 2nd and 4th Saturday afternoons, I.O.O.F. Hall; Mrs. Alta L. Douglas, Rec. Sec.

FRESNO COUNTY.

Fresno No. 187, Fresno—Meets 2nd and 4th Fridays, Pythian Castle, Cor. "R" and Merced Sts.; Mary Aubery, Rec. Sec., 1040 Delphia Ave.

GRAND OFFICERS.

Mrs. Evelyn I. Carlson..........Past Grand President
281 E. Tuscaloosa Ave., Atherton

Mrs. Anna M. Armstrong..........Grand President
Woodland

Mrs. Irma Laird..........Grand Vice-president
Alturas

Mrs. Sallie R. Thaler..........Grand Secretary
555 Baker St., San Francisco

Mrs. Susie K. Christ..........Grand Treasurer
555 Baker St., San Francisco

Mrs. Gladys Noce..........Grand Marshal
Sutter Creek

Mrs. Orinda G. Giannini..........Grand Inside Sentinel
2142 Filbert St., San Francisco

Mrs. Hazel B. Hansen..........Grand Outside Sentinel
501 Griswold St., Glendale

Mrs. Clara Gairaud..........Grand Organist
134 Locust St., San Jose

GRAND TRUSTEES.

Mrs. Florence Boyle..........Oroville
Mrs. Edna Briggs..........1045 Santa Ynez Way, Sacramento
Mrs. Anna Thuesen..........615 38th Ave., San Francisco
Mrs. Ethel Begley..........283 Prospect Ave., San Francisco
Mrs. Minna K. Horn..........Etna
Mrs. Jane Vick..........418 Bath St., Santa Barbara
Mrs. Willow Borba..........330 So. Main St., Sebastopol

GLENN COUNTY.

Berryessa No. 192, Willows—Meets 1st and 3rd Mondays, I.O.O.F. Hall; Mrs. Leonora Neate, Rec. Sec., 338 No. Lassen St.

HUMBOLDT COUNTY.

Occident No. 28, Eureka—Meets 1st and 3rd Wednesdays, N.S.G.W. Hall; Mrs. Eva L. MacDonald, Rec. Sec., 2309 "B" St.

Oneonta No. 71, Ferndale—Meets 2nd and 4th Fridays, I.O.O.F. Hall; Mrs. Myra Rumrill, Rec. Sec., P.O. box 142.

Reichling No. 97, Fortuna—Meets 1st and 3rd Tuesdays, Friendship Hall; Mrs. Grace Swett, Rec. Sec., P. O. box 328.

KERN COUNTY.

Miocene No. 228, Taft—Meets 1st and 3rd Wednesday afternoons, I.O.O.F. Hall; Mrs. Evalyn G. Towne, Rec. Sec., P. O. box 1011.

El Tejon No. 239, Bakersfield—Meets 1st and 3rd Fridays, Eagles Hall, 1714 "G" St.; Mary B. Hampson, Rec. Sec., 908 Quincy St.

Desert Gold No. 250, Mojave—Meets 2nd and 4th Fridays, I.O.O.F. Hall; Jane Lucile Waters, Rec. Sec., Tehachapi.

LAKE COUNTY.

Clear Lake No. 135, Middletown—Meets 2nd and 4th Tuesdays, Herrick Hall; Mrs. Alma E. Snow, Rec. Sec.

LASSEN COUNTY.

Nataqua No. 152, Standish—Meets 1st and 3rd Wednesdays, Foresters Hall; Mrs. Mayda Elledge, Rec. Sec.

Mount Lassen No. 215, Bieber—Meets 2nd and 4th Thursdays, I.O.O.F. Hall; Mrs. Angie C. Kenyon, Rec. Sec.

Susanville No. 243, Susanville—Meets 3rd Thursday, I.O.O.F. Hall; Mildred Hardy, Rec. Sec., P.O. box 425.

LOS ANGELES COUNTY.

Los Angeles No. 124, Los Angeles—Meets 1st and 3rd Wednesdays, I.O.O.F. Hall, Washington and Oak Sts.; Mrs. Mary K. Corcoran, Rec. Sec., 822 No. Van Ness Ave.

Long Beach No. 154, Long Beach—Meets 1st and 3rd Thursdays, K.P. Hall, 341 Pacific Ave.; Mrs. Bertha Hitt, Rec. Sec., 5355 Lime Ave.

Rudecinda No. 230, San Pedro—Meets 2nd and 4th Thursdays, Unity Hall, I.O.O.F. Temple, 10th and Gaffey; Letitia Sarciaux, Rec. Sec., 1054 W. 24th St.

Verdugo No. 240, Glendale—Meets 2nd and 4th Tuesdays, Masonic Temple, 234 So. Brand Blvd.; Miss Etta Fulkerth, Rec. Sec., 526 No. Orange St.

Santa Monica Bay No. 245, Santa Monica—Meets 2nd and 4th Wednesdays, Odd Fellows Hall, 1431 Third St.; Mrs. Rosalie Hyde, Rec. Sec., 738 Flower St., Venice.

Californiana No. 247, Los Angeles—Meets 2nd and 4th Tuesday afternoons, Hollywood Studio Club, 1215 Lodi Place; Mrs. Inez Sitton, Rec. Sec., 4223 Berenice St.

MADERA COUNTY.

Madera No. 244, Madera—Meets 2nd and 4th Thursdays, Masonic Annex; Mrs. Margaret O. Boyle, Rec. Sec., 111 No. "B" St.

MARIN COUNTY.

Sea Point No. 196, Sausalito—Meets 2nd and 4th Mondays, Perry Hall, 50 Caledonia St.; Mrs. Mary B. Smith, Rec. Sec., 47½ Glen Drive.

Marinita No. 198, San Rafael—Meets 2nd and 4th Mondays, 316 "B" St.; Miss Mollye Y. Spaelti, Rec. Sec., 539 4th St.

Fairfax No. 225, Fairfax—Meets 2nd and 4th Tuesdays, Community Hall; Mrs. Marguerite Geary, Rec. Sec.

Tamelpa No. 231, Mill Valley—Meets 1st and 2nd Tuesdays, I.O.O.F. Hall; Mrs. Delphine M. Todt, Rec. Sec., 500 Irwin St., San Rafael.

MARIPOSA COUNTY.

Mariposa No. 63, Mariposa—Meets 1st and 3rd Fridays, I.O.O.F. Hall; Elizabeth E. Johnson, Rec. Sec.

MENDOCINO COUNTY.

Fort Bragg No. 210, Fort Bragg—Meets 1st and 3rd Thursdays, I.O.O.F. Hall; Mrs. Ruth W. Fuller, Rec. Sec.

MERCED COUNTY.

Veritas No. 75, Merced—Meets 1st and 3rd Tuesdays, I.O.O.F. Hall; Miss Flora Fernandes, Rec. Sec., Parkside Apt.

MODOC COUNTY.

Alturas No. 159, Alturas—Meets 1st Thursday, Alturas Civic Club; Mrs. Irma W. Laird, Rec. Sec.

MONTEREY COUNTY.

Aleli No. 102, Salinas—Meets 2nd and 4th Thursdays, Pythian Hall; Miss Rose Rhyner, Rec. Sec., 420 Soledad St.

Junipero No. 141, Monterey—Meets 2nd and 4th Fridays, K. of P. Hall, Main St.; Miss Matilda M. Bergschicker, Rec. Sec., 498 Van Buren St.

NAPA COUNTY.

Eshcol No. 16, Napa—Meets 2nd and 4th Mondays, N.S.G.W. Hall; Mrs. Ella Ingram, Rec. Sec., 2140 Seminary St.

Calistoga No. 145, Calistoga—Meets 2nd and 4th Mondays, I.O.O.F. Hall; Sadie P. Brooks, Rec. Sec.

La Junta No. 203, Saint Helena—Meets 1st and 3rd Tuesdays, N.S.G.W. Hall; Mrs. Marie Signorelli, Rec. Sec., 1341 Madrona Ave.

ATTENTION, SECRETARIES!

THIS DIRECTORY IS PUBLISHED BY AUTHORITY OF THE GRAND PARLOR N.D.G.W., AND ALL NOTICES OF CHANGES MUST BE RECEIVED BY THE GRAND SECRETARY (NOT THE MAGAZINE) ON OR BEFORE THE 20TH OF EACH MONTH TO INSURE CORRECTION IN NEXT PUBLICATION OF DIRECTORY.

NEVADA COUNTY.

Laurel No. 6, Nevada City—Meets 1st and 3rd Wednesdays, I.O.O.F. Hall; Mrs. Nellie E. Clark, Rec. Sec., 412 Pine St.

Manzanita No. 29, Grass Valley—Meets 1st and 3rd Tuesdays, Auditorium; Mrs. Loraine Keast, Rec. Sec., 123 Race St.

Columbia No. 70, French Corral—Meets Fridays, Farrelley Hall; Mrs. Kate Farrelley-Sullivan, Rec. Sec.

Snow Peak No. 176, Truckee—Meets 1st Monday, I.O.O.F. Hall; Mrs. Henrietta M. Eaton, Rec. Sec., P. O. box 116.

ORANGE COUNTY.

Santa Ana No. 235, Santa Ana—Meets 2nd and 4th Mondays, K.C. Hall, 4th and French Sts.; Mrs. Matilda S. Lemon, Rec. Sec., 1628 W. 8th St.

Grace No. 242, Fullerton—Meets 1st and 3rd Thursdays, I.O.O.F. Hall, 116½ E. Commonwealth; Mrs. Mary R. Rothaermel, Rec. Sec., Acacia St. & Commonwealth.

PLACER COUNTY.

Placer No. 138, Lincoln—Meets 2nd Wednesday, I.O.O.F. Hall; Miss Carrie Parlin, Rec. Sec.

La Rosa No. 191, Roseville—Meets 1st and 3rd Tuesdays, Eagles Hall; Mrs. Alice Lee West, Rec. Sec., Rocklin.

Auburn No. 233, Auburn—Meets 2nd and 4th Fridays, Foresters Hall; Mrs. Elsie Patrick, Rec. Sec.

PLUMAS COUNTY.

Plumas Pioneer No. 219, Quincy—Meets 1st and 3rd Mondays, I.O.O.F. Hall; Minnie E. Johnson, Rec. Sec., P. O. box 243.

SACRAMENTO COUNTY.

Califia No. 22, Sacramento—Meets 2nd and 4th Tuesdays, N.S.G.W. Hall; Miss Lulu Gillis, Rec. Sec., 921 8th St.

La Bandera No. 110, Sacramento—Meets 1st and 3rd Fridays, N.S.G.W. Hall; Mrs. Clara Weldon, Rec. Sec., 1310 "O" St.

Sutter No. 111, Sacramento—Meets 1st and 3rd Tuesdays, N.S.G.W. Hall; Mrs. Adele Nix, Rec. Sec., 1238 "S" St.

Fern No. 123, Folsom—Meets 1st and 3rd Tuesdays, K.P. Hall; Elizabeth Ryan, Rec. Sec., Represa.

Chabolla No. 171, Galt—Meets 2nd and 4th Tuesdays, I.O.O.F. Hall; Mrs. Mary Pritchard, Rec. Sec.

Coloma No. 212, Sacramento—Meets 1st and 3rd Tuesdays, I.O.O.F. Hall, Oak Park; Mrs. Nettie Harry, Rec. Sec., 1217 35th St.

Liberty No. 213, Elk Grove—Meets 2nd and 4th Fridays, I.O.O.F. Hall; Mrs. Frances Wackman, Rec. Sec., P. O. box 192.

Victory No. 216, Courtland—Meets 1st Saturday and 3rd Monday, N.S.G.W. Hall; Mrs. Agueda Lample, Rec. Sec.

Rio Rita No. 253, Sacramento—Meets 2nd and 4th Mondays, 902 "J" St.; Dorothea Rourke, Rec. Sec.

SAN BENITO COUNTY.

Copa de Oro No. 105, Hollister—Meets 2nd and 4th Thursdays, Grangers Union Hall; Mrs. Mollie Daveggio, Rec. Sec., 110 San Benito St.

San Juan Bautista No. 179, San Juan Bautista—Meets 1st Wednesday, Mission Corridor Rooms; Miss Gertrude Breen, Rec. Sec.

SAN BERNARDINO COUNTY.

Lugonia No. 241, San Bernardino—Meets 2nd and 4th Wednesdays, Eagles Hall; Miss Lois Poling, Rec. Sec., 295 E. 11th St.

Ontario No. 251, Ontario—Meets 2nd and 4th Thursdays, Ontario Hotel; Miss Helen Hickman, Rec. Sec., 923 No. Laurel Ave.

SAN DIEGO COUNTY.

San Diego No. 208, San Diego—Meets 2nd and 4th Wednesdays, Directors Room, Chamber Commerce Bldg., 499 W. Broadway; Mrs. Elsie Case, Rec. Sec., 3051 Broadway.

SAN FRANCISCO CITY AND COUNTY.

Minerva No. 2, San Francisco—Meets 1st and 3rd Wednesdays, N.S.G.W. Bldg.; Miss Dorothy Finn, Rec. Sec., 90 Princess St., Sausalito.

Alta No. 3, San Francisco—Meets 2nd and 4th Tuesdays, N.S.G.W. Bldg.; Mrs. Agnese L. Hughes, Rec. Sec., 3980 Sacramento St.

Oro Fino No. 9, San Francisco—Meets 1st and 3rd Thursdays, N.S.G.W. Bldg.; Mrs. Josephine B. Morrisey, Rec. Sec., 4441 20th St.

Golden State No. 50, San Francisco—Meets 1st and 3rd Wednesdays, N.D.G.W. Home; Miss Millie Tietjen, Rec. Sec., 328 Lexington Ave.

Orinda No. 56, San Francisco—Meets 2nd, 4th and 5th Fridays, N.D.G.W. Home; Mrs. Anna A. Gruber-Loser, Rec. Sec., 72 Grove Lane, San Anselmo.

Fremont No. 59, San Francisco—Meets 1st and 3rd Tuesdays, N.S.G.W. Bldg.; Miss Hannah Collins, Rec. Sec., 617 Fillmore St.

Buena Vista No. 68, San Francisco—Meets 1st, 3rd and 5th Thursdays, N.D.G.W. Home; Miss Margaret Barrett, Rec. Sec., 3774 20th St.

Las Lomas No. 72, San Francisco—Meets 1st and 3rd Tuesdays, N.D.G.W. Home; Mrs. Marion S. Day, Rec. Sec., 469 Noe St.

Yosemite No. 83, San Francisco—Meets 1st and 3rd Tuesdays, American Hall, 20th and Capp Sts.; Miss Mary Monahan, Rec. Sec., 237 Noe St.

La Estrella No. 89, San Francisco—Meets 2nd and 4th Mondays, N.S.G.W. Bldg.; Miss Birdie Hartman, Rec. Sec., 1018 Jackson St.

Sans Souci No. 96, San Francisco—Meets 2nd and 4th Mondays, N.D.G.W. Home; Mrs. Minnie F. Dobbin, Rec. Sec., 1483 43rd Ave.

Calaveras No. 103, San Francisco—Meets 2nd and 4th Tuesdays, Swedish American Hall, 2174 Market St.; Mary L. Krogh, Rec. Sec., 4235 Cabrillo St.

Darina No. 114, San Francisco—Meets 1st and 3rd Mondays, N.S.G.W. Bldg.; Miss Adele Walsh, Rec. Sec., 479 Page St.

El Vespero No. 118, San Francisco—Meets 2nd and 4th Tuesdays, Masonic Hall, 4705 3rd St.; Mrs. Nell R. Boege, Rec. Sec., 1526 Kirkwood Ave.

Genevieve No. 132, San Francisco—Meets 1st and 3rd Thursdays, N.S.G.W. Bldg.; Miss Branice Peguillan, Rec. Sec., 2434 16th Ave.

Keith No. 137, San Francisco—Meets 2nd and 4th Thursdays, N.S.G.W. Bldg.; Mrs. Helen T. Mann, Rec. Sec., 575 Pierce St., Apt. 206.

Gabrielle No. 139, San Francisco—Meets 2nd and 4th Wednesdays, N.S.G.W. Bldg.; Mrs. Dorothy Wuesterfeld, Rec. Sec., 1020 Munich St.

Presidio No. 148, San Francisco—Meets 2nd and 4th Tuesdays, N.S.G.W. Bldg.; Mrs. Hattie Gaughran, Rec. Sec., 713 Capp St.

Guadalupe No. 153, San Francisco—Meets 2nd and 4th Mondays, Forester Hall, 170 Valencia St.; Miss May A. McCarthy, Rec. Sec., 336 Elsie St.

Golden Gate No. 158, San Francisco—Meets 2nd and 4th Mondays, N.S.G.W. Bldg.; Mrs. Mary Sullivan, Rec. Sec., 83 Cuvier St.

Dolores No. 169, San Francisco—Meets 2nd and 4th Wednesdays, N.S.G.W. Bldg.; Mrs. Ada Saunders, Rec. Sec., 284 Allison St.

Linda Rosa No. 170, San Francisco—Meets 2nd and 4th Wednesdays, Swedish American Hall, 2174 Market St.; Mrs. Eva P. Tyrrel, Rec. Sec., 2629 Mission St.

Portola No. 172, San Francisco—Meets 1st and 3rd Tuesdays, N.S.G.W. Bldg.; Catherine H. Dolly, Rec. Sec., 4125 23rd St.

Castro No. 178, San Francisco—Meets 1st and 3rd Wednesdays, K.C. Bldg., 150 Golden Gate Ave.; Miss Adeline Sandersfeld, Rec Sec., 50 Baker St.

Twin Peaks No. 185, San Francisco—Meets 2nd and 4th Fridays, Druids Temple, 44 Page St.; Mrs. Loretta Cameron, Rec. Sec., 3969 Army St.

James Lick No. 220, San Francisco—Meets 1st and 3rd Wednesdays, N.S.G.W. Bldg.; Mrs. Edna Bishop, Rec. Sec., 3841 24th St.

Mission No. 227, San Francisco—Meets 2nd and 4th Fridays, N.S.G.W. Bldg.; Mrs. Ann Dippel, Rec. Sec., 448 Dewey Blvd.

Bret Harte No. 232, San Francisco—Meets 2nd and 4th Tuesdays, Aloha Hall, 3009 16th St.; Pearl Wedde, Rec. Sec., 225 7th Ave.

La Dorada No. 236, San Francisco—Meets 2nd and 4th Thursdays, N.S.G.W. Hall; Mrs. Theresa R. O'Brien, Rec. Sec., 567 Liberty St.

Balboa No. 249, San Francisco—Meets 1st and 3rd Thursdays, Knights Columbus Hall, 382 18th Ave.; Miss Juan Moffet, Rec. Sec., 476 26th Ave.

Utopia No. 252, San Francisco—Meets 2nd and 4th Tuesdays, American Hall, 20th and Capp Sts.; Miss Lelia M. Little, Rec. Sec., 4450 20th St.

SAN JOAQUIN COUNTY.

Joaquin No. 5, Stockton—Meets 2nd and 4th Tuesdays, N.S.G.W. Hall, 314 E. Main St.; Mrs. Della Garvin, Rec. Sec., 1122 E. Market St.

El Pescadero No. 82, Tracy—Meets 1st and 3rd Fridays, I.O.O.F. Hall; Mrs. Mary A. Hewitson, Rec. Sec., 122 Walnut St.

Ivy No. 88, Lodi—Meets 1st and 3rd Wednesdays, Eagles Hall; Mrs. Mae Corson, Rec. Sec., 109 So. School St.

Calis de Oro No. 206, Stockton—Meets 1st and 3rd Tuesdays, N.S.G.W. Hall, 314 E. Main St.; Mrs. Frances Germain, Rec. Sec., 450 No. Regent.

Phoebe A. Hearst No. 214, Manteca—Meets 2nd and 4th Wednesdays, I.O.O.F. Hall; Mrs. Josie M. Frederick, Rec. Sec., Route A, Box 364, Ripon.

SAN LUIS OBISPO COUNTY.

San Miguel No. 94, San Miguel—Meets 2nd and 4th Wednesday afternoons, Clemon Hall; Mrs. Nellie Wickstrom, Rec. Sec.

San Luisita No. 108, San Luis Obispo—Meets 2nd and 4th Thursdays, W.O.W. Hall; Miss Agnes M. Lee, Rec. Sec., P. O. box 584.

El Pinal No. 163, Cambria—Meets 2nd, 4th and 5th Tuesdays, N.S.G.W. Hall; Kathryn Luchessa, Rec. Sec.

SAN MATEO COUNTY.

Bonita No. 10, Redwood City—Meets 2nd and 4th Thursdays, I.O.O.F. Hall; Mrs. Dora Wilson, Rec. Sec., 518 Middlefield Rd.

Vista del Mar No. 155, Halfmoon Bay—Meets 2nd and 4th Thursdays, I.O.O.F. Hall; Elizabeth Olney, Rec. Sec.

Ano Nuevo No. 180, Pescadero—Meets 1st and 3rd Wednesdays, I.O.O.F. Hall; Mrs. Alice Mattei, Rec. Sec.

El Carmelo No. 181, Daly City—Meets 1st and 3rd Wednesdays, Masonic Hall; Miss Alice Mathias, Rec. Sec., 2218 26th Ave., San Francisco.

Menlo No. 211, Menlo Park—Meets 2nd and 4th Mondays, Masonic Hall; Mrs. Frances E. Maloney, Rec. Sec., P. O. box 626.

San Bruno No. 246, San Bruno—Meets 2nd and 4th Fridays, Legion Hall; Miss Mildred Foley, Rec. Sec., 217 Miller Ave., South San Francisco.

SANTA BARBARA COUNTY.

Reina del Mar No. 126, Santa Barbara—Meets 1st and 3rd Tuesdays, Pythian Castle, 222 W. Carillo St.; Mrs. Dorothy Yule, Rec. Sec., 112 Ocean Ave.

SANTA CLARA COUNTY.

San Jose No. 81, San Jose—Meets Thursdays, Catholic Women Center, 5th and San Fernando Sts.; Mrs. Nellie Fleming, Rec. Sec., Catholic Women Center.

Vendome No. 100, San Jose—Meets Wednesdays, Old Scottish Rite Temple; Miss Marie Buck, Rec. Sec., 245 Hawthorne St.

El Monte No. 205, Mountain View—Meets 2nd and 4th Fridays, American Legion Hall; Miss Elizabeth Spencer, Rec. Sec., 512 Hope St.

Palo Alto No. 229, Palo Alto—Meets 1st and 2nd Mondays, N.S.G.W. Hall; Miss Helena G. Hansen, Rec. Sec., 531 Lytton Ave.

SANTA CRUZ COUNTY.

Santa Cruz No. 26, Santa Cruz—Meets Mondays, N.S.G.W. Hall; Mrs. May L. Williamson, Rec. Sec., 170 Walnut Ave.

El Pajaro No. 35, Watsonville—Meets 1st and 3rd Tuesdays, I.O.O.F. Hall; Miss Ruth E. Wilson, Rec. Sec., 16 Laurel St.

SHASTA COUNTY.

Camellia No. 41, Anderson—Meets 1st and 3rd Tuesdays, Masonic Hall; Mrs. Olga E. Welbourn, Rec. Sec.

Lassen View No. 98, Shasta—Meets 2nd Friday, Masonic Hall; Miss Louise Litsch, Rec. Sec.

Hiawatha No. 140, Redding—Meets 2nd and 4th Wednesdays, Moose Hall; Ruth Presleigh, Rec. Sec., Office County Clerk.

SIERRA COUNTY.

Naomi No. 36, Downieville—Meets 2nd and 4th Wednesdays, I.O.O.F. Hall; Louise O. Dubuque, Rec. Sec.

Imogen No. 134, Sierraville—Meets 2nd and 4th Saturday afternoons, Copren Hall; Mrs. Jennie Copren, Rec. Sec.

SISKIYOU COUNTY.

Eschscholtzia No. 112, Etna—Meets 1st and 3rd Wednesdays, Masonic Hall; Mrs. Bernice E. Smith, Rec. Sec.

Mountain Dawn No. 120, Sawyers Bar—Meets 2nd and last Wednesdays, I.O.O.F. Hall; Miss Edith Dunphy, Rec. Sec.

SOLANO COUNTY.

Vallejo No. 195, Vallejo—Meets 1st and 3rd Wednesdays, K.C. Hall, 820 Marin St.; Mrs. Mary Combs, Rec. Sec., 511 York St.

Mary E. Bell No. 224, Dixon—Meets 2nd and 4th Thursdays, I.O.O.F. Hall; Mary Young, Rec. Sec.

SONOMA COUNTY.

Sonoma No. 209, Sonoma—Meets 2nd and 4th Mondays, I.O.O.F. Hall; Mrs. Mae Norrbom, Rec. Sec., R.F.D., box 171.

Santa Rosa No. 217, Santa Rosa—Meets 1st and 3rd Thursdays, N.S.G.W. Hall; Mrs. Clytie L. Lewis, Rec. Sec., R.F.D. No. 4, Box 345-A.

Petaluma No. 222, Petaluma—Meets 1st and 3rd Tuesdays, Dania Hall; Mrs. Margaret M. Oeltjen, Rec. Sec., 503 Prospect St.

STANISLAUS COUNTY.

Oakdale No. 125, Oakdale—Meets 3rd Monday, McLeod Home; Mrs. Lou Reeder, Rec. Sec.

Morada No. 199, Modesto—Meets 2nd and 4th Wednesdays, I.O.O.F. Hall; Mrs. Susan Sullivan, Rec. Sec., 823 10th St.

Eldora No. 248, Turlock—Meets 1st and 3rd Mondays, Masonic Temple; Effie Lund, Rec. Sec., 312 Mitchell St.

SUTTER COUNTY.

South Butte No. 226, Sutter—Meets 1st and 3rd Mondays, N.D.G.W. Hall; Mrs. Abbie N. Vagedes, Rec. Sec.

TEHAMA COUNTY.

Berendos No. 23, Red Bluff—Meets 1st and 3rd Tuesdays, W.O.W. Hall, 200 Pine St.; Mrs. Lillie Hammer, Rec. Sec., 636 Jackson St.

TRINITY COUNTY.

Eltapome No. 55, Weaverville—Meets 2nd and 4th Thursdays, N.S.G.W. Hall; Mrs. Lou N. Fetzer, Rec. Sec.

TUOLUMNE COUNTY.

Dardanelle No. 66, Sonora—Meets Fridays, I.O.O.F. Hall; Mrs. Nettie Whitto, Rec. Sec., P.O. box 122.

Golden Era No. 99, Columbia—Meets 1st and 3rd Thursdays, N.S.G.W. Hall; Miss Irene Ponce, Rec. Sec.

Anona No. 164, Jamestown—Meets 2nd and 4th Tuesdays, I.O.O.F. Hall; Nellie Hope, Rec. Sec.

YOLO COUNTY.

Woodland No. 90, Woodland—Meets 2nd and 4th Tuesdays, N.S.G.W. Hall; Mrs. Maude Heston, Rec. Sec., 153 College St.

YUBA COUNTY.

Marysville No. 162, Marysville—Meets 2nd and 4th Wednesdays, Liberty Hall; Miss Cecelia C. Gomes, Rec. Sec., 701 6th St.

Camp Far West No. 218, Wheatland—Meets 3rd Tuesday, I.O.O.F. Hall; Mrs. Ethel C. Brock, Rec. Sec., P. O. box 285.

AFFILIATED ORGANIZATIONS.

General Association Past Presidents—Meetings held annually in April at the home-town of Chief President; Mrs. Cora Stobing, 1739 San Jose Ave., San Francisco, Chief President; Mrs. Anna G. Loser, 72 Grove Lane, San Anselmo, Chief Secretary.

Past Presidents Association No. 1—Meets 1st and 3rd Mondays, N.S.G.W. Bldg., 414 Mason St., San Francisco; Mrs. Alice Ogburn, Pres.; Mrs. Leah M. Williams, Rec. Sec., 956 Pierce St., Apt. 104, San Francisco.

Past Presidents Association No. 2—Meets 2nd and 4th Mondays, "Wigwam," Pacific Bldg., 16th and Jefferson, Oakland; Emma Haggerty, Pres.; Mrs. Elizabeth B. Goodman, Rec. Sec., 134 Juana Ave., San Leandro.

Past Presidents Association No. 3 (Santa Clara County)—Meets 2nd Tuesday, Musicians Hall, 114 E. Santa Clara St., San Jose; Augusta Singleton, Pres.; Clara Briggs, Rec. Sec., 1336 Magnolia Ave., San Jose.

Past Presidents Association No. 4 (Sacramento County)—Meets 2nd Monday, N.S.G.W. Hall, 11th and "J" Sts., Sacramento City; Edith Kelley, Pres.; Lily May Tilden, Rec. Sec., 3225 "T" St., Sacramento.

Past Presidents Association No. 5 (Butte County)—Meets 1st Friday, homes of members, Chico and Oroville; Marie Picanco, Pres.; Ruth Brown, Rec. Sec., 1265 Leah Court, Oroville.

Past Presidents Association No. 6 (Nevada County)—Meets 4th Friday, alternately between Nevada City, Pythian Castle, and Grass Valley, Edna Sampson's home; Margaret V. Nolan, Pres.; Vere Hansen, Rec. Sec., R.F.D. No. 2, box 41-C, Grass Valley.

Past Presidents Association No. 7 (Sonoma County)—Meets 2nd Tuesday, Violet Mastrup home, 622 5th St., Petaluma; Viola Mastrup, Pres.; Elizabeth Dillon, Rec. Sec., Petaluma.

Past Presidents Association No. 8 (San Joaquin and Stanislaus Counties)—Meets 2nd Thursday, Red Men Hall, Stockton; Mrs. Lois Armstrong, Pres.; Mrs. Harriet F. Corr, Rec. Sec., 729 E. Sonora St., Stockton.

Native Sons and Native Daughters Central Committee on Homeless Children—Main Office, 955 Phelan Bldg., San Francisco; Mrs. John W. Stirling, Chmn.; Miss Mary E. Brusie, Sec. Los Angeles branch office, 3924 Sunset Blvd.; Dorothy Schlingman, Sec.

(ADVERTISEMENT.)

NATIVE DAUGHTER NEWS

(Continued from Page 19)

March 22. It is made up of active and prospective members of Lugonia and their mothers. It meets the first and third Tuesdays at the members' homes. A flower garden quilt is being made and will be disposed of to raise funds.

Living Pioneer Monuments.

Angels Camp—Princess No. 84 participated in Arbor Day exercises, held April 2 in Utica Park, by planting in the Native Daughter plot of the park two trees as living monuments to "for their untiring efforts in making this state the Pioneers. In dedicating the trees President Hildred Mayo eulogized the California Pioneers the land of safety and prosperity for posterity." The trees were presented to the Parlor by D. Fricat, who raised them in Calaveras County from nuts from a tree growing on the site of the battle of Gettysburg.

Historical Fashion Show.

Chico—Annie K. Bidwell No. 168 had a historical fashion show March 23. Grace Morrow, who originated the idea, read the story as the characters representing the various periods appeared: Spanish, Antoinette Choisser; gold rush, Mabel Marshall; Civil War, Francis Snider; gay nineties, Margaret Polk; Roosevelt, Lila Roohr; World War, Charlotte Boyd; jazz, Minnie Wesbrook; modern, Lucy Girdler. Appropriate selections were sung by Alice Bass, Lois Heberlie and Katherine McEnespy, with Evelyn Boyd as accompanist. Josephine Alexander was chairman of a committee that served refreshments at tables decorated in spring flowers.

No Hall, Account of Quake.

Santa Ana—Santa Ana No. 235 not being able to find a hall since the recent quake, meetings were held March 27 at the home of First Vice-president Mae West and April 10 at the home of Past President Genevieve Hiskey. The thimble club met at the homes of Gertrude Etzold and Ruth Campbell. As the latter is to become a bride April 30, she was given a surprise shower of useful gifts. A cooked-food sale was held April 15, and a card party was given at the Balboa home of Lillian Gant April 18. May 8 the Parlor will sponsor a pioneer tea, and May 22 a potluck dinner.

Members of Santa Ana will always recall the bigheartedness and unassuming sweetness of Grand President Anna Mixon Armstrong. Through her understanding of the Parlor's position after the quake, and through the courtesy of Grace No. 242 (Fullerton), No. 235 was privileged to join with the latter for the official visit.

President Initiates Three Daughters.

San Rafael—At a very impressive ceremony, Grand President Anna Mixon Armstrong paid her official visit to Marinita No. 198 April 10. Preceding the meeting, dinner was served, the banquet hall being beautifully decorated in red and gold. California missions formed the theme for the decorative scheme of the tables, in front of the Grand President being a replica of Mission San Rafael, and at intervals were mission bells, each representing one of the missions from San Diego to Sonoma, also tiny Indian tepees, Indians, friars, etc. California poppies were the flowers used, together with cacti, and the menus were in Spanish. The meeting hall was decorated in red and gold crepe paper, poppies and ferns. Other guests, in addition to representatives of numerous Parlors were: Junior Past Grand Evelyn I. Carlson, Grand Trustees Ethel Begley, Willow Borba, and Annie Thuesen, Grand Inside Sentinel Orinda Giannini, Past Grands Emma G. Foley, Margaret G. Hill and May C. Boldemann, Supervising Deputies Clytie Lewis, Edna Richter, Sadie Brainard and Alice Lane, Deputy Delphine Todt and eleven other deputies.

Grand President Armstrong was escorted to her seat of honor by Marinita's drill team while Antoinette Hecht sang "Our Wishing Song." Seven candidates were initiated, three of them being daughters of President Mary Zappetini, who presided in a very able manner. Mrs. Armstrong commended the officers for their work, and the Parlor for furthering the Order's projects. Numerous gifts were presented and refreshments were served at the meeting's close. The very efficient committee in charge of the affair was headed by Charter Member Anna Spinney.

Bride Showered.

Oroville—A large and enthusiastic crowd attended the vaudeville show of Gold of Ophir No. 190 March 30. Betty Boyle, dressed as a clown, acted as herald and carried the posters announcing the numbers. The committee that worked diligently for the success of the affair included Mae Belle Bills (chairman), Grand Trustee Florence D. Boyle, Verna Parker, Margaret Gilbert, Alta B. Baldwin. April 5 a hobo party proved very unique. Hattie McCoy received first prize for the best sustained character. A real mulligan stew was served following the stunts. In charge were Freda Cole (chairman), Alta Baldwin, Grand Trustee Boyle and Hattie Clark.

April 11, California day, under the chairmanship of Evelyn Joslyn, was observed at the Soroptimist Club, and a program in keeping with the occasion was presented. April 17 a shower was held at the home of Verna Parker for the Parlor's latest bride, Mae Mitchell. Beautiful gifts were presented her. Bridge was the evening's diversion. Mrs. Parker, Francis O'Brien and Mary Slisman were in charge.

(Additional N.D. News Page 15)

N.D.G.W. OFFICIAL DEATH LIST.

Giving the name, the date of death, and the Subordinate Parlor affiliation of all deceased members as reported to Grand Secretary Sallie R. Thaler from March 19, 1933, to April 19, 1933:

McHugh, Myrtle Littleton; February 15; Calis de Oro No. 206.
Lane, Lillian; March 9; Chispa No. 40.
Gundry, Mary V.; March 14; Orinda No. 56.
Gilbert, Sadie; February 21; Fern No. 123.
Wagner, Henrietta Louise; March 13; Joaquin No. 5.
Burley, Clara; March 25; Alta No. 3.
Rose, Frances Wells; March 7; Occident No. 28.
Stolle, Rose Olson; March 15, Alta No. 3.
Clark, Sarah Mooney; March 25; Forrest No. 86.
Walizer, Mildred O'Barr; January 19; Rudecinda No. 230.
Williams, Frances Dolores; March 30; Amapola No. 80.
Barnett, Nellie I.; March 22; Reina del Mar No. 126.

SAN FRANCISCO

PURITANISM, LEISURE, AND LACK OF normal fun and enjoyment are three factors definitely linked with vice and crime, Dr. Herman Adler, professor of psychiatry at the University of California, said in the course of a popular lecture on "Psychiatry and Crime" delivered recently in San Francisco. "In sex, alcohol and drugs, and gambling, factors leading to vice and crime, the common denominator is restlessness and discontent caused by the damming back of natural fundamental impulses. The spirit of adventure which is represented by gambling is a safe one, but it cannot be safely indulged in unless it is directed toward non-criminal goals. Gang activities do not furnish the only possible adventures today. Anything legitimate which counteracts in the individual the feeling that he is shut out and solitary, is desirable, and helps in preventing vicious demoralization. Group adventures, such as experiments in barter, are being worked out today."

Good times do not spell danger, Dr. Adler emphasized. It is the duty of public officials to make possible and organize such good times, the healthy use of leisure. Fun and play are especially desirable right now. Having a good time is much more desirable for the unemployed than to allow them to sit at home in solemn dejection or to wander about aimlessly in search for jobs which do not exist.

"In the changing economic order of things," he commented, "it is apparent that man is going to be faced with increasingly great amounts of time. Two groups will make adjustments without difficulty. The mentally-low-grade man will accept the situation with stolidity. The superior man, the artist, the genius, because of his great gifts, will escape, through his burning interests, the boredom of undirected activity. Between these two groups, however, is the great bulk of humanity which is neither so suggestible as to follow blindly, nor so superior as to be able to ignore lack of environmental compulsion. Individuals in this group are going to be at loose ends. As amount of leisure increases, boredom and frustration can be expected to increase."

RECEPTION FOR N.S. GRAND PRESIDENT.

The San Francisco N.S.G.W. Parlors, through the Extension of the Order Committee, sponsored a reception in honor of Grand President Seth Millington, in the auditorium of Native Sons Building April 28. There was an immense outpouring of members from all the San Francisco Bay district. It was a real oldtime recèption, with fun galore.

A wonderful program of ten high-class acts was presented, and Grand President Millington delivered a brief address. From the auditorium the crowd went to the banquethall, where "A Night at the Dutchman's Corner" was featured. The committee in charge of the evening included Martin Huber (chairman), Frank Foss (master of ceremonies), Charles J. Barry, Wilbur Doyle, Frank Lynch, Al Vlautin and Albert Anderson.

NATIVE DAUGHTER PARLORS BRIEFS.

Preceding the bridge game at the Home April 27, members of Alta Parlor No. 3 and their many friends enjoyed a delicious luncheon. May L. MacDonald, the charming hostess, was assisted by Grand Trustee Anna Thuesen, Angeline Vest and a corps of workers. Not to be outdone by the April committee, the social committee for May, under the leadership of Grand Trustee Thuesen and Mary Schultz, promises an out-of-the-ordinary affair.

Members of Gabrielle Parlor No. 139 turned out in numbers to greet Grand President Anna Mixon Armstrong on her official visit. Among the many visitors was Deputy Muriel Sandell. An Easter atmosphere reigned in the banquetroom. Alice Hornblower was chairwoman of the evening. Gabrille has just formed a drill team.

Golden Gate Parlor No. 158 is always busy with activities in the interest of the Order. It has adopted a baby girl, named Wilma Joy, and has agreed to supply her with milk until taken care of by new parents. Some of the Parlor members have formed a drill team, which recently sponsored a card party that was a great success.

NATIVE SON PARLORS BRIEFS.

Pacific Parlor No. 10 will have its annual picnic and outing at Wildwood, May 14. An elaborate program of games and races, with events included for both young and old, will be among the features of the day. A jazz orchestra will provide music for open-air dancing.

Stanford Parlor No. 76 had its spring dinner-dance April 22; Past President Frank F. Morris was the chairman. The card parties held the last Tuesday of each month continue to grow in popularity. The Parlor's annual picnic will be held June 4 at La Honda; Theo. Schmidt is in charge.

LOYAL CITIZEN PASSES.

George Tourny, president of the San Francisco Bank and a member of the Board of Park Commissioners, died March 21 at the age of 71, survived by a wife and two daughters. Commenting on his demise, Mayor Angelo J. Rossi (El Dorado Parlor No. 52 N.S.G.W.) declared:

"In the death of George Tourny, San Francisco has suffered a great loss. A man of the highest ideals, an executive of rare ability, a man of broad vision, intensely loyal to the interests of San Francisco, Mr. Tourny represented the highest type of American citizen. He gave his great efforts to San Francisco, the city he loved, as a member of the Park Commission for many years."

MEMORIES

(Continued from Page 12)

"opportunity" was theirs. She arrived with Lotta and found that she was to run a boarding house. So, close to Lola's "castle" the Crabtrees held forth in their business venture. Crabtree was happy. His wife did the work, and kept a well-filled table for him to adorn.

Soon Lotta is spending afternoons with Lola at the "big house." This woman of the world was greatly attached to the youthful and winsome Lotta. Lola had been on the stage. She danced well, and has histrionic skill. She recognized talent in the child, and found the youngster an apt and willing pupil. From her mother, Lotta had inherited a bent toward the stage. Soon pupil could outdance her teacher. She soon added singing to her accomplishments, and later banjo playing. How Lotta's mother could have permitted her daughter to have spent these hours with Lola is not quite conceivable, as we now view morals and environment, but that condition perhaps is explained by the thought that Mrs. Crabtree was an innocent woman in the ways of the world and it never dawned upon her the real truth of the rumors she must have heard concerning her neighbor. Or perhaps she knew her daughter was too young to have her morals affected.

The dancing lessons go on, and the mature woman and little child take to riding horseback together, Lola on her mount and Lotta on her pony. It is related that once, when they rode from Grass Valley to Rough and Ready, that there she stood the child on an anvil and Lotta amused a small audience with her songs. The delegates to the Grand Parlor of Native Sons may retrace the road over which Lola and Lotta rode in those forgotten days—days that were filled with delight for the child and companionable amusement for the elder woman. Lotta lived in Grass Valley until she was eight, Lola lived there in all about a year and a half.

From her debut at Rabbit Creek to her death at Boston in 1924, no effort will be made to trace the meteoric career of Lotta. She has left her trace too recent in California to recount the triumphs of a girl blessed by nature with smiling countenance, a pathos that was natural, and an aptness in singing songs that had both heart and music in her voice. Undoubtedly she was like the Al Jolson of a few years ago and sang songs with a tender appeal that brought out the best in them and left an audience with a tugging feeling at the heart strings. Perhaps it was the time and lack of competition that measured a great deal of her success. However, we cannot mitigate her greatness by taking this point of view, for when she grew older she likewise became a favorite on the Chicago stage, although she did not always register in New York, the place of her birth.

Lola left Grass Valley, lingered a time in San Francisco, and took boat to Australia. There she remained for a time, returning to New York, where she died comparatively young, at the age of 43, on January 7, 1861. Paralysis, perhaps the result of having trod the airy, fairy path for too long a spell, caused the death of this beautiful and talented woman. May both of them, the laughing girl and the woman who laughed at life and its codes, be remembered as Native Sons see the scenes their once living eyes beheld at Grass Valley.

This article cannot be concluded without reference to that miner poet, John Rollin Ridge, part Cherokee Indian, whose brilliant pen wrote undying poetry, for we remember that the skull which formerly housed that brain is resting in the eternal sleep in a Grass Valley cemetery. May the memory of this talented man be not forgotten in the lustre of his female contemporaries, and may we honor him as we read a fragment of his beautiful tribute to Mount Shasta:

"Far lifted in the boundless blue, he doth
Encircle with his gaze supreme, the broad
Dominions of the West, which lie beneath
His feet, in pictures of such sublime repose
No artist ever drew. He sees the tall, gigantic
Hills arise in silentness
And peace and in the long review of distance
Range themselves in order grand.
He sees the sunlight
Play upon the golden streams which through
The valleys glide.
He hears the music of the great and solemn sea,
And overlooks the huge old western wall
To view the birthplace of undying melody."

PIONEER NATIVES DEAD

(Brief Notices of the Demise of Men and Women born in California Prior to 1860.)

Mrs. Ella M. Parmer-Beers, born Sacramento City, 1857; died March 17, Santa Cruz City; husband and daughter survive.

Gene Terwilliger, born Siskiyou County, 1855; died March 19, Yreka.

Mrs. Hattie Dally-Ayala, born Santa Barbara County, 1857; died March 19, El Rio, Ventura County; husband and three sons survive.

Jefferson de Angelis, born San Francisco, 1859; died March 20, Orange, New Jersey State. He was a well-known actor.

Mrs. Matilda Peterson-Marvin, born Tuolumne County, 1858; died March 20, San Francisco.

Mrs. Jennie Berryessa-Howe, born Marin County, 1856; died March 21, Olema; four children survive.

Mrs. Alta Elizabeth Lee-Larison, born Plumas County, 1858; died March 24, Quincy; three children survive.

John L. Bannister, born Santa Clara County, 1857; died March 25, San Francisco; wife and five children survive.

Mrs. Mary Scully-Browning, born Sacramento County, 1858; died March 27, Berkeley, Alameda County; three children survive.

Frank M. Silva, born Los Angeles County, 1846; died March 28, Riverside City.

Henry Krim, born Calaveras County, 1855; died March 28, Coalinga, Fresno County; wife and four children survive.

Mrs. Frances Dolores Leon-Williams, born Amador County, 1852; died March 30, Sutter Creek; two sons survive. She was a charter member of Amapola Parlor No. 80 N.D.G.W. (Sutter Creek).

Charles C. Goald, born Alameda County, 1858; died April 1, near Danville, Contra Costa County; wife and daughter survive.

Mrs. Sophie Jeanette Rice-Davidson, born Siskiyou County, 1859; died April 1, King City, Monterey County; three sons survive.

Mrs. Jennie Agard-Westland, born Santa Clara County, 1856; died April 2, Berkeley, Alameda County; husband and daughter survive.

Mrs. Mary Jane Doyle, born Butte County, 1857; died April 7, Sacramento City; four children survive.

Mrs. Adelina Yorba-Carrillo, born Orange County, 1854; died April 11, near Placentia; four children survive.

Joseph Foster, born Sacramento City, 1853; died April 8, San Diego City. For twenty-three years he was a supervisor of San Diego County.

George A. Edgar, born Vallejo, Solano County, July 18, 1859; died April 8, Santa Ana, Orange County; wife and three children survive. He was affiliated with Santa Ana Parlor No. 265 N.S.G.W.

Mrs. Ada Fairfax McDaniel-Nichols, born Yuba County, 1857; died April 9, Los Angeles City; three daughters survive. She was a sister of Judge E. P. McDaniel (Marysville No. 6 N.S.G.W.).

Charles E. Isbell, born San Joaquin County, 1852; died April 11, Livingston, Merced County; wife and two children survive.

John Craig Taylor, born Sonoma City, August 25, 1849; died April 12, Downieville, Sierra County. He was affiliated with Downieville Parlor No. 92 N.S.G.W.

John Samuel Harrison, born Yuba County, 1856; died April 13, Dobbins; wife and daughter survive.

Samuel M. Murray, born Merced County, 1855; died April 15, Madera City; four children survive.

Edward F. Lennon, born San Francisco, 1855; died April 15, Red Bluff, Tehama County; two daughters survive.

Francis Mariam Coval, born Shingle Springs, El Dorado County, 1852; died there April 15; eight children survive.

Thomas Hardin Vestal, born Yuba County, 1854; died April 15, near Pittville, Shasta County; a wife and four children survive.

William Henry Seymour, born Nevada County, 1859; died April 18, Grass Valley.

Lawrence Evans, born Sacramento County, 1858; died April 19, Sacramento City.

NEVADA, CITY OF FOUR HILLS, GOVERNMENT SEAT NEVADA COUNTY, CALIFORNIA

John W. O'Neill

(Hydraulic Parlor No. 56 N.S.G.W.)

NEVADA CITY DIFFERS FROM ANcient Rome in one particular at least, whereas the city by the Tiber sat on seven hills, Nevada City finds four sufficient. Situated in a natural bowl in the mountains, surrounded by the foothills of the Sierras upon which grows the finest stand of second-growth timber in the world, this government-seat of Nevada County of close to 2,000 souls looks serenely down from an elevation of 2,500 feet to "the great Valleys of the Sacramento and the San Joaquin."

Some time in September 1849 the first habitation was built on the site of what is now Nevada City by Captain John Pennington, Thomas Cros and William McCaig, and a month later Dr. A. B. Caldwell built a log hut on the site of the present Washington schoolhouse and here opened the first mercantile establishment of what was destined to become a thriving mining community.

The town was first known as "Deer Creek Dry Diggings" or "Caldwell's Upper Store" until March 1850, when an election under Mexican law was called for the purpose of selecting an alcalde. A Mr. Stamps who, with his wife and sister and family had arrived in the fall of 1849, was elected. There were 250 votes cast, and on the day of the election it was decided to change the name of the camp. "Nevada" was chosen. It means "snowy" in Spanish, and was doubtless chosen because of the fact that the winter before had been one of deep snows. The selection has proved unfortunate, as later-day experience has shown loyal residents of Nevada City and Nevada County, because of the fact that several years later our sister state on the east was named "Nevada," and Nevada City and Nevada County have become associated with that state to the extent that many believe our city and county are a part of Nevada State.

The winter of 1849-50 was an exceedingly severe one, snow falling to the depth of several feet, and it found the hundreds of miners who were working the placers in the near-by streams ill prepared for it. The newly-built roads soon became impassible, and prices of provisions jumped to almost prohibitive demands.

In May 1850 rich deposits of gravel were found in the hills to the north of the town, and thousands of miners came as a result and the population increased rapidly. This brought about a change in the city government, and the authorities at Marysville [Yuba County], the county seat, ordered an election of justice of the peace to supplant the alcalde. A man named Olny, who had been secretary of state in Rhode Island, was elected and he had ways of his own when it came to dispensing justice. He died of tuberculosis a few months after his election, and in his dying hours asked that the "boys" take what money he had after paying funeral expenses and, as he expressed it, "have a jolly good time with it." This same spirit was typical of the men of that time.

The discovery in the gravels of the hills north of the town bearing high gold values, caused a stampede to that section, where a new town, called "Coyoteville," sprang up, lived its short life and became a memory when the gold was all worked out. The town got its name not from the coyote, but from the manner of mining, which consisted of digging shallow shafts or running short drifts, taking out the rich gravel and leaving holes that resembled the burrows of animals.

Nevada City has, in the course of its existence, had several forms of municipal government. In the summer of 1851 an election was held for officers of the newly-formed city created by special act of the Legislature. There were elected a mayor, ten aldermen and a large number of other officials. The first mayor was Moses F. Hoit. His administration, however, was destined to be short lived, for in less than a year the people demanded a change. The Legislature came to their relief, and the law creating the city was repealed, the officers ousted, and an $8,000 indebtedness which they incurred was never paid.

The city government has since operated under different enactments of the Legislature, but it is now being governed as a city of the sixth class, with five councilmen who select their presiding officer, who is designated "mayor," a clerk who is ex-officio assessor, a chief of police who is ex-officio tax collector, and other officials. The present council consists of R. J. Bennetts (mayor), A. Seaman, Fred C. Worth, C. R. Murchie and Wade Armstrong. George H. Calanan is clerk, Mrs. Emma Foley treasurer, and W. G. Robson chief of police.

NEVADA CITY, GOVERNMENT SEAT NEVADA COUNTY, CALIFORNIA.
From an exceptional photograph, taken from an airplane by Allen Chapman (Hydraulic No. 56 N.S.G.W.)

The city owns its own water distributing system, profits from which pay a large part of the expense of the city government. Water comes from the mountain areas and frequent tests made by the University of California have shown it to be almost one hundred percent pure. No disease germs have ever been found in it.

The Pacific Gas & Electric Co. had its beginning in Nevada City. The first organization was known as the "Nevada County Electric Power Co.", with its plant on the South Yuba River five miles from this city, water power coming from a dam farther up the stream. Its first office was in Nevada City. Later the "Bay Counties Power Co." was organized, took over the "Nevada County Electric Co." and built a power house at Colgate, on the Middle Yuba River twenty miles from this city, and from this power house was constructed the first long-distance power transmission line in the world, taking power to San Francisco. The Bay Counties Power Co. was absorbed by the Pacific. The first gas plant was established in the late fifties by Amariah Pierce. It was located in the lower end of Coyote street, and was operated for more than fifty years, when it was dismantled and gas now comes from a plant near Grass Valley.

Benjamin Blanton was the first postmaster of Nevada City. The postoffice was established early in 1851, near where the Nevada County Court House now stands. The city became then and has since continued to be the distributing center for mail to all surrounding towns.

Upon the establishing of the Nevada County government early in 1851 an election was held to determine the location of the county seat, and Nevada City won out over Grass Valley and Rough and Ready. The latter, now just a small village, came within eight votes of being declared the seat of county government.

The first court house, a wooden building, was destroyed in the fire of 1856. The next was of two stories, with the first story of stone and the upper story of brick. This was destroyed in the fire of November 8, 1863. Later the county rebuilt the court house, and purchased near-by lots on which wooden buildings had been erected, as a protection against another fire. To this building was, in 1900, added another story of brick, constituting the court house building of today.

Like all small mining towns, Nevada City has suffered from a number of disastrous fires. The first was on May 11, 1851, and the entire town of about 250 buildings was wiped out. July 19, occurred what is known as the "big fire of '56," which wiped out practically the entire town, including the court house and other public buildings. Ten lives were lost, seven of them people who took refuge in brick buildings, believing them fireproof. November 8, 1863, another big fire occurred, destroying most of the business section, with the court house.

The city now has two active fire companies: Nevada No. 1, organized June 12, 1860, and Pennsylvania No. 2, organized June 13, 1860. They constitute one of the most modern fire departments in the state. The city also has a firealarm system. The water system is capable of supplying fourteen large streams of water at the Plaza at one time, under 180-foot pressure.

One of the greatest disasters in the history of the city was the breaking of the Laird dam on Deer Creek, six miles above the town. The water came down the narrow stream with torrential force, flooding the lower part of the city and destroying a hotel, a theater and other buildings, and causing $50,000 damages.

The first church organized in Nevada City was the Congregational. Rev. James H. Warren was the pastor, and the organization was effected September 28, 1851. It was a small house on Main street built of shakes. Later a brick building was constructed and used by the church until it disorganized about twenty years ago. Of other churches organized in the early fifties, three remain today.

The city has a free library, the building having been dedicated in 1908. It is the successor of the Nevada Library Association and the Odd Fellows Library, and many of the 10,000 books now on the shelves were handed down from these original libraries. Almost from its beginning, Nevada City has had fraternal societies. The Masonic was the first, Nevada Lodge No. 13 having been organized in November 1850. Next was the Independent Order of Odd Fellows, organized in November 1853.

Nevada City has a splendid school system, with the elementary department housed in the Washington school building, and the high school. The latter, destroyed by fire April 6, 1931, was rebuilt. There are 300 pupils in the elementary schools, and 200 in the high school.

Nevada City is situated on both sides of Deer Creek, which flows through the city from east to west. Little Deer Creek makes its confluence with the larger stream in the lower section of the city, and farther south is Gold Run. In the early days all these streams yielded large quotas of gold to the miners who flocked here. Across Deer Creek are three bridges. The largest, now known as the Gait bridge, was built in 1862. It was a suspension bridge, but owing to faulty construction collapsed in June of that year when a heavy oxteam was crossing. It was rebuilt, and remained in use until 1895, when the present steel bridge was erected. The Main and the Broad streets bridges are also of steel construction.

The city has always had splendid newspaper service. The first paper was the "Nevada Journal," established in 1851. Later the "Nevada Democrat," "Gazette," "Transcript" and other papers were established. The "Transcript," the city's first daily, was established September 6, 1863, and continued publication until absorbed by the "Nevada County Miner" in 1900. None of the papers established in Nevada City are now being published. The "Morning Union" of Nevada City and Grass Valley, printed in the latter city, covers the field, and circulates throughout Nevada County and in southern Sierra County. The "Nevada City Nugget," published twice a week, is the only other newspaper.

Nevada City is a modern little city, with hotel, theater, schools, business buildings, churches, library, paved streets, gas, electricity, splendid water, sewer system, sanitarium, and other features that are not always found in cities much larger in size. While mining has been its chief support for many years, it is finding other sources of income. Its fine climate—with winters that are not severe, summers that are not hot, health conditions that are of the best,—is bringing here many summer tourists as well as permanent residents.

It is a distributing center for a wide area extending into southern Sierra County. It is the terminus of the Sacramento, Auburn, Grass Valley state highway, which connects with the Yuba Pass highway to Sierra County points and into the State of Nevada. This highway is through the most beautiful scenery in the world. The Tahoe-Ukiah highway also extends through this city from Ukiah on the west, connecting with the Victory highway to Lake Tahoe on the east. The city has an active Chamber of Commerce, with Fred F. Cassidy, prominent merchant, as president, and W. H. Griffith, experienced promotion man, as secretary. The headquarters are in the Elks Building, where a splendid display of Nevada County products may be found.

In conclusion, Nevada City bids the delegates to the Grand Parlor of the Native Sons of the Golden West convening in Grass Valley a hearty welcome, the typical welcome and hospitality that have come down from the Pioneers. The people urge the delegates to visit this city, get acquainted with its citizens, and investigate its possibilities for the establishing of "homes among the hills," where health and happiness reign supreme.

THE ROUGH AND READY CEMETERY.
(DR. T. RICARDO.)

I wandered through the graveyard
Of this once lively town;
I read the tombstone names
Of Pioneers who gained renown.

I've seen them in their vim and prime;
Seen them up, seen them down;
Seen them smile, seen them frown;
Seen them hue in red this "has been" town.

They came for gold. They got it!
Some kept the gold they found,
But in their wake none did take
An ounce beyond each grassy mound.

Know your home-state, California! Learn of its past history and of its present-day development by reading regularly The Grizzly Bear. $1.50 for one year (12 issues). Subscribe now.

"Friendship is the highest degree of perfection in society."—Montaigne.

"QUEEN OF THE SIERRA"
NEVADA CITY

Edward C. Uren
(Mining Engineer.)

NEVADA CITY DATES ITS EXISTENCE from October 1849, when a Dr. A. B. Caldwell built a store near Gold Run, a tributary of Deer Creek, which passes almost through the center of the city.

By the end of 1850 there were more than 250 buildings and the town was growing rapidly. Gold Run was well named, for it is claimed that the first placer miners who worked the bed of the stream cleaned up as much as a Troy-pound of gold in a day's work, which would represent in currency about $200. The first habitations were located on American Hill, on the west flank of the city, and the accounts of the first public hanging mentions the fact that fully 4,000 people were gathered here to view the spectacle. The site of the scaffold was the highest part of the hill; the victim being brought from the jail with a team and going through the ordeal with true frontier courage.

In 1856, Nevada City had its own flourmill capable of turning out 150 barrels of flour daily, and for several years this mill produced around 15,000 barrels yearly. It possessed a tannery which turned out about $2,000 worth of leather yearly, most of which was used locally for harness and sole leather, for Nevada was at this time the distributing point for many mountain towns and a great amount of teaming and freighting was carried on. In 1867, two daily papers were published here—the "Gazette" and the "Transcript."

The town was destroyed by fire four different times: in 1851, 1856, 1858 and 1863, but each time was rapidly rebuilt. After the fire of 1863 it was agreed that the streets were entirely too narrow and crooked, so they were laid out with what at the time was considered proper lines for modern needs. But the leading citizens of the time could not, of course, foresee the coming of the automobile and modern transportation. They lived in an era of rollicking, bustling good times; of spending and of pleasures of varied degree. Their community life was quite different from what we know today because they, figuratively, had to stay "put." They couldn't jump into a machine and go to outside points on the spur of the moment, because even a trip to Grass Valley, four miles distant, took about forty minutes, and thirty miles meant a whole day behind horses.

And yet, I have often wondered if the citizens of those days didn't get more real enjoyment out of life than we do today. It was but natural that the stay-at-home conditions of the times created more intimate friendships, better fraternalism and a more-active civic pride than exists in these dizzy times, when the ambition of the average human seems to be to spend most of his time away from home. It is true there was gambling, and the saloon was the most popular meetingplace, but I do not believe, indeed I know from my own remembrance of the latter days of pioneer life, that there was less delinquency among minors, that there was less petty crime, and that justice was usually more swift and certain than it is today.

Situated at an altitude of 2,500 feet and surrounded by evergreen hills of pine, spruce, cedar and oak, the city is as charming a spot as can be imagined. It has an excellent supply of pure mountain water fed by the snows of the high Sierra. Its reservoirs are 250 feet above the plaza and as many as fourteen fire streams have been playing at one time from its water mains, affording an ideal system of fire protection.

While the district is decidedly a mining community, it produces an abundance of the finest fruits, among which the Bartlett pear stands out in exceptional quality. Apples, plums and cherries do well at this altitude, and grapes have a much higher sugar content than those raised in the lowlands. Nevada County, in fact, used to produce annually from 10,000 to 20,000 gallons of wines which compared very favorably with the best wines of France and were sold as high as $2 per gallon by the cask.

The new Tahoe-Ukiah highway wends its way for four miles up the slopes of Harmony Ridge, in sight of the city, toward Truckee and the lake region. A most impressive sight of the city is gained from the higher elevations along the route, particularly at night. The ski course is situated nine miles above on the highway at an elevation of 4,200 feet. It is a matter of but twenty minutes ride to go from the usually snow-free streets of Nevada City into from three to four feet of snow in winter.

The thoroughness with which the early placer miner worked the main streams and creek bottoms of the surrounding country in search of the yellow metal is astonishing. Go where you will, anywhere within this area, on any ravine, and you will find evidences of walled-up rock and creek debris which has been overturned in an effort to reach the bedrock.

After the loose placers of the streams had been relieved of their gold, attention was directed to the ancient river channels—those old streams which derived their burden and their values from the ice age. One of them whose rugged scars are seen by all who enter Nevada City from the south, crossed 150 feet over the lowest part of the present Deer Creek basin and passed under the lava to the north of the city. It left large bodies of gravel along the edges to be washed by the hydraulic process, and the first hydraulic mining in Nevada County took place within, or close to, the north city limits on East Broad street.

That the oldtimers did not know at first what the origin of these deposits were is obvious from a quotation from the old "Nevada City Transcript" under date of January 4, 1865, which states: "The lead is of unexplored width, never found above or below certain elevations, and has a decided dip to the north. It averages 30 feet in thickness and the pay dirt about five." These old channels ran nearly east and west, and the first work done on them was apparently along the south rim, so that as they drove through this rim the bedrock dipped toward the lowest part of the trough. Later they found a corresponding rise toward the north rim. When the lava overburden became too deep to handle by hydraulicking, drifting was resorted to, and just north of the Manzanita hydraulic pit the channel has been literally honeycombed with stopes, which in the old Nebraska produced over $2,000,000 within a small area, being one of the richest placer diggings in the state.

Following the depletion of the placers attention was directed to the quartz veins of the district, which were very numerous. The first mill was built on the Gold Tunnel claim, within a quarter-mile of the business part of Nevada City, in 1852. In 1861 a mill was erected on the Murchie mine, which is now—seventy-two years later—being operated by a company of New Yorkers. The Murchie ores have their principal values in the sulphides which are now treated by flotation with an almost perfect recovery. The gold values could not be saved by the old amalgamation process.

Along the so-called "contact" west of the city, where the granite intrusion has thrust through the slate, the Champion and Providence mines were operated over a period of seventy years, and to a depth of 3,000 feet. There were 140 stamps dropping constantly down the creek and 300 men were employed. These old properties are again under option, and they will undoubtedly later be brought into production after a lapse of twelve years in idleness.

Nevada City Basin occupies an area of about fifteen square miles, and in the numerous veins which exist within it, it is safe to say that practically any and all of them contain pay shoots at some point. A good example in proof of this contention is the Hoge mine, one of the most successful and prosperous mines in this district. Starting on a ledge of but a few inches in thickness in the red, oxidized topsoil, at 300 feet it was a veritable bonanza with four to six feet of highly mineralized ore where the overlying surface gives no indications whatever of the riches beneath.

There are many properties idle today which were worked at a profit to a depth of 100 or 200 feet sixty or seventy years ago, when steam power, inefficient pumps and hand drilling only were available. The custom mill retained all the sulphides as a matter of practice; and in many mines the sulphides contain the greater proportion of the values. These properties were not abandoned by their owners or leasers because the values gave out, but rather owing to the handicap of the times. Some of them have a great deal of merit, and with modern flotation can be brought into efficient production.

Just what effect the gold embargo is going to have on gold mining is at the moment problematical, but it would seem that as gold is the very foundation of government credit not only here, but the world over, the effect will be to place gold at a premium, and if such a condition comes to pass, then Nevada City is destined to see an era of prosperity such as has not been known since the '50s.

HYDRAULIC
THE ALWAYS CO-OPERATING

(Compiled by Dr. C. W. CHAPMAN, at The Grizzly Bear's urgent request.)

ALTHOUGH THE NUMBER 56 DOES NOT suggest an early date nor a pioneer rating, yet it should be borne in mind that the first growth of any movement is likely to be rapid. So it was with the organization of the Native Sons of the Golden West.

Hydraulic Parlor No. 56 of Nevada City can be fairly included in that first rapid growth of the Order. It was instituted February 27, 1885, by Grand President John A. Steinbach. Fred H. Greely of Marysville No. 6 was Grand First Vice-president at that time. He is today the senior living Past Grand President, and he still holds the full measure of our affection and esteem.

Nineteen interested native sons met together in the very same hall which has all these years been headquarters for Hydraulic Parlor and determined to institute a parlor in Nevada City.

VERNE E. GLEASON, President.

DR. C. W. CHAPMAN, Recording Secretary.

Seventeen of them were present at the second meeting, and were initiated and granted a charter. LeRoy B. Johnson was the first president, and W. T. Morgan the first secretary. The charter remained open for signatures until fifty-four had been enrolled. There are, after forty-six years, seven of Hydraulic Parlor's charter members still on its rolls—William M. Richards, charter junior past president; J. F. Colley, charter financial secretary; C. W. Chapman, Marcus M. Baruh, Frank T. Nilon, George J. Hothersoll and Levi Kendrick. George A. Black, another charter member, is now affiliated with Santa Barbara Parlor No. 116.

Several names were proposed for the new Parlor, among them that of the chief industry which maintained Nevada City and the surrounding communities. Hydraulic mining, which had its birth within the corporate limits of Nevada City, was at that time being assailed with anti-debris injunction lawsuits, and as a gesture of loyalty to home and loved ones the name "Hydraulic" was chosen.

Hydraulic Parlor has been continuously active, rarely failing a regular meeting. It strongly advocates hewing close to the line and making the Order distinctly patriotic and historical in character. Imbued with civic pride, it has frequently been the moving spirit in public-welfare undertakings, and on numerous occasions the community has looked to Hydraulic and to Laurel Parlor No. 6 N.D.G.W. to conduct its major affairs, either of a social or a business nature.

Hydraulic Parlor contributed sixty-one, two-fifths of its membership, to the American forces in the World War. Its service flag contains four gold stars, four silver stars and one silver star traced with blue. The Parlor remitted dues for all members during their period of service, and kept them eligible for benefits.

It was Hydraulic Parlor that started the fund for the Pioneer monument at Donner Lake, Nevada County, with a subscription of $100. It set that pace because it was specifically the Native Sons and the Native Daughters who should pay the tribute. The sentiment to pay tribute to the sacrifices made by the Pioneers is similar, and is typified by the historic "Lone Grave," located within the jurisdiction of Hydraulic, and the Parlor is endeavoring to fulfill its duty by fostering this enterprise.

Hydraulic Parlor has twice been host to the Grand Parlor, once in 1887 and again in 1898, both sessions being held in Nevada City. The Grand Parlor of 1887 consisted of 147, including delegates and officers. It was entertained at an expense of but $863.45, financed as follows: proceeds from a public ball, $563.00; subscriptions of Hydraulic Parlor members, $135.50; deficiency supplied from Hydraulic Parlor funds, $164.95. Carl B. Schwartz, now but one month deceased, was the Parlor's president then, and Dr. C. W. Chapman was then, as he is today, the recording secretary. At the 1898 Grand Parlor, consisting of 239 members all told, Hydraulic Parlor's delegates opposed limiting membership in the Order to those born in California prior to 1900 and their descendants born in California. They also opposed the adoption of a permanent meetingplace.

Hydraulic Parlor has had the distinction of providing from its membership three grand officers: D. E. Morgan and Fred L. Arbogast, who served several terms as Grand Trustees, and jovial Joe V. Snyder, who was, at the time of his passing, a Past Grand President. Its delegates have also, in many cases, served on important Grand Parlor committees.

It is the proud privilege of Hydraulic Parlor this year to serve, as helpful neighbor, with Quartz Parlor No. 58 of Grass Valley, which is host to the 1933 Grand Parlor. It is in small measure a return for many like favors rendered, and for nearly half a century of cordial and fraternal pooling of interests by the two Parlors.

The present officers of Hydraulic Parlor are: Verne E. Gleason, president; Arthur W. Davis, senior past president; Frank Davis, junior past president; Walter W. Watters, first vice-president; Raglan Tuttle, second vice-president; Leonard C. Foote, third vice-president; Dr. C. W. Chapman, recording secretary; Miles D. Coughlin, financial secretary; Thos. G. Richards, treasurer; R. A. Eddy, marshal; R. L. P. Bigelow, C. J. Scheemer, C. G. Sweeney, trustees; E. J. Baker, inside sentinel; E. J. Kilroy, outside sentinel; Walter H. McLeod, organist.

PREPARE

(Continued from Page 17)

rearing. Go into any county where children have been placed for adoption, and the citizens will tell you that they have known boys and girls who have reached the age when it can be said of them that they are a credit to their foster-parents, to their county, and to California. Other citizens will go farther than that, and point to a second generation of healthy, normal children on their way to good citizenship,—your Central Committee are "grandparents now."

Unquestionably, one will find criticism here and there. A friend may not have been given a baby when a member thought he should have one. A child may not have developed as those who are interested or responsible expect him to. Some of the local committees may forget the prerogatives of the Central Committee in their responsibility for the placing and supervising of every child. Some may question the need of the required number of workers, or the salaries paid, without comparing them with those of other social workers in the same field. But no one seems inclined to attack the standards or the character of the work that is accomplished, and everyone agrees that caring for the homeless child is a fitting obligation for the men and women of California to take wholeheartedly and enthusiastically upon themselves.

When conquering Caesars, flushed with pilfered pelf,
Would placate plebes, for love of show and self,
They showered gold from gilded equipage,
As we do now—but call it patronage.

When feudal barons, home from raiding ride,
Would scatter largesse thru the countryside,
They shared the booty from their brigandage,
As we do now—in party patronage.

In modern politics or war's turmoils,
Still to the victor must belong the spoils;
What is the difference, any place or age,
If it be plunder—or just patronage!

—George S. Holmes.

"QUEEN OF THE YUBA"---DOWNIEVILLE

Ross F. Taylor
(Downieville Parlor No. 92 N.S.G.W.)

DOWNIEVILLE! TO THE CALIFORnian the very name is fraught with romance. Gold, adventure, violence, comedy and love, the camp-followers of pioneer boom days, have more than filled the history of this amazing eighty-four-year-old California town, and more than in any other camp of the placer mining region are the evidences of the days of gold still spread before the eyes of the visitor. For Downieville has never become "civilized." The same old stone buildings that housed the first businesses of the Pioneers are still huddled along her crooked main street, looking with disdain at the few plate-glass fronts that have failed to modernize the ancient thoroughfare.

Downieville is old. The first miners arrived in the summer of 1849, and found here on the forks of the Yuba the richest spot on that unbelievably rich stream. The town began to grow immediately. For a few months it was known as "The Forks of the Yuba" or the "Forks." It was not until 1850, when the four populous "flats" along the stream were consolidated into one town that the name "Downieville" was adopted. Thus did the metropolis of the "northern mines" honor her discoverer and founder, Major William Downie, Pioneer, miner and historian, who was the first White man to plunge his gold-pan into the waters that flow through the town. Within twelve months, five thousand men were wresting a fabulous living from these waters, and in population Downieville was one of the first seven towns in California. Two alcaldes ruled her courts. Scores of saloons and dancehalls lined her narrow streets. Two newspapers dispensed the news of the world to the hundreds of lonely miners late from the "east."

In 1852, the rapidly growing community began to feel the isolation from Marysville, the county-seat of Yuba County, of which Sierra County was then a part. Seventy miles by rough trail down the Yuba was too far to travel to the seat of justice, despite the fact that the stream was said to be so thickly populated that news could be carried from Downieville to Marysville by word of mouth in less than one hour. So, in April 1852, Sierra County, with Downieville as the county-seat, was carved from the mother county. For one year the hall of justice was the famous Craycroft saloon. In 1853 the three supervisors of the county ordered the building of a court house. D. G. Webber undertook to put up the building for a few dollars under $13,000, and in the summer of 1854 he had completed it. It was not until 1855, however, that the supervisors ordered the county court moved into the new building. With but few alterations, this old court house still houses the superior court of Sierra County—the oldest court house in California still in use.

—Courtesy Mountain Messenger.

By 1856, the population of the new county had reached a huge figure. That year 5,404 votes were cast for president. In Downieville, fourteen attorneys were practicing, and six physicians were busy with the ills of the rough mining town. Visitors from Los Angeles County will please be advised that in that same year, 1856, the village of Los Angeles supported but eleven lawyers and four doctors, and the entire county of Los Angeles, now the most populous in the Golden State, cast but 1,377 votes for president. Alameda County did but little better, so the relative importance of the roaring "Forks of the Yuba" may well be imagined.

Through the turbulent sixties, the prosperous seventies and the booming eighties the town roared on. Three fires swept her clean, excepting for the few stone buildings that still stand, sole survivors of a hectic past. But no mere fire served more than to retard for a brief space the young city. Each time she arose from her ashes better built than before. Each time her loyal miners returned again to their diggings, pouring their golden streams into the coffers of the nation, building toward the $200,000,000 that has been credited to Sierra County.

Then came the late '80s, and the injunction. And the town that had defied the fire demon and sneered at floods bowed before a catastrophe greater than anything she had ever before been required to meet—the throttling of her great hydraulic mines by legislation. This was Downieville's deathknell. But a day ago, her hills were crumbling before the streams from a hundred giants,—stripped to the bedrock for the gold that lay mingled with the earth. Then,—silence. But a day ago, scores of prosperous mining camps held the homes of care-free miners and their families. Then,—solitude.

The "Queen of the Yuba" never recovered from the blow dealt her only industry. Men by the hundreds left the stricken town. Building after building closed the iron shutters. Downieville's former glory had faded. Let it not be supposed that the town became deserted. Hundreds engaged in branches of mining other than hydraulic remained, and still remain, happy dwellers in a happy land. But the old Downieville, that once was reckoned with in the world of finance and politics, was no more. The resumption of hydraulic mining has done much to draw investors again to this region of gold; modern highways have brought their hundreds to see and to exclaim over this famous old camp. All that has left Downieville is her once great population. The spirit of '49 is still here; the same buildings are here, the same friendliness, the same gentle lawlessness lives in the hearts of the sons and daughters of the Pioneers.

Today, the visitor from the outside may see in Downieville the ghost of 1850. Even if the highway leading from Grass Valley fifty miles to the Sierra County town led through a drab waste the trip would be worth while. But it is made doubly interesting by the beautiful scenery that spreads lavishly on both hands all along the fifty delightful miles. The three historic forks of the Yuba River, the old mining towns of North San Juan and Camptonville along the route, the Depot Hill hydraulic mine in operation nearly eighty years, at the very roadside just within the borders of Sierra County, make the trip one not soon to be forgotten. And, a brief two hours from Grass Valley, the visitor swings around Cannon Point and looks down upon Downieville. World-traveler though he may be, he has never before had such an introduction to a village. No description could even begin to do it justice—it must be seen; and it will never be forgotten.

Among the interesting sights offered the visitor are the eighty-year-old court house, with its historic court-room; the gallows upon which two murderers of the four legally executed in Sierra County were hanged; the hydraulic diggings reaching to the very edge of the court house square, where more than $5,000,000 in gold was mined; and the ancient plant of the "Mountain Messenger," the third oldest weekly newspaper in California. The "Messenger" was not originally published in Downieville, but it has been a Sierra County institution since 1854. The site of the bridge where the Spanish woman was hanged in 1851 still attracts visitors to whom the recital of the regrettable lynching is new.

The ancient fire-carts, new in 1858, and then the pride of Downieville's fire department; the old fire-bell; the St. Charles Hotel, the oldest business in Downieville, with the rambling old front on Main street unchanged for seventy years; the tiny old churches and the fire-scarred stone buildings, hold the interest of all who love the memory of early California. Visitors may look from the bridge to the old Tin Cup Diggings, where in 1850 each of four partners received for his share of the day's work, a tin cup level-full of gold dust.

In the museum of the Native Sons and Native Daughters, housed in a stone building of forgotten age, have been gathered many relics of Down-

A STREET IN DOWNIEVILLE, SIERRA COUNTY.

leville's past in a most interesting exhibit. Let the Californian of the south, the bay or the great valleys lay aside for a few hours the cares of 1933 and return to 1853. Go back eighty years in the twinkling of an eye, and when you return again to your busy modern cities, depression will seem less real, business cares less heavy. For you will have seen peace that once was roaring activity—Downieville!

SIERRA COUNTY PARLORS.

Downieville Parlor No. 92 N.S.G.W. was instituted August 26, 1886, with twenty charter members, by District Deputy G. W. Starr. F. R. Wehe was the first president, and H. W. Orear the first secretary. The present officers include: J. M. McMahon, past president; Frank H. Turner, president; James Sutherland, first vice-president; Earl Rickard, second vice-president; A. J. Ponta, third vice-president; H. S. Tibbey, secretary; Lee Bessler, marshal; Ralph Costa, inside sentinel; Paul Smith Jr., outside sentinel. The Parlor now has a membership of fifty-two.

Golden Nugget Parlor No. 94 N.S.G.W., at Sierra City, was instituted October 18, 1886, with fifteen charter members, by District Deputy G. W. Starr. George Wood was the first president, and Charles Rich the first secretary. Elmer Thompson is the present president, and Arthur R. Pride the present secretary. The Parlor now has a membership of eighteen.

There are also two Native Daughter Parlors in Sierra County—Naomi No. 36 at Downieville, and Imogen No. 134 at Sierraville.

ADMISSION TO SISTERHOOD STATES

(Continued from Page 16)

the fertile valleys of the Sacramento and San Joaquin stretch for hundreds of miles to north and south, while southern California is golden in wealth and unrivaled in progress. To the east, rising from the valleys, the lofty, snow-capped Sierras gather the life-giving waters of winter, which are stored in canyons and ravines, and in summer released to fertilize and beautify the plains below. Great power plants also gather the electric forces, conserved by the waters of these mountains, and distribute them to the myriad industries which have sprung up throughout the State.

Orange and lemon groves, fruitful orchards, boundless fields of grain and alfalfa, dairy and stock farms are seen on every hand. Herds of the finest bred cattle and flocks of sheep graze o'er valley and hillside, and here have been sired the fastest race horses of the world. Splendid forests of redwood, pine, spruce, fir and other timber clothe the mountain sides, while the magnificent sequoia gigantea, the largest tree and the oldest living object in the world, has for thousands of years lifted its green boughs to the bluest of heavens. No country excels California in the number of well-paved highways, nor do roads anywhere open up more beautiful vistas of coastline, valleys, hills, mountains, streams and lakes. In value of farms and farm products and orchards, and in the percapita wealth of the people living therein, California excels all other states. With the growth of agriculture, manufacturing and commerce have kept pace. Within the manufacturing districts of San Francisco and Los Angeles the yearly value of goods produced has reached a figure of approximately $2,500,000,000, while in the field of commerce the total value of cargoes, foreign and domestic, shipped each year from the ports of these two cities exceeds even that figure.

Over and above all this, however, we place the loyalty of her citizens. Our flag protects the home, the factory and the workshop, the sailor on sea and the man who toils on land; it floats above our schools and universities; learning finds a refuge beneath its folds and knowledge and invention go with it to the bounds of the earth. It reflects the character and nobility of American citizenship. The enemies of organized government, those who preach the overthrow of law and order by force and terrorism, the communist and the anarchist, should find no home on the soil of California. We want none here but loyal men, the lovers of one flag—the American Flag!

For our splendid inheritance of free government, gratitude must be aroused in the hearts of the citizens of this land. The young men and young women in every university, college and school of California should be taught that it is a great privilege and blessing to be an American citizen, understanding and appreciating what constitutional liberty and representative government have done for America. It is for this purpose that the sons of California have associated themselves in a fraternity [the Order of Native Sons of the Golden West], and Admission Day is a day upon which to recall to memory the Pioneers, to pledge ourselves anew to the defense of the Constitution and law and order, and to the crushing out of treason, disloyalty and terrorism in this land of ours.

Grizzly Bear

JUNE — THE ONLY OFFICIAL PUBLICATION OF THE NATIVE SONS AND DAUGHTERS OF THE GOLDEN WEST — 1933

Featuring

GENERAL NEWS OF INTEREST CONCERNING ALL CALIFORNIA, and ORDERS NATIVE SONS and NATIVE DAUGHTERS

Price: 15 Cents

Welcome, Native Daughters

Official Headquarters

Grand Parlor

HOTEL LEAMINGTON

RATES

EUROPEAN PLAN — DAILY

Single Room and Shower...$2.50
Single Room and Bath......$2.50
Double Room and Shower...$3.00 ($1.50 per person)

RATES

EUROPEAN PLAN — DAILY

Double Room and Bath.....$3.00 ($1.50 per person)
Twin Beds with Shower.....$4.00 ($2.00 per person)
Twin Beds with Tub........$4.00 ($2.00 per person)

Greetings to the
Native Daughters:

It is a matter of a great deal of pride to the Hotel Leamington to be selected again as official headquarters for the GRAND PARLOR, NATIVE DAUGHTERS OF THE GOLDEN WEST, and we are all looking forward to an especially fine gathering.

Kindly keep in mind that Hotel Leamington will be the center of all activities during the sessions and also that we are caring for the various dinners and numerous other affairs in connection with the meeting.

From this, you will readily see the advantage of being established in the same hotel.

In specifying the type of reservations you desire, be sure to note that our rates conform with existing conditions and that you have a wide range of accommodations from which to make a selection. We will obviously be thoroughly filled, and for this reason we are obliged to set aside room accommodations in the order of receipt of individual reservation.

Please let us have your room reservations by return mail.

Sincerely,

HOTEL LEAMINGTON

OAKLAND, CALIFORNIA

ughters

Grand

Parlor

"FRATERNITY HAS NOT FAILED, NOR WILL IT FAIL, SO LONG AS LOVE, DEVOTION AND FAITH EXIST!"

Anna Mixon Armstrong
GRAND PRESIDENT N.D.G.W.

A HELPFUL EXPERIENCE IS TO pause occasionally and take stock of any enterprise in which we may be engaged, and balance our accomplishments against possible failures; and, from the balances thus cast, point the way for the future.

This is a necessary procedure in commercial affairs, and is equally important in fraternal. In our retrospective review of our Order of Native Daughters of the Golden West we perceive certain signs that indicate a marking of time, while other indications point to a much brighter record. I shall briefly consider both aspects.

The far-reaching industrial condition, where depression laid its heavy hand upon enterprise, has had its effect upon all fraternal organizations, ours among the rest. Little growth in membership may be noted, but growth in fidelity and spirit has been outstanding, which, after all, is the important matter.

A need for helpfulness to those whom circumstances have embarrassed and saddened, has accentuated and quickened a sometimes latent consciousness of mutual dependence.

Out of this reawakened and revivified innate spirit of human kindness has budded, blossomed and fruited a wonderfully close tie of sisterly concern among our membership, evident in every Parlor of our Order. Verily, adversity has its compensations!

This spirit of true fraternity leads me to express the opinion that the suggestion of some to make of our Order a mere historical society, stripped of those fraternal ties which bind men and women into closely allied cults, would have been a real calamity under the recent situation in which we have been placed.

To comfort, to soothe and to care for our own, is an inherent instinct. To know and feel that these Native Daughters are our own, creates a desire to co-operate with and for the well-being of the whole. Fraternity has not failed, nor will it fail, so long as love, devotion and faith exist!

We welcome the aid of all those who are adopted sons and daughters of California. Their interest in our history and traditions need not suffer, simply because California's daughters by birth elect to maintain a family relationship. Family life holds closely to its own, but it extends the welcoming hand to all who seek its friendship.

Let us maintain our Order on the very highest fraternal plane it is possible to attain. Then are we honoring those Pioneers whom we revere.

The projects of our Order have not suffered during these unsettled months. It would appear from the very fact that unfavorable conditions prevailed, girded our members to extra efforts to "carry on." Their response to every appeal has been most heartening to the officers of the Grand Parlor. In no instance have our humanitarian projects been allowed to suffer. The unflagging interest, state-wide, has been an inspiration that has carried over the hard places all those charged with authority.

Veterans welfare work has had a deeper personal significance than ever before. If money was lacking, then was individual service more pronounced and intensive. After all, the man or woman, hospital bound, gets more real benefit and pleasure from personal contact and heart sympathy than from the few cents or dollars contributed, essential as they are. A kindly word, a friendly handclasp, will roll away the cloud of desolation as will nothing else! A magazine, an interesting book, a handmade convenience of some sort, how cheering they are. Our Daughters have stressed that sort of work this year. They have been happy in doing it, they have made others happy by doing it.

Our work for homeless children is outstanding among all like efforts in our State. Real homes have been found for real children in scores of instances. Imagine a purely historical society in the role of child welfare. To our fraternity, this is one of the most cherished projects.

MRS. ANNA MIXON ARMSTRONG OF WOODLAND, GRAND PRESIDENT N.D.G.W.

Women's hearts are animated by the same sense of responsibility as men's, but it goes further; there is a maternal instinct that sanctifies the home, that sets it apart as a shrine, as the holy mecca from which shall radiate the influences that make for progress and the happiness of the human race. Our Order is large enough of heart, earnest enough of purpose, and virile enough in energy to accept, as a part of its creed, the care of veterans and of children and, at the same time, continue in its accepted work of assisting in the preservation of pioneer landmarks, traditions and sentimental lore. In fact, we are firm in our belief that we can succeed in all our purposes far better as a fraternity than as a historical society.

Our State Home in San Francisco stands as a monument to the energy and loyalty of our entire membership. It was a mighty financial undertaking, but the enthusiasm of its proponents was not to be denied, and now it stands a finished product, substantial, imposing and fully paid for. It is the center of our activities whence our Secretary keeps in touch with each Parlor, where homelike surroundings are afforded those of our members who, through misfortune, may find solace and comfort during the down-hill time of life.

A portion of the Home is also dedicated as a real abiding place for younger members who are circumstanced to pay their way. These young women have mostly come to the metropolis from interior points to seek congenial and remunerative employment, but through lack of acquaintance are, to that extent, dependent. In the Home they find a splendid environment and are afforded every bodily comfort. The Home is a fine adjunct of our work.

It may not be generally known that our Order has, by purchase, acquired a tract of redwoods in Humboldt County. It is forty-six acres in extent and lies contiguous to the famed Redwood Highway, one of the most noted thoroughfares in America. These immense redwood trees, the oldest living things on earth, stand now dedicated to the memory of the Pioneer Men and Women who laid the foundation on which has been builded our State of California.

The members of our Order are also deeply interested in education, and have been a factor in promoting the proper observance of "school week" in every community in which a Parlor is located.

We are also maintaining and sustaining three college scholarships in the State, one at Mills College, one at the University of California at Los Angeles, and one at the University of California at Berkeley.

Because of this activity of our Order, a number of deserving young women have become equipped to go out into the state and impart knowledge and good citizenship to others. The stressful times have not been allowed to interfere with this important purpose of our Order. The progress of these girls is watched with the keenest interest by all members of the several Parlors.

The preservation of the landmarks of early California is stressed in our ritual, and actively practiced by our fraternity. To perpetuate the sentiment and reduce to print as much as possible the ancient lore and song of the mining camp is not neglected. In fact, a number of our members are making that their major activity. In a number of places in the Mother Lode country are located museums where have been accumulated numberless articles of pioneer day interest. Most of these museums are the result of interest manifested by members of our Order.

Especially are we interested in the old Spanish missions given to us through the religious devotion of the early padres. Every year each Parlor contributes of its funds to assist in their rehabilitation and preservation. We look upon them as a glorious heritage, and are proud to join with other forces in saving them for posterity.

Our Order is ever active in marking places of historic interest. We have marked scores of such places up and down the State with suitable bronze plaques properly inscribed and permanently set. It has been my pleasure this year to thus mark a dozen or more such places. All this work is accounted one of our major projects, and no doubt will continue as the years go by.

In my travels over the State during the year on my official visitations I have been

(Continued on Page 4)

CALIFORNIA HAPPENINGS OF FIFTY YEARS AGO

Thomas R. Jones

(COMPILED EXPRESSLY FOR THE GRIZZLY BEAR.)

THE FIRST CARLOAD OF CALIFORNIA deciduous fruit was shipped to the East from Vacaville, Solano County, June 12, 1883, in a ventilated fruit car attached to a passenger train. The fruit was expected to ripen during the five-day trip, and to be put on the market in edible condition. The event was a newspaper headliner. Refrigerator cars and trains came later.

C. W. Ayers, Fresno County farmer, attended June 11 a meeting in San Francisco of the State Railroad Commission called to hear arguments, pro and con, on the proposed reduction of railroad freight and passenger rates. He began a tirade which one of the commissioners attempted to stop. So, Ayers drew from his pocket a generous assortment of overripe eggs and leveled them at the commissioner. The bombarding farmer was arrested, but not prosecuted.

During the first fortnight of June, thermometers in the valleys of the state went to 105 degrees in the shade.

The cornerstone of the new State Fair Pavilion at the corner of Fifteenth and M Streets, Sacramento City, was laid June 5. Preceding the ceremony there was a large parade, one conspicuous division of which was made up of the Society of California Pioneers and Sacramento Parlor No. 3 N.S.G.W.

Stephen H. Meek, a pioneer citizen of Siskiyou County, made the following statement: "The McCloud River was first explored by John McCloud, a factotum of the Hudson Bay Company, in 1828. It was named after him by myself and the other trappers in 1830." An effort was being made by a number of newspaper editors of the day to change the name of the river to "Cloud."

The English dam, built on the boundary line of Sierra and Nevada Counties to impound slickens and furnish a water supply for the mines below it on the Middle Fork of the Yuba River, broke June 18. Several miners were drowned, and everything movable on both banks of the river for forty miles was swept away by the 100-foot-high flood which rushed along at ten miles an hour. The flood reached Marysville, Yuba County, in eight hours, but was there reduced to a hight of four feet. It broke a levee near Marysville, and flooded 5,000 acres of grain.

This dam, said to be the largest in the United States, was 400 feet long and 100 feet high. It cost $100,000 to build, and the flood resulting from its breaking did property damage estimated at $300,000.

The California and Oregon Railroad, being constructed north from Redding, Shasta County, cut through a bed of gravel on the bank of Backbone Creek, June 20. An oldtimer prospected the gravel and in two hours panned $50 in gold dust.

A vein of gold-bearing quartz found this month in the Sierra east of Fresno City had a vein of moss agate paralleling it.

Harry Sutton uncovered a rich quartz vein one mile from the American River, opposite Folsom, Sacramento County.

Billy Miner, a Butte County prospector, found a pocket on Butte Creek from which he took $6,000 in gold dust in two days.

An epidemic of cholera morbus caused the deaths this month of a score of Red Bluff, Tehama County, children.

Steamships arriving during the month from China brought $2,000,000 worth of opium, all consigned to Chinese merchants of the state.

Counting the "cash on hand" in the Alameda County treasury, a shortage of $50,000 was discovered. Where the missing dollars had gone, the county treasurer did not know.

William Jones was hanged in the Lakeport, Lake County, jail June 15 for the murder of his son-in-law during a drunken quarrel in May 1882. Before the noose was adjusted, he delivered a temperance lecture.

Chinese laborers on the California and Oregon Railroad to the number of 1,700, grading the roadbed north of Redding, Shasta County, struck for higher wages June 25, and the railroad temporarily stopped its climb along the Sacramento River. They were being paid $1.25 a day, but wanted "two bittee" more. The company issued the ultimatum, "no workee, no eatee," meaning that unless the Chinks went back to work, no grub would be hauled to them. They ate rice, principally, and they had to get it by rail.

Eugene Casserly, in San Francisco since the '50s, died June 14 at the age of 61. In 1868 he was elected United States Senator from California.

The stage from Ione to Jackson, Amador County, was stopped June 3 by a lone highwayman who took the expressbox, containing about $1,000.

Daggett, San Bernardino County, burned June 5, a business block in San Mateo City was destroyed by fire June 15, causing a loss of $20,000, and Fall River Mills, Shasta County, burned June 24, causing a $40,000 loss.

Fire in San Francisco June 20 destroyed a four-story brick building at the corner of Post and Kearny streets housing the city's leading drygoods emporium and other firms. The loss was estimated at $600,000.

Wm. Keeley was sunstruck while haying near Altamont, Alameda County, June 7, and died.

An infuriated bull on the Colonia Rancho in Ventura County fatally gored Mrs. Michard Kauffman, June 4.

Robert Shearer, 13-year-old lad employed in a minor capacity in a Truckee, Nevada County, sawmill, was June 20 caught in a flywheel making 200 revolutions a minute, and whirled to his death.

Two Red Bluff, Tehama County, editors, Abraham Townsend and Charles F. Montgomery, began a campaign of personal abuse in their respective weekly newspapers. June 10 they met accidentally in a saloon, and Montgomery shot and fatally wounded Townsend.

Anson Stone, a lad gathering mussels at Angel Point, near Santa Cruz City June 18, was engulfed by a huge wave and drowned.

Mrs. M. A. Davis, attempting to extinguish a grass fire near her Rocklin, Placer County, home June 12, was fatally burned.

"FRATERNITY HAS NOT FAILED"

(Continued from Page 3)

impressed at the responsibilities the Parlors have accepted from their localities. Particularly is this true in the smaller communities. Just as an instance, I have in mind a small Parlor in a mountainous district. There the Parlor takes the place of the usual chamber of commerce. It promoted a town library, and has seen it finally located in a fireproof memorial building of attractive architecture and its shelves filled with a wealth of good books; it takes the place of the usual parent-teacher association for the schools; it promotes and directs annual Arbor Day exercises, and has been instrumental in planting many trees; it supports a garden club; it assists a non-denominational religious organization; in fact, it is the leading force in its locality. It is not dictatorial, it is merely helpful. I go to this length in this instance so that you may the more readily understand just what I mean when I say, that a Native Daughters Parlor is an asset to every community where it is located!

We feel that our fathers and mothers, back through the line of ancestry, have placed a torch in our hands that is to light the way for these present-day efforts of ours which, in turn, may write history of worth-while import for those who come after us.

We, as Native Daughters, believe that California is still in the building, and that we of the present time are numbered among its builders. We believe that character must be wrought into the edifice, and that the fellowship of fraternity must adorn it. We believe that religious faith, without sectarianism, must be maintained. We believe that the laws of our State should be respected. We believe that society should be maintained upon a high plane.

For the attainment of these things, we believe organization is required, and with all our hearts we believe the Order of the Native Daughters of the Golden West is peculiarly well fitted to take a commanding place.

Fraternally, we are drawn closely together, and thus, in a spirit of true and friendly comradeship, we are better equipped to accomplish our aims than under any other type of organization.

Under our banner, through our ritual, with our signs and even with our passwords, we expect to carry on all the projects in which we are interested. As time goes on and the need arises, we no doubt shall add others that need succor.

For those things we stand firm, and for them shall we continue to strive!

The Grizzly Bear Magazine

The ALL California Monthly

OWNED, CONTROLLED, PUBLISHED BY GRIZZLY BEAR PUBLISHING CO., (Incorporated)

COMPOSED OF NATIVE SONS.

HERMAN C. LICHTENBERGER, Pres.
JOHN T. NEWELL RAY HOWARD
WM. I. TRAEGER LORENZO F. SOTO
CHAS. R. THOMAS HARRY J. LELANDE
ARTHUR A. SCHMIDT, Vice-Pres.
BOARD OF DIRECTORS

CLARENCE M. HUNT
General Manager and Editor

OFFICIAL ORGAN AND THE ONLY OFFICIAL PUBLICATION OF THE NATIVE SONS AND THE NATIVE DAUGHTERS GOLDEN WEST.

ISSUED FIRST EACH MONTH.
FORMS CLOSE 20th MONTH.
ADVERTISING RATES ON APPLICATION.

SAN FRANCISCO OFFICE:
N.S.G.W. BLDG., 414 MASON ST., RM. 302
(Office Grand Secretary N.S.G.W.)
Telephone: Kearney 1223
SAN FRANCISCO, CALIFORNIA

PUBLICATION OFFICE:
309-15 WILCOX BLDG., 2nd AND SPRING,
Telephone: VAndike 6234
LOS ANGELES, CALIFORNIA

(Entered as second-class matter May 29, 1918, at the Postoffice at Los Angeles, California, under the act of August 24, 1912.)

PUBLISHED REGULARLY SINCE MAY 1907
VOL. LIII (53). WHOLE NO. 314

BIRDS

(With apologies to Joyce Kilmer.)
(ESTHER CRONE.)

I think that I have never heard
A song as sweet as from a bird.
A bird that sits up on a pole
And carrols forth his very soul;
Upon whose head the sun and rain
Does not disturb his glad refrain;
A bird that flirts his floppy tail
And from our chimneys upward sail.
His riot runs through all the night
Until you wish he'd take his flight.
Songs are made of note and word,
But it takes an egg to make a bird.

"Imported" Walnut Cut Down—One of California's oldest known "imported" walnut trees was cut down recently at Fiddletown, Amador County, says the "Amador Ledger" of April 27. The seed, from Missouri, was planted in 1864 by Ann Harrington, who drove an oxteam across the plains to California. The tree measured six feet at the base.

"All higher motives, ideals, conceptions, sentiments in a man are of no account if they do not come forward to strengthen him for the better discharge of the duties which devolve upon him in the ordinary affairs of life."—Henry Ward Beecher.

Salinas Rodeo—The famed California rodeo will be staged at Salinas, Monterey County, June 19-23.

THE SAN FRANCISCO BANK

SAVINGS COMMERCIAL TRUST

INCORPORATED FEBRUARY 10TH, 1868

One of the Oldest Banks in California, the Assets of which have never been increased by mergers or consolidations with other Banks

MEMBER ASSOCIATED SAVINGS BANKS OF SAN FRANCISCO

526 California Street, San Francisco, Cal.

December 31st, 1932

Assets—

United States and Other Bonds, (value $64,171,686.00) on books at	$ 61,081,697.82
Loans on Real Estate	73,596,959.27
Loans on Bonds and Other Securities	1,278,738.75
Bank Buildings and Lots, (value over $2,135,000.00) on books at	1.00
Other Real Estate, (value over $500,000.00) on books at	1.00
Pension Fund, (value over $800,000.00) on books at	1.00
Cash	21,507,228.09
Total	$157,464,626.93

Liabilities—

Due Depositors	$151,114,626.93
Capital Stock	1,000,000.00
Reserve and Contingent Funds	5,350,000.00
Total	$157,464,626.93

The following additional statement may be of interest to the Depositors of the Bank: The Earnings of the Bank for the entire Fiscal Year ending December 31st, 1932 were as follows:

Income	$7,564,580.66
Expenses and Taxes	906,735.60
Net Profits	$6,657,845.06

The above does not include Interest due on Loans but not yet collected

MISSION BRANCH ... Mission and 21st Streets
PARK-PRESIDO BRANCH ... Clement Street and 7th Ave.
HAIGHT STREET BRANCH ... Haight and Belvedere Streets
WEST PORTAL BRANCH ... West Portal Ave. and Ulloa St.

Dividends on Deposits as declared quarterly by the Board of Directors, are Computed Monthly and Compounded Quarterly, and may be withdrawn quarterly.

THE
GRANT D. MILLER
MORTUARIES

Directors of Funerals
OAKLAND, CALIFORNIA

MAIN OFFICE AND CHAPELS
2372 East 14th Street

CATHEDRAL CHAPEL
2850 Telegraph Avenue

MANY
BAY REGION BRANCHES
FOR YOUR
CONVENIENCE
STRONG
CENTRALIZED CONTROL
FOR YOUR
PROTECTION

AMERICAN TRUST COMPANY
SINCE 1854
Member Federal Reserve System

Just
One Way
to Know
Your
California
Read
Regularly
The
GRIZZLY
BEAR
$1.50
the Year

REVIEW OF GRASS VALLEY N.S.G.W. GRAND PARLOR

(CLARENCE M. HUNT.)

THE FIFTY-SIXTH GRAND PARLOR, IN session at Grass Valley, Nevada County, May 15, 16 and 18, went into the annals of the Order of Native Sons of the Golden West as one of the most outstanding, from every viewpoint, in several years. The surroundings were ideal, the arrangements were perfect in every detail, the entertainment was excellent and, above all, the spirit of unadulterated fraternity held sway, both within and without the meetingroom. Grand President Seth Millington of Colusa Parlor No. 69 presided throughout the Grand Parlor deliberations.

The reports of grand officers and committees dealt mostly with matters which heretofore have been given publicity in The Grizzly Bear. A review of the Fifty-sixth Grand Parlor follows:

GRAND PARLOR LAW CHANGES.

Art. V, Sec. 1 amended by changing the designation "Historiographer" to "Grand Historian."

Art. VI, Sec. 4 amended to create a "Grand Parlor Insurance Fund to insure all officers of the Subordinate Parlors required to be bonded by the Constitution or by the bylaws of any Subordinate Parlor."

Art. VIII, Sec. 3, Sub. 3 amended to increase the personnel of the Publicity Committee to ten.

Art. VIII, Sec. 3, Sub. 4 amended to increase the personnel of the History Committee to fifteen.

Art. IX, Sec. 12 amended to provide that no bylaw or amendment to a bylaw of a Subordinate Parlor "shall take effect until approved by the Grand President. If not approved by the Grand President the Board of Grand Officers . . . may, . . . suspend the operation or the taking effect of said bylaw until the next session of the Grand Parlor. In the event of such action taken by the Board of Grand Officers said bylaw shall be passed upon by the Grand Parlor and shall not be of any force or effect until approved by a majority vote of the members of the Grand Parlor."

SUBORDINATE PARLORS LAW CHANGES.

Art. III, Sec. 1 amended by adding: "except in Parlors having a membership of twenty-five or less, three members in good standing shall constitute a quorum."

Art. VI, Secs. 4 and 5 amended to provide that the financial secretary and the treasurer "shall be bonded with the Grand Parlor Insurance Fund in such sums as the Parlor may require."

Art. VI, Sec. 15 amended to require of the outside sentinel: "He shall remain at the outer door during initiations, opening and closing ceremonies. He may take a seat in the body of the Parlor near the inner door when requested by the president directly or through the inside sentinel so to do."

Art. VIII, Sec. 1 amended to provide: "every beneficial member hereunder entitled shall be paid, . . . benefits at least equal to the sum of his monthly dues and charges during the continuance of an illness."

Art. XV amended by adding a new section, No. 11, thereby creating a "Committee on California Institutions whose duty it shall be to (1) actively engage in the promotion of the general welfare of the communities to the end that the State may be benefited; (2) aid, assist and encourage local beneficial enterprise, and for that purpose meet and commune with officials, organizations and their representatives engaged in that work."

Art. XVII, Secs. 2 and 3 amended to provide that no bylaw, rule, regulation or standing resolution, or any amendment thereto, shall become effective until approved "in accordance with the provisions of Sec. 12, Art. IX of the Constitution of the Grand Parlor."

BUDGET AND PERCAPITA TAX.

The Finance Committee presented a budget totaling $29,125, and to raise that amount recommended a $1.10 percapita tax. The Grand Parlor, however, increased the budget by making appropriations of $1,000 for a history fellowship, $500 for relief of Past Grand Dr. Frank I. Gonzalez, injured in an auto accident while serving as Grand President, and approximately $1,050 to assist in financing the Admission Day, September 9, celebration at Santa Rosa, Sonoma County. These additions required a fifteen-cent increase in the percapita.

The percapita tax, therefore, was fixed at $1.25, payable thirty-five cents June 1, 1933; thirty cents September 1, 1933; thirty cents December 1, 1933; thirty cents March 1, 1934. Among others, the approved budget carries these appropriations: organization fund, $3,600; special relief fund, $1,000; landmarks fund, $500; oriental exclusion fund, $250; mileage, Grass Valley session, $4,000.

OTHER BUSINESS TRANSACTED.

Ukiah, Mendocino County, was selected as the meetingplace of the Fifty-seventh (1934) Grand Parlor.

One thousand dollars was appropriated for a "Native Sons of the Golden West Traveling History Fellowship at the University of California," with a proviso that in making the selection preference be given members of the Order.

A proposal to permit "non-ritualistic members" in Subordinate Parlors was referred to a special committee, which recommended a new class of membership, namely "associate," with numerous restrictions as to privileges, in addition to the "beneficial" and "non-beneficial" classes now provided for. After much debate, the recommendation was voted down, decisively.

Fines levied against Ramona No. 109, Tracy No. 186, Dolores No. 208 and Sutter No. 261 were remitted, and the proposal to allow Compton No. 273 a supplies credit of $150 was referred to the incoming Board of Grand Officers.

The charters of Chico No. 21 and Cahuenga No. 268 were revoked, and the surrender of the charter of Rainbow No. 40 was approved.

The granting of charters to six new Parlors—Los Banos No. 206, Visalia No. 19, University No. 272, Compton No. 273, Willows No. 255 and Turlock No. 274—was approved.

The report of the State of the Order Committee, which was unanimously adopted, commended Grand President Seth Millington for the great service rendered during the past year. It concluded with: "We recommend to the delegates that each return to his Parlor with the determination that his Parlor is going to grow in membership during the year 1933. . . . In these trying times, it is our opinion that the majority of the Subordinate Parlors have held up very well, and we hope that with that same determination to carry on, the Parlors will continue their good work in the interests of our Order."

NEW GRAND OFFICERS.

At the election of grand officers May 18, 352 ballots were cast, and the following were selected:

Grand President, Justice Emmet Seawell (Santa Rosa No. 28).

Grand First Vice-president, Chas. A. Koenig (Golden Gate No. 29).

Grand Second Vice-president, Harmon D. Skillin (Castro No. 232).

Grand Third Vice-president, J. Hartley Russell (Stanford No. 76).

Grand Secretary, John T. Regan (South San Francisco No. 157).

EMMET SEAWELL, CALIFORNA SUPREME COURT JUSTICE,
GRAND PRESIDENT ORDER NATIVE SONS OF THE GOLDEN WEST.

Grand Treasurer, John A. Corotto (San Jose No. 22).

Grand Marshal, Gam Hurst (Piedmont No. 120).

Grand Inside Sentinel, William A. Reuter (Sepulveda No. 263).

Grand Outside Sentinel, Walter P. Rothenbush (Stockton No. 7).

Grand Trustees (in order of vote received)—Eldred L. Meyer (Santa Monica Bay No. 267), Henry S. Lyon (Placerville No. 9), Charles H. Spengemann (Hesperian No. 137), Thomas M. Foley (Pacific No. 10), Jesse H. Miller (California No. 1), John M. Burnett (San Jose No. 22), Edward T. Schnarr (Fruitvale No. 252).

They, along with Seth Millington (Colusa No. 69), who automatically became the Junior Past Grand President, were installed by Past Grand John T. Newell, assisted by Clarence M. Hunt (Sacramento No. 3), acting grand secretary, and W. Bernard O'Brien (Alameda No. 47), acting grand marshal.

To complete the list of grand officers, Grand President Seawell, just previous to adjournment, announced the appointment of Leslie Maloche (Arrowhead No. 110) as Grand Organist, and Chester Gannon (Sunset No. 26) as Grand Historian.

RESOLUTIONS ADOPTED.

Regretting the deaths of Past Grand Presidents Dr. Charles W. Decker and William J. Hayes, and directing that engrossed copies of the resolutions be presented the families of the deceased.

Favoring the continuance and the proper maintenance of the California Nautical School, and petitioning the State Legislature "to let no temporary period of restricted governmental activity interfere with the project in view of its obvious importance to the State of California, and to our National Government whose earnest objective is to attain a position of commercial supremacy amongst the nations of the world."

Declaring "The San Francisco Symphony Orchestra is an important cultural asset not only of the City of San Francisco, but of the entire State," and expressing approval of the project and best wishes for its success.

Memorializing "the Congress of the United States of America to encourage the production of gold in this country by relieving individuals and (or) companies engaged in production of gold from the payment of any and (or) all income tax on the gold so produced."

Endorsing "proposed legislation exempting non-profit private schools from taxation."

Petitioning the Federal Congress to pass "a bill calling for an appropriation to be used in transporting Filipinos back to their native islands, free of charge, on United States Government transports, with the stipulation that they will not be permitted to return to the United States of America."

Extending the heartfelt thanks of the Fifty-sixth Grand Parlor "to the Committee on Arrangements, Quartz Parlor No. 58 N.S.G.W., Hydraulic Parlor No. 56 N.S.G.W., Downieville Parlor No. 92 N.S.G.W., Manzanita Parlor No. 29 N.D.G.W., Laurel Parlor No. 6 N.D.G.W., Grass Valley Chamber of Commerce, Grass Valley high school band, the people in general of the City of Grass Valley and of Nevada City, and all those who contributed entertainment; also, for the numerous courtesies extended the officers and delegates of this Grand Parlor and guests accompanying, and especially to the press of the City of Grass Valley for the publicity accorded."

GOODWILL GREETINGS.

Telegrams and letters of greetings from several fraternal and civic organizations, and individuals were received, among the messages being the following resolution adopted by the Knights of Pythias Grand Lodge, in session at Santa Rosa, Sonoma County:

"Whereas, The Grand Parlor of the Native Sons of the Golden West is in convention assembled during this week from May 15th to 19th, 1933, at Grass Valley, California, and whereas, this Grand Lodge Knights of Pythias, also in convention assembled, has for the Grand Parlor of the Native Sons the most sincere regard and fraternal feeling, and is in hearty sympathy with its desire to preserve and foster the romantic history and traditions of our glorious state, and whereas, it has come to our attention that the Honorable Emmet Seawell, Associate Justice of the Supreme Court of California, for whom we entertain a sincere affection, is in line for promotion to the highest executive office of the Grand Parlor, and whereas, this Grand Lodge is desirous of testifying to its high regard, both for the Grand Parlor and for Justice Seawell, now, therefore, be it and it is hereby

"Resolved, That we transmit to Justice Seawell and the Grand Parlor of the Native Sons this resolution of our esteem and good-will; that we etxend to it every good wish for its continued success in fostering, for the people of our great commonwealth, a love for its history and traditions; that we wish for its members in common with all our citizens a speedy return to prosperity and happiness, and a steady growth of fraternal feeling; that a copy hereof be spread upon our permanent records; and that Brother Ira F. Thompson, Grand Tribune, be designated to convey our message of good-will to the Grand Parlor, Native Sons of the Golden West."

MEMORIAL SESSION.

The annual Grand Parlor Memorial Session, held the afternoon of May 15 and opened to the public, was presided over by Past Grand Lewis F. Byington. The program included:

Eulogy, Dr. Charles W. Decker, Past Grand President, by Past Grand Fred H. Greely; eulogy, William J. Hayes, Past Grand President, by Past Grand Edward J. Lynch; eulogy, Edward Van Vranken (Stockton No. 7), former Grand Trustee, by Past Grand Hubert R. McNoble; eulogy, Walter William Greer (Sunset No. 26), former Grand Trustee and Grand Lecturer, by John J. Monteverde (Sunset No. 26); eulogy, Justice Frank M. Angelotti (Mount Tamalpais No. 64), former Grand Trustee, by Grand First Vice-president Justice Emmet Seawell; eulogy, W. Joseph Ford (Glendale No. 264), former Historiographer, by Henry G. Bodkin (Hollywood No. 196); eulogy, former members Grand Parlor, by Past Grand Fletcher A. Cutler; eulogy, all deceased members of the Order, George F. McNoble (Stockton No. 7).

Vocal selections were rendered by Grand Marshal W. Bernard O'Brien, accompanied at the piano by Grand Organist Leslie Maloche.

A NEW YEAR

UNITED ACTION ASSURES SUCCESS

"PERMIT ME, THROUGH OUR OFFICIAL publication,"—writes Justice Emmet Seawell, Grand President of the Order of Native Sons of the Golden West, to The Grizzly Bear editor,—"to extend a word of greeting to the rank and file of our membership. The Fifty-sixth Grand Parlor has closed, and all the delegates and members-at-large are taking stock as to what was accomplished. I am sure that the session marked an important epoch in our Order's history. Some of the important events have never before been equaled by any previous session of the Grand Parlor. The entire membership of the Supreme Court of the State of California, and the Governor of the State, took the pains to pause in their busy and important duties to pay tribute to our Order. This is a recognition of our place in the affairs of the State, which should be appreciated by every member of the Order—an honor without precedent in the State's history of fraternal organizations. Important matters of legislation were earnestly discussed, and while you and myself may have been disappointed in the wisdom of the adoption of some particular measure, nevertheless we bow to the wisdom of the majority and are as sincerely behind the legislation that was adopted as though we had sponsored it.

"I want to say to the membership at large that every member stands on an equal footing with every other member, so far as an opportunity to serve the interest of the Order is concerned, and there will be no class preference shown in any respect. The right to recognition will be extended, so far as I can see it, to those who have by service earned such right.

"We have begun not 'another' year, but a NEW year. Let our enthusiasm for the reasonable possibilities of accomplishment carry us over any temporary obstacles which may serve to block our progress. We are by right and in fact the favored state organization of California. Our advancement into a wider field of influence and usefulness is entirely in our own hands. I call upon the membership to quicken their interest in the welfare of the Order!

"Let every officer who has been appointed for the first time, or re-appointed, awaken to the fact that he is not to perform his duties in a perfunctory manner merely, but he is to enter upon his duties with enthusiastic effort and go forward valiantly in extending the scope of our work. I want to emphasize the importance of entering into the service to which each is assigned in a spirit of an earnest purpose to do the work better than it has ever been done before! The employee who has too anxiously watched the hands of the clock approach the noon hour, or the quitting hour in the afternoon, has never received a promotion at the hands of his employer. The man whose interest has been keenly engrossed with the thought of how much he can accomplish has always been selected for promotion. So it is in every activity of life. The brother who has given earnest service to the Order will advance to the front lines, while the officer who has adopted the 'get by' policy is doomed to fade from the picture.

"We have just begun to make our Order felt in the affairs of the State. We are in a position to go rapidly to the top. By real united action we can easily increase our membership by hundreds during the NEW year. This can be done by beginning at once! It will not do to wait until the three months preceding the meeting of the Grand Parlor. Plans should be laid early. Delay is always dangerous. The Secretaries occupy important offices in the local Parlors, and the success of the Order is with the local Parlors and by no means with the Grand Parlor.

"I expect to give to the Order all the time that it is possible for me to give. I must have the united strength of all Parlors, if we are to carry forward. Brothers, I believe that the time is now at hand for a glorious revival of the spirit which moved our Pioneers to conquer what seemed to be the unconquerable. It was their enthusiasm that won the western empire. We can, and we should, succeed! The basic principles of our Order are right. All we need is men to carry our message to the people. If every Parlor should do what it is capable of doing this NEW year, there can be no question as to a vastly increased membership.

"Let us all pull together for at least one year, and realize the results that may be accomplished. Commence now!"

LANDMARKS REPORT.

The Historic Landmarks Committee reported a contribution of $500 toward the purchase price of the General M. G. Vallejo home near Sonoma City, acquired by the California State Park Commission. "This is, in fact," says the report, "the first real acknowledgment of the great service rendered to this commonwealth by General M. G. Vallejo."

The report also advised that "California, through the State Park Commission and public-spirited citizens, will shortly come into possession of San Juan Plaza, facing San Juan Bautista Mission, located in the old town of San Juan [San Benito County]. It is the one remaining Spanish plaza, typical of those of the early days of California, which maintains its ancient aspect, surrounded on four sides by historic adobe buildings."

The committee will use its best endeavors to have the California State Park Commission make emergency repairs to a noted landmark, the property of the state, sadly in need of attention—the Pio Pico mansion at Whittier, Los Angeles County, the home of the last Mexican governor of California, a portion of which was built in 1826.

NOTES OF THE SESSION.

On behalf of Ukiah Parlor No. 71, Grand First Vice Justice Emmet Seawell presented to the Grand Parlor a redwood gavel, and it was accepted by Grand President Millington.

Past Grand Fletcher Cutler delivered a brief address, extolling the work of the N.S.G.W. and N.D.G.W. Central Homeless Children Committee.

The Past Grand Presidents, at their annual reunion dinner, arranged to mark with a suitably inscribed monument of Nevada County granite the grave of Past Grand Jo V. Snyder in the Greenwood Cemetery, Grass Valley.

Tuesday, the Historic Landmarks Committee marked with a bronze plaque the grave of John Rollin Ridge in Greenwood Cemetery. The inscription reads: "John Rollin Ridge, California Poet. Author of 'Mt. Shasta' and other poems. Born March 19, 1827, in Cherokee Nation, near what is now Rome, Georgia. Died in Grass Valley, October 5, 1867. In grateful memory by Historic Landmarks Committee, Native Sons of the Golden West, May 16, 1933." Speakers included Past Grand Joseph R. Knowland, committee chairman; Grand President Millington; E. G. Kinyon, managing editor "Morning Union;" President Frank Rowe of Quartz Parlor; Past Grand Lewis F. Byington.

United States of America and California State (Bear) Flags were presented Thursday to the high and the grammar schools of Nevada City. Dr. C. W. Chapman (Hydraulic No. 56) introduced Past Grand Byington, who made the presentation address. The flags for the high school were accepted by Warren Chapman and Ruth Rector, and those for the grammar school by Craig Davis and Margaret Chapman. Similar stands of flags were also presented the high and the grammar schools of Grass Valley, Leo V. Youngworth (Ramona No. 109) making the presentation address.

Wednesday, the Downieville-bound caravan stopped at Fiddle Creek to dedicate the "Cannon of Brandy City Monument" to the memory of the "Pioneers of the Placers." District Attorney J. M. McMahon of Sierra County (Downieville No. 92) made the principal address, and with Past Grand Alison F. Watt of the Native Daughters accompanying at the organ, the assemblage sang "The Star Spangled Banner."

ENTERTAINMENT FEATURES.

No Grand Parlor was better entertained than the Fifty-sixth. Hospitality reigned supreme in the Grass Valley-Nevada City area. Quartz No. 58, the host Parlor, had the full co-operation of Hydraulic No. 56, Manzanita No. 29 and Laurel No. 6 N.D.G.W., and the citizens generally. The Native Daughters provided special entertainment features for the visiting womenfolks, and were their guests delighted with each and every event!

At the Monday night reception, James C. Tyrrell presided, and the speakers included Mayor M. J. Brock, Superior Judge Raglan Tuttle, President Frank Rowe of Quartz Parlor and Grand President Seth Millington, all Native Sons; President Mrs. Frank Rowe of Manzanita Parlor, Grand President Anna Mixon Armstrong

(Continued on Page 15)

47th NATIVE DAUGHTER GR

(CLARENCE M. HUNT.)

MONDAY, JUNE 19, AT 9:30 A.M., the Forty-seventh annual Grand Parlor of the Order of Native Daughters of the Golden West will convene at Oakland, Alameda County, for a four-day session. Grand President Anna Mixon Armstrong of Woodland, Yolo County, affiliated with Woodland Parlor No. 90, will preside throughout the deliberations and, at their conclusion, will automatically become the Junior Past Grand President. The sessions of the Grand Parlor will be held daily in the Leamington Hotel, Nineteenth and Franklin streets, which has been selected as the official headquarters and where all the activities will center.

Considering conditions generally, the closing Grand Parlor year has been a successful one. By thorough co-operation of the Subordinate Parlors, the worthwhile projects of the Order have not only been maintained, but advanced. As an organized group, the Native Daughters are successful in all their undertakings because they deserve success. They labor indefatigably to attain each and every goal.

According to information received, on request, direct by The Grizzly Bear from the Subordinate Parlors of the Order, Joaquin No. 5 (Stockton) continues to hold the lead as the strongest Parlor, numerically, having a membership of 269. Other Parlors with a membership in excess of two hundred are: Los Angeles No. 124 (Los Angeles), 235; Twin Peaks No. 185 (San Francisco), 210; Sutter No. 111 (Sacramento), 204.

Parlors with a membership in excess of one hundred are: Marguerite No. 12 (Placerville), 197; Manzanita No. 29 (Grass Valley), 197; Castro No. 178 (San Francisco), 194; Laurel No. 6 (Nevada City), 186; Woodland No. 90 (Woodland), 180; Alta No. 3 (San Francisco), 179; Californiana No. 247 (Los Angeles), 179; Piedmont No. 87 (Oakland), 170; La Bandera No. 110 (Sacramento), 170; Marinita No. 198 (San Rafael), 167; Ursula No. 1 (Jackson), 164; Buena Vista No. 68 (San Francisco), 164; Genevieve No. 132 (San Francisco), 163; Presidio No. 148 (San Francisco), 152; San Jose No. 8 (San Jose), 150; Vendome No. 100 (San Jose), 147; Coloma No. 212 (Sacramento), 141; Reina del Mar No. 126 (Santa Barbara), 139; El Vespero No. 118 (San Francisco), 129; Guadalupe No. 153 (San Francisco), 128; Golden Gate No. 158 (San Francisco), 124; Gabrielle No. 139 (San Francisco), 122; Mission No. 227 (San Francisco), 118; El Pescadero No. 82 (Tracy), 114; Copa de Oro No. 105 (Hollister), 106; Aloha No. 106 (Oakland), 105; El Carmelo No. 181 (Daly City), 105; El Pajaro No. 35 (Watsonville), 104; Santa Cruz No. 26 (Santa Cruz), 103; Lugonia No. 241 (San Bernardino), 103; Califia No. 22 (Sacramento), 101.

RESOLUTIONS TO BE SUBMITTED.

Resolutions proposing changes in the Grand Parlor Constitution will be presented as follows:

By Los Angeles Parlor No. 124, amending Art. III, Sec. 2 to provide that each Subordinate Parlor shall be entitled to one delegate at large and one delegate for "every seventy-five members."

By Californiana Parlor No. 247, amending Art. III, Sec. 5 to read: "No proxies shall be admitted to represent elected delegates, but alternates shall be elected who must possess the same qualifications; that the candidate receiving the next highest number of votes in the election for delegates, after the number of delegates are elected, shall be designated as alternate number one, and so on."

By Golden Gate Parlor No. 158, amending Art. X, Sec. 3, Par. 5 by providing that the death benefit will be paid on the demise of one who "has been a member of the Order for six months."

LosAngeles Parlor is also sponsoring these resolutions: "That the annual Native Daughter Home assessment be reduced in such amount as may seem meet with the financial condition of the Home, at the date of Grand Parlor, 1933." "That all salaries paid by the Grand Parlor be reduced ten percent." "That the Grand Parlor pay no more than fifty dollars per month for the rental of office space for the Grand Secretary."

Californiana Parlor is also sponsoring this resolution: "That the President of a Subordinate Parlor be empowered to appoint a Nominating Committee, whose duty it shall be to select a suitable corps of officers for the ensuing term, same to be submitted to the Parlor at time of nomination of officers; the selection of the Nominating Committee not to exclude members the privilege of nominating from the floor, if they so desire."

GRAND PARLORS OF THE PAST, AND GRAND PRESIDENTS PRESIDING.

1—July	1887,	San Francisco	Tina L. Kane*
2—July	1888,	Stockton	Tina L. Kane*
3—June	1889,	San Francisco	Louise Watson-Morris
4—June	1890,	Santa Rosa	Carrie Roesch-Durham
5—June	1891,	Santa Cruz	Mollie B. Johnson*
6—June	1892,	Sacramento	Clara K. Wittenmyer*
7—June	1893,	Watsonville	Mae B. Wilkin
8—June	1894,	Chico	Minnie Coulter*
9—June	1895,	Grass Valley	Dr. Elizabeth A. Spencer
10—June	1896,	Napa	Dr. Mariana Bertola
11—June	1897,	Sonora	Mary E. Tillman*
12—June	1898,	Woodland	Belle W. Conrad*
13—June	1899,	Stockton	Lena Hilke-Mills†
14—June	1900,	Jackson	Cora B. Sifford
15—June	1901,	Sacramento	Ema Gett*
16—June	1902,	San Francisco	Genevieve Watson-Baker
17—June	1903,	Red Bluff	Eliza D. Keith
18—June	1904,	Pacific Grove	Stella Finkeldey
19—June	1905,	San Jose	Ella E. Caminetti
20—June	1906,	Salinas	Ariana W. Stirling
21—July	1907,	Watsonville	Dr. Eva R. Rasmussen
22—June	1908,	Lodi	Emma Gruber-Foley
23—June	1909,	Del Monte	Anna L. Monroe
24—June	1910,	Santa Barbara	Emma Lou Humphrey
25—June	1911,	Santa Cruz	Mamie G. Peyton
26—June	1912,	San Francisco	Anna F. Lacy*
27—June	1913,	Tallac	Olive Bedford-Matlock
28—June	1914,	Oakland	Alison F. Watt
29—June	1915,	San Francisco	May C. Boldemann
30—June	1916,	Fresno	Margaret Grote-Hill
31—June	1917,	Del Monte	Mamie P. Carmichael
32—June	1918,	Santa Cruz	Grace S. Stoermer
33—June	1919,	Berkeley	Addie L. Mosher
34—June	1920,	San Jose	Mary E. Bell
35—June	1921,	San Francisco	Bertha A. Briggs
36—June	1922,	San Rafael	Dr. Victory A. Derrick*
37—June	1923,	Stockton	Mattie M. Stein
38—June	1924,	Santa Cruz	Amy V. McAvoy
39—June	1925,	Placerville	Catherine E. Gloster
40—June	1926,	Sacramento	Sue J. Irwin
41—June	1927,	Modesto	Pearl Lamb
42—June	1928,	San Francisco	Mae Himes-Noonan
43—June	1929,	Santa Cruz	Dr. Louise C. Heilbron
44—June	1930,	Oakland	Esther R. Sullivan
45—June	1931,	Santa Rosa	Estelle M. Evans
46—June	1932,	Merced	Evelyn I. Carlson

*Deceased.
†Connection with Order severed.

CANDIDATES FOR OFFICE.

By communicating with all the Subordinate Parlors and the many "rumored" candidates, The Grizzly Bear is enabled to announce the candidacies of several aspirants for Grand Parlor office honors. The list is complete, insofar as definite information has been received, but it is not complete if gossip be founded on fact. For, there are whisperings that every elective office, excepting the grand presidency and the grand vice-presidency, will have two, or more, seekers. Be that as it may, here is the authentic "dope" received by The Grizzly Bear:

Grand President—Grand Vice-president Irma Laird (Alturas No. 159) of Alturas.

Grand Vice-president—Grand Marshal Gladys E. Noce (Amapola No. 80) of Sutter Creek.

Grand Secretary—Sallie R. Thaler (Aloha No. 106) of Oakland, incumbent.

Grand Treasurer—Susie K. Christ (Yosemite No. 83) of San Francisco, incumbent.

Grand Marshal—Grand Trustee Anna Thuesen (Alta No. 3) of San Francisco; Grand Trustee Edna B. Briggs (La Bandera No. 110) of Sacramento.

Grand Inside Sentinel—Grand Outside Sentinel Hazel B. Hansen (Verdugo No. 240) of Glendale.

Grand Outside Sentinel—Alice Mathias Oldham (El Carmelo No. 181) of Daly City.

Grand Organist—Clara Gairaud (Vendome No. 100) of San Jose, incumbent.

Grand Trustees (seven to be selected)—Grand Inside Sentinel Orinda Gunther Giannini (Orinda No. 56) of San Francisco; Minna Kane Horn (Eschscholtzia No. 112) of Etna, incumbent; Jane D. Vick (Reina del Mar No. 126) of Santa Barbara, incumbent; Alice M. Lane (Castro No. 178) of San Francisco; Florence Danforth Boyle (Gold of Ophir No. 190) of Oroville, incumbent; Ethel S. Begley (Marinita No. 198) of San Rafael, incumbent; Willow Borba (Santa Rosa No. 217) of Sebastopol, incumbent; Evalyn G. Towne (Miocene No. 228) of Taft.

PROGRAM.

Arrangements for the Oakland Grand Parlor are in the hands of the following general committee: Past Grand Sue J. Irwin, Josephine Clark, Carmelita Luhr, Dora Brayton and Grand

nier, Mary Tuttle, Myrtle Lanini, Constance Lucio.

GRAND PARLOR MAKEUP.

Any member of the Order is privileged to attend the Grand Parlor. Those entitled to a vote, however, include:

Grand Officers—Mrs. Evelyn I. Carlson, Junior Past Grand President; Mrs. Anna M. Armstrong, Grand President; Mrs. Irma Laird, Grand Vice-president; Mrs. Sallie R. Thaler, Grand Secretary; Mrs. Susie K. Christ, Grand Treasurer; Mrs. Gladys Noce, Grand Marshal; Mrs. Orinda G. Giannini, Grand Inside Sentinel; Mrs. Hazel B. Hansen, Grand Outside Sentinel; Mrs. Clara Gairaud, Grand Organist; Mrs. Florence Boyle, Mrs. Edna Briggs, Mrs. Anna Thuesen, Mrs. Ethel Begley, Mrs. Minna K. Horn, Mrs. Jane Vick, Mrs. Willow Borba, Grand Trustees.

Founder of the Order—Lily O. Reichling-Dyer (Ursula No. 1).

Senior Past Grand Presidents—Louise Watson-Morris (Buena Vista No. 68), Carrie Roesch-Durham (Joaquin No. 5), Mae B. Wilkin (Santa Cruz No. 26), Dr. Elizabeth A. Spencer (Buena Vista No. 68), Dr. Mariana Bertola (Buena Vista No. 68), Cora B. Sifford (Reina del Mar No. 126), Genevieve Watson-Baker (Buena Vista No. 68), Eliza D. Keith (Alta No. 3), Stella Finkeldey (Santa Cruz No. 26), Ella E. Caminetti (Ursula No. 1), Ariana W. Stirling (Aleli No. 102), Dr. Eva R. Rasmussen (Coloma No. 212), Emma Gruber-Foley (Orinda No. 56), Anna L. Monroe (Oneonta No. 71), Emma Lou Humphrey (Ivy No. 88), Mamie G. Peyton (Joaquin No. 5), Olive Bedford-Matlock (Camellia No. 41), Alison F. Watt (Manzanita No. 29), May C. Boldemann (La Estrella No. 89), Margaret Grote-Hill (Alta No. 3), Mamie Peirce-Carmichael (Vendome No. 100), Grace S. Stoermer (Los Angeles No. 124), Addie L. Mosher (Piedmont No. 87), Mary E. Bell (Buena Vista No. 68), Bertha A. Briggs (Copa de Oro No. 105), Mattie M. Stein (Ivy No. 88), Amy V. McAvoy (Stirling No. 146), Catherine E. Glaster (Alturas No. 159), Sue J. Irwin (Berkeley No. 150), Pearl Lamb (El Pescadero No. 82), Mae Himes-Noonan (Portola No. 172), Dr. Louise C. Heilbron (San Diego No. 208), Esther R. Sullivan (Marysville No. 162), Estelle M. Evans (Antioch No. 223).

Permanent Members—Grace S. Williams (Alta No. 3), Lizzie Winkley-Pfenninger (Alta No. 3), Josie Hofmeister-Pratt (Marguerite No. 12), Kate Even-Stewart (Eschol No. 16), Mary Hutchings (Buena Vista No. 68), members First Grand Parlor (1887) retaining continuous membership in the Order. Georgia Watson-Cotter-Ryan (Buena Vista No. 68), Laura J. Frakes-Toman (Amapola No. 80), Alice H. Dougherty (Angelita No. 32), former Grand Secretaries.

Ex-officio Members—Mary E. Brusie (Argonaut No. 166), Annie L. Adair (Los Angeles No. 124), secretary and assistant secretary, respectively, of the N.S.G.W. and N.D.G.W. Central Committee on Homeless Children.

Subordinate Parlor Delegates—The list is complete, insofar as Parlors reported, as requested, to The Grizzly Bear up to the time of going to press. Delegates of Parlors not supplying the required information are not listed here:

Ursula No. 1—Henrietta O'Neill, Flora Podesta, Amy Clark Oates, Catherine B. Swensen.

Minerva No. 2—Lena Wall.

Alta No. 3—Angeline Vest, Claire Bolman, May MacDonald, Mary Jordan.

Joaquin No. 5—Esther Osborn, Elvira Sanguinetti, Susie Cooney, Constance Stormes, Harriet Corr, Grace Bessac.

Laurel No. 6—Agnes Worthley, Zoe Tredennick, Addale Tredennick, Adeline O'Connor.

Oro Fino No. 9—Julia Chienzola.

Bonita No. 10—Miss Jessie Leslie, Mrs. Dora Wilson.

Marguerite No. 12—Mrs. Nettie Leonardi, Mrs. Ethel VanVleck, Mrs. Dora Wood, Mrs. Lilla Ziesz.

Eschol No. 16—Miss Edna Blanchard, Mrs. Jane Ezetti.

Laura Loma No. 18—Catherine Plumb.

Califia No. 22—Mrs. Maud Green Cook, Miss Vivian Hall.

Berendos No. 23—Mrs. Mary N. Ray.

Desert Gold No. 25—Mrs. Mae Coffil.

Santa Cruz No. 26—Marjorie Brunjes, Mary Gregory.

Occident No. 28—Caroline Henry, Lena J. Pettingill.

Manzanita No. 29—Anna Rowe, Anne Whiting, Florence George, Caroline Hotchkiss.

Angelita No. 32—Mrs. Margaret Volponi, Mrs. Myrtle Johnson.

El Pajaro No. 35—Dora Zmudowski, Mary Aston, Caroline Hinkle.

Naomi No. 36—Lucille Fogarty.

Chispa No. 40—Esther Gebhardt, Cynthia Phillips.

Camellia No. 41—Mrs. Frankie Miller.

Golden State No. 50—Mrs. Irene Milan, Miss Millie Tietjen.

Orinda No. 56—Mrs. Marie McGrath, Mrs. Emily Fanda, Mrs. Anna G. Loser.

Fremont No. 59—Hannah Collins, Etsie M. Gill.

Dardanelle No. 66—Anna C. Silva, Nettie Whittle.

Buena Vista No. 68—Helen Kennerley, Helen Lebeuk, Sadie Carman, Kittie Schmidt.

Oneonta No. 71—Mrs. Hattie E. Roberts, Mrs. Ann Jespersen.

Las Lomas No. 72—Evelyn Crosby, Katherine Whelan.

Veritas No. 75—Mrs. Zelphia Thomas, Miss Marian Palcifer.

Amapola No. 80—Marea Fontenrose, Edith Murphy, Elsie Hartwick.

San Jose No. 81—Dorothy Koerber, Genevieve Epler, Iola Shannon.

El Pescadero No. 82—Miss Frances Huck, Miss Alice Ritter, Mrs. Mary A. Hewitson.

Yosemite No. 83—Eva Park, Mona Theisen.

Forrest No. 86—Clara Steiner, Evelyn Blake.

Piedmont No. 87—Augusta Huxsol, Nell Moore, Dorothy Hadlen, Dorothy Davis.

Ivy No. 88—Mrs. Thirza E. Hunt, Mrs. Mary Meehl.

La Estrella No. 89—Mrs. Georgie Thurbach.

Woodland No. 90—Mrs. Gladys Evans, Mrs. Edna Richter, Mrs. Geraldine O'Donnell, Miss Lela Ewert.

Sans Souci No. 96—Mrs. Jessie Dobbin Crowley, Mrs. Tessie Pearce.

Reichling No. 97—Madge Heath Evers.

Lassen View No. 98—Mrs. Mabel Thompson.

Vendome No. 100—Dorothy Salas, Gertrude Musser, Alice Roll.

Aleli No. 102—Mrs. Stella Taveruetti, Mrs. Mary McElheran.

Copa de Oro No. 105—Mayme Moran, Rachael Maroney, Rose Guilhamet.

Aloha No. 106—Caroline Schulze, Katherine Walker, Alma O. Lonardi.

San Luisita No. 108—Mae Umbertis, Julia Bell.

La Bandera No. 110—Mrs. Mae Sydenstricker, Mrs. Eva Mordecai, Mrs. Lucy Roberts, Miss Helen Kennedy.

Sutter No. 111—Mrs. Emilie Lachmann, Mrs. Loraine Williams, Mrs. Audrey Brown, Mrs. Lavinia Blakely, Mrs. Belle Brye.

Eschscholtzia No. 112—Laura Wolford, Margaret Weston.

San Andreas No. 113—Florence Hunt, Adeline Squellati.

Darina No. 114—Miss Elise Barth, Miss Anna Barth.

El Vespero No. 118—Miss Gladys J. Casey, Mrs. Ruby D. Bried, Mrs. Nell R. Boege.

Hayward No. 122—Ella M. Knudsen, Ruth M. Gansberger.

Fern No. 123—Mrs. Ruby Bunker.

Los Angeles No. 124—Mattie Labory Gara, Olinda Kerby, Dolores Malis, Grace J. Norton, Grace T. Haven.

Oakdale No. 125—Mrs. Alice Dorroh.

Reina del Mar No. 126—Mrs. Amelia Acres, Miss Marion Arroqui, Mrs. Vera Pacheco Grim.

Genevieve No. 132—Mrs. Elvira Desmond, Mrs. Lillian Neisel, Miss Evelyn Kilkenny, Mrs. Olga Kastelle.

Imogen No. 134—Mrs. Margaret E. Banks.

Clear Lake No. 135—Florence Blume.

Keith No. 137—Helen T. Mann, Gertrude LaFortune.

Placer No. 138—Margaret Kennedy, Adaline Blackie.

Gabrielle No. 139—Mrs. Ernestine Ranzulo, Mrs. Carmelita Diederichsen, Mrs. Helen Sprung.

Hiawatha No. 140—L. Elizabeth Bass, Elizabeth Kise.

Junipero No. 141—Miss Matilda Bergschicker.

Calistoga No. 145—Bretta Lundell, Lillus Kelley.

Stirling No. 146—Margaret Delp.

Richmond No. 147—Maud Arnold.

Presidio No. 148—Emelia Muhlbach, Emilie Clifford, Claire S. Clark, Ella Gilbert.

Bear Flag No. 151—Miss Mabel McGee, Miss Edna Cullisch.

Natoqua No. 152—Mrs. Josie Davis, Mrs. Olive Bouchard.

Guadalupe No. 153—Lula Porter, May McCarthy, Pauline DesRoches.

Long Beach No. 154—Miss Eleanor E. Johnson, Mrs. Gertrude Riddle.

Encinal No. 156—Laura E. Fisher, Barbara Rose.

Brooklyn No. 157—Evelyn Palmer, Elbertha Williams.

Golden Gate No. 158—Mrs. Wilma Creighton, Mrs. Margaret Ramm, Miss Sophie Siebe.

Alturas No. 159—Mildred F. Smith, Irene W. Cummings.

Marysville No. 162—Mrs. Annie Sperbeck, Mrs. Ruth S. Manwell.

El Pinal No. 163—Mrs. Kathryn Luchessa.

Anona No. 164—Laverne Nebra.

Argonaut No. 166—Mrs. Angelina DeLucchi Domaschina, Mrs. Ella Fraters Freitas.

Bahia Vista No. 167—Mrs. Helen O'Connell, Mrs. Carrie Redmayne.

Annie K. Bidwell No. 168—Miss Icel Snider.

Dolores No. 169—Elizabeth Roth, Juanita Blanchfield, Ellen Rabill.

Linda Rosa No. 170—Margaretha McGowan, Helen J. O'Connell.

Chabolla No. 171—Elberta Carpenter.

Portola No. 172—Agnes M. Curry, Nan Kelly, Ethel Hernan.

Fruitvale No. 177—Lorretta Kidd, Oro L. Rogers.

Castro No. 178—Alice Lane, Margaret Griffith, Mae Waring, Sadie Ingham.

San Juan Bautista No. 179—Mrs. Catherine Breen Nyland.

Ano Nuevo No. 180—Emily R. Cardoza.

El Carmelo No. 181—Mrs. Alice Mathias Oldham, Mrs. Alice Anderson, Mrs. Christine Hume.

Twin Peaks No. 185—Merle Sandell, Harriett D. Cate, Kay Jensen, Loretta M. Cameron, Eleanor Walsh.

El Dorado No. 186—Ethel Francis.

Fresno No. 187—Mable Kenkel.

Gold of Ophir No. 190—Mrs. Hattie Clark, Mrs. Pearl Damon.

Berryessa No. 192—Mrs. Avis Evans, Mrs. Aleta Danley.

Donner No. 193—Mrs. Virginia Boitzen.

Colus No. 194—Lillian Clement.

Vallejo No. 195—Mrs. Mabel Thompson, Mrs. Elvena Woodard.

Sea Point No. 196—Miss Helen Sullivan, Miss Minnie Carreiro.

Marinita No. 198—Mary Zappetini, Irene Griffin, Antoinette Hecht, Mollye Y. Spaelti.

Morada No. 199—Lillian Stammerjohan, Minnie Hogin.

La Junta No. 203—Mrs. Wilma Mitchell, Miss Elise Metzner.

El Monte No. 205—Elizabeth Spencer.

Caliz de Oro No. 206—Mrs. Imelda Bowden, Miss Lura Day.

El Cereso No. 207—Mrs. Virginia Marshall, Mrs. Bernice Arbini.

San Diego No. 208—Irma Heilbron, Doris Hoffner.

Sonoma No. 209—Josephine Andreux, Rose Bartoli.

Fort Bragg No. 210—Ruth G. Lyta, Marjorie S. Lyta.

(Continued on Page 17)

LOS ANGELES
CITY AND COUNTY

THE DEATH AT TULARE CITY, APRIL 22, of Mrs. Adriana Johnson-Almon,—whose likeness in later years is here presented—recalls some of the early-day personages of Los Angeles City. She was born here, on the site of the present City Hall, in 1850. According to Charles J. Prudhomme of Ramona Parlor No. 109 N.S.G.W., well versed in the history of Los Angeles:

In 1833, Captain James (Santiago) Johnson, an English sea captain, brought the Guirado family—a brother and three sisters—from Guaymas to Los Angeles, and later married Carmen Guirado. Gertrude Guirado became the wife of Mamuel Requena, and Meves Guirado married Captain Alexander Bell. Among the children of Rafael Guirado was Maria de Jesus, who married John G. Downey, seventh Governor of California.

The children of Captain "Santiago" and Carmen (Guirado) Johnson were Adalaida, who married Francis Mellus; Anita, who married Henry Mellus, who came to California with Dana aboard the "Pilgrim;" Margarita, who married James H. Lander, and Francisco (Pancho) Johnson. Mrs. Almon, whose passing is here recorded, was a daughter of "Pancho" Johnson. She is survived by a daughter, Mrs. Glafira Hawvichrost of Tulare City.

BRIDGE LUNCHEON IN VERDUGO HILLS.

The lovely home of Mr. and Mrs. John Steven McGroarty high up in the green Verdugo hills will be the scene of a bridge luncheon, June 7 at 12:30 p.m., when Californiana Parlor No. 247 N.D.G.W. will be hostess to members and friends. Past President Gertrude Tuttle and a capable committee are in charge of the affair, which promises to be an outstanding social event. The funds derived will be used for Parlor activities. Those who have no means of transportation or have room in their cars are asked to call Mrs. Tuttle, RO. 2450, and make reservations with Mrs. George Parris, RO. 8022.

A large number of members attended a salad bridge May 17 at Balboa, when Grace Parlor No. 242 (Fullerton) was hostess at a delightful party. Mrs. Isabel Lopez Fages was appointed a member of a committee to make investigations at the ancient Pio Pico mansion, a number of Parlors having interested themselves in this valuable landmark. The baby adopted by Californiana, a fine youngster, has been named "Robert Californiana." Mrs. Lelia Tabor, chairman of the homeless children committee, selected the little fellow and will be the visitor at the home of his adoption. The Parlor has sent a letter of appreciation to Grand Outside Sentinel Hazel B. Hansen, felicitating her on the success of the homeless children benefit ball.

Past Grand Grace S. Stoermer was a recent visitor at the Parlor. She voiced her sentiments about the selection of proper officers, and gave valuable advice for the future conduct of No. 247. Dr. Elizabeth Sullivan of the extension department of U.C.L.A. and U.S.C., prominent teacher of philosophy and psychology and a member of Californiana, delivered an instructive lecture on "Psychology in Human Affairs" after the May 9 luncheon. Guests were President Mattie Gara of Los Angeles Parlor No. 124, Miss Wilkins of Spokane, Washington, who plans to make her home here, and Deputy Helen Anderson.—O.L.

PRESENTATIONS.

Compton—At the April 25 meeting of Compton Parlor No. 273 N.S.G.W., President Leslie Packard, on behalf of Los Angeles Parlor No. 45 N.S.G.W., presented Compton with a Holy Bible, and on behalf of Ramona Parlor No. 109 N.S.G.W., Ralph I. Harbison presented a map of California. A large number of visitors were in attendance from all neighboring Parlors, and among the speakers were Past Grand John T. Newell and Grand Trustee Eldred L. Meyer.

SPLENDID EFFORTS FOR NEEDY PRAISED.

Long Beach—Long Beach Parlor No. 154 N.D.G.W., which is temporarily meeting at the home of President Eleonor Johnson, initiated three candidates April 20. Deputy Nellie Kline, a visitor, complimented the officers on their rendition of the ritual, and praised highly the splendid work being done by the Parlor for the needy. A shower was held after the May 4 meeting for Mrs. Leola Temby, who received many lovely gifts. The color scheme was pink and blue. Mms. Mary Stultz, Alice Waldow, Rosa Faust and Kitty Dillon constituted the committee in charge. Following nomination of officers May 18, refreshments were served by Mms. Stultz and Waldow. A benefit card party was held at the home of Mrs. Georgia Pierson May 26.

The Parlor's thimble club, which is busily engaged in making comforts, children's dresses and other garments for the needy, met April 26 at the home of Recording Secretary Bertha Hitt, May 11 at the home of Mrs. Alice Waldow, and May 25 at the home of Mrs. Johanna Reed.

PRIZE WALTZERS REWARDED.

The "hard times" dance sponsored by Los Angeles Parlor No. 45 N.S.G.W. was well attended, and everybody had a good time. First Vice-president Roger Johnson was the director of activities. A presentation was made to Marie Bandurraga and Frank Ziegler (Ramona No. 109) for their prize waltzing. Andy Stodel, off the chicken reservation for the occasion and overall-clad, was given a "hand." The old faithful "Twin Als"—Cron and Metz—dispensed punch.

BAZAR DECIDED SUCCESS.

May 17, Los Angeles Parlor No. 124 N.D.G.W. initiated a class of six young women who were much impressed with the ritual and the projects fostered by the Parlor. Among the speakers were Past Grand Grace S. Stoermer, who congratulated No. 124 on its splendid progress; Grand Outside Sentinel Hazel B. Hansen, Mrs. Lelia Tabor (Californiana No. 247) and the initiates. A letter of congratulations was sent John Steven McGroarty, California's new poet laureate. During the closing Grand Parlor year members of the Parlor, under the guidance of Dolores Malin, have made pilgrimages to Los Angeles County landmarks. A very successful card party was held May 10; Peggy Ambler was in charge.

The May 24 bazar under the competent direction of Grace T. Haven was a decided success. Booths, artistically decorated, were conducted by the following: county store, Ella Steinbeck; cake, Adeline Waite, Mary McAnany; art, Evelyn Howell, Dolores Malin; apron, Ann Schlebusch; fish pond, Sophia Stewart; refreshments, Juanita Porter, Edna Trombatore, Louise McNary, Evelyn Trautwein; fortune telling, Ramona Thoroughgood; fancy work, Sail Joseph; checkroom, Edith Schallmo, Ruth Ruiz. An orchestra furnished splendid music for dancing.

Los Angeles' June calendar includes: 7th, potluck dinner, speaker and election officers. 14th, final party in the bridge tournament; Evelyn Trautwein, Ella Steinbeck, Grace Haven, Peggy Ambler chairmen. 28th, card party for clubhouse fund; Flora Holy chairman.

CONFIDENCE VOICED.

The oldtimers night of Hollywood Parlor No. 196 N.S.G.W., May 8, attracted a goodly crowd, and the "new deal" refreshments were greatly enjoyed. First Vice-preisdent Gene Murphy was master of ceremonies, and a pleasing program was presented. At a brief meeting prior to the show, the Parlor adopted a resolution voicing confidence in Raymond Haight, former State Corporation Commissioner.

Hollywood's June program includes: 5th, open meeting for eligibles. 12th, election of officers. 19th, class initiation in honor of President Henry G. Bodkin. The doors of Hollywood are always ajar for all Native Sons.

NATIVE TREES DEDICATED.

Glendale—Verdugo Parlor No. 240 N.D.G.W. preceded its May 9 meeting with a dinner in honor of Mothers Day. All the past presidents, headed by Betty Sanders, were in charge, and the mothers of the members were presented with corsages. Following dinner a splendid program was given, with Edith Dobson in charge. President Vera Carlson, on behalf of the Parlor, presented her with a beautiful basket of flowers.

May 13 a pair of cedar trees were planted in Fremont Park and dedicated to the present and the Pioneer Mothers and Fathers. These trees, which were accepted by H. Elwyn Davis of the City Parks Commission, were, when very tiny, brought from Grass Valley, Nevada County, by Ada Steele and were given by her to the Parlor.

May 18 a dessert bridge party was given at the Elks Club for the homeless children fund. It was a great success, with more than eighty in attendance. Gussie Anderson was chairman. May 21, Verdugo was hostess to Los Angeles Parlor No. 124 N.D.G.W. at the old Sanchez adobe on the original Verdugo Rancho. This is one of the oldest adobes in Southern California. Evelyn Wilson was chairman of the occasion.

OFF FOR CATALINA!

The stage is all set for the institution anniversary celebration of Ramona Parlor No. 109 N.S.G.W. at Catalina, June 11. "All Californians at heart are supposed to be there," says First Vice-president Charles Straube, who is directing the affair. "Something doing every minute of the day. Make reservations with Secretary John V. Scott not later than June 7. Let us make this the outstanding Native Son and Native Daughter event of all time!"

June 2, Ramona will have an important meeting; re-financing will be the special order, and officers will be elected. June 9, initiation. June 16, monthly birthday dinner and entertainment.

PERSONAL PARAGRAPHS.

Dan Q. Troy (Mission N.S.) of San Francisco was a visitor last month.

Mrs. Mattie Gara (Los Angeles N.D.) and husband were visitors last month to Palm Springs.

Mrs. Juanita Porter (Los Angeles N.D.) and husband have returned from a motor trip to Canada.

Mrs. Mary Noerenberg (Californiana N.D.) has been elected president of the Women's Breakfast Club.

THE DEATH RECORD.

William Thomas, brother of Charles R. Thomas (Ramona N.S.), died April 25.

Mrs. Mattie B. Cheshire, mother of H. Lee Cheshire (Ramona N.S.), died May 12.

William S. Walton, affiliated with Ramona Parlor No. 109 N.S.G.W., died at Sawtelle, May 12, survived by a wife. He was born at Fresno City, July 23, 1887.

Mrs. Alice Masopust, sister of John P. Coyle (Ramona N.S.), died May 16.

Harry G. Andrews, father of Albert E. Andrews (Ramona N.S.), died May 17.

Passing of the California Pioneer

(Confined to Brief Notices of the Demise of Those Men and Women Who Came to California Prior to 1870.)

CHARLES DORMAN ROBINSON, NATIVE of Vermont, 86; came to California in 1850; died at San Rafael, Marin County, survived by a daughter. He was a landscape artist of international renown, and his father, Dr. David Robinson, is said to have built the first theater in San Francisco, the Adelphi.

Ben White, native of New York, 88; came via Panama in 1851 and the following year settled in Amador County; died at Amador City, survived by two daughters.

Mrs. Pauline W. A. Schwarz, 88; crossed the plains in 1851 and resided many years in Sacramento City; died at Oakland, Alameda County, survived by three daughters.

Colonel Constant Benjamin Louis Duhem, native of France, 93; came via Cape Horn in 1852; died at Oroville, Butte County, survived by a wife and a son. He was a veteran of many wars.

Mrs. Ruth Clementina Epps-Cruey-York, native of Missouri, 88; came across the plains in 1854 and settled in Napa County; died at Saint Helena.

Major Lewis Williams, native of Iowa, 80; came in 1855 and resided many years in El Dorado County; died at Copperopolis, Calaveras County.

Mrs. Mary McKinney, native of Missouri, 87; came in 1856; died at Esparto, Yolo County, survived by three children.

Mrs. Dorcas J. Spencer, native of Rhode Island, 94; crossed the plains in 1856 and resided many years in Nevada County; died at Berkeley, Alameda County, survived by four children. She was an author of considerable note, and a noted temperance worker.

Mrs. Evelyn Jeanette Twitchell-Smith, native of Maine, 80; came via Panama in 1862; died at Gridley, Butte County, survived by two children.

William DuBois, 77; came in 1861 and resided in Yolo, Sonoma and Napa Counties; died at Napa City, survived by a wife and three children.

Mrs. Caroline Lane, native of Germany, 93; came in 1863 and resided in El Dorado and Contra Costa Counties; died at Crockett.

Mrs. Sadie Sears-George, native of New York, 74; came via Panama in 1865 and resided many years in San Mateo County; died at Watsonville, Santa Cruz County, survived by a husband and two children.

William Freeborn, native of Minnesota, 82; crossed the plains in 1865 and resided many years in San Luis Obispo County; died at Palo Alto, Santa Clara County, survived by a wife and six children.

Mrs. Catherine Bowers-Beysser, native of Ohio, 92; came in 1865 and resided in San Joaquin and Calaveras Counties; died at Milton, survived by three children.

Mrs. Elizabeth Russell Colquhoun-Ryan, native of British Columbia, 71; since 1865 resident San Francisco, where she died; a son survives.

Mrs. Mary Jane Barron, native of England, 77; since 1867 Tuolumne County resident; died at Soulsbyville, survived by a son.

Mrs. Rachel Dresner, native of Germany, 93; since 1868 resident San Francisco, where she died; five children survive.

Mrs. Caroline Pfeiler, 75; came in 1868 and long resided in Ventura County; died at Los Angeles City, survived by a husband and five children.

Daniel Webster Saylor, native of Indiana, 80; since 1868 resident San Francisco, where he died.

Mrs. Martha Ann Arbuthurst-Johnson, native of Pennsylvania, 90; came across the plains in 1868 and settled in Butte County; died near Cana, survived by three children.

Orin Knight, 71; came across the plains in 1868; died near Los Banos, Merced County, survived by a son.

Mrs. Hester Amanda Brewer, native of Canada, 85; came in 1868 and resided many years in San Francisco; died at Atherton, San Mateo County, survived by a daughter.

Mrs. Florence Lander-Porter, native of Wisconsin, 92; since 1868 resident Turlock, Stanislaus County, where she died; a daughter survives.

Stephen Schuyler Skidmore, native of Texas, 78; came in 1869; died at Downey, Los Angeles County, survived by a wife and a son.

Mannel Senter, native of Azores Islands, 90; came in 1864 and resided in Fresno and Stanislaus Counties; died at Oakdale, survived by six children.

Anton Bagolio, native of Italy, 81; since 1863 resident Mariposa County; died at Merced City, survived by two children.

Mrs. Dulcena Cathey, native of Missouri, 77; since 1863 Humboldt County resident; died at Garberville, survived by three children.

Henry Jackson Triplett, native of Illinois, 74; came via Panama in 1863; died at Petaluma, Sonoma County, survived by a wife and two children.

Mrs. Maria Dornaleche-Avila, native of France, 76; since 1860 resident Los Angeles County; died at Walnut.

Michael J. Burke, native of Missouri, 76; since 1860 resident Sacramento City, where he died; a wife and two daughters survive.

Mrs. Lorena Ellsworth, born in Nebraska in 1858 while her parents were enroute to California; died at San Bernardino City, survived by nine children.

Mrs. Mary Ebbert, native of Iowa, 82; crossed the plains in 1858; died at Ukiah, Mendocino County, survived by six children.

Mrs. Harriet Olive Coates, native of Wisconsin, 83; crossed the plains in 1854; died at Rohnerville, Humboldt County, survived by five children.

David Brush, native of Illinois, 85; crossed the plains in 1853; died at Huntington Beach, Orange County.

Mrs. Florida America Spriggs Griffin, native of Georgia, 85; came in 1853 and resided in El Dorado, Yolo and Colusa Counties; died near Williams, survived by a husband and four children.

Mrs. Marian Scnther-Wood, native of Illinois, 85; crossed the plains in 1852 and resided in San Benito and Santa Clara Counties; died at San Jose, survived by five children.

Thomas Miles Burns, 93; crossed the plains in 1849 and in 1870 settled in Humboldt County; died at Bridgeville, survived by three children.

Charles C. Perry, 88; since 1846 a resident of Santa Cruz City, where he died; a son survives.

Mrs. Susan Merchant-Parrish, native of Australia, 88; since 1856 resident San Bernardino County; died at Oakglen, survived by seven children.

In Memoriam

WALTER E. BRAMLETTE.

"No one hears the door that opens,
When they pass beyond our call;
Soft as loosened leaves of roses,
One by one our loved ones fall."

By the death of Walter E. Bramlette, our State has lost an honored Pioneer, Lower Lake Parlor No. 159 N.S.G.W. a beloved member, and his family a kind and loving husband and father. The charm of his upright character and kindly disposition won for him the respect and love of our membership, who

Resolved, That this tribute of affection be sent to the bereaved family, that a copy be spread upon our records, and that a copy be sent to The Grizzly Bear for publication.

MAX BERLIN JR.,
W. A. CARY,
ALBERT S. KUGELMAN,
Committee.

Lower Lake, May 20, 1933.

UNCOVERING GHOST TOWN CEMETERY RECALLS THE LONG, LONG AGO.

The grim relic of the heartaches and the shattered careers of a pioneer ghost town of Trinity County were recently brought to light, says the "Weekly Trinity Journal" of April 29, when the ruins of the cemetery of the once-prosperous, but long-obsolete and almost-forgotten, town of Ridgeville were uncovered. The mounds of seventeen graves were discovered, but only two had distinguishable markers.

These two had withstood the ravages of time, and their inscriptions bear mute testimony to the sorrow of a Pioneer Father and Mother, in the loss of two of their infant children. The inscriptions read: Frances A. Aber, child of F. T. and E. A. Aber, born October 6, 1852, died July 14, 1856. W. G. Aber, child of F. T. and E. A. Aber, born May 20, 1856, died August 24, 1857. Who the Aber family were, or what became of them, there is no other record.

Ridgeville, also known as Golden City, was at that time (1856) a lively, bustling camp, situated on Digger Creek, about two miles from Minersville, and boasted a population of 800 souls, and the necessary stores, hotels, saloons, etc., to sustain such a population. Most of the inhabitants were making a living working the rich, shallow diggings adjacent to the town, which were paying from $5 to $30 a day to the man. But the mines soon pegged out, and by 1860 the population had dwindled to 150. In a few short years the town was deserted, and its buildings left to decay. A few years later a forest fire wiped out all that remained, and the site grew up with brush. Recently the Trinity County Board of Supervisors decided to clear the site and, in co-operation with the forest service, fence the cemetery and preserve it for posterity, hence the discovery of these pathetic markers of three-fourths of a century ago.

Feminine World's Fads and Fancies

PREPARED ESPECIALLY FOR THE GRIZZLY BEAR BY ANNA STOERMER

THRIFT AND FASHION ARE COMbined when it comes to the new sports clothes which, this season, have become highly specialized. Sports clothes satisfy with even more thoroughness than ever the two great demands put upon them, to be efficient and to do flattering things to the wearer.

There are some combination frocks that might be used for golf or tennis, but the majority are made with their purpose definitely in mind, and, because they are so inexpensive, one can afford the luxury of feeling "dressed for the occasion," whatever the favorite sports. The flattering quality is obtained in the care with which the lines of the body are carried out. Exaggeration is permitted only if it suggests a slightly broader shoulder and so, narrows the hip. Otherwise, the silhouette is slim, although deceptively so. For inverted plaits are discreetly used and open out in action to give all the necessary freedom of legs and arms. An inverted plait is used at center back, and sleeves are slightly wider.

Jackets are a joy, and are handy to carry lipstick, powder and handkerchief in, for all can be accommodated. The fabric is dull dark silk, and is often trimmed with yellow. A new tennis dress is of crisp white pique. Particular attention has been paid to any demand for speed that might be put upon it. The skirt is plaited front and back, but the plaits start from a low-molded yoke. The neckline is high in the back as well as the front, so that the shoulders won't slip off at the decisive swing of the racket. The monogram adds a personal touch. After a hard game, a nice soft wool cardigan is perfect, and for decorative purposes a gay scarf is used. For that white linen suit, use a black, red and white striped cotton blouse and scarf, and tie the scarf under the chin in a pussycat bow.

A charming pajama set for house or beach is fashioned of seersucker, with checked effects in gay colors. A long coat accompanies the outfit, and is made of the same material. A combination both mannish and feminine is achieved when a young person wears flannel slacks and a snug-fitting blouse topped with a short capelet in a light shade.

Jackets, capes and swagger coats are all smart in white silk ensembles. It is a toss-up as to whether the jacket or the cape is smarter. To wear one of the swagger coats is to feel rejuvenated.

White is eternally new and eternally fresh, and this new, fresh and glorious feeling is emphasized by the new style features. Crepe and sheer ensembles are fagoted, and have exquisite lingerie touches. Pique, crinkled crepe and straw combinations contribute to the white mode.

Hats are ambitious to rise in the back, and do so in the most fetching manner. They are simply trimmed, light, summery types of great chic. We have the fine white toyo hats in the tailored mode for summer, and they owe their smartness to precision of design and attention to finishing details. The pointed alpine hat, that reminds of the time when one would laugh at the same, is now proving to be one of the smartest ideas. Its well-chosen companion, in the shape of a soft bag of woolen fabric, is finished with a gold metal bar. The bag is made of a most beguiling two-tone roughish mixture, and the hat also is made of the same.

Flattering hats are made of silk and cotton. Pique and linen hats have smartly stitched brims of various widths in self or contrasting colors. Sailors and turbans come in white pique, and natural, white, linen, navy, brown or black ribbons adorn them. You will find one a necessary adjunct to the summer wardrobe. Pique hats are worn with pique garments. Pique gloves in white may be depended upon to fit perfectly. Novelty meshes with ruffle trims, starched organdy cuffs, the mousquetaire and the pull-ons may all be had in a delightful variety.

Knitted costumes, utterly smart and exceptionally useful, of pure silk and angora can be worn happily in all California seasons. A selection of styles is presented, all combining a one-piece dress with a jacket. The colors are gold, lacquer, blue, green and brown. Gloves, hats and scarfs, all so important, must play their part. This season, the new exotic gloves are fashioned of every conceivable material and design.

A bright, spanking-new idea is the trick of making accessory sets of matching fabrics. Never have we realized how many intriguing things can be done with this and that. Ginghams combined with pique and linens are appearing in perky little sailor hats along with gauntlet gloves, handbags, flowers or maybe a cape to match. This smart assembling goes right around the clock, for you will find gloves made of the same printed silk as a dress, and perhaps a cunning little hat matching. In the evening you will see sets of things in organdy.

Organdy blouses seem more fetching than the last crisp white and pastel blouses. Gay tissue ginghams, equally smart, have frilly collars. Semi-tailored blouses of sheer silk crepe are dainty and cool for summer wear. Some have valenciennes laces and hand-drawn work. Necklines are designed to flatter the wearer and look well under a coat or jacket.

For anything so important as a graduation frock, what could be more flattering or so utterly adorable as the crisp organdy. Choose it in white or pastel, plain, embroidered or matelasse. One always looks well in a polka-dot suit. There is something particularly youthful in the new slenderizing ensembles, with the finger-tip jacket and the tailored frock, in navy or brown, with white dots.

One cannot tell now, by the material, the time of day or the place for which it is intended, and the same thing has happened to colors. The old familiar piques and linens, for instance, that you could depend upon finding in a limited number of delicate shades, now are made in dark, rich colors that widen their appeal and increase their smartness. Black pique is outstanding this year. We see it in beach clothes and for evening wear.

A wrap-around dress is designed for the beach, and has a short, impudent jacket. It is very broad shouldered, due to the two-tiered effect of the capelets, and gives a decided 1933 look. The dress is low-backed, and the blackness is emphasized by large white pearl buttons down the side, which mark the closing. Another black dress, of crepe, has a bodice of the newest string lace. The romance stirring black pique capelet is decorated by a corsage of stiffened crocheted flowers, and a white carded pique collar adds a flattering note. A black satin gown is designed along slender lines, and is topped by a frivolous bolero of black tulle, studded with spangles.

Brevity is the rule for the little wraps, capes generally ending at the elbow line. Jackets fall no lower than the waist. Sleeves are rarely longer than elbow length. A floral frock, pink and white, is worn with a little wrap of shell pink organdy, with frilled circular sleeves.

Native Daughters of the Golden West

MARYSVILLE—THE PRINCIPAL event in this city's observance of Public Schools Week was the dedication, April 26, of Marysville's new primary school building, named Mary Covillaud in memory of the woman whose name is imperishably preserved in the name of the community itself. The ceremonies were in charge of Marysville No. 162, and the main speakers were Past Grand Esther R. Sullivan of the Native Daughters, and Past Grand Fred H. Greely of the Native Sons. Other speakers were Willard Roberts, Principal Walter Kynoch, Willard Will, and Mrs. Charles Sperbeck, president No. 162.

Past Grand Sullivan recounted the history of Mary Covillaud, one of the first women to come to Marysville, in 1847, before the town had been founded. She had come to California at the age of 16, in 1846, with the ill-fated Donner Party, and was taken to Sutter Fort first, and moving to Cordua Ranch, or New Mecklenburg, now Marysville, when nothing but an adobe building used as a trading post occupied the site. Marysville, said Miss Sullivan, was not named for Mary Covillaud because she was the first White woman to come here, nor because she was the most beautiful. It was her spirit of kindliness to the sick and generosity to the unfortunates that made her the beloved of the community, made up mostly of men. Past Grand Greely briefly reviewed the history of Marysville's public schools.

Band of Friendship Strengthened.

Etna—The older mothers of Scott Valley were honor guests Mothers Day at a pleasant entertainment given by Eschscholtzia No. 112. The program, directed by Grand Trustee Minna K. Horn, consisted of two choruses by a group of Native Daughters, words of welcome from Supervising Deputy Margaret E. Weston, readings by Gladys Young, Anita Tucker, Frances Kappler and District Deputy Lettie Lewis, vocal and instrumental numbers by Mildred Young, Margaret Pitman, Helen Lewis, Anita Tucker and Minna K. Horn. At the close of the program refreshments were served by Nancy Smith and a committee at tables attractively decorated with pansies, lilacs and tulips. Some of the Pioneer Mothers, at the request of President Laura Wolford, then entertained with interesting stories reminiscent of early days in Siskiyou County. With mutual expressions of pleasure in this annual reunion, guests and hostesses parted, the bond of friendship strengthened by memories of a happy afternoon.

Anniversary Celebrated.

San Diego—April 26 being the institution anniversary of San Diego No. 208, the past presidents of the Parlor entertained. Past Grand Dr. Louise C. Heilbron, charter past president, was the honor-guest, and on behalf of the Parlor and the past presidents club she was presented with gifts by Pearl Schachtebeck and Sarah Miller. "Souvenirs of Early California," the program feature, was participated in by Pearl Simpson, Rosina Hertzbrun, Elizabeth Case, Alice Damarus, Pearl Schachtebeck, Martha Klindt, Sofia Sharpe, Jane Florentin, Marion Stough, Irma Heilbron, Virginia Burke, Mabel Burgert, Elsie Frank, Ann Wood, Sarah Miller. Refreshments were served.

Honoring Dr. Heilbron, a reception was held at the home of Edith Barngrover the evening of April 25. May 10, the Parlor entertained the past presidents; games were played and refreshments were served. Complimentary to President Isabel Young, Doris Hoffner sponsored a bridge luncheon at her home May 13. Among activities planned for the near-future are a benefit for the homeless children, and an entertainment for the oldtimers. The Parlor is taking an active part in the restoration of El Campo Santo, one of San Diego's oldest cemeteries in which many of the earliest Pioneers were buried.

GRAND PRESIDENT'S OFFICIAL ITINERARY.

Woodland—Grand President Anna Mixon Armstrong's June itinerary includes:

3rd—Deputies' luncheon, San Francisco.

4th—Memorial services, Golden Gate Park, San Francisco.

6th—Tamelpa Parlor No. 231, Mill Valley, official visit.

Mother of Indian Babe Remembered.

Alturas—Twenty-five years ago, when the newly instituted Alturas No. 159 was choosing a design for its official seal, the committee in charge, wishing to have a design typical of the locality, decided on an Indian papoose strapped in its dotjompme, to symbolize the birth of Native Daughter activity in Modoc County. Even at that late date, Modoc Indians were averse to being photographed, considering it a sign of bad luck, but a photograph was necessary for the engraver to copy. Finally a buxom mahala was persuaded to pose her baby. Whether there be any truth in the old Indian superstition may be a mooted question between the Paleface and the Redman, nevertheless the baby did not live long to enjoy further recognition from the Native Daughters. May 10 the mother, Emma Harris, died, a victim of "tick fever." Upon her coffin Alturas placed its floral tribute, in memory of the little babe whose form is stamped upon every official communication emanating from No. 159.

Alturas' contribution to Public Schools Week was an oratorical contest on California history topics. The first prize went to Iris Baldwin of Alturas, and the second to Katherine Wylie of Cedarville. A benefit picture show April 19 and 20 netted satisfactory returns. Maud Sloss is being felicitated on the birth of a daughter, Marilyn Louise; the Parlor presented a silver drinking cup to the little one. A social hour of bridge May 4 was followed by refreshments. The Parlor joined with the American Legion in observance of Memorial Day.

District Meeting.

Oroville—The district meeting May 6 of Butte, Glenn and Plumas Counties Parlors was largely attended. Mrs. Annie Skelly presided, and among the guests were Grand President Anna Mixon Armstrong, Grand Marshal Gladys E. Noce, Grand Trustees Florence D. Boyle and Edna B. Briggs, Past Grands Carrie Roesch-Durham, Dr. Louise C. Heilbron and Esther R. Sullivan, District Deputy Ruth Brown. One candidate was initiated, for Gold of Ophir No. 190.

Grand President Armstrong gave an inspiring address, stating she was in the southland during the recent earthquake and that her faith in the fraternal spirit of the Order was there revivified. Mrs. Vivian Mahon sang "One Hour With You," with words to fit the occasion, and Mrs. Frances Forbes contributed flute solos. At the banquet-board, bedecked with roses, community singing was engaged in with enthusiasm.

Happy Pastime Delights Children.

Oakland—May 11, Piedmont No. 87 joined with Piedmont No. 120 N.S.G.W. in a celebration of Mothers Night at which the mothers of the members of both Parlors were guests. Each mother was presented with a corsage, and refreshments were served. Josephine Collins was chairman of the enjoyable occasion.

Piedmont No. 87 recently made a number very interesting and attractive scrapboo which were distributed to sick children in t local hospitals by President Ella Mullen. T children were delighted with the books, and t members of the Parlor found the making them a happy pastime.

Pioneer Women Guests.

Santa Ana—Twenty members of Santa A No. 235 motored to the Orange County Heal Camp April 27 for a day's sewing—repairi blankets, socks and stockings for the camp ki dies—and accomplished quite a lot of work. noon a covered-dish luncheon was served, a at the day's close the party went on a tour inspection of the camp buildings and equipme The Parlor has adopted a baby and named h Anna Mae, in honor of Grand President An M. Armstrong. Mae West and Margaret Hisk will sponsor a series of card parties for t baby's benefit.

Fifty-one pioneer women of Santa Ana a vicinity attended May 8 the tea given annual by No. 235 in honor of the oldtimers. Mrs. R. Biee, the oldest guest, was presented with lovely boquet. The thimble club met May 11 the Balboa home of Lillian Gant. A citizensh class is scheduled for June and under the chai manship of Matilda S. Lemon the Parlor, carr ing out an annual custom, will present flags the new citizens. A California history speak will be provided, a musical program will be pr sented and dinner will be served.

Hearts of Gold.

Hollister—Copa de Oro No. 105 added a n name to its membership roll April 27, and f lowing the ceremonies contests were he Awards went to Kate Burdg, Marie Rackl Zella Williams and Alice Perry. Deputy Ed Butterfield headed the committee of arran ments, which served particularly dainty refres ments, carrying out the pink and green col scheme in the "eats" as well as the table deco ations.

The Parlor has adopted a homeless baby, an in honor of Past Grand Briggs she has be named Bertha Adele Briggs. The sunshi march at each meeting adds to the funds f the adopted little one. A recent Saturday afte noon a group of little folks, aged 5 to 10, stylin themselves the Good Will Club, put on a circu and at its conclusion marched to the home Past Grand Briggs and gave her the proceed $1.30. The spokesman announced the amou was to be used for the benefit of the adopt baby. Copa de Oro members point with pride this noble gesture, performed on the initiati of the kiddies themselves. Every cent of t contribution represents a heart of gold, and t instigators deserve warm commendation f their unselfish deed.

Pioneer's Grave Plaqued.

Sutter—The memory of Pioneer William Murphy of Donner Party fame was perpetuat in a plaque placed upon his grave in the Yu City Cemetery April 29 by South Butte No. 22 Among the many in attendance at the cer monies were Misses Lulu and Harriet Murph daughters, and Mrs. Harry Cheim, granddaug ter, of the pioneer attorney of Marysville.

The program included: remarks, J. P. C ford; song, "America," audience; address, Pa Grand Esther R. Sullivan; saxophone solo, Love You, California," Ivan Norris; presentati and unveiling of plaque, Mrs. Sadie Winn-Bra ard; song, "The Star Spangled Banner," au ence; remarks, Mrs. A. F. Beecroft, preside South Butte; remarks, Miss Harriet Murphy.

Illustrated Talk on Mexico.

San Bernardino—Lugonia No. 241 celebrat its sixth institution anniversary May 10. Gues were members of Santa Ana No. 235 and Ontar No. 251, and Deputy Margaret Hiskey. Pre dent Noyes cut the birthday cake. Clever j saw puzzles were the placecards. Later in t evening those assembled joined with Arrowhe No. 110 N.S.G.W. in listening to an illustrat talk on Mexico by Roscoe Goodcell. April the Parlor observed Public Schools Week having Margaret Erdt give a talk on art wo in the public schools; Mary Johnson had char of the program.

N.S. GRAND PARLOR

(Continued from Page 7)

and Past Grand Alison F. Watt of the Native Daughters. Mms. Jack Wolff and Gove Cello charmed with delightful vocal solos, the Grass Valley Cornish gold miners' chorus pleased with several selections, and the Grass Valley high school orchestra's contributions were most commendable.

At the grand ball Tuesday night, the grand march was led by Grand President and Mrs. Seth Millington. Excellent music was provided.

The Wednesday outing in the high Sierra! Words are inadequate to describe that pleasure. God's gentle washing of the mountains but added to the gorgeousness of the unexcelled scenery. The caravan paused at Downieville, Sierra County, which had declared a holiday. There the Nevada City high school band entertained, lunch was served by Downieville No. 92, and the townspeople extended every courtesy to the visitors. By the writer, that glorious trip will never be forgotten, thanks to the guidance of Jack Wolff who, while not a native, is intensely interested in the wealth of history that abounds throughout the region traversed. Wouldst be inspired by countless works of Nature unscarred by human hand? Then hit the trail, winding along the forks of the Yuba through ghost towns of the departed but never-to-be-forgotten past, from Grass Valley to the Sierra Buttes!

The banquet Wednesday night was unique, in that six justices of the California Supreme Court—Schenk, Langdon, Preston, Thompson, Curtis and Seawell—sat at the festiveboard in compliment to the latter, who was elevated to the Grand Presidency. Judge George L. Jones was the toastmaster, and the speakers included Mayor M. J. Brock, Justice Ira F. Thompson, Justice John W. Curtis, President Frank Rowe of Quartz Parlor, Grand President Seth Millington, Past Grand Lewis F. Byington and Past Grand Fletcher A. Cutler. Vocal selections were rendered by Chester Prisk and Louis Hooper, and the Grass Valley high school orchestra favored with several numbers. On behalf of the Order, Grand First Vice Justice Emmet Seawell presented a silver service to Grand President Millington, who was also the recipient of a Nevada County gold nugget, presented by Quartz Parlor.

Chairman Loyle Freeman and the arrangements committee worked long and faithfully, and they have the commendation of all who visited Grass Valley for the Fifty-sixth N.S.G.W. Grand Parlor.

In Memoriam

GEORGE HAINES.

To the Officers and Members of Fresno Parlor No. 25 N.S.G.W.—We, your committee appointed to draft resolutions of condolence and respect on the death of Brother George Haines, beg leave to report: that

Whereas, It being the will of Providence that our Brother George Haines should be called by death, thereby depriving this Parlor of one of its most worthy members, one who has been looked upon as a brother devoted unselfishly to the good of the Order and who has worked industriously in the promotion of the work and precepts of the Native Sons of the Golden West. We mourn his loss, but bow in humble subjection to that greater Power that dictates the destinies of all; therefore, be it

Resolved, That the members of Fresno Parlor No. 25 N.S.G.W., in regular session assembled, do hereby proclaim their sorrow over the passing of Brother George Haines, recognizing that in his death one of our most valued members has passed away,—a void that will not, immediately, be filled in the ranks of the Parlor. To his dear wife and daughter we extend our heartfelt sympathy. And be it further resolved, that the foregoing preamble and resolutions be spread upon the minutes of the Parlor, and a copy thereof be sent to the widow of our deceased brother, and that a copy be published in The Grizzly Bear.

Respectfully submitted,

W. C. GUARD,
F. M. LANE,
C. B. HARKNESS,
Committee.

Fresno, May 19, 1933.

MARY KANE MULLALLY.

To the Officers and Members of Aloha Parlor No. 106 Native Daughters of the Golden West—We, your committee appointed to draft a testimonial of respect to the memory of Sister Mary Kane Mullally, respectfully submit the following:

Again our golden chain has been broken, and it is with deep sorrow we bow in humble submission to the will of our Heavenly Father, who has called from our midst our beloved member, Mary Kane Mullally. In her passing our Parlor has lost a most highly respected member, and a husband, a devoted wife.

Resolved, That we extend our sincere and heartfelt sympathy to her bereaved family; and further be it resolved, that a copy of these resolutions be sent to her husband and sister, that a copy in full be spread upon the minutes of this Parlor, and that a copy be sent to The Grizzly Bear for publication.

Respectfully submitted in P.D.F.A.,

GRACE DuPONT,
LURINE MARTIN,
GLADYS FARLEY,
Committee.

Oakland, May 20, 1933.

N.D.G.W. HOME DONATIONS.

San Francisco—Donations to the N.D.G.W. Home since the list last published in The Grizzly Bear include the following, according to Past Grands Dr. Mariana Bertola and Emma G. Foley, chairman and secretary, respectively, of the Grand Parlor Home Committee:

$5 in memory of Josephine Ortega, by LaDorada No. 236. 12 tea towels, 6 table cloths, 3 pot holders, 3 dish cloths, by Grand Trustee Edna Briggs. 12 tea towels, by Mrs. Elinor Taylor of Elitapome No. 55. 2 boxes etched dish cloths and 2 large bundles clean rags, by Past Grand Carrie Roesch Durham. Several dozen magazines, by Mrs. May MacDonald of Alta No. 3. Booklet, "The Romance of Concepcion Arguello," by Mrs. Katherine Jones of Califia No. 22. Books, by Mrs. Ella Osburn of Buena Vista No. 68. 10 books, by Katherine and Sarah Tully of Joaquin No. 5. Metal book ends, by Mrs. Emma Saunders of La Dorada No. 236. Framed picture of Past Grand Dr. Mariana Bertola, by Orinda No. 56. Box of almonds, by Past Grand Carrie Roesch Durham. Box each of almonds, apricots, plums and apples, by Mrs. R. T. V'Rea of Antioch No. 223. 3 large boxes of apricots, by Mrs. Amelia Silva of Dolores No. 169. Plum jam, by Past Grand Mattie M. Stein. 2 gallons jam, by Mrs. Lucie Liegingor of Joaquin No. 5. Box of apples, by Reliance Fruit & Grocery Co. Box of apples, by Mrs. Gladys Simoni of Santa Rosa No. 217. Box of apricots, by Mrs. Myra Rademacher of Antioch No. 223. Sack of onions, by Past Grand Dr. Louise C. Heilbron. Large platter, by Mrs. Evalyn M. Joly of Alta No. 3. 3 hot water pitchers, by Mary E. Rogers of Alta No. 3. Sugar and creamer set, by Miss Emma Dellwig of Buena Vista No. 68. 3 jardinieres, a tray table, and window box for plants, by Mrs. Laura D. Hawkins of Santa Cruz No. 26. 2 sacks leaf mold, by Mrs. Gladys Bennett of Orinda No. 56. Large potted maiden-hair fern, by Grand Trustee Willow Borba. Flowers for the N.D.G.W. Club breakfasts, by Miss Emma Dieckhoff. Flowers, by Past Grand Genevieve W. Baker. Flowers, by N.S. Past Grand Judge Fletcher A. Cutler. Flowers and plant, by Past Grand Emma G. Foley. Crochet work on table linen, by Miss Elizabeth F. Douglass, Mms. Agnes M. Curry and Alice M. Lane. Two volumes, "Memoirs of Ulysses S. Grant," in memory of Margaret A. Wright, by her daughter, Hattie Wright of Galt.

May 13, Lugonia sponsored a dance at Highlands. Several surprise features were introduced. Evelyn Shaddox was chairman of the arrangements committee. The Harmony Club, recently organized, is completing a flower garden quilt and other articles for the coming bazar.

Mothers Entertained.

Salinas—Aleli No. 102 entertained the mothers of its members May 11. A program under the direction of Mrs. W. J. Larkin included: welcome to mothers, Mrs. William Dodd; solo, Miss Henrietta Juhler; trio, songs mother used to sing, Nason sisters, Mrs. Louise Nason-Hatton, Mrs. Frances Nason-Leidig, Mrs. Rose Nason-Rhyner; "The Meaning of Mother's Day," Miss Josephine DeCarli; solo, Mrs. Frances Nason-Leidig; trio, "We Love You Truly," Nason sisters.

During the last number pansy corsages were passed to the visiting mothers. After the program all participated in the game of keno. Refreshments were served at tables prettily decorated with pink roses, carnations and sweetpeas by a committee headed by Mrs. Clara Kalar.

Interesting History Related.

Chico—Annie K. Bidwell No. 168 had a California history period April 27, and Mrs. Laura Anderson told of the coming to California across the plains in 1849 of her grandparents, Mr. and Mrs. Samuel Long. They traversed the Lassen Trail, and at Vina, Tehama County, constructed a raft of green wood and traveled on it to Sacramento. Past Grand Carrie Roesch-Durham was a visitor.

A program May 11 in recognition of Mothers Day was presented by Grace L. Morrow, Katherine McEnespy and Margaret Hudspeth. The latter displayed a map of Chico, made by General John Bidwell, on which the triangle at First and Main streets is designated "Washington Square." Memorial services in honor of departed members were held at the Presbyterian Church May 28.

SUBORDINATE PARLORS BRIEFS.

Sutter Creek—Amapola No. 80 celebrated its thirty-ninth institution anniversary April 27. Mrs. L. L. Cuneo read the minutes of the Parlor's first meeting, held April 26, 1894. Delicious refreshments were served at tables beautifully decorated with iris.

Santa Barbara—Supervising Deputy Anna E. McCaughey and Grand Trustee Jane Vick recently visited San Luis Obispo, where they were entertained by San Luisita No. 108 and San Miguel No. 94 jointly. Miss McCaughey emphasized the importance of program and the carrying out of the principles of the Order, and Mrs. Vick spoke on the White House conference. The visit gave new impetus to the workers of the Parlors.

Modesto—The April card party of Morada No. 199 and Modesto No. 11 N.S.G.W. attracted thirty-two tables of players. Following the play refreshments were served, and then dancing was

(Continued on Page 19)

SAN FRANCISCO

THE ELEVENTH ANNUAL MEETING of the General Association N.D.G.W. Past Presidents was held at the Home April 22. Percapita tax payments showed a membership of 683, in eight associations. A pin designed for Association No. 1 (San Francisco) was adopted as the official emblem of the organization, and a song for the opening ceremonies used by Association No. 4 (Sacramento County) was approved for all associations. Oakland was selected for next year's meeting, Association No. 2 to be the hostess. A vote of thanks was tendered the N.D.G.W. Home Committee for courtesies extended. Officers elected include:

Winifred Halter, chief president; Cora Stobing, junior chief president; Mary Frances Mitchell, chief vice-president; Anna G. Loser, chief secretary; Emma G. Foley, chief treasurer; Margaret G. Hill, chief marshal; Emilie J. Clifford, chief inside sentinel; Mamie Davis, chief outside sentinel; Antha Locklin, chief organist; Edna D. Sampson, Willow Borba, Edith Kelley, Mattie M. Stein, Alice Roll,, directors. In attendance were Founder Leah Magner Williams, Charter Chief Past President Beda Pecheco, Past Chief Presidents Winnie Buckingham, Josephine Schmidt, Susie K. Christ, Millie Tietjen, Lily May Tilden and Josephine Clark, Permanent Members Jennie Brown and Emma G. Foley.

In the evening a program was presented, as follows: Readings, Ann B. Dippel and Margaret Hudspeth; pantomime, "And the Lights Went Out," Association No. 2; kitchen symphony, Association No. 4; musical selections, Clara A. Gairaud and Katherine Kay; skit, "Passing the Buck," Association No. 3; skit, "Mock Marriage in Rhyme," Association No. 1.

MOTHERS DAY AT N.D. HOME.

Mothers Day was observed at the N.D.G.W. Home breakfast Sunday, May 14. The dining-room was beautifully decorated with spring flowers, presented by Portola Parlor No. 172. Past Grand Dr. Mariana Bertola was the chairman, with Mrs. Agnes Curry as co-hostess. Many San Francisco, Marin and Alameda Counties Parlors were represented.

Speakers were Past Grands Bertola, Emma G. Foley, Margaret G. Hill, Bertha Briggs and Dr. Louise C. Heilbron, the latter paying tribute to the Pioneer Mothers; Grand Trustees Anna C. Thuesen and Ethel Begley, Supervising Deputy Alice Lane, and members of the Grand Parlor Home Committee. Ethel Browning of Castro Parlor No. 178 delighted the guests with her golden voice.

GREATER DEEDS FOR CHILDREN PLANNED.

Inspired by the message of Grand President Anna Mixon Armstrong in advocating the adoption of a baby by each Native Daughter Parlor, Alta Parlor No. 3 renewed its interest in the homeless children. At the suggestion of Grand Trustee Anna C. Thuesen, application was made for a baby, a Negro child if possible, and the Parlor is now the proud possessor of a fine baby boy of the desired race, Richard Hall. In addition, Alta has made liberal donations to this great work during the closing Grand Parlor year, and for next year greater deeds are planned.

SONS GUESTS OF DAUGHTERS.

Genevieve Parlor No. 132 N.D.G.W. was hostess to El Dorado Parlor No. 52 N.S.G.W. April 20. Greetings were extended by President Elvira Desmond. The following program was enjoyed: vocal numbers, Evelyn Denike, Alicia O'Day, Theresa Kendall and Ella Collins; specialties, Nora Scheffien; piano selections, Lillian Troy, Betty Marquis; community singing. Through the courtesy of Charles H. Spengemann, Grand Trustee N.S.G.W., music for dancing was furnished by the popular orchestra of Hesperian Parlor No. 137 N.S.G.W. Preceding the dancing delicious homemade refreshments were served by the hospitality committee, Carrie Kerwin, Evelyn Kilkenny, Mayme O'Leary, Edith and Gladys Joorisen, Kathleen Lagrave, Camile Jacobsen, Virginia Lynch, May LaSalle.

April 25, Genevieve held a whist for the Loyalty Pledge, and it was well attended. The Parlor anticipates completing its debt before the Grand Parlor convenes. A beautiful handmade quilt, thirty blocks of which were made by members of the Parlor, will be disposed of for the benefit of members who are unable at the present time to pay their dues. A penny march is held at every meeting for the milk fund of the Parlor. Plans are under way to raise funds for the homeless children.

MANY GREET N.D. GRAND PRESIDENT.

Grand President Anna Mixon Armstrong paid an official visit to Dolores Parlor No. 169 N.D.G.W. April 26. Preceding the meeting a very delightful dinner was served. The meeting-hall, which was beautifully decorated with spring flowers, was filled to overflowing with over 300 members of the Order. The Grand President was escorted through a floral arch made by members of the newly-organized drill team, and was presented with a lovely shower boquet of talisman roses. The ritualistic work was presented in a most commendable manner by President Kittie Mullaney and her capable corps of officers, one candidate being initiated.

Grand President Armstrong expressed pleasure at being present, and complimented the Parlor for its interest in all the projects of the Order. She was the recipient of a beautiful italian luncheon cloth and napkins. Other guests were Grand Organist Clara Gairaud, Grand Trustees Ethel Begley, Anna Thuesen and Edna Briggs, Grand Inside Sentinel Orinda Giannini, Past Grands Margaret Grote Hill, Emma Foley and Mae C. Boldemann, Supervising Deputy Alice Lane, Deputy Agnes McVerry. Tasty refreshments were served in the banquetroom. Junior Past Grand Evelyn I. Carlson was the charming hostess for the evening.

"A COUNTRY COUSIN."

Mothers Day was appropriately celebrated by Castro Parlor No. 178 N.D.G.W. May 17. Twenty-five mothers of the members, as honor-guests, were escorted to the rostrum, introduced by Chairman Cora Stobing and presented with corsages and little souvenirs.

A program, contributed to by the N.D.G.W. Glee Club, Ann Godfrey, Ruby Bried, Elsie Dethlefsen and Barbara Latz, concluded with an original sketch, "A Country Cousin," written by Ruby Bried and presented by the glee club. Dainty refreshments were served at prettily decorated tables.

WELFARE WORK PRAISED.

James Lick Parlor No. 220 N.D.G.W. was paid an official visit May 3 by Grand President Anna Mixon Armstrong. Among other visitors were Past Grands Evelyn I. Carlson and Margaret Hill, Grand Inside Sentinel Orinda Giannini, Grand Trustees Anna Thuesen, Ethel Begley and Edna Briggs. President Margaret Kane presided, and Edna Bishop was chairlady of the evening.

Being introduced to the members, the Grand President was presented with a shower boquet of red roses and pansies, and other grand officers received beautiful compacts. Mrs. Armstrong was pleased with the large class of candidates initiated, and praised the members for the Parlor's progress and its splendid welfare work efforts. A supper brought to a close another perfect evening for the officers, members and friends of James Lick.

MOTHER OF N.D. PAST GRAND PASSES.

Mrs. Catherine Francis Noonan, mother of Mrs. Mae Himes-Noonan, Past Grand President N.D.G.W., passed away April 28. She was a native of Redwood City, San Mateo County, and was affiliated with Portola Parlor No. 172 N.D.G.W.

Cherry Festival—San Leandro, Alameda County, will have its annual cherry festival, June 5-10.

Roundup—The annual Merced City roundup is billed for June 10 and 11.

N.D. DELEGATES

(Continued from Page 9)

Menlo No. 211—Mrs. Grace Berry.
Coloma No. 212—Amy Bartholomew, Berniee Parrott, Nettie Harry.
Liberty No. 213—Evelyn Hale, Helen Hanner.
Phoebe A. Hearst No. 214—Margaret Dempsey.
Victory No. 216—Mrs. Marie Goodman.
Santa Rosa No. 217—Ida Losch, Clytie Lewis.
Plumas Pioneer No. 219—Helen Hall, Elsie Ann Price.
James Lick No. 220—Margaret Kane, Irma Collins.
Las Juntas No. 221—Miss Mabel Nicholson, Miss Winifred Bickel.
Petaluma No. 222—Edna Meadows, Pearl Lopus.
Antioch No. 223—Marguerite Peters, Marguerite Flannery.
Mary E. Bell No. 224—Emma Lawrence, Mabel Podrick.
Fairfax No. 225—Belle Druhan.
South Butte No. 226—Theresa Putman.
Mission No. 227—Hazel Groswird, Estelle Bartholomew, Pearl Anderson.
Miocene No. 228—Evalyn G. Towne.
Palo Alto No. 229—Helena G. Hansen.
Rudecinda No. 230—Letitia Sarelaux, Margaret Kreider.
Bret Harte No. 232—Helen Meyer.
Santa Ana No. 235—Mrs. Mildred Gray, Mrs. Stella Stiffler.
Pleasanton No. 237—Mrs. Julia Cronmie.
Betsy Ross No. 238—Matilda Enos.
Verdugo No. 240—Mrs. Sarah Burleson, Mrs. Margaret Donlan.
Lugonia No. 241—Lucy Mecham, Mary H. Johnson.
Grace No. 242—Mary R. Rothaermel, Helen Anderson.
Susanville No. 243—Mary Gribble.
Madera No. 244—Lois Roach.
Santa Monica Bay No. 245—Mrs. Amada Machado.
Californiana No. 247—Ernestine F. Aylward, Ruth B. Parris, Inez S. Sitton.
Eldora No. 248—Eva B. Bishop.
Balboa No. 249—Mrs. Cecile LeGallee, Mrs. Marge Picetti.
Ontario No. 251—Maude VanFleet.
Utopia No. 252—Alice Cummins.

Fiesta Pageant—The third annual fiesta and pageant, "The Prayer of the Padre," will be staged June 17 and 18 at historic San Fernando Mission, Los Angeles County.

Visalia Rodeo—Visalia, Tulare County, will have a rodeo, June 2-4.

GRIZZLY GROWLS

(CLARENCE M. HUNT.)

The State Legislature came out of a huddle into a recess, but will reconvene in July. A special state election was provided for, to be held June 27, when ten propositions will be submitted to the electorate. Most of those propositions have to do with taxes, directly or indirectly. Voters, and particularly small-home owners, should earnestly and carefully consider each and every one of them, and then go to the polls and cast an intelligent vote! Be not influenced by propaganda, and pleadings of selfish or class interests; vote to reduce the intolerable tax burden, and against any proposal that will relieve a few at added expense to the many. Apropos of conditions in California, the following quotations are pertinent:

"STATE OF CALIFORNIA FACES RECEIVERSHIP UNLESS TAXPAYERS AWAKEN TO SITUATION. The State of California faces a most serious financial situation. The Legislature has recessed without being within striking distance of a balanced budget. A small but heroic band in both houses labored diligently for economy, but the powerful organized groups entrenched in public jobs swarmed the legislative halls. Other interests fought the imposition of new sources of revenue. . . . The gravity of the situation cannot be overstated. . . . Every taxpayer in California must become alive to the problem. . . . The present deplorable condition of State finances can be charged directly to public indifference. With the facts before it, will the public react, or remain complacent until new and undreamed-of burdens are placed upon it?"—Oakland Tribune.

"LEGISLATURE SESSION SHOWS NEED OF PUBLIC AWAKENING IN GOVERNMENT. If one possessed both candor and a caustic pen he could render an exceedingly worthwhile service to his state by writing an expose of the recessed session of the State Legislature. . . . On the bad side of the ledger might be listed: complete breakdown of the economy bloc. . . . Steam-roller and 'star chamber' sessions on many vital issues; . . . lack of leadership and lack of interest in the 'other fellow's problem' were shortcomings all too evident. Many conscientious legislators earnestly trying to do a good job found voters demanding economy and special benefits in the same breath. . . . It would seem, therefore, that California government needs . . . an application of the Golden Rule. But it may require a candid and caustic diagnosis to bring it about."—Van Nuys News.

The additional revelations regarding activities of financial highboys emanating from the National Capital are astounding, but not at all surprising to those who follow the course of events in this country. Those "boys," legalized thieves, have grown gold-fat through feeding by a government which enacted laws to protect them in their thievery.

As frequently stated in these columns, we are, as a people, today suffering because government connived with crooks to enthrone dishonesty. Until honesty again prevails in government, state as well as national, until men of unquestioned honesty and proven ability are chosen to conduct affairs of government, there can be no hope of lasting relief from the conditions which have brought such havoc.

Away back in 1837, when the nation was in distress, the great Daniel Webster remarked: "In times like these, we find ourselves in the midst of a serious financial and industrial crisis. . . . The renewal of confidence and the allaying of violent fear in the minds of the people, which will allow for active buying, rather than money hoarding, must precede business recovery."

That is true today, renewal of confidence must precede recovery. And confidence will not be restored until racketeering, in government, politics, business and society, be obliterated, and the racketeers, high and mighty as well as meek and lowly, be ostracized.

"There has been so much propaganda concerning supposed reductions in public school expenditures in California, that the people paying the bill for the schools should know what actually has been accomplished," says Secretary N. Bradford Trenham of the educational committee of the California Taxpayers Association.

"EXPENDITURES FOR OPERATING THE PUBLIC SCHOOL SYSTEM HAVE BEEN REDUCED LESS THAN FIVE PERCENT BELOW THE PEAK YEAR 1930-31. . . . A sane, dispassionate study of the facts reveals that, taking California as a whole, the schools have been dealt with gently during the depression, when we consider the greatly reduced ability of the public to support any kind of governmental activity."

Asserting "there are a million more men in arms in Europe tonight than on August 1, 1914," and likening Europe to a "smouldering volcano" where the "drift is distinctly toward war," United States Senator William E. Borah declared in a May 20 Washington address: "It will be difficult, if not impossible, to stabilize currencies, adjust tariffs, open markets, and bring trade and commerce back to normal conditions while nations are piling up armaments, making all preparation apparently for war."

Senator Borah commended President Franklin Roosevelt's sagacity and sure grasp of the situation in turning the economic conference from debts to disarmament. "Our troubles lie deeper than dollars and cents," he declared.

Addressing, by invitation, a "dry" meeting in Pasadena, Dr. Kenneth Taber caused an uproar when he remarked he had prescribed whisky for ministers and that they had "thrived on it and lived longer." Asked, "Isn't it true that liquor is a poison?", he replied, "So is food when taken immoderately. Most people dig their graves with their knives and forks." In conclusion, Dr. Taber said young people should be given all the facts of life, if they are to arrive at the truth of any subject.

The Federal Congress has passed and the President has signed a bill providing for suspension of annual assessment work on mining claims. That should benefit California. The suspension, however, does not apply to a mine owner who paid an income tax in 1932.

OTHER PASTURES ARE NO GREENER.

(ADDISON N. CLARK.)

Why should gold in Asia lure you
When there's more in California?
Let an old-time miner warn you
Not to rush to far Manchuria.

Gold in far-off lands comes harder—
Costs you more in human vigor;
So, since net rewards are bigger,
To our own mines give your ardor.

In the depths of our Sierra
Lies a wealth of golden treasure
Yet untouched—in greater measure
Than in days of Padre Serra.

Come and breathe the pine-tree odors
Where our hardy forty-niners
Set a world aflame as miners—
Join us loyal Mother Loders!

Sick of sordid money-shambles,
Daily mankind waxes keener
For new gold—for wealth that's cleaner
Than the gains of tainted gambles.

Brother, if YOUR purse is leaner,
If adversity has torn you,
Mine with us in California—
OTHER PASTURES ARE NO GREENER!

(Addison Clark, San Francisco mining engineer, writer and public relations counsel, knowing the yet-unwon latent gold wealth of the Sierra Nevada's Mother Lode and of the northern Sierra and Coast Range, resents the inane "gold rushes" to supposedly "greener pastures" in remote wildernesses. He has taken this metrical fling at them, emphasizing California's golden opportunities for depression-scarred men today. Through Director Walter W. Bradley of the State Division of Mines, Clark has given the poem to The Grizzly Bear and other California publications, dedicating it to the stimulation of more active development of new, clean PRIMARY wealth—as differentiated from stock-market gambling gains—in the state of his adoption, California.—Editor.)

Know your home-state, California! Learn of its past history and of its present-day development by reading regularly The Grizzly Bear. $1.50 for one year (12 issues). Subscribe now.

AIMS AND OBJECTS of the ORDER OF NATIVE DAUGHTERS OF THE GOLDEN WEST

To cultivate state pride.
To aid state development.
To advance state progress.
To promote the study of California history.
To preserve California's landmarks, relics and traditions.
To honor and keep in memory California's Pioneers.
To stimulate and inspire patriotism.
To assist in the work of americanization.
To encourage higher education for women, as evidenced by the Order's liberal college scholarship.
To guarantee social enjoyment, mental improvement and mutual benefit to members.
To care, conjointly with the Order of Native Sons of the Golden West, for the orphaned children of California, of whatever class, color or creed, by placing them in permanent homes through legal adoption proceedings, thus engaging in the most humanitarian of public welfare work, that of improving the future citizenship of the state.

If YOU were born in California and believe in these principles, you should be a member of the Order of Native Daughters of the Golden West.

Official Directory of Parlors of the N. D. G. W.

ALAMEDA COUNTY.

Angelita No. 32, Livermore—Meets 2nd and 4th Fridays, Foresters Hall; Mrs. Myrtle I. Johnson, Rec. Sec., P.O. box 253.

Piedmont No. 87, Oakland—Meets Thursdays, Corinthian Hall, Pacific Bldg.; Miss Helen Ring, Rec. Sec., 822 11th St.

Aloha No. 106, Oakland—Meets Tuesdays, 4016 Grove St.; Mrs. Lurine Martin, Rec. Sec., 2815 Wallace St., Berkeley.

Hayward No. 122, Hayward—Meets 1st and 3rd Tuesdays, Veterans Memorial Bldg., Main St.; Miss Ruth Gansberger, Rec. Sec., P. O. box 44, Mount Eden.

Berkeley No. 150, Berkeley—Meets 2nd Saturday afternoon, Berkeley City Women's Club, 2315 Durant; Mrs. Lelia B. Baker, Rec. Sec., 915 Contra Costa Ave.

Bear Flag No. 151, Berkeley—Meets 2nd and 4th Wednesdays, Veterans Memorial Bldg., 1931 Center St.; Mrs. Maud Wagner, Rec. Sec., 817 Alcatraz Ave., Oakland.

Encinal No. 156, Alameda—Meets 2nd and 4th Wednesdays, Veterans Memorial Bldg., Central Ave. and Walnut St.; Mrs. Laura E. Fisher, Rec. Sec., 1413 Caroline St.

Brooklyn No. 157, East Oakland—Meets 2nd and 4th Wednesdays, Masonic Temple, 8th Ave. and E. 14th St.; Mrs. Ruth Cooney, Rec. Sec., 3907 14th Ave.

Argonaut No. 166, Oakland—Meets Tuesdays, Klinkner Hall, 59th and San Pablo; Mrs. Ada Spilman, Rec. Sec., 2905 Ellis St., Berkeley.

Bahia Vista No. 167, Oakland—Meets 1st and 3rd Thursdays, Wigwam Hall, Pacific Bldg.; Mrs. Minnie E. Raper, Rec. Sec., 3449 Helen St.

Fruitvale No. 177, Oakland—Meets Fridays, W.O.W. Hall; May E. Barthold, Rec. Sec., 3832 Santa Rita St.

Laura Loma No. 182, Niles—Meets 1st and 3rd Tuesdays, I.O.O.F. Hall; Mrs. Ethel Fournier, Rec. Sec., P. O. box 515.

El Cereso No. 207, San Leandro—Meets 2nd and 4th Tuesdays, Masonic Hall; Mrs. Mary Tuttle, Rec. Sec., P. O. box 56.

Pleasanton No. 237, Pleasanton—Meets 1st Tuesday, I.O.O.F. Hall; Mrs. Myrtle Lanini, Rec. Sec.

Betsy Rose No. 238, Centerville—Meets 1st and 3rd Fridays, Anderson Hall; Miss Constance Lucio, Rec. Sec., P. O. box 187.

AMADOR COUNTY.

Ursula No. 1, Jackson—Meets 2nd and 4th Tuesdays, N.S.G.W. Hall; Mrs. Emma Boarman-Wright, Rec. Sec., 114 Court St.

Chispa No. 40, Ione—Meets 2nd and 4th Fridays, N.S.G.W. Hall; Cynthia Phillips, Rec. Sec.

Amapola No. 80, Sutter Creek—Meets 2nd and 4th Thursdays, N.S.G.W. Bldg.; Mrs. Hazel M. Marre, Rec. Sec.

Forrest No. 86, Plymouth—Meets 2nd and 4th Tuesdays, I.O.O.F. Hall; Mrs. Marguerite Davis, Rec. Sec.

BUTTE COUNTY.

Annie K. Bidwell No. 168, Chico—Meets 2nd and 4th Thursdays, I.O.O.F. Hall; Mrs. Irene Henry, Rec. Sec., 3015 Woodland Ave.

Gold of Ophir No. 190, Oroville—Meets 1st and 3rd Wednesdays, Memorial Hall; Mrs. Ruth Brown, Rec. Sec., 1265 Leah Court.

CALAVERAS COUNTY.

Ruby No. 46, Murphys—Meets 4th Friday, N.S.G.W. Hall; Belle Segale, Rec. Sec.

Princess No. 84, Angels Camp—Meets 2nd and 4th Wednesdays, I.O.O.F. Hall; Mrs. Grace M. Mills, Rec. Sec., P.O. box 313.

San Andreas No. 113, San Andreas—Meets 1st Friday, Fraternal Hall; Miss Doris Treat, Rec. Sec.

COLUSA COUNTY.

Colus No. 194, Colusa—Meets 1st and 3rd Mondays, Eagles Hall; Miss Kate Busch, Rec. Sec., 350 Market St.

CONTRA COSTA COUNTY.

Stirling No. 146, Pittsburg—Meets 1st and 3rd Wednesdays, Veteran Memorial Hall; Mrs. Leslie Clement, Rec. Sec., 466 E. Santa Fe.

Richmond No. 147, Richmond—Meets 1st and 3rd Tuesdays, Richmond Club House, 1125 Nevin Ave.; Grace Curry, Rec. Sec., 932 Ohio Ave.

Donner No. 193, Byron—Meets 1st and 3rd Wednesdays, I.O.O.F. Hall; Mrs. Anna Pendry, Rec. Sec., P.O. box 442, Brentwood.

Las Juntas No. 221, Martinez—Meets 1st and 3rd Mondays, Pythian Castle; Mrs. Lola O. Viera, Rec. Sec., R.F.D. No. 1.

Antioch No. 223, Antioch—Meets 2nd and 4th Tuesdays, I.O.O.F. Hall; Mrs. Estelle Evans, Rec. Sec., 202 E. 5th St., Pittsburg.

Carquinez No. 234, Crockett—Meets 2nd and 4th Wednesdays, I.O.O.F. Hall; Mrs. Cecile Petee, Rec. Sec., 465 Edwards St.

EL DORADO COUNTY.

Marguerite No. 12, Placerville—Meets 1st and 3rd Wednesdays, Masonic Hall; Mrs. Nettie Leonardi, Rec. Sec., 25 Coloma St.

El Dorado No. 186, Georgetown—Meets 2nd and 4th Saturday afternoons, I.O.O.F. Hall; Mrs. Alta L. Douglas, Rec. Sec.

FRESNO COUNTY.

Fresno No. 187, Fresno—Meets 2nd and 4th Fridays, Pythian Castle, Cor. "R" and Merced Sts.; Mary Aubery, Rec. Sec., 1040 Delphia Ave.

GRAND OFFICERS.

Mrs. Evelyn I. Carlson........Past Grand President
281 E. Tuscaloosa Ave., Atherton

Mrs. Anna M. Armstrong........Grand President
Woodland

Mrs. Irma Laird........Grand Vice-president
Alturas

Mrs. Sallie R. Thaler........Grand Secretary
555 Baker St., San Francisco

Mrs. Susie K. Christ........Grand Treasurer
555 Baker St., San Francisco

Mrs. Gladys Noce........Grand Marshal
Sutter Creek

Mrs. Orinda G. Giannini........Grand Inside Sentinel
2142 Filbert St., San Francisco

Mrs. Hazel B. Hansen........Grand Outside Sentinel
501 Griswold St., Glendale

Mrs. Clara Gairaud........Grand Organist
134 Locust St., San Jose

GRAND TRUSTEES.

Mrs. Florence Boyle........Oroville
Mrs. Edna Briggs........1045 Santa Ynez Way, Sacramento
Mrs. Anna Thuesen........615 38th Ave., San Francisco
Mrs. Ethel Begley........233 Prospect Ave., San Francisco
Mrs. Minna K. Horn........Etna
Mrs. Jane Vick........418 Bath St., Santa Barbara
Mrs. Willow Borba........330 So. Main St., Sebastopol

GLENN COUNTY.

Berryessa No. 192, Willows—Meets 1st and 3rd Mondays, I.O.O.F. Hall; Mrs. Leonora Neate, Rec. Sec., 338 No. Lassen St.

HUMBOLDT COUNTY.

Occident No. 28, Eureka—Meets 1st and 3rd Wednesdays, N.S.G.W. Hall; Mrs. Eva L. MacDonald, Rec. Sec., 2309 "B" St.

Oneonta No. 71, Ferndale—Meets 2nd and 4th Fridays, I.O.O.F. Hall; Mrs. Myra Rumrill, Rec. Sec., P.O. box 142.

Reichling No. 97, Fortuna—Meets 1st and 3rd Tuesdays, Friendship Hall; Mrs. Grace Swett, Rec. Sec., P. O. box 328.

KERN COUNTY.

Miocene No. 228, Taft—Meets 1st and 3rd Wednesday afternoons, I.O.O.F. Hall; Mrs. Evalyn G. Towne, Rec. Sec., 301 Woodrow St.

El Tejon No. 239, Bakersfield—Meets 1st and 3rd Fridays, Eagles Hall, 1714 "G" St.; Mary B. Hampson, Rec. Sec., 908 Quincy St.

Desert Gold No. 250, Mojave—Meets 2nd and 4th Fridays, I.O.O.F. Hall; Jane Lucile Waters, Rec. Sec., Tehachapi.

LAKE COUNTY.

Clear Lake No. 135, Middletown—Meets 2nd and 4th Tuesdays, Herrick Hall; Mrs. Alma E. Snow, Rec. Sec.

LASSEN COUNTY.

Nataqua No. 152, Standish—Meets 1st and 3rd Wednesdays, Foresters Hall; Mrs. Mayda Elledge, Rec. Sec.

Mount Lassen No. 215, Bieber—Meets 2nd and 4th Thursdays, I.O.O.F. Hall; Mrs. Angie C. Kenyon, Rec. Sec.

Susanville No. 243, Susanville—Meets 3rd Thursday, I.O.O.F. Hall; Mildred Hardy, Rec. Sec., P.O. box 425.

LOS ANGELES COUNTY.

Los Angeles No. 124, Los Angeles—Meets 1st and 3rd Wednesdays, I.O.O.F. Hall, Washington and Oak Sts.; Mrs. Mary K. Corcoran, Rec. Sec., 322 No. Van Ness Ave.

Long Beach No. 154, Long Beach—Meets 1st and 3rd Thursdays, Home of Eleonor Johnson, 1920 Bermuda St.; Mrs. Bertha Hitt, Rec. Sec., 5355 Lime Ave.

Rudecinda No. 230, San Pedro—Meets 2nd and 4th Thursdays, Unity Hall, I.O.O.F. Temple, 10th and Gaffey; Letitia Sarciaux, Rec. Sec., 1054 W. 24th St.

Verdugo No. 240, Glendale—Meets 2nd and 4th Tuesdays, Masonic Temple, 234 So. Brand Blvd.; Miss Etta Fulkerth, Rec. Sec., 526 No. Orange St.

Santa Monica Bay No. 245, Santa Monica—Meets 2nd and 4th Wednesdays, Odd Fellows Hall, 1431 Third St.; Mrs. Rosalie Hyde, Rec. Sec., 738 Flower St., Venice.

Californiana No. 247, Los Angeles—Meets 2nd and 4th Tuesday afternoons, Hollywood Studio Club, 1215 Lodi Place; Mrs. Inez Sitton, Rec. Sec., 4228 Berenice St.

MADERA COUNTY.

Madera No. 244, Madera—Meets 2nd and 4th Thursdays, Masonic Annex; Mrs. Margaret C. Boyle, Rec. Sec., 111 No. "B" St.

MARIN COUNTY.

Sea Point No. 196, Sausalito—Meets 2nd and 4th Mondays, Perry Hall, 50 Caledonia St.; Mrs. Mary B. Smith, Rec. Sec., 47½ Glen Drive.

Marinita No. 198, San Rafael—Meets 2nd and 4th Mondays, 316 "B" St.; Miss Mollye Y. Spaelti, Rec. Sec., 539 4th St.

Fairfax No. 225, Fairfax—Meets 2nd and 4th Tuesdays, Community Hall; Mrs. Marguerite Geary, Rec. Sec.

Tamelpa No. 231, Mill Valley—Meets 1st and 2nd Tuesdays, I.O.O.F. Hall; Mrs. Delphine M. Todt, Rec. Sec., 500 Irwin St., San Rafael.

MARIPOSA COUNTY.

Mariposa No. 63, Mariposa—Meets 1st and 3rd Fridays, I.O.O.F. Hall; Elizabeth E. Johnson, Rec. Sec.

MENDOCINO COUNTY.

Fort Bragg No. 210, Fort Bragg—Meets 1st Thursday, I.O.O.F. Hall; Mrs. Ruth W. Fuller, Rec. Sec.

MERCED COUNTY.

Veritas No. 75, Merced—Meets 1st and 3rd Tuesdays, I.O.O.F. Hall; Miss Flora Fernandes, Rec. Sec., Parkside Apt.

MODOC COUNTY.

Alturas No. 159, Alturas—Meets 1st Thursday, Alturas Civic Club; Mrs. Irma W. Laird, Rec. Sec.

MONTEREY COUNTY.

Aleli No. 102, Salinas—Meets 2nd and 4th Thursdays, Pythian Hall; Miss Rose Rhyner, Rec. Sec., 420 Soledad St.

Junipero No. 141, Monterey—Meets 2nd and 4th Fridays, K. of P. Hall, Main St.; Miss Matilda M. Bergschicker, Rec. Sec., 498 Van Buren St.

NAPA COUNTY.

Eshcol No. 16, Napa—Meets 2nd and 4th Mondays, N.S.G.W. Hall; Mrs. Ella Ingram, Rec. Sec., 2140 Seminary St.

Calistoga No. 145, Calistoga—Meets 2nd and 4th Mondays, I.O.O.F. Hall; Sadie P. Brooks, Rec. Sec.

La Junta No. 203, Saint Helena—Meets 1st and 3rd Tuesdays, N.S.G.W. Hall; Mrs. Marie Signorelli, Rec. Sec., 1341 Madrona Ave.

ATTENTION, SECRETARIES!

THIS DIRECTORY IS PUBLISHED BY AUTHORITY OF THE GRAND PARLOR N.D.G.W., AND ALL NOTICES OF CHANGES MUST BE RECEIVED BY THE GRAND SECRETARY (NOT THE MAGAZINE) ON OR BEFORE THE 20TH OF EACH MONTH TO INSURE CORRECTION IN NEXT PUBLICATION OF DIRECTORY.

NEVADA COUNTY.

Laurel No. 6, Nevada City—Meets 1st and 3rd Wednesdays, I.O.O.F. Hall; Mrs. Nellie E. Clark, Rec. Sec., 412 Pine St.

Manzanita No. 29, Grass Valley—Meets 1st and 3rd Tuesdays, Auditorium; Mrs. Loraine Keast, Rec. Sec., 123 Race St.

Columbia No. 70, French Corral—Meets Fridays, Farrelley Hall; Mrs. Kate Farrelley-Sullivan, Rec. Sec.

Snow Peak No. 176, Truckee—Meets 1st Monday, I.O.O.F. Hall; Mrs. Henrietta M. Eaton, Rec. Sec., P. O. box 116.

ORANGE COUNTY.

Santa Ana No. 235, Santa Ana—Meets 2nd and 4th Mondays, K.C. Hall, 4th and French Sts.; Mrs. Matilda S. Lemon, Rec. Sec., 1628 W. 5th St.

Grace No. 242, Fullerton—Meets 1st and 3rd Thursdays, I.O.O.F. Hall, 116½ E. Commonwealth; Mrs. Mary R. Rothaermel, Rec. Sec., Acacia St. & Commonwealth.

PLACER COUNTY.

Placer No. 138, Lincoln—Meets 2nd Wednesday, I.O.O.F. Hall; Miss Carrie Parlin, Rec. Sec.

La Rosa No. 191, Roseville—Meets 1st and 3rd Tuesdays, Eagles Hall; Mrs. Alice Lee West, Rec. Sec., Rocklin.

Auburn No. 233, Auburn—Meets 2nd and 4th Fridays, Foresters Hall; Mrs. Elsie Patrick, Rec. Sec.

PLUMAS COUNTY.

Plumas Pioneer No. 219, Quincy—Meets 1st and 3rd Mondays, I.O.O.F. Hall; Minnie E. Johnson, Rec. Sec., P. O. box 243.

SACRAMENTO COUNTY.

Califia No. 22, Sacramento—Meets 2nd and 4th Tuesdays, N.S.G.W. Hall; Miss Lulu Gillis, Rec. Sec., 921 8th St.

La Bandera No. 110, Sacramento—Meets 1st and 3rd Fridays, N.S.G.W. Hall; Mrs. Clara Weldon, Rec. Sec., 1310 "O" St.

Sutter No. 111, Sacramento—Meets 1st and 3rd Tuesdays, N.S.G.W. Hall; Mrs. Adele Nix, Rec. Sec., 1238 "S" St.

Fern No. 123, Folsom—Meets 1st and 3rd Tuesdays, K.P. Hall; Elizabeth Ryan, Rec. Sec., Represa.

Chabolla No. 171, Galt—Meets 2nd and 4th Tuesdays, I.O.O.F. Hall; Mrs. Mary Pritchard, Rec. Sec.

Coloma No. 212, Sacramento—Meets 1st and 3rd Tuesdays, I.O.O.F. Hall, Oak Park; Mrs. Nettie Harry, Rec. Sec., 1217 35th St.

Liberty No. 213, Elk Grove—Meets 2nd and 4th Fridays, I.O.O.F. Hall; Mrs. Frances Wackman, Rec. Sec., P. O. box 192.

Victory No. 216, Courtland—Meets 1st Saturday and 3rd Monday, N.S.G.W. Hall; Mrs. Agneda Lample, Rec. Sec.

Rio Rita No. 253, Sacramento—Meets 1st and 3rd Mondays, 902 "J" St.; Dorothea Rourke, Rec. Sec.

SAN BENITO COUNTY.

Copa de Oro No. 105, Hollister—Meets 2nd and 4th Thursdays, Grangers Union Hall; Mrs. Mollie Daveggio, Rec. Sec., 110 San Benito St.

San Juan Bautista No. 179, San Juan Bautista—Meets 1st Wednesday, Mission Corridor Rooms; Miss Gertrude Breen, Rec. Sec.

SAN BERNARDINO COUNTY.

Lugonia No. 241, San Bernardino—Meets 2nd and 4th Wednesdays, Eagles Hall; Miss Lois Poling, Rec. Sec., 295 E. 11th St.

Ontario No. 251, Ontario—Meets 2nd and 4th Thursdays, Ontario Hotel; Miss Helen Hickman, Rec. Sec., 923 No. Laurel Ave.

SAN DIEGO COUNTY.

San Diego No. 208, San Diego—Meets 2nd and 4th Wednesdays, Directors Room, Chamber Commerce Bldg., 499 W. Broadway; Mrs. Elsie Case, Rec. Sec., 3051 Broadway.

SAN FRANCISCO CITY AND COUNTY.

Minerva No. 2, San Francisco—Meets 1st and 3rd Wednesdays, N.S.G.W. Bldg.; Miss Dorothy Finn, Rec. Sec., 90 Princess St., Sausalito.

Alta No. 3, San Francisco—Meets 2nd and 4th Tuesdays, N.S.G.W. Bldg.; Mrs. Agnese L. Hughes, Rec. Sec., 3980 Sacramento St.

Oro Fino No. 9, San Francisco—Meets 1st and 3rd Thursdays, N.S.G.W. Bldg.; Mrs. Josephine B. Morrisey, Rec. Sec., 4441 20th St.

Golden State No. 50, San Francisco—Meets 1st and 3rd Wednesdays, N.D.G.W. Home; Miss Millie Tietjen, Rec. Sec., 328 Lexington Ave.

Orinda No. 56, San Francisco—Meets 2nd, 4th and 5th Fridays, N.D.G.W. Home; Mrs. Anna A. Gruber-Loser, Rec. Sec., 72 Grove Lane, San Anselmo.

Fremont No. 59, San Francisco—Meets 1st and 3rd Tuesdays, N.S.G.W. Bldg.; Miss Hannah Collins, Rec. Sec., 617 Fillmore St.

Buena Vista No. 68, San Francisco—Meets 1st, 3rd and 5th Thursdays, N.D.G.W. Home; Miss Margaret Barrett, Rec. Sec., 3774 20th St.

Las Lomas No. 72, San Francisco—Meets 1st and 3rd Tuesdays, N.D.G.W. Home; Mrs. Marion S. Day, Rec. Sec., 469 Noe St.

Yosemite No. 83, San Francisco—Meets 1st and 3rd Tuesdays, American Hall, 20th and Capp Sts.; Miss Mary Monahan, Rec. Sec., 237 Noe St.

La Estrella No. 89, San Francisco—Meets 2nd and 4th Mondays, N.S.G.W. Bldg.; Miss Birdie Hartman, Rec. Sec., 1018 Jackson St.

Sans Souci No. 96, San Francisco—Meets 2nd and 4th Mondays, N.D.G.W. Home; Mrs. Minnie F. Dobbin, Rec. Sec., 1483 43rd Ave.

Calaveras No. 103, San Francisco—Meets 2nd and 4th Tuesdays, Swedish American Hall, 2174 Market St.; Mary L. Krogh, Rec. Sec., 4235 Cabrillo St.

Darina No. 114, San Francisco—Meets 1st and 3rd Mondays, N.S.G.W. Bldg.; Miss Adele Walsh, Rec. Sec., 479 Page St.

El Vespero No. 118, San Francisco—Meets 2nd and 4th Tuesdays, Masonic Hall, 4705 3rd St.; Mrs. Nell R. Boege, Rec. Sec., 1626 Kirkwood Ave.

Genevieve No. 132, San Francisco—Meets 1st and 3rd Thursdays, N.S.G.W. Bldg.; Miss Branice Peguillan, Rec. Sec., 2434 16th Ave.

Keith No. 137, San Francisco—Meets 2nd and 4th Thursdays, N.S.G.W. Bldg.; Mrs. Helen T. Mann, Rec. Sec., 575 Pierce St., Apt. 206.

Gabrielle No. 139, San Francisco—Meets 2nd and 4th Wednesdays, N.S.G.W. Bldg.; Mrs. Dorothy Wuesterfeld, Rec. Sec., 1020 Munich St.

Presidio No. 148, San Francisco—Meets 2nd and 4th Tuesdays, N.S.G.W. Bldg.; Mrs. Hattie Gaughran, Rec. Sec., 713 Capp St.

Guadalupe No. 153, San Francisco—Meets 2nd and 4th Mondays, Forester Hall, 170 Valencia St.; Miss May A. McCarthy, Rec. Sec., 336 Elsie St.

Golden Gate No. 158, San Francisco—Meets 2nd and 4th Mondays, N.S.G.W. Bldg.; Mrs. Mary Sullivan, Rec. Sec., 33 Cuvier St.

Dolores No. 169, San Francisco—Meets 2nd and 4th Wednesdays, N.S.G.W. Bldg.; Mrs. Ada Saunders, Rec. Sec., 284 Allison St.

Linda Rosa No. 170, San Francisco—Meets 2nd and 4th Wednesdays, Swedish American Hall, 2174 Market St.; Mrs. Eva P. Tyrrel, Rec. Sec., 2629 Mission St.
Portola No. 172, San Francisco—Meets 1st and 3rd Tuesdays, N.S.G.W. Bldg.; Catherine H. Dolly, Rec. Sec., 4125 23rd St.
Castro No. 178, San Francisco—Meets 1st and 3rd Wednesdays, K.C. Bldg., 150 Golden Gate Ave.; Miss Adeline Saudersfeld, Rec Sec., 50 Baker St.
Twin Peaks No. 185, San Francisco—Meets 2nd and 4th Fridays, Druids Temple, 44 Page St.; Mrs. Loretta Cameron, Rec. Sec., 8969 Army St.
James Lick No. 220, San Francisco—Meets 1st and 3rd Wednesdays, N.S.G.W. Bldg.; Mrs. Edna Bishop, Rec. Sec., 3841 24th St.
Mission No. 227, San Francisco—Meets 2nd and 4th Fridays, N.S.G.W. Bldg.; Mrs. Ann Dippul, Rec. Sec., 443 Dewey Blvd.
Bret Harte No. 232, San Francisco—Meets 2nd and 4th Tuesdays, Aloha Hall, 3009 16th St.; Pearl Wedde, Rec. Sec., 225 7th Ave.
La Dorada No. 236, San Francisco—Meets 2nd and 4th Thursdays, N.S.G.W. Hall; Mrs. Theresa R. O'Brien, Rec. Sec. 567 Liberty St.
Balboa No. 240, San Francisco—Meets 1st and 3rd Thursdays, Knights Columbus Hall, 382 18th Ave.; Miss Jean Moffet, Rec. Sec., 476 26th Ave.
Utopia No. 252, San Francisco—Meets 2nd and 4th Tuesdays, American Hall, 20th and Capp Sts.; Miss Lelia M. Little, Rec. Sec., 4450 20th St.

SAN JOAQUIN COUNTY.

Joaquin No. 5, Stockton—Meets 2nd and 4th Tuesdays, N.S.G.W. Hall, 314 E. Main St.; Mrs. Della Garvin, Rec. Sec., 1122 E. Market St.
El Pescadero No. 82, Tracy—Meets 1st and 3rd Fridays, I.O.O.F. Hall; Mrs. Mary A. Hewitson, Rec. Sec., 122 Walnut St.
Ivy No. 88, Lodi—Meets 1st and 3rd Wednesdays, Eagles Hall; Mrs. Mae Corson, Rec. Sec., 109 So. School St.
Calis de Oro No. 206, Stockton—Meets 1st and 3rd Tuesdays, N.S.G.W. Hall, 314 E. Main St.; Mrs. Frances Germain, Rec. Sec., 450 No. Regent.
Phoebe A. Hearst No. 214, Manteca—Meets 2nd and 4th Wednesdays, I.O.O.F. Hall; Mrs. Josie M. Frederick, Rec. Sec., Route A, Box 364, Ripon.

SAN LUIS OBISPO COUNTY.

San Miguel No. 94, San Miguel—Meets 2nd and 4th Wednesday afternoons, Clemon Hall; Mrs. Nellie Wickstrom, Rec. Sec.
San Luisita No. 108, San Luis Obispo—Meets 2nd and 4th Thursdays, W.O.W. Hall; Miss Agnes M. Lee, Rec. Sec., P. O. box 584.
El Pinal No. 163, Cambria—Meets 2nd, 4th and 5th Tuesdays, N.S.G.W. Hall; Kathryn Luchessa, Rec. Sec.

SAN MATEO COUNTY.

Bonita No. 10, Redwood City—Meets 2nd and 4th Thursdays, I.O.O.F. Hall; Mrs. Dora Wilson, Rec. Sec., 518 Middlefield Rd.
Vista del Mar No. 155, Halfmoon Bay—Meets 2nd Thursday, I.O.O.F. Hall; Elizabeth Olney, Rec. Sec.
Ano Nuevo No. 180, Pescadero—Meets 1st and 3rd Wednesdays, I.O.O.F. Hall; Mrs. Alice Mattei, Rec. Sec.
El Carmelo No. 181, Daly City—Meets 1st and 3rd Wednesdays, Masonic Hall; Mrs. Alice Mathias Oldham, Rec. Sec., 2218 26th Ave., San Francisco.
Menlo No. 211, Menlo Park—Meets 2nd and 4th Mondays, Masonic Hall; Mrs. Frances E. Maloney, Rec. Sec., P. O. box 626.
San Bruno No. 246, San Bruno—Meets 2nd and 4th Fridays, Legion Hall; Miss Mildred Foley, Rec. Sec., 217 Miller Ave., South San Francisco.

SANTA BARBARA COUNTY.

Reina del Mar No. 126, Santa Barbara—Meets 1st and 3rd Tuesdays, Pythian Castle, 222 W. Carillo St.; Mrs. Dorothy Yule, Rec. Sec., 112 Ocean Ave.

SANTA CLARA COUNTY.

San Jose No. 81, San Jose—Meets Thursdays, Catholic Women Center, 5th and San Fernando Sts.; Mrs. Nellie Fleming, Rec. Sec., Catholic Women Center.
Vendome No. 100, San Jose—Meets 2nd and 4th Wednesdays, Old Scottish Rite Temple; Miss Marie Buck, Rec. Sec., 245 Hawthorne St.
El Monte No. 205, Mountain View—Meets 2nd and 4th Fridays, American Legion Hall; Miss Elizabeth Spencer, Rec. Sec., 1620 Villa St.
Palo Alto No. 229, Palo Alto—Meets 1st and 2nd Mondays, N.S.G.W. Hall; Miss Helena G. Hansen, Rec. Sec., 531 Lytton Ave.

SANTA CRUZ COUNTY.

Santa Cruz No. 26, Santa Cruz—Meets Mondays, N.S.G.W. Hall; Mrs. May L. Williamson, Rec. Sec., 170 Walnut Ave.
El Pajaro No. 35, Watsonville—Meets 1st and 3rd Tuesdays, I.O.O.F. Hall; Miss Ruth E. Wilson, Rec. Sec., 16 Laurel St.

SHASTA COUNTY.

Camellia No. 41, Anderson—Meets 1st and 3rd Tuesdays, Masonic Hall; Mrs. Olga E. Welbourn, Rec. Sec.
Lassen View No. 98, Shasta—Meets 2nd Friday, Masonic Hall; Miss Louise Litsch, Rec. Sec.
Hiawatha No. 140, Redding—Meets 2nd and 4th Wednesdays, Moose Hall; Ruth Presleigh, Rec. Sec., Office County Clerk.

SIERRA COUNTY.

Naomi No. 36, Downieville—Meets 2nd and 4th Wednesdays, I.O.O.F. Hall; Louise C. Dubuque, Rec. Sec.
Imogen No. 134, Sierraville—Meets 2nd and 4th Saturday afternoons, Copren Hall; Mrs. Jennie Copren, Rec. Sec.

SISKIYOU COUNTY.

Eschscholtzia No. 112, Etna—Meets 1st and 3rd Wednesdays, Masonic Hall; Mrs. Bernice E. Smith, Rec. Sec.
Mountain Dawn No. 120, Sawyers Bar—Meets 2nd and last Wednesdays, I.O.O.F. Hall; Miss Edith Dunphy, Rec. Sec.

SOLANO COUNTY.

Vallejo No. 195, Vallejo—Meets 1st and 3rd Wednesdays, K.C. Hall, 820 Marin St.; Mrs. Mary Combs, Rec. Sec., 511 York St.
Mary E. Bell No. 224, Dixon—Meets 2nd and 4th Thursdays, I.O.O.F. Hall; Mary Young, Rec. Sec.

SONOMA COUNTY.

Sonoma No. 209, Sonoma—Meets 2nd and 4th Mondays, I.O.O.F. Hall; Mrs. Mae Norrbom, Rec. Sec., R.F.D., box 171.
Santa Rosa No. 217, Santa Rosa—Meets 1st and 3rd Thursdays, N.S.G.W. Hall; Mrs. Clytie L. Lewis, Rec. Sec., R.F.D. No. 4, Box 345-A.
Petaluma No. 222, Petaluma—Meets 1st and 3rd Tuesdays, Dania Hall; Mrs. Margaret M. Oeltjen, Rec. Sec., 503 Prospect St.

STANISLAUS COUNTY.

Oakdale No. 125, Oakdale—Meets 3rd Monday, McLeod Home; Mrs. Lou Reeder, Rec. Sec.
Morada No. 199, Modesto—Meets 2nd and 4th Wednesdays, I.O.O.F. Hall; Mrs. Susan Sullivan, Rec. Sec., 823 10th St.
Eldora No. 248, Turlock—Meets 1st and 3rd Mondays, Masonic Temple; Effie Lund, Rec. Sec., 312 Mitchell St.

SUTTER COUNTY.

South Butte No. 226, Sutter—Meets 1st and 3rd Mondays, N.D.G.W. Hall; Mrs. Abbie N. Vagedes, Rec. Sec.

NATIVE DAUGHTER NEWS

(Continued from Page 15)

in order. Chas. D. Blaine was master of ceremonies, Ann Oleson had charge of the card party arrangements, and Robert Benson and Alice Phoenix were in charge of the social committee. A sociable held April 29 by Morada was directed by Ethel Enos. No. 199 has adopted a homeless baby boy and named him "Jim Morada."

Sonoma—Sonoma No. 209 had a most delightful meeting May 8, when Supervising Deputy Clytie Lewis, Deputy Mary Vogt and Past Grand Margaret Hill, "mother" of the Parlor, were guests. In observance of Mothers Day an appropriate program of songs and recitations was presented. A beautiful basket of choice flowers was presented "Mother" Hill, and the members were greatly rewarded by the lovely response from her. Delicious refreshments were served at beautifully decorated tables. At the place of each past president was a token, in recognition of her past efforts for the Parlor. Among other visitors were Grand Trustees Anna Thuesen and Willow Borba. The evening was unanimously voted a huge success.

Palo Alto—When Grand President Anna Mixon Armstrong officially visited Palo Alto No. 229 she found a small, but happy, group assembled to greet her. A fine fraternal spirit was everywhere evident, and the ritual was exemplified in a commendable manner. Visitors included representatives from ten Parlors, Grand Trustee Anna Thuesen, Grand Organist Clara Gairaud, Past Grand Margaret Hill, Supervising Deputy Katherine Nelson, Deputies Marie Buck, Marie Orinda, Elsie Fisher, Mary Junker. A mystery box was disposed of and brought a neat sum for the homeless children. President Adelaide Freeman, an experienced leader, as hostess of the occasion prepared and donated delicious refreshments for the reception that closed a very profitable and most delightful evening.

N.D.G.W. OFFICIAL DEATH LIST.

Giving the name, the date of death, and the Subordinate Parlor affiliation of all deceased members as reported to Grand Secretary Sallie R. Thaler from April 19, 1933, to May 18, 1933:

Archer, Clara Bass; March 26; Hiawatha No. 140.
Cahill, Nellie; April 20; Linda Rosa No. 170.
Restovich, Ida Mae; April 21; Castro No. 178.
FitzSimmons, Nellie M.; April 22; Alta No. 3.
Bennott, Agnes Christensen; April 21; Angelita No. 32.
Carmichael, Abbie; April 22; Oakdale No. 12[illegible].
Himes, Catherine; April 28; Portola No. 172.
Murray, Abbie L.; April 20; Woodland No. 90.
Myers, Elizabeth; April 29; Alta No. 3.
Zumwalt, Etta Haley; April 25; Ursula No. 1.
Eldridge, Irene; April 15; Joaquin No. 5.

TEHAMA COUNTY.

Berendos No. 23, Red Bluff—Meets 1st and 3rd Tuesdays, W.O.W. Hall, 200 Pine St.; Mrs. Lillie Hammer, Rec. Sec., 636 Jackson St.

TRINITY COUNTY.

Eltapome No. 55, Weaverville—Meets 2nd and 4th Thursdays, N.S.G.W. Hall; Mrs. Lou N. Fetzer, Rec. Sec.

TUOLUMNE COUNTY.

Dardanelle No. 66, Sonora—Meets Fridays, I.O.O.F. Hall; Mrs. Nettie Whitto, Rec. Sec., P.O. box 122.
Golden Era No. 99, Columbia—Meets 1st and 3rd Thursdays, N.S.G.W. Hall; Miss Irene Ponce, Rec. Sec.
Anona No. 164, Jamestown—Meets 2nd and 4th Tuesdays, I.O.O.F. Hall; Nellie Hope, Rec. Sec.

YOLO COUNTY.

Woodland No. 90, Woodland—Meets 2nd and 4th Tuesdays, N.S.G.W. Hall; Mrs. Maude Heaton, Rec. Sec., 153 College St.

YUBA COUNTY.

Marysville No. 162, Marysville—Meets 2nd and 4th Wednesdays, Liberty Hall; Miss Cecelia C. Gomes, Rec. Sec., 701 6th St.
Camp Far West No. 218, Wheatland—Meets 3rd Tuesday, I.O.O.F. Hall; Mrs. Ethel C. Brock, Rec. Sec., P. O. box 285.

AFFILIATED ORGANIZATIONS.

General Association Past Presidents—Meetings held annually in April at the home-town of Chief President; Mrs. Winifred Halter, 465 40th St., Oakland, Chief President; Mrs. Anna G. Loser, 72 Grove Lane, San Anselmo, Chief Secretary.
Past Presidents Association No. 1—Meets 1st and 3rd Mondays, N.S.G.W. Bldg., 414 Mason St., San Francisco; Mrs. Alice Ogburn, Pres.; Mrs. Leah M. Williams, Rec. Sec., 956 Pierce St., Apt. 104, San Francisco.
Past Presidents Association No. 2—Meets 2nd and 4th Mondays, "Wigwam," Pacific Bldg., 16th and Jefferson, Oakland; Anna Enos, Pres.; Mrs. Elizabeth B. Goodman, Rec. Sec., 134 Juana Ave., San Leandro.
Past Presidents Association No. 3 (Santa Clara County)—Meets 2nd Tuesday, Musicians Hall, 114 E. Santa Clara St., San Jose; Augusta Singleton, Pres.; Clara Briggs, Rec. Sec., 1336 Magnolia Ave., San Jose.
Past Presidents Association No. 4 (Sacramento County)—Meets 2nd Monday, N.S.G.W. Hall, 11th and "J" Sts., Sacramento City; Edith Kelley, Pres.; Lily May Tilden, Rec. Sec., 3225 "T" St., Sacramento.
Past Presidents Association No. 5 (Butte County)—Meets 1st Friday, homes of members, Chico and Oroville; Marie Picanco, Pres.; Ruth Brown, Rec. Sec., 1265 Leah Court, Oroville.
Past Presidents Association No. 6 (Nevada County)—Meets 4th Friday, alternately between Nevada City, Pythian Castle, and Grass Valley, Edna Sampson's home; Margaret V. Nolan, Pres.; Vere Hansen, Rec. Sec., R.F.D. No. 2, box 41-C, Grass Valley.
Past Presidents Association No. 7 (Sonoma County)—Meets 2nd Tuesday, Violet Mastrup home, 622 5th St., Petaluma; Viola Mastrup, Pres.; Elizabeth Dillon, Rec. Sec., Petaluma.
Past Presidents Association No. 8 (San Joaquin and Stanislaus Counties)—Meets 2nd Thursday, Red Men Hall, Stockton; Mrs. Lois Armstrong, Pres.; Mrs. Harriet F. Corr, Rec. Sec., 729 E. Sonora St., Stockton.
Native Sons and Native Daughters Central Committee on Homeless Children—Main Office, 955 Phelan Bldg., San Francisco; Mrs. John W. Stirling, Chmn.; Miss Mary E. Brusie, Sec. Los Angeles branch office, 3924 Sunset Blvd.; Dorothy Schlingman, Sec.

(ADVERTISEMENT.)

In Memoriam

CLARA BASS ARCHER.

(Hiawatha Parlor No. 140 N.D.G.W.)

Whereas, Almighty God, in His infinite wisdom, has removed from our midst to the Heavenly Parlor on High our esteemed sister, Clara Bass Archer, and while, in all reverence, we submit our minds and hearts to the will of Him, we mourn our loss and feel the deepest sympathy for the family of our departed sister; therefore, be it

Resolved, That in testimony of our love and esteem for our departed sister, these resolutions be spread upon the minutes of the Parlor; and as evidence of our sympathy for our sister's family, that a copy be sent to them, and a copy sent to The Grizzly Bear Magazine for publication.

"To weary hearts, to mourning homes,
God's meekest angel gently comes;
No power has he to banish pain,
Or give us back our lost again;
And yet in tenderest love, our dear
And Heavenly Father sends him here.

There's quiet in that angel's glance,
There's rest in his still countenance!
He mocks no grief with idle cheer,
Nor wounds with words the mourner's ear;
But ills and woes he may not cure,
He kindly trains us to endure.

Angel of Patience, sent to calm
Our feverish brows with cooling palm;
To lay the storms of hope and fear,
And reconcile life's smile and tear;
The throbs of wounded pride to still
And make our own our Father's will!

Oh! thou who mournest on thy way,
With longings for the close of day,
He walks with thee, that angel kind,
And gently whispers, "Be resigned;
Bear up, bear on, the end shall tell,
The dear Lord ordereth all things well!"

Respectfully submitted,

EDNA SAYGROVER,
BERTHA MERRILL,
AURELIA S. BENTON,
Committee.

Redding, April 26, 1933.

AGNES BENNETT.

To the Officers and Members of Angelita Parlor No. 32 N.D.G.W.—We, your committee appointed to draft resolutions expressing the heartfelt sympathy of the members of the Parlor on the death of our sister, Agnes Bennett, respectfully submit the following:

Whereas, It has pleased our Heavenly Father to take from our midst our beloved sister, Agnes Bennett, and to summon her to a higher life; and whereas, in her passing our Parlor has lost a loyal member and her family a devoted sister and mother; therefore, be it

Resolved, That Angelita Parlor extend sincere sympathy to the family; that a copy of these resolutions be sent to the family of our departed sister; that a copy be spread upon the minutes of the Parlor, and that a copy be sent to The Grizzly Bear for publication.

Submitted in P.D.F.A.,

MYRTLE JOHNSON,
ANNIE McDONALD,
Committee.

Livermore, May 15, 1933.

ONE OF STATE'S LARGEST OAK TREES IS IN TRINITY COUNTY.

Much has been written and told about the size of the famous Hooker oak tree near Chico, Butte County, but how many know we have an oak of no mean proportions right here in Trinity County?

On the old Given ranch, near the mouth of Oregon Gulch, about nine miles from Weaverville, there stands a liveoak tree that has withstood the ravages of the elements for centuries. It has a circumference of 34 feet 4 inches, 16 inches from the ground. The limbs have a spread of 144 feet, and it is 75 feet tall. It is a perfect tree as to shape, and well worth a trip to view.—Trinity Journal, Weaverville.

Orange Selected—"Orange will hereafter be the color of all highway equipment used in California," says an announcement of the State Public Works Department.

"**Alert Motorists—Safe Children**," is the June slogan of the California Public Safety Committee in its campaign to lessen the constantly increasing auto death-toll.

Native Sons of the Golden West

JUSTICE EMMET SEAWELL OF SANTA Rosa No. 28, installed as Grand President just previous to the close of the Grass Valley Grand Parlor, has made the following appointments of committees and district deputy grand presidents. He bespeaks the hearty co-operation not only of these appointees, but of every member of the Order, to the end that the projects sponsored by the Grand Parlor may be advanced notably and that, by the close of his term, the Order will have made a record-breaking gain in numerical strength:

STANDING AND SPECIAL COMMITTEES.

Finance—Joseph Rose (Marshall No. 202), James L. Foley (Twin Peaks No. 214), Harry W. Gaetjen (Golden Gate No. 29).

Board of Appeals—Irving D. Gibson (Sacramento No. 3), Ben Harrison (Arrowhead No. 110), J. M. McMahon (Downieville No. 92), Richard M. Hamb (Piedmont No. 120), Joseph P. Sproul (Hollywood No. 196).

Board of Control—Walter Bammann (Pacific No. 10), John S. Ramsay (Castro No. 232), W. C. Neumiller (Stockton No. 7).

Publicity—William F. Knowland (Halcyon No. 146), Albert V. Mayrhofer (San Diego No. 108), Arthur J. E. Cleu (Fruitvale No. 252), Horace W. Amphlett (Redwood No. 66), Harold J. Zimmerman (Ukiah No. 71), William Peters (Arcata No. 20), Willett Ware (Santa Cruz No. 90), J. J. Monteverde (Sunset No. 26), Joseph J. McShane (Twin Peaks No. 214), Lawrence P. Hart (San Jose No. 22).

Ritual—Seth Millington (Jr.P.G.P.), Thomas J. McKeon (Calistoga No. 86), Burrell D. Neighbours (Ramona No. 109), James F. Stanley (Stanford No. 76), Frank M. Buckley (National No. 118).

Printing and Supplies—Fred H. Nickelson (South San Francisco No. 157), Albert W. Grosskopf (Stanford No. 76), Louis F. Erb (Alcalde No. 154).

History—Edward J. Lynch (P.G.P.), Fletcher A. Cutler (P.G.P.), William P. Caubu (P.G.P.), Hilliard E. Welch (P.G.P.), Frank C. Merritt (Brooklyn No. 151), George H. Barron (Precita No. 187), Henry G. Bodkin (Hollywood No. 196), Charles R. Boden (Pacific No. 10), I. M. Peckham (Stanford No. 76), J. J. Longshore (Sacramento No. 3), Max E. Licht (Bay City No. 104).

Employment (First District)—Joseph B. Keenan (Niantic No. 105), Herman Zimmerman (South San Francisco No. 157), William H. James (California No. 1).

Employment (Second District)—T. J. Simpson (Alder Glen No. 200), Thomas D. Davis (Plymouth No. 48), Thomas McAuliffe (Sacramento No. 3).

Employment (Third District)—George W Burnett (Santa Monica Bay No. 267), H. C. Sweetser (Santa Barbara No. 116), Walter C. Richards (Sepulveda No. 263).

Historic Landmarks—Joseph R. Knowland (P.G.P.), Lewis F. Byington (P.G.P.), Herman C. Lichtenberger (P.G.P.), Clarence E. Jarvis (P.G.P.), J. Harvey McCarthy (Ramona No. 109).

Homeless Children—I. M. Reuter (Yosemite No. 24), Fletcher A. Cutler (P.G.P.), Earl Warren (Fruitvale No. 252).

Laws of Subordinates—Joseph I. McNamara (Stanford No. 76), Adrien M. Hynes (Piedmont No. 120), B. Rey Schauer (Ramona No. 109).

Transportation and Mileage—Joseph Berry (Courtland No 106), Wesley Colgan (Santa Rosa No. 28), Eugene W. Biscailuz (Santa Monica Bay No. 267).

State Board of Relief—D. D. Gibbons (Sequoia No. 160), R. M. Hamb (Piedmont No 120), John J. Ryan (South San Francisco No. 157), Felix Robson (Claremont No. 240), Jesse M. Waterman (Observatory No. 177), John H. Nelson (San Francisco No. 49), Al Cron (Los Angeles No. 45), Ralph I. Harbison (Ramona No. 109), C. H. Rasmussen (Ferndale No. 93).

Admission Day Observance—A. W. Katzenstein (Sutter Fort No. 241), William G. Muntz (Estudillo No. 223), Harry Romick (Castro No. 232), Sidney B. Witkowski (Los Angeles No. 45), Ray B. Felton (Fruitvale No. 252).

Athletics—Al Sandel (Twin Peaks No. 214), R. J. Garrett (Berkeley No. 210), Martin H. Huber (Mission No. 38), F. B. Leonard (Eden No. 113), Edward J. Ginochio (Claremont No. 240).

Lone Grave—C. W. Chapman (Hydraulic No. 56), Peter J. Delay (Marysville No. 6), H. Ray George (Quartz No. 58).

Butano Forest—Oscar A. Foster (Santa Cruz No. 90), Horace W. Amphlett (Redwood No. 66), Edwin A. Meserve (Ramona No. 109), W. A. Gilkey (Los Angeles No. 45), E. A. Shaw (Pebble Beach No. 230).

Education—Peter T. Conmy (Golden Gate No. 29), Roy Cloud (Redwood No. 66), George F. McNoble (Stockton No. 7), John Andreson (Arrowhead No. 110), Lowell Palmer (Saint Helena No. 53).

Forestry and Conservation—R. L. P. Bigelow (Hydraulic No. 56), Southard M. Modry (Bret Harte No. 260), Carl O. Gerhardy (Alder Glen No. 200), N. John Lund (Ferndale No. 93), Robert H. Dewitt (Liberty No. 193).

DISTRICT DEPUTY GRAND PRESIDENTS.

No. 1, Liberty No. 193—John M. Barry (Liberty No. 193).
No. 2, Etna No. 192—L. E. Buchner (Etna No. 192).
No. 3, McCloud No. 149—Arthur Dean (McCloud No. 149).
No. 4, Mount Bally No. 87—R. L. Marshall (Mount Bally No. 87).
No. 5, Humboldt No. 14, Arcata No. 20, Ferndale No. 93—Ralph Jacobsen (Ferndale No. 93).
No. 6, Ukiah No. 71—Harry G. Buchnell (Ukiah No. 71).
No. 7, Broderick No. 117, Alder Glen No. 200—Ralph W. Todd (Alder Glen No. 200).
No. 8, Honey Lake No. 198—Zebnor Johnson (Honey Lake No. 198).
No. 9, Big Valley No. 211—Ben Bunselmeir (Big Valley No. 211).
No. 10, Quincy No. 131, Golden Anchor No. 182, Plumas No. 228—J. D. McLaughlin (Quincy No. 131).
No. 11, Colusa No. 69, Sutter No. 261, Willows No. 255—Elton C. Fitch (Colusa No. 69).
No. 12, Downieville No. 92, Golden Nugget No. 94—August Costa (Downieville No. 92).
No. 13, Hydraulic No. 56, Quartz No. 58, Auburn No. 59—John Thomas (Quartz No. 58).
No. 14, Donner No. 162—M. J. McGwinn (Donner No. 162).
No. 15, Marysville No. 6, Argonaut No. 8—C. R. Macdonald (Argonaut No. 8).
No. 16, Silver Star No. 63, Rocklin No. 233—H. A. Schroeder (Silver Star No. 63).
No. 17, Petaluma No. 27, Glen Ellen No. 102, Santa Rosa No. 28—Louis Bosch (Sonoma No. 111).
No. 18, Sebastopol No. 143, Sonoma No. 111—Wesley Beach (Santa Rosa No. 28).
No. 19, Mount Tamalpais No. 64, Sea Point No. 158, Nicasio No. 183—Chas. Solduvini (Mount Tamalpais No. 64).
No. 20, Mount Diablo No. 101, Byron No. 170, Carquinez No. 205—J. J. Meaney (Carquinez No. 205).
No. 21, General Winn No. 32, Richmond No. 217, Concord No. 245, Diamond No. 246—W. A. Clement (Diamond No. 246).
No. 22, Saint Helena No. 53, Napa No. 62, Calistoga No. 86, Lower Lake No. 159—Harry N. Bunce (Napa No. 62).
No. 23, Solano No. 39, Vallejo No. 77—Melvin F. Brooks (Vallejo No. 77).
No. 24, Sunset No. 26, Elk Grove No. 41, Galt No. 243—J. G. Fitzhenry (Sacramento No. 3).
No. 25, Woodland No. 30, Granite No. 83, Courtland No. 106—J. J. Monteverde (Sunset No. 26).
No. 26, Sacramento No. 3, Sutter Fort No. 241—W. H. Thisby (Courtland No. 106).
No. 27, Placerville No. 9, Georgetown No. 91—Geo. Smith (Placerville No. 9).
No. 28, Amador No. 17, Excelsior No. 31, Ione No. 33, Plymouth No. 48—Thomas D. Davis (Plymouth No. 48).
No. 29, Chispa No. 139—Milton Stevens (Chispa No. 139).
No. 30, Tuolumne No. 144, Columbia No. 258—Rowan Hardin (Tuolumne No. 144).
No. 31, Stockton No. 7, Tracy No. 186—Arthur W. Libhart (Stockton No. 7).
No. 32, Lodi No. 18, Oakdale No. 142, Manteca No. 271—Lawrence D. Buol (Stockton No. 7).
No. 33, Alameda No. 47, Halcyon No. 146—Allen G. Norris (Washington No. 169).
No. 34, Oakland No. 50, Eden No. 113—Frank P. Smith (Piedmont No. 120).
No. 35, Washington No. 169, Pleasanton No. 244—F. B. Leonard (Eden No. 113).
No. 36, Brooklyn No. 151, Fruitvale No. 252—Felix H. Robson (Claremont No. 240).
No. 37, Las Positas No. 96, Piedmont No. 120—Henry E. Uebner (Athens No. 195).
No. 38, Berkeley No. 210, Claremont No. 240—Elwood Fitzgerald (Oakland No. 50).
No. 39, Athens No. 195, Estudillo No. 223—Joseph F. Ehrhart (Fruitvale No. 252).
No. 40, Wisteria No. 127, Niles No. 250—Frank Perry (Brooklyn No. 151).
No. 41, San Jose No. 22, Santa Clara No. 100—A. C. Hansen (Observatory No. 177).
No. 42, Observatory No. 177, Mountain View No. 215—J. J. Trinajstich (Santa Clara No. 100).
No. 43, Redwood No. 66, Menlo No. 185, Palo Alto No. 216—R. J. White (Palo Alto No. 216).
No. 44, Seaside No. 95, Pebble Beach No. 230—M. R. Mattei (Pebble Beach No. 230).
No. 45, Fremont No. 44, Watsonville No. 65, Santa Cruz No. 90—Arnold R. Baldwin (Santa Cruz No. 90).
No. 46, Monterey No. 75, Santa Lucia No. 97, Gabilan No. 132—R. W. Adcock (Santa Lucia No. 97).
No. 47, San Miguel No. 150, Cambria No. 152—Henry Twisselman (San Miguel No. 150).
No. 48, Modesto No. 11, Orestimba No. 247, Turlock No. 274—Ambrose E. Daneri (Yosemite No. 24).
No. 49, Yosemite No. 24, Los Banos No. 206—Appointment pending.
No. 50, Visalia No. 19, Fresno No. 25, Selma No. 107, Madera No. 130—Frank M. Lane (Fresno No. 25).
No. 51, Bakersfield No. 42—George Taylor (Bakersfield No. 42).
No. 52, Cabrillo No. 144, Santa Barbara No. 116—A. C. Dinsmore (Santa Barbara No. 116).
No. 53, Los Angeles No. 45, University No. 272—Arthur Leonard (Santa Monica Bay No. 267).
No. 54, Ramona No. 109, Hollywood No. 196—Walter Fisher (Los Angeles No. 45).
No. 55, Sepulveda No. 263, Glendale No. 264—Walter Baskerville (Ramona No. 109).
No. 56, Long Beach No. 239, Santa Monica Bay No. 267, Compton No. 273—E. Baldwin (Sepulveda No. 263).
No. 57, Santa Ana No. 265—Len Reid (Arrowhead No. 110).
No. 58, Arrowhead No. 110—Walter Hiskey (Santa Ana No. 265).
No. 59, San Diego No. 108—Edward H. Dowell (San Diego No. 108).
No. 60, Pacific No. 10, El Dorado No. 52, Industrial City No. 209—Henry Delagues (South San Francisco No. 157).
No. 61, Mission No. 38, Utopia No. 270—L. A. Werner (Golden Gate No. 29).
No. 62, San Francisco No. 49, Dolores No. 208—Fred A. Hornblower (Rincon No. 72).
No. 63, California No. 1, Stanford No. 76—Thos. M. Dillon (Castro No. 232).
No. 64, South San Francisco No. 157, Precita No. 187—Hubert J. Caveney (Stanford No. 76).
No. 65, Bay City No. 104, Sequoia No. 160—J. W. Smith (Precita No. 187).
No. 66, Hesperian No. 137, Twin Peaks No. 214—Paul Conniff (Pacific No. 10).
No. 67, Marshall No. 202, Castro No. 232—Howard Stewart (Mission No. 38).
No. 68, Presidio No. 194, Balboa No. 234—G. E. Ritter (Hesperian No. 137).
No. 69, Golden Gate No. 29, Rincon No. 72—Robert Donohue (El Dorado No. 52).
No. 70, National No. 118, Alcalde No. 154—Theodore Schmidt (Stanford No. 76).
No. 71, Niantic No. 105, Guadalupe No. 231—Edward J. Wren (National No. 118).
No. 72, El Capitan No. 222, Olympus No. 189—James L. Vizzard (Sequoia No. 160).
No. 73, El Carmelo No. 256, Bret Harte No. 260—Ferdinand Hauck (Alcalde No. 154).

DEPUTY GRAND PRESIDENTS.

Fred Ehlers (California No. 1), Clarence M. Hunt (Sacramento No. 3), L. T. Sinnott (Marysville No. 6), W. H. Hibbard (Argonaut No. 8), Harry Alexander (Pacific No. 10), Walton E. Holmes (Sunset No. 26), Al Cron (Los Angeles No. 45), Alfred Viautin (El Dorado No. 52), Joseph Tinney (Rincon No. 72), I. M. Peckham (Stanford No. 76), C. E. Newton (Santa Clara No. 100), A. V. Mayrhofer (San Diego No. 108), Donald E. VanLuven (Arrowhead No. 110), Walter H. Odemar (Ramona No. 109), Walter Melvin Davis (Piedmont No. 120), Frank Roemer (Piedmont No. 120), R. J. Marraccini (Tracy No. 186), Allan W. Sunkler (Athens No. 195), John J. Ford (Hollywood No. 196), James B. McSheehy (Twin Peaks No. 214), Al Lobree (Castro No. 232), David R. Norris (Fruitvale No. 252), John T. Regan (G.S.).

WHOEVER MAKES A GARDEN

(LAURA NOLIN.)

Whoever makes a garden
Has never worked alone;
The rain has always found it,
The sun has always known,
The wind has blown across it
And helped to scatter seeds.
Whoever makes a garden
Has all the help he needs.

Whoever makes a garden
Should surely not complain;
With someone like the rain
And someone like the breezes
To aid him at his toil,
And someone like the Father
Who gave the garden soil.

Whoever makes a garden
Has O, so many friends,—
The glory of the morning,
The dew when daylight ends,
Wind and rain and sunshine,
And dew and fertile sod.
And he who makes a garden
Works hand in hand with God.

(The above, by Mrs. Laura Nolin, a member of Ontario Parlor No. 251 N.D.G.W., was sent by her to the office of the Grand Secretary N.S.G.W., who forwarded the contribution to The Grizzly Bear.—Editor.)

Old Board Grand Officers Meets.

San Francisco—The Board of Grand Officers met April 29 and transacted much detail business preparatory for the Grass Valley Grand Parlor. In attendance were Grand President Seth Millington, who presided, Grand First Vice Justice Emmet Seawell, Grand Second Vice Chas. A. Koenig, Grand Third Vice Harmon D. Skillin, Grand Secretary John T. Regan, Grand Trustees Jesse H. Miller, Eldred L. Meyer, John M. Burnett, Henry S. Lyon, Joseph J. McShane, Horace J. Leavitt, Chas. H. Spengemann.

An invitation to dedicate the new United States Postoffice building at Marysville, Yuba County, was accepted. An invitation was also received from the San Francisco Grove of Memory Association to attend the memorial services June 4.

A charter was granted to Turlock Parlor No. 274 at Turlock, Stanislaus County. It was voted to recommend that the Grass Valley Grand Parlor take up the charters of Rainbow Parlor No. 40 at Wheatland, Yuba County, and Chico Parlor No. 21 at Chico, Butte County.

Resolutions on the deaths of Past Grand Presidents Dr. Charles W. Decker and William J.

THE LETTER BOX

Comments on subjects of general interest and importance received from readers of The Grizzly Bear.

"FIFTY YEARS AGO" EDITOR DOES NOT INDULGE IN FICTION.

Editor Grizzly Bear—As the Livermore oldtimers dispute the furor caused among the Mexican population in March 1883 by the prediction of a flood that never came, I send you copy of the item published in the "Sacramento Daily Union" of March 6, 1883, giving the news. You can depend upon my articles having a basis, for I do not indulge in fiction to embellish them. The item, telegraphic news from San Francisco, said:

"San Francisco, March 5, 1883—There is an extraordinary exodus among the Spanish families of Livermore Valley who in consequence of a prediction made 100 years ago by Padre Anselmo that Livermore Valley would be flooded this month are hastening to camp upon Cedar Hill near Livermore. Bernal Alviso, an ex-member of the Mexico congress, and about 100 other Spanish and Mexican families fled from the valley Sunday, March 4th, and also encamped on Cedar Hill. Several predictions made by Padre Anselmo have been verified and the fleeing Spanish families say there is to be a great flood. Padre Anselmo predicted the flood that occurred in Livermore Valley in 1838."

THOMAS R. JONES.

Sacramento, April 30, 1933.

BUTTE COUNTY OLDTIMER REMEMBERS TIDAL WAVE SCARE.

Editor Grizzly Bear—Noticed in the March 1933 issue of The Grizzly Bear inquiry for any one who remembers the exodus of people from the lowlands about the [San Francisco] bay, especially Oakland. I remember distinctly about the occurrence, but cannot give the date.

The scare was among the Seventh Day Adventists, whose leaders predicted the end of the world, on a certain day Oakland and vicinity to be destroyed by a tidal wave. Many of the followers of the belief sold or gave away their property for little or nothing, as they knew they would have no use for wealth where they expected to go. The day before the date of the arrival of the expected tidal wave, all the believers—or God's people, particularly those belonging to the church mentioned above,—moved to the high hills back of Oakland and Berkeley, leaving nearly all their belongings behind, and waited patiently for the expected and welcomed end of the world, but it never came, to their sorrow.

One reason why I remember the incident is the fact I had occasion to go to Sacramento that day and some of us on the train kept a close lookout for the mountain of water that was to engulf the whole Sacramento Valley. Sorry I cannot give the date. Wishing The Grizzly Bear much success,

R. J. STRANG.

Oroville, May 7, 1933.

KEEP UP THE GOOD WORK.

Editor Grizzly Bear—Your issue for May is splendid. Keep up the good work. I like the magazine very well, for I can see what other Parlors are doing. I thank you for the good work that is being done by The Grizzly Bear Magazine.

JAMES QUINN.

San Francisco, May 11, 1933.

Hayes were presented and ordered submitted to the Grass Valley Grand Parlor.

Forty-nine Days Essay Prizewinner.

Livermore—Awards in the annual essay contest on California history conducted by Las Positas No. 96 were announced April 26, during the observance of Public School Week. First prize went to Guy Alan Brown, high school student, whose topic was "The Days of Forty-nine." The essay, setting forth important features of the upbuilding of the Golden State during the "gold" days, is "Dedicated to the memory of . . . Elias Perry and other brave and daring frontiersmen who freighted across the great plains in the days of forty-nine."

Prizes, in order, went also to the following: Donald Kennedy, Frank Fales, Roseanna Hansen, Cecelia Azevedo and Ross Hansen.

Membership Standing Largest Parlors.

San Francisco—Grand Secretary John T. Regan reports the standing of the Subordinate Parlors having a membership of over 400 January 1, 1933, as follows, together with their membership figures May 19, 1933:

Parlor	Jan. 1	May 19	Gain	Loss
Ramona No. 109	1032	1033	1	....
South San Francisco No. 157	803	801	....	2
Castro No. 232	764	766	2	....
Stanford No. 76	575	569	....	6
Arrowhead No. 110	573	566	....	7
Stockton No. 7	535	535	....	....
Twin Peaks No. 214	522	517	....	5
Piedmont No. 120	491	490	....	1
Rincon No. 72	418	408	....	10

Birthday Celebrated.

Calistoga—Calistoga No. 86, instituted May 3, 1886, celebrated its anniversary commencing at the meeting May 1, when incidents associated with the first decade of its existence were related by Charter Members A. H. McArthur and C. E. Butler, and C. A. Carroll. The "youngsters" got quite a "kick" out of the tales. Rev. T. J. McKeon gave the final illustrated lecture in his series of California missions talks, the subject being "Mission Carmel." May 7, a birthday dinner was held at Kenny Grove.

New Parlor Instituted.

Turlock—Turlock No. 274 was instituted May 5 by Grand President Seth Millington, assisted by Deputy Grand President Al Lobree. The ritual was exemplified by the officers of Yosemite No. 24 (Merced), and the officers of the new Parlor were installed by District Deputy L. E. Bither, as follows:

Robley Roy Libby, president; Claude Davis Kinser, junior past president; William E. Trent, first vice; Merte W. George, second vice; Leslie Garcia, third vice; Steve A. Carkeet, recording secretary; Harry R. Wilson, treasurer; George H. Witmer, marshal; Lauren Vincent Freitas, inside sentinel; Robert E. Olsen, outside sentinel; Jay Roden Thompson, organist; Joshue M. Lawson, Thomas Theodore Kell, Pat Gamba, trustees.

Oratorical Contest.

Sacramento—Under the auspices of Sacramento No. 3, an oratorical contest on California history for junior college students was conducted in Native Son Hall May 4. Awards, in order, went to Margaret Lazzarone, "James King of William;" Henry Attias, "Broderick," and Clifford Todd, "Broderick." Other participants were Lawrence Schei, "Admission of California;" Alta Jane Allawalt, "Broderick;" Robert Pedder, "Vigilantes of '56;" Edward Williams, "The Forgotten Man;" Robert Holcomb, "History Repeats Itself."

The Parlor had an oldtimers night, preceded by a dinner, May 25. Arrangements were perfected by Tom McAuliffe, June Longshore and Irving Gibson. The annual outing of the Native Sons and Native Daughters of Sacramento and San Joaquin Counties was held at Elk Grove, May 21. Dancing, races and baseball were featured.

The Secret of Success.

San Rafael—Mount Tamalpais No. 64 had as honor-guests at a banquet the basketball team of the Parlor, and in appreciation for having won the championship in a series of spirited contests members of the team were presented with gold basketballs. Assistant District Attorney Harold J. Haley presided, and lauded the team's persistency in the face of many previous discouragements. "This sticktoitiveness," he said, "finally brought home the bacon and glory to Mount Tamalpais." Captain Charles Soldavini responded, and credited the team's success to the loyal support given by members of the Parlor. "That," he said, "is the secret of success at all times, and if the Parlor officers prove worthy through faithful efforts they may alway be assured of loyal support by the members generally."

President Arthur Hecht said that while his term is drawing to a close he will work just as hard for the success of those who follow him. He appointed a "fact finding committee" to formulate plans for creating interest and promoting attendance.

SUBORDINATE PARLORS BRIEFS.

Modesto—T. F. Griffin addressed the members of Modesto No. 11 on "The Money Situation" May 3. Deputy Grand President Al Lobree was a visitor. A delegation from Modesto attended the institution of the Parlor at Turlock.

(Continued on Page 23)

Official Directory of Parlors of the N. S. G. W.

ALAMEDA COUNTY.

Alameda No. 47, Alameda City—R. H. Fallmer, Pres.; Robt. H. Cavanaugh, Sec., 1806 Pacific Ave.; Wednesdays, Veterans Memorial Bldg.

Oakland No. 50, Oakland—F. R. Born, Pres.; F. M. Norris, Sec., 5595 Taft Ave.; Fridays, Native Sons Hall, 11th and Clay Sts.

Las Positas No. 96, Livermore—Dr. Donald M. Fraser, Pres.; John J. Kelly, Sec., P. O. box 841; Thursdays, Foresters Hall.

Eden No. 113, Hayward—John Meincke, Pres.; Filbert M. Soares, Sec., 1487 "B" St.; 2nd and 4th Tuesdays, Memorial Hall, Main St.

Piedmont No. 120, Oakland—Stanley Hadlen, Pres.; Charles Morando, Sec., 906 Vermont St.; Thursdays, Native Sons Hall, 11th and Clay Sts.

Wisteria No. 127, Alvarado—Henry May, Pres.; J. M. Scribner, Sec., Livermore; 1st Thursday, I.O.O.F. Hall.

Halcyon No. 146, Alameda City—S. Chesley Anderson, Pres.; J. C. Bates, Sec., 2139 Buena Vista Ave.; 1st and 3rd Tuesdays, I.O.O.F. Hall, 2329 Santa Clara Ave.

Brooklyn No. 151, Oakland—Frank B. Perry, Pres.; E. W. Cooney, Sec., 3907 14th Ave.; 1st and 3rd Wednesdays, Masonic Temple, 8th Ave. and E. 14th St.

Washington No. 169, Centerville—M. D. Silva, Pres.; Allen G. Norris, Sec., P. O. box 31; 2nd and 4th Tuesdays, Hansen Hall.

Athens No. 195, Oakland—Milton O. Peterson, Pres.; Harold B. Farley, Sec., 4623 Benevides Ave.; Tuesdays, Native Sons Hall, 11th and Clay Sts.

Berkeley No. 210, Berkeley—F. Gohl, Pres.; R. J. Garrett, Sec., 1708 Virginia St.; Tuesdays, Native Sons Hall, 2108 Shattuck Ave.

Estudillo No. 223, San Leandro—E. E. King, Pres.; Albert G. Pacheco, Sec., 1736 E. 14th St.; 1st and 3rd Tuesdays, U.P.E.C. Hall.

Claremont No. 240, Emeryville—Raymond P. Burke, Pres.; E. N. Thienger, Sec., 839 Hearst Ave., Berkeley; Tuesdays, Veterans Memorial Bldg., 43rd and Salem Sts.

Pleasanton No. 244, Pleasanton—Edward Holzreiter, Pres.; Ernest W. Schween, Sec.; 2nd and 4th Thursdays, I.O.O.F. Hall.

Niles No. 250, Niles—M. L. Fournier, Pres.; C. E. Martenstein, Sec.; 2nd Thursday, I.O.O.F. Hall.

Fruitvale No. 252, Oakland—Ernest Perry, Pres.; Ray B. Felton, Sec., 1575 Allce St.; Fridays, W.O.W. Hall, 3256 E. 14th St.

AMADOR COUNTY.

Amador No. 17, Sutter Creek—J. H. Williams, Pres.; F. J. Payne, Sec.; 1st and 3rd Fridays, Native Sons Hall.

Excelsior No. 31, Jackson—Thomas G. Negrich, Pres.; William Going, Sec.; 1st and 3rd Wednesdays, Native Sons Hall, 22 Court St.

Ione No. 33, Ione—Earl Grover, Pres.; Josiah H. Saunders, Sec.; 1st and 3rd Wednesdays, Native Sons Hall.

Plymouth No. 48, Plymouth—Chester G. Johnson, Pres.; Thos. D. Davis, Sec.; 1st and 3rd Saturdays, N.S.G.W. Hall.

BUTTE COUNTY.

Argonaut No. 8, Oroville—Frank H. O'Brien, Pres.; Cyril R. Macdonald, Sec., P. O. box 502; 1st and 3rd Wednesdays, Veterans Memorial Hall.

CALAVERAS COUNTY.

Chispa No. 139, Murphys—Maynard Segale, Pres.; Antone Malaspina, Sec.; Wednesdays, Native Sons Hall.

COLUSA COUNTY.

Colusa No. 69, Colusa City—Rotheus A. Gray, Pres.; Phil J. Humburg, Sec., 223 Parkhill St.; Tuesdays, Eagles Hall.

CONTRA COSTA COUNTY.

General Winn No. 32, Antioch—Edmont T. Uren, Pres.; Joel H. Ford, Sec., P. O. box 311; 2nd and 4th Wednesdays, Union Hall.

Mount Diablo No. 101, Martinez—R. P. Anderson, Pres.; G. T. Barkley, Sec.; 1st and 3rd Mondays, I.O.O.F. Hall.

Byron No. 170, Byron—William E. Bunn, Pres.; H. G. Krumland, Sec.; 1st and 3rd Tuesdays, I.O.O.F. Hall.

Carquinez No. 205, Crockett—John McManns, Pres.; Thomas R. Cox, Sec., P.O. box 721; 1st and 3rd Wednesdays, I.O.O.F. Hall.

Richmond No. 217, Richmond—Frank Weber, Pres.; Lloyd N. Mason, Sec., 11 6th St.; 1st Wednesday, 818 Macdonald Ave.

Concord No. 245, Concord—Chas. H. Gray, Pres.; D. E. Pramberg, Sec., P. O. box 235; 1st Monday, Guy's Parlors.

Diamond No. 246, Pittsburg—Victor Ericsson, Pres.; Francis A. Irving, Sec., 248 E. 5th St.; 1st and 3rd Wednesdays, Veterans Memorial Bldg.

EL DORADO COUNTY.

Placerville No. 9, Placerville—Chris. C. Orelli, Pres.; Clyde R. Berriman, Sec., Wood St.; 2nd and 4th Tuesdays, Masonic Hall.

Georgetown No. 91, Georgetown—George W. Brichler, Pres.; O. F. Irish, Sec.; 2nd and 4th Wednesdays, I.O.O.F. Hall.

FRESNO COUNTY.

Fresno No. 25, Fresno City—Oliver M. Akers, Pres.; W. O. Guard, Sec., R.F.D. No. 2, box 379; 1st and 3rd Fridays, Pythian Castle, Cor. "R" and Merced Sts.

Selma No. 107, Selma—Chester E. Shepard, Pres.; E. C. Laughlin, Sec.; 1st Wednesday, American Legion Hall.

GRAND OFFICERS.

Seth Millington..........Junior Past Grand President
Gridley

Justice Emmet Seawell..........Grand President
State Bldg., San Francisco

Chas. A. Koenig..........Grand First Vice-president
531 35th Ave., San Francisco

Harmon D. Skillin..........Grand Second Vice-president
Mills Bldg., San Francisco

J. Hartley Russell..........Grand Third Vice-president
1025 Russ Bldg., San Francisco

John T. Regan..........Grand Secretary
N.S.G.W. Bldg., 414 Mason St., San Francisco

John A. Corotto..........Grand Treasurer
560 No. 5th St., San Jose

Gam Hurst..........Grand Marshal
5262 Boyd Ave., Oakland

William A. Reuter..........Grand Inside Sentinel
1009 Marine Ave., Wilmington

Walter P. Rothenbush..........Grand Outside Sentinel
N.S.G.W. Club Rooms, Stockton

Leslie Maloche..........Grand Organist
1775 El Cerrito, Los Angeles

Chester Gannon..........Grand Historian
613 Capital Ntl. Bank Bldg., Sacramento

GRAND TRUSTEES.

Eldred L. Meyer..........922 San Vicente Blvd., Santa Monica
Henry S. Lyon..........Placerville
Chas. H. Spengemann..........827 27th Ave., San Francisco
Thos. M. Foley..........Hearst Bldg., San Francisco
Jesse H. Miller..........712 DeYoung Bldg., San Francisco
John M. Burnett..........Bank America Bldg., San Jose
Edward T. Schnarr..........3611 Allendale Ave., Oakland

GLENN COUNTY.

Willows No. 255, Willows—Ralph W. Camper, Pres.; Leon Marshall, Sec., P.O. box 747; 2nd and 4th Tuesdays, I.O.O.F. Hall.

HUMBOLDT COUNTY.

Humboldt No. 14, Eureka—Henry Sundfors, Pres.; Loren M. Nelson, Sec., P.O. box 195; 2nd and 4th Mondays, Native Sons Hall.

Arcata No. 20, Arcata—F. A. Nicholson, Pres.; William Peters, Sec., P. O. box 1117; Thursdays, Native Sons Hall.

Ferndale No. 93, Ferndale—Hans P. Petersen, Pres.; C. H. Rasmussen, Sec., R.F.D., 47-A; 1st and 3rd Mondays, Danish Hall.

KERN COUNTY.

Bakersfield No. 42, Bakersfield—George Taylor, Pres.; Henry A. Bannister, Sec., care Bank of America; 2nd and 4th Fridays, Justice Court, City Hall.

LAKE COUNTY.

Lower Lake No. 159, Lower Lake—LeRoy England, Pres.; Albert Kugelman, Sec.; Thursdays, I.O.O.F. Hall.

LASSEN COUNTY.

Honey Lake No. 198, Standish—Leo T. Davis, Pres.; N. V. Wemple, Sec., Litchfield; 1st and 3rd Wednesdays, Wrede Hall.

Big Valley No. 211, Bieber—Fred Bunselmeier, Pres.; A. W. McKenzie, Sec.; 1st and 3rd Wednesdays, I.O.O.F. Hall.

LOS ANGELES COUNTY.

Los Angeles No. 45, Los Angeles City—Leslie A. Packard, Pres.; Willard F. Allen, Sec., 4955 Los Feliz Blvd.; Thursdays, Merchant Plumbers Hall, 1832 So. Hope.

Ramona No. 109, Los Angeles City—Frank S. Adams, Pres.; John V. Scott, Sec., Patriotic Hall, 1816 So. Figueroa; Fridays, Patriotic Hall, 1816 So. Figueroa.

Hollywood No. 196, Los Angeles City—Henry G. Bodkin, Pres.; E. J. Reilly, Sec., Olive View; Mondays, 1089 No. Oxford Ave.

Long Beach No. 239, Long Beach—Francis H. Gentry, Pres.; W. W. Brady, Sec., 801 Jergins Trust Bldg.; Dept. No. 1 Municipal Court, 8th floor Jergins Trust Bldg.

Sepulveda No. 263, San Pedro—Patrick H. Doran, Pres.; H. E. Fairall, Sec., 1925 So. Pacific Ave.; 1st and 3rd Fridays, Redman Hall, 543 Shepherd St., Point Firmin.

Glendale No. 264, Glendale—Harvey T. Gillette, Pres.; Philip D. Molen, Sec., 222 So. Glendale; 1st and 3rd Thursdays, Starr Heights Recreation Bldg., 3246 Community Place.

Santa Monica Bay No. 267, Santa Monica—Arthur R. Leonard, Pres.; John J. Smith, Sec., 830 Rialto Ave., Venice; 1st and 3rd Wednesdays, Odd Fellows Hall, 1431 Third St.

University No. 272, Los Angeles City—Bernard G. Hiss, Pres.; Martin DeFazio, Sec., 845 W. 53rd St.; Wednesdays, 1008 West Adams St.

Compton No. 273, Compton—Laurence W. Cowan, Pres.; Wm. Don Castillo, Sec., 641 W. Bennett St.; 2nd and 4th Tuesdays, Elks Hall, 6172 No. Long Beach Blvd., North Long Beach.

MADERA COUNTY.

Madera No. 130, Madera City—Cornelius Noble, Pres.; T. P. Cosgrave, Sec.; 1st and 3rd Thursdays, First National Bank Bldg.

MARIN COUNTY.

Mount Tamalpais No. 64, San Rafael—Arthur Hecht, Pres.; Manuel A. Andrade, Sec., 532 Mission Ave.; 1st and 3rd Mondays, "B" Street Hall.

Sea Point No. 158, Sausalito—Wm. W. Taylor, Pres.; Manuel Santos, Sec., 6 Glen Drive; 1st and 3rd Wednesdays, Perry Bldg.

Nicasio No. 183, Nicasio—M. T. Farley, Pres.; R. J. Rogers, Sec.; 2nd and 4th Wednesdays, U.A.O.D. Hall.

MENDOCINO COUNTY.

Ukiah No. 71, Ukiah—W. B. Danis, Pres.; Ben Hofman, Sec., P. O. box 473; 1st and 3rd Mondays, I.O.O.F. Hall.

Broderick No. 117, Point Arena—Ivan Lawson, Pres.; C. J. Buchanan, Sec.; 1st and 3rd Thursdays, Forester Hall.

Alder Glen No. 200, Fort Bragg—Thomas Cooney, Pres.; C. R. Weller, Sec.; 2nd and 4th Fridays, I.O.O.F. Hall.

MERCED COUNTY.

Yosemite No. 24, Merced City—John J. Thronton, Pres.; True W. Fowler, Sec., P. O. box 781; 2nd and 4th Mondays, I.O.O.F. Hall.

Los Banos No. 206, Los Banos—Daniel Pedroni, Pres.; L. E. Sarbo, Sec., R.F.D., box 21; 2nd and 4th Wednesdays, Eagles Hall.

MONTEREY COUNTY.

Monterey No. 75, Monterey City—James Millington, Pres.; T. W. Krieger, Sec., 999 Franklin St.; 1st and 3rd Fridays, Knights Pythias Hall, Main St.

Santa Lucia No. 97, Salinas—Roy Martella, Pres.; R. W. Adcock, Sec., 32 W. Alisal St.; Mondays, Native Sons Hall, 32 W. Alisal St.

Gabilan No. 132, Castroville—B. A. McCoy, Pres.; R. H. Martin, Sec., P. O. box 81; 1st and 3rd Thursdays, Native Sons Hall.

NAPA COUNTY.

Saint Helena No. 53, Saint Helena—Gilman Clark, Pres.; Edw. L. Bonhote, Sec., P. O. box 267; Mondays, Native Sons Hall.

Napa No. 62, Napa City—E. L. Miller, Pres.; H. J. Hoernle, Sec., 1226 Oak St.; Mondays, Native Sons Hall.

Calistoga No. 86, Calistoga—Fred Heitz, Pres.; Louis Carlenzoli, Sec.; 1st and 3rd Mondays, I.O.O.F. Hall.

NEVADA COUNTY.

Hydraulic No. 56, Nevada City—Verne Gleason, Pres.; Dr. C. W. Chapman, Sec.; Tuesdays, Pythian Castle.

Quartz No. 58, Grass Valley—Frank J. Rowe, Pres.; H. Ray George, Sec., 151 Conaway Ave.; Mondays, Auditorium Hall.

Donner No. 162, Truckee—J. F. Lichtenberger, Pres.; H. C. Lichtenberger, Sec.; 2nd and 4th Tuesdays, Native Sons Hall.

ORANGE COUNTY.

Santa Ana No. 265, Santa Ana—Amos Huntzinger, Pres.; E. F. Marks, Sec., 1124 No. Bristol St.; 1st and 3rd Mondays, The Old Time Dance Hall, Grass Valley St., Tustin.

PLACER COUNTY.

Auburn No. 59, Auburn—Hans J. Petersen, Pres.; J. G. Walsh, Sec.; 1st and 3rd Fridays, Foresters Hall.

Silver Star No. 63, Lincoln—Robert P. Dixon, Pres.; Barney G. Barry, Sec., P. O. box 72; 3rd Wednesday, I.O.O.F. Hall.

Rocklin No. 233, Roseville—Wm. La Due, Pres.; M. E. Reed, Sec., 253 W. Duranta; 2nd and 4th Wednesdays, Eagles Hall.

PLUMAS COUNTY.

Quincy No. 131, Quincy—Herbert Hard, Pres.; E. O. Kelsey, Sec.; 2nd Thursday, I.O.O.F. Hall.

Golden Anchor No. 182, La Porte—R. J. McGrath, Pres.; LeRoy J. Post, Sec.; 2nd and 4th Sunday mornings, Native Sons Hall.

Plumas No. 228, Taylorsville—E. E. Sikes, Pres.; George E. Boyden, Sec.; 1st and 3rd Mondays, Native Sons Hall.

SACRAMENTO COUNTY.

Sacramento No. 3, Sacramento City—Parker Kelly, Pres.; J. F. Didion, Sec., 1213 "O" St.; Thursdays, Native Sons Bldg., 11th and "J" Sts.

Sunset No. 26, Sacramento City—Albert Costa, Pres.; Edward E. Reese, Sec., County Treasurer Office; Mondays, Native Sons Bldg., 11th and "J" Sts.

Elk Grove No. 41, Elk Grove—Robert Carr, Pres.; Walter Martin, Sec.; 2nd and 4th Fridays, Masonic Hall.

Granite No. 83, Folsom—Joe Relvas, Pres.; Frank Showers, Sec.; 2nd and 4th Tuesdays, K.P. Hall.

Courtland No. 106, Courtland—N. H. Thisby, Pres.; Jos. Green, Sec.; 1st Saturday and 3rd Monday, Native Sons Hall.

Sutter Fort No. 241, Sacramento City—Ed. T. Goyne, Pres.; C. L. Katzenstein, Sec., P. O. box 914; 2nd and 4th Wednesdays, Native Sons Bldg., 11th and "J" Sts.

Galt No. 243, Galt—Abel G. Stock, Pres.; F. W. Harms, Sec.; 1st and 3rd Mondays, I.O.O.F. Hall.

SAN BENITO COUNTY.

Fremont No. 44, Hollister—S. Churchill, Pres.; J. E. Prendergast Jr., Sec., 1064 Monterey St.; 1st and 3rd Thursdays, Grangers Union Hall.

SAN BERNARDINO COUNTY.

Arrowhead No. 110, San Bernardino City—F. L. McGarvey, Pres.; R. W. Brazelton, Sec., 462 6th St.; Wednesdays, Eagles Hall, 469 4th St.

SAN DIEGO COUNTY.

San Diego No. 108, San Diego City—Martin J. Spangler, Pres.; A. V. Mayrhofer, Sec., 1572 2nd St.; Wednesdays, K.C. Hall, 4th and Elm Sts.

SAN FRANCISCO CITY AND COUNTY.

California No. 1, San Francisco—Joseph Lawlor, Pres.; Ellis A. Blackman, Sec., 1248-A Divisadero St.; Thursdays, Native Sons Bldg., 414 Mason St.

Pacific No. 10, San Francisco—Albert L. Anders, Pres.; J. Henry Bastein, Sec., 426 City Hall; Tuesdays, Native Sons Bldg., 414 Mason St.

Golden Gate No. 29, San Francisco—Ernest H. Allen, Pres.; Adolph Eberhart, Sec., 183 Carl St.; Mondays, Native Sons Bldg., 414 Mason St.

Mission No. 38, San Francisco—Martin H. Huber, Pres.; Thos. J. Stewart, Sec., 419 South Van Ness Ave.; Wednesdays, Redmen Hall, 3053 16th St.

San Francisco No. 49, San Francisco—Robert Hallenbarter, Pres.; David Capurro, Sec., 976 Union St.; Thursdays, Native Sons Bldg., 414 Mason St.

El Dorado No. 52, San Francisco—Fred Ageno, Pres.; Alfred Vlautin, Sec., 1537 Franklin St.; Thursdays, Native Sons Bldg., 414 Mason St.

Rincon No. 72, San Francisco—Frank Granzella, Pres.; John A. Gilmour, Sec., 2069 Golden Gate Ave.; Wednesdays, Native Sons Bldg., 414 Mason St.

Stanford No. 76, San Francisco—Charles J. Barry, Pres.; Charles T. O'Kane, Sec., 2900 Scott St.; Tuesdays, Native Sons Bldg., 414 Mason St.

Bay City No. 104, San Francisco—Jacob A. Helbing, Pres.; Max E. Licht, Sec., 1831 Fulton St.; 2nd and 4th Wednesdays, Native Sons Bldg., 414 Mason St.

Niantic No. 105, San Francisco—A. Furner, Pres.; J. M. Darcy, Sec., 10 Hoffman Ave.; Wednesdays, Native Sons Bldg., 414 Mason St.

National No. 118, San Francisco—Walter J. Murphy, Pres.; Martin M. Ratigan, Sec., 1325 Page St., Apt. 6; Thursdays, 1160 Eddy St.

Hesperian No. 137, San Francisco—N. G. Reimers, Pres.; Albert Carlson, Sec., 379 Justin Dr.; Thursdays, Native Sons Bldg., 414 Mason St.

Alcalde No. 154, San Francisco—Robert DeSparr, Pres.; Harry S. Burke, Sec., 25 Ord St.; 2nd and 4th Wednesdays, Native Sons Bldg., 414 Mason St.

South San Francisco No. 157, San Francisco—Mathew Brady, Pres.; John T. Regan, Sec., 1489 Newcomb Ave.; Wednesdays, Masonic Bldg., 4705 3rd St.

Sequoia No. 160, San Francisco—John Lynch, Pres.; Walter W. Garrett, Sec., 2500 Van Ness Ave.; Mondays, Swedish-American Bldg., 2174 Market St.

Precita No. 187, San Francisco—Leland J. Jenkins, Pres.; Edward Tietjen, Sec., 1367 15th Ave.; Thursdays, Mission Masonic Hall, 2668 Mission St.

Olympus No. 189, San Francisco—Henry H. McGowan, Pres.; Harvey J. Carty, Sec., 1651 Market St., Apt. 505; 2nd and 4th Tuesdays, Independent Redmen Hall, 3053 16th St.

Presidio No. 194, San Francisco—Charles Maker, Pres.; George A. Ducker, Sec., 442 21st Ave.; Mondays, Native Sons Bldg., 414 Mason St.

ATTENTION, SECRETARIES!

THIS DIRECTORY IS PUBLISHED BY AUTHORITY OF THE GRAND PARLOR N.S.G.W., AND ALL NOTICES OF CHANGES MUST BE RECEIVED BY THE GRAND SECRETARY (NOT THE MAGAZINE) ON OR BEFORE THE 20TH OF EACH MONTH TO INSURE CORRECTION IN NEXT ISSUE OF DIRECTORY.

Marshall No. 202, San Francisco—Eugene Biancalona, Pres.; Frank Bacigalupi, Sec., 725 Douglas St.; 1st and 3rd Wednesdays, Native Sons Bldg., 414 Mason St.
Dolores No. 208, San Francisco—Henry J. Adami, Pres.; Edward F. Webb, Sec., 2801 Sacramento St.; 2nd and 4th Tuesdays, Redmen Hall, 3053 16th St.
Twin Peaks No. 214, San Francisco—Oswald Storm, Pres.; Thos. Pendergast, Sec., 278 Douglas St.; Wednesdays, Willopi Hall, 4061 24th St.
El Capitan No. 222, San Francisco—John O. Coomy, Pres.; James Hanna, Sec., 2450 27th Ave.; 1st and 3rd Thursdays, King Soloman Hall, 1739 Fillmore St.
Guadalupe No. 231, San Francisco—Thomas Wall, Pres.; Alvin A. Johnson, Sec., 142 Rousseau St.; Tuesdays, Guadalupe Hall, 4551 Mission St.
Castro No. 232, San Francisco—Roy Lund, Pres.; James H. Hayes, Sec., 4014 18th St.; Tuesdays, Native Sons Bldg., 414 Mason St.
Balboa No. 234, San Francisco—J. E. Killeen, Pres.; E. W. Boyd, Sec., 437 Cherry St.; Thursdays, Maccabee Hall, 5th Ave. and Clement St.
Bret Harte No. 260, San Francisco—Louis S. Merrill, Pres.; A. W. McElhatton, Sec., 1027 Capitol Ave.; Tuesdays, West of Twin Peaks Hall, 233 Legion Court.
Utopia No. 270, San Francisco—A. E. Rosenbaum, Pres.; Herbert H. Schneider, Sec., 3455 16th Ave.; Tuesdays, American Hall, 20th and Capp Sts.

SAN JOAQUIN COUNTY.

Stockton No. 7, Stockton—Ben S. Waller, Pres.; R. D. Dorcey, Sec., P. O. box 388; Mondays, Native Sons Hall.
Lodi No. 18, Lodi—Herbert Osterman, Pres.; Dr. Clyde Bresnan, Sec.; 2nd Wednesday, Eagles Hall.
Tracy No. 186, Tracy—O. S. Seina, Pres.; R. J. Marraccini, Sec., R.F.D. No. 1, box 217, Thursdays, I.O.O.F. Hall.
Manteca No. 271, Manteca—John P. Mulholand, Pres.; Leonard Faria, Sec., R.F.D., box 75, Lathrop; 1st and 3rd Wednesdays, I.O.O.F. Hall.

SAN LUIS OBISPO COUNTY.

San Miguel No. 150, San Miguel—H. Twisselman, Pres.; Otto Kuehl, Sec., Paso Robles; 1st Wednesday, Clemons Hall.
Cambria No. 152, Cambria—N. Sturni, Pres.; A. S. Gay, Sec.; Wednesdays, Rigdon Hall.

SAN MATEO COUNTY.

Redwood No. 66, Redwood City—H. E. Holmquist, Pres.; A. S. Liguori, Sec., P. O. box 212; Thursdays, American Foresters Hall.
Seaside No. 95, Half Moon Bay—Melvin Frey, Pres.; John G. Gilcrest, Sec.; 2nd and 4th Tuesdays, I.O.O.F. Hall.
Menlo No. 185, Menlo Park—C. T. Maloney, Pres.; F. W. Johnson, Sec., P. O. box 601; 1st and 3rd Thursdays, Masonic Hall.
Pebble Beach No. 230, Pescadero—Earle A. Williamson, Pres.; E. A. Shaw, Sec.; 2nd and 4th Wednesdays, I.O.O.F. Hall.
El Carmelo No. 256, Daly City—Harry McDonald, Pres.; Ernest L. Micco, Sec., 639 Morse St., San Francisco; 2nd and 4th Wednesdays, Eagles Hall.
Industrial City No. 269, South San Francisco—John C. Hamilton, Pres.; Geo. A. Roll, Sec., P. O. box 237; 2nd and 4th Mondays, Metropolitan Hall.

SANTA BARBARA COUNTY.

Santa Barbara No. 116, Santa Barbara City—Philip Bradley, Pres.; H. C. Sweetser, Sec., Court House; 1st and 3rd Thursdays, Pythian Castle.

SANTA CLARA COUNTY.

San Jose No. 22, San Jose—Fred Carmichael, Pres.; Joseph Lawrence, Sec., 1095 No. First St.; Mondays, I.O.O.F. Hall.
Santa Clara No. 100, Santa Clara City—A. P. Cunha, Pres.; Clarence Clevenger, Sec., P.O. box 297; 1st and 3rd Wednesdays, Redmen Hall.
Observatory No. 177, San Jose—James J. Flannery, Pres.; A. B. Langford, Sec., Hall Records; Tuesdays, Knights Columbus Hall, 40 No. First St.
Mountain View No. 215, Mountain View—Henry A. Schultze, Pres.; C. A. Antonioli, Sec., 301 Castro St.; 2nd and 4th Wednesdays, Mockbee Hall.
Palo Alto No. 216, Palo Alto—John C. Bernal, Pres.; Albert A. Quinn, Sec., 643 High St.; Mondays, Native Sons Bldg., Hamilton Ave. and Emerson St.

SANTA CRUZ COUNTY.

Watsonville No. 65, Watsonville—J. E. Giacoma, Pres.; E. R. Tindall, Sec., 51 Marchant St.; 2nd and 4th Tuesdays, I.O.O.F. Hall.
Santa Cruz No. 90, Santa Cruz City—W. S. Rodgers, Pres.; T. V. Mathews, Sec., 105 Pacheco Ave.; Fridays, Native Sons Hall, 117 Pacific Ave.

SHASTA COUNTY.

McCloud No. 149, Redding—Roy Hawes, Pres.; Hugh A. Shuffleton, Sec.; 1st and 3rd Thursdays, Moose Hall.

SIERRA COUNTY.

Downieville No. 92, Downieville—Frank H. Turner, Pres.; H. S. Tibbey, Sec.; 2nd and 4th Mondays, I.O.O.F. Hall.
Golden Nugget No. 94, Sierra City—Elmer Thompson, Pres.; Arthur R. Pride, Sec.; 1st and 3rd Wednesdays, Masonic Hall.

SISKIYOU COUNTY.

Etna No. 192, Etna—Frank B. Quigley, Pres.; Harvey A. Green, Sec.; 1st and 3rd Wednesdays, I.O.O.F. Hall.
Liberty No. 193, Sawyers Bar—David H. Bobinson, Pres.; John M. Barry, Sec.; 1st and 3rd Saturdays, I.O.O.F. Hall.

SOLANO COUNTY.

Solano No. 39, Suisun—John S. Cannon, Pres.; J. W. Kinlock, Sec.; 1st and 3rd Tuesdays, I.O.O.F. Hall.
Vallejo No. 77, Vallejo—Frank J. Heidener, Pres.; Werner B. Hallin, Sec., 912 Carolina; 2nd and 4th Tuesdays, San Pablo Hall.

SONOMA COUNTY.

Petaluma No. 27, Petaluma—Clarence Christiansen, Pres.; C. F. Fobes, Sec., 114 Prospect St.; 2nd and 4th Mondays, Druid Hall, Gross Bldg., 41 Main St.
Santa Rosa No. 28, Santa Rosa—George A. Eckman, Pres.; Leland S. Lewis, Sec., Court House; Mondays, Native Sons Hall.
Glen Ellen No. 102, Glen Ellen—Tony Cereghino, Pres.; Frank Kirch, Sec., Route 3, Santa Rosa; 2nd Monday, N.S.G.W. Hall.
Sonoma No. 111, Sonoma City—Chas. E. Bacigalupi, Pres.; L. H. Green, Sec.; 1st and 3rd Mondays, I.O.O.F. Hall.
Sebastopol No. 143, Sebastopol—O. A. McChristian, Pres.; F. G. McFarlane, Sec.; 1st and 3rd Fridays, I.O.O.F. Hall.

STANISLAUS COUNTY.

Modesto No. 11, Modesto—Chas. D. Blaine, Pres.; C. C. Eastin Jr., Sec., P.O. box 898; 1st and 3rd Wednesdays, I.O.O.F. Hall.
Oakdale No. 142, Oakdale—D. W. Tulloch, Pres.; E. T. Gobin, Sec.; 2nd Monday, Legion Hall.
Orestimba No. 247, Crows Landing—Lloyd W. Fink, Pres.; G. W. Fink, Sec.; 1st and 3rd Wednesdays, Community Club Home.
Turlock No. 274, Turlock—Robley R. Libby, Pres.; Steve A. Karkeet, Sec.

SUTTER COUNTY.

Sutter No. 261, Sutter City—Henry Correll, Pres.; Glen R. Haynes, Sec., R.F.D. No. 2, Yuba City; 2nd and 4th Mondays, N.D.G.W. Hall.

NATIVE SON NEWS

(Continued from Page 21)

Colusa—R. G. Powers, representing Colusa No. 69, addressed the graduating class of the local grammar school and told the students that the Parlor, recognizing the fact that local history has been practically lost, is offering a silver cup to the winner of an essay contest to be conducted annually. The subject chosen for this year is "The Colus Indian."

Weaverville—The celebration and outdoor initiation of Fred H. Greely Past Presidents Association, scheduled to be held here June 3 and 4, have been postponed to June 10 and 11, so that several of the grand officers may attend. Mount Bally No. 87 will be the host.

Ferndale—J. A. Shaw, charter member of Ferndale No. 93, has been elected president of the Ferndale Bank, of which he has been a director since its organization in 1893.

In a note to The Grizzly Bear dated Oakland, May 11, City Clerk Frank C. Merritt (Brooklyn No. 151) says: "My subscription is renewed with satisfaction and pleasure for the twenty-fourth consecutive year!"

WIFE N.S. PAST GRAND PASSES.

Sacramento—Mrs. Ruby Steacy-Welch, wife of Hilliard E. Welch, Past Grand President N.S.G.W., passed away May 19. She was a native of Calaveras County, but for many years resided in Lodi, San Joaquin County. In addition to her husband, four children survive.

N.S.G.W. OFFICIAL DEATH LIST.

Containing the name, the date and place of birth, the date of death, and the Subordinate Parlor affiliation of deceased members reported to Grand Secretary John T. Regan from April 20 to May 20, 1933:

Waterman, E. H.; San Francisco, October 2, 1864; March 5, 1933; Pacific No. 10.
Watson, Wm. F.; San Francisco, March 21, 1863; March 24, 1933; Pacific No. 10.
Grimes, George James; San Francisco, November 30, 1901; April 22, 1933; Pacific No. 10.
Philippsen, Jorgen Herbert; Beatrice, September 16, 1904; May 6, 1933; Arcata No. 20.
Day, Charles M.; Petaluma, February 28, 1863; April 7, 1933; Alameda No. 47.
Flanagan, Raymond; San Rafael, November 3, 1899; March 23, 1933; Mount Tamalpais No. 64.

TRINITY COUNTY.

Mount Bally No. 87, Weaverville—H. W. Day, Pres.; E. V. Ryan, Sec.; 1st and 3rd Mondays, Native Sons Hall.

TULARE COUNTY.

Visalia No. 19, Visalia—G. W. Houk, Pres.; C. H. Wenn, Sec.; 2nd and 4th Tuesdays, Woodman Hall.

TUOLUMNE COUNTY.

Tuolumne No. 144, Sonora—Mathew J. Marshall, Pres.; William M. Harrington, Sec., P. O. box 715; 2nd and 4th Fridays, Knights Columbus Hall.
Columbia No. 258, Columbia—Jos. Cadematori, Pres.; Charles E. Grant, Sec.; 2nd and 4th Thursdays, Native Sons Hall.

VENTURA COUNTY.

Cabrillo No. 114, Ventura City—David Bennett, Pres., 1380 Church St.

YOLO COUNTY.

Woodland No. 30, Woodland—J. L. Aronson, Pres.; R. G. Lawson, Sec.; 1st Thursday, Native Sons Hall.

YUBA COUNTY.

Marysville No. 6, Marysville—A. W. Graves, Pres.; Verne Fogarty, Sec., 719 6th St.; 2nd Friday, Foresters Hall.

AFFILIATED ORGANIZATIONS.

San Francisco Extension of the Order Committee, N.S.G.W.—Joseph J. McShane, Chmn.; Harold J. Regan, Sec., 414 Mason St., San Francisco; meets 2nd and 4th Fridays, Grizzly Bear Club, 414 Mason St., San Francisco.
Alameda County Extension of the Order Committee, N.S.G.W.—Gam Hurst, Chmn.; Frank Roemer, Sec., 3297 Morcom Ave., Oakland; meets 1st and 3rd Mondays, N.S.G.W. Hall, 11th and Clay Sts., Oakland.
Interparlor Committee (Southern District), N.S.G.W. and N.D.G.W.—Burrel D. Neighbours, Chmn.; F. J. Burmester, Sec., P. O. box 42, Colton; meets 2nd and 4th Fridays, Patriotic Hall, 1816 So. Figueroa St., Los Angeles.
San Francisco Assembly No. 1 Past Presidents Association N.S.G.W.—Meets 1st and 3rd Fridays, Native Sons Bldg., 414 Mason St., San Francisco; Fred T. Kane, Gov.; J. F. Stanley, Sec., 1175 O'Farrell St., San Francisco.
East Bay Counties Assembly No. 3 Past Presidents Association N.S.G.W.—Meets 4th Monday, Native Sons Hall 11th and Clay Sts., Oakland; M. W. Louden, Gov.; Edgar G. Hanson, Sec., 1260 Russell St., Berkeley.
Marin County Assembly No. 5 Past Presidents Association N.S.G.W.—J. S. Rose Jr., Gov.; L. J. Peter, Sec., Peter Bldg., 4th and "C" Sts., San Rafael.
Fred H. Greely Assembly No. 6 Past Presidents Association N.S.G.W.—Meets monthly with different Parlors comprising district; Peter J. Delay, Gov.; Barney Barry, Sec., P.O. box 72, Lincoln.
San Joaquin Assembly No. 7 Past Presidents Association N.S.G.W.—Meets 1st Friday, Native Sons Hall, Stockton; Clyde H. Gregg, Gov.; R. D. Dorcey, Sec., Native Sons Club, Stockton.
Sonoma County Assembly No. 9 Past President Association N.S.G.W.—Meets monthly at different Parlor headquarters in county; P. A. R. Gambini, Gov.; L. S. Lewis, Sec., Court House, Santa Rosa.
General John A. Sutter Assembly No. 10 Past Presidents Association—C. O. Wachman, Gov.; Jas. J. Longshore, Sec., 514 "J" St., Sacramento.
Grizzly Bear Club—Members all Parlors outside San Francisco at all times welcome. Clubrooms top floor Native Sons Bldg., 414 Mason St., San Francisco.
Native Sons and Native Daughters Central Committee on Homeless Children—Main office, 955 Phelan Bldg., San Francisco; Mrs. John W. Stirling, Chmn.; Miss Mary E. Brusie, Sec. Los Angeles branch office, 3924 Sunset Blvd.; Dorothy Schlingman, Sec.

(ADVERTISEMENT.)

PIONEER NATIVES DEAD

(Brief Notices of the Demise of Men and Women born in California Prior to 1860.)

Joseph E. Shields, born Sierra County, 1855; died recently, Riverside City; wife and three children survive.

Dr. Edward McCabe, born Nevada County, 1854; died April 15, I.O.O.F. Home, Saratoga, Santa Clara County; daughter survives. He was a charter member of Watsonville Parlor No. 65 N.S.G.W.

James D. Helms, born Lake County, 1857; died April 16, Stockton, San Joaquin County.

William A. Rattenberry, born Sacramento City, 1857; died April 21, Los Angeles City. He was a veteran actor.

Mrs. Amelia Carmen McDonald, born Monterey County, 1851; died April 23, near Merced City; nine children survive.

Charles P. Lyndall, born Santa Clara County, 1855; died April 27, Los Angeles City. He was affiliated with Ramona Parlor No. 109 N.S.G.W.

Mrs. Mary Jane Williams, born Shasta County, 1859; died April 28, Redding; four sons survive.

Mrs. Grace Camden Richards, born Shasta County, 1858; died April 28, Oakland, Alameda County.

Mrs. Elizabeth Kirchner-Myers, born Mariposa County, 1857; died April 29, San Francisco; two sons survive. She was a charter member of Alta Parlor No. 3 N.D.G.W. (San Francisco).

Rev. Thomas Ewing Sherman, S.J., born San Francisco, 1858; died April 30, New Orleans, Louisiana State.

Jose Del Carmen Espinosa, born Santa Barbara City, 1849; died there, May 2.

Stephen S. McGarvey, born Stanislaus County, 1858; died May 3, Ukiah, Mendocino County; three children survive.

Mrs. Isabelle Castro-O'Neill, born Contra Costa County, 1848; died May 4, Pinole. She was a daughter of Victor Castro and a granddaughter of Ignacio Martinez, well known in the early days of California.

Mrs. Lavenia Hathaway-Vaughn, born Merced County, 1857; died May 5, Fresno City.

Mrs. Angelo Morano, born Monterey County, 1833; died May 9, Merced City.

Mary Ann Deady, born Calaveras County, 1856; died May 9, Benicia, Solano County.

William R. Arthur, born Placer County, 1854; died May 10, Oakland, Alameda County; three children survive.

Mrs. Kate Brincard, born Shasta County, 1858; died May 10, Los Angeles City; two children survive.

David Sullivan, born San Francisco, 1858; died there May 12; wife and daughter survive.

Emeline A. Mathewson, born El Dorado County, 1859; died May 15, San Francisco.

Mrs. Erolinda Cota-Yorba, born Los Angeles City, 1853; died there May 19; six children survive. Her parents, Francisco and Martino Cota, once owned the great La Ballona Rancho, now the site of Culver City.

Fogelsang, Frank M.; Oroville, birth date missing; April 19, 1933; Colusa No. 69.
Fay, Luke; San Francisco, February 28, 1861; May 2, 1933; Niantic No. 105.
Higuera, Bernardo J.; The Palms, March 28, 1858; April 20, 1933; Ramona No. 109.
Lyndall, Charles P.; Santa Clara, September 1, 1855; April 27, 1933; Ramona No. 109.
Kiesner, William C.; Los Angeles, September 18, 1891; May 5, 1933; Santa Barbara No. 116.
Bramlette, Walter Edward; Downey, December 15, 1900; April 29, 1933; Lower Lake No. 159.
Summervill, Robert P.; San Francisco, August 14, 1898; April 18, 1933; Presidio No. 194.
Crowley, James P.; San Francisco, July, 1879; May 3, 1933; Presidio No. 194.
Kearney, John Richard; Oakland, June 9, 1885; April 26, 1933; Athens No. 195.
Jordan, Wayne Early; Los Angeles, April 15, 1898; April 8, 1933; Hollywood No. 196.
Romani, George C.; San Francisco, May 18, 1889; April 20, 1933; Guadalupe No. 231.
Minehan, Joseph F.; San Francisco, November 19, 1878; February 28, 1933; Balboa No. 234.
Molinari, F. A.; San Francisco, May 9, 1895; April 11, 1933; Balboa No. 234.

Humboldt Helps—Humboldt County produced 6,798,863 pounds of butter-fat in 1932, to help California maintain its reputation as one of the nation's leading dairy states. The production for the entire state totaled 150,682,156 pounds.

Grizzly Bear

JULY THE ONLY OFFICIAL PUBLICATION OF THE NATIVE SONS AND DAUGHTERS OF THE GOLDEN WEST 1933

Featuring

GENERAL NEWS OF INTEREST CONCERNING ALL CALIFORNIA, and ORDERS NATIVE SONS and NATIVE DAUGHTERS

Price: 15 Cents

"When Wig-Wags Warn, Take Heed!" is the July slogan of the California Public Safety Committee in its campaign to lessen the constantly increasing auto death-toll.

The Grizzly Bear Magazine

The ALL California Monthly

OWNED, CONTROLLED, PUBLISHED BY GRIZZLY BEAR PUBLISHING CO., (Incorporated) COMPOSED OF NATIVE SONS.

HERMAN C. LICHTENBERGER, Pres.
JOHN T. NEWELL RAY HOWARD
WM. I. TRAEGER LORENZO F. SOTO
CHAS. R. THOMAS HARRY J. LELANDE
ARTHUR A. SCHMIDT, Vice-Pres.
BOARD OF DIRECTORS

CLARENCE M. HUNT
General Manager and Editor

OFFICIAL ORGAN AND THE ONLY OFFICIAL PUBLICATION OF THE NATIVE SONS AND THE NATIVE DAUGHTERS OF THE GOLDEN WEST.

ISSUED FIRST OF EACH MONTH. FORMS CLOSE 20th MONTH. ADVERTISING RATES ON APPLICATION.

SAN FRANCISCO OFFICE:
N.S.G.W. BLDG., 414 MASON ST., ROOM 302
(Office Grand Secretary N.S.G.W.)
Telephone: KEarny 1223
SAN FRANCISCO, CALIFORNIA

PUBLICATION OFFICE:
309-15 WILCOX BLDG., 2nd AND SPRING,
Telephone: VAndike 6234
LOS ANGELES, CALIFORNIA

(Entered as second-class matter May 29, 1918, at the Postoffice at Los Angeles, California, under the act of August 24, 1912.)

PUBLISHED REGULARLY SINCE MAY 1907

VOL. LIII(53). WHOLE NO. 315

"OLD SPANISH DAYS"
SANTA BARBARA'S HISTORIC FESTIVAL

Clifford F. Rizor

(PUBLICITY CHAIRMAN
SANTA BARBARA PARLOR N.S.G.W.)

"He loved the twilight that surrounds
The border-land of old romance,
Where glitter hauberk, helm and lance,
And banner waves, and trumpet sounds."
—"Tales of a Wayside Inn."

DURING THE FIRST WEEK IN AUGUST, Santa Barbara will again invite the world to participate with her in the tenth annual celebration of "Old Spanish Days." This distinctively Californian production is attracting larger numbers of visitors to the city each year; a factor having much to do with the continued success of the idea fostered ten years ago by several well-known Native Sons and Native Daughters, with the assistance of prominent Santa Barbara artists and civic leaders.

Once again, through the magic of stagecraft and the arts of the make-up box, Santa Barbara will live and move in the lights and shadows of by-gone years. Here, in the course of the work-a-day world, architects have reproduced the storied atmosphere of old Spain: the square towers and iron balconies of Seville, the palm-fronded courts and exotic gardens of Granada; an authentic background for the spirit of the old romantic age, lending a touch of realism to the make-believe. Therefore, it is not difficult to stir memories of the past; to endow California history, through the varied phases of a moving pageant, with a vitality it never possessed in the pages of books.

Reaching back into Santa Barbara's obscure beginnings, the pageantry will afford a glimpse of the glorious adventurers of the Spanish Main, and the plumed knights with their men-at-arms; moving in all the panoplied circumstance of Spain in her day of greatness. For "Old Spanish Days" is the portrayal of a time "when knighthood was in flower;" when music, romance, and the gentle graces of boundless hospitality were the very essence of life in a pastoral world. Cabrillo, carrying the standard of Castilla y Leon to the shores of the western sea; Portola, following the paths of conquest and high adventure; Serra, pressing forward in the high calling of his faith—all, in a sense, were knights errant in an age of chivalry; all will live again, as in the colorful sequences of a drama. The music of the string orchestras, the creaking of the ox-carts, the graceful figures of "La Jota" and "El Jarabe" will speak once more of a world unmarred by the mechanical dissonance and jangle of our own prosaic generation. George Eliot tells the story of a "village where many of the old echoes lingered, undrowned by new voices." These words are perhaps best descriptive of Santa Barbara, as she dons fiesta garb to revive the old, carefree spirit of "la primavera."

It is fitting, in these days, that the padres open the celebration with a reception and entertainment at old Santa Barbara Mission, for the mission was the focal point of all social life in Santa Barbara's early years; it was there that the old-time fiestas had their beginnings.

The historic street parade, brilliant and colorful, is one of the featured events of the fiesta, commemorating the various episodes of Santa Barbara's history. The conquistadores, the pirates and the freebooters; the soldiery of Viscaino, Ortega and Fremont; the sailors, miners and trappers of the later '49 period, all are faithfully represented; an entertainment and instructive spectacle for historian and tourist alike. The equestrian division is worthy of special mention as being an outstanding feature. More than a thousand costumed riders, mounted on California's finest horses (palominos, arabians and other varieties of blooded stock) appear in this section. General Fremont's soldiers, with their smooth-bore muskets and nondescript uniforms, march to the strains of "Oh, Susanna," as their band precedes them down the street.

The stagecoaches, tallyhos and covered wagons which follow are suggestive of the intrusion of the American influence that was so soon to make rude changes in the leisurely tradition of the old-established order; an influence that was to bring "Main Street" to Santa Barbara, jangling its restful harmonies, and shaping it into what it was until very recently—just another rambling, ordinary, American small town, without uniformity or plan. Yet, as we watch the groups of dancers performing in the sunken gardens, surrounded by the beautiful Spanish type buildings of the Santa Barbara County Court House, and hear the string orchestras playing in "El Paseo," it would seem that "Main Street," with its inharmonious angles, had been relegated far into the discard.

No "Spanish Days" would be complete without the historic pageant-play performed each year in Peabody Stadium. This year it is titled "La Entrada de los Americanos," and was written by Charles E. Pressley, who is also the director. This pageant deals with the period of the early American occupation, with General Fremont and Benjamin Foxen as the principal characters. There is also the familiar scene of the wedding celebration at the De La Guerra home in Santa Barbara. The beauty of this pageant is always enhanced by specially arranged orchestration, performed by a full concert orchestra. The famous theme songs of the fiesta, "Song of the Vigilantes" and "Carmelita," constantly recurrent in the incidental music, are compositions of Santa Barbara's own artist-composer, Raymond B. Eldred, who in past years has conducted the orchestra for the pageant and is expected to hold the baton again this year.

It is well to note, in passing, that the impromptu elements of the celebration are very nearly as entertaining as its organized program. The thousands of people who participate in the parade, the pageant and other planned features are perhaps outnumbered by those who take part in the street dancing, or join with the independent groups of singers, dancers and musicians who appear everywhere in the restaurants, hotels, clubs and public places.

FIESTA TIME IN SANTA BARBARA.

As an evidence of the historic research undertaken by the history departments of Santa Barbara Parlor No. 116 N.S.G.W. and Reina Del Mar Parlor No. 126 N.D.G.W. to properly authenticate the various phases of costuming and pageantry, this fiesta should be of intense interest to the members of both Orders. Justifiably, it may be said that "Old Spanish Days" holds the elements of inspiration and uplift for all classes.

So, in conclusion, we invite you to visit Santa Barbara! Sit in your hotel lobby and listen to the sparkling notes of Spanish melody, as only a real Spanish orchestra can produce it. Go out into the street and mingle with the brightly costumed crowd to witness the world-famous street parade. Attend a performance of the historic pageant-play, "La Entrada de los Americanos." Then you will know why "Old Spanish Days" is one of the great civic festivals. It is probable, too, that as the last day is ended, and strolling groups of troubadours pass through the streets at midnight playing "Adios, Adios, Amores," you will feel a very real sense of regret for the passing of the old provincial custom; you will look forward to another year, in confidence that "Old Spanish Days" will bring you back to Santa Barbara.

"DAN" RYAN
JOURNEYS ON

DANIEL ALPHONSUS RYAN, PAST Grand President of the Order of Native Sons of the Golden West and one of California's most brilliant sons, passed into the great beyond from his San Francisco home, June 11. Surviving him are his wife, Mrs. Josephine Cooney-Ryan, and three daughters, Mrs. William Wallace, Mrs. Ward von Tillow and Miss Mary Margaret Ryan.

"Dan" Ryan was born at San Francisco, August 21, 1873, and affiliated with Pacific Parlor No. 10 N.S.G.W. of that city July 14, 1896. As a delegate from Pacific, his first Grand Parlor was the Twenty-first (Nevada City 1898). At the Twenty-seventh Grand Parlor (Vallejo) he was elected a Grand Trustee, and at the Thirty-third Grand Parlor (Lake Tahoe) he became the Grand President and presided at the Thirty-fourth (Santa Cruz) Grand Parlor.

Burial services were conducted June 13 from Saint Mary's Cathedral, one of San Francisco's largest churches, which was crowded to capacity with friends of this talented son of the Golden State. No eulogy was delivered, and naught but a simple church ritual was recited, for "Dan" lived a very active, but unostentatious, life. He numbered his friends by the thousands, and was admired because of his sterling worth as a plain citizen.

DANIEL A. RYAN,
Past Grand President N.S.G.W.

Among the numerous honorary pallbearers were the following Native Sons: Grand President Justice Emmet Seawell; Past Grand Presidents Lewis F. Byington and Herman C. Lichtenberger; Mayor Angelo J. Rossi (El Dorado Parlor No. 52); Supervisors J. Emmet Hayden (Mount Tamalpais Parlor No. 64) and Victor J. Canepa (San Francisco Parlor No. 49); Superior Judges George H. Cabaniss (Pacific Parlor No. 10), Timothy I. Fitzpatrick (Stanford Parlor No. 76), Daniel C. Deasy (Pacific Parlor No. 10) and John J. Van Nostrand (Stanford Parlor No. 76), and Frank J. Klimm (Pacific Parlor No. 10).—C.M.H.

Bridge Ceremonies—Ground-breaking ceremonies for the mammoth San Francisco-Oakland bridge will be held on Yerba Buena Island, July 9.

REVIEW OF OAKLAND N.D.G.W. GRAND PARLOR

(CLARENCE M. HUNT.)

GRAND PRESIDENT ANNA MIXON Armstrong (Woodland No. 90) presided throughout the deliberations of the Forty-seventh Grand Parlor of the Order of Native Daughters of the Golden West, in session at Oakland, Alameda County, June 19, 20, 21 and 22. Concluding a detailed account of her incumbency, Mrs. Armstrong said: "The report of my stewardship is finished. The history of my service has been written day by day, as I have come to you in your own home Parlors. I hope I have not been found wanting. Any failures which may have been made, have certainly been of the head and not of the heart. I have given to the full of my physical strength and my mental measure. No other could do more. One thing I have learned, aside from the fraternal love existing in our Order, is to love California more devotedly than ever before. . . . To California, I pledge fealty, I pledge service, I pledge constant and unflagging love. Will each one of you join me in that pledge? Then will we, as true Native Daughters, have kept the faith. No more fitting words may be found with which to close, than those of our own Past Grand President, Eliza D. Keith:

"CALIFORNIA.
Her poppies fling a cloth of gold
O'er California hills,
Fit emblem of the wealth untold
That hill and dale and plain unfold:
Her fame the Whole world fills."

Then, in compliment to the Grand President, the escort team of Woodland No. 90, under the direction of Captain Lela Ewert, executed an unusual drill, made colorful by beautiful gowns in pastel shades, and baskets of gorgeous spring flowers. The team's personnel included: Dorothy Bigelow, Madeline Hermle, Mary Tillotson, Gladys Neiman, Oleta Wademan, Bernice Braden, Marybelle Pierce, Ramona Roth, Iola Anderson, Leona Sachs, Evelyn Groh, Irene LeCornec, Edna Bailey, Leola Crow, Lena Rominger and Geraldine O'Donnell (accompanist).

The report of Grand Secretary Sallie R. Thaler recounted the numerous transactions of that office. La Dorada No. 236 (San Francisco) surrendered its charter January 26, 1933. Grand Parlor receipts for the year were $20,274.46 and disbursements $18,136.48. The year's cash gain was $2,137.98. The June 1, 1933, worth of the Grand Parlor was $25,636.20, including a cash balance of $20,585. One hundred and nineteen members passed away during the year, and $8,850 was paid from the Grand Parlor death burial fund.

Grand Treasurer Susie K. Christ reported the cash balances in the several Grand Parlor funds as follows, as of June 1, 1933: General, $20,585; Phelan Trust, $10,473.76; Death Benefit, $480; Mills College Scholarship, $595.01; Redwood Memorial Grove, $927.46; University Scholarship, $747.87.

Miss Millie Tietjen (Golden State No. 50), assistant treasurer Grand Parlor Home Committee, reported June 1, 1933, cash balances in the commercial account, $1,120.90, and in the savings account, $9,087.10. Receipts for the year totaled $10,233.99. Loyalty Pledge payments amounted to $3,248.91, and cook book sales amounted to $625.07.

Other reports of grand officers and committees dealt mostly with matters which heretofore have been given publicity in The Grizzly Bear. A review of the Forty-seventh Grand Parlor follows:

CHANGES IN CONSTITUTIONS.

Changes in the governing laws were made as follows, the abbreviations "C.G.P." and "C.S.P." referring, respectively, to the Constitution Grand Parlor and the Constitution Subordinate Parlors:

Art. III, Sec. 2, C.G.P., amended by adding: "Subordinate Parlors must keep a record of attendance of past and present officers."

Art. III, Sec. 5, C.G.P., amended to provide: "No proxies shall be admitted to represent elected [Grand Parlor] delegates, but alternates shall be elected who must possess the same qualifications; that the candidate receiving the next highest number of votes in the election for delegates, after the number of delegates are elected, shall be designated as alternate number one, and so on."

Art. X, Sec. 3, Par. 5, C.G.P., amended to read: "The sum of $75 shall be drawn from this [Death Benefit] Fund upon the receipt of a certificate of death of a sister, providing she has been a member of the Order for six months," etc.

Art. II, Sec. 3b, C.S.P., amended by adding: "In order to be eligible to receive Grand Parlor death benefits, a member must have been affiliated with the Order for six months."

BUSINESS TRANSACTED.

Santa Cruz City was selected as the meeting place of the Forty-eighth (1934) Grand Parlor.

The mileage bill of $1,761.12 for this (Oakland) session was approved.

The percapita tax was reduced from one dollar to fifty cents, payable twenty-five cents in July and twenty-five cents in January. The annual Home assessment was reduced from fifty cents to twenty-five cents.

A resolution prevailed, "That the Grand Parlor pay no more than fifty dollars per month for the rental of office space for the Grand Secretary."

Several changes in the Initiatory Ritual were approved, and a new Installation Ceremony, to become effective January 1, 1934, was adopted.

Several Subordinate Parlors were excused from non-representation at the session, and also exempted from fines.

A motion prevailed that, "whenever possible, the Subordinate Parlors subscribe to and assist in the work of the Veterans Welfare Committee."

Five scholarships were awarded: Winona Laverty (Veritas No. 75) of Merced, and Imogene Gray (Marguerite No. 12) of Placerville,

MRS. IRMA LAIRD,
GRAND PRESIDENT N.D.G.W.

in the University of California at Berkeley; Lois Allen (Los Angeles No. 124) of Los Angeles, in the University of California at Los Angelse; Phyllis Thompson (La Junta No. 203) of Saint Helena, and Jane Alexander of San Francisco, in Mills College.

One hundred dollars was contributed toward the erection of an Easter sunrise service cross on Mount Davidson, San Francisco, and fifty dollars was donated to San Antonio de Padua Mission.

The granting of a charter to Rio Rita No. 253 (Sacramento), instituted April 8, 1933, was ratified.

The Grizzly Bear was re-endorsed as the official organ of the Order, and financial provision was made for the publication therein of the Official Directory.

An invitation was extended John Steven McGroarty of Los Angeles, California's poet laureate, "to attend a Grand Parlor meeting whenever he finds it convenient."

A letter of thanks was ordered sent O. L. Brainard of Sacramento for his kindness in making, at such a low cost, the plaque for the Order's Redwood Memorial Grove in Humboldt County.

A resolution prevailed, that Subordinate Parlors be granted a three-year extension to fulfill their Loyalty Pledge quotas, and that funds be provided "to place the names of all Parlors which have completed their pledges on the Honor Roll plaque in the Native Daughter Home."

On recommendation Grand President Armstrong, ordered "That the Grand Parlor, through its Veterans Welfare Committee, subscribe for one copy of The Grizzly Bear Magazine to each Government Hospital in the State, and that the subscription be paid from the Veterans Welfare fund."

A motion prevailed, that Past Grand Emma G. Foley be given charge of the cook books, and that they be sold, at thirty-five cents each, to Subordinate Parlors, which are authorized to resell them.

A letter of thanks and appreciation was ordered sent Grand Trustee Willow Borba (Santa Rosa No. 217) for her loyal, efficient and unremunerative work in compiling the cook books.

A rising vote of thanks was given Past Grand Dr. Mariana Bertola for her untiring efforts in behalf of the Native Daughter Home.

For her years of service to the Order, Past Grand Emma Gruber-Foley was given a rising vote of thanks. As Grand President, she presided at the Twenty-second (Lodi 1908) Grand Parlor. In responding, Mrs. Foley said the happiest moments of her life "have been given to her by the Order and the friendships she has made."

A resolution—presented by Past Grand Catherine E. Gloster, Elizabeth Spencer (El Monte No. 205), Inez Sitton (Californiana No. 247) and Margeret E. Weston (Eschscholtzia No. 112)—was unanimously adopted, extending thanks to "Worthy Grand President Anna Mixon Armstrong for her gracious and orderly conduct of the Grand Parlor session, and for her fine representation of the highest ideals of the Order throughout the year when she made contacts with the membership of the entire state; to the N.D.G.W. Parlors of Alameda County, which so lavishly provided for the comfort and entertainment of the Grand Parlor; . . . to the management of Hotel Leamington, for the many courtesies extended the Grand Parlor; . . . to the 'Oakland Tribune,' the 'Post-Enquirer' and the 'Call-Bulletin,' for the unstinted and commendable publicity given the Grand Parlor and its personnel; to the General Association Past Presidents, for refreshments served during the session; and to all others who contributed in any way to the wellbeing of this Grand Parlor."

NEW GRAND OFFICERS.

At the election of grand officers Wednesday, 353 ballots were cast, and the following were selected:

Grand President, Irma Laird (Alturas No. 159).

Grand Vice-president, Gladys E. Noce (Amapola No. 80).

Grand Secretary, Sallie R. Thaler (Aloha No. 106).

Grand Treasurer, Susie K. Christ (Yosemite No. 83).

Grand Marshal, Annie C. Thuesen (Alta No. 3).

Grand Inside Sentinel, Hazel B. Hansen (Verdugo No. 240).

Grand Outside Sentinel, Alice Mathias Oldham (El Carmelo No. 181).

Grand Organist, Clara Gairaud (Vendome No. 100).

Grand Trustees (in order of vote received), Orinda G. Giannini (Orinda No. 56), Florence D. Boyle (Gold of Ophir No. 190), Minna Kane-Horn (Eschscholtzia No. 112), Jane Vick (Reina del Mar No. 126), Alice M. Lane (Castro No. 178), Ethel S. Begley (Marinita No. 198) and Willow Borba (Santa Rosa No. 217).

They, along with Anna Mixon Armstrong (Woodland No. 90), who automatically became the Junior Past Grand President, were installed by Past Grand Evelyn I. Carlson as Supreme President, assisted by Edna B. Briggs (La Bandera No. 110) as Supreme Marshal, Emilie Lachman (Amapola No. 80) as Supreme Organist, and Past Grand Estelle M. Evans as Supreme Inside Sentinel. At the conclusion of the ceremonies Past Grand Sue J. Irwin, on the Order's behalf, presented a ruby-and-diamond ring to Mrs. Armstrong, the retiring Grand President.

"WE GO FORTH INTO THE MORROW DEDICATED ANEW TO OUR GREAT CAUSE."

The Publicity Committee, through Past Grand Bertha A. Briggs, reported on the publicity given activities of the Subordinate Parlors, and several scrapbooks of clippings were exhibited. Quoting from this report:

"The yesterday of countless perplexities, of far-reaching anxieties, of seemingly insurmountable problems has brought forth a wider valuation and a deeper appreciation of the ennobling principles of the Native Daughters of the Golden West. Heretofore, we have seemed to see as through a glass darkly, but now a brighter light has come, enabling us to comprehend more clearly, reason more exactly, and strive more constantly and diligently for the furtherance of our established projects and activities. Truly have we grown in understanding and in tolerance, in foresight and in fervor. In spirit and in thought, we have gone steadily forward, and there has been awakened within us a real, a vital and an enduring interest. The point has been reached where, more than ever before, we openly manifest that interest. We go forth into the morrow—calmly and resolutely—dedicated anew to our great cause. Your publicity group points with justifiable pride to the no-small part they have severally played in this awakening to a keener realization that our principles stand now—as they have ever stood—for the development of all that is good, for the promotion of all that lends to encouragement, and for guidance to a state of stability, contentment and clarity. . . .

"To insure the continuation of this keen interest, the individual members of Subordinate Parlors are once again urged to lend their loyal support and financial assistance to our only official organ—The Grizzly Bear. A copy of this strictly California periodical should reach every Native Daughter home each month. Through columns featuring general news of our State and of our Orders of Native Sons and Native Daughters of the Golden West, and filled with valuable facts and references, as well as interesting reading matter, the story of our developmeit and our worthy activities is given to the world. Assuredly, the editor deserves our hearty support. Let it be our determined purpose to make the ensuing twelve months an outstanding year for our own Grizzly Bear—its success is vital to our Order."

RITUAL EXEMPLIFICATION.

The ritual was exemplified the night of June 21 by the district deputies of Alameda County, who were charmingly gowned. Supervising Deputy Mildred Brant Irwin (Berkeley No. 150) was in charge, and was assisted by Deputy Grand President Ellen Hitch (Berkeley No. 150). Seven candidates were initiated. Those officiating were:

Matilda Enos (Betsy Ross No. 238), president; Louise McDougall (Bahia Vista No. 167), past president; Lurine Martin (Aloha No. 106), first vice; Marion White (Piedmont No. 87), second vice; Thelma Schornick (Bear Flag No. 151), third vice; Kathleen Dombrink (Piedmont No. 87), marshal; Martha Watson (Aloha No. 106), recording secretary; Elsie Haven (Bear Flag No. 151), financial secretary; Adelaide Martin (Laura Loma No. 182), treasurer; Ella Freitas (Argonaut No. 166), Grace Curry (Richmond No. 147) and Olinda Kardoza (El Cereso No. 207), trustees; Ann Mello (Fruitvale No. 177), junior past president; Ann Lewis (El Cereso No. 207), senior past president; Florence Shapero (Berkeley No. 150), organist; Kathryn Walde (Hayward No. 122), inside sentinel; Marie Thompson (Berkeley No. 150), outside sentinel.

Dora Brayton (Bahia Vista No. 167), in a most impressive ceremony attesting the friendship of the Alameda County Native Daughters for Grand President Armstrong, presented her with a gift of rock crystal. Marie Cordery, newly initiated member of Aloha No. 106, sang "The End of a Perfect Year."

NOTES OF THE SESSION.

Three charter members of the "mother" Parlor, Ursula No. 1 (Jackson), were in attendance: Founder Lily O. Reichling-Dyer, Mrs. Flora Dunning-Podesta and Mrs. Henrietta Greenhalgh-O'Neill.

Past Grand Carrie Roesch-Durham, who has attended every one of the forty-seven Grand Parlors, again headed the Credentials Committee.

Past Grand Addie L. Mosher, unable, because of serious illness, to attend the session, was visited at her Oakland home by many of her close friends.

Past Grand Catherine E. Gloster and sister, Miss Dorothy Gloster (Alturas No. 159) announced they would depart July 1, via the Panama Canal, on a month's tour of Eastern cities.

Marguerite No. 12 (Placerville) disposed of a baby-crib quilt for the benefit of the homeless children, and it went to Grand Outside Sentinel Alice Mathias-Oldham, a recent bride.

In presenting her annual report, Secretary Mary E. Brusie (Argonaut No. 166) of the N.S.G.W. and N.D.G.W. Central Homeless Children Committee, conducted an imaginary trip through an art gallery wherein were displayed likenesses of many adopted children. Despite depression difficulties, she said, 180 children were placed the past year, a larger number than in any other year, swelling the total number placed to more than 4,200. Members of the Grand Parlor were delighted with Miss Brusie's charming recital of the conduct of this outstand-

(Continued on Page 14)

"IT IS YOUR DUTY TO SELL THE N.D.G.W. ORDER"

MRS. IRMA LAIRD OF ALTURAS, MODOC County, affiliated with Alturas Parlor No. 159, became the Grand President of the Order of Native Daughters of the Golden West at the Oakland Grand Parlor, June 22. Her installation address—her message to the members of the Order and to the women of California eligible to membership in this outstanding fraternal organization—follows:

"The Order of Native Daughters of the Golden West is a unique institution. Membership therein means far more than any other fraternal affiliation. It is an enlistment in a movement which has for its purpose the preservation of the sanctity of the home, the teaching of loyalty to established government, and the cultivation of the spirit of service to Order, State and Nation. Born out of a desire to perpetuate the glorious deeds of our pioneer fathers and mothers and to leave as a heritage to posterity a carefully studied history of California, the Order has steadily grown in strength and prestige until in its maturity it affords common ground for California-born women of every class and creed to labor in the blessed spirit of toleration.

"Tonight, a beloved leader completes her year of service, surrenders her responsibilities and her gavel. They are assumed by a new leader. The example of service set by our Worthy Grand President of the year just closed is truly to me an inspiration which I may well wish to emulate. She has been a worthy successor to the long line of sterling women who have led us in the past, and who still give their time and talents to all that bespeaks progress to California and our Order. Their presence here, year after year, is an indication of their love for and loyalty to those who have honored them in the past.

"It is human for one, new and untried, to hesitate about taking on great responsibilities, not knowing what problems may confront her, or whether she shall have the qualifications and attributes to meet and overcome them in a spirit of justice and charity. I want you to know that I fully realize the import of the time-honored traditions of my office, as well as its opportunity for service; that I keenly appreciate the confidence which prompted you to confer this honor upon me. Nevertheless, it is in a spirit of humility and fraternal love that I accept the office of Grand President of the Order of Native Daughters of the Golden West.

"With each new administration come new and live interests, different viewpoints and a new note of progress. I shall look to every member of the Order to co-operate with the Grand Officers in perpetuating the original aims and objects of our Order, and also in meeting and dealing with the new situations which the Spirit of Progress has forced upon us.

"Due to political machinations or economic changes, there have come times in the history of our nation that have 'tried men's souls.' Such a period obtains today. In all the land few, indeed, have been able to carry on without incurring heavy financial losses. From the country as well as the populous cities has come the cry of hungry mouths that labor cannot fill. There is confusion in our financial world, and confusion in our moral standards!

"Americans, in the days of prosperity, became so inflated with their own success that they forgot the Giver of their blessings, and many abandoned the standards of their fathers and, by their open disregard of the laws of God and Man, brought chaos into our political, economic and social life. This period of enforced idleness, when twelve million men are yet unemployed and suffering privation in this, the richest country in the world, has prepared a fertile field for the fatal seeds of communism and other red elements which will produce a harvest of thorns and thistles to destroy our faith in home, government and religion.

"What are we going to do about it? How can we, possessed of a finer spirit and a keener insight than the average individual, assist those who have lost faith through their contact with adversity, or been contaminated by the enemies of Right and Truth? What can we do to rehabilitate the morale of our country?

"We are the daughters of a race of men and women who have won the admiration of the world for their faith, their courage, their industry and their efficiency. Our pioneer forbears did not falter when obstacles prevented their progress, nor may we. In every community let the Native Daughters be an agency to inspire the citizens with courage, confidence and patriotism, and with respect and reverence for established law and order. Fighting together, we can combat the pernicious influences which seek to destroy our social structure. Through united efforts, we will help restore happiness to our country and to our Golden State! I appeal to each and every member in this Order to help me in keeping this distinctly California organization in the vanguard of the Nation's mighty builders.

"In attacking our new problems, however, we should never lose sight of the original purpose for which our Order was instituted. Other organizations, casting about for some method to popularize themselves and to justify their existence, have undertaken the staging of 'pioneer' celebrations and the marking of historical spots. Let us remember that we are the pioneers in this work, and let us so cover the possibilities in each locality that there will be no room for interlopers.

"I ask that you assist not only in the expansion of the Order but, also, that you strive for the retention of present members. The hard times and lack of employment have made it difficult for many splendid members to keep up their dues. I feel that some plan should be worked out in every Parlor to save these members to the Order. The elimination of certain practices which draw heavily upon the Parlors' surplus funds, such as the payment of sick benefits, might conserve sufficient funds to tide over, during this period, worthy members who are temporarily unable to pay dues and assessments. The Parlors may express their love and sympathy to the sick in many ways which would do far more toward ameliorating the discomforts of sickness than simply drawing a check for a specific sum. The comparatively small amount that Parlors are able to pay in sick benefits is not sufficient to make the practice a drawing card for membership. This is but one of any number of methods that may be used to carry out a plan for the retention of members. Each of you, in your own locality and in your own way, can evolve a workable plan.

"Again, let me admonish you that it is your duty, as well as your privilege, to sell the Order of Native Daughters of the Golden West to the eligible women of your community. For I hold that every California-born woman who honors and reveres the memory of the pioneers and wishes to perpetuate the fruits of their labors; who thrills with pride over California's romantic history; who believes in the preservation of the state's landmarks, relics and traditions; who is interested in civic betterment in her community and the state; who holds high ideals of patriotism; who believes in safeguarding our national welfare by the americanization of the foreign born within our gates; who would encourage higher educational advantages for women; whose heart goes out in loving sympathy to the disabled veteran and the orphaned and homeless children of California, should be a member of the Native Daughters of the Golden West, for these are the principles upon which our great woman's organization stands.

"You have made me your Grand President. The honor thrills me, and yet tonight I am not so much concerned with what the office may do for me, but with what I shall be able to do for the office. Fully aware of my limitations, but confident that I shall have your wholehearted support, I enter upon my term of office with this prayer to Him, who doeth all things well:

"'Make me too brave to waver or to be unkind. Make me too understanding to mind the little hurts companions give; and friends, the careless little hurts that no one quite intends. Make me too thankful to hurt others so. Help me to know the inmost hearts of those for whom I care; their secret wishes, all the loads they bear, that I may add my courage to their own. May I make lonely folks feel less alone, and happy ones a little happier yet. May I forget what ought to be forgotten, and recall unfailingly all that ought to be recalled; each kindly thing, forgetting what might sting. To all upon my way, day after day, let me bring joy and hope, and let me sing'."

CALIFORNIA FIFTY YEARS AGO

Thomas R. Jones

(COMPILED EXPRESSLY FOR THE GRIZZLY BEAR.)

THE ONE HUNDRED AND SEVENTH anniversary of the independence of the United States of America was celebrated in the cities and towns of California July 4, 1883. With a salute of thirteen guns at daybreak, unrestricted firing of firecrackers, bombs and guns during the daytime, the glorious national holiday closed with nighttime exhibitions of fireworks. No disastrous fires ensued from this year's celebration.

At the banquet of the Society of California Pioneers in Sacramento, Governor George Stoneman, in reminiscing, stated he was the grand marshal of Sacramento's first Fourth of July celebration, in 1850.

Members of the Democratic Party had a mass meeting in San Francisco July 8 and adopted resolutions condemning the State Railroad Commission for not reducing railroad passenger and freight rates.

Exports of flour by ocean this month exceeded those of any previous month to date, 132,000 barrels being shipped to foreign countries.

The price of hops declined to 20 cents a pound this month, and the growers viewed the situation with alarm. The hop acreage of the state had been increased to 2,000 this year, and the market was stagnated.

Sale was this month made of 3,300 acres of the Santa Rita Rancho in Alameda County, at an average price of $100 an acre.

July was a month of strikes. The printers on the "San Francisco Call" went out, because they objected to working with non-union printers. Then the Chinese shoemakers, the coopers and the restaurant waiters struck for higher wages. July 25, telegraph operators employed by the Western Union throughout the nation, including those in several California cities, quit their keys.

The 1,700 Chinese laborers on the California and Oregon Railway north of Redding, Shasta County, who struck for more wages, consumed their last bags of rice June 16 and went back to work. The railroad company's edict, "no workee, no eatee," won out.

Typhoid fever was epidemic in Petaluma, Sonoma County, sixty-nine cases being treated there July 31.

The Irish Land League had a state convention July 12 in San Francisco. A report showed that during the year California members had contributed, and sent to Ireland, $50,000. A resolution was adopted forbidding members to purchase goods made in England.

The Fong Tuck Hong, a California Chinese benevolent society, was chartered to begin business July 8. Far ahead of the Americans, its laws provided for unemployment insurance, marriage and birth contributions, and banned divorce.

Sierra County's gold mines came to the front. July 15, the Rainbow struck another of its prolific pockets that yielded over $100,000. The Ruby took out a two-pound nugget July 22, and the Bald Mountain produced eight pounds of the yellow metal in a week.

The stage from Redding, Shasta County, to Weaverville, Trinity County, went off the grade near Old Shasta July 2. The four horses were killed, and several passengers were severely injured.

A state bicycle meet was held in San Francisco July 15, and the hundred and more delegates pedaled from the Ferry Building to the Cliff House and back.

A business block in Lincoln, Placer County, burned July 11, causing a $20,000 loss. The Whitmore Flourmill at Modesto, Stanislaus County, was destroyed by fire July 15; loss, $50,000.

A large portion of Colusa City's business district burned July 25, entailing a $75,000 loss. July 30, fire practically wiped out Tulare City's business section, with a loss of $130,000.

Jonas Spect, Pioneer of 1846 and one of the first men to prospect on the Yuba River in 1849, died at Colusa City July 3.

P. J. Hooper and D. E. Callahan, Pioneers of 1849, died at Sacramento July 22 and 24, respectively. The former was private secretary to Governor John Bigler in 1853, and for many years published the "Folsom Telegraph."

Colonel J. C. Zabriskie, who came from Virginia in 1849, died July 11 at San Francisco at the age of 79. He was Sacramento's first city attorney, and later became prominent in the affairs of the Bay City. His daughter was the wife of Governor J. Neely Johnson.

Miss Ada Fern, aged 16, was thrown from a horse at Adams Springs, Lake County, July 1 and killed.

Tim Flaherty, who mined in Sierra County in 1849, was killed by a cave-in at a Sebastopol, Sonoma County, mine July 13.

A lad named Henderson, herding sheep near Durham, Butte County, July 15 sat upon a railroad tie and fell asleep. He was struck by a train and killed.

Archie McMillan, working on the new State Fair pavilion begin erected in Sacramento City, was accidentally killed July 1.

John Hennesey, in San Francisco, went insane July 7. He found Mrs. Hattie Fellows in her back yard and killed her.

SLIM LAW

• • •

Harry Oliver

FOLSOM BILL CAME BACK TO THE valley, after a three-year absence, with a short haircut and a long black music instrument he calls a bassoon. He told his ma, who we know as the Widow Winchester, that he's been playin' in the town band up state at Folsom. Bill's always been the black sheep of our valley—guess we had to have one since Borego is Mex for sheep—so we all try to keep him out of trouble and took his story for what it was worth, even though he did devil the life out of his ma, makin' things harder with a house full of grandchildren to look after that's been carelessly left her by his older brother.

Well, two weeks ago someone swiped about sixty dollars' worth of groceries from Gopher Joe right after he takes them from my store, and our Deputy Sheriff, Slim Law, comes out of the moth balls and starts lookin' for clews and motives.

Now, it's hard to prove whose can of coffee a can is if everybody uses the same brand like they do here. I stock only one kind in my store—the best, and that's the way it is with the rest of the groceries. Slim starts thinkin' and naturally he thought of Folsom Bill, and as Bill's a great hand to figure himself out of a bad spot, started action at once. Slim puts his kids in his Ford, gets a lot of lollypops at my store and goes over to the widow's like he was makin' a social call for the kiddies' benefit.

Folsom Bill is home, as Slim Law figured he'd be, and he can't very well go because of not having any excuse, so he stays. Slim gets the youngsters to playin' and toward evenin' drifts into the kitchen with Bill. Then one of Slim's kids comes in, warm from play, with his little sweater in his hands as he was told to. Bill turns around to light his pipe by the stove, when Slim takes the sweater and puts it over the kid's head, sayin' loud and gruff, "Now I got ya! Stick 'em up! What you got in here?"

Slim's game works like magic. Bill, without turnin', says, "Not so loud. I'll go with you. Don't tell ma. Kin I take my bassoon along?"

Well, the Widow Winchester was glad when we told her Bill was workin' on the new road that's goin' to help the valley so much. In fact, everything's come out fine. The prisoners at the road camp are glad to have Bill's music. Gopher Joe's glad because he got his groceries back; they never was stolen—he put them in the wrong car by mistake. Slim's glad he got something real on Bill when he found a bottle of booze in his pocket. Bill's glad that the only charge Slim pinched him on was bootleggin' and all's he lost was one quart of his tequila. And I'm glad Bill took his shriekin' bassoon where it's appreciated.

(This contribution to The Grizzly Bear is from Harry Oliver of Palms, Los Angeles County, who hopes to publish in book form a series of his short stories.—Editor.)

Power Bonds—Brawley, Imperial County, citizens have voted $500,000 bonds for a municipal power plant.

Homeless Children

A WORTHWHILE NON-SECTARIAN ENDEAVOR
SPONSORED AND SUPPORTED BY
THE ORDERS OF
NATIVE SONS AND NATIVE DAUGHTERS
OF THE GOLDEN WEST

BERTHA A. BRIGGS, PAST GRAND PRESident N.D.G.W., sent to the San Francisco office of the N.S.G.W. and N.D.G.W. Central Homeless Children Committee the following description of a circus given in Hollister, San Benito County, by boys and girls from 5 to 10 years of age. **This eagerness on the part of young girls and boys to help some child less fortunate than themselves augurs well for the future citizenship of their community:**

STOP READ!
BIG CIRCUS SATURDAY
APRIL 29, 1933 AT
554 4TH ST. AT 10:30 AM
CAUSE FOR HOMELESS
CHILDREN

Saturday afternoon, April 29, a group of ten children appeared at the home of Past Grand President Briggs and presented her with nickels and pennies to the amount of $1.30. This amount covered the proceeds of a circus held by The Good Will Club that morning in the backyard of the home of the president, Genevieve Willson, aged 10 years.

THE GOOD WILL CLUB
Of Hollister, San Benito County.

The Good Will Club learned that Copa de Oro Parlor No. 105 N.D.G.W. had adopted a homeless baby, and these ten little boys and girls and their star performer, "Boots Grant Willson," made up their minds to help the Native Daughters and thought of and planned the whole affair and announced, when making their presentation to Mrs. Briggs, that they wanted the money they had made to be used for the adopted baby. She accepted the gift with due ceremony and gratitude, and wrote a letter of thanks to each member of the club.

Two weeks later, a second circus was held at the home of another member of the club, with several Native Daughters present by special invitation. The proceeds of this performance, amounting to $1.55, were also presented to Mrs. Briggs, at which time an invitation was presented to the members of The Good Will Club to appear at the next meeting of Copa de Oro Parlor to "strut their stuff." Twenty-one performers responded to the invitation and, in the words of Eugene Willson, leader of the cowboy chorus, "We're getting famous!" The stunts consisted of songs, dances, chorus, acrobatic feats, closing with all the performers appearing in "I Love You, California." In this act were indians, cowboys and a covered wagon, and a real holdup was staged.

The three human rights of every child,—a home, a school, and a place to play,—have been given to over 4,200 children through the efforts of the Native Sons and the Native Daughters of the Golden West.

"He who would do some great thing in this short life must apply himself to work with such a concentration of his forces as, to idle spectators who live only to amuse themselves, looks like insanity."—Parkman.

Passing of the California Pioneer

(Confined to Brief Notices of the Demise of Those Men and Women Who Came to California Prior to 1870.)

JONATHAN WATSON, NATIVE OF MISSOURI, 89; came across the plains to California in 1849 and resided a few years in the vicinity of Sacramento; in 1868 he went to what is now Orange County and acquired a vast acreage; died in Santa Ana Canyon, survived by a wife and five children.

Mrs. Anna Cromwell-Reed, native of Missouri, 89; crossed the plains in 1850 and settled in El Dorado County; died at Placerville.

William Henry Kenyon, born in 1853 in Nevada State while his parents were enroute across the plains; resided in El Dorado and Shasta Counties; died at Redding, survived by four daughters.

Joseph Chambers, native of Ireland, 93; came around Cape Horn in 1854 and settled in San Francisco, where he died; seven children survive.

Mrs. Louisa Brown-Fry, native of Massachusetts, 89; came around Cape Horn in 1856 and long resided in Solano County; died at Berkeley, Alameda County, survived by four children.

Mrs. Ellen Cathers-Marcus, native of England, 87; came via Panama in 1857 and long resided in Santa Cruz County; died at Oakland, Alameda County, survived by six children.

Herman L. Judell, native of Germany, 89; in 1858 settled in San Francisco, where he died; four children survive.

Mrs. Eva Price, native of Germany, 99; came in 1860 and resided in El Dorado and Sacramento Counties; died at Sacramento City, survived by four daughters.

Marcus J. Bigelow, native of New York, 92; crossed the plains in 1860 and resided in Sutter and Butte Counties; died near Gridley.

Mrs. Susan Isabella Seely-Meacham, native of Quebec, 89; came in 1862 and resided in Humboldt, Santa Clara, San Luis Obispo and Santa Barbara Counties; died at Santa Maria, survived by four children.

Joseph E. Baird, native of Isle of Man, 83; crossed the plains in 1862 and settled in Yolo County; died at Woodland.

Mrs. Mary A. Young, 83; since 1862 Contra Costa County resident; died near Danville, survived by a husband and two daughters.

Mrs. Emma Janes, native of New Hampshire, 80; since 1865 Humboldt County resident; died at Eureka, survived by a son.

Josiah A. Polhemus, native of Iowa, 74; since 1868 Sacramento County resident; died at Elk Grove, survived by a wife and five children.

William Tomlinson, native of Nova Scotia, 82; came via Panama in 1868; died at Eureka, Humboldt County. He had engaged in newspaper work in various cities.

Mrs. Annie Rebecca Hanson-Harris, native of Ohio, 73; since 1868 resident Colfax, Placer County, where she died.

Charles Lauritsen, native of Denmark, 83; came via Panama in 1868; died at San Luis Obispo City, survived by a wife and four children.

William Thomas Dorral, native of Kentucky, 86; came in 1868 and resided in Calaveras and Stanislaus Counties; died at Oakdale, survived by six children.

Timothy Jerome Horgan, native of Massachusetts, 76; came in 1868; died at Watsonville, Santa Cruz County, survived by a wife.

James Darius Culp, native of New York, 95; came in 1865; died at Pacific Grove, Monterey County, survived by a wife and two sons.

Mrs. Laura Alice Eber, native of Ohio, 80; came in 1865; died at San Leandro, Alameda County, survived by four children.

Mrs. Ann Frances Perry-Aitken, native of Maine, 76; came in 1865; died at Berkeley, Alameda County, survived by two children.

George Meredith Underwood, native of Ohio, 78; crossed the plains in 1862; died at Madera City, survived by a wife and three daughters.

Albert J. Young, 92; since 1862 resident Danville, Contra Costa County, where he died. He was a former state assemblyman.

Mrs. Angela L. Marre, native of Italy, 81; came in 1860; died at San Luis Obispo City, survived by three children.

Joseph K. Jones, native of Ohio, 83; came via Cape Horn in 1855 and except for a few years resided in San Francisco, where he died; a son survives.

PIONEER NATIVES DEAD

(Brief Notices of the Demise of Men and Women born in California Prior to 1860.)

Mrs. Olivia Murphey-LeClert, born Stanislaus County, 1856; died Petaluma, Sonoma County; three children survive.

George Griffitts, born Plumas County, 1856; died near Upper Lake, Lake County; two children survive.

Mrs. Alice Frances Brown, born Sacramento County, 1858; died Sacramento City. She was a daughter of Joseph Grammer, Pioneer of 1849.

George C. Graves, born Calaveras County, 1855; died May 20, San Diego City; wife and two sons survive.

Frank Alexander Payne, born San Joaquin County, 1857; died May 21, Calistoga, Napa County; wife and four sons survive.

Mrs. Margaret Ann Alcorn-Scrivner, born San Joaquin County, 1857; died May 23, Hanford, Kings County; five children survive.

August L. Johnson, born Alameda County, 1857; died May 23, Mount Eden; wife survives. His father, Captain John Johnson, founded Mount Eden in 1850.

George Coughlan, born Nevada County, 1857; died May 23, Nevada City. He was affiliated with Hydraulic Parlor No. 56 N.S.G.W., and for many years was clerk of Nevada County. His parents, Mr. and Mrs. Michael Colgan, were Pioneers of 1849.

Mrs. Wilhelmina Buslach, born Tehama County, 1858; died May 25, San Francisco; wife and son survive.

William H. Nichols, born Santa Cruz County, 1858; died May 25, San Francisco; wife and four children survive.

Mrs. Lucy Gober-Boyd, born Sacramento City, 1857; died there, May 27.

Mrs. Rosa Sparks-Porter, born Santa Barbara County, 1851; died May 28, Covina, Los Angeles County; six children survive.

John C. Luce, born Sacramento City, 1855; died there, May 30; three daughters survive.

Thomas C. Conmy, born Trinity County, 1855; died May 30, San Francisco; wife and three children survive. He was affiliated with Golden Gate Parlor No. 29 N.S.G.W., from which he was a delegate to many Grand Parlors.

Larkin M. Locke, born Alameda County, 1855; died June 1, Pleasanton; wife and daughter survive.

Edwin Meese Sr., born San Francisco, 1857; died June 1, Oakland, Alameda County; wife and two children survive.

Mrs. Mary A. Avery, born Nevada County, 1852; died June 2, Sacramento City; four children survive. Her father, Nathan Hawk, was a Pioneer of 1846.

Mrs. Minnie Davidson, born San Francisco, 1853; died there, June 3; four children survive.

Mrs. Marie Kohler-Koebig, born San Francisco, 1857; died June 4, Los Angeles City; husband and three children survive.

Mrs. Maria Dominguez-Francis, born Los Angeles County, 1847; died June 4, Los Angeles City. She was a daughter of Manuel Dominguez, born at San Diego in 1803, owner of vast land acreages.

Mrs. Ellen Louise Ryder-Staples, born Santa Cruz County, 1854; died June 4, near Soquel; two daughters survive.

Charles L. Abner, born Sacramento County, 1857; died June 9, San Francisco; five children survive.

Charles Henry Phelps, born San Joaquin County, 1853; died New York City; wife and daughter survive.

Mrs. Annie Laurie Reeves-Lutman, born Butte County, 1859; died June 11, Vallejo, Solano County; four children survive.

Mrs. Margaret Sheehan-Juarez, born Napa County, 1859; died June 14, Napa City; six children survive.

Levingston Johnson, born Calaveras County, 1854; died June 15, Sheep Ranch; wife and four children survive.

Mrs. Mary Ann Schultze, born San Joaquin County, 1857; died June 15, Vallejo, Solano County; husband and two daughters survive.

Mrs. Eleanor Haskell-Burns, born Tuolumne County, 1858; died June 18, Merced City; six children survive.

Edward J. McCutchen, born Santa Clara County, 1857; died June 22, Palo Alto; daughter survives.

TABLET DEDICATION RECALLS EARLY-DAY TUOLUMNE HISTORY.

At Sonora, Tuolumne County, a tablet was dedicated May 25 honoring Dr. Lewis C. Gunn, from 1849 to 1861 a prominent citizen of that community, and Mrs. Elizabeth LeBreton-Gunn, a Pioneer Mother, and also marking the first two-story house to be erected in Sonora. The tablet, embellished by a replica of the original house, is inscribed:

"First two-story house in Sonora, built 1850 by Dr. Lewis C. Gunn, '49er physician, druggist, educator, County Recorder, publisher 'Sonora Herald' and promoter of many civic enterprises. Home of Dr. Gunn's family, 1851-1861. County Recorder's office, 1850-1852. Printing office 'Sonora Herald,' first newspaper in the Southern Mines, 1850-1852. Residence of County Clerk P. M. Fisher until 1866. County Hospital, 1866-1897. Erected by Sonora Welfare Club May 25, 1933."

Gas Tax Large—Of all the states of the nation, California in 1932 was the second largest in gas-tax revenue, according to the Federal Agricultural Department. The largest was New York, with $42,528,854; California's revenue amounted to $36,128,854.

"To live in the presence of great truths and eternal laws, that is what keeps a man patient when the world ignores him, and calm and unspoiled when the world praises him."—Balzac.

Native Daughters of the Golden West

SANTA ANA—HONORING TWENTY-three candidates for naturalization, Santa Ana No. 235 and Santa Ana No. 256 N.S.G.W. entertained June 12 with a fine program under the chairmanship of Matilda Lemon. Z. B. West, in a splendid talk on "The Bear Flag," outlined the background and history of California's admission to statehood. J. Frank Burke suggested that, in their citizenship here, the candidates should emulate the lives of the finest people of the country whence they came; he emphasized the spirit of democracy and the value of its institutions. Other speakers were Superior Judge Ames, W. W. Wieman, Mrs. Golden Northcross Weston, Dr. C. E. Price, President Mildred Gray and District Deputy Walter E. Hiskey, the two latter extending the Natives' welcome.

During the evening Principal Edith Ritter (Grace No. 242) of Fremont school presented pupils of the school in a very fine americanization program which was greatly enjoyed. She was ably assisted by Miss Mirrle Wilson, at the piano. Refreshments were served.

Mrs. Mae West has been elected president of No. 235. Mrs. Eunice Fox, in charge of the successful dinnér, had the assistance of a fine committee. Memorial Day was appropriately observed. Recent meetings of the thimble club were held at the homes of Mms. Marsile and Bray.

Grand President Given Nugget.

Georgetown—El Dorado No. 186 received an official visit from Grand President Anna Mixon Armstrong, May 24. Accompanying her were Grand Trustee Edna Briggs and members of Piedmont, La Bandera, Fern and Coloma Parlors. Scotch broom, which grows most profusely in this section, decorated the hall.

The ritual was commendably exemplified, and on the Parlor's behalf Past President Ella Stanton presented a nugget of El Dorado County gold to Mrs. Armstrong. Dainty refreshments were served at poppy-laden tables.

Kiddies Do Their Bit.

Hollister—Copa de Oro No. 105 members were entertained May 27 by The Good Will Club, a group of little people who have arranged and successfully carried out two circus performances of their own planning and conducting. The proceeds on both occasions were donated to the Parlor for the benefit of the homeless baby adopted by it. These kiddies range from 5 to 10 years of age. Their program for the entertainment consisted of acrobatic stunts, dances, wisecracks and cowboy choruses, concluding with "I Love You, California," staging a real holdup with indians, covered wagon and all the necessary features. A trained dog, "Boots," is an important member of the cast of twenty-one.

Following the program, the performers were treated to eskimo pies, with a bone for "Boots." The following day, at the request of Past Grand President Bertha A. Briggs, a group picture was taken and a print has been mailed to each participant in the show. Alberta Jensen gave a most enjoyable bridge tea recently for the benefit of the homeless baby.

Beautiful Blue-and-Gold Decorations.

Chico—Annie K. Bidwell No. 168 was officially visited by Grand President Anna Mixon Armstrong, May 25. One candidate was initiated, and a program, arranged by Mrs. C. A. Wesbrook, was presented by Carmelita Gridler, Arlyne Brooke, Evelyn Boyd, Mary Helen Richards, Eleanor Cummings, Josephine Hall, Rayna Tochterman, Kathryn Jones, Iris Marion. Patty Boyd, the small daughter of President Edna Boyd, dressed as a fairy presented a gift, on the Parlor's behalf, to the Grand President.

Refreshments were served at tables made most beautiful in a blue-and-gold color motif. Maypoles of those colors were placed at intervals along the tables, with gold flower pots of blue larkspur and yellow coreopsis alternating. Golden poppy nutcups had gold nuggets attached to them, and on the nuggets were the letters N.D. in blue. At the officers' table were hand-painted poppy-shaped placecards. Josephine Alexander decorated the tables, and Cora Hintz headed the refreshment committee. At the June 8 meeting of the Parlor, Cora Hintz, in charge of the California history period, gave excerpts from the diary of Pioneer O. B. Coleman, who came via Nicaragua in 1852.

Encouraging Talk.

Elk Grove—The official visit of Grand President Anna Mixon Armstrong, May 26, was an outstanding event in the history of Liberty No. 213. Among the many visitors were Past Grands Mary E. Bell, Dr. Eva R. Rasmussen and Dr. Louise C. Heilbron, Supervising Deputy Bessie Leitch, Deputy Sophia Monteverde and Grand Trustee Edna Briggs. The lodgeroom presented a spring-like scene. One candidate was initiated, and a short service was held in memory of deceased members.

Grand President Armstrong gave a most inspiring and encouraging talk. She was the recipient of numerous gifts, among them a huge boquet of gorgeous flowers, presented by President Nat Core on behalf of Elk Grove No. 41 N.S.G.W., and china, presented by President Hale on behalf of Liberty. A strawberry festival concluded the meeting. Louisa Krull was chairman of the banquet committee, and Muriel Blodgett had charge of the decorations.

Drill Team Appears Flag Day.

Modesto—Morada No. 199 and Modesto No. 11 N.S.G.W. had a joint sociable June 17. Following cards luncheon boxes were auctioned by President Charles Blaine. Robert Benson and Ethel Enos were in charge of arrangements.

Morada's newly organized drill team, directed by Ethel Enos and captained by John Fee, made its initial appearance in the Flag Day parade June 14. Members having birthdays in April, May and June were honor-guests at a banquet June 28. Leila Benson, as president, heads the corps of officers to serve during the July-December term. Agnes Frost is chairman of the first of a series of card parties to be given at the members' homes during the summer season.

Officers' Work Perfect.

Sacramento—Rio Rita No. 253 received an official visit June 5, less than two months following institution. Grand President Anna Mixon Armstrong was escorted through a pathway of roses while Marion Weber sang "Roses are Blooming for You," and was presented with a basket of roses by an escort of four girls. During recess three tiny girls sang a song bidding Mrs. Armstrong "Shuffle Off to the Leamington." The Grand President pronounced the officers' work perfect. In attendance were Grand Trustee Edna B. Briggs, Past Grands Mary E. Bell, Dr. Eva Rasmussen and Dr. Louise C. Heilbron, Supervising Deputies Bessie Leitch and Sadie Winn-Brainard, the latter the organizer of Rio Rita. After the meeting refreshments were served. Kay Jones was general chairman of the occasion.

SUBORDINATE PARLORS BRIEFS.

Oakdale—Oakdale No. 125 had its annual dinner and program for the Pioneers, eleven of whom responded. Colors of the Order were featured in the decorations.

San Bernardino—Lugonia No. 241 elected officers June 14, Mary Johnson being chosen president. A Flag Day program was presented. June 28 delegates to the Oakland Grand Parlor reported. The Harmony Club had its first evening card party June 1 at the home of Lois Poling, and at an all-day session at Mamie Heap's home June 20 plans for a Christmas bazar were discussed.

N.D.G.W. OFFICIAL DEATH LIST.

Giving the name, the date of death, and the Subordinate Parlor affiliation of all deceased members as reported to Grand Secretary Sallie R. Thaler from May 18, 1933, to June 15, 1933:

Hammill, Mary M.; April 4; Dardanelle No. 66.
Schreiner, Louise Evelyn; May 12; Oneonta No. 71.
Johnston, Catherine Kane; May 11; Antioch No. 223.
Hensley, Eva Rodriques Strohmeier; October 22, 1932; Golden Gate No. 158.
Muller, Hattie May; May 18; Marguerite No. 12.
Finley, Susie; May 25; Golden State No. 50.
Mullally, Mary Kane; May 12; Aloha No. 106.
Cooper, Martha Millsaps; May 25; Berryessa No. 192.
Allen, Belle Crane; May 20; Marinita No. 198.

PIONEER MOTHER'S 100TH MILESTONE.

Fort Bragg (Mendocino County)—Mrs. Margaret "Grandma" Wells, celebrated May 27 her one hundredth birthday anniversary. She was born in London, England, May 27, 1833. In 1869, she came via Panama to California, and has ever since resided in Mendocino County, at Mendocino City, Navarro and Fort Bragg. Three of the ten children born to her are now living.

Fire Hazard—Warm summer weather and lack of precipitation have brought back hazard of fire in mountain areas. Those going into forest areas are urged to co-operate in fire prevention work by strictly observing the rules laid down.

Noted California Mother Passes—Mrs. Jennie Kistle, a native of Nevada County aged 41, died May 28 at Fairfax, Marin County. She is survived by her husband and twenty children, ten sons and ten daughters.

"MARK OUR LANDMARKS"

Chester F. Gannon

(GRAND HISTORIAN N.S.G.W.)

"MARK OUR LANDMARKS"

A REVIEW OF THE N.S. GRAND PARLOR

THE DUTY OF A HISTORIAN IS TO record past events. The events of the Native Son Grand Parlor at Grass Valley have gone into the ocean of yesterdays and have thus become part of the history of our Order. To retrace, in thought, the events of those few days the middle of May last, is to recount a pleasant sojourn in the foothills "rising to mountains higher." It is to recall a hospitable community in an especially favored region—one that has no superior for pioneer lore. The Memorial Auditorium lent a good setting to the Grand Parlor deliberations, and its social activities. The limited hotel accommodations were met with generous hospitality on the part of the townspeople, who opened their homes with the same spirit that must have permeated the men and women of an earlier age.

But with all the modernistic atmosphere, the story of the bygone day spoke from every landscape. It spoke loudly, but not as loud as it should have spoken, if the Native Sons for the past twenty-five years had fulfilled the purposes of our Order; and to this end, your Historian, who has been favored with reappointment by Grand President Seawell, will revert as he did at the beginning of his first term. His motto was then and is now, "Mark Our Landmarks!"

There are few, if any, markers on historic spots in and about Grass Valley or Nevada City. The Grand Parlor did rescue the grave of that gifted poet, John Rollin Ridge, from oblivion. But it did nothing more. Why could not the former homes of Lotta Crabtree and Lola Montez have been marked? Despite the fact that the name of Lola Montez is almost disclaimed by many of the present generation, yet she was a woman whose name was emblazoned on the history of her day. She ran the gamut of human emotions and drank from the cup of life as have few women of any age. She stopped in the busy whirl and turmoil of her life to make Grass Valley her home for almost two years. Yet your Historian was told by a prominent Native Daughter of the guest city that her townspeople did not want their community known as having been associated with the life of that notorious woman.

No matter what Lola Montez may have been, she earned a place in the history of early California. Her's is a historical, if not an eminent, name. Good people and bad, make up communities and write history. You cannot write the history of America without the name of Benedict Arnold. Virtue and vice are intermingled in the tide of events. A small plaque where she lived would be appreciated by the lover of history and the romanticist of coming generations.

Why cannot future generations have pointed out to them in Grass Valley the old childhood home of that heaven-blessed child, Lotta Crabtree? Not a finger points to those history-making spots in Grass Valley, and it is for this reason that your Historian again and again calls attention to a deficiency in the accomplishments of the Native Sons.

The body of a recent able man will be more tenderly revered because the Past Grand Presidents decided to suitably mark the last resting place of that buoyant, carefree, likeable Past Grand President Jo V. Snyder, whose grave, near that of Ridge, was practically unmarked by stone or marker until the advent of the Grand Parlor. The Past Grands decreed that one of their rank should not lie unnoticed in his grave.

The trip to Downieville, as part of the entertainment of the local committee, was one of the most enjoyable tendered to delegates anywhere. But once arrived in that tranquil and romantic mountain town, the same remissness was apparent. Where or by what mark could one see that there important pages of the history of the West had been written? There appeared to be but one marker, and that on the old court house. The bridge from which the living body of the young Spanish woman was flung by mob rule,—though classed a legal procedure,—to be strangled to death at the end of the death rope, is unmarked.

At that point was enacted one of the tragic and sorrowful pages of early California. The old bridge felt the gnaw of Time and a new one replaces it, but on the same site. Lewis F. Byington lived at Downieville as a boy. He said that the scene upstream from the bridge, where a few hundred feet away the two Yubas meet to continue their dash to the ocean, looked about the same as in his youth. The only exception was that vegetation was denser. So we may assume that the last sight of that unfortunate woman, as she gazed on the face of hangman and spectators, beheld a landscape pretty much as it appears today.

Where is she buried? Where did she kill the man for whose murder she was executed? What other events were enacted in the long past along those now-quiet streets? These questions are unanswered, because historical spots are not marked. Already, lack of information prevents designation. Soon that will apply to all unmarked historical spots.

Why is the grave of William B. Ide unmarked? Why has no reverence and respect been shown to the grave of the man who was president of California for twenty-three days under the Bear Flag Republic? He was the real organizer of the Bear Flag Party. Yet the Orland Boosters Club is, at this late date, undertaking to pay homage to that character and intends to bury his remains in Orland and make it a historical shrine. A laudable undertaking!

Dr. C. W. Chapman, during one of the days of the Grand Parlor, took the writer to a spot between Grass Valley and Nevada City and pointed out the place where the miner cabin of William Randolph Hearst's father had been. Likewise the site of a similar cabin of MacKay, founder of the Postal Telegraph. No marker designates these spots, made famous by fathers whose sons are now known throughout America. The Native Daughters are evincing an interest in marking places and have already rescued many from oblivion. The Native Sons must meet the challenge which fast-eroding Time flaunts in their faces, and act before it is too late!

Native Sons of the Golden West

WORK---WITH ENTHUSIASM!

TO THE OFFICERS AND MEMBERS OF Subordinate Parlors N.S.G.W.—Dear Sirs and Brothers: I greet you in the name of the Order to which we have all pledged our allegiance.

I am not prompted by any motive of personal pride in making a special effort at this critical moment to bring our Order up to the standard of numerical strength and influence in the affairs of the civic and social life of our state which it is entitled to enjoy. But I am moved by a deep sense of duty and responsibility which rests upon me as Grand President of the only existing order in the state of our nativity that has specially dedicated itself to the promotion of the welfare of our state and the maintenance of our matchless institutions,—which are, after all, but the more expansive structures builded upon the foundations and fashioned after the pattern that was laid and conceived by the founders and builders of this Commonwealth,—to turn our annually recurring losses of membership into a gain. I believe it can be done. If I did not so believe, I would not be engaged in a fruitless task. The members of the Subordinate Parlors are as vitally interested in the reversal of our gain-and-loss figures as are the members of the Grand Parlor.

It has been the custom of the Order during the many years past, except one, 1928, to employ an organizer. I make no criticism of the earnestness with which these loyal officers have applied themselves to their tasks. Whatever arguments may have justified the system in the early periods of our existence fail to justify a continuance of that system in the changed conditions which have existed during the past seven years, beginning with the year 1926 and ending with 1932, as demonstrated by the statistical table herewith appended. It seems so logical as not to require figures to verify the proposition, that a Parlor which can neither increase nor hold its membership, and which habitually relies on a paid organizer to maintain its quota, is doomed, sooner or later, to find itself slipping beyond the possibility of recovery, notwithstanding the heroic efforts which the most experienced organizer can bring to his aid.

Many, if not all, of the most substantial Parlors have never had or requested the service of an organizer. They did their own organization work, effectively, within their membership. It is repugnant to reason that a stranger to the community could arouse the interest and confidence in eligibles of the type that would become lasting members of the local Parlor, as would the members of such Parlor who have business and social and neighborly contact with the eligibles and who are known in the community for probity and good citizenship. If the members of the local Parlors are so indifferent to the growth of their Parlor that they will not exert themselves in its behalf, how may they hope that an organizer who is not a member of their Parlor would be able to induce eligibles to associate themselves with the Parlor that has lost interest in itself!

If an individual is not enthusiastic in his work, he will sooner or later fail. If the members of a Parlor lose their enthusiasm for its ideals and purposes, it is doomed to surrender its charter. We must enter upon our plan of organization with enthusiasm! **Enthusiasm is the motive power which moves men, whether as individuals or in mass formation, to victory.** It has been so from the beginning of organized social life, and before. Every great leader whom the world has immortalized won victory by the impetus of the enthusiasm by which he was moved. The men of abundant enthusiasm are leading the world today. **We can build our Order up to great numbers if we go about the task with enthusiasm.** No order has greater inspirational background or nobler purposes, or more humanity, or more practical objectives, than ours. We can mean much to humanity and the state. When we ourselves fully appreciate the great work to which we are committed, we will move forward with quickened strides to take our place in the first rank of statehood.

We must build from the ground up! The local Parlor is the foundation of our fraternal organization. The Grand Parlor could not exist but for the local Parlors. It is therefore plain that our first interest must be in the success of the local Parlors. To accomplish our primary purpose, some time prior to the meeting of the last Grand Parlor at Grass Valley several conferences were held by the three Grand Vice-presidents for the purpose of discussing ways and means by which the membership of our Order might be restored to its former proportions. Every issue which might affect the result was considered. We unanimously agreed, after several conferences, that the plan adopted by Past Grand President James A. Wilson during his administration, which was successful in 1928, would be peculiarly applicable to this period of business and financial readjustment.

We came to the conclusion that turning back, as far as possible, the sum of $4,000 to the Parlors from which it was taken under a plan which would, at the same time, act as a stimulus to the members of the local Parlors to put forth extra efforts in increasing their membership, was a plan worth giving an earnest, thorough and fair trial. The sum of $2.50, which shall be paid to the brother for each member which he shall bring into his local Parlor under the system hereby adopted, will assist in paying the dues at least of many brothers who find such payments most difficult under existing conditions. We are also of the view that the work of organization will be better handled by the members taking it into their hands, both from the standpoint of increased membership and economy. Further, that a distribution of this fund among the members will have a wholesome effect. After all, the system adopted amounts to compensation paid out for organization purposes.

Space will not permit of further elaboration upon the project. Herewith is appended the table showing the number of initiations and the cost per member beginning with 1926 and ending in 1932. It will be observed that the year 1928 is but one member short of the largest gain, 1927, and surpasses all the other years as shown by the table, save one, by increases varying from 86 to 762. You will please note the small cost percapita during the year 1928, as compared with the years when specially appointed organizers were employed. The table follows:

Year	No. Initiated	Total Cost	Cost per Member
1926	1562	$7694.00	$4.95
1927	1649	6744.00	4.00
1928	1648	4306.00	2.60
1929	1300	6089.00	4.64
1930	1027	5649.00	5.50
1931	1129	4888.00	4.33
1932	896	4355.00	4.85

The above sum [$2.50] is to be paid to the proposer of each candidate who becomes a bonafire member of the local Parlor as a result of such proposal. In no case is payment to exceed the sum of $2.50 on account of the initiation of a single candidate. Said payments are to be made upon the certificate of the secretary of each respective Subordinate Parlor, signed by the president, certifying that the candidate has been initiated into the Parlor upon the proposal of the respective claimant. The above order is to be in effect as and of June 1, 1933.

In addition to the above organization plan, a system of awards or prizes is hereby adopted as follows: There shall be paid out of the treasury of the Grand Parlor the sum of $100 to the Subordinate Parlor which shall, from and including July 1, 1933, to and including December 31, 1933, initiate into its Parlor the largest number of candidates. A second prize in the sum of $50 will be paid in like manner to the Parlor which shall during such period initiate the second largest number of candidates. The minimum number in each case shall not be less than twenty candidates to entitle a Parlor in any case to receive said award. That is to say, that a Parlor must initiate in every case at least twenty members to entitle it to receive said award or prize.

The sum of $100 shall be paid to the Parlor which shall within the period above specified initiate into its Parlor the largest percentage of members based upon the bonafide roll of membership of said respective Parlor as shown by its records as and of July 1, 1933. The sum of $50 shall be paid to the Parlor which shall, within the period above specified, initiate the second largest percentage of members in accordance with the rule last above set out.

The recording secretary and the president of each Subordinate Parlor shall in every case certify to the Grand Secretary the names of the candidates initiated, their sponsors and such other facts as may hereafter be deemed necessary to make a just award. In no case shall the Parlor in either of the above named classes, or in both, be entitled to more than one prize or award. In case of a tie the prize or award shall be distributed equally to the highest tying contenders.

It is the hope of the promoters of the plan this day adopted that it will stimualte a spirit of fraternal rivalry which shall not in the slightest degree mar the good fellowship and brotherly love which are the basis of our Order. All contests must be conducted in a spirit of true friendship and fairness, and to the end that our Order, in the final analysis, will be the principal beneficiary of the efforts of our entire membership.

Finally, brothers, let every Parlor as a united body pull together and make a test of our strength for at least the balance of the year, that we may demonstrate how much may be accomplished with just a little effort on the part of all.

With a feeling of confidence that our efforts will be rewarded with surprising success, I am, fraternally yours,

EMMET SEAWELL,
Grand President N.S.G.W.

Dated: San Francisco, California, June 16, 1933.

SAN FRANCISCO—THE BOARD OF GRAND Officers met June 3. In attendance were Grand President Justice Emmet Seawell, who presided, Grand First Vice Chas. A. Koenig, Grand Second Vice Harmon D. Skillin, Grand Third Vice J. Hartley Russell, Grand Secretary John T. Regan, Grand Trustees Eldred L. Meyer, Henry S. Lyon, Chas. H. Spengemann, Thos. M. Foley, Jesse H. Miller, John M. Burnett and Edward T. Schnarr.

The Crocker First National Bank, the Crocker First Federal Trust, the San Francisco Bank, the Bank of America and the Hibernia Bank were designated as depositories for Grand Parlor funds.

Joseph B. Keenan (Niantic No. 105) and Chas. A. Koenig (Grand First Vice) were nominated as directors of the San Francisco Hall Association, and were authorized to vote the Grand Parlor stock therein.

A motion prevailed that Subordinate Parlors pay the same premium this year for bonds of officers as paid last year.

Considerable routine business was transacted, and Grand President Seawell assigned Subordinate Parlor visiting districts as follows:

No. 1, Harmon D. Skillin, Grand Second Vice-president—Bakersfield No. 42, Los Angeles No. 45, San Diego No. 108, Ramona No. 109, Arrowhead No. 110, Santa Barbara No. 116, Hollywood No. 196, Long Beach No. 239, Sepulveda No. 263, Glendale No. 264, Santa Ana No. 265, Santa Monica Bay No. 267, University No. 272, Compton No. 273.

No. 2, Chas. H. Spengemann, Grand Trustee—San Jose No. 22, Fremont No. 44, Watsonville No. 65, Redwood No. 66, Monterey No. 75, Santa Cruz No. 90, Santa Lucia No. 97, Santa Clara No. 100, Gabilan No. 132, San Miguel No. 150, Cambria No. 152, Observatory No. 177, Menlo No. 185, Mountain View No. 215, Palo Alto No. 216.

No. 3, Edward T. Schnarr, Grand Trustee—Visalia No. 19, Yosemite No. 24, Fresno No. 25, Santa Rosa No. 28, Alameda No. 47, Saint Helena No. 53, Las Positas No. 96, Glen Ellen No. 102, Selma No. 107, Eden No. 113, Wisteria No. 127, Madera No. 130, Brooklyn No. 151, Washington No. 169, Athens No. 195, Berkeley No. 210, Richmond No. 217, Niles No. 250.

No. 4, Chas. A. Koenig, Grand First Vice-president—California No. 1, Pacific No. 10, Petaluma No. 27, General Winn No. 32, Mission No. 38, Elk Grove No. 41, San Francisco No. 49, Mount Tamalpais No. 64, Seaside No. 95, Mount Diablo No. 101, Sebastopol No. 143, Sea Point No. 158, Byron No. 170, Carquinez No. 205.

No. 5, Eldred L. Meyer, Grand Trustee—Oakland No. 50, El Dorado No. 52, Rincon No. 72, Stanford No. 76, Bay City No. 104, Sonoma No. 111, National No. 118, Piedmont No. 120, Halcyon No. 146, Nicasio No. 183, Estudillo No. 223, Pleasanton No. 244, Diamond No. 246, Fruitvale No. 252.

No. 6, Jesse H. Miller, Grand Trustee—Sunset No. 26, Hydraulic No. 56, Quartz No. 58, Napa No. 62, Granite No. 83, Calistoga No. 86, Niantic No. 105, Courtland No. 106, Hesperian No. 137, Alcalde No. 154, Lower Lake No. 159, Sequoia No. 160, Precita No. 187, Pebble Beach No. 230, Claremont No. 240, Galt No. 243.

No. 7, J. Hartley Russell, Grand Third Vice-president—Solano No. 39, Quincy No. 131, Oakdale No. 142, South San Francisco No. 157, Olympus No. 189, Etna No. 192, Presidio No. 194, Honey Lake No. 198, Marshall No. 202, Los Banos No. 206, Plumas No. 228, El Carmelo No. 256, Industrial City No. 269.

AWAKE, FROM THE DEEP

At the close of the Grass Valley, Nevada County, Grand Parlor the Native Sons pictured here took a jaunt, underground, to the 3,600-foot level of the North Star Mine. It was a hurried trip, too, for the skip dropped them at the rate of 1,500 feet a minute. Besides the usual mining operations, they witnessed the firing of a round of holes, and were shown a vein of gold, eight inches wide, that was followed for more than 300 feet. In the group, garbed for underground operations, are, right to left: Grand Second Vice-president Harmon D. Skillin, Mayor M. J. Brock (Quartz Parlor No. 58), Junior Past Grand President Seth Millington, Grand Trustee Eldred L. Meyer, Grand First Vice-president Chas. A. Koenig, and Superintendent Mann of the North Star.

No. 8, Thos. M. Foley, Grand Trustee—Stockton No. 7, Modesto No. 11, Humboldt No. 14, Lodi No. 18, Arcata No. 20, Ukiah No. 71, Vallejo No. 77, Ferndale No. 93, Broderick No. 117, Alder Glen No. 200, Dolores No. 208, El Capitan No. 222, Guadalupe No. 231, Castro No. 232, Orestimba No. 247, Turlock No. 274.

No. 9, John M. Burnett, Grand Trustee—Placerville No. 9, Amador No. 17, Golden Gate No. 29, Excelsior No. 31, Ione No. 33, Plymouth No. 48, Auburn No. 59, Silver Star No. 63, Downieville No. 92, Golden Nugget No. 94, Tracy No. 186, Twin Peaks No. 214, Rocklin No. 233, Balboa No. 234, Bret Harte No. 260, Utopia No. 270.

No. 10, Henry S. Lyon, Grand Trustee—Sacramento No. 3, Marysville No. 6, Argonaut No. 8, Woodland No. 30, Colusa No. 69, Mount Bally No. 87, Georgetown No. 91, Chispa No. 139, Tuolumne No. 144, McCloud No. 149, Big Valley No. 211, Sutter Fort No. 241, Willows No. 255, Columbia No. 258, Sutter No. 261, Manteca No. 271.

Special—Cabrillo No. 114, Donner No. 162, Golden Anchor No. 182, Liberty No. 193, Concord No. 245.

A motion prevailed that the next meeting of the Board be held at Santa Rosa, September 10, at 11 a.m.

The Grand Trustees also met, and organized by the election of Eldred L. Meyer (Santa Monica Bay No. 267), as chairman, and Henry S. Lyon (Placerville No. 9) as secretary.

Faithful Visit Historic Weaverville.

Weaverville—Overlooked by snow-capped peaks, reminder of the late spring, in a God-made amphitheater,—grove that the poet speaks of as the Creator's first temple,—Fred H. Greely Past Presidents Assembly No. 6 held its annual open-air initiation June 6 just outside this historic Trinity County little city. Notables witnessing the scene, some appearing as substitutes in the assembly's ritual team, were Senior Past Grand Charles L. Dodge, Junior Past Grand Seth Millington, Grand First Vice Chas. A. Koenig, Grand Second Vice Harmon D. Skillin, Grand Secretary John T. Regan, Past Governor General June Longshore of the General Past Presidents Association and Grand Third Vice J. Hartley Russell.

Three candidates were initiated, one for Colusa No. 69 and two for Mount Bally No. 87. Conferring the work was the following team: junior past, Robert P. Dixon (Silver Star No. 63); senior past, H. J. Tofft (Silver Star No. 63); president, John P. Colford (Sutter No. 261); first vice, Barney Barry (Silver Star No. 63); second vice, John T. Regan (South San Francisco No. 157); third vice, Harmon D. Skillin (Castro No. 232); marshal, Elton C. Fitch (Colusa No. 69); inside sentinel, Albert Dokken (Colusa No. 69); outside sentinel, Peter J. Delay (Marysville No. 6).

It was a two-day visit to Weaverville for the faithful. The program opened Saturday afternoon with a ball game between teams of Sutter No. 261 and Mount Bally No. 87. The latter won in a closely contested battle, score 4 to 2. Victor and vanquished, in true fraternal spirit, on the following afternoon united to battle with the team of the Moose lodge of Redding on the same grounds. The picked nine won, score 9 to 6. The latter game was preceded by an exhibition drill by the drum corps of Colusa No. 69, which came to Weaverville twenty-two strong in attractive uniforms. It was the first time many Trinity County residents saw a drum corps.

Saturday night there was a reception and dance in Native Sons Hall and Veteran Memorial Auditorium, the latter the first building of its character to be erected in California. Of great interest to the visiting Native Sons was the old fire engine, stationed outside the auditorium as a pioneer-day relic; it is said to have been brought around Cape Horn for use first in San Francisco, later in Sacramento, and finally in Redding. Music for the dance was furnished by the Weaverville high school orchestra.

Following the open-air initiation, and prior to the ball game Sunday afternoon, was the barbecue, midway between the ball park and the scene of the initiatory ceremonies. Here, Horace J. Leavitt of Mount Bally No. 87, head of the general committee, spoke on behalf of the new Grand President of the Order, Justice Emmet Seawell, expressing regret at the inability of the Order's head to attend. Justice Seawell's call to Los Angeles to hold court prevented, Leavitt explained. He introduced as the after-dinner speakers Junior Past Grand Millington and Grand Second Vice Skillin.

On the coming and going trips the visitors found much of interest at old Mount Shasta City and its museum, and at the lone grave at which road engineers shied when laying out the Redding-Weaverville highway.—P.J.D.

Membership Standing Largest Parlors.

San Francisco—Grand Secretary John T. Regan reports the standing of the Subordinate Parlors having a membership of over 400 January 1, 1933, as follows, together with their membership figures June 20, 1933:

Parlor	Jan. 1	June 20	Gain	Loss
Ramona No. 109	1032	1034	2	....
South San Francisco No. 157	803	800	....	3
Castro No. 232	764	765	1	....
Arrowhead No. 110	573	566	....	7
Stanford No. 76	575	563	....	12
Stockton No. 7	535	535	....	....
Twin Peaks No. 214	522	520	....	2
Piedmont No. 120	491	490	....	1
Rincon No. 72	418	406	....	12

Laudable Undertaking.

Santa Barbara—Santa Barbara No. 116 entertained June 10 at a barbecue in Oak Park the officers and members of the California Nautical School's training ship "California State," recently returned to home waters after a trip around the world. The ship visited this city at the invitation of Secretary Harry C. Sweetser and Mayor

(Continued on Page 13)

Official Directory of Parlors of the N. S. G. W.

ALAMEDA COUNTY.

Alameda No. 47, Alameda City—J. F. Hanson, Pres.; Robt. H. Cavanaugh, Sec., 1806 Pacific Ave.; Wednesdays, Veterans Memorial Bldg.

Oakland No. 50, Oakland—T. J. Markert, Pres.; F. M. Norris, Sec., 5595 Taft Ave.; Fridays, Native Sons Hall, 11th and Clay Sts.

Las Positas No. 96, Livermore—Louis J. Volponi, Pres.; John J. Kelly, Sec., P. O. box 341; Thursdays, Foresters Hall.

Eden No. 113, Hayward—John Meincke, Pres.; Filbert M. Soares, Sec., 1437 "B" St.; 2nd and 4th Tuesdays, Memorial Hall, Main St.

Piedmont No. 120, Oakland—George T. Frytz, Pres.; Charles Morando, Sec., 906 Vermont St.; Thursdays, Native Sons Hall, 11th and Clay Sts.

Wisteria No. 127, Alvarado—Henry May, Pres.; J. M. Scribner, Sec., Livermore; 1st Thursday, I.O.O.F. Hall.

Halcyon No. 146, Alameda City—S. Chesley Anderson, Pres.; J. C. Bates, Sec., 2139 Buena Vista Ave.; 1st and 3rd Tuesdays, I.O.O.F. Hall, 2329 Santa Clara Ave.

Brooklyn No. 151, Oakland—Frank B. Perry, Pres.; E. W. Cooney, Sec., 3907 14th Ave.; 1st and 3rd Wednesdays, Masonic Temple, 8th Ave. and E. 14th St.

Washington No. 169, Centerville—Thomas Silva, Pres.; Allen G. Norris, Sec., P. O. box 58; 2nd and 4th Tuesdays, Hansen Hall.

Athens No. 195, Oakland—Fred G. Martin, Pres.; Harold B. Farley, Sec., 4623 Benevides Ave.; Tuesdays, Native Sons Hall, 11th and Clay Sts.

Berkeley No. 210, Berkeley—H. P. Corbett, Pres.; R. J. Garrett, Sec., 1708 Virginia St.; Tuesdays, Native Sons Hall, 2108 Shattuck Ave.

Estudillo No. 223, San Leandro—E. E. King, Pres.; Albert G. Pacheco, Sec., 1736 E. 14th St.; 1st and 3rd Tuesdays, U.P.E.C. Hall.

Claremont No. 240, Emeryville—Edward J. Ginochio, Pres.; E. N. Thienger, Sec., 839 Hearst Ave., Berkeley; Tuesdays, Veterans Memorial Bldg., 43rd and Salem Sts.

Pleasanton No. 244, Pleasanton—Edward Holzreiter, Pres.; Ernest W. Schween, Sec.; 2nd and 4th Thursdays, I.O.O.F. Hall.

Niles No. 250, Niles—M. L. Fournier, Pres.; C. E. Martenstein, Sec.; 2nd Thursday, I.O.O.F. Hall.

Fruitvale No. 252, Oakland—Ernest Perry, Pres.; Ray B. Felton, Sec., 1575 Alice St.; Fridays, W.O.W. Hall, 3256 E. 14th St.

AMADOR COUNTY.

Amador No. 17, Sutter Creek—J. H. Williams, Pres.; F. J. Payne, Sec.; 1st and 3rd Fridays, Native Sons Hall.

Excelsior No. 31, Jackson—Thomas G. Negrich, Pres.; William Going, Sec.; 1st and 3rd Wednesdays, Native Sons Hall, 22 Court St.

Ione No. 33, Ione—Earl Grover, Pres.; Josiah H. Saunders, Sec.; 1st and 3rd Wednesdays, Native Sons Hall.

Plymouth No. 48, Plymouth—D. A. Upton, Pres.; Thos. D. Davis, Sec.; 1st and 3rd Saturdays, N.S.G.W. Hall.

BUTTE COUNTY.

Argonaut No. 8, Oroville—Frank H. O'Brien, Pres.; Cyril R. Macdonald, Sec., P. O. box 502; 1st and 3rd Wednesdays, Veterans Memorial Hall.

CALAVERAS COUNTY.

Chispa No. 139, Murphys—Maynard Segale, Pres.; Antone Malaspina, Sec.; Wednesdays, Native Sons Hall.

COLUSA COUNTY.

Colusa No. 69, Colusa City—Rotheus A. Gray, Pres.; Phil J. Humburg, Sec., 228 Parkhill St.; Tuesdays, Eagles Hall.

CONTRA COSTA COUNTY.

General Winn No. 32, Antioch—Edmont T. Uren, Pres.; Joel H. Ford, Sec., P. O. box 811; 2nd and 4th Wednesdays, Union Hall.

Mount Diablo No. 101, Martinez—R. P. Anderson, Pres.; G. T. Barkley, Sec.; 1st and 3rd Mondays, I.O.O.F. Hall.

Byron No. 170, Byron—William E. Bunn, Pres.; H. G. Krumland, Sec.; 1st and 3rd Tuesdays, I.O.O.F. Hall.

Carquinez No. 205, Crockett—John McManus, Pres.; Thomas R. Cox, Sec., P.O. box 721; 1st and 3rd Wednesdays, I.O.O.F. Hall.

Richmond No. 217, Richmond—Frank Weber, Pres.; Lloyd N. Mason, Sec., 11 6th St.; 1st Wednesday, 818 Macdonald Ave.

Concord No. 245, Concord—C. H. Guy, Pres.; D. E. Pramberg, Sec., P. O. box 235; 1st Tuesday, Guy's Parlors.

Diamond No. 246, Pittsburg—Victor Ericsson, Pres.; Francis A. Irving, Sec., 248 E. 5th St.; 1st and 3rd Wednesdays, Veterans Memorial Bldg.

EL DORADO COUNTY.

Placerville No. 9, Placerville—Chris. C. Orelli, Pres.; Clyde R. Berriman, Sec., Wood St.; 2nd and 4th Tuesdays, Masonic Hall.

Georgetown No. 91, Georgetown—George W. Brichler, Pres.; O. F. Irish, Sec.; 2nd and 4th Wednesdays, I.O.O.F. Hall.

FRESNO COUNTY.

Fresno No. 25, Fresno City—J. H. Sutton, Pres.; W. C. Guard, Sec., R.F.D. No. 2, box 379; 1st and 3rd Fridays, Pythian Castle, Cor. "R" and Merced Sts.

Selma No. 107, Selma—C. R. Snyder, Pres; E. C. Laughlin, Sec.; 1st Wednesday, American Legion Hall.

GRAND OFFICERS.

Seth Millington........................Junior Past Grand President
Gridley
Justice Emmet Seawell........................Grand President
State Bldg., San Francisco
Chas. A. Koenig........................Grand First Vice-president
531 35th Ave., San Francisco
Harmon D. Skillin........................Grand Second Vice-president
Mills Bldg., San Francisco
J. Hartley Russell........................Grand Third Vice-president
1025 Russ Bldg., San Francisco
John T. Regan........................Grand Secretary
N.S.G.W. Bldg., 414 Mason St., San Francisco
John A. Corotto........................Grand Treasurer
560 No. 5th St., San Jose
Gam Hurst........................Grand Marshal
5262 Boyd Ave., Oakland
William A. Reuter........................Grand Inside Sentinel
1009 Marine Ave., Wilmington
Walter P. Rothenbush........................Grand Outside Sentinel
N.S.G.W. Club Rooms, Stockton
Leslie Maloche........................Grand Organist
1775 El Cerrito, Los Angeles
Chester Gannon........................Grand Historian
613 Capital Ntl. Bank Bldg., Sacramento

GRAND TRUSTEES.

Eldred L. Meyer........922 San Vicente Blvd., Santa Monica
Henry S. Lyon........................Placerville
Chas. H. Spengemann..............827 27th Ave., San Francisco
Thos. M. Foley........................Hearst Bldg., San Francisco
Jesse H. Miller..............712 DeYoung Bldg., San Francisco
John M. Burnett..............Bank America Bldg., San Jose
Edward T. Schnarr..............3611 Allendale Ave., Oakland

GLENN COUNTY.

Willows No. 255, Willows—Ralph W. Camper, Pres.; Leon Marshall, Sec., P.O. box 747; 2nd and 4th Tuesdays, I.O.O.F. Hall.

HUMBOLDT COUNTY.

Humboldt No. 14, Eureka—Henry Sundfors, Pres.; Loren M. Nelson, Sec., P.O. box 195; 2nd and 4th Mondays, Native Sons Hall.

Arcata No. 20, Arcata—W. H. Anderson, Pres.; William Peters, Sec., P. O. box 1117; Thursdays, Native Sons Hall.

Ferndale No. 93, Ferndale—C. J. Olsen, Pres.; C. H. Rasmussen, Sec., R.F.D., 47-A; 1st and 3rd Mondays, Danish Hall.

KERN COUNTY.

Bakersfield No. 42, Bakersfield—George Taylor, Pres.; Henry A. Bannister, Sec., care Bank of America; 2nd and 4th Fridays, Justice Court, City Hall.

LAKE COUNTY.

Lower Lake No. 159, Lower Lake—LeRoy England, Pres.; Albert Kugelman, Sec.; Thursdays, I.O.O.F. Hall.

LASSEN COUNTY.

Honey Lake No. 198, Standish—Leo T. Davis, Pres.; N. V. Wemple, Sec., Litchfield; 1st and 3rd Wednesdays, Wrede Hall.

Big Valley No. 211, Bieber—Fred Bunselmeier, Pres.; A. W. McKenzie, Sec.; 1st and 3rd Wednesdays, I.O.O.F. Hall.

LOS ANGELES COUNTY.

Los Angeles No. 45, Los Angeles City—Roger M. Johnson, Pres.; Willard F. Allen, Sec., 4955 Los Feliz Blvd.; Thursdays, Merchant Plumbers Hall, 1832 So. Hope.

Ramona No. 109, Los Angeles City—Charles E. Straube, Pres.; John V. Scott, Sec., Patriotic Hall, 1816 So. Figueroa; Fridays, Patriotic Hall, 1816 So. Figueroa.

Hollywood No. 196, Los Angeles City—Henry G. Bodkin, Pres.; E. J. Reilly, Sec., Olive View; Mondays, 1089 No. Oxford Ave.

Long Beach No. 239, Long Beach—Francis H. Gentry, Pres.; W. W. Brady, Sec., 801 Jergins Trust Bldg.; Dept. No. 1 Municipal Court, 8th floor Jergins Trust Bldg.

Sepulveda No. 263, San Pedro—Walter C. Richards, Pres.; H. E. Fairall, Sec., 1925 So. Pacific Ave.; 1st and 3rd Fridays, Redman Hall, 543 Shepherd St., Point Firmin.

Glendale No. 264, Glendale—Harvey T. Gillette, Pres.; Philip D. Molen, Sec., 222 So. Glendale; 1st and 3rd Thursdays, Starr Heights Recreation Bldg., 3246 Community Place.

Santa Monica Bay No. 267, Santa Monica—J. Edward McCurdy, Pres.; John J. Smith, Sec., 830 Rialto Ave., Venice; 1st and 3rd Wednesdays, Odd Fellows Hall, 1431 Third St.

University No. 272, Los Angeles City—Bernard G. Hiss, Pres.; Martin DeFazio, Sec., 845 W. 53rd St.; Wednesdays, 1008 West Adams St.

Compton No. 273, Compton—Laurence W. Cowan, Pres.; Wm. Don Castillo, Sec., 641 W. Bennett St.; 2nd and 4th Tuesdays, Elks Hall, 6172 No. Long Beach Blvd., North Long Beach.

MADERA COUNTY.

Madera No. 130, Madera City—Cornelius Noble, Pres.; T. P. Cosgrave, Sec.; 1st and 3rd Thursdays, First National Bank Bldg.

MARIN COUNTY.

Mount Tamalpais No. 64, San Rafael—Arthur Hecht, Pres.; Manuel A. Andrade, Sec., 532 Mission Ave.; 1st and 3rd Mondays, "B" Street Hall.

Sea Point No. 158, Sausalito—Clarence D. Ross, Pres.; Manuel Santos, Sec., 6 Glen Drive; 1st and 3rd Wednesdays, Perry Bldg.

Nicasio No. 183, Nicasio—M. T. Farley, Pres.; R. J. Rogers, Sec.; 2nd and 4th Wednesdays, U.A.O.D. Hall.

MENDOCINO COUNTY.

Ukiah No. 71, Ukiah—Kenneth Phillips, Pres.; Ben Hofman, Sec., P.O. box 473; 1st and 3rd Mondays, I.O.O.F. Hall.

Broderick No. 117, Point Arena—Albert Seymour, Pres.; C. J. Buchanan, Sec.; 1st and 3rd Thursdays, Forester Hall.

Alder Glen No. 200, Fort Bragg—Fred LeValley, Pres.; C. R. Weller, Sec.; 2nd and 4th Fridays, I.O.O.F. Hall.

MERCED COUNTY.

Yosemite No. 24, Merced City—Alfred Wm. Petersen, Pres.; True W. Fowler, Sec., P. O. box 781; 2nd and 4th Mondays, I.O.O.F. Hall.

Los Banos No. 206, Los Banos—Daniel Pedroni, Pres.; L. E. Sarbo, Sec., R.F.D., box 21; 2nd and 4th Wednesdays, Eagles Hall.

MONTEREY COUNTY.

Monterey No. 75, Monterey City—James Millington, Pres.; T. W. Krieger, Sec., 999 Franklin St.; 1st and 3rd Fridays, Knights Pythias Hall, Main St.

Santa Lucia No. 97, Salinas—Roy Martella, Pres.; R. W. Adcock, Sec., 32 W. Alisal St.; Mondays, Native Sons Hall, 32 W. Alisal St.

Gabilan No. 132, Castroville—James C. Jordan, Pres.; J. F. Gambetta, Sec., P. O. box 94; 1st and 3rd Thursdays, Native Sons Hall.

NAPA COUNTY.

Saint Helena No. 53, Saint Helena—Gilman Clark, Pres.; Edw. L. Bonhote, Sec., P. O. box 267; Mondays, Native Sons Hall.

Napa No. 62, Napa City—Theodore E. Freitas, Pres.; H. J. Hoernle, Sec., 1226 Oak St.; Mondays, Native Sons Hall.

Calistoga No. 86, Calistoga—James Marchese, Pres.; Louis Carlenzoli, Sec.; 1st and 3rd Mondays, I.O.O.F. Hall.

NEVADA COUNTY.

Hydraulic No. 56, Nevada City—Raglan Tuttle, Pres.; Dr. C. W. Chapman, Sec.; Tuesdays, Pythian Castle.

Quartz No. 58, Grass Valley—Frank G. Hooper, Pres.; H. Ray George, Sec., 151 Conaway Ave.; Mondays, Auditorium Hall.

Donner No. 162, Truckee—J. F. Lichtenberger, Pres.; H. C. Lichtenberger, Sec.; 2nd and 4th Tuesdays, Native Sons Hall.

ORANGE COUNTY.

Santa Ana No. 265, Santa Ana—Ivan H. Harper, Pres.; E. F. Marks, Sec., 1124 No. Bristol St.; 1st and 3rd Mondays, The Old Time Dance Hall, Grass Valley St., Tustin.

PLACER COUNTY.

Auburn No. 59, Auburn—Hans J. Petersen, Pres.; J. G. Walsh, Sec.; 1st and 3rd Fridays, Foresters Hall.

Silver Star No. 63, Lincoln—Robert P. Dixon, Pres.; Barney G. Barry, Sec., P. O. box 72; 3rd Wednesday, I.O.O.F. Hall.

Rocklin No. 233, Roseville—Wm. La Due, Pres.; M. E. Reed, Sec., 253 W. Duranta; 2nd and 4th Wednesdays, Eagles Hall.

PLUMAS COUNTY.

Quincy No. 131, Quincy—Herbert Hard, Pres.; E. O. Kelsey, Sec.; 2nd Thursday, I.O.O.F. Hall.

Golden Anchor No. 182, La Porte—R. J. McGrath, Pres.; LeRoy J. Post, Sec.; 2nd and 4th Sunday mornings, Native Sons Hall.

Plumas No. 228, Taylorsville—E. E. Sikes, Pres.; George E. Boyden, Sec.; 1st and 3rd Mondays, Native Sons Hall.

SACRAMENTO COUNTY.

Sacramento No. 3, Sacramento City—Parker Kelly, Pres.; J. F. Didion, Sec., 1213 "O" St.; Thursdays, Native Sons Bldg., 11th and "J" Sts.

Sunset No. 26, Sacramenot City—William H. Peters, Pres.; Edward E. Reese, Sec., County Treasurer Office; Mondays, Native Sons Bldg., 11th and "J" Sts.

Elk Grove No. 41, Elk Grove—Robert Carr, Pres.; Walter Martin, Sec.; 2nd and 4th Fridays, Masonic Hall.

Granite No. 83, Folsom—Joe Relvas, Pres.; Frank Showers, Sec.; 2nd and 4th Tuesdays, K.P. Hall.

Courtland No. 106, Courtland—N. H. Thisby, Pres.; Jos. Green, Sec.; 1st Saturday and 3rd Monday, Native Sons Hall.

Sutter Fort No. 241, Sacramento City—Ed. T. Goyne, Pres.; C. L. Katzenstein, Sec., P. O. box 914; 2nd and 4th Wednesdays, Native Sons Bldg., 11th and "J" Sts.

Galt No. 243, Galt—Abel G. Stock, Pres.; F. W. Harms, Sec.; 1st and 3rd Mondays, I.O.O.F. Hall.

SAN BENITO COUNTY.

Fremont No. 44, Hollister—S. Churchill, Pres.; J. E. Prendergast Jr., Sec., 1064 Monterey St.; 1st and 3rd Thursdays, Grangers Union Hall.

SAN BERNARDINO COUNTY.

Arrowhead No. 110, San Bernardino City—F. L. McGarvey, Pres.; R. W. Brazelton, Sec., 462 6th St.; Wednesdays, Eagles Hall, 469 4th St.

SAN DIEGO COUNTY.

San Diego No. 108, San Diego City—John P. Murphy, Pres.; A. V. Mayrhofer, Sec., 1572 2nd St.; Wednesdays, K.C. Hall, 4th and Elm Sts.

SAN FRANCISCO CITY AND COUNTY.

California No. 1, San Francisco—Henry F. Ricklefs, Pres.; Ellis A. Blackman, Sec., 1248-A Divisadero St.; Thursdays, Native Sons Bldg., 414 Mason St.

Pacific No. 10, San Francisco—William G. Boyce, Pres.; J. Henry Bastein, Sec., 380 Van Ness Ave. South; Tuesdays, Native Sons Bldg., 414 Mason St.

Golden Gate No. 29, San Francisco—William M. Roll, Pres.; Adolph Eberhart, Sec., 183 Carl St.; Mondays, Native Sons Bldg., 414 Mason St.

Mission No. 38, San Francisco—Martin H. Huber, Pres.; Thos. J. Stewart, Sec., 419 South Van Ness Ave.; Wednesdays, Redmen Hall, 3053 16th St.

San Francisco No. 49, San Francisco—Alfred Watts, Pres.; David Capurro, Sec., 976 Union St.; 2nd and 4th Thursdays, Dante Hall, 1606 Stockton St.

El Dorado No. 52, San Francisco—Robert Foltz, Pres.; Alfred Viautin, Sec., 1587 Franklin St.; Thursdays, Native Sons Bldg., 414 Mason St.

Rincon No. 72, San Francisco—Albert Granzella, Pres.; John A. Gilmour, Sec., 2069 Golden Gate Ave.; Wednesdays, Native Sons Bldg., 414 Mason St.

Stanford No. 76, San Francisco—Urban Morf, Pres.; Charles T. O'Kane, Sec., 2900 Scott St.; Tuesdays, Native Sons Bldg., 414 Mason St.

Bay City No. 104, San Francisco—Jacob A. Helbing, Pres.; Max E. Licht, Sec., 1831 Fulton St.; 2nd and 4th Wednesdays, Native Sons Bldg., 414 Mason St.

Niantic No. 105, San Francisco—A. Furner, Pres.; J. M. Darcy, Sec., 10 Hoffman Ave.; Wednesdays, Native Sons Bldg., 414 Mason St.

National No. 118, San Francisco—Walter J. Murphy, Pres.; Martin M. Ratigan, Sec., 1325 Page St., Apt. 6; Thursdays, 1160 Eddy St.

Hesperian No. 137, San Francisco—N. G. Reimers, Pres.; Albert Carlson, Sec., 379 Justin Dr.; Thursdays, Native Sons Bldg., 414 Mason St.

Alcalde No. 154, San Francisco—Daniel A. Hinell, Pres.; Harry S. Burke, Sec., 637 Shotwell St.; 2nd and 4th Wednesdays, Native Sons Bldg., 414 Mason St.

South San Francisco No. 157, San Francisco—Peter Macarini, Pres.; John T. Regan, Sec., 1489 Newcomb Ave.; Wednesdays, Masonic Bldg., 4705 3rd St.

Sequoia No. 160, San Francisco—Frank Sullivan, Pres.; Walter W. Garrett, Sec., 2500 Van Ness Ave.; 2nd and 4th Mondays, Swedish-American Bldg., 2174 Market St.

Precita No. 187, San Francisco—Edward F. Rom, Pres.; Edward Tietjen, Sec., 1367 15th Ave.; Thursdays, Mission Masonic Hall, 2668 Mission St.

Olympus No. 189, San Francisco—Henry H. McGowan, Pres.; Harvey J. Carty, Sec., 1651 Market St., Apt. 505; 2nd and 4th Tuesdays, Independent Redmen Hall, 3053 16th St.

Presidio No. 194, San Francisco—Charles Maker, Pres.; George A. Ducker, Sec., 442 21st Ave.; Mondays, Native Sons Bldg., 414 Mason St.

ATTENTION, SECRETARIES!

THIS DIRECTORY IS PUBLISHED BY AUTHORITY OF THE GRAND PARLOR N.S.G.W., AND ALL NOTICES OF CHANGES MUST BE RECEIVED BY THE GRAND SECRETARY (NOT THE MAGAZINE) ON OR BEFORE THE 20TH OF EACH MONTH TO INSURE CORRECTION IN NEXT ISSUE OF DIRECTORY.

NATIVE SON NEWS

(Continued from Page 11)

Harvey T. Nielson. About 150 students attended the barbecue.

Addresses were made by Mayor Nielson, Captain Emile V. Topp of the training ship, First Vice-president James E. Sloan and Secretary Sweetser. In the course of his remarks the latter said: "The training of our young men for positions as officers of American vessels is a laudable undertaking, in view of the fact that many of these ships are now officered by men of foreign birth. The curtailment of the nautical school even for a temporary period, and as an economy measure, would be a sacrifice California could ill afford to make." Frank Castro headed the barbecue committee.

To Dedicate Seven Redwoods.

Santa Rosa—Santa Rosa No. 28 voted June 5 to enter a team in the city night indoor baseball league, composed of eight teams. L. S. Lewis is manager of the Parlor team. The opening game, June 27, was preceded by a parade in which the drum corps of No. 28 appeared. June 17 the Parlor's ritual team, headed by President George Eckman, went to Ukiah, accompanied by the drum corps, and initiated two candidates for Ukiah No. 71. This was the start of a drive by the latter Parlor for new members.

In memory of Past President Louis Julliard, a former grand marshal of the Order, Santa Rosa has planted seven redwoods in Julliard Park, recently donated to the "City of Roses" by the Julliard heirs, and they will be dedicated by Grand President Justice Emmet Seawell during the Admission Day celebration. Sonoma County Past Presidents Assembly No. 9 met at Sonoma City June 19 and arranged to do some necessary work at the historic Hooker marker.

SUBORDINATE PARLORS BRIEFS.

Sacramento—Sacramento No. 3 had services June 1 in memory of its 150 deceased members. Irving D. Gibson presided, and Frank E. Michel delivered the eulogy. Musical selections were rendered by Mms. Fred Cippa and Edna Briggs. Arrangements for the ceremonies were made by Thomas W. McAuliffe, June Longshore, John T. Stafford, Roy C. Cothrin, Joseph Lannon, Dr. E. L. Dryden, A. M. Mull Jr., E. Beall, George A. Burns, J. Frank Didion and Parker B. Kelly.

Stockton—George Witherow has been elected president of Stockton No. 7. The joint social affairs with the Native Daughters the first Thursday of each month will be continued. San Joaquin Past President Assembly No. 7 met with the Parlor June 5.

Oroville—Argonaut No. 8 and Gold of Ophir No. 190 N.D.G.W. had their fourteenth annual reunion-dinner for Butte County oldtimers May 31. Presidents Frank O'Brien and Hattie Clark welcomed the guests, among whom were Mms. Harriet Smith, H. G. Baker, Belle Kelly, Mary Abbott, Lucinda Roberts, Emma Danforth, Mary Rogers and Selina Binet; Edwin W. Skinner, T. F. Whipple, L. W. Clark, Gordon Nisbet, James Binet, John H. Hillman, and Miss Fredericka Braden.

Sutter Creek—Amador No. 17 celebrated its fiftieth institution anniversary June 16. Members of Amapola No. 80 N.D.G.W. were guests of honor. A program was presented and refreshments were served.

San Jose—Mario Ponzini has been elected president of San Jose No. 22 for the July-December term. The Parlor has a bowling team, and carpetball games are usually played after meetings. A membership committee, led by Grand Trustee John M. Burnett and Grand Treasurer John A. Corotto, is working to add new names to the rolls.

Ferndale—As has been the custom for many years, Ferndale No. 93 had charge of the Memorial Day observance locally. The committee of arrangements included Joseph Bagnuda (chairman), Emil Calanchini and A. M. Ring. President Hans Petersen presided, and those on the program included Rev. D. Miller, Raymond Grinsell, Francis Givins, Mrs. Rusk, Lora Dedini, Victor Zampatti, Gertrude Moore, Andrew Genzoli, American Legion, John Blackburn, grammar school glee club.

Courtland—Courtland No. 106 had its forty-fourth annual charity ball June 10. The proceeds went to the homeless children. President Thisby had charge of the arrangements, and was assisted by R. J. Heringer, Clifford Smith, Lee Eller, Frank Fawcett, Elwood Bunnell and Bert Schiller. At midnight a chicken supper was served.

San Diego—San Diego No. 108 joined with other organizations in observing Flag Day, June 14. The main feature was a series of flag raisings in Old Town. Among the speakers were Carl Heilbron and President Isabel Young of San Diego No. 208 N.D.G.W. Deputy Grand President Albert V. Mayrhofer was in charge. Officers-elect of No. 108, with John J. Murphy as president, will be installed July 5 by District Deputy Edward H. Dowell.

San Bernardino—Arrowhead No. 110 staged its fifth annual roundup at its Crestline clubhouse June 10. Gene Ward, chairman arrangements committee, had as assistants Henry Peake, Ed Poppett, Ralph Frederickson, G. MacDonald, Gordon Lee, Donald E. VanLuven, Eugene W. Lee, L. D. Case, Elmer Motschman, M. Bellamy, Cecil Webb, Bob Brazelton, Jim Olivas, Harold Davies, John Dexter and Lynn Reed. Independence Day, July 4, will be celebrated at a barbecue at Crestline.

Sonoma City—Sonoma No. 111 and Sonoma No. 209 N.D.G.W. will have their annual picnic-barbecue at Oak Grove, July 16. This is a red-letter date on the calendar of the local Natives. Games and dancing will be featured.

Sebastopol—Guided by W. S. Borba of Sebastopol No. 143, the Native Sons and Native Daughters of Sonoma County had the first of a series of caravans to the numerous historic places in the county June 4. Among the places visited were the site of the first sawmill west of the Rockies, the burial ground of the first christianized Indians on the Pacific Coast, the original Russian flagpole, site of the Captain Smith adobe, and the landing place of Lieutenant Bodega.

Los Banos—Los Banos No. 206 initiated a class of thirteen candidates May 31. President Daniel Pedroni and his corps of officers conducted the ceremonies.

Turlock—Turlock No. 274 initiated six candidates May 26. A team from Modesto No. 11, headed by A. B. Gibson, exemplified the ritual.

You, Too, Will Find It So.

Editor Grizzly Bear—Enclosed is $1.50 for a year's subscription to The Grizzly Bear Magazine. I have read it frequently at Santa Clara Parlor No. 100 N.S.G.W. and find it most interesting. JOHN J. TRINAJSTICH.

Santa Clara, June 5, 1933.

SAN FRANCISCO

THE NATIVE SONS AND THE NATIVE Daughters of San Francisco held their annual memorial services in the beautiful Redwood Memorial Grove of Golden Gate Park, Sunday, June 4. More than five hundred were in attendance, and the ceremonies were most impressive. The program follows:

"Star Spangled Banner;" "Pledge of Allegiance," Troop 82, Boy Scouts of America; invocation, John T. Regan, Grand Secretary N.S.G.W.; address, John Barrett (Rincon No. 72 N.S.G.W.), president Grove of Memory Association; "History of the American Flag," Scout Mulcrevy; address, Angelo J. Rossi (El Dorado No. 52 N.S.G.W.), Mayor of San Francisco; roll call deceased Native Daughters of San Francisco Parlors, Miss Alma Hall (Dolores No. 169 N.D.G.W.), P. Schlesinger (Balboa No. 249 N.S.G.W.); selection, Native Daughter Glee Club, Mrs. Ruby Bried (El vespero No. 118), director; eulogy, Mrs. Anna Mixon Armstrong, Grand President N.D.G.W.; address, Joseph McShane (Twin Peaks No. 214), chairman Extension Order Committee N.S.G.W.; roll call deceased Native Sons of San Francisco Parlors, Alfred Hons (National No. 118 N.S.G.W.), Gladys McCarthy (Twin Peaks No. 185 N.D.G.W.); selection; eulogy, Justice Emmet Seawell, Grand President N.S.G.W.; solo, Irving Kennedy, accompanied by J. Hartley Russell, Grand Third vice-president N.S.G.W.; roll call Gold Star Native Sons of San Francisco Parlors, Jesse Miller, Grand Trustee N.S.G.W.; "The Unknown Soldier," Mrs. Henry Dippell (Mission No. 229 N.D.G.W.); solo, Irving Kennedy, J. Hartley Russell accompanist; memorial address, Joseph E. Tinney (Rincon No. 72 N.S.G.W.; benediction, "The Boy Scout Prayer," Scout Julius Solomons; firing squad, First Combat Train 250th Coast Artillery, California National Guard; "America," Native Daughter Glee Club; taps.

In addition to those participating in the program, these grand officers were in attendance: Grand Trustee Ethel Begley of the Native Daughters; Junior Past Grand Seth Millington, Grand First vice Chas. A. Koenig, Grand Trustees Eldred L. Meyer, Chas. H. Spengemann and Thos. M. Foley of the Native Sons.

N.S.G.W. LIBRARY ENRICHED.

The library of the Grizzly Bear Club in Native Sons Building now has a complete file of the official magazines of the California Fish and Game Commission, entitled "California Fish and Game." This otherwise unobtainable collection is the generous gift of Francis A. Cavagnaro of Stanford Parlor No. 76 N.S.G.W. The Fish and Game Commission has agreed to supply future issues, so that the club will have one of the few complete files of this now-important publication.

As the subject of conservation and propagation of fish and game in the state is of great importance to every Native Son, this collection should prove a valuable source of information. The set commences with Vol. I, issued October 1914, and comprises the eighteen volumes so far issued. A reading of these volumes will give one a complete history of all the work done by the commission since it was instituted in 1871. There are also a number of articles by sportsmen and experts from all parts of the world on matters of breeding, and the care of fish and game for both commercial and sporting use.

MOTHERS BANQUET GUESTS.

At its annual mothers banquet, Orinda Parlor No. 56 N.D.G.W. had as guests sixty-six mothers of members, each of whom was presented with a gift. The dramatic club presented two plays, and the balance of the evening was devoted to games. May 17, the members born in April and May were given a birthday party and President Marie McGrath, on the Parlor's behalf, presented each with a very pretty apron. Mrs. Charlotte Gunther, in honor of her daughter, Grand Inside Sentinel Orinda Giannini, furnished a beautiful birthday cake.

Orinda's June 9 meeting was dedicated to Past Grand President Emma G. Foley, in recognition of her birthday. The officers, beautifully arrayed in evening gowns, made a wonderful picture. A buffet supper was served, and Past Grand Foley was presented with a gift.

Birthday Observed—Monterey City, early-day capital of California, celebrated June 3 its one hundred and sixty-third birthday.

N.D. GRAND PARLOR

(Continued from Page 5)

ing and most deserving endeavor, and they had the pleasure of meeting personally many of the proud foster parents and their babes.

Greetings from the Order of Native Sons of the Golden West were extended by Grand President Justice Emmet Seawell and Grand Secretary John T. Regan. Other "outsiders" who addressed the session were: Grand Trustee Edward T. Schnarr and Grand Marshal Gam Hurst, of the Native Sons; William Hamilton, chairman Alameda County Board Supervisors; William G. Paden, superintendent Alameda County schools, who gave a most interesting address on California history, and Mayor Fred Morcom of Oakland.

Arrangements for the Oakland Grand Parlor were made, and admirably executed, by the Alameda County Parlors, working together. The general committee included Past Grand Sue J. Irwin, Josephine Clark, Carmelita Luhr, Dora Brayton and Grand Secretary Sallie R. Thaler.

PAST GRANDS' ANNUAL GATHERING.

The Past Grand Presidents had their annual supper gathering the evening of June 20. The table was attractively decorated in pastel shades. Mrs. Evelyn I. Carlson was received as the "baby" member, and was presented with a toy, a feed plate and a bib. Mrs. Carrie Roesch-Durham led in prayer, after which Mrs. May C.

MRS. ANNA THUESEN,
Elected N.D. Grand Marshal.

Boldemann, the hostess of the occasion, extended a welcome to those gathered about the festive board. Mrs. Olive Bedford-Matlock was re-elected president, and Mrs. Bertha A. Briggs was retained as secretary.

In attendance were Past Grands Carrie Roesch-Durham, Dr. Mariana Bertola, Cora B. Sifford, Eliza D. Keith, Ariana W. Stirling, Dr. Eva R. Rasmussen, Emma Gruber-Foley, Emma W. Humphrey, Alison F. Watt, Mamie G. Peyton, May C. Boldemann, Margaret Grote-Hill, Mary E. Bell, Bertha A. Briggs, Mattie M. Stein, Catherine E. Gloster, Pearl Lamb, Dr. Louise C. Heilbron, Esther R. Sullivan, Estelle M. Evans and Evelyn I. Carlson.

ENTERTAINMENT—DRILL TEAMS.

At the Monday evening formal reception, Mrs. Dora Brayton (Bahia vista No. 167) chairman, the drill team of Joaquin No. 5 (Stockton), twenty-four in number, appeared in an exhibition wisteria drill. Mrs. Henry H. Drais is chairman of the team, which has appeared at

Highways Aid—Federal Government aid for highways allocated to California for the fiscal year commencing July 1 totals $16,802,000.

many Natives' functions. Bridge and whist followed the program.

At the Tuesday night grand ball, Mrs. Carmelita Luhr (Aloha No. 106) chairman, the grand march was led by Grand President Armstrong and Governor James Rolph (Hesperian No. 137 N.S.G.W.). Several Native Sons were in attendance, and among Mrs. Luhr's assistants were Richard M. Hamb (Piedmont No. 120 N.S.G.W.) and Arthur E. Cleu (Fruitvale No. 252 N.S.G.W.). Excellent music was provided. Previous to the dancing, the large assemblage was entertained by the drill team of Manzanita No. 29 (Grass Valley), composed of Grace Eva, Marie Foote, Vashti Schwartz, Hannabel Daley, Venita Jones, Ruth Lindval, Ethel Foote, Verna Taylor, Mae Merrifield, Inez Hammill, Muriel Rosewall, Vera Hansen, Alice Collins, Sue Harris, Dorothea Dettner, Hazel Jenkins and President Anna Rowe. Ethel Veale was the pianist.

SONOMA COUNTY LANDMARK NOW IN CALIFORNIA'S PARK SYSTEM.

June 5, title to "Lachryma Montis," the historic Sonoma County home of General Mariano G. Vallejo near Sonoma City, passed to the State of California and will be preserved as a landmark under the supervision of the State Park Commission. The property embraces some seventeen acres, and a museum will be a feature of the new state park.

Patriotic citizens contributed one-half the purchase price of the property, and the State subscribed the other half and will bear the cost of upkeep and repair. The Order of Native Sons of the Golden West and Sonoma County were liberal contributors to the purchase-fund.

"Anybody can walk right through the boundaries we ordinarily believe are our limitations." —Henry Ford.

GRIZZLY GROWLS

(CLARENCE M. HUNT.)

THE SPECIAL SESSION OF THE SEVenty-third Federal Congress adjourned June 16. At the suggestion, and on the insistence, of President Franklin Roosevelt it enacted many important bills, which have become laws. The largest peace-time authorizations of expenditures in the history of the nation, characterized the session of the Congress; they were made to aid and to hasten the return of prosperity. Among the enacted legislation is the National Industrial Recovery Act, declared by the President "the most important and far-reaching legislation ever enacted by the American Congress." Following the signing of this bill, he issued a statement; quoting therefrom:

"The law was passed to put people back to work—to let them buy more of the products of farms and factories and start our business at a living rate again. This task is in two stages—first, to get many hundreds of thousands of the unemployed back on the payroll by snowfall and, second, to plan for a better future for the longer pull.

"While we shall not neglect the second, the first stage is an emergency job. It has the right of way. The second part of the Act gives employment by a vast program of public works. Our studies show that we should be able to hire many men at once and to step up to about a million new jobs by October 1, and a much greater number later.

"We must put at the head of our list those works which are fully ready to start now. Our first purpose is to create employment as fast as we can, but we should not pour money into unproved projects. . . .

"In my inaugural address I laid down the simple proposition that nobody is going to starve in this country. It seems to me to be equally plain that no business which depends for existence on paying less than living wages to its workers has any right to continue in this country.

"By 'business' I mean the whole of commerce as well as the whole of industry; by workers I mean all workers—the white-collar class as well as the men in overalls; and by living wages I mean more than bare subsistence level—I mean the wages of decent living.

"Throughout industry, the change from starvation wages and starvation employment to living wages and sustained employment can, in large part, be made by an industrial covenant to which all employers shall subscribe. It is greatly to their interest to do this because decent living, widely spread among our 125,000,000 people, eventually means the opening up to industry of the richest market the world has known.

"It is the only way to utilize the so-called excess capacity of our industrial plants. This is the principle that makes this one of the most important laws that ever came from Congress because, before the passage of this Act, no such industrial covenant was possible. . . .

"It is a challenge to industry, which has long insisted that, given the right to act in unison, it could do much for the general good which has hitherto been unlawful. From today it has that right. Many good men voted this new charter with misgivings. I do not share these doubts. . . .

"This is not a law to foment discord, and it will not be executed as such. This is a time for mutual confidence and help, and we can safely rely on the sense of fair play among all Americans to assure every industry which now moves forward promptly in this united drive against depression that its workers will be with it to a man. . . .

"Finally, this law is a challenge to our whole people. There is no power in America that can force against the public will such action as we require, but there is no group in America that can withstand the force of an aroused public opinion.

"This great co-operation can succeed only if those who bravely go forward to restore jobs have aggressive public support and those who lag are made to feel the full weight of public disapproval. . . .

"As in the great crisis of the World War, it puts a whole people to the simple but vital test: 'Must we go on in many groping, disorganized, separate units to defeat or shall we move as one great team to victory?' "

The Senate fact-finding committe of the California State Legislature, after due and careful investigation, presented several economy measures, designed to aid the burdened taxpayers without inflicting an injustice on any individual or group. The purpose was to lower the costs of government, as they should be lowered, by eliminating notorious extravagances. Most of the measures passed the Legislature, but during the recess of the law-making body they were dealt death-blows by the veto-axe.

Those measures should, in the interest of the tax-burdened farmers and small-home owners of the state, be revived by the Legislature when it reconvenes, and passed over the Governor's veto. That would, of course, be contrary to the desire of the political-racketeers minority, but the tax-paying majority of California citizens demand that it be done. The conduct of the Legislature, in this time of need, will clearly indicate if there be any possibility of relief from state misgovernment, unless the ballot box be resorted to.

Coming, the great national holiday—the Fourth of July! So, give thought to "The American's Creed," written in 1917 by William Tyler Page, clerk of the Federal House of Representatives:

"I believe in the United States of America as a government of the people, by the people, for the people; whose just powers are derived from the consent of the governed; a democracy in a republic; a sovereign nation of many sovereign states; a perfect union, one and inseparable; established upon those principles of freedom, equality, justice and humanity for which American patriots sacrificed their lives and fortunes. I therefore believe it is my duty to my country to love it; to support its Constitution; to obey its laws; to respect its flag, and to defend it against all enemies."

"We have brought about our present unhappy condition by divorcing education, industry, politics, business and economics from morality," declares a statement issued by the National Catholic Welfare Conference, June 7. In other words, dishonesty, the general practice, accounts for most of our ills.

If you have gold, better disgorge it, for the Federal Attorney-General says positively that not only will the hoarders' names be publicized, but they will be prosecuted, also.

"Don't let the Morgan revelations further weaken your faith in government," says the Livingston, Merced County, "Chronicle." "Remember, it is government, a governmental agency, which is revealing to you these hidden secrets involving polite bribery. The Morgan system of having a preferred list of public men . . . involves the same principle as other better-known evils of politics, . . . The idea is to put men in public office under obligations."

Testimony before the Sacramento County Grand Jury indicates willful mismanagement, if not outright crookedness, caused the failure of two of the Capital City's banks. Evidence reflecting unfavorably on the state banking department was included. Considering that fact, and the Beesemeyer building-and-loan thievery, a grave doubt arises as to whether state supervision is of any value—to those who entrust their funds to others.

Be thankful for small favors: July 1, the postage rate on first-class mail for local delivery will be reduced to two cents an ounce.

"How about the accusation that Uncle Sam is dealing niggardly with those who once wore his uniform?", commented the "Bee" of Sacramento, editorially, June 15. "Even under the revised Roosevelt program, the United States Veterans Bureau will be getting an amount exceeding the combined expenditures for such purposes by Great Britain, France, Germany and Italy.

"Compare their casualties and our own with the amount of compensation they have paid thus far and our own. The figures follow: France, casualties, 4,950,000; number assisted by the government, 708,000, or one in seven. Great Britain, casualties, 4,266,000; number compensated, 499,000, or one in eight. United States, casualties, 234,000; compensated 737,000, or three times as many as were actually wounded in battle. On the other hand, if the French program were being followed in America, assistance would be limited to 37,000 cases; or of the British, to 30,000.

"Moreover, the annual expenditure for Veterans' aid in the three countries named last year per casualty case was: France, $51; Great Britain, $38; United States, $2,658. The outlay in the United States was forty-five times that of England, and fifty times that of France. The fact is that history has failed to disclose a government so bountiful in the extension of its largess to former soldiers and sailors as Uncle Sam. He leads the rest of the world combined."

In a certain chain of newspapers there has been unlimited publicity advocating a national sales tax, which proposal, incidentally, was rejected by the national administration. Here's a comment from the Willows, Glenn County, "Journal":

"William Randolph Hearst, mighty publisher, objects strenuously to an increase in income taxes. He favors a sales tax to raise money to pay the interest on several billions of bonds for vast public works to aid unemployment. Hearst is worth many millions. Like most others of great wealth he objects to paying more income tax to aid the poor. He would compel the poor to raise most of the money by imposition of a sales tax. Like a majority of rich men, Hearst is a great patriot as long as his own pocketbook is not touched."

An account of factional uprisings among Tuolumne County Chinese in October 1856 is contained in original letters and documents gathered by Prof. Herbert G. Florcken of the Modesto Junior College history department, reports the Modesto, Stanislaus County, "News Herald." One of the letters, penned at Columbia, October 24, 1856,—then the headquarters of the Second Brigade, Third Division, California State Militia,—was written by Brigadier-General Thomas N. Cazneau to Governor J. Neely Johnson. It says:

"For some time past, serious difficulties have arisen between our Chinese residents, understood to belong to separate factions, which have now assumed a deplorable character. A body of Hong Kong Chinamen estimated at 400 have concentrated at the Rock River Ranch in this (Tuolumne) county, armed with spears, swords, battle cleavers and other war-like implements peculiar to these people, and also with muskets obtained from San Francisco. They have in addition a small brass field piece rudely mounted.

"At Chinese Camp (likewise in this county)

(Continued on Page 19)

Official Directory of Parlors of the N. D. G. W.

ALAMEDA COUNTY.

Angelita No. 32, Livermore—Meets 2nd and 4th Fridays, Foresters Hall; Mrs. Myrtle I. Johnson, Rec. Sec., P.O. box 253.

Piedmont No. 87, Oakland—Meets Thursdays, Corinthian Hall, Pacific Bldg.; Miss Helen Ring, Rec. Sec., 822 11th St.

Aloha No. 106, Oakland—Meets Tuesdays, 4016 Grove St.; Mrs. Lurine Martin, Rec. Sec., 2815 Wallace St., Berkeley.

Hayward No. 122, Hayward—Meets 1st and 3rd Tuesdays, Veterans Memorial Bldg., Main St.; Miss Ruth Gansberger, Rec. Sec., P. O. box 44, Mount Eden.

Berkeley No. 150, Berkeley—Meets 2nd Saturday afternoon, Berkeley City Women's Club, 2315 Durant; Mrs. Lella B. Baker, Rec. Sec., 915 Contra Costa Ave.

Bear Flag No. 151, Berkeley—Meets 2nd and 4th Wednesdays, Veterans Memorial Bldg., 1931 Center St.; Mrs. Maud Wagner, Rec. Sec., 317 Alcatraz Ave., Oakland.

Encinal No. 156, Alameda—Meets 2nd and 4th Wednesdays, Veterans Memorial Bldg., Central Ave. and Walnut St.; Mrs. Laura E. Fisher, Rec. Sec., 1413 Caroline St.

Brooklyn No. 157, East Oakland—Meets 2nd and 4th Wednesdays, Masonic Temple, 8th Ave. and E. 14th St.; Mrs. Ruth Cooney, Rec. Sec., 3907 14th Ave.

Argonaut No. 166, Oakland—Meets Tuesdays, Klinkner Hall, 59th and San Pablo; Mrs. Ada Spilman, Rec. Sec., 2905 Ellis St., Berkeley.

Bahia Vista No. 167, Oakland—Meets 1st and 3rd Thursdays, Wigwam Hall, Pacific Bldg.; Mrs. Minnie E. Raper, Rec. Sec., 3449 Helen St.

Fruitvale No. 177, Oakland—Meets Fridays, W.O.W. Hall; May E. Barthold, Rec. Sec., 3832 Santa Rita St.

Laura Loma No. 182, Niles—Meets 1st and 3rd Tuesdays, I.O.O.F. Hall; Mrs. Ethel Fournier, Rec. Sec., P. O. box 515.

El Cereso No. 207, San Leandro—Meets 2nd and 4th Tuesda s, Masonic Hall; Mrs. Mary Tuttle, Rec. Sec., P. O. box 56.

Pleasanton No. 237, Pleasanton—Meets 1st Tuesday, I.O.O.F. Hall; Mrs. Myrtle Lanini, Rec. Sec.

Betsy Rose No. 238, Centerville—Meets 1st and 3rd Fridays, Anderson Hall; Miss Constance Lucio, Rec. Sec., P. O. box 187.

AMADOR COUNTY.

Ursula No. 1, Jackson—Meets 2nd and 4th Tuesdays, N.S.G.W. Hall; Mrs. Emma Boarman-Wright, Rec. Sec., 114 Court St.

Chispa No. 40, Ione—Meets 2nd and 4th Fridays, N.S.G.W. Hall; Cynthia Phillips, Rec. Sec.

Amapola No. 80, Sutter Creek—Meets 2nd and 4th Thursdays, N.S.G.W. Bldg.; Mrs. Hazel M. Marre, Rec. Sec.

Forrest No. 86, Plymouth—Meets 2nd and 4th Tuesdays, I.O.O.F. Hall; Mrs. Marguerite Davis, Rec. Sec.

BUTTE COUNTY.

Annie K. Bidwell No. 168, Chico—Meets 2nd and 4th Thursdays, I.O.O.F. Hall; Mrs. Irene Henry, Rec. Sec., 3015 Woodland Ave.

Gold of Ophir No. 190, Oroville—Meets 1st and 3rd Wednesdays, Memorial Hall; Mrs. Ruth Brown, Rec. Sec., 1265 Leah Court.

CALAVERAS COUNTY.

Ruby No. 46, Murphys—Meets 4th Friday, N.S.G.W. Hall; Bella Segale, Rec. Sec.

Princess No. 84, Angels Camp—Meets 2nd and 4th Wednesdays, I.O.O.F. Hall; Mrs. Grace M. Mills, Rec. Sec., P.O. box 313.

San Andreas No. 113, San Andreas—Meets 1st Friday, Fraternal Hall; Miss Doris Treat, Rec. Sec.

COLUSA COUNTY.

Colus No. 194, Colusa—Meets 1st and 3rd Mondays, Eagles Hall; Miss Kate Busch, Rec. Sec., 350 Market St.

CONTRA COSTA COUNTY.

Stirling No. 146, Pittsburg—Meets 1st and 3rd Wednesdays, Veteran Memorial Hall; Mrs. Leslie Clement, Rec. Sec., 468 E. Santa Fe.

Richmond No. 147, Richmond—Meets 1st and 3rd Tuesdays, Richmond Club House, 1125 Nevin Ave.; Grace Curry, Rec. Sec., 932 Ohio Ave.

Donner No. 193, Byron—Meets 1st and 3rd Wednesdays, I.O.O.F. Hall; Mrs. Anna Pendry, Rec. Sec., P.O. box 442, Brentwood.

Las Juntas No. 221, Martinez—Meets 1st and 3rd Mondays, Pythian Castle; Mrs. Lola O. Viera, Rec. Sec., R.F.D. No. 1.

Antioch No. 223, Antioch—Meets 2nd and 4th Tuesdays, I.O.O.F. Hall; Mrs. Estelle Evans, Rec. Sec., 202 E. 5th St., Pittsburg.

Carquinez No. 234, Crockett—Meets 2nd and 4th Wednesdays, I.O.O.F. Hall; Mrs. Cecile Petee, Rec. Sec., 465 Edwards St.

EL DORADO COUNTY.

Marguerite No. 12, Placerville—Meets 1st and 3rd Wednesdays, Masonic Hall; Mrs. Nettie Leonardi, Rec. Sec., 25 Coloma St.

El Dorado No. 186, Georgetown—Meets 2nd and 4th Saturday afternoons, I.O.O.F. Hall; Mrs. Alta L. Douglas, Rec. Sec.

FRESNO COUNTY.

Fresno No. 187, Fresno—Meets 2nd and 4th Fridays, Pythian Castle, Cor. "R" and Merced Sts.; Mary Aubery, Rec. Sec., 1040 Delphia Ave.

GRAND OFFICERS.

Mrs. Anna M. Armstrong..........Past Grand President
Woodland
Mrs. Irma Laird..........Grand President
Alturas
Mrs. Gladys Noce..........Grand Vice-president
Sutter Creek
Mrs. Sallie R. Thaler..........Grand Secretary
555 Baker St., San Francisco
Mrs. Susie K. Christ..........Grand Treasurer
555 Baker St., San Francisco
Mrs. Anna Thuesen..........Grand Marshal
615 38th Ave., San Francisco
Mrs. Hazel B. Hansen..........Grand Inside Sentinel
501 Griswold St., Glendale
Mrs. Alice M. Oldham..........Grand Outside Sentinel
2218 26th Ave., San Francisco
Mrs. Clara Gairaud..........Grand Organist
134 Locust St., San Jose

GRAND TRUSTEES.

Mrs. Orinda G. Giannini.....2142 Filbert St., San Francisco
Mrs. Florence D. Boyle..........Oroville
Mrs. Minna K. Horn..........Etna
Mrs. Jane Vick..........418 Bath St., Santa Barbara
Mrs. Alice M. Lane..........191 15th Ave., San Francisco
Mrs. Ethel Begley..........233 Prospect Ave., San Francisco
Mrs. Willow Borba..........330 So. Main St., Sebastopol

GLENN COUNTY.

Berryessa No. 192, Willows—Meets 1st and 3rd Mondays, I.O.O.F. Hall; Mrs. Leonora Neate, Rec. Sec., 338 No. Lassen St.

HUMBOLDT COUNTY.

Occident No. 28, Eureka—Meets 1st and 3rd Wednesdays, N.S.G.W. Hall; Mrs. Eva L. MacDonald, Rec. Sec., 2309 "B" St.

Oneonta No. 71, Ferndale—Meets 2nd and 4th Fridays, I.O.O.F. Hall; Mrs. Myra Rumrill, Rec. Sec., P.O. box 142.

Reichling No. 97, Fortuna—Meets 1st and 3rd Tuesdays, F endship Hall; Mrs. Grace Swett, Rec. Sec., P. O. box 328.

KERN COUNTY.

Miocene No. 228, Taft—Meets 1st and 3rd Wednesday afternoons, I.O.O.F. Hall; Mrs. Evalyn G. Towne, Rec. Sec., 301 Woodrow St.

El Tejon No. 239, Bakersfield—Meets 1st and 3rd Fridays, Eagles Hall, 1714 "G" St.; Mary B. Hampson, Rec. Sec., 908 Quincy St.

Desert Gold No. 250, Mojave—Meets 2nd and 4th Fridays, I.O.O.F. Hall; Jane Lucile Waters, Rec. Sec., Tehachapi.

LAKE COUNTY.

Clear Lake No. 135, Middletown—Meets 2nd and 4th Tuesdays, Herrick Hall; Mrs. Alma E. Snow, Rec. Sec.

LASSEN COUNTY.

Nataqua No. 152, Standish—Meets 1st and 3rd Wednesdays, Foresters Hall; Mrs. Mayda Elledge, Rec. Sec.

Mount Lassen No. 215, Bieber—Meets 2nd and 4th Thursdays, I.O.O.F. Hall; Mrs. Angie C. Kenyon, Rec. Sec.

Susanville No. 243, Susanville—Meets 3rd Thursday, I.O.O.F. Hall; Mildred Hardy, Rec. Sec., P.O. box 425.

LOS ANGELES COUNTY.

Los Angeles No. 124, Los Angeles—Meets 1st and 3rd Wednesdays, I.O.O.F. Hall, Washington and Oak Sts.; Mrs. Mary K. Corcoran, Rec. Sec., 322 No. Van Ness Ave.

Long Beach No. 154, Long Beach—Meets 1st and 3rd Thursdays, Home of Eleonor Johnson, 1920 Bermuda St.; Mrs. Bertha Hitt, Rec. Sec., 5355 Lime Ave.

Rudecinda No. 230, San Pedro—Meets 2nd and 4th Thursdays, Unity Hall, I.O.O.F. Temple, 10th and Gaffey; Letitia Sarciaux, Rec. Sec., 1054 W. 24th St.

Verdugo No. 240, Glendale—Meets 2nd and 4th Tuesdays, Masonic Temple, 234 So. Brand Blvd.; Miss Etta Fulkerth, Rec. Sec., 526 No. Orange St.

Santa Monica Bay No. 245, Santa Monica—Meets 2nd and 4th Wednesdays, Odd Fellows Hall, 1431 Third St.; Mrs. Rosalie Hyde, Rec. Sec., 738 Flower St., Venice.

Californiana No. 247, Los Angeles—Meets 2nd and 4th Tuesday afternoons, Hollywood Studio Club, 1215 Lodi Place; Mrs. Inez Sitton, Rec. Sec., 4223 Berenice St.

MADERA COUNTY.

Madera No. 244, Madera—Meets 2nd and 4th Thursdays, Masonic Annex; Mrs. Margaret C. Boyle, Rec. Sec., 111 No. "B" St.

MARIN COUNTY.

Sea Point No. 196, Sausalito—Meets 2nd and 4th Mondays, Perry Hall, 50 Caledonia St.; Mrs. Mary B. Smith, Rec. Sec., 47½ Glen Drive.

Marinita No. 198, San Rafael—Meets 2nd and 4th Mondays, 316 "B" St.; Lillian Whitmore, Rec. Sec., 337 5th St.

Fairfax No. 225, Fairfax—Meets 2nd and 4th Tuesdays, Community Hall; Mrs. Marguerite Geary, Rec. Sec.

Tamelpa No. 231, Mill Valley—Meets 1st and 2nd Tuesdays, I.O.O.F. Hall; Mrs. Delphine M. Todt, Rec. Sec., 500 Irwin St., San Rafael.

MARIPOSA COUNTY.

Mariposa No. 63, Mariposa—Meets 1st and 3rd Fridays, I.O.O.F. Hall; Elizabeth E. Johnson, Rec. Sec.

MENDOCINO COUNTY.

Fort Bragg No. 210, Fort Bragg—Meets 1st Thursday, I.O.O.F. Hall; Mrs. Ruth W. Fuller, Rec. Sec.

MERCED COUNTY.

Veritas No. 75, Merced—Meets 1st and 3rd Tuesdays, I.O.O.F. Hall; Miss Flora Fernandes, Rec. Sec., 28 19th St.

MODOC COUNTY.

Alturas No. 159, Alturas—Meets 1st Thursday, Alturas Civic Club; Mrs. Irma W. Laird, Rec. Sec.

MONTEREY COUNTY.

Aleli No. 102, Salinas—Meets 2nd and 4th Thursdays, Pythian Hall; Miss Rose Rhyner, Rec. Sec., 420 Soledad St.

Junipero No. 141, Monterey—Meets 2nd and 4th Fridays, K. of P. Hall, Main St.; Miss Matilda M. Bergschicker, Rec. Sec., 498 Van Buren St.

NAPA COUNTY.

Eshcol No. 16, Napa—Meets 2nd and 4th Mondays, N.S.G.W. Hall; Mrs. Ella Ingram, Rec. Sec., 2140 Seminary St.

Calistoga No. 145, Calistoga—Meets 2nd and 4th Mondays, I.O.O.F. Hall; Sadie P. Brooks, Rec. Sec.

La Junta No. 203, Saint Helena—Meets 1st and 3rd Tuesdays, N.S.G.W. Hall; Mrs. Marie Signorelli, Rec. Sec., 1341 Madrona Ave.

ATTENTION, SECRETARIES!

THIS DIRECTORY IS PUBLISHED BY AUTHORITY OF THE GRAND PARLOR N.D.G.W., AND ALL NOTICES OF CHANGES MUST BE RECEIVED BY THE GRAND SECRETARY (NOT THE MAGAZINE) ON OR BEFORE THE 20TH OF EACH MONTH TO INSURE CORRECTION IN NEXT PUBLICATION OF DIRECTORY.

NEVADA COUNTY.

Laurel No. 6, Nevada City—Meets 1st and 3rd Wednesdays, I.O.O.F. Hall; Mrs. Nellie E. Clark, Rec. Sec., 412 Pine St.

Manzanita No. 29, Grass Valley—Meets 1st and 3rd Tuesdays, Auditorium; Mrs. Loraine Keast, Rec. Sec., 123 Race St.

Columbia No. 70, French Corral—Meets Fridays, Farrelley Hall; Mrs. Kate Farrelley-Sullivan, Rec. Sec.

Snow Peak No. 176, Truckee—Meets 1st Monday, I.O.O.F. Hall; Mrs. Henrietta M. Eaton, Rec. Sec., P. O. box 116.

ORANGE COUNTY.

Santa Ana No. 235, Santa Ana—Meets 2nd and 4th Mondays, K.C. Hall, 4th and French Sts.; Mrs. Matilda S. Lemon, Rec. Sec., 1628 W. 8th St.

Grace No. 242, Fullerton—Meets 1st and 3rd Thursdays, I.O.O.F. Hall, 116½ E. Commonwealth; Mrs. Mary R. Rothsermel, Rec. Sec., Acacia St. & Commonwealth.

PLACER COUNTY.

Placer No. 138, Lincoln—Meets 2nd Wednesday, I.O.O.F. Hall; Miss Carrie Parlin, Rec. Sec.

La Rosa No. 191, Roseville—Meets 1st and 3rd Tuesdays, Eagles Hall; Miss Margaret Parrish, Rec. Sec., Atlantic St.

Auburn No. 233, Auburn—Meets 2nd and 4th Fridays, Foresters Hall; Mrs. Elsie Patrick, Rec. Sec.

PLUMAS COUNTY.

Plumas Pioneer No. 219, Quincy—Meets 1st and 3rd Mondays, I.O.O.F. Hall; Minnie E. Johnson, Rec. Sec., P. O. box 243.

SACRAMENTO COUNTY.

Califia No. 22, Sacramento—Meets 2nd and 4th Tuesdays, N.S.G.W. Hall; Miss Lulu Gillis, Rec. Sec., 921 8th St.

La Bandera No. 110, Sacramento—Meets 1st and 3rd Fridays, N.S.G.W. Hall; Mrs. Clara Waldon, Rec. Sec., 1310 "O" St.

Sutter No. 111, Sacramento—Meets 1st and 3rd Tuesdays, N.S.G.W. Hall; Mrs. Adele Nix, Rec. Sec., 1288 "S" St.

Fern No. 123, Folsom—Meets 1st and 3rd Tuesdays, K.P. Hall; Elizabeth Ryan, Rec. Sec., Represa.

Chabolla No. 171, Galt—Meets 2nd and 4th Tuesdays, I.O.O.F. Hall; Mrs. Mary Pritchard, Rec. Sec.

Coloma No. 212, Sacramento—Meets 1st and 3rd Tuesdays, I.O.O.F. Hall, Oak Park; Mrs. Nettie Harry, Rec. Sec., 1217 35th St.

Liberty No. 213, Elk Grove—Meets 2nd and 4th Fridays, I.O.O.F. Hall; Mrs. Frances Wackman, Rec. Sec., P. O. box 192.

Victory No. 216, Courtland—Meets 1st Saturday and 3rd Monday, N.S.G.W. Hall; Mrs. Agneda Lample, Rec. Sec.

Rio Rita No. 253, Sacramento—Meets 1st and 3rd Mondays, 902 "J" St.; Dorothea Rourke, Rec. Sec.

SAN BENITO COUNTY.

Copa de Oro No. 105, Hollister—Meets 2nd and 4th Thursdays, Grangers Union Hall; Mrs. Mollie Daveggio, Rec. Sec., 110 San Benito St.

San Juan Bautista No. 179, San Juan Bautista—Meets 1st Wednesday, Mission Corridor Rooms; Miss Gertrude Breen, Rec. Sec.

SAN BERNARDINO COUNTY.

Lugonia No. 241, San Bernardino—Meets 2nd and 4th Wednesdays, Eagles Hall; Miss Lois Poling, Rec. Sec., 295 E. 11th St.

Ontario No. 251, Ontario—Meets 2nd and 4th Thursdays, Ontario Hotel; Miss Helen Hickman, Rec. Sec., 928 No. Laurel Ave.

SAN DIEGO COUNTY.

San Diego No. 208, San Diego—Meets 2nd and 4th Wednesdays, Directors Room, Chamber Commerce Bldg., 499 W. Broadway; Mrs. Elsie Case, Rec. Sec., 3051 Broadway.

SAN FRANCISCO CITY AND COUNTY.

Minerva No. 2, San Francisco—Meets 1st and 3rd Wednesdays, N.S.G.W. Bldg.; Miss Dorothy Finn, Rec. Sec., 90 Princess St., Sausalito.

Alta No. 3, San Francisco—Meets 2nd and 4th Tuesdays, N.S.G.W. Bldg.; Mrs. Agnese L. Hughes, Rec. Sec., 3980 Sacramento St.

Oro Fino No. 9, San Francisco—Meets 1st and 3rd Thursdays, N.S.G.W. Bldg.; Mrs. Josephine B. Morrisey, Rec. Sec., 4441 20th St.

Golden State No. 50, San Francisco—Meets 1st and 3rd Wednesdays, N.D.G.W. Home; Miss Millie Tietjen, Rec. Sec., 328 Lexington Ave.

Orinda No. 56, San Francisco—Meets 2nd, 4th and 5th Fridays, N.D.G.W. Home; Mrs. Anna A. Gruber-Loser, Rec. Sec., 72 Grove Lane, San Anselmo.

Fremont No. 59, San Francisco—Meets 1st and 3rd Tuesdays, N.S.G.W. Bldg.; Miss Hannah Collins, Rec. Sec., 617 Fillmore St.

Buena Vista No. 68, San Francisco—Meets 1st, 3rd and 5th Thursdays, N.D.G.W. Home; Miss Margaret Barrett, Rec. Sec., 3774 20th St.

Las Lomas No. 72, San Francisco—Meets 1st and 3rd Tuesdays, N.D.G.W. Home; Mrs. Marion S. Day, Rec. Sec., 459 Noe St.

Yosemite No. 83, San Francisco—Meets 1st and 3rd Tuesdays, American Hall, 20th and Capp Sts.; Miss Mary Monahan, Rec. Sec., 237 Noe St.

La Estrella No. 89, San Francisco—Meets 2nd and 4th Mondays, N.S.G.W. Bldg.; Miss Birdie Hartman, Rec. Sec., 1018 Jackson St.

Sans Souci No. 96, San Francisco—Meets 2nd and 4th Mondays, N.D.G.W. Home; Mrs. Minnie F. Dobbin, Rec. Sec., 1483 43rd Ave.

Calaveras No. 103, San Francisco—Meets 2nd and 4th Tuesdays, Swedish American Hall, 2174 Market St.; Mary L. Krogh, Rec. Sec., 4235 Cabrillo St.

Darina No. 114, San Francisco—Meets 1st and 3rd Mondays, N.S.G.W. Bldg.; Miss Adele Walsh, Rec. Sec., 479 Page St.

El Vespero No. 118, San Francisco—Meets 2nd and 4th Tuesdays, Masonic Hall, 4705 3rd St.; Mrs. Nell R. Boege, Rec. Sec., 1526 Kirkwood Ave.

Genevieve No. 132, San Francisco—Meets 1st and 3rd Thursdays, N.S.G.W. Bldg.; Miss Branice Peguillan, Rec. Sec., 2434 16th Ave.

Keith No. 137, San Francisco—Meets 2nd and 4th Thursdays, N.S.G.W. Bldg.; Mrs. Helen T. Mann, Rec. Sec., 575 Pierce St., Apt. 206.

Gabrielle No. 139, San Francisco—Meets 2nd and 4th Wednesdays, N.S.G.W. Bldg.; Mrs. Dorothy Wuesterfeld, Rec. Sec., 1020 Munich St.

Presidio No. 148, San Francisco—Meets 2nd and 4th Tuesdays, N.S.G.W. Bldg.; Mrs. Hattie Gaughran, Rec. Sec., 713 Capp St.

Guadalupe No. 153, San Francisco—Meets 2nd and 4th Mondays, Forester Hall, 170 Valencia St.; Miss May A. McCarthy, Rec. Sec., 336 Elsie St.

Golden Gate No. 158, San Francisco—Meets 2nd and 4th Mondays, N.S.G.W. Bldg.; Mrs. Mary Sullivan, Rec. Sec., 33 Cuvier St.

Dolores No. 169, San Francisco—Meets 2nd and 4th Wednesdays, N.S.G.W. Bldg.; Mrs. Ada Saunders, Rec. Sec., 284 Allison St.

Linda Rosa No. 170, San Francisco—Meets 2nd and 4th Wednesdays, Swedish American Hall, 2174 Market St.; Mrs. Eva P. Tyrrel, Rec. Sec., 2620 Mission St.

Portola No. 172, San Francisco—Meets 1st and 3rd Tuesdays, N.S.G.W. Bldg.; Catherine H. Dolly, Rec. Sec., 4125 23rd St.

Castro No. 178, San Francisco—Meets 1st and 3rd Wednesdays, K.C. Bldg., 150 Golden Gate Ave.; Miss Adeline Sandersfeld, Rec Sec., 50 Baker St.

Twin Peaks No. 185, San Francisco—Meets 2nd and 4th Fridays, Druids Temple, 44 Page St.; Mrs. Loretta Casterton, Rec. Sec., 3969 Army St.

James Lick No. 220, San Francisco—Meets 1st and 3rd Wednesdays, N.S.G.W. Bldg.; Mrs. Edna Bishop, Rec. Sec., 3841 24th St.

Mission No. 227, San Francisco—Meets 2nd and 4th Fridays, N.S.G.W. Bldg.; Mrs. Ann Dippel, Rec. Sec., 448 Dewey Blvd.

Bret Harte No. 232, San Francisco—Meets 2nd and 4th Tuesdays, Aloha Hall, 3009 16th St.; Pearl Wedde, Rec. Sec., 225 7th Ave.

Balboa No. 249, San Francisco—Meets 1st and 3rd Thursdays, Knights Columbus Hall, 382 18th Ave.; Miss Joan Moffet, Rec. Sec., 476 26th Ave.

Utopia No. 252, San Francisco—Meets 2nd and 4th Tuesdays, American Hall, 20th and Capp Sts.; Miss Lelia M. Little, Rec. Sec., 4430 20th St.

SAN JOAQUIN COUNTY.

Joaquin No. 5, Stockton—Meets 2nd and 4th Tuesdays, N.S.G.W. Hall, 314 E. Main St.; Mrs. Della Garvin, Rec. Sec., 1122 E. Market St.

El Pescadero No. 82, Tracy—Meets 1st and 3rd Fridays, I.O.O.F. Hall; Mrs. Mary A. Hewitson, Rec. Sec., 122 Walnut St.

Ivy No. 88, Lodi—Meets 1st and 3rd Wednesdays, Eagles Hall; Mrs. Mae Corson, Rec. Sec., 109 So. School St.

Calix de Oro No. 206, Stockton—Meets 1st and 3rd Tuesdays, N.S.G.W. Hall, 314 E. Main St.; Mrs. Frances Germain, Rec. Sec., 450 No. Regent.

Phoebe A. Hearst No. 214, Manteca—Meets 2nd and 4th Wednesdays, I.O.O.F. Hall; Mrs. Josie M. Frederick, Rec. Sec., Route A, Box 364, Ripon.

SAN LUIS OBISPO COUNTY.

San Miguel No. 94, San Miguel—Meets 2nd and 4th Wednesday afternoons, Clemon Hall; Mrs. Nellie Wickstrom, Rec. Sec.

San Luisita No. 108, San Luis Obispo—Meets 2nd and 4th Thursdays, W.O.W. Hall; Miss Agnes M. Lee, Rec. Sec., P. O. box 584.

El Pinal No. 163, Cambria—Meets 2nd, 4th and 5th Tuesdays, N.S.G.W. Hall; Kathryn Lucheasa, Rec. Sec.

SAN MATEO COUNTY.

Bonita No. 10, Redwood City—Meets 2nd and 4th Thursdays, I.O.O.F. Hall; Mrs. Dora Wilson, Rec. Sec., 518 Middlefield Rd.

Vista del Mar No. 155, Halfmoon Bay—Meets 2nd Thursday, I.O.O.F. Hall; Elizabeth Olney, Rec. Sec.

Ano Nuevo No. 180, Pescadero—Meets 1st and 3rd Wednesdays, I.O.O.F. Hall; Mrs. Alice Mattei, Rec. Sec.

El Carmelo No. 181, Daly City—Meets 1st and 3rd Wednesdays, Masonic Hall; Mrs. Alice Mathias Oldham, Rec. Sec., 2218 26th Ave., San Francisco.

Menlo No. 211, Menlo Park—Meets 2nd and 4th Mondays, Masonic Hall; Mrs. Frances E. Maloney, Rec. Sec., P. O. box 626.

San Bruno No. 246, San Bruno—Meets 2nd and 4th Fridays, Legion Hall; Miss Mildred Foley, Rec. Sec., 217 Miller Ave., South San Francisco.

SANTA BARBARA COUNTY.

Reina del Mar No. 126, Santa Barbara—Meets 1st and 3rd Tuesdays, Pythian Castle, 222 W. Carillo St.; Mrs. Dorothy Yule, Rec. Sec., 112 Ocean Ave.

SANTA CLARA COUNTY.

San Jose No. 81, San Jose—Meets Thursdays, Catholic Women Center, 5th and San Fernando Sts.; Mrs. Nellie Fleming, Rec. Sec., Catholic Women Center.

Vendome No. 100, San Jose—Meets 2nd and 4th Wednesdays, Old Scottish Rite Temple; Miss Marie Buck, Rec. Sec., 245 Hawthorne St.

El Monte No. 205, Mountain View—Meets 2nd and 4th Fridays, American Legion Hall; Miss Elizabeth Spencer, Rec. Sec., 1620 Villa St.

Palo Alto No. 229, Palo Alto—Meets 1st and 2nd Mondays, N.S.G.W. Hall; Miss Helena G. Hansen, Rec. Sec., 531 Lytton Ave.

SANTA CRUZ COUNTY.

Santa Cruz No. 26, Santa Cruz—Meets Mondays, N.S.G.W. Hall; Mrs. May L. Williamson, Rec. Sec., 170 Walnut Ave.

El Pajaro No. 35, Watsonville—Meets 1st and 3rd Tuesdays, I.O.O.F. Hall; Miss Ruth E. Wilson, Rec. Sec., 16 Laurel St.

SHASTA COUNTY.

Camellia No. 41, Anderson—Meets 1st and 3rd Tuesdays, Masonic Hall; Mrs. Olga E. Welbourn, Rec. Sec.

Lassen View No. 98, Shasta—Meets 2nd Friday, Masonic Hall; Miss Louise Litsch, Rec. Sec.

Hiawatha No. 140, Redding—Meets 2nd and 4th Wednesdays, Moose Hall; Ruth Presleigh, Rec. Sec., Office County Clerk.

SIERRA COUNTY.

Naomi No. 36, Downieville—Meets 2nd and 4th Wednesdays, I.O.O.F. Hall; Louise C. Dubuque, Rec. Sec.

Imogen No. 134, Sierraville—Meets 2nd and 4th Saturday afternoons, Copren Hall; Mrs. Jennie Copren, Rec. Sec.

SISKIYOU COUNTY.

Eschscholtzia No. 112, Etna—Meets 1st and 3rd Wednesdays, Masonic Hall; Mrs. Bernice E. Smith, Rec. Sec.

Mountain Dawn No. 120, Sawyers Bar—Meets 2nd and last Wednesdays, I.O.O.F. Hall; Miss Edith Dunphy, Rec. Sec.

SOLANO COUNTY.

Vallejo No. 195, Vallejo—Meets 1st and 3rd Wednesdays, K.C. Hall, 820 Marin St.; Mrs. Mary Combs, Rec. Sec., 511 York St.

Mary E. Bell No. 224, Dixon—Meets 2nd and 4th Thursdays, I.O.O.F. Hall; Mary Young, Rec. Sec.

SONOMA COUNTY.

Sonoma No. 209, Sonoma—Meets 2nd and 4th Mondays, I.O.O.F. Hall; Mrs. Mae Norrbom, Rec. Sec., R.F.D., box 171.

Santa Rosa No. 217, Santa Rosa—Meets 1st and 3rd Thursdays, N.S.G.W. Hall; Mrs. Clytie L. Lewis, Rec. Sec., R.F.D. No. 4, Box 345-A.

Petaluma No. 222, Petaluma—Meets 1st and 3rd Tuesdays, Dania Hall; Mrs. Margaret M. Oeltjen, Rec. Sec., 503 Prospect St.

STANISLAUS COUNTY.

Oakdale No. 125, Oakdale—Meets 3rd Monday, McLeod Home; Mrs. Lou Reeder, Rec. Sec.

Morada No. 199, Modesto—Meets 2nd and 4th Wednesdays, I.O.O.F. Hall; Mrs. Susan Sullivan, Rec. Sec., 823 10th St.

Eldora No. 248, Turlock—Meets 1st and 3rd Mondays, Masonic Temple; Effie Lund, Rec. Sec., 312 Mitchell St.

SUTTER COUNTY.

South Butte No. 226, Sutter—Meets 1st and 3rd Mondays, N.D.G.W. Hall; Mrs. Abbie N. Vagedes, Rec. Sec.

TEHAMA COUNTY.

Berendos No. 23, Red Bluff—Meets 1st and 3rd Tuesdays, W.O.W. Hall, 200 Pine St.; Mrs. Lillie Hammer, Rec. Sec., 636 Jackson St.

In Memoriam

LOUISE EVELYN SCHREINER.

To the Officers and Members of Oneonta Parlor No. 71 N.D.G.W.—We, your committee appointed to draft resolutions of love and respect in memory of our departed sister, Louise Evelyn Schreiner, do submit the following:

Again our Heavenly Father has seen fit to enter our Parlor and take from our midst to the Grand Parlor above our beloved sister and Charter Member, Louise Evelyn Schreiner. Whereas, in view of the loss we have sustained and the greater loss sustained by those who are nearest and dearest to her, be it

Resolved, That though we bow to His divine will, our hearts are saddened by the loss of our dear sister, yet the memory of her noble life will be an inspiration to us for all time.

And at home, in the beautiful hills of God
By the valley of rest so fair,
Some day, some time, when our work is done,
With joy we shall meet her there.

To the bereaved husband and relatives we extend our heartfelt sympathy, and commend them to Him who doeth all things well. Resolved, That our Charter be draped for a period of thirty days; that a copy of these resolutions be sent to the husband of our deceased sister; that a copy be sent to The Grizzly Bear Magazine for publication, and that a copy be spread in full upon the minutes of our Parlor.

Respectfully submitted in P.D.F.A.,

MYRA RUMRILL,
VERNA H. PEERS,
HATTIE E. ROBERTS,
Committee.

Ferndale, May 26, 1933.

N.S.G.W. OFFICIAL DEATH LIST.

Containing the name, the date and the place of birth, the date of death, and the Subordinate Parlor affiliation of deceased members reported to Grand Secretary John T. Regan from May 20 to June 20, 1933:

Bloch, Ellis; San Francisco, February 23, 1861; May 23, 1933; California No. 1.

Pernau, Henry Frank; San Francisco, June 29, 1870; May 29, 1933; California No. 1.

Potts, William; El Dorado, May 4, 1858; May 9, 1933; Placerville No. 9.

Larkin, Warren; Diamond Springs, January 28, 1865; May 26, 1933; Placerville No. 9.

O'Neil, Paul Anthony; Sacramento, August 16, 1899; May 29, 1933; Sacramento No. 3.

Bawden, Richard; Grass Valley, October 14, 1881; June 14, 1933; Sacramento No. 3.

Flaherty, Thomas F.; Napa, August 15, 1880; June 3, 1933; Pacific No. 10.

Haines, George; Woodland, September 29, 1871; June 9, 1933; Fresno No. 25.

Upton, Cassius V.; Elk Grove, May 8, 1869; May 20, 1933; Elk Grove No. 41.

Hodges, Edwin Putnam; Lodi, September 28, 1890; June 6, 1933; Plymouth No. 48.

Schaffer, Henry C.; Woodland, October 2, 1876; June 9, 1933; Saint Helena No. 53.

Coughlan, George; Nevada City, December 23, 1857; May 23, 1933; Hydraulic No. 56.

Rex, Frank M.; Gint Creek, March 17, 1885; June 5, 1933; Quartz No. 58.

Davidson, John Joseph; San Francisco, February 22, 1890; May 25, 1933; Rincon No. 72.

Boden, John F.; San Francisco, May 25, 1866; May 31, 1933; Stanford No. 76.

Lemis, John Francis; Benicia, August 9, 1862; May 22, 1933; Vallejo No. 77.

Licht, Simon Louis; San Francisco, July 27, 1872; June 6, 1933; Bay City No. 104.

Walton, William Shelly; Fresno, July 23, 1887; May 12, 1933; Ramona No. 109.

Denker, Louis Andrew; Los Angeles, September 6, 1884; June 25, 1933; Ramona No. 109.

Minehan, Timothy P.; San Francisco, January 17, 1875; June 12, 1933; Precita No. 187.

Lewis, Harry J.; San Francisco, August 9, 1892; June 1, 1933; Guadalupe No. 231.

Conlon, James Edward; San Francisco, August 12, 1876; May 8, 1933; Castro No. 232.

Plevin, James Ralph; San Francisco, August 21, 1874; June 5, 1933; Castro No. 232.

TRINITY COUNTY.

Eltapome No. 55, Weaverville—Meets 2nd and 4th Thursdays, N.S.G.W. Hall; Mrs. Lou N. Fetzer, Rec. Sec.

TUOLUMNE COUNTY.

Dardanelle No. 66, Sonora—Meets Fridays, I.O.O.F. Hall; Mrs. Nettie Whitto, Rec. Sec., P.O. box 122.

Golden Era No. 99, Columbia—Meets 1st and 3rd Thursdays, N.S.G.W. Hall; Miss Irene Ponce, Rec. Sec.

Anona No. 164, Jamestown—Meets 2nd and 4th Tuesdays, I.O.O.F. Hall; Nellie Hope, Rec. Sec.

YOLO COUNTY.

Woodland No. 90, Woodland—Meets 2nd and 4th Tuesdays, N.S.G.W. Hall; Mrs. Maude Heaton, Rec. Sec., 153 College St.

YUBA COUNTY.

Marysville No. 162, Marysville—Meets 2nd and 4th Wednesdays, Liberty Hall; Miss Cecelia C. Gomes, Rec. Sec., 701 6th St.

Camp Far West No. 218, Wheatland—Meets 3rd Tuesday, I.O.O.F. Hall; Mrs. Ethel C. Brock, Rec. Sec., P. O. box 265.

AFFILIATED ORGANIZATIONS.

General Association Past Presidents—Meetings held annually in April at the home-town of Chief President; Mrs. Winifred Halter, 465 40th St., Oakland, Chief President; Mrs. Anna G. Loser, 72 Grove Lane, San Anselmo, Chief Secretary.

Past Presidents Association No. 1—Meets 1st and 3rd Mondays, N.S.G.W. Bldg., 414 Mason St., San Francisco; Mrs. Alice Ogburn, Pres.; Mrs. Leah M. Williams, Rec. Sec., 956 Pierce St., Apt. 104, San Francisco.

Past Presidents Association No. 2—Meets 2nd and 4th Mondays, "Wigwam," Pacific Bldg., 16th and Jefferson, Oakland; Anna Enos, Pres.; Mrs. Elizabeth B. Goodman, Rec. Sec., 134 Juana Ave., San Leandro.

Past Presidents Association No. 3 (Santa Clara County)—Meets 2nd Tuesday, Musicians Hall, 114 E. Santa Clara St., San Jose; Augusta Singleton, Pres.; Clara Briggs, Rec. Sec., 1336 Magnolia Ave., San Jose.

Past Presidents Association No. 4 (Sacramento County)—Meets 2nd Monday, N.S.G.W. Hall, 11th and "J" Sts., Sacramento City; Edith Kelley, Pres.; Lily May Tilden, Rec. Sec., 3225 "T" St., Sacramento.

Past Presidents Association No. 5 (Butte County)—Meets 1st Friday, homes of members, Chico and Oroville; Marie Picanco, Pres.; Ruth Brown, Rec. Sec., 1265 Leah Court, Oroville.

Past Presidents Association No. 6 (Nevada County)—Meets 4th Friday, alternately between Nevada City, Pythian Castle, and Grass Valley, Edna Sampson's home; Margaret V. Nolan, Pres.; Vere Hansen, Rec. Sec., R.F.D. No. 2, box 41-C, Grass Valley.

Past Presidents Association No. 7 (Sonoma County)—Meets 2nd Tuesday, Ruby Berger home, 327 College Ave., Santa Rosa; Ruby Berger, Pres.; Ann M. Beach, Rec. Sec., R.F.D. No. 4, box 528, Santa Rosa.

Past Presidents Association No. 8 (San Joaquin and Stanislaus Counties)—Meets 2nd Thursday, Red Men Hall, Stockton; Mrs. Lois Armstrong, Pres.; Mrs. Harriet F. Corr, Rec. Sec., 729 E. Sonora St., Stockton.

Native Sons and Native Daughters Central Committee on Homeless Children—Main Office, 955 Phelan Bldg., San Francisco; Mrs. John W. Stirling, Chmn.; Miss Mary E. Brusie, Sec. Los Angeles branch office, 3924 Sunset Blvd.; Dorothy Schlingman, Sec.

(ADVERTISEMENT.)

ADMISSION DAY

SANTA ROSA—SANTA ROSA PARLOR NO. 28 N.S.G.W. is making good progress with its plans for the statewide Admission Day, September 9, celebration to be held in this city by the Native Sons and the Native Daughters. Commencing July 7, the general celebration committee of the Parlor, headed by Wes Colgan, will meet every Friday night. Grand Marshal Gaín Hurst has appointed City Manager Charles O. Dunbar (Santa Rosa No. 28)—just recently named Federal Collector of Customs at San Francisco by President Franklin D. Roosevelt—chief of staff, and Sonoma County Sheriff Mike Flohr (Petaluma No. 27) chief aide.

Dr. W. C. Shipley, chairman of the parade committee, had a meeting June 8 with the marshals of all the Sonoma County Parlors and plans were outlined which have been submitted to the Parlors for approval. Chairman George Gilman of the housing committee reports reservations going fast. Chairman Art Janssen of the competitive drill committee has directed questionaires to all Subordinate Parlors with drum corps or drill teams, and a prompt response is urged.

EAST BAY GETTING READY.

Oakland—Native Son and Native Daughter Parlors of the east San Francisco Bay district have organized to arrange for participation in the Santa Rosa Admission Day celebration. Officers of the joint general committee are Allen N. Sunkler (Athens No. 195), chairman, and Grand Secretary Sallie R. Thaler (Aloha No. 106), secretary. Chairmen of subcommittees include Arnold Halstead, publicity; Grand Trustee Edward T. Schnarr, parade; Adrian Merle Hynes, observance.

Prosperity Sign—Indian legend holds that the great cross of snow that has appeared again this year on the slope of Mount Tallac, overlooking Lake Tahoe, is a sign of prosperity. This white cross has been evident on the mountain in various years for untold centuries, and the story is that summers following its appearance are certain to bring prosperity.

LOS ANGELES
CITY AND COUNTY

THE NATIVE SONS AND THE NATIVE Daughters of Los Angeles had annual Memorial Day services in their Memorial Grove at Griffith Park, May 30. Mrs Mary Noerenberg was chairman of the committee of arrangements, and Henry G. Bodkin presided. The program included:

Salute to The Flag, R.O.T.C. of John Marshall high school, directed by Major D. B. Knape; "Star Spangled Banner," Marybelle Chapman and assemblage; invocation, Rev. Ernest Ford; vocal solo, Miss Mabel Straube, accompanied by Mrs. Clinton Skinner; address, "Pioneer Mothers and Native Daughters," Mrs. Leiland Atherton Irish; address, "Eulogy to the Native Sons," Dwight Crittenden; vocal solo, Mrs. George Sabichi, accompanied by Miss Harriet Seeger; dedication of tree by Mrs. John C. Porter to the memory of her parents, Mr. and Mrs. Benjamin Franklin Lee; dedication of tree by Charles F. Maguire, in behalf of Dr. Frank F. Barham, to the memory of the latter's parents, Richard Marion and Martha Medora (Arnold) Barham, Pioneers of '49; dedication of trees by Dr. George Sabichi to the memory of his father, Frank Sabichi, and his grandfather, William Wolfskill; dedication of tree by Loring E. Kent, on behalf of Glendale Parlor No. 264 N.S.G.W., to the memory of Raymond McGrath; dedication of trees by Henry G. Bodkin, on behalf of Hollywood Parlor No. 196 N.S.G.W., to the memory of W. Joseph Ford, Henry Sloss and Wayne Early Jordan; reminiscences, Pioneer Joseph Messmer; "I Love You, California," Marybelle Chapman and assemblage; benediction, Rev. Lewis Mulvihill. Past Grand Presidents Herman C. Lichtenberger and John T. Newell, and Grand Trustee Eldred L. Meyer of the Native Sons were among the many in attendance.

FLAG DAY AT CASA FIGUEROA.

Flag Day, June 14, four flags were presented to Casa Figueroa—the Spanish, by Mrs. Arrata de Voorhees; the Mexican, by Eugene Plummer; the California State (Bear), by President Mattie Labory Gara on behalf of Los Angeles Parlor No. 124 N.D.G.W.; the United States of America, by Dr. Owen C. Coy, director of the California State Historical Association.

Dr. Coy, the speaker of the day, gave an interesting and educational talk on California history, and stated that history has much more of real romance than any fiction that could be written. Refreshments were served by the casa hostess, Mrs. Anita Begue Packman, assisted by Mrs. Julie Patroli, Florence D. Schoneman, Teresa L. Bouttier, Maria Walsh and others.

ORGANIZE FOR MEMBERSHIP BUILDING.

At the call of Grand Trustee Eldred L. Meyer, the presidents and the first vice-presidents of the Native Son Parlors in Los Angeles County, together with many deputy and district deputy grand presidents, had a very interesting meeting June 20 at which much was accomplished. The group decided to request the Parlors of the county to co-operate in a drive for new members on a large scale. The names of desirable eligibles are to be procured from various sources, and large rallies, at which good programs will be featured, are planned under the auspices of the combined Parlors.

President Henry G. Bodkin of Hollywood No. 196 was appointed chairman of this new Central Membership Committee. A luncheon club was also organized, with President Leslie Packard of Los Angeles No. 45 as chairman. The first gathering was held June 23. All members of the Order are invited to the meetings of the luncheon club.

The group also went on record to urge Parlors in the district to support the statewide Admission Day celebration at Santa Rosa, and to request the local Interparlor N.S.G.W. and N.D.G.W. Committee to prepare for some kind of September 9 celebration in or around Los Angeles for those unable to go to Santa Rosa. A committee was appointed to arrange publicity for the Order of Native Sons in this district. The Central Membership Committee will meet again July 11 at 7:30 p.m. at the office of Henry G. Bodkin.—W.H.O.

OFFICERS TO BE PUBLICLY INSTALLED.

Los Angeles Parlor No. 124 N.D.G.W. elected officers June 7, Miss Dolores Malin being chosen president. Mothers Day was observed May 31, and under the chairmanship of Ann Shiebusch a delightful evening was enjoyed. The final party of the bridge tourney, June 14, was a success in every particular. Flora Holy (chairman), Ruth Ruiz, Lucy Malin, Olinda Kerby, Margaret Carter, Sophia Stewart and Adele White had charge of the clubhouse party June 28; there was a big crowd, and a goodly sum was cleared. The sewing circle spent a pleasant afternoon at the Montebello home of Jennie Raymond; chairman Mildred Ripling presented an attractive box of dainty articles.

Los Angeles' July calendar includes: 5th, initiation. 8th, sewing club meeting at home of Bertha Murray; phone reservations to PL 3268. 12th, beach party; Esther Renne, chairman. 19th, potluck dinner and speaker. 26th, public installation officers.

CO-OPERATION ASSURES GROWTH.

Compton—Compton Parlor No. 273 N.S.G.W., considerably shaken shortly after its institution, is showing the real pioneer spirit and making fine progress. Three candidates were initiated June 13, and the ritual was exemplified by the Parlor officers, headed by President Dr. Laurence W. Cowan, in a very creditable manner. Large delegations were present from Sepulveda Parlor No. 263 and Santa Monica Bay Parlor No. 267, and the former turned over to Compton sixteen dollars, the returns from a dance given for No. 273's benefit. The Parlor and its officers were highly commended by Grand Trustee Eldred L. Meyer, Grand Inside Sentinel William A. Reuter, District Deputy Arthur Leonard and Deputy Grand President Walter Odemar.

"With the wonderful co-operation given by adjacent Parlors and the endeavors of its own members, Compton will keep on growing," says Secretary William Don Castillo.

FIVE INITIATED.

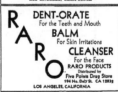

Glendale—The new corps of officers of Ver-go Parlor No. 240 N.D.G.W. will be headed Sarah Burleson, elected president June 13. ve candidates were initiated, and a baby spoon s presented the son of Theresa Dempski. Past esident Betty Sanders came up from Brawley · the initiation. Preceding the meeting, mo-n pictures of the Lake Tahoe region were own.

June 14 the Parlor had a successful bridge rty at Chevy Chase Country Club. Evelyn ilson was in charge. Verdugo has adopted a meless baby, named Hazel Vera, in honor of and Inside Sentinel Hazel Hansen and Presi-nt Vera Carlson.

PAST PRESIDENT HONORED.

Santa Monica—Santa Monica Bay Parlor No. 7 N.S.G.W. June 7 honored Past President J. oward Blanchard at a dinner. Also present ere members of Troop No. 10 Boy Scouts of nerica, sponsored by the Parlor, who put on brief program. Blanchard has been in charge the troop the past five years. Two candidates ere initiated at the meeting following the din-r, President Arthur Leonard and his officers emplifying the ritual. The next past presi-nt to be honored is William Dowsing.

June 21, the Parlor held its annual pioneer ght dance. Three hundred people attended, ostly attired in pioneer costume. Bert Bair's ative Son orchestra furnished the music. A idsummer dinner dance in Santa Monica is eing planned for early August, with an added ature of midnight swimming. Carol Loftner's urteen-piece orchestra will furnish the music. ull particulars in the next issue of The Grizzly ear.

LOVELY YARD SCENE OF ACTIVITIES.

Long Beach—The thimble club of Long Beach arlor No. 154 N.D.G.W. met June 8 in the vely yard at Gussie Taber's home and sewed or the needy, and June 29 a steak bake was eld there for members, their families and iends. June 15 plans were made for a cooked-ood sale at the municipal market July 1. The ommittee in charge includes Alice Waldow chairman), Mabel Emery, Gertrude Riddle and 'iolet Henshilwood.

BIG CROWD AT BIRTHDAY FEAST.

Ramona Parlor No. 109 N.S.G.W. had a very argely attended meeting June 2, when questions f finance were discussed and officers were elect-d. Charles Straube was chosen for president, nd John V. Scott was retained as secretary. 'he institution anniversary outing to Catalina une 11 attracted some 300 and was very en-oyable. Among the assistants of Charles traube, in charge of arrangements, were Ray tehart, Walter Slosson, Homer Chapelle, Walter demar, Ernest Orfila and Walter Baskerville. 'he June birthday dinner, prepared by "Chef" harles Gassagne and assistants, was exception-lly well attended. After the feast came a pro-ram, presented by The California Golden Song irds under the direction of Constance Henry leauer. Scoutmaster Robert E. Dunn wants to orrow equipment for the Yosemite outing of tamona Troop No. 109 Boy Scouts of America.

Ramona's July program includes: 7th, instal-ation officers. 14th, initiation. 21st, monthly irthday dinner, also honoring Grand Trustee ildred L. Meyer; First Vice-president Walter demar, directing, promises a special attraction.

"SYMPHONIES UNDER THE STARS."

The twelfth annual season of "symphonies under the stars" will open Tuesday, July 11, in the Hollywood Bowl. Many innovations on this summer's programs are expected to prove espe-cially attractive to music lovers. Alfred Hertz, "father of the Bowl," will conduct the opening concert, to be followed the remainder of the first week by Nicholas Slonimsky, one of the finest symphonic leaders in the world. The first ballot will be presented Saturday, July 15, when Fan-chon and Marco, nationally-known stage pro-ducers, will off r a colorful spectacle.

One of the innovations this year will be a series of "twilight" concerts late Sunday after-noons. These probably will start between 5 and 7 o'clock, Manager Glenn M. Tindall says. The exact starting hour will be announced later. This is the first time in the Bowl's history that Sunday programs have been a part of the reg-ular season.

Concerts will be presented Tuesday, Thursday and Saturday nights, and Sunday evenings, for eight weeks, concluding September 3. A new scale of admission prices adopted by the Sym-phonies Under the Stars Foundation makes fifty cents the minimum for each program. Season book tickets will be good for all events.

PERSONAL PARAGRAPHS.

A native son arrived at the home of John J. Herlihy (Hollywood N.S.) June 4.

Mrs. Edith B. Schallmo (Los Angeles N.D.) vacationed in San Francisco last month.

Miss Margaret Nash (Los Angeles N.D.) and sister en-joyed a vacation in Honolulu.

Sheriff Eugene W. Biscailuz (Santa Monica Bay N.S.) became a grandfather May 25.

Mrs. Grace Haven (Los Angeles N.D.) visited with rela-tives in Marin County last month.

Herman C. Lichtenberger (Past Grand President N.S.) was a visitor to San Francisco last month.

Mrs. Lily O. R. Dyer (Founder N.D.) after a visit of several months has returned to San Francisco.

A native daughter arrived May 28 at the Long Beach home of Mrs. Leola Temby (Long Beach N.D.).

John R. Quinn (Los Angeles N.S.) has been elected chairman Los Angeles County Board Supervisors.

Justice Emmet Seawell (Grand President N.S.) of the California Supreme Court was a visitor last month.

Mrs. Olive W. Lopez (Californiana N.D.) last month vis-ited the Century of Progress Exposition at Chicago.

Miss Jeanette Hunt and Edward L. Baker, son of Coun-cilman G. W. C. Baker (Ramona N.S.), were wedded June 14.

Miss Dorothy Roche and Charles A. Johnson (Ramona N.S.) were wedded May 29. They are residing in Santa Monica.

Samuel M. Shortridge Jr. (Menlo N.S.) of San Francisco paid a brief visit last month on his way home from Wash-ington, D. C.

Mrs. Kate McFadyen (Long Beach N.D.) has returned to her Long Beach home after a three-month visit with her daughter, Mrs. Marie Monroe, in Pendleton, Oregon.

THE DEATH RECORD.

Mrs. Eliza Gray, mother of Mrs. W. H. Morrow (Long Beach N.D.), died at Downey. She was a native of Illi-nois, aged 84.

Mrs. Marjorie Alice Reinschemidt, sister of John D. Home (Ramona N.S.), died May 24.

William Allen Packard, father of Leslie A. Packard (Los Angeles N.S.), died May 23. He was a native of Maine, aged 88. He was a Civil War veteran, and for many years resided in Napa County.

Louis A. Denker, affiliated with Ramona Parlor No. 109 N.S.G.W., died May 25, survived by two daughters. He was born in Los Angeles, September 6, 1884.

Charles E. Donnatin, father of Mrs. Paul Robinson (Los Angeles N.D.), died June 10. He was a native of Germany, aged 84. At his obsequies, Leo V. Youngworth (Ramona N.S.) delivered a eulogy.

Roger B. Cornell, affiliated with Santa Monica Bay Parlor No. 267 N.S.G.W., died June 22. He was born in Berkeley, Alameda County, July 25, 1884.

United States Marshal Albert C. Sittel, affiliated with Ramona Parlor No. 109 N.S.G.W., died June 23 at Redondo. He was born in Los Angeles, October 1, 1876.

GRIZZLY GROWLS

(Continued from Page 15)

the opposing faction known as the Canton China-men are concentrated to the number of two or three hundreds, armed with implements similar to those in the hands of the Hong Kong men with the exception of muskets. Today a large team, partly loaded with spears, battle axes and provinder started from this town, and large bodies of Chinamen are en route for the scene of expected hostilities."

The letter goes on to say the county sheriff had shown no inclination to interfere. For that reason, Brigadier-General Cazneau sets forth he will have to act himself to keep down the ex-pected battle. "In view of meeting the contin-gency," he wrote, "I have directed Sergeant Throckmorton with Privates Ward and Mullins of the Fusileers to proceed to Chinese Camp with twenty stands of arms." No letter telling how the soldiers fared against the 700 or 800 Chinese has yet been found.

"A decent and manly examination of the acts of government should be not only tolerated but encouraged."—President William Henry Harri-son.

Know your home-state, California! Learn of its past history and of its present-day development by reading regularly The Grizzly Bear. $1.50 for one year (12 issues). Subscribe now.

Feminine World's Fads and Fancies

PREPARED ESPECIALLY FOR THE GRIZZLY BEAR BY ANNA STOERMER

NEW BRIDAL GOWNS VARY IN TYPES. It is a funny thing about wedding dresses. They are alike, and yet different. Most brides wear long and rather high-necked satin or crepe dresses. The veil may or may not be lace. But somehow the ingredients combine in more different ways than there are colors to the rainbow. Therefore, do not let saleswomen or dressmakers tell you what sort of dress you want, if you understand your type. Roughly speaking, there are three sorts—the romantic bride, the very chic and simple bride, and the very feminine bride. All three sorts are charming in the right girl.

The white satin wedding gown with sweeping train and filmy veil is back in the glamorous bridal pageant. The fashionable brides who are sweeping down the aisles of the historic old churches have chosen bridal gowns of dead white, instead of the pale blues and pinks formerly in vogue. Longer trains are the rule; some of them sweep the floor for two yards. Many of the veils trail almost the length of the train, being designed to fall over the bride's face when she enters the church, and to be swept back from it when she leaves.

Guests who attend fashionable weddings should dress as formally as the bride. Rich crepes and velvets make up frocks which are designed on long, slender lines with skirts about ankle length. The most popular wrap is an elbow or waist length cape made of fur or fabric to match the frock.

Hats vary from broad-brimmed straws to small toques trimmed with flowers or lacquered leaves, and are often finished with a nose veil filming the eyes.

The bride's boquet is conventionally round and is made of gardenias. The florists have helpful suggestions. A pretty effect is gotten by attaching sprigs to the silk markers of a prayer book, if one be carried. Flower muffs are also popular, but must be kept small or they will look heavy. Some brides like real orange blossoms worked into the cap which holds the veil. This must be done carefully, to avoid appearing heavy and pretentious.

It is not difficult to find appropriate gifts for the bride who will motor travel on the wedding trip. Articles useful and luxurious are also plentiful for the one who is to prepare a home. The list is endless, from rugs to silver. If the bride cares for color, there is the new cutlery, or to be more modish in expression, the flat ware may be purchased in any favored color.

Cotton has gone grand, for it sweeps everything before it all day long. It started modestly, as the basis of simple evening dresses of the sort worn on a boat, at parties, beach clubs, or home affairs. Now it is the bright particular star of the grandest ball.

Organdie has been jeweled and sequined and generally bedecked, but it is really most successful when it keeps its own character. So flattering is organdie that it is easy to select something in this youthful fabric as a gift for the young girl. It is used for trimmings, blouses, jackets, hats, neckwear and gloves.

The fabric glove is proving very popular, always matching the frock. Gloves are determined to be different from day to day. White gloves have gauntlet tops with black linen applique on the flare. These novel gloves are an excellent accompaniment to the black linen suit or frock.

Black linen is an insistent note in coats, frocks and other feminine apparel. So we find it with white trim in frocks and swagger coats, the newest offering in the way of the somber linen weaves. Linen is generally classed with the cotton family, a little heavier than the handkerchief sort, but very fine and proving how wide the range of color can be.

The plaid is either squared or biased. Plaids of indestructible organdie are a good investment, and may be had in every color of the rainbow. They are seen at all smart affairs. Slim, straight and well fitted, seems to be the general formula for this season's styles, with variations in both fabric and design serving to give the smart and individual touch to the costume.

With the return to favor of cotton materials comes the re-establishment of the all-over cotton lace frock, of coarse design, made over a deep blue voile slip. The dress is sleeveless, and the slip fastens high around the throat instead of turning back with the dress lapels, a note which is quite novel and interesting. A dark belt with a jeweled buckle, a white or blue hat and pumps are worn with this costume.

A new note for cotton is the frock made of string lace. Many beautiful designs are shown in varied colors. Suits are also made of string lace, loosely woven in a sort of homespun effect. These look cool, and may be kept fresh and unmussed.

The loose, informally-cut coat is worn with a crispy striped red-and-white gillet buttoning down the front, and topped with a scarf pinned with a crystal clip. A red-and-white striped hat, and red shoes and bag complete this costume. Who would ever dream that string could make such gorgeous looking frocks?

If you go in for all of the summer sports, your wardrobe will, of course, include a bathing suit and many pairs of slacks and shorts. You will be very modern in stripes or very dashing in solid colors, or you may mix your colors.

Fishing, hunting, hiking, swimming, golfing, tennis and bicycling each calls for its own clothing, which is designed to afford a maximum of exposure to the sun's rays, plus unrestricted freedom of action.

Bathing suits are more colorful than heretofore. It seems yellows are most popular, but the blues are fine. Brilliant hues are among the favorites for the younger set. Suits have been reduced and reduced until now they are as near minimum as the law allows. A sunburn can be most painful and even dangerous, so one must cover up.

White knitted slacks are tailored as a man's. They are worn with a simple red knitted shirt opened at the neck, and are vastly becoming. Shirt and slacks meet with a red-and-white canvas belt.

A WESTERN GARDEN

(EDNA BIGGS.)

Behold the palm, the tropic's pride,
Fanning the fir that stands by her side;
The fir, all drooping and swaying,
Wishing for snow, yet not dismaying.
The pool, with its flowers and fishes,
Stirs the heart like fleeting wishes;
The little rock garden, with cactus and sedum,
Tells of the desert and its dull, lonely freedom.
Rare plants from Africa, China and Asia,
All nod together by the fragrant acacia.
'Round cottage, mansion, on hillside, plain,
The gardens are growing in sunshine and rain;
True altars of beauty, and pride, and love,
Scattering incense to Heaven above.

(This verse came to The Grizzly Bear from Edna Biggs of Martinez, Contra Costa County.—Editor.)

Reforestation Progress—Trees were planted on 24,900 acres of denuded areas in the national forests during 1932, reports the Federal Forest Service.

Intercollegiate Races will be held at the Long Beach Marine Stadium July 7 and 8. Harvard, Yale, Cornell, Washington and California Universities will be represented.

Grizzly Bear

AUGUST THE ONLY OFFICIAL PUBLICATION OF THE NATIVE SONS AND DAUGHTERS OF THE GOLDEN WEST **1933**

Fancies

WESTERN GARDEN

(EDNA BIGGS.)

JULY

edding Sale

Beginning June 26th, is more important this year than ever, with prices rising as they are.

We placed orders for this sale last February, already anticipating this, and offer our patrons all sorts of bedding, mattresses, etc., at genuine

Read the daily papers

"No man is worth his salt who is not ready at all times to risk his body, to risk his well-being, to risk his life, in a great cause."—Theodore Roosevelt.

The Grizzly Bear Magazine

The ALL California Monthly

OWNED, CONTROLLED, PUBLISHED BY GRIZZLY BEAR PUBLISHING CO., (Incorporated) COMPOSED OF NATIVE SONS.

HERMAN C. LICHTENBERGER, Pres.
JOHN T. NEWELL RAY HOWARD
WILLIAM I. TRAEGER
CHAS. R. THOMAS HARRY J. LELANDE
ARTHUR A. SCHMIDT, Vice-Pres.
BOARD OF DIRECTORS

CLARENCE M. HUNT
General Manager and Editor

OFFICIAL ORGAN AND THE ONLY OFFICIAL PUBLICATION OF THE NATIVE SONS AND THE NATIVE DAUGHTERS OF THE GOLDEN WEST.

ISSUED FIRST OF EACH MONTH.
FORMS CLOSE 20th MONTH.
ADVERTISING RATES ON APPLICATION.

SAN FRANCISCO OFFICE:
N.S.G.W. BLDG., 414 MASON ST., ROOM 302
(Office Grand Secretary N.S.G.W.)
Telephone: KEarny 1223
SAN FRANCISCO, CALIFORNIA

PUBLICATION OFFICE:
309-15 WILCOX BLDG., 2nd AND SPRING,
Telephone: VAndike 6234
LOS ANGELES, CALIFORNIA

(Entered as second-class matter May 29, 1918, at the Postoffice at Los Angeles, California, under the act of August 24, 1912.)

PUBLISHED REGULARLY SINCE MAY 1907

VOL. LIII (53). WHOLE NO. 816

GRIZZLY GROWLS

(CLARENCE M. HUNT.)

PRESIDENT FRANKLIN ROOSEVELT has launched his National Industrial Recovery program, and it promises to be, as it should be, a grand success. It is estimated that it will result in the re-employment of at least 2,500,000 now-idle persons, and will add around $34,000,000 to weekly payrolls. The whole program is devoted to the problem of re-employment, and the expressed objective of the national administration is to solve the problem by Labor Day, September 4, of this year. No force will be used in the campaign "except conscience and opinion," —most effective weapons.

"This is a test of patriotism," says a bulletin issued in connection with the program. "It is the time to demonstrate the faith of our fathers and our belief in ourselves. We are a people of disciplined democracy to a self-control—sufficient to unite our purchasing power—our labor power—our management power to carry out this great national covenant with vigor, with determination, but with the calm composure and fair play which should always mark the American way."

July 27, a letter from President Roosevelt was delivered to every employer in the United States along with a form of agreement pledging the employer's acceptance of the re-employment program. "This agreement," he says, "is part of a nation-wide plan to raise wages, create employment, and thus increase purchasing power and restore business. That plan depends wholly on united action by all employers. For this reason I ask you, as an employer, to do your part by signing." What the President is asking of all employers of more than two persons is: that child labor be abolished; that a $14 to $15 minimum wage and a forty-hour week be established for the white-collar class; that a 30 to 40 cents an hour minimum wage and a thirty-five hours maximum week with an eight-hour day maximum be set for factory and mechanical labor.

From recent occurrences, it is presumed that a determined effort will be made to have the next Federal Congress amend the Exclusion Law, so that "immigrants from Japan and certain other countries of the Far East whose nationals are not eligible to citizenship in the United States may be admitted on the same basis as is now open to so-called quota nations."

The yellow-dollar, in the guise of goodwill, is the real impelling motive behind this plan to open the immigration gates to Japs—to make California and the Pacific Coast of the United States safe and sure for Japan! Many powerful organizations, church and civic, are sponsoring the Jap-quota proposal, and unless those having the welfare of California at heart take steps to stop the Jap conquest of American opinion and be constantly on guard, the law will be amended to the satisfaction of the Japs, both yellow and white.

Secretary V. S. McClatchy of the California Joint Immigration Committee cautions: "We should, as does Japan, take care that in inviting the good-will of other nations we do not sacrifice the vital welfare of our own country."

"Tax tigers are eating up the nation's resources," says the "San Francisco Chronicle" editorially. "While business starves, workers take pay slashes and everyone struggles under depleted income, the levies for federal, state, county and city taxes go on virtually unchecked. An incredible number of taxing agencies continue to heap burdens on the people struggling to get back to some normal balance. . . . A very large part of the expenditure that makes up the tax levy is dead weight, charges on public debts gayly assumed in more prosperous days, long-term bonds on which the return is guaranteed by iron clad contracts. . . . The tax tigers got into the corral in better times, purring like house cats and ingratiating themselves with the family. Even in those days it was noticeable that they ate a great deal but they pleaded that it was only scraps from the table. Shrinkage of income has not been accompanied by corresponding reduction of taxes. The lower the income falls, the greater the proportion of the taxes. This is the most serious menace to every program for recovery." The people of California, incidentally, are going to pay more taxes, in one form and another, than ever before. And much of the increased tax-revenue will go to continue financing wasteful extravagances in state, county and city governments. The cost of government must be reduced, by kicking the political racketeers out of government.

Marriages and divorces are decreasing throughout the nation. In California last year the percentage decrease was, respectively, 9.2 and 6.7 percent. That's not to be wondered at. The laws of both God and man are, with general approval and applaud, openly transgressed. Why, therefore, bother about a marriage ceremony, or go to the expense and trouble of obtaining a divorce? As a nation, we are liberal minded. So, eliminate the camouflage and legalize what has, to our shame, become a custom—"free love."

Addressing the National Congress of Parents and Teachers at Seattle, Dr. Anthony Blanks of the University of California pleaded for America to return to basic simplicities and homely living. "Yesterday men frequently spent all their lives with the same wife and dad could snooze on the old horsehair sofa without being disturbed by some crooner from Medicine Hat," Dr. Blanks said. "Today Reno is a national shrine and the old-fashioned three R's have become rouge, rum and runabouts. This apparently frivolous way of stating a very serious situation implies that yesterday we had some standards that were positive. We knew where we were going."

In an address to the Civilian Conservation Corps of 300,000 young men July 17, President Franklin Roosevelt said: "Too much in recent years, large numbers of our population have sought out success as an opportunity to gain money with the least possible work. It is time for each and every one of us to cast away self-destroying, nation-destroying efforts to get something for nothing and to appreciate that satisfying reward and safe reward come only through honest work. That must be the new spirit of the American future."

The Japs and the Mexis in the southland have been having labor troubles among themselves. In a statement, the Mexican Consul called attention "to the intolerable working conditions, the employment of child labor and the inhumanly low wage scale of from 6 cents an hour for children and from 9 to 13 cents for adults paid to Mexican agricultural workers employed by Japanese farmers in Los Angeles and Orange Counties." The Federal Government should cure that sore by deporting all concerned!

The National Railroad Workers' Syndicate of Mexico has asked that government to compel the discharge of Americans employed on railroads in Lower California. The Mexican government should do that very thing, in fairness to its nationals, and the United States Government, in fairness to its nationals, should compel the railroads operating in California to discharge all Mexis employed by them.

It is to laugh! The drug stores are howling because butcher shops, fruit stands and most other lines of business are now retailing drugs. It's all right, of course, for the pillrollers to sell hardware, confections, etc., and to engage in the restaurant business, but it's all wrong, so they contend, for others to butt in on the drug-line. The so-called drug store of today is, in fact, a department store, and should be so classified.

THINK THIS OVER!

The order of Native Sons of the Golden West is, we believe, with the exception of the Order of Native Daughters of the Golden West, the only organization that limits membership exclusively to NATIVE-BORN AMERICANS.

Knowing the serious conditions in this country today, this fact alone should impel every Native Son of California to immediately SEEK AFFILIATION with that American-born and American-operated institution, the man-power and wealth of which are pledged to the protection of American institutions in times of peace as well as in times of war.

Representative Doughton, chairman of the Federal House ways and means committee, assures that "by the January session of Congress we will have plans to stop tax-dodging." Let's hope the plans do not go astray. And the Congress should, also, remove all exemptions, including the horde of public officeholders and employes, from the income tax law.

"Advertising is like liniment," remarks an exchange. "It is not very effective when applied with a feather, but needs to be rubbed in for results. One or two applications should not be expected to bring adequate relief for a sick business"—or organization.

This declaration of the "Livermore Herald" has the right ring: "No sympathy whatsoever will [should] be wasted on those Americans who have lost their happy homes in Europe, Paris especially, because of the drop in the value of United States currency. We will accept them back in this country because we have to, but we would just as soon force them to stay in France if we could and let them struggle along as best they could. If the land of their birth was not good enough for them in their prosperity, it should not be good enough for them in the days of their adversity. But that class was never noted for strength of character, and will now, as usual, take the easiest way out."

Pro-Japists have often given assurance that Japan has done away with dual citizenship, in deference to American opinion. Little credence can be placed, however, on any statement emanating from Jap sources; the Japs promise anything, for publicity effect, and continue on their course. This Associated Press dispatch from Honolulu was dated June 23: "Victor S. K. Houston, former congressional delegate from Hawaii, told a meeting of Japanese-Americans here today the 'real reason' for President Roosevelt's request for authority to appoint a non-resident governor of Hawaii was the preponderance of Japanese residents in the islands. Houston said suspicion had arisen on the mainland because many American citizens of Japanese ancestry here still hold dual allegiance to America and Japan. He urged renunciation of Japanese citizenship by residents of the territory." Many, if not all, Japs in California also still hold that dual allegiance. Why?

These headings appeared recently in newspapers of the state: "You Can Still Have the Sun for $1 a Year." Listens like the croon of a get-rich-quicker. "Be Careful in Driving Over the Holidays." How about humans? The holidays will live on, care or no care. "Many Attend 3 Forks Fete." Many, also, attend no-forks and no-clothes fetes.

A submerged mountain has been found in the Pacific by the Federal Coast and Geodetic Survey. It lies about fifty-two miles southwestward from Point Sur in California, and rises from depths of approximately 2,000 fathoms. The mountain runs in a north and south direction and if the ocean were to be drained it would show up as an isolated mountain 7,500 feet in elevation. The discovery was made by the Survey ship "Guide" which is now engaged in hydrographic surveys off California.

Ray W. Howard, newspaper publisher, arrived in San Francisco July 7 from a tour of the Far East, and expressed the opinion that the American Navy should be brought up to full treaty quota immediately. "The fact is," he said, "that the Japanese public has become convinced that America is too penurious to fight. In that misconception lies real danger. . . . The last two years have demonstrated that so far as the Far East is concerned America's efforts to substitute reason for force in international disagreements were premature." In brief, the pacifists of this nation should be muzzled, and our lights should be brightly burning when the day of reckoning comes, and come it must and will.

"The operations of the government affect the interests of every person living within the jurisdiction of the United States."—President William Howard Taft.

"All the doors that lead inward to the secret place of the Most High are doors outward—out of self, out of smallness, out of wrong."—George Macdonald.

1933 CALIFORNIA STATE FAIR WILL TYPIFY SPIRIT OF PEOPLE

(HAROLD J. McCURRY,
Sacramento Postmaster, Fair Director.)

THE SEVENTY-NINTH ANNUAL CALIFORNIA State Fair, to be held in Sacramento September 2 to 9, will bring to life the days of '49 in a vivid expression of the spirit, past and present, of California. Once, the annual State Fair was a simple harvest festival where people met to display and admire the soil-given wealth of this land of fruits and flowers. But the wealth sources of the state have multiplied since that simple beginning. Today, a California harvest festival must include the harvests of industry as well as the harvests of the soil.

California has a richness that no exhibit of oranges, peaches, cows, or tractors can express. This richness is the spirit of California people. To appreciate that wealth of spirit, you must be one of the thousands who come to the Fair to express joy in the present and confidence in the future. The spirit of California can only be seen in the faces of Californians.

This year, the directors of the Fair searched for a more concrete expression of the spirit of California. September 8 has been dedicated to mining,—California Mining Day. It will include gold-panning contests, a double-hand jack drilling contest, displays of mining machinery, exhibitions of old-time square dances, scenes re-lived from the days of '49. The mining parade will be a vivid picturization of the actual days of '49. Everyone who attends the Fair that day is urged to come dressed in the picturesque costumes of by-gone days.

Mining Day will bring to life the traditions upon which California was founded,—the spirit of '49. But more than that, it will be a modern exhibit of the spirit of today. Today, when once again our streams are lined with patient panners of gold; when once again the whirr of machinery can be heard at our mines. Today, when gold must again be added to the long list of important products of this Golden State. Mining Day is but one of the many features planned for the 1933 California State Fair, to give the largest and most representative display of California resources ever shown.

Yet, four months ago no one knew whether there would be a California State Fair this year. Faced with the most difficult financial problems it has ever faced, the State Legislature seriously considered the abandonment of the Fair until times were better. Faced with the fog of complete economic uncertainty, the people of the state were in no mood for festivities, yet, undaunted, they voted to continue this time-honored institution, their Fair. Slowly the fog lifted. Plans were no longer half-hearted. In every part of the state the great need to rejoice that no longer was California living under an "uncertain tomorrow" found expression in hearty and lavish plans for the State Fair. The day-by-day growth of plans would make a temperature chart of the rising spirits of Californians that even those who run might read and, reading, heartily rejoice.

Sensing the need in the heart of every Californian to gather together and rejoice, the directors of the State Fair have instituted two new policy changes, planning thereby to make the Fair more easily accessible to anyone and everyone.

With the exception of the working press who so faithfully keep all of California informed of the progress of the Fair, and of the exhibitors who actively participate with entries, absolutely no passes will be issued this year. Everyone will pay his small bit for entrance to the Fair.

The companion measure to this "no-pass" policy is a reduction of fifty percent in the admission price. This price reduction in "seeing the fair" is made possible by the pre-sale of scrip books. Patrons can walk through the gates this year for twenty-five cents, instead of fifty cents, provided they have purchased a scrip book. Each book will contain five dollars' worth of admissions, but can be purchased for two dollars and fifty cents any time during August and up to and including the first day of the Fair.

Accompanying all the visible evidence that depressions cannot stem the steady flow of California's basic wealth, will be the entertainment features. Prize contests for young and old, and all of the traditional Fair entertainment will be there. Spelling bees, bicycle races, children's competitions,—there will be things to watch and things to do. But perhaps the most exciting of all entertainment features will be the spectacle of legal betting on horse races, possible for the first time in twenty-eight years. This will have a special meaning to those who hold the past of California close to their hearts. For it was the speed and quality of its race horses, the tense spectacles of its races, that first made California known all over the country as a sunny playground.

All in all, this year's Fair is not a fair to be missed. All will be eager to give an affirmative response to the message from President A. B. Miller of the State Agricultudal Society: "We ask you to make a special effort to visit the Fair this year, for its success depends wholly on you, and especially on those who have in the past so faithfully helped and supported us by exhibiting their stock and products. You will, after your visit, be better informed, and thoroughly satisfied that YOUR State Fair in its seventy-ninth year has lived up to its slogan of BIGGER and BETTER."

THE MINER'S TOAST

I've been over to the Weaver diggins, Jo,
The Camp whar we ust to be
Way back thar in the long ago
In the winter of Sixty-three,
I stood in the same old Cabin, Jo,
That sheltered us oft from Cold
Where the Candle's light full many a night
Shone bright on our pan of gold.

The Cabin has crumbled away, Jo;
It didn't seem quite the same
For the logs that are thar today, Jo,
Are feeding the Campers' flame,
The hearth and Chimney too, Jo,
Have crumbled away to dust
And the pick that belonged to you, Jo,
Is Covered with dirt and rust.

The dirt we used to pan, Jo,
Is only a gravel mound
And the water that ran by it, Jo,
Is sunken beneath the ground.
Thar's part of a rocker near, Jo,
The one we ust to use
And oh it brot many a tear, Jo,
And many a fit of blues.

The pan that hung on the wall, Jo,
The one we left behind,
Is rusted beyond recall, Jo,
Tho it lay where we last had mined.
It seemed to be full of gold, Jo,
As bright as the nuggets then—
As bright as the days of old, Jo,
Which never can come again.

The people I met in Shasta
Were different, new, and strange;
While some have died on the prairies wide
And others upon the range,
But those who were with us then, Jo,
The friends whom we learned to love
Are sorting ore on another shore
And working the mines above.

The few who are living now, Jo,
Are as helpless as you and I;
Death's shadow lies dark on their brow, Jo,
And the angel of death is nigh.
So here's to the good old times, Jo,
And the camp whar we ust to be;
We'll drink to the toast in rhyme, Jo.
To the winter of Sixty-three.

(The above came to The Grizzly Bear from H. H. Noonan, a member of Mount Bally Parlor No. 87 N.S.G.W., Weaverville, Trinity County, with the following notation: "I am enclosing a piece of poetry handed me by Past President E. G. Chapman of Mount Bally Parlor, which he would like to have published in The Grizzly Bear. The poetry is 'anonymous,' author not known."—Editor.)

CALIFORNIA'S WINE FAME CREDITED TO HUNGARIAN-BORN CITIZEN.

"History of Grape Growing in California," is the title of an extended, but most interesting, article in the "Index-Tribune" of Sonoma City, written by Mrs. C. G. Murphy. She says:

"The man responsible for California's vast vineyard and wine area, was Agoston Haraszthy —Hungarian born, a citizen of the United States by adoption. He was the commissioner delegated by Governor J. G. Downey of California in the year 1861 'to report on the improvement and culture of the vine in California' and to make an extended stay in Europe to observe methods of grape growing and wine making.

"To him, California owes the wealth and fame which grapes and wine brought to the Golden State before prohibition. After an eventful era, Haraszthy went to Nicaragua, where he fell into a river and was devoured by an alligator."

"Questions like the tariff and currency are literally of no consequence whatever compared with the vital questions of having the unit of our social life, the home, preserved."—Theodore Roosevelt.

Dairy Meet—The California State Dairy Council will have a convention at Crescent City, Del Norte County, August 17-19.

Homeless Children

A WORTHWHILE NON-SECTARIAN ENDEAVOR
SPONSORED AND SUPPORTED BY
THE ORDERS OF
NATIVE SONS AND NATIVE DAUGHTERS
OF THE GOLDEN WEST

The three human rights of every child—a home, a school, and a chance to play—have been given to 4,242 children through the aid of the Native Sons and the Native Daughters of the Golden West.

A HOME DOES NOT MEAN FOUR WALLS, attractive as the interior may be with luxurious furniture, a radio, one or more high-priced cars in the garage. Nor is Home a place where liquor has taken the greater share of father's earnings, and compelled mother to work in order to help with its upkeep.

Real mothers are not those whose sole aim in life is to be able to provide for their children the choicest of viands, up-to-date clothes, travel and amusements, with social obligations uppermost in their minds and hearts. A real father is not one who is too harassed by economic demands to enjoy the companionship of his wife and children, or to be interested in what each is doing.

A HOME.

When the Native Sons and the Native Daughters Central Committee on Homeless Children refer to a Home, they have in mind the carefully selected home for the homeless child which measures up to all that the word home implies: harmony, affection, morality, refinement, intelligence, and a deep sense of duty to one's church, whatever that church may be. Parents in the home who LIVE the life—rather than prescribe it for the child whom they have taken into their affections—of truthfulness, sobriety and honesty, and who are willing to sustain toward the child all the legal obligations and relations of parent and child, including support, affection, education, maintenance and inheritance.

A School, in which there shall be the heartiest co-operation between teachers and parents, thus assuring a child's advancement.

A Chance to Play which, according to the interpretation of the Native Sons and the Native Daughters, means freedom from work in factory or mill, city streets or asparagus fields, with an accepted responsibility for simple home duties and with time for wholesome play.

A good recipe, in short, to preserve children: "Take one (1) large grassy field, ½ dozen children, 2 or 3 small dogs, a pinch of brook and some pebbles. Mix the children and dogs well, put them in the field, constantly stirring. Pour the brook over the pebbles, sprinkle the field with flowers, spread over a deep, deep blue sky, and bake in the hot sun. When brown, remove and set away to cool in a bathtub. When thoroughly cleansed, place between 2 clean sheets to rest, after flavoring with kisses. The next day, repeat the process, with variations."

"He [Abraham Lincoln] was not a born king of men, ruling by the resistless might of his natural superiority, but a child of the people, who made himself a great persuader, therefore a leader, by dint of firm resolve, and patient effort, and dogged perseverance."—Horace Greeley.

Dahlia Show—The San Francisco Dahlia Society will have its annual display August 18-19.

MURDERER'S BAR

(BETTY L. WHITSELL.)

A town whose name was law
And none ignored that name
Was Murderer's Bar.
And known as peaceful diggings, too,
Both near and far.

A quiet mining camp
Where stealing never paid
And there was peace
For reputations were maintained
Without police.

All theft was held to be
A most disgraceful crime
And hanging meant
Triumphant law in Murderer's Bar
With full consent.

(This is another contribution from Betty L. Whitsell of Burlingame, San Mateo County, whose writings frequently appear in The Grizzly Bear.—Editor.)

WHAT IS REFORESTATION?
PLANTING JOB IN CALIFORNIA BIG ONE.

The word "reforestation" is much before the public nowadays. It is a headline word. President Franklin Roosevelt has done much to popularize it, and it has been dealt with in a congressional act. There is apparently much popular confusion in the use of the word. Just what is "reforestation?"

To the forester, it is a word with a definite and specific meaning. As a technical word, it means the restoring of an area to forest, either by artificial or natural means. That is, either the growing and setting out of young forest trees or seedlings on land which once had forests; or the slow or gradual re-stocking with forest by nature of land once forested. That is the correst or technical meaning. Likewise, afforestation means the planting of a forest on land which has not previously borne forest. Deforestation means the destruction or removal of forest from land with no conscious effort to restock the land.

Of late, however, the word "reforestation" has come to be popularly used to cover a much wider field. In this loose or popular sense, it has come to mean almost any method, means or system whereby forest land is improved, developed or protected, whether the land is cut over or is now bearing mature timber. For example, a system of fire lines or trails, or protection roads, the felling of snags or dead standing trees for fire protection, the thinning out of too-dense tree growth, or even a law to encourage the holding and protection of cut-over lands for future tree crops, have all come to be referred to as "reforestation" measures.

The area of once-forested lands requiring planting in the California pine region is very large. Estimates ranging from 300,000 to 2,000,000 acres serve to emphasize the magnitude of the planting job. On a large part of these lands all timber growth has been swept away by repeated fires, and no chance for natural reproduction remains. For the rest, lumbering followed by fire, and in recent years lumbering alone, have denuded the land quite as thoroughly. Planting with native conifers is the only known possibility of making these areas again productive within several generations.

With so great a job of planting in prospect, efforts of the Forest Service have been concentrated on the areas where reforestation is most urgently needed and will be most effective. This has been done only in an experimental way, with stock grown in the Forest Service nursery at Susanville, Lassen County. The capacity of this nursery will be doubled to make 1,000,000 seedlings available during the life of the reforestation act, but Forest Service officials believe that "reforestation" in California will consist mainly of fire protection measures.

THE FOREST FIRE

(F. G. de STONE, M.D.)

Thou vast primeval mountain chain,
  Ancient verdured in arboreal green,
Thy sides now licked by fierce devouring flame,
  Thy loss so great can ne'er again be seen;
A memory only of the mind, I ween.

Thou low hung scarlet screened sun,
  Though you depart now at the close of day,
And night shall fall and end the smoke murked run,
  No mortal tongue could half so apt portray
Thy blood red symbol of our tragedy.

Horse Show—The seventh annual San Mateo County National Horse Show is billed for August 5-12 at Atherton.

"MARK OUR LANDMARKS"

Chester F. Gannon

(GRAND HISTORIAN N.S.G.W.)

"MARK OUR LANDMARKS"

BITS OF HISTORY

"GOD BLESS YOU! YOUR SOUL'S IN Heaven! God bless you! California has lost her noblest son." An old man, as he touched the pallid forehead of the slain David C. Broderick, uttered the pathetic words just quoted. The body lay in state, surrounded by flowers and flags. A monument, still massive and imposing, marks his resting place at Laurel Hill Cemetery, San Francisco. But the fame of that noble Californian has not endured, and his last resting place has never been a shrine for Native Sons as it should be.

★ ★ ★

"There should be a law compelling all Californians to visit this lake on pain of—being transported to the East. The scenery is nobler than I anticipated, and the situation of the lake is certainly one of the wonders and masterpieces of scenery belonging to our insignificant little globe." This beautiful tribute to Lake Tahoe was written on the 5th day of June, 1863, by Thomas Starr King. He and Father Serra, in the Hall of Fame at Washington, forever represent the manhood of the State of California. He described with much detail, his arduous trip from Placerville to Lake Tahoe. As these warm days are upon us, our minds revert to that beautiful California mountain spot. The lure of vacation ease, health and beauty abound there today as they did when the tired Thomas Starr King left the rostrum from which he was oratorically voicing the cause of the Union. During the Civil War a strong southern influence was forever at work in California. The silver tongue of King helped keep our State loyal. After leaving the lake, he again returned to plunge into his patriotic devotion, which self-imposed duty was too much for his frail form and finally resulted in his death at San Francisco on the 6th of March, 1864.

★ ★ ★

"I decided that it was for me rather to govern events than to be governed by them." With this emphatic declaration on the 15th day of June, 1846, at his camp on the American River near Sacramento, Captain John C. Fremont threw down the gauntlet to the Mexicans, and determined once and for all to stand for American acquisition of California regardless of results. Next day, the Bear Flag Party struck at Sonoma, less than seventy miles from Sacramento. Had Fremont not uttered that memorable sentence and had he not been so close to the scene of hostilities, what would have been the fate of California? Historians resort to conjecture and some believe that the navy of Great Britain would have taken possession of these shores in the name of its king.

★ ★ ★

Fremont relates a rather unhappy incident of the military strife which followed the ejection from California of the Mexicans by Kearny and Commodore Stockton. A Mexican Indian, fighting on the American side in a small skirmish near Los Angeles, was run through the body by the sword of one of the Californians (Mexicans). When the Indian felt the sword go through him, he knew that the wound was fatal and called out in Spanish, "Enough!" "Another time," said the soldier-murderer, and ran him through the body a second time. "There it is," said he. "Yes, senor," said the dying man with the usual stolid submission of an Indian to his fate.

★ ★ ★

An example of the chivalry of the California Mexicans was demonstrated during the siege of General Kearny's army near San Bernardino. General Kearny and his force were surrounded by a Mexican command slightly larger than his own. General Pico, the Mexican leader, had him completely hemmed in. Things looked black and foreboding for the Americans. Pico captured a messenger who had been sent for relief through the Mexican lines to San Diego, forty miles away. As the scout endeavored to return to Kearny with the news that help was on its way, he was captured. From this scout, Godey, Pico learned that Lieutenant Gillespie was wounded. Gillespie was the man who had carried the memorable message from Monterey to Oregon for Fremont. This important message had caused the return of Fremont to California.

Pico was particularly interested in this brave young man, whom he personally knew, and when Godey told him that Gillespie was badly lanced and that his servant in San Diego had made up some supplies consisting of food and medicine for the wounded man, Pico's instant response to this news was to put the supplies under a flag of truce and send them to Gillespie with the invitation for him to come to his camp and receive better treatment than he could get on the dry rocks of the beleaguered army at San Bernardino. This chivalric offer was accepted and Gillespie left his companions-in-arms, went to the Mexican camp, and was treated like a friend.

★ ★ ★

Another incident of that little-known war was enacted at about the same time when General Pico, in seeking to exchange prisoners, sent a detail under a flag of truce toward the American lines. General Kearny, believing that the California Mexicans were treacherous, insisted that the emissary from the American camp go armed to the tryst. The American emissary, a young ensign by the name of Beale, protested against this fear, but complied with orders. As he approached the Mexican line, he was stopped by an outpost at the river. Kearny's beleaguered men had little or no water and were exposed to the burning sun. The Mexican lieutenant who stopped him offered him a drink of water. Beale put the cup to his lips, merely wet them and passed it back as much as to say, "I appreciate the civility of the occasion, but we have plenty of water on the hill."

What a chivalric act on the part of the Mexican, and what an heroic gesture on the part of the thirsty American! When the unarmed Mexican detail appeared to arrange for the exchange of prisoners, the conscience-stricken Beale could not conceal his weapon longer and, taking the weapon from his person, tossed it forty feet away, and thus high honor prevailed and negotiations were honorably and successfully carried on.

★ ★ ★

The very night of the incident just narrated, the same Beale and Kit Carson with stealth crept through the Mexican lines and, after a great deal of suffering, reached San Diego and brought succor to the inexperienced and unhappy Kearny, who had come to conquer the West and almost lost his army through his blundering and inaptness.

★ ★ ★

"Oh Temple! planned with the cunning skill of laborious art, rise in all thy majesty and beauty toward the skies. May thy walls be strength, and all thy tabernacles peace! May the votaries who shall in the long march of centuries enter thy sacred portals, find evermore therein repose, refreshment, peace! May the light of thy sacred altars burn ever like a star! May the 'stranger and sojourner in the land' ever enjoy the blessings of thy welcome and thy shelter; and when the hour of thy decay and dissolution crumbles thee to earth, may there be found thousands of faithful and devoted hearts to raise thee from thy ashes with renewed splendor and more enduring life!"

With this beautiful peroration on the 25th day of June, 1860, Harry M. Gray laid the cornerstone of Masonic Temple at San Francisco. I doubt if there is an orator in California today who could say more beautiful things in reference to a fraternal building than did this pioneer San Francisco orator on that long-forgotten day. And perhaps the most noteworthy thing about this noteworthy man was the fact that he was not an attorney but an eminently successful doctor gifted with polished and fervid oratory.

Unemployment Relief bonds to the amount of $20,000,000 were voted by California's electorate July 27.

"True glory lies in the silent conquest of ourselves."—Thompson.

CALIFORNIA FIFTY YEARS AGO

Thomas R. Jones

(COMPILED EXPRESSLY FOR THE GRIZZLY BEAR.)

GENERAL ANDREW MAVER WINN, California Pioneer of 1849 and Founder of the Order of Native Sons of the Golden West, died August 26, 1883, at his Sonoma County home. He was born in Virginia, April 27, 1810, the first of the twenty-one children of Captain John S. Winn, who commanded a company of American soldiers in the War of 1812, and Anjanet Maver-Winn. In 1850, the California State Legislature organized a state militia, and Governor Peter H. Burnett appointed him Brigadier General. In 1850 also, he was elected the first Mayor of Sacramento.

In 1869, General Winn organized a coterie of native California boys to march in the San Francisco Independence Day parade, of which he was the grand marshal, and this incident resulted in the founding, by him, of what later became the Order of Native Sons. The initial organization, now known as California Parlor No. 1 (San Francisco), was perfected in 1875, with John A. Steinbach as the first president. The funeral of General Winn, in Sacramento, August 28, was largely attended by men prominent in affairs of the state.

The State Board of Agriculture published statistics this month showing the following acreages sowed to grain in California this season: wheat, 2,634,716; barley, 775,405; corn, 65,766; oats, 122,618; rye, 29,251. An eighty percent yield was estimated.

John Lester Kaye, an English baronet, purchased 5,000 acres of overflow Yolo County tule land for $75,000. He sowed 3,500 acres to wheat. A dry winter saved the land from being overflowed by flood waters of the Sacramento River, and he harvested 35,000 sacks of wheat, which he shipped to England and got his investment back.

Hop growers held a convention in San Francisco to organize a state association. The hop acreage was double that of 1882, and the price had dropped from a dollar to twenty-five cents a pound. There was a scarcity of harvest labor, hence the growers were "up against" a bad situation.

A rancher brought into Los Angeles City, August 10, six watermelons totaling 444 pounds in weight, an average of 74 pounds each. August 20 another rancher, from Cahuenga, brought in a melon weighing 95 pounds.

John Wolfskill, a Yolo County fruit grower, this season sold the apricots from 250 trees for $4,800.

California wheat exports during August totaled 996,400 centals, valued at $1,662,000.

Land values in California North were booming. Henry Cutter of Biggs, Butte County, in 1880 tried in vain to sell 100 acres of land for $800. This month he was offered $45 an acre, but refused to sell.

On the William Hamilton ranch in Kern County was a lake which, while filled with water in winter, dried up in the summer and exposed a deposit of pure table salt. It proved a bonanza for its owner, who shipped enormous quantities of the product.

A gigantic irrigation scheme was inaugurated to take water from Kings River to irrigate 30,000,000 acres of land in Fresno and adjacent counties. A dam 25 feet high, 800 feet long and 140 feet thick was being thrown across the river, and the canal was to be 100 feet wide and 15 feet deep.

Cutter Salmon, boring an artesian well seven miles from Stockton, San Joaquin County, at a depth of 1,225 feet struck a flow of water and a gusher of gas. He piped the gas, and with it illuminated his home.

A brilliant violet-hued meteor passed over California South the morning of August 11.

A V-shaped flock of wild geese alighted August 7 in a Butte County grain field, and all of California's weather prognosticators began predicting an early and a wet winter.

Ventura County was seething with excitement over the effort to collect a $150-per-quarter license from every liquor dealer. The citizenry divided on high or low license, and an intensive talk-war was on.

Unmarried women, desirous of obtaining teacher positions in Sacramento City's public schools, made a successful fight and had seven instructors, with husbands able to support them, dropped from the payroll.

Pasadena, Los Angeles County, was building its second public school building, at a cost of $4,500, and was boasting of the fact.

A forest fire along the North Fork of the Feather River was doing immense damage to timber and settlements. Over thirty square miles of territory had been burned over, and the fire was still raging at the end of the month, although a hundred men were fighting it.

In San Francisco, August 4, fire destroyed the Winter Garden theater and several other large buildings, causing a $150,000 loss. The Salinas, Monterey County, flourmill burned August 2; loss, $10,000.

The Southern Pacific bridge across the Yuba River at Marysville, Yuba County, burned August 9. It was 700 feet long, and cost $80,000.

Fire in Red Bluff, Tehama County, August 7 destroyed a dance house in the rear of which lived a Mexican family, named Morales. The mother and a ten-year-old daughter were cremated.

Confidence engine No. 1 of Sacramento City was sold August 3 to a Honolulu fire engine company and shipped there. Built in Philadelphia for the company in 1857 at a cost of $7,500, it was shipped around Cape Horn, and when it arrived in San Francisco, January 1858, the volunteer fire department of that city turned out in full uniform and paraded through the streets with it, then loaded it aboard a chartered steamboat and, accompanied by a large escort, sent it to Sacramento. There the population turned out to receive it, and delegations of volunteer firemen came from Marysville, Placerville and other interior towns to join in a three-day celebration. The engine was christened with twenty baskets of champagne, while additional buckets of the beverage were passed around for everybody to quaff. It cost the Confidence Fire Engine Company over $5,000 to celebrate the engine's arrival.

The Sierra Valley stage was held up by two masked men fifteen miles from Truckee, Nevada County. The express box, containing over $1,000, was taken, and the six passengers were relieved of $160.

The stage from Yosemite Valley was stopped by three road agents, who robbed the seven tourists aboard of money and jewelry. The stage afterward upset, and all the passengers were more or less hurt.

C. C. Peters, founder of Yreka, Siskiyou county, died there August 3, at the age of 71.

Mrs. Margaret Taylor died in Yolo County, August 12. As Mrs. McDowell, in 1847 she gave birth to the first White child born at Sutter Fort. McDowell was killed in the Sacramento squatter riots of 1850.

Joseph H. Austin of Chico, Butte County, aged 82, was a devout spiritualist. August 20 he said he was being called to the spirit-land, and committed suicide.

James G. Fair, Comstock bonanza magnate, was building a mansion at the corner of California and Mason streets, San Francisco. He had just completed, at a cost of $45,000, a granite wall around the street frontage.

Mrs. Ellen M. Colton, widow of General Colton, presented a handsome and commodious schoolhouse to Colton, San Bernardino County, named after the general.

Pioneer D. O. Mills, noted early-day banker, presented to California a marble statue of Christopher Columbus and Queen Isabella of Spain making arrangements for Columbus' voyage of discovery. It arrived in Sacramento City August 20, and was being placed in the State Capitol rotunda.

Charles Crocker, railway millionaire, had a raft anchored in Monterey Bay, 700 feet from shore, and invited San Francisco's elite to a picnic thereon. All had to swim to the raft, however, for no boats were allowed. About sixty, of both sexes, accepted the bid, and on reaching the raft were regaled with a luncheon of tempting edibles washed down with champagne.

Diamonds were being found in the sluiceboxes of the Cherokee, Butte County, mines. The first diamond was found there in 1853, and of the sixty that had been discovered to date the largest, picked up by John Moore, weighed two and three-quarters carats. Zircons and platinum also were frequently found.

A quartz boulder, worn smooth by the action of flowing water, was found in a Gibsonville hydraulic mine. It weighed ninety-nine pounds, and yielded $2,600 in gold.

The United States Mint at San Francisco coined during August 120,000 twenty-dollar gold pieces and 900,000 silver dollars.

Frank Walton of Ventura City, student at the University of California, Berkeley, went home with typhoid fever and died July 27. His father and his mother contracted the malady, and the father died August 2 and the mother the following day.

Sixty Greek fishermen attempted to defy the law declaring a closed season for salmon during August. Constable Jones of Rio Vista, Solano County, was resisted in his efforts to arrest a couple of the law's violators. He shot and killed the reputed leader, and the war ended.

John Droglevich, proprietor of a Santa Clara City winery, fell into an empty wine vat August 22 and was suffocated. Attempting to rescue him, Joseph Brothers met a like fate.

Archie Johnson, aged 12, and the Weber boys, aged 10 and 12, were drowned while swimming in the Sacramento River near the Capital City, August 28.

Wm. Fleming and James Scanlan were driving in a spring wagon near Vallejo, Solano County, August 14. A railroad train struck the conveyance, and both were killed.

Nicholas Skerrit, wealthy San Francisco realtor, was lured to a vacant house and murdered by Wm. Ladue, an ex-convict from Idaho.

Henry Eaton, keeper of the Bonito Point lighthouse at the entrance to the Golden Gate, fell 150 feet off a cliff August 10 and was killed. He had been employed but five days.

"Liberty consists in the power of doing that which is permitted by law."—Cicero.

Feminine World's Fads and Fancies

PREPARED ESPECIALLY FOR THE GRIZZLY BEAR BY ANNA STOERMER

FEELING LOW IN YOUR MIND? PERhaps you need a new dress, and that is a normal sensation this time of the year. The remedy is to buy something new that your friends will exclaim over. No tonic will revive the state of mind with more speed. This being the middle of summer, you are proabbly wearing out the summery things and by now they bore you. Designers have "come across," as they always do, with many new ideas. What we used to consider strictly morning materials, now go dining and dancing, and former high-tea fabrics do the marketing. This paves the way to tell you of two charming dresses.

One is a plaid organdie, the sheerest, finest material imaginable. The other is a dark-brown and red-brown plaid. Instead of sleeves, a ruffled flounce grows fuller and fuller at the shoulder. On the whole, they are quite prim, and very well tailored. Another is of taffeta trimmed in black and white organdie. This, too, is tailored and relies on a wide belt and stiff bow of taffeta for trimming. A white hat is banded in matching plaid or black grosgrain ribbon. The new taffeta gloves would be exactly the right thing to wear with this costume.

Stripes are terribly important this year, not only the simple straight stripes but the wavy ones. For instance, a divided skirt is in dull orange and navy blue heavy cotton. The yoke is of plain navy blue with orange string lacings at the sides. The skirt is cut so that the stripes, running diagonally, form a "v" at the front, the back and the sides. This novel skirt is worn with a smart little cotton blouse which has short cupped sleeves and a novel neckline.

We see much style in the new negligees, such as higher waistlines, the princess silhouette, puffed or capelet sleeves, shoulder crests with width, ruffles and flounces. Some of the current style trends have been incorporated into the newest lingerie and boudoir frocks. Even the materials are of the type used for day frocks.

A negligee is made of french blue triple sheer and has self-ruching at the neck. It closes at the end of a surplice front with a soft sash that ties at the side. The capelet sleeves are trimmed with self-ruching, and the skirt is fitted about the hips, falling in graceful lines to ankle length. Another luxury, in the form of a printed negligee, has made itself so practical, in addition to being bewitchingly charming, that you absolutely must have one. It is most attractive for traveling. It takes up the smallest bit of room and the wrinkles fall out as if by magic.

Another note is the short sassy jacket, to be worn in bed, when comfortably propped against the reading pillow. There are numerous designs. Some, for age sixteen, with ruffles over the shoulders and down the front, are made of dainty flowered print. Others, not unlike the top of the negligee, are merely soft, with a trifle of warmth. These little toplets for the gown are cozy things to possess.

Some activities demand natural freedom of the body, which is a difficult art without especially created undergarments. There must be just enough restraint to confine one's figure, and an airy quality about the fabric so one may feel cool.

Some inspired woman must have dug into friend husband's wardrobe to copy his mannish trunks, downright masculine, but cut to fit the female figure. These are loose enough for active sports and free enough to not hinder long strides. They come in sheer white broadcloth, madras, nainsook and fine mesh. The fitted band which buttons in front is adjustable. In the back there is another amusing idea.

Shorts and skirts (petticoats) are made of bright plaid; in fact, make them of any material. No matter how perfect your limbs, stockings have a way of slipping unless evenly supported by long garters. With hot weather at hand, you will approve of the new garter panties. Two sets of garters are attached to the two-way-stretch waistband, and the panties themselves are of a fine openwork mesh, light as a feather.

Since every smart summer wardrobe is almost entirely of cotton, it is fitting that morning dresses should also be. The joy of it is, that women have such a flock of materials to choose from,—batistes, dotted swisses, ginghams, piques, voiles, linens and muslins. Of course, there are the plaid organdies and polkadots. Others, of flowers, are for those who prefer the floral designs. Nice neat little boquets of field flowers, for instance, come in red, white and blue daisies, pansies, asters and all sorts of blooms, and are printed over a black batiste ground.

A white organdie sailor collar has a girlish ruffled edging. The whole thing is as simple as can be, and is quite flattering. Top the lighter dresses with a floppy hat and cotton accessories. A tailored linen hat, linen gloves and white shoes would be style-proof with the flowered dress.

Deep-toned red proves popular. Costumes of sheer fabrics this year have found a new popularity and, strangely, too, the preference has been given to the dark colors, especially navy blue, brown and deep-toned reds.

The mannish suit has a touch of feminity, and there seems to be no tendency to break away from this season's edict of fashion. The shoulders are severely plain and mannish. The feminine touch, however, is given by the white pique collar and bow tie worn with a blouse of white pique. Gloves, too, match. Straw sailors have black bands or white ribbon. Black pumps complete natty costumes and are as smart as they are simple.

The new swagger coats go slouchy—pleasingly slouchy, instead of form fitting. We are to have the scarf with us for fall. Early showings are featuring scarfs in the new taffetas, rayon crepes and prints. Some show how one may pep up a limited wardrobe. For chic blouses, checks, plaids and stripes are all important. The new materials are silk, rayon, taffeta and cotton.

Krinklvel is a new light-weight velvet, which is very important. It fashions some of the smartest new evening wraps, including various new waistlines and shoulder capes. For color, the new "eel gray" promises to be important. One notes such luscious new colors now as poppy red, spring green, majorca blue and water blue.

Deep suntan is one of the smarter new shades for two-piece pajamas. The coat is finger-tip length and trimmed with buckles of old gold, set with coral and turquoise. One is on the shoulder, and one at the belt front. The sleeves are full from the shoulder to the elbow, then are tight to the wrist, and are made of many-shaped gores. These make very smart lounging garments. Another is of green satin. The body lines are given additional chic by a belt fastened with an ornamental buckle of imitation carved jade. Green satin mules complete the ensemble.

THAT'S CALIFORNIA!

(ROBERT L. HAWKENSEN.)

Fragrant blossoms everywhere,
Melodious song birds flood the air
From lofty snowy mountain peak,
To sun baked sands that bathers seek.
That's California!

The Gateway to the Golden West,
The one great State that's really blest
With sunshine, flowers, birds and bees,
And such a cooling summer breeze.
That's California!

Of all the places that I know,
There's only one to which I'd go;
The grandest spot on all this earth,
Where leadership has had its birth.
That's California!

(This verse came to The Grizzly Bear from Robert L. Hawkensen of Glendale, Los Angeles County.—Editor.)

The Western Writers League will have a convention at Long Beach, Los Angeles County, August 14-19.

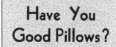

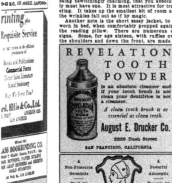

Native Sons of the Golden West

COMB THE FIELDS!

"EDITOR GRIZZLY BEAR: CHEERing news is coming in from all parts of the state in support of the new system of organization. **This is Native Son year in California!** The readjustment period is in our favor. People are thinking more than ever before of the value of companionship, fraternal fellowship, and of the substantial and lasting things of life, and less of the dollar as a source of all happiness.

"Everywhere the auxiliary bodies are making plans for a year of intense activity. The officers of local Parlors, past president associations, committees on the extension of the order, district deputies, lapsation committees and the rank and file of the Order are taking up the work with a zeal and earnestness that has not been equaled in years.

"**The great number of native born of this state offer a fruitful field for recruiting possibilities.** Do you know, brothers, as a matter of fact there are thousands of worthy young men who have never been solicited to join the Order? **Let us comb the fields!** No man is so big that he will not be helped by membership in our Order. Self-interest, as well as loyalty and duty to his native state, are impelling reasons why he should join our ranks, leaving out of the question all other human and practical advantages which the Order offers to its members.

"From one end of the state to the other, both small and large Parlors have expressed determination to make a drive for an increased membership. We expect to have a more definite report from all the Parlors by the first of October. In the meantime, let each Parlor write in to The Grizzly Bear Magazine and give to the other Parlors any good news it may have.

"The Grizzly Bear Magazine wants to be a newsy periodical, as well as an historical publication. It cannot supply the news of the Order unless it is furnished with it by the members of the Order. Make your articles short, but don't fail to report the news. The magazine is our official journal, and it should be heartily supported by the subscriptions of all of the members of the Order.

"Preparations for a bumper celebration at Santa Rosa on September 9th [Admission Day] are engrossing the attention of many Parlors. We will have in line a wonderful group of Native Daughters and Native Sons from every county in California. The eyes of the state will be upon us, and we count upon the magnificent display we will make on California's natal day to greatly help us in building up local Parlors. The official, civic and industrial life of the state will take part in the state celebration. It will be a splendid success! Fraternally,

"EMMET SEAWELL,
"Grand President, N.S.G.W.
"San Francisco, July 17, 1933."

Co-operation's the Needed Thing.

President Ervin J. Beall of Sacramento No. 3, under date of July 12, addressed a letter, overflowing with food for thought, to each member of that Parlor. "With a little co-operation it won't be long before we are again 'sitting on top of the world'," he says, and in commenting on the dues situation—a perplexing question in all Subordinate Parlors—he speaks plainly:

"In going over the financial secretary's books I find two classes of delinquent members. The first is the brother who, through no fault of his own, is absolutely unable to pay. He has been out of employment, unforeseen expenses have arisen, things have gone hay-wire with him in general, but in spite of all he is still anxious and willing to pay his honest obligations. The second is the member who, although steadily employed, has not paid, never has and never expects to. He is perfectly willing to let 'George' carry the load. He is very indignant, and makes the loudest noise when matters do not suit him. He is absolutely worthless as a member. For the first type, I have the greatest respect and, in line with the wishes of our grand officers, the Parlor hopes to be able to carry them on until they get their second wind. They are men enough to realize the Order cannot be run on bluff and wind. For the second type, I have no regard. They will be suspended. They are an expense to the Parlor and we will have no more of them."
—C.M.H.

There is no substitute for membership! Respond to the call of the Grand President for laborers in the eligible field, now ripe for harvest. Work, with ENTHUSIASM!

Officials Well Pleased.

Ukiah—Grand First vice-president Chas. A. Koenig and Grand Secretary John T. Regan, visitors in Ukiah July 15, were entertained at luncheon by Ukiah No. 71. Harold Zimmerman presided, and speakers included President Henry Spurr of the Ukiah Chamber of Commerce, Koenig and Regan. The two latter, after an inspection tour, expressed themselves well pleased with the housing and other accommodations in Ukiah, selected as the meeting place of the 1934 Grand Parlor. Grand Second vice-president Harmon D. Skillin was also in the city, but missed the luncheon.

Officers of the Parlor were installed July 17, Kenneth Phillips becoming president. Plans are already under way for next year's Grand Parlor, and Henry Spurr and Keith C. Eversole have been appointed a general committee of arrangements.

Anniversary Celebrated.

San Bernardino—Arrowhead No. 110 entertained a large crowd at its annual Independence Day barbecue at its Crestline clubhouse in the San Bernardino Mountains. Henry B. Peake was the general chairman. Outdoor sports and dancing were provided. A feature of the occasion was the dedication of two plaques under the direction of Chairman Jerome B. Kavanaugh of the Parlor's history and landmarks committee. One, at the old Mormon springs where, in early days, lumbermen of the San Bernardinos secured water for themselves and their teams. The other, a monitor used by hydraulic miners in the early days, in memory of the late Charles Doyle, who found the relic on one of his many trips over the mountains.

July 26, Arrowhead celebrated its twenty-sixth institution anniversary. Charter Members Joe Rich, Emory Tyler and Albert Burcham were honor-guests. Ben Harrison was the principal speaker of the occasion. Henry B. Peake, as president, heads the Parlor's new corps of officers, installed July 12 by District Deputy Walter E. Hiskey.

There is no substitute for membership! Respond to the call of the Grand President for laborers in the eligible field, now ripe for harvest. Work, with ENTHUSIASM!

Six Initiated.

Sonoma—Sonoma No. 111 added six new names to its membership roll July 3, the ritual being faultlessly exemplified by the officers of South San Francisco No. 157 (San Francisco). There was a very large attendance of visitors, including twenty members of No. 157 and delegations from all the Sonoma County Parlors. A chicken dinner concluded the enthusiastic gathering.

Speakers of the evening included Grand Secretary John T. Regan, Sheriff Mike Flohr and Treasurer James Ramage of Sonoma County, Chairman Wesley Colgan of the Santa Rosa Admission Day committee, and Dr. W. C. Shipley, chairman of the committee arranging for the Admission Day, September 9, parade.

There is no substitute for membership! Respond to the call of the Grand President for laborers in the eligible field, now ripe for harvest. Work, with ENTHUSIASM!

Annual Barbecue.

Santa Barbara—Santa Barbara No. 116 will hold its annual barbecue at Stow's ranch, in Goleta, just west of Santa Barbara, Sunday, August 13. Plans are being arranged for sports, music and dancing, as well as other amusements and good times, both before and after the barbecue, which is held at 12:30 p.m.

Frank Castro and his good of the order com-

FITTING TRIBUTE

(JUDGE FLETCHER A. CUTLER,
Past Grand President N.S.G.W.)

AT THE SESSION OF THE N.S.G.W. Grand Parlor held in Grass Valley, Nevada County, the attention of the delegates was called to the fact that the last resting place there of Past Grand President Jo V. Snyder was unmarked. A motion was made, and carried, that a committee be appointed to decorate the grave with appropriate floral offerings during the session of the Grand Parlor, which was accordingly done.

The Past Grand Presidents attending the Grand Parlor called a meeting to discuss plans for a proper monument to be erected to the memory of Past Grand President Snyder. In accordance therewith, it was arranged that a substantial piece of granite be taken from the

hillsides of his native county, and that a proper inscription be placed thereon. As a result thereof, a piece of granite in the rough, five feet high, was obtained, and on one side there was chiseled a scroll bearing the inscription "Jo V. Snyder, Past Grand President, N.S.G.W., served in 1918."

The monument was unveiled July 30. Grand President Justice Emmet Seawell, accompanied by Fletcher A. Cutler, representing the Past Grand Presidents, and Grand Secretary John T. Regan participated in the ceremonies, which were attended by members of Fred H. Greeley Assembly of Past Presidents and prominent Native Sons of the northern counties of California.

Thus there has been paid a fitting tribute to the memory of one who devoted a large measure of his time and talents to the Order of the Native Sons of the Golden West. No member of the Order ever took a more active interest in its affairs, nor evidenced the sentiment of loyalty that inspired Jo V. Snyder as he traveled about the state while he was passing through the respective stations of a grand officer. His eloquent addresses, his words of encouragement and cheer, and with all his happy, smiling presence, endeared him to all. It will be a source of satisfaction to every member of the Order who came in contact with him to know that "high up in the Sierras," as he loved to refer to his hometown, there is a monument reflecting the affection and esteem in which he was held by all Native Sons.

mittee can and do put on a wonderful affair; in fact, the Natives' barbecue is always one of the most outstanding of the year. All Native Sons and their families are more than welcome.

Membership Standing Largest Parlors.

San Francisco—Grand Secretary John T. Regan reports the standing of the Subordinate Parlors having a membership of over 400 January 1, 1933, as follows, together with their membership figures July 20, 1933:

Parlor.	Jan. 1	July 20	Gain	Loss
Ramona No. 109	1032	1036	4	....
South San Francisco No. 157	803	798	....	5
Castro No. 232	764	765	1	....
Arrowhead No. 110	573	567	....	6
Stanford No. 76	575	566	....	9
Stockton No. 7	535	517	....	18
Twin Peaks No. 214	522	502	....	20
Piedmont No. 120	491	489	....	2
Rincon No. 72	418	404	....	14

There is no substitute for membership! Respond to the call of the Grand President for laborers in the eligible field, now ripe for harvest. Work, with ENTHUSIASM!

NEWSY N.S. PARAGRAPHS.

Sonoma—At the formal dedication as a state park, July 7, of "Lachryma Montis," the historic home of General M. J. Vallejo, speakers included Grand President Justice Emmet Seawell, and Past Grands Lewis F. Byington and Joseph R. Knowland.

Placerville—Officers of Placerville No. 9 and Marguerite No. 12 N.D.G.W. were jointly installed July 11 by District Deputies George Smith and Nettie Leonardi, Milton Orelli and Ruth Baumhoff becoming the respective presidents. A large crowd was in attendance, and delicious refreshments were served. On behalf of Marguerite, Dorian Sutton presented an emblematic pin to Junior Past President Monica McCusker.

Modesto—Modesto No. 11 and Yosemite No. 24 of Merced had joint installation of officers at the latter city July 24. Charles D. Blaine presided. Modesto's arrangements committee included Ben Munson, Myron Moyle and Guy Allen.

There is no substitute for membership! Respond to the call of the Grand President for laborers in the eligible field, now ripe for harvest. Work, with ENTHUSIASM!

Fresno—Officers of Visalia No. 19, Fresno No. 25 and Selma No. 107 were jointly installed July 7. District Deputy Frank M. Lane presided, and Gareth Houk, J. H. Sutton and C. R. Snyder became the respective presidents. There was a large attendance, and among the speakers were David E. Peckinpah, B. W. Gearhart and M. E. Griffith. Refreshments were served.

Nevada City—Hydraulic No. 56, according to Dr. C. W. Chapman, recording secretary, plans to place markers at a number of historic points in Nevada County.

Napa—Napa No. 62 initiated a class of candidates July 31, the ceremonies being held outofdoors, at the Coombs ranch.

San Rafael—Officers of Mount Tamalpais No. 64 were installed July 17 by District Deputy Charles Soldavini Jr. Donald J. Locati became the president, and he contemplates observing the Parlor's forty-eighth institution anniversary with a big class initiation and banquet. Dancing and refreshments concluded the installation ceremonies.

Weaverville—Miss Vivian E. Bennett became the bride, July 9, of Horace J. Leavitt of Mount Bally No. 87, former grand trustee. The attendants were Miss Lois Vitzthum and Edwin J. Regan (South San Francisco No. 157), and the ceremony was performed by Superior Judge C. A. Paulsen. The couple are residing at Hat Creek, Shasta County, where Leavitt is identified with the United States Forest Service.

Santa Barbara—Grand Trustee Henry S. Lyon of Placerville, district attorney El Dorado County, was elected president of the California District Attorneys Association in anunal convention here. He was honor-guest at a dinner party sponsored by Santa Barbara No. 116.

There is no substitute for membership! Respond to the call of the Grand President for laborers in the eligible field, now ripe for harvest. Work, with ENTHUSIASM!

Oakland—Piedmont No. 120 will have its annual picnic, with plenty of entertainment, at Bjornsen Park, Crow Canyon, August 6. F. X. Weber is the chairman and Frank Roemer the secretary of the arrangements committee. Prizes are in charge of Arnold Halstead.

Sausalito—District Deputy Charles Soldavini

(Continued on Page 13)

Know your home-state, California! Learn of its past history and of its present-day development by reading regularly The Grizzly Bear. $1.50 for one year (12 issues). Subscribe now.

SAN FRANCISCO

"EVEN HAD GOLD NEVER BEEN DISCOVERED, California would be today much as it is," declared Secretary Rodney S. Ellsworth of the scientific research section of the San Francisco Commonwealth Club in a recent address. "Early advertising had built up such a picture of California in the minds of Easterners that heavy migration here was bound to come, with or without the lure of gold. Gold merely hastened the process. This migration was so portentious that had there been no Mexican War, the conquest of California was nevertheless on its way."

Ellsworth cited as an example of early advertising an issue of the "American Register," published in 1808, in which an article stated that California was a province "wanting nothing but a vigorous, progressive population." He showed that advertising, through its pulling power, brought to the West the civilization whose inroads caused wild-life depletion.

NATIVE DAUGHTERS DOINGS.

The monthly Native Daughter Home breakfast was held Sunday, July 9, with Mollye Spaelti of Marinita Parlor No. 198 (San Rafael) and Emma O'Meara of Dolores Parlor No. 169 (San Francisco) as hostesses. The dining room and the tables were beautifully decorated with red, white, and blue flowers, in keeping with the Fourth of July. Parlors represented were Orinda, Castro, Buena Vista, Aloha, Alturas, Marinita, Alta, Las Lomas, Dolores, Golden State, Twin Peaks and El Vespero.

Speakers included Hubert Caveney of Stanford Parlor No. 76 N.S.G.W., Past Grands Dr. Mariana Bertola, Evelyn I. Carlson and Emma Foley, Millie Tietjen and Elizabeth Douglas. The Native Daughter Glee Club favored with "My Own United States" and southern selections.

Alta Parlor No. 3—Mrs. Annie C. Thuesen was tendered a reception and banquet by her home-Parlor July 12, in honor of her election to the office of Grand Marshal at the Oakland Grand Parlor. A special song of greeting to the tune of "Smiles" was sung while she was being escorted to a seat of honor at the banquetboard, where she was welcomed by Mrs. May L. MacDonald, chairman and toastmaster on this auspicious occasion. Among the artists who contributed to the success of the program were Mrs. Mary Jordan, Madam M. Marchand and Miss Estelle M. Carr. Grand officers present were Grand Secretary Sallie Thaler, Past Grands Dr. Mariana Bertola, Genevieve W. Baker, Eliza D. Keith and Margaret G. Hill. Among the gifts presented Grand Marshal Thuesen was a set of fine damask napkins. Mrs. Catherine O'Reilly, the mother of Mrs. Thuesen and also a member of Alta, shared her daughter's honors. Officers were publicly installed by Deputy Ida Mesquite July 25, Claire Bolman becoming president.

Genevieve Parlor No. 132—The drum corps and that of Castro Parlor No. 232 N.S.G.W. have arranged for a big whist at Native Sons Building, August 1, and an enjoyable evening is assured. Arrangements are in charge of Misses R. Taube, E. Kilkenny, E. Taube, I. O'Leary, C. Jacobsen, E. Joorisen and G. Joorisen of Genevieve, and Messrs. Bartholomew and Leary of Castro.

Dolores Parlor No. 169—At public ceremonies July 15 attended by 200, officers with Juanita Blanchfield as president were installed. Deputy Pearl Wedde officiated and was assisted by Past Grand Evelyn I. Carlson and members of Bret Harte Parlor No. 232. Junior Past President Alma Hall was presented with an emblematic pin. Among the guests was Mrs. Madge Blanchfield of Guadalupe Parlor No. 153, mother of President Blanchfield. Dancing concluded an enjoyable evening. Dolores' drill team, which will make its first public appearance in the Santa Rosa Admission Day parade, will hold a card party and dance at Native Sons Building August 10.

Linda Rosa Parlor No. 170—An "old fashioned clothes" party was given July 12. The costumes were the center of much merriment, which lasted throughout the evening. Guests and members joined in a virginia reel, and then were served refreshments. Among the honor-guests was Deputy Muller.

Castro Parlor No. 178—A reception was held July 5 in honor of Financial Secretary Alice Lane, elected Grand Trustee at the Oakland Grand Parlor. It was a very pretty affair, and no pains were spared by the able chairman, Cora Stobing, to make it so. An entertainment innovation was the introduction of twelve little charges of Superintendent Tanghe of Russian missions, who appeared in a sketch which was hugely enjoyed. At the banquetboard the new grand officer's place was marked by a floral arch of red, white and blue flowers, and a most delicious cake especially made for "Our Alice." Other table declorations were in keeping with the national holiday.

Past Presidents Association No. 1—At public ceremonies July 17 officers, with Merle Sandell as president, were installed by Junior Past President Louise Cases, assisted by Margaret Grote Hill and Chief President Winnie Halter. Mrs. Cases was presented with an emblematic ring. Several vocal selections were rendered by Marie Vogel and Ann Godfrey. Refreshments were served.

NATIVE SONS DOINGS.

New officers of the Extension of the Order Committee are: Hubert Caveney (Stanford No. 76), chairman; Charles H. Spengemann (Hesperian No. 137), vice-chairman; L. A. Werner (Golden Gate No. 29), treasurer; Harold J. Regan (South San Francisco No. 157), secretary. Since July 7 the committee has been operating, jointly with representatives of the Native Daughter Parlors, as an Admission Day Committee, and meetings are held every Friday night to arrange for participation in the September 9 celebration at Santa Rosa.

A committee headed by Peter T. Conmy has been appointed to arrange for observance of American Education week. The Extension Committee contemplates a monster initiation, probably in October, in honor of Grand President Justice Emmet Seawell; all the local Parlors will participate.

George H. Barron of Precita Parlor No. 187, retired July 1 as curator of the M. H. de Young Memorial Museum in Golden Gate Park after twenty-four years of efficient service. He was born at San Francisco, September 19, 1869. "George" says "I want to rest before I reach the wheel-chair stage. I want to retrace the footsteps of the padres; to re-visit the missions and adobes, and pause again among the historic scenes of California's romantic days. I will travel back through the land of tradition, and it will be a journey of happy memory."

(Continued on Page 11)

Passing of the California Pioneer

(Confined to Brief Notices of the Demise of Those Men and Women Who Came to California Prior to 1870.)

SISTER MARY CATHERINE HANRAHAN, native of Ireland, 93; came to California in 1850 and long resided in Marin County. Died at Benicia, Solano County. She is said to have been the oldest Dominican nun in California, having joined that religious order in 1858.

Mrs. Aurelia Swain-Webber, native of Massachusetts, 86; came in 1851; died at Berkeley, Alameda County, survived by two sons.

Newton G. Finley, native of Missouri, 92; came across the plains in 1852 and resided in Santa Clara and Sonoma Counties; died at Campbell, survived by two children. He was a nephew of Benjamin Campbell, Pioneer of 1846 who founded Campbell.

Mrs. Sarah Baker Skillman, native of Canada, 98; crossed the plains in 1853; died at Eureka, Humboldt County, survived by a son. She was the widow of Archibald Skillman who, in 1870, established the "Eureka Sentinel."

Mrs. Martha A. Justice, born in 1854 while her parents were enroute across the plains to California; died at Montebello, Los Angeles County, survived by six children. She resided fifty-five years in Orange County.

Mrs. Eleanor Whiteside-Batchelder, native of Illinois, 84; came across the plains in 1854 and resided in Yuba and Butte Counties; died at Chico, survived by three children.

Mrs. Anna Amalia Garrecht, native of Germany, 82; came via Cape Horn in 1856 and settled in Shasta County; died at Shasta Town, survived by a son.

Mrs. Carrie Hook Gordon, native of Massachusetts, 83; came in 1856 and settled in San Francisco, where she died; three children survive.

Mrs. Hannah Frances Healy-Brady, 82; came in 1858 and settled in Sierra County; died at Forest City, survived by four children.

George E. Buck, 97; came in 1858 and resided in Tuolumne and Los Angeles Counties; died at Santa Monica, survived by a daughter.

Charles W. Godfrey, native of Maine, 78; came in 1859 and resided in Yuba and Nevada Counties; died at Nevada City, survived by a wife and a daughter.

Mrs. Mary Catherine Bouchard, native of Prussia, 95; came in 1860; died at Adin, Modoc County, survived by three daughters.

Thomas Edwin Bevan, native of New York, 79; came via Cape Horn in 1862 and resided in Sutter and Yuba Counties; died at Benicia, Solano County, survived by two daughters. For nearly forty years he was assessor of Yuba County.

Mrs. Johanna Grasser-Wolf, native of New York, 83; came in 1864 and resided in Alameda and Contra Costa Counties; died at Berkeley, survived by two sons.

Mrs. Sarah Ann Webb-Laughlin, native of Missouri, 81; came in 1864 and resided in Solano, Mendocino and Sonoma Counties; died at Princeton, Colusa County, survived by four children.

Mrs. Hannah Winzer, native of England, 93; came in 1865 and three years later settled in Humboldt County; died at Eureka, survived by seven children.

Adelbert E. Kellogg, native of Vermont, 86; came in 1865; died at San Francisco, survived by four children. For years he was an educator in Marin and Alameda Counties.

Mrs. Mary Callahan, native of New York, 75; since 1865 resident of San Francisco, where she died; six children survive.

George P. Putnam, native of Massachusetts, 73; since 1866 resident Sacramento City, where he died; a wife and a son survive. He was a son of George A. Putnam, Pioneer of 1849.

Mrs. Catherine Agnes Sullivan-Haire, native of New York, 68; came in 1867 and resided many years in San Francisco; died at Saint Helena, Napa County, survived by a husband.

Heny Dedmon, native of Arkansas, 78; since 1868 resident of Plumas County; died at Quincy, survived by a wife and six children.

Sol Dannenbaum, native of Germany, 93; came in 1869 and for some time resided in Solano County; died at San Francisco, survived by a wife and five children.

A. B. Rodaway, native of England, 84; came in 1869; died at Oxnard, Ventura County, survived by a wife.

Alvertis A. Hopkins, native of Indiana, 86; came in 1866 and resided for a time in Sacramento County; died at Los Angeles City, his home for forty-seven years, survived by three sons. He was a Civil War veteran, and in the long-ago operated stages between Los Angeles, San Diego, Santa Barbara and San Bernardino.

Abraham M. Briggs, 81; came via the Kit Carson pass in 1864 and resided in San Joaquin and Stanislaus Counties; died at Modesto, survived by a wife and two children.

Mrs. Anna Foley, native of Ireland; came in 1863 and long resided in Yolo County; died at Sacramento City, survived by a son.

Mrs. Harriet Garner Arthur-Roduner, native of Ohio, 72; came in 1862 and resided in Mariposa and Merced Counties; died at Merced City, survived by eight children.

Mrs. Helena K. Dahneke, 95; since 1860 a resident of North San Juan, Nevada County, where she died; a daughter survives.

George H. Rauchert, native of Massachusetts, 84; came via Cape Horn in 1852 and resided in Solano and San Luis Obispo Counties; died near San Miguel.

Mrs. Louisa Coons, native of Texas, 83; crossed the plains in 1852 and long resided in Kern County; died at Los Angeles City, survived by five children. She was the widow of W. H. Coons, former Kern County sheriff.

PIONEER NATIVES DEAD

(Brief Notices of the Demise of Men and Women born in California Prior to 1860.)

Mrs. Mary Plummer, born Tuolumne County, 1855; died June 26, Jamestown; son survives.

George Hyde, born Solano County, 1853; died June 27, Campbell, Santa Clara County; wife and two sons survive.

Thomas B. Cutler, born San Francisco, 1859; died June 28, Crescent City, Del Norte County; wife and daughter survive. He was a brother of Judge Fletcher A. Cutler (Past Grand President N.S.G.W.).

John W. McKenzie, born San Francisco, 1855; died July 1, Oakland, Alameda County; two daughters survive.

Mrs. Lena Glusen, born Solano County, 1856; died July 1, Cordelia; three children survive.

Francis Ignacio Valencia, born San Francisco, 1845; died July 3, Corte Madera, Marin County; four children survive. He was a son of Jose Valencia, who at one time owned much of the present San Francisco area.

Mrs. Sophia Passet, born Santa Clara County, 1858; died July 4, Oakland, Alameda County; four daughters survive.

Thomas Frederick Miller, born San Francisco, 1854; died July 5, near Graton, Sonoma County; wife survives. He was affiliated with Santa Rosa Parlor No. 28 N.S.G.W.

Maclovio Anthony Botello, born Los Angeles City, 1856; died July 6, Santa Barbara City; wife and five children survive.

Joseph D. Bermudez, born Los Angeles County, 1852; died July 6, San Gabriel; wife and ten children survive.

John C. Woodson, born Humboldt County, 1851; died July 9, Saratoga, Santa Clara County; three children survive. Most of his life was spent in San Joaquin County.

Kewen Hilliard Dorsey, born Los Angeles County, 1857; died July 11, Fontana, San Bernardino County; wife and two children survive. His father, Major Hilliard P. Dorsey, a Mexican War veteran, arrived in Los Angeles in 1848.

Luis Serrano, born San Diego County, 1845; died July 14, San Diego City.

Mrs. Matilda Carteri, born Santa Barbara County, 1856; died July 17, Santa Barbara City; ten children survive. She was a daughter of William B. Foxen, who aided General John C. Fremont in his conquest of California.

Mrs. Mary I. Salinas, born Los Angeles County, 1849; died July 17, Corning, Tehama County; seven children survive.

Charles Victor Hall, born San Francisco, 1854; died July 20, Buena, San Diego County; wife survives.

SAN FRANCISCO

(Continued from Page 10)

Pacific Parlor No. 10—Officers were installed July 18, with William G. Boyce as president. A snappy entertainment program was presented by the good of the order committee, Joe Sugrowe chairman. The drum corps sponsored a whist party July 21.

Golden Gate Parlor No. 29—William McKinley Roll, as president, heads the new corps of officers, installed July 7 by Deputy Robert Donohue. A movement is under way for the consolidation of Olympus Parlor No. 189 with Golden Gate.

Stanford Parlor No. 76—At public ceremonies July 11, officers were installed, Urban Morf becoming president. A program was presented and dancing was then in order. A large membership committee, with Hubert J. Caveney as chairman, has been appointed.

CALIFORNIA FIFTH AMONG STATES OF THE NATION IN POPULATION.

The officially estimated population of the United States July 1, 1933, was 125,693,000, according to an announcement of the Federal Commerce Department's census bureau. This is an increase over the population of 122,775,046 shown by the April 1, 1930, census of 2,917,954.

California, which has now moved up to fifth place in population among the states, is credited with an estimated increase of 384,749. At the time of the 1930 census it had a population of 5,677,251, and each year since the estimated number has increased: 5,848,000 (1931), 5,947,000 (1932), 6,062,000 (1933). The states exceeding California in the July estimate are: New York, 12,965,000; Pennsylvania, 9,787,000; Illinois, 7,826,000; Ohio, 6,798,000.

Humboldt Fair—The annual Humboldt County Fair will be held at Ferndale, August 24-27.

Official Directory of Parlors of the N. S. G. W.

ALAMEDA COUNTY.

Alameda No. 47, Alameda City—J. F. Hanson, Pres.; Robt. H. Cavanaugh, Sec., 1806 Pacific Ave.; Wednesdays, Veterans Memorial Bldg.

Oakland No. 50, Oakland—T. J. Markert, Pres.; F. M. Norris, Sec., 5595 Taft Ave.; Fridays, Native Sons Hall, 11th and Clay Sts.

Las Positas No. 96, Livermore—Louis J. Volponi, Pres.; John J. Kelly, Sec., P. O. box 341; Thursdays, Foresters Hall.

Eden No. 113, Hayward—Leo Wessman, Pres.; Filbert M. Soares, Sec., 1437 "B" St.; 2nd and 4th Tuesdays, Memorial Hall, Main St.

Piedmont No. 120, Oakland—George T. Pryts, Pres.; Charles Morando, Sec., 906 Vermont St.; Thursdays, Native Sons Hall, 11th and Clay Sts.

Wisteria No. 127, Alvarado—Henry May, Pres.; J. M. Scribner, Sec., Livermore; 1st Thursday, I.O.O.F. Hall.

Halcyon No. 146, Alameda City—F. A. Stahl, Pres.; J. C. Bates, Sec., 2139 Buena Vista Ave.; 1st and 3rd Tuesdays, I.O.O.F. Hall, 2329 Santa Clara Ave.

Brooklyn No. 151, Oakland—Henry Barrett, Pres.; E. W. Cudney, Sec., 3907 14th Ave.; 1st and 3rd Wednesdays, Masonic Temple, 8th Ave. and E. 14th St.

Washington No. 169, Centerville—Thomas Silva, Pres.; Allen G. Norris, Sec., P. O. box 58; 2nd and 4th Tuesdays, Hansen Hall.

Athens No. 195, Oakland—Fred G. Martin, Pres.; Harold B. Farley, Sec., 4623 Benevides Ave.; Tuesdays, Native Sons Hall, 11th and Clay Sts.

Berkeley No. 210, Berkeley—H. P. Corbett, Pres.; R. J. Garrett, Sec., 1708 Virginia St.; Tuesdays, Native Sons Hall, 2108 Shattuck Ave.

Estudillo No. 223, San Leandro—E. E. King, Pres.; Albert G. Pacheco, Sec., 1736 E. 14th St.; 1st and 3rd Tuesdays, U.P.E.C. Hall.

Claremont No. 240, Emeryville—Edward J. Ginochio, Pres.; E. N. Thienger, Sec., 839 Hearst Ave., Berkeley; Tuesdays, Veterans Memorial Bldg., 43rd and Salem Sts.

Pleasanton No. 244, Pleasanton—Edward Holzreiter, Pres.; Ernest W. Schween, Sec.; 2nd and 4th Thursdays, I.O.O.F. Hall.

Niles No. 250, Niles—M. L. Fournier, Pres.; O. E. Martenstein, Sec.; 2nd Thursday, I.O.O.F. Hall.

Fruitvale No. 252, Oakland—Ernest Perry, Pres.; Ray B. Felton, Sec., 63 11th St.; Fridays, W.O.W. Hall, 3256 E. 14th St.

AMADOR COUNTY.

Amador No. 17, Sutter Creek—J. H. Williams, Pres.; F. J. Payne, Sec.; 1st and 3rd Fridays, Native Sons Hall.

Excelsior No. 31, Jackson—Thomas G. Negrich, Pres.; William Going, Sec.; 1st and 3rd Wednesdays, Native Sons Hall, 22 Court St.

Ione No. 33, Ione—Earl Grover, Pres.; Josiah H. Saunders, Sec.; 1st and 3rd Wednesdays, Native Sons Hall.

Plymouth No. 48, Plymouth—D. A. Upton, Pres.; Thos. D. Davis, Sec.; 1st and 3rd Saturdays, N.S.G.W. Hall.

BUTTE COUNTY.

Argonaut No. 8, Oroville—Frank H. O'Brien, Pres.; Cyril R. Macdonald, Sec., P. O. box 502; 1st and 3rd Wednesdays, Veterans Memorial Hall.

CALAVERAS COUNTY.

Chispa No. 139, Murphys—Maynard Segale, Pres.; Antone Malaspina, Sec.; Wednesdays, Native Sons Hall.

COLUSA COUNTY.

Colusa No. 69, Colusa City—Thomas F. Busch, Pres.; Phil J. Humburg, Sec., 223 Parkhill St.; Tuesdays, Eagles Hall.

CONTRA COSTA COUNTY.

General Winn No. 32, Antioch—John P. Welch, Pres.; Joel H. Ford, Sec., P. O. box 311; 2nd and 4th Wednesdays, Union Hall.

Mount Diablo No. 101, Martinez—R. P. Anderson, Pres.; G. T. Barkley, Sec.; 1st and 3rd Mondays, I.O.O.F. Hall.

Byron No. 170, Byron—William E. Bunn, Pres.; H. G. Krumland, Sec.; 1st and 3rd Tuesdays, I.O.O.F. Hall.

Carquinez No. 205, Crockett—John McManus, Pres.; Thomas R. Cox, Sec., P.O. box 721; 1st and 3rd Wednesdays, I.O.O.F. Hall.

Richmond No. 217, Richmond—Frank Weber, Pres.; Lloyd N. Mason, Sec., 11 6th St.; 1st Wednesday, 818 Macdonald Ave.

Concord No. 245, Concord—C. H. Guy, Pres.; D. E. Framberg, Sec., P. O. box 235; 1st Tuesday, Guy's Parlors.

Diamond No. 246, Pittsburg—S. E. Caruso, Pres.; Edward Wilson, Sec., 2 Front St.; 1st and 3rd Wednesdays, Veterans Memorial Bldg.

EL DORADO COUNTY.

Placerville No. 9, Placerville—Chris. C. Orelli, Pres.; Clyde R. Berriman, Sec., Wood St.; 2nd and 4th Tuesdays, Masonic Hall.

Georgetown No. 91, Georgetown—George W. Brichler, Pres.; C. F. Irish, Sec.; 2nd and 4th Wednesdays, I.O.O.F. Hall.

FRESNO COUNTY.

Fresno No. 25, Fresno City—J. H. Sutton, Pres.; W. C. Guard, Sec., R.F.D. No. 2, box 379; 1st and 3rd Fridays, Pythian Castle, Cor. "R" and Merced Sts.

Selma No. 107, Selma—C. R. Snyder, Pres.; E. C. Laughlin, Sec.; 1st Wednesday, American Legion Hall.

GRAND OFFICERS.

Seth Millington........Junior Past Grand President
Gridley

Justice Emmet Seawell........Grand President
State Bldg., San Francisco

Chas. A. Koenig........Grand First Vice-president
531 35th Ave., San Francisco

Harmon D. Skillin........Grand Second Vice-president
Mills Bldg., San Francisco

J. Hartley Russell........Grand Third Vice-president
1025 Russ Bldg., San Francisco

John T. Regan........Grand Secretary
N.S.G.W. Bldg., 414 Mason St., San Francisco

John A. Corotto........Grand Treasurer
560 No. 5th St., San Jose

Sam Hurst........Grand Marshal
5262 Boyd Ave., Oakland

William A. Reuter........Grand Inside Sentinel
1009 Marine Ave., Wilmington

Walter P. Rothenbush........Grand Outside Sentinel
N.S.G.W. Club Rooms, Stockton

Leslie Maloche........Grand Organist
1775 El Cerrito, Los Angeles

Chester Gannon........Grand Historian
618 Capital Ntl. Bank Bldg., Sacramento

GRAND TRUSTEES.

Eldred L. Meyer........922 San Vicente Blvd., Santa Monica
Henry S. Lyon........Placerville
Chas. H. Spengemann........827 27th Ave., San Francisco
Thos. M. Foley........Hearst Bldg., San Francisco
Jesse H. Miller........712 DeYoung Bldg., San Francisco
John M. Burnett........Bank America Bldg., San Jose
Edward T. Schnarr........3611 Allendale Ave., Oakland

GLENN COUNTY.

Willows No. 255, Willows—Lee V. Logan, Pres.; Leon Marshall, Sec., P.O. box 747; 2nd and 4th Tuesdays, I.O.O.F. Hall.

HUMBOLDT COUNTY.

Humboldt No. 14, Eureka—Henry Sundfors, Pres.; Loren M. Nelson, Sec., P.O. box 195; 2nd and 4th Mondays, Native Sons Hall.

Arcata No. 20, Arcata—W. H. Anderson, Pres.; William Petes, Sec., P. O. box 1117; Thursdays, Native Sons Hall.

Ferndale No. 93, Ferndale—O. J. Olsen, Pres.; C. H. Rasmussen, Sec., R.F.D., 47-A; 1st and 3rd Mondays, Danish Hall.

KERN COUNTY.

Bakersfield No. 42, Bakersfield—George Taylor, Pres.; Henry A. Bannister, Sec., care Bank of America; 2nd and 4th Fridays, Justice Court, City Hall.

LAKE COUNTY.

Lower Lake No. 159, Lower Lake—LeRoy England, Pres.; Albert Kugelman, Sec.; Thursdays, I.O.O.F. Hall.

LASSEN COUNTY.

Honey Lake No. 198, Standish—Leo T. Davis, Pres.; N. V. Wemple, Sec., Litchfield; 1st and 3rd Wednesdays, Wrede Hall.

Big Valley No. 211, Bieber—Fred Bunselmeier, Pres.; A. W. McKenzie, Sec.; 1st and 3rd Wednesdays, I.O.O.F. Hall.

LOS ANGELES COUNTY.

Los Angeles No. 45, Los Angeles City—Roger M. Johnson, Pres.; Willard F. Allen, Sec., 4955 Los Feliz Blvd.; Thursdays, Merchant Plumbers Hall, 1832 So. Hope.

Ramona No. 109, Los Angeles City—Charles E. Straube, Pres.; John V. Scott, Sec., Patriotic Hall, 1816 So. Figueroa; Fridays, Patriotic Hall, 1816 So. Figueroa.

Hollywood No. 196, Los Angeles City—Henry G. Bodkin, Pres.; E. J. Reilly, Sec., Olive View; Mondays, 1089 No. Oxford Ave.

Long Beach No. 239, Long Beach—Francis H. Gentry, Pres.; W. W. Brady, Sec., 801 Jergins Trust Bldg.; Dept. No. 1 Municipal Court, 8th floor Jergins Trust Bldg.

Sepulveda No. 263, San Pedro—Walter C. Richards, Pres.; H. E. Fairall, Sec., 1925 So. Pacific Ave.; 1st and 3rd Fridays, Redman Hall, 543 Shepherd St., Point Firmin.

Glendale No. 264, Glendale—Harvey T. Gillette, Pres.; Philip D. Molen, Sec., 222 So. Glendale; 1st and 3rd Thursdays, Starr Heights Recreation Bldg., 3246 Community Place.

Santa Monica Bay No. 267, Santa Monica—J. Edward McCurdy, Pres.; John J. Smith, Sec., 830 Rialto Ave., Venice; 1st and 3rd Wednesdays, Odd Fellows Hall, 1431 Third St.

University No. 272, Los Angeles City—Maynard P. Garrison, Pres.; Carl Martin, Sec., 1607 So. Spaulding St.; Wednesdays, Casa de Rosas, Adams and Hoover Sts.

Compton No. 273, Compton—Ray W. Hecock, Pres.; Wm. Don Castillo, Sec., care Police Dept.; 2nd and 4th Tuesdays, Elks Hall, 6172 No. Long Beach Blvd., North Long Beach.

MADERA COUNTY.

Madera No. 130, Madera City—Cornelius Noble, Pres.; T. P. Cosgrave, Sec.; 1st and 3rd Thursdays, First National Bank Bldg.

MARIN COUNTY.

Mount Tamalpais No. 64, San Rafael—Donald J. Locati, Pres.; Manuel A. Andrade, Sec., 532 Mission Ave.; 1st and 3rd Mondays, Portuguese-American Hall.

Sea Point No. 158, Sausalito—Clarence D. Rosa, Pres.; Manuel Santos, Sec., 6 Glen Drive; 1st and 3rd Wednesdays, Perry Bldg.

Nicasio No. 183, Nicasio—M. T. Farley, Pres.; R. J. Rogers, Sec.; 2nd and 4th Wednesdays, U.A.O.D. Hall.

MENDOCINO COUNTY.

Ukiah No. 71, Ukiah—Kenneth Phillips, Pres.; Ben Hofman, Sec., P.O. box 473; 1st and 3rd Mondays, I.O.O.F. Hall.

Broderick No. 117, Point Arena—Albert Seymour, Pres.; C. J. Buchanan, Sec.; 1st and 3rd Thursdays, Forester Hall.

Alder Glen No. 200, Fort Bragg—Fred LeValley, Pres.; C. R. Weller, Sec.; 2nd and 4th Fridays, I.O.O.F. Hall.

MERCED COUNTY.

Yosemite No. 24, Merced City—Alfred Wm. Petersen, Pres.; True W. Fowler, Sec., P. O. box 781; 2nd and 4th Mondays, I.O.O.F. Hall.

Los Banos No. 206, Los Banos—Frank Dambrosio, Pres.; L. E. Sarbo, Sec., R.F.D., box 21; 2nd and 4th Wednesdays, Eagles Hall.

MONTEREY COUNTY.

Monterey No. 75, Monterey City—James Millington, Pres.; T. W. Krieger, Sec., 999 Franklin St.; 1st and 3rd Fridays, Knights Pythias Hall, Main St.

ATTENTION, SECRETARIES!

THIS DIRECTORY IS PUBLISHED BY AUTHORITY OF THE GRAND PARLOR N.S.G.W., AND ALL NOTICES OF CHANGES MUST BE RECEIVED BY THE GRAND SECRETARY (NOT THE MAGAZINE) ON OR BEFORE THE 20TH OF EACH MONTH TO INSURE CORRECTION IN NEXT ISSUE OF DIRECTORY.

Santa Lucia No. 97, Salinas—George S. Miller, Pres.; R. W. Adcock, Sec., R.F.D. No. 2, box 181; Mondays, Native Sons Hall, 32 W. Alisal St.

Gabilan No. 132, Castroville—James C. Jordan, Pres.; J. F. Gambetta, Sec., P. O. box 94; 1st and 3rd Thursdays, Native Sons Hall.

NAPA COUNTY.

Saint Helena No. 53, Saint Helena—J. P. Vasconi Sr., Pres.; Edw. L. Bonhote, Sec., P. O. box 364; Mondays, Native Sons Hall.

Napa No. 62, Napa City—Theodore E. Freitas, Pres.; H. J. Hoernle, Sec., 1226 Oak St.; Mondays, Native Sons Hall.

Calistoga No. 86, Calistoga—James Marchese, Pres.; Louis Carlenzoli, Sec.; 1st and 3rd Mondays, I.O.O.F. Hall.

NEVADA COUNTY.

Hydraulic No. 56, Nevada City—Raglan Tuttle, Pres.; Dr. C. W. Chapman, Sec.; Tuesdays, Pythian Castle.

Quartz No. 58, Grass Valley—Frank G. Hooper, Pres.; H. Ray George, Sec., 151 Conaway Ave.; Mondays, Auditorium Hall.

Donner No. 162, Truckee—J. F. Lichtenberger, Pres.; H. C. Lichtenberger, Sec.; 2nd and 4th Tuesdays, Native Sons Hall.

ORANGE COUNTY.

Santa Ana No. 265, Santa Ana—Ivan H. Harper, Pres.; E. F. Marks, Sec., 1124 No. Bristol St.; 1st and 3rd Mondays, The Old Time Dance Hall, Grass Valley St., Tustin.

PLACER COUNTY.

Auburn No. 59, Auburn—Hans J. Petersen, Pres.; J. G. Walsh, Sec.; 1st and 3rd Fridays, Foresters Hall.

Silver Star No. 63, Lincoln—Robert P. Dixon, Pres.; Barney G. Barry, Sec., P. O. box 72; 3rd Wednesday, I.O.O.F. Hall.

Rocklin No. 233, Roseville—Wm. La Due, Pres.; M. E. Reed, Sec., 253 W. Durante; 2nd and 4th Wednesdays, Eagles Hall.

PLUMAS COUNTY.

Quincy No. 131, Quincy—Herbert Hard, Pres.; E. C. Kelsey, Sec.; 2nd Thursday, I.O.O.F. Hall.

Golden Anchor No. 182, La Porte—R. J. McGrath, Pres.; LeRoy J. Post, Sec.; 2nd and 4th Sunday mornings, Native Sons Hall.

Plumas No. 228, Taylorsville—E. E. Sikes, Pres.; George E. Boyden, Sec.; 1st and 3rd Mondays, Native Sons Hall.

SACRAMENTO COUNTY.

Sacramento No. 3, Sacramento City—Ervin Beall, Pres.; J. F. Didion, Sec., 1213 "O" St.; Thursdays, Native Sons Bldg., 11th and "J" Sts.

Sunset No. 26, Sacramenot City—William H. Peters, Pres.; Edward E. Reese, Sec., County Treasurer Office; Mondays, Native Sons Bldg., 11th and "J" Sts.

Elk Grove No. 41, Elk Grove—Robert Carr, Pres.; Walter Martin, Sec.; 2nd and 4th Fridays, Masonic Hall.

Granite No. 83, Folsom—Joe Relvas, Pres.; Frank Showers, Sec.; 2nd and 4th Tuesdays, K.P. Hall.

Courtland No. 106, Courtland—W. H. Thisby, Pres.; Jos. Green, Sec.; 1st Saturday and 3rd Monday, Native Sons Hall.

Sutter Fort No. 241, Sacramento City—Ed. T. Goyne, Pres.; C. L. Katzenstein, Sec., P. O. box 914; 2nd and 4th Wednesdays, Native Sons Bldg., 11th and "J" Sts.

Galt No. 243, Galt—Abel G. Stock, Pres.; F. W. Harms, Sec.; 1st and 3rd Mondays, I.O.O.F. Hall.

SAN BENITO COUNTY.

Fremont No. 44, Hollister—S. Churchill, Pres.; J. E. Prendergast Jr., Sec., 1064 Monterey St.; 1st and 3rd Thursdays, Grangers Union Hall.

SAN BERNARDINO COUNTY.

Arrowhead No. 110, San Bernardino City—Henry B. Peake, Pres.; R. W. Brazelton, Sec., 462 6th St.; Wednesdays, Eagles Hall, 469 4th St.

SAN DIEGO COUNTY.

San Diego No. 108, San Diego City—John P. Murphy, Pres.; A. V. Mayrhofer, Sec., 1572 2nd St.; Wednesdays, K.C. Hall, 4th and Elm Sts.

SAN FRANCISCO CITY AND COUNTY.

California No. 1, San Francisco—Henry F. Rickleffs, Pres.; Ellis A. Blackman, Sec., 1248-A Divisadero St.; Thursdays, Native Sons Bldg., 414 Mason St.

Pacific No. 10, San Francisco—William G. Boyce, Pres.; J. Henry Bastein, Sec., 380 Van Ness Ave. South; Tuesdays, Native Sons Bldg., 414 Mason St.

Golden Gate No. 29, San Francisco—William M. Roll, Pres.; Adolph Eberhart, Sec., 188 Carl St.; Mondays, Native Sons Bldg., 414 Mason St.

Mission No. 38, San Francisco—Faustino F. Augustine, Pres.; Thos. J. Stewart, Sec., 419 South Van Ness Ave.; Wednesdays, Redmen Hall, 3053 16th St.

San Francisco No. 49, San Francisco—Alfred Watts, Pres.; David Capurro, Sec., 976 Union St.; 2nd and 4th Thursdays, Dante Hall, 1606 Stockton St.

El Dorado No. 52, San Francisco—Robert Foltz, Pres.; Alfred Vlautin, Sec., 1537 Franklin St.; Thursdays, Native Sons Bldg., 414 Mason St.

Rincon No. 72, San Francisco—Albert Granzella, Pres.; John A. Gilmour, Sec., 2069 Golden Gate Ave.; Wednesdays, Native Sons Bldg., 414 Mason St.

Stanford No. 76, San Francisco—Urban Morf, Pres.; Charles T. O'Kane, Sec., 2900 Scott St.; Tuesdays, Native Sons Bldg., 414 Mason St.

Bay City No. 104, San Francisco—Charles L. Licht, Pres.; Max E. Licht, Sec., 1831 Fulton St.; 2nd and 4th Wednesdays, Native Sons Bldg., 414 Mason St.

Niantic No. 105, San Francisco—A. Furner, Pres.; J. M. Darcy, Sec., 10 Hoffman Ave.; Wednesdays, Native Sons Bldg., 414 Mason St.

National No. 118, San Francisco—Walter J. Murphy, Pres.; Martin M. Ratigan, Sec., 1625 Page St., Apt. 6; Thursdays, 1160 Eddy St.

Hesperian No. 137, San Francisco—F. P. Indig, Pres.; Albert Carlson, Sec., 879 Justin Dr.; Thursdays, Native Sons Bldg., 414 Mason St.

Alcalde No. 154, San Francisco—Daniel A. Hinell, Pres.; Harry S. Burke, Sec., 687 Shotwell St.; 2nd and 4th Wednesdays, Native Sons Bldg., 414 Mason St.

South San Francisco No. 157, San Francisco—Peter Macarini, Pres.; John T. Regan, Sec., 1489 Newcomb Ave.; Wednesdays, Masonic Bldg., 4705 3rd St.

Sequoia No. 160, San Francisco—Frank Sullivan, Pres.; Walter W. Garrett, Sec., 2500 Van Ness Ave.; 2nd and 4th Mondays, Swedish-American Bldg., 2174 Market St.

Precita No. 187, San Francisco—Edward F. Rom, Pres.; Edward Tietjen, Sec., 1367 15th Ave.; Thursdays, Mission Masonic Hall, 2668 Mission St.

Olympus No. 189, San Francisco—Henry H. McGowan, Pres.; Harvey J. Carty, Sec., 1651 Market St., Apt. 505; 2nd and 4th Tuesdays, Independent Redmen Hall, 3053 16th St.

Presidio No. 194, San Francisco—Joseph Lenzio, Pres.; George A. Ducker, Sec., 442 21st Ave.; Mondays, Native Sons Bldg., 414 Mason St.

Marshall No. 202, San Francisco—Eugene Biancalona, Pres.; Frank Bacigalupi, Sec., 725 Douglas St.; 1st and 3rd Wednesdays, Native Sons Bldg., 414 Mason St.
Dolores No. 208, San Francisco—Eugene H. O'Donnell, Pres.; Edward F. Webb, Sec., 2801 Sacramento St.; 2nd and 4th Tuesdays, Mission Masonic Hall, 2668 Mission.
Twin Peaks No. 214, San Francisco—Leo Felt, Pres.; Thos. Pendergast, Sec., 278 Douglas St.; Wednesdays, Willopi Hall, 4061 24th St.
El Capitan No. 222, San Francisco—John C. Conmy, Pres.; James Hanna, Sec., 2450 27th Ave.; 1st and 3rd Thursdays, King Soloman Hall, 1739 Fillmore St.
Guadalupe No. 231, San Francisco—Joseph Fay, Pres.; Alvin A. Johnson, Sec., 142 Rousseau St.; Tuesdays, Guadalupe Hall, 4551 Mission St.
Castro No. 232, San Francisco—John J. Qualters, Pres.; James H. Hayes, Sec., 4014 18th St.; Tuesdays, Native Sons Bldg., 414 Mason St.
Balboa No. 234, San Francisco—Jack Killeen, Pres.; E. W. Boyd, Sec., 1046 Lake St.; Thursdays, Maccabee Hall, 5th Ave. and Clement St.
Bret Harte No. 260, San Francisco—Herbert Cline, Pres.; A. W. McElhatton, Sec., 1027 Capitol Ave.; 2nd, 4th and 5th Tuesdays, West of Twin Peaks Hall, 233 Legion Crt.
Utopia No. 270, San Francisco—D. P. Finnegan, Pres.; Herbert H. Schneider, Sec., 2455 14th Ave.; Tuesdays, American Hall, 20th and Capp Sts.

SAN JOAQUIN COUNTY.

Stockton No. 7, Stockton—George Witherow, Pres.; R. D. Dorcey, Sec., P. O. box 388; Mondays, Native Sons Hall.
Lodi No. 18, Lodi—Herbert Osterman, Pres.; Clyde J. Brennan, Sec., Cory Bldg.; 2nd and 4th Wednesdays, Eagles Hall.
Tracy No. 186, Tracy—Frank Vierra, Pres.; R. J. Marraccini, Sec., R.F.D. No. 1, box 217, Thursdays, I.O.O.F. Hall.
Manteca No. 271, Manteca—W. R. Perry, Pres.; Leonard Faria, Sec., R.F.D., box 75, Lathrop; 1st and 3rd Wednesdays, I.O.O.F. Hall.

SAN LUIS OBISPO COUNTY.

San Miguel No. 150, San Miguel—H. Twisselman, Pres.; Otto Kuebl, Sec., Paso Robles; 1st Wednesday, Clemons Hall.
Cambria No. 152, Cambria—Edward Shang, Pres.; A. S. Gay, Sec.; Wednesdays, Rigdon Hall.

SAN MATEO COUNTY.

Redwood No. 66, Redwood City—Seneca R. Coats, Pres.; A. S. Liguori, Sec., P. O. box 212; Thursdays, American Foresters Hall.
Seaside No. 95, Half Moon Bay—H. Locke Nelson, Pres.; John G. Gilcrest, Sec.; 2nd and 4th Tuesdays, I.O.O.F. Hall.
Menlo No. 185, Menlo Park—C. W. Call, Pres.; F. W. Johnson, Sec., P. O. box 601; 1st and 3rd Thursdays, Masonic Hall.
Pebble Beach No. 230, Pescadero—John Souza, Pres.; E. A. Shaw, Sec.; 2nd and 4th Wednesdays, I.O.O.F. Hall.
El Carmelo No. 256, Daly City—Harry McDonald, Pres.; Ernest L. Micco, Sec., 639 Morse St., San Francisco; 2nd and 4th Wednesdays, Eagles Hall.
Industrial City No. 269, South San Francisco—John C. Hamilton, Pres.; Geo. A. Roll, Sec., P. O. box 237; 2nd and 4th Mondays, Metropolitan Hall.

SANTA BARBARA COUNTY.

Santa Barbara No. 116, Santa Barbara City—Philip Bradley, Pres.; H. C. Sweetser, Sec., Court House; 1st and 3rd Thursdays, Pythian Castle.

SANTA CLARA COUNTY.

San Jose No. 22, San Jose—Mario Ponzini, Pres.; Joseph Lawrence, Sec., 1095 No. First St.; Mondays, I.O.O.F. Hall.
Santa Clara No. 100, Santa Clara City—A. P. Cunha, Pres.; Clarence Clevenger, Sec., P.O. box 297; 1st and 3rd Wednesdays, Redmen Hall.
Observatory No. 177, San Jose—Louis V. Dietz, Pres.; A. B. Langford, Sec., Hall Records; Tuesdays, Knights Columbus Hall, 40 No. First St.
Mountain View No. 215, Mountain View—Henry A. Schultze Jr., Pres.; C. A. Antonioli, Sec., 301 Castro St.; 2nd and 4th Wednesdays, Mockbee Hall.
Palo Alto No. 216, Palo Alto—John C. Bernal, Pres.; Albert A. Quinn, Sec., 643 High St.; 2nd and 4th Mondays, N.S.G.W. Bldg., Hamilton Ave. and Emerson St.

SANTA CRUZ COUNTY.

Watsonville No. 65, Watsonville—J. E. Giacoma, Pres.; E. R. Tindall, Sec., 51 Marchant St.; 2nd and 4th Tuesdays, I.O.O.F. Hall.
Santa Cruz No. 90, Santa Cruz City—James H. Griffin Jr., Pres.; T. V. Mathews, Sec., 105 Pacheco Ave.; Fridays, Native Sons Hall, 117 Pacific Ave.

SHASTA COUNTY.

McCloud No. 149, Redding—Melvin Zeis, Pres.; Hugh A. Shuffleton, Sec.; 1st and 3rd Thursdays, Moose Hall.

SIERRA COUNTY.

Downieville No. 92, Downieville—Earl Rickard, Pres.; H. S. Tibbey, Sec.; 2nd and 4th Mondays, I.O.O.F. Hall.
Golden Nugget No. 94, Sierra City—Emil Alleson, Pres.; Arthur R. Pride, Sec.; 1st and 3rd Wednesdays, Masonic Hall.

SISKIYOU COUNTY.

Etna No. 192, Etna—George Wm. Smith, Pres.; Harvey A. Green, Sec.; 1st and 3rd Wednesdays, I.O.O.F. Hall.
Liberty No. 193, Sawyers Bar—David H. Robinson, Pres.; John M. Barry, Sec.; 1st and 3rd Saturdays, I.O.O.F. Hall.

SOLANO COUNTY.

Solano No. 39, Suisun—John S. Cannon, Pres.; J. W. Kinlock, Sec.; 1st and 3rd Tuesdays, I.O.O.F. Hall.
Vallejo No. 77, Vallejo—Frank J. Heidener, Pres.; Werner B. Hallin, Sec., 912 Carolina; 2nd and 4th Tuesdays, San Pablo Hall.

SONOMA COUNTY.

Petaluma No. 27, Petaluma—Walter Christiansen, Pres.; C. F. Fobes, Sec., 114 Prospect St.; 2nd and 4th Mondays, Druid Hall, Gross Bldg., 41 Main St.
Santa Rosa No. 28, Santa Rosa—James Brucker, Pres.; Leland S. Lewis, Sec., Court House; Mondays, Native Sons Hall.
Glen Ellen No. 102, Glen Ellen—Robert Kennedy, Pres.; Frank Kirch, Sec., Route 3, Santa Rosa; 2nd Monday, N.S.G.W. Hall.
Sonoma No. 111, Sonoma City—Antone Barrachi, Pres.; L. H. Green, Sec.; 1st and 3rd Mondays, I.O.O.F. Hall.
Sebastopol No. 143, Sebastopol—T. F. Hyland, Pres.; F. G. McFarlane, Sec.; 1st and 3rd Fridays, I.O.O.F. Hall.

STANISLAUS COUNTY.

Modesto No. 11, Modesto—B. E. Munson, Pres.; C. C. Eastin Jr., Sec., P.O. box 898; 1st and 3rd Wednesdays, I.O.O.F. Hall.
Oakdale No. 142, Oakdale—D. W. Tulloch, Pres.; E. T. Gobin, Sec.; 2nd Monday, Legion Hall.
Orestimba No. 247, Crows Landing—Lloyd W. Fink, Pres.; G. W. Fink, Sec.; 1st and 3rd Wednesdays, Community Club Home.
Turlock No. 274, Turlock—Robley R. Libby, Pres.; Steve A. Karkeet, Sec.

SUTTER COUNTY.

Sutter No. 261, Sutter City—James Putman, Pres.; Glen R. Haynes, Sec., R.F.D. No. 2, Yuba City; 2nd and 4th Mondays, N.D.G.W. Hall.

NATIVE SON NEWS

(Continued from Page 9)

Jr. installed the officers of Sea Point No. 158, July 5, C. D. Rosa becoming president. Present was a large delegation from Mount Tamalpais No. 64 (San Rafael). Grand Third Vice-president J. Hartley Russell commended Sea Point on its activities. A delicious chicken dinner was served.

Sawyers Bar—George Francis Bigelow, a charter member of Liberty No. 193, which was instituted August 11, 1894, died recently. He was born February 15, 1864.

Turlock—Turlock No. 274 had a nightime fishing party at Mills Grove on the Merced River July 5. In charge were Pat Gamba, J. M. Lawson and Wallace Hedell.

Oakland—East Bay Counties Assembly No. 2 N.S. Past Presidents and Past President Association No. 2 N.D. had joint installation of officers July 24. Grand Marshal Gam Hurst became governor of the former, and Mrs. Stanley Hall president of the latter.

There is no substitute for membership! Respond to the call of the Grand President for laborers in the eligible field, now ripe for harvest. Work, with ENTHUSIASM!

N.S.G.W. OFFICIAL DEATH LIST.

Containing the name, the date and the place of birth, the date of death, and the Subordinate Parlor affiliation of deceased members reported to Grand Secretary John T. Regan from June 20 to July 20, 1933:

Ewald, Edward; San Francisco, May 13, 1859; June 16, 1933; California No. 1.
Forbes, Wm. J.; Brandy City, September 5, 1862; April 26, 1933; Marysville No. 6.
Wolleson, W. F.; Mariposa, May 7, 1872; March 16, 1933; Stockton No. 7.
Deady, Wm. George; Kelsey, August 22, 1855; June 12, 1933; Stockton No. 7.
Allard, Chas. A.; Stockton, April 25, 1893; June 22, 1933; Stockton No. 7.
Watts, Albert James; Iowa Hill, May 30, 1882; July 4, 1933; Sunset No. 26.
Miller, Thos. Fred; San Francisco, May 27, 1854; July 5, 1933; Santa Rosa No. 28.
Conmy, Thomas Cherry; Weaverville, January 14, 1855; May 30, 1933; Golden Gate No. 29.
Anderson, William A.; Sacramento, August 6, 1875; January 5, 1933; Woodland No. 30.

TRINITY COUNTY.

Mount Bally No. 87, Weaverville—H. W. Day, Pres.; E. V. Ryan, Sec.; 1st and 3rd Mondays, Native Sons Hall.

TULARE COUNTY.

Visalia No. 19, Visalia—G. W. Houk, Pres.; C. H. Wenn, Sec.; 2nd and 4th Tuesdays, Woodman Hall.

TUOLUMNE COUNTY.

Tuolumne No. 144, Sonora—Mathew J. Marshall, Pres.; William M. Harrington, Sec., P. O. box 715; 2nd and 4th Fridays, Knights Columbus Hall.
Columbia No. 258, Columbia—Jos. Cadematori, Pres.; Charles E. Grant, Sec.; 2nd and 4th Thursdays, Native Sons Hall.

VENTURA COUNTY.

Cabrillo No. 114, Ventura City—David Bennett, Pres., 1380 Church St.

YOLO COUNTY.

Woodland No. 30, Woodland—J. L. Aronson, Pres.; T. G. Hughes, Sec.; 1st Thursday, Native Sons Hall.

YUBA COUNTY.

Marysville No. 6, Marysville—A. W. Graves, Pres.; Verne Fogarty, Sec., 719 6th St.; 2nd Friday, Foresters Hall.

AFFILIATED ORGANIZATIONS.

San Francisco Extension of the Order Committee, N.S.G.W.—Joseph J. McShane, Chmn.; Harold J. Regan, Sec., 414 Mason St., San Francisco; meets 2nd and 4th Fridays, Grizzly Bear Club, 414 Mason St., San Francisco.
Alameda County Extension of the Order Committee, N.S.G.W.—Gam Hurst, Chmn.; Frank Roemer, Sec., 830 30th St., Oakland; meets 1st and 3rd Mondays, N.S.G.W. Hall, 11th and Clay Sts., Oakland.
Interparlor Committee (Southern District), N.S.G.W. and N.D.G.W.—Burrel D. Neighbours, Chmn.; Clyde H. Davis, Sec., 1935 E. 78th St.; meets 3rd Friday, Patriotic Hall, 1816 So. Figueroa St., Los Angeles.
San Francisco Assembly No. 1 Past Presidents Association N.S.G.W.—Meets 1st and 3rd Fridays, Native Sons Bldg., 414 Mason St., San Francisco; John Kirrane, Gov.; J. F. Stanley, Sec., 1175 O'Farrell St., San Francisco.
East Bay Counties Assembly No. 3 Past Presidents Association N.S.G.W.—Meets 4th Monday, Native Sons Hall, 11th and Clay Sts., Oakland; Gam Hurst, Gov.; Edgar G. Hanson, Sec., 1260 Russell St., Berkeley.
Marin County Assembly No. 5 Past Presidents Association N.S.G.W.—J. S. Rose Jr., Gov.; L. J. Peter, Sec., Peter Bldg., 4th and "C" Sts., San Rafael.
Fred H. Greely Assembly No. 6 Past Presidents Association N.S.G.W.—Meets monthly with different Parlors comprising district; Peter J. Delay, Gov.; Barney Barry, Sec., P.O. box 72, Lincoln.
San Joaquin Assembly No. 7 Past Presidents Association N.S.G.W.—Meets 1st Friday, Native Sons Hall, Stockton; Clyde H. Gregg, Gov.; R. D. Dorcey, Sec., Native Sons Club, Stockton.
Sonoma County Assembly No. 9 Past President Association N.S.G.W.—Meets monthly at different Parlor headquarters in county; P. A. R. Gambini, Gov.; L. S. Lewis, Sec., Court House, Santa Rosa.
General John A. Sutter Assembly No. 10 Past Presidents Association—C. C. Wachman, Gov.; Jas. J. Longshore, Sec., 514 "J" St., Sacramento.
Grizzly Bear Club—Members all Parlors outside San Francisco at all times welcome. Clubrooms top floor Native Sons Bldg., 414 Mason St., San Francisco.
Native Sons and Native Daughters Central Committee on Homeless Children—Main office, 955 Phelan Bldg., San Francisco; Mrs. John W. Stirling, Chmn.; Miss Mary E. Brusie, Sec. Los Angeles branch office, 3924 Sunset Blvd.; Dorothy Schlingman, Sec.

(ADVERTISEMENT.)

THE LETTER BOX

Comments on subjects of general interest and importance received from readers of The Grizzly Bear.

INFORMATION SOUGHT BY ONE OF FEW REMAINING "ORIGINAL" NATIVE SONS.

Editor Grizzly Bear—Note in the July issue the passing of Ellis Bloch, a member of California Parlor No. 1. Brother Bloch was No. 19 of the 113 members who joined the Order of Native Sons of the Golden West between July 11, 1875 (the date of its organization), and the date of its incorporation, March 27, 1876.

To the best of my knowledge, the only others still living who joined between those dates are: William M. Josephi, No. 23; R. V. Taylor, No. 31; James V. Stovall, No. 56; A. Gilbert, No. 63; Aaron Heringhi, No. 68; Albert Goldman, No. 81; A. C. Leutgens, No. 100; and the undersigned.

If any member knows of others still living of the original 113, or of any in this list who have passed away, will be glad to receive the information.

CHAS. H. SMITH, No. 4.

Joined July 11, 1875; now a member of Ramona Parlor No. 109. Address P. O. box 1016, Avalon, Catalina Island, California.

There is no substitute for membership! Respond to the call of the Grand President for laborers in the eligible field, now ripe for harvest. Work, with ENTHUSIASM!

EARLY-DAY SLAVE-FREEING DOCUMENT UNCOVERED IN SIERRA.

Searching early-day Sierra County records in the courthouse at Downieville, Clerk Charles F. Belding of Butte County came across several entries unlike anything recorded in recent years, says the "Sacramento Bee." One follows:

"Stone and Campbell to Stephen Campbell: Know all men by these presents, that we, Joe B. Stone and Alfred Campbell, of Sierra County, State of California, A.D. 1853, by virtue of authority delegated to us by S. A. Carignow, administrator of George Campbell, deceased, of Madison County, Missouri, in consideration of the sum of $300, lawful money of the United States, to us in hand paid, receipt of which is hereby acknowledged, have manumitted Stephen Campbell, aforesaid.

"Said Negro is 40 years of age, nearly six feet high, and well made, and at present resides in the county and state aforesaid, and we do by these presents restore, set free, manumit, regenerate, disenthral and declare said Stephen Campbell a free man.

"Witness our hands and seals at Downieville the 5th day of December, 1853. J. B. STONE, ALFRED CAMPBELL."

Rader, John C.; Oleta, October 4, 1864; June 1, 1933; Excelsior No. 31.
Hayden, William; Petaluma, August 7, 1860; January 8, 1933; Fremont No. 44.
Morris, Julius S.; San Francisco, September 30, 1869; June 22, 1933; Los Angeles No. 45.
Boyd, Thomas Patrick; San Rafael, December 12, 1872; January 28, 1933; Mount Tamalpais No. 64.
Licht, Simon Louis; San Francisco, July 27, 1872; June 6, 1933; Bay City No. 104.
Sittel, Albert C.; Los Angeles, October 1, 1876; June 23, 1933; Ramona No. 109.
Viall, Jacob Vanderhuyden; Los Angeles, February 25, 1896; June 27, 1933; Ramona No. 109.
Soto, Lorenzo Francisco; Concord, September 5, 1862; July 7, 1933; Ramona No. 109.
Andrews, Richard H.; San Francisco, August 22, 1867; June 24, 1933; Alcalde No. 154.
Cove, William J.; San Francisco, October 1, 1878; June 6, 1933; Alcalde No. 154.
Linsley, William Edward; San Francisco, November 21, 1866; June 19, 1933; Sequoia No. 160.
Young, Henry; Scott Valley, December 16, 1876; April 1, 1933; Etna No. 192.
Evans, Harry P.; Fort Jones, January 8, 1877; June 1, 1933; Etna No. 192.
Bigelow, George Francis; Sawyers Bar, February 15, 1864; May 24, 1933; Liberty No. 193.
Hayes, Thomas Edward; Oakland, April 30, 1877; June 19, 1933; Athens No. 195.
Riehl, James E.; Oroville, December 22, 1859; June 19, 1933; Palo Alto No. 216.
Costa, Louis; Mokelumne Hill, November 28, 1880; June 21, 1933; Sutter Fort No. 241.
Soares, John Leo; Oakland, November 28, 1907; March 24, 1933; Fruitvale No. 252.
Manning, Lester; Alameda, May 2, 1890; May 6, 1933; Fruitvale No. 252.
Highstreet, Lawrence; Colusa, May 7, 1891; June 2, 1933; Fruitvale No. 252.
Cornell, Roger B.; Berkeley, July 25, 1884; June 22, 1933; Santa Monica Bay No. 267.

"Keep To the Right and Be Right," is the August slogan of the California Public Safety Committee in its campaign to lessen the constantly increasing auto death-toll.

San Joaquin Fair—The annual San Joaquin County Fair will be held at Stockton, August 21-27.

Native Daughters of the Golden West

ALTURAS—GRAND PRESIDENT IRMA Laird announces the appointment of assistants for her term, July 1, 1933, to July 1, 1934,—standing committees, supervising deputies and deputy grand presidents—as follows. The first named of each committee is the chairman thereof:

STANDING COMMITTEES.

Finance—Emma Lou Humphrey (P.G.P.), Sue J. Irwin (P.G.P.), Ariana Stirling (P.G.P.).

Printing and Supplies—Estelle Evans (P.G.P.), Loretta Kidd (Fruitvale No. 177), Katherine Whelan (Las Lomas No. 72).

Laws and Supervision—Gladys E. Noce (G.V.P.), Esther Sullivan (P.G.P.), Nell Boege (El Vespero No. 118), Grace Bessac (Joaquin No. 5), Mollye Spaelti (Marinita No. 198).

Legislation—Emma Lou Humphrey (P.G.P.), Dr. Eva R. Rasmussen (P.G.P.), Cora Sifford (P.G.P.), Helen Anderson (Grace No. 242), Nan Kelly (Portola No. 172).

State of the Order—Catherine E. Gloster (P.G.P.), Mamie P. Carmichael (P.G.P.), Grace Stoermer (P.G.P.), Claire Lindsey (Golden Gate No. 158), Eliza D. Keith (P.G.P.).

Appeals and Grievances—Cora Sifford (P.G.P.), Dr. Eva Rasmussen (P.G.P.), Mattie Stein (P.G.P.), Elinor Taylor (Eltapome No. 55), Inez Sitton (Californiana No. 247).

Petitions—Amy McAvoy (P.G.P.), Margaret Grote Hill (P.G.P.), May C. Boldemann (P.G.P.).

Ritual—Bertha A. Briggs (P.G.P.), May C. Boldemann (P.G.P.), Estelle Evans (P.G.P.), Ruth Gansberger (Hayward No. 122), Florence Shapero (Berkeley No. 150).

Transportation—Emma G. Foley (P.G.P.), Sallie R. Thaler (G.S.), Grace Norton (Los Angeles No. 124).

Credentials—Carrie Roesch Durham (P.G.P.), May Givens (Mariposa No. 63), Olive B. Matlock (P.G.P.).

Homeless Children—Ariana W. Stirling (P.G.P.), Sue J. Irwin (P.G.P.), May Himes Noonan (P.G.P.).

Education—Eliza D. Keith (P.G.P.), Mary Noerenberg (Californiana No. 247), Reta Rust (Lassen View No. 98), Kathryn Ronan (Los Angeles No. 124), Edna Hill (Donner No. 193).

Americanization—Dr. Louise C. Heilbron (P.G.P.), Myra Rumrill (Oneonta No. 71), Dorothy Benjamin (Hiawatha No. 140), Ethel Brock (Camp Far West No. 218), Edna Richter (Woodland No. 90), Melissa Wilson (Mary E. Bell No. 224), Mary Francis Mitchell (San Jose No. 81), Josephine Clark (Piedmont No. 87), May Edwards (Castro No. 178).

Pioneer Roster and Relics—Mamie P. Carmichael (P.G.P.), Edith Kelly (Califia No. 22), Hannah Collins (Fremont No. 59), and one member to be selected by the president of each Subordinate Parlor.

Board of Control—Irma Laird (G.P.), Emma Lou Humphrey (P.G.P.), Ethel Begley (G.T.), Marguerite Sullivan (Alta No. 3), Agnes Curry (Portola No. 172).

Mills College Scholarship—Dr. Mariana Bertola (P.G.P.), Alison F. Watt (P.G.P.), Mazie Roderick (Oro Fino No. 9), Genevieve Watson Baker (P.G.P.), Mae Minear (Hiawatha No. 140).

Publicity—Bertha A. Briggs (P.G.P.), Dorothy Gloster (Alturas No. 159), Ruth Presleigh (Hiawatha No. 140), Evelyn Eby (Reina del Mar No. 126), Olive Lopez (Californiana No. 247), May Givens (Mariposa No. 63), Rita Hayden (Oro Fino No. 9), Irma Murray (Aloha No. 106), Clara Gairaud (Vendome No. 100), Mabel Nicholson (Las Juntas No. 221), Hazel Chicozoli (Ursula No. 1).

Veterans Welfare—Stella Finkeldey (P.G.P.), Oro L. Rogers (Fruitvale No. 177), Eleanor Clark (Presidio No. 148), Ann McDonald (Angelita No. 32), Genevieve Cummerford (Palo Alto No. 229), Margaret Griffith (Castro No. 178), Maude Wagner (Bear Flag No. 151), Alice Kady (Vendome No. 100), Elvina Woodward (Vallejo No. 195), Wiletta Biscailuz (Santa Monica Bay No. 245).

California History and Landmarks—Esther Sullivan (P.G.P.), Henrietta O'Neill (Ursula No. 1), Margaret Griffin (Castro No. 178), Ruby Bunker (Fern No. 123), Eva Bemis (Lugonia No. 241), Irma Heilbron (San Diego No. 208), Ernestine Alward (Californiana No. 247), Mary Gribble (Susanville No. 243), Lola Viera (Las Juntas No. 221), Frankie Miller (Camellia No. 41), Lela Ewert (Woodland No. 90), Mattie Gara (Los Angeles No. 124), Irene Cummings (Alturas No. 159), Catherine Nyland (San Juan Bautista No. 179), E. Mae Rhodes (Madera No. 244).

Extension of the Order—Edith Kelly (Califia No. 22). Alameda County, Carmelita Luhr (Aloha No. 106); Amador County, Emma Boarman-Wright (Ursula No. 1); Butte County, Edna Boyd (Annie K. Bidwell No. 168); Calaveras County, Idell Smith (San Andreas No. 113); El Dorado County, Ethel VanVleck (Marguerite No. 12); Fresno County, Francis Oliver (Fresno No. 187); Glenn County, Neva Wasley (Berryessa No. 192); Humboldt County, Lucile Breeden (Oneonta No. 71); Imperial County, Kathryn Ronan (Los Angeles No. 124); Kern, Kings and Tulare Counties, Ramona Crabtree (Miocene No. 228); Lake County, Dora Herrick (Clear Lake No. 135); Lassen County, Erma Haley (Nataqua No. 152); Los Angeles County, Ora Evans (Californiana No. 247); Madera County, Lois Roach (Madera No. 244); Marin County, Emma Foley (P.G.P.); Mariposa and Tuolumne Counties, Mamie E. Weston (Mariposa No. 63); Mendocino County, Ruth Fuller (Fort Bragg No. 210); Merced County, May Givens (Mariposa No. 63); Modoc County, Katie E. Gloster (Alturas No. 159); Monterey County, Nathalie Clark (Aleli No. 102); Napa County, Ella Ingram (Calistoga No. 145); Nevada County, Adeline O'Connor (Laurel No. 6); Orange County, Nellie Cline (Grace No. 242); Placer County, Laura Goy (Placer No. 138); Plumas County, Rhoda Thompson (Plumas Pioneer No. 219); Riverside County, Mattie Edwards (Grace No. 242); Sacramento County, Kathryn Jones (Rio Rita No. 253); San Benito County, Kathryn B. Nyland (San Juan Bautista No. 179); San Bernardino County, Eva Bemis (Lugonia No. 241); San Diego County, Ann Wood (San Diego No. 208); San Francisco County, Nan Kelly (Portola No. 172); San Joaquin County, Angelina Perry (Phoebe A. Hearst No. 214); San Luis Obispo County, Agnes Lee (San Luisita No. 108); San Mateo County, Ida Thompson (Bonita No. 10); Santa Barbara County, Jane Vick (G.T.); Santa Clara County, Marie Buck (Vendome No. 100); Santa Cruz County, May Williamson (Santa Cruz No. 26); Shasta County, May Minear (Hiawatha No. 140); Sierra County, Jennie Copren (Imogen No. 134); Siskiyou County, Minna Horn (G.T.); Solano County, Mary Bell (P.G.P.); Sonoma County, Florence Anderson (Petaluma No. 222); Stanislaus County, Agnes Frost (Morada No. 199); Sutter County, Theresa Putnam (South Butte No. 226); Tehama County, Dorothy Benjamin (Hiawatha No. 140); Trinity County, Ella Bennett (Eltapome No. 55); Yolo County, Lela Ewert (Woodland No. 90); Yuba County, Annie Sperbeck (Marysville No. 162); Ventura County, Josephine Barboni (Vendome No. 100).

GRAND PRESIDENT'S OFFICIAL ITINERARY.

Alturas—Grand President Irma Laird will officially visit the following Subordinate Parlors on the dates noted. The reference "regular" or "adjourned" is to regular or adjourned meeting of the Parlor:

AUGUST.

16th—Castro No. 178, San Francisco; regular.
17th—Piedmont No. 87, Oakland; regular.
22nd—Presidio No. 148, San Francisco; regular.
23rd—Encinal No. 156, Alameda; regular.
29th—El Pajaro No. 35, Watsonville; adjourned.
30th—Ano Nuevo No. 180, Pescadero; adjourned.

SEPTEMBER.

1st—Ruby No. 46, Murphys; Princess No. 84, Angels Camp; San Andreas No. 113, San Andreas; jointly at San Andreas; regular.
2nd—Victory No. 216, Courtland; regular.
4th—Darina No. 114, San Francisco; regular.
5th—Fern No. 123, Folsom; regular.

SUPERVISING AND DEPUTY GRAND PRESIDENTS.

District No. 1, Del Norte, Humboldt and Mendocino Counties, Hattie E. Roberts supervising deputy. Fort Bragg No. 210, Mae Harmon (Fort Bragg No. 210). Occident No. 28, Oneonta No. 71, Reichling No. 97, Addie Bittencourt (Reichling No. 97).

District No. 2, Siskiyou County, Margaret Weston supervising deputy. Eschscholtzia No. 112, Anita Tucker (Eschscholtzia No. 112). Mountain Dawn No. 120, Essie Skillern (Mountain Dawn No. 120).

District No. 3, Shasta, Tehama and Trinity Counties, Edna Saygrover supervising deputy. Berendos No. 23, Eltapome No. 55, Lassen View No. 98, Olive Endicott (Hiawatha No. 140). Camellia No. 41, Hiawatha No. 140, Rose Machado (Lassen View No. 98).

District No. 4, Modoc and Lassen Counties, Bessie Wemple supervising deputy. Alturas No. 159, Mount Lassen No. 215, Nettie McKenzie (Mount Lassen No. 215). Nataqua No. 152, Susanville No. 234, Lucile Skillern (Nataqua No. 152).

District No. 5, Yuba and Colusa Counties, Cecilia Gomes supervising deputy. Marysville No. 162, Grace Jopson (Camp Far West No. 218). Camp Far West No. 218, Wilhelmina Beecroft (South Butte No. 226). South Butte No. 226, Elsie Schofield (Marysville No. 162). Colus No. 194, Bernice Sperbeck (Marysville No. 162).

District No. 6, Plumas, Butte, Sutter and Glenn Counties, Mae Huston supervising deputy. Annie K. Bidwell No. 168, Lauretta Ross (Gold of Ophir No. 190). Berryessa No. 192, Florence Roe (Colus No. 194). Gold of Ophir No. 190, Frances Snider (Annie K. Bidwell No. 168). Plumas Pioneer No. 219, Helen Hall (Plumas Pioneer No. 219).

District No. 7, Yolo and Solano (part) Counties, Mary E. Bell supervising deputy. Mary E. Bell No. 224, Carrie Congrave (Vallejo No. 195). Vallejo No. 195, Ruth Hickey (Woodland No. 90). Woodland No. 90, Lena Nickum (Mary E. Bell No. 224).

District No. 8, Sonoma County, Clytie Lewis supervising deputy. Sonoma No. 209, Mary Vogt (Orinda No. 56). Petaluma No. 222, Ann Beach (Santa Rosa No. 217). Santa Rosa No. 217, Gertrude Groskopf (Sonoma No. 209).

District No. 9, Marin County, Delphine Todt supervising deputy. Marinita No. 198, Myrtle Divito (Fairfax No. 225). Fairfax No. 225, Lillian Azivido (Sea Point No. 196). Tamelpa No. 231, Irene Griffin (Marinita No. 198). Sea Point No. 196, Anna Loser (Orinda No. 56).

District No. 10, Napa, Lake and Solano (part) Counties, Wilna Mitchell supervising deputy. Clear Lake No. 135, Calistoga No. 145, La Junta No. 203, Lilius Kelly (Calistoga No. 145).

District No. 11, Sierra County, Emma Lou Humphrey supervising deputy. Naomi No. 36, Amelia Sullivan (Naomi No. 36). Snow Peak No. 176, Lotia Bryant (Snow Peak No. 176). Imogen No. 134, Rosa Merrell (Imogen No. 134).

District No. 12, Nevada County, Alison F. Watt supervising deputy. Manzanita No. 29, Columbia No. 70, Clara Phillips (Laurel No. 6). Laurel No. 6, Vanita Jones (Manzanita No. 29).

District No. 13, Placer County, Sadie Brainard supervising deputy. Auburn No. 233, Irma Lohse (La Rosa No. 191). Placer No. 138, La Rosa No. 191, Elizabeth Livingston (Auburn No. 233).

District No. 14, El Dorado County, Beatrice Losse supervising deputy. Marguerite No. 12, El Dorado No. 186, Nettie Leonardi (Marguerite No. 12).

District No. 15, Sacramento County, May Lucas supervising deputy. Liberty No. 213, Myrtle Underhill (Coloma No. 212). Chabolla No. 171, Helen Hanner (Liberty No. 213). Victory No. 216, Alice Carpenter (Chabolla No. 216). Fern No. 123, Lucile Huntoon (La Bandera No. 110). Califia No. 22, Anna Kloss (Liberty No. 213). Coloma No. 212, Edna Brackley (Califia No. 22). La Bandera No. 110, Martha Buckley (Victory No. 216). Sutter No. 111, Esther Mulligan (Califia No. 22). Rio Rita No. 253, Vera Hellinge (Sutter No. 111).

District No. 16, Amador and Calaveras Counties, Emma Boarman Wright supervising deputy. Amapola No. 80, Forrest No. 86, Marie Fontenrose (Amapola No. 80). Ursula No. 1, Chispa No. 40, Esther Gebsardt (Chispa No. 40). Ruby No. 46, Princess No. 84, San Andreas No. 113, Zirda Hertiz (San Andreas No. 113).

District No. 17, Contra Costa (part) County, Mary Ross supervising deputy. Stirling No. 146, Virginia Boltzen (Donner No. 193). Donner No. 193, Margaret Delph (Stirling No. 146). Las Juntas No. 221, Margaret Peters (Antioch No. 223). Antioch No. 223, Mabel Nickelson (Las Juntas No. 221).

District No. 18, San Francisco County, Ann Dippel supervising deputy. Minerva No. 2, Adele Walsh (Darina No. 114). Alta No. 3, Ida Mesquite (Ano Nuevo No. 180). Oro Fino No. 9, Gertrude LaFortune (Keith No. 137). Golden State No. 50, Emma O'Meara (Dolores No. 169). Orinda No. 56, Mae Waring (Castro No. 178). Fremont No. 59, Lena Wall (Minerva No. 2). Buena Vista No. 68, May McDonald (Alta No. 3). Las Lomas No. 72, May Noble (Buena Vista No. 68). Yosemite No. 83, Margaretha McGowan (Linda Rosa No. 170). La Estrella No. 89, Ann Godfrey (El Vespero No. 118). Sans Souci No. 96, Inge Meyer (Mission No. 227). Calaveras No. 103, Mary Hayes (Sans Souci No. 96). Darina No. 114, Mazie Roderick (Oro Fino No. 9). El Vespero No. 118, Emily Ryan (Las Lomas No. 72). Genevieve No. 132, Edna Bishop (James Lick No. 220). Keith No. 137, Alice Bolderman (La Estrella No. 89). Gabrielle No. 139, Merle Sandell (Twin Peaks No. 185). Presidio No. 148, Rena Taube (Genevieve No. 132). Guadalupe No. 153, Nora Stefflin (Genevieve No. 132). Golden Gate No. 158, Alice Schirley (Presidio No. 148). Dolores No. 169, Pearl Wedde (Bret Harte No. 232). Linda Rosa No. 170, Elizabeth Muller (Golden State No. 50). Portola No. 172, Helen Mann (Keith No. 137). Castro No. 178, Agnes Curry (Portola No. 172). Twin Peaks No. 185, May McCarty (Guadalupe No. 153). James Lick No. 220, Loretta Cameron (Twin Peaks No. 185). Mission No. 227, Annie Franzen (Golden Gate No. 158). Bret Harte No. 232, Helen Sprung (Gabrielle No. 139). Balboa No. 249, Nan Kelly (Portola No. 172). Utopia No. 252, Evelyn I. Carlson (Dolores No. 169).

District No. 19, Alameda County, Dora Brayton supervising deputy. Angelita No. 32, Katherine Walde (Hayward No. 122). Aloha No. 106, Pauline Cleu (Fruitvale No. 177). Argonaut No. 166, Agusta Huxsol (Piedmont No. 87). Berkeley No. 150, Lottie Bischoff (Bahia Vista No. 167). Betsy Ross No. 238, Olinda Kardoza (El Cereso No. 207). Laura Loma No. 182, Evelyn Day Garcia (Betsy Ross No. 238). Piedmont No. 87, Thelma Schonick (Bear Flag No. 151). Encinal No. 156, Martha Watson (Aloha No. 106). Bear Flag No. 151, Larine Martin (Aloha No. 106). Brooklyn No. 157, Marion White (Piedmont No. 87). Bahia Vista No. 167, Kathleen Dombrink (Piedmont No. 87). Fruitvale No. 177, Louise McDougal (Bahia Vista No. 167). El Cereso No. 207, Lottie Heritage (Encinal No. 156). Hayward No. 122, Edna Califish (Bear Flag No. 151). Pleasanton No. 237, Evelyn Perry (Brooklyn No. 157). Richmond No. 147, Ella Freites (Argonaut No. 166).

District No. 20, San Joaquin County, Clarice Cook supervising deputy. Joaquin No. 5, Bess Jackson (El Pescadero No. 82). Caliz de Oro No. 206, Norma Hodson (Phoebe A. Hearst No. 214). El Pescadero No. 82, Delia Garvin (Joaquin No. 5). Ivy No. 88, Edna Gormsen (Joaquin No. 5). Phoebe A. Hearst No. 214, Thirza Hunt (Ivy No. 88).

District No. 21, Stanislaus and Tuolumne Counties, Harriet Corr supervising deputy. Morada No. 199, Eldora No. 248, Ethel Enos (Morada No. 199). Oakdale No. 125,

Laura Roberts (Eldora No. 248). Dardanelle No. 66, Golden Era No. 99, Anona No. 164, Anna C. Silva (Dardenelle No. 66).

District No. 22, Merced, Fresno, Madera and Mariposa Counties, May Givens supervising deputy. Mariposa No. 63, Zelphia Thomas (Veritas No. 75). Veritas No. 75, Lois Roach (Madera No. 244). Fresno No. 187, Hazel Laverty (Veritas No. 75). Madera No. 244, Lena Vierra (Fresno No. 187).

District No. 23, San Mateo County, Rena Mathias supervising deputy. Bonita No. 10, Isabelle Lindquist (Menlo No. 211). Menlo No. 211, Hattie Kelly (El Carmelo No. 181). Vista del Mar No. 155, Alice Mattei (Ano Nuevo No. 180). Ano Nuevo No. 180, Gladys Bennett (Orinda No. 56). El Carmelo No. 181, Mona Thiesen (Yosemite No. 83). San Bruno No. 246, Mary Junker (Bonita No. 10).

District No. 24, Santa Clara County, Emeline McDonald supervising deputy. San Jose No. 81, Dolores Collette (El Monte No. 205). Vendome No. 100, Genevieve Eppler (San Jose No. 81). El Monte No. 205, Grace Pearl (Vendome No. 100). Palo Alto No. 229, Marie Burk (Vendome No. 100).

District No. 25, San Benito, Santa Cruz and Monterey Counties, Rose Rhyner supervising deputy. Santa Cruz No. 26, El Pajaro No. 35, Aleli No. 102, Copa de Oro No. 105, Junipero No. 141, San Juan Bautista No. 179, Alberta McCormick (Santa Cruz No. 26).

District No. 26, Kern County, Lou Herrod supervising deputy. Miocene No. 228, El Tejon No. 239, Desert Gold No. 250, Evelyn Town (Miocene No. 228).

District No. 27, San Luis Obispo County, Katie Van Gorden supervising deputy. San Miguel No. 94, San Luisita No. 108, El Pinal No. 163, Elsie Loose (San Miguel No. 94).

District No. 28, Santa Barbara County, Anna McCaughey supervising deputy. Reina del Mar No. 126, Vera Pacheco Grim (Reina del Mar No. 126).

District No. 29, San Diego and Imperial Counties, Marguerite Dickenson supervising deputy. San Diego No. 208, Pearl Adams Simpson (San Diego No. 208).

District No. 30, Los Angeles County, Grace S. Stoermer supervising deputy. Los Angeles No. 124, Marion Crum (Santa Ana No. 235). Long Beach No. 154, Letitia Sarciaux (Rudecinda No. 230). Rudecinda No. 230, Rita Smith (Santa Monica Bay No. 245). Verdugo No. 240, Adele S. Frankish (Ontario No. 251). Santa Monica Bay No. 245, Bulah VanLuven (Verdugo No. 240). Californiana No. 247, Mattie Edwards (Grace No. 242).

District No. 31, San Bernardino, Orange and Riverside Counties, Marvel Thomas supervising deputy. Santa Ana No. 235, Violet Henshelwood (Long Beach No. 154). Lugonia No. 241, Gertrude Tuttle (Californiana No. 247). Grace No. 242, Irene Ederf (Los Angeles No. 124). Ontario No. 251, Gladys Case Baker (Lugonia No. 241).

Anniversary Observed.

Marysville—The twenty-fifth anniversary of the institution of Marysville No. 162 was observed July 12 with a supper and program in the garden of the Sperbeck home. President Anna Sperbeck gave an address of welcome and then called the charter-roll. The following, honor-guests of the evening, responded: Past Grand Esther R. Sullivan, Mabel Kimball-Richards, Martha Sullivan-Boyd, Ina Hedger-Wells, Ada Hedger-Lewis, Anna Noyes-Moncur, Elizabeth Delay and Mary Moncur.

A resume of the outstanding activities of the Parlor constituted the program: Past Grand Sullivan, homeless children work; Mrs. Ina Wells, restoration of missions; Mrs. Ada Lewis, historic building at Timbuctoo; Mrs. Gertrude Cable, markers at Fremont camp, Hock Farm, Mary Covillaud grave, Cortez Square and the Mary Covillaud school; Miss Bernice Sperbeck, tribute to the Pioneers.

Mms. Gertrude Cable and Ruth Manwell had charge of the program, and the refreshments committee included Misses Bernice Sperbeck, Ruth Galligan, Mary Meade, and Mrs. Blanche Tharp. The Parlor was instituted July 10, 1908, by the then Grand President, Mrs. Ema Gett, now deceased. Mrs. Elizabeth Delay was the charter president, and Miss Violet Heyl, now deceased, was the organizer and the first recording secretary.

Marine Band's Co-operation Appreciated.

San Diego—Members of San Diego No. 208 enjoyed a pot-luck supper at which a small sum was cleared for landmarks purposes. Miss Elva Crowley entertained at a bridge luncheon, and the proceeds were donated by the Parlor toward repair of the exposition buildings in Balboa Park. A dessert-bridge at the home of Mrs. Louise Miller and a garden party are planned for the near-future.

June 29 a committee representing the Parlor visited the United States Marine Base and expressed appreciation for the willing assistance of the marine band on many public programs. The aims and objects of the Order were briefly outlined by Miss Marion S. Stough, who presented the score of "I Love You, California," which was played by the band. President Isabel Young presented a large box of home-made candy. Both gifts were accepted by First Sergeant Raymond G. Jones, bandmaster.

Grand Trustee Feted.

San Rafael—Marinita No. 198 observed its twenty-first institution anniversary June 29, and at the same time had a reception in honor of Grand Trustee Ethel S. Begley, a member of the Parlor. She was presented with a gift of silver and a basket of beautiful flowers.

President Mary Zappettini cut the birthday cake, presented by Supervising Deputy Delphine Todt. Among the many in attendance were Past Grand Emma Gruber-Foley, "mother" of Marinita, and Charter Members Anne Andrade, Rita O'Connor, Lillian Whitmore and Myra Murphy. Chairman Ora Perry of the arrangements committee presided during the evening.

Many At Birthday Party.

Sacramento—La Bandera No. 110 celebrated its thirty-fourth institution anniversary July 7, and honored Charter Members Clara Weldon, Grace Sherman, Gene Harges and Sophie Monteverde, also Mrs. Mae K. Sydenstricker, retiring president, to whom, on the Parlor's behalf, Charter President Monteverde presented a gift. Among the 130 present were Past Grands Dr. Eva R. Rasmussen and Dr. Louise C. Heilbron, Deputy Martha Buckley and representatives of Sutter, Coloma, Fern, Liberty, Victory, Rio Rita, San Diego, Rudecinda and Snow Peak Parlors. The arrangements were perfected by a committee which included Mms. Maude Young (chairman), Genevieve Didion, Agnes Ward, Grace Schaden, Amy Meister, Elsie O'Brien, Minnie Frankland, Eva Mordecai, Clara Weldon, Lillian Bragg, Theresa Eberwine and Ruby Lovett.

Officers of La Bandera, with Mrs. Helen Aunger as president, were installed July 21. A program and refreshments followed the ceremonies. The Parlor's drill team of twenty members—Miss Marion Lund supervisor and Miss Hannah Mannerberg captain—will participate in the Santa Rosa Admission Day parade.

NEWSY N.D. PARAGRAPHS.

Napa—Miss Eleonor Simpkins, retiring president, was given a birthday surprise by Eschol No. 16. Members gathered about a horseshoe-shaped table decorated with pink sweetpeas. An impromptu program was enjoyed. Dell Stockman was chairman of the hostess committee. Miss Edna Blanchard succeeds as president.

Lodi—Officers of Ivy No. 88 were installed July 18 by Deputy Edna Gormsen, Mary Meehl becoming president. Past Grands Carrie R. Durham, Mamie G. Peyton and Mattie M. Stein were among the visitors.

Oakland—Aloha No. 106 and Athens No. 195 N.S.G.W. had joint installation of officers July 11. Deputies Pauline Cleu and Joseph Ehrhart officiated, and Katherine Walker and Fred T. Martin became the respective presidents. Grand Secretary Sallie R. Thaler, on Aloha's behalf, presented a past president pin to Thelma D. Rogers. The ceremonies were followed by dancing and refreshments.

Sacramento—Sutter No. 111 honored Mrs. Emilie Lachmann, retiring president, at an affair at which a program was presented and many gifts were given to her. The banquetroom, where an elaborate supper was served, resembled a rose garden. The entrance was through a gate over which hung bowers of roses, and arches of pink roses connected the tables. In charge were Mms. Inez Brown, Ethel Ludwig, Elizabeth Bennetts, Elsie Beskeen, Dora Hubert, Lottie Patterson, Minnie Taylor, Eunice Millman, Adele Nix, Emma Ballew; Misses Garland Taylor, Lorene Patterson, Mayme Sanderson, Margaret Nix.

Chico—Officers of Annie K. Bidwell No. 168 were installed July 13 by Deputy Loretta Ross, Kathryn McEnespy becoming president. Gifts were presented Laura Officer, a recent bride, and the installing officer, and Laura Anderson, outgoing president, was given an emblematic pin. Several members of Gold of Ophir No. 190 (Oroville) were in attendance. A committee composed of Pearl Skelly, Josephine Alexander,

(Continued on Page 17)

Official Directory of Parlors of the N. D. G. W.

ALAMEDA COUNTY.

Angelita No. 32, Livermore—Meets 2nd and 4th Fridays, Foresters Hall; Mrs. Myrtle I. Johnson, Rec. Sec., P.O. box 253.
Piedmont No. 87, Oakland—Meets Thursdays, Corinthian Hall, Pacific Bldg.; Miss Helen Ring, Rec. Sec., 832 11th St.
Aloha No. 106, Oakland—Meets Tuesdays, 4016 Grove St.; Mrs. Lurine Martin, Rec. Sec., 2815 Wallace St., Berkeley.
Hayward No. 122, Hayward—Meets 1st and 3rd Tuesdays, Veterans Memorial Bldg., Main St.; Miss Ruth Gansberger, Rec. Sec., P. O. box 44, Mount Eden.
Berkeley No. 150, Berkeley—Meets 2nd Saturday afternoon, Berkeley City Women's Club, 2315 Durant; Mrs. Lelia B. Baker, Rec. Sec., 915 Contra Costa Ave.
Bear Flag No. 151, Berkeley—Meets 2nd and 4th Wednesdays, Veterans Memorial Bldg., 1931 Center St.; Mrs. Maud Wagner, Rec. Sec., 917 Alcatraz Ave., Oakland.
Encinal No. 156, Alameda—Meets 2nd and 4th Wednesdays, Veterans Memorial Bldg., Central Ave. and Walnut St.; Mrs. Laura E. Fisher, Rec. Sec., 1413 Caroline St.
Brooklyn No. 157, East Oakland—Meets 2nd and 4th Wednesdays, Masonic Temple, 8th Ave. and E. 14th St.; Mrs. Ruth Cooney, Rec. Sec., 3907 14th Ave.
Argonaut No. 166, Oakland—Meets Tuesdays, Klinkner Hall, 59th and San Pablo; Mrs. Ada Spilman, Rec. Sec., 2905 Ellis St., Berkeley.
Bahia Vista No. 167, Oakland—Meets 1st and 3rd Thursdays, Wigwam Hall, Pacific Bldg.; Mrs. Minnie E. Raper, Rec. Sec., 3449 Helen St.
Fruitvale No. 177, Oakland—Meets Fridays, W.O.W. Hall; May E. Barthold, Rec. Sec., 3832 Santa Rita St.
Laura Loma No. 182, Niles—Meets 1st and 3rd Tuesdays, I.O.O.F. Hall; Mrs. Ethel Fournier, Rec. Sec., P. O. box 515.
El Cereso No. 207, San Leandro—Meets 2nd and 4th Tuesdays, Masonic Hall; Mrs. Mary Tuttle, Rec. Sec., P. O. box 56.
Pleasanton No. 237, Pleasanton—Meets 1st Tuesday, I.O.O.F. Hall; Mrs. Myrtle Lanini, Rec. Sec.
Betsy Ross No. 238, Centerville—Meets 1st and 3rd Fridays, Anderson Hall; Miss Constance Lucio, Rec. Sec., P. O. box 187.

AMADOR COUNTY.

Ursula No. 1, Jackson—Meets 2nd and 4th Tuesdays, N.S.G.W. Hall; Mrs. Emma Boarman-Wright, Rec. Sec., 114 Court St.
Chispa No. 40, Ione—Meets 2nd and 4th Fridays, N.S.G.W. Hall; Cynthia Phillips, Rec. Sec.
Amapola No. 80, Sutter Creek—Meets 2nd and 4th Thursdays, N.S.G.W. Bldg.; Mrs. Hazel M. Marre, Rec. Sec.
Forrest No. 86, Plymouth—Meets 2nd and 4th Tuesdays, I.O.O.F. Hall; Mrs. Marguerite Davis, Rec. Sec.

BUTTE COUNTY.

Annie K. Bidwell No. 168, Chico—Meets 2nd and 4th Thursdays, I.O.O.F. Hall; Mrs. Irene Henry, Rec. Sec., 3015 Woodland Ave.
Gold of Ophir No. 190, Oroville—Meets 1st and 3rd Wednesdays, Memorial Hall; Mrs. Ruth Brown, Rec. Sec., 1265 Leah Court.

CALAVERAS COUNTY.

Ruby No. 46, Murphys—Meets 4th Friday, N.S.G.W. Hall; Belle Segale, Rec. Sec.
Princess No. 84, Angels Camp—Meets 2nd and 4th Wednesdays, I.O.O.F. Hall; Mrs. Grace M. Mills, Rec. Sec., P.O. box 312.
San Andreas No. 113, San Andreas—Meets 1st Friday, Fraternal Hall; Miss Doris Treat, Rec. Sec.

COLUSA COUNTY.

Colus No. 194, Colusa—Meets 1st and 3rd Mondays, Eagles Hall; Miss Kate Busch, Rec. Sec., 350 Market St.

CONTRA COSTA COUNTY.

Stirling No. 146, Pittsburg—Meets 1st and 3rd Wednesdays, Veteran Memorial Hall; Mrs. Leslie Clement, Rec. Sec., 468 E. Santa Fe.
Richmond No. 147, Richmond—Meets 1st and 3rd Tuesdays, Richmond Club House, 1125 Nevin Ave.; Grace Curry, Rec. Sec., 932 Ohio Ave.
Donner No. 193, Byron—Meets 1st and 3rd Wednesdays, I.O.O.F. Hall; Mrs. Anna Pendry, Rec. Sec., P.O. box 442, Brentwood.
Las Juntas No. 221, Martinez—Meets 1st and 3rd Mondays, Pythian Castle; Mrs. Lola O. Viera, Rec. Sec., R.F.D. No. 1.
Antioch No. 223, Antioch—Meets 2nd and 4th Tuesdays, I.O.O.F. Hall; Mrs. Estelle Evans, Rec. Sec., 202 E. 5th St., Pittsburg.
Carquinez No. 234, Crockett—Meets 2nd and 4th Wednesdays, I.O.O.F. Hall; Mrs. Cecile Petee, Rec. Sec., 465 Edwards St.

EL DORADO COUNTY.

Marguerite No. 12, Placerville—Meets 1st and 3rd Wednesdays, Masonic Hall; Mrs. Nettie Leonardi, Rec. Sec., 25 Coloma St.
El Dorado No. 186, Georgetown—Meets 2nd and 4th Saturday afternoons, I.O.O.F. Hall; Mrs. Alta L. Douglas, Rec. Sec.

FRESNO COUNTY.

Fresno No. 187, Fresno—Meets 2nd and 4th Fridays, Pythian Castle, Cor. "R" and Merced Sts.; Mary Aubery, Rec. Sec., 1040 Delphia Ave.

GRAND OFFICERS.

Mrs. Anna M. Armstrong..........Past Grand President
Woodland
Mrs. Irma Laird..........Grand President
Alturas
Mrs. Gladys Noce..........Grand Vice-president
Sutter Creek
Mrs. Sallie R. Thaler..........Grand Secretary
555 Baker St., San Francisco
Mrs. Susie K. Christ..........Grand Treasurer
555 Baker St., San Francisco
Mrs. Anna Thuesen..........Grand Marshal
615 38th Ave., San Francisco
Mrs. Hazel B. Hansen..........Grand Inside Sentinel
501 Griswold St., Glendale
Mrs. Alice M. Oldham..........Grand Outside Sentinel
2218 26th Ave., San Francisco
Mrs. Clara Gairaud..........Grand Organist
134 Locust St., San Jose

GRAND TRUSTEES.

Mrs. Orinda G. Giannini......2142 Filbert St., San Francisco
Mrs. Florence D. Boyle..........Oroville
Mrs. Minna K. Horn..........Etna
Mrs. Jane Vick..........418 Bath St., Santa Barbara
Mrs. Alice M. Lane..........191 15th Ave., San Francisco
Mrs. Ethel Begley..........233 Prospect Ave., San Francisco
Mrs. Willow Borba..........330 So. Main St., Sebastopol

GLENN COUNTY.

Berryessa No. 192, Willows—Meets 1st and 3rd Mondays, I.O.O.F. Hall; Mrs. Leonora Neate, Rec. Sec., 338 No. Lassen St.

HUMBOLDT COUNTY.

Occident No. 28, Eureka—Meets 1st and 3rd Wednesdays, N.S.G.W. Hall; Mrs. Eva L. MacDonald, Rec. Sec., 2309 "B" St.
Oneonta No. 71, Ferndale—Meets 2nd and 4th Fridays, I.O.O.F. Hall; Mrs. Myra Rumrill, Rec. Sec., P.O. box 142.
Reichling No. 97, Fortuna—Meets 1st and 3rd Tuesdays, Friendship Hall; Mrs. Grace Swett, Rec. Sec., P. O. box 328.

KERN COUNTY.

Miocene No. 228, Taft—Meets 1st and 3rd Wednesday afternoons, I.O.O.F. Hall; Mrs. Evalyn G. Towne, Rec. Sec., 301 Woodrow St.
El Tejon No. 239, Bakersfield—Meets 1st and 3rd Fridays, Eagles Hall, 1714 "G" St.; Mary B. Hampson, Rec. Sec., 908 Quincy St.
Desert Gold No. 250, Mojave—Meets 2nd and 4th Fridays, I.O.O.F. Hall; Jane Lucile Waters, Rec. Sec., Tehachapi.

LAKE COUNTY.

Clear Lake No. 135, Middletown—Meets 2nd and 4th Tuesdays, Herrick Hall; Mrs. Alma E. Snow, Rec. Sec.

LASSEN COUNTY.

Nataqua No. 152, Standish—Meets 1st and 3rd Wednesdays, Foresters Hall; Mrs. Mayda Elledge, Rec. Sec.
Mount Lassen No. 215, Bieber—Meets 2nd and 4th Thursdays, I.O.O.F. Hall; Mrs. Angie C. Kenyon, Rec. Sec.
Susanville No. 243, Susanville—Meets 3rd Thursday, I.O.O.F. Hall; Mildred Hardy, Rec. Sec., P.O. box 425.

LOS ANGELES COUNTY.

Los Angeles No. 124, Los Angeles—Meets 1st and 3rd Wednesdays, I.O.O.F. Hall, Washington and Oak Sts.; Mrs. Mary K. Corcoran, Rec. Sec., 322 No. Van Ness Ave.
Long Beach No. 154, Long Beach—Meets 1st and 3rd Thursdays, Home of Eleonor Johnson, 1920 Bermuda St.; Mrs. Bertha Hitt, Rec. Sec., 5855 Lime Ave.
Rudecinda No. 230, San Pedro—Meets 1st and 3rd Mondays, Womans Club, Gaffey and "N" Sts.; Letitia Sarciaux, Rec. Sec., 1054 W. 24th St.
Verdugo No. 240, Glendale—Meets 2nd and 4th Tuesdays, Masonic Temple, 234 So. Brand Blvd.; Miss Etta Fulkerth, Rec. Sec., 526 No. Orange St.
Santa Monica Bay No. 245, Santa Monica—Meets 2nd and 4th Wednesdays, Odd Fellows Hall, 1431 Third St.; Mrs. Rosalie Hyde, Rec. Sec., 738 Flower St., Venice.
Californiana No. 247, Los Angeles—Meets 2nd and 4th Tuesday afternoons, Hollywood Studio Club, 1215 Lodi Place; Mrs. Ines Sitton, Rec. Sec., 4228 Berenice St.

MADERA COUNTY.

Madera No. 244, Madera—Meets 2nd and 4th Thursdays, Masonic Annex; Mrs. Margaret O. Boyle, Rec. Sec., 111 No. "B" St.

MARIN COUNTY.

Sea Point No. 196, Sausalito—Meets 2nd and 4th Mondays, Perry Hall, 50 Caledonia St.; Mrs. Mary B. Smith, Rec. Sec., 47½ Glen Drive.
Marinita No. 198, San Rafael—Meets 2nd and 4th Mondays, 316 "B" St.; Lillian Whitmore, Rec. Sec., 337 5th St.
Fairfax No. 225, Fairfax—Meets 2nd and 4th Tuesdays, Community Hall; Mrs. Marguerite Geary, Rec. Sec.
Tamelpa No. 231, Mill Valley—Meets 1st and 2nd Tuesdays, I.O.O.F. Hall; Mrs. Delphine M. Todt, Rec. Sec., 500 Irwin St., San Rafael.

MARIPOSA COUNTY.

Mariposa No. 63, Mariposa—Meets 1st and 3rd Fridays, I.O.O.F. Hall; Elizabeth E. Johnson, Rec. Sec.

MENDOCINO COUNTY.

Fort Bragg No. 210, Fort Bragg—Meets 1st Thursday, I.O.O.F. Hall; Mrs. Ruth W. Fuller, Rec. Sec.

MERCED COUNTY.

Veritas No. 75, Merced—Meets 1st and 3rd Tuesdays, I.O.O.F. Hall; Miss Flora Fernandes, Rec. Sec., 28 19th St.

MODOC COUNTY.

Alturas No. 159, Alturas—Meets 1st Thursday, Alturas Civic Club; Mrs. Irma W. Laird, Rec. Sec.

MONTEREY COUNTY.

Aleli No. 102, Salinas—Meets 2nd and 4th Thursdays, Pythian Hall; Miss Rose Rhyner, Rec. Sec., 420 Soledad St.
Junipero No. 141, Monterey—Meets 2nd and 4th Fridays, K. of P. Hall, Main St.; Miss Matilda M. Bergschicker, Rec. Sec., 498 Van Buren St.

NAPA COUNTY.

Eshcol No. 16, Napa—Meets 2nd and 4th Mondays, N.S.G.W. Hall; Mrs. Ella Ingram, Rec. Sec., 2140 Seminary St.
Calistoga No. 145, Calistoga—Meets 2nd and 4th Mondays, I.O.O.F. Hall; Sadie P. Brooks, Rec. Sec.
La Junta No. 203, Saint Helena—Meets 1st and 3rd Tuesdays, N.S.G.W. Hall; Mrs. Marie Signorelli, Rec. Sec., 1341 Madrona Ave.

ATTENTION, SECRETARIES!

THIS DIRECTORY IS PUBLISHED BY AUTHORITY OF THE GRAND PARLOR N.D.G.W., AND ALL NOTICES OF CHANGES MUST BE RECEIVED BY THE GRAND SECRETARY (NOT THE MAGAZINE) ON OR BEFORE THE 20TH OF EACH MONTH TO INSURE CORRECTION IN NEXT PUBLICATION OF DIRECTORY.

NEVADA COUNTY.

Laurel No. 6, Nevada City—Meets 1st and 3rd Wednesdays, I.O.O.F. Hall; Mrs. Nellie E. Clark, Rec. Sec., 412 Pine St.
Manzanita No. 29, Grass Valley—Meets 1st and 3rd Tuesdays, Auditorium; Mrs. Loraine Keast, Rec. Sec., 123 Race St.
Columbia No. 70, French Corral—Meets Fridays, Farrelley Hall; Mrs. Kate Farrelley-Sullivan, Rec. Sec.
Snow Peak No. 176, Truckee—Meets 1st Monday, I.O.O.F. Hall; Mrs. Henrietta M. Eaton, Rec. Sec., P. O. box 116.

ORANGE COUNTY.

Santa Ana No. 235, Santa Ana—Meets 2nd and 4th Mondays, K.C. Hall, 4th and French Sts.; Mrs. Matilda S. Lemon, Rec. Sec., 1628 W. 8th St.
Grace No. 242, Fullerton—Meets 1st and 3rd Thursdays, I.O.O.F. Hall, 116½ E. Commonwealth; Mrs. Mary R. Rothaermel, Rec. Sec., Acacia St. & Commonwealth.

PLACER COUNTY.

Placer No. 138, Lincoln—Meets 2nd Wednesday, I.O.O.F. Hall; Miss Carrie Parlin, Rec. Sec.
La Rosa No. 191, Roseville—Meets 1st and 3rd Tuesdays, Eagles Hall; Miss Margaret Parrish, Rec. Sec., Atlantic St.
Auburn No. 233, Auburn—Meets 2nd and 4th Fridays, Foresters Hall; Mrs. Elsie Patrick, Rec. Sec.

PLUMAS COUNTY.

Plumas Pioneer No. 219, Quincy—Meets 1st and 3rd Mondays, I.O.O.F. Hall; Minnie E. Johnson, Rec. Sec., P. O. box 243.

SACRAMENTO COUNTY.

Califia No. 22, Sacramento—Meets 2nd and 4th Tuesdays, N.S.G.W. Hall; Miss Lulu Gillis, Rec. Sec., 921 8th St.
La Bandera No. 110, Sacramento—Meets 1st and 3rd Fridays, N.S.G.W. Hall; Mrs. Clara Weldon, Rec. Sec., 1310 "O" St.
Sutter No. 111, Sacramento—Meets 1st and 3rd Tuesdays, N.S.G.W. Hall; Mrs. Adele Nix, Rec. Sec., 1238 "S" St.
Fern No. 123, Folsom—Meets 1st and 3rd Tuesdays, K.P. Hall; Elizabeth Ryan, Rec. Sec., Represa.
Chabolla No. 171, Galt—Meets 2nd and 4th Tuesdays, I.O.O.F. Hall; Mrs. Mary Pritchard, Rec. Sec.
Coloma No. 212, Sacramento—Meets 1st and 3rd Tuesdays, I.O.O.F. Hall, Oak Park; Mrs. Nettie Harry, Rec. Sec., 1217 35th St.
Liberty No. 213, Elk Grove—Meets 2nd and 4th Fridays, I.O.O.F. Hall; Mrs. Frances Wackman, Rec. Sec., P. O. box 192.
Victory No. 216, Courtland—Meets 1st Saturday and 3rd Monday, N.S.G.W. Hall; Mrs. Agneda Lample, Rec. Sec.
Rio Rita No. 253, Sacramento—Meets 1st and 3rd Mondays, 902 "J" St.; Dorothea Rourke, Rec. Sec.

SAN BENITO COUNTY.

Copa de Oro No. 105, Hollister—Meets 2nd and 4th Thursdays, Grangers Union Hall; Mrs. Mollie Daveggio, Rec. Sec., 110 San Benito St.
San Juan Bautista No. 179, San Juan Bautista—Meets 1st Wednesday, Mission Corridor Rooms; Miss Gertrude Breen, Rec. Sec.

SAN BERNARDINO COUNTY.

Lugonia No. 241, San Bernardino—Meets 2nd and 4th Wednesdays, Eagles Hall; Miss Lois Poling, Rec. Sec., 295 E. 11th St.
Ontario No. 251, Ontario—Meets 2nd and 4th Thursdays, Ontario Hotel; Miss Wilma Poole, Rec. Sec., 1102 No. Euclid Ave.

SAN DIEGO COUNTY.

San Diego No. 208, San Diego—Meets 2nd and 4th Wednesdays, Directors Room, Chamber Commerce Bldg., 499 W. Broadway; Mrs. Elsie Case, Rec. Sec., 3051 Broadway.

SAN FRANCISCO CITY AND COUNTY.

Minerva No. 2, San Francisco—Meets 1st and 3rd Wednesdays, N.S.G.W. Bldg.; Miss Dorothy Finn, Rec. Sec., 90 Princess St., Sausalito.
Alta No. 3, San Francisco—Meets 2nd and 4th Tuesdays, N.S.G.W. Bldg.; Mrs. Agnese L. Hughes, Rec. Sec., 3980 Sacramento St.
Oro Fino No. 9, San Francisco—Meets 1st and 3rd Thursdays, N.S.G.W. Bldg.; Mrs. Josephine B. Morrisey, Rec. Sec., 4441 20th St.
Golden State No. 50, San Francisco—Meets 1st and 3rd Wednesdays, N.D.G.W. Home; Miss Millie Tietjen, Rec. Sec., 328 Lexington Ave.
Orinda No. 56, San Francisco—Meets 2nd and 4th Fridays, N.D.G.W. Home; Mrs. Anna A. Gruber-Loser, Rec. Sec., 72 Grove Lane, San Anselmo.
Fremont No. 59, San Francisco—Meets 1st and 3rd Tuesdays, N.S.G.W. Bldg.; Miss Hannah Collins, Rec. Sec., 617 Fillmore St.
Buena Vista No. 68, San Francisco—Meets 1st, 3rd and 5th Thursdays, N.D.G.W. Home; Miss Margaret Barrett, Rec. Sec., 3774 20th St.
Las Lomas No. 72, San Francisco—Meets 1st and 3rd Tuesdays, N.D.G.W. Home; Mrs. Marion S. Day, Rec. Sec., 469 Noe St.
Yosemite No. 83, San Francisco—Meets 1st and 3rd Tuesdays, American Hall, 20th and Capp Sts.; Miss Mary Monahan, Rec. Sec., 287 Noe St.
La Estrella No. 89, San Francisco—Meets 2nd and 4th Mondays, N.S.G.W. Bldg.; Miss Birdie Hartman, Rec. Sec., 1018 Jackson St.
Sans Souci No. 96, San Francisco—Meets 2nd and 4th Mondays, N.D.G.W. Home; Mrs. Minnie F. Dobbin, Rec. Sec., 1483 43rd Ave.
Calaveras No. 103, San Francisco—Meets 2nd and 4th Tuesdays, Swedish American Hall, 2174 Market St.; Mary L. Krogh, Rec. Sec., 4235 Cabrillo St.
Darina No. 114, San Francisco—Meets 1st and 3rd Mondays, N.S.G.W. Bldg.; Miss Adele Walsh, Rec. Sec., 479 Page St.
El Vespero No. 118, San Francisco—Meets 2nd and 4th Tuesdays, Masonic Hall, 4705 3rd St.; Mrs. Nell R. Boage, Rec. Sec., 1526 Kirkwood Ave.
Genevieve No. 132, San Francisco—Meets 1st and 3rd Thursdays, N.S.G.W. Bldg.; Miss Branice Paguillan, Rec. Sec., 2434 16th Ave.
Keith No. 137, San Francisco—Meets 2nd and 4th Thursdays, N.S.G.W. Bldg.; Mrs. Helen T. Mann, Rec. Sec., 575 Pierce St., Apt. 206.
Gabrielle No. 139, San Francisco—Meets 2nd and 4th Wednesdays, N.S.G.W. Bldg.; Mrs. Dorothy Wuesterfeld, Rec. Sec., 1020 Munich St.
Presidio No. 148, San Francisco—Meets 2nd and 4th Tuesdays, N.S.G.W. Bldg.; Mrs. Hattie Gaughran, Rec. Sec., 713 Capp St.
Guadalupe No. 153, San Francisco—Meets 2nd and 4th Mondays, Forester Hall, 170 Valencia St.; Miss May A. McCarthy, Rec. Sec., 336 Elsie St.
Golden Gate No. 158, San Francisco—Meets 2nd and 4th Mondays, N.S.G.W. Bldg.; Mrs. Mary Sullivan, Rec. Sec., 33 Cuvier St.
Dolores No. 169, San Francisco—Meets 2nd and 4th Wednesdays, N.S.G.W. Bldg.; Mrs. Ada Saunders, Rec. Sec., 284 Allison St.

Linda Rosa No. 170, San Francisco—Meets 2nd and 4th Wednesdays, Swedish American Hall, 2174 Market St.; Mrs. Eva P. Tyrrel, Rec. Sec., 2629 Mission St.
Portola No. 172, San Francisco—Meets 1st and 3rd Tuesdays, N.S.G.W. Bldg.; Catherine H. Dolly, Rec. Sec., 4125 23rd St.
Castro No. 178, San Francisco—Meets 1st and 3rd Wednesdays, K.C. Bldg., 150 Golden Gate Ave.; Miss Adeline Sanderefeld, Rec Sec., 50 Baker St.
Twin Peaks No. 185, San Francisco—Meets 2nd and 4th Fridays, Druids Temple, 44 Page St.; Mrs. Loretta Cameron, Rec. Sec., 3969 Army St.
James Lick No. 220, San Francisco—Meets 1st and 3rd Wednesdays, N.S.G.W. Bldg.; Mrs. Edna Bishop, Rec. Sec., 3841 24th St.
Mission No. 227, San Francisco—Meets 2nd and 4th Fridays, N.S.G.W. Bldg.; Mrs. Ann Dippel, Rec. Sec., 448 Dewey Blvd.
Bret Harte No. 232, San Francisco—Meets 2nd and 4th Tuesdays, Aloha Hall, 3009 16th St.; Pearl Wedde, Rec. Sec., 225 7th Ave.
Balboa No. 249, San Francisco—Meets 1st and 3rd Thursdays, Knights Columbus Hall, 382 18th Ave.; Miss Jean Moffet, Rec. Sec., 476 26th Ave.
Utopia No. 252, San Francisco—Meets 2nd and 4th Tuesdays, American Hall, 20th and Capp Sts.; Miss Lelia M. Little, Rec. Sec., 4450 20th St.

SAN JOAQUIN COUNTY.

Joaquin No. 5, Stockton—Meets 2nd and 4th Tuesdays, N.S.G.W, Hall, 314 E. Main St.; Mrs. Della Garvin, Rec. Sec., 1122 E. Market St.
El Pescadero No. 82, Tracy—Meets 1st and 3rd Fridays, I.O.O.F. Hall; Mrs. Mary A. Hewitson, Rec. Sec., 122 Walnut St.
Ivy No. 88, Lodi—Meets 1st and 3rd Tuesdays, Pythian Hall, Cory Bldg., Pine St.; Mrs. Mae Corson, Rec. Sec., 109 So. School St.
Calis de Oro No. 206, Stockton—Meets 1st and 3rd Tuesdays, N.S.G.W. Hall, 314 E. Main St.; Mrs. Frances Germain, Rec. Sec., 450 No. Regent.
Phoebe A. Hearst No. 214, Manteca—Meets 2nd and 4th Wednesdays, I.O.O.F. Hall; Mrs. Josie M. Frederick, Rec. Sec., Route A, Box 364, Ripon.

SAN LUIS OBISPO COUNTY.

San Miguel No. 94, San Miguel—Meets 2nd and 4th Wednesday afternoons, Clemon Hall; Mrs. Nellie Wickstrom, Rec. Sec.
San Luisita No. 108, San Luis Obispo—Meets 2nd and 4th Thursdays, W.O.W. Hall; Miss Agnes M. Lee, Rec. Sec., P. O. box 584.
El Pinal No. 163, Cambria—Meets 2nd, 4th and 5th Tuesdays, N.S.G.W. Hall; Kathryn Luchessa, Rec. Sec.

SAN MATEO COUNTY.

Bonita No. 10, Redwood City—Meets 2nd and 4th Thursdays, I.O.O.F. Hall; Mrs. Dora Wilson, Rec. Sec., 518 Middlefield Rd.
Vista del Mar No. 155, Halfmoon Bay—Meets 2nd Thursday, I.O.O.F. Hall; Elizabeth Olney, Rec. Sec.
Ano Nuevo No. 180, Pescadero—Meets 1st and 3rd Wednesdays, I.O.O.F. Hall; Mrs. Alice Mattei, Rec. Sec.
El Carmelo No. 181, Daly City—Meets 1st and 3rd Wednesdays, Masonic Hall; Mrs. Alice Mathias Oldham, Rec. Sec., 2218 26th Ave., San Francisco.
Menlo No. 211 Menlo Park—Meets 2nd and 4th Mondays, Masonic Hall; Mrs. Frances E. Maloney, Rec. Sec., P. O. box 626.
San Bruno No. 246, San Bruno—Meets 2nd and 4th Fridays, Legion Hall; Miss Mildred Foley, Rec. Sec., 217 Miller Ave., South San Francisco.

SANTA BARBARA COUNTY.

Reina del Mar No. 126, Santa Barbara—Meets 1st and 3rd Tuesdays, Pythian Castle, 222 W. Carillo St.; Mrs. Dorothy Yule, Rec. Sec., 112 Ocean Ave.

SANTA CLARA COUNTY.

San Jose No. 81, San Jose—Meets 1st and 3rd Wednesdays, I.O.O.F. Hall, 3rd and Santa Clara Sts.; Mrs. Nellie Fleming, Rec. Sec., Catholic Women Center.
Vendome No. 100, San Jose—Meets 2nd and 4th Wednesdays, Old Scottish Rite Temple; Miss Marie Buck, Rec. Sec., 245 Hawthorne St.
El Monte No. 205, Mountain View—Meets 2nd and 4th Fridays, American Legion Hall; Miss Elizabeth Spencer, Rec. Sec., 1620 Villa St.
Palo Alto No. 229, Palo Alto—Meets 1st and 2nd Mondays, N.S.G.W. Hall; Miss Helena G. Hansen, Rec. Sec., 581 Lytton Ave.

SANTA CRUZ COUNTY.

Santa Cruz No. 26, Santa Cruz—Meets Mondays, N.S.G.W. Hall; Mrs. May L. Williamson, Rec. Sec., 170 Walnut Ave.
El Pajaro No. 35, Watsonville—Meets 1st and 3rd Tuesdays, I.O.O.F. Hall; Miss Ruth E. Wilson, Rec. Sec., 16 Laurel St.

SHASTA COUNTY.

Camellia No. 41, Anderson—Meets 1st and 3rd Tuesdays, Masonic Hall; Mrs. Olga E. Welbourn, Rec. Sec.
Lassen View No. 98, Shasta—Meets 2nd Friday, Masonic Hall; Miss Louise Litsch, Rec. Sec.
Hiawatha No. 140, Redding—Meets 2nd and 4th Wednesdays, Moose Hall; Ruth Presleigh, Rec. Sec., Office County Clerk.

SIERRA COUNTY.

Naomi No. 36, Downieville—Meets 2nd and 4th Wednesdays, I.O.O.F. Hall; Louise O. Dubuque, Rec. Sec.
Imogen No. 134, Sierraville—Meets 2nd and 4th Saturday afternoons, Copren Hall; Mrs. Jennie Copren, Rec. Sec.

SISKIYOU COUNTY.

Eschscholtzia No. 112, Etna—Meets 1st and 3rd Wednesdays, Masonic Hall; Mrs. Bernice E. Smith, Rec. Sec.
Mountain Dawn No. 120, Sawyers Bar—Meets 2nd and last Wednesdays, I.O.O.F. Hall; Miss Edith Dunphy, Rec. Sec.

SOLANO COUNTY.

Vallejo No. 195, Vallejo—Meets 1st and 3rd Wednesdays, K.C. Hall, 820 Marin St.; Mrs. Mary Combs, Rec. Sec., 511 York St.
Mary E. Bell No. 224, Dixon—Meets 2nd and 4th Thursdays, I.O.O.F. Hall; Mary Young, Rec. Sec.

SONOMA COUNTY.

Sonoma No. 209, Sonoma—Meets 2nd and 4th Mondays, I.O.O.F. Hall; Mrs. Mae Norrbom, Rec. Sec., R.F.D., box 171.
Santa Rosa No. 217, Santa Rosa—Meets 1st and 3rd Thursdays, N.S.G.W. Hall; Mrs. Clytie L. Lewis, Rec. Sec., R.F.D. No. 4, Box 345-A.
Petaluma No. 222, Petaluma—Meets 1st and 3rd Tuesdays, Dania Hall; Mrs. Margaret M. Oeltjen, Rec. Sec., 503 Prospect St.

STANISLAUS COUNTY.

Oakdale No. 125, Oakdale—Meets 3rd Monday, McLeod Home; Mrs. Lou Reeder, Rec. Sec.
Morada No. 199, Modesto—Meets 2nd and 4th Wednesdays, I.O.O.F. Hall; Mrs. Susan Sullivan, Rec. Sec., 823 10th St.
Eldora No. 248, Turlock—Meets 1st and 3rd Mondays, Masonic Temple; Effie Lund, Rec. Sec., 312 Mitchell St.

SUTTER COUNTY.

South Butte No. 226, Sutter—Meets 1st and 3rd Mondays, N.D.G.W. Hall; Mrs. Abbie N. Vagedes, Rec. Sec.

TEHAMA COUNTY.

Berendos No. 23, Red Bluff—Meets 1st and 3rd Tuesdays, W.O.W. Hall, 200 Pine St.; Mrs. Lillie Hammer, Rec. Sec., 686 Jackson St.

NATIVE DAUGHTER NEWS

(Continued from Page 16)

Ethel Estes and Mabel Marshall was named to arrange for the entertainment of oldtimers of the community September 9.

Georgetown—Past President Victoria Knox entertained the officers of El Dorado No. 186 at her home July 1. Singing and games provided amusement, and delicious refreshments were served.

Bieber—Mount Lassen No. 215 had its annual entertainment for the mothers and the fathers. A program was presented, and jigsaw puzzles and guessing games afforded amusement. Refreshments were served at tables decorated with flowers. Officers-elect, with Bessie Chace as president, will be installed in August by Deputy Nettie McKenzie.

Antioch—Antioch No. 223 entertained its past presidents at a "hard times" party. Priscilla Taylor was awarded a prize for the most worn-out costume. Luncheon was served in picnic style. Francis Frodsham was chairman of the doings. In attendance were Past Presidents Mary Ross, Genevieve Field, Alice Bloomfield, Grace Gatter, Myra Rademacher and Edythe Schaller, and Past Grand Estelle M. Evans.

Mill Valley—The drum corps of Tamelpa No. 231 had a barn dance July 6. The purpose was to raise funds with which to purchase new uniforms for the Santa Rosa Admission Day parade.

San Bernardino—Lugonia No. 241 had a sociable July 12; bridge was played and refreshments were served. The Harmony Club met July 11 at the home of Mildred Meyers and worked on articles for the October bazar. Officers were installed July 19, Mary Harris Johnson becoming president.

Fullerton—Grace No. 242 members and their families enjoyed the Parlor's annual summer evening picnic at Irvine Park. President Lena Aspden was in charge. Officers were publicly installed July 20. The arrangements committee included Marie Haiber, Christine McFarland, Grace Hirigoyen, Lydia Oswald and Helen Anderson.

San Jose—Officers of Past Presidents Association No. 3 were installed July 11, Alice Roll becoming president. Amelia Hartman, installing officer, was given a lovely gift. The welfare work of this small group, on a par with that of many larger organizations, will be continued during the winter under the direction of Claire Borchers. The association will observe its ninth anniversary in August, and initiation of a class of candidates will be a feature.

Sacramento—Officers of Past President Association No. 4 were installed July 9 by Mrs. Edna B. Briggs, Mrs. Nettie Harry becoming president. Mrs. Harriet Hall headed the arrangements committee for the social hour. Mrs. Briggs, retiring president, was the recipient of a gift from the association.

TRINITY COUNTY.

Eltapome No. 55, Weaverville—Meets 2nd and 4th Thursdays, N.S.G.W. Hall; Mrs. Lou N. Fetzer, Rec. Sec.

TUOLUMNE COUNTY.

Dardanelle No. 66, Sonora—Meets Fridays, I.O.O.F. Hall; Mrs. Nettie Whitto, Rec. Sec., P.O. box 122.
Golden Era No. 99, Columbia—Meets 1st and 3rd Thursdays, N.S.G.W. Hall; Miss Irene Ponce, Rec. Sec.
Anona No. 164, Jamestown—Meets 2nd and 4th Tuesdays, I.O.O.F. Hall; Nellie Hope, Rec. Sec.

YOLO COUNTY.

Woodland No. 90, Woodland—Meets 2nd and 4th Tuesdays, N.S.G.W. Hall; Mrs. Maude Heaton, Rec. Sec., 153 College St.

YUBA COUNTY.

Marysville No. 162, Marysville—Meets 2nd and 4th Wednesdays, Liberty Hall; Miss Cecelia C. Gomes, Rec. Sec., 701 6th St.
Camp Far West No. 218, Wheatland—Meets 3rd Tuesday, I.O.O.F. Hall; Mrs. Ethel C. Brock, Rec. Sec., P. O. box 285.

AFFILIATED ORGANIZATIONS.

General Association Past Presidents—Meetings held annually in April at the home-town of Chief President; Mrs. Winifred Halter, 465 40th St., Oakland, Chief President; Mrs. Anna G. Loser, 72 Grove Lane, San Anselmo, Chief Secretary.
Past Presidents Association No. 1—Meets 1st and 3rd Mondays, N.S.G.W. Bldg., 414 Mason St., San Francisco; Mrs. Alice Ogburn, Pres.; Mrs. Leah M. Williams, Rec. Sec., 956 Pierce St., Apt. 104, San Francisco.
Past Presidents Association No. 2—Meets 2nd and 4th Mondays, "Wigwam," Pacific Bldg., 16th and Jefferson, Oakland; Anna Enos, Pres.; Mrs. Elizabeth B. Goodman, Rec. Sec., 134 Juana Ave., San Leandro.
Past Presidents Association No. 3 (Santa Clara County)—Meets 2nd Tuesday, Musicians Hall, 114 E. Santa Clara St., San Jose; Alice Roll, Pres.; Clara Briggs, Rec. Sec., 1336 Magnolia Ave., San Jose.
Past Presidents Association No. 4 (Sacramento County)—Meets 2nd Monday, N.S.G.W. Hall, 11th and "J" Sts., Sacramento City; Edith Kelley, Pres.; Lily May Tilden, Rec. Sec., 3225 "T" St., Sacramento.
Past Presidents Association No. 5 (Butte County)—Meets 1st Friday, homes of members, Chico and Oroville; Maria Picanco, Pres.; Ruth Brown, Rec. Sec., 1265 Leah Court, Oroville.
Past Presidents Association No. 6 (Nevada County)—Meets 4th Friday, alternately between Nevada City, Pythian Castle, and Grass Valley, Edna Sampson's home; Margaret V. Nolan, Pres.; Vere Hansen, Rec. Sec., R.F.D. No. 2, box 41-C, Grass Valley.
Past Presidents Association No. 7 (Sonoma County)—Meets 2nd Tuesday, Ruby Berger home, 327 College Ave., Santa Rosa; Ruby Berger, Pres.; Ann M. Beach, Rec. Sec., R.F.D. No. 4, box 528, Santa Rosa.
Past Presidents Association No. 8 (San Joaquin and Stanislaus Counties)—Meets 2nd Thursday, Red Men Hall, Stockton; Mrs. Lois Armstrong, Pres.; Mrs. Harriet F. Corr, Rec. Sec., 729 E. Sonora St., Stockton.
Native Sons and Native Daughters Central Committee on Homeless Children—Main Office, 955 Phelan Bldg., San Francisco; Mrs. John W. Stirling, Chmn.; Miss Mary E. Brusie, Sec. Los Angeles branch office, 3924 Sunset Blvd.; Dorothy Schlingman, Sec.

(ADVERTISEMENT.)

N.D.G.W. OFFICIAL DEATH LIST.

Giving the name, the date of death, and the Subordinate Parlor affiliation of all deceased members as reported to Grand Secretary Sallie R. Thaler from June 15, 1933, to July 18, 1933:

Granger, Mary King; June 9; Bonita No. 10.
Riecken, Dessie L.; June 21; Coloma No. 212.
Lewis, Marie; July 1; Gabrielle No. 139.
Roy, Mary Jane; June 26; Veritas No. 75.
Frame, Mary Eva; May 6; Berendos No. 23.
Donnelly, Laura B.; June 30; San Luisita No. 108.
Gregory, Amanda; June 5; La Rosa No. 191.

In Memoriam

CATHERINE H. HIMES.

(Portola Parlor No. 172 N.D.G.W.)

Whereas, The golden chain of our fraternity has been severed by the loss of our dearly beloved sister, Catherine Himes, we must know that it has pleased our Heavenly Father to call our dear sister to the Eternal Parlor above. Let us think of her as a sweet-scented rose that climbed the garden wall and is blossoming on the other side.

Whereas, God is merciful and just, we bow before His sight, knowing by our faith and trust He doeth all things right. We hold in fond memory her cheerful smile, her loving ways and her sweet disposition. The trials, the sorrows and the disappointments that come in every life, however sheltered, are ended for our beloved sister; she sleeps peacefully. Reverently, then, we must say, "Thy will be done." We here record our love and affection for one whose kindly ways endeared her to all who knew her. Therefore, be it

Resolved, That we extend to her bereaved family our deepest sympathy, with an earnest prayer that God, in His infinite mercy, assuage their grief and send peace into their hearts; be it further resolved, that our charter be draped in mourning in due respect for our dearly beloved sister, that a copy of these resolutions be spread in full upon our minutes, and that a copy be sent to The Grizzly Bear Magazine for publication.

AGNES CURRY,
NAN KELLY,
CATHERINE DOLLY,
Committee.
ETHEL HERNAN,
President.

San Francisco, July 9, 1933.

DOLLIE KING GRANGER.

The Angel of Death has entered the portals of Bonita Parlor No. 10 N.D.G.W. and taken from our midst our sister, Dollie King Granger. She was a loyal Native Daughter and loved California with a true and tender love. Our Order has lost a loved and faithful member. Therefore, be it

Resolved, That our charter be draped in mourning; that a copy of these resolutions be sent to her bereaved family, and that they be published in the "Redwood City Tribune," and that a copy be sent to The Grizzly Bear Magazine for publication.

"May the California winds blow lightly,
May the California sun shine brightly,
May the California rain fall softly,
Where sleeps our Sister dear."

Respectfully submitted in P.D.F.A.,
JESSIE LESLIE,
MAMIE GLENNAN,
DORA WILSON,
Committee.

Redwood City, July 13, 1933.

MINNIE TABER.

To the Officers and Members of Aloha Parlor No. 106, Native Daughters of the Golden West—We, your committee appointed to draft a resolution of respect to the memory of our departed charter member, Minnie Taber, respectfully submit the following:

Whereas, Another of our beloved members, Sister Minnie Taber, has answered the call of our Heavenly Father, it is with deepest sorrow we bow in humble prayer, realizing our loss is the heavenly gain of our dear sister. While we pay loving tribute to her memory, we are not unmindful of the sympathy we owe her loved ones; therefore, be it

Resolved, That we extend to her bereaved family our sincere and heartfelt sympathy; also, that this resolution be recorded in the minutes of our Parlor, that a copy be sent to the family of our deceased sister, and that a copy be sent to The Grizzly Bear for publication.

Respectfully submitted,
GRACE DuPONT,
GLADYS FARLEY,
LURINE MARTIN,
Committee.

Oakland, July 15, 1933.

Goldenrod, the floral outcast to hay-fever sufferers, has been restored to good standing. Ragweed, found in every state, is the true culprit in most hay-fever cases, says the Federal Agricultural Department.

Harbor Day—San Francisco will stage its fifth annual Harbor Day celebration August 17. The purpose is "to let the world know that San Francisco has the finest harbor in the world."

Will Power—Easy ways beget hard roads that must be traveled till the Will becomes strong enough to stand.—Jeanette Nourland.

LOS ANGELES

CITY AND COUNTY

THE N.S.G.W. CENTRAL MEMBERSHIP Committee, Henry G. Bodkin chairman, is progressing in its determination to aid Grand President Justice Emmet Seawell in his campaign to arouse interest among the members of the Order and to enroll thousands of the numerous eligibles. The meetings are well attended and constructive suggestions are given careful thought. Among those active in the conferences are the presidents of all the Los Angeles County Parlors and the district deputies.

As a means of instilling enthusiasm, a monthly series of high-class standard entertainments will be staged, and six Parlors—Los Angeles No. 45, Ramona No. 109, Hollywood No. 196, Sepulveda No. 263, Santa Monica Bay No. 267 and University No. 272—have agreed to finance the enterprise. The shows will be staged by these Parlors, in numerical order, the last meeting night of each month, and there will be no admission fee.

The first of the united Parlors' mammoth entertainments will be staged Thursday, August 31, at the hall of Los Angeles Parlor No. 45, 1832 South Hope street. Every Native Son, regardless of Parlor affiliation, is urged to lend his presence at each of these entertainments and to bring along eligible friends.

SIX INITIATED.

At a largely attended public ceremony July 26, officers of Los Angeles Parlor No. 124 N.D.G.W. were installed by Deputy Marion Crum, Miss Dolores Malin becoming president. The ceremony was very beautiful, the officers-elect being gowned in white and carrying shower hoquets in pastel colors. Dancing and refreshments followed the installation.

Six candidates were initiated July 5. The sewing club met July 8 at the home of Bertha Murray; many garments were completed and delicious refreshments were served. A big crowd enjoyed the "dog" bake at Santa Monica July 12; Esther Rinne was chairman. The drill team is practicing weekly. Los Angeles' August program provides: 9th, swimming party Womens Athletic Club, Edna Trombatore chairman; 23rd, weinie bake, Olinda Kerby in charge. The monthly card parties will be resumed September 13, when Ann Schiebusch will preside.

GOES OVER BIG.

The N.S.G.W. Luncheon Club, originated in June, is a great success, and each week both the attendance and the interest increase. The gathering affords an excellent opportunity to get better acquainted and to "gossip" about affairs generally, including those of the Order. During July the following presided: Leslie Packard (Los Angeles), Ernest Orfila (Ramona), Bernard Hiss (University), John Ford (Hollywood) and "Sid" Witkowski (Los Angeles).

The luncheon club meets every Friday at 12:15 (noon) in the Rosslyn Hotel, Fifth and Main. A separate compartment off from the main diningroom has been set aside for the club's use. All Native Sons and eligibles are welcome. Come on in, the spirit is exhilarating and you will be well repaid.

TO INCREASE NUMBERS AND INTEREST.

Officers of Californiana Parlor No. 247 N.D.G.W. were publicly installed July 25 by Deputy Mattie Edwards, Mrs. Inez Sitton becoming president. Beautiful decorations and the officers' lovely gowns created a charming scene. The occasion was, too, a "home coming day," and many friends were in attendance. Miss Mary Emily Foy was chairman, and Mrs. Edith Adams and the hospitality committee served delicious refreshments.

July 11, Mrs. Irene Blank presented three talented artists in a delightful program—Misses Alice and Margaret Papst and Amado Fernandez. Following luncheon, Treasurer Minnie Behm, on the Parlor's behalf, presented a gift to Past President Gertrude Tuttle in appreciation for outstanding service rendered No. 247. Mrs. Charles Jacobson, third vice-president, entertained the new officers at a charming luncheon at her home.

Californiana will vacation during August, the next meeting to be held Tuesday, September 12. Plans for the future are expected to bring about more interest and to bring into the ranks many oldtime members and scores of new ones. One meeting a month will be given over to the program committee. The history study class will be resumed, and a new section, early California folk lore, has been created under the guidance of Mrs. Isabel Lopez Fages. Tours to historic spots are planned, and members will learn to step the colorful dances of the days of the dons.

OUTING AT CABRILLO BEACH.

President Charles Straube of Ramona Parlor No. 109 N.S.G.W. has long advocated a monthly outing for Native Sons, Native Daughters and their families, where sports will be featured. The first will be held Sunday, August 13, at Cabrillo Beach, shore end of the San Pedro breakwater. Autos will leave Patriotic Hall, 1816 South Figueroa, at 9 a.m. It will be a basket picnic, everyone bringing his own "grub," and baseball, games and swimming will be on the program. "This is not a Ramona affair," says Deputy Grand President Walter E. Odemar, in charge. "We want to make this an event for the enjoyment of all Natives and their families, and we are hopeful that a similar outing, some where, may be held every month."

PRESIDENT GRATEFUL TO ASSISTANTS.

Glendale—July 11, at the last meeting of Verdugo Parlor No. 240 N.D.G.W. at which President Vera Carlson presided, she presented each of her officers with a corsage in colors of red, white and blue. Dorothy Courtney sang "I Love You Truly" and "The End of a Perfect Day." At the meeting's close Mrs. Carlson entertained at her home. The centerpiece of the festive board was a huge cake with the names of all the officers inscribed thereon. A recent bridge party at the home of Dorothy Ravn attracted many players; the hostess was assisted by Maud Molen and Mayme Kirri. Myrtize Tregea and Etta Fulkerth served dainty refreshments June 27.

Newly elected officers of the Parlor, with Sarah Burleson as president, were installed July 25 by Deputy Adele Frankish. At the conclusion of the ceremonies President Burleson entertained.

DINE AND DANCE AT SANTA MONICA.

Santa Monica—Santa Monica Bay Parlor No. 267 N.S.G.W. entertained another big crowd July 19, the occasion being the installation of its officers jointly with those of Glendale Parlor No. 264 and University Parlor No. 272. District Deputy Arthur Leonard officiated, assisted by District Deputy Walter Baskerville and Deputy Grand President Walter Odemar, and the following became presidents: J. Edward McCurdy (No. 267), Harvey Gillette (No. 264), Maynard Garrison (No. 272). Municipal Judge Joseph Call conducted the good of the order, and there were many speakers, including Grand Trustee Eldred Meyer. William M. Dowsing was guest of the evening, Santa Monica thus honoring each month one of its past presidents. Entertainment was provided and refreshments were served.

No. 267 is sponsoring a sports dinner dance in the silver palm room of the Grand Hotel, Santa Monica, August 1 at 7:30 p.m. A splendid orchestra will furnish music, and a midnight swimming party is a promised added attraction. This affair is for the benefit of the Parlor's newly-organized twelve-piece drum corps, which plans to appear in the Santa Rosa Admission Day parade. "A cordial invitation is extended all Natives," says Chairman Clayton Brandt. During August, Santa Monica Bay will honor Past President Harold Barden.

JOINT INSTALLATION.

San Pedro—Officers of Sepulveda Parlor No. 263 and Compton Parlor No. 272 N.S.G.W. were installed at a largely attended joint meeting July 7. District Deputy Walter E. Baskerville officiated, and Walter C. Richards and Ray W. Hecock became the respective presidents. Among the speakers of the evening were Grand Trustee Eldred L. Meyer, Grand Inside Sentinel William A. Reuter and District Deputy Edward E. Baldwin. A tamale supper concluded the ceremonies.

SUNSET BARBECUE.

Santa Monica—Santa Monica Bay Parlor No. 245 N.D.G.W. had several visitors from Long Beach and Verdugo Parlors July 12, among them Deputies Bulah VanLuven and Violet Henshilwood. Lucretia Coates, No. 245's former deputy, was honor-guest, and to her the Parlor, through Deputy Rita Smith, presented a gift. One candidate was initiated, and Chairman Helen Burke of the veterans welfare committee sponsored a shower for "her boys." With Audrea Merritt as hostess, delicious refreshments were served. The favors, in the state's colors, were made by Mrs. Smith.

Kathryn Worsham entertained July 11 with a tea at her home; sewing for the fall bazar was the order of the day. A food sale July 22 was in charge of Hazel McCreary. Mrs. Harold Barden entertained July 28 with a pot-luck luncheon in the gardens of her home. For the Parlor's benefit, President Amada Machado will have a sunset barbecue at her home, 1301 Jefferson boulevard, Culver City, August 5. Music will be furnished by a Spanish trio, and cards will provide entertainment. Admission, 75 cents.

LOS ANGELES NATIVE SONS BRIEFS.

Los Angeles Parlor No. 45 officers were installed July 14 by District Deputy Arthur Leonard, Roger M. Johnson becoming president. The membership campaign aroused considerable discussion, among the many participating being Grand Trustee Eldred L. Meyer, District Deputy Walter Fisher, Owen S. Adams, Sidney B. Witkowski and Ray LeMoine.

Ramona Parlor No. 109 officers were installed by District Deputy Walter Fisher, July 7, Charles Straube becoming president. The July birthday dinner drew a large crowd, including many visitors, and at the festive board Edwin A. Meserve made a brief talk. The affair was also complimentary to Grand Trustee Eldred L. Meyer who, at the meeting, detailed the Order's activities. Ramona's greetings to him were extended by Robert Todd. The athletic committee, Homer Chapelle chairman, is planning activities. Scout Master Robert Martin has arranged to take Ramona Troop No. 109 of Boy Scouts on an outing to Yosemite, August 10-19. The Parlor will hold initiation August 11, and the monthly birthday dinner, with a surprise, is set for August 18.

Hollywood Parlor No. 196 has retained Henry G. Bodkin as president for another term. Several new members have been added to the rolls, among them Paul, the son of Federal Judge McCormick. The Parlor proposes to take up the study of important civic questions, and a lively discussion along that line July 14 was participated in by President Bodkin, Deputy Grand President John Ford, District Deputy Walter Fisher, M. U. Rosenthal, John F. Lieb, W. L. O'Meara and many others. A class of candidates will be initiated August 21.

University Parlor No. 272 initiated six candidates last month, and will have a class of seven August 9. The next dance, at the Casa de Rosas, 1008 West Adams, August 19, will be in charge of William J. Quast (chairman), Howard Babb, Roy Parsons, Lucien A. Griffin, Walter Wells and James Shorten. Carl Martin is the new recording secretary, succeeding Martin DeFazio. The Parlor's baseball nine, under the leadership of James Shorten, promises to give the Santa Rosa team a hard fight on Admission Day.

ADMISSION DAY LOCALLY.

The Interparlor N.S.G.W. and N.D.G.W. Committee elected these officers July 21: Burrel D. Neighbours (Ramona N.S.), chairman; Mary Noerenberg (Californiana N.D.), vice-chairman; Clyde H. Davis (Los Angeles N.S.), secretary; Frank Frank (Los Angeles N.S.), treasurer.

A committee was authorized to arrange for the observance locally of Admission Day, September 9. Gertrude Allen (Los Angeles N.D.) was made chairman, and among her assistants are the first vice-presidents of all Subordinate Parlors. A tentative program includes a basket supper, followed by a program and dancing, at the Breakfast Club, 3213 Riverside drive. Full particulars in The Grizzly Bear for September. The committee will meet August 4 at 8 p.m. in the library of Patriotic Hall, 1816 South Figueroa.

ALL NATIVE SONS INVITED.

The Californians Civic League, recently formed to participate in civic affairs, will have an open meeting at 7:30 p.m. August 1 in Ramona clubrooms, 1816 South Figueroa, to which all Native Sons are invited. "The purpose of the organization, composed entirely of Native Sons, is to further the interest of California for Californians." Sidney B. Witkowski is the chairman, and J. F. Meehan the secretary.

THE DEATH RECORD.

Julius S. Morris, affiliated with Los Angeles Parlor No. 45 N.S.G.W., died June 22. He was born at San Francisco, September 30, 1869.

Jacob Vanderhuyden Viall, affiliated with Ramona Parlor No. 109 N.S.G.W., died June 27 at Sawtelle. He was born at Los Angeles, February 25, 1898.

Mrs. Frances Chandler-Kirkpatrick, wife of Dr. John L. Kirkpatrick (Ramona N.S.), died July 1. She was a native of Los Angeles, aged 43.

Lorenzo Francisco Soto, affiliated with Ramona Parlor No. 109 N.S.G.W., died July 7. He was born at Concord, Contra Costa County, September 5, 1862. Always a gentleman of the old school, Lorenzo was for years active in all Native Son affairs and was a director of the Grizzly Bear Publishing Company, Inc.

George K. Reuter, brother of William A. Reuter (Grand Inside Sentinel N.S.), died July 17 at San Francisco. He was a native of Merced City.

Ray M. Russill, affiliated with Ramona Parlor No. 109 N.S.G.W., died July 22, survived by a wife. He was born at Los Angeles, July 24, 1895, and was a brother of Louis P. and Charles A. Russill (both Ramona N.S.).

PERSONAL PARAGRAPHS.

Mrs. Anita Santo (Los Angeles N.D.) spent her vacation in Yosemite Valley.

Bernard G. Hiss (University N.S.) paid a brief visit last month to Bakersfield.

Henry G. Bodkin (Hollywood N.S.) left last month for a vacation in Honolulu, T. H.

Assemblyman Percy G. West (Sunset N.S.) of Sacramento was a visitor last month.

A native son arrived at the Glendale home of Donald Dewar (Ramona N.S.) July 19.

Frank Regan (Ramona N.S.) made his annual pilgrimage to the Puget Sound country last month.

Miss Margaret Coleman (Californiana N.D.), residing in San Francisco, was a visitor last month.

Walter H. Odemar (Ramona N.S.) last month spent a week's vacation in Sequoia National Park.

Edward E. Baldwin (Sepulveda N.S.) of San Pedro visited last month in Lake and Sonoma Counties.

Leo V. Youngworth (Ramona N.S.) last month attended the Shrine National Conclave at Atlantic City.

Mrs. Alphonse Pages (Californiana N.D.) and husband spent a vacation of two weeks in Yosemite Valley.

Miss Jeanne Clos (Los Angeles N.D.) and mother are enjoying a Panama vacation, and Miss Leonie Clos (Los Angeles N.D.) has gone to Honolulu, T. H., for a visit.

Miss Marjorie Jacobson (Los Angeles N.D.) visited the Century of Progress Exposition at Chicago, and Miss Irene Eden (Los Angeles N.D.) is now there taking in the sights.

A native daughter arrived July 16 at the home of Municipal Judge Leo I. Aggeler (Hollywood N.S.). She is a granddaughter of Superior Judge William T. Aggeler (Ramona N.S.).

Congressman William I. Traeger (Past Grand N.S.) and wife (Los Angeles N.D.) arrived July 1 from Washington, D. C., in San Francisco, and thence departed on a visit to Honolulu, T. H.

"MIRACLE MIDWAY."

Under the auspices of "Los Angeles County Parlors Native Sons of the Golden West, Inc.," the directors of which corporation are J. Edward McCurdy, Eldred L. Meyer, Walter E. Baskerville, Harry Honn, Harvey Gillett, Walter Fisher, William J. Bright, Maynard Garrison and Bernard G. Hiss, a "Miracle Midway" is to be staged for ten days commencing August 26. J. Jack Stanley is the director. Details are being worked out, and the location of the grounds will be made public later.

"He is truly rich who desires nothing, and he is truly poor who covets all."—Solon.

Grizzly Bear

SEPTEMBER THE ONLY OFFICIAL PUBLICATION OF THE NATIVE SONS AND DAUGHTERS OF THE GOLDEN WEST **1933**

ADMISSION DAY (September 9) ANNUAL, Featuring
GENERAL NEWS OF INTEREST CONCERNING
ALL CALIFORNIA, and ORDERS
NATIVE SONS and NATIVE DAUGHTERS

Price: 15 Cents

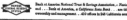

BITS OF HISTORY

"MARK OUR LANDMARKS"

Chester F. Gannon

(GRAND HISTORIAN N.S.G.W.)

"MARK OUR LANDMARKS"

WITH THE ADVENT OF A NEW Admission Day, our thoughts revert to the significance of that event and recall early celebrations connected with California's birth into the sisterhood of states.

Perhaps no state accepted statehood with more joy than did California on that memorable 9th day of September, 1850, when Congress approved her application for admission. It meant to the people on this far-western shore that their property and lives would be protected by the parent government. Prior to that, great uncertainty existed as to the title to lands, and life itself was precarious.

Therefore, when in October 1850 the glad tidings came slowly over the waters that California had become a sovereign state in the federal sisterhood, enthusiastic citizens of San Francisco celebrated the memorable event with great pomp and ceremony.

Then, more so than now, no celebration was complete without the services of the ablest orator to be had. In San Francisco then, lived Pioneer Nathaniel Bennett, miner, lawyer, judge, born in the State of New York in 1818 and who had migrated to California on the whaling vessel, "Mentor," with a group of twenty-five intimate friends. This boat had been chartered by Bennett and friends, who brought with them in a part of the vessel designated as "steerage," fifty other adventuresome souls. After a pleasant voyage 'round the Horn, the vessel finally landed its passengers at San Francisco on June 30, 1849.

Five months had been consumed with the passage from the Atlantic to the Pacific coast. Probably no more intelligent passenger list could have been found in any of the pioneer vessels than those who came with Bennett. The captain and crew were old whalers and well-behaved men, and the cabin passengers were men of integrity and learning, and were well supplied with books, chessboards, cards, etc. During the long five months of the voyage, Bennett spent considerable time every day studying the Spanish language. Almost immediately after landing, Bennett was successful in mining on the Tuolumne River about two miles below Jackson. Even though the strike at this point yielded profitable returns, Bennett was importuned to leave mining and return to the practice of law in San Francisco. This he did, in the fall of 1849.

This was the type of Pioneer who, on October 29, 1850, at San Francisco, was selected on that long-forgotten Admission Day to speak for the people of the West their message of thanksgiving for California's birth, in an oration that must have consumed an hour and a half to deliver. Among other things this brilliant, many-sided Pioneer said,

"To the people of the old States the admission of a new one has always been a source of honest pride. They behold with gratification the spread of the empire of freemen; and their welcome voice has always been heard in the past, as in gay and glittering procession, and laden with varied gifts, State after State has gone thronging up for admission and been marshalled into the lists of the Union. How then could it be otherwise, when California, with her robe glowing with silver and a diadem of gold upon her brow, had so long and patiently waited for the privilege of being allowed to participate with her elder sisterhood in their hopes and fears, to share with them the common benefits and sustain her portion of the common burdens. The numerous manifestations of kindly feelings from our brethren of the East prove that their satisfaction is inferior only to our own—that they receive us into their embrace with sincere friendship, and with warm wishes for our continued prosperity and permanent welfare. . . .

"Californians, natives of the soil! such is the nation, its progress in the past and its prospects for the future, which you have chosen to adopt for your country. You and ourselves stand on common ground. Born and reared under different governments, and speaking different tongues, we nevertheless meet here today as brothers. The same fraternal roof shelters us all. The aegis of the Constitution guards and protects us alike. Though you have been severed from the parent tree, your strength is not sapped nor your leaves withered; but, grafted into a strange branch, you nevertheless spring forth with more than former vigor, and flourish with fresh and unwonted luxuriance."

As your Historian read this brilliant oration by this long-forgotten man whose very existence is unknown to most of us and whose grave perhaps is neglected and unhonored, he thought to himself, "How many of our present-day orators could excel this Admission Day orator? Could Fletcher Cutler, Lewis Byington, Joseph R. Knowland or Justice Emmett Seawell match it with their known and tested ability? Could Charles 'Tears' McLaughlin in his best days have ranked with Bennett?" This question can only be decided by the individual, for we know our older contemporary orators to be very able. Given the same time those old-time orators took to prepare their masterpieces, would not California's present forensic ability have compared with the old school which your Historian has heretofore designated as "California's Golden Age of Oratory"?

★ ★ ★

Homeless Children

A WORTHWHILE NON-SECTARIAN ENDEAVOR SPONSORED AND SUPPORTED BY THE ORDERS OF NATIVE SONS AND NATIVE DAUGHTERS OF THE GOLDEN WEST

SOME VERY INTERESTING STORIES about adopted children have come to the workers of the Native Sons and Native Daughters Central Homeless Children Committee from foster parents. It seems too bad not to share them with the members of the Orders.

One small boy was learning to swear quite proficiently from a boy in the neighborhood, so the foster parents decided it might be well to separate the boys and send their hopeful to kindergarten. The first day of school the foster mother and son arrived in the schoolroom, and the small boy, all dressed up in a pretty blue suit and white collar and with his pompadour all "sta-combed," was introduced to his teacher. By way of acknowledgment and with the idea of making the child feel at ease, the teacher said, "Well, little man, do you know your letters?" and, looking up at her in the most astonished manner he said, "Hell, no! I've only been here five minutes."

A little girl was inclined to be selfish, and her mother was somewhat concerned over this fact. One day as the mother sat sewing, her child and three or four little girls were playing school. The mother noticed that her child usually chose to be teacher, so in quiet tones she said, "Frances, you must let the other children be the teacher once in a while. You must not want to be the teacher all of the time." So Frances said, "All right, Julia, YOU can be the teacher." (The mother was quite pleased over the child's readiness to heed her admonition). "YOU can be the teacher, and I'LL be the PRINCIPAL!"

A small boy had learned in Sundayschool about the wonderful story in the Bible of the great friendship between David and Jonathan. A few weeks later, by way of reviewing the lessons, the teacher asked the children who the two men in the Bible were between whom there was the great friendship, and one small boy spoke up and said, "Potash and Purlmutter."

A little six-year-old girl, reared in the mountains near Yosemite in a home of squalor, was left an orphan and was brought to a San Francisco institution. The Committee was asked to find a home for her. The first Saturday that the child was in the institution she was told by the matron not to make her bed as it was the day to change the sheets. "Change the sheets?" said she, "Who do I change with?"

"Love is a pipe we light at twenty, smoke until forty, and rake the dregs until our exit." This sage philosophy was uttered by the captain of the boat which brought Lola Montez back to England when she left India for the last time. Strange, this exotic woman in whose career romance and love played such a part, died in her forty-third year, soon after the period quoted as the time for the dying of that well-known spark in human breasts.

★ ★ ★

"When Brigham Young gives me a receipt signed by the Lord then, and not until then, will I give him his tithes." This was the terse answer Sam Brannon gave to the messenger which Brigham Young, located at Salt Lake, Utah, sent to California. When the father of the Mormon Church heard of the rich returns from Brannon's mining on Mormon Island in the American River near Folsom he sent this messenger across the miles to collect for the Lord. Sam was too smart for his employer. The proposition of paying one-tenth of all his gold to Brigham Young for the Lord was too much for him. Sam was promptly excommunicated by Brigham Young, but that little bothered the carefree Sam, who went on to make a name for himself as a leader in early California and who died after as exciting and as accomplished a life as any Pioneer ever lived. Your Historian had read that the grave of Brannon is practically unmarked in a San Diego cemetery. If this is the case, then his memory should be commemorated by a suitable marker, and suitable honor paid to the grave of a man whose only fault perhaps occurred in his later years when he took to excessive drink.

★ ★ ★

"You never injured me. Take me across the river and I will pay you for your trouble." This was the answer of Joaquin Murietta to the plea of the old ferryman on the Tuolumne River, when at midnight Joaquin, with gun in hand, awakened him from his rude hut and demanded his money or his life. The frightened man told the bandit king that he had only $100, but that he was welcome to it. Somewhere in the heart of the monster burned the light of chivalry, and instead of robbing the old man of his small belongings made the above reply, which shows a latent goodness in a heart then reeking with blood and cruelty.

★ ★ ★

Native Sons who attended Parlor in the last six months know well what the name of "William B. Ide" was employed for. Few perhaps realized the importance of Ide in the Bear Flag uprising. Ide was the leader of the Pioneers at Sonoma and not only was he a brave man but his letters, intact today, show a man of great breeding and learning. His letter under date of June 15, 1846, addressed to Jno. B. Montgomery, Commander of the United States ship "Portsmouth," lying in San Francisco Bay, concludes with these words:

"Destined as we are to certain destruction should we prove unsuccessful, we have the honor to be your Fellow Countrymen, and whether we conquer or perish we are resolved to approve ourselves not unworthy the kindly regards of those who 'build to the honor and glory of the American Flag.' It is our object and earnest desire to embrace the first opportunity to unite our adopted and rescued country, to the country of our early home. With every consideration and by the will of the people, I have the honor to be, etc., WILLIAM B. IDE."

This letter is comparable to the last message sent out by the leader of the ill-fated garrison in the Alamo at San Antonio, Texas, when in 1836 he appealed vainly to the United States for help from the death which speedily overtook the entire command.

FOREVER ONWARD

(ROBT. L. HAWKENSEN.)

O shifting sand of the desert,
If blest with heart or soul,
I beg that you have mercy on
Men striving toward their goal.

Far across your barren wasteland
The traveler wends his way,
Tramping on till the burning sun
Melts at the close of day.

Then peacefully he goes to sleep,
Out in your arid land,
Dreaming of the glittering gold
Buried in yonder sand.

Morning comes as a brilliant sun
Climbs over distant slope,
And he renews his endless march,
Possessed of love and hope.

CALIFORNIA FIFTY YEARS AGO

Thomas R. Jones

(COMPILED EXPRESSLY FOR THE GRIZZLY BEAR.)

ADMISSION DAY, SEPTEMBER 9, COMING on a Sunday in 1883, the holiday was observed the 10th. The Order of Native Sons of the Golden West had a celebration at Stockton, San Joaquin County, the principal feature of which was a mile-long parade, headed by Grand President A. F. Jones. Participating were Governor George C. Stoneman and staff, a corps of Mexican War veterans, pioneer associations, civic and military organizations and ten Subordinate Parlors of the Order. The San Francisco contingent went by steamboat, accompanied by the First U. S. Artillery band. Arthur L. Levinsky was chairman of the arrangements committee.

In his report of the celebration to the Seventh (Marysville 1884) Grand Parlor, Grand President Jones said: "Every member of the Order should be gratified at the energy and enthusiasm displayed by Stockton Parlor No. 7, which resulted in such a grand success on the 10th of September, 1883. We can only wish for at least an equal occasion each year. To properly celebrate and make the appearance of the Natives uniform on this occasion, I sanctioned the use of the hat and plume worn on that day."

In observance of the day, the Society of California Pioneers, San Francisco, had an outing at Del Monte, Monterey County, and Pioneers of Solano and Napa Counties had enthusiastic celebrations, respectively, at Suisun and Napa City.

The annual California State Fair opened at Sacramento City September 10 for a week's run. Irving M. Scott delivered the address. The receipts were $19,475.80, the largest to date of any fair. To solve the gambling question, the Sacramento Board of City Trustees licensed the games and relegated them to the second floors of buildings. Thirty-five licenses were taken out, and the city collected $3,350 in fees.

Other fairs this month were: California North District at Marysville, Yuba County, and Nevada County, at Grass Valley, the 4th; San Joaquin Valley, at Stockton, the 17th; Santa Clara County, at San Jose, the 24th. A feature at the latter was a fifty-mile riding race between P. Figueroa and Charley Anderson of Los Angeles; the latter won.

Wool growers of the state organized September 12 and elected J. B. Hoyt of Solano County president. It was claimed the industry was in a paralyzed condition.

The Federal Government reduced letter postage from three to two cents September 15, and a special car loaded with the new stamps was sent to California.

The season's first rainstorm prevailed September 29 and 30. The precipitation was .90 of an inch.

Eight steamboats were busy on the Sacramento River towing barges loaded with grain from points south of Colusa City to Port Costa, Contra Costa County.

Charles Martell, at Vaca Valley, Solano County, raised twenty tons of tokay grapes on two acres of vines and sold the product for $1,700.

Frank Kimball of San Diego offered to deed 1,000 acres of land to anyone who would plant half the acreage to grape vines; Arpad Harathy of San Francisco accepted the offer.

Ventura had a ten-seconds shock of earthquake at 4 a.m. of September 5.

The stage from Yreka, Siskiyou County, was robbed by a lone highwayman near Shasta, September 12. The express box was taken.

A woman in Maine died and left an estate valued at $150,000. A brother, who went to California in the '50s was advertised for as the heir. He turned up as a citizen of Downieville, Sierra County, named Walter Plummer, and went East to claim the estate.

Adolph Hartman, secretary of the Humboldt Savings Bank in San Francisco, was short $15,000 in his accounts, and September 20 committed suicide.

Lakeport, Lake County, had a dozen buildings burn September 6; loss, $25,000. A big fire on the Sausalito, Marin County, waterfront September 12 caused a $20,000 loss. Tehama City suffered a $10,000 fire loss September 24.

In a Butte County mine, at a depth of forty feet, the skeleton of a man six feet tall was found. By his side were an ax and a pipe, both of stone.

General George S. Evans, once adjutant-general of the state and a senator from San Joaquin County, died at San Francisco, September 17. The same day, J. F. Chellis, lieutenant-governor of California in 1862-63, died in Oregon State.

Stewart S. Brook, Pioneer of '49 who built the Yreka Canal, claimed to be the longest mining ditch in the state, died September 19 at San Francisco.

Pressley Dunlap, who arrived in Sacramento in August of 1849 and was that county's first clerk, died September 21.

D. M. Kenfield, Tuolumne Pioneer who was treasurer of the county for ten years and state controller from 1879 to 1883, died at San Francisco, September 29.

The Four Hills mine near Downieville, Sierra County, struck a bonanza September 4. Gold streaked the quartz taken out, and one ton yielded over $100,000 worth of the precious metal.

At Sweetland, Nevada County, the Manzanita hydraulic mine cleaned up its sluices after a forty-day run and recovered gold dust valued at $110,000.

Two men, sinking a well on the Santa Maria rancho, San Diego County, put in a blast that threw out a shower of quartz impregnated with gold. As a result, they located a rich ledge.

A pocket containing several large nuggets of pure gold was found September 19 in the Nevill mine, at Middle Bar on the Mokelumne River in Amador County. The find was valued at $90,000.

Wm. A. Gordon, Ventura farmer, committed suicide September 2 by lying down upon a giant-powder cartridge and exploding it. His head was found a hundred feet from where his feet were picked up.

H. H. Harrington of Livermore, Alameda County, September 12 shot and killed 14-year-old Mary Davis, a servant in his home, and then ended his own life.

Redding, Shasta County, had a shooting affray September 11 in which George Finch killed Marion Berry.

Quarreling in Fresno County September 13 over the belling of a cow, Isaac Harris was shot and killed by Charles Slocum, his soninlaw.

At North San Juan, Nevada County, a wagon-load of 185 kegs of powder exploded September 20. Thomas Cleveland, the driver, and four horses were killed.

A powder explosion at the Alameda County works of the California Powder Company, September 30, blew thirty-six Chinamen and a Whiteman to atoms.

H. H. White, working in an Inyo County location, one Sunday rested and, taking his Bible, sat beneath a pine tree on the hillside of a deep ravine. He dozed, the Bible fell off his lap and rolled down the bank about sixty feet, and he descended to pick it up. It was open at the seventh chapter of St. Matthew, where lay a piece of quartz the book had dislodged. The verse beneath the quartz read, "Ask, and it shall be given unto you; seek, and ye shall find," etc. The quartz was gold streaked. He climbed the steep side and found the ledge from which it had been dislodged. The quartz assayed $225 a ton.

Jim Townsend, pioneer miner of Grass Valley, Nevada County, gave an editor this remedy for drinking too much booze: "I don't care if a man is as drunk as a democrat every night for a month, raw beef will cure him. When his stomach is weak at even the looks of cold water, raw beef is a panacea. When feeling groggy, go to a butchershop, get a piece of juicy roundsteak, sprinkle it with salt, then eat it. The gastric juice will flow freely again, and inside of an hour you will feel as solid as a brick house with a slate roof."

A Los Angeles hotel had tacked up in each room the following sign: "No combustibles such as paper, old clothing, empty bottles and oyster cans are to be thrown out of the window."

A man filing his papers in the United States Land Office at San Francisco, wrote his christian name, "Usual." Asked how he came to get such an unusual name, he stated, "I am the seventh son. My parents had hoped for a daughter when I was born. When it was me, my father remarked 'Another son, as usual.' That gave me the name of 'Usual'."

A saloon in Paradise, Butte County, was named "Soretoe Retreat," and one in Yankee Hill was called "Bellywash Castle." "Hog Hollow was the name of a small town near by.

THE LETTER BOX

Comments on subjects of general interest and importance received from readers of The Grizzly Bear.

WOULD SAVE LAUREL HILL FROM GREEDY REAL ESTATE DEALERS.

Editor Grizzly Bear—I have been extremely interested in The Grizzly Bear writings of Mr. Chester F. Gannon on the subject of the duel between Senator Broderick and Judge Terry which my father considered no duel at all, but a dastardly murder. Perhaps I am more interested in this now, because I do not believe there is another person on earth but myself who stood by Mr. Broderick's death bed a few minutes after he breathed his last, and witnessed what was to be the most vivid picture in all my memory. It is a terrible sight to a child to see a man cry, and I was awestruck to see one man with his head bowed over the pillow and another bending over the foot of the bed where was the body of their loved friend lying so calm and peaceful. Both of these gentlemen were sobbing aloud, as were several others, for there were many of Mr. Broderick's friends there that day, overwhelmed with grief. Do you wonder that I could never forget it? We were living on Black Point at that time, and my father, who was a friend of Mr. Broderick, feeling that this was a part of California history, thought it was right for my sister and my older brother and myself to have the memory of this scene. I had never before seen anyone who was dead, but Mr. Broderick was noble looking in death and there was no horror attached to that part of it, only sorrow at seeing such grief.

And this brings me to a subject so near to my heart: the beautiful old [San Francisco] cemetery where nearly all the Pioneers are buried; where there is hardly a foreign name on the stones erected there. We always pause at Mr. Broderick's grave and Col. Baker's when we go to the cemetery. They are both on the way to our lot, and we have often found flowers on Mr. Broderick's grave. I have hoped so much that the Native Sons and Daughters would take an interest in saving Laurel Hill from the greedy real estate dealers and let the Pioneers of our state rest undisturbed! It would make a beautiful park, and perpetuate the memory of many brave and noble men who built California. All power to Mr. Gannon! I wish he might succeed in arousing an interest in saving the burial place of these truly great men.

MRS. ANNA E. WILLEY.

Alameda City, August 10, 1933.

(The writer of the above, Mrs. Anna Cook-Willey, arrived in California via Panama in 1851, at the age of three. She is a daughter of Pioneer Charles W. Cook, deceased, who came to this state aboard the "Oregon" in 1849 and engaged in the banking business in San Francisco under the firm name of Palmer, Cook & Co.—Editor.)

VERY FEW OLDTIME PIONEERS NOW LEFT—SLOWLY THINNING OUT.

Editor Grizzly Bear—Will you please publish these good anecdotes in The Grizzly Bear? Died in Oakland, Mrs. Mariana Sorden de Moreno, August 2, 1933. She was born in Monterey, California, in 1850. Her father was Charles Sorden, who came with Commodore Sloat in 1846. He was one of the men who helped raise the American Flag at the Casa de la Duana, now called Old Custom House, under Commodore Sloat. Her mother was one of the many colonists who came up to Monterey from San Jose del Cabo (Lower California). Her name was Juana Sombreros de Campos, a member of the Hipolito family. Mrs. Moreno had many friends, and was well known to many of the old residents of Monterey. She was baptized at the old Carmel Mission church, was one of the many pupils who went to school at the old Quartel building ("adobe"), and later on lived in Watsonville. Very few now left of those oldtime Pioneers; slowly thinning out.

The writer is also a pioneer of the old town of Monterey, born there in 1858. Mother was a Pioneer of 1848, and father was one of the old side-wheeler passengers who came around the Horn on steamer "Senator" in 1850. We are all good Native Sons and Daughters, believing in the Orders.

ROBT. J. RICHARDS.

Daly City, August 5, 1933.

BOYHOOD DAYS RECALLED.

Editor Grizzly Bear—I see by an article in The Grizzly Bear Magazine of August, under "Fifty Years Ago," about a project to irrigate 30,000,000 acres of land and take the water from Kings River. The notice was pleasing to me.

As a boy 15 years of age I was employed on that survey, as a hunter for fresh meat and a roustabout. We started the survey at Clark's Fork of Kings River, which is on the Laguna De Tache ranch. Thence we ran the line out west to Summit Lake, which they were going to use as a reservoir, and thence north to Tracy. Yours very truly,

FRED W. ZIMMERMAN.

San Francisco, August 20, 1933.

(Fred Zimmerman is the historian of South San Francisco Parlor No. 157 N.S.G.W. and has long been a subscriber to The Grizzly Bear.—Editor.)

Tahoe Rim Drive—A modern paved highway, completely encircling Lake Tahoe, was opened and dedicated August 6.

AMADOR COUNTY'S OPPORTUNITIES EXCELLENT FOR THE GOLD MINER.

Amador County has the deepest and richest gold mines on the North American Continent, says Harold V. Tallon in the "Amador Ledger" of Jackson. Situated in the "Heart of the Mother Lode" and having an enviable mining history since 1850, gives Amador County the right to claim that most excellent opportunities for the gold miner exist here today, as they did yesterday, and as eminent geologists affirm, "will continue for time to come."

The greater part of the gold mining history of the Golden West has been made in Amador County and is being made today. . . . Opportunities for gold miners exist here on every hand, but one cannot be deluded into the thought that plenty of enthusiasm, a few men, a grub stake, and some picks and shovels will produce a good mine over night. Such conditions may have existed in the old placer days of the '49er, but in this day and age things have changed, and mining is no exception. Amador County is primarily a deep-ledge mining section. New operators must be well financed, must have a definite program, and must have mining men of experience and practice to direct developments. After all, gold mining is not magic—it is a business, and an exacting one.

The Grizzly Bear Magazine

The ALL California Monthly

OWNED, CONTROLLED, PUBLISHED BY GRIZZLY BEAR PUBLISHING CO., (Incorporated) COMPOSED OF NATIVE SONS.

CLARENCE M. HUNT
General Manager and Editor

OFFICIAL ORGAN AND THE ONLY OFFICIAL PUBLICATION OF THE NATIVE SONS AND THE NATIVE DAUGHTERS OF THE GOLDEN WEST.

ISSUED FIRST OF EACH MONTH.
FORMS CLOSE 20th MONTH.
ADVERTISING RATES ON APPLICATION.

SAN FRANCISCO OFFICE:
N.S.G.W. BLDG., 414 MASON ST., ROOM 302
(Office Grand Secretary N.S.G.W.)
Telephone: KEarny 1223
SAN FRANCISCO, CALIFORNIA

PUBLICATION OFFICE:
309-15 WILCOX BLDG., 2nd AND SPRING,
Telephone: VAndike 6234
LOS ANGELES, CALIFORNIA

(Entered as second-class matter May 29, 1918, at the Postoffice at Los Angeles, California, under the act of August 24, 1912.)

PUBLISHED REGULARLY SINCE MAY 1907

VOL. LIII (53). WHOLE NO. 317

Rodeo and Pow-wow—Lakeport, Lake County, will stage its annual regatta, rodeo and Indian pow-wow, September 2, 3 and 4.

"Behind the smoke of every great social battle, you will find great minds."—Henry Suzzallo.

Native Sons of the Golden West

"TO THE OFFICERS AND MEMBERS of all Subordinate Parlors of the Native Sons of the Golden West—Dear Sirs and Brothers: Admission Day Greetings!

"Our entire membership is eagerly awaiting the approach of California's eighty-third anniversary. We are already beginning to feel the thrill of the occasion, as we vision marching columns of thousands of California's sons and daughters, arrayed in colorful uniforms, interspersed with drum corps and bands of music, and uniquely designed historical figures, representative of the romance and adventure of a pioneer epoch which has no counterpart in American civilization. Admission Day celebrations and parades have become a fixed pageant feature in the life of our State, and if they should be discontinued it would seem that we were no longer living in California.

"The annual custom of celebrating the ninth day of September was commenced many years ago by our Order. The appropriateness of the annual celebrations of the admission of California into the Union, held by our Order on each succeeding year, grew so strong in public favor

JUSTICE EMMET SEAWELL,
Grand President N.S.G.W.

that the legislature of the State finally included it within the list of national events worthy of State recognition. Our natal day celebrations are distinctively Californian in color, attractiveness, and in spirit. They are solely concepts of Western origin and aptly symbolize the habits, customs, thoughts and ways of the actors who played heroic parts in one of the greatest of all human dramas, which had for its stage settings the vast mountain chains, broad and fertile valleys, great rivers and primeval forests which are now included within our State lines.

"At the fifty-sixth session of our Grand Parlor, Santa Rosa was selected as the place in which the Admission Day celebration is to be held this year. The selection is a happy one, as Santa Rosa is the seat of government of Sonoma County, and but a short distance from Pueblo de Sonoma, where the first decisive action was taken in California to establish a civil government which should in due course of time become annexed to the union of American states. Many exciting and historical events have transpired within this pioneer county. The flags of Spain, Mexico, and Russia have been raised upon its soil as symbols of foreign dominion. Then came the fourth, the Bear flag, and lastly and forever, the Stars and Stripes. In the midst of these hallowed scenes, surely we may befittingly celebrate the day.

"The assuring word comes from every part of the State that the attendance will be the largest that has gathered upon a similar occasion in many years. A revival of the spirit of the Order is sweeping the entire State. Our ideals are unquestionably taking hold of the public mind. We are becoming better understood year by year. The pioneer county of Sonoma bids you thrice welcome. The day will abound in good fellowship and good will greetings.

"Let us join hands again in renewal of our loyalty to the State of California, and to the pledge which we have taken to promote the welfare and happiness of our citizens to the fullest measure of our strength.

"With every good wish for the Order and its members, I am, sincerely and fraternally,

"EMMET SEAWELL,
"Grand President N.S.G.W.
"San Francisco, August 9, 1933."

ATTENTION, NATIVE SONS!

The grand officers, headed by Grand President Justice Emmet Seawell, will dedicate the new Federal Postoffice building at Marysville, Yuba County, Sunday, September 17.

The next meeting of the Board of Grand Officers will be held Sunday, September 10, at 11 a.m., at Santa Rosa, Sonoma County.

Murder Site Marked.

Nevada City—The forenoon of July 30, several Native Sons gathered on the Blue Tent road, about four miles above Nevada City, where Hydraulic No. 56 placed a marker at the site of the murder of Arthur Myers, a stage driver, October 31, 1894. Dr. C. W. Chapman gave the following account:

"The killing of the driver of the stage was due to a trifling peculiar habit he had of always standing with his left hand in his pocket and his right hand resting on his hip while he talked to anyone. He had been breaking in some new horses and shifted a couple of colts from the wheel to the lead. They were doing fairly well but could not be trusted yet, and when he got the order, 'Hands up!', he stuck the left hand with the lines between his knees to keep the colts from bolting and then mechanically put the right hand on his hip. That was fatal. The highwayman mistook it and plugged him just under the heart. He slumped forward into the boot of the stage and onto the lines, drawing them tighter and holding them fast. There was one passenger on the seat with him. That passenger jumped and ran back down the road, where some men were working wtih a plow. Two shots followed him, but missed, and the highwayman took to the woods without finishing the robbery. The workmen hurried to the scene and one of them, Pete Arbogast, drove the stage to town."

WITH ENTHUSIASM, respond to the call of the Grand President and COMB THE FIELDS! Bring into the fold the thousands of ready and willing eligibles. There positively is NO SUBSTITUTE FOR MEMBERSHIP! With numbers, there is no limit to accomplishments.

Twenty-two Initiated.

Hayward—Eden No. 113 initiated a class of twenty-two candidates July 25—less than three weeks after Grand President Justice Emmet Seawell issued his letter calling for action. Entertainment numbers were furnished by Arthur Manter, Gene McBarron and "Doc" Hanley's band, and a dutch lunch was served. Among the many in attendance were Grand Trustee Edward T. Schnarr, Grand Marshal Gam Hurst and Deputy Frank Smith.

The married and the unmarried members of the Parlor engaged in a baseball contest July 30. The latter won, and the former served the barbecue which followed the game. Filbert Soares captained the bachelors.

Grand Officer To Visit in South.

San Francisco—Grand Second Vice-president Harmon D. Skillin announces that he will officially visit the following Subordinate Parlors, on the dates noted:

Arrowhead No. 110 (San Bernardino), September 27.

Long Beach No. 239 (Long Beach), September 28.

Ramona No. 109 (Los Angeles), September 29.

Santa Ana No. 265 (Santa Ana), October 2.

Santa Monica Bay No. 267 (Santa Monica), October 4.

Santa Barbara No. 116 (Santa Barbara), October 5.

Sepulveda No. 263 (San Pedro), October 6.

WITH ENTHUSIASM, respond to the call of the Grand President and COMB THE FIELDS! Bring into the fold the thousands of ready and willing eligibles. There positively is NO SUBSTITUTE FOR MEMBERSHIP! With numbers, there is no limit to accomplishments.

Rounding Up Eligibles.

Santa Rosa—Santa Rosa No. 28, the home-Parlor of Grand President Justice Emmet Seawell, while extremely busy arranging for the statewide Admission Day celebration, finds time to round up eligibles. Three classes of new recruits have been initiated—July 31, August 14 and 28.

The Parlor was officially visited August 14 by Grand Trustee Edward Schnarr, and there were many visitors from the east San Francisco Bay district Parlors. A "buck" feed was enjoyed after the meeting, the chief item on the menu being furnished by Recording Secretary Leland S. Lewis. No. 28 has an athletics committee composed of Matt Rogina, Fred Clark, Art Janssen, Cecil Branstetter and Earl Donner.

NEWSY N.S. PARAGRAPHS.

Grass Valley—The unveiling of the monument above the grave of Past Grand Jo Victor Snyder

MY OLDTIME BURRO

Marysville (Yuba County)—A highly pleasing number on the program rendered August 6 during the annual reunion of residents of Yuba and Sutter Counties in Mosswood Park, Oakland, was the reciting of an original poem—"My Old-Time Burro," dedicated to the young miner of '49—by Miss Eleanor Sooy of San Francisco, former Camptonville girl:

Wasn't any shakes fer beauty,—just a burro, small 'n' gray,—
Tiny thing, an' him a-havin' just a reg'lar jackass bray;
Waked me up most ev'ry mornin',—warm 'n' bright, or wet 'n' raw,—
Chills a-chasin' through my innards when I'd hear that old hee-haw!

Lift! My lord, you should-a seen 'im, with my load upon his back,—
All my tools 'n' other fixin's, 'n' my heavy beddin' pack;
Off he'd march, his long ears pointin', for he knew my word was law,
An' I knew how things were goin', when I'd hear that old hee-haw!

Once I nearly lost th' feller. (Golly! what a life we led)!
Comin' down a river grade, sir,—bluff 'n' danger just ahead;
Slipped, 'n' nearly lost 'is footin',—death fer him was what I saw,—
Trembled,—cowered,—s-t-e-a-d-i-e-d,—started,—with that welcome old hee-haw!

Spirit an' a heart uv oak, sir,—lurkin' devil shore wuz there,—
Hurt me, too, to have to whale 'im, but 'e didn't seem to care,—
Shook 'imself when all wuz over,—in 'is eye endurance raw,—
When he knew I'd bust out cryin', loud would come that old hee-haw!

I wuz just a striplin', mister,—that wuz many years ago,—
My ol' pan 'n' rocker helped me,—made my pile an' saw it go;
Made some more 'n' quit a-minin'; came home; learned respect fer law,—
Lef' my fun 'n' little burro; gee, I missed that old hee-haw!

Him an' me we shore wuz cronies; boy loved beast,—I cared a lot;
Al'ays listened to my stories,—broke or flush it mattered not;
Couldn't bring 'im, so I left 'im where the strength of might was law,
An' I feel he heartened others with that lusty old hee-haw!

Another feature of the gathering was the appearance of Mrs. Sophia Davis, former Sutter County resident, now 99 years of age and determined, she declared, to reach the one hundredth milestone. Five hundred former or present Yubaites and Sutterites attended the reunion.—PETER J. DELAY.

—referred to in The Grizzly Bear last month—was most impressive, and profuse compliments were extended those who arranged the details. Among the many in attendance were Grand President Justice Emmet Seawell, Junior Past Grand Seth Millington, Grand First Vice Chas. A. Koenig, Grand Secretary John T. Regan, Grand Historian Chester Gannon, Past Grands Fred H. Greely, Lewis F. Byington, Judge Fletcher A. Cutler and Charles L. Dodge, and a goodly number of Fred H. Greely Past Presidents Assembly. The monument was unveiled by Mrs. Alison F. Watt, who was Grand President of the Native Daughters when "Jo" headed the Native Sons, and Past Grand Greely.

Sacramento—Sacramento No. 3 sent to three inmates of the El Dorado County Hospital at Placerville—Edmund Cooper, 115, William Bowman, 98, and R. C. Ogilvie, 97,—heart-shaped birthday greeting cards worded: "May this friendly greeting from the Native Sons of the Golden West, to whom 'The story of California is a story where every page glitters with a Golden Glory,' be like a golden thread in your memory, of our thought and best wishes, on this, the anniversary of your birth."

Merced—Officers of Modesto No. 11, Yosemite No. 24 and Los Banos No. 206 were installed at a joint ceremonial conducted by Deputies L. E. Bither and Ambrose Daneri. B. E. Munson, A. W. Peterson and Frank Dambrosia became the respective presidents. Charles D. Blaine, retiring president No. 11, was presented with an emblematic pin. Refreshments followed the ceremonies.

WITH ENTHUSIASM, respond to the call of the Grand President and **COMB THE FIELDS!** Bring into the fold the thousands of ready and willing eligibles. There positively is **NO SUBSTITUTE FOR MEMBERSHIP!** With numbers, there is no limit to accomplishments.

Visalia—Visalia No. 19 has an athletic committee composed of H. W. Kelly, John Mendes, Gilbert Meyers, Gareth Houk and Columbus Baido, appointed to arrange a sports program.

Arcata—Arcata No. 20 will have its annual whiskerino ball Admission Day, September 9. It will be in the nature of a golden jubilee celebration, in recognition of the Parlor's fiftieth institution anniversary. The arrangements committee, appointed by President Wilfred Anderson, includes T. C. Fleckenstein (general chairman), W. H. Anderson, Wm. Peters, C. J. Monroe, J. B. Tilley, H. P. Carr, E. L. Henry, L. Stromberg, F. C. Nicholson, Dr. N. Stromberg.

San Jose—Officers of San Jose No. 22 were installed by Deputy Alfred C. Hansen, Mario Ponzini becoming president. Preceding the ceremonies three candidates were initiated. July 23 the Parlor had a "stag" barbecue at the Frank Nelson ranch.

WITH ENTHUSIASM, respond to the call of the Grand President and **COMB THE FIELDS!** Bring into the fold the thousands of ready and willing eligibles. There positively is **NO SUBSTITUTE FOR MEMBERSHIP!** With numbers, there is no limit to accomplishments.

Fresno—Fresno No. 25 has named F. M. Lane and B. W. Gearhart captains for a membership drive which was inaugurated August 4 with a watermelon "feed."

Saint Helena—Saint Helena No. 53 had its annual barbecue at Lyman Grove July 24. Sheriff Jack Steckter was the toastmaster, and brief addresses were made by Judge Percy S. King, Paul R. Alexander, Julius Goodman, Dr. Herbert L. Byrd, E. A. Erickson, Chris. Mills and Ed. S. Bell. The barbecue committee included Joseph P. Vasconi Sr., Wm. Bulotti, Arnold Metzner, Lucas Haus and Lowell Palmer.

Grass Valley—Officers of Quartz No. 58 and Manzanita No. 29 N.D.G.W. were installed August 7 by Deputies John Thomas and Clara Phillips, Frank Hooper and Ann Whiting becoming the respective presidents. Florence Hart Allen (Californiana No. 247 N.D.G.W.), assisted by her son, entertained with character sketches. A banquet concluded the ceremonies. H. Ray George was the toastmaster, and among the speakers was Past Grand Alison F. Watt.

WITH ENTHUSIASM, respond to the call of the Grand President and **COMB THE FIELDS!** Bring into the fold the thousands of ready and willing eligibles. There positively is **NO SUBSTITUTE FOR MEMBERSHIP!** With numbers, there is no limit to accomplishments.

San Rafael—Mount Tamalpais No. 64 initiated a large class of candidates August 21, the ceremonies being followed by an entertainment. The Parlor's drum and bugle corps will be in the Santa Rosa Admission Day parade. Chairman Frank Kelly announces a dance and card party for the corps' benefit.

Colusa—At the joint installation of officers of Colusa No. 69 and Colus No. 194 N.D.G.W. conducted by Deputies Elton C. Fitch and Bernice Sperbeck, Thomas Busch and Maude Bond became the respective presidents. Gathered about the festive board at the conclusion of the ceremonies, Ben R. Ragain acted as toastmaster.

WITH ENTHUSIASM, respond to the call of the Grand President and **COMB THE FIELDS!** Bring into the fold the thousands of ready and willing eligibles. There positively is **NO SUBSTITUTE FOR MEMBERSHIP!** With numbers, there is no limit to accomplishments.

Ukiah—Ukiah No. 71 had initiation August 21 and heard an address on NRA by Chairman

(Continued on Page 19)

Know your home-state, California! Learn of its past history and of its present-day development by reading regularly The Grizzly Bear. $1.50 for one year (12 issues). Subscribe now.

THE GRIZZLY BEAR
IS REGULARLY ON SALE:
SAN FRANCISCO:
N.S.G.W. Bldg., 414 Mason St., Room 302.
OAKLAND:
Fred M. DeWitt, 620 14th St.
LOS ANGELES:
315 Wilcox Bldg., Second and Spring.

CALIFORNIA'S ANNIVERSARY

THREE-DAY FESTIVAL AT SANTA ROSA

SANTA ROSA, SONOMA COUNTY, HAS ARranged a three-day Admission Day festival which will be participated in by thousands of Native Sons and Native Daughters and other lovers of California from all sections of the state who desire to pay homage to this Gem of the West on the occasion of the eighty-third anniversary of its becoming one of the United States of America.

The main feature of the celebration will be the Admission Day, September 9, parade, directed by Gam Hurst, Grand Marshal N.S.G.W. Nine silver trophies will be awarded competitive drum corps and drill teams appearing in the line, and other prizes will be given for best-appearing floats and marching units.

The parade will start at 10:30 a.m. The Grizzly Bear presents the lineup as received from Grand Marshal Hurst, August 23, with this notation: "This lineup is subject to change, and is in nowise definite."

ADVANCE DIVISION—Detachment State Traffic Police under Capt. Shriver. Gam Hurst, Grand Marshal N.S.G.W.; Mrs. Anna Thuesen, Grand Marshal N.D.G.W.; Richard M. Hamb, adjutant; Charles O. Dunbar, chief of staff; Frank Foss, chief aide; Mike Flohr, chief aide-de-camp; Irving Gibson, Horace Leavitt, Walter M. Davis, Ray Schauer, Fred Flake, Fred Nickelson, Dr. A. P. Toscano, Harry Gaetjen, R. L. P. Bigelow, Ben Harrison, John S. Ramsay, F. B. Leonard, Frank Perry, Albert V. Mayrhofer, aides-de-camp; Frank Lane, Frank Rowe, W. B. O'Brien, Harry G. Williams, Charles Bowden, Joseph S. McShane, Silva Zambelli, Ann Dippel, Art Jensen, Dora Brayton, Peggy Hoffman, Frank Buckley, Stanley E. Hadlen, Art Pohein, aides to Grand Marshal. Santa Rosa Municipal Band. Color Guard with Colors. 3rd Battalion 184th Infantry N.G.C. Forty decorated automobiles for honored guests, including grand officers N.S.G.W. and N.D.G.W., Justices California Supreme Court, Mayor and City Council of Santa Rosa, Sonoma County Board of Supervisors.

FIRST DIVISION—Arthur Cleu, marshal; Frank Smith, Felix Robson, Alice Weber, Martha Watson, aides. Police Escort and Colors: Chief of Jolice James J. Drew, platoon of Oakland Police. Oakland City Officials: Mayor Dr. W. McCracken, City Manager Ossian E. Carr, J. DePaoli, A. Arlett, W. Jacobson, J. Quinn, G. Fitzgerald, Dr. J. M.

GAM HURST,
Grand Marshal N.S.G.W.

Gresham, H. Beach, Dr. J. Slavich. Alameda County Board Supervisors: W. G. Hamilton, Ralph Richmond, Clifford Wixson, Thomas Caldecott, George Janssen. Alameda County N.S.G.W. and N.D.G.W. Parade Committee: Edward T. Schnarr (chairman), Sallie R. Thaler (co-chairman), Gus Nelson, Dr. De Benedetti, Les Ashworth, E. Fitzgerald, F. B. Leonard, Fred Martin, Louise Kehoe, Dorothy Hadlen, Evelyn Perry, Lenore Sunkler, Sam Levy, Frank Smith. Piedmont Parlor No. 120 N.S. Band. Piedmont Parlor No. 120 N.S. Piedmont Parlor No. 87 N.D. Piedmont Parlor No. 120 N.S. Drum Corps. Piedmont Parlor No. 120 N.S. Float. Alameda Parlor No. 47 N.S. Halcyon Parlor No. 146 N.S. Encinal Parlor No. 156 N.D. Berkeley Parlor No. 210 N.S. Brooklyn Parlor No. 157 N.D. Claremont Parlor No. 240 N.S. Drum Corps. Claremont Parlor No. 240 N.S. Argonaut Parlor No. 166 N.D. Washington Parlor No. 169 N.S. Bear Flag Parlor No. 151 N.D. Eden Parlor No. 113 N.S. Past Presidents Association No. 2 N.D. City of Oakland and County of Alameda Float.

SECOND DIVISION—Allan Sunkler, marshal; Adrian Hynes, Lloyd Alexander, Ruth Toussaint, Evelyn Perry, aides. Oakland Parlor No. 50 N.S. Drum Corps. Oakland Parlor No. 50 N.S. Bahia Vista Parlor No. 167 N.D. Estudillo Parlor No. 223 N.S. El Cereso Parlor No. 207 N.D. Athens Parlor No. 195 N.S. Aloha Parlor No. 106 N.D. Las Positas Parlor No. 96 N.S. Fruitvale Parlor No. 252 N.S. Drum Corps. Fruitvale Parlor No. 252 N.S. Fruitvale Parlor No. 177 N.D. Pleasanton Parlor No. 244 N.S. Wisteria Parlor No. 127 N.S.

THIRD DIVISION—Frank A. Biederman (chairman) and San Francisco Parade Committee. Louis F. Erb, marshal; Walter Bamman, Grace Templeton, aides. California Parlor No. 1 N.S. Drum Corps. California Parlor No. 1 N.S. Minerva Parlor No. 2 N.D. Alta Parlor No. 3 N.D. Pacific Parlor No. 10 N.S. Portola Parlor No. 172 N.D. Golden Gate Parlor No. 29 N.S. Golden Gate Parlor No. 158 N.D. Oro Fino Parlor No. 9 N.D. Fremont Parlor No. 59 N.D. San Francisco Parlor No. 49 N.S. Drum and Fife Corps. San Francisco Parlor No. 49 N.S. Keith Parlor No. 137 N.D. Mission Parlor No. 38 N.S. Drum Corps. Mission Parlor No. 38 N.S. Mission Parlor No. 227 N.D. Drum Corps. Golden State Parlor No. 50 N.D.

ADMISSION DAY PROGRAM

Friday, September 8:
Baseball Game
Street Dance and Mardi Gras
Midnite Show and Frolic

Saturday, September 9:
Admission Day Parade
Open House at Headquarters

Sunday, September 10:
Athletic Sports

WESLEY COLGAN,
Chairman Admission Day Committee.

FOURTH DIVISION—Albert Viautin, marshal; Patricia Selinter, Joseph Rose, aides. Rincon Parlor No. 72 N.S. Band. Rincon Parlor No. 72 N.S. Drum Corps. Rincon Parlor No. 72 N.S. Gabrielle Parlor No. 139 N.D. El Dorado Parlor No. 52 N.S. Olympus Parlor No. 189 N.S. Marshall Parlor No. 202 N.S. Bay City Parlor No. 104 N.S. El Capitan Parlor No. 222 N.S. Sequoia Parlor No. 160 N.S. Yosemite Parlor No. 83 N.D. Linda Rosa Parlor No. 170 N.D. La Dorada Parlor No. 236 N.D. Stage Coach. Niantic Parlor No. 105 N.S. Drum Corps. Niantic Parlor No. 105 N.S. Buena Vista Parlor No. 68 N.D. Orinda Parlor No. 56 N.D. Genevieve Parlor No. 132 N.D. Drum Corps. Genevieve Parlor No. 132 N.D.

FIFTH DIVISION—Dr. Vincent V. Hartman, marshal; Milton Lawler, Kitty Mullaney, aides. Stanford Parlor No. 76 N.S. Band. Stanford Parlor No. 76 N.S. La Estrella Parlor No. 89 N.D. Calaveras Parlor No. 103 N.D. San Souci Parlor No. 96 N.D. National Parlor No. 118 N.S. El Vespero Parlor No. 118 N.D. Drill Team. El Vespero Parlor No. 118 N.D. Hesperian Parlor No. 137 N.S. Drum Corps. Hesperian Parlor No. 137 N.S. Precita Parlor No. 187 N.S. Drum Corps. Precita Parlor No. 187 N.S. Las Lomas Parlor No. 72 N.D.

SIXTH DIVISION—Harry Romick, marshal; Clifford Roberts, aide. South San Francisco Parlor No. 157 N.S. Drum and Piccolo Corps. South San Francisco Parlor No. 157 N.S. Stage Coach. South San Francisco Parlor No. 157 N.S. Darina Parlor No. 114 N.D. Alcalde Parlor No. 154 N.S. Drum Corps. Alcalde Parlor No. 154 N.S. James Lick Parlor No. 220 N.D. Presidio Parlor No. 194 N.S. Presidio Parlor No. 148 N.D. Drill Team. Dolores Parlor No. 208 N.S. Dolores Parlor No. 169 N.D. Guadalupe Parlor No. 153 N.D. Drum Corps. Guadalupe Parlor No. 153 N.D.

SEVENTH DIVISION—Twin Peaks Parlor No. 214 N.S. Drum and Fife Corps. Twin Peaks Parlor No. 214 N.S.

LELAND S. LEWIS,
Secretary Admission Day Committee.

Twin Peaks Parlor No. 185 N.D. Drill Team. Twin Peaks Parlor No. 185 N.D. Balboa Parlor No. 234 N.S. Balboa Parlor No. 249 N.D. Bret Harte Parlor No. 260 N.S. Drum Corps. Bret Harte Parlor No. 260 N.S. Bret Harte Parlor No. 282 N.D. Guadalupe Parlor No. 231 N.S. Drum Corps. Guadalupe Parlor No. 231 N.S. Castro Parlor No. 232 Drum and Bugle Corps. Castro Parlor No. 232 N.S. Castro Parlor No. 178 N.D. Utopia Parlor No. 270 N.S. Drum Corps. Utopia Parlor No. 270 N.S. Utopia Parlor No. 252 N.D. Drill Team. Utopia Parlor No. 252 N.D.

EIGHTH DIVISION—William J. Bright, marshal. Los Angeles Parlor No. 45 N.S. Los Angeles Parlor No. 124 N.D. Ramona Parlor No. 109 N.S. Californiana Parlor No. 247 N.D. Hollywood Parlor No. 196 N.S. Long Beach Parlor No. 239 N.S. Long Beach Parlor No. 154 N.D. Sepulveda Parlor No. 263 N.S. Rudecinda Parlor No. 230 N.D. Glendale Parlor No. 264 N.S. Verdugo Parlor No. 240 N.D. Santa Monica Bay Parlor No. 267 N.S. Drum Corps. Santa Monica Bay Parlor No. 267 N.S. Santa Monica Bay Parlor No. 245 N.D. University Parlor No. 272 N.S. Compton Parlor No. 273 N.S. Santa Ana Parlor No. 265 N.S. Arrowhead Parlor No. 110 N.S.

NINTH DIVISION—Frank Nelson, marshal. San Jose Parlor No. 22 N.S. Drum Corps. San Jose Parlor No. 22 N.S. San Jose Parlor No. 81 N.D. Santa Clara Parlor No. 100 N.S. Observatory Parlor No. 177 N.S. Vendome Parlor No. 100 N.D. Redwood Parlor No. 66 N.S. Bonita Parlor No. 10 N.D. El Carmelo Parlor No. 256 N.S. Drum Corps. El Carmelo Parlor No. 256 N.S. El Carmelo Parlor No. 181 N.D. Drill Team. El Carmelo Parlor No. 181 N.D.

TENTH DIVISION—Ray Friedberger, marshal; June Longshore, John Monteverde, Edna Briggs, aides. Stockton Parlor No. 7 N.S. Joaquin Parlor No. 5 N.D. Lodi Parlor No. 18 N.S. Stage Coach. Sacramento Parlor No. 3 N.S. Califia Parlor No. 22 N.D. Sunset Parlor No. 26 N.S. La Bandera Parlor No. 110 N.D. Drill Team. La Bandera Parlor No. 110 N.D. Rocklin Parlor No. 233 N.S. Sutter Parlor No. 111 N.D. Drill Team. Sutter Parlor No. 111 N.D. Courtland Parlor No. 106 N.S. Coloma Parlor No. 212 N.D.

ELEVENTH DIVISION—Frank Harrison, marshal; Joseph F. Rose, Monroe Label, R. R. Veale, aides. Mount Tamalpais Parlor No. 64 N.S. Drum Corps. Mount Tamalpais Parlor No. 64 N.S. Marinita Parlor No. 198 N.D. Sea Point Parlor No. 158 N.S. Sea Point Parlor No. 196 N.D. Nicasio Parlor No. 183 N.S. Fairfax Parlor No. 225 N.D. Tamelpa Parlor No. 231 N.D. Saint Helena Parlor No. 53 N.S. La Junta Parlor No. 203 N.D. Napa Parlor No. 62 N.S. Drum Corps. Napa Parlor No. 62 N.S. Eshcol Parlor No. 16 N.D. Calistoga Parlor No. 86 N.S. Calistoga Parlor No. 145 N.D. Vallejo Parlor No. 77 N.S. Vallejo Parlor No. 195 N.D.

TWELFTH DIVISION—Charles Bacigalupi, marshal; William Borba, Walter Christian, aides. American Legion Band of Santa Rosa. Colors. Petaluma Parlor No. 27 N.S. Float. Petaluma Parlor No. 222 N.D. Sonoma Parlor No. 111 N.S. Float. Sonoma Parlor No. 209 N.D. Sebastopol Parlor No. 143 N.S. Float. Glen Ellen Parlor No. 102 N.S. Santa Rosa Parlor No. 28 N.S. Drum Corps. Santa Rosa Parlor No. 217 N.D. Float. Santa Rosa Parlor No. 28 N.S.

"OPEN HOUSE" HEADQUARTERS.

"Open house" is one of the enjoyable features of every Admission Day celebration. Parlors' headquarters, where open-handed hospitality will be dispensed, will be located in Santa Rosa as follows:

San Francisco N.S.G.W. Extension Order Committee—Elks Temple, Fourth and "A" streets.

Alameda County N.S.G.W. and N.D.G.W.—Churchman Hall, 215 Exchange avenue.

Sonoma County N.S.G.W. and N.D.G.W.—Native Sons Hall, 310 Mendocino avenue.

Rincon Parlor No. 72 N.S.G.W. (San Francisco)—Burbank Hotel.

Stanford Parlor No. 76 N.S.G.W. (San Francisco)—Occidental Hotel.

Precita Parlor No. 187 N.S.G.W. (San Francisco)—Occidental Hotel.

Twin Peaks Parlor No. 214 N.S.G.W. (San Francisco)—I.O.O.F. Hall, 380 Mendocino avenue.

Guadalupe Parlor No. 231 N.S.G.W. (San Francisco)—Moose Hall, 441 Fourth street.

Subscription Order Blank

For Your Convenience

Grizzly Bear Magazine,
309-15 Wilcox Bldg.,
206 South Spring St.,
Los Angeles, California.

For the enclosed remittance of $1.50 enter my subscription to The Grizzly Bear Magazine for one year.

Name..

Street Address..

City or Town..

BASEBALL CONTESTS.

Saturday, September 9, at Doyle Park, there will be a baseball game between teams from University Parlor No. 272 N.S.G.W. (Los Angeles) and Santa Rosa Parlor No. 28 N.S.G.W. Sunday, September 10, at Doyle Park, teams from Castro Parlor No. 232 N.S.G.W. (San Francisco) and Santa Rosa Parlor No. 28 N.S.G.W. will contest.

COMMITTEES IN CHARGE.

Arrangements for the Santa Rosa Admission Day festival have been made under the supervision of Santa Rosa Parlor No. 28 N.S.G.W. The general committee includes Wesley Colgan, chairman; Leland S. Lewis, secretary; Frank Berger, Dr. W. C. Shipley, James Brucker and Wesley Beach. Subcommittees are:

Finance—Frank P. Doyle, John Hawkes, George Colgan and T. J. Hutchinson.

Decorations—Frank Berger, P. Gambini, Sid Kurlander and Wm. Cook.

Parade—Dr. W. C. Shipley, Mike Flohr, E. L. Mangin, Ann Dickson, A. J. Kerner and Larry Walker.

Publicity—James Brucker, Herbert Sweed, Clytie Lewis, Angie Miner and Chas. Bacigalupi.

Housing—Geo. Gilman, Inez Mundell and Ann Beach.

Athletics—Matt Rogina, Tom Grace, Fred Clark and Earl Donner.

Prizes—Walter Andrews, Lee Britton, Irving Kurlander, Ruby Berger and James Grace.

Street Dance—James Bertino, Geo. Beach, Geo. Eckman and Louie Allegrin.

Music—L. H. Harris, Dr. D. W. Barnett and O. G. Pedigo.

Drum and Drill Competition—Arthur Janssen, Wesley Jamison, Carrie Avellar and Ralph Rawson.

REDWOOD TEMPLE

(Memorial Redwood Grove.)

(RUTH PARLE.)

A quiet hush; eternal calm
Is templed here.
Its silent beauty holds heart's balm,
For God is near.

In welcome stand old redwoods high
For those who pray.
Towering spires reach the sky
To clouds of grey.

This, a poem in solemn wood
Memorial to Him
Made in beauteous, revering mood
By faith ne'er dim—
Cathedral peace where love is tood—
Eternal Hymn.

CALIFORNIA STATE MONUMENTS THAT PERPETUATE HISTORY OF LONG AGO.

California has ten state monuments, all of historic interest, administered by the State Park Commission. They include:

Donner Monument—Nevada County, at Donner Lake. A memorial erected by the N.S.G.W. and N.D.G.W. to the ill-fated Donner party, snowbound at Donner Lake in the winter of 1847.

Marshall Monument—El Dorado County, near the site of the cabin of James W. Marshall, discoverer of gold at Coloma, in 1848.

Fort Ross—Sonoma County. Site of a Russian settlement founded in 1812.

Mission San Francisco de Solano—Sonoma City. Most northerly of the Franciscan missions.

General Vallejo Home—Outskirts of Sonoma City. Home-place of General Mariano Guadalupe Vallejo, soldier, statesman and patriot.

First California Theater—Monterey City. Erected in 1843, and used as a place of entertainment.

Junipero Serra Landing Place—Outskirts of Monterey City.

Monterey Custom House—Monterey City. Where Commodore John Drake Sloat raised the American Flag, July 7, 1846.

Hacienda Governor Pio Pico—Whittier, Los Angeles County. Adobe residence of Pio Pico, a governor of California in the days of Mexican rule.

San Pasqual Battlefield—San Diego County. Where American troops defeated Mexican forces, December 5, 1846.

The number of these historic monuments is being increased from time to time. Soon to be added are the San Juan Bautista, San Benito County, Plaza and old buildings facing San Juan Mission.

KNOW HUMBOLDT COUNTY— NUMEROUS HISTORIC PLACES LISTED.

The Humboldt County Board of Trade, with headquarters at Eureka, has prepared for distribution an authoritative list of historical places in Humboldt County. The various sites which have associations with the pioneers of the Redwood Empire are described in detail.

Among the places included in the compilation are Trinidad Head, discovered by Spanish navigators June 9, 1775; Fort Humboldt, near Eureka, where U. S. Grant was stationed in 1853; scenes of fighting with Indians, and many other historic sites. A narrative on the discovery of Humboldt Bay is included, besides a list of books referring to the history of Humboldt County.

This report on the historic places in Humboldt County may be secured from the Humboldt Board of Trade, which has also issued a new strip map showing the route of the redwood highway. The Eureka Chamber of Commerce has published a new illustrated leaflet on Eureka, its advantages and attractions.

Pinnacles Monument Enlarged—Some 5,000 acres have been added to California's Pinnacles National Monument. With the exception of the portion embracing Chalone Mountain, in Monterey County, the Pinnacles area is in San Benito County.

Flower Festival—The ninth annual California Flower Festival is to be held September 14-17 at San Leandro, Alameda County. The largest and most spectacular orchid display ever seen in the West will be a feature.

Native Daughters of the Golden West

"TO THE OFFICERS AND MEMBERS of Subordinate Parlors Native Daughters of the Golden West—From the time when Jason and his Argonauts traveled the Aegean Sea in search of the Golden Fleece, the heart of man has yearned for the 'Golden.' His aspirations were realized in this blessed land, where Golden Sunshine sheds its light upon the hills, covered with the Golden Poppy, and containing precious Golden Metal.

"One has but to understand the meaning of the symbols in the Great Seal of State, to fully appreciate the significance of Admission Day. The tall goddess tells how, Minerva-like, California was born a state, without having gone through the probation of a territory. The grizzly bear feeding upon the grapevine, typifies peculiar characteristics of California; the miner with uplifted pick, toils to gather the rock-bound treasure, picturing industry and the golden wealth of this sun-lit land; the ship points to the situation of the State with respect to commercial greatness; the snowcapped Sierras emphasize the beauty, strength and nobility of California's natural beauty, and the motto 'Eureka' indicates that the Pioneer fathers and mothers after traversing a continent, found in California the wealth and beauty of the world. The golden wealth poured from these western shores in time of civil conflict established the priceless heritage of human liberty.

MRS. IRMA W. LAIRD,
Grand President N.D.G.W.

"In 1881 the people of the State of California by common consent delegated to the Native Sons of the Golden West the privilege of naming the place for holding a state-wide celebration in honor of Admission Day. Since 1887 the Native Daughters of the Golden West have been coworkers with the Native Sons in perpetuating this date as a holiday, a day set aside for the observance of Pioneer customs, songs and traditions. The covered wagon and the oxen have become symbolical of those days of tragedy and romance, the days of '49 when our mothers came, young and unafraid, side by side with the Pioneer fathers, to build this land of the West.

"It is particularly fitting that on this eighty-third anniversary of our Statehood that we should pay special honor to those Pioneers who established our first western homes. It is from them that we inherited our love of home, and we are still close enough to them to have retained at least a little of their pioneering spirit.

"This year upon Admission Day, the Native Sons and Native Daughters will gather in the city of Santa Rosa, the home of the late Luther Burbank. Our thoughts will naturally turn to the well-known plant wizard, who was able to develop the most mediocre varieties of plants, flowers, fruits and vegetables to such an extent that even the thorny cacti of the desert became edible for livestock; drab flowers took on spectral hues and exhaled fragrance; bitter fruit became luscious, and even the lowly tuber developed into an aristocrat of the table.

"Analagous to the remarkable scientific work of Burbank might come the development of 'Better Parades.' We are expecting the usual magnificent and glamorous display, the long line of brilliantly garbed Native Sons and Daughters, and we realize that each individual success shall redound to the honor and credit of the Orders. Each individual in that line of march holds to a degree the reputation of our Order. It is because I believe so profoundly in the Order of the Native Daughters of the Golden West, and because I am so proud of what it is and what it is doing, that I covet for it the best personal character, in ideals and in all personal appearances.

" 'In the land of heaven's peculiar grace, the heritage of nature's noblest race, there is a spot on earth supremely blest, a dearer, sweeter spot than all the rest. Where shall that land, that spot of earth be found? Oh, thou shalt find, howe'er thy footsteps roam, that land thy country, and that spot thy home,'—CALIFORNIA.

"Sincerely and fraternally in P.D.F.A.,
"IRMA W. LAIRD,
"Grand President N.D.G.W.
"Alturas, August 11, 1933."

GRAND PRESIDENT'S OFFICIAL ITINERARY.

Alturas—Grand President Irma W. Laird will, on the dates noted, officially visit the following Subordinate Parlors:

SEPTEMBER.

1st—Ruby No. 46, Murphys; Princess No. 84, Angels Camp; San Andreas No. 113, San Andreas; jointly at Angels Camp.
11th—Sea Point No. 196, Sausalito.
12th—El Vespero No. 118, San Francisco.
13th—Gabrielle No. 139, San Francisco.
14th—Contra Costa County district meeting, at Pittsburg.
15th—Plumas Pioneer No. 219, Quincy.
18th—Colus No. 194, Colusa.
19th—Lassen View No. 98, Shasta; Camellia No. 41, Anderson; Berendos No. 23, Red Bluff; Hiawatha No. 140, Redding; jointly at Anderson.
20th—Susanville No. 243, Susanville; Nataqua No. 152, Standish; jointly at Standish.
23rd—Imogen No. 134, Sierraville; Naomi No. 36, Downieville; jointly at Sierraville.

OCTOBER.

2nd—Berryessa No. 192, Willows.
3rd—Sutter No. 111, Sacramento.
4th—Gold of Ophir No. 190, Oroville.
6th—Alturas No. 159, Alturas; Mount Lassen No. 215, Bieber; jointly at Alturas.

Thirty State Flags Presented Schools.

Editor Grizzly Bear—The inclosed poem was written by a 12-year-old girl attending Bryte school, Yolo County, after she had accepted a California State (Bear) Flag for her class, presented by Woodland No. 90. The Parlor is very interested in presenting the state flag to the schools of the county. To date, thirty have been presented, and the history and landmarks committee is anxious to continue the work. President Lela Ewert has appointed Edna Richter, Rhoda Maxwell and Gladys Nieman to act. I would appreciate having the poem published in The Grizzly Bear, as we are very proud of the interest shown by the children.

EDNA RICHTER.

Woodland, August 14, 1933.

The poem, entitled "Pioneers," by Eunice Quuner, seventh grade pupil of the Bryte, Yolo County, school, follows:

Our Pioneers! Good and great were they,
To make this West of ours.
They did not come in the month of May;
They did not choose the brightest way.
They took this land so large and great;
They did not wait—and wait.
Brave in heart and brave in soul,
They marched straight on to this land of gold!
They built their homes and started trade.
Brave men and women, not afraid!
They left this land to you and me,
Now let us try and keep it free.

Large Crowd at Public Installation.

Fullerton—Some three hundred persons attended the public installation of officers of Grace No. 242, conducted by Deputy Irene Eden. Among the number were Past Grand Grace Stoermer and Mms. A. H. Rothaermel, Nellie Cline, Helen Anderson, Lucanna McFadden, Carrie Ford, Mattie Edwards and Lena Aspden, past presidents of the Parlor. A garden effect was created in the hall by the use of baskets of gladioli in pastel tints, combined with potted ferns and a profusion of shasta daisies.

The assisting installing officers, from Los Angeles No. 124, and the new officers of Grace, headed by President Erma Watts, were gowned in white and carried boquets of gardenias. A program arranged by Helen Anderson included numbers by Mrs. James Sutherland, Kate McCullah, Mary Mason and George Forster. To Lena Aspden was presented a past president ring. Concluding the delightful occasion, refreshments were served at tables beautified with carnations, ferns and scabiosis.

Grand President Visits.

Oakland—At a very interesting meeting August 17, Piedmont No. 87 had as guest of honor Grand President Irma W. Laird. Four candidates were initiated, and President Dorothy Hadlen and her assisting officers were congratulated on the efficient manner in which the ritual was exemplified. All in attendance missed the smiling countenance of Past Grand Addie L. Mosher, who has been very seriously ill for a year.

Among the many visitors were Past Grands Dr. Mariana Bertola, who instituted Piedmont during her term as Grand President, Margaret Grote Hill, May C. Boldeman, Evelyn Carlson and Estelle Evans, Grand Secretary Sallie Thaler and Grand Trustee Orinda Giannini. The Parlor will turn out in strong numbers in the Admission Day, September 9, parade at Santa Rosa.

Fiesta Entries Prize Winners.

Santa Ana—With Mae West as president, officers of Santa Ana No. 235 were installed by Deputy Violet Henshilwood. Among the many visitors were Grand Inside Sentinel Hazel Hansen and the Parlor organizer, Bertha Hitt (Long Beach No. 154). President West was the recipient of many remembrances, and a past president ring was given Mildred Gray. A fine program of entertainment was presented. As a pleasant surprise, members having birthday anniversaries

MANZANITA PARLOR DRILL TEAM

Grass Valley—The drill team of Manzanita No. 29, which was well received at the Oakland Grand Parlor. Upper left: Ethel Foote, Venita Jones, Marie Merrifield, Dorothy Dettner, Alice Collins, Ethel Veale (pianist), Susie Harris, Hazel Jenkins, Ruth Linwall, Inez Hammill, Nettie Myers. Lower row: Vere Hansen, Vashti Schwartz, Grace Eva, Anna Rowe, Beatrice Deward, Marie Foote, Hannibelle Daley, Verne Taylor. The drill team always acts as an escort at all the Parlor's installations. Maurice Studio, Grass Valley, photo.

in August—Marguerite Cramer, Elva Selvidge, Ruth Kotlar—were August 14 honored at refreshment tables decorated in pink and white.

Entries of the Parlor and Santa Ana No. 265 N.S.G.W.—a wagon labeled "Santa Ana or Bust" and a group of "forty-niners"—won first and third prizes in the Fiesta del Oro parade July 27. Mrs. Walter Hiskey was chairman for No. 235. The Parlors had a joint basket picnic, followed by dancing, at Irvine Park the evening of August 23.

Past Grand Honored.

Middletown—Honoring Past Grand Sue J. Irwin, Clear Lake No. 135 held a picnic and card party in the grounds of the beautiful Gordon estate, located in the foothills west of Middletown, August 5. The occasion marked the thirty-first anniversary of the Parlor, which was organized by Cora Brooks-Herrick, and instituted by Grand President Ema Gett, lately deceased, in August of 1902.

The following enjoyed the afternoon at cards and games on the terrace, after partaking of a delicious luncheon prepared by members of Clear Lake: Mr. and Mrs. E. M. Gordon, Miss Sue Irwin, Mms. Mildred Irwin, Addie Penney, Gladys Brooks, Merle Bohn, Helen Herman, Minnie Parrvott, Belle Farmer, Freda Richardson, Bertha Brookins, Millie Danis, Gertie Cofisey, Lelia Davis, Clara Spomer, Anjie Nelson and Cora Herrick.

Barn Dance and Corn Feed.

Oakland—Members of Aloha No. 106, their husbands and friends were the guests August 8 of Athens No. 195 N.S.G.W. at a barn dance and corn feed. Nearly everyone came attired in gingham dress or overalls. A buggy, without a horse, and hay upon the floor gave the hall a barnlike appearance. A corn husking contest was enjoyed, and for refreshments corn on the cob, cake and coffee were served.

Aloha honored Deputy Pauline Cleu, President Katherine Walker and its latest bride, Ortha Buckley, August 15. Each received a gift from the Parlor. The banquet tables were beautifully decorated, and delicious refreshments were enjoyed. Admission Day was the incentive for a dance and card party August 26 under the capable supervision of Past President Martha Watson, chairman September 9 committee.

NEWSY N.D. PARAGRAPHS.

Jackson—Ursula No. 1 sponsored a reception in honor of Grand Vice-president Gladys E. Noce. A short program was presented, and refreshments were served. Henrietta O'Neill, on the Parlor's behalf, presented a gift to Mrs. Noce. Among the large number present were Past Grand Ella Caminetti and Supervising Deputy Emma B. Wright. During the evening Ursula's officers were installed by Deputy Esther Gebhardt, Catherine Swenson becoming president.

Santa Cruz—Santa Cruz No. 26 had a surprise shower July 31 for Mrs. Lillian Smith-Miller, a recent bride. Deputies Alberta McCormick and Horace Burkett officiated at the joint installation July 24 of the officers of the Parlor and those of Santa Cruz No. 90. A potluck supper preceded the ceremonies. Among the speakers of the occasion were Past Grands Stella Finkeldey and Bertha Briggs, and Supervising Deputy Rose Rhyner.

Sacramento—Califia No. 22's officers were installed July 25 by Deputy Anne Kloss, Esther Mulligan becoming president. Gifts were presented Senior Past President Addie DeCoe, Junior Past President Ella Lambert, Past President Sulene Cowan and President Mulligan. Mrs. Addie Gillis-Bowman, a charter member, passed away recently and in memory of her five dollars was donated the veterans welfare to be used for a bed-ridden soldier. Bessie Leitch, chairman of the evening, was assisted by Maude Scott, Hazel Leitch, Ruth Assalena, Fern Edwards, Blanche Schmidt and Lottie Stevens.

Sutter Creek—Amapola No. 80 had a reception in honor of one of its favored members, Grand Vice-president Gladys Noce. Officers were installed by Deputy Marea Fontenrose, Edith Murphy becoming president.

Hayward—With President Ella Knudsen presiding, Hayward No. 122 had a party August 15 honoring Mrs. Jessie McLeod-Dickinson, recent bride. Following cards, the bride, to the tune of Lohengrin's "Wedding March," led the assemblage to the attractively decorated banquetroom, where she received many beautiful gifts. The reception committee included Misses Lena Harder and Eleanor Thorndike, Mms. Henry Powell and Anna Petersen.

Lincoln—Many members attended the installation here August 9 of the officers of the three Placer County Parlors—Placer No. 138 (Lincoln), La Rosa No. 191 (Roseville) and Auburn No. 233. Deputy Irma Lohse officiated, and in attendance were Past Grands Dr. Eva Rasmussen and Dr. Louise Heilbron, and Supervising Deputy Sadie Brainard. The hall and banquetroom were beautifully decorated in yellow. Sev-

(Continued on Page 15)

Passing of the California Pioneer

(Confined to Brief Notices of the Demise of Those Men and Women Who Came to California Prior to 1870.)

MATHEW JACKSON McGAUGH, native of Missouri, 91; came across the plains to California in 1850, experiencing the many hardships endured by the Pioneers of that period; in 1869 he settled in Los Angeles County; died at Norwalk, survived by two daughters.

Auguste Duhem, native of Africa, 86; camé via Cape Horn in 1852 and resided in various places, including San Francisco and Sacramento Cities; died at National City, San Diego County, survived by a daughter.

Mrs. Amanda Dwelly-Wolf, native of Maine, 95; came in 1852 and settled in Stockton, San Joaquin County, where she died. She was the widow of Andrew Wolf, 1849 Pioneer.

Richard Pritchett, native of Illinois, 81; came across the plains in 1853 and resided in Sonoma and Shasta Counties; died at Anderson, survived by a wife and a son.

Mrs. Mary Carter-Shaw, native of Texas, 81; came in 1854 and resided many years in Santa Cruz County; died at Oakland, Alameda County, survived by a daughter.

Richard Cox, native of England, 88; since 1855 a resident of San Francisco, where he died. He was San Francisco's oldest veteran fireman.

John H. Zumwalt, native of Illinois, 95; crossed the plains in 1853 and resided in Sacramento, San Luis Obispo, Tulare and Kern Counties; died near Bakersfield, survived by two daughters.

Mrs. Nannie Kelly-Fay, native of Arkansas, 78; crossed the plains in 1857 and settled in Visalia, Tulare County, where she died; a husband and two children survive.

Dr. William Henry Briggs, 79; came in 1858 and resided in Sonoma and Alameda Counties many years; died at Stockton, San Joaquin County, survived by a son.

Mrs. Rebecca Jessen, native of Germany, 84; since 1859 a resident of Irvington, Alameda County, where she died; five daughters survive.

Mrs. Karolin Korbel, native of Czechoslovakia, 78; came in 1860 and resided in Humboldt and Sonoma Counties; died at Korbel Ranch, Sonoma County, survived by four children.

Mrs. Mary French Martin, native of Missouri, 75; came in 1863; died at Loomis, Placer County.

Mrs. Dolly Collins, 87; came in 1863; died at Sacramento City, survived by a daughter.

Mrs. Mary Jane Martin, native of Ireland, 97; came in 1863; died at Placerville, El Dorado County, survived by four children.

Charles H. Jordan, native of Massachusetts, 77; came via Panama in 1864 and settled in Siskiyou County; died at Fort Jones.

Mrs. Mary Jane Pixley, native of Ohio, 83; came across the plains in 1864 and resided in Stanislaus and San Joaquin Counties; died at Lodi, survived by a daughter.

John Struve, native of Germany, 88; since 1868 Napa County resident; died at Napa City.

Mrs. Mary Ellen Sullivan, native of Ireland, 90; arrived in 1869 aboard the "Golden Empire" and resided in Contra Costa and Alameda Counties; died at Oakland, survived by three children.

Mrs. Florabelle Smith-Gesford, native of Iowa, 73; crossed the plains in 1864 and resided in Sonoma and Yolo Counties; died at Winters, survived by a son.

Isaac B. Barnes, native of Illinois, 88; crossed the plains in 1852 and resided many years in El Dorado and Humboldt Counties; died at San Francisco, survived by two daughters.

Mrs. Minna Duisenberg, native of Germany, 84; since 1869 a resident of San Francisco, where she died; five children survive. She was the widow of Charles A. C. Duisenberg, Pioneer of 1849 and the first German consul in San Francisco.

Robert Gawthorp, native of England, 89; since 1868 a resident of Dutch Flat, Placer County, where he died; a wife and a daughter survive.

Mrs. Anna Louise Otto-Elster, native of Germany, 79; came in 1867 and resided in Santa Cruz, Mendocino and Fresno Counties; died at Fresno City, survived by a son.

Mrs. Alice Cook-Hunter, native of Michigan, 75; came via Panama in 1866 and settled in Humboldt County; died at San Francisco, survived by six children.

William B. Heckart, native of Pennsylvania, 94; settled in Butte County in 1866; died at Oroville.

Mrs. Mary Ellen Croney-Gillespie, native of New York, 91; since 1862 a resident of Suisun, Solano County, where she died.

Mrs. Martha Temperance-Rice, native of Texas, 75; since 1863 a resident of Los Angeles City, where she died; a husband and four children survive.

Byron Everts Williams, native of New York, 73; came in 1864; died at Durham, Butte County.

Mrs. Almira Hall-Eddy, native of New York, 92; came in 1862; died at Santa Barbara City, survived by two children.

Mrs. Mary Jane Hardin-Fowler, native of Kentucky, 94; crossed the plains in 1851 and settled in Sonoma County; died at East Petaluma, survived by three daughters.

Mrs. Ada Cox, native of Louisiana, 91; came in 1847 and settled in Sacramento City, where she died; a son survives. Her father, Captain L. E. Lucket, was a close friend of Captain John Sutter.

PIONEER NATIVES DEAD

(Brief Notices of the Demise of Men and Women born in California Prior to 1860.)

Mrs. Alice Anna Hackley-Fenner, born El Dorado County, 1854; died Sacramento City; husband survives.

James A. Hall, born Monterey County, 1857; died Watsonville, Santa Cruz County; wife and two children survive. He was at various times mayor of Watsonville, district attorney of Santa Cruz County and state assemblyman. His parents, Richard F. and Maria L. (Stinson) Hall, were '49 Pioneers from Virginia.

Mrs. Hanna Harris-Lasar, born San Benito County, 1858; died Los Alamos, Santa Barbara County; son survives.

Ramon J. Belarde, born San Bernardino County, 1858; died Colton; three children survive.

Mrs. Elenor Jane Crooks-Anderson, born Sacramento County, 1856; died July 20, Salmon Falls, El Dorado County; son survives.

Mrs. Mary Jane French-Mitchell, born Yuba County, 1853; died July 21, Grass Valley, Nevada County. She was affiliated with Manzanita Parlor No. 29 N.D.G.W. (Grass Valley), but originally was a charter member of Columbia Parlor No. 70 (French Corral).

Jasper Norton True, born Napa County, 1854; died July 21, Napa City; son survives.

Mrs. Ramona Fainz-McAleer, born Los Angeles County, 1849; died July 21, San Diego City; seven children survive.

Mrs. Fanny Renney, born Santa Clara County, 1859; died July 21, Los Gatos; son survives.

George W. Phipps, born San Joaquin County, 1853; died July 23, Walnut Grove, Sacramento County; wife and ten children survive.

Mrs. Rebecca Ann Williams-Norman, born Colusa County, 1858; died July 26, Dunsmuir, Siskiyou County; two children survive.

Mrs. Lena Schimmelpfenning-LeBallister, born San Francisco, 1854; died July 26, Oakland, Alameda County; two sons survive.

Benjamin F. Wallace, born Napa County, 1856; died July 27, Colusa City.

Calvin Petray, born Sonoma County, 1859; died July 31, Oakland, Alameda County; wife and three children survive. He was well known in educational circles.

Mrs. Dolores Olivas, born Los Angeles County, 1858; died August 2, Glendale; husband and four children survvie.

George M. McPherson, born Merced County, 1858; died August 3, Richmond, Contra Costa County. He was a charter member of Pacific Parlor No. 10 N.S.G.W. (San Francisco).

Theodore G. Disney, born Tuolumne County, 1857; died August 4, Chico, Butte County; seven children survive.

Mrs. Flora Sparks-Harloe, born Santa Barbara County, 1845; died August 4, San Francisco; two children survive.

John W. Thomas, born Santa Clara County, 1853; died August 8, near Palo Alto; wife and six children survive.

Mrs. Martha Porter-Roelke, born El Dorado County, 1859; died August 9, Latrobe.

Mrs. Lucy Brown-Wentworth, born San Diego City, 1857; died there, August 11; a son survives. Her father, Captain John Brown, arrived in San Diego from Connecticut in 1846, while her mother, Mrs. Martina Villar-Brown, was born in San Diego Presidio.

John Murphy, born Placer County, 1858; died August 12, Wheatland, Yuba County; wife survives.

Mrs. Victoria Lopez, born San Francisco, 1855; died August 15, Alameda City; five children survive.

Charles Henry Hughes, born Nevada County, 1855; died August 15, Grass Valley; wife and two children survive.

Myron L. Carrick, born Siskiyou County, 1859; died August 16, Yreka; wife and two children survive.

William A. Beck, born Santa Cruz County, 1854; died August 17, Watsonville; wife and three daughters survive. His father, Thomas Beck, was secretary of state 1875-79.

Mrs. Martha Taylor Allison, born San Francisco, 1848; died August 17, San Rafael, Marin County. Her father, Ben R. Buckelew, sold to the state in 1852 the site of San Quentin Prison.

SANTA BARBARA TREASURER DIES.

Santa Barbara City—Winfield B. Metcalf, affiliated with Santa Barbara Parlor No. 116 N.S.G.W., died July 30, survived by a wife and a son. He was born at Hydesville, Humboldt County, September 3, 1862. Continuously since 1892 and to the time of his death he was treasurer of Santa Barbara County.

"Life indeed must be measured by thought and action, not by time."—Lubbock.

Feminine World's Fads and Fancies

PREPARED ESPECIALLY FOR THE GRIZZLY BEAR BY ANNA STOERMER

WHEREVER SMART WOMEN GATHER, the latest in hats, suits and ensembles will be observed. Satin and velvet are obviously the most popular fabrics this fall, and that is a pleasant surprise to those who love the sheen of these lovely materials. Shirt-waist frocks are new ideas, made in these shiny fabrics. They will be exquisitely tailored, trim and neat, and undoubtedly will win a new popularity. Some very lovely fashions are being seen and many accessory sets of these materials are frankly frivolous, but they are beautiful and quite elegant.

Gloves, scarfs and purses are often sold to go with hats, as a matter of course. One little velvet hat is seen with a stitched fold coming forward to one side. This new idea is used instead of the hat being pulled down over the eyes. When down-in-the-front headgear had narrow brims like visors pulled sharply over the eyes, they would come a bit higher in back. Feathers are sprouting on a large percentage of hats. Black satin dinner hats are slightly dressy, and usually have a curled bunch of feathers perched near the brim. These are worn in the evening. Those cocky, mad, independent crochet hats are still with us. Young girls who hate to look sedate wear these, and feel charmingly absurd.

From all this, it is obvious that whatever is most becoming to you, will be the fashion for you to cultivate. For winter, your choice is endless. It just means, suit yourself. There is need just now of a hat or two to fill the gap between the white hats of summer and the dark hats that the first touch of fall in the air will serve to introduce. The beret type hat of thin black felt or velvet with a jaunty side tip will be one of the most popular with which to start the autumn season.

Bows continue to be a most important feature of this season's styles, which probably accounts for the fact that many women are wearing dark-hued clothes of sheer material during the warm weather, depending upon the fresh looking bows of white pique or organdie to create the effect of coolness. Organdie cuffs are also refreshing. Bows are predicted for the coming autumn season. Large satin ones are being supplemented for those of wash fabrics.

The frantic search for school wardrobes is on. Young girls are picking up pens, pencils and carefully selected clothes to start college life again. True, they need a very special wardrobe, but it is a simple one to put together. Knitted things stand at the head of the class. Nothing better suits the atmosphere, and a good fashion never dies. To date, nothing has been created to overshadow the prominence of knitted clothes. One knit is a bit more tailored than the other.

PACK TRAINS

(BETTY L. WHITSELL.)

A winding file of mules
In slow deliberate climb
Up mountain-side
Has played a part in history
That will abide.

Upon each mule was lashed
Four hundred pounds of freight.
An ominous load!
Yet with true fortitude they climbed
The perilous road.

And eager hungry men
Buried in mining camps
Did love this sight—
That weary train of laden mules
Brought them delight.

These trails are roads today
The mules are motor trucks
Dependable.
For transportation has progressed
Man's miracle!

But in the trackless past
Are forms of shadowy trains
That used to be—
Up long, long paths that some can see
In memory.

For town wear, we see the jacquard combination which will find itself very much at home on the campus. There is something classic about it. As the years go by it becomes evident that this very simple sweater suit with round basque neckline is a fashion that young people insist on wholeheartedly. The new licorice brown, eel gray, bright and purplish navy, green, black and color combinations of woolens and precious silk fabrics are exactly duplicated in yarns. Some of the new weaves are masterpieces in design.

Another good school want that you cannot keep down is the suede jacket. Snoop around until you find the new version, which should be in the shops by this time. They have adjustable slide fasteners, shaped like fashionable frogs, which close the jacket at one side. The whole thing fits well. Many sizes are eliminated because you simply jerk the slides a little to the right or left and the jacket will adjust itself to you.

The newest knitted dresses look more like woolens or sheer tweeds, and that is a part of the plan to fool you. If they are of this year's crop they will catch you, so perfectly do they resemble the woolens and tweeds. Of course, they will shine on campuses in the fall, but before that you and I are going to wear them against all sorts of backgrounds.

This is a most acceptable costume for town and traveling by motor. It is a wise woman who realizes the value of trim lines. They minimize her size. The nice thing about these new knits is the new idea of contrasting colors. For instance, a deep red, tobacco brown and grey striped top has a chic mouse-colored taupe skirt with matching crocheted hat, touched off by a red feather.

Luck is with the woman who has a frock she can make over, for fall has promised us satin in combination with other fabrics, and in addition to a continuation of accented shoulders. One of the newest is made from a black crepe, the kind that does not go to pieces with even two seasons' wearing. The top is made of satin, with the looped sleeves tapering from the elbow to the wrist. The sash, of satin, has a fair-sized bow and quite long ends at the left side. A small bow finishes the high, round neckline.

When any new fabric is launched, look for it in dresses and suits and also in accessories. Which brings us to the point: some of the best looking satin, velvet and taffeta gloves, hats and bags go with dresses of these fabrics. With a black evening dress, look for the new coral beads. Incidentally, with the advent of satin, pearls assume a new significance again. Black, a favorite color for years, is stronger than ever.

Cocktail-hour dresses with long or short tunic tops are important, besides adding a new fashion interest. A two-piece arrangement is a handy one. It allows one to make several costumes from the first foundation. A white lace top would be charming with a black lace skirt. Black and white are tremendously smart again.

Some delightful new coats are being displayed as harbingers of the early fall. They continue to show the broad shoulder effect. A model has huge winglike flaps at the shoulder, which adds a fashionable touch to an otherwise simple garment. While the rough fabrics promise to hold their own in the new fall styles, the smooth-textured materials will be used extensively for very smart and expensive coats.

Capital City's Birthday—Sacramento City reached its ninety-fourth milestone August 12. On that day, in 1839, Captain John Sutter landed at the mouth of the American River and established a settlement designated New Helvetia. It grew, and later became known as Sacramento. Sutter began the construction of his fort in 1841, and it was completed in 1844.

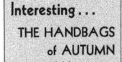

Official Directory of Parlors of the N. D. G. W.

ALAMEDA COUNTY.

Angelita No. 32, Livermore—Meets 2nd and 4th Fridays, Foresters Hall; Mrs. Myrtle I. Johnson, Rec. Sec., P.O. box 253.

Piedmont No. 87, Oakland—Meets Thursdays, Corinthian Hall, Pacific Bldg.; Miss Helen Ring, Rec. Sec., 822 11th St.

Aloha No. 106, Oakland—Meets Tuesdays, 4016 Grove St.; Mrs. Lurine Martin, Rec. Sec., 2815 Wallace St., Berkeley.

Hayward No. 122, Hayward—Meets 1st and 3rd Tuesdays, Veterans Memorial Bldg., Main St.; Miss Ruth Gansberger, Rec. Sec., P. O. box 44, Mount Eden.

Berkeley No. 150, Berkeley—Meets 2nd Saturday afternoon, Berkeley City Women's Club, 2315 Durant; Mrs. Lelia B. Baker, Rec. Sec., 915 Contra Costa Ave.

Bear Flag No. 151, Berkeley—Meets 2nd and 4th Wednesdays, Veterans Memorial Bldg., 1931 Center St.; Mrs. Maud Wagner, Rec. Sec., 817 Alcatraz Ave., Oakland.

Encinal No. 156, Alameda—Meets 2nd and 4th Wednesdays, Veterans Memorial Bldg., Central Ave. and Walnut St.; Mrs. Laura E. Fisher, Rec. Sec., 1413 Caroline St.

Brooklyn No. 157, East Oakland—Meets 2nd and 4th Wednesdays, Masonic Temple, 8th Ave. and E. 14th St.; Mrs. Ruth Cooney, Rec. Sec., 3907 14th Ave.

Argonaut No. 166, Oakland—Meets Tuesdays, Klinkner Hall, 59th and San Pablo; Mrs. Ada Spilman, Rec. Sec., 2905 Ellis St., Berkeley.

Bahia Vista No. 167, Oakland—Meets 1st and 3rd Thursdays, Wigwam Hall, Pacific Bldg.; Mrs. Minnie E. Raper, Rec. Sec., 3449 Helen St.

Fruitvale No. 177, Oakland—Meets Fridays, W.O.W. Hall; May E. Barthold, Rec. Sec., 3832 Santa Rita St.

Laura Loma No. 182, Niles—Meets 1st and 3rd Tuesdays, I.O.O.F. Hall; Mrs. Ethel Fournier, Rec. Sec., P. O. box 515.

El Cereso No. 207, San Leandro—Meets 2nd and 4th Tuesdays, Masonic Hall; Mrs. Mary Tuttle, Rec. Sec., P. O. box 56.

Pleasanton No. 237, Pleasanton—Meets 1st Tuesday, I.O.O.F. Hall; Mrs. Myrtle Lanini, Rec. Sec.

Betsy Ross No. 238, Centerville—Meets 1st and 3rd Fridays, Anderson Hall; Miss Constance Lucio, Rec. Sec., P. O. box 187.

AMADOR COUNTY.

Ursula No. 1, Jackson—Meets 2nd and 4th Tuesdays, N.S.G.W. Hall; Mrs. Emma Boarman-Wright, Rec. Sec., 114 Court St.

Chispa No. 40, Ione—Meets 2nd and 4th Fridays, N.S.G.W. Hall; Cynthia Phillips, Rec. Sec.

Amapola No. 80, Sutter Creek—Meets 2nd and 4th Thursdays, N.S.G.W. Bldg.; Mrs. Hazel M. Marre, Rec. Sec.

Forrest No. 86, Plymouth—Meets 2nd and 4th Tuesdays, I.O.O.F. Hall; Mrs. Marguerite Davis, Rec. Sec.

BUTTE COUNTY.

Annie K. Bidwell No. 168, Chico—Meets 2nd and 4th Thursdays, I.O.O.F. Hall; Mrs. Irene Henry, Rec. Sec., 3015 Woodland Ave.

Gold of Ophir No. 190, Oroville—Meets 1st and 3rd Wednesdays, Memorial Hall; Mrs. Ruth Brown, Rec. Sec., 1365 Leah Court.

CALAVERAS COUNTY.

Ruby No. 46, Murphys—Meets 4th Friday, N.S.G.W. Hall; Belle Segale, Rec. Sec.

Princess No. 84, Angels Camp—Meets 2nd and 4th Wednesdays, I.O.O.F. Hall; Mrs. Grace M. Mills, Rec. Sec., P.O. box 313.

San Andreas No. 113, San Andreas—Meets 1st Friday, Fraternal Hall; Miss Doris Treat, Rec. Sec.

COLUSA COUNTY.

Colus No. 194, Colusa—Meets 1st and 3rd Mondays, Eagles Hall; Miss Kate Busch, Rec. Sec., 350 Market St.

CONTRA COSTA COUNTY.

Stirling No. 146, Pittsburg—Meets 1st and 3rd Wednesdays, Veteran Memorial Hall; Mrs. Leslie Clement, Rec. Sec., 468 E. Santa Fe.

Richmond No. 147, Richmond—Meets 1st and 3rd Tuesdays, Richmond Club House, 1125 Nevin Ave.; Grace Curry, Rec. Sec., 932 Ohio Ave.

Donner No. 193, Byron—Meets 1st and 3rd Wednesdays, I.O.O.F. Hall; Mrs. Anna Pendry, Rec. Sec., P.O. box 442, Brentwood.

Las Juntas No. 221, Martinez—Meets 1st and 3rd Mondays, Pythian Castle; Mrs. Lola O. Viera, Rec. Sec., R.F.D. No. 1.

Antioch No. 223, Antioch—Meets 2nd and 4th Tuesdays, I.O.O.F. Hall; Mrs. Estelle Evans, Rec. Sec., 202 E. 5th St., Pittsburg.

Carquinez No. 234, Crockett—Meets 2nd and 4th Wednesdays, I.O.O.F. Hall; Mrs. Cecile Petee, Rec. Sec., 465 Edwards St.

EL DORADO COUNTY.

Marguerite No. 12, Placerville—Meets 1st and 3rd Wednesdays, Masonic Hall; Mrs. Nettie Leonardi, Rec. Sec., 25 Coloma St.

El Dorado No. 186, Georgetown—Meets 2nd and 4th Saturday afternoons, I.O.O.F. Hall; Mrs. Alta L. Douglas, Rec. Sec.

FRESNO COUNTY.

Fresno No. 187, Fresno—Meets 2nd and 4th Fridays, Pythian Castle, Cor. "R" and Merced Sts.; Mary Aubery, Rec. Sec., 1040 Delphia Ave.

GRAND OFFICERS.

Mrs. Anna M. Armstrong..........Past Grand President
Woodland

Mrs. Irma Laird..........Grand President
Alturas

Mrs. Gladys Noce..........Grand Vice-president
Sutter Creek

Mrs. Sallie R. Thaler..........Grand Secretary
555 Baker St., San Francisco

Mrs. Susie K. Christ..........Grand Treasurer
555 Baker St., San Francisco

Mrs. Anna Thuesen..........Grand Marshal
615 38th Ave., San Francisco

Mrs. Hazel B. Hansen..........Grand Inside Sentinel
501 Griswold St., Glendale

Mrs. Alice M. Oldham..........Grand Outside Sentinel
2218 26th Ave., San Francisco

Mrs. Clara Gairaud..........Grand Organist
134 Locust St., San Jose

GRAND TRUSTEES.

Mrs. Orinda G. Giannini.......2142 Filbert St., San Francisco
Mrs. Florence D. Boyle..........Oroville
Mrs. Minna K. Horn..........Etna
Mrs. Jane Vick..........418 Bath St., Santa Barbara
Mrs. Alice M. Lane..........191 15th Ave., San Francisco
Mrs. Ethel Begley..........233 Prospect Ave., San Francisco
Mrs. Willow Borba..........330 So. Main St., Sebastopol

GLENN COUNTY.

Berryessa No. 192, Willows—Meets 1st and 3rd Mondays, I.O.O.F. Hall; Mrs. Leonora Neate, Rec. Sec., 338 No. Lassen St.

HUMBOLDT COUNTY.

Occident No. 28, Eureka—Meets 1st and 3rd Wednesdays, N.S.G.W. Hall; Mrs. Eva L. MacDonald, Rec. Sec., 2309 "B" St.

Oneonta No. 71, Ferndale—Meets 2nd and 4th Fridays, I.O.O.F. Hall; Mrs. Myra Rumrill, Rec. Sec., P.O. box 142.

Reichling No. 97, Fortuna—Meets 1st and 3rd Tuesdays, Friendship Hall; Mrs. Grace Swett, Rec. Sec., P. O. box 326.

KERN COUNTY.

Miocene No. 228, Taft—Meets 1st and 3rd Wednesday afternoons, I.O.O.F. Hall; Mrs. Evalyn G. Towne, Rec. Sec., 301 Woodrow St.

El Tejon No. 239, Bakersfield—Meets 1st and 3rd Fridays, Eagles Hall, 1714 "G" St.; Mary B. Hampson, Rec. Sec., 908 Quincy St.

Desert Gold No. 250, Mojave—Meets 2nd and 4th Fridays, I.O.O.F. Hall; Jane Lucile Waters, Rec. Sec., Tehachapi.

LAKE COUNTY.

Clear Lake No. 185, Middletown—Meets 2nd and 4th Tuesdays, Herrick Hall; Mrs. Alma E. Snow, Rec. Sec.

LASSEN COUNTY.

Nataqua No. 152, Standish—Meets 1st and 3rd Wednesdays, Foresters Hall; Mrs. Mayda Elledge, Rec. Sec.

Mount Lassen No. 215, Bieber—Meets 2nd and 4th Thursdays, I.O.O.F. Hall; Mrs. Angie C. Kenyon, Rec. Sec.

Susanville No. 243, Susanville—Meets 3rd Thursday, I.O.O.F. Hall; Mildred Hardy, Rec. Sec., P.O. box 425.

LOS ANGELES COUNTY.

Los Angeles No. 124, Los Angeles—Meets 1st and 3rd Wednesdays, I.O.O.F. Hall, Washington and Oak Sts.; Mrs. Mary K. Corcoran, Rec. Sec., 322 No. Van Ness Ave.

Long Beach No. 154, Long Beach—Meets 1st and 3rd Thursdays, Home of Eleanor Johnson, 1920 Bermuda St.; Mrs. Bertha Hitt, Rec. Sec., 5355 Lime Ave.

Rudecinda No. 230, San Pedro—Meets 1st and 3rd Mondays, Womans Club, Gaffey and "N" Sts.; Letitia Sarciaux, Rec. Sec., 1054 W. 24th St.

Verdugo No. 240, Glendale—Meets 2nd and 4th Tuesdays, Masonic Temple, 234 So. Brand Blvd.; Miss Etta Fulkerth, Rec. Sec., 526 No. Orange St.

Santa Monica Bay No. 245, Santa Monica—Meets 2nd and 4th Wednesdays, Odd Fellows Hall, 1431 Third St.; Mrs. Rosalie Hyde, Rec. Sec., 21 Park Ave., Venice.

Californiana No. 247, Los Angeles—Meets 2nd and 4th Tuesday afternoons, Hollywood Studio Club, 1215 Lodi Place; Mrs. Betty Hale, Rec. Sec., 6619 Franklin Ave.

MADERA COUNTY.

Madera No. 244, Madera—Meets 2nd and 4th Thursdays, Masonic Annex; Mrs. Margaret C. Boyle, Rec. Sec., 111 No. "B" St.

MARIN COUNTY.

Sea Point No. 196, Sausalito—Meets 2nd and 4th Mondays, Perry Hall, 50 Caledonia St.; Mrs. Mary B. Smith, Rec. Sec., 47½ Glen Drive.

Marinita No. 198, San Rafael—Meets 2nd and 4th Mondays, 316 "B" St.; Lillian Whitmore, Rec. Sec., 337 5th St.

Fairfax No. 225, Fairfax—Meets 2nd and 4th Tuesdays, Community Hall; Mrs. Marguerite Geary, Rec. Sec.

Tamelpa No. 231, Mill Valley—Meets 1st and 2nd Tuesdays, I.O.O.F. Hall; Mrs. Delphine M. Todt, Rec. Sec., 500 Irwin St., San Rafael.

MARIPOSA COUNTY.

Mariposa No. 63, Mariposa—Meets 1st and 3rd Fridays, I.O.O.F. Hall; Elizabeth E. Johnson, Rec. Sec.

MENDOCINO COUNTY.

Fort Bragg No. 210, Fort Bragg—Meets 1st Thursday, I.O.O.F. Hall; Mrs. Ruth W. Fuller, Rec. Sec.

MERCED COUNTY.

Veritas No. 75, Merced—Meets 1st and 3rd Tuesdays, I.O.O.F. Hall; Miss Flora Fernandes, Rec. Sec., 28 19th St.

MODOC COUNTY.

Alturas No. 159, Alturas—Meets 1st Thursday, Alturas Civic Club; Mrs. Irma W. Laird, Rec. Sec.

MONTEREY COUNTY.

Aleli No. 102, Salinas—Meets 2nd and 4th Thursdays, Pythian Hall; Miss Rose Rhyner, Rec. Sec., 420 Soledad St.

Junipero No. 141, Monterey—Meets 2nd and 4th Fridays, K. of P. Hall, Main St.; Miss Matilda M. Bergschicker, Rec. Sec., 498 Van Buren St.

NAPA COUNTY.

Eshcol No. 16, Napa—Meets 2nd and 4th Mondays, N.S.G.W. Hall; Mrs. Ella Ingram, Rec. Sec., 2140 Seminary St.

Calistoga No. 145, Calistoga—Meets 2nd and 4th Mondays, I.O.O.F. Hall; Sadie P. Brooks, Rec. Sec.

La Junta No. 203, Saint Helena—Meets 1st and 3rd Tuesdays, N.S.G.W. Hall; Mrs. Marie Signorelli, Rec. Sec., 1341 Madrona Ave.

ATTENTION, SECRETARIES!

THIS DIRECTORY IS PUBLISHED BY AUTHORITY OF THE GRAND PARLOR N.D.G.W., AND ALL NOTICES OF CHANGES MUST BE RECEIVED BY THE GRAND SECRETARY (NOT THE MAGAZINE) ON OR BEFORE THE 20TH OF EACH MONTH TO INSURE CORRECTION IN NEXT PUBLICATION OF DIRECTORY.

NEVADA COUNTY.

Laurel No. 6, Nevada City—Meets 1st and 3rd Wednesdays, I.O.O.F. Hall; Mrs. Nellie E. Clark, Rec. Sec., 412 Pine St.

Manzanita No. 29, Grass Valley—Meets 1st and 3rd Tuesdays, Auditorium; Mrs. Loraine Keast, Rec. Sec., 123 Race St.

Columbia No. 70, French Corral—Meets Fridays, Farrelley Hall; Mrs. Kate Farrelley-Sullivan, Rec. Sec.

Snow Peak No. 176, Truckee—Meets 1st Monday, I.O.O.F. Hall; Mrs. Henrietta M. Eaton, Rec. Sec., P. O. box 116.

ORANGE COUNTY.

Santa Ana No. 235, Santa Ana—Meets 2nd and 4th Mondays, K.C. Hall, 4th and French Sts.; Mrs. Matilda S. Lemon, Rec. Sec., 1628 W. 8th St.

Grace No. 242, Fullerton—Meets 1st and 3rd Thursdays, I.O.O.F. Hall, 116½ E. Commonwealth; Mrs. Mary R. Rothaermel, Rec. Sec., Acacia St. & Commonwealth.

PLACER COUNTY.

Placer No. 138, Lincoln—Meets 2nd Wednesday, I.O.O.F. Hall; Miss Carrie Parlin, Rec. Sec.

La Rosa No. 191, Roseville—Meets 1st and 3rd Tuesdays, Eagles Hall; Miss Margaret Parrish, Rec. Sec., Atlantic St.

Auburn No. 233, Auburn—Meets 2nd and 4th Fridays, Foresters Hall; Mrs. Elsie Patrick, Rec. Sec.

PLUMAS COUNTY.

Plumas Pioneer No. 219, Quincy—Meets 1st and 3rd Mondays, I.O.O.F. Hall; Minnie E. Johnson, Rec. Sec., P. O. box 243.

SACRAMENTO COUNTY.

Califia No. 22, Sacramento—Meets 2nd and 4th Tuesdays, N.S.G.W. Hall; Miss Lulu Gillis, Rec. Sec., 921 8th St.

La Bandera No. 110, Sacramento—Meets 1st and 3rd Fridays, N.S.G.W. Hall; Mrs. Clara Weldon, Rec. Sec., 1310 "O" St.

Sutter No. 111, Sacramento—Meets 1st and 3rd Tuesdays, N.S.G.W. Hall; Mrs. Adele Nix, Rec. Sec., 1238 "S" St.

Fern No. 123, Folsom—Meets 1st and 3rd Tuesdays, K.P. Hall; Elizabeth Ryan, Rec. Sec., Represa.

Chabolla No. 171, Galt—Meets 2nd and 4th Tuesdays, I.O.O.F. Hall; Mrs. Mary Pritchard, Rec. Sec.

Coloma No. 212, Sacramento—Meets 1st and 3rd Tuesdays, I.O.O.F. Hall, Oak Park; Mrs. Nettie Harry, Rec. Sec., 1217 35th St.

Liberty No. 213, Elk Grove—Meets 2nd and 4th Fridays, I.O.O.F. Hall; Mrs. Frances Wackman, Rec. Sec., P. O. box 192.

Victory No. 216, Courtland—Meets 1st Saturday and 3rd Monday, N.S.G.W. Hall; Mrs. Agneda Lampie, Rec. Sec.

Rio Rita No. 253, Sacramento—Meets 1st and 3rd Mondays, 902 "J" St.; Katherine L. Jones, Rec. Sec., 2708 Ninth Ave.

SAN BENITO COUNTY.

Copa de Oro No. 105, Hollister—Meets 2nd and 4th Thursdays, Grangers Union Hall; Mrs. Mollie Daveggio, Rec. Sec., 110 San Benito St.

San Juan Bautista No. 179, San Juan Bautista—Meets 1st Wednesday, Mission Corridor Rooms; Miss Gertrude Breen, Rec. Sec.

SAN BERNARDINO COUNTY.

Lugonia No. 241, San Bernardino—Meets 2nd and 4th Wednesdays, Eagles Hall; Miss Lois Poling, Rec. Sec., 295 E. 11th St.

Ontario No. 251, Ontario—Meets 2nd and 4th Thursdays, Ontario Hotel; Miss Wilma Poole, Rec. Sec., 1102 No. Euclid Ave.

SAN DIEGO COUNTY.

San Diego No. 208, San Diego—Meets 2nd and 4th Wednesdays, Directors Room, Chamber Commerce Bldg., 499 W. Broadway; Mrs. Elsie Case, Rec. Sec., 3051 Broadway.

SAN FRANCISCO CITY AND COUNTY.

Minerva No. 2, San Francisco—Meets 1st and 3rd Wednesdays, N.S.G.W. Bldg.; Miss Dorothy Flun, Rec. Sec., 90 Princess St., Sausalito.

Alta No. 3, San Francisco—Meets 2nd and 4th Tuesdays, N.S.G.W. Bldg.; Mrs. Agnese L. Hughes, Rec. Sec., 3980 Sacramento St.

Oro Fino No. 9, San Francisco—Meets 1st and 3rd Thursdays, N.S.G.W. Bldg.; Mrs. Josephine B. Morrissey, Rec. Sec., 4441 20th St.

Golden State No. 50, San Francisco—Meets 1st and 3rd Wednesdays, N.D.G.W. Home; Miss Millie Tietjen, Rec. Sec., 328 Lexington Ave.

Orinda No. 56, San Francisco—Meets 2nd and 4th Fridays, N.D.G.W. Home; Mrs. Anna A. Gruber-Loser, Rec. Sec., 72 Grove Lane, San Anselmo.

Fremont No. 59, San Francisco—Meets 1st and 3rd Tuesdays, N.S.G.W. Bldg.; Miss Hannah Collins, Rec. Sec., 617 Fillmore St.

Buena Vista No. 68, San Francisco—Meets 1st, 3rd and 5th Thursdays, N.D.G.W. Home; Miss Margaret Barrett, Rec. Sec., 3774 20th St.

Las Lomas No. 72, San Francisco—Meets 1st and 3rd Tuesdays, N.D.G.W. Home; Mrs. Marion S. Day, Rec. Sec., 459 Noe St.

Yosemite No. 83, San Francisco—Meets 1st and 3rd Tuesdays, American Hall, 20th and Capp Sts.; Miss Mary Monahan, Rec. Sec., 237 Noe St.

La Estrella No. 89, San Francisco—Meets 2nd and 4th Mondays, N.S.G.W. Bldg.; Miss Birdie Hartman, Rec. Sec., 1018 Jackson St.

Sans Souci No. 96, San Francisco—Meets 2nd and 4th Mondays, N.D.G.W. Home; Mrs. Minnie F. Dobbin, Rec. Sec., 289 Urbano Drive.

Calaveras No. 103, San Francisco—Meets 2nd and 4th Tuesdays, Swedish American Hall, 2174 Market St.; Mary L. Krogh, Rec. Sec., 4235 Cabrillo St.

Darina No. 114, San Francisco—Meets 1st and 3rd Mondays, N.S.G.W. Bldg.; Miss Adele Walsh, Rec. Sec., 479 Page St.

El Vespero No. 118, San Francisco—Meets 2nd and 4th Tuesdays, Masonic Hall, 4705 3rd St.; Mrs. Nell R. Boege, Rec. Sec., 1526 Kirkwood Ave.

Genevieve No. 132, San Francisco—Meets 1st and 3rd Thursdays, N.S.G.W. Bldg.; Miss Branice Pegnillan, Rec. Sec., 2484 16th Ave.

Keith No. 137, San Francisco—Meets 2nd and 4th Thursdays, N.S.G.W. Bldg.; Mrs. Helen T. Mann, Rec. Sec., 575 Pierce St., Apt. 206.

Gabrielle No. 139, San Francisco—Meets 2nd and 4th Wednesdays, N.S.G.W. Bldg.; Mrs. Dorothy Wuesterfeld, Rec. Sec., 1020 Munich St.

Presidio No. 148, San Francisco—Meets 2nd and 4th Tuesdays, N.S.G.W. Bldg.; Mrs. Hattie Gaughran, Rec. Sec., 713 Capp St.

Guadalupe No. 153, San Francisco—Meets 2nd and 4th Mondays, Forester Hall, 170 Valencia St.; Miss May A. McCarthy, Rec. Sec., 336 Elsie St.

Golden Gate No. 158, San Francisco—Meets 2nd and 4th Mondays, N.S.G.W. Bldg.; Mrs. Mary Sullivan, Rec. Sec., 83 Cuvier St.

Dolores No. 169, San Francisco—Meets 2nd and 4th Wednesdays, N.S.G.W. Bldg.; Mrs. Ada Saunders, Rec. Sec., 284 Allison St.

Linda Rosa No. 170, San Francisco—Meets 2nd and 4th Wednesdays, Swedish American Hall, 2174 Market St.; Mrs. Eva P. Tyrrel, Rec. Sec., 2829 Mission St.

Portola No. 172, San Francisco—Meets 1st and 3rd Tuesdays, N.S.G.W. Bldg.; Catherine H. Dolly, Rec. Sec., 4125 23rd St.

Castro No. 178, San Francisco—Meets 1st and 3rd Wednesdays, K.C. Bldg., 150 Golden Gate Ave.; Miss Adeline Sandersfeld, Rec Sec., 50 Baker St.

Twin Peaks No. 185, San Francisco—Meets 2nd and 4th Fridays, Druids Temple, 44 Page St.; Mrs. Loretta Cameron, Rec. Sec., 3969 Army St.

James Lick No. 220, San Francisco—Meets 1st and 3rd Wednesdays, N.S.G.W. Bldg.; Mrs. Edna Bishop, Rec. Sec., 3841 24th St.

Mission No. 227, San Francisco—Meets 2nd and 4th Fridays, N.S.G.W. Bldg.; Mrs. Ann Dippel, Rec. Sec., 448 Dewey Blvd.

Bret Harte No. 232, San Francisco—Meets 2nd and 4th Tuesdays, Aloha Hall, 3009 16th St.; Pearl Wedde, Rec. Sec., 225 7th Ave.

Balboa No. 249, San Francisco—Meets 1st and 3rd Thursdays, Knights Columbus Hall, 382 18th Ave.; Miss Jean Moffet, Rec. Sec., 478 26th Ave.

Utopia No. 252, San Francisco—Meets 2nd and 4th Tuesdays, American Hall, 20th and Capp Sts.; Miss Lelia M. Little, Rec. Sec., 4450 20th St.

SAN JOAQUIN COUNTY.

Joaquin No. 5, Stockton—Meets 2nd and 4th Tuesdays, N.S.G.W. Hall, 314 E. Main St.; Mrs. Della Garvin, Rec. Sec., 1122 E. Market St.

El Pescadero No. 82, Tracy—Meets 1st and 3rd Fridays, I.O.O.F. Hall; Mrs. Mary A. Hewitson, Rec. Sec., 123 Walnut St.

Ivy No. 88, Lodi—Meets 1st and 3rd Tuesdays, Pythian Hall, Cory Bldg., Pine St.; Mrs. Mae Corson, Rec. Sec., 109 So. School St.

Calis de Oro No. 206, Stockton—Meets 1st and 3rd Tuesdays, N.S.G.W. Hall, 314 E. Main St.; Mrs. Frances Germain, Rec. Sec., 450 No. Regent.

Phoebe A. Hearst No. 214, Manteca—Meets 2nd and 4th Wednesdays, I.O.O.F. Hall; Mrs. Josie M. Frederick, Rec. Sec., Route A, Box 384, Ripon.

SAN LUIS OBISPO COUNTY.

San Miguel No. 94, San Miguel—Meets 2nd and 4th Wednesday afternoons, Clemons Hall; Mrs. Nellie Wickstrom, Rec. Sec.

San Luisita No. 108, San Luis Obispo—Meets 2nd and 4th Thursdays, W.O.W. Hall; Miss Agnes M. Lee, Rec. Sec., P. O. box 584.

El Pinal No. 163, Cambria—Meets 2nd, 4th and 5th Tuesdays, N.S.G.W. Hall; Kathryn Luchessa, Rec. Sec.

SAN MATEO COUNTY.

Bonita No. 10, Redwood City—Meets 2nd and 4th Thursdays, I.O.O.F. Hall; Mrs. Dora Wilson, Rec. Sec., 518 Middlefield Rd.

Vista del Mar No. 155, Halfmoon Bay—Meets 2nd Thursday, I.O.O.F. Hall; Elizabeth Olney, Rec. Sec.

Ano Nuevo No. 180, Pescadero—Meets 1st and 3rd Wednesdays, I.O.O.F. Hall; Mrs. Alice Mattei, Rec. Sec.

El Carmelo No. 181, Daly City—Meets 1st and 3rd Wednesdays, Masonic Hall; Mrs. Alice Mathias Oldham, Rec. Sec., 2218 26th Ave., San Francisco.

Menlo No. 211, Menlo Park—Meets 2nd and 4th Mondays, Masonic Hall; Mrs. Frances E. Maloney, Rec. Sec., P. O. box 626.

San Bruno No. 246, San Bruno—Meets 2nd and 4th Fridays, Legion Hall; Miss Mildred Foley, Rec. Sec., 317 Miller Ave., South San Francisco.

SANTA BARBARA COUNTY.

Reina del Mar No. 126, Santa Barbara—Meets 1st and 3rd Tuesdays, Pythian Castle, 222 W. Carillo St.; Mrs. Dorothy Yule, Rec. Sec., 112 Ocean Ave.

SANTA CLARA COUNTY.

San Jose No. 81, San Jose—Meets 1st and 3rd Wednesdays, I.O.O.F. Hall, 3rd and Santa Clara Sts.; Mrs. Nellie Fleming, Rec. Sec., Catholic Women Center.

Vendome No. 100, San Jose—Meets 2nd and 4th Wednesdays, Old Scottish Rite Temple; Miss Marie Buck, Rec. Sec., 245 Hawthorne St.

El Monte No. 205, Mountain View—Meets 2nd and 4th Fridays, American Legion Hall; Miss Elizabeth Spencer, Rec. Sec., 1620 Villa St.

Palo Alto No. 229, Palo Alto—Meets 1st and 2nd Mondays, N.S.G.W. Hall; Miss Helena G. Hansen, Rec. Sec., 531 Lytton Ave.

SANTA CRUZ COUNTY.

Santa Cruz No. 26, Santa Cruz—Meets Mondays, N.S.G.W. Hall; Mrs. May L. Williamson, Rec. Sec., 170 Walnut Ave.

El Pajaro No. 35, Watsonville—Meets 1st and 3rd Tuesdays, I.O.O.F. Hall; Miss Ruth E. Wilson, Rec. Sec., 16 Laurel St.

SHASTA COUNTY.

Camellia No. 41, Anderson—Meets 1st and 3rd Tuesdays, Masonic Hall; Mrs. Olga E. Welbourn, Rec. Sec.

Lassen View No. 98, Shasta—Meets 2nd Friday, Masonic Hall; Miss Louise Litsch, Rec. Sec.

Hiawatha No. 140, Redding—Meets 2nd and 4th Wednesdays, Moose Hall; Ruth Presleigh, Rec. Sec., Office County Clerk.

SIERRA COUNTY.

Naomi No. 36, Downieville—Meets 2nd and 4th Wednesdays, I.O.O.F. Hall; Louise C. Dubuque, Rec. Sec.

Imogen No. 134, Sierraville—Meets 2nd and 4th Saturday afternoons, Copren Hall; Mrs. Jennie Copren, Rec. Sec.

SISKIYOU COUNTY.

Eschscholtzia No. 112, Etna—Meets 1st and 3rd Wednesdays, Masonic Hall; Mrs. Bernice E. Smith, Rec. Sec.

Mountain Dawn No. 120, Sawyers Bar—Meets 2nd and last Wednesdays, I.O.O.F. Hall; Miss Edith Dunphy, Rec. Sec.

SOLANO COUNTY.

Vallejo No. 195, Vallejo—Meets 1st and 3rd Wednesdays, K.C. Hall, 820 Marin St.; Mrs. Mary Combs, Rec. Sec., 511 York St.

Mary E. Bell No. 224, Dixon—Meets 2nd and 4th Thursdays, I.O.O.F. Hall; Mary Young, Rec. Sec.

SONOMA COUNTY.

Sonoma No. 209, Sonoma—Meets 2nd and 4th Mondays, I.O.O.F. Hall; Catherine Bulotti, Rec. Sec.

Santa Rosa No. 217, Santa Rosa—Meets 1st and 3rd Thursdays, N.S.G.W. Hall; Mrs. Clytie L. Lewis, Rec. Sec., R.F.D. No. 4, Box 345-A.

Petaluma No. 222, Petaluma—Meets 1st and 3rd Tuesdays, Dania Hall; Mrs. Margaret M. Oeltjen, Rec. Sec., 503 Prospect St.

STANISLAUS COUNTY.

Oakdale No. 125, Oakdale—Meets 3rd Monday, McLeod Home; Mrs. Lou Reeder, Rec. Sec.

Morada No. 199, Modesto—Meets 2nd and 4th Wednesdays, I.O.O.F. Hall; Mrs. Susan Sullivan, Rec. Sec., 823 10th St.

Eldora No. 248, Turlock—Meets 1st and 3rd Mondays, Masonic Temple; Effie Lund, Rec. Sec., 312 Mitchell St.

SUTTER COUNTY.

South Butte No. 226, Sutter—Meets 1st and 3rd Mondays, N.D.G.W. Hall; Mrs. Abbie N. Varedes, Rec. Sec.

TEHAMA COUNTY.

Berendos No. 23, Red Bluff—Meets 1st and 3rd Tuesdays, W.O.W. Hall, 200 Pine St.; Mrs. Lillie Hammer, Rec. Sec., 636 Jackson St.

NATIVE DAUGHTER NEWS

(Continued from Page 11)

eral gifts were presented, a number of talks were enjoyed, and delicious refreshments were served.

Berkeley—Berkeley No. 150 entertained at a beautiful ceremony in the drawingroom of the Berkeley Women City Club. Supervising Deputy Dora Brayton, assisted by Past Grand Esther R. Sullivan and Grand Secretary Sallie R. Thaler, installed the officers of the Parlor, Florence Shapero becoming president. Past Grand Sue J. Irwin presented Alda Nelson, retiring past president, with an emblematic jewel. Bridge and whist followed buffet refreshments.

Oakland—Fruitvale No. 177's officers were installed by Deputy Louise McDougall, Mae Franklin becoming president. . The hall was prettily decorated with ferns and gladioli. The officers were attired in pastel shades of organdie, and the march was very colorful. A past president emblem was presented Ora Rogers by Pauline Cleu.

Vallejo—Officers of Vallejo No. 195 were installed by Deputy Ruth Hickey, Elizabeth Wassman becoming president. Past Grand Mary Bell and Deputy Lena Nickum were visitors. A past president emblem was presented Edith Gutfeld, and the retiring president, Mabel Thompson, was the recipient of a gift. A banquet was spread, Elizabeth Burns and an able committee in charge.

San Rafael—At the joint installation of officers of Marinita No. 198 and Mount Tamalpais No. 64 N.S.G.W., Deputies Myrtle Divita and Charles Soldavini Jr. officiated, and Dora Cooley and Donald J. Locati became the respective presidents. In appreciation for eight years of efficient service as recording secretary of Marinita, Miss Mollye Y. Spaelti was presented with a fountain pen. Past president emblems were presented Miss Lena Mazza and Monroe E. Peterson. Among the many in attendance were Past Grand Emma Foley and Supervising Deputy Delphine Todt.

San Diego—Mrs. Louise Miller was hostess at a dessert bridge party at her home sponsored by San Diego No. 208. This was the second in a series of affairs given by the Parlor for the benefit of the Balboa Park buildings restoration fund. With Marie James as president, officers were installed by Deputy Pearl Adams Simpson. The Golden Poppy Sewing Club met during August at the homes of President James and Louise Miller, and spent the time sewing and discussing future plans. It was decided to hold a bazar in the fall.

Santa Rosa—At joint ceremonies, officers of Santa Rosa No. 217 and Santa Rosa No. 28 N.S.G.W. were installed by Deputies Gertrude Groskopf and Louis Bosch, Ida Losch and James Brucker becoming the respective presidents. Among the visitors were Past Grand Emma Foley and Grand Trustee Willow Borba.

San Bernardino—Deputy Gertrude Tuttle installed the officers of Lugonia No. 241 July 26, Mary Harris Johnson becoming president. Among the guests was Grand Inside Sentinel Hazel Hansen. With Evelyn Shaddox as chairman, a most successful dance was held at Crestline August 4. The Harmony Club, which has become very popular, made articles for the October Bazar August 15; Kathrine McIntosh is the club president.

Antioch—A number of invited guests witnessed the installation of Antioch No. 223's officers by Deputy Mabel Micholson Huffman, when Marguerite Flannery became president. Past Grand Estelle Evans gave a short talk. Members of the Parlor accompanied Supervising Deputy Mary Ross, a charter member of No. 223, when she attended installations of the officers of Las Juntas No. 221 (Martinez), Stirling No. 146 (Pittsburg) and Donner No. 199 (Byron); at the former, District Deputy Marguerite Peters presided. August 22 a potluck supper was served By Estelle Beasley, Nellie Nicholls, Marguerite Flannery, Mary Ross, Estelle Evans, Abbie Simonds and Emma Lynn.

Sacramento—Officers of Rio Rita No. 253 were installed by Deputy Vera Hellinge, Alpha Filcher becoming president. Gifts were presented Sadie Winn-Brainard, organizer of the Parlor, and Mrs. Hellinge. In attendance were Past Grands Dr. Eva Rasmussen and Dr. Louise Heilbron. Refreshments, carrying out a novel NRA idea, were served, and a delightful entertainment featuring five children was enjoyed. Enthusiastic members are forming a glee club and an escort team.

TRINITY COUNTY.

Eltapome No. 55, Weaverville—Meets 2nd and 4th Thursdays, N.S.G.W. Hall; Mrs. Lou N. Fetzer, Rec. Sec.

TUOLUMNE COUNTY.

Dardanelle No. 66, Sonora—Meets Fridays, I.O.O.F. Hall; Mrs. Nettie Whitte, Rec. Sec., P.O. box 122.

Golden Era No. 99, Columbia—Meets 1st and 3rd Thursdays, N.S.G.W. Hall; Miss Irene Ponce, Rec. Sec.

Anona No. 164, Jamestown—Meets 2nd and 4th Tuesdays, I.O.O.F. Hall; Nellie Hope, Rec. Sec.

YOLO COUNTY.

Woodland No. 90, Woodland—Meets 2nd and 4th Tuesdays, N.S.G.W. Hall; Mrs. Maude Heaton, Rec. Sec., 153 College St.

YUBA COUNTY.

Marysville No. 162, Marysville—Meets 2nd and 4th Wednesdays, Liberty Hall; Miss Cecelia C. Gomes, Rec. Sec., 701 6th St.

Camp Far West No. 218, Wheatland—Meets 3rd Tuesday, I.O.O.F. Hall; Mrs. Ethel C. Brock, Rec. Sec., P. O. box 285.

AFFILIATED ORGANIZATIONS.

General Association Past Presidents—Meetings held annually in April at the home-town of Chief President; Mrs. Winifred Halter, 465 40th St., Oakland, Chief President; Mrs. Anna G. Loser, 72 Grove Lane, San Anselmo, Chief Secretary.

Past Presidents Association No. 1—Meets 1st and 3rd Mondays, N.S.G.W. Bldg., 414 Mason St., San Francisco; Mrs. Merle Sandell, Pres.; Mrs. Leah M. Williams, Rec. Sec., 956 Pierce St., Apt. 104, San Francisco.

Past Presidents Association No. 2—Meets 2nd and 4th Mondays, "Wigwam," Pacific Bldg., 16th and Jefferson, Oakland; Anna Enos, Pres.; Mrs. Elizabeth B. Goodman, Rec. Sec., 134 Juana Ave., San Leandro.

Past Presidents Association No. 3 (Santa Clara County)—Meets 2nd Tuesday, Musicians Hall, 114 E. Santa Clara St., San Jose; Alice Roll, Pres.; Clara Briggs, Rec. Sec., 1336 Magnolia Ave., San Jose.

Past Presidents Association No. 4 (Sacramento County)—Meets 2nd Monday, N.S.G.W. Hall, 11th and "J" Sts., Sacramento City; Edith Kelley, Pres.; Lily May Tilden, Rec. Sec., 3225 "T" St., Sacramento.

Past Presidents Association No. 5 (Butte County)—Meets 1st Friday, homes of members, Chico and Oroville; Marie Picanco, Pres.; Ruth Brown, Rec. Sec., 1365 Leah Court, Oroville.

Past Presidents Association No. 6 (Nevada County)—Meets 4th Friday, alternately between Nevada City, Pythian Castle, and Grass Valley, Edna Sampson's home; Margaret V. Nolan, Pres.; Vere Hansen, Rec. Sec., R.F.D. No. 2, box 41-C, Grass Valley.

Past Presidents Association No. 7 (Sonoma County)—Meets 2nd Tuesday, Ruby Berger home, 327 College Ave., Santa Rosa; Ruby Berger, Pres.; Ann M. Beach, Rec. Sec., R.F.D. No. 4, box 528, Santa Rosa.

Past Presidents Association No. 8 (San Joaquin and Stanislaus Counties)—Meets 2nd Thursday, Red Men Hall, Stockton; Mrs. Lois Armstrong, Pres.; Mrs. Harriet F. Corr, Rec. Sec., 729 E. Sonora St., Stockton.

Native Sons and Native Daughters Central Committee on Homeless Children—Main Office, 955 Phelan Bldg., San Francisco; Mrs. John W. Stirling, Chmn.; Miss Mary E. Brusie, Sec. Los Angeles branch office, 3924 Sunset Blvd.; Dorothy Schlingman, Sec.

(ADVERTISEMENT.)

N.D.G.W. OFFICIAL DEATH LIST.

Giving the name, the date of death, and the Subordinate Parlor affiliation of all deceased members as reported to Grand Secretary Sallie R. Thaler from July 18, 1933, to August 18, 1933:

Bowman, Adda Gillis; July 2; Califia No. 22.
Taber, Minnie; June 17; Aloha No. 106.
Williams, Nora; July 18; Berryessa No. 192.
Linder, Mae Haese; June 12; Brooklyn No. 157.
Brockman, Lillie; June 8; Nataqua No. 152.
Thiele, Dorothea S.; July 23; Las Lomas No. 72.
Sheehy, Harriet; July 3; El Pajaro No. 35.
Blake, Emily; July 7; Mountain Dawn No. 120.
Brophy, Mary F.; July 9; Buena Vista No. 68.
Moore, Mary Dungan; July 17; Santa Ana No. 235.

In Memoriam

MARY ROY.

To the Officers and Members of Veritas Parlor No. 75 N.D.G.W.—We, your committee appointed to draft resolutions of respect on the death of our dearly beloved member, Mary Roy, submit the following:

Whereas, Our Heavenly Father, in His infinite wisdom, has called from our midst our beloved sister, Mary Roy; in her passing a place in our Parlor has been made vacant and we shall greatly miss her ever-cheerful presence.

Resolved, That our heartfelt sympathy be extended to the bereaved relatives, and that it is a tender privilege to pay a loving tribute to the memory of our departed sister whose passing we mourn with deep regret; be it further resolved, that a copy of these resolutions be sent to the bereaved family, that a copy be written in the minutes, and that another copy be sent to The Grizzly Bear.

FLORA FERNANDES,
LEONIE CRAWFORD,
Committee.
ENEZ McDONALD,
President.

Merced, August 11, 1933.

MARY DUNGAN MOORE.

We, your committee appointed to draft a testimonial of respect to the memory of our departed sister, Past President Mary Dungan Moore, do respectfully submit the following:

Once again, our golden chain has been broken and, with deep sorrow, we humbly bow to the will of our Heavenly Father, who has claimed from our midst Sister Mary Dungan Moore, an esteemed member and ardent worker.

In her passing, Santa Ana Parlor No. 235 N.D.G.W. has sustained the loss of a faithful member and friend, and her family a faithful, loving wife and mother. To them, we extend our heartfelt sympathy, commending them to a Higher Power for consolation in their grief.

We ask that a copy of this testimonial be spread upon our minutes, a copy sent to the family, and a copy to The Grizzly Bear for publication.

MATILDA S. LEMON,
ELIZABETH MARSILE,
ROSE FORD,
Committee.

Santa Ana, August 19, 1933.

"School Zones Are as Safe as You Make Them," is the September slogan of the California Public Safety Committee in its campaign to lessen the constantly increasing auto death-toll.

SAN FRANCISCO

SAN FRANCISCO'S NATIVE SONS AND Native Daughters, meeting weekly in joint committee for some time, have completed arrangements for their participation in the celebration at Santa Rosa, September 8, 9 and 10, of Admission Day, the eighty-third anniversary of California's admission to statehood, September 9, 1850. And they will, as usual, be no small contributing factor to the success of the Golden State's birthday festivities in old Sonoma County, where the American California had its beginning, with the raising of the Bear Flag, June 14, 1846.

The joint committee is officered by Hubert J. Caveney, chairman; Charles H. Spengemann, vice-chairman; Harold J. Regan, secretary; L. A. Werner, treasurer. Chairmen of the several Admission Day subcommittees include Herbert De la Rosa, accommodations; Frank Biedermann, parade; Charles H. Spengemann, arrangements; Joseph J. McShane, observance; Al Lobree, publicity; Jack Smith, reception; Jesse H. Miller, finance; Mrs. Lulu Porter, costumes.

Sixteen San Francisco Parlors will have "open house" at Santa Rosa in the Elks Building, the afternoon and evening of September 9. Details have been arranged by a committee composed of Charles H. Spengemann (chairman), Harry Romick, Charles Wolters, Harold J. Regan, Paul Coniff, Albert Vlautin and Nicolas Murphy. Guests will be looked after by a reception committee which includes Jack Smith (chairman), William Bryce, George J. Leahy, Eugene Herzog, Fred Kane, Gus E. Ritter, George Kendall, Helen Cunningham, Louise Sullivan, Gulda Minton, Elise Barth, Evelyn Nopper, Marie Thieubaut, Ursula Lawless, Lea Christern, Claire Bohman, Julia Chicazola, Milton Lawlor, Thomas Dillon and Edward Wren.

FIRST N.D. OFFICIAL VISIT.

The honor of receiving the first official visit in San Francisco from Grand President Irma Laird was accorded Castro Parlor No. 178 N.D.G.W., which showed appreciation by giving a reception perfect in every detail. A delicious dinner preceded the meeting, attended by over 400 members of the Order, including Founder Lily Reichling-Dyer, Grand Secretary Sallie Thaler, Grand Marshal Anna Thuesen, Grand Trustees Alice Lane and Orinda Giannini, Grand Outside Sentinel Alice Oldham, Past Grand Presidents Dr. Marianna Bertola, Dr. Eva Rasmussen, Evelyn Carlson and Emma Foley, four supervising deputies and twenty-seven district deputies.

A feature of the opening ceremonies was the escort of honor, eight young women bearing flower-decked staffs, which they raised to form an arch under which the Grand President was escorted to her station. The exemplification of the ritual was without flaw, each officer being letter perfect, and five young girls were initiated. The N.D.G.W. Glee Club was a feature of the entertainment. Gifts were presented the Grand President, Grand Trustee Lane and Deputy Agnes Curry, and the meeting closed with an inspiring and interesting address by Mrs. Laird. Members and friends then repaired to the banquethall and were served with dainty refreshments. Deft hands had turned the place into a bower of beauty, the pretty little favors, the flowers, the candles set upon pedestals and the ornamental table decorations, all in pastel colors, being most effective. Grand Trustee Lane was chairman and Cora Stobing her assistant for the affair.

SUCCESSFUL MEMBERSHIP DRIVE.

San Francisco Parlor No. 49 N.S.G.W. is conducting a most successful membership drive under the leadership of one of its youngest members, Frank Marini, who has been treasurer for exactly fifty years! He proposed as a first step that the Parlor remove its place of meeting to that part of the city where most of its members have always resided, to the North Beach district, which embraces the old San Francisco founded by Governor Figueroa. This change was made June 8. Then things began to hum. At the meeting June 22 fourteen candidates were initiated. Twenty-three applications were presented, and exactly twenty-two of them were brought in by that young fellow, Frank Marini. Since then, seventeen additional candidates have been initiated, and sixteen of them Marini's finds.

The change of hall to the real neighborhood of the Parlor's membership has increased attendance at the meetings of over 100 percent. The new officers were installed July 27, Alfred Watts becoming president. A banquet followed the ceremonies. Moral: "Keep in touch with your members, and remember that the OLD BOYS are still YOUNG FELLOWS!"—R.P.T.

NATIVE DAUGHTERS NEWS PARAGRAPHS.

Mary Waters (Las Lomas Parlor No. 72) and Harriet Cate (Twin Peaks Parlor No. 185) were hostesses at the Sunday breakfast at the N.D.G.W. Home August 13. The chief speaker, Congresswoman Florence Kahn, related doings in Washington and answered several questions pertaining to national affairs. The program consisted of musical selections by the Native Daughter Glee Club, Kathryn Kay and C. Ray Cate. Among the seventy in attendance were Past Grands Dr. Mariana Bertola, Evelyn Carlson and Margaret Hill, Grand Trustees Orinda Gianini and Alice Lane. Twenty members from Las Lomas took occasion to celebrate the birthday anniversary of Mary Waters.

Orinda Parlor No. 56 held a reception in honor of Grand Trustee Orinda Gunther-Giannini, and the guests assembled represented a goodly number of local Parlors, and included the parents of Mrs. Giannini. President Marie McGrath extended a welcome, and remarks were made by the honor-guest, Grand Trustee Alice M. Lane, Past Grands Stella Finkeldey and Emma G. Foley, and Deputy Mae E. Waring. Vocal selections were rendered by President Alyce R. Gendotti (Fairfax Parlor No. 225). Dancing was a feature of the entertainment. Grand Trustee Giannini was the recipient of many gifts from personal friends and the Parlor.

NATIVE SONS NEWS PARAGRAPHS.

Stanford Parlor No. 76 has an Admission Day "booster" meeting September 5. Dave McCarthy will be general chairman, and Frank Biedermann the irrigation engineer. For the Santa Rosa doings, the Parlor will be quartered at Aqua Caliente. A hike August 20 was in charge of Chas. Roberts, and Frank Morris was chairman of the August 29 whist party. John J. Mazza lectured on "Tramping in the High Sierra" August 15, and initiation was held August 22.

Officers of Sequoia Parlor No. 160 have been installed, with Frank Sullivan as president. With Dr. Wm. Vizzard as master of ceremonies, an elegant repast followed the ceremonies.

John S. Ramsay of Castro Parlor No. 282 has been appointed a member of the State Board of Pharmacy.

WITH ENTHUSIASM, respond to the call of the Grand President and COMB THE FIELDS! Bring into the fold the thousands of ready and willing eligibles. There positively is NO SUBSTITUTE FOR MEMBERSHIP! With numbers, there is no limit to accomplishments.

Know your home-state, California! Learn of its past history and of its present-day development by reading regularly The Grizzly Bear. $1.50 for one year (12 issues). Subscribe now.

GOLD IS KING

Edward Pollock

My friends, and Pioneers, once more to you
My thanks, good wishes, and respects are due;
The circling years, that glide in joy or pain,
But bind us closer in their lengthening chain,
Enclosed more firmly, as we all draw nigh
The grateful solitude where all shall die.
'Tis well this way to notice, as they pass,
The fading moments in reflection's glass,—
To think what friends have fell, what foes have fled,
And, inly grieving for the gallant dead,
Rejoice so many yet in firm array
Remain to fight the battle of the day.
For as in war a strong battalion falls,
Man after man, before beleaguered walls,
The faithful warriors close the ranks, and still
Maintain the combat with determined will,
So we should gather nearer day by day,
And cling the closer as we pass away.
With your good leave, again in earnest rhyme
Your bard would show the spirit of the time.
Half hopeful and half sad must be the strain
Which he shall sing, and sing, perhaps, in vain!

Our youngest statesman, and our future sage
When time has soothed acridity with age,
As harsh and stringent juices of the vine
By years are mellowed into generous wine,
Has lately told us, in his regal way,
Who o'er the land omnipotent hath sway,
What hand with his the royal sceptre sways
Above the masses of these latter days,
What monarch reigns despotic and supreme
In all the realms of life's delusive dream.
Thus hath he said, and echoing nations ring
With, 'tis not cotton, it is Gold is King.

So, long ago, on Syrian plains, there came
A voice of thunder from a haze of flame,
Commanding to His presence him who made
Egyptian priests before their shrines afraid;
Whose strong right hand had made his people free,
Upheld by Aaron's arm and God's decree.
Long days of weary waiting chilled the throng
Whose feet had sought the promised land so long;
Impatient to their priest—to Aaron—cries
From all the wayworn wanderers arise,
"Go, Aaron, make us gods to go before,
For this man Moses we shall see no more."
The priestly man to their appeals gave way,—
For priests their congregation must obey;
The golden treasures that the pilgrims stole
He seeks, he gathers; he dissolves the whole,
And from the crucible on their behalf
Comes out the miracle,—a Golden Calf!
From the low mound he waves his sacred rod,
And cries to Israel's hosts, "Behold, your God."

But from the splintered cliffs of lone Sinai,
Where sulphurous clouds had long obscured the day,
There came, with downcast eyes, but stately pace,
The man who met Jehovah face to face;
Where on the granite summit topped with snow,
While lightnings veiled his splendor from below,
The lines were graven and the words were said
By Him, the Lord, to rule the world He made;
And holy anger filled the prophet's eyes,
A wrath divine succeeding his surprise.
With sacred fury from his hands were thrown
And crashed in dust the consecrated stone;
Struck by his arm, the golden idol fell,
Consigned to fire,—premonitor of hell;
Reduced to ashes, to the saddened wave
The remnant of idolatry he gave;
While all the people shrank before his nod,
To Israel's hosts he said, "Behold, your God!"

Yes, Gold is King, and vices he controls;
King of all sordid and ignoble souls;
Strong to destroy, but powerless to save;
Impotent, save for pleasure and a grave.
But not one generous heart can Gold seduce
To bend its energies to evil use.
Can Gold buy love? I know you blush with shame
That dross should mingle with that sacred name;
Gold may be King in clouded walks by night,
In lawless passions and impure delight;
But the fond heart, the tearful eye, the cheek
That waits the kisses that it fain would seek,—
The rapturous tender pulses of that love
Which shuns the blessed in the realms above,—
Can these be bought?—can these by wealth be made,
Like gold or cotton, articles of trade?
Wealth win one heart-throb from the chaste and true?
O lovely ladies, I appeal to you.

And there are mothers, sisters, daughters, wives,
Who hold their honor as they hold their lives,
Whose firm affections are not bought and sold,
Whose last and least idea would be of Gold.
Thank God, not few are they; in mass they stand,
The health, the wealth, the glory of our land.
Behold the matron, who through want and woes
Still lulls her family in sweet repose,
Relieves the opening soul of griefs and cares,
Her children all the jewels that she wears.
Can wealth buy such? The priceless gem may be
Without a price, my friends, consigned to thee,
And deem its radiance brighter than the day.
Oh, prize it, gaze on its unsullied ray,
'Tis a rich pearl in every good man's eye,
That all the gold of Ophir could not buy.

Can Gold buy friendship? Service, Gold may bring,
And o'er such purchased service Gold is King;
But the strong arm, free heart, and liberal thought
Of noble natures never can be bought.
O stainless charity, immortal faith,
Soother of life, and conqueror of death,
Your places, vacant, Gold cannot supply;
Your priceless services no gold can buy.

Gold is not King; 'tis Virtue that controls
The tides that ebb or swell in noble souls.
The faithless lawyer, statesman, priest, or spy,
Lost to all shame, cupidity may buy;
But there are millions, strong in truth divine,
Who scorn the Yellow Monarch of the Mine,
Who shield the State, and calmly tell the world
This land shall flourish while her flag's unfurled,—
Not hirelings, but our unbought volunteers:
In the first ranks I greet you, Pioneers.

(This poem was delivered before the Society of California Pioneers, San Francisco, Admission Day, September 9, 1858. The thoughts expressed therein, three-quarters of a century back, are most pertinent today, for worship of King Gold unquestionably accounts for the devastating ills sorely afflicting this Nation.—Editor.)

ALAMEDA COUNTY DAUGHTERS WILL BE AT SANTA ROSA IN FORCE.

Albany (Alameda County)—Elaborate plans are being formed by the various Native Daughter Parlors throughout Alameda County to do their part in making the parade to be held September 9 in Santa Rosa a most colorful one. Many beautiful floats and snappy drill teams are being entered in the line of march, with large marching units to swell the ranks.

Much interest is being shown by the large attendance of Native Daughters at the joint committee meeting held with the Native Sons every Monday evening. Grand Secretary Sallie Thaler of Aloha Parlor No. 106 and the supervising deputy of Alameda County, Dora Brayton of Bahia Vista Parlor No. 167, are among the active workers for the Native Daughters. Miss Martha Watson of Aloha Parlor is co-chairman, working with Allen Sunkler of Athens Parlor No. 195 N.S.G.W.—R.L.T.

TRI-COUNTIES N.D.G.W. PARLORS DISTRICT MEET AT SALINAS.

Hollister (San Benito County)—The six Native Daughter Parlors of Monterey, Santa Cruz and San Benito Counties will hold their annual district meeting at Salinas, Saturday evening, September 23, the session opening with dinner at 6:45. Arrangements are in charge of Supervising Deputy Rose Rhyner of Aleli Parlor No. 102 (Salinas).

The theme of the evening will be "California Romance." The program, which will be participated in by every Parlor of the district, will be broadcast by "radio station N.D.G.W." Current events in each of the six Parlors will be announced, and brief talks of interest to the membership will be interspersed with musical numbers appropriate to the theme of the evening.—B.A.B.

AID TO SMALL-SCALE GOLD MINERS.

As an aid to the small-scale placer miners and others interested in the placer-gold resources of the streams of California North, the State Mines Division has issued a new map on which the principal rivers and creeks from which gold was produced in 1932 are indicated and named.

The map covers the area from a line through San Jose, Santa Clara County, to the Oregon State boundary. It is for sale at offices of the mines division in San Francisco, Los Angeles, Sacramento and Redding at twenty cents a copy; by mail, twenty-five cents.

"Reprove your friend in secret, and praise him openly."—Leonardo da Vinci.

Official Directory of Parlors of the N. S. G. W.

ALAMEDA COUNTY.

Alameda No. 47, Alameda City—J. F. Hanson, Pres.; Robt. H. Cavanaugh, Sec., 1806 Pacific Ave.; Wednesdays, Veterans Memorial Bldg.
Oakland No. 50, Oakland—T. J. Markert, Pres.; F. M. Norris, Sec., 5595 Taft Ave.; Fridays, Native Sons Hall, 11th and Clay Sts.
Las Positas No. 96, Livermore—Louis J. Volponi, Pres.; John J. Kelly, Sec., P. O. box 341; Thursdays, Foresters Hall.
Eden No. 113, Hayward—Leo Wessman, Pres.; Filbert M. Soares, Sec., 1437 "B" St.; 2nd and 4th Tuesdays, Memorial Hall, Main St.
Piedmont No. 120, Oakland—George T. Pryts, Pres.; Charles Morando, Sec., 908 Vermont St.; Thursdays, Native Sons Hall, 11th and Clay Sts.
Wisteria No. 127, Alvarado—Henry May, Pres.; J. M. Scribner, Sec., Livermore; 1st Thursday, I.O.O.F. Hall.
Halcyon No. 146, Alameda City—F. A. Stahl, Pres.; J. O. Bates, Sec., 2139 Buena Vista Ave.; 1st and 3rd Tuesdays, I.O.O.F. Hall, 2329 Santa Clara Ave.
Brooklyn No. 151, Oakland—Frank O. Merritt, Pres.; E. W. Cooney, Sec., 3907 14th Ave.; 1st and 3rd Wednesdays, Masonic Temple, 8th Ave. and E. 14th St.
Washington No. 169, Centerville—Thomas Silva, Pres.; Allen G. Norris, Sec., P. O. box 58; 2nd and 4th Tuesdays, Hansen Hall.
Athens No. 195, Oakland—Fred G. Martin, Pres.; Harold B. Farley, Sec., 4623 Benevides Ave.; Tuesdays, Native Sons Hall, 11th and Clay Sts.
Berkeley No. 210, Berkeley—H. P. Corbett, Pres.; R. J. Garrett, Sec., 1708 Virginia St.; Tuesdays, Native Sons Hall, 2108 Shattuck Ave.
Estudillo No. 223, San Leandro—E. E. King, Pres.; Albert G. Pacheco, Sec., 1736 E. 14th St.; 1st and 3rd Tuesdays, U.P.E.C. Hall.
Claremont No. 240, Emeryville—Edward J. Ginocchio, Pres.; E. N. Thienger, Sec., 839 Hearst Ave., Berkeley; Tuesdays, Veterans Memorial Bldg., 43rd and Salem Sts.
Pleasanton No. 244, Pleasanton—P. Edward Holzreiter, Pres.; Ernest W. Schween, Sec.; 2nd and 4th Thursdays, I.O.O.F. Hall.
Niles No. 250, Niles—M. L. Fournier, Pres.; C. E. Martenstein, Sec.; 2nd Thursday, I.O.O.F. Hall.
Fruitvale No. 252, Oakland—Ernest Perry, Pres.; Edward T. Schnarr, Sec., 3611 Allendale Ave.; Fridays, W.O.W. Hall, 3256 E. 14th St.

AMADOR COUNTY.

Amador No. 17, Sutter Creek—J. H. Williams, Pres.; F. J. Payne, Sec.; 1st and 3rd Fridays, Native Sons Hall.
Excelsior No. 31, Jackson—Thomas G. Negrich, Pres.; William Going, Sec.; 1st and 3rd Wednesdays, Native Sons Hall, 22 Court St.
Ione No. 33, Ione—Earl Grover, Pres.; Josiah H. Saunders, Sec.; 1st and 3rd Wednesdays, Native Sons Hall.
Plymouth No. 48, Plymouth—D. A. Upton, Pres.; Thos. D. Davis, Sec.; 1st and 3rd Saturdays, N.S.G.W. Hall.

BUTTE COUNTY.

Argonaut No. 8, Oroville—Frank H. O'Brien, Pres.; Cyril R. Macdonald, Sec., P. O. box 502; 1st and 3rd Wednesdays, Veterans Memorial Hall.

CALAVERAS COUNTY.

Chispa No. 139, Murphys—Maynard Segale, Pres.; Antone Malaspina, Sec.; Wednesdays, Native Sons Hall.

COLUSA COUNTY.

Colusa No. 69, Colusa City—Thomas F. Busch, Pres.; Phil J. Humburg, Sec., 223 Parkhill St.; Tuesdays, Eagles Hall.

CONTRA COSTA COUNTY.

General Winn No. 32, Antioch—John P. Welch, Pres.; Joel H. Ford, Sec., P. O. box 811; 2nd and 4th Wednesdays, Union Hall.
Mount Diablo No. 101, Martinez—R. P. Anderson, Pres.; G. T. Barkley, Sec.; 1st and 3rd Mondays, I.O.O.F. Hall.
Byron No. 170, Byron—William E. Bunn, Pres.; H. G. Krumland, Sec.; 1st and 3rd Tuesdays, I.O.O.F. Hall.
Carquinez No. 205, Crockett—John McManus, Pres.; Thomas B. Cox, Sec., P.O. box 721; 1st and 3rd Wednesdays, I.O.O.F. Hall.
Richmond No. 217, Richmond—Frank Weber, Pres.; Lloyd N. Mason, Sec., 11 6th St.; 1st Wednesday, 818 Macdonald Ave.
Concord No. 245, Concord—C. H. Guy, Pres.; D. E. Pramberg, Sec., P. O. box 235; 1st Tuesday, Guy's Parlors.
Diamond No. 246, Pittsburg—S. E. Caruso, Pres.; Edward Wilson, Sec., 2 Front St.; 1st and 3rd Wednesdays, Veterans Memorial Bldg.

EL DORADO COUNTY.

Placerville No. 9, Placerville—Milton Orelli, Pres.; Clyde R. Berriman, Sec., Wood St.; 2nd and 4th Tuesdays, Masonic Hall.
Georgetown No. 91, Georgetown—George W. Brichler, Pres.; O. F. Irish, Sec.; 2nd and 4th Wednesdays, I.O.O.F. Hall.

FRESNO COUNTY.

Fresno No. 25, Fresno City—J. H. Sutton, Pres.; W. C. Guard, Sec., R.F.D. No. 2, box 879; 1st and 3rd Fridays, Pythian Castle, Cor. "R" and Merced Sts.
Selma No. 107, Selma—C. R. Snyder, Pres; E. C. Laughlin, Sec.; 1st Wednesday, American Legion Hall.

GRAND OFFICERS.

Seth Millington .... Junior Past Grand President
Gridley
Justice Emmet Seawell .... Grand President
State Bldg., San Francisco
Chas. A. Koenig .... Grand First Vice-president
531 35th Ave., San Francisco
Harmon D. Skillin .... Grand Second Vice-president
Mills Bldg., San Francisco
J. Hartley Russell .... Grand Third Vice-president
1025 Russ Bldg., San Francisco
John T. Regan .... Grand Secretary
N.S.G.W. Bldg., 414 Mason St., San Francisco
John A. Corotto .... Grand Treasurer
560 No. 5th St., San Jose
Gam Hurst .... Grand Marshal
5262 Boyd Ave., Oakland
William A. Reuter .... Grand Inside Sentinel
1009 Marine Ave., Wilmington
Walter P. Rothenbush .... Grand Outside Sentinel
N.S.G.W. Club Rooms, Stockton
Leslie Malocha .... Grand Organist
1775 El Cerrito, Los Angeles
Chester Gannon .... Grand Historian
613 Capital Ntl. Bank Bldg., Sacramento

GRAND TRUSTEES.

Eldred L. Meyer .... 922 San Vicente Blvd., Santa Monica
Henry S. Lyon .... Placerville
Chas. H. Spengemann .... 827 27th Ave., San Francisco
Thos. M. Foley .... Hearst Bldg., San Francisco
Jesse H. Miller .... 712 DeYoung Bldg., San Francisco
John M. Burnett .... Bank America Bldg., San Jose
Edward T. Schnarr .... 3611 Allendale Ave., Oakland

GLENN COUNTY.

Willows No. 255, Willows—Lee V. Logan, Pres.; Leon Marshall, Sec., P.O. box 747; 2nd and 4th Tuesdays, I.O.O.F. Hall.

HUMBOLDT COUNTY.

Humboldt No. 14, Eureka—Henry Sundfors, Pres.; Loren M. Nelson, Sec., P.O. box 195; 2nd and 4th Mondays, Native Sons Hall.
Arcata No. 20, Arcata—W. H. Anderson, Pres.; William Peters, Sec., P. O. box 1117; Thursdays, Native Sons Hall.
Ferndale No. 93, Ferndale—C. J. Olsen, Pres.; C. H. Rasmussen, Sec., R.F.D., 47-A; 1st and 3rd Mondays, Danish Hall.

KERN COUNTY.

Bakersfield No. 42, Bakersfield—George Taylor, Pres.; Henry A. Bannister, Sec., care Bank of America; 2nd and 4th Fridays, Justice Court, City Hall.

LAKE COUNTY.

Lower Lake No. 159, Lower Lake—LeRoy England, Pres.; Albert Kugelman, Sec.; Thursdays, I.O.O.F. Hall.

LASSEN COUNTY.

Honey Lake No. 198, Standish—Leo T. Davis, Pres.; N. V. Wemple, Sec., Litchfield; 1st and 3rd Wednesdays, Wrede Hall.
Big Valley No. 211, Bieber—Fred Bunselmeier, Pres.; A. W. McKenzie, Sec.; 1st and 3rd Wednesdays, I.O.O.F. Hall.

LOS ANGELES COUNTY.

Los Angeles No. 45, Los Angeles City—Roger M. Johnson, Pres.; Willard F. Allen, Sec., 4955 Los Feliz Blvd.; Thursdays, Merchant Plumbers Hall, 1832 So. Hope.
Ramona No. 109, Los Angeles City—Charles E. Straube, Pres.; John V. Scott, Sec., Patriotic Hall, 1816 So. Figueroa; Fridays, Patriotic Hall, 1816 So. Figueroa.
Hollywood No. 196, Los Angeles City—Henry G. Bodkin, Pres.; E. J. Reilly, Sec., Olive View; Mondays, 1089 No. Oxford Ave.
Long Beach No. 239, Long Beach—Francis H. Gentry, Pres.; W. W. Brady, Sec., 801 Jergins Trust Bldg.; Dept. No. 1 Municipal Court, 8th floor Jergins Trust Bldg.
Sepulveda No. 263, San Pedro—Walter C. Richards, Pres.; H. E. Fairall, Sec., 1925 So. Pacific Ave.; 1st and 3rd Fridays, Redman Hall, 543 Shepherd St., Point Firmin.
Glendale No. 264, Glendale—Harvey T. Gillette, Pres.; Philip D. Molen, Sec., 222 So. Glendale; 1st and 3rd Thursdays, Starr Heights Recreation Bldg., 3246 Community Place.
Santa Monica Bay No. 267, Santa Monica—J. Edward McCurdy, Pres.; John J. Smith, Sec., 830 Rialto Ave., Venice; 1st and 3rd Wednesdays, Odd Fellows Hall, 1431 Third St.
University No. 272, Los Angeles City—Maynard P. Garrison, Pres.; Carl Martin, Sec., 1607 So. Spaulding St.; Wednesdays, Casa de Rosas, Adams and Hoover Sts.
Compton No. 273, Compton—Ray W. Hecock, Pres.; Wm. Don Castillo, Sec., care Police Dept.; 2nd and 4th Tuesdays, Elks Hall, 6172 No. Long Beach Blvd., North Long Beach.

MADERA COUNTY.

Madera No. 130, Madera City—Cornelius Noble, Pres.; T. P. Cosgrave, Sec.; 1st and 3rd Thursdays, First National Bank Bldg.

MARIN COUNTY.

Mount Tamalpais No. 64, San Rafael—Donald J. Locati, Pres.; Manuel A. Andrade, Sec., 532 Mission Ave.; 1st and 3rd Mondays, Portuguese-American Hall.
Sea Point No. 158, Sausalito—Clarence D. Ross, Pres.; Manuel Santos, Sec., 6 Glen Drive; 1st and 3rd Wednesdays, Perry Bldg.
Nicasio No. 183, Nicasio—M. T. Farley, Pres.; R. J. Rogers, Sec.; 2nd and 4th Wednesdays, U.A.O.D. Hall.

MENDOCINO COUNTY.

Ukiah No. 71, Ukiah—Kenneth Phillips, Pres.; Ben Hofman, Sec., P.O. box 473; 1st and 3rd Mondays, I.O.O.F. Hall.
Broderick No[117, Point Arena—Albert Seymour, Pres.; C. J. Buchanan, Sec.; 1st and 3rd Thursdays, Forester Hall.
Alder Glen No. 200, Fort Bragg—Fred LeValley, Pres.; O. R. Weller, Sec.; 2nd and 4th Fridays, I.O.O.F. Hall.

MERCED COUNTY.

Yosemite No. 24, Merced City—Alfred Wm. Petersen, Pres.; True W. Fowler, Sec., P. O. box 781; 2nd and 4th Mondays, I.O.O.F. Hall.
Los Banos No. 206, Los Banos—Frank Dambrosio, Pres.; L. E. Sarbo, Sec., R.F.D., box 21; 2nd and 4th Wednesdays, Eagles Hall.

MONTEREY COUNTY.

Monterey No. 75, Monterey City—James Millington, Pres.; T. W. Krieger, Sec., 999 Franklin St.; 1st and 3rd Fridays, Knights Pythias Hall, Main St.
Santa Lucia No. 97, Salinas—George S. Miller, Pres.; R. W. Adcock, Sec., R.F.D. No. 2, box 181; Mondays, Native Sons Hall, 32 W. Alisal St.
Gabilan No. 132, Castroville—James C. Jordan, Pres.; J. F. Gambetta, Sec., P. O. box 94; 1st and 3rd Thursdays, Native Sons Hall.

NAPA COUNTY.

Saint Helena No. 53, Saint Helena—J. P. Vasconi Sr., Pres.; Edw. L. Bonhote, Sec., P. O. box 364; Mondays, Native Sons Hall.
Napa No. 62, Napa City—Theodore E. Freitas, Pres.; H. J. Hoernle, Sec., 1226 Oak St.; Mondays, Native Sons Hall.
Calistoga No. 86, Calistoga—James Marchese, Pres.; Louis Carlenzoli, Sec.; 1st and 3rd Mondays, I.O.O.F. Hall.

NEVADA COUNTY.

Hydraulic No. 56, Nevada City—Raglan Tuttle, Pres.; Dr. C. W. Chapman, Sec.; Tuesdays, Pythian Castle.
Quartz No. 58, Grass Valley—Frank G. Hooper, Pres.; H. Ray George, Sec., 151 Conaway Ave.; Mondays, Auditorium Hall.
Donner No. 162, Truckee—J. F. Lichtenberger, Pres.; H. C. Lichtenberger, Sec.; 2nd and 4th Tuesdays, Native Sons Hall.

ORANGE COUNTY.

Santa Ana No. 265, Santa Ana—Ivan H. Harper, Pres.; E. F. Marks, Sec., 1124 No. Bristol St.; 1st and 3rd Mondays, The Old Time Dance Hall, Grass Valley St., Tustin.

PLACER COUNTY.

Auburn No. 59, Auburn—Hans J. Petersen, Pres.; J. G. Walsh, Sec.; 1st and 3rd Fridays, Foresters Hall.
Silver Star No. 63, Lincoln—Robert P. Dixon, Pres.; Barney G. Barry, Sec., P. O. box 72; 3rd Wednesday, I.O.O.F. Hall.
Rocklin No. 233, Roseville—Wm. La Due, Pres.; M. E. Reed, Sec., 253 W. Durante; 2nd and 4th Wednesdays, Eagles Hall.

PLUMAS COUNTY.

Quincy No. 131, Quincy—Herbert Hard, Pres.; E. C. Kelsey, Sec.; 2nd Thursday, I.O.O.F. Hall.
Golden Anchor No. 182, La Porte—R. J. McGrath, Pres.; LeRoy J. Post, Sec.; 2nd and 4th Sunday mornings, Native Sons Hall.
Plumas No. 228, Taylorsville—E. E. Sikes, Pres.; George E. Boyden, Sec.; 1st and 3rd Mondays, Native Sons Hall.

SACRAMENTO COUNTY.

Sacramento No. 3, Sacramento City—Ervin Beall, Pres.; J. F. Didion, Sec., 1213 "O" St.; Thursdays, Native Sons Bldg., 11th and "J" Sts.
Sunset No. 26, Sacramenot City—William H. Peters, Pres.; Edward E. Reese, Sec., County Treasurer Office; Mondays, Native Sons Bldg., 11th and "J" Sts.
Elk Grove No. 41, Elk Grove—George D. Beitzel, Pres.; Walter Martin, Sec.; 2nd and 4th Fridays, Masonic Hall.
Granite No. 83, Folsom—Joe Relvas, Pres.; Frank Showers, Sec.; 2nd and 4th Tuesdays, K.P. Hall.
Courtland No. 106, Courtland—W. H. Thisby, Pres.; Jos. Green, Sec.; 1st Saturday and 3rd Monday, Native Sons Hall.
Sutter Fort No. 241, Sacramento City—Ed. T. Goyne, Pres.; C. L. Katzenstein, Sec., P. O. box 914; 2nd and 4th Wednesdays, Native Sons Bldg., 11th and "J" Sts.
Galt No. 243, Galt—Abel G. Stock, Pres.; F. W. Harms, Sec.; 1st and 3rd Mondays, I.O.O.F. Hall.

SAN BENITO COUNTY.

Fremont No. 44, Hollister—S. Churchill, Pres.; J. E. Prendergast Jr., Sec., 1064 Monterey St.; 1st and 3rd Thursdays, Grangers Union Hall.

SAN BERNARDINO COUNTY.

Arrowhead No. 110, San Bernardino City—Henry B. Peake, Pres.; R. W. Brazelton, Sec., 462 6th St.; Wednesdays, Eagles Hall, 469 4th St.

SAN DIEGO COUNTY.

San Diego No. 108, San Diego City—John P. Murphy, Pres.; A. V. Mayrhofer, Sec., 1572 2nd St.; Wednesdays, K.C. Hall, 4th and Elm Sts.

SAN FRANCISCO CITY AND COUNTY.

California No. 1, San Francisco—Henry F. Rickleffs, Pres.; Ellis A. Blackman, Sec., 1248-A Divisadero St.; Thursdays, Native Sons Bldg., 414 Mason St.
Pacific No. 10, San Francisco—William G. Boyce, Pres.; J. Henry Bastein, Sec., 380 Van Ness Ave. South; Tuesdays, Native Sons Bldg., 414 Mason St.
Golden Gate No. 29, San Francisco—William M. Roll, Pres.; Adolph Eberhart, Sec., 183 Carl St.; Mondays, Native Sons Bldg., 414 Mason St.
Mission No. 38, San Francisco—Faustino F. Augustine, Pres.; Thos. J. Stewart, Sec., 419 South Van Ness Ave.; Wednesdays, Redmen Hall, 3053 16th St.
San Francisco No. 49, San Francisco—Alfred Watts, Pres.; David Capurro, Sec., 976 Union St.; 2nd and 4th Thursdays, Dante Hall, 1606 Stockton St.
El Dorado No. 52, San Francisco—Robert Foltz, Pres.; Alfred Vlautin, Sec., 1537 Franklin St.; Thursdays, Native Sons Bldg., 414 Mason St.
Rincon No. 72, San Francisco—Albert Granzella, Pres.; John A. Gilmour, Sec., 2069 Golden Gate Ave.; Wednesdays, Native Sons Bldg., 414 Mason St.
Stanford No. 76, San Francisco—Urban Mort, Pres.; Charles T. O'Kane, Sec., 2900 Scott St.; Tuesdays, Native Sons Bldg., 414 Mason St.
Bay City No. 104, San Francisco—Charles L. Licht, Pres.; Max E. Licht, Sec., 1881 Fulton St.; 2nd and 4th Wednesdays, Native Sons Bldg., 414 Mason St.
Niantic No. 105, San Francisco—A. Furner, Pres.; J. M. Darcy, Sec., 10 Hoffman Ave.; Wednesdays, Native Sons Bldg., 414 Mason St.
National No. 118, San Francisco—Walter J. Murphy, Pres.; Martin M. Ratigan, Sec., 1825 Page St., Apt. 6; Thursdays, 1160 Eddy St.
Hesperian No. 137, San Francisco—F. P. Indig, Pres.; Albert Carlson, Sec., 379 Justin Dr.; Thursdays, Native Sons Bldg., 414 Mason St.
Alcalde No. 154, San Francisco—Daniel A. Hinell, Pres.; Harry S. Burke, Sec., 637 Shotwell St.; 2nd and 4th Wednesdays, Native Sons Bldg., 414 Mason St.
South San Francisco No. 157, San Francisco—Peter Macarini, Pres.; John T. Regan, Sec., 1489 Newcomb Ave.; Wednesdays, Masonic Bldg., 4705 3rd St.
Sequoia No. 160, San Francisco—Frank Sullivan, Pres.; Walter W. Garrett, Sec., 2500 Van Ness Ave.; 2nd and 4th Mondays, Swedish-American Bldg., 2174 Market St.
Precita No. 187, San Francisco—Edward F. Rom, Pres.; Edward Tietjen, Sec., 1367 15th Ave.; Thursdays, Mission Masonic Hall, 2668 Mission St.
Olympus No. 189, San Francisco—Henry H. McGowan, Pres.; Harvey J. Carty, Sec., 1651 Market St., Apt. 505; 2nd and 4th Tuesdays, Independent Redmen Hall, 3053 16th St.
Presidio No. 194, San Francisco—Joseph Lenzio, Pres.; George A. Ducker, Sec., 442 21st Ave.; Mondays, Native Sons Bldg., 414 Mason St.

ATTENTION, SECRETARIES!

THIS DIRECTORY IS PUBLISHED BY AUTHORITY OF THE GRAND PARLOR N.S.G.W., AND ALL NOTICES OF CHANGES MUST BE RECEIVED BY THE GRAND SECRETARY (NOT THE MAGAZINE) ON OR BEFORE THE 20TH OF EACH MONTH TO INSURE CORRECTION IN NEXT ISSUE OF DIRECTORY.

Marshall No. 202, San Francisco—Eugene Biancalona, Pres.; Frank Bacigalupi, Sec., 725 Douglas St.; 1st and 3rd Wednesdays, Native Sons Bldg., 414 Mason St.
Dolores No. 208, San Francisco—Eugene H. O'Donnell, Pres.; Edward F. Webb, Sec., 2801 Sacramento St.; 2nd and 4th Tuesdays, Mission Masonic Hall, 2668 Mission.
Twin Peaks No. 214, San Francisco—Leo Felt, Pres.; Thos. Pendergast, Sec., 278 Douglas St.; Wednesdays, Willopi Hall, 4061 24th St.
El Capitan No. 222, San Francisco—John C. Conmy, Pres.; James Hanna, Sec., 2450 27th Ave.; 1st and 3rd Thursdays, King Soloman Hall, 1739 Fillmore St.
Guadalupe No. 231, San Francisco—Joseph Fay, Pres.; Alvin A. Johnson, Sec., 142 Rousseau St.; Tuesdays, Guadalupe Hall, 4551 Mission St.
Castro No. 232, San Francisco—John J. Qualters, Pres.; James H. Hayes, Sec., 4014 18th St.; Tuesdays, Native Sons Bldg., 414 Mason St.
Balboa No. 234, San Francisco—Jack Killeen, Pres.; E. W. Boyd, Sec., 1046 Lake St.; Thursdays, Maccabee Hall, 5th Ave. and Clement St.
Bret Harte No. 260, San Francisco—Herbert Cline, Pres.; A. W. McElhatton, Sec., 1027 Capitol Ave.; 2nd, 4th and 5th Tuesdays, West of Twin Peaks Hall, 233 Legion Crt.
Utopia No. 270, San Francisco—D. P. Finnegan, Pres.; Herbert H. Schneider, Sec., 2455 10th Ave.; Tuesdays, American Hall, 20th and Capp Sts.

SAN JOAQUIN COUNTY.

Stockton No. 7, Stockton—George Witherow, Pres.; R. D. Dorcey, Sec., P. O. box 888; Mondays, Native Sons Hall.
Lodi No. 18, Lodi—Herbert Osterman, Pres.; Clyde J. Bresnan, Sec., Cory Bldg.; 2nd and 4th Wednesdays, Eagles Hall.
Tracy No. 186, Tracy—Frank Vierra, Pres.; R. J. Marraccini, Sec., R.F.D. No. 1, box 217, Thursdays, I.O.O.F. Hall.
Manteca No. 271, Manteca—W. R. Perry, Pres.; Leonard Faria, Sec., R.F.D., box 75, Lathrop; 1st and 3rd Wednesdays, I.O.O.F. Hall.

SAN LUIS OBISPO COUNTY.

San Miguel No. 150, San Miguel—H. Twisselman, Pres.; Otto Kuehl, Sec., Paso Robles; 1st Wednesday, Clemons Hall.
Cambria No. 152, Cambria—Edward Shang, Pres.; A. S. Gay, Sec.; Wednesdays, Rigdon Hall.

SAN MATEO COUNTY.

Redwood No. 66, Redwood City—Seneca R. Coats, Pres.; A. S. Liguori, Sec., P. O. box 212; Thursdays, American Foresters Hall.
Seaside No. 95, Half Moon Bay—H. Locke Nelson, Pres.; John G. Gilcrest, Sec.; 2nd and 4th Tuesdays, I.O.O.F. Hall.
Menlo No. 185, Menlo Park—C. W. Call, Pres.; F. W. Johnson, Sec., P. O. box 601; 1st and 3rd Thursdays, Masonic Hall.
Pebble Beach No. 230, Pescadero—John Souza, Pres.; E. A. Shaw, Sec.; 2nd and 4th Wednesdays, I.O.O.F. Hall.
El Carmelo No. 256, Daly City—Harry McDonald, Pres.; Ernest L. Micco, Sec., 639 Morse St., San Francisco; 2nd and 4th Wednesdays, Eagles Hall.
Industrial City No. 269, South San Francisco—John C. Hamilton, Pres.; Geo. A. Roll, Sec., P. O. box 237; 2nd and 4th Mondays, Metropolitan Hall.

SANTA BARBARA COUNTY.

Santa Barbara No. 116, Santa Barbara City—Philip Bradley, Pres.; H. C. Sweetser, Sec., Court House; 1st and 3rd Thursdays, Pythian Castle.

SANTA CLARA COUNTY.

San Jose No. 22, San Jose—Mario Ponzini, Pres.; Joseph Lawrence, Sec., 1095 No. First St.; Mondays, I.O.O.F. Hall.
Santa Clara No. 100, Santa Clara City—A. P. Cunha, Pres.; Clarence Clevenger, Sec., P.O. box 297; 1st and 3rd Wednesdays, Redmen Hall.
Observatory No. 177, San Jose—Louis V. Dietz, Pres.; A. B. Langford, Sec., Hall Records; Tuesdays, Knights Columbus Hall, 40 No. First St.
Mountain View No. 215, Mountain View—Henry A. Schultze Jr., Pres.; C. A. Antonioli, Sec., 301 Castro St.; 2nd and 4th Wednesdays, Mockbee Hall.
Palo Alto No. 216, Palo Alto—John C. Bernal, Pres.; Albert A. Quinn, Sec., 643 High St.; 2nd and 4th Mondays, N.S.G.W. Bldg., Hamilton Ave. and Emerson St.

SANTA CRUZ COUNTY.

Watsonville No. 65, Watsonville—J. E. Giacoma, Pres.; E. R. Tindall, Sec., 51 Marchant St.; 2nd and 4th Tuesdays, I.O.O.F. Hall.
Santa Cruz No. 90, Santa Cruz City—James H. Griffin Jr., Pres.; T. V. Mathews, Sec., 105 Pacheco Ave.; Fridays, Native Sons Hall, 117 Pacific Ave.

SHASTA COUNTY.

McCloud No. 149, Redding—Melvin Zeis, Pres.; Hugh A. Shuffleton, Sec.; 1st and 3rd Thursdays, Moose Hall.

SIERRA COUNTY.

Downieville No. 92, Downieville—Earl Rickard, Pres.; H. S. Tibbey, Sec.; 2nd and 4th Mondays, I.O.O.F. Hall.
Golden Nugget No. 94, Sierra City—Emil Alleson, Pres.; Arthur R. Pride, Sec.; 1st and 3rd Wednesdays, Masonic Hall.

SISKIYOU COUNTY.

Etna No. 192, Etna—George Wm. Smith, Pres.; Harvey A. Green, Sec.; 1st and 3rd Wednesdays, I.O.O.F. Hall.
Liberty No. 193, Sawyers Bar—David H. Robinson, Pres.; John M. Barry, Sec.; 1st and 3rd Saturdays, I.O.O.F. Hall.

SOLANO COUNTY.

Solano No. 39, Suisun—John S. Cannon, Pres.; J. W. Kinlock, Sec.; 1st and 3rd Tuesdays, I.O.O.F. Hall.
Vallejo No. 77, Vallejo—Frank J. Heldener, Pres.; Werner B. Hallin, Sec., 912 Carolina; 2nd and 4th Tuesdays, San Pablo Hall.

SONOMA COUNTY.

Petaluma No. 27, Petaluma—Walter Christiansen, Pres.; C. F. Fobes, Sec., 114 Prospect St.; 2nd and 4th Mondays, Druid Hall, Gross Bldg., 41 Main St.
Santa Rosa No. 28, Santa Rosa—James Brucker, Pres.; Leland S. Lewis, Sec., Court House; Mondays, Native Sons Hall.
Glen Ellen No. 102, Glen Ellen—Robert Kennedy, Pres.; Frank Kirch, Sec., Route 3, Santa Rosa; 2nd Monday, N.S.G.W. Hall.
Sonoma No. 111, Sonoma City—Antone Barrachi, Pres.; L. H. Green, Sec.; 1st and 3rd Mondays, I.O.O.F. Hall.
Sebastopol No. 143, Sebastopol—T. F. Hyland, Pres.; F. G. McFarlane, Sec.; 1st and 3rd Fridays, I.O.O.F. Hall.

STANISLAUS COUNTY.

Modesto No. 11, Modesto—B. E. Munson, Pres.; C. C. Eastin Jr., Sec., P.O. box 898; 1st and 3rd Wednesdays, I.O.O.F. Hall.
Oakdale No. 142, Oakdale—D. W. Tulloch, Pres.; E. T. Gobin, Sec.; 2nd Monday, Legion Hall.
Orestimba No. 247, Crows Landing—Lloyd W. Fink, Pres.; G. W. Fink, Sec.; 1st and 3rd Wednesdays, Community Club Home.
Turlock No. 274, Turlock—Robley R. Libby, Pres.; Steve A. Karkeet, Sec.

SUTTER COUNTY.

Sutter No. 261, Sutter City—James Putman, Pres.; Glen R. Haynes, Sec., R.F.D. No. 2, Yuba City; 2nd and 4th Mondays, N.D.G.W. Hall.

NATIVE SON NEWS

(Continued from Page 7)

Henry Spurr of the 1934 Grand Parlor committee. In the Santa Rosa Admission Day parade, No. 71 will have an Indian float, with real Indians in native costumes. Al Bechtol and Henry Bucknell are in charge of arrangements.

Calistoga—At joint ceremonies, officers of Calistogu No. 86 and Calistoga No. 145 N.D.G.W. were installed by Deputies Harry N. Bunce and Lilius Kelley, J. H. Marchese and Grace Wolt becoming the respective presidents. Refreshments and dancing followed the ceremonies. During the winter months the Parlors will resume their popular dances.

Livermore—Las Positas No. 96's officers were installed by Deputy Henry E. Uebner, L. J. Volponi becoming president. There were many visitors.

San Bernardino—Arrowhead No. 110 had a "stag" at its Crestline clubhouse August 12; Jeff Sawyer was in charge. Fred Kramer conducted the August 23 sociable, for the benefit of the homeless children. The annual watermelon feast was held at Harlem Springs August 30. Three candidates were initiated August 9.

Santa Barbara—In the Old Spanish Days Fiesta parade, August 3, Santa Barbara No. 116 featured the Bear Flag episode; Roy Richardson designed the float. Sheriff Eugene W. Biscailuz (Santa Monica Bay No. 267) of Los Angeles County and his posse appeared in the line and following the parade were entertained at luncheon by the Parlor.

Sebastopol—Native Sons of Sonoma County made a pilgrimage August 6 to Mount Saint Helena's north peak where, in 1844, Russians from Fort Ross placed a plaque naming the peak for Princess Helena. Enroute, luncheon was served at Stevenson monument where, in 1884, Robert Louis Stevenson wrote "The Silverado Squatters." W. S. Borba (Sebastopol No. 143) was chairman of the arrangements committee.

Centerville—Officers of Washington No. 169 were installed August 8 by Deputy T. J. Leonard, Tom Silva becoming president. Entertainment and refreshments followed the ceremonies, which were attended by many Hayward and Oakland visitors.

TRINITY COUNTY.

Mount Bally No. 87, Weaverville—H. W. Day, Pres.; E. V. Ryan, Sec.; 1st and 3rd Mondays, Native Sons Hall.

TULARE COUNTY.

Visalia No. 19, Visalia—G. W. Houk, Pres.; Jack De Alba, Sec., 916 W. Oak St.; 2nd and 4th Tuesdays, Woodman Hall.

TUOLUMNE COUNTY.

Tuolumne No. 144, Sonora—Mathew J. Marshall, Pres.; William M. Harrington, Sec., P. O. box 715; 2nd and 4th Fridays, Knights Columbus Hall.
Columbia No. 258, Columbia—Anthony Solari, Pres.; Charles E. Grant, Sec.; 2nd and 4th Thursdays, Native Sons Hall.

VENTURA COUNTY.

Cabrillo No. 114, Ventura City—David Bennett, Pres., 1380 Church St.

YOLO COUNTY.

Woodland No. 30, Woodland—J. L. Aronson, Pres.; T. G. Hughes, Sec.; 1st Thursday, Native Sons Hall.

YUBA COUNTY.

Marysville No. 6, Marysville—A. W. Graves, Pres.; Verne Fogarty, Sec., 719 6th St.; 2nd Friday, Foresters Hall.

AFFILIATED ORGANIZATIONS.

San Francisco Extension of the Order Committee, N.S.G.W.—Joseph J. McShane, Chmn.; Harold J. Regan, Sec., 414 Mason St., San Francisco; meets 2nd and 4th Fridays, Grizzly Bear Club, 414 Mason St., San Francisco.
Alameda County Extension of the Order Committee, N.S.G.W.—Gam Hurst, Chmn.; Frank Roemer, Sec., 830 30th St., Oakland; meets 1st and 3rd Mondays, N.S.G.W. Hall, 11th and Clay Sts., Oakland.
Interparlor Committee (Southern District), N.S.G.W. and N.D.G.W.—Burrel D. Neighbours, Chmn.; Clyde H. Davis, Sec., 1935 E. 78th St.; meets 3rd Friday, Patriotic Hall, 1816 So. Figueroa St., Los Angeles.
San Francisco Assembly No. 1 Past Presidents Association N.S.G.W.—Meets 1st and 3rd Fridays, Native Sons Bldg., 414 Mason St., San Francisco; John Kirrane, Gov.; J. F. Stanley, Sec., 1175 O'Farrell St., San Francisco.
East Bay Counties Assembly No. 3 Past Presidents Association N.S.G.W.—Meets 4th Monday, Native Sons Hall, 11th and Clay Sts., Oakland; Gam Hurst, Gov.; Edgar G. Hanson, Sec., 1260 Russell St., Berkeley.
Marin County Assembly No. 5 Past Presidents Association N.S.G.W.—J. S. Rose Jr., Gov.; L. J. Peter, Sec., Peter Bldg., 4th and "C" Sts., San Rafael.
Fred H. Greely Assembly No. 6 Past Presidents Association N.S.G.W.—Meets monthly with different Parlors comprising district; Peter J. Delay, Gov.; Barney Barry, Sec., P.O. box 72, Lincoln.
San Joaquin Assembly No. 7 Past Presidents Association N.S.G.W.—Meets 1st Friday, Native Sons Hall, Stockton; Clyde H. Gregg, Gov.; R. D. Dorcey, Sec., Native Sons Club, Stockton.
Sonoma County Assembly No. 9 Past President Association N.S.G.W.—Meets monthly at different Parlor headquarters in county; P. A. R. Gambini, Gov.; L. S. Lewis, Sec., Court House, Santa Rosa.
General John A. Sutter Assembly No. 10 Past Presidents Association—C. O. Wachman, Gov.; Jas. J. Longshore, Sec., 514 "J" St., Sacramento.
Grizzly Bear Club—Members all Parlors outside San Francisco at all times welcome. Clubrooms top floor Native Sons Bldg., 414 Mason St., San Francisco.
Native Sons and Native Daughters Central Committee on Homeless Children—Main office, 955 Phelan Bldg., San Francisco; Mrs. John W. Stirling, Chmn.; Miss Mary E. Brusie, Sec. Los Angeles branch office, 3924 Sunset Blvd.; Dorothy Schlingman, Sec.

(ADVERTISEMENT.)

In Memoriam

MARY FRENCH MITCHELL.

To the Officers and Members of Manzanita Parlor No. 29 N.D.G.W.—We, your committee appointed to prepare a testimonial of love and respect to the memory of our departed sister, Mary French Mitchell, beg to submit the following:

Whereas, Our Heavenly Father has called to her eternal reward our beloved and most charitable sister; and whereas, we note the place made vacant by her absence and miss her cheery smile; be it

Resolved, That Manzanita Parlor No. 29 N.D.G.W. bows to the will of our Heavenly Father in love, and with the confidence that our sister whose earthly birthday is today, on today she enters her happier home in Heaven to live in joy and peace and in greater opportunities for usefulness. For, as Longfellow has beautifully said:

"There is no death.
What seems so is transition.
This life of mortal breath
Is but a suburb of the life elysian
Whose portals we call death.
In that great cloister's stillness and seclusion
By guardian angels led
Safe from temptation, safe from sin's pollution—
She lives—whom we call dead."

Be it further resolved, That through these lines we extend to her bereaved relatives our sincere sympathy in their loss, and also our appreciation of the noble life of our truly pioneer sister; and be it further resolved, that a copy of this memorial be spread upon our minutes, and that a copy be sent to The Grizzly Bear Magazine for publication.

ANNIE F. CONLIN,
LOUISE WALES,
VINITA A. JONES,
Committee.

Grass Valley, August 11, 1933.

EDWIN P. HODGES.

To the Officers and Members of Plymouth Parlor No. 48 N.S.G.W.—Divine Wisdom has seen fit to transfer to the Heavenly Parlor on High our well beloved brother, Edwin P. Hodges, past president and trustee of this Parlor. Brother Hodges was one of our most active members, and in his daily life he exhibited those qualities which make a man a good husband and father, a good neighbor and a good citizen, and which we like to think typify the true spirit of a Native Son. With those of us who had the privilege of working with him, the memory of his unselfish devotion to the interests of our Parlor and the purposes of our Order will remain as an inspiration, undimmed through the passing years.

However, we believe it to be fitting and proper that some permanent and public expression be made of the sentiments of the members of this Parlor; therefore, be it Resolved, That a copy of this statement be sent to his bereaved family as evidence of our sincere sympathy for them; that, in testimony of our sense of loss, our charter be draped in mourning for a period of thirty days; that this statement be spread in full upon the minutes of the Parlor, and that a copy be sent to The Grizzly Bear for publication.

THOS. D. DAVIS,
B. L. CRAIN,
M. N. POOL,
Committee.

Plymouth, August 21, 1933.

N.S.G.W. OFFICIAL DEATH LIST.

Containing the name, the date and the place of birth, the date of death, and the Subordinate Parlor affiliation of deceased members reported to Grand Secretary John T. Regan from July 20 to August 19, 1933:

Nicolaus, Henry Jr.; Sacramento, November 6, 1868; July 31, 1933; Sacramento No. 3.
Scroggs, John Calvin; Sacramento, September 9, 1862; August 9, 1933; Sacramento No. 3.
Hobin, William H.; Turlock, December 22, 1874; July 22, 1933; Stockton No. 7.
Young, Dave E.; Farmington, June 23, 1871; August 1, 1933; Stockton No. 7.
Doyle, Thos. B.; San Francisco, August 8, 1880; January 28, 1933; Pacific No. 10.
Green, George Albert; San Francisco, August 8, 1880; May 13, 1933; Pacific No. 10.
Ryan, Daniel A.; San Francisco, August 21, 1873; June 11, 1933; Pacific No. 10.
McPherson, George W.; Snelling, October 25, 1858; August 3, 1933; Pacific No. 10.
Ferguson, William J.; San Francisco, June 17, 1859; July 3, 1933; Mission No. 38.
Stroh, George M.; Howland Flat, July 2, 1869; July 31, 1933; El Dorado No. 52.
Hothersolle, George; Nevada City, November 18, 1865; July 29, 1933; Hydraulic No. 56.
Watters, Walter Grant; Dutch Flat, November 14, 1865; July 31, 1933; Hydraulic No. 56.
Grace, William Francis; San Francisco, October 20, 1870; August 2, 1933; Rincon No. 72.
Ramke, Arthur; Pleasanton, July 2, 1878; July 4, 1933; Las Positas No. 96.
Edelman, Elmer Bergold; San Francisco, June 1, 1902; June 15, 1933; Niantic No. 105.
Russill, Ray Millard; Los Angeles, July 24, 1895; July 22, 1933; Ramona No. 109.
Botello, Maclovio Antonio; Los Angeles, June 13, 1856; July 6, 1933; Santa Barbara No. 116.
Goix, Thomas; Santa Barbara, September 15, 1863; July 16, 1933; Santa Barbara No. 116.
Metcalf, Winfield B.; Hydesville, September 3, 1862; July 30, 1933; Santa Barbara No. 116.
Gould, Charles A.; San Francisco, February 1, 1868; July 16, 1933; Sequoia No. 160.
Otto, Robert William; San Francisco, August 31, 1866; July 29, 1933; Sequoia No. 160.
Naughton, James Joseph; San Francisco, November 27, 1883; August 5, 1933; Sequoia No. 160.
Tiegeler, Henry R.; San Francisco, August 18, 1880; July 27, 1933; Precita No. 187.
Doyle, Luke Aloysius; Alameda, September 26, 1880; July 10, 1933; Athens No. 195.
Murphy, George L.; San Francisco, November 14, 1899; August 2, 1933; Dolores No. 208.
Botzback, William T.; Lodi, March 6, 1887; August 12, 1933; Galt No. 243.

Mendocino Fair—The Mendocino County Fair is to be held at Ukiah, September 15 to 17. A rodeo will be featured, also a stock show.

LOS ANGELES
CITY AND COUNTY

ADMISSION DAY, SATURDAY, SEPTEMBER 9, will be fittingly observed at an affair, sponsored by the Native Sons and Native Daughters of the Golden West, to be held at the Breakfast Club, 3213 Riverside drive. The general public are cordially invited to join in this recognition of the state's eighty-third birthday anniversary, where genuine old California hospitality will be dispensed. A small admission fee of twenty-five cents will be charged adults; children under 12 years free. Tickets may be secured from the secretary of any Native Son or Native Daughter Parlor.

The festivities will begin in the afternoon, with a family basket supper from 5 to 7 o'clock. Bring your own food, but coffee will be supplied. Then will follow a two-hour entertainment program, the varied talent being supplied through the courtesy of the several Parlors. Los Angeles No. 45 N.S.G.W. will present Roger Johnson in musical saw selections; Los Angeles No. 124 N.D.G.W. a California fiesta scene participated in by Dolores Malin, Marvel Thomas, Leonie Clos, Jeanne Clos, Marie Walsh, Henrietta DeGoede, Bertha Murray, Ascension Simon, Frances Ontiveros, Mercedes Caldwell, Ann Schiebusch, Erlinda Sepulveda, Edna Trombatore, Anita Santo and Lucy Jordan; Californiana No. 247 N.D.G.W., Marybelle Chapman and Alphonse B. Fages in vocal selections, and the Lick sisters in a dance duo; Verdugo No. 240 N.D.G.W., Dorothy Courtney in a vocal number; Santa Monica Bay No. 245 N.D.G.W., a violin soloist; University No. 272 N.S.G.W., specialty dance numbers. The program contributions from the other Parlors had not been announced at the time The Grizzly Bear went to press.

Frank G. Tyrrell, one of California's most gifted orators, will deliver a fifteen-minute talk on "The Significance of Admission Day." This will be followed by dancing until midnight, music being furnished by Burt Bair's Native Son orchestra.

Arrangements for the local Admission Day festival are in charge of a joint committee made up of representatives from all the Los Angeles County Parlors of Native Sons and Native Daughters. Mrs. Gertrude Allen (Los Angeles No. 124 N.D.G.W.) is the general chairman and Mrs. Dorothy Ravn (Verdugo No. 240 N.D.G.W.) the secretary. Miss Flora Holy is in charge of the ticket distribution, Mrs. Ella Steinbeck is attending to the publicity, and Mrs. Olinda Kerby is arranging the program.

"For California's birthday party," says Chairman Allen, "the Natives and their friends will have use of the entire grounds of the Breakfast Club, as well as the pavilion and the arena. A cleaner, shadier and more delightful setting would be hard to find. The family supper will be served under the spreading trees of the Garden of Friendship. Put aside your work and worries, and join with us. You will be glad you came!"

N.S.G.W. CENTRAL MEMBERSHIP ACTIVITIES—NEXT BIG SHOW SEP. 29

The Native Sons Luncheon Club—inaugurated by the N.S.G.W. Central Membership Committee, Henry G. Bodkin (Hollywood No. 196) chairman—has become very popular, and the attendance is on the increase. The club meets every Friday at 12:15 (noon) at the Rosslyn Hotel, Fifth and Main streets, and adjourns promptly at 1:15 p.m. This is not a talkfest, but a happy-go-lucky get-together for the Order's good and the individual's pleasure.

A different chairman presides each week. Those serving in that capacity during August were Sheriff Eugene W. Biscailuz (Santa Monica Bay Parlor No. 267), Lindsay K. Dickey (Santa Monica Bay Parlor No. 267), Charles Straube (Ramona Parlor No. 109) and Harry T. Honn (Santa Monica Bay Parlor No. 267). "All members of the Order are urged to come to these luncheons," says Secretary Walter Odemar, "and participate in true Native Son friendship."

The first of the six monthly big shows provided by the united Los Angeles County Parlors under the auspices of the Central Membership Committee, to aid in the membership drive outlined by Grand President Justice Emmet Seawell, was held at the meetingplace of Los Angeles Parlor No. 45, August 31. Lindsay K. Dickey was the program director, and Burrel D. Neighbours was the speaker.

The second of the united Parlors' shows will be held Friday night, September 29, at the meetingplace of Ramona Parlor No. 109, Patriotic Hall, 1816 South Figueroa. Grand Second Vice-president Harmon D. Skillin will be the sole speaker. Every Native Son should rally to these shows, which feature the highest class talent, and especially should he bring at least one eligible as a guest.

FINAL SYMPHONIES FEATURES.

Saturday, September 2, brings the final ballet production of the "symphonies under the stars" season at the Hollywood Bowl. This colorful feature was devised by Francesca Braggiotti, noted Boston dance creator, who will appear personally. It is "In the Vienna Woods," to the muisc of the Strauss waltz.

The final concert of the year will be the twilight program at 5:15 o'clock of Sunday, September 3. Bernardino Molinari will present an orchestral group including Respighi's "Pines of Rome," and Margaretha Lohmann will appear as piano soloist.

FRIENDS GUESTS OF FRIENDS.

The beautiful South Pasadena home of Herman C. Lichtenberger, Past Grand President N.S.G.W., and wife—La Casa de los Amigos, "The Home of the Friends,"—was the scene of another most delightful gathering August 5. A feast, fit for the gods, of barbecued bullshead and all the accompaniments, was served, and there was a flow of reminiscences as well as an interesting discussion of current events. Friendship was the keynote of the occasion, and hospitality reigned supreme. Guests included:

George Beebe, Henry Carter, Isidore B. Dockweiler, Percy A. Eisen, R. E. Barry, Louis A. Duni, Frank A. Duggan, Clarence M. Hunt, Harry J. Lelande, Lon S. McCoy, John T. Newell, Louis P. Russill, Charles Straube, J. Deacon Taggart, Charles R. Thomas, Robert A. Todd,

Wm. J. Variel, Seth S. Williams, Leo V. Youngworth, Burrell D. Neighbours, Judge B. Ray Schauer, Judge Ruben Schmidt, Judge Joseph P. Sproul, Judge Louis H. Valentine, Judge Fletcher Bowron, John Maitman, William J. Bright, Harry G. Folsom, Father Morris, Father Louis A. Mulvihill, Henry Morrissey, John Carrigan, Ilde Sepulveda, Clyde Johnson, Percy F. Schumacher, Dr. John Schwam, Arthur A. Schmidt, H. L. Burrell, J. H. Rishebarger, Walter Trask, B. A. Garlinghouse, W. A. Anderson, Brodie Hamilton, Paul Kiefer, George M. Holstein, Joe Mesmer, J. Harvey McCarthy.

SPLENDID REPORTS OF EXCELLENT WORK.

At the August 4 meeting of the N.S.G.W. and N.D.G.W. Homeless Children Committee, splendid reports of the excellent work being done were given. Officers were elected as follows: Irving Baxter (Ramona N.S.), chairman; Grace J. Norton (Los Angeles N.D.), vice-chairman; Annie L. Adair (Los Angeles N.D.), recording secretary; John Gower (Sepulveda N.S.), financial secretary; Flora M. Holy (Los Angeles N.D.), treasurer.

An account of the recent benefit ball showed a profit of $400.25. In July, the joint committee turned into the Central Committee $1,000, and a very appreciative letter from General Secretary Mary E. Brusie was read, thanking the local Natives for their liberal contribution to the great work.

WILL FEATURE HISTORY.

Commemorating the day, August 2, 1769, on which Los Angeles was named by Portola's men, Californiana Parlor No. 247 N.D.G.W. had a luncheon at the Women Athletic Club. The event inaugurated a year to be dedicated to the recognition of dates of historical interest, as well as the revival of customs typical of early California. Among the speakers were Past Grand Grace S. Stoermer, Miss Mary Foy, President Inez Sitton, Past Presidents Ora M. Evans, Mary B. Noerenberg and Gertrude Tuttle, Mms. Isabel Lopez-Fages, Charles Decker and Dexter Monroe.

September 4 the Parlor will celebrate the founding of Los Angeles with an informal gathering at the Plaza, wherein is placed the statue of Felipe de Neve, founder of the city, which was donated to Los Angeles by Californiana. Later, dinner and entertainment will be enjoyed in Olvera street. Mrs. Amos O. Evans is in charge of arrangements.

When the Parlor opens September 12 after the summer recess, President Inez Sitton and the chairmen of her many committees will outline a program which, it is hoped, will create an interest making for a most prosperous year. She plans to carry on the projects which have gained statewide recognition for Californiana, and the program includes a history class, talks on historical subjects and other interesting features.

EIGHT INITIATED.

University Parlor No. 272 N.S.G.W. initiated a class of eight candidates, the ritual being splendidly exemplified by the officers of Ramona Parlor No. 109, headed by President Charles Straube. Among the initiates was City Councilman Earl C. Gay. Among the many speakers were Burrel D. Neighbours, who stressed the necessity of membership activity, Grand Trustee Eldred L. Meyer, District Deputy Walter Baskerville, Leo V. Youngworth, Deputy Grand President Walter Odemar, City Councilman John W. Baumgartner, Howard Babb and Ben Hiss. Refreshments were served.

The Parlor sponsored a sports dance August 19; snappy music was provided. University hopes to have its baseball team at Santa Rosa for Admission Day.

N.D.G.W. NEWS PARAGRAPHS.

Los Angeles—The September calendar of Los Angeles Parlor No. 124 includes: 13th, card party, first of bridge tournament; Ann Schiebusch chairman. 20th, initiation. 27th, swimming party, Women Athletic Club, 5:30 p.m. The weinie bake August 23 was a wonderful success and heartily enjoyed; Olinda Kerby headed the active committee. The August 30 dance, Juanita Porter chairman, proved a pleasant affair.

Long Beach—Meeting at the home of President Eleonor Johnson, Long Beach Parlor No. 154 had a visit from Deputy Letitia Sarciaux July 27. Gertrude Riddle and Clara Fay served refreshments August 8. The thimble club met August 3 and 17 at the home of Gussie Tabor. A benefit card party was held August 10 at the home of Kate McFadyen; assisting the hostess were Lois McDougall and Kitty Dillon. A steak dinner is to be held at the home of Gussie Tabor, with Clara Fay as committee chairman.

Glendale—President Sarah Burleson of Verdugo Parlor No. 240 expressed a determination August 8 to have a memory garden, and appointed Betty Sanders chairman of a committee to provide one. A successful card party August 15 was in charge of Ada Steele (chairman), Beulah VanLuven and Vera Carlson; prizes went to Nan Hutchinson, H. Shuck, Earle Steele and Maude Molen. First Vice-president Margaret Donlan sponsored a weinie bake at Hermosa Beach August 22. The Parlor is sending a copy of The Grizzly Bear regularly to each of the four public libraries in Glendale.

Santa Monica—The "sunset" barbecue of Santa Monica Bay Parlor No. 245 at the Machado Culver City residence August 5 was a social and financial success. A delightful afternoon was spent August 11 at the Los Angeles home of Second Vice-president Helen Burke. August 23 a "Emelia Sundquist" night was enjoyed with a complimentary card party. In the near-future Recording Secretary Rosalie F. Hyde will sponsor a "chowder" party at her Venice home.

NATIVE SONS NEWS PARAGRAPHS.

Los Angeles—Los Angeles Parlor No. 45's September program includes: 14th, initiation. 21st, open house, with California Pioneers as guests; refreshments will be served.

Los Angeles—The monthly birthday suppers being featured by Ramona Parlor No. 109 are growing in popularity. All members of the Order are welcome. Four teams have been put in the field to harvest recruits for the Parlor; they are captained by Past Grand Herman C. Lichtenberger, District Deputy Walter E. Baskerville, Leon Leonard and President Charles Straube. Ramona's September schedule includes: 8th, initiation. 15th, birthday dinner, complimentary to the September borns. 29th, official visit of Grand Second Vice-president Harmon D. Skillin; short meeting, beginning at 7:30, and then adjournment to the auditorium for the big show.

Santa Monica—Santa Monica Bay Parlor No. 267 will have a class initiation September 6. Its newly organized drum corps will appear in the Santa Rosa Admission Day parade. The supper

(Continued on Page 23)

GRIZZLY GROWLS

(CLARENCE M. HUNT.)

CALIFORNIA IS IN A DEPLORABLE condition, financially, thanks to the Legislature, which lacked the guts to do that which its members know full well should have been done for the state's best interest, and the executive branch of the government which, it appears, knows nothing of economy and is concerned about tomorrow (next year) rather than today. As a result of the juggling of the legislative and the executive branches of the State Government, a sales tax has been added to the burden of the already near-pauperized majority,—to provide funds for the uninterrupted continuation of the spending orgy—but the income tax, that would have come from the well-able-to-pay minority, has been vetoed by the Governor. Because of these tax measures, the State Government is being severely criticised. Here are some of the comments:

"THE GOVERNOR'S BUM TAX JOKES—When Governor Rolph poses as a friend of economy and low taxation and when he assumes the they-made-me-do-it excuse for signing sales tax and and at the same time refuses to sign the income tax he is indulging in that sport known as drawing the long bow. If the Governor wants to prove that he had a mandate from the public let him dare withdraw his opposition to a popular vote on the law and get his thunderous 'No' from the voters. He had a clear, definite, unmistakable mandate from agriculture and labor to sign the income tax and his gay disregard of that is equaled only by his gay disregard of so many other obligations and duties. Had the Governor said he had a mandate from certain rich supporters not to sign the income tax bill it would have sounded much more convincing. This paper certainly tried to be definite and clear in expressing its opinion about this issue. It suggested that the Riley plan should be voted for only on the stipulation that legislators be instructed to stand staunchly for an income tax if a sales tax were proposed. In other words if a disproportionate burden were laid on folk of moderate means by a sales tax then lay a disproportionate tax on the rich taxdodgers by means of an income tax and thus make every one feel the weight of government and have a pocketbook interest in economy. Governor Rolph now qualifies as a comedian by claiming that the income tax would fall hardest on people of moderate income. That ought to be good for a hollow laugh in which the Governor's own echo would be the only voice to join. Meanwhile the Governor ought to heed seriously—if he has the capacity to be serious—the warning that if a property tax is laid to make up for the deficiencies of the vetoed income tax there may be a tax strike in this state. If the Governor imagines that is an idle threat he should get some one to read to him about Machado of Cuba. All over this state people are paying their sales tax pennies with quips about 'another penny for Rolph's salary,' 'a new silk hat for the Governor,' and similar cracks. These jokes are mirthless. The fact that the Governor refused to cut his own salary and income of approximately $50,000 a year is not a good joke to tax-weighted citizens."—Pacific Rural Press.

"THE SALES TAX IRRITANT AND ITS FUTURE—The average person now paying the sales tax in California would do so gladly if convinced that the money was to be wisely and economically applied to the needs of this great State, but the spectacle of extravagance, waste, experiment and incompetency which politicians have given us in recent years is poor incentive to dig up extra pennies. The psychological effect of pay, pay, pay, taxes, taxes, taxes, we believe, will have the effect of slowing up business in California which had begun to revive and should not be retarded at this critical moment. However, the Legislature had time to think about all of this and if our representatives at Sacramento have blundered, it will result in there being few old faces at the State Capitol next term. Voters will see to that. Most tax wails before the sales tax era were heard only twice a year and from a limited class—real estate owners who bore most of the tax load. After wheezing in April, taxpayers forgot about it until November, when they groaned again. With the advent of the sales tax, an augmented chorus of all-year-round groans should make the sales tax symphony a howling success. . . . Glad-handed politicians, from the Governor to Assemblyman, will find that the old blarney stuff will not win votes so readily in the future. The people will demand a strict accounting of their business at Sacramento, and ability in public servants to administer their affairs when a crisis looms. That is the test of statesmanship—a test which precious few have met. If such public servants cannot be found and elected, the States will revamp their form of government. Floundering representatives and irresponsible governors such as some of the states, including California, have put up with in recent years is a challenge to popular government."—Sonoma Index Tribune.

"ROLPH TRUE TO FORM—Governor Rolph announced yesterday the veto of the income tax bill passed by the recent Legislature as a part of the balanced tax plan under the Riley-Stewart amendment and thereby threatened flippantly to throw away from $10,000,000 to $15,000,000 of much needed revenue. Rolph lives in a past era. He has never awakened to find out what the New Deal means. He still believes in the sanctity and untouchableness of wealth and has utter scorn for the spirit of the hour which is concerned with the underdog. The income tax would take from those who have. The sales tax takes from those least able to pay. If anyone is to be 'soaked,' and all tax-payers are soaked these days, it should be those who can stand the strain of governmental costs. . . . Rolph should not be too severely condemned for his action in this matter. No man should be twitted for being blind and deaf. Loss of sight and hearing is a great misfortune to the persons deprived of them, but it is a disaster to a great state when its executive is totally blind to governmental conditions and deaf to the advice of those in touch with popular sentiment."—Sacramento Union.

"NRA SHOULD NOT BE BLAMED FOR STATE SALES TAX—We have with us Mr. Sales Tax. Have you met the gentleman! You may not realize it, but he is the 'skeleton at the feast'—if feast there be—in every home in California, and he's likely to prove a regular guest for at least two years to come, perhaps more, for there are eighteen months left of the run of your present state administration. . . . No excuses, evasions or alleged exigencies can change the situation as it exists as of today. To blame the Legislature is of no avail. The Legislature did not 'blow in' the state's money. It did not by any 'presto change' necromancy cause a balance in cash of about twenty-nine millions of dollars, . . . to dissolve in air. That Legislature assembled leaderless. . . . All was chaos; out of it all came only chaotic pieces of hardly understandable matter, vague as to sensible and executable details, confusing and, in fact, gravely questionable as to constitutional legality. . . . Unfortunately the great program of the national administration came into active promulgation simultaneously with this California state administration sales tax matter. A lot of citizens are so mixed up that they are blaming the Roosevelt administration; blaming the NRA (National Recovery Act), destined and intended to help us all up on our feet, for this local, state, sales tax measure now in force, instead of placing the blame where it belongs, which is on the shoulders of our state administration, which is the sole responsible agent in this matter. Do not make this mistake. NRA has nothing whatever to do with the sales tax."—Weekly Calistogan.

"EFFICIENCY COULD HAVE MADE NEW STATE SALES TAX LOWER—All this blame being placed upon Governor Rolph for the new sales tax is by no means unjustified or misplaced. True, the Governor did nothing more than sign the bill when it was handed him by the Legislature. It was not in his budget-balancing plan and possibly he does not even approve of it. But, nevertheless, his administration of State affairs is in no small measure responsible for the necessity of the sales tax. Conditions over which the Governor has no control, including the transfer of school support from the counties to the State, were an important factor in the adoption of this tax, but there are millions of dollars involved in the unbalanced budget which could have been eliminated had there been efficient government at Sacramento. A sales tax would probably have been necessary regardless of Governor Rolph, but if he had furnished the State with the right type of administration the tax could have been much less and need not have been the highest, except one, in the entire country. So when purchasers make 'wisecracks' about the pennies going to Governor Rolph they are not missing the mark so very far at that. . . . California's rate is higher than 18 of the other 19 states using a sales tax."—Livermore Herald.

In Remembrance of
THE CALIFORNIA PIONEERS

Admission Day, 1933

Captioned "California Says Hands Off Exclusion Law," an excellent editorial, to which we add a fervent "Amen!," appeared in "The Sacramento Bee" of August 24. Keep ever in mind the warning therein—which has so frequently been sounded in The Grizzly Bear—"necessity for the friends of the present law ever to be on the alert." Here's the editorial, in full:

"A small leak in the dyke is all that is often necessary to bring about its ultimate destruction. A parallel case is the movement now under way so to modify the Asiatic Exclusion Act of 1924 as to give preferential treatment to the Japanese. That act now stands as a staunch barrier to the influx here of all who are ineligible to American citizenship, of those who can never hope to be assimilated into the dominant American racial strain. But begin to tinker with it, make a break in the barrier, however small, and the whole structure will become endangered.

"Hence the necessity for the friends of the present law ever to be on the alert against the insidious propaganda now being widely circulated to secure congressional modification in 1934. Inspiring and directing this propaganda is a curious and strange alliance—returned missionaries, inoculated with the Japanese viewpoint; professional pacifists, ever ready to sacrifice the interests and welfare of their own country to cure some imagined slight to a foreign nation; selfish shipping interests which vision a profit in the return of conditions such as prevailed before 1924; and a coterie of idealists so-called whom President Theodore Roosevelt once fittingly described as the 'lunatic fringe' of the body politic. These are all parroting the idea that somehow Japan has suffered a permanent insult from the present law; and that until proper amends are made the friendly relations between the two countries are endangered.

"That is clotted nonsense. The exclusion issue is today practically as dead an issue in Tokio as it is in Washington. The only thing that keeps it alive is the misguided and misdirected agitation of a group of Californians who ought to know better, men and women who should be thinking first of the welfare and security of their own state instead of advocating a policy so detrimental to her. But even if there were subatantial support for their fears, the sacrifice they call upon the country to make is too great to be given favorable consideration—namely the sacrifice of the principle that America herself must be the sole and exclusive judge of those whom she believes should be welcomed to her shores.

"The simple fact is that the doors of immigration cannot be opened to the Japanese without at the same time giving a like concession to every other Asiatic people. So far as California is concerned, the overwhelming majority of her people feel strongly that it would have been far better and wiser had the act of 1924 been applied a quarter of a century earlier. And they are in no mood to tolerate the undoing of the good job finally accomplished in that year. Keep the dyke intact."

The dailies these days are overcrowded with racketeer dope, the propaganda, however, being directed at the gun-toting variety, the kidnaper, etc. No reference whatever is made to the source and sustenance of the racketeer "profession"—political racketeering, the nation's chief menace; the direct cause of the depression which has exacted and continues to exact a stupendous toll from honest, lawabiding citizens.

The political racketeers in national, state, county, city and municipal governments must be cleaned out of public office before there can be any appreciable relief from existant conditions—confiscatory taxation, etc., and The People, themselves, must do the job. California and its several counties and cities are today suffering more from political racketeering than from any other cause. NOW is the time for elimination of the cause!

The NRA, so advices from the National Capital state, is making satisfactory progress and several thousand people have been given employment through its operation. It was designed for the nation's good, and every loyal American will wholeheartedly, to the extreme of his or her ability, co-operate with President Franklin Roosevelt in putting the blue eagle over the top.

This good news comes from the California State Historical Association through Director Owen C. Coy: "We are glad to report that through the efforts of loyal friends of California history, the legislative measure which proposed to abolish the State Historical Association was held in an Assembly committee. The association is continuing to operate as a part of the State Department of Education. We take this opportunity to express our appreciation of the assistance which has made this continuance possible. We count on your live co-operation to keep the association active and useful."

Here's heartening news from Sacramento: The State Board of Equalization has warned county, municipal and district officials that the Riley-Stewart Tax Act limitations affecting tax rates for 1933-34 will be strictly enforced, and that increases exceeding the legal 5 percent may invalidate the entire levy.

So, Mr. Citizen Taxpayer, scan your tax bill, and if the law has been violated follow the course suggested by the State Equalization Board which, in a public statement, cautions: "Local taxpayers were guaranteed $38,000,000 a year in propetry tax relief by the shifting of school costs to the State, now being defrayed through the sales tax. The new tax rates must actually embody that relief and any attempt to dissipate it will not be tolerated. If any municipality, county or district exceeds by more than 5 percent the total expenditures of the preceding year such overage is invalid and cannot be legally levied.

"Any taxpayer can resist the excess levy and invalidate the entire amount. The taxpayer should tender only the amount legally due and demand a receipt in full. If refused a receipt he can then mandamus the tax collector to issue it, which will effect the cancellation of all overage." It probably would be a blessing if the tax levies were, for one reason or another, invalidated and the mis-governing agencies left without funds to operate. That would, indeed, hasten the end of political racketeering.

This statement, from the Los Angeles Realty Board, appearing in a written protest filed with the Los Angeles County Board of Supervisors against a tax increase should have the earnest consideration of taxpaying citizens, hordes of them bankrupt: "We desire to call your attention to the item set up in the salary fund for 1933-34, amounting to $17,430,716.44, or an increase of $1,340,332.44 over the salary item for 1932-33."

Commenting on this, the "Los Angeles Times" said editorially: "Los Angeles County was well served, most people will agree, in 1925-26. In that fiscal year it spent $7,317,064 for salaries, which went to 7,909 employees. Since 1926 the population has increased about 32 percent; but the proposed budget calls for a salary list of $17,430,000 to go to 13,836 employees—an increase of 140 percent. How such an increase can be justified has not yet been explained. . . . Every plus of public expenditure is balanced by a minus of private expenditure." The increase can, but will not, be explained. To do so would necessitate exposure of the "inner circle." The condition can, if The People so will, be rectified by the recall.

Michimasa Soyeshima of Japan is reported in press dispatches to have stated in Ottawa: "The growth of the United States Navy is becoming a menace to the peace of the world. The fact that her Atlantic fleet is in the Pacific Ocean is causing ill-feeling in Japan. If the United States would remove her navy and repeal the Japanese Exclusion Act it would do much to disarm the minds of the people of Japan."

The tactics of Japan ARE a constant menace to world peace. If the United States Government would operate in accord with the wishes of Japan, everything would be "jake"—for the "rising sun."

A check by the Associated Press, made public August 2, revealed that with the exception of Los Angeles County, there was a marked downturn in relief activities. San Francisco and Alameda County had each cut off approximately 20,000 from the needy list. In Los Angeles County, 11,965 cases were added to the needy rolls during July, and it was officially reported that 485,000, about one-fourth of that county's population, are dependent on Los Angeles for aid. These statements and figures should, also, be given careful consideration by Los Angeles County taxpayers. Why the substantial decrease in San Francisco and Oakland, and the substantial increase in Los Angeles? Why are such a large percentage of that county's residents on the public relief rolls?

In this connection, the State Motor Vehicle Department reported, August 19, 150,000 persons came into California via motor routes the first six months of 1933. And the same day the State Emergency Relief Commission appealed for prompt Federal aid to care for "California's vast army of 100,000 indigent transients." Now, Los Angeles population promoters contend, in their voluminous propaganda, that most of the arriving tourists land in Los Angeles. They are attracted there by enticing advertisements spread broadcast throughout the nation, for the cost of which the Los Angeles County Board of Supervisors annually appropriates thousands of dollars of tax funds. It would appear, therefore, that Los Angeles County, through its generous (with taxpayers' money) Board of Supervisors, spends oodles of money to attract "vast armies," and then provides additional thousands for their relief.

More power to the Minute Men! They should continue, and broaden, their activities, and should be re-inforced by a REAL newspaper!

The State Motor Vehicle Department is authority for the statement that arrests for drunk auto driving have increased some 10 percent in number since the legalization of beer. There will be no lessening, but a continuous increase, of the number, legal or illegal booze, until such time as the courts impartially and promptly enforce the law, which now is not the custom.

The tuna packers of California South are emitting an awful howl because of Japan's "serious inroads into the American tuna market" via the dumping process, a method of commercial warfare extensively practiced by the "nice little yellow boys."

Little sympathy should be wasted on the California tuna packers, for they have steadfastly opposed any and every effort to curb the Jap menace in this state. Let them get a bellyful of the Japs and then, perhaps, they will join forces with those who have the welfare of California at heart and in mind always. It really might be a good idea to purchase the Jap rather than the California tuna, for the most effective way to reach a white-Jap is through the pocketbook.

"Today is the day to live your life; tomorrow's too far away. Today is the day for your honest strife; nor dream of the yesterday."—Ian Emde.

Motor Fees Divided—The California Motor Vehicle Department apportioned August 11 equally between the state highways division and the several counties of the state $4,758,944 in motor registration fees received the first six months of 1933. The apportionment was based on a total registration of 1,929,515 vehicles. Los Angeles County, having 789,691 of the total, received the lion's share of the divvy, $973,844.

Bar Meet—The annual convention of the State Bar of California will be held at Del Monte, Monterey County, September 21-23.

Nurserymen's Meet—The annual convention of the California Nurserymen's Association will be held September 18-20 at Oakland, Alameda County.

Tri-Counties Exposition—The twelfth annual Los Angeles County Fair, combined with the fairs of Riverside and Orange Counties, will be held at Pomona, September 15-24.

LOS ANGELES

(Continued from Page 21)

dance August 2 was well attended and most enjoyable. In compliment to the Los Angeles County Parlors, No. 267 sponsored a dance August 30.

Compton—Compton Parlor No. 273 has, under the supervision of President Ray W. Hecock, inaugurated a constructive program for increasing its membership. Every wanted eligible in Compton will be interviewed.

WITH ENTHUSIASM, respond to the call of the Grand President and COMB THE FIELDS! Bring into the fold the thousands of ready and willing eligibles. There positively is NO SUBSTITUTE FOR MEMBERSHIP! With numbers, there is no limit to accomplishments.

PERSONAL PARAGRAPHS.

John P. Keating (Sacramento N.S.) was a visitor last month.

William G. Newell (Los Angeles N.S.) last month paid a visit to Wyoming.

Mrs. Margaret Carter (Los Angeles N.D.) spent her vacation at Monterey City.

Frank S. Adams (Ramona N.S.) vacationed last month in Sequoia National Park.

Herman C. Lichtenberger (Past Grand N.S.) paid a visit last month to San Francisco.

Frederick J. Batser (Ramona N.S.) departed last month on an extensive Eastern tour.

Mayor Angelo Rossi (El Dorado N.S.) of San Francisco was among last month's visitors.

Superior Judge William T. Aggeler (Ramona N.S.) was a visitor last month to San Jose.

Miss Freda Johnson (Los Angeles N.D.) has returned from a three-week vacation at Chicago.

Mrs. Mae Baird (Los Angeles N.D.) and husband, Judge W. S. Baird, are visiting in Scotland.

Mrs. Bertha Murray (Los Angeles N.D.) and husband were recent visitors to the Grand Canyon.

Mrs. Leola Temby (Long Beach N.D.) of Long Beach was a visitor to Sacramento City last month.

Mrs. Florestina DeGilbert (Los Angeles N.D.) and daughter, Inez O'Shea, vacationed in San Francisco.

E. J. Amar Jr. (Sepulveda N.S.) of San Pedro has been appointed a member of the Harbor Commission.

Thomas J. (Piedmont N.S.) and Edna M. (Piedmont N.D.) Healey of Oakland were visitors last month.

Ramon D. Sepulveda (Sepulveda N.S.) of San Pedro observed his seventy-ninth birthday anniversary August 9.

Misses Evelyn Weldon, Alice Bray and Rose O'Connor (all Los Angeles N.D.) have been visiting in the Orient.

Mrs. Lucy Malin, Miss Marvel Thomas and Miss Dolores Malin (all Los Angeles N.D.) spent fiesta week at Santa Barbara.

THE DEATH RECORD.

Dr. David W. Edelman, affiliated with Hollywood Parlor No. 196 N.S.G.W., died August 6. He was born at Los Angeles City, January 29, 1869.

Edmund F. Ontiveros, husband of Mrs. Frances Ontiveros (Los Angeles N.D.), died August 10.

John B. Stewart, husband of Mrs. Sophia Stewart (Los Angeles N.D.), died August 14.

Joseph Albert Adair, affiliated with Ramona Parlor No. 109 N.S.G.W., died August 19, survived by a wife, Mrs. Annie L. Adair (Los Angeles N.D.) and two sons, Joseph A. Jr. and Aubury L. Adair. He was born at Michigan Flats, El Dorado County, June 2, 1861. He taught school for several years, was associated with the "Mariposa Gazette," and for ten years was district attorney of Mariposa County. Frequently he was a delegate to the N.S.G.W. Grand Parlor. No more loyal Californian, no truer friend ever lived than "Joe" Adair.—C.M.H.

TALENT SOUGHT.

The Paramount Studios are seeking new talent, both adult and juvenile. Says General Director Harry King: "I believe that if many youngsters and talented people are given the opportunity and proper tests, and if directors would take a little more of their valuable time to determine the applicant's possibilities, we would have ample star material right here in Los Angeles for musical and dramatic stage and screen productions." Lon Murray, head of Paramount, is the husband of Mrs. Mary Louise Larkin Murray, a member of Los Angeles Parlor No. 124 N.D.G.W.

N.S.G.W.

Admission Day!

SATURDAY, SEPTEMBER 9, 1933

The Eighty-third Anniversary of California's Recognition as One of the Sovereign Commonwealths of the United States

A LEGAL HOLIDAY

N. D. G. W.

Native and Adopted Sons and Daughters Give Due Recognition to this Important Date in the Romantic and Resourceful History of the State of California

N. S. G W

Close Your Places of Business!

Display the California State (Bear) Flag!

Join in Admisson Day Festivities!

Affiliate with either of California's Two Outstanding Patriotic Orders:
THE NATIVE SONS OF THE GOLDEN WEST
THE NATIVE DAUGHTERS OF THE GOLDEN WEST

BRANCHES (PARLORS) OF BOTH ORDERS ARE NUMEROUS

JOIN TODAY THE BRANCH NEAREST YOUR HOME

Grand Parlor, Native Sons of the Golden West.

N.D.G.W.

Grizzly Bear

OCTOBER — THE ONLY OFFICIAL PUBLICATION OF THE NATIVE SONS AND DAUGHTERS OF THE GOLDEN WEST — 1933

Featuring

GENERAL NEWS OF INTEREST CONCERNING ALL CALIFORNIA, and ORDERS NATIVE SONS and NATIVE DAUGHTERS

THE YEAR, $1.50 — SINGLE COPY, 15c

GRIZZLY GROWLS

(CLARENCE M. HUNT.)

TO AID THE BLUE EAGLE AND hasten the return of substantial prosperity to this land of plenty, the right-thinking, right-living citizens of the nation, who constitute a vast majority of the populace, should unite on and put into immediate effect a N.R.A.—NO RACKETEERS ALLOWED—code for all of the several subdivisions of government. The outstanding need of the country is to relegate to oblivion the racketeers in public office—the leeches who are taking the life-blood of the nation by impoverishing business and small-home owners through excessive taxation. Clear out the political racketeers, and others of that "profession," including the gangsters, will speedily abandon their "calling," for they will have "no friends at court." A vast reduction in over-excessive taxation is as necessary to assure the return of prosperity as are employment and higher prices.

California is paying dearly for political racketeering, in state, county, city and township governments. That condition accounts for bankrupting tax bills; for keeping on the payrolls, at the expense of taxpayers, unnecessary and incompetent employes; for failure to reduce the salaries of over-paid public employes and, in not a few instances, actually increasing salaries; for the creation of special assessment districts and thereby overloading with tax burdens the suffering property owner; for purchasing property at excessive prices, etc., ad infinitum. The costs of government, stupendous and far beyond all honestly necessary requirements, are due, mainly, to political racketeers, in and out of public office. Small in numbers and otherwise, they have, nevertheless, made the majority their slaves.

Are the people of this state desirous of contributing their all for the wellbeing of these political racketeers? Do they choose to remain in slavery? If not, they will proceed to oust the racketeers from public office. NOW IS THE APPOINTED TIME!

The efforts of a "select" few Californians to induce the Federal Congress to so amend the Immigration Act as to enable more Japs to come here via a quota is being extensively publicized in portions of the state press previously silent on the subject, and many publicity seekers are taking advantage of the get-before-the-public opportunity. The quota for Japs, another menace, has been advocated by certain interests for several years, as readers of The Grizzly Bear well know. No new facts have been expounded, but many heretofore presented in these columns have been, and are being, re-published. For lo, these many, many years, The Grizzly Bear has been keeping its readers well informed on the numerous phases of Japan's "peaceful invasion" schemes. Why the sudden awakening of certain dailies? Have they, at last, scented the "rising sun" danger? Whatever the cause, they are welcome in the campaign to keep California White.

President Robert Gordon Sproule of the University of California is one of the clique seeking to open the immigration gates to Japs. "Why should the president of the University of California feel it incumbent upon him," queries the "Bee" of Sacramento, "to rush into print with respect to a public matter so foreign to his own duties and responsibilities? Or is the academic atmosphere of the campus so tainted with a half-baked internationalism that even the heads thereof cannot escape its insidious influence?"

The "Literary Digest" says, "California, that traditional champion of exclusion, has already reversed its attitude." A falsehood, deliberate, or due to ignorance of the situation in this state! The Orders of Native Sons and Native Daughters of the Golden West, the California Grange, the California Labor Federation, the American Legion of California, the Commonwealth Club of San Francisco and numerous other organizations, as well as the California State Legislature, are on record as absolutely opposed to the quota for Japs, and will forcefully oppose any and every attempt to amend the Immigration Act. "It is exceedingly apparent," says the "Post Inquirer" of Oakland, "that California has not reversed its attitude on the subject of Oriental immigration, and has no intention of doing so—no more so, probably, than Japan, which rigidly excludes as immigrants the people of China, Korea and other Oriental countries."

Another red-hot war is on in Los Angeles, generaled by the Minute Men and the District Attorney. It started at a September 20 meeting of the governmental affairs committee of the Chamber of Commerce when, according to published reports, the latter accused the former of being the "greatest allies of the underworld," and said, "if this Chamber of Commerce wants to help fight gangsterism in the community, let it suppress the Junior Chamber and its Minute Men." Minute Man Kegley called the district attorney a liar, and said, "You have listened to the district attorney's dastardly falsehoods long enough without contravention. . . . Los Angeles is infested with political crooks and gangsters in public office."

The following day, at the Del Monte meeting of the State Bar, President Guy Richards Crump, also of the Angel City, charged that politics had, in many instances, made courts a disgrace. "Too many incompetent and inferior men have been appointed to the bench through political pull," he declared. In criticism of superior court judges he said, "Some are good, some are bad; some are learned in the law, some are ignorant of its elementary principles; some are industrious, others indolent; some are guided strictly by the law and the dictates of conscience, a few are otherwise controlled. The trial bench in California, at least in the larger counties, is rapidly deteriorating. In Los Angeles County, for instance, we are getting no better fast."

President Franklin Roosevelt has decided to maintain the Civilian Conservation Corps for another six months. Excellent conclusion, for various reasons! Plans for winter C.C.C. activities in California call for a continuation of truck trail and fire break construction, camp ground clearing and erosion control activities in the southland, and for the building of an 800-mile fire break bordering the national forests in central and northern California.

Urging a code on domestic relations to "minimize the divorce debauch," Rev. Walter A. Maier, Lutheran theologian, made this pertinent suggestion in the course of an address: "If American industry has seen fit to adopt codes for the co-ordination and regulation of American manufacturing and business, there is a hundred times more reason for a code on domestic relations. . . . We have a veritable crazy quilt of divorce laws in our country. A man may be a reputable husband in one state and a bigamist in another. American divorce markets are competing in the sort of cut-throat competition that our industrial codes are seeking to eliminate from the business world."

The Grizzly Bear of last month called attention to the warning sent by the State Board of Equalization to county, municipal and district officials that the Riley-Stewart Tax Act limitations affecting 1933-34 tax rates will be strictly enforced, and that increases exceeding the legal 5 percent may invalidate the entire levy. The oversigned directed an inquiry to Chairman Richard E. Collins of the board, as to whether the lawful 5-percent increase applies to the tax rate or the tax bill, and received this reply:

"In response to your letter of September 6th concerning the 5 percent expenditure limitation imposed on county, municipal, and district expenditures, I wish to state that this limitation applies to the total expenditures of said governmental units, and not to the tax rate. In other words, the Board does not limit tax rates as such, but the limitation applies to the expenditure which, of course, determines the tax rate. For example, if a county, municipality, or school district expended $100,000 last year (1932-33) it would be allowed to expend under the new law $105,000 for the coming year, 1933-34.

"This expenditure limitation was embodied in our new tax law so that the benefits to the taxpayers in the way of reducing their property tax would not be off-set by increased expenditures. I know the plan will work very successfully and will prove a great assistance in relieving real and personal property in this State which we know to be at present greatly over-burdened with taxation."

So, taxpayers, scan the 1933-34 tax bills carefully and see if they are, as they should be, appreciably less than for 1932-33. The shifting of the school costs from counties to state should lower materially the coming tax bills. In some counties and cities, however, where political racketeers govern, the taxpayers will not benefit to any great extent from the shift. Any way, Mr. Taxpayer, you can lawfully refuse to pay this year's tax bill if it exceeds the 5-percent increase limitation.

"Something To Think About" headed this editorial in the "Star" of Saint Helena, Napa County:

"One of our heavily taxed farmers, whose tax bill every year is in three figures, was in a store in St. Helena the other day shopping when two Mexican children entered the store and purchased a package of smoking tobacco of a popular brand. Inquiry brought out the fact that the children were two of a family of ten and that county aid is being extended as the head of the family contends that he is out of employment most of the time. . . . It seems to us that when foreigners or others come into this or any other county and have no visible means of support or do not want to work, they should not be supported by local taxpayers in whole or in part but given their walking papers even to the extent of causing the deportation of those from other lands."

Concurring in the opinion, it is suggested that the course proposed be followed in Los Angeles and other southern counties, so that thousands of near-bankrupt resident citizens may be relieved of the alien-charity tax burden and that employment, now given preferably to Mexis, Japs, Filipinos, etc., may go to deserving Whites.

An A.P. dispatch from Tokio, September 2, says: "The Japanese government today rejected a proposal of an American missionary to establish a branch Christian church at Ogaki in Gifu Prefecture. The rejection was based on the grounds that friction between Christianity and Japan's national faith, Shintoism, might cause disturbances at a time when national feeling is running high."

And yet, we permit the Japs to establish their churches in this country, and allow them numerous other privileges that no alien would be given in Japan. How foolish of us, not the Japs, as time will prove!

According to Dr. T. I. Storer, University California zoology professor, muskrats colonized on a farm in Mud Lake, Fall River Valley, Shasta County, threaten the entire levee system of the Sacramento River and its tributaries. If they should get past the barriers which obstruct their access to the lower Pit River, it would be but a comparatively short time before they would be working in the Sacramento River valley.

Says George H. Dern, Federal Secretary of State:

"There is in effect today a foreign army estimated at 400,000—more than three times the size of the Regular Army of the United States—that is operating in this country, invading the domestic tranquility of our people, invading the security of our homes, and confiscating our property. I say it is a foreign army because it is foreign to everything that is really American—foreign to American principles and institutions—foreign to American ideals and traditions. I refer, of course, to the army of 400,000 men and women in the United States who make their living mostly through crime, constituting what may very appropriately be called 'The Scarlet Army of the United States.' . . . Racketeers are levying tribute, in one form or another, on our business and industry that adds to the cost of the necessities of life of every family in the land. . . . However, I believe with General Pershing that once the American citizen is aroused to the danger that menaces his country in this terrible crime situation, he will gloriously redeem his indifference of the past."

Hasten, Most High, the arousing!

There's a lot of meat for studious thought in this editorial, captioned "But the Bill Must Be Paid," from the "Times" of Los Angeles:

"Advances to California from R.F.C. and Federal public-works funds have reached the surprising total of $870,000,000 and if the allocations to Hoover Dam are counted, as they should be, the total reaches $497,000,000. Among the additional appropriations sought for the State and its subdivisions is a list of preferred projects totaling $421,000,000, and if these are granted the State will have obtained more than $918,000,000 of Federal funds under the R.F.C. and public-works acts. Most of the loans for 'self-liquidating' projects have come to this State, some 61 percent of the total granted. . . . The interest that will have to be paid on money already advanced or definitely allocated amounts to more than $20,000,000 a year and amortization on a fifty-year basis is another $10,000,000 a year. Getting half a billion dollars for more or less needed projects seems to be very helpful, but temporary well-being at the cost of a permanently high tax and interest burden may be purchased too dearly. The total is already very large and it may be time to stop, look and listen before venturing much deeper into debt."

The State Board of Health recommends that subsidies for tubercular patients in sanitoria be limited to American citizens, and presents these excellent reasons why that should be done: "The situation at Weimar [Placer County, where one-quarter of the patients are aliens] is typical of similar institutions over the state, except that in southern counties, with their heavy Mexican population, the percentage of aliens is even greater. The bed capacities, in some instances, are so crowded with aliens that American citizens suffering with tuberculosis cannot be accommodated and are forced to accept places on waiting lists. . . . The state should show preference to its own citizens in paying out these funds." Not only should California first care for unfortunate citizens, but it should deport the alien public charges.

The Stockton "Independent" observes, "Before adjournment, both houses of the California Legislature passed a resolution to 'study' the feasibility of holding a session of the Legislature annually instead of biennially." It suggests to the Commonwealth Club of San Francisco that the club "start a study of a simpler and more economical and efficient form of state government, with a council of state rather than a bicameral legislature, and submit the new state charter to the people for their approval. So long as the present unwieldy, inefficient and scandalously costly system remains there is little hope for lower taxes and better government."

From the records of State Legislature of the past, not excepting the one recently terminated, it is concluded the interests of both the state and the taxpayers would be best conserved and protected if the Legislature met every quarter-century.

Here's cheerful news: Chief J. B. Kincer of the United States Weather Bureau's climate division says there is little probability that the trend toward warmer winters will be broken by exceptionally severe weather this year. He observes, however, that householders should not have too optimistic hopes for small heating bills, as there is always the possibility of a "maverick" cold winter drifting into the grouping of warm winters.

"The California booster," says "Tax Facts," "calls California 'God's country.' God would probably deny the allegation if He could see the condition we are in now. . . . This is our boasted civilization!"

"Hindus captured in car now facing deportation," headed a news article in a city daily. The Hindus, not the car, should be deported.

James J. Garrigan, Santa Barbara County sanitation inspector, suggests the City of Lompoc reduce or eliminate its Mexican and Filipino housing and sanitation problems by effecting a Reconstruction Finance Corporation loan with which to build dwellings for alien occupancy. The R.F.C. should make no loan for any such purpose. Lompoc should oust the Mexis and Filipinos, also the Japs. The alien evil should be completely obliterated, not encouraged, as proposed, or shifted.

The Grizzly Bear Magazine

The ALL California Monthly

OWNED, CONTROLLED, PUBLISHED BY GRIZZLY BEAR PUBLISHING CO., (Incorporated) COMPOSED OF NATIVE SONS.

HERMAN C. LICHTENBERGER, Pres.
JOHN T. NEWELL RAY HOWARD
WILLIAM I. TRAEGER
CHAS. R. THOMAS HARRY J. LELANDE
ARTHUR A. SCHMIDT, Vice-Pres.
BOARD OF DIRECTORS

CLARENCE M. HUNT
General Manager and Editor

OFFICIAL ORGAN AND THE ONLY OFFICIAL PUBLICATION OF THE NATIVE SONS AND THE NATIVE DAUGHTERS OF THE GOLDEN WEST.

ISSUED FIRST OF EACH MONTH.
FORMS CLOSE 20th MONTH.
ADVERTISING RATES ON APPLICATION.

SAN FRANCISCO OFFICE:
N.S.G.W. BLDG., 414 MASON ST., ROOM 302
(Office Grand Secretary N.S.G.W.)
Telephone: KEarny 1223
SAN FRANCISCO, CALIFORNIA

PUBLICATION OFFICE:
309-15 WILCOX BLDG., 2nd AND SPRING,
Telephone: VAndike 6234
LOS ANGELES, CALIFORNIA

(Entered as second-class matter May 29, 1918, at the Postoffice at Los Angeles, California, under the act of August 24, 1912.)

PUBLISHED REGULARLY SINCE MAY 1907

VOL. LIII (53). WHOLE NO. 318

MY GARDEN IN THE RAIN

(MRS. IMOGENE SAILOR.)

Sweet Rose, blushing Rose, droops her head in meek surrender
To the dashing, silvery rain.
But the Lily, white and haughty, fends him off
In sweet disdain.

Poinsettia, gay and flaunting, lures him on with vivid smiles,
Then she shakes her red, red head.
But the Poppy, silly Poppy, tightly folds her yellow cloak
And hies herself to bed.

Mignonette, lovely, fragrant, sentimental Mignonette,
Smiles at him with gestures shy;
But the Rain, the careless Rain, glances at her not at all
As he swiftly passes by.

Thus, my garden in the rain.
The pepper tree, with glistening, emerald branches
Guards the silent fountain underneath.
The gold-fish dart like fiery arrows through the pool,
To elude the pelting drops.
But see—a rift of blue among the hurrying clouds!
A glint of gold, a gentle breeze;
And my flowers, laughing, swaying, sparkling,
Glow in beauty 'neath the sun.

NATIVE SONS HISTORY HONORS GO TO CALIFORNIA SOUTH STUDENTS.

Berkeley (Alameda County)—The two fellowships in Pacific Coast History supported by the Order of Native Sons of the Golden West have been awarded to Vernon Tate of Los Angeles and Theodore E. Treutlein of San Diego. The appointments were made on nominations by Prof. Herbert E. Bolton, chairman of the history department of the University of California. Tate was graduated from the University of California at Los Angeles in 1929, and Treutlein took his bachelor's degree from the San Diego State Teachers College the same year.

These fellowships are awarded annually to the students in the graduate division who give the greatest promise in research in the field of California history.

CALIFORNIA FIFTY YEARS AGO

Thomas R. Jones

(COMPILED EXPRESSLY FOR THE GRIZZLY BEAR.)

TWO MILD STORMS PASSED OVER California during October 1883, dropping .97 of an inch of rain, and making the total rainfall of the season to date 1.89 inches. A cyclone cutting a swath eighty feet wide passed over the farm of George Perley, near Stockton, San Joaquin County, October 6. A barn was carried nearly a mile and wrecked.

An earthquake at 6 a.m. of October 22 caused a bluff 80 feet high and 200 feet long near Merced Falls to cave into the Merced River, which became dammed and cut a new channel. San Mateo, Santa Clara and adjacent counties had a severe shake at 9:10 a.m. of October 30.

A brilliant meteor passed over Nevada County the night of October 13. At 8 p.m. of October 31 a meteor passed over Santa Barbara County and illuminated the sky almost as bright as at noonday.

The State Grange had its annual session at San Jose, Santa Clara County, October 5. Among the many resolutions passed was one calling for an extra session of the Legislature to change the tax laws.

Exports of California grain this month totaled 1,825,000 centals, valued at $3,094,400.

George West and C. A. Wetmore of the Rincon del Diablo Rancho, San Diego County, were preparing to plant 2,000 acres in vines and 1,000 acres in olive trees.

The Natoma Vineyard Company was preparing to plant near Folsom, Sacramento County, 1,000 acres of grapevines during the winter.

Napa Valley had sixty-three wine cellars, and wine grapes were selling there for $30 a ton. The valley's wine yield this season was estimated at 2,150,000 gallons.

The Sherman ranch of 480 acres near Marysville, Yuba County, was unsalable at $5 an acre before hydraulic mining was enjoined. This month it was sold for $15 an acre.

J. P. Whitney, Rocklin, Placer County, rancher, imported from England a carload of Derbyshires, largest and strongest horses in the world. All were two-year-olds, and the stallions weighed 2,500 pounds.

One of the most prolific seasons of horse racing that the turfites of California had ever enjoyed terminated October 27.

The Siskiyou County Fair opened at Yreka October 3, the Los Angeles County Fair at Los Angeles City October 8, the Santa Barbara County Fair at Santa Barbara City and the Lake County Fair at Lakeport October 12, and the Monterey County Fair at Salinas October 20. Race meets began at Gilroy, Santa Clara County, October 8, at Santa Cruz City October 18, and at San Francisco October 20.

There was an exodus of Chinamen during the month. More than 2,000 left California on steamships China-bound. Most of them had round-trip tickets, so were expected to return after celebrating the Chinese New Year in January.

A cable 22,000 feet long, 4 inches in circumference and weighing 130 tons, made in San Francisco for the McAllister street railway, was hauled up market street October 26 by a team of twenty-four horses.

Eastern investors bought the Belmont quartz mine in Placer County, paying $65,000 for the property.

With another dividend payment this month, the Sierra Buttes Mine in Sierra County brought its total to $1,400,300.

During October the United States Mint at San Francisco coined 128,000 twenty-dollar gold pieces and 400,000 silver dollars.

A licensed faro bank in Sacramento City began paying off losses in silver, much to the discomfiture of winners.

A Yuba County judge granted, on complaint of a Butte Creek farmer, a perpetual injunction against the Spring Valley Hydraulic Mining Company at Cherokee, Butte County, operating the state's largest hydraulic mine.

October 16 the Sierra Valley stage was again robbed, evidently by the same old highwayman, near the same old place, about twelve miles from Truckee, Nevada County. The express box, containing $300, was taken and the three passengers were relieved of $20. The robber, subsequently caught in Reno, Nevada State, was tried, convicted and sent to the penitentiary for twenty years.

Blasting operations along the Sacramento River north of Redding, Shasta County, made in building the railroad to Oregon State by the C. & O. Railway, were causing salmon to quit their run up that stream.

San Francisco's streets were being illuminated by 5,500 gas lights, at a cost of 12½ cents a light per night.

Fire at Susanville, Lassen County, October 1 destroyed the grandstand and stables at the fair grounds. The Capital City Brewery at Sacramento burned October 7 with a $20,000 loss. Redding, Shasta County, had a $30,000 conflagration October 18.

San Pedro, Los Angeles County, was partially burned October 8, and Henry Meyers was cremated. A disastrous blaze October 16 at Grass Valley, Nevada County, swept "Battle Row," causing a $20,000 loss.

Horace Adams, who came to California from New Hampshire in 1850 and was prominent in the state's business and political circles, died of yellow fever October 3 at Mazatlan, Mexico, where he had gone on a business trip.

Elizabeth, wife of C. P. Huntington, one of the Central Pacific Railway builders, died October 5 at New York City. She was one of the Pioneer Women who came to California in 1849 and for many years resided in Sacramento City.

Dr. J. F. Montgomery, who came to California in 1850, died at Sacramento City October 8 at the age of 70.

Alex. Forbes, one of Marin County's largest land owners, died October 26 at San Rafael. He came to California in 1850.

James McClatchy, one of the founders of the "Sacramento Bee" in 1857 and the father of C. K., nationally known editor, and V. S. McClatchy, died at Paraiso Springs, Monterey County, October 26. He came to California via Mexico with the father of the compiler [of The Grizzly Bear's "Fifty Years Ago" notes, Thomas R. Jones,] in 1849.

William White, aged 16, was killed while horseback riding near Hollister, San Benito County, October 17. October 1 his father passed away, leaving a widow and eight children.

Hiram W. Doty, mining near Yreka, Siskiyou County, October 3 sat under an 800-pound boulder that fell and broke his neck.

Huram Miller, who killed Dr. Glenn, was tried and found guilty by a Colusa County jury, and sentenced to prison for life.

A Southern Pacific freight train went through a bridge over the Santa Ana River near Colton, San Bernardino County, October 31 and dropped eighteen cars fifteen feet. Two tramps were killed.

A gang of tramps found side tracked at Lancaster, Los Angeles County, a carload of wine, and were drunk on champagne for several days. A special train was run from Los Angeles City with a posse of officers to suppress them.

A Chinaman being called to the witness chair in a Nevada City, Nevada County, court was asked by the judge what kind of an oath would be the most binding on him to tell the truth. He answered: "Me no care. You clack him saucer, you kill him rooster, you blow out him match, you smell him book—allee same me."

J. P. Stanley of Hopland, Mendocino County, found about fifty petrified pumpkins in a ravine near there. They had been washed from a farmer's garden by a freshet and lodged in the ravine that flowed water impregnated with calcareous matter.

Thomas P. Turpen, a well-to-do farmer near Igo, Shasta County, had two noses, one roman and the other pug. The only trouble he had from them was when he caught a cold; that necessitated his blowing four nostrils. His good looks were marred. He came to California from Ohio in 1850.

Abel Jenkins of San Rafael, Marin County, went quail hunting October 5. He shot at a flock and saw one drop in a clump of bushes. This he entered and saw a man stooping, apparently in an effort to pick up the bird, and yelled at him. Getting no response, he went up to him, and discovered a clothed skeleton hanging by a rope from the limb of a tree. The dead man had committed suicide.

It took three Italian fishermen over two hours of tugging to haul in their seine October 19 near Angel Island, in San Francisco Bay. They had caught a big fish, ten feet long and four feet wide, with a mouth twelve inches across. It was called an elephant fish, and was the first to be caught in California waters. It is common in the Mediterranean Sea. This one must have come around Cape Horn or the Cape of Good Hope to get to San Francisco.

Frank Cooper, a lad living in Tehama, Tehama County, had trained two captured sturgeons to pull a boat eighteen feet long up and down the river. He fastened cords to their tails and to the boat for them to pull by. To their heads he attached stout twine, used as reins to guide them. He gave three of his schoolmates rides in the boat every afternoon. The sturgeon steeds were kept in a floating cage made of slats anchored near the river bank.

Homeless Children

A WORTHWHILE NON-SECTARIAN ENDEAVOR
SPONSORED AND SUPPORTED BY
THE ORDERS OF
NATIVE SONS AND NATIVE DAUGHTERS
OF THE GOLDEN WEST

OCTOBER 8 WILL BE CHILDREN'S Day, the time set apart by the Native Sons and Native Daughters of the Golden West and the founder, Fairfax H. Wheelan, for remembering the homeless children. Now that Admission Day in California has been fittingly observed, it is time to think of the Homeless Children and their care and training, in order that they may, in turn, remember their whole duty to California.

There are children needing homes, there are over one thousand families wanting and needing children, and there are trained workers willing, with the help of the members of the Orders, to get the two together. But it cannot be done creditably without funds!

It is not surprising that many Parlors were not able to help as generously as usual during the past three years. Every charity has felt the effects of hard times. Even now, when hope and expectancy and encouragement are in the air, one cannot look for entirely adequate returns from a still-bewildered public.

The real burden of the Homeless Children work rests upon each individual. If every worker will do his utmost to help, even if results are less favorable than he anticipated, and not depend upon a few hard-working, conscientious members to carry the load, the children's work will continue satisfactorily. If the present needs of the work which the Orders have been proud of for twenty-three years could be broadcast over the radio every night of every week, the efficacy of repetition would no doubt be effective, and if 4,400 families could also broadcast the happiness which has come to each home's trinity of occupants,—father, mother and child—there would be such a chorus of gratitude that every Native Son and Native Daughter would say: "I'll do my FULL part this year! Our charity MUST be supported!"

A word of appreciation must here be recorded for all of the Native Daughter Parlors that have met the expense of the milk supply for their adopted children promptly and regularly. Orinda 56, Gabriel 139, Dolores 169, Twin Peaks 185, Supervisor and Deputy Grand Presidents of San Francisco County, Piedmont 87, Aloha 106, Ursula 1, Manzanita 29, Amapola 80, Copa de Ora 105, Reina del Mar 126, El Carmelo 181, Morada 199, Grand Parlor Home Committee, Presidents Assembly, Supervisor and Deputy Grand Presidents of San Mateo County, La Junta 203, Phoebe A. Hearst 214, El Tejon 239, Verdugo 240, and Mr. and Mrs. Clarence M. Hunt have all paid in full for the six weeks' care of a baby. Presidio 148, Portola 172, Castro 178 (twins), La Junta 203 and Phoebe A. Hearst 214 have adopted a second baby. Treasurer Willa Wilson of Phoebe A. Hearst Parlor writes: "It seems to me that having the baby's picture and working for his milk has given our members more interest in the work of the Homeless Children."

TRY IT

(ESTHER CRONE.)

If for something you itch
And wish you was rich,
And could have things
Your neighbors to match,
Just put on a smile
And try humping awhile—
You will win if
You get out and scratch!

Enormous Debt—California, with a property assessed valuation of approximately $6,000,000,000, is weighted with a total bonded indebtedness of $1,009,514,327. The bond-debt of the cities alone is $449,560,928.

BITS OF HISTORY

"MARK OUR LANDMARKS"

Chester F. Gannon
(GRAND HISTORIAN N.S.G.W.)

"MARK OUR LANDMARKS"

FEW PRESENT-DAY CALIFORNIANS ever heard of Henry H. Byrne, District Attorney of the City and County of San Francisco for terms from 1851 to 1854 and 1868 to 1871. No more ardent advocate of justice, no more talented lawyer ever practiced anywhere than this now almost unknown and forgotten man. It is said that only four men in pioneer days ever had more deference, respect and heartfelt sorrow shown at their graves than Byrne. Those exceptions were James King of William, David C. Broderick, General E. D. Baker and Thomas Starr King.

He was known as the most popular man who ever lived in pioneer California. Unquestionably he was much more popular than Baker, whose brilliancy seemed to awe the general public and kept him from having the common touch. Byrne possessed brilliancy and the common touch. Therefore his popularity was greatly enhanced. Many old reviewers believed that only two men ever excelled him in the flow of oratory—Edward D. Baker and Thomas Fitch.

The trial of Mrs. Fair, charged with the murder of the prominent lawyer, A. P. Crittendon, consumed a month in presentment of evidence. At this trial, one of the best jury addresses ever made by an American prosecutor was delivered by Henry H. Byrne. In these days of loose jury duty and indifference to law and order; in these days when criminals are clothed with a halo of leniency, and righteousness is driven from the temple of justice, it is refreshing to look back upon this fearless prosecutor and hear him as he stood before that jury and, in part, said,

"The juror's oath is not a by-play. It is held most solemn by all Christian communities where the jury system prevails. It is that chain which binds the integrity of man to the throne of eternal justice. And when that chain is broken, conscience swings from its moorings, and society is again in a condition to resolve itself back into the original chaos out of which it was carved."

This admonition to juries is as trite today, and more necessary, than it was in that long-forgotten courtroom scene. It should be read and reread by every potential juror and every American citizen who believes in the domination of justice over criminality.

★ ★ ★

"Walk in, gentlemen! Walk in! And take a Thousand Drinks!" This hospitable greeting by General Green, a Senator from Sacramento, who had rented a room adjoining the Senate Chamber, earned for the first California Legislature in the year 1850 at San Jose, the reputation of being the "Legislature of a Thousand Drinks." The generous Senator little thought when he engaged in convivial drinking with his legislative friends that he would put such a wet stamp upon that Legislature and becloud its sober members with the reputation of being inebriates.

The first Legislature of the State of California convened at San Jose, December 16, 1849. On December 20, four days later, Peter H. Burnett was inaugurated first Governor of California. John C. Fremont and William M. Gwin were elected United States Senators.

How ironic! Fremont, now little honored by the Native Sons for a military breach committed in 1847, was held in high esteem by the Pioneers, whose opinions were not prompted by prejudice or misunderstanding and who could view the man close up rather than in retrospective.

★ ★ ★

Some of the great orators of pioneer days were Matthew P. Deady, George Gordon, Matthew Hall McAllister, Joseph W. Winans, Edward J. C. Kewen, Eugene Casserly, Hugh Campbell Murray, Henry M. Gray, Tod Robinson, Joseph R. McConnell, Nathaniel Bennett, Edmund Randolph, Hugh P. Gallagher, Henry Huntly Haight, Stephen J. Field, James A. McDougall, Tom Fitch, Edward D. Baker and Henry H. Byrne. Nearly all of the above men of brilliant minds are buried in San Francisco. Their graves, as well as their living worth, are unknown to the present Californian.

★ ★ ★

The following address of J. B. Crockett at the Democratic State Convention at San Francisco in June of 1867 nominated Henry Huntly Haight, a lawyer, later elected in September of 1869 over his Republican opponent, Geo. C. Gorham:

"I rise to perform an agreeable duty in presenting for the high office of Governor of the State of California a gentleman whom I have known from his boyhood. I have known him twenty years; and I can say, truthfully say, that I have never known a truer, better, more upright man than he whose name I will present to the convention; a man distinguished for his integrity and perfect uprightness of character, in all the walks of life; a man against whom not a word of reproach has been or is likely to be uttered; a man in whose keeping the honor and welfare of the State will be perfectly safe; a man who will be a party to no scheme, who will not yield to any corrupt influences, and who will administer the government of the State with ability, in the spirit of the constitution and the laws; and who will do honor to the office and to the party which elects him. And I do now nominate for the office of Governor of California, Henry H. Haight."

This nomination is not presented for its superior forensic strength, but rather to recall the incident of nomination, the names of the nominator and the nominee as men who did their part when California was young. There is little difference in that speech than in dozens of others made before or since; it simply marks the enthusiasm of one man for the character and ability of his friend.

★ ★ ★

An interesting event occurred at Sacramento on September 8, 1933, when Howard Driggs, chairman of the Oregon Trail Marker Association, visited the Capital City and, on Second Street between J and K at the western terminal of the Pony Express, placed a bronze marker depicting an express rider galloping at full speed. The occasion was almost glorified by the presence of William Campbell of Stockton. At the age of 92 years, he is the only known surviving Pony Express rider. He spoke intelligently and well of his experiences in riding his 100 mile lap in Wyoming. Strangely, it was not the Indians who gave him his severest test, but the cruel elements which swept with unabated fury against man and beast and obliterated the trail and chilled the stoutest heart. Joseph R. Knowland, Past Grand President N.S.G.W., attended and spoke.

Driggs is an exceptional student of the Oregon Trail history and gave a splendid address. He is an English teacher at New York University and engages in the marking work for no remuneration but to follow his love for years—marking that grand old trail and its subsidiary branches.

★ ★ ★

The Californian who hasn't read Dana's "Two Years Before The Mast" fails to comprehend the romance and color of early California life. If one has read it, it bears reading and re-reading. This autobiography, written in fascinating style, gives a beautiful picture of California, such as no other book has ever recorded of that romantic period from 1836 to the discovery of gold. Your Historian also recommends "Troupers of the Gold Coast" by Rourke. This is an interesting story of Edwin Booth, Lola Montez, Lotta Crabtree and other histrionic lights of that era.

ADMISSION DAY

MEMBERS OF THE ORDERS OF Native Sons and Native Daughters of the Golden West by the thousands and from every section of the state invaded Santa Rosa, Sonoma County, being attracted by the three-day Admission Day festival arranged by Santa Rosa Parlor No. 28 N.S.G.W. in observance of the eighty-third anniversary of California's admission to statehood. It was a splendid celebration, and if anyone failed to have a good time, the fault was his or her own, for opportunities aplenty, to satisfy the desire and the inclination of any and every one, were abundant and available to all.

The main event of the celebration was the most excellent Admission Day, September 9, parade in which the Native hordes, colorfully uniformed and accompanied by their bands, drum corps and drill teams, glorified their heritage, California. The makeup of the parade was given in detail in The Grizzly Bear for September. It was directed by Gam Hurst and Mrs. Anna Thuesen, Grand Marshals, respectively, of the Native Sons and Native Daughters. Heading the parade were Mrs. Irma Laird, Grand President N.D.G.W., and Justice Emmet Seawell, Grand President N.S.G.W. and a charter member of Santa Rosa Parlor.

Some very attractive floats were in line, too. Those from San Francisco and Alameda County were particularly elaborate works of decorative art. That from San Francisco was a Viking galley, done entirely in greenery and flowers and featuring the N.R.A. blue eagle emblem. That of Alameda County, also of gorgeous flowers, featured the United States of America and the California State (Bear) Flags. Among the many other floats were the Great Seal of State, from Saint Helena; the historic Vallejo Adobe, from Petaluma; the Valley of the Moon, featuring Mission San Francisco de Solano, from Sonoma; the mining days of '49, from Santa Rosa; the Gravenstein apple tree, from Sebastopol; the replica of a stone house built in 1835, from Contra Costa County; the "baby" N.D.G.W. Parlor, from Sacramento; the golden bear, from Napa.

Novel entries in the parade were the keg drum corps of Hydraulic No. 56 (Nevada City) and Quartz No. 58 (Grass Valley) Parlors N.S.G.W., and the clown band of Eden No. 113 (Hayward) Parlor N.S.G.W. The former beat time on nail kegs, and the latter created a lot of merriment both during and following the march. The "walking maypole" of Marinita No. 198 (San Rafael) Parlor N.D.G.W. was new and very attractive, every color of the rainbow being represented. The Natives of San Francisco and Alameda County are deserving of special commendation for their great contributions, in numbers and outstanding features, to the success of the parade. They never fail!

Prize-winning entries of the parade, selected by Colonel E. K. Johnstone and Lieutenant H. E. Jacob, the judges, were announced late in the afternoon from the Sonoma County Court House steps by Chas. A. Koenig, Grand First Vice-president N.S.G.W. Silver cups went to:

Best float—Calistoga Parlor No. 86 N.S.G.W. and Calistoga Parlor No. 145 N.D.G.W., stagecoach, drawn by six white horses.

Best Native Son drum corps without field music—Oakland Parlor No. 50, first; Piedmont Parlor No. 120 (Oakland), second; San Jose Parlor No. 22, third.

Best Native Son drum corps with field music—Napa Parlor No. 62.

Best appearing Native Son marching unit—Twin Peaks Parlor No. 214 (San Francisco).

Best Native Daughter drill team—Dolores Parlor No. 169 (San Francisco), first; Presidio Parlor No. 148 (San Francisco), second; Gabrielle Parlor No. 139 (San Francisco), third.

Best Native Daughter drum corps—Tamelpa Parlor No. 231 (Mill Valley).

Best appearing Native Daughter marching unit—Marinita Parlor No. 198 (San Rafael).

Largest competing unit from greatest distance—Santa Monica Bay Parlor No. 267 N.S.G.W. (Santa Monica) drum corps.

Admission Day evening, under the auspices of the San Francisco N.S.G.W. Extension of the Order Committee, a program, arranged by Grand Trustee Charles H. Spengemann, was presented. Chairman Hubert J. Caveney of the committee presided, and introduced the speakers: Chas. A. Koenig, Grand First Vice-president N.S.G.W., who delivered a welcome message; Mrs. Irma Laird, Grand President N.D.G.W., and Justice Emmet Seawell, Grand President N.S.G.W. Vocal selections were rendered by Miss Maria Vogel, her closing selection being "I Love You, California."

Baseball contests attracted large crowds. September 9, teams from University Parlor No. 272 N.S.G.W. (Los Angeles) and Santa Rosa Parlor No. 28 N.S.G.W. contested, the latter winning with a score of 9 to 1. September 10, the hometown (Santa Rosa) boys lost to the team from Castro Parlor No. 232 N.S.G.W. (San Francisco), the score being 6 to 2.

All in all, it was a great celebration of a holiday—Admission Day—which should be respected and observed by every loyal resident of California, regardless of birthplace, for in the history of this glorious Golden State September 9, Admission Day, has a significance equivalent to that of July 4, Independence Day, in the history of the United States of America.—C.M.H.

Native Sons of the Golden West

"EDITOR GRIZZLY BEAR: I FEEL THAT it is proper to say a word to the members of our Order with respect to the celebration of last Admission Day, held at Santa Rosa, under the leadership of the Native Sons and Native Daughters of the Golden West.

"It has won for both Orders the praise of the entire state. The celebration was held at an opportune time, and it is hailed as a civic triumph. It was the longest line of men and women and the finest display of the unconquerable spirit of Americanism that will be seen in marching form in California during the year 1933. The line was perfect, from the first to the last division. It was inspirational. The example of what our Order has done in re-establishing faith in our people is of inestimable value, not only to the state, but also to the nation. The State of California is proud of its Sons and Daughters, who exemplified the kind of courage which gave to the Union California and to the world the United States of America. From all parts of the state comes the word that the Native Sons and Native Daughters have done their full part by demonstrating in a profound manner their faith in and loyalty to the principles upon which our government is founded.

"We have set a splendid example to all the citizens of the state at an opportune time. We have taken a long stride, and have responded nobly to the call of patriotic duty which is ringing throughout the nation. It was one of the most colorful and picturesque parades, bristling with patriotic sentiment, that was ever held in this state. Much of the credit must be given to the tireless work done by the Extension of the Order bodies of San Francisco and the East Bay districts. Weekly meetings were held, beginning months before the date of celebration. Men and women gave their time and labor unsparingly to the success of the celebration. The attendance upon these meetings grew in numbers at each successive meeting, until the spacious halls became too small to accommodate the increased attendance. The interest grew greater at each meeting, climaxing in the wonderful parade and celebration on September 9th.

"Santa Rosa Parlor and the citizens of the City of Roses devoted themselves unceasingly to the success of the day. Parlors from the far south and north and from the valleys and mountains all had a part in honoring the state in a fitting and stately manner. The Grizzly Bear Magazine, the Parlor bulletins, the local press of Santa Rosa and the metropolitan and interior press cheerfully gave publicity to our program. We are much indebted to the press of the state and to every Parlor of the state for the support which they gave to the celebration of California's natal day. Both the Order of the Native Sons and the Order of the Native Daughters have gained much prestige throughout the state. We can go forth in our work for increased membership with a much better heart and with greater hope for success than we could have gone about our work before our great display of patriotism and good cheer at Santa Rosa.

"Our first great purpose of the year has been accomplished. LET US NOW TURN TO THE GREATER WORK OF INCREASING OUR MEMBERSHIP! By devoting the same energy and enthusiasm to increasing our membership that was exerted in making the celebration a success, we will be richly rewarded by a surprising increase in our ranks. Every Parlor and every member of the Order should feel stimulated and encouraged by the results of the last two months and enter the serious campaign which is now before us with increased enthusiasm. It will require organization and effort to accomplish the results, but they can be accomplished by united effort and co-operation by the membership throughout the state.

"LET US NOW DEVOTE OURSELVES TO THE REMAINING TASK OF THE YEAR OF STRENGTHENING OUR ORDER, BOTH IN NUMBERS AND PRESTIGE. We occupy a splendid position in the favor of the people of our native state.

"EMMET SEAWELL,
"Grand President N.S.G.W.
"San Francisco, September 21, 1933."

INCREASED MEMBERSHIP, of substantial quality, is TODAY'S OUTSTANDING NEED of the Order of Native Sons. COMB THE FIELDS, urges the Grand President, who solicits NOW the co-operation of every Native Son. Bear in mind always, THERE IS NO SUBSTITUTE FOR MEMBERSHIP, and rally to the cause.

Foresight of Pioneers Extolled.

Marysville—September 17 was a red letter day here for the Native Sons and Daughters of the Golden West, the occasion being the dedication of Marysville's $150,000 Federal building and postoffice by the grand officers of the two bodies. Incidentally, the members of the Sacramento Valley Postmasters Association figured, that body being in session here in regular quarterly meeting. With a vast assemblage of Yuba and Sutter Counties residents, the postmasters and their wives witnessed the impressive proceedings—a flag ceremony by the Native Daughters and the placing of the usual plaque by the Native Sons.

The latter ceremony was participated in by Grand President Justice Emmet Seawell, Grand First Vice Chas. A. Koenig, Grand Second Vice Harmon D. Skillin and Grand Secretary John T. Regan. Prior to the ceremony, Grand President Seawell delivered an address extolling the foresight of the forty-eight members of California's First Constitutional Convention, held in Monterey in 1848. He pointed out that the constitution there framed sufficed excellently until 1879, when the Second Constitutional Convention was called. Justice Seawell was followed by Grand Second Vice Skillin, who interpreted the significance of the wording on the plaque used by the Native Sons in the dedication of public buildings: "This Building Dedicated to Truth, Liberty, Toleration, by the Native Sons of the Golden West. September 17, 1933."

During the flag ceremony, and following an address by Grand President Irma Laird of the Native Daughters, Past Grand Esther R. Sullivan impressively related the history of California's flags through the Spanish, Mexican and Bear Flag eras to the present day. This was followed by the dedication of the flag that will float over the new postoffice building by President Anna Sperbeck of Marysville No. 162, who was assisted by a score of that Parlor's members. In both ceremonies the Marysville municipal band ably assisted by playing appropriate airs.

During the session Jefferson D. Wilcoxon, now a Yuba City, Sutter County, resident, was introduced by the master of ceremonies, Peter J. Delay, as the only surviving charter member of Marysville No. 6, organized in 1879. C. F. Parker formally presented the keys of the postoffice building to Postmaster James M. Cremin, who accepted them on behalf of the Federal Government. He was followed by Acting Mayor Leo J. Smith, who accepted the structure on behalf of the people of Marysville. In her address, Grand President Irma Laird attested her faith in the Golden State, built by the Pioneer Fathers and Mothers in the face of almost insurmountable difficulties. The ceremony concluded with a benediction by Rev. Raymond M. Huston; Rev. Jesse R. Rudkin delivered the invocation.

The following Native Daughters, visiting Marysville for the occasion, were introduced at the joint luncheon of the Native Sons and Native Daughters: Past Grands Anna Mixon Armstrong, Dr. Louise Heilbron, Margaret Grote Hill and Alison Watt, and Grand President Laird. Others introduced were Supervising Deputy Celia Gomes and President Anna Sperbeck. Reminiscing members of the local Parlors recalled during the day the list of the city's postmasters through the years since 1852, the date of the founding of Marysville, beginning with Phil W. Keyser, who later became judge of the Superior Court of Yuba and Sutter Counties. The others were Wm. C. Daugherty, Barney Eilerman, J. Fred Eastman, Charles Hapgood, Emma Hapgood, Thomas Farrell, A. S. Smith, J. M. Cremin (first term), John P. Swift, Oscar L. Meek, Thomas Fogarty, Ed Lewis and J. M. Cremin (second term). A dozen places were enumerated as occupied during the years as leased postoffice premises. At the close of the program the new building was opened to the public for inspection.—P.J.D.

INCREASED MEMBERSHIP, of substantial quality, is TODAY'S OUTSTANDING NEED of the Order of Native Sons. COMB THE FIELDS, urges the Grand President, who solicits NOW the co-operation of every Native Son. Bear in mind always, THERE IS NO SUBSTITUTE FOR MEMBERSHIP, and rally to the cause.

State's History Not Provincial.

San Diego—San Diego No. 108 had a rousing good meeting September 6, when oldtimers night was featured. Members whose fathers were Pioneers answered the rollcall. President John P. Murphy, Henry U. Emery, Joseph Kelley and Peter Rask perfected the arrangements.

Deputy Grand President Albert V. Mayrhofer explained the program of marking the oldest commercial highway in the West, between Mission San Diego de Alcala and Ballast Point, Point Loma, and spoke on three historic Point Loma places which were formally marked September 9: where Cabrillo landed in 1542; the site of Fort Guijarros, built in 1800; the site of the old whaling station which was at its peak of activity in 1830. Several members of the Parlor participated in these marking ceremonies and in the evening attended the Admission Day dinner sponsored by the San Diego Historical Society. The main speaker was Dr. Owen C. Coy, director California State Historical Association, whose subject was "California's Admission as a State."

Dr. Coy stressed the importance of California's history, "in no way provincial, but touching the fringes of world history. To study the past, to study history, is to become interested in the problems of the present, is to help one to solve the problems of the present, is to make for better citizenship now. The history of each locality is different. San Diego's story, the story of Los Angeles and that of San Francisco, all are different. And the story of the mining towns in the mountains is altogether different from any of these. The Spanish nomenclature here in the south is one of our great assets and I think we do well to preserve it in all its aspects. The nomenclature of the mining towns also is most interesting and should be preserved." Dr. Coy traced the history of the rise of government in California from the ancient laws of the Indians, through California pueblo life to the first American attempts at self-government, and then the beginnings of the independent state which, September 9, 1850, was admitted as a free state.

Fiftieth Anniversary Observed.

Arcata—In recognition of Admission Day, Arcata No. 20 sponsored a public program at the Plaza September 9. The occasion also marked the Parlor's fiftieth institution anniversary. Honored guests were four surviving charter members of No. 20—James B. Hill, Albert Nelson, Howard Barter and David Wood—and F. E. Herrick, the sole remaining charter member of Humboldt No. 14 (Eureka), who was present at the institution of Arcata in 1883. Len Yocom was master of ceremonies, the Arcata Union high school band rendered selections and E. V. Jeffers favored with vocal solos.

John Lund of Ferndale No. 93 was the speaker of the day. He stressed the importance of California history, not only to Californians but to the entire United States, and paid a splendid tribute to the Pioneers who made the state's illustrious record. Referring to local fascinating history, he described the adventures of the Gregg party, who ate Christmas dinner in 1849 at a spring not far from the northeast corner of the Arcata Plaza. The first store building was erected by Major Murdock in 1850; a hall on the second floor provided a social center for the community. The first stone building was erected by A. Jacoby in 1850. In conclusion, Lund recounted the history of Arcata Parlor.

INCREASED MEMBERSHIP, of substantial quality, is TODAY'S OUTSTANDING NEED of the Order of Native Sons. COMB THE FIELDS, urges the Grand President, who solicits NOW the co-operation of every Native Son. Bear in mind always, THERE IS NO SUBSTITUTE FOR MEMBERSHIP, and rally to the cause.

Flags Presented Museum.

Oroville—In commemoration of the eighty-third anniversary of California's admission to statehood, Argonaut No. 8 September 9 presented United States of America and California State (Bear) Flags to the Butte County Pioneer Memorial Museum. Arrangements for the presentation were made by a committee composed of District Deputy C. R. Macdonald, W. K. Palmer, Earl Ward, Ed Shreve and Robert Strang.

Trustee Charles F. Belding made the presentation on the Parlor's behalf and in the course of his remarks said: "Perhaps no state accepted statehood with more joy than did California on that memorable 9th day of September, 1850, when C gress approved her application for admission. It meant to the people on this far-western shore that their property and lives would be protected by the parent government. Prior to that, great uncertainty existed as to the title to lands, and life itself was precarious." In accepting the flags for the museum association, President Marlton Parker thanked the donor, Argonaut Parlor, and concluded with: "This place is sacred indeed. God bless these flags, God bless this building, and God bless you."

INCREASED MEMBERSHIP, of substantial quality, is TODAY'S OUTSTANDING NEED of the Order of Native Sons. COMB THE FIELDS, urges the Grand President, who solicits NOW the co-operation of every Native Son. Bear in mind always, THERE IS NO SUBSTITUTE FOR MEMBERSHIP, and rally to the cause.

Grand Officer Visiting Southland.

San Francisco—Grand Second Vice-president Harmon D. Skillin will, during October, continue his official visits to Subordinate Parlors of the southland. The itinerary includes:

Glendale No. 264 (Glendale), 3rd.
Santa Monica Bay No. 267 (Santa Monica), 4th.
Santa Barbara No. 116 (Santa Barbara), 5th.
Sepulveda No. 263 (San Pedro), 6th.
Hollywood No. 196 (Los Angeles), 9th.
University No. 272 (Los Angeles) and Compton No. 273 (Compton), 10th, jointly at Compton.
San Diego No. 108 (San Diego), 11th.
Los Angeles No. 45 (Los Angeles), 12th.
Bakersfield No. 42 (Bakersfield), 13th.

Board Grand Officers Meets.

Santa Rosa—The Board of Grand Officers met September 10, with Grand President Justice Emmet Seawell presiding. Others in attendance were Junior Past Grand Seth Millington, Grand First Vice Chas. A. Koenig, Grand Second Vice Harmon D. Skillin, Grand Third Vice J. Hartley Russell, Grand Secretary John T. Regan, Grand Trustees Eldred L. Meyer, Charles H. Spengemann, Thomas M. Foley, Jesse H. Miller, John M. Burnett and Edward T. Schnarr.

Letters of appreciation for sympathies extended were received from the widows of Past Grands Daniel A. Ryan and William J. Hayes.

Approval was given action taken by the District Grand Lodge of Bnai Brith in requesting "President Franklin D. Roosevelt to do all in his power to voice the disapproval of the American people to the unwarranted attacks of the Nazi government upon the Jewish people in Germany."

Grand Trustee Foley brought up the matter of insurance for visiting grand officers and district deputies, and on motion a committee composed of Grand Trustees Miller, Burnett and Foley, and Junior Past Grand Millington was appointed to investigate and report.

J. M. Waterman (Observatory No. 177) advised that a member of that Parlor contemplates preparing a map of California featuring the locations of historical spots marked by the Order, and requested assistance in fixing the locations. A motion prevailed that every assistance be given.

Letters pertaining to certain affairs affecting San Miguel No. 150, Concord No. 245 and University No. 272 (Los Angeles) were referred to visiting grand officers in whose districts the Parlors are located.

At the urge of William Borba (Sebastopol No. 143), the Grand Secretary was directed to communicate with the Subordinate Parlors and request them to furnish names of speakers who would, when called on, represent the Order before service clubs, etc. The idea is to have a speakers bureau.

(Continued on Page 18)

INCREASED MEMBERSHIP, of substantial quality, is TODAY'S OUTSTANDING NEED of the Order of Native Sons. COMB THE FIELDS, urges the Grand President, who solicits NOW the co-operation of every Native Son. Bear in mind always, THERE IS NO SUBSTITUTE FOR MEMBERSHIP, and rally to the cause.

Know your home-state, California! Learn of its past history and of its present-day development by reading regularly The Grizzly Bear. $1.50 for one year (12 issues). Subscribe now.

THE GRIZZLY BEAR
IS REGULARLY ON SALE:
SAN FRANCISCO:
N.S.G.W. Bldg., 414 Mason St., Room 302.
OAKLAND:
Fred M. DeWitt, 620 14th St.
LOS ANGELES:
315 Wilcox Bldg., Second and Spring.

Native Daughters of the Golden West

"TO THE OFFICERS AND MEMBERS of Subordinate Parlors Native Daughters of the Golden West—Dear Sisters: It was four hundred forty-one years ago this month that Columbus and his men sailed out in their frail ships from the eastward and set foot upon the land of the Western Hemisphere. Few events in history have been freighted with greater significance. Forces were set in motion by Almighty God destined to change and to give new direction to man's conception of his world, and to give new direction to his ambitions.

"Mighty though the deeds of Columbus were, back of them was yet a mightier force; and that was his Faith. The Faith to try, the Faith to carry on through storm and calm over an uncharted sea;—a quality that has been instilled and refined within the brave heart and the inspired soul of a man. This Faith, revealed in deed, rises far above the mighty thing it brought to pass.

"The Native Daughters of the Golden West have undertaken an ambitious program. I am of the opinion that our united effort, our combined energies should be directed toward the realization of the dreams and ideals of an earnest, sincere and patriotic womanhood, the perfect instrumentality of service.

"We know our strength in numbers and wealth. We know our proud record of humanitarian endeavor and patriotic practice. We know of the unselfish devotion demanded for successful administration. We appreciate the competitive forces, factors and distractions of modern life.

"We know that we must sell the Native Daughters of the Golden West to those whose names already appear upon the rolls of our membership, before we can carry on to greater heights of achievement.

"Sell the Order to Native Daughters! Astonishing statement—yes. And what does it mean?

"It means everlasting application on the part of all Grand Officers, Committeemen and Deputies; extraordinary effort on the part of each Subordinate President. It demands that those IN authority speak WITH authority to the ghosts of depression and pessimism that are abroad in the land, to the end that the Native Daughters of the Golden West may 'Know and Be Known.'

" 'The World stands out on either side,
No wider than the heart is wide.'

"Sincerely and fraternally in P.D.F.A.,
"IRMA W. LAIRD,
'Grand President N.D.G.W.
"Alturas, September 16, 1933."

Increased Membership Urged.

San Andreas—A most enjoyable gathering of Calaveras County members was held at Angels Camp September 1, when Ruby No. 46 (Murphys), Princess No. 84 (Angels Camp) and San Andreas No. 113 (San Andreas) met in joint session to welcome Grand President Irma Laird on her official visit. Accompanying her was Grand Secretary Sallie R. Thaler, and other grand officers in attendance were Grand Vice-president Gladys Noce, Supervising Deputy

GRAND PRESIDENT'S OFFICIAL ITINERARY.

Alturas—Grand President Irma W. Laird will, on the dates noted, officially visit the following Subordinate Parlors:

OCTOBER.

6th—Alturas No. 159, Alturas; Mount Lassen No. 215, Bieber; jointly at Alturas.

7th—Eschscholtzia No. 112, Etna; Mountain Dawn No. 120, Sawyers Bar; jointly at Etna.

9th—Eschol No. 16, Napa. Regular meeting.

10th—Argonaut No. 166, Oakland. Regular meeting.

11th—Linda Rosa No. 170, San Francisco. Regular meeting.

12th—Bonita No. 10, Redwood City. Regular meeting.

13th—Orinda No. 56, San Francisco. Regular meeting.

16th—James Lick No. 220, San Francisco. Adjourned meeting.

17th—La Rosa No. 191, Roseville. Regular meeting.

18th—Vallejo No. 195, Vallejo. Regular meeting.

19th—Bahia Vista No. 167, Oakland. Regular meeting.

20th—El Pescadero No. 82, Tracy. Regular meeting.

24th—Fairfax No. 225, Fairfax. Regular meeting.

25th—Brooklyn No. 157, Oakland. Regular meeting.

26th—Aleli No. 102, Salinas. Regular meeting.

27th—Junipero No. 141, Monterey. Regular meeting.

30th—San Francisco deputies district meeting.

31st—Las Lomas No. 72, San Francisco. Adjourned meeting.

NOVEMBER.

1st—Donner No. 193, Byron. Regular meeting.

2nd—Buena Vista No. 68, San Francisco. Regular meeting.

3rd—Fruitvale No. 177, Oakland. Regular meeting.

Emma Boarman Wright and Deputy Zaida Hertzig. Visitors from Joaquin, El Pescadero, Ursula and Amapola also attended. President Lilla Bisbee of Princess presided, and the ritual was exemplified in portions assigned to the three Parlors.

In an inspiring address, Grand President Laird pointed to the projects of the Order, including care of homeless children, veterans welfare, historical and landmarking activities and the Home, and she urged loyalty of members in attracting increased membership. Other grand officers and representatives of visiting delegations also spoke briefly. A banquet concluded the evening, more than sixty-five members being seated at tables decorated with autumn flowers.

Reminiscent of Old California.

Fullerton—Grace No. 242 members and their friends enjoyed an outdoor supper on the beautiful grounds of Mrs. Kate Hill's home in Placentia August 24. Cards were palyed later in the spacious rooms and refreshments were served. Reminiscent of old California was the spanish night fiesta August 31 at the beautiful Tuffree hacienda in Placentia. A fine program of Spanish music and dances was enjoyed. Mary Belle Chapman of Californiana Parlor added to the entertainment with two solos. Grace, acting as co-hostesses with Mr. and Mrs. John Tuffree, assisted by serving refreshments throughout the evening. A candy booth and fortune telling were financial benefits to No. 242.

September 7 the Parlor had a very interesting meeting. Supervising Deputy Marvel Thomas and Deputy Irene Eden were guests. Lena Wagner and her committee served coffee, cake and sandwiches. September 9 a number of members attended the Admission Day celebration at the Breakfast Club in Los Angeles. As its share of the program, Grace presented George "Bud" Forster in two vocal numbers.

Anniversary Observed.

Saint Helena—A long-to-be-remembered event in the annals of La Junta No. 203 was the celebration of the Parlor's twentieth institution anniversary. Among the guests were Past Grand May Boldemann who, as Grand President, instituted the Parlor, Supervising Deputy Wilna Mitchell, Deputy Lilius Kelley and ten members of Eschol. President Elise Metzner presided. A humorous skit was presented, and then came a fashion show, all the costumes being of twenty years or more back. Refreshments were served, and the enjoyable evening closed with the singing of "I Love You, California."

Two recent brides of La Junta—Mms. William L. Sanborn (nee Florence Waldeck) and Cecil Agivie (nee Gretchen Graff)—were honor guests of the Parlor September 5. Hearts was played, the prize going to Miss Martha Klubescheidt. Large decorated baskets, containing lovely and useful gifts, were presented the brides. Light refreshments were served.

Great Deed for Children Planned.

Oakland—Inspired by the message from Grand President Irma Laird in advocating some act of kindness in our community, Fruitvale No. 177, at the suggestion of Financial Secretary Chrissie Harrison, will adopt the cripple class of Mrs. Sheridan and Treasurer Nell Crowley of the Hawthorne school. A committee is now preparing gifts, and at a later date the Parlor will visit the school and be entertained by these little children.—L.K.

San Mateo Meet.

Daly City—The annual district meeting of the San Mateo County Parlors was held August 19. In honor of Supervising Deputy Rena Mathias and her daughter, Grand Outside Sentinel Alice Oldham, the gathering was designated Rena-Alice Parlor. Deputies Gladys Bennett, Isabel Lindquist, Alice Mattei, Hattie Kelly, Mana Theisen and Mary Junker, assisted by members from the county's six Parlors, exemplified the ritual in a most creditable manner and were highly complimented.

Among the many in attendance were Grand President Irma Laird, Grand Marshal Anna Thuesen, Grand Outside Sentinel Alice Oldham, Grand Organist Clara Gairaud, Past Grands Emma Foley, Margaret Hill, May Himes Noonan, Estelle Evans and Evelyn Carlson. Grand President Laird was presented with a silver gift, and a traveling bag was presented Supervising Deputy Mathias. Dainty refreshments were served. The expenses were met by contributions from the participating Parlors and the surplus was turned over to the Central Homeless Children Committee.

Benefit for Homeless Children.

Hollister—Copa de Oro No. 105 held a most entertaining meeting September 14, the first following the summer recess. A potluck dinner was served at 6:30, during which musical numbers were rendered by Mrs. Effa Hawkins and little Miss Marilyn Frost. The banquet and meeting halls were especially attractive with a profusion of bright autumn blossoms. Deputy Alberta McCormick installed the officers. The installing officers carried beautiful sprays of asters and ferns, while the officers-elect carried colorful french boquets. Deputy McCormick, Retiring President Rose Guilhamet and Past

PRIZE WINNING NATIVE DAUGHTER DRILL TEAM

San Francisco—The drill team of Dolores Parlor No. 169 in snappy uniforms of red and white won first honors in that classification in the Admission Day celebration at Santa Rosa. Captain Helen Lokken and her team were delighted to receive such a beautiful loving cup. This was the first public appearance of the team, and Dolores feels highly honored for having such a splendid group of young women. The members of the team are: Helen Lokken (captain), Alvina Burkhardt (lieutenant), Gladys Carroll, Gertrude Penaluna, Yvonne Evans, Gladys Lynch, Lenore Lynch, Rose Spaelti, Margaret Uhlmann, Mabel Hinton, Madeline Jacobsen, Louise Nau, Hazel Nelson, Alice Kane, Alfa Nelson, Pauline Laurel, Charlotte Lacoste. The sponsors of the team are Past Grand Evelyn I. Carlson, Ada Saunders and Emma O'Meara. James F. O'Rourke of Hesperian No. 137 N.S.G.W. is the drillmaster.—E.J.M.

Grand Bertha A. Briggs were presented with gifts and flowers. Guests were present from Santa Cruz, San Juan Bautista and San Luisita Parlors.

The homeless children committee announced the date of the annual benefit to be Thursday evening, October 19. Plans were formulated for participation in the tri-county district meeting September 23 at Salinas.

Faithful Secretary Honored.

Sacramento—La Bandera No. 110 had as special guests September 15 members of Fern No. 123 (Folsom) and that Parlor's deputy, Lucille Huntoon, affiliated with No. 110. Decorations for the banquetroom carried out a "century of progress" idea, and the lodgeroom was adorned with seasonal flowers. Among the many present were Past Grand Dr. Louise C. Heilbron, Supervising Deputy May F. Lucas, Deputy Martha Buckley and representatives of Califia, Sutter, Manzanita, Victory, Rio Rita, Liberty and Coloma Parlors. Mrs. Edna B. Briggs, general chairman, was assisted in making arrangements by Mms. Ada Appleton, Nellie Nordstrom, Jane Klumpp, Azeta Johnson, Frances Voss, Mae King and Margaret Lumpkins; Misses Phyllis Howard, Dorothy Howard, Frances Fisher and Marion Lund.

On this occasion also, Mrs. Clara Weldon was honored with a birthday surprise party. For thirty-five years she has faithfully served La Bandera as recording secretary.

Admission Day Program.

Oakland—The Ninth of September dance given August 26 by Aloha No. 106, Past President Martha Watson chairman, was a social and financial success. Whist and bridge was enjoyed by those who did not wish to dance. Honored guests were Grand President Irma Laird and Grand Secretary Sallie Thaler, and Grand Trustee Edward Schnarr and Grand Marshal Gam Hurst of the Native Sons. Plans are under way for another dance in the near-future.

Aloha was entertained September 5 with an Admission Day program, presented by the literary committee, as follows: Essay on California, Past President Caroline Schulze, chairman; vocal solo, "Queen of the West," Marie Cordery; California poem, Edith Hoover; harmonica and piano solo, Eda Steuer. The monthly whist was held September 22 at the home of Johnina Lindblad.

Open Meeting Draws Large Crowd.

Pittsburg—A joint meeting of the eastern Contra Costa County Parlors was held September 14. All Native Sons and Native Daughters and their friends had been invited, and there was a large attendance. Supervising Deputy Mary Ross made the opening remarks, and Mayor High H. Donovan extended a welcome. Orchestral and vocal selections were rendered, Past Grand Estelle M. Evans accompanying the singers.

Speakers included Mrs. Irma Laird, N.D. Grand President; Justice Emmet Seawell, N.S. Grand President; B. O. Wilson, superintendent county schools; Dr. Mariana Bertola, N.D. Past Grand; John T. Regan, N.S. Grand Secretary, and Edna Hill. Parlors active in arranging the open meeting were Stirling No. 146 (Pittsburg), Donner No. 193 (Byron), Las Juntas No. 221 (Martinez) and Antioch No. 223.

Grand President To Visit Home Parlor.

Alturas—Past Grand Catherine E. Gloster has been appointed chairman of the women's division of the N.R.A. for Modoc County. Pioneers here were visited Admission Day by members of Alturas No. 159, who carried to them gifts and greetings. Past Grand Gloster had an appreciative audience when, at the September 7 meeting, she recounted the trip taken by her sister, Miss Dorothy Gloster, and herself east through the Panama Canal and west via the Canadian Rockies.

The Parlor is making great plans for the official visit of Grand President Irma Laird, affiliated with No. 159, October 6. The local Masonic lodge has departed from the rule that none other than a Masonic organization may use its beautiful new temple, and as a tribute to Mrs. Laird the use of the structure for the occasion was extended the Native Daughters.

NEWSY N.D. PARAGRAPHS.

Placerville—Grand President Irma Laird paid an official visit to Marguerite No. 12 September 6. Present also were Grand Vice-president Gladys Noce, Supervising Deputy Emma B. Wright and members of Ursula, Amapola and El Dorado Parlors. President Ruth Baumhoff presided and two candidates were initiated. Grand President Laird briefly outlined the work she thought Subordinate Parlors should take up, and stressed increased numbers, urging each member to secure a candidate. Refreshments were served under the chairmanship of Lily Zeisz, and a delightful program was presented by the entertainment committee, Agnes Scheff chairman.

Grass Valley—Manzanita No. 29 commemorated the state's birthday with a program, a pageant and a banquet September 5. Miss Jean Rowe, wearing a robe of golden satin, represented California. President Ann Whiting recited a poem, "Pioneers," Past President Louise Wales spoke on "Admission Day," and anecdotes of the past were related by Past Grand Alison F. Watt. Participating in the pageant, representing three periods of California history, were Irene Whiting, Beatrice George, Hilda Sandow, Bernice Deward, Peggy Hoffman, Josephine Carveth, Ann Whiting, Olive Vincent, Lorraine Keast, Melita Hutchinson, Isabelle Hooper, Florence George, Caroline Hotchkiss, Anna Rowe, Vashti Schwartz, Muriel Rosewald, Vera Hansen, Hazel Jenkins, Vinita Jones, Sue Harris and Grace Eva.

San Jose—Mrs. Mary Frances Mitchell, affiliated with San Jose No. 81, died September 3 survived by a daughter. She was a former Grand Trustee and Grand Marshal, and was active in the past presidents association.

Lodi—A largely attended card party was held August 31 at the lovely country home of Mr. and Mrs. C. E. Keslar for the benefit of Bruella Troop, Boy Scouts of America. Mrs. Keslar is a member of Ivy No. 88. September 5 the Parlor enjoyed a program and refreshments arranged for by Mirza Hunt, Elfrieda Landback and Eunice Spenker. A public food sale was held September 16.

Marysville—Past President Bernice Sperbeck of Marysville No. 162, following a visit to the Century of Progress Exposition at Chicago, sent this message to her mother: "California State exhibit is outstanding in comparison with other

(Continued on Page 11)

Official Directory of Parlors of the N. D. G. W.

ALAMEDA COUNTY.

Angelita No. 32, Livermore—Meets 2nd and 4th Fridays, Foresters Hall; Mrs. Myrtle I. Johnson, Rec. Sec., P.O. box 253.

Piedmont No. 87, Oakland—Meets Thursdays, Corinthian Hall, Pacific Bldg.; Miss Helen Ring, Rec. Sec., 822 11th St.

Aloha No. 106, Oakland—Meets Tuesdays, 4016 Grove St.; Mrs. Lurine Martin, Rec. Sec., 2815 Wallace St., Berkeley.

Hayward No. 122, Hayward—Meets 1st and 3rd Tuesdays, Veterans Memorial Bldg., Main St.; Miss Ruth Gansberger, Rec. Sec., P. O. box 44, Mount Eden.

Berkeley No. 150, Berkeley—Meets 2nd Saturday afternoon, Berkeley City Women's Club, 2315 Durant; Mrs. Leha B. Baker, Rec. Sec., 915 Contra Costa Ave.

Bear Flag No. 151, Berkeley—Meets 2nd and 4th Wednesdays, Veterans Memorial Bldg., 1931 Center St.; Mrs. Maud Wagner, Rec. Sec., 317 Alcatraz Ave., Oakland.

Encinal No. 156, Alameda—Meets 2nd and 4th Wednesdays, Veterans Memorial Bldg., Central Ave. and Walnut St.; Mrs. Laura E. Fisher, Rec. Sec., 1413 Caroline St.

Brooklyn No. 157, East Oakland—Meets 2nd and 4th Wednesdays, Masonic Temple, 8th Ave. and E. 14th St.; Mrs. Ruth Cooney, Rec. Sec., 3907 14th Ave.

Argonaut No. 166, Oakland—Meets Tuesdays, Klinkner Hall, 59th and San Pablo; Mrs. Ada Spilman, Rec. Sec., 2905 Ellis St., Berkeley.

Bahia Vista No. 167, Oakland—Meets 1st and 3rd Thursdays, Wigwam Hall, Pacific Bldg.; Mrs. Minnie E. Raper, Rec. Sec., 3449 Helen St.

Fruitvale No. 177, Oakland—Meets Fridays, W.O.W. Hall; May E. Barthold, Rec. Sec., 3832 Santa Rita St.

Laura Loma No. 182, Niles—Meets 1st and 3rd Tuesdays, I.O.O.F. Hall; Mrs. Ethel Fournier, Rec. Sec., P. O. box 515.

El Cereso No. 207, San Leandro—Meets 2nd and 4th Tuesdays, Masonic Hall; Mrs. Mary Tuttle, Rec. Sec., P. O. box 56.

Pleasanton No. 237, Pleasanton—Meets 1st Tuesday, I.O.O.F. Hall; Mrs. Myrtle Lanini, Rec. Sec.

Betsy Ross No. 238, Centerville—Meets 1st and 3rd Fridays, Anderson Hall; Miss Constance Lucio, Rec. Sec., P. O. box 187.

AMADOR COUNTY.

Ursula No. 1, Jackson—Meets 2nd and 4th Tuesdays, N.S.G.W. Hall; Mrs. Emma Boarman-Wright, Rec. Sec., 114 Court St.

Chispa No. 40, Ione—Meets 2nd and 4th Fridays, N.S.G.W. Hall; Cynthia Phillips, Rec. Sec.

Amapola No. 80, Sutter Creek—Meets 2nd and 4th Thursdays, N.S.G.W. Bldg.; Mrs. Hazel M. Marre, Rec. Sec.

Forrest No. 86, Plymouth—Meets 2nd and 4th Tuesdays, I.O.O.F. Hall; Mrs. Marguerite Davis, Rec. Sec.

BUTTE COUNTY.

Annie K. Bidwell No. 168, Chico—Meets 2nd and 4th Thursdays, I.O.O.F. Hall; Mrs. Irene Henry, Rec. Sec., 3015 Woodland Ave.

Gold of Ophir No. 190, Oroville—Meets 1st and 3rd Wednesdays, Memorial Hall; Mrs. Ruth Brown, Rec. Sec., 1265 Leah Court.

CALAVERAS COUNTY.

Ruby No. 46, Murphys—Meets 4th Friday, N.S.G.W. Hall; Belle Segale, Rec. Sec.

Princess No. 84, Angels Camp—Meets 2nd and 4th Wednesdays, I.O.O.F. Hall; Mrs. Grace M. Mills, Rec. Sec., P.O. box 313.

San Andreas No. 113, San Andreas—Meets 1st Friday, Fraternal Hall; Miss Doris Treat, Rec. Sec.

COLUSA COUNTY.

Colus No. 194, Colusa—Meets 1st and 3rd Mondays, Eagles Hall; Miss Kate Busch, Rec. Sec., 850 Market St.

CONTRA COSTA COUNTY.

Stirling No. 146, Pittsburg—Meets 1st and 3rd Wednesdays, Veteran Memorial Hall; Mrs. Leslie Clement, Rec. Sec., 468 E. Santa Fe.

Richmond No. 147, Richmond—Meets 1st and 3rd Tuesdays, Richmond Club House, 1125 Nevin Ave.; Grace Curry, Rec. Sec., 932 Ohio Ave.

Donner No. 193, Byron—Meets 1st and 3rd Wednesdays, I.O.O.F. Hall; Mrs. Anna Pendry, Rec. Sec., P.O. box 442, Brentwood.

Las Juntas No. 221, Martinez—Meets 1st and 3rd Mondays, Pythian Castle; Mrs. Lois O. Viera, Rec. Sec., R.F.D. No. 1.

Antioch No. 223, Antioch—Meets 2nd and 4th Tuesdays, I.O.O.F. Hall; Mrs. Estelle Evans, Rec. Sec., 202 E. 5th St., Pittsburg.

Carquinez No. 234, Crockett—Meets 2nd and 4th Wednesdays, I.O.O.F. Hall; Mrs. Cecile Petee, Rec. Sec., 465 Edwards St.

EL DORADO COUNTY.

Marguerite No. 12, Placerville—Meets 1st and 3rd Wednesdays, Masonic Hall; Mrs. Nettie Leonardi, Rec. Sec., 25 Coloma St.

El Dorado No. 186, Georgetown—Meets 2nd and 4th Saturday afternoons, I.O.O.F. Hall; Mrs. Alta L. Douglas, Rec. Sec.

FRESNO COUNTY.

Fresno No. 187, Fresno—Meets 2nd and 4th Fridays, Pythian Castle, Cor. "R" and Merced Sts.; Mary Anbery, Rec. Sec., 1040 Delphia Ave.

GRAND OFFICERS.

Mrs. Anna M. Armstrong........Past Grand President
Woodland
Mrs. Irma Laird........Grand President
Alturas
Mrs. Gladys Noce........Grand Vice-president
Sutter Creek
Mrs. Sallie R. Thaler........Grand Secretary
555 Baker St., San Francisco
Mrs. Susie K. Christ........Grand Treasurer
555 Baker St., San Francisco
Mrs. Anna Thuesen........Grand Marshal
615 38th Ave., San Francisco
Mrs. Hazel B. Hansen........Grand Inside Sentinel
301 Griswold St., Glendale
Mrs. Alice M. Oldham........Grand Outside Sentinel
2218 26th Ave., San Francisco
Mrs. Clara Gairaud........Grand Organist
134 Locust St., San Jose

GRAND TRUSTEES.

Mrs. Orinda G. Giannini....2142 Filbert St., San Francisco
Mrs. Florence D. Boyle........Oroville
Mrs. Minna K. Horn........Etna
Mrs. Jane Vick........418 Bath St., Santa Barbara
Mrs. Alice M. Lane........191 15th Ave., San Francisco
Mrs. Ethel Begley........233 Prospect Ave., San Francisco
Mrs. Willow Borba........330 So. Main St., Sebastopol

GLENN COUNTY.

Berryessa No. 192, Willows—Meets 1st and 3rd Mondays, I.O.O.F. Hall; Mrs. Leonora Neate, Rec. Sec., 338 No. Lassen St.

HUMBOLDT COUNTY.

Occident No. 28, Eureka—Meets 1st and 3rd Wednesdays, N.S.G.W. Hall; Mrs. Eva L. MacDonald, Rec. Sec., 2309 "B" St.

Oneonta No. 71, Ferndale—Meets 2nd and 4th Fridays, I.O.O.F. Hall; Mrs. Myra Rumrill, Rec. Sec., P.O. box 142.

Reichling No. 97, Fortuna—Meets 1st and 3rd Tuesdays, Friendship Hall; Mrs. Grace Swett, Rec. Sec., P. O. box 328.

KERN COUNTY.

Miocene No. 228, Taft—Meets 1st and 3rd Wednesday afternoons, I.O.O.F. Hall; Mrs. Evalyn G. Towne, Rec. Sec., 801 Woodrow St.

El Tejon No. 239, Bakersfield—Meets 1st and 3rd Fridays, Eagles Hall, 1714 "G" St.; Mary B. Hampson, Rec. Sec., 908 Quincy St.

Desert Gold No. 250, Mojave—Meets 2nd and 4th Fridays, I.O.O.F. Hall; Jane Lucile Waters, Rec. Sec., Tehachapi.

LAKE COUNTY.

Clear Lake No. 185, Middletown—Meets 2nd and 4th Tuesdays, Herrick Hall; Mrs. Alma E. Snow, Rec. Sec.

LASSEN COUNTY.

Nataqua No. 152, Standish—Meets 1st and 3rd Wednesdays, Foresters Hall; Mrs. Mayda Elledge, Rec. Sec.

Mount Lassen No. 215, Bieber—Meets 2nd and 4th Thursdays, I.O.O.F. Hall; Mrs. Angie C. Kenyon, Rec. Sec.

Susanville No. 243, Susanville—Meets 3rd Thursday, I.O.O.F. Hall; Mildred Hardy, Rec. Sec., P.O. box 435.

LOS ANGELES COUNTY.

Los Angeles No. 124, Los Angeles—Meets 1st and 3rd Wednesdays, I.O.O.F. Hall, Washington and Oak Sts.; Mrs. Mary K. Corcoran, Rec. Sec., 322 No. Van Ness Ave.

Long Beach No. 154, Long Beach—Meets 1st and 3rd Thursdays, Home of Eleonor Johnson, 1920 Bermuda St.; Mrs. Bertha Hitt, Rec. Sec., 5355 Lime Ave.

Rudecinda No. 230, San Pedro—Meets 1st and 3rd Mondays, Womans Club, Gaffey and "N" Sts.; Letitia Sarciaux, Rec. Sec., 973 W. 10th St.

Verdugo No. 240, Glendale—Meets 2nd and 4th Tuesdays, Masonic Temple, 234 So. Brand Blvd.; Miss Etta Fulkerth, Rec. Sec., 526 No. Orange St.

Santa Monica Bay No. 245, Santa Monica—Meets 2nd and 4th Wednesdays, Odd Fellows Hall, 1431 Third St.; Mrs. Rosalie Hyde, Rec. Sec., 21 Park Ave., Venice.

Californiana No. 247, Los Angeles—Meets 2nd and 4th Tuesday afternoons, Hollywood Studio Club, 1215 Lodi Place; Miss Betty Hale, Rec. Sec., 6619 Franklin Ave.

MADERA COUNTY.

Madera No. 244, Madera—Meets 2nd and 4th Thursdays, Masonic Annex; Mrs. Margaret O. Boyle, Rec. Sec., 111 No. "B" St.

MARIN COUNTY.

Sea Point No. 196, Sausalito—Meets 2nd and 4th Mondays, Perry Hall, 50 Caledonia St.; Mrs. Mary B. Smith, Rec. Sec., 47½ Glen Drive.

Marinita No. 198, San Rafael—Meets 2nd and 4th Mondays, 316 "B" St.; Lillian Whitmore, Rec. Sec., 837 5th St.

Fairfax No. 225, Fairfax—Meets 2nd and 4th Tuesdays, Community Hall; Mrs. Marguerite Geary, Rec. Sec.

Tamelpa No. 231, Mill Valley—Meets 1st and 2nd Tuesdays, I.O.O.F. Hall; Mrs. Delphine M. Todt, Rec. Sec., 500 Irwin St., San Rafael.

MARIPOSA COUNTY.

Mariposa No. 63, Mariposa—Meets 1st and 3rd Fridays, I.O.O.F. Hall; Elizabeth E. Johnson, Rec. Sec.

MENDOCINO COUNTY.

Fort Bragg No. 210, Fort Bragg—Meets 1st Thursday, I.O.O.F. Hall; Mrs. Ruth W. Fuller, Rec. Sec.

MERCED COUNTY.

Veritas No. 75, Merced—Meets 1st and 3rd Tuesdays, I.O.O.F. Hall; Miss Flora Fernandes, Rec. Sec., 28 19th St.

MODOC COUNTY.

Alturas No. 159, Alturas—Meets 1st Thursday, Alturas Civic Club; Mrs. Irma W. Laird, Rec. Sec.

MONTEREY COUNTY.

Aleli No. 102, Salinas—Meets 2nd and 4th Thursdays, Pythian Hall; Miss Rose Rhyner, Rec. Sec., 420 Soledad St.

Junipero No. 141, Monterey—Meets 2nd and 4th Fridays, K. of P. Hall, Main St.; Miss Matilda M. Bergschicker, Rec. Sec., 498 Van Buren St.

NAPA COUNTY.

Eshcol No. 16, Napa—Meets 2nd and 4th Mondays, N.S.G.W. Hall; Mrs. Ella Ingram, Rec. Sec., 2140 Seminary St.

Calistoga No. 145, Calistoga—Meets 2nd and 4th Mondays, I.O.O.F. Hall; Sadie P. Brooks, Rec. Sec.

La Junta No. 203, Saint Helena—Meets 1st and 3rd Tuesdays, N.S.G.W. Hall; Mrs. Marie Signorelli, Rec. Sec., 1341 Madrona Ave.

ATTENTION, SECRETARIES!

THIS DIRECTORY IS PUBLISHED BY AUTHORITY OF THE GRAND PARLOR N.D.G.W., AND ALL NOTICES OF CHANGES MUST BE RECEIVED BY THE GRAND SECRETARY (NOT THE MAGAZINE) ON OR BEFORE THE 20TH OF EACH MONTH TO INSURE CORRECTION IN NEXT PUBLICATION OF DIRECTORY.

NEVADA COUNTY.

Laurel No. 6, Nevada City—Meets 1st and 3rd Wednesdays, I.O.O.F. Hall; Mrs. Nellie E. Clark, Rec. Sec., 412 Pine St.

Manzanita No. 29, Grass Valley—Meets 1st and 3rd Tuesdays, Auditorium; Mrs. Loraine Keast, Rec. Sec., 123 Race St.

Columbia No. 70, French Corral—Meets Fridays, Farrelley Hall; Mrs. Kate Farrelley-Sullivan, Rec. Sec.

Snow Peak No. 176, Truckee—Meets 1st Monday, I.O.O.F. Hall; Mrs. Henrietta M. Eaton, Rec. Sec., P. O. box 116.

ORANGE COUNTY.

Santa Ana No. 235, Santa Ana—Meets 2nd and 4th Mondays, K.C. Hall, 4th and French Sts.; Mrs. Matilda S. Lemon, Rec. Sec., 1628 W. 8th St.

Grace No. 242, Fullerton—Meets 1st and 3rd Thursdays, I.O.O.F. Hall, 116½ E. Commonwealth; Mrs. Mary R. Rothaermel, Rec. Sec., Acacia St. & Commonwealth.

PLACER COUNTY.

Placer No. 138, Lincoln—Meets 2nd Wednesday, I.O.O.F. Hall; Miss Carrie Parlin, Rec. Sec.

La Rosa No. 191, Roseville—Meets 1st and 3rd Tuesdays, Moose Hall; Mrs. Gertrude Gerza, Rec. Sec., 527 Oak St.

Auburn No. 233, Auburn—Meets 2nd and 4th Fridays, Foresters Hall; Mrs. Elsie Patrick, Rec. Sec.

PLUMAS COUNTY.

Plumas Pioneer No. 219, Quincy—Meets 1st and 3rd Mondays, I.O.O.F. Hall; Minnie E. Johnson, Rec. Sec., P. O. box 248.

SACRAMENTO COUNTY.

Califia No. 22, Sacramento—Meets 2nd and 4th Tuesdays, N.S.G.W. Hall; Miss Lulu Gillis, Rec. Sec., 921 8th St.

La Bandera No. 110, Sacramento—Meets 1st and 3rd Fridays, N.S.G.W. Hall; Mrs. Clara Weldon, Rec. Sec., 1310 "O" St.

Sutter No. 111, Sacramento—Meets 1st and 3rd Tuesdays, N.S.G.W. Hall; Mrs. Adele Nix, Rec. Sec., 1238 "S" St.

Fern No. 123, Folsom—Meets 1st and 3rd Tuesdays, K.P. Hall; Elizabeth Ryan, Rec. Sec., Represa.

Chabolla No. 171, Galt—Meets 2nd and 4th Tuesdays, I.O.O.F. Hall; Mrs. Mary Pritchard, Rec. Sec.

Coloma No. 212, Sacramento—Meets 1st and 3rd Tuesdays, I.O.O.F. Hall, Oak Park; Mrs. Nettie Harry, Rec. Sec., 1217 35th St.

Liberty No. 213, Elk Grove—Meets 2nd and 4th Fridays, I.O.O.F. Hall; Mrs. Frances Wackman, Rec. Sec., P. O. box 192.

Victory No. 216, Courtland—Meets 1st Saturday and 3rd Monday, N.S.G.W. Hall; Mrs. Agneda Lample, Rec. Sec.

Rio Rita No. 253, Sacramento—Meets 1st and 3rd Mondays, 902 "J" St.; Katherine L. Jones, Rec. Sec., 2708 Ninth Ave.

SAN BENITO COUNTY.

Copa de Oro No. 105, Hollister—Meets 2nd and 4th Thursdays, Grangers Union Hall; Mrs. Mollie Daveggio, Rec. Sec., 110 San Benito St.

San Juan Bautista No. 179, San Juan Bautista—Meets 1st Wednesday, Mission Corridor Rooms; Miss Gertrude Breen, Rec. Sec.

SAN BERNARDINO COUNTY.

Lugonia No. 241, San Bernardino—Meets 2nd and 4th Wednesdays, Eagles Hall; Miss Lois Poling, Rec. Sec., 295 E. 11th St.

Ontario No. 251, Ontario—Meets 2nd and 4th Thursdays, Ontario Hotel; Miss Wilma Poole, Rec. Sec., 1102 No. Euclid Ave.

SAN DIEGO COUNTY.

San Diego No. 208, San Diego—Meets 2nd and 4th Wednesdays, Directors Room, Chamber Commerce Bldg., 499 W. Broadway; Mrs. Elsie Case, Rec. Sec., 3051 Broadway.

SAN FRANCISCO CITY AND COUNTY.

Minerva No. 2, San Francisco—Meets 1st and 3rd Wednesdays, N.S.G.W. Bldg.; Miss Dorothy Finn, Rec. Sec., 90 Princess St., Sausalito.

Alta No. 3, San Francisco—Meets 2nd and 4th Tuesdays, N.S.G.W. Bldg.; Mrs. Aguese L. Hughes, Rec. Sec., 3980 Sacramento St.

Oro Fino No. 9, San Francisco—Meets 1st and 3rd Thursdays, N.S.G.W. Bldg.; Mrs. Josephine B. Morrissey, Rec. Sec., 4441 20th St.

Golden State No. 50, San Francisco—Meets 1st and 3rd Wednesdays, N.D.G.W. Home; Miss Millie Tietjen, Rec. Sec., 328 Lexington Ave.

Orinda No. 56, San Francisco—Meets 2nd and 4th Fridays, N.D.G.W. Home; Mrs. Anna A. Gruber-Loser, Rec. Sec., 72 Grove Lane, San Anselmo.

Fremont No. 59, San Francisco—Meets 1st and 3rd Tuesdays, N.S.G.W. Bldg.; Miss Hannah Collins, Rec. Sec., 617 Fillmore St.

Buena Vista No. 68, San Francisco—Meets 1st, 3rd and 5th Thursdays, N.D.G.W. Home; Miss Margaret Barrett, Rec. Sec., 3774 20th St.

Las Lomas No. 72, San Francisco—Meets 1st and 3rd Tuesdays, N.D.G.W. Home; Mrs. Marion S. Day, Rec. Sec., 469 Noe St.

Yosemite No. 83, San Francisco—Meets 1st and 3rd Tuesdays, American Hall, 20th and Capp Sts.; Miss Mary Monahan, Rec. Sec., 237 Noe St.

La Estrella No. 89, San Francisco—Meets 2nd and 4th Mondays, N.S.G.W. Bldg.; Miss Birdie Hartman, Rec. Sec., 1018 Jackson St.

Sans Souci No. 96, San Francisco—Meets 2nd and 4th Mondays, N.D.G.W. Home; Mrs. Minnie F. Dobbin, Rec. Sec., 289 Urbana Drive.

Calaveras No. 103, San Francisco—Meets 2nd and 4th Tuesdays, Swedish American Hall, 2174 Market St.; Mary L. Krogh, Rec. Sec., 4235 Cabrillo St.

Darina No. 114, San Francisco—Meets 1st and 3rd Mondays, N.S.G.W. Bldg.; Miss Adele Walsh, Rec. Sec., 479 Page St.

El Vespero No. 118, San Francisco—Meets 2nd and 4th Tuesdays, Masonic Hall, 4705 3rd St.; Mrs. Nell R. Boege, Rec. Sec., 1526 Kirkwood Ave.

Genevieve No. 132, San Francisco—Meets 1st and 3rd Thursdays, N.S.G.W. Bldg.; Miss Branice Peguillan, Rec. Sec., 2494 16th Ave.

Keith No. 137, San Francisco—Meets 2nd and 4th Thursdays, N.S.G.W. Bldg.; Mrs. Helen T. Mann, Rec. Sec., 575 Pierce St., Apt. 206.

Gabrielle No. 139, San Francisco—Meets 2nd and 4th Wednesdays, N.S.G.W. Bldg.; Mrs. Dorothy Wuesterfeld, Rec. Sec., 1020 Munich St.

Presidio No. 148, San Francisco—Meets 2nd and 4th Tuesdays, N.S.G.W. Bldg.; Mrs. Hattie Gaughran, Rec. Sec., 713 Capp St.

Guadalupe No. 153, San Francisco—Meets 2nd and 4th Mondays, Forester Hall, 170 Valencia St.; Miss May A. McCarthy, Rec. Sec., 336 Elsie St.

Golden Gate No. 158, San Francisco—Meets 2nd and 4th Mondays, N.S.G.W. Bldg.; Mrs. Mary Sullivan, Rec. Sec., 33 Cuvier St.

Dolores No. 169, San Francisco—Meets 2nd and 4th Wednesdays, N.S.G.W. Bldg.; Mrs. Ada Saunders, Rec. Sec., 264 Allison St.

Linda Rosa No. 170, San Francisco—Meets 2nd and 4th Wednesdays, Swedish American Hall, 2174 Market St.; Mrs. Eva P. Tyrrel, Rec. Sec., 2629 Mission St.
Portola No. 172, San Francisco—Meets 1st and 3rd Tuesdays, N.S.G.W. Bldg.; Catherine H. Dolly, Rec. Sec., 4125 23rd St.
Castro No. 178, San Francisco—Meets 1st and 3rd Wednesdays, K.C. Bldg., 150 Golden Gate Ave.; Miss Adeline Sanderefeld, Rec Sec., 60 Baker St.
Twin Peaks No. 185, San Francisco—Meets 2nd and 4th Fridays, Druids Temple, 44 Page St.; Mrs. Loretta Cameron, Rec. Sec., 3959 Army St.
James Lick No. 220, San Francisco—Meets 1st and 3rd Wednesdays, N.S.G.W. Bldg.; Mrs. Edna Bishop, Rec. Sec., 3841 24th St.
Mission No. 227, San Francisco—Meets 2nd and 4th Fridays, N.S.G.W. Bldg.; Mrs. Ann Dippel, Rec. Sec., 448 Dewey Blvd.
Bret Harte No. 232, San Francisco—Meets 2nd and 4th Tuesdays, Aloha Hall, 3009 16th St.; Pearl Wedde, Rec. Sec., 225 7th Ave.
Balboa No. 249, San Francisco—Meets 1st and 3rd Thursdays, Knights Columbus Hall, 332 18th Ave.; Miss Jean Moffet, Rec. Sec., 476 28th Ave.
Utopia No. 252, San Francisco—Meets 2nd and 4th Tuesdays, American Hall, 20th and Capp Sts.; Miss Lelia M. Little, Rec. Sec., 4450 20th St.

SAN JOAQUIN COUNTY.

Joaquin No. 5, Stockton—Meets 2nd and 4th Tuesdays, N.S.G.W. Hall, 314 E. Main St.; Mrs. Della Garvin, Rec. Sec., 1122 E. Market St.
El Pescadero No. 82, Tracy—Meets 1st and 3rd Fridays, I.O.O.F. Hall; Mrs. Mary A. Hewitson, Rec. Sec., 122 Walnut St.
Ivy No. 88, Lodi—Meets 1st and 3rd Tuesdays, Pythian Hall, Cory Bldg., Pine St.; Mrs. Mae Corson, Rec. Sec., 109 So. School St.
Calle de Oro No. 206, Stockton—Meets 1st and 3rd Tuesdays, N.S.G.W. Hall, 314 E. Main St.; Mrs. Frances Germain, Rec. Sec., 450 No. Regent.
Phoebe A. Hearst No. 214, Manteca—Meets 2nd and 4th Wednesdays, I.O.O.F. Hall; Mrs. Josie M. Frederick, Rec. Sec., Route A, Box 364, Ripon.

SAN LUIS OBISPO COUNTY.

San Miguel No. 94, San Miguel—Meets 2nd and 4th Wednesday afternoons, Clemon Hall; Mrs. Nellie Wickstrom, Rec. Sec.
San Luisita No. 108, San Luis Obispo—Meets 2nd and 4th Thursdays, W.O.W. Hall; Miss Agnes M. Lee, Rec. Sec., P. O. box 584.
El Pinal No. 163, Cambria—Meets 2nd, 4th and 5th Tuesdays, N.S.G.W. Hall; Kathryn Luchessa, Rec. Sec.

SAN MATEO COUNTY.

Bonita No. 10, Redwood City—Meets 2nd and 4th Thursdays, I.O.O.F. Hall; Mrs. Dora Wilson, Rec. Sec., 518 Middlefield Rd.
Vista del Mar No. 155, Halfmoon Bay—Meets 2nd Thursday, I.O.O.F. Hall; Elizabeth Olney, Rec. Sec.
Ano Nuevo No. 180, Pescadero—Meets 1st and 3rd Wednesdays, I.O.O.F. Hall; Mrs. Alice Mattei, Rec. Sec.
El Carmelo No. 181, Daly City—Meets 1st and 3rd Wednesdays, Masonic Hall; Mrs. Alice Mathias Oldham, Rec. Sec., 2218 26th Ave., San Francisco.
Menlo No. 211, Menlo Park—Meets 2nd and 4th Mondays, Masonic Hall; Mrs. Frances E. Maloney, Rec. Sec., P. O. box 626.
San Bruno No. 246, San Bruno—Meets 2nd and 4th Fridays, Legion Hall; Miss Mildred Foley, Rec. Sec., 217 Miller Ave., South San Francisco.

SANTA BARBARA COUNTY.

Reina del Mar No. 126, Santa Barbara—Meets 1st and 3rd Tuesdays, Pythian Castle, 222 W. Carillo St.; Mrs. Dorothy Yule, Rec. Sec., 1632 Olive St.

SANTA CLARA COUNTY.

San Jose No. 81, San Jose—Meets 1st and 3rd Wednesdays, I.O.O.F. Hall, 3rd and Santa Clara Sts.; Mrs. Nellie Fleming, Rec. Sec., 75 No. Third St.
Vendome No. 100, San Jose—Meets 2nd and 4th Wednesdays, Old Scottish Rite Temple; Miss Marie Buck, Rec. Sec., 245 Hawthorne St.
El Monte No. 205, Mountain View—Meets 2nd and 4th Fridays, American Legion Hall; Miss Elizabeth Spencer, Rec. Sec., 1620 Villa St.
Palo Alto No. 229, Palo Alto—Meets 1st and 2nd Mondays, N.S.G.W. Hall; Miss Helena G. Hansen, Rec. Sec., 531 Lytton Ave.

SANTA CRUZ COUNTY.

Santa Cruz No. 26, Santa Cruz—Meets Mondays, N.S.G.W. Hall; Mrs. May L. Williamson, Rec. Sec., 170 Walnut Ave.
El Pajaro No. 35, Watsonville—Meets 1st and 3rd Tuesdays, I.O.O.F. Hall; Miss Ruth E. Wilson, Rec. Sec., 15 Laurel St.

SHASTA COUNTY.

Camellia No. 41, Anderson—Meets 1st and 3rd Tuesdays, Masonic Hall; Mrs. Olga E. Welbourn, Rec. Sec.
Lassen View No. 98, Shasta—Meets 2nd Friday, Masonic hall; Miss Louise Litsch, Rec. Sec.
Hiawatha No. 140, Redding—Meets 2nd and 4th Wednesdays, Moose Hall; Ruth Presleigh, Rec. Sec., Office County Clerk.

SIERRA COUNTY.

Naomi No. 36, Downieville—Meets 2nd and 4th Wednesdays, I.O.O.F. Hall; Louise C. Dubuque, Rec. Sec.
Imogen No. 134, Sierraville—Meets 2nd and 4th Saturday afternoons, Copren Hall; Mrs. Jennie Copren, Rec. Sec.

SISKIYOU COUNTY.

Eschscholtzia No. 112, Etna—Meets 1st and 3rd Wednesdays, Masonic Hall; Mrs. Bernice E. Smith, Rec. Sec.
Mountain Dawn No. 120, Sawyers Bar—Meets 2nd and last Wednesdays, I.O.O.F. Hall; Miss Edith Dunphy, Rec. Sec.

SOLANO COUNTY.

Vallejo No. 195, Vallejo—Meets 1st and 3rd Wednesdays, K.P. Hall, 820 Marin St.; Mrs. Mary Combs, Rec. Sec., 511 York St.
Mary E. Bell No. 224, Dixon—Meets 2nd and 4th Thursdays, I.O.O.F. Hall; Mary Young, Rec. Sec.

SONOMA COUNTY.

Sonoma No. 209, Sonoma—Meets 2nd and 4th Mondays, I.O.O.F. Hall; Catherine Bulotti, Rec. Sec.
Santa Rosa No. 217, Santa Rosa—Meets 1st and 3rd Thursdays, N.S.G.W. Hall; Mrs. Clytie L. Lewis, Rec. Sec., R.F.D. No. 4, Box 345-A.
Petaluma No. 222, Petaluma—Meets 1st and 3rd Tuesdays, Dania Hall; Mrs. Margaret M. Oeltjen, Rec. Sec., 503 Prospect St.

STANISLAUS COUNTY.

Oakdale No. 125, Oakdale—Meets 3rd Monday, McLeod Home; Mrs. Lou Reeder, Rec. Sec.
Morada No. 199, Modesto—Meets 2nd and 4th Wednesdays, I.O.O.F. Hall; Mrs. Susan Sullivan, Rec. Sec., 823 10th St.
Eldora No. 248, Turlock—Meets 1st and 3rd Mondays, Masonic Temple; Effie Lund, Rec. Sec., 312 Mitchell St.

SUTTER COUNTY.

South Butte No. 226, Sutter—Meets 1st and 3rd Mondays, N.D.G.W. Hall; Mrs. Abbie N. Vagedes, Rec. Sec.

TEHAMA COUNTY.

Berendos No. 23, Red Bluff—Meets 1st and 3rd Tuesdays, W.O.W. Hall, 200 Pine St.; Mrs. Lillie Hammer, Rec. Sec., 636 Jackson St.

TRINITY COUNTY.

Eltapome No. 55, Weaverville—Meets 2nd and 4th Thursdays, N.S.G.W. Hall; Mrs. Lou N. Fetzer, Rec. Sec.

TUOLUMNE COUNTY.

Dardanelle No. 66, Sonora—Meets Fridays, I.O.O.F. Hall; Mrs. Nettie Whitto, Rec. Sec., P.O. box 122.
Golden Era No. 99, Columbia—Meets 1st and 3rd Thursdays, N.S.G.W. Hall; Miss Irene Ponce, Rec. Sec.
Anona No. 164, Jamestown—Meets 2nd and 4th Tuesdays, I.O.O.F. Hall; Nellie Hope, Rec. Sec.

YOLO COUNTY.

Woodland No. 90, Woodland—Meets 2nd and 4th Tuesdays, N.S.G.W. Hall; Mrs. Maude Heaton, Rec. Sec., 153 College St.

YUBA COUNTY.

Marysville No. 162, Marysville—Meets 2nd and 4th Wednesdays, Liberty Hall; Miss Cecelia C. Gomes, Rec. Sec., 701 6th St.
Camp Far West No. 218, Wheatland—Meets 3rd Tuesday, I.O.O.F. Hall; Mrs. Ethel C. Brock, Rec. Sec., P. O. box 285.

AFFILIATED ORGANIZATIONS.

General Association Past Presidents—Meetings held annually in April at the home-town of Chief President; Mrs. Winifred Halter, 465 40th St., Oakland, Chief President; Mrs. Anna G. Loser, 72 Grove Lane, San Anselmo, Chief Secretary.
Past Presidents Association No. 1—Meets 1st and 3rd Mondays, N.S.G.W. Bldg., 414 Mason St., San Francisco; Mrs. Merle Sandell, Pres.; Mrs. Leah M. Williams, Rec. Sec., 956 Pierce St., Apt. 104, San Francisco.
Past Presidents Association No. 2—Meets 2nd and 4th Mondays, "Wigwam," Pacific Bldg., 16th and Jefferson, Oakland; Anna Ehob, Pres.; Mrs. Elizabeth B. Goodman, Rec. Sec., 134 Juana Ave., San Leandro.
Past Presidents Association No. 3 (Santa Clara County)—Meets 2nd Tuesday, Musicians Hall, 114 E. Santa Clara St., San Jose; Alice Roll, Pres.; Clara Briggs, Rec. Sec., 1536 Magnolia Ave., San Jose.
Past Presidents Association No. 4 (Sacramento County)—Meets 2nd Monday, N.S.G.W. Hall, 11th and "J" Sts., Sacramento City; Edith Kelley, Pres.; Lily May Tilden, Rec. Sec., 3225 "T" St., Sacramento.
Past Presidents Association No. 5 (Butte County)—Meets 1st Friday, homes of members, Chico and Oroville; Emma Logan, Pres.; Mae Belle Bills, Rec. Sec., 1234 Leah Court, Oroville.
Past Presidents Association No. 6 (Nevada County)—Meets 4th Friday, alternately between Nevada City, Pythian Castle, and Grass Valley, Edna Sampson's home; Margaret V. Nolan, Pres.; Vere Hansen, Rec. Sec., R.F.D. No. 2, box 41-C, Grass Valley.
Past Presidents Association No. 7 (Sonoma County)—Meets 2nd Tuesday, Ruby Berger home, 327 College Ave., Santa Rosa; Ruby Berger, Pres.; Ann M. Beach, Rec. Sec., R.F.D. No. 4, box 528, Santa Rosa.
Past Presidents Association No. 8 (San Joaquin and Stanislaus Counties)—Meets 2nd Thursday, Red Men Hall, Stockton; Mrs. Lois Armstrong, Pres.; Mrs. Harriet F. Corr, Rec. Sec., 729 E. Sonora St., Stockton.
Native Sons and Native Daughters Central Committee on Homeless Children—Main Office, 955 Phelan Bldg., San Francisco; Mrs. John W. Stirling, Chmn.; Miss Mary E. Brusie, Sec. Los Angeles branch office, 3924 Sunset Blvd.; Dorothy Schlingman, Sec.

(ADVERTISEMENT.)

NATIVE DAUGHTER NEWS

(Continued from Page 9)

state exhibits. After viewing a number of our united states I cherish more than ever my heritage of being a native daughter of the Golden West."

Chico—Annie K. Bidwell No. 168 entertained the local Pioneers September 9. Mrs. B. F. Hudspeth delivered an address of welcome. Mr. and Mrs. D. T. Thatcher, who recently celebrated their seventieth wedding anniversary, were presented with a basket of old-fashioned flowers. A program was presented and refreshments were served.

Pescadero—Ano Nuevo No. 180 received an official visit from Grand President Irma Laird August 30. Preceding the meeting fifty-four enjoyed a banquet. Mrs. Laird gave a very instructive address and complimented the Parlor officers. Among those present were Grand Secretary Sallie Thaler, Grand Marshal Anna Thuesen, Grand Trustee Orinda Giannini, Grand Organist Clara Gairaud, Grand Outside Sentinel Alice Oldham, Past Grand Emma Foley, Supervising Deputy Rena Mathias, Deputy Gladys Bennett and representatives of fourteen Parlors. Gifts were presented Grand President Laird and Deputy Bennett.

Modesto—Morada No. 199 had a visit August 24 from Past Grand Emma Foley, who entertained with a brief talk. Mrs. Ann Sargent headed a committee which served refreshments at flower-bedecked tables. August 30 a picnic outing was held on the Tuolumne River. Morada's drill team, which performs at various large meetings and public social affairs, will enter the local Armistice Day parade.

San Diego—Mrs. Edith Barngrover entertained for San Diego No. 208 with a garden party at her home. Bridge and other games were enjoyed. The Golden Poppy Sewing Club had its September meeting at the home of Mrs. Mabel Burgert.

Bieber—Mount Lassen No. 215 had its annual dinner for the oldtime residents of Big Valley September 9. Robert G. Vestal of Pittville carried off the honors for length of residence. Talks on oldtime topics were made by J. J. Potter, T. J. Durwee, W. B. Philliber, Mrs. Carrie Kellogg, Andrew Babcock and Ben Bath. Mms. Nettie McKenzie, Marie Walsh and Annye Mitchell composed the committee in charge. Officers of the Parlor were installed by Deputy Nettie McKenzie August 24, Bessie Chace becoming president.

Santa Ana—Santa Ana No. 235 had as visitors September 10 Deputy Violet Henshilwood and several members of Long Beach and Grace Parlors. A gift was presented Mrs. Guy Gilbert of Grace, a recent bride. A benefit public card party was held September 22 at the San Joaquin ranch home of Mrs. Ray Lambert.

San Bernardino—The Harmony Club of Lugonia No. 241 had an all-day meeting September 7 with Ada McInerney. Admission Day, September 9, was honored with an appropriate program. Officers of the Parlor sponsored a dinner September 27 at which the members were guests. A short program was presented.

Mojave—Desert Gold No. 250 celebrated Admission Day by giving a dance. The balmy breezes enticed a large crowd, who enjoyed every minute of the evening. Supervisor Perry Brite escorted a large crowd from Bakersfield. Prizes for the oldest native daughter and native son went to Mrs. Geo. J. Haigh, 72, born in Tuolumne County, and Louis Boden, 58, born in Kern County. Visitors were present from Miocene and El Tejon Parlors. President Gertrude Phelps was in charge of all arrangements, and a neat sum was realized to help Desert Gold carry on.

San Francisco—Chief President Winifred Halter of the Past Presidents Association has accepted the following dates for official visits to subordinate associations: No. 4, Sacramento, October 9; No. 8, Stockton, October 12; No. 5, Oroville, November 2; No. 1, San Francisco, November 6.

N.D.G.W. OFFICIAL DEATH LIST.

Giving the name, the date of death, and the Subordinate Parlor affiliation of all deceased members as reported to Grand Secretary Sallie R. Thaler from August 18, 1933, to September 18, 1933:

Getz, Minnie W.; August 28; Alta No. 3.

Mitchell, Mary Frances; September 3; San Jose No. 81.

Stoddard, Agnes; September 6; Reina del Mar No. 126.

In Memoriam

EMELIA SUNQUIST.

To the Officers and Members of Santa Monica Bay Parlor No. 245 Native Daughters of the Golden West: Again, the Angel of Death has entered the portals of our Parlor and our Heavenly Father, in His Infinite wisdom, has called from our midst our beloved sister, Emelia Sunquist.

Resolved, That we extend to her bereaved family our deepest sympathy. It is our earnest prayer that God, in His Mercy, assuage their deep grief and send peace to their hearts, for she is not dead to those who love her; not lost, but gone before. She lives with us in memory, and will forever more. We shall hold in fond remembrance her cheerful smile, her loving ways and always helping hand. Be it further resolved, that our charter be draped for thirty days, and that a copy of this resolution be spread upon the minutes, a copy sent to the bereaved family and a copy sent to The Grizzly Bear for publication.

Respectfully submitted in Friendship, Loyalty and Charity.

ANNA PIERCE,
MARY MEYER,
MYRTLE BARDEN,
Committee.

Santa Monica, September 12, 1933.

A Tribute to the Memory of MARY FRANCES MITCHELL By San Jose Parlor No. 81 N.D.G.W.

Again our Golden Chain has been broken and a loved member has Crossed the Bar. Always working for the best interests of the Native Daughters of the Golden West, her love of Country and devotion to our Flag will never be forgotten by those who knew her well.

While bowing in humble submission to the will of our Heavenly Father, who has taken our loved sister, Mary Frances Mitchell, from our midst, we realize that San Jose Parlor No. 81 has lost a faithful member and her family a devoted mother, grandmother and great-grandmother. To these, we extend our deep sympathy, and commend them to a Higher Power for consolation in their grief. Their loved one has passed on to that Beautiful Home that awaits us all.

"Where the River of Life flows soft and sweet
Through the Garden of God so fair,
He has taken the loved ones, those broken ties.
We shall find them waiting there."

CLAIRE BORCHERS,
MARGARET A. GILLERAN,
NELLIE FLEMING,
Committee.

San Jose, September 20, 1933.

A JEST

(N. H. DUNNING.)

He gave the world a friendly nod,
And asked of it a little space
In which to keep the modern pace.
Yet, save a speedy fall from grace,
It only frowned a bit and said,
"Keep off the grass!"

Again he said, "Dear World, how odd
Indeed. I'll chance a little fall,
If you can make it rational.
The thing I said was just a 'stall'."
The world replied, "Just go ahead.
I'm sure you'll pass!"

Official Directory of Parlors of the N. S. G. W.

ALAMEDA COUNTY.

Alameda No. 47, Alameda City—J. F. Hanson, Pres.; Robt. H. Cavanaugh, Sec., 1806 Pacific Ave.; Wednesdays, Veterans Memorial Bldg.

Oakland No. 50, Oakland—T. J. Markert, Pres.; F. M. Norris, Sec., 5595 Taft Ave.; Fridays, Native Sons Hall, 11th and Clay Sts.

Las Positas No. 96, Livermore—Louis J. Volponi, Pres.; John J. Kelly, Sec., P. O. box 341; Thursdays, Foresters Hall.

Eden No. 113, Hayward—Leo Wessman, Pres.; Filbert M. Soares, Sec., 1437 "B" St.; 2nd and 4th Tuesdays, Memorial Hall, Main St.

Piedmont No. 120, Oakland—George T. Pryts, Pres.; Charles Morando, Sec., 906 Vermont St.; Thursdays, Native Sons Hall, 11th and Clay Sts.

Wisteria No. 127, Alvarado—Henry May, Pres.; J. M. Scribner, Sec., Livermore; 1st Thursday, I.O.O.F. Hall.

Halcyon No. 146, Alameda City—F. A. Stahl, Pres.; J. C. Bates, Sec., 2139 Buena Vista Ave.; 1st and 3rd Tuesdays, I.O.O.F. Hall, 2329 Santa Clara Ave.

Brooklyn No. 151, Oakland—Frank C. Merritt, Pres.; E. W. Cooney, Sec., 3907 14th Ave.; 1st and 3rd Wednesdays, Masonic Temple, 8th Ave. and E. 14th St.

Washington No. 169, Centerville—Thomas Silva, Pres.; Allen G. Norris, Sec., P. O. box 58; 2nd and 4th Tuesdays, Hansen Hall.

Athens No. 195, Oakland—Fred G. Martin, Pres.; Harold B. Farley, Sec., 4623 Benevides Ave.; Tuesdays, Native Sons Hall, 11th and Clay Sts.

Berkeley No. 210, Berkeley—H. P. Corbett, Pres.; R. J. Garrett, Sec., 1708 Virginia St.; Tuesdays, Native Sons Hall, 2108 Shattuck Ave.

Estudillo No. 223, San Leandro—E. B. King, Pres.; Albert G. Pacheco, Sec., 1736 E. 14th St.; 1st and 3rd Tuesdays, U.P.E.C. Hall.

Claremont No. 240, Emeryville—Edward J. Ginocchio, Pres.; E. N. Thienger, Sec., 839 Hearst Ave., Berkeley; Tuesdays, Veterans Memorial Bldg., 43rd and Salem Sts.

Pleasanton No. 244, Pleasanton—P. Edward Holzreiter, Pres.; Ernest W. Schween, Sec.; 2nd and 4th Thursdays, I.O.O.F. Hall.

Niles No. 250, Niles—M. L. Fournier, Pres.; C. E. Martenstein, Sec.; 2nd Thursday, I.O.O.F. Hall.

Fruitvale No. 252, Oakland—Ernest Perry, Pres.; Edward T. Schnarr, Sec., 3611 Allendale Ave.; Fridays, W.O.W. Hall, 3256 E. 14th St.

AMADOR COUNTY.

Amador No. 17, Sutter Creek—J. H. Williams, Pres.; F. J. Payne, Sec.; 1st and 3rd Fridays, Native Sons Hall.

Excelsior No. 31, Jackson—Thomas G. Negrich, Pres.; William Going, Sec.; 1st and 3rd Wednesdays, Native Sons Hall, 22 Court St.

Ione No. 33, Ione—Earl Grover, Pres.; Josiah H. Saunders, Sec.; 1st and 3rd Wednesdays, Native Sons Hall.

Plymouth No. 48, Plymouth—D. A. Upton, Pres.; Thos. D. Davis, Sec.; 1st and 3rd Saturdays, N.S.G.W. Hall.

BUTTE COUNTY.

Argonaut No. 8, Oroville—Frank H. O'Brien, Pres.; Cyril R. Macdonald, Sec., P. O. box 502; 1st and 3rd Wednesdays, Veterans Memorial Hall.

CALAVERAS COUNTY.

Chispa No. 139, Murphys—Maynard Segale, Pres.; Antone Malaspina, Sec.; Wednesdays, Native Sons Hall.

COLUSA COUNTY.

Colusa No. 69, Colusa City—Thomas F. Busch, Pres.; Phil J. Humburg, Sec., 223 Parkhill St.; Tuesdays, Eagles Hall.

CONTRA COSTA COUNTY.

General Winn No. 32, Antioch—John P. Welch, Pres.; Joel H. Ford, Sec., P. O. box 311; 2nd and 4th Wednesdays, Union Hall.

Mount Diablo No. 101, Martinez—R. P. Anderson, Pres.; G. T. Barkley, Sec.; 1st and 3rd Mondays, I.O.O.F. Hall.

Byron No. 170, Byron—William E. Bunn, Pres.; H. G. Krumland, Sec.; 1st and 3rd Tuesdays, I.O.O.F. Hall.

Carquinez No. 205, Crockett—John McManus, Pres.; Thomas R. Cox, Sec., P.O. box 721; 1st and 3rd Wednesdays, I.O.O.F. Hall.

Richmond No. 217, Richmond—Frank Weber, Pres.; Lloyd N. Mason, Sec., 11 6th St.; 1st Wednesday, 818 Macdonald Ave.

Concord No. 245, Concord—C. H. Guy, Pres.; D. E. Pramberg, Sec., P. O. box 235; 1st Tuesday, Guy's Parlors.

Diamond No. 246, Pittsburg—S. E. Caruso, Pres.; Edward Wilson, Sec., 2 Front St.; 1st and 3rd Wednesdays, Veterans Memorial Bldg.

EL DORADO COUNTY.

Placerville No. 9, Placerville—Milton Orelli, Pres.; Clyde R. Berriman, Sec., Wood St.; 2nd and 4th Tuesdays, Masonic Hall.

Georgetown No. 91, Georgetown—George W. Brichler, Pres.; C. F. Irish, Sec.; 2nd and 4th Wednesdays, I.O.O.F. Hall.

FRESNO COUNTY.

Fresno No. 25, Fresno City—J. H. Sutton, Pres.; W. C. Guard, Sec., R.F.D. No. 2, box 879; 1st and 3rd Fridays, Pythian Castle, Cor. "R" and Merced Sts.

Selma No. 107, Selma—C. R. Snyder, Pres; E. C. Laughlin, Sec.; 1st Wednesday, American Legion Hall.

GRAND OFFICERS.

Seth Millington.................Junior Past Grand President
Gridley

Justice Emmet Seawell.................Grand President
State Bldg., San Francisco

Chas. A. Koenig.................Grand First Vice-president
531 35th Ave., San Francisco

Harmon D. Skillin.................Grand Second Vice-president
1070 Mills Bldg., San Francisco

J. Hartley Russell.................Grand Third Vice-president
1025 Russ Bldg., San Francisco

John T. Regan.................Grand Secretary
N.S.G.W. Bldg., 414 Mason St., San Francisco

John A. Corotto.................Grand Treasurer
560 No. 5th St., San Jose

Gam Hurst.................Grand Marshal
5262 Boyd Ave., Oakland

William A. Reuter.................Grand Inside Sentinel
1009 Marine Ave., Wilmington

Walter P. Rothenbush.................Grand Outside Sentinel
N.S.G.W. Club Rooms, Stockton

Leslie Maloche.................Grand Organist
1775 El Cerrito, Los Angeles

Chester Gannon.................Grand Historian
613 Capital Ntl. Bank Bldg., Sacramento

GRAND TRUSTEES.

Eldred L. Meyer.......922 San Vicente Blvd., Santa Monica
Henry S. Lyon.................Placerville
Chas. H. Spengemann.........827 27th Ave., San Francisco
Thos. M. Foley.................Hearst Bldg., San Francisco
Jesse H. Miller.............712 DeYoung Bldg., San Francisco
John M. Burnett.................Bank America Bldg., San Jose
Edward T. Schnarr.................3611 Allendale Ave., Oakland

GLENN COUNTY.

Willows No. 255, Willows—Lee V. Logan, Pres.; Leon Marshall, Sec., P.O. box 747; 2nd and 4th Tuesdays, I.O.O.F. Hall.

HUMBOLDT COUNTY.

Humboldt No. 14, Eureka—Henry Sundfors, Pres.; Loren M. Nelson, Sec., P.O. box 195; 2nd and 4th Mondays, Native Sons Hall.

Arcata No. 20, Arcata—W. H. Anderson, Pres.; William Peters, Sec., P. O. box 1117; Thursdays, Native Sons Hall.

Ferndale No. 93, Ferndale—O. J. Olsen, Pres.; C. H. Rasmussen, Sec., R.F.D., 47-A; 1st and 3rd Mondays, Danish Hall.

KERN COUNTY.

Bakersfield No. 42, Bakersfield—George Taylor, Pres.; Henry A. Bannister, Sec., care Bank of America; 2nd and 4th Fridays, Justice Court, City Hall.

LAKE COUNTY.

Lower Lake No. 159, Lower Lake—LeRoy England, Pres.; Albert Kugelman, Sec.; Thursdays, I.O.O.F. Hall.

LASSEN COUNTY.

Honey Lake No. 198, Standish—Leo T. Davis, Pres.; N. V. Wemple, Sec., Litchfield; 1st and 3rd Wednesdays, Wrede Hall.

Big Valley No. 211, Bieber—Fred Bunselmeier, Pres.; A. W. McKenzie, Sec.; 1st and 3rd Wednesdays, I.O.O.F. Hall.

LOS ANGELES COUNTY.

Los Angeles No. 45, Los Angeles City—Roger M. Johnson, Pres.; Willard F. Allen, Sec., 4955 Los Feliz Blvd.; Thursdays, Merchant Plumbers Hall, 1832 So. Hope.

Ramona No. 109, Los Angeles City—Charles E. Straube, Pres.; John V. Scott, Sec., Patriotic Hall, 1816 So. Figueroa; Fridays, Patriotic Hall, 1816 So. Figueroa.

Hollywood No. 196, Los Angeles City—Henry G. Bodkin, Pres.; E. J. Reilly, Sec., Olive View; Mondays, 1089 No. Oxford Ave.

Long Beach No. 239, Long Beach—Francis H. Gentry, Pres.; W. W. Brady, Sec., 801 Jergins Trust Bldg.; Dept. No. 1 Municipal Court, 8th floor Jergins Trust Bldg.

Sepulveda No. 263, San Pedro—Walter C. Richards, Pres.; H. E. Fairall, Sec., 1925 So. Pacific Ave.; 1st and 3rd Fridays, Redman Hall, 543 Shepherd St., Point Firmin.

Glendale No. 264, Glendale—Harvey T. Gillette, Pres.; Philip D. Molen, Sec., 222 So. Glendale; 1st and 3rd Thursdays, Starr Heights Recreation Bldg., 3311 Downing Ave.

Santa Monica Bay No. 267, Santa Monica—J. Edward McCurdy, Pres.; John J. Smith, Sec., 830 Rialto Ave., Venice; 1st and 3rd Wednesdays, Odd Fellows Hall, 1431 Third St.

University No. 272, Los Angeles City—Maynard P. Garrison, Pres.; Carl Martin, Sec., 1607 So. Spaulding St.; Wednesdays, Casa de Rosas, Adams and Hoover Sts.

Compton No. 273, Compton—Ray W. Hecock, Pres.; Wm. Don Castillo, Sec., care Police Dept.; 2nd and 4th Tuesdays, Elks Hall, 6172 No. Long Beach Blvd., North Long Beach.

MADERA COUNTY.

Madera No. 130, Madera City—Cornelius Noble, Pres.; T. P. Cosgrave, Sec.; 1st and 3rd Thursdays, First National Bank Bldg.

MARIN COUNTY.

Mount Tamalpais No. 64, San Rafael—Donald J. Locati, Pres.; Manuel A. Andrade, Sec., 532 Mission Ave.; 1st and 3rd Mondays, Portuguese-American Hall.

Sea Point No. 158, Sausalito—Clarence D. Ross, Pres.; Manuel Santos, Sec., 6 Glen Drive; 1st and 3rd Wednesdays, Perry Bldg.

Nicasio No. 183, Nicasio—M. T. Farley, Pres.; R. J. Rogers, Sec.; 2nd and 4th Wednesdays, U.A.O.D. Hall.

MENDOCINO COUNTY.

Ukiah No. 71, Ukiah—Kenneth Phillips, Pres.; Ben Hofman, Sec., P.O. box 473; 1st and 3rd Mondays, I.O.O.F. Hall.

Broderick No. 117, Point Arena—Albert Seymour, Pres.; C. J. Buchanan, Sec.; 1st and 3rd Thursdays, Forester Hall.

Alder Glen No. 200, Fort Bragg—Fred LeValley, Pres.; C. R. Weller, Sec.; 2nd and 4th Fridays, I.O.O.F. Hall.

MERCED COUNTY.

Yosemite No. 24, Merced City—Alfred Wm. Petersen, Pres.; True W. Fowler, Sec., P. O. box 781; 2nd and 4th Mondays, I.O.O.F. Hall.

Los Banos No. 206, Los Banos—Frank Dambrosio, Pres.; L. E. Sarbo, Sec., R.F.D., box 21; 2nd and 4th Wednesdays, Eagles Hall.

MONTEREY COUNTY.

Monterey No. 75, Monterey City—James Millington, Pres.; T. W. Krieger, Sec., 999 Franklin St.; 1st and 3rd Fridays, Knights Pythias Hall, Main St.

Santa Lucia No. 97, Salinas—George S. Miller, Pres.; R. W. Adcock, Sec., R.F.D. No. 2, box 181; Mondays, Native Sons Hall, 32 W. Alisal St.

Gabilan No. 132, Castroville—James C. Jordan, Pres.; J. F. Gambetta, Sec., P. O. box 94; 1st and 3rd Thursdays, Native Sons Hall.

NAPA COUNTY.

Saint Helena No. 53, Saint Helena—J. P. Vasconi Sr., Pres.; Edw. L. Bonhote, Sec., P. O. box 364; Mondays, Native Sons Hall.

Napa No. 62, Napa City—Theodore E. Freitas, Pres.; H. J. Hoernle, Sec., 1226 Oak St.; Mondays, Native Sons Hall.

Calistoga No. 86, Calistoga—James Marchese, Pres.; Louis Carlenzoli, Sec.; 1st and 3rd Mondays, I.O.O.F. Hall.

NEVADA COUNTY.

Hydraulic No. 56, Nevada City—Raglan Tuttle, Pres.; Dr. C. W. Chapman, Sec.; Tuesdays, Pythian Castle.

Quartz No. 58, Grass Valley—Frank G. Hooper, Pres.; H. Ray George, Sec., 151 Conaway Ave.; Mondays, Auditorium Hall.

Donner No. 162, Truckee—J. F. Lichtenberger, Pres.; H. C. Lichtenberger, Sec.; 2nd and 4th Tuesdays, Native Sons Hall.

ORANGE COUNTY.

Santa Ana No. 265, Santa Ana—Ivan H. Harper, Pres.; E. F. Marks, Sec., 1124 No. Bristol St.; 1st and 3rd Mondays, Gonzales Hall, 206½ E. 4th St.

PLACER COUNTY.

Auburn No. 59, Auburn—Hans J. Petersen, Pres.; J. G. Walsh, Sec.; 1st and 3rd Fridays, Foresters Hall.

Silver Star No. 63, Lincoln—Robert P. Dixon, Pres.; Barney G. Barry, Sec., P. O. box 72; 3rd Wednesday, I.O.O.F. Hall.

Rocklin No. 233, Roseville—Wm. La Due, Pres.; M. E. Reed, Sec., 253 W. Duranta; 2nd and 4th Wednesdays, Eagles Hall.

PLUMAS COUNTY.

Quincy No. 131, Quincy—Herbert Hard, Pres.; E. C. Kelsey, Sec.; 2nd Thursday, I.O.O.F. Hall.

Golden Anchor No. 182, La Porte—R. J. McGrath, Pres.; LeRoy J. Post, Sec.; 2nd and 4th Sunday mornings, Native Sons Hall.

Plumas No. 228, Taylorsville—E. E. Sikes, Pres.; George E. Boyden, Sec.; 1st and 3rd Mondays, Native Sons Hall.

SACRAMENTO COUNTY.

Sacramento No. 3, Sacramento City—Ervin Beall, Pres.; J. F. Didion, Sec., 1213 "O" St.; Thursdays, Native Sons Bldg., 11th and "J" Sts.

Sunset No. 26, Sacramenot City—William H. Peters, Pres.; Edward E. Reese, Sec., County Treasurer Office; Mondays, Native Sons Bldg., 11th and "J" Sts.

Elk Grove No. 41, Elk Grove—George D. Beitzel, Pres.; Walter Martin, Sec.; 2nd and 4th Fridays, Masonic Hall.

Granite No. 83, Folsom—Joe Relvas, Pres.; Frank Showers, Sec.; 2nd and 4th Tuesdays, K.P. Hall.

Courtland No. 106, Courtland—W. H. Thisby, Pres.; Joe. Green, Sec.; 1st Saturday and 3rd Monday, Native Sons Hall.

Sutter Fort No. 241, Sacramento City—Ed. T. Goyne, Pres.; C. L. Katzenstein, Sec., P. O. box 914; 2nd and 4th Wednesdays, Native Sons Bldg., 11th and "J" Sts.

Galt No. 243, Galt—Abel G. Stock, Pres.; F. W. Harms, Sec.; 1st and 3rd Mondays, I.O.O.F. Hall.

SAN BENITO COUNTY.

Fremont No. 44, Hollister—S. Churchill, Pres.; J. E. Prendergast Jr., Sec., 1064 Monterey St.; 1st and 3rd Thursdays, Grangers Union Hall.

SAN BERNARDINO COUNTY.

Arrowhead No. 110, San Bernardino City—Henry B. Peake, Pres.; R. W. Braselton, Sec., 462 5th St.; Wednesdays, Eagles Hall, 469 4th St.

SAN DIEGO COUNTY.

San Diego No. 108, San Diego City—John P. Murphy, Pres.; A. V. Mayrhofer, Sec., 1572 2nd St.; Wednesdays, K.C. Hall, 4th and Elm Sts.

SAN FRANCISCO CITY AND COUNTY.

California No. 1, San Francisco—Henry F. Rickleffs, Pres.; Ellis A. Blackman, Sec., 1248-A Divisadero St.; Thursdays, Native Sons Bldg., 414 Mason St.

Pacific No. 10, San Francisco—William G. Boyce, Pres.; J. Henry Bastein, Sec., 380 Van Ness Ave. South; Tuesdays, Native Sons Bldg., 414 Mason St.

Golden Gate No. 29, San Francisco—William M. Roll, Pres.; Adolph Eberhart, Sec., 183 Carl St.; Mondays, Native Sons Bldg., 414 Mason St.

Mission No. 38, San Francisco—Faustino F. Augustine, Pres.; Thos. J. Stewart, Sec., 419 South Van Ness Ave.; Wednesdays, Redmen Hall, 3053 16th St.

San Francisco No. 49, San Francisco—Alfred Watts, Pres.; David Capurro, Sec., 976 Union St.; 2nd and 4th Thursdays, Dante Hall, 1606 Stockton St.

El Dorado No. 52, San Francisco—Robert Foltz, Pres.; Alfred Vlautin, Sec., 1537 Franklin St.; Thursdays, Native Sons Bldg., 414 Mason St.

Rincon No. 72, San Francisco—Albert Granzella, Pres.; John A. Gilmour, Sec., 3069 Golden Gate Ave.; Wednesdays, Native Sons Bldg., 414 Mason St.

Stanford No. 76, San Francisco—Urban Morf, Pres.; Charles T. O'Kane, Sec., 2900 Scott St.; Tuesdays, Native Sons Bldg., 414 Mason St.

Bay City No. 104, San Francisco—Charles L. Licht, Pres.; Max E. Licht, Sec., 1881 Fulton St.; 2nd and 4th Wednesdays, Native Sons Bldg., 414 Mason St.

Niantic No. 105, San Francisco—A. Furner, Pres.; J. M. Darcy, Sec., 10 Hoffman Ave.; Wednesdays, Native Sons Bldg., 414 Mason St.

National No. 118, San Francisco—Walter J. Murphy, Pres.; Martin M. Raligan, Sec., 1825 Page St., Apt. 8; Thursdays, 1160 Eddy St.

Hesperian No. 137, San Francisco—F. P. Indig, Pres.; Albert Carlson, Sec., 379 Justin Dr.; Thursdays, Native Sons Bldg., 414 Mason St.

Alcalde No. 154, San Francisco—Daniel A. Hinell, Pres.; Harry S. Burke, Sec., 687 Shotwell St.; 2nd and 4th Wednesdays, Native Sons Bldg., 414 Mason St.

South San Francisco No. 157, San Francisco—Peter Macarini, Pres.; John T. Regan, Sec., 1489 Newcomb Ave.; Wednesdays, Masonic Bldg., 4705 3rd St.

Sequoia No. 160, San Francisco—Frank Sullivan, Pres.; Walter W. Garrett, Sec., 2500 Van Ness Ave.; 2nd and 4th Mondays, Swedish-American Bldg., 2174 Market St.

Precita No. 187, San Francisco—Edward P. Rom, Pres.; Edward Tietjen, Sec., 1367 15th Ave.; Thursdays, Mission Masonic Hall, 2668 Mission St.

Presidio No. 194, San Francisco—Joseph Lenzio, Pres.; George A. Ducker, Sec., 442 21st Ave.; Mondays, Native Sons Bldg., 414 Mason St.

Marshall No. 202, San Francisco—Eugene Biancalona, Pres.; Frank Bacigalupi, Sec., 725 Douglas St.; 1st and 3rd Wednesdays, Native Sons Bldg., 414 Mason St.

ATTENTION, SECRETARIES!

THIS DIRECTORY IS PUBLISHED BY AUTHORITY OF THE GRAND PARLOR N.S.G.W., AND ALL NOTICES OF CHANGES MUST BE RECEIVED BY THE GRAND SECRETARY (NOT THE MAGAZINE) ON OR BEFORE THE 20TH OF EACH MONTH TO INSURE CORRECTION IN NEXT ISSUE OF DIRECTORY.

Dolores No. 208, San Francisco—Eugene H. O'Donnell, Pres.; Edward F. Webb, Sec., 2801 Sacramento St.; 2nd and 4th Tuesdays, Mission Masonic Hall, 2668 Mission.
Twin Peaks No. 214, San Francisco—Leo Felt, Pres.; Thos. Pendergast, Sec., 278 Douglas St.; Wednesdays, Willopi Hall, 4061 24th St.
El Capitan No. 222, San Francisco—John C. Conmy, Pres.; James Hanna, Sec., 2450 27th Ave.; 1st and 3rd Thursdays, King Soloman Hall, 1739 Fillmore St.
Guadalupe No. 231, San Francisco—Joseph Fay, Pres.; Alvin A. Johnson, Sec., 142 Rousseau St.; Tuesdays, Guadalupe Hall, 4551 Mission St.
Castro No. 232, San Francisco—John J. Qualters, Pres.; James H. Hayes, Sec., 4014 18th St.; Tuesdays, Native Sons Bldg., 414 Mason St.
Balboa No. 234, San Francisco—Jack Killeen, Pres.; E. W. Boyd, Sec., 1046 Lake St.; Thursdays, Maccabee Hall, 5th Ave. and Clement St.
Bret Harte No. 260, San Francisco—Herbert Cline, Pres.; A. W. McElhatton, Sec., 1027 Capitol Ave.; 2nd, 4th and 5th Tuesdays, West of Twin Peaks Hall, 238 Legion Crt.
Utopia No. 270, San Francisco—D. P. Finnegan, Pres.; Herbert H. Schneider, Sec., 2455 16th Ave.; Tuesdays, American Hall, 20th and Capp Sts.

SAN JOAQUIN COUNTY.

Stockton No. 7, Stockton—George Witherow, Pres.; R. D. Dorcey, Sec., P. O. box 886; Mondays, Native Sons Hall.
Lodi No. 18, Lodi—Herbert Osterman, Pres.; Clyde J. Brennan, Sec., Cory Bldg.; 2nd and 4th Wednesdays, Eagles Hall.
Tracy No. 186, Tracy—Frank Vierra, Pres.; R. J. Marraccini, Sec., R.F.D. No. 1, box 217, Thursdays, I.O.O.F. Hall.
Manteca No. 271, Manteca—W. R. Perry, Pres.; Leonard Faria, Sec., R.F.D., box 75, Lathrop; 1st and 3rd Wednesdays, I.O.O.F. Hall.

SAN LUIS OBISPO COUNTY.

San Miguel No. 150, San Miguel—H. Twisselman, Pres.; Otto Kuehl, Sec., Paso Robles; 1st Wednesday, Clemons Hall.
Cambria No. 152, Cambria—Edward Shang, Pres.; A. S. Gay, Sec.; Wednesdays, Rigdon Hall.

SAN MATEO COUNTY.

Redwood No. 66, Redwood City—Seneca R. Coats, Pres.; A. S. Liguori, Sec., P. O. box 212; Thursdays, American Foresters Hall.
Seaside No. 95, Half Moon Bay—H. Locke Nelson, Pres.; John G. Gilcrest, Sec.; 2nd and 4th Tuesdays, I.O.O.F. Hall.
Menlo No. 185, Menlo Park—C. W. Call, Pres.; F. W. Johnson, Sec., P. O. box 601; 1st and 3rd Thursdays, Masonic Hall.
Pebble Beach No. 230, Pescadero—John Souza, Pres.; E. A. Shaw, Sec.; 2nd and 4th Wednesdays, I.O.O.F. Hall.
El Carmelo No. 256, Daly City—Harry McDonald, Pres.; Ernest L. Micco, Sec., 639 Morse St., San Francisco; 2nd and 4th Wednesdays, Eagles Hall.
Industrial City No. 269, South San Francisco—John C. Hamilton, Pres.; Geo. A. Roll, Sec., P. O. box 237; 2nd and 4th Mondays, Metropolitan Hall.

SANTA BARBARA COUNTY.

Santa Barbara No. 116, Santa Barbara City—Philip Bradley, Pres.; H. C. Sweetser, Sec., Court House; 1st and 3rd Thursdays, Pythian Castle.

SANTA CLARA COUNTY.

San Jose No. 22, San Jose—Mario Ponzini, Pres.; Joseph Lawrence, Sec., 1095 No. First St.; Mondays, I.O.O.F. Hall.
Santa Clara No. 100, Santa Clara City—A. P. Cunha, Pres.; Clarence Clevenger, Sec., P.O. box 297; 1st and 3rd Wednesdays, Redmen Hall.
Observatory No. 177, San Jose—Louis V. Dietz, Pres.; A. B. Langford, Sec., Hall Records; Tuesdays, Knights Columbus Hall, 40 No. First St.
Mountain View No. 215, Mountain View—Henry A. Schultze Jr., Pres.; C. A. Antonioli, Sec., 301 Castro St.; 2nd and 4th Wednesdays, Mockbee Hall.
Palo Alto No. 216, Palo Alto—John C. Bernal, Pres.; Albert A. Quinn, Sec., 643 High St.; 2nd and 4th Mondays, N.S.G.W. Bldg., Hamilton Ave. and Emerson St.

SANTA CRUZ COUNTY.

Watsonville No. 65, Watsonville—J. E. Giacoma, Pres.; E. R. Tindall, Sec., 51 Marchant St.; 2nd and 4th Tuesdays, I.O.O.F. Hall.
Santa Cruz No. 90, Santa Cruz City—James H. Griffin Jr., Pres.; T. V. Mathews, Sec., 105 Pacheco Ave.; Fridays, Native Sons Hall, 117 Pacific Ave.

SHASTA COUNTY.

McCloud No. 149, Redding—Melvin Zeis, Pres.; Hugh A. Shuffleton, Sec.; 1st and 3rd Thursdays, Moose Hall.

SIERRA COUNTY.

Downieville No. 92, Downieville—Earl Rickard, Pres.; H. S. Tibbey, Sec.; 2nd and 4th Mondays, I.O.O.F. Hall.
Golden Nugget No. 94, Sierra City—Emil Alleson, Pres.; Arthur R. Pride, Sec.; 1st and 3rd Wednesdays, Masonic Hall.

SISKIYOU COUNTY.

Etna No. 192, Etna—George Wm. Smith, Pres.; Harvey A. Green, Sec.; 1st and 3rd Wednesdays, I.O.O.F. Hall.
Liberty No. 193, Sawyers Bar—David H. Bobinson, Pres.; John M. Barry, Sec.; 1st and 3rd Saturdays, I.O.O.F. Hall.

SOLANO COUNTY.

Solano No. 39, Suisun—John S. Cannon, Pres.; J. W. Kinlock, Sec.; 1st and 3rd Tuesdays, I.O.O.F. Hall.
Vallejo No. 77, Vallejo—Frank J. Heldener, Pres.; Werner B. Hallin, Sec., 912 Carolina; 2nd and 4th Tuesdays, San Pablo Hall.

SONOMA COUNTY.

Petaluma No. 27, Petaluma—Walter Christiansen, Pres.; C. F. Fobes, Sec., 114 Prospect St.; 2nd and 4th Mondays, Druid Hall, Gross Bldg., 41 Main St.
Santa Rosa No. 28, Santa Rosa—James Brucker, Pres.; Leland S. Lewis, Sec., Court House; Mondays, Native Sons Hall.
Glen Ellen No. 102, Glen Ellen—Robert Kennedy, Pres.; Frank Kirch, Sec., Route 3, Santa Rosa; 2nd Monday, N.S.G.W. Hall.
Sonoma No. 111, Sonoma City—Antone Barrachi, Pres.; L. H. Green, Sec.; 1st and 3rd Mondays, I.O.O.F. Hall.
Sebastopol No. 143, Sebastopol—T. F. Hyland, Pres.; F. G. McFarlane, Sec.; 1st and 3rd Fridays, I.O.O.F. Hall.

STANISLAUS COUNTY.

Modesto No. 11, Modesto—B. E. Munson, Pres.; C. C. Eastin Jr., Sec., P.O. box 898; 1st and 3rd Wednesdays, I.O.O.F. Hall.
Oakdale No. 142, Oakdale—D. W. Tulloch, Pres.; E. T. Gobin, Sec.; 2nd Monday, Legion Hall.
Orestimba No. 247, Crows Landing—Lloyd W. Fink, Pres.; G. W. Fink, Sec.; 1st and 3rd Wednesdays, Community Club Home.
Turlock No. 274, Turlock—Robley R. Libby, Pres.; Steve A. Karkeet, Sec.

SUTTER COUNTY.

Sutter No. 261, Sutter City—James Putman, Pres.; Glen R. Haynes, Sec., R.F.D. No. 2, Yuba City; 2nd and 4th Mondays, N.D.G.W. Hall.

TRINITY COUNTY.

Mount Bally No. 87, Weaverville—H. W. Day, Pres.; E. V. Ryan, Sec.; 1st and 3rd Mondays, Native Sons Hall.

TULARE COUNTY.

Visalia No. 19, Visalia—G. W. Houk, Pres.; Jack De Alba, Sec., 916 W. Oak St.; 2nd and 4th Tuesdays, Woodman Hall.

TUOLUMNE COUNTY.

Tuolumne No. 144, Sonora—T. M. Wilzinski, Pres.; William M. Harrington, Sec., P. O. box 715; 1st and 3rd Tuesdays, Columbus Hall.
Columbia No. 258, Columbia—Anthony Solari, Pres.; Charles E. Grant, Sec.; 2nd and 4th Thursdays, Native Sons Hall.

VENTURA COUNTY.

Cabrillo No. 114, Ventura City—David Bennett, Pres., 1880 Church St.

YOLO COUNTY.

Woodland No. 30, Woodland—J. L. Aronson, Pres.; T. G. Hughes, Sec.; 1st Thursday, Native Sons Hall.

YUBA COUNTY.

Marysville No. 6, Marysville—A. W. Graves, Pres.; Verne Fogarty, Sec., 719 6th St.; 2nd Friday, Foresters Hall.

AFFILIATED ORGANIZATIONS.

San Francisco Extension of the Order Committee, N.S.G.W.—Hubert J. Caveney, Chmn.; Harold J. Regan, Sec., 414 Mason St., San Francisco; meets 2nd and 4th Fridays, Grizzly Bear Club, 414 Mason St., San Francisco.
Alameda County Extension of the Order Committee, N.S.G.W.—Gam Hurst, Chmn.; Frank Roemer, Sec., 830 30th St., Oakland; meets 1st and 3rd Mondays, N.S.G.W. Hall, 11th and Clay Sts., Oakland.
Interparlor Committee (Southern District), N.S.G.W. and N.D.G.W.—Burrel D. Neighbours, Chmn.; Clyde H. Davis, Sec., 1935 E. 78th St.; meets 3rd Friday, Patriotic Hall, 1816 So. Figueroa St., Los Angeles.
San Francisco Assembly No. 1 Past Presidents Association N.S.G.W.—Meets 1st and 3rd Fridays, Native Sons Bldg., 414 Mason St., San Francisco; John Kirrane, Gov.; J. F. Stanley, Sec., 1175 O'Farrell St., San Francisco.
East Bay Counties Assembly No. 3 Past Presidents Association N.S.G.W.—Meets 4th Monday, Native Sons Hall, 11th and Clay Sts., Oakland; Gam Hurst, Gov.; Edgar G. Hanson, Sec., 1260 Russell St., Berkeley.
Marin County Assembly No. 5 Past Presidents Association N.S.G.W.—J. S. Rose Jr., Gov.; L. J. Petar, Sec., Petar Bldg., 4th and "C" Sts., San Rafael.
Fred H. Greely Assembly No. 6 Past Presidents Association N.S.G.W.—Meets monthly with different Parlors comprising district; Peter J. Delay, Gov.; Barney Barry, Sec., P.O. box 72, Lincoln.
San Joaquin Assembly No. 7 Past Presidents Association N.S.G.W.—Meets 1st Friday, Native Sons Hall, Stockton; Clyde H. Gregg, Gov.; R. D. Dorcey, Sec., Native Sons Club, Stockton.
Sonoma County Assembly No. 9 Past President Association N.S.G.W.—Meets monthly at different Parlor headquarters in county; P. A. R. Gambini, Gov.; L. S. Lewis, Sec., Court House, Santa Rosa.
General John A. Sutter Assembly No. 10 Past Presidents Association—C. C. Wachman, Gov.; Jas. J. Longshore, Sec., 514 "J" St., Sacramento.
Grizzly Bear Club—Members all Parlors outside San Francisco at all times welcome. Clubrooms top floor Native Sons Bldg., 414 Mason St., San Francisco.
Native Sons and Native Daughters Central Committee on Homeless Children—Main office, 955 Phelan Bldg., San Francisco; Mrs. John W. Stirling, Chmn.; Miss Mary E. Brusie, Sec. Los Angeles branch office, 3924 Sunset Blvd.; Dorothy Schlingman, Sec.

(ADVERTISEMENT.)

NATIVE SON NEWS

(Continued from Page 7)

On motion, seven cents was fixed as the mileage that will be allowed those traveling the highways on official business of the Grand Parlor.

Other business of minor importance was transacted, and the Board adjourned to the call of Grand President Seawell.

INCREASED MEMBERSHIP, of substantial quality, is TODAY'S OUTSTANDING NEED of the Order of Native Sons. COMB THE FIELDS, urges the Grand President, who solicits NOW the co-operation of every Native Son. Bear in mind always, THERE IS NO SUBSTITUTE FOR MEMBERSHIP, and rally to the cause.

NEWSY N.S. BRIEFS.

Forceful pre-Admission Day addresses were delivered at Santa Rosa by Grand Trustee Jesse H. Miller and I. M. Peckham (Stanford No. 76).

Grand Historian Chester F. Gannon departed last month for a visit to New York City, and Past Grand Lewis F. Byington left for Chicago to "take in" the Century of Progress Exposition.

Sacramento—George Vice, affiliated with Sacramento No. 3, has been appointed by President Franklin Roosevelt United States Marshal for the northern district of California.

Modesto—At a largely attended meeting of Modesto No. 11, September 6, presided over by President B. E. Munson, much interest was displayed in proposed plans to inaugurate a campaign for new members. Arrangements were made to hold an entertainment of local talent September 20, and George Hansen, Dr. F. G. de Stone and Arthur Crabb were appointed to look after details. It was voted to send a large delegation to the postoffice dedication ceremonies at Marysville September 17. The Parlor plans to hold its annual anniversary party the first meeting night in November.

Santa Rosa—Santa Rosa No. 28 September 11 planned a party in honor of the general committee and all the subcommittees that arranged for the Admission Day festival. President James Brucker named as the arrangements committee for the social affair Art Janssen (chairman), Al Maroni, Earl Donner, Joe Pisenti and Mat Rogina.

Downieville—At a largely attended ritual exemplification September 12 at which Downieville No. 92 was host to visitors from Grass Valley, Nevada City and Sierra City, four candidates were initiated, two for No. 92, and one each for Quartz No. 58 and Hydraulic No. 56. A program of music was presented and a delicious chicken supper was served.

San Bernardino—Arrowhead No. 110 received September 27 an official visit from Grand Second Vice-president Harmon D. Skillin, who extolled the Order for its accomplishments and urged increased membership. Several candidates were initiated, and many visitors were in attendance.

Sebastopol—W. S. Borba of Sebastopol No. 143, chairman Sonoma County history committee, has been giving California history talks in which he has told about the Natives and their work. In October, the committee hopes to place a marker at Bodega.

INCREASED MEMBERSHIP, of substantial quality, is TODAY'S OUTSTANDING NEED of the Order of Native Sons. COMB THE FIELDS, urges the Grand President, who solicits NOW the co-operation of every Native Son. Bear in mind always, THERE IS NO SUBSTITUTE FOR MEMBERSHIP, and rally to the cause.

GOLDEN STATE HOTEL, SAN FRANCISCO, HAS NEW MANAGER.

The Golden State Hotel in San Francisco, situated at Powell and Ellis streets, is now under the management of Abe Jacobs, who for many years managed the Manx, and who is well known all over the Pacific Coast. The Golden State contains two hundred newly-furnished rooms, with tub and shower baths, and is noted for its wonderful location, right in the heart of everything, close to all the leading department stores and theatres, and only one block from Market street. It has free garage facilities for guests.

STATE OFFICIAL, NATIVE SON, DIES.

San Quentin (Marin County)—Charles L. Neumiller, chairman State Board Prison Director, died suddenly September 18. His home was in Stockton, where he was affiliated with Stockton Parlor No. 7 N.S.G.W. He was a brother of William L. Neumiller, tax collector San Joaquin County and well known in Native Son circles.

N.S.G.W. OFFICIAL DEATH LIST.

Containing the name, the date and the place of birth, the date of death, and the Subordinate Parlor affiliation of deceased members reported to Grand Secretary John T. Regan from August 20 to September 20, 1933:

Soracco, Lawrence B.; Sutter Creek, December 23, 1874; August 25, 1933; Amador No. 17.

Toothaker, Edward C.; Vallejo, August 19, 1862; August 4, 1933; Woodland No. 30.

Kean, William C.; Nevada County, November 23, 1864; August 23, 1933; Woodland No. 30.

Williams, Frank Andrew; Marysville, February 1, 1863; August 5, 1933; Alameda No. 47.

Cornepa, John Herman; San Francisco, August 23, 1858; August 10, 1933; San Francisco No. 49.

Schonfeld, Louis C.; San Francisco, August 30, 1890; August 28, 1933; El Dorado No. 52.

Moenning, Herman A.; San Francisco, April 3, 1870; September 3, 1933; El Dorado No. 52.

Phippen, Fred Warner; North San Juan, January 18, 1881; September 1, 1933; Hydraulic No. 56.

Mann, Jeff Lary; San Jose, January 5, 1863; August 7, 1933; Watsonville No. 65.

Beeson, Willis W.; Pescadero, January 11, 1855; August 10, 1933; Redwood No. 66.

Mead, William H.; Downieville, July 7, 1876; July 11, 1933; Stanford No. 76.

Connolly, Thomas W.; Petaluma, October 14, 1874; August 6, 1933; Stanford No. 76.

Leonetto, Frank Henry; Crescent Mills, February 12, 1886; June 9, 1933; Santa Cruz No. 90.

Lyons, Hugo Joseph; San Francisco, July 14, 1869; August 21, 1933; Bay City No. 104.

Adair, Joseph A. Sr.; El Dorado County, June 2, 1861; August 19, 1933; Ramona No. 109.

Kruckeberg, Hal S.; Los Angeles, August 29, 1888; September 8, 1933; Ramona No. 109.

West, Charles Clifton; Glendora, March 22, 1880; September 15, 1933; Ramona No. 109.

Wilkens, Herman; San Francisco, June 26, 1874; January 14, 1933; Piedmont No. 120.

Thompson, Charles; Angels Camp, January 6, 1874; September 2, 1933; Chispa No. 139.

Edelman, David W.; Los Angeles, January 29, 1869; August 6, 1933; Hollywood No. 196.

Kaupert, Rudolph Bertrom; San Francisco, October 1, 1889; August 12, 1933; Dolores No. 208.

Bartlett, Ed C.; San Francisco, July 6, 1860; September 15, 1933; Berkeley No. 210.

Winkler, William Francis; San Francisco, January 7, 1896; September 1, 1933; Twin Peaks No. 214.

Millions for Schools—California funds to the amount of $69,430,350 were September 11 apportioned by the State Education Department to public school districts for the 1933-34 term. Los Angeles County received the largest slice. Alameda County came next, and San Francisco was third.

"Your Life's at Stake With a Faulty Brake," is the October slogan of the California Public Safety Conference in its campaign to lessen the constantly increasing auto death-toll.

SAN FRANCISCO

"THIS IS SUPPOSED TO BE A GOVernment of the people," said Chairman William J. Locke in an address before the municipal government section of the Commonwealth Club. "But when you come right down to it, this is a government of a very small part of the people. It's only too easy to sit down at home evenings instead of going out to take part in public activities. This has been the practice of many citizens during times of prosperity—so long as these men were making money they didn't care who governed or how.

"A question which the Club might well study would be, 'Are our cities governed by organized minorities?' I believe a minority of less than ten percent can put over things opposed to the interest of the other nine-tenths of the people. Somehow, the fact that a group is organized and has an interest at stake makes it very powerful.

"It may be that the new sales tax will interest people more in their government—because when you hit a man over the head or put your hand in his pocket he immediately becomes interested in finding out what it's all about."

PATRIOTISM RENEWED.

At the monthly Native Daughter Home breakfast September 17, Josephine Parker of Buena Vista Parlor No. 68 and Ethel Browning of Castro Parlor No. 178 were the hostesses. Joseph Tinney was the principal speaker, his topic being "What Are the Native Daughters of the Golden West Going To Do for the Government," and his address renewed the patriotism and the pride of his hearers.

Other speakers were Past Grands Grace S. Stoermer, Dr. Mariana Bertola, Genevieve Watson-Baker and Mary E. Bell, Josephine Cereghino and Natalie Clark. A skit, entitled "I Cannot Sing the Old, Old Songs I Sang so Long Ago," composed by Ruby Bried and her daughter, Esther, both of El Vespero Parlor No. 118, was presented by them, assisted by the San Francisco N.D. Glee Club. Mrs. Bried, attired in a dress belonging to her great-grandmother, described the songs to her daughter, who represented a little child, and the glee club hummed the tunes.

PERFECT IN EVERY DETAIL.

The official visit of Grand President Irma W. Laird to El Vespero Parlor No. 118 N.D.G.W., eagerly looked forward to by the members, was successfully carried out in every detail by them. Past President Agnes Ryan was chairman of the meeting, while President Mary J. Casey conducted the opening ceremonies. Immediately afterward, while bells rang merrily, the Grand President was escorted and introduced as the San Francisco Glee Club, led by Past President Ruby Bried of El Vespero, and members sang a special greeting song. Two candidates were initiated. Among those present were representatives of every San Francisco Parlor, many of the Bay counties district deputies, Past Grands Margaret Hill, Mae Boldemann and Evelyn Carlson, Grand Marshal Anna Thuesen, Grand Secretary Sallie Thaler, Grand Outside Sentinel Alice Oldham, Grand Trustee Orinda Giannini, Supervising Deputies Ann Dippel, Sadie Brainard and Rena Matthias.

After the meeting, which the Grand President termed perfect in every detail, Past President Evelyn Ford, chairman of the official visit, and her assistants entertained more than two hundred at a beautifully decorated table with a splendidly served repast. Articles of silver were presented the Grand President and Deputy Emily Ryan, and the glee club and all visiting grand officers were given souvenirs of the occasion. Merited praise was bestowed on the "mother" of the Parlor, Mrs. Nell R. Boege, who has been an officer ever since El Vespero was organized by her thirty-three years ago. In a letter to the Parlor since the official visit, Grand President Laird tells El Vespero "it was one of the most beautiful and dignified of fraternal occasions that it has ever been my pleasure to experience. The evening was everything that could be desired; as near perfection as human efforts could make it." Past President Ann Godfrey of No. 118 is deputy this term for La Estrella Parlor No. 89.—N.R.B.

ANNIVERSARIES OBSERVED.

Orinda Parlor No. 56 N.D.G.W. celebrated its forty-third institution anniversary August 31. The evening was also dedicated to Past Grand Emma G. Foley, in honor of the twenty-fifth anniversary of her Grand Presidency. All charter members, those being affiliated with Orinda twenty-five years and more, Grand President Irma Laird, Past Grands Genevieve Baker and Foley, Grand Trustee Orinda Giannini and Deputy Mae Warring were special guests.

Charter Members Foley, Kate Jewell, Kate Britschgi and Anna Loser related the Parlor's history. A fashion show presented by the dramatic club displayed garments worn during the past quarter-century by Past Grand Foley, who was presented with a brief case. A skit, "The Family Photographer," was also presented by the dramatic club.

PROUD.

Members of Gabrielle Parlor No. 139 N.D.G.W. greeted Grand President Irma Laird on her official visit, September 13, as a proud Parlor. Its drill team was one of the cup winners at Santa Rosa, September 9. This was the team's first public appearance. Many visitors were present, among them Deputy Merle Sandell.

N.D.G.W. DISTRICT MEET.

Honoring Grand President Irma W. Laird, the district meeting of the San Francisco N.D.G.W. deputies will be held the evening of October 30 in Native Son Auditorium under the direction of Supervising Deputy Ann Dippel. The following will officiate: Emily Ryan, as president, Emma Omeara, Ann Godfrey, Edna Bishop, Mae Warring, Inga Meyer, Ida Mesquite, Alice Shirley, Adele Walsh, Lena Wall, Mazie Roderick, Ernestine McCormick, Mae Noble, Margaret McGowen, Merle Sandell, May McDonald and Gertrude LaFortune.

NATIVE SON BRIEFS.

The Extension of the Order Committee, at a meeting September 22, inaugurated a campaign for new members.

Stanford Parlor No. 76 enjoyed September 19 snappy, up-to-the-minute motion pictures of the Century of Progress Exposition at Chicago.

Olympus Parlor No. 189 has been consolidated with Golden Gate Parlor No. 29.

Among the many new names recently added to the membership-roll of Castro Parlor No. 232 is Gerald J. Kenny, public defender.

Plans are being made for an entertainment and ball for the benefit of the Homeless Children, to be held in the Civic Auditorium, Thanksgiving Eve.

Grand Trustee Eldred L. Meyer of Santa Monica was a Friday Luncheon Club visitor, September 8.

INCREASED MEMBERSHIP, of substantial quality, is TODAY'S OUTSTANDING NEED of the Order of Native Sons. COMB THE FIELDS, urges the Grand President, who solicits NOW the co-operation of every Native Son. Bear in mind always, THERE IS NO SUBSTITUTE FOR MEMBERSHIP, and rally to the cause.

Navy Day—Under the auspices of the United States Navy League, Navy Day will be celebrated October 27.

Redwood Meet—The thirteenth annual convention of the Redwood Empire Association will be held October 13 and 14 at Santa Rosa, Sonoma County.

Record Broken—The attendance record of the State Fair, which closed at Sacramento September 9, was broken this year, when 326,965 persons passed through the gates.

Know your home-state, California! Learn of its past history and of its present-day development by reading regularly The Grizzly Bear. $1.50 for one year (12 issues). Subscribe now.

Feminine World's Fads and Fancies

PREPARED ESPECIALLY FOR THE GRIZZLY BEAR BY ANNA STOERMER

WOOLEN COSTUMES ARE IMPORtant in the fashion picture this season. A paramount example of the current styles is the one-piece dress with a detachable cape of rich, dark gray; warm, but extremely soft and light in weight. It is flecked with silvery bits of rabbit hair and made on slim, straight lines. The frock achieves distinction through simplicity. The detachable cape fastens at the throat with two gunmetal buttons which are darker than the dress and add a note of contrast. Complementing such a costume is an ingenious version of the beret, fashioned of soft duvetyn and trimmed with a jaunty cockade of feathers. Black suede gloves, bag and shoes are suitable accessories.

Other modern costumes of dull woolens are accented with trimmings of satin, and advanced styles also feature combinations with plaid. Short or finger-tip jackets complete many of these costumes. Sheer woolen dresses with matching jackets are shown with tops of striped tie silk.

Other one-piece dresses have sleeveless boleros of fur. Furs are more varied than ever before, but they must be good furs. The fur trimming on coats is concentrated all at one place—neck and sleeves, or skirt, but not in two places at once.

It is a great suit year, but not for the simple little mannish jacket suits, either with short or three-quarters fitted coats. If I was going to have only one fall suit, I would not let the shoulders extend or even bulge. I might have a hip basque, because I could take that off when ever I tired of it.

The lingerie touch is definitely out. No more little collars of organdie, or linen, or frills. If there must be a touch of white on fall clothes, it will be in silk, satin, wool or fur, and it must be just a touch.

Colors are either dark and rich, or dark and grayed, but they are all dark, so after all the new colors, the smart person chooses black. Satin is especially good this year, the all-silk variety being particularly good looking. It is soft and supple and has a wonderful sheen that has not been evident for years. An all-black satin or crepe is smart, but many prefer a bit of contrasting color or material.

Taffeta is excellent for lapels and the newer features of the mode, and now that the repeal is practically upon us the speakeasy gown of last season has become the cocktail party dress of today. This means that you may wear a five-o'clock cocktail party costume on through the dinner at six, the theatre at eight and the night club at twelve, and be appropriately dressed at all times.

One of the newest outfits points with pride to its Gibson-girl lines and flaunts a dust ruffle beneath its floor-length hem. It is of black velvet, with a long sweeping skirt and a tight little basque bodice, buttoned up to its high neckline with flashing crystal buttons. Full sleeves are gathered on to a slightly dropped shoulder line, and become tightly fitted from elbow to wrist. With it, one may wear a brimmed black velvet hat with a trimming of ostrich plumes, and be ready to sail in on any gathering.

Another gay-nineties gown, intended for dinner and theater wear, is also of black velvet. It is fitted closely to the figure and has that off-the-shoulder line which was so popular long ago. Wide, crisp, black net ruching finishes the bodice top, and the gown is held on by narrow shoulder straps, but they hardly show behind the ruching. This, too, may be worn with a big brimmed hat of black velvet and plumes, black velvet gloves edged with ostrich, and gobs of rhinestone bracelets.

Evening wraps are gracefully long and warm. Velvet gives an added stately effect when trimmed with white fur or squirrel and fitted around the shoulders instead of the neck. Coquetry, too, returns with frills, furbelows and fans. The new collars are designed to give the beguiling lines of 1910. Silhouette and shoulder widths are achieved in a variety of ingenious ways.

It is the little things in fashion that make or mar the costume. Accessories are to the mode what the frame is to the picture. Neither can function without the other. There was a time when the average woman could manage fairly well with two sets of accessories, one for day-time and one for evening. Today, a dozen sets are not too many. The more jewelry one wears today, the smarter she appears.

Rhinestone and cut-steel shoe buckles are back in vogue, and once more jeweled clips are worn on gowns, bags, hats, and even belts. There is great use for exotic costume jewelry such as bracelets, necklaces and earrings. "Button, button, who has the button?" Buttons are just one of the features of fall fashion. Everything has buttons on it, and it looks as if designers are lying awake nights trying to find new uses for them.

Velvets in new beret types have fine stitchings, draped crowns, rhinestone clips, face veils and drooped brims. Fabric hats have self-trimming ribbon bands and feathers. Felt hats come in ingenious designs and colors such as black, brown, navy blue, green, eel and light gray.

Lovely evening bags are beaded with synthetic pearls, crystal beads and rhinestones, or with all-black beads. Several designs are offered, including the pouch style, having frames inlaid with synthetic pearls and brilliants. Many new ornaments accent handbags, and the jeweled mirror clips reflect fashion's favor. The quilted satin style is new. The smooth, dull calfskin is accented with bright metal and has much style merit.

By all means, buy velvet gloves for evening. Bright velvet gloves in elbow length will be a fashionable note this fall and will be worn with white or black evening gowns. Imported velvet gloves with soft leather palms for better fit are shown in bright green, red, black and some pastel shades.

Fine shoes in new designs are masterpieces of artistry and workmanship. Superior quality leathers make possible greater beauty. Satin-finished kidskin complements sheer fabrics and satins. Brown crocodile in the vamp and heel, with brown suede uppers, correctly complements rough crepes and tweed costumes.

Color is important in autumn and fall hosiery. A new clocked ingrain chiffon is favored for afternoon occasions in alibaba, vichy or afton. Hosiery is shown without clocks in brown, biscayne, friars brown, jungle and spice brown.

The football season has already started, so one has to consider a coat for this occasion. Nothing is nicer than tweeds. One is of dark brown and beige, with a huge collar of natural raccoon, exaggerated sleeves, and a very wide belt. Another is of dark gray worsted, with sleeves and collar of shaded krimmer. It is slightly fitted and buttoned with three bone buttons, and is worn with a duvetyn beret which has a floppy bow on the top and over the right eye. Light gray doeskin gloves and dark gray suede pumps or oxfords complete this outfit.

A favorite shade for fall is what is called a red henna. It is very near the old so-called burnt orange—that gorgeous warm color which makes one look so alive. This color is lovely on both blondes and brunettes.

"**Back To Good Times**" is the slogan for the twenty-ninth annual convention of California realtors, to be held October 4-7 at Riverside City.

Diamond Jubilee—Wilmington, Los Angeles County, celebrated with a fiesta September 23 the seventy-fifth anniversary of its beginning.

School Bonds—Long Beach, Los Angeles County, has voted $4,930,000 bonds for public schools construction.

Grape Festival—The thirtieth annual Marin County Grape Festival will be held at Kentfield, October 7.

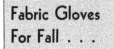

RED OCEAN

William A. Evans

THE FISHING BOAT "AMERICA" WAS the neatest looking boat tied at Fisherman's Wharf. Her grey painted hull was scrubbed clean; the deck washed and swabbed dry. Her bait tanks were milling with lively sardines. Plenty of fresh water was aboard, and her fuel tank was full. She was ready to go, and there was nothing to do now but wait until the sportsfellows arrived.

Joe Bonimi, her owner, hired the boat out by the day to small parties of men who wished to try their luck at the big fish outside the kelp beds. Joe was standing on the aft bait tank picking off dead sardines with a small net. There were so many in the tanks that the weaker ones died off. When they floated belly-up, Joe scooped down with his net and flicked them into the bay.

Sig Larson was Joe's only helper. Sig was sixteen, and every summer when school let out he went to work on the "America." He was husky and well built for his age, although a little too short. His shoulders were unusually wide for a boy's; his arms were those of a big man's and covered with a thick crop of yellow hair. Sitting on an upturned bucket at the port side of the cabin he looked like a squatting gorilla, his uncombed shock of blonde hair giving a wild look. He was scraping the rust from a large fishhook with his pocketknife.

"I got to quit and go back to school next week," he said.

"Yes?" said Joe. "Well, that's okay. I got my kid-brother coming back on the 'Florance.' They been down for tuna."

"Joe," said Sig, "are you sure Mr. Kelly is bringing his daughter with him this time?"

"That's what he said. Why you so interested?"

"I knew her at school," said Sig. "She didn't know me, though."

"Stuck up like most of these rich guy's kids."

"No," said Sig. "She just never saw me. Runs with some rich kid with a classy roadster. I got an old Ford."

"If you land a jewfish today she'll see you plenty."

Sig scratched his neck below his chin with the fishhook and shook his head from side to side.

"I think they all been caught," he said. "I didn't get a strike this summer yet."

A car honked above them on the wharf. Sig looked up and saw a large sedan draw over by the edge and stop. Five men got out. They were dressed in white trousers and sport coats.

"Hello, Mr. Kelly," said Joe in a loud voice, then swooped down and flicked up a floating sardine from the tank.

"Good-morning," said Mr. Kelly.

He was a large man with a round, bloated stomach that held his shirt stretched out in front. His panama hat had a blue and red band around it.

The five men stood on the edge of the wharf and looked down at the "America." While they stood there the chauffeur untied their fishing poles from the side of the car and handed them down to Sig. Next he passed down several large baskets filled with lunch. Sig stood the poles by the cabin and put the baskets inside.

Later, after the men had climbed down the ladder and were aboard, a blue roadster pulled up and parked in back of the sedan. A girl in a sailor hat and sport dress jumped from the car. She was followed by a young fellow about Sig's age dressed in knickers and a red sweater.

"About time they showed up," said Kelly. "Been fooling along the way."

When the couple climbed down the ladder and stood on the deck Kelly introduced them to the other men as his daughter, Lucelle, and her boy friend, Ted Wilson.

"All set to go?" Kelly asked Joe.

"Sure, sure," said Joe, grinning.

"We're off, then."

"Cut her loose, Sig," said Joe, "while I kick over the engine."

The "America" threw up a lot of water at her stern, then slowly drew away from the wharf and moved toward the center of the harbor. Her bow was pointed in the direction of Point Loma and the Pacific Ocean beyond.

As soon as the boat was well under way Sig went into the cabin and put on a clean shirt. Then he wet his hair with some water from a bucket sitting in the corner. When he had finished combing his hair he hid the comb under one of the mattresses where he always kept it, then went out to keep an eye on the bait.

The sun had been up but a short while, and the air was still damp and coolish from a foggy night. Later, the air would be hot and sticky, but now it was pleasant. The bow, cutting cleanly through the water, left a long, white line on either side of the boat.

When they reached the south end of the kelp beds Joe swung north along the outer edge and headed for La Jolla. All ready there were scores of fishing boats moving in the same line. Some were moving slowly, trawling lines out, jigs skipping behind. Others chummed with sardines, trying to spot the yellowtail and barracuda schools.

Joe kept a sharp lookout ahead for seagulls swooping down in gangs; when they ganged up it was a good sign of the big fish chasing the sardines to the surface. He slowed down the boat as they neared the kelp break off La Jolla, then cut off the engine and ran forward to kick loose the anchor. A moment or so later and the "America" swung on her anchor, motionless save for a long, easy heave from side to side.

As soon as Sig had passed out bait to the men and cleared the tanks of dead fish he went into the cabin and got his jewfish outfit. For bait he used a dead mackerel that he unwrapped from a newspaper. The mackerel was two days old and had started to rot.

"Good," said Joe, coming up behind Sig. "The more it stinks the better the jewfish likes it."

"That's the way I figure," said Sig. "I left it out in the sun all yesterday afternoon so it would be good and ripe."

He dropped the hook over the side, letting it run through his fingers. The bolt that acted as a sinker carried it down with a rush. A sudden slackening told him he had touched bottom and he hauled the line back several feet, then made it fast to the boat.

"Listen," said Joe. "Go up in the bow and ask Mr. Kelly's kid and her feller if they want to fish. You can rig them up with outfits from the box. I'll take the first trick at passing out the bait to these guys."

Sig nodded and went up forward. He found the couple seated on the chain locker. The girl was laughing and talking, but the boy was silent, his mouth drooping at the corners.

"Want to fish?" asked Sig. "I'll rig you up with a couple outfits."

The girl smiled and started to nod her head, but her companion made a sudden movement toward the rail and leaned far over. He stayed there for a few moments, then straightened, his face a greenish white.

"Pardon," he said to the girl. "I thought I was going to be ill but I guess it was only a notion. We don't want to mess about with fishing, do we?"

Lucelle was looking sideways at Sig and did not answer. Finally she said, "Haven't I seen you at school?"

"Sure," said Sig.

"Don't you remember him, Ted?"

Ted looked at Sig for a moment, then nodded. "Kind of," he said.

He turned away and stared down at the water as if trying to remember, then suddenly leaned over and started to vomit. Presently he took his handkerchief from his pocket and wiped the outside of his lips.

"Want to lay down?" asked Sig. "There's a pair of bunks in the cabin. Use either of them."

Without answering him, Ted got up from beside Lucelle and walked toward the cabin, steadying himself with the rail. He went inside without looking back.

"He'll be all right," said Sig. "I used to heave once in a while like that."

Lucelle gave him a quick look, then stared down at her hands, which were palms up in her lap. The thumbs lay in the palms and the fingers were pressed tightly about them. She kept her head bowed for a while, but finally gave a little shrug and looked up at him.

"I'd like to fish," she said, "but you'll have to show me how."

Sig ran over to the cabin and pulled one of the bamboo poles out of a rack. He fastened a reel to the pole, then went back to the bait tanks to get a sardine.

"I'm going to show her how to fish," he said to Joe.

Joe tossed a sardine at him and winked meaningly.

"I see you got her feller off his feet," he said.

"If I get my jewfish," Sig said, "that guy won't have a chance."

With the wriggling sardine held tightly in one hand he went back to Lucelle in the bow. While she watched, he slipped the hook through the fish's nose, then cast out a short distance. The bait wheeled about in small circles, then dropped lower, carried down by the weight of the line.

"Now we just stand and wait," said Sig. "Pretty soon you get a little tug. That's a yellowtail killing the bait. Then he'll draw back and grab the whole thing with a rush. You set the hook with a yank, then let him run until he gets pooped."

"Oh!"

Sig handed her the pole.

"Lay your thumb on the reel like that," he said.

She looked deeply interested and held the pole carefully, the way he had shown her. The butt of the pole was pressed lightly in the pit of her arm; the thumb of her left hand lay gently on the reel.

Sig sat down on the chain locker and leaned back on his elbows. Lucelle was standing quite close to him, and he stared hard at her back, then down at her legs, which were stockingless. They were skinny, but well shaped, and a good coat of tan covered them—tan the color of a sea trout's back.

Lucelle gave a sudden cry and jerked violently on the pole. The next second the reel was humming as the line shot out from it.

"Here," she cried, "I can't hold it."

Sig grabbed the pole from her and tightened up the drag. The reel slowed down and he was able to draw the fish in for a ways, but it turned and started for the bottom. He let it go with the drag fairly tight, then started to reel in slowly.

"I nearly got it," he said over his shoulder. "It's about ripe to jerk in."

It was nearly five minutes before he could bring the fish to the surface and lift its head clear of the water. Then, with the line wrapped around one hand, he swung down with a gaff and stuck the fish in back of the head. The next moment it was threshing about the deck.

"Twenty pound yellowtail," said Sig. "Not bad."

Lucelle hopped from one foot to the other. She was excited and could hardly wait to get her line into the water again and start fishing. Her face was flushed and she was giggling as if catching the fish had made her intoxicated.

When the bait had been put on the hook and tossed out, she moved closer to Sig. For a moment she stood there looking down at the wheeling sardine, then slipped one hand through the crook of his arm. Sig's face got red and he stared down at the bait, trying not to notice her hand.

"I wish Ted could fish," she said. "He can't do a thing but play golf."

Sig laughed loudly. "It takes a man to fish."

"Yes," said Lucelle, nodding, "I guess you're right."

They watched the sardine for a while without speaking. Finally Sig rubbed his shin-bone with the other knee, then turned his face so as to look straight at her.

"What do you want to go with a guy that gets sick for?" he asked. "I wouldn't if I was you."

"Oh, Ted," said Lucelle. "Why, we've been friends ever since grammar-school days."

"Well, I could teach you a lot of things about fishing."

"Yes, I guess you could, all right."

"Say, then," said Sig. "What's the matter with me coming out to see you or something?"

Lucelle wrinkled up her nose and started to laugh. But she stopped suddenly and looked at him soberly, her nostrils twitching.

"I'll tell you," she said. "You said that fish weighed twenty pounds. Well, if you can get one, say about a hundred pounds, you can come out and see me. Why, I might even tell Ted to stay home that night."

At this Sig turned and looked at his jewfish line, then gave a sudden start. It was taut and stood out from the side of the boat. He jumped away from Lucelle and made a grab for the line, just as Ted, his face drained of all color, lurched from the cabin and leaned over the railing.

"Joe," yelled Sig, "I got it!"

Joe leaped down from the bait tank and ran into the cabin. He came out with a rusty shotgun in his hand and leaned it against the railing. Then he and Sig took a good hold on the line and started to haul in the fish. It was hard work; they made little headway at first. Gradually, though, the great fish weakened. Presently they could see it swimming back and forth below them. It loomed up as big as a house, and was a flashing silver in color. There was no fight in it; merely a powerful pull in the opposite direction.

"Brace yourself," said Joe, panting. "I'm letting go to grab the gun."

Sig took a fresh hold and heaved upwards with all his might. Joe held the gun pointed down at the water and the instant the jewfish's head broke through he fired.

(Continued on Page 20)

Passing of the California Pioneer

(Confined to Brief Notices of the Demise of Those Men and Women Who Came to California Prior to 1870.)

ARTHUR BENTON SHEARER, NATIVE of Missouri, 90; came across the plains to California via the southern route in 1849 and resided in various San Joaquin Valley communities; died at Merced City, survived by a wife and six children. He is said to have been one of the state's first telegraphers, and to have established, with his father, the first newspaper in Visalia, Tulare County.

Mrs. Anna Bell-Leach, native of Missouri, 92; crossed the plains via the Lassen Trail in 1849 and resided in Amador, Tulare and Shasta Counties; died at Redding, survived by five children.

Mrs. Harriet Elizabeth Cuthbert, 84; crossed the plains in 1851; died at Burlingame, San Mateo County, survived by a husband and five children.

Mrs. Emma Louise Drew-Mead, native of Iowa, 82; came in 1852 and resided in Calaveras, Tehama, San Joaquin and Stanislaus Counties; died at Oakdale, survived by two daughters.

Mrs. Jane Rohrer-Lane, native of Missouri, 85; came in 1852 and settled in Sonoma County; died at San Francisco.

Milan Williams, native of Texas, 80; came in 1853 and resided in Orange and Los Angeles Counties; died at Bellflower, survived by six children.

Mrs. Emily Adelia Dozier, native of Tennessee, 100; came in 1853 and resided in Kern and Los Angeles Counties; died at Temple City, survived by three daughters.

George Beanston, native of Scotland, 88; came via Cape Horn in 1853; died at Piedmont, Alameda County, survived by four sons.

Richard B. Flowers, native of Maine, 87; came in 1855; died at Placerville, El Dorado County, survived by two children.

Mrs. Frances Casey-DeShields, native of Texas, 83; came across the plains in 1857 and resided many years in Los Angeles County; died at San Diego City, survived by six children, among them L. M. DeShields (Fresno Parlor No. 25 N.S.G.W.).

Mrs. Ellen Riley, 97; since 1857 a resident of San Jose, Santa Clara County, where she died; three children survive.

John Riley Garner, native of Missouri, 95; came in 1857; died near Lakeport, Lake County, survived by six sons.

Mrs. Lora Turner-Boyce, native of Missouri, 82; came via Panama in 1857 and settled in San Joaquin County; died at Lodi, survived by a daughter.

Joseph A. Parker, native of Arkansas, 84; crossed the plains in 1857 and settled in Visalia, Tulare Cunty, where he died.

James C. Horsley, native of Indiana, 84; came via Panama in 1857 and resided most of the time since in Stanislaus County; died at Waterford.

Mrs. Augusta Ingham, native of Ohio, 94; came in 1858; died at Mountain View, Santa Clara County, survived by a daughter.

Mrs. Nancy Johnson (Negress), native of Tennessee, 84; came via Panama in 1858 and settled in Marysville, Yuba County, where she died; two daughters survive.

Wright Thompson Covell, native of New York, 74; came in 1860 and resided in Alameda, San Joaquin and Stanislaus Counties; died at Modesto, survived by three sons.

Mrs. Elizabeth Goodspeed, native of Maine, 98; since 1860 a resident of San Mateo County; died at San Mateo City, survived by a daughter.

Mrs. Mattie Jewell-Perry, native of Vermont; came via Panama in 1860 and settled in San Francisco, where she died; four sons survive.

Mrs. Hannah Sweeney, native of Ireland, 88; came in 1861 and resided many years in Sacramento City; died at Los Angeles City, survived by three children.

Robert E. Saint, native of Iowa, 78; crossed the plains in 1862 and resided in Colusa and Fresno Counties; died at Fresno City, survived by a wife and five children.

Captain William J. Gray, native of New York, 83; since 1862 a resident of San Francisco, where he died; a wife and two sons survive.

Mrs. Flora W. DeNure, native of Virginia, 79; crossed the plains in 1862 and long resided in Ventura County; died at Eagle Rock, Los Angeles County, survived by five children.

Mrs. Birdie Wilson-Robinson, native of Wisconsin, 72; came across the plains in 1862 and resided in Lassen, Modoc and Butte Counties; died at Sacramento City, survived by a husband and two children.

Charles Herbert Wilbur, native of Massachusetts, 79; came via Panama in 1864 and resided in Riverside, Orange and Stanislaus Counties; died at Modesto, survived by a wife and nine children.

Mrs. Medora Prouty-Amick, 77; crossed the plains in 1860 and long resided in Amador County; died at Sacramento City, survived by six children.

Albert Hierchman, native of New York, 89; came in 1864; died at Oakland, Alameda County, survived by a daughter.

Mrs. Elizabeth Jarrett, native of Missouri, 83; came in 1865 and resided sixty-two years in Placer County; died near Woodland, Yolo County, survived by four children.

Mrs. Harriet Richardson-Keiting, native of England, 93; came in 1867 and resided in Marin and San Mateo Counties; died at Redwood City, survived by three children.

William Crewderman, native of Michigan, 79; came in 1867; died at Thermalito, Butte County.

Mrs. Jane Hally, native of Connecticut; since 1867 a resident of Alameda City, where she died; three daughters survive.

Mrs. Julia Bent-Wilson, native of Canada, 84; came in 1867; died at Benicia, Solano County, survived by a daughter.

George Henry Clark, native of Iowa, 86; since 1868 Napa County resident; died at Napa City, survived by three sons.

Oscar Romer, native of Germany, 85; came in 1868 and resided many years in San Francisco; died at Mill Valley, Marin County, survived by six children.

Emanuel Santerfo, native of Italy, 83; since 1869 resident of Amador County; died at Volcano, survived by three children.

Mrs. Mary J. Grasee, native of Massachusetts, 81; since 1862 resident Oakland, Alameda County, where she died; a daughter survives.

Mrs. Sarah Angeline Dickinson-Shartel, native of Missouri, 80; crossed the plains in 1854 and settled in the Sacramento Valley; died at Mentone, San Bernardino County, survived by three sons.

Mrs. Flora Scott-Stefani, native of Illinois, 83; came via Panama in 1852 and in 1863 settled in Monterey County; died at Salinas, survived by two daughters.

PIONEER NATIVES DEAD

(Brief Notices of the Demise of Men and Women born in California Prior to 1860.)

Willis Warren Beeson, born San Mateo County, 1855; died Petaluma, Sonoma County; wife and two children survive. He was affiliated with Redwood Parlor No. 66 N.S.G.W.

Mrs. Louisa Marie Hanke-Huck, born Solano County, 1857; died Sanger, Fresno County; seven children survive.

Emil Charles Albers, born Tuolumne County, 1849; died August 20, Stockton, San Joaquin County; wife and six children survive.

Thomas J. Watson, born San Benito (then Monterey) County, 1856; died August 21, Monterey City. He was a descendant of Jim Watson, once owner of Rancho San Benito, comprising nearly all of what is now San Benito County.

Mrs. Sonoma Tatham, born Sonoma County, 1855; died August 22, Saint Helena, Napa County; four children survive.

Mrs. Mary Lovejoy, born El Dorado County, 1858; died August 23, Cool; husband survives.

Mrs. Mary Elizabeth Wixom-Hidden, born San Bernardino County, 1853; died August 25, Los Angeles City.

Mrs. Nellie Gage-Darling, born Shasta County, 1851; died August 25, Penryn, Placer County.

Mrs. Sarah Gallagher-Furlong, born San Joaquin County, 1854; died August 26, Sebastopol, Sonoma Cunty; twelve children survive.

Mrs. Mary A. Sanders, born Santa Clara County, 1852; died August 30, Oakland, Alameda County; five children survive. She was a daughter of Thomas Shannon, member of the Jayhawker Party which came to California via Death Valley.

Mrs. Isaac Thompson, born Napa County, 1848; died August 30, Kerby, Oregon State.

Julian Berryessa, born Napa County, 1853; died September 3, West Acres, Yolo County; wife and five children survive. He was a son of Cisto Berryessa who, in 1825, took up a land grant extending from Napa County to Lake County.

Mrs. Isabel French-Gaddie, born Alameda County, 1854; died September 3, Oakland; son survives.

Clay Meredith Greene, born San Francisco, 1850; died there, September 5; wife and two daughters survive. He was a son of Colonel William Greene, president of San Francisco's first Board of Aldermen, and is said to have been the first boy of American parentage born in the Bay City; he was a playwright, author and poet of national renown.

Mrs. Luisa Botiller-Foxen, born Santa Barbara County, 1854; died September 5, Los Angeles City; eight children survive. She was the widow of Fred Foxen, whose father, Benjamin Foxen, in 1846 saved the forces of General Fremont from destruction in Gaviota Pass.

Mrs. Isabel Fairchild Howell, born Santa Cruz County, 1856; died September 5, Saint Helena, Napa County; three children survive.

Mrs. Mary Edith Moore-Jennings, born San Mateo County, 1854; died September 6, San Mateo City; three sons survive.

Mrs. Margaret Mahler-Preddy, born El Dorado County, 1850; died September 6, San Francisco; two sons survive. Her parents, the Mahlers, settled in Coloma in 1849, and she is said to have been the first White child born in El Dorado County.

Thomas Franklin Sanger, born Amador County, 1856; died September 9, Eureka, Humboldt County.

Mrs. Conrad Mosner, born Calaveras County, 1858; died September 9, Altaville; five children survive.

Frank R. Wehe, born Sierra County, 1854; died September 11, Berkeley, Alameda County; wife and daughter survive. He was a charter member of Downieville Parlor No. 92 N.S.G.W. and a former Grand Trustee.

Mrs. Rachel Milvina Knipschild, born Napa County, 1855; died September 12, Saint Helena; husband and son survive.

"Slight not what's near, through aiming at what's far."—Euripedes.

LOS ANGELES CITY AND COUNTY

THE CELEBRATION OF ADMISSION Day, September 9, arranged by a joint committee representing all the Los Angeles County Native Daughters and Native Sons Parlors, was a wonderful success in every particular and attracted a large crowd. Mrs. Gertrude Allen of Los Angeles Parlor No. 124 N.D.G.W. was the general chairman.

A pioneer reception in the afternoon was attended by many in costumes of the '49 period. Then came the outofdoors basket supper, which was followed by an elaborate program of entertainment, talent for which was contributed by the various Parlors. The program opened with the assemblage enthusiastically singing "I Love You, California," President Roger Johnson of Los Angeles Parlor No. 45 N.S.G.W. accompanying at the piano.

Frank G. Tyrrell of Ramona Parlor No. 109 N.S.G.W. gave a stirring address on "The Significance of Admission Day," and stressed its relation to the patriotic duty of citizens of today. His forceful and eloquent address was listened to with marked attention, and at its conclusion he was greeted with rounds of applause. Dancing concluded the Admission Day festivities, which are generally declared to have been the very best ever featured locally.

NATIVE SONS UNITED ACTIVITIES.

The Luncheon Club, a creation of Grand Trustee Eldred L. Meyer, has become well established and each Friday the gatherings become more popular. September chairmen were Past Grand Herman C. Lichtenberger, M. U. Rosenthal and Robert E. Ford (Hollywood No. 196), Clarence M. Hunt (Sacramento No. 3) and Grand Trustee Meyer. At the September 29 meeting Grand Second Vice-president Harmon D. Skillin gave an inspiring talk on the Order.

The club assembles every Friday at 12:15 (noon) at the Rosslyn Hotel, and adjourns promptly at 1:15. Join the "gang" and get a real "kick" out of goodfellowship.

The Central Membership Committee, Henry G. Bodkin (Hollywood No. 196) chairman, is fostering the united Parlors' monthly vaudeville shows, and is receiving congratulations for its efforts to increase the membership of the Los Angeles County Parlors. Bring your eligible friends to these excellent shows, the purpose of which is to interest native Californians in the worthwhileness of affiliation with the Order of Native Sons.

The third in the series of monthly shows, which will be continued throughout the year, will be held at the meetingplace of Hollywood Parlor No. 196, 1089 North Oxford avenue.—W.E.O.

PILGRIMAGE TO SAN GABRIEL.

Los Angeles Parlor No. 124 N.D.G.W. started another series of its enjoyable and successful card parties September 13; Ann Schiebusch was chairman. A Sunday morning breakfast was enjoyed at Ferndell Canyon September 17. Edna Holcomb and Mary McAnany were in charge, and after the splendid meal served in the open a pilgrimage was made to San Gabriel Mission.

Six candidates were initiated September 20, and the splendid ritual rendition by President Dolores Malin and her officers was greatly enjoyed. Among the many visitors were Grand Inside Sentinel Hazel Hansen and Deputy Marian Crum. The Parlor was congratulated on its activities and success. Delicious refreshments were served by an able committee headed by Kate Williams. President Malin, Mattie L. Gara and Mary McAnany will represent the Parlor at an advertising conference. Ann Schlebusch, Edna Trombatore and Rose Graffia have been appointed a committee to present plans for a supper.

Los Angeles' October calendar: 3rd, sewing club meeting at the home of Leonie and Jeanne Clos, 1939 Virginia road, 7 p.m. 11th, card party, second of tournament. 18th, potluck dinner, with Marie Walsh as the speaker.

NEWSY N.S. PARAGRAPHS.

Los Angeles—Los Angeles Parlor No. 45 entertained September 21 California Pioneers, many of whom responded to the invitation. Past Grand John T. Newell presided and extended a welcome, and Joe Messmer, president Los Angeles County Pioneer Society, responded for the guests. Dr. Owen C. Coy, director California State Historical Association, delivered an interesting history talk, and entertainment was provided under the supervision of President Roger Johnson. Refreshments were served. The occasion was most enjoyable. The Parlor will receive an official visit from Grand Second Vice-president Harmon D. Skillin October 12.

Los Angeles—President Charles E. Straube of Ramona Parlor No. 109, with the co-operation of the officers and members, is endeavoring to put over a plan whereby the Parlor will acquire land in the close-by mountains and build thereon a clubhouse for the members' free use. It is planned, also, to have an auto campsite on the shoreline, probably between Los Angeles and San Diego. "It is hoped," says Straube, "these splendid inducements will interest the present members and attract many new ones." Ramona will have initiation October 13, and the birthday dinner for the Oct ber boys will be featured October 28. These birthday dinners, originated by Past President Frank Adams, have become very popular.

Los Angeles—Hollywood Parlor No. 196 will feature one of its noted "stag" parties October 9, when Grand Second Vice-president Harmon D. Skillin pays an official visit; Harold Thomas heads the arrangements committee. October 30, Hollywood will sponsor the third of the united Parlors' entertainments to promote interest in the Order. An especially good program is promised. "Bring your eligibles," urges Deputy Grand President John J. Ford.

Glendale—Glendale Parlor No. 264 will have a special meeting October 3 at its meetingplace, 3311 Downing avenue, to receive Grand Second Vice-president Harmon D. Skillin on his official visit. All members of the Order are invited.

Santa Monica—Santa Monica Bay Parlor No. 267 will initiate a class of candidates October 4, when Grand Second Vice-president Harmon D. Skillin makes his official visit.

Los Angeles—University Parlor No. 272 initiated five candidates September 20; refreshments followed the ceremony. The Parlor will join with Compton Parlor No. 273, at the latter's meetingplace, for the official visit of Grand Second Vice-president Harmon D. Skillin. "By all means don't make any prior dates for the night of October 28," is Recording Secretary Carl Martin's urge on the members of the Order, "for University has its first birthday and plans a huge event that you cannot afford to miss. Details will be announced in your Parlor shortly."

INCREASED MEMBERSHIP, of substantial quality, is TODAY'S OUTSTANDING NEED of the Order of Native Sons. COMB THE FIELDS, urges the Grand President, who solicits NOW the co-operation of every Native Son. Bear in mind always, THERE IS NO SUBSTITUTE FOR MEMBERSHIP, and rally to the cause.

HISTORY CLASS DRAWING CARD.

The history and landmarks class of Californiana Parlor No. 247 N.D.G.W. proved a drawing card for September 12. Early California explorers were studied, and books were allotted for review at the October meeting. Isabel Lopez Fages is the chairman. Program Chairman Martha Decker provided two interesting speakers following luncheon—Miss Florence Woodhead and Mrs. Arthur Clark.

The one hundred and fifty-second anniversary of the founding of Los Angeles was celebrated by the Parlor visiting September 4 the Felipe de Neve statue in the Plaza. In preparation for the bazar to be held in December for the benefit of the homeless children, the sewing circle had two delightful meetings during the month. Miss Mary E. Foy presided with delightful oldtime hospitality at a tea following the September 26 meeting; many guests attended. An autumn bridge was held at the home of Mrs. Oscar Schmidt September 28; Past President Gertrude Tuttle was in charge.

NEWSY N.D. PARAGRAPHS.

Long Beach—Meetings of Long Beach Parlor No. 154 were held at the home of President Eleonor Johnson September 7 and 21. August 31 a steak bake was held at Gussie Tabor's home; Clara Fay chairman. The thimble club had a special meeting at the home of Kate McFadyen, August 29, and completed school dresses for several children. The club met September 4 at the home of Lucretia Coats.

San Pedro—Rudecinda Parlor No. 230 has been very active lately, sponsoring several card parties, and its sewing club has featured picnics at the beaches and in the parks. A large number attended the two-act play presented by the Women's Aid of Terminal Island. Verniece Durant was chairman of the arrangements committee.

Glendale—An all-day party at the home of Grand Inside Sentinel Hazel Hansen September 27, in behalf of Verdugo Parlor No. 240, was well attended. Luncheon was followed by cards, and at 6:30 p.m. supper was served. The proceeds are to be used to purchase a California State (Bear) Flag for Glendale's new postoffice. Ada Steele had charge of the luncheon, and Vera Carlson of the dinner. Verdugo is making plans for a dinner dance and bazar to be held November 18.

Santa Monica—Recording Secretary Rosalie F. Hyde sponsored a "chowder" bridge September 23 at her Venice home for the benefit of Santa Monica Bay Parlor No. 245.

PERSONAL N.S. AND N.D. PARAGRAPHS.

Thelma Stengel (Los Angeles N.D.) enjoyed a motor trip through Oregon.

Mrs. Grace Bessac (Joaquin N.D.) of Stockton is visiting here with relatives.

Margaret Baldwin (Los Angeles N.D.) has returned from a vacation in Texas.

Marje Walsh (Los Angeles N.D.) has returned from a visit to San Francisco.

Lucile Duncan (Los Angeles N.D.) has returned from a month's visit to Balboa.

Supervisor John R. Quinn (Los Angeles N.S.) left last month for an Eastern visit.

Clyde H. Foot (Sepulveda N.S.) of San Pedro was a recent visitor to Milwaukee.

Walter T. Richards (Sepulveda N.S.) of San Pedro recently joined the ranks of the benedicts.

John R. Spring (Ramona N.S.) has been appointed secretary of the Board of Fire Commissioners.

Ernestine Aylward (Californiana N.D.) has been elected president of the American Legion Auxiliary.

Maybelle Lunn Roy (Los Angeles N.D.) has returned from a motor trip to Chicago and New York.

Hampton Neergard (Sepulveda N.S.) and wife of San Pedro vacationed last month in Shasta County.

Justice Emmet Seawell (Grand President N.S.) of the California Supreme Court was a visitor last month.

Louis J. Peter (Mount Tamalpais N.S.) and daughter, Miss Marie, of San Rafael were visitors last month.

Carvel P. Hunt (Ramona N.S.) and wife left late last month for a vacation in San Francisco and Sacramento.

Harmon D. Skillin (Grand Second Vice-president N.S.), assistant district attorney of San Francisco, is a visitor.

Evelyn Trautwein (Los Angeles N.D.) and husband are enjoying a motor trip to Chicago, New York and Florida.

Olinda Kerby and Louise McNary (both Los Angeles N.D.) and their husbands were recent Monterey City visitors.

Mrs. Gertrude Riddle (Long Beach N.D.) has returned to her Long Beach home from a visit to New York and Chicago.

Miss Betty Hall (Californiana N.D.) became the bride of R. C. Quizenberry at a secret ceremony in Ventura City last June.

Miss Grace S. Stoermer (Past Grand N.D.) last month attended the annual convention of the Association of Bank Women at Chicago.

Andrew M. Stodel (Los Angeles N.S.) has been elected a director of the recently organized California State Fair Poultry Association.

Donald Gunn (Sepulveda N.S.), now residing in New York, was a visitor last month to his old homes in San Pedro and Long Beach.

William A. Reuter (Grand Inside Sentinel N.S.) of Wilmington had as a recent guest his brother, I. H. Reuter (Yosemite N.S.) of Merced City.

THE DEATH RECORD.

Charles Powers, husband of Mrs. Mercy Powers (Rudecinda N.D.), died at San Pedro. He was a native of Sweden, aged 71.

Jean Emile Sentous, son of Louis Sentous (Ramona N.S.), died August 25.

John B. Amestoy, affiliated with Ramona Parlor No. 109 N.S.G.W., died August 26, survived by a wife and three children. He was born at Los Angeles, July 4, 1869.

Anthony Schwamm, affiliated with Ramona Parlor No. 109 N.S.G.W., died September 5, survived by a wife and four children, among them Dr. John A. Schwamm (Ramona N.S.). He was born at San Francisco, March 29, 1865.

Hal S. Kruckeberg, affiliated with Ramona Parlor No. 109 N.S.G.W., died September 8, survived by a wife and two children. He was born at Los Angeles, August 29, 1888.

Mrs. Mabelle Locke-Meserve, wife of Edwin A. Meserve (Ramona N.S.), died September 9. She was a native of Massachusetts, aged 69.

Anastisco A. Avila, brother of Felipe A. Avila (Ramona N.S.), died September 14, at the age of 72.

Charles Clifton West, affiliated with Ramona Parlor No. 109 N.S.G.W., died September 15 at Atascadero, San Luis Obispo County, survived by a wife. He was born at Glendora, March 22, 1880.

Charles S. Simpson, affiliated with Hollywood Parlor No. 196 N.S.G.W., died September 18, survived by a wife and two children. He was born in Merced County, March 15, 1874.

Dr. James Hovey Bullard, father of John A. Bullard (Ramona N.S.), died September 20. A native of Massachusetts, aged 77, he came to California in 1883 and for several years practiced medicine in Orange and Los Angeles Counties, later becoming prominently identified with construction financing. Dr. Bullard was most charitable, being a very liberal contributor to all public agencies, and a dispenser, without blare of trumpet, of financial aid to numerous individuals and charitable organizations of his own choosing.—C.M.H.

RED OCEAN

(Continued from Page 16)

There was no struggle; only a sudden bursting from the water of a great massive body. It lay still, belly-up, and a great red hole showed where the shots had ripped through the head. The water around it turned a deep red as the blood ran out.

"Give us a hand," said Joe to the men leaning over the railing near them.

He stuck two gaffs into the fish, and the men took hold. Sig reached down with one hand and shoved his fingers in under the fish's left eyeball. Together they worked the four-hundred-pound ocean scavenger up over the railing and let it slide down to the deck.

Only once did Sig look at Lucelle. She was watching him, her lips parted, eyes very wide. Her face was quite pale. He smiled at her, then turned and ran into the cabin to return with a short butcherknife in one hand.

"Hey, there," said Joe. "What's the idea? It'll get sunburnt if you clean it now. Wait until we start back."

"Aw, listen," said Sig in a half-whisper. "I got to beat that other kid's time somehow. I want to show her what a real man can do while she's in the mind to watch.

Joe shrugged. "You're nuts," he said, "but it's your fish."

Without a word Sig peeled off his shirt and, naked to the waist, kneeled by the scaled mass. He slid the point of his knife from the head down a distance of three feet, leaving a gaping hole in the belly. Into this he plunged his arms to the elbows and brought out an armful of entrails. He laid his burden on the deck and slashed loose the long yellow tubes that connected the mass of quivering substance to the inside of the fish. Then, piece by piece, he flung the chunks over the side. Each separate piece he held aloft for a second and called aloud its name, so the men grouped about would better understand.

When the jewfish was cleaned Sig fastened a stout cord in back of its gills. A beam extended from the top of the cabin and attached to it was a block and tackle. Sig hauled his fish up until only its tail touched the deck. Then, with buckets of sea-water he slushed off the blood, both inside and out.

"Fourteen minutes," said Joe. "Big Pete always took seventeen or more and he never did tell the sportsfellows the names of the guts."

Sig laughed and drew back to better view the fish. Blood was smeared the whole of his torso and on his arms were flecks of entrails; bits of stringy stuff.

He looked around for Lucelle and found that she no longer watched him. He found her up in the bow. She was watching the shoreline, and with her was young Ted Wilson.

Sig brushed the hair back from his forehead, then went up behind the couple.

"Why don't you come and look at it?" he said. "I'll make you a present of it, Lucelle."

They turned to look at him. Lucelle moved as far away as possible and stood up in the very point of the bow.

"I don't want it," she said in a low voice.

"It'll pass a hundred and then some," said Sig. "Why, it'll hit four hundred at least. Remember what you said?"

Lucelle had her back to him, but she turned her head slightly to look. Her teeth began to chatter together, and her shoulders shook. Then suddenly she made a queer sound with her mouth and leaned away out over the railing.

Sig stood there for a moment, perplexed at her sudden change. Then, shrugging, he went back to look at the jewfish again.

(This story is a contribution to The Grizzly Bear from William A. Evans of San Diego, well known short story writer affiliated with San Diego Parlor No. 108 N.S.G.W. "Uncle Jim's Farm," another of his stories which appeared in The Grizzly Bear for January 1932, was received with much favor by the magazine's readers. —Editor.)

Subscription Order Blank

For Your Convenience

Grizzly Bear Magazine,
309-15 Wilcox Bldg.,
206 South Spring St.,
Los Angeles, California.

For the enclosed remittance of $1.50 enter my subscription to The Grizzly Bear Magazine for one year.

Name..

Street Address..

City or Town..

Lightning Source UK Ltd.
Milton Keynes UK
UKHW020607120219
337137UK00005B/732/P

9 780260 162700